J. W. McKENZIE

12 …
Ewell, E… KT19 0QT

Tel: 0181-393 7700 Fax: 0181-393 1694

Specialists in Antiquarian,
Secondhand Cricket Books
Wisdens, and Memorabilia

Catalogue Sent on Request

You are welcome to visit our well-stocked shop
premises at the above address
Hours: 9am–5pm Monday–Friday
Most Saturdays 10am–1pm
For your own convenience, please ring beforehand

We are always pleased to hear of Books and
Collections for Sale

134TH YEAR

WISDEN

CRICKETERS' ALMANACK

1997

EDITED BY MATTHEW ENGEL

PUBLISHED BY JOHN WISDEN & CO LTD

Cased edition ISBN 0 947766 38 3 £26
Soft cover edition ISBN 0 947766 39 1 £26
Leather bound edition ISBN 0 947766 40 5 £200
(Limited edition of 150)

JOHN WISDEN & CO LTD
25 Down Road, Merrow, Guildford, Surrey GU1 2PY
Tel: 01483 570358 Fax: 01483 533153

WISDEN CRICKETERS' ALMANACK

Editor: Matthew Engel, The Oaks, Newton St Margarets, Herefordshire HR2 0QN.
Assistant editor: Harriet Monkhouse. Production editor: Christine Forrest.
Editorial assistant: Simon Briggs.
General manager: Christopher Lane. Advertisement manager: Colin Ackehurst.

Computer typeset by Spottiswoode Ballantyne Ltd, Colchester

Printed and bound in Great Britain by Clays Ltd, St Ives plc
Distributed by The Penguin Group

PREFACE

There is one important innovation in the 1997 *Wisden*. For the first time the Almanack includes a Register of Players, giving biographical information for almost a thousand of the world's leading cricketers.

Births and Deaths of Cricketers was first included in the 1867 *Wisden*, and 130 is normally considered a rather advanced age for breeding. But the new spin-off from this venerable feature will enable *Wisden* to give more information on more players. The plan is that Births and Deaths will concentrate on retired cricketers; the current generation will be contained in the Register. For now, there is a lot of overlap, which should be removed once readers have become accustomed to the new system.

No one – myself included – got used to Births and Deaths' most recent positioning, lost between Cricket Records and the English season. The Register, Births and Deaths and other related material are now stowed further forward in a new Part Two of *Wisden* devoted to The Players.

There are also changes to the qualifications for entry into Births and Deaths. Some players from the recent past have been deleted; others, often more distinguished, but more distant, have been restored. It seemed to me incongruous that being dead for ten years should be a reason for removal from this section, and I hope those readers most resistant to any change in *Wisden* will share the sentiment. I am grateful to Philip Bailey and Robert Brooke for their work in these departments.

The 134th *Wisden* contains a more direct affront to tradition. Two years ago in this space I reaffirmed the criteria for selection of the Five Cricketers of the Year. I have now felt obliged to modify them to include a player who was not a participant in the last English season: Sanath Jayasuriya of Sri Lanka.

The diminishing status of English cricket has been a fact for a long time. But now even the home fixture list fails to reflect the realities of the world game. Despite the impact the Sri Lankans have had on cricket, their players can expect minimal opportunities to play in England. Jayasuriya's performances in the World Cup reverberated everywhere and earned him the right to be in our hall of fame.

Wisden, like everyone else, has to recognise that each year the cricketing world revolves a little less round St John's Wood. This subject is necessarily a theme of the 1997 Almanack. I hope we can bring to the debate more light and less hot air than has been available elsewhere.

It has also been a year of change within John Wisden and Co. David Frith's retirement, after 17 distinguished years as editor of *Wisden Cricket Monthly*, has led to a revamped magazine under Tim de Lisle's editorship and a much stronger connection between the magazine and the Almanack. I am grateful to the board and management committee of John Wisden & Co for their enlightened and progressive stewardship. My special thanks also to Harriet Monkhouse, Christine Forrest, Simon Briggs, Christopher Lane and Colin Ackehurst of the *Wisden* staff; to Peter Bather and Mike Smith of Spottiswoode Ballantyne, our typesetters; to our distributors Penguin; to Gordon Burling, Bill Frindall, John Kitchin and Roy Smart; and – most profoundly – to Hilary and Laurie, my wife and son.

MATTHEW ENGEL

Newton St Margarets, Herefordshire,
January 1997

LIST OF CONTRIBUTORS

Jonathan Agnew
Neale Andrew
Andy Arlidge
Chris Aspin
Jack Bailey
Philip Bailey
Mark Baldwin
Jack Bannister
Brian Bearshaw
Mike Berry
Scyld Berry
Edward Bevan
J. Watson Blair
Mihir Bose
Trent Bouts
Robert Brooke
Philip Brown
Colin Bryden
John Callaghan
D. J. Cameron
Frank Coppi
Tony Cozier
John Curtis
Geoffrey Dean
Ralph Dellor
Norman de Mesquita
Patrick Eagar
John Etheridge
Sebastian Faulks
David Field
David Foot
Bill Frindall
David Frith
Nigel Fuller
Andrew Gidley
Chris Goddard
Paul Haigh
David Hallett
David Hardy
Peter S. Hargreaves
Norman Harris
Michael Henderson
Eric Hill
Philip Hoare
Grenville Holland
David Hopps
Gerald Howat
Martin Johnson
Peter Johnson
Winston Jordan
Abid Ali Kazi
John Kelland
Ross Kinnaird
John Kitchin
Alan Lee
Tony Lewis
David Llewellyn
David Lloyd
Nick Lucy
Steven Lynch
David McKie
John MacKinnon
Lord MacLaurin
Ashley Mallett
Vic Marks
Christopher Martin-Jenkins
Peter Mason
R. Mohan
Graham Morris
Gerald Mortimer
David Munden
Brian Murgatroyd
Adrian Murrell
Mike Neasom
David Norrie
Terry Power
Qamar Ahmed
Andrew Radd
Peter Robinson
Carol Salmon
Andrew Samson
Derek Scott
Mike Selvey
Bill Smith
Barney Spender
Ivo Tennant
Sa'adi Thawfeeq
Andrew Tong
Chris Turvey
Sudhir Vaidya
Gerry Vaidyasekera
John Ward
David Warner
Paul Weaver
Tim Wellock
Graeme Wright

Round the World: Trevor Bayley, Olivier de Braekeleer, David de Silva, Brian Fell, T. J. Finlayson, Tony Fisher, Simone Gambino, Maurice F. Hankey, Simon Hewitt, Anthony Letts, Russell Mawhinney, Guy Parker, Stanley Perlman, Fraser M. Simm, Andrew Simpson-Parker, Jasmer Singh, Stephen Spawls, Derek Thursby, S. J. Vickery, Rajah M. Wickremesinhe and Clive Woodbridge.

Thanks are accorded to the following for checking the scorecards of first-class matches: John Blondel, Keith Booth, Caroline Byatt, Len Chandler, Bill Davies, Alex Davis, Byron Denning, Jack Foley, Keith Gerrish, Peter Gordon, Brian Hunt, Vic Isaacs, David Kendix, Tony Kingston, Reg May, David Oldam, Gordon Stringfellow, Stan Tacey, Tony Weld, Roy Wilkinson and Graham York.

The editor also acknowledges with gratitude assistance from the following: Barry Abraham, the ACS e-mail group, Bill Andersson, Keith Andrew, David Armstrong, Keith Armstrong, Simon Barnes, Carl Bell, Tim Bible, Rob Bishop, Dick Brittenden, Richard Colbey, Geoffrey Copinger, Mike Coward, Nick Cowley, Brian Croudy, Prakash Dahatonde, Gareth A. Davies, Frank Duckworth, Robert Eastaway, Richard England, Ric Finlay, Sujoy Ghosh, Ghulam Mustafa Khan, David C. Gibbs, Bob Harragan, Les Hatton, Col. Malcolm Havergal, Faith Hawkins, Ruth Hayman, Ken Ingman, Mohammad Ali Jafri, Kate Jenkins, Rajesh Kumar, David Lacey, Malcolm Lorimer, Dave Luxton, Mahendra Mapagunaratne, Mohandas Menon, Allan Miller, P. S. Mukhopadhyay, John Murray, Vasant Naik, Francis Payne, S. Pervez Qaiser, Mark Ray, Rex Roberts, Major R. W. K. Ross-Hurst, Peter Sallis, Geoffrey Saulez, Michael Snook, Philip Snow, Karen Spink, Richard Streeton, Mike Turner, David Walsh, Alan Weedy, Wendy Wimbush, Robert Winder, John Woodcock and Peter Wynne-Thomas.

The production of *Wisden* would not be possible without the support and co-operation of many other cricket officials, writers and lovers of the game. To them all, many thanks.

CONTENTS

Part One: Comment

Notes by the Editor 9
The Wisden World Championship 18
English Cricket: A Manifesto by Lord MacLaurin 20
A Wind Blows From the East by Mihir Bose 21
If You Can Meet With Triumph and Disaster 25
Sri Lanka: Years of Preparation . . . by Gerry Vaidyasekera 30
. . . A Night to Remember by David Hopps 31
The Man Who Stole the Show by Tony Lewis 33
A Spin-Doctor Writes by Ashley Mallett 37
Fifty Sheffield Shield Years by David Frith and Philip Bailey 39
Years of the Fox by Martin Johnson 41
Five Cricketers of the Year
Sanath Jayasuriya 44
Mushtaq Ahmed 46
Saeed Anwar 47
Phil Simmons 49
Sachin Tendulkar 51

Part Two: The Players

Test Cricketers 1877-1996 53
Births and Deaths of Cricketers 104
Register of Players 150
Wisden's Cricketers of the Year, 1889-1997 167
Post-War Cricketers of the Year 170

Part Three: Records

Index to Records 171
First-Class Records
Batting 175
Bowling 198
All-Round 206
Wicket-Keeping 209
Fielding 211
Teams 212
Test Match Records
Batting 217
Bowling 229
All-Round 235
Wicket-Keeping 236
Fielding 238
Teams 239
Captaincy 244
Umpires 244
Test Series 245
Limited-Overs International Records 325
Miscellaneous 336

Part Four: English Cricket in 1996

Features of 1996 342
Statistics
First-Class Averages 348
Individual Scores of 100 and Over 356
Ten Wickets in a Match 360

The Indians in England 363
The Pakistanis in England 389
South Africa A in England 417
Britannic Assurance County Championship
Review 429
Past Champions and Statistics 432
TCCB County Pitches Table of Merit 437
Derbyshire 438
Durham 453
Essex 467
Glamorgan 480
Gloucestershire 494
Hampshire 509
Kent 523
Lancashire 538
Leicestershire 552
Middlesex 565
Northamptonshire 578
Nottinghamshire 592
Somerset 606
Surrey 620
Sussex 634
Warwickshire 649
Worcestershire 662
Yorkshire 677
NatWest Trophy 693
Benson and Hedges Cup 720
Sunday League 762
The Universities
Oxford 865
Cambridge 876
The University Match 886
BUSA Championship 888
Other First-Class Matches 891
MCC Matches 893
Other Matches 895
The Minor Counties 897
Second Eleven Cricket
Championship 911
Bain Hogg Trophy 932
Career Figures 934
League Cricket
The Lancashire Leagues 936
League Cricket in England and Wales 938
National Club Championship 941
National Village Championship 942
Irish Cricket 944
Scottish Cricket 945
New Zealand Under-19 in England 946
NAYC Under-19 County Festivals 952
Lombard World Under-15 Challenge 954
Schools Cricket
MCC Schools Festival 957
Eton v Harrow 961
Reports and Averages 962
Youth Cricket 1003
Women's Cricket
New Zealand Women in England 1004
English Women's Cricket 1007

Part Five: Overseas Cricket in 1995-96

Features of 1995-96 ... 1009
The World Cup, 1996 ... 1015
England in South Africa ... 1050
England A in Pakistan ... 1076
The Sri Lankans in Pakistan ... 1086
The New Zealanders in India ... 1096
The South Africans in Zimbabwe ... 1106
The Pakistanis in Australia and New Zealand ... 1110
The Sri Lankans in Australia ... 1124
The West Indians in Australia ... 1132
The Zimbabweans in New Zealand ... 1134
The New Zealanders in the West Indies ... 1143
The Sri Lankans in the West Indies ... 1153
Singer Champions Trophy ... 1155
Benson and Hedges World Series ... 1161
Singer Cup ... 1172
Pepsi Cup ... 1177
England Under-19 in Zimbabwe ... 1183
English Counties Overseas ... 1187
England Women in India ... 1191
Domestic Cricket
- Cricket in Australia ... 1195
- Cricket in South Africa ... 1208
- Cricket in the West Indies ... 1222
- Cricket in New Zealand ... 1232
- Cricket in India ... 1240
- Cricket in Pakistan ... 1254
- Cricket in Sri Lanka ... 1270
- Cricket in Zimbabwe ... 1285
- Cricket in Denmark ... 1291
- Cricket in The Netherlands ... 1292
- The European Championship, 1996 ... 1293
- Cricket Round the World ... 1294

Part Six: Administration and Laws

Administration
- The International Cricket Council ... 1303
- The England and Wales Cricket Board ... 1304
- The Marylebone Cricket Club ... 1304
- European Cricket Federation ... 1305
- Addresses of Representative Bodies and Counties ... 1305

Laws
- The Laws of Cricket ... 1309
- Regulations of the International Cricket Council ... 1338
- ICC Code of Conduct ... 1342
- Regulations for First-Class Matches in Britain, 1996 ... 1342

Meetings and Decisions in 1996 ... 1345

Part Seven: Miscellaneous

Chronicle of 1996 ... 1349
Cricket Books, 1996 ... 1357
Cricket Videos, 1996 ... 1375
Cricket and the Media, 1996 ... 1376
Cricket and the Law in 1996 ... 1378
Cricketana in 1996 ... 1381
Cricket Equipment in 1996 ... 1383

Umpiring in 1996 1384
Cricket Grounds in 1996 1386
Blind Cricket in 1996 1387
Charities in 1996 1388
Grant Aid for Cricket, 1996 1389
Cricket in the Classroom in 1996 1390
Cricket and Betting in 1996 1391
Cricket People in 1996 1392
Directory of Book Dealers 1394
Directory of Cricket Suppliers 1395
Obituary 1399
Index to Test Matches 1419
Index of Unusual Occurrences 1420
Test Matches, 1996-97 1421
Fixtures, 1997 1429

Addresses of first-class and minor counties can now be found on pages 1307-1308.

A more detailed index to Cricket Records appears on pages 171-175. The index to the Laws may be found on pages 1309-1310 and an index of Test matches played in 1995-96 on pages 1419-1420.

Index of Fillers and Inserts

Ashes, The, *216*.
Biggest Falls in the County Championship, *591*
Biggest Leaps in the County Championship, *428*
CEAT Cricketer of the Year, *1253*
Champions, The, *648*
Coca-Cola Cricket Week, *1182*
Coopers & Lybrand Awards, *347*
Coopers & Lybrand Ratings, The, *361*
Cornhill Insurance England Player of the Year, *347*
County Benefits Awarded For 1997, *508*
County Caps Awarded in 1996, *508*
County Membership, *493*
Cricket Society Awards, *951*
Cricket Society Literary Award, *1374*
Cricketers in ICC Associate Countries, *1290*
Duckworth/Lewis Method, The, *719*
England's International Schedule, *1085*
Errata in *Wisden*, *1142*
Fielding in 1996, *452*
Fifty Years Ago, *940*
Highest Championship First-Wicket Partnerships, *590*
Highest Partnerships for Yorkshire, *484*
Highest Scores for Losing Side, *547*
Highest Totals Against Yorkshire, *685*
Honours' List, 1996-97, *1231*
I Zingari Results, 1996, *910*
ICC Code – Breaches and Penalties, *1176*
International Schedule, 1997-98, *1154*
International Umpires' Panel, *1308*
Longest County Championship Innings, *547*
Longest Innings for England, *1061*
Most Wickets in a Sunday League Season, *840*
One Hundred Years Ago, *1190*
Peter Smith Memorial Award, *1284*
Presidents of MCC Since 1946, *149*
Professionals' Awards, 1996, *691*
Ridley Wicket, *347*
Sheffield Shield Player of the Year, *1207*
Umpires for 1997, *933*
Walter Lawrence Trophy, *347*
West Indies Youth in Pakistan, *1123*
Whyte & Mackay Rankings, The, *605*
Winless Championship Seasons Since the War, *452*
Wombwell Cricket Lovers' Society Awards, 1996, *691*
Worst Seasonal Records in the Sunday League, *776*
Young Cricketer of the Year, *466*
Youngest Players to Score 200 in First-Class Cricket, *672*

PART ONE: COMMENT

NOTES BY THE EDITOR

One evening last July I was sitting at Worcester watching Durham, who were bottom of the County Championship, play Worcestershire, who were then 15th. It was precisely the sort of cricket match people who never watch the game keep saying is entirely worthless.

After tea on the first day, the Durham spearhead Simon Brown reduced Worcestershire to 11 for four. Only Graeme Hick stood between Durham and probable victory. Both men were playing for a place in the Test team against Pakistan the following week. Hick had also made himself unpopular with some Worcestershire members by missing the previous home match, pleading exhaustion. This was the very stuff of cricket: wheels within wheels, confrontations within the confrontation, games within the game. I thought it was utterly enthralling. In the event, Hick stood in Brown's way through the evening and much of the next day as well; the supporters decided they loved him again; and so did the England selectors, who chose both him and Brown for the next Test – then dropped them.

At the end of August, I was at Bristol for an even deader match: Gloucestershire playing Northamptonshire, two counties going nowhere. There was a young off-spinner, Jeremy Snape, bowling to an old slogger, Courtney Walsh, with three men on the leg-side boundary while Walsh tried to give them jumping practice; there too was an even younger batsman, Alec Swann – apparently impassive behind his grille but heart pounding – facing the master bowler Walsh, as he played his very first innings in county cricket.

At Taunton a few days later, I saw Derbyshire, thirsting for their first Championship in sixty years, bounding on to the field in bright sunshine with their hyperactive wicket-keeper Karl Krikken shouting "keep working" even before a ball had been bowled – and his captain, Dean Jones, then providing a running commentary which became noticeably more intermittent as the Somerset score moved towards 194 for one.

The 1996 cricket season in England was in some respects the most depressing in memory, almost entirely due to the continual disasters that afflicted the national team. A calendar year which began with the dreadful conclusion to the tour of South Africa, and a wretched performance in the World Cup, ended with England's glum failures in Zimbabwe. An indifferent summer was sandwiched in between; and a pall of gloom descended on the game. But every time I went to a county match I enjoyed myself hugely, no matter how few people might have been around to share that enjoyment.

The debate in English cricket is sometimes said to be between conservatives and radicals. Yet it seems to me that every true cricket lover is, in a sense, a conservative, or at any rate that the game represents the conservative side of our nature: our love of summer days and our youth. More often, the debate – such as it is – goes on between sleepwalkers on one side and hysterics on the other. Fleet Street cricket correspondents no longer report the game as such. Nearly all the time they just cover the soap opera of the England team: *EastEnders* without the varying storylines. Before contemplating the future of cricket – and, most daunting of all, English cricket – it makes sense to pause, and to give thanks for a wonderful game. It needs to change; but it has to be changed with care and love.

Tomorrow the world?

Taking a global perspective, the game of cricket is thriving. Sri Lanka's success in the World Cup has sent a whole country cricket-crazy. Between harvests, when the rice paddies are dry, they are said to be filled with youngsters playing with any implements that approximate to bats and balls; indeed, elsewhere in *Wisden* we record the concern of doctors there about the injuries being done by flying stones. In rural South Africa, you see black people – women as well as men – playing impromptu versions of a game that was once effectively denied them. In Australia, the national team's success has helped restore cricket's role as the country's most potent unifying factor. In India, a remarkable proportion of the national income is now being channelled into the game, and the players' pockets.

In the subcontinent the success of the one-day game has wreaked havoc in other directions; the 1996-97 Duleep Trophy final in Mohali, a first-class match of some significance, was said to have begun with an attendance of one. But South Africa has shown that people can be won back to traditional cricket. When India visited there for the first post-isolation Tests in 1992-93, crowds varied between the patchy and the pitiful; four years on, when India returned, the support was tremendous.

The buzzword among optimists now is "globalisation", the belief that cricket can and must colonise new lands where the game is little-known. It happened once before (through imperialism rather than television), which is why cricket is an international sport and not a quaint Olde English pastime. The evidence that it can happen again is not overwhelming. Thus far only two new countries, Kenya and Bangladesh, remotely look as if they might be able to stage Test cricket in the foreseeable future – though the ICC Trophy in Malaysia will shortly provide further evidence on this point. The fear is that what globalisation might actually mean is more and more piddling one-day tournaments staged in more and more recherché places for the benefit of Asian satellite TV. This is exacerbated by the perception that Indian cricket is keener on short-term financial gains than the long-term welfare of the game.

These considerations have informed a year of intense debate among the members of the International Cricket Council, following the failure of the controversial secretary of the Indian board, Jagmohan Dalmiya, to be elected ICC chairman at the 1996 meeting. Mihir Bose discusses these issues on page 21. The past few months have been taken up with intense negotiations over a plan devised by Sir John Anderson, the chairman of New Zealand Cricket, to put a new executive committee in place, with devolved powers to sub-committees covering cricket, finance and marketing, and development. In the long run, that is likely to mean a beefed-up secretariat, with less power for the non-Test-playing countries, and perhaps less importance attached to the post of chairman.

Within ICC, there are faint glimmerings of a consensus, particularly over the need to get a balance between one-day internationals and Tests. Two years ago, in these Notes, I made the case for an ongoing World Championship of

Test cricket. *Wisden's* own version of this now exists (see pages 18-19) and has gathered a gratifying amount of interest throughout the cricketing world. The principle of a World Championship now seems to command overwhelming support, whether or not ICC, who are due to debate the subject this year, ever manage to reach agreement on establishing one in practice.

If there were a Test Championship, it would be reasonable to consider a similar framework for international one-day cricket. South Africa has floated the idea of staging the World Cup every two years instead of four; others are interested in an ongoing one-day Championship culminating in a mini-World Cup between, say, the top four teams. The World Cup provides cricket with a showcase for the most popular form of the game, and it would certainly be preferable to clone that rather than continue with the present absurd situation in which meaningless trilateral and quadilaterial tournaments fill the international calendar and TV time to no sporting purpose whatever.

Whichever way this goes, part of the pattern is clear: a more seamless year, with cricket in many countries even during the English summer; and shorter, more intense, competitions that may render the concept of "touring" obsolete. Indeed, while the English were earnestly debating whether or not overseas players should be allowed to play county cricket, hardly anyone seemed to notice that the decision was being taken for them because the players were rapidly becoming unavailable. More than ever, one suspects, leading international cricketers will be just that and nothing else – they will be representing their country, or preparing to do so, or recovering and resting.

The English disease

Early in 1997, Archie Henderson, sports editor of a South African newspaper, the *Cape Argus,* wrote a column enthusing about the role television has played in the cricketing boom there. "Cricket, once seemingly destined for extinction, has learned to sell itself," he wrote. "While rugby and soccer have rested on their laurels, cricket has exploited the medium with imaginative innovations. This has extended the audience from largely white and male . . . the marketing gurus behind the sport have taken every little nuance of a game that is full of nuances and turned them into sub-plots of the greater drama."

Such a column might also be written in Britain, with the word "not" strategically inserted throughout. And this is only in part because the production values of the BBC TV coverage now seem so stereotyped and dated. Amid the general global mood of cricketing expansionism, England is a spectacular and potentially catastrophic exception.

In 1996-97 the national team reached a point where even the good days were bad. They were one run short of victory in the Bulawayo Test and one wicket short at Auckland. It felt as though the English, who were once presumed to have won first prize in the lottery of life, were now on the receiving end of some cosmic practical joke.

At the 1996 World Cup, the England squad resembled a bad-tempered grandmother attending a teenage rave; British delegations at European summits have sometimes behaved in a similar fashion. Unable to comprehend what was happening – on the field or off it – the players just lingered, looking sullen as well as incompetent. They conveyed as bad an impression in

Zimbabwe at the end of the year. And, though they appeared to have learned to display a little grace under pressure by the time they reached New Zealand in January 1997, that merely emphasised their earlier petulance. The captain, Mike Atherton, and coach, David Lloyd, were culpable in failing to understand the importance of their roles as public figures. But it was hardly surprising. Until the end of 1996, they were paid by the Test and County Cricket Board, a body that found public relations so difficult that for its last couple of years it simply gave up on the whole business.

All this was merely the superficial expression of a far deeper mess. In England, football has always been more popular than cricket. Ten years ago, when Ian Botham and David Gower were more instantly recognisable than any footballer, and soccer was struggling against the ravages of hooliganism, the gap was a narrow one. It is now a yawning chasm. Play in the Lord's Test was stopped by the roar of delight among the spectators when they heard that England had beaten Spain in the European Championship quarter-final. The idea that the reverse might ever happen at Wembley is unthinkable.

The consistent failure of the England team is the biggest single cause of the crisis, but it is not the crisis itself. The blunt fact is that cricket in the UK has become unattractive to the overwhelming majority of the population. The game is widely perceived as elitist, exclusionist and dull. The authorities have been accused of worrying too much about "marketing". In fact their idea of marketing has usually consisted of sucking up to corporate sponsors and TV executives. If anyone has devoted serious thought to finding innovative ways of bringing young people into cricket grounds, then it must be one of those secrets of which the old TCCB was so fond.

The fixtures are either unpopular or, in some cases, too popular to be accessible. "One of the joys of an Oval Test," wrote Terence Rattigan in 1965, "is always the presence in force of the very young." How many young people does anyone suppose will be at the 1997 Oval Test when all the tickets will have been sold six months before the event? Equally, how many will be at the many other games where tickets are available and unwanted? Very little has been done to make grounds welcoming and attractive to the young. The message is merely, "Sit down and shut up."

Of course, the biggest possible fillip English cricket could receive is success. It would be tremendous if, by the time they reach The Oval, England have won, are still contesting or even have not utterly disgraced themselves in the fight for the Ashes. But this will not be enough on its own.

RIP, TCCB

Amid this atmosphere of crisis, the start of 1997 marked the end, after 29 years, of the Test and County Cricket Board and its replacement with something formally called the England and Wales Cricket Board, to be known by the acronym ECB. This in itself is not a promising start for an organisation that is supposedly going to cut through sectional interests and provide a clear path to the future. The "and Wales" appears to be a sop to David Morgan, the Glamorgan chairman, who was one of the key figures in the development of the new Board's structure. Since Mr Morgan is not insisting that the national team be known as "England and Wales" it is hard to see the point of this piece of confusion.

This is detail. People are waiting to see whether the new chairman and chief executive, Lord MacLaurin and Tim Lamb, will give the game clear leadership, and whether the ECB's streamlined policy-making system will prove more responsive than the old, clogged, TCCB methods.

MacLaurin's arrival was well received. He has been a successful chairman of the supermarket group Tesco and, from this summer, will be free to devote himself to cricket. He appears to be a man of sufficient calibre to do the job justice. One sensed some cricket writers thrilling to the idea of someone who might boss everyone about. Dictatorship is always an attractive option at times of crisis. Indeed, Lamb has talked cheerfully about the game being "de-democratised". There is a danger here. Successful businessmen are sometimes thoroughly accustomed to giving orders and getting them obeyed. That is not English cricket's need. It does require clearer leadership and bolder decision-making. But it needs, if anything, to be more democratically accountable – and, above all, transparent – not less.

There is an attractive, but not especially hopeful, idea being floated for a National Cricket Membership Scheme. But cricket needs to involve as members not only the 150,000-plus people who belong to the major clubs, but the hundreds of thousands more who play the game. One of the objects of the ECB is to integrate the amateur and professional sides of cricket. This needs to be done formally, at grassroots level, so that anyone who belongs to a village club has an instant affiliation to their county club – and a stake in what is happening at Lord's.

Above all, what English cricket needs is something that Lord MacLaurin is better qualified than anyone to provide. It needs Tesco-isation. The game needs to become an attractive product sold in an imaginative manner at competitive prices.

"O, these eclipses do portend these divisions"

But, whenever England lose a Test match, and the squealing starts, the demands for change focus narrowly on the structure of the English professional game. A few years ago, four-day cricket was going to be the answer. Now anyone who attempts to argue with the proposition of a two-division Championship is widely presumed to be a nincompoop.

Some people think this could lead to the County Championship becoming as competitive as the FA Premiership, with the big matches being contested before a packed house like Manchester United v Liverpool. It sounds great. But very often the same people insist that the chairman of Test selectors should have the right to pick county sides.

They can't have it both ways. Cricket in England is a long game with a short season. There is, and has to be, a tacit compromise whereby the demands of county cricket are subsidiary to the needs of the national team. Soon England may follow the international pattern and play more home one-day internationals, making current Test players even less available for the counties. Even a two-division season with only eight Championship matches per team is not going to change that reality.

County cricket needs rapid reform: less one-day cricket; the end of the benefit system balanced by far more attractive payments for success; an

Academy (though, preferably, a winter one based somewhere warm rather than one that competes with the counties for talent) to help build what coaches at the Australian original call "a focus on achieving"; a smoother flow of players from lower down the system; and, yes, more combative county matches. I have an instant suggestion for that. The first-class counties should pay a fee of at least £25,000 to enter the Championship. The resulting £450,000 would be distributed to the players, in addition to the sponsors' money, in accordance with their position in the table, right down to second-last place, with huge differences between the pay-outs to the leading counties and the also-rans. That would put a stop to the dead end-of-season matches which cause so much irritation.

But the changes have to be realistic, and the idea that there is any instant cure for England's habit of losing Test matches is nonsense. English cricket's deepest attitudes have to change. It has to make use of all the country's human resources. Britain has 35,000 schools and a hundred universities; cricket seems to work on the principle that the correct figures are a couple of dozen, and two. Above all, it has to be ambitious for itself.

Panic is not the answer. The closure of long-established county cricket clubs – a very possible result of two divisions – is an idea greeted with relish by some reformers. They like to talk about pruning the branches to preserve the main stem. I suspect it's the wrong metaphor. They would be blocking the tributaries, and then the river would dry up.

Alas, poor Raymond

In the face of all this, it hardly matters who moves the pawns on the England chessboard. As I write, the jury remains out on David Lloyd's contribution as coach and the leadership of Atherton, who has drawn close to Peter May's record number of matches as captain without ever inspiring public confidence. Atherton's own heroic batting enabled England to finish their 1996-97 Tests well, with a 2-0 series win over a weak New Zealand and the bonus of an apparently settled side, something that was never allowed to develop when Ray Illingworth was in command. Illingworth's three-year reign as chairman of selectors, and briefer period as all-purpose supremo, will not be remembered kindly. It was sad to watch a man whose career embodied so many of the strengths of English cricket flail around and have his failings exposed so hopelessly in the World Cup. He had no long-term strategy, merely faith in his own instincts. It was not enough. A teacher friend of mine has a motto on his wall from an unknown American educator: "In times of change, learners inherit the earth, while the learned find themselves beautifully equipped to deal with the world which no longer exists." It can serve as Illy's cricketing epitaph.

The out-grounds go out

And so to smaller concerns. One of the minor sadnesses of modern county cricket is the way in which the game is being withdrawn from so many of the out-grounds, and moving closer towards the point when nearly all the matches will be played at the 18 county headquarters. In 1996, most drastically, Yorkshire abolished their traditional fixtures in three of Britain's largest cities – Sheffield, Bradford and Middlesbrough – and one of its liveliest festival grounds, Harrogate. Simultaneously, Somerset made the long-expected decision to abandon the Weston-super-Mare festival. Further retrenchment is expected elsewhere in the years ahead.

Any argument against these changes is usually dismissed as soppy sentimentalism by county officials who like to present themselves as shrewd managers making sensible economic decisions in keeping with cricket's modern needs. The reverse is the case. Of all branches of the game, county cricket is the one that has most dismally failed to market itself – hence its appalling public image.

The festival games have long been the one great exception, the time when county cricket comes alive, and draws in a wider public. In Yorkshire's case, it would have been one thing to get rid of their outposts in the context of a move to a spanking new stadium, which everyone would want to experience. They hope to move to Wakefield by 2000. This may or may not happen; it will be terrific for English cricket if it does. But for the next few seasons they will be playing almost all their cricket at Headingley, which they have effectively condemned. Unless the team is very successful indeed, at least three very downbeat years are in prospect; it is impossible to see how this can work to the advantage of either Yorkshire or cricket – except in the narrow terms of saving small amounts of cash. I hope Lord MacLaurin tells them Tesco did not succeed by closing down shops without opening new ones.

Sorry, Notts and Glos

The Schleswig-Holstein question, Lord Palmerston said, was only understood by three people. One was dead, one was mad and he was the third, and he'd forgotten. The pre-1890 County Championship may well come into the same category. None the less, it has been necessary to investigate it, and to change *Wisden's* position on this matter.

Until 1962 the Almanack carried a traditional list of champions dating back to 1873. The following year my late predecessor, Norman Preston, printed an amended list, starting in 1864, which ended, for instance, the romantic notion that Derbyshire were the 1874 champions. He was influenced by the arguments put forward in the 1959 Almanack by the historian Rowland Bowen and, perhaps, tempted by the thought of listing all the champions from *Wisden's* first year. But all Bowen did was to sift – very conscientiously – the conflicting opinions of various contemporary sources. His champions were not necessarily acknowledged by *Wisden* at the time. It is impossible to come up with a definitive champion until 1890, after the counties' representatives had met and agreed a points system.

Wisden has a historic mission to separate cricketing fact from fiction and opinion, and it seemed to me that we were failing in our duty. We will continue to publish Bowen's champions, but they cannot be equated with the real champions of 1890 onwards.

If county cricket still arouses passions – and I hope it does – I expect to be burned in effigy in Mansfield Woodhouse and Wotton-under-Edge, since the effect is to strip Nottinghamshire of ten outright Championships and five shared ones, and to reduce Gloucestershire to none at all – the county of the Graces joining the disgraces, I am afraid to say. I am sorry if this upsets two historic and congenial cricketing counties, but I can see no honest alternative.

The Young Ones – or not

Sometimes contemporary facts are even more elusive. During the Pakistan tour last summer, the fast bowler Waqar Younis was quoted in *The Sun* as confirming what many people in cricket had long suspected, that he was not born on November 16, 1971, as recorded in *Wisden* and in every other reference book. He said he was two years older than that.

I then approached Waqar for confirmation of *The Sun* story. He did not deny it, but said the date should be left alone, and demanded to know why it mattered. There was no ready answer to that. After all, there is no age limit in Test cricket. He is not cheating anyone; why should it matter? When Waqar signed for Glamorgan, he stuck to the 1971 date on his registration form, so there it must rest.

There are circumstances, however, in which it definitely would matter. In 1996 the first Under-15 World Cup was held in England, and Pakistan reached the final: some journalists wrote about players who performed with "maturity beyond their years". If anyone in this competition had lied about his age, that clearly would be cheating. Later in the year, there was an intriguing development. In October, Hassan Raza, Pakistan's top scorer in the final, was picked for the Test team against Zimbabwe, aged – according to the records – 14 years 227 days, making him the youngest Test player in history.

However, after the game, the Pakistan Cricket Board themselves rejected Raza's age, and announced that a test on his wrist – a "bone-age study" – showed he was 15, which came as a surprise to those of us unaware that the human wrist had the same qualities as the rings of a tree-trunk.

It also came as a surprise to Dr Jamil Mohsin, a radiologist working at the Westchester County Medical Center in Valhalla, New York, who wrote to me – backing his arguments with impressive quotes from Greulich and Pyle's *Radiographic Atlas of Skeletal Development of the Hand and Wrist* (second edition), the *Wisden* of such matters – insisting that this test could never be regarded as exact, and that it was only intended to show whether someone's growth was in accordance with their age, not to prove how old they actually were.

There are rumours that some of the old-time Australian players also liked to knock a year or so off their age, so this problem may not be unique to Pakistan. It certainly looks as though it might take a while to sort this one out. In the meantime, let's just say that Hassan Raza, however old he is, does seem to be an awfully good player – an awfully good, young, player.

What's in an initial?

One of the Cricketers of the Year exactly a hundred years ago was the wicket-keeper Arthur Augustus "Dick" Lilley, "far and away the greatest cricketer Warwickshire has yet produced", as *Wisden* 1897 put it. Throughout a lengthy county and Test career he was always A. A. Lilley. Sometime after his death in 1929, some researcher appears to have discovered that he had an additional middle name of Frederick, and thus the laborious process began of transforming A. A. Lilley into A. F. A. Lilley.

I expect if A. A. Lilley had wanted to be known in cricket scorecards and records as A. F. A. Lilley, then at some point during his 416 first-class matches he might have mentioned it. Perhaps he hated the name Frederick; perhaps he was unaware of it; but he has the right not to have it forced on him just because it is on his birth certificate.

Cricketers are entitled to call themselves whatever they want, provided they do not use a name for fraudulent purposes, and they are certainly entitled to suppress initials they find embarrassing. Lilley is not the only cricketer who has mysteriously acquired extra initials after retirement or death. It will take a while to make the whole of *Wisden* consistent, but I shall do my best to remove them. Posterity ought to remember cricketers under the names they used in their careers, otherwise posterity is going to be mighty confused.

Curiouser and curiouser

Alert readers will have noticed that of late *Wisden* has become assiduous at collecting the ludicrous incidents which attach themselves so much more readily to cricket than to any other game. In 1994 we instituted the Chronicle of each year, and in 1996 the Index of Unusual Occurrences (and may I reiterate my plea, especially to more far-flung readers, for appropriate newspaper cuttings).

It is good to be reassured that this merely reinstates one of the game's richest traditions. Roger Heavens, a Cambridgeshire publisher and enthusiast, has just indexed *Wisden's* honoured ancestor, *Scores and Biographies.* He has included the index compiled in 1885 by A. L. Ford, called simply Curiosities of Cricket.

These included: "ball caught on knife of spectator"; "long-stop padded with sack of straw"; "ball passed through long-stop's coat and killed dog on other side"; "ball rolled one-sixth of mile after delivery"; "batsman batted with two bats, one larger than the other, to play fast bowler"; and "ball never hit during whole of match" (a single-wicket contest).

I believe the 1997 crop of eccentricities is well up to standard: the fielder who returned by bus, the team who played the wrong opposition, the golden retriever elected club vice-president and the British businessman, held hostage in the Colombian jungle, who taught his captors cricket. There's globalisation for you! Unfortunately, the terrorists and his fellow-captives were all very relieved when the bat broke. They much preferred football, apparently. More fool them.

THE WISDEN WORLD CHAMPIONSHIP

By MATTHEW ENGEL

The idea of a World Championship of Test cricket is hardly brand-new. In 1912 the three major playing nations of the time – England, Australia and South Africa – gathered in England for the Triangular Tournament, and played a nine-Test round-robin.

The combination of a very wet summer, a boycott by the leading Australians, and a weak South African team proved disastrous. The 1913 *Wisden* warned the experiment might not be repeated "in this generation". This was optimistic. The number of Test cricketing nations grew, but South Africa's apartheid policies (and such lesser difficulties as the trans-Tasman snobbery that stopped Australia playing New Zealand) meant that only England had a playing relationship with all the teams. And even that ceased with South Africa's exile from the game after 1970.

Thus the idea went to sleep. Cricket had other problems and priorities. The one-day World Cup began in 1975, but for some years the West Indians were so dominant in Test cricket that the question of who might be champions rarely caused much discussion.

In the 1990s the situation changed. The emergence of the new South Africa and the promotion of Zimbabwe brought the number of Test countries to nine. At the same time, West Indies ceased to be cricket's undisputed superpower. When Australia took the Frank Worrell Trophy in May 1995 for the first time in almost two decades, they were widely described as the new world champions. But this judgment was complicated by the steady form of the South Africans, the spasmodic brilliance of Pakistan and India's near-invincibility at home.

Sometimes a Test World Cup was suggested, but the logistics were horrendous: everyone would have to gather in one place for months. It took a while to work round that. But in my Editor's Notes in the 1995 *Wisden*, I suggested an ongoing Championship, using normal Test fixtures. The thought was well-received, but brought forth no official response. Then, in the November 1996 edition of *Wisden Cricket Monthly*, I argued the case in greater detail, calling for minor changes to the international fixture list so that such a Championship could be formally started. Wisden also set up a prototype, unofficial, table using the present incomplete schedule.

On this occasion the timing was right. The United Cricket Board of South Africa formally endorsed the Wisden plan and said it would recommend its adoption at ICC in 1997. Administrators from other countries reacted more guardedly but, in almost every case, sympathetically. There was by now a growing recognition of the need to ensure the safety of traditional cricket in countries where the popularity of the one-day game was in danger of overwhelming it. And respected figures across the cricketing world were coming up with similar thoughts. Clive Lloyd called for a Championship. Sir Richard Hadlee and Ian Chappell independently proposed not dissimilar schemes for what Hadlee called "Supertests", leading to a grand final every four years. The former Australian batsman Ross Edwards suggested a points system involving the top six nations. These ideas have the drawback of requiring substantial reconstruction of the fixture list and, in some cases, are rather complex.

The Wisden Championship has the advantages of simplicity, practicality – and a working model. The proposal is that each country should agree to play the other eight in at least one Test – home and away – every four years, the existing cycle for the traditional confrontations such as England v Australia. A handful of extra Tests would be needed on top of current schedules.

Each "series" of whatever length – counting a one-off game as a series – would be worth the same: two points for winning the series, one for drawing and none for losing. The competition would be continuous, like the world ranking systems in golf and tennis, but every time a series was contested it would replace the corresponding one in the table.

The system used in the prototype Wisden Championship is identical. But since not every country has played everyone else (e.g. Australia and West Indies have yet to play Tests against Zimbabwe), the difference between points gained and series played determines the standings. Series not renewed since 1990 are also excluded; this date will be subject to periodic review.

In January 1997 Australia's success in their home series against West Indies made them undisputed leaders of the Wisden table. This fact was prominently reported not merely in many papers across the cricketing world but at the top of the sports page in the *International Herald Tribune*, which is aimed primarily at expatriate Americans.

This helps back up Wisden's contention that a World Championship offers the chance to ignite interest in Test matches even among non-cricketers. I believe it could secure the future of the traditional game, and offer the authorities and players commercial opportunities beyond the easy pickings of one-day internationals. I hope ICC will take the small steps necessary to make the competition official. It has been a while since 1912. In the meantime, *Wisden* will continue to publish its own Championship table.

THE WISDEN CHAMPIONSHIP TABLE

(as at March 14, 1997)

	Series played	*Points*	*Difference*
1. Australia	14	21	+7
2. South Africa	12	17	+5
3. India	13	17	+4
4. West Indies	11	14	+3
5. Pakistan	12	14	+2
6. Sri Lanka	14	12	−2
7. England	14	11	−3
8. Zimbabwe	10	4	−6
9. New Zealand	16	6	−10

Previous leaders: October 13–December 12, 1996 South Africa; December 12–January 28, 1997 Australia, South Africa and West Indies (joint).

The standings are updated regularly in *Wisden Cricket Monthly*.

ENGLISH CRICKET: A MANIFESTO

By LORD MACLAURIN

Where is cricket going to be in 20 or 30 years? We're under pressure from a host of activities – passive and active. My belief is that the prime task of the new Board is to ensure that, by the time we get to the 2020s, cricket in England and Wales is at least as healthy as it is at the moment. And that it remains the national summer sport.

That may sound unadventurous. Obviously we want to grow, to get more and more people playing and watching the game. But we're in an increasingly competitive market-place – something I've had to cope with in the retail trade – with new leisure activities coming in all the time. Just to stay where we are will be a very sizeable achievement.

How do we ensure that? The main message that Tim Lamb, the new chief executive, and I have been taking to the counties is that the top priority has to be a successful national side. That's the key to our cricket and to our business. I remember when my own son was nine or ten: it is so much easier to capture kids' attention if they've got heroes they can look up to, and try to emulate.

Yet it's been so rare for England to win Test matches that people can almost remember where they were when it happened. We need more results like last year's soccer – England 4 Holland 1 – which will capture the public imagination. Tetley's announcement of their withdrawal from England team sponsorship was depressing. There were all kinds of reasons involving corporate restructuring that were behind that decision, but it can't have been entirely coincidental that England had been so unsuccessful for so long. There are some amber lights flashing over our game, and we have to respond.

In so many ways we have so much going for us. There are as many people playing cricket as have ever played it. Although there is less school cricket, there are now 4,000 clubs with colts' sections. And our finances have never been in better shape. We are a £65 million business, and more than £20 million in Lottery funds have been distributed to the game in one form or another. But to maintain the support of TV, sponsors and the public, the flagship – the England team – has to be successful. People want to be associated with winners.

This doesn't mean the whole of our game is going to be sacrificed on the altar of national success. County cricket is an important, integral part of the game, and of the fabric of the country. So is village cricket. And we wouldn't dream of changing that. But now the whole of cricket is run under one roof, we can give the game a strategic plan and a framework that will move us forward.

Tim Lamb and I are a new team, and we have a blank sheet of paper. We're prepared to talk to the counties about issues that in the past might have been filed under "too hard": the amount of one-day cricket, uncovered wickets, two divisions, anything. Perhaps we will have a more radical agenda than people expect. But, clearly, we've got to get it right at the top level, so all the other levels can thrive.

Lord MacLaurin of Knebworth is chairman of the new England and Wales Cricket Board. He retires this summer as chairman of Tesco.

A WIND BLOWS FROM THE EAST

By MIHIR BOSE

Napoleon's warning that the world should beware when China awakes has, in the last year, been translated into a wholly unexpected warning for the cricket world from another part of Asia – the Indian subcontinent. It has happened, not on the cricket field, but off it. On the field, the subcontinent has been a major power since 1971, when India won back-to-back series away from home in the West Indies and England. Sri Lanka's recent rise has merely confirmed this trend: three of the last four World Cups have been won by the subcontinent.

However, it is the money that the subcontinent can now generate through cricket that is posing a challenge to the established power centres. It is transforming the traditional image of the subcontinent as the land of magical spinners, wristy batsmen and (in Pakistan) devilish fast bowlers, into a place whose rich cricket administrators can dictate the future of the game.

This sounds like a contradiction. With a combined population of well over a billion, South Asia remains one of the poorest regions of the world. But, while much of this population lives just above the poverty line, there is also a well-off nation within the poor one. Six hundred million Indians may not get more than a square meal a day; but India also has 250 million people – almost the population of the United States – with a standard of living not far behind that of the West. Inside the subcontinent's thin man, there is a fat man trying to get out – and desperate to advertise his wealth.

A hint of this had come in 1993 when India, Pakistan and Sri Lanka, after the most fractious meeting ever of the International Cricket Council, won the right to stage the 1996 World Cup. The key to victory was the way the three countries got the ICC's Associate Members – hitherto treated much as the Soviet Union used to treat its eastern European satellites – on their side by promising them £100,000 each. England, who believed they had a gentleman's agreement guaranteeing them the 1996 tournament, had offered £60,000 each, and throughout the meeting seemed to assume this was yet another cosy old boys' gathering. The Asians wheeled in politicians and lawyers and treated the event as if it were an American presidential convention. They outflanked England, and won a rich prize. How rich only became evident when the 1996 World Cup began.

Unlike the Olympic Games, or soccer's World Cup and European Championships, the cricket World Cup is not an event owned by the international authority that runs the game. The country staging it, in effect, owns the competition. In five previous World Cups this had made little difference: the host country had made money, but not so much as to raise eyebrows. The 1996 World Cup changed everything.

As soon as they had won the competition the hosts set about selling it. Their biggest success was auctioning the television rights for a staggering $US14 million, using a hitherto unknown agent of Indian extraction based in the United States, Mark Mascarenhas. The UK rights alone fetched $7.5 million, compared to $1 million in 1992. In addition the tournament was marketed on a scale never before seen in cricket. There was an official sponsor for every conceivable product, including the official World Cup chewing gum.

A few years earlier, the world's most famous soft drink manufacturers had not even been allowed to sell their products in India. Now Coca-Cola and Pepsi-Cola battled it out to be the official drink supplier. Coke won – but they had to pay $3.8 million, more than Benson and Hedges paid the Australians to be the main sponsor of the 1992 World Cup. That role went to Wills, the Indian tobacco offshoot of BAT, who paid $12 million.

The organisers loved the rivalry. They were aware that they could keep all the profits, once they had met their expenses, which included a fee of £250,000 to each of the competing Test countries. This amount did not even cover the expenses of some of the teams, but the hosts pocketed a profit of almost $50 million. Contrast this with the 1996 European Soccer Championship in England: where UEFA, as owners of the championships, made a profit of £69 million, England, the hosts, made a loss of £1.7 million.

It could be argued that the cricket administrators of the rest of the world were naive to agree to such an arrangement. But in five previous World Cups nobody had sought, let alone achieved, such commercial success. Not everyone on the subcontinent foresaw it. The Sri Lankans, co-hosts of the tournament along with India and Pakistan, clearly had doubts: they did not agree to underwrite the costs, so did not participate in any of the profits.

The man who drove the commercial juggernaut was Jagmohan Dalmiya, secretary of the Indian Board. He hails from the Marwari community of India whose business skills are both feared and respected. The joke in India is that a Marwari can do business with a Scotsman and a Jew and still make money. The other joke, less flattering, is that if you should see a Marwari and a tiger together in the jungle, you should shoot the Marwari first. Even within the Indian Board, there are some who are less than enamoured of Dalmiya. He was responsible for the opening ceremony in Calcutta, which was widely regarded as a disaster. But few have ever had doubts about his financial acumen.

Had the subcontinent been content with its World Cup killing, this would have been an interesting marketing story. What has made it an explosive cricketing one is the use the triumphant administrators made of their new-found financial power. They launched a two-pronged attack. The short-term aim was to make Dalmiya chairman of ICC. The long-term aim was to make sure that the subcontinent was at the centre of the cricket world.

The first battle came to a head during the annual ICC meeting at Lord's in July. With Sir Clyde Walcott coming to the end of his term, Dalmiya stood for the chairmanship, along with Malcolm Gray from Australia and Krish Mackerdhuj of South Africa. On the basis of a simple majority, Dalmiya, bolstered by the Associate countries, had the votes. But he did not command the majority of the Test-playing countries. The rules were less than clear, but the Indians, having taken the advice of a QC, contended that the election should be decided by a simple majority. Walcott argued that any successful chairman must have the backing of a two-thirds majority of the Test-playing countries: six out of nine. Underlying this was concern about what a Dalmiya chairmanship might do. Before the meeting, his thoughts on the future development of the game had been extensively

[*Patrick Eagar*

Jagmohan Dalmiya – the most powerful figure in Indian cricket.

quoted in the media. These included a suggestion that Tests should become more like one-day matches, with every innings limited to certain numbers of overs.

The meeting ended in stalemate. Various suggestions to resolve it, including a second term for Walcott or for future chairmen to rotate country-by-country, were left hanging. But as 1996 turned into 1997, intense negotiations suggested a possible compromise framework: a rotating short-term chairmanship (probably starting with Dalmiya), a new, authoritative executive committee, less power for the Associates. In the meantime Walcott carried on. The wider issue remains: how can ICC accommodate the new power? The Asians want to be at the top table. As one administrator put it: ''We do not want to come to Lord's for ICC and just nod our heads like little schoolboys as we used to. Now we come with fully prepared plans and want to be heard as equals.''

It is interesting to note that on this issue the old racial solidarity displayed when ICC tackled apartheid in South Africa no longer holds. In subcontinental eyes the West Indies are part of the old power structure, marshalled by England and Australia. Cricket has evolved no mechanism to cope with a changing situation. In 1974 the world football body FIFA elected the Brazilian, Joao Havelange, as president. He defeated Sir Stanley Rous, the symbol of the old European control, by shrewdly aligning the footballing centres of Latin America with the emerging countries. The Europeans have never been totally reconciled to him, but coexistence has been possible because Europe is still the economic powerhouse of the game. New centres such as Africa have come through and football has flourished.

Cricket has never had to cope with a Havelange. The ICC may no longer be a creature of the MCC, but its offices are still at Lord's. And the two men who have presided over it since the MCC President stopped being automatically head of ICC, Sir Colin Cowdrey and Sir Clyde Walcott, have been old-world figures. In such a setting, Dalmiya is seen as a *parvenu* out to wreck the game. As one (non-Asian) administrator put it: "Dalmiya, personally, may not have been acceptable, and his tactics of trying to storm the citadel were probably wrong. But we have to realise that the subcontinent is a major power in world cricket. The television market there alone makes it very important."

The fear is that if Asia is not kept sweet, it could use its money to seduce Test-playing countries into something like a rival cricket circuit. Here cricket's very structure could be a help. The game is still organised in the 19th century way. Apart from the World Cup every four years, and England's regular series with Australia, there are no fixed dates on the calendar. This means entrepreneurs can, almost at will, construct lucrative cricket tournaments. In 1996 the cricket boards of India and Pakistan, together with Mark McCormack's company TWI, staged five one-day matches in Toronto, the first time official internationals had been played in North America. The enterprise was underpinned by the ability to sell television rights, at $1 million a match, to a satellite company keen to broadcast to the subcontinent.

In May 1997 the Indians are planning to hold a tournament to celebrate 50 years of their independence. Traditionally, the idea of playing in India in May was considered preposterous. But in order to avoid the worst of the intense heat, the Indians intend to start matches at about 3.30 in the afternoon and play until midnight. The Indians can contemplate this because the profits of the World Cup have helped them install lights on most of their grounds. And they know the TV rights will fetch large sums of money. Already, cricket in Sri Lanka from August has cut into the latter half of the northern summer, which used to be the exclusive cricket preserve of England. A tournament in May will be another dent.

The end result could be a far more powerful ICC – more like FIFA or the International Olympic Committee than the present small-scale set-up consisting of David Richards, the chief executive, a couple of assistants and a few phones. The subcontinent may not even want such an outcome: its bid for power should be seen as more akin to the barons at Runnymede extracting concessions from King John. But just as Magna Carta led to consequences undreamt of by the barons, so this could make ICC the real powerhouse of cricket.

But is this what cricket wants, or needs? At present the game has no centralised bureaucracy, no Havelange at its helm. Does it really want to exchange the cosy club – admittedly biased in favour of the older cricketing countries – for an elective dictatorship at the mercy of the richest? In such a situation the subcontinent may even find that it has created an animal it cannot always control.

Mihir Bose writes on sports politics for the Daily Telegraph. *Among his books is* A History of Indian Cricket.

IF YOU CAN MEET WITH TRIUMPH AND DISASTER . . .

PRESS REACTIONS TO THE 1996 WORLD CUP

EAST AFRICAN
Standard
No. 25436, Friday, March 1, 1996
Price: 20/00

A MIRACLE!

By Special Correspondent

THE sports world was last night in total shock as "little" Kenya yesterday humbled the mighty West Indies cricket team in the 1996 World Cup in Pune, India.

Kenya stuns the world

Full report see Page 2
More colour on Back Page

The Barbados
Advocate
Friday, March 1, 1996 • $1.50c

LOTTO
Winning numbers: 1, 8, 13, 26, 31
Free ticket letter: M

WHAT I GONE AND DO?

SHAME!

Kenya rub salt in wide open wounds of West Indies

RANK outsiders Kenya caused the biggest upset in World Cup cricket history when they beat twice former champions West Indies by 73 runs on Thursday.

Highest individual figure

Kenyans will not stop at anything in the sporting arena. That we are record breakers and history makers was repeated on Thursday when our national team caused the greatest upset in World Cup history in beating fancied West Indies . . . the cricket side, besides really doing this nation proud, has proved that determination alongside proper organisation can move mountains, contrary to the age-old excuses of lack of facilities and funds reminiscent of our other sporting organisations.

Leader, *East African Standard*, Nairobi, March 2

The World Cup encounters have brought West Indies cricket to a new low, nothing unusual for Mr [Richie] Richardson. ... Can he not hear those thousands, perhaps millions, of voices screaming in agony at his disastrous leadership and pleading for his removal?

Editorial, *Barbados Advocate*, March 2

Asante sana, Kenya. In Swahili that means "Thank you, Kenya". ... For the past three or four years we have watched with horror, frustration and disbelief as the structure and ethos of West Indian cricket have crumbled before our eyes. ... But it took a team of part-time cricketers from a country where the majority still remains blissfully unaware that there is any such thing as a cricket World Cup to lead us out of the encircling darkness. Now, assuredly, even the blind who have been leading us will be able to see their way clear. It is the door marked "Out".

Oliver Jackman, *Sunday Sun*, Barbados, March 3

England walked to the gallows [against New Zealand] like criminals rather than martyrs. There must be surer heads in inter-school cricket than this bunch of Englishmen.

Indian Express, February 15

END OF THE WORLD FOR PATHETIC ENGLAND

Headline, *Sunday Mirror*, March 10

HAPLESS, HOPELESS, HUMILIATED

Headline, *Independent on Sunday*, March 10

WE MUST GET RID OF LORD'S LOSERS

Headline, *News of the World*, March 10

The England team and the system which produces it is a heavy lorry in the slow lane being passed by a succession of sports cars.

Christopher Martin-Jenkins, *Daily Telegraph*, March 11

There appears to be no spirit of adventure left in English cricket, either on or off the field.

Derek Pringle, *The Independent*, March 11

Winston Jordan, *Sunday Sun*, Barbados, March 3

Annihilation by that mighty cricketing nation Sri Lanka – one of the most predictable results of the World Cup – brought the usual demands for mass sackings, promises of fresh starts and threats of revolution. We have heard them all before – and seen English cricket plod on, blind to the rest of the world, still running and playing the game for the benefit of the pensioners who take their Thermos flasks and Marmite sandwiches to our barren county grounds.

Peter Johnson, *Daily Mail*, March 11

A WAVE OF GRIEF HAS SWEPT THE COUNTRY –
WE HAVE LOST OUR GLOBAL HONOUR

Headline, *Al Akhbar*, Islamabad, March 10

Pakistan cricket fans smashed television sets and one committed suicide amid national gloom over Pakistan's defeat by arch-rivals India in the World Cup quarter-finals. . . . College student Jaffer Khan fired a burst of Kalashnikov bullets into a television screen in the town of Mardan in the North-West Frontier Province. . . . A front-page cartoon in the English-language *Frontier Post* showed freshly dug graves with a sign reading "a plot for each player" – a reference to incentives of land and cash offered by

Prime Minister Benazir Bhutto's husband, Asif Ali Zardari, to Pakistan players if they retained the cup. . . . Several papers said teenaged girls had called their offices in tears. . . . The Urdu-language *Nawa-E-Waqt* quoted a Muslim religious cleric, Maulana Naqahbandi, as blaming the débâcle on what he called Pakistan's "obscene" imitation of Indian culture. He also said Pakistan could not expect to win as long as it was governed by women. "Any nation which made a woman its ruler never prospered," said Naqahbandi, apparently ignoring England's quarter-final humiliation by Sri Lanka, whose President and Prime Minister are both women.

The Hindu, Madras, March 11

The shocking defeat of the Pakistani team dominated the proceedings of the Senate in Islamabad yesterday. Senators cited different factors behind the defeat including gambling, political affiliations and the wrath of the Almighty Allah because of obscenity spread through cultural shows at Pakistan Television.

The Muslim, Islamabad, March 11

Pakistan lost the quarter-final in Bangalore because on that particular day India played better than Pakistan. It is as simple as that.

Mir Jamil-ur-Rahman, *The News*, Lahore, March 16

The usually appreciative Eden Gardens crowd disgraced the country when it went on a rampage as India plunged towards defeat in the World Cup semi-final against Sri Lanka.

The Telegraph, Calcutta, March 14

It is impossible today to be Indian and not be ashamed.

Shekhar Gupta, *Indian Express*, March 14

India has succeeded in establishing the point that it deserves to be excommunicated from the world of cricket. Cricket is civilisation. India, let us have the grace to admit, has yet to attain that level of civility. We are a primitive tribe incapable of accepting the harshness of the world.

Ashok Mitra, *The Telegraph*, Calcutta, March 14

Nearly 50 years after the British Empire has faded into history, people in the subcontinent still say "It's not cricket," meaning something is not fair . . . but in the past month, all across the region, cricket's inherited culture has come under challenge . . . cricket, enveloped in distinctly un-English passions on and off the field, and in playing techniques that resemble baseball more than the traditional cricket game, has changed in ways that the stalwarts of yore would scarcely have recognised – so much so that old-timers might say that cricket itself is "not cricket" any more.

John F. Burns, *New York Times*, March 16

32 Pages

Daily News

The English Daily with the largest circulation in Sri Lanka

AVAILABLE ON THE WORLD WIDE WEB OF THE INTERNET

Late City

VOL. 79 NO. 67 — Established: 3-1-1918 — MONDAY MARCH 18, 1996 — PRICE: Rupees 12.00 — Registered as a Newspaper in Sri Lanka

Aravinda de Silva man-of-the-match

Lanka conquer cricket's Mount Everest

Bash the Aussies by 7 wickets

Congratulations from President

President Chandrika Bandaranaike Kumaratunga in a congratulatory message to the victorious Sri Lankan cricket team on the historic occasion of winning the World Cup said: "Please accept my heartiest congratulations on this great victory which was achieved by overcoming many obstacles. By this victory you have shown the whole world that Sri Lanka possesses a strong and talented team. Although we are a tiny country we have proved to be world beaters and you have brought honour and fame to our country.

Vavuniya public servants get quarters

Sri Lanka, who were given a horror time in Australia during the World Series games, proved that they are the rightful champions and that given neutral umpires they could beat any team in the world.

Elmo Rodrigopulle, *Daily News*, Colombo, March 18

The lions roared in Lahore
And put the kangaroo to flight
This was to be expected
As the latter was always in fright

The fright was evident down under
When the ball tampering story began
And then the false claim for chucking
Against Muttiah Muralitharan . . .

. . . There is a little moral
As I come to the end of my lay
The lion is bold and honourable
Unlike the off-shoots of Botany Bay.

Poem "The Lion Roars" by Premnath Moraes, *Daily News*, Colombo, March 18

Make no mistake, the best team won cricket's World Cup. Beyond question Sri Lanka were the most outstanding team of this tournament. It dared to be different; it dared to be itself.

Greg Baum, *The Age*, Melbourne, March 19

SRI LANKA: YEARS OF PREPARATION . . .

By GERRY VAIDYASEKERA

Nearly fifty years ago, the British ceased to rule Ceylon. They left behind their democratic form of Parliamentary Government, their literature and that lovely summer game of theirs, cricket, for us to cherish and treasure.

When our cold regions were converted into tea estates, several well-known cricketers, including county players and University Blues, came over to work as planters. Naturally, they played among themselves, formed clubs and taught the game to others. The game had been played on the island as early as 1832.

Men like Dr Bailey, Archdeacon of Colombo, introduced cricket at the Colombo Academy, later known as Royal College, over 150 years ago. (His son, George, toured England with the Australian team of 1878.) Royal College produced Dr Churchill Hector Gunasekera, who played regularly for Middlesex after the First World War. Around that time many of our cricketers were studying in England and played in the University Trials. Most failed to win Blues, like our late Prime Minister, Dudley Senanayaka, who played for the Indian Gymkhana Club at Osterley Park against the 1932 All Indian team. The first player who did win a Blue, F. C. de Saram of Oxford in 1934 and 1935, was an old Royalist, as was Gamini Goonesena, who later captained Cambridge.

Between the World Wars, cricket flourished in Colombo's public schools, and the newly formed Ceylon Cricket Association controlled the game. A three-day match was played, usually in August, between the Ceylonese and the Europeans. The Ceylonese won more often than they lost. Fortunately, Ceylon lay on the shipping route between Britain and Australia, and this gave us the golden opportunity of watching world-famed stars in action, if only for a few hours. These "limb looseners" were raised to Test status by our press, and crowds flocked there. Our cricketers deemed it a great honour to play against the greats.

After the Second World War, cricket flourished in the rural schools as well. The Ministry of Sports encouraged this growth. As cricket implements were costly, boys played with tennis balls. But the spirit, rules and the tempo were the same.

The sun has blessed us with cricket during the whole year, and the paddy fields began to echo with shouting when anyone brought out a bat and ball. Then, as TV sets started to disturb the peace of the countryside, cricket became even more popular, pushing soccer into second place. I live close to a High School and, whenever a game was being shown, boys and girls would flock round my set to watch their heroes.

Eventually, the boys demanded to switch from softball cricket to the real game. With the help of two firms from Colombo, we laid down a concrete practice area. The boys were thrilled at wearing pads and gloves for the first time; but they were shy of being hurt by the ball. When coaching them, I was surprised to find them playing graceful strokes, not taught by anyone, but copied from seeing Aravinda de Silva, Sanath Jayasuriya, Arjuna Ranatunga and Roshan Mahanama on the TV screen.

And now Sri Lanka has proved to the cricket world that it is a force to be reckoned with. In this hour of triumph and joy, we remember the English people who taught us the game and the Lankans – then called Ceylonese – who first brought honour to the country and absorbed the lessons that cricket teaches.

In the 1950s, after an election, I called on the defeated Prime Minister, General Sir John Kotelawala, to compliment him on the manner in which he took defeat. I shall never forget his reply. "Gerry," he said, "I HAVE PLAYED CRICKET."

Gerry Vaidyasekera has been Wisden*'s Sri Lanka correspondent since 1966.*

. . . A NIGHT TO REMEMBER

By DAVID HOPPS

Colombo had known much grief in the weeks leading up to the World Cup final. The bomb on January 31 that killed about 90 people had brought terrorism back to the heart of the capital. And it undermined Sri Lanka's hopes that their co-hosting of the tournament would promote tourism and investment, as well as providing funds for an expansion of cricket facilities throughout the country.

Australia, having just been involved in a bitter series against Sri Lanka, had already voiced some reluctance to fulfil their fixtures in the country, on the grounds that some of their players had received hate mail and feared for their safety, for reasons connected with cricket rather than politics. The atrocity in Colombo justified their quick withdrawal. Even the pleas of the Sri Lankan Government, whose array of security measures included an offer to fly the team in from Madras or The Maldives, failed to change their minds.

West Indies soon followed Australia's example, without bothering to consult their players, leaving only two relatively minor sides, Kenya and Zimbabwe, to play fixtures which passed off without incident. That was only some compensation. In the early stages of the tournament, the mood in this most gracious and easy-going of countries was one of demoralisation and betrayal.

The night of March 17 provided handsome recompense. To be on Galle Face Green, a traditional Colombo meeting point overlooking the Indian Ocean, shortly after Sri Lanka's triumph over Australia in the final in Lahore was to witness a joyful outpouring of national pride. With most Sri Lankans preferring to watch the final in small family groups, the capital was eerily deserted for much of the day but, as night fell, the streets abruptly came alive to the blaring of car horns and the explosion of fireworks.

Some people had privately expressed their reluctance to join the Galle Face parade, fearing that there could be no more crushing time for the Tamil Tigers to launch another attack than at the moment of the country's greatest sporting achievement. But many suppressed their fears as tens of thousands streamed along the sea-front in just about every form of transport known to man.

Even in its most harrowing times, Sri Lanka has rung to the sound of laughter and it was impossible to walk a few yards along Galle Face Green without another invitation to join an impromptu street party. The walk back to the hotel as the sun began to rise was made more unsteadily. Whisky and arrack (the local firewater distilled from coconut) flowed, and Bob Marley music blared from the back of cars and open-top trucks, upon which rapturous youngsters danced precariously. Among the most soulful songs was "This Land Belongs to Us", and such lyrics cannot be sung in Sri Lanka without a sense of underlying weariness caused by years of terrorist warfare.

Cricket had always been a unifying force, offering recreation for Sinhalese, Tamil, Moslem and Christian alike. Now it had given the nation a chance to forget. The schools in Colombo had only just reopened after the Tigers' warning to the Government to "build smaller coffins". Now young children wandered freely and ecstatically through the throng.

According to Sri Lankan folklore, Nadiya – the jackal – is despised as the lowest of all animals, because of its willingness to eat the crow, which is regarded as the dustbin of Sri Lanka. Australia's forfeit of their group match in Colombo had caused their High Commissioner to be greeted with the call of Nadiya – "Hu, Hu, Hu" – at the prize-giving ceremony following Sri Lanka's victory against Kenya in Kandy. As televisions focused on a defeated Australian team, the jackal sounded for a final time. It was the response of a country getting even, and relishing every minute of it.

David Hopps is a cricket writer on The Guardian.

THE MAN WHO STOLE THE SHOW

By TONY LEWIS

Harold Dennis Bird, known to the cricket world as Dickie, retired from Test match umpiring in 1996, aged 63. He had completed 23 years at the top and his 66 Tests were a record; he stood in three World Cup finals and 71 one-day internationals. His career coincided with the advent of television coverage of cricket by satellite to many parts of the world; consequently his fame was global. Frank Chester, who umpired in England between 1924 and 1955, was once described as "the most famous of all umpires". There is no doubt that this accolade now belongs to Dickie Bird.

Personal celebrity, however, was never thought to sit easily alongside excellence in a professional cricket umpire, and so Bird's retirement provoked debate. Was he television-made? Was he better known for his eccentric, theatrical behaviour than for his wise judgments? Administrators of the British game used to throw their hands to their faces, hoping to mask the sight of Dickie running to the boundary behind the bowler's arm to deliver loud Yorkshire strictures to someone disturbing the batsman's concentration. Hands on hips, he would address a hospitality box three floors above, informing them that their open glass door was reflecting sunshine into a player's eyes. Everything he said was in the manner of the lugubrious northern over-the-garden-wall comedian. "Shut that door. Shut it. Where d'yer think you are?"

Sometimes he himself seemed to be the interruption. When he prepared to umpire in Sharjah, in the Gulf, for the first time, he was advised not to subject his eyes to the dazzle of the sun which bounced up off the shiny pitch. Instead he was told to look away from the playing surface between balls, and to divert his eyes to the grassy surrounds. So after the first ball from his end, he set off on a crouching, circular walk, like someone searching for a lost contact lens within a 15-yard radius of the stumps, and kept that up all day. Afterwards, he thanked his adviser: "Me eyes were great, they were. Great they were, me eyes." The conclusion was that he was not performing theatricals but that it was "just Dickie".

In Frank Chester's day, umpires were seen but rarely heard. They had been brought up as players on ground staffs in counties captained by amateurs but heavily influenced by the senior professional. There was hierarchy and discipline, and so the control they exerted as umpires was by the odd word to the captain or senior pro – and perhaps only a whisper: "Have a word with your fast bowler. He's pushing his luck with that appealing."

Chester virtually created the modern profession of umpiring by his serious approach to the smallest detail. After him, Syd Buller was outstanding: massively unobtrusive, entirely dependable. His decisions were quick and clean. Players were happy with his judgments; even if they had not been, no one would have dared leave the field with a shaking head. Charlie Elliott, another protector of the spirit of cricket, was often Buller's companion in Tests, and also operated without fuss or palaver. And so it

[*Neale Andrew*

[*Adrian Murrell/Allsport*

Dickie Bird (*left*), as captured in bronze by sculptor Neale Andrew, son of former England wicket-keeper Keith, and (*right*) in one of the poses cricket lovers will remember.

must have been a fascinating umpires' room at Headingley in England's Third Test against New Zealand in 1973 when Elliott, of the old school, welcomed Dickie Bird to Test cricket.

"I have never seen anyone so nervous in my life," Elliott recalled. "I thought he would never make it to the middle let alone give good decisions. Then I saw something which was a clue to his future reputation. He gave Ray Illingworth out lbw. The bowler was the New Zealand seamer Bruce Taylor and he was bowling round the wicket. I thought from square leg – 'How can that be out? A seamer bowling right-arm round the wicket?' But I saw it later on television and I liked what I saw. Dickie was absolutely correct: the ball had moved back into Illingworth from the line of off stump. It was a top-class instant decision."

There are not many secret corners to Dickie Bird's life; he has written autobiographies and has been the subject of many written and broadcast profiles. Son of a Barnsley miner, still cared for by his sister; nervous, dithery off the field, highly strung. A former Leicestershire team-mate of his, Ray Julian, remembers how Bird needed help to strap on his pads and put his sausage-fingered gloves on the right hands before walking out to bat. "And not a lot has changed when we share an umpires' dressing-room now." Julian, like Charlie Elliott, talks of a different Dickie once he is crouched behind the stumps.

There is no doubt that his failure to become an established county cricketer heightened his appreciation of being an umpire. But it was the cricket he did play – from 1956 to 1959 with Yorkshire, from 1960 to 1964 with Leicestershire – that helped him become such an outstanding umpire. So has it been with most first-class umpires in England. Bird carried over from his playing days a strong sympathy for the legion of cricketers who plied their daily trade. He cared for professional standards.

Everyone agrees that he has been a very good umpire for a long time. It is the other little choices he has always found so difficult. But there is a special relationship between Bird and other umpires. His colleagues have been willing to take over when Bird's nerves are twanging at the thought of making tricky decisions about bad light or resuming play after rain. Where Dickie has been unique is in his rapport with players, and with the crowds watching at the ground or on television. The message emanating from Bird's whole being is his complete understanding of the spirit of the game, and his ability to preserve sporting play. Charlie Elliott agrees that international umpiring is more difficult these days. There is far more shouting, far more concerted appealing; as fielders, protected by helmets and padding, have moved in closer to the bat, the appeals for catches off bat and pad are now acted out in order to deceive the umpire. This is cheating.

If there was similar trouble in the old days, Buller or Elliott or Harry Baldwin would simply address the captain and tell him to control his players; the captain, after all, is responsible for preserving the spirit of the game. Bird, however, was able to chide individuals who specialised in sledging opponents and cursing umpires. He had their respect. Merv Hughes, Dennis Lillee and Javed Miandad, who were all verbally bellicose, accepted that he could laugh with them and yet caution them. They knew Dickie Bird put cricket above his own life.

As he leaves the Test match scene, the job has become more and more burdensome. Decisions made by humans in white coats are checked endlessly against technology on television and they are sometimes proved wrong. The use of a third umpire to pass judgment may bring about correct decisions but it undermines the authority of the umpire in the middle and erodes his confidence.

We are left looking back at the Dickie Bird phenomenon. His huge appeal was based on his personal vulnerability. He was a magnet for minor disasters. But the watching world was affectionate; old ladies wanted to mother him. Here was a real character, fun to observe in days when the cricketers themselves had become anonymous under helmets and behind visors. In a busy main street in Colombo he once got out of a car on the wrong side and found himself in the middle of hooting Ambassador cars, fast bicycles, slow ox-carts, and listing Leyland buses, all bearing down on him. Suddenly everyone stopped. They began pointing and shouting: "Mr Dickie Bird." He played to the crowd and gave them his funny hunched run to safety, repeating louder than any of them, "Mr Dickie Bird. Mr Dickie Bird."

His final exit at Lord's, 1996, was incredible. He was given a Hollywood-style reception which has never been afforded to any player, let alone an umpire. Don Bradman and Viv Richards were applauded to the crease when they played their last innings in England, and The Don was given three cheers. Umpire Bird walked out of the Long Room and the whole of Lord's stood and applauded. Even more, the players of the England and India sides were out on the grass to form a corridor of appreciation. Frank Chester would not have recognised the scene nor, I guess, would he and his contemporaries have approved the elevation of an umpire so far above the real craftsmen who bat, bowl and field.

But if you wanted the essence of Dickie Bird encapsulated in a few minutes, you could have seen it that day. One moment he was dabbing at his tears with a handkerchief; then at the fifth ball of the match he gave a rock-solid decision for lbw against Mike Atherton, the England captain. It is probably true that Dickie was a natural character who became a conscious character. But he never allowed anything to stand in the way of the fair conduct of the game. This is why he retained the trust of the players and stayed at the top so long.

Tony Lewis captained Glamorgan and England. He is a journalist and broadcaster.

A SPIN-DOCTOR WRITES

By ASHLEY MALLETT

The genius of Shane Warne has led to a surge of interest in spin bowling. Warne keeps his method simple – walk-up start, eyes focused, wrist cocked and an enormous surge of power through the crease. Until he came along, many feared wrist-spin was a lost art, gone the way of the dinosaurs, who vanished years ago when Planet Earth failed to duck a cosmic bumper.

Yet, at the same time, finger-spinners have been finding it harder than ever to take wickets. People advance all kinds of reasons for this, like heavy bats. I don't believe this. A heavier bat might mean bigger sixes and harder-hit boundaries, but it also means more mis-hits and edges that carry into fielders' hands. Any off-spinner worth his salt would love to bowl to batsmen like Graeme Hick and Robin Smith – and Mark Taylor and Steve Waugh. But the modern generation of finger-spinners is simply inadequate.

Spin bowling lost favour in the early 1970s. John Snow won the Ashes for England, led by Ray Illingworth, in 1970-71 and pace dominated the epic series of 1972. Illingworth was a masterful captain. He used Snow brilliantly and had Derek Underwood to tie down one end. On a rain-affected wicket, Underwood lived up to his nickname of "Deadly". But on a flat wicket, which was more normal in Test cricket, he kept things tight as a drum. And Illingworth's use of him greatly influenced other captains round the world: a barrage of pace with a slowie to keep up an end was the less than subtle trend. A spinner was let loose in attack only on a spinning minefield.

Then, after West Indies were crushed 5-1 by the Australian pacemen in 1975-76, things moved a stage further when Clive Lloyd developed his strategy of using four fast bowlers in a system of constant quality pace, with rest periods built in for the bowlers, but no respite for the batsmen. Applied to the letter, the plan allowed for each bowler to deliver 18 six-ball overs.

Spinners could not be part of such a scheme. Even outside West Indies, Test spinners soon became support staff, useful for keeping things tight while the quicks were rotated at the other end. I have first-hand experience of this. In 23 Tests from 1968 to 1975 I took 100 wickets, yet only 32 in 15 from 1975 to 1980. When they were given the odd chance, spinners suffered by bowling to wicket-keepers picked primarily for their ability to bat: batting line-ups had to be bolstered to withstand the pace barrage. To retain a Test place (outside India) in the mid-1970s, slow men usually had to double as batsmen, or field like Trojans, or both. A mind-set was established. Emerging spinners were urged to "keep it tight", a trend increased by the growth of one-day cricket.

Most of the spinners who emerged in this climate were "rollers" who gave the ball a gentle release rather than a real tweak. They would turn the ball adequately on the soft pitches of England or New Zealand, or the flat plasticine wickets of Sydney grade cricket, but in Adelaide or Perth the ball would go through cannonball straight.

But what that meant was a generation of top batsmen who did not know how to confront great spin when it arrived. It took an unusual piece of cricket to prove the rule. In 1988-89 Allan Border took 11 for 96 at Sydney. It was, admittedly, a poor track, but if a roller like Border, who would never get wickets on a true surface, could do that, it told us that batsmanship against spin had sunk to the depths.

Then came Warne. He bowled the leg-break with over-spin, the flipper and the top-spinner; he did not need to bowl the wrong 'un too often. Instead of the googly against the left-hander beating the bat by a fair margin, his top-spinner took the edge. Smart. Above all, he was accurate. During the bleak years for spin, the idea was that finger-spinners were more accurate and could be trusted. Turn to history and you will find that many of the most accurate bowlers of all time were leg-spinners: Grimmett, Wright, O'Reilly, Barnes, Gupte, Benaud, Kumble, Warne.

The wrist-spinner can sometimes get away with a shortish delivery, anyway, because of the work he achieves on the ball, given that he is using a combination of fingers, wrist and arm. The ball bounces high and often tucks the batsman up. The delivery might cost him one run whereas an orthodox spinner's short one would not usually have steepling bounce and would get the full treatment. And when the ball is wet, the wrist-spinner has a decided advantage. Offies hold the ball very tightly, with fingers widely spaced across the seam; that makes purchase very difficult.

Warne has also re-asserted mastery in the air. During the 1960-61 West Indies v Australia series, Garry Sobers and Norman O'Neill often blocked half-volleys from the spinners, then launched into stinging drives against seemingly identical deliveries. I thought they were merely resting: block one, belt one. But in 1967 I found myself in Clarrie Grimmett's back garden in Adelaide. He was 75, I was 22. After I bowled two balls at him and he middled them both, he called down the pitch: "Son, give up bowling and become a batsman. I could play you blindfolded!" Then he talked good sense about flight.

Grimmett knew how easily a batsman could read the exact spot a flat-trajectory ball would pitch as soon as it left the hand. If he is looking down on the ball, he holds all the aces, like a fighter pilot diving out of the sun on his prey. I realised that O'Neill and Sobers were blocking only the balls that had genuinely beaten them in flight. Such balls are spun hard, dipping acutely from above eye-level.

This is the lesson. A spinner must try to make things happen, not merely bowl accurately and wait for the batsman to make a mistake. In this sense, there is no difference between finger-spin and wrist-spin. Many people believe that one is easy and the other difficult. But the off-break with maximum spin is just as hard to bowl with control as a leg-break – and it takes greater toll on the fingers. Men like Lance Gibbs and Jim Laker had huge calluses. Warne's problems have been with ligaments; he does not appear to damage his skin so much. The philosophies are the same. It just happens that right now there are more good leg-spinners than finger-spinners.

They need not despair. Their turn will come, and when the right bowler emerges he will find modern batsmen ripe for the plucking. But the bowlers need to learn to attack and contain simultaneously; and their coaches need to get out of the belief that the two types of spin are so different that the coaching of them has to be segregated. The principles are the same. And the real secret of both is flair.

Ashley Mallett is director of Spin Australia, which encourages and promotes the art of spin bowling. He played 38 Tests for Australia as an off-spinner.

FIFTY SHEFFIELD SHIELD YEARS

By DAVID FRITH and PHILIP BAILEY

It has been called the toughest domestic cricket competition in the world, a claim that defies serious argument even nowadays, when current Test players appear only rarely. You have to look at the players on the fringe of the Australian side who move into the English game, and compare the way they prosper with the struggles of some of the West Indians. Sheffield Shield runs and wickets have often been harder to secure than certain Test match runs and wickets. Australians who prosper in the Shield are clearly made of the right stuff.

All along, Shield matches have demanded penetrative bowling. They have been played over four days since 1930-31 (originally, they were timeless). They are usually played on well-prepared pitches, nearly always on Test grounds; and they involve batsmen who get comparatively few innings (compared to their English county counterparts, who constantly fight fatigue and staleness) and will therefore not easily be shifted. The outstanding feats of the past fifty years make dazzling reading, even compared to the golden batting age pre-war when Bradman and co. beat the life out of cricket balls.

David Hookes towers from the peaceful Adelaide Oval with the fastest century (34 balls), a triple-century in a stand of 462 (with Wayne Phillips) and four centuries in two matches within 11 days. The Waugh brothers beat that stand by putting on 464 for New South Wales, finishing extraordinarily fresh as their captain declared. Barry Richards scored 356 for South Australia against a Western Australia attack that included Lillee, McKenzie and Lock, after missing the first ball of the day and causing Rod Marsh to stage-whisper, "I thought this bloke was supposed to be able to play a bit?"

But in many ways the stars of the Shield have been those who have rarely or never made it into the Test team. Indeed, there have been batsmen as good as Ray Flockton, who emerged from 12th man duty with the New South Wales team of 1959-60 to make an unbeaten 264 against South Australia. There was Les Favell, who captained South Australia with the same panache that Stuart Surridge brought to leading Surrey. And there are modern players like the Queenslander Trevor Barsby and the South Australian captain Jamie Siddons, who would walk into most national teams.

Philip Bailey's survey of the first fifty seasons since the war, 1946-47 to 1995-96, shows that New South Wales are the champions of the post-war Sheffield Shield. But this does not tell the whole story. New South Wales dominated the first two decades after the war, when Keith Miller led his adopted state like some Douglas Fairbanks in flannels, and began a run of nine successive Shields from 1953-54 to 1961-62.

New South Wales won almost half their matches (71 out of 146) in those first twenty years, but since the mid-1960s Western Australia have been the dominant team in the Shield. They were not even in the competition until 1947-48 when they took part on a restricted basis, won two of their first four matches and took the Shield at their first attempt.

Before the war the combination of tyrannical distance and an absence of star players meant the West did not take part in the Shield. And after their initial triumph, they often struggled until Tony Lock's drive and two generations of great players turned them into the most feared team in the country. Though Western Australia is more than ten times the size of Britain, most of the players come from the small area round Perth, comparable to Barbados as a fertile patch of cricketing talent.

There is a special fighting spirit in the West that goes beyond cricket. But perhaps it was more significant that the Perth pitch has long been so fast it has intimidated many players from the eastern states.

Victoria, the most traditionally minded of states, have shunned imports and succeeded patchily. South Australia – the state that had Garry Sobers as well as Ian Chappell – have made major contributions to the history of the Shield, and won it seven times in the fifty years, without ever retaining it.

Queensland tried year after year to buy the extra talent that would win them the Shield, until weight of expectation became their greatest problem. Finally, under Stuart Law's captaincy, they broke through in 1994-95, 68 years after their first attempt. Tasmania, since they joined in 1977-78, have been the Durham of this competition. They had a heady few seasons under Jack Simmons's leadership and Queensland's success has encouraged them. But the axiom that one star will never be enough holds true, especially when that star – David Boon – has usually been unavailable.

Despite all the quality, and the intense competitiveness of the play, the crowds are seldom much more than enough to cover the gatemen's wages, though the institution of the final from 1982-83 has created an upturn in interest. As elsewhere, the revenue from one-day cricket has covered the costs of staging the domestic first-class competition. Only the most fervent limited-overs fan would begrudge this. It is the very making of the Test team, which has hardly ever been out of the top three in the world. – D.F.

SHEFFIELD SHIELD 1946-47–1995-96

		P	*W*	*L*	*D*	*T*	*% W*	*Shields*
1	New South Wales	427	163	107	156	1	38.17	20
2	Western Australia	394	131	112	151	0	33.24	13
3	Victoria	421	131	104	185	1	31.11	9
4	Queensland	426	114	133	178	1	26.76	1
5	South Australia	422	111	156	154	1	26.30	7
6	Tasmania	166	22	60	84	0	13.25	0
		2,256	672	672	908	4	29.78	50

YEARS OF THE FOX

By MARTIN JOHNSON

Homespun, unfashionable, unglamorous, prosaic . . . all these descriptions were applied to Leicestershire in 1996, and when the County Championship went to Grace Road, it was greeted with the kind of embarrassed silence associated with a rag-and-bone man's horse winning the Derby. In fact, if they ever built a ring road next to Leicestershire's ground, they would probably have to call it the Charisma By-Pass.

Not that there were ever many traffic jams when Leicestershire were playing. They won the Championship by using only 13 players all season, and were roared on towards the coveted pennant by much the same number of spectators. Not the least of Leicestershire's achievements was in clinching the title against Middlesex at home in their final game, when they faced the unfamiliar pressure of performing in front of an audience which almost qualified as a crowd.

It was a long way removed from Leicestershire's only previous Championship, in 1975, even though there were parallels involved, such as having a Yorkshireman as captain and losing only once, to Surrey at The Oval. However, if James Whitaker became known for orchestrating the mid-pitch "huddle", the only time Raymond Illingworth was ever likely to call for a huddle was when a bit of loose change dropped out of his trouser pocket.

Under Illingworth, the 1975 side was as close to glamorous as Leicestershire have ever got. Apart from Illy, they had players of the stature of Ken Higgs, Graham McKenzie, Brian Davison, Roger Tolchard, and the embryonic David Gower. There were times in those days when getting around the ground was harder work than elbowing your way through Marks and Spencer on Christmas Eve, whereas the average 1996 spectator required a loud-hailer to converse with his neighbour. This had more than a little to do with the side being all but ignored by the local evening newspaper, for whom sport appeared to begin and end at Filbert Street. A booking for Leicester City's No. 5 would be greeted with the largest headline available, while a double-century for Vince Wells could just about be located with the aid of a magnifying glass.

There was a different atmosphere in 1975, when no home match was complete without a local character nicknamed The Foghorn, who would announce his impending presence from the front door of his house a couple of hundred yards away. "I'm on me way!" he'd bellow, at about five past eleven, and would regularly circumnavigate the ground clutching (or to be more accurate, spilling) a pint of mild, yelling: "Get Birky on!" He knew full well, of course, that Jack Birkenshaw, the present manager, would be bowling only if Illy had first ascertained that the pitch was in no danger of taking spin.

Those were the days when Leicestershire not only had crowds, but sponsored marquees on the outfield. Illy protested on a daily basis that "t'bloody tents" were compromising the long boundaries he demanded for a team that had no less than five decent spin bowlers, and, on one memorable occasion when a down-the-order slogger had launched him into a plate of salmon mousse, Illy stalked up to the committee balcony and launched into a five-minute, finger-wagging tirade.

They were also the days, long gone now, one imagines, when players used to combine two professional sports. Graham Cross was Leicester City's centre half as well as a county player, and when Leicestershire won the Championship in their final match at Chesterfield, Chris Balderstone interrupted an innings of 51 not out at close of play, dashed up the M1 to play soccer for Doncaster Rovers, and returned to complete his century the following morning.

After Illingworth left in 1978, Leicestershire had their moments, but made more headlines for the number of players heading for the exit gate than for their exploits on the field. Nick Cook, Phillip DeFreitas, Chris Lewis, Peter Such and, finally, David Gower, all left for various reasons, and Leicestershire slipped back into their previous existence as a team with no stars. The structure known as The Meet, a sort of cross between an aircraft hangar and a farmer's barn, symbolised a kind of cobwebbed decrepitude, where a handful of elderly punters peered through opaque windows, swapping stories about the good old days.

It was this general perception of a run-down club that masked a succession of highly respectable seasons in the early nineties, and presumably persuaded some bookmakers to quote them at 40 to 1 for the 1996 Championship. Even when they began the season well, and remained at or near the top of the table as it went on, the general belief was that they would eventually slide away into mid-table anonymity.

Their failure to do so had a lot to do with the newly elected captain. Admirable cricketer though Nigel Briers, Whitaker's predecessor, had been, he was a more naturally cautious leader than the gung-ho Whitaker, who, as a youngster in his first season, had greeted the first three deliveries that Ian Botham had ever sent down to him with thundering off-drives for four. Leicestershire are known as the Fox County, and if Briers and Whitaker had both belonged to the Quorn Hunt, Whitaker would have been out front with the bugle, while Briers would have been more practically engaged at the back, collecting fertiliser for the roses.

Whitaker had taken inspiration from the idiosyncratic methods employed to such good effect by Dermot Reeve at Warwickshire, and also concluded (partly as a slightly nervous newcomer to captaincy) that team spirit would best be fostered by democracy rather than dictatorship. This led to the famous "huddle", as Leicestershire plotted their tactics for the next man in. Quite how and when the huddle first started, even Whitaker is not sure, though he thought it might have been against Yorkshire. "They were top of the table at the time, but we posted a massive first-innings total and then started running through them. Everyone was on such a high that suddenly we all had our arms around one another, and would start talking about how to bowl at the next man in."

There were times, Whitaker admits, when the conversation ran along more traditional lines, such as: "Where shall we go for dinner tonight?" or "Have you seen that girl in front of the pavilion?" But mostly, he said, it was about tactics. "It was never planned, it just happened. I like to think it reflected the way we all played for one another, and how everyone was made to feel that their input was important."

Whitaker also backed his admiration for Vince Wells – an apparently workaday cricketer transferred from Kent as someone who could bowl a bit, bat a bit, and keep wicket a bit – by promoting him to open the batting. Wells then proceeded to make two double-centuries and a 197 in the space of six weeks. David Millns and Alan Mullally formed a formidable new-ball partnership. Meanwhile, Gordon Parsons, whose one-time belief that he was at least 40 m.p.h. quicker than Jeff Thomson was rarely shaken, even when he had to wait for the ball to be thrown back by a pedestrian from the adjacent Milligan Road, had developed into a cagey, and highly effective, medium-pacer. However, the individual who most of all turned Leicestershire from an averagely decent side into a title-winning one was, according to Whitaker, the West Indian Phil Simmons. He made runs, took a lot of wickets with his deceptive pace, and had flypaper hands in the slips, but it was his infectious enthusiasm and tactical input that made him so valuable.

Birkenshaw reckoned that the 1996 side would have been more than decent opposition for the one he played for in 1975; as someone who watched them both, I would take minor issue with that. However, I would not quibble with his contention that the 1996 model was out in front in terms of team spirit.

As for Whitaker, he missed the boat as a Test player after winning his one and only cap in Australia on Mike Gatting's 1986-87 Ashes tour. But he now regards himself as a cricketer fulfilled. "If I had to point to one single factor for our success," he said, "it would be enthusiasm. At the start of the season we sat down and asked ourselves why we were all playing professional cricket, and the answer was obvious. To enjoy it. Once you've focused in on that, the game doesn't seem half so difficult."

In 1975, Martin Johnson was cricket correspondent of the Leicester Mercury. *He is now a sports feature writer on the* Daily Telegraph.

FIVE CRICKETERS OF THE YEAR

SANATH JAYASURIYA

Great players invariably possess an individuality that imprints itself forever on the memory: the ethereal grace of David Gower's strokeplay, the brightly scrubbed, soap-opera fantasy of Australia's leg-spinner, Shane Warne, or the brooding and intelligent menace of the West Indian fast bowler, Malcolm Marshall. Techniques might be largely unchanging, or at least evolve only slowly, but those who scale the heights do so in a distinctive manner that forever sets them apart.

Sanath Jayasuriya cannot yet be classified as a great player, which makes his influence in 1996 all the more remarkable. His World Cup exploits in an unexpected Sri Lankan triumph did not just assure him of a lasting place in the game's history, but promised – indeed, for a few heady weeks, insisted – that the course of the game would change forever. Few of The Greats have ever achieved that.

It is a mark of cricket's changing emphasis that Jayasuriya is celebrated not for years of consistent achievement in five-day Tests, but for a brief outpouring of intemperate strokeplay in a one-day tournament in the emotive atmosphere of the subcontinent. Traditionalists may be wary of the accolade. But all those who witnessed Jayasuriya's audacious attacking batsmanship – most particularly against India, in a group match in Delhi, and England, in the quarter-final in Faisalabad – gaped in admiration.

This was combustible strokeplay that challenged our assumptions. Steady starts . . . playing yourself in . . . wickets in hand . . . such tenets had been adapted, for sure, to the demands of one-day cricket, but never so freely abandoned. Jayasuriya's method of playing himself in seemed to consist of taking three steps down the pitch and carving the ball high over cover. He was batting as if in a baseball diamond, entirely overtaken by attacking intent. The defensive policy adopted by England's openers, Geoff Boycott and Mike Brearley, in the second World Cup final at Lord's in 1979 seemed the stuff of a different age.

It was the introduction of artificial attacking fields for the first 15 overs of a one-day international, combined with reliable batting surfaces, that provided the conditions for Jayasuriya to flourish. The term "pinch-hitter" was stolen from baseball to define an opening batsman specifically given the licence to adopt a high-risk approach in the opening overs. The very word caused some offence, but no one summoned up a more vivid description. And while other countries, notably England, viewed the new tactics suspiciously or half-heartedly, no batsmen accepted their roles with more alacrity than Jayasuriya and his opening partner, Romesh Kaluwitharana.

Their joyous, uninhibited style brought starts in the first 15 overs of 90 against Zimbabwe, 117 against India (42 in the first three overs), 123 against Kenya and 121 against England. Sri Lanka were merely tapping their inclinations. As their captain, Arjuna Ranatunga, said: "They are playing their natural game. They can hit over the in-field, so we get the maximum out of them." It was Jayasuriya who was by far the classier and more successful of the two. England attempted to quell him by opening with Richard Illingworth's left-arm spin, but Illingworth was struck out of the attack within two overs as Jayasuriya breezed to 82 in 44 balls. Even after the World Cup, he was not spent, recording the fastest one-day international century, from 48 balls, and then the fastest fifty, from 17, both against Pakistan at Singapore's Padang ground in April. Pakistan did gain rich recompense six months later, however, when Shahid Afridi hit Jayasuriya for 41 in two overs on his way to an even faster 37-ball hundred in Nairobi. One-day cricket recognises few barriers.

SANATH TERAN JAYASURIYA was born on June 30, 1969, in Matara, a fishing town which rests at the end of Sri Lanka's south-west coast railway, 100 miles from the capital, Colombo. Renowned for its local delicacy of curd and treacle, only in the last decade has it begun to make a consistent contribution to Sri Lankan cricket as the game has expanded beyond the traditional base provided by the leading Colombo colleges. His cricketing pedigree was scant: his father, Dunstan, who worked for Matara Council as a sanitary supervisor, had no active involvement in the game, and his brother, Chandana, abandoned it as a teenager to work in the council's fisheries department. St Servatius College in Matara, where Jayasuriya studied from the age of nine, also had a limited cricketing background, but the enthusiasm of the college's principal, G. L. Galappathie, and his first coach, Lionel Wagasinghe, ensured that his talents flourished.

In the late 1980s, Sri Lanka was in the grip of civil unrest. The government had invited Indian peace-keeping forces on to the island to try to suppress the terrorist activities of the LTTE, the Tamil Tigers, and that fuelled a further backlash from nationalist groups. Cricket tours to the island were being cancelled. It was no time to be considering an international sporting career, but in such pressing circumstances the Sri Lankan cricket authorities stalled a mass overseas migration of their top players by establishing the first-class game more firmly.

Jayasuriya, at 19, was the discovery of the first season of the new system, 1988-89. He hit successive double-centuries, in Lahore and Karachi, on a B tour of Pakistan; a Test debut followed in Hamilton on Sri Lanka's 1990-91 tour of New Zealand; and, at Lord's the following summer, he registered his first, typically enterprising, Test half-century. It was against Australia at the Adelaide Oval in 1995-96 that his maiden Test hundred finally followed, the ground's short square boundaries encouraging the jubilant square-of-the-wicket shots that have become his hallmark.

Jayasuriya's Test record remains modest, if improving. After Sri Lanka's series with Zimbabwe in September 1996, he had 830 runs in 19 Tests at an average of 34.58. Allied to that, he is a useful left-arm spinner and excellent close catcher. He has already played more than 100 one-day internationals, although only comparatively recently has he been freed from the frustrations of the lower middle order.

However unexpected his World Cup exploits were, he is no overnight sensation. Rather more, this is the story of a man who persevered in the face of considerable hardships and, when success finally came, enthralled millions. – DAVID HOPPS.

MUSHTAQ AHMED

By taking 45 wickets in six Tests for Pakistan between November 1995 and August 1996 Mushtaq Ahmed confirmed his status as the final member – alongside Shane Warne and Anil Kumble – of a glittering triumvirate of wrist-spinners who adorn the modern game. Mushtaq is the most enchanting of the lot.

Warne's success stems from prodigious spin and accuracy, Kumble's from prodigious bounce and accuracy; like superbly schooled sheepdogs, both pen batsmen down before picking them off with clinical ruthlessness. Mushtaq prefers to lure batsmen to their end in the traditional manner. He is the arch-deceiver, possessing every nefarious variation in the wrist-spinner's armoury. Unlike the others, he has a googly which is indecipherable to most international batsmen. His instincts are to outwit opponents rather than wear them down.

He is the most impetuous of the trio, which is often betrayed by the frenzied nature of his appealing. He cannot hide his exasperation when a batsman thrusts his front leg down the pitch in the pretence of playing a shot without being penalised by umpires, who are often equally bamboozled by his spin. "Sometimes," he says, "I tell the umpire a straight one is coming, so watch out" – a ploy that has yet to meet with conspicuous success. He has usually been the most expensive of the three in his headlong pursuit of wickets rather than maidens. Indeed, at Brisbane in November 1995, this profligacy led to his omission from the Test team.

Sometimes his variations were too pronounced and too frequent. When he was at Somerset in 1995, many opponents, following the advice of Martin Crowe, started to play him as an off-spinner because he impatiently bowled so many googlies. For a while his county colleagues nicknamed him "Tauseef" after the Pakistani off-spinner of the 1980s. In Australia he talked to Warne, more about the mental approach to wrist-spinning than the mechanics. Warne stressed the benefits of restricting batsmen and of preying on their frustration. Mushtaq took note.

Recalled for the two Tests in Hobart and Sydney, he gathered 18 wickets; there were ten more at Christchurch against New Zealand. But his maturity was confirmed in the three-Test series against England in the summer of 1996. He spun Pakistan to victory on the final afternoons at Lord's and The Oval. His innate competitiveness was now allied to patience, and this became clear to all at Lord's. Having bowled 48 overs since taking a wicket in England's first innings, he suddenly mesmerised the batsmen, conjuring figures of five for 11 from 57 balls between lunch and tea.

On the last day at The Oval, he bowled 30 overs unchanged from the Vauxhall End to take six for 67, which he regards as his finest Test spell yet. He recognised that Mike Atherton was the key English batsman, and on both final days he dismissed him when bowling – Warne-style – from around the wicket. Once Atherton was gone, the rest of the English order was nonplussed as Mushtaq whirled out an assortment of unrecognisable deliveries. In the glow of victory, his grateful captain, Wasim Akram, proclaimed that Mushtaq was better than Warne.

His conversations with Warne had been productive, but his first role model was inevitably Abdul Qadir, Pakistan's impish leg-spinner of the 1980s. As a nine-year-old in Sahiwal, where MUSHTAQ AHMED was born on June 28, 1970, he would bounce up to the wicket aping Qadir and he soon discovered that he could torment much larger schoolfriends with his looping, teasing tweakers. He first haunted English batsmen at the age of 17 during the notorious 1987-88 tour by Mike Gatting's side, taking six for 81 for the Punjab Chief Minister's XI in his home town.

In January 1990, he flew out to Australia to replace Abdul Qadir and made his Test debut in Adelaide. However, his first international excursion was notable for the wrong reasons; in the next match, a state game in Melbourne, he was warned for running on the pitch by umpire Robin Bailhache, who eventually instructed the captain for the day, Ramiz Raja, to remove Mushtaq from the attack. The Pakistan team refused to accept this ruling and walked off the ground; play could be resumed only after an uneasy compromise had been hatched. The 1992 World Cup in Australia and New Zealand prompted happier memories. Pakistan won the tournament and Mushtaq's bag of 16 wickets was a vital contribution. In the final against England he took three crucial wickets – Hick, who was completely baffled by that googly, Gooch and Reeve. Curiously, at this stage of his career Mushtaq, despite being a wrist-spinner, was more effective – and more secure – in Pakistan's one-day team.

During the victorious 1992 tour of England, during which he captured 15 Test wickets, he was signed up by Somerset. He quickly proved to be an inspired recruit. In two and a half seasons he took 217 Championship wickets. He became as popular as any of his illustrious predecessors at Taunton – in the dressing-room, the committee rooms, the kitchens and the members' stand. Cricket chairman Brian Rose recalls: "The whole process of signing him took five minutes – he was so keen to come. He has been the model overseas player; he wins matches for the club and adds members." At Taunton, he is happy to bowl all day and he usually does; in the absence of Waqar Younis he is even allowed the luxury of bowling at the tail.

But a 40-over spell from Mushtaq is never dull; every over is an adventure. One of his ambitions is to take 100 wickets in a season for Somerset – his best haul so far is 92. He is also the most entertaining of tailenders, who once won a Test with his bat, when he added 57 with Inzamam-ul-Haq for the last wicket to defeat Australia in Karachi in 1994-95. His batting, like his motoring, should be keenly observed; it is erratic and potentially destructive. – VIC MARKS.

SAEED ANWAR

If the most handsome batting of the English summer came from Sachin Tendulkar, the most beautiful innings was surely Saeed Anwar's century at The Oval. After he had scored 74 and 88 in the opening Test at Lord's, England conceived the policy of bowling wide of the left-hander's off stump, to tempt him into impetuosities in the gully area, and it worked on the uneven pitch at Headingley. At The Oval, Anwar moved his front foot and head well across, then his wrists hovered, hawk-like, over the advancing ball, extending further and further as if they were elastic if the ball was slanted ever more away from him, before the bat flowed into a square-drive to the boundary.

England's strategy sped him to his highest Test score of 176. The same line in the one-day international series, to a 6-3 field, did not keep him quiet either: in his three innings he scored 151 runs off 159 balls, his timing rising above a paceless Old Trafford pitch when his equally belligerent partner Aamir Sohail could not get the ball off the patchy square. More conventional bowling methods at the start of the tour were to little avail: he made 219 not out against Glamorgan on his debut here and two more hundreds in his next three first-class games. Although his experience of cricket in England had been limited to a couple of league games in Bristol in 1992, his predisposition to front-foot play enabled him to finish with 1,224 runs at 68.00 to top the Pakistanis' first-class tour averages. His brilliance, and the capable young understudy Shadab Kabir, minimised the effects of the wrist injury to Sohail; and on a personal level he demonstrated, once and for all, that he was not merely a one-day batsman.

SAEED ANWAR was born in Karachi on September 6, 1968, and came close to never playing cricket at all. In 1973 his father, an engineer, moved to a job in Teheran, and his family stayed there with him until the beginnings of pre-revolutionary turmoil drove them away in 1977. In that time the boy's only sport was football. When his father took his next job in Saudi Arabia, Anwar returned to Karachi to live with his grandparents.

His father was a talented club cricketer when business allowed. Aged 45, he played in a club match with his son and straight-drove a ball which, his son says, "almost cleared two grounds". Anwar thinks he may have inherited some of his wrist-power from his father. He developed it by playing squash (daily) and table tennis; he became a slow left-arm bowler too; and, above all, he practised batting in the garage of his Karachi home. The bowler was not his much younger brother, Javed Anwar, who has played for Lahore Under-19, but often Rashid Latif, Pakistan's future wicket-keeper, who lived nearby. His reflexes were heightened by batting against a tennis ball covered in tape and bowled from 14 or 15 yards.

Anwar attended Malir Cantonment College and progressed into the Malir Gymkhana team during his first year at N. E. D. University in Karachi. Starting his club career as a spinner and No. 9 batsman, he soon moved up to the middle order where his capacity for strokeplay found expression on pitches of matting laid over cement that were "quick but straight". He graduated in computer systems engineering and would probably have joined numerous university classmates in going to the United States to do a Masters in networking or systems analysis, but for his cricket.

His rapid run-scoring led to selection against the touring Australians in 1988-89 at Peshawar for the NWFP Governor's XI: batting at No. 5 Anwar does not seem to have been overawed as he scored his 127 from 156 balls. He was chosen for the short tour of Australia and New Zealand a few months later and he did make his debut in one-day internationals, but was

i

THE WORLD TURNED UPSIDE DOWN (1)

[*Patrick Eagar*

Father Time is temporarily removed from Lord's before the demolition of the old Grand Stand.

THE YOUNG ONES

[*Patrick Eagar*

[*Empics*

Hassan Raza batting in the World Under-15 final at Lord's. In October he made his Test debut for Pakistan, but the Pakistani board cast doubt on initial reports that he was still only 14. Liam Botham (*right*) outshone even his own father, Ian, by taking five for 67 on his first-class debut for Hampshire against Middlesex. But he later announced that he would concentrate on playing rugby.

THE WORLD TURNED UPSIDE DOWN (2)

[*Ross Kinnaird/Allsport*

Arjuna Ranatunga and Asanka Gurusinha celebrate with the trophy in Lahore after Sri Lanka astonished cricket by winning the World Cup.

DOUBLE HUDDLE

[*Ross Kinnaird/Allsport*

As the Leicestershire players celebrate another wicket on their way to the Championship and go into their traditional huddle, umpires Peter Willey and Barrie Leadbeater do their own version.

SMASHING SHOT

[*John Kelland*

The winning picture in the Veuve Clicquot Champagne Moment photograph of the season competition. "Smiling through" – Neil Garland of Armoury finds humour in adversity in the Bristol and District League Division III. His team had just been dismissed for 43.

A GAME OF PAD AND BALL

[*Frank Coppi*

Dermot Reeve of Warwickshire jettisons his bat while facing the Hampshire slow left-armer Rajesh Maru, bowling into the rough at Edgbaston. Reeve played this non-shot 15 times and MCC later advised that it could be construed as obstruction.

LARGER THAN LIFE

[*Philip Brown*

Neil Williams of Essex bowls at Edgbaston with a giant advert for Texaco behind him.

FIVE CRICKETERS OF THE YEAR

[*Chris Turvey*

SANATH JAYASURIYA

FIVE CRICKETERS OF THE YEAR

[*Graham Morris*

MUSHTAQ AHMED

FIVE CRICKETERS OF THE YEAR

[*Patrick Eagar*

SAEED ANWAR

FIVE CRICKETERS OF THE YEAR

[*Graham Morris*

PHIL SIMMONS

FIVE CRICKETERS OF THE YEAR

[*Adrian Murrell/Allsport*

SACHIN TENDULKAR

sent home after one first-class game in Australia as Pakistan needed an opener. He was back on the Test tour of Australia a year later. There was little opportunity in the middle order, but when he was promoted to open halfway through the World Series, he scored 126 off only 99 balls against Sri Lanka. His one-day career was launched.

His beginning in Test matches was stickier: against West Indies at Faisalabad in 1990-91, he bagged a pair as an opener, but it was Curtly Ambrose and Ian Bishop who dismissed him and he can laugh about it in retrospect. The one-day runs continued in profusion, but further Test opportunities did not arise, and the "one-day batsman" label applied by Pakistan's press and public stuck ever more tightly. It was with some relief that in February 1994, in his third Test, he scored 169 against New Zealand at Wellington. "It was the most thrilling time of my life. I was really happy to have proved all those people wrong."

His tour captain last summer, Wasim Akram, thought that marriage also had a hand in Anwar's maturing as a Test cricketer. He was married in March 1996 to a cousin and doctor, Lubna, who had nursed him through the attack of what might have been malaria or typhoid that led him to miss most of 1995. He was cured only just in time for the last World Cup. It all came together in England last summer, and the only disappointment – other than for England's bowlers – was that a three-Test series was too short for a full appreciation of Test cricket's new delight. – SCYLD BERRY.

PHIL SIMMONS

There has never been a shortage of talented cricketers at Leicestershire. Any number of them have been and gone over the last 20 years or so. Often they have chosen to go because of the alarming absence of team spirit. Therefore it came as no surprise to the Grace Road faithful when they tuned in to BBC Radio Leicester last spring to hear James Whitaker, Leicestershire's new captain, refer to his team-mate, Phil Simmons, as "an absolute prick".

One could almost hear the collective groan echoing throughout the hunting county as the members shrugged their shoulders and contemplated another season of unfulfilled potential. Little did they know that Leicestershire would win English cricket's most coveted prize, the County Championship, for only the second time in their 117-year history. Whitaker, in fact, had been widely misheard and his actual phrase – "an absolute brick" – turned out to be uncannily accurate. Simmons was the cornerstone upon whom Leicestershire built their success.

PHILIP VERANT SIMMONS was born on April 18, 1963, in Arima, Trinidad. His first home was 16 miles from Port-of-Spain, just two houses away from Larry Gomes, the former West Indies batsman. At school, Simmons was an enthusiastic participant in all sports, but at cricket he was outstanding. Soon he was playing regional cricket for East Zone and it was the arrival there of Rohan Kanhai as coach which fuelled Simmons's ambition to follow the career of another early role model, Harold Joseph, and represent Trinidad & Tobago.

That dream was realised in 1983, the year after he had toured England with West Indies Under-19. Five years later, in 1988, he returned to England with the full West Indies team under Viv Richards's captaincy. Gordon Greenidge and Desmond Haynes were established as the leading opening partnership in the world. Greenidge was Simmons's hero: "Everyone loved Viv but I admired Gordon for his technique, his aggression and his positive outlook."

Simmons would probably not have got many chances on that tour anyway. As it turned out, he only played one first-class match, against Gloucestershire. It very nearly proved to be his last ever.

"It was one of those typical English days," he recalls. "It started off bright and sunny but then got progressively darker and the umpires eventually offered us the light. I wanted some practice, so I turned it down. But a couple of balls later it got totally dark. I just saw the bowler, David Lawrence, go up. I never saw the ball come out of his hand."

That hostile delivery struck Simmons on the head. He was rushed to hospital, and his heart stopped for a short while; after he was revived, an emergency operation was carried out to relieve pressure from around his brain. "I thank God that I was so close to Frenchay Hospital in Bristol because it is one of the leading hospitals in Europe for head injuries. I still keep in touch with the surgeon who saved my life, Nigel Rawlinson. He has become a good friend."

Simmons's confidence remained unshaken, and he returned to England in 1991 for what turned out to be his greatest disappointment. Opening the innings in all five Tests, he barely averaged 18, and after his first-ball dismissal in the second innings at Headingley when, with his team desperately in need of a solid start, he dragged on a wide, short ball from DeFreitas, some West Indian onlookers were prompted to doubt his international future. Though he scored a Test century, in defeat, at Melbourne at the end of 1992, his place in the West Indies team was never secure, and he began to look towards county cricket.

His first season with Leicestershire in 1994 began amazingly with a double-century on his debut against Northamptonshire, but that was the only time he was to reach three figures. Again, he fell short of expectations. Having failed to make the West Indies touring party of England in 1995 (although he scored two centuries in his three innings as a late replacement), he returned to Leicestershire in the spring of 1996 with a point to prove. This time, he achieved his aim spectacularly.

Four Championship centuries and the small matter of 56 wickets at an average of 18.23 tell their own tale, but do not quite express how much his presence meant to his team-mates. He batted with something like the disdain of Greenidge himself. He had developed his upper-body strength, which transformed a former medium-paced trundler into a bowler capable of delivering at genuine pace. His six for 14 against hapless Durham, in the penultimate match of the season, was vital in settling the Championship. His unbeaten 142 against Middlesex in the final match made certain.

As the crowd gathered beneath the players' balcony and the singing began, one name was almost immediately chanted in unison. "Simmo! Simmo!" Reluctantly, it seemed, the giant figure stepped forward. Having carefully poured a generous measure of champagne into the Championship trophy, Simmons tilted his head back and, to the biggest cheer of the day, quaffed the lot. While the debate about the value of overseas players in county cricket continues to rage, do not expect to receive a rational answer from Grace Road. The Leicestershire public love the genial character who has helped to put their county back on the cricketing map. – JONATHAN AGNEW.

SACHIN TENDULKAR

It was one brief moment in time. The World Cup, India versus West Indies in Gwalior, and a single stroke of such exquisiteness that the old maharajah surely would have had it carved in ivory and placed on a plinth. In essence, it was no more than a leg-side flick to the boundary and, in a competition that gorged itself on hitting, might have been worth only transient acclaim. But this was a gem: a length ball from a high-class pace bowler met initially with a straight blade, and then, at the last nanosecond, turned away with a roll of the wrist and such an irresistible alliance of power, timing and placement that first of all it eluded the fingertips of a mid-wicket fielder diving to his right, and then it did the same to the boundary runner haring and plunging to his left. Skill, technique, confidence, awareness, vision: pure genius, and four more runs to Sachin Tendulkar.

The young man is probably the most famous and feted man in India, outglitzing even the stars of Bollywood movies. With endorsements over the next five years estimated to be worth at least $US75 million, he is also the highest earner in cricket. He has become public property in a country of enthusiasms that can spill over into the fanatical, but has managed to maintain a dignified, mature outlook, remaining aware of his responsibilities while protecting his privacy. When he married Anjali, a doctor and friend from his childhood, he rejected massive sums from satellite TV for live coverage, keeping the ceremony a family affair. He knows his worth, and is wealthy beyond the dreams of almost a billion Indians, but he is not a grabber. His father, a university professor, imparted a sense of perspective and a work ethic.

Tendulkar averages over 50 in Tests and is the supreme right-hander, if not quite the finest batsman, on the planet. He is a focused technician, who offers a counterpoint to Brian Lara's more eye-catching destruction, fuelled on flair and ego. He has, it seems, been around for ever. In the Third Test at Trent Bridge last summer, he scored 177, the tenth century of his Test career and his second of the series: yet remarkably, at 23, Tendulkar was younger than any member of the England team, with only Dominic Cork and Min Patel born even in the same decade. His figures have been achieved despite a lack of Test cricket, particularly at home. Seven of his centuries had been scored before his 21st birthday, a unique record. Had India not rationalised their Test match programme so much that, prior to last summer, they had played just one three-match series, heavily affected by rain, against New Zealand, in the previous 18 months, there is no telling what he might already have achieved. With time on his side and a return to a full Test programme, he could prove Sunil Gavaskar right and rewrite the records.

SACHIN RAMESH TENDULKAR was born in Bombay on April 24, 1973, and, since childhood, has trodden a steady, almost inevitable, path to greatness. He attended the city's Sharadashram Vidyamandir school, where the Harris Memorial Challenge Shield, a competition for Under-17s, provided the chance to bat for hours. From the age of 12, when he scored his first century for the school and came to notice as a special talent, he indulged himself. When 14, he compiled not out scores of 207, 329 and 346 in the space of five innings, one of them contributing to an unbroken partnership of 664 with Vinod Kambli, a record in any form of cricket.

He was 16 years and 205 days old when he made his Test debut, in November 1989, in the National Stadium in Karachi – for a young Indian, perhaps the most fiery baptism of all. The following year, at Old Trafford, he hit his first Test century – not a scintillating innings, but an exercise in technique, concentration and application beyond his tender years, which saved a game that might have been lost. Had it come 31 days earlier, he would have been the youngest century-maker in Test history. During the winter of 1991-92, he went to Australia, where they still talk in awe of the centuries he scored in Sydney and in Perth.

A few days after his 19th birthday, Tendulkar came back to England: to Yorkshire, no less, as the county's first overseas player. It would have been a massive responsibility for anyone, let alone a teenager from India, and it did not quite work. Tendulkar assumed the mantle conscientiously, and posed with cloth cap and pint of bitter, impressing colleagues and supporters alike with his understanding of public relations. But, in the end, he failed to come to terms with the county game, scoring only one century and barely scraping past 1,000 runs in his only season. Hindsight would tell him that it was part of his education, but a mistake none the less.

In 1996 he returned to England, a teenage prodigy no longer, but a seasoned Test batsman fit to stand alongside his first hero, Gavaskar. The pair have much in common: Gavaskar was slight of build and, of necessity, a supreme judge of length. Tendulkar, too, is short. There is a lot of bottom hand, but he drives strongly, on the rise, such is his strength of wrist and the control in his hands, while he is devastating off his legs, pulls well and – given good bounce – can cut wide bowling to ribbons. If the delicate and unexpected talents of Sourav Ganguly provided a distraction last season, then Tendulkar's two hundreds in three Tests were ample demonstration of the team's premier batsman leading from the front. The first of them – at Edgbaston, where he made 122 out of 219 – was a stunning display of virtuosity in adversity.

In August, aged 23, Tendulkar succeeded Mohammad Azharuddin as captain of his country. Had he craved it and pursued it with a passion, he would surely have got the job earlier, perhaps even while a teenager. Rather, it was a position that was being held in abeyance until the time was right. His leadership has a firm base of experience to it now. His first Test in charge was against Australia. He made ten and nought but India won, just as one almost assumed they would. Some things just seem part of a wider plan. – MIKE SELVEY.

PART TWO: THE PLAYERS

TEST CRICKETERS

FULL LIST FROM 1877 TO AUGUST 26, 1996

These lists have been compiled on a home and abroad basis, appearances abroad being printed in *italics*.

Abbreviations. E: England. A: Australia. SA: South Africa. WI: West Indies. NZ: New Zealand. In: India. P: Pakistan. SL: Sri Lanka. Z: Zimbabwe.

All appearances are placed in this order of seniority. Hence, any England cricketer playing against Australia in England has that achievement recorded first and the remainder of his appearances at home (if any) set down before passing to matches abroad. The figures immediately following each name represent the total number of appearances in *all* Tests.

No Tests from the 1996-97 season have been included.

Where the season embraces two different years, the first year is given; i.e. 1876 indicates 1876-77.

ENGLAND

Number of Test cricketers: 582

Abel, R. 13: v A 1888 (3) 1896 (3) 1902 (2); *v A 1891 (3); v SA 1888 (2)*
Absolom, C. A. 1: *v A 1878*
Agnew, J. P. 3: v A 1985 (1); v WI 1984 (1); v SL 1984 (1)
Allen, D. A. 39: v A 1961 (4) 1964 (1); v SA 1960 (2); v WI 1963 (2) 1966 (1); v P 1962 (4); *v A 1962 (1) 1965 (4); v SA 1964 (4); v WI 1959 (5); v NZ 1965 (3); v In 1961 (5); v P 1961 (3)*
Allen, G. O. B. 25: v A 1930 (1) 1934 (2); v WI 1933 (1); v NZ 1931 (3); v In 1936 (3); *v A 1932 (5) 1936 (5); v WI 1947 (3); v NZ 1932 (2)*
Allom, M. J. C. 5: *v SA 1930 (1); v NZ 1929 (4)*
Allott, P. J. W. 13: v A 1981 (1) 1985 (4); v WI 1984 (3); v In 1982 (2); v SL 1984 (1); *v In 1981 (1); v SL 1981 (1)*
Ames, L. E. G. 47: v A 1934 (5) 1938 (2); v SA 1929 (1) 1935 (4); v WI 1933 (3); v NZ 1931 (3) 1937 (3); v In 1932 (1); *v A 1932 (5) 1936 (5); v SA 1938 (5); v WI 1929 (4) 1934 (4); v NZ 1932 (2)*
Amiss, D. L. 50: v A 1968 (1) 1975 (2) 1977 (2); v WI 1966 (1) 1973 (3) 1976 (1); v NZ 1973 (3); v In 1967 (2) 1971 (1) 1974 (3); v P 1967 (1) 1971 (3) 1974 (3); *v A 1974 (5) 1976 (1); v WI 1973 (5); v NZ 1974 (2); v In 1972 (3) 1976 (5); v P 1972 (3)*
Andrew, K. V. 2: v WI 1963 (1); *v A 1954 (1)*
Appleyard, R. 9: v A 1956 (1); v SA 1955 (1); v P 1954 (1); *v A 1954 (4); v NZ 1954 (2)*
Archer, A. G. 1: *v SA 1898*
Armitage, T. 2: *v A 1876 (2)*
Arnold, E. G. 10: v A 1905 (4); v SA 1907 (2); *v A 1903 (4)*
Arnold, G. G. 34: v A 1972 (3) 1975 (1); v WI 1973 (3); v NZ 1969 (1) 1973 (3); v In 1974 (2); v P 1967 (2) 1974 (3); *v A 1974 (4); v WI 1973 (3); v NZ 1974 (2); v In 1972 (4); v P 1972 (3)*
Arnold, J. 1: v NZ 1931
Astill, W. E. 9: *v SA 1927 (5); v WI 1929 (4)*
Atherton, M. A. 62: v A 1989 (2) 1993 (6); v SA 1994 (3); v WI 1991 (5) 1995 (6); v NZ 1990 (3) 1994 (3); v In 1990 (3) 1996 (3); v P 1992 (3) 1996 (3); *v A 1990 (5) 1994 (5); v SA 1995 (5); v WI 1993 (5); v In 1992 (1); v SL 1992 (1)*
Athey, C. W. J. 23: v A 1980 (1); v WI 1988 (1); v NZ 1986 (3); v In 1986 (2); v P 1987 (4); *v A 1986 (5) 1987 (1); v WI 1980 (2); v NZ 1987 (1); v P 1987 (3)*
Attewell, W. 10: v A 1890 (1); *v A 1884 (5) 1887 (1) 1891 (3)*

Bailey, R. J. 4: v WI 1988 (1); *v WI 1989 (3)*
Bailey, T. E. 61: v A 1953 (5) 1956 (4); v SA 1951 (2) 1955 (5); v WI 1950 (2) 1957 (4); v NZ 1949 (4) 1958 (4); v P 1954 (3); *v A 1950 (4) 1954 (5) 1958 (5); v SA 1956 (5); v WI 1953 (5); v NZ 1950 (2) 1954 (2)*

Bairstow, D. L. 4: v A 1980 (1); v WI 1980 (1); v In 1979 (1); *v WI 1980 (1)*
Bakewell, A. H. 6: v SA 1935 (2); v WI 1933 (1); v NZ 1931 (2); *v In 1933 (1)*
Balderstone, J. C. 2: v WI 1976 (2)
Barber, R. W. 28: v A 1964 (1) 1968 (1); v SA 1960 (1) 1965 (3); v WI 1966 (2); v NZ 1965 (3); *v A 1965 (5); v SA 1964 (4); v In 1961 (5); v P 1961 (3)*
Barber, W. 2: v SA 1935 (2)
Barlow, G. D. 3: v A 1977 (1); *v In 1976 (2)*
Barlow, R. G. 17: v A 1882 (1) 1884 (3) 1886 (3); *v A 1881 (4) 1882 (4) 1886 (2)*
Barnes, S. F. 27: v A 1902 (1) 1909 (3) 1912 (3); v SA 1912 (3); *v A 1901 (3) 1907 (5) 1911 (5); v SA 1913 (4)*
Barnes, W. 21: v A 1880 (1) 1882 (1) 1884 (2) 1886 (2) 1888 (3) 1890 (2); *v A 1882 (4) 1884 (5) 1886 (1)*
Barnett, C. J. 20: v A 1938 (3) 1948 (1); v SA 1947 (3); v WI 1933 (1); v NZ 1937 (3); v In 1936 (1); *v A 1936 (5); v In 1933 (3)*
Barnett, K. J. 4: v A 1989 (3); v SL 1988 (1)
Barratt, F. 5: v SA 1929 (1); *v NZ 1929 (4)*
Barrington, K. F. 82: v A 1961 (5) 1964 (5) 1968 (3); v SA 1955 (2) 1960 (4) 1965 (3); v WI 1963 (5) 1966 (2); v NZ 1965 (2); v In 1959 (5) 1967 (3); v P 1962 (4) 1967 (3); *v A 1962 (5) 1965 (5); v SA 1964 (5); v WI 1959 (5) 1967 (5); v NZ 1962 (3); v In 1961 (5) 1963 (1); v P 1961 (2)*
Barton, V. A. 1: *v SA 1891*
Bates, W. 15: *v A 1881 (4) 1882 (4) 1884 (5) 1886 (2)*
Bean, G. 3: *v A 1891 (3)*
Bedser, A. V. 51: v A 1948 (5) 1953 (5); v SA 1947 (2) 1951 (5) 1955 (1); v WI 1950 (3); v NZ 1949 (2); v In 1946 (3) 1952 (4); v P 1954 (2); *v A 1946 (5) 1950 (5) 1954 (1); v SA 1948 (5); v NZ 1946 (1) 1950 (2)*
Benjamin, J. E. 1: v SA 1994
Benson, M. R. 1: v In 1986
Berry, R. 2: v WI 1950 (2)
Bicknell, M. P. 2: v A 1993 (2)
Binks, J. G. 2: *v In 1963 (2)*
Bird, M. C. 10: *v SA 1909 (5) 1913 (5)*
Birkenshaw, J. 5: *v WI 1973 (2); v In 1972 (2); v P 1972 (1)*
Blakey, R. J. 2: *v In 1992 (2)*
Bligh, Hon. I. F. W. 4: *v A 1882 (4)*
Blythe, C. 19: v A 1905 (1) 1909 (2); v SA 1907 (3); *v A 1901 (5) 1907 (1); v SA 1905 (5) 1909 (2)*
Board, J. H. 6: *v SA 1898 (2) 1905 (4)*
Bolus, J. B. 7: v WI 1963 (2); *v In 1963 (5)*
Booth, M. W. 2: *v SA 1913 (2)*
Bosanquet, B. J. T. 7: v A 1905 (3); *v A 1903 (4)*
Botham, I. T. 102: v A 1977 (2) 1980 (1) 1981 (6) 1985 (6) 1989 (3); v WI 1980 (5) 1984 (5) 1991 (1); v NZ 1978 (3) 1983 (4) 1986 (1); v In 1979 (4) 1982 (3); v P 1978 (3) 1982 (3) 1987 (5) 1992 (2); v SL 1984 (1) 1991 (1); *v A 1978 (6) 1979 (3) 1982 (5) 1986 (4); v WI 1980 (4) 1985 (5); v NZ 1977 (3) 1983 (3) 1991 (1); v In 1979 (1) 1981 (6); v P 1983 (1); v SL 1981 (1)*
Bowden, M. P. 2: *v SA 1888 (2)*
Bowes, W. E. 15: v A 1934 (3) 1938 (2); v SA 1935 (4); v WI 1939 (2); v In 1932 (1) 1946 (1); *v A 1932 (1); v NZ 1932 (1)*
Bowley, E. H. 5: v SA 1929 (2); *v NZ 1929 (3)*
Boycott, G. 108: v A 1964 (4) 1968 (3) 1972 (2) 1977 (3) 1980 (1) 1981 (6); v SA 1965 (2); v WI 1966 (4) 1969 (3) 1973 (3) 1980 (5); v NZ 1965 (2) 1969 (3) 1973 (3) 1978 (2); v In 1967 (2) 1971 (1) 1974 (1) 1979 (4); v P 1967 (1) 1971 (2); *v A 1965 (5) 1970 (5) 1978 (6) 1979 (3); v SA 1964 (5); v WI 1967 (5) 1973 (5) 1980 (4); v NZ 1965 (2) 1977 (3); v In 1979 (1) 1981 (4); v P 1977 (3)*
Bradley, W. M. 2: v A 1899 (2)
Braund, L. C. 23: v A 1902 (5); v SA 1907 (3); *v A 1901 (5) 1903 (5) 1907 (5)*
Brearley, J. M. 39: v A 1977 (5) 1981 (4); v WI 1976 (2); v NZ 1978 (3); v In 1979 (4); v P 1978 (3); *v A 1976 (1) 1978 (6) 1979 (3); v In 1976 (5) 1979 (1); v P 1977 (2)*
Brearley, W. 4: v A 1905 (2) 1909 (1); v SA 1912 (1)
Brennan, D. V. 2: v SA 1951 (2)
Briggs, John 33: v A 1886 (3) 1888 (3) 1893 (2) 1896 (1) 1899 (1); *v A 1884 (5) 1886 (2) 1887 (1) 1891 (3) 1894 (5) 1897 (5); v SA 1888 (2)*
Broad, B. C. 25: v A 1989 (2); v WI 1984 (4) 1988 (2); v P 1987 (4); v SL 1984 (1); *v A 1986 (5) 1987 (1); v NZ 1987 (3); v P 1987 (3)*
Brockwell, W. 7: v A 1893 (1) 1899 (1); *v A 1894 (5)*

Bromley-Davenport, H. R. 4: *v SA 1895 (3) 1898 (1)*
Brookes, D. 1: *v WI 1947*
Brown, A. 2: *v In 1961 (1); v P 1961 (1)*
Brown, D. J. 26: v A 1968 (4); v SA 1965 (2); v WI 1966 (1) 1969 (3); v NZ 1969 (1); v In 1967 (2): *v A 1965 (4); v WI 1967 (4); v NZ 1965 (2); v P 1968 (3)*
Brown, F. R. 22: v A 1953 (1); v SA 1951 (5); v WI 1950 (1); v NZ 1931 (2) 1937 (1) 1949 (2); v In 1932 (1); *v A 1950 (5); v NZ 1932 (2) 1950 (2)*
Brown, G. 7: v A 1921 (3); *v SA 1922 (4)*
Brown, J. T. 8: v A 1896 (2) 1899 (1); *v A 1894 (5)*
Brown, S. J. E. 1: v P 1996
Buckenham, C. P. 4: *v SA 1909 (4)*
Butcher, A. R. 1: v In 1979
Butcher, R. O. 3: *v WI 1980 (3)*
Butler, H. J. 2: v SA 1947 (1); *v WI 1947 (1)*
Butt, H. R. 3: *v SA 1895 (3)*

Caddick, A. R. 9: v A 1993 (4); v P 1996 (1); *v WI 1993 (4)*
Calthorpe, Hon. F. S. G. 4: *v WI 1929 (4)*
Capel, D. J. 15: v A 1989 (1); v WI 1988 (2); v P 1987 (1); *v A 1987 (1); v WI 1989 (4); v NZ 1987 (3); v P 1987 (3)*
Carr, A. W. 11: v A 1926 (4); v SA 1929 (2); *v SA 1922 (5)*
Carr, D. B. 2: *v In 1951 (2)*
Carr, D. W. 1: v A 1909
Cartwright, T. W. 5: v A 1964 (2); v SA 1965 (1); v NZ 1965 (1); *v SA 1964 (1)*
Chapman, A. P. F. 26: v A 1926 (4) 1930 (4); v SA 1924 (2); v WI 1928 (3); *v A 1924 (4) 1928 (4); v SA 1930 (5)*
Charlwood, H. R. J. 2: *v A 1876 (2)*
Chatterton, W. 1: *v SA 1891*
Childs, J. H. 2: v WI 1988 (2)
Christopherson, S. 1: v A 1884
Clark, E. W. 8: v A 1934 (2); v SA 1929 (1); v WI 1933 (2); *v In 1933 (3)*
Clay, J. C. 1: v SA 1935
Close, D. B. 22: v A 1961 (1); v SA 1955 (1); v WI 1957 (2) 1963 (5) 1966 (1) 1976 (3); v NZ 1949 (1); v In 1959 (1) 1967 (3); v P 1967 (3); *v A 1950 (1)*
Coldwell, L. J. 7: v A 1964 (2); v P 1962 (2); *v A 1962 (2); v NZ 1962 (1)*
Compton, D. C. S. 78: v A 1938 (4) 1948 (5) 1953 (5) 1956 (1); v SA 1947 (5) 1951 (4) 1955 (5); v WI 1939 (3) 1950 (1); v NZ 1937 (1) 1949 (4); v In 1946 (3) 1952 (2); v P 1954 (4); *v A 1946 (5) 1950 (4) 1954 (4); v SA 1948 (5) 1956 (5); v WI 1953 (5); v NZ 1946 (1) 1950 (2)*
Cook, C. 1: v SA 1947
Cook, G. 7: v In 1982 (3); *v A 1982 (3); v SL 1981 (1)*
Cook, N. G. B. 15: v A 1989 (3); v WI 1984 (3); v NZ 1983 (2); *v NZ 1983 (1); v P 1983 (3) 1987 (3)*
Cope, G. A. 3: *v P 1977 (3)*
Copson, W. H. 3: v SA 1947 (1); v WI 1939 (2)
Cork, D. G. 16: v WI 1995 (5); v In 1996 (3); v P 1996 (3); *v SA 1995 (5)*
Cornford, W. L. 4: *v NZ 1929 (4)*
Cottam, R. M. H. 4: *v In 1972 (2); v P 1968 (2)*
Coventry, Hon. C. J. 2: *v SA 1888 (2)*
Cowans, N. G. 19: v A 1985 (1); v WI 1984 (1); v NZ 1983 (4); *v A 1982 (4); v NZ 1983 (2); v In 1984 (5); v P 1983 (2)*
Cowdrey, C. S. 6: v WI 1988 (1); *v In 1984 (5)*
Cowdrey, M. C. 114: v A 1956 (5) 1961 (4) 1964 (3) 1968 (4); v SA 1955 (1) 1960 (5) 1965 (3); v WI 1957 (5) 1963 (2) 1966 (4); v NZ 1958 (4) 1965 (3); v In 1959 (5); v P 1962 (4) 1967 (2) 1971 (1); *v A 1954 (5) 1958 (5) 1962 (5) 1965 (4) 1970 (3) 1974 (5); v SA 1956 (5); v WI 1959 (5) 1967 (5); v NZ 1954 (2) 1958 (2) 1962 (3) 1965 (3) 1970 (1); v In 1963 (3); v P 1968 (3)*
Coxon, A. 1: v A 1948
Cranston, J. 1: v A 1890
Cranston, K. 8: v A 1948 (1); v SA 1947 (3); *v WI 1947 (4)*
Crapp, J. F. 7: v A 1948 (3); *v SA 1948 (4)*
Crawford, J. N. 12: v SA 1907 (2); *v A 1907 (5); v SA 1905 (5)*
Crawley, J. P. 12: v SA 1994 (3); v WI 1995 (3); v P 1996 (2); *v A 1994 (3); v SA 1995 (1)*
Croft, R. D. B. 1: v P 1996

Curtis, T. S. 5: v A 1989 (3); v WI 1988 (2)
Cuttell, W. R. 2: *v SA 1898 (2)*

Dawson, E. W. 5: *v SA 1927 (1); v NZ 1929 (4)*
Dean, H. 3: v A 1912 (2); v SA 1912 (1)
DeFreitas, P. A. J. 44: v A 1989 (1) 1993 (1); v SA 1994 (3); v WI 1988 (3) 1991 (5) 1995 (1); v NZ 1990 (2) 1994 (3); v P 1987 (1) 1992 (2); v SL 1991 (1); *v A 1986 (4) 1990 (3) 1994 (4); v WI 1989 (2); v NZ 1987 (2) 1991 (3); v In 1992 (1); v P 1987 (2)*
Denness, M. H. 28: v A 1975 (1); v NZ 1969 (1); v In 1974 (3); v P 1974 (3); *v A 1974 (5); v WI 1973 (5); v NZ 1974 (2); v In 1972 (5); v P 1972 (3)*
Denton, D. 11: v A 1905 (1); *v SA 1905 (5) 1909 (5)*
Dewes, J. G. 5: v A 1948 (1); v WI 1950 (2); *v A 1950 (2)*
Dexter, E. R. 62: v A 1961 (5) 1964 (5) 1968 (2); v SA 1960 (5); v WI 1963 (5); v NZ 1958 (1) 1965 (2); v In 1959 (2); v P 1962 (5); *v A 1958 (2) 1962 (5); v SA 1964 (5); v WI 1959 (5); v NZ 1958 (2) 1962 (3); v In 1961 (5); v P 1961 (3)*
Dilley, G. R. 41: v A 1981 (3) 1989 (2); v WI 1980 (3) 1988 (4); v NZ 1983 (1) 1986 (2); v In 1986 (2); v P 1987 (4); *v A 1979 (2) 1986 (4) 1987 (1); v WI 1980 (4); v NZ 1987 (3); v In 1981 (4); v P 1983 (1) 1987 (1)*
Dipper, A. E. 1: v A 1921
Doggart, G. H. G. 2: v WI 1950 (2)
D'Oliveira, B. L. 44: v A 1968 (2) 1972 (5); v WI 1966 (4) 1969 (3); v NZ 1969 (3); v In 1967 (2) 1971 (3); v P 1967 (3) 1971 (3); *v A 1970 (6); v WI 1967 (5); v NZ 1970 (2); v P 1968 (3)*
Dollery, H. E. 4: v A 1948 (2); v SA 1947 (1); v WI 1950 (1)
Dolphin, A. 1: *v A 1920*
Douglas, J. W. H. T. 23: v A 1912 (1) 1921 (5); v SA 1924 (1); *v A 1911 (5) 1920 (5) 1924 (1); v SA 1913 (5)*
Downton, P. R. 30: v A 1981 (1) 1985 (6); v WI 1984 (5) 1988 (3); v In 1986 (1); v SL 1984 (1); *v WI 1980 (3) 1985 (5); v In 1984 (5)*
Druce, N. F. 5: *v A 1897 (5)*
Ducat, A. 1: v A 1921
Duckworth, G. 24: v A 1930 (5); v SA 1924 (1) 1929 (4) 1935 (1); v WI 1928 (1); v In 1936 (3); *v A 1928 (5); v SA 1930 (3); v NZ 1932 (1)*
Duleepsinhji, K. S. 12: v A 1930 (4); v SA 1929 (1); v NZ 1931 (3); *v NZ 1929 (4)*
Durston, F. J. 1: v A 1921

Ealham, M. A. 2: v In 1996 (1); v P 1996 (1)
Edmonds, P. H. 51: v A 1975 (2) 1985 (5); v NZ 1978 (3) 1983 (2) 1986 (3); v In 1979 (4) 1982 (3) 1986 (2); v P 1978 (3) 1987 (5); *v A 1978 (1) 1986 (5); v WI 1985 (3); v NZ 1977 (3); v In 1984 (5); v P 1977 (2)*
Edrich, J. H. 77: v A 1964 (3) 1968 (5) 1972 (5) 1975 (4); v SA 1965 (1); v WI 1963 (3) 1966 (1) 1969 (3) 1976 (2); v NZ 1965 (1) 1969 (3); v In 1967 (2) 1971 (3) 1974 (3); v P 1971 (3) 1974 (3); *v A 1965 (5) 1970 (6) 1974 (4); v WI 1967 (5); v NZ 1965 (3) 1970 (2) 1974 (2); v In 1963 (2); v P 1968 (3)*
Edrich, W. J. 39: v A 1938 (4) 1948 (5) 1953 (3); v SA 1947 (4); v WI 1950 (2); v NZ 1949 (4); v In 1946 (1); v P 1954 (1); *v A 1946 (5) 1954 (4); v SA 1938 (5); v NZ 1946 (1)*
Elliott, H. 4: v WI 1928 (1); *v SA 1927 (1); v In 1933 (2)*
Ellison, R. M. 11: v A 1985 (2); v WI 1984 (1); v In 1986 (1); v SL 1984 (1); *v WI 1985 (3); v In 1984 (3)*
Emburey, J. E. 64: v A 1980 (1) 1981 (4) 1985 (6) 1989 (3) 1993 (1); v WI 1980 (3) 1988 (3) 1995 (1); v NZ 1978 (1) 1986 (2); v In 1986 (3); v P 1987 (4); v SL 1988 (1); *v A 1978 (4) 1986 (5) 1987 (1); v WI 1980 (4) 1985 (4); v NZ 1987 (3); v In 1979 (1) 1981 (3) 1992 (1); v P 1987 (3); v SL 1981 (1) 1992 (1)*
Emmett, G. M. 1: v A 1948
Emmett, T. 7: *v A 1876 (2) 1878 (1) 1881 (4)*
Evans, A. J. 1: v A 1921
Evans, T. G. 91: v A 1948 (5) 1953 (5) 1956 (5); v SA 1947 (5) 1951 (3) 1955 (3); v WI 1950 (3) 1957 (5); v NZ 1949 (4) 1958 (5); v In 1946 (1) 1952 (4) 1959 (2); v P 1954 (4); *v A 1946 (4) 1950 (5) 1954 (4) 1958 (3); v SA 1948 (3) 1956 (5); v WI 1947 (4) 1953 (4); v NZ 1946 (1) 1950 (2) 1954 (2)*

Fagg, A. E. 5: v WI 1939 (1); v In 1936 (2); *v A 1936 (2)*
Fairbrother, N. H. 10: v NZ 1990 (3); v P 1987 (1); *v NZ 1987 (2); v In 1992 (2); v P 1987 (1); v SL 1992 (1)*

Fane, F. L. 14: *v A 1907 (4); v SA 1905 (5) 1909 (5)*
Farnes, K. 15: v A 1934 (2) 1938 (4); *v A 1936 (2); v SA 1938 (5); v WI 1934 (2)*
Farrimond, W. 4: v SA 1935 (1); *v SA 1930 (2); v WI 1934 (1)*
Fender, P. G. H. 13: v A 1921 (2); v SA 1924 (2) 1929 (1); *v A 1920 (3); v SA 1922 (5)*
Ferris, J. J. 1: *v SA 1891*
Fielder, A. 6: *v A 1903 (2) 1907 (4)*
Fishlock, L. B. 4: v In 1936 (2) 1946 (1); *v A 1946 (1)*
Flavell, J. A. 4: v A 1961 (2) 1964 (2)
Fletcher, K. W. R. 59: v A 1968 (1) 1972 (1) 1975 (2); v WI 1973 (3); v NZ 1969 (2) 1973 (3); v In 1971 (2) 1974 (3); v P 1974 (3); *v A 1970 (5) 1974 (5) 1976 (1); v WI 1973 (4); v NZ 1970 (1) 1974 (2); v In 1972 (5) 1976 (3) 1981 (6); v P 1968 (3) 1972 (3); v SL 1981 (1)*
Flowers, W. 8: v A 1893 (1); *v A 1884 (5) 1886 (2)*
Ford, F. G. J. 5: *v A 1894 (5)*
Foster, F. R. 11: v A 1912 (3); v SA 1912 (3); *v A 1911 (5)*
Foster, N. A. 29: v A 1985 (1) 1989 (3) 1993 (1); v WI 1984 (1) 1988 (2); v NZ 1983 (1) 1986 (1); v In 1986 (1); v P 1987 (5); v SL 1988 (1); *v A 1987 (1); v WI 1985 (3); v NZ 1983 (2); v In 1984 (2); v P 1983 (2) 1987 (2)*
Foster, R. E. 8: v SA 1907 (3); *v A 1903 (5)*
Fothergill, A. J. 2: *v SA 1888 (2)*
Fowler, G. 21: v WI 1984 (5); v NZ 1983 (2); v P 1982 (1); v SL 1984 (1); *v A 1982 (3); v NZ 1983 (2); v In 1984 (5); v P 1983 (2)*
Fraser, A. R. C. 32: v A 1989 (3) 1993 (1); v SA 1994 (2); v WI 1995 (5); v NZ 1994 (3); v In 1990 (3); *v A 1990 (3) 1994 (3); v SA 1995 (3); v WI 1989 (2) 1993 (4)*
Freeman, A. P. 12: v SA 1929 (3); v WI 1928 (3); *v A 1924 (2); v SA 1927 (4)*
French, B. N. 16: v NZ 1986 (3); v In 1986 (2); v P 1987 (4); *v A 1987 (1); v NZ 1987 (3); v P 1987 (3)*
Fry, C. B. 26: v A 1899 (5) 1902 (3) 1905 (4) 1909 (3) 1912 (3); v SA 1907 (3) 1912 (3); *v SA 1895 (2)*

Gallian, J. E. R. 3: v WI 1995 (2); *v SA 1995 (1)*
Gatting, M. W. 79: v A 1980 (1) 1981 (6) 1985 (6) 1989 (1) 1993 (2); v WI 1980 (4) 1984 (1) 1988 (2); v NZ 1983 (2) 1986 (3); v In 1986 (3); v P 1982 (3) 1987 (5); *v A 1986 (5) 1987 (1) 1994 (5); v WI 1980 (1) 1985 (1); v NZ 1977 (1) 1983 (2) 1987 (3); v In 1981 (5) 1984 (5) 1992 (3); v P 1977 (1) 1983 (3) 1987 (3); v SL 1992 (1)*
Gay, L. H. 1: *v A 1894*
Geary, G. 14: v A 1926 (2) 1930 (1) 1934 (2); v SA 1924 (1) 1929 (2); *v A 1928 (4); v SA 1927 (2)*
Gibb, P. A. 8: v In 1946 (2); *v A 1946 (1); v SA 1938 (5)*
Gifford, N. 15: v A 1964 (2) 1972 (3); v NZ 1973 (2); v In 1971 (2); v P 1971 (2); *v In 1972 (2); v P 1972 (2)*
Gilligan, A. E. R. 11: v SA 1924 (4); *v A 1924 (5); v SA 1922 (2)*
Gilligan, A. H. H. 4: *v NZ 1929 (4)*
Gimblett, H. 3: v WI 1939 (1); v In 1936 (2)
Gladwin, C. 8: v SA 1947 (2); v NZ 1949 (1); *v SA 1948 (5)*
Goddard, T. W. 8: v A 1930 (1); v WI 1939 (2); v NZ 1937 (2); *v SA 1938 (3)*
Gooch, G. A. 118: v A 1975 (2) 1980 (1) 1981 (5) 1985 (6) 1989 (5) 1993 (6); v SA 1994 (3); v WI 1980 (5) 1988 (5) 1991 (5); v NZ 1978 (3) 1986 (3) 1990 (3) 1994 (3); v In 1979 (4) 1986 (3) 1990 (3); v P 1978 (2) 1992 (5); v SL 1988 (1) 1991 (1); *v A 1978 (6) 1979 (2) 1990 (4) 1994 (5); v WI 1980 (4) 1985 (5) 1989 (2); v NZ 1991 (3); v In 1979 (1) 1981 (6) 1992 (2); v P 1987 (3); v SL 1981 (1)*
Gough, D. 12: v SA 1994 (3); v WI 1995 (3); v NZ 1994 (1); *v A 1994 (3); v SA 1995 (2)*
Gover, A. R. 4: v NZ 1937 (2); v In 1936 (1) 1946 (1)
Gower, D. I. 117: v A 1980 (1) 1981 (5) 1985 (6) 1989 (6); v WI 1980 (1) 1984 (5) 1988 (4); v NZ 1978 (3) 1983 (4) 1986 (3); v In 1979 (4) 1982 (3) 1986 (2) 1990 (3); v P 1978 (3) 1982 (3) 1987 (5) 1992 (3); v SL 1984 (1); *v A 1978 (6) 1979 (3) 1982 (5) 1986 (5) 1990 (5); v WI 1980 (4) 1985 (5); v NZ 1983 (3); v In 1979 (1) 1981 (6) 1984 (5); v P 1983 (3); v SL 1981 (1)*
Grace, E. M. 1: v A 1880
Grace, G. F. 1: v A 1880
Grace, W. G. 22: v A 1880 (1) 1882 (1) 1884 (3) 1886 (3) 1888 (3) 1890 (2) 1893 (2) 1896 (3) 1899 (1); *v A 1891 (3)*
Graveney, T. W. 79: v A 1953 (5) 1956 (2) 1968 (5); v SA 1951 (1) 1955 (5); v WI 1957 (4) 1966 (4) 1969 (1); v NZ 1958 (4); v In 1952 (4) 1967 (3); v P 1954 (3) 1962 (4) 1967 (3); *v A 1954 (2) 1958 (5) 1962 (3); v WI 1953 (5) 1967 (5); v NZ 1954 (2) 1958 (2); v In 1951 (4); v P 1968 (3)*
Greenhough, T. 4: v SA 1960 (1); v In 1959 (3)

Greenwood, A. 2: *v A 1876 (2)*
Greig, A. W. 58: v A 1972 (5) 1975 (4) 1977 (5); v WI 1973 (3) 1976 (5); v NZ 1973 (3); v In 1974 (3); v P 1974 (3); *v A 1974 (6) 1976 (1); v WI 1973 (5); v NZ 1974 (2); v In 1972 (5) 1976 (5); v P 1972 (3)*
Greig, I. A. 2: v P 1982 (2)
Grieve, B. A. F. 2: *v SA 1888 (2)*
Griffith, S. C. 3: *v SA 1948 (2); v WI 1947 (1)*
Gunn, G. 15: v A 1909 (1); *v A 1907 (5) 1911 (5); v WI 1929 (4)*
Gunn, J. 6: v A 1905 (1); *v A 1901 (5)*
Gunn, W. 11: v A 1888 (2) 1890 (2) 1893 (3) 1896 (1) 1899 (1); *v A 1886 (2)*

Haig, N. E. 5: v A 1921 (1); *v WI 1929 (4)*
Haigh, S. 11: v A 1905 (2) 1909 (1) 1912 (1); *v SA 1898 (2) 1905 (5)*
Hallows, C. 2: v A 1921 (1); v WI 1928 (1)
Hammond, W. R. 85: v A 1930 (5) 1934 (5) 1938 (4); v SA 1929 (4) 1935 (5); v WI 1928 (3) 1933 (3) 1939 (3); v NZ 1931 (3) 1937 (3); v In 1932 (1) 1936 (2) 1946 (3); *v A 1928 (5) 1932 (5) 1936 (5) 1946 (4); v SA 1927 (5) 1930 (5) 1938 (5); v WI 1934 (4); v NZ 1932 (2) 1946 (1)*
Hampshire, J. H. 8: v A 1972 (1) 1975 (1); v WI 1969 (2); *v A 1970 (2); v NZ 1970 (2)*
Hardinge, H. T. W. 1: v A 1921
Hardstaff, J. 5: *v A 1907 (5)*
Hardstaff, J. jun. 23: v A 1938 (2) 1948 (1); v SA 1935 (1); v WI 1939 (3); v NZ 1937 (3); v In 1936 (2) 1946 (2); *v A 1936 (5) 1946 (1); v WI 1947 (3)*
Harris, Lord 4: v A 1880 (1) 1884 (2); *v A 1878 (1)*
Hartley, J. C. 2: *v SA 1905 (2)*
Hawke, Lord 5: *v SA 1895 (3) 1898 (2)*
Hayes, E. G. 5: v A 1909 (1); v SA 1912 (1); *v SA 1905 (3)*
Hayes, F. C. 9: v WI 1973 (3) 1976 (2); *v WI 1973 (4)*
Hayward, T. W. 35: v A 1896 (2) 1899 (5) 1902 (1) 1905 (5) 1909 (1); v SA 1907 (3); *v A 1897 (5) 1901 (5) 1903 (5); v SA 1895 (3)*
Hearne, A. 1: *v SA 1891*
Hearne, F. 2: *v SA 1888 (2)*
Hearne, G. G. 1: *v SA 1891*
Hearne, J. T. 12: v A 1896 (3) 1899 (3); *v A 1897 (5); v SA 1891 (1)*
Hearne, J. W. 24: v A 1912 (3) 1921 (1) 1926 (1); v SA 1912 (2) 1924 (3); *v A 1911 (5) 1920 (2) 1924 (4); v SA 1913 (3)*
Hemmings, E. E. 16: v A 1989 (1); v NZ 1990 (3); v In 1990 (3); v P 1982 (2); *v A 1982 (3) 1987 (1) 1990 (1); v NZ 1987 (1); v P 1987 (1)*
Hendren, E. H. 51: v A 1921 (2) 1926 (5) 1930 (2) 1934 (4); v SA 1924 (5) 1929 (4); v WI 1928 (1); *v A 1920 (5) 1924 (5) 1928 (5); v SA 1930 (5); v WI 1929 (4) 1934 (4)*
Hendrick, M. 30: v A 1977 (3) 1980 (1) 1981 (2); v WI 1976 (2) 1980 (2); v NZ 1978 (2); v In 1974 (3) 1979 (4); v P 1974 (2); *v A 1974 (2) 1978 (5); v NZ 1974 (1) 1977 (1)*
Heseltine, C. 2: *v SA 1895 (2)*
Hick, G. A. 46: v A 1993 (3); v SA 1994 (3); v WI 1991 (4) 1995 (5); v NZ 1994 (3); v In 1996 (3); v P 1992 (4) 1996 (1); *v A 1994 (3); v SA 1995 (5); v WI 1993 (5); v NZ 1991 (3); v In 1992 (3); v SL 1992 (1)*
Higgs, K. 15: v A 1968 (1); v WI 1966 (5); v SA 1965 (1); v In 1967 (1); v P 1967 (3); *v A 1965 (1); v NZ 1965 (3)*
Hill, A. 2: *v A 1876 (2)*
Hill, A. J. L. 3: *v SA 1895 (3)*
Hilton, M. J. 4: v SA 1951 (1); v WI 1950 (1); *v In 1951 (2)*
Hirst, G. H. 24: v A 1899 (1) 1902 (4) 1905 (3) 1909 (4); v SA 1907 (3); *v A 1897 (4) 1903 (5)*
Hitch, J. W. 7: v A 1912 (1) 1921 (1); v SA 1912 (1); *v A 1911 (3) 1920 (1)*
Hobbs, J. B. 61: v A 1909 (3) 1912 (3) 1921 (1) 1926 (5) 1930 (5); v SA 1912 (3) 1924 (4) 1929 (1); v WI 1928 (2); *v A 1907 (4) 1911 (5) 1920 (5) 1924 (5) 1928 (5); v SA 1909 (5) 1913 (5)*
Hobbs, R. N. S. 7: v In 1967 (3); v P 1967 (1) 1971 (1); *v WI 1967 (1); v P 1968 (1)*
Hollies, W. E. 13: v A 1948 (1); v SA 1947 (3); v WI 1950 (2); v NZ 1949 (4); *v WI 1934 (3)*
Holmes, E. R. T. 5: v SA 1935 (1); *v WI 1934 (4)*
Holmes, P. 7: v A 1921 (1); v In 1932 (1); *v SA 1927 (5)*
Hone, L. 1: *v A 1878*
Hopwood, J. L. 2: v A 1934 (2)
Hornby, A. N. 3: v A 1882 (1) 1884 (1); *v A 1878 (1)*
Horton, M. J. 2: v In 1959 (2)

Howard, N. D. 4: *v In 1951 (4)*
Howell, H. 5: v A 1921 (1); v SA 1924 (1); *v A 1920 (3)*
Howorth, R. 5: v SA 1947 (1); *v WI 1947 (4)*
Humphries, J. 3: *v A 1907 (3)*
Hunter, J. 5: *v A 1884 (5)*
Hussain, N. 12: v A 1993 (4); v In 1996 (3); v P 1996 (2); *v WI 1989 (3)*
Hutchings, K. L. 7: v A 1909 (2); *v A 1907 (5)*
Hutton, L. 79: v A 1938 (3) 1948 (4) 1953 (5); v SA 1947 (5) 1951 (5); v WI 1939 (3) 1950 (3); v NZ 1937 (3) 1949 (4); v In 1946 (3) 1952 (4); v P 1954 (2); *v A 1946 (5) 1950 (5) 1954 (5); v SA 1938 (4) 1948 (5); v WI 1947 (2) 1953 (5); v NZ 1950 (2) 1954 (2)*
Hutton, R. A. 5: v In 1971 (3); v P 1971 (2)

Iddon, J. 5: v SA 1935 (1); *v WI 1934 (4)*
Igglesden, A. P. 3: v A 1989 (1); *v WI 1993 (2)*
Ikin, J. T. 18: v SA 1951 (3) 1955 (1); v In 1946 (2) 1952 (2); *v A 1946 (5); v NZ 1946 (1); v WI 1947 (4)*
Illingworth, R. 61: v A 1961 (2) 1968 (3) 1972 (5); v SA 1960 (4); v WI 1966 (2) 1969 (3) 1973 (3); v NZ 1958 (1) 1965 (1) 1969 (3) 1973 (3); v In 1959 (2) 1967 (3) 1971 (3); v P 1962 (1) 1967 (1) 1971 (3); *v A 1962 (2) 1970 (6); v WI 1959 (5); v NZ 1962 (3) 1970 (2)*
Illingworth, R. K. 9: v WI 1991 (2) 1995 (4); *v SA 1995 (3)*
Ilott, M. C. 5: v A 1993 (3); *v SA 1995 (2)*
Insole, D. J. 9: v A 1956 (1); v SA 1955 (1); v WI 1950 (1) 1957 (1); *v SA 1956 (5)*
Irani, R. C. 2: v In 1996 (2)

Jackman, R. D. 4: v P 1982 (2); *v WI 1980 (2)*
Jackson, F. S. 20: v A 1893 (2) 1896 (3) 1899 (5) 1902 (5) 1905 (5)
Jackson, H. L. 2: v A 1961 (1); v NZ 1949 (1)
Jameson, J. A. 4: v In 1971 (2); *v WI 1973 (2)*
Jardine, D. R. 22: v WI 1928 (2) 1933 (2); v NZ 1931 (3); v In 1932 (1); *v A 1928 (5) 1932 (5); v NZ 1932 (1); v In 1933 (3)*
Jarvis, P. W. 9: v A 1989 (2); v WI 1988 (2); *v NZ 1987 (2); v In 1992 (2), v SL 1992 (1)*
Jenkins, R. O. 9: v WI 1950 (2); v In 1952 (2); *v SA 1948 (5)*
Jessop, G. L. 18: v A 1899 (1) 1902 (4) 1905 (1) 1909 (2); v SA 1907 (3) 1912 (2); *v A 1901 (5)*
Jones, A. O. 12: v A 1899 (1) 1905 (2) 1909 (2); *v A 1901 (5) 1907 (2)*
Jones, I. J. 15: v WI 1966 (2); *v A 1965 (4); v WI 1967 (5); v NZ 1965 (3); v In 1963 (1)*
Jupp, H. 2: *v A 1876 (2)*
Jupp, V. W. C. 8: v A 1921 (2); v WI 1928 (2); *v SA 1922 (4)*

Keeton, W. W. 2: v A 1934 (1); v WI 1939 (1)
Kennedy, A. S. 5: *v SA 1922 (5)*
Kenyon, D. 8: v A 1953 (2); v SA 1955 (3); *v In 1951 (3)*
Killick, E. T. 2: v SA 1929 (2)
Kilner, R. 9: v A 1926 (4); v SA 1924 (2); *v A 1924 (3)*
King, J. H. 1: v A 1909
Kinneir, S. P. 1: *v A 1911*
Knight, A. E. 3: *v A 1903 (3)*
Knight, B. R. 29: v A 1968 (2); v WI 1966 (1) 1969 (3); v NZ 1969 (2); v P 1962 (2); *v A 1962 (1) 1965 (2); v NZ 1962 (3) 1965 (2); v In 1961 (4) 1963 (5); v P 1961 (2)*
Knight, D. J. 2: v A 1921 (2)
Knight, N. V. 6: v WI 1995 (2); v In 1996 (1); v P 1996 (3)
Knott, A. P. E. 95: v A 1968 (5) 1972 (5) 1975 (4) 1977 (5) 1981 (2); v WI 1969 (3) 1973 (3) 1976 (5) 1980 (4); v NZ 1969 (3) 1973 (3); v In 1971 (3) 1974 (3); v P 1967 (2) 1971 (3) 1974 (3); *v A 1970 (6) 1974 (6) 1976 (1); v WI 1967 (2) 1973 (5); v NZ 1970 (1) 1974 (2); v In 1972 (5) 1976 (5); v P 1968 (3) 1972 (3)*
Knox, N. A. 2: v SA 1907 (2)

Laker, J. C. 46: v A 1948 (3) 1953 (3) 1956 (5); v SA 1951 (2) 1955 (1); v WI 1950 (1) 1957 (4); v NZ 1949 (1) 1958 (4); v In 1952 (4); v P 1954 (1); *v A 1958 (4); v SA 1956 (5); v WI 1947 (4) 1953 (4)*
Lamb, A. J. 79: v A 1985 (6) 1989 (1); v WI 1984 (5) 1988 (4) 1991 (4); v NZ 1983 (4) 1986 (1) 1990 (3); v In 1982 (3) 1986 (2) 1990 (3); v P 1982 (3) 1992 (2); v SL 1984 (1) 1988 (1); *v A 1982 (5) 1986 (5) 1990 (3); v WI 1985 (5) 1989 (4); v NZ 1983 (3) 1991 (3); v In 1984 (5); v P 1983 (3)*

Langridge, James 8: v SA 1935 (1); v WI 1933 (2); v In 1936 (1) 1946 (1); *v In 1933 (3)*
Larkins, W. 13: v A 1981 (1); v WI 1980 (3); *v A 1979 (1) 1990 (3); v WI 1989 (4); v In 1979 (1)*
Larter, J. D. F. 10: v SA 1965 (2); v NZ 1965 (1); v P 1962 (1); *v NZ 1962 (3); v In 1963 (3)*
Larwood, H. 21: v A 1926 (2) 1930 (3); v SA 1929 (3); v WI 1928 (2); v NZ 1931 (1); *v A 1928 (5) 1932 (5)*
Lathwell, M. N. 2: v A 1993 (2)
Lawrence, D. V. 5: v WI 1991 (2); v SL 1988 (1) 1991 (1); *v NZ 1991 (1)*
Leadbeater, E. 2: *v In 1951 (2)*
Lee, H. W. 1: *v SA 1930*
Lees, W. S. 5: *v SA 1905 (5)*
Legge, G. B. 5: *v SA 1927 (1); v NZ 1929 (4)*
Leslie, C. F. H. 4: *v A 1882 (4)*
Lever, J. K. 21: v A 1977 (3); v WI 1980 (1); v In 1979 (1) 1986 (1); *v A 1976 (1) 1978 (1) 1979 (1); v NZ 1977 (1); v In 1976 (5) 1979 (1) 1981 (2); v P 1977 (3)*
Lever, P. 17: v A 1972 (1) 1975 (1); v In 1971 (1); v P 1971 (3); *v A 1970 (5) 1974 (2); v NZ 1970 (2) 1974 (2)*
Leveson Gower, H. D. G. 3: *v SA 1909 (3)*
Levett, W. H. V. 1: *v In 1933*
Lewis, A. R. 9: v NZ 1973 (1); *v In 1972 (5); v P 1972 (3)*
Lewis, C. C. 32: v A 1993 (2); v WI 1991 (2); v NZ 1990 (1); v In 1990 (2) 1996 (3); v P 1992 (5) 1996 (2); v SL 1991 (1); *v A 1990 (1) 1994 (2); v WI 1993 (5); v NZ 1991 (2); v In 1992 (3); v SL 1992 (1)*
Leyland, M. 41: v A 1930 (3) 1934 (5) 1938 (1); v SA 1929 (5) 1935 (4); v WI 1928 (1) 1933 (1); v In 1936 (2); *v A 1928 (1) 1932 (5) 1936 (5); v SA 1930 (5); v WI 1934 (3)*
Lilley, A. A. 35: v A 1896 (3) 1899 (4) 1902 (5) 1905 (5) 1909 (5); v SA 1907 (3); *v A 1901 (5) 1903 (5)*
Lillywhite, James jun. 2: *v A 1876 (2)*
Lloyd, D. 9: v In 1974 (2); v P 1974 (3); *v A 1974 (4)*
Lloyd, T. A. 1: v WI 1984
Loader, P. J. 13: v SA 1955 (1); v WI 1957 (2); v NZ 1958 (3); v P 1954 (1); *v A 1958 (2); v SA 1956 (4)*
Lock, G. A. R. 49: v A 1953 (2) 1956 (4) 1961 (3); v SA 1955 (3); v WI 1957 (3) 1963 (3); v NZ 1958 (5); v In 1952 (2); v P 1962 (3); *v A 1958 (4); v SA 1956 (1); v WI 1953 (5) 1967 (2); v NZ 1958 (2); v In 1961 (5); v P 1961 (2)*
Lockwood, W. H. 12: v A 1893 (2) 1899 (1) 1902 (4); *v A 1894 (5)*
Lohmann, G. A. 18: v A 1886 (3) 1888 (3) 1890 (2) 1896 (1); *v A 1886 (2) 1887 (1) 1891 (3); v SA 1895 (3)*
Lowson, F. A. 7: v SA 1951 (2) 1955 (1); *v In 1951 (4)*
Lucas, A. P. 5: v A 1880 (1) 1882 (1) 1884 (2); *v A 1878 (1)*
Luckhurst, B. W. 21: v A 1972 (4); v WI 1973 (2); v In 1971 (3); v P 1971 (3); *v A 1970 (5) 1974 (2); v NZ 1970 (2)*
Lyttelton, Hon. A. 4: v A 1880 (1) 1882 (1) 1884 (2)

Macaulay, G. G. 8: v A 1926 (1); v SA 1924 (1); v WI 1933 (2); *v SA 1922 (4)*
MacBryan, J. C. W. 1: v SA 1924
McCague, M. J. 3: v A 1993 (2); *v A 1994 (1)*
McConnon, J. E. 2: v P 1954 (2)
McGahey, C. P. 2: *v A 1901 (2)*
MacGregor, G. 8: v A 1890 (2) 1893 (3); *v A 1891 (3)*
McIntyre, A. J. W. 3: v SA 1955 (1); v WI 1950 (1); *v A 1950 (1)*
MacKinnon, F. A. 1: *v A 1878*
MacLaren, A. C. 35: v A 1896 (2) 1899 (4) 1902 (5) 1905 (4) 1909 (5); *v A 1894 (5) 1897 (5) 1901 (5)*
McMaster, J. E. P. 1: *v SA 1888*
Makepeace, J. W. H. 4: *v A 1920 (4)*
Malcolm, D. E. 36: v A 1989 (1) 1993 (1); v SA 1994 (1); v WI 1991 (2) 1995 (2); v NZ 1990 (3) 1994 (1); v In 1990 (3); v P 1992 (3); *v A 1990 (5) 1994 (4); v SA 1995 (2); v WI 1989 (4) 1993 (1); v In 1992 (2); v SL 1992 (1)*
Mallender, N. A. 2: v P 1992 (2)
Mann, F. G. 7: v NZ 1949 (2); *v SA 1948 (5)*
Mann, F. T. 5: *v SA 1922 (5)*
Marks, V. J. 6: v NZ 1983 (1); v P 1982 (1); *v NZ 1983 (1); v P 1983 (3)*

Marriott, C. S. 1: v WI 1933
Martin, F. 2: v A 1890 (1); *v SA 1891 (1)*
Martin, J. W. 1: v SA 1947
Martin, P. J. 7: v WI 1995 (3); v In 1996 (1); *v SA 1995 (3)*
Mason, J. R. 5: *v A 1897 (5)*
Matthews, A. D. G. 1: v NZ 1937
May, P. B. H. 66: v A 1953 (2) 1956 (5) 1961 (4); v SA 1951 (2) 1955 (5); v WI 1957 (5); v NZ 1958 (5); v In 1952 (4) 1959 (3); v P 1954 (4); *v A 1954 (5) 1958 (5); v SA 1956 (5); v WI 1953 (5) 1959 (3); v NZ 1954 (2) 1958 (2)*
Maynard, M. P. 4: v A 1993 (2); v WI 1988 (1); *v WI 1993 (1)*
Mead, C. P. 17: v A 1921 (2); *v A 1911 (4) 1928 (1); v SA 1913 (5) 1922 (5)*
Mead, W. 1: v A 1899
Midwinter, W. E. 4: *v A 1881 (4)*
Milburn, C. 9: v A 1968 (2); v WI 1966 (4); v In 1967 (1); v P 1967 (1); *v P 1968 (1)*
Miller, A. M. 1: *v SA 1895*
Miller, G. 34: v A 1977 (2); v WI 1976 (1) 1984 (2); v NZ 1978 (2); v In 1979 (3) 1982 (1); v P 1978 (3) 1982 (1); *v A 1978 (6) 1979 (1) 1982 (5); v WI 1980 (1); v NZ 1977 (3); v P 1977 (3)*
Milligan, F. W. 2: *v SA 1898 (2)*
Millman, G. 6: v P 1962 (2); *v In 1961 (2); v P 1961 (2)*
Milton, C. A. 6: v NZ 1958 (2); v In 1959 (2); *v A 1958 (2)*
Mitchell, A. 6: v SA 1935 (2); v In 1936 (1); *v In 1933 (3)*
Mitchell, F. 2: *v SA 1898 (2)*
Mitchell, T. B. 5: v A 1934 (2); v SA 1935 (1); *v A 1932 (1); v NZ 1932 (1)*
Mitchell-Innes, N. S. 1: v SA 1935
Mold, A. W. 3: v A 1893 (3)
Moon, L. J. 4: *v SA 1905 (4)*
Morley, F. 4: v A 1880 (1); *v A 1882 (3)*
Morris, H. 3: v WI 1991 (2); v SL 1991 (1)
Morris, J. E. 3: v In 1990 (3)
Mortimore, J. B. 9: v A 1964 (1); v In 1959 (2); *v A 1958 (1); v NZ 1958 (2); v In 1963 (3)*
Moss, A. E. 9: v A 1956 (1); v SA 1960 (2); v In 1959 (3); *v WI 1953 (1) 1959 (2)*
Moxon, M. D. 10: v A 1989 (1); v WI 1988 (2); v NZ 1986 (2); v P 1987 (1); *v A 1987 (1); v NZ 1987 (3)*
Mullally, A. D. 6: v In 1996 (3); v P 1996 (3)
Munton, T. A. 2: v P 1992 (2)
Murdoch, W. L. 1: *v SA 1891*
Murray, J. T. 21: v A 1961 (5); v WI 1966 (1); v In 1967 (3); v P 1962 (3) 1967 (1); *v A 1962 (1); v SA 1964 (1); v NZ 1962 (1) 1965 (1); v In 1961 (3); v P 1961 (1)*

Newham, W. 1: *v A 1887*
Newport, P. J. 3: v A 1989 (1); v SL 1988 (1); *v A 1990 (1)*
Nichols, M. S. 14: v A 1930 (1); v SA 1935 (4); v WI 1933 (1) 1939 (1); *v NZ 1929 (4); v In 1933 (3)*

Oakman, A. S. M. 2: v A 1956 (2)
O'Brien, Sir T. C. 5: v A 1884 (1) 1888 (1); *v SA 1895 (3)*
O'Connor, J. 4: v SA 1929 (1); *v WI 1929 (3)*
Old, C. M. 46: v A 1975 (3) 1977 (2) 1980 (1) 1981 (2); v WI 1973 (1) 1976 (2) 1980 (1); v NZ 1973 (2) 1978 (1); v In 1974 (3); v P 1974 (3) 1978 (3); *v A 1974 (2) 1976 (1) 1978 (1); v WI 1973 (4) 1980 (1); v NZ 1974 (1) 1977 (2); v In 1972 (4) 1976 (4); v P 1972 (1) 1977 (1)*
Oldfield, N. 1: v WI 1939

Padgett, D. E. V. 2: v SA 1960 (2)
Paine, G. A. E. 4: *v WI 1934 (4)*
Palairet, L. C. H. 2: v A 1902 (2)
Palmer, C. H. 1: *v WI 1953*
Palmer, K. E. 1: *v SA 1964*
Parfitt, P. H. 37: v A 1964 (4) 1972 (3); v SA 1965 (2); v WI 1969 (1); v NZ 1965 (2); v P 1962 (5); *v A 1962 (2); v SA 1964 (5); v NZ 1962 (3) 1965 (3); v In 1961 (2) 1963 (3); v P 1961 (2)*
Parker, C. W. L. 1: v A 1921
Parker, P. W. G. 1: v A 1981
Parkhouse, W. G. A. 7: v WI 1950 (2); v In 1959 (2); *v A 1950 (2); v NZ 1950 (1)*

Parkin, C. H. 10: v A 1921 (4); v SA 1924 (1); *v A 1920 (5)*
Parks, J. H. 1: v NZ 1937
Parks, J. M. 46: v A 1964 (5); v SA 1960 (5) 1965 (3); v WI 1963 (4) 1966 (4); v NZ 1965 (3); v P 1954 (1); *v A 1965 (5); v SA 1964 (5); v WI 1959 (1) 1967 (3); v NZ 1965 (2); v In 1963 (5)*
Pataudi sen., Nawab of, 3: v A 1934 (1); *v A 1932 (2)*
Patel, M. M. 2: v In 1996 (2)
Paynter, E. 20: v A 1938 (4); v WI 1939 (2); v NZ 1931 (1) 1937 (2); v In 1932 (1); *v A 1932 (3); v SA 1938 (5); v NZ 1932 (2)*
Peate, E. 9: v A 1882 (1) 1884 (3) 1886 (1); *v A 1881 (4)*
Peebles, I. A. R. 13: v A 1930 (2); v NZ 1931 (3); *v SA 1927 (4) 1930 (4)*
Peel, R. 20: v A 1888 (3) 1890 (1) 1893 (1) 1896 (1); *v A 1884 (5) 1887 (1) 1891 (3) 1894 (5)*
Penn, F. 1: v A 1880
Perks, R. T. D. 2: v WI 1939 (1); *v SA 1938 (1)*
Philipson, H. 5: *v A 1891 (1) 1894 (4)*
Pigott, A. C. S. 1: *v NZ 1983*
Pilling, R. 8: v A 1884 (1) 1886 (1) 1888 (1); *v A 1881 (4) 1887 (1)*
Place, W. 3: *v WI 1947 (3)*
Pocock, P. I. 25: v A 1968 (1); v WI 1976 (2) 1984 (2); v SL 1984 (1); *v WI 1967 (2) 1973 (4); v In 1972 (4) 1984 (5); v P 1968 (1) 1972 (3)*
Pollard, R. 4: v A 1948 (2); v In 1946 (1); *v NZ 1946 (1)*
Poole, C. J. 3: *v In 1951 (3)*
Pope, G. H. 1: v SA 1947
Pougher, A. D. 1: *v SA 1891*
Price, J. S. E. 15: v A 1964 (2) 1972 (1); v In 1971 (3); v P 1971 (1); *v SA 1964 (4); v In 1963 (4)*
Price, W. F. F. 1: v A 1938
Prideaux, R. M. 3: v A 1968 (1); *v P 1968 (2)*
Pringle, D. R. 30: v A 1989 (2); v WI 1984 (3) 1988 (4) 1991 (4); v NZ 1986 (1); v In 1982 (3) 1986 (3); v P 1982 (1) 1992 (3); v SL 1988 (1); *v A 1982 (3); v NZ 1991 (2)*
Pullar, G. 28: v A 1961 (5); v SA 1960 (3); v In 1959 (3); v P 1962 (2); *v A 1962 (4); v WI 1959 (5); v In 1961 (3); v P 1961 (3)*

Quaife, W. G. 7: v A 1899 (2); *v A 1901 (5)*

Radford, N. V. 3: v NZ 1986 (1); v In 1986 (1); *v NZ 1987 (1)*
Radley, C. T. 8: v NZ 1978 (3); v P 1978 (3); *v NZ 1977 (2)*
Ramprakash, M. R. 19: v A 1993 (1); v WI 1991 (5) 1995 (2); v P 1992 (3); v SL 1991 (1); *v A 1994 (1); v WI 1993 (4); v SA 1995 (2)*
Randall, D. W. 47: v A 1977 (5); v WI 1984 (1); v NZ 1983 (3); v In 1979 (3) 1982 (3); v P 1982 (3); *v A 1976 (1) 1978 (6) 1979 (2) 1982 (4); v NZ 1977 (3) 1983 (3); v In 1976 (4); v P 1977 (3) 1983 (3)*
Ranjitsinhji, K. S. 15: v A 1896 (2) 1899 (5) 1902 (3); *v A 1897 (5)*
Read, H. D. 1: v SA 1935
Read, J. M. 17: v A 1882 (1) 1890 (2) 1893 (1); *v A 1884 (5) 1886 (2) 1887 (1) 1891 (3); v SA 1888 (2)*
Read, W. W. 18: v A 1884 (2) 1886 (3) 1888 (3) 1890 (2) 1893 (2); *v A 1882 (4) 1887 (1); v SA 1891 (1)*
Reeve, D. A. 3: *v NZ 1991 (3)*
Relf, A. E. 13: v A 1909 (1); *v A 1903 (2); v SA 1905 (5) 1913 (5)*
Rhodes, H. J. 2: v In 1959 (2)
Rhodes, S. J. 11: v SA 1994 (3); v NZ 1994 (3); *v A 1994 (5)*
Rhodes, W. 58: v A 1899 (3) 1902 (5) 1905 (4) 1909 (4) 1912 (3) 1921 (1) 1926 (1); v SA 1912 (3); *v A 1903 (5) 1907 (5) 1911 (5) 1920 (5); v SA 1909 (5) 1913 (5); v WI 1929 (4)*
Richards, C. J. 8: v WI 1988 (2); v P 1987 (1); *v A 1986 (5)*
Richardson, D. W. 1: v WI 1957
Richardson, P. E. 34: v A 1956 (5); v WI 1957 (5) 1963 (1); v NZ 1958 (4); *v A 1958 (4); v SA 1956 (5); v NZ 1958 (2); v In 1961 (5); v P 1961 (3)*
Richardson, T. 14: v A 1893 (1) 1896 (3); *v A 1894 (5) 1897 (5)*
Richmond, T. L. 1: v A 1921
Ridgway, F. 5: *v In 1951 (5)*
Robertson, J. D. 11: v SA 1947 (1); v NZ 1949 (1); *v WI 1947 (4); v In 1951 (5)*
Robins, R. W. V. 19: v A 1930 (2); v SA 1929 (1) 1935 (3); v WI 1933 (2); v NZ 1931 (1) 1937 (3); v In 1932 (1) 1936 (2); *v A 1936 (4)*

Robinson, R. T. 29: v A 1985 (6) 1989 (1); v In 1986 (1); v P 1987 (5); v SL 1988 (1); *v A 1987 (1); v WI 1985 (4); v NZ 1987 (3); v In 1984 (5); v P 1987 (2)*
Roope, G. R. J. 21: v A 1975 (1) 1977 (2); v WI 1973 (1); v NZ 1973 (3) 1978 (1); v P 1978 (3); *v NZ 1977 (3); v In 1972 (2); v P 1972 (2) 1977 (3)*
Root, C. F. 3: v A 1926 (3)
Rose, B. C. 9: v WI 1980 (3); *v WI 1980 (1); v NZ 1977 (2); v P 1977 (3)*
Royle, V. P. F. A. 1: *v A 1878*
Rumsey, F. E. 5: v A 1964 (1); v SA 1965 (1); v NZ 1965 (3)
Russell, A. C. 10: v A 1921 (2); *v A 1920 (4); v SA 1922 (4)*
Russell, R. C. 49: v A 1989 (6); v WI 1991 (4) 1995 (3); v NZ 1990 (3); v In 1990 (3) 1996 (3); v P 1992 (3) 1996 (2); v SL 1988 (1) 1991 (1); *v A 1990 (3); v SA 1995 (5); v WI 1989 (4) 1993 (5); v NZ 1991 (3)*
Russell, W. E. 10: v SA 1965 (1); v WI 1966 (2); v P 1967 (1); *v A 1965 (1); v NZ 1965 (3); v In 1961 (1); v P 1961 (1)*

Salisbury, I. D. K. 9: v SA 1994 (1); v P 1992 (2) 1996 (2); *v WI 1993 (2); v In 1992 (2)*
Sandham, A. 14: v A 1921 (1); v SA 1924 (2); *v A 1924 (2); v SA 1922 (5); v WI 1929 (4)*
Schultz, S. S. 1: *v A 1878*
Scotton, W. H. 15: v A 1884 (1) 1886 (3); *v A 1881 (4) 1884 (5) 1886 (2)*
Selby, J. 6: *v A 1876 (2) 1881 (4)*
Selvey, M. W. W. 3: v WI 1976 (2); *v In 1976 (1)*
Shackleton, D. 7: v SA 1951 (1); v WI 1950 (1) 1963 (4); *v In 1951 (1)*
Sharp, J. 3: v A 1909 (3)
Sharpe, J. W. 3: v A 1890 (1); *v A 1891 (2)*
Sharpe, P. J. 12: v A 1964 (2); v WI 1963 (3) 1969 (3); v NZ 1969 (3); *v In 1963 (1)*
Shaw, A. 7: v A 1880 (1); *v A 1876 (2) 1881 (4)*
Sheppard, Rev. D. S. 22: v A 1956 (2); v WI 1950 (1) 1957 (2); v In 1952 (2); v P 1954 (2) 1962 (2); *v A 1950 (2) 1962 (5); v NZ 1950 (1) 1963 (3)*
Sherwin, M. 3: v A 1888 (1); *v A 1886 (2)*
Shrewsbury, A. 23: v A 1884 (3) 1886 (3) 1890 (2) 1893 (3); *v A 1881 (4) 1884 (5) 1886 (2) 1887 (1)*
Shuter, J. 1: v A 1888
Shuttleworth, K. 5: v P 1971 (1); *v A 1970 (2); v NZ 1970 (2)*
Sidebottom, A. 1: v A 1985
Simpson, R. T. 27: v A 1953 (3); v SA 1951 (3); v WI 1950 (3); v NZ 1949 (2); v In 1952 (2); v P 1954 (3); *v A 1950 (5) 1954 (1); v SA 1948 (1); v NZ 1950 (2) 1954 (2)*
Simpson-Hayward, G. H. 5: *v SA 1909 (5)*
Sims, J. M. 4: v SA 1935 (1); v In 1936 (1); *v A 1936 (2)*
Sinfield, R. A. 1: v A 1938
Slack, W. N. 3: v In 1986 (1); *v WI 1985 (2)*
Smailes, T. F. 1: v In 1946
Small, G. C. 17: v A 1989 (1); v WI 1988 (1); v NZ 1986 (2) 1990 (3); *v A 1986 (2) 1990 (4); v WI 1989 (4)*
Smith, A. C. 6: *v A 1962 (4); v NZ 1962 (2)*
Smith, C. A. 1: *v SA 1888*
Smith, C. I. J. 5: v NZ 1937 (1); *v WI 1934 (4)*
Smith, C. L. 8: v NZ 1983 (2); v In 1986 (1); *v NZ 1983 (2); v P 1983 (3)*
Smith, D. 2: v SA 1935 (2)
Smith, D. M. 2: *v WI 1985 (2)*
Smith, D. R. 5: *v In 1961 (5)*
Smith, D. V. 3: v WI 1957 (3)
Smith, E. J. 11: v A 1912 (3); v SA 1912 (3); *v A 1911 (4); v SA 1913 (1)*
Smith, H. 1: v WI 1928
Smith, M. J. K. 50: v A 1961 (1) 1972 (3); v SA 1960 (4) 1965 (3); v WI 1966 (1); v NZ 1958 (3) 1965 (3); v In 1959 (2); *v A 1965 (5); v SA 1964 (5); v WI 1959 (5); v NZ 1965 (3); v In 1961 (4) 1963 (5); v P 1961 (3)*
Smith, R. A. 62: v A 1989 (5) 1993 (5); v WI 1988 (2) 1991 (4) 1995 (4); v NZ 1990 (3) 1994 (3); v In 1990 (3); v P 1992 (5); v SL 1988 (1) 1991 (1); *v A 1990 (5); v SA 1995 (5); v WI 1989 (4) 1993 (5); v NZ 1991 (3); v In 1992 (3); v SL 1992 (1)*
Smith, T. P. B. 4: v In 1946 (1); *v A 1946 (2); v NZ 1946 (1)*
Smithson, G. A. 2: *v WI 1947 (2)*

Snow, J. A. 49: v A 1968 (5) 1972 (5) 1975 (4); v SA 1965 (1); v WI 1966 (3) 1969 (3) 1973 (1) 1976 (3); v NZ 1965 (1) 1969 (2) 1973 (3); v In 1967 (3) 1971 (2); v P 1967 (1); *v A 1970 (6); v WI 1967 (4); v P 1968 (2)*
Southerton, J. 2: *v A 1876 (2)*
Spooner, R. H. 10: v A 1905 (2) 1909 (2) 1912 (3); v SA 1912 (3)
Spooner, R. T. 7: v SA 1955 (1); *v In 1951 (5); v WI 1953 (1)*
Stanyforth, R. T. 4: *v SA 1927 (4)*
Staples, S. J. 3: *v SA 1927 (3)*
Statham, J. B. 70: v A 1953 (1) 1956 (3) 1961 (4); v SA 1951 (2) 1955 (4) 1960 (5) 1965 (1); v WI 1957 (3) 1963 (2); v NZ 1958 (2); v In 1959 (3); v P 1954 (4) 1962 (3); *v A 1954 (5) 1958 (4) 1962 (5); v SA 1956 (4); v WI 1953 (4) 1959 (3); v NZ 1950 (1) 1954 (2); v In 1951 (5)*
Steel, A. G. 13: v A 1880 (1) 1882 (1) 1884 (3) 1886 (3) 1888 (1); *v A 1882 (4)*
Steele, D. S. 8: v A 1975 (3); v WI 1976 (5)
Stephenson, J. P. 1: v A 1989
Stevens, G. T. S. 10: v A 1926 (2); *v SA 1922 (1) 1927 (5); v WI 1929 (2)*
Stevenson, G. B. 2: *v WI 1980 (1); v In 1979 (1)*
Stewart, A. J. 58: v A 1993 (6); v SA 1994 (3); v WI 1991 (1) 1995 (3); v NZ 1990 (3) 1994 (3); v In 1996 (2); v P 1992 (5) 1996 (3); v SL 1991 (1); *v A 1990 (5) 1994 (2); v SA 1995 (5); v WI 1989 (4) 1993 (5); v NZ 1991 (3); v In 1992 (3); v SL 1992 (1)*
Stewart, M. J. 8: v WI 1963 (4); v P 1962 (2); *v In 1963 (2)*
Stoddart, A. E. 16: v A 1893 (3) 1896 (2); *v A 1887 (1) 1891 (3) 1894 (5) 1897 (2)*
Storer, W. 6: v A 1899 (1); *v A 1897 (5)*
Street, G. B. 1: *v SA 1922*
Strudwick, H. 28: v A 1921 (2) 1926 (5); v SA 1924 (1); *v A 1911 (1) 1920 (4) 1924 (5); v SA 1909 (5) 1913 (5)*
Studd, C. T. 5: v A 1882 (1); *v A 1882 (4)*
Studd, G. B. 4: *v A 1882 (4)*
Subba Row, R. 13: v A 1961 (5); v SA 1960 (4); v NZ 1958 (1); v In 1959 (1); *v WI 1959 (2)*
Such, P. M. 8: v A 1993 (5); v NZ 1994 (3)
Sugg, F. H. 2: v A 1888 (2)
Sutcliffe, H. 54: v A 1926 (5) 1930 (4) 1934 (4); v SA 1924 (5) 1929 (5) 1935 (2); v WI 1928 (3) 1933 (2); v NZ 1931 (2); v In 1932 (1); *v A 1924 (5) 1928 (4) 1932 (5); v SA 1927 (5); v NZ 1932 (2)*
Swetman, R. 11: v In 1959 (3); *v A 1958 (2); v WI 1959 (4); v NZ 1958 (2)*

Tate, F. W. 1: v A 1902
Tate, M. W. 39: v A 1926 (5) 1930 (5); v SA 1924 (5) 1929 (3) 1935 (1); v WI 1928 (3); v NZ 1931 (1); *v A 1924 (5) 1928 (5); v SA 1930 (5); v NZ 1932 (1)*
Tattersall, R. 16: v A 1953 (1); v SA 1951 (5); v P 1954 (1); *v A 1950 (2); v NZ 1950 (2); v In 1951 (5)*
Tavaré, C. J. 31: v A 1981 (2) 1989 (1); v WI 1980 (2) 1984 (1); v NZ 1983 (4); v In 1982 (3); v P 1982 (3); v SL 1984 (1); *v A 1982 (5); v NZ 1983 (2); v In 1981 (6); v SL 1981 (1)*
Taylor, J. P. 2: v NZ 1994 (1); *v In 1992 (1)*
Taylor, K. 3: v A 1964 (1); v In 1959 (2)
Taylor, L. B. 2: v A 1985 (2)
Taylor, R. W. 57: v A 1981 (3); v NZ 1978 (3) 1983 (4); v In 1979 (3) 1982 (3); v P 1978 (3) 1982 (3); *v A 1978 (6) 1979 (3) 1982 (5); v NZ 1970 (1) 1977 (3) 1983 (3); v In 1979 (1) 1981 (6); v P 1977 (3) 1983 (3); v SL 1981 (1)*
Tennyson, Hon. L. H. 9: v A 1921 (4); *v SA 1913 (5)*
Terry, V. P. 2: v WI 1984 (2)
Thomas, J. G. 5: v NZ 1986 (1); *v WI 1985 (4)*
Thompson, G. J. 6: v A 1909 (1); *v SA 1909 (5)*
Thomson, N. I. 5: *v SA 1964 (5)*
Thorpe, G. P. 32: v A 1993 (3); v SA 1994 (2); v WI 1995 (6); v In 1996 (3); v P 1996 (3); *v A 1994 (5); v SA 1995 (5); v WI 1993 (5)*
Titmus, F. J. 53: v A 1964 (5); v SA 1955 (2) 1965 (3); v WI 1963 (4) 1966 (3); v NZ 1965 (3); v P 1962 (2) 1967 (2); *v A 1962 (5) 1965 (5) 1974 (4); v SA 1964 (5); v WI 1967 (2); v NZ 1962 (3); v In 1963 (5)*
Tolchard, R. W. 4: *v In 1976 (4)*
Townsend, C. L. 2: v A 1899 (2)
Townsend, D. C. H. 3: *v WI 1934 (3)*
Townsend, L. F. 4: *v WI 1929 (1); v In 1933 (3)*
Tremlett, M. F. 3: *v WI 1947 (3)*

Trott, A. E. 2: *v SA 1898 (2)*
Trueman, F. S. 67: v A 1953 (1) 1956 (2) 1961 (4) 1964 (4); v SA 1955 (1) 1960 (5); v WI 1957 (5) 1963 (5); v NZ 1958 (5) 1965 (2); v In 1952 (4) 1959 (5); v P 1962 (4); *v A 1958 (3) 1962 (5); v WI 1953 (3) 1959 (5); v NZ 1958 (2) 1962 (2)*
Tufnell, N. C. 1: *v SA 1909*
Tufnell, P. C. R. 22: v A 1993 (2); v SA 1994 (1); v WI 1991 (1); v P 1992 (1); v SL 1991 (1); *v A 1990 (4) 1994 (4); v WI 1993 (2); v NZ 1991 (3); v In 1992 (2); v SL 1992 (1)*
Turnbull, M. J. 9: v WI 1933 (2); v In 1936 (1); *v SA 1930 (5); v NZ 1929 (1)*
Tyldesley, E. 14: v A 1921 (3) 1926 (1); v SA 1924 (1); v WI 1928 (3); *v A 1928 (1): v SA 1927 (5)*
Tyldesley, J. T. 31: v A 1899 (2) 1902 (5) 1905 (5) 1909 (4); v SA 1907 (3); *v A 1901 (5) 1903 (5); v SA 1898 (2)*
Tyldesley, R. K. 7: v A 1930 (2); v SA 1924 (4); *v A 1924 (1)*
Tylecote, E. F. S. 6: v A 1886 (2); *v A 1882 (4)*
Tyler, E. J. 1: *v SA 1895*
Tyson, F. H. 17: v A 1956 (1); v SA 1955 (2); v P 1954 (1); *v A 1954 (5) 1958 (2); v SA 1956 (2); v NZ 1954 (2) 1958 (2)*

Ulyett, G. 25: v A 1882 (1) 1884 (3) 1886 (3) 1888 (2) 1890 (1); *v A 1876 (2) 1878 (1) 1881 (4) 1884 (5) 1887 (1); v SA 1888 (2)*
Underwood, D. L. 86: v A 1968 (4) 1972 (2) 1975 (4) 1977 (5); v WI 1966 (2) 1969 (2) 1973 (3) 1976 (5) 1980 (1); v NZ 1969 (3) 1973 (1); v In 1971 (1) 1974 (3); v P 1967 (2) 1971 (1) 1974 (3); *v A 1970 (5) 1974 (5) 1976 (1) 1979 (3); v WI 1973 (4); v NZ 1970 (2) 1974 (2); v In 1972 (4) 1976 (5) 1979 (1) 1981 (6); v P 1968 (3) 1972 (2); v SL 1981 (1)*

Valentine, B. H. 7: *v SA 1938 (5); v In 1933 (2)*
Verity, H. 40: v A 1934 (5) 1938 (4); v SA 1935 (4); v WI 1933 (2) 1939 (1); v NZ 1931 (2) 1937 (1); v In 1936 (3); *v A 1932 (4) 1936 (5); v SA 1938 (5); v NZ 1932 (1); v In 1933 (3)*
Vernon, G. F. 1: *v A 1882*
Vine, J. 2: *v A 1911 (2)*
Voce, W. 27: v NZ 1931 (1) 1937 (1); v In 1932 (1) 1936 (1) 1946 (1); *v A 1932 (4) 1936 (5) 1946 (2); v SA 1930 (5); v WI 1929 (4); v NZ 1932 (2)*

Waddington, A. 2: *v A 1920 (2)*
Wainwright, E. 5: v A 1893 (1); *v A 1897 (4)*
Walker, P. M. 3: v SA 1960 (3)
Walters, C. F. 11: v A 1934 (5); v WI 1933 (3); *v In 1933 (3)*
Ward, A. 5: v WI 1976 (1); v NZ 1969 (3); v P 1971 (1)
Ward, A. 7: v A 1893 (2); *v A 1894 (5)*
Wardle, J. H. 28: v A 1953 (3) 1956 (1); v SA 1951 (2) 1955 (3); v WI 1950 (1) 1957 (1); v P 1954 (4); *v A 1954 (4); v SA 1956 (4); v WI 1947 (1) 1953 (2); v NZ 1954 (2)*
Warner, P. F. 15: v A 1909 (1) 1912 (1); v SA 1912 (1); *v A 1903 (5); v SA 1898 (2) 1905 (5)*
Warr, J. J. 2: *v A 1950 (2)*
Warren, A. R. 1: v A 1905
Washbrook, C. 37: v A 1948 (4) 1956 (3); v SA 1947 (5); v WI 1950 (2); v NZ 1937 (1) 1949 (2); v In 1946 (3); *v A 1946 (5) 1950 (5); v SA 1948 (5); v NZ 1946 (1) 1950 (1)*
Watkin, S. L. 3: v A 1993 (1); v WI 1991 (2)
Watkins, A. J. 15: v A 1948 (1); v NZ 1949 (1); v In 1952 (3); *v SA 1948 (5); v In 1951 (5)*
Watkinson, M. 4: v WI 1995 (3); *v SA 1995 (1)*
Watson, W. 23: v A 1953 (3) 1956 (2); v SA 1951 (5) 1955 (1); v NZ 1958 (2); v In 1952 (1); *v A 1958 (2); v WI 1953 (5); v NZ 1958 (2)*
Webbe, A. J. 1: *v A 1878*
Wellard, A. W. 2: v A 1938 (1); v NZ 1937 (1)
Wells, A. P. 1: v WI 1995
Wharton, A. 1: v NZ 1949
Whitaker, J. J. 1: *v A 1986*
White, C. 6: v SA 1994 (1); v WI 1995 (2); v NZ 1994 (3)
White, D. W. 2: v *P 1961 (2)*
White, J. C. 15: v A 1921 (1) 1930 (1); v SA 1929 (3); v WI 1928 (1); *v A 1928 (5); v SA 1930 (4)*
Whysall, W. W. 4: v A 1930 (1); *v A 1924 (3)*
Wilkinson, L. L. 3: *v SA 1938 (3)*
Willey, P. 26: v A 1980 (1) 1981 (4) 1985 (1); v WI 1976 (2) 1980 (5); v NZ 1986 (1); v In 1979 (1); *v A 1979 (3); v WI 1980 (4) 1985 (4)*

Williams, N. F. 1: v In 1990
Willis, R. G. D. 90: v A 1977 (5) 1981 (6); v WI 1973 (1) 1976 (2) 1980 (4) 1984 (3); v NZ 1978 (3) 1983 (4); v In 1974 (1) 1979 (3) 1982 (3); v P 1974 (1) 1978 (3) 1982 (2); *v A 1970 (4) 1974 (5) 1976 (1) 1978 (6) 1979 (3) 1982 (5); v WI 1973 (3); v NZ 1970 (1) 1977 (3) 1983 (3); v In 1976 (5) 1981 (5); v P 1977 (3) 1983 (1); v SL 1981 (1)*
Wilson, C. E. M. 2: *v SA 1898 (2)*
Wilson, D. 6: *v NZ 1970 (1); v In 1963 (5)*
Wilson, E. R. 1: *v A 1920*
Wood, A. 4: v A 1938 (1); v WI 1939 (3)
Wood, B. 12: v A 1972 (1) 1975 (3); v WI 1976 (1); v P 1978 (1); *v NZ 1974 (2); v In 1972 (3); v P 1972 (1)*
Wood, G. E. C. 3: v SA 1924 (3)
Wood, H. 4: v A 1888 (1); *v SA 1888 (2) 1891 (1)*
Wood, R. 1: *v A 1886*
Woods S. M. J. 3: *v SA 1895 (3)*
Woolley, F. E. 64: v A 1909 (1) 1912 (3) 1921 (5) 1926 (5) 1930 (2) 1934 (1); v SA 1912 (3) 1924 (5) 1929 (3); v NZ 1931 (1); v In 1932 (1); *v A 1911 (5) 1920 (5) 1924 (5); v SA 1909 (5) 1913 (5) 1922 (5); v NZ 1929 (4)*
Woolmer, R. A. 19: v A 1975 (2) 1977 (5) 1981 (2); v WI 1976 (5) 1980 (2); *v A 1976 (1); v In 1976 (2)*
Worthington, T. S. 9: v In 1936 (2); *v A 1936 (3); v NZ 1929 (4)*
Wright, C. W. 3: *v SA 1895 (3)*
Wright, D. V. P. 34: v A 1938 (3) 1948 (1); v SA 1947 (4); v WI 1939 (3) 1950 (1); v NZ 1949 (1); v In 1946 (2); *v A 1946 (5) 1950 (5); v SA 1938 (3) 1948 (3); v NZ 1946 (1) 1950 (2)*
Wyatt, R. E. S. 40: v A 1930 (1) 1934 (4); v SA 1929 (2) 1935 (5); v WI 1933 (2); v In 1936 (1); *v A 1932 (5) 1936 (2); v SA 1927 (5) 1930 (5); v WI 1929 (2) 1934 (4); v NZ 1932 (2)*
Wynyard, E. G. 3: v A 1896 (1); *v SA 1905 (2)*

Yardley, N. W. D. 20: v A 1948 (5); v SA 1947 (5); v WI 1950 (3); *v A 1946 (5); v SA 1938 (1); v NZ 1946 (1)*
Young, H. I. 2: v A 1899 (2)
Young, J. A. 8: v A 1948 (3); v SA 1947 (1); v NZ 1949 (2); *v SA 1948 (2)*
Young, R. A. 2: *v A 1907 (2)*

AUSTRALIA

Number of Test cricketers: 366

a'Beckett, E. L. 4: v E 1928 (2); v SA 1931 (1); *v E 1930 (1)*
Alderman, T. M. 41: v E 1982 (1) 1990 (4); v WI 1981 (2) 1984 (3) 1988 (2); v NZ 1989 (1); v P 1981 (3) 1989 (2); v SL 1989 (2); *v E 1981 (6) 1989 (6); v WI 1983 (3) 1990 (1); v NZ 1981 (3) 1989 (1); v P 1982 (1)*
Alexander, G. 2: v E 1884 (1); *v E 1880 (1)*
Alexander, H. H. 1: v E 1932
Allan, F. E. 1: v E 1878
Allan, P. J. 1: v E 1965
Allen, R. C. 1: v E 1886
Andrews, T. J. E. 16: v E 1924 (3); *v E 1921 (5) 1926 (5); v SA 1921 (3)*
Angel, J. 4: v E 1994 (1); v WI 1992 (1); *v P 1994 (2)*
Archer, K. A. 5: v E 1950 (3); v WI 1951 (2)
Archer, R. G. 19: v E 1954 (4); v SA 1952 (1); *v E 1953 (3) 1956 (5); v WI 1954 (5); v P 1956 (1)*
Armstrong, W. W. 50: v E 1901 (4) 1903 (3) 1907 (5) 1911 (5) 1920 (5); v SA 1910 (5); *v E 1902 (5) 1905 (5) 1909 (5) 1921 (5); v SA 1902 (3)*

Badcock, C. L. 7: v E 1936 (3); *v E 1938 (4)*
Bannerman, A. C. 28: v E 1878 (1) 1881 (3) 1882 (4) 1884 (4) 1886 (1) 1887 (1) 1891 (3); *v E 1880 (1) 1882 (1) 1884 (3) 1888 (3) 1893 (3)*
Bannerman, C. 3: v E 1876 (2) 1878 (1)
Bardsley, W. 41: v E 1911 (4) 1920 (5) 1924 (3); v SA 1910 (5); *v E 1909 (5) 1912 (3) 1921 (5) 1926 (5); v SA 1912 (3) 1921 (3)*

Barnes, S. G. 13: v E 1946 (4); v In 1947 (3); *v E 1938 (1) 1948 (4); v NZ 1945 (1)*
Barnett, B. A. 4: *v E 1938 (4)*
Barrett, J. E. 2: *v E 1890 (2)*
Beard, G. R. 3: *v P 1979 (3)*
Benaud, J. 3: v P 1972 (2); *v WI 1972 (1)*
Benaud, R. 63: v E 1954 (5) 1958 (5) 1962 (5); v SA 1952 (4) 1963 (4); v WI 1951 (1) 1960 (5); *v E 1953 (3) 1956 (5) 1961 (4); v SA 1957 (5); v WI 1954 (5); v In 1956 (3) 1959 (5); v P 1956 (1) 1959 (3)*
Bennett, M. J. 3: v WI 1984 (2); *v E 1985 (1)*
Bevan, M. G. 6: v E 1994 (3); *v P 1994 (3)*
Blackham, J. McC. 35: v E 1876 (2) 1878 (1) 1881 (4) 1882 (4) 1884 (2) 1886 (1) 1887 (1) 1891 (3) 1894 (1); *v E 1880 (1) 1882 (1) 1884 (3) 1886 (3) 1888 (3) 1890 (2) 1893 (3)*
Blackie, D. D. 3: v E 1928 (3)
Blewett, G. S. 9: v E 1994 (2); v P 1995 (3); *v WI 1994 (4)*
Bonnor, G. J. 17: v E 1882 (4) 1884 (3); *v E 1880 (1) 1882 (1) 1884 (3) 1886 (2) 1888 (3)*
Boon, D. C. 107: v E 1986 (4) 1987 (1) 1990 (5) 1994 (5); v SA 1993 (3); v WI 1984 (3) 1988 (5) 1992 (5); v NZ 1985 (3) 1987 (3) 1989 (1) 1993 (3); v In 1985 (3) 1991 (5); v P 1989 (2) 1995 (3); v SL 1987 (1) 1989 (2) 1995 (3); *v E 1985 (4) 1989 (6) 1993 (6); v SA 1993 (3); v WI 1990 (5) 1994 (4); v NZ 1985 (3) 1989 (1) 1992 (3); v In 1986 (3); v P 1988 (3) 1994 (3); v SL 1992 (3)*
Booth, B. C. 29: v E 1962 (5) 1965 (3); v SA 1963 (4); v P 1964 (1); *v E 1961 (2) 1964 (5); v WI 1964 (5); v In 1964 (3); v P 1964 (1)*
Border, A. R. 156: v E 1978 (3) 1979 (3) 1982 (5) 1986 (5) 1987 (1) 1990 (5); v SA 1993 (3); v WI 1979 (3) 1981 (3) 1984 (5) 1988 (5) 1992 (5); v NZ 1980 (3) 1985 (3) 1987 (3) 1989 (1) 1993 (3); v In 1980 (3) 1985 (3) 1991 (5); v P 1978 (2) 1981 (3) 1983 (5) 1989 (3); v SL 1987 (1) 1989 (2); *v E 1980 (1) 1981 (6) 1985 (6) 1989 (6) 1993 (6); v SA 1993 (3); v WI 1983 (5) 1990 (5); v NZ 1981 (3) 1985 (3) 1989 (1) 1992 (3); v In 1979 (6) 1986 (3); v P 1979 (3) 1982 (3) 1988 (3); v SL 1982 (1) 1992 (3)*
Boyle, H. F. 12: v E 1878 (1) 1881 (4) 1882 (1) 1884 (1); *v E 1880 (1) 1882 (1) 1884 (3)*
Bradman, D. G. 52: v E 1928 (4) 1932 (4) 1936 (5) 1946 (5); v SA 1931 (5); v WI 1930 (5); v In 1947 (5); *v E 1930 (5) 1934 (5) 1938 (4) 1948 (5)*
Bright, R. J. 25: v E 1979 (1); v WI 1979 (1); v NZ 1985 (1); v In 1985 (3); *v E 1977 (3) 1980 (1) 1981 (5); v NZ 1985 (2); v In 1986 (3); v P 1979 (3) 1982 (2)*
Bromley, E. H. 2: v E 1932 (1); *v E 1934 (1)*
Brown, W. A. 22: v E 1936 (2); v In 1947 (3); *v E 1934 (5) 1938 (4) 1948 (2); v SA 1935 (5); v NZ 1945 (1)*
Bruce, W. 14: v E 1884 (2) 1891 (3) 1894 (4); *v E 1886 (2) 1893 (3)*
Burge, P. J. 42: v E 1954 (1) 1958 (1) 1962 (3) 1965 (4); v SA 1963 (5); v WI 1960 (2); *v E 1956 (3) 1961 (5) 1964 (5); v SA 1957 (1); v WI 1954 (1); v In 1956 (3) 1959 (2) 1964 (3); v P 1959 (2) 1964 (1)*
Burke, J. W. 24: v E 1950 (2) 1954 (2) 1958 (5); v WI 1951 (1); *v E 1956 (5); v SA 1957 (5); v In 1956 (3); v P 1956 (1)*
Burn, K. E. 2: *v E 1890 (2)*
Burton, F. J. 2: v E 1886 (1) 1887 (1)

Callaway, S. T. 3: v E 1891 (2) 1894 (1)
Callen, I. W. 1: v In 1977
Campbell, G. D. 4: v P 1989 (1); v SL 1989 (1); *v E 1989 (1); v NZ 1989 (1)*
Carkeek, W. 6: *v E 1912 (3); v SA 1912 (3)*
Carlson, P. H. 2: v E 1978 (2)
Carter, H. 28: v E 1907 (5) 1911 (5) 1920 (2); v SA 1910 (5); *v E 1909 (5) 1921 (4); v SA 1921 (2)*
Chappell, G. S. 87: v E 1970 (5) 1974 (6) 1976 (1) 1979 (3) 1982 (5); v WI 1975 (6) 1979 (3) 1981 (3); v NZ 1973 (3) 1980 (3); v In 1980 (3); v P 1972 (3) 1976 (3) 1981 (3) 1983 (5); *v E 1972 (5) 1975 (4) 1977 (5) 1980 (1); v WI 1972 (5); v NZ 1973 (3) 1976 (2) 1981 (3); v P 1979 (3); v SL 1982 (1)*
Chappell, I. M. 75: v E 1965 (2) 1970 (6) 1974 (6) 1979 (2); v WI 1968 (5) 1975 (6) 1979 (1); v NZ 1973 (3); v In 1967 (4); v P 1964 (1) 1972 (3); *v E 1968 (5) 1972 (5) 1975 (4); v SA 1966 (5) 1969 (4); v WI 1972 (5); v NZ 1973 (3); v In 1969 (5)*
Chappell, T. M. 3: *v E 1981 (3)*
Charlton, P. C. 2: *v E 1890 (2)*
Chipperfield, A. G. 14: v E 1936 (3); *v E 1934 (5) 1938 (1); v SA 1935 (5)*
Clark, W. M. 10: v In 1977 (5); v P 1978 (1); *v WI 1977 (4)*
Colley, D. J. 3: *v E 1972 (3)*

Collins, H. L. 19: v E 1920 (5) 1924 (5); *v E 1921 (3) 1926 (3); v SA 1921 (3)*
Coningham, A. 1: v E 1894
Connolly, A. N. 29: v E 1965 (1) 1970 (1); v SA 1963 (3); v WI 1968 (5); v In 1967 (3); *v E 1968 (5); v SA 1969 (4); v In 1964 (2) 1969 (5)*
Cooper, B. B. 1: v E 1876
Cooper, W. H. 2: v E 1881 (1) 1884 (1)
Corling, G. E. 5: *v E 1964 (5)*
Cosier, G. J. 18: v E 1976 (1) 1978 (2); v WI 1975 (3); v In 1977 (4); v P 1976 (3); *v WI 1977 (3); v NZ 1976 (2)*
Cottam, J. T. 1: v E 1886
Cotter, A. 21: v E 1903 (2) 1907 (2) 1911 (4); v SA 1910 (5); *v E 1905 (3) 1909 (5)*
Coulthard, G. 1: v E 1881
Cowper, R. M. 27: v E 1965 (4); v In 1967 (4); v P 1964 (1); *v E 1964 (1) 1968 (4); v SA 1966 (5); v WI 1964 (5); v In 1964 (2); v P 1964 (1)*
Craig, I. D. 11: v SA 1952 (1); *v E 1956 (2); v SA 1957 (5); v In 1956 (2); v P 1956 (1)*
Crawford, P. 4: *v E 1956 (1); v In 1956 (3)*

Darling, J. 34: v E 1894 (5) 1897 (5) 1901 (3); *v E 1896 (3) 1899 (5) 1902 (5) 1905 (5); v SA 1902 (3)*
Darling, L. S. 12: v E 1932 (2) 1936 (1); *v E 1934 (4); v SA 1935 (5)*
Darling, W. M. 14: v E 1978 (4); v In 1977 (1); v P 1978 (1); *v WI 1977 (3); v In 1979 (5)*
Davidson, A. K. 44: v E 1954 (3) 1958 (5) 1962 (5); v WI 1960 (4); *v E 1953 (5) 1956 (2) 1961 (5); v SA 1957 (5); v In 1956 (1) 1959 (5); v P 1956 (1) 1959 (3)*
Davis, I. C. 15: v E 1976 (1); v NZ 1973 (3); v P 1976 (3); *v E 1977 (3); v NZ 1973 (3) 1976 (2)*
Davis, S. P. 1: *v NZ 1985*
De Courcy, J. H. 3: *v E 1953 (3)*
Dell, A. R. 2: v E 1970 (1); v NZ 1973 (1)
Dodemaide, A. I. C. 10: v E 1987 (1); v WI 1988 (2); v NZ 1987 (1); v SL 1987 (1); *v P 1988 (3); v SL 1992 (2)*
Donnan, H. 5: v E 1891 (2); *v E 1896 (3)*
Dooland, B. 3: v E 1946 (2); v In 1947 (1)
Duff, R. A. 22: v E 1901 (4) 1903 (5); *v E 1902 (5) 1905 (5); v SA 1902 (3)*
Duncan, J. R. F. 1: v E 1970
Dyer, G. C. 6: v E 1986 (1) 1987 (1); v NZ 1987 (3); v SL 1987 (1)
Dymock, G. 21: v E 1974 (1) 1978 (3) 1979 (3); v WI 1979 (2); v NZ 1973 (1); v P 1978 (1); *v NZ 1973 (2); v In 1979 (5); v P 1979 (3)*
Dyson, J. 30: v E 1982 (5); v WI 1981 (2) 1984 (3); v NZ 1980 (3); v In 1977 (3) 1980 (3); *v E 1981 (5); v NZ 1981 (3); v P 1982 (3)*

Eady, C. J. 2: v E 1901 (1); *v E 1896 (1)*
Eastwood, K. H. 1: v E 1970
Ebeling, H. I. 1: *v E 1934*
Edwards, J. D. 3: *v E 1888 (3)*
Edwards, R. 20: v E 1974 (5); v P 1972 (2); *v E 1972 (4) 1975 (4); v WI 1972 (5)*
Edwards, W. J. 3: v E 1974 (3)
Emery, P. A. 1: *v P 1994*
Emery, S. H. 4: *v E 1912 (2); v SA 1912 (2)*
Evans, E. 6: v E 1881 (2) 1882 (1) 1884 (1); *v E 1886 (2)*

Fairfax, A. G. 10: v E 1928 (1); v WI 1930 (5); *v E 1930 (4)*
Favell, L. E. 19: v E 1954 (4) 1958 (2); v WI 1960 (4); *v WI 1954 (2); v In 1959 (4); v P 1959 (3)*
Ferris, J. J. 8: v E 1886 (2) 1887 (1); *v E 1888 (3) 1890 (2)*
Fingleton, J. H. 18: v E 1932 (3) 1936 (5); v SA 1931 (1); *v E 1938 (4); v SA 1935 (5)*
Fleetwood-Smith, L. O'B. 10: v E 1936 (3); *v E 1938 (4); v SA 1935 (3)*
Fleming, D. W. 4: v E 1994 (3); *v P 1994 (1)*
Francis, B. C. 3: *v E 1972 (3)*
Freeman, E. W. 11: v WI 1968 (4); v In 1967 (2); *v E 1968 (2); v SA 1969 (2); v In 1969 (1)*
Freer, F. W. 1: v E 1946

Gannon, J. B. 3: v In 1977 (3)
Garrett, T. W. 19: v E 1876 (2) 1878 (1) 1881 (3) 1882 (3) 1884 (3) 1886 (2) 1887 (1); *v E 1882 (1) 1886 (3)*
Gaunt, R. A. 3: v SA 1963 (1); *v E 1961 (1); v SA 1957 (1)*

Gehrs, D. R. A. 6: v E 1903 (1); v SA 1910 (4); *v E 1905 (1)*
Giffen, G. 31: v E 1881 (3) 1882 (4) 1884 (3) 1891 (3) 1894 (5); *v E 1882 (1) 1884 (3) 1886 (3) 1893 (3) 1896 (3)*
Giffen, W. F. 3: v E 1886 (1) 1891 (2)
Gilbert, D. R. 9: v NZ 1985 (3); v In 1985 (2); *v E 1985 (1); v NZ 1985 (1); v In 1986 (2)*
Gilmour, G. J. 15: v E 1976 (1); v WI 1975 (5); v NZ 1973 (2); v P 1976 (3); *v E 1975 (1); v NZ 1973 (1) 1976 (2)*
Gleeson, J. W. 29: v E 1970 (5); v WI 1968 (5); v In 1967 (4); *v E 1968 (5) 1972 (3); v SA 1969 (4); v In 1969 (3)*
Graham, H. 6: v E 1894 (2); *v E 1893 (3) 1896 (1)*
Gregory, D. W. 3: v E 1876 (2) 1878 (1)
Gregory, E. J. 1: v E 1876
Gregory, J. M. 24: v E 1920 (5) 1924 (5) 1928 (1); *v E 1921 (5) 1926 (5); v SA 1921 (3)*
Gregory, R. G. 2: v E 1936 (2)
Gregory, S. E. 58: v E 1891 (1) 1894 (5) 1897 (5) 1901 (5) 1903 (4) 1907 (2) 1911 (1); *v E 1890 (2) 1893 (3) 1896 (3) 1899 (5) 1902 (5) 1905 (3) 1909 (5) 1912 (3); v SA 1902 (3) 1912 (3)*
Grimmett, C. V. 37: v E 1924 (1) 1928 (5) 1932 (3); v SA 1931 (5); v WI 1930 (5); *v E 1926 (3) 1930 (5) 1934 (5); v SA 1935 (5)*
Groube, T. U. 1: *v E 1880*
Grout, A. T. W. 51: v E 1958 (5) 1962 (2) 1965 (5); v SA 1963 (5); v WI 1960 (5); *v E 1961 (5) 1964 (5); v SA 1957 (5); v WI 1964 (5); v In 1959 (4) 1964 (1); v P 1959 (3) 1964 (1)*
Guest, C. E. J. 1: v E 1962

Hamence, R. A. 3: v E 1946 (1); v In 1947 (2)
Hammond, J. R. 5: *v WI 1972 (5)*
Harry, J. 1: v E 1894
Hartigan, R. J. 2: v E 1907 (2)
Hartkopf, A. E. V. 1: v E 1924
Harvey, M. R. 1: v E 1946
Harvey, R. N. 79: v E 1950 (5) 1954 (5) 1958 (5) 1962 (5); v SA 1952 (5); v WI 1951 (5) 1960 (4); v In 1947 (2); *v E 1948 (2) 1953 (5) 1956 (5) 1961 (5); v SA 1949 (5) 1957 (4); v WI 1954 (5); v In 1956 (3) 1959 (5); v P 1956 (1) 1959 (3)*
Hassett, A. L. 43: v E 1946 (5) 1950 (5); v SA 1952 (5); v WI 1951 (4); v In 1947 (4); *v E 1938 (4) 1948 (5) 1953 (5); v SA 1949 (5); v NZ 1945 (1)*
Hawke, N. J. N. 27: v E 1962 (1) 1965 (4); v SA 1963 (4); v In 1967 (1); v P 1964 (1); *v E 1964 (5) 1968 (2); v SA 1966 (2); v WI 1964 (5); v In 1964 (1); v P 1964 (1)*
Hayden, M. L. 1: *v SA 1993*
Hazlitt, G. R. 9: v E 1907 (2) 1911 (1); *v E 1912 (3); v SA 1912 (3)*
Healy, I. A. 79: v E 1990 (5) 1994 (5); v SA 1993 (3); v WI 1988 (5) 1992 (5); v NZ 1989 (1) 1993 (3); v In 1991 (5); v P 1989 (3) 1995 (3); v SL 1989 (2) 1995 (3); *v E 1989 (6) 1993 (6); v SA 1993 (3); v WI 1990 (5) 1994 (4); v NZ 1989 (1) 1992 (3); v P 1988 (3) 1994 (2); v SL 1992 (3)*
Hendry, H. L. 11: v E 1924 (1) 1928 (4); *v E 1921 (4); v SA 1921 (2)*
Hibbert, P. A. 1: v In 1977
Higgs, J. D. 22: v E 1978 (5) 1979 (1); v WI 1979 (1); v NZ 1980 (3); v In 1980 (2); *v WI 1977 (4); v In 1979 (6)*
Hilditch, A. M. J. 18: v E 1978 (1); v WI 1984 (2); v NZ 1985 (1); v P 1978 (2); *v E 1985 (6); v In 1979 (6)*
Hill, C. 49: v E 1897 (5) 1901 (5) 1903 (5) 1907 (5) 1911 (5); v SA 1910 (5); *v E 1896 (3) 1899 (3) 1902 (5) 1905 (5); v SA 1902 (3)*
Hill, J. C. 3: *v E 1953 (2); v WI 1954 (1)*
Hoare, D. E. 1: v WI 1960
Hodges, J. 2: v E 1876 (2)
Hogan, T. G. 7: v P 1983 (1); *v WI 1983 (5); v SL 1982 (1)*
Hogg, R. M. 38: v E 1978 (6) 1982 (3); v WI 1979 (2) 1984 (4); v NZ 1980 (2); v In 1980 (2); v P 1978 (2) 1983 (4); *v E 1981 (2); v WI 1983 (4); v In 1979 (6); v SL 1982 (1)*
Hohns, T. V. 7: v WI 1988 (2); *v E 1989 (5)*
Hole, G. B. 18: v E 1950 (1) 1954 (3); v SA 1952 (4); v WI 1951 (5); *v E 1953 (5)*
Holland, R. G. 11: v WI 1984 (3); v NZ 1985 (3); v In 1985 (1); *v E 1985 (4)*
Hookes, D. W. 23: v E 1976 (1) 1982 (5); v WI 1979 (1); v NZ 1985 (2); v In 1985 (2); *v E 1977 (5); v WI 1983 (5); v P 1979 (1); v SL 1982 (1)*
Hopkins, A. J. 20: v E 1901 (2) 1903 (5); *v E 1902 (5) 1905 (3) 1909 (2); v SA 1902 (3)*
Horan, T. P. 15: v E 1876 (1) 1878 (1) 1881 (4) 1882 (4) 1884 (4); *v E 1882 (1)*

Hordern, H. V. 7: v E 1911 (5); v SA 1910 (2)
Hornibrook, P. M. 6: v E 1928 (1); *v E 1930 (5)*
Howell, W. P. 18: v E 1897 (3) 1901 (4) 1903 (3); *v E 1899 (5) 1902 (1); v SA 1902 (2)*
Hughes, K. J. 70: v E 1978 (6) 1979 (3) 1982 (5); v WI 1979 (3) 1981 (3) 1984 (4); v NZ 1980 (3); v In 1977 (2) 1980 (3); v P 1978 (2) 1981 (3) 1983 (5); *v E 1977 (1) 1980 (1) 1981 (6); v WI 1983 (5); v NZ 1981 (3); v In 1979 (6); v P 1979 (3) 1982 (3)*
Hughes, M. G. 53: v E 1986 (4) 1990 (4); v WI 1988 (4) 1992 (5); v NZ 1987 (1) 1989 (1); v In 1985 (1) 1991 (5); v P 1989 (3); v SL 1987 (1) 1989 (2); *v E 1989 (6) 1993 (6); v SA 1993 (2); v WI 1990 (5); v NZ 1992 (3)*
Hunt, W. A. 1: v SA 1931
Hurst, A. G. 12: v E 1978 (6); v NZ 1973 (1); v In 1977 (1); v P 1978 (2); *v In 1979 (2)*
Hurwood, A. 2: v WI 1930 (2)

Inverarity, R. J. 6: v WI 1968 (1); *v E 1968 (2) 1972 (3)*
Iredale, F. A. 14: v E 1894 (5) 1897 (4); *v E 1896 (2) 1899 (3)*
Ironmonger, H. 14: v E 1928 (2) 1932 (4); v SA 1931 (4); v WI 1930 (4)
Iverson, J. B. 5: v E 1950 (5)

Jackson, A. A. 8: v E 1928 (2); v WI 1930 (4); *v E 1930 (2)*
Jarman, B. N. 19: v E 1962 (3); v WI 1968 (4); v In 1967 (4); v P 1964 (1); *v E 1968 (4); v In 1959 (1) 1964 (2)*
Jarvis, A. H. 11: v E 1884 (3) 1894 (4); *v E 1886 (2) 1888 (2)*
Jenner, T. J. 9: v E 1970 (2) 1974 (2); v WI 1975 (1); *v WI 1972 (4)*
Jennings, C. B. 6: *v E 1912 (3); v SA 1912 (3)*
Johnson I. W. 45: v E 1946 (4) 1950 (5) 1954 (4); v SA 1952 (1); v WI 1951 (4); v In 1947 (4); *v E 1948 (4) 1956 (5); v SA 1949 (5); v WI 1954 (5); v NZ 1945 (1); v In 1956 (2); v P 1956 (1)*
Johnson, L. J. 1: v In 1947
Johnston W. A. 40: v E 1950 (5) 1954 (4); v SA 1952 (5); v WI 1951 (5); v In 1947 (4); *v E 1948 (5) 1953 (3); v SA 1949 (5); v WI 1954 (4)*
Jones, D. M. 52: v E 1986 (5) 1987 (1) 1990 (5); v WI 1988 (3); v NZ 1987 (3) 1989 (1); v In 1991 (5); v P 1989 (3); v SL 1987 (1) 1989 (2); *v E 1989 (6); v WI 1983 (2) 1990 (5); v NZ 1989 (1); v In 1986 (3); v P 1988 (3); v SL 1992 (3)*
Jones, E. 19: v E 1894 (1) 1897 (5) 1901 (2); *v E 1896 (3) 1899 (5) 1902 (2); v SA 1902 (1)*
Jones, S. P. 12: v E 1881 (2) 1884 (4) 1886 (1) 1887 (1); *v E 1882 (1) 1886 (3)*
Joslin, L. R. 1: v In 1967
Julian, B. P. 7: v SL 1995 (1); *v E 1993 (2); v WI 1994 (4)*

Kelleway, C. 26: v E 1911 (4) 1920 (5) 1924 (5) 1928 (1); v SA 1910 (5); *v E 1912 (3); v SA 1912 (3)*
Kelly, J. J. 36: v E 1897 (5) 1901 (5) 1903 (5); *v E 1896 (3) 1899 (5) 1902 (5) 1905 (5); v SA 1902 (3)*
Kelly, T. J. D. 2: v E 1876 (1) 1878 (1)
Kendall, T. 2: v E 1876 (2)
Kent, M. F. 3: *v E 1981 (3)*
Kerr, R. B. 2: v NZ 1985 (2)
Kippax, A. F. 22: v E 1924 (1) 1928 (5) 1932 (1); v SA 1931 (4); v WI 1930 (5); *v E 1930 (5) 1934 (1)*
Kline L. F. 13: v E 1958 (2); v WI 1960 (2); *v SA 1957 (5); v In 1959 (3); v P 1959 (1)*

Laird, B. M. 21: v E 1979 (2); v WI 1979 (3) 1981 (3); v P 1981 (3); *v E 1980 (1); v NZ 1981 (3); v P 1979 (3) 1982 (3)*
Langer, J. L. 6: v WI 1992 (2); *v NZ 1992 (3); v P 1994 (1)*
Langley, G. R. A. 26: v E 1954 (2); v SA 1952 (5); v WI 1951 (5); *v E 1953 (4) 1956 (3); v WI 1954 (4); v In 1956 (2); v P 1956 (1)*
Laughlin, T. J. 3: v E 1978 (1); *v WI 1977 (2)*
Laver, F. 15: v E 1901 (1) 1903 (1); *v E 1899 (4) 1905 (5) 1909 (4)*
Law, S. G. 1: v SL 1995
Lawry, W. M. 67: v E 1962 (5) 1965 (5) 1970 (5); v SA 1963 (5); v WI 1968 (5); v In 1967 (4); v P 1964 (1); *v E 1961 (5) 1964 (5) 1968 (4); v SA 1966 (5) 1969 (4); v WI 1964 (5); v In 1964 (3) 1969 (5); v P 1964 (1)*
Lawson, G. F. 46: v E 1982 (5) 1986 (1); v WI 1981 (1) 1984 (5) 1988 (1); v NZ 1980 (1) 1985 (2) 1989 (1); v P 1983 (5); v SL 1989 (1); *v E 1981 (3) 1985 (6) 1989 (6); v WI 1983 (5); v P 1982 (3)*
Lee, P. K. 2: v E 1932 (1); v SA 1931 (1)

Lillee, D. K. 70: v E 1970 (2) 1974 (6) 1976 (1) 1979 (3) 1982 (1); v WI 1975 (5) 1979 (3) 1981 (3); v NZ 1980 (3); v In 1980 (3); v P 1972 (3) 1976 (3) 1981 (3) 1983 (5); *v E 1972 (5) 1975 (4) 1980 (1) 1981 (6); v WI 1972 (1); v NZ 1976 (2) 1981 (3); v P 1979 (3); v SL 1982 (1)*
Lindwall, R. R. 61: v E 1946 (4) 1950 (5) 1954 (4) 1958 (2); v SA 1952 (4); v WI 1951 (5); v In 1947 (5); *v E 1948 (5) 1953 (5) 1956 (4); v SA 1949 (4); v WI 1954 (5); v NZ 1945 (1); v In 1956 (3) 1959 (2); v P 1956 (1) 1959 (2)*
Love, H. S. B. 1: v E 1932
Loxton, S. J. E. 12: v E 1950 (3); v In 1947 (1); *v E 1948 (3); v SA 1949 (5)*
Lyons, J. J. 14: v E 1886 (1) 1891 (3) 1894 (3) 1897 (1); *v E 1888 (1) 1890 (2) 1893 (3)*

McAlister, P. A. 8: v E 1903 (2) 1907 (4); *v E 1909 (2)*
Macartney, C. G. 35: v E 1907 (5) 1911 (1) 1920 (2); v SA 1910 (4); *v E 1909 (5) 1912 (3) 1921 (5) 1926 (5); v SA 1912 (3) 1921 (2)*
McCabe, S. J. 39: v E 1932 (5) 1936 (5); v SA 1931 (5); v WI 1930 (5); *v E 1930 (5) 1934 (5) 1938 (4); v SA 1935 (5)*
McCool, C. L. 14: v E 1946 (5); v In 1947 (3); *v SA 1949 (5); v NZ 1945 (1)*
McCormick, E. L. 12: v E 1936 (4); *v E 1938 (3); v SA 1935 (5)*
McCosker, R. B. 25: v E 1974 (3) 1976 (1) 1979 (2); v WI 1975 (4) 1979 (1); v P 1976 (3); *v E 1975 (4) 1977 (5); v NZ 1976 (2)*
McDermott, C. J. 71: v E 1986 (1) 1987 (1) 1990 (2) 1994 (5); v SA 1993 (3); v WI 1984 (2) 1988 (2) 1992 (5); v NZ 1985 (2) 1987 (3) 1993 (3); v In 1985 (2) 1991 (5); v P 1995 (3); v SL 1987 (1) 1995 (3); *v E 1985 (6) 1993 (2); v SA 1993 (3); v WI 1990 (5); v NZ 1985 (2) 1992 (3); v In 1986 (2); v P 1994 (2); v SL 1992 (3)*
McDonald, C. C. 47: v E 1954 (2) 1958 (5); v SA 1952 (5); v WI 1951 (1) 1960 (5); *v E 1956 (5) 1961 (3); v SA 1957 (5); v WI 1954 (5); v In 1956 (2) 1959 (5); v P 1956 (1) 1959 (3)*
McDonald, E. A. 11: v E 1920 (3); *v E 1921 (5); v SA 1921 (3)*
McDonnell, P. S. 19: v E 1881 (4) 1882 (3) 1884 (2) 1886 (2) 1887 (1); *v E 1880 (1) 1884 (3) 1888 (3)*
McGrath, G. D. 19: v E 1994 (2); v SA 1993 (1); v NZ 1993 (2); v P 1995 (3); v SL 1995 (3); *v SA 1993 (2); v WI 1994 (4); v P 1994 (2)*
McIlwraith, J. 1: *v E 1886*
McIntyre, P. E. 1: v E 1994
Mackay, K. D. 37: v E 1958 (5) 1962 (3); v WI 1960 (5); *v E 1956 (3) 1961 (5); v SA 1957 (5); v In 1956 (3) 1959 (5); v P 1959 (3)*
McKenzie, G. D. 60: v E 1962 (5) 1965 (4) 1970 (3); v SA 1963 (5); v WI 1968 (5); v In 1967 (2); v P 1964 (1); *v E 1961 (3) 1964 (5) 1968 (5); v SA 1966 (5) 1969 (3); v WI 1964 (5); v In 1964 (3) 1969 (5); v P 1964 (1)*
McKibbin, T. R. 5: v E 1894 (1) 1897 (2); *v E 1896 (2)*
McLaren, J. W. 1: v E 1911
Maclean, J. A. 4: v E 1978 (4)
McLeod, C. E. 17: v E 1894 (1) 1897 (5) 1901 (2) 1903 (3); *v E 1899 (1) 1905 (5)*
McLeod, R. W. 6: v E 1891 (3); *v E 1893 (3)*
McShane, P. G. 3: v E 1884 (1) 1886 (1) 1887 (1)
Maddocks, L. V. 7: v E 1954 (3); *v E 1956 (2); v WI 1954 (1); v In 1956 (1)*
Maguire, J. N. 3: v P 1983 (1); *v WI 1983 (2)*
Mailey, A. A. 21: v E 1920 (5) 1924 (5); *v E 1921 (3) 1926 (5); v SA 1921 (3)*
Mallett, A. A. 38: v E 1970 (2) 1974 (5) 1979 (1); v WI 1968 (1) 1975 (6) 1979 (1); v NZ 1973 (3); v P 1972 (2); *v E 1968 (1) 1972 (2) 1975 (4) 1980 (1); v SA 1969 (1); v NZ 1973 (3); v In 1969 (5)*
Malone, M. F. 1: *v E 1977*
Mann, A. L. 4: v In 1977 (4)
Marr, A. P. 1: v E 1884
Marsh, G. R. 50: v E 1986 (5) 1987 (1) 1990 (5); v WI 1988 (5); v NZ 1987 (3); v In 1985 (3) 1991 (4); v P 1989 (2); v SL 1987 (1); *v E 1989 (6); v WI 1990 (5); v NZ 1985 (3) 1989 (1); v In 1986 (3); v P 1988 (3)*
Marsh, R. W. 96: v E 1970 (6) 1974 (6) 1976 (1) 1979 (3) 1982 (5); v WI 1975 (6) 1979 (3) 1981 (3); v NZ 1973 (3) 1980 (3); v In 1980 (3); v P 1972 (3) 1976 (3) 1981 (3) 1983 (5); *v E 1972 (5) 1975 (4) 1977 (5) 1980 (1) 1981 (6); v WI 1972 (5); v NZ 1973 (3) 1976 (2) 1981 (3); v P 1979 (3) 1982 (3)*
Martin, J. W. 8: v SA 1963 (1); v WI 1960 (3); *v SA 1966 (1); v In 1964 (2); v P 1964 (1)*
Martyn, D. R. 7: v SA 1993 (2); v WI 1992 (4); *v NZ 1992 (1)*
Massie, H. H. 9: v E 1881 (4) 1882 (3) 1884 (1); *v E 1882 (1)*
Massie, R. A. L. 6: v P 1972 (2); *v E 1972 (4)*

Matthews, C. D. 3: v E 1986 (2); v WI 1988 (1)
Matthews, G. R. J. 33: v E 1986 (4) 1990 (5); v WI 1984 (1) 1992 (2); v NZ 1985 (3); v In 1985 (3); v P 1983 (2); *v E 1985 (1); v WI 1983 (1) 1990 (2); v NZ 1985 (3); v In 1986 (3); v SL 1992 (3)*
Matthews, T. J. 8: v E 1911 (2); *v E 1912 (3); v SA 1912 (3)*
May, T. B. A. 24: v E 1994 (3); v SA 1993 (3); v WI 1988 (3) 1992 (1); v NZ 1987 (1) 1993 (2); *v E 1993 (5); v SA 1993 (1); v P 1988 (3) 1994 (2)*
Mayne, E. R. 4: *v E 1912 (1); v SA 1912 (1) 1921 (2)*
Mayne, L. C. 6: *v SA 1969 (2); v WI 1964 (3); v In 1969 (1)*
Meckiff, I. 18: v E 1958 (4); v SA 1963 (1); v WI 1960 (2); *v SA 1957 (4); v In 1959 (5); v P 1959 (2)*
Meuleman, K. D. 1: *v NZ 1945*
Midwinter, W. E. 8: v E 1876 (2) 1882 (1) 1886 (2); *v E 1884 (3)*
Miller, K. R. 55: v E 1946 (5) 1950 (5) 1954 (4); v SA 1952 (4); v WI 1951 (5); v In 1947 (5); *v E 1948 (5) 1953 (5) 1956 (5); v SA 1949 (5); v WI 1954 (5); v NZ 1945 (1); v P 1956 (1)*
Minnett, R. B. 9: v E 1911 (5); *v E 1912 (1); v SA 1912 (3)*
Misson, F. M. 5: v WI 1960 (3); *v E 1961 (2)*
Moody, T. M. 8: v NZ 1989 (1); v In 1991 (1); v P 1989 (1); v SL 1989 (2); *v SL 1992 (3)*
Moroney, J. 7: v E 1950 (1); v WI 1951 (1); *v SA 1949 (5)*
Morris, A. R. 46: v E 1946 (5) 1950 (5) 1954 (4); v SA 1952 (5); v WI 1951 (4); v In 1947 (4); *v E 1948 (5) 1953 (5); v SA 1949 (5); v WI 1954 (4)*
Morris, S. 1: v E 1884
Moses, H. 6: v E 1886 (2) 1887 (1) 1891 (2) 1894 (1)
Moss, J. K. 1: v P 1978
Moule, W. H. 1: *v E 1880*
Murdoch, W. L. 18: v E 1876 (1) 1878 (1) 1881 (4) 1882 (4) 1884 (1); *v E 1880 (1) 1882 (1) 1884 (3) 1890 (2)*
Musgrove, H. 1: v E 1884

Nagel, L. E. 1: v E 1932
Nash, L. J. 2: v E 1936 (1); v SA 1931 (1)
Nitschke, H. C. 2: v SA 1931 (2)
Noble, M. A. 42: v E 1897 (4) 1901 (5) 1903 (5) 1907 (5); *v E 1899 (5) 1902 (5) 1905 (5) 1909 (5); v SA 1902 (3)*
Noblet, G. 3: v SA 1952 (1); v WI 1951 (1); *v SA 1949 (1)*
Nothling, O. E. 1: v E 1928

O'Brien, L. P. J. 5: v E 1932 (2) 1936 (1); *v SA 1935 (2)*
O'Connor, J. D. A. 4: v E 1907 (3); *v E 1909 (1)*
O'Donnell, S. P. 6: v NZ 1985 (1); *v E 1985 (5)*
Ogilvie, A. D. 5: v In 1977 (3); *v WI 1977 (2)*
O'Keeffe, K. J. 24: v E 1970 (2) 1976 (1); v NZ 1973 (3); v P 1972 (2) 1976 (3); *v E 1977 (3); v WI 1972 (5); v NZ 1973 (3) 1976 (2)*
Oldfield, W. A. 54: v E 1920 (3) 1924 (5) 1928 (5) 1932 (4) 1936 (5); v SA 1931 (5); v WI 1930 (5); *v E 1921 (1) 1926 (5) 1930 (5) 1934 (5); v SA 1921 (1) 1935 (5)*
O'Neill, N. C. 42: v E 1958 (5) 1962 (5); v SA 1963 (4); v WI 1960 (5); *v E 1961 (5) 1964 (4); v WI 1964 (4); v In 1959 (5) 1964 (2); v P 1959 (3)*
O'Reilly, W. J. 27: v E 1932 (5) 1936 (5); v SA 1931 (2); *v E 1934 (5) 1938 (4); v SA 1935 (5); v NZ 1945 (1)*
Oxenham, R. K. 7: v E 1928 (3); v SA 1931 (1); v WI 1930 (3)

Palmer, G. E. 17: v E 1881 (4) 1882 (4) 1884 (2); *v E 1880 (1) 1884 (3) 1886 (3)*
Park, R. L. 1: v E 1920
Pascoe, L. S. 14: v E 1979 (2); v WI 1979 (1) 1981 (1); v NZ 1980 (3); v In 1980 (3); *v E 1977 (3) 1980 (1)*
Pellew, C. E. 10: v E 1920 (4); *v E 1921 (5); v SA 1921 (1)*
Phillips, W. B. 27: v WI 1984 (2); v NZ 1985 (3); v In 1985 (3); v P 1983 (5); *v E 1985 (6); v WI 1983 (5); v NZ 1985 (3)*
Phillips, W. N. 1: v In 1991
Philpott, P. I. 8: v E 1965 (3); *v WI 1964 (5)*
Ponsford, W. H. 29: v E 1924 (5) 1928 (2) 1932 (3); v SA 1931 (4); v WI 1930 (5); *v E 1926 (2) 1930 (4) 1934 (4)*

Ponting, R. T. 3: v SL 1995 (3)
Pope, R. J. 1: v E 1884

Rackemann, C. G. 12: v E 1982 (1) 1990 (1); v WI 1984 (1); v NZ 1989 (1); v P 1983 (2) 1989 (3); v SL 1989 (1); *v WI 1983 (1); v NZ 1989 (1)*
Ransford, V. S. 20: v E 1907 (5) 1911 (5); v SA 1910 (5); *v E 1909 (5)*
Redpath, I. R. 66: v E 1965 (1) 1970 (6) 1974 (6); v SA 1963 (1); v WI 1968 (5) 1975 (6); v In 1967 (3); v P 1972 (3); *v E 1964 (5) 1968 (5); v SA 1966 (5) 1969 (4); v WI 1972 (5); v NZ 1973 (3); v In 1964 (2) 1969 (5); v P 1964 (1)*
Reedman, J. C. 1: v E 1894
Reid, B. A. 27: v E 1986 (5) 1990 (4); v WI 1992 (1); v NZ 1987 (2); v In 1985 (3) 1991 (2); *v WI 1990 (2); v NZ 1985 (3); v In 1986 (2); v P 1988 (3)*
Reiffel, P. R. 21: v SA 1993 (2); v NZ 1993 (2); v In 1991 (1); v P 1995 (3); v SL 1995 (2); *v E 1993 (3); v SA 1993 (1); v WI 1994 (4); v NZ 1992 (3)*
Renneberg, D. A. 8: v In 1967 (3); *v SA 1966 (5)*
Richardson, A. J. 9: v E 1924 (4); *v E 1926 (5)*
Richardson, V. Y. 19: v E 1924 (3) 1928 (2) 1932 (5); *v E 1930 (4); v SA 1935 (5)*
Rigg, K. E. 8: v E 1936 (3); v SA 1931 (4); v WI 1930 (1)
Ring, D. T. 13: v SA 1952 (5); v WI 1951 (5); v In 1947 (1); *v E 1948 (1) 1953 (1)*
Ritchie, G. M. 30: v E 1986 (4); v WI 1984 (1); v NZ 1985 (3); v In 1985 (2); *v E 1985 (6); v WI 1983 (5); v NZ 1985 (3); v In 1986 (3); v P 1982 (3)*
Rixon, S. J. 13: v WI 1984 (3); v In 1977 (5); *v WI 1977 (5)*
Robertson, W. R. 1: v E 1884
Robinson, R. D. 3: *v E 1977 (3)*
Robinson, R. H. 1: v E 1936
Rorke, G. F. 4: v E 1958 (2); *v In 1959 (2)*
Rutherford, J. W. 1: *v In 1956*
Ryder, J. 20: v E 1920 (5) 1924 (3) 1928 (5); *v E 1926 (4); v SA 1921 (3)*

Saggers, R. A. 6: *v E 1948 (1); v SA 1949 (5)*
Saunders, J. V. 14: v E 1901 (1) 1903 (2) 1907 (5); *v E 1902 (4); v SA 1902 (2)*
Scott, H. J. H. 8: v E 1884 (2); *v E 1884 (3) 1886 (3)*
Sellers, R. H. D. 1: *v In 1964*
Serjeant, C. S. 12: v In 1977 (4); *v E 1977 (3); v WI 1977 (5)*
Sheahan, A. P. 31: v E 1970 (2); v WI 1968 (5); v NZ 1973 (2); v In 1967 (4); v P 1972 (2); *v E 1968 (5) 1972 (2); v SA 1969 (4); v In 1969 (5)*
Shepherd, B. K. 9: v E 1962 (2); v SA 1963 (4); v P 1964 (1); *v WI 1964 (2)*
Sievers, M. W. 3: v E 1936 (3)
Simpson, R. B. 62: v E 1958 (1) 1962 (5) 1965 (3); v SA 1963 (5); v WI 1960 (5); v In 1967 (3) 1977 (5); v P 1964 (1); *v E 1961 (5) 1964 (5); v SA 1957 (5) 1966 (5); v WI 1964 (5) 1977 (5); v In 1964 (3); v P 1964 (1)*
Sincock, D. J. 3: v E 1965 (1); v P 1964 (1); *v WI 1964 (1)*
Slater, K. N. 1: v E 1958
Slater, M. J. 33: v E 1994 (5); v SA 1993 (3); v NZ 1993 (3); v P 1995 (3); v SL 1995 (3); *v E 1993 (6); v SA 1993 (3); v WI 1994 (4); v P 1994 (3)*
Sleep, P. R. 14: v E 1986 (3) 1987 (1); v NZ 1987 (3); v P 1978 (1) 1989 (1); v SL 1989 (1); *v In 1979 (2); v P 1982 (1) 1988 (1)*
Slight, J. 1: *v E 1880*
Smith, D. B. M. 2: *v E 1912 (2)*
Smith, S. B. 3: *v WI 1983 (3)*
Spofforth, F. R. 18: v E 1876 (1) 1878 (1) 1881 (1) 1882 (4) 1884 (3) 1886 (1); *v E 1882 (1) 1884 (3) 1886 (3)*
Stackpole, K. R. 43: v E 1965 (2) 1970 (6); v WI 1968 (5); v NZ 1973 (3); v P 1972 (1); *v E 1972 (5); v SA 1966 (5) 1969 (4); v WI 1972 (4); v NZ 1973 (3); v In 1969 (5)*
Stevens, G. B. 4: *v In 1959 (2); v P 1959 (2)*

Taber, H. B. 16: v WI 1968 (1); *v E 1968 (1); v SA 1966 (5) 1969 (4); v In 1969 (5)*
Tallon, D. 21: v E 1946 (5) 1950 (5); v In 1947 (5); *v E 1948 (4) 1953 (1); v NZ 1945 (1)*
Taylor, J. M. 20: v E 1920 (5) 1924 (5); *v E 1921 (5) 1926 (3); v SA 1921 (2)*
Taylor, M. A. 72: v E 1990 (5) 1994 (5); v SA 1993 (3); v WI 1988 (2) 1992 (4); v NZ 1989 (1) 1993 (3); v In 1991 (5); v P 1989 (3) 1995 (3); v SL 1989 (2) 1995 (3); *v E 1989 (6) 1993 (6); v SA 1993 (2); v WI 1990 (5) 1994 (4); v NZ 1989 (1) 1992 (3); v P 1994 (3); v SL 1992 (3)*

Taylor, P. L. 13: v E 1986 (1) 1987 (1); v WI 1988 (2); v In 1991 (2); v P 1989 (2); v SL 1987 (1); *v WI 1990 (1); v NZ 1989 (1); v P 1988 (2)*
Thomas, G. 8: v E 1965 (3); *v WI 1964 (5)*
Thoms, G. R. 1: v WI 1951
Thomson, A. L. 4: v E 1970 (4)
Thomson, J. R. 51: v E 1974 (5) 1979 (1) 1982 (4); v WI 1975 (6) 1979 (1) 1981 (2); v In 1977 (5); v P 1972 (1) 1976 (1) 1981 (3); *v E 1975 (4) 1977 (5) 1985 (2); v WI 1977 (5); v NZ 1981 (3); v P 1982 (3)*
Thomson, N. F. D. 2: v E 1876 (2)
Thurlow, H. M. 1: v SA 1931
Toohey, P. M. 15: v E 1978 (5) 1979 (1); v WI 1979 (1); v In 1977 (5); *v WI 1977 (3)*
Toshack, E. R. H. 12: v E 1946 (5); v In 1947 (2); *v E 1948 (4); v NZ 1945 (1)*
Travers, J. P. F. 1: v E 1901
Tribe, G. E. 3: v E 1946 (3)
Trott, A. E. 3: v E 1894 (3)
Trott, G. H. S. 24: v E 1891 (3) 1894 (5) 1897 (5); *v E 1888 (3) 1890 (2) 1893 (3) 1896 (3)*
Trumble, H. 32: v E 1894 (1) 1897 (5) 1901 (5) 1903 (4); *v E 1890 (2) 1893 (3) 1896 (3) 1899 (5) 1902 (3); v SA 1902 (1)*
Trumble, J. W. 7: v E 1884 (4); *v E 1886 (3)*
Trumper, V. T. 48: v E 1901 (5) 1903 (5) 1907 (5) 1911 (5); v SA 1910 (5); *v E 1899 (5) 1902 (5) 1905 (5) 1909 (5); v SA 1902 (3)*
Turner, A. 14: v WI 1975 (6); v P 1976 (3); *v E 1975 (3); v NZ 1976 (2)*
Turner, C. T. B. 17: v E 1886 (2) 1887 (1) 1891 (3) 1894 (3); *v E 1888 (3) 1890 (2) 1893 (3)*

Veivers, T. R. 21: v E 1965 (4); v SA 1963 (3); v P 1964 (1); *v E 1964 (5); v SA 1966 (4); v In 1964 (3); v P 1964 (1)*
Veletta, M. R. J. 8: v E 1987 (1); v WI 1988 (2); v NZ 1987 (3); v P 1989 (1); v SL 1987 (1)

Waite, M. G. 2: *v E 1938 (2)*
Walker, M. H. N. 34: v E 1974 (6) 1976 (1); v WI 1975 (3); v NZ 1973 (1); v P 1972 (2) 1976 (2); *v E 1975 (4) 1977 (5); v WI 1972 (5); v NZ 1973 (3) 1976 (2)*
Wall, T. W. 18: v E 1928 (1) 1932 (4); v SA 1931 (3); v WI 1930 (1); *v E 1930 (5) 1934 (4)*
Walters, F. H. 1: v E 1884
Walters, K. D. 74: v E 1965 (5) 1970 (6) 1974 (6) 1976 (1); v WI 1968 (4); v NZ 1973 (3) 1980 (3); v In 1967 (2) 1980 (3); v P 1972 (1) 1976 (3); *v E 1968 (5) 1972 (4) 1975 (4) 1977 (5); v SA 1969 (4); v WI 1972 (5); v NZ 1973 (3) 1976 (2); v In 1969 (5)*
Ward, F. A. 4: v E 1936 (3); *v E 1938 (1)*
Warne, S. K. 44: v E 1994 (5); v SA 1993 (3); v WI 1992 (4); v NZ 1993 (3); v In 1991 (2); v P 1995 (3); v SL 1995 (3); *v E 1993 (6); v SA 1993 (3); v WI 1994 (4); v NZ 1992 (3); v P 1994 (3); v SL 1992 (2)*
Watkins, J. R. 1: v P 1972
Watson, G. D. 5: *v E 1972 (2); v SA 1966 (3)*
Watson, W. J. 4: v E 1954 (1); *v WI 1954 (3)*
Waugh, M. E. 54: v E 1990 (2) 1994 (5); v SA 1993 (3); v WI 1992 (5); v NZ 1993 (3); v In 1991 (4); v P 1995 (3); v SL 1995 (3); *v E 1993 (6); v SA 1993 (3); v WI 1990 (5) 1994 (4); v NZ 1992 (2); v P 1994 (3); v SL 1992 (3)*
Waugh, S. R. 81: v E 1986 (5) 1987 (1) 1990 (3) 1994 (5); v SA 1993 (1); v WI 1988 (5) 1992 (5); v NZ 1987 (3) 1989 (1) 1993 (3); v In 1985 (2); v P 1989 (3) 1995 (3); v SL 1987 (1) 1989 (2) 1995 (2); *v E 1989 (6) 1993 (6); v SA 1993 (3); v WI 1990 (2) 1994 (4); v NZ 1985 (3) 1989 (1) 1992 (3); v In 1986 (3); v P 1988 (3) 1994 (2)*
Wellham, D. M. 6: v E 1986 (1); v WI 1981 (1); v P 1981 (2); *v E 1981 (1) 1985 (1)*
Wessels, K. C. 24: v E 1982 (4); v WI 1984 (5); v NZ 1985 (1); v P 1983 (5); *v E 1985 (6); v WI 1983 (2); v SL 1982 (1)*
Whatmore, D. F. 7: v P 1978 (2); *v In 1979 (5)*
Whitney, M. R. 12: v WI 1988 (1) 1992 (1); v NZ 1987 (1); v In 1991 (3); *v E 1981 (2); v WI 1990 (2); v SL 1992 (2)*
Whitty, W. J. 14: v E 1911 (2); v SA 1910 (5); *v E 1909 (1) 1912 (3); v SA 1912 (3)*
Wiener, J. M. 6: v E 1979 (2); v WI 1979 (2); *v P 1979 (2)*
Wilson, J. W. 1: *v In 1956*
Wood, G. M. 59: v E 1978 (6) 1982 (1); v WI 1981 (3) 1984 (5) 1988 (3); v NZ 1980 (3); v In 1977 (1) 1980 (3); v P 1978 (1) 1981 (3); *v E 1980 (1) 1981 (6) 1985 (5); v WI 1977 (5) 1983 (1); v NZ 1981 (3); v In 1979 (2); v P 1982 (3) 1988 (3); v SL 1982 (1)*

Woodcock, A. J. 1: v NZ 1973
Woodfull, W. M. 35: v E 1928 (5) 1932 (5); v SA 1931 (5); v WI 1930 (5); *v E 1926 (5) 1930 (5) 1934 (5)*
Woods, S. M. J. 3: *v E 1888 (3)*
Woolley, R. D. 2: *v WI 1983 (1); v SL 1982 (1)*
Worrall, J. 11: v E 1884 (1) 1887 (1) 1894 (1) 1897 (1); *v E 1888 (3) 1899 (4)*
Wright, K. J. 10: v E 1978 (2); v P 1978 (2); *v In 1979 (6)*

Yallop, G. N. 39: v E 1978 (6); v WI 1975 (3) 1984 (1); v In 1977 (1); v P 1978 (1) 1981 (1) 1983 (5); *v E 1980 (1) 1981 (6); v WI 1977 (4); v In 1979 (6); v P 1979 (3); v SL 1982 (1)*
Yardley, B. 33: v E 1978 (4) 1982 (5); v WI 1981 (3); v In 1977 (1) 1980 (2); v P 1978 (1) 1981 (3); *v WI 1977 (5); v NZ 1981 (3); v In 1979 (3); v P 1982 (2); v SL 1982 (1)*

Zoehrer, T. J. 10: v E 1986 (4); *v NZ 1985 (3); v In 1986 (3)*

SOUTH AFRICA

Number of Test cricketers: 263

Adams, P. R. 2: v E 1995 (2)
Adcock, N. A. T. 26: v E 1956 (5); v A 1957 (5); v NZ 1953 (5) 1961 (2); *v E 1955 (4) 1960 (5)*
Anderson, J. H. 1: v A 1902
Ashley, W. H. 1: v E 1888

Bacher, A. 12: v A 1966 (5) 1969 (4); *v E 1965 (3)*
Balaskas, X. C. 9: v E 1930 (2) 1938 (1); v A 1935 (3); *v E 1935 (1); v NZ 1931 (2)*
Barlow, E. J. 30: v E 1964 (5); v A 1966 (5) 1969 (4); v NZ 1961 (5); *v E 1965 (3); v A 1963 (5); v NZ 1963 (3)*
Baumgartner, H. V. 1: v E 1913
Beaumont, R. 5: v E 1913 (2); *v E 1912 (1); v A 1912 (2)*
Begbie, D. W. 5: v E 1948 (3); v A 1949 (2)
Bell, A. J. 16: v E 1930 (3); *v E 1929 (3) 1935 (3); v A 1931 (5); v NZ 1931 (2)*
Bisset, M. 3: v E 1898 (2) 1909 (1)
Bissett, G. F. 4: v E 1927 (4)
Blanckenberg, J. M. 18: v E 1913 (5) 1922 (5); v A 1921 (3); *v E 1924 (5)*
Bland, K. C. 21: v E 1964 (5); v A 1966 (1); v NZ 1961 (5); *v E 1965 (3); v A 1963 (4); v NZ 1963 (3)*
Bock, E. G. 1: v A 1935
Bond, G. E. 1: v E 1938
Bosch, T. 1: *v WI 1991*
Botten, J. T. 3: *v E 1965 (3)*
Brann, W. H. 3: v E 1922 (3)
Briscoe, A. W. 2: v E 1938 (1); v A 1935 (1)
Bromfield, H. D. 9: v E 1964 (3); v NZ 1961 (5); *v E 1965 (1)*
Brown, L. S. 2: *v A 1931 (1); v NZ 1931 (1)*
Burger, C. G. de V. 2: v A 1957 (2)
Burke, S. F. 2: v E 1964 (1); v NZ 1961 (1)
Buys, I. D. 1: v E 1922

Cameron, H. B. 26: v E 1927 (5) 1930 (5); *v E 1929 (4) 1935 (5); v A 1931 (5); v NZ 1931 (2)*
Campbell, T. 5: v E 1909 (4); *v E 1912 (1)*
Carlstein, P. R. 8: v A 1957 (1); *v E 1960 (5); v A 1963 (2)*
Carter, C. P. 10: v E 1913 (2); v A 1921 (3); *v E 1912 (2) 1924 (3)*
Catterall, R. H. 24: v E 1922 (5) 1927 (5) 1930 (4); *v E 1924 (5) 1929 (5)*
Chapman, H. W. 2: v E 1913 (1); v A 1921 (1)
Cheetham, J. E. 24: v E 1948 (1); v A 1949 (3); v NZ 1953 (5); *v E 1951 (5) 1955 (3); v A 1952 (5); v NZ 1952 (2)*
Chevalier, G. A. 1: v A 1969
Christy, J. A. J. 10: v E 1930 (1); *v E 1929 (2); v A 1931 (5); v NZ 1931 (2)*
Chubb, G. W. A. 5: *v E 1951 (5)*

Cochran, J. A. K. 1: v E 1930
Coen, S. K. 2: v E 1927 (2)
Commaille, J. M. M. 12: v E 1909 (5) 1927 (2); *v E 1924 (5)*
Commins, J. B. 3: v NZ 1994 (2); v P 1994 (1)
Conyngham, D. P. 1: v E 1922
Cook, F. J. 1: v E 1895
Cook, S. J. 3: v In 1992 (2); *v SL 1993 (1)*
Cooper, A. H. C. 1: v E 1913
Cox, J. L. 3: v E 1913 (3)
Cripps, G. 1: v E 1891
Crisp, R. J. 9: v A 1935 (4); *v E 1935 (5)*
Cronje, W. J. 27: v E 1995 (5); v A 1993 (3); v NZ 1994 (3); v In 1992 (3); v P 1994 (1); *v E 1994 (3); v A 1993 (3); v WI 1991 (1); v NZ 1994 (1); v SL 1993 (3); v Z 1995 (1)*
Cullinan, D. J. 19: v E 1995 (5); v NZ 1994 (3); v In 1992 (1); v P 1994 (1); *v E 1994 (1); v A 1993 (3); v NZ 1994 (1); v SL 1993 (3); v Z 1995 (1)*
Curnow, S. H. 7: v E 1930 (3); *v A 1931 (4)*

Dalton, E. L. 15: v E 1930 (1) 1938 (4); v A 1935 (1); *v E 1929 (1) 1935 (4); v A 1931 (2); v NZ 1931 (2)*
Davies, E. Q. 5: v E 1938 (3); v A 1935 (2)
Dawson, O. C. 9: v E 1948 (4); *v E 1947 (5)*
Deane, H. G. 17: v E 1927 (5) 1930 (2); *v E 1924 (5) 1929 (5)*
de Villiers, P. S. 14: v A 1993 (3); v NZ 1994 (3); v P 1994 (1); *v E 1994 (3); v A 1993 (3); v NZ 1994 (1)*
Dixon, C. D. 1: v E 1913
Donald, A. A. 25: v E 1995 (5); v A 1993 (3); v In 1992 (4); v P 1994 (1); *v E 1994 (3); v A 1993 (3); v WI 1991 (1); v NZ 1994 (1); v SL 1993 (3); v Z 1995 (1)*
Dower, R. R. 1: v E 1898
Draper, R. G. 2: v A 1949 (2)
Duckworth, C. A. R. 2: v E 1956 (2)
Dumbrill, R. 5: v A 1966 (2); *v E 1965 (3)*
Duminy, J. P. 3: v E 1927 (2); *v E 1929 (1)*
Dunell, O. R. 2: v E 1888 (2)
Du Preez, J. H. 2: v A 1966 (2)
Du Toit, J. F. 1: v E 1891
Dyer, D. V. 3: *v E 1947 (3)*

Eksteen, C. E. 6: v E 1995 (1); v NZ 1994 (2); v P 1994 (1); *v NZ 1994 (1); v SL 1993 (1)*
Elgie, M. K. 3: v NZ 1961 (3)
Endean, W. R. 28: v E 1956 (5); v A 1957 (5); v NZ 1953 (5); *v E 1951 (1) 1955 (5); v A 1952 (5); v NZ 1952 (2)*

Farrer, W. S. 6: v NZ 1961 (3); *v NZ 1963 (3)*
Faulkner, G. A. 25: v E 1905 (5) 1909 (5); *v E 1907 (3) 1912 (3) 1924 (1); v A 1910 (5) 1912 (3)*
Fellows-Smith, J. P. 4: *v E 1960 (4)*
Fichardt, C. G. 2: v E 1891 (1) 1895 (1)
Finlason, C. E. 1: v E 1888
Floquet, C. E. 1: v E 1909
Francis, H. H. 2: v E 1898 (2)
Francois, C. M. 5: v E 1922 (5)
Frank, C. N. 3: v A 1921 (3)
Frank, W. H. B. 1: v E 1895
Fuller, E. R. H. 7: v A 1957 (1); *v E 1955 (2); v A 1952 (2); v NZ 1952 (2)*
Fullerton, G. M. 7: v A 1949 (2); *v E 1947 (2) 1951 (3)*
Funston, K. J. 18: v E 1956 (3); v A 1957 (5); v NZ 1953 (3); *v A 1952 (5); v NZ 1952 (2)*

Gamsy, D. 2: v A 1969 (2)
Gleeson, R. A. 1: v E 1895
Glover, G. K. 1: v E 1895
Goddard, T. L. 41: v E 1956 (5) 1964 (5); v A 1957 (5) 1966 (5) 1969 (3); *v E 1955 (5) 1960 (5); v A 1963 (5); v NZ 1963 (3)*
Gordon, N. 5: v E 1938 (5)

Graham, R. 2: v E 1898 (2)
Grieveson, R. E. 2: v E 1938 (2)
Griffin, G. M. 2: *v E 1960 (2)*

Hall, A. E. 7: v E 1922 (4) 1927 (2) 1930 (1)
Hall, G. G. 1: v E 1964
Halliwell, E. A. 8: v E 1891 (1) 1895 (3) 1898 (1); v A 1902 (3)
Halse, C. G. 3: *v A 1963 (3)*
Hands, P. A. M. 7: v E 1913 (5); v A 1921 (1); *v E 1924 (1)*
Hands, R. H. M. 1: v E 1913
Hanley, M. A. 1: v E 1948
Harris, T. A. 3: v E 1948 (1); *v E 1947 (2)*
Hartigan, G. P. D. 5: v E 1913 (3); *v E 1912 (1); v A 1912 (1)*
Harvey, R. L. 2: v A 1935 (2)
Hathorn, C. M. H. 12: v E 1905 (5); v A 1902 (3); *v E 1907 (3); v A 1910 (1)*
Hearne, F. 4: v E 1891 (1) 1895 (3)
Hearne, G. A. L. 3: v E 1922 (2); *v E 1924 (1)*
Heine, P. S. 14: v E 1956 (5); v A 1957 (4); v NZ 1961 (1); *v E 1955 (4)*
Henry, O. 3: v In 1992 (3)
Hime, C. F. W. 1: v E 1895
Hudson, A. C. 25: v E 1995 (5); v A 1993 (3); v NZ 1994 (2); v In 1992 (4); *v E 1994 (2); v A 1993 (3); v WI 1991 (1); v NZ 1994 (1); v SL 1993 (3); v Z 1995 (1)*
Hutchinson, P. 2: v E 1888 (2)

Ironside, D. E. J. 3: v NZ 1953 (3)
Irvine, B. L. 4: v A 1969 (4)

Jack, S. D. 2: v NZ 1994 (2)
Johnson, C. L. 1: v E 1895

Kallis, J. H. 2: v E 1995 (2)
Keith, H. J. 8: v E 1956 (3); *v E 1955 (4); v A 1952 (1)*
Kempis, G. A. 1: v E 1888
Kirsten, G. 20: v E 1995 (5); v A 1993 (3); v NZ 1994 (3); v P 1994 (1); *v E 1994 (3); v A 1993 (3); v NZ 1994 (1); v Z 1995 (1)*
Kirsten, P. N. 12: v A 1993 (3); v In 1992 (4); *v E 1994 (3); v A 1993 (1); v WI 1991 (1)*
Kotze, J. J. 3: v A 1902 (2); *v E 1907 (1)*
Kuiper, A. P. 1: *v WI 1991*
Kuys, F. 1: v E 1898

Lance, H. R. 13: v A 1966 (5) 1969 (3); v NZ 1961 (2); *v E 1965 (3)*
Langton, A. B. C. 15: v E 1938 (5); v A 1935 (5); *v E 1935 (5)*
Lawrence, G. B. 5: v NZ 1961 (5)
le Roux, F. L. 1: v E 1913
Lewis, P. T. 1: v E 1913
Lindsay, D. T. 19: v E 1964 (3); v A 1966 (5) 1969 (2); *v E 1965 (3); v A 1963 (3); v NZ 1963 (3)*
Lindsay, J. D. 3: *v E 1947 (3)*
Lindsay, N. V. 1: v A 1921
Ling, W. V. S. 6: v E 1922 (3); v A 1921 (3)
Llewellyn, C. B. 15: v E 1895 (1) 1898 (1); v A 1902 (3); *v E 1912 (3); v A 1910 (5) 1912 (2)*
Lundie, E. B. 1: v E 1913

Macaulay, M. J. 1: v E 1964
McCarthy, C. N. 15: v E 1948 (5); v A 1949 (5); *v E 1951 (5)*
McGlew, D. J. 34: v E 1956 (1); v A 1957 (5); v NZ 1953 (5) 1961 (5); *v E 1951 (2) 1955 (5) 1960 (5); v A 1952 (4); v NZ 1952 (2)*
McKinnon, A. H. 8: v E 1964 (2); v A 1966 (2); v NZ 1961 (1); *v E 1960 (1) 1965 (2)*
McLean, R. A. 40: v E 1956 (5) 1964 (2); v A 1957 (4); v NZ 1953 (4) 1961 (5); *v E 1951 (3) 1955 (5) 1960 (5); v A 1952 (5); v NZ 1952 (2)*
McMillan, B. M. 23: v E 1995 (5); v A 1993 (3); v NZ 1994 (3); v In 1992 (4); v P 1994 (1); *v E 1994 (3); v A 1993 (1); v SL 1993 (2); v Z 1995 (1)*
McMillan, Q. 13: v E 1930 (5); *v E 1929 (2); v A 1931 (4); v NZ 1931 (2)*

Mann, N. B. F. 19: v E 1948 (5); v A 1949 (5); *v E 1947 (5) 1951 (4)*
Mansell, P. N. F. 13: *v E 1951 (2) 1955 (4); v A 1952 (5); v NZ 1952 (2)*
Markham, L. A. 1: v E 1948
Marx, W. F. E. 3: v A 1921 (3)
Matthews, C. R. 18: v E 1995 (3); v A 1993 (3); v NZ 1994 (2); v In 1992 (3); *v E 1994 (3); v A 1993 (2); v NZ 1994 (1); v Z 1995 (1)*
Meintjes, D. J. 2: v E 1922 (2)
Melle, M. G. 7: v A 1949 (2); *v E 1951 (1); v A 1952 (4)*
Melville, A. 11: v E 1938 (5) 1948 (1); *v E 1947 (5)*
Middleton, J. 6: v E 1895 (2) 1898 (2); v A 1902 (2)
Mills, C. 1: v E 1891
Milton, W. H. 3: v E 1888 (2) 1891 (1)
Mitchell, B. 42: v E 1930 (5) 1938 (5) 1948 (5); v A 1935 (5); *v E 1929 (5) 1935 (5) 1947 (5); v A 1931 (5); v NZ 1931 (2)*
Mitchell, F. 3: *v E 1912 (1); v A 1912 (2)*
Morkel, D. P. B. 16: v E 1927 (5); *v E 1929 (5); v A 1931 (5); v NZ 1931 (1)*
Murray, A. R. A. 10: v NZ 1953 (4); *v A 1952 (4); v NZ 1952 (2)*

Nel, J. D. 6: v A 1949 (5) 1957 (1)
Newberry, C. 4: v E 1913 (4)
Newson, E. S. 3: v E 1930 (1) 1938 (2)
Nicholson, F. 4: v A 1935 (4)
Nicolson, J. F. W. 3: v E 1927 (3)
Norton, N. O. 1: v E 1909
Nourse, A. D. 34: v E 1938 (5) 1948 (5); v A 1935 (5) 1949 (5); *v E 1935 (4) 1947 (5) 1951 (5)*
Nourse, A. W. 45: v E 1905 (5) 1909 (5) 1913 (5) 1922 (5); v A 1902 (3) 1921 (3); *v E 1907 (3) 1912 (3) 1924 (5); v A 1910 (5) 1912 (3)*
Nupen, E. P. 17: v E 1922 (4) 1927 (5) 1930 (3); v A 1921 (2) 1935 (1); *v E 1924 (2)*

Ochse, A. E. 2: v E 1888 (2)
Ochse, A. L. 3: v E 1927 (1); *v E 1929 (2)*
O'Linn, S. 7: v NZ 1961 (2); *v E 1960 (5)*
Owen-Smith, H. G. 5: *v E 1929 (5)*

Palm, A. W. 1: v E 1927
Parker, G. M. 2: *v E 1924 (2)*
Parkin, D. C. 1: v E 1891
Partridge, J. T. 11: v E 1964 (3); *v A 1963 (5); v NZ 1963 (3)*
Pearse, O. C. 3: *v A 1910 (3)*
Pegler, S. J. 16: v E 1909 (1); *v E 1912 (3) 1924 (5); v A 1910 (4) 1912 (3)*
Pithey, A. J. 17: v E 1956 (3) 1964 (5); *v E 1960 (2); v A 1963 (4); v NZ 1963 (3)*
Pithey, D. B. 8: v A 1966 (2); *v A 1963 (3); v NZ 1963 (3)*
Plimsoll, J. B. 1: *v E 1947*
Pollock, P. M. 28: v E 1964 (5); v A 1966 (5) 1969 (4); v NZ 1961 (3); *v E 1965 (3); v A 1963 (5); v NZ 1963 (3)*
Pollock, R. G. 23: v E 1964 (5); v A 1966 (5) 1969 (4); *v E 1965 (3); v A 1963 (5); v NZ 1963 (1)*
Pollock, S. M. 5: v E 1995 (5)
Poore, R. M. 3: v E 1895 (3)
Pothecary, J. E. 3: *v E 1960 (3)*
Powell, A. W. 1: v E 1898
Prince, C. F. H. 1: v E 1898
Pringle, M. W. 4: v E 1995 (1); v In 1992 (2); *v WI 1991 (1)*
Procter, M. J. 7: v A 1966 (3) 1969 (4)
Promnitz, H. L. E. 2: v E 1927 (2)

Quinn, N. A. 12: v E 1930 (1); *v E 1929 (4); v A 1931 (5); v NZ 1931 (2)*

Reid, N. 1: v A 1921
Rhodes, J. N. 27: v E 1995 (5); v A 1993 (3); v NZ 1994 (3); v In 1992 (4); v P 1994 (1); *v E 1994 (3); v A 1993 (3); v NZ 1994 (1); v SL 1993 (3); v Z 1995 (1)*
Richards, A. R. 1: v E 1895
Richards, B. A. 4: v A 1969 (4)

Richards, W. H. 1: v E 1888
Richardson, D. J. 28: v E 1995 (5); v A 1993 (3); v NZ 1994 (3); v In 1992 (4); v P 1994 (1); *v E 1994 (3); v A 1993 (3); v WI 1991 (1); v NZ 1994 (1); v SL 1993 (3); v Z 1995 (1)*
Robertson, J. B. 3: v A 1935 (3)
Rose-Innes, A. 2: v E 1888 (2)
Routledge, T. W. 4: v E 1891 (1) 1895 (3)
Rowan, A. M. B. 15: v E 1948 (5); *v E 1947 (5) 1951 (5)*
Rowan, E. A. B. 26: v E 1938 (4) 1948 (4); v A 1935 (3) 1949 (5); *v E 1935 (5) 1951 (5)*
Rowe, G. A. 5: v E 1895 (2) 1898 (2); v A 1902 (1)
Rushmere, M. W. 1: *v WI 1991*

Samuelson, S. V. 1: v E 1909
Schultz, B. N. 7: v E 1995 (1); v In 1992 (2); *v SL 1993 (3); v Z 1995 (1)*
Schwarz, R. O. 20: v E 1905 (5) 1909 (4); *v E 1907 (3) 1912 (1); v A 1910 (5) 1912 (2)*
Seccull, A. W. 1: v E 1895
Seymour, M. A. 7: v E 1964 (2); v A 1969 (1); *v A 1963 (4)*
Shalders, W. A. 12: v E 1898 (1) 1905 (5); v A 1902 (3); *v E 1907 (3)*
Shepstone, G. H. 2: v E 1895 (1) 1898 (1)
Sherwell, P. W. 13: v E 1905 (5); *v E 1907 (3); v A 1910 (5)*
Siedle, I. J. 18: v E 1927 (1) 1930 (5); v A 1935 (5); *v E 1929 (3) 1935 (4)*
Sinclair, J. H. 25: v E 1895 (3) 1898 (2) 1905 (5) 1909 (4); v A 1902 (3); *v E 1907 (3); v A 1910 (5)*
Smith, C. J. E. 3: v A 1902 (3)
Smith, F. W. 3: v E 1888 (2) 1895 (1)
Smith, V. I. 9: v A 1949 (3) 1957 (1); *v E 1947 (4) 1955 (1)*
Snell, R. P. 5: v NZ 1994 (1); *v A 1993 (1); v WI 1991 (1); v SL 1993 (2)*
Snooke, S. D. 1: *v E 1907*
Snooke, S. J. 26: v E 1905 (5) 1909 (5) 1922 (3); *v E 1907 (3) 1912 (3); v A 1910 (5) 1912 (2)*
Solomon, W. R. 1: v E 1898
Stewart, R. B. 1: v E 1888
Steyn, P. J. R. 3: v NZ 1994 (1); v P 1994 (1); *v NZ 1994 (1)*
Stricker, L. A. 13: v E 1909 (4); *v E 1912 (2); v A 1910 (5) 1912 (2)*
Susskind, M. J. 5: *v E 1924 (5)*
Symcox, P. L. 6: *v A 1993 (2); v SL 1993 (3); v Z 1995 (1)*

Taberer, H. M. 1: v A 1902
Tancred, A. B. 2: v E 1888 (2)
Tancred, L. J. 14: v E 1905 (5) 1913 (1); v A 1902 (3); *v E 1907 (1) 1912 (2); v A 1912 (2)*
Tancred, V. M. 1: v E 1898
Tapscott, G. L. 1: v E 1913
Tapscott, L. E. 2: v E 1922 (2)
Tayfield, H. J. 37: v E 1956 (5); v A 1949 (5) 1957 (5); v NZ 1953 (5); *v E 1955 (5) 1960 (5); v A 1952 (5); v NZ 1952 (2)*
Taylor, A. I. 1: v E 1956
Taylor, D. 2: v E 1913 (2)
Taylor, H. W. 42: v E 1913 (5) 1922 (5) 1927 (5) 1930 (4); v A 1921 (3); *v E 1912 (3) 1924 (5) 1929 (3); v A 1912 (3) 1931 (5); v NZ 1931 (1)*
Theunissen, N. H. 1: v E 1888
Thornton, P. G. 1: v A 1902
Tomlinson, D. S. 1: *v E 1935*
Traicos, A. J. 3: v A 1969 (3)
Trimborn, P. H. J. 4: v A 1966 (3) 1969 (1)
Tuckett, L. 9: v E 1948 (4); *v E 1947 (5)*
Tuckett, L. R. 1: v E 1913
Twentyman-Jones, P. S. 1: v A 1902

van der Bijl, P. G. V. 5: v E 1938 (5)
Van der Merwe, E. A. 2: v A 1935 (1); *v E 1929 (1)*
Van der Merwe, P. L. 15: v E 1964 (2); v A 1966 (5); *v E 1965 (3); v A 1963 (3); v NZ 1963 (2)*
Van Ryneveld, C. B. 19: v E 1956 (5); v A 1957 (4); v NZ 1953 (5); *v E 1951 (5)*
Varnals, G. D. 3: v E 1964 (3)
Viljoen, K. G. 27: v E 1930 (3) 1938 (4) 1948 (2); v A 1935 (4); *v E 1935 (4) 1947 (5); v A 1931 (4); v NZ 1931 (1)*

Vincent, C. L. 25: v E 1927 (5) 1930 (5); *v E 1929 (4) 1935 (4); v A 1931 (5); v NZ 1931 (2)*
Vintcent, C. H. 3: v E 1888 (2) 1891 (1)
Vogler, A. E. E. 15: v E 1905 (5) 1909 (5); *v E 1907 (3); v A 1910 (2)*

Wade, H. F. 10: v A 1935 (5); *v E 1935 (5)*
Wade, W. W. 11: v E 1938 (3) 1948 (5); v A 1949 (3)
Waite, J. H. B. 50: v E 1956 (5) 1964 (2); v A 1957 (5); v NZ 1953 (5) 1961 (5); *v E 1951 (4) 1955 (5) 1960 (5); v A 1952 (5) 1963 (4); v NZ 1952 (2) 1963 (3)*
Walter, K. A. 2: v NZ 1961 (2)
Ward, T. A. 23: v E 1913 (5) 1922 (5); v A 1921 (3); *v E 1912 (2) 1924 (5); v A 1912 (3)*
Watkins, J. C. 15: v E 1956 (2); v A 1949 (3); v NZ 1953 (3); *v A 1952 (5); v NZ 1952 (2)*
Wesley, C. 3: *v E 1960 (3)*
Wessels, K. C. 16: v A 1993 (3); v In 1992 (4); *v E 1994 (3); v A 1993 (2); v WI 1991 (1); SL 1993 (3)*
Westcott, R. J. 5: v A 1957 (2); v NZ 1953 (3)
White, G. C. 17: v E 1905 (5) 1909 (4); *v E 1907 (3) 1912 (2); v A 1912 (3)*
Willoughby, J. T. 2: v E 1895 (2)
Wimble, C. S. 1: v E 1891
Winslow, P. L. 5: v A 1949 (2); *v E 1955 (3)*
Wynne, O. E. 6: v E 1948 (3); v A 1949 (3)

Zulch, J. W. 16: v E 1909 (5) 1913 (3); v A 1921 (3); *v A 1910 (5)*

WEST INDIES

Number of Test cricketers: 212

Achong, E. 6: v E 1929 (1) 1934 (2); *v E 1933 (3)*
Adams, J. C. 24: v E 1993 (5); v A 1994 (4); v SA 1991 (1); v NZ 1995 (2); *v E 1995 (4); v A 1992 (3); v NZ 1994 (2); v In 1994 (3)*
Alexander, F. C. M. 25: v E 1959 (5); v P 1957 (5); *v E 1957 (2); v A 1960 (5); v In 1958 (5); v P 1958 (3)*
Ali, Imtiaz 1: v In 1975
Ali, Inshan 12: v E 1973 (2); v A 1972 (3); v In 1970 (1); v P 1976 (1); v NZ 1971 (3); *v E 1973 (1); v A 1975 (1)*
Allan, D. W. 5: v A 1964 (1); v In 1961 (2); *v E 1966 (2)*
Allen, I. B. A. 2: *v E 1991 (2)*
Ambrose, C. E. L. 61: v E 1989 (3) 1993 (5); v A 1990 (5) 1994 (4); v SA 1991 (1); v NZ 1995 (2); v In 1988 (4); v P 1987 (3) 1992 (3); *v E 1988 (5) 1991 (5) 1995 (5); v A 1988 (5) 1992 (5); v NZ 1994 (2); v P 1990 (3); v SL 1993 (1)*
Arthurton, K. L. T. 33: v E 1993 (5); v A 1994 (3); v SA 1991 (1); v In 1988 (4); v P 1992 (3); *v E 1988 (1) 1995 (5); v A 1992 (5); v NZ 1994 (2); v In 1994 (3); v SL 1993 (1)*
Asgarali, N. 2: *v E 1957 (2)*
Atkinson, D. St E. 22: v E 1953 (4); v A 1954 (4); v P 1957 (1); *v E 1957 (2); v A 1951 (2); v NZ 1951 (1) 1955 (4); v In 1948 (4)*
Atkinson, E. St E. 8: v P 1957 (3); *v In 1958 (3); v P 1958 (2)*
Austin, R. A. 2: v A 1977 (2)

Bacchus, S. F. A. F. 19: v A 1977 (2); *v E 1980 (5); v A 1981 (2); v In 1978 (6); v P 1980 (4)*
Baichan, L. 3: *v A 1975 (1); v P 1974 (2)*
Baptiste, E. A. E. 10: v E 1989 (1); v A 1983 (3); *v E 1984 (5); v In 1983 (1)*
Barrett, A. G. 6: v E 1973 (2); v In 1970 (2); *v In 1974 (2)*
Barrow, I. 11: v E 1929 (1) 1934 (1); *v E 1933 (3) 1939 (1); v A 1930 (5)*
Bartlett, E. L. 5: *v E 1928 (1); v A 1930 (4)*
Benjamin, K. C. G. 21: v E 1993 (5); v A 1994 (4); v SA 1991 (1); *v E 1995 (5); v A 1992 (1); v NZ 1994 (2); v In 1994 (3)*
Benjamin, W. K. M. 21: v E 1993 (5); v A 1994 (4); v In 1988 (1); v P 1987 (3) 1992 (2); *v E 1988 (3); v NZ 1994 (1); v In 1987 (1); v SL 1993 (1)*
Best, C. A. 8: v E 1985 (3) 1989 (3); *v P 1990 (2)*
Betancourt, N. 1: v E 1929

Binns, A. P. 5: v A 1954 (1); v In 1952 (1); *v NZ 1955 (3)*
Birkett, L. S. 4: *v A 1930 (4)*
Bishop, I. R. 26: v E 1989 (4); v NZ 1995 (2); v In 1988 (4); v P 1992 (2); *v E 1995 (6); v A 1992 (5); v P 1990 (3)*
Boyce, K. D. 21: v E 1973 (4); v A 1972 (4); v In 1970 (1); *v E 1973 (3); v A 1975 (4); v In 1974 (3); v P 1974 (2)*
Browne, C. O. 5: v A 1994 (1); v NZ 1995 (2); *v E 1995 (2)*
Browne, C. R. 4: v E 1929 (2); *v E 1928 (2)*
Butcher, B. F. 44: v E 1959 (2) 1967 (5); v A 1964 (5); *v E 1963 (5) 1966 (5) 1969 (3); v A 1968 (5); v NZ 1968 (3); v In 1958 (5) 1966 (3); v P 1958 (3)*
Butler, L. 1: v A 1954
Butts, C. G. 7: v NZ 1984 (1); *v NZ 1986 (1); v In 1987 (3); v P 1986 (2)*
Bynoe, M. R. 4: *v In 1966 (3); v P 1958 (1)*

Camacho, G. S. 11: v E 1967 (5); v In 1970 (2); *v E 1969 (2); v A 1968 (2)*
Cameron, F. J. 5: *v In 1948 (5)*
Cameron, J. H. 2: *v E 1939 (2)*
Campbell, S. L. 11: v A 1994 (1); v NZ 1995 (2); *v E 1995 (6); v NZ 1994 (2)*
Carew, G. M. 4: v E 1934 (1) 1947 (2); *v In 1948 (1)*
Carew, M. C. 19: v E 1967 (1); v NZ 1971 (3); v In 1970 (3); *v E 1963 (2) 1966 (1) 1969 (1); v A 1968 (5); v NZ 1968 (3)*
Challenor, G. 3: *v E 1928 (3)*
Chanderpaul, S. 11: v E 1993 (4); v NZ 1995 (2); *v E 1995 (2); v NZ 1994 (2); v In 1994 (1)*
Chang, H. S. 1: *v In 1978*
Christiani, C. M. 4: v E 1934 (4)
Christiani, R. J. 22: v E 1947 (4) 1953 (1); v In 1952 (2); *v E 1950 (4); v A 1951 (5); v NZ 1951 (1); v In 1948 (5)*
Clarke, C. B. 3: *v E 1939 (3)*
Clarke, S. T. 11: v A 1977 (1); *v A 1981 (1); v In 1978 (5); v P 1980 (4)*
Constantine, L. N. 18: v E 1929 (3) 1934 (3); *v E 1928 (3) 1933 (1) 1939 (3); v A 1930 (5)*
Croft, C. E. H. 27: v E 1980 (4); v A 1977 (2); v P 1976 (5); *v E 1980 (3); v A 1979 (3) 1981 (3); v NZ 1979 (3); v P 1980 (4)*
Cuffy, C. E. 2: *v In 1994 (2)*
Cummins, A. C. 5: v P 1992 (2); *v A 1992 (1); v In 1994 (2)*

Da Costa, O. C. 5: v E 1929 (1) 1934 (1); *v E 1933 (3)*
Daniel, W. W. 10: v A 1983 (2); v In 1975 (1); *v E 1976 (4); v In 1983 (3)*
Davis, B. A. 4: v A 1964 (4)
Davis, C. A. 15: v A 1972 (2); v NZ 1971 (5); v In 1970 (4); *v E 1969 (3); v A 1968 (1)*
Davis, W. W. 15: v A 1983 (1); v NZ 1984 (2); v In 1982 (1); *v E 1984 (1); v In 1983 (6) 1987 (4)*
De Caires, F. I. 3: v E 1929 (3)
Depeiza, C. C. 5: v A 1954 (3); *v NZ 1955 (2)*
Dewdney, T. 9: v A 1954 (2); v P 1957 (3); *v E 1957 (1); v NZ 1955 (3)*
Dhanraj, R. 4: v NZ 1995 (1); *v E 1995 (1); v NZ 1994 (1); v In 1994 (1)*
Dowe, U. G. 4: v A 1972 (1); v NZ 1971 (1); v In 1970 (2)
Dujon, P. J. L. 81: v E 1985 (4) 1989 (4); v A 1983 (5) 1990 (5); v NZ 1984 (4); v In 1982 (5) 1988 (4); v P 1987 (3); *v E 1984 (5) 1988 (5) 1991 (5); v A 1981 (3) 1984 (5) 1988 (5); v NZ 1986 (3); v In 1983 (6) 1987 (4); v P 1986 (3) 1990 (3)*

Edwards, R. M. 5: *v A 1968 (2); v NZ 1968 (3)*

Ferguson, W. 8: v E 1947 (4) 1953 (1); *v In 1948 (3)*
Fernandes, M. P. 2: v E 1929 (1); *v E 1928 (1)*
Findlay, T. M. 10: v A 1972 (1); v NZ 1971 (5); v In 1970 (2); *v E 1969 (2)*
Foster, M. L. C. 14: v E 1973 (1); v A 1972 (4) 1977 (1); v NZ 1971 (3); v In 1970 (2); v P 1976 (1); *v E 1969 (1) 1973 (1)*
Francis, G. N. 10: v E 1929 (1); *v E 1928 (3) 1933 (1); v A 1930 (5)*
Frederick, M. 1: v E 1953
Fredericks, R. C. 59: v E 1973 (5); v A 1972 (5); v NZ 1971 (5); v In 1970 (4) 1975 (4); v P 1976 (5); *v E 1969 (3) 1973 (3) 1976 (5); v A 1968 (4) 1975 (6); v NZ 1968 (3); v In 1974 (5); v P 1974 (2)*

Fuller, R. L. 1: v E 1934
Furlonge, H. A. 3: v A 1954 (1); *v NZ 1955 (2)*

Ganteaume, A. G. 1: v E 1947
Garner, J. 58: v E 1980 (4) 1985 (5); v A 1977 (2) 1983 (5); v NZ 1984 (4); v In 1982 (4); v P 1976 (5); *v E 1980 (5) 1984 (5); v A 1979 (3) 1981 (3) 1984 (5); v NZ 1979 (3) 1986 (2); v P 1980 (3)*
Gaskin, B. B. M. 2: v E 1947 (2)
Gibbs, G. L. 1: v A 1954
Gibbs, L. R. 79: v E 1967 (5) 1973 (5); v A 1964 (5) 1972 (5); v NZ 1971 (2); v In 1961 (5) 1970 (1); v P 1957 (4); *v E 1963 (5) 1966 (5) 1969 (3) 1973 (3); v A 1960 (3) 1968 (5) 1975 (6); v NZ 1968 (3); v In 1958 (1) 1966 (3) 1974 (5); v P 1958 (3) 1974 (2)*
Gibson, O. D. 1: *v E 1995*
Gilchrist, R. 13: v P 1957 (5); *v E 1957 (4); v In 1958 (4)*
Gladstone, G. 1: v E 1929
Goddard, J. D. C. 27: v E 1947 (4); *v E 1950 (4) 1957 (5); v A 1951 (4); v NZ 1951 (2) 1955 (3); v In 1948 (5)*
Gomes, H. A. 60: v E 1980 (4) 1985 (5); v A 1977 (3) 1983 (2); v NZ 1984 (4); v In 1982 (5); *v E 1976 (2) 1984 (5); v A 1981 (3) 1984 (5); v NZ 1986 (3); v In 1978 (6) 1983 (6); v P 1980 (4) 1986 (3)*
Gomez, G. E. 29: v E 1947 (4) 1953 (4); v In 1952 (4); *v E 1939 (2) 1950 (4); v A 1951 (5); v NZ 1951 (1); v In 1948 (5)*
Grant, G. C. 12: v E 1934 (4); *v E 1933 (3); v A 1930 (5)*
Grant, R. S. 7: v E 1934 (4); *v E 1939 (3)*
Gray, A. H. 5: *v NZ 1986 (2); v P 1986 (3)*
Greenidge, A. E. 6: v A 1977 (2); *v In 1978 (4)*
Greenidge, C. G. 108: v E 1980 (4) 1985 (5) 1989 (4); v A 1977 (2) 1983 (5) 1990 (5); v NZ 1984 (4); v In 1982 (5) 1988 (4); v P 1976 (5) 1987 (3); *v E 1976 (5) 1980 (5) 1984 (5) 1988 (4); v A 1975 (2) 1979 (3) 1981 (2) 1984 (5) 1988 (5); v NZ 1979 (3) 1986 (3); v In 1974 (5) 1983 (6) 1987 (3); v P 1986 (3) 1990 (3)*
Greenidge, G. A. 5: v A 1972 (3); v NZ 1971 (2)
Grell, M. G. 1: v E 1929
Griffith, C. C. 28: v E 1959 (1) 1967 (4); v A 1964 (5); *v E 1963 (5) 1966 (5); v A 1968 (3); v NZ 1968 (2); v In 1966 (3)*
Griffith, H. C. 13: v E 1929 (3); *v E 1928 (3) 1933 (2); v A 1930 (5)*
Guillen, S. C. 5: *v A 1951 (3); v NZ 1951 (2)*

Hall, W. W. 48: v E 1959 (5) 1967 (4); v A 1964 (5); v In 1961 (5); *v E 1963 (5) 1966 (5); v A 1960 (5) 1968 (2); v NZ 1968 (1); v In 1958 (5) 1966 (3); v P 1958 (3)*
Harper, R. A. 25: v E 1985 (2); v A 1983 (4); v NZ 1984 (1); *v E 1984 (5) 1988 (3); v A 1984 (2) 1988 (1); v In 1983 (2) 1987 (1); v P 1986 (3); v SL 1993 (1)*
Haynes, D. L. 116: v E 1980 (4) 1985 (5) 1989 (4) 1993 (4); v A 1977 (2) 1983 (5) 1990 (5); v SA 1991 (1); v NZ 1984 (4); v In 1982 (5) 1988 (4); v P 1987 (3) 1992 (3); *v E 1980 (5) 1984 (5) 1988 (4) 1991 (5); v A 1979 (3) 1981 (3) 1984 (5) 1988 (5) 1992 (5); v NZ 1979 (3) 1986 (3); v In 1983 (6) 1987 (4); v P 1980 (4) 1986 (3) 1990 (3); v SL 1993 (1)*
Headley, G. A. 22: v E 1929 (4) 1934 (4) 1947 (1) 1953 (1); *v E 1933 (3) 1939 (3); v A 1930 (5); v In 1948 (1)*
Headley, R. G. A. 2: *v E 1973 (2)*
Hendriks, J. L. 20: v A 1964 (4); v In 1961 (1); *v E 1966 (3) 1969 (1); v A 1968 (5); v NZ 1968 (3); v In 1966 (3)*
Hoad, E. L. G. 4: v E 1929 (1); *v E 1928 (1) 1933 (2)*
Holder, V. A. 40: v E 1973 (1); v A 1972 (3) 1977 (3); v NZ 1971 (4); v In 1970 (3) 1975 (1); v P 1976 (1); *v E 1969 (3) 1973 (2) 1976 (4); v A 1975 (3); v In 1974 (4) 1978 (6); v P 1974 (2)*
Holding, M. A. 60: v E 1980 (4) 1985 (4); v A 1983 (3); v NZ 1984 (3); v In 1975 (4) 1982 (5); *v E 1976 (4) 1980 (5) 1984 (4); v A 1975 (5) 1979 (3) 1981 (3) 1984 (3); v NZ 1979 (3) 1986 (1); v In 1983 (6)*
Holford, D. A. J. 24: v E 1967 (4); v NZ 1971 (5); v In 1970 (1) 1975 (2); v P 1976 (1); *v E 1966 (5); v A 1968 (2); v NZ 1968 (3); v In 1966 (1)*
Holt, J. K. 17: v E 1953 (5); v A 1954 (5); *v In 1958 (5); v P 1958 (2)*
Hooper, C. L. 52: v E 1989 (3); v A 1990 (5) 1994 (4); v P 1987 (3) 1992 (3); *v E 1988 (5) 1991 (5) 1995 (5); v A 1988 (5) 1992 (4); v In 1987 (3) 1994 (3); v P 1990 (3); v SL 1993 (1)*
Howard, A. B. 1: v NZ 1971

Hunte, C. C. 44: v E 1959 (5); v A 1964 (5); v In 1961 (5); v P 1957 (5); *v E 1963 (5) 1966 (5); v A 1960 (5); v In 1958 (5) 1966 (3); v P 1958 (1)*
Hunte, E. A. C. 3: v E 1929 (3)
Hylton, L. G. 6: v E 1934 (4); *v E 1939 (2)*

Johnson, H. H. H. 3: v E 1947 (1); *v E 1950 (2)*
Johnson, T. F. 1: *v E 1939*
Jones, C. M. 4: v E 1929 (1) 1934 (3)
Jones, P. E. 9: v E 1947 (1); *v E 1950 (2); v A 1951 (1); v In 1948 (5)*
Julien, B. D. 24: v E 1973 (5); v In 1975 (4); v P 1976 (1); *v E 1973 (3) 1976 (2); v A 1975 (3); v In 1974 (4); v P 1974 (2)*
Jumadeen, R. R. 12: v A 1972 (1) 1977 (2); v NZ 1971 (1); v In 1975 (4); v P 1976 (1); *v E 1976 (1); v In 1978 (2)*

Kallicharran, A. I. 66: v E 1973 (5); v A 1972 (5) 1977 (5); v NZ 1971 (2); v In 1975 (4); v P 1976 (5); *v E 1973 (3) 1976 (3) 1980 (5); v A 1975 (6) 1979 (3); v NZ 1979 (3); v In 1974 (5) 1978 (6); v P 1974 (2) 1980 (4)*
Kanhai, R. B. 79: v E 1959 (5) 1967 (5) 1973 (5); v A 1964 (5) 1972 (5); v In 1961 (5) 1970 (5); v P 1957 (5); *v E 1957 (5) 1963 (5) 1966 (5) 1973 (3); v A 1960 (5) 1968 (5); v In 1958 (5) 1966 (3); v P 1958 (3)*
Kentish, E. S. M. 2: v E 1947 (1) 1953 (1)
King, C. L. 9: v P 1976 (1); *v E 1976 (3) 1980 (1); v A 1979 (1); v NZ 1979 (3)*
King, F. M. 14: v E 1953 (3); v A 1954 (4); v In 1952 (5); *v NZ 1955 (2)*
King, L. A. 2: v E 1967 (1); v In 1961 (1)

Lambert, C. B. 1: *v E 1991*
Lara, B. C. 33: v E 1993 (5); v A 1994 (4); v SA 1991 (1); v NZ 1995 (2); v P 1992 (3); *v E 1995 (6); v A 1992 (5); v NZ 1994 (2); v In 1994 (3); v P 1990 (1); v SL 1993 (1)*
Lashley, P. D. 4: *v E 1966 (2); v A 1960 (2)*
Legall, R. 4: v In 1952 (4)
Lewis, D. M. 3: v In 1970 (3)
Lloyd, C. H. 110: v E 1967 (5) 1973 (5) 1980 (4); v A 1972 (3) 1977 (2) 1983 (4); v NZ 1971 (2); v In 1970 (5) 1975 (4) 1982 (5); v P 1976 (5); *v E 1969 (3) 1973 (3) 1976 (5) 1980 (4) 1984 (5); v A 1968 (4) 1975 (6) 1979 (2) 1981 (3) 1984 (5); v NZ 1968 (3) 1979 (3); v In 1966 (3) 1974 (5) 1983 (6); v P 1974 (2) 1980 (4)*
Logie, A. L. 52: v E 1989 (3); v A 1983 (1) 1990 (5); v NZ 1984 (4); v In 1982 (5) 1988 (4); v P 1987 (3); *v E 1988 (5) 1991 (4); v A 1988 (5); v NZ 1986 (3); v In 1983 (3) 1987 (4); v P 1990 (3)*

McMorris, E. D. A. St J. 13: v E 1959 (4); v In 1961 (4); v P 1957 (1); *v E 1963 (2) 1966 (2)*
McWatt, C. A. 6: v E 1953 (5); v A 1954 (1)
Madray, I. S. 2: v P 1957 (2)
Marshall, M. D. 81: v E 1980 (1) 1985 (5) 1989 (2); v A 1983 (4) 1990 (5); v NZ 1984 (4); v In 1982 (5) 1988 (3); v P 1987 (2); *v E 1980 (4) 1984 (4) 1988 (5) 1991 (5); v A 1984 (5) 1988 (5); v NZ 1986 (3); v In 1978 (3) 1983 (6); v P 1980 (4) 1986 (3) 1990 (3)*
Marshall, N. E. 1: v A 1954
Marshall, R. E. 4: *v A 1951 (2); v NZ 1951 (2)*
Martin, F. R. 9: v E 1929 (1); *v E 1928 (3); v A 1930 (5)*
Martindale, E. A. 10: v E 1934 (4); *v E 1933 (3) 1939 (3)*
Mattis, E. H. 4: v E 1980 (4)
Mendonca, I. L. 2: v In 1961 (2)
Merry, C. A. 2: *v E 1933 (2)*
Miller, R. 1: v In 1952
Moodie, G. H. 1: v E 1934
Moseley, E. A. 2: v E 1989 (2)
Murray, D. A. 19: v E 1980 (4); v A 1977 (3); *v A 1981 (2); v In 1978 (6); v P 1980 (4)*
Murray, D. L. 62: v E 1967 (5) 1973 (5); v A 1972 (4) 1977 (2); v In 1975 (4); v P 1976 (5); *v E 1963 (5) 1973 (3) 1976 (5) 1980 (5); v A 1975 (6) 1979 (3); v NZ 1979 (3); v In 1974 (5); v P 1974 (2)*
Murray, J. R. 24: v E 1993 (5); v A 1994 (3); v P 1992 (3); *v E 1995 (4); v A 1992 (3); v NZ 1994 (2); v In 1994 (3); v SL 1993 (1)*

Nanan, R. 1: *v P 1980*
Neblett, J. M. 1: v E 1934
Noreiga, J. M. 4: v In 1970 (4)
Nunes, R. K. 4: v E 1929 (1); *v E 1928 (3)*
Nurse, S. M. 29: v E 1959 (1) 1967 (5); v A 1964 (4); v In 1961 (1); *v E 1966 (5); v A 1960 (3) 1968 (5); v NZ 1968 (3); v In 1966 (2)*

Padmore, A. L. 2: v In 1975 (1); *v E 1976 (1)*
Pairaudeau, B. H. 13: v E 1953 (2); v In 1952 (5): *v E 1957 (2); v NZ 1955 (4)*
Parry, D. R. 12: v A 1977 (5); *v NZ 1979 (1); v In 1978 (6)*
Passailaigue, C. C. 1: v E 1929
Patterson, B. P. 28: v E 1985 (5) 1989 (1); v A 1990 (5); v SA 1991 (1); v P 1987 (1); *v E 1988 (2) 1991 (3); v A 1988 (4) 1992 (1); v In 1987 (4); v P 1986 (1)*
Payne, T. R. O. 1: v E 1985
Phillip, N. 9: v A 1977 (3); *v In 1978 (6)*
Pierre, L. R. 1: v E 1947

Rae, A. F. 15: v In 1952 (2); *v E 1950 (4); v A 1951 (3); v NZ 1951 (1); v In 1948 (5)*
Ramadhin, S. 43: v E 1953 (5) 1959 (4); v A 1954 (4); v In 1952 (4); *v E 1950 (4) 1957 (5); v A 1951 (5) 1960 (2); v NZ 1951 (2) 1955 (4); v In 1958 (2); v P 1958 (2)*
Richards, I. V. A. 121: v E 1980 (4) 1985 (5) 1989 (3); v A 1977 (2) 1983 (5) 1990 (5); v NZ 1984 (4); v In 1975 (4) 1982 (5) 1988 (4); v P 1976 (5) 1987 (2); *v E 1976 (4) 1980 (5) 1984 (5) 1988 (5) 1991 (5); v A 1975 (6) 1979 (3) 1981 (3) 1984 (5) 1988 (5); v NZ 1986 (3); v In 1974 (5) 1983 (6) 1987 (4); v P 1974 (2) 1980 (4) 1986 (3)*
Richardson, R. B. 86: v E 1985 (5) 1989 (4) 1993 (4); v A 1983 (5) 1990 (5) 1994 (4); v SA 1991 (1); v NZ 1984 (4); v In 1988 (4); v P 1987 (3) 1992 (3); *v E 1988 (3) 1991 (5) 1995 (6); v A 1984 (5) 1988 (5) 1992 (5); v NZ 1986 (3); v In 1983 (1) 1987 (4); v P 1986 (3) 1990 (3); v SL 1993 (1)*
Rickards, K. R. 2: v E 1947 (1); *v A 1951 (1)*
Roach, C. A. 16: v E 1929 (4) 1934 (1); *v E 1928 (3) 1933 (3); v A 1930 (5)*
Roberts, A. M. E. 47: v E 1973 (1) 1980 (3); v A 1977 (2); v In 1975 (2) 1982 (5); v P 1976 (5); *v E 1976 (5) 1980 (3); v A 1975 (5) 1979 (3) 1981 (2); v NZ 1979 (2); v In 1974 (5) 1983 (2); v P 1974 (2)*
Roberts, A. T. 1: *v NZ 1955*
Rodriguez, W. V. 5: v E 1967 (1); v A 1964 (1); v In 1961 (2); *v E 1963 (1)*
Rowe, L. G. 30: v E 1973 (5); v A 1972 (3); v NZ 1971 (4); v In 1975 (4); *v E 1976 (2); v A 1975 (6) 1979 (3); v NZ 1979 (3)*

St Hill, E. L. 2: v E 1929 (2)
St Hill, W. H. 3: v E 1929 (1); *v E 1928 (2)*
Samuels, R. G. 2: v NZ 1995 (2)
Scarlett, R. O. 3: v E 1959 (3)
Scott, A. P. H. 1: v In 1952
Scott, O. C. 8: v E 1929 (1); *v E 1928 (2); v A 1930 (5)*
Sealey, B. J. 1: *v E 1933*
Sealy, J. E. D. 11: v E 1929 (2) 1934 (4); *v E 1939 (3); v A 1930 (2)*
Shepherd, J. N. 5: v In 1970 (2); *v E 1969 (3)*
Shillingford, G. C. 7: v NZ 1971 (2); v In 1970 (3); *v E 1969 (2)*
Shillingford, I. T. 4: v A 1977 (1); v P 1976 (3)
Shivnarine, S. 8: v A 1977 (3); *v In 1978 (5)*
Simmons, P. V. 24: v E 1993 (2); v SA 1991 (1); v NZ 1995 (2); v P 1987 (1) 1992 (3); *v E 1991 (5); v A 1992 (5); v In 1987 (1) 1994 (3); v SL 1993 (1)*
Singh, C. K. 2: v E 1959 (2)
Small, J. A. 3: v E 1929 (1); *v E 1928 (2)*
Small, M. A. 2: v A 1983 (1); *v E 1984 (1)*
Smith, C. W. 5: v In 1961 (1); *v A 1960 (4)*
Smith, O. G. 26: v A 1954 (4); v P 1957 (5); *v E 1957 (5); v NZ 1955 (4); v In 1958 (5); v P 1958 (3)*
Sobers, G. S. 93: v E 1953 (1) 1959 (5) 1967 (5) 1973 (4); v A 1954 (4) 1964 (5); v NZ 1971 (5); v In 1961 (5) 1970 (5); v P 1957 (5); *v E 1957 (5) 1963 (5) 1966 (5) 1969 (3) 1973 (3); v A 1960 (5) 1968 (5); v NZ 1955 (4) 1968 (3); v In 1958 (5) 1966 (3); v P 1958 (3)*
Solomon, J. S. 27: v E 1959 (2); v A 1964 (4); v In 1961 (4); *v E 1963 (5); v A 1960 (5); v In 1958 (4); v P 1958 (3)*
Stayers, S. C. 4: v In 1961 (4)

Stollmeyer, J. B. 32: v E 1947 (2) 1953 (5); v A 1954 (2); v In 1952 (5); *v E 1939 (3) 1950 (4); v A 1951 (5); v NZ 1951 (2); v In 1948 (4)*
Stollmeyer, V. H. 1: *v E 1939*

Taylor, J. 3: v P 1957 (1); *v In 1958 (1); v P 1958 (1)*
Thompson, P. I. C. 1: v NZ 1995
Trim, J. 4: v E 1947 (1); *v A 1951 (1); v In 1948 (2)*

Valentine, A. L. 36: v E 1953 (3); v A 1954 (3); v In 1952 (5) 1961 (2); v P 1957 (1); *v E 1950 (4) 1957 (2); v A 1951 (5) 1960 (5); v NZ 1951 (2) 1955 (4)*
Valentine, V. A. 2: *v E 1933 (2)*

Walcott, C. L. 44: v E 1947 (4) 1953 (5) 1959 (2); v A 1954 (5); v In 1952 (5); v P 1957 (4); *v E 1950 (4) 1957 (5); v A 1951 (3); v NZ 1951 (2); v In 1948 (5)*
Walcott, L. A. 1: v E 1929
Walsh, C. A. 82: v E 1985 (1) 1989 (3) 1993 (5); v A 1990 (5) 1994 (4); v SA 1991 (1); v NZ 1984 (1) 1995 (2); v In 1988 (4); v P 1987 (3) 1992 (3); *v E 1988 (5) 1991 (5) 1995 (6); v A 1984 (5) 1988 (5) 1992 (5); v NZ 1986 (3) 1994 (2); v In 1987 (4) 1994 (3); v P 1986 (3) 1990 (3); v SL 1993 (1)*
Watson, C. 7: v E 1959 (5); v In 1961 (1); *v A 1960 (1)*
Weekes, E. D. 48: v E 1947 (4) 1953 (4); v A 1954 (5) v In 1952 (5); v P 1957 (5); *v E 1950 (4) 1957 (5); v A 1951 (5); v NZ 1951 (2) 1955 (4); v In 1948 (5)*
Weekes, K. H. 2: *v E 1939 (2)*
White, W. A. 2: v A 1964 (2)
Wight, C. V. 2: v E 1929 (1); *v E 1928 (1)*
Wight, G. L. 1: v In 1952
Wiles, C. A. 1: *v E 1933*
Willett, E. T. 5: v A 1972 (3); *v In 1974 (2)*
Williams, A. B. 7: v A 1977 (3); *v In 1978 (4)*
Williams, D. 3: v SA 1991 (1); *v A 1992 (2)*
Williams, E. A. V. 4: v E 1947 (3); *v E 1939 (1)*
Williams, S. C. 12: v E 1993 (1); v A 1994 (4); *v E 1995 (2); v NZ 1994 (2); v In 1994 (3)*
Wishart, K. L. 1: v E 1934
Worrell, F. M. M. 51: v E 1947 (3) 1953 (4) 1959 (4); v A 1954 (4); v In 1952 (5) 1961 (5); *v E 1950 (4) 1957 (5) 1963 (5); v A 1951 (5) 1960 (5); v NZ 1951 (2)*

NEW ZEALAND

Number of Test cricketers: 199

Alabaster, J. C. 21: v E 1962 (2); v WI 1955 (1); v In 1967 (4); *v E 1958 (2); v SA 1961 (5); v WI 1971 (2); v In 1955 (4); v P 1955 (1)*
Allcott, C. F. W. 6: v E 1929 (2); v SA 1931 (1); *v E 1931 (3)*
Allott, G. I. 2: v Z 1995 (2)
Anderson, R. W. 9: v E 1977 (3); *v E 1978 (3); v P 1976 (3)*
Anderson, W. M. 1: v A 1945
Andrews, B. 2: *v A 1973 (2)*
Astle, N. J. 4: v Z 1995 (2); *v WI 1995 (2)*

Badcock, F. T. 7: v E 1929 (3) 1932 (2); v SA 1931 (2)
Barber, R. T. 1: v WI 1955
Bartlett, G. A. 10: v E 1965 (2); v In 1967 (2); v P 1964 (1); *v SA 1961 (5)*
Barton, P. T. 7: v E 1962 (3); *v SA 1961 (4)*
Beard, D. D. 4: v WI 1951 (2) 1955 (2)
Beck, J. E. F. 8: v WI 1955 (4); *v SA 1953 (4)*
Bell, W. 2: *v SA 1953 (2)*
Bilby, G. P. 2: v E 1965 (2)
Blain, T. E. 11: v A 1992 (2); v P 1993 (3); *v E 1986 (1); v A 1993 (3); v In 1988 (2)*
Blair, R. W. 19: v E 1954 (1) 1958 (2) 1962 (2); v SA 1952 (2) 1963 (3); v WI 1955 (2); *v E 1958 (3); v SA 1953 (4)*
Blunt, R. C. 9: v E 1929 (4); v SA 1931 (2); *v E 1931 (3)*

Bolton, B. A. 2: v E 1958 (2)
Boock, S. L. 30: v E 1977 (3) 1983 (2) 1987 (1); v WI 1979 (3) 1986 (2); v P 1978 (3) 1984 (2) 1988 (1); *v E 1978 (3); v A 1985 (1); v WI 1984 (3); v P 1984 (3); v SL 1983 (3)*
Bracewell, B. P. 6: v P 1978 (1) 1984 (1); *v E 1978 (3); v A 1980 (1)*
Bracewell, J. G. 41: v E 1987 (3); v A 1985 (2) 1989 (1); v WI 1986 (3); v In 1980 (1) 1989 (2); v P 1988 (2); *v E 1983 (4) 1986 (3) 1990 (3); v A 1980 (3) 1985 (2) 1987 (3); v WI 1984 (1); v In 1988 (3); v P 1984 (2); v SL 1983 (2) 1986 (1)*
Bradburn, G. E. 5: v SL 1990 (1); *v P 1990 (3); v SL 1992 (1)*
Bradburn, W. P. 2: v SA 1963 (2)
Brown, V. R. 2: *v A 1985 (2)*
Burgess, M. G. 50: v E 1970 (1) 1977 (3); v A 1973 (1) 1976 (2); v WI 1968 (2); v In 1967 (4) 1975 (3); v P 1972 (3) 1978 (3); *v E 1969 (2) 1973 (3) 1978 (3); v A 1980 (3); v WI 1971 (5); v In 1969 (3) 1976 (3); v P 1969 (3) 1976 (3)*
Burke, C. 1: v A 1945
Burtt, T. B. 10: v E 1946 (1) 1950 (2); v SA 1952 (1); v WI 1951 (2); *v E 1949 (4)*
Butterfield, L. A. 1: v A 1945

Cairns, B. L. 43: v E 1974 (1) 1977 (1) 1983 (3); v A 1976 (1) 1981 (3); v WI 1979 (3); v In 1975 (1) 1980 (3); v P 1978 (3) 1984 (3); v SL 1982 (2); *v E 1978 (2) 1983 (4); v A 1973 (1) 1980 (3) 1985 (1); v WI 1984 (2); v In 1976 (2); v P 1976 (2); v SL 1983 (2)*
Cairns, C. L. 16: v E 1991 (3); v A 1992 (2); v P 1993 (1) 1995 (1); v SL 1990 (1); v Z 1995 (2); *v A 1989 (1) 1993 (2); v In 1995 (3)*
Cameron, F. J. 19: v E 1962 (3); v SA 1963 (3); v P 1964 (3); *v E 1965 (2); v SA 1961 (5); v In 1964 (1); v P 1964 (2)*
Cave, H. B. 19: v E 1954 (2); v WI 1955 (3); *v E 1949 (4) 1958 (2); v In 1955 (5); v P 1955 (3)*
Chapple, M. E. 14: v E 1954 (1) 1965 (1); v SA 1952 (1) 1963 (3); v WI 1955 (1); *v SA 1953 (5) 1961 (2)*
Chatfield, E. J. 43: v E 1974 (1) 1977 (1) 1983 (3) 1987 (3); v A 1976 (2) 1981 (1) 1985 (3); v WI 1986 (3); v P 1984 (3) 1988 (2); v SL 1982 (2); *v E 1983 (3) 1986 (1); v A 1985 (2) 1987 (2); v WI 1984 (4); v In 1988 (3); v P 1984 (1); v SL 1983 (2) 1986 (1)*
Cleverley, D. C. 2: v SA 1931 (1); v A 1945 (1)
Collinge, R. O. 35: v E 1970 (2) 1974 (2) 1977 (3); v A 1973 (3); v In 1967 (2) 1975 (3); v P 1964 (3) 1972 (2); *v E 1965 (3) 1969 (1) 1973 (3) 1978 (1); v In 1964 (2) 1976 (1); v P 1964 (2) 1976 (2)*
Colquhoun, I. A. 2: v E 1954 (2)
Coney, J. V. 52: v E 1983 (3); v A 1973 (2) 1981 (3) 1985 (3); v WI 1979 (3) 1986 (3); v In 1980 (3); v P 1978 (3) 1984 (3); v SL 1982 (2); *v E 1983 (4) 1986 (3); v A 1973 (2) 1980 (2) 1985 (3); v WI 1984 (4); v P 1984 (3); v SL 1983 (3)*
Congdon, B. E. 61: v E 1965 (3) 1970 (2) 1974 (2) 1977 (3); v A 1973 (3) 1976 (2); v WI 1968 (3); v In 1967 (4) 1975 (3); v P 1964 (3) 1972 (3); *v E 1965 (3) 1969 (3) 1973 (3) 1978 (3); v A 1973 (3); v WI 1971 (5); v In 1964 (3) 1969 (3); v P 1964 (1) 1969 (3)*
Cowie, J. 9: v E 1946 (1); v A 1945 (1); *v E 1937 (3) 1949 (4)*
Cresswell G. F. 3: v E 1950 (2); *v E 1949 (1)*
Cromb, I. B. 5: v SA 1931 (2); *v E 1931 (3)*
Crowe, J. J. 39: v E 1983 (3) 1987 (2); v A 1989 (1); v WI 1986 (3); v P 1984 (3) 1988 (2); v SL 1982 (2); *v E 1983 (2) 1986 (3); v A 1985 (3) 1987 (3) 1989 (1); v WI 1984 (4); v P 1984 (3); v SL 1983 (3) 1986 (1)*
Crowe, M. D. 77: v E 1983 (3) 1987 (3) 1991 (3); v A 1981 (3) 1985 (3) 1992 (3); v SA 1994 (1); v WI 1986 (3); v In 1989 (3); v P 1984 (3) 1988 (2); v SL 1990 (2); *v E 1983 (4) 1986 (3) 1990 (3) 1994 (3); v A 1985 (3) 1987 (3) 1989 (1) 1993 (1); v SA 1994 (3); v WI 1984 (4); v In 1995 (3); v P 1984 (3) 1990 (3); v SL 1983 (3) 1986 (1) 1992 (2); v Z 1992 (2)*
Cunis, R. S. 20: v E 1965 (3) 1970 (2); v SA 1963 (1); v WI 1968 (3); *v E 1969 (1); v WI 1971 (5); v In 1969 (3); v P 1969 (2)*

D'Arcy, J. W. 5: *v E 1958 (5)*
Davis, H. T. 1: *v E 1994*
de Groen, R. P. 5: v P 1993 (2); *v A 1993 (2); v SA 1994 (1)*
Dempster, C. S. 10: v E 1929 (4) 1932 (2); v SA 1931 (2); *v E 1931 (2)*
Dempster, E. W. 5: v SA 1952 (1); *v SA 1953 (4)*
Dick, A. E. 17: v E 1962 (3); v SA 1963 (2); v P 1964 (2); *v E 1965 (2); v SA 1961 (5); v P 1964 (3)*
Dickinson, G. R. 3: v E 1929 (2); v SA 1931 (1)
Donnelly, M. P. 7: *v E 1937 (3) 1949 (4)*
Doull, S. B. 11: v WI 1994 (2); v P 1993 (3); *v A 1993 (2); v SA 1994 (3); v Z 1992 (1)*

Dowling, G. T. 39: v E 1962 (3) 1970 (2); v SA 1963 (1); v WI 1968 (3); v In 1967 (4); v P 1964 (2); *v E 1965 (3) 1969 (3); v SA 1961 (4); v WI 1971 (2); v In 1964 (4) 1969 (3); v P 1964 (2) 1969 (3)*
Dunning, J. A. 4: v E 1932 (1); *v E 1937 (3)*

Edgar, B. A. 39: v E 1983 (3); v A 1981 (3) 1985 (3); v WI 1979 (3); v In 1980 (3); v P 1978 (3); v SL 1982 (2); *v E 1978 (3) 1983 (4) 1986 (3); v A 1980 (3) 1985 (3); v P 1984 (3)*
Edwards, G. N. 8: v E 1977 (1); v A 1976 (2); v In 1980 (3); *v E 1978 (2)*
Emery, R. W. G. 2: v WI 1951 (2)

Fisher, F. E. 1: v SA 1952
Fleming, S. P. 20: v SA 1994 (1); v WI 1994 (2); v In 1993 (1); v P 1995 (1); v SL 1994 (2); v Z 1995 (2); *v E 1994 (3); SA 1994 (3); v WI 1995 (2); v In 1995 (3)*
Foley, H. 1: v E 1929
Franklin, T. J. 21: v E 1987 (3); v A 1985 (1) 1989 (1); v In 1989 (3); v SL 1990 (3); *v E 1983 (1) 1990 (3); v In 1988 (3); v P 1990 (3)*
Freeman, D. L. 2: v E 1932 (2)

Gallichan, N. 1: *v E 1937*
Gedye, S. G. 4: v SA 1963 (3); v P 1964 (1)
Germon, L. K. 8: v P 1995 (1); v Z 1995 (2); *v WI 1995 (2); v In 1995 (3)*
Gillespie, S. R. 1: v A 1985
Gray, E. J. 10: *v E 1983 (2) 1986 (3); v A 1987 (1); v In 1988 (1); v P 1984 (2); v SL 1986 (1)*
Greatbatch, M. J. 39: v E 1987 (2) 1991 (1); v A 1989 (1) 1992 (3); v In 1989 (3) 1993 (1); v P 1988 (1) 1992 (1) 1993 (3); v SL 1990 (2) 1994 (2); *v E 1990 (3) 1994 (1); v A 1989 (1) 1993 (3); v In 1988 (3) 1995 (3); v P 1990 (3); v Z 1992 (2)*
Guillen, S. C. 3: v WI 1955 (3)
Guy, J. W. 12: v E 1958 (2); v WI 1955 (2); *v SA 1961 (2); v In 1955 (5); v P 1955 (1)*

Hadlee, D. R. 26: v E 1974 (2) 1977 (1); v A 1973 (3) 1976 (1); v In 1975 (3); v P 1972 (2); *v E 1969 (2) 1973 (3); v A 1973 (3); v In 1969 (3); v P 1969 (3)*
Hadlee, R. J. 86: v E 1977 (3) 1983 (3) 1987 (1); v A 1973 (2) 1976 (2) 1981 (3) 1985 (3) 1989 (1); v WI 1979 (3) 1986 (3); v In 1975 (2) 1980 (3) 1989 (3); v P 1972 (1) 1978 (3) 1984 (3) 1988 (2); v SL 1982 (2); *v E 1973 (1) 1978 (3) 1983 (4) 1986 (3) 1990 (3); v A 1973 (3) 1980 (3) 1985 (3) 1987 (3); v WI 1984 (4); v In 1976 (3) 1988 (3); v P 1976 (3); v SL 1983 (3) 1986 (1)*
Hadlee, W. A. 11: v E 1946 (1) 1950 (2); v A 1945 (1); *v E 1937 (3) 1949 (4)*
Harford, N. S. 8: *v E 1958 (4); v In 1955 (2); v P 1955 (2)*
Harford, R. I. 3: v In 1967 (3)
Harris, C. Z. 7: v A 1992 (1); v P 1992 (1); *v A 1993 (1); v WI 1995 (2); v SL 1992 (2)*
Harris, P. G. Z. 9: v P 1964 (1); *v SA 1961 (5); v In 1955 (1); v P 1955 (2)*
Harris, R. M. 2: v E 1958 (2)
Hart, M. N. 14: v SA 1994 (1); v WI 1994 (2); v In 1993 (1); v P 1993 (2); *v E 1994 (3); v SA 1994 (3); v In 1995 (2)*
Hartland, B. R. 9: v E 1991 (3); v In 1993 (1); v P 1992 (1) 1993 (1); *v E 1994 (1); v SL 1992 (2)*
Haslam, M. J. 4: *v In 1995 (2); v Z 1992 (2)*
Hastings, B. F. 31: v E 1974 (2); v A 1973 (3); v WI 1968 (3); v In 1975 (1); v P 1972 (3); *v E 1969 (3) 1973 (3); v A 1973 (3); v WI 1971 (5); v In 1969 (2); v P 1969 (3)*
Hayes, J. A. 15: v E 1950 (2) 1954 (1); v WI 1951 (2); *v E 1958 (4); v In 1955 (5); v P 1955 (1)*
Henderson, M. 1: v E 1929
Horne, P. A. 4: v WI 1986 (1); *v A 1987 (1); v P 1990 (1); v SL 1986 (1)*
Hough, K. W. 2: v E 1958 (2)
Howarth, G. P. 47: v E 1974 (2) 1977 (3) 1983 (3); v A 1976 (2) 1981 (3); v WI 1979 (3); v In 1980 (3); v P 1978 (3) 1984 (3); v SL 1982 (2); *v E 1978 (3) 1983 (4); v A 1980 (2); v WI 1984 (4); v In 1976 (2); v P 1976 (2); v SL 1983 (3)*
Howarth, H. J. 30: v E 1970 (2) 1974 (2); v A 1973 (3) 1976 (2); v In 1975 (2); v P 1972 (3); *v E 1969 (3) 1973 (2); v WI 1971 (5); v In 1969 (3); v P 1969 (3)*

James, K. C. 11: v E 1929 (4) 1932 (2); v SA 1931 (2); *v E 1931 (3)*
Jarvis, T. W. 13: v E 1965 (1); v P 1972 (3); *v WI 1971 (4); v In 1964 (2); v P 1964 (3)*
Jones, A. H. 39: v E 1987 (1) 1991 (3); v A 1989 (1) 1992 (3); v WI 1994 (2); v In 1989 (3); v P 1988 (2) 1992 (1) 1993 (3); v SL 1990 (3); *v E 1990 (3); v A 1987 (3) 1993 (3); v In 1988 (3); v SL 1986 (1) 1992 (2); v Z 1992 (2)*

Kennedy, R. J. 4: v Z 1995 (2); *v WI 1995 (2)*
Kerr, J. L. 7: v E 1932 (2); v SA 1931 (1); *v E 1931 (2) 1937 (2)*
Kuggeleijn, C. M. 2: *v In 1988 (2)*

Larsen, G. R. 8: v SA 1994 (1); v P 1995 (1); v SL 1994 (2); v Z 1995 (1); *v E 1994 (1); v WI 1995 (2)*
Latham, R. T. 4: v E 1991 (1); v P 1992 (1); *v Z 1992 (2)*
Lees, W. K. 21: v E 1977 (2); v A 1976 (1); v WI 1979 (3); v P 1978 (3); v SL 1982 (2); *v E 1983 (2); v A 1980 (2); v In 1976 (3); v P 1976 (3)*
Leggat, I. B. 1: *v SA 1953*
Leggat, J. G. 9: v E 1954 (1); v SA 1952 (1); v WI 1951 (1) 1955 (1); *v In 1955 (3); v P 1955 (2)*
Lissette, A. F. 2: v WI 1955 (2)
Loveridge, G. R. 1: v Z 1995
Lowry, T. C. 7: v E 1929 (4); *v E 1931 (3)*

McEwan, P. E. 4: v WI 1979 (1); *v A 1980 (2); v P 1984 (1)*
MacGibbon, A. R. 26: v E 1950 (2) 1954 (2); v SA 1952 (1); v WI 1955 (3); *v E 1958 (5); v SA 1953 (5); v In 1955 (5); v P 1955 (3)*
McGirr, H. M. 2: v E 1929 (2)
McGregor, S. N. 25: v E 1954 (2) 1958 (2); v SA 1963 (3); v WI 1955 (4); v P 1964 (2); *v SA 1961 (5); v In 1955 (4); v P 1955 (3)*
McLeod E. G. 1: v E 1929
McMahon T. G. 5: v WI 1955 (1); *v In 1955 (3); v P 1955 (1)*
McRae, D. A. N. 1: v A 1945
Matheson, A. M. 2: v E 1929 (1); *v E 1931 (1)*
Meale, T. 2: *v E 1958 (2)*
Merritt, W. E. 6: v E 1929 (4); *v E 1931 (2)*
Meuli, E. M. 1: v SA 1952
Milburn, B. D. 3: v WI 1968 (3)
Miller, L. S. M. 13: v SA 1952 (2); v WI 1955 (3); *v E 1958 (4); v SA 1953 (4)*
Mills, J. E. 7: v E 1929 (3) 1932 (1); *v E 1931 (3)*
Moir, A. M. 17: v E 1950 (2) 1954 (2) 1958 (2); v SA 1952 (1); v WI 1951 (2) 1955 (1); *v E 1958 (2); v In 1955 (2); v P 1955 (3)*
Moloney D. A. R. 3: *v E 1937 (3)*
Mooney, F. L. H. 14: v E 1950 (2); v SA 1952 (2); v WI 1951 (2); *v E 1949 (3); v SA 1953 (5)*
Morgan, R. W. 20: v E 1965 (2) 1970 (2); v WI 1968 (1); v P 1964 (2); *v E 1965 (3); v WI 1971 (3); v In 1964 (4); v P 1964 (3)*
Morrison, B. D. 1: v E 1962
Morrison, D. K. 47: v E 1987 (3) 1991 (3); v A 1989 (1) 1992 (3); v SA 1994 (1); v WI 1994 (2); v In 1989 (3) 1993 (1); v P 1988 (1) 1992 (1) 1993 (2) 1995 (1); v SL 1990 (3) 1994 (1); *v E 1990 (3); v A 1987 (3) 1989 (1) 1993 (3); v SA 1994 (2); v WI 1995 (2); v In 1988 (1) 1995 (3); v P 1990 (3)*
Morrison, J. F. M. 17: v E 1974 (2); v A 1973 (3) 1981 (3); v In 1975 (3); *v A 1973 (3); v In 1976 (1); v P 1976 (2)*
Motz, R. C. 32: v E 1962 (2) 1965 (3); v SA 1963 (2); v WI 1968 (3); v In 1967 (4); v P 1964 (3); *v E 1965 (3) 1969 (3); v SA 1961 (5); v In 1964 (3); v P 1964 (1)*
Murray, B. A. G. 13: v E 1970 (1); v In 1967 (4); *v E 1969 (2); v In 1969 (3); v P 1969 (3)*
Murray, D. J. 8: v SA 1994 (1); v WI 1994 (2); v SL 1994 (2); *v SA 1994 (3)*

Nash, D. J. 14: v SA 1994 (1); v WI 1994 (1); v In 1993 (1); v P 1995 (1); v SL 1994 (1); *v E 1994 (3); v SA 1994 (1); v In 1995 (3); v SL 1992 (1); v Z 1992 (1)*
Newman J. 3: v E 1932 (2); v SA 1931 (1)

O'Sullivan, D. R. 11: v In 1975 (1); v P 1972 (1); *v A 1973 (3); v In 1976 (3); v P 1976 (3)*
Overton, G. W. F. 3: *v SA 1953 (3)*
Owens, M. B. 8: v A 1992 (2); v P 1992 (1) 1993 (1); *v E 1994 (2); v SL 1992 (2)*

Page, M. L. 14: v E 1929 (4) 1932 (2); v SA 1931 (2); *v E 1931 (3) 1937 (3)*
Parker, J. M. 36: v E 1974 (2) 1977 (3); v A 1973 (3) 1976 (2); v WI 1979 (3); v In 1975 (3); v P 1972 (1) 1978 (2); *v E 1973 (3) 1978 (2); v A 1973 (3) 1980 (3); v In 1976 (3); v P 1976 (3)*
Parker, N. M. 3: *v In 1976 (2); v P 1976 (1)*

Parore, A. C. 27: v E 1991 (1); v A 1992 (1); v SA 1994 (1); v WI 1994 (2); v In 1993 (1); v P 1992 (1) 1995 (1); v SL 1994 (2); v Z 1995 (2); *v E 1990 (1) 1994 (3); v SA 1994 (3); v WI 1995 (1); v In 1995 (3); v SL 1992 (2); v Z 1992 (2)*

Patel, D. N. 31: v E 1991 (3); v A 1992 (3); v SA 1994 (1); v WI 1986 (3); v P 1988 (1) 1992 (1) 1995 (1); v SL 1990 (2) 1994 (1); v Z 1995 (2); *v A 1987 (3) 1989 (1) 1993 (3); v WI 1995 (1); v P 1990 (3); v Z 1992 (2)*

Petherick, P. J. 6: v A 1976 (1); *v In 1976 (3); v P 1976 (2)*

Petrie, E. C. 14: v E 1958 (2) 1965 (3); *v E 1958 (5); v In 1955 (2); v P 1955 (2)*

Playle, W. R. 8: v E 1962 (3); *v E 1958 (5)*

Pocock, B. A. 6: v P 1993 (2); *v E 1994 (1); v A 1993 (3)*

Pollard, V. 32: v E 1965 (3) 1970 (1); v WI 1968 (3); v In 1967 (4); v P 1972 (1); *v E 1965 (3) 1969 (3) 1973 (3); v In 1964 (4) 1969 (1); v P 1964 (3) 1969 (3)*

Poore, M. B. 14: v E 1954 (1); v SA 1952 (1); *v SA 1953 (5); v In 1955 (4); v P 1955 (3)*

Priest, M. W. 1: *v E 1990*

Pringle, C. 14: v E 1991 (1); v In 1993 (1); v P 1993 (1); v SL 1990 (2) 1994 (1); *v E 1994 (2); v SA 1994 (2); v P 1990 (3); v SL 1992 (1)*

Puna, N. 3: v E 1965 (3)

Rabone, G. O. 12: v E 1954 (2); v SA 1952 (1); v WI 1951 (2); *v E 1949 (4); v SA 1953 (3)*

Redmond, R. E. 1: v P 1972

Reid, J. F. 19: v A 1985 (3); v In 1980 (3); v P 1978 (1) 1984 (3); *v A 1985 (3); v P 1984 (3); v SL 1983 (3)*

Reid, J. R. 58: v E 1950 (2) 1954 (2) 1958 (2) 1962 (3); v SA 1952 (2) 1963 (3); v WI 1951 (2) 1955 (4); v P 1964 (3); *v E 1949 (2) 1958 (5) 1965 (3); v SA 1953 (5) 1961 (5); v In 1955 (5) 1964 (4); v P 1955 (3) 1964 (3)*

Roberts, A. D. G. 7: v In 1975 (2); *v In 1976 (3); v P 1976 (2)*

Roberts, A. W. 5: v E 1929 (1); v SA 1931 (2); *v E 1937 (2)*

Robertson, G. K. 1: v A 1985

Rowe, C. G. 1: v A 1945

Rutherford, K. R. 56: v E 1987 (2) 1991 (2); v A 1985 (3) 1989 (1) 1992 (3); v SA 1994 (1); v WI 1986 (2) 1994 (2); v In 1989 (3) 1993 (1); v P 1992 (1) 1993 (3); v SL 1990 (3) 1994 (2); *v E 1986 (1) 1990 (2) 1994 (3); v A 1987 (1) 1993 (3); v SA 1994 (3); v WI 1984 (4); v In 1988 (2); v P 1990 (3); v SL 1986 (1) 1992 (2); v Z 1992 (2)*

Scott, R. H. 1: v E 1946

Scott, V. J. 10: v E 1946 (1) 1950 (2); v A 1945 (1); v WI 1951 (2); *v E 1949 (4)*

Shrimpton, M. J. F. 10: v E 1962 (2) 1965 (3) 1970 (2); v SA 1963 (1); *v A 1973 (2)*

Sinclair, B. W. 21: v E 1962 (3) 1965 (3); v SA 1963 (3); v In 1967 (2); v P 1964 (2); *v E 1965 (3); v In 1964 (2); v P 1964 (3)*

Sinclair, I. M. 2: v WI 1955 (2)

Smith, F. B. 4: v E 1946 (1); v WI 1951 (1); *v E 1949 (2)*

Smith, H. D. 1: v E 1932

Smith, I. D. S. 63: v E 1983 (3) 1987 (3) 1991 (2); v A 1981 (3) 1985 (3) 1989 (1); v WI 1986 (3); v In 1980 (3) 1989 (3); v P 1984 (3) 1988 (2); v SL 1990 (3); *v E 1983 (2) 1986 (2) 1990 (2); v A 1980 (1) 1985 (3) 1987 (3) 1989 (1); v WI 1984 (4); v In 1988 (3); v P 1984 (3) 1990 (3); v SL 1983 (3) 1986 (1)*

Snedden, C. A. 1: v E 1946

Snedden, M. C. 25: v E 1983 (1) 1987 (2); v A 1981 (3) 1989 (1); v WI 1986 (1); v In 1980 (3) 1989 (3); v SL 1982 (2); *v E 1983 (1) 1990 (3); v A 1985 (1) 1987 (1) 1989 (1); v In 1988 (1); v SL 1986 (1)*

Sparling, J. T. 11: v E 1958 (2) 1962 (1); v SA 1963 (2); *v E 1958 (3); v SA 1961 (3)*

Spearman, C. M. 5: v P 1995 (1); v Z 1995 (2); *v WI 1995 (2)*

Stirling, D. A. 6: *v E 1986 (2); v WI 1984 (1); v P 1984 (3)*

Su'a, M. L. 13: v E 1991 (2); v A 1992 (2); v WI 1994 (1); v P 1992 (1); v SL 1994 (1); *v A 1993 (2); v SL 1992 (2); v Z 1992 (2)*

Sutcliffe, B. 42: v E 1946 (1) 1950 (2) 1954 (2) 1958 (2); v SA 1952 (2); v WI 1951 (2) 1955 (2); *v E 1949 (4) 1958 (4) 1965 (1); v SA 1953 (5); v In 1955 (5) 1964 (4); v P 1955 (3) 1964 (3)*

Taylor, B. R. 30: v E 1965 (1); v WI 1968 (3); v In 1967 (3); v P 1972 (3); *v E 1965 (2) 1969 (2) 1973 (3); v WI 1971 (4); v In 1964 (3) 1969 (2); v P 1964 (3) 1969 (1)*

Taylor, D. D. 3: v E 1946 (1); v WI 1955 (2)

Thomson, K. 2: v In 1967 (2)

Thomson, S. A. 19: v E 1991 (1); v WI 1994 (2); v In 1989 (1) 1993 (1); v P 1993 (3); v SL 1990 (2) 1994 (1); *v E 1994 (3); v SA 1994 (3); v In 1995 (2)*
Tindill, E. W. T. 5: v E 1946 (1); v A 1945 (1); *v E 1937 (3)*
Troup, G. B. 15: v A 1981 (2) 1985 (2); v WI 1979 (3); v In 1980 (2); v P 1978 (2); *v A 1980 (2); v WI 1984 (1); v In 1976 (1)*
Truscott, P. B. 1: v P 1964
Turner, G. M. 41: v E 1970 (2) 1974 (2); v A 1973 (3) 1976 (2); v WI 1968 (3); v In 1975 (3); v P 1972 (3); v SL 1982 (2); *v E 1969 (2) 1973 (3); v A 1973 (2); v WI 1971 (5); v In 1969 (3) 1976 (3); v P 1969 (1) 1976 (2)*
Twose, R. G. 7: v P 1995 (1); v Z 1995 (2); *v WI 1995 (2); v In 1995 (2)*

Vance, R. H. 4: v E 1987 (1); v P 1988 (2); *v A 1989 (1)*
Vaughan, J. T. C. 3: *v WI 1995 (2); v SL 1992 (1)*
Vivian, G. E. 5: *v WI 1971 (4); v In 1964 (1)*
Vivian, H. G. 7: v E 1932 (1); v SA 1931 (1); *v E 1931 (2) 1937 (3)*

Wadsworth, K. J. 33: v E 1970 (2) 1974 (2); v A 1973 (3); v In 1975 (3); v P 1972 (3); *v E 1969 (3) 1973 (3); v A 1973 (3); v WI 1971 (5); v In 1969 (3); v P 1969 (3)*
Wallace, W. M. 13: v E 1946 (1) 1950 (2); v A 1945 (1); v SA 1952 (2); *v E 1937 (3) 1949 (4)*
Walmsley, K. P. 2: v SL 1994 (2)
Ward, J. T. 8: v SA 1963 (1); v In 1967 (1); v P 1964 (1); *v E 1965 (1); v In 1964 (4)*
Watson, W. 15: v E 1991 (1); v A 1992 (2); v SL 1990 (3); *v E 1986 (2); v A 1989 (1) 1993 (1); v P 1990 (3); v Z 1992 (2)*
Watt, L. 1: v E 1954
Webb, M. G. 3: v E 1970 (1); v A 1973 (1); *v WI 1971 (1)*
Webb, P. N. 2: v WI 1979 (2)
Weir, G. L. 11: v E 1929 (3) 1932 (2); v SA 1931 (2); *v E 1931 (3) 1937 (1)*
White, D. J. 2: *v P 1990 (2)*
Whitelaw, P. E. 2: v E 1932 (2)
Wright, J. G. 82: v E 1977 (3) 1983 (3) 1987 (3) 1991 (3); v A 1981 (3) 1985 (2) 1989 (1) 1992 (3); v WI 1979 (3) 1986 (3); v In 1980 (3) 1989 (3); v P 1978 (3) 1984 (3) 1988 (2); v SL 1982 (2) 1990 (3); *v E 1978 (2) 1983 (3) 1986 (3) 1990 (3); v A 1980 (3) 1985 (3) 1987 (3) 1989 (1); v WI 1984 (4); v In 1988 (3); v P 1984 (3); v SL 1983 (3) 1992 (2)*

Young, B. A. 18: v SA 1994 (1); v WI 1994 (2); v In 1993 (1); v P 1993 (3) 1995 (1); v SL 1994 (2); *v E 1994 (3); v A 1993 (1); v SA 1994 (3); v In 1995 (1)*
Yuile, B. W. 17: v E 1962 (2); v WI 1968 (3); v In 1967 (1); v P 1964 (3); *v E 1965 (1); v In 1964 (3) 1969 (1); v P 1964 (1) 1969 (2)*

INDIA

Number of Test cricketers: 207

Abid Ali, S. 29: v E 1972 (4); v A 1969 (1); v WI 1974 (2); v NZ 1969 (3); *v E 1971 (3) 1974 (3); v A 1967 (4); v WI 1970 (5); v NZ 1967 (4)*
Adhikari, H. R. 21: v E 1951 (3); v A 1956 (2); v WI 1948 (5) 1958 (1); v P 1952 (2); *v E 1952 (3); v A 1947 (5)*
Amarnath, L. 24: v E 1933 (3) 1951 (3); v WI 1948 (5); v P 1952 (5); *v E 1946 (3); v A 1947 (5)*
Amarnath, M. 69: v E 1976 (2) 1984 (5); v A 1969 (1) 1979 (1) 1986 (3); v WI 1978 (2) 1983 (3) 1987 (3); v NZ 1976 (3); v P 1983 (2) 1986 (5); v SL 1986 (2); *v E 1979 (2) 1986 (2); v A 1977 (5) 1985 (3); v WI 1975 (4) 1982 (5); v NZ 1975 (3); v P 1978 (3) 1982 (6) 1984 (2); v SL 1985 (2)*
Amarnath, S. 10: v E 1976 (2): *v WI 1975 (2); v NZ 1975 (3); v P 1978 (3)*
Amar Singh 7: v E 1933 (3); *v E 1932 (1) 1936 (3)*
Amir Elahi 1: *v A 1947*
Amre, P. K. 11: v E 1992 (3); v Z 1992 (1); *v SA 1992 (4); v SL 1993 (3)*
Ankola, S. A. 1: *v P 1989*
Apte, A. L. 1: *v E 1959*
Apte, M. L. 7: v P 1952 (2); *v WI 1952 (5)*
Arshad Ayub 13: v WI 1987 (4); v NZ 1988 (3); *v WI 1988 (4); v P 1989 (2)*
Arun, B. 2: v SL 1986 (2)

Arun Lal 16: v WI 1987 (4); v NZ 1988 (3); v P 1986 (1); v SL 1982 (1); *v WI 1988 (4); v P 1982 (3)*
Azad, K. 7: v E 1981 (3); v WI 1983 (2); v P 1983 (1); *v NZ 1980 (1)*
Azharuddin, M. 71: v E 1984 (3) 1992 (3); v A 1986 (3); v WI 1987 (3) 1994 (3); v NZ 1988 (3) 1995 (3); v P 1986 (5); v SL 1986 (1) 1990 (1) 1993 (3); v Z 1992 (1); *v E 1986 (3) 1990 (3) 1996 (3); v A 1985 (3) 1991 (5); v SA 1992 (4); v WI 1988 (3); v NZ 1989 (3) 1993 (1); v P 1989 (4); v SL 1985 (3) 1993 (3); v Z 1992 (1)*

Baig, A. A. 10: v A 1959 (3); v WI 1966 (2); v P 1960 (3); *v E 1959 (2)*
Banerjee, S. A. 1: v WI 1948
Banerjee, S. N. 1: v WI 1948
Banerjee, S. T. 1: *v A 1991*
Baqa Jilani, M. 1: *v E 1936*
Bedi, B. S. 67: v E 1972 (5) 1976 (5); v A 1969 (5); v WI 1966 (2) 1974 (4) 1978 (3); v NZ 1969 (3) 1976 (3); *v E 1967 (3) 1971 (3) 1974 (3) 1979 (3); v A 1967 (2) 1977 (5); v WI 1970 (5) 1975 (4); v NZ 1967 (4) 1975 (2); v P 1978 (3)*
Bhandari, P. 3: v A 1956 (1); v NZ 1955 (1); *v P 1954 (1)*
Bhat, A. R. 2: v WI 1983 (1); v P 1983 (1)
Binny, R. M. H. 27: v E 1979 (1); v WI 1983 (6); v P 1979 (6) 1983 (2) 1986 (3); *v E 1986 (3); v A 1980 (1) 1985 (2); v NZ 1980 (1); v P 1984 (1); v SL 1985 (1)*
Borde, C. G. 55: v E 1961 (5) 1963 (5); v A 1959 (5) 1964 (3) 1969 (1); v WI 1958 (4) 1966 (3); v NZ 1964 (4); v P 1960 (5); *v E 1959 (4) 1967 (3); v A 1967 (4); v WI 1961 (5); v NZ 1967 (4)*

Chandrasekhar, B. S. 58: v E 1963 (4) 1972 (5) 1976 (5); v A 1964 (2); v WI 1966 (3) 1974 (4) 1978 (4); v NZ 1964 (2) 1976 (3); *v E 1967 (3) 1971 (3) 1974 (2) 1979 (1); v A 1967 (2) 1977 (5); v WI 1975 (4); v NZ 1975 (3); v P 1978 (3)*
Chauhan, C. P. S. 40: v E 1972 (2); v A 1969 (1) 1979 (6); v WI 1978 (6); v NZ 1969 (2); v P 1979 (6); *v E 1979 (4); v A 1977 (4) 1980 (3); v NZ 1980 (3); v P 1978 (3)*
Chauhan, R. K. 15: v E 1992 (3); v WI 1994 (2); v NZ 1995 (2); v SL 1993 (3); v Z 1992 (1); *v NZ 1993 (1); v SL 1993 (3)*
Chowdhury, N. R. 2: v E 1951 (1); v WI 1948 (1)
Colah, S. H. M. 2: v E 1933 (1); *v E 1932 (1)*
Contractor, N. J. 31: v E 1961 (5); v A 1956 (1) 1959 (5); v WI 1958 (5); v NZ 1955 (4); v P 1960 (5); *v E 1959 (4); v WI 1961 (2)*

Dani, H. T. 1: v P 1952
Desai, R. B. 28: v E 1961 (4) 1963 (2); v A 1959 (3); v WI 1958 (1); v NZ 1964 (3); v P 1960 (5); *v E 1959 (5); v A 1967 (1); v WI 1961 (3); v NZ 1967 (1)*
Dilawar Hussain 3: v E 1933 (2); *v E 1936 (1)*
Divecha, R. V. 5: v E 1951 (2); v P 1952 (1); *v E 1952 (2)*
Doshi, D. R. 33: v E 1979 (1) 1981 (6); v A 1979 (6); v P 1979 (6) 1983 (1); v SL 1982 (1); *v E 1982 (3); v A 1980 (3); v NZ 1980 (2); v P 1982 (4)*
Dravid, R. 2: *v E 1996 (2)*
Durani, S. A. 29: v E 1961 (5) 1963 (5) 1972 (3); v A 1959 (1) 1964 (3); v WI 1966 (1); v NZ 1964 (3); *v WI 1961 (5) 1970 (3)*

Engineer, F. M. 46: v E 1961 (4) 1972 (5); v A 1969 (5); v WI 1966 (1) 1974 (5); v NZ 1964 (4) 1969 (2); *v E 1967 (3) 1971 (3) 1974 (3); v A 1967 (4); v WI 1961 (3); v NZ 1967 (4)*

Gadkari, C. V. 6: *v WI 1952 (3); v P 1954 (3)*
Gaekwad, A. D. 40: v E 1976 (4) 1984 (3); v WI 1974 (3) 1978 (5) 1983 (6); v NZ 1976 (3); v P 1983 (3); *v E 1979 (2); v A 1977 (1); v WI 1975 (3) 1982 (5); v P 1984 (2)*
Gaekwad, D. K. 11: v WI 1958 (1); v P 1952 (2) 1960 (1); *v E 1952 (1) 1959 (4); v WI 1952 (2)*
Gaekwad, H. G. 1: v P 1952
Gandotra, A. 2: v A 1969 (1); v NZ 1969 (1)
Ganguly, S. C. 2: *v E 1996 (2)*
Gavaskar, S. M. 125: v E 1972 (5) 1976 (5) 1979 (1) 1981 (6) 1984 (5); v A 1979 (6) 1986 (3); v WI 1974 (2) 1978 (6) 1983 (6); v NZ 1976 (3); v P 1979 (6) 1983 (3) 1986 (4); v SL 1982 (1) 1986 (3); *v E 1971 (3) 1974 (3) 1979 (4) 1982 (3) 1986 (3); v A 1977 (5) 1980 (3) 1985 (3); v WI 1970 (4) 1975 (4) 1982 (5); v NZ 1975 (3) 1980 (3); v P 1978 (3) 1982 (6) 1984 (2); v SL 1985 (3)*
Ghavri, K. D. 39: v E 1976 (3) 1979 (1); v A 1979 (6); v WI 1974 (3) 1978 (6); v NZ 1976 (2); v P 1979 (6); *v E 1979 (4); v A 1977 (3) 1980 (3); v NZ 1980 (1); v P 1978 (1)*

Ghorpade, J. M. 8: v A 1956 (1); v WI 1958 (1); v NZ 1955 (1); *v E 1959 (3); v WI 1952 (2)*
Ghulam Ahmed 22: v E 1951 (2); v A 1956 (2); v WI 1948 (3) 1958 (2); v NZ 1955 (1); v P 1952 (4); *v E 1952 (4); v P 1954 (4)*
Gopalan, M. J. 1: v E 1933
Gopinath, C. D. 8: v E 1951 (3); v A 1959 (1); v P 1952 (1); *v E 1952 (1); v P 1954 (2)*
Guard, G. M. 2: v A 1959 (1); v WI 1958 (1)
Guha, S. 4: v A 1969 (3); *v E 1967 (1)*
Gul Mahomed 8: v P 1952 (2); *v E 1946 (1); v A 1947 (5)*
Gupte, B. P. 3: v E 1963 (1); v NZ 1964 (1); v P 1960 (1)
Gupte, S. P. 36: v E 1951 (1) 1961 (2); v A 1956 (3); v WI 1958 (5); v NZ 1955 (5); v P 1952 (2) 1960 (3); *v E 1959 (5); v WI 1952 (5); v P 1954 (5)*
Gursharan Singh 1: *v NZ 1989*

Hafeez, A. 3: *v E 1946 (3)*
Hanumant Singh 14: v E 1963 (2); v A 1964 (3); v WI 1966 (2); v NZ 1964 (4) 1969 (1); *v E 1967 (2)*
Hardikar, M. S. 2: v WI 1958 (2)
Hazare, V. S. 30: v E 1951 (5); v WI 1948 (5); v P 1952 (3); *v E 1946 (3) 1952 (4); v A 1947 (5); v WI 1952 (5)*
Hindlekar, D. D. 4: *v E 1936 (1) 1946 (3)*
Hirwani, N. D. 15: v WI 1987 (1); v NZ 1988 (3) 1995 (1); v SL 1990 (1); *v E 1990 (3); v WI 1988 (3); v NZ 1989 (3)*

Ibrahim, K. C. 4: v WI 1948 (4)
Indrajitsinhji, K. S. 4: v A 1964 (3); v NZ 1969 (1)
Irani, J. K. 2: *v A 1947 (2)*

Jadeja, A. D. 8: v NZ 1995 (3); *v E 1996 (2); v SA 1992 (3)*
Jahangir Khan, M. 4: *v E 1932 (1) 1936 (3)*
Jai, L. P. 1: v E 1933
Jaisimha, M. L. 39: v E 1961 (5) 1963 (5); v A 1959 (1) 1964 (3); v WI 1966 (2); v NZ 1964 (4) 1969 (1); v P 1960 (4); *v E 1959 (1); v A 1967 (2); v WI 1961 (4) 1970 (3); v NZ 1967 (4)*
Jamshedji, R. J. 1: v E 1933
Jayantilal, K. 1: *v WI 1970*
Joshi, P. G. 12: v E 1951 (2); v A 1959 (1); v WI 1958 (1); v P 1952 (1) 1960 (1); *v E 1959 (3); v WI 1952 (3)*
Joshi, S. B. 1: *v E 1996*

Kambli, V. G. 17: v E 1992 (3); v WI 1994 (3); v NZ 1995 (3); v SL 1993 (3); v Z 1992 (1); *v NZ 1993 (1); v SL 1993 (3)*
Kanitkar, H. S. 2: v WI 1974 (2)
Kapil Dev 131: v E 1979 (1) 1981 (6) 1984 (4) 1992 (3); v A 1979 (6) 1986 (3); v WI 1978 (6) 1983 (6) 1987 (4); v NZ 1988 (3); v P 1979 (6) 1983 (3) 1986 (5); v SL 1982 (1) 1986 (3) 1990 (1) 1993 (3); v Z 1992 (1); *v E 1979 (4) 1982 (3) 1986 (3) 1990 (3); v A 1980 (3) 1985 (3) 1991 (5); v SA 1992 (4); v WI 1982 (5) 1988 (4); v NZ 1980 (3) 1989 (3) 1993 (1); v P 1978 (3) 1982 (6) 1984 (2) 1989 (4); v SL 1985 (3) 1993 (3); v Z 1992 (1)*
Kapoor, A. R. 2: v WI 1994 (1); v NZ 1995 (1)
Kardar, A. H. (*see* Hafeez)
Kenny, R. B. 5: v A 1959 (4); v WI 1958 (1)
Kirmani, S. M. H. 88: v E 1976 (5) 1979 (1) 1981 (6) 1984 (5); v A 1979 (6); v WI 1978 (6) 1983 (6); v NZ 1976 (3); v P 1979 (6) 1983 (3); v SL 1982 (1); *v E 1982 (3); v A 1977 (5) 1980 (3) 1985 (3); v WI 1975 (4) 1982 (5); v NZ 1975 (3) 1980 (3); v P 1978 (3) 1982 (6) 1984 (2)*
Kischenchand, G. 5: v P 1952 (1); *v A 1947 (4)*
Kripal Singh, A. G. 14: v E 1961 (3) 1963 (2); v A 1956 (2) 1964 (1); v WI 1958 (1); v NZ 1955 (4); *v E 1959 (1)*
Krishnamurthy, P. 5: *v WI 1970 (5)*
Kulkarni, R. R. 3: v A 1986 (1); v P 1986 (2)
Kulkarni, U. N. 4: *v A 1967 (3); v NZ 1967 (1)*
Kumar, V. V. 2: v E 1961 (1); v P 1960 (1)
Kumble, A. 26: v E 1992 (3); v WI 1994 (3); v NZ 1995 (3); v SL 1993 (3); v Z 1992 (1); *v E 1990 (1) 1996 (3); v SA 1992 (4); v NZ 1993 (1); v SL 1993 (3); v Z 1992 (1)*

Kunderan, B. K. 18: v E 1961 (1) 1963 (5); v A 1959 (3); v WI 1966 (2); v NZ 1964 (1); v P 1960 (2); *v E 1967 (2); v WI 1961 (2)*

Lall Singh 1: *v E 1932*
Lamba, R. 4: v WI 1987 (1); v SL 1986 (3)

Madan Lal 39: v E 1976 (2) 1981 (6); v WI 1974 (2) 1983 (3); v NZ 1976 (1); v P 1983 (3); v SL 1982 (1); *v E 1974 (2) 1982 (3) 1986 (1); v A 1977 (2); v WI 1975 (4) 1982 (2); v NZ 1975 (3); v P 1982 (3) 1984 (1)*
Maka, E. S. 2: v P 1952 (1); *v WI 1952 (1)*
Malhotra, A. 7: v E 1981 (2) 1984 (1); v WI 1983 (3); *v E 1982 (1)*
Maninder Singh 35: v A 1986 (3); v WI 1983 (4) 1987 (3); v P 1986 (4); v SL 1986 (3); v Z 1992 (1); *v E 1986 (3); v WI 1982 (3); v P 1982 (5) 1984 (1) 1989 (3); v SL 1985 (2)*
Manjrekar, S. V. 36: v WI 1987 (1) 1994 (3); v NZ 1995 (1); v SL 1990 (1) 1993 (3); *v E 1990 (3) 1996 (2); v A 1991 (5); v SA 1992 (4); v WI 1988 (4); v NZ 1989 (3) 1993 (1); v P 1989 (4); v Z 1992 (1)*
Manjrekar, V. L. 55: v E 1951 (2) 1961 (5) 1963 (4); v A 1956 (3) 1964 (3); v WI 1958 (4); v NZ 1955 (5) 1964 (1); v P 1952 (3) 1960 (5); *v E 1952 (4) 1959 (2); v WI 1952 (4) 1961 (5); v P 1954 (5)*
Mankad, A. V. 22: v E 1976 (1); v A 1969 (5); v WI 1974 (1); v NZ 1969 (2) 1976 (3); *v E 1971 (3) 1974 (1); v A 1977 (3); v WI 1970 (3)*
Mankad, V. 44: v E 1951 (5); v A 1956 (3); v WI 1948 (5) 1958 (2); v NZ 1955 (4); v P 1952 (4); *v E 1946 (3) 1952 (3); v A 1947 (5); v WI 1952 (5); v P 1954 (5)*
Mansur Ali Khan (*see* Pataudi)
Mantri, M. K. 4: v E 1951 (1); *v E 1952 (2); v P 1954 (1)*
Meherhomji, K. R. 1: *v E 1936*
Mehra, V. L. 8: v E 1961 (1) 1963 (2); v NZ 1955 (2); *v WI 1961 (3)*
Merchant, V. M. 10: v E 1933 (3) 1951 (1); *v E 1936 (3) 1946 (3)*
Mhambrey, P. L. 2: *v E 1996 (2)*
Milkha Singh, A. G. 4: v E 1961 (1); v A 1959 (1); v P 1960 (2)
Modi, R. S. 10: v E 1951 (1); v WI 1948 (5); v P 1952 (1); *v E 1946 (3)*
Mongia, N. R. 13: v WI 1994 (3); v NZ 1995 (3); v SL 1993 (3); *v E 1996 (3); v NZ 1993 (1)*
More, K. S. 49: v E 1992 (3); v A 1986 (2); v WI 1987 (4); v NZ 1988 (3); v P 1986 (5); v SL 1986 (3) 1990 (1); *v E 1986 (3) 1990 (3); v A 1991 (3); v SA 1992 (4); v WI 1988 (4); v NZ 1989 (3); v P 1989 (4); v SL 1993 (3); v Z 1992 (1)*
Muddiah, V. M. 2: v A 1959 (1); v P 1960 (1)
Mushtaq Ali, S. 11: v E 1933 (2) 1951 (1); v WI 1948 (3); *v E 1936 (3) 1946 (2)*

Nadkarni, R. G. 41: v E 1961 (1) 1963 (5); v A 1959 (5) 1964 (3); v WI 1958 (1) 1966 (1); v NZ 1955 (1) 1964 (4); v P 1960 (4); *v E 1959 (4); v A 1967 (3); v WI 1961 (5); v NZ 1967 (4)*
Naik, S. S. 3: v WI 1974 (2); *v E 1974 (1)*
Naoomal Jeoomal 3: v E 1933 (2); *v E 1932 (1)*
Narasimha Rao, M. V. 4: v A 1979 (2); v WI 1978 (2)
Navle, J. G. 2: v E 1933 (1); *v E 1932 (1)*
Nayak, S. V. 2: *v E 1982 (2)*
Nayudu, C. K. 7: v E 1933 (3); *v E 1932 (1) 1936 (3)*
Nayudu, C. S. 11: v E 1933 (2) 1951 (1); *v E 1936 (2) 1946 (2); v A 1947 (4)*
Nazir Ali, S. 2: v E 1933 (1); *v E 1932 (1)*
Nissar, Mahomed 6: v E 1933 (2); *v E 1932 (1) 1936 (3)*
Nyalchand, S. 1: v P 1952

Pai, A. M. 1: v NZ 1969
Palia, P. E. 2: *v E 1932 (1) 1936 (1)*
Pandit, C. S. 5: v A 1986 (2); *v E 1986 (1); v A 1991 (2)*
Parkar, G. A. 1: *v E 1982*
Parkar, R. D. 2: v E 1972 (2)
Parsana, D. D. 2: v WI 1978 (2)
Patankar, C. T. 1: v NZ 1955
Pataudi sen., Nawab of, 3: *v E 1946 (3)*
Pataudi jun., Nawab of (now Mansur Ali Khan) 46: v E 1961 (3) 1963 (5) 1972 (3); v A 1964 (3) 1969 (5); v WI 1966 (3) 1974 (4); v NZ 1964 (4) 1969 (3); *v E 1967 (3); v A 1967 (3); v WI 1961 (3); v NZ 1967 (4)*

Patel, B. P. 21: v E 1976 (5); v WI 1974 (3); v NZ 1976 (3); *v E 1974 (2); v A 1977 (2); v WI 1975 (3); v NZ 1975 (3)*
Patel, J. M. 7: v A 1956 (2) 1959 (3); v NZ 1955 (1); *v P 1954 (1)*
Patel, R. 1: v NZ 1988
Patiala, Yuvraj of, 1: v E 1933
Patil, S. M. 29: v E 1979 (1) 1981 (4) 1984 (2); v WI 1983 (2); v P 1979 (2) 1983 (3); v SL 1982 (1); *v E 1982 (2); v A 1980 (3); v NZ 1980 (3); v P 1982 (4) 1984 (2)*
Patil, S. R. 1: v NZ 1955
Phadkar, D. G. 31: v E 1951 (4); v A 1956 (1); v WI 1948 (4) 1958 (1); v NZ 1955 (4); v P 1952 (2); *v E 1952 (4); v A 1947 (4); v WI 1952 (4); v P 1954 (3)*
Prabhakar, M. 39: v E 1984 (2) 1992 (3); v WI 1994 (3); v NZ 1995 (3); v SL 1990 (1) 1993 (3); v Z 1992 (1); *v E 1990 (3); v A 1991 (5); v SA 1992 (4); v NZ 1989 (3); v P 1989 (4); v SL 1993 (3); v Z 1992 (1)*
Prasad, B. K. V. 3: *v E 1996 (3)*
Prasanna, E. A. S. 49: v E 1961 (1) 1972 (3) 1976 (4); v A 1969 (5); v WI 1966 (1) 1974 (5); v NZ 1969 (3); *v E 1967 (3) 1974 (2); v A 1967 (4) 1977 (4); v WI 1961 (1) 1970 (3) 1975 (1); v NZ 1967 (4) 1975 (3); v P 1978 (2)*
Punjabi, P. H. 5: *v P 1954 (5)*

Rai Singh, K. 1: *v A 1947*
Rajinder Pal 1: v E 1963
Rajindernath, V. 1: v P 1952
Rajput, L. S. 2: *v SL 1985 (2)*
Raju, S. L. V. 24: v E 1992 (3); v WI 1994 (3); v NZ 1995 (2); v SL 1990 (1) 1993 (3); *v E 1996 (1); v A 1991 (4); v SA 1992 (2); v NZ 1989 (2) 1993 (1); v SL 1993 (1); v Z 1992 (1)*
Raman, W. V. 8: v WI 1987 (1); v NZ 1988 (1); *v SA 1992 (1); v WI 1988 (1); v NZ 1989 (3); v Z 1992 (1)*
Ramaswami, C. 2: *v E 1936 (2)*
Ramchand, G. S. 33: v A 1956 (3) 1959 (5); v WI 1958 (3); v NZ 1955 (5); v P 1952 (3); *v E 1952 (4); v WI 1952 (5); v P 1954 (5)*
Ramji, L. 1: v E 1933
Rangachari, C. R. 4: v WI 1948 (2); *v A 1947 (2)*
Rangnekar, K. M. 3: *v A 1947 (3)*
Ranjane, V. B. 7: v E 1961 (3) 1963 (1); v A 1964 (1); v WI 1958 (1); *v WI 1961 (1)*
Rathore, V. 3: *v E 1996 (3)*
Razdan, V. 2: *v P 1989 (2)*
Reddy, B. 4: *v E 1979 (4)*
Rege, M. R. 1: v WI 1948
Roy, A. 4: v A 1969 (2); v NZ 1969 (2)
Roy, Pankaj 43: v E 1951 (5); v A 1956 (3) 1959 (5); v WI 1958 (5); v NZ 1955 (3); v P 1952 (3) 1960 (1); *v E 1952 (4) 1959 (5); v WI 1952 (4); v P 1954 (5)*
Roy, Pranab 2: v E 1981 (2)

Sandhu, B. S. 8: v WI 1983 (1); *v WI 1982 (4); v P 1982 (3)*
Sardesai, D. N. 30: v E 1961 (1) 1963 (5) 1972 (1); v A 1964 (3) 1969 (1); v WI 1966 (2); v NZ 1964 (3); *v E 1967 (1) 1971 (3); v A 1967 (2); v WI 1961 (3) 1970 (5)*
Sarwate, C. T. 9: v E 1951 (1); v WI 1948 (2); *v E 1946 (1); v A 1947 (5)*
Saxena, R. C. 1: *v E 1967*
Sekar, T. A. P. 2: *v P 1982 (2)*
Sen, P. 14: v E 1951 (2); v WI 1948 (5); v P 1952 (2); *v E 1952 (2); v A 1947 (3)*
Sen Gupta, A. K. 1: v WI 1958
Sharma, Ajay 1: v WI 1987
Sharma, Chetan 23: v E 1984 (3); v A 1986 (2); v WI 1987 (3); v SL 1986 (2); *v E 1986 (2); v A 1985 (2); v WI 1988 (4); v P 1984 (2); v SL 1985 (3)*
Sharma, Gopal 5: v E 1984 (1); v P 1986 (2); v SL 1990 (1); *v SL 1985 (1)*
Sharma, P. 5: v E 1976 (2); v WI 1974 (2); *v WI 1975 (1)*
Sharma, Sanjeev 2: v NZ 1988 (1); *v E 1990 (1)*
Shastri, R. J. 80: v E 1981 (6) 1984 (5); v A 1986 (3); v WI 1983 (6) 1987 (4); v NZ 1988 (3); v P 1983 (2) 1986 (5); v SL 1986 (3) 1990 (1); *v E 1982 (3) 1986 (3) 1990 (3); v A 1985 (3) 1991 (3); v SA 1992 (3); v WI 1982 (5) 1988 (4); v NZ 1980 (3); v P 1982 (2) 1984 (2) 1989 (4); v SL 1985 (3); v Z 1992 (1)*
Shinde, S. G. 7: v E 1951 (3); v WI 1948 (1); *v E 1946 (1) 1952 (2)*

Shodhan, R. H. 3: v P 1952 (1); *v WI 1952 (2)*
Shukla, R. C. 1: v SL 1982
Sidhu, N. S. 36: v E 1992 (3); v WI 1983 (2) 1994 (3); v NZ 1988 (3) 1995 (2); v SL 1993 (3); v Z 1992 (1); *v E 1990 (3); v A 1991 (3); v WI 1988 (4); v NZ 1989 (1) 1993 (1); v P 1989 (4); v SL 1993 (3)*
Sivaramakrishnan, L. 9: v E 1984 (5); *v A 1985 (2); v WI 1982 (1); v SL 1985 (1)*
Sohoni, S. W. 4: v E 1951 (1); *v E 1946 (2); v A 1947 (1)*
Solkar, E. D. 27: v E 1972 (5) 1976 (1); v A 1969 (4); v WI 1974 (4); v NZ 1969 (1); *v E 1971 (3) 1974 (3); v WI 1970 (5) 1975 (1)*
Sood, M. M. 1: v A 1959
Srikkanth, K. 43: v E 1981 (4) 1984 (2); v A 1986 (3); v WI 1987 (4); v NZ 1988 (3); v P 1986 (5); v SL 1986 (3); *v E 1986 (3); v A 1985 (3) 1991 (4); v P 1982 (2) 1989 (4); v SL 1985 (3)*
Srinath, J. 21: v WI 1994 (3); v NZ 1995 (3); *v E 1996 (3); v A 1991 (5); v SA 1992 (3); v NZ 1993 (1); v SL 1993 (2); v Z 1992 (1)*
Srinivasan, T. E. 1: *v NZ 1980*
Subramanya, V. 9: v WI 1966 (2); v NZ 1964 (1); *v E 1967 (2); v A 1967 (2); v NZ 1967 (2)*
Sunderram, G. 2: v NZ 1955 (2)
Surendranath, R. 11: v A 1959 (2); v WI 1958 (2); v P 1960 (2); *v E 1959 (5)*
Surti, R. F. 26: v E 1963 (1); v A 1964 (2) 1969 (1); v WI 1966 (2); v NZ 1964 (1) 1969 (2); v P 1960 (2); *v E 1967 (2); v A 1967 (4); v WI 1961 (5); v NZ 1967 (4)*
Swamy, V. N. 1: v NZ 1955

Tamhane, N. S. 21: v A 1956 (3) 1959 (1); v WI 1958 (4); v NZ 1955 (4); v P 1960 (2); *v E 1959 (2); v P 1954 (5)*
Tarapore, K. K. 1: v WI 1948
Tendulkar, S. R. 41: v E 1992 (3); v WI 1994 (3); v NZ 1995 (3); v SL 1990 (1) 1993 (3); v Z 1992 (1); *v E 1990 (3) 1996 (3); v A 1991 (5); v SA 1992 (4); v NZ 1989 (3) 1993 (1); v P 1989 (4); v SL 1993 (3); v Z 1992 (1)*

Umrigar, P. R. 59: v E 1951 (5) 1961 (4); v A 1956 (3) 1959 (3); v WI 1948 (1) 1958 (5); v NZ 1955 (5); v P 1952 (5) 1960 (5); *v E 1952 (4) 1959 (4); v WI 1952 (5) 1961 (5); v P 1954 (5)*

Vengsarkar, D. B. 116: v E 1976 (1) 1979 (1) 1981 (6) 1984 (5); v A 1979 (6) 1986 (2); v WI 1978 (6) 1983 (5) 1987 (3); v NZ 1988 (3); v P 1979 (5) 1983 (1) 1986 (5); v SL 1982 (1) 1986 (3) 1990 (1); *v E 1979 (4) 1982 (3) 1986 (3) 1990 (3); v A 1977 (5) 1980 (3) 1985 (3) 1991 (5); v WI 1975 (2) 1982 (5) 1988 (4); v NZ 1975 (3) 1980 (3) 1989 (2); v P 1978 (3) 1982 (6) 1984 (2); v SL 1985 (3)*
Venkataraghavan, S. 57: v E 1972 (2) 1976 (1); v A 1969 (5) 1979 (3); v WI 1966 (2) 1974 (2) 1978 (6); v NZ 1964 (4) 1969 (2) 1976 (3); v P 1983 (2); *v E 1967 (1) 1971 (3) 1974 (2) 1979 (4); v A 1977 (1); v WI 1970 (5) 1975 (3) 1982 (5); v NZ 1975 (1)*
Venkataramana, M. 1: *v WI 1988*
Viswanath, G. R. 91: v E 1972 (5) 1976 (5) 1979 (1) 1981 (6); v A 1969 (4) 1979 (6); v WI 1974 (5) 1978 (6); v NZ 1976 (3); v P 1979 (6); v SL 1982 (1); *v E 1971 (3) 1974 (3) 1979 (4) 1982 (3); v A 1977 (5) 1980 (3); v WI 1970 (3) 1975 (4); v NZ 1975 (3) 1980 (3); v P 1978 (3) 1982 (6)*
Viswanath, S. 3: *v SL 1985 (3)*
Vizianagram, Maharaj Kumar of, Sir Vijay A. 3: *v E 1936 (3)*

Wadekar, A. L. 37: v E 1972 (5); v A 1969 (5); v WI 1966 (2); v NZ 1969 (3); *v E 1967 (3) 1971 (3) 1974 (3); v A 1967 (4); v WI 1970 (5); v NZ 1967 (4)*
Wassan, A. S. 4: *v E 1990 (1); v NZ 1989 (3)*
Wazir Ali, S. 7: v E 1933 (3); *v E 1932 (1) 1936 (3)*

Yadav, N. S. 35: v E 1979 (1) 1981 (1) 1984 (4); v A 1979 (5) 1986 (3); v WI 1983 (3); v P 1979 (5) 1986 (4); v SL 1986 (2); *v A 1980 (2) 1985 (3); v NZ 1980 (1); v P 1984 (1)*
Yadav, V. S. 1: v Z 1992
Yajurvindra Singh 4: v E 1976 (2); v A 1979 (1); *v E 1979 (1)*
Yashpal Sharma 37: v E 1979 (1) 1981 (2); v A 1979 (6); v WI 1983 (1); v P 1979 (6) 1983 (3); v SL 1982 (1); *v E 1979 (3) 1982 (3); v A 1980 (3); v WI 1982 (5); v NZ 1980 (1); v P 1982 (2)*
Yograj Singh 1: *v NZ 1980*

Note: Hafeez, on going later to Oxford University, took his correct name, Kardar.

PAKISTAN

Number of Test cricketers: 137

Aamer Malik 14: v E 1987 (2); v A 1988 (1) 1994 (1); v WI 1990 (1); v In 1989 (4); *v A 1989 (2); v WI 1987 (1); v NZ 1988 (2)*
Aamir Nazir 6: v SL 1995 (1); *v SA 1994 (1); v WI 1992 (1); v NZ 1993 (1); v Z 1994 (2)*
Aamir Sohail 32: v A 1994 (3); v SL 1995 (3); v Z 1993 (3); *v E 1992 (5) 1996 (2); v A 1995 (3); v SA 1994 (1); v WI 1992 (2); v NZ 1992 (1) 1993 (3) 1995 (1); v SL 1994 (2); v Z 1994 (3)*
Abdul Kadir 4: v A 1964 (1); *v A 1964 (1); v NZ 1964 (2)*
Abdul Qadir 67: v E 1977 (3) 1983 (3) 1987 (3); v A 1982 (3) 1988 (3); v WI 1980 (2) 1986 (3) 1990 (2); v NZ 1984 (3) 1990 (2); v In 1982 (5) 1984 (1) 1989 (4); v SL 1985 (3); *v E 1982 (3) 1987 (4); v A 1983 (5); v WI 1987 (3); v NZ 1984 (2) 1988 (2); v In 1979 (3) 1986 (3); v SL 1985 (2)*
Afaq Hussain 2: v E 1961 (1); *v A 1964 (1)*
Aftab Baloch 2: v WI 1974 (1); v NZ 1969 (1)
Aftab Gul 6: v E 1968 (2); v NZ 1969 (1); *v E 1971 (3)*
Agha Saadat Ali 1: v NZ 1955
Agha Zahid 1: v WI 1974
Akram Raza 9: v A 1994 (2); v WI 1990 (1); v In 1989 (1); v SL 1991 (1); *v NZ 1993 (2); v SL 1994 (1); v Z 1994 (1)*
Alim-ud-Din 25: v E 1961 (2); v A 1956 (1) 1959 (1); v WI 1958 (1); v NZ 1955 (3); v In 1954 (5); *v E 1954 (3) 1962 (3); v WI 1957 (5); v In 1960 (1)*
Amir Elahi 5: *v In 1952 (5)*
Anil Dalpat 9: v E 1983 (3); v NZ 1984 (3); *v NZ 1984 (3)*
Anwar Hussain 4: *v In 1952 (4)*
Anwar Khan 1: *v NZ 1978*
Aqib Javed 21: v A 1994 (1); v NZ 1990 (3); v SL 1991 (3) 1995 (3); *v E 1992 (5); v A 1989 (1); v SA 1994 (1); v NZ 1988 (1) 1992 (1); v Z 1994 (2)*
Arif Butt 3: *v A 1964 (1); v NZ 1964 (2)*
Ashfaq Ahmed 1: v Z 1993
Ashraf Ali 8: v E 1987 (3); v In 1984 (2); v SL 1981 (2) 1985 (1)
Asif Iqbal 58: v E 1968 (3) 1972 (3); v A 1964 (1); v WI 1974 (2); v NZ 1964 (3) 1969 (3) 1976 (3); v In 1978 (3); *v E 1967 (3) 1971 (3) 1974 (3); v A 1964 (1) 1972 (3) 1976 (3) 1978 (2); v WI 1976 (5); v NZ 1964 (3) 1972 (3) 1978 (2); v In 1979 (6)*
Asif Masood 16: v E 1968 (2) 1972 (1); v WI 1974 (2); v NZ 1969 (1); *v E 1971 (3) 1974 (3); v A 1972 (3) 1976 (1)*
Asif Mujtaba 23: v E 1987 (1); v WI 1986 (2); v Z 1993 (3); *v E 1992 (5) 1996 (2); v SA 1994 (1); v WI 1992 (3); v NZ 1992 (1) 1993 (2); v SL 1994 (2); v Z 1994 (1)*
Ata-ur-Rehman 13: v SL 1995 (1); v Z 1993 (3); *v E 1992 (1) 1996 (2); v WI 1992 (3); v NZ 1993 (2) 1995 (1)*
Atif Rauf 1: *v NZ 1993*
Azeem Hafeez 18: v E 1983 (2); v NZ 1984 (3); v In 1984 (2); *v A 1983 (5); v NZ 1984 (3); v In 1983 (3)*
Azhar Khan 1: v A 1979
Azmat Rana 1: v A 1979

Basit Ali 19: v A 1994 (2); v SL 1995 (1); v Z 1993 (3); *v A 1995 (3); v WI 1992 (3); v NZ 1993 (3) 1995 (1); v SL 1994 (2); v Z 1994 (1)*
Burki, J. 25: v E 1961 (3); v A 1964 (1); v NZ 1964 (3) 1969 (1); *v E 1962 (5) 1967 (3); v A 1964 (1); v NZ 1964 (3); v In 1960 (5)*

D'Souza, A. 6: v E 1961 (2); v WI 1958 (1); *v E 1962 (3)*

Ehtesham-ud-Din 5: v A 1979 (1); *v E 1982 (1); v In 1979 (3)*

Farooq Hamid 1: *v A 1964*
Farrukh Zaman 1: v NZ 1976
Fazal Mahmood 34: v E 1961 (1); v A 1956 (1) 1959 (2); v WI 1958 (3); v NZ 1955 (2); v In 1954 (4); *v E 1954 (4) 1962 (2); v WI 1957 (5); v In 1952 (5) 1960 (5)*

Ghazali, M. E. Z. 2: *v E 1954 (2)*
Ghulam Abbas 1: *v E 1967*
Gul Mahomed 1: v A 1956

Hanif Mohammad 55: v E 1961 (3) 1968 (3); v A 1956 (1) 1959 (3) 1964 (1); v WI 1958 (1); v NZ 1955 (3) 1964 (3) 1969 (1); v In 1954 (5); *v E 1954 (4) 1962 (5) 1967 (3); v A 1964 (1); v WI 1957 (5); v NZ 1964 (3); v In 1952 (5) 1960 (5)*
Haroon Rashid 23: v E 1977 (3); v A 1979 (2) 1982 (3); v In 1982 (1); v SL 1981 (2); *v E 1978 (3) 1982 (1); v A 1976 (1) 1978 (1); v WI 1976 (5); v NZ 1978 (1)*
Haseeb Ahsan 12: v E 1961 (2); v A 1959 (1); v WI 1958 (1); *v WI 1957 (3); v In 1960 (5)*

Ibadulla, K. 4: v A 1964 (1); *v E 1967 (2); v NZ 1964 (1)*
Ijaz Ahmed, sen. 30: v E 1987 (3); v A 1988 (3) 1994 (1); v WI 1990 (3); *v E 1987 (4) 1996 (3); v A 1989 (3) 1995 (2); v SA 1994 (1); v WI 1987 (2); v NZ 1995 (1); v In 1986 (1); v Z 1994 (3)*
Ijaz Ahmed, jun. 2: v SL 1995 (2)
Ijaz Butt 8: v A 1959 (2); v WI 1958 (3); *v E 1962 (3)*
Ijaz Faqih 5: v WI 1980 (1); *v A 1981 (1); v WI 1987 (2); v In 1986 (1)*
Imran Khan 88: v A 1979 (2) 1982 (3); v WI 1980 (4) 1986 (3) 1990 (3); v NZ 1976 (3); v In 1978 (3) 1982 (6) 1989 (4); v SL 1981 (1) 1985 (3) 1991 (3); *v E 1971 (1) 1974 (3) 1982 (3) 1987 (5); v A 1976 (3) 1978 (2) 1981 (3) 1983 (2) 1989 (3); v WI 1976 (5) 1987 (3); v NZ 1978 (2) 1988 (2); v In 1979 (5) 1986 (5); v SL 1985 (3)*
Imtiaz Ahmed 41: v E 1961 (3); v A 1956 (1) 1959 (3); v WI 1958 (3); v NZ 1955 (3); v In 1954 (5); *v E 1954 (4) 1962 (4); v WI 1957 (5); v In 1952 (5) 1960 (5)*
Intikhab Alam 47: v E 1961 (2) 1968 (3) 1972 (3); v A 1959 (1) 1964 (1); v WI 1974 (2); v NZ 1964 (3) 1969 (3) 1976 (3); *v E 1962 (3) 1967 (3) 1971 (3) 1974 (3); v A 1964 (1) 1972 (3); v WI 1976 (1); v NZ 1964 (3) 1972 (3); v In 1960 (3)*
Inzamam-ul-Haq 33: v A 1994 (3); v SL 1995 (3); v Z 1993 (3); *v E 1992 (4) 1996 (3); v A 1995 (3); v SA 1994 (1); v WI 1992 (3); v NZ 1992 (1) 1993 (3) 1995 (1); v SL 1994 (2); v Z 1994 (3)*
Iqbal Qasim 50: v E 1977 (3) 1987 (3); v A 1979 (3) 1982 (2) 1988 (3); v WI 1980 (4); v NZ 1984 (3); v In 1978 (3) 1982 (2); v SL 1981 (3); *v E 1978 (3); v A 1976 (3) 1981 (2); v WI 1976 (2); v NZ 1984 (1); v In 1979 (6) 1983 (1) 1986 (3)*
Israr Ali 4: v A 1959 (2); *v In 1952 (2)*

Jalal-ud-Din 6: v A 1982 (1); v In 1982 (2) 1984 (2); v SL 1985 (1)
Javed Akhtar 1: *v E 1962*
Javed Miandad 124: v E 1977 (3) 1987 (3); v A 1979 (3) 1982 (3) 1988 (3); v WI 1980 (4) 1986 (3) 1990 (2); v NZ 1976 (3) 1984 (3) 1990 (3); v In 1978 (3) 1982 (6) 1984 (2) 1989 (4); v SL 1981 (3) 1985 (3) 1991 (3); v Z 1993 (3); *v E 1978 (3) 1982 (3) 1987 (5) 1992 (5); v A 1976 (3) 1978 (2) 1981 (3) 1983 (5) 1989 (3); v WI 1976 (1) 1987 (3) 1992 (3); v NZ 1978 (3) 1984 (3) 1988 (2) 1992 (1); v In 1979 (6) 1983 (3) 1986 (4); v SL 1985 (3)*

Kabir Khan 4: *v SA 1994 (1); v SL 1994 (1); v Z 1994 (2)*
Kardar, A. H. 23: v A 1956 (1); v NZ 1955 (3); v In 1954 (5); *v E 1954 (4); v WI 1957 (5); v In 1952 (5)*
Khalid Hassan 1: *v E 1954*
Khalid Wazir 2: *v E 1954 (2)*
Khan Mohammad 13: v A 1956 (1); v NZ 1955 (3); v In 1954 (4); *v E 1954 (2); v WI 1957 (2); v In 1952 (1)*

Liaqat Ali 5: v E 1977 (2); v WI 1974 (1); *v E 1978 (2)*

Mahmood Hussain 27: v E 1961 (1); v WI 1958 (3); v NZ 1955 (1); v In 1954 (5); *v E 1954* (2) *1962 (3); v WI 1957 (3); v In 1952 (4) 1960 (5)*
Majid Khan 63: v E 1968 (3) 1972 (3); v A 1964 (1) 1979 (3); v WI 1974 (2) 1980 (4); v NZ 1964 (3) 1976 (3); v In 1978 (3) 1982 (1); v SL 1981 (1); *v E 1967 (3) 1971 (2) 1974 (3) 1982 (1); v A 1972 (3) 1976 (3) 1978 (2) 1981 (3); v WI 1976 (5); v NZ 1972 (3) 1978 (2); v In 1979 (6)*
Mansoor Akhtar 19: v A 1982 (3); v WI 1980 (2); v In 1982 (3); v SL 1981 (1); *v E 1982 (3) 1987 (5); v A 1981 (1) 1989 (1)*
Manzoor Elahi 6: v NZ 1984 (1); v In 1984 (1); *v In 1986 (2); v Z 1994 (2)*
Maqsood Ahmed 16: v NZ 1955 (2); v In 1954 (5); *v E 1954 (4); v In 1952 (5)*

Masood Anwar 1: v WI 1990
Mathias, Wallis 21: v E 1961 (1); v A 1956 (1) 1959 (2); v WI 1958 (3); v NZ 1955 (1); *v E 1962 (3); v WI 1957 (5); v In 1960 (5)*
Miran Bux 2: v In 1954 (2)
Mohammad Akram 5: v SL 1995 (2); *v E 1996 (1); v A 1995 (2)*
Mohammad Aslam 1: *v E 1954*
Mohammad Farooq 7: v NZ 1964 (3); *v E 1962 (2); v In 1960 (2)*
Mohammad Ilyas 10: v E 1968 (2); v NZ 1964 (3); *v E 1967 (1); v A 1964 (1); v NZ 1964 (3)*
Mohammad Munaf 4: v E 1961 (2); v A 1959 (2)
Mohammad Nazir 14: v E 1972 (1); v WI 1980 (4); v NZ 1969 (3); *v A 1983 (3); v In 1983 (3)*
Mohsin Kamal 9: v E 1983 (1); v A 1994 (2); v SL 1985 (1); *v E 1987 (4); v SL 1985 (1)*
Mohsin Khan 48: v E 1977 (1) 1983 (3); v A 1982 (3); v WI 1986 (3); v NZ 1984 (2); v In 1982 (6) 1984 (2); v SL 1981 (2) 1985 (2); *v E 1978 (3) 1982 (3); v A 1978 (1) 1981 (2) 1983 (5); v NZ 1978 (1) 1984 (3); v In 1983 (3); v SL 1985 (3)*
Moin Khan 20: v A 1994 (1); v WI 1990 (2); v SL 1991 (3) 1995 (3); *v E 1992 (4) 1996 (2); v A 1995 (2); v SA 1994 (1); v WI 1992 (2)*
Mudassar Nazar 76: v E 1977 (3) 1983 (1) 1987 (3); v A 1979 (3) 1982 (3) 1988 (3); v WI 1986 (2); v NZ 1984 (3); v In 1978 (2) 1982 (6) 1984 (2); v SL 1981 (1) 1985 (3) ; *v E 1978 (3) 1982 (3) 1987 (5); v A 1976 (1) 1978 (1) 1981 (3) 1983 (5); v WI 1987 (3); v NZ 1978 (1) 1984 (3) 1988 (2); v In 1979 (5) 1983 (3); v SL 1985 (3)*
Mufasir-ul-Haq 1: *v NZ 1964*
Munir Malik 3: v A 1959 (1); *v E 1962 (2)*
Mushtaq Ahmed 24: v A 1994 (3); v WI 1990 (2); v Z 1993 (2); *v E 1992 (5) 1996 (3); v A 1989 (1) 1995 (2); v WI 1992 (1); v NZ 1992 (1) 1993 (1) 1995 (1); v SL 1994 (2)*
Mushtaq Mohammad 57: v E 1961 (3) 1968 (3) 1972 (3); v WI 1958 (1) 1974 (2); v NZ 1969 (2) 1976 (3); v In 1978 (3); *v E 1962 (5) 1967 (3) 1971 (3) 1974 (3); v A 1972 (3) 1976 (3) 1978 (2); v WI 1976 (5); v NZ 1972 (2) 1978 (3); v In 1960 (5)*

Nadeem Abbasi 3: v In 1989 (3)
Nadeem Ghauri 1: *v A 1989*
Nadeem Khan 1: *v WI 1992*
Nasim-ul-Ghani 29: v E 1961 (2); v A 1959 (2) 1964 (1); v WI 1958 (3); *v E 1962 (5) 1967 (2); v A 1964 (1) 1972 (1); v WI 1957 (5); v NZ 1964 (3); v In 1960 (4)*
Naushad Ali 6: v NZ 1964 (3); *v NZ 1964 (3)*
Naved Anjum 2: v NZ 1990 (1); v In 1989 (1)
Nazar Mohammad 5: *v In 1952 (5)*
Nazir Junior (*see* Mohammad Nazir)
Niaz Ahmed 2: v E 1968 (1); *v E 1967 (1)*

Pervez Sajjad 19: v E 1968 (1) 1972 (2); v A 1964 (1); v NZ 1964 (3) 1969 (3); *v E 1971 (3); v NZ 1964 (3) 1972 (3)*

Qasim Omar 26: v E 1983 (3); v WI 1986 (3); v NZ 1984 (3); v In 1984 (2); v SL 1985 (3); *v A 1983 (5); v NZ 1984 (3); v In 1983 (1); v SL 1985 (3)*

Ramiz Raja 55: v E 1983 (2) 1987 (3); v A 1988 (3); v WI 1986 (3) 1990 (2); v NZ 1990 (3); v In 1989 (4); v SL 1985 (1) 1991 (3) 1995 (3); *v E 1987 (2) 1992 (5); v A 1989 (2) 1995 (3); v WI 1987 (3) 1992 (3); v NZ 1992 (1) 1995 (1); v In 1986 (5); v SL 1985 (3)*
Rashid Khan 4: v SL 1981 (2); *v A 1983 (1); v NZ 1984 (1)*
Rashid Latif 19: v A 1994 (2); v Z 1993 (3); *v E 1992 (1) 1996 (1); v A 1995 (1); v WI 1992 (1); v NZ 1992 (1) 1993 (3) 1995 (1); v SL 1994 (2); v Z 1994 (3)*
Rehman, S. F. 1: *v WI 1957*
Rizwan-uz-Zaman 11: v WI 1986 (1); v SL 1981 (2); *v A 1981 (1); v NZ 1988 (2); v In 1986 (5)*

Sadiq Mohammad 41: v E 1972 (3) 1977 (2); v WI 1974 (1) 1980 (3); v NZ 1969 (3) 1976 (3); v In 1978 (1); *v E 1971 (3) 1974 (3) 1978 (3); v A 1972 (3) 1976 (2); v WI 1976 (5); v NZ 1972 (3); v In 1979 (3)*
Saeed Ahmed 41: v E 1961 (3) 1968 (3); v A 1959 (3) 1964 (1); v WI 1958 (3); v NZ 1964 (3); *v E 1962 (5) 1967 (3) 1971 (1); v A 1964 (1) 1972 (2); v WI 1957 (5); v NZ 1964 (3); v In 1960 (5)*
Saeed Anwar 17: v A 1994 (3); v WI 1990 (1); v SL 1995 (2); *v E 1996 (3); v SA 1994 (1); v NZ 1993 (3); v SL 1994 (2); v Z 1994 (2)*

Salah-ud-Din 5: v E 1968 (1); v NZ 1964 (3) 1969 (1)

Saleem Jaffer 14: v E 1987 (1); v A 1988 (2); v WI 1986 (1); v NZ 1990 (2); v In 1989 (1); v SL 1991 (2); *v WI 1987 (1); v NZ 1988 (2); v In 1986 (2)*

Salim Altaf 21: v E 1972 (3); v NZ 1969 (2); v In 1978 (1); *v E 1967 (2) 1971 (2); v A 1972 (3) 1976 (2); v WI 1976 (3); v NZ 1972 (3)*

Salim Elahi 2: *v A 1995 (2)*

Salim Malik 90: v E 1983 (3) 1987 (3); v A 1988 (3) 1994 (3); v WI 1986 (1) 1990 (3); v NZ 1984 (3) 1990 (3); v In 1982 (6) 1984 (2) 1989 (4); v SL 1981 (2) 1985 (3) 1991 (3); *v E 1987 (5) 1992 (5) 1996 (3); v A 1983 (3) 1989 (1) 1995 (2); v SA 1994 (1); v WI 1987 (3); v NZ 1984 (3) 1988 (2) 1992 (1) 1993 (3) 1995 (1); v In 1983 (2) 1986 (5); v SL 1985 (3) 1994 (2); v Z 1994 (3)*

Salim Yousuf 32: v A 1988 (3); v WI 1986 (3) 1990 (1); v NZ 1990 (3); v In 1989 (1); v SL 1981 (1) 1985 (2); *v E 1987 (5); v A 1989 (3); v WI 1987 (3); v NZ 1988 (2); v In 1986 (5)*

Saqlain Mushtaq 4: v SL 1995 (2); *v A 1995 (2)*

Sarfraz Nawaz 55: v E 1968 (1) 1972 (2) 1977 (2) 1983 (3); v A 1979 (3); v WI 1974 (2) 1980 (2); v NZ 1976 (3); v In 1978 (3) 1982 (6); *v E 1974 (3) 1978 (2) 1982 (1); v A 1972 (2) 1976 (2) 1978 (2) 1981 (3) 1983 (3); v WI 1976 (4); v NZ 1972 (3) 1978 (3)*

Shadab Kabir 2: *v E 1996 (2)*

Shafiq Ahmed 6: v E 1977 (3); v WI 1980 (2); *v E 1974 (1)*

Shafqat Rana 5: v E 1968 (2); v A 1964 (1); v NZ 1969 (2)

Shahid Israr 1: v NZ 1976

Shahid Mahboob 1: v In 1989

Shahid Mahmood 1: *v E 1962*

Shahid Saeed 1: v In 1989

Shakeel Ahmed 3: *v WI 1992 (1); v Z 1994 (2)*

Sharpe, D. 3: v A 1959 (3)

Shoaib Mohammad 45: v E 1983 (1) 1987 (1); v A 1988 (3); v WI 1990 (3); v NZ 1984 (1) 1990 (3); v In 1989 (4); v SL 1985 (1) 1991 (3) 1995 (3); v Z 1993 (3); *v E 1987 (4) 1992 (1); v A 1989 (3); v WI 1987 (3); v NZ 1984 (1) 1988 (2); v In 1983 (2) 1986 (3)*

Shuja-ud-Din 19: v E 1961 (2); v A 1959 (3); v WI 1958 (3); v NZ 1955 (3); v In 1954 (5); *v E 1954 (3)*

Sikander Bakht 26: v E 1977 (2); v WI 1980 (1); v NZ 1976 (1); v In 1978 (2) 1982 (1); *v E 1978 (3) 1982 (2); v A 1978 (2) 1981 (3); v WI 1976 (1); v NZ 1978 (3); v In 1979 (5)*

Tahir Naqqash 15: v A 1982 (3); v In 1982 (2); v SL 1981 (3); *v E 1982 (2); v A 1983 (1); v NZ 1984 (1); v In 1983 (3)*

Talat Ali 10: v E 1972 (3); *v E 1978 (2); v A 1972 (1); v NZ 1972 (1) 1978 (3)*

Taslim Arif 6: v A 1979 (3); v WI 1980 (2); *v In 1979 (1)*

Tauseef Ahmed 34: v E 1983 (2) 1987 (2); v A 1979 (3) 1988 (3); v WI 1986 (3); v NZ 1984 (1) 1990 (2); v In 1984 (1); v SL 1981 (3) 1985 (1); v Z 1993 (1); *v E 1987 (2); v A 1989 (3); v NZ 1988 (1); v In 1986 (4); v SL 1985 (2)*

Waqar Hassan 21: v A 1956 (1) 1959 (1); v WI 1958 (1); v NZ 1955 (3); v In 1954 (5); *v E 1954 (4); v WI 1957 (1); v In 1952 (5)*

Waqar Younis 41: v A 1994 (2); v WI 1990 (3); v NZ 1990 (3); v In 1989 (2); v SL 1991 (3) 1995 (1); v Z 1993 (3); *v E 1992 (5) 1996 (3); v A 1989 (3) 1995 (3); v WI 1992 (3); v NZ 1992 (1) 1993 (3) 1995 (1); v SL 1994 (2)*

Wasim Akram 70: v E 1987 (2); v A 1994 (2); v WI 1986 (2) 1990 (3); v NZ 1990 (2); v In 1989 (4); v SL 1985 (3) 1991 (3) 1995 (2); v Z 1993 (2); *v E 1987 (5) 1992 (4) 1996 (3); v A 1989 (3) 1995 (3); v SA 1994 (1); v WI 1987 (3) 1992 (3); v NZ 1984 (2) 1992 (1) 1993 (3) 1995 (1); v In 1986 (5); v SL 1985 (3) 1994 (2); v Z 1994 (3)*

Wasim Bari 81: v E 1968 (3) 1972 (3) 1977 (3); v A 1982 (3); v WI 1974 (2) 1980 (2); v NZ 1969 (3) 1976 (2); v In 1978 (3) 1982 (6); *v E 1967 (3) 1971 (3) 1974 (3) 1978 (3) 1982 (3); v A 1972 (3) 1976 (3) 1978 (2) 1981 (3) 1983 (5); v WI 1976 (5); v NZ 1972 (3) 1978 (3); v In 1979 (6) 1983 (3)*

Wasim Raja 57: v E 1972 (1) 1977 (3) 1983 (3); v A 1979 (3); v WI 1974 (2) 1980 (4); v NZ 1976 (1) 1984 (1); v In 1982 (1) 1984 (1); v SL 1981 (3); *v E 1974 (2) 1978 (3) 1982 (1); v A 1978 (1) 1981 (3) 1983 (2); v WI 1976 (5); v NZ 1972 (3) 1978 (3) 1984 (2); v In 1979 (6) 1983 (3)*

Wazir Mohammad 20: v A 1956 (1) 1959 (1); v WI 1958 (3); v NZ 1955 (2); v In 1954 (5); *v E 1954 (2); v WI 1957 (5); v In 1952 (1)*

Younis Ahmed 4: v NZ 1969 (2); *v In 1986 (2)*

Zaheer Abbas 78: v E 1972 (2) 1983 (3); v A 1979 (2) 1982 (3); v WI 1974 (2) 1980 (3); v NZ 1969 (1) 1976 (3) 1984 (3); v In 1978 (3) 1982 (6) 1984 (2); v SL 1981 (1) 1985 (2); *v E 1971 (3) 1974 (3) 1982 (3); v A 1972 (3) 1976 (3) 1978 (2) 1981 (2) 1983 (5); v WI 1976 (3); v NZ 1972 (3) 1978 (2) 1984 (2); v In 1979 (5) 1983 (3)*
Zahid Fazal 9: v A 1994 (2); v WI 1990 (3); v SL 1991 (3) 1995 (1)
Zakir Khan 2: v In 1989 (1); *v SL 1985 (1)*
Zulfiqar Ahmed 9: v A 1956 (1); v NZ 1955 (3); *v E 1954 (2); v In 1952 (3)*
Zulqarnain 3: *v SL 1985 (3)*

SRI LANKA

Number of Test cricketers: 65

Ahangama, F. S. 3: v In 1985 (3)
Amalean, K. N. 2: v P 1985 (1); *v A 1987 (1)*
Amerasinghe, A. M. J. G. 2: v NZ 1983 (2)
Anurasiri, S. D. 17: v A 1992 (3); v WI 1993 (1); v NZ 1986 (1) 1992 (2); v P 1985 (2); *v E 1991 (1); v In 1986 (1) 1993 (3); v P 1991 (3)*
Atapattu, M. S. 3: v A 1992 (1); *v In 1990 (1) 1993 (1)*

Dassanayake, P. B. 11: v SA 1993 (3); v WI 1993 (1); v P 1994 (2); *v In 1993 (3); v Z 1994 (2)*
de Alwis, R. G. 11: v A 1982 (1); v NZ 1983 (3); v P 1985 (2); *v A 1987 (1); v NZ 1982 (1); v In 1986 (3)*
de Mel, A. L. F. 17: v E 1981 (1); v A 1982 (1); v In 1985 (3); v P 1985 (3); *v E 1984 (1); v In 1982 (1) 1986 (1); v P 1981 (3) 1985 (3)*
de Silva, A. M. 3: v E 1992 (1); v In 1993 (2)
de Silva, D. S. 12: v E 1981 (1); v A 1982 (1); v NZ 1983 (3); *v E 1984 (1); v NZ 1982 (2); v In 1982 (1); v P 1981 (3)*
de Silva, E. A. R. 10: v In 1985 (1); v P 1985 (1); *v A 1989 (2); v NZ 1990 (3); v In 1986 (3)*
de Silva, G. R. A. 4: v E 1981 (1); *v In 1982 (1); v P 1981 (2)*
de Silva, P. A. 53: v E 1992 (1); v A 1992 (3); v SA 1993 (3); v WI 1993 (1); v NZ 1992 (2); v In 1985 (3) 1993 (3); v P 1985 (3) 1994 (2); *v E 1984 (1) 1988 (1) 1991 (1); v A 1987 (1) 1989 (2) 1995 (3); v NZ 1990 (3) 1994 (2); v In 1986 (3) 1990 (1) 1993 (3); v P 1985 (3) 1991 (3) 1995 (2); v Z 1994 (3)*
Dharmasena, H. D. P. K. 10: v SA 1993 (2); v P 1994 (2); *v A 1995 (2); v P 1995 (2); v Z 1994 (2)*
Dias, R. L. 20: v E 1981 (1); v A 1982 (1); v NZ 1983 (2) 1986 (1); v In 1985 (3); v P 1985 (1); *v E 1984 (1); v In 1982 (1) 1986 (3); v P 1981 (3) 1985 (3)*
Dunusinghe, C. I. 5: *v NZ 1994 (2); v P 1995 (3)*

Fernando, E. R. N. S. 5: v A 1982 (1); v NZ 1983 (2); *v NZ 1982 (2)*

Goonatillake, H. M. 5: v E 1981 (1); *v In 1982 (1); v P 1981 (3)*
Gunasekera, Y. 2: *v NZ 1982 (2)*
Guneratne, R. P. W. 1: v A 1982
Gurusinha, A. P. 39: v E 1992 (1); v A 1992 (3); v SA 1993 (1); v NZ 1986 (1) 1992 (2); v In 1993 (3); v P 1985 (2) 1994 (1); *v E 1991 (1); v A 1989 (2) 1995 (3); v NZ 1990 (3) 1994 (2); v In 1986 (3) 1990 (1); v P 1985 (1) 1991 (3) 1995 (3); v Z 1994 (3)*

Hathurusinghe, U. C. 24: v E 1992 (1); v A 1992 (3); v SA 1993 (3); v NZ 1992 (2); v In 1993 (3); *v E 1991 (1); v A 1995 (3); v NZ 1990 (2); v P 1991 (3) 1995 (3)*

Jayasekera, R. S. A. 1: *v P 1981*
Jayasuriya S. T. 17: v E 1992 (1); v A 1992 (2); v SA 1993 (2); v WI 1993 (1); v In 1993 (1); v P 1994 (1); *v E 1991 (1); v A 1995 (1); v NZ 1990 (2); v In 1993 (1); v P 1991 (3); v Z 1994 (1)*
Jeganathan, S. 2: *v NZ 1982 (2)*
John, V. B. 6: v NZ 1983 (3); *v E 1984 (1); v NZ 1982 (2)*
Jurangpathy, B. R. 2: v In 1985 (1); *v In 1986 (1)*

Kalpage, R. S. 8: v SA 1993 (1); v WI 1993 (1); v In 1993 (1); v P 1994 (1); *v In 1993 (3); v Z 1994 (1)*

Kaluperuma, L. W. 2: v E 1981 (1); *v P 1981 (1)*
Kaluperuma, S. M. S. 4: v NZ 1983 (3); *v A 1987 (1)*
Kaluwitharana, R. S. 6: v A 1992 (2); v In 1993 (1); *v A 1995 (3)*
Kuruppu, D. S. B. P. 4: v NZ 1986 (1); *v E 1988 (1) 1991 (1); v A 1987 (1)*
Kuruppuarachchi, A. K. 2: v NZ 1986 (1); v P 1985 (1)

Labrooy, G. F. 9: *v E 1988 (1); v A 1987 (1) 1989 (2); v NZ 1990 (3); v In 1986 (1) 1990 (1)*
Liyanage, D. K. 8: v A 1992 (2); v SA 1993 (1); v NZ 1992 (2); v In 1993 (2); *v In 1993 (1)*

Madugalle, R. S. 21: v E 1981 (1); v A 1982 (1); v NZ 1983 (3) 1986 (1); v In 1985 (3); *v E 1984 (1) 1988 (1); v A 1987 (1); v NZ 1982 (2); v In 1982 (1); v P 1981 (3) 1985 (3)*
Madurasinghe, A. W. R. 3: v A 1992 (1); *v E 1988 (1); v In 1990 (1)*
Mahanama, R. S. 37: v E 1992 (1); v A 1992 (3); v SA 1993 (3); v WI 1993 (1); v NZ 1986 (1) 1992 (2); v In 1993 (3); v P 1985 (2) 1994 (2); *v E 1991 (1); v A 1987 (1) 1989 (2) 1995 (2); v NZ 1990 (1); v In 1990 (1) 1993 (3); v P 1991 (2) 1995 (3); v Z 1994 (3)*
Mendis, L. R. D. 24: v E 1981 (1); v A 1982 (1); v NZ 1983 (3) 1986 (1); v In 1985 (3); v P 1985 (3); *v E 1984 (1) 1988 (1); v In 1982 (1) 1986 (3); v P 1981 (3) 1985 (3)*
Muralitharan, M. 23: v E 1992 (1); v A 1992 (2); v SA 1993 (3); v WI 1993 (1); v NZ 1992 (1); v In 1993 (2); v P 1994 (1); *v A 1995 (2); v NZ 1994 (2); v In 1993 (3); v P 1995 (3); v Z 1994 (2)*

Pushpakumara, K. R. 7: v P 1994 (1); *v A 1995 (1); v NZ 1994 (2); v P 1995 (1); v Z 1994 (2)*

Ramanayake, C. P. H. 18: v E 1992 (1); v A 1992 (3); v SA 1993 (2); v NZ 1992 (1); v In 1993 (1); *v E 1988 (1) 1991 (1); v A 1987 (1) 1989 (2); v NZ 1990 (3); v P 1991 (2)*
Ranasinghe, A. N. 2: *v In 1982 (1); v P 1981 (1)*
Ranatunga, A. 62: v E 1981 (1) 1992 (1); v A 1982 (1) 1992 (3); v SA 1993 (3); v WI 1993 (1); v NZ 1983 (3) 1986 (1) 1992 (2); v In 1985 (3) 1993 (3); v P 1985 (3) 1994 (2); *v E 1984 (1) 1988 (1); v A 1987 (1) 1989 (2) 1995 (3); v NZ 1990 (3) 1994 (2); v In 1982 (1) 1986 (3) 1990 (1) 1993 (3); v P 1981 (2) 1985 (3) 1991 (3) 1995 (3); v Z 1994 (3)*
Ranatunga, D. 2: *v A 1989 (2)*
Ranatunga, S. 7: v P 1994 (1); *v NZ 1994 (2); v P 1995 (1); v Z 1994 (3)*
Ratnayake, R. J. 23: v A 1982 (1); v NZ 1983 (1) 1986 (1); v In 1985 (3); v P 1985 (1); *v E 1991 (1); v A 1989 (1); v NZ 1982 (2) 1990 (3); v In 1986 (2) 1990 (1); v P 1985 (3) 1991 (3)*
Ratnayeke, J. R. 22: v NZ 1983 (2) 1986 (1); v P 1985 (3); *v E 1984 (1) 1988 (1); v A 1987 (1) 1989 (2); v NZ 1982 (2); v In 1982 (1) 1986 (3); v P 1981 (2) 1985 (3)*

Samarasekera, M. A. R. 4: *v E 1988 (1); v A 1989 (1); v In 1990 (1); v P 1991 (1)*
Samaraweera, D. P. 7: v WI 1993 (1); v P 1994 (1); *v NZ 1994 (2); v In 1993 (3)*
Senanayake, C. P. 3: *v NZ 1990 (3)*
Silva, K. J. 1: *v A 1995*
Silva, S. A. R. 9: v In 1985 (3); v P 1985 (1); *v E 1984 (1) 1988 (1); v NZ 1982 (1); v P 1985 (2)*

Tillekeratne, H. P. 36: v E 1992 (1); v A 1992 (1); v SA 1993 (3); v WI 1993 (1); v NZ 1992 (2); v In 1993 (3); v P 1994 (2); *v E 1991 (1); v A 1989 (1) 1995 (3); v NZ 1990 (3) 1994 (2); v In 1990 (1) 1993 (3); v P 1991 (3) 1995 (3); v Z 1994 (3)*

Vaas, W. P. U. J. C. 12: v P 1994 (1); *v A 1995 (3); v NZ 1994 (2); v P 1995 (3); v Z 1994 (3)*

Warnapura, B. 4: v E 1981 (1); *v In 1982 (1); v P 1981 (2)*
Warnaweera, K. P. J. 10: v E 1992 (1); v NZ 1992 (2); v In 1993 (3); v P 1985 (1) 1994 (1); *v NZ 1990 (1); v In 1990 (1)*
Weerasinghe, C. D. U. S. 1: v In 1985
Wettimuny, M. D. 2: *v NZ 1982 (2)*
Wettimuny, S. 23: v E 1981 (1); v A 1982 (1); v NZ 1983 (3); v In 1985 (3); v P 1985 (3); *v E 1984 (1); v NZ 1982 (2); v In 1986 (3); v P 1981 (3) 1985 (3)*
Wickremasinghe, A. G. D. 3: v NZ 1992 (2); *v A 1989 (1)*
Wickremasinghe, G. P. 23: v A 1992 (1); v SA 1993 (2); v WI 1993 (1); v In 1993 (2); v P 1994 (1); *v A 1995 (3); v NZ 1994 (2); v In 1993 (3); v P 1991 (3) 1995 (3); v Z 1994 (2)*
Wijegunawardene, K. I. W. 2: *v E 1991 (1); v P 1991 (1)*
Wijesuriya, R. G. C. E. 4: *v P 1981 (1) 1985 (3)*
Wijetunge, P. K. 1: v SA 1993

ZIMBABWE

Number of Test cricketers: 29

Arnott, K. J. 4: v NZ 1992 (2); v In 1992 (1); *v In 1992 (1)*
Brain, D. H. 9: v NZ 1992 (1); v P 1994 (3); v SL 1994 (2); *v In 1992 (1); v P 1993 (2)*
Brandes, E. A. 8: v NZ 1992 (1); v In 1992 (1); *v NZ 1995 (2); v In 1992 (1); v P 1993 (3)*
Briant, G. A. 1: *v In 1992*
Bruk-Jackson, G. K. 2: *v P 1993 (2)*
Burmester, M. G. 3: v NZ 1992 (2); v In 1992 (1)
Butchart, I. P. 1: v P 1994
Campbell, A. D. R. 16: v SA 1995 (1); v NZ 1992 (2); v In 1992 (1); v P 1994 (3); v SL 1994 (3); *v NZ 1995 (2); v In 1992 (1); v P 1993 (3)*
Carlisle, S. V. 5: v P 1994 (3); *v NZ 1995 (2)*
Crocker, G. J. 3: v NZ 1992 (2); v In 1992 (1)
Dekker, M. H. 9: v SA 1995 (1); v P 1994 (2); v SL 1994 (3); *v P 1993 (3)*
Flower, A. 16: v SA 1995 (1); v NZ 1992 (2); v In 1992 (1); v P 1994 (3); v SL 1994 (3); *v NZ 1995 (2); v In 1992 (1); v P 1993 (3)*
Flower, G. W. 16: v SA 1995 (1); v NZ 1992 (2); v In 1992 (1); v P 1994 (3); v SL 1994 (3); *v NZ 1995 (2); v In 1992 (1); v P 1993 (3)*
Houghton, D. L. 16: v SA 1995 (1); v NZ 1992 (2); v In 1992 (1); v P 1994 (3); v SL 1994 (3); *v NZ 1995 (2); v In 1992 (1); v P 1993 (3)*
James, W. R. 4: v SL 1994 (3); *v P 1993 (1)*
Jarvis, M. P. 5: v NZ 1992 (1); v In 1992 (1); v SL 1994 (3)
Lock, A. C. I. 1: v SA 1995
Olonga, H. K. 2: v P 1994 (1); *v NZ 1995 (1)*
Peall, S. G. 4: v SL 1994 (2); *v P 1993 (2)*
Pycroft, A. J. 3: v NZ 1992 (2); v In 1992 (1)
Ranchod, U. 1: *v In 1992*
Rennie, J. A. 3: v SL 1994 (1); *v P 1993 (2)*
Shah, A. H. 2: v NZ 1992 (1); *v In 1992 (1)*
Strang, B. C. 5: v SA 1995 (1); v P 1994 (2); *v NZ 1995 (2)*
Strang, P. A. 7: v SA 1995 (1); v P 1994 (3); v SL 1994 (1); *v NZ 1995 (2)*
Streak, H. H. 12: v SA 1995 (1); v P 1994 (3); v SL 1994 (3); *v NZ 1995 (2); v P 1993 (3)*
Traicos, A. J. 4: v NZ 1992 (2); v In 1992 (1); *v In 1992 (1)*
Whittall, G. J. 12: v SA 1995 (1); v P 1994 (3); v SL 1994 (3); *v NZ 1995 (2); v P 1993 (3)*
Wishart, C. B. 2: v SA 1995 (1); *v NZ 1995 (1)*

TWO COUNTRIES

Fourteen cricketers have appeared for two countries in Test matches, namely:

Amir Elahi, *India and Pakistan.*
J. J. Ferris, *Australia and England.*
S. C. Guillen, *West Indies and NZ.*
Gul Mahomed, *India and Pakistan.*
F. Hearne, *England and South Africa.*
A. H. Kardar, *India and Pakistan.*
W. E. Midwinter, *England and Australia.*
F. Mitchell, *England and South Africa.*
W. L. Murdoch, *Australia and England.*
Nawab of Pataudi, sen., *England and India.*
A. J. Traicos, *South Africa and Zimbabwe.*
A. E. Trott, *Australia and England.*
K. C. Wessels, *Australia and South Africa.*
S. M. J. Woods, *Australia and England.*

ENGLAND v REST OF THE WORLD

In 1970, owing to the cancellation of the South African tour to England, a series of matches was arranged, with the trappings of a full Test series, between England and the Rest of the World. It was played for the Guinness Trophy.

The following were awarded England caps for playing against the Rest of the World in that series, although the five matches played are now generally considered not to have rated as full Tests: D. L. Amiss (1), G. Boycott (2), D. J. Brown (2), M. C. Cowdrey (4), M. H. Denness (1), B. L. D'Oliveira (4), J. H. Edrich (2), K. W. R. Fletcher (4), A. W. Greig (3), R. Illingworth (5), A. Jones (1), A. P. E. Knott (5), P. Lever (1), B. W. Luckhurst (5), C. M. Old (2), P. J. Sharpe (1), K. Shuttleworth (1), J. A. Snow (5), D. L. Underwood (3), A. Ward (1), D. Wilson (2).

The following players represented the Rest of the World: E. J. Barlow (5), F. M. Engineer (2), L. R. Gibbs (4), Intikhab Alam (5), R. B. Kanhai (5), C. H. Lloyd (5), G. D. McKenzie (3), D. L. Murray (3), Mushtaq Mohammad (2), P. M. Pollock (1), R. G. Pollock (5), M. J. Procter (5), B. A. Richards (5), G. S. Sobers (5).

LIMITED-OVERS INTERNATIONAL CRICKETERS

The following players have appeared for Test-playing countries in limited-overs internationals but had not represented their countries in Test matches by September 7, 1996:

England A. D. Brown, I. J. Gould, D. W. Headley, A. J. Hollioake, G. W. Humpage, T. E. Jesty, G. D. Lloyd, J. D. Love, M. A. Lynch, M. J. Smith, N. M. K. Smith, S. D. Udal, C. M. Wells.

Australia G. A. Bishop, J. N. Gillespie, S. F. Graf, G. B. Hogg, M. S. Kasprowicz, S. Lee, D. S. Lehmann, R. J. McCurdy, K. H. MacLeay, G. D. Porter, G. R. Robertson, J. D. Siddons, G. S. Trimble, A. K. Zesers.

South Africa N. Boje, D. J. Callaghan, D. N. Crookes, L. Klusener, G. F. J. Liebenberg, S. J. Palframan, C. E. B. Rice, M. J. R. Rindel, D. B. Rundle, T. G. Shaw, E. O. Simons, E. L. R. Stewart, P. J. R. Steyn, C. J. P. G. van Zyl, M. Yachad.

West Indies H. A. G. Anthony, B. St A. Browne, V. C. Drakes, R. S. Gabriel, R. C. Haynes, R. I. C. Holder, R. D. Jacobs, M. R. Pydanna, P. A. Wallace, L. R. Williams.

New Zealand B. R. Blair, P. G. Coman, M. W. Douglas, B. G. Hadlee, R. T. Hart, R. L. Hayes, B. J. McKechnie, E. B. McSweeney, J. P. Millmow, R. G. Petrie, R. B. Reid, S. J. Roberts, L. W. Stott, R. J. Webb, J. W. Wilson.

G. R. Larsen appeared for New Zealand in 55 limited-overs internationals before making his Test debut.

India A. C. Bedade, Bhupinder Singh, sen., G. Bose, V. B. Chandrasekhar, U. Chatterjee, R. S. Ghai, S. C. Khanna, S. P. Mukherjee, A. K. Patel, Randhir Singh, R. P. Singh, R. R. Singh, Sudhakar Rao, P. S. Vaidya.

Pakistan Aamer Hameed, Aamer Hanif, Arshad Khan, Arshad Pervez, Ghulam Ali, Haafiz Shahid, Hasan Jamil, Iqbal Sikandar, Irfan Bhatti, Javed Qadir, Mahmood Hamid, Mansoor Rana, Maqsood Rana, Masood Iqbal, Moin-ul-Atiq, Naeem Ahmed, Naeem Ashraf, Naseer Malik, Parvez Mir, Saadat Ali, Saeed Azad, Sajid Ali, Sajjad Akbar, Salim Pervez, Shahid Anwar, Shahid Nazir, Shakil Khan, Sohail Fazal, Tanvir Mehdi, Wasim Haider, Zafar Iqbal, Zahid Ahmed.

Sri Lanka U. U. Chandana, D. L. S. de Silva, G. N. de Silva, E. R. Fernando, T. L. Fernando, U. N. K. Fernando, J. C. Gamage, F. R. M. Goonatillake, A. A. W. Gunawardene, P. D. Heyn, S. A. Jayasinghe, S. H. U. Karnain, C. Mendis, M. Munasinghe, A. R. M. Opatha, S. P. Pasqual, K. G. Perera, H. S. M. Pieris, S. K. Ranasinghe, N. Ranatunga, N. L. K. Ratnayake, A. P. B. Tennekoon, M. H. Tissera, E. A. Upashantha, D. M. Vonhagt, A. P. Weerakkody, S. R. de S. Wettimuny, R. P. A. H. Wickremaratne.

Zimbabwe R. D. Brown, K. M. Curran, S. G. Davies, K. G. Duers, E. A. Essop-Adam, C. N. Evans, D. A. G. Fletcher, J. G. Heron, V. R. Hogg, G. C. Martin, M. A. Meman, G. A. Paterson, G. E. Peckover, P. W. E. Rawson, A. C. Waller, A. R. Whittall.

BIRTHS AND DEATHS OF CRICKETERS

The qualifications for inclusion are as follows:

1. All players who have appeared in a Test match or a one-day international for a Test-match playing country.

2. County players who appeared in 200 or more first-class matches during their careers, or 100 after the Second World War.

3. English county captains who captained their county in three seasons or more since 1890.

4. All players chosen as *Wisden* Cricketers of the Year, including the Public Schoolboys chosen for the 1918 and 1919 Almanacks. Cricketers of the Year are identified by the italic notation *CY* and year of appearance. A list of the Cricketers of the Year from 1889 to 1997 appears on pages 167-170.

5. Players or personalities not otherwise qualified who are thought to be of sufficient interest to merit inclusion.

Key to abbreviations and symbols

CU – Cambridge University, OU – Oxford University.

Australian states: NSW – New South Wales, Qld – Queensland, S. Aust. – South Australia, Tas. – Tasmania, Vic. – Victoria, W. Aust. – Western Australia.

Indian teams: Eur. – Europeans, Guj. – Gujarat, H'bad – Hyderabad, Ind. Rlwys – Indian Railways, Ind. Serv. – Indian Services, J/K – Jammu and Kashmir, Karn. – Karnataka (Mysore to 1972-73), M. Pradesh – Madhya Pradesh (Central India [C. Ind.] to 1939-40, Holkar to 1954-55, Madhya Bharat to 1956-57), M'tra – Maharashtra, Naw. – Nawanagar, Raja. – Rajasthan, S'tra – Saurashtra (West India [W. Ind.] to 1945-46, Kathiawar to 1949-50), S. Punjab – Southern Punjab (Patiala to 1958-59, Punjab since 1968-69), TC – Travanacore-Cochin (Kerala since 1956-57), TN – Tamil Nadu (Madras to 1959-60), U. Pradesh – Uttar Pradesh (United Provinces [U. Prov.] to 1948-49), Vidarbha (CP & Berar to 1949-50, Madhya Pradesh to 1956-57).

New Zealand provinces: Auck. – Auckland, Cant. – Canterbury, C. Dist. – Central Districts, N. Dist. – Northern Districts, Wgtn – Wellington.

Pakistani teams: ADBP – Agricultural Development Bank of Pakistan, B'pur – Bahawalpur, F'bad – Faisalabad, HBFC – House Building Finance Corporation, HBL – Habib Bank Ltd, I'bad – Islamabad, IDBP – Industrial Development Bank of Pakistan, Kar. – Karachi, MCB – Muslim Commercial Bank, NBP – National Bank of Pakistan, NWFP – North-West Frontier Province, PACO – Pakistan Automobile Corporation, Pak. Rlwys – Pakistan Railways, Pak. Us – Pakistan Universities, PIA – Pakistan International Airlines, PNSC – Pakistan National Shipping Corporation, PWD – Public Works Department, R'pindi – Rawalpindi, UBL – United Bank Ltd, WAPDA – Water and Power Development Authority.

South African provinces: E. Prov. – Eastern Province, E. Tvl – Eastern Transvaal, Griq. W. – Griqualand West, N. Tvl – Northern Transvaal, NE Tvl – North-Eastern Transvaal, OFS – Orange Free State, Rhod. – Rhodesia, Tvl – Transvaal, W. Prov. – Western Province, W. Tvl – Western Transvaal.

Sri Lankan teams: Ant. – Antonians, Bloom. – Bloomfield Cricket and Athletic Club, BRC – Burgher Recreation Club, CCC – Colombo Cricket Club, Mor. – Moratuwa Sports Club, NCC – Nondescripts Cricket Club, Pan. – Panadura Sports Club, Seb. – Sebastianites, SLAF – Air Force, SSC – Sinhalese Sports Club, TU – Tamil Union Cricket and Athletic Club, Under-23 – Board Under-23 XI, WPC – Western Province (City), WPN – Western Province (North), WPS – Western Province (South).

West Indies islands: B'dos – Barbados, BG – British Guiana (Guyana since 1966), Comb. Is. – Combined Islands, Jam. – Jamaica, T/T – Trinidad & Tobago.
Zimbabwean teams: Mash. – Mashonaland, Mat. – Matabeleland, MCD – Mashonaland Country Districts, Under-24 – Mashonaland Under-24, Zimb. – Zimbabwe.

** Denotes Test player. ** Denotes appeared for two countries. There is a list of Test players country by country from page 53.*
† Denotes also played for team under its previous name.

Aamer Hameed (Pak. Us, Lahore, Punjab & OU) b Oct. 18, 1954
Aamer Hanif (Kar., PACO & Allied Bank) b Oct. 4, 1971
*Aamer Malik (ADBP, PIA, Multan & Lahore) b Jan. 3, 1963
*Aamir Nazir (I'bad, Lahore & Allied Bank) b Jan. 2, 1971
*Aamir Sohail (HBL, Sargodha, Lahore & Allied Bank) b Sept. 14, 1966
Abberley, R. N. (Warwicks) b April 22, 1944
*a'Beckett, E. L. (Vic.) b Aug. 11, 1907, d June 2, 1989
*Abdul Kadir (Kar. & NBP) b May 10, 1944
*Abdul Qadir (HBL, Lahore & Punjab) b Sept. 15, 1955
*Abel, R. (Surrey; *CY 1890*) b Nov. 30, 1857, d Dec. 10, 1936
*Abid Ali, S. (H'bad) b Sept. 9, 1941
Abrahams, J. (Lancs) b July 21, 1952
*Absolom, C. A. (CU & Kent) b June 7, 1846, d July 30, 1889
Acfield, D. L. (CU & Essex) b July 24, 1947
*Achong, E. (T/T) b Feb. 16, 1904, d Aug. 29, 1986
Ackerman, H. M. (Border, NE Tvl, Northants, Natal & W. Prov.) b April 28, 1947
Adam, Sir Ronald, 2nd Bt (Pres. MCC 1946-47) b Oct. 30, 1885, d Dec. 26, 1982
Adams, C. J. (Derbys) b May 6, 1970
*Adams, J. C. (Jam. & Notts) b Jan. 9, 1968
*Adams, P. R. (W. Prov.) b Jan. 20, 1977
Adams, P. W. (Cheltenham & Sussex; *CY 1919*) b Sept. 5, 1900, d Sept. 28, 1962
*Adcock, N. A. T. (Tvl & Natal; *CY 1961*) b March 8, 1931
*Adhikari, H. R. (Guj., Baroda & Ind. Serv.) b July 31, 1919
*Afaq Hussain (Kar., Pak Us, PIA & PWD) b Dec. 31, 1939
Afford, J. A. (Notts) b May 12, 1964
*Aftab Baloch (PWD, Kar., Sind, NBP & PIA) b April 1, 1953
*Aftab Gul (Punjab U., Pak. Us & Lahore) b March 31, 1946
*Agha Saadat Ali (Pak. Us, Punjab, B'pur & Lahore) b June 21, 1929, d Oct. 26, 1995
*Agha Zahid (Pak Us, Punjab, Lahore & HBL) b Jan. 7, 1953
*Agnew, J. P. (Leics; *CY 1988;* broadcaster) b April 4, 1960
*Ahangama, F. S. (SSC) b Sept. 14, 1959
Aird, R. (CU & Hants; Sec. MCC 1953-62, Pres. MCC 1968-69) b May 4, 1902, d Aug. 16, 1986
Aislabie, B. (Surrey, Hants, Kent & Sussex; Sec. MCC 1822-42) b Jan. 14, 1774, d June 2, 1842
Aitchison, Rev. J. K. (Scotland) b May 26, 1920, d Feb. 13, 1994
*Akram Raza (Lahore, Sargodha, WAPDA & HBL) b Nov. 22, 1964
*Alabaster, J. C. (Otago) b July 11, 1930
Alcock, C. W. (Sec. Surrey CCC 1872-1907; Editor *Cricket* 1882-1907) b Dec. 2, 1842, d Feb. 26, 1907
Alderman, A. E. (Derbys) b Oct. 30, 1907, d June 4, 1990
*Alderman, T. M. (W. Aust., Kent & Glos; *CY 1982*) b June 12, 1956
Alexander of Tunis, 1st Lord (Pres. MCC 1955-56) b Dec. 10, 1891, d June 16, 1969
*Alexander, F. C. M. (CU & Jam.) b Nov. 2, 1928
*Alexander, G. (Vic.) b April 22, 1851, d Nov. 6, 1930
*Alexander, H. H. (Vic.) b June 9, 1905, d April 15, 1993
Alikhan, R. I. (Sussex, PIA, Surrey & PNSC) b Dec. 28, 1962
*Alim-ud-Din (Rajputana, Guj., Sind, B'pur, Kar. & PWD) b Dec. 15, 1930
*Allan, D. W. (B'dos) b Nov. 5, 1937
*Allan, F. E. (Vic.) b Dec. 2, 1849, d Feb. 9, 1917
Allan, J. M. (OU, Kent, Warwicks & Scotland) b April 2, 1932
*Allan, P. J. (Qld) b Dec. 31, 1935
*Allcott, C. F. W. (Auck.) b Oct. 7, 1896, d Nov. 19, 1973
Allen, B. O. (CU & Glos) b Oct. 13, 1911, d May 1, 1981
*Allen, D. A. (Glos) b Oct. 29, 1935
*Allen, Sir George O. B. (CU & Middx; Pres. MCC 1963-64) b July 31, 1902, d Nov. 29, 1989
*Allen, I. B. A. (Windwards) b Oct. 6, 1965
Allen, M. H. J. (Northants & Derbys) b Jan. 7, 1933, d Oct. 6, 1995
*Allen, R. C. (NSW) b July 2, 1858, d May 2, 1952
Alletson, E. B. (Notts) b March 6, 1884, d July 5, 1963
Alley, W. E. (NSW & Som; Test umpire; *CY 1962*) b Feb. 3, 1919

Alleyne, M. W. (Glos) b May 23, 1968
*Allom, M. J. C. (CU & Surrey; Pres. MCC 1969-70) b March 23, 1906, d April 8, 1995
*Allott, G. I. (Cant.) b Dec. 24, 1971
*Allott, P. J. W. (Lancs & Wgtn) b Sept. 14, 1956
Altham, H. S. (OU, Surrey & Hants; historian; Pres. MCC 1959-60) b Nov. 30, 1888, d March 11, 1965
*Amalean, K. N. (SL) b April 7, 1965
*Amarnath, Lala (N. B.) (N. Ind., S. Punjab, Guj., Patiala, U. Pradesh & Ind. Rlwys) b Sept. 11, 1911
*Amarnath, M. (Punjab & Delhi; *CY 1984*) b Sept. 24, 1950
*Amarnath, S. (Punjab & Delhi) b Dec. 30, 1948
*Amar Singh, L. (Patiala, W. Ind. & Naw.) b Dec. 4, 1910, d May 20, 1940
*Ambrose, C. E. L. (Leewards & Northants; *CY 1992*) b Sept. 21, 1963
*Amerasinghe, A. M. J. G. (Nomads & Ant.) b Feb. 2, 1954
*Ames, L. E. G. (Kent; *CY 1929*) b Dec. 3, 1905, d Feb. 26, 1990
**Amir Elahi (Baroda, N. Ind., S. Punjab & B'pur) b Sept. 1, 1908, d Dec. 28, 1980
*Amiss, D. L. (Warwicks; *CY 1975*) b April 7, 1943
*Amre, P. K. (Ind. Rlwys, Raja. & Bombay) b Aug. 14, 1968
Anderson, I. S. (Derbys & Boland) b April 24, 1960
*Anderson, J. H. (W. Prov.) b April 26, 1874, d March 11, 1926
*Anderson, R. W. (Cant., N. Dist., Otago & C. Dist.) b Oct. 2, 1948
*Anderson, W. M. (Cant.) b Oct. 8, 1919, d Dec. 21, 1979
*Andrew, K. V. (Northants) b Dec. 15, 1929
*Andrews, B. (Cant., C. Dist. & Otago) b April 4, 1945
*Andrews, T. J. E. (NSW) b Aug. 26, 1890, d Jan. 28, 1970
Andrews, W. H. R. (Som) b April 14, 1908, d Jan. 9, 1989
*Angel, J. (W. Aust.) b April 22, 1968
Angell, F. L. (Som) b June 29, 1922
*Anil Dalpat (Kar. & PIA) b Sept. 20, 1963
*Ankola, S. A. (M'tra & Bombay) b March 1, 1968
Anthony, H. A. G. (Leewards & Glam) b Jan. 16, 1971
*Anurasiri, S. D. (Pan. & WPS) b Feb. 25, 1966
*Anwar Hussain (N. Ind., Bombay, Sind & Kar.) b July 16, 1920
*Anwar Khan (Kar., Sind & NBP) b Dec. 24, 1955
*Appleyard, R. (Yorks; *CY 1952*) b June 27, 1924
*Apte, A. L. (Ind. Us, Bombay & Raja.) b Oct. 24, 1934
*Apte, M. L. (Bombay & Bengal) b Oct. 5, 1932
*Aqib Javed (Lahore, PACO, Hants, I'bad & Allied Bank) b Aug. 5, 1972
*Archer, A. G. (Worcs) b Dec. 6, 1871, d July 15, 1935
*Archer, K. A. (Qld) b Jan. 17, 1928
*Archer, R. G. (Qld) b Oct. 25, 1933
*Arif Butt (Lahore & Pak. Rlwys) b May 17, 1944
Arlott, John (Writer & broadcaster) b Feb. 25, 1914, d Dec. 14, 1991
*Armitage, T. (Yorks) b April 25, 1848, d Sept. 21, 1922
Armstrong, N. F. (Leics) b Dec. 22, 1892, d Jan. 19, 1990
*Armstrong, W. W. (Vic.; *CY 1903*) b May 22, 1879, d July 13, 1947
Arnold, A. P. (Cant. & Northants) b Oct. 16, 1926
*Arnold, E. G. (Worcs) b Nov. 7, 1876, d Oct. 25, 1942
*Arnold, G. G. (Surrey & Sussex; *CY 1972*) b Sept. 3, 1944
*Arnold, J. (Hants) b Nov. 30, 1907, d April 4, 1984
*Arnott, K. J. (MCD) b March 8, 1961
Arnott, T. (Glam) b Feb. 16, 1902, d Feb. 2, 1975
*Arshad Ayub (H'bad) b Aug. 2, 1958
Arshad Khan (Peshawar, I'bad, Pak. Rlwys & Allied Bank) b March 22, 1971
Arshad Pervez (Sargodha, Lahore, Pak. Us, Servis Ind., HBL & Punjab) b Oct. 1, 1952
*Arthurton, K. L. T. (Leewards) b Feb. 21, 1965
*Arun, B. (TN) b Dec. 14, 1962
*Arun Lal (Delhi & Bengal) b Aug. 1 1955
*Asgarali, N. (T/T) b Dec. 28, 1920
Ashdown, W. H. (Kent) b Dec. 27, 1898, d Sept. 15, 1979
*Ashfaq Ahmed (PACO & PIA) b June 6, 1973
*Ashley, W. H. (W. Prov.) b Feb. 10, 1862, d July 14, 1930
*Ashraf Ali (Lahore, Income Tax, Pak. Us, Pak. Rlways & UBL) b April 22, 1958
Ashton, C. T. (CU & Essex) b Feb. 19, 1901, d Oct. 31, 1942
Ashton, G. (CU & Worcs) b Sept. 27, 1896, d Feb. 6, 1981
Ashton, Sir Hubert (CU & Essex; *CY 1922;* Pres. MCC 1960-61) b Feb. 13, 1898, d June 17, 1979
Asif Din, M. (Warwicks) b Sept. 21, 1960
*Asif Iqbal (H'bad, Kar., Kent, PIA & NBP; *CY 1968*) b June 6, 1943
*Asif Masood (Lahore, Punjab U. & PIA) b Jan. 23, 1946
*Asif Mujtaba (Kar. & PIA) b Nov. 4, 1967
Aslett, D. G. (Kent) b Feb. 12, 1958
*Astill, W. E. (Leics; *CY 1933*) b March 1, 1888, d Feb. 10, 1948

*Astle, N. J. (Cant.) b Sept. 15, 1971
*Atapattu, M. S. (SSC & WPC) b Nov. 22, 1972
*Ata-ur-Rehman (Lahore, PACO & Allied Bank) b March 28, 1975
*Atherton, M. A. (CU & Lancs; *CY 1991*) b March 23, 1968
*Athey, C. W. J. (Yorks, Glos & Sussex) b Sept. 27, 1957
*Atif Rauf (I'bad & ADBP) b March 3, 1964
Atkinson, C. R. M. (Som) b July 23, 1931, d June 25, 1991
*Atkinson, D. St E. (B'dos & T/T) b Aug. 9, 1926
*Atkinson, E. St E. (B'dos) b Nov. 6, 1927
Atkinson, G. (Som & Lancs) b March 29, 1938
*Attewell, W. (Notts; *CY 1892*) b June 12, 1861, d June 11, 1927
Austin, Sir Harold B. G. (B'dos) b July 15, 1877, d July 27, 1943
*Austin, R. A. (Jam.) b Sept. 5, 1954
Avery, A. V. (Essex) b Dec. 19, 1914
Aylward, James (Hants & All-England) b 1741, *buried* Dec. 27, 1827
Aymes, A. N. (Hants) b June 4, 1964
*Azad, K. (Delhi) b Jan. 2, 1959
*Azeem Hafeez (Kar., Allied Bank & PIA) b July 29, 1963
*Azhar Khan (Lahore, Punjab, Pak. Us, PIA & HBL) b Sept. 7, 1955
*Azharuddin, M. (H'bad & Derbys; *CY 1991*) b Feb. 8, 1963
*Azmat Rana (B'pur, PIA, Punjab, Lahore & MCB) b Nov. 3, 1951

*Bacchus, S. F. A. F. (Guyana, W. Prov. & Border) b Jan. 31, 1954
*Bacher, Dr A. (Tvl; Managing Director UCBSA) b May 24, 1942
*Badcock, C. L. (Tas. & S. Aust.) b April 10, 1914, d Dec. 13, 1982
*Badcock, F. T. (Wgtn & Otago) b Aug. 9, 1895, d Sept. 19, 1982
Baggallay, R. R. C. (Derbys) b May 4, 1884, d Dec. 12, 1975
*Baichan, L. (Guyana) b May 12, 1946
*Baig, A. A. (H'bad, OU & Som) b March 19, 1939
Bailey, J. (Hants) b April 6, 1908, d Feb. 9, 1988
Bailey, J. A. (Essex & OU; Sec. MCC 1974-87) b June 22, 1930
*Bailey, R. J. (Northants) b Oct. 28, 1963
*Bailey, T. E. (Essex & CU; *CY 1950*) b Dec. 3, 1923
Baillie, A. W. (Sec. MCC 1858-63) b June 22, 1830, d May 10, 1867
Bainbridge, H. W. (Surrey, CU & Warwicks) b Oct. 29, 1862, d March 3, 1940
Bainbridge, P. (Glos & Durham; *CY 1986*) b April 16, 1958
*Bairstow, D. L. (Yorks & Griq. W.) b Sept. 1, 1951
Baker, C. S. (Warwicks) b Jan. 5, 1883, d Dec. 16, 1976
Baker, G. R. (Yorks & Lancs) b April 18, 1862, d Dec. 6, 1938
*Bakewell, A. H. (Northants; *CY 1934*) b Nov. 2, 1908, d Jan. 23, 1983
*Balaskas, X. C. (Griq. W., Border, W. Prov., Tvl & NE Tvl) b Oct. 15, 1910, d May 12, 1994
*Balderstone, J. C. (Yorks & Leics) b Nov. 16, 1940
Baldry, D. O. (Middx & Hants) b Dec. 26, 1931
*Banerjee, S. A. (Bengal & Bihar) b Nov. 1, 1919, d Sept. 14, 1992
*Banerjee, S. N. (Bengal, Naw., Bihar & M. Pradesh) b Oct. 3, 1911, d Oct. 14, 1980
*Banerjee, S. T. (Bihar) b Feb. 13, 1969
*Bannerman, A. C. (NSW) b March 22, 1854, d Sept. 19, 1924
*Bannerman, Charles (NSW) b July 23, 1851, d Aug. 20, 1930
Bannister, J. D. (Warwicks) b Aug. 23, 1930
*Baptiste, E. A. E. (Kent, Leewards, Northants & E. Prov.) b March 12, 1960
*Baqa Jilani, M. (N. Ind.) b July 20, 1911, d July 2, 1941
*Barber, R. T. (Wgton & C. Dist.) b June 3, 1925
*Barber, R. W. (Lancs, CU & Warwicks; *CY 1967*) b Sept. 26, 1935
*Barber, W. (Yorks) b April 18, 1901, d Sept. 10, 1968
Barclay, J. R. T. (Sussex & OFS) b Jan. 22, 1954
*Bardsley, W. (NSW; *CY 1910*) b Dec. 6, 1882, d Jan. 20, 1954
Barker, G. (Essex) b July 6, 1931
Barling, T. H. (Surrey) b Sept. 1, 1906, d Jan. 2, 1993
*Barlow, E. J. (Tvl, E. Prov., W. Prov., Derbys & Boland) b Aug. 12, 1940
*Barlow, G. D. (Middx) b March 26, 1950
*Barlow, R. G. (Lancs) b May 28, 1851, d July 31, 1919
Barnard, H. M. (Hants) b July 18, 1933
Barnes, A. R. (Sec. Aust. Cricket Board 1960-81) b Sept. 12, 1916, d March 14, 1989
*Barnes, S. F. (Warwicks & Lancs; *CY 1910*) b April 19, 1873, d Dec. 26, 1967
*Barnes, S. G. (NSW) b June 5, 1916, d Dec. 16, 1973
*Barnes, W. (Notts; *CY 1890*) b May 27, 1852, d March 24, 1899
*Barnett, B. A. (Vic.) b March 23, 1908, d June 29, 1979
*Barnett, C. J. (Glos; *CY 1937*) b July 3, 1910, d May 28, 1993

*Barnett, K. J. (Derbys & Boland; *CY 1989*) b July 17, 1960
Baroda, Maharaja of (Manager, Ind. in Eng. 1959) b April 2, 1930, d Sept. 1, 1988
*Barratt, F. (Notts) b April 12, 1894, d Jan. 29, 1947
*Barrett, A. G. (Jam.) b April 5, 1942
*Barrett, Dr J. E. (Vic.) b Oct. 15, 1866, d Feb. 6, 1916
Barrick, D. W. (Northants) b April 28, 1926
*Barrington, K. F. (Surrey; *CY 1960*) b Nov. 24, 1930, d March 14, 1981
Barron, W. (Lancs & Northants) b Oct. 26, 1917
*Barrow, I. (Jam.) b Jan. 6, 1911, d April 2, 1979
*Bartlett, E. L. (B'dos) b March 10, 1906, d Dec. 21, 1976
*Bartlett, G. A. (C. Dist. & Cant.) b Feb. 3, 1941
Bartlett, H. T. (CU, Surrey & Sussex; *CY 1939*) b Oct. 7, 1914, d June 26, 1988
Bartley, T. J. (Test umpire) b March 19, 1908, d April 2, 1964
Barton, M. R. (OU & Surrey) b Oct. 14, 1914
*Barton, P. T. (Wgtn) b Oct. 9, 1935
*Barton, V. A. (Kent & Hants) b Oct. 6, 1867, d March 23, 1906
Barwick, S. R. (Glam) b Sept. 6, 1960
Base, S. J. (W. Prov., Glam, Derbys, Boland & Border) b Jan. 2, 1960
*Basit Ali (Kar. & UBL) b Dec. 13, 1970
Bates, D. L. (Sussex) b May 10, 1933
Bates, L. A. (Warwicks) b March 20, 1895, d March 11, 1971
*Bates, W. (Yorks) b Nov. 19, 1855, d Jan. 8, 1900
Bates, W. E. (Yorks & Glam) b March 5, 1884, d Jan. 17, 1957
*Baumgartner, H. V. (OFS & Tvl) b Nov. 17, 1883, d April 8, 1938
*Bean, G. (Notts & Sussex) b March 7, 1864, d March 16, 1923
Bear, M. J. (Essex & Cant.) b Feb. 23, 1934
*Beard, D. D. (C. Dist. & N. Dist.) b Jan. 14, 1920, d July 15, 1982
*Beard, G. R. (NSW) b Aug. 19, 1950
Beauclerk, Lord Frederick (Middx, Surrey & MCC) b May 8, 1873, d April 22, 1950.
Beaufort, 10th Duke of (Pres. MCC 1952-53) b April 4, 1900, d Feb. 5, 1984
*Beaumont, R. (Tvl) b Feb. 4, 1884, d May 25, 1958
*Beck, J. E. F. (Wgtn) b Aug. 1, 1934
Bedade, A. C. (Baroda) b Sept. 24, 1966
*Bedi, B. S. (N. Punjab, Delhi & Northants) b Sept. 25, 1946
*Bedser, Sir Alec V. (Surrey; *CY 1947*) b July 4, 1918
Bedser, E. A. (Surrey) b July 4, 1918
Beet, G. (Derbys; Test umpire) b April 24, 1886, d Dec. 13, 1946
*Begbie, D. W. (Tvl) b Dec. 12, 1914
Beldham, W. (Hambledon & Surrey) b Feb. 5, 1766, d Feb. 20, 1862
*Bell, A. J. (W. Prov. & Rhod.) b April 15, 1906, d Aug. 1, 1985
Bell, R. V. (Middx & Sussex) b Jan. 7, 1931, d Oct. 26, 1989
*Bell, W. (Cant.) b Sept. 5, 1931
Bellamy, B. W. (Northants) b April 22, 1891, d Dec. 22, 1985
*Benaud, J. (NSW) b May 11, 1944
*Benaud, R. (NSW; *CY 1962*) b Oct. 6, 1930
*Benjamin, J. E. (Warwicks & Surrey) b Feb. 2, 1961
*Benjamin, K. C. G. (Leewards & Worcs) b April 8, 1967
*Benjamin, W. K. M. (Leewards, Leics & Hants) b Dec. 31, 1964
Bencraft, Sir H. W. Russell (Hants) b March 4, 1858, d Dec. 25, 1943
Bennett, D. (Middx) b Dec. 18, 1933
*Bennett, M. J. (NSW) b Oct. 6, 1956
*Benson, M. R. (Kent) b July 6, 1958
Berry, L. G. (Leics) b April 28, 1906, d Feb. 5, 1985
*Berry, R. (Lancs, Worcs & Derbys) b Jan. 29, 1926
*Best, C. A. (B'dos & W. Prov.) b May 14, 1959
Bestwick, W. (Derbys) b Feb. 24, 1875, d May 2, 1938
*Betancourt, N. (T/T) b June 4, 1887, d Oct. 12, 1947
*Bevan, M. G. (NSW & Yorks) b May 8, 1970
Bhalekar, R. B. (M'tra) b Feb. 17, 1952
*Bhandari, P. (Delhi & Bengal) b Nov. 27, 1935
*Bhat, A. R. (Karn.) b April 16, 1958
Bhupinder Singh, (Punjab) b April 1, 1965
Bick, D. A. (Middx) b Feb. 22, 1936, d Jan. 13, 1992
Bicknell, D. J. (Surrey) b June 24, 1967
*Bicknell, M. P. (Surrey) b Jan. 14, 1969
*Bilby, G. P. (Wgtn) b May 7, 1941
*Binks, J. G. (Yorks; *CY 1969*) b Oct. 5, 1935
*Binns, A. P. (Jam.) b July 24, 1929
*Binny, R. M. H. (Karn.) b July 19, 1955
Birch, J. D. (Notts) b June 18, 1955
Bird, H. D. (Yorks & Leics; Test umpire) b April 19, 1933
*Bird, M. C. (Lancs & Surrey) b March 25, 1888, d Dec. 9, 1933
Bird, R. E. (Worcs) b April 4, 1915, d Feb. 20, 1985
*Birkenshaw, J. (Yorks, Leics & Worcs) b Nov. 13, 1940
*Birkett, L. S. (B'dos, BG & T/T; *oldest living Test cricketer at end 1996*) b April 14, 1904
Bishop, G. A. (S. Aust.) b Feb. 25, 1960
*Bishop, I. R. (T/T & Derbys) b Oct. 24, 1967
*Bisset, Sir Murray (M.) (W. Prov.) b April 14, 1876, d Oct. 24, 1931

*Bissett, G. F. (Griq. W., W. Prov. & Tvl) b Nov. 5, 1905, d Nov. 14, 1965
Bissex, M. (Glos) b Sept. 28, 1944
*Blackham, J. McC. (Vic; *CY 1891*) b May 11, 1854, d Dec. 28, 1932
*Blackie, D. D. (Vic.) b April 5, 1882, d April 18, 1955
*Blain, T. E. (C. Dist.) b Feb. 17, 1962
Blair, B. R. (Otago) b Dec. 27, 1957
*Blair, R. W. (Wgtn & C. Dist.) b June 23, 1932
*Blakey, R. J. (Yorks) b Jan. 15, 1967
*Blanckenberg, J. M. (W. Prov. & Natal) b Dec. 31, 1892, dead
*Bland, K. C. (Rhod., E. Prov. & OFS; *CY 1966*) b April 5, 1938
Blenkiron, W. (Warwicks) b July 21, 1942
*Blewett, G. S. (S. Aust.) b Oct. 29, 1971
*Bligh, Hon. Ivo (I. F. W.) (8th Earl of Darnley) (CU & Kent; Pres. MCC 1900) b March 13, 1859, d April 10, 1927
*Blunt, R. C. (Cant. & Otago; *CY 1928*) b Nov. 3, 1900, d June 22, 1966
*Blythe, C. (Kent; *CY 1904*) b May 30, 1879, d Nov. 8, 1917
*Board, J. H. (Glos) b Feb. 23, 1867, d April 15, 1924
*Bock, E. G. (Griq. W., Tvl & W. Prov.) b Sept. 17, 1908, d Sept. 5, 1961
Boje, N. (OFS) b March 20, 1973
*Bolton, B. A. (Cant. & Wgtn) b May 31, 1935
*Bolus, J. B. (Yorks, Notts & Derbys) b Jan. 31, 1934
*Bond, G. E. (W. Prov.) b April 5, 1909, d Aug. 27, 1965
Bond, J. D. (Lancs & Notts; *CY 1971*) b May 6, 1932
*Bonnor, G. J. (Vic. & NSW) b Feb. 25, 1855, d June 27, 1912
*Boock, S. L. (Otago & Cant.) b Sept. 20, 1951
*Boon, D. C. (Tas.; *CY 1994*) b Dec. 29, 1960
Boon, T. J. (Leics) b Nov. 1, 1961
*Booth, B. C. (NSW) b Oct. 19, 1933
Booth, B. J. (Lancs & Leics) b Dec. 3, 1935
Booth, C. (CU & Hants) b May 11, 1842, d July 14, 1926
*Booth, M. W. (Yorks; *CY 1914*) b Dec. 10, 1886, d July 1, 1916
Booth, R. (Yorks & Worcs) b Oct. 1, 1926
*Borde, C. G. (Baroda & M'tra) b July 21, 1933
*Border, A. R. (NSW, Glos, Qld & Essex; *CY 1982*) b July 27, 1955
Bore, M. K. (Yorks & Notts) b June 2, 1947
Borrington, A. J. (Derbys) b Dec. 8, 1948
*Bosanquet, B. J. T. (OU & Middx; *CY 1905*) b Oct. 13, 1877, d Oct. 12, 1936
*Bosch, T. (N. Tvl & Natal) b March 14, 1966
Bose, G. (Bengal) b May 20, 1947
Boshier, B. S. (Leics) b March 6, 1932
*Botham, I. T. (Som, Worcs, Durham & Qld; *CY 1978*) b Nov. 24, 1955
*Botten, J. T. (NE Tvl & N. Tvl) b June 21, 1938
Boucher, J. C. (Ireland) b Dec. 22, 1910, d Dec. 25, 1995
Bowden, J. (Derbys) b Oct. 8, 1884, d March 1, 1958
*Bowden, M. P. (Surrey & Tvl) b Nov. 1, 1865, d Feb. 19, 1892
Bowell, A. (Hants) b April 27, 1880, d Aug. 28, 1957
*Bowes, W. E. (Yorks; *CY 1932*) b July 25, 1908, d Sept. 5, 1987
Bowler, P. D. (Leics, Tas., Derbys & Som) b July 30, 1963
*Bowley, E. H. (Sussex & Auck.; *CY 1930*) b June 6, 1890, d July 9, 1974
Bowley, F. L. (Worcs) b Nov. 9 1873, d May 31, 1943
Box, T. (Sussex) b Feb. 7, 1808, d July 12, 1876
*Boyce, K. D. (B'dos & Essex; *CY 1974*) b Oct. 11, 1943, d Oct. 11, 1996
*Boycott, G. (Yorks & N. Tvl; *CY 1965*) b Oct. 21, 1940
Boyd-Moss, R. J. (CU & Northants) b Dec. 16, 1959
Boyes, G. S. (Hants) b March 31, 1899, d Feb. 11, 1973
*Boyle, H. F. (Vic.) b Dec. 10, 1847, d Nov. 21, 1907
*Bracewell, B. P. (C. Dist., Otago & N. Dist.) b Sept. 14, 1959
*Bracewell, J. G. (Otago & Auck.) b April 15, 1958
*Bradburn, G. E. (N. Dist.) b May 26, 1966
*Bradburn, W. P. (N. Dist.) b Nov. 24, 1938
*Bradley, W. M. (Kent) b Jan. 2, 1875, d June 19, 1944
*Bradman, Sir Donald G. (NSW & S. Aust.; *CY 1931*) b Aug. 27, 1908
Brain, B. M. (Worcs & Glos) b Sept. 13, 1940
*Brain, D. H. (Mash.) b Oct. 4, 1964
Bramall, Field-Marshal The Lord (Pres. MCC 1988-89) b Dec. 18, 1923
*Brandes, E. A. (MCD) b March 5, 1963
Brann, G. (Sussex) b April 23, 1865, d June 14, 1954
*Brann, W. H. (E. Prov.) b April 4, 1899, d Sept. 22, 1953
Brassington, A. J. (Glos) b Aug. 9, 1954
*Braund, L. C. (Surrey & Som; *CY 1902*) b Oct. 18, 1875, d Dec. 23, 1955
Bray, C. (Essex) b April 6, 1898, d Sept. 12, 1993
Brayshaw, I. J. (W. Aust.) b Jan. 14, 1942
Breakwell, D. (Northants & Som) b July 2, 1948
*Brearley, J. M. (CU & Middx; *CY 1977*) b April 28, 1942
*Brearley, W. (Lancs; *CY 1909*) b March 11, 1876, d Jan. 13, 1937

*Brennan, D. V. (Yorks) b Feb. 10, 1920, d Jan. 9, 1985
*Briant, G. A. (Mash.) b April 11, 1969
Bridges, J. J. (Som) b June 28, 1887, d Sept. 26, 1966
Brierley, T. L. (Glam, Lancs & Canada) b June 15, 1910, d Jan. 7, 1989
Briers, N. E. (Leics; *CY 1993*) b Jan. 15, 1955
*Briggs, John (Lancs; *CY 1889*) b Oct. 3, 1862, d Jan. 11, 1902
*Bright, R. J. (Vic.) b July 13, 1954
*Briscoe, A. W. (Tvl) b Feb. 6, 1911, d April 22, 1941
*Broad, B. C. (Glos & Notts) b Sept. 29, 1957
Broadbent, R. G. (Worcs) b June 21, 1924, d April 26, 1993
*Brockwell, W. (Surrey & Kimberley; *CY 1895*) b Jan. 21, 1865, d June 30, 1935
Broderick, V. (Northants) b Aug. 17, 1920
*Bromfield, H. D. (W. Prov.) b June 26, 1932
*Bromley, E. H. (W. Aust. & Vic.) b Sept. 2, 1912, d Feb. 1, 1967
*Bromley-Davenport, H. R. (CU, Eur., & Middx) b Aug. 18, 1870, d May 23, 1954
*Brookes, D. (Northants; *CY 1957*) b Oct. 29, 1915
Brookes, Wilfrid H. (Editor of *Wisden* 1936-39) b Dec. 5, 1894, d May 28, 1955
*Brown, A. (Kent) b Oct. 17, 1935
Brown, A. D. (Surrey) b Feb. 11, 1970
Brown, A. S. (Glos) b June 24, 1936
*Brown, D. J. (Warwicks) b Jan. 30, 1942
*Brown, F. R. (CU, Surrey & Northants; *CY 1933;* Pres. MCC 1971-72) b Dec. 16, 1910, d July 24, 1991
*Brown, G. (Hants) b Oct. 6, 1887, d Dec. 3, 1964
Brown, J. (Scotland) b Sept. 24, 1931
*Brown, J. T. (Yorks; *CY 1895*) b Aug. 20, 1869, d Nov. 4, 1904
Brown, K. R. (Middx) b March 18, 1963
*Brown, L. S. (Tvl, NE Tvl & Rhod.) b Nov. 24, 1910, d Sept. 1, 1983
Brown, R. D. (Mash.) b March 11, 1951
*Brown, S. J. E. (Northants & Durham) b June 29, 1969
Brown, S. M. (Middx) b Dec. 8, 1917, d Dec. 28, 1987
*Brown, V. R. (Cant. & Auck.) b Nov. 3, 1959
*Brown, W. A. (NSW & Qld; *CY 1939*) b July 31, 1912
Brown, W. C. (Northants) b Nov. 13, 1900, d Jan. 20, 1986
Browne, B. St A (Guyana) b Sept. 16, 1967
*Browne, C. O. (B'dos) b Dec. 7, 1970
*Browne, C. R. (B'dos & BG) b Oct. 8, 1890, d Jan. 12, 1964
*Bruce, W. (Vic.) b May 22, 1864, d Aug. 3, 1925
*Bruk-Jackson, G. K. (MCD) b April 25, 1969
Bryan, G. J. (Kent) b Dec. 29, 1902, d April 4, 1991
Bryan, J. L. (CU & Kent; *CY 1922*) b May 26, 1896, d April 23, 1985
Bryan, R. T. (Kent) b July 30, 1898, d July 27, 1970
*Buckenham, C. P. (Essex) b Jan. 16, 1876, d Feb. 23, 1937
Buckston, R. H. R. (Derbys) b Oct. 10, 1908, d May 16, 1967
Budd, E. H. (Middx & All-England) b Feb. 23, 1785, d March 29, 1875
Budd, W. L. (Hants; Test umpire) b Oct. 25, 1913, d Aug. 23, 1986
Bull, F. G. (Essex; *CY 1898*) b April 2, 1875, d Sept. 16, 1910
Buller, J. S. (Yorks & Worcs; Test umpire) b Aug. 23, 1909, d Aug. 7, 1970
Burden, M. D. (Hants) b Oct. 4, 1930, d Nov. 9, 1987
*Burge, P. J. (Qld; *CY 1965*) b May 17, 1932
*Burger, C. G. de V. (Natal) b July 12, 1935
Burgess, G. I. (Som) b May 5, 1943
*Burgess, M. G. (Auck.) b July 17, 1944
*Burke, C. (Auck.) b March 22, 1914
*Burke, J. W. (NSW; *CY 1957*) b June 12, 1930, d Feb. 2, 1979
*Burke, S. F. (NE Tvl & OFS) b March 11, 1934
*Burki, Javed (Pak. Us, OU, Punjab, Lahore, Kar., R'pindi & NWFP) b May 8, 1938
*Burmester, M. G. (Mash.) b Jan. 24, 1968
*Burn, K. E. (Tas.) b Sept. 17, 1862, d July 20, 1956
Burns, N. D. (Essex, W. Prov., Som) b Sept. 19, 1965
Burns, W. B. (Worcs) b Aug. 29, 1883, d July 7, 1916
Burnup, C. J. (CU & Kent; *CY 1903*) b Nov. 21, 1875, d April 5, 1960
Burrough, H. D. (Som) b Feb. 6, 1909, d April 9, 1994
Burrows, R. D. (Worcs) b June 6, 1871, d Feb. 12, 1943
Burton, D. C. F. (Yorks) b Sept. 13, 1887, d Sept. 24, 1971
*Burton, F. J. (Vic. & NSW) b Nov. 2, 1865, d Aug. 25, 1929
*Burtt, T. B. (Cant.) b Jan. 22, 1915, d May 24, 1988
Buse, H. T. F. (Som) b Aug. 5, 1910, d Feb. 23, 1992
Buss, A. (Sussex) b Sept. 1, 1939
Buss, M. A. (Sussex & OFS) b Jan. 24, 1944
*Butchart, I. P. (MCD) b May 9, 1960
*Butcher, A. R. (Surrey & Glam; *CY 1991*) b Jan. 7, 1954
*Butcher, B. F. (Guyana; *CY 1970*) b Sept. 3, 1933
Butcher, I. P. (Leics & Glos) b July 1, 1962
*Butcher, R. O. (Middx, B'dos & Tas.) b Oct. 14, 1953
*Butler, H. J. (Notts) b March 12, 1913, d July 17, 1991

*Butler, L. (T/T) b Feb. 9, 1929
*Butt, H. R. (Sussex) b Dec. 27, 1865, d Dec. 21, 1928
*Butterfield, L. A. (Cant.) b Aug. 29, 1913
*Butts, C. G. (Guyana) b July 8, 1957
Buxton, I. R. (Derbys) b April 17, 1938
*Buys, I. D. (W. Prov.) b Feb. 3, 1895, dead
Byas, D. (Yorks) b Aug. 26, 1963
*Bynoe, M. R. (B'dos) b Feb. 23, 1941
Byrne, J. F. (Warwicks) b June 19, 1871, d May 10, 1954

Caccia, Lord (Pres. MCC 1973-74) b Dec. 21, 1905, d Oct. 31, 1990
*Caddick, A. R. (Som) b Nov. 21, 1968
Cadman, S. (Derbys) b Jan. 29, 1877, d May 6, 1952
Caesar, Julius (Surrey & All-England) b March 25, 1830, d March 6, 1878
Caffyn, W. (Surrey & NSW) b Feb. 2, 1828, d Aug. 28, 1919
Caine, C. Stewart (Editor of *Wisden* 1926-33) b Oct. 28, 1861, d April 15, 1933
*Cairns, B. L. (C. Dist., Otago & N. Dist.) b Oct. 10, 1949
*Cairns, C. L. (N. Dist., Notts & Cant.) b June 13, 1970
Calder, H. L. (Cranleigh; *CY 1918*) b Jan. 24, 1901, d Sept. 15, 1995
*Callaway, S. T. (NSW & Cant.) b Feb. 6, 1868, d Nov. 25, 1923
*Callen, I. W. (Vic. & Boland) b May 2, 1955
*Calthorpe, Hon. F. S. Gough- (CU, Sussex & Warwicks) b May 27, 1892, d Nov. 19, 1935
*Camacho, G. S. (Guyana; Chief Exec. WICB) b Oct. 15, 1945
*Cameron, F. J. (Jam.) b June 22, 1923, d Feb. 1995
*Cameron, F. J. (Otago) b June 1, 1932
*Cameron, H. B. (Tvl, E. Prov. & W. Prov.; *CY 1936*) b July 5, 1905, d Nov. 2, 1935
*Cameron, J. H. (CU, Jam. & Som) b April 8, 1914
*Campbell, A. D. R. (MCD & Mash.) b Sept. 23, 1972
*Campbell, G. D. (Tas.) b March 10, 1964
*Campbell, S. L. (B'dos & Durham) b Nov. 1, 1970
*Campbell, T. (Tvl) b Feb. 9, 1882, d Oct. 5, 1924
Cannings, V. H. D. (Warwicks & Hants) b April 3, 1919
*Capel, D. J. (Northants & E. Prov.) b Feb. 6, 1963
Cardus, Sir Neville (Writer) b April 3, 1888, d Feb. 27, 1975
*Carew, G. M. (B'dos) b June 4, 1910, d Dec. 9, 1974
*Carew, M. C. (T/T) b Sept. 15, 1937
*Carkeek, W. (Vic.) b Oct. 17, 1878, d Feb. 20, 1937
*Carlisle, S. V. (Zimb. U-24) b May 10, 1972
*Carlson, P. H. (Qld) b Aug. 8, 1951
*Carlstein, P. R. (OFS, Tvl, Natal & Rhod.) b Oct. 28, 1938
Carpenter, D. (Glos) b Sept. 12, 1935
Carpenter, H. A. (Essex) b July 12, 1869, d Dec. 12, 1933
Carpenter, R. (Cambs & Utd England XI) b Nov. 18, 1830, d July 13, 1901
*Carr, A. W. (Notts; *CY 1923*) b May 21, 1893, d Feb. 7, 1963
*Carr, D. B. (OU & Derbys; *CY 1960;* Sec. TCCB 1974-86) b Dec. 28, 1926
*Carr, D. W. (Kent; *CY 1910*) b March 17, 1872, d March 23, 1950
Carr, J. D. (OU & Middx) b June 15, 1963
Carrick, P. (Yorks & E. Prov.) b July 16, 1952
*Carter, C. P. (Natal & Tvl) b April 23, 1881, d Nov. 8, 1952
*Carter, H. (NSW) b March 15, 1878, d June 8, 1948
Carter, R. G. M. (Worcs) b July 11, 1937
*Cartwright, T. W. (Warwicks, Som & Glam) b July 22, 1935
Case, C. C. C. (Som) b Sept. 7, 1895, d Nov. 11, 1969
Cass, G. R. (Essex, Worcs & Tas.) b April 23, 1940
Catt, A. W. (Kent & W. Prov.) b Oct. 2, 1933
*Catterall, R. H. (Tvl, Rhod., Natal & OFS; *CY 1925*) b July 10, 1900, d Jan. 3, 1961
*Cave, H. B. (Wgtn & C. Dist.) b Oct. 10, 1922, d Sept. 15, 1989
Chalk, F. G. H. (OU & Kent) b Sept. 7, 1910, d Feb. 17, 1943
*Challenor, G. (B'dos) b June 28, 1888, d July 30, 1947
Chamberlain, W. R. F. (Northants; Chairman TCCB 1990-94) b April 13, 1925
Chandana, U. U. (TU) b Sept. 3, 1972
*Chanderpaul, S. (Guyana) b Aug. 18, 1974
*Chandrasekhar, B. S. (†Karn.; *CY 1972*) b May 17, 1945
Chandrasekhar, V. B. (TN) b Aug. 21, 1961
*Chang, H. S. (Jam.) b July 22, 1952
Chaplin, H. P. (Sussex & Eur.) b March 1, 1883, d March 6, 1970
*Chapman, A. P. F. (Uppingham, OU & Kent; *CY 1919*) b Sept. 3, 1900, d Sept. 16, 1961
*Chapman, H. W. (Natal) b June 30, 1890, d Dec. 1, 1941
Chapman, J. (Derbys) b March 11, 1877, d Aug. 12, 1956
*Chappell, G. S. (S. Aust., Som & Qld; *CY 1973*) b Aug. 7, 1948
*Chappell, I. M. (S. Aust. & Lancs; *CY 1976*) b Sept. 26, 1943
*Chappell, T. M. (S. Aust., W. Aust. & NSW) b Oct. 21, 1952
*Chapple, M. E. (Cant. & C. Dist.) b July 25, 1930, d July 31, 1985

Charlesworth, C. (Warwicks) b Feb. 12, 1875, d June 15, 1953
*Charlton, P. C. (NSW) b April 9, 1867, d Sept. 30, 1954
*Charlwood, H. R. J. (Sussex) b Dec. 19, 1846, d June 6, 1888
*Chatfield, E. J. (Wgtn) b July 3, 1950
Chatterjee, U. (Bengal) b July 13, 1964
*Chatterton, W. (Derbys) b Dec. 27, 1861, d March 19, 1913
*Chauhan, C. P. S. (M'tra & Delhi) b July 21, 1947
*Chauhan, R. K. (M. Pradesh) b Dec. 19, 1966
*Cheetham, J. E. (W. Prov.) b May 26, 1920, d Aug. 21, 1980
Chester, F. (Worcs; Test umpire) b Jan. 20, 1895, d April 8, 1957
*Chevalier, G. A. (W. Prov.) b March 9, 1937
*Childs, J. H. (Glos & Essex; *CY 1987*) b Aug. 15, 1951
*Chipperfield, A. G. (NSW) b Nov. 17, 1905, d July 29, 1987
Chisholm, R. H. E. (Scotland) b May 22, 1927
*Chowdhury, N. R. (Bihar & Bengal) b May 23, 1923, d Dec. 14, 1979
*Christiani, C. M. (BG) b Oct. 28, 1913, d April 4, 1938
*Christiani, R. J. (BG) b July 19, 1920
*Christopherson, S. (Kent; Pres. MCC 1939-45) b Nov. 11, 1861, d April 6, 1949
*Christy, J. A. J. (Tvl & Qld) b Dec. 12, 1904, d Feb. 1, 1971
*Chubb, G. W. A. (Border & Tvl) b April 12, 1911, d Aug. 28, 1982
Clark, D. G. (Kent; Pres. MCC 1977-78) b Jan. 27, 1919
Clark, E. A. (Middx) b April 15, 1937
*Clark, E. W. (Northants) b Aug. 9, 1902, d April 28, 1982
Clark, T. H. (Surrey) b Oct. 5, 1924, d June 14, 1981
*Clark, W. M. (W. Aust.) b Sept. 19, 1953
*Clarke, Dr C. B. (B'dos, Northants & Essex) b April 7, 1918, d Oct. 14, 1993
Clarke, R. W. (Northants) b April 22, 1924, d Aug. 3, 1981
*Clarke, S. T. (B'dos, Surrey, Tvl, OFS & N. Tvl) b Dec. 11, 1954
Clarke, William (Notts; founded All-England XI & Trent Bridge ground) b Dec. 24, 1798, d Aug. 25, 1856
Clarkson, A. (Yorks & Som) b Sept. 5, 1939
*Clay, J. C. (Glam) b March 18, 1898, d Aug. 12, 1973
Clay, J. D. (Notts) b Oct. 15, 1924
Clayton, G. (Lancs & Som) b Feb. 3, 1938
*Cleverley, D. C. (Auck.) b Dec. 23, 1909
Clift, Patrick B. (Rhod., Leics & Natal) b July 14, 1953, d Sept. 2, 1996
Clift, Phil B. (Glam) b Sept. 3, 1918
Clinton, G. S. (Kent, Surrey & Zimb.-Rhod.) b May 5, 1953
*Close, D. B. (Yorks & Som; *CY 1964*) b Feb. 24, 1931
Cobb, R. A. (Leics & N. Tvl) b May 18, 1961
Cobham, 10th Visct (Hon. C. J. Lyttelton) (Worcs; Pres. MCC 1954) b Aug. 8, 1909, d March 20, 1977
*Cochrane, J. A. K. (Tvl & Griq. W.) b July 15, 1909, d June 15, 1987
Coe, S. (Leics) b June 3, 1873, d Nov. 4, 1955
*Coen, S. K. (OFS, W. Prov., Tvl & Border) b Oct. 14, 1902, d Jan. 28, 1967
*Colah, S. M. H. (Bombay, W. Ind. & Naw.) b Sept. 22, 1902, d Sept. 11, 1950
Colchin, Robert ("Long Robin") (Kent & All-England) b Nov. 1713, d April 1750
*Coldwell, L. J. (Worcs) b Jan. 10, 1933, d Aug. 6, 1996
*Colley, D. J. (NSW) b March 15, 1947
*Collinge, R. O. (C. Dist., Wgtn & N. Dist.) b April 2, 1946
Collins, A. E. J. (Clifton Coll. & Royal Engineers) b Aug. 18, 1885, d Nov. 11, 1914
Collins, G. C. (Kent) b Sept. 21, 1889, d Jan. 23, 1949
*Collins, H. L. (NSW) b Jan. 21, 1888, d May 28, 1959
Collins, R. (Lancs) b March 10, 1934
*Colquhoun, I. A. (C. Dist.) b June 8, 1924
Coman, P. G. (Cant.) b April 13, 1943
*Commaille, J. M. M. (W. Prov., Natal, OFS & Griq. W.) b Feb. 21, 1883, d July 28, 1956
*Commins, J. B. (Boland & W. Prov.) b Feb. 19, 1965
*Compton, D. C. S. (Middx & Holkar; *CY 1939*) b May 23, 1918
Compton, L. H. (Middx) b Sept. 12, 1912, d Dec. 27, 1984
*Coney, J. V. (Wgtn; *CY 1984*) b June 21, 1952
*Congdon, B. E. (C. Dist., Wgtn, Otago & Cant.; *CY 1974*) b Feb. 11, 1938
*Coningham, A. (NSW & Qld) b July 14, 1863, d June 13, 1939
*Connolly, A. N. (Vic. & Middx) b June 29, 1939
Connor, C. A. (Hants) b March 24, 1961
Constable, B. (Surrey) b Feb. 19, 1921
Constant, D. J. (Kent & Leics; Test umpire) b Nov. 9, 1941
*Constantine, L. N. (later Baron) (T/T & B'dos; *CY 1940*) b Sept. 21, 1902, d July 1, 1971
Constantine, L. S. (T/T) b May 25, 1874, d Jan. 5, 1942
*Contractor, N. J. (Guj. & Ind. Rlwys) b March 7, 1934
*Conyngham, D. P. (Natal, Tvl & W. Prov.) b May 10, 1897, d July 7, 1979
*Cook, C. (Glos) b Aug. 23, 1921, d Sept. 4, 1996
*Cook, F. J. (E. Prov.) b 1870, d Nov. 30, 1914
*Cook, G. (Northants & E. Prov.) b Oct. 9, 1951

Cook, L. W. (Lancs) b March 28, 1885, d Dec. 2, 1933
*Cook, N. G. B. (Leics & Northants) b June 17, 1956
*Cook, S. J. (Tvl & Som; *CY 1990*) b July 31, 1953
Cook, T. E. R. (Sussex) b Jan. 5, 1901, d Jan. 15, 1950
*Cooper, A. H. C. (Tvl) b Sept. 2, 1893, d July 18, 1963
*Cooper, B. B. (Middx, Kent & Vic.) b March 15, 1844, d Aug. 7, 1914
Cooper, E. (Worcs) b Nov. 30, 1915, d Oct. 29, 1968
Cooper, F. S. Ashley- (Historian) b March 17, 1877, d Jan. 31, 1932
Cooper, G. C. (Sussex) b Sept. 2, 1936
Cooper, K. E. (Notts & Glos) b Dec. 27, 1957
*Cooper, W. H. (Vic.) b Sept. 11, 1849, d April 5, 1939
*Cope, G. A. (Yorks) b Feb. 23, 1947
*Copson, W. H. (Derbys; *CY 1937*) b April 27, 1908, d Sept. 14, 1971
Cordle, A. E. (Glam) b Sept. 21, 1940
*Cork, D. G. (Derbys; *CY 1996*) b Aug. 7, 1971
*Corling, G. E. (NSW) b July 13, 1941
Cornford, J. H. (Sussex) b Dec. 9, 1911, d June 17, 1985
*Cornford, W. L. (Sussex) b Dec. 25, 1900, d Feb. 6, 1964
Cornwallis, W. S. (later 2nd Baron) (Kent) b March 14, 1892, d Jan. 4, 1982
Corrall, P. (Leics) b July 16, 1906, d Feb. 1994
Corran, A. J. (OU & Notts) b Nov. 25, 1936
*Cosier, G. J. (Vic., S. Aust. & Qld) b April 25, 1953
*Cottam, J. T. (NSW) b Sept. 5, 1867, d Jan. 30, 1897
*Cottam, R. M. H. (Hants & Northants) b Oct. 16, 1944
*Cotter, A. (NSW) b Dec. 3, 1884, d Oct. 31, 1917
Cottey, P. A. (Glam & E. Tvl) b June 2, 1966
Cotton, J. (Notts & Leics) b Nov. 7, 1940
*Coulthard, G. (Vic.; Test umpire) b Aug. 1, 1856, d Oct. 22, 1883
*Coventry, Hon. C. J. (Worcs) b Feb. 26, 1867, d June 2, 1929
*Cowans, N. G. (Middx & Hants) b April 17, 1961
*Cowdrey, C. S. (Kent & Glam) b Oct. 20, 1957
Cowdrey, G. R. (Kent) b June 27, 1964
*Cowdrey, Sir M. Colin (OU & Kent; *CY 1956;* Pres. MCC 1986-87) b Dec. 24, 1932
*Cowie, J. (Auck.) b March 30, 1912, d June 3, 1994
Cowley, N. G. (Hants & Glam) b March 1, 1953
*Cowper, R. M. (Vic. & W. Aust.) b Oct. 5, 1940
Cox, A. L. (Northants) b July 22, 1907, d Nov. 13, 1986
Cox, G., jun. (Sussex) b Aug. 23, 1911, d March 30, 1985
Cox, G., sen. (Sussex) b Nov. 29, 1873, d March 24, 1949
*Cox, J. L. (Natal) b June 28, 1886, d July 4, 1971
*Coxon, A. (Yorks) b Jan. 18, 1916
*Craig, I. D. (NSW) b June 12, 1935
Cranfield, L. M. (Glos) b Aug. 29, 1909, d Nov. 18, 1993
Cranmer, P. (Warwicks & Eur.) b Sept. 10, 1914, d May 29, 1994
*Cranston, J. (Glos) b Jan. 9, 1859, d Dec. 10, 1904
*Cranston, K. (Lancs) b Oct. 20, 1917
*Crapp, J. F. (Glos; Test umpire) b Oct. 14, 1912, d Feb. 15, 1981
*Crawford, J. N. (Surrey, S. Aust., Wgtn & Otago; *CY 1907*) b Dec. 1, 1886, d May 2, 1963
*Crawford, P. (NSW) b Aug. 3, 1933
Crawford, V. F. S. (Surrey & Leics) b April 11, 1879, d Aug. 21, 1922
Crawley, A. M. (OU & Kent; Pres. MCC 1972-73) b April 10, 1908, d Nov. 3, 1993
*Crawley, J. P. (Lancs & CU) b Sept. 21, 1971
Cray, S. J. (Essex) b May 29, 1921
Creese, W. L. (Hants) b Dec. 27, 1907, d March 9, 1974
*Cresswell, G. F. (Wgtn & C. Dist.) b March 22, 1915, d Jan. 10, 1966
*Cripps, G. (W. Prov.) b Oct. 19, 1865, d July 27, 1943
*Crisp, R. J. (Rhod., W. Prov. & Worcs) b May 28, 1911, d March 3, 1994
*Crocker, G. J. (MCD) b May 16, 1962
*Croft, C. E. H. (Guyana & Lancs) b March 15, 1953
*Croft, R. D. B. (Glam) b May 25, 1970
*Cromb, I. B. (Cant.) b June 25, 1905, d March 6, 1984
*Cronje, W. J. (OFS & Leics) b Sept. 25, 1969
Crookes, D. N. (Natal) b March 5, 1969
Croom, A. J. (Warwicks) b May 23, 1896, d Aug. 16, 1947
*Crowe, J. J. (S. Aust. & Auck.) b Sept. 14, 1958
*Crowe, M. D. (Auck., C. Dist., Som & Wgtn; *CY 1985*) b Sept. 22, 1962
Crump, B. S. (Northants) b April 25, 1938
Cuffe, J. A. (NSW & Worcs) b June 26, 1880, d May 16, 1931
*Cuffy, C. E. (Windwards & Surrey) b Feb. 8, 1970
*Cullinan, D. J. (Border, W. Prov., Tvl & Derbys) b March 4, 1967
Cumbes, J. (Lancs, Surrey, Worcs & Warwicks) b May 4, 1944
*Cummins, A. C. (B'dos & Durham) b May 7, 1966

*Cunis, R. S. (Auck. & N. Dist.) b Jan. 5, 1941
*Curnow, S. H. (Tvl) b Dec. 16, 1907, d July 28, 1986
Curran, K. M. (Glos, Zimb., Natal, Northants & Boland) b Sept. 7, 1959
*Curtis, T. S. (Worcs & CU) b Jan. 15, 1960
Cutmore, J. A. (Essex) b Dec. 28, 1898, d Nov. 30, 1985
*Cuttell, W. R. (Lancs; *CY 1898*) b Sept. 13, 1864, d Dec. 9, 1929

*Da Costa, O. C. (Jam.) b Sept. 11, 1907, d Oct. 1, 1936
Dacre, C. C. (Auck. & Glos) b May 15, 1899, d Nov. 2, 1975
Daft, H. B. (Notts) b April 5, 1866, d Jan. 12, 1945
Daft, Richard (Notts & All-England) b Nov. 2, 1835, d July 18, 1900
Dale, A. (Glam) b Oct. 24, 1968
Dalmeny, Lord (later 6th Earl of Rosebery) (Middx, Surrey & Scotland) b Jan. 8, 1882, d May 30, 1974
*Dalton, E. L. (Natal) b Dec. 2, 1906, d June 3, 1981
*Dani, H. T. (M'tra & Ind. Serv.) b May 24, 1933
*Daniel, W. W. (B'dos, Middx & W. Aust.) b Jan. 16, 1956
*D'Arcy, J. W. (Cant., Wgtn & Otago) b April 23, 1936
Dare, R. (Hants) b Nov. 26, 1921
*Darling, J. (S. Aust.; *CY 1900*) b Nov. 21, 1870, d Jan. 2, 1946
*Darling, L. S. (Vic.) b Aug. 14, 1909, d June 24, 1992
*Darling, W. M. (S. Aust.) b May 1, 1957
*Dassanayake, P. B. (Bloom. & C. Prov.) b July 11, 1970
Davey, J. (Glos) b Sept. 4, 1944
*Davidson, A. K. (NSW; *CY 1962*) b June 14, 1929
Davidson, G. (Derbys) b June 29, 1866, d Feb. 8, 1899
Davies, Dai (Glam; Test umpire) b Aug. 26, 1896, d July 16, 1976
Davies, Emrys (Glam; Test umpire) b June 27, 1904, d Nov. 10, 1975
*Davies, E. Q. (E. Prov., Tvl & NE Tvl) b Aug. 26, 1909, d Nov. 11, 1976
Davies, H. G. (Glam) b April 23, 1912, d Sept. 4, 1993
Davies, J. G. W. (CU & Kent; Pres. MCC 1985-86) b Sept. 10, 1911, d Nov. 5, 1992
Davies, S. G. (Mat.) b May 12, 1977
Davies, T. (Glam) b Oct. 25, 1960
*Davis, B. A. (T/T & Glam) b May 2, 1940
*Davis, C. A. (T/T) b Jan. 1, 1944
Davis, E. (Northants) b March 8, 1922
*Davis, H. T. (Wgtn) b Nov. 30, 1971
*Davis, I. C. (NSW & Qld) b June 25, 1953
Davis, P. (Northants) b May 24, 1915
Davis, R. C. (Glam) b Jan. 1, 1946
Davis, R. P. (Kent, Warwicks & Glos) b March 18, 1966
*Davis, S. P. (Vic.) b Nov. 8, 1959
*Davis, W. W. (Windwards, Glam, Tas., Northants & Wgtn) b Sept. 18, 1958
Davison, B. F. (Rhod., Leics, Tas. & Glos) b Dec. 21, 1946
Davison, I. J. (Notts) b Oct. 4, 1937
Dawkes, G. O. (Leics & Derbys) b July 19, 1920
*Dawson, E. W. (CU & Leics) b Feb. 13, 1904, d June 4, 1979
*Dawson, O. C. (Natal & Border) b Sept. 1, 1919
Day, A. P. (Kent; *CY 1910*) b April 10, 1885, d Jan. 22, 1969
*de Alwis, R. G. (SSC) b Feb. 15, 1959
*Dean, H. (Lancs) b Aug. 13, 1884, d March 12, 1957
Dean, J., sen. (Sussex) b Jan. 4, 1816, d Dec. 25, 1881
*Deane, H. G. (Natal & Tvl) b July 21, 1895, d Oct. 21, 1939
*De Caires, F. I. (BG) b May 12, 1909, d Feb. 2, 1959
*De Courcy, J. H. (NSW) b April 18, 1927
*DeFreitas, P. A. J. (Leics, Lancs, Boland & Derbys; *CY 1992*) b Feb. 18, 1966
*de Groen, R. P. (Auck. & N. Dist.) b Aug. 5, 1962
*Dekker, M. H. (Mat.) b Dec. 5, 1969
*Dell, A. R. (Qld) b Aug. 6, 1947
*de Mel, A. L. F. (SL) b May 9, 1959
*Dempster, C. S. (Wgtn, Leics, Scotland & Warwicks; *CY 1932*) b Nov. 15, 1903, d Feb. 14, 1974
*Dempster, E. W. (Wgtn) b Jan. 25, 1925
*Denness, M. H. (Scotland, Kent & Essex; *CY 1975*) b Dec. 1, 1940
Dennett, G. (Glos) b April 27, 1880, d Sept. 14, 1937
Denning, P. W. (Som) b Dec. 16, 1949
Dennis, F. (Yorks) b June 11, 1907
Dennis, S. J. (Yorks, OFS & Glam) b Oct. 18, 1960
*Denton, D. (Yorks; *CY 1906*) b July 4, 1874, d Feb. 16, 1950
Deodhar, D. B. (M'tra) b Jan. 14, 1892, d Aug. 24, 1993
*Depeiza, C. C. (B'dos) b Oct. 10, 1928, d Nov. 10, 1995
*Desai, R. B. (Bombay) b June 20, 1939
*de Silva, A. M. (CCC) b Dec. 3, 1963
de Silva, D. L. S. (SL) b Nov. 17, 1956, d April 12, 1980
*de Silva, D. S. (Bloom.) b June 11, 1942
*de Silva, E. A. R. (NCC & Galle) b March 28, 1956
de Silva, G. N. (SL) b March 12, 1955
*de Silva, G. R. A. (SL) b Dec. 12, 1952

*de Silva, P. A. (NCC & Kent; *CY 1996*) b Oct. 17, 1965
de Smidt, R. W. (W. Prov.; *believed to be longest-lived first-class cricketer*) b Nov. 24, 1883, d Aug. 3, 1986
De Trafford, C. E. (Lancs & Leics) b May 21, 1864, d Nov. 11, 1951
Devereux, L. N. (Middx, Worcs & Glam) b Oct. 20, 1931
*de Villiers, P. S. (N. Tvl & Kent) b Oct. 13, 1964
*Dewdney, C. T. (Jam.) b Oct. 23, 1933
*Dewes, J. G. (CU & Middx) b Oct. 11, 1926
Dews, G. (Worcs) b June 5, 1921
*Dexter, E. R. (CU & Sussex; *CY 1961*) b May 15, 1935
*Dhanraj, R. (T/T) b Feb. 6, 1969
*Dharmasena, H. D. P. K. (TU, Ant. & Bloom.) b April 24, 1971
*Dias, R. L. (CCC) b Oct. 18, 1952
Dibbs, A. H. A. (Pres. MCC 1983-84) b Dec. 9, 1918, d Nov. 28, 1985
*Dick, A. E. (Otago & Wgtn) b Oct. 10, 1936
*Dickinson, G. R. (Otago) b March 11, 1903, d March 17, 1978
*Dilawar Hussain (C. Ind. and U. Prov.) b March 19, 1907, d Aug. 26, 1967
*Dilley, G. R. (Kent, Natal & Worcs) b May 18, 1959
Dillon, E. W. (Kent & OU) b Feb. 15, 1881, d April 20, 1941
*Dipper, A. E. (Glos) b Nov. 9, 1885, d Nov. 7, 1945
*Divecha, R. V. (Bombay, OU, Northants, Vidarbha & S'tra) b Oct. 18, 1927
Diver, A. J. D. (Cambs., Middx, Notts & All-England) b June 6, 1824, d March 25, 1876
Diver, E. J. (Surrey & Warwicks) b March 20, 1861, d Dec. 27, 1924
Dixon, A. L. (Kent) b Nov. 27, 1933
*Dixon, C. D. (Tvl) b Feb. 12, 1891, d Sept. 9, 1969
Dixon, J. A. (Notts) b May 27, 1861, d June 8, 1931
Dodds, T. C. (Essex) b May 29, 1919
*Dodemaide, A. I. C. (Vic. & Sussex) b Oct. 5, 1963
*Doggart, G. H. G. (CU & Sussex; Pres. MCC 1981-82) b July 18, 1925
*D'Oliveira, B. L. (Worcs; *CY 1967*) b Oct. 4, 1931
D'Oliveira, D. B. (Worcs) b Oct. 19, 1960
*Dollery, H. E. (Warwicks & Wgtn; *CY 1952*) b Oct. 14, 1914, d Jan. 20, 1987
*Dolphin, A. (Yorks) b Dec. 24, 1885, d Oct. 23, 1942
*Donald, A. A. (OFS & Warwicks; *CY 1992*) b Oct. 20, 1966
*Donnan, H. (NSW) b Nov. 12, 1864, d Aug. 13, 1956
*Donnelly, M. P. (Wgtn, Cant., OU, Middx & Warwicks; *CY 1948*) b Oct. 17, 1917
*Dooland, B. (S. Aust. & Notts; *CY 1955*) b Nov. 1, 1923, d Sept. 8, 1980
Dorrinton, W. (Kent & All-England) b April 29, 1809, d Nov. 8, 1848
Dorset, 3rd Duke of (Kent) b March 24, 1745, d July 19, 1799
*Doshi, D. R. (Bengal, Notts, Warwicks & S'tra) b Dec. 22, 1947
*Douglas, J. W. H. T. (Essex; *CY 1915*) b Sept. 3, 1882, d Dec. 19, 1930
Douglas, M. W. (C. Dist. & Wgtn) b Oct. 20, 1968
*Doull, S. B. (N. Dist.) b Aug. 6, 1969
Dovey, R. R. (Kent) b July 18, 1920, d Dec. 27, 1974
*Dowe, U. G. (Jam.) b March 29, 1949
*Dower, R. R. (E. Prov.) b June 4, 1876, d Sept. 15, 1964
*Dowling, G. T. (Cant.) b March 4, 1937
*Downton, P. R. (Kent & Middx) b April 4, 1957
Drakes, V. C. (B'dos & Sussex) b Aug. 5, 1969
*Draper, R. G. (E. Prov & Griq. W.) b Dec. 24, 1926
*Dravid, R. S. (Karn.) b Jan. 11, 1973
Dredge, C. H. (Som) b Aug. 4, 1954
*Druce, N. F. (CU & Surrey; *CY 1898*) b Jan. 1, 1875, d Oct. 27, 1954
Drybrough, C. D. (OU & Middx) b Aug. 31, 1938
*D'Souza, A. (Kar., Peshawar & PIA) b Jan. 17, 1939
*Ducat, A. (Surrey; *CY 1920*) b Feb. 16, 1886, d July 23, 1942
*Duckworth, C. A. R. (Natal & Rhod.) b March 22, 1933
*Duckworth, G. (Lancs; *CY 1929*) b May 9, 1901, d Jan. 5, 1966
Dudleston, B. (Leics, Glos & Rhod.; Test umpire) b July 16, 1945
Duers, K. G. (Mash.) b June 30, 1960
*Duff, R. A. (NSW) b Aug. 17, 1878, d Dec. 13, 1911
*Dujon, P. J. L. (Jam.; *CY 1989*) b May 28, 1956
*Duleepsinhji, K. S. (CU & Sussex; *CY 1930*) b June 13, 1905, d Dec. 5, 1959
*Dumbrill, R. (Natal & Tvl) b Nov. 19, 1938
*Duminy, J. P. (OU, W. Prov. & Tvl) b Dec. 16, 1897, d Jan. 31, 1980
*Duncan, J. R. F. (Qld & Vic.) b March 25, 1944
*Dunell, O. R. (E. Prov.) b July 15, 1856, d Oct. 21, 1929
*Dunning, J. A. (Otago & OU) b Feb. 6, 1903, d June 24, 1971
*Dunusinghe, C. I. (Ant.) b Oct. 19, 1970
*Du Preez, J. H. (Rhod. & Zimb.) b Nov. 14, 1942
*Durani, S. A. (S'tra, Guj. & Raja.) b Dec. 11, 1934

*Durston, F. J. (Middx) b July 11, 1893, d April 8, 1965
*Du Toit, J. F. (SA) b April 5, 1868, d July 10, 1909
Dye, J. C. J. (Kent, Northants & E. Prov.) b July 24, 1942
*Dyer, D. V. (Natal) b May 2, 1914, d June 18, 1990
*Dyer, G. C. (NSW) b March 16, 1959
*Dymock, G. (Qld) b July 21, 1945
Dyson, A. H. (Glam) b July 10, 1905, d June 7, 1978
Dyson, Jack (Lancs) b July 8, 1934
*Dyson, John (NSW) b June 11, 1954

*Eady, C. J. (Tas.) b Oct. 29, 1870, d Dec. 20, 1945
Eagar, E. D. R. (OU, Glos & Hants) b Dec. 8, 1917, d Sept. 13, 1977
Ealham, A. G. E. (Kent) b Aug. 30, 1944
*Ealham, M. A. (Kent) b Aug. 27, 1969
East, D. E. (Essex) b July 27, 1959
East, R. E. (Essex) b June 20, 1947
Eastman, L. C. (Essex & Otago) b June 3, 1897, d April 17, 1941
*Eastwood, K. H. (Vic.) b Nov. 23, 1935
*Ebeling, H. I. (Vic.) b Jan. 1, 1905, d Jan. 12, 1980
Eckersley, P. T. (Lancs) b July 2, 1904, d Aug. 13, 1940
*Edgar, B. A. (Wgtn) b Nov. 23, 1956
Edinburgh, HRH Duke of (Pres. MCC 1948-49, 1974-75) b June 10, 1921
Edmeades, B. E. A. (Essex) b Sept. 17, 1941
*Edmonds, P. H. (CU, Middx & E. Prov.) b March 8, 1951
Edrich, B. R. (Kent & Glam) b Aug. 18, 1922
Edrich, E. H. (Lancs) b March 27, 1914, d July 9, 1993
Edrich, G. A. (Lancs) b July 13, 1918
*Edrich, J. H. (Surrey; *CY 1966*) b June 21, 1937
*Edrich, W. J. (Middx; *CY 1940*) b March 26, 1916, d April 24, 1986
*Edwards, G. N. (C. Dist.) b May 27, 1955
*Edwards, J. D. (Vic.) b June 12, 1862, d July 31, 1911
Edwards, M. J. (CU & Surrey) b March 1, 1940
*Edwards, R. (W. Aust. & NSW) b Dec. 1, 1942
*Edwards, R. M. (B'dos) b June 3, 1940
*Edwards, W. J. (W. Aust.) b Dec. 23, 1949
*Ehtesham-ud-Din (Lahore, Punjab, PIA, NBP & UBL) b Sept. 4, 1950
*Eksteen, C. E. (Tvl) b Dec. 2, 1966
*Elgie, M. K. (Natal) b March 6, 1933
Elliott, C. S. (Derbys; Test umpire) b April 24, 1912
Elliott, Harold (Lancs; Test umpire) b June 15, 1904, d April 15, 1969
Elliott, Harry (Derbys) b Nov. 2, 1891, d Feb. 2, 1976
*Ellison, R. M. (Kent & Tas.; *CY 1986*) b Sept. 21, 1959
*Emburey, J. E. (Middx, W. Prov. & Northants; *CY 1984*) b Aug. 20, 1952
*Emery, P. A. (NSW) b June 25, 1964
*Emery, R. W. G. (Auck. & Cant.) b March 28, 1915, d Dec. 18, 1982
*Emery, S. H. (NSW) b Oct. 16, 1885, d Jan. 7, 1967
*Emmett, G. M. (Glos) b Dec. 2, 1912, d Dec. 18, 1976
*Emmett, T. (Yorks) b Sept. 3, 1841, d June 30, 1904
*Endean, W. R. (Tvl) b May 31, 1924
*Engineer, F. M. (Bombay & Lancs) b Feb. 25, 1938
Enthoven, H. J. (CU & Middx) b June 4, 1903, d June 29, 1975
Essop-Adam, E. A. (Mash.) b Nov. 16, 1968
*Evans, A. J. (OU, Hants & Kent) b May 1, 1889, d Sept. 18, 1960
Evans, C. N. (Mash. & Mat.) b Nov. 29, 1969
Evans, D. G. L. (Glam; Test umpire) b July 27, 1933, d March 25, 1990
*Evans, E. (NSW) b March 26, 1849, d July 2, 1921
Evans, K. P. (Notts) b Sept. 10, 1963
*Evans, T. G. (Kent; *CY 1951*) b Aug. 18, 1920
Evershed, Sir Sydney H. (Derbys) b Jan. 13, 1861, d March 7, 1937
Every, T. (Glam) b Dec. 19, 1909, d Jan. 20, 1990
Eyre, T. J. P. (Derbys) b Oct. 17, 1939

*Fagg, A. E. (Kent; Test umpire) b June 18, 1915, d Sept. 13, 1977
*Fairbrother, N. H. (Lancs & Tvl) b Sept. 9, 1963
*Fairfax, A. G. (NSW) b June 16, 1906, d May 17, 1955
Fairservice, W. J. (Kent) b May 16, 1881, d June 26, 1971
*Fane, F. L. (OU & Essex) b April 27, 1875, d Nov. 27, 1960
*Farnes, K. (CU & Essex; *CY 1939*) b July 8, 1911, d Oct. 20, 1941
*Farooq Hamid (Lahore & PIA) b March 3, 1945
*Farrer, W. S. (Border) b Dec. 8, 1936
*Farrimond, W. (Lancs) b May 23, 1903, d Nov. 14, 1979
*Farrukh Zaman (Peshawar, NWFP, Punjab & MCB) b April 2, 1956
*Faulkner, G. A. (Tvl) b Dec. 17, 1881, d Sept. 10, 1930
*Favell, L. E. (S. Aust.) b Oct. 6, 1929, d June 14, 1987
*Fazal Mahmood (N. Ind., Punjab & Lahore; *CY 1955*) b Feb. 18, 1927

Fearnley, C. D. (Worcs; bat-maker) b April 12, 1940
Featherstone, N. G. (Tvl, N. Tvl, Middx & Glam) b Aug. 20, 1949
'Felix', N. (Wanostrocht) (Kent, Surrey & All-England) b Oct. 4, 1804, d Sept. 3, 1876
*Fellows-Smith, J. P. (OU, Tvl & Northants) b Feb. 3, 1932
Feltham, M. A. (Surrey & Middx) b June 26, 1963
Felton, N. A. (Som & Northants) b Oct. 24, 1960
*Fender, P. G. H. (Sussex & Surrey; *CY 1915*) b Aug. 22, 1892, d June 15, 1985
*Ferguson, W. (T/T) b Dec. 14, 1917, d Feb. 23, 1961
*Fernandes, M. P. (BG) b Aug. 12, 1897, d May 8, 1981
Fernando, E. R. (SL) b Feb. 22, 1944
*Fernando, E. R. N. S. (SLAF) b Dec. 19, 1955
Fernando, T. L. (Colts & BRC) b Dec. 27, 1962
Fernando, U. N. K. (SSC) b March 10, 1970
Ferreira, A. M. (N. Tvl & Warwicks) b April 13, 1955
**Ferris, J. J. (NSW, Glos & S. Aust.; *CY 1889*) b May 21, 1867, d Nov. 21, 1900
*Fichardt, C. G. (OFS) b March 20, 1870, d May 30, 1923
Fiddling, K. (Yorks & Northants) b Oct. 13, 1917, d June 19, 1992
Field, F. E. (Warwicks) b Sept. 23, 1874, d Aug. 25, 1934
*Fielder, A. (Kent; *CY 1907*) b July 19, 1877, d Aug. 30, 1949
*Findlay, T. M. (Comb. Is. & Windwards) b Oct. 19, 1943
Findlay, W. (OU & Lancs; Sec. Surrey CCC 1907-19; Sec. MCC 1926-36) b June 22, 1880, d June 19, 1953
*Fingleton, J. H. (NSW) b April 28, 1908, d Nov. 22, 1981
*Finlason, C. E. (Tvl & Griq. W.) b Feb. 19, 1860, d July 31, 1917
Finney, R. J. (Derbys) b Aug. 2, 1960
Firth, Canon J. D'E. E. (Winchester, OU & Notts; *CY 1918*) b Jan. 21, 1900, d Sept. 21, 1957
Firth, J. (Yorks & Leics) b June 27, 1917, d Sept. 7, 1981
*Fisher, F. E. (Wgtn & C. Dist.) b July 28, 1924, d June 19, 1996
*Fishlock, L. B. (Surrey; *CY 1947*) b Jan. 2, 1907, d June 26, 1986
Fishwick, T. S. (Warwicks) b July 24, 1876, d Feb. 21, 1950
Fitzgerald, R. A. (CU & Middx; Sec. MCC 1863-76) b Oct. 1, 1834, d Oct. 28, 1881
Fitzroy-Newdegate, Hon. J. M. (Northants) b March 20, 1897, d May 7, 1976
*Flavell, J. A. (Worcs; *CY 1965*) b May 15, 1929
*Fleetwood-Smith, L. O'B. (Vic.) b March 30, 1908, d March 16, 1971
*Fleming, D. W. (Vic.) b April 24, 1970
Fleming, M. V. (Kent) b Dec. 12, 1964
*Fleming, S. P. (Cant.) b April 1, 1973
Fletcher, D. A. G. (Rhod. & Zimb.) b Sept. 27, 1948
Fletcher, D. G. W. (Surrey) b July 6, 1924
*Fletcher, K. W. R. (Essex; *CY 1974*) b May 20, 1944
Fletcher, S. D. (Yorks & Lancs) b June 8, 1964
*Floquet, C. E. (Tvl) b Nov. 3, 1884, d Nov. 22, 1963
*Flower, A. (Mash.) b April 28, 1968
*Flower, G. W. (Mash.) b Dec. 20, 1970
*Flowers, W. (Notts) b Dec. 7, 1856, d Nov. 1, 1926
*Foley, H. (Wgtn) b Jan. 28, 1906, d Oct. 16, 1948
Folley, I. (Lancs & Derbys) b Jan. 9, 1963, d Aug. 30, 1993
Forbes, C. (Notts) b Aug. 9, 1936
*Ford, F. G. J. (CU & Middx) b Dec. 14, 1866, d Feb. 7, 1940
Fordham, A. (Northants) b Nov. 9, 1964
Foreman, D. J. (W. Prov. & Sussex) b Feb. 1, 1933
*Foster, F. R. (Warwicks; *CY 1912*) b Jan. 31, 1889, d May 3, 1958
Foster, G. N. (OU, Worcs & Kent) b Oct. 16, 1884, d Aug. 11, 1971
Foster, H. K. (OU & Worcs; *CY 1911*) b Oct. 30, 1873, d June 23, 1950
Foster, M. K. (Worcs) b Jan. 1, 1889, d Dec. 3, 1940
*Foster, M. L. C. (Jam.) b May 9, 1943
*Foster, N. A. (Essex & Tvl; *CY 1988*) b May 6, 1962
*Foster, R. E. (OU & Worcs; *CY 1901*) b April 16, 1878, d May 13, 1914
*Fothergill, A. J. (Som) b Aug. 26, 1854, d Aug. 1, 1932
Fowke, G. H. S. (Leics) b Oct. 14, 1880, d June 24, 1946
*Fowler, G. (Lancs & Durham) b April 20, 1957
*Francis, B. C. (NSW & Essex) b Feb. 18, 1948
Francis, D. A. (Glam) b Nov. 29, 1953
*Francis, G. N. (B'dos) b Dec. 11, 1897, d Jan. 7, 1942
*Francis, H. H. (Glos & W. Prov.) b May 26, 1868, d Jan. 7, 1936
Francke, F. M. (SL & Qld) b March 29, 1941
*Francois, C. M. (Griq. W.) b June 20, 1897, d May 26, 1944
*Frank, C. N. (Tvl) b Jan. 27, 1891, d Dec. 25, 1961
*Frank, W. H. B. (SA) b Nov. 23, 1872, d Feb. 16, 1945
*Franklin, T. J. (Auck.) b March 18, 1962

*Fraser, A. R. C. (Middx; *CY 1996*) b Aug. 8, 1965
*Frederick, M. (B'dos, Derbys & Jam.) b May 6, 1927
*Fredericks, R. C. (†Guyana & Glam; *CY 1974*) b Nov. 11, 1942
*Freeman, A. P. (Kent; *CY 1923*) b May 17, 1888, d Jan. 28, 1965
*Freeman, D. L. (Wgtn) b Sept. 8, 1914, d May 31, 1994
*Freeman, E. W. (S. Aust.) b July 13, 1944
Freeman, J. R. (Essex) b Sept. 3, 1883, d Aug. 8, 1958
*Freer, F. W. (Vic.) b Dec. 4, 1915
*French, B. N. (Notts) b Aug. 13, 1959
Frost, G. (Notts) b Jan. 15, 1947
*Fry, C. B. (OU, Sussex & Hants; *CY 1895*) b April 25, 1872, d Sept. 7, 1956
*Fuller, E. R. H. (W. Prov.) b Aug. 2, 1931
*Fuller, R. L. (Jam.) b Jan. 30, 1913, d May 3, 1987
*Fullerton, G. M. (Tvl) b Dec. 8, 1922
*Funston, K. J. (NE Tvl, OFS & Tvl) b Dec. 3, 1925
*Furlonge, H. A. (T/T) b June 19, 1934

Gabriel, R. S. (T/T) b June 5, 1952
*Gadkari, C. V. (M'tra & Ind. Serv.) b Feb. 3, 1928
*Gaekwad, A. D. (Baroda) b Sept. 23, 1952
*Gaekwad, D. K. (Baroda) b Oct. 27, 1928
*Gaekwad, H. G. (†M. Pradesh) b Aug. 29, 1923
Gale, R. A. (Middx) b Dec. 10, 1933
*Gallian, J. E. R. (Lancs & OU) b June 25, 1971
*Gallichan, N. (Wgtn) b June 3, 1906, d March 25, 1969
Gamage, J. C. (Galle) b April 17, 1964
*Gamsy, D. (Natal) b Feb. 17, 1940
*Gandotra, A. (Delhi & Bengal) b Nov. 24, 1948
*Ganguly, S. C. (Bengal) b July 8, 1972
*Gannon, J. B. (W. Aust.) b Feb. 8, 1947
*Ganteaume, A. G. (T/T) b Jan. 22, 1921
Gard, T. (Som) b June 2, 1957
Gardner, F. C. (Warwicks) b June 4, 1922, d Jan. 12, 1979
Gardner, L. R. (Leics) b Feb. 23, 1934
Garland-Wells, H. M. (OU & Surrey) b Nov. 14, 1907, d May 28, 1993
Garlick, R. G. (Lancs & Northants) b April 11, 1917, d May 16, 1988
*Garner, J. (B'dos, Som & S. Aust.; *CY 1980*) b Dec. 16, 1952
Garnham, M. A. (Glos, Leics & Essex) b Aug. 20, 1960
*Garrett, T. W. (NSW) b July 26, 1858, d Aug. 6, 1943
*Gaskin, B. B. M. (BG) b March 21, 1908, d May 1, 1979
*Gatting, M. W. (Middx; *CY 1984*) b June 6, 1957
*Gaunt, R. A. (W. Aust. & Vic.) b Feb. 26, 1934
*Gavaskar, S. M. (Bombay & Som; *CY 1980*) b July 10, 1949
*Gay, L. H. (CU, Hants & Som) b March 24, 1871, d Nov. 1, 1949
*Geary, G. (Leics; *CY 1927*) b July 9, 1893, d March 6, 1981
*Gedye, S. G. (Auck.) b May 2, 1929
*Gehrs, D. R. A. (S. Aust.) b Nov. 29, 1880, d June 25, 1953
*Germon, L. K. (Cant.) b Nov. 4, 1968
Ghai, R. S. (Punjab) b June 12, 1960
*Ghavri, K. D. (S'tra & Bombay) b Feb. 28, 1951
*Ghazali, M. E. Z. (M'tra & Pak. Serv.) b June 15, 1924
*Ghorpade. J. M. (Baroda) b Oct. 2, 1930, d March 29, 1978
*Ghulam Abbas (Kar., NBP & PIA) b May 1, 1947
*Ghulam Ahmed (H'bad) b July 4, 1922
Ghulam Ali (Kar. & PACO) b Sept. 8, 1966
*Gibb, P. A. (CU, Scotland, Yorks & Essex) b July 11, 1913, d Dec. 7, 1977
Gibbons, H. H. (Worcs) b Oct. 10, 1904, d Feb. 16, 1973
*Gibbs, G. L. (BG) b Dec. 27, 1925, d Feb. 21, 1979
*Gibbs, L. R. (†Guyana, S. Aust. & Warwicks; *CY 1972*) b Sept. 29, 1934
Gibbs, P. J. K. (OU & Derbys) b Aug. 17, 1944
Gibson, C. H. (Eton, CU & Sussex; *CY 1918*) b Aug. 23, 1900, d Dec. 31, 1976
Gibson, D. (Surrey) b May 1, 1936
*Gibson, O. D. (B'dos, Border & Glam) b March 16, 1969
*Giffen, G. (S. Aust.; *CY 1894*) b March 27, 1859, d Nov. 29, 1927
*Giffen, W. F. (S. Aust.) b Sept. 20, 1861, d June 29, 1949
*Gifford, N. (Worcs & Warwicks; *CY 1975*) b March 30, 1940
*Gilbert, D. R. (NSW, Tas. & Glos) b Dec. 29, 1960
*Gilchrist, R. (Jam. & H'bad) b June 28, 1934
Giles, R. J. (Notts) b Oct. 17, 1919
Gilhouley, K. (Yorks & Notts) b Aug. 8, 1934
*Gillespie, S. R. (Auck.) b March 2, 1957
Gilliat, R. M. C. (OU & Hants) b May 20, 1944
*Gilligan, A. E. R. (CU, Surrey & Sussex; *CY 1924;* Pres. MCC 1967-68) b Dec. 23, 1894, d Sept. 5, 1976
*Gilligan, A. H. H. (Sussex) b June 29, 1896, d May 5, 1978
Gilligan, F. W. (OU & Essex) b Sept. 20, 1893, d May 4, 1960

Gillingham, Canon F. H. (Essex) b Sept. 6, 1875, d April 1, 1953
*Gilmour, G. J. (NSW) b June 26, 1951
*Gimblett, H. (Som; *CY 1953*) b Oct. 19, 1914, d March 30, 1978
*Gladstone, G (*see* Marais, G. G.)
*Gladwin, Cliff (Derbys) b April 3, 1916, d April 10, 1988
*Gleeson, J. W. (NSW & E. Prov.) b March 14, 1938
*Gleeson, R. A. (E. Prov.) b Dec. 6, 1873, d Sept. 27, 1919
Glover, A. C. S. (Warwicks) b April 19, 1872, d May 22, 1949
*Glover, G. K. (Kimberley & Griq. W.) b May 13, 1870, d Nov. 15, 1938
*Goddard, J. D. C. (B'dos) b April 21, 1919, d Aug. 26, 1987
*Goddard, T. L. (Natal & NE Tvl) b Aug. 1, 1931
*Goddard, T. W. (Glos; *CY 1938*) b Oct. 1, 1900, d May 22, 1966
Goel, R. (Patiala & Haryana) b Sept. 29, 1942
*Gomes, H. A. (T/T & Middx; *CY 1985*) b July 13, 1953
*Gomez, G. E. (T/T) b Oct. 10, 1919, d Aug. 6, 1996
*Gooch, G. A. (Essex & W. Prov.; *CY 1980*) b July 23, 1953
Goodwin, K. (Lancs) b June 25, 1938
Goodwin, T. J. (Leics) b Jan. 22, 1929
Goonatillake, F. R. M. de S. (SL) b Aug. 15, 1951
*Goonatillake, H. M. (SL) b Aug. 16, 1952
Goonesena, G. (Ceylon, Notts, CU & NSW) b Feb. 16, 1931
*Gopalan, M. J. (Madras) b June 6, 1909
*Gopinath, C. D. (Madras) b March 1, 1930
*Gordon, N. (Tvl) b Aug. 6, 1911
Gore, A. C. (Eton & Army; *CY 1919*) b May 14, 1900, d June 7, 1990
*Gough, D. (Yorks) b Sept. 18, 1970
Gould, I. J. (Middx, Auck. & Sussex) b Aug. 19, 1957
*Gover, A. R. (Surrey; *CY 1937; oldest surviving CY*) b Feb. 29, 1908
*Gower, D. I. (Leics & Hants; *CY 1979*) b April 1, 1957
Gowrie, 1st Lord (Pres. MCC 1948-49) b July 6, 1872, d May 2, 1955
Grace, C. B. (London County; son of W. G.) b March 1882, d June 6, 1938
*Grace, Dr E. M. (Glos; brother of W. G.) b Nov. 28, 1841, d May 20, 1911
*Grace, G. F. (Glos; brother of W. G.) b Dec. 13, 1850, d Sept. 22, 1880
Grace, Dr Henry (Glos; brother of W. G.) b Jan. 31, 1833, d Nov. 15, 1895
Grace, Dr H. M. (father of W. G.) b Feb. 21, 1808, d Dec. 23, 1871
Grace, Mrs H. M. (mother of W. G.) b July 18, 1812, d July 25, 1884
*Grace, Dr W. G. (Glos; *CY 1896*) b July 18, 1848, d Oct. 23, 1915
Grace, W. G., jun. (CU & Glos; son of W. G.) b July 6, 1874, d March 2, 1905
Graf, S. F. (Vic., W. Aust. & Hants) b May 19, 1957
*Graham, H. (Vic. & Otago) b Nov. 22, 1870, d Feb. 7, 1911
Graham, J. N. (Kent) b May 8, 1943
*Graham, R. (W. Prov.) b Sept. 16, 1877, d April 21, 1946
*Grant, G. C. (CU, T/T & Rhod.) b May 9, 1907, d Oct. 26, 1978
*Grant, R. S. (CU & T/T) b Dec. 15, 1909, d Oct. 18, 1977
Graveney, D. A. (Glos, Som & Durham) b Jan. 2, 1953
Graveney, J. K. (Glos) b Dec. 16, 1924
*Graveney, T. W. (Glos, Worcs & Qld; *CY 1953*) b June 16, 1927
Graves, P. J. (Sussex & OFS) b May 19, 1946
*Gray, A. H. (T/T, Surrey & W. Tvl) b May 23, 1963
*Gray, E. J. (Wgtn) b Nov. 18, 1954
Gray, J. R. (Hants) b May 19, 1926
Gray, L. H. (Middx) b Dec. 15, 1915, d Jan. 3, 1983
*Greatbatch, M. J. (C. Dist.) b Dec. 11, 1963
Green, A. M. (Sussex & OFS) b May 28, 1960
Green, D. M. (OU, Lancs & Glos; *CY 1969*) b Nov. 10, 1939
Green, Major L. (Lancs) b Feb. 1, 1890, d March 2, 1963
*Greenhough, T. (Lancs) b Nov. 9, 1931
*Greenidge, A. E. (B'dos) b Aug. 20, 1956
*Greenidge, C. G. (Hants & B'dos; *CY 1977*) b May 1, 1951
*Greenidge, G. A. (B'dos & Sussex) b May 26, 1948
Greensmith, W. T. (Essex) b Aug. 16, 1930
*Greenwood, A. (Yorks) b Aug. 20, 1847, d Feb. 12, 1889
Greetham, C. (Som) b Aug. 28, 1936
*Gregory, D. W. (NSW; first Australian captain) b April 15, 1845, d Aug. 4, 1919
*Gregory, E. J. (NSW) b May 29, 1839, d April 22, 1899
*Gregory, J. M. (NSW; *CY 1922*) b Aug. 14, 1895, d Aug. 7, 1973
*Gregory, R. G. (Vic.) b Feb. 28, 1916, d June 10, 1942
Gregory, R. J. (Surrey) b Aug. 26, 1902, d Oct. 6, 1973
*Gregory, S. E. (NSW; *CY 1897*) b April 14, 1870, d Aug. 1, 1929
*Greig, A. W. (Border, E. Prov. & Sussex; *CY 1975*) b Oct. 6, 1946
*Greig, I. A. (CU, Border, Sussex & Surrey) b Dec. 8, 1955
*Grell, M. G. (T/T) b Dec. 18, 1899, d Jan. 11, 1976

*Grieve, B. A. F. (Eng.) b May 28, 1864, d Nov. 19, 1917
Grieves, K. J. (NSW & Lancs) b Aug. 27, 1925, d Jan. 3, 1992
*Grieveson, R. E. (Tvl) b Aug. 24, 1909
*Griffin, G. M. (Natal & Rhod.) b June 12, 1939
*Griffith, C. C. (B'dos; *CY 1964*) b Dec. 14, 1938
Griffith, G. ("Ben") (Surrey & Utd England XI) b Dec. 20, 1833, d May 3, 1879
*Griffith, H. C. (B'dos) b Dec. 1, 1893, d March 18, 1980
Griffith, M. G. (CU & Sussex) b Nov. 25, 1943
*Griffith, S. C. (CU, Surrey & Sussex; Sec. MCC 1962-74; Pres. MCC 1979-80) b June 16, 1914, d April 7, 1993
Griffiths, B. J. (Northants) b June 13, 1949
Griffiths, W. H. (later Rt Hon. The Lord) (CU & Glam; Pres. MCC 1990-91) b Sept. 26, 1923
*Grimmett, C. V. (Wgtn, Vic., & S. Aust.; *CY 1931*) b Dec. 25, 1891, d May 2, 1980
*Groube, T. U. (Vic.) b Sept. 2, 1857, d Aug. 5, 1927
*Grout, A. T. W. (Qld) b March 30, 1927, d Nov. 9, 1968
Grove, C. W. (Warwicks & Worcs) b Dec. 16, 1912, d Feb. 15, 1982
Grundy, James (Notts & Utd England XI) b March 5, 1824, d Nov. 24, 1873
*Guard, G. M. (Bombay & Guj.) b Dec. 12, 1925, d March 13, 1978
*Guest, C. E. J. (Vic. & W. Aust.) b Oct. 7, 1937
*Guha, S. (Bengal) b Jan. 31, 1946
**Guillen, S. C. (T/T & Cant.) b Sept. 24, 1924
**Gul Mahomed (N. Ind., Baroda, H'bad, Punjab & Lahore) b Oct. 15, 1921, d May 8, 1992
*Gunasekera, Y. (SL) b Nov. 8, 1957
Gunawardene, A. A. W. (SSC) b March 31, 1969
*Guneratne, R. P. W. (Nomads) b Jan. 26, 1962
*Gunn, G. (Notts; *CY 1914*) b June 13, 1879, d June 29, 1958
Gunn, G. V. (Notts) b June 21, 1905, d Oct. 14, 1957
*Gunn, J. (Notts; *CY 1904*) b July 19, 1876, d Aug. 21, 1963
*Gunn, W. (Notts; *CY 1890*) b Dec. 4, 1858, d Jan. 29, 1921
*Gupte, B. P. (Bombay, Bengal & Ind. Rlwys) b Aug. 30, 1934
*Gupte, S. P. (Bombay, Bengal, Raja. & T/T) b Dec. 11, 1929
*Gursharan Singh (Punjab) b March 8, 1863
*Gurusinha, A. P. (SSC & NCC) b Sept. 16, 1966
*Guy, J. W. (C. Dist., Wgtn, Northants, Cant., Otago & N. Dist.) b Aug. 29, 1934

Haafiz Shahid (WAPDA) b May 10, 1963
Hadlee, B. G. (Cant.) b Dec. 14, 1941
*Hadlee, D. R. (Cant.) b Jan. 6, 1948
*Hadlee, Sir Richard J. (Cant., Notts & Tas.; *CY 1982*) b July 3, 1951
*Hadlee, W. A. (Cant. & Otago) b June 4, 1915
*Hafeez, A. (*see* Kardar)
*Haig, N. E. (Middx) b Dec. 12, 1887, d Oct. 27, 1966
*Haigh, S. (Yorks; *CY 1901*) b March 19, 1871, d Feb. 27, 1921
Halfyard, D. J. (Kent & Notts) b April 3, 1931, d Aug. 23, 1996
*Hall, A. E. (Tvl & Lancs) b Jan. 23, 1896, d Jan. 1, 1964
*Hall, G. G. (NE Tvl & E. Prov.) b May 24, 1938, d June 26, 1987
Hall, I. W. (Derbys) b Dec. 27, 1939
Hall, L. (Yorks; *CY 1890*) b Nov. 1, 1852, d Nov. 19, 1915
*Hall, W. W. (B'dos, T/T & Qld) b Sept. 12, 1937
Hallam, A. W. (Lancs & Notts; *CY 1908*) b Nov. 12, 1869, d July 24, 1940
Hallam, M. R. (Leics) b Sept. 10, 1931
Halliday, H. (Yorks) b Feb. 9, 1920, d Aug. 27, 1967
*Halliwell, E. A. (Tvl & Middx; *CY 1905*) b Sept. 7, 1864, d Oct. 2, 1919
*Hallows, C. (Lancs; *CY 1928*) b April 4, 1895, d Nov. 10, 1972
Hallows, J. (Lancs; *CY 1905*) b Nov. 14, 1873, d May 20, 1910
*Halse, C. G. (Natal) b Feb. 28, 1935
*Hamence, R. A. (S. Aust.) b Nov. 25, 1915
Hamer, A. (Yorks & Derbys) b Dec. 8, 1916, d Nov. 3, 1993
*Hammond, J. R. (S. Aust.) b April 19, 1950
*Hammond, W. R. (Glos; *CY 1928*) b June 19, 1903, d July 1, 1965
*Hampshire, J. H. (Yorks, Derbys & Tas.; Test umpire) b Feb. 10, 1941
*Hands, P. A. M. (W. Prov.) b March 18, 1890, d April 27, 1951
*Hands, R. H. M. (W. Prov.) b July 26, 1888, d April 20, 1918
*Hanif Mohammad (B'pur, Kar. & PIA; *CY 1968*) b Dec. 21, 1934
*Hanley, M. A. (Border & W. Prov.) b Nov. 10, 1918
*Hanumant Singh (M. Pradesh & Raja.) b March 29, 1939
Harden, R. J. (Som & C. Dist.) b Aug. 16, 1965
Hardie, B. R. (Scotland & Essex) b Jan. 14, 1950
*Hardikar, M. S. (Bombay) b Feb. 8, 1936, d Feb. 4, 1995
*Hardinge, H. T. W. (Kent; *CY 1915*) b Feb. 25, 1886, d May 8, 1965
*Hardstaff, J. (Notts; Test umpire) b Nov. 9, 1882, d April 2, 1947

*Hardstaff, J., jun. (Notts & Auck.; *CY 1938*) b July 3, 1911, d Jan. 1, 1990
Hardy, J. J. E. (Hants, Som, W. Prov. & Glos) b Oct. 2, 1960
*Harford, N. S. (C. Dist. & Auck.) b Aug. 30, 1930, d March 30, 1981
*Harford, R. I. (Auck.) b May 30, 1936
Hargreave, S. (Warwicks) b Sept. 22, 1875, d Jan. 1, 1929
Harman, R. (Surrey) b Dec. 28, 1941
*Haroon Rashid (Kar., Sind, NBP, PIA & UBL) b March 25, 1953
*Harper, R. A. (Guyana & Northants) b March 17, 1963
*Harris, 4th Lord (OU & Kent; Pres. MCC 1895) b Feb. 3, 1851, d March 24, 1932
Harris, C. B. (Notts) b Dec. 6, 1907, d Aug. 8, 1954
*Harris, C. Z. (Cant.) b Nov. 20, 1969
Harris, David (Hants & All-England) b 1755, d May 19, 1803
Harris, M. J. (Middx, Notts, E. Prov. & Wgtn) b May 25, 1944
*Harris, P. G. Z. (Cant.) b July 18, 1927, d Dec. 1, 1991
*Harris, R. M. (Auck.) b July 27, 1933
*Harris, T. A. (Griq. W. & Tvl) b Aug. 27, 1916, d March 7, 1993
Harrison, L. (Hants) b June 8, 1922
*Harry, J. (Vic.) b Aug. 1, 1857, d Oct. 27, 1919
*Hart, M. N. (N. Dist.) b May 16, 1972
Hart, R. T. (C. Dist. & Wgtn) b Nov. 7, 1961
*Hartigan, G. P. D. (Border) b Dec. 30, 1884, d Jan. 7, 1955
*Hartigan, R. J. (NSW & Qld) b Dec. 12, 1879, d June 7, 1958
*Hartkopf, A. E. V. (Vic.) b Dec. 28, 1889, d May 20, 1968
*Hartland, B. R. (Cant.) b Oct. 22, 1966
Hartley, A. (Lancs; *CY 1911*) b April 11, 1879, d Oct. 9, 1918
*Hartley, J. C. (OU & Sussex) b Nov. 15, 1874, d March 8, 1963
Hartley, P. J. (Warwicks & Yorks) b April 18, 1960
Hartley, S. N. (Yorks & OFS) b March 18, 1956
Harvey, J. F. (Derbys) b Sept. 27, 1939
*Harvey, M. R. (Vic.) b April 29, 1918, d March 20, 1995
Harvey, P. F. (Notts) b Jan. 15, 1923
*Harvey, R. L. (Natal) b Sept. 14, 1911
*Harvey, R. N. (Vic. & NSW; *CY 1954*) b Oct. 8, 1928
Hasan Jamil, (Kalat, Kar., Pak. Us & PIA) b July 25, 1952
*Haseeb Ahsan (Peshawar, Pak. Us, Kar. & PIA) b July 15, 1939
*Haslam, M. J. (Auck.) b Sept. 26, 1972
Hassan, B. (Notts) b March 24, 1944
*Hassett, A. L. (Vic.; *CY 1949*) b Aug. 28, 1913, d June 16, 1993
*Hastings, B. F. (Wgtn, C. Dist. & Cant.) b March 23, 1940
*Hathorn, C. M. H. (Tvl) b April 7, 1878, d May 17, 1920
*Hathurusinghe, U. C. (TU) b Sept. 13, 1968
*Hawke, 7th Lord (CU & Yorks; *CY 1909;* Pres. MCC 1914-18) b Aug. 16, 1860, d Oct. 10, 1938
*Hawke, N. J. N. (W. Aust., S. Aust. & Tas.) b June 27, 1939
Hawker, Sir Cyril (Essex; Pres. MCC 1970-71) b July 21, 1900, d Feb. 22, 1991
Hawkins, D. G. (Glos) b May 18, 1935
*Hayden, M. L. (Qld) b Oct. 29, 1971
*Hayes, E. G. (Surrey & Leics; *CY 1907*) b Nov. 6, 1876, d Dec. 2, 1953
*Hayes, F. C. (Lancs) b Dec. 6, 1946
*Hayes, J. A. (Auck. & Cant.) b Jan. 11, 1927
Hayes, R. L. (N. Dist.) b May 9, 1971
Haygarth, A. (Sussex; Historian) b Aug. 4, 1825, d May 1, 1903
Hayhurst, A. N. (Lancs & Som) b Nov. 23, 1962
*Haynes, D. L. (B'dos, Middx & W. Prov.; *CY 1991*) b Feb. 15, 1956
Haynes, R. C. (Jam.) b Nov. 11, 1964
Hayward, T. (Cambs. & All-England) b March 21, 1835, d July 21, 1876
*Hayward, T. W. (Surrey; *CY 1895*) b March 29, 1871, d July 19, 1939
*Hazare, V. S. (M'tra, C. Ind. & Baroda) b March 11, 1915
Hazell, H. L. (Som) b Sept. 30, 1909, d March 31, 1990
Hazlerigg, Sir A. G. Bt (later 1st Lord) (Leics) b Nov. 17, 1878, d May 25, 1949
Hazlitt, G. R. (Vic. & NSW) b Sept. 4, 1888, d Oct. 30, 1915
Headley, D. W. (Middx & Kent) b Jan. 27, 1970
*Headley, G. A. (Jam.; *CY 1934*) b May 30, 1909, d Nov. 30, 1983
*Headley, R. G. A. (Worcs & Jam.) b June 29, 1939
*Healy, I. A. (Qld; *CY 1994*) b April 30, 1964
Heane, G. F. H. (Notts) b Jan. 2, 1904, d Oct. 24, 1969
Heap, J. S. (Lancs) b Aug. 12, 1882, d Jan. 30, 1951
Hearn, P. (Kent) b Nov. 18, 1925
*Hearne, A. (Kent; *CY 1894*) b July 22, 1863, d May 16, 1952
**Hearne, F. (Kent & W. Prov.) b Nov. 23, 1858, d July 14, 1949
*Hearne, G. A. L. (W. Prov.) b March 27, 1888, d Nov. 13, 1978
*Hearne, G. G. (Kent) b July 7, 1856, d Feb. 13, 1932
*Hearne, J. T. (Middx; *CY 1892*) b May 3, 1867, d April 17, 1944

*Hearne, J. W. (Middx; *CY 1912*) b Feb. 11, 1891, d Sept. 14, 1965
Hearne, T. (Middx) b Sept. 4, 1826, d May 13, 1900
Heath, G. E. M. (Hants) b Feb. 20, 1913
Heath, M. (Hants) b March 9, 1934
Hedges, B. (Glam) b Nov. 10, 1927
Hedges, L. P (Tonbridge, OU, Kent & Glos; *CY 1919*) b July 13, 1900, d Jan. 12, 1933
Hegg, W. K. (Lancs) b Feb. 23, 1968
*Heine, P. S. (NE Tvl, OFS & Tvl) b June 28, 1928
*Hemmings, E. E. (Warwicks, Notts & Sussex) b Feb. 20, 1949
Hemsley, E. J. O. (Worcs) b Sept. 1, 1943
*Henderson, M. (Wgtn) b Aug. 2, 1895, d June 17, 1970
Henderson, R. (Surrey; *CY 1890*) b March 30, 1865, d Jan. 29, 1931
*Hendren, E. H. (Middx; *CY 1920*) b Feb. 5, 1889, d Oct. 4, 1962
*Hendrick, M. (Derbys & Notts; *CY 1978*) b Oct. 22, 1948
*Hendriks, J. L. (Jam.) b Dec. 21, 1933
*Hendry, H. L. (NSW & Vic.) b May 24, 1895, d Dec. 16, 1988
*Henry, O. (W. Prov., Boland, OFS & Scotland) b Jan. 23, 1952
Herman, O. W. (Hants) b Sept. 18, 1907, d June 24, 1987
Herman, R. S. (Middx, Border, Griq. W. & Hants) b Nov. 30, 1946
Heron, J. G. (Zimb.) b Nov. 8, 1948
*Heseltine, C. (Hants) b Nov. 26, 1869, d June 13, 1944
Hever, N. G. (Middx & Glam) b Dec. 17, 1924, d Sept. 11, 1987
Hewett, H. T. (OU & Som; *CY 1893*) b May 25, 1864, d March 4, 1921.
Heyhoe-Flint, Rachael (England Women) b June 11, 1939
Heyn, P. D. (SL) b June 26, 1945
*Hibbert, P. A. (Vic.) b July 23, 1952
*Hick, G. A. (Worcs, Zimb., N. Dist. & Qld; *CY 1987*) b May 23, 1966
*Higgs, J. D. (Vic.) b July 11, 1950
*Higgs, K. (Lancs & Leics; *CY 1968*) b Jan. 14, 1937
Hignell, A. J. (CU & Glos) b Sept. 4, 1955
*Hilditch, A. M. J. (NSW & S. Aust.) b May 20, 1956
Hill, Alan (Derbys & OFS) b June 29, 1950
*Hill, Allen (Yorks) b Nov. 14, 1843, d Aug. 29, 1910
*Hill, A. J. L. (CU & Hants) b July 26, 1871, d Sept. 6, 1950
*Hill, C. (S. Aust.; *CY 1900*) b March 18, 1877, d Sept. 5, 1945
Hill, E. (Som) b July 9, 1923
Hill, G. (Hants) b April 15, 1913
*Hill, J. C. (Vic.) b June 25, 1923, d Aug. 11, 1974
Hill, M. (Notts, Derbys & Som) b Sept. 14, 1935
Hill, N. W. (Notts) b Aug. 22, 1935
Hill, W. A. (Warwicks) b April 27, 1910, d Aug. 11, 1995
Hill-Wood, Sir Samuel H. (Derbys) b March 21, 1872, d Jan. 4, 1949
Hillyer, W. R. (Kent & Surrey) b March 5, 1813, d Jan. 8, 1861
Hilton, C. (Lancs & Essex) b Sept. 26, 1937
*Hilton, M. J. (Lancs; *CY 1957*) b Aug. 2, 1928, d July 8, 1990
*Hime, C. F. W. (Natal) b Oct. 24, 1869, d Dec. 6, 1940
*Hindlekar, D. D. (Bombay) b Jan. 1, 1909, d March 30, 1949
Hinks, S. G. (Kent & Glos) b Oct. 12, 1960
Hipkin, A. B. (Essex) b Aug. 8, 1900, d Feb. 11, 1957
*Hirst, G. H. (Yorks; *CY 1901*) b Sept. 7, 1871, d May 10, 1954
*Hirwani, N. D. (M. Pradesh) b Oct. 18, 1968
*Hitch, J. W. (Surrey; *CY 1914*) b May 7, 1886, d July 7, 1965
Hitchcock, R. E. (Cant. & Warwicks) b Nov. 28, 1929
*Hoad, E. L. G. (B'dos) b Jan. 29, 1896, d March 5, 1986
*Hoare, D. E. (W. Aust.) b Oct. 19, 1934
*Hobbs, Sir John B. "Jack" (Surrey; *CY 1909, special portrait 1926*) b Dec. 16, 1882, d Dec. 21, 1963
*Hobbs, R. N. S. (Essex & Glam) b May 8, 1942
*Hodges, J. (Vic.) b Aug. 11, 1855, death unknown
Hodgson, A. (Northants) b Oct. 27, 1951
Hodgson, G. D. (Glos) b Oct. 22, 1966
*Hogan, T. G. (W. Aust.) b Sept. 23, 1956
*Hogg, R. M. (S. Aust.) b March 5, 1951
*Hohns, T. V. (Qld) b Jan. 23, 1954
Holder, J. W. (Hants; Test umpire) b March 19, 1945
Holder, R. I. C. (B'dos) b Dec. 22, 1967
*Holder, V. A. (B'dos, Worcs & OFS) b Oct. 8, 1945
*Holding, M. A. (Jam., Lancs, Derbys, Tas. & Cant.; *CY 1977*) b Feb. 16, 1954
*Hole, G. B. (NSW & S. Aust.) b Jan. 6, 1931, d Feb. 14, 1990
*Holford, D. A. J. (B'dos & T/T) b April 16, 1940
Holland, F. C. (Surrey) b Feb. 10, 1876, d Feb. 5, 1957
*Holland, R. G. (NSW & Wgtn) b Oct. 19, 1946
*Hollies, W. E. (Warwicks; *CY 1955*) b June 5, 1912, d April 16, 1981
Holmes, Gp Capt. A. J. (Sussex) b June 30, 1899, d May 21, 1950
*Holmes, E. R. T. (OU & Surrey; *CY 1936*) b Aug. 21, 1905, d Aug. 16, 1960

Holmes, G. C. (Glam) b Sept. 16, 1958
*Holmes, P. (Yorks; *CY 1920*) b Nov. 25, 1886, d Sept. 3, 1971
Holt, A. G. (Hants) b April 8, 1911, d July 28, 1994
*Holt, J. K., jun. (Jam.) b Aug. 12, 1923
Home of the Hirsel, Lord (Middx; Pres. MCC 1966-67) b July 2, 1903, d Oct. 9, 1995
*Hone, L. (MCC) b Jan. 30, 1853, d Dec. 31, 1896
Hooker, R. W. (Middx) b Feb. 22, 1935
*Hookes, D. W. (S. Aust.) b May 3, 1955
*Hooper, C. L. (Guyana & Kent) b Dec. 15, 1966
*Hopkins, A. J. (NSW) b May 3, 1874, d April 25, 1931
Hopkins, J. A. (Glam & E. Prov.) b June 16, 1953
*Hopwood, J. L. (Lancs) b Oct. 30, 1903, d June 15, 1985
*Horan, T. P. (Vic.) b March 8, 1854, d April 16, 1916
*Hordern, Dr H. V. (NSW & Philadelphia) b Feb. 10, 1884, d June 17, 1938
Hornby, A. H. (CU & Lancs) b July 29, 1877, d Sept. 6, 1952
*Hornby, A. N. (Lancs) b Feb. 10, 1847, d Dec. 17, 1925
*Horne, P. A. (Auck.) b Jan. 21, 1960
Horner, N. F. (Yorks & Warwicks) b May 10, 1926
*Hornibrook, P. M. (Qld) b July 27, 1899, d Aug. 25, 1976
Horsfall, R. (Essex & Glam) b June 26, 1920, d Aug. 25, 1981
Horton, H. (Worcs & Hants) b April 18, 1923
*Horton, M. J. (Worcs & N. Dist.) b April 21, 1934
*Hough, K. W. (Auck.) b Oct. 24, 1928
*Houghton, D. L. (Mash.) b June 23, 1957
*Howard, A. B. (B'dos) b Aug. 27, 1946
*Howard, N. D. (Lancs) b May 18, 1925, d May 31, 1979
Howard, Major R. (Lancs; MCC Team Manager) b April 17, 1890, d Sept. 10, 1967
*Howarth, G. P. (Auck., Surrey & N. Dist.) b March 29, 1951
*Howarth, H. J. (Auck.) b Dec. 25, 1943
*Howell, H. (Warwicks) b Nov. 29, 1890, d July 9, 1932
*Howell, W. P. (NSW) b Dec. 29, 1869, d July 14, 1940
*Howorth, R. (Worcs) b April 26, 1909, d April 2, 1980
Hubble, J. C. (Kent) b Feb. 10, 1881, d Feb. 26, 1965
*Hudson, A. C. (Natal) b March 17, 1965
Huggins, H. J. (Glos) b March 15, 1877, d Nov. 20, 1942
Hughes, D. P. (Lancs & Tas.; *CY 1988*) b May 13, 1947
*Hughes, K. J. (W. Aust. & Natal; *CY 1981*) b Jan. 26, 1954
*Hughes, M. G. (Vic. & Essex; *CY 1994*) b Nov. 23, 1961
Hughes, S. P. (Middx, N. Tvl & Durham) b Dec. 20, 1959
Huish, F. H. (Kent) b Nov. 15, 1869, d March 16, 1957
Hulme, J. H. A. (Middx) b Aug. 26, 1904, d Sept. 26, 1991
Humpage, G. W. (Warwicks & OFS; *CY 1985*) b April 24, 1954
Humphrey, T. (Surrey) b Jan. 16, 1839, d Sept. 3, 1878
Humphreys, E. (Kent & Cant.) b Aug. 24, 1881, d Nov. 6, 1949
Humphreys, W. A. (Sussex & Hants) b Oct. 28, 1849, d March 23, 1924
Humphries, D. J. (Leics & Worcs) b Aug. 6, 1953
*Humphries, J. (Derbys) b May 19, 1876, d May 7, 1946
Hunt, A. V. (Scotland & Bermuda) b Oct. 1, 1910
Hunt, G. E. (Som) b Sept. 30, 1896, d Jan. 22, 1959
*Hunt, W. A. (NSW) b Aug. 26, 1908, d Dec. 30, 1983
*Hunte, C. C. (B'dos; *CY 1964*) b May 9, 1932
*Hunte, E. A. C. (T/T) b Oct. 3, 1905, d June 26, 1967
Hunter, D. (Yorks) b Feb. 23, 1860, d Jan. 11, 1927
*Hunter, J. (Yorks) b Aug. 3, 1855, d Jan. 4, 1891
*Hurst, A. G. (Vic.) b July 15, 1950
Hurst, R. J. (Middx) b Dec. 29, 1933, d Feb. 10, 1996
*Hurwood, A. (Qld) b June 17, 1902, d Sept. 26, 1982
*Hussain, N. (Essex) b March 28, 1968
*Hutchings, K. L. (Kent; *CY 1907*) b Dec. 7, 1882, d Sept. 3, 1916
Hutchinson, J. M. (Derbys; *believed to be oldest living county cricketer at end 1996*) b Nov. 29, 1896
*Hutchinson, P. (SA) b Jan. 26, 1862, d Sept. 30, 1925
*Hutton, Sir Leonard (Yorks; *CY 1938*) b June 23, 1916, d Sept. 6, 1990
*Hutton, R. A. (CU, Yorks & Tvl) b Sept. 6, 1942
*Hylton, L. G. (Jam.) b March 29, 1905, d May 17, 1955

*Ibadulla, K. (Punjab, Warwicks, Tas. & Otago) b Dec. 20, 1935
*Ibrahim, K. C. (Bombay) b Jan. 26, 1919
Iddison, R. (Yorks & Lancs) b Sept. 15, 1834, d March 19, 1890
*Iddon, J. (Lancs) b Jan. 8, 1902, d April 17, 1946

*Igglesden, A. P. (Kent & W. Prov.) b Oct. 8, 1964
*Ijaz Ahmed, sen. (Gujranwala, PACO, HBL, I'bad & Lahore) b Sept. 20, 1968
*Ijaz Ahmed, jun. (F'bad, ADBP & Pak. Rlwys) b Feb. 2, 1969
*Ijaz Butt (Pak. Us, Punjab, Lahore, R'pindi & Multan) b March 10, 1938
*Ijaz Faqih (Kar., Sind, PWD & MCB) b March 24, 1956
*Ikin, J. T. (Lancs) b March 7, 1918, d Sept. 15, 1984
*Illingworth, R. (Yorks & Leics; *CY 1960*) b June 8, 1932
*Illingworth, R. K. (Worcs & Natal) b Aug. 23, 1963
*Ilott, M. C. (Essex) b Aug. 27, 1970
*Imran Khan (Lahore, Dawood, Worcs, OU, PIA, Sussex & NSW; *CY 1983*) b Nov. 25, 1952
*Imtiaz Ahmed (N. Ind., Comb. Us, NWFP, Pak. Servs, Peshawar & PAF) b Jan. 5, 1928
*Imtiaz Ali (T/T) b July 28, 1954
Inchmore, J. D. (Worcs & N. Tvl) b Feb. 22, 1949
*Indrajitsinhji, K. S. (S'tra & Delhi) b June 15, 1937
Ingle, R. A. (Som) b Nov. 5, 1903, d Dec. 19, 1992
Ingleby-Mackenzie, A. C. D. (Hants; Pres. MCC 1996-) b Sept. 15, 1933
Inman, C. C. (Ceylon & Leics) b Jan. 29, 1936
*Inshan Ali (T/T) b Sept. 25, 1949, d June 24, 1995
*Insole, D. J. (CU & Essex; *CY 1956*) b April 18, 1926
*Intikhab Alam (Kar., PIA, Surrey, PWD, Sind, Punjab) b Dec. 28, 1941
*Inverarity, R. J. (W. Aust. & S. Aust.) b Jan. 31, 1944
*Inzamam-ul-Haq (Multan & UBL) b March 3, 1970
*Iqbal Qasim (Kar., Sind & NBP) b Aug. 6, 1953
Iqbal Sikandar (Kar. & PIA) b Dec. 19, 1958
*Irani, J. K. (Sind) b Aug. 18, 1923, d Feb. 25, 1982
*Irani, R. C. (Lancs & Essex) b Oct. 26, 1971
*Iredale, F. A. (NSW) b June 19, 1867, d April 15, 1926
Iremonger, J. (Notts; *CY 1903*) b March 5, 1876, d March 25, 1956
Irfan Bhatti (R'pindi) b Sept. 28, 1964
*Ironmonger, H. (Qld & Vic.) b April 7, 1882, d June 1, 1971
*Ironside, D. E. J. (Tvl) b May 2, 1925
*Irvine, B. L. (W. Prov., Natal, Essex & Tvl) b March 9, 1944
*Israr Ali (S. Punjab, B'pur & Multan) b May 1, 1927
*Iverson, J. B. (Vic.) b July 27, 1915, d Oct. 24, 1973
*Jack, S. D. (Tvl) b Aug. 4, 1970
*Jackman, R. D. (Surrey, W. Prov. & Rhod.; *CY 1981*) b Aug. 13, 1945
*Jackson, A. A. (NSW) b Sept. 5, 1909, d Feb. 16, 1933
Jackson, A. B. (Derbys) b Aug. 21, 1933
*Jackson, Rt Hon. Sir F. Stanley (CU & Yorks; *CY 1894;* Pres. MCC 1921) b Nov. 21, 1870, d March 9, 1947
Jackson, G. R. (Derbys) b June 23, 1896, d Feb. 21, 1966
*Jackson, H. L. (Derbys; *CY 1959*) b April 5, 1921
Jackson, J. (Notts & All-England) b May 21, 1833, d Nov. 4, 1901
Jackson, P. F. (Worcs) b May 11, 1911
Jackson, V. E. (NSW & Leics) b Oct. 25, 1916, d Jan. 30, 1965
Jacobs, R. D. (Leewards) b Nov. 26, 1967
*Jadeja, A. D. (Haryana) b Feb. 1, 1971
*Jahangir Khan (N. Ind. & CU) b Feb. 1, 1910, d July 23, 1988
*Jai, L. P. (Bombay) b April 1, 1902, d Jan. 29, 1968
*Jaisimha, M. L. (H'bad) b March 3, 1939
Jakeman, F. (Yorks & Northants) b Jan. 10, 1920, d May 18, 1986
*Jalal-ud-Din (PWD, Kar., IDBP & Allied Bank) b June 12, 1959
James, A. E. (Sussex) b Aug. 7, 1924
James, C. L. R. (Writer) b Jan. 4, 1901, d May 31, 1989
*James, K. C. (Wgtn & Northants) b March 12, 1904, d Aug. 21, 1976
James, K. D. (Middx, Hants & Wgtn) b March 18, 1961
James, S. P. (Glam, CU & Mash.) b Sept. 7, 1967
*James, W. R. (Mat.) b Aug. 27, 1965
*Jameson, J. A. (Warwicks) b June 30, 1941
*Jamshedji, R. J. (Bombay) b Nov. 18, 1892, d April 5, 1976
*Jardine, D. R. (OU & Surrey; *CY 1928*) b Oct. 23, 1900, d June 18, 1958
*Jarman, B. N. (S. Aust.) b Feb. 17, 1936
*Jarvis, A. H. (S. Aust.) b Oct. 19, 1860, d Nov. 15, 1933
Jarvis, K. B. S. (Kent & Glos) b April 23, 1953
*Jarvis, M. P. (Mash.) b Dec. 6, 1955
*Jarvis, P. W. (Yorks & Sussex) b June 29, 1965
*Jarvis, T. W. (Auck. & Cant.) b July 29, 1944
*Javed Akhtar (R'pindi & Pak. Serv.) b Nov. 21, 1940
*Javed Miandad (Kar., Sind, Sussex, HBL & Glam; *CY 1982*) b June 12, 1957
Javed Qadir (PIA) b Aug. 25, 1976
*Jayantilal, K. (H'bad) b Jan. 13, 1948
*Jayasekera, R. S. A. (SL) b Dec. 7, 1957
Jayasinghe, S. (Ceylon & Leics) b Jan. 19, 1931

Jayasinghe, S. A. (SL) b July 15, 1955, d April 20, 1995
*Jayasuriya, S. T. (CCC & Bloom.; *CY 1997*) b June 30, 1969
Jeeves, P. (Warwicks) b March 5, 1888, d July 22, 1916
Jefferies, S. T. (W. Prov., Derbys, Lancs, Hants & Boland) b Dec. 8, 1959
*Jeganathan, S. (SL) b July 11, 1951, d May 14, 1996
*Jenkins, R. O. (Worcs; *CY 1950*) b Nov. 24, 1918, d July 21, 1995
*Jenner, T. J. (W. Aust. & S. Aust.) b Sept. 8, 1944
*Jennings, C. B. (S. Aust.) b June 5, 1884, d June 20, 1950
Jennings, R. V. (Tvl & N. Tvl) b Aug. 9, 1954
Jephson, D. L. A. (CU & Surrey) b Feb. 23, 1871, d Jan. 19, 1926
Jepson, A. (Notts; Test umpire) b July 12, 1915
*Jessop, G. L. (CU & Glos; *CY 1898*) b May 19, 1874, d May 11, 1955
Jesty, T. E. (Hants, Border, Griq. W., Cant., Surrey & Lancs; *CY 1983*) b June 2, 1948
Jewell, Major M. F. S. (Worcs & Sussex) b Sept. 15, 1885, d May 28, 1978
*John, V. B. (SL) b May 27, 1960
*Johnson, C. L. (Tvl) b 1871, d May 31, 1908
Johnson, G. W. (Kent & Tvl) b Nov. 8, 1946
*Johnson, H. H. H. (Jam.) b July 17, 1910, d June 24, 1987
Johnson, H. L. (Derbys) b Nov. 8, 1927
*Johnson, I. W. (Vic.) b Dec. 8, 1917
Johnson, L. A. (Northants) b Aug. 12, 1936
*Johnson, L. J. (Qld) b March 18, 1919, d April 20, 1977
Johnson, P. (Notts) b April 24, 1965
Johnson, P. R. (CU & Som) b Aug. 5, 1880, d July 1, 1959
*Johnson, T. F. (T/T) b Jan. 10, 1917, d April 5, 1985
Johnston, Brian A. (Broadcaster) b June 24, 1912, d Jan. 5, 1994
*Johnston, W. A. (Vic.; *CY 1949*) b Feb. 26, 1922
Jones, A. (Glam, W. Aust., N. Tvl & Natal; *CY 1978*) b Nov. 4, 1938
Jones, A. A. (Sussex, Som, Middx, Glam, N. Tvl & OFS) b Dec. 9, 1947
*Jones, A. H. (Wgtn & C. Dist.) b May 9, 1959
Jones, A. L. (Glam) b June 1, 1957
Jones, A. N. (Sussex, Border & Som) b July 22, 1961
*Jones, A. O. (Notts & CU; *CY 1900*) b Aug. 16, 1872, d Dec. 21, 1914
*Jones, C. M. (BG) b Nov. 3, 1902, d Dec. 10, 1959
*Jones, D. M. (Vic., Durham & Derbys; *CY 1990*) b March 24, 1961
*Jones, Ernest (S. Aust. & W. Aust.) b Sept. 30, 1869, d Nov. 23, 1943
Jones, E. W. (Glam) b June 25, 1942
*Jones, I. J. (Glam) b Dec. 10, 1941
Jones, K. V. (Middx) b March 28, 1942
*Jones, P. E. (T/T) b June 6, 1917, d Nov. 21, 1991
Jones, P. H. (Kent) b June 19, 1935
*Jones, S. P. (NSW, Qld & Auck.) b Aug. 1, 1861, d July 14, 1951
Jones, W. E. (Glam) b Oct. 31, 1916, d July 25, 1996
Jordon, R. C. (Vic.) b Feb. 17, 1937
*Joshi, P. G. (M'tra) b Oct. 27, 1926, d Jan. 8, 1987
*Joshi, S. (Karn.) b June 6, 1969
Joshi, U. C. (S'tra, Ind. Rlwys, Guj. & Sussex) b Dec. 23, 1944
*Joslin, L. R. (Vic.) b Dec. 13, 1947
*Julian, B. P. (W. Aust. & Surrey) b Aug. 10, 1970
Julian, R. (Leics) b Aug. 23, 1936
*Julien, B. D. (T/T & Kent) b March 13, 1950
*Jumadeen, R. R. (T/T) b April 12, 1948
*Jupp, H. (Surrey) b Nov. 19, 1841, d April 8, 1889
*Jupp, V. W. C. (Sussex & Northants; *CY 1928*) b March 27, 1891, d July 9, 1960
*Jurangpathy, B. R. (CCC) b June 25, 1967

*Kabir Khan (HBFC) b April 12, 1974
*Kallicharran, A. I. (Guyana, Warwicks, Qld, Tvl & OFS; *CY 1983*) b March 21, 1949
*Kallis, J. H. (W. Prov.) b Oct. 16, 1975
*Kalpage, R. S. (NCC & Bloom.) b Feb. 19, 1970
*Kaluperuma, L. W. (SL) b May 25, 1949
*Kaluperuma, S. M. S. (SL) b Oct. 22, 1961
*Kaluwitharana, R. S. (Seb. & Galle) b Nov. 24, 1969
*Kambli, V. G. (Bombay) b Jan. 18, 1972
*Kanhai, R. B. (†Guyana, T/T, W. Aust., Warwicks & Tas.; *CY 1964*) b Dec. 26, 1935
*Kanitkar, H. S. (M'tra) b Dec. 8, 1942
*Kapil Dev (Haryana, Northants & Worcs; *CY 1983*) b Jan. 6, 1959
*Kapoor, A. R. (TN & Punjab) b March 25, 1971
**Kardar, A. H. (formerly Abdul Hafeez) (N. Ind., OU, Warwicks & Pak. Serv.) b Jan. 17, 1925, d April 21, 1996
Karnain, S. H. U. (NCC & Moors) b Aug. 11, 1962
Kasprowicz, M. S. (Qld & Essex) b Feb. 10, 1972
*Keeton, W. W. (Notts; *CY 1940*) b April 30, 1905, d Oct. 10, 1980
*Keith, H. J. (Natal) b Oct. 25, 1927
*Kelleway, C. (NSW) b April 25, 1886, d Nov. 16, 1944
*Kelly, J. J. (NSW; *CY 1903*) b May 10, 1867, d Aug. 14, 1938

Kelly, J. M. (Lancs & Derbys) b March 19, 1922, d Nov. 13, 1979
*Kelly, T. J. D. (Vic.) b May 3, 1844, d July 20, 1893
*Kempis, G. A. (Natal) b Aug. 4, 1865, d May 19, 1890
*Kendall, T. (Vic. & Tas.) b Aug. 24, 1851, d Aug. 17, 1924
Kennedy, A. (Lancs) b Nov. 4, 1949
*Kennedy, A. S. (Hants; *CY 1933*) b Jan. 24, 1891, d Nov. 15, 1959
*Kennedy, R. J. (Otago) b June 3, 1972
*Kenny, R. B. (Bombay & Bengal) b Sept. 29, 1930, d Nov. 21, 1985
*Kent, M. F. (Qld) b Nov. 23, 1953
*Kentish, E. S. M. (Jam. & OU) b Nov. 21, 1916
*Kenyon, D. (Worcs; *CY 1963*) b May 15, 1924, d Nov. 12, 1996
Kenyon, M. N. (Lancs) b Dec. 25, 1886, d Nov. 21, 1960
*Kerr, J. L. (Cant.) b Dec. 28, 1910
*Kerr, R. B. (Qld) b June 16, 1961
Key, Sir Kingsmill J. (Surrey & OU) b Oct. 11, 1864, d Aug. 9, 1932
*Khalid Hassan (Punjab & Lahore) b July 14, 1937
*Khalid Wazir (Pak.) b April 27, 1936
*Khan Mohammad (N. Ind., Pak. Us, Som, B'pur, Sind, Kar. & Lahore) b Jan. 1, 1928
Khanna, S. C. (Delhi) b June 3, 1956
Killick, E. H. (Sussex) b Jan. 17, 1875, d Sept. 29, 1948
*Killick, Rev. E. T. (CU & Middx) b May 9, 1907, d May 18, 1953
Kilner, N. (Yorks & Warwicks) b July 21, 1895, d April 28, 1979
*Kilner, R. (Yorks; *CY 1924*) b Oct. 17, 1890, d April 5, 1928
King, B. P. (Worcs & Lancs) b April 22, 1915, d March 31, 1970
*King, C. L. (B'dos, Glam, Worcs & Natal) b June 11, 1951
*King, F. M. (B'dos) b Dec. 14, 1926, d Dec. 23, 1990
King, J. B. (Philadelphia) b Oct. 19, 1873, d Oct. 17, 1965
*King, J. H. (Leics) b April 16, 1871, d Nov. 18, 1946
*King, L. A. (Jam. & Bengal) b Feb. 27, 1939
*Kinneir, S. P. (Warwicks; *CY 1912*) b May 13, 1871, d Oct. 16, 1928
*Kippax, A. F. (NSW) b May 25, 1897, d Sept. 4, 1972
Kirby, D. (CU & Leics) b Jan. 18, 1939
*Kirmani, S. M. H. (†Karn.) b Dec. 29, 1949
*Kirsten, G. (W. Prov.) b Nov. 23, 1967
*Kirsten, P. N. (W. Prov., Sussex, Derbys & Border) b May 14, 1955
*Kischenchand, G. (W. Ind., Guj. & Baroda) b April 14, 1925
Kitchen, M. J. (Som; Test umpire) b Aug. 1, 1940
*Kline, L. F. (Vic.) b Sept. 29, 1934
Klusener, L. (Natal) b Sept. 4, 1971
*Knight, A. E. (Leics; *CY 1904*) b Oct. 8, 1872, d April 25, 1946
*Knight, B. R. (Essex & Leics) b Feb. 18, 1938
*Knight, D. J. (OU & Surrey; *CY 1915*) b May 12, 1894, d Jan. 5, 1960
*Knight, N. V. (Essex & Warwicks) b Nov. 28, 1969
Knight, R. D. V. (CU, Surrey, Glos & Sussex; Sec. MCC 1994-) b Sept. 6, 1946
Knight, W. H. (Editor of *Wisden* 1870-79) b Nov. 29, 1812, d Aug. 16, 1879
*Knott, A. P. E. (Kent & Tas.; *CY 1970*) b April 9, 1946
Knott, C. J. (Hants) b Nov. 26, 1914
*Knox, N. A. (Surrey; *CY 1907*) b Oct. 10, 1884, d March 3, 1935
Kortright, C. J. (Essex) b Jan. 9, 1871, d Dec. 12, 1952
*Kotze, J. J. (Tvl & W. Prov.) b Aug. 7, 1879, d July 7, 1931
Krikken, K. M. (Derbys) b April 9, 1969
*Kripal Singh, A. G. (Madras & H'bad) b Aug. 6, 1933, d July 23, 1987
*Krishnamurthy, P. (H'bad) b July 12, 1947
*Kuggeleijn, C. M. (N. Dist.) b May 10, 1956
*Kuiper, A. P. (W. Prov., Derbys & Boland) b Aug. 24, 1959
*Kulkarni, R. R. (Bombay) b Sept. 25, 1962
*Kulkarni, U. N. (Bombay) b March 7, 1942
*Kumar, V. V. (†TN) b June 22, 1935
*Kumble, A. (Karn. & Northants; *CY 1996*) b Oct. 17, 1970
*Kunderan, B. K. (Ind. Rlwys & Mysore) b Oct. 2, 1939
*Kuruppu, D. S. B. P. (BRC) b Jan. 5, 1962
*Kuruppuarachchi, A. K. (NCC) b Nov. 1, 1964
*Kuys, F. (W. Prov.) b March 21, 1870, d Sept. 12, 1953
Kynaston, R. (Middx; Sec. MCC 1846-58) b Nov. 5, 1805, d June 21, 1874

*Labrooy, G. F. (CCC) b June 7, 1964
Lacey, Sir Francis E. (CU & Hants; Sec. MCC 1898-1926) b Oct. 19, 1859, d May 26, 1946
*Laird, B. M. (W. Aust.) b Nov. 21, 1950
*Laker, J. C. (Surrey, Auck. & Essex; *CY 1952*) b Feb. 9, 1922, d April 23, 1986
*Lall Singh (S. Punjab) b Dec. 16, 1909, d Nov. 19, 1985
*Lamb, A. J. (W. Prov., Northants & OFS; *CY 1981*) b June 20, 1954
Lamb, Hon. T. M. (OU, Middx & Northants; Chief Exec. ECB, 1997-) b March 24, 1953
*Lamba, R. (Delhi) b Jan. 2, 1958
*Lambert, C. B. (Guyana & N. Tvl) b Feb. 10, 1962

Lambert, G. E. (Glos & Som) b May 11, 1918, d Oct. 31, 1991
Lambert, R. H. (Ireland) b July 18, 1874, d March 24, 1956
Lambert, Wm (Surrey) b 1779, d April 19, 1851
Lampitt, S. R. (Worcs) b July 29, 1966
*Lance, H. R. (NE Tvl & Tvl) b June 6, 1940
Langdon, T. (Glos) b Jan. 8, 1879, d Nov. 30, 1944
*Langer, J. L. (W. Aust.) b Nov. 21, 1970
Langford, B. A. (Som) b Dec. 17, 1935
*Langley, G. R. A. (S. Aust.; *CY 1957*) b Sept. 14, 1919
*Langridge, James (Sussex; *CY 1932*) b July 10, 1906, d Sept. 10, 1966
Langridge, John (Sussex; Test umpire; *CY 1950*) b Feb. 10, 1910
Langridge, R. J. (Sussex) b April 13, 1939
*Langton, A. B. C. (Tvl) b March 2, 1912, d Nov. 27, 1942
*Lara, B. C. (T/T & Warwicks; *CY 1995*) b May 2, 1969
*Larkins, W. (Northants, E. Prov. & Durham) b Nov. 22, 1953
*Larsen, G. R. (Wgtn) b Sept. 27, 1962
*Larter, J. D. F. (Northants) b April 24, 1940
*Larwood, H. (Notts; *CY 1927*) b Nov. 14, 1904, d July 22, 1995
*Lashley, P. D. (B'dos) b Feb. 11, 1937
Latchman, H. C. (Middx & Notts) b July 26, 1943
*Latham, R. T. (Cant.) b June 12, 1961
*Lathwell, M. N. (Som) b Dec. 26, 1971
*Laughlin, T. J. (Vic.) b Jan. 30, 1951
*Laver, F. (Vic.) b Dec. 7, 1869, d Sept. 24, 1919
Lavis, G. (Glam) b Aug. 17, 1908, d July 29, 1956
*Law, S. G. (Qld & Essex) b Oct. 18, 1968
*Lawrence, D. V. (Glos) b Jan. 28, 1964
*Lawrence, G. B. (Rhod. & Natal) b March 31, 1932
Lawrence, J. (Som) b March 29, 1914, d Dec. 10, 1988
*Lawry, W. M. (Vic.; *CY 1962*) b Feb. 11, 1937
*Lawson, G. F. (NSW & Lancs) b Dec. 7, 1957
Lawton, A. E. (Derbys & Lancs) b March 31, 1879, d Dec. 25, 1955
Leach, G. (Sussex) b July 18, 1881, d Jan. 10, 1945
Leadbeater, B. (Yorks) b Aug. 14, 1943
*Leadbeater, E. (Yorks & Warwicks) b Aug. 15, 1927
Leary, S. E. (Kent) b April 30, 1933, d Aug. 21, 1988
Leatherdale, D. A. (Worcs) b Nov. 26, 1967
Lee, C. (Yorks & Derbys) b March 17, 1924
Lee, F. S. (Middx & Som; Test umpire) b July 24, 1905, d March 30, 1982
Lee, G. M. (Notts & Derbys) b June 7, 1887, d Feb. 29, 1976
*Lee, H. W. (Middx) b Oct. 26, 1890, d April 21, 1981
Lee, J. W. (Middx & Som) b Feb. 1, 1904, d June 20, 1944
Lee, P. G. (Northants & Lancs; *CY 1976*) b Aug. 27, 1945
*Lee, P. K. (S. Aust.) b Sept. 15, 1904, d Aug. 9, 1980
Lee, S. (NSW & Som) b Aug. 8, 1973
*Lees, W. K. (Otago) b March 19, 1952
*Lees, W. S. (Surrey; *CY 1906*) b Dec. 25, 1875, d Sept. 10, 1924
Leese, Sir Oliver, Bt (Pres. MCC 1965-66) b Oct. 27, 1894, d Jan. 20, 1978
Lefebvre, R. P. (Holland, Som, Cant. & Glam) b Feb. 7, 1963
*Legall, R. (B'dos & T/T) b Dec. 1, 1925
*Leggat, I. B. (C. Dist.) b June 7, 1930
*Leggat, J. G. (Cant.) b May 27, 1926, d March 9, 1973
*Legge, G. B. (OU & Kent) b Jan. 26, 1903, d Nov. 21, 1940
Lenham, L. J. (Sussex) b May 24, 1936
Lenham, N. J. (Sussex) b Dec. 17, 1965
*le Roux, F. L. (Tvl & E. Prov.) b Feb. 5, 1882, d Sept. 22, 1963
le Roux, G. S. (W. Prov. & Sussex) b Sept. 4, 1955
*Leslie, C. F. H. (OU & Middx) b Dec. 8, 1861, d Feb. 12, 1921
Lester, E. (Yorks) b Feb. 18, 1923
Lester, G. (Leics) b Dec. 27, 1915
Lester, Dr J. A. (Philadelphia) b Aug. 1, 1871, d Sept. 3, 1969
*Lever, J. K. (Essex & Natal; *CY 1979*) b Feb. 24, 1949
*Lever, P. (Lancs & Tas.) b Sept. 17, 1940
*Leveson Gower, Sir H. D. G. (OU & Surrey) b May 8, 1873, d Feb. 1, 1954
*Levett, W. H. V. (Kent) b Jan. 25, 1908, d Nov. 30, 1995
*Lewis, A. R. (Glam & CU) b July 6, 1938
Lewis, A. E. (Som) b Jan. 20, 1877, d Feb. 22, 1956
Lewis, C. (Kent) b July 27, 1908, d April 26, 1993
*Lewis, C. C. (Leics, Notts & Surrey) b Feb. 14, 1968
*Lewis, D. M. (Jam.) b Feb. 21, 1946
Lewis, E. J. (Glam & Sussex) b Jan. 31, 1942
*Lewis, P. T. (W. Prov.) b Oct. 2, 1884, d Jan. 30, 1976
*Leyland, M. (Yorks; *CY 1929*) b July 20, 1900, d Jan. 1, 1967
*Liaqat Ali (Kar., Sind, HBL & PIA) b May 21, 1955
Liebenberg, G. F. J. (Griq. W. & OFS) b April 7, 1972
Lightfoot, A. (Northants) b Jan. 8, 1936
*Lillee, D. K. (W. Aust., Tas. & Northants; *CY 1973*) b July 18, 1949

*Lilley, A. A. (Warwicks; *CY 1897*) b Nov. 28, 1866, d Nov. 17, 1929
Lilley, A. W. (Essex) b May 8, 1959
Lilley, B. (Notts) b Feb. 11, 1895, d Aug. 4, 1950
Lillywhite, Fred (Sussex; Editor of *Lillywhite's Guide to Cricketers*) b July 23, 1829, d Sept. 15, 1866
Lillywhite, F. W. ("William") (Sussex) b June 13, 1792, d Aug. 21, 1854
*Lillywhite, James, jun. (Sussex) b Feb. 23, 1842, d Oct. 25, 1929
*Lindsay, D. T. (NE Tvl, N. Tvl & Tvl) b Sept. 4, 1939
*Lindsay, J. D. (Tvl & NE Tvl) b Sept. 8, 1909, d Aug. 31, 1990
*Lindsay, N. V. (Tvl & OFS) b July 30, 1886, d Feb. 2, 1976
*Lindwall, R. R. (NSW & Qld; *CY 1949*) b Oct. 3, 1921, d June 23, 1996
*Ling, W. V. S. (Griq. W. & E. Prov.) b Oct. 3, 1891, d Sept. 26, 1960
*Lissette, A. F. (Auck. & N. Dist.) b Nov. 6, 1919, d Jan. 24, 1973
Lister, W. H. L. (CU & Lancs) b Oct. 7, 1911
Livingston, L. (NSW & Northants) b May 3, 1920
Livingstone, D. A. (Hants) b Sept. 21, 1933, d Sept. 8, 1988
Livsey, W. H. (Hants) b Sept. 23, 1893, d Sept. 12, 1978
*Liyanage, D. K. (Colts & WPS) b June 6, 1972
*Llewellyn, C. B. (Natal & Hants; *CY 1911*) b Sept. 26, 1876, d June 7, 1964
Llewellyn, M. J. (Glam) b Nov. 27, 1953
Lloyd, B. J. (Glam) b Sept. 6, 1953
*Lloyd, C. H. (†Guyana & Lancs; *CY 1971*) b Aug. 31, 1944
*Lloyd, D. (Lancs) b March 18, 1947
Lloyd, G. D. (Lancs) b July 1, 1969
*Lloyd, T. A. (Warwicks & OFS) b Nov. 5, 1956
Lloyds, J. W. (Som, OFS & Glos) b Nov. 17, 1954
*Loader, P. J. (Surrey & W. Aust.; *CY 1958*) b Oct. 25, 1929
Lobb, B. (Warwicks & Som) b Jan. 11, 1931
*Lock, A. C. I. (MCD) b Sept. 10, 1962
*Lock, G. A. R. (Surrey, W. Aust. & Leics; *CY 1954*) b July 5, 1929, d March 29, 1995
Lockwood, Ephraim (Yorks) b April 4, 1845, d Dec. 19, 1921
*Lockwood, W. H. (Notts & Surrey; *CY 1899*) b March 25, 1868, d April 26, 1932
Lockyer, T. (Surrey & All-England) b Nov. 1, 1826, d Dec. 22, 1869
Logan, J. D., jun. (SA) b June 24, 1880, d Jan. 3, 1960
*Logie, A. L. (T/T) b Sept. 28, 1960
*Lohmann, G. A. (Surrey, W. Prov. & Tvl; *CY 1889*) b June 2, 1865, d Dec. 1, 1901
Lomax, J. G. (Lancs & Som) b May 5, 1925, d May 21, 1992
Long, A. (Surrey & Sussex) b Dec. 18, 1940
Longrigg, E. F. (Som & CU) b April 16, 1906, d July 23, 1974
Lord, Thomas (Middx; founder of Lord's) b Nov. 23, 1755, d Jan. 13, 1832
*Love, H. S. B. (NSW & Vic.) b Aug. 10, 1895, d July 22, 1969
Love, J. D. (Yorks) b April 22, 1955
*Loveridge, G. R. (C. Dist.) b Jan. 15, 1975
*Lowry, T. C. (Wgtn, CU & Som) b Feb. 17, 1898, d July 20, 1976
*Lowson, F. A. (Yorks) b July 1, 1925, d Sept. 8, 1984
*Loxton, S. J. E. (Vic.) b March 29, 1921
*Lucas, A. P. (CU, Surrey, Middx & Essex) b Feb. 20, 1857, d Oct. 12, 1923
Luckes, W. T. (Som) b Jan. 1, 1901, d Oct. 27, 1982
*Luckhurst, B. W. (Kent; *CY 1971*) b Feb. 5, 1939
Lumb, R. G. (Yorks) b Feb. 27, 1950
*Lundie, E. B. (E. Prov., W. Prov. & Tvl) b March 15, 1888, d Sept. 12, 1917
Lupton, A. W. (Yorks) b Feb. 23, 1879, d April 14, 1944
Lynch, M. A. (Surrey, Guyana & Glos) b May 21, 1958
Lyon, B. H. (OU & Glos; *CY 1931*) b Jan. 19, 1902, d June 22, 1970
Lyon, M. D. (CU & Som) b April 22, 1898, d Feb. 17, 1964
*Lyons, J. J. (S. Aust.) b May 21, 1863, d July 21, 1927
*Lyttelton, Hon. Alfred (CU & Middx; Pres. MCC 1898) b Feb. 7, 1857, d July 5, 1913
Lyttelton, Rev. Hon. C. F. (CU & Worcs) b Jan. 26, 1887, d Oct. 3, 1931
Lyttelton, Hon. C. G. (CU) b Oct. 27, 1842, d June 9, 1922
Lyttelton, Hon. C. J. (*see* 10th Visct Cobham)

*McAlister, P. A. (Vic.) b July 11, 1869, d May 10, 1938
*Macartney, C. G. (NSW & Otago; *CY 1922*) b June 27, 1886, d Sept. 9, 1958
*Macaulay, G. G. (Yorks; *CY 1924*) b Dec. 7, 1897, d Dec. 13, 1940
*Macaulay, M. J. (Tvl, W. Prov., OFS, NE Tvl & E. Prov.) b April 1939
*MacBryan, J. C. W. (CU & Som; *CY 1925*) b July 22, 1892, d July 14, 1983
*McCabe, S. J. (NSW; *CY 1935*) b July 16, 1910, d Aug. 25, 1968
*McCague, M. J. (Kent & W. Aust.) b May 24, 1969
*McCarthy, C. N. (Natal & CU) b March 24, 1929
*McConnon, J. E. (Glam) b June 21, 1922
*McCool, C. L. (NSW, Qld & Som) b Dec. 9, 1916, d April 5, 1986

McCorkell, N. (Hants) b March 23, 1912
*McCormick, E. L. (Vic.) b May 16, 1906, d June 28, 1991
*McCosker, R. B. (NSW; *CY 1976*) b Dec. 11, 1946
McCurdy, R. J. (Vic., Derbys, S. Aust., E. Prov. & Natal) b Dec. 30, 1959
*McDermott, C. J. (Qld; *CY 1986*) b April 14, 1965
*McDonald, C. C. (Vic.) b Nov. 17, 1928
*McDonald, E. A. (Tas., Vic. & Lancs; *CY 1922*) b Jan. 6, 1891, d July 22, 1937
*McDonnell, P. S. (Vic., NSW & Qld) b Nov. 13, 1858, d Sept. 24, 1896
McEwan, K. S. (E. Prov., W. Prov., Essex & W. Aust.; *CY 1978*) b July 16, 1952
*McEwan, P. E. (Cant.) b Dec. 19, 1953
*McGahey, C. P. (Essex; *CY 1902*) b Feb. 12, 1871, d Jan. 10, 1935
*MacGibbon, A. R. (Cant.) b Aug. 28, 1924
McGilvray, A. D. (NSW; broadcaster) b Dec. 6, 1909, d July 16, 1996
*McGirr, H. M. (Wgtn) b Nov. 5, 1891, d April 14, 1964
*McGlew, D. J. (Natal; *CY 1956*) b March 11, 1929
*McGrath, G. D. (NSW) b Fb. 9, 1970
*MacGregor, G. (CU & Middx; *CY 1891*) b Aug. 31, 1869, d Aug. 20, 1919
*McGregor, S. N. (Otago) b Dec. 18, 1931
*McIlwraith, J. (Vic.) b Sept. 7, 1857, d July 5, 1938
*McIntyre, A. J. (Surrey; *CY 1958*) b May 14, 1e918
*McIntyre, P. E. (S. Aust.) b April 27, 1966
*Mackay, K. D. (Qld) b Oct. 24, 1925, d June 13, 1982
McKechnie, B. J. (Otago) b Nov. 6, 1953
*McKenzie, G. D. (W. Aust. & Leics; *CY 1965*) b June 24, 1941
*McKibbin, T. R. (NSW) b Dec. 10, 1870, d Dec. 15, 1939
*McKinnon, A. H. (E. Prov. & Tvl) b Aug. 20, 1932, d Dec. 1, 1983
*MacKinnon, F. A. (CU & Kent; *believed to be longest-lived Test cricketer*) b April 9, 1848, d Feb. 27, 1947
*MacLaren, A. C. (Lancs; *CY 1895*) b Dec. 1, 1871, d Nov. 17, 1944
*McLaren, J. W. (Qld) b Dec. 24, 1887, d Nov. 17, 1921
MacLaurin of Knebworth, Lord (Chairman ECB 1997-) b March 30, 1937
*Maclean, J. A. (Qld) b April 27, 1946
*McLean, R. A. (Natal; *CY 1961*) b July 9, 1930
MacLeay, K. H. (W. Aust. & Som) b April 2, 1959
*McLeod, C. E. (Vic.) b Oct. 24, 1869, d Nov. 26, 1918
*McLeod, E. G. (Auck. & Wgtn) b Oct. 14, 1900, d Sept. 14, 1989
*McLeod, R. W. (Vic.) b Jan. 19, 1868, d June 14, 1907
McMahon, J. W. (Surrey & Som) b Dec. 28, 1919
*McMahon, T. G. (Wgtn) b Nov. 8, 1929
*McMaster, J. E. P. (Eng.) b March 16, 1861, d June 7, 1929
*McMillan, B. M. (Tvl, W. Prov. & Warwicks) b Dec. 22, 1963
*McMillan, Q. (Tvl) b June 23, 1904, d July 3, 1948
*McMorris, E. D. A. (Jam.) b April 4, 1935
*McRae, D. A. N. (Cant.) b Dec. 25, 1912, d Aug. 10, 1986
*McShane, P. G. (Vic.) b 1857, d Dec. 11, 1903
McSweeney, E. B. (C. Dist. & Wgtn) b March 8, 1957
McVicker, N. M. (Warwicks & Leics) b Nov. 4, 1940
*McWatt, C. A. (BG) b Feb. 1, 1922
*Madan Lal (Punjab & Delhi) b March 20, 1951
*Maddocks, L. V. (Vic. & Tas.) b May 24, 1926
*Madray, I. S. (BG) b July 2, 1934
*Madugalle, R. S. (NCC) b April 22, 1959
*Madurasinghe, A. W. R. (Kurunegala & NWP) b Jan. 30, 1961
*Maguire, J. N. (Qld, E. Prov. & Leics) b Sept. 15, 1956
*Mahanama, R. S. (CCC & Bloom.) b May 31, 1966
Maher, B. J. M. (Derbys) b Feb. 11, 1958
Mahmood Hamid (Kar. & UBL) b Jan. 19, 1969
*Mahmood Hussain (Pak. Us, Punjab, Kar., E. Pak. & NTB) b April 2, 1932, d Dec. 25, 1991
*Mailey, A. A. (NSW) b Jan. 3, 1886, d Dec. 31, 1967
*Majid Khan (Lahore, Pak. Us, CU, Glam, PIA, Qld, Punjab; *CY 1970*) b Sept. 28, 1946
*Maka, E. S. (Bombay) b March 5, 1922
*Makepeace, H. (Lancs) b Aug. 22, 1881, d Dec. 19, 1952
*Malcolm, D. E. (Derbys; *CY 1995*) b Feb. 22, 1963
*Malhotra, A. (Haryana & Bengal) b Jan. 26, 1957
*Mallender, N. A. (Northants, Otago & Som) b Aug. 13, 1961
*Mallett, A. A. (S. Aust.) b July 13, 1945
*Malone, M. F. (W. Aust. & Lancs) b Oct. 9, 1950
*Maninder Singh (Delhi) b June 13, 1965
*Manjrekar, S. V. (Bombay) b July 12, 1965
*Manjrekar, V. L. (Bombay, Bengal, Andhra, U. Pradesh, Raja. & M'tra) b Sept. 26, 1931, d Oct. 18, 1983
*Mankad, A. V. (Bombay) b Oct. 12, 1946

*Mankad, V. (M. H.) (W. Ind., Naw., M'tra, Guj., Bengal, Bombay & Raja.; *CY 1947*) b April 12, 1917, d Aug. 21, 1978
*Mann, A. L. (W. Aust.) b Nov. 8, 1945
*Mann, F. G. (CU & Middx; Pres. MCC 1984-85) b Sept. 6, 1917
*Mann, F. T. (CU & Middx) b March 3, 1888, d Oct. 6, 1964
*Mann, N. B. F. (Natal & E. Prov.) b Dec. 28, 1920, d July 31, 1952
Manning, J. S. (S. Aust. & Northants) b June 11, 1924, d May 5, 1988
Manning, T. E. (Northants) b Sept. 2, 1884, d Nov. 22, 1975
*Mansell, P. N. F. (Rhod.) b March 16, 1920, d May 9, 1995
*Mansoor Akhtar (Kar., UBL & Sind) b Dec. 25, 1956
Mansoor Rana (ADBP & Lahore) b Dec. 27, 1962
Mansur Ali Khan (*see* Pataudi, Mansur Ali, Nawab of)
*Mantri, M. K. (Bombay & M'tra) b Sept. 1, 1921
*Manzoor Elahi (Multan, Pak. Rlwys & IDBP) b April 15, 1963
*Maqsood Ahmed (S. Punjab, R'pindi & Kar.) b March 26, 1925
Maqsood Rana (Lahore, NBP & R'pindi) b Aug. 1, 1972
*Marais, G. G. ("G. Gladstone") (Jam.) b Jan. 14, 1901, d May 19, 1978
Marchant, F. (Kent & CU) b May 22, 1864, d April 13, 1946
*Markham, L. A. (Natal) b Sept. 12, 1924
*Marks, V. J. (OU, Som & W. Aust.) b June 25, 1955
Marlar, R. G. (CU & Sussex) b Jan. 2, 1931
Marlow, F. W. (Sussex) b Oct. 8, 1867, d Aug. 7, 1952
Marner, P. T. (Lancs & Leics) b March 31, 1936
*Marr, A. P. (NSW) b March 28, 1962, d March 15, 1940
*Marriott, C. S. (CU, Lancs & Kent) b Sept. 14, 1895, d Oct. 13, 1966
Marsden, Tom (Eng.) b 1805, d Feb. 27, 1843
*Marsh, G. R. (W. Aust.) b Dec. 31, 1958
*Marsh, R. W. (W. Aust.; *CY 1982*) b Nov. 11, 1947
Marsh, S. A. (Kent) b Jan. 27, 1961
Marshal, Alan (Qld & Surrey; *CY 1909*) b June 12, 1883, d July 23, 1915
*Marshall, M. D. (B'dos, Hants & Natal; *CY 1983*) b April 18, 1958
*Marshall, N. E. (B'dos & T/T) b Feb. 27, 1924
*Marshall, R. E. (B'dos & Hants; *CY 1959*) b April 25, 1930, d Oct. 27, 1992
Marsham, C. H. B. (OU & Kent) b Feb. 10, 1879, d July 19, 1928
Martin, E. J. (Notts) b Aug. 17, 1925
*Martin, F. (Kent; *CY 1892*) b Oct. 12, 1861, d Dec. 13, 1921
*Martin, F. R. (Jam.) b Oct. 12, 1893, d Nov. 23, 1967
Martin, G. C. (Mash.) b May 30, 1966
*Martin, J. W. (NSW & S. Aust.) b July 28, 1931, d July 16, 1992
*Martin, J. W. (Kent) b Feb. 16, 1917, d Jan. 4, 1987
*Martin, P. J. (Lancs) b Nov. 15, 1968
Martin, S. H. (Worcs, Natal & Rhod.) b Jan. 11, 1909, d Feb. 1988
*Martindale, E. A. (B'dos) b Nov. 25, 1909, d March 17, 1972
Martin-Jenkins, Christopher (Writer & broadcaster) b Jan. 20, 1945
*Martyn, D. R. (W. Aust.) b Oct. 21, 1971
Maru, R. J. (Middx & Hants) b Oct. 28, 1962
*Marx, W. F. E. (Tvl) b July 4, 1895, d June 2, 1974
*Mason, J. R. (Kent; *CY 1898*) b March 26, 1874, d Oct. 15, 1958
*Masood Anwar (UBL, Multan & F'bad) b Dec. 12, 1967
Masood Iqbal (Lahore, Punjab U., Pak. Us & HBL) b April 17, 1952
*Massie, H. H. (NSW) b April 11, 1854, d Oct. 12, 1938
*Massie, R. A. L. (W. Aust.; *CY 1973*) b April 14, 1947
*Matheson, A. M. (Auck.) b Feb. 27, 1906, d Dec. 31, 1985
*Mathias, Wallis (Sind, Kar. & NBP) b Feb. 4, 1935, d Sept. 1, 1994
*Matthews, A. D. G. (Northants & Glam) b May 3, 1904, d July 29, 1977
*Matthews, C. D. (W. Aust. & Lancs) b Sept. 22, 1962
*Matthews, C. R. (W. Prov.) b Feb. 15, 1965
*Matthews, G. R. J. (NSW) b Dec. 15, 1959
*Matthews, T. J. (Vic.) b April 3, 1884, d Oct. 14, 1943
*Mattis, E. H. (Jam.) b April 11, 1957
*May, P. B. H. (CU & Surrey; *CY 1952;* Pres. MCC 1980-81) b Dec. 31, 1929, d Dec. 27, 1994
*May, T. B. A. (S. Aust.) b Jan. 26, 1962
Mayer, J. H. (Warwicks) b March 2, 1902, d Sept. 6, 1981
Maynard, C. (Warwicks & Lancs) b April 8, 1958
*Maynard, M. P. (Glam & N. Dist.) b March 21, 1966
*Mayne, E. R. (S. Aust. & Vict.) b July 2, 1882, d Oct. 26, 1961
*Mayne, L. C. (W. Aust.) b Jan. 23, 1942
*Mead, C. P. (Hants; *CY 1912*) b March 9, 1887, d March 26, 1958
*Mead, W. (Essex; *CY 1904*) b March 25, 1868, d March 18, 1954
Meads, E. A. (Notts) b Aug. 17, 1916
*Meale, T. (Wgtn) b Nov. 11, 1928

*Meckiff, I. (Vic.) b Jan. 6, 1935
Medlycott, K. T. (Surrey & N. Tvl) b May 12, 1965
*Meherhomji, K. R. (W. Ind. & Bombay) b Aug. 9, 1911, d Feb. 10, 1982
*Mehra, V. L. (E. Punjab, Ind. Rlwys & Delhi) b March 12, 1938
*Meintjes, D. J. (Tvl) b June 9, 1890, d July 17, 1979
*Melle, M. G. (Tvl & W. Prov.) b June 3, 1930
Melluish, M. E. L. (CU & Middx; Pres. MCC 1991-92) b June 13, 1932
*Melville, A. (OU, Sussex, Natal & Tvl; *CY 1948*) b May 19, 1910, d April 18, 1983
Mendis, G. D. (Sussex & Lancs) b April 20, 1955
*Mendis, L. R. D. (SSC) b Aug. 25, 1952
Mendis, M. C. (Colts) b Dec. 28, 1968
*Mendonca, I. L. (BG) b July 13, 1934
Mercer, J. (Sussex, Glam & Northants; *CY 1927*) b April 22, 1895, d Aug. 31, 1987
*Merchant, V. M. (Bombay; *CY 1937*) b Oct. 12, 1911, d Oct. 27, 1987
*Merritt, W. E. (Cant. & Northants) b Aug. 18, 1908, d June 9, 1977
*Merry, C. A. (T/T) b Jan. 20, 1911, d April 19, 1964
Metcalfe, A. A. (Yorks, OFS & Notts) b Dec. 25, 1963
Metson, C. P. (Middx & Glam) b July 2, 1963
*Meuleman, K. D. (Vic. & W. Aust.) b Sept. 5, 1923
*Meuli, E. M. (C. Dist.) b Feb. 20, 1926
Meyer, B. J. (Glos; Test umpire) b Aug. 21, 1932
Meyer, R. J. O. (CU, Som & W. Ind.) b March 15, 1905, d March 9, 1991
*Mhambrey, P. L. (Bombay) b June 20, 1972
Mian Mohammed Saeed (N. India, Patiala & S. Punjab) b Aug. 31, 1910, d Aug. 23, 1979
*Middleton, J. (W. Prov.) b Sept. 30, 1865, d Dec. 23, 1913
Middleton, T. C. (Hants) b Feb. 1, 1964
**Midwinter, W. E. (Vic. & Glos) b June 19, 1851, d Dec. 3, 1890
*Milburn, B. D. (Otago) b Nov. 24, 1943
*Milburn, C. (Northants & W. Aust.; *CY 1967*) b Oct. 23, 1941, d Feb. 28, 1990
*Milkha Singh, A. G. (Madras) b Dec. 31, 1941
*Miller, A. M. (Eng.) b Oct. 19, 1869, d June 26, 1959
Miller, F. P. (Surrey) b July 29, 1828, d Nov. 22, 1875
*Miller, G. (Derbys, Natal & Essex) b Sept. 8, 1952
*Miller, K. R. (Vic., NSW & Notts; *CY 1954*) b Nov. 28, 1919
*Miller, L. S. M. (C. Dist. & Wgtn) b March 31, 1923, d Dec. 17, 1996
Miller, R. (Warwicks) b Jan. 6, 1941, d May 7, 1996
*Miller, R. C. (Jam.) b Dec. 24, 1924
*Milligan, F. W. (Yorks) b March 19, 1870, d March 31, 1900
*Millman, G. (Notts) b Oct. 2, 1934
Millmow, J. P. (Wgtn) b Sept. 22, 1967
Millns, D. J. (Notts & Leics) b Feb. 27, 1965
*Mills, C. H. (Surrey, Kimberley & W. Prov.) b Nov. 26, 1867, d July 26, 1948
*Mills, J. E. (Auck.) b Sept. 3, 1905, d Dec. 11, 1972
Mills, P. T. (Glos) b May 7, 1879, d Dec. 8, 1950
*Milton, C. A. (Glos; *CY 1959*) b March 10, 1928
*Milton, Sir William H. (W. Prov.) b Dec. 3, 1854, d March 6, 1930
*Minnett, R. B. (NSW) b June 13, 1888, d Oct. 21, 1955
Minshull, John (scorer of first recorded century) b *circa* 1741, d Oct. 1793
*Miran Bux (Pak. Serv., Punjab & R'pindi) b April 20, 1907, d Feb. 8, 1991
*Misson, F. M. (NSW) b Nov. 19, 1938
*Mitchell, A. (Yorks) b Sept. 13, 1902, d Dec. 25, 1976
*Mitchell, B. (Tvl; *CY 1936*) b Jan. 8, 1909, d July 2, 1995
**Mitchell, F. (CU, Yorks & Tvl; *CY 1902*) b Aug. 13, 1872, d Oct. 11, 1935
*Mitchell, T. B. (Derbys) b Sept. 4, 1902, d Jan. 27, 1996
*Mitchell-Innes, N. S. (OU & Som) b Sept. 7, 1914
*Modi, R. S. (Bombay) b Nov. 11, 1924, d May 17, 1996
*Mohammad Akram (R'pindi) b Sept. 10, 1974
*Mohammad Aslam (N. Ind. & Pak. Rlwys) b Jan. 5, 1920
*Mohammad Farooq (Kar.) b April 8, 1938
*Mohammad Ilyas (Lahore & PIA) b March 19, 1946
*Mohammad Munaf (Sind, E. Pak., Kar. & PIA) b Nov. 2, 1935
*Mohammad Nazir (Pak. Rlwys) b March 8, 1946
*Mohsin Kamal (Lahore, Allied Bank & PNSC) b June 16, 1963
*Mohsin Khan (Pak. Rlwys, Kar., Sind, Pak. Us & HBL) b March 15, 1955
*Moin Khan (Kar. & PIA) b Sept. 23, 1971
Moin-ul-Atiq (UBL, Kar. & HBL) b Aug. 5, 1964
*Moir, A. M. (Otago) b July 17, 1919
*Mold, A. (Lancs; *CY 1892*) b May 27, 1863, d April 29, 1921
Moles, A. J. (Warwicks & Griq. W.) b Feb. 12, 1961
*Moloney, D. A. R. (Wgtn, Otago & Cant.) b Aug. 11, 1910, d July 15, 1942
Monckton of Brenchley, 1st Visct (Pres. MCC 1956-57) b Jan. 17, 1891, d Jan. 9, 1965
*Mongia, N. R. (Baroda) b Dec. 19, 1969
*Moodie, G. H. (Jam.) b Nov. 25, 1915

*Moody, T. M. (W. Aust., Warwicks & Worcs) b Oct. 2, 1965
*Moon, L. J. (CU & Middx) b Feb. 9, 1878, d Nov. 23, 1916
*Mooney, F. L. H. (Wgtn) b May 26, 1921
Moore, H. I. (Notts) b Feb. 28, 1941
Moore, R. H. (Hants) b Nov. 14, 1913
Moores, P. (Worcs, Sussex & OFS) b Dec. 18, 1962
Moorhouse, R. (Yorks) b Sept. 7, 1866, d Jan. 7, 1921
*More, K. S. (Baroda) b Sept. 4, 1962
Morgan, D. C. (Derbys) b Feb. 26, 1929
*Morgan, R. W. (Auck.) b Feb. 12, 1941
*Morkel, D. P. B. (W. Prov.) b Jan. 25, 1906, d Oct. 6, 1980
*Morley, F. (Notts) b Dec. 16, 1850, d Sept. 28, 1884
*Moroney, J. (NSW) b July 24, 1917
*Morris, A. R. (NSW; *CY 1949*) b Jan. 19, 1922
*Morris, H. (Glam) b Oct. 5, 1963
Morris, H. M. (Essex & CU) b April 16, 1898, d Nov. 18, 1984
*Morris, J. E. (Derbys, Griq. W. & Durham) b April 1, 1964
*Morris, S. (Vic.) b June 22, 1855, d Sept. 20, 1931
*Morrison, B. D. (Wgtn) b Dec. 17, 1933
*Morrison, D. K. (Auck. & Lancs) b Feb. 3, 1966
*Morrison, J. F. M. (C. Dist. & Wgtn) b Aug. 27, 1947
Mortensen, O. H. (Denmark & Derbys) b Jan. 29, 1958
*Mortimore, J. B. (Glos) b May 14, 1933
Mortlock, W. (Surrey & Utd Eng. XI) b July 18, 1832, d Jan. 23, 1884
Morton, A., jun. (Derbys) b May 7, 1883, d Dec. 19, 1935
*Moseley, E. A. (B'dos, Glam, E. Prov. & N. Tvl) b Jan. 5, 1958
Moseley, H. R. (B'dos & Som) b May 28, 1948
*Moses, H. (NSW) b Feb. 13, 1858, d Dec. 7, 1938
*Moss, A. E. (Middx) b Nov. 14, 1930
*Moss, J. K. (Vic.) b June 29, 1947
*Motz, R. C. (Cant.; *CY 1966*) b Jan. 12, 1940
*Moule, W. H. (Vic.) b Jan. 31, 1858, d Aug. 24, 1939
*Moxon, M. D. (Yorks & Griq. W.; *CY 1993*) b May 4, 1960
*Mudassar Nazar (Lahore, Punjab, Pak. Us, HBL, PIA & UBL) b April 6, 1956
*Muddiah, V. M. (Mysore & Ind. Servs) b June 8, 1929
*Mufasir-ul-Haq (Kar., Dacca, PWD, E. Pak. & NBP) b Aug. 16, 1944, d July 27, 1983
Mukherjee, S. P. (Bengal) b Oct. 5, 1964
*Mullally, A. D. (W. Aust., Vic., Hants & Leics) b July 12, 1969
Munasinghe, M. (SSC) b Dec. 10, 1971
Muncer, B. L. (Glam & Middx) b Oct. 23, 1913, d Jan. 18, 1982
Munden, V. S. (Leics) b Jan. 2, 1928
*Munir Malik (Punjab, R'pindi, Pak. Serv. & Kar.) b July 10, 1934
*Munton, T. A. (Warwicks; *CY 1995*) b July 30, 1965
*Muralitharan, M. (TU) b April 17, 1972
**Murdoch, W. L. (NSW & Sussex) b Oct. 18, 1854, d Feb. 18, 1911
*Murray, A. R. A. (E. Prov.) b April 30, 1922, d April 17, 1995
*Murray, B. A. G. (Wgtn) b Sept. 18, 1940
*Murray, D. A. (B'dos) b Sept. 29, 1950
*Murray, D. J. (Cant.) b Sept. 4, 1967
*Murray, D. L. (T/T, CU, Notts & Warwicks) b May 20, 1943
*Murray, J. R. (Windwards) b Jan. 20, 1968
*Murray, J. T. (Middx; *CY 1967*) b April 1, 1935
Murrell, H. R. (Kent & Middx) b Nov. 19, 1879, d Aug. 15, 1952
*Musgrove, H. (Vic.) b Nov. 27, 1860, d Nov. 2, 1931
*Mushtaq Ahmed (UBL, Multan & Som; *CY 1997*) b June 28, 1970
*Mushtaq Ali, S. (C. Ind., Guj., †M. Pradesh & U. Pradesh) b Dec. 17, 1914
*Mushtaq Mohammad (Kar., Northants & PIA; *CY 1963*) b Nov. 22, 1943
Mynn, Alfred (Kent & All-Eng.) b Jan. 19, 1807, d Oct. 31, 1861

*Nadkarni, R. G. (M'tra & Bombay) b April 4, 1932
*Nadeem Abbasi (R'pindi) b April 15, 1964
*Nadeem Ghauri (Lahore, Pak. Rlwys & HBL) b Oct. 12, 1962
*Nadeem Khan (Kar. & NBP) b Dec. 10, 1969
Naeem Ahmed, (Kar., Pak Us, NBP, UBL & PIA) b Sept. 20, 1952
Naeem Ahmed (Sargodha & HBL) b April 14, 1971
Naeem Ashraf (Lahore & NBP) b Nov. 10, 1972
*Nagel, L. E. (Vic.) b March 6, 1905, d Nov. 23, 1971
*Naik, S. S. (Bombay) b Feb. 21, 1945
*Nanan, R. (T/T) b May 29, 1953
*Naoomal Jeoomal, M. (N. Ind. & Sind) b April 17, 1904, d July 18, 1980
*Narasimha Rao, M. V. (H'bad) b Aug. 11, 1954
Naseer Malik (Khairpair & NBP) b Feb. 1, 1950
*Nash, D. J. (N. Dist., Otago & Middx) b Nov. 20, 1971
*Nash, L. J. (Tas. & Vic.) b May 2, 1910, d July 24, 1986
Nash, M. A. (Glam) b May 9, 1945
*Nasim-ul-Ghani (Kar., Pak. Us, Dacca, E. Pak., PWD & NBP) b May 14, 1941

*Naushad Ali (Kar., E. Pak., R'pindi, Peshawar, NWFP, Punjab & Pak. Serv.) b Oct. 1, 1943
*Naved Anjum (Lahore, UBL & HBL) b July 27, 1963
*Navle, J. G. (Rajputna, C. Ind., Holkar & Gwalior) b Dec. 7, 1902, d Sept. 7, 1979
*Nayak, S. V. (Bombay) b Oct. 20, 1954
*Nayudu, Col. C. K. (C. Ind., Andhra, U. Pradesh & Holkar; *CY 1933*) b Oct. 31, 1895, d Nov. 14, 1967
*Nayudu, C. S. (C. Ind., Holkar, Baroda, Bengal, Andhra & U. Pradesh) b April 18, 1914.
*Nazar Mohammad (N. Ind. & Punjab) b March 5, 1921, d July 12, 1996
*Nazir Ali, S. (S. Punjab & Sussex) b June 8, 1906, d Feb. 18, 1975
Neale, P. A. (Worcs; *CY 1989*) b June 5, 1954
Neale, W. L. (Glos) b March 3, 1904, d Oct. 26, 1955
*Neblett, J. M. (B'dos & BG) b Nov. 13, 1901, d March 28, 1959
Needham, A. (Surrey & Middx) b March 23, 1957
*Nel, J. D. (W. Prov.) b July 10, 1928
Nelson, R. P. (Middx, CU & Northants) b Aug. 7, 1912, d Oct. 29, 1940
*Newberry, C. (Tvl) b 1889, d Aug. 1, 1916
Newell, M. (Notts) b Feb. 25, 1965
*Newham, W. (Sussex) b Dec. 12, 1860, d June 26, 1944
Newland, Richard (Sussex) b *circa* 1718, d May 29, 1791
*Newman, Sir Jack (Wgtn & Cant.) b July 3, 1902, d Sept. 23, 1996
Newman, J. A. (Hants & Cant.) b Nov. 12, 1884, d Dec. 21, 1973
Newman, P. G. (Derbys) b Jan. 10, 1959
*Newport, P. J. (Worcs, Boland & N. Tvl) b Oct. 11, 1962
*Newson, E. S. (Tvl & Rhod.) b Dec. 2, 1910, d April 24, 1988
Newstead, J. T. (Yorks; *CY 1909*) b Sept. 8, 1877, d March 25, 1952
Newton, A. E. (OU & Som) b Sept. 12, 1862, d Sept. 15, 1952
*Niaz Ahmed (Dacca, E. Pak., PWD & Pak. Rlwys) b Nov. 11, 1945
Nicholas, M. C. J. (Hants) b Sept. 29, 1957
Nicholls, D. (Kent) b Dec. 8, 1943
Nicholls, R. B. (Glos) b Dec. 4, 1933, d July 21, 1994
*Nichols, M. S. (Essex; *CY 1934*) b Oct. 6, 1900, d Jan. 26, 1961
Nicholson, A. G. (Yorks) b June 25, 1938, d Nov. 4, 1985
*Nicholson, F. (Griq. W.) b Sept. 17, 1909, d July 30, 1982
*Nicolson, J. F. W. (Natal & OU) b July 19, 1899, d Dec. 13, 1935
*Nissar, Mahomed (Patiala, S. Punjab & U. Pradesh) b Aug. 1, 1910, d March 11, 1963
*Nitschke, H. C. (S. Aust.) b April 14, 1905, d Sept. 29, 1982
Nixon, P. A. (Leics) b Oct. 21, 1970
*Noble, M. A. (NSW; *CY 1900*) b Jan. 28, 1873, d June 22, 1940
*Noblet, G. (S. Aust.) b Sept. 14, 1916
*Noreiga, J. M. (T/T) b April 15, 1936
Norfolk, 16th Duke of (Pres. MCC 1957-58) b May 30, 1908, d Jan. 31, 1975
Norman, M. E. J. C. (Northants & Leics) b Jan. 19, 1933
*Norton, N. O. (W. Prov. & Border) b May 11, 1881, d June 27, 1968
*Nothling, O. E. (NSW & Qld) b Aug. 1, 1900, d Sept. 26, 1965
*Nourse, A. D. ("Dudley") (Natal; *CY 1948*) b Nov. 12, 1910, d Aug. 14, 1981
*Nourse, A. W. ("Dave") (Natal, Tvl & W. Prov.) b Jan. 26, 1878, d July 8, 1948
Nugent, 1st Lord (Pres. MCC 1962-63) b Aug. 11, 1895, d April 27, 1973
*Nunes, R. K. (Jam.) b June 7, 1894, d July 22, 1958
*Nupen, E. P. (Tvl) b Jan. 1, 1902, d Jan. 29, 1977
*Nurse, S. M. (B'dos; *CY 1967*) b Nov. 10, 1933
Nutter, A. E. (Lancs & Northants) b June 28, 1913, d June 3, 1996
*Nyalchand, S. (W. Ind., Kathiawar, Guj., & S'tra) b Sept. 14, 1919, d Jan. 1, 1997
Nyren, John (Hants) b Dec. 15, 1764, d June 28, 1937
Nyren, Richard (Hants & Sussex; Proprietor Bat & Ball Inn, Broadhalfpenny Down) b 1734, d April 25, 1797

Oakes, C. (Sussex) b Aug. 10, 1912
Oakes, J. (Sussex) b March 3, 1916
*Oakman, A. S. M. (Sussex) b April 20, 1930
Oates, T. W. (Notts) b Aug. 9, 1875, d June 18, 1949
Oates, W. F. (Yorks & Derbys) b June 11, 1929
*O'Brien, L. P. J. (Vic.) b July 2, 1907
*O'Brien, Sir Timothy C. (OU & Middx) b Nov. 5, 1861, d Dec. 9, 1948
*Ochse, A. E. (Tvl) b March 11, 1870, d April 11, 1918
*Ochse, A. L. (E. Prov.) b Oct. 11, 1899, d May 5, 1949
*O'Connor, J. (Essex) b Nov. 6, 1897, d Feb. 22, 1977
*O'Connor, J. D. A. (NSW & S. Aust.) b Sept. 9, 1875, d Aug. 23, 1941
*O'Donnell, S. P. (Vic.) b Jan. 26, 1963
*Ogilvie, A. D. (Qld) b June 3, 1951
O'Gorman, T. J. G. (Derbys) b May 15, 1967
*O'Keeffe, K. J. (NSW & Som) b Nov. 25, 1949

*Old, C. M. (Yorks, Warwicks & N. Tvl; *CY 1979*) b Dec. 22, 1948
*Oldfield, N. (Lancs & Northants; Test umpire) b May 5, 1911, d April 19, 1996
Oldfield, W. A. (NSW; *CY 1927*) b Sept. 9, 1894, d Aug. 10, 1976
Oldham, S. (Yorks & Derbys) b July 26, 1948
Oldroyd, E. (Yorks) b Oct. 1, 1888, d Dec. 27, 1964
*O'Linn, S. (Kent, W. Prov. & Tvl) b May 5, 1927
Oliver, L. (Derbys) b Oct. 18, 1886, d Jan. 22, 1948
*Olonga, H. K. (Mat.) b July 3, 1976
*O'Neill, N. C. (NSW; *CY 1962*) b Feb. 19, 1937
Ontong, R. C. (Border, Tvl, N. Tvl & Glam) b Sept. 9, 1955
Opatha, A. R. M. (SL) b Aug. 5, 1947
Ord, J. S. (Warwicks) b July 12, 1912
*O'Reilly, W. J. (NSW; *CY 1935*) b Dec. 20, 1905, d Oct. 6, 1992
Ormrod, J. A. (Worcs & Lancs) b Dec. 22, 1942
Oscroft, W. (Notts) b Dec. 16, 1843, d Oct. 10, 1905
O'Shaughnessy, S. J. (Lancs & Worcs) b Sept. 9, 1961
Oslear, D. O. (Test umpire) b March 3, 1929
Ostler, D. P. (Warwicks) b July 15, 1970
*O'Sullivan, D. R. (C. Dist. & Hants) b Nov. 16, 1944
Outschoorn, L. (Worcs) b Sept. 26, 1918, d Jan. 9, 1994
*Overton, G. W. F. (Otago) b June 8, 1919, d Sept. 7, 1993
Owen, H. G. P. (CU & Essex) b May 19, 1859, d Oct. 20, 1912
*Owens, M. B. (Cant.) b Nov. 11, 1969
*Owen-Smith, H. G. (W. Prov., OU & Middx; *CY 1930*) b Feb. 18, 1909, d Feb. 28, 1990
Owen-Thomas, D. R. (CU & Surrey) b Sept. 20, 1948
*Oxenham, R. K. (Qld) b July 28, 1891, d Aug. 16, 1939

*Padgett, D. E. V. (Yorks) b July 20, 1934
*Padmore, A. L. (B'dos) b Dec. 17, 1946
Page, J. C. T. (Kent) b May 20, 1930, d Dec. 14, 1990
Page, M. H. (Derbys) b June 17, 1941
*Page, M. L. (Cant.) b May 8, 1902, d Feb. 13, 1987
*Pai, A. M. (Bombay) b April 28, 1945
*Paine, G. A. E. (Middx & Warwicks; *CY 1935*) b June 11, 1908, d March 30, 1978
*Pairaudeau, B. H. (BG & N. Dist.) b April 14, 1931
*Palairet, L. C. H. (OU & Som; *CY 1893*) b May 27, 1870, d March 27, 1933
Palairet, R. C. N. (OU & Som) b June 25, 1871, d Feb. 11, 1955
*Palia, P. E. (Parsis, Madras, U. Prov., Bombay, Mysore & Bengal) b Sept. 5, 1910, d Sept. 9, 1981
Palframan, S. J. (E. Prov. & Border) b May 12, 1970
*Palm, A. W. (W. Prov.) b June 8, 1901, d Aug. 17, 1966
*Palmer, C. H. (Worcs & Leics; Pres. MCC 1978-79) b May 15, 1919
*Palmer, G. E. (Vic. & Tas.) b Feb. 22, 1859, d Aug. 22, 1910
*Palmer, K. E. (Som; Test umpire) b April 22, 1937
Palmer, R. (Som; Test umpire) b July 12, 1942
*Pandit, C. S. (Bombay, M. Pradesh & Assam) b Sept. 30, 1961
Pardon, Charles F. (Editor of *Wisden* 1887-90) b March 28, 1850, d April 18, 1890
Pardon, Sydney H. (Editor of *Wisden* 1891-1925) b Sept. 23, 1855, d Nov. 20, 1925
*Parfitt, P. H. (Middx; *CY 1963*) b Dec. 8, 1936
Paris, C. G. A. (Hants; Pres. MCC 1975-76) b Aug. 30, 1911
Parish, R. J. (Aust. Administrator) b May 7, 1916
*Park, Dr R. L. (Vic.) b July 30, 1892, d Jan. 23, 1947
*Parkar, G. A. (Bombay) b Oct. 24, 1955
*Parkar, R. D. (Bombay) b Oct. 31, 1946
Parkar, Z. (Bombay) b Nov. 22, 1957
*Parker, C. W. L. (Glos; *CY 1923*) b Oct. 14, 1882, d July 11, 1959
*Parker, G. M. (SA) b May 27, 1899, d May 1, 1969
Parker, J. F. (Surrey) b April 23, 1913, d Jan. 27, 1983
*Parker, J. M. (N. Dist. & Worcs) b Feb. 21, 1951
*Parker, N. M. (Otago & Cant.) b Aug. 28, 1948
*Parker, P. W. G. (CU, Sussex, Natal & Durham) b Jan. 15, 1956
*Parkhouse, W. G. A. (Glam) b Oct. 12, 1925
*Parkin, C. H. (Yorks & Lancs; *CY 1924*) b Feb. 18, 1886, d June 15, 1943
*Parkin, D. C. (E. Prov., Tvl & Griq. W.) b Feb. 20, 1873, d March 20, 1936
Parks, H. W. (Sussex) b July 18, 1906, d May 7, 1984
*Parks, J. H. (Sussex & Cant.; *CY 1938*) b May 12, 1903, d Nov. 21, 1980
*Parks, J. M. (Sussex & Som; *CY 1968*) b Oct. 21, 1931
Parks, R. J. (Hants & Kent) b June 15, 1959
*Parore, A. C. (Auck.) b Jan. 23, 1971
Parr, George (Notts & All-England) b May 22, 1826, d June 23, 1891
*Parry, D. R. (Comb. Is. & Leewards) b Dec. 22, 1954
*Parsana, D. D. (S'tra, Ind. Rlwys & Guj.) b Dec. 2, 1947

Parsons, A. B. D. (CU & Surrey) b Sept. 20, 1933
Parsons, G. J. (Leics, Warwicks, Boland, Griq. W. & OFS) b Oct. 17, 1959
Parsons, Canon J. H. (Warwicks) b May 30, 1890, d Feb. 2, 1981
*Partridge, J. T. (Rhod.) b Dec. 9, 1932, d June 7, 1988
Partridge, N. E. (Malvern, CU & Warwicks; *CY 1919*) b Aug. 10, 1900, d March 10, 1982
Partridge, R. J. (Northants) b Feb. 11, 1912
Parvez Mir (R'pindi, Lahore, Punjab, Pak. Us, Derbys, HBL & Glam) b Sept. 24, 1953
*Pascoe, L. S. (NSW) b Feb. 13, 1950
Pasqual, S. P. (SL) b Oct. 15, 1961
*Passailaigue, C. C. (Jam.) b Aug. 1902, d Jan. 7, 1972
*Patankar, C. T. (Bombay) b Nov. 24, 1930
**Pataudi, Iftiqar Ali, Nawab of (OU, Worcs, Patiala, N. Ind. & S. Punjab; *CY 1932*) b March 16, 1910, d Jan. 5, 1952
*Pataudi, Mansur Ali, Nawab of (Sussex, OU, Delhi & H'bad; *CY 1968*) b Jan. 5, 1941
Patel, A. K. (S'tra) b March 6, 1957
*Patel, B. P. (Karn.) b Nov. 24, 1952
*Patel, D. N. (Worcs & Auck.) b Oct. 25, 1958
*Patel, J. M. (Guj.) b Nov. 26, 1924, d Dec. 12, 1992
*Patel, M. M. (Kent) b July 7, 1970
*Patel, R. (Baroda) b June 1, 1964
*Patiala, Maharaja of (N. Ind., Patiala & S. Punjab) b Jan. 17, 1913, d June 17, 1974
*Patil, S. M. (Bombay & M. Pradesh) b Aug. 18, 1956
*Patil, S. R. (M'tra) b Oct. 10, 1933
*Patterson, B. P. (Jam., Tas. & Lancs) b Sept. 15, 1961
Patterson, W. H. (OU & Kent) b March 11, 1859, d May 3, 1946
*Payne, T. R. O. (B'dos) b Feb. 13, 1957
*Paynter, E. (Lancs; *CY 1938*) b Nov. 5, 1901, d Feb. 5, 1979
Payton, W. R. D. (Notts) b Feb. 13, 1882, d May 2, 1943
Peach, H. A. (Surrey) b Oct. 6, 1890, d Oct. 8, 1961
*Peall, S. G. (MCD) b Sept. 2, 1969
Pearce, T. N. (Essex) b Nov. 3, 1905, d April 10, 1994
*Pearse, O. C. (Natal) b Oct. 10, 1884, d May 7, 1953
Pearson, F. (Worcs & Auck.) b Sept. 23, 1880, d Nov. 10, 1963
*Peate, E. (Yorks) b March 2, 1855, d March 11, 1900
*Peebles, I. A. R. (OU, Middx & Scotland; writer; *CY 1931*) b Jan. 20, 1908, d Feb. 28, 1980
*Peel, R. (Yorks; *CY 1889*) b Feb. 12, 1857, d Aug. 12, 1941
*Pegler, S. J. (Tvl) b July 28, 1888, d Sept. 10, 1972
*Pellew, C. E. (S. Aust.) b Sept. 21, 1893, d May 9, 1981
Penn, C. (Kent) b June 19, 1963
*Penn, F. (Kent) b March 7, 1851, d Dec. 26, 1916
Penney, T. L. (Boland, Warwicks & Mash.) b June 11, 1968
Pepper, C. G. (NSW & Aust. Serv.; umpire) b Sept. 15, 1916, d March 24, 1993
Perera, K. G. (Mor.) b May 22, 1964
Perkins, H. (CU & Cambs; Sec. MCC 1876-97) b Dec. 10, 1832, d May 6, 1916
*Perks, R. T. D. (Worcs) b Oct. 4, 1911, d Nov. 22, 1977
Perrin, P. A. (Essex; *CY 1905*) b May 26, 1876, d Nov. 20, 1945
Perryman, S. P. (Warwicks & Worcs) b Oct. 22, 1955
*Pervez Sajjad (Lahore, PIA & Kar.) b Aug. 30, 1942
*Petherick, P. J. (Otago & Wgtn) b Sept. 25, 1942
*Petrie, E. C. (Auck. & N. Dist.) b May 22, 1927
Petrie, R. G. (Cant & Wgtn) b Aug. 23, 1967
Pettiford, J. (NSW & Kent) b Nov. 29, 1919, d Oct. 11, 1964
*Phadkar, D. G. (M'tra, Bombay, Bengal & Ind. Rlwys) b Dec. 10, 1925, d March 17, 1985
Phebey, A. H. (Kent) b Oct. 1, 1924
Phelan, P. J. (Essex) b Feb. 9, 1938
*Philipson, H. (OU & Middx) b June 8, 1866, d Dec. 4, 1935
*Phillip, N. (Comb. Is., Windwards & Essex) b June 12, 1948
Phillips, H. (Sussex) b Oct. 14, 1844, d July 3, 1919
Phillips, R. B. (NSW & Qld) b May 23, 1954
*Phillips, W. B. (S. Aust.) b March 1, 1958
*Phillips, W. N. (Vic.) b Nov. 7, 1962
Phillipson, C. P. (Sussex) b Feb. 10, 1952
Phillipson, W. E. (Lancs; Test umpire) b Dec. 3, 1910, d Aug. 24, 1991
*Philpott, P. I. (NSW) b Nov. 21, 1934
Pick, R. A. (Notts & Wgtn) b Nov. 19, 1963
Pieris, H. S. M. (SL) b Feb. 16, 1946
*Pierre, L. R. (T/T) b June 5, 1921, d April 14, 1989
Pierson, A. R. K. (Warwicks & Leics) b July 21, 1963
*Pigott, A. C. S. (Sussex, Wgtn & Surrey) b June 4, 1958
Pilch, Fuller (Norfolk & Kent) b March 17, 1804, d May 1, 1870
Pilling, H. (Lancs) b Feb. 23, 1943
*Pilling, R. (Lancs; *CY 1891*) b July 5, 1855, d March 28, 1891
Piper, K. J. (Warwicks) b Dec. 18, 1969

*Pithey, A. J. (Rhod. & W. Prov.) b July 17, 1933
*Pithey, D. B. (Rhod., OU, Northants, W. Prov., Natal & Tvl) b Oct. 4, 1936
*Place, W. (Lancs) b Dec. 7, 1914
Platt, R. K. (Yorks & Northants) b Dec. 21, 1932
*Playle, W. R. (Auck. & W. Aust.) b Dec. 1, 1938
Pleass, J. E. (Glam) b May 21, 1923
Plews, N. T. (Test umpire) b Sept. 5, 1934
*Plimsoll, J. B. (W. Prov. & Natal) b Oct. 27, 1917
*Pocock, B. A. (N. Dist.) b June 18, 1971
Pocock, N. E. J. (Hants) b Dec. 15, 1951
*Pocock, P. I. (Surrey & N. Tvl) b Sept. 24, 1946
Pollard, P. R. (Notts) b Sept. 24, 1968
*Pollard, R. (Lancs) b June 19, 1912, d Dec. 16, 1985
*Pollard, V. (C. Dist. & Cant.) b Sept. 7, 1945
*Pollock, P. M. (E. Prov.; *CY 1966*) b June 30, 1941
*Pollock, R. G. (E. Prov. & Tvl; *CY 1966*) b Feb. 27, 1944
*Pollock, S. M. (Natal & Warwicks) b July 16, 1973
*Ponsford, W. H. (Vic.; *CY 1935*) b Oct. 19, 1900, d April 6, 1991
Pont, K. R. (Essex) b Jan. 16, 1953
*Ponting, R. T. (Tas.) b Dec. 19, 1974
*Poole, C. J. (Notts) b March 13, 1921, d Feb. 11, 1996
Pooley, E. (Surrey & first England tour) b Feb. 13, 1838, d July 18, 1907
*Poore, M. B. (Cant.) b June 1, 1930
*Poore, Brig-Gen. R. M. (Hants & SA; *CY 1900*) b March 20, 1866, d July 14, 1938
Pope, A. V. (Derbys) b Aug. 15, 1909, d May 11, 1996
*Pope, G. H. (Derbys) b Jan. 27, 1911, d Oct. 29, 1993
*Pope, Dr R. J. (NSW) b Feb. 18, 1864, d July 27, 1952
Popplewell, N. F. M. (CU & Som) b Aug. 8, 1957
Portal of Hungerford, 1st Lord (Pres. MCC 1958-59) b May 21, 1893, d April 22, 1971
Porter, G. D. (W. Aust.) b March 18, 1955
Pothecary, A. E. (Hants) b March 1, 1906, d May 21, 1991
*Pothecary, J. E. (W. Prov.) b Dec. 6, 1933
Potter, L. (Kent, Griq. W., Leics & OFS) b Nov. 7, 1962
*Pougher, A. D. (Leics) b April 19, 1865, d May 20, 1926
*Powell, A. W. (Griq. W.) b July 18, 1873, d Sept. 11, 1948
*Prabhakar, M. (Delhi & Durham) b April 15, 1963
Prasad, B. K. V. (TN & Karn.) b Aug. 5, 1969
*Prasanna, E. A. S. (†Karn.) b May 22, 1940
Prentice, F. T. (Leics) b April 22, 1912, d July 10, 1978
Pressdee, J. S. (Glam & NE Tvl) b June 19, 1933
Preston, Hubert (Editor of *Wisden* 1944-51) b Dec. 16, 1868, d Aug. 6, 1960
Preston, K. C. (Essex) b Aug. 22, 1925
Preston, Norman (Editor of *Wisden* 1952-80) b March 18, 1903, d March 6, 1980
Pretlove, J. F. (CU & Kent) b Nov. 23, 1932
*Price, J. S. E. (Middx) b July 22, 1937
*Price, W. F. (Middx; Test umpire) b April 25, 1902, d Jan. 13, 1969
Prichard, P. J. (Essex) b Jan. 7, 1965
*Prideaux, R. M. (CU, Kent, Northants, Sussex & OFS) b July 31, 1939
Pridgeon, A. P. (Worcs) b Feb. 22, 1954
*Priest, M. W. (Cant.) b Aug. 12, 1961
*Prince, C. F. H. (W. Prov., Border & E. Prov.) b Sept. 11, 1874, d Feb. 2, 1949
*Pringle, C. (Auck.) b Jan. 26, 1968
*Pringle, D. R. (CU & Essex) b Sept. 18, 1958
*Pringle, M. W. (OFS & W. Prov.) b June 22, 1966
Pritchard, T. L. (Wgtn, Warwicks & Kent) b March 10, 1917
*Procter, M. J. (Glos, Natal, W. Prov., Rhod. & OFS; *CY 1970*) b Sept. 15, 1946
Prodger, J. M. (Kent) b Sept. 1, 1935
*Promnitz, H. L. E. (Border, Griq. W. & OFS) b Feb. 23, 1904, d Sept. 7, 1983
*Pullar, G. (Lancs & Glos; *CY 1960*) b Aug. 1, 1935
*Puna, N. (N. Dist.) b Oct. 28, 1929, d June 7, 1996
*Punjabi, P. H. (Sind & Guj.) b Sept. 20, 1921
*Pushpakumara, K. R. (NCC) b July 21, 1975
*Pycroft, A. J. (Zimb.) b June 6, 1956
Pydanna, M. R. (Guyana) b Jan. 27, 1950

*Qasim Omar (Kar. & MCB) b Feb. 9, 1957
Quaife, B. W. (Warwicks & Worcs) b Nov. 24, 1899, d Nov. 28, 1984
Quaife, Walter (Sussex & Warwicks) b April 1, 1864, d Jan. 18, 1943
*Quaife, William (W. G.) (Warwicks & Griq. W.; *CY 1902*) b March 17, 1872, d Oct. 13, 1951
*Quinn, N. A. (Griq. W. & Tvl) b Feb. 21, 1908, d Aug. 5, 1934

*Rabone, G. O. (Wgtn & Auck.) b Nov. 6, 1921
*Rackemann, C. G. (Qld & Surrey) b June 3, 1960
Radcliffe, Sir Everard J. Bt (Yorks) b Jan. 27, 1884, d Nov. 23, 1969
*Radford, N. V. (Lancs, Tvl & Worcs; *CY 1986*) b June 7, 1957
*Radley, C. T. (Middx; *CY 1979*) b May 13, 1944
*Rae, A. F. (Jam.) b Sept. 30, 1922
Raees Mohammad (Kar.) b Dec. 24, 1932

*Rai Singh, K. (S. Punjab & Ind. Serv.) b Feb. 24, 1922
Rait Kerr, Col. R. S. (Eur.; Sec. MCC 1936-52) b April 13, 1891, d April 2, 1961
Rajadurai, B. E. A. (SSC) b Aug. 24, 1965
*Rajindernath, V. (N. Ind., U. Prov., S. Punjab, Bihar & E. Punjab) b Jan. 7, 1928, d Nov. 22, 1989
*Rajinder Pal (Delhi, S. Punjab & Punjab) b Nov. 18, 1937
*Rajput, L. S. (Bombay) b Dec. 18, 1961
*Raju, S. L. V. (H'bad) b July 9, 1969
Ralph, L. H. R. (Essex) b May 22, 1920
*Ramadhin, S. (T/T & Lancs; *CY 1951*) b May 1, 1929
*Raman, W. V. (TN) b May 23, 1965
*Ramanayake, C. P. H. (TU) b Jan. 8, 1965
*Ramaswami, C. (Madras) b June 18, 1896, presumed dead.
*Ramchand, G. S. (Sind, Bombay & Raja.) b July 26, 1927
*Ramiz Raja (Lahore, Allied Bank, PNSC & I'bad) b July 14, 1962
*Ramji, L. (W. Ind.) b Oct. 2, 1902, d Dec. 20, 1948
*Ramprakash, M. R. (Middx) b Sept. 5, 1969
*Ranasinghe, A. N. (BRC) b Oct. 13, 1956
Ranasinghe, S. K. (SL) b July 4, 1962
*Ranatunga, A. (SSC) b Dec. 1, 1963
*Ranatunga, D. (SSC) b Oct. 12, 1962
Ranatunga, N. (WPN) b Jan. 22, 1966
*Ranatunga, S. (NCC) b April 25, 1969
*Ranchod, U. (Mash.) b May 17, 1969
*Randall, D. W. (Notts; *CY 1980*) b Feb. 24, 1951
Randhir Singh (Orissa & Bihar) b Aug. 16, 1957
*Rangachari, C. R. (Madras) b April 14, 1916, d Oct. 9, 1993
*Rangnekar, K. M. (M'tra, Bombay & †M. Pradesh) b June 27, 1917, d Oct. 11, 1984
*Ranjane, V. B. (M'tra & Ind. Rlwys) b July 22, 1937
*Ranjitsinhji, K. S., afterwards H. H. the Jam Sahib of Nawanagar (CU & Sussex; *CY 1897*) b Sept. 10, 1872, d April 2, 1933
*Ransford, V. S. (Vic.; *CY 1910*) b March 20, 1885, d March 19, 1958
*Rashid Khan (PWD, Kar. & PIA) b Dec. 15, 1959
*Rashid Latif (Kar. & UBL) b Oct. 14, 1968
*Rathore, V. (Punjab) b March 26, 1969
Ratnayake, N. L. K. (SSC) b Nov. 22, 1968
*Ratnayake, R. J. (NCC) b Jan. 2, 1964
*Ratnayeke, J. R. (NCC) b May 2, 1960
Rawlin, J. T. (Yorks & Middx) b Nov. 10, 1856, d Jan. 19, 1924
Rawson, P. W. E. (Zimb. & Natal) b May 25, 1957
Rayment, A. W. H. (Hants) b May 29, 1928
*Razdan, V. (Delhi) b Aug. 25, 1969
*Read, H. D. (Surrey & Essex) b Jan. 28, 1910
*Read, J. M. (Surrey; *CY 1890*) b Feb. 9, 1859, d Feb. 17, 1929
*Read, W. W. (Surrey; *CY 1893*) b Nov. 23, 1855, d Jan. 6, 1907
*Reddy, B. (TN) b Nov. 12, 1954
*Redmond, R. E. (Wgtn & Auck.) b Dec. 29, 1944
*Redpath, I. R. (Vic.) b May 11, 1941
Reed, B. L. (Hants) b Sept. 17, 1937
*Reedman, J. C. (S. Aust.) b Oct. 9, 1865, d March 25, 1924
Rees, A. (Glam) b Feb. 17, 1938
*Reeve, D. A. (Sussex & Warwicks; *CY 1996*) b April 2, 1963
Reeves, W. (Essex; Test umpire) b Jan. 22, 1875, d March 22, 1944
*Rege, M. R. (M'tra) b March 18, 1924
*Rehman, S. F. (Punjab, Pak. Us & Lahore) b June 11, 1935
*Reid, B. A. (W. Aust.) b March 14, 1963
*Reid, J. F. (Auck.) b March 3, 1956
*Reid, J. R. (Wgtn & Otago; *CY 1959*) b June 3, 1928
*Reid, N. (W. Prov.) b Dec. 26, 1890, d June 6, 1947
Reid, R. B. (Wgtn & Auck.) b Dec. 3, 1958
Reidy, B. W. (Lancs) b Sept. 18, 1953
*Reiffel, P. R. (Vic.) b April 19, 1966
*Relf, A. E. (Sussex & Auck.; *CY 1914*) b June 26, 1874, d March 26, 1937
Relf, R. R. (Sussex) b Sept. 1, 1883, d April 28, 1965
*Renneburg, D. A. (NSW) b Sept. 23, 1942
*Rennie, J. A. (Mat.) b July 29, 1970
Revill, A. C. (Derbys & Leics) b March 27, 1923
Reynolds, B. L. (Northants) b June 10, 1932
Rhodes, A. E. G. (Derbys; Test umpire) b Oct. 10, 1916, d Oct. 18, 1983
*Rhodes, H. J. (Derbys) b July 22, 1936
*Rhodes, J. N. (Natal) b July 26, 1969
*Rhodes, S. J. (Yorks & Worcs; *CY 1995*) b June 17, 1964
*Rhodes, W. (Yorks; *CY 1899*) b Oct. 29, 1877, d July 8, 1973
Rice, C. E. B. (Tvl & Notts; *CY 1981*) b July 23, 1949
Rice, J. M. (Hants) b Oct. 23, 1949
*Richards, A. R. (W. Prov.) b Dec. 14, 1867, d Jan. 9, 1904
*Richards, B. A. (Natal, Glos, Hants & S. Aust.; *CY 1969*) b July 21, 1945
*Richards, C. J. (Surrey & OFS) b Aug. 10, 1958
Richards, D. L. (Chief Exec. ICC 1993-) b July 28, 1946
Richards, G. (Glam) b Nov. 29, 1951
*Richards, I. V. A. (Comb. Is., Leewards, Som, Qld & Glam; *CY 1977*) b March 7, 1952
*Richards, W. H. (SA) b March 26, 1862, d Jan. 4, 1903

*Richardson, A. J. (S. Aust.) b July 24, 1888, d Dec. 23, 1973
Richardson, A. W. (Derbys) b March 4, 1907, d July 29, 1983
*Richardson, D. J. (E. Prov. & N. Tvl) b Sept. 16, 1959
*Richardson, D. W. (Worcs) b Nov. 3, 1934
*Richardson, P. E. (Worcs & Kent; *CY 1957*) b July 4, 1931
*Richardson, R. B. (Leewards & Yorks; *CY 1992*) b Jan. 12, 1962
*Richardson, T. (Surrey & Som; *CY 1897*) b Aug. 11, 1870, d July 2, 1912
*Richardson, V. Y. (S. Aust.) b Sept. 7, 1894, d Oct. 29, 1969
Riches, N. V. H. (Glam) b June 9, 1883, d Nov. 6, 1975
*Richmond, T. L. (Notts) b June 23, 1890, d Dec. 29, 1957
*Rickards, K. R. (Jam. & Essex) b Aug. 23, 1923, d Aug. 21, 1995
Riddington, A. (Leics) b Dec. 22, 1911
*Ridgway, F. (Kent) b Aug. 10, 1923
*Rigg, K. E. (Vic.) b May 21, 1906, d Feb. 28, 1995
Rindel, M. J. R. (Tvl & N. Tvl) b Feb. 9, 1963
*Ring, D. T. (Vic.) b Oct. 14, 1918
Ripley, D. (Northants) b Sept. 13, 1966
*Ritchie, G. M. (Qld) b Jan. 23, 1960
*Rixon, S. J. (NSW) b Feb. 25, 1954
*Rizwan-uz-Zaman (Kar. & PIA) b Sept. 4, 1962
*Roach, C. A. (T/T) b March 13, 1904, d April 16, 1988
*Roberts, A. D. G. (N. Dist.) b May 6, 1947, d Oct. 26, 1989
*Roberts, A. M. E. (Comb. Is., Leewards, Hants, NSW & Leics; *CY 1975*) b Jan. 29, 1951
*Roberts, A. T. (Windwards & T/T) b Sept. 18, 1937, d July 24, 1996
*Roberts, A. W. (Cant. & Otago) b Aug. 20, 1909, d May 13, 1978
Roberts, B. (Tvl & Derbys) b May 30, 1962
Roberts, The Hon. Sir Denys (Pres. MCC 1989-90) b Jan. 19, 1923
Roberts, F. G. (Glos) b April 1, 1862, d April 7, 1936
Roberts, S. J. (Cant.) b March 22, 1965
Roberts, W. B. (Lancs & Victory Tests) b Sept. 27, 1914, d Aug. 24, 1951
*Robertson, G. K. (C. Dist.) b July 15, 1960
Robertson, G. R. (NSW) b May 28, 1966
*Robertson, J. B. (W. Prov.) b June 5, 1906, d July 5, 1985
*Robertson, J. D. (Middx; *CY 1948*) b Feb. 22, 1917, d Oct. 12, 1996
*Robertson, W. R. (Vic.) b Oct. 6, 1861, d June 24, 1938
Robertson-Glasgow, R. C. (OU & Som; writer) b July 15, 1901, d March 4, 1965
Robins, D. H. (Warwicks) b June 26, 1914
*Robins, R. W. V. (CU & Middx; *CY 1930*) b June 3, 1906, d Dec. 12, 1968
Robinson, D. C. (Glos & Essex) b April 20, 1884, d July 29, 1963
Robinson, E. (Yorks) b Nov. 16, 1883, d Nov. 17, 1969
Robinson, E. P. (Yorks & Som) b Aug. 10, 1911
Robinson, Sir Foster G. (Glos) b Sept. 19, 1880, d Oct. 31, 1967
Robinson, M. A. (Northants & Yorks) b Nov. 23, 1966
Robinson, P. E. (Yorks & Leics) b Aug. 3, 1963
Robinson, P. J. (Worcs & Som) b Feb. 9, 1943
*Robinson, R. D. (Vic.) b June 8, 1946
*Robinson, R. H. (NSW, S. Aust. & Otago) b March 26, 1914, d Aug. 10, 1965
*Robinson, R. T. (Notts; *CY 1986*) b Nov. 21, 1958
Robson, C. (Hants) b June 20, 1859, d Sept. 27, 1943
Robson, E. (Som) b May 1, 1870, d May 23, 1924
*Rodriguez, W. V. (T/T) b June 25, 1934
Roe, B. (Som) b Jan. 27, 1939
Roebuck, P. M. (CU & Som; *CY 1988*) b March 6, 1956
Rogers, N. H. (Hants) b March 9, 1918
Rogers, S. S. (Eur. & Som) b March 18, 1923, d Nov. 6, 1969
Romaines, P. W. (Northants, Glos & Griq. W.) b Dec. 25, 1955
*Roope, G. R. J. (Surrey & Griq. W.) b July 12, 1946
*Root, C. F. (Derbys & Worcs) b April 16, 1890, d Jan. 20, 1954
*Rorke, G. F. (NSW) b June 27, 1938
*Rose, B. C. (Som; *CY 1980*) b June 4, 1950
Rose, G. D. (Middx & Som) b April 12, 1964
Roseberry, M. A. (Middx & Durham) b Nov. 28, 1966
*Rose-Innes, A. (Kimberley & Tvl) b Feb. 16, 1868, d Nov. 22, 1946
Rotherham, G. A. (Rugby, CU, Warwicks & Wgtn.; *CY 1918*) b May 28, 1899, d Jan. 31, 1985
Rouse, S. J. (Warwicks) b Jan. 20, 1949
*Routledge, T. W. (W. Prov. & Tvl) b April 18, 1867, d May 9, 1927
*Rowan, A. M. B. (Tvl) b Feb. 7, 1921
*Rowan, E. A. B. (Tvl; *CY 1952*) b July 20, 1909, d April 30, 1993
Rowbotham, J. (Yorks; Test umpire) b July 8, 1831, d Dec. 22, 1899
*Rowe, C. G. (Wgtn & C. Dist.) b June 30, 1915, d June 9, 1995
Rowe, C. J. C. (Kent & Glam) b Nov. 11, 1951
Rowe, E. J. (Notts) b July 21, 1920, d Dec. 17, 1989

*Rowe, G. A. (W. Prov.) b June 15, 1874, d Jan. 8, 1950
*Rowe, L. G. (Jam. & Derbys) b Jan. 8, 1949
*Roy, A. (Bengal) b June 5, 1945
*Roy, Pankaj (Bengal) b May 31, 1928
*Roy, Pranab (Bengal) b Feb. 10, 1957
*Royle, Rev. V. P. F. A. (OU & Lancs) b Jan. 29, 1854, d May 21, 1929
*Rumsey, F. E. (Worcs, Som & Derbys) b Dec. 4, 1935
Rundle, D. B. (W. Prov.) b Sept. 25, 1965
Rushby, T. (Surrey) b Sept. 6, 1880, d July 13, 1962
*Rushmere, M. W. (E. Prov. & Tvl) b Jan. 7, 1965
*Russell, A. C. (Essex; *CY 1923*) b Oct. 7, 1887, d March 23, 1961
Russell, P. E. (Derbys) b May 9, 1944
*Russell, R. C. (Glos; *CY 1990*) b Aug. 15, 1963
Russell, S. E. J. (Middx & Glos) b Oct. 4, 1937, d June 18, 1994
*Russell, W. E. (Middx) b July 3, 1936
*Rutherford, J. W. (W. Aust.) b Sept. 25, 1929
*Rutherford, K. R. (Otago & Tvl) b Oct. 26, 1965
Ryan, F. (Hants & Glam) b Nov. 14, 1888, d Jan. 5, 1954
Ryan, M. (Yorks) b June 23, 1933
*Ryder, J. (Vic.) b Aug. 8, 1889, d April 3, 1977

Saadat Ali (Lahore, UBL & HBFC) b Feb. 6, 1955
*Sadiq Mohammad (Kar., PIA, Tas., Essex, Glos & UBL) b May 3, 1945
*Saeed Ahmed (Punjab, Pak. Us, Lahore, PIA, Kar., PWD & Sind) b Oct. 1, 1937
*Saeed Anwar (Kar., UBL & ADBP; *CY 1997*) b Sept. 6, 1968
Saeed Azad (NBP & Kar.) b Aug. 14, 1967
*Saggers, R. A. (NSW) b May 15, 1917, d March 17, 1987
Sainsbury, P. J. (Hants; *CY 1974*) b June 13, 1934
*St Hill, E. L. (T/T) b March 9, 1904, d May 21, 1957
*St Hill, W. H. (T/T) b July 6, 1893, d *circa* 1957
Sajid Ali (Kar. & NBP) b July 1, 1963
Sajjad Akbar (Lahore, PNSC & Sargodha) b March 1, 1961
*Salah-ud-Din (Kar., PIA & Pak. Us) b Feb. 14, 1947
*Saleem Altaf (Lahore & PIA) b April 19, 1944
*Saleem Jaffer (Kar. & UBL) b Nov. 19, 1962
*Salim Elahi (Lahore) b Nov. 21, 1976
*Salim Malik (Lahore, HBL & Essex; *CY 1988*) b April 16, 1963
Salim Pervez (NBP) b Sept. 9, 1947
*Salim Yousuf (Sind, Kar., IDBP, Allied Bank & Customs) b Dec. 7, 1959
*Salisbury, I. D. K. (Sussex; *CY 1993*) b Jan. 21, 1970
Samaranayake, A. D. A. (SL) b Feb. 25, 1962
*Samarasekera, M. A. R. (CCC) b Aug. 5, 1961
*Samaraweera, D. P. (Colts) b Feb. 12, 1972
Sampson, H. (Yorks & All-England) b March 13, 1813, d March 29, 1885
*Samuels, R. G. (Jam.) b March 13, 1971
*Samuelson, S. V. (Natal) b Nov. 21, 1883, d Nov. 18, 1958
*Sandham, A. (Surrey; *CY 1923*) b July 6, 1890, d April 20, 1982
*Sandhu, B. S. (Bombay) b Aug. 3, 1956
Santall, F. R. (Warwicks) b July 12, 1903, d Nov. 3, 1950
Santall, S. (Warwicks) b June 10, 1873, d March 19, 1957
*Saqlain Mushtaq (I'bad & PIA) b Nov. 27, 1976
*Sardesai, D. N. (Bombay) b Aug. 8, 1940
*Sarfraz Nawaz (Lahore, Punjab, Northants, Pak. Rlwys & UBL) b Dec. 1, 1948
*Sarwate, C. T. (CP & B, M'tra, Bombay & †M. Pradesh) b June 22, 1920
*Saunders, J. V. (Vic. & Wgtn) b March 21, 1876, Dec. 21, 1927
Savage, J. S. (Leics & Lancs) b March 3, 1929
Savill, L. A. (Essex) b June 30, 1935
Saville, G. J. (Essex) b Feb. 5, 1944
Saxelby, K. (Notts) b Feb. 23, 1959
*Saxena, R. C. (Delhi & Bihar) b Sept. 20, 1944
Sayer, D. M. (OU & Kent) b Sept. 19, 1936
*Scarlett, R. O. (Jam.) b Aug. 15, 1934
*Schultz, B. N. (E. Prov.) b Aug. 26, 1970
*Schultz, S. S. (CU & Lancs) b Aug. 29, 1857, d Dec. 18, 1937
*Schwarz, R. O. (Middx & Natal; *CY 1908*) b May 4, 1875, d Nov. 18, 1918
*Scott, A. P. H. (Jam.) b July 29, 1934
Scott, C. J. (Glos) b May 1, 1919, d Nov. 22, 1992
Scott, C. W. (Notts & Durham) b Jan. 23, 1964
*Scott, H. J. H. (Vic.) b Dec. 26, 1858, d Sept. 23, 1910
Scott, M. E. (Northants) b May 8, 1936
*Scott, O. C. (Jam.) b Aug. 14, 1893, d June 15, 1961
*Scott, R. H. (Cant.) b March 6, 1917
Scott, S. W. (Middx; *CY 1893*) b March 24, 1854, d Dec. 8, 1933
*Scott, V. J. (Auck.) b July 31, 1916, d Aug. 2, 1980
*Scotton, W. H. (Notts) b Jan. 15, 1856, d July 9, 1893
*Sealey, B. J. (T/T) b Aug. 12, 1899, d Sept. 12, 1963
*Sealy, J. E. D. (B'dos & T/T) b Sept. 11, 1912, d Jan. 3, 1982
*Seccull, A. W. (Kimberley, W. Prov. & Tvl) b Sept. 14, 1868, d July 20, 1945

*Sekar, T. A. P. (TN) b March 28, 1955
*Selby, J. (Notts) b July 1, 1849, d March 11, 1894
Sellers, A. B. (Yorks; *CY 1940*) b March 5, 1907, d Feb. 20, 1981
*Sellers, R. H. D. (S. Aust.) b Aug. 20, 1940
*Selvey, M. W. W. (CU, Surrey, Middx, Glam & OFS) b April 25, 1948
*Sen, P. (Bengal) b May 31, 1926, d Jan. 27, 1970
*Sen Gupta, A. K. (Ind. Serv.) b Aug. 3, 1939
*Senanayake, C. P. (CCC) b Dec. 19, 1962
*Serjeant, C. S. (W. Aust.) b Nov. 1, 1951
Seymour, James (Kent) b Oct. 25, 1879, d Sept. 30, 1930
*Seymour, M. A. (W. Prov.) b June 5, 1936
*Shackleton, D. (Hants; *CY 1959*) b Aug. 12, 1924
*Shadab Kabir (Kar.) b Nov. 12, 1977
*Shafiq Ahmed (Lahore, Punjab, NBP & UBL) b March 28, 1949
*Shafqat Rana (Lahore & PIA) b Aug. 10, 1943
*Shah, A. H. (Mash.) b Aug. 7, 1959
Shahid Anwar (NBP) b July 5, 1968
*Shahid Israr (Kar. & Sind) b March 1, 1950
*Shahid Mahboob (Kar., Quetta, R'pindi, PACO & Allied Bank) b Aug. 25, 1962
*Shahid Mahmoud (Kar., Pak. Us & PWD) b March 17, 1939
Shahid Nazir (F'bad) b Dec. 4, 1977
*Shahid Saeed (HBFC, Lahore & PACO) b Jan. 6, 1966
*Shakeel Ahmed (B'pur, HBL & I'bad) b Nov. 12, 1971
Shakil Khan (WAPDA, HBL, R'pindi & I'bad) b May 28, 1968
*Shalders, W. A. (Griq. W. & Tvl) b Feb. 12, 1880, d March 18, 1917
*Sharma, Ajay (Delhi) b April 3, 1964
*Sharma, Chetan (Haryana & Bengal) b Jan. 3, 1966
*Sharma, Gopal (U. Pradesh) b Aug. 3, 1960
*Sharma, P. (Raja.) b Jan. 5, 1948
Sharma, Sanjeev (Delhi) b Aug. 25, 1965
Sharp, G. (Northants; Test umpire) b March 12, 1950
Sharp, H. P. (Middx) b Oct. 6, 1917, d Jan. 15, 1995
*Sharp, J. (Lancs) b Feb. 15, 1878, d Jan. 28, 1938
Sharp, K. (Yorks & Griq. W.) b April 6, 1959
*Sharpe, D. (Punjab, Pak. Rlwys, Lahore & S. Aust.) b Aug. 3, 1937
*Sharpe, J. W. (Surrey & Notts; *CY 1892*) b Dec. 9, 1866, d June 19, 1936
*Sharpe, P. J. (Yorks & Derbys; *CY 1963*) b Dec. 27, 1936
*Shastri, R. J. (Bombay & Glam) b May 27, 1962
*Shaw, Alfred (Notts & Sussex) b Aug. 29, 1842, d Jan. 16, 1907
Shaw, T. G. (E. Prov.) b July 5, 1959
*Sheahan, A. P. (Vic.) b Sept. 30, 1946
Sheffield, J. R. (Essex & Wgtn) b Nov. 19, 1906
*Shepherd, B. K. (W. Aust.) b April 23, 1937
Shepherd, D. J. (Glam; *CY 1970*) b Aug. 12, 1927
Shepherd, D. R. (Glos; Test umpire) b Dec. 27, 1940
*Shepherd, J. N. (B'dos, Kent, Rhod. & Glos; *CY 1979*) b Nov. 9, 1943
Shepherd, T. F. (Surrey) b Dec. 5, 1889, d Feb. 13, 1957
*Sheppard, Rt Rev. D. S. (Bishop of Liverpool) (CU & Sussex; *CY 1953*) b March 6, 1929
*Shepstone, G. H. (Tvl) b April 9, 1876, d July 3, 1940
*Sherwell, P. W. (Tvl) b Aug. 17, 1880, d April 17, 1948
*Sherwin, M. (Notts; *CY 1891*) b Feb. 26, 1851, d July 3, 1910
Shields, J. (Leics) b Feb. 1, 1882, d May 11, 1960
*Shillingford, G. C. (Comb. Is. & Windwards) b Sept. 25, 1944
*Shillingford, I. T. (Comb. Is. & Windwards) b April 18, 1944
*Shinde, S. G. (Baroda, M'tra & Bombay) b Aug. 18, 1923, d June 22, 1955
Shipman, A. W. (Leics) b March 7, 1901, d Dec. 12, 1979
Shirreff, A. C. (CU, Hants, Kent & Som) b Feb. 12, 1919
*Shivnarine, S. (Guyana) b May 13, 1952
*Shoaib Mohammad (Kar. & PIA) b Jan. 8, 1961
*Shodhan, R. H. (Guj. & Baroda) b Oct. 18, 1928
*Shrewsbury, A. (Notts; *CY 1890*) b April 11, 1856, d May 19, 1903
*Shrimpton, M. J. F. (C. Dist. & N. Dist.) b June 23, 1940
*Shuja-ud-Din, Col. (N. Ind., Pak. Us, Pak. Serv., B'pur & R'pindi) b April 10, 1930
*Shukla, R. C. (Bihar & Delhi) b Feb. 4, 1948
*Shuter, J. (Kent & Surrey) b Feb. 9, 1855, d July 5, 1920
*Shuttleworth, K. (Lancs & Leics) b Nov. 13, 1944
Sibbles, F. M. (Lancs) b March 15, 1904, d July 20, 1973
Siddons, J. D. (Vic. & S. Aust.) b April 25, 1964
*Sidebottom, A. (Yorks & OFS) b April 1, 1954
*Sidhu, N. S. (Punjab) b Oct. 20, 1963
Sidwell, T. E. (Leics) b Jan. 30, 1888, d Dec. 8, 1958
*Siedle, I. J. (Natal) b Jan. 11, 1903, d Aug. 24, 1982
*Sievers, M. W. (Vic.) b April 13, 1912, d May 10, 1968

*Sikander Bakht (PWD, PIA, Sind, Kar. & UBL) b Aug. 25, 1957
Silk, D. R. W. (CU & Som; Pres. MCC 1992-94; Chairman TCCB 1994-96) b Oct. 8, 1931
*Silva, K. J. (Bloom.) b June 2, 1973
*Silva, S. A. R. (NCC) b Dec. 12, 1960
Sime, W. A. (OU & Notts) b Feb. 8, 1909, d May 5, 1983
Simmons, J. (Lancs & Tas.; *CY 1985*) b March 28, 1941
*Simmons, P. V. (T/T, Border & Leics; *CY 1997*) b April 18, 1963
Simons, E. O. (W. Prov. & N. Tvl) b March 9, 1962
*Simpson, R. B. (NSW & W. Aust.; *CY 1965*) b Feb. 3, 1936
*Simpson, R. T. (Sind & Notts; *CY 1950*) b Feb. 27, 1920
*Simpson-Hayward, G. H. (Worcs) b June 7, 1875, d Oct. 2, 1936
Sims, Sir Arthur (Cant.) b July 22, 1877, d April 27, 1969
*Sims, J. M. (Middx) b May 13, 1903, d April 27, 1973
*Sinclair, B. W. (Wgtn) b Oct. 23, 1936
*Sinclair, I. M. (Cant.) b June 1, 1933
*Sinclair, J. H. (Tvl) b Oct. 16, 1876, d Feb. 23, 1913
*Sincock, D. J. (S. Aust.) b Feb. 1, 1942
*Sinfield, R. A. (Glos) b Dec. 24, 1900, d March 17, 1988
*Singh, Charan K. (T/T) b Nov. 27, 1935
Singh, "Robin" (R. R.) (TN) b Sept. 14, 1963
Singh, R. P. (U. Pradesh) b Jan. 6, 1963
Singleton, A. P. (OU, Worcs & Rhod.) b Aug. 5, 1914
*Sivaramakrishnan, L. (TN) b Dec. 31, 1965
Skelding, A. (Leics; umpire) b Sept. 5, 1886, d April 17, 1960
*Slack, W. N. (Middx & Windwards) b Dec. 12, 1954, d Jan. 15, 1989
Slade, D. N. F. (Worcs) b Aug. 24, 1940
Slater, A. G. (Derbys) b Nov. 22, 1890, d July 22, 1949
*Slater, K. N. (W. Aust.) b March 12, 1935
*Slater, M. J. (NSW) b Feb. 21, 1970
*Sleep, P. R. (S. Aust.) b May 4, 1957
*Slight, J. (Vic.) b Oct. 20, 1855, d Dec. 9, 1930
Slocombe, P. A. (Som) b Sept. 6, 1954
*Smailes, T. F. (Yorks) b March 27, 1910, d Dec. 1, 1970
Smales, K. (Yorks & Notts) b Sept. 15, 1927
*Small, G. C. (Warwicks & S. Aust.) b Oct. 18, 1961
Small, John, sen. (Hants & All-England) b April 19, 1737, d Dec. 31, 1826
*Small, J. A. (T/T) b Nov. 3, 1892, d April 26, 1958
*Small, M. A. (B'dos) b Feb. 12, 1964
Smart, C. C. (Warwicks & Glam) b July 23, 1898, d May 21, 1975
Smart, J. A. (Warwicks) b April 12, 1891, d Oct. 3, 1979
Smedley, M. J. (Notts) b Oct. 28, 1941
*Smith, A. C. (OU & Warwicks; Chief Exec. TCCB 1987-96) b Oct. 25, 1936
*Smith, Sir C. Aubrey (CU, Sussex & Tvl) b July 21, 1863, d Dec. 20, 1948
*Smith, C. I. J. (Middx; *CY 1935*) b Aug. 25, 1906, d Feb. 9, 1979
*Smith, C. J. E. (Tvl) b Dec. 25, 1872, d March 27, 1947
*Smith, C. L. (Natal, Glam & Hants; *CY 1984*) b Oct. 15, 1958
Smith, C. L. A. (Sussex) b Jan. 1, 1879, d Nov. 22, 1949
Smith, C. S. (later Sir Colin Stansfield-) (CU & Lancs) b Oct. 1, 1932
*Smith, C. W. (B'dos) b July 29, 1933
*Smith, Denis (Derbys; *CY 1936*) b Jan. 24, 1907, d Sept. 12, 1979
*Smith, D. B. M. (Vic.) b Sept. 14, 1884, d July 29, 1963
Smith, D. H. K. (Derbys & OFS) b June 29, 1940
*Smith, D. M. (Surrey, Worcs & Sussex) b Jan. 9, 1956
*Smith, D. R. (Glos) b Oct. 5, 1934
*Smith, D. V. (Sussex) b June 14, 1923
Smith, Edwin (Derbys) b Jan. 2, 1934
Smith, Ernest (OU & Yorks) b Oct. 19, 1869, d April 9, 1945
*Smith, E. J. (Warwicks) b Feb. 6, 1886, d Aug. 31, 1979
*Smith, F. B. (Cant.) b March 13, 1922
*Smith, F. W. (Tvl) b unknown, d 1913
Smith, G. J. (Essex) b April 2, 1935
*Smith, Harry (Glos) b May 21, 1890, d Nov. 12, 1937
Smith, H. A. (Leics) b March 29, 1901, d Aug. 7, 1948
*Smith, H. D. (Otago & Cant.) b Jan. 8, 1913, d Jan. 25, 1986
*Smith, I. D. S. (C. Dist. & Auck.) b Feb. 28, 1957
Smith, K. D. (Warwicks) b July 9, 1956
Smith, M. J. (Middx) b Jan. 4, 1942
*Smith, M. J. K. (Leics, OU & Warwicks; *CY 1960*) b June 30, 1933
Smith, N. (Yorks & Essex) b April 1, 1949
Smith, N. M. K. (Warwicks) b July 27, 1967
*Smith, O. G. ("Collie") (Jam.; *CY 1958*) b May 5, 1933, d Sept. 9, 1959
Smith, P. A. (Warwicks) b April 5, 1964
Smith, Ray (Essex) b Aug. 10, 1914, d Feb. 21, 1996
Smith, Roy (Som) b April 14, 1930
*Smith, R. A. (Natal & Hants; *CY 1990*) b Sept. 13, 1963
Smith, R. C. (Leics) b Aug. 3, 1935
*Smith, S. B. (NSW & Tvl) b Oct. 18, 1961

Smith, S. G. (T/T, Northants & Auck.; *CY 1915*) b Jan. 15, 1881, d Oct. 25, 1963
*Smith, T. P. B. (Essex; *CY 1947*) b Oct. 30, 1908, d Aug. 4, 1967
*Smith, V. I. (Natal) b Feb. 23, 1925
Smith, W. A. (Surrey) b Sept. 15, 1937
Smith, W. C. (Surrey; *CY 1911*) b Oct. 4, 1877, d July 16, 1946
*Smithson, G. A. (Yorks & Leics) b Nov. 1, 1926, d Sept. 6, 1970
*Snedden, C. A. (Auck.) b Jan. 7, 1918, d May 19, 1993
*Snedden, M. C. (Auck.) b Nov. 23, 1958
*Snell, R. P. (Natal, Tvl & Som) b Sept. 12, 1968
Snellgrove, K. L. (Lancs) b Nov. 12, 1941
*Snooke, S. D. (W. Prov. & Tvl) b Nov. 11, 1878, d April 6, 1959
*Snooke, S. J. (Border, W. Prov. & Tvl) b Feb. 1, 1881, d Aug. 14, 1966
*Snow, J. A. (Sussex; *CY 1973*) b Oct. 13, 1941
*Sobers, Sir Garfield S. (B'dos, S. Aust. & Notts; *CY 1964*) b July 28, 1936
Sohail Fazal (Lahore & HBL) b Nov. 11, 1967
*Sohoni, S. W. (M'tra, Baroda & Bombay) b March 5, 1918, d May 19, 1993
*Solkar, E. D. (Bombay & Sussex) b March 18, 1948
*Solomon, J. S. (BG) b Aug. 26, 1930
*Solomon, W. R. (Tvl & E. Prov.) b April 23, 1872, d July 12, 1964
*Sood, M. M. (Delhi) b July 6, 1939
Southern, J. W. (Hants) b Sept. 2, 1952
*Southerton, James (Surrey, Hants & Sussex) b Nov. 16, 1827, d June 16, 1880
Southerton, S. J. (Editor of *Wisden* 1934-35) b July 7, 1874, d March 12, 1935
*Sparling, J. T. (Auck.) b July 24, 1938
Speak, N. J. (Lancs) b Nov. 21, 1966
*Spearman, C. M. (Auck.) b July 4, 1972
Speight, M. P. (Sussex & Wgtn) b Oct. 24, 1967
Spencer, C. T. (Leics) b Aug. 18, 1931
Spencer, J. (CU & Sussex) b Oct. 6, 1949
Spencer, T. W. (Kent; Test umpire) b March 22, 1914
Sperry, J. (Leics) b March 19, 1910
*Spofforth, F. R. (NSW & Vic.) b Sept. 9, 1853, d June 4, 1926
*Spooner, R. H. (Lancs; *CY 1905*) b Oct. 21, 1880, d Oct. 2, 1961
*Spooner, R. T. (Warwicks) b Dec. 30, 1919
Springall, J. D. (Notts) b Sept. 19, 1932
Sprot, E. M. (Hants) b Feb. 4, 1872, d Oct. 8, 1945
Squires, H. S. (Surrey) b Feb. 22, 1909, d Jan. 24, 1950
*Srikkanth, K. (TN) b Dec. 21, 1959
*Srinath, J. (Karn. & Glos) b Aug. 31, 1969
*Srinivasan, T. E. (TN) b Oct. 26, 1950
*Stackpole, K. R. (Vic.; *CY 1973*) b July 10, 1940
Standen, J. A. (Worcs) b May 30, 1935
*Stanyforth, Lt-Col. R. T. (Yorks) b May 30, 1892, d Feb. 20, 1964
Staples, A. (Notts) b Feb. 4, 1899, d Sept. 9, 1965
*Staples, S. J. (Notts; *CY 1929*) b Sept. 18, 1892, d June 4, 1950
*Statham, J. B. (Lancs; *CY 1955*) b June 17, 1930
*Stayers, S. C. (†Guyana & Bombay) b June 9, 1937
Stead, B. (Yorks, Essex, Notts & N. Tvl) b June 21, 1939, d April 15, 1980
*Steel, A. G. (CU & Lancs; Pres. MCC 1902) b Sept. 24, 1858, d June 15, 1914
*Steele, D. S. (Northants & Derbys; *CY 1976*) b Sept. 29, 1941
Steele, J. F. (Leics, Natal & Glam) b July 23, 1946
Stemp, R. D. (Worcs & Yorks) b Dec. 11, 1967
Stephens, E. J. (Glos) b March 23, 1909, d April 3, 1983
Stephenson, F. D. (B'dos, Glos, Tas., Notts, Sussex & OFS; *CY 1989*) b April 8, 1959
Stephenson, G. R. (Derbys & Hants) b Nov. 19, 1942
Stephenson, H. H. (Surrey & All-England) b May 3, 1832, d Dec. 17, 1896
Stephenson, H. W. (Som) b July 18, 1920
*Stephenson, J. P. (Essex, Boland & Hants) b March 14, 1965
Stephenson, Lt-Col. J. R. (Sec. MCC 1987-93) b Feb. 25, 1931
Stevens, Edward ("Lumpy") (Hants) b *circa* 1735, d Sept. 7, 1819
*Stevens, G. B. (S. Aust.) b Feb. 29, 1932
*Stevens, G. T. S. (UCS, OU & Middx; *CY 1918*) b Jan. 7, 1901, d Sept. 19, 1970
*Stevenson, G. B. (Yorks & Northants) b Dec. 16, 1955
Stevenson, K. (Derbys & Hants) b Oct. 6, 1950
*Stewart, A. J. (Surrey; *CY 1993*) b April 8, 1963
Stewart, E. L. R. (Natal) b July 30, 1969
*Stewart, M. J. (Surrey; *CY 1958*) b Sept. 16, 1932
*Stewart, R. B. (SA) b Sept. 3, 1856, d Sept. 12, 1913
Stewart, W. J. (Warwicks & Northants) b Oct. 31, 1934
*Steyn, P. J. R. (Griq. W., OFS & Natal) b June 30, 1967
*Stirling, D. A. (C. Dist.) b Oct. 5, 1961
Stocks, F. W. (Notts) b Nov. 6, 1918, d Feb. 23, 1996
*Stoddart, A. E. (Middx; *CY 1893*) b March 11, 1863, d April 3, 1915
*Stollmeyer, J. B. (T/T) b April 11, 1921, d Sept. 10, 1989
*Stollmeyer, V. H. (T/T) b Jan. 24, 1916

Stone, J. (Hants & Glam) b Nov. 29, 1876, d Nov. 15, 1942
Storer, H. jun. (Derbys) b Feb. 2, 1898, d Sept. 1, 1967
*Storer, W. (Derbys; *CY 1899*) b Jan. 25, 1867, d Feb. 28, 1912
Storey, S. J. (Surrey & Sussex) b Jan. 6, 1941
Stott, L. W. (Auck.) b Dec. 8, 1946
Stott, W. B. (Yorks) b July 18, 1934
Stovold, A. W. (Glos & OFS) b March 19, 1953
*Strang, B. C. (MCD) b June 9, 1972
*Strang, P. A. (MCD) b July 28, 1970
*Streak, H. H. (Mat. & Hants) b March 16, 1974
*Street, G. B. (Sussex) b Dec. 6, 1889, d April 24, 1924
*Stricker, L. A. (Tvl) b May 26, 1884, d Feb. 5, 1960
*Strudwick, H. (Surrey; *CY 1912*) b Jan. 28, 1880, d Feb. 14, 1970
*Studd, C. T. (CU & Middx) b Dec. 2, 1860, d July 16, 1931
*Studd, G. B. (CU & Middx) b Oct. 20, 1859, d Feb. 13, 1945
Studd, Sir J. E. Kynaston (Middx & CU; Pres. MCC 1930) b July 26, 1858, d Jan. 14, 1944
*Su'a, M. L. (N. Dist. & Auck.) b Nov. 7, 1966
*Subba Row, R. (CU, Surrey & Northants; *CY 1961*) b Jan. 29, 1932
*Subramanya, V. (Mysore) b July 16, 1936
*Such, P. M. (Notts, Leics & Essex) b June 12, 1964
Sudhakar Rao, R. (Karn.) b Aug. 8, 1952
Sueter, T. (Hants & Surrey) b *circa* 1749, d Feb. 17, 1827
*Sugg, F. H. (Yorks, Derbys & Lancs; *CY 1890*) b Jan. 11, 1862, d May 29, 1933
Sullivan, J. (Lancs) b Feb. 5, 1945
Sully, H. (Som & Northants) b Nov. 1, 1939
*Sunderram, G. (Bombay & Raja.) b March 29, 1930
*Surendranath, R. (Ind. Serv.) b Jan. 4, 1937
Surridge, W. S. (Surrey; *CY 1953*) b Sept. 3, 1917, d April 13, 1992
*Surti, R. F. (Guj., Raja., & Qld) b May 25, 1936
*Susskind, M. J. (CU, Middx & Tvl) b June 8, 1891, d July 9, 1957
*Sutcliffe, B. (Auck., Otago & N. Dist.; *CY 1950*) b Nov. 17, 1923
*Sutcliffe, H. (Yorks; *CY 1920*) b Nov. 24, 1894, d Jan. 22, 1978
Sutcliffe, W. H. H. (Yorks) b Oct. 10, 1926
Suttle, K. G. (Sussex) b Aug. 25, 1928
*Swamy, V. N. (Ind. Serv.) b May 23, 1924, d May 1, 1983
Swanton, E. W. (Middx; writer & broadcaster) b Feb. 11, 1907
Swarbrook, F. W. (Derbys, Griq. W. & OFS) b Dec. 17, 1950
Swart, P. D. (Rhod., W. Prov., Glam & Boland) b April 27, 1946
*Swetman, R. (Surrey, Notts & Glos) b Oct. 25, 1933
Sydenham, D. A. D. (Surrey) b April 6, 1934
*Symcox, P. L. (Griq. W., Natal & N. Tvl) b April 14, 1960

*Taber, H. B. (NSW) b April 29, 1940
*Taberer, H. M. (OU & Natal) b Oct. 7, 1870, d June 5, 1932
*Tahir Naqqash (Servis Ind., MCB, Punjab & Lahore) b July 6, 1959
*Talat Ali (Lahore, PIA & UBL) b May 29, 1950
*Tallon, D. (Qld; *CY 1949*) b Feb. 17, 1916, d Sept. 7, 1984
*Tamhane, N. S. (Bombay) b Aug. 4, 1931
*Tancred, A. B. (Kimberley, Griq. W. & Tvl) b Aug. 20, 1865, d Nov. 23, 1911
*Tancred, L. J. (Tvl) b Oct. 7, 1876, d July 28, 1934
*Tancred, V. M. (Tvl) b July 7, 1875, d June 3, 1904
Tanvir Mehdi (Lahore & UBL) b Nov. 7, 1972
*Tapscott, G. L. (Griq. W.) b Nov. 7, 1889, d Dec. 13, 1940
*Tapscott, L. E. (Griq. W.) b March 18, 1894, d July 7, 1934
*Tarapore, K. K. (Bombay) b Dec. 17, 1910, d June 15, 1986
Tarbox, C. V. (Worcs) b July 2, 1891, d June 15, 1978
Tarrant, F. A. (Vic., Middx & Patiala; *CY 1908*) b Dec. 11, 1880, d Jan. 29, 1951
Tarrant, G. F. (Cambs. & All-England) b Dec. 7, 1838, d July 2, 1870
*Taslim Arif (Kar., Sind & NBP) b May 1, 1954
*Tate, F. W. (Sussex) b July 24, 1867, d Feb. 24, 1943
*Tate, M. W. (Sussex; *CY 1924*) b May 30, 1895, d May 18, 1956
*Tattersall, R. (Lancs) b Aug. 17, 1922
*Tauseef Ahmed (PWD, UBL & Kar.) b May 10, 1958
*Tavaré, C. J. (OU, Kent & Som) b Oct. 27, 1954
*Tayfield, H. J. (Natal, Rhod. & Tvl; *CY 1956*) b Jan. 30, 1929, d Feb. 25, 1994
*Taylor, A. I. (Tvl) b July 25, 1925
Taylor, B. (Essex; *CY 1972*) b June 19, 1932
*Taylor, B. R. (Cant. & Wgtn) b July 12, 1943
Taylor, C. G. (CU & Sussex) b Nov. 21, 1816, d Sept. 10, 1869
*Taylor, Daniel (Natal) b Jan. 9, 1887, d Jan. 24, 1957
*Taylor, D. D. (Auck. & Warwicks) b March 2, 1923, d Dec. 5, 1980
Taylor, D. J. S. (Surrey, Som & Griq. W.) b Nov. 12, 1942

*Taylor, H. W. (Natal, Tvl & W. Prov.; *CY 1925*) b May 5, 1889, d Feb. 8, 1973
*Taylor, J. (T/T) b Jan. 3, 1932
*Taylor, J. M. (NSW) b Oct. 10, 1895, d May 12, 1971
*Taylor, J. P. (Derbys & Northants) b Aug. 8, 1964
*Taylor, K. (Yorks & Auck.) b Aug. 21, 1935
*Taylor, L. B. (Leics & Natal) b Oct. 25, 1953
*Taylor, M. A. (NSW; *CY 1990*) b Oct. 27, 1964
Taylor, M. N. S. (Notts & Hants) b Nov. 12, 1942
Taylor, N. R. (Kent) b July 21, 1959
*Taylor, P. L. (NSW & Qld) b Aug. 22, 1956
*Taylor, R. W. (Derbys; *CY 1977*) b July 17, 1941
Taylor, R. M. (Essex) b Nov. 30, 1909, d Jan. 7, 1984
Taylor, T. L. (CU & Yorks; *CY 1901*) b May 25, 1878, d March 16, 1960
*Tendulkar, S. R. (Bombay & Yorks; *CY 1997*) b April 24, 1973
Tennekoon, A. P. B. (SL) b Oct. 29, 1946
*Tennyson, 3rd Lord (Hon. L. H.) (Hants; *CY 1914*) b Nov. 7, 1889, d June 6, 1951
*Terry, V. P. (Hants) b Jan. 14, 1959
*Theunissen, N. H. (W. Prov.) b May 4, 1867, d Nov. 9, 1929
Thomas, A. E. (Northants) b June 7, 1893, d March 21, 1965
Thomas, D. J. (Surrey, N. Tvl, Natal & Glos) b June 30, 1959
*Thomas, G. (NSW) b March 21, 1938
*Thomas, J. G. (Glam, Border, E. Prov. & Northants) b Aug. 12, 1960
Thompson, A. (Middx) b April 17, 1916
*Thompson, G. J. (Northants; Test umpire; *CY 1906*) b Oct. 27, 1877, d March 3, 1943
Thompson, R. G. (Warwicks) b Sept. 26, 1932
*Thoms, G. R. (Vic.) b March 22, 1927
*Thomson, A. L. (Vic.) b Dec. 2, 1945
*Thomson, J. R. (NSW, Qld & Middx) b Aug. 16, 1950
*Thomson, K. (Cant.) b Feb. 26, 1941
*Thomson, N. F. D. (NSW) b May 29, 1839, d Sept. 2, 1896
*Thomson, N. I. (Sussex) b Jan. 23, 1929
*Thomson, P. I. C. (B'dos) b Sept. 26, 1971
*Thomson, S. A. (N. Dist.) b Jan. 27, 1969
Thornton, C. I. (CU, Kent & Middx) b March 20, 1850, d Dec. 10, 1929
*Thornton, Dr P. G. (Yorks, Middx & SA) b Dec. 24, 1867, d Jan. 31, 1939
*Thorpe, G. P. (Surrey) b Aug. 1, 1969
*Thurlow, H. M. (Qld) b Jan. 10, 1903, d Dec. 3, 1975
*Tillekeratne, H. P. (NCC) b July 14, 1967
Timms, B. S. V. (Hants & Warwicks) b Dec. 17, 1940
Timms, J. E. (Northants) b Nov. 3, 1906, d May 18, 1980
Tindall, R. A. E. (Surrey) b Sept. 23, 1935
*Tindill, E. W. T. (Wgtn) b Dec. 18, 1910
Tissera, M. H. (SL) b March 23, 1939
*Titmus, F. J. (Middx, Surrey & OFS; *CY 1963*) b Nov. 24, 1932
Todd, L. J. (Kent) b June 19, 1907, d Aug. 20, 1967
Todd, P. A. (Notts & Glam) b March 12, 1953
*Tolchard, R. W. (Leics) b June 15, 1946
Tomlins, K. P. (Middx & Glos) b Oct. 23, 1957
*Tomlinson, D. S. (Rhod. & Border) b Sept. 4, 1910, d July 11, 1993
Tompkin, M. (Leics) b Feb. 17, 1919, d Sept. 27, 1956
*Toohey, P. M. (NSW) b April 20, 1954
Topley, T. D. (Surrey, Essex & Griq. W.) b Feb. 25, 1964
*Toshack, E. R. H. (NSW) b Dec. 15, 1914
Townsend, A. (Warwicks) b Aug. 26, 1921
Townsend, A. F. (Derbys) b March 29, 1912, d Feb. 25, 1994
*Townsend, C. L. (Glos; *CY 1899*) b Nov. 7, 1876, d Oct. 17, 1958
*Townsend, D. C. H. (OU) b April 20, 1912, d Jan. 27, 1997
*Townsend, L. F. (Derbys & Auck.; *CY 1934*) b June 8, 1903, d Feb. 17, 1993
**Traicos, A. J. (Rhod. & Mash.) b May 17, 1947
*Travers, J. P. F. (S. Aust.) b Jan. 10, 1871, d Sept. 15, 1942
*Tremlett, M. F. (Som & C. Dist.) b July 5, 1923, d July 30, 1984
Tremlett, T. M. (Hants) b July 26, 1956
*Tribe, G. E. (Vic. & Northants; *CY 1955*) b Oct. 4, 1920
*Trim, J. (BG) b Jan. 25, 1915, d Nov. 12, 1960
Trimble, G. S. (Qld) b Jan. 1, 1963
*Trimborn, P. H. J. (Natal) b May 18, 1940
**Trott, A. E. (Vic., Middx & Hawkes Bay; *CY 1899*) b Feb. 6, 1873, d July 30, 1914
*Trott, G. H. S. (Vic.; *CY 1894*) b Aug. 5, 1866, d Nov. 10, 1917
Troughton, L. H. W. (Kent) b May 17, 1879, d Aug. 31, 1933
*Troup, G. B. (Auck.) b Oct. 3, 1952
*Trueman, F. S. (Yorks; *CY 1953*) b Feb. 6, 1931
*Trumble, H. (Vic.; *CY 1897*) b May 12, 1867, d Aug. 14, 1938
*Trumble, J. W. (Vic.) b Sept. 16, 1863, d Aug. 17, 1944
Trump, H. R. J. (Som) b Oct. 11, 1968
*Trumper, V. T. (NSW; *CY 1903*) b Nov. 2, 1877, d June 28, 1915
*Truscott, P. B. (Wgtn) b Aug. 14, 1941
*Tuckett, L. (OFS) b Feb. 6, 1919
*Tuckett, L. R. (Natal & OFS) b April 19, 1885, d April 8, 1963
*Tufnell, N. C. (CU & Surrey) b June 13, 1887, d Aug. 3, 1951
*Tufnell, P. C. R. (Middx) b April 29, 1966

Tuke, Sir Anthony (Pres. MCC 1982-83) b Aug. 22, 1920
Tunnicliffe, C. J. (Derbys) b Aug. 11, 1951
Tunnicliffe, J. (Yorks; *CY 1901*) b Aug. 26, 1866. d July 11, 1948
*Turnbull, M. J. (CU & Glam; *CY 1931*) b March 16, 1906, d Aug. 5, 1944
*Turner, A. (NSW) b July 23, 1950
Turner, C. (Yorks) b Jan. 11, 1902, d Nov. 19, 1968
*Turner, C. T. B. (NSW; *CY 1889*) b Nov. 16, 1862, d Jan. 1, 1944
Turner, D. R. (Hants & W. Prov.) b Feb. 5, 1949
Turner, F. M. (Leics) b Aug. 8, 1934
*Turner, G. M. (Otago, N. Dist. & Worcs; *CY 1971*) b May 26, 1947
Turner, R. J. (CU & Som) b Nov. 25, 1967
Turner, S. (Essex & Natal) b July 18, 1943
*Twentyman-Jones, P. S. (W. Prov.) b Sept. 13, 1876, d March 8, 1954
Twining, R. H. (OU & Middx; Pres. MCC 1964-65) b Nov. 3, 1889, d Jan. 3, 1979
*Twose, R. G. (Warwicks, N. Dist., C. Dist. & Wgtn) b April 17, 1968
*Tyldesley, E. (Lancs; *CY 1920*) b Feb. 5, 1889, d May 5, 1962
*Tyldesley, J. T. (Lancs; *CY 1902*) b Nov. 22, 1873, d Nov. 27, 1930
*Tyldesley, R. K. (Lancs; *CY 1925*) b March 11, 1897, d Sept. 17, 1943
*Tylecote, E. F. S. (OU & Kent) b June 23, 1849, d March 15, 1938
*Tyler, E. J. (Som) b Oct. 13, 1864, d Jan. 25, 1917
*Tyson, F. H. (Northants; *CY 1956*) b June 6, 1930

Udal, S. D. (Hants) b March 18, 1969
Ufton, D. G. (Kent) b May 31, 1928
*Ulyett, G. (Yorks) b Oct. 21, 1851, d June 18, 1898
*Umrigar, P. R. (Bombay & Guj.) b March 28, 1926
*Underwood, D. L. (Kent; *CY 1969*) b June 8, 1945
Upashantha, E. A. (NWP) b June 10, 1972

*Vaas, W. P. U. J. C. (Colts) b Jan. 27, 1975
Vaidya, P. S. (Bengal) b Sept. 23, 1967
*Valentine, A. L. (Jam.; *CY 1951*) b April 29, 1930
*Valentine, B. H. (CU & Kent) b Jan. 17, 1908, d Feb. 2, 1983
*Valentine, V. A. (Jam.) b April 4, 1908, d July 6, 1972
*Vance, R. H. (Wgtn) b March 31, 1955
*van der Bijl, P. G. (W. Prov. & OU) b Oct. 21, 1907, d Feb. 16, 1973
van der Bijl, V. A. P. (Natal, Middx & Tvl; *CY 1981*) b March 19, 1948
*Van der Merwe, E. A. (Tvl) b Nov. 9, 1904, d Feb. 26, 1971
*Van der Merwe, P. L. (W. Prov. & E. Prov.) b March 14, 1937
van Geloven, J. (Yorks & Leics) b Jan. 4, 1934
*Van Ryneveld, C. B. (W. Prov. & OU) b March 19, 1928
van Troost, A. P. (Holland & Som) b Oct. 2, 1972
*Varnals, G. D. (E. Prov., Tvl & Natal) b July 24, 1935
*Vaughan, J. T. C. (Auck.) b Aug. 30, 1967
*Veivers, T. R. (Qld) b April 6, 1937
*Veletta, M. R. J. (W. Aust.) b Oct. 30, 1963
*Vengsarkar, D. B. (Bombay; *CY 1987*) b April 6, 1956
*Venkataraghavan, S. (†TN & Derbys; Test umpire) b April 21, 1946
*Venkataramana, M. (TN) b April 24, 1966
*Verity, H. (Yorks; *CY 1932*) b May 18, 1905, d July 31, 1943
*Vernon, G. F. (Middx) b June 20, 1856, d Aug. 10, 1902
Vials, G. A. T. (Northants) b March 18, 1887, d April 26, 1974
Vigar, F. H. (Essex) b July 7, 1917
*Viljoen, K. G. (Griq. W., OFS & Tvl) b May 14, 1910, d Jan. 21, 1974
*Vincent, C. L. (Tvl) b Feb. 16, 1902, d Aug. 24, 1968
*Vine, J. (Sussex; *CY 1906*) b May 15, 1875, d April 25, 1946
*Vintcent, C. H. (Tvl & Griq. W.) b Sept. 2, 1866, d Sept. 28, 1943
Virgin, R. T. (Som, Northants & W. Prov.; *CY 1971*) b Aug. 26, 1939
*Viswanath, G. R. (†Karn.) b Feb. 12, 1949
*Viswanath, S. (Karn.) b Nov. 29, 1962
*Vivian, G. E. (Auck.) b Feb. 28, 1946
*Vivian, H. G. (Auck.) b Nov. 4, 1912, d Aug. 12, 1983
*Vizianagram, Maharaj Kumar of, Sir Vijay A., (U. Prov.) b Dec. 28, 1905, d Dec. 2, 1965
*Voce, W. (Notts; *CY 1933*) b Aug. 8, 1909, d June 6, 1984
*Vogler, A. E. E. (Middx, Natal, Tvl & E. Prov.; *CY 1908*) b Nov. 28, 1876, d Aug. 9, 1946
Vonhagt, D. M. (Moors) b March 31, 1965

*Waddington, A. (Yorks) b Feb. 4, 1893, d Oct. 28, 1959
*Wade, H. F. (Natal) b Sept. 14, 1905, d Nov. 23, 1980
Wade, T. H. (Essex) b Nov. 24, 1910, d July 25, 1987
*Wade, W. W. (Natal) b June 18, 1914
*Wadekar, A. L. (Bombay) b April 1, 1941
*Wadsworth, K. J. (C. Dist. & Cant.) b Nov. 30, 1946, d Aug. 19, 1976
*Wainwright, E. (Yorks; *CY 1894*) b April 8, 1865, d Oct. 28, 1919

*Waite, J. H. B. (E. Prov. & Tvl) b Jan. 19, 1930
*Waite, M. G. (S. Aust.) b Jan. 7, 1911, d Dec. 16, 1985
*Walcott, Sir Clyde L. (B'dos & BG; *CY 1958*) b Jan. 17, 1926
*Walcott, L. A. (B'dos) b Jan. 18, 1894, d Feb. 27, 1984
Walden, F. (Northants; Test umpire) b March 1, 1888, d May 3, 1949
Walker, A. (Northants & Durham) b July 7, 1962
Walker, C. (Yorks & Hants) b June 27, 1919, d Dec. 3, 1992
Walker, I. D. (Middx) b Jan. 8, 1844, d July 6, 1898
*Walker, M. H. N. (Vic.) b Sept. 12, 1948
*Walker, P. M. (Glam, Tvl & W. Prov.) b Feb. 17, 1936
Walker, V. E. (Middx) b April 20, 1837, d Jan. 3, 1906
Walker, W. (Notts) b Nov. 24, 1892, d Dec. 3, 1991
*Wall, T. W. (S. Aust.) b May 13, 1904, d March 25, 1981
Wallace, P. A. (B'dos) b Aug. 2, 1970
*Wallace, W. M. (Auck.) b Dec. 19, 1916
Waller, A. C. (MCD) b Sept. 25, 1959
Waller, C. E. (Surrey & Sussex) b Oct. 3, 1948
*Walmsley, K. P. (Auck.) b Aug. 23, 1973
*Walsh, C. A. (Jam. & Glos; *CY 1987*) b Oct. 30, 1962
Walsh, J. E. (NSW & Leics) b Dec. 4, 1912, d May 20, 1980
*Walter, K. A. (Tvl) b Nov. 5, 1939
*Walters, C. F. (Glam & Worcs; *CY 1934*) b Aug. 28, 1905, d Dec. 23, 1992
*Walters, F. H. (Vic. & NSW) b Feb. 9, 1860, d June 1, 1922
*Walters, K. D. (NSW) b Dec. 21, 1945
*Waqar Hassan (Pak. Us, Punjab, Pak. Serv. & Kar.) b Sept. 12, 1932
*Waqar Younis (Multan, UBL & Surrey; *CY 1992*) b Nov. 16, 1971
*Ward, Alan (Derbys, Leics & Border) b Aug. 10, 1947
*Ward, Albert (Yorks & Lancs; *CY 1890*) b Nov. 21, 1865, d Jan. 6, 1939
Ward, B. (Essex) b Feb. 28, 1944
Ward, D. (Glam) b Aug. 30, 1934
Ward, D. M. (Surrey) b Feb. 10, 1961
*Ward, F. A. (S. Aust.) b Feb. 23, 1906, d March 25, 1974
*Ward, J. T. (Cant.) b March 11, 1937
*Ward, T. A. (Tvl) b Aug. 2, 1887, d Feb. 16, 1936
Ward, T. R. (Kent) b Jan. 18, 1968
Ward, William (MCC & Hants) b July 24, 1787, d June 30, 1849
*Wardle, J. H. (Yorks; *CY 1954*) b Jan. 8, 1923, d July 23, 1985
*Warnapura, B. (SL) b March 1, 1953
*Warnaweera, K. P. J. (Galle) b Nov. 23, 1960
*Warne, S. K. (Vic.; *CY 1994*) b Sept. 13, 1969
Warner, A. E. (Worcs & Derbys) b May 12, 1959
*Warner, Sir Pelham F. (OU & Middx; *CY 1904, special portrait 1921;* Pres. MCC 1950-51) b Oct. 2, 1873, d Jan. 30, 1963
*Warr, J. J. (CU & Middx; Pres. MCC 1987-88) b July 16, 1927
*Warren, A. R. (Derbys) b April 2, 1875, d Sept. 3, 1951
*Washbrook, C. (Lancs; *CY 1947*) b Dec. 6, 1914
*Wasim Akram (Lahore, PACO, PNSC, PIA & Lancs; *CY 1993*) b June 3, 1966
*Wasim Bari (Kar., PIA & Sind) b March 23, 1948
Wasim Haider (F'bad & PIA) b June 6, 1967
*Wasim Raja (Lahore, Sargodha, Pak. Us, PIA, Punjab & NBP) b July 3, 1952
Wass, T. G. (Notts; *CY 1908*) b Dec. 26, 1873, d Oct. 27, 1953
*Wassan, A. S. (Delhi) b March 23, 1968
Wassell, A. (Hants) b April 15, 1940
*Watkin, S. L. (Glam; *CY 1994*) b Sept. 15, 1964
*Watkins, A. J. (Glam) b April 21, 1922
*Watkins, J. C. (Natal) b April 10, 1923
*Watkins, J. R. (NSW) b April 16, 1943
*Watkinson, M. (Lancs) b Aug. 1, 1961
Watson, A. (Lancs) b Nov. 4, 1844, d Oct. 26, 1920
*Watson, C. (Jam. & Delhi) b July 1, 1938
Watson, F. (Lancs) b Sept. 17, 1898, d Feb. 1, 1976
*Watson, G. D. (Vic., W. Aust. & NSW) b March 8, 1945
Watson, G. S. (Kent & Leics) b April 10, 1907, d April 1, 1974
*Watson, W. (Yorks & Leics; *CY 1954*) b March 7, 1920
*Watson, W. (Auck.) b Aug. 31, 1965
*Watson, W. J. (NSW) b Jan. 31, 1931
Watt, A. E. (Kent) b June 19, 1907, d Feb. 3, 1974
*Watt, L. (Otago) b Sept. 17, 1924, d Nov. 15, 1996
Watts, E. A. (Surrey) b Aug. 1, 1911, d May 2, 1982
Watts, P. D. (Northants & Notts) b March 31, 1938
Watts, P. J. (Northants) b June 16, 1940
*Waugh, M. E. (NSW & Essex; *CY 1991*) b June 2, 1965
*Waugh, S. R. (NSW & Som; *CY 1989*) b June 2, 1965
*Wazir, Ali, S. (C. Ind., S. Punjab & Patiala) b Sept. 15, 1903, d June 17, 1950
*Wazir Mohammad (B'pur & Kar.) b Dec. 22, 1929
*Webb, M. G. (Otago & Cant.) b June 22, 1947
*Webb, P. N. (Auck.) b July 14, 1957

Webb, R. J. (Otago) b Sept. 15, 1952
Webb, R. T. (Sussex) b July 11, 1922
*Webbe, A. J. (OU & Middx) b Jan. 16, 1855, d Feb. 19, 1941
Webster, W. H. (CU & Middx; Pres. MCC 1976-77) b Feb. 22, 1910, d June 19, 1986
*Weekes, Sir Everton D. (B'dos; *CY 1951*) b Feb. 26, 1925
*Weekes, K. H. (Jam.) b Jan. 24, 1912
Weeks, R. T. (Warwicks) b April 30, 1930
Weerakkody, A. P. (NCC) b Oct. 1, 1970
*Weerasinghe, C. D. U. S. (TU & NCC) b March 1, 1968
Weigall, G. J. V. (CU & Kent) b Oct. 19, 1870, d May 17, 1944
*Weir, G. L. (Auck.) b June 2, 1908
*Wellard, A. W. (Som; *CY 1936*) b April 8, 1902, d Dec. 31, 1980
*Wellham, D. M. (NSW, Tas. & Qld) b March 13, 1959
*Wells, A. P. (Sussex & Border) b Oct. 2, 1961
Wells, B. D. (Glos & Notts) b July 27, 1930
Wells, C. M. (Sussex, Border, W. Prov. & Derbys) b March 3, 1960
Wells, W. (Northants) b March 14, 1881, d March 18, 1939
Wenman, E. G. (Kent & England) b Aug. 18, 1803, d Dec. 31, 1879
Wensley, A. F. (Sussex, Auck., Naw. & Eur.) b May 23, 1898, d June 17, 1970
*Wesley, C. (Natal) b Sept. 5, 1937
**Wessels, K. C. (OFS, W. Prov., N. Tvl, Sussex, Qld & E. Prov.; *CY 1995*) b Sept. 14, 1957
West, G. H. (Editor of *Wisden* 1880-86) b 1851, d Oct. 6, 1896
*Westcott, R. J. (W. Prov.) b Sept. 19, 1927
Weston, M. J. (Worcs) b April 8, 1959
*Wettimuny, M. D. (SL) b June 11, 1951
*Wettimuny, S. (SL; *CY 1985*) b Aug. 12, 1956
Wettimuny, S. R. de S. (SL) b Feb. 7, 1949
*Wharton, A. (Lancs & Leics) b April 30, 1923, d Aug. 26, 1993
*Whatmore, D. F. (Vic.) b March 16, 1954
Wheatley, O. S. (CU, Warwicks & Glam; *CY 1969*) b May 28, 1935
Whitaker, Haddon (Editor of *Wisden* 1940-43) b Aug. 30, 1908, d Jan. 5, 1982
*Whitaker, J. J. (Leics; *CY 1987*) b May 5, 1962
White, A. F. T. (CU, Warwicks & Worcs) b Sept. 5, 1915, d March 16, 1993
White, Sir Archibald W. 4th Bt (Yorks) b Oct. 14, 1877, d Dec. 16, 1945
*White, C. (Vic. & Yorks) b Dec. 16, 1969
*White, D. J. (N. Dist.) b June 26, 1961
*White, D. W. (Hants & Glam) b Dec. 14, 1935
*White, G. C. (Tvl) b Feb. 5, 1882, d Oct. 17, 1918
*White, J. C. (Som; *CY 1929*) b Feb. 19, 1891, d May 2, 1961
White, Hon. L. R. (5th Lord Annaly) (Middx & Victory Test) b March 15, 1927, d Sept. 30, 1990
White, R. A. (Middx & Notts) b Oct. 6, 1936
White, R. C. (CU, Glos & Tvl) b Jan. 29, 1941
*White, W. A. (B'dos) b Nov. 20, 1938
Whitehead, A. G. T. (Som; Test umpire) b Oct. 28, 1940
Whitehead, H. (Leics) b Sept. 19, 1874, d Sept. 14, 1944
Whitehouse, J. (Warwicks) b April 8, 1949
*Whitelaw, P. E. (Auck.) b Feb. 10, 1910, d Aug. 28, 1988
Whiteside, J. P. (Lancs & Leics) b June 11, 1861, d March 8, 1946
Whitington, R. S. (S. Aust. & Victory Tests; writer) b June 30, 1912, d March 13, 1984
*Whitney, M. R. (NSW & Glos) b Feb. 24, 1959
Whittaker, G. J. (Surrey) b May 29, 1916
*Whittall, G. J. (Mat.) b Sept. 5, 1972
Whitticase, P. (Leics) b March 15, 1965
Whittingham, N. B. (Notts) b Oct. 22, 1940
*Whitty, W. J. (S. Aust.) b Aug. 15, 1886, d Jan. 30, 1974
*Whysall, W. W. (Notts; *CY 1925*) b Oct. 31, 1887, d Nov. 11, 1930
Wickremaratne, R. P. A. H. (SSC) b Feb. 21, 1971
*Wickremasinghe, A. G. D. (NCC) b Dec. 27, 1965
*Wickremasinghe, G. P. (BRC & SSC) b Aug. 14, 1971
*Wiener, J. M. (Vic.) b May 1, 1955
*Wight, C. V. (BG) b July 28, 1902, d Oct. 4, 1969
*Wight, G. L. (BG) b May 28, 1929
Wight, P. B. (BG, Som & Cant.) b June 25, 1930
*Wijegunawardene, K. I. W. (CCC) b Nov. 23, 1964
*Wijesuriya, R. G. C. E. (Mor. & Colts) b Feb. 18, 1960
*Wijetunge, P. K. (SSC) b Aug. 6, 1971
Wilcox, D. R. (Essex & CU) b June 4, 1910, d Feb. 6, 1953
Wild, D. J. (Northants) b Nov. 28, 1962
*Wiles, C. A. (B'dos & T/T) b Aug. 11, 1892, d Nov. 4, 1957
Wilkins, C. P. (Derbys, Border, E. Prov. & Natal) b July 31, 1944
Wilkinson, C. T. A. (Surrey) b Oct. 4, 1884, d Dec. 16, 1970
*Wilkinson, L. L. (Lancs) b Nov. 5, 1916
Willatt, G. L. (CU, Notts & Derbys) b May 7, 1918
*Willett, E. T. (Comb. Is. & Leewards) b May 1, 1953
Willett, M. D. (Surrey) b April 21, 1933
*Willey, P. (Northants, E. Prov. & Leics; Test umpire) b Dec. 6, 1949
*Williams, A. B. (Jam.) b Nov. 21, 1949

*Williams, D. (T/T) b Nov. 4, 1963
Williams, D. L. (Glam) b Nov. 20, 1946
*Williams, E. A. V. (B'dos) b April 10, 1914
Williams, L. R. (Jam.) b Dec. 12, 1968
*Williams, N. F. (Middx, Windwards, Tas. & Essex) b July 2, 1962
Williams, R. G. (Northants) b Aug. 10, 1957
*Williams, S. C. (Leewards) b Aug. 12, 1969
*Willis, R. G. D. (Surrey, Warwicks & N. Tvl; *CY 1978*) b May 30, 1949
*Willoughby, J. T. (SA) b Nov. 7, 1874, d March 11, 1952
Willsher, E. (Kent & All-England) b Nov. 22, 1828, d Oct. 7, 1885
Wilson, A. (Lancs) b April 24, 1921
Wilson, A. E. (Middx & Glos) b May 18, 1910
*Wilson, Rev. C. E. M. (CU & Yorks) b May 15, 1875, d Feb. 8, 1944
*Wilson, D. (Yorks) b Aug. 7, 1937
*Wilson, E. R. (CU & Yorks) b March 25, 1879, d July 21, 1957
Wilson, G. (CU & Yorks) b Aug. 21, 1895, d Nov. 29, 1960
Wilson, H. L. (Sussex) b June 27, 1881, d March 15, 1937
Wilson, J. V. (Yorks; *CY 1961*) b Jan. 17, 1921
Wilson, J. W. (Otago) b Oct. 24, 1973
*Wilson, J. W. (Vic. & S. Aust.) b Aug. 20, 1921, d Oct. 13, 1985
Wilson, R. C. (Kent) b Feb. 18, 1928
*Wimble, C. S. (Tvl) b April 22, 1861, d Jan. 28, 1930
Windows, A. R. (Glos & CU) b Sept. 25, 1942
Winfield, H. M. (Notts) b June 13, 1933
Winrow, H. F. (Notts) b Jan. 17, 1916, d Aug. 19, 1973
*Winslow, P. L. (Sussex, Tvl & Rhod.) b May 21, 1929
Wisden, John (Sussex; founder John Wisden & Co and *Wisden's Cricketers' Almanack*) b Sept. 5, 1826, d April 5, 1884
*Wishart, C. B. (Mash.) b Jan. 9, 1974
*Wishart, K. L. (BG) b Nov. 28, 1908, d Oct. 18, 1972
Wolton, A. V. (Warwicks) b June 12, 1919, d Sept. 9, 1990
*Wood, A. (Yorks; *CY 1939*) b Aug. 25, 1898, d April 1, 1973
*Wood, B. (Yorks, Lancs, Derbys & E. Prov.) b Dec. 26, 1942
Wood, C. J. B. (Leics) b Nov. 21, 1875, d June 5, 1960
Wood, D. J. (Sussex) b May 19, 1914, d March 12, 1989
*Wood, G. E. C. (CU & Kent) b Aug. 22, 1893, d March 18, 1971
*Wood, G. M. (W. Aust.) b Nov. 6, 1956
*Wood, H. (Kent & Surrey; *CY 1891*) b Dec. 14, 1854, d April 30, 1919
*Wood, R. (Lancs & Vic.) b March 7, 1860, d Jan. 6, 1915
*Woodcock, A. J. (S. Aust.) b Feb. 27, 1948
Woodcock, John C. (Writer; Editor of *Wisden* 1981-86) b Aug. 7, 1926
*Woodfull, W. M. (Vic.; *CY 1927*) b Aug. 22, 1897, d Aug. 11, 1965
Woodhead, F. G. (Notts) b Oct. 30, 1912, d May 24, 1991
**Woods, S. M. J. (CU & Som; *CY 1889*) b April 13, 1867, d April 30, 1931
Wooller, W. (CU & Glam) b Nov. 20, 1912
Woolley, C. N. (Glos & Northants) b May 5, 1886, d Nov. 3, 1962
*Woolley, F. E. (Kent; *CY 1911*) b May 27, 1887, d Oct. 18, 1978
*Woolley, R. D. (Tas.) b Sept. 16, 1954
*Woolmer, R. A. (Kent, Natal & W. Prov.; *CY 1976*) b May 14, 1948
*Worrall, J. (Vic.) b June 21, 1861, d Nov. 17, 1937
*Worrell, Sir Frank M. M. (B'dos & Jam.; *CY 1951*) b Aug. 1, 1924, d March 13, 1967
Worsley, D. R. (OU & Lancs) b July 18, 1941
Worsley, Sir W. A. 4th Bt (Yorks; Pres. MCC 1961-62) b April 5, 1890, d Dec. 4, 1973
*Worthington, T. S. (Derbys; *CY 1937*) b Aug. 21, 1905, d Aug. 31, 1973
Wrathall, H. (Glos) b Feb. 1, 1869, d June 1, 1944
Wright, A. C. (Kent) b April 4, 1895, d May 26, 1959
Wright, A. J. (Glos) b July 27, 1962
*Wright, C. W. (CU & Notts) b May 27, 1863, d Jan. 10, 1936
*Wright, D. V. P. (Kent; *CY 1940*) b Aug. 21, 1914
Wright, Graeme A. (Editor of *Wisden* 1987-92) b April 23, 1943
*Wright, J. G. (N. Dist., Derbys, Cant. & Auck.) b July 5, 1954
*Wright, K. J. (W. Aust. & S. Aust.) b Dec. 27, 1953
Wright, L. G. (Derbys; *CY 1906*) b June 15, 1862, d Jan. 11, 1953
Wright, W. (Notts & Kent) b Feb. 29, 1856, d March 22, 1940
*Wyatt, R. E. S. (Warwicks & Worcs; *CY 1930*) b May 2, 1901, d April 20, 1995
*Wynne, O. E. (Tvl & W. Prov.) b June 1, 1919, d July 13, 1975
*Wynyard, E. G. (Hants) b April 1, 1861, d Oct. 30, 1936

*Yadav, N. S. (H'bad) b Jan. 26, 1957
*Yadav, V. S. (Haryana) b March 14, 1967
*Yajurvindra Singh (M'tra & S'tra) b Aug. 1, 1952
*Yallop, G. N. (Vic.) b Oct. 7, 1952
*Yardley, B. (W. Aust.) b Sept. 5, 1947
*Yardley, N. W. D. (CU & Yorks; *CY 1948*) b March 19, 1915, d Oct. 4, 1989

Yardley, T. J. (Worcs & Northants) b Oct. 27, 1946
Yarnold, H. (Worcs) b July 6, 1917, d Aug. 13, 1974
*Yashpal Sharma (Punjab) b Aug. 11, 1954
Yawar Saeed (Som & Punjab) b Jan. 22, 1935
*Yograj Singh (Haryana & Punjab) b March 25, 1958
Young, A. (Som) b Nov. 6, 1890, d April 2, 1936
*Young, B. A. (N. Dist.) b Nov. 3, 1964
Young, D. M. (Worcs & Glos) b April 15, 1924, d June 18, 1993
*Young, H. I. (Essex) b Feb. 5, 1876, d Dec. 12, 1964
*Young, J. A. (Middx) b Oct. 14, 1912, d Feb. 5, 1993
*Young, R. A. (CU & Sussex) b Sept. 16, 1885, d July 1, 1968
*Younis Ahmed (Lahore, Kar., Surrey, PIA, S. Aust., Worcs & Glam) b Oct. 20, 1947
*Yuile, B. W. (C. Dist.) b Oct. 29, 1941

Zafar Iqbal (Kar., NBP & Lahore) b March 6, 1969
*Zaheer Abbas (Kar., Glos, PWD, Dawood Ind., Sind & PIA; *CY 1972*) b July 24, 1947
Zahid Ahmed (PIA, Peshawar & F'bad) b Nov. 15, 1961
*Zahid Fazal (PACO, PIA & Lahore) b Nov. 10, 1973
*Zakir Khan (Sind, Peshawar & ADBP) b April 3, 1963
Zesers, A. K. (S. Aust.) b March 11, 1967
*Zoehrer, T. J. (W. Aust.) b Sept. 25, 1961
*Zulch, J. W. (Tvl) b Jan. 2, 1886, d May 19, 1924
*Zulfiqar Ahmed (B'pur & PIA) b Nov. 22, 1926
*Zulqarnain (Pak. Rlwys, Lahore, HBFC & PACO) b May 25, 1962

PRESIDENTS OF MCC SINCE 1946

1946	General Sir Ronald Adam, Bart
1947	Captain Lord Cornwallis
1948	Brig.-Gen. The Earl of Gowrie
1949	HRH The Duke of Edinburgh
1950	Sir Pelham Warner
1951-52	W. Findlay
1952-53	The Duke of Beaufort
1953-54	The Earl of Rosebery
1954-55	Viscount Cobham
1955-56	Field Marshal Earl Alexander of Tunis
1956-57	Viscount Monckton of Brenchley
1957-58	The Duke of Norfolk
1958-59	Marshal of the RAF Viscount Portal of Hungerford
1959-60	H. S. Altham
1960-61	Sir Hubert Ashton
1961-62	Col. Sir William Worsley, Bart
1962-63	Lt-Col. Lord Nugent
1963-64	G. O. B. Allen
1964-65	R. H. Twining
1965-66	Lt-Gen. Sir Oliver Leese, Bart
1966-67	Sir Alec Douglas-Home
1967-68	A. E. R. Gilligan
1968-69	R. Aird
1969-70	M. J. C. Allom
1970-71	Sir Cyril Hawker
1971-72	F. R. Brown
1972-73	A. M. Crawley
1973-74	Lord Caccia
1974-75	HRH The Duke of Edinburgh
1975-76	C. G. A. Paris
1976-77	W. H. Webster
1977-78	D. G. Clark
1978-79	C. H. Palmer
1979-80	S. C. Griffith
1980-81	P. B. H. May
1981-82	G. H. G. Doggart
1982-83	Sir Anthony Tuke
1983-84	A. H. A. Dibbs
1984-85	F. G. Mann
1985-86	J. G. W. Davies
1986-87	M. C. Cowdrey
1987-88	J. J. Warr
1988-89	Field Marshal The Lord Bramhall
1989-90	The Hon. Sir Denys Roberts
1990-91	The Rt Hon. The Lord Griffiths
1991-92	M. E. L. Melluish
1992-94	D. R. W. Silk
1994-96	The Hon. Sir Oliver Popplewell
1996-	A. C. D. Ingleby-Mackenzie

Since 1951, Presidents of MCC have taken office on October 1. Previously they took office immediately after the annual general meeting at the start of the season. Since 1992, Presidents have been eligible for two consecutive years of office.

REGISTER OF PLAYERS

The qualifications for inclusion are as follows:

1. All players who appeared in Tests or one-day internationals for a Test-playing country in 1995-96 or 1996.
2. All players who appeared in the County Championship in 1996.
3. All players who appeared in the Sheffield Shield, Castle Cup, Red Stripe Cup and Duleep Trophy in 1995-96.
4. All players who appeared in first-class domestic cricket in New Zealand, Pakistan, Sri Lanka and Zimbabwe in 1995-96, who have also played in Tests or one-day international cricket.

Notes: The forename by which the player is known is underlined if it is not his first name.

Teams are those played for in 1995-96 and/or 1996.

Countries are those for which players are qualified.

The country of birth is given if it is not the one for which a player is qualified. It is also given to differentiate between nations in the Leeward and Windward Islands, and where it is essential for clarity.

* *Denotes Test player.*

	Team	*Country*	*Born*	*Birthplace*
Aamer Hanif	Karachi/Allied Bank	P	4.10.71	*Karachi*
***Aamer Malik**	Lahore/PIA	P	3.1.63	*Mandi Bahauddin*
***Aamir Nazir**	Allied Bank	P	2.1.71	*Lahore*
***Aamir Sohail**	Allied Bank	P	14.9.66	*Lahore*
***Abdul Qadir**	Habib Bank	P	15.9.55	*Lahore*
Ackerman Hylton Deon	Western Province	SA	14.2.73	*Cape Town*
Adams Christopher John	Derbyshire	E	6.5.70	*Whitwell*
***Adams** James Clive	Jamaica	WI	9.1.68	*Port Maria*
***Adams** Paul Regan	Western Province	SA	20.1.77	*Cape Town*
Afford John Andrew	Nottinghamshire	E	12.5.64	*Crowland*
Afzaal Usman	Nottinghamshire	E	9.6.77	*Rawalpindi, Pakistan*
***Ahangama** Franklyn Saliya	Sinhalese	SL	14.9.59	*Colombo*
***Akram Raza**	Lahore	P	22.11.64	*Lahore*
Aldred Paul	Derbyshire	E	4.2.69	*Chellaston*
***Allen** Ian Basil Alston	Windward Islands	WI	6.10.65	*Coull's Hill, St Vincent*
Alleyne Mark Wayne	Gloucestershire	E	23.5.68	*Tottenham*
***Allott** Geoffrey Ian	Canterbury	NZ	24.12.71	*Christchurch*
Altree Darren Anthony	Warwickshire	E	30.9.74	*Rugby*
***Ambrose** Curtly Elconn Lynwall	Leeward I./Northants	WI	21.9.63	*Swetes Village, Antigua*
Amm Philip Geoffrey	Eastern Province	SA	2.4.64	*Grahamstown*
***Amre** Pravin Kalyan	Rajasthan	I	14.8.68	*Bombay*
Andrew Stephen Jon Walter	Essex	E	27.1.66	*London*
***Angel** Jo	Western Australia	A	22.4.68	*Subiaco*
***Ankola** Salil Ashok	Bombay	I	1.3.68	*Sholapur*
Anthony Hamish Arbeb Gervais	Leeward Islands	WI	16.1.71	*Urlings Village, Antigua*
Antoine Eugene Clifford	Trinidad & Tobago	WI	8.4.67	*Trinidad*
***Anurasiri** Sangarange Don	Panadura	SL	25.2.66	*Panadura*
***Anwar Khan**	Bahawalpur	P	24.12.55	*Karachi*
***Aqib Javed**	Allied Bank	P	5.8.72	*Sheikhupura*
Archer Graeme Francis	Nottinghamshire	E	26.9.70	*Carlisle*
Armstrong Sean Hussain	Barbados	WI	11.5.73	*Barbados*
Arnberger Jason Lee	New South Wales	A	18.11.72	*Penrith*
Arshad Khan	Peshawar/Allied Bank	P	22.3.71	*Peshawar*
***Arthurton** Keith Lloyd Thomas	Leeward Islands	WI	21.2.65	*Charlestown, Nevis*
***Arun Lal**	Bengal	I	1.8.55	*Moradabad*
***Asif Mujtaba**	Karachi/PIA	P	4.11.67	*Karachi*
***Astle** Nathan John	Canterbury	NZ	15.9.71	*Christchurch*
***Atapattu** Marvan Samson	Sinhalese	SL	22.11.72	*Kalutara*
***Ata-ur-Rehman**	Allied Bank	P	28.3.75	*Lahore*
***Atherton** Michael Andrew	Lancashire	E	23.3.68	*Manchester*

	Team	Country	Born	Birthplace
***Athey** Charles William Jeffrey	Sussex	E	27.9.57	*Middlesbrough*
***Atif Rauf**	ADBP	P	3.3.64	*Lahore*
Atkinson Mark Neville	Tasmania	A	11.2.69	*Sydney*
Austin Ian David	Lancashire	E	30.5.66	*Haslingden*
Aymes Adrian Nigel	Hampshire	E	4.6.64	*Southampton*
Ayres Warren Geoffrey	Victoria	A	25.10.65	*Moorabbin*
***Azharuddin** Mohammad	Hyderabad	I	8.2.63	*Hyderabad*
Bacher Adam Marc	Transvaal	SA	29.10.73	*Johannesburg*
Badenhorst Alan	Eastern Province	SA	10.7.70	*Cape Town*
Baguley Bryan Charles	Boland	SA	25.3.71	*Cape Town*
Bahutule Sairaj Vasant	Bombay	I	6.1.73	*Bombay*
***Bailey** Robert John	Northamptonshire	E	28.10.63	*Biddulph*
Bailey Tobin Michael Barnaby	Northamptonshire	E	28.8.76	*Kettering*
Bainbridge Philip	Durham	E	16.4.58	*Stoke-on-Trent*
Baker Robert Michael	Western Australia	A	24.7.75	*Osborne Park*
Bakker Jason Richard	Victoria	A	12.11.67	*Geelong*
Bakkes Herman Charles	Free State	SA	24.12.69	*Port Elizabeth*
Ball Martyn Charles John	Gloucestershire	E	26.4.70	*Bristol*
Balliram Anil	Trinidad & Tobago	WI	27.2.74	*Trinidad*
***Banerjee** Subroto Tara	Bihar	I	13.2.69	*Patna*
***Baptiste** Eldine Ashworth Elderfield	Eastern Province	SA	12.3.60	*Liberta, Antigua*
***Barnett** Kim John	Derbyshire	E	17.7.60	*Stoke-on-Trent*
Barry Neil Erwyn Fitzgerald	Guyana	WI	6.8.66	*Victoria*
Barsby Trevor John	Queensland	A	16.1.64	*Herston*
Barwick Stephen Royston	Glamorgan	E	6.9.60	*Neath*
Base Simon John	Derbyshire	E	2.1.60	*Maidstone*
***Basit Ali**	United Bank	P	13.12.70	*Karachi*
Bates Richard Terry	Nottinghamshire	E	17.6.72	*Stamford*
Batty Jeremy David	Somerset	E	15.5.71	*Bradford*
Beamish Michael Gwynne	Eastern Province	SA	30.7.69	*King William's Town*
Bedade Atul Chandrakant	Baroda	I	24.9.66	*Bombay*
Bedi Arun	Punjab	I	10.11.65	*Hoshiapur*
***Benjamin** Joseph Emmanuel	Surrey	E	2.2.61	*Christ Church, St Kitts*
***Benjamin** Kenneth Charlie Griffith	Leeward Islands	WI	8.4.67	*St John's, Antigua*
***Benjamin** Winston Keithroy Matthew	Hampshire	E	31.12.64	*All Saints, Antigua*
Benkenstein Dale Martin	Natal	SA	9.6.74	*Salisbury, Rhodesia*
Berry Darren Shane	Victoria	A	10.12.69	*Melbourne*
Betts Melvyn Morris	Durham	E	26.3.75	*Sacriston*
***Bevan** Michael Gwyl	NSW/Yorkshire	A	8.5.70	*Belconnen*
Bhave Surendra Shriram	Maharashtra	I	30.3.66	*Poona*
Bhupinder Singh. sen.	Punjab	I	1.4.65	*Hoshiapur*
Bhupinder Singh. jun.	Punjab	I	19.11.70	*Tarantaran*
Bichel Andrew John	Queensland	A	27.8.70	*Laidley*
Bicknell Darren John	Surrey	E	24.6.67	*Guildford*
***Bicknell** Martin Paul	Surrey	E	14.1.69	*Guildford*
Birbeck Shaun David	Durham	E	26.7.72	*Easington Lane*
***Bishop** Ian Raphael	Trinidad & Tobago	WI	24.10.67	*Port-of-Spain*
Biswal Ranjib Basantkumar	Orissa	I	21.9.70	*Cuttack*
***Blakey** Richard John	Yorkshire	E	15.1.67	*Huddersfield*
Blenkiron Darren Andrew	Durham	E	4.2.74	*Solihull*
***Blewett** Gregory Scott	South Australia	A	29.10.71	*Adelaide*
Boden David Jonathan Peter	Gloucestershire	E	26.11.70	*Eccleshall*
Bodoe Mahadeo	Trinidad & Tobago	WI	3.12.66	*Trinidad*
Boiling James	Durham	E	8.4.68	*New Delhi, India*
Boje Nico	Free State	SA	20.3.73	*Bloemfontein*
***Boon** David Clarence	Tasmania	A	29.12.60	*Launceston*
***Border** Allan Robert	Queensland	A	27.7.55	*Cremorne*
***Bosch** Tertius	Natal	SA	14.3.66	*Vereeniging*
Boswell Scott Antony John	Northamptonshire	E	11.9.74	*Fulford*
Botha Lodewikus Daniel	Eastern Province	SA	11.4.68	*Elsburg*

	Team	Country	Born	Birthplace
Botha Peterus Johannes	Border	SA	28.9.66	*Vereeniging*
Botham Liam James	Hampshire	E	26.8.77	*Doncaster*
Boucher Mark Verdon	Border	SA	3.12.76	*East London*
Bovill James Noel Bruce	Hampshire	E	2.6.71	*High Wycombe*
Bowen Mark Nicholas	Nottinghamshire	E	6.12.67	*Redcar*
Bowler Peter Duncan	Somerset	E	30.7.63	*Plymouth*
***Bradburn** Grant Eric	Northern Districts	NZ	26.5.66	*Hamilton*
***Brain** David Hayden	Mashonaland	Z	4.10.64	*Salisbury*
***Brandes** Eddo Andre	Mashonaland Co. Dists	Z	5.3.63	*Port Shepstone, SA*
Brayshaw James Antony	South Australia	A	11.5.67	*Subiaco*
Breese Gareth Rohan	Jamaica	WI	9.1.76	*Montego Bay*
***Briant** Gavin Aubrey	Mashonaland	Z	11.4.69	*Salisbury*
Brimson Matthew Thomas	Leicestershire	E	1.12.70	*Plumstead*
Brink Mechiel Matthys	Boland	SA	10.6.75	*Baberton*
Broster Paul Alexander	Victoria	A	31.1.73	*Wangaratta*
Brown Alistair Duncan	Surrey	E	11.2.70	*Beckenham*
Brown Douglas Robert	Warwicks/Wellington	E	29.10.69	*Stirling, Scotland*
Brown Jason Fred	Northamptonshire	E	10.10.74	*Newcastle-under-Lyme*
Brown Keith Robert	Middlesex	E	18.3.63	*Edmonton*
Brown Robin David	Mashonaland Co. Dists	Z	11.3.51	*Gatooma*
***Brown** Simon John Emmerson	Durham	E	29.6.69	*Cleadon*
Browne Barrington St Aubyn	Guyana	WI	16.9.67	*Georgetown*
***Browne** Courtney Oswald	Barbados	WI	7.12.70	*London, England*
Browne Robin Eusi	Guyana	WI	26.5.70	*Guyana*
***Bruk-Jackson** Glen Keith	Mashonaland Co. Dists	Z	25.4.69	*Salisbury*
Bruyns Mark Lloyd	Natal	SA	8.11.73	*Pietermaritzburg*
Bryan Henderson Ricardo	Barbados	WI	21.3.70	*Barbados*
Bryson Rudi Edwin	Northern Transvaal	SA	25.7.68	*Springs*
Buch Valmik Nalinkant	Baroda	I	29.8.75	*Rajkot*
***Burmester** Mark Grenville	Mashonaland	Z	24.1.68	*Durban, South Africa*
Burns Michael	Warwickshire	E	2.6.69	*Barrow-in-Furness*
Burton Shimei Nathaniel	Jamaica	WI	3.2.75	*Manchester (Jamaica)*
Butcher Gary Paul	Glamorgan	E	11.3.75	*Clapham*
Butcher Mark Alan	Surrey	E	23.8.72	*Croydon*
Byas David	Yorkshire	E	26.8.63	*Kilham*
***Caddick** Andrew Richard	Somerset	E	21.11.68	*Christchurch, NZ*
***Cairns** Christopher Lance	Canterbury/Notts	NZ	13.6.70	*Picton*
Callaghan David John	Eastern Province	SA	1.2.65	*Queenstown*
***Campbell** Alistair Douglas Ross	Mashonaland Co. Dists	Z	23.9.72	*Salisbury*
Campbell Colin Lockley	Durham	E	11.8.77	*Newcastle-upon-Tyne*
***Campbell** Sherwin Legay	Barbados/Durham	WI	1.11.70	*Bridgetown*
Cannonier Colin Darren	Leeward Islands	WI	22.5.73	*St Kitts*
***Capel** David John	Northamptonshire	E	6.2.63	*Northampton*
***Carlisle** Stuart Vance	Mashonaland	Z	10.5.72	*Salisbury*
Carr John Donald	Middlesex	E	15.6.63	*St John's Wood*
Cary Sean Ross	Western Australia	A	10.3.71	*Subiaco*
Chandana Umagiliyedurage Upul	Tamil Union	SL	3.9.72	*Galle*
***Chanderpaul** Shivnarine	Guyana	WI	18.8.74	*Unity Village*
Chandrasekhar Vakkadai Biksheswaran	Goa	I	21.8.61	*Madras*
Chapple Glen	Lancashire	E	23.1.74	*Skipton*
Chatterjee Utpal	Bengal	I	13.7.64	*Calcutta*
***Chauhan** Rajesh Kumar	Madhya Pradesh	I	19.12.66	*Ranchi*
Chee Quee Richard	New South Wales	A	4.1.71	*Camperdown*
***Childs** John Henry	Essex	E	15.8.51	*Plymouth*
Church Matthew John	Worcestershire	E	26.7.72	*Guildford*
Cilliers Alexander	Western Province	SA	6.6.71	*Klerksdorp*
Collingwood Paul David	Durham	E	26.5.76	*Shotley Bridge*
***Commins** John Brian	Western Province	SA	19.2.65	*East London*
Connor Cardigan Adolphus	Hampshire	E	24.3.61	*The Valley, Anguilla*

	Team	*Country*	*Born*	*Birthplace*
Cook Simon Hewitt	New South Wales	A	29.1.72	*Hastings*
Cooper Kevin Edwin	Gloucestershire	E	27.12.57	*Hucknall*
Corbett Troy Frederick	Victoria	A	11.10.72	*Ouyen*
***Cork** Dominic Gerald	Derbyshire	E	7.8.71	*Newcastle-under-Lyme*
Cosker Dean Andrew	Glamorgan	E	7.1.78	*Weymouth*
Cottam Andrew Colin	Somerset	E	14.7.73	*Northampton*
Cottey Phillip Anthony	Glamorgan	E	2.6.66	*Swansea*
Coulson Craig Edward	Western Australia	A	13.6.67	*South Perth*
Cowan Ashley Preston	Essex	E	7.5.75	*Hitchin*
Cowdrey Graham Robert	Kent	E	27.6.64	*Farnborough, Kent*
Cox David Mathew	Durham	E	2.3.72	*Southall*
Cox Jamie	Tasmania	A	15.10.69	*Burnie*
Craven Christiaan Frans	Free State	SA	6.12.70	*Dundee*
***Crawley** John Paul	Lancashire	E	21.9.71	*Maldon*
***Croft** Robert Damien Bale	Glamorgan	E	25.5.70	*Morriston*
Cronje Frans Johannes Cornelius	Border	SA	15.5.67	*Bloemfontein*
Cronje Schalk Grove	Free State	SA	6.9.70	*Bloemfontein*
***Cronje** Wessel Johannes	Free State	SA	25.9.69	*Bloemfontein*
Crookes Derek Norman	Natal	SA	5.3.69	*Mariannhill*
***Crowe** Martin David	Wellington	NZ	22.9.62	*Auckland*
***Cuffy** Cameron Eustace	Windward Islands	WI	8.2.70	*South Rivers, St Vincent*
***Cullinan** Daryll John	Border	SA	4.3.67	*Kimberley*
***Cummins** Anderson Cleophas	Barbados	WI	7.5.66	*Packer's Valley*
Cunliffe Robert John	Gloucestershire	E	8.11.73	*Oxford*
Curran Kevin Malcolm	Northamptonshire	E	7.9.59	*Rusape, Rhodesia*
***Curtis** Timothy Stephen	Worcestershire	E	15.1.60	*Chislehurst*
Cush Lennox Joseph	Guyana	WI	12.1.74	*Guyana*
Dale Adrian	Glamorgan	E	24.10.68	*Germiston, South Africa*
Daley James Arthur	Durham	E	24.9.73	*Sunderland*
Daly Anthony John	Tasmania	A	25.7.69	*Newcastle*
Das Shiv Sunder	Orissa	I	5.11.77	*Bhubaneshwar*
***Dassanayake** Pubudu Bathiya	Bloomfield	SL	11.7.70	*Kandy*
Davids Faiek	Cape Town	SA	1.9.64	*Cape Town*
Davies Sean Gerard	Mashonaland	Z	15.10.73	*Salisbury*
Davis Casper Andre	Windward Islands	WI	14.3.66	*St Vincent*
***Davis** Heath Te-Ihi-O-Te-Rangi	Wellington	NZ	30.11.71	*Lower Hutt*
Davis Mark Jeffrey Gonrow	N. Transvaal	SA	10.10.71	*Port Elizabeth*
Davis Richard Peter	Gloucestershire	E	18.3.66	*Margate*
Davison John Michael	Victoria	A	9.5.70	*Campbell River, Canada*
Davison Rodney John	New South Wales	A	26.6.69	*Kogarah*
Dawson Alan Charles	Western Province	SA	27.11.69	*Cape Town*
Dawson Robert Ian	Gloucestershire	E	29.3.70	*Exmouth*
Dean Kevin James	Derbyshire	E	16.10.75	*Derby*
***DeFreitas** Phillip Anthony Jason	Derbyshire/Boland	E	18.2.66	*Scotts Head, Dominica*
***de Groen** Richard Paul	Northern Districts	NZ	5.8.62	*Otorohanga*
De Groot Nicholas Alexander	Guyana	WI	22.10.75	*Guyana*
***Dekker** Mark Hamilton	Matabeleland	Z	5.12.69	*Gatooma*
Denton Gerard John	Tasmania	A	7.8.75	*Mount Isa*
***de Silva** Ashley Matthew	Colombo	SL	3.12.63	*Colombo*
***de Silva** Ellawalakankanamge Asoka Ranjit	Galle	SL	28.3.56	*Kalutara*
***de Silva** Pinnaduwage Aravinda	Nondescripts	SL	17.10.65	*Colombo*
***de Villiers** Petrus Stephanus	N. Transvaal	SA	13.10.64	*Vereeniging*
***Dhanraj** Rajindra	Trinidad & Tobago	WI	6.2.69	*Barrackpore*
Dharmani Pankaj	Punjab	I	27.9.74	*Delhi*
***Dharmasena** Handunettige Deepthi Priyantha Kumara	Bloomfield	SL	24.4.71	*Colombo*
Dighe Samir Sudhakar	Bombay	I	8.10.68	*Bombay*
Dippenaar Hendrik Human	Free State	SA	14.6.77	*Kimberley*
Di Venuto Michael James	Tasmania	A	12.12.73	*Hobart*

	Team	Country	Born	Birthplace
***Dodemaide** Anthony Ian Christopher	Victoria	A	5.10.63	*Williamstown*
***Donald** Allan Anthony	Free State	SA	20.10.66	*Bloemfontein*
Doshi Manish Surendra	Vidarbha	I	8.3.73	*Nagpur*
***Doull** Simon Blair	Northern Districts	NZ	6.8.69	*Pukekohe*
Dowman Mathew Peter	Nottinghamshire	E	10.5.74	*Grantham*
Doyle Bryan Bernard John	Victoria	A	20.10.68	*Seymour*
Drakes Vasbert Conniel	Barbados/Sussex	WI	5.8.69	*St James*
***Dravid** Rahul	Karnataka	I	11.1.73	*Indore*
Drew Bryan John	Boland	SA	23.1.71	*Durban*
***Dunusinghe** Chamara Iroshan	Antonians	SL	19.10.70	*Colombo*
Dutch Keith Philip	Middlesex	E	21.3.73	*Harrow*
***Ealham** Mark Alan	Kent	E	27.8.69	*Willesborough*
Ecclestone Simon Charles	Somerset	E	16.7.71	*Great Dunmow*
Edmond Michael Denis	Warwickshire	E	30.7.69	*Barrow-in-Furness*
***Eksteen** Clive Edward	Transvaal	SA	2.12.66	*Johannesburg*
Elliott Matthew Thomas Gray	Victoria	A	28.9.71	*Chelsea*
Ellis Scott William Kenneth	Worcestershire	E	3.10.75	*Newcastle-under-Lyme*
Elworthy Steven	N. Transvaal/Lancs	SA	23.2.65	*Bulawayo, Rhodesia*
***Emburey** John Ernest	Northamptonshire	E	20.8.52	*Peckham*
***Emery** Philip Allen	New South Wales	A	25.6.64	*St Ives*
Emslie Peter Arthur Norman	Border	SA	21.10.68	*Grahamstown*
Erasmus Marais	Boland	SA	27.2.64	*George*
Essop-Adam Ebrahim Ali	Mashonaland	Z	16.11.68	*Salisbury*
Evans Alun Wyn	Glamorgan	E	20.8.75	*Fishguard*
Evans Craig Neil	Mashonaland Co. Dists	Z	29.11.69	*Salisbury*
Evans Kevin Paul	Nottinghamshire	E	10.9.63	*Calverton*
***Fairbrother** Neil Harvey	Lancashire	E	9.9.63	*Warrington*
Farrell Michael Graeme	Tasmania	A	24.9.68	*Melbourne*
***Farrukh Zaman**	Peshawar	P	2.4.56	*Peshawar*
Fay Richard Anthony	Middlesex	E	14.5.74	*Kilburn*
Feltham Mark Andrew	Middlesex	E	26.6.63	*St John's Wood*
Fernando Ungamandalige Nisal Kumudusiri	Sinhalese	SL	10.3.70	*Colombo*
Ferreira Lloyd Douglas	Boland	SA	6.5.74	*Johannesburg*
***Fleming** Damien William	Victoria	A	24.4.70	*Bentley*
Fleming Matthew Valentine	Kent	E	12.12.64	*Macclesfield*
***Fleming** Stephen Paul	Canterbury	NZ	1.4.73	*Christchurch*
***Flower** Andrew	Mashonaland	Z	28.4.68	*Cape Town, SA*
***Flower** Grant William	Young Mashonaland	Z	20.12.70	*Salisbury*
Foley Geoffrey Ian	Queensland	A	11.10.67	*Jandowae*
Follett David	Middlesex	E	14.10.68	*Newcastle-under-Lyme*
Ford Shane George Bancroft	Jamaica	WI	8.9.69	*Jamaica*
Forde Keith Adrian	Natal	SA	12.7.69	*Pietermaritzburg*
Fordham Alan	Northamptonshire	E	9.11.64	*Bedford*
Foster Michael James	Durham	E	17.9.72	*Leeds*
Fourie Brenden Craig	Border	SA	13.4.70	*East London*
Francis Nigel Bernard	Trinidad & Tobago	WI	6.9.71	*Trinidad*
Franks Paul John	Nottinghamshire	E	3.2.79	*Mansfield*
***Fraser** Angus Robert Charles	Middlesex	E	8.8.65	*Billinge*
Freedman David Andrew	New South Wales	A	19.6.64	*Sydney*
Fulton David Paul	Kent	E	15.11.71	*Lewisham*
***Gallian** Jason Edward Riche	Lancashire	E	25.6.71	*Sydney, Australia*
Gamage Janak Champika	Galle	SL	17.4.64	*Matara*
Gandhe Pritam Vithal	Vidarbha	I	6.8.71	*Nagpur*
Gandhi Devang	Bengal	I	6.9.71	*Bhavnagar*
***Ganguly** Sourav Chandidas	Bengal	I	8.7.72	*Calcutta*
Gardiner Grant Bruce	Victoria	A	26.2.65	*Melbourne*

	Team	Country	Born	Birthplace
***Gatting** Michael William	Middlesex	E	6.6.57	*Kingsbury*
George Shane Peter	South Australia	A	20.10.70	*Adelaide*
Germishuys Louis-Marc	Boland	SA	23.3.67	*Cape Town*
***Germon** Lee Kenneth	Canterbury	NZ	4.11.68	*Christchurch*
Ghare Yogesh Trimbak	Vidarbha	I	5.7.71	*Nagpur*
Ghayas Feroze	Delhi	I	3.5.73	*Delhi*
Ghulam Ali	Karachi/PIA	P	8.9.66	*Karachi*
Gibbs Herschelle Herman	Western Province	SA	23.2.74	*Cape Town*
Gibbs Marlon Christopher	Jamaica	WI	30.3.71	*Jamaica*
***Gibson** Ottis Delroy	Barbados/Glamorgan	WI	16.3.69	*Sion Hill*
Giddins Edward Simon Hunter	Sussex	E	20.7.71	*Eastbourne*
Gilchrist Adam Craig	Western Australia	A	14.11.71	*Bellingen*
Giles Ashley Fraser	Warwickshire	E	19.3.73	*Chertsey*
Gillespie Jason Neil	South Australia	A	19.4.75	*Darlinghurst*
***Gooch** Graham Alan	Essex	E	23.7.53	*Leytonstone*
Goodchild David John	Middlesex	E	17.9.76	*Harrow*
***Gough** Darren	Yorkshire	E	18.9.70	*Barnsley*
Grant Joseph Benjamin	Jamaica	WI	17.12.68	*Jamaica*
Grayson Adrian Paul	Essex	E	31.3.71	*Ripon*
***Greatbatch** Mark John	Central Districts	NZ	11.12.63	*Auckland*
Green Richard James	Lancashire	E	13.3.76	*Warrington*
Greenfield Keith	Sussex	E	6.12.68	*Brighton*
Griffith Adrian Frank Gordon	Barbados	WI	19.11.71	*Barbados*
Gunawardene Aruna Alwis Wijesiri	Sinhalese	SL	31.3.69	*Colombo*
Gupta Ashwini	Jammu and Kashmir	I	13.11.67	*Jammu*
***Gurusinha** Asanka Pradeep	Sinhalese	SL	16.9.66	*Colombo*
Habib Aftab	Leicestershire	E	7.2.72	*Reading*
Hall James William	Sussex	E	30.3.68	*Chichester*
Hamilton Gavin Mark	Yorkshire	E	16.9.74	*Broxburn, Scotland*
Hancock Timothy Harold Coulter	Gloucestershire	E	20.4.72	*Reading*
Haniff Zaheer Abbass	Guyana	WI	13.4.74	*Guyana*
Harden Richard John	Somerset	E	16.8.65	*Bridgwater*
Harmison Stephen James	Durham	E	23.10.78	*Ashington*
***Harper** Roger Andrew	Guyana	WI	17.3.63	*Georgetown*
Harrigan Lanville Allonie	Leeward Islands	WI	26.9.67	*Anguilla*
Harris Andrew James	Derbyshire	E	26.6.73	*Ashton-under-Lyne*
***Harris** Chris Zinzan	Canterbury	NZ	20.11.69	*Christchurch*
Harrison Jason Christian	Middlesex	E	15.1.72	*Amersham*
Harrity Mark Andrew	South Australia	A	9.3.74	*Semaphore*
Hart Jamie Paul	Nottinghamshire	E	31.12.75	*Blackpool*
***Hart** Matthew Norman	Northern Districts	NZ	16.5.72	*Hamilton*
***Hartland** Blair Robert	Canterbury	NZ	22.10.66	*Christchurch*
Hartley Peter John	Yorkshire	E	18.4.60	*Keighley*
Harvey Ian Joseph	Victoria	A	10.4.72	*Wonthaggi*
***Haslam** Mark James	Auckland	NZ	26.9.72	*Bury, England*
***Hathurusinghe** Upul Chandika	Tamil Union	SL	13.9.68	*Colombo*
Hatton Mark Aaron	Tasmania	A	24.1.74	*Waverley*
***Hayden** Matthew Lawrence	Queensland	A	29.10.71	*Kingaroy*
Hayes Roydon Leslie	Northern Districts	NZ	9.5.71	*Paeroa*
Hayhurst Andrew Neil	Somerset	E	23.11.62	*Manchester*
***Haynes** Desmond Leo	Western Province	SA	15.2.56	*Holders Hill, Barbados*
Haynes Jamie Jonathan	Lancashire	E	5.7.74	*Bristol*
Haywood Martin Thomas	New South Wales	A	7.10.69	*Tamworth*
Headley Dean Warren	Kent	E	27.1.70	*Stourbridge*
***Healy** Ian Andrew	Queensland	A	30.4.64	*Spring Hill*
Hegg Warren Kevin	Lancashire	E	23.2.68	*Whitefield*
Hemp David Lloyd	Glamorgan	E	8.11.70	*Hamilton, Bermuda*
Henderson Claude William	Boland	SA	14.6.72	*Worcester*
Hewett Ian Stephen Louis	Victoria	A	24.1.76	*East Melbourne*

	Team	Country	Born	Birthplace
Hewitt James Peter	Middlesex	E	26.2.76	*Southwark*
Hewson Dominic Robert	Gloucestershire	E	3.10.74	*Cheltenham*
***Hick** Graeme Ashley	Worcestershire	E	23.5.66	*Salisbury, Rhodesia*
Hills Dene Fleetwood	Tasmania	A	27.8.70	*Wynyard*
***Hirwani** Narendra Deepchand	Madhya Pradesh	I	18.10.68	*Gorakhpur*
Hodge Bradley John	Victoria	A	29.12.74	*Sandringham*
Hogg George Bradley	Western Australia	A	6.2.71	*Narrogin*
Holder Roland Irwin Christopher	Barbados	WI	22.12.67	*Port-of-Spain, Trinidad*
Holdstock Adrian Thomas	Boland	SA	27.4.70	*Cape Town*
Holdsworth Wayne John	New South Wales	A	5.10.68	*Paddington*
Hollioake Adam John	Surrey	E	5.9.71	*Melbourne, Australia*
Hollioake Benjamin Caine	Surrey	E	11.11.77	*Melbourne, Australia*
Holloway Piran Charles Laity	Somerset	E	1.10.70	*Helston*
***Hooper** Carl Llewellyn	Guyana/Kent	WI	15.12.66	*Georgetown*
Horan Brendan Patrick	Border	SA	17.9.74	*Cape Town*
***Houghton** David Laud	Mashonaland	Z	23.6.57	*Bulawayo*
Howard Craig	Victoria	A	8.4.74	*Lilydale*
Howell Ian Lester	Border	SA	20.5.58	*Port Elizabeth*
Hoyte Ricardo Lawrence	Barbados	WI	15.10.69	*Bridgetown*
Huckle Adam George	Eastern Province	SA	21.9.71	*Bulawayo, Rhodesia*
***Hudson** Andrew Charles	Natal	SA	17.3.65	*Eshowe*
Hughes John Gareth	Northamptonshire	E	3.5.71	*Wellingborough*
Hurley Ryan O'Neal	Barbados	WI	13.9.75	*Barbados*
***Hussain** Nasser	Essex	E	28.3.68	*Madras, India*
Hussey Michael Edward	Western Australia	A	27.5.75	*Morley*
Hutton Stewart	Durham	E	30.11.69	*Stockton-on-Tees*
***Ijaz Ahmed**, sen.	Habib Bank	P	20.9.68	*Sialkot*
***Ijaz Ahmed**, jun.	Faisalabad/Allied Bank	P	2.2.69	*Lyallpur*
***Illingworth** Richard Keith	Worcestershire	E	23.8.63	*Bradford*
***Ilott** Mark Christopher	Essex	E	27.8.70	*Watford*
Innes Kevin John	Northamptonshire	E	24.9.75	*Wellingborough*
***Inzamam-ul-Haq**	United Bank	P	3.3.70	*Multan*
Iqbal Sikandar	Hyderabad	P	19.12.58	*Karachi*
***Irani** Ronald Charles	Essex	E	26.10.71	*Leigh*
Irfan Bhatti	Rawalpindi	P	28.9.64	*Peshawar*
***Jack** Steven Douglas	Transvaal	SA	4.8.70	*Durban*
Jackson Kenneth Charles	Boland	SA	16.8.64	*Kitwe, Zambia*
Jackson Paul William	Queensland	A	1.11.61	*East Melbourne*
Jacobs Ridley Detamore	Leeward Islands	WI	26.11.67	*Antigua*
Jacobs Stefan	Transvaal	SA	11.3.66	*Virginia*
***Jadeja** Ajaysinhji	Haryana	I	1.2.71	*Jamnagar*
Jain Pradeep	Haryana	I	22.5.65	*Delhi*
James Kevan David	Hampshire	E	18.3.61	*Lambeth*
James Stephen Peter	Glamorgan	E	7.9.67	*Lydney*
***James** Wayne Robert	Matabeleland	Z	27.8.65	*Bulawayo*
Jamieson Warren Edwin	Eastern Province	SA	2.7.66	*Port Elizabeth*
***Jarvis** Paul William	Sussex	E	29.6.65	*Redcar*
***Javed Miandad**	Habib Bank	P	12.6.57	*Karachi*
Javed Qadeer	Karachi/PIA	P	25.8.76	*Karachi*
***Jayasuriya** Sanath Teran	Bloomfield	SL	30.6.69	*Matara*
Joglekar Manoj Vijay	Bombay	I	1.11.73	*Bombay*
Johnson Benjamin Andrew	South Australia	A	1.8.73	*Naracoorte*
Johnson David Jude	Karnataka	I	16.10.71	*Arasikere*
Johnson Neil Clarkson	Natal	SA	24.1.70	*Salisbury, Rhodesia*
Johnson Paul	Nottinghamshire	E	24.4.65	*Newark*
Johnson Richard Leonard	Middlesex	E	29.12.74	*Chertsey*
***Jones** Andrew Howard	Central Districts	NZ	9.5.59	*Wellington*
***Jones** Dean Mervyn	Victoria/Derbyshire	A	24.3.61	*Coburg*
Jordaan Deon	Free State	SA	3.12.70	*Bloemfontein*
Joseph David Rolston Emmanuel	Leeward Islands	WI	15.11.69	*Antigua*

	Team	*Country*	*Born*	*Birthplace*
Joseph Dawnley Alister	Windward Islands	WI	20.8.66	*Stubbs, St Vincent*
Joseph Jenson Eugene Simon	Leeward Islands	WI	7.10.66	*Antigua*
***Joshi** Sunil Bandacharya	Karnataka	I	6.6.69	*Gadag*
***Julian** Brendon Paul	W. Australia/Surrey	A	10.8.70	*Hamilton, New Zealand*
***Kabir Khan**	Peshawar/Habib Bank	P	12.4.74	*Peshawar*
Kale Abhijit Vasant	Maharashtra	I	3.7.73	*Ahmednagar*
***Kallis** Jacques Henry	Western Province	SA	16.10.75	*Cape Town*
***Kalpage** Ruwan Senani	Bloomfield	SL	19.2.70	*Kandy*
***Kaluwitharana** Romesh Shantha	Galle	SL	24.11.69	*Colombo*
Kalyani Shrikant Jagannath	Bengal	I	21.8.64	*Poona*
***Kambli** Vinod Ganpat	Bombay	I	18.1.72	*Bombay*
Kanwaljit Singh	Hyderabad	I	15.4.63	*Secunderabad*
***Kapoor** Aashish Rakesh	Punjab	I	25.3.71	*Madras*
Karim Syed Saba	Bengal	I	14.11.67	*Patna*
Karnain Shaul Hameed Uvais	Moors	SL	11.8.62	*Colombo*
Kasprowicz Michael Scott	Queensland	A	10.2.72	*South Brisbane*
Keech Matthew	Hampshire	E	21.10.70	*Hampstead*
Keedy Gary	Lancashire	E	27.11.74	*Wakefield*
Kendall William Salwey	Hampshire/Oxford U.	E	18.12.73	*Wimbledon*
Kendrick Neil Michael	Glamorgan	E	11.11.67	*Bromley*
***Kennedy** Robert John	Otago	NZ	3.6.72	*Dunedin*
Kerr Jason Ian Douglas	Somerset	E	7.4.74	*Bolton*
Kersey Graham James *Died January 1, 1997.*	Surrey	E	19.5.71	*Plumstead*
Kettleborough Richard Allan	Yorkshire	E	15.3.73	*Sheffield*
Khan Gul Abbass	Derbyshire/Oxford U.	E	31.12.73	*Gujrat, Pakistan*
Khan Wasim Gulzar	Warwickshire	E	26.2.71	*Birmingham*
Khoda Gagan Kishanlal	Rajasthan	I	24.10.74	*Barmer*
Khullar Vinod	Bihar	I	11.7.64	*Jamshedpur*
Khurasia Amay Ramsevak	Madhya Pradesh	I	18.5.72	*Jabalpur*
Kidwell Errol Wayne	Transvaal	SA	6.6.75	*Vereeniging*
Killeen Neil	Durham	E	17.10.75	*Shotley Bridge*
King Reon Dane	Guyana	WI	6.10.75	*Guyana*
Kinikar Hemant Anand	Maharashtra	I	6.12.71	*Poona*
***Kirsten** Gary	Western Province	SA	23.11.67	*Cape Town*
Kirsten Paul	Western Province	SA	30.10.69	*Cape Town*
***Kirsten** Peter Noel	Border	SA	14.5.55	*Pietermaritzburg*
Kirtley Robert James	Sussex	E	10.1.75	*Eastbourne*
Klusener Lance	Natal	SA	4.9.71	*Durban*
***Knight** Nicholas Verity	Warwickshire	E	28.11.69	*Watford*
Koen Louis Johannes	Eastern Province	SA	28.3.67	*Paarl*
Koenig Sven Gaetan	Western Province	SA	9.12.73	*Durban*
Krikken Karl Matthew	Derbyshire	E	9.4.69	*Bolton*
Krishnakumar Pudiyangum	Rajasthan	I	1.1.74	*Palghat*
Krug Murray Clayton	Northern Transvaal	SA	30.4.72	*East London*
Kruis Gideon Jacobus	Northern Transvaal	SA	9.5.74	*Pretoria*
***Kuiper** Adrian Paul	Boland	SA	24.8.59	*Johannesburg*
Kulkarni Milind Shripath	Maharashtra	I	12.12.69	*Koregaon*
Kulkarni Nilesh Moreshwar	Bombay	I	3.4.73	*Dombivili*
Kumar Avinash	Bihar	I	14.12.62	*Patna*
***Kumble** Anil	Karnataka	I	17.10.70	*Bangalore*
Kuruvilla Abey	Bombay	I	8.8.68	*Mannar*
Laing Dean Ralph	Transvaal	SA	18.9.70	*Durban*
***Lamba** Raman	Delhi	I	2.1.60	*Meerut*
***Lambert** Clayton Benjamin	Northern Transvaal	WI	10.2.62	*New Amsterdam, Guyana*
Lampitt Stuart Richard	Worcestershire	E	29.7.66	*Wolverhampton*
Laney Jason Scott	Hants/Matabeleland	E	27.4.73	*Winchester*
***Langer** Justin Lee	Western Australia	A	21.11.70	*Perth*
***Lara** Brian Charles	Trinidad & Tobago	WI	2.5.69	*Santa Cruz*
Larkin Rohan Patrick	Victoria	A	19.10.69	*Seymour*

	Team	Country	Born	Birthplace
***Larsen** Gavin Rolf	Wellington	NZ	27.9.62	*Wellington*
***Lathwell** Mark Nicholas	Somerset	E	26.12.71	*Bletchley*
Lavender Mark Philip	Western Australia	A	28.8.67	*Madras, India*
Law Danny Richard	Sussex	E	15.7.75	*London*
***Law** Stuart Grant	Queensland/Essex	A	18.10.68	*Herston*
Lawrence Andre	Trinidad & Tobago	WI	4.5.69	*Trinidad*
Lawson Andrew Grant	Eastern Province	SA	4.3.67	*Durban*
Laxman Vangipurappu Venkata Sai	Hyderabad	I	1.11.74	*Hyderabad*
Lazard Terence Nicholas	Boland	SA	19.10.65	*Cape Town*
Leatherdale David Antony	Worcestershire	E	26.11.67	*Bradford*
Lee Shane	NSW/Somerset	A	8.8.73	*Wollongong*
Lehmann Darren Scott	South Australia	A	5.2.70	*Gawler*
Lenham Neil John	Sussex	E	17.12.65	*Worthing*
***Lewis** Clairmonte Christopher	Surrey	E	14.2.68	*Georgetown, Guyana*
Lewis Jonathan	Gloucestershire	E	26.8.75	*Aylesbury*
Lewis Jonathan James Benjamin	Essex	E	21.5.70	*Isleworth*
Lewis Rawl Nicholas	Windward Islands	WI	5.9.74	*Grenada*
Lewry Jason David	Sussex	E	2.4.71	*Worthing*
Liburd Merlin Dave	Leeward Islands	WI	15.12.69	*Nevis*
Liebenberg Gerhardus Frederick Johannes	Free State	SA	7.4.72	*Upington*
Ligertwood David George Coutts	Durham	E	16.5.69	*Oxford*
Light Craig	Free State	SA	23.9.72	*Randburg*
***Liyanage** Dulip Kapila	Colts	SL	6.6.72	*Kalutara*
Llong Nigel James	Kent	E	11.2.69	*Ashford, Kent*
Lloyd Graham David	Lancashire	E	1.7.69	*Accrington*
***Lock** Alan Charles Ingram	Mashonaland Co. Dists	Z	10.9.62	*Marondellas*
Longley Jonathan Ian	Durham	E	12.4.69	*New Brunswick, NJ, USA*
Love Martin Lloyd	Queensland	A	30.3.74	*Mundubbera*
***Loveridge** Greg Riaka	Central Districts	NZ	15.1.75	*Palmerston North*
Loye Malachy Bernard	Northamptonshire	E	27.9.72	*Northampton*
Lugsden Steven	Durham	E	10.7.76	*Gateshead*
Lyle Rowan Andrew	Transvaal	SA	1.12.68	*Kokstad*
Lynch Monte Alan	Gloucestershire	E	21.5.58	*Georgetown, Brit. Guiana*
***McCague** Martin John	Kent	E	24.5.69	*Larne, Northern Ireland*
***McDermott** Craig John	Queensland	A	14.4.65	*Ipswich*
McGarrell Neil Christopher	Guyana	WI	12.7.72	*Guyana*
McGinty Adam David	Victoria	A	24.3.71	*Melbourne*
McGrath Anthony	Yorkshire	E	6.10.75	*Bradford*
***McGrath** Glenn Donald	New South Wales	A	9.2.70	*Dubbo*
MacHelm Dean Quinton	Western Province	SA	18.4.71	*Kuils River*
***McIntyre** Peter Edward	South Australia	A	27.4.66	*Gisborne*
McKenzie Denville St Delmo	Jamaica	WI	4.12.75	*Little London*
McKenzie Neil Douglas	Transvaal	SA	24.11.75	*Johannesburg*
McKeown Patrick Christopher	Lancashire	E	1.6.76	*Liverpool*
McLean Nixon Alexei McNamara	Windward Islands	WI	28.7.73	*St Vincent*
***McMillan** Brian Mervin	Western Province	SA	22.12.63	*Welkom*
Macmillan Gregor Innes	Leicestershire	E	7.8.69	*Guildford*
McNamara Bradley Edward	New South Wales	A	30.12.65	*Sydney*
Maddy Darren Lee	Leicestershire	E	23.5.74	*Leicester*
***Madurasinghe** Arachchige Wijaysiri Ranjith	Kurunegala Youth	SL	30.1.61	*Kurunegala*
***Mahanama** Roshan Siriwardene	Bloomfield	SL	31.5.66	*Colombo*
Maher James Patrick	Queensland	A	27.2.74	*Innistail*
Mahmood Hamid	Karachi/PIA	P	19.1.69	*Karachi*
***Malcolm** Devon Eugene	Derbyshire	E	22.2.63	*Kingston, Jamaica*
Malhotra Akash	Delhi	I	12.12.72	*Delhi*
***Mallender** Neil Alan	Northamptonshire	E	13.8.61	*Kirk Sandall*
Manbodhe Naresh Kumar	Guyana	WI	15.7.72	*Guyana*
***Manjrekar** Sanjay Vijay	Bombay	I	12.7.65	*Mangalore*

	Team	*Country*	*Born*	*Birthplace*
***Mansoor Akhtar**	United Bank	P	25.12.57	*Karachi*
Mansoor Rana	ADBP	P	27.12.62	*Lahore*
***Manzoor Elahi**	Lahore/ADBP	P	15.4.63	*Sahiwal*
Maqsood Rana	National Bank	P	1.8.72	*Lahore*
Marquet Joshua Phillip	Tasmania	A	3.12.69	*Melbourne*
Marsh Steven Andrew	Kent	E	27.1.61	*London*
***Marshall** Malcolm Denzil	Natal	WI	18.4.58	*Bridgetown*
Marshall Roy Ashworth	Windward Islands	WI	1.4.65	*St Joseph, Dominica*
Martin Gary Charles	Mashonaland	Z	30.5.66	*Marondellas*
Martin Jacob Joseph	Baroda	I	11.5.72	*Baroda*
***Martin** Peter James	Lancashire	E	15.11.68	*Accrington*
Martyn Aubrey	Western Province	SA	23.6.72	*Pretoria*
***Martyn** Damien Richard	Western Australia	A	21.10.71	*Darwin*
Maru Rajesh Jamandass	Hampshire	E	28.10.62	*Nairobi, Kenya*
Mascarenhas Adrian Dimitri	Hampshire	E	30.10.77	*London*
Mason Keno	Trinidad & Tobago	WI	13.11.72	*Trinidad*
***Masood Anwar**	Faisalabad	P	12.12.67	*Khanewal*
***Matthews** Craig Russell	Western Province	SA	15.2.65	*Cape Town*
***Matthews** Gregory Richard John	New South Wales	A	15.12.59	*Newcastle*
Maxwell Neil Donald	New South Wales	A	12.6.67	*Lautoka, Fiji*
May Michael Robert	Derbyshire	E	22.7.71	*Chesterfield*
***May** Timothy Brian Alexander	South Australia	A	26.1.62	*North Adelaide*
Maynard Dayne Romano	Barbados	WI	1.4.69	*Barbados*
***Maynard** Matthew Peter	Glamorgan	E	21.3.66	*Oldham*
Mehra Ajay	Punjab	I	5.1.69	*Delhi*
Mendis Chaminda	Colts	SL	28.12.68	*Galle*
Metcalfe Ashley Anthony	Nottinghamshire	E	25.12.63	*Horsforth*
Metson Colin Peter	Glamorgan	E	2.7.63	*Goffs Oak*
***Mhambrey** Paras Laxmikant	Bombay	I	20.6.72	*Bombay*
Mike Gregory Wentworth	Nottinghamshire	E	14.7.66	*Nottingham*
Milburn Stuart Mark	Hampshire	E	29.9.72	*Harrogate*
Miller Colin Reid	Tasmania	A	6.2.64	*Footscray*
Millns David James	Leicestershire	E	27.2.65	*Clipstone*
***Mohammad Akram**	Rawalpindi	P	10.9.74	*Islamabad*
Mohammad Aslam	Rajasthan	I	7.8.74	*Jaipur*
***Mohsin Kamal**	PNSC	P	16.6.63	*Lyallpur*
***Moin Khan**	Karachi	P	23.9.71	*Rawalpindi*
Moin-ul-Atiq	Karachi/Habib Bank	P	5.8.64	*Karachi*
Moles Andrew James	Warwickshire	E	12.2.61	*Solihull*
***Mongia** Nayan Ramlal	Baroda	I	19.12.69	*Baroda*
Montgomerie Richard Robert	Northamptonshire	E	3.7.71	*Rugby*
***Moody** Thomas Masson	W. Australia/Worcs	A	2.10.65	*Adelaide*
Moores Peter	Sussex	E	18.12.62	*Macclesfield*
***More** Kiran Shankar	Baroda	I	4.9.62	*Baroda*
Morgan Delroy Simeon	Jamaica	WI	4.3.67	*Rollington Town*
Morgan Grant	Eastern Province	SA	19.5.71	*Port Elizabeth*
Morris Alexander Corfield	Yorkshire	E	4.10.76	*Barnsley*
***Morris** Hugh	Glamorgan	E	5.10.63	*Cardiff*
***Morris** John Edward	Durham	E	1.4.64	*Crewe*
Morris Robert Sean Milner	Hampshire	E	10.9.68	*Great Horwood*
***Morrison** Daniel Kyle	Auckland	NZ	3.2.66	*Auckland*
Mott Matthew Peter	Queensland	A	3.10.73	*Charleville*
***Moxon** Martyn Douglas	Yorkshire	E	4.5.60	*Barnsley*
Mukherjee Saradindu Purnendu	Bengal	I	5.10.64	*Calcutta*
***Mullally** Alan David	Leicestershire	E	12.7.69	*Southend-on-Sea*
Munasinghe Arachchige Manjula Nishantha	Sinhalese	SL	10.12.71	*Colombo*
***Munton** Timothy Alan	Warwickshire	E	30.7.65	*Melton Mowbray*
***Muralitharan** Muttiah	Tamil Union	SL	17.4.72	*Kandy*
Murphy Brian Samuel	Jamaica	WI	7.4.73	*Jamaica*
***Murray** Junior Randalph	Windward Islands	WI	20.1.68	*St Georges, Grenada*

	Team	Country	Born	Birthplace
***Mushtaq Ahmed**	United Bank	P	28.6.70	*Sahiwal*
Muzumdar Amol Anil	Bombay	I	11.11.74	*Bombay*
Nackerdien Mugammad Salieg	Boland	SA	19.7.63	*Paarl*
***Nadeem Abbasi**	Rawalpindi	P	15.4.64	*Rawalpindi*
***Nadeem Ghauri**	Habib Bank	P	12.10.62	*Lahore*
***Nadeem Khan**	Karachi/PIA	P	10.12.69	*Rawalpindi*
Nagamootoo Mahendra Veeren	Guyana	WI	9.10.75	*Guyana*
Nagamootoo Vishal	Guyana	WI	7.1.77	*Guyana*
***Nash** Dion Joseph	N. Districts/Middlesex	NZ	20.11.71	*Auckland*
***Naved Anjum**	Habib Bank	P	27.7.63	*Lahore*
Nayyar Rajiv	Himachal Pradesh	I	28.3.70	*Delhi*
Nedd Gavin Hilton	Guyana	WI	21.7.72	*Guyana*
Newell Keith	Sussex/Matabeleland	E	25.3.72	*Crawley*
Newell Mark	Sussex	E	19.12.73	*Crawley*
***Newport** Philip John	Worcestershire	E	11.10.62	*High Wycombe*
Nielsen Timothy John	South Australia	A	5.5.68	*Forest Gate, England*
Nixon Paul Andrew	Leicestershire	E	21.10.70	*Carlisle*
Nobes Paul Christopher	South Australia	A	20.4.64	*West Heidelberg*
Noon Wayne Michael	Nottinghamshire	E	5.2.71	*Grimsby*
Nosworthy David Owen	Border	SA	25.12.67	*Johannesburg*
Ntini Makhaya	Border	SA	6.7.77	*Zwelitsha*
Odedra Nilesh Rambhai	Saurashtra	I	15.4.73	*Porbandar*
O'Gorman Timothy Joseph Gerard	Derbyshire	E	15.5.67	*Woking*
Oldroyd Bradley John	Western Australia	A	5.11.73	*Bentley*
***Olonga** Henry Khaaba	Matabeleland	Z	3.7.76	*Lusaka, Zambia*
Ostler Dominic Piers	Warwickshire	E	15.7.70	*Solihull*
Owen John Edward	Derbyshire	E	7.8.71	*Derby*
***Owens** Michael Barry	Canterbury	NZ	11.11.69	*Christchurch*
Padmanabhan K. Narayanaiyer Anantha	Kerala	I	8.9.69	*Trivandrum*
Palframan Steven John	Border	SA	12.5.70	*East London*
Pandey Gyanendrakumar Kedarnath	Uttar Pradesh	I	12.8.72	*Lucknow*
***Pandit** Chandrakant Sitaram	Madhya Pradesh	I	30.9.61	*Bombay*
Parker Bradley	Yorkshire	E	30.1.66	*Mirfield*
Parkin Owen Thomas	Glamorgan	E	24.9.72	*Coventry*
***Parore** Adam Craig	Northern Districts	NZ	23.1.71	*Auckland*
Parsana Hitesh Jayarambhai	Saurashtra	I	20.2.70	*Rajkot*
Parsons Gordon James	Leicestershire	E	17.10.59	*Slough*
Parsons Keith Alan	Somerset	E	2.5.73	*Taunton*
***Patel** Dipak Narshibhai	Auckland	NZ	25.10.58	*Nairobi, Kenya*
***Patel** Minal Mahesh	Kent	E	7.7.70	*Bombay, India*
***Patel** Rashid	Baroda	I	1.6.64	*Sabarkantha*
Peake Clinton John	Victoria	A	25.3.77	*Geelong*
***Peall** Stephen Guy	Mashonaland Co. Dists	Z	2.9.69	*Salisbury*
Pearson Richard Michael	Surrey	E	27.1.72	*Batley*
Penberthy Anthony Leonard	Northamptonshire	E	1.9.69	*Troon*
Pennett David Barrington	Nottinghamshire	E	26.10.69	*Leeds*
Penney Trevor Lionel	Warwickshire	E	12.6.68	*Salisbury, Rhodesia*
Percival Andre Ricardo	Guyana	WI	5.1.75	*New Amsterdam*
Perera Kahawelage Gamini	Moratuwa	SL	22.5.64	*Colombo*
Perry Nehemiah Odolphus	Jamaica	WI	16.6.68	*Jamaica*
Peters Stephen David	Essex	E	10.12.78	*Harold Wood*
Petrie Richard George	Wellington	NZ	23.8.67	*Christchurch*
Phillip Warrington Dexter	Leeward Islands	WI	23.7.68	*Nevis*
Phillips Ben James	Kent	E	30.9.74	*Lewisham*
Phillips Nicholas Charles	Sussex	E	10.5.74	*Pembury*

	Team	*Country*	*Born*	*Birthplace*
Pick Robert Andrew	Nottinghamshire	E	19.11.63	*Nottingham*
Pienaar Roy Francois	Northern Transvaal	SA	17.7.61	*Johannesburg*
Pierre Andrew Jones	Windward Islands	WI	5.10.63	*Goodwill, Dominica*
Pierson Adrian Roger Kirshaw	Leicestershire	E	21.7.63	*Enfield*
Piper Keith John	Warwickshire	E	18.12.69	*Leicester*
Pistorius Ivan	Northern Transvaal	SA	8.7.70	*Durban*
Player Bradley Thomas	Free State	SA	18.1.67	*Benoni*
***Pocock** Blair Andrew	Northern Districts	NZ	18.6.71	*Papakura*
Pollard Paul Raymond	Nottinghamshire	E	24.9.68	*Nottingham*
Pollock Graeme Anthony	Transvaal	SA	7.4.73	*Port Elizabeth*
***Pollock** Shaun Maclean	Natal/Warwickshire	SA	16.7.73	*Port Elizabeth*
***Ponting** Ricky Thomas	Tasmania	A	19.12.74	*Launceston*
Pooley Jason Calvin	Middlesex	E	8.8.69	*Hammersmith*
Pope Steven Charles	Border	SA	15.11.72	*East London*
Pope Uzzah	Windward Islands	WI	3.1.71	*St Vincent*
Pothas Nic	Transvaal	SA	18.11.73	*Johannesburg*
Powell Michael James	Warwickshire	E	5.4.75	*Bolton*
Powell Ronald Malcolm	Leeward Islands	WI	5.3.68	*Nevis*
Powell Tony Orlando	Jamaica	WI	22.12.72	*Jamaica*
***Prabhakar** Manoj	Delhi	I	15.4.63	*Ghaziabad*
***Prasad** Bapu Krishnarao Venkatesh	Karnataka	I	5.8.69	*Bangalore*
Prasad Mannava Srikanth K.	Andhra	I	24.4.75	*Guntur*
Preece Benjamin Edward Ashley	Worcestershire	E	8.11.76	*Birmingham*
Preston Nicholas William	Kent	E	22.1.72	*Dartford*
Pretorius Nicolaas Willem	Free State	SA	8.3.69	*Ventersdorp*
Prichard Paul John	Essex	E	7.1.65	*Billericay*
***Priest** Mark Wellings	Canterbury	NZ	12.8.61	*Greymouth*
Prince Ashwell Gavin	Eastern Province	SA	28.5.77	*Port Elizabeth*
***Pringle** Christopher	Auckland	NZ	26.1.68	*Auckland*
***Pringle** Meyrick Wayne	Western Province	SA	22.6.66	*Adelaide*
Proverbs Ahmed Edward	Barbados	WI	28.1.70	*Barbados*
Puckerin Livingstone Kenneth	Barbados	WI	19.6.69	*Rosegate*
***Pushpakumara** Karuppiahyage Ravindra	Nondescripts	SL	21.7.75	*Panadura*
***Rackemann** Carl Gray	Queensland	A	3.6.60	*Wondai*
Radford Toby Alexander	Sussex	E	31.12.71	*Caerphilly*
Radley Philip Johannes Lourens	Free State	SA	7.2.69	*Bloemfontein*
Ragoonath Suruj	Trinidad & Tobago	WI	22.3.68	*Trinidad*
***Raju** Sagi Lakshmi Venkatapathy	Hyderabad	I	9.7.69	*Hyderabad*
***Raman** Woorkeri Venkat	Tamil Nadu	I	23.5.65	*Madras*
***Ramanayake** Champaka Priyadarshana Hewage	Tamil Union	SL	8.1.65	*Colombo*
***Ramiz Raja**	Allied Bank	P	14.8.62	*Lyallpur*
***Ramprakash** Mark Ravin	Middlesex	E	5.9.69	*Bushey*
Ramnarine Dinanth	Trinidad & Tobago	WI	4.6.75	*Trinidad*
***Ranatunga** Arjuna	Sinhalese	SL	1.12.63	*Colombo*
***Ranatunga** Dammika	Sinhalese	SL	12.10.62	*Colombo*
Ranatunga Nishantha	Colts	SL	22.1.66	*Gampaha*
***Ranatunga** Sanjeeva	Nondescripts	SL	25.4.69	*Colombo*
***Ranchod** Ujesh	Mashonaland	Z	17.5.69	*Salisbury*
Rao Kashireddi Var Prasad	Bihar	I	21.11.65	*Jamshedpur*
Rao Rajesh Krishnakant	Sussex	E	9.12.74	*Park Royal*
Rashid Umer Bin Abdul	Middlesex	E	6.2.76	*Southampton*
***Rashid Latif**	United Bank	P	14.10.68	*Karachi*
Ratcliffe Jason David	Surrey	E	19.6.69	*Solihull*
***Rathore** Vikram	Punjab	I	26.3.69	*Jullundur*
***Ratnayake** Romesh Joseph	Nondescripts	SL	2.1.64	*Colombo*
Raul Sanjay	Orissa	I	6.10.76	*Cuttack*
Rawnsley Matthew James	Worcestershire	E	8.6.76	*Birmingham*

	Team	Country	Born	Birthplace
***Reeve** Dermot Alexander	Warwickshire	E	2.4.63	*Kowloon, Hong Kong*
***Reid** Bruce Anthony	Western Australia	A	14.3.63	*Osborne Park*
Reid Winston Emmerson	Barbados	WI	29.9.62	*Bank Hall*
Reifer Floyd Lamonte	Barbados	WI	23.7.72	*Barbados*
***Reiffel** Paul Ronald	Victoria	A	19.4.66	*Box Hill*
***Rennie** John Alexander	Matabeleland	Z	29.7.70	*Fort Victoria*
Renshaw Simon John	Hampshire	E	6.3.74	*Bebington*
***Rhodes** Jonathan Neil	Natal	SA	26.7.69	*Pietermaritzburg*
***Rhodes** Steven John	Worcestershire	E	17.6.64	*Bradford*
Ricci Brendan Paul	Victoria	A	24.4.65	*Fitzroy*
Richards Corey John	New South Wales	A	25.8.75	*Camden*
Richards O'Neil Rohan	Jamaica	WI	7.7.76	*St Catherine*
***Richardson** David John	Eastern Province	SA	16.9.59	*Johannesburg*
***Richardson** Richard Benjamin	Leeward Islands	WI	12.1.62	*Five Islands, Antigua*
Ridgway Mark William	Tasmania	A	21.5.63	*Warragul*
Rindel Michael John Raymond	Northern Transvaal	SA	9.2.63	*Durban*
Ripley David	Northamptonshire	E	13.9.66	*Leeds*
***Rizwan-uz-Zaman**	PIA	P	4.9.61	*Karachi*
Roach Peter John	Victoria	A	19.5.75	*Kew*
Roberts Andrew Richard	Northamptonshire	E	16.4.71	*Kettering*
Roberts David James	Northamptonshire	E	29.12.76	*Truro*
Roberts Glenn Martin	Derbyshire	E	4.11.73	*Huddersfield*
Roberts Kevin Joseph	New South Wales	A	25.7.72	*North Sydney*
Roberts Lincoln Abraham	Trinidad & Tobago	WI	4.9.74	*Tobago*
Roberts Stuart John	Canterbury	NZ	22.3.65	*Christchurch*
Robinson Darren David John	Essex	E	2.3.73	*Braintree*
***Robinson** Robert Timothy	Nottinghamshire	E	21.11.58	*Sutton-in-Ashfield*
Roe Garth Anthony	Eastern Province	SA	9.7.73	*Port Elizabeth*
Rollins Adrian Stewart	Derbyshire	E	8.2.72	*Barking*
Rollins Robert John	Essex	E	30.1.74	*Plaistow*
Rose Graham David	Somerset	E	12.4.64	*Tottenham*
Roseberry Michael Anthony	Durham	E	28.11.66	*Sunderland*
Rossouw Daniel	Eastern Province	SA	30.4.70	*Port Elizabeth*
Rowell Gregory John	Queensland	A	1.9.66	*Lindfield*
Rule Kevin John	Northern Transvaal	SA	28.3.63	*Johannesburg*
Rundle David Bryan	Western Province	SA	25.9.65	*Cape Town*
***Rushmere** Mark Weir	Transvaal	SA	7.1.65	*Port Elizabeth*
***Russell** Robert Charles	Gloucestershire	E	15.8.63	*Stroud*
***Rutherford** Kenneth Robert	Transvaal	SA	26.10.65	*Dunedin, New Zealand*
***Saeed Anwar**	ADBP	P	6.9.68	*Karachi*
Saeed Azad	Karachi/National Bank	P	14.8.66	*Karachi*
Saggers Martin John	Durham	E	23.5.72	*King's Lynn*
Saint John Michael	Tasmania	A	31.1.69	*Auburn*
Sajid Ali	Karachi/National Bank	P	1.7.63	*Karachi*
Sajjad Akbar	PNSC	P	1.3.61	*Lahore*
Saker David James	Victoria	A	29.6.66	*Oakleigh*
***Saleem Jaffer**	United Bank	P	19.11.62	*Karachi*
Sales David John	Northamptonshire	E	3.12.77	*Carshalton*
***Salim Elahi**	United Bank	P	21.11.76	*Sahiwal*
***Salim Malik**	Habib Bank	P	16.4.63	*Lahore*
***Salisbury** Ian David Kenneth	Sussex	E	21.1.70	*Northampton*
***Samaraweera** Dulip Prasanna	Colts	SL	12.2.72	*Colombo*
Samaroo Avidesh	Trinidad & Tobago	WI	22.1.78	*Trinidad*
***Samuels** Robert George	Jamaica	WI	13.3.71	*Jamaica*
***Saqlain Mushtaq**	PIA	P	27.11.76	*Lahore*
Sarkar Arindam	Bengal	I	12.8.73	*Calcutta*
Sarwan Ramnaresh	Guyana	WI	23.6.80	*Guyana*
***Schultz** Brett Nolan	Eastern Province	SA	26.8.70	*East London*
Scott Christopher Wilmot	Durham	E	23.1.64	*Thorpe-on-the-Hill*
Seccombe Wade Anthony	Queensland	A	30.10.71	*Murgon*

	Team	Country	Born	Birthplace
Semple Keith Fitzpatrick	Guyana	WI	21.8.70	*Georgetown*
Seymore Andre Johan	Northern Transvaal	SA	16.2.75	*Rustenburg*
***Shadab Kabir**	Karachi	P	12.11.77	*Karachi*
***Shah** Ali Hassimshah	Mashonaland	Z	7.8.59	*Salisbury*
Shah Owais Alam	Middlesex	E	22.10.78	*Karachi, Pakistan*
Shahid Nadeem	Surrey	E	23.4.69	*Karachi, Pakistan*
Shahid Anwar	National Bank	P	5.7.68	*Multan*
***Shahid Mahboob**	Islamabad/Allied Bank	P	25.8.62	*Karachi*
Shahid Nazir	Faisalabad/Nat. Bank	P	4.12.77	*Faisalabad*
***Shahid Saeed**	Lahore	P	6.1.66	*Lahore*
***Shakeel Ahmed**	Rawalpindi/Habib Bank	P	12.11.71	*Daska*
Shakeel Khan	Habib Bank	P	28.5.68	*Lahore*
Shamshad Rizwan	Uttar Pradesh	I	19.11.72	*Aligarh*
Sharath Sridharan	Madras	I	31.10.72	*Madras*
Sharma Abhay	Railways	I	30.4.67	*Delhi*
***Sharma** Ajay	Delhi	I	3.4.64	*Delhi*
***Sharma** Chetan	Bengal	I	3.1.66	*Ludhiana*
Shaw Adrian David	Glamorgan	E	17.2.72	*Neath*
***Shaw** Timothy Gower	Eastern Province	SA	5.7.59	*Empangeni*
Sheriyar Alamgir	Worcestershire	E	15.11.73	*Birmingham*
Shine Kevin James	Somerset	E	22.2.69	*Bracknell*
***Shoaib Mohammad**	Karachi/PIA	P	8.1.61	*Karachi*
Shukla Saurabh Anand	Uttar Pradesh	I	24.11.67	*Lucknow*
Siddons James Darren	South Australia	A	25.4.64	*Robinvale*
***Sidhu** Navjot Singh	Punjab	I	20.10.63	*Patiala*
Silva Kelaniyage Jayantha	Sinhalese	SL	2.6.73	*Kalutara*
Silva Sampathwaduge Amal Rohitha	Nondescripts	SL	12.12.60	*Moratuwa*
Silverwood Christopher Eric Wilfred	Yorkshire	E	5.3.75	*Pontefract*
***Simmons** Philip Verant	T & T/Leicestershire	WI	18.4.63	*Arima*
Simons Eric Owen	Western Province	SA	9.3.62	*Cape Town*
Singh Anurag	Warwicks/Camb. U.	E	9.9.75	*Kanpur, India*
Singh Rabindra Ramanarayan	Tamil Nadu	I	14.9.63	*Princes Town, Trinidad*
Singh Rudra Pratap	Uttar Pradesh	I	6.1.63	*Lucknow*
***Slater** Michael Jonathon	New South Wales	A	21.2.70	*Wagga Wagga*
***Small** Gladstone Cleophas	Warwickshire	E	18.10.61	*St George, Barbados*
Smith Andrew Michael	Gloucestershire	E	1.10.67	*Dewsbury*
Smith Benjamin Francis	Leicestershire	E	3.4.72	*Corby*
Smith Edward Thomas	Kent/Cambridge U.	E	19.7.77	*Pembury*
Smith Gregory James	Northern Transvaal	SA	30.10.71	*Pretoria*
Smith Neil Michael Knight	Warwickshire	E	27.7.67	*Birmingham*
Smith Paul Andrew	Warwickshire	E	15.4.64	*Jesmond*
Smith Richard Andrew Mortimer	Trinidad & Tobago	WI	17.7.71	*Trinidad*
***Smith** Robin Arnold	Hampshire	E	13.9.63	*Durban, South Africa*
Snape Jeremy Nicholas	Northamptonshire	E	27.4.73	*Stoke-on-Trent*
***Snell** Richard Peter	Transvaal	SA	12.9.68	*Durban*
Sohail Fazal	Habib Bank	P	11.11.67	*Lahore*
Solanki Vikram Singh	Worcestershire	E	1.4.76	*Udaipur, India*
Sommerville Blaise Justin	Northern Transvaal	SA	25.5.67	*Pretoria*
Speak Nicholas Jason	Lancashire	E	21.11.66	*Manchester*
***Spearman** Craig Murray	Auckland	NZ	4.7.72	*Auckland*
Speight Martin Peter	Sussex	E	24.10.67	*Walsall*
Spilhaus Carl Fredric	Border	SA	11.11.63	*Cape Town*
Spiring Karl Reuben	Worcestershire	E	13.11.74	*Southport*
Sridhar Maruti Venkat	Hyderabad	I	2.8.65	*Vijayawada*
***Srinath** Javagal	Karnataka	I	31.8.69	*Mysore*
Stacey Bradley John	Victoria	A	11.6.72	*Geelong*
Stanford Edward John	Kent	E	21.1.71	*Dartford*
Stapleton Bertram Bennett	Windward Islands	WI	19.10.70	*St Vincent*
Stelling William Frederick	Boland	SA	30.6.69	*Johannesburg*

	Team	Country	Born	Birthplace
Stemp Richard David	Yorkshire	E	11.12.67	*Birmingham*
Stephenson Franklyn Dacosta	Free State	SA	8.4.59	*St James, Barbados*
***Stephenson** John Patrick	Hampshire	E	14.3.65	*Stebbing*
***Stewart** Alec James	Surrey	E	8.4.63	*Merton*
Stewart Errol Leslie Rae	Natal	SA	30.7.69	*Durban*
***Steyn** Philippus Jeremia Rudolf	Kimberley	SA	30.6.67	*Kimberley*
Still Quentin Raxham	Border	SA	8.8.74	*Pietermaritzburg*
Storey Keith Graham	Natal	SA	25.1.69	*Salisbury, Rhodesia*
***Strang** Bryan Colin	Mashonaland Co. Dists	Z	9.6.72	*Bulawayo*
***Strang** Paul Andrew	Mashonaland Co. Dists	Z	28.7.70	*Bulawayo*
***Streak** Heath Hilton	Matabeleland	Z	16.3.74	*Bulawayo*
Strydom Pieter Coenraad	Border	SA	10.6.69	*Somerset East*
Stuart Anthony Mark	New South Wales	A	2.1.70	*Newcastle*
Stuart Colin Ellsworth Laurie	Guyana	WI	28.9.73	*Guyana*
***Su'a** Murphy Logo	Auckland	NZ	7.11.66	*Wanganui*
Subramaniam Satyanarayana	Services	I	20.7.62	*Mysore*
***Such** Peter Mark	Essex	E	12.6.64	*Helensburgh, Scotland*
Sugwekar Shantanu Sharad	Maharashtra	I	18.12.66	*Poona*
Swain Brett Andrew	South Australia	A	14.2.74	*Stirling*
Swann Alec James	Northamptonshire	E	26.10.76	*Northampton*
Sylvester John Anthony Rodney	Windward Islands	WI	6.10.69	*Grenada*
Sylvester Kester Kenneth	Windward Islands	WI	5.12.73	*Grenada*
***Symcox** Patrick Leonard	Natal	SA	14.4.60	*Kimberley*
Symonds Andrew	Glos/Queensland	E/A	9.6.75	*Birmingham*
***Tauseef Ahmed**	United Bank	P	10.5.60	*Karachi*
***Taylor** Jonathan Paul	Northamptonshire	E	8.8.64	*Ashby-de-la-Zouch*
***Taylor** Mark Anthony	New South Wales	A	27.10.64	*Leeton*
Tazelaar Dirk	Queensland	A	13.1.63	*Ipswich*
Telemachus Roger	Boland	SA	27.3.73	*Stellenbosch*
***Tendulkar** Sachin Ramesh	Bombay	I	24.4.73	*Bombay*
***Terry** Vivian Paul	Hampshire	E	14.1.59	*Osnabruck, Germany*
Thakur Iqbal Abubakker	Railways	I	8.12.66	*Bombay*
Thomas Dennison	Windward Islands	WI	3.3.68	*Grenada*
Thomas Paul Anthony	Worcestershire	E	3.6.71	*Birmingham*
Thomas Stuart Darren	Glamorgan	E	25.1.75	*Morriston*
Thompson Julian Barton DeCourcy	Kent	E	28.10.68	*Cape Town, SA*
***Thompson** Patterson Ian Chesterfield	Barbados	WI	26.9.71	*Barbados*
Thompson Scott Michael	New South Wales	A	4.5.72	*Bankstown*
***Thomson** Shane Alexander	Northern Districts	NZ	27.1.69	*Hamilton*
***Thorpe** Graham Paul	Surrey	E	1.8.69	*Farnham*
Thursfield Martin John	Hampshire	E	14.12.71	*South Shields*
Tikolo Steven	Boland	K	25.6.71	*Nairobi*
***Tillekeratne** Hashan Prasantha	Nondescripts	SL	14.7.67	*Colombo*
Titchard Stephen Paul	Lancashire	E	17.12.67	*Warrington*
Tolley Christopher Mark	Nottinghamshire	E	30.12.67	*Kidderminster*
Trainor Nicholas James	Gloucestershire	E	29.6.75	*Gateshead*
Trescothick Marcus Edward	Somerset	E	25.12.75	*Keynsham*
Trump Harvey Russell John	Somerset	E	11.10.68	*Taunton*
Tucker Rodney James	Tasmania	A	28.8.64	*Auburn*
Tuckett Carl McArthur	Leeward Islands	WI	18.5.70	*Nevis*
***Tufnell** Philip Charles Roderick	Middlesex	E	29.4.66	*Barnet*
Turner Robert Julian	Somerset	E	25.11.67	*Malvern*
Tweats Timothy Andrew	Derbyshire	E	18.4.74	*Stoke-on-Trent*
***Twose** Roger Graham	Wellington	NZ	17.4.68	*Torquay, England*
Udal Shaun David	Hampshire	E	18.3.69	*Farnborough, Hants*
Upashantha Eric Amila	Colts	SL	10.6.72	*Kurunegala*

	Team	Country	Born	Birthplace
***Vaas** Warnakulasooriya Patabendige Ushantha Joseph Chaminda	Colts	SL	27.1.74	*Mattumagala*
Vaidya Avinash	Karnataka	I	24.1.69	*Hubli*
Vaidya Prashant Sridhar	Bengal	I	23.9.67	*Nagpur*
Vandrau Matthew James	Derbys/Transvaal B	SA/E	22.7.69	*Epsom*
van Jaarsveld Martin	Northern Transvaal	SA	18.6.74	*Klerksdorp*
van Noordwyk Chris	Northern Transvaal	SA	4.11.70	*Durban*
van Troost Adrianus Pelrus	Somerset	E	2.10.72	*Schiedam, Netherlands*
van Zyl Daniel Jacobús	Northern Transvaal	SA	8.1.71	*Pretoria*
Vasu Divakar	Tamil Nadu	I	11.12.67	*Coonoor*
***Vaughan** Justin Thomas Caldwell	Auckland	NZ	30.8.67	*Hereford, England*
Vaughan Michael Paul	Yorkshire	E	29.10.74	*Manchester*
Veenstra Ross Edward	Natal	SA	22.4.72	*Estcourt*
***Venkataramana** Margashayam	Tamil Nadu	I	24.4.66	*Secunderabad*
Venter Jacobus Francois	Free State	SA	1.10.69	*Bloemfontein*
Ventura Mario Dimitri	Jamaica	WI	21.4.74	*Jamaica*
Victor Gavin Charles	Eastern Province	SA	11.8.66	*Port Elizabeth*
Vij Bharati	Punjab	I	9.1.67	*Ludhiana*
Vimpani Graeme Ronald	Victoria	A	27.1.72	*Brisbane*
Volsteedt Andre Kenne	Boland	SA	6.5.75	*Bloemfontein*
Wait Clayton Clement	Eastern Province	SA	6.8.69	*Port Elizabeth*
Wallace Philo Alphonso	Barbados	WI	2.8.70	*Around-the-town*
Walker Alan	Durham	E	7.7.62	*Emley*
Walker Lyndsay Nicholas Paton	Nottinghamshire	E	22.6.74	*Armidale, Australia*
Walker Matthew Jonathan	Kent	E	2.1.74	*Gravesend*
Waller Andrew Christopher	Mashonaland Co. Dists	Z	25.9.59	*Salisbury*
***Walmsley** Kerry Peter	Auckland	NZ	23.8.73	*Dunedin*
***Walsh** Courtney Andrew	Jamaica/Glos	WI	30.10.62	*Kingston*
Walton Timothy Charles	Northamptonshire	E	8.11.72	*Low Head*
***Waqar Younis**	United Bank	P	16.11.71	*Vehari*
Ward David Mark	Surrey	E	10.2.61	*Croydon*
Ward Trevor Robert	Kent	E	18.1.68	*Farningham*
***Warnaweera** Kahakatchchi Patabandige Jayananda	Galle	SL	23.11.60	*Matara*
***Warne** Shane Keith	Victoria	A	13.9.69	*Ferntree Gully*
Warren Russell John	Northamptonshire	E	10.9.71	*Northampton*
***Wasim Akram**	PIA	P	3.6.66	*Lahore*
Wasim Haider	PIA	P	6.6.67	*Lyallpur*
***Wassan** Atul Satish	Delhi	I	23.3.68	*Delhi*
***Watkin** Steven Llewellyn	Glamorgan	E	15.9.64	*Maesteg*
***Watkinson** Michael	Lancashire	E	1.8.61	*Westhoughton*
Watson Douglas James	Natal	SA	15.5.73	*Pietermaritzburg*
Waugh Dean Parma	New South Wales	A	3.2.69	*Campsie*
***Waugh** Mark Edward	New South Wales	A	2.6.65	*Sydney*
***Waugh** Stephen Rodger	New South Wales	A	2.6.65	*Sydney*
Webber Darren Scott	South Australia	A	18.8.71	*Barnside*
Webster Trevor Craig	Transvaal	SA	4.10.69	*Johannesburg*
Weekes Lesroy Charlesworth	Leeward Islands	WI	19.7.71	*Montserrat*
Weekes Paul Nicholas	Middlesex	E	8.7.69	*Hackney*
Weerakkody Ajith Priyantha	Nondescripts	SL	1.10.70	*Colombo*
***Weerasinghe** Colombage Don Udesh Sanjeewa	Nondescripts	SL	1.3.68	*Colombo*
Welch Graeme	Warwickshire	E	21.3.72	*Durham*
Wellings Peter Edward	Middlesex	E	5.3.70	*Wolverhampton*
***Wells** Alan Peter	Sussex	E	2.10.61	*Newhaven*
Wells Colin Mark	Derbyshire	E	3.3.60	*Newhaven*
Wells Vincent John	Leicestershire	E	6.8.65	*Dartford*
Wessels Andrew	Boland	SA	13.5.74	*Pietermaritzburg*
***Wessels** Kepler Christoffel	Eastern Province	SA	14.9.57	*Bloemfontein*
Weston Robin Michael Swann	Durham	E	7.6.75	*Durham*

	Team	Country	Born	Birthplace
Weston William Philip Christopher	Worcestershire	E	16.6.73	*Durham*
Wharf Alexander George	Yorkshire	E	4.6.75	*Bradford*
***Whitaker** John James	Leicestershire	E	5.5.62	*Skipton*
Whitaker Paul Robert	Hampshire	E	28.6.73	*Keighley*
White Brad Middleton	Transvaal	SA	15.5.70	*Johannesburg*
***White** Craig	Yorkshire	E	16.12.69	*Morley*
White Giles William	Hampshire	E	23.3.72	*Barnstaple*
***Whittall** Guy James	Matabeleland	Z	5.9.72	*Chipinga*
Wiblin Wayne	Border	SA	13.2.69	*Grahamstown*
Wickremaratne Ranasinghe Pattikirikoralalage Aruna Hemantha	Sinhalese	SL	21.2.71	*Colombo*
***Wickremasinghe** Anguppulige Gamini Dayantha	Nondescripts	SL	27.12.65	*Colombo*
***Wickremasinghe** Gallage Pramodya	Sinhalese	SL	14.8.71	*Matara*
Wigney Bradley Neil	South Australia	A	30.6.65	*Leongatha*
***Wijetunge** Piyal Kashwapa	Bloomfield	SL	6.8.71	*Badulla*
Wilkinson Louis Johannes	Free State	SA	19.11.66	*Vereeniging*
Williams Brad Andrew	Victoria	A	20.11.74	*Frankston*
Williams David	Trinidad & Tobago	WI	4.11.63	*San Fernando*
Williams Harwood Wycum	Leeward Islands	WI	17.1.70	*St Kitts*
Williams Henry Smith	Boland	SA	11.6.67	*Stellenbosch*
Williams Joseph Henderson	Barbados	WI	1.9.74	*Barbados*
Williams Laurie Rohan	Jamaica	WI	12.12.68	*Jamaica*
***Williams** Neil FitzGerald	Essex	E	2.7.62	*Hope Well, St Vincent*
Williams Richard Charles James	Gloucestershire	E	8.8.69	*Bristol*
***Williams** Stuart Clayton	Leeward Islands	WI	12.8.69	*Government Road, Nevis*
Willis Simon Charles	Kent	E	19.3.74	*Greenwich*
Willoughby Charl Myles	Boland	SA	3.12.74	*Cape Town*
Wilson Jeffrey William	Otago	NZ	24.10.73	*Invercargill*
Wilson Paul	South Australia	A	12.1.72	*Newcastle*
Windows Matthew Guy Norman	Gloucestershire	E	5.4.73	*Bristol*
***Wishart** Craig Brian	Young Mashonaland	Z	9.1.74	*Salisbury*
Wong Kenneth Arthur	Guyana	WI	22.5.73	*Guyana*
Wood John	Durham	E	22.7.70	*Crofton*
Wood Nathan Theodore	Lancashire	E	4.10.74	*Thornhill Edge*
Wren Timothy Neil	Kent	E	26.3.70	*Folkestone*
Wright Anthony John	Gloucestershire	E	27.6.62	*Stevenage*
Wylie Andrew Robert	Boland	SA	31.12.71	*Pietermaritzburg*
***Yadav** Vijay Singh	Haryana	I	14.3.67	*Gonda*
Yates Gary	Lancashire	E	20.9.67	*Ashton-under-Lyne*
***Young** Bryan Andrew	Northern Districts	NZ	3.11.64	*Whangarei*
Young Shaun	Tasmania	A	13.6.70	*Burnie*
Zafar Iqbal	Karachi/Nat. Bank	P	6.3.69	*Karachi*
Zahid Ahmed	PIA	P	15.11.61	*Karachi*
***Zahid Fazal**	Lahore/PIA	P	10.11.73	*Sialkot*
Zaidi Ashish Winston	Uttar Pradesh	I	16.9.71	*Allahabad*

WISDEN'S CRICKETERS OF THE YEAR, 1889-1997

1889	*Six Great Bowlers of the Year:* J. Briggs, J. J. Ferris, G. A. Lohmann, R. Peel, C. T. B. Turner, S. M. J. Woods.
1890	*Nine Great Batsmen of the Year:* R. Abel, W. Barnes, W. Gunn, L. Hall, R. Henderson, J. M. Read, A. Shrewsbury, F. H. Sugg, A. Ward.
1891	*Five Great Wicket-Keepers:* J. McC. Blackham, G. MacGregor, R. Pilling, M. Sherwin, H. Wood.
1892	*Five Great Bowlers:* W. Attewell, J. T. Hearne, F. Martin, A. W. Mold, J. W. Sharpe.
1893	*Five Batsmen of the Year:* H. T. Hewett, L. C. H. Palairet, W. W. Read, S. W. Scott, A. E. Stoddart.
1894	*Five All-Round Cricketers:* G. Giffen, A. Hearne, F. S. Jackson, G. H. S. Trott, E. Wainwright.
1895	*Five Young Batsmen of the Season:* W. Brockwell, J. T. Brown, C. B. Fry, T. W. Hayward, A. C. MacLaren.
1896	W. G. Grace.
1897	*Five Cricketers of the Season:* S. E. Gregory, A. A. Lilley, K. S. Ranjitsinhji, T. Richardson, H. Trumble.
1898	*Five Cricketers of the Year:* F. G. Bull, W. R. Cuttell, N. F. Druce, G. L. Jessop, J. R. Mason.
1899	*Five Great Players of the Season:* W. H. Lockwood, W. Rhodes, W. Storer, C. L. Townsend, A. E. Trott.
1900	*Five Cricketers of the Season:* J. Darling, C. Hill, A. O. Jones, M. A. Noble, Major R. M. Poore.
1901	*Mr R. E. Foster and Four Yorkshiremen:* R. E. Foster, S. Haigh, G. H. Hirst, T. L. Taylor, J. Tunnicliffe.
1902	L. C. Braund, C. P. McGahey, F. Mitchell, W. G. Quaife, J. T. Tyldesley.
1903	W. W. Armstrong, C. J. Burnup, J. Iremonger, J. J. Kelly, V. T. Trumper.
1904	C. Blythe, J. Gunn, A. E. Knight, W. Mead, P. F. Warner.
1905	B. J. T. Bosanquet, E. A. Halliwell, J. Hallows, P. A. Perrin, R. H. Spooner.
1906	D. Denton, W. S. Lees, G. J. Thompson, J. Vine, L. G. Wright.
1907	J. N. Crawford, A. Fielder, E. G. Hayes, K. L. Hutchings, N. A. Knox.
1908	A. W. Hallam, R. O. Schwarz, F. A. Tarrant, A. E. E. Vogler, T. G. Wass.
1909	*Lord Hawke and Four Cricketers of the Year:* W. Brearley, Lord Hawke, J. B. Hobbs, A. Marshal, J. T. Newstead.
1910	W. Bardsley, S. F. Barnes, D. W. Carr, A. P. Day, V. S. Ransford.
1911	H. K. Foster, A. Hartley, C. B. Llewellyn, W. C. Smith, F. E. Woolley.
1912	*Five Members of the MCC's Team in Australia:* F. R. Foster, J. W. Hearne, S. P. Kinneir, C. P. Mead, H. Strudwick.
1913	John Wisden: Personal Recollections.
1914	M. W. Booth, G. Gunn, J. W. Hitch, A. E. Relf, Hon. L. H. Tennyson.
1915	J. W. H. T. Douglas, P. G. H. Fender, H. T. W. Hardinge, D. J. Knight, S. G. Smith.
1916-17	No portraits appeared.
1918	*School Bowlers of the Year:* H. L. Calder, J. E. D'E. Firth, C. H. Gibson, G. A. Rotherham, G. T. S. Stevens.
1919	*Five Public School Cricketers of the Year:* P. W. Adams, A. P. F. Chapman, A. C. Gore, L. P. Hedges, N. E. Partridge.
1920	*Five Batsmen of the Year:* A. Ducat, E. H. Hendren, P. Holmes, H. Sutcliffe, E. Tyldesley.
1921	P. F. Warner.
1922	H. Ashton, J. L. Bryan, J. M. Gregory, C. G. Macartney, E. A. McDonald.
1923	A. W. Carr, A. P. Freeman, C. W. L. Parker, A. C. Russell, A. Sandham.
1924	*Five Bowlers of the Year:* A. E. R. Gilligan, R. Kilner, G. G. Macaulay, C. H. Parkin, M. W. Tate.
1925	R. H. Catterall, J. C. W. MacBryan, H. W. Taylor, R. K. Tyldesley, W. W. Whysall.
1926	J. B. Hobbs.

1927	G. Geary, H. Larwood, J. Mercer, W. A. Oldfield, W. M. Woodfull.
1928	R. C. Blunt, C. Hallows, W. R. Hammond, D. R. Jardine, V. W. C. Jupp.
1929	L. E. G. Ames, G. Duckworth, M. Leyland, S. J. Staples, J. C. White.
1930	E. H. Bowley, K. S. Duleepsinhji, H. G. Owen-Smith, R. W. V. Robins, R. E. S. Wyatt.
1931	D. G. Bradman, C. V. Grimmett, B. H. Lyon, I. A. R. Peebles, M. J. Turnbull.
1932	W. E. Bowes, C. S. Dempster, James Langridge, Nawab of Pataudi sen., H. Verity.
1933	W. E. Astill, F. R. Brown, A. S. Kennedy, C. K. Nayudu, W. Voce.
1934	A. H. Bakewell, G. A. Headley, M. S. Nichols, L. F. Townsend, C. F. Walters.
1935	S. J. McCabe, W. J. O'Reilly, G. A. E. Paine, W. H. Ponsford, C. I. J. Smith.
1936	H. B. Cameron, E. R. T. Holmes, B. Mitchell, D. Smith, A. W. Wellard.
1937	C. J. Barnett, W. H. Copson, A. R. Gover, V. M. Merchant, T. S. Worthington.
1938	T. W. J. Goddard, J. Hardstaff jun., L. Hutton, J. H. Parks, E. Paynter.
1939	H. T. Bartlett, W. A. Brown, D. C. S. Compton, K. Farnes, A. Wood.
1940	L. N. Constantine, W. J. Edrich, W. W. Keeton, A. B. Sellers, D. V. P. Wright.
1941-46	No portraits appeared.
1947	A. V. Bedser, L. B. Fishlock, V. (M. H.) Mankad, T. P. B. Smith, C. Washbrook.
1948	M. P. Donnelly, A. Melville, A. D. Nourse, J. D. Robertson, N. W. D. Yardley.
1949	A. L. Hassett, W. A. Johnston, R. R. Lindwall, A. R. Morris, D. Tallon.
1950	T. E. Bailey, R. O. Jenkins, J. G. Langridge, R. T. Simpson, B. Sutcliffe.
1951	T. G. Evans, S. Ramadhin, A. L. Valentine, E. D. Weekes, F. M. M. Worrell.
1952	R. Appleyard, H. E. Dollery, J. C. Laker, P. B. H. May, E. A. B. Rowan.
1953	H. Gimblett, T. W. Graveney, D. S. Sheppard, W. S. Surridge, F. S. Trueman.
1954	R. N. Harvey, G. A. R. Lock, K. R. Miller, J. H. Wardle, W. Watson.
1955	B. Dooland, Fazal Mahmood, W. E. Hollies, J. B. Statham, G. E. Tribe.
1956	M. C. Cowdrey, D. J. Insole, D. J. McGlew, H. J. Tayfield, F. H. Tyson.
1957	D. Brookes, J. W. Burke, M. J. Hilton, G. R. A. Langley, P. E. Richardson.
1958	P. J. Loader, A. J. McIntyre, O. G. Smith, M. J. Stewart, C. L. Walcott.
1959	H. L. Jackson, R. E. Marshall, C. A. Milton, J. R. Reid, D. Shackleton.
1960	K. F. Barrington, D. B. Carr, R. Illingworth, G. Pullar, M. J. K. Smith.
1961	N. A. T. Adcock, E. R. Dexter, R. A. McLean, R. Subba Row, J. V. Wilson.
1962	W. E. Alley, R. Benaud, A. K. Davidson, W. M. Lawry, N. C. O'Neill.
1963	D. Kenyon, Mushtaq Mohammad, P. H. Parfitt, P. J. Sharpe, F. J. Titmus.
1964	D. B. Close, C. C. Griffith, C. C. Hunte, R. B. Kanhai, G. S. Sobers.
1965	G. Boycott, P. J. Burge, J. A. Flavell, G. D. McKenzie, R. B. Simpson.
1966	K. C. Bland, J. H. Edrich, R. C. Motz, P. M. Pollock, R. G. Pollock.
1967	R. W. Barber, B. L. D'Oliveira, C. Milburn, J. T. Murray, S. M. Nurse.
1968	Asif Iqbal, Hanif Mohammad, K. Higgs, J. M. Parks, Nawab of Pataudi jun.
1969	J. G. Binks, D. M. Green, B. A. Richards, D. L. Underwood, O. S. Wheatley.
1970	B. F. Butcher, A. P. E. Knott, Majid Khan, M. J. Procter, D. J. Shepherd.
1971	J. D. Bond, C. H. Lloyd, B. W. Luckhurst, G. M. Turner, R. T. Virgin.
1972	G. G. Arnold, B. S. Chandrasekhar, L. R. Gibbs, B. Taylor, Zaheer Abbas.
1973	G. S. Chappell, D. K. Lillee, R. A. L. Massie, J. A. Snow, K. R. Stackpole.
1974	K. D. Boyce, B. E. Congdon, K. W. R. Fletcher, R. C. Fredericks, P. J. Sainsbury.
1975	D. L. Amiss, M. H. Denness, N. Gifford, A. W. Greig, A. M. E. Roberts.
1976	I. M. Chappell, P. G. Lee, R. B. McCosker, D. S. Steele, R. A. Woolmer.
1977	J. M. Brearley, C. G. Greenidge, M. A. Holding, I. V. A. Richards, R. W. Taylor.
1978	I. T. Botham, M. Hendrick, A. Jones, K. S. McEwan, R. G. D. Willis.
1979	D. I. Gower, J. K. Lever, C. M. Old, C. T. Radley, J. N. Shepherd.
1980	J. Garner, S. M. Gavaskar, G. A. Gooch, D. W. Randall, B. C. Rose.
1981	K. J. Hughes, R. D. Jackman, A. J. Lamb, C. E. B. Rice, V. A. P. van der Bijl.
1982	T. M. Alderman, A. R. Border, R. J. Hadlee, Javed Miandad, R. W. Marsh.
1983	Imran Khan, T. E. Jesty, A. I. Kallicharran, Kapil Dev, M. D. Marshall.
1984	M. Amarnath, J. V. Coney, J. E. Emburey, M. W. Gatting, C. L. Smith.
1985	M. D. Crowe, H. A. Gomes, G. W. Humpage, J. Simmons, S. Wettimuny.
1986	P. Bainbridge, R. M. Ellison, C. J. McDermott, N. V. Radford, R. T. Robinson.
1987	J. H. Childs, G. A. Hick, D. B. Vengsarkar, C. A. Walsh, J. J. Whitaker.
1988	J. P. Agnew, N. A. Foster, D. P. Hughes, P. M. Roebuck, Salim Malik.
1989	K. J. Barnett, P. J. L. Dujon, P. A. Neale, F. D. Stephenson, S. R. Waugh.

1990	S. J. Cook, D. M. Jones, R. C. Russell, R. A. Smith, M. A. Taylor.
1991	M. A. Atherton, M. Azharuddin, A. R. Butcher, D. L. Haynes, M. E. Waugh.
1992	C. E. L. Ambrose, P. A. J. DeFreitas, A. A. Donald, R. B. Richardson, Waqar Younis.
1993	N. E. Briers, M. D. Moxon, I. D. K. Salisbury, A. J. Stewart, Wasim Akram.
1994	D. C. Boon, I. A. Healy, M. G. Hughes, S. K. Warne, S. L. Watkin.
1995	B. C. Lara, D. E. Malcolm, T. A. Munton, S. J. Rhodes, K. C. Wessels.
1996	D. G. Cork, P. A. de Silva, A. R. C. Fraser, A. Kumble, D. A. Reeve.
1997	S. T. Jayasuriya, Mushtaq Ahmed, Saeed Anwar, P. V. Simmons, S. R. Tendulkar.

POST-WAR CRICKETERS OF THE YEAR

The five players chosen to be Cricketers of the Year for 1997 bring the number chosen since selection resumed in 1947 after the wartime hiatus to 255. The 255 have been chosen from 26 different teams as follows:

Derbyshire	7	Lancashire	12	Sussex	8	South Africans	11
Durham	–	Leicestershire	5	Warwickshire	13	West Indians	21
Essex	12	Middlesex	11	Worcestershire	11	New Zealanders	5
Glamorgan	7	Northants	9	Yorkshire	13	Indians	9
Gloucestershire	7	Nottinghamshire	7	Oxford Univ.	1	Pakistanis	10
Hampshire	9	Somerset	10	Cambridge Univ.	2	Sri Lankans	2
Kent	10	Surrey	15	Australians	33	Zimbabweans	–

Note: The total of sides comes to 260 because five players played regularly for two teams in the year for which they were chosen: K. D. Boyce (Essex and West Indians), Imran Khan (Sussex and Pakistanis), Kapil Dev (Northamptonshire and Indians), P. B. H. May (Surrey and Cambridge University) and D. S. Sheppard (Sussex and Cambridge University).

S. T. Jayasuriya of Sri Lanka, in 1997, is the first player to be chosen who did not play in England the previous season.

Types of players

Of the 255 Cricketers of the Year, 140 are best classified as batsmen, 73 as bowlers, 26 as all-rounders and 16 as wicket-keepers.

Nationalities

At the time they were chosen, 129 (50.59 per cent) were qualified to play for England, 38 for Australia, 33 West Indies, 19 South Africa, 13 Pakistan, 10 India, 9 New Zealand, 3 Sri Lanka and 1 Zimbabwe.

A. J. Lamb (1981) and G. A. Hick (1987) were chosen when they were regarded as South African and Zimbabwean respectively, though they subsequently played Test cricket for England.

No England-qualified players were chosen in 1949, 1962, 1982 and 1997.

Non-Test players

The following post-War Cricketers of the Year never appeared in Test cricket: W. E. Alley (1962), P. Bainbridge (1986), J. D. Bond (1971), N. E. Briers (1993), D. M. Green (1969), D. P. Hughes (1988), G. W. Humpage (1985), T. E. Jesty (1983), A. Jones (1978), J. G. Langridge (1950), P. G. Lee (1976), K. S. McEwan (1978), P. A. Neale (1989), C. E. B. Rice (1981), P. M. Roebuck (1988), P. J. Sainsbury (1974), D. J. Shepherd (1970), J. Simmons (1985), F. D. Stephenson (1989), W. S. Surridge (1953), B. Taylor (1972), V. A. P. van der Bijl (1981), R. T. Virgin (1971), O. S. Wheatley (1969), J. V. Wilson (1961).

All the above were England-qualified except for Alley (Australian), McEwan, Rice and van der Bijl (South African) and Stephenson (West Indian).

PART THREE: RECORDS

CRICKET RECORDS

Test match and first-class records amended by BILL FRINDALL to end of the 1996 season in England

Unless stated to be of a minor character, all records apply only to first-class cricket. This is traditionally considered to have started in 1815, after the Napoleonic War.

* Denotes not out or an unbroken partnership.

(A), (SA), (WI), (NZ), (I), (P), (SL) or (Z) indicates either the nationality of the player, or the country in which the record was made.

FIRST-CLASS RECORDS

BATTING RECORDS

Highest Individual Scores 175
Double-Hundred on Debut 176
Two Separate Hundreds on Debut 177
Hundred on Debut in Britain 178
Two Double-Hundreds in a Match 179
Triple-Hundred and Hundred in a Match 179
Double-Hundred and Hundred in a Match 179
Two Separate Hundreds in a Match 180
Four Hundreds or More in Succession 180
Most Hundreds in a Season 181
Most Double-Hundreds in a Season 181
Most Hundreds in a Career 181
3,000 Runs in a Season 183
2,000 Runs in a Season (since 1969) 184
1,000 Runs in a Season Most Times 184
Highest Aggregates Outside England 185
Leading Batsmen in an English Season 185
25,000 Runs in a Career 186
Current Players with 20,000 Runs 189
Career Average Over 50 190
Fast Scoring 191
300 Runs in One Day 191
1,000 Runs in May 191
1,000 Runs in April and May 192
1,000 Runs in Two Separate Months 192
Most Runs Scored off One Over 192
Most Sixes in an Innings 193
Most Sixes in a Match 193
Most Sixes in a Season 193
Most Boundaries in an Innings 193
Highest Partnerships 194
Highest Partnerships for Each Wicket 195
Unusual Dismissals 197

BOWLING RECORDS

Ten Wickets in an Innings 198
Outstanding Analyses 200
Most Wickets in a Match 200
Sixteen or More Wickets in a Day 200
Four Wickets with Consecutive Balls 201

Hat-Tricks 201
250 Wickets in a Season 202
Leading Bowlers in an English Season 203
100 Wickets in a Season (since 1969) 204
100 Wickets in a Season Most Times 204
100 Wickets in a Season Outside England 204
1,500 Wickets in a Career 205
Current Players with 1,000 Wickets 206

ALL-ROUND RECORDS

Hundred and Ten Wickets in an Innings 206
Two Hundred Runs and Sixteen Wickets 206
Hundred in Each Innings and Five Wickets Twice 206
Hundred in Each Innings and Ten Wickets 207
Hundred and Four Wickets with Consecutive Balls 207
Hundred and Hat-Trick 207
Season Doubles 207
20,000 Runs and 2,000 Wickets in a Career 208

WICKET-KEEPING RECORDS

Most Dismissals in an Innings 209
Wicket-Keepers' Hat-Tricks 210
Most Dismissals in a Match 210
Most Dismissals in a Season 210
Most Dismissals in a Career 210
Current Players with 500 Dismissals 211

FIELDING RECORDS

Most Catches in an Innings 211
Most Catches in a Match 211
Most Catches in a Season 212
Most Catches in a Career 212
Most Catches by Current Players 212

TEAM RECORDS

Highest Totals 212
Lowest Totals 213
Highest Match Aggregates 214
Lowest Aggregate in a Completed Match 214
Highest Fourth-Innings Totals 214
Largest Victories 215
Tied Matches 215
Matches Begun and Finished on First Day 216

TEST MATCH RECORDS

BATTING RECORDS

Highest Individual Innings 217
Hundred on Test Debut 217
300 Runs in First Test 219

Two Separate Hundreds in a Test 219
Triple-Hundred and Hundred in Same Test 219
Double-Hundred and Hundred in Same Test 219
Most Runs in a Series 219
Most Test Runs in a Calendar Year 220
Most Runs in a Career 220
Highest Career Averages 224
Most Hundreds 224
Carrying Bat Through Test Innings 225
Fastest Fifties 226
Fastest Hundreds 226
Fastest Double-Hundreds 226
Fastest Triple-Hundreds 227
Most Runs in a Day by a Batsman 227
Slowest Individual Batting 227
Slowest Hundreds 227
Highest Partnerships for Each Wicket 228
Partnerships of 300 and Over 228

BOWLING RECORDS

Most Wickets in an Innings 229
Outstanding Analyses 230
Most Wickets in a Match 230
Most Wickets in a Series 231
Most Wickets in a Career 231
Wicket with First Ball in Test Cricket 234
Hat-Tricks 234
Four Wickets in Five Balls 234
Most Balls Bowled in a Test 235

ALL-ROUND RECORDS

100 Runs and Five Wickets in an Innings 235
100 Runs and Five Dismissals in an Innings 235
100 Runs and Ten Wickets in a Test 236
1,000 Runs and 100 Wickets in a Career 236
1,000 Runs, 100 Wickets and 100 Catches 236

WICKET-KEEPING RECORDS

Most Dismissals in an Innings 236
Most Dismissals in a Test 237
Most Dismissals in a Series 237
Most Dismissals in a Career 238

FIELDING RECORDS

Most Catches in an Innings 238
Most Catches in a Test 238
Most Catches in a Series 239
Most Catches in a Career 239

TEAM RECORDS

Highest Innings Totals 239
Highest Fourth-Innings Totals 240
Most Runs in a Day (Both Sides and One Side) 240
Most Wickets in a Day 240
Highest Match Aggregates 240
Lowest Innings Totals 241
Fewest Runs in a Full Day's Play 241
Lowest Match Aggregates 241
Youngest Test Players 242
Oldest Players on Test Debut 242
Oldest Test Players 243
Most Test Appearances 243
Most Consecutive Test Appearances 243

CAPTAINCY

Most Tests as Captain 244

UMPIRING

Most Test Matches 244

TEST SERIES

Summary of All Test Matches 245
England v Australia 246
England v South Africa 256
England v West Indies 260
England v New Zealand 264
England v India 267
England v Pakistan 270
England v Sri Lanka 273
Australia v South Africa 274
Australia v West Indies 276
Australia v New Zealand 280
Australia v India 282
Australia v Pakistan 285
Australia v Sri Lanka 288
South Africa v West Indies 289
South Africa v New Zealand 290
South Africa v India 292
South Africa v Pakistan 293
South Africa v Sri Lanka 294
South Africa v Zimbabwe 295
West Indies v New Zealand 296
West Indies v India 297
West Indies v Pakistan 301
West Indies v Sri Lanka 303
New Zealand v India 304
New Zealand v Pakistan 306
New Zealand v Sri Lanka 308
New Zealand v Zimbabwe 310
India v Pakistan 311
India v Sri Lanka 313
India v Zimbabwe 315
Pakistan v Sri Lanka 316

Pakistan v Zimbabwe 318
Sri Lanka v Zimbabwe 319
Test Match Grounds 320
Families in Test Cricket 322

LIMITED-OVERS INTERNATIONAL RECORDS

Summary of All Limited-Overs Internationals 325
Most Runs 326
Highest Individual Scores 327
Most Hundreds 327
Highest Partnership for Each Wicket 327
Most Wickets 328
Best Analyses 328
Hat-Tricks 329
Wicket-keeping and Fielding Records 329
All-Round 330
Highest Innings Totals 331
Highest Totals Batting Second 331
Highest Match Aggregates 331
Lowest Innings Totals 331
Largest Victories 332
Tied Matches 332
Most Appearances 332
World Cup Records 333
Limited-Overs International Captains 335

MISCELLANEOUS

Large Attendances 336
Lord's Cricket Ground 337
Highest Individual Scores in Minor Cricket 338
Highest Partnership in Minor Cricket 338
Record Hit 338
Throwing the Cricket Ball 338
Formation Dates of County and Minor County Clubs 339
Constitution of County Championship 339
Most County Championship Appearances 340
Most Consecutive County Championship Appearances 340
Most County Championship Appearances by Umpires 341
Most Seasons on First-Class Umpires' List 341

FIRST-CLASS RECORDS

BATTING RECORDS

HIGHEST INDIVIDUAL SCORES

501*	B. C. Lara	Warwickshire v Durham at Birmingham	1994
499	Hanif Mohammad	Karachi v Bahawalpur at Karachi	1958-59
452*	D. G. Bradman	NSW v Queensland at Sydney	1929-30

443*	B. B. Nimbalkar	Maharashtra v Kathiawar at Poona	1948-49
437	W. H. Ponsford	Victoria v Queensland at Melbourne	1927-28
429	W. H. Ponsford	Victoria v Tasmania at Melbourne	1922-23
428	Aftab Baloch	Sind v Baluchistan at Karachi	1973-74
424	A. C. MacLaren	Lancashire v Somerset at Taunton	1895
405*	G. A. Hick	Worcestershire v Somerset at Taunton	1988
385	B. Sutcliffe	Otago v Canterbury at Christchurch	1952-53
383	C. W. Gregory	NSW v Queensland at Brisbane	1906-07
377	S. V. Manjrekar	Bombay v Hyderabad at Bombay	1990-91
375	B. C. Lara	West Indies v England at St John's	1993-94
369	D. G. Bradman	South Australia v Tasmania at Adelaide	1935-36
366	N. H. Fairbrother	Lancashire v Surrey at The Oval	1990
366	M. V. Sridhar	Hyderabad v Andhra at Secunderabad	1993-94
365*	C. Hill	South Australia v NSW at Adelaide	1900-01
365*	G. S. Sobers	West Indies v Pakistan at Kingston	1957-58
364	L. Hutton	England v Australia at The Oval	1938
359*	V. M. Merchant	Bombay v Maharashtra at Bombay	1943-44
359	R. B. Simpson	NSW v Queensland at Brisbane	1963-64
357*	R. Abel	Surrey v Somerset at The Oval	1899
357	D. G. Bradman	South Australia v Victoria at Melbourne	1935-36
356	B. A. Richards	South Australia v Western Australia at Perth	1970-71
355*	G. R. Marsh	Western Australia v South Australia at Perth	1989-90
355	B. Sutcliffe	Otago v Auckland at Dunedin	1949-50
352	W. H. Ponsford	Victoria v NSW at Melbourne	1926-27
350	Rashid Israr	Habib Bank v National Bank at Lahore	1976-77
345	C. G. Macartney	Australians v Nottinghamshire at Nottingham	1921
344*	G. A. Headley	Jamaica v Lord Tennyson's XI at Kingston	1931-32
344	W. G. Grace	MCC v Kent at Canterbury	1876
343*	P. A. Perrin	Essex v Derbyshire at Chesterfield	1904
341	G. H. Hirst	Yorkshire v Leicestershire at Leicester	1905
340*	D. G. Bradman	NSW v Victoria at Sydney	1928-29
340	S. M. Gavaskar	Bombay v Bengal at Bombay	1981-82
338*	R. C. Blunt	Otago v Canterbury at Christchurch	1931-32
338	W. W. Read	Surrey v Oxford University at The Oval	1888
337*	Pervez Akhtar	Railways v Dera Ismail Khan at Lahore	1964-65
337*	D. J. Cullinan	Transvaal v Northern Transvaal at Johannesburg	1993-94
337†	Hanif Mohammad	Pakistan v West Indies at Bridgetown	1957-58
336*	W. R. Hammond	England v New Zealand at Auckland	1932-33
336	W. H. Ponsford	Victoria v South Australia at Melbourne	1927-28
334	D. G. Bradman	Australia v England at Leeds	1930
333	K. S. Duleepsinhji	Sussex v Northamptonshire at Hove	1930
333	G. A. Gooch	England v India at Lord's	1990
332	W. H. Ashdown	Kent v Essex at Brentwood	1934
331*	J. D. Robertson	Middlesex v Worcestershire at Worcester	1949
325*	H. L. Hendry	Victoria v New Zealanders at Melbourne	1925-26
325	A. Sandham	England v West Indies at Kingston	1929-30
325	C. L. Badcock	South Australia v Victoria at Adelaide	1935-36
324*	D. M. Jones	Victoria v South Australia at Melbourne	1994-95
324	J. B. Stollmeyer	Trinidad v British Guiana at Port-of-Spain	1946-47
324	Waheed Mirza	Karachi Whites v Quetta at Karachi	1976-77
323	A. L. Wadekar	Bombay v Mysore at Bombay	1966-67
322	E. Paynter	Lancashire v Sussex at Hove	1937
322	I. V. A. Richards	Somerset v Warwickshire at Taunton	1985
321	W. L. Murdoch	NSW v Victoria at Sydney	1881-82
320	R. Lamba	North Zone v West Zone at Bhilai	1987-88
319	Gul Mahomed	Baroda v Holkar at Baroda	1946-47
318*	W. G. Grace	Gloucestershire v Yorkshire at Cheltenham	1876
317	W. R. Hammond	Gloucestershire v Nottinghamshire at Gloucester	1936
317	K. R. Rutherford	New Zealanders v D. B. Close's XI at Scarborough	1986
316*	J. B. Hobbs	Surrey v Middlesex at Lord's	1926

316*	V. S. Hazare	Maharashtra v Baroda at Poona	1939-40
316	R. H. Moore	Hampshire v Warwickshire at Bournemouth	1937
315*	T. W. Hayward	Surrey v Lancashire at The Oval	1898
315*	P. Holmes	Yorkshire v Middlesex at Lord's	1925
315*	A. F. Kippax	NSW v Queensland at Sydney	1927-28
314*	C. L. Walcott	Barbados v Trinidad at Port-of-Spain	1945-46
313*	S. J. Cook	Somerset v Glamorgan at Cardiff	1990
313	H. Sutcliffe	Yorkshire v Essex at Leyton	1932
313	W. V. Raman	Tamil Nadu v Goa at Panjim	1988-89
312*	W. W. Keeton	Nottinghamshire v Middlesex at The Oval‡	1939
312*	J. M. Brearley	MCC Under-25 v North Zone at Peshawar	1966-67
312	R. Lamba	Delhi v Himachal Pradesh at Delhi	1994-95
312	J. E. R. Gallian	Lancashire v Derbyshire at Manchester	1996
311*	G. M. Turner	Worcestershire v Warwickshire at Worcester	1982
311	J. T. Brown	Yorkshire v Sussex at Sheffield	1897
311	R. B. Simpson	Australia v England at Manchester	1964
311	Javed Miandad	Karachi Whites v National Bank at Karachi	1974-75
310*	J. H. Edrich	England v New Zealand at Leeds	1965
310	H. Gimblett	Somerset v Sussex at Eastbourne	1948
309	V. S. Hazare	The Rest v Hindus at Bombay	1943-44
308*	F. M. M. Worrell	Barbados v Trinidad at Bridgetown	1943-44
307*	T. N. Lazard	Boland v W. Province at Worcester, Cape Province	1993-94
307	M. C. Cowdrey	MCC v South Australia at Adelaide	1962-63
307	R. M. Cowper	Australia v England at Melbourne	1965-66
306*	A. Ducat	Surrey v Oxford University at The Oval	1919
306*	E. A. B. Rowan	Transvaal v Natal at Johannesburg	1939-40
306*	D. W. Hookes	South Australia v Tasmania at Adelaide	1986-87
305*	F. E. Woolley	MCC v Tasmania at Hobart	1911-12
305*	F. R. Foster	Warwickshire v Worcestershire at Dudley	1914
305*	W. H. Ashdown	Kent v Derbyshire at Dover	1935
304*	A. W. Nourse	Natal v Transvaal at Johannesburg	1919-20
304*	P. H. Tarilton	Barbados v Trinidad at Bridgetown	1919-20
304*	E. D. Weekes	West Indians v Cambridge University at Cambridge	1950
304	R. M. Poore	Hampshire v Somerset at Taunton	1899
304	D. G. Bradman	Australia v England at Leeds	1934
303*	W. W. Armstrong	Australians v Somerset at Bath	1905
303*	Mushtaq Mohammad	Karachi Blues v Karachi University at Karachi	1967-68
303*	Abdul Azeem	Hyderabad v Tamil Nadu at Hyderabad	1986-87
303*	S. Chanderpaul	Guyana v Jamaica at Kingston	1995-96
302*	P. Holmes	Yorkshire v Hampshire at Portsmouth	1920
302*	W. R. Hammond	Gloucestershire v Glamorgan at Bristol	1934
302*	Arjan Kripal Singh	Tamil Nadu v Goa at Panjim	1988-89
302	W. R. Hammond	Gloucestershire v Glamorgan at Newport	1939
302	L. G. Rowe	West Indies v England at Bridgetown	1973-74
301*	E. H. Hendren	Middlesex v Worcestershire at Dudley	1933
301	W. G. Grace	Gloucestershire v Sussex at Bristol	1896
300*	V. T. Trumper	Australians v Sussex at Hove	1899
300*	F. B. Watson	Lancashire v Surrey at Manchester	1928
300*	Imtiaz Ahmed	PM's XI v Commonwealth XI at Bombay	1950-51
300	J. T. Brown	Yorkshire v Derbyshire at Chesterfield	1898
300	D. C. S. Compton	MCC v N. E. Transvaal at Benoni	1948-49
300	R. Subba Row	Northamptonshire v Surrey at The Oval	1958
300	Ramiz Raja	Allied Bank v Habib Bank at Lahore	1994-95

† *Hanif Mohammad is now believed to have batted for 16 hours 39 minutes – the longest innings in first-class cricket.*

‡ *Played at The Oval because Lord's was required for Eton v Harrow.*

Note: W. V. Raman (313) and Arjan Kripal Singh (302*) provide the only instance of two triple-hundreds in the same innings.

DOUBLE-HUNDRED ON DEBUT

227	T. Marsden	Sheffield & Leicester v Nottingham at Sheffield	1826
207	N. F. Callaway†	New South Wales v Queensland at Sydney	1914-15
240	W. F. E. Marx	Transvaal v Griqualand West at Johannesburg	1920-21
200*	A. Maynard	Trinidad v MCC at Port-of-Spain	1934-35
232*	S. J. E. Loxton	Victoria v Queensland at Melbourne	1946-47
215*	G. H. G. Doggart	Cambridge University v Lancashire at Cambridge	1948
202	J. Hallebone	Victoria v Tasmania at Melbourne	1951-52
230	G. R. Viswanath	Mysore v Andhra at Vijayawada	1967-68
260	A. A. Muzumdar	Bombay v Haryana at Faridabad	1993-94
209*	A. Pandey	Madhya Pradesh v Uttar Pradesh at Bhilai	1995-96
210*	D. J. Sales	Northants v Worcestershire at Kidderminster	1996

† *In his only first-class innings. He was killed in action in France in 1917.*

TWO SEPARATE HUNDREDS ON DEBUT

148 and 111	A. R. Morris	New South Wales v Queensland at Sydney	1940-41
152 and 102*	N. J. Contractor	Gujarat v Baroda at Baroda	1952-53
132* and 110	Aamer Malik	Lahore "A" v Railways at Lahore	1979-80

Notes: J. S. Solomon, British Guiana, scored a hundred in each of his first three innings in first-class cricket: 114* v Jamaica; 108 v Barbados in 1956-57; 121 v Pakistanis in 1957-58.

R. Watson-Smith, Border, scored 310 runs before he was dismissed in first-class cricket, including not-out centuries in his first two innings: 183* v Orange Free State and 125* v Griqualand West in 1969-70.

G. R. Viswanath and D. M. Wellham alone have scored a hundred on their debut in both first-class cricket and Test cricket. Viswanath scored 230 for Mysore v Andhra in 1967-68 and 137 for India v Australia in 1969-70. Wellham scored 100 for New South Wales v Victoria in 1980-81 and 103 for Australia v England in 1981.

HUNDRED ON DEBUT IN BRITAIN

(The following list does not include instances of players who have previously appeared in first-class cricket outside the British Isles or who performed the feat before 1965. Full lists of earlier instances are in *Wisdens* prior to 1984.)

108	D. R. Shepherd	Gloucestershire v Oxford University at Oxford	1965
110*	A. J. Harvey-Walker†	Derbyshire v Oxford University at Burton upon Trent	1971
173	J. Whitehouse	Warwickshire v Oxford University at Oxford	1971
106	J. B. Turner	Minor Counties v Pakistanis at Jesmond	1974
112	J. A. Claughton†	Oxford University v Gloucestershire at Oxford	1976
100*	A. W. Lilley†	Essex v Nottinghamshire at Nottingham	1978
146*	J. S. Johnson	Minor Counties v Indians at Wellington	1979
110	N. R. Taylor	Kent v Sri Lankans at Canterbury	1979
146*	D. G. Aslett	Kent v Hampshire at Bournemouth	1981
116	M. D. Moxon†	Yorkshire v Essex at Leeds	1981
100	D. A. Banks	Worcestershire v Oxford University at Oxford	1983
122	A. A. Metcalfe	Yorkshire v Nottinghamshire at Bradford	1983
117* 101*	K. T. Medlycott‡ N. J. Falkner ‡	Surrey v Cambridge University at Banstead	1984
106	A. C. Storie†	Northamptonshire v Hampshire at Northampton	1985
102	M. P. Maynard	Glamorgan v Yorkshire at Swansea	1985
117*	R. J. Bartlett	Somerset v Oxford University at Oxford	1986
100*	P. D. Bowler	Leicestershire v Hampshire at Leicester	1986
145	I. L. Philip	Scotland v Ireland at Glasgow	1986
114*	P. D. Atkins	Surrey v Cambridge University at The Oval	1988
100	B. M. W. Patterson	Scotland v Ireland at Dumfries	1988

116*	J. J. B. Lewis	Essex v Surrey at The Oval	1990
117	J. D. Glendenen	Durham v Oxford University at Oxford	1992
109	J. R. Wileman	Nottinghamshire v Cambridge U. at Nottingham	1992
123	A. J. Hollioake†	Surrey v Derbyshire at Ilkeston	1993
101	E. T. Smith	Cambridge University v Glamorgan at Cambridge	1996
110	S. D. Peters	Essex v Cambridge University at Cambridge	1996
210*	D. J. Sales†	Northamptonshire v Worcestershire at Kidderminster	1996

† *In his second innings.*
‡ *The only instance in England of two players performing the feat in the same match.*

TWO DOUBLE-HUNDREDS IN A MATCH

A. E. Fagg	244	202*	Kent v Essex at Colchester	1938

TRIPLE-HUNDRED AND HUNDRED IN A MATCH

G. A. Gooch	333	123	England v India at Lord's	1990

DOUBLE-HUNDRED AND HUNDRED IN A MATCH

C. B. Fry	125	229	Sussex v Surrey at Hove	1900
W. W. Armstrong	157*	245	Victoria v South Australia at Melbourne	1920-21
H. T. W. Hardinge	207	102*	Kent v Surrey at Blackheath	1921
C. P. Mead	113	224	Hampshire v Sussex at Horsham	1921
K. S. Duleepsinhji	115	246	Sussex v Kent at Hastings	1929
D. G. Bradman	124	225	Woodfull's XI v Ryder's XI at Sydney	1929-30
B. Sutcliffe	243	100*	New Zealanders v Essex at Southend	1949
M. R. Hallam	210*	157	Leicestershire v Glamorgan at Leicester	1959
M. R. Hallam	203*	143*	Leicestershire v Sussex at Worthing	1961
Hanumant Singh	109	213*	Rajasthan v Bombay at Bombay	1966-67
Salah-ud-Din	256	102*	Karachi v East Pakistan at Karachi	1968-69
K. D. Walters	242	103	Australia v West Indies at Sydney	1968-69
S. M. Gavaskar	124	220	India v West Indies at Port-of-Spain	1970-71
L. G. Rowe	214	100*	West Indies v New Zealand at Kingston	1971-72
G. S. Chappell	247*	133	Australia v New Zealand at Wellington	1973-74
L. Baichan	216*	102	Berbice v Demerara at Georgetown	1973-74
Zaheer Abbas	216*	156*	Gloucestershire v Surrey at The Oval	1976
Zaheer Abbas	230*	104*	Gloucestershire v Kent at Canterbury	1976
Zaheer Abbas	205*	108*	Gloucestershire v Sussex at Cheltenham	1977
Saadat Ali	141	222	Income Tax v Multan at Multan	1977-78
Talat Ali	214*	104	PIA v Punjab at Lahore	1978-79
Shafiq Ahmad	129	217*	National Bank v MCB at Karachi	1978-79
D. W. Randall	209	146	Notts. v Middlesex at Nottingham	1979
Zaheer Abbas	215*	150*	Gloucestershire v Somerset at Bath	1981
Qasim Omar	210*	110	MCB v Lahore at Lahore	1982-83
A. I. Kallicharran	200*	117*	Warwicks. v Northants at Birmingham	1984
Rizwan-uz-Zaman	139	217*	PIA v PACO at Lahore	1989-90
G. A. Hick	252*	100*	Worcs. v Glamorgan at Abergavenny	1990
N. R. Taylor	204	142	Kent v Surrey at Canterbury	1990
N. R. Taylor	111	203*	Kent v Sussex at Hove	1991
W. V. Raman	226	120	Tamil Nadu v Haryana at Faridabad	1991-92
A. J. Lamb	209	107	Northants v Warwicks. at Northampton	1992
G. A. Gooch	101	205	Essex v Worcestershire at Worcester	1994
P. A. de Silva	255	116	Kent v Derbyshire at Maidstone	1995
C. Mendis	111	200*	Colts CC v Singha SC at Colombo	1995-96

TWO SEPARATE HUNDREDS IN A MATCH

Eight times: Zaheer Abbas.
Seven times: W. R. Hammond.
Six times: J. B. Hobbs, G. M. Turner.
Five times: C. B. Fry, G. A. Gooch.
Four times: D. G. Bradman, G. S. Chappell, J. H. Edrich, L. B. Fishlock, T. W. Graveney, C. G. Greenidge, H. T. W. Hardinge, E. H. Hendren, Javed Miandad, G. L. Jessop, H. Morris, P. A. Perrin, B. Sutcliffe, H. Sutcliffe.
Three times: Agha Zahid, L. E. G. Ames, Basit Ali, G. Boycott, I. M. Chappell, D. C. S. Compton, S. J. Cook, M. C. Cowdrey, D. Denton, K. S. Duleepsinhji, R. E. Foster, R. C. Fredericks, S. M. Gavaskar, W. G. Grace, G. Gunn, M. R. Hallam, Hanif Mohammad, M. J. Harris, T. W. Hayward, V. S. Hazare, D. W. Hookes, L. Hutton, A. Jones, D. M. Jones, P. N. Kirsten, R. B. McCosker, P. B. H. May, C. P. Mead, T. M. Moody, M. H. Parmar, Rizwan-uz-Zaman, R. T. Robinson, A. C. Russell, Sadiq Mohammad, J. T. Tyldesley, K. C. Wessels.
Twice: Ali Zia, D. L. Amiss, C. W. J. Athey, L. Baichan, D. C. Boon, A. R. Border, B. J. T. Bosanquet, R. J. Boyd-Moss, A. R. Butcher, M. D. Crowe, C. C. Dacre, G. M. Emmett, A. E. Fagg, L. E. Favell, H. Gimblett, C. Hallows, R. A. Hamence, A. L. Hassett, M. L. Hayden, D. L. Haynes, G. A. Headley, G. A. Hick, A. I. Kallicharran, J. H. King, A. F. Kippax, A. J. Lamb, J. G. Langridge, S. G. Law, H. W. Lee, E. Lester, C. B. Llewellyn, C. G. Macartney, M. P. Maynard, C. A. Milton, A. R. Morris, P. H. Parfitt, Nawab of Pataudi jun., E. Paynter, C. Pinch, R. G. Pollock, R. T. Ponting, R. M. Prideaux, Qasim Omar, M. R. Ramprakash, W. Rhodes, B. A. Richards, I. V. A. Richards, Pankaj Roy, Salim Malik, James Seymour, Shafiq Ahmad, R. B. Simpson, C. L. Smith, G. S. Sobers, M. V. Sridhar, M. A. Taylor, N. R. Taylor, E. Tyldesley, C. L. Walcott, T. R. Ward, W. W. Whysall, G. N. Yallop.

Notes: W. Lambert scored 107 and 157 for Sussex v Epsom at Lord's in 1817 and it was not until W. G. Grace made 130 and 102* for South of the Thames v North of the Thames at Canterbury in 1868 that the feat was repeated.

C. J. B. Wood, 107* and 117* for Leicestershire v Yorkshire at Bradford in 1911, and S. J. Cook, 120* and 131* for Somerset v Nottinghamshire at Nottingham in 1989, are alone in carrying their bats and scoring hundreds in each innings.

FOUR HUNDREDS OR MORE IN SUCCESSION

Six in succession: D. G. Bradman 1938-39; C. B. Fry 1901; M. J. Procter 1970-71.
Five in succession: B. C. Lara 1993-94/1994; E. D. Weekes 1955-56.
Four in succession: C. W. J. Athey 1987; M. Azharuddin 1984-85; M. G. Bevan 1990-91; A. R. Border 1985; D. G. Bradman 1931-32, 1948/1948-49; D. C. S. Compton 1946-47; N. J. Contractor 1957-58; S. J. Cook 1989; K. S. Duleepsinhji 1931; C. B. Fry 1911; C. G. Greenidge 1986; W. R. Hammond 1936-37, 1945/1946; H. T. W. Hardinge 1913; T. W. Hayward 1906; J. B. Hobbs 1920, 1925; D. W. Hookes 1976-77; Ijaz Ahmed, jun. 1994-95; P. N. Kirsten 1976-77; J. G. Langridge 1949; C. G. Macartney 1921; K. S. McEwan 1977; P. B. H. May 1956-57; V. M. Merchant 1941-42; A. Mitchell 1933; Nawab of Pataudi sen. 1931; Rizwan-uz-Zaman 1989-90; L. G. Rowe 1971-72; Pankaj Roy 1962-63; Sadiq Mohammad 1976; Saeed Ahmed 1961-62; M. V. Sridhar 1990-91/1991-92; H. Sutcliffe 1931, 1939; S. R. Tendulkar 1994-95; E. Tyldesley 1926; W. W. Whysall 1930; F. E. Woolley 1929; Zaheer Abbas 1970-71, 1982-83.

Notes: T. W. Hayward (Surrey v Nottinghamshire and Leicestershire) and D. W. Hookes (South Australia v Queensland and New South Wales) are the only players listed above to score two hundreds in two successive matches. Hayward scored his in six days, June 4-9, 1906.

The most fifties in consecutive innings is ten – by E. Tyldesley in 1926, by D. G. Bradman in the 1947-48 and 1948 seasons and by R. S. Kaluwitharana in 1994-95.

MOST HUNDREDS IN A SEASON

Eighteen: D. C. S. Compton 1947.
Sixteen: J. B. Hobbs 1925.
Fifteen: W. R. Hammond 1938.
Fourteen: H. Sutcliffe 1932.
Thirteen: G. Boycott 1971, D. G. Bradman 1938, C. B. Fry 1901, W. R. Hammond 1933 and 1937, T. W. Hayward 1906, E. H. Hendren 1923, 1927 and 1928, C. P. Mead 1928, H. Sutcliffe 1928 and 1931.

Since 1969 (excluding G. Boycott – above)

Twelve: G. A. Gooch 1990.
Eleven: S. J. Cook 1991, Zaheer Abbas 1976.
Ten: G. A. Hick 1988, H. Morris 1990, M. R. Ramprakash 1995, G. M. Turner 1970, Zaheer Abbas 1981.

MOST DOUBLE-HUNDREDS IN A SEASON

Six: D. G. Bradman 1930.
Five: K. S. Ranjitsinhji 1900; E. D. Weekes 1950.
Four: Arun Lal 1986-87; C. B. Fry 1901; W. R. Hammond 1933, 1934; E. H. Hendren 1929-30; V. M. Merchant 1944-45; G. M. Turner 1971-72.
Three: L. E. G. Ames 1933; Arshad Pervez 1977-78; D. G. Bradman 1930-31, 1931-32, 1934, 1935-36, 1936-37, 1938, 1939-40; W. J. Edrich 1947; C. B. Fry 1903, 1904; M. W. Gatting 1994; G. A. Gooch 1994; W. R. Hammond 1928, 1928-29, 1932-33, 1938; J. Hardstaff jun. 1937, 1947; V. S. Hazare 1943-44; E. H. Hendren 1925; J. B. Hobbs 1914, 1926; L. Hutton 1949; D. M. Jones 1991-92; A. I. Kallicharran 1982; V. G. Kambli 1992-93; P. N. Kirsten 1980; R. S. Modi 1944-45; Nawab of Pataudi sen. 1933; W. H. Ponsford 1927-28, 1934; W. V. Raman 1988-89; M. R. Ramprakash 1995; K. S. Ranjitsinhji 1901; I. V. A. Richards 1977; R. B. Simpson 1963-64; P. R. Umrigar 1952, 1959; F. B. Watson 1928.

MOST HUNDREDS IN A CAREER

(35 or more)

		100s	Total Inns	100th 100 Season	100th 100 Inns	400+	300+	200+
1	J. B. Hobbs	197	1,315	1923	821	0	1	16
2	E. H. Hendren	170	1,300	1928-29	740	0	1	22
3	W. R. Hammond	167	1,005	1935	679	0	4	36
4	C. P. Mead	153	1,340	1927	892	0	0	13
5	G. Boycott	151	1,014	1977	645	0	0	10
6	H. Sutcliffe	149	1,088	1932	700	0	1	17
7	F. E. Woolley	145	1,532	1929	1,031	0	1	9
8	L. Hutton	129	814	1951	619	0	1	11
9	**G. A. Gooch**	**128**	**971**	**1992-93**	**820**	**0**	**1**	**13**
10	W. G. Grace	126	1,493	1895	1,113	0	3	13
11	D. C. S. Compton	123	839	1952	552	0	1	9
12	T. W. Graveney	122	1,223	1964	940	0	0	7
13	D. G. Bradman	117	338	1947-48	295	1	6	37
14	I. V. A. Richards	114	796	1988-89	658	0	1	10
15	Zaheer Abbas	108	768	1982-83	658	0	0	10
16	A. Sandham	107	1,000	1935	871	0	1	11
16	M. C. Cowdrey	107	1,130	1973	1,035	0	1	3

		100s	Total Inns	100th 100 Season	100th 100 Inns	400+	300+	200+
18	T. W. Hayward	104	1,138	1913	1,076	0	1	8
19	J. H. Edrich	103	979	1977	945	0	1	4
	G. M. Turner	103	792	1982	779	0	1	10
21	E. Tyldesley	102	961	1934	919	0	0	7
	L. E. G. Ames	102	951	1950	915	0	0	9
	D. L. Amiss	102	1,139	1986	1,081	0	0	3

E. H. Hendren, D. G. Bradman and I. V. A. Richards scored their 100th hundreds in Australia, G. A. Gooch scored his in India. His record includes his century in South Africa in 1981-82, which is no longer accepted by ICC. Zaheer Abbas scored his in Pakistan. Zaheer Abbas and G. Boycott did so in Test matches.

Most double-hundreds scored by batsmen not included in the above list:

Sixteen: C. B. Fry.

Fourteen: C. G. Greenidge, K. S. Ranjitsinhji.

Thirteen: W. H. Ponsford (including two 400s and two 300s), J. T. Tyldesley.

Twelve: P. Holmes, Javed Miandad, R. B. Simpson.

Eleven: J. W. Hearne, V. M. Merchant.

Ten: S. M. Gavaskar, J. Hardstaff, jun., V. S. Hazare, A. Shrewsbury, R. T. Simpson.

J. W. Hearne	96
C. B. Fry	94
C. G. Greenidge	92
M. W. Gatting	**90**
G. A. Hick	**90**
A. J. Lamb	89
A. I. Kallicharran	87
W. J. Edrich	86
G. S. Sobers	86
J. T. Tyldesley	86
P. B. H. May	85
R. E. S. Wyatt	85
J. Hardstaff, jun.	83
R. B. Kanhai	83
S. M. Gavaskar	81
Javed Miandad	80
M. Leyland	80
B. A. Richards	80
C. H. Lloyd	79
K. F. Barrington	76
J. G. Langridge	76
C. Washbrook	76
H. T. W. Hardinge	75
R. Abel	74
G. S. Chappell	74
D. Kenyon	74
K. S. McEwan	74
Majid Khan	73
Mushtaq Mohammad	72
J. O'Connor	72
W. G. Quaife	72
K. S. Ranjitsinhji	72
D. Brookes	71
M. D. Crowe	**71**
A. C. Russell	71
A. R. Border	**70**
D. Denton	69
M. J. K. Smith	69
R. E. Marshall	68
R. N. Harvey	67
P. Holmes	67
J. D. Robertson	67
P. A. Perrin	66
S. J. Cook	64
R. G. Pollock	64
R. T. Simpson	64
K. W. R. Fletcher	63
G. Gunn	62
R. T. Robinson	**61**
D. L. Haynes	**60**
V. S. Hazare	60
G. H. Hirst	60
R. B. Simpson	60
P. F. Warner	60
K. C. Wessels	**60**
D. C. Boon	**59**
I. M. Chappell	59
A. L. Hassett	59
W. Larkins	59
A. Shrewsbury	59
M. E. Waugh	**59**
J. G. Wright	59
A. E. Fagg	58
P. H. Parfitt	58
W. Rhodes	58
L. B. Fishlock	56
A. Jones	56
C. A. Milton	56
C. Hallows	55
Hanif Mohammad	55
P. N. Kirsten	**55**
D. B. Vengsarkar	55
W. Watson	55
C. W. J. Athey	**54**
D. J. Insole	54
W. W. Keeton	54
W. Bardsley	53
B. F. Davison	53
A. E. Dipper	53
D. I. Gower	53
G. L. Jessop	53
James Seymour	53
Shafiq Ahmad	53
E. H. Bowley	52
D. B. Close	52
A. Ducat	52
D. W. Randall	52
E. R. Dexter	51
J. M. Parks	51
R. A. Smith	**51**
W. W. Whysall	51
B. C. Broad	50
G. Cox, jun.	50
H. E. Dollery	50
K. S. Duleepsinhji	50
H. Gimblett	50
D. M. Jones	**50**
W. M. Lawry	50
T. M. Moody	**50**
Sadiq Mohammad	50
F. B. Watson	50
K. J. Barnett	**49**
C. G. Macartney	49
H. Morris	**49**
M. J. Stewart	49
K. G. Suttle	49
P. R. Umrigar	49
W. M. Woodfull	49
C. J. Barnett	48
M. R. Benson	48
W. Gunn	48

E. G. Hayes 48
B. W. Luckhurst 48
M. J. Procter 48
C. E. B. Rice 48
C. J. Tavaré 48
A. C. MacLaren 47
P. W. G. Parker 47
W. H. Ponsford 47
C. L. Smith 47
A. R. Butcher 46
J. Iddon 46
A. R. Morris 46
C. T. Radley 46
Younis Ahmed 46
W. W. Armstrong 45
Asif Iqbal 45
L. G. Berry 45
J. M. Brearley 45
A. W. Carr 45
C. Hill 45
N. C. O'Neill 45
E. Paynter 45
Rev. D. S. Sheppard... 45
K. D. Walters 45
M. Azharuddin 44
H. H. Gibbons 44
V. M. Merchant 44
A. Mitchell 44
M. D. Moxon 44
P. E. Richardson 44
B. Sutcliffe 44
G. R. Viswanath 44
P. Willey 44
E. J. Barlow 43
B. L. D'Oliveira 43
J. H. Hampshire 43
A. F. Kippax 43
J. W. H. Makepeace .. 43
A. P. Wells 43
James Langridge 42
J. E. Morris 42
Mudassar Nazar 42
H. W. Parks 42
T. F. Shepherd 42
N. R. Taylor 42
V. T. Trumper 42
M. A. Atherton 41
M. J. Harris 41
G. D. Mendis 41
K. R. Miller 41
A. D. Nourse 41
J. H. Parks 41
R. M. Prideaux 41
G. Pullar 41
W. E. Russell 41
R. C. Fredericks 40
J. Gunn 40
M. P. Maynard 40
M. J. Smith 40
C. L. Walcott 40
D. M. Young 40
Arshad Pervez 39
W. H. Ashdown 39
R. J. Bailey 39
J. B. Bolus 39
W. A. Brown 39
T. S. Curtis 39
R. J. Gregory 39
M. A. Lynch 39
W. R. D. Payton 39
J. R. Reid 39
Salim Malik 39
F. M. M. Worrell 39
I. T. Botham 38
F. L. Bowley 38
P. J. Burge 38
J. F. Crapp 38
D. Lloyd 38
V. L. Manjrekar 38
A. W. Nourse 38
N. Oldfield 38
Rev. J. H. Parsons 38
W. W. Read 38
Rizwan-uz-Zaman 38
J. Sharp 38
V. P. Terry 38
L. J. Todd 38
S. R. Waugh 38
J. Arnold 37
G. Brown 37
G. Cook 37
G. M. Emmett 37
H. W. Lee 37
M. A. Noble 37
B. P. Patel 37
R. B. Richardson 37
H. S. Squires 37
R. T. Virgin 37
C. J. B. Wood 37
N. F. Armstrong 36
G. Fowler 36
M. C. J. Nicholas 36
E. Oldroyd 36
W. Place 36
A. J. Stewart 36
A. L. Wadekar 36
E. D. Weekes 36
C. S. Dempster 35
N. H. Fairbrother 35
D. R. Jardine 35
T. E. Jesty 35
B. H. Valentine 35
G. M. Wood 35

Bold type denotes those who played in 1995-96 and 1996 seasons.

3,000 RUNS IN A SEASON

	Season	*I*	*NO*	*R*	*HS*	*100s*	*Avge*
D. C. S. Compton	1947	50	8	3,816	246	18	90.85
W. J. Edrich	1947	52	8	3,539	267*	12	80.43
T. W. Hayward	1906	61	8	3,518	219	13	66.37
L. Hutton	1949	56	6	3,429	269*	12	68.58
F. E. Woolley	1928	59	4	3,352	198	12	60.94
H. Sutcliffe	1932	52	7	3,336	313	14	74.13
W. R. Hammond	1933	54	5	3,323	264	13	67.81
E. H. Hendren	1928	54	7	3,311	209*	13	70.44
R. Abel	1901	68	8	3,309	247	7	55.15
W. R. Hammond	1937	55	5	3,252	217	13	65.04
M. J. K. Smith	1959	67	11	3,245	200*	8	57.94
E. H. Hendren	1933	65	9	3,186	301*	11	56.89
C. P. Mead	1921	52	6	3,179	280*	10	69.10
T. W. Hayward	1904	63	5	3,170	203	11	54.65
K. S. Ranjitsinhji	1899	58	8	3,159	197	8	63.18
C. B. Fry	1901	43	3	3,147	244	13	78.67

	Season	I	NO	R	HS	100s	Avge
K. S. Ranjitsinhji	1900	40	5	3,065	275	11	87.57
L. E. G. Ames	1933	57	5	3,058	295	9	58.80
J. T. Tyldesley	1901	60	5	3,041	221	9	55.29
C. P. Mead	1928	50	10	3,027	180	13	75.67
J. B. Hobbs	1925	48	5	3,024	266*	16	70.32
E. Tyldesley	1928	48	10	3,024	242	10	79.57
W. E. Alley	1961	64	11	3,019	221*	11	56.96
W. R. Hammond	1938	42	2	3,011	271	15	75.27
E. H. Hendren	1923	51	12	3,010	200*	13	77.17
H. Sutcliffe	1931	42	11	3,006	230	13	96.96
J. H. Parks	1937	63	4	3,003	168	11	50.89
H. Sutcliffe	1928	44	5	3,002	228	13	76.97

Notes: W. G. Grace scored 2,739 runs in 1871 – the first batsman to reach 2,000 runs in a season. He made ten hundreds and twice exceeded 200, with an average of 78.25 in all first-class matches.

The highest aggregate in a season since the reduction of County Championship matches in 1969 is 2,755 by S. J. Cook (42 innings) in 1991.

2,000 RUNS IN A SEASON

Since Reduction of Championship Matches in 1969

Five times: G. A. Gooch 2,746 (1990), 2,559 (1984), 2,324 (1988), 2,208 (1985), 2,023 (1993).

Three times: D. L. Amiss 2,239 (1984), 2,110 (1976), 2,030 (1978); S. J. Cook 2,755 (1991), 2,608 (1990), 2,241 (1989); M. W. Gatting 2,257 (1984), 2,057 (1991), 2,000 (1992); G. A. Hick 2,713 (1988), 2,347 (1990), 2,004 (1986); G. M. Turner 2,416 (1973), 2,379 (1970), 2,101 (1981).

Twice: G. Boycott 2,503 (1971), 2,051 (1970); J. H. Edrich 2,238 (1969), 2,031 (1971); A. I. Kallicharran 2,301 (1984), 2,120 (1982); Zaheer Abbas 2,554 (1976), 2,306 (1981).

Once: M. Azharuddin 2,016 (1991); J. B. Bolus 2,143 (1970); P. D. Bowler 2,044 (1992); B. C. Broad 2,226 (1990); A. R. Butcher 2,116 (1990); C. G. Greenidge 2,035 (1986); M. J. Harris 2,238 (1971); D. L. Haynes 2,346 (1990); Javed Miandad 2,083 (1981); A. J. Lamb 2,049 (1981); B. C. Lara 2,066 (1994); K. S. McEwan 2,176 (1983); Majid Khan 2,074 (1972); A. A. Metcalfe 2,047 (1990); H. Morris 2,276 (1990); M. R. Ramprakash 2,258 (1995); D. W. Randall 2,151 (1985); I. V. A. Richards 2,161 (1977); R. T. Robinson 2,032 (1984); M. A. Roseberry 2,044 (1992); C. L. Smith 2,000 (1985); R. T. Virgin 2,223 (1970); D. M. Ward 2,072 (1990); M. E. Waugh 2,072 (1990).

1,000 RUNS IN A SEASON MOST TIMES

(Includes Overseas Tours and Seasons)

28 times: W. G. Grace 2,000 (6); F. E. Woolley 3,000 (1), 2,000 (12).

27 times: M. C. Cowdrey 2,000 (2); C. P. Mead 3,000 (2), 2,000 (9).

26 times: G. Boycott 2,000 (3); J. B. Hobbs 3,000 (1), 2,000 (16).

25 times: E. H. Hendren 3,000 (3), 2,000 (12).

24 times: D. L. Amiss 2,000 (3); W. G. Quaife 2,000 (1); H. Sutcliffe 3,000 (3), 2,000 (12).

23 times: A. Jones.

22 times: T. W. Graveney 2,000 (7); W. R. Hammond 3,000 (3), 2,000 (9).

21 times: D. Denton 2,000 (5); J. H. Edrich 2,000 (6); G. A. Gooch 2,000 (5); W. Rhodes 2,000 (2).

20 times: D. B. Close; K. W. R. Fletcher; G. Gunn; T. W. Hayward 3,000 (2), 2,000 (8); James Langridge 2,000 (1); J. M. Parks 2,000 (3); A. Sandham 2,000 (8); M. J. K. Smith 3,000 (1), 2,000 (5); C. Washbrook 2,000 (2).

19 times: J. W. Hearne 2,000 (4); G. H. Hirst 2,000 (3); D. Kenyon 2,000 (7); E. Tyldesley 3,000 (1), 2,000 (5); J. T. Tyldesley 3,000 (1), 2,000 (4).

18 times: L. G. Berry 2,000 (1); M. W. Gatting 2,000 (3); H. T. W. Hardinge 2,000 (5); R. E. Marshall 2,000 (6); P. A. Perrin; G. M. Turner 2,000 (3); R. E. S. Wyatt 2,000 (5).

17 times: L. E. G. Ames 3,000 (1), 2,000 (5); T. E. Bailey 2,000 (1); D. Brookes 2,000 (6); D. C. S. Compton 3,000 (1), 2,000 (5); C. G. Greenidge 2,000 (1); L. Hutton 3,000 (1), 2,000 (8); J. G. Langridge 2,000 (11); M. Leyland 2,000 (3); I. V. A. Richards 2,000 (1); K. G. Suttle 2,000 (1); Zaheer Abbas 2,000 (2).

16 times: D. G. Bradman 2,000 (4); D. E. Davies 2,000 (1); E. G. Hayes 2,000 (2); C. A. Milton 2,000 (1); J. O'Connor 2,000 (4); C. T. Radley; James Seymour 2,000 (1); C. J. Tavaré.

15 times: G. Barker; K. F. Barrington 2,000 (3); E. H. Bowley 2,000 (4); M. H. Denness; A. E. Dipper 2,000 (5); H. E. Dollery 2,000 (2); W. J. Edrich 3,000 (1), 2,000 (8); J. H. Hampshire; P. Holmes 2,000 (7); Mushtaq Mohammad; R. B. Nicholls 2,000 (1); P. H. Parfitt 2,000 (3); W. G. A. Parkhouse 2,000 (1); B. A. Richards 2,000 (1); J. D. Robertson 2,000 (9); G. S. Sobers; M. J. Stewart 2,000 (1).

Notes: F. E. Woolley reached 1,000 runs in 28 consecutive seasons (1907-1938), C. P. Mead in 27 (1906-1936).

Outside England, 1,000 runs in a season has been reached most times by D. G. Bradman (in 12 seasons in Australia).

Three batsmen have scored 1,000 runs in a season in each of four different countries: G. S. Sobers in West Indies, England, India and Australia; M. C. Cowdrey and G. Boycott in England, South Africa, West Indies and Australia.

HIGHEST AGGREGATES OUTSIDE ENGLAND

	Season	*I*	*NO*	*R*	*HS*	*100s*	*Avge*
In Australia							
D. G. Bradman	1928-29	24	6	1,690	340*	7	93.88
In South Africa							
J. R. Reid	1961-62	30	2	1,915	203	7	68.39
In West Indies							
E. H. Hendren	1929-30	18	5	1,765	254*	6	135.76
In New Zealand							
M. D. Crowe	1986-87	21	3	1,676	175*	8	93.11
In India							
C. G. Borde	1964-65	28	3	1,604	168	6	64.16
In Pakistan							
Saadat Ali	1983-84	27	1	1,649	208	4	63.42
In Sri Lanka							
R. P. Arnold	1995-96	24	3	1,475	217*	5	70.23
In Zimbabwe							
G. W. Flower........	1994-95	20	3	983	201*	4	57.82

Note: In more than one country, the following aggregates of over 2,000 runs have been recorded:

M. Amarnath (P/I/WI)	1982-83	34	6	2,234	207	9	79.78
J. R. Reid (SA/A/NZ).	1961-62	40	2	2,188	203	7	57.57
S. M. Gavaskar (I/P)	1978-79	30	6	2,121	205	10	88.37
R. B. Simpson (I/P/A/WI)	1964-65	34	4	2,063	201	8	68.76

LEADING BATSMEN IN AN ENGLISH SEASON

(Qualification: 8 completed innings)

Season	*Leading scorer*	*Runs*	*Avge*	*Top of averages*	*Runs*	*Avge*
1946	D. C. S. Compton ...	2,403	61.61	W. R. Hammond ...	1,783	84.90
1947	D. C. S. Compton ...	3,816	90.85	D. C. S. Compton ..	3,816	90.85
1948	L. Hutton	2,654	64.73	D. G. Bradman.....	2,428	89.92
1949	L. Hutton	3,429	68.58	J. Hardstaff........	2,251	72.61

Season	*Leading scorer*	*Runs*	*Avge*	*Top of averages*	*Runs*	*Avge*
1950	R. T. Simpson	2,576	62.82	E. Weekes	2,310	79.65
1951	J. D. Robertson	2,917	56.09	P. B. H. May	2,339	68.79
1952	L. Hutton	2,567	61.11	D. S. Sheppard	2,262	64.62
1953	W. J. Edrich	2,557	47.35	R. N. Harvey	2,040	65.80
1954	D. Kenyon	2,636	51.68	D. C. S. Compton	1,524	58.61
1955	D. J. Insole	2,427	42.57	D. J. McGlew	1,871	58.46
1956	T. W. Graveney	2,397	49.93	K. Mackay	1,103	52.52
1957	T. W. Graveney	2,361	49.18	P. B. H. May	2,347	61.76
1958	P. B. H. May	2,231	63.74	P. B. H. May	2,231	63.74
1959	M. J. K. Smith	3,245	57.94	V. L. Manjrekar	755	68.63
1960	M. J. K. Smith	2,551	45.55	R. Subba Row	1,503	55.66
1961	W. E. Alley	3,019	56.96	W. M. Lawry	2,019	61.18
1962	J. H. Edrich	2,482	51.70	R. T. Simpson	867	54.18
1963	J. B. Bolus	2,190	41.32	G. S. Sobers	1,333	47.60
1964	T. W. Graveney	2,385	54.20	K. F. Barrington	1,872	62.40
1965	J. H. Edrich	2,319	62.67	M. C. Cowdrey	2,093	63.42
1966	A. R. Lewis	2,198	41.47	G. S. Sobers	1,349	61.31
1967	C. A. Milton	2,089	46.42	K. F. Barrington	2,059	68.63
1968	B. A. Richards	2,395	47.90	G. Boycott	1,487	64.65
1969	J. H. Edrich	2,238	69.93	J. H. Edrich	2,238	69.93
1970	G. M. Turner	2,379	61.00	G. S. Sobers	1,742	75.73
1971	G. Boycott	2,503	100.12	G. Boycott	2,503	100.12
1972	Majid Khan	2,074	61.00	G. Boycott	1,230	72.35
1973	G. M. Turner	2,416	67.11	G. M. Turner	2,416	67.11
1974	R. T. Virgin	1,936	56.94	C. H. Lloyd	1,458	63.39
1975	G. Boycott	1,915	73.65	R. B. Kanhai	1,073	82.53
1976	Zaheer Abbas	2,554	75.11	Zaheer Abbas	2,554	75.11
1977	I. V. A. Richards	2,161	65.48	G. Boycott	1,701	68.04
1978	D. L. Amiss	2,030	53.42	C. E. B. Rice	1,871	66.82
1979	K. C. Wessels	1,800	52.94	G. Boycott	1,538	102.53
1980	P. N. Kirsten	1,895	63.16	A. J. Lamb	1,797	66.55
1981	Zaheer Abbas	2,306	88.69	Zaheer Abbas	2,306	88.69
1982	A. I. Kallicharran	2,120	66.25	G. M. Turner	1,171	90.07
1983	K. S. McEwan	2,176	64.00	I. V. A. Richards	1,204	75.25
1984	G. A. Gooch	2,559	67.34	C. G. Greenidge	1,069	82.23
1985	G. A. Gooch	2,208	71.22	I. V. A. Richards	1,836	76.50
1986	C. G. Greenidge	2,035	67.83	C. G. Greenidge	2,035	67.83
1987	G. A. Hick	1,879	52.19	M. D. Crowe	1,627	67.79
1988	G. A. Hick	2,713	77.51	R. A. Harper	622	77.75
1989	S. J. Cook	2,241	60.56	D. M. Jones	1,510	88.82
1990	G. A. Gooch	2,746	101.70	G. A. Gooch	2,746	101.70
1991	S. J. Cook	2,755	81.02	C. L. Hooper	1,501	93.81
1992	P. D. Bowler	2,044	65.93	Salim Malik	1,184	78.93
	M. A. Roseberry	2,044	56.77			
1993	G. A. Gooch	2,023	63.21	D. C. Boon	1,437	75.63
1994	B. C. Lara	2,066	89.82	J. D. Carr	1,543	90.76
1995	M. R. Ramprakash	2,258	77.86	M. R. Ramprakash	2,258	77.86
1996	G. A. Gooch	1,944	67.03	S. C. Ganguly	762	95.25

Notes: The highest average recorded in an English season was 115.66 (2,429 runs, 26 innings) by D. G. Bradman in 1938.

In 1953 W. A. Johnston averaged 102.00 from 17 innings, 16 not out.

25,000 RUNS IN A CAREER

Dates in italics denote the first half of an overseas season; i.e. *1945* denotes the 1945-46 season.

		Career	*R*	*I*	*NO*	*HS*	*100s*	*Avge*
1	J. B. Hobbs	1905-34	61,237	1,315	106	316*	197	50.65
2	F. E. Woolley	1906-38	58,969	1,532	85	305*	145	40.75
3	E. H. Hendren	1907-38	57,611	1,300	166	301*	170	50.80

		Career	*R*	*I*	*NO*	*HS*	*100s*	*Avge*
4	C. P. Mead	1905-36	55,061	1,340	185	280*	153	47.67
5	W. G. Grace	1865-1908	54,896	1,493	105	344	126	39.55
6	W. R. Hammond	1920-51	50,551	1,005	104	336*	167	56.10
7	H. Sutcliffe	1919-45	50,138	1,088	123	313	149	51.95
8	G. Boycott	1962-86	48,426	1,014	162	261*	151	56.83
9	T. W. Graveney	1948-*71*	47,793	1,223	159	258	122	44.91
10	**G. A. Gooch**	**1973-96**	**44,472**	**971**	**74**	**333**	**128**	**49.57**
11	T. W. Hayward	1893-1914	43,551	1,138	96	315*	104	41.79
12	D. L. Amiss	1960-87	43,423	1,139	126	262*	102	42.86
13	M. C. Cowdrey	1950-76	42,719	1,130	134	307	107	42.89
14	A. Sandham	1911-*37*	41,284	1,000	79	325	107	44.82
15	L. Hutton	1934-60	40,140	814	91	364	129	55.51
16	M. J. K. Smith	1951-75	39,832	1,091	139	204	69	41.84
17	W. Rhodes	1898-1930	39,802	1,528	237	267*	58	30.83
18	J. H. Edrich	1956-78	39,790	979	104	310*	103	45.47
19	R. E. S. Wyatt	1923-57	39,405	1,141	157	232	85	40.04
20	D. C. S. Compton	1936-64	38,942	839	88	300	123	51.85
21	E. Tyldesley	1909-36	38,874	961	106	256*	102	45.46
22	J. T. Tyldesley	1895-1923	37,897	994	62	295*	86	40.66
23	K. W. R. Fletcher	1962-88	37,665	1,167	170	228*	63	37.77
24	C. G. Greenidge	1970-92	37,354	889	75	273*	92	45.88
25	J. W. Hearne	1909-36	37,252	1,025	116	285*	96	40.98
26	L. E. G. Ames	1926-51	37,248	951	95	295	102	43.51
27	D. Kenyon	1946-67	37,002	1,159	59	259	74	33.63
28	W. J. Edrich	1934-58	36,965	964	92	267*	86	42.39
29	J. M. Parks	1949-76	36,673	1,227	172	205*	51	34.76
30	D. Denton	1894-1920	36,479	1,163	70	221	69	33.37
31	G. H. Hirst	1891-1929	36,323	1,215	151	341	60	34.13
32	I. V. A. Richards	*1971*-93	36,212	796	63	322	114	49.40
33	A. Jones	1957-83	36,049	1,168	72	204*	56	32.89
34	W. G. Quaife	1894-1928	36,012	1,203	185	255*	72	35.37
35	R. E. Marshall	*1945*-72	35,725	1,053	59	228*	68	35.94
36	G. Gunn	1902-32	35,208	1,061	82	220	62	35.96
37	D. B. Close	1949-86	34,994	1,225	173	198	52	33.26
38	Zaheer Abbas	*1965-86*	34,843	768	92	274	108	51.54
39	J. G. Langridge	1928-55	34,380	984	66	250*	76	37.45
40	**M. W. Gatting**	**1975-96**	**34,357**	**803**	**118**	**258**	**90**	**50.15**
41	G. M. Turner	*1964-82*	34,346	792	101	311*	103	49.70
42	C. Washbrook	1933-64	34,101	906	107	251*	76	42.67
43	M. Leyland	1920-48	33,660	932	101	263	80	40.50
44	H. T. W. Hardinge	1902-33	33,519	1,021	103	263*	75	36.51
45	R. Abel	1881-1904	33,124	1,007	73	357*	74	35.46
46	A. I. Kallicharran	*1966*-90	32,650	834	86	243*	87	43.64
47	A. J. Lamb	*1972*-95	32,502	772	108	294	89	48.94
48	C. A. Milton	1948-74	32,150	1,078	125	170	56	33.73
49	J. D. Robertson	1937-59	31,914	897	46	331*	67	37.50
50	J. Hardstaff, jun.	1930-55	31,847	812	94	266	83	44.35
51	James Langridge	1924-53	31,716	1,058	157	167	42	35.20
52	K. F. Barrington	1953-68	31,714	831	136	256	76	45.63
53	C. H. Lloyd	*1963*-86	31,232	730	96	242*	79	49.26
54	Mushtaq Mohammad	*1956*-85	31,091	843	104	303*	72	42.07
55	C. B. Fry	1892-*1921*	30,886	658	43	258*	94	50.22
56	D. Brookes	1934-59	30,874	925	70	257	71	36.10
57	P. Holmes	1913-35	30,573	810	84	315*	67	42.11
58	R. T. Simpson	*1944*-63	30,546	852	55	259	64	38.32
59	L. G. Berry	1924-51	30,225	1,056	57	232	45	30.25
	K. G. Suttle	1949-71	30,225	1,064	92	204*	49	31.09
61	P. A. Perrin	1896-1928	29,709	918	91	343*	66	35.92

		Career	*R*	*I*	*NO*	*HS*	*100s*	*Avge*
62	P. F. Warner	1894-1929	29,028	875	75	244	60	36.28
63	R. B. Kanhai	*1954-81*	28,774	669	82	256	83	49.01
64	J. O'Connor	1921-39	28,764	903	79	248	72	34.90
65	Javed Miandad	*1973-93*	28,647	631	95	311	80	53.44
66	T. E. Bailey	1945-67	28,641	1,072	215	205	28	33.42
67	D. W. Randall	1972-93	28,456	827	81	237	52	38.14
68	E. H. Bowley	1912-34	28,378	859	47	283	52	34.94
69	B. A. Richards	*1964-82*	28,358	576	58	356	80	54.74
70	G. S. Sobers	*1952*-74	28,315	609	93	365*	86	54.87
71	A. E. Dipper	1908-32	28,075	865	69	252*	53	35.27
72	D. G. Bradman	*1927-48*	28,067	338	43	452*	117	95.14
73	J. H. Hampshire	1961-84	28,059	924	112	183*	43	34.55
74	P. B. H. May	1948-63	27,592	618	77	285*	85	51.00
75	B. F. Davison	*1967-87*	27,453	766	79	189	53	39.96
76	Majid Khan	*1961-84*	27,444	700	62	241	73	43.01
77	A. C. Russell	1908-30	27,358	717	59	273	71	41.57
78	E. G. Hayes	1896-1926	27,318	896	48	276	48	32.21
79	A. E. Fagg	1932-57	27,291	803	46	269*	58	36.05
80	James Seymour	1900-26	27,237	911	62	218*	53	32.08
81	W. Larkins	1972-95	27,142	842	54	252	59	34.44
82	**A. R. Border**	***1976-95***	**27,131**	**625**	**97**	**205**	**70**	**51.38**
83	P. H. Parfitt	1956-*73*	26,924	845	104	200*	58	36.33
84	**G. A. Hick**	***1983-96***	**26,895**	**535**	**53**	**405***	**90**	**55.79**
85	G. L. Jessop	1894-1914	26,698	855	37	286	53	32.63
86	K. S. McEwan	*1972-91*	26,628	705	67	218	74	41.73
87	D. E. Davies	1924-54	26,564	1,032	80	287*	32	27.90
88	A. Shrewsbury	1875-1902	26,505	813	90	267	59	36.65
89	M. J. Stewart	1954-72	26,492	898	93	227*	49	32.90
90	C. T. Radley	1964-87	26,441	880	134	200	46	35.44
91	D. I. Gower	1975-93	26,339	727	70	228	53	40.08
92	C. E. B. Rice	*1969-93*	26,331	766	123	246	48	40.95
93	Younis Ahmed	*1961-86*	26,073	762	118	221*	46	40.48
94	P. E. Richardson	1949-65	26,055	794	41	185	44	34.60
95	M. H. Denness	1959-80	25,886	838	65	195	33	33.48
96	S. M. Gavaskar	*1966*-87	25,834	563	61	340	81	51.46
97	J. W. H. Makepeace	1906-30	25,799	778	66	203	43	36.23
98	W. Gunn	1880-1904	25,691	850	72	273	48	33.02
99	W. Watson	1939-64	25,670	753	109	257	55	39.86
100	**R. T. Robinson**	**1978-96**	**25,667**	**668**	**78**	**220***	**61**	**43.50**
101	G. Brown	1908-33	25,649	1,012	52	232*	37	26.71
102	G. M. Emmett	1936-59	25,602	865	50	188	37	31.41
103	J. B. Bolus	1956-75	25,598	833	81	202*	39	34.03
104	W. E. Russell	1956-72	25,525	796	64	193	41	34.87
105	**D. L. Haynes**	***1976-95***	**25,430**	**626**	**71**	**255***	**60**	**45.81**
106	C. J. Barnett	1927-*53*	25,389	821	45	259	48	32.71
107	L. B. Fishlock	1931-52	25,376	699	54	253	56	39.34
108	D. J. Insole	1947-63	25,241	743	72	219*	54	37.61
109	J. M. Brearley	1961-83	25,185	768	102	312*	45	37.81
110	J. Vine	1896-1922	25,171	920	79	202	34	29.92
111	R. M. Prideaux	1958-*74*	25,136	808	75	202*	41	34.29
112	J. H. King	1895-1925	25,122	988	69	227*	34	27.33
113	J. G. Wright	*1975-92*	25,073	636	44	192	59	42.35

Bold type denotes those who played in 1995-96 and 1996 seasons.

Note: Some works of reference provide career figures which differ from those in this list, owing to the exclusion or inclusion of matches recognised or not recognised as first-class by *Wisden*.

Current Players with 20,000 Runs

	Career	R	I	NO	HS	100s	Avge
C. W. J. Athey	1976-96	24,771	763	69	184	54	35.69
K. J. Barnett	1979-96	23,272	646	59	239*	49	39.64
K. C. Wessels	*1973-95*	22,757	498	44	254	60	50.12
P. N. Kirsten	*1973-95*	21,969	551	58	271	55	44.56
R. A. Smith	*1980*-96	20,727	545	77	209*	51	44.28
M. D. Moxon	1981-96	20,572	523	47	274*	44	43.21
T. S. Curtis	1979-96	20,083	556	66	248	39	40.98

CAREER AVERAGE OVER 50

(Qualification: 10,000 runs)

Avge		Career	I	NO	R	HS	100s
95.14	D. G. Bradman	*1927-48*	338	43	28,067	452*	117
71.22	V. M. Merchant	*1929-51*	229	43	13,248	359*	44
65.18	W. H. Ponsford	*1920-34*	235	23	13,819	437	47
64.99	W. M. Woodfull	*1921-34*	245	39	13,388	284	49
58.24	A. L. Hassett	*1932-53*	322	32	16,890	232	59
58.19	V. S. Hazare	*1934-66*	365	45	18,621	316*	60
57.22	A. F. Kippax	*1918-35*	256	33	12,762	315*	43
56.83	G. Boycott	1962-86	1,014	162	48,426	261*	151
56.55	C. L. Walcott	*1941-63*	238	29	11,820	314*	40
56.37	K. S. Ranjitsinhji	1893-1920	500	62	24,692	285*	72
56.22	R. B. Simpson	*1952-77*	436	62	21,029	359	60
56.10	W. R. Hammond	1920-51	1,005	104	50,551	336*	167
56.02	**M. D. Crowe**	***1979-95***	**412**	**62**	**19,608**	**299**	**71**
55.79	**G. A. Hick**	***1983*-96**	**535**	**53**	**26,895**	**405***	**90**
55.51	L. Hutton	1934-60	814	91	40,140	364	129
55.34	E. D. Weekes	*1944-64*	241	24	12,010	304*	36
55.24	**M. E. Waugh**	***1985-95***	**375**	**48**	**18,065**	**229***	**59**
54.87	G. S. Sobers	*1952*-74	609	93	28,315	365*	86
54.74	B. A. Richards	*1964-82*	576	58	28,358	356	80
54.67	R. G. Pollock	*1960-86*	437	54	20,940	274	64
54.24	F. M. M. Worrell	*1941*-64	326	49	15,025	308*	39
53.78	R. M. Cowper	*1959-69*	228	31	10,595	307	26
53.67	A. R. Morris	*1940-63*	250	15	12,614	290	46
53.44	Javed Miandad	*1973-93*	631	95	28,647	311	80
52.86	D. B. Vengsarkar	*1975-91*	390	52	17,868	284	55
52.62	**D. M. Jones**	***1981*-96**	**369**	**40**	**17,313**	**324***	**50**
52.47	**M. Azharuddin**	***1981*-96**	**275**	**30**	**12,857**	**226**	**44**
52.32	Hanif Mohammad	*1951-75*	371	45	17,059	499	55
52.27	P. R. Umrigar	*1944-67*	350	41	16,154	252*	49
52.20	G. S. Chappell	*1966-83*	542	72	24,535	247*	74
51.95	H. Sutcliffe	1919-45	1,088	123	50,138	313	149
51.85	D. C. S. Compton	1936-64	839	88	38,942	300	123
51.54	Zaheer Abbas	*1965-86*	768	92	34,843	274	108
51.53	A. D. Nourse	*1931-52*	269	27	12,472	260*	41
51.46	S. M. Gavaskar	*1966*-87	563	61	25,834	340	81
51.44	W. A. Brown	*1932-49*	284	15	13,838	265*	39
51.38	**A. R. Border**	***1976-95***	**625**	**97**	**27,131**	**205**	**70**
51.27	**S. R. Waugh**	***1984-95***	**322**	**58**	**13,537**	**216***	**38**
51.00	P. B. H. May	1948-63	618	77	27,592	285*	85
50.95	N. C. O'Neill	*1955-67*	306	34	13,859	284	45
50.93	R. N. Harvey	*1946-62*	461	35	21,699	231*	67
50.90	W. M. Lawry	*1955-71*	417	49	18,734	266	50

Avge		*Career*	*I*	*NO*	*R*	*HS*	*100s*
50.90	A. V. Mankad	*1963-82*	326	71	12,980	265	31
50.80	E. H. Hendren	1907-38	1,300	166	57,611	301*	170
50.65	J. B. Hobbs	1905-34	1,315	106	61,237	316*	197
50.58	S. J. Cook	*1972-94*	475	57	21,143	313*	64
50.22	C. B. Fry	1892-*1921*	658	43	30,886	258*	94
50.15	**M. W. Gatting**	**1975-96**	**803**	**118**	**34,357**	**258**	**90**
50.12	**K. C. Wessels**	***1973-95***	**498**	**44**	**22,757**	**254**	**60**
50.01	Shafiq Ahmad	*1967-90*	449	58	19,555	217*	53

Note: G. A. Headley (*1927*-1954) scored 9,921 runs, average 69.86.

Bold type denotes those who played in 1995-96 and 1996 seasons.

FASTEST FIFTIES

Minutes			
11	C. I. J. Smith (66)	Middlesex v Gloucestershire at Bristol	1938
14	S. J. Pegler (50)	South Africans v Tasmania at Launceston	1910-11
14	F. T. Mann (53)	Middlesex v Nottinghamshire at Lord's	1921
14	H. B. Cameron (56)	Transvaal v Orange Free State at Johannesburg	1934-35
14	C. I. J. Smith (52)	Middlesex v Kent at Maidstone	1935

Note: The following fast fifties were scored in contrived circumstances when runs were given from full tosses and long hops to expedite a declaration: C. C. Inman (8 minutes), Leicestershire v Nottinghamshire at Nottingham, 1965; G. Chapple (10 minutes), Lancashire v Glamorgan at Manchester, 1993; T. M. Moody (11 minutes), Warwickshire v Glamorgan at Swansea, 1990; A. J. Stewart (14 minutes), Surrey v Kent at Dartford, 1986; M. P. Maynard (14 minutes), Glamorgan v Yorkshire at Cardiff, 1987.

FASTEST HUNDREDS

Minutes			
35	P. G. H. Fender (113*)	Surrey v Northamptonshire at Northampton	1920
40	G. L. Jessop (101)	Gloucestershire v Yorkshire at Harrogate	1897
40	Ahsan-ul-Haq (100*)	Muslims v Sikhs at Lahore	1923-24
42	G. L. Jessop (191)	Gentlemen of South v Players of South at Hastings	1907
43	A. H. Hornby (106)	Lancashire v Somerset at Manchester	1905
43	D. W. Hookes (107)	South Australia v Victoria at Adelaide	1982-83
44	R. N. S. Hobbs (100)	Essex v Australians at Chelmsford	1975

Notes: The fastest recorded authentic hundred in terms of balls received was scored off 34 balls by D. W. Hookes (above).

Research of the scorebook has shown that P. G. H. Fender scored his hundred from between 40 and 46 balls. He contributed 113 to an unfinished sixth-wicket partnership of 171 in 42 minutes with H. A. Peach.

E. B. Alletson (Nottinghamshire) scored 189 out of 227 runs in 90 minutes against Sussex at Hove in 1911. It has been estimated that his last 139 runs took 37 minutes.

The following fast hundreds were scored in contrived circumstances when runs were given from full tosses and long hops to expedite a declaration: G. Chapple (21 minutes), Lancashire v Glamorgan at Manchester, 1993; T. M. Moody (26 minutes), Warwickshire v Glamorgan at Swansea, 1990; S. J. O'Shaughnessy (35 minutes), Lancashire v Leicestershire at Manchester, 1983; C. M. Old (37 minutes), Yorkshire v Warwickshire at Birmingham, 1977; N. F. M. Popplewell (41 minutes), Somerset v Gloucestershire at Bath, 1983.

FASTEST DOUBLE-HUNDREDS

Minutes			
113	R. J. Shastri (200*)	Bombay v Baroda at Bombay	1984-85
120	G. L. Jessop (286)	Gloucestershire v Sussex at Hove	1903
120	C. H. Lloyd (201*)	West Indians v Glamorgan at Swansea	1976
130	G. L. Jessop (234)	Gloucestershire v Somerset at Bristol	1905
131	V. T. Trumper (293)	Australians v Canterbury at Christchurch	1913-14

FASTEST TRIPLE-HUNDREDS

Minutes			
181	D. C. S. Compton (300)	MCC v N. E. Transvaal at Benoni	1948-49
205	F. E. Woolley (305*)	MCC v Tasmania at Hobart	1911-12
205	C. G. Macartney (345)	Australians v Nottinghamshire at Nottingham	1921
213	D. G. Bradman (369)	South Australia v Tasmania at Adelaide	1935-36

300 RUNS IN ONE DAY

390*	B. C. Lara	Warwickshire v Durham at Birmingham	1994
345	C. G. Macartney	Australians v Nottinghamshire at Nottingham	1921
334	W. H. Ponsford	Victoria v New South Wales at Melbourne	1926-27
333	K. S. Duleepsinhji	Sussex v Northamptonshire at Hove	1930
331*	J. D. Robertson	Middlesex v Worcestershire at Worcester	1949
325*	B. A. Richards	S. Australia v W. Australia at Perth	1970-71
322†	E. Paynter	Lancashire v Sussex at Hove	1937
322	I. V. A. Richards	Somerset v Warwickshire at Taunton	1985
318	C. W. Gregory	New South Wales v Queensland at Brisbane	1906-07
317	K. R. Rutherford	New Zealanders v D. B. Close's XI at Scarborough	1986
316†	R. H. Moore	Hampshire v Warwickshire at Bournemouth	1937
315*	R. C. Blunt	Otago v Canterbury at Christchurch	1931-32
312*	J. M. Brearley	MCC Under-25 v North Zone at Peshawar	1966-67
311*	G. M. Turner	Worcestershire v Warwickshire at Worcester	1982
311*	N. H. Fairbrother	Lancashire v Surrey at The Oval	1990
309*	D. G. Bradman	Australia v England at Leeds	1930
307*	W. H. Ashdown	Kent v Essex at Brentwood	1934
306*	A. Ducat	Surrey v Oxford University at The Oval	1919
305*	F. R. Foster	Warwickshire v Worcestershire at Dudley	1914

† *E. Paynter's 322 and R. H. Moore's 316 were scored on the same day: July 28, 1937.*

These scores do not necessarily represent the complete innings. *See pages 175-177.*

1,000 RUNS IN MAY

	Runs	*Avge*
W. G. Grace, May 9 to May 30, 1895 (22 days):		
13, 103, 18, 25, 288, 52, 257, 73*, 18, 169	1,016	112.88
Grace was within two months of completing his 47th year.		
W. R. Hammond, May 7 to May 31, 1927 (25 days):		
27, 135, 108, 128, 17, 11, 99, 187, 4, 30, 83, 7, 192, 14	1,042	74.42
Hammond scored his 1,000th run on May 28, thus equalling Grace's record of 22 days.		
C. Hallows, May 5 to May 31, 1928 (27 days):		
100, 101, 51*, 123, 101*, 22, 74, 104, 58, 34*, 232	1,000	125.00

1,000 RUNS IN APRIL AND MAY

	Runs	*Avge*
T. W. Hayward, April 16 to May 31, 1900: 120*, 55, 108, 131*, 55, 193, 120, 5, 6, 3, 40, 146, 92	1,074	97.63
D. G. Bradman, April 30 to May 31, 1930: 236, 185*, 78, 9, 48*, 66, 4, 44, 252*, 32, 47*	1,001	143.00
On April 30 Bradman was 75 not out.		
D. G. Bradman, April 30 to May 31, 1938: 258, 58, 137, 278, 2, 143, 145*, 5, 30*	1,056	150.85
Bradman scored 258 on April 30, and his 1,000th run on May 27.		
W. J. Edrich, April 30 to May 31, 1938: 104, 37, 115, 63, 20*, 182, 71, 31, 53*, 45, 15, 245, 0, 9, 20*	1,010	84.16
Edrich was 21 not out on April 30. All his runs were scored at Lord's.		
G. M. Turner, April 24 to May 31, 1973: 41, 151*, 143, 85, 7, 8, 17*, 81, 13, 53, 44, 153*, 3, 2, 66*, 30, 10*, 111	1,018	78.30
G. A. Hick, April 17 to May 29, 1988: 61, 37, 212, 86, 14, 405*, 8, 11, 6, 7, 172	1,019	101.90
Hick scored a record 410 runs in April, and his 1,000th run on May 28.		

1,000 RUNS IN TWO SEPARATE MONTHS

Only four batsmen, C. B. Fry, K. S. Ranjitsinhji, H. Sutcliffe and L. Hutton, have scored over 1,000 runs in each of two months in the same season. L. Hutton, by scoring 1,294 in June 1949, made more runs in a single month than anyone else. He also made 1,050 in August 1949.

MOST RUNS SCORED OFF ONE OVER

(All instances refer to six-ball overs)

36	G. S. Sobers	off M. A. Nash, Nottinghamshire v Glamorgan at Swansea (six sixes)	1968
36	R. J. Shastri	off Tilak Raj, Bombay v Baroda at Bombay (six sixes)	1984-85
34	E. B. Alletson	off E. H. Killick, Nottinghamshire v Sussex at Hove (46604446; including two no-balls)	1911
34	F. C. Hayes	off M. A. Nash, Lancashire v Glamorgan at Swansea (646666)	1977
32	I. T. Botham	off I. R. Snook, England XI v Central Districts at Palmerston North (466466)	1983-84
32	P. W. G. Parker	off A. I. Kallicharran, Sussex v Warwickshire at Birmingham (466664)	1982
32	I. R. Redpath	off N. Rosendorff, Australians v Orange Free State at Bloemfontein (666644)	1969-70
32	C. C. Smart	off G. Hill, Glamorgan v Hampshire at Cardiff (664664)	1935

Notes: The following instances have been excluded from the above table because of the bowlers' compliance: 34 – M. P. Maynard off S. A. Marsh, Glamorgan v Kent at Swansea, 1992; 34 – G. Chapple off P. A. Cottey, Lancashire v Glamorgan at Manchester, 1993; 32 – C. C. Inman off N. W. Hill, Leicestershire v Nottinghamshire at Nottingham, 1965; 32 – T. E. Jesty off R. J. Boyd-Moss, Hampshire v Northamptonshire at Southampton, 1984; 32 – G. Chapple off P. A. Cottey, Lancashire v Glamorgan at Manchester, 1993. Chapple's 34 and 32 came off successive overs from Cottey.

The greatest number of runs scored off an eight-ball over is 34 (40446664) by R. M. Edwards off M. C. Carew, Governor-General's XI v West Indians at Auckland, 1968-69.

In a Shell Trophy match against Canterbury at Christchurch in 1989-90, R. H. Vance (Wellington), acting on the instructions of his captain, deliberately conceded 77 runs in an over of full tosses which contained 17 no-balls and, owing to the umpire's understandable miscalculation, only five legitimate deliveries.

MOST SIXES IN AN INNINGS

16	A. Symonds (254*)	Gloucestershire v Glamorgan at Abergavenny	1995
15	J. R. Reid (296)	Wellington v N. Districts at Wellington	1962-63
14	Shakti Singh (128)	Himachal Pradesh v Haryana at Dharmsala	1990-91
13	Majid Khan (147*)	Pakistanis v Glamorgan at Swansea	1967
13	C. G. Greenidge (273*)	D. H. Robins' XI v Pakistanis at Eastbourne	1974
13	C. G. Greenidge (259)	Hampshire v Sussex at Southampton	1975
13	G. W. Humpage (254)	Warwickshire v Lancashire at Southport	1982
13	R. J. Shastri (200*)	Bombay v Baroda at Bombay	1984-85
12	Gulfraz Khan (207)	Railways v Universities at Lahore	1976-77
12	I. T. Botham (138*)	Somerset v Warwickshire at Birmingham	1985
12	R. A. Harper (234)	Northamptonshire v Gloucestershire at Northampton	1986
12	D. M. Jones (248)	Australians v Warwickshire at Birmingham	1989
12	D. N. Patel (204)	Auckland v Northern Districts at Auckland	1991-92
12	W. V. Raman (206)	Tamil Nadu v Kerala at Madras	1991-92
11	C. K. Nayudu (153)	Hindus v MCC at Bombay	1926-27
11	C. J. Barnett (194)	Gloucestershire v Somerset at Bath	1934
11	R. Benaud (135)	Australians v T. N. Pearce's XI at Scarborough	1953
11	R. Bora (126)	Assam v Tripura at Gauhati	1987-88
11	G. A. Hick (405*)	Worcestershire v Somerset at Taunton	1988

MOST SIXES IN A MATCH

20	A. Symonds (254*, 76)	Gloucestershire v Glamorgan at Abergavenny	1995
17	W. J. Stewart (155, 125)	Warwickshire v Lancashire at Blackpool	1959

MOST SIXES IN A SEASON

80	I. T. Botham	1985
66	A. W. Wellard	1935
57	A. W. Wellard	1936
57	A. W. Wellard	1938
51	A. W. Wellard	1933
49	I. V. A. Richards	1985
48	A. W. Carr	1925
48	J. H. Edrich	1965
48	A. Symonds	1995

MOST BOUNDARIES IN AN INNINGS

	4s/6s			
72	62/10	B. C. Lara (501*)	Warwickshire v Durham at Birmingham	1994
68	68/–	P. A. Perrin (343*)	Essex v Derbyshire at Chesterfield	1904
64	64/–	Hanif Mohammad (499)	Karachi v Bahawalpur at Karachi	1958-59
63	62/1	A. C. MacLaren (424)	Lancashire v Somerset at Taunton	1895
57	52/5	J. H. Edrich (310*)	England v New Zealand at Leeds	1965
55	55/–	C. W. Gregory (383)	NSW v Queensland at Brisbane	1906-07
55	53/2	G. R. Marsh (355*)	W. Australia v S. Australia at Perth	1989-90
54	53/1	G. H. Hirst (341)	Yorkshire v Leicestershire at Leicester	1905
54	51/2†	S. V. Manjrekar (377)	Bombay v Hyderabad at Bombay	1990-91
53	53/–	A. W. Nourse (304*)	Natal v Transvaal at Johannesburg	1919-20
53	45/8	K. R. Rutherford (317)	New Zealanders v D. B. Close's XI at Scarborough	1986
52	47/5	N. H. Fairbrother (366)	Lancashire v Surrey at The Oval	1990
51	47/4	C. G. Macartney (345)	Australians v Notts. at Nottingham	1921
51	50/1	B. B. Nimbalkar (443*)	Maharashtra v Kathiawar at Poona	1948-49
50	46/4	D. G. Bradman (369)	S. Australia v Tasmania at Adelaide	1935-36
50	47/–‡	A. Ducat (306*)	Surrey v Oxford U. at The Oval	1919
50	35/15	J. R. Reid (296)	Wellington v N. Districts at Wellington	1962-63
50	42/8	I. V. A. Richards (322)	Somerset v Warwickshire at Taunton	1985

† Plus one five.
‡ Plus three fives.

HIGHEST PARTNERSHIPS

577	V. S. Hazare (288) and Gul Mahomed (319), fourth wicket, Baroda v Holkar at Baroda	1946-47
574*	F. M. M. Worrell (255*) and C. L. Walcott (314*), fourth wicket, Barbados v Trinidad at Port-of-Spain	1945-46
561	Waheed Mirza (324) and Mansoor Akhtar (224*), first wicket, Karachi Whites v Quetta at Karachi	1976-77
555	P. Holmes (224*) and H. Sutcliffe (313), first wicket, Yorkshire v Essex at Leyton	1932
554	J. T. Brown (300) and J. Tunnicliffe (243), first wicket, Yorkshire v Derbyshire at Chesterfield	1898
502*	F. M. M. Worrell (308*) and J. D. C. Goddard (218*), fourth wicket, Barbados v Trinidad at Bridgetown	1943-44
490	E. H. Bowley (283) and J. G. Langridge (195), first wicket, Sussex v Middlesex at Hove	1933
487*	G. A. Headley (344*) and C. C. Passailaigue (261*), sixth wicket, Jamaica v Lord Tennyson's XI at Kingston	1931-32
475	Zahir Alam (257) and L. S. Rajput (239), second wicket, Assam v Tripura at Gauhati	1991-92
470	A. I. Kallicharran (230*) and G. W. Humpage (254), fourth wicket, Warwickshire v Lancashire at Southport	1982

HIGHEST PARTNERSHIPS FOR EACH WICKET

The following lists include all stands above 400; otherwise the top ten for each wicket.

First Wicket

561	Waheed Mirza and Mansoor Akhtar, Karachi Whites v Quetta at Karachi	1976-77
555	P. Holmes and H. Sutcliffe, Yorkshire v Essex at Leyton	1932
554	J. T. Brown and J. Tunnicliffe, Yorkshire v Derbyshire at Chesterfield	1898
490	E. H. Bowley and J. G. Langridge, Sussex v Middlesex at Hove	1933
464	R. Sehgal and R. Lamba, Delhi v Himachal Pradesh at Delhi	1994-95
456	E. R. Mayne and W. H. Ponsford, Victoria v Queensland at Melbourne	1923-24
451*	S. Desai and R. M. H. Binny, Karnataka v Kerala at Chikmagalur	1977-78
431	M. R. J. Veletta and G. R. Marsh, Western Australia v South Australia at Perth	1989-90
428	J. B. Hobbs and A. Sandham, Surrey v Oxford University at The Oval	1926
424	I. J. Siedle and J. F. W. Nicolson, Natal v Orange Free State at Bloemfontein	1926-27
421	S. M. Gavaskar and G. A. Parkar, Bombay v Bengal at Bombay	1981-82
418	Kamal Najamuddin and Khalid Alvi, Karachi v Railways at Karachi	1980-81
413	V. Mankad and Pankaj Roy, India v New Zealand at Madras	1955-56
405	C. P. S. Chauhan and M. S. Gupte, Maharashtra v Vidarbha at Poona	1972-73

Second Wicket

475	Zahir Alam and L. S. Rajput, Assam v Tripura at Gauhati	1991-92
465*	J. A. Jameson and R. B. Kanhai, Warwicks. v Gloucestershire at Birmingham	1974
455	K. V. Bhandarkar and B. B. Nimbalkar, Maharashtra v Kathiawar at Poona	1948-49
451	W. H. Ponsford and D. G. Bradman, Australia v England at The Oval	1934
446	C. C. Hunte and G. S. Sobers, West Indies v Pakistan at Kingston	1957-58
429*	J. G. Dewes and G. H. G. Doggart, Cambridge U. v Essex at Cambridge	1949
426	Arshad Pervez and Mohsin Khan, Habib Bank v Income Tax at Lahore	1977-78

415	A. D. Jadeja and S. V. Manjrekar, Indians v Bowl XI at Springs	1992-93
403	G. A. Gooch and P. J. Prichard, Essex v Leicestershire at Chelmsford	1990
398	A. Shrewsbury and W. Gunn, Nottinghamshire v Sussex at Nottingham	1890

Third Wicket

467	A. H. Jones and M. D. Crowe, New Zealand v Sri Lanka at Wellington	1990-91
456	Khalid Irtiza and Aslam Ali, United Bank v Multan at Karachi	1975-76
451	Mudassar Nazar and Javed Miandad, Pakistan v India at Hyderabad	1982-83
445	P. E. Whitelaw and W. N. Carson, Auckland v Otago at Dunedin	1936-37
434	J. B. Stollmeyer and G. E. Gomez, Trinidad v British Guiana at Port-of-Spain	1946-47
424*	W. J. Edrich and D. C. S. Compton, Middlesex v Somerset at Lord's	1948
413	D. J. Bicknell and D. M. Ward, Surrey v Kent at Canterbury	1990
410*	R. S. Modi and L. Amarnath, India in England v The Rest at Calcutta	1946-47
405	A. D. Jadeja and A. S. Kaypee, Haryana v Services at Faridabad	1991-92
399	R. T. Simpson and D. C. S. Compton, MCC v N. E. Transvaal at Benoni	1948-49

Fourth Wicket

577	V. S. Hazare and Gul Mahomed, Baroda v Holkar at Baroda	1946-47
574*	C. L. Walcott and F. M. M. Worrell, Barbados v Trinidad at Port-of-Spain	1945-46
502*	F. M. M. Worrell and J. D. C. Goddard, Barbados v Trinidad at Bridgetown	1943-44
470	A. I. Kallicharran and G. W. Humpage, Warwicks. v Lancs. at Southport	1982
462*	D. W. Hookes and W. B. Phillips, South Australia v Tasmania at Adelaide	1986-87
448	R. Abel and T. W. Hayward, Surrey v Yorkshire at The Oval	1899
425*	A. Dale and I. V. A. Richards, Glamorgan v Middlesex at Cardiff	1993
424	I. S. Lee and S. O. Quin, Victoria v Tasmania at Melbourne	1933-34
411	P. B. H. May and M. C. Cowdrey, England v West Indies at Birmingham	1957
410	G. Abraham and P. Balan Pandit, Kerala v Andhra at Palghat	1959-60
402	W. Watson and T. W. Graveney, MCC v British Guiana at Georgetown	1953-54
402	R. B. Kanhai and K. Ibadulla, Warwicks. v Notts. at Nottingham	1968

Fifth Wicket

464*	M. E. Waugh and S. R. Waugh, New South Wales v Western Australia at Perth	1990-91
405	S. G. Barnes and D. G. Bradman, Australia v England at Sydney	1946-47
397	W. Bardsley and C. Kelleway, New South Wales v South Australia at Sydney	1920-21
393	E. G. Arnold and W. B. Burns, Worcestershire v Warwickshire at Birmingham	1909
391	A. Malhotra and S. Dogra, Delhi v Services at Delhi	1995-96
360	U. M. Merchant and M. N. Raiji, Bombay v Hyderabad at Bombay	1947-48
355	Altaf Shah and Tariq Bashir, HBFC v Multan at Multan	1976-77
355	A. J. Lamb and J. J. Strydom, OFS v Eastern Province at Bloemfontein	1987-88
347	D. Brookes and D. W. Barrick, Northamptonshire v Essex at Northampton	1952
344	M. C. Cowdrey and T. W. Graveney, MCC v South Australia at Adelaide	1962-63

Sixth Wicket

487*	G. A. Headley and C. C. Passailaigue, Jamaica v Lord Tennyson's XI at Kingston	1931-32
428	W. W. Armstrong and M. A. Noble, Australians v Sussex at Hove	1902
411	R. M. Poore and E. G. Wynyard, Hampshire v Somerset at Taunton	1899
376	R. Subba Row and A. Lightfoot, Northamptonshire v Surrey at The Oval	1958
371	V. M. Merchant and R. S. Modi, Bombay v Maharashtra at Bombay	1943-44
356	W. V. Raman and A. Kripal Singh, Tamil Nadu v Goa at Panjim	1988-89
353	Salah-ud-Din and Zaheer Abbas, Karachi v East Pakistan at Karachi	1968-69
346	J. H. W. Fingleton and D. G. Bradman, Australia v England at Melbourne	1936-37
337	R. R. Montgomerie and D. J. Capel, Northamptonshire v Kent at Canterbury	1995
332	N. G. Marks and G. Thomas, New South Wales v South Australia at Sydney	1958-59

Seventh Wicket

460	Bhupinder Singh, jun. and P. Dharmani, Punjab v Delhi at Delhi	1994-95
347	D. St E. Atkinson and C. C. Depeiza, West Indies v Australia at Bridgetown	1954-55
344	K. S. Ranjitsinhji and W. Newham, Sussex v Essex at Leyton	1902
340	K. J. Key and H. Philipson, Oxford University v Middlesex at Chiswick Park	1887
336	F. C. W. Newman and C. R. N. Maxwell, Sir J. Cahn's XI v Leicestershire at Nottingham	1935
335	C. W. Andrews and E. C. Bensted, Queensland v New South Wales at Sydney	1934-35
325	G. Brown and C. H. Abercrombie, Hampshire v Essex at Leyton	1913
323	E. H. Hendren and L. F. Townsend, MCC v Barbados at Bridgetown	1929-30
308	Waqar Hassan and Imtiaz Ahmed, Pakistan v New Zealand at Lahore	1955-56
301	C. C. Lewis and B. N. French, Nottinghamshire v Durham at Chester-le-Street	1993

Eighth Wicket

433	V. T. Trumper and A. Sims, A. Sims' Aust. XI v Canterbury at Christchurch	1913-14
292	R. Peel and Lord Hawke, Yorkshire v Warwickshire at Birmingham	1896
270	V. T. Trumper and E. P. Barbour, New South Wales v Victoria at Sydney	1912-13
263	D. R. Wilcox and R. M. Taylor, Essex v Warwickshire at Southend	1946
255	E. A. V. Williams and E. A. Martindale, Barbados v Trinidad at Bridgetown	1935-36
249*	Shaukat Mirza and Akram Raza, Habib Bank v PNSC at Lahore	1993-94
246	L. E. G. Ames and G. O. B. Allen, England v New Zealand at Lord's	1931
243	R. J. Hartigan and C. Hill, Australia v England at Adelaide	1907-08
242*	T. J. Zoehrer and K. H. MacLeay, W. Australia v New South Wales at Perth	1990-91
240	Gulfraz Khan and Raja Sarfraz, Railways v Universities at Lahore	1976-77

Ninth Wicket

283	J. Chapman and A. Warren, Derbyshire v Warwickshire at Blackwell	1910
268	J. B. Commins and N. Boje, South Africa A v Mashonaland at Harare	1994-95
251	J. W. H. T. Douglas and S. N. Hare, Essex v Derbyshire at Leyton	1921
245	V. S. Hazare and N. D. Nagarwalla, Maharashtra v Baroda at Poona	1939-40
244*	Arshad Ayub and M. V. Ramanamurthy, Hyderabad v Bihar at Hyderabad	1986-87
239	H. B. Cave and I. B. Leggat, Central Districts v Otago at Dunedin	1952-53
232	C. Hill and E. Walkley, South Australia v New South Wales at Adelaide	1900-01
231	P. Sen and J. Mitter, Bengal v Bihar at Jamshedpur	1950-51
230	D. A. Livingstone and A. T. Castell, Hampshire v Surrey at Southampton	1962
226	C. Kelleway and W. A. Oldfield, New South Wales v Victoria at Melbourne	1925-26

Tenth Wicket

307	A. F. Kippax and J. E. H. Hooker, New South Wales v Victoria at Melbourne	1928-29
249	C. T. Sarwate and S. N. Banerjee, Indians v Surrey at The Oval	1946
235	F. E. Woolley and A. Fielder, Kent v Worcestershire at Stourbridge	1909
233	Ajay Sharma and Maninder Singh, Delhi v Bombay at Bombay	1991-92
230	R. W. Nicholls and W. Roche, Middlesex v Kent at Lord's	1899
228	R. Illingworth and K. Higgs, Leicestershire v Northamptonshire at Leicester	1977
218	F. H. Vigar and T. P. B. Smith, Essex v Derbyshire at Chesterfield	1947
211	M. Ellis and T. J. Hastings, Victoria v South Australia at Melbourne	1902-03
196*	Nadim Yousuf and Maqsood Kundi, MCB v National Bank at Lahore	1981-82
192	H. A. W. Bowell and W. H. Livsey, Hampshire v Worcs. at Bournemouth	1921

Note: Three of the above partnerships were affected by TCCB or ACB regulations governing no-balls. The stand between A. Dale and I. V. A. Richards (fourth wicket) included 13 runs for no-balls instead of the five that would have applied under the Laws of Cricket; between M. E. and S. R. Waugh (fifth wicket) 20 instead of seven; between R. R. Montgomerie and D. J. Capel (sixth wicket) nine instead of four.

UNUSUAL DISMISSALS

Handled the Ball

J. Grundy	MCC v Kent at Lord's	1857
G. Bennett	Kent v Sussex at Hove	1872
W. H. Scotton	Smokers v Non-Smokers at East Melbourne	1886-87
C. W. Wright	Nottinghamshire v Gloucestershire at Bristol	1893
E. Jones	South Australia v Victoria at Melbourne	1894-95
A. W. Nourse	South Africans v Sussex at Hove	1907
E. T. Benson	MCC v Auckland at Auckland	1929-30
A. W. Gilbertson	Otago v Auckland at Auckland	1952-53
W. R. Endean	South Africa v England at Cape Town	1956-57
P. J. Burge	Queensland v New South Wales at Sydney	1958-59
Dildar Awan	Services v Lahore at Lahore	1959-60
M. Mehra	Railways v Delhi at Delhi	1959-60
Mahmood-ul-Hasan	Karachi University v Railways-Quetta at Karachi	1960-61
Ali Raza	Karachi Greens v Hyderabad at Karachi	1961-62
Mohammad Yusuf	Rawalpindi v Peshawar at Peshawar	1962-63
A. Rees	Glamorgan v Middlesex at Lord's	1965
Pervez Akhtar	Multan v Karachi Greens at Sahiwal	1971-72
Javed Mirza	Railways v Punjab at Lahore	1972-73
R. G. Pollock	Eastern Province v Western Province at Cape Town	1973-74
C. I. Dey	Northern Transvaal v Orange Free State at Bloemfontein	1973-74
Nasir Valika	Karachi Whites v National Bank at Karachi	1974-75
Haji Yousuf	National Bank v Railways at Lahore	1974-75
Masood-ul-Hasan	PIA v National Bank B at Lyallpur	1975-76
D. K. Pearse	Natal v Western Province at Cape Town	1978-79
A. M. J. Hilditch	Australia v Pakistan at Perth	1978-79
Musleh-ud-Din	Railways v Lahore at Lahore	1979-80
Jalal-ud-Din	IDBP v Habib Bank at Bahawalpur	1981-82
Mohsin Khan	Pakistan v Australia at Karachi	1982-83
D. L. Haynes	West Indies v India at Bombay	1983-84
K. Azad	Delhi v Punjab at Amritsar	1983-84
Athar A. Khan	Allied Bank v HBFC at Sialkot	1983-84
A. N. Pandya	Saurashtra v Baroda at Baroda	1984-85
G. L. Linton	Barbados v Windward Islands at Bridgetown	1985-86
R. B. Gartrell	Tasmania v Victoria at Melbourne	1986-87
R. Nayyar	Himachal Pradesh v Punjab at Una	1988-89
R. Weerawardene	Moratuwa v Nomads SC at Colombo	1988-89
A. M. Kane	Vidarbha v Railways at Nagpur	1989-90
P. Bali	Jammu and Kashmir v Services at Delhi	1991-92
M. J. Davis	Northern Transvaal B v OFS B at Bloemfontein	1991-92
J. T. C. Vaughan	Emerging Players v England XI at Hamilton	1991-92
G. A. Gooch	England v Australia at Manchester	1993
A. C. Waller	Mashonaland CD v Mashonaland Under-24 at Harare	1994-95
K. M. Krikken	Derbyshire v Indians at Derby	1996

Obstructing the Field

C. A. Absolom	Cambridge University v Surrey at The Oval	1868
T. Straw	Worcestershire v Warwickshire at Worcester	1899
T. Straw	Worcestershire v Warwickshire at Birmingham	1901
J. P. Whiteside	Leicestershire v Lancashire at Leicester	1901
L. Hutton	England v South Africa at The Oval	1951
J. A. Hayes	Canterbury v Central Districts at Christchurch	1954-55
D. D. Deshpande	Madhya Pradesh v Uttar Pradesh at Benares	1956-57
K. Ibadulla	Warwickshire v Hampshire at Coventry	1963
Qaiser Khan	Dera Ismail Khan v Railways at Lahore	1964-65
Ijaz Ahmed	Lahore Greens v Lahore Blues at Lahore	1973-74

Qasim Feroze	Bahawalpur v Universities at Lahore	1974-75
T. Quirk	Northern Transvaal v Border at East London	1978-79
Mahmood Rashid	United Bank v Muslim Commercial Bank at Bahawalpur	1981-82
Arshad Ali	Sukkur v Quetta at Quetta	1983-84
H. R. Wasu	Vidarbha v Rajasthan at Akola	1984-85
Khalid Javed	Railways v Lahore at Lahore	1985-86
C. Binduhewa	Singha SC v Sinhalese SC at Colombo	1990-91
S. J. Kalyani	Bengal v Orissa at Calcutta	1994-95

Hit the Ball Twice

H. E. Bull	MCC v Oxford University at Lord's	1864
H. R. J. Charlwood	Sussex v Surrey at Hove	1872
R. G. Barlow	North v South at Lord's	1878
P. S. Wimble	Transvaal v Griqualand West at Kimberley	1892-93
G. B. Nicholls	Somerset v Gloucestershire at Bristol	1896
A. A. Lilley	Warwickshire v Yorkshire at Birmingham	1897
J. H. King	Leicestershire v Surrey at The Oval	1906
A. P. Binns	Jamaica v British Guiana at Georgetown	1956-57
K. Bhavanna	Andhra v Mysore at Guntur	1963-64
Zaheer Abbas	PIA A v Karachi Blues at Karachi	1969-70
Anwar Miandad	IDBP v United Bank at Lahore	1979-80
Anwar Iqbal	Hyderabad v Sukkur at Hyderabad	1983-84
Iqtidar Ali	Allied Bank v Muslim Commercial Bank at Lahore	1983-84
Aziz Malik	Lahore Division v Faisalabad at Sialkot	1984-85
Javed Mohammad	Multan v Karachi Whites at Sahiwal	1986-87
Shahid Pervez	Jammu and Kashmir v Punjab at Srinagar	1986-87

BOWLING RECORDS

TEN WICKETS IN AN INNINGS

	O	*M*	*R*		
E. Hinkly (Kent)				v England at Lord's	1848
*J. Wisden (North)				v South at Lord's	1850
V. E. Walker (England)	43	17	74	v Surrey at The Oval	1859
V. E. Walker (Middlesex)	44.2	5	104	v Lancashire at Manchester	1865
G. Wootton (All England)	31.3	9	54	v Yorkshire at Sheffield	1865
W. Hickton (Lancashire)	36.2	19	46	v Hampshire at Manchester	1870
S. E. Butler (Oxford)	24.1	11	38	v Cambridge at Lord's	1871
James Lillywhite (South)	60.2	22	129	v North at Canterbury	1872
A. Shaw (MCC)	36.2	8	73	v North at Lord's	1874
E. Barratt (Players)	29	11	43	v Australians at The Oval	1878
G. Giffen (Australian XI)	26	10	66	v The Rest at Sydney	1883-84
W. G. Grace (MCC)	36.2	17	49	v Oxford University at Oxford	1886
G. Burton (Middlesex)	52.3	25	59	v Surrey at The Oval	1888
†A. E. Moss (Canterbury)	21.3	10	28	v Wellington at Christchurch	1889-90
S. M. J. Woods (Cambridge U.)	31	6	69	v Thornton's XI at Cambridge	1890
T. Richardson (Surrey)	15.3	3	45	v Essex at The Oval	1894
H. Pickett (Essex)	27	11	32	v Leicestershire at Leyton	1895
E. J. Tyler (Somerset)	34.3	15	49	v Surrey at Taunton	1895
W. P. Howell (Australians)	23.2	14	28	v Surrey at The Oval	1899
C. H. G. Bland (Sussex)	25.2	10	48	v Kent at Tonbridge	1899
J. Briggs (Lancashire)	28.5	7	55	v Worcestershire at Manchester	1900
A. E. Trott (Middlesex)	14.2	5	42	v Somerset at Taunton	1900
A. Fielder (Players)	24.5	1	90	v Gentlemen at Lord's	1906
E. G. Dennett (Gloucestershire)	19.4	7	40	v Essex at Bristol	1906
A. E. E. Vogler (E. Province)	12	2	26	v Griqualand W. at Johannesburg	1906-07

	O	M	R		
C. Blythe (Kent)	16	7	30	v Northants at Northampton	1907
A. Drake (Yorkshire)	8.5	0	35	v Somerset at Weston-s-Mare	1914
W. Bestwick (Derbyshire)	19	2	40	v Glamorgan at Cardiff	1921
A. A. Mailey (Australians)	28.4	5	66	v Gloucestershire at Cheltenham	1921
C. W. L. Parker (Glos.)	40.3	13	79	v Somerset at Bristol	1921
T. Rushby (Surrey)	17.5	4	43	v Somerset at Taunton	1921
J. C. White (Somerset)	42.2	11	76	v Worcestershire at Worcester	1921
G. C. Collins (Kent)	19.3	4	65	v Nottinghamshire at Dover	1922
H. Howell (Warwickshire)	25.1	5	51	v Yorkshire at Birmingham	1923
A. S. Kennedy (Players)	22.4	10	37	v Gentlemen at The Oval	1927
G. O. B. Allen (Middlesex)	25.3	10	40	v Lancashire at Lord's	1929
A. P. Freeman (Kent)	42	9	131	v Lancashire at Maidstone	1929
G. Geary (Leicestershire)	16.2	8	18	v Glamorgan at Pontypridd	1929
C. V. Grimmett (Australians)	22.3	8	37	v Yorkshire at Sheffield	1930
A. P. Freeman (Kent)	30.4	8	53	v Essex at Southend	1930
H. Verity (Yorkshire)	18.4	6	36	v Warwickshire at Leeds	1931
A. P. Freeman (Kent)	36.1	9	79	v Lancashire at Manchester	1931
V. W. C. Jupp (Northants)	39	6	127	v Kent at Tunbridge Wells	1932
H. Verity (Yorkshire)	19.4	16	10	v Nottinghamshire at Leeds	1932
T. W. Wall (South Australia)	12.4	2	36	v New South Wales at Sydney	1932-33
T. B. Mitchell (Derbyshire)	19.1	4	64	v Leicestershire at Leicester	1935
J. Mercer (Glamorgan)	26	10	51	v Worcestershire at Worcester	1936
T. W. J. Goddard (Glos.)	28.4	4	113	v Worcestershire at Cheltenham	1937
T. F. Smailes (Yorkshire)	17.1	5	47	v Derbyshire at Sheffield	1939
E. A. Watts (Surrey)	24.1	8	67	v Warwickshire at Birmingham	1939
*W. E. Hollies (Warwickshire)	20.4	4	49	v Notts at Birmingham	1946
J. M. Sims (East)	18.4	2	90	v West at Kingston	1948
T. E. Bailey (Essex)	39.4	9	90	v Lancashire at Clacton	1949
J. K. Graveney (Glos.)	18.4	2	66	v Derbyshire at Chesterfield	1949
R. Berry (Lancashire)	36.2	9	102	v Worcestershire at Blackpool	1953
S. P. Gupte (President's XI)	24.2	7	78	v Combined XI at Bombay	1954-55
J. C. Laker (Surrey)	46	18	88	v Australians at The Oval	1956
J. C. Laker (England)	51.2	23	53	v Australia at Manchester	1956
G. A. R. Lock (Surrey)	29.1	18	54	v Kent at Blackheath	1956
K. Smales (Nottinghamshire)	41.3	20	66	v Gloucestershire at Stroud	1956
P. M. Chatterjee (Bengal)	19	11	20	v Assam at Jorhat	1956-57
J. D. Bannister (Warwickshire)	23.3	11	41	v Comb. Services at Birmingham‡	1959
A. J. G. Pearson (Cambridge U.)	30.3	8	78	v Leics at Loughborough	1961
N. I. Thomson (Sussex)	34.2	19	49	v Warwickshire at Worthing	1964
P. J. Allan (Queensland)	15.6	3	61	v Victoria at Melbourne	1965-66
I. J. Brayshaw (W. Australia)	17.6	4	44	v Victoria at Perth	1967-68
Shahid Mahmood (Karachi Whites)	25	5	58	v Khairpur at Karachi	1969-70
E. E. Hemmings (International XI)	49.3	14	175	v West Indies XI at Kingston	1982-83
P. Sunderam (Rajasthan)	22	5	78	v Vidarbha at Jodhpur	1985-86
S. T. Jefferies (W. Province)	22.5	7	59	v Orange Free State at Cape Town	1987-88
Imran Adil (Bahawalpur)	22.5	3	92	v Faisalabad at Faisalabad	1989-90
G. P. Wickremasinghe (Sinhalese SC)	19.2	5	41	v Kalutara at Colombo (SSC)	1991-92
R. L. Johnson (Middlesex)	18.5	6	45	v Derbyshire at Derby	1994
Naeem Akhtar (Rawalpindi B)	21.3	10	28	v Peshawar at Peshawar	1995-96

Note: The following instances were achieved in 12-a-side matches:

E. M. Grace (MCC)	32.2	7	69	v Gents of Kent at Canterbury	1862
W. G. Grace (MCC)	46.1	15	92	v Kent at Canterbury	1873
†D. C. S. Hinds (A. B. St Hill's XII)	19.1	6	36	v Trinidad at Port-of-Spain	1900-01

* *J. Wisden and W. E. Hollies achieved the feat without the direct assistance of a fielder. Wisden's ten were all bowled; Hollies bowled seven and had three lbw.*

† *On debut in first-class cricket.* ‡ *Mitchells & Butlers Ground.*

OUTSTANDING ANALYSES

	O	M	R	W		
H. Verity (Yorkshire)	19.4	16	10	10	v Nottinghamshire at Leeds	1932
G. Elliott (Victoria)	19	17	2	9	v Tasmania at Launceston	1857-58
Ahad Khan (Railways)	6.3	4	7	9	v Dera Ismail Khan at Lahore	1964-65
J. C. Laker (England)	14	12	2	8	v The Rest at Bradford	1950
D. Shackleton (Hampshire)	11.1	7	4	8	v Somerset at Weston-s-Mare	1955
E. Peate (Yorkshire)	16	11	5	8	v Surrey at Holbeck	1883
F. R. Spofforth (Australians)	8.3	6	3	7	v England XI at Birmingham	1884
W. A. Henderson (N.E. Transvaal)	9.3	7	4	7	v Orange Free State at Bloemfontein	1937-38
Rajinder Goel (Haryana)	7	4	4	7	v Jammu and Kashmir at Chandigarh	1977-78
V. I. Smith (South Africans)	4.5	3	1	6	v Derbyshire at Derby	1947
S. Cosstick (Victoria)	21.1	20	1	6	v Tasmania at Melbourne	1868-69
Israr Ali (Bahawalpur)	11	10	1	6	v Dacca U. at Bahawalpur	1957-58
A. D. Pougher (MCC)	3	3	0	5	v Australians at Lord's	1896
G. R. Cox (Sussex)	6	6	0	5	v Somerset at Weston-s-Mare	1921
R. K. Tyldesley (Lancashire)	5	5	0	5	v Leicestershire at Manchester	1924
P. T. Mills (Gloucestershire)	6.4	6	0	5	v Somerset at Bristol	1928

MOST WICKETS IN A MATCH

19-90	J. C. Laker	England v Australia at Manchester	1956
17-48	C. Blythe	Kent v Northamptonshire at Northampton	1907
17-50	C. T. B. Turner	Australians v England XI at Hastings	1888
17-54	W. P. Howell	Australians v Western Province at Cape Town	1902-03
17-56	C. W. L. Parker	Gloucestershire v Essex at Gloucester	1925
17-67	A. P. Freeman	Kent v Sussex at Hove	1922
17-89	W. G. Grace	Gloucestershire v Nottinghamshire at Cheltenham	1877
17-89	F. C. L. Matthews	Nottinghamshire v Northants at Nottingham	1923
17-91	H. Dean	Lancashire v Yorkshire at Liverpool	1913
17-91	H. Verity	Yorkshire v Essex at Leyton	1933
17-92	A. P. Freeman	Kent v Warwickshire at Folkestone	1932
17-103	W. Mycroft	Derbyshire v Hampshire at Southampton	1876
17-106	G. R. Cox	Sussex v Warwickshire at Horsham	1926
17-106	T. W. J. Goddard	Gloucestershire v Kent at Bristol	1939
17-119	W. Mead	Essex v Hampshire at Southampton	1895
17-137	W. Brearley	Lancashire v Somerset at Manchester	1905
17-159	S. F. Barnes	England v South Africa at Johannesburg	1913-14
17-201	G. Giffen	South Australia v Victoria at Adelaide	1885-86
17-212	J. C. Clay	Glamorgan v Worcestershire at Swansea	1937

SIXTEEN OR MORE WICKETS IN A DAY

17-48	C. Blythe	Kent v Northamptonshire at Northampton	1907
17-91	H. Verity	Yorkshire v Essex at Leyton	1933
17-106	T. W. J. Goddard	Gloucestershire v Kent at Bristol	1939
16-38	T. Emmett	Yorkshire v Cambridgeshire at Hunslet	1869
16-52	J. Southerton	South v North at Lord's	1875
16-69	T. G. Wass	Nottinghamshire v Lancashire at Liverpool	1906
16-38	A. E. E. Vogler	E. Province v Griqualand West at Johannesburg	1906-07
16-103	T. G. Wass	Nottinghamshire v Essex at Nottingham	1908
16-83	J. C. White	Somerset v Worcestershire at Bath	1919

FOUR WICKETS WITH CONSECUTIVE BALLS

J. Wells	Kent v Sussex at Brighton	1862
G. Ulyett	Lord Harris's XI v New South Wales at Sydney	1878-79
G. Nash	Lancashire v Somerset at Manchester	1882
J. B. Hide	Sussex v MCC and Ground at Lord's	1890
F. J. Shacklock	Nottinghamshire v Somerset at Nottingham	1893
A. D. Downes	Otago v Auckland at Dunedin	1893-94
F. Martin	MCC and Ground v Derbyshire at Lord's	1895
A. W. Mold	Lancashire v Nottinghamshire at Nottingham	1895
W. Brearley†	Lancashire v Somerset at Manchester	1905
S. Haigh	MCC v Army XI at Pretoria	1905-06
A. E. Trott‡	Middlesex v Somerset at Lord's	1907
F. A. Tarrant	Middlesex v Gloucestershire at Bristol	1907
A. Drake	Yorkshire v Derbyshire at Chesterfield	1914
S. G. Smith	Northamptonshire v Warwickshire at Birmingham	1914
H. A. Peach	Surrey v Sussex at The Oval	1924
A. F. Borland	Natal v Griqualand West at Kimberley	1926-27
J. E. H. Hooker†	New South Wales v Victoria at Sydney	1928-29
R. K. Tyldesley†	Lancashire v Derbyshire at Derby	1929
R. J. Crisp	Western Province v Griqualand West at Johannesburg	1931-32
R. J. Crisp	Western Province v Natal at Durban	1933-34
A. R. Gover	Surrey v Worcestershire at Worcester	1935
W. H. Copson	Derbyshire v Warwickshire at Derby	1937
W. A. Henderson	N.E. Transvaal v Orange Free State at Bloemfontein	1937-38
F. Ridgway	Kent v Derbyshire at Folkestone	1951
A. K. Walker§	Nottinghamshire v Leicestershire at Leicester	1956
S. N. Mohol	President's XI v Combined XI at Poona	1965-66
P. I. Pocock	Surrey v Sussex at Eastbourne	1972
S. S. Saini†	Delhi v Himachal Pradesh at Delhi	1988-89
D. Dias	W. Province (Suburbs) v Central Province at Colombo	1990-91
Ali Gauhar	Karachi Blues v United Bank at Peshawar	1994-95
K. D. James**	Hampshire v Indians at Southampton	1996

† *Not all in the same innings.*
‡ *Trott achieved another hat-trick in the same innings of this, his benefit match.*
§ *Having bowled Firth with the last ball of the first innings, Walker achieved a unique feat by dismissing Lester, Tompkin and Smithson with the first three balls of the second.*
** *James also scored a century, a unique double.*

Notes: In their match with England at The Oval in 1863, Surrey lost four wickets in the course of a four-ball over from G. Bennett.

Sussex lost five wickets in the course of the final (six-ball) over of their match with Surrey at Eastbourne in 1972. P. I. Pocock, who had taken three wickets in his previous over, captured four more, taking in all seven wickets with 11 balls, a feat unique in first-class matches. (The eighth wicket fell to a run-out.)

HAT-TRICKS

Double Hat-Trick

Besides Trott's performance, which is given in the preceding section, the following instances are recorded of players having performed the hat-trick twice in the same match, Rao doing so in the same innings.

A. Shaw	Nottinghamshire v Gloucestershire at Nottingham	1884
T. J. Matthews	Australia v South Africa at Manchester	1912
C. W. L. Parker	Gloucestershire v Middlesex at Bristol	1924
R. O. Jenkins	Worcestershire v Surrey at Worcester	1949
J. S. Rao	Services v Northern Punjab at Amritsar	1963-64
Amin Lakhani	Combined XI v Indians at Multan	1978-79

Five Wickets in Six Balls

W. H. Copson	Derbyshire v Warwickshire at Derby	1937
W. A. Henderson	N.E. Transvaal v Orange Free State at Bloemfontein	1937-38
P. I. Pocock	Surrey v Sussex at Eastbourne	1972

Most Hat-Tricks

Seven times: D. V. P. Wright.

Six times: T. W. J. Goddard, C. W. L. Parker.

Five times: S. Haigh, V. W. C. Jupp, A. E. G. Rhodes, F. A. Tarrant.

Four times: R. G. Barlow, J. T. Hearne, J. C. Laker, G. A. R. Lock, G. G. Macaulay, T. J. Matthews, M. J. Procter, T. Richardson, F. R. Spofforth, F. S. Trueman.

Three times: W. M. Bradley, H. J. Butler, S. T. Clarke, W. H. Copson, R. J. Crisp, J. W. H. T. Douglas, J. A. Flavell, A. P. Freeman, G. Giffen, D. W. Headley, K. Higgs, A. Hill, W. A. Humphreys, R. D. Jackman, R. O. Jenkins, A. S. Kennedy, W. H. Lockwood, E. A. McDonald, T. L. Pritchard, J. S. Rao, A. Shaw, J. B. Statham, M. W. Tate, H. Trumble, D. Wilson, G. A. Wilson.

Twice (current players only): D. G. Cork, M. D. Marshall, P. A. Smith.

HAT-TRICK ON DEBUT

H. Hay	South Australia v Lord Hawke's XI at Unley, Adelaide	1902-03
H. A. Sedgwick	Yorkshire v Worcestershire at Hull	1906
V. B. Ranjane	Maharashtra v Saurashtra at Poona	1956-57
J. S. Rao	Services v Jammu & Kashmir at Delhi	1963-64
R. O. Estwick	Barbados v Guyana at Bridgetown	1982-83
S. A. Ankola	Maharashtra v Gujarat at Poona	1988-89
J. Srinath	Karnataka v Hyderabad at Secunderabad	1989-90
S. P. Mukherjee	Bengal v Hyderabad at Secunderabad	1989-90

Notes: R. R. Phillips (Border) took a hat-trick in his first over in first-class cricket (v Eastern Province at Port Elizabeth, 1939-40) having previously played in four matches without bowling.

J. S. Rao took two more hat-tricks in his next match.

250 WICKETS IN A SEASON

	Season	*O*	*M*	*R*	*W*	*Avge*
A. P. Freeman	1928	1,976.1	423	5,489	304	18.05
A. P. Freeman	1933	2,039	651	4,549	298	15.26
T. Richardson	1895‡	1,690.1	463	4,170	290	14.37
C. T. B. Turner**	1888†	2,427.2	1,127	3,307	283	11.68
A. P. Freeman	1931	1,618	360	4,307	276	15.60
A. P. Freeman	1930	1,914.3	472	4,632	275	16.84
T. Richardson	1897‡	1,603.4	495	3,945	273	14.45
A. P. Freeman	1929	1,670.5	381	4,879	267	18.27
W. Rhodes	1900	1,553	455	3,606	261	13.81
J. T. Hearne	1896	2,003.1	818	3,670	257	14.28
A. P. Freeman	1932	1,565.5	404	4,149	253	16.39
W. Rhodes	1901	1,565	505	3,797	251	15.12

† *Indicates 4-ball overs;* ‡ *5-ball overs.*
** *Exclusive of matches not reckoned as first-class.*

Notes: In four consecutive seasons (1928-31), A. P. Freeman took 1,122 wickets, and in eight consecutive seasons (1928-35), 2,090 wickets. In each of these eight seasons he took over 200 wickets.

T. Richardson took 1,005 wickets in four consecutive seasons (1894-97).

In 1896, J. T. Hearne took his 100th wicket as early as June 12. In 1931, C. W. L. Parker did the same and A. P. Freeman obtained his 100th wicket a day later.

LEADING BOWLERS IN AN ENGLISH SEASON

(Qualification: 10 wickets in 10 innings)

Season	*Leading wicket-taker*	*Wkts*	*Avge*	*Top of averages*	*Wkts*	*Avge*
1946	W. E. Hollies	184	15.60	A. Booth	111	11.61
1947	T. W. J. Goddard	238	17.30	J. C. Clay	65	16.44
1948	J. E. Walsh	174	19.56	J. C. Clay	41	14.17
1949	R. O. Jenkins	183	21.19	T. W. J. Goddard	160	19.18
1950	R. Tattersall	193	13.59	R. Tattersall	193	13.59
1951	R. Appleyard	200	14.14	R. Appleyard	200	14.14
1952	J. H. Wardle	177	19.54	F. S. Trueman	61	13.78
1953	B. Dooland	172	16.58	C. J. Knott	38	13.71
1954	B. Dooland	196	15.48	J. B. Statham	92	14.13
1955	G. A. R. Lock	216	14.49	R. Appleyard	85	13.01
1956	D. J. Shepherd	177	15.36	G. A. R. Lock	155	12.46
1957	G. A. R. Lock	212	12.02	G. A. R. Lock	212	12.02
1958	G. A. R. Lock	170	12.08	H. L. Jackson	143	10.99
1959	D. Shackleton	148	21.55	J. B. Statham	139	15.01
1960	F. S. Trueman	175	13.98	J. B. Statham	135	12.31
1961	J. A. Flavell	171	17.79	J. A. Flavell	171	17.79
1962	D. Shackleton	172	20.15	C. Cook	58	17.13
1963	D. Shackleton	146	16.75	C. C. Griffith	119	12.83
1964	D. Shackleton	142	20.40	J. A. Standen	64	13.00
1965	D. Shackleton	144	16.08	H. J. Rhodes	119	11.04
1966	D. L. Underwood	157	13.80	D. L. Underwood	157	13.80
1967	T. W. Cartwright	147	15.52	D. L. Underwood	136	12.39
1968	R. Illingworth	131	14.36	O. S. Wheatley	82	12.95
1969	R. M. H. Cottam	109	21.04	A. Ward	69	14.82
1970	D. J. Shepherd	106	19.16	Majid Khan	11	18.81
1971	L. R. Gibbs	131	18.89	G. G. Arnold	83	17.12
1972	T. W. Cartwright B. Stead	98 98	18.64 20.38	I. M. Chappell	10	10.60
1973	B. S. Bedi	105	17.94	T. W. Cartwright	89	15.84
1974	A. M. E. Roberts	119	13.62	A. M. E. Roberts	119	13.62
1975	P. G. Lee	112	18.45	A. M. E. Roberts	57	15.80
1976	G. A. Cope	93	24.13	M. A. Holding	55	14.38
1977	M. J. Procter	109	18.04	R. A. Woolmer	19	15.21
1978	D. L. Underwood	110	14.49	D. L. Underwood	110	14.49
1979	D. L. Underwood J. K. Lever	106 106	14.85 17.30	J. Garner	55	13.83
1980	R. D. Jackman	121	15.40	J. Garner	49	13.93
1981	R. J. Hadlee	105	14.89	R. J. Hadlee	105	14.89
1982	M. D. Marshall	134	15.73	R. J. Hadlee	61	14.57
1983	J. K. Lever D. L. Underwood	106 106	16.28 19.28	Imran Khan	12	7.16
1984	R. J. Hadlee	117	14.05	R. J. Hadlee	117	14.05
1985	N. V. Radford	101	24.68	R. M. Ellison	65	17.20
1986	C. A. Walsh	118	18.17	M. D. Marshall	100	15.08
1987	N. V. Radford	109	20.81	R. J. Hadlee	97	12.64
1988	F. D. Stephenson	125	18.31	M. D. Marshall	42	13.16
1989	D. R. Pringle S. L. Watkin	94 94	18.64 25.09	T. M. Alderman	70	15.64
1990	N. A. Foster	94	26.61	I. R. Bishop	59	19.05
1991	Waqar Younis	113	14.65	Waqar Younis	113	14.65
1992	C. A. Walsh	92	15.96	C. A. Walsh	92	15.96
1993	S. L. Watkin	92	22.80	Wasim Akram	59	19.27
1994	M. M. Patel	90	22.86	C. E. L. Ambrose	77	14.45
1995	A. Kumble	105	20.40	A. A. Donald	89	16.07
1996	C. A. Walsh	85	16.84	C. E. L. Ambrose	43	16.67

100 WICKETS IN A SEASON

Since Reduction of Championship Matches in 1969

Five times: D. L. Underwood 110 (1978), 106 (1979), 106 (1983), 102 (1971), 101 (1969).
Four times: J. K. Lever 116 (1984), 106 (1978), 106 (1979), 106 (1983).
Twice: B. S. Bedi 112 (1974), 105 (1973); T. W. Cartwright 108 (1969), 104 (1971); N. A. Foster 105 (1986), 102 (1991); N. Gifford 105 (1970), 104 (1983); R. J. Hadlee 117 (1984), 105 (1981); P. G. Lee 112 (1975), 101 (1973); M. D. Marshall 134 (1982), 100 (1986); M. J. Procter 109 (1977), 108 (1969); N. V. Radford 109 (1987), 101 (1985); F. J. Titmus 105 (1970), 104 (1971).
Once: J. P. Agnew 101 (1987); I. T. Botham 100 (1978); K. E. Cooper 101 (1988); R. M. H. Cottam 109 (1969); D. R. Doshi 101 (1980); J. E. Emburey 103 (1983); L. R. Gibbs 131 (1971); R. N. S. Hobbs 102 (1970); Intikhab Alam 104 (1971); R. D. Jackman 121 (1980); A. Kumble 105 (1995); A. M. E. Roberts 119 (1974); P. J. Sainsbury 107 (1971); Sarfraz Nawaz 101 (1975); M. W. W. Selvey 101 (1978); D. J. Shepherd 106 (1970); F. D. Stephenson 125 (1988); C. A. Walsh 118 (1986); Waqar Younis 113 (1991); D. Wilson 102 (1969).

100 WICKETS IN A SEASON MOST TIMES

(Includes Overseas Tours and Seasons)

23 times: W. Rhodes 200 wkts (3).
20 times: D. Shackleton (In successive seasons – 1949 to 1968 inclusive).
17 times: A. P. Freeman 300 wkts (1), 200 wkts (7).
16 times: T. W. J. Goddard 200 wkts (4), C. W. L. Parker 200 wkts (5), R. T. D. Perks, F. J. Titmus.
15 times: J. T. Hearne 200 wkts (3), G. H. Hirst 200 wkts (1), A. S. Kennedy 200 wkts (1).
14 times: C. Blythe 200 wkts (1), W. E. Hollies, G. A. R. Lock 200 wkts (2), M. W. Tate 200 wkts (3), J. C. White.
13 times: J. B. Statham.
12 times: J. Briggs, E. G. Dennett 200 wkts (1), C. Gladwin, D. J. Shepherd, N. I. Thomson, F. S. Trueman.
11 times: A. V. Bedser, G. Geary, S. Haigh, J. C. Laker, M. S. Nichols, A. E. Relf.
10 times: W. Attewell, W. G. Grace, R. Illingworth, H. L. Jackson, V. W. C. Jupp, G. G. Macaulay 200 wkts (1), W. Mead, T. B. Mitchell, T. Richardson 200 wkts (3), J. Southerton 200 wkts (1), R. K. Tyldesley, D. L. Underwood, J. H. Wardle, T. G. Wass, D. V. P. Wright.
9 times: W. E. Astill, T. E. Bailey, W. E. Bowes, C. Cook, R. Howorth, J. Mercer, A. W. Mold 200 wkts (2), J. A. Newman, C. F. Root 200 wkts (1), A. Shaw 200 wkts (1), H. Verity 200 wkts (3).
8 times: T. W. Cartwright, H. Dean, J. A. Flavell, A. R. Gover 200 wkts (2), H. Larwood, G. A. Lohmann 200 wkts (3), R. Peel, J. M. Sims, F. A. Tarrant, R. Tattersall, G. J. Thompson, G. E. Tribe, A. W. Wellard, F. E. Woolley, J. A. Young.

100 WICKETS IN A SEASON OUTSIDE ENGLAND

W		*Season*	*Country*	*R*	*Avge*
116	M. W. Tate	1926-27	India/Ceylon	1,599	13.78
107	Ijaz Faqih	1985-86	Pakistan	1,719	16.06
106	C. T. B. Turner	1887-88	Australia	1,441	13.59
106	R. Benaud	1957-58	South Africa	2,056	19.39
105	Murtaza Hussain	1995-96	Pakistan	1,882	17.92
104	S. F. Barnes	1913-14	South Africa	1,117	10.74
104	Sajjad Akbar	1989-90	Pakistan	2,328	22.38
103	Abdul Qadir	1982-83	Pakistan	2,367	22.98

1,500 WICKETS IN A CAREER

Dates in italics denote the first half of an overseas season; i.e. *1970* denotes the 1970-71 season.

		Career	*W*	*R*	*Avge*
1	W. Rhodes	1898-1930	4,187	69,993	16.71
2	A. P. Freeman	1914-36	3,776	69,577	18.42
3	C. W. L. Parker	1903-35	3,278	63,817	19.46
4	J. T. Hearne	1888-1923	3,061	54,352	17.75
5	T. W. J. Goddard	1922-52	2,979	59,116	19.84
6	W. G. Grace	1865-1908	2,876	51,545	17.92
7	A. S. Kennedy	1907-36	2,874	61,034	21.23
8	D. Shackleton	1948-69	2,857	53,303	18.65
9	G. A. R. Lock	1946-*70*	2,844	54,709	19.23
10	F. J. Titmus	1949-82	2,830	63,313	22.37
11	M. W. Tate	1912-37	2,784	50,571	18.16
12	G. H. Hirst	1891-1929	2,739	51,282	18.72
13	C. Blythe	1899-1914	2,506	42,136	16.81
14	D. L. Underwood	1963-87	2,465	49,993	20.28
15	W. E. Astill	1906-39	2,431	57,783	23.76
16	J. C. White	1909-37	2,356	43,759	18.57
17	W. E. Hollies	1932-57	2,323	48,656	20.94
18	F. S. Trueman	1949-69	2,304	42,154	18.29
19	J. B. Statham	1950-68	2,260	36,999	16.37
20	R. T. D. Perks	1930-55	2,233	53,770	24.07
21	J. Briggs	1879-1900	2,221	35,431	15.95
22	D. J. Shepherd	1950-72	2,218	47,302	21.32
23	E. G. Dennett	1903-26	2,147	42,571	19.82
24	T. Richardson	1892-1905	2,104	38,794	18.43
25	T. E. Bailey	1945-67	2,082	48,170	23.13
26	R. Illingworth	1951-83	2,072	42,023	20.28
27	N. Gifford	1960-88	2,068	48,731	23.56
	F. E. Woolley	1906-38	2,068	41,066	19.85
29	G. Geary	1912-38	2,063	41,339	20.03
30	D. V. P. Wright	1932-57	2,056	49,307	23.98
31	J. A. Newman	1906-30	2,032	51,111	25.15
32	†A. Shaw	1864-97	2,027	24,580	12.12
33	S. Haigh	1895-1913	2,012	32,091	15.94
34	H. Verity	1930-39	1,956	29,146	14.90
35	W. Attewell	1881-1900	1,951	29,896	15.32
36	J. C. Laker	1946-*64*	1,944	35,791	18.41
37	A. V. Bedser	1939-60	1,924	39,279	20.41
38	W. Mead	1892-1913	1,916	36,388	18.99
39	A. E. Relf	1900-21	1,897	39,724	20.94
40	P. G. H. Fender	1910-36	1,894	47,458	25.05
41	J. W. H. T. Douglas	1901-30	1,893	44,159	23.32
42	J. H. Wardle	1946-*67*	1,846	35,027	18.97
43	G. R. Cox	1895-1928	1,843	42,136	22.86
44	G. A. Lohmann	1884-*97*	1,841	25,295	13.73
45	J. W. Hearne	1909-36	1,839	44,926	24.42
46	G. G. Macaulay	1920-35	1,837	32,440	17.65
47	M. S. Nichols	1924-39	1,833	39,666	21.63
48	J. B. Mortimore	1950-75	1,807	41,904	23.18
49	C. Cook	1946-64	1,782	36,578	20.52
50	R. Peel	1882-99	1,752	28,442	16.23
51	H. L. Jackson	1947-63	1,733	30,101	17.36
52	J. K. Lever	1967-89	1,722	41,772	24.25
53	T. P. B. Smith	1929-52	1,697	45,059	26.55
54	J. Southerton	1854-79	1,681	24,290	14.44
55	A. E. Trott	*1892*-1911	1,674	35,317	21.09
56	A. W. Mold	1889-1901	1,673	26,010	15.54

		Career	W	R	Avge
57	T. G. Wass	1896-1920	1,666	34,092	20.46
58	V. W. C. Jupp	1909-38	1,658	38,166	23.01
59	C. Gladwin	1939-58	1,653	30,265	18.30
60	**M. D. Marshall**	***1977-95***	**1,651**	**31,548**	**19.10**
61	W. E. Bowes	1928-47	1,639	27,470	16.76
62	A. W. Wellard	1927-50	1,614	39,302	24.35
63	P. I. Pocock	1964-86	1,607	42,648	26.53
64	**J. E. Emburey**	**1973-96**	**1,604**	**41,699**	**25.99**
65	N. I. Thomson	1952-72	1,597	32,867	20.58
66	J. Mercer	1919-47	1,591	37,210	23.38
	G. J. Thompson	1897-1922	1,591	30,058	18.89
68	J. M. Sims	1929-53	1,581	39,401	24.92
69	T. Emmett	1866-88	1,571	21,314	13.56
	Intikhab Alam	*1957*-82	1,571	43,474	27.67
71	B. S. Bedi	*1961-81*	1,560	33,843	21.69
72	W. Voce	1927-52	1,558	35,961	23.08
73	A. R. Gover	1928-48	1,555	36,753	23.63
74	T. W. Cartwright	1952-77	1,536	29,357	19.11
	K. Higgs	1958-86	1,536	36,267	23.61
76	James Langridge	1924-53	1,530	34,524	22.56
77	J. A. Flavell	1949-67	1,529	32,847	21.48
78	E. E. Hemmings	1966-95	1,515	44,403	29.30
79	C. F. Root	1910-33	1,512	31,933	21.11
	F. A. Tarrant	*1898-1936*	1,512	26,450	17.49
81	R. K. Tyldesley	1919-35	1,509	25,980	17.21

Bold type denotes those who played in 1995-96 and 1996 seasons.

† *The figures for A. Shaw exclude one wicket for which no analysis is available.*

Note: Some works of reference provide career figures which differ from those in this list, owing to the exclusion or inclusion of matches recognised or not recognised as first-class by *Wisden*.

Current Players with 1,000 Wickets

	Career	W	R	Avge
C. A. Walsh	*1981*-96	1,404	31,022	22.09
J. H. Childs	1975-96	1,028	30,600	29.76

ALL-ROUND RECORDS

HUNDRED AND TEN WICKETS IN AN INNINGS

V. E. Walker, England v Surrey at The Oval; 20*, 108, ten for 74, and four for 17. 1859
W. G. Grace, MCC v Oxford University at Oxford; 104, two for 60, and ten for 49. 1886

Note: E. M. Grace, for MCC v Gentlemen of Kent in a 12-a-side match at Canterbury in 1862, scored 192* and took five for 77 and ten for 69.

TWO HUNDRED RUNS AND SIXTEEN WICKETS

G. Giffen, South Australia v Victoria at Adelaide; 271, nine for 96, and seven for 70. 1891-92

HUNDRED IN EACH INNINGS AND FIVE WICKETS TWICE

G. H. Hirst, Yorkshire v Somerset at Bath; 111, 117*, six for 70, and five for 45. 1906

HUNDRED IN EACH INNINGS AND TEN WICKETS

B. J. T. Bosanquet, Middlesex v Sussex at Lord's; 103, 100*, three for 75, and eight for 53 ... 1905
F. D. Stephenson, Nottinghamshire v Yorkshire at Nottingham; 111, 117, four for 105, and seven for 117 ... 1988

HUNDRED AND FOUR WICKETS WITH CONSECUTIVE BALLS

K. D. James, Hampshire v Indians at Southampton; 103 and five for 74 including four wickets with consecutive balls ... 1996

HUNDRED AND HAT-TRICK

G. Giffen, Australians v Lancashire at Manchester; 13, 113, and six for 55 including hat-trick ... 1884
W. E. Roller, Surrey v Sussex at The Oval; 204, four for 28 including hat-trick, and two for 16. (Unique instance of 200 and hat-trick.) ... 1885
W. B. Burns, Worcestershire v Gloucestershire at Worcester; 102*, three for 56 including hat-trick, and two for 21 ... 1913
V. W. C. Jupp, Sussex v Essex at Colchester; 102, six for 61 including hat-trick, and six for 78 ... 1921
R. E. S. Wyatt, MCC v Ceylon at Colombo; 124 and five for 39 including hat-trick. 1926-27
L. N. Constantine, West Indians v Northamptonshire at Northampton; seven for 45 including hat-trick, 107, and six for 67 ... 1928
D. E. Davies, Glamorgan v Leicestershire at Leicester; 139, four for 27, and three for 31 including hat-trick ... 1937
V. M. Merchant, Dr C. R. Pereira's XI v Sir Homi Mehta's XI at Bombay; 1, 142, three for 31 including hat-trick, and no wicket for 17 ... 1946-47
M. J. Procter, Gloucestershire v Essex at Westcliff-on-Sea; 51, 102, three for 43, and five for 30 including hat-trick (all lbw) ... 1972
M. J. Procter, Gloucestershire v Leicestershire at Bristol; 122, no wkt for 32, and seven for 26 including hat-trick ... 1979

Note: W. G. Grace, for MCC v Kent in a 12-a-side match at Canterbury in 1874, scored 123 and took five for 82 and six for 47 including a hat-trick.

SEASON DOUBLES

2,000 Runs and 200 Wickets

1906 G. H. Hirst 2,385 runs and 208 wickets

3,000 Runs and 100 Wickets

1937 J. H. Parks 3,003 runs and 101 wickets

2,000 Runs and 100 Wickets

	Season	R	W
W. G. Grace	1873	2,139	106
W. G. Grace	1876	2,622	129
C. L. Townsend	1899	2,440	101
G. L. Jessop	1900	2,210	104
G. H. Hirst	1904	2,501	132
G. H. Hirst	1905	2,266	110
W. Rhodes	1909	2,094	141
W. Rhodes	1911	2,261	117
F. A. Tarrant	1911	2,030	111
J. W. Hearne	1913	2,036	124
J. W. Hearne	1914	2,116	123
F. E. Woolley	1914	2,272	125
J. W. Hearne	1920	2,148	142
V. W. C. Jupp	1921	2,169	121
F. E. Woolley	1921	2,101	167
F. E. Woolley	1922	2,022	163
F. E. Woolley	1923	2,091	101
L. F. Townsend	1933	2,268	100
D. E. Davies	1937	2,012	103
James Langridge	1937	2,082	101
T. E Bailey	1959	2,011	100

1,000 Runs and 200 Wickets

	Season	R	W		Season	R	W
A. E. Trott	1899	1,175	239	M. W. Tate	1923	1,168	219
A. E. Trott	1900	1,337	211	M. W. Tate	1924	1,419	205
A. S. Kennedy	1922	1,129	205	M. W. Tate	1925	1,290	228

1,000 Runs and 100 Wickets

Sixteen times: W. Rhodes.
Fourteen times: G. H. Hirst.
Ten times: V. W. C. Jupp.
Nine times: W. E. Astill.
Eight times: T. E. Bailey, W. G. Grace, M. S. Nichols, A. E. Relf, F. A. Tarrant, M. W. Tate†, F. J. Titmus, F. E. Woolley.
Seven times: G. E. Tribe.
Six times: P. G. H. Fender, R. Illingworth, James Langridge.
Five times: J. W. H. T. Douglas, J. W. Hearne, A. S. Kennedy, J. A. Newman.
Four times: E. G. Arnold, J. Gunn, R. Kilner, B. R. Knight.
Three times: W. W. Armstrong (Australians), L. C. Braund, G. Giffen (Australians), N. E. Haig, R. Howorth, C. B. Llewellyn, J. B. Mortimore, Ray Smith, S. G. Smith, L. F. Townsend, A. W. Wellard.

† *M. W. Tate also scored 1,193 runs and took 116 wickets for MCC in first-class matches on the 1926-27 MCC tour of India and Ceylon.*

Note: R. J. Hadlee (1984) and F. D. Stephenson (1988) are the only players to perform the feat since the reduction of County Championship matches. A complete list of those performing the feat before then will be found on p. 202 of the 1982 *Wisden*.

Wicket-Keeper's Double

	Season	R	D
L. E. G. Ames	1928	1,919	122
L. E. G. Ames	1929	1,795	128
L. E. G. Ames	1932	2,482	104
J. T. Murray	1957	1,025	104

20,000 RUNS AND 2,000 WICKETS IN A CAREER

	Career	R	Avge	W	Avge	Doubles
W. E. Astill	1906-39	22,731	22.55	2,431	23.76	9
T. E. Bailey	1945-67	28,641	33.42	2,082	23.13	8
W. G. Grace	1865-1908	54,896	39.55	2,876	17.92	8
G. H. Hirst	1891-1929	36,323	34.13	2,739	18.72	14
R. Illingworth	1951-83	24,134	28.06	2,072	20.28	6
W. Rhodes	1898-1930	39,802	30.83	4,187	16.71	16
M. W. Tate	1912-37	21,717	25.01	2,784	18.16	8
F. J. Titmus	1949-82	21,588	23.11	2,830	22.37	8
F. E. Woolley	1906-38	58,969	40.75	2,068	19.85	8

WICKET-KEEPING RECORDS

MOST DISMISSALS IN AN INNINGS

9 (8ct, 1st)	Tahir Rashid	Habib Bank v PACO at Gujranwala	1992-93
9 (7ct, 2st)	W. R. James*	Matabeleland v Mashonaland CD at Bulawayo	1995-96
8 (all ct)	A. T. W. Grout	Queensland v Western Australia at Brisbane	1959-60
8 (all ct)†	D. E. East	Essex v Somerset at Taunton	1985
8 (all ct)	S. A. Marsh‡	Kent v Middlesex at Lord's	1991
8 (6ct, 2st)	T. J. Zoehrer	Australians v Surrey at The Oval	1993
7 (4ct, 3st)	E. J. Smith	Warwickshire v Derbyshire at Birmingham	1926
7 (6ct, 1st)	W. Farrimond	Lancashire v Kent at Manchester	1930
7 (all ct)	W. F. F. Price	Middlesex v Yorkshire at Lord's	1937
7 (3ct, 4st)	D. Tallon	Queensland v Victoria at Brisbane	1938-39
7 (all ct)	R. A. Saggers	New South Wales v Combined XI at Brisbane	1940-41
7 (1ct, 6st)	H. Yarnold	Worcestershire v Scotland at Dundee	1951
7 (4ct, 3st)	J. Brown	Scotland v Ireland at Dublin	1957
7 (6ct, 1st)	N. Kirsten	Border v Rhodesia at East London	1959-60
7 (all ct)	M. S. Smith	Natal v Border at East London	1959-60
7 (all ct)	K. V. Andrew	Northamptonshire v Lancashire at Manchester	1962
7 (all ct)	A. Long	Surrey v Sussex at Hove	1964
7 (all ct)	R. M. Schofield	Central Districts v Wellington at Wellington	1964-65
7 (all ct)	R. W. Taylor	Derbyshire v Glamorgan at Derby	1966
7 (6ct, 1st)	H. B. Taber	New South Wales v South Australia at Adelaide	1968-69
7 (6ct, 1st)	E. W. Jones	Glamorgan v Cambridge University at Cambridge	1970
7 (6ct, 1st)	S. Benjamin	Central Zone v North Zone at Bombay	1973-74
7 (all ct)	R. W. Taylor	Derbyshire v Yorkshire at Chesterfield	1975
7 (6ct, 1st)	Shahid Israr	Karachi Whites v Quetta at Karachi	1976-77
7 (4ct, 3st)	Wasim Bari	PIA v Sind at Lahore	1977-78
7 (all ct)	J. A. Maclean	Queensland v Victoria at Melbourne	1977-78
7 (5ct, 2st)	Taslim Arif	National Bank v Punjab at Lahore	1978-79
7 (all ct)	Wasim Bari	Pakistan v New Zealand at Auckland	1978-79
7 (all ct)	R. W. Taylor	England v India at Bombay	1979-80
7 (all ct)	D. L. Bairstow	Yorkshire v Derbyshire at Scarborough	1982
7 (6ct, 1st)	R. B. Phillips	Queensland v New Zealanders at Bundaberg	1982-83
7 (3ct, 4st)	Masood Iqbal	Habib Bank v Lahore at Lahore	1982-83
7 (3ct, 4st)	Arif-ud-Din	United Bank v PACO at Sahiwal	1983-84
7 (6ct, 1st)	R. J. East	OFS v Western Province B at Cape Town	1984-85
7 (all ct)	B. A. Young	Northern Districts v Canterbury at Christchurch	1986-87
7 (all ct)	D. J. Richardson	Eastern Province v OFS at Bloemfontein	1988-89
7 (6ct, 1st)	Dildar Malik	Multan v Faisalabad at Sahiwal	1988-89
7 (all ct)	W. K. Hegg	Lancashire v Derbyshire at Chesterfield	1989
7 (all ct)	Imran Zia	Bahawalpur v Faisalabad at Faisalabad	1989-90
7 (all ct)	I. D. S. Smith	New Zealand v Sri Lanka at Hamilton	1990-91
7 (all ct)	J. F. Holyman	Tasmania v Western Australia at Hobart	1990-91
7 (all ct)	P. J. L. Radley	OFS v Western Province at Cape Town	1990-91
7 (all ct)	C. P. Metson	Glamorgan v Derbyshire at Chesterfield	1991
7 (all ct)	H. M. de Vos	W. Transvaal v E. Transvaal at Potchefstroom	1993-94
7 (all ct)	P. Kirsten	Griqualand West v W. Transvaal at Potchefstroom	1993-94
7 (6ct, 1st)	S. A. Marsh	Kent v Durham at Canterbury	1994
7 (all ct)	K. J. Piper	Warwickshire v Essex at Birmingham	1994
7 (6ct, 1st)	K. J. Piper	Warwickshire v Derbyshire at Chesterfield	1994
7 (all ct)	H. H. Devapriya	Colts CC v Sinhalese SC at Colombo	1995-96
7 (all ct)	D. J. R. Campbell	Mashonaland CD v Matabeleland at Bulawayo	1995-96
7 (all ct)	A. C. Gilchrist	Western Australia v South Australia at Perth	1995-96
7 (all ct)	C. W. Scott	Durham v Yorkshire at Chester-le-Street	1996

* *W. R. James also scored 99 and 99 not out.* † *The first eight wickets to fall.* ‡ *S. A. Marsh also scored 108 not out.*

WICKET-KEEPERS' HAT-TRICKS

W. H. Brain, Gloucestershire v Somerset at Cheltenham, 1893 – three stumpings off successive balls from C. L. Townsend.

G. O. Dawkes, Derbyshire v Worcestershire at Kidderminster, 1958 – three catches off successive balls from H. L. Jackson.

R. C. Russell, Gloucestershire v Surrey at The Oval, 1986 – three catches off successive balls from C. A. Walsh and D. V. Lawrence (2).

MOST DISMISSALS IN A MATCH

13 (11ct, 2st)	W. R. James*	Matabeleland v Mashonaland CD at Bulawayo	1995-96
12 (8ct, 4st)	E. Pooley	Surrey v Sussex at The Oval	1868
12 (9ct, 3st)	D. Tallon	Queensland v New South Wales at Sydney	1938-39
12 (9ct, 3st)	H. B. Taber	New South Wales v South Australia at Adelaide.	1968-69
11 (all ct)	A. Long	Surrey v Sussex at Hove	1964
11 (all ct)	R. W. Marsh	Western Australia v Victoria at Perth	1975-76
11 (all ct)	D. L. Bairstow	Yorkshire v Derbyshire at Scarborough	1982
11 (all ct)	W. K. Hegg	Lancashire v Derbyshire at Chesterfield	1989
11 (all ct)	A. J. Stewart	Surrey v Leicestershire at Leicester	1989
11 (all ct)	T. J. Nielsen	South Australia v Western Australia at Perth	1990-91
11 (10ct, 1st)	I. A. Healy	Australians v N. Transvaal at Verwoerdburg	1993-94
11 (10ct, 1st)	K. J. Piper	Warwickshire v Derbyshire at Chesterfield	1994
11 (all ct)	D. S. Berry	Victoria v Pakistanis at Melbourne	1995-96
11 (10ct, 1st)	W. A. Seccombe	Queensland v Western Australia at Brisbane	1995-96
11 (all ct)	R. C. Russell	England v South Africa (Second Test) at Johannesburg	1995-96

* *W. R. James also scored 99 and 99 not out.*

MOST DISMISSALS IN A SEASON

128 (79ct, 49st)	L. E. G. Ames	Kent	1929
122 (70ct, 52st)	L. E. G. Ames	Kent	1928
110 (63ct, 47st)	H. Yarnold	Worcestershire	1949
107 (77ct, 30st)	G. Duckworth	Lancashire	1928
107 (96ct, 11st)	J. G. Binks	Yorkshire	1960
104 (40ct, 64st)	L. E. G. Ames	Kent	1932
104 (82ct, 22st)	J. T. Murray	Middlesex	1957
102 (69ct, 33st)	F. H. Huish	Kent	1913
102 (95ct, 7st)	J. T. Murray	Middlesex	1960
101 (62ct, 39st)	F. H. Huish	Kent	1911
101 (85ct, 16st)	R. Booth	Worcestershire	1960
100 (91ct, 9st)	R. Booth	Worcestershire	1964

MOST DISMISSALS IN A CAREER

Dates in italics denote the first half of an overseas season; i.e. *1914* denotes the 1914-15 season.

		Career	*M*	*Ct*	*St*	*Total*
1	R. W. Taylor	1960-88	639	1,473	176	1,649
2	J. T. Murray	1952-75	635	1,270	257	1,527
3	H. Strudwick	1902-27	675	1,242	255	1,497
4	A. P. E. Knott	1964-85	511	1,211	133	1,344
5	F. H. Huish	1895-1914	497	933	377	1,310
6	B. Taylor	1949-73	572	1,083	211	1,294
7	D. Hunter	1889-1909	548	906	347	1,253

		Career	*M*	*Ct*	*St*	*Total*
8	H. R. Butt	1890-1912	550	953	275	1,228
9	J. H. Board	1891-*1914*	525	852	355	1,207
10	H. Elliott	1920-47	532	904	302	1,206
11	J. M. Parks	1949-76	739	1,088	93	1,181
12	R. Booth	1951-70	468	948	178	1,126
13	L. E. G. Ames	1926-51	593	703	418†	1,121
14	D. L. Bairstow	1970-90	459	961	138	1,099
15	G. Duckworth	1923-47	504	753	343	1,096
16	H. W. Stephenson	1948-64	462	748	334	1,082
17	J. G. Binks	1955-75	502	895	176	1,071
18	T. G. Evans	1939-69	465	816	250	1,066
19	A. Long	1960-80	452	922	124	1,046
20	G. O. Dawkes	1937-61	482	895	148	1,043
21	R. W. Tolchard	1965-83	483	912	125	1,037
22	W. L. Cornford	1921-47	496	675	342	1,017

† *Record.*

Current Players with 500 Dismissals

	Career	*M*	*Ct*	*St*	*Total*
R. C. Russell	1981-96	347	838	104	942
S. J. Rhodes	1981-96	309	773	104	877
C. P. Metson	1981-96	230	557	50	607
S. A. Marsh	1982-96	242	557	48	605
D. Ripley	1984-96	230	496	67	563
D. J. Richardson	*1977-95*	177	512	35	547
W. K. Hegg	1986-96	203	485	61	546
I. A. Healy	*1986-95*	156	478	44	522
R. J. Blakey	1985-96	240	468	42	510
P. Moores	1983-96	211	464	44	508

FIELDING RECORDS

(Excluding wicket-keepers)

MOST CATCHES IN AN INNINGS

7	M. J. Stewart	Surrey v Northamptonshire at Northampton	1957
7	A. S. Brown	Gloucestershire v Nottinghamshire at Nottingham	1966

MOST CATCHES IN A MATCH

10	W. R. Hammond†	Gloucestershire v Surrey at Cheltenham	1928
8	W. B. Burns	Worcestershire v Yorkshire at Bradford	1907
8	F. G. Travers	Europeans v Parsees at Bombay	1923-24
8	A. H. Bakewell	Northamptonshire v Essex at Leyton	1928
8	W. R. Hammond	Gloucestershire v Worcestershire at Cheltenham	1932
8	K. J. Grieves	Lancashire v Sussex at Manchester	1951
8	C. A. Milton	Gloucestershire v Sussex at Hove	1952
8	G. A. R. Lock	Surrey v Warwickshire at The Oval	1957
8	J. M. Prodger	Kent v Gloucestershire at Cheltenham	1961
8	P. M. Walker	Glamorgan v Derbyshire at Swansea	1970
8	Masood Anwar	Rawalpindi v Lahore Division at Rawalpindi	1983-84
8	M. C. J. Ball	Gloucestershire v Yorkshire at Cheltenham	1994

† *Hammond also scored a hundred in each innings.*

MOST CATCHES IN A SEASON

78	W. R. Hammond	1928
77	M. J. Stewart	1957
73	P. M. Walker	1961
71	P. J. Sharpe	1962
70	J. Tunnicliffe	1901
69	J. G. Langridge	1955
69	P. M. Walker	1960
66	J. Tunnicliffe	1895
65	W. R. Hammond	1925
65	P. M. Walker	1959
65	D. W. Richardson	1961
64	K. F. Barrington	1957
64	G. A. R. Lock	1957
63	J. Tunnicliffe	1896
63	J. Tunnicliffe	1904
63	K. J. Grieves	1950
63	C. A. Milton	1956
61	J. V. Wilson	1955
61	M. J. Stewart	1958

Note: The most catches by a fielder since the reduction of County Championship matches in 1969 is 49 by C. J. Tavaré in 1978.

MOST CATCHES IN A CAREER

Dates in italics denote the first half of an overseas season; i.e. *1970* denotes the 1970-71 season.

1,018	F. E. Woolley (1906-38)
887	W. G. Grace (1865-1908)
830	G. A. R. Lock (1946-*70*)
819	W. R. Hammond (1920-51)
813	D. B. Close (1949-86)
784	J. G. Langridge (1928-55)
764	W. Rhodes (1898-1930)
758	C. A. Milton (1948-74)
754	E. H. Hendren (1907-38)

Most Catches by Current Players

543	G. A. Gooch (1973-96)
458	J. E. Emburey (1973-96)
451	M. W. Gatting (1975-96)
420	C. W. J. Athey (1976-96)

TEAM RECORDS

HIGHEST TOTALS

1,107	Victoria v New South Wales at Melbourne	1926-27
1,059	Victoria v Tasmania at Melbourne	1922-23
951-7 dec.	Sind v Baluchistan at Karachi	1973-74
944-6 dec.	Hyderabad v Andhra at Secunderabad	1993-94
918	New South Wales v South Australia at Sydney	1900-01
912-8 dec.	Holkar v Mysore at Indore	1945-46
912-6 dec.†	Tamil Nadu v Goa at Panjim	1988-89
910-6 dec.	Railways v Dera Ismail Khan at Lahore	1964-65
903-7 dec.	England v Australia at The Oval	1938
887	Yorkshire v Warwickshire at Birmingham	1896
868†	North Zone v West Zone at Bhilai	1987-88
863	Lancashire v Surrey at The Oval	1990
855-6 dec.†	Bombay v Hyderabad at Bombay	1990-91
849	England v West Indies at Kingston	1929-30
843	Australians v Oxford & Cambridge U P & P at Portsmouth	1893
839	New South Wales v Tasmania at Sydney	1898-99
826-4	Maharashtra v Western India States at Poona	1948-49
824	Lahore Greens v Bahawalpur at Lahore	1965-66
821-7 dec.	South Australia v Queensland at Adelaide	1939-40
815	New South Wales v Victoria at Sydney	1908-09
811	Surrey v Somerset at The Oval	1899
810-4 dec.	Warwickshire v Durham at Birmingham	1994

807	New South Wales v South Australia at Adelaide	1899-1900
805	New South Wales v Victoria at Melbourne	1905-06
803-4 dec.	Kent v Essex at Brentwood	1934
803	Non-Smokers v Smokers at East Melbourne	1886-87
802-8 dec.	Karachi Blues v Lahore City at Peshawar	1994-95
802	New South Wales v South Australia at Sydney	1920-21
801	Lancashire v Somerset at Taunton	1895

† Tamil Nadu's total of 912-6 dec. included 52 penalty runs from their opponents' failure to meet the required bowling rate. North Zone's total of 868 included 68 and Bombay's total of 855-6 dec. included 48.

LOWEST TOTALS

12	Oxford University v MCC and Ground at Oxford	†1877
12	Northamptonshire v Gloucestershire at Gloucester	1907
13	Auckland v Canterbury at Auckland	1877-78
13	Nottinghamshire v Yorkshire at Nottingham	1901
14	Surrey v Essex at Chelmsford	1983
15	MCC v Surrey at Lord's	1839
15	Victoria v MCC at Melbourne	†1903-04
15	Northamptonshire v Yorkshire at Northampton	†1908
15	Hampshire v Warwickshire at Birmingham (Following on, Hampshire scored 521 and won by 155 runs.)	1922
16	MCC and Ground v Surrey at Lord's	1872
16	Derbyshire v Nottinghamshire at Nottingham	1879
16	Surrey v Nottinghamshire at The Oval	1880
16	Warwickshire v Kent at Tonbridge	1913
16	Trinidad v Barbados at Bridgetown	1942-43
16	Border v Natal at East London (first innings)	1959-60
17	Gentlemen of Kent v Gentlemen of England at Lord's	1850
17	Gloucestershire v Australians at Cheltenham	1896
18	The Bs v England at Lord's	1831
18	Kent v Sussex at Gravesend	†1867
18	Tasmania v Victoria at Melbourne	1868-69
18	Australians v MCC and Ground at Lord's	†1896
18	Border v Natal at East London (second innings)	1959-60
19	Sussex v Surrey at Godalming	1830
19	Sussex v Nottinghamshire at Hove	†1873
19	MCC and Ground v Australians at Lord's	1878
19	Wellington v Nelson at Nelson	1885-86

† Signifies that one man was absent.

Note: At Lord's in 1810, The Bs, with one man absent, were dismissed by England for 6.

LOWEST TOTAL IN A MATCH

34	(16 and 18) Border v Natal at East London	1959-60
42	(27 and 15) Northamptonshire v Yorkshire at Northampton	1908

Note: Northamptonshire batted one man short in each innings.

HIGHEST MATCH AGGREGATES

2,376 for 37 wickets	Maharashtra v Bombay at Poona	1948-49
2,078 for 40 wickets	Bombay v Holkar at Bombay	1944-45
1,981 for 35 wickets	England v South Africa at Durban	1938-39
1,945 for 18 wickets	Canterbury v Wellington at Christchurch	1994-95
1,929 for 39 wickets	New South Wales v South Australia at Sydney	1925-26
1,911 for 34 wickets	New South Wales v Victoria at Sydney	1908-09
1,905 for 40 wickets	Otago v Wellington at Dunedin	1923-24

In Britain

1,808 for 20 wickets	Sussex v Essex at Hove	1993
1,723 for 31 wickets	England v Australia at Leeds	1948
1,650 for 19 wickets	Surrey v Lancashire at The Oval	1990
1,642 for 29 wickets	Nottinghamshire v Kent at Nottingham	1995
1,641 for 16 wickets	Glamorgan v Worcestershire at Abergavenny	1990
1,614 for 30 wickets	England v India at Manchester	1990
1,606 for 34 wickets	Somerset v Derbyshire at Taunton	1996
1,603 for 28 wickets	England v India at Lord's	1990
1,601 for 29 wickets	England v Australia at Lord's	1930
1,601 for 35 wickets	Kent v Surrey at Canterbury	1995

LOWEST AGGREGATE IN A COMPLETED MATCH

105 for 31 wickets	MCC v Australians at Lord's	1878

Note: The lowest aggregate since 1900 is 157 for 22 wickets, Surrey v Worcestershire at The Oval, 1954.

HIGHEST FOURTH-INNINGS TOTALS

(Unless otherwise stated, the side making the runs won the match.)

654-5	England v South Africa at Durban (After being set 696 to win. The match was left drawn on the tenth day.)	1938-39
604	Maharashtra v Bombay at Poona (After being set 959 to win.)	1948-49
576-8	Trinidad v Barbados at Port-of-Spain (After being set 672 to win. Match drawn on fifth day.)	1945-46
572	New South Wales v South Australia at Sydney (After being set 593 to win.)	1907-08
529-9	Combined XI v South Africans at Perth (After being set 579 to win. Match drawn on fourth day.)	1963-64
518	Victoria v Queensland at Brisbane (After being set 753 to win.)	1926-27
507-7	Cambridge University v MCC and Ground at Lord's	1896
506-6	South Australia v Queensland at Adelaide	1991-92
502-6	Middlesex v Nottinghamshire at Nottingham (Game won by an unfinished stand of 271; a county record.)	1925
502-8	Players v Gentlemen at Lord's	1900
500-7	South African Universities v Western Province at Stellenbosch	1978-79

LARGEST VICTORIES

Largest Innings Victories

Inns and 851 runs:	Railways (910-6 dec.) v Dera Ismail Khan (Lahore)	1964-65
Inns and 666 runs:	Victoria (1,059) v Tasmania (Melbourne)	1922-23
Inns and 656 runs:	Victoria (1,107) v New South Wales (Melbourne)	1926-27
Inns and 605 runs:	New South Wales (918) v South Australia (Sydney)	1900-01
Inns and 579 runs:	England (903-7 dec.) v Australia (The Oval)	1938
Inns and 575 runs:	Sind (951-7 dec.) v Baluchistan (Karachi)	1973-74
Inns and 527 runs:	New South Wales (713) v South Australia (Adelaide)	1908-09
Inns and 517 runs:	Australians (675) v Nottinghamshire (Nottingham)	1921

Largest Victories by Runs Margin

685 runs:	New South Wales (235 and 761-8 dec.) v Queensland (Sydney)	1929-30
675 runs:	England (521 and 342-8 dec.) v Australia (Brisbane)	1928-29
638 runs:	New South Wales (304 and 770) v South Australia (Adelaide)	1920-21
625 runs:	Sargodha (376 and 416) v Lahore Municipal Corporation (Faisalabad)	1978-79
609 runs:	Muslim Commercial Bank (575 and 282-0 dec.) v WAPDA (Lahore).	1977-78
573 runs:	Sinhalese SC (395-7 dec. and 350-2 dec.) v Sebastianites C and AC (63 and 109) at Colombo	1990-91
571 runs:	Victoria (304 and 649) v South Australia (Adelaide)	1926-27
562 runs:	Australia (701 and 327) v England (The Oval)	1934

Victory Without Losing a Wicket

Lancashire (166-0 dec. and 66-0) beat Leicestershire by ten wickets (Manchester)	1956
Karachi A (277-0 dec.) beat Sind A by an innings and 77 runs (Karachi)	1957-58
Railways (236-0 dec. and 16-0) beat Jammu and Kashmir by ten wickets (Srinagar)	1960-61
Karnataka (451-0 dec.) beat Kerala by an innings and 186 runs (Chikmagalur)	1977-78

TIED MATCHES IN FIRST-CLASS CRICKET

Since 1948 a tie has been recognised only when the scores are level with all the wickets down in the fourth innings.

The following are the instances since then:

D. G. Bradman's XI v A. L. Hassett's XI at Melbourne	1948-49
Hampshire v Kent at Southampton	1950
Sussex v Warwickshire at Hove	1952
Essex v Lancashire at Brentwood	1952
Northamptonshire v Middlesex at Peterborough	1953
Yorkshire v Leicestershire at Huddersfield	1954
Sussex v Hampshire at Eastbourne	1955
Victoria v New South Wales at Melbourne	1956-57
T. N. Pearce's XI v New Zealanders at Scarborough	1958
Essex v Gloucestershire at Leyton	1959
Australia v West Indies (First Test) at Brisbane	1960-61
Bahawalpur v Lahore B at Bahawalpur	1961-62
Hampshire v Middlesex at Portsmouth	1967
England XI v England Under-25 XI at Scarborough	1968
Yorkshire v Middlesex at Bradford	1973
Sussex v Essex at Hove	1974
South Australia v Queensland at Adelaide	1976-77
Central Districts v England XI at New Plymouth	1977-78
Victoria v New Zealanders at Melbourne	1982-83
Muslim Commercial Bank v Railways at Sialkot	1983-84
Sussex v Kent at Hastings	1984
Northamptonshire v Kent at Northampton	1984
Eastern Province B v Boland at Albany SC, Port Elizabeth	1985-86

Natal B v Eastern Province B at Pietermaritzburg	1985-86
India v Australia (First Test) at Madras	1986-87
Gloucestershire v Derbyshire at Bristol	1987
Bahawalpur v Peshawar at Bahawalpur	1988-89
Wellington v Canterbury at Wellington	1988-89
Sussex v Kent at Hove	†1991
Nottinghamshire v Worcestershire at Nottingham	1993

† *Sussex (436) scored the highest total to tie a first-class match.*

MATCHES BEGUN AND FINISHED ON FIRST DAY

Since 1900. A fuller list may be found in the Wisden *of 1981 and preceding editions.*

Yorkshire v Worcestershire at Bradford, May 7	1900
MCC and Ground v London County at Lord's, May 20	1903
Transvaal v Orange Free State at Johannesburg, December 30	1906
Middlesex v Gentlemen of Philadelphia at Lord's, July 20	1908
Gloucestershire v Middlesex at Bristol, August 26	1909
Eastern Province v Orange Free State at Port Elizabeth, December 26	1912
Kent v Sussex at Tonbridge, June 21	1919
Lancashire v Somerset at Manchester, May 21	1925
Madras v Mysore at Madras, November 4	1934
Ireland v New Zealanders at Dublin, September 11	1937
Derbyshire v Somerset at Chesterfield, June 11	1947
Lancashire v Sussex at Manchester, July 12	1950
Surrey v Warwickshire at The Oval, May 16	1953
Somerset v Lancashire at Bath, June 6 (H. F. T. Buse's benefit)	1953
Kent v Worcestershire at Tunbridge Wells, June 15	1960

THE ASHES

"In affectionate remembrance of English cricket which died at The Oval, 29th August, 1882. Deeply lamented by a large circle of sorrowing friends and acquaintances, R.I.P. N.B. The body will be cremated and the Ashes taken to Australia."

Australia's first victory on English soil over the full strength of England, on August 29, 1882, inspired a young London journalist, Reginald Shirley Brooks, to write this mock "obituary". It appeared in the *Sporting Times*.

Before England's defeat at The Oval, by seven runs, arrangements had already been made for the Hon. Ivo Bligh, afterwards Lord Darnley, to lead a team to Australia. Three weeks later they set out, now with the popular objective of recovering the Ashes. In the event, Australia won the First Test by nine wickets, but with England winning the next two it became generally accepted that they brought back the Ashes.

It was long accepted that the real Ashes – a small urn believed to contain the ashes of a bail used in the third match – were presented to Bligh by a group of Melbourne women. At the time of the 1982 centenary of The Oval Test match, however, evidence was produced which suggested that these ashes were the remains of a ball and that they were given to the England captain by Sir William Clarke, the presentation taking place before the Test matches in Australia in 1883. The certain origin of the Ashes, therefore, is the subject of some dispute.

After Lord Darnley's death in 1927, the urn was given to MCC by Lord Darnley's Australian-born widow, Florence. It can be seen in the cricket museum at Lord's, together with a red and gold velvet bag, made specially for it, and the scorecard of the 1882 match.

TEST MATCH RECORDS

Note: This section covers all Tests up to August 26, 1996.

BATTING RECORDS

HIGHEST INDIVIDUAL INNINGS

375	B. C. Lara	West Indies v England at St John's	1993-94
365*	G. S. Sobers	West Indies v Pakistan at Kingston	1957-58
364	L. Hutton	England v Australia at The Oval	1938
337	Hanif Mohammad	Pakistan v West Indies at Bridgetown	1957-58
336*	W. R. Hammond	England v New Zealand at Auckland	1932-33
334	D. G. Bradman	Australia v England at Leeds	1930
333	G. A. Gooch	England v India at Lord's	1990
325	A. Sandham	England v West Indies at Kingston	1929-30
311	R. B. Simpson	Australia v England at Manchester	1964
310*	J. H. Edrich	England v New Zealand at Leeds	1965
307	R. M. Cowper	Australia v England at Melbourne	1965-66
304	D. G. Bradman	Australia v England at Leeds	1934
302	L. G. Rowe	West Indies v England at Bridgetown	1973-74
299*	D. G. Bradman	Australia v South Africa at Adelaide	1931-32
299	M. D. Crowe	New Zealand v Sri Lanka at Wellington	1990-91
291	I. V. A. Richards	West Indies v England at The Oval	1976
287	R. E. Foster	England v Australia at Sydney	1903-04
285*	P. B. H. May	England v West Indies at Birmingham	1957
280*	Javed Miandad	Pakistan v India at Hyderabad	1982-83
278	D. C. S. Compton	England v Pakistan at Nottingham	1954
277	B. C. Lara	West Indies v Australia at Sydney	1992-93
274	R. G. Pollock	South Africa v Australia at Durban	1969-70
274	Zaheer Abbas	Pakistan v England at Birmingham	1971
271	Javed Miandad	Pakistan v New Zealand at Auckland	1988-89
270*	G. A. Headley	West Indies v England at Kingston	1934-35
270	D. G. Bradman	Australia v England at Melbourne	1936-37
268	G. N. Yallop	Australia v Pakistan at Melbourne	1983-84
267	P. A. de Silva	Sri Lanka v New Zealand at Wellington	1990-91
266	W. H. Ponsford	Australia v England at The Oval	1934
266	D. L. Houghton	Zimbabwe v Sri Lanka at Bulawayo	1994-95
262*	D. L. Amiss	England v West Indies at Kingston	1973-74
261	F. M. M. Worrell	West Indies v England at Nottingham	1950
260	C. C. Hunte	West Indies v Pakistan at Kingston	1957-58
260	Javed Miandad	Pakistan v England at The Oval	1987
259	G. M. Turner	New Zealand v West Indies at Georgetown	1971-72
258	T. W. Graveney	England v West Indies at Nottingham	1957
258	S. M. Nurse	West Indies v New Zealand at Christchurch	1968-69
256	R. B. Kanhai	West Indies v India at Calcutta	1958-59
256	K. F. Barrington	England v Australia at Manchester	1964
255*	D. J. McGlew	South Africa v New Zealand at Wellington	1952-53
254	D. G. Bradman	Australia v England at Lord's	1930
251	W. R. Hammond	England v Australia at Sydney	1928-29
250	K. D. Walters	Australia v New Zealand at Christchurch	1976-77
250	S. F. A. F. Bacchus	West Indies v India at Kanpur	1978-79

The highest individual innings for India is:

236*	S. M. Gavaskar	India v West Indies at Madras	1983-84

HUNDRED ON TEST DEBUT

C. Bannerman (165*)	Australia v England at Melbourne	1876-77
W. G. Grace (152)	England v Australia at The Oval	1880
H. Graham (107)	Australia v England at Lord's	1893
†K. S. Ranjitsinhji (154*)	England v Australia at Manchester	1896

†P. F. Warner (132*)	England v South Africa at Johannesburg	1898-99
†R. A. Duff (104)	Australia v England at Melbourne	1901-02
R. E. Foster (287)	England v Australia at Sydney	1903-04
G. Gunn (119)	England v Australia at Sydney	1907-08
†R. J. Hartigan (116)	Australia v England at Adelaide	1907-08
†H. L. Collins (104)	Australia v England at Sydney	1920-21
W. H. Ponsford (110)	Australia v England at Sydney	1924-25
A. A. Jackson (164)	Australia v England at Adelaide	1928-29
†G. A. Headley (176)	West Indies v England at Bridgetown	1929-30
J. E. Mills (117)	New Zealand v England at Wellington	1929-30
Nawab of Pataudi sen. (102)	England v Australia at Sydney	1932-33
B. H. Valentine (136)	England v India at Bombay	1933-34
†L. Amarnath (118)	India v England at Bombay	1933-34
†P. A. Gibb (106)	England v South Africa at Johannesburg	1938-39
S. C. Griffith (140)	England v West Indies at Port-of-Spain	1947-48
A. G. Ganteaume (112)	West Indies v England at Port-of-Spain	1947-48
†J. W. Burke (101*)	Australia v England at Adelaide	1950-51
P. B. H. May (138)	England v South Africa at Leeds	1951
R. H. Shodhan (110)	India v Pakistan at Calcutta	1952-53
B. H. Pairaudeau (115)	West Indies v India at Port-of-Spain	1952-53
†O. G. Smith (104)	West Indies v Australia at Kingston	1954-55
A. G. Kripal Singh (100*)	India v New Zealand at Hyderabad	1955-56
C. C. Hunte (142)	West Indies v Pakistan at Bridgetown	1957-58
C. A. Milton (104*)	England v New Zealand at Leeds	1958
†A. A. Baig (112)	India v England at Manchester	1959
Hanumant Singh (105)	India v England at Delhi	1963-64
Khalid Ibadulla (166)	Pakistan v Australia at Karachi	1964-65
B. R. Taylor (105)	New Zealand v India at Calcutta	1964-65
K. D. Walters (155)	Australia v England at Brisbane	1965-66
J. H. Hampshire (107)	England v West Indies at Lord's	1969
†G. R. Viswanath (137)	India v Australia at Kanpur	1969-70
G. S. Chappell (108)	Australia v England at Perth	1970-71
‡L. G. Rowe (214, 100*)	West Indies v New Zealand at Kingston	1971-72
A. I. Kallicharran (100*)	West Indies v New Zealand at Georgetown	1971-72
R. E. Redmond (107)	New Zealand v Pakistan at Auckland	1972-73
†F. C. Hayes (106*)	England v West Indies at The Oval	1973
†C. G. Greenidge (107)	West Indies v India at Bangalore	1974-75
†L. Baichan (105*)	West Indies v Pakistan at Lahore	1974-75
G. J. Cosier (109)	Australia v West Indies at Melbourne	1975-76
S. Amarnath (124)	India v New Zealand at Auckland	1975-76
Javed Miandad (163)	Pakistan v New Zealand at Lahore	1976-77
†A. B. Williams (100)	West Indies v Australia at Georgetown	1977-78
†D. M. Wellham (103)	Australia v England at The Oval	1981
†Salim Malik (100*)	Pakistan v Sri Lanka at Karachi	1981-82
K. C. Wessels (162)	Australia v England at Brisbane	1982-83
W. B. Phillips (159)	Australia v Pakistan at Perth	1983-84
§M. Azharuddin (110)	India v England at Calcutta	1984-85
D. S. B. P. Kuruppu (201*)	Sri Lanka v New Zealand at Colombo (CCC)	1986-87
†M. J. Greatbatch (107*)	New Zealand v England at Auckland	1987-88
M. E. Waugh (138)	Australia v England at Adelaide	1990-91
A. C. Hudson (163)	South Africa v West Indies at Bridgetown	1991-92
R. S. Kaluwitharana (132*)	Sri Lanka v Australia at Colombo (SSC)	1992-93
D. L. Houghton (121)	Zimbabwe v India at Harare	1992-93
P. K. Amre (103)	India v South Africa at Durban	1992-93
†G. P. Thorpe (114*)	England v Australia at Nottingham	1993
G. S. Blewett (102*)	Australia v England at Adelaide	1994-95
S. C. Ganguly (131)	India v England at Lord's	1996

† *In his second innings of the match.*
‡ *L. G. Rowe is the only batsman to score a hundred in each innings on debut.*
§ *M. Azharuddin is the only batsman to score hundreds in each of his first three Tests.*

Note: L. Amarnath and S. Amarnath were father and son.

300 RUNS IN FIRST TEST

314	L. G. Rowe (214, 100*)	West Indies v New Zealand at Kingston	1971-72
306	R. E. Foster (287, 19)	England v Australia at Sydney	1903-04

TWO SEPARATE HUNDREDS IN A TEST

Three times: S. M. Gavaskar v West Indies (1970-71), v Pakistan (1978-79), v West Indies (1978-79).

Twice in one series: C. L. Walcott v Australia (1954-55).

Twice: H. Sutcliffe v Australia (1924-25), v South Africa (1929); G. A. Headley v England (1929-30 and 1939); G. S. Chappell v New Zealand (1973-74), v West Indies (1975-76); ‡A. R. Border v Pakistan (1979-80), v New Zealand (1985-86).

Once: W. Bardsley v England (1909); A. C. Russell v South Africa (1922-23); W. R. Hammond v Australia (1928-29); E. Paynter v South Africa (1938-39); D. C. S. Compton v Australia (1946-47); A. R. Morris v England (1946-47); A. Melville v England (1947); B. Mitchell v England (1947); D. G. Bradman v India (1947-48); V. S. Hazare v Australia (1947-48); E. D. Weekes v India (1948-49); J. Moroney v South Africa (1949-50); G. S. Sobers v Pakistan (1957-58); R. B. Kanhai v Australia (1960-61); Hanif Mohammad v England (1961-62); R. B. Simpson v Pakistan (1964-65); K. D. Walters v West Indies (1968-69); †L. G. Rowe v New Zealand (1971-72); I. M. Chappell v New Zealand (1973-74); G. M. Turner v Australia (1973-74); C. G. Greenidge v England (1976); G. P. Howarth v England (1977-78); L. R. D. Mendis v India (1982-83); Javed Miandad v New Zealand (1984-85); D. M. Jones v Pakistan (1989-90); G. A. Gooch v India (1990); A. H. Jones v Sri Lanka (1990-91); A. P. Gurusinha v New Zealand (1990-91); A. J. Stewart v West Indies (1993-94).

† *L. G. Rowe's two hundreds were on his Test debut.*

‡ *A. R. Border scored 150* and 153 against Pakistan to become the first batsman to score 150 in each innings of a Test match.*

TRIPLE-HUNDRED AND HUNDRED IN SAME TEST

G. A. Gooch (England)	333 and 123 v India at Lord's	1990

The only instance in first-class cricket.

DOUBLE-HUNDRED AND HUNDRED IN SAME TEST

K. D. Walters (Australia)	242 and 103 v West Indies at Sydney	1968-69
S. M. Gavaskar (India)	124 and 220 v West Indies at Port-of-Spain	1970-71
†L. G. Rowe (West Indies)	214 and 100* v New Zealand at Kingston	1971-72
G. S. Chappell (Australia)	247* and 133 v New Zealand at Wellington	1973-74

† *On Test debut.*

MOST RUNS IN A SERIES

	T	*I*	*NO*	*R*	*HS*	*100s*	*Avge*		
D. G. Bradman	5	7	0	974	334	4	139.14	A v E	1930
W. R. Hammond	5	9	1	905	251	4	113.12	E v A	1928-29
M. A. Taylor	6	11	1	839	219	2	83.90	A v E	1989
R. N. Harvey	5	9	0	834	205	4	92.66	A v SA	1952-53
I. V. A. Richards	4	7	0	829	291	3	118.42	WI v E	1976
C. L. Walcott	5	10	0	827	155	5	82.70	WI v A	1954-55

	T	I	NO	R	HS	100s	Avge		
G. S. Sobers	5	8	2	824	365*	3	137.33	WI v P	1957-58
D. G. Bradman	5	9	0	810	270	3	90.00	A v E	1936-37
D. G. Bradman	5	5	1	806	299*	4	201.50	A v SA	1931-32
B. C. Lara	5	8	0	798	375	2	99.75	WI v E	1993-94
E. D. Weekes	5	7	0	779	194	4	111.28	WI v I	1948-49
†S. M. Gavaskar	4	8	3	774	220	4	154.80	I v WI	1970-71
B. C. Lara	6	10	1	765	179	3	85.00	WI v E	1995
Mudassar Nazar	6	8	2	761	231	4	126.83	P v I	1982-83
D. G. Bradman	5	8	0	758	304	2	94.75	A v E	1934
D. C. S. Compton	5	8	0	753	208	4	94.12	E v SA	1947
‡G. A. Gooch	3	6	0	752	333	3	125.33	E v I	1990

† *Gavaskar's aggregate was achieved in his first Test series.*
‡ *G. A. Gooch is alone in scoring 1,000 runs in Test cricket during an English season with 1,058 runs in 11 innings against New Zealand and India in 1990.*

MOST TEST RUNS IN A CALENDAR YEAR

	T	I	NO	R	HS	100s	Avge	Year
I. V. A. Richards (WI)	11	19	0	1,710	291	7	90.00	1976
S. M. Gavaskar (I)	18	27	1	1,555	221	5	59.80	1979
G. R. Viswanath (I)	17	26	3	1,388	179	5	60.34	1979
R. B. Simpson (A)	14	26	3	1,381	311	3	60.04	1964
D. L. Amiss (E)	13	22	2	1,379	262*	5	68.95	1974
S. M. Gavaskar (I)	18	32	4	1,310	236*	5	46.78	1983
G. A. Gooch (E)	9	17	1	1,264	333	4	79.00	1990
D. C. Boon (A)	16	25	5	1,241	164*	4	62.05	1993
B. C. Lara (WI)	12	20	2	1,222	179	4	67.77	1995
M. A. Taylor (A)	11	20	1	1,219	219	4	64.15	1989†

† *The year of his debut.*

Notes: M. Amarnath reached 1,000 runs in 1983 on May 3.
The only batsman to score 1,000 runs in a year before World War II was C. Hill of Australia: 1,061 in 1902.

MOST RUNS IN A CAREER

(Qualification: 2,000 runs)

ENGLAND

		T	I	NO	R	HS	100s	Avge
1	G. A. Gooch	118	215	6	8,900	333	20	42.58
2	D. I. Gower	117	204	18	8,231	215	18	44.25
3	G. Boycott	108	193	23	8,114	246*	22	47.72
4	M. C. Cowdrey	114	188	15	7,624	182	22	44.06
5	W. R. Hammond	85	140	16	7,249	336*	22	58.45
6	L. Hutton	79	138	15	6,971	364	19	56.67
7	K. F. Barrington	82	131	15	6,806	256	20	58.67
8	D. C. S. Compton	78	131	15	5,807	278	17	50.06
9	J. B. Hobbs	61	102	7	5,410	211	15	56.94
10	I. T. Botham	102	161	6	5,200	208	14	33.54
11	J. H. Edrich	77	127	9	5,138	310*	12	43.54
12	T. W. Graveney	79	123	13	4,882	258	11	44.38
13	A. J. Lamb	79	139	10	4,656	142	14	36.09
14	**M. A. Atherton**	**62**	**114**	**3**	**4,627**	**185***	**10**	**41.68**
15	H. Sutcliffe	54	84	9	4,555	194	16	60.73
16	P. B. H. May	66	106	9	4,537	285*	13	46.77
17	E. R. Dexter	62	102	8	4,502	205	9	47.89
18	M. W. Gatting	79	138	14	4,409	207	10	35.55

		T	*I*	*NO*	*R*	*HS*	*100s*	*Avge*
19	A. P. E. Knott	95	149	15	4,389	135	5	32.75
20	**R. A. Smith**	**62**	**112**	**15**	**4,236**	**175**	**9**	**43.67**
21	**A. J. Stewart**	**58**	**103**	**6**	**3,935**	**190**	**8**	**40.56**
22	D. L. Amiss	50	88	10	3,612	262*	11	46.30
23	A. W. Greig	58	93	4	3,599	148	8	40.43
24	E. H. Hendren	51	83	9	3,525	205*	7	47.63
25	F. E. Woolley	64	98	7	3,283	154	5	36.07
26	K. W. R. Fletcher	59	96	14	3,272	216	7	39.90
27	M. Leyland	41	65	5	2,764	187	9	46.06
28	**G. A. Hick**	**46**	**80**	**6**	**2,672**	**178**	**4**	**36.10**
29	C. Washbrook	37	66	6	2,569	195	6	42.81
30	B. L. D'Oliveira	44	70	8	2,484	158	5	40.06
31	D. W. Randall	47	79	5	2,470	174	7	33.37
32	W. J. Edrich	39	63	2	2,440	219	6	40.00
33	T. G. Evans	91	133	14	2,439	104	2	20.49
34	L. E. G. Ames	47	72	12	2,434	149	8	40.56
35	W. Rhodes	58	98	21	2,325	179	2	30.19
36	T. E. Bailey	61	91	14	2,290	134*	1	29.74
37	M. J. K. Smith	50	78	6	2,278	121	3	31.63
38	**G. P. Thorpe**	**32**	**59**	**5**	**2,194**	**123**	**2**	**40.62**
39	P. E. Richardson	34	56	1	2,061	126	5	37.47

AUSTRALIA

		T	*I*	*NO*	*R*	*HS*	*100s*	*Avge*
1	A. R. Border	156	265	44	11,174	205	27	50.56
2	**D. C. Boon**	**107**	**190**	**20**	**7,422**	**200**	**21**	**43.65**
3	G. S. Chappell	87	151	19	7,110	247*	24	53.86
4	D. G. Bradman	52	80	10	6,996	334	29	99.94
5	R. N. Harvey	79	137	10	6,149	205	21	48.41
6	**M. A. Taylor**	**72**	**129**	**9**	**5,502**	**219**	**14**	**45.85**
7	K. D. Walters	74	125	14	5,357	250	15	48.26
8	I. M. Chappell	75	136	10	5,345	196	14	42.42
9	W. M. Lawry	67	123	12	5,234	210	13	47.15
10	**S. R. Waugh**	**81**	**125**	**26**	**5,002**	**200**	**11**	**50.52**
11	R. B. Simpson	62	111	7	4,869	311	10	46.81
12	I. R. Redpath	66	120	11	4,737	171	8	43.45
13	K. J. Hughes	70	124	6	4,415	213	9	37.41
14	R. W. Marsh	96	150	13	3,633	132	3	26.51
15	D. M. Jones	52	89	11	3,631	216	11	46.55
16	**M. E. Waugh**	**54**	**86**	**4**	**3,627**	**140**	**10**	**44.23**
17	A. R. Morris	46	79	3	3,533	206	12	46.48
18	C. Hill	49	89	2	3,412	191	7	39.21
19	G. M. Wood	59	112	6	3,374	172	9	31.83
20	V. T. Trumper	48	89	8	3,163	214*	8	39.04
21	C. C. McDonald	47	83	4	3,107	170	5	39.32
22	A. L. Hassett	43	69	3	3,073	198*	10	46.56
23	K. R. Miller	55	87	7	2,958	147	7	36.97
24	W. W. Armstrong	50	84	10	2,863	159*	6	38.68
25	G. R. Marsh	50	93	7	2,854	138	4	33.18
26	K. R. Stackpole	43	80	5	2,807	207	7	37.42
27	**I. A. Healy**	**79**	**117**	**14**	**2,803**	**113***	**2**	**27.21**
28	N. C. O'Neill	42	69	8	2,779	181	6	45.55
29	G. N. Yallop	39	70	3	2,756	268	8	41.13
30	S. J. McCabe	39	62	5	2,748	232	6	48.21
31	**M. J. Slater**	**33**	**57**	**3**	**2,611**	**219**	**7**	**48.35**
32	W. Bardsley	41	66	5	2,469	193*	6	40.47
33	W. M. Woodfull	35	54	4	2,300	161	7	46.00
34	P. J. Burge	42	68	8	2,290	181	4	38.16
35	S. E. Gregory	58	100	7	2,282	201	4	24.53
36	R. Benaud	63	97	7	2,201	122	3	24.45
37	C. G. Macartney	35	55	4	2,131	170	7	41.78
38	W. H. Ponsford	29	48	4	2,122	266	7	48.22
39	R. M. Cowper	27	46	2	2,061	307	5	46.84

SOUTH AFRICA

		T	*I*	*NO*	*R*	*HS*	*100s*	*Avge*
1	B. Mitchell	42	80	9	3,471	189*	8	48.88
2	A. D. Nourse	34	62	7	2,960	231	9	53.81
3	H. W. Taylor	42	76	4	2,936	176	7	40.77
4	E. J. Barlow	30	57	2	2,516	201	6	45.74
	T. L. Goddard	41	78	5	2,516	112	1	34.46
6	D. J. McGlew	34	64	6	2,440	255*	7	42.06
7	J. H. B. Waite	50	86	7	2,405	134	4	30.44
8	R. G. Pollock	23	41	4	2,256	274	7	60.97
9	A. W. Nourse	45	83	8	2,234	111	1	29.78
10	R. A. McLean	40	73	3	2,120	142	5	30.28

K. C. Wessels scored 2,788 runs in 40 Tests: 1,761 (average 42.95) in 24 Tests for Australia, and 1,027 (average 38.03) in 16 Tests for South Africa.

WEST INDIES

		T	*I*	*NO*	*R*	*HS*	*100s*	*Avge*
1	I. V. A. Richards	121	182	12	8,540	291	24	50.23
2	G. S. Sobers	93	160	21	8,032	365*	26	57.78
3	C. G. Greenidge	108	185	16	7,558	226	19	44.72
4	C. H. Lloyd	110	175	14	7,515	242*	19	46.67
5	D. L. Haynes	116	202	25	7,487	184	18	42.29
6	R. B. Kanhai	79	137	6	6,227	256	15	47.53
7	R. B. Richardson	86	146	12	5,949	194	16	44.39
8	E. D. Weekes	48	81	5	4,455	207	15	58.61
9	A. I. Kallicharran	66	109	10	4,399	187	12	44.43
10	R. C. Fredericks	59	109	7	4,334	169	8	42.49
11	F. M. M. Worrell	51	87	9	3,860	261	9	49.48
12	C. L. Walcott	44	74	7	3,798	220	15	56.68
13	P. J. L. Dujon	81	115	11	3,322	139	5	31.94
14	C. C. Hunte	44	78	6	3,245	260	8	45.06
15	**B. C. Lara**	**33**	**55**	**2**	**3,197**	**375**	**7**	**60.32**
16	H. A. Gomes	60	91	11	3,171	143	9	39.63
17	B. F. Butcher	44	78	6	3,104	209*	7	43.11
18	C. L. Hooper	52	87	7	2,548	178*	5	31.85
19	S. M. Nurse	29	54	1	2,523	258	6	47.60
20	A. L. Logie	52	78	9	2,470	130	2	35.79
21	G. A. Headley	22	40	4	2,190	270*	10	60.83
22	J. B. Stollmeyer	32	56	5	2,159	160	4	42.33
23	L. G. Rowe	30	49	2	2,047	302	7	43.55

NEW ZEALAND

		T	*I*	*NO*	*R*	*HS*	*100s*	*Avge*
1	**M. D. Crowe**	**77**	**131**	**11**	**5,444**	**299**	**17**	**45.36**
2	J. G. Wright	82	148	7	5,334	185	12	37.82
3	B. E. Congdon	61	114	7	3,448	176	7	32.22
4	J. R. Reid	58	108	5	3,428	142	6	33.28
5	R. J. Hadlee	86	134	19	3,124	151*	2	27.16
6	G. M. Turner	41	73	6	2,991	259	7	44.64
7	A. H. Jones	39	74	8	2,922	186	7	44.27
8	B. Sutcliffe	42	76	8	2,727	230*	5	40.10
9	M. G. Burgess	50	92	6	2,684	119*	5	31.20
10	J. V. Coney	52	85	14	2,668	174*	3	37.57
11	G. P. Howarth	47	83	5	2,531	147	6	32.44
12	K. R. Rutherford	56	99	8	2,465	107*	3	27.08
13	G. T. Dowling	39	77	3	2,306	239	3	31.16

INDIA

		T	I	NO	R	HS	100s	Avge
1	S. M. Gavaskar	125	214	16	10,122	236*	34	51.12
2	D. B. Vengsarkar	116	185	22	6,868	166	17	42.13
3	G. R. Viswanath	91	155	10	6,080	222	14	41.93
4	Kapil Dev	131	184	15	5,248	163	8	31.05
5	M. Amarnath	69	113	10	4,378	138	11	42.50
6	**M. Azharuddin**	**71**	**101**	**4**	**4,362**	**199**	**14**	**44.96**
7	R. J. Shastri	80	121	14	3,830	206	11	35.79
8	P. R. Umrigar	59	94	8	3,631	223	12	42.22
9	V. L. Manjrekar	55	92	10	3,208	189*	7	39.12
10	C. G. Borde	55	97	11	3,061	177*	5	35.59
11	**S. R. Tendulkar**	**41**	**60**	**7**	**2,911**	**179**	**10**	**54.92**
12	Nawab of Pataudi jun.	46	83	3	2,793	203*	6	34.91
13	S. M. H. Kirmani	88	124	22	2,759	102	2	27.04
14	F. M. Engineer	46	87	3	2,611	121	2	31.08
15	Pankaj Roy	43	79	4	2,442	173	5	32.56
16	V. S. Hazare	30	52	6	2,192	164*	7	47.65
17	A. L. Wadekar	37	71	3	2,113	143	1	31.07
18	V. Mankad	44	72	5	2,109	231	5	31.47
19	**N. S. Sidhu**	**36**	**54**	**2**	**2,087**	**124**	**6**	**40.13**
20	C. P. S. Chauhan	40	68	2	2,084	97	0	31.57
21	K. Srikkanth	43	72	3	2,062	123	2	29.88
22	M. L. Jaisimha	39	71	4	2,056	129	3	30.68
23	**S. V. Manjrekar**	**36**	**59**	**6**	**2,004**	**218**	**4**	**37.81**
24	D. N. Sardesai	30	55	4	2,001	212	5	39.23

PAKISTAN

		T	I	NO	R	HS	100s	Avge
1	Javed Miandad	124	189	21	8,832	280*	23	52.57
2	**Salim Malik**	**90**	**134**	**21**	**5,101**	**237**	**14**	**45.14**
3	Zaheer Abbas	78	124	11	5,062	274	12	44.79
4	Mudassar Nazar	76	116	8	4,114	231	10	38.09
5	Majid Khan	63	106	5	3,931	167	8	38.92
6	Hanif Mohammad	55	97	8	3,915	337	12	43.98
7	Imran Khan	88	126	25	3,807	136	6	37.69
8	Mushtaq Mohammad	57	100	7	3,643	201	10	39.17
9	Asif Iqbal	58	99	7	3,575	175	11	38.85
10	Saeed Ahmed	41	78	4	2,991	172	5	40.41
11	Wasim Raja	57	92	14	2,821	125	4	36.16
12	**Ramiz Raja**	**55**	**91**	**5**	**2,747**	**122**	**2**	**31.94**
13	Mohsin Khan	48	79	6	2,709	200	7	37.10
14	**Shoaib Mohammad**	**45**	**68**	**7**	**2,705**	**203***	**7**	**44.34**
15	Sadiq Mohammad	41	74	2	2,579	166	5	35.81
16	**Inzamam-ul-Haq**	**33**	**57**	**7**	**2,367**	**148**	**5**	**47.34**
17	Imtiaz Ahmed	41	72	1	2,079	209	3	29.28
18	**Aamir Sohail**	**32**	**59**	**2**	**2,037**	**205**	**2**	**35.73**

SRI LANKA

		T	I	NO	R	HS	100s	Avge
1	**A. Ranatunga**	**61**	**104**	**6**	**3,471**	**135***	**4**	**35.41**
2	**P. A. de Silva**	**53**	**93**	**4**	**3,176**	**267**	**8**	**35.68**
3	**A. P. Gurusinha**	**39**	**68**	**7**	**2,312**	**143**	**7**	**37.90**
4	**H. P. Tillekeratne**	**36**	**61**	**8**	**2,166**	**119**	**4**	**40.86**

ZIMBABWE: The highest aggregate is 1,113, average 48.39, by **D. L. Houghton** in 16 Tests.

Bold type denotes those who played Test cricket in 1995-96 and 1996 seasons.

HIGHEST CAREER AVERAGES

(Qualification: 20 innings)

Avge		*T*	*I*	*NO*	*R*	*HS*	*100s*
99.94	D. G. Bradman (A)	52	80	10	6,996	334	29
66.10	**J. C. Adams (WI)**	**24**	**37**	**9**	**1,851**	**208***	**5**
60.97	R. G. Pollock (SA)	23	41	4	2,256	274	7
60.83	G. A. Headley (WI)	22	40	4	2,190	270*	10
60.73	H. Sutcliffe (E)	54	84	9	4,555	194	16
60.32	**B. C. Lara (WI)**	**33**	**55**	**2**	**3,197**	**375**	**7**
59.23	E. Paynter (E)	20	31	5	1,540	243	4
58.67	K. F. Barrington (E)	82	131	15	6,806	256	20
58.61	E. D. Weekes (WI)	48	81	5	4,455	207	15
58.45	W. R. Hammond (E)	85	140	16	7,249	336*	22
57.78	G. S. Sobers (WI)	93	160	21	8,032	365*	26
56.94	J. B. Hobbs (E)	61	102	7	5,410	211	15
56.68	C. L. Walcott (WI)	44	74	7	3,798	220	15
56.67	L. Hutton (E)	79	138	15	6,971	364	19
55.00	E. Tyldesley (E)	14	20	2	990	122	3
54.92	**S. R. Tendulkar (I)**	**41**	**60**	**7**	**2,911**	**179**	**10**
54.20	C. A. Davis (WI)	15	29	5	1,301	183	4
54.20	**V. G. Kambli (I)**	**17**	**21**	**1**	**1,084**	**227**	**4**
53.86	G. S. Chappell (A)	87	151	19	7,110	247*	24
53.81	A. D. Nourse (SA)	34	62	7	2,960	231	9
52.57	Javed Miandad (P)	124	189	21	8,832	280*	23
51.62	J. Ryder (A)	20	32	5	1,394	201*	3
51.12	S. M. Gavaskar (I)	125	214	16	10,122	236*	34
50.56	A. R. Border (A)	156	265	44	11,174	205	27
50.52	**S. R. Waugh (A)**	**81**	**125**	**26**	**5,002**	**200**	**11**
50.23	I. V. A. Richards (WI)	121	182	12	8,540	291	24
50.06	D. C. S. Compton (E)	78	131	15	5,807	278	17

Bold type denotes those who played Test cricket in 1995-96 and 1996 seasons.

MOST HUNDREDS

				Opponents								
	Total	*200+*	*Inns*	*E*	*A*	*SA*	*WI*	*NZ*	*I*	*P*	*SL*	*Z*
S. M. Gavaskar (I) ..	34	4	214	4	8	–	13	2	–	5	2	–
D. G. Bradman (A) ..	29	12	80	19	–	4	2	–	4	–	–	–
A. R. Border (A)	27	2	265	8	–	–	3	5	4	6	1	–
G. S. Sobers (WI) ...	26	2	160	10	4	–	–	1	8	3	–	–
G. S. Chappell (A) ..	24	4	151	9	–	–	5	3	1	6	0	–
I. V. A. Richards (WI)	24	3	182	8	5	–	–	1	8	2	–	–
Javed Miandad (P) ..	23	6	189	2	6	–	2	7	5	–	1	–
G. Boycott (E)	22	1	193	–	7	1	5	2	4	3	–	–
M. C. Cowdrey (E) ..	22	0	188	–	5	3	6	2	3	3	–	–
W. R. Hammond (E).	22	7	140	–	9	6	1	4	2	–	–	–
D. C. Boon (A)	**21**	**1**	**190**	**7**	**–**	**–**	**3**	**3**	**6**	**1**	**1**	**–**
R. N. Harvey (A) ...	21	2	137	6	–	8	3	–	4	0	–	–
K. F. Barrington (E) .	20	1	131	–	5	2	3	3	3	4	–	–
G. A. Gooch (E)	20	2	215	–	4	–	5	4	5	1	1	–
C. G. Greenidge (WI)	19	4	185	7	4	–	–	2	5	1	–	–
L. Hutton (E)	19	4	138	–	5	4	5	3	2	0	–	–
C. H. Lloyd (WI)....	19	1	175	5	6	–	–	0	7	1	–	–
D. I. Gower (E)	18	2	204	–	9	–	1	4	2	2	0	–
D. L. Haynes (WI) ..	18	0	202	5	5	0	–	3	2	3	–	–
D. C. S. Compton (E)	17	2	131	–	5	7	2	2	0	1	–	–
M. D. Crowe (NZ)...	**17**	**1**	**131**	**5**	**3**	**–**	**3**	**–**	**1**	**2**	**2**	**1**
D. B. Vengsarkar (I) .	17	0	185	5	2	–	6	0	–	2	2	–
R. B. Richardson (WI)	16	0	146	4	9	0	–	1	2	0	–	–

				Opponents								
	Total	*200+*	*Inns*	*E*	*A*	*SA*	*WI*	*NZ*	*I*	*P*	*SL*	*Z*
H. Sutcliffe (E)......	16	0	84	–	8	6	0	2	0	–	–	–
J. B. Hobbs (E).....	15	1	102	–	12	2	1	–	–	–	–	–
R. B. Kanhai (WI) ..	15	2	137	5	5	–	–	–	4	1	–	–
C. L. Walcott (WI) ..	15	1	74	4	5	–	–	1	4	1	–	–
K. D. Walters (A) ...	15	2	125	4	–	0	6	3	1	1	–	–
E. D. Weekes (WI) ..	15	2	81	3	1	–	–	3	7	1	–	–

Notes: The most hundreds for Sri Lanka is 8 by **P. A. de Silva** in 93 innings and for Zimbabwe 4 by **D. L. Houghton** in 25 innings.

The most double-hundreds by batsmen not qualifying for the above list is four by Zaheer Abbas (12 hundreds for Pakistan) and three by R. B. Simpson (10 hundreds for Australia).

Bold type denotes those who played Test cricket in 1995-96 and 1996 seasons. Dashes indicate that a player did not play against the country concerned.

CARRYING BAT THROUGH TEST INNINGS

(Figures in brackets show side's total)

A. B. Tancred......	26*	(47)	South Africa v England at Cape Town ..	1888-89
J. E. Barrett	67*	(176)	Australia v England at Lord's	1890
R. Abel	132*	(307)	England v Australia at Sydney	1891-92
P. F. Warner	132*	(237)	England v South Africa at Johannesburg .	1898-99
W. W. Armstrong ..	159*	(309)	Australia v South Africa at Johannesburg	1902-03
J. W. Zulch........	43*	(103)	South Africa v England at Cape Town ..	1909-10
W. Bardsley	193*	(383)	Australia v England at Lord's	1926
W. M. Woodfull	30*	(66)‡	Australia v England at Brisbane	1928-29
W. M. Woodfull	73*	(193)†	Australia v England at Adelaide	1932-33
W. A. Brown	206*	(422)	Australia v England at Lord's	1938
L. Hutton	202*	(344)	England v West Indies at The Oval	1950
L. Hutton	156*	(272)	England v Australia at Adelaide	1950-51
Nazar Mohammad ..	124*	(331)	Pakistan v India at Lucknow	1952-53
F. M. M. Worrell ...	191*	(372)	West Indies v England at Nottingham ...	1957
T. L. Goddard	56*	(99)	South Africa v Australia at Cape Town ..	1957-58
D. J. McGlew......	127*	(292)	South Africa v New Zealand at Durban .	1961-62
C. C. Hunte	60*	(131)	West Indies v Australia at Port-of-Spain .	1964-65
G. M. Turner	43*	(131)	New Zealand v England at Lord's	1969
W. M. Lawry	49*	(107)	Australia v India at Delhi	1969-70
W. M. Lawry	60*	(116)†	Australia v England at Sydney	1970-71
G. M. Turner	223*	(386)	New Zealand v West Indies at Kingston .	1971-72
I. R. Redpath	159*	(346)	Australia v New Zealand at Auckland ...	1973-74
G. Boycott.........	99*	(215)	England v Australia at Perth...........	1979-80
S. M. Gavaskar	127*	(286)	India v Pakistan at Faisalabad	1982-83
Mudassar Nazar	152*	(323)	Pakistan v India at Lahore	1982-83
S. Wettimuny	63*	(144)	Sri Lanka v New Zealand at Christchurch	1982-83
D. C. Boon	58*	(103)	Australia v New Zealand at Auckland ...	1985-86
D. L. Haynes	88*	(211)	West Indies v Pakistan at Karachi	1986-87
G. A. Gooch.......	154*	(252)	England v West Indies at Leeds	1991
D. L. Haynes	75*	(176)	West Indies v England at The Oval	1991
A. J. Stewart.......	69*	(175)	England v Pakistan at Lord's	1992
D. L. Haynes	143*	(382)	West Indies v Pakistan at Port-of-Spain..	1992-93
M. H. Dekker......	68*	(187)	Zimbabwe v Pakistan at Rawalpindi	1993-94

† *One man absent.* ‡ *Two men absent.*

Notes: G. M. Turner (223*) holds the record for the highest score by a player carrying his bat through a Test innings. He is also the youngest player to do so, being 22 years 63 days old when he first achieved the feat (1969).

G. A. Gooch (61.11%) holds the record for the highest percentage of a side's total by anyone carrying his bat throughout a Test innings.

Nazar Mohammad and Mudassar Nazar were father and son.

D. L. Haynes, who is alone in achieving this feat on three occasions, also opened the batting and was last man out in each innings for West Indies v New Zealand at Dunedin, 1979-80.

FASTEST FIFTIES

Minutes			
28	J. T. Brown	England v Australia at Melbourne	1894-95
29	S. A. Durani	India v England at Kanpur	1963-64
30	E. A. V. Williams	West Indies v England at Bridgetown	1947-48
30	B. R. Taylor	New Zealand v West Indies at Auckland	1968-69
33	C. A. Roach	West Indies v England at The Oval	1933
34	C. R. Browne	West Indies v England at Georgetown	1929-30

The fastest fifties in terms of balls received (where recorded) are:

Balls			
30	Kapil Dev	India v Pakistan at Karachi (2nd Test)	1982-83
32	I. V. A. Richards	West Indies v India at Kingston	1982-83
32	I. T. Botham	England v New Zealand at The Oval	1986
33	R. C. Fredericks	West Indies v Australia at Perth	1975-76
33	Kapil Dev	India v Pakistan at Karachi	1978-79
33	Kapil Dev	India v England at Manchester	1982
33	A. J. Lamb	England v New Zealand at Auckland	1991-92

FASTEST HUNDREDS

Minutes			
70	J. M. Gregory	Australia v South Africa at Johannesburg	1921-22
75	G. L. Jessop	England v Australia at The Oval	1902
78	R. Benaud	Australia v West Indies at Kingston	1954-55
80	J. H. Sinclair	South Africa v Australia at Cape Town	1902-03
81	I. V. A. Richards	West Indies v England at St John's	1985-86
86	B. R. Taylor	New Zealand v West Indies at Auckland	1968-69

The fastest hundreds in terms of balls received (where recorded) are:

Balls			
56	I. V. A. Richards	West Indies v England at St John's	1985-86
67	J. M. Gregory	Australia v South Africa at Johannesburg	1921-22
71	R. C. Fredericks	West Indies v Australia at Perth	1975-76
74	Majid Khan	Pakistan v New Zealand at Karachi	1976-77
74	Kapil Dev	India v Sri Lanka at Kanpur	1986-87
76	G. L. Jessop	England v Australia at The Oval	1902

FASTEST DOUBLE-HUNDREDS

Minutes			
214	D. G. Bradman	Australia v England at Leeds	1930
223	S. J. McCabe	Australia v England at Nottingham	1938
226	V. T. Trumper	Australia v South Africa at Adelaide	1910-11
234	D. G. Bradman	Australia v England at Lord's	1930
240	W. R. Hammond	England v New Zealand at Auckland	1932-33
241	S. E. Gregory	Australia v England at Sydney	1894-95
245	D. C. S. Compton	England v Pakistan at Nottingham	1954

The fastest double-hundreds in terms of balls received (where recorded) are:

Balls			
220	I. T. Botham	England v India at The Oval	1982
232	C. G. Greenidge	West Indies v England at Lord's	1984
240	C. H. Lloyd	West Indies v India at Bombay	1974-75
241	Zaheer Abbas	Pakistan v India at Lahore	1982-83
242	D. G. Bradman	Australia v England at The Oval	1934
242	I. V. A. Richards	West Indies v Australia at Melbourne	1984-85

FASTEST TRIPLE-HUNDREDS

Minutes			
288	W. R. Hammond	England v New Zealand at Auckland	1932-33
336	D. G. Bradman	Australia v England at Leeds	1930

MOST RUNS IN A DAY BY A BATSMAN

309	D. G. Bradman	Australia v England at Leeds	1930
295	W. R. Hammond	England v New Zealand at Auckland	1932-33
273	D. C. S. Compton	England v Pakistan at Nottingham	1954
271	D. G. Bradman	Australia v England at Leeds	1934

SLOWEST INDIVIDUAL BATTING

2* in 81 minutes	P. C. R. Tufnell, England v India at Bombay	1992-93
3* in 100 minutes	J. T. Murray, England v Australia at Sydney	1962-63
5 in 102 minutes	Nawab of Pataudi jun., India v England at Bombay	1972-73
6 in 106 minutes	D. R. Martyn, Australia v South Africa at Sydney	1993-94
7 in 123 minutes	G. Miller, England v Australia at Melbourne	1978-79
9 in 132 minutes	R. K. Chauhan, India v Sri Lanka at Ahmedabad	1993-94
10* in 133 minutes	T. G. Evans, England v Australia at Adelaide	1946-47
16* in 147 minutes	D. B. Vengsarkar, India v Pakistan at Kanpur	1979-80
17* in 166 minutes	G. M. Ritchie, Australia v India at Sydney	1985-86
18 in 194 minutes	W. R. Playle, New Zealand v England at Leeds	1958
19 in 217 minutes	M. D. Crowe, New Zealand v Sri Lanka at Moratuwa	1983-84
25 in 242 minutes	D. K. Morrison, New Zealand v Pakistan at Faisalabad	1990-91
28* in 250 minutes	J. W. Burke, Australia v England at Brisbane	1958-59
29* in 277 minutes	R. C. Russell, England v South Africa at Johannesburg	1995-96
35 in 332 minutes	C. J. Tavaré, England v India at Madras	1981-82
55 in 336 minutes	B. A. Edgar, New Zealand v Australia at Wellington	1981-82
57 in 346 minutes	G. S. Camacho, West Indies v England at Bridgetown	1967-68
58 in 367 minutes	Ijaz Butt, Pakistan v Australia at Karachi	1959-60
60 in 390 minutes	D. N. Sardesai, India v West Indies at Bridgetown	1961-62
62 in 408 minutes	Ramiz Raja, Pakistan v West Indies at Karachi	1986-87
68 in 458 minutes	T. E. Bailey, England v Australia at Brisbane	1958-59
99 in 505 minutes	M. L. Jaisimha, India v Pakistan at Kanpur	1960-61
105 in 575 minutes	D. J. McGlew, South Africa v Australia at Durban	1957-58
114 in 591 minutes	Mudassar Nazar, Pakistan v England at Lahore	1977-78
120* in 609 minutes	J. J. Crowe, New Zealand v Sri Lanka, Colombo (CCC)	1986-87
146* in 655 minutes	M. J. Greatbatch, New Zealand v Australia at Perth	1989-90
163 in 720 minutes	Shoaib Mohammad, Pakistan v New Zealand at Wellington	1988-89
201* in 777 minutes	D. S. B. P. Kuruppu, Sri Lanka v New Zealand at Colombo (CCC)	1986-87
337 in 999 minutes	Hanif Mohammad, Pakistan v West Indies at Bridgetown.	1957-58

Note: The longest any batsman in all first-class innings has taken to score his first run is 97 minutes by T. G. Evans for England against Australia at Adelaide, 1946-47.

SLOWEST HUNDREDS

557 minutes	Mudassar Nazar, Pakistan v England at Lahore	1977-78
545 minutes	D. J. McGlew, South Africa v Australia at Durban	1957-58
535 minutes	A. P. Gurusinha, Sri Lanka v Zimbabwe at Harare	1994-95
516 minutes	J. J. Crowe, New Zealand v Sri Lanka at Colombo (CCC)	1986-87
500 minutes	S. V. Manjrekar, India v Zimbabwe at Harare	1992-93
488 minutes	P. E. Richardson, England v South Africa at Johannesburg	1956-57

Notes: The slowest hundred for any Test in England is 458 minutes (329 balls) by K. W. R. Fletcher, England v Pakistan, The Oval, 1974.

The slowest double-hundred in a Test was scored in 777 minutes (548 balls) by D. S. B. P. Kuruppu for Sri Lanka v New Zealand at Colombo (CCC), 1986-87, on his debut. It is also the slowest-ever first-class double-hundred.

HIGHEST PARTNERSHIPS FOR EACH WICKET

413 for 1st	V. Mankad (231)/Pankaj Roy (173)........	I v NZ	Madras	1955-56
451 for 2nd	W. H. Ponsford (266)/D. G. Bradman (244).	A v E	The Oval	1934
467 for 3rd	A. H. Jones (186)/M. D. Crowe (299)......	NZ v SL	Wellington	1990-91
411 for 4th	P. B. H. May (285*)/M. C. Cowdrey (154)..	E v WI	Birmingham	1957
405 for 5th	S. G. Barnes (234)/D. G. Bradman (234) ...	A v E	Sydney	1946-47
346 for 6th	J. H. W. Fingleton (136)/D. G. Bradman (270)	A v E	Melbourne	1936-37
347 for 7th	D. St E. Atkinson (219)/C. C. Depeiza (122)	WI v A	Bridgetown	1954-55
246 for 8th	L. E. G. Ames (137)/G. O. B. Allen (122) ..	E v NZ	Lord's	1931
190 for 9th	Asif Iqbal (146)/Intikhab Alam (51)	P v E	The Oval	1967
151 for 10th	B. F. Hastings (110)/R. O. Collinge (68*)...	NZ v P	Auckland	1972-73

PARTNERSHIPS OF 300 AND OVER

467	for 3rd	A. H. Jones (186)/M. D. Crowe (299)	NZ v SL	Wellington	1990-91
451	for 2nd	W. H. Ponsford (266)/D. G. Bradman (244) ...	A v E	The Oval	1934
451	for 3rd	Mudassar Nazar (231)/Javed Miandad (280*) ..	P v I	Hyderabad	1982-83
446	for 2nd	C. C. Hunte (260)/G. S. Sobers (365*)........	WI v P	Kingston	1957-58
413	for 1st	V. Mankad (231)/Pankaj Roy (173)	I v NZ	Madras	1955-56
411	for 4th	P. B. H. May (285*)/M. C. Cowdrey (154)	E v WI	Birmingham	1957
405	for 5th	S. G. Barnes (234)/D. G. Bradman (234)......	A v E	Sydney	1946-47
399	for 4th	G. S. Sobers (226)/F. M. M. Worrell (197*) ...	WI v E	Bridgetown	1959-60
397	for 3rd	Qasim Omar (206)/Javed Miandad (203*)	P v SL	Faisalabad	1985-86
388	for 4th	W. H. Ponsford (181)/D. G. Bradman (304) ...	A v E	Leeds	1934
387	for 1st	G. M. Turner (259)/T. W. Jarvis (182)........	NZ v WI	Georgetown	1971-72
382	for 2nd	L. Hutton (364)/M. Leyland (187)............	E v A	The Oval	1938
382	for 1st	W. M. Lawry (210)/R. B. Simpson (201)	A v WI	Bridgetown	1964-65
370	for 3rd	W. J. Edrich (189)/D. C. S. Compton (208)....	E v SA	Lord's	1947
369	for 2nd	J. H. Edrich (310*)/K. F. Barrington (163)	E v NZ	Leeds	1965
359	for 1st	L. Hutton (158)/C. Washbrook (195)	E v SA	Johannesburg	1948-49
351	for 2nd	G. A. Gooch (196)/D. I. Gower (157)	E v A	The Oval	1985
350	for 4th	Mushtaq Mohammad (201)/Asif Iqbal (175) ...	P v NZ	Dunedin	1972-73
347	for 7th	D. St E. Atkinson (219)/C. C. Depeiza (122)...	WI v A	Bridgetown	1954-55
346	for 6th	J. H. Fingleton (136)/D. G. Bradman (270)....	A v E	Melbourne	1936-37
344*	for 2nd	S. M. Gavaskar (182*)/D. B. Vengsarkar (157*)	I v WI	Calcutta	1978-79
341	for 3rd	E. J. Barlow (201)/R. G. Pollock (175)........	SA v A	Adelaide	1963-64
338	for 3rd	E. D. Weekes (206)/F. M. M. Worrell (167) ...	WI v E	Port-of-Spain	1953-54
336	for 4th	W. M. Lawry (151)/K. D. Walters (242)	A v WI	Sydney	1968-69
332*	for 5th	A. R. Border (200*)/S. R. Waugh (157*)	A v E	Leeds	1993
331	for 2nd	R. T. Robinson (148)/D. I. Gower (215)	E v A	Birmingham	1985
329	for 1st	G. R. Marsh (138)/M. A. Taylor (219)........	A v E	Nottingham	1989
323	for 1st	J. B. Hobbs (178)/W. Rhodes (179)	E v A	Melbourne	1911-12
322	for 4th	Javed Miandad (153*)/Salim Malik (165)......	P v E	Birmingham	1992
319	for 3rd	A. Melville (189)/A. D. Nourse (149).........	SA v E	Nottingham	1947
316†	for 3rd	G. R. Viswanath (222)/Yashpal Sharma (140)..	I v E	Madras	1981-82
308	for 7th	Waqar Hassan (189)/Imtiaz Ahmed (209)	P v NZ	Lahore	1955-56
308	for 3rd	R. B. Richardson (154)/I. V. A. Richards (178).	WI v A	St John's	1983-84
308	for 3rd	G. A. Gooch (333)/A. J. Lamb (139)	E v I	Lord's	1990
303	for 3rd	I. V. A. Richards (232)/A. I. Kallicharran (97) .	WI v E	Nottingham	1976
303	for 3rd	M. A. Atherton (135)/R. A. Smith (175)	E v WI	St John's	1993-94
301	for 2nd	A. R. Morris (182)/D. G. Bradman (173*).....	A v E	Leeds	1948

† 415 runs were scored for this wicket in two separate partnerships: D. B. Vengsarkar retired hurt when he and Viswanath had added 99 runs.

BOWLING RECORDS

MOST WICKETS IN AN INNINGS

10-53	J. C. Laker	England v Australia at Manchester	1956
9-28	G. A. Lohmann	England v South Africa at Johannesburg	1895-96
9-37	J. C. Laker	England v Australia at Manchester	1956
9-52	R. J. Hadlee	New Zealand v Australia at Brisbane	1985-86
9-56	Abdul Qadir	Pakistan v England at Lahore	1987-88
9-57	D. E. Malcolm	England v South Africa at The Oval	1994
9-69	J. M. Patel	India v Australia at Kanpur	1959-60
9-83	Kapil Dev	India v West Indies at Ahmedabad	1983-84
9-86	Sarfraz Nawaz	Pakistan v Australia at Melbourne	1978-79
9-95	J. M. Noreiga	West Indies v India at Port-of-Spain	1970-71
9-102	S. P. Gupte	India v West Indies at Kanpur	1958-59
9-103	S. F. Barnes	England v South Africa at Johannesburg	1913-14
9-113	H. J. Tayfield	South Africa v England at Johannesburg	1956-57
9-121	A. A. Mailey	Australia v England at Melbourne	1920-21
8-7	G. A. Lohmann	England v South Africa at Port Elizabeth	1895-96
8-11	J. Briggs	England v South Africa at Cape Town	1888-89
8-29	S. F. Barnes	England v South Africa at The Oval	1912
8-29	C. E. H. Croft	West Indies v Pakistan at Port-of-Spain	1976-77
8-31	F. Laver	Australia v England at Manchester	1909
8-31	F. S. Trueman	England v India at Manchester	1952
8-34	I. T. Botham	England v Pakistan at Lord's	1978
8-35	G. A. Lohmann	England v Australia at Sydney	1886-87
8-38	L. R. Gibbs	West Indies v India at Bridgetown	1961-62
8-43†	A. E. Trott	Australia v England at Adelaide	1894-95
8-43	H. Verity	England v Australia at Lord's	1934
8-43	R. G. D. Willis	England v Australia at Leeds	1981
8-45	C. E. L. Ambrose	West Indies v England at Bridgetown	1989-90
8-51	D. L. Underwood	England v Pakistan at Lord's	1974
8-52	V. Mankad	India v Pakistan at Delhi	1952-53
8-53	G. B. Lawrence	South Africa v New Zealand at Johannesburg	1961-62
8-53†	R. A. L. Massie	Australia v England at Lord's	1972
8-55	V. Mankad	India v England at Madras	1951-52
8-56	S. F. Barnes	England v South Africa at Johannesburg	1913-14
8-58	G. A. Lohmann	England v Australia at Sydney	1891-92
8-58	Imran Khan	Pakistan v Sri Lanka at Lahore	1981-82
8-59	C. Blythe	England v South Africa at Leeds	1907
8-59	A. A. Mallett	Australia v Pakistan at Adelaide	1972-73
8-60	Imran Khan	Pakistan v India at Karachi	1982-83
8-61†	N. D. Hirwani	India v West Indies at Madras	1987-88
8-65	H. Trumble	Australia v England at The Oval	1902
8-68	W. Rhodes	England v Australia at Melbourne	1903-04
8-69	H. J. Tayfield	South Africa v England at Durban	1956-57
8-69	Sikander Bakht	Pakistan v India at Delhi	1979-80
8-70	S. J. Snooke	South Africa v England at Johannesburg	1905-06
8-71	G. D. McKenzie	Australia v West Indies at Melbourne	1968-69
8-71	S. K. Warne	Australia v England at Brisbane	1994-95
8-71	A. A. Donald	South Africa v Zimbabwe at Harare	1995-96
8-72	S. Venkataraghavan	India v New Zealand at Delhi	1964-65
8-75†	N. D. Hirwani	India v West Indies at Madras	1987-88
8-75	A. R. C. Fraser	England v West Indies at Bridgetown	1993-94
8-76	E. A. S. Prasanna	India v New Zealand at Auckland	1975-76
8-79	B. S. Chandrasekhar	India v England at Delhi	1972-73
8-81	L. C. Braund	England v Australia at Melbourne	1903-04
8-83	J. R. Ratnayeke	Sri Lanka v Pakistan at Sialkot	1985-86
8-84†	R. A. L. Massie	Australia v England at Lord's	1972
8-85	Kapil Dev	India v Pakistan at Lahore	1982-83
8-86	A. W. Greig	England v West Indies at Port-of-Spain	1973-74

8-87	M. G. Hughes	Australia v West Indies at Perth	1988-89
8-92	M. A. Holding	West Indies v England at The Oval	1976
8-94	T. Richardson	England v Australia at Sydney	1897-98
8-97	C. J. McDermott	Australia v England at Perth	1990-91
8-103	I. T. Botham	England v West Indies at Lord's	1984
8-104†	A. L. Valentine	West Indies v England at Manchester	1950
8-106	Kapil Dev	India v Australia at Adelaide	1985-86
8-107	B. J. T. Bosanquet	England v Australia at Nottingham	1905
8-107	N. A. Foster	England v Pakistan at Leeds	1987
8-112	G. F. Lawson	Australia v West Indies at Adelaide	1984-85
8-126	J. C. White	England v Australia at Adelaide	1928-29
8-141	C. J. McDermott	Australia v England at Manchester	1985
8-143	M. H. N. Walker	Australia v England at Melbourne	1974-75

† *On Test debut.*
Note: The best for Zimbabwe is 6-90 by **H. H. Streak** against Pakistan at Harare in 1994-95.

OUTSTANDING ANALYSES

	O	*M*	*R*	*W*		
J. C. Laker (E)	51.2	23	53	10	v Australia at Manchester	1956
G. A. Lohmann (E)	14.2	6	28	9	v South Africa at Johannesburg	1895-96
J. C. Laker (E)	16.4	4	37	9	v Australia at Manchester	1956
G. A. Lohmann (E)	9.4	5	7	8	v South Africa at Port Elizabeth	1895-96
J. Briggs (E)	14.2	5	11	8	v South Africa at Cape Town	1888-89
J. Briggs (E)	19.1	11	17	7	v South Africa at Cape Town	1888-89
M. A. Noble (A)	7.4	2	17	7	v England at Melbourne	1901-02
W. Rhodes (E)	11	3	17	7	v Australia at Birmingham	1902
A. E. R. Gilligan (E)	6.3	4	7	6	v South Africa at Birmingham	1924
S. Haigh (E)	11.4	6	11	6	v South Africa at Cape Town	1898-99
D. L. Underwood (E)	11.6	7	12	6	v New Zealand at Christchurch	1970-71
S. L. V. Raju (I)	17.5	13	12	6	v Sri Lanka at Chandigarh	1990-91
H. J. Tayfield (SA)	14	7	13	6	v New Zealand at Johannesburg	1953-54
C. T. B. Turner (A)	18	11	15	6	v England at Sydney	1886-87
M. H. N. Walker (A)	16	8	15	6	v Pakistan at Sydney	1972-73
E. R. H. Toshack (A)	2.3	1	2	5	v India at Brisbane	1947-48
H. Ironmonger (A)	7.2	5	6	5	v South Africa at Melbourne	1931-32
T. B. A. May (A)	6.5	3	9	5	v West Indies at Adelaide	1992-93
Pervez Sajjad (P)	12	8	5	4	v New Zealand at Rawalpindi	1964-65
K. Higgs (E)	9	7	5	4	v New Zealand at Christchurch	1965-66
P. H. Edmonds (E)	8	6	6	4	v Pakistan at Lord's	1978
J. C. White (E)	6.3	2	7	4	v Australia at Brisbane	1928-29
J. H. Wardle (E)	5	2	7	4	v Australia at Manchester	1953
R. Appleyard (E)	6	3	7	4	v New Zealand at Auckland	1954-55
R. Benaud (A)	3.4	3	0	3	v India at Delhi	1959-60

MOST WICKETS IN A MATCH

19-90	J. C. Laker	England v Australia at Manchester	1956
17-159	S. F. Barnes	England v South Africa at Johannesburg	1913-14
16-136†	N. D. Hirwani	India v West Indies at Madras	1987-88
16-137†	R. A. L. Massie	Australia v England at Lord's	1972
15-28	J. Briggs	England v South Africa at Cape Town	1888-89
15-45	G. A. Lohmann	England v South Africa at Port Elizabeth	1895-96
15-99	C. Blythe	England v South Africa at Leeds	1907
15-104	H. Verity	England v Australia at Lord's	1934
15-123	R. J. Hadlee	New Zealand v Australia at Brisbane	1985-86
15-124	W. Rhodes	England v Australia at Melbourne	1903-04
14-90	F. R. Spofforth	Australia v England at The Oval	1882

14-99	A. V. Bedser	England v Australia at Nottingham	1953
14-102	W. Bates	England v Australia at Melbourne	1882-83
14-116	Imran Khan	Pakistan v Sri Lanka at Lahore	1981-82
14-124	J. M. Patel	India v Australia at Kanpur	1959-60
14-144	S. F. Barnes	England v South Africa at Durban	1913-14
14-149	M. A. Holding	West Indies v England at The Oval	1976
14-199	C. V. Grimmett	Australia v South Africa at Adelaide	1931-32

† *On Test debut.*

Notes: The best for South Africa is 13-165 by H. J. Tayfield against Australia at Melbourne, 1952-53; for Sri Lanka 10-90 by W. P. U. J. C. Vaas against New Zealand at Napier, 1994-95; for Zimbabwe 9-105 by H. H. Streak against Pakistan at Harare, 1994-95.

MOST WICKETS IN A SERIES

	T	*R*	*W*	*Avge*		
S. F. Barnes	4	536	49	10.93	England v South Africa	1913-14
J. C. Laker	5	442	46	9.60	England v Australia	1956
C. V. Grimmett	5	642	44	14.59	Australia v South Africa	1935-36
T. M. Alderman	6	893	42	21.26	Australia v England	1981
R. M. Hogg	6	527	41	12.85	Australia v England	1978-79
T. M. Alderman	6	712	41	17.36	Australia v England	1989
Imran Khan	6	558	40	13.95	Pakistan v India	1982-83
A. V. Bedser	5	682	39	17.48	England v Australia	1953
D. K. Lillee	6	870	39	22.30	Australia v England	1981
M. W. Tate	5	881	38	23.18	England v Australia	1924-25
W. J. Whitty	5	632	37	17.08	Australia v South Africa	1910-11
H. J. Tayfield	5	636	37	17.18	South Africa v England	1956-57
A. E. E. Vogler	5	783	36	21.75	South Africa v England	1909-10
A. A. Mailey	5	946	36	26.27	Australia v England	1920-21
G. A. Lohmann	3	203	35	5.80	England v South Africa	1895-96
B. S. Chandrasekhar	5	662	35	18.91	India v England	1972-73
M. D. Marshall	5	443	35	12.65	West Indies v England	1988

Notes: The most for New Zealand is 33 by R. J. Hadlee against Australia in 1985-86, for Sri Lanka 20 by R. J. Ratnayake against India in 1985-86, and for Zimbabwe 22 by H. H. Streak against Pakistan in 1994-95.

MOST WICKETS IN A CAREER

(Qualification: 100 wickets)

ENGLAND

		T	*Balls*	*R*	*W*	*Avge*	*5W/i*	*10W/m*
1	I. T. Botham	102	21,815	10,878	383	28.40	27	4
2	R. G. D. Willis	90	17,357	8,190	325	25.20	16	—
3	F. S. Trueman	67	15,178	6,625	307	21.57	17	3
4	D. L. Underwood	86	21,862	7,674	297	25.83	17	6
5	J. B. Statham	70	16,056	6,261	252	24.84	9	1
6	A. V. Bedser	51	15,918	5,876	236	24.89	15	5
7	J. A. Snow	49	12,021	5,387	202	26.66	8	1
8	J. C. Laker	46	12,027	4,101	193	21.24	9	3
9	S. F. Barnes	27	7,873	3,106	189	16.43	24	7
10	G. A. R. Lock	49	13,147	4,451	174	25.58	9	3
11	M. W. Tate	39	12,523	4,055	155	26.16	7	1
12	F. J. Titmus	53	15,118	4,931	153	32.22	7	—
13	J. E. Emburey	64	15,391	5,646	147	38.40	6	—

		T	Balls	R	W	Avge	5W/i	10W/m
14	H. Verity	40	11,173	3,510	144	24.37	5	2
15	C. M. Old	46	8,858	4,020	143	28.11	4	—
16	A. W. Greig	58	9,802	4,541	141	32.20	6	2
17	P. A. J. DeFreitas	44	9,838	4,700	140	33.57	4	—
18	G. R. Dilley	41	8,192	4,107	138	29.76	6	—
19	T. E. Bailey	61	9,712	3,856	132	29.21	5	1
20	W. Rhodes	58	8,231	3,425	127	26.96	6	1
21	P. H. Edmonds	51	12,028	4,273	125	34.18	2	—
22	D. A. Allen	39	11,297	3,779	122	30.97	4	—
	R. Illingworth	61	11,934	3,807	122	31.20	3	—
	D. E. Malcolm	**36**	**7,922**	**4,441**	**122**	**36.40**	**5**	**2**
25	**A. R. C. Fraser**	**32**	**7,967**	**3,509**	**119**	**29.48**	**8**	**—**
26	J. Briggs	33	5,332	2,095	118	17.75	9	4
27	G. G. Arnold	34	7,650	3,254	115	28.29	6	—
28	G. A. Lohmann	18	3,821	1,205	112	10.75	9	5
29	D. V. P. Wright	34	8,135	4,224	108	39.11	6	1
30	J. H. Wardle	28	6,597	2,080	102	20.39	5	1
31	R. Peel	20	5,216	1,715	101	16.98	5	1
32	C. Blythe	19	4,546	1,863	100	18.63	9	4

AUSTRALIA

		T	Balls	R	W	Avge	5W/i	10W/m
1	D. K. Lillee	70	18,467	8,493	355	23.92	23	7
2	**C. J. McDermott**	**71**	**16,586**	**8,332**	**291**	**28.63**	**14**	**2**
3	R. Benaud	63	19,108	6,704	248	27.03	16	1
4	G. D. McKenzie	60	17,681	7,328	246	29.78	16	3
5	R. R. Lindwall	61	13,650	5,251	228	23.03	12	—
6	C. V. Grimmett	37	14,513	5,231	216	24.21	21	7
7	M. G. Hughes	53	12,285	6,017	212	28.38	7	1
8	**S. K. Warne**	**44**	**13,118**	**4,870**	**207**	**23.52**	**10**	**3**
9	J. R. Thomson	51	10,535	5,601	200	28.00	8	—
10	A. K. Davidson	44	11,587	3,819	186	20.53	14	2
11	G. F. Lawson	46	11,118	5,501	180	30.56	11	2
12	K. R. Miller	55	10,461	3,906	170	22.97	7	1
	T. M. Alderman	41	10,181	4,616	170	27.15	14	1
14	W. A. Johnston	40	11,048	3,826	160	23.91	7	—
15	W. J. O'Reilly	27	10,024	3,254	144	22.59	11	3
16	H. Trumble	32	8,099	3,072	141	21.78	9	3
17	M. H. N. Walker	34	10,094	3,792	138	27.47	6	—
18	A. A. Mallett	38	9,990	3,940	132	29.84	6	1
19	B. Yardley	33	8,909	3,986	126	31.63	6	1
20	R. M. Hogg	38	7,633	3,503	123	28.47	6	2
21	M. A. Noble	42	7,159	3,025	121	25.00	9	2
22	B. A. Reid	27	6,244	2,784	113	24.63	5	2
23	I. W. Johnson	45	8,780	3,182	109	29.19	3	—
24	G. Giffen	31	6,457	2,791	103	27.09	7	1
25	A. N. Connolly	29	7,818	2,981	102	29.22	4	—
26	C. T. B. Turner	17	5,179	1,670	101	16.53	11	2

SOUTH AFRICA

		T	Balls	R	W	Avge	5W/i	10W/m
1	H. J. Tayfield	37	13,568	4,405	170	25.91	14	2
2	T. L. Goddard	41	11,736	3,226	123	26.22	5	—
3	P. M. Pollock	28	6,522	2,806	116	24.18	9	1
4	**A. A. Donald**	**25**	**5,781**	**2,836**	**114**	**24.87**	**6**	**2**
5	N. A. T. Adcock	26	6,391	2,195	104	21.10	5	—

WEST INDIES

		T	*Balls*	*R*	*W*	*Avge*	*5W/i*	*10W/m*
1	M. D. Marshall	81	17,584	7,876	376	20.94	22	4
2 {	L. R. Gibbs	79	27,115	8,989	309	29.09	18	2
	C. A. Walsh	**82**	**17,578**	**7,738**	**309**	**25.04**	**11**	**2**
4	**C. E. L. Ambrose**	**61**	**14,319**	**5,658**	**266**	**21.27**	**14**	**3**
5	J. Garner	58	13,169	5,433	259	20.97	7	—
6	M. A. Holding	60	12,680	5,898	249	23.68	13	2
7	G. S. Sobers	93	21,599	7,999	235	34.03	6	—
8	A. M. E. Roberts	47	11,136	5,174	202	25.61	11	2
9	W. W. Hall	48	10,421	5,066	192	26.38	9	1
10	S. Ramadhin	43	13,939	4,579	158	28.98	10	1
11	A. L. Valentine	36	12,953	4,215	139	30.32	8	2
12	C. E. H. Croft	27	6,165	2,913	125	23.30	3	—
13	**I. R. Bishop**	**26**	**5,742**	**2,565**	**117**	**21.92**	**6**	**—**
14	V. A. Holder	40	9,095	3,627	109	33.27	3	—

NEW ZEALAND

		T	*Balls*	*R*	*W*	*Avge*	*5W/i*	*10W/m*
1	R. J. Hadlee	86	21,918	9,612	431	22.29	36	9
2	**D. K. Morrison**	**47**	**9,916**	**5,445**	**157**	**34.68**	**10**	**—**
3	B. L. Cairns	43	10,628	4,280	130	32.92	6	1
4	E. J. Chatfield	43	10,360	3,958	123	32.17	3	1
5	R. O. Collinge	35	7,689	3,392	116	29.24	3	—
6	B. R. Taylor	30	6,334	2,953	111	26.60	4	—
7	J. G. Bracewell	41	8,403	3,653	102	35.81	4	1
8	R. C. Motz	32	7,034	3,148	100	31.48	5	—

INDIA

		T	*Balls*	*R*	*W*	*Avge*	*5W/i*	*10W/m*
1	Kapil Dev	131	27,740	12,867	434	29.64	23	2
2	B. S. Bedi	67	21,364	7,637	266	28.71	14	1
3	B. S. Chandrasekhar	58	15,963	7,199	242	29.74	16	2
4	E. A. S. Prasanna	49	14,353	5,742	189	30.38	10	2
5	V. Mankad	44	14,686	5,236	162	32.32	8	2
6	S. Venkataraghavan	57	14,877	5,634	156	36.11	3	1
7	R. J. Shastri	80	15,751	6,185	151	40.96	2	—
8	S. P. Gupte	36	11,284	4,403	149	29.55	12	1
9	D. R. Doshi	33	9,322	3,502	114	30.71	6	—
10	**A. Kumble**	**26**	**7,883**	**2,996**	**114**	**26.28**	**6**	**1**
11	K. D. Ghavri	39	7,042	3,656	109	33.54	4	—
12	N. S. Yadav	35	8,349	3,580	102	35.09	3	—

PAKISTAN

		T	*Balls*	*R*	*W*	*Avge*	*5W/i*	*10W/m*
1	Imran Khan	88	19,458	8,258	362	22.81	23	6
2	**Wasim Akram**	**70**	**16,034**	**6,874**	**300**	**22.91**	**20**	**3**
3	Abdul Qadir	67	17,126	7,742	236	32.80	15	5
4	**Waqar Younis**	**41**	**8,483**	**4,553**	**216**	**21.07**	**19**	**4**
5	Sarfraz Nawaz	55	13,927	5,798	177	32.75	4	1
6	Iqbal Qasim	50	13,019	4,807	171	28.11	8	2
7	Fazal Mahmood	34	9,834	3,434	139	24.70	13	4
8	Intikhab Alam	47	10,474	4,494	125	35.95	5	2

SRI LANKA: The highest aggregate is 81 wickets, average 33.88, by **M. Muralitharan** in 23 Tests.

ZIMBABWE: The highest aggregate is 58 wickets, average 21.67, by **H. H. Streak** in 12 Tests.

Bold type denotes those who played Test cricket in 1995-96 and 1996 seasons.

WICKET WITH FIRST BALL IN TEST CRICKET

	Batsman dismissed			
A. Coningham	A. C. MacLaren	A v E	Melbourne	1894-95
W. M. Bradley	F. Laver	E v A	Manchester	1899
E. G. Arnold	V. T. Trumper	E v A	Sydney	1903-04
G. G. Macaulay	G. A. L. Hearne	E v SA	Cape Town	1922-23
M. W. Tate	M. J. Susskind	E v SA	Birmingham	1924
M. Henderson	E. W. Dawson	NZ v E	Christchurch	1929-30
H. D. Smith	E. Paynter	NZ v E	Christchurch	1932-33
T. F. Johnson	W. W. Keeton	WI v E	The Oval	1939
R. Howorth	D. V. Dyer	E v SA	The Oval	1947
Intikhab Alam	C. C. McDonald	P v A	Karachi	1959-60
R. K. Illingworth	P. V. Simmons	E v WI	Nottingham	1991

HAT-TRICKS

F. R. Spofforth	Australia v England at Melbourne	1878-79
W. Bates	England v Australia at Melbourne	1882-83
J. Briggs	England v Australia at Sydney	1891-92
G. A. Lohmann	England v South Africa at Port Elizabeth	1895-96
J. T. Hearne	England v Australia at Leeds	1899
H. Trumble	Australia v England at Melbourne	1901-02
H. Trumble	Australia v England at Melbourne	1903-04
T. J. Matthews† / T. J. Matthews	Australia v South Africa at Manchester	1912
M. J. C. Allom‡	England v New Zealand at Christchurch	1929-30
T. W. J. Goddard	England v South Africa at Johannesburg	1938-39
P. J. Loader	England v West Indies at Leeds	1957
L. F. Kline	Australia v South Africa at Cape Town	1957-58
W. W. Hall	West Indies v Pakistan at Lahore	1958-59
G. M. Griffin	South Africa v England at Lord's	1960
L. R. Gibbs	West Indies v Australia at Adelaide	1960-61
P. J. Petherick‡	New Zealand v Pakistan at Lahore	1976-77
C. A. Walsh§	West Indies v Australia at Brisbane	1988-89
M. G. Hughes§	Australia v West Indies at Perth	1988-89
D. W. Fleming‡	Australia v Pakistan at Rawalpindi	1994-95
S. K. Warne	Australia v England at Melbourne	1994-95
D. G. Cork	England v West Indies at Manchester	1995

† *T. J. Matthews did the hat-trick in each innings of the same match.*
‡ *On Test debut.*
§ *Not all in the same innings.*

FOUR WICKETS IN FIVE BALLS

M. J. C. Allom	England v New Zealand at Christchurch *On debut, in his eighth over: W-WWW*	1929-30
C. M. Old	England v Pakistan at Birmingham *Sequence interrupted by a no-ball: WW-WW*	1978
Wasim Akram	Pakistan v West Indies at Lahore (*WW-WW*)	1990-91

MOST BALLS BOWLED IN A TEST

S. Ramadhin (West Indies) sent down 774 balls in 129 overs against England at Birmingham, 1957. It was the most delivered by any bowler in a Test, beating H. Verity's 766 for England against South Africa at Durban, 1938-39. In this match Ramadhin also bowled the most balls (588) in any single first-class innings, including Tests.

ALL-ROUND RECORDS

100 RUNS AND FIVE WICKETS IN AN INNINGS

England					
A. W. Greig	148	6-164	v West Indies	Bridgetown	1973-74
I. T. Botham	103	5-73	v New Zealand	Christchurch	1977-78
I. T. Botham	108	8-34	v Pakistan	Lord's	1978
I. T. Botham	114	6-58 } 7-48	v India	Bombay	1979-80
I. T. Botham	149*	6-95	v Australia	Leeds	1981
I. T. Botham	138	5-59	v New Zealand	Wellington	1983-84
Australia					
C. Kelleway	114	5-33	v South Africa	Manchester	1912
J. M. Gregory	100	7-69	v England	Melbourne	1920-21
K. R. Miller	109	6-107	v West Indies	Kingston	1954-55
R. Benaud	100	5-84	v South Africa	Johannesburg	1957-58
South Africa					
J. H. Sinclair	106	6-26	v England	Cape Town	1898-99
G. A. Faulkner	123	5-120	v England	Johannesburg	1909-10
West Indies					
D. St E. Atkinson	219	5-56	v Australia	Bridgetown	1954-55
O. G. Smith	100	5-90	v India	Delhi	1958-59
G. S. Sobers	104	5-63	v India	Kingston	1961-62
G. S. Sobers	174	5-41	v England	Leeds	1966
New Zealand					
B. R. Taylor†	105	5-86	v India	Calcutta	1964-65
India					
V. Mankad	184	5-196	v England	Lord's	1952
P. R. Umrigar	172*	5-107	v West Indies	Port-of-Spain	1961-62
Pakistan					
Mushtaq Mohammad	201	5-49	v New Zealand	Dunedin	1972-73
Mushtaq Mohammad	121	5-28	v West Indies	Port-of-Spain	1976-77
Imran Khan	117	6-98 } 5-82	v India	Faisalabad	1982-83
Wasim Akram	123	5-100	v Australia	Adelaide	1989-90

† *On debut.*

Note: In 1996-97, after the deadline for inclusion in this section, P. A. Strang achieved 106* and 5-212 for Zimbabwe v Pakistan at Sheikhupura.

100 RUNS AND FIVE DISMISSALS IN AN INNINGS

D. T. Lindsay	182	6ct	SA v A	Johannesburg	1966-67
I. D. S. Smith	113*	4ct, 1st	NZ v E	Auckland	1983-84
S. A. R. Silva	111	5ct	SL v I	Colombo (PSS)	1985-86

100 RUNS AND TEN WICKETS IN A TEST

A. K. Davidson	44 80	5-135 6-87	A v WI	Brisbane	1960-61
I. T. Botham	114	6-58 7-48	E v I	Bombay	1979-80
Imran Khan	117	6-98 5-82	P v I	Faisalabad	1982-83

1,000 RUNS AND 100 WICKETS IN A CAREER

	Tests	*Runs*	*Wkts*	*Tests for Double*
England				
T. E. Bailey	61	2,290	132	47
†I. T. Botham	102	5,200	383	21
J. E. Emburey	64	1,713	147	46
A. W. Greig	58	3,599	141	37
R. Illingworth	61	1,836	122	47
W. Rhodes	58	2,325	127	44
M. W. Tate	39	1,198	155	33
F. J. Titmus	53	1,449	153	40
Australia				
R. Benaud	63	2,201	248	32
A. K. Davidson	44	1,328	186	34
G. Giffen	31	1,238	103	30
M. G. Hughes	53	1,032	212	52
I. W. Johnson	45	1,000	109	45
R. R. Lindwall	61	1,502	228	38
K. R. Miller	55	2,958	170	33
M. A. Noble	42	1,997	121	27
South Africa				
T. L. Goddard	41	2,516	123	36
West Indies				
M. D. Marshall	81	1,810	376	49
†G. S. Sobers	93	8,032	235	48
New Zealand				
J. G. Bracewell	41	1,001	102	41
R. J. Hadlee	86	3,124	431	28
India				
Kapil Dev	131	5,248	434	25
V. Mankad	44	2,109	162	23
R. J. Shastri	80	3,830	151	44
Pakistan				
Abdul Qadir	67	1,029	236	62
Imran Khan	88	3,807	362	30
Intikhab Alam	47	1,493	125	41
Sarfraz Nawaz	55	1,045	177	55
Wasim Akram	**70**	**1,652**	**300**	**45**

Bold type denotes those who played Test cricket in 1995-96 and 1996 seasons.

† I. T. Botham (120 catches) and G. S. Sobers (109) are the only players to have achieved the treble of 1,000 runs, 100 wickets and 100 catches.

WICKET-KEEPING RECORDS

Most Dismissals in an Innings

7 (all ct)	Wasim Bari	Pakistan v New Zealand at Auckland	1978-79
7 (all ct)	R. W. Taylor	England v India at Bombay	1979-80

7 (all ct)	I. D. S. Smith	New Zealand v Sri Lanka at Hamilton	1990-91
6 (all ct)	A. T. W. Grout	Australia v South Africa at Johannesburg	1957-58
6 (all ct)	D. T. Lindsay	South Africa v Australia at Johannesburg	1966-67
6 (all ct)	J. T. Murray	England v India at Lord's	1967
6 (5ct, 1st)	S. M. H. Kirmani	India v New Zealand at Christchurch	1975-76
6 (all ct)	R. W. Marsh	Australia v England at Brisbane	1982-83
6 (all ct)	S. A. R. Silva	Sri Lanka v India at Colombo (SSC)	1985-86
6 (all ct)	R. C. Russell	England v Australia at Melbourne	1990-91
6 (all ct)	R. C. Russell	England v South Africa at Johannesburg	1995-96

Note: The most stumpings in an innings is 5 by K. S. More for India v West Indies at Madras in 1987-88.

Most Dismissals in a Test

11 (all ct)	R. C. Russell	England v South Africa at Johannesburg	1995-96
10 (all ct)	R. W. Taylor	England v India at Bombay	1979-80
9 (8ct, 1st)	G. R. A. Langley	Australia v England at Lord's	1956
9 (all ct)	D. A. Murray	West Indies v Australia at Melbourne	1981-82
9 (all ct)	R. W. Marsh	Australia v England at Brisbane	1982-83
9 (all ct)	S. A. R. Silva	Sri Lanka v India at Colombo (SSC)	1985-86
9 (8ct, 1st)	S. A. R. Silva	Sri Lanka v India at Colombo (PSS)	1985-86
9 (all ct)	D. J. Richardson	South Africa v India at Port Elizabeth	1992-93
9 (all ct)	Rashid Latif	Pakistan v New Zealand at Auckland	1993-94
9 (all ct)	I. A. Healy	Australia v England at Brisbane	1994-95
9 (all ct)	C. O. Browne	West Indies v England at Nottingham	1995
9 (7ct, 2st)	R. C. Russell	England v South Africa at Port Elizabeth	1995-96

Notes: S. A. R. Silva made 18 dismissals in two successive Tests.

The most stumpings in a match is 6 by K. S. More for India v West Indies at Madras in 1987-88.

J. J. Kelly (8ct) for Australia v England in 1901-02 and L. E. G. Ames (6ct, 2st) for England v West Indies in 1933 were the only wicket-keepers to make eight dismissals in a Test before World War II.

Most Dismissals in a Series

(*Played in 5 Tests unless otherwise stated*)

28 (all ct)	R. W. Marsh	Australia v England	1982-83
27 (25ct, 2st)	R. C. Russell	England v South Africa	1995-96
26 (23ct, 3st)	J. H. B. Waite	South Africa v New Zealand	1961-62
26 (all ct)	R. W. Marsh	Australia v West Indies (6 Tests)	1975-76
26 (21ct, 5st)	I. A. Healy	Australia v England (6 Tests)	1993
25 (23ct, 2st)	I. A. Healy	Australia v England	1994-95
24 (22ct, 2st)	D. L. Murray	West Indies v England	1963
24 (all ct)	D. T. Lindsay	South Africa v Australia	1966-67
24 (21ct, 3st)	A. P. E. Knott	England v Australia (6 Tests)	1970-71
24 (all ct)	I. A. Healy	Australia v England	1990-91
23 (16ct, 7st)	J. H. B. Waite	South Africa v New Zealand	1953-54
23 (22ct, 1st)	F. C. M. Alexander	West Indies v England	1959-60
23 (20ct, 3st)	A. T. W. Grout	Australia v West Indies	1960-61
23 (21ct, 2st)	A. E. Dick	New Zealand v South Africa	1961-62
23 (21ct, 2st)	R. W. Marsh	Australia v England	1972
23 (22ct, 1st)	A. P. E. Knott	England v Australia (6 Tests)	1974-75
23 (all ct)	R. W. Marsh	Australia v England (6 Tests)	1981
23 (all ct)	P. J. L. Dujon	West Indies v Australia	1990-91
23 (19ct, 4st)	I. A. Healy	Australia v West Indies	1992-93
22 (all ct)	S. J. Rixon	Australia v India	1977-78
22 (21ct, 1st)	S. A. R. Silva	Sri Lanka v India (3 Tests)	1985-86

Notes: G. R. A. Langley made 20 dismissals (16ct, 4st) in four Tests for Australia v West Indies in 1954-55.

H. Strudwick, with 21 (15ct, 6st) for England v South Africa in 1913-14, was the only wicket-keeper to make as many as 20 dismissals in a series before World War II.

Most Dismissals in a Career

		T	Ct	St	Total
1	R. W. Marsh (Australia)	96	343	12	355
2	**I. A. Healy (Australia)**	**79**	**255**	**20**	**275**
3	P. J. L. Dujon (West Indies)	81	267	5	272
4	A. P. E. Knott (England)	95	250	19	269
5	Wasim Bari (Pakistan)	81	201	27	228
6	T. G. Evans (England)	91	173	46	219
7	S. M. H. Kirmani (India)	88	160	38	198
8	D. L. Murray (West Indies)	62	181	8	189
9	A. T. W. Grout (Australia)	51	163	24	187
10	I. D. S. Smith (New Zealand)	63	168	8	176
11	R. W. Taylor (England)	57	167	7	174
12	**R. C. Russell (England)**	**49**	**141**	**11**	**152**
13	J. H. B. Waite (South Africa)	50	124	17	141
14	K. S. More (India)	49	110	20	130
14	W. A. S. Oldfield (Australia)	54	78	52	130
16	J. M. Parks (England)	46	103	11	114
17	**D. J. Richardson (South Africa)**	**28**	**107**	**0**	**107**
18	Salim Yousuf (Pakistan)	32	91	13	104

Notes: The records for P. J. L. Dujon and J. M. Parks each include two catches taken when not keeping wicket in two and three Tests respectively.

The most dismissals for other countries are Sri Lanka 34 (S. A. R. Silva 33ct, 1st in 9 Tests) and Zimbabwe 36 (**A. Flower** 34ct, 2st in 12 Tests as wicket-keeper).

Bold type denotes those who played Test cricket in 1995-96 and 1996 seasons.

FIELDING RECORDS

(Excluding wicket-keepers)

Most Catches in an Innings

5	V. Y. Richardson	Australia v South Africa at Durban	1935-36
5	Yajurvindra Singh	India v England at Bangalore	1976-77
5	M. Azharuddin	India v Pakistan at Karachi	1989-90
5	K. Srikkanth	India v Australia at Perth	1991-92

Most Catches in a Test

7	G. S. Chappell	Australia v England at Perth	1974-75
7	Yajurvindra Singh	India v England at Bangalore	1976-77
7	H. P. Tillekeratne	Sri Lanka v New Zealand at Colombo (SSC)	1992-93
6	A. Shrewsbury	England v Australia at Sydney	1887-88
6	A. E. E. Vogler	South Africa v England at Durban	1909-10
6	F. E. Woolley	England v Australia at Sydney	1911-12
6	J. M. Gregory	Australia v England at Sydney	1920-21
6	B. Mitchell	South Africa v Australia at Melbourne	1931-32
6	V. Y. Richardson	Australia v South Africa at Durban	1935-36
6	R. N. Harvey	Australia v England at Sydney	1962-63
6	M. C. Cowdrey	England v West Indies at Lord's	1963
6	E. D. Solkar	India v West Indies at Port-of-Spain	1970-71
6	G. S. Sobers	West Indies v England at Lord's	1973
6	I. M. Chappell	Australia v New Zealand at Adelaide	1973-74
6	A. W. Greig	England v Pakistan at Leeds	1974
6	D. F. Whatmore	Australia v India at Kanpur	1979-80
6	A. J. Lamb	England v New Zealand at Lord's	1983
6	G. A. Hick	England v Pakistan at Leeds	1992
6	B. A. Young	New Zealand v Pakistan at Auckland	1993-94
6	J. C. Adams	West Indies v England at Kingston	1993-94

Most Catches in a Series

15	J. M. Gregory	Australia v England	1920-21
14	G. S. Chappell	Australia v England (6 Tests)	1974-75
13	R. B. Simpson	Australia v South Africa	1957-58
13	R. B. Simpson	Australia v West Indies	1960-61

Most Catches in a Career

A. R. Border (Australia)	156 in 156 matches
G. S. Chappell (Australia)	122 in 87 matches
I. V. A. Richards (West Indies)	122 in 121 matches
I. T. Botham (England)	120 in 102 matches
M. C. Cowdrey (England)	120 in 114 matches
R. B. Simpson (Australia)	110 in 62 matches
W. R. Hammond (England)	110 in 85 matches
G. S. Sobers (West Indies)	109 in 93 matches
S. M. Gavaskar (India)	108 in 125 matches
M. A. Taylor (Australia)	**105 in 72 matches**
I. M. Chappell (Australia)	105 in 75 matches
G. A. Gooch (England)	103 in 118 matches

Bold type denotes those who played Test cricket in 1995-96 and 1996 seasons.

TEAM RECORDS

HIGHEST INNINGS TOTALS

903-7 dec.	England v Australia at The Oval	1938
849	England v West Indies at Kingston	1929-30
790-3 dec.	West Indies v Pakistan at Kingston	1957-58
758-8 dec.	Australia v West Indies at Kingston	1954-55
729-6 dec.	Australia v England at Lord's	1930
708	Pakistan v England at The Oval	1987
701	Australia v England at The Oval	1934
699-5	Pakistan v India at Lahore	1989-90
695	Australia v England at The Oval	1930
692-8 dec.	West Indies v England at The Oval	1995
687-8 dec.	West Indies v England at The Oval	1976
681-8 dec.	West Indies v England at Port-of-Spain	1953-54
676-7	India v Sri Lanka at Kanpur	1986-87
674-6	Pakistan v India at Faisalabad	1984-85
674	Australia v India at Adelaide	1947-48
671-4	New Zealand v Sri Lanka at Wellington	1990-91
668	Australia v West Indies at Bridgetown	1954-55
660-5 dec.	West Indies v New Zealand at Wellington	1994-95
659-8 dec.	Australia v England at Sydney	1946-47
658-8 dec.	England v Australia at Nottingham	1938
657-8 dec.	Pakistan v West Indies at Bridgetown	1957-58
656-8 dec.	Australia v England at Manchester	1964
654-5	England v South Africa at Durban	1938-39
653-4 dec.	England v India at Lord's	1990
653-4 dec.	Australia v England at Leeds	1993
652-7 dec.	England v India at Madras	1984-85
652-8 dec.	West Indies v England at Lord's	1973
652	Pakistan v India at Faisalabad	1982-83
650-6 dec.	Australia v West Indies at Bridgetown	1964-65

The highest innings for the countries not mentioned above are:

622-9 dec.	South Africa v Australia at Durban	1969-70
547-8 dec.	Sri Lanka v Australia at Colombo (SSC)	1992-93
544-4 dec.	Zimbabwe v Pakistan at Harare	1994-95

HIGHEST FOURTH-INNINGS TOTALS

To win

406-4	India (needing 403) v West Indies at Port-of-Spain	1975-76
404-3	Australia (needing 404) v England at Leeds	1948
362-7	Australia (needing 359) v West Indies at Georgetown	1977-78
348-5	West Indies (needing 345) v New Zealand at Auckland	1968-69
344-1	West Indies (needing 342) v England at Lord's	1984

To tie

347	India v Australia at Madras	1986-87

To draw

654-5	England (needing 696 to win) v South Africa at Durban	1938-39
429-8	India (needing 438 to win) v England at The Oval	1979
423-7	South Africa (needing 451 to win) v England at The Oval	1947
408-5	West Indies (needing 836 to win) v England at Kingston	1929-30

To lose

445	India (lost by 47 runs) v Australia at Adelaide	1977-78
440	New Zealand (lost by 38 runs) v England at Nottingham	1973
417	England (lost by 45 runs) v Australia at Melbourne	1976-77
411	England (lost by 193 runs) v Australia at Sydney	1924-25

MOST RUNS IN A DAY (BOTH SIDES)

588	England (398-6), India (190-0) at Manchester (2nd day)	1936
522	England (503-2), South Africa (19-0) at Lord's (2nd day)	1924
508	England (221-2), South Africa (287-6) at The Oval (3rd day)	1935

MOST RUNS IN A DAY (ONE SIDE)

503	England (503-2) v South Africa at Lord's (2nd day)	1924
494	Australia (494-6) v South Africa at Sydney (1st day)	1910-11
475	Australia (475-2) v England at The Oval (1st day)	1934
471	England (471-8) v India at The Oval (1st day)	1936
458	Australia (458-3) v England at Leeds (1st day)	1930
455	Australia (455-1) v England at Leeds (2nd day)	1934

MOST WICKETS IN A DAY

27	England (18-3 to 53 out and 62) v Australia (60) at Lord's (2nd day)	1888
25	Australia (112 and 48-5) v England (61) at Melbourne (1st day)	1901-02

HIGHEST MATCH AGGREGATES

Runs	*Wkts*			*Days played*
1,981	35	South Africa v England at Durban	1938-39	10†
1,815	34	West Indies v England at Kingston	1929-30	9‡
1,764	39	Australia v West Indies at Adelaide	1968-69	5
1,753	40	Australia v England at Adelaide	1920-21	6

Runs	*Wkts*			*Days played*
1,723	31	England v Australia at Leeds	1948	5
1,661	36	West Indies v Australia at Bridgetown	1954-55	6

† *No play on one day.* ‡ *No play on two days.*

LOWEST INNINGS TOTALS

26	New Zealand v England at Auckland	1954-55
30	South Africa v England at Port Elizabeth	1895-96
30	South Africa v England at Birmingham	1924
35	South Africa v England at Cape Town	1898-99
36	Australia v England at Birmingham	1902
36	South Africa v Australia at Melbourne	1931-32
42	Australia v England at Sydney	1887-88
42	New Zealand v Australia at Wellington	1945-46
42†	India v England at Lord's	1974
43	South Africa v England at Cape Town	1888-89
44	Australia v England at The Oval	1896
45	England v Australia at Sydney	1886-87
45	South Africa v Australia at Melbourne	1931-32
46	England v West Indies at Port-of-Spain	1993-94
47	South Africa v England at Cape Town	1888-89
47	New Zealand v England at Lord's	1958

The lowest innings for the countries not mentioned above are:

53	West Indies v Pakistan at Faisalabad	1986-87
62	Pakistan v Australia at Perth	1981-82
71	Sri Lanka v Pakistan at Kandy	1994-95
134	Zimbabwe v Pakistan at Karachi (DS)	1993-94

† *Batted one man short.*

FEWEST RUNS IN A FULL DAY'S PLAY

95 At Karachi, October 11, 1956. Australia 80 all out; Pakistan 15 for two (first day, 5½ hours).

104 At Karachi, December 8, 1959. Pakistan 0 for no wicket to 104 for five v Australia (fourth day, 5½ hours).

106 At Brisbane, December 9, 1958. England 92 for two to 198 all out v Australia (fourth day, 5 hours). *England were dismissed five minutes before the close of play, leaving no time for Australia to start their second innings.*

112 At Karachi, October 15, 1956. Australia 138 for six to 187 all out; Pakistan 63 for one (fourth day, 5½ hours).

115 At Karachi, September 19, 1988. Australia 116 for seven to 165 all out and 66 for five following on v Pakistan (fourth day, 5½ hours).

117 At Madras, October 19, 1956. India 117 for five v Australia (first day, 5½ hours).

117 At Colombo (SSC), March 21, 1984. New Zealand 6 for no wicket to 123 for four (fifth day, 5 hours 47 minutes).

In England

151 At Lord's, August 26, 1978. England 175 for two to 289 all out; New Zealand 37 for seven (third day, 6 hours).

159 At Leeds, July 10, 1971. Pakistan 208 for four to 350 all out; England 17 for one (third day, 6 hours).

LOWEST MATCH AGGREGATES

(For a completed match)

Runs	*Wkts*			*Days played*
234	29	Australia v South Africa at Melbourne	1931-32	3†
291	40	England v Australia at Lord's	1888	2

Runs	Wkts			Days played
295	28	New Zealand v Australia at Wellington	1945-46	2
309	29	West Indies v England at Bridgetown	1934-35	3
323	30	England v Australia at Manchester	1888	2

† *No play on one day.*

YOUNGEST TEST PLAYERS

Years	Days			
15	124	Mushtaq Mohammad	Pakistan v West Indies at Lahore	1958-59
16	189	Aqib Javed	Pakistan v New Zealand at Wellington	1988-89
16	205	S. R. Tendulkar	India v Pakistan at Karachi	1989-90
16	221	Aftab Baloch	Pakistan v New Zealand at Dacca	1969-70
16	248	Nasim-ul-Ghani	Pakistan v West Indies at Bridgetown	1957-58
16	352	Khalid Hassan	Pakistan v England at Nottingham	1954
17	5	Zahid Fazal	Pakistan v West Indies at Karachi	1990-91
17	69	Ata-ur-Rehman	Pakistan v England at Birmingham	1992
17	118	L. Sivaramakrishnan	India v West Indies at St John's	1982-83
17	122	J. E. D. Sealy	West Indies v England at Bridgetown	1929-30
17	189	C. D. U. S. Weerasinghe	Sri Lanka v India at Colombo (PSS)	1985-86
17	193	Maninder Singh	India v Pakistan at Karachi	1982-83
17	239	I. D. Craig	Australia v South Africa at Melbourne	1952-53
17	245	G. S. Sobers	West Indies v England at Kingston	1953-54
17	265	V. L. Mehra	India v New Zealand at Bombay	1955-56
17	300	Hanif Mohammad	Pakistan v India at Delhi	1952-53
17	341	Intikhab Alam	Pakistan v Australia at Karachi	1959-60
17	364	Waqar Younis	Pakistan v India at Karachi	1989-90

Note: The youngest Test players for countries not mentioned above are: England – D. B. Close, 18 years 149 days, v New Zealand at Manchester, 1949; New Zealand – D. L. Freeman, 18 years 197 days, v England at Christchurch, 1932-33; South Africa – P. R. Adams, 18 years 340 days v England at Port Elizabeth, 1995-96; Zimbabwe – H. R. Olonga, 18 years 212 days, v Pakistan at Harare, 1994-95.

On October 24, 1996 after the deadline for inclusion in this section, Hassan Raza reportedly became the youngest ever Test player when he appeared for Pakistan against Zimbabwe at Faisalabad, aged "14 years 227 days". The Pakistan Cricket Board subsequently rejected this figure and said medical tests showed Raza was "about 15". Accurate information is awaited.

OLDEST PLAYERS ON TEST DEBUT

Years	Days			
49	119	J. Southerton	England v Australia at Melbourne	1876-77
47	284	Miran Bux	Pakistan v India at Lahore	1954-55
46	253	D. D. Blackie	Australia v England at Sydney	1928-29
46	237	H. Ironmonger	Australia v England at Brisbane	1928-29
42	242	N. Betancourt	West Indies v England at Port-of-Spain	1929-30
41	337	E. R. Wilson	England v Australia at Sydney	1920-21
41	27	R. J. D. Jamshedji	India v England at Bombay	1933-34
40	345	C. A. Wiles	West Indies v England at Manchester	1933
40	295	O. Henry	South Africa v India at Durban	1992-93
40	216	S. P. Kinneir	England v Australia at Sydney	1911-12
40	110	H. W. Lee	England v South Africa at Johannesburg	1930-31
40	56	G. W. A. Chubb	South Africa v England at Nottingham	1951
40	37	C. Ramaswami	India v England at Manchester	1936

Note: The oldest Test player on debut for New Zealand was H. M. McGirr, 38 years 101 days, v England at Auckland, 1929-30; for Sri Lanka, D. S. de Silva, 39 years 251 days, v England at Colombo (PSS), 1981-82; for Zimbabwe, M. P. Jarvis, 36 years 317 days, v India at Harare, 1992-93. A. J. Traicos was 45 years 154 days old when he made his debut for Zimbabwe (v India at Harare, 1992-93) having played 3 Tests for South Africa in 1969-70.

OLDEST TEST PLAYERS

(Age on final day of their last Test match)

Years	*Days*			
52	165	W. Rhodes	England v West Indies at Kingston	1929-30
50	327	H. Ironmonger	Australia v England at Sydney	1932-33
50	320	W. G. Grace	England v Australia at Nottingham	1899
50	303	G. Gunn	England v West Indies at Kingston	1929-30
49	139	J. Southerton	England v Australia at Melbourne	1876-77
47	302	Miran Bux	Pakistan v India at Peshawar	1954-55
47	249	J. B. Hobbs	England v Australia at The Oval	1930
47	87	F. E. Woolley	England v Australia at The Oval	1934
46	309	D. D. Blackie	Australia v England at Adelaide	1928-29
46	206	A. W. Nourse	South Africa v England at The Oval	1924
46	202	H. Strudwick	England v Australia at The Oval	1926
46	41	E. H. Hendren	England v West Indies at Kingston	1934-35
45	304	A. J. Traicos	Zimbabwe v India at Delhi	1992-93
45	245	G. O. B. Allen	England v West Indies at Kingston	1947-48
45	215	P. Holmes	England v India at Lord's	1932
45	140	D. B. Close	England v West Indies at Manchester	1976

MOST TEST APPEARANCES

156	A. R. Border (Australia)
131	Kapil Dev (India)
125	S. M. Gavaskar (India)
124	Javed Miandad (Pakistan)
121	I. V. A. Richards (West Indies)
118	G. A. Gooch (England)
117	D. I. Gower (England)
116	D. L. Haynes (West Indies)
116	D. B. Vengsarkar (India)
114	M. C. Cowdrey (England)
110	C. H. Lloyd (West Indies)
108	G. Boycott (England)
108	C. G. Greenidge (West Indies)
107	**D. C. Boon (Australia)**
102	I. T. Botham (England)

The most appearances for New Zealand is 86 by R. J. Hadlee, for South Africa 50 by J. H. B. Waite, for Sri Lanka 61 by **A. Ranatunga** and for Zimbabwe 16 by **A. D. R. Campbell**, **A. Flower**, **G. W. Flower** and **D. L. Houghton**.

Bold type denotes those who played Test cricket in 1995-96 and 1996 seasons.

MOST CONSECUTIVE TEST APPEARANCES

153	A. R. Border (Australia)	March 1979 to March 1994
106	S. M. Gavaskar (India)	January 1975 to February 1987
87	G. R. Viswanath (India)	March 1971 to February 1983
85	G. S. Sobers (West Indies)	April 1955 to April 1972
72	D. L. Haynes (West Indies)	December 1979 to June 1988
71	I. M. Chappell (Australia)	January 1966 to February 1976
66	Kapil Dev (India)	October 1978 to December 1984
65	I. T. Botham (England)	February 1978 to March 1984
65	Kapil Dev (India)	January 1985 to March 1994
65	A. P. E. Knott (England)	March 1971 to August 1977

The most consecutive Test appearances for the countries not mentioned above are:

58†	J. R. Reid (New Zealand)	July 1949 to July 1965
53	Javed Miandad (Pakistan)	December 1977 to January 1984
45†	A. W. Nourse (South Africa)....	October 1902 to August 1924
35	P. A. de Silva (Sri Lanka)	February 1988 to March 1995

The most for Zimbabwe is 16 (as above).

† *Indicates complete Test career.*

CAPTAINCY

MOST TESTS AS CAPTAIN

	P	*W*	*L*	*D*
A. R. Border (A)	93	32	22	38*
C. H. Lloyd (WI)	74	36	12	26
I. V. A. Richards (WI)	50	27	8	15
G. S. Chappell (A)	48	21	13	14
Imran Khan (P)	48	14	8	26
S. M. Gavaskar (I)	47	9	8	30
P. B. H. May (E)	41	20	10	11
Nawab of Pataudi jun. (I)	40	9	19	12
R. B. Simpson (A)	39	12	12	15
G. S. Sobers (WI)	39	9	10	20
M. Azharuddin (I)	**37**	**11**	**9**	**17**
M. A. Atherton (E)	**35**	**8**	**13**	**14**
G. A. Gooch (E)	34	10	12	12
Javed Miandad (P)	34	14	6	14
Kapil Dev (I)	34	4	7	22*
A. Ranatunga (SL)	**34**	**5**	**13**	**16**
J. R. Reid (NZ)	34	3	18	13
D. I. Gower (E)	32	5	18	9
J. M. Brearley (E)	31	18	4	9
R. Illingworth (E)	31	12	5	14
I. M. Chappell (A)	30	15	5	10
E. R. Dexter (E)	30	9	7	14
G. P. Howarth (NZ)	30	11	7	12

* *One match tied.*

Most Tests as captain of countries not mentioned above:

	P	*W*	*L*	*D*
H. W. Taylor (SA)	18	1	10	7
A. Flower (Z)	**12**	**1**	**5**	**6**

Notes: A. R. Border captained Australia in 93 consecutive Tests.

W. W. Armstrong (Australia) captained his country in the most Tests without being defeated: ten matches with eight wins and two draws.

I. T. Botham (England) captained his country in the most Tests without ever winning: 12 matches with eight draws and four defeats.

Bold type denotes those who were captains in 1995-96 and 1996 seasons.

UMPIRING

MOST TEST MATCHES

		First Test	*Last Test*
66	**H. D. Bird (England)**	**1973**	**1996**
48	F. Chester (England)	1924	1955
42	C. S. Elliott (England)	1957	1974
36	D. J. Constant (England)	1971	1988
33	J. S. Buller (England)	1956	1969
33	A. R. Crafter (Australia)	1978-79	1991-92
33	**Khizar Hayat (Pakistan)**	**1979-80**	**1995-96**
32	R. W. Crockett (Australia)	1901-02	1924-25
31	D. Sang Hue (West Indies)	1961-62	1980-81
30	**D. R. Shepherd (England)**	**1985**	**1996**

Bold type indicates an umpire who stood in 1995-96 or 1996 seasons.

SUMMARY OF ALL TEST MATCHES

To August 26, 1996

	Opponents	Tests	Won by E	A	SA	WI	NZ	I	P	SL	Z	Tied	Drawn
England	Australia	285	90	111	–	–	–	–	–	–	–	–	84
	South Africa	110	47	–	20	–	–	–	–	–	–	–	43
	West Indies	115	27	–	–	48	–	–	–	–	–	–	40
	New Zealand	75	34	–	–	–	4	–	–	–	–	–	37
	India	84	32	–	–	–	–	14	–	–	–	–	38
	Pakistan	55	14	–	–	–	–	–	9	–	–	–	32
	Sri Lanka	5	3	–	–	–	–	–	–	1	–	–	1
Australia	South Africa	59	–	31	13	–	–	–	–	–	–	–	15
	West Indies	81	–	32	–	27	–	–	–	–	–	1	21
	New Zealand	32	–	13	–	–	7	–	–	–	–	–	12
	India	50	–	24	–	–	–	8	–	–	–	1	17
	Pakistan	40	–	14	–	–	–	–	11	–	–	–	15
	Sri Lanka	10	–	7	–	–	–	–	–	0	–	–	3
South Africa	West Indies	1	–	–	0	1	–	–	–	–	–	–	–
	New Zealand	21	–	–	12	–	3	–	–	–	–	–	6
	India	4	–	–	1	–	–	0	–	–	–	–	3
	Pakistan	1	–	–	1	–	–	–	0	–	–	–	–
	Sri Lanka	3	–	–	1	–	–	–	–	0	–	–	2
	Zimbabwe	1	–	–	1	–	–	–	–	–	0	–	–
West Indies	New Zealand	28	–	–	–	10	4	–	–	–	–	–	14
	India	65	–	–	–	27	–	7	–	–	–	–	31
	Pakistan	31	–	–	–	12	–	–	7	–	–	–	12
	Sri Lanka	1	–	–	–	0	–	–	–	0	–	–	1
New Zealand	India	35	–	–	–	–	6	13	–	–	–	–	16
	Pakistan	37	–	–	–	–	4	–	17	–	–	–	16
	Sri Lanka	13	–	–	–	–	4	–	–	2	–	–	7
	Zimbabwe	4	–	–	–	–	1	–	–	–	0	–	3
India	Pakistan	44	–	–	–	–	–	4	7	–	–	–	33
	Sri Lanka	14	–	–	–	–	–	7	–	1	–	–	6
	Zimbabwe	2	–	–	–	–	–	1	–	–	0	–	1
Pakistan	Sri Lanka	17	–	–	–	–	–	–	9	3	–	–	5
	Zimbabwe	6	–	–	–	–	–	–	4	–	1	–	1
Sri Lanka	Zimbabwe	3	–	–	–	–	–	–	–	0	0	–	3
		1,332	247	232	49	125	33	54	64	7	1	2	518

	Tests	Won	Lost	Drawn	Tied	Toss Won
England	729	247	207	275	–	359
Australia	557	232	156	167	2	277
South Africa	200	49	82	69	–	96
West Indies	322	125	77	119	1	168
New Zealand	245	33	101	111	–	125
India	298	54	98	145	1	151
Pakistan	231	64	53	114	–	115
Sri Lanka	66	7	31	28	–	33
Zimbabwe	16	1	7	8	–	8

ENGLAND v AUSTRALIA

Season	Captains: England	Australia	T	E	A	D
1876-77	James Lillywhite	D. W. Gregory	2	1	1	0
1878-79	Lord Harris	D. W. Gregory	1	0	1	0
1880	Lord Harris	W. L. Murdoch	1	1	0	0
1881-82	A. Shaw	W. L. Murdoch	4	0	2	2
1882	A. N. Hornby	W. L. Murdoch	1	0	1	0

THE ASHES

Season	Captains: England	Australia	T	E	A	D	Held by
1882-83	Hon. Ivo Bligh	W. L. Murdoch	4*	2	2	0	E
1884	Lord Harris[1]	W. L. Murdoch	3	1	0	2	E
1884-85	A. Shrewsbury	T. P. Horan[2]	5	3	2	0	E
1886	A. G. Steel	H. J. H. Scott	3	3	0	0	E

Season	England (Captains)	Australia (Captains)	T	E	A	D	Held by
1886-87	A. Shrewsbury	P. S. McDonnell	2	2	0	0	E
1887-88	W. W. Read	P. S. McDonnell	1	1	0	0	E
1888	W. G. Grace[3]	P. S. McDonnell	3	2	1	0	E
1890†	W. G. Grace	W. L. Murdoch	2	2	0	0	E
1891-92	W. G. Grace	J. McC. Blackham	3	1	2	0	A
1893	W. G. Grace[4]	J. McC. Blackham	3	1	0	2	E
1894-95	A. E. Stoddart	G. Giffen[5]	5	3	2	0	E
1896	W. G. Grace	G. H. S. Trott	3	2	1	0	E
1897-98	A. E. Stoddart[6]	G. H. S. Trott	5	1	4	0	A
1899	A. C. MacLaren[7]	J. Darling	5	0	1	4	A
1901-02	A. C. MacLaren	J. Darling[8]	5	1	4	0	A
1902	A. C. MacLaren	J. Darling	5	1	2	2	A
1903-04	P. F. Warner	M. A. Noble	5	3	2	0	E
1905	Hon. F. S. Jackson	J. Darling	5	2	0	3	E
1907-08	A. O. Jones[9]	M. A. Noble	5	1	4	0	A
1909	A. C. MacLaren	M. A. Noble	5	1	2	2	A
1911-12	J. W. H. T. Douglas	C. Hill	5	4	1	0	E
1912	C. B. Fry	S. E. Gregory	3	1	0	2	E
1920-21	J. W. H. T. Douglas	W. W. Armstrong	5	0	5	0	A
1921	Hon. L. H. Tennyson[10]	W. W. Armstrong	5	0	3	2	A
1924-25	A. E. R. Gilligan	H. L. Collins	5	1	4	0	A
1926	A. W. Carr[11]	H. L. Collins[12]	5	1	0	4	E
1928-29	A. P. F. Chapman[13]	J. Ryder	5	4	1	0	E
1930	A. P. F. Chapman[14]	W. M. Woodfull	5	1	2	2	A
1932-33	D. R. Jardine	W. M. Woodfull	5	4	1	0	E
1934	R. E. S. Wyatt[15]	W. M. Woodfull	5	1	2	2	A
1936-37	G. O. B. Allen	D. G. Bradman	5	2	3	0	A
1938†	W. R. Hammond	D. G. Bradman	4	1	1	2	A
1946-47	W. R. Hammond[16]	D. G. Bradman	5	0	3	2	A
1948	N. W. D. Yardley	D. G. Bradman	5	0	4	1	A
1950-51	F. R. Brown	A. L. Hassett	5	1	4	0	A
1953	L. Hutton	A. L. Hassett	5	1	0	4	E
1954-55	L. Hutton	I. W. Johnson[17]	5	3	1	1	E
1956	P. B. H. May	I. W. Johnson	5	2	1	2	E
1958-59	P. B. H. May	R. Benaud	5	0	4	1	A
1961	P. B. H. May[18]	R. Benaud[19]	5	1	2	2	A
1962-63	E. R. Dexter	R. Benaud	5	1	1	3	A
1964	E. R. Dexter	R. B. Simpson	5	0	1	4	A
1965-66	M. J. K. Smith	R. B. Simpson[20]	5	1	1	3	A
1968	M. C. Cowdrey[21]	W. M. Lawry[22]	5	1	1	3	A
1970-71†	R. Illingworth	W. M. Lawry[23]	6	2	0	4	E
1972	R. Illingworth	I. M. Chappell	5	2	2	1	E
1974-75	M. H. Denness[24]	I. M. Chappell	6	1	4	1	A
1975	A. W. Greig[25]	I. M. Chappell	4	0	1	3	A
1976-77‡	A. W. Greig	G. S. Chappell	1	0	1	0	—
1977	J. M. Brearley	G. S. Chappell	5	3	0	2	E
1978-79	J. M. Brearley	G. N. Yallop	6	5	1	0	E
1979-80‡	J. M. Brearley	G. S. Chappell	3	0	3	0	—
1980‡	I. T. Botham	G. S. Chappell	1	0	0	1	—
1981	J. M. Brearley[26]	K. J. Hughes	6	3	1	2	E
1982-83	R. G. D. Willis	G. S. Chappell	5	1	2	2	A
1985	D. I. Gower	A. R. Border	6	3	1	2	E
1986-87	M. W. Gatting	A. R. Border	5	2	1	2	E
1987-88‡	M. W. Gatting	A. R. Border	1	0	0	1	—
1989	D. I. Gower	A. R. Border	6	0	4	2	A
1990-91	G. A. Gooch[27]	A. R. Border	5	0	3	2	A
1993	G. A. Gooch[28]	A. R. Border	6	1	4	1	A
1994-95	M. A. Atherton	M. A. Taylor	5	1	3	1	A
	In Australia		150	52	73	25	
	In England		135	38	38	59	
	Totals		285	90	111	84	

* *The Ashes were awarded in 1882-83 after a series of three matches which England won 2-1. A fourth match was played and this was won by Australia.*

† *The matches at Manchester in 1890 and 1938 and at Melbourne (Third Test) in 1970-71 were abandoned without a ball being bowled and are excluded.*

‡ *The Ashes were not at stake in these series.*

Notes: The following deputised for the official touring captain or were appointed by the home authority for only a minor proportion of the series:
[1]A. N. Hornby (First). [2]W. L. Murdoch (First), H. H. Massie (Third), J. McC. Blackham (Fourth). [3]A. G. Steel (First). [4]A. E. Stoddart (First). [5]J. McC. Blackham (First). [6]A. C. MacLaren (First, Second and Fifth). [7]W. G. Grace (First). [8]H. Trumble (Fourth and Fifth). [9]F. L. Fane (First, Second and Third). [10]J. W. H. T. Douglas (First and Second). [11]A. P. F. Chapman (Fifth). [12]W. Bardsley (Third and Fourth). [13]J. C. White (Fifth). [14]R. E. S. Wyatt (Fifth). [15]C. F. Walters (First). [16]N. W. D. Yardley (Fifth). [17]A. R. Morris (Second). [18]M. C. Cowdrey (First and Second). [19]R. N. Harvey (Second). [20]B. C. Booth (First and Third). [21]T. W. Graveney (Fourth). [22]B. N. Jarman (Fourth). [23]I. M. Chappell (Seventh). [24]J. H. Edrich (Fourth). [25]M. H. Denness (First). [26]I. T. Botham (First and Second). [27]A. J. Lamb (First). [28]M. A. Atherton (Fifth and Sixth).

HIGHEST INNINGS TOTALS

For England in England: 903-7 dec. at The Oval 1938
in Australia: 636 at Sydney 1928-29

For Australia in England: 729-6 dec. at Lord's 1930
in Australia: 659-8 dec. at Sydney 1946-47

LOWEST INNINGS TOTALS

For England in England: 52 at The Oval 1948
in Australia: 45 at Sydney 1886-87

For Australia in England: 36 at Birmingham 1902
in Australia: 42 at Sydney 1887-88

INDIVIDUAL HUNDREDS

For England (201)

R. Abel (1)
132*‡ Sydney 1891-92
L. E. G. Ames (1)
120 Lord's 1934
M. A. Atherton (1)
105 Sydney 1990-91
R. W. Barber (1)
185 Sydney 1965-66
W. Barnes (1)
134 Adelaide 1884-85
C. J. Barnett (2)
129 Adelaide 1936-37
126 Nottingham . 1938
K. F. Barrington (5)
132* Adelaide 1962-63
101 Sydney 1962-63
256 Manchester.. 1964
102 Adelaide 1965-66
115 Melbourne .. 1965-66
I. T. Botham (4)
119* Melbourne .. 1979-80
149* Leeds 1981
118 Manchester.. 1981
138 Brisbane 1986-87
G. Boycott (7)
113 The Oval.... 1964
142* Sydney 1970-71
119* Adelaide 1970-71
107 Nottingham . 1977
191 Leeds 1977
128* Lord's 1980
137 The Oval.... 1981
L. C. Braund (2)
103* Adelaide 1901-02
102 Sydney 1903-04
J. Briggs (1)
121 Melbourne .. 1884-85
B. C. Broad (4)
162 Perth....... 1986-87
116 Adelaide 1986-87
112 Melbourne .. 1986-87
139 Sydney 1987-88
J. T. Brown (1)
140 Melbourne .. 1894-95
A. P. F. Chapman (1)
121 Lord's 1930
D. C. S. Compton (5)
102† Nottingham . 1938
147 }
103* } Adelaide 1946-47
184 Nottingham . 1948
145* Manchester.. 1948

M. C. Cowdrey (5)
102 Melbourne .. 1954-55
100* Sydney 1958-59
113 Melbourne .. 1962-63
104 Melbourne .. 1965-66
104 Birmingham . 1968

M. H. Denness (1)
188 Melbourne .. 1974-75

E. R. Dexter (2)
180 Birmingham . 1961
174 Manchester .. 1964

B. L. D'Oliveira (2)
158 The Oval 1968
117 Melbourne .. 1970-71

K. S. Duleepsinhji (1)
173† Lord's 1930

J. H. Edrich (7)
120† Lord's 1964
109 Melbourne .. 1965-66
103 Sydney 1965-66
164 The Oval 1968
115* Perth 1970-71
130 Adelaide 1970-71
175 Lord's 1975

W. J. Edrich (2)
119 Sydney 1946-47
111 Leeds 1948

K. W. R. Fletcher (1)
146 Melbourne .. 1974-75

R. E. Foster (1)
287† Sydney 1903-04

C. B. Fry (1)
144 The Oval 1905

M. W. Gatting (4)
160 Manchester .. 1985
100* Birmingham . 1985
100 Adelaide 1986-87
117 Adelaide 1994-95

G. A. Gooch (4)
196 The Oval 1985
117 Adelaide 1990-91
133 Manchester .. 1993
120 Nottingham . 1993

D. I. Gower (9)
102 Perth 1978-79
114 Adelaide 1982-83
166 Nottingham . 1985
215 Birmingham . 1985
157 The Oval 1985
136 Perth 1986-87
106 Lord's 1989
100 Melbourne .. 1990-91
123 Sydney 1990-91

W. G. Grace (2)
152† The Oval 1880
170 The Oval 1886

T. W. Graveney (1)
111 Sydney 1954-55

A. W. Greig (1)
110 Brisbane 1974-75

G. Gunn (2)
119† Sydney 1907-08
122* Sydney 1907-08

W. Gunn (1)
102* Manchester .. 1893

W. R. Hammond (9)
251 Sydney 1928-29
200 Melbourne .. 1928-29
119* }
177 } Adelaide 1928-29
113 Leeds 1930
112 Sydney 1932-33
101 Sydney 1932-33
231* Sydney 1936-37
240 Lord's 1938

J. Hardstaff jun. (1)
169* The Oval 1938

T. W. Hayward (2)
130 Manchester .. 1899
137 The Oval 1899

J. W. Hearne (1)
114 Melbourne .. 1911-12

E. H. Hendren (3)
127* Lord's 1926
169 Brisbane 1928-29
132 Manchester .. 1934

J. B. Hobbs (12)
126* Melbourne .. 1911-12
187 Adelaide 1911-12
178 Melbourne .. 1911-12
107 Lord's 1912
122 Melbourne .. 1920-21
123 Adelaide 1920-21
115 Sydney 1924-25
154 Melbourne .. 1924-25
119 Adelaide 1924-25
119 Lord's 1926
100 The Oval 1926
142 Melbourne .. 1928-29

K. L. Hutchings (1)
126 Melbourne .. 1907-08

L. Hutton (5)
100† Nottingham . 1938
364 The Oval 1938
122* Sydney 1946-47
156*‡ Adelaide 1950-51
145 Lord's 1953

Hon. F. S. Jackson (5)
103 The Oval 1893
118 The Oval 1899
128 Manchester .. 1902
144* Leeds 1905
113 Manchester .. 1905

G. L. Jessop (1)
104 The Oval 1902

A. P. E. Knott (2)
106* Adelaide 1974-75
135 Nottingham . 1977

A. J. Lamb (1)
125 Leeds 1989

M. Leyland (7)
137† Melbourne .. 1928-29
109 Lord's 1934
153 Manchester .. 1934
110 The Oval 1934
126 Brisbane 1936-37
111* Melbourne .. 1936-37
187 The Oval 1938

B. W. Luckhurst (2)
131 Perth 1970-71
109 Melbourne .. 1970-71

A. C. MacLaren (5)
120 Melbourne .. 1894-95
109 Sydney 1897-98
124 Adelaide 1897-98
116 Sydney 1901-02
140 Nottingham . 1905

J. W. H. Makepeace (1)
117 Melbourne .. 1920-21

P. B. H. May (3)
104 Sydney 1954-55
101 Leeds 1956
113 Melbourne .. 1958-59

C. P. Mead (1)
182* The Oval 1921

Nawab of Pataudi sen. (1)
102† Sydney 1932-33

E. Paynter (1)
216* Nottingham . 1938

D. W. Randall (3)
174† Melbourne .. 1976-77
150 Sydney 1978-79
115 Perth 1982-83

K. S. Ranjitsinhji (2)
154*† Manchester .. 1896
175 Sydney 1897-98

W. W. Read (1)
117 The Oval 1884

W. Rhodes (1)
179 Melbourne .. 1911-12

C. J. Richards (1)
133 Perth 1986-87

P. E. Richardson (1)
104 Manchester .. 1956

R. T. Robinson (2)
175† Leeds 1985
148 Birmingham . 1985

A. C. Russell (3)
135* Adelaide 1920-21
101 Manchester .. 1921
102* The Oval 1921

R. C. Russell (1)
128* Manchester .. 1989

J. Sharp (1)
105 The Oval 1909

Rev. D. S. Sheppard (2)
113 Manchester .. 1956
113 Melbourne .. 1962-63

A. Shrewsbury (3)
105* Melbourne .. 1884-85
164 Lord's 1886
106 Lord's 1893

R. T. Simpson (1)
156* Melbourne .. 1950-51

R. A. Smith (2)
143 Manchester .. 1989
101 Nottingham . 1989

A. G. Steel (2)
135* Sydney 1882-83
148 Lord's 1884

A. E. Stoddart (2)
134 Adelaide 1891-92
173 Melbourne 1894-95
R. Subba Row (2)
112† Birmingham 1961
137 The Oval 1961
H. Sutcliffe (8)
115† Sydney 1924-25
176 } Melbourne 1924-25
127 }
143 Melbourne 1924-25
161 The Oval 1926
135 Melbourne 1928-29
161 The Oval 1930
194 Sydney 1932-33
G. P. Thorpe (2)
114*† Nottingham 1993
123 Perth 1994-95
J. T. Tyldesley (3)
138 Birmingham 1902
100 Leeds 1905
112* The Oval 1905
G. Ulyett (1)
149 Melbourne 1881-82
A. Ward (1)
117 Sydney 1894-95
C. Washbrook (2)
112 Melbourne 1946-47
143 Leeds 1948
W. Watson (1)
109† Lord's 1953
F. E. Woolley (2)
133* Sydney 1911-12
123 Sydney 1924-25
R. A. Woolmer (3)
149 The Oval 1975
120 Lord's 1977
137 Manchester 1977

† *Signifies hundred on first appearance in England–Australia Tests.*
‡ *Carried his bat.*

For Australia (232)

W. W. Armstrong (4)
133* Melbourne 1907-08
158 Sydney 1920-21
121 Adelaide 1920-21
123* Melbourne 1920-21
C. L. Badcock (1)
118 Melbourne 1936-37
C. Bannerman (1)
165*† Melbourne 1876-77
W. Bardsley (3)
136 } The Oval 1909
130 }
193*‡ Lord's 1926
S. G. Barnes (2)
234 Sydney 1946-47
141 Lord's 1948
G. S. Blewett (2)
102*† Adelaide 1994-95
115 Perth 1994-95
G. J. Bonnor (1)
128 Sydney 1884-85
D. C. Boon (7)
103 Adelaide 1986-87
184* Sydney 1987-88
121 Adelaide 1990-91
164* Lord's 1993
101 Nottingham 1993
107 Leeds 1993
131 Melbourne 1994-95
B. C. Booth (2)
112 Brisbane 1962-63
103 Melbourne 1962-63
A. R. Border (8)
115 Perth 1979-80
123* Manchester 1981
106* The Oval 1981
196 Lord's 1985
146* Manchester 1985
125 Perth 1986-87
100* Adelaide 1986-87
200* Leeds 1993
D. G. Bradman (19)
112 Melbourne 1928-29
123 Melbourne 1928-29
131 Nottingham 1930
254 Lord's 1930
334 Leeds 1930
232 The Oval 1930
103* Melbourne 1932-33
304 Leeds 1934
244 The Oval 1934
270 Melbourne 1936-37
212 Adelaide 1936-37
169 Melbourne 1936-37
144* Nottingham 1938
102* Lord's 1938
103 Leeds 1938
187 Brisbane 1946-47
234 Sydney 1946-47
138 Nottingham 1948
173* Leeds 1948
W. A. Brown (3)
105 Lord's 1934
133 Nottingham 1938
206*‡ Lord's 1938
P. J. Burge (4)
181 The Oval 1961
103 Sydney 1962-63
160 Leeds 1964
120 Melbourne 1965-66
J. W. Burke (1)
101*† Adelaide 1950-51
G. S. Chappell (9)
108† Perth 1970-71
131 Lord's 1972
113 The Oval 1972
144 Sydney 1974-75
102 Melbourne 1974-75
112 Manchester 1977
114 Melbourne 1979-80
117 Perth 1982-83
115 Adelaide 1982-83
I. M. Chappell (4)
111 Melbourne 1970-71
104 Adelaide 1970-71
118 The Oval 1972
192 The Oval 1975
H. L. Collins (3)
104† Sydney 1920-21
162 Adelaide 1920-21
114 Sydney 1924-25
R. M. Cowper (1)
307 Melbourne 1965-66
J. Darling (3)
101 Sydney 1897-98
178 Adelaide 1897-98
160 Sydney 1897-98
R. A. Duff (2)
104† Melbourne 1901-02
146 The Oval 1905
J. Dyson (1)
102 Leeds 1981
R. Edwards (2)
170* Nottingham 1972
115 Perth 1974-75
J. H. Fingleton (2)
100 Brisbane 1936-37
136 Melbourne 1936-37
G. Giffen (1)
161 Sydney 1894-95
H. Graham (2)
107† Lord's 1893
105 Sydney 1894-95
J. M. Gregory (1)
100 Melbourne 1920-21
S. E. Gregory (4)
201 Sydney 1894-95
103 Lord's 1896
117 The Oval 1899
112 Adelaide 1903-04
R. J. Hartigan (1)
116† Adelaide 1907-08

R. N. Harvey (6)
112† Leeds 1948
122 Manchester 1953
162 Brisbane 1954-55
167 Melbourne 1958-59
114 Birmingham 1961
154 Adelaide 1962-63
A. L. Hassett (4)
128 Brisbane 1946-47
137 Nottingham 1948
115 Nottingham 1953
104 Lord's 1953
I. A. Healy (1)
102* Manchester 1993
H. L. Hendry (1)
112 Sydney 1928-29
A. M. J. Hilditch (1)
119 Leeds 1985
C. Hill (4)
188 Melbourne 1897-98
135 Lord's 1899
119 Sheffield 1902
160 Adelaide 1907-08
T. P. Horan (1)
124 Melbourne 1881-82
K. J. Hughes (3)
129 Brisbane 1978-79
117 Lord's 1980
137 Sydney 1982-83
F. A. Iredale (2)
140 Adelaide 1894-95
108 Manchester 1896
A. A. Jackson (1)
164† Adelaide 1928-29
D. M. Jones (3)
184* Sydney 1986-87
157 Birmingham 1989
122 The Oval 1989
C. Kelleway (1)
147 Adelaide 1920-21
A. F. Kippax (1)
100 Melbourne 1928-29
W. M. Lawry (7)
130 Lord's 1961
102 Manchester 1961
106 Manchester 1964
166 Brisbane 1965-66
119 Adelaide 1965-66
108 Melbourne 1965-66
135 The Oval 1968
R. R. Lindwall (1)
100 Melbourne 1946-47
J. J. Lyons (1)
134 Sydney 1891-92
C. G. Macartney (5)
170 Sydney 1920-21
115 Leeds 1921
133* Lord's 1926
151 Leeds 1926
109 Manchester 1926

S. J. McCabe (4)
187* Sydney 1932-33
137 Manchester 1934
112 Melbourne 1936-37
232 Nottingham 1938
C. L. McCool (1)
104* Melbourne 1946-47
R. B. McCosker (2)
127 The Oval 1975
107 Nottingham 1977
C. C. McDonald (2)
170 Adelaide 1958-59
133 Melbourne 1958-59
P. S. McDonnell (3)
147 Sydney 1881-82
103 The Oval 1884
124 Adelaide 1884-85
C. E. McLeod (1)
112 Melbourne 1897-98
G. R. Marsh (2)
110† Brisbane 1986-87
138 Nottingham 1989
R. W. Marsh (1)
110* Melbourne 1976-77
G. R. J. Matthews (1)
128 Sydney 1990-91
K. R. Miller (3)
141* Adelaide 1946-47
145* Sydney 1950-51
109 Lord's 1953
A. R. Morris (8)
155 Melbourne 1946-47
122 }
124* } Adelaide 1946-47
105 Lord's 1948
182 Leeds 1948
196 The Oval 1948
206 Adelaide 1950-51
153 Brisbane 1954-55
W. L. Murdoch (2)
153* The Oval 1880
211 The Oval 1884
M. A. Noble (1)
133 Sydney 1903-04
N. C. O'Neill (2)
117 The Oval 1961
100 Adelaide 1962-63
C. E. Pellew (2)
116 Melbourne 1920-21
104 Adelaide 1920-21
W. H. Ponsford (5)
110† Sydney 1924-25
128 Melbourne 1924-25
110 The Oval 1930
181 Leeds 1934
266 The Oval 1934
V. S. Ransford (1)
143* Lord's 1909
I. R. Redpath (2)
171 Perth 1970-71
105 Sydney 1974-75

A. J. Richardson (1)
100 Leeds 1926
V. Y. Richardson (1)
138 Melbourne 1924-25
G. M. Ritchie (1)
146 Nottingham 1985
J. Ryder (2)
201* Adelaide 1924-25
112 Melbourne 1928-29
H. J. H. Scott (1)
102 The Oval 1884
R. B. Simpson (2)
311 Manchester 1964
225 Adelaide 1965-66
M. J. Slater (4)
152 Lord's 1993
176 Brisbane 1994-95
103 Sydney 1994-95
124 Perth 1994-95
K. R. Stackpole (3)
207 Brisbane 1970-71
136 Adelaide 1970-71
114 Nottingham 1972
J. M. Taylor (1)
108 Sydney 1924-25
M. A. Taylor (5)
136† Leeds 1989
219 Nottingham 1989
124 Manchester 1993
111 Lord's 1993
113 Sydney 1994-95
G. H. S. Trott (1)
143 Lord's 1896
V. T. Trumper (6)
135* Lord's 1899
104 Manchester 1902
185* Sydney 1903-04
113 Adelaide 1903-04
166 Sydney 1907-08
113 Sydney 1911-12
K. D. Walters (4)
155† Brisbane 1965-66
115 Melbourne 1965-66
112 Brisbane 1970-71
103 Perth 1974-75
M. E. Waugh (3)
138† Adelaide 1990-91
137 Birmingham 1993
140 Brisbane 1994-95
S. R. Waugh (3)
177* Leeds 1989
152* Lord's 1989
157* Leeds 1993
D. M. Wellham (1)
103† The Oval 1981
K. C. Wessels (1)
162† Brisbane 1982-83
G. M. Wood (3)
100 Melbourne 1978-79
112 Lord's 1980
172 Nottingham 1985

W. M. Woodfull (6)		
141	Leeds	1926
117	Manchester	1926
111	Sydney	1928-29
107	Melbourne	1928-29
102	Melbourne	1928-29
155	Lord's	1930
G. N. Yallop (3)		
102†	Brisbane	1978-79
121	Sydney	1978-79
114	Manchester	1981

† *Signifies hundred on first appearance in England–Australia Tests.*
‡ *Carried his bat.*

RECORD PARTNERSHIPS FOR EACH WICKET

For England

323 for 1st	J. B. Hobbs and W. Rhodes at Melbourne	1911-12
382 for 2nd†	L. Hutton and M. Leyland at The Oval	1938
262 for 3rd	W. R. Hammond and D. R. Jardine at Adelaide	1928-29
222 for 4th	W. R. Hammond and E. Paynter at Lord's	1938
206 for 5th	E. Paynter and D. C. S. Compton at Nottingham	1938
215 for 6th	L. Hutton and J. Hardstaff jun. at The Oval	1938
	G. Boycott and A. P. E. Knott at Nottingham	1977
143 for 7th	F. E. Woolley and J. Vine at Sydney	1911-12
124 for 8th	E. H. Hendren and H. Larwood at Brisbane	1928-29
151 for 9th	W. H. Scotton and W. W. Read at The Oval	1884
130 for 10th†	R. E. Foster and W. Rhodes at Sydney	1903-04

For Australia

329 for 1st	G. R. Marsh and M. A. Taylor at Nottingham	1989
451 for 2nd†	W. H. Ponsford and D. G. Bradman at The Oval	1934
276 for 3rd	D. G. Bradman and A. L. Hassett at Brisbane	1946-47
388 for 4th†	W. H. Ponsford and D. G. Bradman at Leeds	1934
405 for 5th†‡	S. G. Barnes and D. G. Bradman at Sydney	1946-47
346 for 6th†	J. H. Fingleton and D. G. Bradman at Melbourne	1936-37
165 for 7th	C. Hill and H. Trumble at Melbourne	1897-98
243 for 8th†	R. J. Hartigan and C. Hill at Adelaide	1907-08
154 for 9th†	S. E. Gregory and J. McC. Blackham at Sydney	1894-95
127 for 10th†	J. M. Taylor and A. A. Mailey at Sydney	1924-25

† *Denotes record partnership against all countries.*
‡ *Record fifth-wicket partnership in first-class cricket.*

MOST RUNS IN A SERIES

England in England	732 (average 81.33)	D. I. Gower	1985
England in Australia	905 (average 113.12)	W. R. Hammond	1928-29
Australia in England	974 (average 139.14)	D. G. Bradman	1930
Australia in Australia	810 (average 90.00)	D. G. Bradman	1936-37

TEN WICKETS OR MORE IN A MATCH

For England (36)

13-163 (6-42, 7-121)	S. F. Barnes, Melbourne	1901-02
14-102 (7-28, 7-74)	W. Bates, Melbourne	1882-83
10-105 (5-46, 5-59)	A. V. Bedser, Melbourne	1950-51
14-99 (7-55, 7-44)	A. V. Bedser, Nottingham	1953

11-102 (6-44, 5-58)	C. Blythe, Birmingham	1909
11-176 (6-78, 5-98)	I. T. Botham, Perth	1979-80
10-253 (6-125, 4-128)	I. T. Botham, The Oval	1981
11-74 (5-29, 6-45)	J. Briggs, Lord's	1886
12-136 (6-49, 6-87)	J. Briggs, Adelaide	1891-92
10-148 (5-34, 5-114)	J. Briggs, The Oval	1893
10-104 (6-77, 4-27)†	R. M. Ellison, Birmingham	1985
10-179 (5-102, 5-77)†	K. Farnes, Nottingham	1934
10-60 (6-41, 4-19)	J. T. Hearne, The Oval	1896
11-113 (5-58, 6-55)	J. C. Laker, Leeds	1956
19-90 (9-37, 10-53)	J. C. Laker, Manchester	1956
10-124 (5-96, 5-28)	H. Larwood, Sydney	1932-33
11-76 (6-48, 5-28)	W. H. Lockwood, Manchester	1902
12-104 (7-36, 5-68)	G. A. Lohmann, The Oval	1886
10-87 (8-35, 2-52)	G. A. Lohmann, Sydney	1886-87
10-142 (8-58, 2-84)	G. A. Lohmann, Sydney	1891-92
12-102 (6-50, 6-52)†	F. Martin, The Oval	1890
11-68 (7-31, 4-37)	R. Peel, Manchester	1888
15-124 (7-56, 8-68)	W. Rhodes, Melbourne	1903-04
10-156 (5-49, 5-107)†	T. Richardson, Manchester	1893
11-173 (6-39, 5-134)	T. Richardson, Lord's	1896
13-244 (7-168, 6-76)	T. Richardson, Manchester	1896
10-204 (8-94, 2-110)	T. Richardson, Sydney	1897-98
11-228 (6-130, 5-98)†	M. W. Tate, Sydney	1924-25
11-88 (5-58, 6-30)	F. S. Trueman, Leeds	1961
10-130 (4-45, 6-85)	F. H. Tyson, Sydney	1954-55
10-82 (4-37, 6-45)	D. L. Underwood, Leeds	1972
11-215 (7-113, 4-102)	D. L. Underwood, Adelaide	1974-75
15-104 (7-61, 8-43)	H. Verity, Lord's	1934
10-57 (6-41, 4-16)	W. Voce, Brisbane	1936-37
13-256 (5-130, 8-126)	J. C. White, Adelaide	1928-29
10-49 (5-29, 5-20)	F. E. Woolley, The Oval	1912

For Australia (39)

10-151 (5-107, 5-44)	T. M. Alderman, Leeds	1989
10-239 (4-129, 6-110)	L. O'B. Fleetwood-Smith, Adelaide	1936-37
10-160 (4-88, 6-72)	G. Giffen, Sydney	1891-92
11-82 (5-45, 6-37)†	C. V. Grimmett, Sydney	1924-25
10-201 (5-107, 5-94)	C. V. Grimmett, Nottingham	1930
10-122 (5-65, 5-57)	R. M. Hogg, Perth	1978-79
10-66 (5-30, 5-36)	R. M. Hogg, Melbourne	1978-79
12-175 (5-85, 7-90)†	H. V. Hordern, Sydney	1911-12
10-161 (5-95, 5-66)	H. V. Hordern, Sydney	1911-12
10-164 (7-88, 3-76)	E. Jones, Lord's	1899
11-134 (6-47, 5-87)	G. F. Lawson, Brisbane	1982-83
10-181 (5-58, 5-123)	D. K. Lillee, The Oval	1972
11-165 (6-26, 5-139)	D. K. Lillee, Melbourne	1976-77
11-138 (6-60, 5-78)	D. K. Lillee, Melbourne	1979-80
11-159 (7-89, 4-70)	D. K. Lillee, The Oval	1981
11-85 (7-58, 4-27)	C. G. Macartney, Leeds	1909
11-157 (8-97, 3-60)	C. J. McDermott, Perth	1990-91
10-302 (5-160, 5-142)	A. A. Mailey, Adelaide	1920-21
13-236 (4-115, 9-121)	A. A. Mailey, Melbourne	1920-21
16-137 (8-84, 8-53)†	R. A. L. Massie, Lord's	1972
10-152 (5-72, 5-80)	K. R. Miller, Lord's	1956
13-77 (7-17, 6-60)	M. A. Noble, Melbourne	1901-02
11-103 (5-51, 6-52)	M. A. Noble, Sheffield	1902
10-129 (5-63, 5-66)	W. J. O'Reilly, Melbourne	1932-33
11-129 (4-75, 7-54)	W. J. O'Reilly, Nottingham	1934
10-122 (5-66, 5-56)	W. J. O'Reilly, Leeds	1938

11-165 (7-68, 4-97)	G. E. Palmer, Sydney	1881-82
10-126 (7-65, 3-61)	G. E. Palmer, Melbourne	1882-83
13-148 (6-97, 7-51)	B. A. Reid, Melbourne	1990-91
13-110 (6-48, 7-62)	F. R. Spofforth, Melbourne	1878-79
14-90 (7-46, 7-44)	F. R. Spofforth, The Oval	1882
11-117 (4-73, 7-44)	F. R. Spofforth, Sydney	1882-83
10-144 (4-54, 6-90)	F. R. Spofforth, Sydney	1884-85
12-89 (6-59, 6-30)	H. Trumble, The Oval	1896
10-128 (4-75, 6-53)	H. Trumble, Manchester	1902
12-173 (8-65, 4-108)	H. Trumble, The Oval	1902
12-87 (5-44, 7-43)	C. T. B. Turner, Sydney	1887-88
10-63 (5-27, 5-36)	C. T. B. Turner, Lord's	1888
11-110 (3-39, 8-71)	S. K. Warne, Brisbane	1994-95

† *Signifies ten wickets or more on first appearance in England–Australia Tests.*

Note: J. Briggs, J. C. Laker, T. Richardson in 1896, R. M. Hogg, A. A. Mailey, H. Trumble and C. T. B. Turner took ten wickets or more in successive Tests. J. Briggs was omitted, however, from the England team for the first Test match in 1893.

MOST WICKETS IN A SERIES

England in England	46 (average 9.60)	J. C. Laker	1956
England in Australia	38 (average 23.18)	M. W. Tate	1924-25
Australia in England	42 (average 21.26)	T. M. Alderman (6 Tests)	1981
Australia in Australia	41 (average 12.85)	R. M. Hogg (6 Tests)	1978-79

WICKET-KEEPING – MOST DISMISSALS

	M	*Ct*	*St*	*Total*
†R. W. Marsh (Australia)	42	141	7	148
A. P. E. Knott (England)	34	97	8	105
†W. A. Oldfield (Australia)	38	59	31	90
I. A. Healy (Australia)	22	82	7	89
A. A. Lilley (England)	32	65	19	84
A. T. W. Grout (Australia)	22	69	7	76
T. G. Evans (England)	31	63	12	75

† *The number of catches by R. W. Marsh (141) and stumpings by W. A. Oldfield (31) are respective records in England–Australia Tests.*

SCORERS OF OVER 2,000 RUNS

	T	*I*	*NO*	*R*	*HS*	*Avge*
D. G. Bradman	37	63	7	5,028	334	89.78
J. B. Hobbs	41	71	4	3,636	187	54.26
A. R. Border	47	82	19	3,548	200*	56.31
D. I. Gower	42	77	4	3,269	215	44.78
G. Boycott	38	71	9	2,945	191	47.50
W. R. Hammond	33	58	3	2,852	251	51.85
H. Sutcliffe	27	46	5	2,741	194	66.85
C. Hill	41	76	1	2,660	188	35.46
J. H. Edrich	32	57	3	2,644	175	48.96
G. A. Gooch	42	79	0	2,632	196	33.31
G. S. Chappell	35	65	8	2,619	144	45.94
M. C. Cowdrey	43	75	4	2,433	113	34.26
L. Hutton	27	49	6	2,428	364	56.46

	T	I	NO	R	HS	Avge
R. N. Harvey	37	68	5	2,416	167	38.34
V. T. Trumper	40	74	5	2,263	185*	32.79
D. C. Boon	31	57	8	2,237	184*	45.65
W. M. Lawry	29	51	5	2,233	166	48.54
S. E. Gregory	52	92	7	2,193	201	25.80
W. W. Armstrong	42	71	9	2,172	158	35.03
I. M. Chappell	30	56	4	2,138	192	41.11
K. F. Barrington	23	39	6	2,111	256	63.96
A. R. Morris	24	43	2	2,080	206	50.73

BOWLERS WITH 100 WICKETS

	T	Balls	R	W	5W/i	Avge
D. K. Lillee	29	8,516	3,507	167	11	21.00
I. T. Botham	36	8,479	4,093	148	9	27.65
H. Trumble	31	7,895	2,945	141	9	20.88
R. G. D. Willis	35	7,294	3,346	128	7	26.14
M. A. Noble	39	6,845	2,860	115	9	24.86
R. R. Lindwall	29	6,728	2,559	114	6	22.44
W. Rhodes	41	5,791	2,616	109	6	24.00
S. F. Barnes	20	5,749	2,288	106	12	21.58
C. V. Grimmett	22	9,224	3,439	106	11	32.44
D. L. Underwood	29	8,000	2,770	105	4	26.38
A. V. Bedser	21	7,065	2,859	104	7	27.49
G. Giffen	31	6,457	2,791	103	7	27.09
W. J. O'Reilly	19	7,864	2,587	102	8	25.36
R. Peel	20	5,216	1,715	101	5	16.98
C. T. B. Turner	17	5,195	1,670	101	11	16.53
T. M. Alderman	17	4,717	2,117	100	11	21.17
J. R. Thomson	21	4,951	2,418	100	5	24.18

RESULTS ON EACH GROUND

In England

THE OVAL (31)

England (14) 1880, 1886, 1888, 1890, 1893, 1896, 1902, 1912, 1926, 1938, 1953, 1968, 1985, 1993.

Australia (5) 1882, 1930, 1934, 1948, 1972.

Drawn (12) 1884, 1899, 1905, 1909, 1921, 1956, 1961, 1964, 1975, 1977, 1981, 1989.

MANCHESTER (26)

England (7) 1886, 1888, 1905, 1956, 1972, 1977, 1981.

Australia (6) 1896, 1902, 1961, 1968, 1989, 1993.

Drawn (13) 1884, 1893, 1899, 1909, 1912, 1921, 1926, 1930, 1934, 1948, 1953, 1964, 1985.

The scheduled matches in 1890 and 1938 were abandoned without a ball bowled and are excluded.

LORD'S (30)

England (5) 1884, 1886, 1890, 1896, 1934.

Australia (12) 1888, 1899, 1909, 1921, 1930, 1948, 1956, 1961, 1972, 1985, 1989, 1993.

Drawn (13) 1893, 1902, 1905, 1912, 1926, 1938, 1953, 1964, 1968, 1975, 1977, 1980, 1981.

NOTTINGHAM (17)

England (3) 1905, 1930, 1977.

Australia (5) 1921, 1934, 1948, 1981, 1989.

Drawn (9) 1899, 1926, 1938, 1953, 1956, 1964, 1972, 1985, 1993.

LEEDS (21)

England (6) 1956, 1961, 1972, 1977, 1981, 1985.

Australia (7) 1909, 1921, 1938, 1948, 1964, 1989, 1993.

Drawn (8) 1899, 1905, 1926, 1930, 1934, 1953, 1968, 1975.

BIRMINGHAM (9)

England (3) 1909, 1981, 1985.

Australia (2) 1975, 1993.

Drawn (4) 1902, 1961, 1968, 1989.

SHEFFIELD (1)

Australia (1) 1902.

In Australia

MELBOURNE (50)

England (18) *1876*, *1882*, *1884*(2), *1894*(2), *1903*, *1907*, *1911*(2), *1924*, *1928*, *1950*, *1954*, *1962*, *1974*, *1982*, *1986*.

Australia (25) *1876*, *1878*, *1882*, *1891*, *1897*(2), *1901*(2), *1903*, *1907*, *1920*(2), *1924*, *1928*, *1932*, *1936*(2), *1950*, *1958*(2), *1976*, *1978*, *1979*, *1990*, *1994*.

Drawn (7) *1881*(2), *1946*, *1965*(2), *1970*, *1974*.

One scheduled match in 1970-71 was abandoned without a ball bowled and is excluded.

SYDNEY (50)

England (20) *1882*, *1886*(2), *1887*, *1894*, *1897*, *1901*, *1903*(2), *1911*, *1928*, *1932*(2), *1936*, *1954*, *1965*, *1970*(2), *1978*(2).

Australia (23) *1881*(2), *1882*, *1884*(2), *1891*, *1894*, *1897*, *1901*, *1907*(2), *1911*, *1920*(2), *1924*(2), *1946*(2), *1950*, *1962*, *1974*, *1979*, *1986*.

Drawn (7) *1954*, *1958*, *1962*, *1982*, *1987*, *1990*, *1994*.

ADELAIDE (26)

England (8) *1884*, *1891*, *1911*, *1928*, *1932*, *1954*, *1978*, *1994*.

Australia (13) *1894*, *1897*, *1901*, *1903*, *1907*, *1920*, *1924*, *1936*, *1950*, *1958*, *1965*, *1974*, *1982*.

Drawn (5) *1946*, *1962*, *1970*, *1986*, *1990*.

BRISBANE Exhibition Ground (1)

England (1) *1928*.

BRISBANE Woolloongabba (15)

England (4) *1932*, *1936*, *1978*, *1986*.

Australia (8) *1946*, *1950*, *1954*, *1958*, *1974*, *1982*, *1990*, *1994*.

Drawn (3) *1962*, *1965*, *1970*.

PERTH (8)

England (1) *1978*.

Australia (4) *1974*, *1979*, *1990*, *1994*.

Drawn (3) *1970*, *1982*, *1986*.

For Tests in Australia the first year of the season is given in italics; i.e. *1876* denotes the 1876-77 season.

ENGLAND v SOUTH AFRICA

	Captains					
Season	*England*	*South Africa*	*T*	*E*	*SA*	*D*
1888-89	C. A. Smith[1]	O. R. Dunell[2]	2	2	0	0
1891-92	W. W. Read	W. H. Milton	1	1	0	0
1895-96	Lord Hawke[3]	E. A. Halliwell[4]	3	3	0	0
1898-99	Lord Hawke	M. Bisset	2	2	0	0
1905-06	P. F. Warner	P. W. Sherwell	5	1	4	0
1907	R. E. Foster	P. W. Sherwell	3	1	0	2
1909-10	H. D. G. Leveson Gower[5]	S. J. Snooke	5	2	3	0
1912	C. B. Fry	F. Mitchell[6]	3	3	0	0
1913-14	J. W. H. T. Douglas	H. W. Taylor	5	4	0	1
1922-23	F. T. Mann	H. W. Taylor	5	2	1	2
1924	A. E. R. Gilligan[7]	H. W. Taylor	5	3	0	2
1927-28	R. T. Stanyforth[8]	H. G. Deane	5	2	2	1
1929	J. C. White[9]	H. G. Deane	5	2	0	3
1930-31	A. P. F. Chapman	H. G. Deane[10]	5	0	1	4
1935	R. E. S. Wyatt	H. F. Wade	5	0	1	4
1938-39	W. R. Hammond	A. Melville	5	1	0	4
1947	N. W. D. Yardley	A. Melville	5	3	0	2
1948-49	F. G. Mann	A. D. Nourse	5	2	0	3
1951	F. R. Brown	A. D. Nourse	5	3	1	1
1955	P. B. H. May	J. E. Cheetham[11]	5	3	2	0
1956-57	P. B. H. May	C. B. van Ryneveld[12]	5	2	2	1
1960	M. C. Cowdrey	D. J. McGlew	5	3	0	2
1964-65	M. J. K. Smith	T. L. Goddard	5	1	0	4
1965	M. J. K. Smith	P. L. van der Merwe	3	0	1	2
1994	M. A. Atherton	K. C. Wessels	3	1	1	1
1995-96	M. A. Atherton	W. J. Cronje	5	0	1	4
	In South Africa		63	25	14	24
	In England		47	22	6	19
	Totals		110	47	20	43

Notes: The following deputised for the official touring captain or were appointed by the home authority for only a minor proportion of the series:

[1]M. P. Bowden (Second). [2]W. H. Milton (Second). [3]Sir T. C. O'Brien (First). [4]A. R. Richards (Third). [5]F. L. Fane (Fourth and Fifth). [6]L. J. Tancred (Second and Third). [7]J. W. H. T. Douglas (Fourth). [8]G. T. S. Stevens (Fifth). [9]A. W. Carr (Fourth and Fifth). [10]E. P. Nupen (First), H. B. Cameron (Fourth and Fifth). [11]D. J. McGlew (Third and Fourth). [12]D. J. McGlew (Second).

HIGHEST INNINGS TOTALS

For England in England: 554-8 dec. at Lord's 1947
in South Africa: 654-5 at Durban 1938-39

For South Africa in England: 538 at Leeds 1951
in South Africa: 530 at Durban 1938-39

LOWEST INNINGS TOTALS

For England in England: 76 at Leeds 1907
in South Africa: 92 at Cape Town 1898-99

For South Africa in England: 30 at Birmingham 1924
in South Africa: 30 at Port Elizabeth 1895-96

INDIVIDUAL HUNDREDS

For England (90)

R. Abel (1)
120 Cape Town . . 1888-89
L. E. G. Ames (2)
148* The Oval. . . . 1935
115 Cape Town . . 1938-39
M. A. Atherton (1)
185* Johannesburg 1995-96
K. F. Barrington (2)
148* Durban 1964-65
121 Johannesburg 1964-65
G. Boycott (1)
117 Pt Elizabeth . 1964-65
L. C. Braund (1)
104† Lord's 1907
D. C. S. Compton (7)
163† Nottingham . 1947
208 Lord's 1947
115 Manchester . . 1947
113 The Oval. . . . 1947
114 Johannesburg 1948-49
112 Nottingham . 1951
158 Manchester . . 1955
M. C. Cowdrey (3)
101 Cape Town . . 1956-57
155 The Oval. . . . 1960
105 Nottingham . 1965
D. Denton (1)
104 Johannesburg 1909-10
E. R. Dexter (1)
172 Johannesburg 1964-65
J. W. H. T. Douglas (1)
119† Durban 1913-14
W. J. Edrich (3)
219 Durban 1938-39
189 Lord's 1947
191 Manchester . . 1947
F. L. Fane (1)
143 Johannesburg 1905-06
C. B. Fry (1)
129 The Oval. . . . 1907
P. A. Gibb (2)
106† Johannesburg 1938-39
120 Durban 1938-39
W. R. Hammond (6)
138* Birmingham . 1929
101* The Oval. . . . 1929
136* Durban 1930-31
181 Cape Town . . 1938-39
120 Durban 1938-39
140 Durban 1938-39
T. W. Hayward (1)
122 Johannesburg 1895-96
E. H. Hendren (2)
132 Leeds 1924
142 The Oval. . . . 1924
G. A. Hick (2)
110 Leeds 1994
141 Centurion . . . 1995-96
A. J. L. Hill (1)
124 Cape Town . . 1895-96
J. B. Hobbs (2)
187 Cape Town . . 1909-10
211 Lord's 1924
L. Hutton (4)
100 Leeds 1947
158 Johannesburg 1948-49
123 Johannesburg 1948-49
100 Leeds 1951
D. J. Insole (1)
110* Durban 1956-57
M. Leyland (2)
102 Lord's 1929
161 The Oval. . . . 1935
F. G. Mann (1)
136* Pt Elizabeth . 1948-49
P. B. H. May (3)
138† Leeds 1951
112 Lord's 1955
117 Manchester . . 1955
C. P. Mead (3)
102 Johannesburg 1913-14
117 Pt Elizabeth . 1913-14
181 Durban 1922-23
P. H. Parfitt (1)
122* Johannesburg 1964-65
J. M. Parks (1)
108* Durban 1964-65
E. Paynter (3)
117 }
100 } †Johannesburg 1938-39
243 Durban 1938-39
G. Pullar (1)
175 The Oval. . . . 1960
W. Rhodes (1)
152 Johannesburg 1913-14
P. E. Richardson (1)
117† Johannesburg 1956-57
R. W. V. Robins (1)
108 Manchester . . 1935
A. C. Russell (2)
140 }
111 } Durban 1922-23
R. T. Simpson (1)
137 Nottingham . 1951
M. J. K. Smith (1)
121 Cape Town . . 1964-65
R. H. Spooner (1)
119† Lord's 1912
H. Sutcliffe (6)
122 Lord's 1924
102 Johannesburg 1927-28
114 Birmingham . 1929
100 Lord's 1929
104 }
109* } The Oval. . . . 1929
M. W. Tate (1)
100* Lord's 1929
E. Tyldesley (2)
122 Johannesburg 1927-28
100 Durban 1927-28
J. T. Tyldesley (1)
112 Cape Town . . 1898-99
B. H. Valentine (1)
112 Cape Town . . 1938-39
P. F. Warner (1)
132*†‡Johannesburg 1898-99
C. Washbrook (1)
195 Johannesburg 1948-49
A. J. Watkins (1)
111 Johannesburg 1948-49
H. Wood (1)
134* Cape Town . . 1891-92
F. E. Woolley (3)
115* Johannesburg 1922-23
134* Lord's 1924
154 Manchester . . 1929
R. E. S. Wyatt (2)
113 Manchester . . 1929
149 Nottingham . 1935

For South Africa (62)

E. J. Barlow (1)		
138	Cape Town . .	1964-65
K. C. Bland (2)		
144*	Johannesburg	1964-65
127	The Oval	1965
R. H. Catterall (3)		
120	Birmingham .	1924
120	Lord's	1924
119	Durban	1927-28
E. L. Dalton (2)		
117	The Oval	1935
102	Johannesburg	1938-39
W. R. Endean (1)		
116*	Leeds	1955
G. A. Faulkner (1)		
123	Johannesburg	1909-10
T. L. Goddard (1)		
112	Johannesburg	1964-65
C. M. H. Hathorn (1)		
102	Johannesburg	1905-06
G. Kirsten (1)		
110	Johannesburg	1995-96
P. N. Kirsten (1)		
104	Leeds	1994
D. J. McGlew (2)		
104*	Manchester . .	1955
133	Leeds	1955
R. A. McLean (3)		
142	Lord's	1955
100	Durban	1956-57
109	Manchester . .	1960
B. M. McMillan (1)		
100*	Johannesburg	1995-96
A. Melville (4)		
103	Durban	1938-39
189 }	Nottingham .	1947
104* }	Nottingham .	1947
117	Lord's	1947
B. Mitchell (7)		
123	Cape Town . .	1930-31
164*	Lord's	1935
128	The Oval	1935
109	Durban	1938-39
120 }	The Oval	1947
189* }	The Oval	1947
120	Cape Town . .	1948-49
A. D. Nourse (7)		
120	Cape Town . .	1938-39
103	Durban	1938-39
149	Nottingham .	1947
115	Manchester . .	1947
112	Cape Town . .	1948-49
129*	Johannesburg	1948-49
208	Nottingham .	1951
H. G. Owen-Smith (1)		
129	Leeds	1929
A. J. Pithey (1)		
154	Cape Town . .	1964-65
R. G. Pollock (2)		
137	Pt Elizabeth .	1964-65
125	Nottingham .	1965
E. A. B. Rowan (2)		
156*	Johannesburg	1948-49
236	Leeds	1951
P. W. Sherwell (1)		
115	Lord's	1907
I. J. Siedle (1)		
141	Cape Town . .	1930-31
J. H. Sinclair (1)		
106	Cape Town . .	1898-99
H. W. Taylor (7)		
109	Durban	1913-14
176	Johannesburg	1922-23
101	Johannesburg	1922-23
102	Durban	1922-23
101	Johannesburg	1927-28
121	The Oval	1929
117	Cape Town . .	1930-31
P. G. V. van der Bijl (1)		
125	Durban	1938-39
K. G. Viljoen (1)		
124	Manchester . .	1935
W. W. Wade (1)		
125	Pt Elizabeth .	1948-49
J. H. B. Waite (1)		
113	Manchester . .	1955
K. C. Wessels (1)		
105†	Lord's	1994
G. C. White (2)		
147	Johannesburg	1905-06
118	Durban	1909-10
P. L. Winslow (1)		
108	Manchester . .	1955

† *Signifies hundred on first appearance in England–South Africa Tests. K. C. Wessels had earlier scored 162 on his Test debut for Australia against England at Brisbane in 1982-83.*

‡ *P. F. Warner carried his bat through the second innings.*

A. Melville's four hundreds were made in successive Test innings.

H. Wood scored the only hundred of his career in a Test match.

RECORD PARTNERSHIP FOR EACH WICKET

For England

359	for 1st†	L. Hutton and C. Washbrook at Johannesburg	1948-49
280	for 2nd	P. A. Gibb and W. J. Edrich at Durban	1938-39
370	for 3rd†	W. J. Edrich and D. C. S. Compton at Lord's	1947
197	for 4th	W. R. Hammond and L. E. G. Ames at Cape Town	1938-39
237	for 5th	D. C. S. Compton and N. W. D. Yardley at Nottingham	1947
206*	for 6th	K. F. Barrington and J. M. Parks at Durban	1964-65
115	for 7th	J. W. H. T. Douglas and M. C. Bird at Durban	1913-14
154	for 8th	C. W. Wright and H. R. Bromley-Davenport at Johannesburg . .	1895-96
71	for 9th	H. Wood and J. T. Hearne at Cape Town	1891-92
92	for 10th	A. C. Russell and A. E. R. Gilligan at Durban	1922-23

For South Africa

260	for 1st†	B. Mitchell and I. J. Siedle at Cape Town	1930-31
198	for 2nd†	E. A. B. Rowan and C. B. van Ryneveld at Leeds	1951
319	for 3rd	A. Melville and A. D. Nourse at Nottingham	1947
214	for 4th†	H. W. Taylor and H. G. Deane at The Oval	1929
157	for 5th†	A. J. Pithey and J. H. B. Waite at Johannesburg	1964-65
171	for 6th	J. H. B. Waite and P. L. Winslow at Manchester	1955
123	for 7th	H. G. Deane and E. P. Nupen at Durban	1927-28

109* for 8th	B. Mitchell and L. Tuckett at The Oval	1947
137 for 9th†	E. L. Dalton and A. B. C. Langton at The Oval	1935
103 for 10th†	H. G. Owen-Smith and A. J. Bell at Leeds	1929

† *Denotes record partnership against all countries.*

MOST RUNS IN A SERIES

England in England	753 (average 94.12)	D. C. S. Compton	1947
England in South Africa	653 (average 81.62)	E. Paynter	1938-39
South Africa in England	621 (average 69.00)	A. D. Nourse	1947
South Africa in South Africa	582 (average 64.66)	H. W. Taylor	1922-23

TEN WICKETS OR MORE IN A MATCH

For England (24)

11-110 (5-25, 6-85)†	S. F. Barnes, Lord's	1912
10-115 (6-52, 4-63)	S. F. Barnes, Leeds	1912
13-57 (5-28, 8-29)	S. F. Barnes, The Oval	1912
10-105 (5-57, 5-48)	S. F. Barnes, Durban	1913-14
17-159 (8-56, 9-103)	S. F. Barnes, Johannesburg	1913-14
14-144 (7-56, 7-88)	S. F. Barnes, Durban	1913-14
12-112 (7-58, 5-54)	A. V. Bedser, Manchester	1951
11-118 (6-68, 5-50)	C. Blythe, Cape Town	1905-06
15-99 (8-59, 7-40)	C. Blythe, Leeds	1907
10-104 (7-46, 3-58)	C. Blythe, Cape Town	1909-10
15-28 (7-17, 8-11)	J. Briggs, Cape Town	1888-89
13-91 (6-54, 7-37)†	J. J. Ferris, Cape Town	1891-92
10-207 (7-115, 3-92)	A. P. Freeman, Leeds	1929
12-171 (7-71, 5-100)	A. P. Freeman, Manchester	1929
12-130 (7-70, 5-60)	G. Geary, Johannesburg	1927-28
11-90 (6-7, 5-83)	A. E. R. Gilligan, Birmingham	1924
10-119 (4-64, 6-55)	J. C. Laker, The Oval	1951
15-45 (7-38, 8-7)†	G. A. Lohmann, Port Elizabeth	1895-96
12-71 (9-28, 3-43)	G. A. Lohmann, Johannesburg	1895-96
10-138 (1-81, 9-57)	D. E. Malcolm, The Oval	1994
11-97 (6-63, 5-34)	J. B. Statham, Lord's	1960
12-101 (7-52, 5-49)	R. Tattersall, Lord's	1951
12-89 (5-53, 7-36)	J. H. Wardle, Cape Town	1956-57
10-175 (5-95, 5-80)	D. V. P. Wright, Lord's	1947

For South Africa (6)

11-112 (4-49, 7-63)†	A. E. Hall, Cape Town	1922-23
11-150 (5-63, 6-87)	E. P. Nupen, Johannesburg	1930-31
10-87 (5-53, 5-34)	P. M. Pollock, Nottingham	1965
12-127 (4-57, 8-70)	S. J. Snooke, Johannesburg	1905-06
13-192 (4-79, 9-113)	H. J. Tayfield, Johannesburg	1956-57
12-181 (5-87, 7-94)	A. E. E. Vogler, Johannesburg	1909-10

† *Signifies ten wickets or more on first appearance in England–South Africa Tests.*

Note: S. F. Barnes took ten wickets or more in his first five Tests v South Africa and in six of his seven Tests v South Africa. A. P. Freeman and G. A. Lohmann took ten wickets or more in successive matches.

MOST WICKETS IN A SERIES

England in England	34 (average 8.29)	S. F. Barnes	1912
England in South Africa	49 (average 10.93)	S. F. Barnes	1913-14
South Africa in England	26 (average 21.84)	H. J. Tayfield	1955
South Africa in England	26 (average 22.57)	N. A. T. Adcock	1960
South Africa in South Africa	37 (average 17.18)	H. J. Tayfield	1956-57

ENGLAND v WEST INDIES

Season	Captains England	West Indies	T	E	WI	D
1928	A. P. F. Chapman	R. K. Nunes	3	3	0	0
1929-30	Hon. F. S. G. Calthorpe	E. L. G. Hoad[1]	4	1	1	2
1933	D. R. Jardine[2]	G. C. Grant	3	2	0	1
1934-35	R. E. S. Wyatt	G. C. Grant	4	1	2	1
1939	W. R. Hammond	R. S. Grant	3	1	0	2
1947-48	G. O. B. Allen[3]	J. D. C. Goddard[4]	4	0	2	2
1950	N. W. D. Yardley[5]	J. D. C. Goddard	4	1	3	0
1953-54	L. Hutton	J. B. Stollmeyer	5	2	2	1
1957	P. B. H. May	J. D. C. Goddard	5	3	0	2
1959-60	P. B. H. May[6]	F. C. M. Alexander	5	1	0	4

THE WISDEN TROPHY

Season	Captains England	West Indies	T	E	WI	D	Held by
1963	E. R. Dexter	F. M. M. Worrell	5	1	3	1	WI
1966	M. C. Cowdrey[7]	G. S. Sobers	5	1	3	1	WI
1967-68	M. C. Cowdrey	G. S. Sobers	5	1	0	4	E
1969	R. Illingworth	G. S. Sobers	3	2	0	1	E
1973	R. Illingworth	R. B. Kanhai	3	0	2	1	WI
1973-74	M. H. Denness	R. B. Kanhai	5	1	1	3	WI
1976	A. W. Greig	C. H. Lloyd	5	0	3	2	WI
1980	I. T. Botham	C. H. Lloyd[8]	5	0	1	4	WI
1980-81†	I. T. Botham	C. H. Lloyd	4	0	2	2	WI
1984	D. I. Gower	C. H. Lloyd	5	0	5	0	WI
1985-86	D. I. Gower	I. V. A. Richards	5	0	5	0	WI
1988	J. E. Emburey[9]	I. V. A. Richards	5	0	4	1	WI
1989-90‡	G. A. Gooch[10]	I. V. A. Richards[11]	4	1	2	1	WI
1991	G. A. Gooch	I. V. A. Richards	5	2	2	1	WI
1993-94	M. A. Atherton	R. B. Richardson[12]	5	1	3	1	WI
1995	M. A. Atherton	R. B. Richardson	6	2	2	2	WI
	In England		65	18	28	19	
	In West Indies		50	9	20	21	
	Totals		115	27	48	40	

† The Second Test, at Georgetown, was cancelled owing to political pressure and is excluded.
‡ The Second Test, at Georgetown, was abandoned without a ball being bowled and is excluded.

Notes: The following deputised for the official touring captain or were appointed by the home authority for only a minor proportion of the series:

[1]N. Betancourt (Second), M. P. Fernandes (Third), R. K. Nunes (Fourth). [2]R. E. S. Wyatt (Third). [3]K. Cranston (First). [4]G. A. Headley (First), G. E. Gomez (Second). [5]F. R. Brown (Fourth). [6]M. C. Cowdrey (Fourth and Fifth). [7]M. J. K. Smith (First), D. B. Close (Fifth). [8]I. V. A. Richards (Fifth). [9]M. W. Gatting (First), C. S. Cowdrey (Fourth), G. A. Gooch (Fifth). [10]A. J. Lamb (Fourth and Fifth). [11]D. L. Haynes (Third). [12]C. A. Walsh (Fifth).

HIGHEST INNINGS TOTALS

For England in England: 619-6 dec. at Nottingham 1957
in West Indies: 849 at Kingston 1929-30

For West Indies in England: 692-8 dec. at The Oval 1995
in West Indies: 681-8 dec. at Port-of-Spain 1953-54

LOWEST INNINGS TOTALS

For England in England: 71 at Manchester 1976
in West Indies: 46 at Port-of-Spain 1993-94

For West Indies in England: 86 at The Oval 1957
in West Indies: 102 at Bridgetown 1934-35

INDIVIDUAL HUNDREDS

For England (95)

L. E. G. Ames (3)
105 Port-of-Spain 1929-30
149 Kingston.... 1929-30
126 Kingston.... 1934-35

D. L. Amiss (4)
174 Port-of-Spain 1973-74
262* Kingston.... 1973-74
118 Georgetown . 1973-74
203 The Oval.... 1976

M. A. Atherton (3)
144 Georgetown . 1993-94
135 St John's.... 1993-94
113 Nottingham . 1995

A. H. Bakewell (1)
107† The Oval.... 1933

K. F. Barrington (3)
128† Bridgetown.. 1959-60
121 Port-of-Spain 1959-60
143 Port-of-Spain 1967-68

G. Boycott (5)
116 Georgetown . 1967-68
128 Manchester.. 1969
106 Lord's...... 1969
112 Port-of-Spain 1973-74
104* St John's.... 1980-81

D. C. S. Compton (2)
120† Lord's...... 1939
133 Port-of-Spain 1953-54

M. C. Cowdrey (6)
154† Birmingham . 1957
152 Lord's...... 1957
114 Kingston.... 1959-60
119 Port-of-Spain 1959-60
101 Kingston.... 1967-68
148 Port-of-Spain 1967-68

E. R. Dexter (2)
136*† Bridgetown.. 1959-60
110 Georgetown . 1959-60

J. H. Edrich (1)
146 Bridgetown.. 1967-68

T. G. Evans (1)
104 Manchester.. 1950

K. W. R. Fletcher (1)
129* Bridgetown.. 1973-74

G. Fowler (1)
106 Lord's...... 1984

G. A. Gooch (5)
123 Lord's...... 1980
116 Bridgetown.. 1980-81
153 Kingston.... 1980-81
146 Nottingham . 1988
154*‡ Leeds 1991

D. I. Gower (1)
154* Kingston.... 1980-81

T. W. Graveney (5)
258 Nottingham . 1957
164 The Oval.... 1957
109 Nottingham . 1966
165 The Oval.... 1966
118 Port-of-Spain 1967-68

A. W. Greig (3)
148 Bridgetown.. 1973-74
121 Georgetown . 1973-74
116 Leeds 1976

S. C. Griffith (1)
140† Port-of-Spain 1947-48

W. R. Hammond (1)
138 The Oval.... 1939

J. H. Hampshire (1)
107† Lord's...... 1969

F. C. Hayes (1)
106*† The Oval.... 1973

E. H. Hendren (2)
205* Port-of-Spain 1929-30
123 Georgetown . 1929-30

G. A. Hick (1)
118* Nottingham . 1995

J. B. Hobbs (1)
159 The Oval.... 1928

L. Hutton (5)
196† Lord's...... 1939
165* The Oval.... 1939
202*‡ The Oval.... 1950
169 Georgetown . 1953-54
205 Kingston.... 1953-54

R. Illingworth (1)
113 Lord's...... 1969

D. R. Jardine (1)
127 Manchester.. 1933

A. P. E. Knott (1)
116 Leeds 1976

A. J. Lamb (6)
110 Lord's...... 1984
100 Leeds 1984
100* Manchester.. 1984
113 Lord's...... 1988
132 Kingston.... 1989-90
119 Bridgetown.. 1989-90

P. B. H. May (3)
135 Port-of-Spain 1953-54
285* Birmingham . 1957
104 Nottingham . 1957

C. Milburn (1)
126* Lord's...... 1966

J. T. Murray (1)
112† The Oval.... 1966

J. M. Parks (1)
101*† Port-of-Spain 1959-60

W. Place (1)
107 Kingston.... 1947-48

P. E. Richardson (2)
126 Nottingham . 1957
107 The Oval.... 1957

J. D. Robertson (1)
133 Port-of-Spain 1947-48

A. Sandham (2)
152† Bridgetown.. 1929-30
325 Kingston.... 1929-30

M. J. K. Smith (1)
108 Port-of-Spain 1959-60

R. A. Smith (3)
148* Lord's...... 1991
109 The Oval ... 1991
175 St John's.... 1993-94

D. S. Steele (1)
106† Nottingham . 1976

A. J. Stewart (2)
118 } Bridgetown.. 1993-94
143 }

R. Subba Row (1)
100† Georgetown . 1959-60

E. Tyldesley (1)
122† Lord's...... 1928

C. Washbrook (2)
114† Lord's...... 1950
102 Nottingham . 1950

W. Watson (1)
116† Kingston.... 1953-54

P. Willey (2)
100* The Oval.... 1980
102* St John's.... 1980-81

For West Indies (107)

J. C. Adams (1)
137 Georgetown . 1993-94
K. L. T. Arthurton (1)
126 Kingston.... 1993-94
I. Barrow (1)
105 Manchester.. 1933
C. A. Best (1)
164 Bridgetown.. 1989-90
B. F. Butcher (2)
133 Lord's...... 1963
209* Nottingham . 1966
G. M. Carew (1)
107 Port-of-Spain 1947-48
C. A. Davis (1)
103 Lord's...... 1969
P. J. L. Dujon (1)
101 Manchester.. 1984
R. C. Fredericks (3)
150 Birmingham . 1973
138 Lord's...... 1976
109 Leeds...... 1976
A. G. Ganteaume (1)
112† Port-of-Spain 1947-48
H. A. Gomes (2)
143 Birmingham . 1984
104* Leeds...... 1984
C. G. Greenidge (7)
134 } Manchester.. 1976
101 }
115 Leeds...... 1976
214* Lord's...... 1984
223 Manchester.. 1984
103 Lord's...... 1988
149 St John's.... 1989-90
D. L. Haynes (5)
184 Lord's...... 1980
125 The Oval.... 1984
131 St John's.... 1985-86
109 Bridgetown.. 1989-90
167 St John's.... 1989-90
G. A. Headley (8)
176† Bridgetown.. 1929-30
114 } Georgetown . 1929-30
112 }
223 Kingston.... 1929-30
169* Manchester.. 1933
270* Kingston.... 1934-35
106 } Lord's...... 1939
107 }
D. A. J. Holford (1)
105* Lord's...... 1966
J. K. Holt (1)
166 Bridgetown.. 1953-54
C. L. Hooper (2)
111 Lord's...... 1991
127 The Oval ... 1995
C. C. Hunte (3)
182 Manchester.. 1963
108* The Oval.... 1963
135 Manchester.. 1966
B. D. Julien (1)
121 Lord's...... 1973
A. I. Kallicharran (2)
158 Port-of-Spain 1973-74
119 Bridgetown.. 1973-74
R. B. Kanhai (5)
110 Port-of-Spain 1959-60
104 The Oval.... 1966
153 Port-of-Spain 1967-68
150 Georgetown . 1967-68
157 Lord's...... 1973
B. C. Lara (5)
167 Georgetown . 1993-94
375 St John's.... 1993-94
145 Manchester.. 1995
152 Nottingham . 1995
179 The Oval ... 1995
C. H. Lloyd (5)
118† Port-of-Spain 1967-68
113* Bridgetown.. 1967-68
132 The Oval.... 1973
101 Manchester.. 1980
100 Bridgetown.. 1980-81
S. M. Nurse (2)
137 Leeds...... 1966
136 Port-of-Spain 1967-68
A. F. Rae (2)
106 Lord's...... 1950
109 The Oval.... 1950
I. V. A. Richards (8)
232† Nottingham . 1976
135 Manchester.. 1976
291 The Oval.... 1976
145 Lord's...... 1980
182* Bridgetown.. 1980-81
114 St John's.... 1980-81
117 Birmingham . 1984
110* St John's.... 1985-86
R. B. Richardson (4)
102 Port-of-Spain 1985-86
160 Bridgetown.. 1985-86
104 Birmingham . 1991
121 The Oval ... 1991
C. A. Roach (2)
122 Bridgetown.. 1929-30
209 Georgetown . 1929-30
L. G. Rowe (3)
120 Kingston.... 1973-74
302 Bridgetown.. 1973-74
123 Port-of-Spain 1973-74
O. G. Smith (2)
161† Birmingham . 1957
168 Nottingham . 1957
G. S. Sobers (10)
226 Bridgetown.. 1959-60
147 Kingston.... 1959-60
145 Georgetown . 1959-60
102 Leeds...... 1963
161 Manchester.. 1966
163* Lord's...... 1966
174 Leeds...... 1966
113* Kingston.... 1967-68
152 Georgetown . 1967-68
150* Lord's...... 1973
C. L. Walcott (4)
168* Lord's...... 1950
220 Bridgetown.. 1953-54
124 Port-of-Spain 1953-54
116 Kingston.... 1953-54
E. D. Weekes (3)
141 Kingston.... 1947-48
129 Nottingham . 1950
206 Port-of-Spain 1953-54
K. H. Weekes (1)
137 The Oval.... 1939
F. M. M. Worrell (6)
131* Georgetown . 1947-48
261 Nottingham . 1950
138 The Oval.... 1950
167 Port-of-Spain 1953-54
191*‡ Nottingham . 1957
197* Bridgetown.. 1959-60

† Signifies hundred on first appearance in England–West Indies Tests. S. C. Griffith provides the only instance for England of a player hitting his maiden century in first-class cricket in his first Test.
‡ Carried his bat.

RECORD PARTNERSHIPS FOR EACH WICKET

For England

212	for 1st	C. Washbrook and R. T. Simpson at Nottingham	1950
266	for 2nd	P. E. Richardson and T. W. Graveney at Nottingham	1957
303	for 3rd	M. A. Atherton and R. A. Smith at St John's	1993-94

411	for 4th†	P. B. H. May and M. C. Cowdrey at Birmingham	1957
150	for 5th	A. J. Stewart and G. P. Thorpe at Bridgetown	1993-94
163	for 6th	A. W. Greig and A. P. E. Knott at Bridgetown	1973-74
197	for 7th†	M. J. K. Smith and J. M. Parks at Port-of-Spain	1959-60
217	for 8th	T. W. Graveney and J. T. Murray at The Oval	1966
109	for 9th	G. A. R. Lock and P. I. Pocock at Georgetown	1967-68
128	for 10th	K. Higgs and J. A. Snow at The Oval	1966

For West Indies

298	for 1st†	C. G. Greenidge and D. L. Haynes at St John's	1989-90
287*	for 2nd	C. G. Greenidge and H. A. Gomes at Lord's	1984
338	for 3rd†	E. D. Weekes and F. M. M. Worrell at Port-of-Spain	1953-54
399	for 4th†	G. S. Sobers and F. M. M. Worrell at Bridgetown	1959-60
265	for 5th†	S. M. Nurse and G. S. Sobers at Leeds	1966
274*	for 6th†	G. S. Sobers and D. A. J. Holford at Lord's	1966
155*	for 7th‡	G. S. Sobers and B. D. Julien at Lord's	1973
99	for 8th	C. A. McWatt and J. K. Holt at Georgetown	1953-54
150	for 9th	E. A. E. Baptiste and M. A. Holding at Birmingham	1984
67*	for 10th	M. A. Holding and C. E. H. Croft at St John's	1980-81

† *Denotes record partnership against all countries.*

‡ *231 runs were added for this wicket in two separate partnerships: G. S. Sobers retired ill and was replaced by K. D. Boyce when 155 had been added.*

TEN WICKETS OR MORE IN A MATCH

For England (11)

11-98 (7-44, 4-54)	T. E. Bailey, Lord's	1957
10-93 (5-54, 5-39)	A. P. Freeman, Manchester	1928
13-156 (8-86, 5-70)	A. W. Greig, Port-of-Spain	1973-74
11-48 (5-28, 6-20)	G. A. R. Lock, The Oval	1957
10-137 (4-60, 6-77)	D. E. Malcolm, Port-of-Spain	1989-90
11-96 (5-37, 6-59)†	C. S. Marriott, The Oval	1933
10-142 (4-82, 6-60)	J. A. Snow, Georgetown	1967-68
10-195 (5-105, 5-90)†	G. T. S. Stevens, Bridgetown	1929-30
11-152 (6-100, 5-52)	F. S. Trueman, Lord's	1963
12-119 (5-75, 7-44)	F. S. Trueman, Birmingham	1963
11-149 (4-79, 7-70)	W. Voce, Port-of-Spain	1929-30

For West Indies (14)

10-127 (2-82, 8-45)	C. E. L. Ambrose, Bridgetown	1989-90
11-84 (5-60, 6-24)	C. E. L. Ambrose, Port-of-Spain	1993-94
10-174 (5-105, 5-69)	K. C. G. Benjamin, Nottingham	1995
11-147 (5-70, 6-77)†	K. D. Boyce, The Oval	1973
11-229 (5-137, 6-92)	W. Ferguson, Port-of-Spain	1947-48
11-157 (5-59, 6-98)†	L. R. Gibbs, Manchester	1963
10-106 (5-37, 5-69)	L. R. Gibbs, Manchester	1966
14-149 (8-92, 6-57)	M. A. Holding, The Oval	1976
10-96 (5-41, 5-55)†	H. H. H. Johnson, Kingston	1947-48
10-92 (6-32, 4-60)	M. D. Marshall, Lord's	1988
11-152 (5-66, 6-86)	S. Ramadhin, Lord's	1950
10-123 (5-60, 5-63)	A. M. E. Roberts, Lord's	1976
11-204 (8-104, 3-100)†	A. L. Valentine, Manchester	1950
10-160 (4-121, 6-39)	A. L. Valentine, The Oval	1950

† *Signifies ten wickets or more on first appearance in England–West Indies Tests.*

Note: F. S. Trueman took ten wickets or more in successive matches.

ENGLAND v NEW ZEALAND

Season	*Captains* *England*	*New Zealand*	*T*	*E*	*NZ*	*D*
1929-30	A. H. H. Gilligan	T. C. Lowry	4	1	0	3
1931	D. R. Jardine	T. C. Lowry	3	1	0	2
1932-33	D. R. Jardine[1]	M. L. Page	2	0	0	2
1937	R. W. V. Robins	M. L. Page	3	1	0	2
1946-47	W. R. Hammond	W. A. Hadlee	1	0	0	1
1949	F. G. Mann[2]	W. A. Hadlee	4	0	0	4
1950-51	F. R. Brown	W. A. Hadlee	2	1	0	1
1954-55	L. Hutton	G. O. Rabone	2	2	0	0
1958	P. B. H. May	J. R. Reid	5	4	0	1
1958-59	P. B. H. May	J. R. Reid	2	1	0	1
1962-63	E. R. Dexter	J. R. Reid	3	3	0	0
1965	M. J. K. Smith	J. R. Reid	3	3	0	0
1965-66	M. J. K. Smith	B. W. Sinclair[3]	3	0	0	3
1969	R. Illingworth	G. T. Dowling	3	2	0	1
1970-71	R. Illingworth	G. T. Dowling	2	1	0	1
1973	R. Illingworth	B. E. Congdon	3	2	0	1
1974-75	M. H. Denness	B. E. Congdon	2	1	0	1
1977-78	G. Boycott	M. G. Burgess	3	1	1	1
1978	J. M. Brearley	M. G. Burgess	3	3	0	0
1983	R. G. D. Willis	G. P. Howarth	4	3	1	0
1983-84	R. G. D. Willis	G. P. Howarth	3	0	1	2
1986	M. W. Gatting	J. V. Coney	3	0	1	2
1987-88	M. W. Gatting	J. J. Crowe[4]	3	0	0	3
1990	G. A. Gooch	J. G. Wright	3	1	0	2
1991-92	G. A. Gooch	M. D. Crowe	3	2	0	1
1994	M. A. Atherton	K. R. Rutherford	3	1	0	2
	In New Zealand		35	13	2	20
	In England		40	21	2	17
	Totals		75	34	4	37

Notes: The following deputised for the official touring captain or were appointed by the home authority for only a minor proportion of the series:
[1]R. E. S. Wyatt (Second). [2]F. R. Brown (Third and Fourth). [3]M. E. Chapple (First). [4]J. G. Wright (Third).

HIGHEST INNINGS TOTALS

For England in England: 567-8 dec. at Nottingham 1994
in New Zealand: 593-6 dec. at Auckland 1974-75

For New Zealand in England: 551-9 dec. at Lord's 1973
in New Zealand: 537 at Wellington 1983-84

LOWEST INNINGS TOTALS

For England in England: 158 at Birmingham 1990
in New Zealand: 64 at Wellington 1977-78

For New Zealand in England: 47 at Lord's 1958
in New Zealand: 26 at Auckland 1954-55

INDIVIDUAL HUNDREDS

For England (79)

G. O. B. Allen (1)
122† Lord's 1931
L. E. G. Ames (2)
137† Lord's 1931
103 Christchurch 1932-33
D. L. Amiss (2)
138*† Nottingham 1973
164* Christchurch 1974-75
M. A. Atherton (3)
151† Nottingham 1990
101 Nottingham 1994
111 Manchester 1994
T. E. Bailey (1)
134* Christchurch 1950-51
K. F. Barrington (3)
126† Auckland 1962-63
137 Birmingham 1965
163 Leeds 1965
I. T. Botham (3)
103 Christchurch 1977-78
103 Nottingham 1983
138 Wellington 1983-84
E. H. Bowley (1)
109 Auckland 1929-30
G. Boycott (2)
115 Leeds 1973
131 Nottingham 1978
B. C. Broad (1)
114† Christchurch 1987-88
D. C. S. Compton (2)
114 Leeds 1949
116 Lord's 1949
M. C. Cowdrey (2)
128* Wellington 1962-63
119 Lord's 1965
M. H. Denness (1)
181 Auckland 1974-75
E. R. Dexter (1)
141 Christchurch 1958-59
B. L. D'Oliveira (1)
100 Christchurch 1970-71

K. S. Duleepsinhji (2)
117 Auckland 1929-30
109 The Oval 1931
J. H. Edrich (3)
310*† Leeds 1965
115 Lord's 1969
155 Nottingham 1969
W. J. Edrich (1)
100 The Oval 1949
K. W. R. Fletcher (2)
178 Lord's 1973
216 Auckland 1974-75
G. Fowler (1)
105† The Oval 1983
M. W. Gatting (1)
121 The Oval 1986
G. A. Gooch (4)
183 Lord's 1986
154 Birmingham 1990
114 Auckland 1991-92
210 Nottingham 1994
D. I. Gower (4)
111† The Oval 1978
112* Leeds 1983
108 Lord's 1983
131 The Oval 1986
A. W. Greig (1)
139† Nottingham 1973
W. R. Hammond (4)
100* The Oval 1931
227 Christchurch 1932-33
336* Auckland 1932-33
140 Lord's 1937
J. Hardstaff jun. (2)
114† Lord's 1937
103 The Oval 1937
L. Hutton (3)
100 Manchester 1937
101 Leeds 1949
206 The Oval 1949

B. R. Knight (1)
125† Auckland 1962-63
A. P. E. Knott (1)
101 Auckland 1970-71
A. J. Lamb (3)
102*† The Oval 1983
137* Nottingham 1983
142 Wellington 1991-92
G. B. Legge (1)
196 Auckland 1929-30
P. B. H. May (3)
113* Leeds 1958
101 Manchester 1958
124* Auckland 1958-59
C. A. Milton (1)
104*† Leeds 1958
P. H. Parfitt (1)
131*† Auckland 1962-63
C. T. Radley (1)
158 Auckland 1977-78
D. W. Randall (2)
164 Wellington 1983-84
104 Auckland 1983-84
P. E. Richardson (1)
100† Birmingham 1958
J. D. Robertson (1)
121† Lord's 1949
P. J. Sharpe (1)
111 Nottingham 1969
R. T. Simpson (1)
103† Manchester 1949
A. J. Stewart (3)
148 Christchurch 1991-92
107 Wellington 1991-92
119 Lord's 1994
H. Sutcliffe (2)
117† The Oval 1931
109* Manchester 1931
C. J. Tavaré (1)
109† The Oval 1983
C. Washbrook (1)
103* Leeds 1949

For New Zealand (38)

J. G. Bracewell (1)
110 Nottingham 1986
M. G. Burgess (2)
104 Auckland 1970-71
105 Lord's 1973
J. V. Coney (1)
174* Wellington 1983-84
B. E. Congdon (3)
104 Christchurch 1965-66
176 Nottingham 1973
175 Lord's 1973

J. J. Crowe (1)
128 Auckland 1983-84
M. D. Crowe (5)
100 Wellington 1983-84
106 Lord's 1986
143 Wellington 1987-88
142 Lord's 1994
115 Manchester 1994
C. S. Dempster (2)
136 Wellington 1929-30
120 Lord's 1931
M. P. Donnelly (1)
206 Lord's 1949

T. J. Franklin (1)
101 Lord's 1990
M. J. Greatbatch (1)
107*† Auckland 1987-88
W. A. Hadlee (1)
116 Christchurch 1946-47
G. P. Howarth (3)
122 }
102 } Auckland 1977-78
123 Lord's 1978
A. H. Jones (1)
143 Wellington 1991-92

J. E. Mills (1)
117† Wellington .. 1929-30
M. L. Page (1)
104 Lord's 1931
J. M. Parker (1)
121 Auckland ... 1974-75
V. Pollard (2)
116 Nottingham . 1973
105* Lord's 1973

J. R. Reid (1)
100 Christchurch. 1962-63
K. R. Rutherford (1)
107* Wellington .. 1987-88
B. W. Sinclair (1)
114 Auckland ... 1965-66
I. D. S. Smith (1)
113* Auckland ... 1983-84

B. Sutcliffe (2)
101 Manchester.. 1949
116 Christchurch. 1950-51
J. G. Wright (4)
130 Auckland ... 1983-84
119 The Oval.... 1986
103 Auckland ... 1987-88
116 Wellington .. 1991-92

† *Signifies hundred on first appearance in England–New Zealand Tests.*

RECORD PARTNERSHIPS FOR EACH WICKET

For England

223	for 1st	G. Fowler and C. J. Tavaré at The Oval	1983
369	for 2nd	J. H. Edrich and K. F. Barrington at Leeds	1965
245	for 3rd	J. Hardstaff jun. and W. R. Hammond at Lord's	1937
266	for 4th	M. H. Denness and K. W. R. Fletcher at Auckland	1974-75
242	for 5th	W. R. Hammond and L. E. G. Ames at Christchurch	1932-33
240	for 6th†	P. H. Parfitt and B. R. Knight at Auckland	1962-63
149	for 7th	A. P. E. Knott and P. Lever at Auckland	1970-71
246	for 8th†	L. E. G. Ames and G. O. B. Allen at Lord's	1931
163*	for 9th†	M. C. Cowdrey and A. C. Smith at Wellington	1962-63
59	for 10th	A. P. E. Knott and N. Gifford at Nottingham	1973

For New Zealand

276	for 1st	C. S. Dempster and J. E. Mills at Wellington	1929-30
241	for 2nd†	J. G. Wright and A. H. Jones at Wellington	1991-92
210	for 3rd	B. A. Edgar and M. D. Crowe at Lord's	1986
155	for 4th	M. D. Crowe and M. J. Greatbatch at Wellington	1987-88
180	for 5th	M. D. Crowe and S. A. Thomson at Lord's	1994
141	for 6th	M. D. Crowe and A. C. Parore at Manchester	1994
117	for 7th	D. N. Patel and C. L. Cairns at Christchurch	1991-92
104	for 8th	D. A. R. Moloney and A. W. Roberts at Lord's	1937
118	for 9th	J. V. Coney and B. L. Cairns at Wellington	1983-84
57	for 10th	F. L. H. Mooney and J. Cowie at Leeds	1949

† *Denotes record partnership against all countries.*

TEN WICKETS OR MORE IN A MATCH

For England (8)

11-140 (6-101, 5-39)	I. T. Botham, Lord's	1978
10-149 (5-98, 5-51)	A. W. Greig, Auckland	1974-75
11-65 (4-14, 7-51)	G. A. R. Lock, Leeds	1958
11-84 (5-31, 6-53)	G. A. R. Lock, Christchurch	1958-59
11-147 (4-100, 7-47)†	P. C. R. Tufnell, Christchurch	1991-92
11-70 (4-38, 7-32)†	D. L. Underwood, Lord's	1969
12-101 (6-41, 6-60)	D. L. Underwood, The Oval	1969
12-97 (6-12, 6-85)	D. L. Underwood, Christchurch	1970-71

For New Zealand (5)

10-144 (7-74, 3-70)	B. L. Cairns, Leeds	1983
10-140 (4-73, 6-67)	J. Cowie, Manchester	1937
10-100 (4-74, 6-26)	R. J. Hadlee, Wellington	1977-78
10-140 (6-80, 4-60)	R. J. Hadlee, Nottingham	1986
11-169 (6-76, 5-93)	D. J. Nash, Lord's	1994

† *Signifies ten wickets or more on first appearance in England–New Zealand Tests.*

Note: D. L. Underwood took 12 wickets in successive matches against New Zealand in 1969 and 1970-71.

HAT-TRICK AND FOUR WICKETS IN FIVE BALLS

M. J. C. Allom, in his first Test match, v New Zealand at Christchurch in 1929-30, dismissed C. S. Dempster, T. C. Lowry, K. C. James, and F. T. Badcock to take four wickets in five balls (w-www).

ENGLAND v INDIA

Season	*Captains* England	*Captains* India	*T*	*E*	*I*	*D*
1932	D. R. Jardine	C. K. Nayudu	1	1	0	0
1933-34	D. R. Jardine	C. K. Nayudu	3	2	0	1
1936	G. O. B. Allen	Maharaj of Vizianagram	3	2	0	1
1946	W. R. Hammond	Nawab of Pataudi sen.	3	1	0	2
1951-52	N. D. Howard[1]	V. S. Hazare	5	1	1	3
1952	L. Hutton	V. S. Hazare	4	3	0	1
1959	P. B. H. May[2]	D. K. Gaekwad[3]	5	5	0	0
1961-62	E. R. Dexter	N. J. Contractor	5	0	2	3
1963-64	M. J. K. Smith	Nawab of Pataudi jun.	5	0	0	5
1967	D. B. Close	Nawab of Pataudi jun.	3	3	0	0
1971	R. Illingworth	A. L. Wadekar	3	0	1	2
1972-73	A. R. Lewis	A. L. Wadekar	5	1	2	2
1974	M. H. Denness	A. L. Wadekar	3	3	0	0
1976-77	A. W. Greig	B. S. Bedi	5	3	1	1
1979	J. M. Brearley	S. Venkataraghavan	4	1	0	3
1979-80	J. M. Brearley	G. R. Viswanath	1	1	0	0
1981-82	K. W. R. Fletcher	S. M. Gavaskar	6	0	1	5
1982	R. G. D. Willis	S. M. Gavaskar	3	1	0	2
1984-85	D. I. Gower	S. M. Gavaskar	5	2	1	2
1986	M. W. Gatting[4]	Kapil Dev	3	0	2	1
1990	G. A. Gooch	M. Azharuddin	3	1	0	2
1992-93	G. A. Gooch[5]	M. Azharuddin	3	0	3	0
1996	M. A. Atherton	M. Azharuddin	3	1	0	2
	In England		41	22	3	16
	In India		43	10	11	22
	Totals		84	32	14	38

Notes: The 1932 Indian touring team was captained by the Maharaj of Porbandar but he did not play in the Test match.

The following deputised for the official touring captain or were appointed by the home authority for only a minor proportion of the series:

[1]D. B. Carr (Fifth). [2]M. C. Cowdrey (Fourth and Fifth). [3]Pankaj Roy (Second). [4]D. I. Gower (First). [5]A. J. Stewart (Second).

HIGHEST INNINGS TOTALS

For England in England: 653-4 dec. at Lord's 1990
in India: 652-7 dec. at Madras 1984-85

For India in England: 606-9 dec. at The Oval 1990
in India: 591 at Bombay 1992-93

LOWEST INNINGS TOTALS

For England in England: 101 at The Oval 1971
in India: 102 at Bombay 1981-82

For India in England: 42 at Lord's 1974
in India: 83 at Madras 1976-77

INDIVIDUAL HUNDREDS

For England (76)

D. L. Amiss (2)
188 Lord's 1974
179 Delhi 1976-77
M. A. Atherton (2)
131 Manchester 1990
160 Nottingham 1996
K. F. Barrington (3)
151* Bombay 1961-62
172 Kanpur 1961-62
113* Delhi 1961-62
I. T. Botham (5)
137 Leeds 1979
114 Bombay 1979-80
142 Kanpur 1981-82
128 Manchester 1982
208 The Oval 1982
G. Boycott (4)
246*† Leeds 1967
155 Birmingham 1979
125 The Oval 1979
105 Delhi 1981-82
M. C. Cowdrey (3)
160 Leeds 1959
107 Calcutta 1963-64
151 Delhi 1963-64
M. H. Denness (2)
118 Lord's 1974
100 Birmingham 1974
E. R. Dexter (1)
126* Kanpur 1961-62
B. L. D'Oliveira (1)
109† Leeds 1967
J. H. Edrich (1)
100* Manchester 1974
T. G. Evans (1)
104 Lord's 1952
K. W. R. Fletcher (2)
113 Bombay 1972-73
123* Manchester 1974
G. Fowler (1)
201 Madras 1984-85
M. W. Gatting (3)
136 Bombay 1984-85
207 Madras 1984-85
183* Birmingham 1986
G. A. Gooch (5)
127 Madras 1981-82
114 Lord's 1986
333 } Lord's 1990
123 }
116 Manchester 1990
D. I. Gower (2)
200*† Birmingham 1979
157* The Oval 1990
T. W. Graveney (2)
175† Bombay 1951-52
151 Lord's 1967
A. W. Greig (3)
148 Bombay 1972-73
106 Lord's 1974
103 Calcutta 1976-77
W. R. Hammond (2)
167 Manchester 1936
217 The Oval 1936
J. Hardstaff jun. (1)
205* Lord's 1946
G. A. Hick (1)
178 Bombay 1992-93
N. Hussain (2)
128† Birmingham 1996
107* Nottingham 1996
L. Hutton (2)
150 Lord's 1952
104 Manchester 1952
R. Illingworth (1)
107 Manchester 1971
B. R. Knight (1)
127 Kanpur 1963-64
A. J. Lamb (3)
107 The Oval 1982
139 Lord's 1990
109 Manchester 1990
A. R. Lewis (1)
125 Kanpur 1972-73
C. C. Lewis (1)
117 Madras 1992-93
D. Lloyd (1)
214* Birmingham 1974
B. W. Luckhurst (1)
101 Manchester 1971
P. B. H. May (1)
106 Nottingham 1959
P. H. Parfitt (1)
121 Kanpur 1963-64
G. Pullar (2)
131 Manchester 1959
119 Kanpur 1961-62
D. W. Randall (1)
126 Lord's 1982
R. T. Robinson (1)
160 Delhi 1984-85
R. C. Russell (1)
124 Lord's 1996
D. S. Sheppard (1)
119 The Oval 1952
M. J. K. Smith (1)
100† Manchester 1959
R. A. Smith (2)
100*† Lord's 1990
121* Manchester 1990
C. J. Tavaré (1)
149 Delhi 1981-82
B. H. Valentine (1)
136† Bombay 1933-34
C. F. Walters (1)
102 Madras 1933-34
A. J. Watkins (1)
137*† Delhi 1951-52
T. S. Worthington (1)
128 The Oval 1936

For India (64)

L. Amarnath (1)
118† Bombay 1933-34
M. Azharuddin (6)
110† Calcutta 1984-85
105 Madras 1984-85
122 Kanpur 1984-85
121 Lord's 1990
179 Manchester 1990
182 Calcutta 1992-93
A. A. Baig (1)
112† Manchester 1959
F. M. Engineer (1)
121 Bombay 1972-73
S. C. Ganguly (2)
131† Lord's 1996
136 Nottingham 1996
S. M. Gavaskar (4)
101 Manchester 1974
108 Bombay 1976-77
221 The Oval 1979
172 Bangalore 1981-82
Hanumant Singh (1)
105† Delhi 1963-64
V. S. Hazare (2)
164* Delhi 1951-52
155 Bombay 1951-52
M. L. Jaisimha (2)
127 Delhi 1961-62
129 Calcutta 1963-64
V. G. Kambli (1)
224 Bombay 1992-93
Kapil Dev (2)
116 Kanpur 1981-82
110 The Oval 1990
S. M. H. Kirmani (1)
102 Bombay 1984-85
B. K. Kunderan (2)
192 Madras 1963-64
100 Delhi 1963-64

V. L. Manjrekar (3)
133 Leeds 1952
189* Delhi 1961-62
108 Madras 1963-64
V. Mankad (1)
184 Lord's 1952
V. M. Merchant (3)
114 Manchester .. 1936
128 The Oval 1946
154 Delhi 1951-52
Mushtaq Ali (1)
112 Manchester .. 1936
R. G. Nadkarni (1)
122* Kanpur 1963-64
Nawab of Pataudi jun. (3)
103 Madras 1961-62
203* Delhi 1963-64
148 Leeds 1967

S. M. Patil (1)
129* Manchester .. 1982
D. G. Phadkar (1)
115 Calcutta 1951-52
Pankaj Roy (2)
140 Bombay 1951-52
111 Madras 1951-52
R. J. Shastri (4)
142 Bombay 1984-85
111 Calcutta 1984-85
100 Lord's 1990
187 The Oval ... 1990
N. S. Sidhu (1)
106 Madras 1992-93
S. R. Tendulkar (4)
119* Manchester .. 1990
165 Madras 1992-93
122 Birmingham . 1996
177 Nottingham . 1996

P. R. Umrigar (3)
130* Madras 1951-52
118 Manchester .. 1959
147* Kanpur 1961-62
D. B. Vengsarkar (5)
103 Lord's 1979
157 Lord's 1982
137 Kanpur 1984-85
126* Lord's 1986
102* Leeds 1986
G. R. Viswanath (4)
113 Bombay 1972-73
113 Lord's 1979
107 Delhi 1981-82
222 Madras 1981-82
Yashpal Sharma (1)
140 Madras 1981-82

† *Signifies hundred on first appearance in England–India Tests.*

Notes: G. A. Gooch's match aggregate of 456 (333 and 123) for England at Lord's in 1990 is the record in Test matches and provides the only instance of a batsman scoring a triple-hundred and a hundred in the same first-class match. His 333 is the highest innings in any match at Lord's.

M. Azharuddin scored hundreds in each of his first three Tests.

RECORD PARTNERSHIPS FOR EACH WICKET

For England

225 for 1st	G. A. Gooch and M. A. Atherton at Manchester	1990
241 for 2nd	G. Fowler and M. W. Gatting at Madras	1984-85
308 for 3rd	G. A. Gooch and A. J. Lamb at Lord's	1990
266 for 4th	W. R. Hammond and T. S. Worthington at The Oval	1936
254 for 5th†	K. W. R. Fletcher and A. W. Greig at Bombay	1972-73
171 for 6th	I. T. Botham and R. W. Taylor at Bombay	1979-80
125 for 7th	D. W. Randall and P. H. Edmonds at Lord's	1982
168 for 8th	R. Illingworth and P. Lever at Manchester	1971
83 for 9th	K. W. R. Fletcher and N. Gifford at Madras	1972-73
70 for 10th	P. J. W. Allott and R. G. D. Willis at Lord's	1982

For India

213 for 1st	S. M. Gavaskar and C. P. S. Chauhan at The Oval	1979
192 for 2nd	F. M. Engineer and A. L. Wadekar at Bombay	1972-73
316 for 3rd†‡	G. R. Viswanath and Yashpal Sharma at Madras	1981-82
222 for 4th†	V. S. Hazare and V. L. Manjrekar at Leeds	1952
214 for 5th†	M. Azharuddin and R. J. Shastri at Calcutta	1984-85
130 for 6th	S. M. H. Kirmani and Kapil Dev at The Oval	1982
235 for 7th†	R. J. Shastri and S. M. H. Kirmani at Bombay	1984-85
128 for 8th	R. J. Shastri and S. M. H. Kirmani at Delhi	1981-82
104 for 9th	R. J. Shastri and Madan Lal at Delhi	1981-82
51 for 10th	R. G. Nadkarni and B. S. Chandrasekhar at Calcutta	1963-64
	S. M. H. Kirmani and Chetan Sharma at Madras	1984-85

† *Denotes record partnership against all countries.*

‡ *415 runs were added between the fall of the 2nd and 3rd wickets: D. B. Vengsarkar retired hurt when he and Viswanath had added 99 runs.*

TEN WICKETS OR MORE IN A MATCH

For England (7)

10-78 (5-35, 5-43)†	G. O. B. Allen, Lord's	1936
11-145 (7-49, 4-96)†	A. V. Bedser, Lord's	1946
11-93 (4-41, 7-52)	A. V. Bedser, Manchester	1946
13-106 (6-58, 7-48)	I. T. Botham, Bombay	1979-80
11-163 (6-104, 5-59)†	N. A. Foster, Madras	1984-85
10-70 (7-46, 3-24)†	J. K. Lever, Delhi	1976-77
11-153 (7-49, 4-104)	H. Verity, Madras	1933-34

For India (4)

10-177 (6-105, 4-72)	S. A. Durani, Madras	1961-62
12-108 (8-55, 4-53)	V. Mankad, Madras	1951-52
10-188 (4-130, 6-58)	Chetan Sharma, Birmingham	1986
12-181 (6-64, 6-117)†	L. Sivaramakrishnan, Bombay	1984-85

† *Signifies ten wickets or more on first appearance in England–India Tests.*

Note: A. V. Bedser took 11 wickets in a match in each of the first two Tests of his career.

ENGLAND v PAKISTAN

	Captains					
Season	*England*	*Pakistan*	*T*	*E*	*P*	*D*
1954	L. Hutton[1]	A. H. Kardar	4	1	1	2
1961-62	E. R. Dexter	Imtiaz Ahmed	3	1	0	2
1962	E. R. Dexter[2]	Javed Burki	5	4	0	1
1967	D. B. Close	Hanif Mohammad	3	2	0	1
1968-69	M. C. Cowdrey	Saeed Ahmed	3	0	0	3
1971	R. Illingworth	Intikhab Alam	3	1	0	2
1972-73	A. R. Lewis	Majid Khan	3	0	0	3
1974	M. H. Denness	Intikhab Alam	3	0	0	3
1977-78	J. M. Brearley[3]	Wasim Bari	3	0	0	3
1978	J. M. Brearley	Wasim Bari	3	2	0	1
1982	R. G. D. Willis[4]	Imran Khan	3	2	1	0
1983-84	R. G. D. Willis[5]	Zaheer Abbas	3	0	1	2
1987	M. W. Gatting	Imran Khan	5	0	1	4
1987-88	M. W. Gatting	Javed Miandad	3	0	1	2
1992	G. A. Gooch	Javed Miandad	5	1	2	2
1996	M. A. Atherton	Wasim Akram	3	0	2	1
	In England		37	13	7	17
	In Pakistan		18	1	2	15
	Totals		55	14	9	32

Notes: The following deputised for the official touring captain or were appointed by the home authority for only a minor proportion of the series:

[1]D. S. Sheppard (Second and Third). [2]M. C. Cowdrey (Third). [3]G. Boycott (Third). [4]D. I. Gower (Second). [5]D. I. Gower (Second and Third).

HIGHEST INNINGS TOTALS

For England in England:	558-6 dec. at Nottingham	1954
in Pakistan:	546-8 dec. at Faisalabad	1983-84
For Pakistan in England:	708 at The Oval	1987
in Pakistan:	569-9 dec. at Hyderabad	1972-73

LOWEST INNINGS TOTALS

For England	in England: 130 at The Oval	1954
	in Pakistan: 130 at Lahore	1987-88
For Pakistan	in England: 87 at Lord's	1954
	in Pakistan: 191 at Faisalabad	1987-88

INDIVIDUAL HUNDREDS

For England (47)

D. L. Amiss (3)
112 Lahore 1972-73
158 Hyderabad 1972-73
183 The Oval 1974
C. W. J. Athey (1)
123 Lord's 1987
K. F. Barrington (4)
139† Lahore 1961-62
148 Lord's 1967
109* Nottingham 1967
142 The Oval 1967
I. T. Botham (2)
100† Birmingham 1978
108 Lord's 1978
G. Boycott (3)
121* Lord's 1971
112 Leeds 1971
100* Hyderabad 1977-78
B. C. Broad (1)
116 Faisalabad 1987-88
D. C. S. Compton (1)
278 Nottingham 1954
M. C. Cowdrey (3)
159† Birmingham 1962
182 The Oval 1962
100 Lahore 1968-69
J. P. Crawley (1)
106 The Oval 1996
E. R. Dexter (2)
205 Karachi 1961-62
172 The Oval 1962
B. L. D'Oliveira (1)
114* Dacca 1968-69
K. W. R. Fletcher (1)
122 The Oval 1974
M. W. Gatting (2)
124 Birmingham 1987
150* The Oval 1987
G. A. Gooch (1)
135 Leeds 1992
D. I. Gower (2)
152 Faisalabad 1983-84
173* Lahore 1983-84
T. W. Graveney (3)
153 Lord's 1962
114 Nottingham 1962
105 Karachi 1968-69
N. V. Knight (1)
113 Leeds 1996
A. P. E. Knott (1)
116 Birmingham 1971
B. W. Luckhurst (1)
108*† Birmingham 1971
C. Milburn (1)
139 Karachi 1968-69
P. H. Parfitt (4)
111 Karachi 1961-62
101* Birmingham 1962
119 Leeds 1962
101* Nottingham 1962
G. Pullar (1)
165 Dacca 1961-62
C. T. Radley (1)
106† Birmingham 1978
D. W. Randall (1)
105 Birmingham 1982
R. T. Robinson (1)
166† Manchester 1987
R. T. Simpson (1)
101 Nottingham 1954
R. A. Smith (1)
127† Birmingham 1992
A. J. Stewart (2)
190† Birmingham 1992
170 Leeds 1996

For Pakistan (38)

Aamir Sohail (1)
205 Manchester 1992
Alim-ud-Din (1)
109 Karachi 1961-62
Asif Iqbal (3)
146 The Oval 1967
104* Birmingham 1971
102 Lahore 1972-73
Hanif Mohammad (3)
111 } Dacca 1961-62
104 }
187* Lord's 1967
Haroon Rashid (2)
122† Lahore 1977-78
108 Hyderabad 1977-78
Ijaz Ahmed, sen. (1)
141 Leeds 1996
Imran Khan (1)
118 The Oval 1987
Intikhab Alam (1)
138 Hyderabad 1972-73
Inzamam-ul-Haq (1)
148 Lord's 1996
Javed Burki (3)
138† Lahore 1961-62
140 Dacca 1961-62
101 Lord's 1962
Javed Miandad (2)
260 The Oval 1987
153* Birmingham 1992
Mohsin Khan (2)
200 Lord's 1982
104 Lahore 1983-84
Moin Khan (1)
105 Leeds 1996
Mudassar Nazar (3)
114† Lahore 1977-78
124 Birmingham 1987
120 Lahore 1987-88
Mushtaq Mohammad (3)
100* Nottingham 1962
100 Birmingham 1971
157 Hyderabad 1972-73
Nasim-ul Ghani (1)
101 Lord's 1962

Sadiq Mohammad (1)
119 Lahore 1972-73
Saeed Anwar (1)
176 The Oval ... 1996
Salim Malik (4)
116 Faisalabad .. 1983-84
102 The Oval.... 1987
165 Birmingham . 1992
100* The Oval ... 1996
Wasim Raja (1)
112 Faisalabad .. 1983-84
Zaheer Abbas (2)
274† Birmingham . 1971
240 The Oval.... 1974

† *Signifies hundred on first appearance in England–Pakistan Tests.*

Note: Three batsmen – Majid Khan, Mushtaq Mohammad and D. L. Amiss – were dismissed for 99 at Karachi, 1972-73: the only instance in Test matches.

RECORD PARTNERSHIPS FOR EACH WICKET

For England

198	for 1st	G. Pullar and R. W. Barber at Dacca	1961-62
248	for 2nd	M. C. Cowdrey and E. R. Dexter at The Oval	1962
227	for 3rd	A. J. Stewart and R. A. Smith at Birmingham	1992
188	for 4th	E. R. Dexter and P. H. Parfitt at Karachi	1961-62
192	for 5th	D. C. S. Compton and T. E. Bailey at Nottingham	1954
153*	for 6th	P. H. Parfitt and D. A. Allen at Birmingham	1962
167	for 7th	D. I. Gower and V. J. Marks at Faisalabad	1983-84
99	for 8th	P. H. Parfitt and D. A. Allen at Leeds	1962
76	for 9th	T. W. Graveney and F. S. Trueman at Lord's	1962
79	for 10th	R. W. Taylor and R. G. D. Willis at Birmingham	1982

For Pakistan

173	for 1st	Mohsin Khan and Shoaib Mohammad at Lahore	1983-84
291	for 2nd†	Zaheer Abbas and Mushtaq Mohammad at Birmingham	1971
180	for 3rd	Mudassar Nazar and Haroon Rashid at Lahore	1977-78
322	for 4th	Javed Miandad and Salim Malik at Birmingham	1992
197	for 5th	Javed Burki and Nasim-ul-Ghani at Lord's	1962
145	for 6th	Mushtaq Mohammad and Intikhab Alam at Hyderabad	1972-73
112	for 7th	Asif Mujtaba and Moin Khan at Leeds	1996
130	for 8th†	Hanif Mohammad and Asif Iqbal at Lord's	1967
190	for 9th†	Asif Iqbal and Intikhab Alam at The Oval	1967
62	for 10th	Sarfraz Nawaz and Asif Masood at Leeds	1974

† *Denotes record partnership against all countries.*

TEN WICKETS OR MORE IN A MATCH

For England (2)

11-83 (6-65, 5-18)†	N. G. B. Cook, Karachi	1983-84
13-71 (5-20, 8-51)	D. L. Underwood, Lord's	1974

For Pakistan (6)

10-194 (5-84, 5-110)	Abdul Qadir, Lahore	1983-84
10-211 (7-96, 3-115)	Abdul Qadir, The Oval	1987
13-101 (9-56, 4-45)	Abdul Qadir, Lahore	1987-88
10-186 (5-88, 5-98)	Abdul Qadir, Karachi	1987-88
12-99 (6-53, 6-46)	Fazal Mahmood, The Oval	1954
10-77 (3-37, 7-40)	Imran Khan, Leeds	1987

† *Signifies ten wickets or more on first appearance in England–Pakistan Tests.*

FOUR WICKETS IN FIVE BALLS

C. M. Old, v Pakistan at Birmingham in 1978, dismissed Wasim Raja, Wasim Bari, Iqbal Qasim and Sikander Bakht to take four wickets in five balls (ww-ww).

ENGLAND v SRI LANKA

Season	England (Captains)	Sri Lanka (Captains)	T	E	SL	D
1981-82	K. W. R. Fletcher	B. Warnapura	1	1	0	0
1984	D. I. Gower	L. R. D. Mendis	1	0	0	1
1988	G. A. Gooch	R. S. Madugalle	1	1	0	0
1991	G. A. Gooch	P. A. de Silva	1	1	0	0
1992-93	A. J. Stewart	A. Ranatunga	1	0	1	0
	In England		3	2	0	1
	In Sri Lanka		2	1	1	0
	Totals		5	3	1	1

HIGHEST INNINGS TOTALS

For England in England: 429 at Lord's 1988
in Sri Lanka: 380 at Colombo (SSC) 1992-93

For Sri Lanka in England: 491-7 dec. at Lord's 1984
in Sri Lanka: 469 at Colombo (SSC) 1992-93

LOWEST INNINGS TOTALS

For England in England: 282 at Lord's 1991
in Sri Lanka: 223 at Colombo (PSS) 1981-82

For Sri Lanka in England: 194 at Lord's 1988
in Sri Lanka: 175 at Colombo (PSS) 1981-82

INDIVIDUAL HUNDREDS

For England (4)

G. A. Gooch (1)
174 Lord's 1991

A. J. Lamb (1)
107† Lord's 1984

R. A. Smith (1)
128 Colombo (SSC) 1992-93

A. J. Stewart (1)
113*† Lord's 1991

For Sri Lanka (3)

L. R. D. Mendis (1)
111 Lord's 1984

S. A. R. Silva (1)
102*† Lord's 1984

S. Wettimuny (1)
190 Lord's 1984

† *Signifies hundred on first appearance in England–Sri Lanka Tests.*

BEST BOWLING

Best bowling in an innings for England: 7-70 by P. A. J. DeFreitas at Lord's ... 1991
for Sri Lanka: 5-69 by R. J. Ratnayake at Lord's 1991

RECORD PARTNERSHIPS FOR EACH WICKET

For England

78 for 1st	G. A. Gooch and H. Morris at Lord's	1991
139 for 2nd	G. A. Gooch and A. J. Stewart at Lord's	1991
112 for 3rd	R. A. Smith and G. A. Hick at Colombo (SSC)	1992-93
122 for 4th	R. A. Smith and A. J. Stewart at Colombo (SSC)	1992-93

40 for 5th	A. J. Stewart and I. T. Botham at Lord's	1991
87 for 6th	A. J. Lamb and R. M. Ellison at Lord's	1984
63 for 7th	A. J. Stewart and R. C. Russell at Lord's	1991
20 for 8th	J. E. Emburey and P. W. Jarvis at Colombo (SSC)	1992-93
37 for 9th	P. J. Newport and N. A. Foster at Lord's	1988
40 for 10th	J. E. Emburey and D. E. Malcolm at Colombo (SSC)	1992-93

For Sri Lanka

99 for 1st	R. S. Mahanama and U. C. Hathurusinghe at Colombo (SSC)	1992-93
83 for 2nd	B. Warnapura and R. L. Dias at Colombo (PSS)	1981-82
101 for 3rd	S. Wettimuny and R. L. Dias at Lord's	1984
148 for 4th	S. Wettimuny and A. Ranatunga at Lord's	1984
150 for 5th†	S. Wettimuny and L. R. D. Mendis at Lord's	1984
138 for 6th†	S. A. R. Silva and L. R. D. Mendis at Lord's	1984
74 for 7th	U. C. Hathurusinghe and R. J. Ratnayake at Lord's	1991
29 for 8th	R. J. Ratnayake and C. P. H. Ramanayake at Lord's	1991
83 for 9th†	H. P. Tillekeratne and M. Muralitharan at Colombo (SSC)	1992-93
64 for 10th†	J. R. Ratnayeke and G. F. Labrooy at Lord's	1988

† *Denotes record partnership against all countries.*

AUSTRALIA v SOUTH AFRICA

	Captains					
Season	*Australia*	*South Africa*	*T*	*A*	*SA*	*D*
1902-03*S*	J. Darling	H. M. Taberer[1]	3	2	0	1
1910-11*A*	C. Hill	P. W. Sherwell	5	4	1	0
1912*E*	S. E. Gregory	F. Mitchell[2]	3	2	0	1
1921-22*S*	H. L. Collins	H. W. Taylor	3	1	0	2
1931-32*A*	W. M. Woodfull	H. B. Cameron	5	5	0	0
1935-36*S*	V. Y. Richardson	H. F. Wade	5	4	0	1
1949-50*S*	A. L. Hassett	A. D. Nourse	5	4	0	1
1952-53*A*	A. L. Hassett	J. E. Cheetham	5	2	2	1
1957-58*S*	I. D. Craig	C. B. van Ryneveld[3]	5	3	0	2
1963-64*A*	R. B. Simpson[4]	T. L. Goddard	5	1	1	3
1966-67*S*	R. B. Simpson	P. L. van der Merwe	5	1	3	1
1969-70*S*	W. M. Lawry	A. Bacher	4	0	4	0
1993-94*A*	A. R. Border	K. C. Wessels[5]	3	1	1	1
1993-94*S*	A. R. Border	K. C. Wessels	3	1	1	1
	In South Africa		33	16	8	9
	In Australia		23	13	5	5
	In England		3	2	0	1
	Totals		59	31	13	15

S Played in South Africa. A Played in Australia. E Played in England.

Notes: The following deputised for the official touring captain or were appointed by the home authority for only a minor proportion of the series:

[1]J. H. Anderson (Second), E. A. Halliwell (Third). [2]L. J. Tancred (Third). [3]D. J. McGlew (First). [4]R. Benaud (First). [5]W. J. Cronje (Third).

HIGHEST INNINGS TOTALS

For Australia in Australia: 578 at Melbourne	1910-11
in South Africa: 549-7 dec. at Port Elizabeth	1949-50
For South Africa in Australia: 595 at Adelaide	1963-64
in South Africa: 622-9 dec. at Durban	1969-70

LOWEST INNINGS TOTALS

For Australia in Australia:	111 at Sydney	1993-94
in South Africa:	75 at Durban	1949-50
For South Africa in Australia:	36† at Melbourne	1931-32
in South Africa:	85‡ at Johannesburg	1902-03
	85‡ at Cape Town	1902-03

† *Scored 45 in the second innings giving the smallest aggregate of 81 (12 extras) in Test cricket.*
‡ *In successive innings.*

INDIVIDUAL HUNDREDS

For Australia (58)

W. W. Armstrong (2)
159*‡ Johannesburg 1902-03
132 Melbourne 1910-11
W. Bardsley (3)
132† Sydney 1910-11
121 Manchester 1912
164 Lord's 1912
R. Benaud (2)
122 Johannesburg 1957-58
100 Johannesburg 1957-58
B. C. Booth (2)
169† Brisbane 1963-64
102* Sydney 1963-64
D. G. Bradman (4)
226† Brisbane 1931-32
112 Sydney 1931-32
167 Melbourne 1931-32
299* Adelaide 1931-32
W. A. Brown (1)
121 Cape Town 1935-36
J. W. Burke (1)
189 Cape Town 1957-58
A. G. Chipperfield (1)
109† Durban 1935-36
H. L. Collins (1)
203 Johannesburg 1921-22
J. H. Fingleton (3)
112 Cape Town 1935-36
108 Johannesburg 1935-36
118 Durban 1935-36
J. M. Gregory (1)
119 Johannesburg 1921-22
R. N. Harvey (8)
178 Cape Town 1949-50
151* Durban 1949-50
100 Johannesburg 1949-50
116 Pt Elizabeth 1949-50
109 Brisbane 1952-53
190 Sydney 1952-53
116 Adelaide 1952-53
205 Melbourne 1952-53
A. L. Hassett (3)
112† Johannesburg 1949-50
167 Pt Elizabeth 1949-50
163 Adelaide 1952-53
C. Hill (3)
142† Johannesburg 1902-03
191 Sydney 1910-11
100 Melbourne 1910-11
C. Kelleway (2)
114 Manchester 1912
102 Lord's 1912
W. M. Lawry (1)
157 Melbourne 1963-64
S. J. E. Loxton (1)
101† Johannesburg 1949-50
C. G. Macartney (2)
137 Sydney 1910-11
116 Durban 1921-22
S. J. McCabe (2)
149 Durban 1935-36
189* Johannesburg 1935-36
C. C. McDonald (1)
154 Adelaide 1952-53
J. Moroney (2)
118 }
101* } Johannesburg 1949-50
A. R. Morris (2)
111 Johannesburg 1949-50
157 Pt Elizabeth 1949-50
K. E. Rigg (1)
127† Sydney 1931-32
J. Ryder (1)
142 Cape Town 1921-22
R. B. Simpson (1)
153 Cape Town 1966-67
K. R. Stackpole (1)
134 Cape Town 1966-67
M. A. Taylor (1)
170† Melbourne 1993-94
V. T. Trumper (2)
159 Melbourne 1910-11
214* Adelaide 1910-11
M. E. Waugh (1)
113* Durban 1993-94
S. R. Waugh (1)
164† Adelaide 1993-94
W. M. Woodfull (1)
161 Melbourne 1931-32

For South Africa (38)

E. J. Barlow (5)
114† Brisbane 1963-64
109 Melbourne 1963-64
201 Adelaide 1963-64
127 Cape Town 1969-70
110 Johannesburg 1969-70
K. C. Bland (1)
126 Sydney 1963-64
W. J. Cronje (1)
122 Johannesburg 1993-94
W. R. Endean (1)
162* Melbourne 1952-53
G. A. Faulkner (3)
204 Melbourne 1910-11
115 Adelaide 1910-11
122* Manchester 1912
C. N. Frank (1)
152 Johannesburg 1921-22
A. C. Hudson (1)
102 Cape Town 1993-94
B. L. Irvine (1)
102 Pt Elizabeth 1969-70
D. T. Lindsay (3)
182 Johannesburg 1966-67
137 Durban 1966-67
131 Johannesburg 1966-67
D. J. McGlew (2)
108 Johannesburg 1957-58
105 Durban 1957-58
A. D. Nourse (2)
231 Johannesburg 1935-36
114 Cape Town 1949-50
A. W. Nourse (1)
111 Johannesburg 1921-22
R. G. Pollock (5)
122 Sydney 1963-64
175 Adelaide 1963-64
209 Cape Town 1966-67
105 Pt Elizabeth 1966-67
274 Durban 1969-70
B. A. Richards (2)
140 Durban 1969-70

126	Pt Elizabeth	1969-70
E. A. B. Rowan (1)		
143	Durban	1949-50
J. H. Sinclair (2)		
101	Johannesburg	1902-03
104	Cape Town	1902-03
S. J. Snooke (1)		
103	Adelaide	1910-11
K. G. Viljoen (1)		
111	Melbourne	1931-32
J. H. B. Waite (2)		
115	Johannesburg	1957-58
134	Durban	1957-58
J. W. Zulch (2)		
105	Adelaide	1910-11
150	Sydney	1910-11

† *Signifies hundred on first appearance in Australia–South Africa Tests.*
‡ *Carried his bat.*

RECORD PARTNERSHIPS FOR EACH WICKET

For Australia

233 for 1st	J. H. Fingleton and W. A. Brown at Cape Town	1935-36
275 for 2nd	C. C. McDonald and A. L. Hassett at Adelaide	1952-53
242 for 3rd	C. Kelleway and W. Bardsley at Lord's	1912
169 for 4th	M. A. Taylor and M. E. Waugh at Melbourne	1993-94
208 for 5th	A. R. Border and S. R. Waugh at Adelaide	1993-94
108 for 6th	S. R. Waugh and I. A. Healy at Cape Town	1993-94
160 for 7th	R. Benaud and G. D. McKenzie at Sydney	1963-64
83 for 8th	A. G. Chipperfield and C. V. Grimmett at Durban	1935-36
78 for 9th	D. G. Bradman and W. J. O'Reilly at Adelaide	1931-32
	K. D. Mackay and I. Meckiff at Johannesburg	1957-58
82 for 10th	V. S. Ransford and W. J. Whitty at Melbourne	1910-11

For South Africa

176 for 1st	D. J. McGlew and T. L. Goddard at Johannesburg	1957-58
173 for 2nd	L. J. Tancred and C. B. Llewellyn at Johannesburg	1902-03
341 for 3rd†	E. J. Barlow and R. G. Pollock at Adelaide	1963-64
206 for 4th	C. N. Frank and A. W. Nourse at Johannesburg	1921-22
129 for 5th	J. H. B. Waite and W. R. Endean at Johannesburg	1957-58
200 for 6th†	R. G. Pollock and H. R. Lance at Durban	1969-70
221 for 7th	D. T. Lindsay and P. L. van der Merwe at Johannesburg	1966-67
124 for 8th†	A. W. Nourse and E. A. Halliwell at Johannesburg	1902-03
85 for 9th	R. G. Pollock and P. M. Pollock at Cape Town	1966-67
53 for 10th	L. A. Stricker and S. J. Pegler at Adelaide	1910-11

† *Denotes record partnership against all countries.*

TEN WICKETS OR MORE IN A MATCH

For Australia (6)

14-199 (7-116, 7-83)	C. V. Grimmett, Adelaide	1931-32
10-88 (5-32, 5-56)	C. V. Grimmett, Cape Town	1935-36
10-110 (3-70, 7-40)	C. V. Grimmett, Johannesburg	1935-36
13-173 (7-100, 6-73)	C. V. Grimmett, Durban	1935-36
11-24 (5-6, 6-18)	H. Ironmonger, Melbourne	1931-32
12-128 (7-56, 5-72)	S. K. Warne, Sydney	1993-94

For South Africa (3)

10-123 (4-80, 6-43)	P. S. de Villiers, Sydney	1993-94
10-116 (5-43, 5-73)	C. B. Llewellyn, Johannesburg	1902-03
13-165 (6-84, 7-81)	H. J. Tayfield, Melbourne	1952-53

Note: C. V. Grimmett took ten wickets or more in three consecutive matches in 1935-36.

AUSTRALIA v WEST INDIES

	Captains						
Season	*Australia*	*West Indies*	*T*	*A*	*WI*	*T*	*D*
1930-31*A*	W. M. Woodfull	G. C. Grant	5	4	1	0	0
1951-52*A*	A. L. Hassett[1]	J. D. C. Goddard[2]	5	4	1	0	0
1954-55*W*	I. W. Johnson	D. St E. Atkinson[3]	5	3	0	0	2

THE FRANK WORRELL TROPHY

Season	*Captains* *Australia*	*West Indies*	*T*	*A*	*WI*	*T*	*D*	*Held by*
1960-61*A*	R. Benaud	F. M. M. Worrell	5	2	1	1	1	A
1964-65*W*	R. B. Simpson	G. S. Sobers	5	1	2	0	2	WI
1968-69*A*	W. M. Lawry	G. S. Sobers	5	3	1	0	1	A
1972-73*W*	I. M. Chappell	R. B. Kanhai	5	2	0	0	3	A
1975-76*A*	G. S. Chappell	C. H. Lloyd	6	5	1	0	0	A
1977-78*W*	R. B. Simpson	A. I. Kallicharran[4]	5	1	3	0	1	WI
1979-80*A*	G. S. Chappell	C. H. Lloyd[5]	3	0	2	0	1	WI
1981-82*A*	G. S. Chappell	C. H. Lloyd	3	1	1	0	1	WI
1983-84*W*	K. J. Hughes	C. H. Lloyd[6]	5	0	3	0	2	WI
1984-85*A*	A. R. Border[7]	C. H. Lloyd	5	1	3	0	1	WI
1988-89*A*	A. R. Border	I. V. A. Richards	5	1	3	0	1	WI
1990-91*W*	A. R. Border	I. V. A. Richards	5	1	2	0	2	WI
1992-93*A*	A. R. Border	R. B. Richardson	5	1	2	0	2	WI
1994-95*W*	M. A. Taylor	R. B. Richardson	4	2	1	0	1	A
	In Australia		47	22	16	1	8	
	In West Indies		34	10	11	0	13	
	Totals		81	32	27	1	21	

A Played in Australia. W Played in West Indies.

Notes: The following deputised for the official touring captain or were appointed by the home authority for only a minor proportion of the series:

[1]A. R. Morris (Third). [2]J. B. Stollmeyer (Fifth). [3]J. B. Stollmeyer (Second and Third). [4]C. H. Lloyd (First and Second). [5]D. L. Murray (First). [6]I. V. A. Richards (Second). [7]K. J. Hughes (First and Second).

HIGHEST INNINGS TOTALS

For Australia in Australia: 619 at Sydney 1968-69
in West Indies: 758-8 dec. at Kingston 1954-55

For West Indies in Australia: 616 at Adelaide 1968-69
in West Indies: 573 at Bridgetown 1964-65

LOWEST INNINGS TOTALS

For Australia in Australia: 76 at Perth 1984-85
in West Indies: 90 at Port-of-Spain 1977-78

For West Indies in Australia: 78 at Sydney 1951-52
in West Indies: 109 at Georgetown 1972-73

INDIVIDUAL HUNDREDS

For Australia (76)

R. G. Archer (1)
128 Kingston 1954-55
R. Benaud (1)
121 Kingston 1954-55
D. C. Boon (3)
149 Sydney 1988-89
109* Kingston 1990-91
111 Brisbane 1992-93
B. C. Booth (1)
117 Port-of-Spain 1964-65
A. R. Border (3)
126 Adelaide 1981-82
100* Port-of-Spain 1983-84
110 Melbourne .. 1992-93
D. G. Bradman (2)
223 Brisbane 1930-31
152 Melbourne .. 1930-31
G. S. Chappell (5)
106 Bridgetown .. 1972-73
123, 109* ‡Brisbane ... 1975-76
182* Sydney 1975-76
124 Brisbane 1979-80
I. M. Chappell (5)
117† Brisbane 1968-69
165 Melbourne .. 1968-69
106* Bridgetown .. 1972-73
109 Georgetown . 1972-73
156 Perth 1975-76
G. J. Cosier (1)
109† Melbourne .. 1975-76
R. M. Cowper (2)
143 Port-of-Spain 1964-65
102 Bridgetown .. 1964-65

J. Dyson (1)
127*† Sydney 1981-82
R. N. Harvey (3)
133 Kingston 1954-55
133 Port-of-Spain 1954-55
204 Kingston 1954-55
A. L. Hassett (2)
132 Sydney 1951-52
102 Melbourne .. 1951-52
A. M. J. Hilditch (1)
113† Melbourne .. 1984-85
K. J. Hughes (2)
130*† Brisbane 1979-80
100* Melbourne .. 1981-82
D. M. Jones (1)
216 Adelaide 1988-89
A. F. Kippax (1)
146† Adelaide 1930-31
W. M. Lawry (4)
210 Bridgetown .. 1964-65
105 Brisbane 1968-69
205 Melbourne .. 1968-69
151 Sydney 1968-69
R. R. Lindwall (1)
118 Bridgetown .. 1954-55
R. B. McCosker (1)
109* Melbourne .. 1975-76
C. C. McDonald (2)
110 Port-of-Spain 1954-55
127 Kingston 1954-55
K. R. Miller (4)
129 Sydney 1951-52
147 Kingston 1954-55
137 Bridgetown .. 1954-55
109 Kingston 1954-55
A. R. Morris (1)
111 Port-of-Spain 1954-55
N. C. O'Neill (1)
181† Brisbane 1960-61
W. B. Phillips (1)
120 Bridgetown .. 1983-84
W. H. Ponsford (2)
183 Sydney 1930-31
109 Brisbane 1930-31
I. R. Redpath (4)
132 Sydney 1968-69
102 Melbourne .. 1975-76
103 Adelaide 1975-76
101 Melbourne .. 1975-76
C. S. Serjeant (1)
124 Georgetown . 1977-78
R. B. Simpson (1)
201 Bridgetown .. 1964-65
K. R. Stackpole (1)
142 Kingston 1972-73
M. A. Taylor (1)
144 St John's 1990-91
P. M. Toohey (1)
122 Kingston 1977-78
A. Turner (1)
136 Adelaide 1975-76
K. D. Walters (6)
118 Sydney 1968-69
110 Adelaide 1968-69
242 } Sydney 1968-69
103 }
102* Bridgetown .. 1972-73
112 Port-of-Spain 1972-73
M. E. Waugh (3)
139* St John's 1990-91
112 Melbourne .. 1992-93
126 Kingston 1994-95
S. R. Waugh (2)
100 Sydney 1992-93
200 Kingston 1994-95
K. C. Wessels (1)
173 Sydney 1984-85
G. M. Wood (2)
126 Georgetown . 1977-78
111 Perth 1988-89

For West Indies (78)

F. C. M. Alexander (1)
108 Sydney 1960-61
K. L. T. Arthurton (1)
157*† Brisbane 1992-93
D. St E. Atkinson (1)
219 Bridgetown .. 1954-55
B. F. Butcher (3)
117 Port-of-Spain 1964-65
101 Sydney 1968-69
118 Adelaide 1968-69
C. C. Depeiza (1)
122 Bridgetown .. 1954-55
P. J. L. Dujon (2)
130 Port-of-Spain 1983-84
139 Perth 1984-85
M. L. C. Foster (1)
125† Kingston 1972-73
R. C. Fredericks (1)
169 Perth 1975-76
H. A. Gomes (6)
101† Georgetown . 1977-78
115 Kingston 1977-78
126 Sydney 1981-82
124* Adelaide 1981-82
127 Perth 1984-85
120* Adelaide 1984-85
C. G. Greenidge (4)
120* Georgetown . 1983-84
127 Kingston 1983-84
104 Adelaide 1988-89
226 Bridgetown .. 1990-91
D. L. Haynes (5)
103* Georgetown . 1983-84
145 Bridgetown .. 1983-84
100 Perth 1988-89
143 Sydney 1988-89
111 Georgetown . 1990-91
G. A. Headley (2)
102* Brisbane 1930-31
105 Sydney 1930-31
C. C. Hunte (1)
110 Melbourne .. 1960-61
A. I. Kallicharran (4)
101 Brisbane 1975-76
127 Port-of-Spain 1977-78
126 Kingston 1977-78
106 Adelaide 1979-80
R. B. Kanhai (5)
117 } Adelaide 1960-61
115 }
129 Bridgetown .. 1964-65
121 Port-of-Spain 1964-65
105 Bridgetown .. 1972-73
B. C. Lara (1)
277 Sydney 1992-93
C. H. Lloyd (6)
129† Brisbane 1968-69
178 Georgetown . 1972-73
149 Perth 1975-76
102 Melbourne .. 1975-76
121 Adelaide 1979-80
114 Brisbane 1984-85
F. R. Martin (1)
123* Sydney 1930-31
S. M. Nurse (2)
201 Bridgetown .. 1964-65
137 Sydney 1968-69
I. V. A. Richards (5)
101 Adelaide 1975-76
140 Brisbane 1979-80
178 St John's 1983-84
208 Melbourne .. 1984-85
146 Perth 1988-89
R. B. Richardson (9)
131* Bridgetown .. 1983-84
154 St John's 1983-84
138 Brisbane 1984-85
122 Melbourne .. 1988-89
106 Adelaide 1988-89
104* Kingston 1990-91
182 Georgetown . 1990-91
109 Sydney 1992-93
100 Kingston 1994-95
L. G. Rowe (1)
107 Brisbane 1975-76
P. V. Simmons (1)
110 Melbourne .. 1992-93
O. G. Smith (1)
104† Kingston 1954-55
G. S. Sobers (4)
132 Brisbane 1960-61
168 Sydney 1960-61
110 Adelaide 1968-69
113 Sydney 1968-69

J. B. Stollmeyer (1)
104 Sydney 1951-52
C. L. Walcott (5)
108 Kingston.... 1954-55
126 } Port-of-Spain 1954-55
110 }
155 } Kingston.... 1954-55
110 }
E. D. Weekes (1)
139 Port-of-Spain 1954-55
A. B. Williams (1)
100† Georgetown . 1977-78
F. M. M. Worrell (1)
108 Melbourne .. 1951-52

† *Signifies hundred on first appearance in Australia–West Indies Tests.*
‡ *G. S. Chappell is the only player to score hundreds in both innings of his first Test as captain.*

Note: F. C. M. Alexander and C. C. Depeiza scored the only hundreds of their careers in a Test match.

RECORD PARTNERSHIPS FOR EACH WICKET

For Australia

382 for 1st†	W. M. Lawry and R. B. Simpson at Bridgetown	1964-65
298 for 2nd	W. M. Lawry and I. M. Chappell at Melbourne	1968-69
295 for 3rd†	C. C. McDonald and R. N. Harvey at Kingston	1954-55
336 for 4th	W. M. Lawry and K. D. Walters at Sydney	1968-69
220 for 5th	K. R. Miller and R. G. Archer at Kingston	1954-55
206 for 6th	K. R. Miller and R. G. Archer at Bridgetown	1954-55
134 for 7th	A. K. Davidson and R. Benaud at Brisbane	1960-61
137 for 8th	R. Benaud and I. W. Johnson at Kingston	1954-55
114 for 9th	D. M. Jones and M. G. Hughes at Adelaide	1988-89
97 for 10th	T. G. Hogan and R. M. Hogg at Georgetown	1983-84

For West Indies

250* for 1st	C. G. Greenidge and D. L. Haynes at Georgetown	1983-84
297 for 2nd	D. L. Haynes and R. B. Richardson at Georgetown	1990-91
308 for 3rd	R. B. Richardson and I. V. A. Richards at St John's	1983-84
198 for 4th	L. G. Rowe and A. I. Kallicharran at Brisbane	1975-76
210 for 5th	R. B. Kanhai and M. L. C. Foster at Kingston	1972-73
165 for 6th	R. B. Kanhai and D. L. Murray at Bridgetown	1972-73
347 for 7th†‡	D. St E. Atkinson and C. C. Depeiza at Bridgetown	1954-55
87 for 8th	P. J. L. Dujon and C. E. L. Ambrose at Port-of-Spain	1990-91
122 for 9th	D. A. J. Holford and J. L. Hendriks at Adelaide	1968-69
56 for 10th	J. Garner and C. E. H. Croft at Brisbane	1979-80

† *Denotes record partnership against all countries.*
‡ *Record seventh-wicket partnership in first-class cricket.*

TEN WICKETS OR MORE IN A MATCH

For Australia (11)

11-96 (7-46, 4-50)	A. R. Border, Sydney	1988-89
11-222 (5-135, 6-87)†	A. K. Davidson, Brisbane	1960-61
11-183 (7-87, 4-96)†	C. V. Grimmett, Adelaide	1930-31
10-115 (6-72, 4-43)	N. J. N. Hawke, Georgetown	1964-65
10-144 (6-54, 4-90)	R. G. Holland, Sydney	1984-85
13-217 (5-130, 8-87)	M. G. Hughes, Perth	1988-89
11-79 (7-23, 4-56)	H. Ironmonger, Melbourne	1930-31
11-181 (8-112, 3-69)	G. F. Lawson, Adelaide	1984-85
10-127 (7-83, 3-44)	D. K. Lillee, Melbourne	1981-82
10-159 (8-71, 2-88)	G. D. McKenzie, Melbourne	1968-69
10-185 (3-87, 7-98)	B. Yardley, Sydney	1981-82

For West Indies (4)

10-120 (6-74, 4-46)	C. E. L. Ambrose, Adelaide	1992-93
10-113 (7-55, 3-58)	G. E. Gomez, Sydney	1951-52
11-107 (5-45, 6-62)	M. A. Holding, Melbourne	1981-82
10-107 (5-69, 5-38)	M. D. Marshall, Adelaide	1984-85

† *Signifies ten wickets or more on first appearance in Australia–West Indies Tests.*

AUSTRALIA v NEW ZEALAND

	Captains					
Season	*Australia*	*New Zealand*	*T*	*A*	*NZ*	*D*
1945-46*N*	W. A. Brown	W. A. Hadlee	1	1	0	0
1973-74*A*	I. M. Chappell	B. E. Congdon	3	2	0	1
1973-74*N*	I. M. Chappell	B. E. Congdon	3	1	1	1
1976-77*N*	G. S. Chappell	G. M. Turner	2	1	0	1
1980-81*A*	G. S. Chappell	G. P. Howarth[1]	3	2	0	1
1981-82*N*	G. S. Chappell	G. P. Howarth	3	1	1	1

TRANS-TASMAN TROPHY

	Captains						
Season	*Australia*	*New Zealand*	*T*	*A*	*NZ*	*D*	*Held by*
1985-86*A*	A. R. Border	J. V. Coney	3	1	2	0	NZ
1985-86*N*	A. R. Border	J. V. Coney	3	0	1	2	NZ
1987-88*A*	A. R. Border	J. J. Crowe	3	1	0	2	A
1989-90*A*	A. R. Border	J. G. Wright	1	0	0	1	A
1989-90*N*	A. R. Border	J. G. Wright	1	0	1	0	NZ
1992-93*N*	A. R. Border	M. D. Crowe	3	1	1	1	NZ
1993-94*A*	A. R. Border	M. D. Crowe[2]	3	2	0	1	A
	In Australia		16	8	2	6	
	In New Zealand		16	5	5	6	
	Totals		32	13	7	12	

A Played in Australia. N Played in New Zealand.

Note: The following deputised for the official touring captain: [1]M. G. Burgess (Second). [2]K. R. Rutherford (Second and Third).

HIGHEST INNINGS TOTALS

For Australia in Australia: 607-6 dec. at Brisbane		1993-94
in New Zealand: 552 at Christchurch		1976-77
For New Zealand in Australia: 553-7 dec. at Brisbane		1985-86
in New Zealand: 484 at Wellington		1973-74

LOWEST INNINGS TOTALS

For Australia in Australia: 162 at Sydney	1973-74
in New Zealand: 103 at Auckland	1985-86
For New Zealand in Australia: 121 at Perth	1980-81
in New Zealand: 42 at Wellington	1945-46

INDIVIDUAL HUNDREDS

For Australia (30)

D. C. Boon (3)
143 Brisbane 1987-88
200 Perth 1989-90
106 Hobart 1993-94
A. R. Border (5)
152* Brisbane 1985-86
140, 114* Christchurch. 1985-86
205 Adelaide 1987-88
105 Brisbane 1993-94
G. S. Chappell (3)
247*, 133 Wellington . . 1973-74
176 Christchurch. 1981-82
I. M. Chappell (2)
145, 121 Wellington . . 1973-74

G. J. Gilmour (1)
101 Christchurch. 1976-77
I. A. Healy (1)
113* Perth 1993-94
G. R. Marsh (1)
118 Auckland . . . 1985-86
R. W. Marsh (1)
132 Adelaide 1973-74
G. R. J. Matthews (2)
115† Brisbane 1985-86
130 Wellington . . 1985-86
I. R. Redpath (1)
159*‡ Auckland . . . 1973-74
M. J. Slater (1)
168 Hobart 1993-94

K. R. Stackpole (1)
122† Melbourne . . 1973-74
M. A. Taylor (1)
142* Perth 1993-94
K. D. Walters (3)
104* Auckland . . . 1973-74
250 Christchurch. 1976-77
107 Melbourne . . 1980-81
M. E. Waugh (1)
111 Hobart 1993-94
S. R. Waugh (1)
147* Brisbane 1993-94
G. M. Wood (2)
111† Brisbane 1980-81
100 Auckland . . . 1981-82

For New Zealand (19)

J. V. Coney (1)
101* Wellington . . 1985-86
B. E. Congdon (2)
132 Wellington . . 1973-74
107* Christchurch. 1976-77
M. D. Crowe (3)
188 Brisbane 1985-86
137 Christchurch. 1985-86
137 Adelaide 1987-88
B. A. Edgar (1)
161 Auckland . . . 1981-82

M. J. Greatbatch (1)
146*† Perth 1989-90
B. F. Hastings (1)
101 Wellington . . 1973-74
A. H. Jones (2)
150 Adelaide 1987-88
143 Perth 1993-94
J. F. M. Morrison (1)
117 Sydney 1973-74
J. M. Parker (1)
108 Sydney 1973-74

J. F. Reid (1)
108† Brisbane 1985-86
K. R. Rutherford (1)
102 Christchurch. 1992-93
G. M. Turner (2)
101, 110* Christchurch. 1973-74
J. G. Wright (2)
141 Christchurch. 1981-82
117* Wellington . . 1989-90

† *Signifies hundred on first appearance in Australia–New Zealand Tests.*
‡ *Carried his bat.*

Notes: G. S. and I. M. Chappell at Wellington in 1973-74 provide the only instance in Test matches of brothers both scoring a hundred in each innings and in the same Test.

RECORD PARTNERSHIPS FOR EACH WICKET

For Australia

198 for 1st	M. J. Slater and M. A. Taylor at Perth	1993-94
235 for 2nd	M. J. Slater and D. C. Boon at Hobart	1993-94
264 for 3rd	I. M. Chappell and G. S. Chappell at Wellington	1973-74
150 for 4th	M. E. Waugh and A. R. Border at Hobart	1993-94
213 for 5th	G. M. Ritchie and G. R. J. Matthews at Wellington	1985-86
197 for 6th	A. R. Border and G. R. J. Matthews at Brisbane	1985-86
217 for 7th†	K. D. Walters and G. J. Gilmour at Christchurch	1976-77
93 for 8th	G. J. Gilmour and K. J. O'Keeffe at Auckland	1976-77
69 for 9th	I. A. Healy and C. J. McDermott at Perth	1993-94
60 for 10th	K. D. Walters and J. D. Higgs at Melbourne	1980-81

For New Zealand

111 for 1st	M. J. Greatbatch and J. G. Wright at Wellington	1992-93
128* for 2nd	J. G. Wright and A. H. Jones at Wellington	1989-90
224 for 3rd	J. F. Reid and M. D. Crowe at Brisbane	1985-86
229 for 4th†	B. E. Congdon and B. F. Hastings at Wellington	1973-74
88 for 5th	J. V. Coney and M. G. Burgess at Perth	1980-81
109 for 6th	K. R. Rutherford and J. V. Coney at Wellington	1985-86
132* for 7th	J. V. Coney and R. J. Hadlee at Wellington	1985-86
88* for 8th	M. J. Greatbatch and M. C. Snedden at Perth	1989-90
73 for 9th	H. J. Howarth and D. R. Hadlee at Christchurch	1976-77
124 for 10th	J. G. Bracewell and S. L. Boock at Sydney	1985-86

† *Denotes record partnership against all countries.*

TEN WICKETS OR MORE IN A MATCH

For Australia (2)

10-174 (6-106, 4-68)	R. G. Holland, Sydney	1985-86
11-123 (5-51, 6-72)	D. K. Lillee, Auckland	1976-77

For New Zealand (4)

10-106 (4-74, 6-32)	J. G. Bracewell, Auckland	1985-86
15-123 (9-52, 6-71)	R. J. Hadlee, Brisbane	1985-86
11-155 (5-65, 6-90)	R. J. Hadlee, Perth	1985-86
10-176 (5-109, 5-67)	R. J. Hadlee, Melbourne	1987-88

AUSTRALIA v INDIA

	Captains						
Season	*Australia*	*India*	*T*	*A*	*I*	*T*	*D*
1947-48*A*	D. G. Bradman	L. Amarnath	5	4	0	0	1
1956-57*I*	I. W. Johnson[1]	P. R. Umrigar	3	2	0	0	1
1959-60*I*	R. Benaud	G. S. Ramchand	5	2	1	0	2
1964-65*I*	R. B. Simpson	Nawab of Pataudi jun.	3	1	1	0	1
1967-68*A*	R. B. Simpson[2]	Nawab of Pataudi jun.[3]	4	4	0	0	0
1969-70*I*	W. M. Lawry	Nawab of Pataudi jun.	5	3	1	0	1
1977-78*A*	R. B. Simpson	B. S. Bedi	5	3	2	0	0
1979-80*I*	K. J. Hughes	S. M. Gavaskar	6	0	2	0	4
1980-81*A*	G. S. Chappell	S. M. Gavaskar	3	1	1	0	1
1985-86*A*	A. R. Border	Kapil Dev	3	0	0	0	3
1986-87*I*	A. R. Border	Kapil Dev	3	0	0	1	2
1991-92*A*	A. R. Border	M. Azharuddin	5	4	0	0	1
	In Australia		25	16	3	0	6
	In India		25	8	5	1	11
	Totals		50	24	8	1	17

A Played in Australia. I Played in India.

Notes: The following deputised for the official touring captain or were appointed by the home authority for only a minor proportion of the series:

[1]R. R. Lindwall (Second). [2]W. M. Lawry (Third and Fourth). [3]C. G. Borde (First).

HIGHEST INNINGS TOTALS

For Australia	in Australia: 674 at Adelaide	1947-48
	in India: 574-7 dec. at Madras	1986-87
For India	in Australia: 600-4 dec. at Sydney	1985-86
	in India: 517-5 dec. at Bombay	1986-87

LOWEST INNINGS TOTALS

For Australia	in Australia: 83 at Melbourne	1980-81
	in India: 105 at Kanpur	1959-60
For India	in Australia: 58 at Brisbane	1947-48
	in India: 135 at Delhi	1959-60

INDIVIDUAL HUNDREDS

For Australia (51)

S. G. Barnes (1)
112 Adelaide 1947-48
D. C. Boon (6)
123† Adelaide 1985-86
131 Sydney 1985-86
122 Madras 1986-87
129* Sydney 1991-92
135 Adelaide 1991-92
107 Perth 1991-92
A. R. Border (4)
162† Madras 1979-80
124 Melbourne 1980-81
163 Melbourne 1985-86
106 Madras 1986-87
D. G. Bradman (4)
185† Brisbane 1947-48
132 } Melbourne 1947-48
127* } Melbourne 1947-48
201 Adelaide 1947-48
J. W. Burke (1)
161 Bombay 1956-57
G. S. Chappell (1)
204† Sydney 1980-81
I. M. Chappell (2)
151 Melbourne 1967-68
138 Delhi 1969-70
R. M. Cowper (2)
108 Adelaide 1967-68
165 Sydney 1967-68
L. E. Favell (1)
101 Madras 1959-60
R. N. Harvey (4)
153 Melbourne 1947-48
140 Bombay 1956-57
114 Delhi 1959-60
102 Bombay 1959-60
A. L. Hassett (1)
198* Adelaide 1947-48
K. J. Hughes (2)
100 Madras 1979-80
213 Adelaide 1980-81
D. M. Jones (2)
210† Madras 1986-87
150* Perth 1991-92
W. M. Lawry (1)
100 Melbourne 1967-68
A. L. Mann (1)
105 Perth 1977-78
G. R. Marsh (1)
101 Bombay 1986-87
G. R. J. Matthews (1)
100* Melbourne 1985-86
T. M. Moody (1)
101† Perth 1991-92
A. R. Morris (1)
100* Melbourne 1947-48
N. C. O'Neill (2)
163 Bombay 1959-60
113 Calcutta 1959-60
G. M. Ritchie (1)
128† Adelaide 1985-86
A. P. Sheahan (1)
114 Kanpur 1969-70
R. B. Simpson (4)
103 Adelaide 1967-68
109 Melbourne 1967-68
176 Perth 1977-78
100 Adelaide 1977-78
K. R. Stackpole (1)
103† Bombay 1969-70
M. A. Taylor (1)
100 Adelaide 1991-92
K. D. Walters (1)
102 Madras 1969-70
G. M. Wood (1)
125 Adelaide 1980-81
G. N. Yallop (2)
121† Adelaide 1977-78
167 Calcutta 1979-80

For India (35)

M. Amarnath (2)
100 Perth 1977-78
138 Sydney 1985-86
M. Azharuddin (1)
106 Adelaide 1991-92
N. J. Contractor (1)
108 Bombay 1959-60
S. M. Gavaskar (8)
113† Brisbane 1977-78
127 Perth 1977-78
118 Melbourne .. 1977-78
115 Delhi 1979-80
123 Bombay 1979-80
166* Adelaide 1985-86
172 Sydney 1985-86
103 Bombay 1986-87
V. S. Hazare (2)
116 }
145 } Adelaide 1947-48

M. L. Jaisimha (1)
101 Brisbane 1967-68
Kapil Dev (1)
119 Madras 1986-87
S. M. H. Kirmani (1)
101* Bombay 1979-80
V. Mankad (2)
116 Melbourne .. 1947-48
111 Melbourne .. 1947-48
Nawab of Pataudi jun. (1)
128*† Madras 1964-65
S. M. Patil (1)
174 Adelaide 1980-81
D. G. Phadkar (1)
123 Adelaide 1947-48
G. S. Ramchand (1)
109 Bombay 1956-57

R. J. Shastri (2)
121* Bombay 1986-87
206 Sydney 1991-92
K. Srikkanth (1)
116 Sydney 1985-86
S. R. Tendulkar (2)
148* Sydney 1991-92
114 Perth 1991-92
D. B. Vengsarkar (2)
112 Bangalore ... 1979-80
164* Bombay 1986-87
G. R. Viswanath (4)
137† Kanpur 1969-70
161* Bangalore ... 1979-80
131 Delhi 1979-80
114 Melbourne .. 1980-81
Yashpal Sharma (1)
100* Delhi 1979-80

† *Signifies hundred on first appearance in Australia–India Tests.*

RECORD PARTNERSHIPS FOR EACH WICKET

For Australia

217	for 1st	D. C. Boon and G. R. Marsh at Sydney	1985-86
236	for 2nd	S. G. Barnes and D. G. Bradman at Adelaide	1947-48
222	for 3rd	A. R. Border and K. J. Hughes at Madras	1979-80
178	for 4th	D. M. Jones and A. R. Border at Madras	1986-87
223*	for 5th	A. R. Morris and D. G. Bradman at Melbourne	1947-48
151	for 6th	T. R. Veivers and B. N. Jarman at Bombay	1964-65
66	for 7th	G. R. J. Matthews and R. J. Bright at Melbourne	1985-86
73	for 8th	T. R. Veivers and G. D. McKenzie at Madras	1964-65
87	for 9th	I. W. Johnson and W. P. A. Crawford at Madras	1956-57
77	for 10th	A. R. Border and D. R. Gilbert at Melbourne	1985-86

For India

192	for 1st	S. M. Gavaskar and C. P. S. Chauhan at Bombay	1979-80
224	for 2nd	S. M. Gavaskar and M. Amarnath at Sydney	1985-86
159	for 3rd	S. M. Gavaskar and G. R. Viswanath at Delhi	1979-80
159	for 4th	D. B. Vengsarkar and G. R. Viswanath at Bangalore	1979-80
196	for 5th	R. J. Shastri and S. R. Tendulkar at Sydney	1991-92
298*	for 6th†	D. B. Vengsarkar and R. J. Shastri at Bombay	1986-87
132	for 7th	V. S. Hazare and H. R. Adhikari at Adelaide	1947-48
127	for 8th	S. M. H. Kirmani and K. D. Ghavri at Bombay	1979-80
81	for 9th	S. R. Tendulkar and K. S. More at Perth	1991-92
94	for 10th	S. M. Gavaskar and N. S. Yadav at Adelaide	1985-86

† *Denotes record partnership against all countries.*

TEN WICKETS OR MORE IN A MATCH

For Australia (11)

11-105 (6-52, 5-53)	R. Benaud, Calcutta	1956-57
12-124 (5-31, 7-93)	A. K. Davidson, Kanpur	1959-60

12-166 (5-99, 7-67)	G. Dymock, Kanpur	1979-80
10-168 (5-76, 5-92)	C. J. McDermott, Adelaide	1991-92
10-91 (6-58, 4-33)†	G. D. McKenzie, Madras	1964-65
10-151 (7-66, 3-85)	G. D. McKenzie, Melbourne	1967-68
10-144 (5-91, 5-53)	A. A. Mallett, Madras	1969-70
10-249 (5-103, 5-146)	G. R. J. Matthews, Madras	1986-87
12-126 (6-66, 6-60)	B. A. Reid, Melbourne	1991-92
11-31 (5-2, 6-29)†	E. R. H. Toshack, Brisbane	1947-48
11-95 (4-68, 7-27)	M. R. Whitney, Perth	1991-92

For India (6)

10-194 (5-89, 5-105)	B. S. Bedi, Perth	1977-78
12-104 (6-52, 6-52)	B. S. Chandrasekhar, Melbourne	1977-78
10-130 (7-49, 3-81)	Ghulam Ahmed, Calcutta	1956-57
11-122 (5-31, 6-91)	R. G. Nadkarni, Madras	1964-65
14-124 (9-69, 5-55)	J. M. Patel, Kanpur	1959-60
10-174 (4-100, 6-74)	E. A. S. Prasanna, Madras	1969-70

† *Signifies ten wickets or more on first appearance in Australia–India Tests.*

AUSTRALIA v PAKISTAN

	Captains					
Season	*Australia*	*Pakistan*	*T*	*A*	*P*	*D*
1956-57*P*	I. W. Johnson	A. H. Kardar	1	0	1	0
1959-60*P*	R. Benaud	Fazal Mahmood[1]	3	2	0	1
1964-65*P*	R. B. Simpson	Hanif Mohammad	1	0	0	1
1964-65*A*	R. B. Simpson	Hanif Mohammad	1	0	0	1
1972-73*A*	I. M. Chappell	Intikhab Alam	3	3	0	0
1976-77*A*	G. S. Chappell	Mushtaq Mohammad	3	1	1	1
1978-79*A*	G. N. Yallop[2]	Mushtaq Mohammad	2	1	1	0
1979-80*P*	G. S. Chappell	Javed Miandad	3	0	1	2
1981-82*A*	G. S. Chappell	Javed Miandad	3	2	1	0
1982-83*P*	K. J. Hughes	Imran Khan	3	0	3	0
1983-84*A*	K. J. Hughes	Imran Khan[3]	5	2	0	3
1988-89*P*	A. R. Border	Javed Miandad	3	0	1	2
1989-90*A*	A. R. Border	Imran Khan	3	1	0	2
1994-95*P*	M. A. Taylor	Salim Malik	3	0	1	2
1995-96*A*	M. A. Taylor	Wasim Akram	3	2	1	0
	In Pakistan		17	2	7	8
	In Australia		23	12	4	7
	Totals		40	14	11	15

A Played in Australia. P Played in Pakistan.

Notes: The following deputised for the official touring captain or were appointed by the home authority for only a minor proportion of the series:

[1]Imtiaz Ahmed (Second). [2]K. J. Hughes (Second). [3]Zaheer Abbas (First, Second and Third).

HIGHEST INNINGS TOTALS

For Australia in Australia: 585 at Adelaide	1972-73
in Pakistan: 617 at Faisalabad	1979-80
For Pakistan in Australia: 624 at Adelaide	1983-84
in Pakistan: 537 at Rawalpindi	1994-95

LOWEST INNINGS TOTALS

For Australia	in Australia: 125 at Melbourne	1981-82
	in Pakistan: 80 at Karachi	1956-57
For Pakistan	in Australia: 62 at Perth	1981-82
	in Pakistan: 134 at Dacca	1959-60

INDIVIDUAL HUNDREDS

For Australia (42)

J. Benaud (1)
142 Melbourne .. 1972-73
D. C. Boon (1)
114* Karachi 1994-95
A. R. Border (6)
105† Melbourne .. 1978-79
150*, 153 Lahore 1979-80
118 Brisbane 1983-84
117* Adelaide 1983-84
113* Faisalabad .. 1988-89
G. S. Chappell (6)
116* Melbourne .. 1972-73
121 Melbourne .. 1976-77
235 Faisalabad .. 1979-80
201 Brisbane 1981-82
150* Brisbane 1983-84
182 Sydney 1983-84
I. M. Chappell (1)
196 Adelaide 1972-73
G. J. Cosier (1)
168 Melbourne .. 1976-77
I. C. Davis (1)
105† Adelaide 1976-77
K. J. Hughes (2)
106 Perth....... 1981-82
106 Adelaide 1983-84
D. M. Jones (2)
116, 121* Adelaide 1989-90
R. B. McCosker (1)
105 Melbourne .. 1976-77
R. W. Marsh (1)
118† Adelaide 1972-73
N. C. O'Neill (1)
134 Lahore...... 1959-60
W. B. Phillips (1)
159† Perth....... 1983-84
I. R. Redpath (1)
135 Melbourne .. 1972-73
G. M. Ritchie (1)
106* Faisalabad .. 1982-83
A. P. Sheahan (1)
127 Melbourne .. 1972-73
R. B. Simpson (2)
153, 115 †Karachi 1964-65
M. J. Slater (1)
110 Rawalpindi .. 1994-95
M. A. Taylor (3)
101† Melbourne .. 1989-90
101* Sydney 1989-90
123 Hobart 1995-96
K. D. Walters (1)
107 Adelaide 1976-77
M. E. Waugh (1)
116 Sydney 1995-96
S. R. Waugh (1)
112* Brisbane 1995-96
K. C. Wessels (1)
179 Adelaide 1983-84
G. M. Wood (1)
100 Melbourne .. 1981-82
G. N. Yallop (3)
172 Faisalabad .. 1979-80
141 Perth 1983-84
268 Melbourne .. 1983-84

For Pakistan (36)

Aamir Sohail (1)
105 Lahore 1994-95
Asif Iqbal (3)
152* Adelaide 1976-77
120 Sydney 1976-77
134* Perth....... 1978-79
Hanif Mohammad (2)
101* Karachi 1959-60
104 Melbourne .. 1964-65
Ijaz Ahmed, sen. (3)
122 Faisalabad .. 1988-89
121 Melbourne .. 1989-90
137 Sydney 1995-96
Imran Khan (1)
136 Adelaide ... 1989-90
Javed Miandad (6)
129* Perth....... 1978-79
106* Faisalabad .. 1979-80
138 Lahore 1982-83
131 Adelaide 1983-84
211 Karachi 1988-89
107 Faisalabad .. 1988-89
Khalid Ibadulla (1)
166† Karachi 1964-65
Majid Khan (3)
158 Melbourne .. 1972-73
108 Melbourne .. 1978-79
110* Lahore 1979-80
Mansoor Akhtar (1)
111 Faisalabad .. 1982-83
Mohsin Khan (3)
135 Lahore 1982-83
149 Adelaide 1983-84
152 Melbourne .. 1983-84
Moin Khan (1)
115*† Lahore 1994-95
Mushtaq Mohammad (1)
121 Sydney 1972-73
Qasim Omar (1)
113 Adelaide 1983-84
Sadiq Mohammad (2)
137 Melbourne .. 1972-73
105 Melbourne .. 1976-77
Saeed Ahmed (1)
166 Lahore 1959-60
Salim Malik (2)
237 Rawalpindi .. 1994-95
143 Lahore 1994-95
Taslim Arif (1)
210* Faisalabad .. 1979-80
Wasim Akram (1)
123 Adelaide 1989-90
Zaheer Abbas (2)
101 Adelaide 1976-77
126 Faisalabad .. 1982-83

† *Signifies hundred on first appearance in Australia–Pakistan Tests.*

RECORD PARTNERSHIPS FOR EACH WICKET

For Australia

176 for 1st	M. A. Taylor and M. J. Slater at Rawalpindi	1994-95
259 for 2nd	W. B. Phillips and G. N. Yallop at Perth	1983-84
203 for 3rd	G. N. Yallop and K. J. Hughes at Melbourne	1983-84
217 for 4th	G. S. Chappell and G. N. Yallop at Faisalabad	1979-80
171 for 5th	G. S. Chappell and G. J. Cosier at Melbourne	1976-77
	A. R. Border and G. S. Chappell at Brisbane	1983-84
139 for 6th	R. M. Cowper and T. R. Veivers at Melbourne	1964-65
185 for 7th	G. N. Yallop and G. R. J. Matthews at Melbourne	1983-84
117 for 8th	G. J. Cosier and K. J. O'Keeffe at Melbourne	1976-77
83 for 9th	J. R. Watkins and R. A. L. Massie at Sydney	1972-73
52 for 10th	D. K. Lillee and M. H. N. Walker at Sydney	1976-77
	G. F. Lawson and T. M. Alderman at Lahore	1982-83

For Pakistan

249 for 1st†	Khalid Ibadulla and Abdul Kadir at Karachi	1964-65
233 for 2nd	Mohsin Khan and Qasim Omar at Adelaide	1983-84
223* for 3rd	Taslim Arif and Javed Miandad at Faisalabad	1979-80
155 for 4th	Mansoor Akhtar and Zaheer Abbas at Faisalabad	1982-83
186 for 5th	Javed Miandad and Salim Malik at Adelaide	1983-84
196 for 6th	Salim Malik and Aamir Sohail at Lahore	1994-95
104 for 7th	Intikhab Alam and Wasim Bari at Adelaide	1972-73
111 for 8th	Majid Khan and Imran Khan at Lahore	1979-80
56 for 9th	Intikhab Alam and Afaq Hussain at Melbourne	1964-65
87 for 10th	Asif Iqbal and Iqbal Qasim at Adelaide	1976-77

† *Denotes record partnership against all countries.*

TEN WICKETS OR MORE IN A MATCH

For Australia (4)

10-111 (7-87, 3-24)†	R. J. Bright, Karachi	1979-80
10-135 (6-82, 4-53)	D. K. Lillee, Melbourne	1976-77
11-118 (5-32, 6-86)†	C. G. Rackemann, Perth	1983-84
11-77 (7-23, 4-54)	S. K. Warne, Brisbane	1995-96

For Pakistan (6)

11-218 (4-76, 7-142)	Abdul Qadir, Faisalabad	1982-83
13-114 (6-34, 7-80)†	Fazal Mahmood, Karachi	1956-57
12-165 (6-102, 6-63)	Imran Khan, Sydney	1976-77
11-118 (4-69, 7-49)	Iqbal Qasim, Karachi	1979-80
11-125 (2-39, 9-86)	Sarfraz Nawaz, Melbourne	1978-79
11-160 (6-62, 5-98)†	Wasim Akram, Melbourne	1989-90

† *Signifies ten wickets or more on first appearance in Australia–Pakistan Tests.*

AUSTRALIA v SRI LANKA

	Captains					
Season	*Australia*	*Sri Lanka*	*T*	*A*	*SL*	*D*
1982-83*S*	G. S. Chappell	L. R. D. Mendis	1	1	0	0
1987-88*A*	A. R. Border	R. S. Madugalle	1	1	0	0
1989-90*A*	A. R. Border	A. Ranatunga	2	1	0	1
1992-93*S*	A. R. Border	A. Ranatunga	3	1	0	2
1995-96*A*	M. A. Taylor	A. Ranatunga[1]	3	3	0	0
	In Australia		6	5	0	1
	In Sri Lanka		4	2	0	2
	Totals		10	7	0	3

A Played in Australia. S Played in Sri Lanka.

Note: The following deputised for the official touring captain:
[1]P. A. de Silva (Third).

HIGHEST INNINGS TOTALS

For Australia in Australia: 617-5 dec. at Perth 1995-96
in Sri Lanka: 514-4 dec. at Kandy 1982-83

For Sri Lanka in Australia: 418 in Brisbane 1989-90
in Sri Lanka: 547-8 dec. at Colombo (SSC) 1992-93

LOWEST INNINGS TOTALS

For Australia in Australia: 224 at Hobart 1989-90
in Sri Lanka: 247 at Colombo (KS) 1992-93

For Sri Lanka in Australia: 153 at Perth 1987-88
in Sri Lanka: 164 at Colombo (SSC) 1992-93

INDIVIDUAL HUNDREDS

For Australia (15)

D. C. Boon (1)
110 Melbourne .. 1995-96
A. R. Border (1)
106 Moratuwa... 1992-93
D. W. Hookes (1)
143*† Kandy...... 1982-83
D. M. Jones (3)
102† Perth....... 1987-88
118* Hobart 1989-90
100* Colombo (KS) 1992-93
T. M. Moody (1)
106† Brisbane 1989-90
M. J. Slater (1)
219† Perth....... 1995-96
M. A. Taylor (2)
164† Brisbane 1989-90
108 Hobart 1989-90
M. E. Waugh (1)
111 Perth....... 1995-96
S. R. Waugh (3)
134* Hobart 1989-90
131* Melbourne .. 1995-96
170 Adelaide 1995-96
K. C. Wessels (1)
141† Kandy...... 1982-83

For Sri Lanka (7)

P. A. de Silva (1)
167 Brisbane 1989-90
A. P. Gurusinha (2)
137 Colombo (SSC) 1992-93
143 Melbourne .. 1995-96
S. T. Jayasuriya (1)
112 Adelaide 1995-96
R. S. Kaluwitharana (1)
132*† Colombo (SSC) 1992-93
A. Ranatunga (1)
127 Colombo (SSC) 1992-93
H. P. Tillekeratne (1)
119 Perth....... 1995-96

† *Signifies hundred on first appearance in Australia–Sri Lanka Tests.*

RECORD PARTNERSHIPS FOR EACH WICKET

For Australia

228	for 1st	M. J. Slater and M. A. Taylor at Perth	1995-96
170	for 2nd	K. C. Wessels and G. N. Yallop at Kandy	1982-83
158	for 3rd	T. M. Moody and A. R. Border at Brisbane	1989-90
163	for 4th	M. A. Taylor and A. R. Border at Hobart	1989-90
155*	for 5th	D. W. Hookes and A. R. Border at Kandy	1982-83
260*	for 6th	D. M. Jones and S. R. Waugh at Hobart	1989-90
129	for 7th	G. R. J. Matthews and I. A. Healy at Moratuwa	1992-93
56	for 8th	G. R. J. Matthews and C. J. McDermott at Colombo (SSC)	1992-93
45	for 9th	I. A. Healy and S. K. Warne at Colombo (SSC)	1992-93
49	for 10th	I. A. Healy and M. R. Whitney at Colombo (SSC)	1992-93

For Sri Lanka

110	for 1st	R. S. Mahanama and U. C. Hathurusinghe at Colombo (KS)	1992-93
92	for 2nd	R. S. Mahanama and A. P. Gurusinha at Colombo (SSC)	1992-93
125	for 3rd	S. T. Jayasuriya and S. Ranatunga at Adelaide	1995-96
230	for 4th	A. P. Gurusinha and A. Ranatunga at Colombo (SSC)	1992-93
116	for 5th	H. P. Tillekeratne and A. Ranatunga at Moratuwa	1992-93
96	for 6th	A. Ranatunga and R. S. Kaluwitharana at Colombo (SSC)	1992-93
144	for 7th†	P. A. de Silva and J. R. Ratnayeke at Brisbane	1989-90
33	for 8th	A. Ranatunga and C. P. H. Ramanayake at Perth	1987-88
44*	for 9th	R. S. Kaluwitharana and A. W. R. Madurasinghe at Colombo (SSC)	1992-93
27	for 10th	P. A. de Silva and C. P. H. Ramanayake at Brisbane	1989-90

† *Denotes record partnership against all countries.*

BEST MATCH BOWLING ANALYSES

For Australia

8-156 (3-68, 5-88) M. G. Hughes, Hobart 1989-90

For Sri Lanka

8-157 (5-82, 3-75) C. P. H. Ramanayake, Moratuwa 1992-93

SOUTH AFRICA v WEST INDIES

	Captains					
Season	*South Africa*	*West Indies*	*T*	*SA*	*WI*	*D*
1991-92*W*	K. C. Wessels	R. B. Richardson	1	0	1	0

W Played in West Indies.

HIGHEST INNINGS TOTALS

For South Africa: 345 at Bridgetown 1991-92

For West Indies: 283 at Bridgetown 1991-92

INDIVIDUAL HUNDREDS

For South Africa (1)

A. C. Hudson (1)
163† Bridgetown . . 1991-92

Highest score for West Indies: 79* at Bridgetown 1991-92 by J. C. Adams.
† *Signifies hundred on first appearance in South Africa–West Indies Tests.*

HIGHEST PARTNERSHIPS

For South Africa

125 for 2nd A. C. Hudson and K. C. Wessels at Bridgetown 1991-92

For West Indies

99 for 1st D. L. Haynes and P. V. Simmons at Bridgetown 1991-92

BEST MATCH BOWLING ANALYSES

For South Africa

8-158 (4-84, 4-74) R. P. Snell, Bridgetown 1991-92

For West Indies

8-81 (2-47, 6-34) C. E. L. Ambrose, Bridgetown 1991-92

SOUTH AFRICA v NEW ZEALAND

	Captains					
Season	*South Africa*	*New Zealand*	*T*	*SA*	*NZ*	*D*
1931-32*N*	H. B. Cameron	M. L. Page	2	2	0	0
1952-53*N*	J. E. Cheetham	W. M. Wallace	2	1	0	1
1953-54*S*	J. E. Cheetham	G. O. Rabone[1]	5	4	0	1
1961-62*S*	D. J. McGlew	J. R. Reid	5	2	2	1
1963-64*N*	T. L. Goddard	J. R. Reid	3	0	0	3
1994-95*S*	W. J. Cronje	K. R. Rutherford	3	2	1	0
1994-95*N*	W. J. Cronje	K. R. Rutherford	1	1	0	0
	In New Zealand		8	4	0	4
	In South Africa		13	8	3	2
	Totals		21	12	3	6

N Played in New Zealand. S Played in South Africa.

Note: The following deputised for the official touring captain:
[1]B. Sutcliffe (Fourth and Fifth).

HIGHEST INNINGS TOTALS

For South Africa in South Africa: 464 at Johannesburg 1961-62
in New Zealand: 524-8 at Wellington 1952-53

For New Zealand in South Africa: 505 at Cape Town 1953-54
in New Zealand: 364 at Wellington 1931-32

LOWEST INNINGS TOTALS

For South Africa in South Africa: 148 at Johannesburg 1953-54
in New Zealand: 223 at Dunedin 1963-64

For New Zealand in South Africa: 79 at Johannesburg 1953-54
in New Zealand: 138 at Dunedin 1963-64

INDIVIDUAL HUNDREDS

For South Africa (14)

X. C. Balaskas (1)
122* Wellington .. 1931-32
J. A. J. Christy (1)
103† Christchurch. 1931-32
W. J. Cronje (2)
112 Cape Town . 1994-95
101 Auckland ... 1994-95
W. R. Endean (1)
116 Auckland ... 1952-53
D. J. McGlew (3)
255*† Wellington .. 1952-53
127*‡ Durban 1961-62
120 Johannesburg 1961-62
R. A. McLean (2)
101 Durban 1953-54
113 Cape Town . 1961-62
B. Mitchell (1)
113† Christchurch. 1931-32
A. R. A. Murray (1)
109† Wellington .. 1952-53
D. J. Richardson (1)
109 Cape Town . 1994-95
J. H. B. Waite (1)
101 Johannesburg 1961-62

For New Zealand (7)

P. T. Barton (1)
109 Pt Elizabeth . 1961-62
P. G. Z. Harris (1)
101 Cape Town.. 1961-62
G. O. Rabone (1)
107 Durban 1953-54
J. R. Reid (2)
135 Cape Town.. 1953-54
142 Johannesburg 1961-62
B. W. Sinclair (1)
138 Auckland ... 1963-64
H. G. Vivian (1)
100† Wellington .. 1931-32

† *Signifies hundred on first appearance in South Africa–New Zealand Tests.*
‡ *Carried his bat.*

RECORD PARTNERSHIPS FOR EACH WICKET

For South Africa

196 for 1st	J. A. J. Christy and B. Mitchell at Christchurch	1931-32
97 for 2nd	G. Kirsten and J. B. Commins at Durban	1994-95
112 for 3rd	D. J. McGlew and R. A. McLean at Johannesburg	1961-62
135 for 4th	K. J. Funston and R. A. McLean at Durban	1953-54
130 for 5th	W. R. Endean and J. E. Cheetham at Auckland	1952-53
83 for 6th	K. C. Bland and D. T. Lindsay at Auckland	1963-64
246 for 7th†	D. J. McGlew and A. R. A. Murray at Wellington	1952-53
95 for 8th	J. E. Cheetham and H. J. Tayfield at Cape Town	1953-54
60 for 9th	P. M. Pollock and N. A. T. Adcock at Port Elizabeth	1961-62
47 for 10th	D. J. McGlew and H. D. Bromfield at Port Elizabeth	1961-62

For New Zealand

126 for 1st	G. O. Rabone and M. E. Chapple at Cape Town	1953-54
72 for 2nd	D. J. Murray and S. P. Fleming at Johannesburg	1994-95
94 for 3rd	M. B. Poore and B. Sutcliffe at Cape Town	1953-54
171 for 4th	B. W. Sinclair and S. N. McGregor at Auckland	1963-64
174 for 5th	J. R. Reid and J. E. F. Beck at Cape Town	1953-54
100 for 6th	H. G. Vivian and F. T. Badcock at Wellington	1931-32
84 for 7th	J. R. Reid and G. A. Bartlett at Johannesburg	1961-62
74 for 8th	S. A. Thomson and D. J. Nash at Johannesburg	1994-95
69 for 9th	C. F. W. Allcott and I. B. Cromb at Wellington	1931-32
57 for 10th	S. B. Doull and R. P. de Groen at Johannesburg	1994-95

† *Denotes record partnership against all countries.*

TEN WICKETS OR MORE IN A MATCH

For South Africa (1)

11-196 (6-128, 5-68)† S. F. Burke, Cape Town 1961-62

† *Signifies ten wickets or more on first appearance in South Africa–New Zealand Tests.*

Note: The best match figures by a New Zealand bowler are 8-134 (3-57, 5-77), M. N. Hart at Johannesburg, 1994-95.

SOUTH AFRICA v INDIA

Season	*Captains South Africa*	*India*	*T*	*SA*	*I*	*D*
1992-93*S*	K. C. Wessels	M. Azharuddin	4	1	0	3

S Played in South Africa.

HIGHEST INNINGS TOTALS

For South Africa: 360-9 dec. at Cape Town 1992-93

For India: 277 at Durban 1992-93

INDIVIDUAL HUNDREDS

For South Africa (2)

W. J. Cronje (1)
135 Pt Elizabeth . 1992-93

K. C. Wessels (1)
118† Durban 1992-93

For India (3)

P. K. Amre (1)
103† Durban 1992-93

Kapil Dev (1)
129 Pt Elizabeth . 1992-93

S. R. Tendulkar (1)
111 Johannesburg 1992-93

† *Signifies hundred on first appearance in South Africa–India Tests.*

HUNDRED PARTNERSHIPS

For South Africa

117 for 2nd A. C. Hudson and W. J. Cronje at Port Elizabeth 1992-93

For India

101 for 8th P. K. Amre and K. S. More at Durban 1992-93

TEN WICKETS OR MORE IN A MATCH

For South Africa (1)

12-139 (5-55, 7-84) A. A. Donald at Port Elizabeth 1992-93

Note: The best match figures by an Indian bowler are 8-113 (2-60, 6-53), A. Kumble at Johannesburg, 1992-93.

SOUTH AFRICA v PAKISTAN

	Captains					
Season	*South Africa*	*Pakistan*	*T*	*SA*	*P*	*D*
1994-95*S*	W. J. Cronje	Salim Malik	1	1	0	0

S Played in South Africa.

HIGHEST INNINGS TOTALS

For South Africa: 460 at Johannesburg 1994-95

For Pakistan: 230 at Johannesburg 1994-95

INDIVIDUAL HUNDREDS

For South Africa (1)

B. M. McMillan (1)
113† Johannesburg 1994-95

Highest score for Pakistan: 99 by Salim Malik at Johannesburg 1994-95.

† *Signifies hundred on first appearance in South Africa–Pakistan Tests.*

HUNDRED PARTNERSHIP

For South Africa

157 for 6th J. N. Rhodes and B. M. McMillan at Johannesburg 1994-95

Note: The highest partnership for Pakistan is 93 for the 4th wicket between Asif Mujtaba and Inzamam-ul-Haq at Johannesburg, 1994-95.

TEN WICKETS OR MORE IN A MATCH

For South Africa (1)

10-108 (6-81, 4-27)† P. S. de Villiers, Johannesburg 1994-95

Note: The best match figures for Pakistan are 5-184 (3-102, 2-82), Aqib Javed at Johannesburg, 1994-95.

† *Signifies ten wickets or more on first appearance in South Africa–Pakistan Tests.*

SOUTH AFRICA v SRI LANKA

	Captains					
Season	*South Africa*	*Sri Lanka*	*T*	*SA*	*SL*	*D*
1993-94*SL*	K. C. Wessels	A. Ranatunga	3	1	0	2

SL Played in Sri Lanka.

HIGHEST INNINGS TOTALS

For South Africa: 495 at Colombo (SSC) 1993-94

For Sri Lanka: 331 at Moratuwa 1993-94

INDIVIDUAL HUNDREDS

For South Africa (3)

W. J. Cronje (1)
122 Colombo (SSC) 1993-94

D. J. Cullinan (1)
102 Colombo (PSS) 1993-94

J. N. Rhodes (1)
101*† Moratuwa... 1993-94

For Sri Lanka (1)

A. Ranatunga (1)
131† Moratuwa... 1993-94

† *Signifies hundred on first appearance in South Africa–Sri Lanka Tests.*

HUNDRED PARTNERSHIPS

For South Africa

137 for 1st	K. C. Wessels and A. C. Hudson at Colombo (SSC)	1993-94
122 for 6th	D. J. Cullinan and D. J. Richardson at Colombo (PSS)	1993-94
105 for 3rd	W. J. Cronje and D. J. Cullinan at Colombo (SSC)	1993-94
104 for 1st	K. C. Wessels and A. C. Hudson at Moratuwa	1993-94

For Sri Lanka

121 for 5th	P. A. de Silva and A. Ranatunga at Moratuwa	1993-94
103 for 6th	A. Ranatunga and H. P. Tillekeratne at Moratuwa	1993-94
101 for 4th	P. A. de Silva and A. Ranatunga at Colombo (PSS)	1993-94

BEST MATCH BOWLING ANALYSES

For South Africa

9-106 (5-48, 4-58) B. N. Schultz, Colombo (SSC) 1993-94

For Sri Lanka

6-152 (5-104, 1-48) M. Muralitharan, Moratuwa 1993-94

SOUTH AFRICA v ZIMBABWE

	Captains					
Season	*South Africa*	*Zimbabwe*	*T*	*SA*	*Z*	*D*
1995-96*Z*	W. J. Cronje	A. Flower	1	1	0	0

Z Played in Zimbabwe.

HIGHEST INNINGS TOTALS

For South Africa: 346 at Harare 1995-96

For Zimbabwe: 283 at Harare 1995-96

INDIVIDUAL HUNDREDS

For South Africa (1)

A. C. Hudson (1)
135† Harare 1995-96

Highest score for Zimbabwe: 63 by A. Flower at Harare 1995-96.

† *Signifies hundred on first appearance in South Africa–Zimbabwe Tests.*

HUNDRED PARTNERSHIP

For South Africa

101 for 6th A. C. Hudson and B. M. McMillan at Harare 1995-96

Note: The highest partnership for Zimbabwe is 97 for the 5th wicket between A. Flower and G. J. Whittall at Harare, 1995-96.

TEN WICKETS OR MORE IN A MATCH

For South Africa (1)

11-113 (3-42, 8-71)† A. A. Donald, Harare 1995-96

Note: The best match figures for Zimbabwe are 5-105 (3-68, 2-37) by A. C. I. Lock at Harare, 1995-96.

† *Signifies ten wickets or more on first appearance in South Africa–Zimbabwe Tests.*

WEST INDIES v NEW ZEALAND

	Captains					
Season	*West Indies*	*New Zealand*	*T*	*WI*	*NZ*	*D*
1951-52*N*	J. D. C. Goddard	B. Sutcliffe	2	1	0	1
1955-56*N*	D. St E. Atkinson	J. R. Reid[1]	4	3	1	0
1968-69*N*	G. S. Sobers	G. T. Dowling	3	1	1	1
1971-72*W*	G. S. Sobers	G. T. Dowling[2]	5	0	0	5
1979-80*N*	C. H. Lloyd	G. P. Howarth	3	0	1	2
1984-85*W*	I. V. A. Richards	G. P. Howarth	4	2	0	2
1986-87*N*	I. V. A. Richards	J. V. Coney	3	1	1	1
1993-94*N*	C. A. Walsh	K. R. Rutherford	2	1	0	1
1995-96*W*	C. A. Walsh	L. K. Germon	2	1	0	1
	In New Zealand		17	7	4	6
	In West Indies		11	3	0	8
	Totals		28	10	4	14

N Played in New Zealand. W Played in West Indies.

Notes: The following deputised for the official touring captain or were appointed by the home authority for only a minor proportion of the series:
[1]H. B. Cave (First). [2]B. E. Congdon (Third, Fourth and Fifth).

HIGHEST INNINGS TOTALS

For West Indies in West Indies: 564-8 at Bridgetown 1971-72
in New Zealand: 660-5 dec. at Wellington 1994-95

For New Zealand in West Indies: 543-3 dec. at Georgetown 1971-72
in New Zealand: 460 at Christchurch 1979-80

LOWEST INNINGS TOTALS

For West Indies in West Indies: 133 at Bridgetown 1971-72
in New Zealand: 77 at Auckland 1955-56

For New Zealand in West Indies: 94 at Bridgetown 1984-85
in New Zealand: 74 at Dunedin 1955-56

INDIVIDUAL HUNDREDS

By West Indies (31)

J. C. Adams (2)
151 Wellington .. 1994-95
208* St John's.... 1995-96
S. L. Campbell (1)
208 Bridgetown .. 1995-96
M. C. Carew (1)
109† Auckland ... 1968-69
C. A. Davis (1)
183 Bridgetown .. 1971-72
R. C. Fredericks (1)
163 Kingston.... 1971-72
C. G. Greenidge (2)
100 Port-of-Spain 1984-85
213 Auckland ... 1986-87
D. L. Haynes (3)
105† Dunedin 1979-80
122 Christchurch. 1979-80
121 Wellington .. 1986-87
A. I. Kallicharran (2)
100*† Georgetown . 1971-72
101 Port-of-Spain 1971-72
C. L. King (1)
100* Christchurch. 1979-80
B. C. Lara (1)
147 Wellington .. 1994-95
J. R. Murray (1)
101* Wellington .. 1994-95
S. M. Nurse (2)
168† Auckland ... 1968-69
258 Christchurch. 1968-69
I. V. A. Richards (1)
105 Bridgetown .. 1984-85
R. B. Richardson (1)
185 Georgetown . 1984-85
L. G. Rowe (3)
214 }
100* } †Kingston... 1971-72
100 Christchurch. 1979-80
R. G. Samuels (1)
125 St John's.... 1995-96
G. S. Sobers (1)
142 Bridgetown .. 1971-72
J. B. Stollmeyer (1)
152 Auckland ... 1951-52
C. L. Walcott (1)
115 Auckland ... 1951-52
E. D. Weekes (3)
123 Dunedin 1955-56
103 Christchurch. 1955-56
156 Wellington .. 1955-56
F. M. M. Worrell (1)
100 Auckland ... 1951-52

By New Zealand (20)

N. J. Astle (2)
125† Bridgetown .. 1995-96
103 St John's.... 1995-96
M. G. Burgess (1)
101 Kingston.... 1971-72
B. E. Congdon (2)
166* Port-of-Spain 1971-72
126 Bridgetown .. 1971-72
J. J. Crowe (1)
112 Kingston.... 1984-85
M. D. Crowe (3)
188 Georgetown . 1984-85
119 Wellington .. 1986-87
104 Auckland ... 1986-87
B. A. Edgar (1)
127 Auckland ... 1979-80
R. J. Hadlee (1)
103 Christchurch. 1979-80
B. F. Hastings (2)
117* Christchurch. 1968-69
105 Bridgetown .. 1971-72
G. P. Howarth (1)
147 Christchurch. 1979-80
T. W. Jarvis (1)
182 Georgetown . 1971-72
A. C. Parore (1)
100*† Christchurch. 1994-95
B. R. Taylor (1)
124† Auckland ... 1968-69
G. M. Turner (2)
223*‡ Kingston.... 1971-72
259 Georgetown . 1971-72
J. G. Wright (1)
138 Wellington .. 1986-87

† *Signifies hundred on first appearance in West Indies–New Zealand Tests.*
‡ *Carried his bat.*

Notes: E. D. Weekes in 1955-56 made three hundreds in consecutive innings.

L. G. Rowe and A. I. Kallicharran each scored hundreds in their first two innings in Test cricket, Rowe being the only batsman to do so in his first match.

RECORD PARTNERSHIPS FOR EACH WICKET

For West Indies

225 for 1st	C. G. Greenidge and D. L. Haynes at Christchurch	1979-80
269 for 2nd	R. C. Fredericks and L. G. Rowe at Kingston	1971-72
221 for 3rd	B. C. Lara and J. C. Adams at Wellington	1994-95
162 for 4th	E. D. Weekes and O. G. Smith at Dunedin	1955-56
	C. G. Greenidge and A. I. Kallicharran at Christchurch	1979-80
189 for 5th	F. M. M. Worrell and C. L. Walcott at Auckland	1951-52
254 for 6th	C. A. Davis and G. S. Sobers at Bridgetown	1971-72
143 for 7th	D. St E. Atkinson and J. D. C. Goddard at Christchurch	1955-56
83 for 8th	I. V. A. Richards and M. D. Marshall at Bridgetown	1984-85
70 for 9th	M. D. Marshall and J. Garner at Bridgetown	1984-85
31 for 10th	T. M. Findlay and G. C. Shillingford at Bridgetown	1971-72

For New Zealand

387	for 1st†	G. M. Turner and T. W. Jarvis at Georgetown	1971-72
210	for 2nd	G. P. Howarth and J. J. Crowe at Kingston	1984-85
241	for 3rd	J. G. Wright and M. D. Crowe at Wellington	1986-87
175	for 4th	B. E. Congdon and B. F. Hastings at Bridgetown	1971-72
144	for 5th	N. J. Astle and J. T. C. Vaughan at Bridgetown	1995-96
220	for 6th	G. M. Turner and K. J. Wadsworth at Kingston	1971-72
143	for 7th	M. D. Crowe and I. D. S. Smith at Georgetown	1984-85
136	for 8th†	B. E. Congdon and R. S. Cunis at Port-of-Spain	1971-72
62*	for 9th	V. Pollard and R. S. Cunis at Auckland	1968-69
45	for 10th	D. K. Morrison and R. J. Kennedy at Bridgetown	1995-96

† *Denotes record partnership against all countries.*

TEN WICKETS OR MORE IN A MATCH

For West Indies (2)

11-120 (4-40, 7-80)	M. D. Marshall, Bridgetown	1984-85
13-55 (7-37, 6-18)	C. A. Walsh, Wellington	1994-95

For New Zealand (3)

10-124 (4-51, 6-73)†	E. J. Chatfield, Port-of-Spain	1984-85
11-102 (5-34, 6-68)†	R. J. Hadlee, Dunedin	1979-80
10-166 (4-71, 6-95)	G. B. Troup, Auckland	1979-80

† *Signifies ten wickets or more on first appearance in West Indies–New Zealand Tests.*

WEST INDIES v INDIA

	Captains					
Season	*West Indies*	*India*	*T*	*WI*	*I*	*D*
1948-49*I*	J. D. C. Goddard	L. Amarnath	5	1	0	4
1952-53*W*	J. B. Stollmeyer	V. S. Hazare	5	1	0	4
1958-59*I*	F. C. M. Alexander	Ghulam Ahmed[1]	5	3	0	2
1961-62*W*	F. M. M. Worrell	N. J. Contractor[2]	5	5	0	0
1966-67*I*	G. S. Sobers	Nawab of Pataudi jun.	3	2	0	1
1970-71*W*	G. S. Sobers	A. L. Wadekar	5	0	1	4
1974-75*I*	C. H. Lloyd	Nawab of Pataudi jun.[3]	5	3	2	0
1975-76*W*	C. H. Lloyd	B. S. Bedi	4	2	1	1
1978-79*I*	A. I. Kallicharran	S. M. Gavaskar	6	0	1	5
1982-83*W*	C. H. Lloyd	Kapil Dev	5	2	0	3
1983-84*I*	C. H. Lloyd	Kapil Dev	6	3	0	3
1987-88*I*	I. V. A. Richards	D. B. Vengsarkar[4]	4	1	1	2
1988-89*W*	I. V. A. Richards	D. B. Vengsarkar	4	3	0	1
1994-95*I*	C. A. Walsh	M. Azharuddin	3	1	1	1
	In India		37	14	5	18
	In West Indies		28	13	2	13
	Totals		65	27	7	31

I Played in India. W Played in West Indies.

Notes: The following deputised for the official touring captain or were appointed by the home authority for only a minor proportion of the series:

[1]P. R. Umrigar (First), V. Mankad (Fourth), H. R. Adhikari (Fifth). [2]Nawab of Pataudi jun. (Third, Fourth and Fifth). [3]S. Venkataraghavan (Second). [4]R. J. Shastri (Fourth).

HIGHEST INNINGS TOTALS

For West Indies in West Indies: 631-8 dec. at Kingston 1961-62
in India: 644-8 dec. at Delhi 1958-59

For India in West Indies: 469-7 at Port-of-Spain 1982-83
in India: 644-7 dec. at Kanpur 1978-79

LOWEST INNINGS TOTALS

For West Indies in West Indies: 214 at Port-of-Spain 1970-71
in India: 127 at Delhi 1987-88

For India in West Indies: 97† at Kingston 1975-76
in India: 75 at Delhi 1987-88

† *Five men absent hurt. The lowest with 11 men batting is 98 at Port-of-Spain, 1961-62.*

INDIVIDUAL HUNDREDS

For West Indies (78)

J. C. Adams (2)
125* Nagpur 1994-95
174* Mohali 1994-95
S. F. A. F. Bacchus (1)
250 Kanpur 1978-79
B. F. Butcher (2)
103 Calcutta 1958-59
142 Madras 1958-59
R. J. Christiani (1)
107† Delhi 1948-49
C. A. Davis (2)
125* Georgetown . 1970-71
105 Port-of-Spain 1970-71
P. J. L. Dujon (1)
110 St John's 1982-83
R. C. Fredericks (2)
100 Calcutta 1974-75
104 Bombay 1974-75
H. A. Gomes (1)
123 Port-of-Spain 1982-83
G. E. Gomez (1)
101† Delhi 1948-49
C. G. Greenidge (5)
107† Bangalore ... 1974-75
154* St John's 1982-83
194 Kanpur 1983-84
141 Calcutta 1987-88
117 Bridgetown . 1988-89
D. L. Haynes (2)
136 St John's 1982-83
112* Bridgetown . 1988-89
J. K. Holt (1)
123 Delhi 1958-59
C. L. Hooper (1)
100* Calcutta 1987-88
C. C. Hunte (1)
101 Bombay 1966-67

A. I. Kallicharran (3)
124† Bangalore ... 1974-75
103* Port-of-Spain 1975-76
187 Bombay 1978-79
R. B. Kanhai (4)
256 Calcutta 1958-59
138 Kingston ... 1961-62
139 Port-of-Spain 1961-62
158* Kingston ... 1970-71
C. H. Lloyd (7)
163 Bangalore ... 1974-75
242* Bombay 1974-75
102 Bridgetown . 1975-76
143 Port-of-Spain 1982-83
106 St John's 1982-83
103 Delhi 1983-84
161* Calcutta 1983-84
A. L. Logie (2)
130 Bridgetown . 1982-83
101 Calcutta 1987-88
E. D. A. McMorris (1)
125† Kingston ... 1961-62
B. H. Pairaudeau (1)
115† Port-of-Spain 1952-53
A. F. Rae (2)
104 Bombay 1948-49
109 Madras 1948-49
I. V. A. Richards (8)
192* Delhi 1974-75
142 Bridgetown . 1975-76
130 Port-of-Spain 1975-76
177 Port-of-Spain 1975-76
109 Georgetown . 1982-83
120 Bombay 1983-84
109* Delhi 1987-88
110 Kingston ... 1988-89

R. B. Richardson (2)
194 Georgetown . 1988-89
156 Kingston ... 1988-89
O. G. Smith (1)
100 Delhi 1958-59
G. S. Sobers (8)
142*† Bombay 1958-59
198 Kanpur 1958-59
106* Calcutta 1958-59
153 Kingston ... 1961-62
104 Kingston ... 1961-62
108* Georgetown . 1970-71
178* Bridgetown . 1970-71
132 Port-of-Spain 1970-71
J. S. Solomon (1)
100* Delhi 1958-59
J. B. Stollmeyer (2)
160 Madras 1948-49
104* Port-of-Spain 1952-53
C. L. Walcott (4)
152† Delhi 1948-49
108 Calcutta 1948-49
125 Georgetown . 1952-53
118 Kingston ... 1952-53
E. D. Weekes (7)
128† Delhi 1948-49
194 Bombay 1948-49
162, 101 } Calcutta 1948-49
207 Port-of-Spain 1952-53
161 Port-of-Spain 1952-53
109 Kingston ... 1952-53
A. B. Williams (1)
111 Calcutta 1978-79
F. M. M. Worrell (1)
237 Kingston ... 1952-53

For India (58)

H. R. Adhikari (1)
114*† Delhi 1948-49
M. Amarnath (3)
101* Kanpur 1978-79
117 Port-of-Spain 1982-83
116 St John's 1982-83
M. L. Apte (1)
163* Port-of-Spain 1952-53
C. G. Borde (3)
109 Delhi 1958-59
121 Bombay 1966-67
125 Madras 1966-67
S. A. Durani (1)
104 Port-of-Spain 1961-62
F. M. Engineer (1)
109 Madras 1966-67
A. D. Gaekwad (1)
102 Kanpur 1978-79
S. M. Gavaskar (13)
116 Georgetown . 1970-71
117* Bridgetown . 1970-71
124 } Port-of-Spain 1970-71
220 }
156 Port-of-Spain 1975-76
102 Port-of-Spain 1975-76
205 Bombay 1978-79
107 } Calcutta 1978-79
182* }
120 Delhi 1978-79
147* Georgetown . 1982-83
121 Delhi 1983-84
236* Madras 1983-84
V. S. Hazare (2)
134* Bombay 1948-49
122 Bombay 1948-49
Kapil Dev (3)
126* Delhi 1978-79
100* Port-of-Spain 1982-83
109 Madras 1987-88
S. V. Manjrekar (1)
108 Bridgetown . 1988-89
V. L. Manjrekar (1)
118 Kingston ... 1952-53
R. S. Modi (1)
112 Bombay 1948-49
Mushtaq Ali (1)
106† Calcutta 1948-49
B. P. Patel (1)
115* Port-of-Spain 1975-76
M. Prabhakar (1)
120 Mohali 1994-95
Pankaj Roy (1)
150 Kingston ... 1952-53
D. N. Sardesai (3)
212 Kingston ... 1970-71
112 Port-of-Spain 1970-71
150 Bridgetown . 1970-71
R. J. Shastri (2)
102 St John's 1982-83
107 Bridgetown . 1988-89
N. S. Sidhu (2)
116 Kingston ... 1988-89
107 Nagpur 1994-95
E. D. Solkar (1)
102 Bombay 1974-75
S. R. Tendulkar (1)
179 Nagpur 1994-95
P. R. Umrigar (3)
130 Port-of-Spain 1952-53
117 Kingston ... 1952-53
172* Port-of-Spain 1961-62
D. B. Vengsarkar (6)
157* Calcutta 1978-79
109 Delhi 1978-79
159 Delhi 1983-84
100 Bombay 1983-84
102 Delhi 1987-88
102* Calcutta 1987-88
G. R. Viswanath (4)
139 Calcutta 1974-75
112 Port-of-Spain 1975-76
124 Madras 1978-79
179 Kanpur 1978-79

† *Signifies hundred on first appearance in West Indies–India Tests.*

RECORD PARTNERSHIPS FOR EACH WICKET

For West Indies

296	for 1st	C. G. Greenidge and D. L. Haynes at St John's	1982-83
255	for 2nd	E. D. A. McMorris and R. B. Kanhai at Kingston	1961-62
220	for 3rd	I. V. A. Richards and A. I. Kallicharran at Bridgetown	1975-76
267	for 4th	C. L. Walcott and G. E. Gomez at Delhi	1948-49
219	for 5th	E. D. Weekes and B. H. Pairaudeau at Port-of-Spain	1952-53
250	for 6th	C. H. Lloyd and D. L. Murray at Bombay	1974-75
130	for 7th	C. G. Greenidge and M. D. Marshall at Kanpur	1983-84
124	for 8th†	I. V. A. Richards and K. D. Boyce at Delhi	1974-75
161	for 9th†	C. H. Lloyd and A. M. E. Roberts at Calcutta	1983-84
98*	for 10th	F. M. M. Worrell and W. W. Hall at Port-of-Spain	1961-62

For India

153	for 1st	S. M. Gavaskar and C. P. S. Chauhan at Bombay	1978-79
344*	for 2nd†	S. M. Gavaskar and D. B. Vengsarkar at Calcutta	1978-79
177	for 3rd	N. S. Sidhu and S. R. Tendulkar at Nagpur	1994-95
172	for 4th	G. R. Viswanath and A. D. Gaekwad at Kanpur	1978-79
204	for 5th	S. M. Gavaskar and B. P. Patel at Port-of-Spain	1975-76
170	for 6th	S. M. Gavaskar and R. J. Shastri at Madras	1983-84
186	for 7th	D. N. Sardesai and E. D. Solkar at Bridgetown	1970-71
107	for 8th	Yashpal Sharma and B. S. Sandhu at Kingston	1982-83
143*	for 9th	S. M. Gavaskar and S. M. H. Kirmani at Madras	1983-84
64	for 10th	J. Srinath and S. L. V. Raju at Mohali	1994-95

† *Denotes record partnership against all countries.*

TEN WICKETS OR MORE IN A MATCH

For West Indies (4)

11-126 (6-50, 5-76)	W. W. Hall, Kanpur	1958-59
11-89 (5-34, 6-55)	M. D. Marshall, Port-of-Spain	1988-89
12-121 (7-64, 5-57)	A. M. E. Roberts, Madras	1974-75
10-101 (6-62, 4-39)	C. A. Walsh, Kingston	1988-89

For India (4)

11-235 (7-157, 4-78)†	B. S. Chandrasekhar, Bombay	1966-67
10-223 (9-102, 1-121)	S. P. Gupte, Kanpur	1958-59
16-136 (8-61, 8-75)†	N. D. Hirwani, Madras	1987-88
10-135 (1-52, 9-83)	Kapil Dev, Ahmedabad	1983-84

† *Signifies ten wickets or more on first appearance in West Indies–India Tests.*

WEST INDIES v PAKISTAN

Season	*West Indies* (Captains)	*Pakistan* (Captains)	*T*	*WI*	*P*	*D*
1957-58*W*	F. C. M. Alexander	A. H. Kardar	5	3	1	1
1958-59*P*	F. C. M. Alexander	Fazal Mahmood	3	1	2	0
1974-75*P*	C. H. Lloyd	Intikhab Alam	2	0	0	2
1976-77*W*	C. H. Lloyd	Mushtaq Mohammad	5	2	1	2
1980-81*P*	C. H. Lloyd	Javed Miandad	4	1	0	3
1986-87*P*	I. V. A. Richards	Imran Khan	3	1	1	1
1987-88*W*	I. V. A. Richards[1]	Imran Khan	3	1	1	1
1990-91*P*	D. L. Haynes	Imran Khan	3	1	1	1
1992-93*W*	R. B. Richardson	Wasim Akram	3	2	0	1
	In West Indies		16	8	3	5
	In Pakistan		15	4	4	7
	Totals		31	12	7	12

P Played in Pakistan. W Played in West Indies.

Note: The following was appointed by the home authority for only a minor proportion of the series:

[1]C. G. Greenidge (First).

HIGHEST INNINGS TOTALS

For West Indies in West Indies: 790-3 dec. at Kingston	1957-58
in Pakistan: 493 at Karachi	1974-75
For Pakistan in West Indies: 657-8 dec. at Bridgetown	1957-58
in Pakistan: 406-8 dec. at Karachi	1974-75

LOWEST INNINGS TOTALS

For West Indies in West Indies: 127 at Port-of-Spain	1992-93
in Pakistan: 53 at Faisalabad	1986-87
For Pakistan in West Indies: 106 at Bridgetown	1957-58
in Pakistan: 77 at Lahore	1986-87

INDIVIDUAL HUNDREDS

For West Indies (24)

L. Baichan (1)
105*† Lahore 1974-75
P. J. L. Dujon (1)
106* Port-of-Spain 1987-88
R. C. Fredericks (1)
120 Port-of-Spain 1976-77
C. G. Greenidge (1)
100 Kingston.... 1976-77
D. L. Haynes (3)
117 Karachi 1990-91
143*‡ Port-of-Spain 1992-93
125 Bridgetown.. 1992-93

C. L. Hooper (2)
134 Lahore 1990-91
178* St John's.... 1992-93
C. C. Hunte (3)
142† Bridgetown.. 1957-58
260 Kingston.... 1957-58
114 Georgetown . 1957-58
B. D. Julien (1)
101 Karachi 1974-75
A. I. Kallicharran (1)
115 Karachi 1974-75
R. B. Kanhai (1)
217 Lahore 1958-59
C. H. Lloyd (1)
157 Bridgetown.. 1976-77

I. V. A. Richards (2)
120* Multan 1980-81
123 Port-of-Spain 1987-88
I. T. Shillingford (1)
120 Georgetown . 1976-77
G. S. Sobers (3)
365* Kingston.... 1957-58
125 } Georgetown . 1957-58
109* }
C. L. Walcott (1)
145 Georgetown . 1957-58
E. D. Weekes (1)
197† Bridgetown.. 1957-58

For Pakistan (18)

Asif Iqbal (1)
135 Kingston.... 1976-77
Hanif Mohammad (2)
337† Bridgetown.. 1957-58
103 Karachi 1958-59
Imtiaz Ahmed (1)
122 Kingston.... 1957-58
Imran Khan (1)
123 Lahore 1980-81
Inzamam-ul-Haq (1)
123 St John's.... 1992-93

Javed Miandad (2)
114 Georgetown . 1987-88
102 Port-of-Spain 1987-88
Majid Khan (2)
100 Karachi 1974-75
167 Georgetown . 1976-77
Mushtaq Mohammad (2)
123 Lahore 1974-75
121 Port-of-Spain 1976-77

Saeed Ahmed (1)
150 Georgetown . 1957-58
Salim Malik (1)
102 Karachi 1990-91
Wasim Raja (2)
107* Karachi 1974-75
117* Bridgetown.. 1976-77
Wazir Mohammad (2)
106 Kingston.... 1957-58
189 Port-of-Spain 1957-58

† Signifies hundred on first appearance in West Indies–Pakistan Tests.
‡ Carried his bat.

RECORD PARTNERSHIPS FOR EACH WICKET

For West Indies

182	for 1st	R. C. Fredericks and C. G. Greenidge at Kingston	1976-77
446	for 2nd†	C. C. Hunte and G. S. Sobers at Kingston	1957-58
169	for 3rd	D. L. Haynes and B. C. Lara at Port-of-Spain	1992-93
188*	for 4th	G. S. Sobers and C. L. Walcott at Kingston	1957-58
185	for 5th	E. D. Weekes and O. G. Smith at Bridgetown	1957-58
151	for 6th	C. H. Lloyd and D. L. Murray at Bridgetown	1976-77
70	for 7th	C. H. Lloyd and J. Garner at Bridgetown	1976-77
60	for 8th	C. L. Hooper and A. C. Cummins at St John's	1992-93
61*	for 9th	P. J. L. Dujon and W. K. M. Benjamin at Bridgetown	1987-88
106	for 10th†	C. L. Hooper and C. A. Walsh at St John's	1992-93

For Pakistan

159	for 1st[1]	Majid Khan and Zaheer Abbas at Georgetown	1976-77
178	for 2nd	Hanif Mohammad and Saeed Ahmed at Karachi	1958-59
169	for 3rd	Saeed Ahmed and Wazir Mohammad at Port-of-Spain	1957-58
174	for 4th	Shoaib Mohammad and Salim Malik at Karachi	1990-91
88	for 5th	Basit Ali and Inzamam-ul-Haq at St John's	1992-93
166	for 6th	Wazir Mohammad and A. H. Kardar at Kingston	1957-58
128	for 7th[2]	Wasim Raja and Wasim Bari at Karachi	1974-75

94 for 8th	Salim Malik and Salim Yousuf at Port-of-Spain	1987-88
96 for 9th	Inzamam-ul-Haq and Nadeem Khan at St John's	1992-93
133 for 10th†	Wasim Raja and Wasim Bari at Bridgetown	1976-77

† Denotes record partnership against all countries.

[1] *219 runs were added for this wicket in two separate partnerships: Sadiq Mohammad retired hurt and was replaced by Zaheer Abbas when 60 had been added. The highest partnership by two opening batsmen is 152 by Hanif Mohammad and Imtiaz Ahmed at Bridgetown, 1957-58.*

[2] *Although the seventh wicket added 168 runs against West Indies at Lahore in 1980-81, this comprised two partnerships with Imran Khan adding 72* with Abdul Qadir (retired hurt) and a further 96 with Sarfraz Nawaz.*

TEN WICKETS OR MORE IN A MATCH

For Pakistan (2)

12-100 (6-34, 6-66)	Fazal Mahmood, Dacca	1958-59
11-121 (7-80, 4-41)	Imran Khan, Georgetown	1987-88

Note: The best match figures by a West Indian bowler are 9-95 (8-29, 1-66) by C. E. H. Croft at Port-of-Spain, 1976-77.

WEST INDIES v SRI LANKA

	Captains					
Season	*West Indies*	*Sri Lanka*	*T*	*WI*	*SL*	*D*
1993-94*S*	R. B. Richardson	A. Ranatunga	1	0	0	1

S Played in Sri Lanka.

HIGHEST INNINGS TOTALS

For West Indies: 204 at Moratuwa	1993-94
For Sri Lanka: 190 at Moratuwa	1993-94

Highest score for West Indies: 62 by C. L. Hooper at Moratuwa.
Highest score for Sri Lanka: 53 by P. A. de Silva at Moratuwa.

HIGHEST PARTNERSHIPS

For West Indies

84 for 5th	R. B. Richardson and C. L. Hooper at Moratuwa	1993-94

For Sri Lanka

51 for 7th	R. S. Kalpage and P. B. Dassanayake at Moratuwa	1993-94

BEST MATCH BOWLING ANALYSES

For West Indies

5-51 (4-46, 1-5)	W. K. M. Benjamin, Moratuwa	1993-94

For Sri Lanka

4-47 (4-47)	M. Muralitharan, Moratuwa	1993-94

NEW ZEALAND v INDIA

Season	Captains New Zealand	India	T	NZ	I	D
1955-56*I*	H. B. Cave	P. R. Umrigar[1]	5	0	2	3
1964-65*I*	J. R. Reid	Nawab of Pataudi jun.	4	0	1	3
1967-68*N*	G. T. Dowling[2]	Nawab of Pataudi jun.	4	1	3	0
1969-70*I*	G. T. Dowling	Nawab of Pataudi jun.	3	1	1	1
1975-76*N*	G. M. Turner	B. S. Bedi[3]	3	1	1	1
1976-77*I*	G. M. Turner	B. S. Bedi	3	0	2	1
1980-81*N*	G. P. Howarth	S. M. Gavaskar	3	1	0	2
1988-89*I*	J. G. Wright	D. B. Vengsarkar	3	1	2	0
1989-90*N*	J. G. Wright	M. Azharuddin	3	1	0	2
1993-94*N*	K. R. Rutherford	M. Azharuddin	1	0	0	1
1995-96*I*	L. K. Germon	M. Azharuddin	3	0	1	2
	In India		21	2	9	10
	In New Zealand		14	4	4	6
	Totals		35	6	13	16

I Played in India. N Played in New Zealand.

Notes: The following deputised for the official touring captain or were appointed by the home authority for a minor proportion of the series:
[1]Ghulam Ahmed (First). [2]B. W. Sinclair (First). [3]S. M. Gavaskar (First).

HIGHEST INNINGS TOTALS

For New Zealand in New Zealand: 502 at Christchurch 1967-68
in India: 462-9 dec. at Calcutta 1964-65

For India in New Zealand: 482 at Auckland 1989-90
in India: 537-3 dec. at Madras 1955-56

LOWEST INNINGS TOTALS

For New Zealand in New Zealand: 100 at Wellington 1980-81
in India: 124 at Hyderabad 1988-89

For India in New Zealand: 81 at Wellington 1975-76
in India: 88 at Bombay 1964-65

INDIVIDUAL HUNDREDS

For New Zealand (21)

M. D. Crowe (1)
113 Auckland ... 1989-90
G. T. Dowling (3)
129 Bombay 1964-65
143 Dunedin 1967-68
239 Christchurch. 1967-68
J. W. Guy (1)
102† Hyderabad .. 1955-56
G. P. Howarth (1)
137* Wellington .. 1980-81
A. H. Jones (1)
170* Auckland ... 1989-90
J. M. Parker (1)
104 Bombay 1976-77
J. F. Reid (1)
123* Christchurch. 1980-81
J. R. Reid (2)
119* Delhi....... 1955-56
120 Calcutta 1955-56
I. D. S. Smith (1)
173 Auckland ... 1989-90
B. Sutcliffe (3)
137*† Hyderabad .. 1955-56
230* Delhi....... 1955-56
151* Calcutta 1964-65
B. R. Taylor (1)
105† Calcutta 1964-65
G. M. Turner (2)
117 Christchurch. 1975-76
113 Kanpur..... 1976-77
J. G. Wright (3)
110 Auckland ... 1980-81
185 Christchurch. 1989-90
113* Napier 1989-90

For India (22)

S. Amarnath (1)
124† Auckland ... 1975-76
M. Azharuddin (1)
192 Auckland ... 1989-90
C. G. Borde (1)
109 Bombay 1964-65
S. M. Gavaskar (2)
116† Auckland ... 1975-76
119 Bombay 1976-77
A. G. Kripal Singh (1)
100*† Hyderabad .. 1955-56
V. L. Manjrekar (3)
118† Hyderabad .. 1955-56
177 Delhi....... 1955-56
102* Madras 1964-65
V. Mankad (2)
223 Bombay 1955-56
231 Madras 1955-56
Nawab of Pataudi jun. (2)
153 Calcutta 1964-65
113 Delhi....... 1964-65
G. S. Ramchand (1)
106* Calcutta 1955-56
Pankaj Roy (2)
100 Calcutta 1955-56
173 Madras 1955-56
D. N. Sardesai (2)
200* Bombay 1964-65
106 Delhi....... 1964-65
N. S. Sidhu (1)
116† Bangalore ... 1988-89
P. R. Umrigar (1)
223† Hyderabad .. 1955-56
G. R. Viswanath (1)
103* Kanpur..... 1976-77
A. L. Wadekar (1)
143 Wellington .. 1967-68

† *Signifies hundred on first appearance in New Zealand–India Tests. B. R. Taylor provides the only instance for New Zealand of a player scoring his maiden hundred in first-class cricket in his first Test.*

RECORD PARTNERSHIPS FOR EACH WICKET

For New Zealand

149	for 1st	T. J. Franklin and J. G. Wright at Napier	1989-90
155	for 2nd	G. T. Dowling and B. E. Congdon at Dunedin	1967-68
222*	for 3rd	B. Sutcliffe and J. R. Reid at Delhi	1955-56
125	for 4th	J. G. Wright and M. J. Greatbatch at Christchurch	1989-90
119	for 5th	G. T. Dowling and K. Thomson at Christchurch	1967-68
87	for 6th	J. W. Guy and A. R. MacGibbon at Hyderabad	1955-56
163	for 7th	B. Sutcliffe and B. R. Taylor at Calcutta	1964-65
103	for 8th	R. J. Hadlee and I. D. S. Smith at Auckland	1989-90
136	for 9th†	I. D. S. Smith and M. C. Snedden at Auckland	1989-90
61	for 10th	J. T. Ward and R. O. Collinge at Madras	1964-65

For India

413	for 1st†	V. Mankad and Pankaj Roy at Madras	1955-56
204	for 2nd	S. M. Gavaskar and S. Amarnath at Auckland	1975-76
238	for 3rd	P. R. Umrigar and V. L. Manjrekar at Hyderabad	1955-56
171	for 4th	P. R. Umrigar and A. G. Kripal Singh at Hyderabad	1955-56
127	for 5th	V. L. Manjrekar and G. S. Ramchand at Delhi	1955-56
193*	for 6th	D. N. Sardesai and Hanumant Singh at Bombay	1964-65
128	for 7th	S. R. Tendulkar and K. S. More at Napier	1989-90
143	for 8th†	R. G. Nadkarni and F. M. Engineer at Madras	1964-65
105	for 9th	S. M. H. Kirmani and B. S. Bedi at Bombay	1976-77
		S. M. H. Kirmani and N. S. Yadav at Auckland	1980-81
57	for 10th	R. B. Desai and B. S. Bedi at Dunedin	1967-68

† *Denotes record partnership against all countries.*

TEN WICKETS OR MORE IN A MATCH

For New Zealand (2)

11-58 (4-35, 7-23)	R. J. Hadlee, Wellington	1975-76
10-88 (6-49, 4-39)	R. J. Hadlee, Bombay	1988-89

For India (2)

11-140 (3-64, 8-76)	E. A. S. Prasanna, Auckland	1975-76
12-152 (8-72, 4-80)	S. Venkataraghavan, Delhi	1964-65

NEW ZEALAND v PAKISTAN

	Captains					
Season	*New Zealand*	*Pakistan*	*T*	*NZ*	*P*	*D*
1955-56*P*	H. B. Cave	A. H. Kardar	3	0	2	1
1964-65*N*	J. R. Reid	Hanif Mohammad	3	0	0	3
1964-65*P*	J. R. Reid	Hanif Mohammad	3	0	2	1
1969-70*P*	G. T. Dowling	Intikhab Alam	3	1	0	2
1972-73*N*	B. E. Congdon	Intikhab Alam	3	0	1	2
1976-77*P*	G. M. Turner[1]	Mushtaq Mohammad	3	0	2	1
1978-79*N*	M. G. Burgess	Mushtaq Mohammad	3	0	1	2
1984-85*P*	J. V. Coney	Zaheer Abbas	3	0	2	1
1984-85*N*	G. P. Howarth	Javed Miandad	3	2	0	1
1988-89*N*†	J. G. Wright	Imran Khan	2	0	0	2
1990-91*P*	M. D. Crowe	Javed Miandad	3	0	3	0
1992-93*N*	K. R. Rutherford	Javed Miandad	1	0	1	0
1993-94*N*	K. R. Rutherford	Salim Malik	3	1	2	0
1995-96*N*	L. K. Germon	Wasim Akram	1	0	1	0
	In Pakistan		18	1	11	6
	In New Zealand		19	3	6	10
	Totals		37	4	17	16

N Played in New Zealand. P Played in Pakistan.
† *The First Test at Dunedin was abandoned without a ball being bowled and is excluded.*

Note: The following deputised for the official touring captain:
[1]J. M. Parker (Third).

HIGHEST INNINGS TOTALS

For New Zealand	in New Zealand: 492 at Wellington	1984-85
	in Pakistan: 482-6 dec. at Lahore	1964-65
For Pakistan	in New Zealand: 616-5 dec. at Auckland	1988-89
	in Pakistan: 565-9 dec. at Karachi	1976-77

LOWEST INNINGS TOTALS

For New Zealand	in New Zealand: 93 at Hamilton	1992-93
	in Pakistan: 70 at Dacca	1955-56
For Pakistan	in New Zealand: 169 at Auckland	1984-85
	in Pakistan: 102 at Faisalabad	1990-91

INDIVIDUAL HUNDREDS

For New Zealand (21)

M. G. Burgess (2)
119* Dacca 1969-70
111 Lahore 1976-77
J. V. Coney (1)
111* Dunedin 1984-85
M. D. Crowe (2)
174 Wellington 1988-89
108* Lahore 1990-91
B. A. Edgar (1)
129† Christchurch 1978-79
M. J. Greatbatch (1)
133 Hamilton 1992-93
B. F. Hastings (1)
110 Auckland 1972-73
G. P. Howarth (1)
114 Napier 1978-79
W. K. Lees (1)
152 Karachi 1976-77
S. N. McGregor (1)
111 Lahore 1955-56
R. E. Redmond (1)
107† Auckland 1972-73
J. F. Reid (3)
106 Hyderabad 1984-85
148 Wellington 1984-85
158* Auckland 1984-85
J. R. Reid (1)
128 Karachi 1964-65
B. W. Sinclair (1)
130 Lahore 1964-65
S. A. Thomson (1)
120* Christchurch 1993-94
G. M. Turner (1)
110† Dacca 1969-70
J. G. Wright (1)
107 Karachi 1984-85
B. A. Young (1)
120 Christchurch 1993-94

For Pakistan (38)

Asif Iqbal (3)
175 Dunedin 1972-73
166 Lahore 1976-77
104 Napier 1978-79
Basit Ali (1)
103 Christchurch 1993-94
Hanif Mohammad (3)
103 Dacca 1955-56
100* Christchurch. 1964-65
203* Lahore 1964-65
Ijaz Ahmed, sen. (1)
103 Christchurch. 1995-96
Imtiaz Ahmed (1)
209 Lahore 1955-56
Inzamam-ul-Haq (1)
135* Wellington .. 1993-94
Javed Miandad (7)
163† Lahore 1976-77
206 Karachi 1976-77
160* Christchurch. 1978-79
104 } Hyderabad .. 1984-85
103* }
118 Wellington .. 1988-89
271 Auckland ... 1988-89
Majid Khan (3)
110 Auckland ... 1972-73
112 Karachi 1976-77
119* Napier 1978-79
Mohammad Ilyas (1)
126 Karachi 1964-65
Mudassar Nazar (1)
106 Hyderabad .. 1984-85
Mushtaq Mohammad (3)
201 Dunedin 1972-73
101 Hyderabad .. 1976-77
107 Karachi 1976-77
Sadiq Mohammad (2)
166 Wellington .. 1972-73
103* Hyderabad .. 1976-77
Saeed Ahmed (1)
172 Karachi 1964-65
Saeed Anwar (1)
169 Wellington .. 1993-94
Salim Malik (2)
119* Karachi 1984-85
140 Wellington .. 1993-94
Shoaib Mohammad (5)
163 Wellington .. 1988-89
112 Auckland ... 1988-89
203* Karachi 1990-91
105 Lahore 1990-91
142 Faisalabad .. 1990-91
Waqar Hassan (1)
189 Lahore 1955-56
Zaheer Abbas (1)
135 Auckland ... 1978-79

† *Signifies hundred on first appearance in New Zealand–Pakistan Tests.*

Notes: Mushtaq and Sadiq Mohammad, at Hyderabad in 1976-77, provide the fourth instance in Test matches, after the Chappells (thrice), of brothers each scoring hundreds in the same innings.

RECORD PARTNERSHIPS FOR EACH WICKET

For New Zealand

159 for 1st	R. E. Redmond and G. M. Turner at Auckland	1972-73
195 for 2nd	J. G. Wright and G. P. Howarth at Napier	1978-79
178 for 3rd	B. W. Sinclair and J. R. Reid at Lahore	1964-65
128 for 4th	B. F. Hastings and M. G. Burgess at Wellington	1972-73
183 for 5th†	M. G. Burgess and R. W. Anderson at Lahore	1976-77
145 for 6th	J. F. Reid and R. J. Hadlee at Wellington	1984-85
186 for 7th†	W. K. Lees and R. J. Hadlee at Karachi	1976-77
100 for 8th	B. W. Yuile and D. R. Hadlee at Karachi	1969-70
96 for 9th	M. G. Burgess and R. S. Cunis at Dacca	1969-70
151 for 10th†	B. F. Hastings and R. O. Collinge at Auckland	1972-73

For Pakistan

172 for 1st	Ramiz Raja and Shoaib Mohammad at Karachi	1990-91
140 for 2nd	Ijaz Ahmed, sen. and Inzamam-ul-Haq at Christchurch	1995-96
248 for 3rd	Shoaib Mohammad and Javed Miandad at Auckland	1988-89
350 for 4th†	Mushtaq Mohammad and Asif Iqbal at Dunedin	1972-73
281 for 5th†	Javed Miandad and Asif Iqbal at Lahore	1976-77
217 for 6th†	Hanif Mohammad and Majid Khan at Lahore	1964-65
308 for 7th†	Waqar Hassan and Imtiaz Ahmed at Lahore	1955-56
89 for 8th	Anil Dalpat and Iqbal Qasim at Karachi	1984-85
52 for 9th	Intikhab Alam and Arif Butt at Auckland	1964-65
65 for 10th	Salah-ud-Din and Mohammad Farooq at Rawalpindi	1964-65

† *Denotes record partnership against all countries.*

TEN WICKETS OR MORE IN A MATCH

For New Zealand (1)

11-152 (7-52, 4-100)	C. Pringle, Faisalabad	1990-91

For Pakistan (8)

10-182 (5-91, 5-91)	Intikhab Alam, Dacca	1969-70
11-130 (7-52, 4-78)	Intikhab Alam, Dunedin	1972-73
10-171 (3-115, 7-56)	Mushtaq Ahmed, Christchurch	1995-96
10-106 (3-20, 7-86)	Waqar Younis, Lahore	1990-91
12-130 (7-76, 5-54)	Waqar Younis, Faisalabad	1990-91
10-128 (5-56, 5-72)	Wasim Akram, Dunedin	1984-85
11-179 (4-60, 7-119)	Wasim Akram, Wellington	1993-94
11-79 (5-37, 6-42)†	Zulfiqar Ahmed, Karachi	1955-56

† *Signifies ten wickets or more on first appearance in New Zealand–Pakistan Tests.*

Note: Waqar Younis's performances were in successive matches.

NEW ZEALAND v SRI LANKA

	Captains					
Season	*New Zealand*	*Sri Lanka*	*T*	*NZ*	*SL*	*D*
1982-83*N*	G. P. Howarth	D. S. de Silva	2	2	0	0
1983-84*S*	G. P. Howarth	L. R. D. Mendis	3	2	0	1
1986-87*S*†	J. J. Crowe	L. R. D. Mendis	1	0	0	1
1990-91*N*	M. D. Crowe[1]	A. Ranatunga	3	0	0	3
1992-93*S*	M. D. Crowe	A. Ranatunga	2	0	1	1
1994-95*N*	K. R. Rutherford	A. Ranatunga	2	0	1	1
	In New Zealand		7	2	1	4
	In Sri Lanka		6	2	1	3
	Totals		13	4	2	7

N Played in New Zealand. S Played in Sri Lanka.

† *The Second and Third Tests were cancelled owing to civil disturbances.*

Note: The following was appointed by the home authority for only a minor proportion of the series:

[1]I. D. S. Smith (Third).

HIGHEST INNINGS TOTALS

For New Zealand	in New Zealand: 671-4 at Wellington	1990-91
	in Sri Lanka: 459 at Colombo (CCC)	1983-84
For Sri Lanka	in New Zealand: 497 at Wellington	1990-91
	in Sri Lanka: 397-9 dec. at Colombo (CCC)	1986-87

LOWEST INNINGS TOTALS

For New Zealand	in New Zealand: 109 at Napier	1994-95
	in Sri Lanka: 102 at Colombo (SSC)	1992-93
For Sri Lanka	in New Zealand: 93 at Wellington	1982-83
	in Sri Lanka: 97 at Kandy	1983-84

INDIVIDUAL HUNDREDS

For New Zealand (10)

J. J. Crowe (1)
120* Colombo (CCC) 1986-87
M. D. Crowe (2)
299 Wellington .. 1990-91
107 Colombo (SSC) 1992-93

R. J. Hadlee (1)
151* Colombo (CCC) 1986-87
A. H. Jones (3)
186 Wellington .. 1990-91
122 }
100* } Hamilton ... 1990-91

J. F. Reid (1)
180 Colombo (CCC) 1983-84
K. R. Rutherford (1)
105 Moratuwa ... 1992-93
J. G. Wright (1)
101 Hamilton ... 1990-91

For Sri Lanka (10)

P. A. de Silva (2)
267† Wellington .. 1990-91
123 Auckland ... 1990-91
R. L. Dias (1)
108† Colombo (SSC) 1983-84

A. P. Gurusinha (3)
119 }
102 } Hamilton ... 1990-91
127 Dunedin 1994-95
D. S. B. P. Kuruppu (1)
201*† Colombo (CCC) 1986-87

R. S. Mahanama (2)
153 Moratuwa ... 1992-93
109 Colombo (SSC) 1992-93
H. P. Tillekeratne (1)
108 Dunedin 1994-95

† *Signifies hundred on first appearance in New Zealand–Sri Lanka Tests.*

Note: A. P. Gurusinha and A. H. Jones at Hamilton in 1990-91 provided the second instance of a player on each side hitting two separate hundreds in a Test match.

RECORD PARTNERSHIPS FOR EACH WICKET

For New Zealand

161	for 1st	T. J. Franklin and J. G. Wright at Hamilton	1990-91
76	for 2nd	J. G. Wright and A. H. Jones at Auckland	1990-91
467	for 3rd†‡	A. H. Jones and M. D. Crowe at Wellington	1990-91
82	for 4th	J. F. Reid and S. L. Boock at Colombo (CCC)	1983-84
151	for 5th	K. R. Rutherford and C. Z. Harris at Moratuwa	1992-93
246*	for 6th†	J. J. Crowe and R. J. Hadlee at Colombo (CCC)	1986-87
47	for 7th	D. N. Patel and M. L. Su'a at Dunedin	1994-95
79	for 8th	J. V. Coney and W. K. Lees at Christchurch	1982-83
42	for 9th	W. K. Lees and M. C. Snedden at Christchurch	1982-83
52	for 10th	W. K. Lees and E. J. Chatfield at Christchurch	1982-83

For Sri Lanka

102	for 1st	R. S. Mahanama and U. C. Hathurusinghe at Colombo (SSC)	1992-93
138	for 2nd	R. S. Mahanama and A. P. Gurusinha at Moratuwa	1992-93
159*	for 3rd[1]	S. Wettimuny and R. L. Dias at Colombo (SSC)	1983-84
192	for 4th	A. P. Gurusinha and H. P. Tillekeratne at Dunedin	1994-95
130	for 5th	R. S. Madugalle and D. S. de Silva at Wellington	1982-83
109*	for 6th[2]	R. S. Madugalle and A. Ranatunga at Colombo (CCC)	1983-84
89	for 7th	C. I. Dunusinghe and W. P. U. J. C. Vaas at Napier	1994-95
69	for 8th†	H. P. Tillekeratne and S. D. Anurasiri at Colombo (SSC)	1992-93
31	for 9th	G. F. Labrooy and R. J. Ratnayake at Auckland	1990-91
31	for 9th	S. T. Jayasuriya and R. J. Ratnayake at Auckland	1990-91
60	for 10th	V. B. John and A. M. J. G. Amerasinghe at Kandy	1983-84

† *Denotes record partnership against all countries.*
‡ *Record third-wicket partnership in first-class cricket.*
[1] *163 runs were added for this wicket in two separate partnerships: S. Wettimuny retired hurt and was replaced by L. R. D. Mendis when 159 had been added.*
[2] *119 runs were added for this wicket in two separate partnerships: R. S. Madugalle retired hurt and was replaced by D. S. de Silva when 109 had been added.*

TEN WICKETS OR MORE IN A MATCH

For New Zealand (1)

10-102 (5-73, 5-29) R. J. Hadlee, Colombo (CCC) 1983-84

For Sri Lanka (1)

10-90 (5-47, 5-43)† W. P. U. J. C. Vaas, Napier 1994-95

† *Signifies ten wickets or more on first appearance in New Zealand–Sri Lanka Tests.*

NEW ZEALAND v ZIMBABWE

	Captains					
Season	*New Zealand*	*Zimbabwe*	*T*	*NZ*	*Z*	*D*
1992-93*Z*	M. D. Crowe	D. L. Houghton	2	1	0	1
1995-96*N*	L. K. Germon	A. Flower	2	0	0	2
	In New Zealand		2	0	0	2
	In Zimbabwe		2	1	0	1
	Totals		4	1	0	3

NZ Played in New Zealand. Z Played in Zimbabwe.

HIGHEST INNINGS TOTALS

For New Zealand in New Zealand: 441-5 dec. at Auckland 1995-96
in Zimbabwe: 335 at Harare 1992-93

For Zimbabwe in New Zealand: 326 at Auckland 1995-96
in Zimbabwe: 283-9 dec. at Harare 1992-93

LOWEST INNINGS TOTALS

For New Zealand in New Zealand: 251 at Auckland 1995-96
in Zimbabwe: 335 at Harare 1992-93

For Zimbabwe in New Zealand: 196 at Hamilton 1995-96
in Zimbabwe: 137 at Harare 1992-93

INDIVIDUAL HUNDREDS

For New Zealand (4)

C. L. Cairns (1)
120 Auckland ... 1995-96
M. D. Crowe (1)
140 Harare 1992-93
R. T. Latham (1)
119† Bulawayo ... 1992-93
C. M. Spearman (1)
112 Auckland ... 1995-96

For Zimbabwe (2)

K. J. Arnott (1)
101*† Bulawayo ... 1992-93
D. L. Houghton (1)
104* Auckland ... 1995-96

† *Signifies hundred on first appearance in New Zealand–Zimbabwe Tests.*

HUNDRED PARTNERSHIPS

For New Zealand

214 for 1st	C. M. Spearman and R. G. Twose at Auckland	1995-96
116 for 1st	M. J. Greatbatch and R. T. Latham at Bulawayo	1992-93
102 for 1st	M. J. Greatbatch and R. T. Latham at Bulawayo	1992-93
127 for 2nd	R. T. Latham and A. H. Jones at Bulawayo	1992-93
168 for 4th	M. D. Crowe and K. R. Rutherford at Harare	1992-93
166 for 5th	A. C. Parore and C. L. Cairns at Auckland	1995-96
130 for 5th	K. R. Rutherford and D. N. Patel at Harare	1992-93

For Zimbabwe

120 for 1st†	G. W. Flower and S. V. Carlisle at Auckland	1995-96
107 for 2nd	K. J. Arnott and A. D. R. Campbell at Harare	1992-93
105* for 2nd	K. J. Arnott and A. D. R. Campbell at Bulawayo	1992-93

† *Denotes record partnership against all countries.*

BEST MATCH BOWLING ANALYSES

For New Zealand

8-131 (2-81, 6-50) D. N. Patel, Harare 1992-93

For Zimbabwe

7-160 (3-50, 4-110) H. H. Streak, Auckland 1995-96

INDIA v PAKISTAN

	Captains					
Season	*India*	*Pakistan*	*T*	*I*	*P*	*D*
1952-53*I*	L. Amarnath	A. H. Kardar	5	2	1	2
1954-55*P*	V. Mankad	A. H. Kardar	5	0	0	5
1960-61*I*	N. J. Contractor	Fazal Mahmood	5	0	0	5
1978-79*P*	B. S. Bedi	Mushtaq Mohammad	3	0	2	1
1979-80*I*	S. M. Gavaskar[1]	Asif Iqbal	6	2	0	4
1982-83*P*	S. M. Gavaskar	Imran Khan	6	0	3	3
1983-84*I*	Kapil Dev	Zaheer Abbas	3	0	0	3
1984-85*P*	S. M. Gavaskar	Zaheer Abbas	2	0	0	2
1986-87*I*	Kapil Dev	Imran Khan	5	0	1	4
1989-90*P*	K. Srikkanth	Imran Khan	4	0	0	4
	In India		24	4	2	18
	In Pakistan		20	0	5	15
	Totals		44	4	7	33

I Played in India. P Played in Pakistan.

Note: The following was appointed by the home authority for only a minor proportion of the series:

[1]G. R. Viswanath (Sixth).

HIGHEST INNINGS TOTALS

For India in India: 539-9 dec. at Madras 1960-61
in Pakistan: 509 at Lahore 1989-90

For Pakistan in India: 487-9 dec. at Madras 1986-87
in Pakistan: 699-5 at Lahore 1989-90

LOWEST INNINGS TOTALS

For India in India: 106 at Lucknow 1952-53
in Pakistan: 145 at Karachi 1954-55

For Pakistan in India: 116 at Bangalore 1986-87
in Pakistan: 158 at Dacca 1954-55

INDIVIDUAL HUNDREDS

For India (31)

M. Amarnath (4)
109* Lahore 1982-83
120 Lahore 1982-83
103* Karachi 1982-83
101* Lahore 1984-85
M. Azharuddin (3)
141 Calcutta 1986-87
110 Jaipur 1986-87
109 Faisalabad .. 1989-90
C. G. Borde (1)
177* Madras 1960-61
A. D. Gaekwad (1)
201 Jullundur ... 1983-84
S. M. Gavaskar (5)
111 } Karachi 1978-79
137 }
166 Madras 1979-80
127*‡ Faisalabad .. 1982-83
103* Bangalore ... 1983-84
V. S. Hazare (1)
146* Bombay 1952-53
S. V. Manjrekar (2)
113*† Karachi 1989-90
218 Lahore 1989-90
S. M. Patil (1)
127 Faisalabad .. 1984-85
R. J. Shastri (3)
128 Karachi 1982-83
139 Faisalabad .. 1984-85
125 Jaipur 1986-87
R. H. Shodhan (1)
110† Calcutta 1952-53
K. Srikkanth (1)
123 Madras 1986-87
P. R. Umrigar (5)
102 Bombay 1952-53
108 Peshawar ... 1954-55
115 Kanpur 1960-61
117 Madras 1960-61
112 Delhi 1960-61
D. B. Vengsarkar (2)
146* Delhi 1979-80
109 Ahmedabad . 1986-87
G. R. Viswanath (1)
145† Faisalabad .. 1978-79

For Pakistan (41)

Aamer Malik (2)
117 Faisalabad .. 1989-90
113 Lahore 1989-90
Alim-ud-Din (1)
103* Karachi 1954-55
Asif Iqbal (1)
104† Faisalabad .. 1978-79
Hanif Mohammad (2)
142 Bahawalpur . 1954-55
160 Bombay 1960-61
Ijaz Faqih (1)
105† Ahmedabad . 1986-87
Imtiaz Ahmed (1)
135 Madras 1960-61
Imran Khan (3)
117 Faisalabad .. 1982-83
135* Madras 1986-87
109* Karachi 1989-90
Javed Miandad (5)
154*† Faisalabad .. 1978-79
100 Karachi 1978-79
126 Faisalabad .. 1982-83
280* Hyderabad .. 1982-83
145 Lahore 1989-90
Mohsin Khan (1)
101*† Lahore 1982-83
Mudassar Nazar (6)
126 Bangalore ... 1979-80
119 Karachi 1982-83
231 Hyderabad .. 1982-83
152*‡ Lahore 1982-83
152 Karachi 1982-83
199 Faisalabad .. 1984-85
Mushtaq Mohammad (1)
101 Delhi 1960-61
Nazar Mohammad (1)
124*‡ Lucknow ... 1952-53
Qasim Omar (1)
210 Faisalabad .. 1984-85
Ramiz Raja (1)
114 Jaipur 1986-87
Saeed Ahmed (2)
121† Bombay 1960-61
103 Madras 1960-61
Salim Malik (3)
107 Faisalabad .. 1982-83
102* Faisalabad .. 1984-85
102* Karachi 1989-90
Shoaib Mohammad (2)
101 Madras 1986-87
203* Lahore 1989-90
Wasim Raja (1)
125 Jullundur ... 1983-84
Zaheer Abbas (6)
176† Faisalabad .. 1978-79
235* Lahore 1978-79
215 Lahore 1982-83
186 Karachi 1982-83
168 Faisalabad .. 1982-83
168* Lahore 1984-85

† *Signifies hundred on first appearance in India–Pakistan Tests.*
‡ *Carried his bat.*

RECORD PARTNERSHIPS FOR EACH WICKET

For India

200 for 1st	S. M. Gavaskar and K. Srikkanth at Madras	1986-87
135 for 2nd	N. S. Sidhu and S. V. Manjrekar at Karachi	1989-90
190 for 3rd	M. Amarnath and Yashpal Sharma at Lahore	1982-83
186 for 4th	S. V. Manjrekar and R. J. Shastri at Lahore	1989-90
200 for 5th	S. M. Patil and R. J. Shastri at Faisalabad	1984-85
143 for 6th	M. Azharuddin and Kapil Dev at Calcutta	1986-87
155 for 7th	R. M. H. Binny and Madan Lal at Bangalore	1983-84
122 for 8th	S. M. H. Kirmani and Madan Lal at Faisalabad	1982-83
149 for 9th†	P. G. Joshi and R. B. Desai at Bombay	1960-61
109 for 10th†	H. R. Adhikari and Ghulam Ahmed at Delhi	1952-53

For Pakistan

162 for 1st	Hanif Mohammad and Imtiaz Ahmed at Madras	1960-61
250 for 2nd	Mudassar Nazar and Qasim Omar at Faisalabad	1984-85
451 for 3rd†	Mudassar Nazar and Javed Miandad at Hyderabad	1982-83
287 for 4th	Javed Miandad and Zaheer Abbas at Faisalabad	1982-83
213 for 5th	Zaheer Abbas and Mudassar Nazar at Karachi	1982-83
207 for 6th	Salim Malik and Imran Khan at Faisalabad	1982-83
154 for 7th	Imran Khan and Ijaz Faqih at Ahmedabad	1986-87
112 for 8th	Imran Khan and Wasim Akram at Madras	1986-87
60 for 9th	Wasim Bari and Iqbal Qasim at Bangalore	1979-80
104 for 10th	Zulfiqar Ahmed and Amir Elahi at Madras	1952-53

† *Denotes record partnership against all countries.*

TEN WICKETS OR MORE IN A MATCH

For India (3)

11-146 (4-90, 7-56)	Kapil Dev, Madras	1979-80
10-126 (7-27, 3-99)	Maninder Singh, Bangalore	1986-87
13-131 (8-52, 5-79)†	V. Mankad, Delhi	1952-53

For Pakistan (5)

12-94 (5-52, 7-42)	Fazal Mahmood, Lucknow	1952-53
11-79 (3-19, 8-60)	Imran Khan, Karachi	1982-83
11-180 (6-98, 5-82)	Imran Khan, Faisalabad	1982-83
10-175 (4-135, 6-40)	Iqbal Qasim, Bombay	1979-80
11-190 (8-69, 3-121)	Sikander Bakht, Delhi	1979-80

† *Signifies ten wickets or more on first appearance in India–Pakistan Tests.*

INDIA v SRI LANKA

	Captains					
Season	*India*	*Sri Lanka*	*T*	*I*	*SL*	*D*
1982-83*I*	S. M. Gavaskar	B. Warnapura	1	0	0	1
1985-86*S*	Kapil Dev	L. R. D. Mendis	3	0	1	2
1986-87*I*	Kapil Dev	L. R. D. Mendis	3	2	0	1
1990-91*I*	M. Azharuddin	A. Ranatunga	1	1	0	0
1993-94*S*	M. Azharuddin	A. Ranatunga	3	1	0	2
1993-94*I*	M. Azharuddin	A. Ranatunga	3	3	0	0
	In India		8	6	0	2
	In Sri Lanka		6	1	1	4
	Totals		14	7	1	6

I Played in India. S Played in Sri Lanka.

HIGHEST INNINGS TOTALS

For India in India: 676-7 at Kanpur	1986-87
in Sri Lanka: 446 at Colombo (PSS)	1993-94
For Sri Lanka in India: 420 at Kanpur	1986-87
in Sri Lanka: 385 at Colombo (PSS)	1985-86

LOWEST INNINGS TOTALS

For India in India: 288 at Chandigarh	1990-91
in Sri Lanka: 198 at Colombo (PSS)	1985-86
For Sri Lanka in India: 82 at Chandigarh	1990-91
in Sri Lanka: 198 at Kandy	1985-86

INDIVIDUAL HUNDREDS

For India (17)

M. Amarnath (2)
116* Kandy 1985-86
131 Nagpur 1986-87
176 Kanpur 1986-87

V. G. Kambli (2)
125 Colombo (SSC) 1993-94
120 Colombo (PSS) 1993-94

M. Azharuddin (3)
199 Kanpur 1986-87
108 Bangalore ... 1993-94
152 Ahmedabad . 1993-94

S. M. Gavaskar (2)
155† Madras 1982-83

Kapil Dev (1)
163 Kanpur 1986-87

S. M. Patil (1)
114*† Madras 1982-83

N. S. Sidhu (2)
104 Colombo (SSC) 1993-94
124 Lucknow 1993-94

S. R. Tendulkar (2)
104* Colombo (SSC) 1993-94
142 Lucknow 1993-94

D. B. Vengsarkar (2)
153 Nagpur 1986-87
166 Cuttack 1986-87

For Sri Lanka (9)

P. A. de Silva (1)
148 Colombo (PSS) 1993-94

R. L. Dias (1)
106 Kandy 1985-86

R. S. Madugalle (1)
103 Colombo (SSC) 1985-86

R. S. Mahanama (1)
151 Colombo (PSS) 1993-94

L. R. D. Mendis (3)
105, 105 †Madras 1982-83
124 Kandy 1985-86

A. Ranatunga (1)
111 Colombo (SSC) 1985-86

S. A. R. Silva (1)
111 Colombo (PSS) 1985-86

† *Signifies hundred on first appearance in India–Sri Lanka Tests.*

RECORD PARTNERSHIPS FOR EACH WICKET

For India

171	for 1st	M. Prabhakar and N. S. Sidhu at Colombo (SSC)	1993-94
173	for 2nd	S. M. Gavaskar and D. B. Vengsarkar at Madras	1982-83
173	for 3rd	M. Amarnath and D. B. Vengsarkar at Nagpur	1986-87
163	for 4th	S. M. Gavaskar and M. Azharuddin at Kanpur	1986-87
87	for 5th	M. Azharuddin and S. V. Manjrekar at Bangalore	1993-94
272	for 6th	M. Azharuddin and Kapil Dev at Kanpur	1986-87
78*	for 7th	S. M. Patil and Madan Lal at Madras	1982-83
70	for 8th	Kapil Dev and L. Sivaramakrishnan at Colombo (PSS)	1985-86
67	for 9th	M. Azharuddin and R. K. Chauhan at Ahmedabad	1993-94
29	for 10th	Kapil Dev and Chetan Sharma at Colombo (PSS)	1985-86

For Sri Lanka

159	for 1st†	S. Wettimuny and J. R. Ratnayeke at Kanpur	1986-87
95	for 2nd	S. A. R. Silva and R. S. Madugalle at Colombo (PSS)	1985-86
153	for 3rd	R. L. Dias and L. R. D. Mendis at Madras	1982-83
216	for 4th	R. L. Dias and L. R. D. Mendis at Kandy	1985-86
144	for 5th	R. S. Madugalle and A. Ranatunga at Colombo (SSC)	1985-86
89	for 6th	L. R. D. Mendis and A. N. Ranasinghe at Madras	1982-83
77	for 7th	R. S. Madugalle and D. S. de Silva at Madras	1982-83
40*	for 8th	P. A. de Silva and A. L. F. de Mel at Kandy	1985-86
60	for 9th	H. P. Tillekeratne and A. W. R. Madurasinghe at Chandigarh	1990-91
44	for 10th	R. J. Ratnayake and E. A. R. de Silva at Nagpur	1986-87

† *Denotes record partnership against all countries.*

TEN WICKETS OR MORE IN A MATCH

For India (3)

11-128 (4-69, 7-59)	A. Kumble, Lucknow	1993-94
10-107 (3-56, 7-51)	Maninder Singh, Nagpur	1986-87
11-125 (5-38, 6-87)	S. L. V. Raju, Ahmedabad	1993-94

Note: The best match figures by a Sri Lankan bowler are 9-125 (4-76, 5-49) by R. J. Ratnayake against India at Colombo (PSS), 1985-86.

INDIA v ZIMBABWE

	Captains					
Season	*India*	*Zimbabwe*	*T*	*I*	*Z*	*D*
1992-93*Z*	M. Azharuddin	D. L. Houghton	1	0	0	1
1992-93*I*	M. Azharuddin	D. L. Houghton	1	1	0	0
	In India		1	1	0	0
	In Zimbabwe		1	0	0	1
	Totals		2	1	0	1

I Played in India. Z Played in Zimbabwe.

HIGHEST INNINGS TOTALS

For India: 536-7 dec. at Delhi 1992-93

For Zimbabwe: 456 at Harare 1992-93

INDIVIDUAL HUNDREDS

For India (2)

V. G. Kambli (1)
227† Delhi....... 1992-93

S. V. Manjrekar (1)
104† Harare 1992-93

For Zimbabwe (2)

A. Flower (1)
115 Delhi....... 1992-93

D. L. Houghton (1)
121† Harare 1992-93

† *Signifies hundred on first appearance in India–Zimbabwe Tests.*

HUNDRED PARTNERSHIPS

For India

107 for 2nd	N. S. Sidhu and V. G. Kambli at Delhi	1992-93
137 for 3rd	V. G. Kambli and S. R. Tendulkar at Delhi	1992-93
107 for 4th	V. G. Kambli and M. Azharuddin at Delhi	1992-93

For Zimbabwe

100 for 1st	K. J. Arnott and G. W. Flower at Harare	1992-93
192 for 4th	G. W. Flower and A. Flower at Delhi	1992-93
165 for 6th†	D. L. Houghton and A. Flower at Harare	1992-93

† *Denotes record partnership against all countries.*

BEST MATCH BOWLING ANALYSES

For India

8-160 (3-90, 5-70)	A. Kumble, Delhi	1992-93

For Zimbabwe

5-86 (5-86)	A. J. Traicos, Harare	1992-93

PAKISTAN v SRI LANKA

	Captains					
Season	*Pakistan*	*Sri Lanka*	*T*	*P*	*SL*	*D*
1981-82*P*	Javed Miandad	B. Warnapura[1]	3	2	0	1
1985-86*P*	Javed Miandad	L. R. D. Mendis	3	2	0	1
1985-86*S*	Imran Khan	L. R. D. Mendis	3	1	1	1
1991-92*P*	Imran Khan	P. A. de Silva	3	1	0	2
1994-95*S*†	Salim Malik	A. Ranatunga	2	2	0	0
1995-96*P*	Ramiz Raja	A. Ranatunga	3	1	2	0
	In Pakistan		12	6	2	4
	In Sri Lanka		5	3	1	1
	Totals		17	9	3	5

P Played in Pakistan. S Played in Sri Lanka.

† *One Test was cancelled owing to the threat of civil disturbances following a general election.*
Note: The following deputised for the official touring captain:
[1]L. R. D. Mendis (Second).

HIGHEST INNINGS TOTALS

For Pakistan in Pakistan: 555-3 at Faisalabad	1985-86
in Sri Lanka: 390 at Colombo (PSS)	1994-95
For Sri Lanka in Pakistan: 479 at Faisalabad	1985-86
in Sri Lanka: 323-3 at Colombo (PSS)	1985-86

LOWEST INNINGS TOTALS

For Pakistan in Pakistan: 209 at Faisalabad	1995-96
in Sri Lanka: 132 at Colombo (CCC)	1985-86
For Sri Lanka in Pakistan: 149 at Karachi	1981-82
in Sri Lanka: 71 at Kandy	1994-95

INDIVIDUAL HUNDREDS

For Pakistan (11)

Haroon Rashid (1)
153† Karachi 1981-82
Inzamam-ul-Haq (1)
100* Kandy...... 1994-95
Javed Miandad (1)
203* Faisalabad .. 1985-86
Mohsin Khan (1)
129 Lahore 1981-82

Moin Khan (1)
117* Sialkot 1995-96
Qasim Omar (1)
206† Faisalabad .. 1985-86
Ramiz Raja (1)
122 Colombo (PSS)....... 1985-86

Saeed Anwar (1)
136† Colombo (PSS)....... 1994-95
Salim Malik (2)
100*† Karachi 1981-82
101 Sialkot 1991-92
Zaheer Abbas (1)
134† Lahore 1981-82

For Sri Lanka (9)

P. A. de Silva (4)
122† Faisalabad .. 1985-86
105 Karachi 1985-86
127 Colombo (PSS)....... 1994-95
105 Faisalabad .. 1995-96

R. L. Dias (1)
109 Lahore 1981-82
A. P. Gurusinha (1)
116* Colombo (PSS)....... 1985-86

A. Ranatunga (1)
135* Colombo (PSS)....... 1985-86
H. P. Tillekeratne (1)
157 Faisalabad .. 1995-96
S. Wettimuny (1)
157 Faisalabad .. 1981-82

† *Signifies hundred on first appearance in Pakistan–Sri Lanka Tests.*

RECORD PARTNERSHIPS FOR EACH WICKET

For Pakistan

128 for 1st	Ramiz Raja and Shoaib Mohammad at Sialkot	1991-92
	Saeed Anwar and Aamir Sohail at Colombo (PSS)	1994-95
151 for 2nd	Mohsin Khan and Majid Khan at Lahore	1981-82
397 for 3rd	Qasim Omar and Javed Miandad at Faisalabad	1985-86
162 for 4th	Salim Malik and Javed Miandad at Karachi	1981-82
132 for 5th	Salim Malik and Imran Khan at Sialkot	1991-92
100 for 6th	Zaheer Abbas and Imran Khan at Lahore	1981-82
104 for 7th	Haroon Rashid and Tahir Naqqash at Karachi	1981-82
33 for 8th	Inzamam-ul-Haq and Wasim Akram at Kandy	1994-95
127 for 9th	Haroon Rashid and Rashid Khan at Karachi	1981-82
65 for 10th	Moin Khan and Aamir Nazir at Sialkot	1995-96

For Sri Lanka

81 for 1st	R. S. Mahanama and U. C. Hathurusinghe at Faisalabad	1991-92
217 for 2nd†	S. Wettimuny and R. L. Dias at Faisalabad	1981-82
176 for 3rd†	U. C. Hathurusinghe and P. A. de Silva at Faisalabad	1995-96
240* for 4th†	A. P. Gurusinha and A. Ranatunga at Colombo (PSS)	1985-86
125 for 5th	A. Ranatunga and H. P. Tillekeratne at Peshawar	1995-96
121 for 6th	A. Ranatunga and P. A. de Silva at Faisalabad	1985-86
131 for 7th	H. P. Tillekeratne and R. S. Kalpage at Kandy	1994-95
65 for 8th	H. D. P. K. Dharmasena and W. P. U. J. C. Vaas at Faisalabad	1995-96
52 for 9th	P. A. de Silva and R. J. Ratnayake at Faisalabad	1985-86
36 for 10th	R. J. Ratnayake and R. G. C. E. Wijesuriya at Faisalabad	1985-86

† *Denotes record partnership against all countries.*

TEN WICKETS OR MORE IN A MATCH

For Pakistan (2)

14-116 (8-58, 6-58)	Imran Khan, Lahore	1981-82
11-119 (6-34, 5-85)	Waqar Younis, Kandy	1994-95

Note: The best match figures by a Sri Lankan bowler are 9-162 (4-103, 5-59), D. S. de Silva at Faisalabad, 1981-82.

PAKISTAN v ZIMBABWE

	Captains					
Season / *Pakistan*		*Zimbabwe*	*T*	*P*	*Z*	*D*
1993-94*P* Wasim Akram[1]		A. Flower	3	2	0	1
1994-95*Z* Salim Malik		A. Flower	3	2	1	0
	In Pakistan		3	2	0	1
	In Zimbabwe		3	2	1	0
	Totals		6	4	1	1

P Played in Pakistan. Z Played in Zimbabwe.

Note: The following was appointed by the home authority for only a minor proportion of the series:

[1]Waqar Younis (First).

HIGHEST INNINGS TOTALS

For Pakistan in Pakistan: 423-8 dec. at Karachi (DS) 1993-94
in Zimbabwe: 322 at Harare 1994-95

For Zimbabwe in Pakistan: 289 at Karachi (DS) 1993-94
in Zimbabwe: 544-4 dec. at Harare 1994-95

LOWEST INNINGS TOTALS

For Pakistan in Pakistan: 147 at Lahore 1993-94
in Zimbabwe: 158 at Harare 1994-95

For Zimbabwe in Pakistan: 134 at Karachi (DS) 1993-94
in Zimbabwe: 139 at Harare 1994-95

INDIVIDUAL HUNDREDS

For Pakistan (1)

Inzamam-ul-Haq (1)
101 Harare 1994-95

For Zimbabwe (3)

A. Flower (1)
156 Harare 1994-95

G. W. Flower (1)
201* Harare 1994-95

G. J. Whittall (1)
113* Harare 1994-95

RECORD PARTNERSHIPS FOR EACH WICKET

For Pakistan

95	for 1st	Aamir Sohail and Shoaib Mohammad at Karachi (DS)	1993-94
118*	for 2nd	Shoaib Mohammad and Asif Mujtaba at Lahore	1993-94
83	for 3rd	Shoaib Mohammad and Javed Miandad at Karachi (DS)	1993-94
116	for 4th	Inzamam-ul-Haq and Ijaz Ahmed, sen. at Harare	1994-95
76	for 5th	Ijaz Ahmed, sen. and Inzamam-ul-Haq at Harare	1994-95
96	for 6th	Inzamam-ul-Haq and Rashid Latif at Harare	1994-95
120	for 7th	Ijaz Ahmed, sen. and Inzamam-ul-Haq at Harare	1994-95
46	for 8th	Inzamam-ul-Haq and Wasim Akram at Harare	1994-95
60*	for 9th	Rashid Latif and Tausif Ahmed at Karachi (DS)	1993-94
28	for 10th	Inzamam-ul-Haq and Aamir Nazir at Harare	1994-95

For Zimbabwe

20	for 1st	G. W. Flower and S. V. Carlisle at Harare	1994-95
135	for 2nd†	M. H. Dekker and A. D. R. Campbell at Rawalpindi	1993-94
61	for 3rd	A. D. R. Campbell and D. L. Houghton at Karachi (DS)	1993-94
269	for 4th†	G. W. Flower and A. Flower at Harare	1994-95
233*	for 5th†	G. W. Flower and G. J. Whittall at Harare	1994-95
72	for 6th	M. H. Dekker and G. J. Whittall at Rawalpindi	1993-94
48	for 7th	A. D. R. Campbell and P. A. Strang at Bulawayo	1994-95
46	for 8th	A. Flower and D. H. Brain at Lahore	1993-94
40	for 9th	P. A. Strang and D. H. Brain at Harare	1994-95
29	for 10th	E. A. Brandes and S. G. Peall at Rawalpindi	1993-94

† *Denotes record partnership against all countries.*

TEN WICKETS OR MORE IN A MATCH

For Pakistan (1)

13-135 (7-91, 6-44)†	Waqar Younis, Karachi (DS)	1993-94

Note: The best match figures for Zimbabwe are 9-105 (6-90, 3-15) by H. H. Streak at Harare, 1994-95.

† *Signifies ten wickets or more on first appearance in Pakistan–Zimbabwe Tests.*

SRI LANKA v ZIMBABWE

	Captains					
Season	*Sri Lanka*	*Zimbabwe*	*T*	*SL*	*Z*	*D*
1994-95Z	A. Ranatunga	A. Flower	3	0	0	3

Z Played in Zimbabwe.

HIGHEST INNINGS TOTALS

For Sri Lanka: 402 at Harare	1994-95
For Zimbabwe: 462-9 dec. at Bulawayo	1994-95

LOWEST INNINGS TOTALS

For Sri Lanka: 218 at Bulawayo	1994-95
For Zimbabwe: 375 at Harare	1994-95

INDIVIDUAL HUNDREDS

For Sri Lanka (4)

A. P. Gurusinha (1)
128† Harare 1994-95

S. Ranatunga (2)
118† Harare 1994-95
100* Bulawayo ... 1994-95

H. P. Tillekeratne (1)
116 Harare 1994-95

For Zimbabwe (2)

D. L. Houghton (2)
266 Bulawayo ... 1994-95
142 Harare 1994-95

† *Signifies hundred on first appearance in Sri Lanka–Zimbabwe Tests.*

HUNDRED PARTNERSHIPS

For Sri Lanka

217 for 2nd†	A. P. Gurusinha and S. Ranatunga at Harare	1994-95

For Zimbabwe

113 for 1st	G. W. Flower and M. H. Dekker at Harare	1994-95
194 for 3rd†	A. D. R. Campbell and D. L. Houghton at Harare	1994-95
121 for 4th	D. L. Houghton and A. Flower at Bulawayo	1994-95
100 for 6th	D. L. Houghton and W. R. James at Bulawayo	1994-95

† *Denotes record partnership against all countries.*

BEST MATCH BOWLING ANALYSES

For Sri Lanka

7-116 (7-116)	K. R. Pushpakumara, Harare	1994-95

For Zimbabwe

5-129 (4-97, 1-32)	H. H. Streak, Harare	1994-95

TEST MATCH GROUNDS

In Chronological Sequence

	City and Ground	*First Test Match*		*Tests*
1	Melbourne, Melbourne Cricket Ground	March 15, 1877	A v E	88
2	London, Kennington Oval	September 6, 1880	E v A	79
3	Sydney, Sydney Cricket Ground (No. 1)	February 17, 1882	A v E	82
4	Manchester, Old Trafford	July 11, 1884	E v A	62

	City and Ground	*First Test Match*		*Tests*
5	London, Lord's	July 21, 1884	E v A	95
6	Adelaide, Adelaide Oval	December 12, 1884	A v E	54
7	Port Elizabeth, St George's Park	March 12, 1889	SA v E	14
8	Cape Town, Newlands	March 25, 1889	SA v E	28
9	Johannesburg, Old Wanderers	March 2, 1896	SA v E	22
	Now the site of Johannesburg Railway Station.			
10	Nottingham, Trent Bridge	June 1, 1899	E v A	44
11	Leeds, Headingley	June 29, 1899	E v A	58
12	Birmingham, Edgbaston	May 29, 1902	E v A	32
13	Sheffield, Bramall Lane	July 3, 1902	E v A	1
	Sheffield United Football Club have built a stand over the cricket pitch.			
14	Durban, Lord's	January 21, 1910	SA v E	4
	Ground destroyed and built on.			
15	Durban, Kingsmead	January 18, 1923	SA v E	23
16	Brisbane, Exhibition Ground	November 30, 1928	A v E	2
	No longer used for cricket.			
17	Christchurch, Lancaster Park	January 10, 1930	NZ v E	34
18	Bridgetown, Kensington Oval	January 11, 1930	WI v E	32
19	Wellington, Basin Reserve	January 24, 1930	NZ v E	30
20	Port-of-Spain, Queen's Park Oval	February 1, 1930	WI v E	44
21	Auckland, Eden Park	February 17, 1930	NZ v E	38
22	Georgetown, Bourda	February 21, 1930	WI v E	23
23	Kingston, Sabina Park	April 3, 1930	WI v E	31
24	Brisbane, Woolloongabba	November 27, 1931	A v SA	38
25	Bombay, Gymkhana Ground	December 15, 1933	I v E	1
	No longer used for first-class cricket.			
26	Calcutta, Eden Gardens	January 5, 1934	I v E	27
27	Madras, Chepauk (Chidambaram Stadium)	February 10, 1934	I v E	22
28	Delhi, Feroz Shah Kotla	November 10, 1948	I v WI	23
29	Bombay, Brabourne Stadium	December 9, 1948	I v WI	17
	Rarely used for first-class cricket.			
30	Johannesburg, Ellis Park	December 27, 1948	SA v E	6
	Mainly a rugby stadium, no longer used for cricket.			
31	Kanpur, Green Park (Modi Stadium)	January 12, 1952	I v E	16
32	Lucknow, University Ground	October 25, 1952	I v P	1
	Ground destroyed, now partly under a river bed.			
33	Dacca, Dacca Stadium	January 1, 1955	P v I	7
	Ceased staging Tests after East Pakistan seceded and became Bangladesh.			
34	Bahawalpur, Dring (now Bahawal) Stadium	January 15, 1955	P v I	1
	Still used for first-class cricket.			
35	Lahore, Lawrence Gardens (Bagh-i-Jinnah)	January 29, 1955	P v I	3
	Still used for club and occasional first-class matches.			
36	Peshawar, Services Ground	February 13, 1955	P v I	1
	Superseded by new stadium.			
37	Karachi, National Stadium	February 26, 1955	P v I	30
38	Dunedin, Carisbrook	March 11, 1955	NZ v E	9
39	Hyderabad, Fateh Maidan (Lal Bahadur Stadium)	November 19, 1955	I v NZ	3
40	Madras, Corporation Stadium	January 6, 1956	I v NZ	9
	Superseded by rebuilt Chepauk Stadium.			
41	Johannesburg, Wanderers	December 24, 1956	SA v E	16
42	Lahore, Gaddafi Stadium	November 21, 1959	P v A	27
43	Rawalpindi, Pindi Club Ground	March 27, 1965	P v NZ	1
	Superseded by new stadium.			
44	Nagpur, Vidarbha C.A. Ground	October 3, 1969	I v NZ	4
45	Perth, Western Australian C.A. Ground	December 11, 1970	A v E	23
46	Hyderabad, Niaz Stadium	March 16, 1973	P v E	5
47	Bangalore, Karnataka State C.A. Ground (Chinnaswamy Stadium)	November 22, 1974	I v WI	11
48	Bombay, Wankhede Stadium	January 23, 1975	I v WI	15

	City and Ground	*First Test Match*		*Tests*
49	Faisalabad, Iqbal Stadium	October 16, 1978	P v I	17
50	Napier, McLean Park	February 16, 1979	NZ v P	3
51	Multan, Ibn-e-Qasim Bagh Stadium	December 30, 1980	P v WI	1
52	St John's (Antigua), Recreation Ground	March 27, 1981	WI v E	10
53	Colombo, P. Saravanamuttu Stadium	February 17, 1982	SL v E	6
54	Kandy, Asgiriya Stadium	April 22, 1983	SL v A	6
55	Jullundur, Burlton Park	September 24, 1983	I v P	1
56	Ahmedabad, Gujarat Stadium	November 12, 1983	I v WI	3
57	Colombo, Sinhalese Sports Club Ground	March 16, 1984	SL v NZ	7
58	Colombo, Colombo Cricket Club Ground	March 24, 1984	SL v NZ	3
59	Sialkot, Jinnah Stadium	October 27, 1985	P v SL	4
60	Cuttack, Barabati Stadium	January 4, 1987	I v SL	2
61	Jaipur, Sawai Mansingh Stadium	February 21, 1987	I v P	1
62	Hobart, Bellerive Oval	December 16, 1989	A v SL	3
63	Chandigarh, Sector 16 Stadium	November 23, 1990	I v SL	1
	Superseded by Mohali ground			
64	Hamilton, Trust Bank (Seddon) Park	February 22, 1991	NZ v SL	4
65	Gujranwala, Municipal Stadium	December 20, 1991	P v SL	1
66	Colombo, R. Premadasa (Khettarama) Stadium	August 28, 1992	SL v A	1
67	Moratuwa, Tyronne Fernando Stadium	September 8, 1992	SL v A	4
68	Harare, Harare Sports Club	October 18, 1992	Z v I	7
69	Bulawayo, Bulawayo Athletic Club	November 1, 1992	Z v NZ	1
	Superseded by Queens Sports Club ground.			
70	Karachi, Defence Stadium	December 1, 1993	P v Z	2
71	Rawalpindi, Rawalpindi Cricket Stadium	December 9, 1993	P v Z	2
72	Lucknow, K. D. "Babu" Singh Stadium	January 18, 1994	I v SL	1
73	Bulawayo, Queens Sports Club	October 20, 1994	Z v SL	2
74	Mohali, Punjab Cricket Association Stadium	December 10, 1994	I v WI	1
75	Peshawar, Arbab Niaz Stadium	September 8, 1995	P v SL	1
76	Centurion (*formerly Verwoerdburg*), Centurion Park	November 16, 1995	SA v E	1

Note: The Sheikhupura Cricket Stadium, Sheikhupura, became the 77th Test ground on October 17, 1996, after the deadline for this section, when Pakistan played Zimbabwe.

FAMILIES IN TEST CRICKET

FATHERS AND SONS

England

M. C. Cowdrey (114 Tests, 1954-55–1974-75) and C. S. Cowdrey (6 Tests, 1984-85–1988).
J. Hardstaff (5 Tests, 1907-08) and J. Hardstaff jun. (23 Tests, 1935–1948).
L. Hutton (79 Tests, 1937–1954-55) and R. A. Hutton (5 Tests, 1971).
F. T. Mann (5 Tests, 1922-23) and F. G. Mann (7 Tests, 1948-49–1949).
J. H. Parks (1 Test, 1937) and J. M. Parks (46 Tests, 1954–1967-68).
M. J. Stewart (8 Tests, 1962–1963-64) and A. J. Stewart (58 Tests, 1989-90–1996).
F. W. Tate (1 Test, 1902) and M. W. Tate (39 Tests, 1924–1935).
C. L. Townsend (2 Tests, 1899) and D. C. H. Townsend (3 Tests, 1934-35).

Australia

E. J. Gregory (1 Test, 1876-77) and S. E. Gregory (58 Tests, 1890–1912).

South Africa

F. Hearne (4 Tests, 1891-92–1895-96) and G. A. L. Hearne (3 Tests, 1922-23–1924).
F. Hearne also played 2 Tests for England in 1888-89.
J. D. Lindsay (3 Tests, 1947) and D. T. Lindsay (19 Tests, 1963-64–1969-70).
A. W. Nourse (45 Tests, 1902-03–1924) and A. D. Nourse (34 Tests, 1935–1951).
P. M. Pollock (28 Tests, 1961-62–1969-70) and S. M. Pollock (5 Tests, 1995-96).
L. R. Tuckett (1 Test, 1913-14) and L. Tuckett (9 Tests, 1947–1948-49).

West Indies

G. A. Headley (22 Tests, 1929-30–1953-54) and R. G. A. Headley (2 Tests, 1973).
O. C. Scott (8 Tests, 1928–1930-31) and A. P. H. Scott (1 Test, 1952-53).

New Zealand

W. M. Anderson (1 Test, 1945-46) and R. W. Anderson (9 Tests, 1976-77–1978).
W. P. Bradburn (2 Tests, 1963-64) and G. E. Bradburn (4 Tests, 1990-91).
B. L. Cairns (43 Tests, 1973-74–1985-86) and C. L. Cairns (16 Tests, 1989-90–1995-96).
W. A. Hadlee (11 Tests, 1937–1950-51) and D. R. Hadlee (26 Tests, 1969–1977-78); R. J. Hadlee (86 Tests, 1972-73–1990).
P. G. Z. Harris (9 Tests, 1955-56–1964-65) and C. Z. Harris (7 Tests, 1993-94–1995-96).
H. G. Vivian (7 Tests, 1931–1937) and G. E. Vivian (5 Tests, 1964-65–1971-72).

India

L. Amarnath (24 Tests, 1933-34–1952-53) and M. Amarnath (69 Tests, 1969-70–1987-88); S. Amarnath (10 Tests, 1975-76–1978-79).
D. K. Gaekwad (11 Tests, 1952–1960-61) and A. D. Gaekwad (40 Tests, 1974-75–1984-85).
Nawab of Pataudi (Iftikhar Ali Khan) (3 Tests, 1946) and Nawab of Pataudi (Mansur Ali Khan) (46 Tests, 1961-62–1974-75).
Nawab of Pataudi sen. also played 3 Tests for England, 1932-33–1934.
V. L. Manjrekar (55 Tests, 1951-52–1964-65) and S. V. Manjrekar (36 Tests, 1987-88–96).
V. Mankad (44 Tests, 1946–1958-59) and A. V. Mankad (22 Tests, 1969-70–1977-78).
Pankaj Roy (43 Tests, 1951-52–1960-61) and Pranab Roy (2 Tests, 1981-82).

India and Pakistan

M. Jahangir Khan (4 Tests, 1932–1936) and Majid Khan (63 Tests, 1964-65–1982-83).
S. Wazir Ali (7 Tests, 1932–1936) and Khalid Wazir (2 Tests, 1954).

Pakistan

Hanif Mohammad (55 Tests, 1954–1969-70) and Shoaib Mohammad (45 Tests, 1983-84–1995-96).
Nazar Mohammad (5 Tests, 1952-53) and Mudassar Nazar (76 Tests, 1976-77–1988-89).

GRANDFATHERS AND GRANDSONS

Australia

V. Y. Richardson (19 Tests, 1924-25–1935-36) and G. S. Chappell (87 Tests, 1970-71–1983-84); I. M. Chappell (75 Tests, 1964-65–1979-80); T. M. Chappell (3 Tests, 1981).

GREAT-GRANDFATHER AND GREAT-GRANDSON

Australia

W. H. Cooper (2 Tests, 1881-82 and 1884-85) and A. P. Sheahan (31 Tests, 1967-68–1973-74).

BROTHERS IN SAME TEST TEAM

England

E. M., G. F. and W. G. Grace: 1 Test, 1880; C. T. and G. B. Studd: 4 Tests, 1882-83; A. and G. G. Hearne: 1 Test, 1891-92. *F. Hearne, their brother, played in this match for South Africa*; D. W. and P. E. Richardson: 1 Test, 1957.

Australia

E. J. and D. W. Gregory: 1 Test, 1876-77; C. and A. C. Bannerman: 1 Test, 1878-79; G. and W. F. Giffen: 2 Tests, 1891-92; G. H. S. and A. E. Trott: 3 Tests, 1894-95; I. M. and G. S. Chappell: 43 Tests, 1970-71–1979-80; S. R. and M. E. Waugh: 38 Tests, 1990-91–1995-96 – the first instance of twins appearing together.

South Africa

S. J. and S. D. Snooke: 1 Test, 1907; D. and H. W. Taylor: 2 Tests, 1913-14; R. H. M. and P. A. M. Hands: 1 Test, 1913-14; E. A. B. and A. M. B. Rowan: 9 Tests, 1948-49–1951; P. M. and R. G. Pollock: 23 Tests, 1963-64–1969-70; A. J. and D. B. Pithey: 5 Tests, 1963-64; P. N. and G. Kirsten: 7 Tests, 1993-94–1994.

West Indies

G. C. and R. S. Grant: 4 Tests, 1934-35; J. B. and V. H. Stollmeyer: 1 Test, 1939; D. St E. and E. St E. Atkinson: 1 Test, 1957-58.

New Zealand

D. R. and R. J. Hadlee: 10 Tests, 1973–1977-78; H. J. and G. P. Howarth: 4 Tests, 1974-75–1976-77; J. M. and N. M. Parker: 3 Tests, 1976-77; B. P. and J. G. Bracewell: 1 Test, 1980-81; J. J. and M. D. Crowe: 34 Tests, 1983–1989-90.

India

S. Wazir Ali and S. Nazir Ali: 2 Tests, 1932–1933-34; L. Ramji and Amar Singh: 1 Test, 1933-34; C. K. and C. S. Nayudu: 4 Tests, 1933-34–1936; A. G. Kripal Singh and A. G. Milkha Singh: 1 Test, 1961-62; S. and M. Amarnath: 8 Tests, 1975-76–1978-79.

Pakistan

Wazir and Hanif Mohammad: 18 Tests, 1952-53–1959-60; Wazir and Mushtaq Mohammad: 1 Test, 1958-59; Hanif and Mushtaq Mohammad: 19 Tests, 1960-61–1969-70; Hanif, Mushtaq and Sadiq Mohammad: 1 Test, 1969-70; Mushtaq and Sadiq Mohammad: 26 Tests, 1969-70–1978–79; Wasim and Ramiz Raja: 2 Tests, 1983-84.

Sri Lanka

M. D. and S. Wettimuny: 2 Tests, 1982-83; A. and D. Ranatunga: 2 Tests, 1989-90; A. and S. Ranatunga: 7 Tests, 1994-95–1995-96.

Zimbabwe

A. and G. W. Flower: 16 Tests, 1992-93–1995-96; P. A. and B. C. Strang: 5 Tests, 1994-95–1995-96.

LIMITED-OVERS INTERNATIONAL RECORDS

Note: Limited-overs international matches do not have first-class status.

SUMMARY OF ALL LIMITED-OVERS INTERNATIONALS

1970-71 to September 23, 1996

	Opponents	*Matches*	*Won by*										*Tied*	*NR*
			E	*A*	*SA*	*WI*	*NZ*	*I*	*P*	*SL*	*Z*	*Ass*		
England	Australia	**57**	26	29	–	–	–	–	–	–	–	–	1	1
	South Africa	**12**	5	–	7	–	–	–	–	–	–	–	–	–
	West Indies	**51**	22	–	–	27	–	–	–	–	–	–	–	2
	New Zealand	**42**	21	–	–	–	18	–	–	–	–	–	–	3
	India	**32**	18	–	–	–	–	13	–	–	–	–	–	1
	Pakistan	**40**	25	–	–	–	–	–	14	–	–	–	–	1
	Sri Lanka	**12**	8	–	–	–	–	–	–	4	–	–	–	–
	Zimbabwe	**3**	1	–	–	–	–	–	–	–	2	–	–	–
	Associates	**4**	4	–	–	–	–	–	–	–	–	0	–	–
Australia	South Africa	**20**	–	12	8	–	–	–	–	–	–	–	–	–
	West Indies	**80**	–	31	–	47	–	–	–	–	–	–	1	1
	New Zealand	**63**	–	44	–	–	17	–	–	–	–	–	–	2
	India	**45**	–	26	–	–	–	16	–	–	–	–	–	3
	Pakistan	**42**	–	21	–	–	–	–	18	–	–	–	1	2
	Sri Lanka	**35**	–	22	–	–	–	–	–	11	–	–	–	2
	Zimbabwe	**9**	–	8	–	–	–	–	–	–	1	–	–	–
	Associates	**3**	–	3	–	–	–	–	–	–	–	0	–	–
South Africa	West Indies	**9**	–	–	4	5	–	–	–	–	–	–	–	–
	New Zealand	**8**	–	–	4	–	4	–	–	–	–	–	–	–
	India	**17**	–	–	11	–	–	6	–	–	–	–	–	–
	Pakistan	**14**	–	–	7	–	–	–	7	–	–	–	–	–
	Sri Lanka	**7**	–	–	3	–	–	–	–	3	–	–	–	1
	Zimbabwe	**4**	–	–	3	–	–	–	–	–	0	–	–	1
	Associates	**2**	–	–	2	–	–	–	–	–	–	0	–	–
West Indies	New Zealand	**24**	–	–	–	18	4	–	–	–	–	–	–	2
	India	**51**	–	–	–	32	–	18	–	–	–	–	1	–
	Pakistan	**75**	–	–	–	51	–	–	22	–	–	–	2	–
	Sri Lanka	**27**	–	–	–	19	–	–	–	7	–	–	–	1
	Zimbabwe	**5**	–	–	–	5	–	–	–	–	0	–	–	–
	Associates	**1**	–	–	–	0	–	–	–	–	–	1*	–	–
New Zealand	India	**41**	–	–	–	–	18	23	–	–	–	–	–	–
	Pakistan	**41**	–	–	–	–	16	–	23	–	–	–	1	1
	Sri Lanka	**32**	–	–	–	–	22	–	–	8	–	–	–	2
	Zimbabwe	**8**	–	–	–	–	7	–	–	–	1	–	–	–
	Associates	**4**	–	–	–	–	4	–	–	–	–	0	–	–
India	Pakistan	**50**	–	–	–	–	–	16	32	–	–	–	–	2
	Sri Lanka	**42**	–	–	–	–	–	25	–	14	–	–	–	3
	Zimbabwe	**12**	–	–	–	–	–	11	–	–	0	–	1	–
	Associates	**6**	–	–	–	–	–	6	–	–	–	0	–	–
Pakistan	Sri Lanka	**57**	–	–	–	–	–	–	41	14	–	–	–	2
	Zimbabwe	**9**	–	–	–	–	–	–	7	–	1	–	1	–
	Associates	**7**	–	–	–	–	–	–	7	–	–	0	–	–
Sri Lanka	Zimbabwe	**8**	–	–	–	–	–	–	–	7	1	–	–	–
	Associates	**5**	–	–	–	–	–	–	–	5	–	0	–	–
Zimbabwe	Associates	**2**	–	–	–	–	–	–	–	–	1	0	–	1
Associate	Associates	**1**	–	–	–	–	–	–	–	–	–	1†	–	–
		1,119	130	196	49	204	110	134	171	73	7	2	9	34

* *Kenya beat West Indies in the 1996 World Cup.*
† *United Arab Emirates beat Holland in the 1996 World Cup.*

Note: Current Associate Members of ICC who have played one-day internationals are Bangladesh, Canada, East Africa, Holland, Kenya and United Arab Emirates. Sri Lanka and Zimbabwe also played one-day internationals before being given Test status; these are not included among the Associates' results.

RESULTS SUMMARY OF ALL LIMITED-OVERS INTERNATIONALS

1970-71 to September 23, 1996 (1,116 matches)

	Matches	*Won*	*Lost*	*Tied*	*No Result*	*% Won (excl. NR)*
West Indies	323	204	109	4	6	64.35
Australia	354	196	144	3	11	57.14
South Africa	93	49	42	–	2	53.84
England	253	130	114	1	8	53.06
Pakistan	335	171	151	5	8	52.29
India	296	134	151	2	9	46.68
New Zealand	263	110	142	1	10	43.47
Sri Lanka	225	73	141	–	11	34.11
Kenya	6	1	4	–	1	20.00
United Arab Emirates	7	1	6	–	–	14.28
Zimbabwe	60	7	49	2	2	12.06
Canada	3	–	3	–	–	–
East Africa	3	–	3	–	–	–
Holland	5	–	5	–	–	–
Bangladesh	12	–	12	–	–	–

Note: ICC has ruled that matches abandoned and started again should now count as official internationals in their own right, contrary to its previous ruling.

MOST RUNS

	M	*I*	*NO*	*R*	*HS*	*100s*	*Avge*
D. L. Haynes (West Indies)	238	237	28	8,648	152*	17	41.37
Javed Miandad (Pakistan)	233	218	41	7,381	119*	8	41.70
I. V. A. Richards (West Indies)	187	167	24	6,721	189*	11	47.00
A. R. Border (Australia)	273	252	39	6,524	127*	3	30.62
R. B. Richardson (West Indies)	224	217	30	6,249	122	5	33.41
M. Azharuddin (India)	225	208	41	6,091	108*	3	36.47
D. M. Jones (Australia)	164	161	25	6,068	145	7	44.61
Salim Malik (Pakistan)	235	212	34	6,012	102	5	33.77
D. C. Boon (Australia)	181	177	16	5,964	122	5	37.04
P. A. de Silva (Sri Lanka)	190	184	20	5,661	145	6	34.51
Ramiz Raja (Pakistan)	177	176	14	5,386	119*	9	33.24
A. Ranatunga (Sri Lanka)	193	182	35	5,250	102*	2	35.71
C. G. Greenidge (West Indies)	128	127	13	5,134	133*	11	45.03
M. D. Crowe (New Zealand)	143	141	19	4,704	107*	4	38.55
S. R. Waugh (Australia)	200	180	42	4,420	102*	1	32.02
S. R. Tendulkar (India)	127	124	13	4,389	137	9	39.54
G. R. Marsh (Australia)	117	115	6	4,357	126*	9	39.97
B. C. Lara (West Indies)	104	103	9	4,332	169	9	46.08
G. A. Gooch (England)	125	122	6	4,290	142	8	36.98
K. Srikkanth (India)	146	145	4	4,092	123	4	29.02
A. J. Lamb (England)	122	118	16	4,010	118	4	39.31
Leading aggregates for other Test-playing countries:							
W. J. Cronje (South Africa)	88	84	12	2,681	112	2	37.23
D. L. Houghton (Zimbabwe)	47	45	1	1,279	142	1	29.06

HIGHEST INDIVIDUAL SCORES

189*	I. V. A. Richards	West Indies v England at Manchester	1984
188*	G. Kirsten	South Africa v UAE at Rawalpindi	1995-96
181	I. V. A. Richards	West Indies v Sri Lanka at Karachi	1987-88
175*	Kapil Dev	India v Zimbabwe at Tunbridge Wells	1983
171*	G. M. Turner	New Zealand v East Africa at Birmingham	1975
169*	D. J. Callaghan	South Africa v New Zealand at Verwoerdburg	1994-95
169	B. C. Lara	West Indies v Sri Lanka at Sharjah	1995-96
167*	R. A. Smith	England v Australia at Birmingham	1993
161	A. C. Hudson	South Africa v Holland at Rawalpindi	1995-96
158	D. I. Gower	England v New Zealand at Brisbane	1982-83
153*	I. V. A. Richards	West Indies v Australia at Melbourne	1979-80
153	B. C. Lara	West Indies v Pakistan at Sharjah	1993-94
152*	D. L. Haynes	West Indies v India at Georgetown	1988-89

Highest individual scores for other Test-playing countries:

145	D. M. Jones	Australia v England at Brisbane	1990-91
145	P. A. de Silva	Sri Lanka v Kenya at Kandy	1995-96
142	D. L. Houghton	Zimbabwe v New Zealand at Hyderabad, India	1987-88
137*	Inzamam-ul-Haq	Pakistan v New Zealand at Sharjah	1993-94

MOST HUNDREDS

Total		*E*	*A*	*SA*	*WI*	*NZ*	*I*	*P*	*SL*	*Z*	*Ass*
17	D. L. Haynes (West Indies)	2	6	0	–	2	2	4	1	0	–
11	C. G. Greenidge (West Indies)	0	1	–	–	3	3	2	1	1	–
11	I. V. A. Richards (West Indies)	3	3	–	–	1	3	0	1	0	–
9	B. C. Lara (West Indies)	0	1	2	–	2	0	3	1	0	0
9	G. R. Marsh (Australia)	1	–	0	2	2	3	1	0	0	–
9	Ramiz Raja (Pakistan)	1	0	0	2	3	0	–	3	0	0
9	S. R. Tendulkar (India)	0	1	0	1	1	–	2	3	0	1
8	G. A. Gooch (England)	–	4	0	1	1	1	1	0	0	0
8	Javed Miandad (Pakistan)	1	0	1	1	0	3	–	2	0	0
8	Saeed Anwar (Pakistan)	0	1	0	1	1	0	–	4	1	0
8	M. E. Waugh (Australia)	1	–	1	0	2	1	1	1	0	1
7	D. I. Gower (England)	–	2	–	0	3	0	1	1	–	0
7	D. M. Jones (Australia)	3	–	0	0	2	0	1	1	0	0
7	Zaheer Abbas (Pakistan)	0	2	–	0	1	3	–	1	–	0

Note: Ass = Associate Members.

HIGHEST PARTNERSHIP FOR EACH WICKET

212	for 1st	G. R. Marsh and D. C. Boon	A v I	Jaipur	1986-87
263	for 2nd	Aamir Sohail and Inzamam-ul-Haq	P v NZ	Sharjah	1993-94
224*	for 3rd	D. M. Jones and A. R. Border	A v SL	Adelaide	1984-85
173	for 4th	D. M. Jones and S. R. Waugh	A v P	Perth	1986-87
159	for 5th	R. T. Ponting and M. G. Bevan	A v SL	Melbourne	1995-96
154	for 6th	R. B. Richardson and P. J. L. Dujon	WI v P	Sharjah	1991-92
115	for 7th	P. J. L. Dujon and M. D. Marshall	WI v P	Gujranwala	1986-87
119	for 8th	P. R. Reiffel and S. K. Warne	A v SA	Port Elizabeth	1993-94
126*	for 9th	Kapil Dev and S. M. H. Kirmani	I v Z	Tunbridge Wells	1983
106*	for 10th	I. V. A. Richards and M. A. Holding	WI v E	Manchester	1984

MOST WICKETS

	M	Balls	R	W	BB	4W/i	Avge
Wasim Akram (Pakistan)	206	10,635	6,707	297	5-15	16	22.58
Kapil Dev (India)	224	11,202	6,945	253	5-43	4	27.45
Waqar Younis (Pakistan)	133	6,618	4,992	220	6-26	17	22.69
C. J. McDermott (Australia)	138	7,461	5,018	203	5-44	5	24.71
C. E. L. Ambrose (West Indies)	133	7,105	4,129	184	5-17	9	22.44
C. A. Walsh (West Indies)	162	8,554	5,484	182	5-1	6	30.13
Imran Khan (Pakistan)	175	7,461	4,845	182	6-14	4	26.62
S. R. Waugh (Australia)	200	7,692	5,710	170	4-33	2	33.58
R. J. Hadlee (New Zealand)	115	6,182	3,407	158	5-25	6	21.56
M. Prabhakar (India)	130	6,360	4,535	157	5-33	6	28.88
M. D. Marshall (West Indies)	136	7,175	4,233	157	4-18	6	26.96
J. Srinath (India)	108	5,558	3,991	148	5-24	4	26.96
J. Garner (West Indies)	98	5,330	2,752	146	5-31	5	18.84
Aqib Javed (Pakistan)	134	6,673	4,667	146	7-37	3	31.96
I. T. Botham (England)	116	6,271	4,139	145	4-31	3	28.54
M. A. Holding (West Indies)	102	5,473	3,034	142	5-26	6	21.36
E. J. Chatfield (New Zealand)	114	6,065	3,618	140	5-34	4	25.84
A. Kumble (India)	97	5,234	3,544	133	6-12	6	26.64
Abdul Qadir (Pakistan)	104	5,100	3,453	132	5-44	6	26.15
C. L. Hooper (West Indies)	141	5,626	4,107	129	4-34	1	31.83
R. J. Shastri (India)	150	6,613	4,650	129	5-15	3	36.04
Mushtaq Ahmed (Pakistan)	106	5,429	3,981	124	5-36	2	32.10
I. V. A. Richards (West Indies)	187	5,644	4,228	118	6-41	3	35.83
D. K. Morrison (New Zealand)	92	4,382	3,316	117	5-46	2	28.34
P. A. J. DeFreitas (England)	101	5,610	3,693	115	4-35	1	32.11
M. C. Snedden (New Zealand)	93	4,525	3,237	114	4-34	1	28.39
Mudassar Nazar (Pakistan)	122	4,855	3,432	111	5-28	2	30.91
I. R. Bishop (West Indies)	75	3,919	2,777	110	5-25	8	25.24
S. P. O'Donnell (Australia)	87	4,350	3,102	108	5-13	6	28.72
D. K. Lillee (Australia)	63	3,593	2,145	103	5-34	6	20.82
C. Pringle (New Zealand)	64	3,314	2,455	103	5-45	3	23.83
W. K. M. Benjamin (West Indies)	85	4,442	3,079	100	5-22	1	30.79
R. A. Harper (West Indies)	105	5,175	3,431	100	4-40	3	34.31

Leading aggregates for other Test-playing countries:

	M	Balls	R	W	BB	4W/i	Avge
J. R. Ratnayeke (Sri Lanka)	78	3,573	2,866	85	4-23	1	33.71
A. A. Donald (South Africa)	61	3,266	2,195	89	5-29	3	24.66
S. T. Jayasuriya (Sri Lanka)	114	3,759	3,004	85	6-29	3	35.34
H. H. Streak (Zimbabwe)	30	1,525	1,077	34	4-25	2	31.67
E. A. Brandes (Zimbabwe)	30	1,495	1,258	34	4-21	1	37.00

BEST ANALYSES

7-37	Aqib Javed	Pakistan v India at Sharjah	1991-92
7-51	W. W. Davis	West Indies v Australia at Leeds	1983
6-12	A. Kumble	India v West Indies at Calcutta	1993-94
6-14	G. J. Gilmour	Australia v England at Leeds	1975
6-14	Imran Khan	Pakistan v India at Sharjah	1984-85
6-15	C. E. H. Croft	West Indies v England at Arnos Vale	1980-81
6-26	Waqar Younis	Pakistan v Sri Lanka at Sharjah	1989-90
6-29	B. P. Patterson	West Indies v India at Nagpur	1987-88
6-29	S. T. Jayasuriya	Sri Lanka v England at Moratuwa	1992-93
6-30	Waqar Younis	Pakistan v New Zealand at Auckland	1993-94
6-39	K. H. MacLeay	Australia v India at Nottingham	1983
6-41	I. V. A. Richards	West Indies v India at Delhi	1989-90
6-50	A. H. Gray	West Indies v Australia at Port-of-Spain	1990-91

Best analyses for other Test-playing countries:

5-20	V. J. Marks	England v New Zealand at Wellington	1983-84
5-21	P. A. Strang	Zimbabwe v Kenya at Patna	1995-96
5-22	M. N. Hart	New Zealand v West Indies at Margao	1994-95
5-29	A. A. Donald	South Africa v India at Calcutta	1991-92

HAT-TRICKS

Jalal-ud-Din	Pakistan v Australia at Hyderabad	1982-83
B. A. Reid	Australia v New Zealand at Sydney	1985-86
Chetan Sharma	India v New Zealand at Nagpur	1987-88
Wasim Akram	Pakistan v West Indies at Sharjah	1989-90
Wasim Akram	Pakistan v Australia at Sharjah	1989-90
Kapil Dev	India v Sri Lanka at Calcutta	1990-91
Aqib Javed	Pakistan v India at Sharjah	1991-92
D. K. Morrison	New Zealand v India at Napier	1993-94
Waqar Younis	Pakistan v New Zealand at East London	1994-95

MOST DISMISSALS IN AN INNINGS

5 (all ct)	R. W. Marsh	Australia v England at Leeds	1981
5 (all ct)	R. G. de Alwis	Sri Lanka v Australia at Colombo (PSS)	1982-83
5 (all ct)	S. M. H. Kirmani	India v Zimbabwe at Leicester	1983
5 (3ct, 2st)	S. Viswanath	India v England at Sydney	1984-85
5 (3ct, 2st)	K. S. More	India v New Zealand at Sharjah	1987-88
5 (all ct)	H. P. Tillekeratne	Sri Lanka v Pakistan at Sharjah	1990-91
5 (3ct, 2st)	N. R. Mongia	India v New Zealand at Auckland	1993-94
5 (3ct, 2st)	A. C. Parore	New Zealand v West Indies at Margao	1994-95
5 (all ct)	D. J. Richardson	South Africa v Pakistan at Johannesburg	1994-95
5 (all ct)	Moin Khan	Pakistan v Zimbabwe at Harare	1994-95
5 (4ct, 1st)	R. S. Kaluwitharana	Sri Lanka v Pakistan at Sharjah	1994-95
5 (all ct)	D. J. Richardson	South Africa v Zimbabwe at Harare	1995-96
5 (all ct)	A. Flower	Zimbabwe v South Africa at Harare	1995-96
5 (all ct)	C. O. Browne	West Indies v Sri Lanka at Brisbane	1995-96
5 (4 ct, 1 st)	J. C. Adams	West Indies v Kenya at Pune	1995-96
5 (4 ct, 1 st)	Rashid Latif	Pakistan v New Zealand at Lahore	1995-96
5 (3 ct, 2 st)	N. R. Mongia	India v Pakistan at Toronto	1996

MOST DISMISSALS IN A CAREER

	M	*Ct*	*St*	*Total*
I. A. Healy (Australia)	150	181	32	213
P. J. L. Dujon (West Indies)	169	183	21	204
R. W. Marsh (Australia)	92	120	4	124
D. J. Richardson (South Africa)	82	108	13	121
Rashid Latif (Pakistan)	84	81	22	103
Salim Yousuf (Pakistan)	86	81	22	103

MOST CATCHES IN AN INNINGS

(Excluding wicket-keepers)

5	J. N. Rhodes	South Africa v West Indies at Bombay	1993-94
4	Salim Malik	Pakistan v New Zealand at Sialkot	1984-85
4	S. M. Gavaskar	India v Pakistan at Sharjah	1984-85
4	R. B. Richardson	West Indies v England at Birmingham	1991
4	K. C. Wessels	South Africa v West Indies at Kingston	1991-92
4	M. A. Taylor	Australia v West Indies at Sydney	1992-93
4	C. L. Hooper	West Indies v Pakistan at Durban	1992-93
4	K. R. Rutherford	New Zealand v India at Napier	1994-95
4	P. V. Simmons	West Indies v Sri Lanka at Sharjah	1995-96
4	R. A. Harper	West Indies v New Zealand at Georgetown	1995-96

Note: While fielding as substitute, J. G. Bracewell held 4 catches for New Zealand v Australia at Adelaide, 1980-81.

MOST CATCHES IN A CAREER

	M	*Ct*
A. R. Border (A)	273	127
I. V. A. Richards (WI)	187	101
M. Azharuddin (I)	224	94
R. S. Mahanama (SL)	148	75
R. B. Richardson (WI)	224	75
Kapil Dev (I)	224	71
S. R. Waugh (A)	200	70

ALL-ROUND

1,000 Runs and 100 Wickets

	M	*R*	*W*
I. T. Botham (England)	116	2,113	145
R. J. Hadlee (New Zealand)	115	1,751	158
C. L. Hooper (West Indies)	141	3,270	129
Imran Khan (Pakistan)	175	3,709	182
Kapil Dev (India)	224	3,783	253
Mudassar Nazar (Pakistan)	122	2,653	111
S. P. O'Donnell (Australia)	87	1,242	108
M. Prabhakar (India)	130	1,858	157
I. V. A. Richards (West Indies)	187	6,721	118
R. J. Shastri (India)	150	3,108	129
Wasim Akram (Pakistan)	206	1,894	297
S. R. Waugh (Australia)	200	4,420	170

1,000 Runs and 100 Dismissals

	M	*R*	*D*
P. J. L. Dujon (West Indies)	169	1,945	204
I. A. Healy (Australia)	150	1,593	213
R. W. Marsh (Australia)	92	1,225	124

TEAM RECORDS

HIGHEST INNINGS TOTALS

398-5	(50 overs)	Sri Lanka v Kenya at Kandy	1995-96
363-7	(55 overs)	England v Pakistan at Nottingham	1992
360-4	(50 overs)	West Indies v Sri Lanka at Karachi	1987-88
349-9	(50 overs)	Sri Lanka v Pakistan at Singapore	1995-96
348-8	(50 overs)	New Zealand v India at Nagpur	1995-96
338-4	(50 overs)	New Zealand v Bangladesh at Sharjah	1989-90
338-5	(60 overs)	Pakistan v Sri Lanka at Swansea	1983
334-4	(60 overs)	England v India at Lord's	1975
333-7	(50 overs)	West Indies v Sri Lanka at Sharjah	1995-96
333-8	(45 overs)	West Indies v India at Jamshedpur	1983-84
333-9	(60 overs)	England v Sri Lanka at Taunton	1983
332-3	(50 overs)	Australia v Sri Lanka at Sharjah	1989-90
330-6	(60 overs)	Pakistan v Sri Lanka at Nottingham	1975

Highest totals by other Test-playing countries:

328-3	(50 overs)	South Africa v Holland at Rawalpindi	1995-96
312-4	(50 overs)	Zimbabwe v Sri Lanka at New Plymouth	1991-92
305-5	(50 overs)	India v Pakistan at Sharjah	1995-96

HIGHEST TOTALS BATTING SECOND

329	(49.3 overs) (*Lost by 4 runs*)	Sri Lanka v West Indies at Sharjah	1995-96
315	(49.4 overs) (*Lost by 34 runs*)	Pakistan v Sri Lanka at Singapore	1995-96
313-7	(49.2 overs) (*Won by 3 wickets*)	Sri Lanka v Zimbabwe at New Plymouth	1991-92

HIGHEST MATCH AGGREGATES

664-19	(99.4 overs)	Pakistan v Sri Lanka at Singapore	1995-96
662-17	(99.3 overs)	Sri Lanka v West Indies at Sharjah	1995-96
652-12	(100 overs)	Sri Lanka v Kenya at Kandy	1995-96
626-14	(120 overs)	Pakistan v Sri Lanka at Swansea	1983
625-11	(99.2 overs)	Sri Lanka v Zimbabwe at New Plymouth	1991-92

LOWEST INNINGS TOTALS

43	(19.5 overs)	Pakistan v West Indies at Cape Town	1992-93
45	(40.3 overs)	Canada v England at Manchester	1979
55	(28.3 overs)	Sri Lanka v West Indies at Sharjah	1986-87
63	(25.5 overs)	India v Australia at Sydney	1980-81
64	(35.5 overs)	New Zealand v Pakistan at Sharjah	1985-86
69	(28 overs)	South Africa v Australia at Sydney	1993-94
70	(25.2 overs)	Australia v England at Birmingham	1977
70	(26.3 overs)	Australia v New Zealand at Adelaide	1985-86

Note: This section does not take into account those matches in which the number of overs was reduced.

Lowest totals by other Test-playing countries:

87	(29.3 overs)	West Indies v Australia at Sydney	1992-93
93	(36.2 overs)	England v Australia at Leeds	1975
99	(36.3 overs)	Zimbabwe v West Indies at Hyderabad, India	1993-94

LARGEST VICTORIES

232 runs	Australia (323-2 in 50 overs) v Sri Lanka (91 in 35.5 overs) at Adelaide	1984-85
206 runs	New Zealand (276-7 in 50 overs) v Australia (70 in 26.3 overs) at Adelaide	1985-86
202 runs	England (334-4 in 60 overs) v India (132-3 in 60 overs) at Lord's	1975

By ten wickets: There have been nine instances of victory by ten wickets.

TIED MATCHES

West Indies 222-5 (50 overs) v Australia 222-9 (50 overs) at Melbourne	1983-84
England 226-5 (55 overs) v Australia 226-8 (55 overs) at Nottingham	1989
West Indies 186-5 (39 overs) v Pakistan 186-9 (39 overs) at Lahore	1991-92
India 126 (47.4 overs) v West Indies 126 (41 overs) at Perth	1991-92
Australia 228-7 (50 overs) v Pakistan 228-9 (50 overs) at Hobart	1992-93
Pakistan 244-6 (50 overs) v West Indies 244-5 (50 overs) at Georgetown	1992-93
India 248-5 (50 overs) v Zimbabwe 248 (50 overs) at Indore	1993-94
Pakistan 161-9 (50 overs) v New Zealand 161 (49.4 overs) at Auckland	1993-94
Zimbabwe 219-9 (50 overs) v Pakistan 219 (49.5 overs) at Harare	1994-95

MOST APPEARANCES

(200 or more)

	Total	*E*	*A*	*SA*	*WI*	*NZ*	*I*	*P*	*SL*	*Z*	*Ass*
A. R. Border (A)	273	43	–	15	61	52	38	34	23	5	2
D. L. Haynes (WI)	238	35	64	8	–	13	36	65	14	3	–
Salim Malik (P)	235	24	24	14	45	36	37	–	43	8	4
Javed Miandad (P)	233	27	35	3	64	24	35	–	35	6	4
M. Azharuddin (I)	225	21	33	16	37	29	–	37	37	10	5
Kapil Dev (I)	224	23	41	13	42	29	–	32	33	9	2
R. B. Richardson (WI)	224	35	51	9	–	11	32	61	21	3	1
Wasim Akram (P)	206	24	25	10	46	21	33	–	32	9	6
S. R. Waugh (A)	200	23	–	18	37	40	31	24	20	5	2

Most appearances for other Test-playing countries:

A. Ranatunga (SL)	193	10	28	7	20	27	38	51	–	8	4
J. G. Wright (NZ)	149	30	42	–	11	–	21	18	24	2	1
G. A. Gooch (E)	125	–	32	1	32	16	18	16	6	3	1
W. J. Cronje (SA)	88	12	20	–	8	8	15	13	6	4	2
A. Flower (Z)	48	3	5	4	3	6	8	9	8	–	2

WORLD CUP RECORDS 1975-1996

WORLD CUP FINALS

1975	WEST INDIES (291-8) beat Australia (274) by 17 runs	Lord's
1979	WEST INDIES (286-9) beat England (194) by 92 runs	Lord's
1983	INDIA (183) beat West Indies (140) by 43 runs	Lord's
1987-88	AUSTRALIA (253-5) beat England (246-8) by seven runs	Calcutta
1991-92	PAKISTAN (249-6) beat England (227) by 22 runs	Melbourne
1995-96	SRI LANKA (245-3) beat Australia (241-7) by seven wickets	Lahore

RESULTS SUMMARY

	Played	*Won*	*Lost*	*No Result*
West Indies	38	25	12	1
England	40	25	14	1
Australia	37	22	15	0
Pakistan	37	21	15	1
New Zealand	35	19	16	0
India	36	18	17	1
South Africa	15	10	5	0
Sri Lanka	32	10	20	2
Zimbabwe	25	3	22	0
Kenya	5	1	4	0
UAE	5	1	4	0
Canada	3	0	3	0
East Africa	3	0	3	0
Holland	5	0	5	0

BATTING RECORDS

Most Runs

	M	*I*	*NO*	*R*	*HS*	*100s*	*Avge*
Javed Miandad (P)	33	30	5	1,083	103	1	43.32
I. V. A. Richards (WI)	23	21	5	1,013	181	3	63.31
G. A. Gooch (E)	21	21	1	897	115	1	44.85
M. D. Crowe (NZ)	21	21	5	880	100*	1	55.00
D. L. Haynes (WI)	25	25	2	854	105	1	37.13
A. Ranatunga (SL)	25	24	8	835	88*	0	52.18
D. C. Boon (A)	16	16	1	815	100	2	54.33
S. R. Tendulkar (I)	15	14	2	806	137	2	67.16

Highest Score

188* G. Kirsten South Africa v United Arab Emirates at Rawalpindi 1995-96

Hundred Before Lunch

101 A. Turner Australia v Sri Lanka at The Oval 1975

Most Hundreds

3 I. V. A. Richards (WI), Ramiz Raja (P), M. E. Waugh (A)

Highest Partnership for Each Wicket

186	for 1st	G. Kirsten and A. C. Hudson	SA v H	Rawalpindi	1995-96
176	for 2nd	D. L. Amiss and K. W. R. Fletcher	E v I	Lord's	1975
207	for 3rd	M. E. Waugh and S. R. Waugh	A v K	Vishakhapatnam	1995-96
168	for 4th	L. K. Germon and C. Z. Harris	NZ v A	Madras	1995-96
145*	for 5th	A. Flower and A. C. Waller	Z v SL	New Plymouth	1991-92
144	for 6th	Imran Khan and Shahid Mahboob	P v SL	Leeds	1983
75*	for 7th	D. A. G. Fletcher and I. P. Butchart	Z v A	Nottingham	1983
117	for 8th	D. L. Houghton and I. P. Butchart	Z v NZ	Hyderabad (India)	1987-88
126*	for 9th	Kapil Dev and S. M. H. Kirmani	I v Z	Tunbridge Wells	1983
71	for 10th	A. M. E. Roberts and J. Garner	WI v I	Manchester	1983

BOWLING RECORDS

Most Wickets

	O	*R*	*W*	*BB*	*4W/i*	*Avge*
Imran Khan (P)	169.3	655	34	4-37	2	19.26
I. T. Botham (E)	222	762	30	4-31	1	25.40
Kapil Dev (I)	237	892	28	5-43	1	31.85
Wasim Akram (P)	186.2	768	28	4-32	1	27.42
C. J. McDermott (A)	149	599	27	5-44	2	22.18
Mushtaq Ahmed (P)	135	549	26	3-16	0	21.11
A. M. E. Roberts (WI)	170.1	552	26	3-32	0	21.23

Best Bowling

7-51 W. W. Davis West Indies v Australia at Leeds 1983

Hat-Trick

Chetan Sharma India v New Zealand at Nagpur 1987-88

Most Economical Bowling

12-8-6-1 B. S. Bedi India v East Africa at Leeds 1975

Most Expensive Bowling

12-1-105-2 M. C. Snedden New Zealand v England at The Oval......... 1983

WICKET-KEEPING RECORDS

Most Dismissals

Wasim Bari (P)	22	(18 ct, 4 st)
P. J. L. Dujon (WI)	20	(19 ct, 1 st)
I. A. Healy (A)	20	(17 ct, 3 st)
R. W. Marsh (A)	18	(17 ct, 1 st)
K. S. More (I)	18	(12 ct, 6 st)
D. L. Murray (WI)	16	(16 ct)
D. J. Richardson (SA)	15	(14 ct, 1 st)

Most Dismissals in an Innings

5 (5 ct)	S. M. H. Kirmani	India v Zimbabwe at Leicester	1983
5 (4 ct, 1st)	J. C. Adams	West Indies v Kenya at Pune	1995-96
5 (4 ct, 1st)	Rashid Latif	Pakistan v New Zealand at Lahore	1995-96

FIELDING RECORDS

Most Catches

12 C. H. Lloyd (WI), Kapil Dev (I), D. L. Haynes (WI)
11 C. L. Cairns (NZ)
10 I. T. Botham (E), A. R. Border (A)

MOST APPEARANCES

33 Javed Miandad (P)
28 Imran Khan (P)
26 Kapil Dev (I)
25 A. R. Border (A), D. L. Haynes (WI), A. Ranatunga (SL)

TEAM RECORDS

Highest Total	398-5	Sri Lanka v Kenya	Kandy	1995-96
Batting Second	313-7	Sri Lanka v Zimbabwe	New Plymouth	1991-92
Lowest Total	45	Canada v England	Manchester	1979
Highest Aggregate	652-12	Sri Lanka v Kenya	Kandy	1995-96
Largest Victories	10 wkts	India beat East Africa	Leeds	1975
	10 wkts	West Indies beat Zimbabwe	Birmingham	1983
	10 wkts	West Indies beat Pakistan	Melbourne	1991-92
	202 runs	England beat India	Lord's	1975
Narrowest Victories	1 wkt	West Indies beat Pakistan	Birmingham	1975
	1 wkt	Pakistan beat West Indies	Lahore	1987-88
	1 run	Australia beat India	Madras	1987-88
	1 run	Australia beat India	Brisbane	1991-92

CAPTAINCY

LIMITED-OVERS INTERNATIONAL CAPTAINS

England (253 matches; 19 captains)

G. A. Gooch 50; M. W. Gatting 37; M. A. Atherton 33; R. G. D. Willis 29; J. M. Brearley 25; D. I. Gower 24; M. H. Denness 12; I. T. Botham 9; A. J. Stewart 7; K. W. R. Fletcher 5; J. E. Emburey 4; A. J. Lamb 4; D. B. Close 3; R. Illingworth 3; G. Boycott 2; N. Gifford 2; A. W. Greig 2; J. H. Edrich 1; A. P. E. Knott 1.

Australia (354 matches; 12 captains)

A. R. Border 178; M. A. Taylor 50; G. S. Chappell 49; K. J. Hughes 49; I. M. Chappell 11; I. A. Healy 4; G. R. Marsh 4; G. N. Yallop 4; R. B. Simpson 2; R. J. Bright 1; D. W. Hookes 1; W. M. Lawry 1.

South Africa (93 matches; 3 captains)

K. C. Wessels 52; W. J. Cronje 38; C. E. B. Rice 3.

West Indies (323 matches; 12 captains)

I. V. A. Richards 108; R. B. Richardson 87; C. H. Lloyd 81; C. A. Walsh 22; C. G. Greenidge 8; D. L. Haynes 7; M. A. Holding 2; R. B. Kanhai 2; B. C. Lara 2; D. L. Murray 2; P. J. L. Dujon 1; A. I. Kallicharran 1.

New Zealand (263 matches; 12 captains)

G. P. Howarth 60; M. D. Crowe 44; K. R. Rutherford 37; J. G. Wright 31; J. V. Coney 25; L. K. Germon 23; J. J. Crowe 16; M. G. Burgess 8; G. M. Turner 8; B. E. Congdon 6; G. R. Larsen 3; A. H. Jones 2.

India (296 matches; 13 captains)

M. Azharuddin 119; Kapil Dev 74; S. M. Gavaskar 37; D. B. Vengsarkar 18; K. Srikkanth 13; R. J. Shastri 11; S. R. Tendulkar 8; S. Venkataraghavan 7; B. S. Bedi 4; A. L. Wadekar 2; M. Amarnath 1; S. M. H. Kirmani 1; G. R. Viswanath 1.

Pakistan (335 matches; 17 captains)

Imran Khan 139; Javed Miandad 62; Wasim Akram 40; Salim Malik 34; Zaheer Abbas 13; Aamir Sohail 9; Ramiz Raja 8; Asif Iqbal 6; Abdul Qadir 5; Wasim Bari 5; Mushtaq Mohammad 4; Intikhab Alam 3; Majid Khan 2; Moin Khan 2; Saeed Anwar 1; Sarfraz Nawaz 1; Waqar Younis 1.

Sri Lanka (225 matches; 9 captains)

A. Ranatunga 117; L. R. D. Mendis 61; P. A. de Silva 18; R. S. Madugalle 13; B. Warnapura 8; A. P. B. Tennekoon 4; R. S. Mahanama 2; D. S. de Silva 1; J. R. Ratnayeke 1.

Zimbabwe (60 matches; 5 captains)

A. Flower 28; D. L. Houghton 17; D. A. G. Fletcher 6; A. J. Traicos 6; A. D. R. Campbell 3.

Associate Members (36 matches; 10 captains)

Gazi Ashraf (Bangladesh) 7; Sultan M. Zarawani (UAE) 7; M. Odumbe (Kenya) 6; S. W. Lubbers (Holland) 4; B. M. Mauricette (Canada) 3; Harilal R. Shah (East Africa) 3; Akram Khan (Bangladesh) 2; Minhaz-ul-Abedin (Bangladesh) 2; Athar Ali Khan (Bangladesh) 1; R. P. Lefebvre (Holland) 1.

MISCELLANEOUS

LARGE ATTENDANCES

Test Series

943,000	Australia v England (5 Tests)	1936-37
In England		
549,650	England v Australia (5 Tests)	1953

Test Matches

†350,534	Australia v England, Melbourne (Third Test)	1936-37
325,000+	India v England, Calcutta (Second Test)	1972-73
In England		
158,000+	England v Australia, Leeds (Fourth Test)	1948
137,915	England v Australia, Lord's (Second Test)	1953

Test Match Day

90,800	Australia v West Indies, Melbourne (Fifth Test, 2nd day)	1960-61

Other First-Class Matches in England

93,000	England v Australia, Lord's (Fourth Victory Match, 3 days)	1945
80,000+	Surrey v Yorkshire, The Oval (3 days)	1906
78,792	Yorkshire v Lancashire, Leeds (3 days)	1904
76,617	Lancashire v Yorkshire, Manchester (3 days)	1926

Limited-Overs Internationals

‡100,000	India v South Africa, Calcutta	1993-94
‡100,000	India v West Indies, Calcutta	1993-94
‡100,000	India v Sri Lanka, Calcutta (World Cup semi-final)	1995-96
‡100,000	India v West Indies, Calcutta	1994-95
‡90,000	India v Pakistan, Calcutta	1986-87
‡90,000	India v South Africa, Calcutta	1991-92
87,182	England v Pakistan, Melbourne (World Cup final)	1991-92
86,133	Australia v West Indies, Melbourne	1983-84

† *Although no official figures are available, the attendance at the Fourth Test between India and England at Calcutta, 1981-82, was thought to have exceeded this figure.*

‡ *No official attendance figures were issued for these games, but capacity is believed to have reached 100,000 following rebuilding in 1993.*

LORD'S CRICKET GROUND

Lord's and the MCC were founded in 1787. The Club has enjoyed an uninterrupted career since that date, but there have been three grounds known as Lord's. The first (1787-1810) was situated where Dorset Square now is; the second (1809-13), at North Bank, had to be abandoned owing to the cutting of the Regent's Canal; and the third, opened in 1814, is the present one at St John's Wood. It was not until 1866 that the freehold of Lord's was secured by the MCC. The present pavilion was erected in 1890 at a cost of £21,000.

HIGHEST INDIVIDUAL SCORES MADE AT LORD'S

333	G. A. Gooch	England v India	1990
316*	J. B. Hobbs	Surrey v Middlesex	1926
315*	P. Holmes	Yorkshire v Middlesex	1925

Note: The longest innings in a first-class match at Lord's was played by S. Wettimuny (636 minutes, 190 runs) for Sri Lanka v England, 1984.

HIGHEST TOTALS AT LORD'S

First-Class Matches

729-6 dec.	Australia v England	1930
665	West Indians v Middlesex	1939
653-4 dec.	England v India	1990
652-8 dec.	West Indies v England	1973

Minor Match

735-9 dec. MCC and Ground v Wiltshire 1888

BIGGEST HIT AT LORD'S

The only known instance of a batsman hitting a ball over the present pavilion at Lord's occurred when A. E. Trott, appearing for MCC against Australians on July 31, August 1, 2, 1899, drove M. A. Noble so far and high that the ball struck a chimney pot and fell behind the building.

MINOR CRICKET

HIGHEST INDIVIDUAL SCORES

628* A. E. J. Collins, Clark's House v North Town at Clifton College. (A Junior House match. His innings of 6 hours 50 minutes was spread over four afternoons.) 1899
566 C. J. Eady, Break-o'-Day v Wellington at Hobart.................... 1901-02
515 D. R. Havewalla, B.B. and C.I. Rly v St Xavier's at Bombay............ 1933-34
506* J. C. Sharp, Melbourne GS v Geelong College at Melbourne 1914-15
502* Chaman Lal, Mehandra Coll., Patiala v Government Coll., Rupar at Patiala 1956-57
485 A. E. Stoddart, Hampstead v Stoics at Hampstead.................... 1886
475* Mohammad Iqbal, Muslim Model HS v Islamia HS, Sialkot at Lahore 1958-59
466* G. T. S. Stevens, Beta v Lambda (University College School House match) at Neasden.. 1919
459 J. A. Prout, Wesley College v Geelong College at Geelong 1908-09

Note: The highest score in a Minor County match is 323* by F. E. Lacey for Hampshire v Norfolk at Southampton in 1887; the highest in the Minor Counties Championship is 282 by E. Garnett for Berkshire v Wiltshire at Reading in 1908.

HIGHEST PARTNERSHIP

664* for 3rd V. G. Kambli and S. R. Tendulkar, Sharadashram Vidyamandir School v St Xavier's High School at Bombay 1987-88

RECORD HIT

The Rev. W. Fellows, while at practice on the Christ Church ground at Oxford in 1856, drove a ball bowled by Charles Rogers 175 yards from hit to pitch.

THROWING THE CRICKET BALL

140 yards 2 feet, Robert Percival, on the Durham Sands racecourse, Co. Durham c1882
140 yards 9 inches, Ross Mackenzie, at Toronto.............................. 1872
140 yards, "King Billy" the Aborigine at Clermont, Queensland............... 1872

Note: Extensive research has shown that these traditional records are probably authentic, if not necessarily wholly accurate. Modern competitions have failed to produce similar distances although Ian Pont, the Essex all-rounder who also played baseball, was reported to have thrown 138 yards in Cape Town in 1981. There have been speculative reports attributing throws of 150 yards or more to figures as diverse at the South African Test player Colin Bland, the Latvian javelin thrower Janis Lusis, who won a gold medal for the Soviet Union in the 1968 Olympics, and the British sprinter Charley Ransome. The definitive record is still awaited.

DATES OF FORMATION OF FIRST-CLASS COUNTIES

		Present Club		
County	*First known organisation*	*Original date*	*Reorganisation, if substantial*	*First-class status from*
Derbyshire	1870	1870	—	1871
Durham	1874	1882	1991	1992
Essex	By 1790	1876	—	1895
Glamorgan	1861	1888	—	1921
Gloucestershire	1863	1871	—	1870
Hampshire	1849	1863	1879	1864
Kent	1842	1859	1870	1864
Lancashire	1864	1864	—	1865
Leicestershire	By 1820	1879	—	1895
Middlesex	1863	1864	—	1864
Northamptonshire	1820	1878	—	1905
Nottinghamshire	1841	1841	1866	1864
Somerset	1864	1875	—	1882
Surrey	1845	1845	—	1864
Sussex	1836	1839	1857	1864
Warwickshire	1826	1882	—	1895
Worcestershire	1844	1865	—	1899
Yorkshire	1861	1863	1891	1864

Note: Derbyshire lost first-class status from 1888 to 1894, Hampshire between 1886 and 1894 and Somerset between 1886 and 1890.

DATES OF FORMATION OF CLUBS IN THE CURRENT MINOR COUNTIES CHAMPIONSHIP

County	*First known organisation*	*Present Club*
Bedfordshire	1847	1899
Berkshire	By 1841	1895
Buckinghamshire	1864	1891
Cambridgeshire	1844	1891
Cheshire	1819	1908
Cornwall	1813	1894
Cumberland	1884	1948
Devon	1824	1899
Dorset	1862 *or* 1871	1896
Herefordshire	1836	1991
Hertfordshire	1838	1876
Lincolnshire	1853	1906
Norfolk	1827	1876
Northumberland	1834	1895
Oxfordshire	1787	1921
Shropshire	1819 or 1829	1956
Staffordshire	1871	1871
Suffolk	1864	1932
Wales Minor Counties	1988	1988
Wiltshire	1881	1893

CONSTITUTION OF COUNTY CHAMPIONSHIP

At least four possible dates have been given for the start of county cricket in England. The first, patchy, references began in 1825. The earliest mention in any cricket publication is in 1864 and eight counties have come to be regarded as first-class from that date, including Cambridgeshire, who dropped out after 1871. For many years, the County Championship was considered to have started in 1873, when regulations governing qualification first applied; indeed, a special commemorative stamp was issued by the Post Office in 1973. However, the Championship was not formally organised until 1890 and before then champions were proclaimed by the press; sometimes publications differed in their views and no definitive list of champions can start before that date. Eight teams contested the 1890 competition – Gloucestershire, Kent, Lancashire, Middlesex, Nottinghamshire, Surrey, Sussex and Yorkshire. Somerset joined in the following year, and in 1895 the Championship began to acquire something of its modern shape when Derbyshire, Essex, Hampshire, Leicestershire and Warwickshire were added. At that point MCC officially recognised the competition's existence. Worcestershire, Northamptonshire and Glamorgan were admitted to the Championship in 1899, 1905 and 1921 respectively and are regarded as first-class from these dates. An invitation in 1921 to Buckinghamshire to enter the Championship was declined, owing to the lack of necessary playing facilities, and an application by Devon in 1948 was unsuccessful. Durham were admitted to the Championship in 1992 and were granted first-class status prior to their pre-season tour of Zimbabwe.

MOST COUNTY CHAMPIONSHIP APPEARANCES

762	W. Rhodes	Yorkshire	1898-1930
707	F. E. Woolley	Kent	1906-38
668	C. P. Mead	Hampshire	1906-36
617	N. Gifford	Worcestershire (484), Warwickshire (133)	1960-88
611	W. G. Quaife	Warwickshire	1895-1928
601	G. H. Hirst	Yorkshire	1891-1921

The most appearances for counties not mentioned singly above are:

594	F. J. Titmus	Middlesex	1949-82
591	W. E. Astill	Leicestershire	1906-39
589	D. J. Shepherd	Glamorgan	1950-72
571	C. W. L. Parker	Gloucestershire	1905-35
561	J. Langridge	Sussex	1924-53
544	G. Gunn	Nottinghamshire	1902-32
538	D. Kenyon	Worcestershire	1946-67
536	J. B. Hobbs	Surrey	1905-34
529	K. W. R. Fletcher	Essex	1962-88
526	E. Tyldesley	Lancashire	1909-36
506	D. C. Morgan	Derbyshire	1950-69
479	B. A. Langford	Somerset	1953-74
464	D. Brookes	Northamptonshire	1934-59
82	S. J. E. Brown	Durham	1992-96

Notes: F. J. Titmus also played one match for Surrey (1978). The most appearances by a captain is 407 by Lord Hawke for Yorkshire (1883-1909), by a wicket-keeper 506 by H. Strudwick for Surrey (1902-27) and by an amateur 496 by P. A. Perrin for Essex (1896-1928).

MOST CONSECUTIVE COUNTY CHAMPIONSHIP APPEARANCES

423	K. G. Suttle	Sussex	1954-69
412	J. G. Binks	Yorkshire	1955-69
399	J. Vine	Sussex	1899-1914
344	E. H. Killick	Sussex	1898-1912
326	C. N. Woolley	Northamptonshire	1913-31
305	A. H. Dyson	Glamorgan	1930-47
301	B. Taylor	Essex	1961-72

Notes: J. Vine made 417 consecutive appearances for Sussex in all first-class matches between July 1900 and September 1914.

J. G. Binks did not miss a Championship match for Yorkshire between making his debut in June 1955 and retiring at the end of the 1969 season.

UMPIRES

MOST COUNTY CHAMPIONSHIP APPEARANCES

569	T. W. Spencer	1950-1980
533	F. Chester	1922-1955
516	H. G. Baldwin	1932-1962
481	P. B. Wight	1966-1995
457	A. Skelding	1931-1958

MOST SEASONS ON FIRST-CLASS LIST

31	T. W. Spencer	1950-1980
30	P. B. Wight	1966-1995
28	F. Chester	1922-1955
28	**D. J. Constant**	**1969-1996**
27	**H. D. Bird**	**1970-1996**
27	J. Moss	1899-1929
27	**A. G. T. Whitehead**	**1970-1996**
26	W. A. J. West	1896-1925
25	H. G. Baldwin	1932-1962
25	A. Jepson	1960-1984
25	**R. Julian**	**1972-1996**
25	J. G. Langridge	1956-1980
25	**K. E. Palmer**	**1972-1996**

Bold type denotes umpires who stood in the 1996 season.

PART FOUR: ENGLISH CRICKET IN 1996

FEATURES OF 1996

Double-Hundreds (24)

312	J. E. R. Gallian	Lancashire v Derbyshire at Manchester.
275*	M. J. Walker	Kent v Somerset at Canterbury.
241	G. D. Lloyd	Lancashire v Essex at Chelmsford.
239	C. J. Adams	Derbyshire v Hampshire at Southampton.
235	S. P. James	Glamorgan v Nottinghamshire at Worksop.
219*	Saeed Anwar	Pakistanis v Glamorgan at Pontypridd.
218†	J. J. Whitaker	Leicestershire v Yorkshire at Bradford.
215	A. Habib	Leicestershire v Worcestershire at Leicester.
215	G. A. Hick	Worcestershire v Indians at Worcester.
214*	D. M. Jones	Derbyshire v Yorkshire at Sheffield.
214	M. P. Maynard	Glamorgan v Lancashire at Cardiff.
213	M. D. Moxon	Yorkshire v Glamorgan at Cardiff.
212	T. M. Moody	Worcestershire v Nottinghamshire at Worcester.
210*	D. J. Sales	Northamptonshire v Worcestershire at Kidderminster.
207	P. D. Bowler	Somerset v Surrey at Taunton.
205	M. B. Loye	Northamptonshire v Yorkshire at Northampton.
204	N. H. Fairbrother	Lancashire v Warwickshire at Birmingham.
204	V. J. Wells§	Leicestershire v Northamptonshire at Leicester.
203	P. A. Cottey	Glamorgan v Leicestershire at Swansea.
202*	H. Morris	Glamorgan v Yorkshire at Cardiff.
201*	R. J. Warren	Northamptonshire v Glamorgan at Northampton.
201	G. A. Gooch	Essex v Somerset at Taunton.
200*	K. J. Barnett	Derbyshire v Leicestershire at Derby.
200†	V. J. Wells§	Leicestershire v Yorkshire at Bradford.

† *V. J. Wells and J. J. Whitaker scored double-hundreds in the same innings.*
§ *V. J. Wells scored two double-hundreds.*

Hundred on First-Class Debut in Britain

105*	A. Jadeja	Indians v Worcestershire at Worcester.
110	S. D. Peters	Essex v Cambridge University at Cambridge.
165	V. Rathore	Indians v Worcestershire at Worcester.
219*	Saeed Anwar	Pakistanis v Glamorgan at Pontypridd.
210*	D. J. Sales	Northamptonshire v Worcestershire at Kidderminster.
101	E. T. Smith	Cambridge University v Glamorgan at Cambridge.

Hundred in Each Innings of a Match

C. J. Adams	125	136*	Derbyshire v Middlesex at Derby.
A. J. Hollioake	128	117*	Surrey v Somerset at Taunton.
T. M. Moody	106	169	Worcestershire v Northamptonshire at Kidderminster.
P. N. Weekes	171*	160	Middlesex v Somerset at Uxbridge.

Fastest Hundred

G. D. Lloyd .... 70 balls Lancashire v Essex at Chelmsford.

Hundred Before Lunch

G. A. Gooch	62* to 170*	Essex v Glamorgan at Chelmsford (2nd day).
W. J. House	117*	Cambridge University v Derbyshire at Cambridge (2nd day).
N. V. Knight	115*	Warwickshire v Sussex at Hove (1st day).
S. G. Law (2)	104*	Essex v Indians at Chelmsford (2nd day).
	27* to 161*	Essex v Durham at Hartlepool (3rd day).
G. D. Lloyd	42* to 142	Lancashire v Glamorgan at Cardiff (3rd day).
M. P. Maynard	19* to 128*	Glamorgan v Yorkshire at Cardiff (3rd day).
Saeed Anwar	111*	Pakistanis v Warwickshire at Birmingham (1st day).
P. V. Simmons	28* to 133*	Leicestershire v Durham at Chester-le-Street (2nd day).

First to 1,000 Runs

M. G. Bevan (Yorkshire) on June 24.

2,000 Runs

No batsman scored 2,000 runs. The highest aggregate was 1,944 by G. A. Gooch (Essex).

Carrying Bat Through Completed Innings

D. J. Bicknell	129*	Surrey (299) v Worcestershire at The Oval.
A. S. Rollins	78*	Derbyshire (220) v Sussex at Hove.
W. P. C. Weston	100*	Worcestershire (238) v Derbyshire at Chesterfield.

Unusual Dismissals

Handled the ball	K. M. Krikken, Derbyshire v Indians at Derby.
Stumped by a substitute (W. M. Noon)	H. H. Gibbs, South Africa A v Nottinghamshire at Nottingham.

Notable Partnerships

First Wicket

372† R. R. Montgomerie/M. B. Loye, Northamptonshire v Yorkshire at Northampton.
362 M. D. Moxon/M. P. Vaughan, Yorkshire v Glamorgan at Cardiff.
334*† S. Hutton/M. A. Roseberry, Durham v Oxford University at Oxford.
255* R. R. Montgomerie/A. Fordham, Northamptonshire v Pakistanis at Northampton.
255 W. P. C. Weston/M. J. Church, Worcestershire v Oxford University at Oxford.

Second Wicket

300† W. P. C. Weston/G. A. Hick, Worcestershire v Indians at Worcester.
298 A. S. Rollins/C. J. Adams, Derbyshire v Hampshire at Southampton.

Third Wicket

362* Saeed Anwar/Inzamam-ul-Haq, Pakistanis v Glamorgan at Pontypridd.
269 T. S. Curtis/T. M. Moody, Worcestershire v Northamptonshire at Kidderminster.
255 S. C. Ganguly/S. R. Tendulkar, India v England (Third Test) at Nottingham.

Fourth Wicket

358† S. P. Titchard/G. D. Lloyd, Lancashire v Essex at Chelmsford.
278 D. M. Jones/J. E. Owen, Derbyshire v Yorkshire at Sheffield.
272 D. Byas/A. McGrath, Yorkshire v Hampshire at Harrogate.
251* M. P. Maynard/P. A. Cottey, Glamorgan v Gloucestershire at Bristol.
251 N. J. Speak/G. D. Lloyd, Lancashire v Glamorgan at Cardiff.

Fifth Wicket

320†	J. J. Whitaker/A. Habib, Leicestershire v Worcestershire at Leicester.
239	R. J. Warren/D. J. Capel, Northamptonshire v Glamorgan at Northampton.
226	K. M. Curran/A. L. Penberthy, Northamptonshire v Leicestershire at Leicester.

Sixth Wicket

284†	P. V. Simmons/P. A. Nixon, Leicestershire v Durham at Chester-le-Street.
252	C. White/R. J. Blakey, Yorkshire v Lancashire at Leeds.

Seventh Wicket

278*†	S. Lee/R. J. Turner, Somerset v Worcestershire at Bath.
211†	P. A. Cottey/O. D. Gibson, Glamorgan v Leicestershire at Swansea.

Eighth Wicket

198†	K. M. Krikken/D. G. Cork, Derbyshire v Lancashire at Manchester.
172†	P. A. Nixon/D. J. Millns, Leicestershire v Lancashire at Manchester.

Ninth Wicket

127†	D. G. C. Ligertwood/S. J. E. Brown, Durham v Surrey at Stockton-on-Tees.

Tenth Wicket

141†	A. F. Giles/T. A. Munton, Warwickshire v Worcestershire at Worcester.
113	P. J. Hartley/R. D. Stemp, Yorkshire v Middlesex at Lord's.
112	P. V. Simmons/A. D. Mullally, Leicestershire v Middlesex at Leicester.
110	C. E. W. Silverwood/R. D. Stemp, Yorkshire v Durham at Chester-le-Street.
105	A. R. K. Pierson/A. D. Mullally, Leicestershire v Surrey at The Oval.
103†	M. M. Betts/D. M. Cox, Durham v Sussex at Hove.
101*	J. D. Carr/P. C. R. Tufnell, Middlesex v Worcestershire at Lord's.

* *Unbroken partnership.* † *County record for that wicket.*

Twelve or More Wickets in a Match (5)

13-88	G. D. Rose	Somerset v Nottinghamshire at Taunton.
13-123	P. C. R. Tufnell ..	Middlesex v Lancashire at Manchester.
13-159	T. M. Moody.....	Worcestershire v Gloucestershire at Worcester.
12-83	A. J. Harris	Derbyshire v Middlesex at Derby.
12-135	P. M. Such	Essex v Somerset at Taunton.

Eight or More Wickets in an Innings (9)

9-38	C. A. Connor.....	Hampshire v Gloucestershire at Southampton.
8-22	D. Follett	Middlesex v Durham at Lord's.
8-22	G. M. Gilder	South Africa A v Worcestershire at Worcester.
8-36	M. A. Ealham	Kent v Warwickshire at Birmingham.
8-39	P. N. Weekes	Middlesex v Glamorgan at Lord's.
8-73	A. M. Smith	Gloucestershire v Middlesex at Lord's.
8-75	I. D. K. Salisbury .	Sussex v Essex at Chelmsford.
8-98	D. W. Headley ...	Kent v Derbyshire at Derby.
8-118	P. M. Such	Essex v Yorkshire at Leeds.

Hat-Tricks

A. P. Cowan	Essex v Gloucestershire at Colchester.
D. W. Headley	Kent v Derbyshire at Derby.
D. W. Headley	Kent v Worcestershire at Canterbury.
‡D. W. Headley	Kent v Hampshire at Canterbury.
K. D. James†	Hampshire v Indians at Southampton.
‡M. J. McCague..........	Kent v Hampshire at Canterbury.

† *Also four wickets in four balls.* ‡ *In the same match.*

Wicket with First Ball in First-Class Cricket

P. D. Collingwood	Durham v Northamptonshire at Chester-le-Street.
J. P. Hewitt..............	Middlesex v Gloucestershire at Lord's.
R. W. Tennent	Cambridge University v Sussex at Hove.

100 Wickets

No bowler took 100 wickets. The highest aggregate was 85 by C. A. Walsh (Gloucestershire).

Most Overs Bowled in an Innings

68.3–18–174–2 ...	A. F. Giles	Warwickshire v Yorkshire at Leeds.

Hundred and Four Wickets with Consecutive Balls (Unique instance)

K. D. James................	Hampshire v Indians at Southampton.

Nine or More Wicket-Keeping Dismissals in a Match

10 ct†.....	C. W. Scott	Durham v Yorkshire at Chester-le-Street.
9 ct......	G. J. Kersey	Surrey v Durham at Stockton-on-Tees.
9 ct......	R. J. Turner	Somerset v Yorkshire at Scarborough.

† *County record.*

Six or More Wicket-Keeping Dismissals in an Innings

7 ct†.....	C. W. Scott	Durham v Yorkshire at Chester-le-Street.
6 ct......	W. K. Hegg	Lancashire v Durham at Chester-le-Street.
6 ct......	G. J. Kersey	Surrey v Durham at Stockton-on-Tees.
5 ct, 1 st .	D. G. C. Ligertwood	Durham v Kent at Maidstone.
4 ct, 2 st .	L. N. P. Walker	Nottinghamshire v Gloucestershire at Nottingham.

† *County record.*

Match Double (100 Runs and 10 Wickets)

D. J. Millns	103; 4-74, 6-54	Leicestershire v Essex at Leicester.

No Byes Conceded in Total of 500 or More

S. J. Rhodes	Worcestershire v Leicestershire (638-8 dec.) at Leicester.
R. J. Rollins	Essex v Kent (590) at Ilford.
C. P. Metson	Glamorgan v Yorkshire (536-8 dec.) at Cardiff.
D. G. C. Ligertwood..	Durham v Leicestershire (516-6 dec.) at Chester-le-Street.
W. M. Noon	Nottinghamshire v Hampshire (513-4 dec.) at Southampton.
D. R. H. Churton	Cambridge University v Oxford University (513-6 dec.) at Lord's.
W. K. Hegg.........	Lancashire v Essex (509) at Chelmsford.

Highest Innings Totals

686 .... Lancashire v Essex at Chelmsford.
681-7 dec. .... Leicestershire v Yorkshire at Bradford.
645-7 dec. .... Warwickshire v Sussex at Hove.
638-8 dec. .... Leicestershire v Worcestershire at Leicester.
616-7 dec. .... Kent v Somerset at Canterbury.
601-9 dec. .... Northamptonshire v Nottinghamshire at Nottingham.
597 .... Lancashire v Warwickshire at Birmingham.
590 .... Kent v Essex at Ilford.
587-9 dec. .... Lancashire v Derbyshire at Manchester.
569 .... Gloucestershire v Warwickshire at Cheltenham.
564 .... England v India (Third Test) at Nottingham.
561 .... Yorkshire v Derbyshire at Sheffield.
558 .... Somerset v Surrey at Taunton.
552-8 dec. .... Sussex v Durham at Hove.

Highest Fourth-Innings Totals

449-9 .... Worcestershire v Somerset at Bath (set 446).

Lowest Innings Totals

67 .... Durham v Middlesex at Lord's.
71 .... Gloucestershire v Leicestershire at Cheltenham.
77 .... Worcestershire v South Africa A at Worcester.
83 .... Somerset v Leicestershire at Leicester
85 .... Middlesex v Sussex at Horsham.
89 .... Derbyshire v Leicestershire at Derby.
97 .... Nottinghamshire v Essex at Chelmsford.
98† .... Nottinghamshire v Derbyshire at Derby.
98 .... Derbyshire v Northamptonshire at Northampton.

† *One batsman retired hurt.*

Match Aggregates of 1,500 Runs

Runs	*Wkts*	
1,606	34	Somerset v Derbyshire at Taunton.
1,537	32	Surrey v Derbyshire at The Oval.
1,523	28	Lancashire v Derbyshire at Manchester.
1,523	36	Hampshire v Essex at Southampton.
1,512	27	Worcestershire v Northamptonshire at Kidderminster.

Four Hundreds in an Innings

Glamorgan (509-3 dec.) v Gloucestershire at Bristol:
S. P. James 118, H. Morris 108, M. P. Maynard 145*, P. A. Cottey 101*.

Eleven Bowlers in an Innings

Kent v Yorkshire (223-4) at Canterbury.

Most Extras in an Innings

	b	*l-b*	*w*	*n-b*	
79	5	16	4	54	Somerset (558) v Surrey at Taunton.
72	3	25	3	41	Derbyshire (409) v Indians at Derby.
67	34	15	2	16	Lancashire (597) v Warwickshire at Birmingham.
60	1	22	3	34	Leicestershire (454-9 dec.) v Essex at Leicester.

Under TCCB regulations, two extras were scored for every no-ball, in addition to any runs scored off that ball, except in Tests. There were 11 further instances of 50 or more extras in an innings.

Career Aggregate Milestones†

25,000 runs .... R. T. Robinson.
20,000 runs .... T. S. Curtis, M. D. Moxon, R. A. Smith.
15,000 runs .... M. A. Atherton, P. Johnson, D. M. Jones, T. M. Moody, D. N. Patel, J. J. Whitaker.
10,000 runs .... R. J. Blakey, A. Fordham, N. Hussain, S. J. Rhodes, T. R. Ward.
500 wickets .... A. I. C. Dodemaide, P. J. Hartley, Mushtaq Ahmed.
500 dismissals .... R. J. Blakey, I. A. Healy, W. K. Hegg, P. Moores.

† *Achieved since September 1995.*

WALTER LAWRENCE TROPHY

The Walter Lawrence Trophy for the fastest first-class century in 1996 was won by Graham Lloyd of Lancashire, who reached 100 in 70 balls against Essex. He received £1,000.

RIDLEY WICKET

No bowler took 100 first-class wickets in 1996 to claim the Ridley Wicket, a silver stump, but the Ridley Plate was awarded to Courtney Walsh of Gloucestershire, the leading wicket-taker with 85. He received £1,000.

CORNHILL INSURANCE ENGLAND PLAYER OF THE YEAR

The Cornhill Insurance England Player of the Year Award was won in April 1996 by Dominic Cork of Derbyshire. He received £7,500.

COOPERS & LYBRAND AWARDS

The Coopers & Lybrand International Test Player of the Year Trophy was won in 1996 by Steve Waugh of Australia for his all-round performances against West Indies, Pakistan and Sri Lanka. Waugh was also voted Test Player of the Year in a Coopers & Lybrand poll carried out on the Internet, gaining 39 per cent of the vote. The award for the England player who had made the biggest impact in the Coopers & Lybrand Ratings in the 12 months to April 1996 was won by Graeme Hick, who had climbed to seventh in the world rankings for batsmen.

FIRST-CLASS AVERAGES, 1996

BATTING

(Qualification: 8 completed innings)

* *Signifies not out.* † *Denotes a left-handed batsman.*

		M	*I*	*NO*	*R*	*HS*	*100s*	*50s*	*Avge*
1	†S. C. Ganguly (*Indians*)	9	14	6	762	136	3	4	95.25
2	†Saeed Anwar (*Pakistanis*)	10	19	1	1,224	219*	5	4	68.00
3	G. A. Gooch (*Essex*)	17	30	1	1,944	201	8	6	67.03
4	H. H. Gibbs (*South Africa A*)	8	14	1	867	183	2	5	66.69
5	A. J. Hollioake (*Surrey*)	17	29	6	1,522	129	5	8	66.17
6	Inzamam-ul-Haq (*Pakistanis*)	9	14	2	792	169*	3	4	66.00
7	†M. G. Bevan (*Yorks*)	12	22	3	1,225	160*	3	8	64.47
8	S. R. Tendulkar (*Indians*)	7	11	0	707	177	2	5	64.27
9	†G. P. Thorpe (*Surrey*)	16	29	4	1,569	185	6	7	62.76
10	M. P. Maynard (*Glam*)	17	30	4	1,610	214	6	6	61.92
11	S. Lee (*Somerset*)	17	25	4	1,300	167*	5	5	61.90
12	S. G. Law (*Essex*)	15	26	1	1,545	172	6	5	61.80
13	†M. J. Walker (*Kent*)	8	13	3	606	275*	1	2	60.60
14	K. M. Curran (*Northants*)	15	28	7	1,242	150	2	8	59.14
15	D. N. Crookes (*South Africa A*)	7	11	1	566	155*	2	3	56.60
16	P. V. Simmons (*Leics*)	17	24	2	1,244	171	4	7	56.54
17	†H. Morris (*Glam*)	18	32	2	1,666	202*	6	9	55.53
18	W. S. Kendall (*OU & Hants*)	12	23	4	1,045	145*	3	6	55.00
19	J. J. Whitaker (*Leics*)	16	23	3	1,093	218	4	2	54.65
20	†N. H. Fairbrother (*Lancs*)	12	20	0	1,068	204	2	8	53.40
21	C. J. Adams (*Derbys*)	20	36	3	1,742	239	6	8	52.78
22	†W. J. House (*CU*)	8	15	5	526	136	2	2	52.60
23	D. M. Jones (*Derbys*)	19	34	5	1,502	214*	4	7	51.79
24	†M. A. Butcher (*Surrey*)	18	34	3	1,604	160	3	13	51.74
25	P. A. Cottey (*Glam*)	20	36	6	1,543	203	4	9	51.43
26	T. M. Moody (*Worcs*)	19	31	3	1,427	212	7	4	50.96
27	R. Dravid (*Indians*)	9	16	5	553	101*	1	4	50.27
28	J. P. Crawley (*Lancs*)	15	25	3	1,102	112*	3	8	50.09
29	D. Ripley (*Northants*)	11	16	7	448	88*	0	3	49.77
30	G. D. Lloyd (*Lancs*)	15	25	1	1,194	241	3	4	49.75
	J. B. Commins (*South Africa A*)	9	15	3	597	114*	1	5	49.75
32	M. R. Ramprakash (*Middx*)	17	31	2	1,441	169	4	8	49.68
33	†I. D. Austin (*Lancs*)	10	12	3	437	95*	0	3	48.55
34	†D. M. Cox (*Durham*)	7	13	4	434	95*	0	4	48.22
35	R. A. Smith (*Hants*)	17	31	2	1,396	179	3	8	48.13
36	E. T. Smith (*CU & Kent*)	7	12	0	576	101	2	4	48.00
37	†N. V. Knight (*Warwicks*)	15	28	3	1,196	132	4	5	47.84
38	B. F. Smith (*Leics*)	20	29	3	1,243	190	3	4	47.80
39	S. P. James (*Glam*)	20	38	1	1,766	235	7	6	47.72
40	C. L. Hooper (*Kent*)	17	29	2	1,287	155	3	9	47.66
41	Ijaz Ahmed, sen. (*Pakistanis*)	9	16	2	664	141	2	4	47.42
42	V. Rathore (*Indians*)	10	17	0	805	165	1	7	47.35
43	C. M. Gupte (*OU*)	11	14	1	606	132	2	3	46.61
44	†A. C. Ridley (*OU*)	7	9	0	417	155	2	1	46.33
45	N. Hussain (*Essex*)	18	31	1	1,386	158	3	7	46.20
46	M. B. Loye (*Northants*)	14	25	2	1,048	205	2	5	45.56
47	K. J. Barnett (*Derbys*)	18	34	2	1,456	200*	3	9	45.50
48	Salim Malik (*Pakistanis*)	9	14	4	450	104*	2	1	45.00

		M	*I*	*NO*	*R*	*HS*	*100s*	*50s*	*Avge*
49	R. T. Robinson (*Notts*)	17	31	2	1,302	184	3	6	44.89
50	S. P. Titchard (*Lancs*)	13	23	2	939	163	2	5	44.71
51	†Asif Mujtaba (*Pakistanis*)	10	16	6	445	100*	1	2	44.50
52	G. A. Hick (*Worcs*)	17	29	1	1,245	215	5	3	44.46
53	J. E. R. Gallian (*Lancs*)	15	29	3	1,156	312	3	3	44.46
54	A. Jadeja (*Indians*)	8	13	2	489	112*	2	2	44.45
55	V. J. Wells (*Leics*)	20	30	0	1,331	204	4	3	44.36
56	M. Keech (*Hants*)	12	21	3	793	104	1	7	44.05
57	M. N. Lathwell (*Somerset*)	18	32	4	1,224	109	2	7	43.71
	G. F. Archer (*Notts*)	13	24	3	918	143	2	5	43.71
59	M. D. Moxon (*Yorks*)	14	25	3	961	213	2	5	43.68
60	†W. P. C. Weston (*Worcs*)	20	37	5	1,389	171*	4	7	43.40
61	T. L. Penney (*Warwicks*)	19	34	4	1,295	134	3	8	43.16
62	A. J. Stewart (*Surrey*)	14	24	1	966	170	1	7	42.00
63	T. R. Ward (*Kent*)	18	31	1	1,252	161	2	9	41.73
64	K. R. Spiring (*Worcs*)	18	32	6	1,084	144	3	7	41.69
65	K. Greenfield (*Sussex*)	14	26	4	916	154*	3	3	41.63
66	S. V. Manjrekar (*Indians*)	9	15	2	540	101	1	4	41.53
67	P. D. Bowler (*Somerset*)	19	34	4	1,228	207	2	7	40.93
68	H. D. Ackerman (*South Africa A*)	7	11	0	447	99	0	4	40.63
69	K. M. Krikken (*Derbys*)	19	29	7	882	104	1	3	40.09
70	A. N. Aymes (*Hants*)	19	32	12	801	113	2	2	40.05
71	†P. A. Nixon (*Leics*)	20	27	5	880	106	3	4	40.00
72	M. Azharuddin (*Indians*)	8	13	2	439	111*	1	3	39.90
73	V. S. Solanki (*Worcs*)	14	24	3	828	90	0	6	39.42
74	C. L. Cairns (*Notts*)	16	29	5	946	114	1	6	39.41
75	S. J. Rhodes (*Worcs*)	19	29	5	939	110	1	8	39.12
76	J. S. Laney (*Hants*)	17	30	0	1,163	112	4	5	38.76
77	M. P. Vaughan (*Yorks*)	18	32	2	1,161	183	3	6	38.70
78	M. A. Atherton (*Lancs*)	15	26	1	963	160	1	7	38.52
79	R. C. Irani (*Essex*)	19	31	4	1,039	110*	1	7	38.48
80	†N. J. Llong (*Kent*)	14	22	2	763	130	2	5	38.15
81	C. M. Wells (*Derbys*)	12	19	3	609	165	1	3	38.06
82	R. R. Montgomerie (*Northants*)	18	34	3	1,178	168	4	4	38.00
	G. A. Khan (*OU & Derbys*)	13	18	2	608	101*	1	4	38.00
84	V. P. Terry (*Hants*)	7	12	2	379	87*	0	3	37.90
85	A. Symonds (*Glos*)	18	30	1	1,097	127	3	4	37.82
86	A. W. Evans (*Glam*)	7	13	3	376	71*	0	2	37.60
87	W. K. Hegg (*Lancs*)	17	25	6	713	134	1	3	37.52
88	O. D. Gibson (*Glam*)	9	15	3	449	97	0	3	37.41
89	T. J. G. O'Gorman (*Derbys*)	11	20	3	636	109*	1	6	37.41
90	†I. J. Sutcliffe (*OU & Leics*)	8	12	0	443	83	0	5	36.91
91	†P. N. Weekes (*Middx*)	19	35	2	1,218	171*	4	4	36.90
92	†D. L. Hemp (*Glam*)	8	13	2	405	103*	1	1	36.81
93	A. P. Wells (*Sussex*)	19	35	2	1,206	122	2	6	36.54
94	N. R. Mongia (*Indians*)	7	12	2	364	85	0	2	36.40
95	B. P. Julian (*Surrey*)	16	23	2	759	119	2	3	36.14
96	A. J. Moles (*Warwicks*)	13	25	0	903	176	2	4	36.12
	N. J. Lenham (*Sussex*)	16	28	3	903	145	2	5	36.12
98	R. J. Bailey (*Northants*)	12	22	2	722	163	1	3	36.10
99	M. W. Gatting (*Middx*)	16	25	0	901	171	1	8	36.04
100	A. Habib (*Leics*)	16	24	2	792	215	1	2	36.00
101	A. Singh (*CU & Warwicks*)	12	22	2	718	157	2	1	35.90
102	S. L. Campbell (*Durham*)	16	29	0	1,041	118	1	7	35.89
103	†P. C. L. Holloway (*Somerset*)	10	16	1	535	168	1	3	35.66
104	R. J. Harden (*Somerset*)	12	20	1	676	136	1	5	35.57
105	A. S. Rollins (*Derbys*)	19	36	5	1,101	131	3	5	35.51
106	†Shadab Kabir (*Pakistanis*)	7	12	1	390	99	0	3	35.45
107	K. R. Brown (*Middx*)	18	31	5	917	83	0	8	35.26

		M	I	NO	R	HS	100s	50s	Avge
108	D. D. J. Robinson (*Essex*)	12	23	2	738	97	0	8	35.14
109	A. A. Metcalfe (*Notts*)	12	22	0	771	128	1	3	35.04
110	R. J. Blakey (*Yorks*)	19	30	6	839	109*	1	5	34.95
111	A. P. Grayson (*Essex*)	17	30	3	939	140	2	3	34.77
112	†D. J. Bicknell (*Surrey*)	17	31	3	969	129*	2	3	34.60
113	†R. C. Russell (*Glos*)	19	30	5	858	124	1	7	34.32
114	P. Bainbridge (*Durham*)	11	19	1	617	83	0	5	34.27
115	D. L. Maddy (*Leics*)	20	30	2	958	101*	1	4	34.21
116	†R. A. Kettleborough (*Yorks*)	7	9	0	307	108	1	1	34.11
117	N. J. Speak (*Lancs*)	12	21	4	579	138*	1	3	34.05
118	G. P. Butcher (*Glam*)	14	24	4	679	89	0	5	33.95
119	D. G. Cork (*Derbys*)	18	29	6	779	101*	1	5	33.86
120	†S. Hutton (*Durham*)	14	26	2	812	172*	2	1	33.83
121	D. A. Leatherdale (*Worcs*)	11	18	2	539	122	1	4	33.68
122	T. C. Walton (*Northants*)	6	10	1	302	58	0	4	33.55
123	†K. D. James (*Hants*)	13	23	1	738	118*	2	3	33.54
124	A. Fordham (*Northants*)	10	18	3	502	144*	1	2	33.46
125	N. Shahid (*Surrey*)	11	19	3	535	101	1	4	33.43
126	A. F. Giles (*Warwicks*)	17	27	9	600	106*	1	4	33.33
127	J. E. Owen (*Derbys*)	9	15	0	499	105	2	2	33.26
128	C. W. J. Athey (*Sussex*)	18	33	0	1,091	111	3	5	33.06
129	J. D. Ratcliffe (*Surrey*)	9	16	1	494	69	0	4	32.93
130	M. W. Alleyne (*Glos*)	18	30	3	887	149	1	3	32.85
131	T. S. Curtis (*Worcs*)	17	31	2	952	118	2	5	32.82
132	C. White (*Yorks*)	19	30	1	949	181	1	7	32.72
133	R. Q. Cake (*CU*)	9	16	3	425	102*	1	1	32.69
134	M. A. Ealham (*Kent*)	14	23	4	618	74	0	5	32.52
135	G. F. J. Liebenberg (*S. Africa A*)	8	14	0	453	123	1	2	32.35
136	R. K. Illingworth (*Worcs*)	19	23	10	420	66*	0	1	32.30
137	A. McGrath (*Yorks*)	19	33	2	999	137	2	5	32.22
138	K. P. Evans (*Notts*)	14	18	3	482	71	0	4	32.13
139	†P. R. Pollard (*Notts*)	13	25	2	737	86	0	6	32.04
140	C. C. Lewis (*Surrey*)	14	22	2	639	94	0	4	31.95
141	R. J. Turner (*Somerset*)	18	27	6	668	100*	1	3	31.80
142	P. Johnson (*Notts*)	19	33	2	980	109	2	6	31.61
143	D. P. Fulton (*Kent*)	17	30	3	852	134*	1	5	31.55
144	G. R. Cowdrey (*Kent*)	11	17	0	529	111	1	3	31.11
145	†D. Byas (*Yorks*)	19	32	2	933	138	1	5	31.10
146	G. W. White (*Hants*)	13	24	3	652	73	0	6	31.04
147	P. J. Prichard (*Essex*)	19	31	0	959	108	1	6	30.93
148	M. A. Lynch (*Glos*)	11	19	1	553	72	0	5	30.72
149	M. V. Fleming (*Kent*)	18	30	2	855	116	2	3	30.53
150	S. M. Pollock (*Warwicks*)	13	21	1	606	150*	2	1	30.30
151	J. N. Batty (*OU*)	10	13	3	302	56	0	2	30.20
152	S. R. Lampitt (*Worcs*)	19	27	5	658	88	0	3	29.90
153	D. P. Ostler (*Warwicks*)	18	32	3	863	90	0	8	29.75
154	T. H. C. Hancock (*Glos*)	15	27	3	709	116	1	4	29.54
155	M. G. N. Windows (*Glos*)	9	17	2	443	184	1	1	29.53
156	†U. Afzaal (*Notts*)	6	10	1	264	67*	0	2	29.33
157	K. Newell (*Sussex*)	5	9	1	234	105*	1	0	29.25
158	K. A. Parsons (*Somerset*)	8	15	1	408	83*	0	4	29.14
159	D. J. Capel (*Northants*)	16	30	2	814	103	1	4	29.07
160	J. D. Carr (*Middx*)	17	28	1	783	94	0	4	29.00
161	A. Dale (*Glam*)	15	25	1	690	120	1	4	28.75
162	R. J. Warren (*Northants*)	11	18	1	486	201*	1	1	28.58
163	†J. P. Hewitt (*Middx*)	10	15	4	312	72	0	1	28.36
164	†P. R. Whitaker (*Hants*)	12	22	3	535	67*	0	4	28.15
165	P. Moores (*Sussex*)	19	32	4	782	185	2	1	27.92
166	†S. C. Ecclestone (*Somerset*)	8	13	1	334	94	0	3	27.83
166	†Aamir Sohail (*Pakistanis*)	8	14	2	334	49	0	0	27.83

		M	*I*	*NO*	*R*	*HS*	*100s*	*50s*	*Avge*
168	†M. E. Trescothick (*Somerset*)	15	26	0	720	178	1	2	27.69
169	†J. C. Pooley (*Middx*)	18	34	2	881	138*	2	4	27.53
170	†W. G. Khan (*Warwicks*)	15	28	1	738	130	3	2	27.33
171	N. M. K. Smith (*Warwicks*)	16	27	4	626	74	0	3	27.21
172	M. P. Speight (*Sussex*)	11	21	2	514	122*	1	3	27.05
173	V. C. Drakes (*Sussex*)	15	27	3	649	145*	2	4	27.04
174	R. D. B. Croft (*Glam*)	20	30	6	647	78	0	5	26.95
175	Moin Khan (*Pakistanis*)	5	9	1	215	105	1	0	26.87
176	M. A. Roseberry (*Durham*)	17	30	2	744	145*	1	3	26.57
177	J. P. Stephenson (*Hants*)	15	25	2	611	85	0	5	26.56
178	J. A. Daley (*Durham*)	12	21	3	477	76	0	1	26.50
	O. A. Shah (*Middx*)	5	9	1	212	75	0	2	26.50
180	J. J. B. Lewis (*Essex*)	6	11	2	238	69	0	2	26.44
181	†Wasim Akram (*Pakistanis*)	7	9	1	211	68	0	1	26.37
182	M. P. Bicknell (*Surrey*)	16	18	5	333	59*	0	1	25.61
183	G. D. Rose (*Somerset*)	15	21	5	408	93*	0	2	25.50
	C. M. Tolley (*Notts*)	9	14	2	306	67	0	1	25.50
185	M. J. Church (*Worcs*)	6	11	0	280	152	1	0	25.45
186	†A. L. Penberthy (*Northants*)	18	29	4	635	87	0	3	25.40
187	J. W. Hall (*Sussex*)	7	13	0	330	93	0	3	25.38
188	R. J. Maru (*Hants*)	11	17	5	303	55*	0	1	25.25
189	G. J. Kersey (*Surrey*)	15	20	4	402	68*	0	3	25.12
190	M. Burns (*Warwicks*)	8	15	1	345	81	0	3	24.64
191	A. J. Wright (*Glos*)	9	17	0	415	106	1	3	24.41
192	A. D. Brown (*Surrey*)	16	26	3	555	79	0	5	24.13
193	†M. P. Dowman (*Notts*)	9	14	0	337	107	1	0	24.07
194	H. S. Malik (*OU*)	10	13	3	240	61	0	1	24.00
195	R. J. Rollins (*Essex*)	21	34	4	719	74*	0	3	23.96
196	M. Watkinson (*Lancs*)	17	28	1	645	64	0	2	23.88
197	D. R. Hewson (*Glos*)	6	12	1	261	87	0	3	23.72
198	†D. A. Blenkiron (*Durham*)	9	16	2	328	130	2	0	23.42
199	P. D. Collingwood (*Durham*)	11	20	0	464	91	0	2	23.20
200	C. W. Scott (*Durham*)	7	10	1	208	59	0	2	23.11
201	R. J. Cunliffe (*Glos*)	6	11	0	252	82	0	2	22.90
202	D. Gough (*Yorks*)	16	25	3	501	121	1	2	22.77
203	M. J. Powell (*Warwicks*)	4	8	0	182	39	0	0	22.75
204	P. J. Hartley (*Yorks*)	16	24	3	476	89	0	3	22.66
205	D. R. Brown (*Warwicks*)	19	32	2	671	76	0	3	22.36
206	†D. J. Millns (*Leics*)	19	20	1	424	103	1	1	22.31
207	J. E. Emburey (*Northants*)	11	13	4	200	67*	0	1	22.22
208	D. R. Law (*Sussex*)	17	28	0	619	97	0	3	22.10
209	R. S. M. Morris (*Hants*)	5	9	0	195	112	1	0	21.66
210	K. J. Piper (*Warwicks*)	13	22	2	429	82	0	1	21.45
211	J. N. Snape (*Northants*)	10	16	3	277	64	0	1	21.30
212	S. D. Udal (*Hants*)	17	25	4	447	58	0	2	21.28
213	†A. C. Morris (*Yorks*)	6	9	0	189	60	0	1	21.00
214	I. D. K. Salisbury (*Sussex*)	18	30	3	562	83	0	3	20.81
215	S. A. Marsh (*Kent*)	15	24	1	478	127	1	2	20.78
216	A. D. Mullally (*Leics*)	17	17	5	249	75	0	2	20.75
217	S. Elworthy (*Lancs*)	12	16	2	288	88	0	1	20.57
218	D. G. C. Ligertwood (*Durham*)	12	23	5	367	56	0	1	20.38
219	A. R. K. Pierson (*Leics*)	20	23	10	263	44	0	0	20.23
220	S. G. Koenig (*South Africa A*)	7	11	0	221	46	0	0	20.09
221	N. J. Trainor (*Glos*)	8	14	1	261	67	0	2	20.07
222	P. J. Martin (*Lancs*)	13	18	4	278	42	0	0	19.85
223	M. A. Wagh (*OU*)	11	13	3	198	43	0	0	19.80
224	D. W. Headley (*Kent*)	12	16	3	253	63*	0	1	19.46
225	G. Chapple (*Lancs*)	16	23	6	329	37*	0	0	19.35
226	M. J. McCague (*Kent*)	18	26	7	357	63*	0	1	18.78

		M	I	NO	R	HS	100s	50s	Avge
227	A. N. Hayhurst (*Somerset*)	9	13	1	224	96	0	2	18.66
228	W. M. Noon (*Notts*)	13	21	3	332	57	0	1	18.44
229	G. I. Macmillan (*Leics*)	7	12	1	201	41	0	0	18.27
230	P. C. R. Tufnell (*Middx*)	18	26	10	290	67*	0	1	18.12
231	J. C. Harrison (*Middx*)	7	13	2	199	40	0	0	18.09
232	S. M. Milburn (*Hants*)	10	12	2	180	54*	0	1	18.00
233	P. A. J. DeFreitas (*Derbys*)	14	22	0	394	60	0	1	17.90
234	J. E. Benjamin (*Surrey*)	13	14	6	141	38*	0	0	17.62
	A. R. Roberts (*Northants*)	6	8	0	141	39	0	0	17.62
236	M. J. Vandrau (*Derbys*)	10	16	6	175	34*	0	0	17.50
237	R. D. Stemp (*Yorks*)	19	24	9	260	65	0	2	17.33
238	†J. P. Taylor (*Northants*)	17	23	9	242	57	0	1	17.28
239	M. M. Betts (*Durham*)	14	21	3	308	57*	0	1	17.11
240	R. O. Jones (*CU*)	8	13	1	205	61	0	1	17.08
241	N. F. Williams (*Essex*)	12	16	3	221	39	0	0	17.00
242	†R. C. J. Williams (*Glos*)	5	8	0	133	44	0	0	16.62
243	A. M. Smith (*Glos*)	16	25	3	364	55*	0	1	16.54
244	A. D. Shaw (*Glam*)	13	18	1	281	74	0	2	16.52
245	R. T. Bates (*Notts*)	11	15	1	229	34	0	0	16.35
246	†G. J. Parsons (*Leics*)	18	23	5	290	53	0	2	16.11
247	J. D. Batty (*Somerset*)	16	24	4	321	44	0	0	16.05
248	P. M. Such (*Essex*)	19	22	11	176	54	0	1	16.00
	J. Srinath (*Indians*)	7	9	1	128	52	0	1	16.00
250	†M. C. Ilott (*Essex*)	17	24	2	343	58	0	1	15.59
251	C. A. Connor (*Hants*)	10	12	3	140	42	0	0	15.55
252	S. J. E. Brown (*Durham*)	19	31	5	404	60	0	1	15.53
253	M. M. Patel (*Kent*)	18	23	5	278	33	0	0	15.44
254	R. P. Davis (*Glos*)	15	22	2	308	43	0	0	15.40
255	†S. D. Thomas (*Glam*)	11	16	3	199	48	0	0	15.30
256	Mushtaq Ahmed (*Pakistanis*)	7	9	1	118	38	0	0	14.75
257	J. E. Morris (*Durham*)	17	31	1	429	83	0	3	14.30
258	C. A. Walsh (*Glos*)	15	24	13	154	25	0	0	14.00
259	M. C. J. Ball (*Glos*)	13	21	4	236	46	0	0	13.88
260	A. P. Cowan (*Essex*)	15	20	6	188	34	0	0	13.42
261	A. R. Caddick (*Somerset*)	15	20	5	199	38	0	0	13.26
262	G. Welch (*Warwicks*)	13	17	1	210	45	0	0	13.12
263	R. L. Johnson (*Middx*)	11	20	1	243	37*	0	0	12.78
264	A. Kumble (*Indians*)	8	10	1	112	59*	0	1	12.44
265	T. A. Radford (*Sussex*)	5	8	0	97	53	0	1	12.12
266	R. T. Ragnauth (*CU*)	6	11	1	121	29	0	0	12.10
267	R. I. Dawson (*Glos*)	7	13	1	141	21	0	0	11.75
268	†J. D. Lewry (*Sussex*)	10	15	3	138	28*	0	0	11.50
269	M. J. Saggers (*Durham*)	5	9	1	89	18	0	0	11.12
270	C. E. W. Silverwood (*Yorks*)	16	24	6	198	45*	0	0	11.00
	K. J. Shine (*Somerset*)	12	15	4	121	40	0	0	11.00
272	S. L. Watkin (*Glam*)	18	20	6	153	34	0	0	10.92
273	A. R. C. Fraser (*Middx*)	18	28	6	238	33	0	0	10.81
274	M. N. Bowen (*Notts*)	13	18	2	173	22	0	0	10.81
275	†C. E. L. Ambrose (*Northants*)	9	13	2	116	25*	0	0	10.54
276	J. Lewis (*Glos*)	10	16	2	119	22*	0	0	8.50
277	†R. A. Pick (*Notts*)	6	8	0	66	32	0	0	8.25
278	A. J. Harris (*Derbys*)	12	16	3	102	17	0	0	7.84
279	J. N. B. Bovill (*Hants*)	14	19	2	131	29	0	0	7.70
280	S. J. W. Andrew (*Essex*)	10	14	6	61	13	0	0	7.62
281	D. E. Malcolm (*Derbys*)	18	23	7	119	21	0	0	7.43
282	R. A. Fay (*Middx*)	15	24	2	163	26	0	0	7.40
283	J. Wood (*Durham*)	9	16	2	97	35*	0	0	6.92
284	E. S. H. Giddins (*Sussex*)	14	16	6	55	11	0	0	5.50
285	J. A. Afford (*Notts*)	18	24	14	34	11*	0	0	3.40
286	R. J. Kirtley (*Sussex*)	8	12	4	22	7*	0	0	2.75

BOWLING

(Qualification: 10 wickets in 10 innings)

† *Denotes a left-arm bowler.*

		O	M	R	W	BB	5W/i	Avge
1	C. E. L. Ambrose (*Northants*)	284.4	80	717	43	6-26	5	16.67
2	C. A. Walsh (*Glos*)	526.3	144	1,432	85	6-22	7	16.84
3	P. V. Simmons (*Leics*)	364.4	87	1,021	56	6-14	3	18.23
4	Mushtaq Ahmed (*Pakistanis*)	325	85	861	41	7-91	5	21.00
5	M. A. Ealham (*Kent*)	401.4	130	995	47	8-36	3	21.17
6	Waqar Younis (*Pakistanis*)	195.1	42	654	30	5-42	1	21.80
7	C. A. Connor (*Hants*)	362.4	99	1,071	49	9-38	2	21.85
8	†P. C. R. Tufnell (*Middx*)	839.1	273	1,712	78	7-49	6	21.94
9	N. J. Llong (*Kent*)	80.5	23	249	11	5-21	1	22.63
10	D. Gough (*Yorks*)	573.3	142	1,535	67	6-36	2	22.91
11	†J. D. Lewry (*Sussex*)	302	59	942	41	6-44	4	22.97
12	†D. J. Bicknell (*Surrey*)	124.2	21	368	16	3-7	0	23.00
13	D. J. Millns (*Leics*)	538.1	133	1,659	72	6-54	2	23.04
14	G. D. Rose (*Somerset*)	393.2	98	1,218	50	7-47	3	24.36
15	M. W. Alleyne (*Glos*)	458.1	123	1,316	54	5-32	2	24.37
16	†Wasim Akram (*Pakistanis*)	271.5	67	787	32	5-58	1	24.59
17	M. P. Bicknell (*Surrey*)	568.1	146	1,633	66	5-17	3	24.74
18	M. J. McCague (*Kent*)	590	117	1,897	76	6-51	3	24.96
19	E. S. H. Giddins (*Sussex*)	367.4	66	1,204	48	6-47	2	25.08
20	†A. F. Giles (*Warwicks*)	633.3	191	1,615	64	6-45	3	25.23
21	L. Klusener (*South Africa A*)	232.3	44	783	31	5-74	1	25.25
22	†A. D. Mullally (*Leics*)	628.5	166	1,774	70	6-47	3	25.34
23	T. M. Moody (*Worcs*)	319.5	86	956	37	7-92	3	25.83
24	A. J. Harris (*Derbys*)	379.1	76	1,380	53	6-40	2	26.03
25	P. A. J. DeFreitas (*Derbys*)	545.2	105	1,687	64	7-101	4	26.35
26	P. J. Martin (*Lancs*)	427.4	106	1,161	44	7-50	1	26.38
27	P. M. Such (*Essex*)	771.4	190	2,164	82	8-118	6	26.39
28	S. L. Watkin (*Glam*)	616.4	159	1,797	67	4-28	0	26.82
29	M. V. Fleming (*Kent*)	168.2	32	484	18	3-6	0	26.88
30	†A. M. Smith (*Glos*)	487.3	114	1,615	60	8-73	3	26.91
31	†S. J. E. Brown (*Durham*)	642.1	109	2,130	79	6-77	5	26.96
32	D. W. Headley (*Kent*)	423	69	1,387	51	8-98	2	27.19
33	R. J. Green (*Lancs*)	187.5	36	599	22	6-41	1	27.22
34	†J. P. Taylor (*Northants*)	549.2	116	1,766	64	7-88	3	27.59
35	A. R. Caddick (*Somerset*)	604.1	131	2,029	73	7-83	6	27.79
36	R. J. Kirtley (*Sussex*)	193.4	32	756	27	5-51	1	28.00
37	R. C. Irani (*Essex*)	395	74	1,320	47	5-27	1	28.08
38	S. M. Pollock (*Warwicks*)	446.4	115	1,183	42	6-56	1	28.16
39	G. C. Small (*Warwicks*)	164	35	536	19	4-41	0	28.21
40	J. P. Hewitt (*Middx*)	179.3	38	681	24	3-27	0	28.37
41	†J. A. Afford (*Notts*)	579.5	165	1,471	51	6-51	2	28.84
42	†B. P. Julian (*Surrey*)	447.4	86	1,762	61	6-37	3	28.88
43	I. D. K. Salisbury (*Sussex*)	505	109	1,506	52	8-75	3	28.96
44	D. R. Law (*Sussex*)	320.4	45	1,221	42	5-33	2	29.07
45	I. D. Austin (*Lancs*)	223.4	64	645	22	5-116	1	29.31
46	B. K. V. Prasad (*Indians*)	252.3	59	734	25	5-76	1	29.36
47	†K. D. James (*Hants*)	301.1	57	882	30	5-74	1	29.40
48	V. J. Wells (*Leics*)	255.1	69	765	26	4-44	0	29.42
49	†K. J. Dean (*Derbys*)	144.1	32	471	16	3-47	0	29.43
50	P. J. Hartley (*Yorks*)	459.2	96	1,602	54	6-67	2	29.66
51	C. White (*Yorks*)	299.2	51	1,100	37	4-15	0	29.72
52	C. L. Hooper (*Kent*)	321.3	83	789	26	4-7	0	30.34

		O	M	R	W	BB	5W/i	Avge
53	G. Welch (*Warwicks*)	275.5	42	1,035	34	4-50	0	30.44
54	J. P. Stephenson (*Hants*)	336.4	73	1,098	36	6-48	3	30.50
55	C. E. W. Silverwood (*Yorks*)	404.3	79	1,442	47	5-72	2	30.68
56	P. W. Jarvis (*Sussex*)	168	27	592	19	4-60	0	31.15
57	A. Symonds (*Glos*)	118.3	25	374	12	2-21	0	31.16
58	T. A. Munton (*Warwicks*)	404	116	1,092	35	4-41	0	31.20
59	J. E. Benjamin (*Surrey*)	375.3	83	1,217	39	4-17	0	31.20
60	J. Srinath (*Indians*)	233.3	68	628	20	4-103	0	31.40
61	†M. T. Brimson (*Leics*)	360.2	76	1,106	35	5-12	2	31.60
62	D. E. Malcolm (*Derbys*)	639.2	98	2,597	82	6-52	6	31.67
63	A. L. Penberthy (*Northants*)	352.2	68	1,077	34	5-92	1	31.67
64	V. S. Solanki (*Worcs*)	215.2	37	863	27	5-69	3	31.96
65	N. W. Preston (*Kent*)	130.5	27	352	11	4-68	0	32.00
66	G. J. Parsons (*Leics*)	555	170	1,536	47	4-21	0	32.68
67	R. D. B. Croft (*Glam*)	955.4	237	2,486	76	6-78	4	32.71
68	N. M. K. Smith (*Warwicks*)	486.4	115	1,417	43	5-76	3	32.95
69	N. F. Williams (*Essex*)	331.4	59	1,160	35	5-43	2	33.14
70	D. G. Cork (*Derbys*)	589	121	1,891	57	5-113	1	33.17
71	†M. C. Ilott (*Essex*)	550.2	118	1,666	50	5-53	2	33.32
72	A. R. C. Fraser (*Middx*)	592.4	138	1,636	49	5-55	2	33.38
73	G. Chapple (*Lancs*)	477.1	94	1,671	50	5-64	2	33.42
74	V. C. Drakes (*Sussex*)	454.3	79	1,675	50	5-47	2	33.50
75	D. J. Capel (*Northants*)	348.1	57	1,181	35	4-60	0	33.74
76	†R. K. Illingworth (*Worcs*)	717.1	208	1,721	51	6-75	3	33.74
77	Mohammad Akram (*Pakistanis*)	128.2	21	473	14	7-51	1	33.78
78	P. N. Weekes (*Middx*)	371	75	1,082	32	8-39	2	33.81
79	†D. M. Cox (*Durham*)	306	87	883	26	5-97	2	33.96
80	S. C. Ganguly (*Indians*)	85.4	10	340	10	3-71	0	34.00
81	K. J. Shine (*Somerset*)	276.3	44	1,209	35	6-95	2	34.54
82	D. A. Leatherdale (*Worcs*)	105.5	21	384	11	4-75	0	34.90
83	R. L. Johnson (*Middx*)	242.5	36	878	25	5-29	1	35.12
84	D. R. Brown (*Warwicks*)	407.2	81	1,410	40	6-52	2	35.25
85	P. J. Newport (*Worcs*)	187.3	44	670	19	6-100	1	35.26
86	J. N. B. Bovill (*Hants*)	328	62	1,199	34	5-58	1	35.26
87	C. C. Lewis (*Surrey*)	488.2	98	1,597	45	5-25	2	35.48
88	S. R. Lampitt (*Worcs*)	520.5	102	1,919	54	5-58	2	35.53
89	A. R. K. Pierson (*Leics*)	544.2	108	1,710	48	6-158	2	35.62
90	J. E. R. Gallian (*Lancs*)	150.4	28	574	16	6-115	1	35.87
91	R. A. Fay (*Middx*)	360	84	1,121	31	4-53	0	36.16
92	†R. D. Stemp (*Yorks*)	566	165	1,537	42	5-38	2	36.59
93	A. P. Cowan (*Essex*)	409.2	67	1,464	40	5-68	1	36.60
94	J. E. Emburey (*Northants*)	396.2	94	1,042	27	4-48	0	38.59
95	M. N. Bowen (*Notts*)	366.2	64	1,281	33	5-53	2	38.81
96	A. Dale (*Glam*)	141.1	36	470	12	4-52	0	39.16
97	G. P. Butcher (*Glam*)	199.1	30	826	21	7-77	1	39.33
98	C. L. Cairns (*Notts*)	427.3	73	1,461	37	6-110	1	39.48
99	M. M. Betts (*Durham*)	389.5	48	1,753	44	5-68	2	39.84
100	†J. H. Childs (*Essex*)	222.4	56	765	19	4-99	0	40.26
101	K. P. Evans (*Notts*)	412.4	99	1,217	30	5-30	2	40.56
102	M. Watkinson (*Lancs*)	433	78	1,501	37	5-15	1	40.56
103	†R. J. Maru (*Hants*)	306.2	101	734	18	3-50	0	40.77
104	†N. M. Kendrick (*Glam*)	236	74	706	17	4-89	0	41.52
105	S. Elworthy (*Lancs*)	308.1	43	1,165	28	4-80	0	41.60
106	Ata-ur-Rehman (*Pakistanis*)	184.4	24	710	17	4-50	0	41.76
107	†A. P. Grayson (*Essex*)	264.3	58	759	18	4-82	0	42.16
108	K. J. Barnett (*Derbys*)	139.2	15	507	12	3-26	0	42.25
109	P. R. Whitaker (*Hants*)	118.2	26	423	10	3-36	0	42.30
110	S. J. W. Andrew (*Essex*)	198.4	47	641	15	3-67	0	42.73
111	M. P. Vaughan (*Yorks*)	187.3	28	728	17	4-62	0	42.82
112	O. T. Parkin (*Glam*)	224.4	47	744	17	3-22	0	43.76
113	J. N. Snape (*Northants*)	313.3	62	1,013	23	4-42	0	44.04

		O	M	R	W	BB	5W/i	Avge
114	S. Lee (*Somerset*)	418.3	66	1,770	40	4-52	0	44.25
115	†A. Sheriyar (*Worcs*)	460	78	1,661	37	6-99	1	44.89
116	†R. P. Davis (*Glos*)	314.2	70	1,053	23	4-93	0	45.78
117	R. T. Bates (*Notts*)	278.2	46	969	21	3-42	0	46.14
118	S. D. Udal (*Hants*)	497.4	101	1,582	34	5-82	1	46.52
119	N. Boje (*South Africa A*)	160.4	30	562	12	5-58	1	46.83
120	J. Lewis (*Glos*)	276	65	846	18	3-74	0	47.00
121	†M. M. Patel (*Kent*)	586	176	1,554	33	6-97	2	47.09
122	R. M. Pearson (*Surrey*)	475	101	1,509	31	5-142	1	48.67
123	J. Wood (*Durham*)	291.3	46	1,266	26	4-60	0	48.69
124	S. W. K. Ellis (*Worcs*)	170	27	686	14	3-29	0	49.00
125	J. D. Batty (*Somerset*)	486.4	99	1,572	32	5-85	1	49.12
126	M. C. J. Ball (*Glos*)	225	61	639	13	3-40	0	49.15
127	M. J. Vandrau (*Derbys*)	226	30	789	16	6-34	1	49.31
128	S. J. Renshaw (*Hants*)	206.5	51	743	15	4-56	0	49.53
129	O. D. Gibson (*Glam*)	254	41	1,040	20	3-43	0	52.00
130	†G. Keedy (*Lancs*)	475.1	131	1,215	23	3-45	0	52.82
131	S. G. Law (*Essex*)	208.4	46	760	14	3-100	0	54.28
132	S. M. Milburn (*Hants*)	257	44	939	17	3-47	0	55.23
133	A. Kumble (*Indians*)	281	73	739	13	4-111	0	56.84
134	†C. M. Tolley (*Notts*)	216	37	804	14	4-68	0	57.42
135	K. M. Curran (*Northants*)	180	34	641	11	3-75	0	58.27
136	S. D. Thomas (*Glam*)	295	33	1,175	20	5-121	1	58.75
137	N. C. Phillips (*Sussex*)	224	50	778	13	2-54	0	59.84
138	M. A. Wagh (*OU*)	187.3	31	632	10	3-82	0	63.20
139	A. J. Hollioake (*Surrey*)	236	45	793	12	3-80	0	66.08
140	H. S. Malik (*OU*)	197	23	826	10	3-119	0	82.60
141	A. R. Whittall (*CU*)	274.3	56	932	10	3-103	0	93.20

The following bowlers took ten wickets but bowled in fewer than ten innings:

	O	M	R	W	BB	5W/i	Avge
Shahid Nazir (*Pakistanis*)	47	8	164	12	4-43	0	13.66
Saqlain Mushtaq (*Pakistanis*)	166.5	43	456	29	6-52	2	15.72
A. D. Mascarenhas (*Hants*)	92	21	297	16	6-88	1	18.56
G. M. Gilder (*South Africa A*)	94.4	29	243	13	8-22	1	18.69
S. Lugsden (*Durham*)	70.3	9	262	11	3-45	0	23.81
B. C. Hollioake (*Surrey*)	65	12	252	10	4-74	0	25.20
D. Follett (*Middx*)	147.2	26	589	23	8-22	3	25.60
G. J. Smith (*South Africa A*)	125.2	24	402	15	4-70	0	26.80
N. D. Hirwani (*Indians*)	115.3	24	375	12	6-60	1	31.25
M. J. Saggers (*Durham*)	101	12	443	13	6-65	1	34.07
N. Killeen (*Durham*)	114.5	22	434	12	4-57	0	36.16
†D. A. Cosker (*Glam*)	155.4	38	622	16	4-60	0	38.87
†P. R. Adams (*South Africa A*)	108.4	19	390	10	4-116	0	39.00
M. W. Pringle (*South Africa A*)	172.4	40	579	14	4-90	0	41.35
P. A. Thomas (*Worcs*)	121	14	575	12	4-33	0	47.91
A. R. Roberts (*Northants*)	172.5	44	527	10	3-57	0	52.70
J. I. D. Kerr (*Somerset*)	131	16	586	11	3-108	0	53.27

INDIVIDUAL SCORES OF 100 AND OVER

There were 335 three-figure innings in 204 first-class matches in 1996, 12 fewer than in 1995 when 201 matches were played. Of these, 24 were double-hundreds, compared with 15 in 1995. The list includes 247 hundreds hit in the County Championship, compared with 260 in 1995.

* *Signifies not out.*

G. A. Gooch (8)
130 Essex v Hants, Southampton
101 Essex v Lancs, Chelmsford
128 Essex v Northants, Chelmsford
149 Essex v Surrey, Southend
201 Essex v Somerset, Taunton
111 Essex v Glos, Colchester
147 Essex v Warwicks, Birmingham
170* Essex v Glam, Chelmsford

S. P. James (7)
102* Glam v Cambridge U., Cambridge
110 Glam v Somerset, Swansea
118 Glam v Glos, Bristol
235 Glam v Notts, Worksop
148 Glam v Warwicks, Birmingham
103 Glam v Hants, Southampton
131 Glam v Surrey, Cardiff

T. M. Moody (7)
104 Worcs v Leics, Leicester
138* Worcs v Hants, Worcester
212 Worcs v Notts, Worcester
108 Worcs v Lancs, Manchester
106 }
169 } Worcs v Northants, Kidderminster
124 Worcs v Middx, Lord's

C. J. Adams (6)
239 Derbys v Hants, Southampton
125 }
136* } Derbys v Middx, Derby
119 Derbys v Lancs, Manchester
106 Derbys v Notts, Derby
123 Derbys v Worcs, Chesterfield

S. G. Law (6)
143 Essex v Hants, Southampton
115 Essex v Kent, Ilford
153 Essex v Indians, Chelmsford
144 Essex v Lancs, Chelmsford
125 Essex v Surrey, Southend
172 Essex v Durham, Hartlepool

M. P. Maynard (6)
100* Glam v Cambridge U., Cambridge
136 Glam v Yorks, Cardiff
112 Glam v Sussex, Hove
145* Glam v Glos, Bristol
214 Glam v Lancs, Cardiff
122 Glam v Essex, Chelmsford

H. Morris (6)
126* Glam v Cambridge U., Cambridge
202* Glam v Yorks, Cardiff
108 Glam v Glos, Bristol
106 Glam v Leics, Swansea
118 Glam v Kent, Cardiff
149 Glam v Essex, Chelmsford

G. P. Thorpe (6)
141* The Rest v England A, Chelmsford
100* Surrey v Somerset, Taunton
185 Surrey v Derbys, The Oval
154 Surrey v Leics, The Oval
143 Surrey v Essex, Southend
130 Surrey v Sussex, Guildford

G. A. Hick (5)
215 Worcs v Indians, Worcester
123 Worcs v Hants, Worcester
150 Worcs v Durham, Worcester
148 Worcs v Kent, Canterbury
106 Worcs v Glos, Worcester

A. J. Hollioake (5)
128 }
117* } Surrey v Somerset, Taunton
128 Surrey v Essex, Southend
104* Surrey v Hants, Southampton
129 Surrey v Northants, The Oval

S. Lee (5)
113* Somerset v Northants, Taunton
167* Somerset v Worcs, Bath
134 Somerset v Yorks, Scarborough
110 Somerset v Derbys, Taunton
126 Somerset v Sussex, Hove

Saeed Anwar (5)
219* Pakistanis v Glam, Pontypridd
130 Pakistanis v Somerset, Taunton
131 Pakistanis v Warwicks, Birmingham
102 Pakistanis v Essex, Chelmsford
176 Pakistan v England, The Oval

P. A. Cottey (4)
135* Glam v Derbys, Cardiff
112 Glam v Somerset, Swansea
101* Glam v Glos, Bristol
203 Glam v Leics, Swansea

D. M. Jones (4)
214* Derbys v Yorks, Sheffield
100* Derbys v Middx, Derby
107 Derbys v Lancs, Manchester
105 Derbys v Notts, Derby

N. V. Knight (4)
128 Warwicks v Cambridge U., Cambridge
132 Warwicks v Sussex, Hove
113 England v Pakistan, Leeds
103 Warwicks v Lancs, Birmingham

J. S. Laney (4)
112 Hants v Oxford U., Oxford
100 Hants v Indians, Southampton
102 Hants v Glam, Southampton
105 Hants v Kent, Canterbury

R. R. Montgomerie (4)
126 Northants v Oxford U., Oxford
120 Northants v Essex, Chelmsford
168 Northants v Pakistanis, Northampton
127 Northants v Yorks, Northampton

M. R. Ramprakash (4)
134 Middx v Yorks, Lord's
169 Middx v Warwicks, Lord's
108 Middx v Hants, Portsmouth
110 Middx v Somerset, Uxbridge

P. V. Simmons (4)
143* Leics v Warwicks, Birmingham
108 Leics v Hants, Leicester
171 Leics v Durham, Chester-le-Street
142* Leics v Middx, Leicester

P. N. Weekes (4)
108 Middx v Kent, Canterbury
140 Middx v Northants, Northampton
171* }
160 } Middx v Somerset, Uxbridge

V. J. Wells (4)
200 Leics v Yorks, Bradford
197 Leics v Essex, Leicester
204 Leics v Northants, Leicester
119 Leics v Notts, Nottingham

W. P. C. Weston (4)
121* Worcs v Glam, Abergavenny
124 Worcs v Oxford U., Oxford
171* Worcs v Lancs, Manchester
100* Worcs v Derbys, Chesterfield

J. J. Whitaker (4)
110 Leics v Derbys, Derby
168 Leics v Worcs, Leicester
218 Leics v Yorks, Bradford
129 Leics v Notts, Nottingham

C. W. J. Athey (3)
102 Sussex v Durham, Hove
100 Sussex v Yorks, Eastbourne
111 Sussex v Lancs, Hove

K. J. Barnett (3)
200* Derbys v Leics, Derby
103 Derbys v Notts, Derby
141 Derbys v Somerset, Taunton

M. G. Bevan (3)
136 Yorks v Derbys, Sheffield
107 Yorks v Middx, Lord's
160* Yorks v Surrey, Middlesbrough

M. A. Butcher (3)
112 Surrey v Yorks, Middlesbrough
120 Surrey v Leics, The Oval
160 Surrey v Durham, Stockton-on-Tees

J. P. Crawley (3)
100* Lancs v Hants, Manchester
106 England v Pakistan, The Oval
112* Lancs v Sussex, Hove

J. E. R. Gallian (3)
140 Lancs v Worcs, Manchester
312 Lancs v Derbys, Manchester
113 Lancs v Northants, Northampton

S. C. Ganguly (3)
131 India v England, Lord's
100* Indians v Hants, Southampton
136 India v England, Nottingham

K. Greenfield (3)
141* Sussex v Indians, Hove
124* Sussex v Durham, Hove
154* Sussex v Glam, Hove

C. L. Hooper (3)
155 Kent v Essex, Ilford
105 Kent v Durham, Maidstone
103 Kent v Derbys, Derby

N. Hussain (3)
128 England v India, Birmingham
107* England v India, Nottingham
158 Essex v Yorks, Leeds

Inzamam-ul-Haq (3)
169* Pakistanis v Glam, Pontypridd
148 Pakistan v England, Lord's
106 Pakistanis v Essex, Chelmsford

W. S. Kendall (3)
119 Oxford U. v Kent, Canterbury
145* Oxford U. v Cambridge U., Lord's
103* Hants v Notts, Southampton

W. G. Khan (3)
108 Warwicks v Cambridge U., Cambridge
130 Warwicks v Durham, Birmingham
126 Warwicks v Essex, Birmingham

G. D. Lloyd (3)
241 Lancs v Essex, Chelmsford
142 Lancs v Glam, Cardiff
113 Lancs v Warwicks, Birmingham

P. A. Nixon (3)
100* Leics v Oxford U., Oxford
106 Leics v Lancs, Manchester
103* Leics v Durham, Chester-le-Street

T. L. Penney (3)
134 Warwicks v Sussex, Hove
125 Warwicks v Yorks, Leeds
101 Warwicks v Middx, Lord's

R. T. Robinson (3)
122 Notts v Lancs, Nottingham
184 Notts v Durham, Nottingham
111* Notts v Worcs, Worcester

A. S. Rollins (3)
112 Derbys v Cambridge U., Cambridge
131 Derbys v Hants, Southampton
127 Derbys v Somerset, Taunton

B. F. Smith (3)
123* Leics v Oxford U., Oxford
174* Leics v Kent, Leicester
190 Leics v Glam, Swansea

R. A. Smith (3)
141 Hants v Derbys, Southampton
179 Hants v Northants, Basingstoke
161 Hants v Notts, Southampton

K. R. Spiring (3)
144 Worcs v Hants, Worcester
109 Worcs v Yorks, Worcester
130* Worcs v Derbys, Chesterfield

A. Symonds (3)
120* Glos v Indians, Bristol
117 Glos v Notts, Nottingham
127 Glos v Warwicks, Cheltenham

M. P. Vaughan (3)
183 Yorks v Glam, Cardiff
135 Yorks v Surrey, Middlesbrough
183 Yorks v Northants, Northampton

G. F. Archer (2)
143 Notts v Surrey, Nottingham
120 Notts v Hants, Southampton

A. N. Aymes (2)
113 Hants v Essex, Southampton
100* Hants v Worcs, Worcester

D. J. Bicknell (2)
106 Surrey v Durham, Stockton-on-Tees
129* Surrey v Worcs, The Oval

D. A. Blenkiron (2)
102* Durham v Hants, Portsmouth
130 Durham v Notts, Nottingham

P. D. Bowler (2)
207 Somerset v Surrey, Taunton
112 Somerset v Worcs, Bath

D. N. Crookes (2)
105 South Africa A v Glam, Cardiff
155* South Africa A v Somerset, Taunton

K. M. Curran (2)
150 Northants v Leics, Leicester
117 Northants v Sussex, Northampton

T. S. Curtis (2)
107 Worcs v Northants, Kidderminster
118 Worcs v Middx, Lord's

V. C. Drakes (2)
103 Sussex v Worcs, Worcester
145* Sussex v Essex, Chelmsford

N. H. Fairbrother (2)
144 Lancs v Somerset, Manchester
204 Lancs v Warwicks, Birmingham

M. V. Fleming (2)
114 Kent v Leics, Leicester
116 Kent v Derbys, Derby

H. H. Gibbs (2)
183 South Africa A v MCC, Shenley Park
178 South Africa A v Surrey, The Oval

A. P. Grayson (2)
129 Essex v Lancs, Chelmsford
140 Essex v Middx, Lord's

C. M. Gupte (2)
113* Oxford U. v Durham, Oxford
132 Oxford U. v Worcs, Oxford

W. J. House (2)
136 Cambridge U. v Derbys, Cambridge
127 Cambridge U. v Middx, Cambridge

S. Hutton (2)
172* Durham v Oxford U., Oxford
143* Durham v Glos, Chester-le-Street

Ijaz Ahmed, sen. (2)
136* Pakistanis v Kent, Canterbury
141 Pakistan v England, Leeds

A. Jadeja (2)
105* Indians v Worcs, Worcester
112* Indians v British Universities, Cambridge

K. D. James (2)
118* Hants v Warwicks, Birmingham
103 Hants v Indians, Southampton

P. Johnson (2)
103 Notts v Northants, Nottingham
109 Notts v Hants, Southampton

B. P. Julian (2)
119 Surrey v Lancs, Southport
117 Surrey v Northants, The Oval

M. N. Lathwell (2)
108 Somerset v South Africa A, Taunton
109 Somerset v Derbys, Taunton

N. J. Lenham (2)
100* Sussex v Notts, Nottingham
145 Sussex v Northants, Northampton

N. J. Llong (2)
116 Kent v Derbys, Derby
130 Kent v Hants, Canterbury

M. B. Loye (2)
114 Northants v Somerset, Taunton
205 Northants v Yorks, Northampton

A. McGrath (2)
101 Yorks v Kent, Canterbury
137 Yorks v Hants, Harrogate

A. J. Moles (2)
164 Warwicks v Northants, Northampton
176 Warwicks v Middx, Lord's

P. Moores (2)
185 Sussex v Cambridge U., Hove
119* Sussex v Surrey, Guildford

M. D. Moxon (2)
213 Yorks v Glam, Cardiff
131 Yorks v Warwicks, Leeds

J. E. Owen (2)
101 Derbys v Yorks, Sheffield
105 Derbys v Glam, Cardiff

S. M. Pollock (2)
107 Warwicks v Northants, Northampton
150* Warwicks v Glam, Birmingham

J. C. Pooley (2)
138* Middx v Cambridge U., Cambridge
111 Middx v Hants, Portsmouth

A. C. Ridley (2)
104 Oxford U. v Leics, Oxford
155 Oxford U. v Cambridge U., Lord's

Salim Malik (2)
104* Pakistanis v Essex, Chelmsford
100* Pakistan v England, The Oval

A. Singh (2)
101 Cambridge U. v Hants, Cambridge
157 Cambridge U. v Sussex, Hove

E. T. Smith (2)
101 Cambridge U. v Glam, Cambridge
100 Cambridge U. v Sussex, Hove

S. R. Tendulkar (2)
122 India v England, Birmingham
177 India v England, Nottingham

S. P. Titchard (2)
163 Lancs v Essex, Chelmsford
121* Lancs v Somerset, Manchester

T. R. Ward (2)
106 Kent v Lancs, Canterbury
161 Kent v Yorks, Canterbury

A. P. Wells (2)
113 Sussex v Durham, Hove
122 Sussex v Essex, Chelmsford

The following each played one three-figure innings:

M. W. Alleyne, 149, Glos v Worcs, Worcester; Asif Mujtaba, 100*, Pakistanis v Essex, Chelmsford; M. A. Atherton, 160, England v India, Nottingham; M. Azharuddin, 111*, Indians v Leics, Leicester.

R. J. Bailey, 163, Northants v Notts, Nottingham; W. K. M. Benjamin, 117, Hants v Essex, Southampton; R. J. Blakey, 109*, Yorks v Lancs, Leeds; D. Byas, 138, Yorks v Hants, Harrogate.

C. L. Cairns, 114, Notts v Glos, Nottingham; R. Q. Cake, 102*, Cambridge U. v Derbys, Cambridge; S. L. Campbell, 118, Durham v Notts, Nottingham; D. J. Capel, 103, Northants v Worcs, Kidderminster; M. J. Church, 152, Worcs v Oxford U., Oxford; J. B. Commins, 114*, South Africa A v MCC, Shenley Park; D. G. Cork, 101*, Derbys v Cambridge U., Cambridge; G. R. Cowdrey, 111, Kent v Essex, Ilford.

A. Dale, 120, Glam v Northants, Northampton; M. P. Dowman, 107, Notts v Surrey, Nottingham; R. Dravid, 101*, Indians v British Universities, Cambridge.

A. Fordham, 144*, Northants v Pakistanis, Northampton; D. P. Fulton, 134*, Kent v Oxford U., Canterbury.

M. W. Gatting, 171, Middx v Durham, Lord's; A. F. Giles, 106*, Warwicks v Lancs, Birmingham; D. Gough, 121, Yorks v Warwicks, Leeds.

A. Habib, 215, Leics v Worcs, Leicester; T. H. C. Hancock, 116, Glos v Surrey, Gloucester; R. J. Harden, 136, Somerset v Kent, Canterbury; W. K. Hegg, 134, Lancs v Leics, Manchester; D. L. Hemp, 103*, Glam v Cambridge U., Cambridge; P. C. L. Holloway, 168, Somerset v Middx, Uxbridge.

R. C. Irani, 110*, Essex v Worcs, Worcester.

M. Keech, 104, Hants v Sussex, Arundel; R. A. Kettleborough, 108, Yorks v Essex, Leeds; G. A. Khan, 101*, Oxford U. v Kent, Canterbury; K. M. Krikken, 104, Derbys v Lancs, Manchester.

D. A. Leatherdale, 122, Worcs v Sussex, Worcester; G. F. J. Liebenberg, 123, South Africa A v Derbys, Chesterfield.

D. L. Maddy, 101*, Leics v Northants, Leicester; S. V. Manjrekar, 101, Indians v British Universities, Cambridge; S. A. Marsh, 127, Kent v Essex, Ilford; A. A. Metcalfe, 128, Notts v Glam, Worksop; D. J. Millns, 103, Leics v Essex, Leicester; Moin Khan, 105, Pakistan v England, Leeds; R. S. M. Morris, 112, Hants v Cambridge U., Cambridge.

K. Newell, 105*, Sussex v Cambridge U., Hove.

T. J. G. O'Gorman, 109*, Derbys v Worcs, Chesterfield.

S. D. Peters, 110, Essex v Cambridge U., Cambridge; I. L. Philip, 110, Scotland v Ireland, Linlithgow; P. J. Prichard, 108, Essex v Warwicks, Birmingham; M. W. Pringle, 105, South Africa A v Worcs, Worcester.

V. Rathore, 165, Indians v Worcs, Worcester; D. A. Reeve, 168*, Warwicks v Sussex, Hove; S. J. Rhodes, 110, Worcs v Sussex, Worcester; M. A. Roseberry, 145*, Durham v Oxford U., Oxford; R. C. Russell, 124, England v India, Lord's.

D. J. Sales, 210*, Northants v Worcs, Kidderminster; G. Salmond, 181, Scotland v Ireland, Linlithgow; N. Shahid, 101, Surrey v Hants, Southampton; N. S. Sidhu, 115, Indians v Glos, Bristol; N. J. Speak, 138*, Lancs v Glam, Cardiff; M. P. Speight, 122*, Sussex v Derbys, Hove; A. J. Stewart, 170, England v Pakistan, Leeds.

M. E. Trescothick, 178, Somerset v Hants, Taunton; R. J. Turner, 100*, Somerset v Worcs, Bath.

M. J. Walker, 275*, Kent v Somerset, Canterbury; R. J. Warren, 201*, Northants v Glam, Northampton; C. M. Wells, 165, Derbys v Glam, Cardiff; C. White, 181, Yorks v Lancs, Leeds; M. G. N. Windows, 184, Glos v Warwicks, Cheltenham; A. J. Wright, 106, Glos v Middx, Lord's.

TEN WICKETS IN A MATCH

There were 29 instances of bowlers taking ten or more wickets in a match in first-class cricket in 1996, 15 fewer than in 1995. The list includes 27 in the County Championship. Twice, two bowlers achieved the feat in the same match, when D. R. Brown took 11 wickets for Warwickshire and M. A. Ealham ten for Kent at Birmingham, and when D. E. Malcolm took 11 for Derbyshire and D. W. Headley 11 for Kent at Derby.

A. R. Caddick (3)
10-161, Somerset v Warwicks, Taunton; 11-234, Somerset v Worcs, Bath; 10-180, Somerset v Sussex, Hove.

D. E. Malcolm (2)
11-205, Derbys v Kent, Derby; 10-215, Derbys v Sussex, Hove.

The following each took ten wickets in a match on one occasion:

C. E. L. Ambrose, 11-70, Northants v Derbys, Northampton.

D. R. Brown, 11-120, Warwicks v Kent, Birmingham.

D. M. Cox, 10-236, Durham v Warwicks, Birmingham.

M. A. Ealham, 10-74, Kent v Warwicks, Birmingham.

D. Follett, 10-87, Middx v Durham, Lord's; A. R. C. Fraser, 10-134, Middx v Hants, Portsmouth.

G. M. Gilder, 10-65, South Africa A v Worcs, Worcester.

A. J. Harris, 12-83, Derbys v Middx, Derby; P. J. Hartley, 10-153, Yorks v Sussex, Eastbourne; D. W. Headley, 11-165, Kent v Derbys, Derby.
J. D. Lewry, 11-147, Sussex v Leics, Leicester.
D. J. Millns, 10-128, Leics v Essex, Leicester; T. M. Moody, 13-159, Worcs v Glos, Worcester; A. D. Mullally, 11-130, Leics v Derbys, Derby; Mushtaq Ahmed, 10-108, Pakistanis v Somerset, Taunton.
M. M. Patel, 10-225, Kent v Essex, Ilford.
G. D. Rose, 13-88, Somerset v Notts, Taunton.
I. D. K. Salisbury, 11-169, Sussex v Essex, Chelmsford; A. M. Smith, 10-118, Glos v Middx, Lord's; V. S. Solanki, 10-256, Worcs v Lancs, Manchester; P. M. Such, 12-135, Essex v Somerset, Taunton.
J. P. Taylor, 11-104, Northants v Middx, Northampton; P. C. R. Tufnell, 13-123, Middx v Lancs, Manchester.
C. A. Walsh, 11-117, Glos v Warwicks, Cheltenham.

THE COOPERS & LYBRAND RATINGS

Introduced in 1987, the Coopers & Lybrand Ratings (formerly the Deloitte Ratings) rank Test cricketers on a scale up to 1,000 according to their performances in Test matches. The ratings take into account playing conditions, the quality of the opposition and the result of the matches. A player cannot get a full rating until he has played 30 innings or taken 70 wickets in Tests.

The leading 20 batsmen and bowlers in the Ratings after the 1996 series between England and Pakistan which ended on August 26 were:

	Batsmen	*Rating*		*Bowlers*	*Rating*
1.	S. R. Waugh (*Aus.*)	927	1.	C. E. L. Ambrose (*WI*)	871
2.	B. C. Lara (*WI*)	872	2.	S. K. Warne (*Aus.*)	838
3.	Inzamam-ul-Haq (*Pak.*)	831	3.	H. H. Streak (*Zimb.*)	788†
4.	J. C. Adams (*WI*)	820	4.	A. A. Donald (*SA*)	787
5.	S. R. Tendulkar (*Ind.*)	800	5.	Wasim Akram (*Pak.*)	783
6.	M. E. Waugh (*Aus.*)	781	6.	Mushtaq Ahmed (*Pak.*)	779
7. {	Ijaz Ahmed, sen. (*Pak.*)	719	7.	G. D. McGrath (*Aus.*)	760
	M. J. Slater (*Aus.*)	719	8.	I. R. Bishop (*WI*)	757
9.	M. A. Taylor (*Aus.*)	714	9.	A. Kumble (*Ind.*)	743
10.	M. A. Atherton (*Eng.*)	708	10.	C. A. Walsh (*WI*)	741
11.	A. J. Stewart (*Eng.*)	699	11.	Waqar Younis (*Pak.*)	729
12.	H. P. Tillekeratne (*SL*)	691	12.	W. P. U. J. C. Vaas (*SL*)	720†
13.	G. Kirsten (*SA*)	684	13.	K. C. G. Benjamin (*WI*)	696
14.	B. M. McMillan (*SA*)	682	14.	P. R. Reiffel (*Aus.*)	695†
15.	Salim Malik (*Pak.*)	680	15.	S. L. V. Raju (*Ind.*)	661
16.	G. P. Thorpe (*Eng.*)	671	16.	C. J. McDermott (*Aus.*)	655
17.	Saeed Anwar (*Pak.*)	666	17.	D. G. Cork (*Eng.*)	646†
18.	S. L. Campbell (*WI*)	665*	18.	B. M. McMillan (*SA*)	590†
19.	A. Flower (*Zimb.*)	644*	19.	B. N. Schultz (*SA*)	574†
20.	D. J. Cullinan (*SA*)	633	20.	A. R. C. Fraser (*Eng.*)	558

* *Signifies the batsman has played fewer than 30 Test innings.*
† *Signifies the bowler has taken fewer than 70 wickets.*

The following players have topped the ratings since they were launched on June 17, 1987. The date shown is that on which they first went top; those marked by an asterisk have done so more than once.

Batting: D. B. Vengsarkar, June 17, 1987; Javed Miandad*, February 28, 1989; R. B. Richardson*, November 20, 1989; M. A. Taylor, October 23, 1990; G. A. Gooch*, June 10, 1991; D. L. Haynes, May 6, 1993; B. C. Lara, April 21, 1994; S. R. Tendulkar, December 5, 1994; J. C. Adams, December 14, 1994; S. R. Waugh, May 3, 1995.

Bowling: R. J. Hadlee*, June 17, 1987; M. D. Marshall*, June 21, 1988; Waqar Younis*, December 17, 1991; C. E. L. Ambrose*, July 26, 1992; S. K. Warne*, November 29, 1994.

THE INDIAN TOURING PARTY

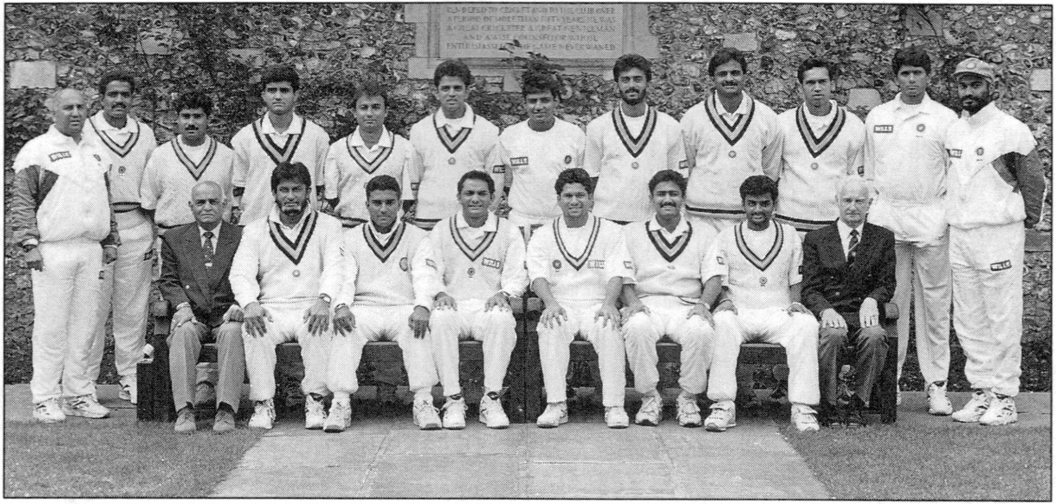

[*Patrick Eagar*

Back row: A. Irani (*physiotherapist*), S. B. Joshi, N. D. Hirwani, S. C. Ganguly, N. R. Mongia, R. Dravid, A. Jadeja, V. Rathore, J. Srinath, P. L. Mhambrey, B. K. V. Prasad, N. S. Sidhu. *Front row:* C. Nagaraj (*manager*), S. M. Patil (*coach*), S. V. Manjrekar, M. Azharuddin (*captain*), S. R. Tendulkar, A. Kumble, S. L. V. Raju, J. Blondel (*scorer*).

THE INDIANS IN ENGLAND, 1996

For Mohammad Azharuddin, a man of dignity and a fine batsman to boot, India's 13th tour of England could scarcely have been a more harrowing experience. He was burdened by problems before the team even arrived and they escalated during the next ten weeks. India were comprehensively outclassed in the one-day internationals, beaten in the Test series and failed to win a single first-class match.

There is more. One of the team's leading players, Navjot Singh Sidhu, flew home in a huff after a bitter disagreement with his captain before the Test matches started. Azharuddin was accused of poor communications and being distant from his players, and endured mutterings about his personal life. He had left his wife and two children a few months previously and his girlfriend, a glamorous product of the "Bollywood" film industry, was by his side for much of the tour. His form with the bat virtually evaporated: he scored just 42 runs in five Test innings.

Ultimately, though, it could have been worse. Having suffered an emphatic beating by eight wickets on an unreliable pitch in the First Test at Edgbaston, India had much the better of things at Lord's and more than held their own at Trent Bridge. Sourav Ganguly emerged as a batsman of impressive technique and temperament, Rahul Dravid was not far behind him, Javagal Srinath and Venkatesh Prasad established themselves as one of the best new-ball attacks in the world and Sachin Tendulkar confirmed what most people already knew: he stands alongside Brian Lara as the world's premier batsman. So, although Azharuddin's personal star barely flickered, he could at least take satisfaction from some elements of his team's performance.

The innings that changed the series was played by Ganguly at Lord's. Facing England's first-innings total of 344, the rest of India's top six struggled, only Tendulkar reaching 30. But Ganguly grew in confidence and stature as he approached his century. Had Dravid not fallen five short, two team-mates would have made hundreds on debut in the same match for the first time in Test history. Left-handed and nimble on his feet, Ganguly presents the full face of the bat and plays his cover-drive with a particular flourish. He scored another century at Trent Bridge and thus became only the third batsman – after Alvin Kallicharran and Lawrence Rowe, both in 1971-72 – to reach three figures in his first two innings in Test cricket. The only mystery was why he and Dravid had not played at Edgbaston.

The World Cup two months earlier exercised a profound influence over the tour. Effigies of Azharuddin had been burned following India's semi-final defeat by Sri Lanka, when the crowd at Eden Gardens rioted. The pressure on Azharuddin was not the only fall-out: Vinod Kambli, despite a Test average in excess of 50, did not tour, amid rumours of late-night indiscretions; Manoj Prabhakar, the seam-bowling all-rounder, had already retired from international cricket after being dropped during the World Cup.

Kambli aside, India made errors in selection, bringing four spinners and only three quicker bowlers. They recognised the mistake quickly enough, though, summoning seamer Salil Ankola from league cricket in Northumberland, rather than another batsman, to replace Sidhu. A team bulging with spinners needed warm and dry conditions. Such weather was denied them; they spent the early weeks of the tour swathed in sweaters and buttressed against the cold. They even suffered stomach upsets – Brummy tummy rather than Delhi belly perhaps. As Sanjay Manjrekar put it: "You just can't trust this English food."

The Arctic winds were crucial because India's slow men – and Anil Kumble in particular – failed to slip into an immediate rhythm, and were always below their best. Kumble was disappointing. In 1995, playing for Northamptonshire, he was the only bowler in the country to take 100 wickets. His selection of snaking, sliding top-spinners and flippers confounded the best and he was expected to be India's most potent weapon. But he took just five wickets in three Tests. The suspicion was that England's batsmen had benefited more from his season in county cricket than Kumble himself; they had him sussed. One left-armer, Sunil Joshi, broke a bone in the First Test and took no further part in the tour. Another, Venkatapathy Raju, took one wicket in his only Test. The back-up wrist-spinner, Narendra Hirwani, played no Tests at all.

If the slow bowlers were ineffective, Srinath and Prasad were magnificent. They were the best bowlers on either side and, with more fortune, could have inflicted greater damage on England's batting. Rarely can a bowler have endured worse luck than Srinath. He consistently moved the ball, beat the bat and showed unflagging stamina. But dropped catches, poor umpiring and endless playing and missing conspired against him. Eleven wickets at 39.36 did him no sort of justice. Prasad, playing in his first Test series, was only a fraction behind Srinath and finished with 15 at 25.00. He, too, deviated the ball almost at will and showed a deceptive turn of speed. On this evidence, Srinath and Prasad are perhaps surpassed as a combination only by Wasim Akram and Waqar Younis and whichever pair West Indies choose to play. Paras Mhambrey was an inadequate third seamer, though Ganguly did his bit; if his bat was golden, his arm also had a fair lustre and he collected half a dozen Test wickets.

Azharuddin's failures left a large hole in the batting. On India's previous tour to England in 1990, he scored two dazzling centuries with wrists as strong as tungsten and as supple as rubber. This time there were weaknesses on and around leg stump. For all his problems, Azharuddin never lost his dignity or his rag in public. After an abject defeat by ten wickets at Derby, however, he delivered a fearful broadside to his players in the sanctuary of their dressing-room.

Vikram Rathore began with a torrent of runs, gleefully crashing anything over-pitched through the covers. But David Lloyd, England's new coach, who had every ball of India's early matches filmed, spotted a weakness and his bowlers duly exploited it. Rathore was caught either at the wicket or in the slips in every Test innings. With Sidhu gone, Ajay Jadeja and Nayan Mongia, the vociferous wicket-keeper, each had a go at opening the batting with Rathore, but neither combination worked. India's highest first-wicket partnership was 25. Manjrekar made fifty at Trent Bridge, but not much besides, after twisting his ankle at Edgbaston and missing Lord's.

Which leaves Tendulkar. Ah, Tendulkar! For a man who had his 23rd birthday just days before arriving in England and whose country has been starved of Test cricket, it is astonishing to think he scored his tenth Test century at Trent Bridge. It was a masterpiece, although not as good as his hundred in a losing cause at Edgbaston. Tendulkar's technical perfection, insatiable run-hunger and unwavering concentration would put him in the top bracket in any era of batsmanship. Anything remotely loose – and plenty that is not – is despatched with power and precision generated by his muscular, 5ft 5in frame.

Tendulkar's contract with the American media company, WorldTel, makes him the highest-earning cricketer in the world at a reported £1 million a year. But he has still managed to remember the team ethos; nobody was surprised when he succeeded Azharuddin as captain in August.

The problems in the Indian team became public after the third one-day international when Sidhu was omitted and then flew home. His parting shot brooked no debate: "I promised my father on his death-bed that I would live my life with integrity and respect. As long as I stay on this tour, I cannot do that." He hinted that he might play under another captain, but the Indian board responded by banning him from international cricket until October 14 and confiscating half his tour fee. Azharuddin and Sandeep Patil, the team manager, continued to insist that their players were united, but Sidhu's huffy exit indicated serious cracks. Just as important, India badly missed his experience and skill at the top of the order. At this point the teams were a long way apart. Each of the one-dayers was affected by rain. Had the first been completed, England would surely have won 3-0. Their team, picked specifically for limited-overs cricket, was unrecognisable from the one which performed so feebly in the World Cup. New coach Lloyd brought a smile and uncomplicated motivational tools. Signs around the dressing-room, carrying such words as "WIN" and "COMMITMENT", and tapes of Winston Churchill and "Land of Hope and Glory" were designed to inspire the players, and in the short run apparently did.

England did make progress under their new regime, although not as much as Lloyd's upbeat pronouncements would have had people believe. They overcame a moderate Indian side by virtue of victory on a substandard surface at Edgbaston. It was, however, England's first series win since they beat New Zealand, also 1-0, two years earlier, so it was not to be sneezed at. Nasser Hussain, playing his first Tests for three years, made a dramatic impact with two centuries, while Chris Lewis also returned successfully and took 15 wickets. Ronnie Irani and Mark Ealham showed glimpses of an appetite for Test cricket, while a third new face, left-arm bowler Alan Mullally, brought a variation of line without the desired in-swing. Graeme Hick was England's greatest concern. He made a double-century for Worcestershire in the tourists' traditional opening first-class fixture, but struggled woefully in the Tests. All the old doubts resurfaced: he scored just 35 in four innings.

Following the disappointing winter in South Africa and the subcontinent, senior players such as Robin Smith, Angus Fraser and Devon Malcolm were cast aside. On his return from South Africa, Malcolm had made some unflattering remarks about Raymond Illingworth, and the saga of Illingworth's response to those, in his book *One-Man Committee*, provided an unedifying distraction from the series. In June, Illingworth was fined £2,000 by the Test and County Cricket Board, after much delay and secrecy. It was unprecedented for somebody in his position to be docked money by his employers, and the decision was overturned in September. Illingworth became increasingly disillusioned with the Board and cricket in general. He had already stood down as manager in March, though he remained chairman of selectors. By midsummer, he was a fringe figure, ticking off the days to the end of the season so that he could "clear off to my house in Spain and put my feet up". – JOHN ETHERIDGE.

INDIAN TOURING PARTY

M. Azharuddin (Hyderabad) (*captain*), S. R. Tendulkar (Bombay) (*vice-captain*), R. Dravid (Karnataka), S. C. Ganguly (Bengal), N. D. Hirwani (Madhya Pradesh), A. Jadeja (Haryana), S. B. Joshi (Karnataka), A. Kumble (Karnataka), S. V. Manjrekar (Bombay), P. L. Mhambrey (Bombay), N. R. Mongia (Baroda), B. K. V. Prasad (Karnataka), S. L. V. Raju (Hyderabad), V. Rathore (Punjab), N. S. Sidhu (Punjab), J. Srinath (Karnataka).

S. A. Ankola (Bombay) joined the party as a replacement for Sidhu, who left the tour after the limited-overs internationals.

Manager: C. Nagaraj. *Coach:* S. M. Patil.

INDIAN TOUR RESULTS

Test matches – Played 3: Lost 1, Drawn 2.
First-class matches – Played 11: Lost 2, Drawn 9.
Losses – England, Derbyshire.
Draws – England (2), Worcestershire, Gloucestershire, Sussex, Essex, Leicestershire, British Universities, Hampshire.
One-day internationals – Played 3: Lost 2, No result 1.
Other non-first-class matches – Played 4: Won 3, Lost 1. *Wins* – Duke of Norfolk's XI, England NCA, Middlesex. *Loss* – Northamptonshire.

TEST MATCH AVERAGES

ENGLAND – BATTING

	T	*I*	*NO*	*R*	*HS*	*100s*	*Avge*	*Ct*
N. Hussain	3	5	1	318	128	2	79.50	3
M. A. Atherton	3	5	1	263	160	1	65.75	2
G. P. Thorpe	3	5	1	193	89	0	48.25	5
A. J. Stewart	2	3	0	136	66	0	45.33	3
R. C. Russell	3	4	0	162	124	1	40.50	8
C. C. Lewis	3	4	1	78	31	0	26.00	1
R. C. Irani	2	3	0	76	41	0	25.33	0
A. D. Mullally	3	4	3	15	14*	0	15.00	0
D. G. Cork	3	4	1	37	32*	0	12.33	2
G. A. Hick	3	4	0	35	20	0	8.75	2

Played in two Tests: M. M. Patel 18, 27 (2 ct). Played in one Test: M. A. Ealham 51; N. V. Knight 27, 14 (4 ct); P. J. Martin 4, 23.

* *Signifies not out.*

BOWLING

	O	*M*	*R*	*W*	*BB*	*5W/i*	*Avge*
M. A. Ealham	43	14	111	6	4-21	0	18.50
C. C. Lewis	131.4	33	356	15	5-72	1	23.73
A. D. Mullally	129	40	298	12	3-60	0	24.83
D. G. Cork	120.4	26	369	10	4-61	0	36.90

Also bowled: G. A. Hick 19–6–51–0; R. C. Irani 21–7–74–2; P. J. Martin 34–10–70–1; M. M. Patel 46–8–180–1; G. P. Thorpe 1–0–3–0.

INDIA – BATTING

	T	*I*	*NO*	*R*	*HS*	*100s*	*Avge*	*Ct*
S. C. Ganguly	2	3	0	315	136	2	105.00	0
S. R. Tendulkar	3	5	0	428	177	2	85.60	2
R. Dravid	2	3	0	187	95	0	62.33	1
P. L. Mhambrey	2	3	1	58	28	0	29.00	1
S. V. Manjrekar	2	4	0	105	53	0	26.25	2
N. R. Mongia	3	5	0	107	45	0	21.40	8
J. Srinath	3	5	0	76	52	0	15.20	3
V. Rathore	3	4	0	46	20	0	11.50	5
B. K. V. Prasad	3	5	3	17	13	0	8.50	0
M. Azharuddin	3	5	0	42	16	0	8.40	1
A. Kumble	3	5	0	36	15	0	7.20	0
A. Jadeja	2	3	0	16	10	0	5.33	1

Played in one Test: S. B. Joshi 12, 12; S. L. V. Raju 1*, 0.

* *Signifies not out.*

BOWLING

	O	*M*	*R*	*W*	*BB*	*5W/i*	*Avge*
S. C. Ganguly	37.5	4	125	6	3-71	0	20.83
B. K. V. Prasad	142.3	39	375	15	5-76	1	25.00
J. Srinath	152.1	37	433	11	4-103	0	39.36
A. Kumble	147	36	334	5	3-90	0	66.80

Also bowled: P. L. Mhambrey 43–6–148–2; S. L. V. Raju 43–12–76–1; S. R. Tendulkar 9–1–29–0.

INDIAN TOUR AVERAGES – FIRST-CLASS MATCHES

BATTING

	M	*I*	*NO*	*R*	*HS*	*100s*	*Avge*	*Ct/St*
S. C. Ganguly	9	14	6	762	136	3	95.25	1
S. R. Tendulkar	7	11	0	707	177	2	64.27	5
R. Dravid	9	16	5	553	101*	1	50.27	6/1
V. Rathore	10	17	0	805	165	1	47.35	9
A. Jadeja	8	13	2	489	112*	2	44.45	6
N. S. Sidhu	2	4	0	171	115	1	42.75	0
S. V. Manjrekar	9	15	2	540	101	1	41.53	4
M. Azharuddin	8	13	2	439	111*	1	39.90	3
N. R. Mongia	7	12	2	364	85	0	36.40	13/1
P. L. Mhambrey	8	9	4	111	28	0	22.20	2
J. Srinath	7	9	1	128	52	0	16.00	3
A. Kumble	8	10	1	112	59*	0	12.44	1
S. B. Joshi	5	7	1	67	22	0	11.16	0
S. L. V. Raju	8	6	3	33	31	0	11.00	0
B. K. V. Prasad	7	7	4	25	13	0	8.33	4

Played in five matches: N. D. Hirwani did not bat (1 ct). Played in four matches: S. A. Ankola 45, 0, 8.

* *Signifies not out.*

BOWLING

	O	*M*	*R*	*W*	*BB*	*5W/i*	*Avge*
B. K. V. Prasad	252.3	59	734	25	5-76	1	29.36
N. D. Hirwani	115.3	24	375	12	6-60	1	31.25
J. Srinath	233.3	68	628	20	4-103	0	31.40
S. C. Ganguly	85.4	10	340	10	3-71	0	34.00
S. A. Ankola	76	9	285	8	4-120	0	35.62
A. Kumble	281	73	739	13	4-111	0	56.84
S. B. Joshi	67.3	9	317	5	2-41	0	63.40
P. L. Mhambrey	146	25	572	8	2-23	0	71.50
S. L. V. Raju	172	47	464	5	1-10	0	92.80

Also bowled: A. Jadeja 11–2–31–0; S. R. Tendulkar 28–5–109–1.

Note: Matches in this section which were not first-class are signified by a dagger.

†DUKE OF NORFOLK'S XI v INDIANS

At Arundel, May 5. Indians won by nine wickets. Toss: Indians.

The Indians won comfortably in the traditional tour-opener at Arundel Castle, though their opponents had undergone a name-change. Following the death of Lavinia, Duchess of Norfolk, who had presided over the fixture for 20 years, the home team played under the aegis of the 17th Duke, her late husband's cousin. (His son, the Earl of Arundel, had taken over the presidency of the Arundel club.) Rajesh Rao of Sussex and Smith put on 99 for the second wicket, but apart from them only Randall reached double figures; Srinath was especially economical. On a chilly day, rain shortened the match slightly, but the Indians won with 13 overs to spare after Sidhu and Tendulkar opened with 139. Tendulkar reached three figures in 97 balls and finished the game with a six.

Duke of Norfolk's XI

R. K. Rao b Joshi	47
J. S. Laney b Srinath	4
R. A. Smith c and b Joshi	60
D. W. Randall b Joshi	17
*M. C. J. Nicholas c Sidhu b Jadeja	7
A. I. C. Dodemaide b Jadeja	9
†A. N. Aymes b Kumble	0
R. J. Maru st Mongia b Kumble	4
C. A. Connor not out	1
J. H. Childs c Manjrekar b Kumble	1
L-b 7, w 6, n-b 5	18
1/7 2/106 3/138 4/145 5/155 6/157 7/166 8/166 9/168 (9 wkts, 48 overs)	168

R. J. Kirtley did not bat.

Bowling: Srinath 7–2–8–1; Mhambrey 8–0–49–0; Kumble 8–1–15–3; Raju 8–0–26–0; Joshi 9–0–28–3; Jadeja 8–0–35–2.

Indians

N. S. Sidhu b Connor	47
*S. R. Tendulkar not out	108
S. V. Manjrekar not out	14
W 4	4
1/139 (1 wkt, 35 overs)	173

R. Dravid, A. Jadeja, †N. R. Mongia, S. B. Joshi, A. Kumble, J. Srinath, P. L. Mhambrey and S. L. V. Raju did not bat.

Bowling: Connor 9–2–19–1; Dodemaide 7–0–33–0; Kirtley 8–0–38–0; Maru 6–0–29–0; Childs 4–0–43–0; Nicholas 1–0–11–0.

Umpires: J. H. Harris and B. J. Meyer.

†ENGLAND NCA v INDIANS

At Uxbridge, May 6. Indians won by 114 runs. Toss: Indians.

The tourists continued to strike form, with Rathore scoring a run-a-ball 103 and Azharuddin 119 in 113 balls. Their stand of 167 for the second wicket set up a target of nearly six an over which was quite beyond their opponents. The amateurs did well to recover from losing two of their top three for ducks, as Luckhurst and Roberts put on 100. Srinath again bowled very tightly; in these two matches, he conceded just 17 runs in 13 overs.

Indians

V. Rathore c Dean b Arnold	103	S. C. Ganguly not out	7
N. S. Sidhu b Roshier	10	L-b 3, w 8, n-b 1	12
*M. Azharuddin b Arnold	119		—
†S. V. Manjrekar c Luckhurst b Robinson	23	1/22 2/189 (4 wkts, 50 overs)	290
R. Dravid not out	16	3/236 4/278	

S. B. Joshi, B. K. V. Prasad, J. Srinath, N. D. Hirwani and P. L. Mhambrey did not bat.

Bowling: Roshier 9–0–44–1; Arnold 10–1–41–2; Foster 7–1–51–0; Robinson 8–0–57–1; Evans 10–0–48–0; Snellgrove 6–0–46–0.

England NCA

S. J. Dean c Manjrekar b Srinath	0	P. G. Roshier c Ganguly b Prasad	6
S. Luckhurst b Hirwani	45	R. A. Evans not out	0
S. Foster lbw b Mhambrey	0		
*M. J. Roberts c Ganguly b Joshi	46	B 2, l-b 25, w 9, n-b 1	37
D. R. Clarke c Azharuddin b Dravid	20		—
J. D. Robinson run out	8	1/4 2/18 3/118 (8 wkts, 50 overs)	176
D. Snellgrove lbw b Hirwani	0	4/129 5/151 6/151	
†C. W. Taylor not out	14	7/155 8/170	

K. A. Arnold did not bat.

Bowling: Srinath 6–3–9–1; Mhambrey 6–2–13–1; Prasad 10–1–36–1; Ganguly 5–0–25–0; Joshi 10–3–28–1; Hirwani 10–2–28–2; Dravid 3–1–10–1.

Umpires: P. Adams and D. R. Shepherd.

WORCESTERSHIRE v INDIANS

At Worcester, May 8, 9, 10. Drawn. Toss: Indians.

Rathore launched the Indians' first-class programme on another bitterly cold day. Caught off a no-ball on 16, he went on to a model 165 in five hours. But he was upstaged by Hick, who made his tenth double-century. In all, he faced 195 balls and plundered 27 in one over from Hirwani, whom he hit for six sixes. There were also 30 fours. He outscored Weston by more than two to one in their stand of 300 in 61 overs, which beat Worcestershire's previous second-wicket record of 287, set by Hick and Curtis ten years before. Hirwani and fellow leg-spinner Kumble conceded 239 between them in 53 overs. Indian team manager Sandeep Patil criticised Worcestershire for delaying their declaration until the third morning, but home coach David Houghton argued that batting practice was a priority for his out-of-form side. The tourists resumed 127 behind, but openers Rathore and Jadeja cleared that with ease.

Close of play: First day, Worcestershire 18-0 (T. S. Curtis 11*, W. P. C. Weston 4*); Second day, Worcestershire 440-4 (S. J. Rhodes 38*, D. A. Leatherdale 7*).

Indians

V. Rathore c Curtis b Sheriyar	165 – (2) c Curtis b Lampitt	72
A. Jadeja c Rhodes b Sheriyar	22 – (1) not out	105
S. V. Manjrekar c Spiring b Sheriyar	0 – b Moody	27
S. R. Tendulkar c Leatherdale b Thomas	52	
*M. Azharuddin b Leatherdale	68	
S. C. Ganguly not out	19 – (4) not out	14
†N. R. Mongia not out	11	
L-b 3, w 1, n-b 8	12 B 4, l-b 7, w 1, n-b 10	22
1/57 2/63 3/187 4/308 5/327 (5 wkts dec.)	349 1/146 2/203 (2 wkts)	240

A. Kumble, P. L. Mhambrey, B. K. V. Prasad and N. D. Hirwani did not bat.

Bowling: *First Innings*—Sheriyar 22–3–64–3; Thomas 23–6–89–1; Lampitt 18–4–70–0; Illingworth 15–2–52–0; Leatherdale 7–0–34–1; Hick 7–0–37–0. *Second Innings*—Sheriyar 6–1–21–0; Thomas 14–1–48–0; Leatherdale 12–3–53–0; Lampitt 12–5–30–1; Illingworth 12–3–37–0; Weston 6–0–35–0; Moody 6–2–5–1.

Worcestershire

T. S. Curtis c Azharuddin b Mhambrey	19
W. P. C. Weston lbw b Ganguly	98
G. A. Hick c Rathore b Prasad	215
K. R. Spiring b Kumble	45
†S. J. Rhodes b Kumble	53
D. A. Leatherdale c Mongia b Prasad	28
S. R. Lampitt not out	0
B 5, l-b 5, n-b 8	18
1/45 2/345 3/351 4/424 5/474 6/476 (6 wkts dec.)	476

*T. M. Moody, R. K. Illingworth, P. A. Thomas and A. Sheriyar did not bat.

Bowling: Prasad 29–5–93–2; Mhambrey 23–5–103–1; Kumble 32–4–123–2; Hirwani 21–3–116–0; Ganguly 7–2–13–1; Jadeja 5–1–18–0.

Umpires: D. J. Constant and P. Willey.

GLOUCESTERSHIRE v INDIANS

At Bristol, May 11, 12, 13. Drawn. Toss: Gloucestershire. First-class debut: D. R. Hewson.

The Indians considered this a more purposeful match than the previous one at Worcester. Alleyne declared 155 behind on the final morning, and the tourists in turn at lunch. There were two hundreds of varying character. Sidhu's was circumspect in the making until the arrival of spin elicited a more enterprising approach. The Anglo-Australian Symonds scored his century in a mature and attractive fashion, guaranteed to renew questions about his international allegiance. He continued to parry enquiries, but when a resourceful Indian journalist did obtain a brief, visible interview, he earned a round of applause on his return to the press box. There was no ambiguity about Symonds's batting, an unbeaten 120 in 138 balls. In contrast, newcomer Dominic Hewson grafted impressively for a three-hour fifty; he had earlier held a spectacular catch at mid-wicket to dismiss Rathore. For India, Srinath took three wickets in ten balls against the county he served so well the previous summer.

Close of play: First day, Indians 282-4 (R. Dravid 20*, S. C. Ganguly 0*); Second day, Gloucestershire 251-4 (A. Symonds 120*, M. W. Alleyne 43*).

Indians

V. Rathore c Hewson b Alleyne	63	– c Hancock b Sheeraz	1
N. S. Sidhu b Alleyne	115	– c Davis b Lewis	16
S. V. Manjrekar c and b Alleyne	55		
†R. Dravid not out	86	– st Williams b Davis	28
*M. Azharuddin lbw b Dawson	13	– c and b Davis	10
S. C. Ganguly c Lynch b Lewis	0	– (3) not out	64
S. B. Joshi c Davis b Alleyne	15	– (6) c Lewis b Alleyne	2
A. Kumble lbw b Alleyne	6	– (7) c sub (M. C. J. Ball) b Alleyne	1
J. Srinath c Symonds b Davis	29	– (8) not out	21
B. K. V. Prasad c Alleyne b Davis	2		
S. L. V. Raju run out	0		
B 2, l-b 12, w 8	22	W 1	1
1/93 2/230 3/255 4/278 5/290 6/328 7/338 8/398 9/405	406	1/2 2/22 3/73 4/87 5/108 6/110 (6 wkts dec.)	144

Bowling: *First Innings*—Lewis 34–8–86–1; Sheeraz 32–5–101–0; Boden 6–0–19–0; Alleyne 29.1–5–81–5; Davis 26–2–88–2; Hancock 5–0–14–0; Dawson 2–0–3–1. *Second Innings*—Lewis 8–4–17–1; Sheeraz 7–1–41–1; Davis 8–0–60–2; Alleyne 7–3–26–2.

Gloucestershire

R. I. Dawson c Rathore b Srinath	15	– c Dravid b Prasad	3
D. R. Hewson b Kumble	53	– b Prasad	2
M. A. Lynch c Dravid b Srinath	4	– b Srinath	1
T. H. C. Hancock b Srinath	4	– c Prasad b Raju	33
A. Symonds not out	120	– lbw b Ganguly	28
*M. W. Alleyne not out	43	– b Prasad	13
†R. C. J. Williams (did not bat)		– b Srinath	9
R. P. Davis (did not bat)		– c Ganguly b Srinath	16
J. Lewis (did not bat)		– not out	22
K. P. Sheeraz (did not bat)		– not out	3
B 5, l-b 7	12	B 21, l-b 1, n-b 6	28
1/28 2/34 3/38 4/178 (4 wkts dec.)	251	1/3 2/6 3/6 4/65 5/83 6/109 7/113 8/150 (8 wkts)	158

D. J. P. Boden did not bat.

Bowling: *First Innings*—Srinath 16–5–58–3; Prasad 14–2–40–0; Raju 8–1–35–0; Kumble 18–2–59–1; Joshi 8–2–47–0. *Second Innings*—Srinath 19–8–27–3; Prasad 17–3–38–3; Ganguly 6–0–37–1; Raju 10–4–10–1; Kumble 10–5–16–0; Joshi 3–1–8–0.

Umpires: R. Julian and A. G. T. Whitehead.

SUSSEX v INDIANS

At Hove, May 16, 17, 18. Drawn. Toss: Sussex.

Some quality strokeplay from Tendulkar and Greenfield enlivened a match played in temperatures barely touching double figures. The Indians fielded in five or six layers, and some stuffed cotton wool in their ears for extra warmth; if the pitifully few spectators were in search of earmuffs, they had the opportunity to take up an unprecedented offer of match commentary on stereo headphones. On the second day Tendulkar unveiled his full repertoire of cuts, pulls, glances and drives, making 85 in 72 balls before declaring 62 behind. Greenfield – who needed 12 overs to get off the mark in the first innings – then batted almost as freely, particularly against the spinners, who had trouble gripping the ball with chilly fingers. His second fifty took just 34 balls and he finished on a career-best 141 not out. Wells set a target of 297 in at least 46 overs: Tendulkar took up the challenge with a rapid 67, but the chase was called off after Phillips snared him for the second time.

Close of play: First day, Sussex 190-1 (C. W. J. Athey 74*, M. P. Speight 16*); Second day, Sussex 29-0 (C. W. J. Athey 15*, K. Greenfield 10*).

Sussex

C. W. J. Athey lbw b Ganguly	80	– st Dravid b Joshi	31
K. Greenfield b Tendulkar	65	– not out	141
M. P. Speight b Hirwani	46	– b Joshi	5
*A. P. Wells b Hirwani	1	– not out	48
N. J. Lenham not out	8		
B 1, l-b 5, w 1, n-b 40	47	L-b 3, n-b 6	9
1/154 2/205 3/206 4/247 (4 wkts dec.)	247	1/79 2/85 (2 wkts dec.)	234

D. R. Law, †P. Moores, J. D. Lewry, N. C. Phillips, P. W. Jarvis and E. S. H. Giddins did not bat.

Bowling: *First Innings*—Srinath 12–7–26–0; Mhambrey 7–1–34–0; Ganguly 12–1–70–1; Joshi 13–2–33–0; Hirwani 10.4–4–21–2; Raju 13–3–19–0; Tendulkar 9–1–28–1; Jadeja 3–0–10–0. *Second Innings*—Mhambrey 13–3–27–0; Ganguly 1–0–8–0; Srinath 4–3–4–0; Hirwani 9–1–28–0; Raju 11–3–58–0; Joshi 14–1–84–2; Tendulkar 3–0–20–0; Jadeja 1–0–2–0.

Indians

A. Jadeja b Lewry	6	– c Moores b Lewry	0
N. S. Sidhu c Speight b Jarvis	14	– (3) c Speight b Law	26
S. V. Manjrekar not out	66	– (4) c Greenfield b Giddins	1
*S. R. Tendulkar c Greenfield b Phillips	85	– (2) st Moores b Phillips	67
†R. Dravid not out	7	– not out	44
S. C. Ganguly (did not bat)		– not out	35
L-b 2, w 5	7	L-b 3, n-b 8	11
1/10 2/26 3/159 (3 wkts dec.)	185	1/0 2/69 3/82 4/110 (4 wkts)	184

S. B. Joshi, J. Srinath, P. L. Mhambrey, S. L. V. Raju and N. D. Hirwani did not bat.

Bowling: *First Innings*—Lewry 4–1–17–1; Jarvis 12–2–31–1; Giddins 9–0–52–0; Law 9–1–45–0; Phillips 5–1–38–1. *Second Innings*—Lewry 8–2–31–1; Jarvis 9–0–51–0; Law 8–0–27–1; Giddins 8–1–28–1; Phillips 9–3–44–1.

Umpires: A. A. Jones and M. J. Kitchen.

†MIDDLESEX v INDIANS

At Lord's, May 19. Indians won on scoring-rate. Toss: Middlesex.

Middlesex felt they had a good chance of victory until they were interrupted by rain. They were needing 77 off 57 balls, with Weekes going well, when a 25-minute break revised their target to 58 off 33 balls, which was never on. The tourists did not bat with much authority, only Azharuddin reaching 50. They made a dreadful start; after ten overs they were 11 for two, and did not hit their stride until the last 20 overs, which brought 136. In contrast, the Middlesex openers, Weekes and Ramprakash, put on 98 in 28 overs. The later batting was not as fluent, but Weekes might have pulled it off but for the interruption.

Indians

V. Rathore lbw b Hewitt	0
S. R. Tendulkar c Carr b Fraser	7
N. S. Sidhu c Fraser b Weekes	45
*M. Azharuddin b Tufnell	73
S. V. Manjrekar c Gatting b Tufnell	38
A. Jadeja c Carr b Tufnell	31
S. C. Ganguly b Follett	21
†N. R. Mongia c Hewitt b Weekes	1
J. Srinath not out	3
A. Kumble not out	3
L-b 3, w 5, n-b 2	10
1/1 2/10 3/110 4/161 5/177 6/212 7/226 8/226 (8 wkts, 50 overs)	232

B. K. V. Prasad did not bat.

Bowling: Fraser 10–2–32–1; Hewitt 10–1–26–1; Follett 10–0–50–1; Carr 4–0–17–0; Tufnell 10–0–66–3; Weekes 6–0–38–2.

Middlesex

P. N. Weekes b Kumble	81	J. P. Hewitt b Srinath	0
M. R. Ramprakash b Ganguly	41	A. R. C. Fraser not out	0
*M. W. Gatting b Kumble	24	L-b 8, w 4, n-b 6	18
J. D. Carr st Mongia b Tendulkar	5		—
J. C. Pooley c Tendulkar b Kumble	11	1/98 2/141 3/150 (7 wkts, 46 overs)	192
†K. R. Brown not out	9	4/177 5/180	
O. A. Shah c Sidhu b Srinath	3	6/190 7/190	

P. C. R. Tufnell and D. Follett did not bat.

Bowling: Srinath 10–0–30–2; Prasad 7–2–13–0; Kumble 10–0–44–3; Ganguly 7–0–39–1; Tendulkar 10–1–41–1; Jadeja 2–0–17–0.

Umpires: J. D. Bond and G. Sharp.

†NORTHAMPTONSHIRE v INDIANS

At Luton, May 21. Northamptonshire won by five wickets. Toss: Northamptonshire.

The tourists suffered their first defeat in another rain-affected game on the eve of the international season. Northamptonshire – who had no players in England's squad, despite having won all their one-day games in 1996 – successfully chased a revised target of 192 in 42 overs. It was their first win over the Indians since 1911, on the first tour by an All-Indian team. Loye, who revealed his full range of attacking strokes, was the architect of victory, hitting nine fours in his 95-ball 83. Tidy bowling, especially by Taylor and Mallender, and fielding kept the visitors in check, although Tendulkar threatened to cut loose until an attempted sharp single brought about his downfall. Penberthy claimed three wickets in the last over.

Indians

V. Rathore c Warren b Mallender	4	A. Kumble c Warren b Penberthy	2
S. R. Tendulkar run out	88	P. L. Mhambrey b Penberthy	0
N. S. Sidhu c Emburey b Curran	26	B. K. V. Prasad not out	1
*M. Azharuddin c Warren b Penberthy	26	L-b 5, w 10	15
S. V. Manjrekar c Bailey b Taylor	37		—
A. Jadeja c Walton b Taylor	10	1/16 2/69 3/119 (9 wkts, 50 overs)	228
†N. R. Mongia not out	6	4/174 5/202 6/204	
S. B. Joshi b Penberthy	13	7/225 8/227 9/227	

Bowling: Taylor 10–2–30–2; Mallender 10–2–35–1; Curran 10–1–48–1; Capel 7–0–41–0; Emburey 4–0–27–0; Penberthy 9–0–42–4.

Northamptonshire

D. J. Capel b Mhambrey	3	†R. J. Warren not out	10
R. R. Montgomerie c Joshi b Prasad	12		
T. C. Walton c Manjrekar b Mhambrey	8	L-b 6, w 2, n-b 4	12
M. B. Loye c Joshi b Kumble	83		—
*R. J. Bailey run out	41	1/4 2/30 3/41 (5 wkts, 40.5 overs)	195
K. M. Curran not out	26	4/134 5/179	

A. L. Penberthy, J. E. Emburey, N. A. Mallender and J. P. Taylor did not bat.

Bowling: Prasad 10–1–37–1; Mhambrey 10–0–39–2; Joshi 6–0–28–0; Kumble 9–0–46–1; Tendulkar 5.5–0–39–0.

Umpires: B. Leadbeater and M. K. Reed.

†ENGLAND v INDIA

First One-Day International

At The Oval, May 23, 24. No result. Toss: England. International debuts: A. D. Brown, M. A. Ealham, R. C. Irani; P. L. Mhambrey.

A new-look England team put their disastrous winter form behind them. Their sequence of nine successive defeats against major countries ended only with a washout, but England were clearly ahead on points before the first day's play was abandoned. Persistent rain prevented any restart on the reserve day. The star was Lewis, who resumed his perplexing international career on what had lately become his home pitch with one of his most compelling performances; he was one of four Surrey players in the England team. India started their quest for 292 in the ferocious style perfected by Sri Lanka during the World Cup: they were 54 without loss in the sixth over. Lewis was on the receiving end at first, but he dismissed Rathore and Kumble – promoted to slog – inside three balls before bowling both Sidhu and Manjrekar, giving him four for six in 21 balls. In between, Martin had Tendulkar leg before on the back foot, putting India in an almost impossible position, even though they were up with the asking-rate. England's batting had relied heavily on Hick, at his most commanding. Two of the newcomers made good scores: Brown's innings was patchy, but Ealham hit two sixes and looked instantly at home. This was the first international in England played on the new worldwide standard of 50 overs a side with a break between innings rather than lunch and tea.

Man of the Match: C. C. Lewis. *Attendance:* 15,639; *receipts* £451,926.

Close of play: India 96-5 (17.1 overs) (M. Azharuddin 15*, A. Jadeja 11*).

England

*M. A. Atherton c Mongia b Prasad	13
A. D. Brown b Mhambrey	37
N. M. K. Smith c Tendulkar b Mhambrey	17
G. A. Hick c Manjrekar b Srinath	91
G. P. Thorpe c Mongia b Jadeja	26
†A. J. Stewart run out	3
R. C. Irani c Prasad b Kumble	11
M. A. Ealham b Kumble	40
C. C. Lewis not out	29
D. G. Cork not out	0
B 1, l-b 11, w 11, n-b 1	24
(8 wkts, 50 overs)	291

1/31 (1) 2/57 (3) 3/85 (2) 4/141 (5) 5/147 (6) 6/176 (7) 7/252 (8) 8/276 (4)

Score at 15 overs: 64-2

P. J. Martin did not bat.

Bowling: Srinath 10–1–45–1; Prasad 10–1–63–1; Mhambrey 9–0–69–2; Kumble 10–1–29–2; Tendulkar 6–0–44–0; Jadeja 5–0–29–1.

India

V. Rathore lbw b Lewis	23
S. R. Tendulkar lbw b Martin	30
A. Kumble c Hick b Lewis	0
N. S. Sidhu b Lewis	3
*M. Azharuddin not out	15
S. V. Manjrekar b Lewis	3
A. Jadeja not out	11
B 4, l-b 2, w 4, n-b 1	11
(5 wkts, 17.1 overs)	96

1/54 (1) 2/54 (3) 3/56 (2) 4/62 (4) 5/68 (6)

Score at 15 overs: 90-5

†N. R. Mongia, J. Srinath, P. L. Mhambrey and B. K. V. Prasad did not bat.

Bowling: Cork 3–0–21–0; Lewis 8.1–0–40–4; Martin 6–0–29–1.

Umpires: R. Julian and P. Willey. Referee: C. W. Smith (West Indies).

†ENGLAND v INDIA

Second One-Day International

At Leeds, May 25. England won by six wickets. Toss: England.

England rediscovered the habit of winning one-day internationals on a dank day at Headingley. The rain came early this time, forcing the match – in the absence of a reserve day – to be compressed to 42 overs a side, but giving England the chance to assert their superiority over an Indian team who looked thoroughly miserable after suffering a very cold English May. In contrast, the natural optimism of the new England coach David Lloyd seemed to be having its effect on players who only a few months earlier seemed terminally defeatist. Their ebullient fielding provided India with almost as many problems as the seamers' canny use of a helpful pitch. England's batting stuttered and they were in trouble at 23 for three, and again at 68 for four, when Maynard, living up to his reputation, got himself run out on the verge of assuming command. But Thorpe and Stewart made no mistake and England won easily.

Man of the Match: G. P. Thorpe. *Attendance:* 13,237; *receipts* £337,176.

India

V. Rathore c Thorpe b Cork	7	P. L. Mhambrey not out	7
S. R. Tendulkar run out	6	B. K. V. Prasad c Stewart b Martin	1
N. S. Sidhu run out	20	L-b 1, w 5	6
*M. Azharuddin c Brown b Martin	40		—
S. V. Manjrekar run out	24	1/16 (2) 2/17 (1)	(40.2 overs) 158
A. Jadeja c Martin b Cork	33	3/58 (3) 4/94 (4)	
†N. R. Mongia c Atherton b Cork	9	5/113 (5) 6/145 (7)	
A. Kumble c Stewart b Martin	0	7/145 (6) 8/149 (8)	
J. Srinath c Cork b Gough	5	9/155 (9) 10/158 (11)	Score at 12 overs: 38-2

Bowling: Cork 9–1–46–3; Lewis 9–1–30–0; Martin 8.2–1–34–3; Gough 8–1–24–1; Ealham 6–0–23–0.

England

*M. A. Atherton c Tendulkar b Prasad	7	†A. J. Stewart not out	47
A. D. Brown lbw b Srinath	0	L-b 5, w 8, n-b 2	15
G. A. Hick lbw b Prasad	0		—
G. P. Thorpe not out	79	1/1 (2) 2/2 (3)	(4 wkts, 39.3 overs) 162
M. P. Maynard run out	14	3/23 (1) 4/68 (5)	Score at 12 overs: 23-3

M. A. Ealham, C. C. Lewis, D. G. Cork, D. Gough and P. J. Martin did not bat.

Bowling: Srinath 9–4–18–1; Prasad 9–2–33–2; Kumble 9–0–36–0; Mhambrey 6–0–29–0; Tendulkar 3–0–15–0; Jadeja 3–0–22–0; Manjrekar 0.3–0–4–0.

Umpires: M. J. Kitchen and A. G. T. Whitehead. Referee: C. W. Smith (West Indies).

†ENGLAND v INDIA

Third One-Day International

At Manchester, May 26, 27. England won by four wickets. Toss: India.

England won the first Texaco Trophy of the summer with their second successive win, this time masterminded by Alistair Brown, the Surrey batsman, whose debut four days earlier had been marked by heavy criticism because he stayed in long enough to have his limitations exposed. In the second match, he was luckier because he failed quickly. This time he batted almost throughout, and after a solid start – not at all in the 1996 pinch-hitter's fashion – scored 118 in a manner that gave signs of high quality. Its impact was diminished because it came on the second day, after yet more rain, and because the contest was overshadowed by politics on both sides. It was announced that Ray Illingworth, the England chairman of selectors, would be brought before the TCCB disciplinary committee because of his attack on Devon Malcolm in his recent book. On the Indian side Navjot Sidhu walked out of the tour after being dropped. India made three changes and two of the newcomers, Ganguly and Dravid, played their part in an improved batting performance. After some early legwork from Rathore, Azharuddin showed glimpses of his best form, scored 73 in 64 balls and took India to 236 for four. Atherton was out cheaply, for the third time out of three, before rain forced a halt. But next day Brown was in powerful form. He faced 137 balls, hit ten fours and two sixes and, with help from Hick and Thorpe, gave England a victory that came with seven balls to spare. It was England's 250th limited-overs international, and their 128th win against 113 defeats.

Man of the Match: A. D. Brown. *Attendance:* 20,310; *receipts* £509,392.

Men of the Series: C. C. Lewis and M. Azharuddin.

Close of play: England 2-1 (1 over) (A. D. Brown 1*, N. M. K. Smith 0*).

India

V. Rathore c Cork b Thorpe	54	R. Dravid not out	22
S. R. Tendulkar c Hick b Cork	1	B 1, l-b 4, w 6	11
S. C. Ganguly st Stewart b Thorpe	46		—
*M. Azharuddin not out	73	1/11 (2) 2/103 (1) (4 wkts, 50 overs)	236
A. Jadeja c Stewart b Cork	29	3/118 (3) 4/190 (5) Score at 15 overs: 38-1	

†N. R. Mongia, A. Kumble, J. Srinath, B. K. V. Prasad and S. L. V. Raju did not bat.

Bowling: Cork 10–3–35–2; Lewis 10–1–49–0; Gough 10–1–43–0; Martin 10–0–50–0; Smith 6–0–39–0; Thorpe 4–0–15–2.

England

*M. A. Atherton lbw b Srinath	0	C. C. Lewis not out	4
A. D. Brown c Dravid b Srinath	118		
N. M. K. Smith c and b Prasad	11	L-b 10, w 8	18
G. A. Hick c Dravid b Prasad	32		—
G. P. Thorpe run out	29	1/2 (1) 2/32 (3) (6 wkts, 48.5 overs)	239
M. P. Maynard lbw b Kumble	14	3/117 (4) 4/186 (5)	
†A. J. Stewart not out	13	5/217 (2) 6/226 (6) Score at 15 overs: 48-2	

D. G. Cork, D. Gough and P. J. Martin did not bat.

Bowling: Srinath 10–1–35–2; Prasad 10–1–26–2; Kumble 10–0–52–1; Raju 9.5–1–50–0; Ganguly 2–0–14–0; Tendulkar 2–0–22–0; Jadeja 5–0–30–0.

Umpires: D. J. Constant and A. A. Jones. Referee: C. W. Smith (West Indies).

ESSEX v INDIANS

At Chelmsford, May 28, 29, 30. Drawn. Toss: Indians.

Rathore and Tendulkar both batted fluently, hitting four and five sixes respectively, before departing while on the attack, but it was Law, awarded his county cap during the match, whose innings really caught the eye. He completed his first 50 from 43 balls, reached his third hundred of the season in another 41 – before lunch on the second day – and went on to 153, his best yet for Essex, collecting 26 fours and one six in 147 balls. After an entertaining 87 from Jadeja, Essex were set a target of 275 for victory in 51 overs, but settled for a draw when Hussain was sixth out with 89 required from ten overs. The main action during the last two days was off the field, as the Indian management tried unsuccessfully to persuade Sidhu, offended by being dropped for a one-day international, to change his mind about retiring and returning home. Seamer Salil Ankola was summoned from north-eastern league cricket.

Close of play: First day, Essex 1-0 (D. D. J. Robinson 1*, A. P. Grayson 0*); Second day, Indians 81-1 (A. Jadeja 55*, S. V. Manjrekar 8*).

Indians

A. Jadeja c Rollins b Andrew	7	– (2) c Such b Childs	87
V. Rathore c Such b Childs	95	– (1) c Rollins b Such	18
S. V. Manjrekar b Childs	32	– c Irani b Childs	48
*S. R. Tendulkar c Such b Law	74	– (7) c Irani b Andrew	1
†R. Dravid b Irani	17	– (6) st Rollins b Childs	6
S. C. Ganguly c Prichard b Irani	51	– (4) not out	34
S. B. Joshi lbw b Irani	22	– (5) c sub (A. J. E. Hibbert) b Childs	0
B. K. V. Prasad not out	6		
P. L. Mhambrey c Law b Irani	1	– (8) not out	24
S. L. V. Raju not out	1		
L-b 5, w 3, n-b 6	14	L-b 1, n-b 4	5
1/7 2/99 3/146 4/210 5/252 6/312 7/313 8/319 (8 wkts dec.)	320	1/47 2/128 3/175 4/175 5/188 6/189 (6 wkts dec.)	223

N. D. Hirwani did not bat.

Bowling: *First Innings*—Cowan 17–3–57–0; Andrew 7–1–15–1; Irani 15–3–37–4; Such 17–1–75–0; Law 9–2–26–1; Childs 16–3–72–2; Grayson 4–0–33–0. *Second Innings*—Cowan 14–4–45–0; Andrew 17–5–44–1; Such 5–0–25–1; Childs 22–3–99–4; Irani 4–0–9–0.

Essex

D. D. J. Robinson c Tendulkar b Mhambrey	1	– lbw b Prasad	2
A. P. Grayson c Jadeja b Prasad	2	– (8) not out	1
N. Hussain c Tendulkar b Mhambrey	7	– b Hirwani	85
S. G. Law c Prasad b Hirwani	153	– c Manjrekar b Joshi	13
*P. J. Prichard c Prasad b Raju	53	– (6) c and b Hirwani	13
R. C. Irani not out	29	– (5) c Mhambrey b Joshi	29
†R. J. Rollins not out	15	– (2) c Dravid b Prasad	33
A. P. Cowan (did not bat)		– (7) not out	22
B 5, n-b 4	9	B 8, l-b 1	9
1/1 2/3 3/47 4/216 5/228 (5 wkts dec.)	269	1/2 2/70 3/91 4/142 5/169 6/186 (6 wkts)	207

P. M. Such, S. J. W. Andrew and J. H. Childs did not bat.

Bowling: *First Innings*—Prasad 11–2–57–1; Mhambrey 10–5–23–2; Raju 19–6–62–1; Ganguly 4–0–19–0; Joshi 14–3–50–0; Hirwani 16–3–53–1; Tendulkar 1–1–0–0. *Second Innings*—Prasad 14–1–63–2; Mhambrey 8–1–24–0; Ganguly 3–0–12–0; Joshi 8–0–41–2; Raju 7–2–27–0; Hirwani 9–4–24–2; Tendulkar 2–1–7–0.

Umpires: H. D. Bird and D. R. Shepherd.

LEICESTERSHIRE v INDIANS

At Leicester, June 1, 2, 3. Drawn. Toss: Indians. First-class debut: D. Williamson.

Batsmen on both sides took advantage of a good pitch to entertain a decent crowd, none more than the Indian opener Rathore, who warmed up for the First Test with innings of 71 and 91, and Azharuddin, who hit a magnificent unbeaten 111 – in which he struck six sixes – and 72. Leicestershire also filled their boots, with Habib holding centre stage. He was run out ten short of his hundred, but the Indians and umpire Bird said the 24-year-old was the best young batsman they had seen on the circuit. In the end, the match petered out to be abandoned as a draw at lunch on the final day because of rain. But there were fireworks off the field. Azharuddin, who had retired with a painful elbow, was so badly stung by criticism at home, where effigies of him were being burned following Sidhu's decision to quit, that he made a public statement saying the team was behind him.

Close of play: First day, Leicestershire 38-0 (V. J. Wells 22*, D. L. Maddy 14*); Second day, Indians 123-2 (S. V. Manjrekar 0*, R. Dravid 8*).

Indians

V. Rathore c Pierson b Millns	71	– st Nixon b Brimson	91
†N. R. Mongia c Simmons b Williamson	22	– lbw b Pierson	24
S. V. Manjrekar c Simmons b Wells	40	– not out	65
R. Dravid not out	58	– lbw b Brimson	12
*M. Azharuddin not out	111	– retired hurt	72
S. B. Joshi (did not bat)		– not out	4
W 1, n-b 2	3	B 4, l-b 1	5
1/62 2/116 3/152 (3 wkts dec.)	305	1/115 2/115 3/136 (3 wkts dec.)	273

A. Kumble, J. Srinath, S. A. Ankola, P. L. Mhambrey and S. L. V. Raju did not bat.

In the second innings M. Azharuddin retired hurt at 260.

Bowling: *First Innings*—Millns 18–4–57–1; Mullally 8–0–28–0; Williamson 12–4–32–1; Pierson 20–0–103–0; Wells 6–1–21–1; Brimson 10–2–64–0. *Second Innings*—Millns 7–0–20–0; Wells 4–1–9–0; Williamson 17–4–63–0; Pierson 22–3–81–1; Brimson 22–3–80–2; Maddy 4–1–15–0.

Leicestershire

V. J. Wells c Manjrekar b Srinath	52	†P. A. Nixon not out	24
D. L. Maddy c Dravid b Kumble	61	B 5, l-b 14, n-b 12	31
B. F. Smith lbw b Srinath	2		
A. Habib run out	90	1/72 2/86 3/166 (5 wkts dec.)	318
*P. V. Simmons c Mongia b Joshi	58	4/269 5/318	

D. J. Millns, A. R. K. Pierson, D. Williamson, A. D. Mullally and M. T. Brimson did not bat.

Bowling: Srinath 15–4–44–2; Ankola 10–2–37–0; Raju 16–5–52–0; Kumble 18–4–55–1; Mhambrey 7–0–57–0; Joshi 7.3–0–54–1.

Umpires: H. D. Bird and G. Sharp.

ENGLAND v INDIA

First Cornhill Test

At Birmingham, June 6, 7, 8, 9. England won by eight wickets. Toss: India. Test debuts: R. C. Irani, A. D. Mullally, M. M. Patel; S. B. Joshi, P. L. Mhambrey, B. K. V. Prasad, V. Rathore.

In a match of seven debutants, it was England's revamped team – picked by a revamped selection committee – who proved easily superior. The game belonged, above all, to Hussain, recalled after a three-year absence and given the responsibility of England's troublesome No. 3 position. He made his first Test hundred, 128, which enabled England to take a first-innings lead of 99 and win a low-scoring game by eight wickets. Predictably, however, the best batting came from Tendulkar, on the third afternoon: as wickets tumbled around him, he made a century of rare brilliance. Neither he nor Srinath deserved to number among the vanquished but they were undone by the poor efforts of their colleagues, a less than satisfactory pitch and some indifferent umpiring.

Cork aside, England's attack was totally changed from the one that allowed the South African tail to snatch the Cape Town Test five months earlier. Malcolm, Martin, Fraser and Watkinson were dropped, along with Stewart and Smith; Mullally of Leicestershire, Irani of Essex and Patel of Kent were the newcomers and Knight, Hussain and Lewis had second chances. The two Lancastrians, Martin and Crawley, were both omitted from England's 13.

Azharuddin had chosen to bat, but India were dismissed an hour after tea on the first day for 214. Lewis, rejuvenated by his move to The Oval, took the first wicket, though Cork returned the best figures, four for 61, with Tendulkar among his victims. The medium-pacer Irani, brought on before lunch, found success with his fifth ball when Azharuddin sought runs with his favourite leg flick and saw Knight take a superb catch at short mid-wicket. Atherton had positioned him there for such a stroke, and his deployment of bowlers and fielders alike was impressive throughout. This was Atherton's best match as England captain.

Had it not been for Srinath's half-century, India would have struggled to reach 200. They were also in Srinath's debt for his superb spell on the second morning, which had England on the rack. It earned him the wickets of Knight and Thorpe and should have ended Hussain's innings on 14 when the batsman seemed to glove a leg-side catch to Mongia, the wicket-keeper, only to be reprieved by Darrell Hair, the Australian umpire. Thereafter Hussain grew in confidence and went to his century in 193 balls, assisted first by Irani, who struck seven boundaries in a forceful run-a-ball 34, and latterly by Patel and Mullally, who boosted the last two wickets by a crucial 98 runs. Hussain was last out, having batted for 282 minutes.

Faced with the task of setting England a testing fourth-innings target, India collapsed to 219. Tendulkar alone stood between them and defeat inside three days. As the European football championships kicked off at Wembley on that Saturday afternoon, the little master from Bombay tried to distract attention by making his ninth Test hundred with a scintillating display of strokes all round the wicket. Before he skied Lewis to Thorpe he scored 122 from 176 balls. The next-best score was Manjrekar's 18 – made with the help of a runner, after he sprained his ankle in the first innings. Lewis, who had retained his place from the one-day internationals, took five wickets in India's second innings. Once again, though, it was Cork who took the spoils, and made headlines. On the first day he waved Kumble goodbye after dismissing him, in a manner that some took to be unnecessary, although coach David Lloyd insisted later that he wanted his players to show aggression. Cork's first wicket in the second innings, that of Rathore, was his 50th in his 11th Test. Within a year of making his Test debut he had become the main attacking bowler in the side, and the only unchallenged bowling selection.

Rathore was unconvinced by his dismissal, as were many of those who digested the television replay, which showed that Hick, at second slip, caught the ball as it kissed the turf. Taking into account a leg-before appeal against Atherton in England's brief second innings, and that early reprieve for Hussain, India had every reason to curse their luck – though Azharuddin chose not to do so. It was a poor game for the Indian captain, who was bowled round his legs for a duck by Mullally as his team batted to save the game on that fatal third day. Mullally ended the match with five wickets, though there was little evidence of his ability to swing the ball back in to the right-hander. Kumble, India's potential match-winner, found his wrist-spin treated with less deference than he is used to and the match ended with Srinath, in a final burst of defiance and frustration, flinging bumpers at Atherton, who saw England home with a careful unbeaten half-century. It was all over before lunch on Sunday, having lasted a day longer than the previous year's débâcle against West Indies, but prompting further queries about the suitability of Edgbaston's pitches for Test cricket. The strip used was the second choice, after the one first proposed had been rejected as unsuitable a fortnight earlier. – MICHAEL HENDERSON.

Man of the Match: N. Hussain. *Attendance:* 45,490; *receipts* £822,011.

Close of play: First day, England 60-0 (N. V. Knight 27*, M. A. Atherton 31*); Second day, India 5-0 (V. Rathore 5*, A. Jadeja 0*); Third day, England 73-1 (M. A. Atherton 29*, N. Hussain 18*).

India

V. Rathore c Knight b Cork	20	– c Hick b Cork	7
A. Jadeja c Atherton b Lewis	0	– c Russell b Lewis	6
S. V. Manjrekar c Atherton b Lewis	23	– (7) c Knight b Lewis	18
S. R. Tendulkar b Cork	24	– c Thorpe b Lewis	122
*M. Azharuddin c Knight b Irani	13	– b Mullally	0
†N. R. Mongia b Mullally	20	– (3) c Hussain b Cork	9
S. B. Joshi c Thorpe b Mullally	12	– (6) c Russell b Mullally	12
A. Kumble c Knight b Cork	5	– run out	15
J. Srinath c Russell b Mullally	52	– lbw b Lewis	1
P. L. Mhambrey c Thorpe b Cork	28	– b Lewis	15
B. K. V. Prasad not out	0	– not out	0
B 3, l-b 10, n-b 4	17	B 4, l-b 9, n-b 1	14
1/8 (2) 2/41 (1) 3/64 (5) 4/93 (4) 5/103 (6) 6/118 (3) 7/127 (8) 8/150 (7) 9/203 (9) 10/214 (10)	214	1/15 (1) 2/17 (2) 3/35 (3) 4/36 (5) 5/68 (6) 6/127 (7) 7/185 (8) 8/193 (9) 9/208 (4) 10/219 (10)	219

In the first innings S. V. Manjrekar, when 10, retired hurt at 40 and resumed at 103.

Bowling: *First Innings*—Lewis 18–2–44–2; Cork 20.1–5–61–4; Mullally 22–7–60–3; Irani 7–4–22–1; Patel 2–0–14–0. *Second Innings*—Lewis 22.4–6–72–5; Cork 19–5–40–2; Mullally 15–4–43–2; Irani 2–0–21–0; Patel 8–3–18–0; Hick 4–1–12–0.

THE ENGLAND TEAM FOR THE EDGBASTON TEST

[*Patrick Eagar*

Back row: N. V. Knight, D. G. Cork, R. C. Irani, A. D. Mullally, N. Hussain, M. M. Patel. *Front row:* C. C. Lewis, G. A. Hick, M. A. Atherton (*captain*), R. C. Russell, G. P. Thorpe.

England

N. V. Knight c Mongia b Srinath	27	lbw b Prasad	14
*M. A. Atherton c Rathore b Mhambrey	33	not out	53
N. Hussain c sub (R. Dravid) b Srinath	128	c Srinath b Prasad	19
G. P. Thorpe b Srinath	21	not out	17
G. A. Hick c Mhambrey b Prasad	8		
R. C. Irani c Mongia b Srinath	34		
†R. C. Russell b Prasad	0		
C. C. Lewis c Rathore b Prasad	0		
D. G. Cork c Jadeja b Prasad	4		
M. M. Patel lbw b Kumble	18		
A. D. Mullally not out	14		
B 16, l-b 3, n-b 7	26	B 8, l-b 7, w 1, n-b 2	18
1/60 (1) 2/72 (2) 3/109 (4) 4/149 (5) 5/195 (6) 6/205 (7) 7/205 (8) 8/215 (9) 9/264 (10) 10/313 (3)	313	1/37 (1) 2/77 (3) (2 wkts)	121

Bowling: *First Innings*—Srinath 28.2–5–103–4; Prasad 28–9–71–4; Kumble 24–4–77–1; Mhambrey 10–0–43–1. *Second Innings*—Srinath 14.5–3–47–0; Prasad 14–0–50–2; Kumble 5–3–9–0.

Umpires: D. B. Hair (Australia) and D. R. Shepherd. Referee: C. W. Smith (West Indies).

DERBYSHIRE v INDIANS

At Derby, June 13, 14, 15. Derbyshire won by ten wickets. Toss: Derbyshire. First-class debuts: K. J. Dean, M. R. May.

The Indians reached the nadir of their tour after being sent into full retreat by Derbyshire, who beat them for the first time since 1932, with a day and a half to spare. (Unusually for a tourists' match, it was scheduled for four days.) It was a dreadful performance by the tourists: they came a poor second in "batting, bowling, fielding and attitude" as their manager, Patil, admitted. Mongia redeemed the first innings, helping the last two wickets to add 119, more than half of an inadequate total. Derbyshire's 409, their highest score against the Indians, owed much to Jones and Krikken. The innings ended when Krikken chopped a ball from Srinath into the ground and, as it bounced towards the stumps, handled it – the first such dismissal in Derbyshire's history. Malcolm, who took eight for 110 in the match, hurried the Indians towards defeat and provided the final embarrassment when he moved from perennial No. 11 to open the innings, hitting 12 of the 13 runs required.

Close of play: First day, Derbyshire 80-3 (D. M. Jones 14*, J. E. Owen 11*); Second day, Indians 86-1 (V. Rathore 16*, S. C. Ganguly 33*).

Indians

A. Jadeja c DeFreitas b Harris	17	(2) lbw b Dean	26
V. Rathore c Krikken b Malcolm	2	(1) c Adams b Harris	16
S. C. Ganguly b Malcolm	14	lbw b Dean	64
R. Dravid lbw b Harris	0	lbw b DeFreitas	7
†N. R. Mongia not out	74	run out	20
*M. Azharuddin lbw b DeFreitas	21	c Krikken b Malcolm	29
A. Kumble c Adams b Dean	5	c Krikken b Malcolm	5
J. Srinath c Adams b Malcolm	1	c DeFreitas b Malcolm	1
P. L. Mhambrey c Adams b Harris	4	c DeFreitas b Harris	1
S. A. Ankola c DeFreitas b Dean	45	c Jones b Malcolm	0
S. L. V. Raju c Krikken b Malcolm	31	not out	0
B 1, l-b 4, w 2, n-b 8	15	B 4, l-b 9, n-b 10	23
1/5 2/25 3/25 4/39 5/63 6/76 7/87 8/110 9/168	229	1/36 2/93 3/108 4/148 5/162 6/178 7/191 8/192 9/192	192

Bowling: *First Innings*—Malcolm 21–6–60–4; Harris 17–3–67–3; Dean 13–2–45–2; DeFreitas 13–1–40–1; Adams 1–0–4–0; Jones 1–0–8–0. *Second Innings*—Malcolm 16.1–5–50–4; Harris 11–4–31–2; Dean 15–1–61–2; DeFreitas 10–1–37–1.

BRITISH UNIVERSITIES v INDIANS

At Cambridge, June 26, 27, 28. Drawn. Toss: Indians. First-class debuts: J. Bahl, S. A. J. Boswell.

The tourists seemed unwilling to treat this match as anything more than an extended net, declining to enforce the follow-on and batting so slowly on the final day that they added only 229 runs. A declaration brought the game to a close once Dravid had completed the hundred that eluded him at Lord's. Manjrekar, returning after a sprained ankle ruled him out at Lord's, and Jadeja had scored centuries in the first innings, and all the top seven made at least 50 in one innings or the other. The students, on the other hand, struggled from the moment that Gupte was bowled by a yorker, the first ball of their innings. Only Singh and Khan managed significant contributions as leg-spinner Hirwani took six for 60, conceding just two an over.

Close of play: First day, Indians 391-5 (A. Jadeja 95*, S. C. Ganguly 31*); Second day, Indians 2-0 (V. Rathore 0*, N. R. Mongia 2*).

Indians

V. Rathore c Wagh b Boswell	54	– c Wagh b Boswell	16
†N. R. Mongia c Boswell b Marc	21	– c Wagh b Sutcliffe	85
S. V. Manjrekar c Boswell b Dibden	101		
*M. Azharuddin c sub (W. J. House) b Dibden	73		
A. Jadeja not out	112		
R. Dravid b Marc	0	– (3) not out	101
S. C. Ganguly c Bahl b Marc	52		
P. L. Mhambrey not out	15	– (5) not out	8
S. A. Ankola (did not bat)		– (4) c Singh b Wagh	8
B 12, l-b 12, w 3, n-b 2	29	B 7, w 6	13
1/43 2/153 3/217 4/291 5/292 6/427	(6 wkts dec.) 457	1/30 2/190 3/213	(3 wkts dec.) 231

N. D. Hirwani and S. L. V. Raju did not bat.

Bowling: *First Innings*—Martin-Jenkins 27–7–60–0; Boswell 10–2–26–1; Marc 25–3–91–3; Dibden 31–1–148–2; Wagh 15–1–89–0; Khan 2–0–19–0. *Second Innings*—Martin-Jenkins 14–5–33–0; Marc 8–4–14–0; Wagh 17–0–74–1; Boswell 8–0–21–1; Dibden 5–0–16–0; Gupte 7–0–26–0; Sutcliffe 8–0–39–1; Singh 1–0–1–0.

British Universities

C. M. Gupte (*Oxford*) b Mhambrey	0
I. J. Sutcliffe (*Oxford*) b Ankola	19
A. Singh (*Cambridge*) b Ankola	49
G. A. Khan (*Oxford*) c Azharuddin b Hirwani	56
*R. Q. Cake (*Cambridge*) c Rathore b Hirwani	18
M. A. Wagh (*Oxford*) c Mongia b Hirwani	29
R. S. C. Martin-Jenkins (*Durham*) st Mongia b Hirwani	20
K. Marc (*St Martin's, London*) lbw b Hirwani	0
R. R. Dibden (*Loughborough*) b Raju	1
S. A. J. Boswell (*Wolverhampton*) b Hirwani	0
†J. Bahl (*Brighton*) not out	0
B 12, l-b 6, w 1, n-b 6	25
1/0 2/62 3/91 4/143 5/176 6/204 7/204 8/215 9/215	217

Bowling: Mhambrey 10–1–38–1; Ankola 12–2–37–2; Ganguly 2–0–19–0; Raju 21–8–45–1; Hirwani 29.5–8–60–6.

Umpires: N. G. Cowley and J. H. Harris.

HAMPSHIRE v INDIANS

At Southampton, June 29, 30, July 1. Drawn. Toss: Hampshire.

This will go down in history as Kevan James's match. The 35-year-old left-arm seamer, who had begun the season in the Second Eleven, became the first man ever to take four wickets with successive balls and score a century in the same game. For the rest, it was largely forgettable, and rain ended proceedings shortly before lunch on the final day. James's four-in-four came on Saturday afternoon; the Indians had advanced smoothly to 207 for one when he struck in his 16th over. Rathore was stumped down the leg side; Tendulkar's inside edge gave a simple catch to short leg; Dravid played down the wrong line and Manjrekar nicked to slip. After that, normality returned, as the immaculate Ganguly completed a wristy century and put on 155 with Kumble. Laney then hit a mature hundred, but James took centre stage again as he scored 103, with three sixes off Hirwani and ten fours. Hampshire closed the second day 21 ahead, with one wicket remaining. But, with the Indians spurning a contrived finish, Stephenson instructed his last pair to bat as long as possible. They survived to lunch, with No. 11 Milburn completing a maiden fifty in 54 balls. Then the weather took over.

Close of play: First day, Hampshire 49-2 (J. S. Laney 23*, K. D. James 2*); Second day, Hampshire 383-9 (M. J. Thursfield 22*, S. M. Milburn 1*).

Indians

A. Jadeja c Keech b James	91	A. Kumble not out	59
V. Rathore st Aymes b James	95		
S. C. Ganguly not out	100	B 2, l-b 6, w 1, n-b 8	17
*S. R. Tendulkar c Laney b James	0		
†R. Dravid lbw b James	0	1/192 2/207 3/207 (5 wkts dec.)	362
S. V. Manjrekar c Terry b James	0	4/207 5/207	

B. K. V. Prasad, S. A. Ankola, N. D. Hirwani and S. L. V. Raju did not bat.

Bowling: Milburn 18.2–2–72–0; Bovill 15–3–66–0; Thursfield 18–0–86–0; James 25–4–74–5; Stephenson 4–0–22–0; Udal 6–0–34–0.

Hampshire

*J. P. Stephenson c Prasad b Ankola 14	S. D. Udal c Dravid b Prasad 9
J. S. Laney c Tendulkar b Hirwani 100	M. J. Thursfield not out................ 37
J. N. B. Bovill c Rathore b Ankola 8	S. M. Milburn not out 54
K. D. James c Kumble b Raju 103	B 23, l-b 28, w 2, n-b 4 57
V. P. Terry b Ankola.................. 20	——
M. Keech c Jadeja b Ankola............ 36	1/33 2/45 3/220 (9 wkts) 458
P. R. Whitaker lbw b Prasad 19	4/254 5/262 6/337
†A. N. Aymes c Jadeja b Ganguly....... 1	7/341 8/351 9/367

Bowling: Prasad 25–7–68–2; Ankola 30–3–120–4; Kumble 17–7–41–0; Hirwani 20–1–73–1; Raju 23–3–75–1; Ganguly 5–3–5–1; Tendulkar 4–1–25–0.

Umpires: J. H. Hampshire and K. J. Lyons.

ENGLAND v INDIA

Third Cornhill Test

At Nottingham, July 4, 5, 6, 8, 9. Drawn. Toss: India. Test debut: M. A. Ealham.

Reports that showers would seriously disrupt the final Test proved to be incorrect, but the forecast that a flat and slowish pitch would prevent a result was more accurate. The match was duly drawn, although England persevered commendably to dismiss India in 69 overs on the fifth day. India were bowled out 168 ahead, bringing down the curtain on a match graced by the batting artistry of Tendulkar and Ganguly, their precocious left-handed discovery. For England, it was marked by the continued success of Hussain in England's problem berth at No. 3, and by Atherton's determined service.

The draw was an odds-on favourite before the start, and history also discouraged India's hopes of squaring the series. In 37 series of three Tests in England, no visiting team had managed to pull level in the final game after conceding the early advantage. England claimed the series by virtue of their eight-wicket triumph at Birmingham, only their fourth home series win out of the last 14 (excuding two one-off wins over Sri Lanka) since Australia's defeat in 1985.

Azharuddin, under pressure to retain the captaincy he had held with distinction since 1990, won the toss for the third time and elected to bat on a cloudy, blustery day. He needed no second look at a solid surface which had driven many a bowler to frustration during the first half of the summer. India replaced the seamer Mhambrey with the left-armer Raju to augment the strength and variety of the spin attack, omitted Jadeja and brought back experienced middle-order batsman Manjrekar, absent at Lord's because of an ankle injury. England fielded the two Kent players, Ealham and Patel, instead of Irani and Martin. Irani, along with Salisbury, had been in the 13.

The home side quickly claimed the wickets of Rathore, one ball before a half-hour rain delay, and Mongia soon after. But that was no prelude to an Indian collapse, though it threatened when Tendulkar gave a chance before scoring; Atherton failed to hold it at gully. Instead, Tendulkar and the cool, stylish Ganguly settled in to bat beautifully for the rest of the first day and, by the close, the partnership was an unbeaten 254. England bowled tidily, without too much threat, but the pitch was proving to be an old-fashioned "shirtfront" as expected. Tendulkar completed his tenth Test hundred, and fourth against England, with 15 fours, while Ganguly joined an elite club formed by West Indians Lawrence Rowe and Alvin Kallicharran, the only batsmen who had previously scored centuries in their first two Test innings. (They had done it in the same series, against New Zealand in 1971-72.) Ganguly took it philosophically. "What's important is how well I do in the rest of my Test career," he said.

His aim was to help India bat into the third day, but he made no addition to his overnight 136. In a fine piece of aggressive left-arm bowling, Mullally jammed Ganguly's hand against the bat handle with a sharp lifter. After he received on-field treatment, the next ball was fast and further up. Ganguly played an expansive open-faced drive and was taken at third slip by Hussain. He had batted for six hours and 268 balls. Tendulkar lasted for seven and a half hours, making a superb 177, Manjrekar contributed a solid half-century, then Dravid followed up his 95 on debut with 84, to confirm that discoveries of talent and temperament can still surface in a series defeat. As at Lord's, Dravid's bat had a mellow ring to it and even his defensive strokes had the hallmark of class.

Determined bowling had kept India to 521, a formidable total, but less than England had feared. In reply, they reached 32 from 11 overs that evening and the opening pair were doubtless pleased to walk off together; it had been tough going, despite the quality of the pitch. Atherton had escaped on nought when Dravid let a slip chance elude him (like Tendulkar, he was to make the opposition pay dearly) and Stewart did his fair share of playing and missing against India's skilled new-ball partners, Srinath and Prasad. Atherton gave another hard chance to Azharuddin at slip on 34; Stewart, on the other hand, looked unlucky to be given caught behind by Sri Lankan umpire K. T. Francis after a hard-fought fifty.

That brought in Hussain, who epitomised the confident batsman. Driving fluently and enjoying the feel-good factor, he scored 25 from his first 16 balls and completed his second hundred in three Tests, although some Indian fieldsmen were convinced he had been caught behind off Tendulkar when 74. Atherton had reached his tenth Test century – his fourth at Nottingham – 90 minutes after lunch, without ever looking convincing. He was beaten a fair number of times, but stuck to his task throughout the third day. England had averted the follow-on just before the close, consigning the match to stalemate. They had lost only the one wicket, though they were effectively deprived of another when Hussain fractured his right index finger in the last over. He failed a net try-out on Monday morning and retired hurt on 107. Atherton remained, reaching 160, his second highest Test score, in seven and a half hours before being taken at slip. Thorpe lacked his usual fluency and Hick laboured long and fruitlessly, but Ealham struck 51 on debut and the tail secured a lead of 43.

This had little consequence, though Ealham's promising start continued when his lively seam bowling picked up four wickets in India's second innings. Tendulkar had time to strike a polished 74, and Ganguly was dismissed by Cork halfway to history, in pursuit of a unique third hundred in his first three Test innings. – DAVID FIELD.

Man of the Match: S. C. Ganguly. *Attendance:* 37,589; *receipts* £740,810.

Men of the Series: England – N. Hussain; India – S. C. Ganguly.

Close of play: First day, India 287-2 (S. C. Ganguly 136*, S. R. Tendulkar 123*); Second day, England 32-0 (M. A. Atherton 21*, A. J. Stewart 10*); Third day, England 322-1 (M. A. Atherton 145*, N. Hussain 107*); Fourth day, England 550-7 (D. G. Cork 24*, M. M. Patel 22*).

India

V. Rathore c Russell b Cork	4	– absent hurt	
†N. R. Mongia c Russell b Lewis	9	– (1) c Lewis b Mullally	45
S. C. Ganguly c Hussain b Mullally	136	– b Cork	48
S. R. Tendulkar c Patel b Ealham	177	– c Stewart b Lewis	74
S. V. Manjrekar c Hick b Patel	53	– (2) c Stewart b Lewis	11
*M. Azharuddin c Patel b Lewis	5	– c Cork b Ealham	8
R. Dravid c Russell b Ealham	84	– (5) c Thorpe b Mullally	8
A. Kumble lbw b Mullally	0	– (7) lbw b Ealham	2
J. Srinath c Cork b Lewis	1	– (8) c Thorpe b Ealham	3
B. K. V. Prasad run out	13	– (9) not out	0
S. L. V. Raju not out	1	– (10) c sub (N. A. Gie) b Ealham	0
B 6, l-b 12, w 7, n-b 13	38	B 1, l-b 1, w 1, n-b 9	12
1/7 (1) 2/33 (2) 3/288 (3) 4/377 (4) 5/385 (6) 6/446 (5) 7/447 (8) 8/453 (9) 9/513 (10) 10/521 (7)	521	1/17 (2) 2/103 (3) 3/140 (1) 4/160 (5) 5/204 (6) 6/208 (4) 7/208 (7) 8/211 (8) 9/211 (10)	211

Bowling: *First Innings*—Lewis 37–10–89–3; Cork 32–6–124–1; Mullally 40–12–88–2; Ealham 29–9–90–2; Patel 24–2–101–1; Hick 4–1–8–0; Thorpe 1–0–3–0. *Second Innings*—Lewis 14–4–50–2; Cork 7–0–32–1; Mullally 13–3–36–2; Ealham 14–5–21–4; Patel 12–3–47–0; Hick 9–4–23–0.

England

*M. A. Atherton c Manjrekar b Prasad	160
A. J. Stewart c Mongia b Srinath	50
N. Hussain retired hurt	107
G. P. Thorpe lbw b Ganguly	45
G. A. Hick c Srinath b Raju	20
M. A. Ealham c sub (A. Jadeja) b Srinath	51
†R. C. Russell c Mongia b Prasad	0
C. C. Lewis lbw b Kumble	21
D. G. Cork not out	32
M. M. Patel c Manjrekar b Ganguly	27
A. D. Mullally c Mongia b Ganguly	1
B 18, l-b 18, n-b 14	50
1/130 (2) 2/360 (1) 3/396 (4) 4/444 (5) 5/444 (7) 6/491 (8) 7/497 (6) 8/558 (10) 9/564 (11)	564

N. Hussain retired hurt at 322.

Bowling: Srinath 47–12–131–2; Prasad 43–12–124–2; Kumble 39–6–98–1; Raju 43–12–76–1; Ganguly 19.5–2–71–3; Tendulkar 7–0–28–0.

Umpires: K. T. Francis (Sri Lanka) and G. Sharp. Referee: C. W. Smith (West Indies).

THE PAKISTANIS IN ENGLAND, 1996

No tour – save, perhaps, the Australians' first visit after Bodyline – can ever have needed more delicate handling than this one. Yet Pakistan achieved the remarkable feat of spreading goodwill while winning a Test series and administering two hefty defeats on England. When they left England in 1992, feeling falsely accused and deeply insulted, Imran Khan predicted in print that no official Pakistan team would ever set foot in the country again. Though that prophecy always seemed a mite over-emotional, the sentiment was understandable. There was so much mutual mistrust that sporting relations between the two nations could not have survived another series ablaze with accusations of ball-tampering, sweater-throwing and umpire-baiting.

The fact that Pakistan managed to play their usual exhilarating, strong-arm, glamorous cricket, yet still kept the peace, was a diplomatic triumph which must be attributed to tour manager Yawar Saeed and, even more so, to captain Wasim Akram. There was little starch in Yawar's approach to public relations. Unlike the early-season Indian tourists, Pakistan had no internal troubles to hide. The players were encouraged to mingle, talk and, above all, entertain. They did all three. The world's most fractious team seemed to have found an unprecedented unity since the Pakistan public turned on them after the defeat by India in the World Cup just over three months earlier.

Wasim had been the most cruelly hounded. He was subjected to outrageous insults in local newspapers and effigies of him were burned in the streets. He kept his job and his dignity and, in the process, earned the kind of respect he never enjoyed when his first misguided spell as captain was ended by a players' rebellion. There were, paradoxically, few times during the tour when Wasim looked, with either ball or bat, the great all-rounder he undoubtedly is. Perhaps he expended so much energy damping down emotions that his own game never caught fire. He began the three-match series needing 11 wickets to become only the 11th bowler to take 300 Test wickets. He did not reach that target until a perfect yorker bowled Alan Mullally and ended England's innings in the final Test at The Oval. He finished on his knees, arms upraised in a gesture that was part triumph, part prayer of thanksgiving. Throughout the tour he said he was unworried by his own lack of form. It never got in the way of his job as manipulator of a team so obviously superior that only a freak English pitch or their own suspect temperament threatened to defeat them. He has learned a lot since he first walked into the traditionally down-to-earth, classless, Lancashire dressing-room in 1988 – not only about English conditions but about English attitudes. Nowadays, he is not a man to take offence easily. His leadership is the antithesis of the posturing and confrontational style that made Javed Miandad the detonator for so many of the 1992 explosions. Wasim was always quick to intervene to calm jangling Pakistan nerves, but never theatrical.

Quite a few landmines were laid in his path. Allan Lamb, whose ball-tampering accusations had caused the major crisis on the previous tour, had strategically resigned from Northamptonshire so that Test and County Cricket Board rules could not prevent him raking over the old ashes in a ghosted autobiography; the newspaper serialisation was timed to coincide with the tour. In the event, those embers were cold, grey and unenlightening. The real, hurtful mud was being slung daily in the High Court where, by some mischievous quirk of the legal calendar, the libel case brought against Imran Khan by Ian Botham

THE PAKISTANI TOURING PARTY

[*Patrick Eagar*

Back row: Mushtaq Ahmed, Saeed Anwar, Rashid Latif, Saqlain Mushtaq, Inzamam-ul-Haq, Shahid Anwar, Mohammad Akram, Ata-ur-Rehman, Shahid Nazir, Moin Khan, Shadab Kabir, Dan Kiesel (*physiotherapist*). *Front row:* Ijaz Ahmed, Waqar Younis, Aamir Sohail, Yawar Saeed (*manager*), Wasim Akram (*captain*), Nasim-ul-Ghani (*assistant manager*), Salim Malik, Asif Mujtaba.

and Lamb provided a lurid and, at times, unintentionally hilarious curtain-raiser to the First Test at Lord's. England captain Mike Atherton and coach David Lloyd were the most reluctant witnesses, called on the eve of the Test. Lloyd, in particular, protested that it interfered with England's preparations. To his credit, he did not offer that as an excuse for the defeat which settled the course of the series.

There had always been a suspicion that England's 1-0 series win over an under-prepared and disorganised India was something of a false dawn, and that reality would be restored once they were confronted by a team with three world-class bowlers – Wasim, Waqar Younis and Mushtaq Ahmed – and a handful of batsmen of dazzling, if vulnerable, brilliance. So it proved. Though Pakistan may be gloriously unpredictable, England are not. They lost the opening Test through a hopeless batting collapse, drew the second by wasting heaven-sent conditions at Headingley and were overwhelmed by weight of runs and Mushtaq's unrelenting spin at The Oval.

Pakistan had arrived while English cricket's other great *cause célèbre* of 1996 – the Illingworth–Malcolm Affair – was still rumbling through the TCCB's own judicial system. And through the Pakistan series, the "hands-on" chairman of selectors, dignity badly bruised though still cussed, kept a deliberately low profile – so bland that it was no longer possible to assess how much influence the once omnipotent Illingworth had on selection or policy. Bowling coach Peter Lever, his first lieutenant in the campaign to smooth out Malcolm's action, submitted his resignation on the eve of the Second Test and later threatened, somewhat vaguely, to "tell all" about the political manoeuvrings behind the scenes.

All this left Lloyd with greater responsibility for the day-to-day running of the team, an authority that was to be confirmed by the regrading of his job in the report of the Acfield working party. He had bubbled with infectious enthusiasm through the early part of the summer, but, like the team and an expectant public, wilted a bit on the last day at Lord's. In that match, England never recovered from the third-wicket stand of 130 between Saeed Anwar and Inzamam-ul-Haq which rescued Pakistan's first innings. The left-handed Anwar's 74 typified the uninhibitedness of modern Pakistani batsmanship. Inzamam, almost two stones lighter since he was ordered on a crash diet after the World Cup, batted with the same freedom to make 148. He was the first of five Pakistanis to make hundreds in the series, being followed by Ijaz Ahmed, Moin Khan, Anwar and, eventually, Salim Malik, at the end of an undistinguished summer by his standards. Opener Aamir Sohail, the batting revelation of their last tour, hurt his finger in the First Test and was relatively subdued when he came back for the last.

Though admiring, Lloyd called Pakistan's batsmen "get-out-able", but England spent half the summer searching for an attack able to justify the phrase. The main problem was that Cork, their only potential match-winner, was palpably worn out, so jaded by overwork and persistent knee trouble that even his appealing lost some of its hysteria. Still unprepared to trust Darren Gough, their biggest hope barely a year earlier, England gave one Test to Durham's journeyman pace bowler Simon Brown and, odder still, only one to the rejuvenated Andrew Caddick. Though he was the pick of the four seamers who failed at Headingley, Caddick was left out of the final Test because of Atherton's misguided belief that Chris Lewis's latest revival would last the summer. In fact, his comeback ended in controversy. Lewis was late reporting at The Oval on Sunday – he blamed it on a flat tyre – and was crossed out of the squad for the three one-day matches and, inevitably, out of the winter tour of

Zimbabwe and New Zealand. With hindsight, the Lewis question should have been faced before it had such a damaging effect.

The other question, concerning the future of Graeme Hick, was resolved at Lord's when Waqar twice exposed his frailty against high-quality fast bowling. Waqar may no longer have the devastating pace of his youth (the new and occasionally accurate electronic speed-gun introduced to measure all the bowlers rarely rated him much above 80 m.p.h.). But he has a unique ability to swing the ball which can no longer be tarnished by disbelieving stares and insinuations of illegality. The umpires did have trouble with the ball, but only because it kept losing its shape. Waqar took eight wickets in the First Test and, when Atherton and Stewart threatened to drag out England's second innings long enough to save the match, Mushtaq produced the bowling spell which reduced England from 168 for one to an all-out 243. Mushtaq's years with Somerset have hardened him, increased his variety and improved what now seems an inexhaustible patience – all the more galling for England, who spent the summer bemoaning the absence of a genuine, home-grown spinner. The relaunch of leg-spinner Ian Salisbury was scuttled by the brutality of Pakistan's batting and they did not put their trust in the steadiness of off-spinner Robert Croft until their sixth Test of the summer. By then, Mushtaq had a hypnotic hold on England, finishing with 17 wickets, including the six for 78 which won the final Test. It was difficult to accept the Pakistanis' belief that he had overtaken a fully-fit Shane Warne as the world's premier wrist-spinner; he does not, for a start, turn the ball as wickedly as the Australian. Yet his accuracy is immaculate and his subtlety boundless.

Encouragingly, England came through the series in some ways toughened rather than demoralised by defeat. The top six looked, at least temperamentally, stronger than it had for years. Stewart, dismissing the notion that he was over the hill, flourished, winning back his place as opener and making 170 at Headingley. Nick Knight hit his maiden Test century in the same match and John Crawley, a talent held back by injury, followed suit at The Oval. England, though, were no nearer finding a true Test all-rounder or of unearthing bowlers with the bite or the know-how to live with top-class opposition.

Pakistan, in contrast, looked capable of growing into the best, most entertaining side in the world. They have never been scared to throw in young talent, and three of this summer's crop, all officially less than 20, seemed destined for greater things. Off-spinner Saqlain Mushtaq, already rated, at 19, the best of his type in the game, could not squeeze into the side until the anticlimactic one-day matches. Shadab Kabir showed nerve and a sound technique when he deputised as opener for Sohail. And Shahid Nazir, who bowls surprisingly quickly off a disarmingly gentle run-up, launched what could be a distinguished international career by leaving Atherton wincing with pain after being hit on the thumb by the youngster's second ball. That was during Pakistan's only win in the three limited-overs internationals.

Those two one-day defeats by England, and one inflicted by Warwickshire over three days, were the only minor blemishes on Pakistan's record. They went home fully expecting to be garlanded by the very people who had abused them only months earlier. If there had been a cross word all tour, it must have been muttered under their breath – even though there were more questionable umpiring decisions than on their previous explosive visit. Some of the mistakes were glaring, some crucial, but they were fairly evenly spread between the two sides. Pakistan, who had campaigned vociferously for neutral umpires, might now be convinced that neutrality does not mean infallibility. And Lord's might question the cricketing, if not financial, wisdom of allowing huge video screens to undermine the umpires' confidence. Once, we were assured that no controversial incidents would be played back. Now they are shown repeatedly and have encouraged a new form of player dissent. Batsmen dissatisfied with their dismissal walk off craning their necks to make sure the replay proves their point. One day, perhaps, one will be provoked into going back to plead his case with photographic evidence. – PETER JOHNSON.

PAKISTANI TOURING PARTY

Wasim Akram (PIA) (*captain*), Aamir Sohail (Lahore/Allied Bank) (*vice-captain*), Asif Mujtaba (Karachi/PIA), Ata-ur-Rehman (Lahore/Allied Bank), Ijaz Ahmed, sen. (Lahore/Habib Bank), Inzamam-ul-Haq (United Bank), Mohammad Akram (Rawalpindi), Moin Khan (Karachi/PIA), Mushtaq Ahmed (Islamabad/United Bank), Rashid Latif (Karachi/United Bank), Saeed Anwar (ADBP), Salim Malik (Habib Bank), Saqlain Mushtaq (Islamabad/PIA), Shadab Kabir (Karachi), Shahid Anwar (Lahore/National Bank), Shahid Nazir (Faisalabad), Waqar Younis (United Bank).

Tour manager: Yawar Saeed. *Assistant manager:* Nasim-ul-Ghani.

PAKISTANI TOUR RESULTS

Test matches – Played 3: Won 2, Drawn 1.
First-class matches – Played 11: Won 7, Lost 1, Drawn 3.
Wins – England (2), Somerset, Kent, Durham, Leicestershire, Essex.
Loss – Warwickshire.
Draws – England, Glamorgan, Northamptonshire.
One-day internationals – Played 3: Won 1, Lost 2.
Other non-first-class matches – Played 4: Won 4. *Wins* – England NCA, Minor Counties, MCC, Scotland.

TEST MATCH AVERAGES

ENGLAND – BATTING

	T	*I*	*NO*	*R*	*HS*	*100s*	*Avge*	*Ct/St*
A. J. Stewart	3	5	0	396	170	1	79.20	2/1
J. P. Crawley	2	3	0	178	106	1	59.33	1
N. V. Knight	3	5	0	190	113	1	38.00	1
N. Hussain	2	3	0	111	51	0	37.00	1
M. A. Atherton	3	5	0	162	64	0	32.40	3
G. P. Thorpe	3	5	0	159	77	0	31.80	2
R. C. Russell	2	3	1	51	41*	0	25.50	9
I. D. K. Salisbury	2	4	1	50	40	0	16.66	0
D. G. Cork	3	5	0	58	26	0	11.60	3
A. D. Mullally	3	5	1	39	24	0	9.75	0
C. C. Lewis	2	3	0	18	9	0	6.00	1

Played in one Test: S. J. E. Brown 1, 10* (1 ct); A. R. Caddick 4; R. D. B. Croft 5*, 6 (1 ct); M. A. Ealham 25, 5 (1 ct); G. A. Hick 4, 4 (1 ct).

* *Signifies not out.*

BOWLING

	O	M	R	W	BB	5W/i	Avge
A. R. Caddick	57.2	10	165	6	3-52	0	27.50
D. G. Cork	131	23	434	12	5-113	1	36.16
A. D. Mullally	150.3	36	377	10	3-44	0	37.70

Also bowled: M. A. Atherton 7–1–20–1; S. J. E. Brown 33–4–138–2; R. D. B. Croft 47.4–10–125–2; M. A. Ealham 37–8–81–1; G. A. Hick 13–2–42–1; C. C. Lewis 71–10–264–1; I. D. K. Salisbury 61.2–8–221–2; G. P. Thorpe 13–4–19–0.

PAKISTAN – BATTING

	T	I	NO	R	HS	100s	Avge	Ct
Moin Khan	2	3	1	158	105	1	79.00	3
Ijaz Ahmed, sen.....	3	6	1	344	141	1	68.80	1
Salim Malik........	3	5	2	195	100*	1	65.00	0
Inzamam-ul-Haq	3	5	0	320	148	1	64.00	2
Saeed Anwar	3	6	0	362	176	1	60.33	2
Aamir Sohail	2	3	1	77	46	0	38.50	1
Asif Mujtaba	2	3	0	90	51	0	30.00	1
Wasim Akram	3	5	1	98	40	0	24.50	1
Shadab Kabir.......	2	4	0	87	35	0	21.75	2
Mushtaq Ahmed	3	5	1	44	20	0	11.00	3
Waqar Younis	3	3	1	11	7	0	5.50	1

Played in two Tests: Ata-ur-Rehman 10*, 0*. Played in one Test: Mohammad Akram did not bat; Rashid Latif 45 (3 ct).

* *Signifies not out.*

BOWLING

	O	M	R	W	BB	5W/i	Avge
Mushtaq Ahmed ...	195	52	447	17	6-78	2	26.29
Waqar Younis	125	25	431	16	4-69	0	26.93
Wasim Akram	128	29	350	11	3-67	0	31.81
Ata-ur-Rehman	48.4	6	173	5	4-50	0	34.60

Also bowled: Aamir Sohail 11–3–24–0; Asif Mujtaba 7–5–6–0; Mohammad Akram 22–4–71–1; Salim Malik 1–0–1–0; Shadab Kabir 1–0–9–0.

PAKISTANI TOUR AVERAGES – FIRST-CLASS MATCHES

BATTING

	M	I	NO	R	HS	100s	Avge	Ct/St
Saeed Anwar.......	10	19	1	1,224	219*	5	68.00	6
Inzamam-ul-Haq	9	14	2	792	169*	3	66.00	6
Ijaz Ahmed, sen. ...	9	16	2	664	141	2	47.42	2
Salim Malik	9	14	4	450	104*	2	45.00	1
Asif Mujtaba.......	10	16	6	445	100*	1	44.50	8
Shadab Kabir	7	12	1	390	99	0	35.45	6
Shahid Anwar	3	6	1	166	89	0	33.20	0
Rashid Latif	7	7	0	232	61	0	33.14	17/4

	M	*I*	*NO*	*R*	*HS*	*100s*	*Avge*	*Ct/St*
Aamir Sohail	8	14	2	334	49	0	27.83	12
Moin Khan	5	9	1	215	105	1	26.87	5/2
Wasim Akram	7	9	1	211	68	0	26.37	4
Saqlain Mushtaq	5	7	2	130	78	0	26.00	3
Mushtaq Ahmed	7	9	1	118	38	0	14.75	4
Ata-ur-Rehman	9	8	2	61	30	0	10.16	5
Waqar Younis	7	7	2	19	8	0	3.80	2
Mohammad Akram	6	5	5	7	4*	0	–	4

Played in three matches: Shahid Nazir 3, 13, 5*.

* *Signifies not out.*

BOWLING

	O	*M*	*R*	*W*	*BB*	*5W/i*	*Avge*
Shahid Nazir	47	8	164	12	4-43	0	13.66
Saqlain Mushtaq	166.5	43	456	29	6-52	2	15.72
Mushtaq Ahmed	325	85	861	41	7-91	5	21.00
Waqar Younis	195.1	42	654	30	5-42	1	21.80
Wasim Akram	271.5	67	787	32	5-58	1	24.59
Mohammad Akram	128.2	21	473	14	7-51	1	33.78
Ata-ur-Rehman	184.4	24	710	17	4-50	0	41.76

Also bowled: Aamir Sohail 65.4–14–205–3; Asif Mujtaba 32–7–104–3; Ijaz Ahmed, sen. 4.5–0–27–0; Inzamam-ul-Haq 4–0–24–0; Moin Khan 9–0–78–2; Rashid Latif 5–1–26–0; Salim Malik 7–1–24–1; Shadab Kabir 5–0–27–0; Shahid Anwar 7.3–2–46–2.

Note: Matches in this section which were not first-class are signified by a dagger.

†ENGLAND NCA v PAKISTANIS

At Trowbridge, June 27. Pakistanis won by eight wickets. Toss: England NCA.

The tourists won in such comfort that they had nearly 20 overs in hand. Vice-captain Aamir Sohail and Saeed Anwar had opened with 131 in 18 overs, and Sohail was run out only four short of victory, after striking a 77-ball century with three sixes and 14 fours. England NCA chose to bat, but their top four contributed only 33 between them. Clarke and Laudat fought back with 72 in 13 overs, but it was hard work for the amateurs. Saqlain Mushtaq marked his English debut by bowling ten overs for just 14 runs and two wickets.

England NCA

S. J. Dean b Saqlain Mushtaq . . . 9
S. Foster b Shahid Nazir . . . 12
S. Luckhurst b Mushtaq Ahmed . . . 7
*M. J. Roberts c Salim Malik b Saqlain Mushtaq . 5
D. R. Clarke not out . . . 65
S. V. Laudat c Salim Malik b Mushtaq Ahmed . 39
J. D. Robinson c Saqlain Mushtaq b Wasim Akram . 8
†C. W. Taylor not out . . . 8
L-b 12, w 5, n-b 12 . . . 29

1/29 2/31 3/40 4/65 5/137 6/164 (6 wkts, 50 overs) 182

K. A. Arnold, P. G. Roshier and R. Ellwood did not bat.

Bowling: Wasim Akram 10–2–38–1; Waqar Younis 10–2–47–0; Saqlain Mushtaq 10–4–14–2; Shahid Nazir 10–1–45–1; Mushtaq Ahmed 10–2–26–2.

Pakistanis

Aamir Sohail run out	104
Saeed Anwar b Laudat	46
Ijaz Ahmed, sen. not out	12
Inzamam-ul-Haq not out	0
L-b 9, w 10, n-b 2	21
1/131 2/179 (2 wkts, 30.4 overs)	183

Salim Malik, *Wasim Akram, †Rashid Latif, Waqar Younis, Mushtaq Ahmed, Saqlain Mushtaq and Shahid Nazir did not bat.

Bowling: Roshier 4–0–28–0; Arnold 7–0–34–0; Robinson 2–0–29–0; Ellwood 6–0–52–0; Laudat 8–1–24–1; Foster 3.4–0–7–0.

Umpires: J. F. Steele and R. A. White.

GLAMORGAN v PAKISTANIS

At Pontypridd, June 29, 30, July 1. Drawn. Toss: Glamorgan.

The Pakistanis declared that they wanted to win all their county games, and they were well placed when rain terminated the final day after seven overs. Glamorgan still trailed by 97 and had lost both openers. Their batsmen had scored an encouraging 304 on the opening day, when Ata-ur-Rehman claimed four wickets and Aamir Sohail four catches at slip. But Saeed Anwar and Inzamam-ul-Haq took control of the game with an unbroken third-wicket partnership of 362. It was an all-wicket record for any Pakistani side in England, and equalled the biggest stand ever conceded by Glamorgan – to Yorkshire openers Moxon and Vaughan a few weeks earlier. Anwar scored 219 not out in 286 balls, striking a six and 31 fours, while the aggressive Inzamam hit two sixes and 24 fours in 220 balls. Wasim Akram declared before the close to keep the initiative, and might have succeeded but for the weather.

Close of play: First day, Pakistanis 74-0 (Aamir Sohail 34*, Saeed Anwar 32*); Second day, Glamorgan 34-1 (S. P. James 8*, A. P. Davies 0*).

Glamorgan

S. P. James c Aamir Sohail b Ata-ur-Rehman	79	– c Rashid Latif b Ata-ur-Rehman	9
A. W. Evans lbw b Ata-ur-Rehman	39	– c Aamir Sohail b Wasim Akram	18
D. L. Hemp c Rashid Latif b Ata-ur-Rehman	4		
G. P. Butcher c Inzamam-ul-Haq b Mushtaq Ahmed	35	– not out	14
A. J. Dalton c Salim Malik b Mushtaq Ahmed	5		
*M. P. Maynard c Rashid Latif b Ata-ur-Rehman	40		
R. D. B. Croft st Rashid Latif b Mushtaq Ahmed	14		
†A. D. Shaw c Aamir Sohail b Waqar Younis	22		
S. D. Thomas c Aamir Sohail b Waqar Younis	9		
A. P. Davies c Aamir Sohail b Wasim Akram	8	– (3) not out	11
O. T. Parkin not out	5		
B 4, l-b 8, w 2, n-b 30	44	W 1, n-b 7	8
1/75 2/83 3/168 4/188 5/194 6/245 7/254 8/277 9/295	304	1/29 2/42 (2 wkts)	60

Bowling: *First Innings*—Wasim Akram 16.5–1–64–1; Waqar Younis 18–4–70–2; Ata-ur-Rehman 20–3–82–4; Mushtaq Ahmed 25–5–76–3. *Second Innings*—Wasim Akram 10–1–34–1; Waqar Younis 4–1–8–0; Mushtaq Ahmed 2–1–1–0; Ata-ur-Rehman 3.1–0–17–1.

Pakistanis

Aamir Sohail c Evans b Thomas	49
Saeed Anwar not out	219
Ijaz Ahmed, sen. c Croft b Thomas	0
Inzamam-ul-Haq not out	169
B 8, l-b 6, w 3, n-b 7	24
1/99 2/99 (2 wkts dec.)	461

Salim Malik, Asif Mujtaba, †Rashid Latif, *Wasim Akram, Mushtaq Ahmed, Waqar Younis and Ata-ur-Rehman did not bat.

Bowling: Parkin 22–4–59–0; Thomas 23–1–110–2; Davies 15–2–75–0; Croft 27–3–129–0; Butcher 10–1–74–0.

Umpires: M. J. Kitchen and B. Leadbeater.

SOMERSET v PAKISTANIS

At Taunton, July 3, 4, 5. Pakistanis won by 105 runs. Toss: Somerset. First-class debut: I. E. Bishop.

Somerset were outclassed by the batting of Saeed Anwar and the bowling of Mushtaq Ahmed, who took ten for 108, but compensated his opponents by signing a contract to bring him back to the county for another two years. Rain interrupted the first two days, but Saeed Anwar followed up his double-hundred three days earlier with 130 in 143 balls in the first innings and 60 from 63 in the second. He received useful help from Asif Mujtaba on the opening day, while Inzamam-ul-Haq scored a lively 42-ball fifty on the last morning. Somerset, already hit by injury, could offer nothing to match. Bowler contributed two half-centuries and looked composed against the seamers, while Shine struck a few lusty blows to save the follow-on. But only Ecclestone suggested that he might be coming to terms with Mushtaq. A target of 316 in 78 overs was well beyond their reach.

Close of play: First day, Pakistanis 253-5 (Shadab Kabir 10*, Rashid Latif 14*); Second day, Pakistanis 107-1 (Aamir Sohail 28*, Shahid Anwar 8*).

Pakistanis

First innings		Second innings	
*Aamir Sohail c Turner b Shine	0	retired hurt	28
Saeed Anwar b Lee	130	c Turner b Batty	60
Shahid Anwar lbw b Shine	21	not out	17
Asif Mujtaba lbw b Lee	54		
Inzamam-ul-Haq c Turner b Lee	4	(4) not out	51
Shadab Kabir not out	21		
†Rashid Latif c Lathwell b Parsons	38		
Mushtaq Ahmed c Bishop b Lee	12		
Waqar Younis not out	0		
B 4, w 4, n-b 12	20	L-b 1, w 1, n-b 16	18
1/2 2/51 3/208 4/214 5/223 6/278 7/300 (7 wkts dec.)	300	1/91 (1 wkt dec.)	174

Ata-ur-Rehman and Mohammad Akram did not bat.

In the second innings Aamir Sohail retired hurt at 107.

Bowling: *First Innings*—Shine 15–0–77–2; Lee 21–4–65–4; van Troost 10.1–0–41–0; Batty 26–7–60–0; Parsons 5–1–24–1; Bishop 7–0–29–0. *Second Innings*—van Troost 5–0–35–0; Shine 11–0–64–0; Batty 12.5–1–61–1; Lathwell 6–0–13–0.

Somerset

First innings		Second innings	
M. N. Lathwell c and b Waqar Younis	0	c Shadab Kabir b Mohammad Akram	25
*P. D. Bowler c Mohammad Akram b Mushtaq Ahmed	68	lbw b Asif Mujtaba	52
M. E. Trescothick c Shadab Kabir b Mushtaq Ahmed	27	lbw b Aamir Sohail	4
K. A. Parsons c Aamir Sohail b Mushtaq Ahmed	0	c Asif Mujtaba b Mushtaq Ahmed	9
S. C. Ecclestone run out	18	c Shadab Kabir b Mushtaq Ahmed	57
S. Lee retired hurt	0	(7) c Inzamam-ul-Haq b Mushtaq Ahmed	0
†R. J. Turner c Asif Mujtaba b Mushtaq Ahmed	14	(6) c Saeed Anwar b Mushtaq Ahmed	9
J. D. Batty b Waqar Younis	0	c Saeed Anwar b Mushtaq Ahmed	27
K. J. Shine not out	19	c Aamir Sohail b Ata-ur-Rehman	6
A. P. van Troost st Rashid Latif b Mushtaq Ahmed	0	not out	5
I. E. Bishop lbw b Waqar Younis	2	lbw b Ata-ur-Rehman	2
B 8, l-b 1, n-b 2	11	B 6, l-b 6, n-b 2	14
1/0 2/67 3/73 4/121 5/125 6/132 7/144 8/144 9/159	159	1/53 2/75 3/98 4/98 5/124 6/124 7/188 8/203 9/203	210

In the first innings S. Lee retired hurt at 121-4.

Bowling: *First Innings*—Waqar Younis 15.1–0–59–3; Ata-ur-Rehman 6–1–24–0; Mohammad Akram 6–0–31–0; Mushtaq Ahmed 13–5–36–5. *Second Innings*—Waqar Younis 3–1–10–0; Mohammad Akram 6–0–34–1; Ata-ur-Rehman 7.5–1–29–2; Mushtaq Ahmed 23–6–72–5; Aamir Sohail 15–2–41–1; Asif Mujtaba 4–0–12–1.

Umpires: V. A. Holder and D. R. Shepherd.

NORTHAMPTONSHIRE v PAKISTANIS

At Northampton, July 6, 7, 8. Drawn. Toss: Northamptonshire.

Left to score 226 in 33 overs after an agreement between the captains, the Pakistanis made good progress through Shadab Kabir and Ijaz Ahmed, while Moin Khan scored a spectacular 39 off 23 balls, but the target proved just beyond reach. The price for the interesting finish was a session of gift bowling, after Fordham and Montgomerie had effectively saved the match by lunch on the final day. They scored 188 genuine runs for the first wicket and Fordham had completed his century against the front-line bowlers. The remaining 67 runs of their stand had little meaning and Fordham retired. This was subsequently, and unconvincingly, attributed to "eye trouble", which attracted adverse comment since some felt Law 2.9 ("retired out") might have applied. On the opening day, Wasim Akram undermined Northamptonshire with five for 14 in 40 balls, all given out lbw by umpire Willey. But the Pakistanis were in trouble at 140 for seven before Shadab and Saqlain Mushtaq added 171, an eighth-wicket record against the county, beating the 151 put on by Wilfred Payton and Harold Larwood for Nottinghamshire in 1925. Shadab was dismissed one short of an eye-catching century after hitting two sixes and 11 fours.

Close of play: First day, Pakistanis 79-1 (Shahid Anwar 26*, Ijaz Ahmed 24*); Second day, Northamptonshire 71-0 (R. R. Montgomerie 23*, A. Fordham 40*).

Northamptonshire

R. R. Montgomerie lbw b Wasim Akram	43	c Asif Mujtaba b Moin Khan	168
A. Fordham lbw b Wasim Akram	37	retired hurt	144
R. J. Warren lbw b Shahid Nazir	1		
M. B. Loye lbw b Wasim Akram	1	(3) c Rashid Latif b Moin Khan	6
*R. J. Bailey b Shahid Nazir	7	(4) c Rashid Latif b Shahid Anwar	29
D. J. Capel lbw b Wasim Akram	2	not out	9
J. N. Snape lbw b Wasim Akram	8	not out	4
†D. Ripley c Wasim Akram b Mohammad Akram	13		
J. G. Hughes c Rashid Latif b Shahid Nazir	8	(5) c Mohammad Akram b Shahid Anwar	6
N. A. Mallender lbw b Shahid Nazir	7		
S. A. J. Boswell not out	2		
B 5, l-b 7, w 3, n-b 8	23	B 3, l-b 11, n-b 16	30
1/89 2/94 3/96 4/105 5/107 6/116 7/120 8/143 9/145	152	1/306 2/353 3/373 4/392 (4 wkts dec.)	396

In the second innings A. J. Fordham retired hurt at 255.

Bowling: *First Innings*—Wasim Akram 20–5–58–5; Mohammad Akram 15–4–39–1; Shahid Nazir 16.4–5–43–4. *Second Innings*—Wasim Akram 15–4–46–0; Mohammad Akram 13–2–49–0; Shahid Nazir 7–1–27–0; Saqlain Mushtaq 9–1–27–0; Rashid Latif 5–1–26–0; Asif Mujtaba 9–0–52–0; Shadab Kabir 4–0–18–0; Ijaz Ahmed 2–0–13–0; Moin Khan 9–0–78–2; Shahid Anwar 7.3–2–46–2.

Pakistanis

Saeed Anwar lbw b Hughes	20	(8) c Montgomerie b Snape	8
Shahid Anwar c Capel b Boswell	26	(1) c Loye b Boswell	12
Ijaz Ahmed, sen. lbw b Boswell	29	run out	39
Asif Mujtaba run out	15	(5) not out	31
Shadab Kabir c Ripley b Capel	99	(2) c Bailey b Snape	52
*Wasim Akram b Snape	21	(4) b Capel	12
Rashid Latif lbw b Capel	3	(6) b Snape	0
†Moin Khan c Montgomerie b Capel	1	(7) c Montgomerie b Boswell	39
Saqlain Mushtaq b Capel	78	c Warren b Bailey	2
Shahid Nazir run out	3		
Mohammad Akram not out	2		
L-b 8, n-b 18	26	B 4, l-b 3, w 1, n-b 2	10
1/30 2/86 3/91 4/108 5/131 6/138 7/140 8/311 9/321	323	1/33 2/103 3/114 4/128 5/129 6/192 7/201 8/205 (8 wkts)	205

Bowling: *First Innings*—Mallender 2–0–20–0; Boswell 23–3–77–2; Hughes 22–5–82–1; Capel 17.1–1–60–4; Snape 23–7–63–1; Bailey 6–3–13–0. *Second Innings*—Boswell 9–0–52–2; Hughes 7–2–46–0; Snape 9–0–63–3; Capel 7–1–34–1; Bailey 0.5–0–3–1.

Umpires: T. E. Jesty and P. Willey.

†MINOR COUNTIES v PAKISTANIS

At Stone, July 11. Pakistanis won by 170 runs. Toss: Pakistanis.

The tourists took easy revenge for their unexpected defeat by the Minor Counties in 1992. Aamir Sohail scored 133 in 102 balls, with 21 fours and two sixes, and Inzamam-ul-Haq made 41 from 28 balls before retiring, complaining of a "dizzy spell". Laudat took two wickets in successive balls but conceded 82, injured his hand and could not bat. The only bowler to escape unscathed was Marcus Sharp, who was later top scorer, with 37 not out; coming in at 77 for eight, effectively their last man, he and Potter almost doubled the total.

Pakistanis

Aamir Sohail c Cockbain b Fell	133
Shadab Kabir c K. Sharp b Laudat	21
Ijaz Ahmed, sen. c Batty b Laudat	0
Inzamam-ul-Haq retired hurt	41
Salim Malik c K. Sharp b Fell	4
*Wasim Akram c M. A. Sharp b Saggers	43
†Rashid Latif c Potter b Laudat	27
Saqlain Mushtaq not out	17
Mushtaq Ahmed run out	1
Waqar Younis not out	14
L-b 4, w 5	9
1/90 2/90 3/186 4/209 5/274 6/280 7/290 (7 wkts, 50 overs)	310

Ata-ur-Rehman did not bat.

Inzamam-ul-Haq retired hurt at 171.

Bowling: Saggers 8–1–64–1; M. A. Sharp 8–2–22–0; Myles 10–0–46–0; Laudat 10–0–82–3; Potter 6–0–47–0; Fell 8–0–45–2.

Minor Counties

S. J. Dean c Mushtaq Ahmed b Waqar Younis	18
R. J. Evans lbw b Waqar Younis	6
K. Sharp b Wasim Akram	6
M. A. Fell c Mushtaq Ahmed b Saqlain Mushtaq	11
*I. Cockbain c sub b Saqlain Mushtaq	11
S. D. Myles c sub b Mushtaq Ahmed	4
L. Potter not out	20
†J. N. Batty lbw b Mushtaq Ahmed	3
M. J. Saggers c Rashid Latif b Saqlain Mushtaq	1
M. A. Sharp not out	37
L-b 3, w 6, n-b 14	23
1/24 2/35 3/39 4/64 5/68 6/72 7/76 8/77 (8 wkts, 50 overs)	140

S. V. Laudat did not bat.

Bowling: Wasim Akram 10–3–41–1; Waqar Younis 7–2–19–2; Saqlain Mushtaq 10–4–9–3; Ata-ur-Rehman 10–2–29–0; Mushtaq Ahmed 10–3–26–2; Aamir Sohail 3–0–13–0.

Umpires: D. L. Burden and C. Stone.

†MCC v PAKISTANIS

At Shenley Park, July 14. Pakistanis won on scoring-rate. Toss: Pakistanis.

MCC were dismissed with more than six overs to spare after rain reduced their target to 148 from 32 and livened up the pitch. Two players were struck on the hand and had to retire, and only the Zimbabwean, Flower, and Extras reached double figures. The Pakistanis also had a shaky start, with Silverwood of Yorkshire and Dodemaide of Victoria reducing them to 48 for four. But Wasim Akram rescued the innings, put on 112 with Moin Khan and set MCC a task which turned out to be well beyond their capacity.

Pakistanis

Aamir Sohail c Barton b Silverwood	9
Shadab Kabir c Blakey b Silverwood	0
Ijaz Ahmed, sen. c Barton b Dodemaide	11
Inzamam-ul-Haq c Munton b Dodemaide	12
Salim Malik c Venter b Giles	26
*Wasim Akram c Byas b Munton	74
†Moin Khan c Venter b Bishop	46
Mushtaq Ahmed not out	13
Saqlain Mushtaq not out	4
B 1, l-b 13, w 13, n-b 8	35
1/1 2/21 3/37 4/48 5/98 6/210 7/211 (7 wkts, 50 overs)	230

Waqar Younis and Mohammad Akram did not bat.

Bowling: Bishop 10–0–42–1; Silverwood 10–2–29–2; Dodemaide 10–0–51–2; Munton 10–1–40–1; Giles 10–0–54–1.

MCC

J. F. Venter b Waqar Younis	0
A. Flower retired hurt	15
*D. Byas b Wasim Akram	0
K. L. T. Arthurton retired hurt	0
H. D. Barton c Moin Khan b Mohammad Akram	4
†R. J. Blakey c Saqlain Mushtaq b Mohammad Akram	7
A. I. C. Dodemaide b Mushtaq Ahmed	8
I. R. Bishop c Inzamam-ul-Haq b Mushtaq Ahmed	6
A. F. Giles b Saqlain Mushtaq	0
C. E. W. Silverwood c Salim Malik b Saqlain Mushtaq	6
T. A. Munton not out	1
L-b 4, w 6, n-b 6	16
1/10 2/15 3/30 4/42 5/54 6/55 7/61 8/63 (25.4 overs)	63

K. L. T. Arthurton retired hurt at 19 and A. Flower at 36.

Bowling: Wasim Akram 7–2–15–1; Waqar Younis 7–1–16–1; Mohammad Akram 5–0–18–2; Saqlain Mushtaq 4–0–6–2; Mushtaq Ahmed 2.4–1–4–2.

Umpires: A. Clarkson and B. Dudleston.

WARWICKSHIRE v PAKISTANIS

At Birmingham, July 17, 18, 19. Warwickshire won by seven wickets. Toss: Pakistanis.

The Pakistanis' only first-class defeat of the tour was the result of poor batting; afterwards, captain Wasim Akram said: "We had a meeting and the batsmen apologised." Saeed Anwar could be excused; he scored a hundred before lunch on the first day, his third century in six innings. He finished with 131 at a run a ball, including 20 fours and three sixes. His dismissal began a collapse of eight wickets for 75. But Mushtaq Ahmed took seven wickets himself, limiting Warwickshire's lead to 13 and compensating for a hamstring injury to Waqar Younis. Only Brown and Penney enabled the county to reach 300, through a sixth-wicket partnership of 142. The tourists soon collapsed again, losing their last nine for 69; Anwar batted at No. 8

because of a stomach infection. Warwickshire needed only 146 and took the £7,500 prize money by 2 p.m., thanks to an unbeaten 90 from Knight in 94 balls. The way he punished Mushtaq ensured his recall to the England side after injury. But the home side were shaken to learn that their captain, Dermot Reeve, was to retire at once after an unsuccessful hip operation.

Close of play: First day, Warwickshire 99-2 (N. V. Knight 42*, A. F. Giles 14*); Second day, Pakistanis 147-8 (Saeed Anwar 20*, Waqar Younis 4*).

Pakistanis

*Aamir Sohail lbw b Welch	30	– c Brown b Altree	4
Saeed Anwar c Burns b Brown	131	– (8) c Burns b Altree	23
Ijaz Ahmed, sen. lbw b Brown	10	– (2) st Burns b Smith	52
Inzamam-ul-Haq c Burns b Altree	51	– lbw b Giles	4
Salim Malik lbw b Brown	0	– (6) c Burns b Smith	9
Asif Mujtaba c Ostler b Welch	38	– (3) c Ostler b Smith	34
†Moin Khan lbw b Altree	0	– (5) c Ostler b Giles	4
Mushtaq Ahmed c Knight b Welch	18	– (7) b Giles	6
Waqar Younis b Giles	0	– (10) run out	8
Ata-ur-Rehman b Giles	0	– (9) c Welch b Altree	1
Mohammad Akram not out	0	– not out	4
L-b 3, n-b 16	19	B 5, n-b 4	9
1/72 2/93 3/222 4/222 5/244 6/244 7/293 8/293 9/293	297	1/6 2/89 3/100 4/106 5/106 6/117 7/121 8/141 9/154	158

Bowling: *First Innings*—Altree 15–0–72–2; Munton 16–5–46–0; Brown 21–4–86–3; Welch 14.4–2–58–3; Smith 3–0–30–0; Giles 4–3–2–2. *Second Innings*—Altree 12–1–41–3; Munton 7–2–17–0; Giles 26–13–39–3; Smith 20–5–56–3.

Warwickshire

N. V. Knight lbw b Ata-ur-Rehman	45	– not out	90
A. Singh c Saeed Anwar b Mohammad Akram	4	– lbw b Mushtaq Ahmed	9
†M. Burns c Moin Khan b Mushtaq Ahmed	36	– st Moin Khan b Aamir Sohail	4
A. F. Giles lbw b Mushtaq Ahmed	28		
D. P. Ostler lbw b Ata-ur-Rehman	3	– (4) b Salim Malik	23
T. L. Penney b Mushtaq Ahmed	66	– (5) not out	7
D. R. Brown c Aamir Sohail b Mushtaq Ahmed	76		
N. M. K. Smith st Moin Khan b Mushtaq Ahmed	23		
G. Welch b Mushtaq Ahmed	9		
*T. A. Munton not out	5		
D. A. Altree b Mushtaq Ahmed	0		
B 6, l-b 5, n-b 4	15	B 8, l-b 1, n-b 6	15
1/4 2/69 3/117 4/121 5/125 6/267 7/282 8/297 9/310	310	1/48 2/61 3/126 (3 wkts)	148

Bowling: *First Innings*—Waqar Younis 3–1–8–0; Mohammad Akram 14–2–64–1; Ata-ur-Rehman 16–3–63–2; Mushtaq Ahmed 28–6–91–7; Aamir Sohail 15–3–73–0. *Second Innings*—Mohammad Akram 4–0–21–0; Ata-ur-Rehman 3–0–9–0; Mushtaq Ahmed 10–1–47–1; Aamir Sohail 7–2–29–1; Inzamam-ul-Haq 4–0–24–0; Salim Malik 3–1–9–1.

Umpires: J. W. Holder and P. Willey.

KENT v PAKISTANIS

At Canterbury, July 20, 21, 22. Pakistanis won by eight wickets. Toss: Kent.

The tourists won, thanks to the best innings of the match from Ijaz Ahmed. His undefeated 136 came off 163 balls, with four sixes and 19 fours. He shared a second-wicket stand of 186 with the promising Shadab Kabir, which all but saw their side through to victory on a glorious day at the St Lawrence Ground. Ealham made a useful all-round contribution, scoring fifty in Kent's first innings and taking four wickets when the Pakistanis replied. They lost half their side for 59 in 25 overs before Latif's valuable half-century helped reduce Kent's lead to 68. Saqlain Mushtaq then finished Kent off for 200, and the county could not rediscover their bowling form of the first day. Seven bowlers were used, with even Cowdrey called upon to pick up a rare but savoured first-class victim – and a good one at that in Shadab, who was to make his Test debut three days later.

Close of play: First day, Pakistanis 74-5 (Salim Malik 22*, Rashid Latif 3*); Second day, Kent 200.

Kent

D. P. Fulton c Ata-ur-Rehman b Saqlain Mushtaq	58	– b Wasim Akram	17
M. V. Fleming lbw b Wasim Akram	26	– lbw b Ata-ur-Rehman	15
T. R. Ward b Saqlain Mushtaq	58	– lbw b Wasim Akram	3
N. J. Llong b Wasim Akram	15	– c Rashid Latif b Shahid Nazir	29
G. R. Cowdrey c Aamir Sohail b Wasim Akram	1	– lbw b Shahid Nazir	22
M. A. Ealham c Rashid Latif b Shahid Nazir	57	– c Inzamam-ul-Haq b Saqlain Mushtaq	28
*S. A. Marsh b Wasim Akram	1	– b Wasim Akram	28
M. J. McCague b Saqlain Mushtaq	1	– b Saqlain Mushtaq	9
D. W. Headley lbw b Shahid Nazir	13	– c Inzamam-ul-Haq b Saqlain Mushtaq	14
†S. C. Willis b Shahid Nazir	0	– c Wasim Akram b Saqlain Mushtaq	12
M. M. Patel not out	4	– not out	5
B 8, l-b 6, n-b 14	28	B 4, l-b 3, w 6, n-b 5	18
1/49 2/116 3/167 4/168 5/183 6/187 7/194 8/257 9/257	262	1/27 2/34 3/39 4/82 5/109 6/127 7/155 8/179 9/183	200

Bowling: *First Innings*—Wasim Akram 23–5–74–4; Ata-ur-Rehman 13–1–74–0; Shahid Nazir 7.1–1–32–3; Saqlain Mushtaq 26–8–59–3; Aamir Sohail 2–0–9–0. *Second Innings*—Wasim Akram 17–6–56–3; Ata-ur-Rehman 7–0–32–1; Shahid Nazir 10–0–42–2; Saqlain Mushtaq 17.3–4–63–4.

Pakistanis

Aamir Sohail lbw b Headley	12	– c Cowdrey b Headley	30
Shadab Kabir c Willis b McCague	3	– c Ward b Cowdrey	84
Ijaz Ahmed, sen. c Willis b Ealham	19	– not out	136
Inzamam-ul-Haq c Headley b Ealham	9		
Salim Malik lbw b Patel	37		
Asif Mujtaba c Fleming b Ealham	6	– (4) not out	5
†Rashid Latif b Patel	61		
*Wasim Akram c Ward b Ealham	12		
Saqlain Mushtaq not out	14		
Ata-ur-Rehman c Ealham b Headley	4		
Shahid Nazir c and b Fleming	13		
B 1, l-b 1, n-b 2	4	B 8, l-b 4, n-b 2	14
1/5 2/29 3/42 4/45 5/59 6/115 7/148 8/162 9/173	194	1/54 2/240 (2 wkts)	269

Bowling: *First Innings*—McCague 16–2–42–1; Headley 17–3–43–2; Ealham 16–4–48–4; Patel 26–13–59–2; Fleming 0.2–0–0–1. *Second Innings*—McCague 10–1–40–0; Headley 15–2–48–1; Ealham 10–3–29–0; Patel 18–5–66–0; Fleming 5–1–12–0; Llong 7–0–43–0; Cowdrey 3.3–0–19–1.

Umpires: J. C. Balderstone and D. R. Shepherd.

ENGLAND v PAKISTAN

First Cornhill Test

At Lord's, July 25, 26, 27, 28, 29. Pakistan won by 164 runs. Toss: Pakistan. Test debuts: S. J. E. Brown; Shadab Kabir.

Having beaten India 1-0, England were losers all the way down the line on their second visit of the summer to Lord's. They lost coach David Lloyd and captain Atherton for part of the eve of Test practice session (both being required to give evidence in the Botham and Lamb v Imran libel trial), lost Hussain and Lewis to injuries before the match, lost the toss for choice of ball, lost the principal toss when both teams were anxious to bat first and, finally, lost nine for 75 in little more than two hours on the last afternoon.

Bad luck? England experienced more than their fair share in a match not memorable for outstanding umpiring, but no one could deny Pakistan were worthy winners. Inzamam-ul-Haq's fifth and highest Test century would have captured many a Man of the Match award. But it was overshadowed by some wonderful fast bowling from Waqar Younis, who returned eight for 154.

England's problems had begun in the Trent Bridge Test against India, where Hussain cracked his right index finger after making his second hundred of the series. The selectors retained him in a squad of 13, but both he and Lewis, who had strained his thigh, withdrew after unconvincing net sessions. Knight, who had also broken a finger, in the Edgbaston Test seven weeks earlier, returned and there was a first cap for Durham's left-arm swing bowler Simon Brown.

Having already captured 56 first-class wickets for struggling Durham, Brown deserved his chance. It took him only ten balls to claim his 57th, thanks to Aamir Sohail padding up. When Cork – a veteran in this attack, having made his debut here 13 months earlier – plucked out Ijaz Ahmed's middle stump as the batsman went walkabout, Pakistan were 12 for two, in danger of wasting near-perfect batting conditions. Inzamam's arrival put that right, however, and 130 more runs came before his partner, Saeed Anwar, edged an attempted cut against Hick. Had Inzamam, rather than Salim Malik, been run out when both batsmen finished at the same end, England might still have taken control. Instead, Inzamam more than doubled his 64, reaching 148 from 218 balls before being bowled via an inside edge. His innings included 19 fours and, most memorably, an on-driven six off Hick that took him to three figures. Even so, closing on 290 for nine, Pakistan were 50 runs short of par. They had lost wickets regularly after a ball change, the first of six replacements ordered by umpires Bucknor and Willey as the Reader balls Pakistan had chosen lost their shape. But the only significant swing on the second morning was in the tourists' direction: last pair Rashid Latif and Ata-ur-Rehman put together a match-tilting stand which gave Pakistan those extra 50 runs.

Detained in the field for an hour more than he wanted, Atherton spent barely 20 minutes at the crease, losing a dubious lbw decision to Wasim Akram. Umpire Willey, standing in his first home Test, later sparked more debate by awarding Knight two runs during the tea interval for an edge originally signalled as leg-byes, a ruling which lifted him from 49 to 51. With Waqar's wicked swing and Mushtaq Ahmed's teasing spin providing the toughest challenge of the summer so far, England needed all of Thorpe's skill and determination to limit their second-day losses to five wickets. Yet it was his failure on the third morning to turn another solid half-century into something more substantial (the 17th time out of 19 he had passed 50 in a Test without getting to 100) that gave Pakistan the encouragement they needed. Playing back to Rehman with a slightly crooked bat, Thorpe deflected a lifting delivery into his stumps. Despite Russell's continued resolution, England lost their last five wickets for 25.

Any hope they had of overcoming a deficit of 55 disappeared during a stand of 136 between Anwar and teenage debutant Shadab Kabir, deputising as opener because Sohail had damaged his wrist dropping Knight's "leg-byes". While Shadab toiled diligently, Anwar dashed into the eighties until he was caught behind off the economical Mullally – the first of three wickets in fading evening light. Ample batting remained, though, and Wasim made his fourth-afternoon declaration after putting some explosive finishing touches to the sound work of Ijaz and Inzamam.

Eight hours remained, but only 27 minutes had passed when Knight fell lbw to Waqar. Atherton was dropped soon after that, but he and Stewart guided England through to the close, then lifted their team's spirits by seeing out the fifth morning. However, Pakistan have often shown that one success can generate unstoppable momentum. This time it stemmed from Mushtaq's switch to round the wicket; Atherton edged a leg-break to slip while trying to play against the spin. The door was only ajar, but the visitors barged through so forcefully that seven wickets fell in 75 balls while 18 runs were added. Mushtaq had Stewart caught off a glove, bowled Ealham behind his legs and won a fortunate lbw decision against Thorpe. At the other end, Waqar extended Hick's summer nightmare by bowling him for the second time in the match, found the outside edge of Russell's bat after a couple of welcoming bouncers and beat Cork for pace. Spin and swing had combined superbly. It was left to Wasim to wrap up victory just before tea when Salisbury edged a pull. Atherton remarked that the pitch suited Pakistan's attack more than his own through "offering turn but not much help for the seamers", and suggested "the Dukes ball is better for us, the Reader for them," but made both comments only after stating, quite properly: "We were outplayed." – DAVID LLOYD (*Evening Standard*).

Man of the Match: Waqar Younis. *Attendance:* 91,485; *receipts* £2,183,917.

Close of play: First day, Pakistan 290-9 (Rashid Latif 7*); Second day, England 200-5 (G. P. Thorpe 43*, R. C. Russell 4*); Third day, Pakistan 162-3 (Ijaz Ahmed 20*, Inzamam-ul-Haq 0*); Fourth day, England 74-1 (M. A. Atherton 24*, A. J. Stewart 46*).

Pakistan

Aamir Sohail lbw b Brown	2		
Saeed Anwar c Russell b Hick	74	– (1) c Russell b Mullally	88
Ijaz Ahmed, sen. b Cork	1	– lbw b Cork	76
Inzamam-ul-Haq b Mullally	148	– (5) c Ealham b Cork	70
Salim Malik run out	7	– (6) not out	27
Shadab Kabir lbw b Cork	17	– (2) c Russell b Cork	33
*Wasim Akram lbw b Ealham	10	– not out	34
†Rashid Latif c Hick b Salisbury	45		
Mushtaq Ahmed c Russell b Mullally	11	– (4) c Thorpe b Brown	5
Waqar Younis c Brown b Mullally	4		
Ata-ur-Rehman not out	10		
B 3, l-b 5, n-b 3	11	B 4, l-b 14, n-b 1	19
1/7 (1) 2/12 (3) 3/142 (2) 4/153 (5) 5/209 (6) 6/257 (7) 7/267 (4) 8/280 (9) 9/290 (10) 10/340 (8)	340	1/136 (1) 2/136 (2) 3/161 (4) 4/279 (3) 5/308 (5) (5 wkts dec.)	352

Bowling: *First Innings*—Cork 28–6–100–2; Brown 17–2–78–1; Mullally 24–8–44–3; Salisbury 12.2–1–42–1; Ealham 21–4–42–1; Hick 6–0–26–1. *Second Innings*—Cork 24–4–86–3; Brown 16–2–60–1; Salisbury 20–4–63–0; Mullally 30.2–9–70–1; Hick 7–2–16–0; Ealham 16–4–39–0.

England

N. V. Knight lbw b Waqar Younis	51	– lbw b Waqar Younis	1
*M. A. Atherton lbw b Wasim Akram	12	– c sub (Asif Mujtaba) b Mushtaq Ahmed	64
A. J. Stewart lbw b Mushtaq Ahmed	39	– c sub (Moin Khan) b Mushtaq Ahmed	89
G. P. Thorpe b Ata-ur-Rehman	77	– lbw b Mushtaq Ahmed	3
G. A. Hick b Waqar Younis	4	– b Waqar Younis	4
M. A. Ealham c Rashid Latif b Ata-ur-Rehman	25	– b Mushtaq Ahmed	5
†R. C. Russell not out	41	– c Rashid Latif b Waqar Younis	1
D. G. Cork c Saeed Anwar b Ata-ur-Rehman	3	– b Waqar Younis	3
I. D. K. Salisbury lbw b Waqar Younis	5	– c Rashid Latif b Wasim Akram	40
A. D. Mullally b Waqar Younis	0	– c sub (Moin Khan) b Mushtaq Ahmed	6
S. J. E. Brown b Ata-ur-Rehman	1	– not out	10
B 9, l-b 13, w 1, n-b 4	27	B 6, l-b 7, n-b 4	17
1/27 (2) 2/107 (1) 3/107 (3) 4/116 (5) 5/180 (6) 6/260 (4) 7/264 (8) 8/269 (9) 9/269 (10) 10/285 (11)	285	1/14 (1) 2/168 (2) 3/171 (3) 4/176 (5) 5/181 (6) 6/182 (7) 7/186 (8) 8/186 (4) 9/208 (10) 10/243 (9)	243

Bowling: *First Innings*—Wasim Akram 22–4–49–1; Waqar Younis 24–6–69–4; Mushtaq Ahmed 38–5–92–1; Ata-ur-Rehman 15.4–3–50–4; Aamir Sohail 3–1–3–0. *Second Innings*—Wasim Akram 21.1–5–45–1; Waqar Younis 25–3–85–4; Mushtaq Ahmed 38–15–57–5; Ata-ur-Rehman 11–2–33–0; Salim Malik 1–0–1–0; Shadab Kabir 1–0–9–0.

Umpires: S. A. Bucknor (West Indies) and P. Willey.
Referee: P. L. van der Merwe (South Africa).

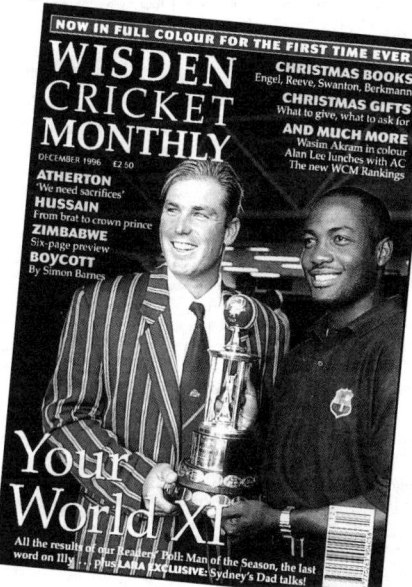

†SCOTLAND v PAKISTANIS

At Raeburn Place, Edinburgh, August 1. Pakistanis won by 108 runs. Toss: Scotland.

Shadab Kabir scored a 119-ball century after the tourists were invited to bat. Supported by Asif Mujtaba, with whom he put on 118, he was chiefly responsible for setting the Scots a target approaching six an over. Philip, their experienced opener, made 50, but the next-highest contribution was 29 from Extras. The innings disintegrated quickly when Saqlain Mushtaq took four wickets in four overs; Shahid Nazir also claimed four as he finished the hosts off with 27 balls to spare.

Pakistanis

Shahid Anwar b Williamson	23
Shadab Kabir c Patterson b Thomson	135
Saeed Anwar b Williamson	9
*Ijaz Ahmed, sen. c Stanger b Sheridan	25
Asif Mujtaba not out	63
†Moin Khan c Stanger b Williamson	3
Mushtaq Ahmed not out	4
L-b 5, w 7, n-b 12	24
1/57 2/81 3/144 4/262 5/281 (5 wkts, 50 overs)	286

Saqlain Mushtaq, Ata-ur-Rehman, Mohammad Akram and Shahid Nazir did not bat.

Bowling: Thomson 10–1–49–1; Stanger 7–0–48–0; Gourlay 10–1–52–0; Williamson 10–0–51–3; Reifer 3–0–21–0; Sheridan 10–0–60–1.

Scotland

I. L. Philip lbw b Shahid Nazir	50
B. G. Lockie c Asif Mujtaba b Ata-ur-Rehman	0
G. N. Reifer lbw b Shahid Nazir	19
B. M. W. Patterson c Moin Khan b Saqlain Mushtaq	27
*G. Salmond c Shahid Anwar b Saqlain Mushtaq	27
J. G. Williamson c Mushtaq Ahmed b Saqlain Mushtaq	6
I. M. Stanger st Moin Khan b Saqlain Mushtaq	1
†A. G. Davies lbw b Mushtaq Ahmed	10
S. Gourlay c Asif Mujtaba b Shahid Nazir	3
K. L. P. Sheridan b Shahid Nazir	6
K. Thomson not out	0
B 3, l-b 6, w 8, n-b 12	29
1/5 2/80 3/94 4/144 5/146 6/155 7/158 8/170 9/175 (45.3 overs)	178

Bowling: Ata-ur-Rehman 4–0–24–1; Mohammad Akram 7–2–38–0; Mushtaq Ahmed 9–2–21–1; Shahid Nazir 9.3–1–31–4; Saqlain Mushtaq 10–0–35–4; Asif Mujtaba 6–1–20–0.

Umpires: D. M. Potter and D. Walker.

DURHAM v PAKISTANIS

At Chester-le-Street, August 3, 4, 5. Pakistanis won by seven wickets. Toss: Durham.

Brown responded to hearing that he had been dropped after one Test with five first-innings wickets against the tourists. By removing four of the top six, he reduced them to 157 for six, still 150 behind. But Rashid Latif and Wasim Akram put on 129 and they eventually led by two. The Pakistanis scored at five an over, compensating for the fact that Durham's all-seam attack bowled only 12.3 an hour. But the home side's received wisdom that the Riverside Ground offers no turn was undermined by teenage off-spinner Saqlain Mushtaq, who claimed three in each innings. It was Wasim who finally settled the direction of this game, taking four for 19 in 18.4 overs to destroy Durham's second attempt; the tourists knocked off a target of 134 inside 26 overs, even though Asif Mujtaba batted throughout for just 19. But Roseberry earned the match award for his brave 93 not out and 48, mostly scored after Wasim broke his finger.

Close of play: First day, Pakistanis 29-0 (Saeed Anwar 16*, Shadab Kabir 5*); Second day, Durham 96-7 (M. A. Roseberry 30*, S. J. E. Brown 0*).

Durham

S. L. Campbell c Ata-ur-Rehman b Shahid Nazir	22	– b Ata-ur-Rehman	0
S. Hutton b Shahid Nazir	34	– b Wasim Akram	7
J. E. Morris c Asif Mujtaba b Shahid Nazir	12	– c Rashid Latif b Ata-ur-Rehman	0
J. A. Daley c Rashid Latif b Wasim Akram	27	– c Rashid Latif b Wasim Akram	5
*M. A. Roseberry not out	93	– (7) b Saqlain Mushtaq	48
R. M. S. Weston lbw b Wasim Akram	0	– (5) c Asif Mujtaba b Saqlain Mushtaq	15
†D. G. C. Ligertwood c Wasim Akram b Asif Mujtaba	16	– (6) lbw b Asif Mujtaba	27
J. Wood c Ijaz Ahmed b Saqlain Mushtaq	21	– lbw b Saqlain Mushtaq	0
S. J. E. Brown c and b Saqlain Mushtaq	1	– c sub (Moin Khan) b Wasim Akram	3
M. J. Saggers b Saqlain Mushtaq	7	– b Wasim Akram	13
N. Killeen b Wasim Akram	32	– not out	0
B 7, l-b 2, n-b 33	42	B 3, l-b 8, n-b 6	17
1/62 2/69 3/92 4/157 5/170 6/195 7/245 8/248 9/262	307	1/5 2/5 3/14 4/15 5/47 6/87 7/88 8/103 9/131	135

In the first innings M. A. Roseberry, when 41, retired hurt at 157-3 and resumed at 195.

Bowling: *First Innings*—Wasim Akram 23.2–6–86–3; Ata-ur-Rehman 16–0–67–0; Saqlain Mushtaq 34–6–89–3; Shahid Nazir 6.1–1–20–3; Ijaz Ahmed 2.5–0–14–0; Asif Mujtaba 7–1–22–1. *Second Innings*—Wasim Akram 18.4–10–19–4; Ata-ur-Rehman 18–3–59–2; Asif Mujtaba 3–0–8–1; Saqlain Mushtaq 16–7–37–3; Salim Malik 1–0–1–0.

Pakistanis

Saeed Anwar b Brown	20	– c Ligertwood b Brown	36
Shadab Kabir c Ligertwood b Brown	18		
Ijaz Ahmed, sen. c Morris b Saggers	17	– lbw b Brown	12
Inzamam-ul-Haq c Ligertwood b Saggers	44	– c Ligertwood b Killeen	34
Salim Malik c Ligertwood b Brown	30	– not out	17
Asif Mujtaba c Hutton b Brown	0	– (2) not out	19
†Rashid Latif c Daley b Wood	55		
*Wasim Akram b Wood	68		
Saqlain Mushtaq lbw b Brown	0		
Ata-ur-Rehman b Saggers	15		
Shahid Nazir not out	5		
B 1, l-b 5, w 3, n-b 28	37	N-b 16	16
1/45 2/48 3/92 4/125 5/144 6/157 7/286 8/287 9/287	309	1/48 2/60 3/101	(3 wkts) 134

Bowling: *First Innings*—Brown 20–1–88–5; Wood 20–4–105–2; Killeen 12–3–56–0; Saggers 10.1–2–54–3. *Second Innings*—Brown 7–1–19–2; Wood 8–1–49–0; Saggers 3–1–17–0; Killeen 6.3–0–43–1; Weston 1–0–6–0.

Umpires: G. I. Burgess and N. T. Plews.

ENGLAND v PAKISTAN

Second Cornhill Test

At Leeds, August 8, 9, 10, 11, 12. Drawn. Toss: England.

This game never took off as a contest but spectators were saved from total boredom by four splendid centuries – from Ijaz Ahmed and Moin Khan for Pakistan, Stewart and Knight for England. Once England decided to field four seam bowlers and no recognised spinner, it seemed highly unlikely that they would have enough variety to bowl out Pakistan twice, and so it proved. The load on the shoulders of Caddick, Mullally, Lewis and Cork was too heavy; it was something of a surprise that at least one of them did not break down.

The all-seam policy was an obvious mistake by England's selectors. But they could claim that their decision to include six batsmen – rather than trying to find a No. 6 who could bowl – was justified. Stewart relished his return to the opener's role, while Knight, displaced to No. 6, calmly responded with a maiden Test hundred. Although their hopes of getting more than a draw surfaced only briefly, on the final day, England came out of the game with the greater credit: their batsmen showed that Wasim Akram and Waqar Younis could be tamed. Each of the famous pair took three wickets – but each paid with over 100 runs.

Once again, a Headingley Test was marred by trouble on the now infamous Western Terrace. Around 200 people were ejected on Friday and Saturday for unruly behaviour, widely reported to have racist overtones. Yorkshire president Sir Lawrence Byford, formerly Chief Inspector of Constabulary, witnessed the trouble at first hand on Saturday and, shaken by what he saw, admitted that Headingley could lose Test cricket if the hooliganism was not stopped. A member of the TCCB executive committee, he found himself having to prepare a report for that body on the disturbances and what action Yorkshire intended to take.

England's squad had three changes from the one for Lord's, with Crawley, Caddick and Irani replacing Hick, Brown and Ealham. This time, Lewis and Hussain were fit; Irani and Salisbury were left out. On winning the toss, Atherton had to decide whether to bat, risking a damaging assault from Wasim and Waqar on a slightly green pitch, or hope that his own, lesser, bowlers could make an impact. He chose the second course, which looked promising when Mullally had Saeed Anwar caught cutting and Caddick bowled an excellent opening spell in his first Test since April 1994. Caddick caused problems for both Shadab Kabir and Ijaz. But Ijaz soon exposed the limitations of England's resources. After losing Shadab and Inzamam-ul-Haq, he settled into a 130-run stand with Salim Malik, who grafted hard for his first fifty of the tour. Ijaz had scored 141 out of 233 when he chased a slower ball from Cork which started wide and was going wider. He had batted for 279 minutes and 201 balls, striking 20 fours and two sixes, and made the first Test century at Headingley for Pakistan, but Moin Khan was soon working his way towards the second. He was a last-minute selection, because Rashid Latif was injured, but seized his chance by becoming the first Pakistan wicket-keeper to score a hundred against England. Moin was given several chances, however. He was still on his overnight eight when Mullally dropped him at long leg off Caddick; on 18, Stewart caught him off a Mullally no-ball and he was dropped again on 84, playing a return drive to Cork's left. By that time, he had added 112 with the unwavering Asif Mujtaba, a seventh-wicket record for Pakistan against England. But the next statistical landmark was for England, when Moin's opposite number, Russell, caught him to reach 150 Test dismissals. Cork, always expecting a wicket, was rewarded for his enthusiasm with five, but he did not outbowl Caddick, who deserved better than his three. The other two wickets went to Mullally; Lewis gave away 100 runs without ever looking as if he would do much.

England's innings was in its third over when a high-class delivery from Wasim nipped back and found Atherton's inside edge. But Stewart and Hussain rattled along nicely, and Saturday, after a rain-delayed start, belonged to Stewart. His wristy play, his early sighting of the ball and his urgency at the crease all combined to blunt Pakistan's pace attack and prevent Mushtaq Ahmed from gaining the initiative – though he did claim the only wicket to fall in the afternoon session, that of Thorpe. Meanwhile, Stewart went to his century. His sheer joy spilled over as he got to the milestone with a three off Wasim, but the press were more excited by what they fancied was merely lukewarm applause from Ray Illingworth, the chairman of selectors.

With Crawley gone for an enterprising 53, Knight began to establish himself in a stand of 108 in 21 overs until Stewart, growing tired, drove back to Mushtaq. He had made 170 from 315 balls with 24 fours, overtaking Ijaz's two-day-old record for the highest score in England–Pakistan Tests at Leeds. Rain made deeper inroads on the fourth day; England could not resume until 12.45 p.m. and then Pakistan were unable to begin their second innings. Between the showers, Knight reached 113, helping England to a creditable 501 and a lead of 53. This time, Illingworth greeted the century by climbing on a chair to make sure his enthusiasm was appreciated.

Pakistan looked fallible on the final morning. Shadab, dropped at slip off Mullally's fourth ball, was caught and bowled by Lewis, and when Cork had Anwar taken behind, the score was 34 for two. Another quick wicket could have had the tourists in difficulties but Inzamam's forceful 65 killed off England's hopes. – DAVID WARNER.

Man of the Match: A. J. Stewart. *Attendance:* 43,423; *receipts* £893,659.

Close of play: First day, Pakistan 281-6 (Asif Mujtaba 19*, Moin Khan 8*); Second day, England 104-1 (A. J. Stewart 52*, N. Hussain 37*); Third day, England 373-5 (N. V. Knight 51*, R. C. Russell 0*); Fourth day, Pakistan 0-0 (Saeed Anwar 0*, Shadab Kabir 0*).

Pakistan

Saeed Anwar c Atherton b Mullally	1	– c Russell b Cork	22
Shadab Kabir lbw b Caddick	35	– c and b Lewis	2
Ijaz Ahmed, sen. c Russell b Cork	141	– c Russell b Caddick	52
Inzamam-ul-Haq c Atherton b Mullally	2	– c Stewart b Caddick	65
Salim Malik b Cork	55	– c Cork b Caddick	6
Asif Mujtaba c Thorpe b Cork	51	– run out	26
*Wasim Akram c Russell b Caddick	7	– lbw b Atherton	7
†Moin Khan c Russell b Cork	105	– not out	30
Mushtaq Ahmed c Atherton b Caddick	20	– not out	6
Waqar Younis c and b Cork	7		
Ata-ur-Rehman not out	0		
B 4, l-b 10, n-b 10	24	B 4, l-b 12, n-b 10	26
1/1 (1) 2/98 (2) 3/103 (4) 4/233 (3) 5/252 (5) 6/266 (7) 7/378 (6) 8/434 (8) 9/444 (10) 10/448 (9)	448	1/16 (2) 2/34 (1) 3/132 (4) 4/142 (5) 5/188 (6) 6/201 (3) 7/221 (7)	(7 wkts dec.) 242

Bowling: *First Innings*—Caddick 40.2–6–113–3; Mullally 41–10–99–2; Lewis 32–4–100–0; Cork 37–6–113–5; Thorpe 3–1–9–0. *Second Innings*—Mullally 15–2–43–0; Lewis 16–3–52–1; Caddick 17–4–52–3; Cork 16–2–49–1; Thorpe 10–3–10–0; Atherton 7–1–20–1.

England

*M. A. Atherton c Moin Khan b Wasim Akram	12
A. J. Stewart c and b Mushtaq Ahmed	170
N. Hussain c and b Waqar Younis	48
G. P. Thorpe c Shadab Kabir b Mushtaq Ahmed	16
J. P. Crawley c Moin Khan b Ata-ur-Rehman	53
N. V. Knight c Mushtaq Ahmed b Waqar Younis	113
†R. C. Russell b Wasim Akram	9
C. C. Lewis b Mushtaq Ahmed	9
D. G. Cork c Shadab Kabir b Wasim Akram	26
A. R. Caddick b Waqar Younis	4
A. D. Mullally not out	9
B 7, l-b 23, n-b 2	32
1/14 (1) 2/121 (3) 3/168 (4) 4/257 (5) 5/365 (2) 6/402 (7) 7/441 (8) 8/465 (6) 9/471 (10) 10/501 (9)	501

Bowling: Wasim Akram 39.5–10–106–3; Waqar Younis 33–7–127–3; Ata-ur-Rehman 22–1–90–1; Mushtaq Ahmed 55–17–142–3; Asif Mujtaba 7–5–6–0.

Umpires: S. A. Bucknor (West Indies) and D. R. Shepherd.
Referee: P. L. van der Merwe (South Africa).

LEICESTERSHIRE v PAKISTANIS

At Leicester, August 14, 15, 16. Pakistanis won by 101 runs. Toss: Pakistanis.

With the Championship in their sights, Leicestershire did not relish this fixture. Resting three top players – Whitaker, Simmons and Mullally – they were bowled out cheaply twice on a dry pitch that turned from the first day, beaten by a combination of pace and spin. The lively Mohammad Akram destroyed their first innings, with seven for 51, and match figures of nine for 99 earned him a place in the Third Test. Off-spinner Saqlain Mushtaq did the damage on the final day, taking six for 52. Leicestershire had the Pakistanis in trouble at 142 for eight on the opening day, thanks to the spinners, Pierson and Brimson. But a ninth-wicket stand of 79 in 22 overs between Mushtaq Ahmed and Ata-ur-Rehman helped them to a respectable first-innings 221. They batted much better second time round, led by Shahid Anwar, with 89, and ultimately won at a canter.

Close of play: First day, Leicestershire 28-1 (D. L. Maddy 8*); Second day, Pakistanis 221-3 (Shahid Anwar 86*, Salim Malik 20*).

Pakistanis

Shadab Kabir b Brimson	25	(2) lbw b Parsons	1
Shahid Anwar c Nixon b Millns	1	(3) lbw b Parsons	89
Saeed Anwar st Nixon b Brimson	22	(4) lbw b Parsons	69
*Aamir Sohail b Brimson	30	(1) b Clarke	34
Salim Malik c Parsons b Pierson	32	run out	22
Asif Mujtaba c Smith b Pierson	14	not out	12
†Moin Khan c and b Pierson	2	c Clarke b Pierson	11
Saqlain Mushtaq c Nixon b Parsons	4	not out	11
Mushtaq Ahmed c Nixon b Parsons	38		
Ata-ur-Rehman c Smith b Brimson	30		
Mohammad Akram not out	0		
B 5, l-b 13, w 1, n-b 4	23	B 10, l-b 1, w 2	13
1/5 2/53 3/62 4/99 5/129 6/131 7/142 8/142 9/221	221	1/8 2/71 3/189 4/223 5/226 6/245	(6 wkts dec.) 262

Bowling: *First Innings*—Millns 18–3–50–1; Parsons 23–9–42–2; Wells 5–2–18–0; Pierson 20–8–44–3; Brimson 21–9–39–4; Clarke 4–1–10–0. *Second Innings*—Millns 5–0–15–0; Parsons 21–8–62–3; Brimson 19–0–74–0; Clarke 7–0–42–1; Pierson 16–2–58–1.

Leicestershire

D. L. Maddy lbw b Mohammad Akram	31	c Moin Khan b Mushtaq Ahmed	16
I. J. Sutcliffe b Mohammad Akram	15	c Mushtaq Ahmed b Mohammad Akram	1
B. F. Smith c and b Mohammad Akram	7	lbw b Saqlain Mushtaq	43
A. Habib c Shadab Kabir b Mushtaq Ahmed	23	(5) c Mohammad Akram b Saqlain Mushtaq	27
†P. A. Nixon c sub (Ijaz Ahmed, sen.) b Saqlain Mushtaq	6	(6) c Aamir Sohail b Saqlain Mushtaq	21
V. P. Clarke b Mohammad Akram	43	(7) c Asif Mujtaba b Saqlain Mushtaq	0
*V. J. Wells c Saqlain Mushtaq b Mushtaq Ahmed	17	(8) c Ata-ur-Rehman b Saqlain Mushtaq	0
D. J. Millns lbw b Mohammad Akram	9	(9) lbw b Aamir Sohail	26
G. J. Parsons b Mohammad Akram	0	(4) lbw b Mohammad Akram	10
A. R. K. Pierson b Mohammad Akram	4	c Asif Mujtaba b Saqlain Mushtaq	11
M. T. Brimson not out	4	not out	10
B 21, l-b 5, w 4, n-b 10	40	B 7, l-b 9, n-b 2	18
1/28 2/49 3/68 4/93 5/105 6/139 7/173 8/173 9/182	199	1/6 2/48 3/62 4/80 5/113 6/113 7/125 8/128 9/150	183

Bowling: *First Innings*—Ata-ur-Rehman 10–2–30–0; Mohammad Akram 19.2–4–51–7; Mushtaq Ahmed 13–4–44–2; Saqlain Mushtaq 12–2–48–1. *Second Innings*—Ata-ur-Rehman 4–1–12–0; Mohammad Akram 13–2–48–2; Mushtaq Ahmed 16–5–47–1; Asif Mujtaba 2–1–4–0; Saqlain Mushtaq 25–7–52–6; Aamir Sohail 6.4–2–4–1.

Umpires: M. J. Kitchen and G. Sharp.

ESSEX v PAKISTANIS

At Chelmsford, August 17, 18, 19. Pakistanis won by 271 runs. Toss: Pakistanis.

A below-strength Essex side were no match for Waqar Younis and off-spinner Saqlain Mushtaq, each of whom finished with nine-wicket hauls. With all day to chase 390, Essex lost their last eight wickets for 32 in the space of 14 overs – with Prichard unable to bat because of a migraine. Robinson, with two solid half-centuries, and Hyam, with a determined career-best 49 in the first innings, were the only county batsmen to offer much resistance. Four Pakistanis completed centuries. Inzamam-ul-Haq retired with a sore knee but returned with a runner to punish the Essex attack with 106 off 110 balls, while Asif Mujtaba added an unbeaten hundred containing many flowing strokes. Next day, their second innings was dominated by Saeed Anwar, whose 102 came from only 96 deliveries, and Salim Malik, who took his first century of the tour off his former county.

Close of play: First day, Essex 29-3 (D. D. J. Robinson 14*, B. J. Hyam 1*); Second day, Pakistanis 277-2 (Salim Malik 104*, Asif Mujtaba 27*).

Pakistanis

*Aamir Sohail b Ilott	0	(2) b Childs	40
Saeed Anwar c Robinson b Andrew	22	(1) c Robinson b Irani	102
Ijaz Ahmed, sen. lbw b Ilott	6		
Inzamam-ul-Haq c Childs b Irani	106		
Salim Malik c Hyam b Irani	4	(3) not out	104
Asif Mujtaba not out	100	(4) not out	27
†Rashid Latif lbw b Irani	30		
Saqlain Mushtaq lbw b Such	21		
Waqar Younis c Ilott b Such	0		
Ata-ur-Rehman lbw b Irani	1		
Mohammad Akram not out	1		
B 8, l-b 4	12	B 2, l-b 1, w 1	4
1/0 2/8 3/50 4/63 5/127 6/172 7/172 8/292 9/298 (9 wkts dec.)	303	1/82 2/177 (2 wkts dec.)	277

In the first innings Inzamam-ul-Haq, when 22, retired hurt at 48 and resumed at 172-7.

Bowling: *First Innings*—Ilott 12–5–45–2; Andrew 18–3–62–1; Such 26–13–35–2; Irani 14.5–0–67–4; Childs 14–2–82–0. *Second Innings*—Ilott 10–1–39–0; Andrew 10–0–79–0; Such 8–0–26–0; Childs 9–0–63–1; Irani 6–2–27–1; Robinson 5–0–24–0; Lewis 4–0–16–0.

Essex

D. D. J. Robinson c Ata-ur-Rehman b Mohammad Akram	57	c and b Saqlain Mushtaq	55
A. J. E. Hibbert c Rashid Latif b Waqar Younis	5	c Rashid Latif b Waqar Younis	4
J. J. B. Lewis b Waqar Younis	2	c sub b Saqlain Mushtaq	21
S. D. Peters b Waqar Younis	5	c Aamir Sohail b Saqlain Mushtaq	0
†B. J. Hyam c Shadab Kabir b Saqlain Mushtaq	49	(6) lbw b Waqar Younis	8
R. C. Irani c Ata-ur-Rehman b Saqlain Mushtaq	32	(5) st Rashid Latif b Saqlain Mushtaq	17
*P. J. Prichard b Saqlain Mushtaq	16	absent ill	
M. C. Ilott c Saeed Anwar b Waqar Younis	0	(7) b Waqar Younis	0
P. M. Such not out	5	(8) b Waqar Younis	3
S. J. W. Andrew c Rashid Latif b Waqar Younis	3	(9) st Rashid Latif b Saqlain Mushtaq	2
J. H. Childs b Saqlain Mushtaq	0	(10) not out	0
B 1, l-b 11, w 1, n-b 4	17	L-b 6, n-b 2	8
1/10 2/12 3/24 4/117 5/150 6/173 7/182 8/182 9/186	191	1/31 2/86 3/86 4/89 5/110 6/112 7/116 8/116 9/118	118

Bowling: *First Innings*—Waqar Younis 16–5–42–5; Mohammad Akram 12–2–51–1; Ata-ur-Rehman 8–3–18–0; Saqlain Mushtaq 14–3–47–4; Aamir Sohail 4–0–8–0; Salim Malik 2–0–13–0. *Second Innings*—Waqar Younis 11–5–26–4; Mohammad Akram 4–1–14–0; Ata-ur-Rehman 4–0–21–0; Saqlain Mushtaq 13.2–5–34–5; Aamir Sohail 5–2–17–0.

Umpires: P. Adams and J. H. Hampshire.

ENGLAND v PAKISTAN

Third Cornhill Test

At The Oval, August 22, 23, 24, 25, 26. Pakistan won by nine wickets. Toss: England. Test debut: R. D. B. Croft.

In a predictable repeat of the Lord's Test, England's batting sank to the leg-spin of Mushtaq Ahmed on the final afternoon after they appeared to be in sight of land at lunch-time. This collapse left Pakistan comfortable winners of their fifth successive series over England. While Mushtaq collected his fifth five-wicket haul in his last six Tests and Pakistan captain Wasim Akram celebrated his 300th Test wicket, retiring chairman of selectors Ray Illingworth suffered his first home series defeat after three years in charge.

For Illingworth, coach David Lloyd and captain Mike Atherton it was a dismal end to a Test summer that had started promisingly at Edgbaston. The long-term worries and discussions centred on England's continuing fast-bowling shortcomings. Yet, badly as they bowled on Friday afternoon, that would not have led to defeat if their batsmen had not played poorly twice on a good pitch. England complained before, during and after the Test that it suited the tourists, but it was difficult to imagine a surface that would have delivered them victory over a side superior in all aspects. Where they must stop handing away the advantage is over the choice of match ball. Once again, Wasim called correctly and chose the Reader ball. For that reason alone, England would have preferred the Dukes. Everywhere else in the world, the home side nominates the type of ball to be used.

Once again, Russell was the first casualty of England's bid to level the series. Atherton's statement after Headingley that they would not sacrifice the wicket-keeper showed that a week in sport is about as long as seven days in politics. He was not even in the squad. With Stewart behind the stumps for the first time in Test cricket since July 1995, England were able to field five bowlers. Irani was dropped from the party, replaced by Glamorgan of-spinner Robert Croft. Either Croft or Lewis had been expected to miss out but, after it was decided to field both spinners – Croft and Salisbury – Atherton played a hunch about Lewis, leaving Caddick as surprised as anyone that his Headingley form did not merit a longer return to the England scene. Aamir Sohail returned for Pakistan, Mohammad Akram came in for Ata-ur-Rehman and Moin Khan retained the gloves although Rashid Latif was fit again.

Crawley's majestic first-day innings failed to disguise the fact that his team-mates had missed their opportunity after Atherton won the toss. Thorpe received a harsh lbw decision and Knight was unlucky to see the ball hit his pad, arm and wicket, but the others also got starts, and got out. Rain kept Crawley waiting until the next afternoon for the six runs he needed for his maiden Test hundred. After that, it was a bad Friday for England. Their total looked woefully inadequate as Saeed Anwar launched into some wayward bowling; the one exception was the new boy, Croft, who showed good skill, temperament, class and a clear pointer to England's spinning future. Pakistan finished the day less than a hundred adrift with only Sohail back in the pavilion. Anwar was already 116, which he took to a Test-best 176 on Saturday, when only 38.3 overs were permitted by rain. England's frustration was evident as Cork pushed Anwar out of the way while fielding the ball. The referee, Peter van der Merwe, spoke to both players, Cork apologised and the matter was closed.

The ingredients of Sunday's principal drama were a puncture on a Mercedes convertible and the late arrival of the most naturally talented and irritating England cricketer of recent times. Lewis's only appearance at The Oval at the correct time was on Illingworth's list for the one-day squad, announced an hour before the start. The man himself appeared 25 minutes later. After a meeting with Atherton, who then discussed the matter with Illingworth and Lloyd, Lewis was replaced in the one-day squad by Kent's Dean Headley. The big crime for the England management was his failure to ring in, even though all the players had been given mobile phones by a sponsor, for just such an eventuality. Lewis's brilliant run-out of Mujtaba later in the day served only to emphasise general bewilderment at his unfulfilled talent and irresponsibility.

On the field, Salim Malik capitalised on Anwar's work with a steady century, his 14th in Tests. Wasim declared 195 ahead; Atherton and Stewart had to survive the 23 overs remaining on the fourth day. They were still together at the close, which came at 7.18 p.m., because of rain, after a hostile barrage from the Pakistan fast bowlers. Mushtaq had come on to deliver the tenth over, from the Vauxhall End, and he bowled unchanged until 4.20 p.m. on the final afternoon when the innings ended. England had reached 158 for two at lunch – reminiscent of Lord's, where they were 152 for one. This time, they seemed to be in a stronger position, just 37 runs away from making the tourists bat again. But Mushtaq was already bowling round the wicket and Atherton had already gone. England's last eight wickets went down for 76 in 27 overs. Hussain received no benefit of the doubt from Sri Lankan umpire B. C. Cooray, and Crawley's concentration was disturbed by two streakers, but, generally, it was a sorry display. When Mushtaq bowled Cork to leave England 238 for eight, Wasim had to take the final two wickets to become the 11th member of the 300-club in his 70th Test. This he did in style, dismissing Croft and Mullally with successive balls; he fell to his knees as his team-mates ran to congratulate him. Pakistan completed the formality of scoring 48 to win in less than seven overs.

Groundsman Paul Brind was one of the few Englishmen to come out with any credit. Richie Benaud described his pitch as the perfect Test wicket because, as Pakistan proved, there was something for bowlers with ability who were prepared to bend their backs. England could cope with neither the pitch nor the Pakistanis, which offered Atherton and Lloyd little comfort for the future. – DAVID NORRIE.

Man of the Match: Mushtaq Ahmed. *Attendance:* 66,704; *receipts* £1,546,751.

Men of the Series: England – A. J. Stewart; Pakistan – Mushtaq Ahmed.

Close of play: First day, England 278-6 (J. P. Crawley 94*, I. D. K. Salisbury 1*); Second day, Pakistan 229-1 (Saeed Anwar 116*, Ijaz Ahmed 58*); Third day, Pakistan 339-4 (Salim Malik 2*, Asif Mujtaba 1*); Fourth day, England 74-0 (M. A. Atherton 26*, A. J. Stewart 40*).

England

*M. A. Atherton b Waqar Younis	31	– c Inzamam-ul-Haq b Mushtaq Ahmed	43
†A. J. Stewart b Mushtaq Ahmed	44	– c Asif Mujtaba b Mushtaq Ahmed	54
N. Hussain c Saeed Anwar b Waqar Younis	12	– lbw b Mushtaq Ahmed	51
G. P. Thorpe lbw b Mohammad Akram	54	– c Wasim Akram b Mushtaq Ahmed	9
J. P. Crawley b Waqar Younis	106	– c Aamir Sohail b Wasim Akram	19
N. V. Knight b Mushtaq Ahmed	17	– c and b Mushtaq Ahmed	8
C. C. Lewis b Wasim Akram	5	– lbw b Waqar Younis	4
I. D. K. Salisbury c Inzamam-ul-Haq b Wasim Akram	5	– (10) not out	0
D. G. Cork c Moin Khan b Waqar Younis	0	– (8) b Mushtaq Ahmed	26
R. D. B. Croft not out	5	– (9) c Ijaz Ahmed b Wasim Akram	6
A. D. Mullally b Wasim Akram	24	– b Wasim Akram	0
L-b 12, w 1, n-b 10	23	B 6, l-b 2, w 1, n-b 13	22
1/64 (2) 2/85 (3) 3/116 (1) 4/205 (4) 5/248 (6) 6/273 (7) 7/283 (8) 8/284 (9) 9/295 (5) 10/326 (11)	326	1/96 (2) 2/136 (1) 3/166 (4) 4/179 (3) 5/187 (6) 6/205 (7) 7/220 (5) 8/238 (8) 9/242 (9) 10/242 (11)	242

Bowling: *First Innings*—Wasim Akram 29.2–9–83–3; Waqar Younis 25–6–95–4; Mohammad Akram 12–1–41–1; Mushtaq Ahmed 27–5–78–2; Aamir Sohail 6–1–17–0. *Second Innings*—Wasim Akram 15.4–1–67–3; Waqar Younis 18–3–55–1; Mushtaq Ahmed 37–10–78–6; Aamir Sohail 2–1–4–0; Mohammad Akram 10–3–30–0.

Pakistan

Saeed Anwar c Croft b Cork	176	– c Knight b Mullally	1
Aamir Sohail c Cork b Croft	46	– not out	29
Ijaz Ahmed, sen. c Stewart b Mullally	61	– not out	13
Inzamam-ul-Haq c Hussain b Mullally	35		
Salim Malik not out	100		
Asif Mujtaba run out	13		
*Wasim Akram st Stewart b Croft	40		
†Moin Khan b Salisbury	23		
Mushtaq Ahmed c Crawley b Mullally	2		
Waqar Younis not out	0		
B 4, l-b 5, n-b 16	25	N-b 5	5
1/106 (2) 2/239 (3) 3/334 (4) 4/334 (1) 5/365 (6) 6/440 (7) 7/502 (8) 8/519 (9)	(8 wkts dec.) 521	1/7 (1)	(1 wkt) 48

Mohammad Akram did not bat.

Bowling: *First Innings*—Lewis 23–3–112–0; Mullally 37.1–7–97–3; Croft 47–10–116–2; Cork 23–5–71–1; Salisbury 29–3–116–1. *Second Innings*—Cork 3–0–15–0; Mullally 3–0–24–1; Croft 0.4–0–9–0.

Umpires: B. C. Cooray (Sri Lanka) and M. J. Kitchen.
Referee: P. L. van der Merwe (South Africa).

†ENGLAND v PAKISTAN

First One-Day International

At Manchester, August 29. England won by five wickets. Toss: Pakistan. International debuts: D. W. Headley, G. D. Lloyd.

England's batsmen fought back bravely after their humiliation at The Oval three days earlier to attain a modest target of 226. Revenge was particularly sweet against Mushtaq Ahmed, who took none for 52 in ten inaccurate overs. Pakistan had been restricted partly by consistent line and length, despite an inexperienced England attack – only Gough had bowled in a limited-overs international before – but mainly by their own apprehension at batting on a cracked, uneven pitch. The first-wicket stand brought up 82 in 24 overs, and Aamir Sohail's 48 dragged on for 117 balls. By contrast, England's choice of Knight and Stewart to open together for the first time was rewarded by a stand of 57 at almost six an over. Atherton dropped to No. 3 and his unruffled 65 put the playing surface into perspective, despite groundsman Peter Marron's comment that he would have been unhappy staging even a Sunday League match on it. Graham Lloyd's debut meant that, like Alec Stewart, he began playing for England while his father was in charge of the team. Dean Headley followed both his father, Ron, and grandfather, George, into international cricket, but for England, not West Indies.

Man of the Match: M. A. Atherton. *Attendance:* 20,686; *receipts* £531,780.

Pakistan

Saeed Anwar c Mullally b Irani	57
Aamir Sohail b Croft	48
Ijaz Ahmed, sen. c Irani b Mullally	48
*Wasim Akram b Croft	6
Inzamam-ul-Haq not out	37
†Moin Khan b Gough	10
Salim Malik not out	6
B 2, l-b 4, w 7	13
1/82 (1) 2/141 (2) 3/160 (4) 4/174 (3) 5/203 (6)	(5 wkts, 50 overs) 225
	Score at 15 overs: 38-0

Mushtaq Ahmed, Waqar Younis, Ata-ur-Rehman and Saqlain Mushtaq did not bat.

Bowling: Gough 10–0–44–1; Mullally 10–3–31–1; Headley 10–0–52–0; Irani 10–0–56–1; Croft 10–1–36–2.

England

N. V. Knight c Moin Khan b Wasim Akram	26
†A. J. Stewart lbw b Waqar Younis	48
*M. A. Atherton b Wasim Akram	65
G. P. Thorpe st Moin Khan b Aamir Sohail	23
M. P. Maynard b Wasim Akram	41
G. D. Lloyd not out	2
R. C. Irani not out	6
L-b 4, w 7, n-b 4	15
1/57 (1) 2/98 (2) 3/146 (4) 4/200 (3) 5/220 (5)	(5 wkts, 46.4 overs) 226
	Score at 15 overs: 77-1

R. D. B. Croft, D. Gough, D. W. Headley and A. D. Mullally did not bat.

Bowling: Wasim Akram 9.4–1–45–3; Waqar Younis 7–0–28–1; Saqlain Mushtaq 10–1–54–0; Ata-ur-Rehman 3–0–14–0; Mushtaq Ahmed 10–0–52–0; Aamir Sohail 7–1–29–1.

Umpires: N. T. Plews and G. Sharp. Referee: P. L. van der Merwe (South Africa).

†ENGLAND v PAKISTAN

Second One-Day International

At Birmingham, August 31. England won by 107 runs. Toss: Pakistan. International debut: A. J. Hollioake.

England tied up the series with a crushing victory, and continued to reverse the trend of the Tests by demolishing Pakistan's fast bowlers. Knight and Stewart showed that the Sri Lankan method of kick-starting an innings could work in English conditions after all, racing from 30 to 103 in six overs. Mushtaq Ahmed rediscovered his rhythm well enough to remove both Stewart and Atherton in his first over, but Knight changed tack, steering the ball into gaps to bring up a memorable century, 113 in 132 balls on his county ground. Pakistan's hopes were virtually eliminated by the second over of their innings, when Moin Khan, promoted ill-advisedly above his station, followed Aamir Sohail back to the pavilion with the score just six. Ijaz Ahmed made England wait with a run-a-ball 79, but he was plucked out by Croft, and Hollioake picked up four wickets on his international debut through subtle changes of pace.

Man of the Match: N. V. Knight. *Attendance:* 19,074; *receipts* £487,524.

England

N. V. Knight st Moin Khan b Saqlain Mushtaq	113	R. D. B. Croft b Waqar Younis	15
†A. J. Stewart b Mushtaq Ahmed	46	D. W. Headley not out	3
*M. A. Atherton lbw b Mushtaq Ahmed	1	L-b 25, w 4, n-b 3	32
G. P. Thorpe lbw b Ata-ur-Rehman	21		—
M. P. Maynard run out	1	1/103 (2) 2/105 (3) (8 wkts, 50 overs)	292
R. C. Irani not out	45	3/163 (4) 4/168 (5)	
A. J. Hollioake run out	15	5/221 (1) 6/257 (7)	
D. Gough run out	0	7/257 (8) 8/286 (9) Score at 15 overs: 111-2	

A. D. Mullally did not bat.

Bowling: Wasim Akram 10–0–50–0; Waqar Younis 9–0–54–1; Ata-ur-Rehman 6–0–40–1; Saqlain Mushtaq 10–0–59–1; Mushtaq Ahmed 10–0–33–2; Aamir Sohail 5–0–31–0.

Pakistan

Saeed Anwar c Stewart b Gough	33	Waqar Younis lbw b Gough	4
Aamir Sohail c Croft b Gough	0	Ata-ur-Rehman c Knight b Hollioake	2
†Moin Khan lbw b Mullally	0	L-b 2, n-b 1	3
Ijaz Ahmed, sen. b Croft	79		—
Inzamam-ul-Haq c Maynard b Croft	6	1/1 (2) 2/6 (3) 3/54 (1) (37.5 overs)	185
Salim Malik c Stewart b Hollioake	23	4/104 (5) 5/137 (4)	
*Wasim Akram c Knight b Hollioake	21	6/164 (7) 7/164 (6)	
Mushtaq Ahmed not out	14	8/168 (9) 9/177 (10)	
Saqlain Mushtaq b Hollioake	0	10/185 (11) Score at 15 overs: 89-3	

Bowling: Gough 8–0–39–3; Mullally 6–0–30–1; Headley 7–0–32–0; Irani 2–0–22–0; Croft 8–0–37–2; Hollioake 6.5–1–23–4.

Umpires: M. J. Kitchen and P. Willey. Referee: P. L. van der Merwe (South Africa).

†ENGLAND v PAKISTAN

Third One-Day International

At Nottingham, September 1. Pakistan won by two wickets. Toss: England. International debuts: Shahid Anwar, Shahid Nazir.

Knight's second hundred in two days (a feat previously achieved in limited-overs internationals only by Dean Jones and Saeed Anwar) was made in a losing cause against a drastically rebuilt Pakistan side. He carried his bat, but no one was able to stay with him long. Atherton was the next-highest scorer, with 30, although his innings was interrupted by an unpleasant blow on the right thumb from Shahid Nazir's second ball. In reply, Pakistan's opening pair of unrelated Anwars and the prolific Ijaz Ahmed reached 177 for two before the middle order subsided, losing four wickets for 22, three to Hollioake. The result hinged on a run-out decision in the 48th over, when Rashid Latif seemed to have been beaten by Atherton's under-arm throw. The third umpire, Ray Julian, gave him not out, apparently on the suspicion that the bails had been dislodged by Stewart's pads fractionally before the ball hit the stumps. Latif went on to cut the winning runs off Hollioake with two balls remaining.

Men of the Match: Pakistan team. *Attendance:* 12,955; *receipts* £337,936.

Men of the Series: N. V. Knight and Ijaz Ahmed.

England

N. V. Knight not out	125
†A. J. Stewart c and b Wasim Akram	3
*M. A. Atherton c Shahid Nazir b Wasim Akram	30
M. P. Maynard b Shahid Nazir	24
G. D. Lloyd c Shadab Kabir b Saqlain Mushtaq	15
R. C. Irani b Shahid Nazir	0
A. J. Hollioake c Ijaz Ahmed b Saqlain Mushtaq	13
D. Gough b Wasim Akram	5
R. D. B. Croft b Waqar Younis	0
P. J. Martin run out	6
A. D. Mullally b Waqar Younis	2
B 2, l-b 8, w 9, n-b 4	23
1/10 (2) 2/108 (4) 3/137 (5) 4/139 (6) 5/178 (7) 6/216 (3) 7/226 (8) 8/231 (9) 9/240 (10) 10/246 (11)	(50 overs) 246

Score at 15 overs: 66-1

M. A. Atherton, when 14, retired hurt at 55 and resumed at 178.

Bowling: Wasim Akram 10–1–45–3; Waqar Younis 10–1–49–2; Shahid Nazir 10–0–47–2; Asif Mujtaba 5–0–27–0; Saqlain Mushtaq 10–0–35–2; Aamir Sohail 5–0–33–0.

Pakistan

Saeed Anwar b Martin	61
Shahid Anwar lbw b Martin	37
Ijaz Ahmed, sen. c Lloyd b Gough	59
Aamir Sohail b Croft	29
Shadab Kabir c Irani b Hollioake	0
Asif Mujtaba b Hollioake	2
*Wasim Akram lbw b Hollioake	5
†Rashid Latif not out	31
Saqlain Mushtaq c Maynard b Hollioake	12
Waqar Younis not out	0
L-b 5, w 6	11
1/93 (2) 2/114 (1) 3/177 (4) 4/182 (5) 5/187 (6) 6/199 (7) 7/219 (3) 8/240 (9)	(8 wkts, 49.4 overs) 247

Score at 15 overs: 92-0

Shahid Nazir did not bat.

Bowling: Gough 10–1–43–1; Mullally 9–0–66–0; Martin 10–0–38–2; Croft 10–0–38–1; Irani 2–0–12–0; Hollioake 8.4–0–45–4.

Umpires: J. W. Holder and D. R. Shepherd.
Referee: P. L. van der Merwe (South Africa).

SOUTH AFRICA A IN ENGLAND, 1996

By BARNEY SPENDER

Overshadowed by the presence in England of India and Pakistan, not to mention the alternative attractions of European Championship soccer, Wimbledon and the Olympics, the South Africa A tour was about as low-key as they come.

Those who did take an interest were poorly rewarded by an almost blanket decision by the counties to send out weakened teams. In many cases this may have been justifiable, although Surrey's decision to field just one player who had appeared in the NatWest Trophy quarter-final immediately beforehand bordered on the insulting. Still more frustrating was the fact that there was no A team Test series. If the TCCB felt it was asking too much to put out a representative side, then they might have shown some imagination by pitting the South Africans against the Indian or Pakistani tourists. The climax of the tour was a four-day game against the TCCB XI, but even that side was chosen strictly from players whose counties were not involved in the concurrent round of Championship games.

Nevertheless, the South Africans kept up their enthusiasm throughout, even if the lack of testing cricket ultimately let them down when they lost their unbeaten record with a day to spare in that final match against the TCCB XI at Chester-le-Street. Their record of three wins, over Glamorgan, Surrey and Worcestershire, and one defeat from nine first-class matches was not to be sniffed at, especially as injuries and the weather denied them probable wins over Somerset and Nottinghamshire. They also had a full complement of one-day wins, over Wales, Gloucestershire and Essex.

The South Africans arrived in the country with four Test players in their ranks. The captain John Commins, the only tourist over 30, had last played against Pakistan in 1994-95, while Brett Schultz, Jacques Kallis and Paul Adams had all figured in the recent series against England. Kallis and Adams had also gone to the World Cup, as had wicket-keeper Steve Palframan, and of the remainder, Derek Crookes, Lance Klusener, Nicky Boje and Gerhardus Liebenberg had all played one-day international cricket for South Africa in 1995-96. Injuries midway through the tour deprived the party of Roger Telemachus (torn stomach muscle), Schultz (broken bone in right foot) and Kallis (stress fracture of lower back), leading to call-ups for another Test player, Meyrick Pringle, who was playing League cricket for Kendal, as well as Gary Gilder, who had yet to make his debut in the Castle Cup.

The first game against Yorkshire was more of an acclimatisation experience than a cricket match. The first day was washed out and the next two were spent shivering in bitterly cold July weather. By the second game in Chesterfield the weather was beginning to warm up, and so were the players. The batsmen, with the exception of Sven Koenig, who struggled for form and did not reach 50, all made the most of good pitches and some friendly bowling attacks. Herschelle Gibbs and Crookes hit two hundreds each while Commins, Liebenberg and Pringle also made centuries. Otherwise H. D. Ackerman, Nic Pothas, Boje and Klusener all contributed with the bat, although there was a general tendency to get out when set. Liebenberg, who toured England with the full South African side in 1994, went through one nightmare patch when he collected a pair against Nottinghamshire and followed it with six and one against Surrey, but otherwise he batted with a style and consistency which suggested a bright future at Test level. Commins also did his chances of a recall no harm, with an assured tour as middle-order batsman and captain. His 114 not out against MCC was a fine innings – despite being upstaged by a blistering 183 from Gibbs at the other end – and he ended the tour with a superbly crafted 85 against the TCCB XI.

But the two to catch the eye were Crookes and Gibbs. Crookes, whose father Norman toured England in 1965, missed the first two matches because of the death of his mother-in-law, but then justified his reputation as a hitter of note. With the South Africans struggling on 41 for four against Glamorgan, he smashed a century from 77 balls; in the next game against Somerset he got off the mark with a six before helping himself to 155 not out. It was spectacular stuff, but he may well find himself pigeon-holed as a one-day specialist. The 22-year-old Gibbs, just beginning to bloom though he had made his first-class debut in 1990-91, was a delight to watch. He made two big hundreds and five half-centuries to end the tour with 867 runs at an average of 66.69. His 183 against MCC, made in adversity while following on, was a study in concentration and showed genuine class and temperament. Gibbs is not a big man but his 178 against Surrey later in the tour was both clinical and cheeky. With four men positioned on the leg-side boundary for the left-armer Richard Nowell, Gibbs took up the challenge by twice hitting him over mid-wicket into the tenth row of seating.

The bowlers, though, all struggled to find the right length. For the first half of the tour, Klusener carried the attack. He bowled with pace and heart and enough venom to have left several county batsmen with a greater understanding of Zulu oaths. Unfortunately, his aggression ran out of control against Surrey and earned him a rebuke from the umpires. Klusener's form dipped at the end, but he still picked up wickets and finished with 31 at an average of 25.25.

The only first-class game he missed was against Worcestershire, when the Natal left-arm seamer Gilder announced himself with a superb spell of bowling, taking eight for 22. Slow left-armer Boje was the pick of the spinners, while the 19-year-old Adams, the "frog in a blender" who had risen with dizzying speed into the ranks of Test cricketers, was happy to find some equilibrium out of the spotlight and enjoy the touring experience.

SOUTH AFRICA A TOURING PARTY

J. B. Commins (Boland) (*captain*), H. D. Ackerman (Western Province), P. R. Adams (Western Province), N. Boje (Free State), D. N. Crookes (Natal), H. H. Gibbs (Western Province), J. H. Kallis (Western Province), L. Klusener (Natal), S. G. Koenig (Western Province), G. F. J. Liebenberg (Free State), S. J. Palframan (Border), N. Pothas (Transvaal), B. N. Schultz (Eastern Province), G. J. Smith (Northern Transvaal), R. Telemachus (Boland).

G. M. Gilder (Natal) and M. W. Pringle (Western Province) joined the party after Kallis, Telemachus and Schultz were injured.

Manager: G. Rajah. *Coach:* D. A. G. Fletcher.

SOUTH AFRICA A TOUR RESULTS

First-class matches – Played 9: Won 3, Lost 1, Drawn 5.
Wins – Glamorgan, Surrey, Worcestershire.
Loss – TCCB XI.
Draws – Yorkshire, Derbyshire, MCC, Somerset, Nottinghamshire.
Other non-first-class matches – Played 3: Won 3. *Wins* – Wales, Gloucestershire, Essex.

SOUTH AFRICA A TOUR AVERAGES – FIRST-CLASS MATCHES

BATTING

	M	*I*	*NO*	*R*	*HS*	*100s*	*Avge*	*Ct/St*
H. H. Gibbs	8	14	1	867	183	2	66.69	9
D. N. Crookes	7	11	1	566	155*	2	56.60	8
J. B. Commins	9	15	3	597	114*	1	49.75	2
N. Pothas	6	9	2	309	90	0	44.14	15
N. Boje	7	9	2	289	89	0	41.28	5
H. D. Ackerman	7	11	0	447	99	0	40.63	3
L. Klusener	8	8	3	171	79	0	34.20	4
G. F. J. Liebenberg	8	14	0	453	123	1	32.35	8
J. H. Kallis	4	4	0	128	92	0	32.00	1
P. R. Adams	4	5	3	63	27	0	31.50	1
M. W. Pringle	4	6	0	170	105	1	28.33	0
S. G. Koenig	7	11	0	221	46	0	20.09	3
S. J. Palframan	5	7	1	104	55	0	17.33	10/1
G. M. Gilder	4	6	0	43	23	0	7.16	1
G. J. Smith	5	5	3	7	5	0	3.50	1

Played in three matches: B. N. Schultz 9, 3 (1 ct); R. Telemachus 0, 8 (2 ct).

** Signifies not out.*

BOWLING

	O	*M*	*R*	*W*	*BB*	*5W/i*	*Avge*
G. M. Gilder	94.4	29	243	13	8-22	1	18.69
J. H. Kallis	56.3	19	145	6	4-31	0	24.16
L. Klusener	232.3	44	783	31	5-74	1	25.25
G. J. Smith	125.2	24	402	15	4-70	0	26.80
R. Telemachus	40	5	188	7	4-99	0	26.85
P. R. Adams	108.4	19	390	10	4-116	0	39.00
M. W. Pringle	172.4	40	579	14	4-90	0	41.35
N. Boje	160.4	30	562	12	5-58	1	46.83
B. N. Schultz	67	6	297	6	2-45	0	49.50

Also bowled: H. D. Ackerman 5–1–10–0; D. N. Crookes 84–16–259–3; H. H. Gibbs 12–2–43–3; S. G. Koenig 3–2–5–0; G. F. J. Liebenberg 3–2–1–0; N. Pothas 1–0–5–0.

Note: Matches in this section which were not first-class are signified by a dagger.

YORKSHIRE v SOUTH AFRICA A

At Leeds, July 3, 4, 5. Drawn. Toss: Yorkshire. First-class debut: M. J. Hoggard.

Once rain had washed out the opening day, the game was always likely to be a draw. Yorkshire, resting six leading players, batted first and made 331, thanks to a bright partnership of 123 between Blakey and White. A great deal of interest centred on the left-arm chinamen of Adams, who struggled to find a length as he bowled into a stiff westerly wind. He was hit for 21 in one over, but later settled to take four for 116. South Africa A got into trouble at 92 for six, but Klusener scored an unbeaten 46 as the tail hit out. They assumed they had saved the follow-on, unaware that they had to reduce the deficit to 99, not 149, because the match had been cut to two days. They were just short, but Byas opted for batting practice anyway.

Close of play: First day, No play; Second day, South Africa A 21-3 (G. F. J. Liebenberg 8*).

Yorkshire

	First innings		Second innings
A. McGrath c Telemachus b Schultz	3	– not out	50
*D. Byas lbw b Telemachus	16	– not out	27
C. White b Adams	77		
†R. J. Blakey lbw b Klusener	64		
R. A. Kettleborough c Kallis b Klusener	0		
B. Parker c Liebenberg b Adams	59		
A. C. Morris c Palframan b Telemachus	33		
A. G. Wharf b Klusener	10		
G. M. Hamilton c Koenig b Adams	1		
R. D. Stemp not out	22		
M. J. Hoggard b Adams	10		
L-b 6, w 4, n-b 26	36	L-b 5, n-b 8	13
1/24 2/24 3/147 4/159 5/193 6/248 7/270 8/275 9/314	331	(no wkt dec.)	90

Bowling: *First Innings*—Schultz 15–1–53–1; Telemachus 11–1–54–2; Kallis 15–3–45–0; Klusener 17–2–57–3; Adams 23–4–116–4. *Second Innings*—Schultz 7–0–35–0; Telemachus 5–2–13–0; Klusener 4–2–5–0; Adams 8–3–23–0; Kallis 5–3–9–0.

South Africa A

S. G. Koenig c Byas b Hamilton	11
G. F. J. Liebenberg b Hoggard	29
J. H. Kallis lbw b Hamilton	0
R. Telemachus lbw b Stemp	0
H. D. Ackerman lbw b Morris	35
*J. B. Commins c Morris b Wharf	6
H. H. Gibbs c Byas b Stemp	28
†S. J. Palframan c Blakey b Stemp	14
L. Klusener not out	46
P. R. Adams c Hamilton b Stemp	27
B. N. Schultz st Blakey b Stemp	9
B 7, l-b 4, n-b 10	21
1/18 2/20 3/21 4/59 5/74 6/92 7/125 8/136 9/194	226

Bowling: Hamilton 15–3–46–2; Hoggard 15–3–41–1; Stemp 25.2–7–69–5; Wharf 7–3–13–1; Morris 5–1–24–1; White 4–1–22–0.

Umpires: B. J. Meyer and P. Willey.

DERBYSHIRE v SOUTH AFRICA A

At Chesterfield, July 6, 7, 8. Drawn. Toss: South Africa A. County debut: G. A. Khan.

A slow, flat Queen's Park pitch and a late declaration from the South Africans on the last afternoon consigned this game to a dull draw as Derbyshire, without seven first-team regulars, declined to chase Commins's target of 342 in a minimum of 55 overs. Derbyshire coach Les Stillman criticised the tourists' caution. The batsmen dominated, with 1,148 runs scored for the loss of 15 wickets. There were 11 scores of 50 and over, and Derbyshire's acting-captain, Adams, became the fourth player to pass 1,000 runs for the summer during his 66. Liebenberg recorded the first hundred of the South Africans' tour, a fluent second-innings 123.

Close of play: First day, Derbyshire 50-0 (T. J. G. O'Gorman 26*, J. E. Owen 18*); Second day, South Africa A 128-0 (S. G. Koenig 42*, G. F. J. Liebenberg 79*).

South Africa A

	First innings		Second innings
S. G. Koenig c Rollins b Vandrau	46	– b Dean	43
G. F. J. Liebenberg b Vandrau	45	– b Aldred	123
J. H. Kallis lbw b Griffith	92		
H. D. Ackerman c May b Aldred	79		
*J. B. Commins not out	27	– (4) not out	59
H. H. Gibbs not out	27	– (3) c Rollins b Vandrau	68
†N. Pothas (did not bat)		– (5) not out	28
L-b 6	6	L-b 10, n-b 4	14
1/65 2/115 3/250 4/274	(4 wkts dec.) 322	1/132 2/209 3/283	(3 wkts dec.) 335

N. Boje, L. Klusener, G. J. Smith and B. N. Schultz did not bat.

Bowling: *First Innings*—Dean 20–3–69–0; Aldred 22–2–63–1; Griffith 20–1–70–1; Wells 3–0–12–0; Vandrau 24–4–82–2; Khan 2–0–20–0. *Second Innings*—Dean 11–3–32–1; Aldred 20–2–86–1; Vandrau 16–0–71–1; Griffith 7–0–67–0; Wells 7–3–17–0; Adams 3–0–8–0; Rollins 3–0–25–0; May 3–0–19–0.

Derbyshire

T. J. G. O'Gorman c Gibbs b Smith	53	– not out	68
J. E. Owen c Gibbs b Schultz	23	– c Liebenberg b Smith	1
*C. J. Adams c Smith b Boje	66		
G. A. Khan c Pothas b Klusener	10	– c Liebenberg b Schultz	15
C. M. Wells c Pothas b Klusener	61		
M. R. May not out	63	– (5) not out	32
†A. S. Rollins not out	7	– (3) c Pothas b Schultz	50
B 4, l-b 15, n-b 14	33	L-b 1, n-b 8	9
1/64 2/135 3/173 4/180 5/291 (5 wkts dec.)	316	1/2 2/76 3/100 (3 wkts)	175

M. J. Vandrau, P. Aldred, F. A. Griffith and K. J. Dean did not bat.

Bowling: *First Innings*—Schultz 18–2–68–1; Smith 15–1–62–1; Boje 27–4–85–1; Kallis 7–2–32–0; Klusener 19–4–50–2. *Second Innings*—Schultz 12–0–81–2; Smith 8–2–22–1; Boje 16–4–43–0; Klusener 3–0–12–0; Liebenberg 3–2–1–0; Ackerman 5–1–10–0; Koenig 3–2–5–0.

Umpires: K. J. Lyons and J. F. Steele.

MCC v SOUTH AFRICA A

At Shenley Park, July 10, 11, 12. Drawn. Toss: MCC.

The South Africans collected their third successive draw, after being forced to follow on. MCC produced some fine, aggressive batting to reach 391 for seven. The most exhilarating hitting came from the West Indian, Arthurton, who scored 82 in 78 balls, with 68 in boundaries. Zimbabwe Test opener Grant Flower made 98 and his brother Andy an attractive 70. The South Africans collapsed after lunch on the second day, with the Trinidadian, Francis, taking four, and followed on 187 behind. In their second innings, their batsmen redeemed themselves. Openers Liebenberg and Pothas scored confident half-centuries and Commins an accomplished 114 not out. The best batting came from Gibbs, however, who struck 25 fours and five sixes in a career-best 183. It was the opening first-class match at the charming Shenley ground near Radlett in Hertfordshire, which was renamed the Denis Compton Ground during the game. MCC used the venue because Lord's was being prepared for the Benson and Hedges Cup final.

Close of play: First day, South Africa A 31-2 (H. H. Gibbs 5*, N. Boje 2*); Second day, South Africa A 133-1 (G. F. J. Liebenberg 51*, H. H. Gibbs 14*).

MCC

G. W. Flower b Smith	98
*H. Morris c Ackerman b Telemachus	10
A. G. Lawson c Gibbs b Klusener	12
K. L. T. Arthurton c Palframan b Telemachus	82
G. I. Foley c Telemachus b Boje	14
†A. Flower c Gibbs b Telemachus	70
A. I. C. Dodemaide not out	62
R. D. B. Croft c Klusener b Telemachus	2
P. A. Strang not out	13
B 2, l-b 4, w 2, n-b 20	28
1/28 2/55 3/205 4/233 5/247 6/365 7/371 (7 wkts dec.)	391

B. St A. Browne and N. B. Francis did not bat.

Bowling: Smith 18–5–52–1; Telemachus 20–2–99–4; Klusener 21–1–83–1; Crookes 15–0–55–0; Boje 18–2–96–1.

South Africa A

G. F. J. Liebenberg c A. Flower b Francis	7	– lbw b Strang	73
N. Pothas lbw b Francis	3	– b Foley	62
H. H. Gibbs c Lawson b Croft	57	– b Dodemaide	183
N. Boje c G. W. Flower b Francis	5		
H. D. Ackerman b Foley	31	– (4) c G. W. Flower b Francis	22
*J. B. Commins c G. W. Flower b Francis	13	– (5) not out	114
†S. J. Palframan run out	9	– (6) not out	10
D. N. Crookes c Strang b Browne	16		
L. Klusener c and b Croft	5		
R. Telemachus c Francis b Strang	8		
G. J. Smith not out	0		
B 9, l-b 21, n-b 20	50	B 14, l-b 6, n-b 6	26
1/13 2/22 3/52 4/116 5/152 6/154 7/169 8/186 9/200	204	1/89 2/189 3/240 4/479 (4 wkts dec.)	490

Bowling: *First Innings*—Francis 17–8–34–4; Browne 13–3–55–1; Croft 11–2–26–2; Dodemaide 6–2–20–0; Foley 9–3–22–1; Strang 11.3–3–17–1. *Second Innings*—Francis 20–5–67–1; Browne 16–4–56–0; Dodemaide 27–7–92–1; Croft 5–0–20–0; Strang 35–7–117–1; Foley 28–2–118–1.

Umpires: R. Julian and N. T. Plews.

†At Swansea, July 14. South Africa A won by 125 runs. Toss: South Africa A. South Africa A 277 for five (50 overs) (S. G. Koenig 66, J. H. Kallis 106, H. H. Gibbs 57 not out); Wales 152 for seven (50 overs) (J. H. Langworth 42; N. Boje three for 14).

GLAMORGAN v SOUTH AFRICA A

At Cardiff, July 17, 18. South Africa A won by an innings and 44 runs. Toss: South Africa A.

The South Africans stepped up a gear and comprehensively beat Glamorgan inside two days. Their victory was set up on the first day by some positive batting from Crookes, after they had slipped to 41 for four in the first 14 overs. Crookes savaged the Glamorgan bowling with a hundred from 77 balls. He shared a partnership of 180 with Ackerman, who remained with Pothas to steer the South Africans towards 346. The Glamorgan batting, missing only Morris and Maynard, then fell apart twice as Klusener and Kallis found some movement off the right length. Glamorgan were dismissed 181 behind and did even worse following on, when Watkin top-scored with 22. Klusener took seven for 81 in the match.

Close of play: First day, Glamorgan 96-5 (A. Dale 26*, O. D. Gibson 0*).

South Africa A

S. G. Koenig lbw b Watkin	0
G. F. J. Liebenberg c Shaw b Parkin	33
J. H. Kallis c Shaw b Watkin	2
H. D. Ackerman st Shaw b Barwick	99
*J. B. Commins lbw b Parkin	0
D. N. Crookes b Parkin	105
†N. Pothas c Dale b Hemp	64
N. Boje c James b Hemp	25
L. Klusener not out	4
P. R. Adams b Hemp	0
B. N. Schultz c Watkin b Barwick	3
B 5, l-b 1, w 1, n-b 4	11
1/8 2/16 3/41 4/41 5/221 6/277 7/332 8/337 9/337	346

Bowling: Watkin 15–3–52–2; Gibson 11–0–49–0; Parkin 14–1–69–3; Barwick 26.4–4–81–2; Kendrick 10–1–66–0; Hemp 6–1–23–3.

Glamorgan

S. P. James c Pothas b Klusener	14	lbw b Klusener	18
A. W. Evans lbw b Klusener	21	c Koenig b Boje	13
D. L. Hemp c Pothas b Kallis	12	c Pothas b Boje	19
A. Dale c Ackerman b Kallis	37	lbw b Adams	13
*P. A. Cottey c Pothas b Kallis	4	c Commins b Adams	15
†A. D. Shaw c Pothas b Kallis	11	b Klusener	0
O. D. Gibson b Schultz	30	c Schultz b Adams	11
N. M. Kendrick not out	5	b Kallis	10
S. L. Watkin c sub (H. H. Gibbs) b Schultz	7	not out	22
S. R. Barwick b Klusener	1	c and b Klusener	1
O. T. Parkin b Klusener	0	lbw b Kallis	0
L-b 12, w 1, n-b 10	23	B 4, l-b 7, w 2, n-b 2	15
1/25 2/44 3/59 4/71 5/95 6/134 7/142 8/158 9/161	165	1/17 2/40 3/63 4/85 5/85 6/85 7/100 8/125 9/136	137

Bowling: *First Innings*—Schultz 11–2–45–2; Klusener 7.4–2–39–4; Kallis 15–5–31–4; Adams 13–1–38–0. *Second Innings*—Schultz 4–1–15–0; Kallis 7.3–3–10–2; Klusener 10–3–42–3; Boje 9–2–17–2; Adams 13–3–37–3; Crookes 4–1–5–0.

Umpires: J. H. Hampshire and T. E. Jesty.

SOMERSET v SOUTH AFRICA A

At Taunton, July 20, 21, 22. Drawn. Toss: South Africa A.

A gripping game played in fierce heat looked likely to end in victory for the South Africans at tea, when Somerset led by only five, with four wickets in hand. But an aggressive seventh-wicket partnership of 123 between Rose and Kerr saved the game. The South Africans were limping towards the finish line, with three strike bowlers injured; Telemachus and Kallis broke down during the first innings and Smith in the second. The tireless Klusener finished with match figures of seven for 169 from 54.5 overs, and their fitness expert Paddy Upton fielded for much of the last day. Nevertheless, they did well to bowl out Somerset for 301 on the first day, after Lathwell had made his first hundred of the season. They then scored at five an over to reach 509 for seven, Crookes finishing on 155 not out, his second hundred of the week. Night-watchman Boje also batted forthrightly for 89, with all but seven coming in boundaries: 19 fours and a six.

Close of play: First day, South Africa A 39-1 (S. G. Koenig 13*, N. Boje 4*); Second day, Somerset 42-0 (M. N. Lathwell 16*, M. E. Trescothick 22*).

Somerset

M. N. Lathwell run out	108	lbw b Crookes	32
*P. D. Bowler b Telemachus	1	(4) c Crookes b Klusener	32
K. A. Parsons c sub (H. D. Ackerman) b Boje	62	c Crookes b Smith	5
M. E. Trescothick st Palframan b Boje	6	(2) c Boje b Smith	55
S. C. Ecclestone c Pothas b Boje	7	c Crookes b Klusener	15
†P. C. L. Holloway c Boje b Klusener	45	c Palframan b Smith	8
G. D. Rose c Crookes b Klusener	6	not out	64
J. I. D. Kerr lbw b Klusener	4	c and b Gibbs	56
J. D. Batty b Klusener	18	lbw b Gibbs	0
A. R. Caddick lbw b Klusener	0	not out	8
K. J. Shine not out	5		
B 2, l-b 8, w 1, n-b 28	39	B 8, l-b 11, w 1, n-b 14	34
1/12 2/137 3/159 4/175 5/230 6/236 7/266 8/294 9/294	301	1/91 2/91 3/102 4/142 5/154 6/163 7/286 8/286	(8 wkts) 309

Bowling: *First Innings*—Smith 20–2–81–0; Telemachus 4–0–22–1; Kallis 7–3–18–0; Klusener 27.4–8–74–5; Boje 29–8–68–3; Crookes 10–2–28–0. *Second Innings*—Smith 11.5–2–34–3; Klusener 27.1–7–95–2; Boje 18–5–56–0; Crookes 27–4–86–1; Gibbs 6–2–14–2; Pothas 1–0–5–0.

South Africa A

S. G. Koenig b Batty	27	†S. J. Palframan c Shine b Lathwell	55
H. H. Gibbs lbw b Caddick	8		
N. Boje c Lathwell b Caddick	89	B 5, l-b 6, w 4, n-b 26	41
*J. B. Commins c Lathwell b Batty	73		
D. N. Crookes not out	155	1/29 2/94 3/221 (7 wkts dec.)	509
N. Pothas c Holloway b Kerr	27	4/235 5/310	
J. H. Kallis lbw b Shine	34	6/379 7/509	

L. Klusener, R. Telemachus and G. J. Smith did not bat.

Bowling: Caddick 22–1–121–2; Shine 12–1–61–1; Batty 36–3–153–2; Rose 11–2–47–0; Kerr 15–2–74–1; Parsons 4–0–28–0; Lathwell 1.4–0–14–1.

Umpires: J. W. Holder and A. G. T. Whitehead.

†At Cheltenham, July 24. South Africa A won by 28 runs. Toss: Gloucestershire. South Africa A 297 for eight (50 overs) (H. H. Gibbs 55, J. H. Kallis 60, H. D. Ackerman 47, D. N. Crookes 66, N. Pothas 31 not out); Gloucestershire 269 (48 overs) (M. A. Lynch 52, A. Symonds 84, M. C. J. Ball 33, J. Lewis 33).

NOTTINGHAMSHIRE v SOUTH AFRICA A

At Nottingham, July 26, 27, 28, 29. Drawn. Toss: South Africa A.

Rain on the last morning washed out any real chance of a result. Injuries had ruled out Schultz and Kallis from the South African line-up and both left for home during the match. Gilder, who had arrived in place of Telemachus, made his first appearance, as did Pringle. The home side was hampered by an injury to wicket-keeper Walker, whose broken thumb prevented him from batting; substitute Noon was allowed to take over behind the stumps. Most of the tourists' middle order made accomplished half-centuries against a weak Nottinghamshire attack before giving away their wickets. The South Africans took a first-innings lead of 115 and more positive batting from Gibbs extended that to 295 by the third-day close. Rain, though, ruled out play before lunch on the final day and, despite Commins's declaration, the game drifted to a draw.

Close of play: First day, South Africa A 396-6 (N. Pothas 63*, L. Klusener 65*); Second day, Nottinghamshire 273-4 (G. F. Archer 78*, C. M. Tolley 19*); Third day, South Africa A 180-6 (N. Pothas 8*, L. Klusener 0*).

South Africa A

S. G. Koenig c Walker b Bates	15	– c sub (W. M. Noon) b Mike	22
G. F. J. Liebenberg c Mike b Chapman	0	– c Pollard b Chapman	0
H. H. Gibbs c Archer b Chapman	95	– st sub (W. M. Noon) b Afzaal	85
H. D. Ackerman c Mike b Chapman	66	– c sub (W. M. Noon) b Tolley	6
*J. B. Commins c Afzaal b Afford	2	– run out	34
D. N. Crookes c Walker b Bates	59	– c Archer b Mike	18
†N. Pothas c Chapman b Afford	90	– not out	8
L. Klusener c Pollard b Afford	79	– not out	0
M. W. Pringle c Bates b Afford	0		
P. R. Adams not out	11		
G. M. Gilder lbw b Chapman	4		
B 7, l-b 2, w 2, n-b 23	34	L-b 2, w 1, n-b 4	7
1/0 2/50 3/190 4/200 5/200 6/282 7/435 8/435 9/446	455	1/1 2/63 3/84 4/146 5/158 6/178 (6 wkts dec.)	180

Bowling: *First Innings*—Mike 23–7–106–0; Chapman 23.5–3–109–4; Tolley 12–2–50–0; Bates 23–5–74–2; Afford 28–9–66–4; Afzaal 7–2–27–0; Dowman 4–1–14–0. *Second Innings*—Mike 11.5–1–34–2; Chapman 4–0–24–1; Tolley 11–1–45–1; Afzaal 12–0–52–1; Afford 8–1–23–0.

Nottinghamshire

P. R. Pollard c Koenig b Adams	34	– not out	72
M. P. Dowman lbw b Pringle	27	– c Commins b Pringle	22
G. F. Archer run out	87	– retired hurt	12
U. Afzaal lbw b Crookes	47	– run out	26
*P. Johnson c Gilder b Adams	26		
C. M. Tolley b Klusener	43	– (5) not out	0
R. T. Bates c Pothas b Klusener	15		
G. W. Mike not out	13		
R. J. Chapman c Pothas b Klusener	0		
J. A. Afford c Pothas b Adams	0		
†L. N. P. Walker absent hurt			
B 18, l-b 10, n-b 20	48	L-b 10, n-b 2	12
1/61 2/85 3/196 4/243 5/286 6/314 7/335 8/339 9/340	340	1/45 2/139	(2 wkts) 144

In the second innings G. F. Archer retired hurt at 71.

Bowling: *First Innings*—Pringle 23–5–65–1; Gilder 17–8–33–0; Klusener 21–6–42–3; Adams 32.4–3–125–3; Crookes 16–5–47–1. *Second Innings*—Pringle 18–8–39–1; Gilder 11–2–42–0; Klusener 6–2–14–0; Adams 14–4–39–0.

Umpires: A. A. Jones and J. W. Lloyds.

SURREY v SOUTH AFRICA A

At The Oval, August 1, 2, 3, 4. South Africa A won by 157 runs. Toss: South Africa A. First-class debut: M. W. Patterson.

Surrey's team was little more than a second eleven; only Brown had appeared in the NatWest quarter-final which finished the previous morning, and Lewis was returning after injury. Irish trialist Mark Patterson took six for 80 in the first innings, the best figures by a Surrey bowler on first-class debut, but the game will be remembered principally for the batting of Gibbs, who hit an electrifying 178 on the third day. It was his second hundred of the tour and included eight sixes and 19 fours. It took him just 24 balls to go from 100 to 150. Set 433, Surrey lost four wickets by the close and Brown early on the fourth morning. Shahid made a sound 84 but left-arm spinner Boje took the last five. The South Africans' success was marred by the umpires' complaints about their behaviour in the field.

Close of play: First day, Surrey 10-0 (J. D. Ratcliffe 5*, G. J. Kennis 2*); Second day, South Africa A 62-2 (H. H. Gibbs 10*, H. D. Ackerman 33*); Third day, Surrey 193-4 (N. Shahid 67*, A. D. Brown 32*).

South Africa A

S. G. Koenig b Nowell	33	– c Brown b Lewis	18
G. F. J. Liebenberg b Lewis	6	– b Patterson	1
H. H. Gibbs c Kennis b Patterson	58	– st Knott b Shahid	178
H. D. Ackerman c Brown b Ratcliffe	48	– c Knott b Shahid	57
*J. B. Commins lbw b Patterson	55	– lbw b Ratcliffe	24
D. N. Crookes c Brown b Nowell	70	– c Brown b Shahid	29
N. Boje not out	58	– not out	23
†S. J. Palframan c Knott b Patterson	5		
L. Klusener b Patterson	12		
M. W. Pringle b Patterson	8		
G. M. Gilder c Shahid b Patterson	0		
B 5, l-b 3, w 2, n-b 16	26	B 8, l-b 1	9
1/10 2/104 3/104 4/187 5/260 6/325 7/349 8/365 9/379	379	1/19 2/19 3/132 4/187 5/290 6/339	(6 wkts dec.) 339

Bowling: *First Innings*—Lewis 16–5–46–1; Patterson 17.3–4–80–6; Kenlock 12–2–40–0; Ward 7–2–21–0; Nowell 18–2–76–2; Shahid 4–0–22–0; Ratcliffe 13–4–54–1; Smith 4–0–32–0. *Second Innings*—Patterson 10–3–44–1; Lewis 9–0–42–1; Nowell 13–3–57–0; Shahid 29.1–2–93–3; Ratcliffe 10–0–37–1; Ward 2–0–28–0; Smith 3–0–29–0.

Surrey

J. D. Ratcliffe run out	69	– lbw b Klusener	22
G. J. Kennis retired hurt	2	– (8) b Boje	1
N. Shahid lbw b Gilder	3	– (4) c Liebenberg b Boje	84
A. W. Smith c Crookes b Klusener	7	– (3) c Gibbs b Pringle	16
*C. C. Lewis c Gibbs b Pringle	52	– c Crookes b Gibbs	49
I. J. Ward c Liebenberg b Klusener	15	– (2) c Palframan b Gilder	4
A. D. Brown c Ackerman b Pringle	69	– (6) lbw b Klusener	32
†J. A. Knott c Palframan b Klusener	3	– (7) not out	49
R. W. Nowell not out	28	– c Palframan b Boje	0
S. G. Kenlock c Crookes b Gilder	0	– c Liebenberg b Boje	5
M. W. Patterson lbw b Pringle	4	– lbw b Boje	2
B 9, l-b 10, w 1, n-b 14	34	B 2, l-b 2, w 1, n-b 6	11
1/28 2/47 3/144 4/173 5/173 6/205 7/265 8/269 9/286	286	1/16 2/39 3/53 4/128 5/194 6/238 7/253 8/253 9/267	275

In the first innings G. J. Kennis retired hurt at 10.

Bowling: *First Innings*—Pringle 31.4–8–92–3; Gilder 22–7–48–2; Klusener 21–3–63–3; Boje 10–0–40–0; Crookes 8–4–24–0. *Second Innings*—Pringle 29–7–89–1; Gilder 6–0–20–1; Klusener 18–2–90–2; Boje 18.5–4–58–5; Gibbs 2–0–14–1.

Umpires: P. Adams and K. E. Palmer.

†At Chelmsford, August 6. South Africa A won by 11 runs. Toss: South Africa A. South Africa A 287 for six (50 overs) (G. F. J. Liebenberg 73, H. H. Gibbs 48, D. N. Crookes 31, N. Boje 39, N. Pothas 36 not out); Essex 276 for six (50 overs) (J. J. B. Lewis 48, R. J. Rollins 31, D. G. Wilson 52 not out, M. C. Ilott 42 not out, Extras 35).

D. G. Wilson was making his first-team debut for Essex.

WORCESTERSHIRE v SOUTH AFRICA A

At Worcester, August 9, 10, 11, 12. South Africa A won by 172 runs. Toss: South Africa A. First-class debuts: M. Amjad, J. T. Ralph.

Although 26 wickets fell on the opening day, South Africa A did not complete their third first-class win until the final morning. Rain washed out play after tea on the second day and limited it on the third. On the opening day, South Africa A collapsed after lunch, losing eight for 34 as Thomas and Preece swung the ball in overcast conditions. Gilder then did the same to take a career-best eight for 22, the best return by a touring bowler at New Road, hustling Worcestershire out for 77. The South Africans lost another six before the close as the ball continued to move and the batsmen continued to play poor shots. Neither side blamed the pitch, though both teams' coaches – the Zimbabweans Duncan Fletcher and Dave Houghton – thought the players had been surprised by a little extra bounce. But Pringle tightened their grip next morning as he hit a rustic maiden century, from 108 balls, and added 90 with last man Adams. His one scare came on 99: Adams edged to third slip, but Solanki put it down. Worcestershire needed 451, an impossible task, despite some gutsy resistance from Leatherdale and Rhodes.

Close of play: First day, South Africa A 160-6 (D. N. Crookes 50*, M. W. Pringle 18*); Second day, Worcestershire 96-3 (V. S. Solanki 27*, D. A. Leatherdale 12*); Third day, Worcestershire 239-6 (S. J. Rhodes 41*, S. W. K. Ellis 5*).

South Africa A

S. G. Koenig b Thomas	6	– c Leatherdale b Thomas	0
G. F. J. Liebenberg c Rhodes b Church	48	– c Rhodes b Leatherdale	33
H. H. Gibbs c Leatherdale b Thomas	47	– c Ralph b Ellis	5
*J. B. Commins run out	61	– b Leatherdale	22
D. N. Crookes lbw b Thomas	5	– c Spiring b Preece	62
N. Boje lbw b Preece	0	– c Spiring b Leatherdale	4
†S. J. Palframan c Rhodes b Thomas	5	– b Leatherdale	6
M. W. Pringle c Rhodes b Preece	0	– c Rhodes b Thomas	105
G. J. Smith c Spiring b Preece	0	– b Thomas	5
G. M. Gilder c Weston b Preece	5	– c Rhodes b Preece	23
P. R. Adams not out	0	– not out	25
L-b 1, w 6, n-b 18	25	L-b 14, w 3, n-b 18	35
1/32 2/82 3/168 4/179 5/183 6/196 7/197 8/197 9/197	202	1/0 2/11 3/76 4/87 5/96 6/114 7/185 8/194 9/235	325

Bowling: *First Innings*—Thomas 12–3–33–4; Ellis 6–0–34–0; Preece 15.2–0–79–4; Church 4–1–11–1; Leatherdale 8–0–37–0; Solanki 4–1–7–0. *Second Innings*—Thomas 20–0–109–3; Ellis 5–1–22–1; Preece 16–1–80–2; Leatherdale 16–2–75–4; Amjad 4–0–25–0.

Worcestershire

W. P. C. Weston c Palframan b Gilder	3	– c Boje b Smith	17
M. J. Church b Gilder	0	– c sub (N. Pothas) b Smith	31
K. R. Spiring c Boje b Smith	33	– c Liebenberg b Gilder	4
V. S. Solanki c Palframan b Gilder	14	– lbw b Gilder	29
D. A. Leatherdale c Palframan b Gilder	2	– c sub (N. Pothas) b Pringle	73
J. T. Ralph b Gilder	0	– c Liebenberg b Pringle	0
*†S. J. Rhodes lbw b Gilder	0	– lbw b Pringle	51
S. W. K. Ellis c Adams b Gilder	4	– b Pringle	13
P. A. Thomas c Crookes b Smith	8	– c Gibbs b Smith	1
M. Amjad c Palframan b Gilder	1	– c sub (H. D. Ackerman) b Smith	7
B. E. A. Preece not out	0	– not out	3
L-b 1, w 3, n-b 8	12	B 18, l-b 7, w 2, n-b 22	49
1/4 2/9 3/33 4/41 5/51 6/51 7/59 8/69 9/75	77	1/29 2/34 3/54 4/100 5/107 6/232 7/259 8/260 9/268	278

Bowling: *First Innings*—Pringle 7–1–41–0; Gilder 10–5–22–8; Smith 3.5–1–13–2. *Second Innings*—Gilder 19–5–43–2; Smith 25–5–70–4; Pringle 26–5–90–4; Adams 5–1–12–0; Crookes 1–0–7–0; Gibbs 4–0–15–0; Boje 3–0–16–0.

Umpires: N. G. Cowley and B. Leadbeater.

TCCB XI v SOUTH AFRICA A

At Chester-le-Street, August 15, 16, 17. TCCB XI won by eight wickets. Toss: South Africa A.

South Africa A ended their tour with their only defeat. They were beaten with a day and a half to spare by a TCCB XI made up of players from the five counties not otherwise engaged. Only the Sussex pair, Wells and Salisbury, had Test experience. But it was their team-mate James Kirtley, a late replacement for the injured Simon Brown, who stole the headlines in his fifth first-class match. The South Africans were in a strong position at 152 for one on the opening day, but Kirtley and Salisbury hit back to dismiss them for 302. Daley and Alistair Brown, both desperately searching for form, shared a partnership of 130 to give the TCCB XI the initiative, but Pringle and Klusener restricted the lead to just 36. Then Kirtley made the decisive breakthrough when the South Africans resumed. He removed Liebenberg, Gibbs and Ackerman with just five on the board, and they also lost Pothas before clearing the deficit. With the ball moving around and Kirtley taking five for 51 – improving his career-best for the second time in the match – Commins played a captain's innings of genuine class. But no one could stay with him, and the TCCB XI needed only 157.

Close of play: First day, TCCB XI 81-1 (R. R. Montgomerie 24*, A. P. Wells 12*); Second day, South Africa A 150-6 (J. B. Commins 60*, N. Boje 20*).

South Africa A

G. F. J. Liebenberg lbw b Kirtley	54	– c Rollins b Kirtley	1
N. Boje b Cowan	65	– (8) lbw b Kirtley	20
H. H. Gibbs c Law b Salisbury	27	– b Kirtley	1
H. D. Ackerman c Brown b Kirtley	4	– c Rollins b Kirtley	0
*J. B. Commins lbw b Law	22	– c Kirtley b Cowan	85
D. N. Crookes lbw b Salisbury	14	– c Montgomerie b Law	33
†N. Pothas c Brown b Law	16	– (2) b Cowan	11
L. Klusener lbw b Kirtley	13	– (7) c Montgomerie b Law	12
M. W. Pringle c Brown b Salisbury	52	– b Kirtley	5
G. M. Gilder c Wells b Salisbury	1	– lbw b Salisbury	10
G. J. Smith not out	1	– not out	1
B 9, l-b 14, n-b 10	33	L-b 12, w 1	13
1/131 2/152 3/156 4/188 5/208 6/228 7/231 8/288 9/289	302	1/1 2/5 3/5 4/29 5/80 6/102 7/151 8/157 9/191	192

Bowling: *First Innings*—Cowan 15–2–64–1; Kirtley 15–4–48–3; Law 15–1–86–2; Hollioake 7–1–19–0; Salisbury 23.4–2–62–4. *Second Innings*—Cowan 15–2–36–2; Kirtley 16–2–51–5; Law 7–1–36–2; Salisbury 10.4–2–47–1; Hollioake 3–0–10–0.

TCCB XI

R. R. Montgomerie run out	48	– c Klusener b Smith	19
M. A. Butcher c Pothas b Smith	26	– b Crookes	38
A. P. Wells c sub (S. J. Palframan) b Klusener	27	– not out	58
J. A. Daley c Pothas b Smith	76		
A. D. Brown c Boje b Pringle	79	– (4) not out	14
*A. J. Hollioake lbw b Pringle	1		
†R. J. Rollins lbw b Pringle	0		
D. R. Law c Gibbs b Pringle	10		
I. D. K. Salisbury c Pothas b Klusener	1		
A. P. Cowan c and b Klusener	11		
R. J. Kirtley not out	7		
B 7, l-b 8, w 1, n-b 36	52	B 5, l-b 3, w 1, n-b 20	29
1/52 2/119 3/134 4/264 5/270 6/286 7/300 8/309 9/323	338	1/36 2/134	(2 wkts) 158

Bowling: *First Innings*—Pringle 30–5–123–4; Gilder 3.4–1–9–0; Smith 16.4–5–56–2; Klusener 24–1–98–3; Boje 7–1–37–0. *Second Innings*—Smith 7–1–12–1; Gilder 6–1–26–0; Pringle 8–1–40–0; Klusener 6–1–19–0; Boje 4.5–0–46–0; Crookes 3–0–7–1.

Umpires: H. D. Bird and M. J. Harris.

BIGGEST LEAPS IN THE COUNTY CHAMPIONSHIP

15 places	Worcestershire	17th to second	1993
	Warwickshire	16th to first	1994
14 places	Gloucestershire	16th to second	1969
	Kent	18th to fourth	1996
13 places	Warwickshire	14th to first	1911
	Worcestershire	14th to first	1964
	Gloucestershire	16th to third	1976
	Kent	14th to first equal	1977
	Surrey	16th to third	1979
	Worcestershire	15th to second	1979
	Middlesex	14th to first	1980
	Hampshire	15th to second	1985
	Lancashire	15th to second	1987

BRITANNIC ASSURANCE COUNTY CHAMPIONSHIP, 1996

James Whitaker

The 1996 County Championship was won, in the end, confidently and convincingly by Leicestershire, for the second time in their not always distinguished history. But their triumph came after a tense and surprising struggle. Six different teams led the table in the last two months. But the top four from 1995 were not among them, and all finished down the field.

Leicestershire's challenge looked more obvious in retrospect than in advance. They were runners-up in 1994, and in 1996 found consistency, bite in attack, a settled team – they used only 13 players all summer – plus a touch of inspiration from both their overseas player, Phil Simmons, and their new captain, James Whitaker, who gave the team an almost mystical sense of destiny, most visible in the team huddle which marked the fall of every wicket.

Continued overleaf

BRITANNIC ASSURANCE CHAMPIONSHIP

					Bonus points		
Win = 16 pts Draw = 3 pts	*Played*	*Won*	*Lost*	*Drawn*	*Batting*	*Bowling*	*Points*
1 – Leicestershire (7)	17	10	1	6	57	61	296
2 – Derbyshire (14)	17	9	3	5	52	58	269
3 – Surrey (12)	17	8	2	7	49	64	262
4 – Kent (18)	17	9	2	6	47	52	261
5 – Essex (5)	17	8	5	4	58	57	255
6 – Yorkshire (8)	17	8	5	4	50	58	248
7 – Worcestershire (10)	17	6	4	7	45	60	222
8 – Warwickshire (1)	17	7	6	4	39	55	218
9 – Middlesex (2)	17	7	6	4	30	59	213
10 – Glamorgan (16)	17	6	5	6	50	43	207
11 – Somerset (9)	17	5	6	6	38	61	197
12 – Sussex (15)	17	6	9	2	36	58	196
13 – Gloucestershire (6)	17	5	7	5	23	59	177
14 – Hampshire (13)	17	3	7	7	41	56	166
15 – Lancashire (4)	17	2	6	9	49	52	160
16 – Northamptonshire (3)	17	3	8	6	36	57	159
17 – Nottinghamshire (11)	17	1	9	7	42	52	131
18 – Durham (17)	17	0	12	5	22	60	97

1995 positions are shown in brackets.

Surrey were the only team to beat Leicestershire all summer – as happened, coincidentally, in their other Championship season, 1975. But that defeat, in mid-June, was followed by a burst of four successive wins which took them to the top of the table. Leicestershire suffered in August, twice finishing one wicket short of victory – then won their last four games to end 27 points clear, a far larger gap than anyone had opened up all season. Six of their ten wins were by an innings, and three were completed in two days.

Surrey's failure in their last match meant they eventually finished third, behind Derbyshire, who had their best Championship season in 60 years and looked probable champions after winning all four of their August matches before their sequence came to an end on a bland wicket at Taunton. Both Derbyshire and Surrey were revitalised by Australian influence: Dean Jones and Les Stillman, the captain-coach team brought to Derby from Melbourne, made the team both combative and notably talkative on the field. Surrey, coached by Dave Gilbert and heavily influenced by both their overseas signing Brendon Julian and the Australian-born vice-captain Adam Hollioake, put together results to match their obvious talent after a sluggish start. They won six games out of seven between early July and early September.

Kent, bottom in 1995, redeemed themselves by surging 14 places and still theoretically had a chance of the title until the very last game. But when September started, the most likely champions seemed to be Essex, who had looked set to win six games in a row, until a disastrous day at Headingley, when Richard Kettleborough and the Yorkshire tail transformed the match and sent Essex hurtling out of the race. They finished fifth, just ahead of Yorkshire, who had been leaders themselves after winning what is meant to be their last-ever match at Harrogate. They lost their next three games, and finished with a familiar feeling of promise unfulfilled.

Worcestershire, bottom in mid-June, hit a late run of form to come seventh, ahead of the 1995 champions and runners-up, Warwickshire and Middlesex, neither of whom found the consistency to put together any kind of challenge. Glamorgan's in-form batsmen helped them into the top ten, for only the fourth time in 26 seasons, ahead of Somerset and Sussex – both beset by internal difficulties – and Gloucestershire, who surprised everyone in 1995 but now reverted to familiar mediocrity.

Hampshire were in the bottom third for the fifth year running, but managed to finish clear of Lancashire, whose miserable Championship form was in stark contrast to their Cup successes, Northamptonshire, who chopped and changed but were never able to find a combination that could reproduce their 1995 form, and Nottinghamshire, who lost eight of their last ten matches at a time when they were winning even more consistently in the Sunday League. None of these, however, were in danger of finishing bottom. Durham became the first team to endure a winless season in 14 years and, since they lost 12 of their matches and won only one game against a first-class county in the other main competitions, arguably had the worst of all post-war seasons.

Fifty of the 153 Championship matches were drawn, a return to more normal proportions after the number slid to only 29 in 1995. This was partly due to worse weather, and partly to the three points for a draw which made counties slightly less willing to do deals or to fold up when the cause was hopeless. Of the 103 games with a result, 37 were over inside three days, and six of these inside two.

Under TCCB playing conditions, two extras were scored for every no-ball bowled whether scored off or not. Any runs scored off the bat were credited to the batsman, while byes and leg-byes were counted as no-balls, in accordance with Law 24.9, in addition to the initial penalty.

Pre-season betting (William Hill): 9-4 Warwickshire; 9-2 Middlesex; 6-1 Lancashire; 7-1 Northamptonshire; 10-1 Essex; 14-1 Worcestershire; 16-1 Surrey; 20-1 Kent, LEICESTERSHIRE and Somerset; 22-1 Gloucestershire and Yorkshire; 25-1 Derbyshire and Nottinghamshire; 50-1 Hampshire and Sussex; 66-1 Glamorgan; 200-1 Durham.

Leaders: from May 20 Leicestershire; June 3 Kent; June 10 Yorkshire; June 24 Kent; July 1 Yorkshire; July 8 Kent; July 22 Yorkshire; July 29 Leicestershire; August 12 Surrey; August 19 Derbyshire; August 26 Essex and Kent; September 2 Kent; September 6 onwards Leicestershire. Leicestershire became champions on September 21.

Bottom place: from May 20 Worcestershire; June 24 Northamptonshire; July 1 onwards Durham.

Prize money

First (Leicestershire)	£65,000
Second (Derbyshire)	£30,000
Third (Surrey)	£15,000
Fourth (Kent)	£10,000
Fifth (Essex)	£9,000
Sixth (Yorkshire)	£8,000
Seventh (Worcestershire)	£7,000
Eighth (Warwickshire)	£6,000
Ninth (Middlesex)	£5,000
Winner of each match	£1,000

Scoring of Points

(*a*) For a win, 16 points plus any points scored in the first innings.

(*b*) In a tie, each side scores eight points, plus any points scored in the first innings.

(*c*) In a drawn match, each side to score three points, plus any points scored in the first innings (see also paragraph (*f*)).

(*d*) If the scores are equal in a drawn match, the side batting in the fourth innings scores eight points, plus any points scored in the first innings, and the opposing side scores three points plus any points scored in the first innings.

(*e*) First-innings points (awarded only for performances in the first 120 overs of each first innings and retained whatever the result of the match).

(i) A maximum of four batting points to be available: 200 to 249 runs – 1 point; 250 to 299 runs – 2 points; 300 to 349 – 3 points; 350 runs or over – 4 points.

(ii) A maximum of four bowling points to be available: 3 or 4 wickets taken – 1 point; 5 or 6 wickets taken – 2 points; 7 or 8 wickets taken – 3 points; 9 or 10 wickets taken – 4 points.

(*f*) If play starts when less than eight hours' playing time remains and a one-innings match is played, no first-innings points shall be scored. The side winning on the one innings scores 12 points. In a tie, each side scores six points. In a drawn match, each side scores three points. If the scores are equal in a drawn match, the side batting in the second innings scores six points and the opposing side scores three points.

(*g*) A county which is adjudged to have prepared a pitch unsuitable for first-class cricket shall be liable to have 25 points deducted. In addition, a penalty of ten or 15 points may in certain circumstances be imposed on a county in respect of a poor pitch.

(*h*) The side which has the highest aggregate of points shall be the Champion County. Should any sides in the Championship table be equal on points, the side with most wins will have priority.

COUNTY CHAMPIONS

The Championship was not formally organised until 1890. Champions before that date were decided by the sporting press, which was not always unanimous. Since 1963, *Wisden* has formally accepted the list of champions "most generally selected" by contemporaries, as researched by the late Rowland Bowen (See *Wisden* 1959, pp 91-98). This appears to be the most accurate available list but has no official status. The county champions from 1864 to 1890 were, according to Bowen:

1864 Surrey; 1865 Nottinghamshire; 1866 Middlesex; 1867 Yorkshire; 1868 Nottinghamshire; 1869 Nottinghamshire and Yorkshire; 1870 Yorkshire; 1871 Nottinghamshire; 1872 Nottinghamshire; 1873 Gloucestershire and Nottinghamshire; 1874 Gloucestershire; 1875 Nottinghamshire; 1876 Gloucestershire; 1877 Gloucestershire; 1878 undecided; 1879 Lancashire and Nottinghamshire; 1880 Nottinghamshire; 1881 Lancashire; 1882 Lancashire and Nottinghamshire; 1883 Nottinghamshire; 1884 Nottinghamshire; 1885 Nottinghamshire; 1886 Nottinghamshire; 1887 Surrey; 1888 Surrey; 1889 Lancashire, Nottinghamshire and Surrey.

Official champions

1890	Surrey
1891	Surrey
1892	Surrey
1893	Yorkshire
1894	Surrey
1895	Surrey
1896	Yorkshire
1897	Lancashire
1898	Yorkshire
1899	Surrey
1900	Yorkshire
1901	Yorkshire
1902	Yorkshire
1903	Middlesex
1904	Lancashire
1905	Yorkshire
1906	Kent
1907	Nottinghamshire
1908	Yorkshire
1909	Kent
1910	Kent
1911	Warwickshire
1912	Yorkshire
1913	Kent
1914	Surrey
1919	Yorkshire
1920	Middlesex
1921	Middlesex
1922	Yorkshire
1923	Yorkshire
1924	Yorkshire
1925	Yorkshire
1926	Lancashire
1927	Lancashire
1928	Lancashire
1929	Nottinghamshire
1930	Lancashire
1931	Yorkshire
1932	Yorkshire
1933	Yorkshire
1934	Lancashire
1935	Yorkshire
1936	Derbyshire
1937	Yorkshire
1938	Yorkshire
1939	Yorkshire
1946	Yorkshire
1947	Middlesex
1948	Glamorgan
1949	Middlesex Yorkshire
1950	Lancashire Surrey
1951	Warwickshire
1952	Surrey
1953	Surrey
1954	Surrey
1955	Surrey
1956	Surrey
1957	Surrey
1958	Surrey
1959	Yorkshire
1960	Yorkshire
1961	Hampshire
1962	Yorkshire
1963	Yorkshire
1964	Worcestershire
1965	Worcestershire
1966	Yorkshire
1967	Yorkshire
1968	Yorkshire
1969	Glamorgan
1970	Kent
1971	Surrey
1972	Warwickshire
1973	Hampshire
1974	Worcestershire
1975	Leicestershire
1976	Middlesex
1977	Middlesex Kent
1978	Kent
1979	Essex
1980	Middlesex
1981	Nottinghamshire
1982	Middlesex
1983	Essex
1984	Essex
1985	Middlesex
1986	Essex
1987	Nottinghamshire
1988	Worcestershire
1989	Worcestershire
1990	Middlesex
1991	Essex
1992	Essex
1993	Middlesex
1994	Warwickshire
1995	Warwickshire
1996	Leicestershire

Notes: Since the championship was constituted in 1890 it has been won outright as follows: Yorkshire 29 times, Surrey 15, Middlesex 10, Lancashire 7, Essex and Kent 6, Warwickshire and Worcestershire 5, Nottinghamshire 4, Glamorgan, Hampshire and Leicestershire 2, Derbyshire 1.

The title has been shared three times since 1890, involving Middlesex twice, Kent, Lancashire, Surrey and Yorkshire.

Wooden Spoons: Since the major expansion of the Championship from nine teams to 14 in 1895, the counties have finished outright bottom as follows: Derbyshire, Northamptonshire and Somerset 11; Glamorgan 9; Nottinghamshire 8; Leicestershire 7; Gloucestershire,

Sussex and Worcestershire 6; Hampshire 5; Durham and Warwickshire 3; Kent 2; Essex and Yorkshire 1. Lancashire, Middlesex and Surrey have never finished bottom. Leicestershire have also shared bottom place twice, once with Hampshire and once with Somerset.

From 1977 to 1983 the Championship was sponsored by Schweppes and since 1984 by Britannic Assurance.

BRITANNIC ASSURANCE CHAMPIONSHIP STATISTICS FOR 1996

	For			*Against*		
County	*Runs*	*Wickets*	*Avge*	*Runs*	*Wickets*	*Avge*
Derbyshire	9,699	272	35.65	9,200	283	32.50
Durham	6,912	299	23.11	8,833	244	36.20
Essex	9,527	256	37.21	9,545	275	34.70
Glamorgan	9,895	252	39.26	9,322	251	37.13
Gloucestershire	7,145	276	25.88	7,452	268	27.80
Hampshire	8,687	271	32.05	9,226	257	35.89
Kent	8,384	251	33.40	8,057	277	29.08
Lancashire	9,725	245	39.69	8,940	239	37.40
Leicestershire	8,645	216	40.02	8,135	316	25.74
Middlesex	8,128	287	28.32	8,142	261	31.19
Northamptonshire	8,883	264	33.64	8,691	255	34.08
Nottinghamshire	8,325	269	30.94	8,788	210	41.84
Somerset	8,348	239	34.92	9,108	250	36.43
Surrey	9,686	238	40.69	9,304	282	32.99
Sussex	7,977	293	27.22	7,860	255	30.82
Warwickshire	8,721	278	31.37	8,500	259	32.81
Worcestershire	9,319	242	38.50	9,170	254	36.10
Yorkshire	9,282	265	35.02	9,015	277	32.54
	157,288	4,713	33.37	157,288	4,713	33.37

COUNTY CHAMPIONSHIP – MATCH RESULTS, 1864-1996

County	*Years of Play*	*Played*	*Won*	*Lost*	*Tied*	*Drawn*
Derbyshire	1871-87; 1895-1996	2,224	554	809	1	860
Durham	1992-1996	90	12	55	0	23
Essex	1895-1996	2,186	634	632	5	915
Glamorgan	1921-1996	1,721	376	589	0	756
Gloucestershire	1870-1996	2,460	726	912	2	820
Hampshire	1864-85; 1895-1996	2,296	597	792	4	903
Kent	1864-1996	2,584	934	780	5	865
Lancashire	1865-1996	2,662	985	556	3	1,118
Leicestershire	1895-1996	2,154	482	797	1	874
Middlesex	1864-1996	2,364	887	594	5	878
Northamptonshire	1905-1996	1,921	473	671	3	774
Nottinghamshire	1864-1996	2,493	757	662	1	1,073
Somerset	1882-85; 1891-1996	2,194	519	885	3	787
Surrey	1864-1996	2,741	1,081	610	4	1,046
Sussex	1864-1996	2,633	734	908	6	985
Warwickshire	1895-1996	2,167	588	632	1	946
Worcestershire	1899-1996	2,108	527	732	2	847
Yorkshire	1864-1996	2,761	1,226	476	2	1,057
Cambridgeshire	1864-69; 1871	19	8	8	0	3
		19,889	12,100	12,100	24	7,765

Notes: Matches abandoned without a ball bowled are wholly excluded.

Counties participated in the years shown, except that there were no matches in the years 1915-18 and 1940-45; Hampshire did not play inter-county matches in 1868-69, 1871-74 and 1879; Worcestershire did not take part in the Championship in 1919.

OVERS BOWLED AND RUNS SCORED IN THE BRITANNIC ASSURANCE CHAMPIONSHIP, 1996

County	*Over-rate per hour*	*Run-rate/ 100 balls*
*Derbyshire (2)	15.79	61.16
*Durham (18)	15.92	50.13
Essex (5)	16.14	58.82
Glamorgan (10)	16.74	59.30
Gloucestershire (13)	16.00	51.28
Hampshire (14)	16.14	51.57
Kent (4)	16.33	56.44
Lancashire (15)	16.19	57.60
Leicestershire (1)	16.10	58.14
Middlesex (9)	16.11	52.74
Northamptonshire (16)	16.17	54.86
Nottinghamshire (17)	16.46	51.24
†Somerset (11)	15.27	54.02
*Surrey (3)	15.55	59.71
Sussex (12)	16.03	51.20
Warwickshire (8)	16.41	55.95
Worcestershire (7)	16.60	54.59
Yorkshire (6)	16.28	57.50
1996 average rate	16.12	55.35

1996 Championship positions are shown in brackets.
* £4,000 fine.
† £6,000 fine.

SUMMARY OF RESULTS, 1996

	Derbyshire	Durham	Essex	Glamorgan	Gloucestershire	Hampshire	Kent	Lancashire	Leicestershire	Middlesex	Northamptonshire	Nottinghamshire	Somerset	Surrey	Sussex	Warwickshire	Worcestershire	Yorkshire
Derbyshire	—	**W**	**D**	*W*	**W**	*W*	**D**	*W*	**L**	**W**	*L*	**W**	*D*	*D*	*W*	**L**	**W**	*D*
Durham	*L*	—	**L**	**L**	**D**	*D*	*L*	**L**	**L**	*L*	**D**	*D*	*D*	**L**	*L*	*L*	*L*	**L**
Essex	*D*	*W*	—	**L**	**W**	*W*	**L**	**D**	*L*	*W*	**D**	**W**	*W*	**D**	**L**	*W*	*W*	*L*
Glamorgan	**L**	*W*	*W*	—	*D*	*D*	**D**	**W**	**D**	*L*	*W*	*W*	**W**	**D**	*L*	*L*	**D**	**L**
Gloucestershire	*L*	*D*	*L*	**D**	—	*L*	**W**	*D*	**L**	*W*	**W**	*L*	**D**	**D**	**L**	**W**	*L*	**W**
Hampshire	**L**	**D**	**L**	**D**	**W**	—	*L*	*D*	*D*	**L**	**W**	**D**	*L*	**L**	*D*	*W*	*D*	*L*
Kent	*D*	**W**	*W*	*D*	*L*	**W**	—	**W**	*D*	**D**	*W*	**W**	**W**	*D*	**W**	*W*	**L**	**D**
Lancashire	**L**	*W*	*D*	*L*	**D**	**D**	*L*	—	**D**	**L**	*L*	*D*	**D**	**L**	*W*	*D*	**D**	*D*
Leicestershire	*W*	*W*	**W**	*D*	*W*	**D**	**D**	*D*	—	**W**	**D**	*W*	**W**	*L*	**W**	*D*	**W**	*W*
Middlesex	*L*	**W**	**L**	**W**	**L**	*W*	*D*	*W*	*L*	—	*W*	*W*	**D**	*L*	*L*	**D**	**D**	**W**
Northamptonshire	**W**	*D*	*D*	**L**	*L*	*L*	**L**	**W**	*D*	**L**	—	*D*	*L*	*L*	**W**	**L**	*D*	**D**
Nottinghamshire	*L*	**D**	*L*	**L**	**W**	*D*	*L*	**D**	**L**	**L**	**D**	—	*L*	**D**	**D**	*L*	*D*	*L*
Somerset	**D**	**D**	**L**	*L*	*D*	**W**	*L*	*D*	*L*	*D*	**W**	**W**	—	**D**	*W*	**L**	**L**	*W*
Surrey	**D**	*W*	*D*	*D*	*D*	*W*	**D**	*W*	**W**	**W**	**W**	*D*	*D*	—	**W**	**W**	**L**	*L*
Sussex	**L**	**W**	*W*	**W**	*W*	**D**	*L*	**L**	*L*	**W**	*L*	*D*	**L**	*L*	—	**L**	*L*	**W**
Warwickshire	*W*	**W**	**L**	**W**	*L*	**L**	**L**	**D**	**D**	*D*	*W*	**W**	*W*	*L*	*W*	—	*D*	*L*
Worcestershire	*L*	**W**	**L**	*D*	**W**	**D**	*W*	*D*	*L*	*D*	**D**	**D**	*W*	*W*	**W**	**D**	—	**L**
Yorkshire	**D**	*W*	**W**	*W*	*L*	**W**	*D*	**D**	**L**	*L*	*D*	**W**	**L**	**W**	*L*	**W**	*W*	—

Home games in bold, away games in italics. W = Won, L = Lost, D = Drawn.

COUNTY CHAMPIONSHIP – FINAL POSITIONS, 1890-1996

	Derbyshire	Essex	Glamorgan	Gloucestershire	Hampshire	Kent	Lancashire	Leicestershire	Middlesex	Northamptonshire	Nottinghamshire	Somerset	Surrey	Sussex	Warwickshire	Worcestershire	Yorkshire
1890	—	—	—	6	—	3	2	—	7	—	5	—	1	8	—	—	3
1891	—	—	—	9	—	5	2	—	3	—	4	5	1	7	—	—	8
1892	—	—	—	7	—	7	4	—	5	—	2	3	1	9	—	—	6
1893	—	—	—	9	—	4	2	—	3	—	6	8	5	7	—	—	1
1894	—	—	—	9	—	4	4	—	3	—	7	6	1	8	—	—	2
1895	5	9	—	4	10	14	2	12	6	—	12	8	1	11	6	—	3
1896	7	5	—	10	8	9	2	13	3	—	6	11	4	14	12	—	1
1897	14	3	—	5	9	12	1	13	8	—	10	11	2	6	7	—	4
1898	9	5	—	3	12	7	6	13	2	—	8	13	4	9	9	—	1
1899	15	6	—	9	10	8	4	13	2	—	10	13	1	5	7	12	3
1900	13	10	—	7	15	3	2	14	7	—	5	11	7	3	6	12	1
1901	15	10	—	14	7	7	3	12	2	—	9	12	6	4	5	11	1
1902	10	13	—	14	15	7	5	11	12	—	3	7	4	2	6	9	1
1903	12	8	—	13	14	8	4	14	1	—	5	10	11	2	7	6	3
1904	10	14	—	9	15	3	1	7	4	—	5	12	11	6	7	13	2
1905	14	12	—	8	16	6	2	5	11	13	10	15	4	3	7	8	1
1906	16	7	—	9	8	1	4	15	11	11	5	11	3	10	6	14	2
1907	16	7	—	10	12	8	6	11	5	15	1	14	4	13	9	2	2
1908	14	11	—	10	9	2	7	13	4	15	8	16	3	5	12	6	1
1909	15	14	—	16	8	1	2	13	6	7	10	11	5	4	12	8	3
1910	15	11	—	12	6	1	4	10	3	9	5	16	2	7	14	13	8
1911	14	6	—	12	11	2	4	15	3	10	8	16	5	13	1	9	7
1912	12	15	—	11	6	3	4	13	5	2	8	14	7	10	9	16	1
1913	13	15	—	9	10	1	8	14	6	4	5	16	3	7	11	12	2
1914	12	8	—	16	5	3	11	13	2	9	10	15	1	6	7	14	4
1919	9	14	—	8	7	2	5	9	13	12	3	5	4	11	15	—	1
1920	16	9	—	8	11	5	2	13	1	14	7	10	3	6	12	15	4
1921	12	15	17	7	6	4	5	11	1	13	8	10	2	9	16	14	3
1922	11	8	16	13	6	4	5	14	7	15	2	10	3	9	12	17	1
1923	10	13	16	11	7	5	3	14	8	17	2	9	4	6	12	15	1
1924	17	15	13	6	12	5	4	11	2	16	6	8	3	10	9	14	1
1925	14	7	17	10	9	5	3	12	6	11	4	15	2	13	8	16	1
1926	11	9	8	15	7	3	1	13	6	16	4	14	5	10	12	17	2
1927	5	8	15	12	13	4	1	7	9	16	2	14	6	10	11	17	3
1928	10	16	15	5	12	2	1	9	8	13	3	14	6	7	11	17	4
1929	7	12	17	4	11	8	2	9	6	13	1	15	10	4	14	16	2
1930	9	6	11	2	13	5	1	12	16	17	4	13	8	7	15	10	3
1931	7	10	15	2	12	3	6	16	11	17	5	13	8	4	9	14	1
1932	10	14	15	13	8	3	6	12	10	16	4	7	5	2	9	17	1
1933	6	4	16	10	14	3	5	17	12	13	8	11	9	2	7	15	1
1934	3	8	13	7	14	5	1	12	10	17	9	15	11	2	4	16	5
1935	2	9	13	15	16	10	4	6	3	17	5	14	11	7	8	12	1
1936	1	9	16	4	10	8	11	15	2	17	5	7	6	14	13	12	3
1937	3	6	7	4	14	12	9	16	2	17	10	13	8	5	11	15	1
1938	5	6	16	10	14	9	4	15	2	17	12	7	3	8	13	11	1
1939	9	4	13	3	15	5	6	17	2	16	12	14	8	10	11	7	1
1946	15	8	6	5	10	6	3	11	2	16	13	4	11	17	14	8	1
1947	5	11	9	2	16	4	3	14	1	17	11	11	6	9	15	7	7
1948	6	13	1	8	9	15	5	11	3	17	14	12	2	16	7	10	4
1949	15	9	8	7	16	13	11	17	1	6	11	9	5	13	4	3	1

	Derbyshire	Durham	Essex	Glamorgan	Gloucestershire	Hampshire	Kent	Lancashire	Leicestershire	Middlesex	Northamptonshire	Nottinghamshire	Somerset	Surrey	Sussex	Warwickshire	Worcestershire	Yorkshire
1950	5	—	17	11	7	12	9	1	16	14	10	15	7	1	13	4	6	3
1951	11	—	8	5	12	9	16	3	15	7	13	17	14	6	10	1	4	2
1952	4	—	10	7	9	12	15	3	6	5	8	16	17	1	13	10	14	2
1953	6	—	12	10	6	14	16	3	3	5	11	8	17	1	2	9	15	12
1954	3	—	15	4	13	14	11	10	16	7	7	5	17	1	9	6	11	2
1955	8	—	14	16	12	3	13	9	6	5	7	11	17	1	4	9	15	2
1956	12	—	11	13	3	6	16	2	17	5	4	8	15	1	9	14	9	7
1957	4	—	5	9	12	13	14	6	17	7	2	15	8	1	9	11	16	3
1958	5	—	6	15	14	2	8	7	12	10	4	17	3	1	13	16	9	11
1959	7	—	9	6	2	8	13	5	16	10	11	17	12	3	15	4	14	1
1960	5	—	6	11	8	12	10	2	17	3	9	16	14	7	4	15	13	1
1961	7	—	6	14	5	1	11	13	9	3	16	17	10	15	8	12	4	2
1962	7	—	9	14	4	10	11	16	17	13	8	15	6	5	12	3	2	1
1963	17	—	12	2	8	10	13	15	16	6	7	9	3	11	4	4	14	1
1964	12	—	10	11	17	12	7	14	16	6	3	15	8	4	9	2	1	5
1965	9	—	15	3	10	12	5	13	14	6	2	17	7	8	16	11	1	4
1966	9	—	16	14	15	11	4	12	8	12	5	17	3	7	10	6	2	1
1967	6	—	15	14	17	12	2	11	2	7	9	15	8	4	13	10	5	1
1968	8	—	14	3	16	5	2	6	9	10	13	4	12	15	17	11	7	1
1969	16	—	6	1	2	5	10	15	14	11	9	8	17	3	7	4	12	13
1970	7	—	12	2	17	10	1	3	15	16	14	11	13	5	9	7	6	4
1971	17	—	10	16	8	9	4	3	5	6	14	12	7	1	11	2	15	13
1972	17	—	5	13	3	9	2	15	6	8	4	14	11	12	16	1	7	10
1973	16	—	8	11	5	1	4	12	9	13	3	17	10	2	15	7	6	14
1974	17	—	12	16	14	2	10	8	4	6	3	15	5	7	13	9	1	11
1975	15	—	7	9	16	3	5	4	1	11	8	13	12	6	17	14	10	2
1976	15	—	6	17	3	12	14	16	4	1	2	13	7	9	10	5	11	8
1977	7	—	6	14	3	11	1	16	5	1	9	17	4	14	8	10	13	12
1978	14	—	2	13	10	8	1	12	6	3	17	7	5	16	9	11	15	4
1979	16	—	1	17	10	12	5	13	6	14	11	9	8	3	4	15	2	7
1980	9	—	8	13	7	17	16	15	10	1	12	3	5	2	4	14	11	6
1981	12	—	5	14	13	7	9	16	8	4	15	1	3	6	2	17	11	10
1982	11	—	7	16	15	3	13	12	2	1	9	4	6	5	8	17	14	10
1983	9	—	1	15	12	3	7	12	4	2	6	14	10	8	11	5	16	17
1984	12	—	1	13	17	15	5	16	4	3	11	2	7	8	6	9	10	14
1985	13	—	4	12	3	2	9	14	16	1	10	8	17	6	7	15	5	11
1986	11	—	1	17	2	6	8	15	7	12	9	4	16	3	14	12	5	10
1987	6	—	12	13	10	5	14	2	3	16	7	1	11	4	17	15	9	8
1988	14	—	3	17	10	15	2	9	8	7	12	5	11	4	16	6	1	13
1989	6	—	2	17	9	6	15	4	13	3	5	11	14	12	10	8	1	16
1990	12	—	2	8	13	3	16	6	7	1	11	13	15	9	17	5	4	10
1991	3	—	1	12	13	9	6	8	16	15	10	4	17	5	11	2	6	14
1992	5	18	1	14	10	15	2	12	8	11	3	4	9	13	7	6	17	16
1993	15	18	11	3	17	13	8	13	9	1	4	7	5	6	10	16	2	12
1994	17	16	6	18	12	13	9	10	2	4	5	3	11	7	8	1	15	13
1995	14	17	5	16	6	13	18	4	7	2	3	11	9	12	15	1	10	8
1996	2	18	5	10	13	14	4	15	1	9	16	17	11	3	12	8	7	6

Note: From 1969 onwards, positions have been given in accordance with the Championship regulations which state that "Should *any* sides in the table be equal on points the side with most wins will have priority".

TCCB COUNTY PITCHES TABLE OF MERIT

First-Class Matches

		Points	*Matches*	*Average in 1996*	*Average in 1995*
1	Surrey (5)	100	10	5.00	4.77
	Somerset (8)	110	11	5.00	4.55
3	Derbyshire (10)	108	11	4.91	4.50
4	Sussex (3)	106	11	4.82	4.90
5	Gloucestershire (1)	96	10	4.80	5.00
	Glamorgan (12)	96	10	4.80	4.40
7	Hampshire (1)	93	10	4.65	5.00
	Leicestershire (8)	93	10	4.65	4.55
9	Middlesex (17)	102	11	4.64	3.96
10	Northamptonshire (12)	82	9	4.56	4.40
11	Kent (11)	98	11	4.45	4.45
	Nottinghamshire (14)	98	11	4.45	4.28
	Yorkshire (6)	98	11	4.45	4.73
14	Essex (7)	97	11	4.41	4.70
15	Durham (16)	87	10	4.35	4.00
16	Worcestershire (15)	104	12	4.33	4.10
17	Warwickshire (17)	84	10	4.20	3.96
18	Lancashire (4)	64	8	4.00	4.80
	Oxford University	72	8	4.50	4.94
	Cambridge University	58	7	4.14	4.33

One-Day Matches

		Points	*Matches*	*Average in 1996*	*Average in 1995*
1	Somerset (10)	135	13	5.19	4.50
2	Sussex (1)	113	11	5.14	5.08
3	Derbyshire (5)	132	13	5.08	4.85
4	Surrey (2)	158	16	4.94	5.00
5	Worcestershire (18)	98	10	4.90	3.62
6	Essex (7)	137	14	4.89	4.81
7	Middlesex (15)	127	13	4.88	4.08
8	Kent (6)	117	12	4.88	4.83
9	Leicestershire (16)	114	12	4.75	4.04
10	Gloucestershire (12)	94	10	4.70	4.42
11	Northamptonshire (14)	120	13	4.62	4.25
12	Nottinghamshire (3)	110	12	4.58	4.96
13	Hampshire (4)	97	11	4.41	4.91
14	Lancashire (8)	156	18	4.33	4.73
15	Warwickshire (9)	109	13	4.19	4.54
16	Yorkshire (11)	110	14	3.93	4.44
17	Durham (17)	93	12	3.88	3.67
18	Glamorgan (13)	80	11	3.64	4.32
	Oxford University	24	2	6.00	5.00
	Cambridge University	18	2	4.50	4.75

In both tables 1995 positions are shown in brackets. Each umpire in a game marks the pitch on the following scale of merit: 6 – very good; 5 – good; 4 – above average; 3 – below average; 2 – poor; 1 – unfit.

The tables, provided by the TCCB, cover all major matches, including Tests etc., played on grounds under the county's jurisdiction. Middlesex pitches at Lord's are the responsibility of MCC.

Dean Jones

DERBYSHIRE

President: J. W. Moss
Chairman: M. A. Horton
Chairman, Cricket Committee: B. Holling
Secretary/General Manager: S. Edwards
Captain: D. M. Jones
Coach: W. L. Stillman
Head Groundsman: B. Marsh
Scorer: S. W. Tacey

As the Championship moved into September, Derbyshire were in position to dictate the outcome. They had won four consecutive matches and, were they to win the remaining three, could afford to drop seven of the 24 available bonus points. Their ambition was thwarted by an excess of caution at Taunton, where the teams compiled a record aggregate for a Derbyshire match, 1,606 runs, and destroyed by Warwickshire's victory at Derby. Dominic Cork was injured while batting against Warwickshire and unable to bowl in either innings. This was a crucial blow as resources were already stretched. Derbyshire won their last game, to complete a miserable summer for Durham, and other results confirmed them as runners-up.

Not since their solitary title in 1936 had Derbyshire finished so high. Although disappointed that the Championship escaped, supporters felt they had been treated to purposeful and rewarding cricket. Dean Jones, as captain, and Les Stillman, as coach, inspired the whole club. They came as a pair from Australia after a difficult season at Victoria, where Jones had lost the captaincy and Stillman's contract was not renewed. Here, they blended effectively: Jones insisting that all things were possible, and ready to confront problems head on; Stillman, with a drier, more detached personality, offering a longer-term perspective. It helped that Jones remained a high-class player. He averaged 51.79 in first-class cricket and scored 1,151 runs, a Derbyshire record, in one-day games at an average of 67.70. His four Sunday centuries equalled Tom Moody's achievement for Worcestershire in 1991 and his unbeaten 100 at Old Trafford was a boundary save by Neil Fairbrother away from eliminating Lancashire from the NatWest Trophy.

An unbeaten 214 at Abbeydale Park was Jones's most important Championship innings; having lost their opening game to Leicestershire, Derbyshire faced a Yorkshire total of 561. Collapse could have set the tone for a difficult season, but a partnership of 278 between Jones and John Owen, who scored his maiden century and followed it with another in the victory over Glamorgan, enabled them to save the follow-on with ease. They had a chance of winning but the draw, along with others against Essex, Surrey and Kent, helped to shape the final table. Cork saved the game at The Oval with an unbeaten 82 and help from some courageous assistants. Colin Wells, who was to be released at the end of the season, hobbled painfully with a foot injury and, unable to face the pavilion steps, took tea in the middle. When he was out, Paul Aldred survived 87 minutes with a broken wrist.

The most extraordinary victory was at Old Trafford. Jason Gallian's painstaking 312 lasted into the sixth session and only Percy Perrin, with 343 not out for Essex at Chesterfield in 1904, has ever scored more against Derbyshire. Like Perrin, Gallian finished on the losing side; a county record eighth-wicket stand of 198 between Cork and Karl Krikken saved the follow-on and Derbyshire were able to chase a target on the final day. A straight six off Steve Elworthy broke the record, made sure Lancashire would bat again and took Krikken to his maiden century. At county level, Cork established himself as a genuine all-rounder and his 97 against Nottinghamshire was masterful in the way he bent the attack to his will. Krikken, noisily restless as ever, had a wonderful year as batsman and wicket-keeper. His stumping of Peter Bowler at Taunton, standing up to DeFreitas, was the work of an artist, but he was also utterly reliable.

On the face of it, nobody felt the benefit of the new regime more than Chris Adams. He responded to technical adjustments suggested by Stillman, scored six centuries at No. 3 and held 34 catches in a side whose close catching improved sharply, but the England selectors took no notice, and although Adams praised both Stillman and Jones, his demands to leave the club became more insistent. He offered to buy himself out of his contract and, when this was rejected, threatened to take Derbyshire to the European Court.

Other players' preoccupations seemed far more routine. After 13 years as captain, Kim Barnett settled happily into the ranks and, at the end of May, passed Denis Smith's total of 20,516 runs to put himself at the top of the Derbyshire list. He completed 1,000 runs for the 13th time, another new county mark, and, though he did not quite retain the dash of old, often timed the ball beautifully. There were some sound starts, even if he and Adrian Rollins managed only one century opening stand in the Championship. When Owen faded, Tim O'Gorman revived but, apart from three Sunday assaults, Phillip DeFreitas was disappointing with the bat. One feature among most of the batsmen was increased alertness between the wickets.

Cork's bowling contribution was limited by international calls but the rapid development of Andrew Harris compensated. With only six first-class matches behind him, Harris found extra pace, and bowled straight. He took 12 for 83 against Middlesex, was capped at Taunton and deservedly picked for England A. Devon Malcolm's 82 wickets represented a magnificent recovery from the problems of his South African winter. At one stage, he took 32 in four games and, although expensive near the end, he made a massive contribution. So did DeFreitas, with 64, once he had fully recovered from an elbow operation. Kevin Dean, a left-arm seamer, showed promise. During the season, Allan Warner and Simon Base announced their retirement and Frank Griffith, final-over hero of the 1993 Benson and Hedges Cup final, left the county.

It would not be Derbyshire without controversy, even in a good year. As well as the Adams business, there was a committee-room row. Following a three-hour emergency meeting, the resignation of former Derbyshire and England bowler Harold Rhodes from the committee was unanimously accepted. The meeting followed a petition by members during the Durham game, expressing concern about an alleged dispute with Stillman. – GERALD MORTIMER.

DERBYSHIRE 1996

[*Bill Smith*

Back row: S. J. Base, T. A. Tweats, M. J. Vandrau, A. S. Rollins, K. J. Dean, B. L. Spendlove, M. E. Cassar, S. P. Griffiths. *Middle row:* R. G. Taylor (*secretary/general manager*), J. D. Brown (*youth coach*), A. Hill (*development officer*), P. Aldred, F. A. Griffith, T. J. G. O'Gorman, C. M. Wells, S. J. Lacey, A. J. Harris, J. E. Owen, M. R. May, A. Brentnall (*physiotherapist*), S. W. Tacey (*scorer*). *Front row:* K. M. Krikken, C. J. Adams, D. E. Malcolm, D. M. Jones (*captain*), W. L. Stillman (*coach*), K. J. Barnett, D. G. Cork, A. E. Warner.

DERBYSHIRE RESULTS

All first-class matches – Played 20: Won 10, Lost 3, Drawn 7.

County Championship matches – Played 17: Won 9, Lost 3, Drawn 5.

Competition placings – Britannic Assurance County Championship, 2nd; NatWest Trophy, q-f; Benson and Hedges Cup, 4th in Group A; AXA Equity & Law League, 11th.

COUNTY CHAMPIONSHIP AVERAGES

BATTING

Cap		*M*	*I*	*NO*	*R*	*HS*	*100s*	*50s*	*Avge*	*Ct/St*
1992	C. J. Adams†	17	32	2	1,590	239	6	6	53.00	30
1996	D. M. Jones§	17	32	5	1,338	214*	4	5	49.55	13
1982	K. J. Barnett	17	33	2	1,436	200*	3	9	46.32	4
1993	D. G. Cork	11	19	4	583	97	0	5	38.86	7
1992	K. M. Krikken	17	27	7	776	104	1	2	38.80	60/3
	J. E. Owen†	7	12	0	434	105	2	2	36.16	3
1995	C. M. Wells	10	17	2	512	165	1	2	34.13	4
1995	A. S. Rollins	16	31	4	905	131	2	4	33.51	9
1992	T. J. G. O'Gorman	10	18	2	515	109*	1	4	32.18	7
1994	P. A. J. DeFreitas	13	21	0	356	60	0	1	16.95	8
	P. Aldred†	4	5	2	50	33	0	0	16.66	2
	M. J. Vandrau	8	15	5	141	29	0	0	14.10	4
1996	A. J. Harris	11	15	3	102	17	0	0	8.50	3
	T. A. Tweats	2	4	0	33	26	0	0	8.25	4
1989	D. E. Malcolm	16	21	5	98	21	0	0	6.12	1
	K. J. Dean†	6	7	1	29	12	0	0	4.83	1
	G. A. Khan	2	4	0	10	4	0	0	2.50	4

Also batted: (cap 1990) S. J. Base (1 match) 1; M. R. May† (1 match) 16; G. M. Roberts (1 match) 52 (1 ct).

* *Signifies not out.* † *Born in Derbyshire.* § *Overseas player.*

BOWLING

	O	*M*	*R*	*W*	*BB*	*5W/i*	*Avge*
K. J. Dean	85.1	23	264	11	3-47	0	24.00
P. A. J. DeFreitas	522.2	103	1,610	62	7-101	4	25.96
A. J. Harris	351.1	69	1,282	48	6-40	2	26.70
D. G. Cork	323.2	70	1,039	35	4-53	0	29.68
D. E. Malcolm	586.1	86	2,407	73	6-52	6	32.97
K. J. Barnett	126.2	11	458	10	3-26	0	45.80
M. J. Vandrau	162	23	546	10	6-34	1	54.60

Also bowled: C. J. Adams 10–1–32–0; P. Aldred 97.5–17–388–6; S. J. Base 23.2–4–105–1; D. M. Jones 76.4–11–313–9; G. M. Roberts 36–18–73–1; A. S. Rollins 2–0–25–0; C. M. Wells 154–37–411–9.

COUNTY RECORDS

Highest score for:	274	G. Davidson v Lancashire at Manchester	1896
Highest score against:	343*	P. A. Perrin (Essex) at Chesterfield	1904
Best bowling for:	10-40	W. Bestwick v Glamorgan at Cardiff	1921
Best bowling against:	10-45	R. L. Johnson (Middlesex) at Derby	1994
Highest total for:	645	v Hampshire at Derby	1898
Highest total against:	662	by Yorkshire at Chesterfield	1898
Lowest total for:	16	v Nottinghamshire at Nottingham	1879
Lowest total against:	23	by Hampshire at Burton upon Trent	1958

At Cambridge, April 20, 21, 22. DERBYSHIRE drew with CAMBRIDGE UNIVERSITY.

DERBYSHIRE v LEICESTERSHIRE

At Derby, May 2, 3, 4, 6. Leicestershire won by six wickets. Leicestershire 22 pts, Derbyshire 8 pts. Toss: Leicestershire.

After a blank first day, Barnett marked his 350th first-class appearance for Derbyshire with his third double-century: only Peter Kirsten, with six, has more for the county. Barnett hit 24 fours, two of them all-run, and shared hundred stands with Wells and Krikken. But it was not enough to earn victory. Having taken a first-innings lead of 47, Derbyshire threw away the game on the third evening when, in 25 overs from Millns and Mullally, they subsided to 68 for six. Bowling unchanged, Leicestershire's pace pair converted that into 89 all out on Monday. By keeping a full length and moving the ball, Mullally achieved his best match figures, 11 for 130. Leicestershire required 137. They lost two early wickets but Habib batted with poise and, with his captain, Whitaker, completed victory shortly after tea. Whitaker had kept his team in the match in their first innings; given too many chances to cut and drive, he scored his 31st century, and his seventh against Derbyshire.

Close of play: First day, No play; Second day, Leicestershire 11-0 (G. I. Macmillan 7*, D. L. Maddy 4*); Third day, Derbyshire 68-6 (C. M. Wells 4*, P. A. J. DeFreitas 8*).

Derbyshire

K. J. Barnett not out	200	– b Millns	8
A. S. Rollins c Nixon b Mullally	4	– c Pierson b Millns	18
C. J. Adams c Wells b Parsons	31	– c Wells b Mullally	1
*D. M. Jones c Parsons b Pierson	27	– b Mullally	14
T. A. Tweats c Nixon b Mullally	3	– b Millns	4
C. M. Wells c Smith b Mullally	40	– c Maddy b Mullally	4
P. A. J. DeFreitas c Nixon b Mullally	0	– (8) c Habib b Mullally	19
D. G. Cork c Wells b Mullally	0	– (9) c Parsons b Mullally	8
†K. M. Krikken b Parsons	43	– (10) not out	1
P. Aldred (did not bat)		– (7) c Millns b Mullally	4
D. E. Malcolm (did not bat)		– c Habib b Millns	0
B 2, l-b 7, w 3, n-b 2	14	B 3, l-b 5	8
1/15 2/79 3/132 4/151 5/252 6/258 7/258 8/362	(8 wkts dec.) 362	1/10 2/11 3/37 4/43 5/51 6/57 7/68 8/88 9/89	89

Bonus points – Derbyshire 4, Leicestershire 3.

Bowling: *First Innings*—Millns 19–0–97–0; Mullally 24–3–83–5; Parsons 16.4–1–59–2; Wells 14–2–41–0; Pierson 16–4–63–1; Maddy 7–3–10–0. *Second Innings*—Millns 17.5–5–34–4; Mullally 17–4–47–6.

Leicestershire

G. I. Macmillan c Aldred b Cork	41	– c Krikken b Cork	0
D. L. Maddy c DeFreitas b Aldred	43	– c Adams b DeFreitas	39
B. F. Smith lbw b Cork	0	– c Krikken b Malcolm	3
*J. J. Whitaker c Cork b Malcolm	110	– (5) not out	24
V. J. Wells c Krikken b Aldred	0	– (4) c Krikken b Aldred	24
A. Habib c Krikken b Cork	27	– not out	42
†P. A. Nixon c Jones b Cork	31		
D. J. Millns c Adams b Barnett	9		
A. R. K. Pierson not out	20		
A. D. Mullally lbw b Barnett	1		
G. J. Parsons c Krikken b Barnett	21		
B 2, l-b 3, w 1, n-b 6	12	L-b 1, n-b 4	5
1/74 2/74 3/110 4/110 5/181 6/249 7/265 8/265 9/266	315	1/2 2/13 3/67 4/69	(4 wkts) 137

Bonus points – Leicestershire 3, Derbyshire 4.

Bowling: *First Innings*—Malcolm 22–2–82–1; Cork 26–5–96–4; Aldred 16–4–65–2; DeFreitas 9–1–41–0; Barnett 10.2–1–26–3. *Second Innings*—Cork 16–1–49–1; Malcolm 13–1–42–1; Barnett 1–0–5–0; Aldred 11.1–5–16–1; DeFreitas 7–1–17–1; Jones 1–0–7–0.

Umpires: J. C. Balderstone and R. Palmer.

At Sheffield, May 9, 10, 11, 13. DERBYSHIRE drew with YORKSHIRE.

At Cardiff, May 16, 17, 18, 20. DERBYSHIRE beat GLAMORGAN by 110 runs.

DERBYSHIRE v ESSEX

At Derby, May 23, 24, 25, 27. Drawn. Derbyshire 9 pts, Essex 11 pts. Toss: Essex.

Essex drew a Championship match for the first time since September 1994, as the unpleasant weather left neither team room to manoeuvre. There was no play after tea on the first day, none at all on the second and a washed-out morning on the fourth. The game was played against the background of Derbyshire's feud with Ray Illingworth, England's chairman of selectors, over his criticisms of Malcolm in his new book. Malcolm, fresh from his county-best analysis in Cardiff, restricted his comment on the subject to bowling Gooch, newly elected to the selection panel, in both innings. Steady batting through the order enabled Essex to declare with maximum points, then Owen continued his impressive form – 290 in five innings – for Derbyshire.

Close of play: First day, Essex 225-3 (S. G. Law 30*, P. J. Prichard 12*); Second day, No play; Third day, Derbyshire 215-3 (D. M. Jones 38*, J. E. Owen 37*).

Essex

G. A. Gooch b Malcolm	17	– b Malcolm	0
D. D. J. Robinson c Krikken b Jones	74	– not out	18
N. Hussain lbw b Harris	81		
S. G. Law c Krikken b Harris	30		
*P. J. Prichard c Wells b Base	44		
A. P. Grayson c Adams b Jones	27	– (3) not out	24
†R. J. Rollins not out	46		
M. C. Ilott c Barnett b Harris	6		
N. F. Williams not out	15		
L-b 1, n-b 12	13	B 1, w 1	2
1/21 2/179 3/179 4/225 5/276 6/297 7/310 (7 wkts dec.)	353	1/0 (1 wkt)	44

P. M. Such and A. P. Cowan did not bat.

Bonus points – Essex 4, Derbyshire 3.

Bowling: *First Innings*—Malcolm 23–3–87–1; Harris 30–9–87–3; Base 23.2–4–105–1; Aldred 8–1–37–0; Wells 10–2–12–0; Jones 8–2–24–2. *Second Innings*—Malcolm 4–0–18–1; Aldred 8–1–17–0; Jones 6–2–8–0.

Derbyshire

K. J. Barnett c Rollins b Williams	39
A. S. Rollins c Williams b Such	27
C. J. Adams b Ilott	58
*D. M. Jones c Gooch b Ilott	43
J. E. Owen lbw b Cowan	78
C. M. Wells lbw b Ilott	5
†K. M. Krikken c Law b Williams	22
P. Aldred st Rollins b Such	1
A. J. Harris run out	9
S. J. Base c Rollins b Cowan	1
D. E. Malcolm not out	7
B 5, l-b 11, w 1, n-b 8	25
1/61 2/103 3/154 4/237 5/243 6/284 7/285 8/300 9/302	315

Bonus points – Derbyshire 3, Essex 4.

Bowling: Ilott 29–7–87–3; Cowan 28.3–3–105–2; Such 11–4–24–2; Williams 16–2–69–2; Grayson 6–2–14–0.

Umpires: J. D. Bond and K. J. Lyons.

At The Oval, May 30, 31, June 1, 3. DERBYSHIRE drew with SURREY.

At Southampton, June 6, 7, 8, 10. DERBYSHIRE beat HAMPSHIRE by 54 runs.

At Derby, June 13, 14, 15. DERBYSHIRE beat INDIANS by ten wickets (See Indian tour section).

DERBYSHIRE v MIDDLESEX

At Derby, June 20, 21, 22, 24. Derbyshire won by 363 runs. Derbyshire 23 pts, Middlesex 4 pts. Toss: Derbyshire. Championship debuts: K. J. Dean, M. R. May.

Two outstanding performances steered Derbyshire to one of the most conclusive victories in their history. Their previous biggest margin for a match going into four innings was 317 runs over Warwickshire in 1933. Adams scored twin centuries, the first instance for Derbyshire since John Morris at Taunton in 1990, and Harris took 12 for 83. Adams played with great authority; he thanked coach Les Stillman for adjusting his technique. Harris also bolstered his growing reputation; he had improved on his career-best figures in the victories over Glamorgan and Hampshire, and improved them twice more here. Tufnell bowled splendidly for Middlesex, a factor in Jones's decision not to enforce the follow-on. Instead, he scored a hundred himself and shared an unbroken stand of 208 in 30 overs with Adams before setting Middlesex 540 to win. They survived less than half an hour into the fourth day.

Close of play: First day, Derbyshire 321; Second day, Derbyshire 118-1 (A. S. Rollins 49*, C. J. Adams 10*); Third day, Middlesex 157-6 (K. R. Brown 20*, R. A. Fay 0*).

Derbyshire

K. J. Barnett b Tufnell	53	– c Carr b Fay	55
A. S. Rollins lbw b Fay	14	– c Carr b Fraser	79
C. J. Adams lbw b Fay	125	– not out	136
*D. M. Jones b Fay	10	– not out	100
J. E. Owen c Pooley b Feltham	9		
M. R. May c Harrison b Tufnell	16		
P. A. J. DeFreitas c Brown b Tufnell	18		
†K. M. Krikken not out	46		
A. J. Harris lbw b Tufnell	0		
K. J. Dean lbw b Fraser	7		
D. E. Malcolm lbw b Tufnell	11		
L-b 12	12	B 6, l-b 7	13
1/28 2/186 3/207 4/212 5/227 6/248 7/265 8/269 9/294	321	1/98 2/175 (2 wkts dec.)	383

Bonus points – Derbyshire 3, Middlesex 4.

Bowling: *First Innings*—Fraser 27–6–78–1; Fay 17–1–71–3; Feltham 14–3–48–1; Weekes 10–2–40–0; Tufnell 40.3–14–72–5. *Second Innings*—Fraser 13–1–55–1; Fay 25–8–84–1; Feltham 19–1–75–0; Weekes 12–2–42–0; Tufnell 30–6–85–0; Ramprakash 1–0–4–0; Gatting 4–0–25–0.

Middlesex

P. N. Weekes b Harris	1	– c Krikken b Harris	58
J. C. Harrison lbw b Harris	4	– c Krikken b Harris	0
M. R. Ramprakash c Krikken b Harris	6	– c Adams b Dean	16
*M. W. Gatting c Krikken b Dean	29	– b Harris	24
J. D. Carr b Harris	36	– c DeFreitas b Malcolm	9
J. C. Pooley b Harris	35	– b Barnett	10
†K. R. Brown c Krikken b DeFreitas	1	– not out	29
M. A. Feltham lbw b DeFreitas	0	– (9) lbw b Harris	1
R. A. Fay b DeFreitas	0	– (8) c Krikken b Harris	0
A. R. C. Fraser not out	24	– b Harris	2
P. C. R. Tufnell b Harris	17	– run out	7
B 4, l-b 3, w 1, n-b 4	12	B 4, l-b 5, w 3, n-b 8	20
1/5 2/10 3/23 4/56 5/106 6/107 7/107 8/107 9/127	165	1/6 2/46 3/104 4/121 5/127 6/151 7/158 8/166 9/168	176

Bonus points – Derbyshire 4.

Bowling: *First Innings*—Malcolm 12–5–31–0; Harris 14.3–4–43–6; Dean 11–4–33–1; DeFreitas 14–3–50–3; Jones 2–1–1–0. *Second Innings*—Malcolm 18.1–4–60–1; Harris 16–4–40–6; Dean 7–2–30–1; DeFreitas 10–3–20–0; Barnett 4–0–17–1.

Umpires: D. J. Constant and R. Julian.

At Northampton, June 27, 28, 29. DERBYSHIRE lost to NORTHAMPTONSHIRE by four wickets.

At Chesterfield, July 6, 7, 8. DERBYSHIRE drew with SOUTH AFRICA A (See South Africa A tour section).

At Manchester, July 18, 19, 20, 22. DERBYSHIRE beat LANCASHIRE by two wickets.

DERBYSHIRE v KENT

At Derby, July 25, 26, 27, 29. Drawn. Derbyshire 8 pts, Kent 11 pts. Toss: Kent. Championship debuts: G. A. Khan; E. T. Smith.

Malcolm took two wickets in his first four overs but Hooper, Llong and Fleming all scored centuries on the first day to put Kent on top. They lost their last five for 55 next day and Marsh cracked a finger facing Malcolm, but Headley immediately increased Kent's advantage with a hat-trick in his first over. He had Barnett and Adams caught by Fulton, the stand-in wicket-keeper, and Jones lbw offering no stroke. Headley bowled fast, straight and most impressively to go on to his best figures, eight for 98, but Derbyshire's last five wickets added 216. They were just four short of saving the follow-on. Kent, however, declined to enforce it, a decision called into question when only 11 overs were possible on the final day. Derbyshire survived with five wickets down; Headley finished with 11 wickets, as did Malcolm. Kent learned on Monday that their captain, Benson, was retiring because of the knee injury that had been keeping him out of the team.

Close of play: First day, Kent 381-5 (N. J. Llong 108*, M. M. Patel 3*); Second day, Kent 30-2 (E. T. Smith 11*, C. L. Hooper 0*); Third day, Derbyshire 121-5 (D. M. Jones 23*, A. J. Harris 2*).

Kent

D. P. Fulton c Krikken b Malcolm	0	– c Krikken b Malcolm	0
E. T. Smith c Adams b Wells	31	– c Adams b Malcolm	26
T. R. Ward c Krikken b Malcolm	9	– c Krikken b Harris	16
C. L. Hooper c Wells b Harris	103	– c Khan b Malcolm	5
N. J. Llong b DeFreitas	116	– c Adams b Malcolm	51
M. V. Fleming c Malcolm b Jones	116	– c Khan b DeFreitas	27
M. M. Patel c Adams b Malcolm	10	– (9) c Krikken b Barnett	33
*†S. A. Marsh c Wells b Malcolm	7	– (11) c Adams b Malcolm	15
M. J. McCague c Khan b DeFreitas	27	– (7) c Krikken b Harris	4
D. W. Headley c Krikken b Malcolm	12	– (8) c DeFreitas b Malcolm	38
N. W. Preston not out	2	– (10) not out	17
B 5, l-b 5, n-b 2	12	L-b 5, n-b 8	13
1/0 2/14 3/86 4/186 5/377 6/390 7/398 8/416 9/442	445	1/0 2/30 3/40 4/50 5/87 6/100 7/177 8/182 9/219	245

Bonus points – Kent 4, Derbyshire 3 (Score at 120 overs: 431-8).

Bowling: *First Innings*—Malcolm 37.2–3–116–5; Harris 20–4–78–1; Wells 17–3–47–1; DeFreitas 29–6–123–2; Vandrau 15–3–43–0; Barnett 7–0–22–0; Jones 1–0–6–1. *Second Innings*—Malcolm 25.2–4–89–6; DeFreitas 26.1–9–52–1; Harris 12.5–1–42–2; Vandrau 5–1–16–0; Wells 12–4–34–0; Barnett 6–3–7–1.

Derbyshire

K. J. Barnett c Fulton b Headley	11	– b Headley	54
M. J. Vandrau c Fulton b Headley	26	– lbw b Headley	10
C. J. Adams c Fulton b Headley	0	– c Llong b McCague	13
*D. M. Jones lbw b Headley	0	– not out	43
G. A. Khan c Hooper b McCague	2	– c Hooper b Headley	4
T. J. G. O'Gorman c Hooper b Headley	62	– c Fulton b McCague	2
C. M. Wells c Ward b Preston	52		
P. A. J. DeFreitas c Hooper b Headley	47		
†K. M. Krikken not out	45		
A. J. Harris c Fulton b Headley	11	– (7) not out	15
D. E. Malcolm c sub b Headley	6		
B 5, l-b 6, w 1, n-b 18	30	B 10, l-b 3, n-b 8	21
1/15 2/15 3/15 4/22 5/76 6/152 7/208 8/245 9/266	292	1/40 2/89 3/97 4/102 5/109	(5 wkts) 162

Bonus points – Derbyshire 2, Kent 4.

Bowling: *First Innings*—McCague 16–1–85–1; Headley 18.3–1–98–8; Preston 11–1–40–1; Fleming 5–1–22–0; Patel 5–0–36–0. *Second Innings*—McCague 19–1–79–2; Headley 16–2–67–3; Preston 2.4–0–3–0.

Umpires: J. H. Hampshire and M. J. Kitchen.

DERBYSHIRE v GLOUCESTERSHIRE

At Derby, August 1, 2, 3. Derbyshire won by seven wickets. Derbyshire 23 pts, Gloucestershire 5 pts. Toss: Gloucestershire.

Derbyshire maintained their control from the first ball of the match, when Malcolm dismissed Trainor, until they won on the third afternoon. For the first time since an elbow operation, DeFreitas had figures to match the quality of his bowling, assisted by an immaculate display from Krikken, standing up to the stumps. Walsh also bowled splendidly but Gloucestershire lost Smith to back trouble and conceded a lead of 118. Cork and DeFreitas eliminated any possibility of a Gloucestershire recovery by working through the second innings. Smith, batting with a runner because of his back, was run out in an unusual way on the third morning; he was in his crease when Krikken broke the stumps with the runner, Symonds, out of his ground. Umpire Sharp's original decision, stumped, was later amended to run out after much discussion of Law 2.7 and a ruling from Lord's. Derbyshire required 84 and won inside 24 overs.

Close of play: First day, Derbyshire 166-4 (D. M. Jones 38*, D. G. Cork 1*); Second day, Gloucestershire 156-6 (M. W. Alleyne 24*, J. Lewis 2*).

Gloucestershire

N. J. Trainor lbw b Malcolm	0	– b Malcolm	2
M. G. N. Windows c Krikken b DeFreitas	76	– c Krikken b Cork	25
T. H. C. Hancock b Dean	27	– lbw b DeFreitas	14
M. A. Lynch lbw b Dean	1	– c DeFreitas b Cork	48
M. W. Alleyne c Cork b Malcolm	25	– not out	50
A. Symonds c Krikken b DeFreitas	10	– c Jones b Cork	19
†R. C. Russell c Krikken b DeFreitas	15	– (9) c Cork b DeFreitas	0
R. P. Davis c Krikken b DeFreitas	16	– (7) c Rollins b Cork	5
A. M. Smith c Adams b Cork	1	– (11) run out	10
J. Lewis c Jones b DeFreitas	11	– (8) b Malcolm	8
*C. A. Walsh not out	17	– (10) b DeFreitas	0
L-b 6, n-b 12	18	L-b 6, n-b 14	20
1/0 2/59 3/61 4/114 5/129 6/162 7/181 8/182 9/194	217	1/14 2/53 3/69 4/118 5/144 6/152 7/176 8/185 9/185	201

Bonus points – Gloucestershire 1, Derbyshire 4.

Bowling: *First Innings*—Malcolm 13–3–38–2; Cork 17–2–72–1; DeFreitas 26–10–72–5; Dean 10–2–29–2. *Second Innings*—Malcolm 14–6–25–2; DeFreitas 27.4–5–93–3; Cork 26–9–53–4; Dean 6–2–24–0.

Derbyshire

K. J. Barnett lbw b Alleyne	65	– c Lynch b Lewis	31
A. S. Rollins c Russell b Walsh	0	– not out	31
C. J. Adams b Walsh	15		
*D. M. Jones c Lynch b Walsh	69	– (5) not out	14
T. J. G. O'Gorman b Symonds	21	– (3) c Russell b Lewis	0
D. G. Cork run out	71		
C. M. Wells c Trainor b Lewis	22	– (4) b Alleyne	1
P. A. J. DeFreitas c Davis b Lewis	13		
†K. M. Krikken c sub b Lewis	17		
K. J. Dean c Davis b Walsh	3		
D. E. Malcolm not out	4		
B 8, l-b 11, n-b 16	35	L-b 9, w 1	10
1/1 2/29 3/121 4/155 5/265 6/293 7/311 8/311 9/331	335	1/52 2/52 3/57	(3 wkts) 87

Bonus points – Derbyshire 3, Gloucestershire 4.

Bowling: *First Innings*—Walsh 28–6–110–4; Smith 7–0–33–0; Alleyne 19–5–60–1; Lewis 21.1–6–74–3; Symonds 2–0–11–1; Davis 10–2–28–0. *Second Innings*—Walsh 7–0–33–0; Lewis 11.1–2–37–2; Alleyne 5–1–8–1.

Umpires: J. H. Harris and G. Sharp.

At Hove, August 8, 9, 10, 12. DERBYSHIRE beat SUSSEX by 47 runs.

DERBYSHIRE v NOTTINGHAMSHIRE

At Derby, August 15, 16, 17, 19. Derbyshire won by 303 runs. Derbyshire 23 pts, Nottinghamshire 7 pts. Toss: Derbyshire.

An overwhelming win put Derbyshire on top of the Championship table. They were given a good start by Jones, who was put down three times on the way to his 50th first-class century, and Cork played a majestic 97. He manipulated the bowling skilfully as the last three wickets added 146; Dean, sensibly closing an end, contributed only three to a stand of 87. Johnson and Cairns put on an exhilarating 129 in 22 overs to keep the deficit to 24, but the game ran away from Nottinghamshire on the third day. Barnett, who had earlier completed 1,000 runs for the 13th time, a county record, and Adams added 177 in a surge that enabled Jones to set a target of 402. Malcolm and DeFreitas took four wickets on the third evening – effectively five, as Pollard, hit on the head ducking into a ball from Malcolm, was unable to resume. On the final morning, Nottinghamshire feebly lost their remaining five in 50 minutes for their fifth successive Championship defeat.

Close of play: First day, Derbyshire 310-8 (D. G. Cork 73*, K. J. Dean 3*); Second day, Derbyshire 49-0 (K. J. Barnett 29*, M. J. Vandrau 16*); Third day, Nottinghamshire 72-4 (C. L. Cairns 13*, M. N. Bowen 4*).

Derbyshire

K. J. Barnett b Bowen	32	– c Metcalfe b Afford	103
A. S. Rollins c Noon b Evans	4	– (9) not out	1
C. J. Adams lbw b Cairns	1	– c Cairns b Afford	106
*D. M. Jones lbw b Bowen	105	– c Evans b Afford	36
T. J. G. O'Gorman b Cairns	34	– c Tolley b Afford	58
M. J. Vandrau b Bowen	7	– (2) c Robinson b Cairns	22
†K. M. Krikken c Bowen b Afford	22	– c and b Afford	10
P. A. J. DeFreitas c Johnson b Afford	0	– (6) st Noon b Afford	15
D. G. Cork c Johnson b Bowen	97	– (8) run out	4
K. J. Dean not out	3		
D. E. Malcolm b Bowen	1		
B 10, l-b 9, n-b 16	35	B 9, l-b 13	22
1/8 2/9 3/61 4/124 5/133 6/191 7/195 8/252 9/339	341	1/68 2/245 3/261 4/311 5/330 6/369 7/376 8/377 (8 wkts dec.)	377

Bonus points – Derbyshire 3, Nottinghamshire 4.

Bowling: *First Innings*—Cairns 29–8–105–2; Evans 22–3–74–1; Bowen 30.2–10–53–5; Tolley 21–2–67–0; Afford 9–2–23–2. *Second Innings*—Cairns 12–2–42–1; Bowen 24–2–100–0; Afford 33.5–8–87–6; Evans 20–3–57–0; Tolley 7–0–59–0; Afzaal 2–0–10–0.

Nottinghamshire

P. R. Pollard c sub b DeFreitas	2	– retired hurt	14
R. T. Robinson c Krikken b DeFreitas	53	– b Malcolm	15
A. A. Metcalfe lbw b Dean	16	– (4) c Adams b DeFreitas	3
*P. Johnson c Krikken b Malcolm	82	– (3) c Adams b DeFreitas	0
U. Afzaal lbw b DeFreitas	0	– b Malcolm	7
C. L. Cairns c O'Gorman b Malcolm	75	– c Rollins b Malcolm	20
C. M. Tolley b DeFreitas	27	– (8) b Malcolm	0
K. P. Evans c Adams b Dean	9	– (9) b DeFreitas	1
†W. M. Noon not out	9	– (10) c Rollins b Malcolm	7
M. N. Bowen lbw b Dean	4	– (7) c Jones b DeFreitas	14
J. A. Afford lbw b DeFreitas	0	– not out	0
B 15, l-b 3, w 2, n-b 20	40	L-b 2, w 5, n-b 10	17
1/12 2/56 3/115 4/115 5/244 6/281 7/301 8/303 9/312	317	1/43 2/43 3/46 4/66 5/79 6/79 7/80 8/98 9/98	98

Bonus points – Nottinghamshire 3, Derbyshire 4.

In the second innings P. R. Pollard retired hurt at 43-1.

Bowling: *First Innings*—Malcolm 19–1–108–2; DeFreitas 20.5–4–54–5; Cork 14–2–53–0; Dean 17–4–47–3; Vandrau 1–0–17–0; Barnett 7–2–20–0. *Second Innings*—Malcolm 16–2–43–5; DeFreitas 15.3–3–53–4.

Umpires: K. E. Palmer and R. A. White.

DERBYSHIRE v WORCESTERSHIRE

At Chesterfield, August 29, 30, 31. Derbyshire won by nine wickets. Derbyshire 24 pts, Worcestershire 5 pts. Toss: Derbyshire. Championship debut: B. E. A. Preece.

Despite fine centuries by Weston and Spiring, Derbyshire had more than four sessions to spare in their fourth consecutive Championship victory. Weston carried his bat through Worcestershire's first innings, which mustered only 238. In reply, Barnett timed his strokes superbly, sharing Derbyshire's first century opening partnership of the season with Rollins. Then Adams scored his sixth century of 1996 and O'Gorman his first for two years, before Moody wrapped up the innings. The centurions both held brilliant close catches as Derbyshire took five wickets on the second evening. Spiring and Rhodes batted through the third morning to avoid an innings defeat, Spiring going on to a determined unbeaten century, but once DeFreitas – acting-captain because Jones had bruised his ribs facing Sheriyar – dismissed Rhodes, Derbyshire were in sight of a victory which made them bookmakers' favourites for the title, a point behind leaders Kent with a game in hand.

Close of play: First day, Derbyshire 166-1 (K. J. Barnett 83*, C. J. Adams 23*); Second day, Worcestershire 133-5 (K. R. Spiring 29*, S. J. Rhodes 1*).

Worcestershire

T. S. Curtis c Krikken b Malcolm	0	– lbw b Malcolm	8
W. P. C. Weston not out	100	– lbw b DeFreitas	18
G. A. Hick lbw b DeFreitas	9	– c O'Gorman b DeFreitas	30
*T. M. Moody b DeFreitas	4	– c Krikken b Cork	12
K. R. Spiring run out	12	– not out	130
V. S. Solanki c Cork b Malcolm	58	– c Adams b Cork	31
†S. J. Rhodes c Cork b Harris	24	– c O'Gorman b DeFreitas	57
S. R. Lampitt lbw b Cork	1	– lbw b Malcolm	1
R. K. Illingworth c Jones b Harris	0	– absent ill	
A. Sheriyar c Krikken b Harris	13	– (9) c Dean b DeFreitas	2
B. E. A. Preece b Harris	0	– (10) c Krikken b Cork	2
L-b 6, w 1, n-b 10	17	B 2, l-b 1, w 1, n-b 8	12
1/0 2/13 3/23 4/44 5/133 6/193 7/194 8/195 9/238	238	1/24 2/28 3/62 4/77 5/129 6/275 7/276 8/285 9/303	303

Bonus points – Worcestershire 1, Derbyshire 4.

Bowling: *First Innings*—Malcolm 14–2–95–2; DeFreitas 10–1–44–2; Harris 8.5–1–31–4; Cork 17–4–57–1; Dean 2–0–5–0. *Second Innings*—Malcolm 20–1–102–2; DeFreitas 25.3–3–70–4; Harris 13–4–54–0; Cork 22.1–6–60–3; Barnett 1.3–0–14–0.

Derbyshire

K. J. Barnett c Rhodes b Sheriyar	87	– not out	27
A. S. Rollins c Illingworth b Lampitt	39	– b Curtis	41
C. J. Adams c Solanki b Illingworth	123	– not out	1
*D. M. Jones b Preece	9		
T. J. G. O'Gorman not out	109		
D. G. Cork c Preece b Moody	10		
†K. M. Krikken b Moody	0		
P. A. J. DeFreitas c Hick b Moody	38		
A. J. Harris c and b Moody	6		
K. J. Dean c Lampitt b Moody	12		
D. E. Malcolm b Moody	0		
B 3, l-b 4, w 1, n-b 30	38	L-b 1, w 1	2
1/108 2/181 3/230 4/360 5/381 6/385 7/427 8/434 9/471	471	1/70	(1 wkt) 71

Bonus points – Derbyshire 4, Worcestershire 4.

Bowling: *First Innings*—Sheriyar 29–5–95–1; Preece 15–0–84–1; Moody 16.5–3–82–6; Lampitt 18–2–105–1; Illingworth 24–10–71–1; Solanki 9–3–27–0. *Second Innings*—Sheriyar 5–0–22–0; Preece 5–0–47–0; Curtis 0.3–0–1–1.

Umpires: B. Dudleston and T. E. Jesty.

At Taunton, September 3, 4, 5, 6. DERBYSHIRE drew with SOMERSET.

DERBYSHIRE v WARWICKSHIRE

At Derby, September 12, 13, 14. Warwickshire won by four wickets. Warwickshire 21 pts, Derbyshire 5 pts. Toss: Warwickshire.

After drawing at Taunton, Derbyshire had to beat Warwickshire to retain an interest in the title. But they were short of bowling. With Dean and Wells unfit, they then lost Cork who was hit on the left shoulder by Brown in the first innings, suffered a hairline fracture of the humerus and was unable to bowl, although he was strapped up to bat again. That reduced Derbyshire to three front-line bowlers and, of those, Malcolm was unduly expensive. In conditions assisting seam, 15 wickets fell on the first day. Adams held the home county together, then DeFreitas bowled unchanged for seven wickets, his best return for Derbyshire. But Welch and Munton added 62 for the last wicket to restrict the deficit to 11 and the match began to lean Warwickshire's way. Chasing 267 in the final innings, Warwickshire slumped to 84 for five, but Penney and Giles were prepared to wait for bowlers to wilt and shared an unbroken partnership of 129. As Jones admitted, Derbyshire had no punches left to throw.

Close of play: First day, Warwickshire 131-5 (D. R. Brown 19*, K. J. Piper 5*); Second day, Derbyshire 189-6 (K. M. Krikken 14*, P. A. J. DeFreitas 12*).

Derbyshire

K. J. Barnett c Piper b Welch	27	– lbw b Small	14
A. S. Rollins lbw b Brown	27	– b Munton	5
C. J. Adams b Small	80	– c and b Munton	24
*D. M. Jones lbw b Munton	9	– st Piper b Giles	39
T. J. G. O'Gorman c Knight b Brown	4	– b Brown	66
G. A. Khan c Piper b Brown	0	– run out	4
D. G. Cork c Knight b Small	29	– (9) c Brown b Welch	23
†K. M. Krikken not out	32	– (7) not out	30
P. A. J. DeFreitas c Piper b Welch	0	– (8) c Welch b Munton	23
A. J. Harris c Penney b Small	2	– c Penney b Welch	3
D. E. Malcolm b Welch	13	– run out	4
B 2, l-b 11, w 4, n-b 2	19	L-b 10, n-b 10	20
1/53 2/73 3/126 4/133 5/135 6/184 7/195 8/196 9/203	242	1/20 2/26 3/47 4/128 5/146 6/175 7/201 8/236 9/244	255

Bonus points – Derbyshire 1, Warwickshire 4.

Bowling: *First Innings*—Small 18–6–41–3; Munton 19–5–57–1; Welch 17.5–2–62–3; Brown 15–5–69–3. *Second Innings*—Welch 18.5–2–59–2; Munton 33–8–79–3; Small 12–3–28–1; Brown 16–2–46–1; Burns 3–0–13–0; Giles 14–6–20–1.

Warwickshire

N. V. Knight c Krikken b DeFreitas	54	– c Rollins b Malcolm	41
A. J. Moles b Harris	28	– c DeFreitas b Malcolm	15
W. G. Khan lbw b DeFreitas	1	– lbw b Harris	8
M. Burns b DeFreitas	0	– c Adams b Harris	1
T. L. Penney c Krikken b DeFreitas	12	– not out	83
D. R. Brown b DeFreitas	27	– lbw b DeFreitas	4
†K. J. Piper b DeFreitas	16	– b Barnett	32
A. F. Giles c Krikken b Harris	9	– not out	67
G. Welch c Khan b Harris	45		
G. C. Small lbw b DeFreitas	0		
*T. A. Munton not out	26		
L-b 5, n-b 8	13	L-b 10, w 1, n-b 8	19
1/79 2/88 3/93 4/96 5/115 6/142 7/159 8/159 9/169	231	1/29 2/48 3/60 4/77 5/84 6/141	(6 wkts) 270

Bonus points – Warwickshire 1, Derbyshire 4.

Bowling: *First Innings*—Malcolm 8–0–62–0; DeFreitas 32–7–101–7; Harris 24.5–4–63–3. *Second Innings*—Malcolm 24–2–104–2; DeFreitas 21–7–43–1; Harris 15–1–82–2; Barnett 12.3–2–31–1.

Umpires: M. J. Kitchen and B. Leadbeater.

DERBYSHIRE v DURHAM

At Derby, September 19, 20, 21. Derbyshire won by eight wickets. Derbyshire 22 pts, Durham 4 pts. Toss: Durham.

Durham's abominable season got even worse when it was announced that they had suspended Blenkiron and Birbeck because of an incident after a party when two club cars were damaged. On the field, they batted better than normal in the second innings but still slumped predictably to their 12th defeat, enabling Derbyshire to finish as runners-up, their best placing since they won in 1936. Durham began with their usual batting collapse and suffered as Adams, with 81 from 60 balls, batted gloriously with Jones. But Derbyshire missed a chance to take total control when the last eight wickets added only 116. In the second innings, Morris and Roseberry completed distressing seasons with only eight runs between them in the match, but Hutton and then Cox, carving effectively past gully, gave Durham a glimmer of hope. However, Derbyshire made light work of their target of 219 and, appropriately, captain Jones hit the winning runs to round off a satisfying if not quite triumphant season.

Close of play: First day, Derbyshire 136-2 (C. J. Adams 77*, D. M. Jones 39*); Second day, Durham 206-5 (S. Hutton 85*, D. M. Cox 51*).

Durham

S. Hutton c Adams b Malcolm	19	– run out	86
J. E. Morris c Adams b DeFreitas	5	– c O'Gorman b Malcolm	0
J. A. Daley c Adams b DeFreitas	35	– b Harris	33
M. A. Roseberry lbw b DeFreitas	2	– c Adams b Dean	1
P. D. Collingwood c Krikken b DeFreitas	5	– c Krikken b Malcolm	34
†D. G. C. Ligertwood b DeFreitas	0	– c Krikken b Malcolm	0
D. M. Cox c Jones b Harris	22	– c Krikken b DeFreitas	91
M. M. Betts b Dean	32	– b DeFreitas	26
*S. J. E. Brown c Adams b Harris	3	– lbw b DeFreitas	44
M. J. Saggers b Harris	12	– c O'Gorman b DeFreitas	7
A. Walker not out	1	– not out	4
B 1, l-b 4, w 1	6	L-b 4, w 2	6
1/6 2/38 3/47 4/67 5/67 6/80 7/104 8/117 9/135	142	1/1 2/72 3/73 4/138 5/138 6/219 7/270 8/285 9/299	332

Bonus points – Derbyshire 4.

Bowling: *First Innings*—Malcolm 11–2–41–1; DeFreitas 21–2–60–5; Harris 12–4–32–3; Dean 1.1–0–4–1. *Second Innings*—Malcolm 29–2–141–3; DeFreitas 20.2–3–54–4; Wells 15–5–40–0; Harris 23–7–80–1; Dean 8–4–13–1.

Derbyshire

K. J. Barnett c Ligertwood b Betts	16	– c Collingwood b Brown	4
A. S. Rollins lbw b Betts	4	– not out	69
C. J. Adams c Ligertwood b Betts	81	– c Ligertwood b Cox	64
*D. M. Jones b Saggers	77	– not out	71
T. J. G. O'Gorman lbw b Betts	11		
C. M. Wells lbw b Saggers	19		
†K. M. Krikken not out	29		
P. A. J. DeFreitas b Cox	10		
A. J. Harris lbw b Brown	1		
K. J. Dean c Collingwood b Brown	0		
D. E. Malcolm run out	1		
L-b 3, w 4	7	B 4, l-b 6, n-b 2	12
1/8 2/47 3/140 4/180 5/211 6/216 7/245 8/246 9/246	256	1/4 2/104 (2 wkts)	220

Bonus points – Derbyshire 2, Durham 4.

Bowling: *First Innings*—Brown 14–3–55–2; Betts 17–1–69–4; Walker 11–4–46–0; Saggers 9–0–60–2; Cox 6–1–23–1. *Second Innings*—Brown 9–1–51–1; Betts 9–1–54–0; Walker 9–2–31–0; Saggers 5–1–19–0; Cox 14.3–2–55–1.

Umpires: J. C. Balderstone and J. H. Harris.

FIELDING IN 1996

(Qualification: 20 dismissals)

67	K. M. Krikken (64 ct, 3 st)	33	W. M. Noon (30 ct, 3 st)
67	R. J. Turner (64 ct, 3 st)	33	A. D. Shaw (28 ct, 5 st)
62	P. A. Nixon (56 ct, 6 st)	32	D. Byas
62	R. J. Rollins (56 ct, 6 st)	28	J. D. Carr
61	K. R. Brown (60 ct, 1 st)	27	K. J. Piper (21 ct, 6 st)
55	W. K. Hegg (50 ct, 5 st)	25	†D. P. Fulton
52	P. Moores (50 ct, 2 st)	25	S. G. Law
51	R. C. Russell (48 ct, 3 st)	23	D. Ripley
48	S. J. Rhodes (40 ct, 8 st)	22	G. J. Parsons
46	G. J. Kersey (45 ct, 1 st)	22	J. C. Pooley
45	A. N. Aymes (42 ct, 3 st)	21	A. D. Brown
44	R. J. Blakey (40 ct, 4 st)	21	M. A. Butcher
36	D. G. C. Ligertwood (31 ct, 5 st)	21	*Rashid Latif (17 ct, 4 st)
35	D. P. Ostler	20	M. P. Maynard
35	P. V. Simmons	20	C. W. Scott
34	C. J. Adams	20	*R. J. Warren (19 ct, 1 st)
34	*S. A. Marsh (28 ct, 6 st)	20	V. J. Wells
33	C. L. Hooper	20	W. P. Weston

** S. A. Marsh and Rashid Latif each took one catch in the field and R. J. Warren took eight.*
† D. P. Fulton took five catches as wicket-keeper.

WINLESS CHAMPIONSHIP SEASONS SINCE THE WAR

		P	*W*	*L*	*D*	*Position*
1967	Nottinghamshire	28	0	4	24	16
1979	Glamorgan	21	0	10	11	17
1982	Warwickshire	22	0	8	14	17
1996	Durham	17	0	12	5	18

Note: In 1967 Nottinghamshire finished ahead of Gloucestershire, who had three wins.

Simon Brown

DURHAM

Patrons: Sir Donald Bradman and A. W. Austin
President: D. W. Midgley
Chairman: J. D. Robson
Director of Cricket: G. Cook
Chief Executive: M. Candlish
Coach: N. Gifford
Captain: 1996 – M. A. Roseberry
1997 – D. C. Boon
Head Groundsman: T. Flintoft
Scorer: B. Hunt

Durham could scarcely have endured a more disastrous season. Other than the two victories which earned them the Costcutter Cup at Harrogate, their only win against first-class opposition was in a Sunday League match against Essex. Generally they were outplayed in one-day combat even more comprehensively than in the Championship, as their lack of all-rounders and hard-hitting batsmen was exposed. The cutlery drawer began to bulge as the third wooden spoon in five years in the Championship was joined by the first from the Sunday League.

Yet Simon Brown was one of the leading bowlers in the country, with 79 wickets, and only three counties picked up more bowling points than Durham's 60. David Cox and Melvyn Betts made big advances with bat and ball, and Paul Collingwood's initial impact, in his first season on the staff, was hugely encouraging. But the senior batsmen failed to provide the necessary pillars of support for the developing youngsters.

Mike Roseberry and John Morris, captain and vice-captain, had to score heavily if Durham's transition from a team of seasoned imports to one of local talent was to succeed. But the two contested signings, both on six-year contracts, managed a joint Championship tally of 868 runs. Morris had previously enjoyed two reasonably successful seasons for Durham, but for Roseberry it was his second year of failure. He resigned the captaincy at the end of August. Three days later, it was announced that the Australian batsman, David Boon, would take over in 1997. Surrendering the captaincy did nothing for Roseberry's form, however, and, under the reluctant leadership of Brown, Durham finished the season in rudderless disarray.

It had begun brightly enough, with moral victories against Hampshire and Nottinghamshire, but, after the NatWest Trophy second-round mauling by Essex, Durham went into terminal decline. They used 25 players in the Championship, including two young pace bowlers, Martin Saggers and Stephen Harmison, who were hurriedly registered in time for first-class debuts. This was necessitated largely by injuries, the first of which cut short a promising start by Michael Foster, the Leeds-born all-rounder who had spent two years with Yorkshire and one with Northamptonshire. He was awarded a two-year contract only to suffer a stress fracture of the back. Similar ailments had kept Steve Lugsden and John Wood out of action the previous season and both succumbed to further injuries after showing brief glimpses of their potential. Collingwood, who took a wicket with his first ball and made 91 on debut, quickly developed a back problem, which prevented him from bowling, and the other young all-rounder, Shaun Birbeck, played only one Championship match before he was also sidelined and subsequently released. This left Phil Bainbridge as the only all-rounder fit to bowl, and even that was questionable. Although he performed admirably with the bat, he brought forward his retirement as aches and pains took their toll.

At least he retired on the back of a testimonial season. Wicket-keeper Chris Scott, another survivor from Durham's debut season in 1992, was allowed to drift away after losing his place through injury in June. Scott, a quiet battler who earned the members' respect, made his final appearance for the club in the Bain Hogg Trophy final defeat at Leicester, which was the culmination of another successful season for the Second Eleven. Also released was Jon Longley, at his own request, after it became clear he did not feature in the first team's plans.

It was after the failure to beat Nottinghamshire, at Trent Bridge in early June, having enforced the follow-on, that things began to go wrong. In the next match, at Hove, Durham's young batsmen were mesmerised by Ian Salisbury, who took six for 15 to put Sussex on the way to an innings victory. Further drubbings by Lancashire and Surrey followed. Although Gloucestershire might have been beaten but for the rain, it was merely a blip on the downward curve; in five of their last eight innings, Durham failed to muster 150.

The biggest revelation was the batting of Cox. Brought in as a slow left-armer at Hove, he made 67 batting at No. 11 and he twice ventured into the nineties to finish comfortably top of the batting averages with 434 runs at 48.22. He gave most of the credit for his progress to the new coach, Norman Gifford. Darren Blenkiron began with two hundreds but barely reached double figures after his confrontation with Salisbury. The only other Championship centuries were scored by Stewart Hutton and Sherwin Campbell, with one each. Hutton otherwise failed to make significant progress; the same applied to Jimmy Daley, whose season was again interrupted by a broken finger suffered at the Riverside Ground. Campbell had a top score there of 39. He prospered elsewhere, but nothing like as much as everyone expected after his double-century for West Indies in April and, despite a few stunning slip catches, he was largely anonymous on the field.

Roseberry's failings were all the more disappointing because of the unanimous welcome his appointment received in 1995. He could not be faulted for effort, and remained unfailingly courteous throughout his troubles, but always felt that playing on immature surfaces hindered his developing side. While the umpires' marks suggested that the Riverside pitches had improved, a deep distrust was embedded in the Durham batsmen's minds, which clearly sapped their confidence. Nick Speak and Jonathan Lewis, the new signings from Lancashire and Essex, will need to be optimists. The management were also convinced that the pitches would not take spin and persevered with a futile policy of fielding an all-seam attack at Chester-le-Street.

Gifford acted as team manager as well as coach, and this allowed Geoff Cook, the director of cricket, to adopt a lower profile, concentrating on youth development. He had plenty to work with, but the members were growing increasingly impatient. And the general sense of embarrassment was summed up when even the end-of-season party ended in disaster: two players, Birbeck and Blenkiron, were suspended for damaging club cars. – TIM WELLOCK.

DURHAM 1996

[*Bill Smith*

Back row: J. I. Longley, A. Pratt, J. Wood, D. G. C. Ligertwood, S. D. Birbeck, M. M. Betts, S. Lugsden, I. Jones, N. Killeen, D. M. Cox, D. A. Blenkiron, J. P. Searle, C. L. Campbell, P. D. Collingwood, J. A. Daley. *Front row:* S. J. E. Brown, A. Walker, J. E. Morris, M. A. Roseberry (*captain*), P. Bainbridge, J. Boiling, S. Hutton, C. W. Scott. *Inset:* S. L. Campbell.

DURHAM RESULTS

All first-class matches – Played 19: Lost 13, Drawn 6.

County Championship matches – Played 17: Lost 12, Drawn 5.

Competition placings – Britannic Assurance County Championship, 18th; NatWest Trophy, 2nd round; Benson and Hedges Cup, 5th in Group A; AXA Equity & Law League, 18th.

COUNTY CHAMPIONSHIP AVERAGES

BATTING

	M	*I*	*NO*	*R*	*HS*	*100s*	*50s*	*Avge*	*Ct/St*
D. M. Cox	7	13	4	434	95*	0	4	48.22	2
S. L. Campbell§	15	27	0	1,019	118	1	7	37.74	15
P. Bainbridge	11	19	1	617	83	0	5	34.27	10
S. Hutton†	12	23	1	599	143*	1	1	27.22	5
J. A. Daley†	9	17	2	357	36	0	0	23.80	6
D. A. Blenkiron	9	16	2	328	130	2	0	23.42	4
P. D. Collingwood†	11	20	0	464	91	0	2	23.20	6
C. W. Scott	6	10	1	208	59	0	2	23.11	19
D. G. C. Ligertwood	11	21	5	324	56	0	1	20.25	26/5
M. M. Betts†	13	21	3	308	57*	0	1	17.11	4
M. A. Roseberry†	15	27	0	458	60	0	2	16.96	6
S. J. E. Brown†	16	27	4	389	60	0	1	16.91	3
J. E. Morris	15	28	0	410	83	0	3	14.64	8
M. J. Saggers	4	7	1	69	18	0	0	11.50	0
J. Boiling	7	11	4	79	31*	0	0	11.28	8
M. J. Foster	3	6	0	67	25	0	0	11.16	0
A. Walker	3	6	3	25	20	0	0	8.33	0
J. Wood	8	14	2	76	35*	0	0	6.33	4
S. Lugsden†	3	5	1	19	9	0	0	4.75	1
N. Killeen†	3	5	0	8	6	0	0	1.60	1

Also batted: S. D. Birbeck† (1 match) 0, 8; C. L. Campbell (1 match) 7; S. J. Harmison (1 match) 6, 4; J. I. Longley (1 match) 2, 4; R. M. S. Weston† (2 matches) 3, 9, 2 (1 ct).

* *Signifies not out.* † *Born in Durham.* § *Overseas player.*
Durham have awarded all playing staff caps.

BOWLING

	O	*M*	*R*	*W*	*BB*	*5W/i*	*Avge*
S. Lugsden	70.3	9	262	11	3-45	0	23.81
S. J. E. Brown	567.1	98	1,859	69	6-77	4	26.94
N. Killeen	83.2	18	293	10	4-57	0	29.30
D. M. Cox	306	87	883	26	5-97	2	33.96
M. J. Saggers	87.5	9	372	10	6-65	1	37.20
M. M. Betts	375.5	48	1,708	44	5-68	2	38.81
J. Wood	263.3	41	1,112	24	4-60	0	46.33

Also bowled: P. Bainbridge 123.3–23–382–7; S. D. Birbeck 31–9–88–3; D. A. Blenkiron 37.5–9–123–5; J. Boiling 237.1–77–532–8; C. L. Campbell 15.2–3–44–1; S. L. Campbell 16.4–3–60–1; P. D. Collingwood 55.2–7–181–3; M. J. Foster 93.3–5–311–8; S. J. Harmison 9–1–77–0; J. E. Morris 1–0–10–0; A. Walker 80–13–277–2; R. M. S. Weston 1–1–0–0.

COUNTY RECORDS

Highest score for:	204	J. E. Morris v Warwickshire at Birmingham	1994
Highest score against:	501*	B. C. Lara (Warwickshire) at Birmingham	1994
Best bowling for:	8-118	A. Walker v Essex at Chelmsford	1995
Best bowling against:	8-22	D. Follett (Middlesex) at Lord's	1996
Highest total for:	625-6 dec.	v Derbyshire at Chesterfield	1994
Highest total against:	810-4 dec.	by Warwickshire at Birmingham	1994
Lowest total for:	67	v Middlesex at Lord's	1996
Lowest total against:	73	by Oxford University at Oxford	1994

At Oxford, April 17, 18, 19. DURHAM drew with OXFORD UNIVERSITY.

DURHAM v NORTHAMPTONSHIRE

At Chester-le-Street, May 2, 3, 4, 6. Drawn. Durham 8 pts, Northamptonshire 9 pts. Toss: Durham. First-class debut: P. D. Collingwood.

After the opening day was washed out, Northamptonshire's first innings spread into the third day. But they reached 320 and had hopes of enforcing the follow-on when they reduced Durham to 44 for three. Paul Collingwood, however, made an assured 91 to continue a remarkable debut: he had bowled Capel with his first ball in first-class cricket, a feat not achieved in the Championship for 15 years until Jamie Hewitt of Middlesex the previous day. Roseberry made his highest Championship score for Durham – a four-hour 59 – and declared 99 behind. On the final day, Northamptonshire lost three men cheaply in the search for quick runs. After another interruption for rain they set a target of 222 in 44 overs. But Durham concentrated on avoiding defeat; when a brief acceleration was accompanied by the loss of wickets, they called a halt to the chase. The visiting captain, Bailey, commented, "If that's the way they want to play cricket, good luck to them." There was another debutant in the match, besides Collingwood; John Emburey was making his first first-class appearance for Northamptonshire. But it was his 500th first-class game in all. His debut for Middlesex was in 1973, three years before Collingwood was born.

Close of play: First day, No play; Second day, Northamptonshire 273-7 (K. M. Curran 47*, D. Ripley 12*); Third day, Durham 221-7 (P. Bainbridge 25*).

Northamptonshire

R. R. Montgomerie c Collingwood b Foster	22	– not out	55
A. Fordham c Scott b Betts	40		
*R. J. Bailey c Brown b Betts	45	– c Boiling b Brown	3
M. B. Loye lbw b Betts	4	– c Bainbridge b Betts	11
R. J. Warren c Morris b Betts	34	– (2) c Scott b Brown	2
D. J. Capel b Collingwood	14	– (5) c Bainbridge b Collingwood	40
K. M. Curran c Collingwood b Brown	68	– (6) not out	10
A. L. Penberthy b Boiling	31		
†D. Ripley b Brown	34		
J. E. Emburey c Betts b Brown	1		
J. P. Taylor not out	0		
L-b 6, w 1, n-b 20	27	L-b 1	1
1/69 2/69 3/76 4/144 5/176 6/178 7/247 8/315 9/320	320	1/7 2/13 3/26 4/101 (4 wkts dec.)	122

Bonus points – Northamptonshire 3, Durham 4.

Bowling: *First Innings*—Brown 29.4–5–78–3; Betts 29–5–120–4; Foster 22–4–59–1; Bainbridge 9–4–14–0; Boiling 21–10–30–1; Collingwood 7–2–13–1. *Second Innings*—Brown 8–1–36–2; Betts 6–0–21–1; Foster 4–0–28–0; Boiling 5–0–22–0; Collingwood 2.2–0–14–1.

Durham

S. Hutton lbw b Taylor	0	– c Montgomerie b Emburey	16
*M. A. Roseberry c Loye b Taylor	59	– c Capel b Penberthy	33
J. A. Daley b Curran	13	– (7) not out	20
J. E. Morris c Ripley b Curran	7	– (3) c sub b Penberthy	35
P. D. Collingwood c Curran b Penberthy	91	– c Warren b Taylor	16
P. Bainbridge not out	25	– lbw b Taylor	19
M. J. Foster b Emburey	6	– (4) c Warren b Penberthy	12
†C. W. Scott b Penberthy	5	– b Taylor	4
J. Boiling (did not bat)		– not out	2
B 5, l-b 6, n-b 4	15	L-b 5, n-b 6	11
1/0 2/34 3/44 4/151 5/203 6/210 7/221 (7 wkts dec.)	221	1/31 2/70 3/90 4/110 5/134 6/144 7/150 (7 wkts)	168

S. J. E. Brown and M. M. Betts did not bat.

Bonus points – Durham 1, Northamptonshire 3.

Bowling: *First Innings*—Taylor 20–4–47–2; Capel 17–0–46–0; Curran 14–3–34–2; Emburey 25–8–53–1; Penberthy 12.4–3–30–2. *Second Innings*—Taylor 11–2–29–3; Curran 4–1–9–0; Emburey 14–1–54–1; Capel 7–0–32–0; Penberthy 7–0–37–3; Bailey 0.4–0–2–0.

Umpires: K. J. Lyons and A. G. T. Whitehead.

At Lord's, May 9, 10, 11, 13. DURHAM lost to MIDDLESEX by 306 runs.

DURHAM v YORKSHIRE

At Chester-le-Street, May 16, 17, 18. Yorkshire won by 144 runs. Yorkshire 23 pts, Durham 5 pts. Toss: Yorkshire.

A match in which the four opening partnerships produced a grand total of 15 runs also saw a last-wicket stand of 110. Yorkshire were 225 for nine when Stemp joined Silverwood, but Stemp smashed 65 in 69 balls – his maiden half-century. This transformed the game, and Yorkshire's pace attack had Durham on eight for three before the first-day close. While the new ball created difficulties on an unpredictable pitch, Bevan had the class to counter the inconsistencies, scoring 90 and 51. Morris's 83 for Durham proved to be a false dawn for a disappointing season. None of his team-mates reached 50 and they failed to survive into a fourth day. Hartley had match figures of eight for 99, exploiting the variable bounce in Durham's second innings to trap Campbell lbw with a shooter and inflict Daley's third broken finger in 12 months at the Riverside ground. Durham's opening bowlers, Brown and Betts, shared 17 wickets, while Scott broke his own county records behind the stumps with seven catches in the first innings and ten in all.

Close of play: First day, Durham 19-3 (J. E. Morris 9*, J. A. Daley 3*); Second day, Yorkshire 149-7 (A. C. Morris 21*, P. J. Hartley 12*).

Yorkshire

A. McGrath c Scott b Betts	0	– c Daley b Brown	27
M. P. Vaughan c Scott b Brown	1	– lbw b Brown	0
*D. Byas lbw b Boiling	22	– b Betts	7
M. G. Bevan c Scott b Betts	90	– lbw b Brown	51
C. White c Scott b Foster	5	– c Scott b Betts	15
†R. J. Blakey c Scott b Brown	27	– c Scott b Brown	7
A. C. Morris lbw b Brown	0	– c Boiling b Betts	40
D. Gough b Boiling	43	– c Scott b Brown	0
P. J. Hartley c Scott b Brown	14	– b Betts	38
C. E. W. Silverwood not out	45	– not out	1
R. D. Stemp c Scott b Betts	65	– c Daley b Betts	14
B 1, l-b 5, w 1, n-b 16	23	B 4, l-b 1, w 1, n-b 4	10
1/3 2/5 3/58 4/84 5/146 6/146 7/189 8/215 9/225	335	1/1 2/10 3/52 4/83 5/116 6/117 7/119 8/189 9/196	210

Bonus points – Yorkshire 3, Durham 4.

Bowling: *First Innings*—Brown 26–3–93–4; Betts 16.2–3–96–3; Boiling 34–15–69–2; Foster 16–1–49–1; Collingwood 3–0–22–0. *Second Innings*—Brown 20–6–54–5; Betts 23.4–4–87–5; Foster 11–1–37–0; Boiling 12–7–27–0.

Durham

S. L. Campbell lbw b Gough	0	– lbw b Hartley	6
*M. A. Roseberry lbw b Hartley	3	– c Byas b Silverwood	37
J. Boiling lbw b Hartley	4	– (9) lbw b Gough	5
J. E. Morris c and b Gough	83	– (3) run out	5
J. A. Daley c Byas b Silverwood	28	– (4) retired hurt	6
J. I. Longley c Blakey b Hartley	2	– (5) b Hartley	4
P. D. Collingwood lbw b Morris	6	– (6) c Morris b Hartley	48
M. J. Foster b Hartley	25	– (7) c Byas b Hartley	12
†C. W. Scott not out	15	– (8) c Hartley b Gough	42
S. J. E. Brown b Gough	28	– b Silverwood	6
M. M. Betts c Hartley b Stemp	2	– not out	0
L-b 5, n-b 14	19	B 1, l-b 10, n-b 4	15
1/0 2/7 3/8 4/76 5/85 6/102 7/150 8/180 9/210	215	1/11 2/26 3/49 4/87 5/111 6/129 7/169 8/180 9/186	186

Bonus points – Durham 1, Yorkshire 4.

In the second innings J. A. Daley retired hurt at 45.

Bowling: *First Innings*—Gough 20–3–57–3; Hartley 18–2–67–4; Silverwood 9–3–20–1; Morris 5–0–28–1; White 5–1–11–0; Stemp 4.4–0–27–1. *Second Innings*—Gough 16–6–36–2; Hartley 22–7–32–4; White 5–1–12–0; Silverwood 13.5–3–40–2; Stemp 7–2–23–0; Bevan 6–2–24–0; Vaughan 1–0–8–0.

Umpires: D. J. Constant and T. E. Jesty.

At Portsmouth, May 23, 24, 25, 27. DURHAM drew with HAMPSHIRE.

At Nottingham, May 30, 31, June 1, 3. DURHAM drew with NOTTINGHAMSHIRE.

At Hove, June 6, 7, 8, 10. DURHAM lost to SUSSEX by an innings and 67 runs.

DURHAM v LANCASHIRE

At Chester-le-Street, June 13, 14, 15. Lancashire won by 345 runs. Lancashire 22 pts, Durham 4 pts. Toss: Lancashire.

Both teams were hunting their first Championship win of the season and Lancashire looked anything but a safe bet at 115 for six just after lunch on the first day. They were rescued by Austin, who had been preferred to Keedy, thus producing a match devoid of spin. Austin made 95 not out and 91 at No. 8, then finished the match with a spell of four for 20 in five overs. His seventh-wicket stand of 175 in 31 overs with Hegg in the second innings put the game well beyond Durham's reach as they suffered for dropping Hegg on nought. Earlier, they had been hampered by Betts's no-ball problems – he bowled 16 plus a wide in six first-innings overs – while Lancashire profited from high-quality exploitation by Chapple and Martin of another untrustworthy Riverside pitch. Eighteen wickets fell on the first day before Lancashire consolidated their lead on the Friday. Durham were set 525 for victory and Chapple removed Roseberry and Morris without a run on the board. Lancashire won in time to watch the European Championship soccer match between England and Scotland; Durham had a lengthy team meeting.

Close of play: First day, Durham 138-8 (D. G. C. Ligertwood 11*, S. J. E. Brown 1*); Second day, Lancashire 395-8 (S. Elworthy 3*, G. Chapple 4*).

Lancashire

M. A. Atherton c Ligertwood b Brown	16	– lbw b Lugsden	37
N. J. Speak lbw b Brown	12	– c Bainbridge b Wood	8
S. P. Titchard c Ligertwood b Betts	12	– c Betts b Lugsden	60
N. H. Fairbrother c Ligertwood b Lugsden	21	– c Ligertwood b Brown	18
G. D. Lloyd lbw b Lugsden	12	– c Campbell b Wood	29
*M. Watkinson c Bainbridge b Wood	5	– c Blenkiron b Bainbridge	25
†W. K. Hegg c Morris b Betts	37	– c Brown b Wood	89
I. D. Austin not out	95	– b Lugsden	91
S. Elworthy c Morris b Brown	3	– not out	17
G. Chapple lbw b Bainbridge	12	– not out	30
P. J. Martin b Lugsden	0		
L-b 2, w 5, n-b 32	39	B 2, l-b 14, w 17, n-b 4	37
1/28 2/29 3/63 4/82 5/89 6/115 7/192 8/197 9/263	264	1/26 2/75 3/103 4/153 5/187 6/213 7/388 8/390	(8 wkts dec.) 441

Bonus points – Lancashire 2, Durham 4.

Bowling: *First Innings*—Brown 19–3–75–3; Wood 16–1–61–1; Betts 6–0–65–2; Lugsden 11.3–2–45–3; Bainbridge 7–1–16–1. *Second Innings*—Brown 20–1–100–1; Wood 23–0–96–3; Lugsden 23–1–91–3; Betts 14–4–72–0; Bainbridge 14–0–52–1; Blenkiron 3–0–14–0.

Durham

S. L. Campbell lbw b Chapple	7	– lbw b Chapple	39
*M. A. Roseberry c Hegg b Chapple	2	– c Hegg b Chapple	0
J. E. Morris c Hegg b Elworthy	52	– lbw b Chapple	0
D. A. Blenkiron c Hegg b Martin	2	– c Fairbrother b Martin	10
P. Bainbridge b Martin	41	– c Atherton b Elworthy	53
P. D. Collingwood lbw b Chapple	4	– c Fairbrother b Austin	21
M. M. Betts c Hegg b Chapple	0	– (8) c Watkinson b Austin	4
†D. G. C. Ligertwood not out	31	– (7) c Fairbrother b Martin	10
J. Wood b Chapple	5	– c Fairbrother b Austin	0
S. J. E. Brown c Hegg b Martin	17	– not out	10
S. Lugsden c Hegg b Elworthy	1	– b Austin	7
L-b 11, w 2, n-b 6	19	B 6, l-b 7, w 4, n-b 8	25
1/6 2/31 3/38 4/83 5/112 6/112 7/120 8/129 9/159	181	1/0 2/0 3/11 4/101 5/109 6/148 7/152 8/152 9/162	179

Bonus points – Lancashire 4.

Bowling: *First Innings*—Martin 21–6–44–3; Chapple 22–6–64–5; Elworthy 9–1–37–2; Austin 6–1–25–0. *Second Innings*—Martin 14–6–33–2; Chapple 14–4–46–3; Austin 10.3–4–33–4; Elworthy 11–1–54–1.

Umpires: J. C. Balderstone and B. Leadbeater.

DURHAM v SURREY

At Stockton-on-Tees, June 20, 21, 22, 24. Surrey won by eight wickets. Surrey 24 pts, Durham 7 pts. Toss: Durham.

Even with Stewart, Thorpe and Lewis on Test duty, Surrey were able to take the greater advantage of a batsman-friendly pitch. Benjamin undermined Durham's good start with four wickets in 16 balls, before a ninth-wicket stand of 127, a county record, between Brown and Ligertwood, repaired the damage. However, Surrey's openers responded with 245, the highest opening stand against Durham, with Butcher making a delightfully fluent 160. His century came off 125 balls and included 20 fours, while Darren Bicknell batted more than six hours to reach

106. Surrey subsided from 376 for three to 440 all out on Bicknell's exit, but the lead of 63 proved valuable. Durham batted woefully in their second innings, leaving Surrey to score just 141 on the last day. With Simon Brown absent because of back trouble and Wood developing a knee injury, the back-up bowlers could not stop Surrey securing victory before lunch.

Close of play: First day, Surrey 27-0 (D. J. Bicknell 5*, M. A. Butcher 21*); Second day, Surrey 382-4 (A. D. Brown 28*, G. J. Kersey 0*); Third day, Durham 203.

Durham

S. L. Campbell c Ratcliffe b M. P. Bicknell	69	– c Kersey b Julian	34
S. Hutton c Kersey b Pearson	47	– c Julian b M. P. Bicknell	6
*J. E. Morris c Kersey b M. P. Bicknell	23	– c Brown b M. P. Bicknell	4
D. A. Blenkiron c Kersey b Pearson	3	– lbw b Benjamin	1
P. Bainbridge c Kersey b Benjamin	35	– c Butcher b Pearson	18
P. D. Collingwood c Julian b Benjamin	25	– c Kersey b M. P. Bicknell	21
†D. G. C. Ligertwood c Kersey b Julian	56	– c Kersey b Hollioake	44
J. Boiling c Kersey b Benjamin	0	– not out	12
J. Wood b Benjamin	0	– c and b Hollioake	2
S. J. E. Brown c Butcher b Pearson	60	– b Julian	18
S. Lugsden not out	1	– b Julian	1
B 9, l-b 12, w 1, n-b 36	58	B 1, l-b 5, w 4, n-b 32	42
1/130 2/161 3/179 4/201 5/237 6/244 7/244 8/244 9/371	377	1/21 2/37 3/40 4/77 5/81 6/142 7/168 8/178 9/201	203

Bonus points – Durham 4, Surrey 4.

Bowling: *First Innings*—M. P. Bicknell 20–3–73–2; Julian 15.1–1–72–1; Hollioake 11–1–39–0; Benjamin 19–3–69–4; Pearson 31–7–103–3. *Second Innings*—M. P. Bicknell 18–5–40–3; Benjamin 19–3–33–1; Pearson 15–4–42–1; Julian 12.5–3–38–3; Ratcliffe 2–0–12–0; Shahid 1–1–0–0; Butcher 1–0–6–0; Hollioake 10–4–26–2.

Surrey

D. J. Bicknell c Ligertwood b Lugsden	106	– lbw b Lugsden	4
M. A. Butcher c Lugsden b Bainbridge	160	– c Boiling b Lugsden	9
J. D. Ratcliffe c Ligertwood b Lugsden	51	– not out	68
N. Shahid lbw b Bainbridge	0	– not out	52
A. D. Brown b Wood	28		
†G. J. Kersey run out	0		
*A. J. Hollioake b Boiling	19		
B. P. Julian b Boiling	31		
M. P. Bicknell b Wood	5		
R. M. Pearson c sub b Lugsden	1		
J. E. Benjamin not out	0		
B 8, l-b 11, w 10, n-b 10	39	L-b 3, w 2, n-b 4	9
1/245 2/345 3/347 4/376 5/382 6/385 7/413 8/424 9/438	440	1/4 2/36	(2 wkts) 142

Bonus points – Surrey 4, Durham 3 (Score at 120 overs: 424-7).

Bowling: *First Innings*—Brown 23–3–78–0; Wood 28–5–113–2; Lugsden 28.2–5–96–3; Bainbridge 14.4–2–44–2; Boiling 35.1–7–90–2. *Second Innings*—Lugsden 7–1–28–2; Wood 5–0–30–0; Boiling 12–4–45–0; Bainbridge 6.5–0–26–0; Morris 1–0–10–0.

Umpires: G. I. Burgess and G. Sharp.

DURHAM v GLOUCESTERSHIRE

At Chester-le-Street, June 27, 28, 29, July 1. Drawn. Durham 7 pts, Gloucestershire 7 pts. Toss: Gloucestershire. First-class debut: C. L. Campbell.

Rain robbed Durham of the chance of their first win of the season. Chasing 395, Gloucestershire were 113 for two at lunch on the final day; torrential rain prevented further play until 4.30. Despite the absence of Walsh, who had flown to Jamaica for a funeral, the visitors bowled

Durham out for 175 on the opening day, when 15 wickets fell. As in the previous Riverside match, against Lancashire, when 18 fell, the umpires blamed poor batting. Durham achieved a nine-run lead, though Gloucestershire's innings began unhappily for them when Lugsden was carried off with a torn hamstring after bowling four balls in the third match of his comeback; he missed 1995 with a back injury. Lugsden's agony quickly gave way to ecstasy for another young pace bowler, 18-year-old Colin Campbell, who completed the over and bowled Wright with his fourth ball in first-class cricket, three balls slower than his team-mate Paul Collingwood's perfect start earlier in the season. Hutton batted with careful application for eight hours for a Championship best 143 not out. He received valuable support from Bainbridge, who made his highest score for nearly three years. Symonds bolstered Gloucestershire's attack by bowling seam for the first time and took two wickets.

Close of play: First day, Gloucestershire 90-5 (T. H. C. Hancock 33*, R. C. Russell 10*); Second day, Durham 92-1 (S. Hutton 34*, J. E. Morris 39*); Third day, Gloucestershire 39-0 (A. J. Wright 28*, N. J. Trainor 7*).

Durham

S. L. Campbell lbw b Smith	8	lbw b Smith	14
S. Hutton c Ball b Lewis	4	not out	143
*J. E. Morris b Boden	12	c Ball b Symonds	68
D. A. Blenkiron c Boden b Smith	11	c Russell b Symonds	4
P. Bainbridge lbw b Alleyne	34	b Ball	83
P. D. Collingwood c Russell b Alleyne	2	c Russell b Alleyne	28
†D. G. C. Ligertwood lbw b Smith	23	c Hancock b Alleyne	8
M. M. Betts lbw b Smith	16	(9) c Lewis b Smith	8
S. J. E. Brown not out	39	(8) c and b Smith	2
C. L. Campbell c Russell b Alleyne	7		
S. Lugsden c Wright b Lewis	9		
B 1, l-b 3, n-b 6	10	B 4, l-b 13, n-b 10	27
1/12 2/12 3/33 4/49 5/66 6/87 7/115 8/118 9/131	175	1/22 2/139 3/147 4/280 5/349 6/372 7/375 8/385 (8 wkts dec.)	385

Bonus points – Gloucestershire 4.

Bowling: *First Innings*—Smith 20–8–39–4; Lewis 16.4–5–42–2; Boden 13–4–50–1; Alleyne 21–8–40–3. *Second Innings*—Smith 31.3–9–81–3; Lewis 21–7–48–0; Alleyne 26–5–83–2; Boden 18–1–71–0; Ball 13–5–28–1; Symonds 17–5–40–2; Hancock 2–0–17–0.

Gloucestershire

A. J. Wright b C. L. Campbell	5	run out	58
N. J. Trainor run out	12	lbw b Brown	7
T. H. C. Hancock not out	65	not out	59
R. I. Dawson lbw b Betts	0	not out	14
A. Symonds lbw b Brown	15		
M. W. Alleyne c Ligertwood b Betts	8		
*†R. C. Russell c S. L. Campbell b Betts	20		
M. C. J. Ball b Betts	17		
A. M. Smith c Blenkiron b Brown	13		
D. J. P. Boden c Ligertwood b Brown	1		
J. Lewis b Betts	1		
L-b 4, w 1, n-b 4	9	L-b 3, w 1, n-b 8	12
1/12 2/22 3/29 4/46 5/57 6/117 7/137 8/164 9/165	166	1/39 2/113 (2 wkts)	150

Bonus points – Durham 4.

Bowling: *First Innings*—Brown 20–4–59–3; Lugsden 0.4–0–2–0; C. L. Campbell 9.2–1–29–1; Betts 18.1–0–68–5; Bainbridge 4–1–4–0. *Second Innings*—Brown 17–1–52–1; Betts 15–2–76–0; C. L. Campbell 6–2–15–0; Bainbridge 4–2–2–0; Collingwood 1–0–2–0.

Umpires: B. Dudleston and V. A. Holder.

At Maidstone, July 4, 5, 6, 8. DURHAM lost to KENT by 83 runs.

At Worcester, July 18, 19, 20. DURHAM lost to WORCESTERSHIRE by nine wickets.

DURHAM v ESSEX

At Hartlepool, July 25, 26, 27. Essex won by 292 runs. Essex 23 pts, Durham 4 pts. Toss: Essex. First-class debut: M. J. Saggers.

With Brown making his Test debut and three seamers injured, Durham rushed through the registration of Martin Saggers, from Norfolk, who had a testing first-class baptism. Durham did well to restrict Essex to 334 on the small ground but, after their openers put on 86 in reply, they went into steep decline. Ilott exploited thickening cloud on the second afternoon with a spell of five for 11 in 27 balls; Durham avoided the follow-on only because Saggers, as last man, helped Wood add 31. Essex took full advantage of Durham's weakening resolve, with Law providing a magnificent lead. His 172 in 170 balls, his sixth and biggest century of the season, included 134 before lunch on the third day and featured seven sixes. Campbell hit 72 as Durham made another good start, pursuing an unlikely 517, but their second innings was almost a replica of the first.

Close of play: First day, Durham 8-0 (S. L. Campbell 6*, S. Hutton 1*); Second day, Essex 121-2 (A. P. Grayson 44*, S. G. Law 27*).

Essex

G. A. Gooch lbw b Killeen	22	– b Cox	33
D. D. J. Robinson c Campbell b Cox	38	– c Killeen b Saggers	9
A. P. Grayson c Roseberry b Killeen	74	– c Ligertwood b Bainbridge	85
S. G. Law c Ligertwood b Wood	73	– c Ligertwood b Killeen	172
*P. J. Prichard c Hutton b Killeen	0	– st Ligertwood b Cox	23
R. C. Irani lbw b Wood	56	– c Morris b Killeen	12
†R. J. Rollins b Wood	1	– c Hutton b Cox	0
M. C. Ilott c Wood b Killeen	17	– c Bainbridge b Killeen	13
N. F. Williams c Roseberry b Cox	23	– not out	6
P. M. Such not out	10		
S. J. W. Andrew c Campbell b Cox	1		
B 4, l-b 7, n-b 8	19	B 4, l-b 7, w 6	17
1/53 2/93 3/165 4/165 5/256 6/260 7/281 8/312 9/332	334	1/21 2/76 3/241 4/338 5/344 6/344 7/352 8/370 (8 wkts dec.)	370

Bonus points – Essex 3, Durham 4.

Bowling: *First Innings*—Wood 21–4–89–3; Saggers 12–0–69–0; Killeen 21–6–57–4; Bainbridge 7–3–25–0; Cox 39.4–14–83–3. *Second Innings*—Wood 13–1–77–0; Killeen 19.3–4–72–3; Saggers 12–0–53–1; Cox 28–5–103–3; Campbell 1–0–4–0; Bainbridge 10–0–50–1.

Durham

S. L. Campbell b Such	56	– c Rollins b Ilott	72
S. Hutton c Rollins b Ilott	31	– b Williams	23
J. E. Morris c Gooch b Ilott	13	– c Robinson b Such	6
J. A. Daley b Such	5	– b Williams	21
*M. A. Roseberry lbw b Ilott	1	– c Law b Irani	19
P. Bainbridge c Rollins b Irani	16	– c Law b Williams	3
†D. G. C. Ligertwood lbw b Ilott	1	– b Such	1
D. M. Cox c Gooch b Ilott	5	– b Law	52
J. Wood not out	35	– c Grayson b Such	0
N. Killeen c Grayson b Such	0	– b Such	0
M. J. Saggers c Rollins b Irani	11	– not out	10
L-b 8, w 1, n-b 5	14	L-b 13, n-b 4	17
1/86 2/105 3/110 4/116 5/118 6/119 7/127 8/154 9/157	188	1/82 2/100 3/118 4/154 5/154 6/157 7/186 8/186 9/212	224

Bonus points – Essex 4.

Bowling: *First Innings*—Ilott 21–4–53–5; Andrew 5–1–22–0; Williams 6–0–20–0; Irani 12.3–2–33–2; Such 22–4–52–3. *Second Innings*—Ilott 19–2–81–1; Andrew 2–1–8–0; Such 22–9–49–4; Williams 10–3–33–3; Irani 12–5–31–1; Law 3.1–0–9–1.

Umpires: B. Dudleston and D. R. Shepherd.

At Chester-le-Street, August 3, 4, 5. DURHAM lost to PAKISTANIS by seven wickets (See Pakistani tour section).

At Birmingham, August 8, 9, 10, 12. DURHAM lost to WARWICKSHIRE by 282 runs.

At Weston-super-Mare, August 21, 22, 23, 24. DURHAM drew with SOMERSET.

DURHAM v GLAMORGAN

At Chester-le-Street, August 28, 29, 30, 31. Glamorgan won by 141 runs. Glamorgan 22 pts, Durham 4 pts. Toss: Durham.

Roseberry announced his resignation as Durham captain on the final morning. Geoff Cook, the director of cricket, was in Tasmania offering the job to David Boon, but Roseberry denied any knowledge of this. He explained he could help the team best by concentrating on his batting. Brown, rather than vice-captain Morris, took over for the remainder of the season. Glamorgan were without Maynard and Croft, on one-day international duty, but effectively won inside three days: no play was possible until 4.40 p.m. on the first day. On a pitch helping the seamers, Saggers returned six for 65, the best figures by a Durham bowler in 1996, to keep Glamorgan down to 259. But woeful batting saw Durham's last seven go for 20 as they replied with 114. Sensing victory was in the bag after a third-wicket stand of 111 between Morris and Dale, Glamorgan threw wickets away, enabling medium-pacer Blenkiron to claim a career-best four for 43.

Close of play: First day, Glamorgan 73-3 (A. Dale 1*, P. A. Cottey 11*); Second day, Glamorgan 8-0 (S. P. James 2*, H. Morris 3*); Third day, Durham 81-3 (J. A. Daley 17*, M. A. Roseberry 11*).

Glamorgan

S. P. James lbw b Brown	4	– lbw b Brown	2
H. Morris c Morris b Betts	25	– c Campbell b Blenkiron	69
D. L. Hemp c Campbell b Walker	28	– b Brown	12
A. Dale c Campbell b Saggers	29	– c Morris b Blenkiron	69
*P. A. Cottey b Betts	81	– c Hutton b Betts	14
G. P. Butcher b Saggers	19	– hit wkt b Betts	12
†A. D. Shaw c Roseberry b Saggers	0	– c Ligertwood b Blenkiron	0
O. D. Gibson b Saggers	41	– c Daley b Blenkiron	2
D. A. Cosker lbw b Saggers	3	– run out	4
S. L. Watkin c Roseberry b Saggers	0	– b Brown	9
O. T. Parkin not out	9	– not out	0
B 5, l-b 5, w 6, n-b 4	20	L-b 5, w 5, n-b 4	14
1/11 2/58 3/58 4/131 5/200 6/200 7/216 8/242 9/242	259	1/13 2/35 3/146 4/169 5/177 6/179 7/193 8/193 9/204	207

Bonus points – Glamorgan 2, Durham 4.

Bowling: *First Innings*—Brown 21–3–62–1; Saggers 16.1–2–65–6; Walker 21–2–50–1; Betts 17–1–71–2; Blenkiron 2–1–1–0. *Second Innings*—Brown 10.1–0–38–3; Saggers 12–3–39–0; Walker 12–1–33–0; Betts 15–1–47–2; Blenkiron 18–5–43–4; Campbell 3–1–2–0.

Durham

S. L. Campbell c James b Parkin	22	– b Gibson	23
S. Hutton c Butcher b Watkin	4	– lbw b Gibson	19
J. E. Morris c Morris b Parkin	10	– c Shaw b Dale	3
J. A. Daley lbw b Watkin	36	– b Parkin	33
*M. A. Roseberry c Shaw b Gibson	23	– c Shaw b Parkin	20
D. A. Blenkiron run out	0	– c James b Watkin	6
†D. G. C. Ligertwood b Dale	4	– not out	33
M. M. Betts c and b Watkin	6	– lbw b Gibson	5
S. J. E. Brown c Dale b Parkin	2	– c Cosker b Dale	6
M. J. Saggers c Shaw b Watkin	0	– lbw b Parkin	11
A. Walker not out	0	– c Gibson b Watkin	20
B 4, l-b 1, n-b 2	7	B 3, l-b 16, w 1, n-b 12	32
1/17 2/36 3/51 4/94 5/98 6/105 7/111 8/114 9/114	114	1/39 2/44 3/49 4/97 5/112 6/116 7/133 8/140 9/184	211

Bonus points – Glamorgan 4.

Bowling: *First Innings*—Watkin 15–6–28–4; Gibson 12–4–40–1; Parkin 9.4–3–22–3; Dale 11–6–19–1. *Second Innings*—Watkin 23.5–7–71–2; Gibson 20–4–59–3; Dale 11–6–15–2; Parkin 15–5–32–3; Cosker 2–0–3–0; Cottey 1–0–4–0; Butcher 1–0–8–0.

Umpires: R. Julian and R. Palmer.

DURHAM v LEICESTERSHIRE

At Chester-le-Street, September 12, 13. Leicestershire won by an innings and 251 runs. Leicestershire 24 pts, Durham 2 pts. Toss: Durham. First-class debut: S. J. Harmison.

Leicestershire increased their lead at the top of the Championship table to 14 points with one game left as they brushed Durham, already certain of the wooden spoon, contemptuously aside in two days. They had won all their six Championship matches against Durham, the last four by an innings. It was Durham's biggest ever defeat. Simmons followed up career-best figures of six for 14 with a magnificent 171 off 170 balls, the highest individual score at the Riverside, while Leicestershire's 516 for six was the highest total. More injuries persuaded Durham to register another pace bowler, 17-year-old Stephen Harmison, from Ashington. But he went for more than eight an over, adding to the disbelief that slow left-armer David Cox had been ignored again. Leicestershire scored throughout at more than five an over: Simmons and Nixon put on 284, breaking the county's 85-year-old sixth-wicket record, 262, set by A. T. Sharpe and G. H. S. Fowke against Derbyshire. Durham's second innings offered little semblance of resistance as Wells destroyed the top order and Mullally cleaned up the tail.

Close of play: First day, Leicestershire 253-5 (P. V. Simmons 28*, P. A. Nixon 2*).

Durham

S. L. Campbell c Nixon b Millns	35	– c Nixon b Millns	0
S. Hutton c Wells b Simmons	30	– lbw b Wells	17
†D. G. C. Ligertwood lbw b Wells	1	– lbw b Wells	9
J. A. Daley c Pierson b Simmons	14	– c Nixon b Wells	29
J. E. Morris run out	1	– c Millns b Wells	0
M. A. Roseberry lbw b Simmons	0	– c Nixon b Mullally	27
D. A. Blenkiron b Mullally	3	– not out	23
M. M. Betts b Simmons	1	– b Mullally	7
A. Walker c Nixon b Simmons	0	– c Nixon b Mullally	0
*S. J. E. Brown not out	18	– b Mullally	8
S. J. Harmison b Simmons	6	– b Mullally	4
L-b 4, w 3, n-b 10	17	B 1, l-b 8, n-b 6	15
1/50 2/51 3/91 4/94 5/94 6/95 7/97 8/97 9/101	126	1/0 2/34 3/41 4/49 5/90 6/92 7/99 8/99 9/121	139

Bonus points – Leicestershire 4.

Bowling: *First Innings*—Mullally 13–4–47–1; Parsons 11–3–36–0; Millns 5–1–16–1; Wells 4–2–7–1; Simmons 9.3–3–14–6; Pierson 4–2–2–0. *Second Innings*—Millns 8–2–24–1; Parsons 8–0–35–0; Wells 14–3–44–4; Mullally 15–5–27–5.

Leicestershire

V. J. Wells b Walker	28	†P. A. Nixon not out	103
D. L. Maddy lbw b Betts	82		
B. F. Smith b Betts	70	L-b 10, w 5, n-b 44	59
G. I. Macmillan c Daley b Blenkiron	0		—
P. V. Simmons b Campbell	171	1/61 2/209 3/212 (6 wkts dec.)	516
*J. J. Whitaker c Ligertwood b Brown	3	4/216 5/232 6/516	

A. R. K. Pierson, G. J. Parsons, D. J. Millns and A. D. Mullally did not bat.

Bonus points – Leicestershire 4, Durham 2.

Bowling: Brown 26–4–106–1; Betts 18–0–117–2; Walker 27–4–117–1; Harmison 9–1–77–0; Blenkiron 13–3–51–1; Campbell 6.2–1–38–1.

Umpires: D. J. Constant and A. A. Jones.

At Derby, September 19, 20, 21. DURHAM lost to DERBYSHIRE by eight wickets.

YOUNG CRICKETER OF THE YEAR

(Elected by the Cricket Writers' Club)

1950	R. Tattersall	1974	P. H. Edmonds
1951	P. B. H. May	1975	A. Kennedy
1952	F. S. Trueman	1976	G. Miller
1953	M. C. Cowdrey	1977	I. T. Botham
1954	P. J. Loader	1978	D. I. Gower
1955	K. F. Barrington	1979	P. W. G. Parker
1956	B. Taylor	1980	G. R. Dilley
1957	M. J. Stewart	1981	M. W. Gatting
1958	A. C. D. Ingleby-Mackenzie	1982	N. G. Cowans
1959	G. Pullar	1983	N. A. Foster
1960	D. A. Allen	1984	R. J. Bailey
1961	P. H. Parfitt	1985	D. V. Lawrence
1962	P. J. Sharpe	1986	A. A. Metcalfe
1963	G. Boycott		J. J. Whitaker
1964	J. M. Brearley	1987	R. J. Blakey
1965	A. P. E. Knott	1988	M. P. Maynard
1966	D. L. Underwood	1989	N. Hussain
1967	A. W. Greig	1990	M. A. Atherton
1968	R. M. H. Cottam	1991	M. R. Ramprakash
1969	A. Ward	1992	I. D. K. Salisbury
1970	C. M. Old	1993	M. N. Lathwell
1971	J. Whitehouse	1994	J. P. Crawley
1972	D. R. Owen-Thomas	1995	A. Symonds
1973	M. Hendrick	1996	C. E. W. Silverwood

An additional award, in memory of Norman Preston, Editor of *Wisden* from 1951 to 1980, was made to C. W. J. Athey in 1980.

Stuart Law

ESSEX

President: D. J. Insole

Chairman: D. L. Acfield

Chairman, Cricket Committee: G. J. Saville

Secretary/General Manager: P. J. Edwards

Captain: P. J. Prichard

Head Groundsman: S. Kerrison

Scorer: C. F. Driver

Two consecutive Saturdays ruined what was otherwise a season of achievement and progress for Essex. The first came at Headingley after a surge of five successive victories – three with a day to spare – had carried Essex from halfway up the Championship to joint top with four games to go. They established a first-innings lead of 82 and reduced Yorkshire to 91 for five. But the bowlers lost their grip, Essex went down to a 98-run defeat and never recaptured their momentum. They eventually finished fifth.

A week later came a far more public humiliation. Batting second in the NatWest final, the traditional route to victory, they were bowled out by Lancashire for just 57, with Lord's packed and the nation watching.

But the season deserves to be remembered for more than this. Essex did extremely well in a year when they were seldom able to field a settled side. Injury and Test demands deprived them of Nasser Hussain for six Championship matches, while Ronnie Irani's elevation to the England team removed him from three games, none of which Essex won. There was immense satisfaction at Hussain's advancement. After a long, patient period knocking on England's door for a recall, he came back and grasped the opportunity to score two centuries against India, confirming the talent everyone knew he possessed, which hitherto had not been accompanied by a reliable temperament. Hussain damaged his hand during the second hundred and scored less freely when he returned to play Pakistan. But his new maturity and self-belief won him the vice-captaincy on the tour of Zimbabwe and New Zealand.

Whatever failings Irani might have, lack of confidence is not one of them. Like Ian Botham, he has a purpose bordering on arrogance when he strides out to bat. He underlined that in the opening game at Worcester, where Essex lost half their side for 32 in pursuit of 187. Irani's response was to plunder five sixes and 12 fours in an unbeaten 110 from 86 balls. That innings, and another match-winning effort a week later against Hampshire, earned him England recognition – and an eventual place on the winter tour.

Graham Gooch began his 24th season by being appointed an England selector and ended it by accepting an invitation to coach England A in Australia – though he later withdrew because of his father's health. He also announced he would play on in 1997, unless he was elected chairman of selectors. Though he had turned 43, no batsman on the circuit could match his authority, class or dedication: he regularly appeared in the nets a couple of hours before the start of play. The older Gooch has got, the easier he has made batting look. He was the country's leading run-scorer, with 1,944 at 67.03, and scored eight Championship hundreds. That took his total to 128, ninth in the list of century-makers, just above W. G. Grace. Gooch also entered the top ten for total runs scored, with an aggregate of 44,472. For good measure, he became the first batsman to reach 30,000 runs for Essex after passing Keith Fletcher's 29,434.

The biggest compliment that can be paid to Stuart Law is that he did not suffer in comparison. Brought over from Queensland with little reputation in England, he surpassed all expectations with an avalanche of runs, including a dozen centuries in all cricket, even though he missed a month of the season during Australia's short tour of Sri Lanka. Law destroyed attacks with a brashness and brutality that left even the better bowlers looking ordinary and, in some cases, shocked. His first-class average was 61.80 from an aggregate of 1,545.

The others could not match the consistency of Gooch and Law. Paul Prichard, whose captaincy was efficient rather than exciting, had the additional burden of his benefit, probably one reason why he failed to top 1,000 runs and scored just one century. Darren Robinson lost his place mid-way through the summer; he marked his recall with three successive first-class fifties, before Courtney Walsh ended his Championship season by breaking his finger. Paul Grayson joined the list of players who have revitalised their careers with Essex. His decision to move from Yorkshire was rewarded with 939 runs and his cap, and he also looked a promising left-arm spinner.

Off-spinner Peter Such did more than any bowler to sustain the campaign, enjoying his best season yet – 82 wickets at 26.39. He did not win a Test recall but was picked for the England A tour. What Essex missed was a genuine strike bowler. Mark Ilott lacked his usual cutting edge, returning a modest haul of 50 wickets, which was still the biggest total among the seam attack. Irani was the next most successful, with 40 for the county, followed by Ashley Cowan and Neil Williams. But 21-year-old Cowan, tall, brisk in pace and big-hearted, suggested a rewarding future once he tightens up his control. And the arrival of Danny Law from Sussex in 1997 may help. Robert Rollins was again satisfactory behind the stumps but failed to develop his batting promise. Steve Peters, one of several newcomers, marked his debut against Cambridge by becoming the county's youngest century-maker, aged 17. Yet in three other first-class games he scored only 20, a harsh reminder of what is required at a higher level.

In the Benson and Hedges Cup, Essex again failed to qualify for the quarter-finals, while their Sunday form was pathetic, the players too often lacking interest and resolve. They lost nine of the final ten matches, and were spared the wooden spoon only by the lamentable form of Durham – whom they provided with their sole first-class scalp of 1996 in a senior competition. Even allowing for international calls and the fact that Gooch missed half the Sunday season on selection duties, their performances were unacceptable.

John Childs's retirement ended a career which brought him 1,028 wickets and two Test caps. After ten seasons with Gloucestershire, he joined Essex in 1985 and became a key figure in three Championship-winning sides. One of *Wisden's* Five Cricketers of the Year in 1987, Childs was not only a superb left-arm spinner, but also one of the most popular players ever to pull on a cricket sweater. – NIGEL FULLER.

ESSEX 1996

[*Bill Smith*

Back row: G. J. A. Goodwin, J. C. Powell, S. D. Peters, J. J. B. Lewis, J. O. Grove, D. W. Ayres, T. P. Hodgson, A. J. E. Hibbert. *Middle row:* J. S. W. Davis (*physiotherapist*), A. P. Grayson, N. A. Derbyshire, D. M. Cousins, S. J. W. Andrew, A. P. Cowan, B. J. Hyam, D. D. J. Robinson, R. J. Rollins, A. R. Butcher (*coach*). *Front row:* N. F. Williams, S. G. Law, P. M. Such, G. A. Gooch, P. J. Prichard (*captain*), N. Hussain, J. H. Childs, M. C. Ilott, R. C. Irani.

ESSEX RESULTS

All first-class matches – Played 20: Won 9, Lost 6, Drawn 5.

County Championship matches – Played 17: Won 8, Lost 5, Drawn 4.

Competition placings – Britannic Assurance County Championship, 5th; NatWest Trophy, finalists; Benson and Hedges Cup, 3rd in Group C; AXA Equity & Law League, 17th.

COUNTY CHAMPIONSHIP AVERAGES

BATTING

Cap		*M*	*I*	*NO*	*R*	*HS*	*100s*	*50s*	*Avge*	*Ct/St*
1975	G. A. Gooch†	17	30	1	1,944	201	8	6	67.03	18
1996	S. G. Law§	14	24	1	1,379	172	5	5	59.95	24
1989	N. Hussain	11	19	0	811	158	1	5	42.68	12
1994	R. C. Irani	14	23	3	816	110*	1	7	40.80	6
1994	J. J. B. Lewis	4	7	2	181	69	0	2	36.20	10
1996	A. P. Grayson	16	28	2	936	140	2	3	36.00	19
	D. D. J. Robinson†	9	17	2	515	75	0	5	34.33	3
1986	P. J. Prichard†	17	28	0	877	108	1	5	31.32	11
1995	R. J. Rollins†	17	28	3	541	74*	0	2	21.64	47/5
1993	M. C. Ilott	15	22	2	343	58	0	1	17.15	3
1996	N. F. Williams	12	16	3	221	39	0	0	17.00	2
1991	P. M. Such	16	20	10	168	54	0	1	16.80	8
	A. P. Cowan	13	18	5	155	34	0	0	11.92	6
	S. J. W. Andrew	7	11	5	53	13	0	0	8.83	2

Also batted: (cap 1986) J. H. Childs (3 matches) 1*, 0*, 0; S. D. Peters† (2 matches) 4, 0, 11 (2 ct).

* *Signifies not out.* † *Born in Essex.* § *Overseas player.*

BOWLING

	O	*M*	*R*	*W*	*BB*	*5W/i*	*Avge*
P. M. Such	680	168	1,914	70	8-118	5	27.34
N. F. Williams	331.4	59	1,160	35	5-43	2	33.14
R. C. Irani	308.2	57	1,029	31	5-27	1	33.19
M. C. Ilott	505.2	105	1,526	45	5-53	2	33.91
A. P. Cowan	348.2	56	1,262	37	5-68	1	34.10
S. J. W. Andrew	132.4	33	398	10	3-67	0	39.80
A. P. Grayson	260.3	58	726	18	4-82	0	40.33
S. G. Law	199.4	44	734	13	3-100	0	56.46

Also bowled: J. H. Childs 122.4–33–357–8; G. A. Gooch 21–7–57–2.

COUNTY RECORDS

Highest score for:	343*	P. A. Perrin v Derbyshire at Chesterfield	1904
Highest score against:	332	W. H. Ashdown (Kent) at Brentwood	1934
Best bowling for:	10-32	H. Pickett v Leicestershire at Leyton	1895
Best bowling against:	10-40	E. G. Dennett (Gloucestershire) at Bristol	1906
Highest total for:	761-6 dec.	v Leicestershire at Chelmsford	1990
Highest total against:	803-4 dec.	by Kent at Brentwood	1934
Lowest total for:	30	v Yorkshire at Leyton	1901
Lowest total against:	14	by Surrey at Chelmsford	1983

At Worcester, May 2, 3, 4, 6. ESSEX beat WORCESTERSHIRE by five wickets.

At Southampton, May 9, 10, 11, 13. ESSEX beat HAMPSHIRE by four wickets.

ESSEX v KENT

At Ilford, May 16, 17, 18, 20. Kent won by an innings and 66 runs. Kent 24 pts, Essex 5 pts. Toss: Kent. First-class debut: N. W. Preston.

Kent celebrated an easy victory by lunch on the final day after Essex lost their last seven wickets for 21 in 83 deliveries. Although the pitch offered generous help to spin, the batsmen played a series of rash strokes. Kent's first innings was nourished by three centurions. Hooper led the way with 155 from 174 balls, hitting 20 fours and three sixes – his third hundred in successive Championship matches against Essex – Cowdrey struck a solid 111 and Marsh helped himself to a career-best 127. Nick Preston's first-class career began with a first-ball duck. Despite entertaining half-centuries from Gooch and Irani, Essex never looked like gathering the 441 needed to avoid the follow-on against unrelenting pressure from Hooper and Patel – who bowled all but 20 of the 198 overs Essex faced in this game. Law then followed up his 143 the previous week with 115, and Robinson helped him add 157. But once they were separated the innings fell apart. Patel's match haul was ten for 225.

Close of play: First day, Kent 323-4 (G. R. Cowdrey 90*, M. A. Ealham 2*); Second day, Essex 70-2 (G. A. Gooch 45*, N. Hussain 5*); Third day, Essex 111-2 (D. D. J. Robinson 53*, S. G. Law 50*).

Kent

D. P. Fulton b Such	34
M. V. Fleming c Rollins b Such	19
T. R. Ward c Rollins b Childs	12
C. L. Hooper c Hussain b Childs	155
G. R. Cowdrey c Law b Irani	111
M. A. Ealham c Irani b Ilott	37
*†S. A. Marsh c sub b Gooch	127
J. B. D. Thompson c Hussain b Such	37
M. J. McCague b Such	28
M. M. Patel not out	12
N. W. Preston lbw b Such	0
L-b 8, n-b 10	18
1/30 2/49 3/89 4/313 5/371 6/390 7/540 8/562 9/590	590

Bonus points – Kent 4, Essex 2 (Score at 120 overs: 397-6).

Bowling: Ilott 33–9–107–1; Williams 16–1–89–0; Such 50.5–8–145–5; Childs 26–5–108–2; Irani 20–2–75–1; Law 6–1–33–0; Gooch 6–1–25–1.

Essex

G. A. Gooch st Marsh b Patel	74	– c Hooper b Ealham	1
D. D. J. Robinson st Marsh b Hooper	17	– b Patel	75
P. M. Such c Ward b Hooper	3	– (10) b Hooper	4
N. Hussain c Marsh b Hooper	36	– (3) lbw b Patel	3
S. G. Law c Ealham b Patel	9	– (4) c Fulton b Patel	115
*P. J. Prichard b Hooper	41	– (5) c Marsh b Patel	1
R. C. Irani c Preston b Patel	50	– (6) c Hooper b Patel	0
†R. J. Rollins c Ealham b Patel	34	– (7) b Hooper	5
M. C. Ilott c Ward b McCague	23	– (8) lbw b Hooper	1
N. F. Williams c Cowdrey b McCague	14	– (9) c Fleming b Patel	0
J. H. Childs not out	1	– not out	0
L-b 4	4	B 5, l-b 4, n-b 4	13
1/48 2/62 3/120 4/136 5/149 6/220 7/234 8/275 9/305	306	1/9 2/12 3/169 4/197 5/199 6/208 7/209 8/214 9/218	218

Bonus points – Essex 3, Kent 4.

Bowling: *First Innings*—McCague 4.5–0–16–2; Thompson 1–0–7–0; Patel 51–17–128–4; Hooper 54–10–151–4. *Second Innings*—McCague 6–2–28–0; Ealham 5–3–5–1; Patel 37.3–8–97–6; Hooper 35–9–67–3; Ward 1–0–5–0; Preston 2–1–7–0.

Umpires: V. A. Holder and B. Leadbeater.

At Derby, May 23, 24, 25, 27. ESSEX drew with DERBYSHIRE.

At Chelmsford, May 28, 29, 30. ESSEX drew with INDIANS (See Indian tour section).

ESSEX v LANCASHIRE

At Chelmsford, June 6, 7, 8, 10. Drawn. Essex 9 pts, Lancashire 9 pts. Toss: Essex. First-class debut: N. T. Wood.

A placid pitch produced 1,127 runs and a crop of records on the first three days, though Lancashire were able to set off a few alarms on Monday before the game finally settled into deadlock. The home team were well satisfied with their first innings, when Gooch, Grayson and Law all scored centuries – Grayson's was a career-best and his first for Essex. Next, they reduced Lancashire to 55 for three, with an early departure for debutant Nathan Wood, son of former county opener Barry. But that brought in a member of another Lancashire dynasty, Graham Lloyd (son of David), who reached his first hundred in 70 balls – the fastest of the season – and his second in 71. He hit 12 sixes, beating the county record of ten, struck by Graeme Fowler against joke Leicestershire bowling in 1983, and 25 fours before he was finally out for 241 from 187 balls, surpassing his previous highest score by 109. Titchard followed, more slowly, to a career-best 163; they shared a stand of 358, beating the Lancashire fourth-wicket record set by Archie MacLaren and Johnny Tyldesley at Trent Bridge in 1904, and only 13 short of their all-wicket best. The final total, 686, was the county's third biggest ever. Though 40 overs were wiped out by rain on the third day, Lancashire eventually took the lead to 177, and Essex lost five wickets before passing that as Lewis steered them to safety.

Close of play: First day, Essex 448-6 (J. J. B. Lewis 33*, M. C. Ilott 9*); Second day, Lancashire 387-3 (S. P. Titchard 112*, G. D. Lloyd 227*); Third day, Lancashire 618-9 (I. D. Austin 45*, G. Keedy 5*).

Essex

G. A. Gooch c Austin b Keedy	101	– b Watkinson	21
D. D. J. Robinson lbw b Chapple	0	– c Speak b Watkinson	50
A. P. Grayson b Keedy	129	– b Keedy	27
S. G. Law c Elworthy b Austin	144	– b Keedy	3
*P. J. Prichard c Titchard b Austin	2	– c Speak b Keedy	31
J. J. B. Lewis c Speak b Austin	69	– not out	54
†R. J. Rollins c Elworthy b Watkinson	9	– c Hegg b Chapple	22
M. C. Ilott c Crawley b Austin	22	– retired hurt	0
A. P. Cowan c Keedy b Austin	0	– not out	12
P. M. Such b Chapple	4		
S. J. W. Andrew not out	8		
L-b 7, n-b 14	21	L-b 5, n-b 4	9
1/3 2/178 3/383 4/390 5/401 6/425 7/480 8/480 9/501	509	1/45 2/104 3/108 4/108 5/169 6/204	(6 wkts) 229

Bonus points – Essex 4, Lancashire 2 (Score at 120 overs: 464-6).

In the second innings M. C. Ilott retired hurt at 208.

Bowling: *First Innings*—Chapple 20.1–1–110–2; Elworthy 21–3–78–0; Austin 31–5–116–5; Watkinson 28–6–105–1; Keedy 34–11–75–2; Speak 5–0–18–0. *Second Innings*—Chapple 9–1–32–1; Elworthy 9–0–38–0; Austin 5–3–9–0; Watkinson 28–4–91–2; Keedy 29–13–45–3; Speak 1–0–9–0.

Lancashire

N. J. Speak b Such	29	S. Elworthy c Prichard b Such	19
N. T. Wood c Rollins b Cowan	1	G. Chapple c Grayson b Such	10
J. P. Crawley c Law b Ilott	1	G. Keedy c Cowan b Andrew	26
S. P. Titchard c Lewis b Such	163		
G. D. Lloyd c Rollins b Cowan	241	B 3, l-b 19, n-b 14	36
*M. Watkinson st Rollins b Grayson	34		
†W. K. Hegg c Grayson b Cowan	37	1/10 2/13 3/55 4/413 5/472	686
I. D. Austin not out	89	6/530 7/536 8/577 9/595	

Bonus points – Lancashire 4, Essex 2 (Score at 120 overs: 528-5).

Bowling: Ilott 32–5–124–1; Cowan 32–3–135–3; Such 42–12–178–4; Andrew 22.4–2–91–1; Grayson 22–2–106–1; Law 6–0–30–0.

Umpires: R. A. White and P. Willey.

ESSEX v NORTHAMPTONSHIRE

At Chelmsford, June 13, 14, 15, 17. Drawn. Essex 10 pts, Northamptonshire 8 pts. Toss: Northamptonshire. Championship debut: D. J. Roberts.

Essex never attempted a target of 389 in a minimum of 78 overs – even though Northamptonshire squeezed in 95 in their bid to pull off their first Championship win of the summer. Earlier, they seemed more likely to achieve their fourth defeat when they were bowled out for 214 and Essex reached 202 for one. But once Gooch departed for 128, the innings rapidly declined. The collapse followed the retrieval of the original ball, which had been mislaid after Hussain hit it into a nearby garden; Taylor suddenly made it swing and claimed five for 16 in 48 balls. Northamptonshire's openers easily cleared the arrears of 94: the 19-year-old debutant David Roberts scored 73 to follow his first-innings 41 and Montgomerie went on to 120, displaying determination and concentration for nearly five hours. After Bailey declared, spinners Emburey and Andy Roberts reduced Essex to 200 for eight before time ran out. On the second day, spectators were briefly diverted when a muntjac fawn appeared from under the parked covers, jumped into the members' enclosure and then into the river. It was found later, safe but scared, in a nearby churchyard.

Close of play: First day, Essex 63-0 (G. A. Gooch 38*, A. P. Grayson 21*); Second day, Northamptonshire 133-0 (D. J. Roberts 46*, R. R. Montgomerie 81*); Third day, Northamptonshire 419-7 (A. L. Penberthy 45*, J. E. Emburey 10*).

Northamptonshire

D. J. Roberts c Grayson b Cowan	41	– c Gooch b Andrew	73
R. R. Montgomerie c Gooch b Andrew	4	– b Such	120
*R. J. Bailey c Rollins b Cowan	16	– c Law b Andrew	10
M. B. Loye c Rollins b Andrew	42	– st Rollins b Grayson	40
†R. J. Warren c Prichard b Cowan	0	– run out	45
D. J. Capel c Rollins b Irani	6	– lbw b Grayson	37
A. L. Penberthy c Law b Childs	8	– not out	66
A. R. Roberts c Law b Childs	37	– lbw b Such	0
J. E. Emburey c Rollins b Childs	2	– c Irani b Childs	40
N. A. Mallender c Andrew b Irani	13	– c Such b Childs	11
J. P. Taylor not out	38		
B 1, n-b 6	7	B 19, l-b 9, n-b 12	40
1/10 2/43 3/105 4/109 5/111 6/124 7/136 8/148 9/163	214	1/185 2/203 3/237 4/283 5/346 6/354 7/355 8/462 9/482 (9 wkts dec.)	482

Bonus points – Northamptonshire 1, Essex 4.

Bowling: *First Innings*—Cowan 22–6–66–3; Andrew 20–7–35–2; Irani 16.2–4–42–2; Law 10–4–27–0; Childs 15–5–31–3; Such 5–0–12–0. *Second Innings*—Cowan 18–1–74–0; Andrew 21–5–50–2; Irani 12–2–44–0; Such 46–13–110–2; Childs 39.4–10–102–2; Law 9–0–41–0; Grayson 22–9–33–2.

Essex

G. A. Gooch lbw b Taylor	128	– c Warren b Emburey	40
A. P. Grayson c Warren b Taylor	30	– b Capel	17
N. Hussain lbw b Taylor	53	– lbw b A. R. Roberts	46
S. G. Law c A. R. Roberts b Penberthy	40	– c Warren b Emburey	23
*P. J. Prichard c Capel b Taylor	0	– c Warren b Emburey	45
R. C. Irani c Bailey b Taylor	2	– st Warren b A. R. Roberts	2
†R. J. Rollins c Mallender b Capel	4	– lbw b A. R. Roberts	14
A. P. Cowan b Taylor	0	– not out	5
P. M. Such not out	31	– c Montgomerie b Emburey	0
S. J. W. Andrew c Taylor b Penberthy	13	– not out	4
J. H. Childs c Bailey b Taylor	0		
B 5, l-b 1, w 1	7	B 1, l-b 3, n-b 4	8
1/98 2/202 3/230 4/230 5/236 6/249 7/254 8/279 9/299	308	1/48 2/85 3/133 4/133 5/137 6/174 7/200 8/200 (8 wkts)	204

Bonus points – Essex 3, Northamptonshire 4.

Bowling: *First Innings*—Taylor 22.2–2–88–7; Mallender 17–3–73–0; Emburey 8–1–32–0; Penberthy 16–4–57–2; Capel 16–2–52–1. *Second Innings*—Taylor 12–3–31–0; Mallender 7–2–17–0; Capel 7–1–19–1; Penberthy 6–3–9–0; Emburey 32–16–48–4; A. R. Roberts 29–10–70–3; Bailey 2–0–6–0.

Umpires: G. I. Burgess and B. J. Meyer.

At Cambridge, June 21, 22, 23. ESSEX beat CAMBRIDGE UNIVERSITY by 122 runs.

ESSEX v SURREY

At Southend, June 27, 28, 29, July 1. Drawn. Essex 8 pts, Surrey 10 pts. Toss: Surrey.

A torrential thunderstorm after tea ended a match already condemned to a draw on a pitch lacking pace and bounce. Thorpe and Hollioake provided the cornerstone of Surrey's innings with a stand of 201 for the fourth wicket. Thorpe hit a six and 14 fours in his fifth century of the season, which took him past 1,000 runs, three days after Michael Bevan of Yorkshire. But Gooch and Law trumped them with a partnership of 232 after Essex's reply had stumbled with the loss of three wickets for three runs. Law's century was his fifth of the summer and he struck a six and 15 fours; Gooch was more subdued than usual, but he defied the visiting attack for seven hours and a fourth hundred. There was speculation that Ray Illingworth, the chairman of selectors, had wanted Gooch, as a member of his panel, to watch elsewhere rather than play. Before the weather closed in, there was time for the in-form Butcher to join Thorpe in reaching 1,000 runs.

Close of play: First day, Surrey 345-3 (G. P. Thorpe 137*, A. J. Hollioake 78*); Second day, Essex 134-3 (G. A. Gooch 46*); Third day, Essex 425-8 (M. C. Ilott 9*, P. M. Such 0*).

Surrey

D. J. Bicknell c Grayson b Irani	30	– c Hussain b Law	30
M. A. Butcher c Law b Childs	53	– not out	85
G. P. Thorpe b Such	143	– (4) not out	11
A. D. Brown c Law b Such	31		
A. J. Hollioake c Hussain b Cowan	128		
B. P. Julian lbw b Ilott	36		
†G. J. Kersey c Rollins b Irani	8		
*A. J. Stewart lbw b Ilott	2	– (3) c Law b Such	33
M. P. Bicknell not out	10		
J. E. Benjamin not out	2		
B 3, l-b 21, w 5, n-b 4	33	B 3, l-b 5	8
1/75 2/97 3/156 4/357 5/444 6/446 7/464 8/466 (8 wkts dec.)	476	1/62 2/133 (2 wkts)	167

R. M. Pearson did not bat.

Bonus points – Surrey 4, Essex 1 (Score at 120 overs: 373-4).

Bowling: *First Innings*—Ilott 27.4–3–78–2; Cowan 17–3–63–1; Irani 13–1–47–2; Childs 42–13–116–1; Such 38–11–102–2; Grayson 12–1–35–0; Law 2–0–11–0. *Second Innings*—Ilott 3–1–4–0; Cowan 2–0–8–0; Grayson 15–2–42–0; Such 24–5–66–1; Law 11–3–39–1.

Essex

G. A. Gooch c Butcher b Pearson	149
A. P. Grayson c Stewart b Pearson	62
A. P. Cowan b Pearson	0
N. Hussain c Butcher b D. J. Bicknell	0
S. G. Law lbw b M. P. Bicknell	125
*P. J. Prichard lbw b Pearson	7
R. C. Irani b Pearson	17
†R. J. Rollins b Julian	12
M. C. Ilott not out	9
P. M. Such c sub b Julian	0
B 9, l-b 11, n-b 24	44
1/131 2/133 3/134 4/366 5/381 6/394 7/405 8/417 9/425 (9 wkts dec.)	425

J. H. Childs did not bat.

Bonus points – Essex 4, Surrey 3 (Score at 120 overs: 407-7).

Bowling: M. P. Bicknell 25–7–63–1; Benjamin 16–6–65–0; Pearson 46–11–142–5; Julian 22.2–5–84–2; D. J. Bicknell 12–2–42–1; Hollioake 4–1–9–0.

Umpires: A. Clarkson and D. J. Constant.

At Leicester, July 4, 5, 6, 8. ESSEX lost to LEICESTERSHIRE by an innings and 44 runs.

ESSEX v NOTTINGHAMSHIRE

At Chelmsford, July 18, 19, 20, 22. Essex won by six wickets. Essex 24 pts, Nottinghamshire 4 pts. Toss: Nottinghamshire.

Essex won just before lunch on the final day, though their path to victory was more tortuous than they might have expected when they bowled out Nottinghamshire for 97 on the opening day and then took a first-innings lead of 271. Nottinghamshire had chosen to bat and Gooch quickly stifled any complaints about the pitch by almost matching their total on his own. Further evidence came when Nottinghamshire scored 415 themselves, with five men making half-centuries. Essex wobbled on the third evening. But Such came in as night-watchman at 19 for two and scored the second fifty of his career in partnership with the boisterous Rollins, who completed the win after Gooch was out for a duck. Gooch had not batted on the Saturday because of a selectors' meeting. There was another absentee on Monday: umpire Constant was summoned to the Botham and Lamb v Imran libel case.

Close of play: First day, Essex 234-4 (P. J. Prichard 21*, R. C. Irani 23*); Second day, Nottinghamshire 152-1 (P. R. Pollard 72*, R. T. Bates 10*); Third day, Essex 26-2 (R. J. Rollins 14*, P. M. Such 2*).

Nottinghamshire

P. R. Pollard b Irani	14	– c Grayson b Law	86
R. T. Robinson c Rollins b Ilott	38	– c and b Law	51
*P. Johnson c Irani b Williams	1	– (5) c Rollins b Williams	61
A. A. Metcalfe c Rollins b Irani	7	– b Ilott	43
U. Afzaal c Rollins b Irani	3	– (6) c Rollins b Andrew	5
C. L. Cairns c Prichard b Ilott	3	– (7) c Law b Such	51
K. P. Evans not out	21	– (8) c Rollins b Ilott	56
†W. M. Noon c Grayson b Ilott	0	– (9) b Such	2
R. T. Bates lbw b Ilott	0	– (3) c and b Law	17
M. N. Bowen c Rollins b Irani	4	– not out	11
J. A. Afford c Rollins b Irani	1	– c and b Ilott	0
L-b 1, n-b 4	5	B 8, l-b 9, w 5, n-b 10	32
1/40 2/41 3/64 4/64 5/70 6/70 7/74 8/74 9/93	97	1/133 2/171 3/180 4/281 5/285 6/307 7/373 8/375 9/415	415

Bonus points – Essex 4.

Bowling: *First Innings*—Ilott 13–5–31–4; Andrew 6–2–20–0; Williams 6–2–18–1; Irani 11.3–3–27–5. *Second Innings*—Ilott 22.5–2–62–3; Williams 25–9–51–1; Irani 7–2–23–0; Andrew 8–1–27–1; Such 34–12–80–2; Grayson 21–8–55–0; Law 27–8–100–3.

Essex

G. A. Gooch c Noon b Afford	91	– (5) c Pollard b Bates	0
D. D. J. Robinson c Noon b Bowen	29	– (1) b Afford	8
A. P. Grayson b Bates	17	– (2) b Bowen	0
S. G. Law c Johnson b Afford	45	– (6) not out	1
*P. J. Prichard c Noon b Evans	80		
R. C. Irani c Afzaal b Bowen	36		
†R. J. Rollins c Johnson b Bowen	0	– (3) not out	74
M. C. Ilott b Bowen	2		
N. F. Williams not out	34		
P. M. Such lbw b Evans	2	– (4) c Afford b Bates	54
S. J. W. Andrew c Cairns b Bowen	12		
L-b 3, n-b 17	20	L-b 2, n-b 6	8
1/104 2/134 3/190 4/194 5/269 6/271 7/273 8/343 9/345	368	1/0 2/19 3/129 4/129	(4 wkts) 145

Bonus points – Essex 4, Nottinghamshire 4.

Bowling: *First Innings*—Cairns 8–3–13–0; Evans 26–5–83–2; Bowen 31.5–3–119–5; Bates 21–1–88–1; Afford 32–14–62–2; Afzaal 1–1–0–0. *Second Innings*—Evans 7–3–10–0; Bowen 8–1–31–1; Bates 13–1–36–2; Afford 15–3–45–1; Afzaal 3–0–21–0.

Umpires: D. J. Constant and G. Sharp.
A. A. Jones deputised for D. J. Constant on the 4th day.

At Hartlepool, July 25, 26, 27. ESSEX beat DURHAM by 292 runs.

At Lord's, August 1, 2, 3. ESSEX beat MIDDLESEX by an innings and 51 runs.

At Chelmsford, August 6. ESSEX lost to SOUTH AFRICA A by 11 runs (See South Africa A tour section).

At Taunton, August 8, 9, 10. ESSEX beat SOMERSET by an innings and 11 runs.

At Chelmsford, August 17, 18, 19. ESSEX lost to PAKISTANIS by 271 runs (See Pakistani tour section).

ESSEX v GLOUCESTERSHIRE

At Colchester, August 22, 23, 24, 26. Essex won by an innings and 64 runs. Essex 24 pts, Gloucestershire 3 pts. Toss: Gloucestershire.

Claiming their fifth successive Championship victory early on the final afternoon, Essex found themselves top of the table with Kent. The 21-year-old seamer Cowan helped bring Gloucestershire's first innings to a swift conclusion by becoming the first Essex player to achieve a hat-trick at Castle Park – and taking five in an innings for the first time. Gooch, with his sixth century of the summer, and Robinson opened with 194 before Robinson retired with his finger broken by a delivery from Walsh; Prichard and Irani also scored freely as Essex built up a first-innings lead of 252. Gloucestershire were soon in disarray, losing half their side for 30 at their second attempt. Lynch and Russell, with his second half-century of the match, ensured a little respectability, but Williams, returning his best figures for the county, was leading Essex's celebrations before long.

Close of play: First day, Essex 72-0 (G. A. Gooch 33*, D. D. J. Robinson 35*); Second day, Essex 194-0 (G. A. Gooch 105*, D. D. J. Robinson 72*); Third day, Gloucestershire 27-4 (M. A. Lynch 10*, R. P. Davis 5*).

Gloucestershire

D. R. Hewson c Lewis b Williams	37	– b Ilott	1
M. G. N. Windows b Ilott	33	– b Williams	1
A. Symonds c Lewis b Ilott	52	– c Grayson b Williams	0
T. H. C. Hancock lbw b Cowan	15	– b Ilott	8
M. A. Lynch c Rollins b Irani	18	– c Rollins b Cowan	50
M. W. Alleyne c Lewis b Such	22	– (7) c Cowan b Irani	23
†R. C. Russell c Irani b Cowan	63	– (8) c sub b Cowan	57
R. P. Davis c Grayson b Cowan	5	– (6) c Such b Williams	7
M. C. J. Ball c Lewis b Cowan	1	– b Williams	9
A. M. Smith b Cowan	0	– c Grayson b Williams	7
*C. A. Walsh not out	3	– not out	13
B 2, l-b 9, n-b 20	31	B 4, l-b 4, n-b 4	12
1/57 2/113 3/134 4/165 5/173 6/242 7/257 8/263 9/263	280	1/4 2/4 3/4 4/17 5/30 6/84 7/104 8/136 9/144	188

Bonus points – Gloucestershire 2, Essex 4.

Bowling: *First Innings*—Ilott 16–1–47–2; Williams 16–2–62–1; Irani 11–0–53–1; Cowan 16–3–68–5; Such 15–7–25–1; Grayson 3–0–14–0. *Second Innings*—Ilott 15–6–35–2; Williams 17–3–43–5; Cowan 17–0–76–2; Irani 7–1–25–1; Such 1–0–1–0.

Essex

G. A. Gooch hit wkt b Walsh	111
D. D. J. Robinson retired hurt	72
A. P. Grayson lbw b Ball	45
*P. J. Prichard c Hancock b Alleyne	88
R. C. Irani run out	91
J. J. B. Lewis run out	15
†R. J. Rollins c Windows b Alleyne	33
M. C. Ilott c Hancock b Alleyne	33
N. F. Williams c Davis b Alleyne	1
A. P. Cowan not out	10
B 16, l-b 5, n-b 12	33
1/223 2/336 3/346 4/406 5/465 6/510 7/515 8/532 (8 wkts dec.)	532

P. M. Such did not bat.

Bonus points – Essex 4, Gloucestershire 1 (Score at 120 overs: 434-4).

D. D. J. Robinson retired hurt at 194.

Bowling: Walsh 28.1–3–102–1; Smith 27–4–118–0; Alleyne 30–8–80–4; Davis 26–2–129–0; Ball 24–5–72–1; Symonds 4–0–10–0.

Umpires: J. D. Bond and K. E. Palmer.

At Leeds, August 29, 30, 31, September 2. ESSEX lost to YORKSHIRE by 98 runs.

At Birmingham, September 3, 4, 5, 6. ESSEX beat WARWICKSHIRE by 170 runs.

ESSEX v SUSSEX

At Chelmsford, September 12, 13, 14, 16. Sussex won by 137 runs. Sussex 24 pts, Essex 8 pts. Toss: Sussex.

On a pitch offering some help, but not as much as his figures suggest, Salisbury returned a career-best eight for 75 to send Essex to a defeat which ended their hopes of a seventh title in 18 years. They started encouragingly enough in pursuit of a daunting 421-run target, but were then teased into submission. Wells had shored up Sussex's first innings, and Drakes scored an unbeaten 145 in the second, making a century in successive Championship matches, before the declaration arrived. Some Essex players let their frustrations boil over. Law and Prichard showed blatant dissent when umpire Whitehead rejected a bat-pad appeal against Drakes on the third day, while Such showed his anger on the final morning when Phillips survived a similar appeal. The match ended with last man Andrew greeting his dismissal with a glare and great reluctance to remove himself from the crease.

Close of play: First day, Sussex 361-8 (I. D. K. Salisbury 69*, N. C. Phillips 15*); Second day, Sussex 2-0 (N. J. Lenham 0*, C. W. J. Athey 0*); Third day, Sussex 335-8 (V. C. Drakes 105*, N. C. Phillips 0*).

Sussex

N. J. Lenham c Grayson b Such	55	– c Such b Andrew	44
C. W. J. Athey lbw b Cowan	6	– c Hussain b Law	74
K. Greenfield b Such	36	– lbw b Law	37
*A. P. Wells lbw b Grayson	122	– lbw b Such	46
K. Newell b Irani	11	– c Cowan b Law	0
V. C. Drakes run out	19	– not out	145
†P. Moores c Gooch b Law	13	– b Such	4
I. D. K. Salisbury b Irani	70	– b Such	5
D. R. Law c Cowan b Such	0	– c Hussain b Such	0
N. C. Phillips not out	15	– not out	40
R. J. Kirtley c Law b Cowan	1		
L-b 15	15	B 4, l-b 10, n-b 8	22
1/14 2/95 3/112 4/135 5/183 6/248 7/324 8/329 9/362	363	1/77 2/154 3/165 (8 wkts dec.) 4/169 5/281 6/289 7/299 8/327	417

Bonus points – Sussex 4, Essex 4.

Bowling: *First Innings*—Ilott 12–1–52–0; Cowan 16.1–2–58–2; Irani 19–3–62–2; Andrew 14–5–45–0; Such 28–6–95–3; Law 5–0–17–1; Grayson 8–1–19–1. *Second Innings*—Cowan 14–3–30–0; Such 49–11–149–4; Ilott 13–1–38–0; Irani 15–2–47–0; Andrew 5–2–14–1; Grayson 8–3–12–0; Law 25–4–113–3.

Essex

G. A. Gooch c and b Kirtley	82	– c Wells b Salisbury	41
A. P. Grayson lbw b Salisbury	16	– c Moores b Drakes	29
N. Hussain c Moores b Drakes	44	– c Moores b Salisbury	35
S. G. Law c Lenham b Phillips	64	– b Salisbury	28
*P. J. Prichard lbw b Kirtley	2	– b Phillips	14
R. C. Irani c Salisbury b Kirtley	43	– c Wells b Salisbury	0
†R. J. Rollins c Phillips b Kirtley	27	– c Lenham b Salisbury	59
M. C. Ilott lbw b Phillips	2	– c Newell b Salisbury	16
A. P. Cowan b Salisbury	34	– c Phillips b Salisbury	21
P. M. Such b Salisbury	19	– not out	9
S. J. W. Andrew not out	4	– c Greenfield b Salisbury	0
B 2, l-b 14, w 1, n-b 6	23	B 13, l-b 1, w 1, n-b 16	31
1/54 2/135 3/167 4/171 5/248 6/268 7/279 8/299 9/351	360	1/60 2/111 3/138 4/167 5/167 6/167 7/218 8/263 9/279	283

Bonus points – Essex 4, Sussex 4.

Bowling: *First Innings*—Drakes 14–2–57–1; Law 11–3–39–0; Kirtley 23–3–94–4; Salisbury 28.2–3–94–3; Phillips 21–4–54–2; Lenham 2–0–6–0. *Second Innings*—Drakes 10–1–56–1; Kirtley 3–0–22–0; Phillips 34–8–116–1; Salisbury 29.4–9–75–8.

Umpires: J. H. Harris and A. G. T. Whitehead.

ESSEX v GLAMORGAN

At Chelmsford, September 19, 20, 21, 22. Glamorgan won by seven wickets. Glamorgan 24 pts, Essex 6 pts. Toss: Essex.

A masterful 149 from 203 balls by Morris destroyed Essex's hopes of the runners-up spot in the Championship. They had to settle for fifth as Glamorgan, chasing 284, cruised to victory. Morris shared an opening stand of 199 in 48 overs with James, who made 78 after being dropped by Gooch at slip before scoring. Gooch had dominated Essex's first innings before retiring at lunch on the second day to accompany his father to hospital. He had scored 170 from 253 balls with 114 in boundaries; the umpires had agreed he could resume later, but Essex lost their last five for 21 to deprive him of the chance. Maynard replied with a superb 122, featuring 17 fours, and put on 222 with Hemp; he declared after reaching their fourth batting point. Then the 18-year-old left-arm spinner, Cosker, undermined the home side's second innings by claiming the prize wickets of Gooch, Hussain and Law.

Close of play: First day, Essex 148-1 (G. A. Gooch 62*, N. Hussain 60*); Second day, Glamorgan 55-2 (D. L. Hemp 11*, M. P. Maynard 22*); Third day, Essex 143-3 (S. G. Law 16*, G. A. Gooch 16*).

Essex

G. A. Gooch retired not out	170	– (5) c Dale b Cosker	25
A. P. Grayson c Shaw b Watkin	12	– lbw b Watkin	7
N. Hussain c Hemp b Watkin	68	– c Croft b Cosker	64
S. G. Law b Parkin	66	– c Hemp b Cosker	26
*P. J. Prichard c Shaw b Dale	14	– (1) c and b Croft	38
R. C. Irani c Shaw b Dale	10	– b Dale	20
†R. J. Rollins c Shaw b Watkin	0	– b Croft	46
M. C. Ilott c Cosker b Dale	5	– c Parkin b Cosker	30
A. P. Cowan lbw b Dale	5	– c Hemp b Croft	6
P. M. Such not out	1		
S. J. W. Andrew c Maynard b Watkin	0	– (10) not out	1
L-b 6, n-b 10	16	B 2, l-b 2, n-b 2	6
1/33 2/182 3/280 4/346 5/346 6/360 7/361 8/366 9/367	367	1/13 2/110 3/112 4/158 5/163 6/202 7/256 8/268 9/269 (9 wkts dec.)	269

Bonus points – Essex 4, Glamorgan 4.

In the first innings G. A. Gooch retired not out at 346-4.

Bowling: *First Innings*—Watkin 22.5–6–64–4; Parkin 19–2–59–1; Hemp 2–0–28–0; Dale 16–4–52–4; Croft 23–3–102–0; Cosker 10–0–56–0. *Second Innings*—Watkin 10–2–39–1; Parkin 3–0–30–0; Dale 10–2–51–1; Croft 23–5–79–3; Cosker 19.4–4–66–4.

Glamorgan

S. P. James c Hussain b Cowan	12	– c Rollins b Law	78
H. Morris c Andrew b Cowan	10	– b Law	149
D. L. Hemp b Law	95	– not out	33
*M. P. Maynard c Prichard b Ilott	122	– c Cowan b Such	9
P. A. Cottey not out	69	– not out	6
A. Dale c Prichard b Grayson	23		
†A. D. Shaw c Law b Such	4		
R. D. B. Croft not out	5		
B 2, l-b 11	13	B 2, l-b 5, n-b 2	9
1/17 2/24 3/246 4/260 5/305 6/318 (6 wkts dec.)	353	1/199 2/254 3/275 (3 wkts)	284

D. A. Cosker, S. L. Watkin and O. T. Parkin did not bat.

Bonus points – Glamorgan 4, Essex 2.

Bowling: *First Innings*—Ilott 19–4–68–1; Cowan 20–4–56–2; Irani 7–0–47–0; Andrew 7–2–19–0; Such 11–0–60–1; Law 18–2–69–1; Grayson 6–1–21–1. *Second Innings*—Ilott 7–2–17–0; Cowan 4–1–19–0; Irani 5–0–21–0; Such 20–0–87–1; Grayson 14–1–52–0; Law 13.3–0–81–2.

Umpires: J. W. Holder and R. Julian.

Steve James

GLAMORGAN

Patron: HRH The Prince of Wales
President: W. Wooller
Chairman: F. D. Morgan
Chairman, Cricket Committee: H. D. Davies
Secretary: M. J. Fatkin
Captain: M. P. Maynard
Director of Coaching: A. Jones
First Eleven Coach: D. A. G. Fletcher
Grounds Supervisor: L. A. Smith
Scorer: B. T. Denning

Glamorgan had an unspectacular season until they broke the news late in August that they had signed the Pakistani fast bowler Waqar Younis as their overseas player for 1997. The capture of Waqar – described by club captain Matthew Maynard as "possibly the best signing Glamorgan have ever made" – was a credit to the club's negotiating skills. He was apparently offered more money by Surrey, his previous county, but chose Glamorgan, saying he hoped to emulate Viv Richards, whose presence had provided them with such inspiration and success.

Glamorgan were short of inspiration in 1996, but advanced in a quiet way. They moved six places up the Championship table to tenth, despite finishing with only 43 bowling points, fewer than any other county. They won six games and were well placed to beat Gloucestershire by an innings at Bristol, but for rain, while they forfeited another likely victory by failing to take the last two Hampshire wickets at Southampton. That, they hoped, would not be a problem in 1997, with Waqar available to unleash his in-swinging yorkers at opposing tailenders.

Maynard had set six Championship wins as a target during his first season as captain, but his objectives in the one-day competitions were not achieved. Glamorgan headed their group in the Benson and Hedges Cup but – as in the 1995 NatWest – were knocked out by Warwickshire at Cardiff. They seemed to be cruising to victory until losing their last five wickets for 11 runs – after Maynard and Ottis Gibson had shared a record-breaking 136 for the sixth wicket. They were also beaten at home in the opening round of the NatWest, by Worcestershire, and lacked consistency in the Sunday League, where the batting order was constantly reshuffled and the team rarely played to a pattern. Gibson, who arrived in April with a serious groin injury which restricted his appearances and affected his performances, was a huge disappointment. He underwent a hernia operation at the end of May and his bowling never measured up to his international status. He rarely used his long run and gave the impression – especially after hearing that Waqar was to replace him – that he was not interested, an attitude confirmed when he asked to be left out of the two final Championship games.

Bowling resources in 1996 were further depleted by Roland Lefebvre's enforced retirement before the start of the season, following a serious injury he had suffered the previous summer. The Dutch bowler had contributed much to Glamorgan's one-day success with his economical strike-rate and outstanding fielding. So once again they depended heavily on the willing work force of

Steve Watkin and Robert Croft, who became Glamorgan's 14th Test cricketer when he played against Pakistan at The Oval. The two bowlers combined figures of 1,508 overs and 139 wickets for the county reflected their heavy responsibility, but Waqar's arrival should assist Watkin, whose dependable qualities have carried an under-strength attack for several seasons.

Darren Thomas, who had promised much but achieved little since taking five wickets on his debut as a 17-year-old in 1992, was given numerous opportunities. But, ignoring length and line to rely on pace, he conceded too many runs; figures of 20 wickets at 58.75 reflected his erratic performances. In contrast, Owen Parkin, a young seamer who recovered from a serious back injury in 1995, emerged as a bowler of considerable promise, taking five for 28 on his Sunday League debut at Hove and removing Worcestershire's top three – including Graeme Hick – in the NatWest Trophy two days later. Dean Cosker, an 18-year-old left-arm spinner, also made an immediate impression, taking six wickets on his first Championship appearance against Lancashire and dismissing three of Essex's Test batsmen in the final match. Glamorgan won both games. Gary Butcher, who was given an extended run due to injuries, responded by taking seven for 77 against Gloucestershire and scoring 679 runs in his first full season.

There was no shortage of runs. Steve James, Hugh Morris, Tony Cottey and Maynard all exceeded 1,500 and between them struck 23 centuries. James, who scored a career-best 235 against Nottinghamshire, was the leading run-scorer with 1,766, an aggregate exceeded only by Graham Gooch. The other three also struck double-hundreds and, after scoring 149 against Essex, Morris only requires a hundred against Surrey to complete his set of Championship centuries against every other county.

Among the other batsmen, David Hemp played in only five Championship games after suffering a serious injury at Fenner's in April, when he collided in the outfield with Morris. Hemp, who broke four ribs and also punctured a lung, took time to adjust when he returned two months later and began to feel out of sorts with the county. He signed for Warwickshire in November. A broken finger disrupted Adrian Dale's season after he had scored a brilliant 120 in a run-chase at Northampton, but the young batsman Alun Evans showed considerable promise after making his debut at Oxford. Evans, who was MCC's Young Cricketer of the Year in 1995, struck an unbeaten 50 on his Sunday League debut against Gloucestershire and looked as though he might blossom into a player of substance. Glamorgan succumbed to the current trend of including wicket-keeper/batsmen when they replaced Colin Metson – one of the best in the business – with Adrian Shaw because of Shaw's run-scoring potential. He responded with two half-centuries in September, but needed to work hard at his craft to emulate Metson, who has been awarded a benefit in 1997.

The season ended with an embarrassing row when three players – Steve Barwick, a Glamorgan player for 16 years, Alistair Dalton and Neil Kendrick – learned of their release during the Second Eleven game against Worcestershire. They refused to field the following day, and the match was lost. But, with Waqar on his way, and the plans for the rebuilding of Sophia Gardens starting to take shape, Glamorgan looked to 1997 in optimistic mood. – EDWARD BEVAN.

GLAMORGAN 1996

[*Bill Smith*

Back row: A. W. Evans, D. A. Cosker, G. P. Butcher, A. P. Davies, O. T. Parkin, N. M. Kendrick, J. R. A. Williams, A. J. Dalton. *Middle row:* B. T. Denning (*First Eleven scorer*), D. O. Conway (*physiotherapist*), A. D. Shaw, A. Dale, O. D. Gibson, D. L. Hemp, R. P. Lefebvre, S. D. Thomas, G. R. Stone (*secretary*), G. N. Lewis (*Second Eleven scorer*). *Front row:* J. Derrick (*coach*), R. D. B. Croft, S. L. Watkin, S. R. Barwick, H. Morris, M. P. Maynard (*captain*), C. P. Metson, S. P. James, P. A. Cottey, A. Jones (*director of coaching*).

GLAMORGAN RESULTS

All first-class matches – Played 21: Won 6, Lost 6, Drawn 9.

County Championship matches – Played 17: Won 6, Lost 5, Drawn 6.

Competition placings – Britannic Assurance County Championship, 10th; NatWest Trophy, 1st round; Benson and Hedges Cup, q-f; AXA Equity & Law League, 13th.

COUNTY CHAMPIONSHIP AVERAGES

BATTING

Cap		*M*	*I*	*NO*	*R*	*HS*	*100s*	*50s*	*Avge*	*Ct/St*
1992	P. A. Cottey†	17	31	6	1,476	203	4	9	59.04	14
1987	M. P. Maynard	15	28	3	1,470	214	5	6	58.80	20
1986	H. Morris†	16	30	1	1,530	202*	5	9	52.75	14
1992	S. P. James	17	32	0	1,532	235	6	5	47.87	14
1994	O. D. Gibson§	8	13	3	408	97	0	3	40.80	6
1994	D. L. Hemp	5	9	1	267	95	0	1	33.37	5
	G. P. Butcher	12	21	3	547	89	0	4	30.38	8
1992	A. Dale	12	21	1	585	120	1	3	29.25	4
1992	R. D. B. Croft†	15	24	4	543	78	0	4	27.15	12
	A. W. Evans†	4	7	1	148	48*	0	0	24.66	3
	O. T. Parkin	7	9	6	60	14	0	0	20.00	3
	A. D. Shaw†	10	13	1	234	74	0	2	19.50	24/4
	S. D. Thomas†	8	13	2	175	48	0	0	15.90	2
1989	S. L. Watkin†	16	18	5	124	34	0	0	9.53	7
	D. A. Cosker	5	6	1	45	24	0	0	9.00	3
1987	S. R. Barwick†	5	5	1	32	20*	0	0	8.00	2
1987	C. P. Metson	7	11	4	53	18*	0	0	7.57	12/2
	N. M. Kendrick	8	8	4	19	16*	0	0	4.75	4

* *Signifies not out.* † *Born in Wales.* § *Overseas player.*

BOWLING

	O	*M*	*R*	*W*	*BB*	*5W/i*	*Avge*
S. L. Watkin	580.4	149	1,692	63	4-28	0	26.85
R. D. B. Croft	807.5	205	2,050	67	6-78	4	30.59
G. P. Butcher	180.1	27	716	20	7-77	1	35.80
A. Dale	137.1	35	466	12	4-52	0	38.83
D. A. Cosker	155.4	38	622	16	4-60	0	38.87
N. M. Kendrick	188	63	516	13	4-89	0	39.69
O. T. Parkin	174.4	41	553	13	3-22	0	42.53
O. D. Gibson	243	41	991	20	3-43	0	49.55
S. D. Thomas	228	25	924	16	5-121	1	57.75

Also bowled: S. R. Barwick 114.3–39–286–2; P. A. Cottey 34–3–107–4; D. L. Hemp 9–0–60–0; M. P. Maynard 7.3–4–7–0.

COUNTY RECORDS

Highest score for:	287*	D. E. Davies v Gloucestershire at Newport	1939
Highest score against:	313*	S. J. Cook (Somerset) at Cardiff	1990
Best bowling for:	10-51	J. Mercer v Worcestershire at Worcester	1936
Best bowling against:	10-18	G. Geary (Leicestershire) at Pontypridd	1929
Highest total for:	587-8 dec.	v Derbyshire at Cardiff	1951
Highest total against:	657-7 dec.	by Warwickshire at Birmingham	1994
Lowest total for:	22	v Lancashire at Liverpool	1924
Lowest total against:	33	by Leicestershire at Ebbw Vale	1965

At Cambridge, April 17, 18, 19. GLAMORGAN drew with CAMBRIDGE UNIVERSITY.

GLAMORGAN v YORKSHIRE

At Cardiff, May 2, 3, 4, 6. Yorkshire won by 43 runs. Yorkshire 22 pts, Glamorgan 5 pts. Toss: Yorkshire.

A match of batting records ended with a collapse that gave Yorkshire victory with nine balls to spare. Glamorgan seemed likely winners at 202 for three, needing 58 from nine overs. But Gough and White demolished the last seven for 14 runs. No wickets fell on the opening day, when Moxon and Vaughan piled up 316. Two of the most famous statistics in cricket, the Yorkshire opening stands of 555 and 554, appeared under threat. And the partnership reached 362 – an all-wicket record for any team playing Glamorgan, and the fourth-highest stand for Yorkshire – before Vaughan was dismissed next morning for a career-best 183. Moxon scored 213, hitting 24

HIGHEST PARTNERSHIPS FOR YORKSHIRE

555	P. Holmes and H. Sutcliffe v Essex at Leyton	1932
554	J. T. Brown and J. Tunnicliffe v Derbyshire at Chesterfield	1898
378	J. T. Brown and J. Tunnicliffe v Sussex at Sheffield	1897
362	**M. D. Moxon and M. P. Vaughan v Glamorgan at Cardiff**	**1996**
351	G. Boycott and M. D. Moxon v Worcestershire at Worcester	1985

All the above were for the first wicket.

fours in eight and a half hours and 424 balls. It was the first double-century ever in Yorkshire–Glamorgan matches, but the second arrived next day, when Morris made an unbeaten 202 from 368 balls, with 28 fours. Surprisingly, it was his maiden double-hundred – Moxon, who like Morris made his debut in 1981, had scored his fifth. But, going back to September, it was Morris's fourth unbeaten century in successive first-class innings in Great Britain; in between, he scored 77 and 0 against Northern Transvaal. Maynard hit a dominant 136 as he and Morris put on 228. Yorkshire were in trouble at 32 for four until Bevan and night-watchman Wharf set up the declaration with a stand of 133.

Close of play: First day, Yorkshire 316-0 (M. D. Moxon 150*, M. P. Vaughan 156*); Second day, Glamorgan 132-2 (H. Morris 59*, M. P. Maynard 19*); Third day, Yorkshire 32-4 (M. G. Bevan 14*, A. G. Wharf 0*).

Yorkshire

M. D. Moxon c Watkin b Croft	213	– lbw b Thomas	10
M. P. Vaughan c Dale b Butcher	183	– lbw b Watkin	3
*D. Byas lbw b Watkin	12	– c and b Croft	2
M. G. Bevan st Metson b Croft	15	– run out	77
A. McGrath c James b Croft	9	– lbw b Watkin	2
C. White c Morris b Croft	1	– (7) not out	14
†R. J. Blakey c Butcher b Croft	38	– (8) lbw b Thomas	2
D. Gough not out	31	– (9) not out	19
P. J. Hartley b Watkin	10		
A. G. Wharf (did not bat)		– (6) run out	62
L-b 22, n-b 2	24	B 2, l-b 5, w 1, n-b 6	14
1/362 2/385 3/404 4/416 5/424 6/476 7/510 8/536 (8 wkts dec.)	536	1/13 2/14 3/23 4/32 5/165 6/167 7/169 (7 wkts dec.)	205

R. D. Stemp did not bat.

Bonus points – Yorkshire 4, Glamorgan 1 (Score at 120 overs: 416-4).

Bowling: *First Innings*—Watkin 28.5–6–101–2; Thomas 26–3–89–0; Butcher 12–1–62–1; Barwick 29–12–70–0; Croft 45–11–133–5; Dale 7–0–44–0; Cottey 3–0–15–0. *Second Innings*—Watkin 17–4–64–2; Thomas 13–0–47–2; Croft 24–7–47–1; Barwick 5–1–19–0; Butcher 2–0–21–0.

Glamorgan

S. P. James c Blakey b Hartley	40	– b Stemp	62
H. Morris not out	202	– b Hartley	51
A. Dale c Blakey b Hartley	5	– c Hartley b Stemp	23
*M. P. Maynard c Blakey b White	136	– lbw b Gough	27
P. A. Cottey lbw b White	1	– run out	21
G. P. Butcher c Moxon b Hartley	25	– c Gough b White	0
R. D. B. Croft c Moxon b Gough	12	– b Gough	0
S. D. Thomas c Stemp b Wharf	18	– lbw b White	4
†C. P. Metson not out	12	– not out	2
S. L. Watkin (did not bat)		– lbw b White	0
S. R. Barwick (did not bat)		– lbw b White	4
B 13, l-b 8, w 2, n-b 8	31	B 8, l-b 14	22
1/76 2/92 3/320 4/328 5/385 6/421 7/456	(7 wkts dec.) 482	1/113 2/135 3/153 4/202 5/202 6/202 7/204 8/212 9/212	216

Bonus points – Glamorgan 4, Yorkshire 2 (Score at 120 overs: 422-6).

Bowling: *First Innings*—Gough 26–5–66–1; Hartley 26–6–104–3; Wharf 18–1–121–1; Stemp 29–10–68–0; White 20–6–44–2; Vaughan 11–3–30–0; Bevan 4–0–28–0. *Second Innings*—Gough 14–5–34–2; Hartley 10–1–56–1; White 8.3–2–33–4; Stemp 16–2–71–2.

Umpires: J. D. Bond and P. Willey.

At Northampton, May 9, 10, 11, 13. GLAMORGAN beat NORTHAMPTONSHIRE by five wickets.

GLAMORGAN v DERBYSHIRE

At Cardiff, May 16, 17, 18, 20. Derbyshire won by 110 runs. Derbyshire 22 pts, Glamorgan 6 pts. Toss: Derbyshire.

As in the previous home game, Glamorgan crumbled on the final day. They required only 218, but began disastrously, losing their top four for just three runs. Cottey steered them past their worst total against Derbyshire – 49 in 1967 – but Glamorgan were all out inside 22 overs. Malcolm took six for 52, his best figures for his county, and Harris four for 55, his best ever. There had been no shortage of first-innings runs for either side after Derbyshire rallied from some early losses. Owen reached his second hundred in successive matches and Wells made 165, his biggest score since leaving Sussex. Butcher took a career-best four for 28 and later scored 61, helping Cottey to put on 154 for the sixth wicket before Maynard declared 85 behind. But the final day saw Derbyshire lose nine wickets for 98 before Glamorgan's own collapse.

Close of play: First day, Derbyshire 334-5 (C. M. Wells 102*, D. G. Cork 4*); Second day, Glamorgan 12-0 (S. P. James 6*, C. P. Metson 2*); Third day, Derbyshire 34-1 (K. J. Barnett 17*, C. J. Adams 15*).

Derbyshire

K. J. Barnett c Metson b Watkin	0	– b Butcher	22
A. S. Rollins c Butcher b Croft	73	– lbw b Thomas	2
C. J. Adams c Maynard b Thomas	7	– c Maynard b Butcher	37
*D. M. Jones c Cottey b Butcher	22	– c Metson b Butcher	12
J. E. Owen c Butcher b Croft	105	– c Croft b Watkin	0
C. M. Wells c Thomas b Butcher	165	– c Morris b Watkin	3
D. G. Cork c Cottey b Croft	10	– lbw b Watkin	12
†K. M. Krikken lbw b Butcher	51	– not out	26
M. J. Vandrau c Metson b Croft	2	– c James b Watkin	0
A. J. Harris lbw b Butcher	1	– c Morris b Croft	17
D. E. Malcolm not out	2	– b Thomas	1
B 1, l-b 8, w 1, n-b 16	26		
1/0 2/9 3/51 4/152 5/303 6/355 7/452 8/461 9/461	464	1/8 2/56 3/68 4/73 5/73 6/84 7/93 8/97 9/124	132

Bonus points – Derbyshire 4, Glamorgan 2 (Score at 120 overs: 364-6).

Bowling: *First Innings*—Watkin 25–8–55–1; Thomas 27–3–129–1; Butcher 17.4–5–28–4; Dale 11–0–43–0; Croft 55–12–122–4; Kendrick 28–8–78–0; Maynard 1–1–0–0. *Second Innings*—Watkin 18–2–61–4; Thomas 7–2–12–2; Kendrick 5–1–10–0; Croft 6–2–14–1; Butcher 9–3–30–3; Dale 4–2–5–0.

Glamorgan

S. P. James c Krikken b Malcolm	7	– c Krikken b Harris	0
†C. P. Metson c Krikken b Malcolm	2	– (10) b Malcolm	0
H. Morris b Harris	90	– (2) lbw b Harris	0
A. Dale c Wells b Cork	26	– (3) b Malcolm	3
*M. P. Maynard c Krikken b Cork	35	– (4) c Krikken b Malcolm	0
P. A. Cottey not out	135	– (5) b Malcolm	45
G. P. Butcher not out	61	– (6) b Harris	7
R. D. B. Croft (did not bat)		– (7) b Malcolm	8
S. D. Thomas (did not bat)		– (8) c Krikken b Harris	28
N. M. Kendrick (did not bat)		– (9) b Malcolm	0
S. L. Watkin (did not bat)		– not out	16
B 4, l-b 6, w 7, n-b 6	23		
1/13 2/14 3/67 4/127 5/225 (5 wkts dec.)	379	1/0 2/3 3/3 4/3 5/23 6/48 7/77 8/79 9/79	107

Bonus points – Glamorgan 4, Derbyshire 2.

Bowling: *First Innings*—Malcolm 20–4–91–2; Cork 17.1–4–40–2; Harris 23–5–104–1; Wells 12–3–49–0; Vandrau 13–2–64–0; Barnett 6–2–21–0; Jones 1–1–0–0. *Second Innings*—Malcolm 11–3–52–6; Harris 10.4–1–55–4.

Umpires: D. R. Shepherd and A. G. T. Whitehead.

GLAMORGAN v WORCESTERSHIRE

At Abergavenny, May 23, 24, 25, 27. Drawn. Glamorgan 6 pts, Worcestershire 8 pts. Toss: Worcestershire. First-class debut: M. J. Rawnsley.

Abergavenny's sequence of tremendous matches in sunny weather was washed away over a wet bank holiday. Half the opening day and all of the second were rained off, and a vehicle transporting temporary stands turned part of the parking area into a quagmire. Moody and Cottey, who was leading Glamorgan while Maynard took part in the one-day internationals, both declared to give Worcestershire a run-chase of 323 from a minimum of 60 overs. Once Watkin reduced them to 11 for three in an eight-ball burst, the visitors' ambitions were restricted to saving the game. They lost their fifth wicket with 26 overs left, but Rhodes batted patiently for two and a half hours, supported by Lampitt, to see out time. On the third day, Glamorgan's lower order had rescued them from an unpromising 157 for six, adding 171 for the last four wickets; in Worcestershire's reply, Weston scored 121 not out, his highest innings yet, before the declaration came 128 behind.

Close of play: First day, Glamorgan 148-5 (A. D. Shaw 3*); Second day, No play; Third day, Glamorgan 8-1 (S. P. James 2*, S. L. Watkin 0*).

Glamorgan

S. P. James b Newport	20	– st Rhodes b Illingworth	89
H. Morris c Illingworth b Sheriyar	4	– lbw b Sheriyar	4
A. Dale c Moody b Newport	29		
G. P. Butcher b Newport	73	– c Sheriyar b Lampitt	42
*P. A. Cottey c Rawnsley b Newport	2	– c Rhodes b Lampitt	3
†A. D. Shaw b Newport	8		
R. D. B. Croft not out	73	– not out	9
O. D. Gibson c Rhodes b Illingworth	51	– (6) not out	34
S. D. Thomas c Illingworth b Rawnsley	23		
S. L. Watkin c Rhodes b Newport	17	– (3) b Sheriyar	0
S. R. Barwick run out	1		
B 2, l-b 7, n-b 18	27	L-b 9, n-b 4	13
1/24 2/26 3/127 4/137 5/148 6/157 7/227 8/264 9/317	328	1/8 2/33 3/106 4/117 5/161 (5 wkts dec.)	194

Bonus points – Glamorgan 3, Worcestershire 4.

Bowling: *First Innings*—Newport 28–7–100–6; Sheriyar 14–1–56–1; Lampitt 15.1–4–62–0; Illingworth 30–11–46–1; Rawnsley 14–3–55–1. *Second Innings*—Newport 9–4–41–0; Sheriyar 12–2–57–2; Illingworth 8–0–34–1; Lampitt 9–1–43–2; Rawnsley 2–0–10–0.

Worcestershire

T. S. Curtis not out	62	– c Shaw b Thomas	42
W. P. C. Weston not out	121	– b Watkin	1
K. R. Spiring (did not bat)		– lbw b Watkin	0
*T. M. Moody (did not bat)		– c James b Watkin	1
D. A. Leatherdale (did not bat)		– lbw b Butcher	30
†S. J. Rhodes (did not bat)		– not out	53
S. R. Lampitt (did not bat)		– not out	31
B 5, l-b 4, n-b 8	17	B 2, l-b 6, n-b 6	14
(no wkt dec.)	200	1/7 2/7 3/11 4/54 5/97 (5 wkts)	172

P. J. Newport, R. K. Illingworth, A. Sheriyar and M. J. Rawnsley did not bat.

Bonus point – Worcestershire 1.

Bowling: *First Innings*—Watkin 7–3–24–0; Thomas 11.4–2–62–0; Gibson 2–0–13–0; Croft 11–4–25–0; Butcher 5–0–30–0; Barwick 7–3–13–0; Dale 5–1–24–0. *Second Innings*—Watkin 14–3–41–3; Thomas 11–0–43–1; Croft 19–1–57–0; Barwick 11–8–4–0; Butcher 5–1–19–1.

Umpires: V. A. Holder and N. T. Plews.

At Oxford, June 1, 3, 4. GLAMORGAN drew with OXFORD UNIVERSITY.

At Lord's, June 6, 7, 8. GLAMORGAN lost to MIDDLESEX by nine wickets.

GLAMORGAN v SOMERSET

At Swansea, June 13, 14, 15, 17. Glamorgan won by 173 runs. Glamorgan 22 pts, Somerset 7 pts. Toss: Glamorgan.

Glamorgan's spinners set up their second Championship win by dismissing Somerset with 14 overs remaining. A dry pitch was skilfully exploited by slow left-armer Kendrick and, especially, off-spinner Croft; they took 14 wickets between them in the match. Somerset must have regretted including only one slow bowler, Batty. Nevertheless, they reduced Glamorgan to 158 for five on the opening day before a century from Cottey enabled the home side to recover to 310. Hayhurst then occupied the crease for five hours, falling four short of his hundred, to set up a lead of 28. But Glamorgan's top order batted well at their second attempt, with James scoring 110 after his first-day duck and Cottey again prominent. They declared an hour into the final morning, leaving Somerset to score 327 from a minimum of 79 overs. There was little chance of that after the visitors lost three wickets on 59.

Close of play: First day, Somerset 2-1 (M. N. Lathwell 0*); Second day, Somerset 299-7 (R. J. Turner 27*, G. D. Rose 6*); Third day, Glamorgan 275-3 (S. P. James 100*, P. A. Cottey 45*).

Glamorgan

S. P. James c Trescothick b Caddick	0	– c Caddick b Batty	110
H. Morris lbw b Rose	54	– c Turner b Rose	31
A. Dale c Turner b Rose	35	– b Shine	62
*M. P. Maynard c Holloway b Shine	1	– c Turner b Caddick	13
P. A. Cottey c Lathwell b Caddick	112	– c Trescothick b Batty	61
G. P. Butcher c Bowler b Rose	15	– not out	33
R. D. B. Croft c Holloway b Rose	37	– c Turner b Shine	7
†A. D. Shaw b Batty	15	– c Lathwell b Batty	3
S. D. Thomas c Turner b Caddick	12	– not out	1
N. M. Kendrick lbw b Batty	2		
S. L. Watkin not out	0		
B 2, l-b 13, w 4, n-b 8	27	B 4, l-b 8, w 1, n-b 20	33
1/0 2/69 3/79 4/126 5/158 6/241 7/292 8/296 9/302	310	1/51 2/155 3/205 (7 wkts dec.) 4/297 5/310 6/330 7/341	354

Bonus points – Glamorgan 3, Somerset 4.

Bowling: *First Innings*—Caddick 28–8–92–3; Shine 14–5–50–1; Batty 29–9–80–2; Rose 23–4–45–4; Hayhurst 4–1–17–0; Parsons 3–1–11–0. *Second Innings*—Caddick 24–4–70–1; Shine 22–3–123–2; Batty 37–13–107–3; Rose 15–3–40–1; Parsons 3–2–2–0.

Somerset

J. D. Batty b Watkin	2	– (9) not out	19
M. N. Lathwell b Kendrick	68	– (1) c Croft b Thomas	10
*A. N. Hayhurst c Cottey b Kendrick	96	– (5) c Cottey b Croft	0
M. E. Trescothick c and b Kendrick	9	– b Watkin	11
P. C. L. Holloway c and b Croft	3	– (3) c Cottey b Croft	20
K. A. Parsons c Cottey b Kendrick	2	– b Croft	18
P. D. Bowler lbw b Croft	73	– (2) b Kendrick	25
†R. J. Turner c Shaw b Watkin	31	– (7) lbw b Kendrick	21
G. D. Rose c Shaw b Watkin	18	– (8) b Croft	23
A. R. Caddick not out	16	– lbw b Croft	1
K. J. Shine c Dale b Watkin	6	– b Croft	1
B 7, l-b 4, w 1, n-b 2	14	B 4	4
1/2 2/104 3/130 4/141 5/146 6/221 7/293 8/311 9/324	338	1/15 2/59 3/59 4/59 5/79 6/99 7/132 8/136 9/147	153

Bonus points – Somerset 3, Glamorgan 3 (Score at 120 overs: 307-7).

Bowling: *First Innings*—Watkin 27.5–13–47–4; Croft 51–11–113–2; Thomas 10–2–53–0; Butcher 5–0–16–0; Kendrick 33–8–89–4; Cottey 4–1–9–0. *Second Innings*—Watkin 9–1–28–1; Thomas 5–1–9–1; Croft 33.2–12–78–6; Kendrick 28–16–34–2.

Umpires: J. W. Holder and K. J. Lyons.

At Hove, June 20, 21, 22, 24. GLAMORGAN lost to SUSSEX by an innings and seven runs.

At Pontypridd, June 29, 30, July 1. GLAMORGAN drew with PAKISTANIS (See Pakistani tour section).

At Bristol, July 4, 5, 6, 8. GLAMORGAN drew with GLOUCESTERSHIRE.

At Cardiff, July 17, 18. GLAMORGAN lost to SOUTH AFRICA A by an innings and 44 runs (See South Africa A tour section).

GLAMORGAN v LANCASHIRE

At Cardiff, July 25, 26, 27, 29. Glamorgan won by 48 runs. Glamorgan 22 pts, Lancashire 7 pts. Toss: Glamorgan. First-class debut: D. A. Cosker.

Debutant slow left-armer Dean Cosker shared nine wickets with his spin partner Croft as Glamorgan gained their third Championship win with 15 minutes remaining. Play did not resume on the final day until 2.15 p.m. when Lancashire were set 287 in what became 57 overs. They began well, but lost five mid-innings wickets for 22 in 29 balls. Chapple and Martin put on 50 for the ninth wicket, but could not quite salvage the draw. Cosker, a former Millfield student, took four for 60, while Croft advanced his claim for an England place with five for 47. During the first two days, Maynard had scored the third double-century of his career, which included 22 fours and three sixes. It was also his third hundred in successive Championship innings. Then Speak, with his first Championship century for two years, and Lloyd – who scored a hundred before lunch on the third day – shared a partnership of 251, before Lancashire declared 27 behind, thus setting up the tense finish.

Close of play: First day, Glamorgan 359-3 (M. P. Maynard 147*, P. A. Cottey 74*); Second day, Lancashire 280-3 (N. J. Speak 87*, G. D. Lloyd 42*); Third day, Glamorgan 259-3 (M. P. Maynard 68*, P. A. Cottey 55*).

Glamorgan

S. P. James b Chapple	18	– c Gallian b Keedy	49
H. Morris c Hegg b Martin	71	– c Gallian b Martin	61
G. P. Butcher c Hegg b Watkinson	35	– b Martin	3
*M. P. Maynard b Austin	214	– not out	68
P. A. Cottey c Gallian b Martin	74	– not out	55
†A. D. Shaw lbw b Martin	0		
O. D. Gibson c Hegg b Chapple	19		
R. D. B. Croft lbw b Chapple	0		
D. A. Cosker st Hegg b Watkinson	24		
S. L. Watkin c Hegg b Watkinson	11		
S. R. Barwick not out	20		
B 1, l-b 16, n-b 2	19	B 14, l-b 7, n-b 2	23
1/38 2/100 3/166 4/359 5/359 6/378 7/378 8/463 9/484	505	1/103 2/112 3/139 (3 wkts dec.)	259

Bonus points – Glamorgan 4, Lancashire 3 (Score at 120 overs: 402-7).

Bowling: *First Innings*—Chapple 33–8–122–3; Martin 32–8–115–3; Gallian 14–5–51–0; Austin 23–6–57–1; Keedy 28–5–70–0; Watkinson 22.2–3–73–3. *Second Innings*—Martin 14–2–47–2; Chapple 8–1–46–0; Watkinson 12–0–59–0; Austin 7–0–36–0; Keedy 16–4–50–1.

Lancashire

J. E. R. Gallian c Shaw b Watkin	13	– (3) st Shaw b Cosker	29
S. P. Titchard c and b Watkin	67	– b Croft	42
J. P. Crawley b Croft	46	– (4) c James b Croft	25
N. J. Speak not out	138	– (6) c Shaw b Cosker	6
G. D. Lloyd c Watkin b Cosker	142	– c Barwick b Cosker	15
*M. Watkinson c and b Cosker	1	– (1) b Watkin	22
†W. K. Hegg not out	24	– b Croft	28
I. D. Austin (did not bat)		– c Morris b Croft	0
G. Chapple (did not bat)		– not out	21
P. J. Martin (did not bat)		– lbw b Cosker	34
G. Keedy (did not bat)		– lbw b Croft	0
B 15, l-b 9, w 1, n-b 22	47	B 7, l-b 3, n-b 6	16
1/22 2/108 3/181 4/432 5/434 (5 wkts dec.)	478	1/40 2/84 3/128 4/139 5/143 6/149 7/150 8/187 9/237	238

Bonus points – Lancashire 4, Glamorgan 2.

Bowling: *First Innings*—Watkin 20–3–82–2; Gibson 17.4–0–112–0; Croft 33–6–97–1; Cosker 25–6–90–2; Barwick 12–0–48–0; Butcher 4–0–25–0. *Second Innings*—Watkin 11–0–54–1; Gibson 7–0–54–0; Butcher 3–0–13–0; Cosker 16–4–60–4; Croft 17.1–6–47–5.

Umpires: B. J. Meyer and R. Palmer.

At Worksop, August 1, 2, 3, 5. GLAMORGAN beat NOTTINGHAMSHIRE by eight wickets.

GLAMORGAN v LEICESTERSHIRE

At Swansea, August 8, 9, 10, 12. Drawn. Glamorgan 9 pts, Leicestershire 11 pts. Toss: Leicestershire.

Glamorgan's last pair survived the final eight balls with ten men round the bat, denying Leicestershire the win that would have put them 12 points clear in the Championship table. The home attack, already weakened by the absence of Watkin, also lost Kendrick, who split the webbing in his hand, and conceded 536 to Leicestershire. Smith scored a career-best 190 and put on 200 with Simmons. But Cottey took four in an innings for the first time with his rarely used off-breaks and then rescued his side from 127 for six with a maiden double-hundred, hitting 32 fours and a six in 333 balls. He was the fourth Glamorgan batsman to score a double-century in 1996; this had been achieved only twice before, by Essex and Northamptonshire, both in 1990. Cottey put on a county record 211 for the seventh wicket with Gibson, who fell three short of his first hundred in England. Leicestershire trebled their first-innings lead before setting Glamorgan 335 from 86 overs. But an earlier declaration might have given them a better chance of dismissing the opposition on a turning pitch.

Close of play: First day, Leicestershire 298-3 (B. F. Smith 82*, P. V. Simmons 79*); Second day, Glamorgan 133-6 (P. A. Cottey 58*, O. D. Gibson 6*); Third day, Leicestershire 141-3 (B. F. Smith 27*, A. Habib 23*).

Leicestershire

V. J. Wells b Croft	44	– c sub b Croft	46
D. L. Maddy c Gibson b Butcher	43	– b Thomas	2
G. I. Macmillan b Butcher	18	– c Metson b Thomas	31
B. F. Smith c and b Cottey	190	– run out	32
*P. V. Simmons c Maynard b Croft	92	– (6) c sub b Croft	34
A. Habib c Morris b Thomas	34	– (5) lbw b Croft	28
†P. A. Nixon c Croft b Cottey	42	– not out	27
D. J. Millns c sub b Croft	6	– c Evans b Croft	11
G. J. Parsons c Morris b Cottey	0	– not out	6
A. R. K. Pierson not out	13		
M. T. Brimson c Evans b Cottey	4		
B 2, l-b 8, w 10, n-b 30	50	B 4, l-b 7, w 1, n-b 2	14
1/89 2/95 3/124 4/324 5/395 6/485 7/494 8/496 9/527	536	1/14 2/66 3/99 4/151 5/161 6/200 7/220	(7 wkts dec.) 231

Bonus points – Leicestershire 4, Glamorgan 2 (Score at 120 overs: 453-5).

Bowling: *First Innings*—Gibson 24–4–131–0; Thomas 21–1–97–1; Butcher 26–2–112–2; Croft 52–8–137–3; Kendrick 1.3–1–0–0; Maynard 0.3–0–0–0; Cottey 17–2–49–4. *Second Innings*—Gibson 11–0–78–0; Thomas 9–0–51–2; Croft 17–2–47–4; Butcher 2–0–16–0; Cottey 7–0–22–0; Maynard 2–0–6–0.

Glamorgan

S. P. James c Wells b Millns	5	– lbw b Simmons	29
H. Morris run out	8	– lbw b Pierson	106
A. W. Evans c Simmons b Wells	13	– c Simmons b Pierson	23
*M. P. Maynard b Simmons	21	– st Nixon b Brimson	33
P. A. Cottey b Simmons	203	– b Brimson	10
G. P. Butcher c Wells b Simmons	3	– run out	15
†C. P. Metson b Brimson	1	– (10) not out	1
O. D. Gibson b Pierson	97	– (7) b Macmillan	42
R. D. B. Croft lbw b Simmons	29	– c Wells b Brimson	0
S. D. Thomas c Parsons b Simmons	4	– (8) b Macmillan	13
N. M. Kendrick not out	0	– not out	0
B 6, l-b 11, w 1, n-b 31	49	B 13, l-b 14	27
1/8 2/28 3/35 4/104 5/118 6/127 7/338 8/402 9/418	433	1/82 2/115 3/165 4/195 5/228 6/240 7/280 8/287 9/299	(9 wkts) 299

Bonus points – Glamorgan 4, Leicestershire 4.

Bowling: *First Innings*—Millns 20–1–115–1; Parsons 17–5–55–0; Wells 13–1–42–1; Simmons 22.3–4–62–5; Brimson 30–6–98–1; Pierson 15–1–44–1. *Second Innings*—Millns 5–1–19–0; Parsons 6–1–15–0; Pierson 20–4–75–2; Brimson 27–6–86–3; Wells 6–4–3–0; Simmons 10–4–30–1; Macmillan 12–2–44–2.

Umpires: A. A. Jones and R. A. White.

At Birmingham, August 15, 16, 17, 19. GLAMORGAN lost to WARWICKSHIRE by two wickets.

GLAMORGAN v KENT

At Cardiff, August 22, 23, 24, 26. Drawn. Glamorgan 5 pts, Kent 6 pts. Toss: Kent.

Rain badly affected the first two days and the third was washed out, so that Kent did not complete their first innings until 11.55 on the final morning. After Fulton and Walker had put on 122 on the opening day and Hooper and Llong took their fourth-wicket stand to 147, a declaration and two forfeits left Glamorgan a target of 324 from 80 overs. When rain caused two further interruptions, the captains agreed that Glamorgan should be fed 50 more runs and then chase 108 in 11 overs. But once Morris was out, Gibson declined to attack the bowling. Kent, chasing the Championship, were unhappy about this, but they did not help their cause by posting eight men on the boundary for Headley and McCague, or by allowing Patel only one more over, which he bowled over the wicket into the rough.

Close of play: First day, Kent 128-1 (D. P. Fulton 53*, T. R. Ward 2*); Second day, Kent 255-3 (C. L. Hooper 52*, N. J. Llong 33*); Third day, No play.

Kent

D. P. Fulton c James b Gibson	64	*†S. A. Marsh not out	3
M. J. Walker c James b Dale	59		
T. R. Ward c Watkin b Barwick	25	B 8, l-b 2, w 1, n-b 12	23
C. L. Hooper lbw b Watkin	77		
N. J. Llong c Maynard b Barwick	63	1/122 2/157 3/163 4/310 5/312	(5 wkts dec.) 323
M. V. Fleming not out	9		

D. W. Headley, M. M. Patel, M. J. McCague and T. N. Wren did not bat.

Bonus points – Kent 3, Glamorgan 2.

Bowling: Watkin 19–3–56–1; Gibson 16–3–40–1; Dale 15–2–70–1; Barwick 30.3–10–85–2; Hemp 5–0–21–0; Kendrick 5–0–37–0; Cottey 1–0–4–0.

Kent forfeited their second innings.

Glamorgan

Glamorgan forfeited their first innings.

S. P. James lbw b McCague	3
H. Morris c Fleming b McCague	118
D. L. Hemp b Headley	4
*M. P. Maynard b Hooper	47
P. A. Cottey c Ward b Headley	70
A. Dale not out	11
O. D. Gibson not out	12
B 2, l-b 3, w 1, n-b 2	8
1/10 2/15 3/109 4/245 5/249 (5 wkts)	273

N. M. Kendrick, †A. D. Shaw, S. L. Watkin and S. R. Barwick did not bat.

Bowling: McCague 14–4–46–2; Headley 18–1–82–2; Patel 7–0–38–0; Wren 6–0–30–0; Hooper 10.1–4–29–1; Fleming 2–0–5–0; Fulton 1–0–19–0; Walker 1–0–19–0.

Umpires: B. Dudleston and G. Sharp.

At Chester-le-Street, August 28, 29, 30, 31. GLAMORGAN beat DURHAM by 141 runs.

At Southampton, September 3, 4, 5, 6. GLAMORGAN drew with HAMPSHIRE.

GLAMORGAN v SURREY

At Cardiff, September 12, 13, 14, 16. Drawn. Glamorgan 9 pts, Surrey 11 pts. Toss: Glamorgan.

Glamorgan thwarted Surrey's hopes of a win which would have kept them a point behind leaders Leicestershire, though Stewart would have been set a more realistic target to chase on the fourth day had he declared Surrey's first innings after gaining maximum batting points. He elected to bat on for a lead of 107, and Maynard felt he had no option but to extend Glamorgan's second innings into the final afternoon. Glamorgan lost three wickets in clearing the deficit before James, with his sixth Championship hundred of the season, and Cottey shared a fourth wicket partnership of 168. Stewart used ten bowlers – including himself – hoping Maynard would declare earlier, but elicited no response. Surrey were eventually set 336 from what became 51 overs; once they slipped to 88 for four in the 11th over, they settled for the draw.

Close of play: First day, Glamorgan 351-9 (S. L. Watkin 3*, O. T. Parkin 10*); Second day, Surrey 273-4 (N. Shahid 66*, A. J. Hollioake 45*); Third day, Glamorgan 218-3 (S. P. James 84*, P. A. Cottey 64*).

Glamorgan

S. P. James c D. J. Bicknell b M. P. Bicknell	4	– c Thorpe b Shahid	131
H. Morris c Stewart b Lewis	6	– c Stewart b Julian	17
D. L. Hemp lbw b M. P. Bicknell	47	– b Benjamin	8
*M. P. Maynard c Pearson b Benjamin	82	– c Lewis b Pearson	16
P. A. Cottey lbw b D. J. Bicknell	25	– b Shahid	83
A. Dale b Pearson	90	– c Stewart b Shahid	11
†A. D. Shaw b Benjamin	19	– c Lewis b Butcher	74
R. D. B. Croft b Pearson	25	– c Lewis b Butcher	38
D. A. Cosker lbw b Julian	0	– not out	8
S. L. Watkin not out	8	– c sub b Butcher	0
O. T. Parkin c Stewart b Lewis	12	– not out	8
L-b 9, w 5, n-b 32	46	B 5, l-b 20, w 5, n-b 18	48
1/14 2/14 3/123 4/166 5/208 6/279 7/317 8/322 9/336	364	1/47 2/56 3/94 4/262 5/286 6/311 7/390 8/434 9/434 (9 wkts dec.)	442

Bonus points – Glamorgan 4, Surrey 4.

Bowling: *First Innings*—M. P. Bicknell 19–8–49–2; Lewis 21.2–2–86–2; Julian 15–3–54–1; Benjamin 20–4–53–2; Pearson 21–6–59–2; D. J. Bicknell 15–0–54–1. *Second Innings*—M. P. Bicknell 12–2–37–0; Lewis 14–4–46–0; Julian 8–1–40–1; Benjamin 10–2–25–1; Hollioake 5–1–12–0; Pearson 34–7–88–1; D. J. Bicknell 5–0–26–0; Shahid 29–5–96–3; Butcher 5–0–23–3; Stewart 2–0–24–0.

Surrey

D. J. Bicknell st Shaw b Croft	30	– (6) not out	27
M. A. Butcher c Maynard b Cosker	31	– c Shaw b Parkin	9
*†A. J. Stewart run out	10	– (7) c Cottey b Cosker	2
G. P. Thorpe c Morris b Watkin	77	– (8) c Hemp b Cosker	10
N. Shahid lbw b Watkin	79	– (9) not out	24
A. J. Hollioake c Morris b Watkin	51	– (3) lbw b Croft	85
C. C. Lewis b Cosker	57	– (4) st Shaw b Croft	40
B. P. Julian lbw b Cosker	41	– (1) c Hemp b Watkin	0
M. P. Bicknell not out	59	– (5) c and b Croft	2
J. E. Benjamin c Parkin b Cosker	5		
R. M. Pearson not out	8		
B 11, l-b 8, n-b 4	23	B 1, l-b 3, n-b 2	6
1/69 2/71 3/102 4/201 5/291 6/296 7/383 8/426 9/448	(9 wkts dec.) 471	1/0 2/15 3/84 4/88 5/154 6/157 7/171	(7 wkts) 205

Bonus points – Surrey 4, Glamorgan 2 (Score at 120 overs: 359-6).

Bowling: *First Innings*—Watkin 26–4–85–3; Parkin 14–3–55–0; Croft 56–11–158–1; Cosker 34–10–142–4; Dale 8–4–12–0. *Second Innings*—Watkin 3.4–0–26–1; Parkin 3–0–42–1; Croft 22–6–49–3; Cosker 20–6–80–2; Maynard 1–1–0–0; Cottey 1–0–4–0.

Umpires: J. C. Balderstone and A. Clarkson.

At Chelmsford, September 19, 20, 21, 22. GLAMORGAN beat ESSEX by seven wickets.

COUNTY MEMBERSHIP

	1986	*1995*	*1996*
Derbyshire	1,420	2,580	2,555
Durham	—	5,795	5,876
Essex	8,954	7,502	7,237
Glamorgan	2,877	11,893	10,812
Gloucestershire	3,764	4,672	5,339
Hampshire	4,536	4,790	4,394
Kent	5,121	5,657	5,960
Lancashire	10,853	13,638	14,044
Leicestershire	3,470	4,878	4,591
Middlesex	8,287	8,581	8,810
Northamptonshire	1,886	2,296	4,121
Nottinghamshire	4,077	4,861	5,145
Somerset	4,911	5,517	5,736
Surrey	6,062	6,588	7,051
Sussex	4,604	5,243	6,067
Warwickshire	8,453	14,441	15,081
Worcestershire	3,045	5,141	5,869
Yorkshire	10,250	9,190	9,201
MCC	19,925	19,808	19,860
Total	112,495	143,071	147,749

Note: In 1996, Durham, Northamptonshire, Somerset, Sussex and Worcestershire began to quote their membership in terms of the total number of individuals affiliated to their clubs. Fifteen counties now follow this practice: only Derbyshire, Kent and Yorkshire continue to register corporate or joint membership as representing one person.

Courtney Walsh

GLOUCESTERSHIRE

Patron: Lord Vestey
President: J. A. Horne
Chairman: J. C. Higson
Chief Executive: C. L. Sexstone
Cricket Secretary: P. G. M. August
Captain: C. A. Walsh
Coach: A. W. Stovold
Assistant Coach: P. W. Romaines
Head Groundsman: D. Bridle
Scorer: K. T. Gerrish

You could hardly blame the pace attack for Gloucestershire's patently unfulfilled season. Courtney Walsh bowled for most of the time like a dream. That deceptively languorous action had a succession of batsmen ducking or sparring helplessly to slip. He took 85 wickets, more than anyone else on the county circuit. He was again a popular and respected captain, though no more communicative than usual when the locals began to worry about whether he would be coming back. In the end came the verbal promise – and relief all round, until it became clear that West Indies' heavy 1997 schedule made the best intentions unsustainable.

It was difficult to imagine how the county might ever have bowled out oppositions without Walsh in 1996. But, of course, Mike Smith – less spectacularly and with less venom – did his share. In the right conditions he had prodigious in-swing. Short himself and awkward to play, he earned his 60 Championship wickets by honest left-arm graft, and increasing craft. At Lord's, in the opening match, his eight for 73 in Middlesex's second innings was an exhibition fitting for headquarters. So, in their varying ways, were his six wickets against Leicestershire at Cheltenham and his five against Northamptonshire at Bristol. There was also valued medium-paced backing from Mark Alleyne. The slow bowlers, Richard Davis and Martyn Ball, alas, took only 32 Championship wickets between them. Gloucestershire suffered at times from an imbalance when it was their turn to bowl. The captain needed more penetrative and effective options than were available to him.

Yet it was the batsmen who let the county down. And this was supposed to be the summer when half a dozen young batsmen of unquestionable ability, at least at the lower levels of the game, were due to establish themselves in first-class cricket. Rob Cunliffe might have done, if he had not been given compassionate leave because of family illness. Matt Windows came up with a memorable 184 in the Warwickshire match at Cheltenham; Tim Hancock raised high hopes with his hundred against Surrey at Gloucester; Dominic Hewson nearly got there at Southampton.

For too long, however, the batting failures mounted. The county actually went eight weeks without picking up a batting point. Tony Wright, in his benefit year, scored one solid century before injury and subsequent loss of form. Alleyne sustained his reputation as the eternal riddle. Repeatedly he had just started to construct handsome innings when he was out. At Worcester, he dominated his side's innings with a well-fashioned 149. Why, everyone at Nevil Road asks, do such gems not come more frequently?

One of the most eloquent commentaries of all was that Jack Russell headed the Championship batting averages. It reflects his qualities of application, but also the failings of the others. Russell is a middle-order batsman, still searching for 1,000 runs in a season: a bonny fighter with a repertoire of shots acquired, we can only believe, in the undulating byways of the Cotswolds. But there are specialist batsmen in the county who should be scoring twice as many runs.

Andrew Symonds was the only Gloucestershire batsman to reach 1,000 runs in all first-class cricket. In five or six matches he batted quite superbly. Maybe too much was expected of him. Was he, just occasionally, burdened by a little too much technical advice? Was he needlessly caught up in the tactical complexes of the English game? Symonds is still young; he is also an instinctive player, at his best when the head is buzzing with adventure and the shots are queuing up. His decision to play for Australia A in the winter made it virtually certain he would not return, as it meant the loss of his England qualification. He will be badly missed. His Gloucestershire cap was well deserved, as was one for "Reggie" Williams, the second wicket-keeper. Williams contemplated moving, especially when Russell appeared to be permanently out of favour with the England selectors. But he remained patient and has proved an efficient deputy – and, like Jack, not at all a bad batsman in a crisis.

Gloucestershire slipped from sixth to 13th in the table and their final destination would have been more depressing but for a late-season flourish. They had started the summer in high spirits with their win over Middlesex. Wright, Cunliffe and Smith all appeared to have run into immediate form. The flags were fluttering excitedly back in Bristol. After that, the county went miserably into decline until the closing weeks.

The added resolve could be traced, as if one didn't know, to Cheltenham. There, Gloucestershire had Leicestershire on the run but, in an embarrassing match – not least for those who looked after corporate hospitality – it was all over in two days, and not in Gloucestershire's favour. The home county had actually dismissed the ultimate champions in the 150s in both innings. They had, however, perished in 27 overs at their own first attempt, for 71, and there was really no coming back in this surprisingly low-scoring fixture on a pitch that was not capricious.

Cheltenham still celebrated a Championship victory: Warwickshire were outplayed and went down by an innings. Back at Bristol, Yorkshire lost by ten wickets, and so did Kent. The faithful were left to ponder what might have been. The disquieting pattern of Gloucestershire's season was that, because of the limp and fibreless quality of much of the early batting, regular and unreasonable burdens were placed on the middle order. It must have been dispiriting for the successful bowlers who saw their sweaty labours being eroded.

The county's one-day endeavours again lacked imagination – and points. Gloucestershire ended two from the bottom of the Sunday League, with no more than four wins, and went out of the NatWest Trophy as soon as they met first-class opposition. Their utter failure to adjust technical standards and attitudes again worked against them: they are not the only set of players who, in recent years when the game has demanded conflicting and confusing skills, have got understandably lost in the text-book wilderness. – DAVID FOOT.

GLOUCESTERSHIRE 1996

[*Bill Smith*

Back row: D. R. Hewson, R. J. Cunliffe, K. P. Sheeraz, M. C. J. Ball, R. I. Dawson, T. H. C. Hancock, R. C. J. Williams. *Middle row:* M. A. Lynch, A. M. Smith, R. P. Davis, J. G. Whitby-Coles, M. J. Cawdron, A. Symonds, D. J. P. Boden, J. Lewis, K. E. Cooper, K. T. Gerrish (*scorer*). *Front row:* P. W. Romaines (*assistant coach*), M. W. Alleyne, R. C. Russell (*vice-captain*), J. C. Higson (*chairman*), A. J. Wright, A. W. Stovold (*coach*). *Inset:* C. A. Walsh (*captain*).

GLOUCESTERSHIRE RESULTS

All first-class matches – Played 18: Won 5, Lost 7, Drawn 6.

County Championship matches – Played 17: Won 5, Lost 7, Drawn 5.

Competition placings – Britannic Assurance County Championship, 13th; NatWest Trophy, 2nd round; Benson and Hedges Cup, q-f; AXA Equity & Law League, 16th.

COUNTY CHAMPIONSHIP AVERAGES

BATTING

Cap		*M*	*I*	*NO*	*R*	*HS*	*100s*	*50s*	*Avge*	*Ct/St*
1985	R. C. Russell†	13	21	4	634	75	0	7	37.29	31/2
1995	M. A. Lynch	10	17	1	548	72	0	5	34.25	9
1996	A. Symonds	17	28	0	949	127	2	4	33.89	8
1990	M. W. Alleyne	17	28	2	831	149	1	3	31.96	14
	T. H. C. Hancock	14	25	3	672	116	1	4	30.54	10
	M. G. N. Windows†	9	17	2	443	184	1	1	29.53	4
1987	A. J. Wright	9	17	0	415	106	1	3	24.41	11
	R. J. Cunliffe	6	11	0	252	82	0	2	22.90	1
	D. R. Hewson†	5	10	1	206	87	0	2	22.88	1
	N. J. Trainor	8	14	1	261	67	0	2	20.07	5
1996	R. C. J. Williams†	4	7	0	124	44	0	0	17.71	12
1995	A. M. Smith	16	25	3	364	55*	0	1	16.54	2
	R. P. Davis	14	21	2	292	43	0	0	15.36	15
1985	C. A. Walsh§	15	24	13	154	25	0	0	14.00	7
1996	M. C. J. Ball†	13	21	4	236	46	0	0	13.88	15
	R. I. Dawson	6	11	1	123	21	0	0	12.30	0
	J. Lewis	9	15	1	97	20	0	0	6.92	3

Also batted: D. J. P. Boden (1 match) 1 (1 ct); (cap 1995) K. E. Cooper (1 match) 5.

* *Signifies not out.* † *Born in Gloucestershire.* § *Overseas player.*

BOWLING

	O	*M*	*R*	*W*	*BB*	*5W/i*	*Avge*
C. A. Walsh	526.3	144	1,432	85	6-22	7	16.84
M. W. Alleyne	422	115	1,209	47	5-32	1	25.72
A. M. Smith	487.3	114	1,615	60	8-73	3	26.91
A. Symonds	118.3	25	374	12	2-21	0	31.16
J. Lewis	234	53	743	16	3-74	0	46.43
R. P. Davis	280.2	68	905	19	4-93	0	47.63
M. C. J. Ball	225	61	639	13	3-40	0	49.15

Also bowled: D. J. P. Boden 31–5–121–1; K. E. Cooper 39–12–82–5; R. I. Dawson 0.2–0–4–0; T. H. C. Hancock 13–4–46–0; N. J. Trainor 1–0–4–0.

COUNTY RECORDS

Highest score for:	318*	W. G. Grace v Yorkshire at Cheltenham	1876
Highest score against:	296	A. O. Jones (Nottinghamshire) at Nottingham	1903
Best bowling for:	10-40	E. G. Dennett v Essex at Bristol	1906
Best bowling against:	10-66	A. A. Mailey (Australians) at Cheltenham	1921
Highest total for:	653-6 dec.	v Glamorgan at Bristol	1928
Highest total against:	774-7 dec.	by Australians at Bristol	1948
Lowest total for:	17	v Australians at Cheltenham	1896
Lowest total against:	12	by Northamptonshire at Gloucester	1907

At Lord's, May 2, 3, 4. GLOUCESTERSHIRE beat MIDDLESEX by five wickets.

At Bristol, May 11, 12, 13. GLOUCESTERSHIRE drew with INDIANS (See Indian tour section).

GLOUCESTERSHIRE v SOMERSET

At Bristol, May 16, 17, 18, 20. Drawn. Gloucestershire 9 pts, Somerset 9 pts. Toss: Somerset.

Most of the drama came at the end, when Batty and Shine, Somerset's ninth-wicket pair, survived 12 overs, with Walsh at his most aggressive. Walsh was back from West Indian duties for his first Championship match since 1994; he followed three wickets in the first innings with five in the second, leaving Somerset with bruised knuckles, apprehensive looks to complement their courage and, in Bowler's case, hospital treatment for a cut near the eye. Bowler rushed back, arriving in time for the final over, but Batty and Shine made sure he was not needed. Refreshingly, there were no complaints, merely praise for Walsh's skill. Gloucestershire batted badly in the first innings, when Hancock and Russell offered the only serious resistance. But, after rain and bad light cut the second day to just 30 overs, they still took a four-run lead. Lee, Somerset's new recruit from New South Wales, demonstrated his all-round skills, while Caddick's progress – following his shin injury – was carefully monitored by Test selector David Graveney.

Close of play: First day, Somerset 53-2 (M. N. Lathwell 30*, R. J. Harden 14*); Second day, Somerset 131-4 (R. J. Harden 53*, S. Lee 3*); Third day, Gloucestershire 136-6 (R. J. Cunliffe 0*, M. C. J. Ball 2*).

Gloucestershire

A. J. Wright c Lee b Caddick	11	– c Turner b Caddick	17
R. J. Cunliffe b Shine	3	– (7) lbw b Caddick	25
T. H. C. Hancock lbw b Lee	89	– c and b Shine	9
A. Symonds c and b Lee	18	– lbw b Batty	47
M. W. Alleyne c Turner b Lee	1	– lbw b Lee	27
†R. C. Russell c Caddick b Shine	63	– c Rose b Batty	1
M. C. J. Ball c Lathwell b Lee	19	– (8) c Turner b Lee	22
R. P. Davis c Turner b Rose	19	– (2) c Turner b Shine	31
J. Lewis b Caddick	0	– lbw b Batty	20
A. M. Smith b Rose	16	– c and b Shine	25
*C. A. Walsh not out	3	– not out	11
B 8, w 3, n-b 10	21	B 1, l-b 3, w 2, n-b 4	10
1/6 2/30 3/66 4/80 5/205 6/209 7/228 8/228 9/260	263	1/48 2/50 3/66 4/127 5/133 6/133 7/177 8/189 9/215	245

Bonus points – Gloucestershire 2, Somerset 4.

Bowling: *First Innings*—Caddick 18–6–43–2; Shine 11–0–63–2; Rose 13–2–44–2; Lee 14–4–55–4; Batty 20–5–50–0. *Second Innings*—Caddick 22–4–83–2; Shine 14.4–0–50–3; Batty 13–3–29–3; Lee 15–3–59–2; Rose 5–1–20–0.

Somerset

M. N. Lathwell c Davis b Walsh	49	– c Russell b Walsh	29
P. D. Bowler c Russell b Walsh	1	– retired hurt	12
*A. N. Hayhurst c Hancock b Walsh	6	– c Wright b Lewis	1
R. J. Harden run out	54	– c Wright b Walsh	7
P. C. L. Holloway run out	14	– lbw b Ball	14
S. Lee c sub b Smith	65	– lbw b Walsh	35
†R. J. Turner c Alleyne b Ball	50	– c Lewis b Walsh	4
G. D. Rose c sub b Smith	7	– b Ball	5
J. D. Batty c Russell b Ball	4	– not out	36
A. R. Caddick not out	0	– b Walsh	2
K. J. Shine c Alleyne b Smith	0	– not out	5
L-b 2, w 1, n-b 6	9	B 4, l-b 12, w 1, n-b 4	21
1/3 2/15 3/77 4/112 5/139 6/231 7/252 8/259 9/259	259	1/39 2/44 3/65 4/65 5/102 6/108 7/116 8/122	(8 wkts) 171

Bonus points – Somerset 2, Gloucestershire 4.

In the second innings P. D. Bowler retired hurt at 44-2, and R. J. Turner, when 0, retired hurt at 69 and resumed at 108.

Bowling: *First Innings*—Walsh 24–6–73–3; Smith 21.3–6–55–3; Lewis 19–7–46–0; Davis 9–0–44–0; Alleyne 5–1–15–0; Ball 7–0–24–2. *Second Innings*—Walsh 21–3–69–5; Smith 7–3–18–0; Lewis 6–1–21–1; Ball 12–2–38–2; Davis 1–0–9–0.

Umpires: B. J. Meyer and N. T. Plews.

GLOUCESTERSHIRE v SURREY

At Gloucester, May 23, 24, 25, 27. Drawn. Gloucestershire 9 pts, Surrey 8 pts. Toss: Gloucestershire. First-class debut: N. J. Trainor.

After the weather restricted the opening two days to 86 overs, Surrey declared 145 behind on the third evening, and were eventually set 309 in a minimum of 64 overs; they never approached the target and had only two wickets remaining at the end. Nick Trainor, who had failed sufficiently to impress his native Durham, and had written in vain to several other clubs, had been invited to prove himself in the West Country, and responded with a half-century in each innings, scored with a discerning technique. Hancock, too, had searched for form and recognition the previous season, but bounced back with a hundred. For Surrey, who had lost four players to England's one-day squad, pugnacious hitting by Ward prevented the possibility of the follow-on. Their best bowling came from Julian, who took five for the first time in Championship cricket. One awkward delivery of his hit Lynch on the thumb; nomadic by nature at the crease, Lynch wandered unwisely from his ground and was run out by Ratcliffe.

Close of play: First day, Gloucestershire 223-4 (T. H. C. Hancock 43*, M. W. Alleyne 5*); Second day, Gloucestershire 303-5 (T. H. C. Hancock 93*, R. C. Russell 18*); Third day, Surrey 228-6 dec.

Gloucestershire

A. J. Wright lbw b Julian	51	– c Julian b Benjamin	32
N. J. Trainor lbw b Julian	67	– b Benjamin	57
M. A. Lynch run out	0	– not out	46
T. H. C. Hancock c Kersey b Ratcliffe	116	– not out	19
A. Symonds c Kersey b M. P. Bicknell	32		
M. W. Alleyne b Julian	11		
†R. C. Russell c Shahid b Julian	42		
R. P. Davis c Hollioake b M. P. Bicknell	0		
M. C. J. Ball not out	7		
A. M. Smith c Hollioake b M. P. Bicknell	0		
*C. A. Walsh c and b Julian	8		
L-b 7, w 2, n-b 30	39	L-b 1, w 2, n-b 6	9
1/111 2/111 3/146 4/199 5/232 6/349 7/358 8/358 9/358	373	1/90 2/115	(2 wkts dec.) 163

Bonus points – Gloucestershire 4, Surrey 4.

Bowling: *First Innings*—M. P. Bicknell 29–6–98–3; Julian 30.5–7–97–5; Hollioake 8–1–25–0; Benjamin 21–4–77–0; Pearson 18–2–62–0; Ratcliffe 2–1–7–1. *Second Innings*—M. P. Bicknell 6–0–31–0; Julian 5–1–22–0; Pearson 11–0–58–0; Benjamin 8–0–37–2; Hollioake 2–0–14–0.

Surrey

D. J. Bicknell lbw b Smith	30	– lbw b Smith	0
M. A. Butcher c Lynch b Alleyne	38	– c Alleyne b Ball	58
J. D. Ratcliffe run out	29	– c Ball b Alleyne	1
*A. J. Hollioake st Russell b Ball	17	– b Walsh	52
N. Shahid c Wright b Walsh	0	– lbw b Ball	7
D. M. Ward not out	64	– lbw b Walsh	0
B. P. Julian lbw b Smith	9	– b Ball	32
†G. J. Kersey not out	34	– c Hancock b Walsh	6
M. P. Bicknell (did not bat)		– not out	6
R. M. Pearson (did not bat)		– not out	1
L-b 6, w 1	7	B 4, l-b 3, n-b 4	11
1/47 2/75 3/104 4/113 5/126 6/137	(6 wkts dec.) 228	1/7 2/30 3/114 4/122 5/124 6/158 7/161 8/167	(8 wkts) 174

J. E. Benjamin did not bat.

Bonus points – Surrey 1, Gloucestershire 2.

Bowling: *First Innings*—Walsh 19–7–43–1; Smith 13–2–31–2; Davis 13–4–37–0; Alleyne 14–5–40–1; Ball 17–5–41–1; Hancock 2–0–10–0; Symonds 1.4–0–20–0. *Second Innings*—Walsh 18–3–52–3; Smith 10–2–33–1; Alleyne 7–2–23–1; Ball 23–12–40–3; Davis 7–1–19–0.

Umpires: H. D. Bird and T. E. Jesty.

At Manchester, May 30, 31, June 1, 3. GLOUCESTERSHIRE drew with LANCASHIRE.

GLOUCESTERSHIRE v SUSSEX

At Bristol, June 13, 14, 15. Sussex won by three runs. Sussex 20 pts, Gloucestershire 4 pts. Toss: Sussex.

It would have been hard for Sussex to orchestrate a more exciting and unlikely result. Drakes dismissed Davis lbw to complete victory after Gloucestershire, 12 runs short and with three wickets in hand, had appeared clear favourites. An obdurate fifty by Wright and a calculated 71 by Alleyne counted for nothing. There had been wayward batting from both sides and, on the first day, 18 wickets fell. Sussex were 40 for five by lunch and Alleyne returned a career-best five for 32, with only Lenham showing much fibre. Gloucestershire in turn sank to 72 for eight on a Nevil Road pitch offering far less help to the bowlers than the scoring suggested. A total collapse was averted by the ninth-wicket pair, Ball and Smith. Law made a capable 97, his highest Championship score, after the top order crumpled against Walsh to set up the tense climax. Russell took his 600th catch for Gloucestershire, coinciding neatly with the announcement of his MBE.

Close of play: First day, Gloucestershire 138-8 (M. C. J. Ball 21*, A. M. Smith 42*); Second day, Gloucestershire 18-0 (N. J. Trainor 3*, A. J. Wright 8*).

Sussex

C. W. J. Athey lbw b Walsh	0	– c Wright b Walsh	4
T. A. Radford c Russell b Alleyne	11	– c Russell b Walsh	14
*A. P. Wells c Ball b Walsh	1	– c Ball b Walsh	36
K. Greenfield c Alleyne b Smith	10	– c Russell b Walsh	2
N. J. Lenham c Alleyne b Davis	70	– c Ball b Walsh	6
D. R. Law c Wright b Walsh	0	– c Russell b Smith	97
†P. Moores c Ball b Alleyne	28	– c Russell b Alleyne	8
I. D. K. Salisbury lbw b Alleyne	4	– run out	24
V. C. Drakes b Alleyne	0	– b Walsh	6
J. D. Lewry c Walsh b Alleyne	10	– c Hancock b Alleyne	10
E. S. H. Giddins not out	6	– not out	4
L-b 3, n-b 14	17	B 8, l-b 4, w 2, n-b 6	20
1/2 2/8 3/25 4/37 5/37 6/123 7/129 8/141 9/141	157	1/14 2/27 3/33 4/59 5/82 6/124 7/176 8/184 9/219	231

Bonus points – Gloucestershire 4.

Bowling: *First Innings*—Walsh 15.4–6–48–3; Smith 18.2–5–58–1; Alleyne 17–6–32–5; Hancock 3–2–3–0; Davis 5–1–13–1. *Second Innings*—Walsh 27–9–57–6; Smith 22.1–4–73–1; Alleyne 17–5–48–2; Ball 7–3–10–0; Davis 16–5–31–0.

Gloucestershire

N. J. Trainor b Drakes	4	– lbw b Lewry	6
A. J. Wright c Moores b Drakes	12	– lbw b Drakes	51
R. J. Cunliffe b Law	10	– b Law	6
T. H. C. Hancock c Moores b Law	3	– b Giddins	17
A. Symonds c Law b Giddins	11	– c Moores b Giddins	9
M. W. Alleyne lbw b Giddins	6	– c Moores b Law	71
†R. C. Russell c Greenfield b Giddins	14	– c Moores b Lewry	13
R. P. Davis c Greenfield b Law	5	– lbw b Drakes	13
M. C. J. Ball not out	26	– c Athey b Giddins	9
A. M. Smith c Salisbury b Giddins	48	– lbw b Drakes	2
*C. A. Walsh c Salisbury b Giddins	2	– not out	1
B 1, l-b 5, n-b 4	10	B 8, l-b 11, w 2, n-b 15	36
1/4 2/23 3/28 4/31 5/43 6/53 7/72 8/72 9/145	151	1/26 2/33 3/63 4/81 5/160 6/202 7/204 8/226 9/231	234

Bonus points – Sussex 4.

Bowling: *First Innings*—Drakes 9–2–27–2; Lewry 9–1–26–0; Law 13–4–35–3; Giddins 15.2–3–53–5; Salisbury 2–0–4–0. *Second Innings*—Drakes 23.4–4–66–3; Giddins 20–5–45–3; Lewry 15–1–41–2; Law 12–1–36–2; Salisbury 14–1–27–0.

Umpires: J. H. Hampshire and R. A. White.

At Nottingham, June 20, 21, 22. GLOUCESTERSHIRE lost to NOTTINGHAMSHIRE by an innings and three runs.

At Chester-le-Street, June 27, 28, 29, July 1. GLOUCESTERSHIRE drew with DURHAM.

GLOUCESTERSHIRE v GLAMORGAN

At Bristol, July 4, 5, 6, 8. Drawn. Gloucestershire 4 pts, Glamorgan 11 pts. Toss: Glamorgan.

For the first time, four Glamorgan batsmen scored a hundred in the same innings – which Maynard declared at 509 for three. It was an easy pitch and the bowling was innocuous; Walsh's contributions were restricted by flu, and Gloucestershire patently needed him. After the morning had been lost to rain, James and Morris reached 233 without being parted on the first day. After them came Maynard, in his crispest form, and Cottey, to share a fourth-wicket stand of 251, a county record against Gloucestershire. Only 20-year-old Alun Evans missed out. In contrast, Gloucestershire revealed their batting shortcomings again, leaving Butcher to savour career-best figures of seven for 77. There was a deficit of 328 as Glamorgan were left to bowl out the home team on the final day, the only one not shortened by rain. A Glamorgan win looked likely when Watkin used the second new ball to take three wickets without conceding a run, but they were frustrated by the ninth-wicket pair, Ball and Lewis.

Close of play: First day, Glamorgan 233-0 (S. P. James 114*, H. Morris 103*); Second day, Gloucestershire 13-0 (A. J. Wright 0*, R. J. Cunliffe 13*); Third day, Gloucestershire 181.

Glamorgan

S. P. James b Smith 118
H. Morris c Wright b Smith 108
A. W. Evans c Ball b Smith 4
*M. P. Maynard not out 145
P. A. Cottey not out 101
B 5, l-b 5, w 1, n-b 22 33

1/240 2/247 3/258 (3 wkts dec.) 509

G. P. Butcher, R. D. B. Croft, †A. D. Shaw, O. T. Parkin, N. M. Kendrick and S. L. Watkin did not bat.

Bonus points – Glamorgan 4, Gloucestershire 1 (Score at 120 overs: 419-3).

Bowling: Walsh 15–5–33–0; Smith 26–3–113–3; Lewis 26–6–88–0; Alleyne 20–3–78–0; Ball 33–7–111–0; Symonds 12.3–1–62–0; Hancock 4–1–14–0.

Gloucestershire

A. J. Wright c Maynard b Butcher	15	–	lbw b Butcher	30
R. J. Cunliffe b Watkin	18	–	c Butcher b Croft	82
T. H. C. Hancock lbw b Butcher	5	–	b Croft	6
R. I. Dawson c Shaw b Butcher	11	–	c Shaw b Croft	18
A. Symonds c Morris b Watkin	8	–	c James b Croft	30
M. W. Alleyne c Shaw b Butcher	27	–	lbw b Watkin	29
†R. C. J. Williams c Shaw b Watkin	44	–	c Shaw b Watkin	13
M. C. J. Ball c Evans b Butcher	6	–	not out	0
A. M. Smith not out	18	–	b Watkin	0
J. Lewis c Croft b Butcher	8	–	not out	1
*C. A. Walsh c Maynard b Butcher	2			
L-b 7, n-b 12	19		B 7, l-b 4, n-b 4	15
1/35 2/39 3/54 4/63 5/63 6/130 7/142 8/156 9/175	181		1/51 2/78 3/143 4/144 5/185 6/220 7/223 8/223 (8 wkts)	224

Bonus points – Glamorgan 4.

Bowling: *First Innings*—Watkin 24–8–64–3; Parkin 16–4–26–0; Butcher 23.3–4–77–7; Croft 6–4–7–0; Kendrick 2–2–0–0. *Second Innings*—Watkin 24.5–10–37–3; Parkin 17–6–58–0; Butcher 15–2–54–1; Croft 36–20–39–4; Kendrick 12–7–25–0; Maynard 2–2–0–0.

Umpires: G. I. Burgess and J. H. Harris.

GLOUCESTERSHIRE v LEICESTERSHIRE

At Cheltenham, July 18, 19. Leicestershire won by 102 runs. Leicestershire 20 pts, Gloucestershire 4 pts. Toss: Leicestershire.

A two-day win made Leicestershire Championship leaders, but only for 24 hours. It also left Gloucestershire an estimated £5,000 down on gate money; officials hastily organised a makeshift match with their Second Eleven on Saturday. Remarkably, 25 wickets fell on the first day, a reflection on poor batting and penetrative bowling rather than a capricious pitch. Leicestershire's opening innings revolved round the two Smiths. At No. 3, Ben batted untroubled for more than three hours, emphasising the technical flaws of the players around him. Mike took six for 55 with consistent swing: his first three were lbw, the others caught behind the stumps and at slip. But Gloucestershire collapsed for 71 in 27 overs, against steady rather than menacing seam bowling, and Leicestershire lost another five by the close, including Simmons for a first-day pair, twice lbw to Smith. They recovered to a modest 150, which left Gloucestershire to score 239. They never looked like countering Mullally and Millns, though Lynch, recalled to the side, offered flickering hope, scoring all but two of his 38 in boundaries.

Close of play: First day, Leicestershire 80-5 (J. J. Whitaker 12*, A. R. K. Pierson 12*).

Leicestershire

V. J. Wells lbw b Smith	5	– lbw b Smith	13
D. L. Maddy lbw b Smith	31	– c Symonds b Walsh	14
B. F. Smith not out	68	– run out	7
P. V. Simmons lbw b Smith	0	– (5) lbw b Smith	0
*J. J. Whitaker c Russell b Walsh	5	– (6) c Smith b Walsh	31
A. Habib c Russell b Smith	0	– (4) lbw b Walsh	4
†P. A. Nixon c Russell b Smith	4	– (8) c Windows b Walsh	3
D. J. Millns c Wright b Smith	0	– (9) c Russell b Alleyne	21
G. J. Parsons c Wright b Lewis	13	– (10) not out	10
A. R. K. Pierson c Ball b Lewis	0	– (7) c Russell b Alleyne	16
A. D. Mullally c and b Alleyne	1	– b Alleyne	1
B 5, l-b 10, w 1, n-b 16	32	B 8, l-b 1, w 1, n-b 20	30
1/7 2/78 3/78 4/85 5/86 6/114 7/120 8/156 9/156	159	1/37 2/39 3/44 4/48 5/62 6/109 7/114 8/127 9/140	150

Bonus points – Gloucestershire 4.

Bowling: *First Innings*—Walsh 16–3–42–1; Smith 18–3–55–6; Lewis 9–5–19–2; Alleyne 11–3–23–1; Ball 4–2–5–0. *Second Innings*—Walsh 18–6–40–4; Smith 14–2–60–2; Ball 2–0–8–0; Alleyne 8.3–5–12–3; Lewis 5–0–21–0.

Gloucestershire

M. G. N. Windows lbw b Millns	0	– c Nixon b Millns	4
A. J. Wright c Simmons b Millns	0	– c Nixon b Simmons	7
T. H. C. Hancock c Simmons b Mullally	4	– c and b Simmons	18
M. A. Lynch c Simmons b Mullally	18	– c Nixon b Mullally	38
A. Symonds lbw b Simmons	3	– b Parsons	2
M. W. Alleyne c Millns b Parsons	20	– c Wells b Millns	14
†R. C. Russell c Nixon b Simmons	0	– not out	19
M. C. J. Ball run out	4	– b Mullally	11
A. M. Smith c Simmons b Parsons	0	– b Mullally	0
J. Lewis b Mullally	6	– c Nixon b Mullally	4
*C. A. Walsh not out	1	– b Millns	4
L-b 2, w 5, n-b 8	15	L-b 5, n-b 10	15
1/0 2/1 3/9 4/26 5/35 6/35 7/43 8/43 9/65	71	1/4 2/30 3/35 4/54 5/98 6/98 7/109 8/109 9/123	136

Bonus points – Leicestershire 4.

Bowling: *First Innings*—Millns 8–3–14–2; Mullally 8–4–16–3; Simmons 5–0–19–2; Parsons 6–1–20–2. *Second Innings*—Millns 11.3–3–41–3; Mullally 12–5–22–4; Parsons 10–4–27–1; Simmons 9–2–41–2.

Umpires: B. Dudleston and N. T. Plews.

At Cheltenham, July 24. GLOUCESTERSHIRE lost to SOUTH AFRICA A by 28 runs (See South Africa A tour section).

GLOUCESTERSHIRE v WARWICKSHIRE

At Cheltenham, July 25, 26, 27. Gloucestershire won by an innings and 116 runs. Gloucestershire 24 pts, Warwickshire 3 pts. Toss: Gloucestershire.

Warwickshire's surprising defeat against a county without a batting point since May signalled that a third successive Championship title was beyond them. The match was a triumph for Walsh, who took six wickets inside 15 overs in the first innings and ended with 11 for 117. This was exceptional bowling, an amalgam of deceptive pace and bounce. But his batsmen were just as important, scoring 569, the highest total in matches between these counties. Windows made an efficient maiden Championship hundred, almost a double, in spite of being given run out in the late eighties; umpire Bird then decided the wicket-keeper had taken two attempts to displace the bails, and that Windows was in by the time he succeeded. So he called him back. Symonds's century – 127 in 107 balls – was more spectacular because that is the man's style. Warwickshire never looked like averting defeat, as they succumbed to Walsh and followed on 353 behind. Ostler played two defiant innings; Pollock's late 53 was a brave gesture.

Close of play: First day, Gloucestershire 331-3 (M. G. N. Windows 162*, R. P. Davis 14*); Second day, Warwickshire 206-7 (D. P. Ostler 69*, A. F. Giles 3*).

Gloucestershire

N. J. Trainor c Burns b Small	6
M. G. N. Windows c Burns b Pollock	184
T. H. C. Hancock c Burns b Small	57
M. A. Lynch c Pollock b Small	69
R. P. Davis c Burns b Brown	23
M. W. Alleyne c Brown b Small	30
A. Symonds c Burns b Brown	127
†R. C. J. Williams c Singh b Giles	10
M. C. J. Ball c Singh b Munton	12
A. M. Smith c Smith b Munton	15
*C. A. Walsh not out	12
B 5, l-b 19	24
1/18 2/166 3/306 4/362 5/362 6/422 7/439 8/492 9/518	569

Bonus points – Gloucestershire 4, Warwickshire 2 (Score at 120 overs: 370-5).

Bowling: Pollock 29–7–71–1; Munton 33–13–85–2; Small 24–3–99–4; Brown 22.4–4–97–2; Smith 16–2–62–0; Giles 31–4–131–1.

Warwickshire

A. J. Moles lbw b Walsh	16	– lbw b Smith	0
N. M. K. Smith b Davis	41	– c Williams b Walsh	14
†M. Burns c Williams b Walsh	2	– c Trainor b Smith	0
D. P. Ostler c and b Walsh	73	– c Trainor b Davis	90
T. L. Penney c and b Alleyne	26	– c Williams b Walsh	0
A. Singh c Trainor b Walsh	13	– (7) c and b Walsh	10
S. M. Pollock c Walsh b Ball	4	– (8) c Ball b Davis	53
D. R. Brown b Davis	6	– (6) c Williams b Ball	39
A. F. Giles c Symonds b Walsh	6	– c Trainor b Walsh	18
G. C. Small not out	2	– c Ball b Walsh	0
*T. A. Munton b Walsh	0	– not out	6
B 1, l-b 9, n-b 17	27	L-b 1, n-b 6	7
1/58 2/68 3/74 4/137 5/157 6/167 7/188 8/213 9/216	216	1/1 2/15 3/23 4/24 5/111 6/132 7/174 8/227 9/227	237

Bonus points – Warwickshire 1, Gloucestershire 4.

Bowling: *First Innings*—Walsh 14.5–6–26–6; Smith 9–2–66–0; Davis 20–8–63–2; Alleyne 9–3–31–1; Ball 6–2–20–1. *Second Innings*—Walsh 21–2–91–5; Smith 15–3–59–2; Alleyne 6–2–10–0; Davis 18.4–5–46–2; Ball 9–2–30–1.

Umpires: H. D. Bird and B. Leadbeater.

At Derby, August 1, 2, 3. GLOUCESTERSHIRE lost to DERBYSHIRE by seven wickets.

At Southampton, August 8, 9, 10, 12. GLOUCESTERSHIRE lost to HAMPSHIRE by 63 runs.

GLOUCESTERSHIRE v YORKSHIRE

At Bristol, August 15, 16. Gloucestershire won by ten wickets. Gloucestershire 23 pts, Yorkshire 4 pts. Toss: Yorkshire.

This was only Gloucestershire's third win of the season, but again it helped to dash the Championship aspirations of a county well above them in the table. Yorkshire succumbed in two days, and already seemed to be heading for their third defeat in a row by the seventh over, when they had lost five wickets with only 15 scored. There was no more than a mild measure of dampness in the pitch. That the innings reached 166, in 43 troubled overs, was attributable to two and a half hours of defiance by White, who was in some pain after several blows on his hands from Walsh. Walsh's bowling was once more in another class, even though he was not fully fit and had to limp off at one point. He took six for 22 in the first innings and three more in the second. Smith picked up five with his in-swing, passing 200 first-class wickets, and might have had more; twice in the match, he dismissed Blakey with a no-ball. Gloucestershire scored steadily down the order to back up Symonds's 75, and in such a contest they had more than enough.

Close of play: First day, Gloucestershire 211-6 (R. P. Davis 13*, M. W. Alleyne 1*).

Yorkshire

M. D. Moxon c Symonds b Walsh	1	– c Symonds b Walsh	1
M. P. Vaughan lbw b Smith	1	– c Symonds b Alleyne	35
*D. Byas c Hancock b Walsh	9	– c Alleyne b Walsh	3
A. McGrath lbw b Smith	0	– b Smith	3
R. A. Kettleborough b Walsh	2	– lbw b Walsh	7
C. White b Walsh	74	– b Smith	20
†R. J. Blakey c Lynch b Davis	38	– not out	52
D. Gough b Walsh	3	– b Smith	4
P. J. Hartley c Alleyne b Davis	20	– c Alleyne b Davis	38
C. E. W. Silverwood b Walsh	0	– c and b Davis	0
R. D. Stemp not out	2	– c Walsh b Davis	0
L-b 4, n-b 12	16	L-b 4, n-b 12	16
1/4 2/4 3/13 4/13 5/15 6/113 7/116 8/149 9/153	166	1/3 2/7 3/22 4/38 5/58 6/104 7/108 8/171 9/171	179

Bonus points – Gloucestershire 4.

Bowling: *First Innings*—Walsh 14.2–8–22–6; Smith 10–1–46–2; Lewis 6–0–21–0; Alleyne 7–1–31–0; Davis 6–0–42–2. *Second Innings*—Smith 13–2–56–3; Walsh 12–2–37–3; Alleyne 12–5–29–1; Lewis 7–2–17–0; Davis 8.2–1–31–3; Symonds 1–0–5–0.

Gloucestershire

D. R. Hewson lbw b Gough	0	– not out	6
M. G. N. Windows c Kettleborough b Silverwood	40	– not out	10
A. Symonds c Kettleborough b Gough	75		
T. H. C. Hancock b Silverwood	29		
M. A. Lynch b White	36		
R. P. Davis c Byas b Silverwood	19		
J. Lewis b Silverwood	0		
M. W. Alleyne c Blakey b Hartley	25		
†R. C. Russell not out	26		
A. M. Smith c Blakey b Hartley	19		
*C. A. Walsh b Silverwood	25		
B 13, l-b 4, n-b 18	35	W 1	1
1/0 2/108 3/135 4/193 5/199 6/199 7/234 8/249 9/275	329	(no wkt)	17

Bonus points – Gloucestershire 3, Yorkshire 4.

Bowling: *First Innings*—Gough 24–3–72–2; Silverwood 24.5–5–78–5; Hartley 20–2–76–2; Stemp 7–0–27–0; White 14–0–59–1. *Second Innings*—Gough 2.1–0–7–0; Silverwood 2–0–10–0.

Umpires: G. I. Burgess and A. A. Jones.

At Colchester, August 22, 23, 24, 26. GLOUCESTERSHIRE lost to ESSEX by an innings and 64 runs.

GLOUCESTERSHIRE v NORTHAMPTONSHIRE

At Bristol, August 29, 30, 31, September 2. Gloucestershire won by 15 runs. Gloucestershire 20 pts, Northamptonshire 4 pts. Toss: Gloucestershire. Championship debut: A. J. Swann.

A match that seemed meaningless on the fixture list actually turned into a mini-classic with cricket that was rarely high-class but always tight. Northamptonshire's last pair, Snape and Taylor, battled though extra time on Saturday night and the first few overs of Monday to score 26 of the 42 they needed, before Gloucestershire broke the stand and secured the win. The match had turned in Gloucestershire's favour when Russell, doggedly discriminate as ever and relying on his personalised repertoire of shots, completed his fourth half-century in succession in a noteworthy stand of 115 with Davis. After conceding a seven-run lead in the first innings, Gloucestershire appeared to be on their way to defeat at 95 for six – their second collapse – before that resolute rescue operation. Afterwards, they were close to bowling out a young Northamptonshire team on the third day. They claimed the extra half-hour but it was curtailed by bad light. The last pair resumed on Monday needing 25 and had added nine when Snape was leg-before in the sixth over to Smith's third appeal in four balls.

Close of play: First day, Northamptonshire 123-4 (K. M. Curran 51*, A. L. Penberthy 13*); Second day, Gloucestershire 185-6 (R. C. Russell 56*, R. P. Davis 39*); Third day, Northamptonshire 218-9 (J. N. Snape 32*, J. P. Taylor 7*).

Gloucestershire

D. R. Hewson c Innes b Ambrose	0	– lbw b Taylor	3
M. G. N. Windows c Ripley b Ambrose	6	– c Ripley b Capel	4
A. Symonds lbw b Penberthy	38	– c Innes b Taylor	21
R. I. Dawson lbw b Capel	21	– c Ripley b Capel	20
M. A. Lynch c Ripley b Capel	6	– lbw b Ambrose	9
M. W. Alleyne c Ambrose b Penberthy	0	– lbw b Innes	23
†R. C. Russell c Ambrose b Capel	50	– c Montgomerie b Snape	75
R. P. Davis c Sales b Curran	7	– c and b Penberthy	43
M. C. J. Ball b Penberthy	7	– (10) b Ambrose	4
A. M. Smith c Ripley b Taylor	15	– (11) not out	19
*C. A. Walsh not out	10	– (9) lbw b Snape	12
B 1, l-b 7, w 1, n-b 14	23	B 4, l-b 8, n-b 4	16
1/0 2/19 3/69 4/75 5/78 6/86 7/131 8/152 9/158	183	1/3 2/27 3/31 4/48 5/62 6/95 7/210 8/212 9/226	249

Bonus points – Northamptonshire 4.

Bowling: *First Innings*—Ambrose 16–4–34–2; Taylor 18.5–9–38–1; Capel 13–2–34–3; Penberthy 16–1–50–3; Curran 6–2–19–1. *Second Innings*—Ambrose 22.2–9–35–2; Taylor 21–5–61–2; Capel 13–1–37–2; Penberthy 17–5–43–1; Innes 5–0–17–1; Curran 6–2–21–0; Snape 14–5–23–2.

Northamptonshire

R. R. Montgomerie lbw b Alleyne	20	– b Smith	5
A. J. Swann lbw b Smith	2	– lbw b Alleyne	14
D. J. Capel c Ball b Alleyne	18	– c Russell b Walsh	39
D. J. Sales c Lynch b Alleyne	10	– c Russell b Alleyne	2
*K. M. Curran c Russell b Walsh	52	– c Hewson b Symonds	13
A. L. Penberthy c Davis b Smith	19	– lbw b Symonds	2
K. J. Innes lbw b Smith	3	– (8) b Alleyne	20
†D. Ripley not out	20	– (7) c Lynch b Walsh	36
J. N. Snape lbw b Smith	9	– lbw b Smith	33
C. E. L. Ambrose lbw b Smith	11	– c Lynch b Walsh	11
J. P. Taylor b Walsh	6	– not out	13
B 4, l-b 4, n-b 12	20	B 12, l-b 9, w 2, n-b 16	39
1/6 2/39 3/48 4/81 5/125 6/130 7/143 8/157 9/173	190	1/7 2/47 3/49 4/62 5/66 6/108 7/151 8/179 9/201	227

Bonus points – Gloucestershire 4.

Bowling: *First Innings*—Walsh 21–8–44–2; Smith 24–11–68–5; Alleyne 16–4–69–3; Ball 1–0–1–0. *Second Innings*—Walsh 28–9–62–3; Smith 18.4–6–40–2; Alleyne 23–9–49–3; Symonds 10–4–21–2; Ball 11–3–34–0.

Umpires: B. Leadbeater and R. A. White.

At Worcester, September 12, 13, 14, 16. GLOUCESTERSHIRE lost to WORCESTERSHIRE by five wickets.

GLOUCESTERSHIRE v KENT

At Bristol, September 19, 20, 21. Gloucestershire won by ten wickets. Gloucestershire 21 pts, Kent 4 pts. Toss: Kent.

Kent's Championship prize money appeared to decrease by the over. They started the match only 15 points behind leaders Leicestershire, but had to settle for fourth place and £10,000 after only their second defeat. It was Gloucestershire's fourth successive home win. Kent soon regretted choosing to bat as the pitch's uneven bounce was a constant worry. On the opening day, they lost five wickets before lunch, and the pattern of apprehension was set. Their innings was saved only by Ward's dependability over three and a half hours. The pitch did not entirely excuse Kent's failure to obtain any batting points. Nor did Walsh's bowling, but he had a good deal to do with it. In the first innings, he took three wickets in six balls, and three for two in 13 balls in the second; he finished as the season's leading wicket-taker, with 85. Symonds, switching from modest spin to gentle seam, dismissed Hooper and Llong in one over. Russell held several spectacular catches and was, less happily, bowled off his visor. Trainor revealed application over four hours while Lynch went to his fifty by a typically direct route.

Close of play: First day, Gloucestershire 9-0 (N. J. Trainor 6*, M. G. N. Windows 2*); Second day, Kent 21-1 (M. J. Walker 11*, M. J. McCague 6*).

Kent

M. V. Fleming c Lynch b Alleyne	21	– b Smith	0
M. J. Walker lbw b Walsh	0	– lbw b Walsh	11
T. R. Ward c Walsh b Alleyne	86	– (4) lbw b Walsh	6
C. L. Hooper lbw b Symonds	6	– (5) b Walsh	0
N. J. Llong b Symonds	0	– (6) b Symonds	8
M. A. Ealham c Russell b Smith	11	– (7) c Russell b Alleyne	17
G. R. Cowdrey c Ball b Walsh	4	– (8) c Windows b Symonds	35
*†S. A. Marsh c Russell b Walsh	0	– (9) b Smith	4
M. M. Patel c Russell b Walsh	0	– (10) b Walsh	1
M. J. McCague not out	12	– (3) lbw b Smith	22
D. W. Headley c Russell b Smith	1	– not out	0
L-b 4, w 1, n-b 8	13	B 1, l-b 2, w 2, n-b 8	13
1/1 2/49 3/62 4/62 5/87 6/101 7/101 8/101 9/150	154	1/3 2/28 3/44 4/44 5/46 6/65 7/85 8/106 9/111	117

Bonus points – Gloucestershire 4.

Bowling: *First Innings*—Walsh 15–3–50–4; Smith 14.4–5–36–2; Alleyne 10–1–30–2; Symonds 17–6–31–2; Ball 3–2–3–0. *Second Innings*—Walsh 15–6–21–4; Smith 15–2–43–3; Alleyne 8–2–19–1; Symonds 7.2–2–31–2.

Gloucestershire

N. J. Trainor st Marsh b Patel	48	– not out	20
M. G. N. Windows c Hooper b McCague	8	– not out	8
A. Symonds c Marsh b Headley	14		
R. I. Dawson b Headley	5		
M. A. Lynch run out	54		
M. W. Alleyne c Llong b Patel	23		
†R. C. Russell b Headley	8		
R. P. Davis c Hooper b Headley	6		
A. M. Smith b McCague	28		
M. C. J. Ball b McCague	20		
*C. A. Walsh not out	12		
B 8, l-b 5, n-b 2	15	W 5	5
1/27 2/53 3/69 4/141 5/153 6/174 7/174 8/196 9/216	241		(no wkt) 33

Bonus points – Gloucestershire 1, Kent 4.

Bowling: *First Innings*—McCague 19.3–5–50–3; Headley 27–8–65–4; Ealham 26–8–70–0; Fleming 6–3–10–0; Patel 11–4–33–2. *Second Innings*—Llong 2–0–10–0; Fleming 1–0–4–0; Ward 2–0–14–0; Patel 1.2–1–5–0.

Umpires: D. J. Constant and T. E. Jesty.

COUNTY CAPS AWARDED IN 1996

Derbyshire	A. J. Harris, D. M. Jones.
Essex	A. P. Grayson, S. G. Law, N. F. Williams.
Gloucestershire	M. C. J. Ball, A. Symonds, R. C. J. Williams.
Hampshire	J. S. Laney.
Leicestershire	D. L. Maddy.
Somerset	S. Lee.
Surrey	M. A. Butcher, B. P. Julian, G. J. Kersey.
Sussex	V. C. Drakes, K. Greenfield, D. R. Law, J. D. Lewry.
Warwickshire	A. F. Giles, S. M. Pollock.
Yorkshire	C. E. W. Silverwood, R. D. Stemp.

No caps were awarded by Glamorgan, Kent, Lancashire, Middlesex, Northamptonshire, Nottinghamshire or Worcestershire. Durham gave caps to all their playing staff.

COUNTY BENEFITS AWARDED FOR 1997

Derbyshire	D. E. Malcolm.
Essex	A. W. Lilley.
Glamorgan	C. P. Metson.
Gloucestershire	Gloucestershire CCC.
Hampshire	C. A. Connor.
Kent	G. R. Cowdrey.
Lancashire	M. A. Atherton.
Leicestershire	R. A. Cobb and P. Whitticase.
Middlesex	A. R. C. Fraser.
Northamptonshire	D. Ripley.
Somerset	G. D. Rose.
Surrey	M. P. Bicknell.
Warwickshire	A. J. Moles.
Worcestershire	R. K. Illingworth.

No benefit was awarded by Durham, Nottinghamshire, Sussex or Yorkshire.

Kevan James

HAMPSHIRE

President: W. J. Weld
Chairman: B. G. Ford
Chairman, Cricket Committee: J. R. Gray
Chief Executive: A. F. Baker
Captain: J. P. Stephenson
Director of Cricket: T. M. Tremlett
Coach: M. D. Marshall
Head Groundsman: N. Gray
Scorer: V. H Isaacs

Transition can be painful, and Hampshire are in the midst of transition. Under a new captain, John Stephenson, and a new coach, their former star bowler Malcolm Marshall, they slipped one place down the Championship table, winning just three games to finish 14th. They climbed three places from the foot of the Sunday League, while neither knockout competition held much satisfaction. Yet the summer was lifted out of the mundane by four individual performances. Two were by players in the late stages of honest, salt-of-the-earth careers, two by lads just setting out.

First, Kevan James entered cricket's record books with a unique match double. His previous claim to fame had been his six for 22 to dismiss the 1985 Australians for 76. This time it was the Indians who got the James treatment. On a sunny afternoon in June, they had eased to an impressive 207 for one. Seven minutes later, it was 207 for five. In four deliveries, left-arm seamer James removed Rathore, Tendulkar, Dravid and Manjrekar – the first four in four in Hampshire's history. Next day, James completed a century, and a place in cricket's hall of fame was his.

Six weeks later, it was Cardigan Connor's turn, as he destroyed Gloucestershire with nine for 38 at Southampton. Those were the best figures by any bowler in 1996, the best for the county in Northlands Road's 112-year history and the fifth-best ever for Hampshire. It took him to 49 for the season and 599 in his career; sadly, injury decreed that he finished the season still on 599.

Connor's knee problem helped two younger characters to step into the spotlight as the season drew to a close. Hampshire had lost Winston Benjamin and Stuart Milburn as well, and their bowling resources were so stretched that, when Middlesex visited Portsmouth, they turned to Liam Botham, at such short notice that the national press had no time to descend on the ground. They missed a treat. Two days past his 19th birthday, Ian's son showed he possessed his old man's sense of the dramatic by taking five for 67 – Mike Gatting was his first success.

In the next match, Botham was eclipsed by someone two months younger. Dimitri Mascarenhas had arrived in Southampton in April on the recommendation of Paul Terry, who had seen him playing club cricket in Western Australia. He had performed moderately for the Second Eleven but, as the injury crisis continued, he was pitched into the meeting with Glamorgan in early September. His tight and accurate right-arm seam returned six for 88. In the second innings, he took three for 62; in the next match, at Canterbury, he took another seven. By the time he flew back to Perth, he had a two-year contract tucked in his baggage, as well as the ball, neatly mounted, with which he had skittled Glamorgan. Hampshire only hoped that Australia would not end his English status – he was born in London, to Sri Lankan parents, though raised in Perth – by selecting him for representative cricket.

Mascarenhas could help Hampshire to re-emerge as winners. Botham, however, decided in the autumn that he would rather concentrate on playing Rugby Union for West Hartlepool, where his father's shadow might be a little less overpowering. There were still four batsmen in their twenties who offered hope in an unsatisfactory summer.

Top of the list was Jason Laney, a powerfully built opener, who hit centuries off Glamorgan and Kent in successive games and swept to 1,000 first-class runs. Will Kendall also passed that barrier, in the final match, although his first 444 runs were for Oxford. Two more batsmen wintered with "almost there" pencilled across their CVs. Matthew Keech had joined from Middlesex in 1994, but had under-achieved until he was sent into action at Arundel with the assurance that he had four or five matches to prove himself. He responded with a maiden hundred and his next nine innings contained five fifties – though all too often a reckless streak and his failure to judge a run cut him off in full flight. A fractured wrist ended his season early, but the breakthrough seemed imminent. Meanwhile, Giles White suggested he had a future: given the chance to open regularly towards the end of the summer, he took it solidly.

Inevitably, the batting hinged on Robin Smith, who led the way with 1,396 runs. But it was encouraging to see Keech, Kendall and Laney occupying high places in the first-class averages, along with the dependable wicket-keeper Adrian Aymes. The bowling generally disappointed. Connor was the leading wicket-taker, with 49 at 21.85, while Stephenson chipped in with 36, compensation for a lean time with the bat. Shaun Udal had his worst summer since breaking into the team, finishing with 34 at a costly 46.52.

But the real story of the season was of injury. The West Indian overseas player, Benjamin, appeared in just two Championship matches before damaging a shoulder. He continued for a while as a one-day batsman – he hit a spectacular century to rush Northamptonshire to Sunday defeat at Basingstoke – until sloping off into premature retirement. Hampshire engaged Queensland batsman Matthew Hayden as his replacement for 1997, hoping he would not find favour again with the Australian selectors.

Benjamin was the major casualty, but at times the team had the look of an emergency ward. Stephenson, Smith, Laney and Keech all suffered broken bones; Milburn played ten matches before injury and then surgery for appendicitis ended his involvement; while Jim Bovill, Terry and Sean Morris all had back problems.

The end of Terry's career saddened many supporters. Hampshire began the season with a give-youth-its-head policy. When that faltered, they recalled the likes of James. But in the later stages they reverted. The 37-year-old Terry was told he was surplus to requirements, would not play again, and would not get another contract. He was sadly disaffected as he took his wife and family to a new life in Western Australia. Terry had served Hampshire well, scoring more than 16,000 runs, and deserved a better exit-line. – MIKE NEASOM.

HAMPSHIRE 1996

[*Bill Smith*

Back row: W. S. Kendall, J. N. B. Bovill, G. W. White, S. R. G. Francis, L. J. Botham, R. R. Dibden, S. M. Milburn. *Middle row:* M. D. Marshall (*coach*), G. R. Treagus, P. R. Whitaker, R. S. M. Morris, W. K. M. Benjamin, M. J. Thursfield, K. D. James, S. J. Renshaw, M. Keech, J. S. Laney, T. M. Tremlett (*coach*). *Front row:* D. M. Thomas, A. N. Aymes, R. J. Maru, R. A. Smith, J. P. Stephenson (*captain*), V. P. Terry, C. A. Connor, S. D. Udal, M. Garaway.

HAMPSHIRE RESULTS

All first-class matches – Played 20: Won 4, Lost 7, Drawn 9.

County Championship matches – Played 17: Won 3, Lost 7, Drawn 7.

Competition placings – Britannic Assurance County Championship, 14th; NatWest Trophy, q-f; Benson and Hedges Cup, 3rd in Group D; AXA Equity & Law League, 15th.

COUNTY CHAMPIONSHIP AVERAGES

BATTING

Cap		*M*	*I*	*NO*	*R*	*HS*	*100s*	*50s*	*Avge*	*Ct/St*
1985	R. A. Smith	16	29	2	1,348	179	3	8	49.92	1
	W. S. Kendall	8	16	2	601	103*	1	4	42.92	11
1991	A. N. Aymes†	17	30	12	770	113	2	2	42.77	39/1
	M. Keech	10	18	2	644	104	1	6	40.25	8
1983	V. P. Terry	5	9	1	301	87*	0	3	37.62	10
1996	J. S. Laney†	14	26	0	932	105	2	5	35.84	8
	W. K. M. Benjamin§	2	4	0	140	117	1	0	35.00	3
	G. W. White	11	21	2	579	73	0	6	30.47	12
1989	K. D. James	12	22	1	635	118*	1	3	30.23	6
1995	J. P. Stephenson	13	23	2	550	85	0	5	26.19	6
1986	R. J. Maru	11	17	5	303	55*	0	1	25.25	17
	P. R. Whitaker	9	17	1	385	67*	0	3	24.06	4
1992	S. D. Udal†	14	21	3	374	50*	0	1	20.77	11
1988	C. A. Connor	9	12	3	140	42	0	0	15.55	0
	S. M. Milburn	8	10	0	109	25	0	0	10.90	0
	J. N. B. Bovill	12	18	2	123	29	0	0	7.68	0
	R. S. M. Morris	3	6	0	44	11	0	0	7.33	2
	S. J. Renshaw	6	7	5	10	9*	0	0	5.00	3

Also batted: L. J. Botham (3 matches) 30, 1, 0 (2 ct); A. D. Mascarenhas (2 matches) 10, 14, 0; M. J. Thursfield (2 matches) 4, 18.

* *Signifies not out.* † *Born in Hampshire.* § *Overseas player.*

BOWLING

	O	*M*	*R*	*W*	*BB*	*5W/i*	*Avge*
A. D. Mascarenhas	92	21	297	16	6-88	1	18.56
C. A. Connor	342.4	91	1,033	48	9-38	2	21.52
J. P. Stephenson	314.4	68	1,035	36	6-48	3	28.75
K. D. James	276.1	53	808	25	3-17	0	32.32
J. N. B. Bovill	288	52	1,047	31	5-58	1	33.77
R. J. Maru	306.2	101	734	18	3-50	0	40.77
S. M. Milburn	215.4	39	791	17	3-47	0	46.52
S. J. Renshaw	192.5	48	689	14	4-56	0	49.21
S. D. Udal	416.5	85	1,333	26	5-82	1	51.26

Also bowled: W. K. M. Benjamin 69.2–13–201–6; L. J. Botham 55–9–268–8; M. Keech 18–3–46–0; W. S. Kendall 14–1–47–2; J. S. Laney 14–2–61–0; M. J. Thursfield 40–5–158–0; P. R. Whitaker 81–14–311–3; G. W. White 17–2–75–0.

COUNTY RECORDS

Highest score for:	316	R. H. Moore v Warwickshire at Bournemouth	1937
Highest score against:	302*	P. Holmes (Yorkshire) at Portsmouth	1920
Best bowling for:	9-25	R. M. H. Cottam v Lancashire at Manchester	1965
Best bowling against:	10-46	W. Hickton (Lancashire) at Manchester	1870
Highest total for:	672-7 dec.	v Somerset at Taunton	1899
Highest total against:	742	by Surrey at The Oval	1909
Lowest total for:	15	v Warwickshire at Birmingham	1922
Lowest total against:	23	by Yorkshire at Middlesbrough	1965

At Oxford, May 2, 3, 4. HAMPSHIRE drew with OXFORD UNIVERSITY.

HAMPSHIRE v ESSEX

At Southampton, May 9, 10, 11, 13. Essex won by four wickets. Essex 23 pts, Hampshire 8 pts. Toss: Essex.

Prichard had the last laugh after three days during which his decision to field first looked decidedly suspect. Hampshire looked well placed after scoring 539, their biggest ever total against Essex, on a bland pitch. They owed much to a proficient seventh-wicket partnership of 178 between Aymes and Benjamin, whose century was his first for the county; both scored career-bests. Gooch responded with his fifth hundred in six innings against Hampshire, and Law with his first in Championship cricket. But a late-order collapse gave the home side a lead of 107. Thanks largely to a solid, unbeaten half-century from Whitaker, they were able to leave a target of 329 in 69 overs. Essex were an unpromising 168 for four. But Prichard and Irani ran up 112 in just 16 overs and Irani saw them home with 12 balls to spare.

Close of play: First day, Hampshire 381-6 (A. N. Aymes 51*, W. K. M. Benjamin 102*); Second day, Essex 209-2 (G. A. Gooch 121*, S. G. Law 40*); Third day, Hampshire 135-7 (P. R. Whitaker 29*, S. D. Udal 4*).

Hampshire

*J. P. Stephenson lbw b Williams	50	– c Law b Such	36
J. S. Laney c Rollins b Irani	31	– c Robinson b Such	28
R. S. M. Morris c Rollins b Irani	0	– c Hussain b Such	11
R. A. Smith c Law b Such	50	– b Grayson	9
G. W. White c Robinson b Ilott	0	– lbw b Such	1
P. R. Whitaker c Hussain b Such	55	– not out	67
†A. N. Aymes lbw b Such	113	– run out	4
W. K. M. Benjamin c Rollins b Williams	117	– c and b Such	5
S. D. Udal b Grayson	38	– c Law b Grayson	16
S. M. Milburn run out	13	– (11) c Gooch b Grayson	22
C. A. Connor not out	25	– (10) c Irani b Grayson	14
B 6, l-b 14, w 1, n-b 26	47	B 4, l-b 2, n-b 2	8
1/83 2/83 3/99 4/114 5/194 6/225 7/403 8/501 9/501	539	1/62 2/69 3/86 4/88 5/89 6/106 7/113 8/160 9/194	221

Bonus points – Hampshire 4, Essex 3 (Score at 120 overs: 435-7).

Bowling: *First Innings*—Ilott 37–8–111–1; Williams 28.2–3–106–2; Law 9–0–39–0; Irani 21–1–103–2; Such 35–10–108–3; Grayson 13–2–52–1. *Second Innings*—Ilott 4–0–20–0; Williams 3–0–27–0; Such 32–7–74–5; Irani 3–1–12–0; Grayson 28.3–5–82–4.

Essex

G. A. Gooch b Benjamin	130	– c Morris b Connor	21
D. D. J. Robinson b Milburn	18	– run out	18
N. Hussain lbw b Connor	22	– c Benjamin b Connor	60
S. G. Law b Benjamin	143	– c Aymes b Milburn	44
*P. J. Prichard c Whitaker b Udal	23	– c Benjamin b Milburn	69
R. C. Irani c Aymes b Whitaker	25	– not out	81
A. P. Grayson c Aymes b Benjamin	17	– b Connor	8
†R. J. Rollins b Benjamin	7	– not out	25
M. C. Ilott c Aymes b Milburn	13		
N. F. Williams c Aymes b Milburn	15		
P. M. Such not out	1		
L-b 16, w 2	18	L-b 5	5
1/65 2/106 3/238 4/307 5/375 6/375 7/385 8/412 9/416	432	1/33 2/49 3/113 4/168 5/280 6/293	(6 wkts) 331

Bonus points – Essex 4, Hampshire 4.

Bowling: *First Innings*—Benjamin 33–9–96–4; Connor 23–8–73–1; Milburn 27–6–104–3; Stephenson 11–2–63–0; Udal 14–2–56–1; Whitaker 8–3–24–1. *Second Innings*—Benjamin 16–2–63–0; Milburn 15–0–81–2; Connor 16–2–73–3; Udal 14–0–86–0; Whitaker 6–0–23–0.

Umpires: A. A. Jones and D. R. Shepherd.

At Birmingham, May 16, 17, 18, 20. HAMPSHIRE beat WARWICKSHIRE by 122 runs.

HAMPSHIRE v DURHAM

At Portsmouth, May 23, 24, 25, 27. Drawn. Hampshire 7 pts, Durham 10 pts. Toss: Hampshire.

Stephenson batted first, but was having second thoughts in minutes: Brown had him and fellow-opener Laney caught behind in the first over. On a juicy pitch, the Durham seamers – including Wood, in his first Championship game for exactly 12 months – reduced Hampshire to 111 for eight. But Aymes and Connor put on 54 in 11 overs and the last two wickets added 95 to avert total disaster. After half the first day and all the second had been lost to rain, Durham's batting was almost as shaky until Blenkiron and Collingwood compiled a solid fifth-wicket stand of 156. Blenkiron completed an impressive unbeaten century after being marooned in the nineties for ten overs. The visitors led by 97 and, despite the weather's intrusions, looked like forcing an unlikely innings victory when Hampshire slumped to 59 for five. Then Aymes, again, and White dug in and steered their side to safety.

Close of play: First day, Hampshire 192-9 (A. N. Aymes 41*, S. M. Milburn 12*); Second day, No play; Third day, Durham 174-4 (D. A. Blenkiron 69*, P. D. Collingwood 24*).

Hampshire

*J. P. Stephenson c Scott b Brown	0	– c Boiling b Brown	6
J. S. Laney c Scott b Brown	0	– b Betts	0
R. S. M. Morris lbw b Brown	8	– b Wood	9
K. D. James c Blenkiron b Betts	23	– lbw b Brown	13
P. R. Whitaker c Morris b Wood	8	– c and b Wood	10
G. W. White b Wood	19	– (7) not out	16
†A. N. Aymes not out	48	– (6) not out	21
S. D. Udal lbw b Betts	5		
R. J. Maru lbw b Wood	8		
C. A. Connor c Boiling b Brown	42		
S. M. Milburn c Bainbridge b Wood	19		
L-b 1, w 5, n-b 20	26	B 2, l-b 8, n-b 12	22
1/0 2/1 3/8 4/27 5/64 6/70 7/91 8/111 9/165	206	1/2 2/16 3/20 4/44 5/59	(5 wkts) 97

Bonus points – Hampshire 1, Durham 4.

Bowling: *First Innings*—Brown 20–2–55–4; Betts 19–1–83–2; Wood 17.4–3–60–4; Collingwood 3–0–7–0. *Second Innings*—Brown 15–6–19–2; Betts 8–0–27–1; Wood 9.2–5–34–2; Boiling 11–6–7–0.

Durham

S. L. Campbell c Aymes b Milburn	9
*M. A. Roseberry lbw b James	10
J. E. Morris c Maru b Stephenson	35
D. A. Blenkiron not out	102
P. Bainbridge c Laney b Udal	16
P. D. Collingwood b Connor	80
†C. W. Scott c Stephenson b Milburn	10
J. Wood c Morris b Milburn	14
S. J. E. Brown run out	3
J. Boiling not out	0
B 8, l-b 12, w 2, n-b 2	24
1/13 2/39 3/67 4/106 5/262 6/275 7/296 8/299	(8 wkts dec.) 303

M. M. Betts did not bat.

Bonus points – Durham 3, Hampshire 3.

Bowling: Connor 27.5–7–82–1; Milburn 32–8–79–3; Stephenson 9–0–22–1; James 13–3–34–1; Udal 18–5–37–1; Maru 13–3–29–0.

Umpires: J. W. Holder and K. E. Palmer.

At Worcester, May 30, 31, June 1, 3. HAMPSHIRE drew with WORCESTERSHIRE.

HAMPSHIRE v DERBYSHIRE

At Southampton, June 6, 7, 8, 10. Derbyshire won by 54 runs. Derbyshire 24 pts, Hampshire 6 pts. Toss: Derbyshire.

Frailty against spin saw Hampshire crash to defeat in a curious match. Both sides scored big first-innings totals. Then, as the weather deteriorated, the ball held sway. Derbyshire's 472 was built round a partnership of 298 between Adams and Rollins – an all-wicket county record against Hampshire. Adams was given out caught behind on 115, but stood his ground and, after consulting his colleague at square leg, umpire Sharp decided it had not carried, allowing Adams to advance to a personal best of 239, with five sixes and 27 fours off 338 balls in 407 minutes. Thanks to Smith hitting his first century of the summer and a valuable fifty from Aymes, Hampshire still took a lead of 22. Unexpectedly, the visitors' most successful bowler was their captain, Jones, who had never taken more than one wicket in a first-class innings but managed five here with his off-breaks. The second innings was very different: Derbyshire folded against the pace of Connor and Udal's off-spin, and the target was only 171. But a similar double-pronged attack – Vandrau's off-spin and Harris's swing – punished some limp batting. Both returned career-best figures as Derbyshire won in comfort.

Close of play: First day, Derbyshire 389-4 (C. J. Adams 213*, J. E. Owen 8*); Second day, Hampshire 291-5 (R. A. Smith 98*, R. J. Maru 2*); Third day, Derbyshire 145-5 (T. A. Tweats 0*, P. A. J. DeFreitas 20*).

Derbyshire

K. J. Barnett b Connor	7	– c White b James	49
A. S. Rollins c Whitaker b Udal	131	– c Udal b Bovill	7
C. J. Adams lbw b Udal	239	– lbw b Connor	5
*D. M. Jones lbw b James	19	– c Laney b Udal	19
T. A. Tweats c White b James	0	– (6) c Maru b Udal	26
J. E. Owen c Maru b Connor	20	– (5) c Whitaker b Udal	33
P. A. J. DeFreitas c James b Udal	11	– c Stephenson b Connor	29
†K. M. Krikken lbw b Connor	6	– lbw b Connor	1
M. J. Vandrau not out	8	– c Laney b Udal	1
A. J. Harris c White b Udal	11	– not out	8
D. E. Malcolm b Maru	4	– c sub b Connor	0
B 1, l-b 15	16	L-b 10, w 2, n-b 2	14
1/26 2/324 3/360 4/360 5/414 6/442 7/449 8/449 9/467	472	1/16 2/27 3/72 4/118 5/124 6/165 7/167 8/172 9/191	192

Bonus points – Derbyshire 4, Hampshire 2 (Score at 120 overs: 423-5).

Bowling: *First Innings*—Connor 22–5–70–3; Bovill 15–4–64–0; James 22–2–53–2; Stephenson 8–1–32–0; Udal 40–11–127–4; Maru 22.3–5–56–1; Whitaker 3–0–20–0; White 6–0–34–0. *Second Innings*—Connor 19.3–3–64–4; Bovill 9–2–43–1; Udal 27–10–44–4; James 9–2–31–1.

Hampshire

*J. P. Stephenson c Rollins b Jones	85	– c Tweats b Harris	5
J. S. Laney lbw b Malcolm	21	– b Harris	7
K. D. James lbw b Vandrau	28	– c Tweats b Vandrau	25
R. A. Smith c DeFreitas b Jones	141	– c Harris b Vandrau	17
P. R. Whitaker b Jones	27	– b Harris	0
G. W. White b DeFreitas	7	– (9) not out	8
R. J. Maru c Tweats b Jones	34	– (10) st Krikken b Vandrau	4
†A. N. Aymes not out	55	– (6) c Jones b Vandrau	0
S. D. Udal c Tweats b DeFreitas	42	– (7) c Krikken b Vandrau	17
C. A. Connor b Harris	8	– (8) c Jones b Vandrau	15
J. N. B. Bovill c Owen b Jones	20	– c DeFreitas b Harris	8
B 6, l-b 5, w 1, n-b 14	26	L-b 2, w 2, n-b 6	10
1/41 2/103 3/208 4/264 5/289 6/367 7/368 8/436 9/464	494	1/8 2/16 3/51 4/52 5/57 6/76 7/96 8/97 9/103	116

Bonus points – Hampshire 4, Derbyshire 4.

Bowling: *First Innings*—Malcolm 19–1–93–1; DeFreitas 28–1–103–2; Harris 12–1–59–1; Vandrau 23–3–73–1; Barnett 12–1–43–0; Jones 23.5–2–112–5. *Second Innings*—Malcolm 9–2–32–0; Harris 15.5–2–48–4; Vandrau 19–4–34–6.

Umpires: B. J. Meyer and G. Sharp.

At Cambridge, June 14, 15, 16. HAMPSHIRE beat CAMBRIDGE UNIVERSITY by 114 runs.

HAMPSHIRE v NORTHAMPTONSHIRE

At Basingstoke, June 19, 20, 21. Hampshire won by an innings and 72 runs. Hampshire 24 pts, Northamptonshire 4 pts. Toss: Hampshire.

Smith's 50th first-class century, allied to good seam bowling, swept Hampshire to a massive victory with a day to spare. Smith batted for 292 minutes and 264 balls and hit 27 fours and two sixes. His 144-run stand with Laney gave Hampshire the initiative and, after heavy rain on the second morning, they went on to 394. Northamptonshire were suspicious of the unpredictable bounce of what Bailey called "a club wicket" and slid to 58 for six by the close. There was no contest after that. Only a spiky fifty from Curran averted humiliation as they were bowled out 247 behind. The second innings was another procession, though once more Curran and Penberthy brought some respectability with a breezy 48 runs for the seventh wicket. Hampshire suffered only one blow, when Curran hit the ball to short leg and struck Laney on the larynx – he was taken to hospital for a check-up.

Close of play: First day, Hampshire 329-6 (A. N. Aymes 11*, S. D. Udal 7*); Second day, Northamptonshire 58-6 (D. J. Capel 5*, K. M. Curran 1*).

Hampshire

*J. P. Stephenson b Penberthy	16
J. S. Laney c Curran b Emburey	81
K. D. James c Warren b Capel	9
R. A. Smith b Taylor	179
V. P. Terry c Bailey b Emburey	19
M. Keech c Bailey b Penberthy	1
†A. N. Aymes not out	37
S. D. Udal c Warren b Taylor	8
R. J. Maru c Warren b Penberthy	8
C. A. Connor c Warren b Penberthy	0
J. N. B. Bovill c Penberthy b Capel	29
L-b 7	7
1/37 2/52 3/196 4/256 5/265 6/320 7/330 8/341 9/349	394

Bonus points – Hampshire 4, Northamptonshire 4 (Score at 120 overs: 356-9).

Bowling: Taylor 28–3–117–2; Penberthy 27–8–54–4; Curran 11–4–30–0; Capel 17.4–4–64–2; Emburey 38–9–81–2; A. R. Roberts 8–2–38–0; Bailey 1–0–3–0.

Northamptonshire

D. J. Roberts lbw b Stephenson	23	– (2) c Keech b James	29
R. R. Montgomerie c Maru b Connor	0	– (1) c Keech b Connor	0
*R. J. Bailey c Laney b James	11	– c Stephenson b Bovill	11
M. B. Loye b Connor	1	– c Aymes b Bovill	0
J. P. Taylor c Terry b Stephenson	10	– (11) c Terry b Stephenson	1
†R. J. Warren lbw b James	0	– (5) c Maru b Stephenson	8
D. J. Capel c Laney b Bovill	9	– (6) c Terry b James	18
K. M. Curran b Stephenson	53	– (7) lbw b James	49
A. L. Penberthy lbw b Stephenson	20	– (8) lbw b Connor	30
A. R. Roberts b Stephenson	10	– (9) c Maru b Udal	2
J. E. Emburey not out	0	– (10) not out	11
B 5, l-b 2, w 1, n-b 2	10	B 4, l-b 10, n-b 2	16
1/1 2/34 3/35 4/44 5/48 6/56 7/93 8/121 9/146	147	1/0 2/15 3/22 4/50 5/74 6/75 7/123 8/138 9/174	175

Bonus points – Hampshire 4.

Bowling: *First Innings*—Connor 17–8–38–2; Bovill 12–3–45–1; Stephenson 14.2–4–27–5; James 10–3–30–2. *Second Innings*—Connor 16–7–34–2; Bovill 11–3–35–2; James 11–3–27–3; Stephenson 9.1–1–48–2; Udal 6–1–17–1.

Umpires: J. H. Hampshire and R. Palmer.

At Southampton, June 29, 30, July 1. HAMPSHIRE drew with INDIANS (See Indian tour section).

At Arundel, July 3, 4, 5, 6. HAMPSHIRE drew with SUSSEX.

At Harrogate, July 18, 19, 20. HAMPSHIRE lost to YORKSHIRE by ten wickets.

HAMPSHIRE v SURREY

At Southampton, July 25, 26, 27, 29. Surrey won by five wickets. Surrey 23 pts, Hampshire 8 pts. Toss: Hampshire.

Stephenson challenged Surrey to score 330 at six an over, which at first sight looked cautious. But he had reckoned without the inspired aggression of Hollioake and Shahid. They came together in the 24th over, with Surrey toiling at 119 for four. Suddenly, the balance shifted. Helped by some indifferent fielding – Hollioake was missed three times – they added a brutal 195 in only 28 overs. When Stephenson bowled Shahid, Surrey needed only 16; they hit the winning runs with five balls to spare. Hollioake finished unbeaten on 104 from 93 balls. Neither side quite succeeded in exploiting a placid pitch during the first two days. Hampshire took a 28-run first-innings lead, which they extended chiefly through Smith and Terry, who added 154 in 33 overs to set up the declaration. Smith reached 20,000 first-class runs when 50; Terry's half-century proved a sadder landmark, as this turned out to be his final home Championship appearance.

Close of play: First day, Hampshire 332-7 (S. D. Udal 19*, R. J. Maru 7*); Second day, Hampshire 0-0 (R. J. Maru 0*, J. S. Laney 0*); Third day, Hampshire 150-4 (R. A. Smith 13*, V. P. Terry 1*).

Hampshire

*J. P. Stephenson c Kersey b M. P. Bicknell	61	– (3) c Hollioake b Julian	62
J. S. Laney lbw b M. P. Bicknell	8	– c Hollioake b M. P. Bicknell	8
K. D. James lbw b M. P. Bicknell	49	– (4) b Benjamin	27
R. A. Smith c Kersey b Hollioake	54	– (5) not out	70
V. P. Terry c and b Pearson	57	– (6) not out	87
M. Keech run out	15		
†A. N. Aymes b Pearson	27		
S. D. Udal c Shahid b Benjamin	31		
R. J. Maru not out	14	– (1) c Butcher b Julian	27
S. M. Milburn c Hollioake b Benjamin	8		
J. N. B. Bovill c Shahid b M. P. Bicknell	0		
B 1, l-b 4, n-b 30	35	B 2, l-b 3, w 1, n-b 14	20
1/13 2/128 3/137 4/213 5/239 6/291 7/304 8/346 9/358	359	1/17 2/71 3/117 4/147 (4 wkts dec.)	301

Bonus points – Hampshire 4, Surrey 4.

Bowling: *First Innings*—M. P. Bicknell 22.4–3–64–4; Benjamin 21–3–73–2; Hollioake 19–5–44–1; Julian 15–1–71–0; Pearson 29–3–80–2; D. J. Bicknell 4–1–18–0; Shahid 2–0–4–0. *Second Innings*—M. P. Bicknell 21–6–66–1; Benjamin 18–5–38–1; Julian 15–4–49–2; Hollioake 9–0–43–0; Shahid 5–0–32–0; Pearson 10–0–60–0; D. J. Bicknell 2–0–8–0.

Surrey

D. J. Bicknell c Keech b Maru	48	– lbw b Stephenson	26
M. A. Butcher c and b James	58	– run out	53
J. D. Ratcliffe c Udal b Stephenson	23	– lbw b Udal	26
N. Shahid lbw b Stephenson	14	– b Stephenson	101
A. D. Brown c Aymes b Bovill	20	– c Terry b Maru	0
*A. J. Hollioake lbw b Stephenson	83	– not out	104
B. P. Julian c Maru b Milburn	12	– not out	4
†G. J. Kersey c Maru b Milburn	0		
M. P. Bicknell not out	15		
R. M. Pearson c Aymes b Milburn	6		
J. E. Benjamin c Keech b Bovill	28		
B 1, l-b 7, n-b 16	24	B 2, l-b 13, w 1, n-b 2	18
1/87 2/124 3/146 4/150 5/210 6/253 7/257 8/285 9/292	331	1/58 2/115 3/119 4/119 5/314	(5 wkts) 332

Bonus points – Surrey 3, Hampshire 4.

Bowling: *First Innings*—Milburn 21–4–85–3; Bovill 16.3–3–63–2; Udal 15–1–47–0; James 9–1–35–1; Stephenson 18–2–64–3; Maru 12–2–29–1. *Second Innings*—Milburn 9–0–71–0; Bovill 5–1–23–0; Stephenson 10.1–0–59–2; James 3–0–12–0; Udal 14–0–83–1; Maru 12–2–69–1.

Umpires: V. A. Holder and A. G. T. Whitehead.

At Taunton, August 1, 2, 3. HAMPSHIRE lost to SOMERSET by an innings and 151 runs.

HAMPSHIRE v GLOUCESTERSHIRE

At Southampton, August 8, 9, 10, 12. Hampshire won by 63 runs. Hampshire 20 pts, Gloucestershire 4 pts. Toss: Hampshire. Championship debut: D. R. Hewson.

This was Cardigan Connor's match. The performance of his life – "I just tried to bowl straight" – brought him nine for 38, the last four for nought in six balls. Only four Hampshire bowlers had bettered his return and no one had taken nine for the county in the 112 years' cricket at Northlands Road. Ironically, a long-standing knee injury was about to end Connor's season; he bowled at half-pace in the second innings and could not take the one wicket he needed for both 50 in the season and 600 in his first-class career. But his figures were to remain the best of 1996. Connor's efforts earned a narrow first-innings lead even though the hostile Walsh had dismissed Hampshire for 186. Both sides did better the second time: Hampshire batted steadily to extend their lead to 378, while Championship newcomer Dominic Hewson scored his second fifty of the match for Gloucestershire. But Udal claimed the final wicket, his fifth, with one ball to spare.

Close of play: First day, Gloucestershire 138-4 (D. R. Hewson 87*, A. Symonds 22*); Second day, Hampshire 145-3 (K. D. James 34*, W. S. Kendall 0*); Third day, Gloucestershire 27-0 (D. R. Hewson 9*, M. G. N. Windows 15*).

Hampshire

*J. P. Stephenson c Ball b Walsh	0	– c Williams b Lewis	0
J. S. Laney c Williams b Lewis	0	– c Williams b Walsh	27
K. D. James c Walsh b Davis	42	– c Ball b Davis	50
R. A. Smith c Davis b Alleyne	26	– c Davis b Walsh	77
W. S. Kendall c Davis b Walsh	42	– lbw b Walsh	63
M. Keech c Symonds b Walsh	55	– c Hancock b Alleyne	61
†A. N. Aymes lbw b Walsh	0	– b Alleyne	7
S. D. Udal c Hancock b Davis	8	– not out	28
R. J. Maru c Williams b Walsh	9	– c Williams b Alleyne	5
C. A. Connor not out	0	– c Williams b Alleyne	24
J. N. B. Bovill b Davis	1	– run out	0
L-b 1, n-b 2	3	B 6, l-b 6, n-b 2	14
1/0 2/12 3/60 4/78 5/153 6/153 7/176 8/176 9/185	186	1/1 2/33 3/145 4/170 5/285 6/289 7/292 8/312 9/354	356

Bonus points – Gloucestershire 4.

Bowling: *First Innings*—Walsh 17–7–34–5; Lewis 10–2–40–1; Alleyne 12–4–49–1; Davis 13.2–3–54–3; Ball 5–1–8–0. *Second Innings*—Walsh 29–9–55–3; Lewis 17–3–52–1; Alleyne 22.2–5–86–4; Davis 27–8–79–1; Ball 18–1–72–0.

Gloucestershire

D. R. Hewson c Laney b Connor	87	– b Maru	58
M. G. N. Windows c Kendall b Bovill	0	– c Udal b James	38
T. H. C. Hancock b Connor	3	– (4) b Maru	9
M. A. Lynch b Connor	0	– (5) c and b Udal	13
M. W. Alleyne b Connor	17	– (6) lbw b Udal	45
A. Symonds c Aymes b Connor	26	– (3) st Aymes b Maru	90
†R. C. J. Williams b Connor	16	– run out	1
R. P. Davis lbw b Connor	6	– (9) not out	37
M. C. J. Ball c Maru b Connor	0	– (10) lbw b Udal	0
J. Lewis c Aymes b Connor	0	– (11) c Keech b Udal	6
*C. A. Walsh not out	0	– (8) c sub b Udal	0
L-b 4, w 1, n-b 4	9	B 7, l-b 4, w 1, n-b 6	18
1/8 2/15 3/19 4/76 5/142 6/143 7/163 8/163 9/163	164	1/64 2/166 3/202 4/205 5/248 6/253 7/253 8/271 9/277	315

Bonus points – Hampshire 4.

Bowling: *First Innings*—Connor 18.1–8–38–9; Bovill 5–0–21–1; Stephenson 10–3–30–0; James 11–5–18–0; Maru 6–3–17–0; Udal 8–2–18–0; Keech 6–0–18–0. *Second Innings*—Connor 24–3–96–0; Stephenson 12–1–43–0; Udal 30.5–7–82–5; Maru 33–17–50–3; James 15–5–33–1.

Umpires: J. C. Balderstone and P. Willey.

At Manchester, August 15, 16, 17, 19. HAMPSHIRE drew with LANCASHIRE.

At Leicester, August 22, 23, 24, 26. HAMPSHIRE drew with LEICESTERSHIRE.

HAMPSHIRE v MIDDLESEX

At Portsmouth, August 28, 29, 30, 31. Middlesex won by 188 runs. Middlesex 20 pts, Hampshire 5 pts. Toss: Middlesex. First-class debut: L. J. Botham.

Liam Botham made a dramatic entrance in the true family tradition, although even his father Ian had failed to start like this. Two days after his 19th birthday, Botham junior was summoned from a Second Eleven match because Stephenson was unfit, wrong-footing journalists, who would have flocked to Portsmouth had the event been well signalled. The game had just begun when he arrived. Coming on second change, he dismissed Gatting with his seventh ball – a leg-side half-volley – and finished with figures of five for 67. His bowling showed the aggression of his father at his best – and his mysterious ability to take wickets with bad balls. Botham scored a commendable 30 to help Hampshire take the lead, but he was not able to bring them victory. For the rest of the match, Fraser took charge. He bowled with controlled hostility on a lively pitch to claim ten for 134. After Pooley and Ramprakash had put Middlesex on top with a second-wicket stand of 187 in 49 overs, Fraser and Tufnell completed the job before lunch on the final day.

Close of play: First day, Hampshire 105-4 (W. S. Kendall 11*, R. J. Maru 1*); Second day, Middlesex 226-1 (J. C. Pooley 106*, M. R. Ramprakash 81*); Third day, Hampshire 109-5 (A. N. Aymes 8*, R. J. Maru 9*).

Middlesex

P. N. Weekes lbw b Bovill	28 – c Botham b Bovill	24
J. C. Pooley lbw b Renshaw	1 – c Aymes b Renshaw	111
M. R. Ramprakash c Udal b Bovill	46 – b James	108
*M. W. Gatting c Keech b Botham	8 – c James b Bovill	83
J. D. Carr c Aymes b Botham	10 – lbw b Botham	4
†K. R. Brown lbw b James	57 – c Udal b Maru	0
O. A. Shah c Maru b James	17 – not out	38
R. L. Johnson c and b Botham	1 – c Udal b Bovill	15
R. A. Fay c White b Botham	4 – c Kendall b Maru	5
A. R. C. Fraser not out	2 – c Kendall b James	7
P. C. R. Tufnell c Aymes b Botham	17 – b James	7
W 2, n-b 6	8 B 9, l-b 6, w 3, n-b 6	24
1/6 2/36 3/55 4/69 5/140 6/172 7/174 8/178 9/178	199 1/49 2/236 3/282 4/336 5/339 6/368 7/384 8/395 9/413	426

Bonus points – Hampshire 4.

Bowling: *First Innings*—Bovill 14–1–40–2; Renshaw 11–2–33–1; James 13–4–23–2; Botham 15–1–67–5; Udal 5–1–27–0; Maru 2–0–9–0. *Second Innings*—Bovill 23–2–91–3; Renshaw 26–5–103–1; Udal 8–2–19–0; Botham 15–3–83–1; James 15.2–1–64–3; Maru 23–8–50–2; Kendall 1–0–1–0.

Hampshire

G. W. White c Pooley b Fraser	32 – c Carr b Tufnell	20
K. D. James c Brown b Fay	1 – c Carr b Fraser	4
M. Keech c Pooley b Fay	13 – c Gatting b Weekes	12
*R. A. Smith b Fay	42 – c Brown b Fraser	28
W. S. Kendall c Brown b Fraser	24 – lbw b Tufnell	18
R. J. Maru c Pooley b Fay	33 – (7) c Ramprakash b Fraser	38
†A. N. Aymes c Gatting b Fraser	27 – (6) c Brown b Fraser	41
L. J. Botham c Pooley b Johnson	30 – c Weekes b Tufnell	1
S. D. Udal c Brown b Fraser	9 – c Fay b Tufnell	18
J. N. B. Bovill c Johnson b Fraser	5 – c Brown b Fraser	9
S. J. Renshaw not out	0 – not out	0
L-b 4, n-b 12	16 B 10, l-b 6	16
1/4 2/18 3/66 4/104 5/124 6/168 7/217 8/217 9/231	232 1/5 2/36 3/36 4/76 5/93 6/169 7/178 8/180 9/205	205

Bonus points – Hampshire 1, Middlesex 4.

Bowling: *First Innings*—Fraser 28–8–55–5; Fay 28–9–77–4; Johnson 26–5–87–1; Tufnell 3–1–5–0; Weekes 2–0–4–0. *Second Innings*—Fraser 22–5–79–5; Fay 6–3–9–0; Tufnell 24.1–10–39–4; Weekes 25–6–62–1.

Umpires: A. Clarkson and A. G. T. Whitehead.

HAMPSHIRE v GLAMORGAN

At Southampton, September 3, 4, 5, 6. Drawn. Hampshire 11 pts, Glamorgan 8 pts. Toss: Glamorgan. First-class debut: A. D. Mascarenhas.

First Liam Botham, then Dimitri Mascarenhas. An 18-year-old seamer, born in London of Sri Lankan parentage and raised in Australia, Mascarenhas claimed six for 88 – the best analysis by a Hampshire bowler on first-class debut since 1899. On a pitch offering little real help, he dismissed James and Morris, and then Dale, in quick succession after a superb opening stand of 177, and kept Glamorgan down to a comparatively modest 401. After Laney replied with a maiden Championship hundred, Hampshire declared 49 behind to keep the game alive. Maynard responded vigorously, with a magnificent array of shots – five sixes and seven fours – as he scored 69 from 44 balls. Glamorgan's declaration challenged the home side to make 331 on the final day. While Smith and Kendall were adding 156 in 31 overs, they had a chance. But once those two were dismissed, Hampshire abandoned the chase, and Keech, playing down the order because of a damaged wrist, had to bat out time at No. 10.

Close of play: First day, Glamorgan 229-5 (A. D. Shaw 16*, D. A. Cosker 3*); Second day, Hampshire 193-2 (J. S. Laney 102*, R. J. Maru 3*); Third day, Glamorgan 281-6 (O. D. Gibson 62*, R. D. B. Croft 23*).

Glamorgan

S. P. James lbw b Mascarenhas	103	– c Kendall b Mascarenhas	24
H. Morris c White b Mascarenhas	80	– c sub b Mascarenhas	35
A. Dale c Aymes b Mascarenhas	0	– b Botham	11
*M. P. Maynard c and b Renshaw	15	– run out	69
P. A. Cottey c Aymes b Botham	8	– c sub b Mascarenhas	41
†A. D. Shaw b Mascarenhas	53	– c Renshaw b Maru	11
D. A. Cosker b Mascarenhas	6		
O. D. Gibson c Aymes b Mascarenhas	14	– (7) not out	62
R. D. B. Croft b Maru	67	– (8) not out	23
S. L. Watkin run out	34		
O. T. Parkin not out	13		
L-b 4, n-b 4	8	L-b 3, w 2	5
1/177 2/177 3/194 4/198 5/226 6/256 7/271 8/288 9/358	401	1/32 2/65 3/108 4/148 5/171 6/242 (6 wkts dec.)	281

Bonus points – Glamorgan 4, Hampshire 4 (Score at 120 overs: 397-9).

Bowling: *First Innings*—Renshaw 30–7–110–1; Thursfield 18–3–75–0; Maru 19.5–9–45–1; Botham 14–2–59–1; Mascarenhas 32–8–88–6; Keech 7–2–20–0. *Second Innings*—Mascarenhas 16–2–62–3; Renshaw 9–1–46–0; Thursfield 7–1–20–0; Botham 6–2–33–1; Maru 12–1–71–1; White 9–1–37–0; Laney 2–0–9–0.

Hampshire

G. W. White c Watkin b Croft	70	– lbw b Watkin	14
J. S. Laney c Morris b Watkin	102	– c Maynard b Gibson	11
M. Keech c Morris b Croft	12	– (10) not out	26
R. J. Maru not out	55	– (9) not out	7
*R. A. Smith c Maynard b Croft	54	– (4) c Cottey b Parkin	91
W. S. Kendall not out	43	– (5) c Shaw b Parkin	71
†A. N. Aymes (did not bat)		– (3) c Shaw b Gibson	0
L. J. Botham (did not bat)		– (6) c Maynard b Gibson	0
A. D. Mascarenhas (did not bat)		– (7) c Shaw b Watkin	10
M. J. Thursfield (did not bat)		– (8) c Gibson b Watkin	18
B 5, l-b 8, w 1, n-b 2	16	B 4, l-b 8, w 1	13
1/153 2/179 3/193 4/279 (4 wkts dec.)	352	1/20 2/22 3/39 4/195 5/200 6/200 7/216 8/231 (8 wkts)	261

S. J. Renshaw did not bat.

Bonus points – Hampshire 4, Glamorgan 1.

Bowling: *First Innings*—Watkin 14–0–60–1; Gibson 15–3–75–0; Parkin 17–4–38–0; Croft 31–11–51–3; Cosker 20–4–98–0; Dale 4.1–1–17–0. *Second Innings*—Watkin 21.5–6–49–3; Gibson 25–6–74–3; Croft 23–9–41–0; Parkin 17–3–51–2; Dale 3–1–7–0; Cosker 9–4–27–0.

Umpires: G. I. Burgess and D. J. Constant.

At Canterbury, September 12, 13, 14, 16. HAMPSHIRE lost to KENT by 148 runs.

HAMPSHIRE v NOTTINGHAMSHIRE

At Southampton, September 19, 20, 21, 22. Drawn. Hampshire 8 pts, Nottinghamshire 8 pts. Toss: Hampshire. First-class debut: P. J. Franks.

A disappointing season for both counties drifted into hibernation as Nottinghamshire cold-shouldered a challenge to score 304 in a minimum of 52 overs. There was some satisfaction for two of Hampshire's younger generation. Laney was awarded his county cap, having joined Smith in the previous game as the only batsmen to score 1,000 runs for the county. Kendall also completed his thousand – he had made 444 for Oxford – during a maiden Championship hundred. The innings of the match, however, was a pugnacious century by Smith. Nottinghamshire replied to Hampshire's 513 for four – the biggest total in meetings between these two sides – with 391 for four, Archer and Johnson scoring rapid hundreds off the nine bowlers used. But the visitors' decision to declare 122 behind failed to bring the desired response. Although Johnson himself bowled and wicket-keeper Noon trundled down four overs, Smith delayed his declaration so long that the target held little interest for Nottinghamshire. A chilled, tiny audience was desperately short-changed.

Close of play: First day, Hampshire 213-2 (J. S. Laney 76*, R. A. Smith 42*); Second day, Hampshire 513-4 dec.; Third day, Hampshire 39-1 (G. W. White 4*, P. R. Whitaker 0*).

Hampshire

G. W. White b Franks	73	– c and b Johnson	53
J. S. Laney c Cairns b Afzaal	97	– lbw b Archer	25
P. R. Whitaker c Noon b Franks	0	– c Noon b Franks	6
*R. A. Smith c Archer b Bowen	161	– (7) not out	31
W. S. Kendall not out	103	– (4) c Noon b Archer	22
†A. N. Aymes not out	38	– not out	29
S. D. Udal (did not bat)		– (5) lbw b Archer	2
L-b 18, w 1, n-b 22	41	L-b 6, w 1, n-b 6	13
1/147 2/149 3/305 4/400 (4 wkts dec.)	513	1/35 2/52 3/102 4/116 5/124 (5 wkts dec.)	181

L. J. Botham, R. J. Maru, J. N. B. Bovill and S. J. Renshaw did not bat.

Bonus points – Hampshire 4, Nottinghamshire 1 (Score at 120 overs: 434-4).

Bowling: *First Innings*—Cairns 19–3–70–0; Bowen 31–4–120–1; Tolley 25–5–80–0; Franks 28–9–65–2; Afford 25–6–79–0; Dowman 4–0–29–0; Afzaal 6–0–31–1; Archer 4–1–21–0. *Second Innings*—Bowen 4–0–17–0; Franks 13–5–37–1; Archer 11–3–18–3; Johnson 12–2–51–1; Dowman 7–4–8–0; Tolley 4–0–22–0; Noon 4–1–22–0.

Nottinghamshire

R. T. Robinson c Maru b Bovill	39		
M. P. Dowman c Aymes b Bovill	21	– (1) lbw b Maru	20
G. F. Archer c Aymes b Kendall	120	– c Aymes b Udal	63
*P. Johnson c Renshaw b Kendall	109	– (7) not out	7
U. Afzaal not out	67	– (2) b Udal	19
C. L. Cairns not out	23	– (5) c Aymes b Udal	3
C. M. Tolley (did not bat)		– (4) b Maru	11
†W. M. Noon (did not bat)		– (6) not out	25
B 4, l-b 8	12	L-b 3, w 1	4
1/29 2/174 3/185 4/342 (4 wkts dec.)	391	1/29 2/63 3/98 4/109 5/132 (5 wkts)	152

M. N. Bowen, P. J. Franks and J. A. Afford did not bat.

Bonus points – Nottinghamshire 4, Hampshire 1.

Bowling: *First Innings*—Bovill 9–2–25–2; Renshaw 17–6–78–0; Botham 5–1–26–0; Udal 13–2–50–0; Maru 20–6–46–0; Kendall 13–1–46–2; Laney 10–2–49–0; Whitaker 11–2–55–0; White 2–1–4–0. *Second Innings*—Bovill 3–2–2–0; Udal 30–8–93–3; Maru 20–8–38–2; Renshaw 7–4–16–0.

Umpires: G. I. Burgess and V. A. Holder.

Dean Headley

KENT

Patron: HRH The Duke of Kent
President: 1996 – R. Baker White
1997 – P. Edgley
Chairman: D. S. Kemp
Chairman, Cricket Committee: D. G. Ufton
Secretary: S. T. W. Anderson
Captain: 1996 – M. R. Benson
1997 – S. A. Marsh
Cricket Administrator: Ms L. Walters
Head Groundsman: B. A. Fitch
Scorer: J. C. Foley

It was a great pity that Kent's season should finish on a note of anticlimax, with a ten-wicket defeat in two and a half days by Gloucestershire at Bristol. They arrived in the West Country with high hopes; three days before, they had produced arguably the most remarkable half-hour's county cricket of the entire season to beat Hampshire, a result which kept them in with an outside chance of being champions. But defeat pushed them down to fourth.

It would have been astonishing had they triumphed. A year earlier, Kent came rock bottom in the Championship while winning the Sunday League. The players claimed they were not given enough credit for their success, with too much emphasis on the failure. But at the annual meeting the members made it clear where their priorities lay.

Much of the criticism was aimed at captain Mark Benson, cricket committee chairman Derek Ufton and coach Daryl Foster. Sadly, it got rather personal. Benson's tactics and Foster's role came under fire from an audience that was ambivalent about Kent's first trophy for 17 years. "Must do better" was the clear message left by the meeting, and the team did. Kent's jump of 14 Championship places has been surpassed only twice in history. But, in contrast, they had a modest season in all the one-day competitions.

As it turned out, Benson would never again captain the side anyway. He suffered a knee injury playing football in pre-season training; and though he hoped to play, he never did. He resigned as captain at the end of July, and the county announced his release, with a year of his contract still left. He went into hospital in October for another operation. In Benson's absence, vice-captain Steve Marsh led the side and he was confirmed in the position at the end of the season. In fact, Kent had five captains during the year; while Marsh was out with a broken finger in August, Carl Hooper took charge against Worcestershire. After leading the side to Kent's first Championship defeat in 1996, he stepped down and Trevor Ward steered them to victory in the next two games. Min Patel was captain against Oxford.

Like Benson, the former England fast bowler Alan Igglesden was also unable to play. He missed the start of the season with a back problem and then ankle and hamstring trouble caused further setbacks. He was also released from his contract, but could return in 1997 on a match-to-match basis. Igglesden promised to dedicate his winter to fitness, after a season he described as the lowest point in his 11-year – and frequently injury-plagued – career.

Neil Taylor also left. He seemed resigned to his fate weeks before the news was confirmed but, with Benson sidelined, it was a mistake to overlook Taylor completely; he continued to lead the Second Eleven, scoring freely, and eventually found a berth at Sussex. He departed at the same time as Benson; they had made their debuts within a year of each other and a total of just over 36,000 first-class runs in nearly 600 matches was testimony to the contribution they had made to Kent cricket. The gap in experience will be filled by the arrival of the displaced Sussex captain, Alan Wells, who was given a five-year contract that will take him through until he is 40. Benson's departure was followed by the news that his sister, Tina, was to leave after five years as marketing manager to start her own public relations and corporate entertainment business.

Kent's dramatic improvement in the Championship was built on their spirit and determination to succeed. With Igglesden missing and Dean Headley's hip problem keeping him out early on, Martin McCague carried the burden of front-line bowler on his broad shoulders. He appeared in all Kent's Championship matches, looking lean and hungry, and bowled with great enthusiasm and no little hostility. A total of 76 first-class wickets earned him the Player of the Year Award. But Headley made up for lost time by equalling the world record of three hat-tricks in a season – against Derbyshire, his native Worcestershire and Hampshire. McCague also took a hat-trick as Hampshire lost eight wickets for seven runs in the memorable game at Canterbury.

Headley finished with 51 first-class wickets and also earned a well-deserved call-up to England's one-day squad against Pakistan. But like colleague Mark Ealham, he was disappointed only to make the A team, rather than the senior tour to Zimbabwe and New Zealand. Ealham had made his one-day international debut against India and appeared in two Tests, but strained a rib muscle, an untimely injury in a period when the position of England's No. 1 all-rounder was so open. Patel's two Tests were disappointing and seemed to have an adverse effect on his county form and confidence.

Hooper scored more than 2,000 runs in Championship and one-day cricket and Ward once again passed 1,000 runs. Nigel Llong produced several important scores late in the season to secure his middle-order spot. In his third Championship match of the season, Matthew Walker scored 275 not out against Somerset, the fourth-highest score ever by a Kent batsman and the highest ever for Kent at Canterbury. With Walker opening and Matthew Fleming dropping down the order, it was Graham Cowdrey – Kent's beneficiary in 1997 – who lost his place. Will House was named Kent's most promising uncapped player, in a year when youngsters were given their chance: Ed Smith, House's fellow Cambridge University student, earned a first-class debut, as did Ben Phillips and Nick Preston. But early in 1997, Kent suddenly had the problem of finding someone to guide all these youngsters; Foster said he would not be returning as coach for "personal reasons". – ANDREW GIDLEY.

KENT 1996

[*Bill Smith*

Back row: E. J. Stanford, N. W. Preston, D. P. Fulton, J. B. D. Thompson, B. J. Phillips, D. J. Spencer, S. C. Willis. *Middle row:* J. C. Foley (*scorer*), F. Errington (*physiotherapist*), M. J. Walker, N. J. Llong, D. W. Headley, T. N. Wren, M. A. Ealham, M. M. Patel. *Front row:* M. J. McCague, T. R. Ward, N. R. Taylor, M. R. Benson (*captain*), S. A. Marsh, G. R. Cowdrey, M. V. Fleming. *Insets:* C. L. Hooper, A. P. Igglesden.

KENT RESULTS

All first-class matches – Played 19: Won 9, Lost 3, Drawn 7.

County Championship matches – Played 17: Won 9, Lost 2, Drawn 6.

Competition placings – Britannic Assurance County Championship, 4th; NatWest Trophy, 2nd round; Benson and Hedges Cup, q-f; AXA Equity & Law League, 10th.

COUNTY CHAMPIONSHIP AVERAGES

BATTING

Cap		*M*	*I*	*NO*	*R*	*HS*	*100s*	*50s*	*Avge*	*Ct/St*
	M. J. Walker†	7	13	3	606	275*	1	2	60.60	2
1992	C. L. Hooper§	17	29	2	1,287	155	3	9	47.66	33
	S. C. Willis	3	4	1	129	78	0	1	43.00	6
1989	T. R. Ward†	17	29	1	1,191	161	2	8	42.53	10
1993	N. J. Llong†	12	20	2	719	130	2	5	39.94	12
1988	G. R. Cowdrey†	10	15	0	506	111	1	3	33.73	4
1992	M. A. Ealham†	11	18	4	452	74	0	3	32.28	5
1990	M. V. Fleming	17	28	2	814	116	2	3	31.30	7
	D. P. Fulton	15	27	2	643	88	0	4	25.72	24
1986	S. A. Marsh	14	22	1	449	127	1	2	21.38	28/6
1993	D. W. Headley	10	14	3	226	63*	0	1	20.54	3
1992	M. J. McCague	17	24	7	347	63*	0	1	20.41	10
	J. B. D. Thompson	4	5	0	89	37	0	0	17.80	0
1994	M. M. Patel	14	19	3	224	33	0	0	14.00	6
	N. W. Preston†	7	11	4	63	17*	0	0	9.00	3
	T. N. Wren†	6	5	2	15	8	0	0	5.00	2

Also batted: B. J. Phillips (3 matches) 2, 1, 2 (1 ct); E. T. Smith† (1 match) 31, 26; E. J. Stanford† (2 matches) 0*, 10*, 2* (1 ct).

* *Signifies not out.* † *Born in Kent.* § *Overseas player.*

BOWLING

	O	*M*	*R*	*W*	*BB*	*5W/i*	*Avge*
M. A. Ealham	295.4	101	726	36	8-36	3	20.16
M. J. McCague	564	114	1,815	75	6-51	3	24.20
D. W. Headley	364	59	1,235	45	8-98	2	27.44
M. V. Fleming	163	31	472	17	3-6	0	27.76
C. L. Hooper	321.3	83	789	26	4-7	0	30.34
N. W. Preston	119.5	25	326	10	4-68	0	32.60
M. M. Patel	469	142	1,186	29	6-97	2	40.89

Also bowled: G. R. Cowdrey 8–3–23–0; D. P. Fulton 4–1–28–0; N. J. Llong 52.5–17–135–9; S. A. Marsh 6–4–5–0; B. J. Phillips 40–12–109–4; E. J. Stanford 67.3–22–158–5; J. B. D. Thompson 75.2–14–268–7; M. J. Walker 1–0–19–0; T. R. Ward 9–3–29–2; T. N. Wren 92–17–347–8.

COUNTY RECORDS

Highest score for:	332	W. H. Ashdown v Essex at Brentwood	1934
Highest score against:	344	W. G. Grace (MCC) at Canterbury	1876
Best bowling for:	10-30	C. Blythe v Northamptonshire at Northampton	1907
Best bowling against:	10-48	C. H. G. Bland (Sussex) at Tonbridge	1899
Highest total for:	803-4 dec.	v Essex at Brentwood	1934
Highest total against:	676	by Australians at Canterbury	1921
Lowest total for:	18	v Sussex at Gravesend	1867
Lowest total against:	16	by Warwickshire at Tonbridge	1913

KENT v LANCASHIRE

At Canterbury, May 2, 3, 4, 6. Kent won by 64 runs. Kent 19 pts, Lancashire 4 pts. Toss: Lancashire. Championship debut: S. Elworthy.

Wooden spoon holders Kent produced an unexpected victory shortly after 5 o'clock on a gorgeous bank holiday afternoon. It was their first Championship win for 11 months and the first time in 23 seasons they had won their opening game. Collusion between the two captains – Marsh, standing in for the injured Benson, and Watkinson – was necessary after rain halted play at 12.25 on the first day and washed out all of Friday. Two contrived declarations turned the contest into virtually a one-innings affair, with Lancashire left to chase 340 in 96 overs on the final day. When Fairbrother and Atherton added 140 in 101 minutes, reaching 190 for two, the visitors looked favourites. But once Fairbrother went, Patel bowled Kent to victory, taking his Championship record against Lancashire to 31 wickets in six innings.

Close of play: First day, Kent 63-2 (T. R. Ward 31*, C. L. Hooper 15*); Second day, No play; Third day, Kent 66-3 dec.

Kent

D. P. Fulton lbw b Chapple	5	– lbw b Martin	1
M. V. Fleming lbw b Chapple	8	– c Chapple b Watkinson	18
T. R. Ward c and b Austin	106	– c Speak b Watkinson	25
C. L. Hooper lbw b Austin	54	– not out	17
G. R. Cowdrey c Elworthy b Gallian	52		
M. A. Ealham not out	48	– (5) not out	5
*†S. A. Marsh c Watkinson b Elworthy	10		
J. B. D. Thompson c Speak b Watkinson	0		
M. J. McCague c Speak b Watkinson	0		
M. M. Patel lbw b Watkinson	5		
T. N. Wren c Fairbrother b Austin	8		
B 1, l-b 8, w 3, n-b 12	24		
1/13 2/14 3/141 4/230 5/260 6/278 7/285 8/285 9/293	320	1/10 2/20 3/60 (3 wkts dec.)	66

Bonus points – Kent 3, Lancashire 4.

Bowling: *First Innings*—Martin 20–6–55–0; Chapple 20–5–57–2; Austin 18.1–3–79–3; Elworthy 23–3–78–1; Watkinson 8–1–25–3; Gallian 9–3–17–1. *Second Innings*—Martin 6–0–19–1; Watkinson 5.3–0–47–2.

Lancashire

M. A. Atherton b Thompson	11	– b Patel	98
J. E. R. Gallian not out	18	– c Marsh b Thompson	12
G. Chapple not out	18	– (10) not out	7
J. P. Crawley (did not bat)		– (3) b Fleming	5
N. H. Fairbrother (did not bat)		– (4) c Hooper b McCague	85
N. J. Speak (did not bat)		– (5) c Fulton b McCague	4
*M. Watkinson (did not bat)		– (6) b Wren	21
†W. K. Hegg (did not bat)		– (7) b Patel	2
I. D. Austin (did not bat)		– (8) c McCague b Patel	0
S. Elworthy (did not bat)		– (9) c and b Patel	10
P. J. Martin (did not bat)		– lbw b Patel	20
		B 1, l-b 4, n-b 6	11
1/23 (1 wkt dec.)	47	1/30 2/50 3/190 4/194 5/223 6/232 7/232 8/242 9/247	275

Bowling: *First Innings*—McCague 3–1–11–0; Thompson 5.1–0–28–1; Wren 3–1–8–0. *Second Innings*—McCague 23–3–75–2; Thompson 16–4–44–1; Wren 12–3–44–1; Fleming 7–0–37–1; Patel 28.2–13–65–5; Hooper 1–0–5–0.

Umpires: A. A. Jones and R. Julian.

At The Oval, May 9, 10, 11, 13. KENT drew with SURREY.

At Ilford, May 16, 17, 18, 20. KENT beat ESSEX by an innings and 66 runs.

KENT v YORKSHIRE

At Canterbury, May 23, 24, 25, 27. Drawn. Kent 8 pts, Yorkshire 11 pts. Toss: Yorkshire.

By refusing to open up the game on the final day, Yorkshire won few friends and the game finished in a manner as dreary as the bank holiday weather. Marsh, who had made unsuccessful overtures to Byas earlier in the day, gave his entire side the opportunity to bowl. There was sympathy for young McGrath, who made use of the opportunity to reach his maiden Championship hundred, though the sense of frustration grew when he spent half an hour on 92 as Llong bowled eight successive maidens. When bad light took the players off at 4.25, Byas defended his strategy: "I understand spectators complaining, but I was not going to gift Kent a victory." He also pointed to Kent's failure to declare on Saturday. Bad weather had prolonged Yorkshire's first innings into Saturday morning. Ward then scored 161 in four hours, but Kent's late order crumbled to White.

Close of play: First day, Yorkshire 261-5 (R. J. Blakey 32*, A. C. Morris 13*); Second day, Yorkshire 320-7 (R. J. Blakey 56*, A. G. Wharf 16*); Third day, Yorkshire 29-1 (A. McGrath 19*, D. Byas 8*).

Yorkshire

A. McGrath c Hooper b Preston	40	– c Marsh b Ward	101
M. P. Vaughan c Hooper b McCague	24	– c Fleming b McCague	1
*D. Byas c Marsh b Preston	44	– b Fleming	79
M. G. Bevan c Llong b Preston	80	– not out	15
C. White c Hooper b McCague	13	– c Fleming b Ward	7
†R. J. Blakey not out	60	– not out	0
A. C. Morris c Fulton b Patel	27		
P. J. Hartley b Preston	5		
A. G. Wharf b McCague	41		
C. E. W. Silverwood not out	0		
B 2, l-b 3, w 1, n-b 10	16	B 12, l-b 6, n-b 2	20
1/60 2/68 3/196 4/211 5/217 6/284 7/295 8/349 (8 wkts dec.)	350	1/11 2/174 3/209 4/221 (4 wkts)	223

R. D. Stemp did not bat.

Bonus points – Yorkshire 4, Kent 3.

Bowling: *First Innings*—McCague 33–7–97–3; Thompson 15–4–66–0; Preston 25–5–68–4; Fleming 11–3–30–0; Patel 29.1–7–84–1. *Second Innings*—McCague 10–2–43–1; Thompson 9–3–33–0; Patel 30–15–28–0; Hooper 13–7–22–0; Cowdrey 8–3–23–0; Fulton 3–1–9–0; Preston 5–0–11–0; Fleming 3–0–12–1; Llong 12–8–9–0; Ward 6–3–10–2; Marsh 6–4–5–0.

Kent

D. P. Fulton lbw b Silverwood	34
M. V. Fleming c Morris b Hartley	17
T. R. Ward b White	161
C. L. Hooper c Byas b Silverwood	0
G. R. Cowdrey c Byas b Stemp	7
N. J. Llong c Byas b Morris	10
*†S. A. Marsh b White	4
J. B. D. Thompson b White	28
M. J. McCague c Hartley b Stemp	4
M. M. Patel c Morris b White	0
N. W. Preston not out	4
B 1, l-b 7, n-b 22	30
1/29 2/86 3/86 4/136 5/177 6/188 7/283 8/290 9/290	299

Bonus points – Kent 2, Yorkshire 4.

Bowling: Hartley 14–5–46–1; Silverwood 17–3–85–2; White 12.2–3–42–4; Wharf 13–4–45–0; Stemp 15–5–50–2; Morris 8–2–23–1.

Umpires: A. Clarkson and R. Palmer.

KENT v SUSSEX

At Tunbridge Wells, May 30, 31. Kent won by ten wickets. Kent 22 pts, Sussex 4 pts. Toss: Sussex. First-class debut: B. J. Phillips.

Kent won in two days to go top of the table, though some home supporters' delight was mixed with disappointment: the Mayor of Tunbridge Wells, for instance, had invited a number of guests for lunch in a marquee on the Saturday. Wells had no hesitation in batting, but Sussex were dismissed before tea and never recovered. Kent had their problems too, losing six wickets to Drakes and Law by the close: three fell in the last 13 balls of the day and then Marsh went first ball in the morning. But their lead was already 58 and Ealham, supported by McCague, extended that to 138. Sussex batted poorly again, and their frustrations seemed to get the better of Wells, who hit the ball away and waved his bat when he was given out lbw by umpire Burgess. Kent passed their target of 27 inside four overs. Marsh attributed victory to the "most disciplined bowling performance by a Kent side for a long time"; Ealham was the star, with match figures of eight for 71.

Close of play: First day, Kent 200-6 (M. A. Ealham 0*).

Sussex

C. W. J. Athey lbw b Preston	16	– lbw b Fleming	34
J. W. Hall c McCague b Ealham	10	– b Phillips	23
M. P. Speight b Preston	10	– b Phillips	5
N. J. Lenham c Hooper b Ealham	9	– (5) c Marsh b McCague	10
*A. P. Wells c McCague b Ealham	5	– (4) lbw b Ealham	45
D. R. Law c Marsh b Phillips	17	– c Hooper b Ealham	33
†P. Moores c Marsh b McCague	13	– lbw b Ealham	2
I. D. K. Salisbury c Hooper b Fleming	18	– lbw b Ealham	1
V. C. Drakes b Preston	23	– c McCague b Phillips	3
P. W. Jarvis c and b McCague	5	– not out	1
E. S. H. Giddins not out	2	– c Cowdrey b Ealham	4
L-b 4, n-b 10	14	B 1, l-b 2	3
1/28 2/38 3/46 4/55 5/58 6/89 7/100 8/124 9/134	142	1/55 2/63 3/77 4/102 5/136 6/140 7/148 8/157 9/159	164

Bonus points – Kent 4.

Bowling: *First Innings*—McCague 12.2–3–36–2; Phillips 12–3–22–1; Preston 14–2–46–3; Ealham 16–12–16–3; Patel 3–0–5–0; Fleming 6–1–13–1. *Second Innings*—McCague 14–4–43–1; Phillips 14–5–34–3; Ealham 18.2–4–55–5; Preston 7–3–9–0; Fleming 6–2–10–1; Hooper 1–0–4–0; Patel 1–0–6–0.

Kent

D. P. Fulton c Jarvis b Law	6	– not out	17
M. V. Fleming lbw b Law	41	– not out	8
T. R. Ward b Law	51		
C. L. Hooper lbw b Drakes	72		
N. W. Preston lbw b Law	5		
G. R. Cowdrey c Law b Drakes	0		
M. A. Ealham not out	31		
*†S. A. Marsh lbw b Drakes	0		
M. J. McCague b Giddins	32		
M. M. Patel c Law b Jarvis	6		
B. J. Phillips lbw b Law	2		
L-b 9, w 1, n-b 24	34	W 1, n-b 4	5
1/58 2/61 3/188 4/200 5/200 6/200 7/200 8/254 9/261	280		(no wkt) 30

Bonus points – Kent 2, Sussex 4.

Bowling: *First Innings*—Drakes 17–4–65–3; Jarvis 15–1–59–1; Law 18.5–3–62–5; Giddins 14–4–46–1; Salisbury 5–0–39–0. *Second Innings*—Drakes 2–0–16–0; Jarvis 1.3–0–14–0.

Umpires: G. I. Burgess and K. E. Palmer.

At Leicester, June 5, 6, 7, 8. KENT drew with LEICESTERSHIRE.

KENT v MIDDLESEX

At Canterbury, June 13, 14, 15, 17. Drawn. Kent 9 pts, Middlesex 10 pts. Toss: Middlesex. First-class debut: P. E. Wellings.

Kent had to fight off the threat of Tufnell on the final afternoon. Set 299 to win in what became 68 overs, Kent were 152 for two, then lost four wickets in six overs on a turning pitch. Tufnell got three, his reward for a marathon stint bowling into the rough, including Hooper, who was bowled after a delivery seemed to bounce off his shoulder on to the stumps. Ealham and McCague survived several loud appeals as Middlesex scented victory – Tufnell was so frustrated at seeing one rejected that he threw down his cap and was given a quiet warning by umpire Plews. In the first innings, Weekes scored his century off 159 balls, Peter Wellings, Middlesex's fifth Championship newcomer of the season, narrowly missed his fifty and Fraser and Tufnell shared a frustrating last-wicket stand of 48. Wellings, brought in to replace the indisposed Gatting, added 41 not out on the last morning, when occasional off-spinner Llong took four wickets in 21 balls. The Middlesex wicket-keeper Brown caused some comment by keeping to the spinners in a helmet.

Close of play: First day, Middlesex 358-5 (K. R. Brown 20*, P. E. Wellings 29*); Second day, Kent 215-4 (G. R. Cowdrey 23*, M. A. Ealham 43*); Third day, Middlesex 123-3 (J. D. Carr 39*, J. C. Pooley 13*).

Middlesex

P. N. Weekes b Headley	108	– c Llong b Patel	14
J. C. Harrison lbw b Patel	40	– c Fulton b McCague	10
M. R. Ramprakash b Fleming	66	– run out	30
*J. D. Carr c Llong b Ealham	6	– b Patel	49
J. C. Pooley c McCague b Hooper	67	– c Ward b Patel	20
†K. R. Brown c Hooper b McCague	21	– st Marsh b Llong	30
P. E. Wellings c Ward b Patel	48	– not out	41
M. A. Feltham c Marsh b McCague	0	– c Fulton b Llong	0
R. A. Fay c Fleming b McCague	12	– c Fulton b Llong	0
A. R. C. Fraser lbw b Ealham	31	– c Hooper b Llong	9
P. C. R. Tufnell not out	17	– c Headley b Llong	6
B 5, l-b 5, w 1, n-b 14	25	B 24, l-b 10, n-b 4	38
1/110 2/182 3/199 4/299 5/311 6/359 7/359 8/391 9/393	441	1/25 2/25 3/100 4/139 5/155 6/207 7/213 8/213 9/237	247

Bonus points – Middlesex 4, Kent 3 (Score at 120 overs: 392-8).

Bowling: *First Innings*—McCague 30–6–84–3; Headley 28–5–101–1; Ealham 16.1–4–46–2; Patel 27–6–104–2; Hooper 11–1–53–1; Fleming 16–1–43–1. *Second Innings*—McCague 15–4–47–1; Headley 8–1–34–0; Patel 37–14–77–3; Ealham 10–4–15–0; Hooper 4–0–19–0; Llong 8.5–2–21–5.

Kent

D. P. Fulton c Carr b Feltham	32	– c Carr b Fay	11
M. V. Fleming c Tufnell b Fay	31	– run out	59
T. R. Ward lbw b Feltham	41	– c Harrison b Fraser	45
C. L. Hooper c Harrison b Tufnell	33	– b Tufnell	25
G. R. Cowdrey c Brown b Fraser	51		
M. A. Ealham c Harrison b Tufnell	59	– (5) not out	23
N. J. Llong not out	63	– (6) c Carr b Tufnell	0
*†S. A. Marsh c Brown b Feltham	20	– (7) c Brown b Tufnell	0
M. J. McCague c Brown b Tufnell	34	– (8) not out	24
M. M. Patel not out	0		
B 10, l-b 8, n-b 8	26	L-b 10, n-b 8	18
1/46 2/78 3/139 4/149 5/265 6/267 7/314 8/385 (8 wkts dec.)	390	1/21 2/97 3/152 4/162 5/162 6/164 (6 wkts)	205

D. W. Headley did not bat.

Bonus points – Kent 3, Middlesex 3 (Score at 120 overs: 322-7).

Bowling: *First Innings*—Fraser 31–8–72–1; Fay 24–5–73–1; Tufnell 50–17–126–3; Feltham 24–10–62–3; Weekes 13–2–39–0. *Second Innings*—Fraser 12–0–41–1; Fay 4–1–19–1; Tufnell 27.3–9–60–3; Weekes 17–5–63–0; Ramprakash 7–4–12–0.

Umpires: T. E. Jesty and N. T. Plews.

At Birmingham, June 20, 21, 22. KENT beat WARWICKSHIRE by 32 runs.

KENT v OXFORD UNIVERSITY

At Canterbury, June 29, 30, July 1. Drawn. Toss: Kent. First-class debuts: J. A. Ford, C. D. Walsh.

Rain washed out the final afternoon, preventing Kent from starting the chase for 311. Three centuries – by Fulton, Kendall and Khan – provided the highlights for the sparse crowd. Fulton's century was his third against University teams in successive years. He and debutant Chris Walsh shared an unbroken stand of 200, an emphatic reply to Oxford's first-innings 294, before acting-captain Patel declared behind. Khan, about to join Derbyshire, took full advantage of some friendly bowling to make his maiden hundred; Kendall, on Hampshire's books, had scored his second earlier in the match.

Close of play: First day, Oxford University 209-5 (W. S. Kendall 72*, H. S. Malik 3*); Second day, Oxford University 28-1 (C. M. Gupte 7*).

Oxford University

*C. M. Gupte c Patel b Headley	6	b Llong	7
I. J. Sutcliffe c Willis b Llong	83	c Willis b Wren	17
A. C. Ridley c Walsh b Headley	0	run out	24
G. A. Khan c Wren b Thompson	34	not out	101
W. S. Kendall c Walsh b Headley	119	c and b Fulton	43
†J. N. Batty c Willis b Patel	5	not out	20
H. S. Malik run out	10		
M. A. Wagh c Ford b Thompson	0		
R. B. Thomson not out	11		
S. P. du Preez b Preston	9		
A. W. Maclay not out	1		
L-b 4, n-b 12	16	N-b 4	4
1/16 2/16 3/76 4/174 5/183 6/233 7/253 8/265 9/282	(9 wkts dec.) 294	1/28 2/28 3/65 4/138	(4 wkts dec.) 216

Bowling: *First Innings*—Headley 20–3–48–3; Wren 13–3–47–0; Thompson 16–2–68–2; Preston 11–2–26–1; Patel 27–8–63–1; Llong 13–4–38–1. *Second Innings*—Headley 7–2–13–0; Wren 7–2–15–1; Llong 8–2–33–1; Walsh 12–0–64–0; Ford 11.2–1–54–0; Fulton 7–0–37–1.

Kent

D. P. Fulton not out	134
C. D. Walsh not out	56
L-b 2, n-b 8	10
(no wkt dec.)	200

M. J. Walker, N. J. Llong, J. A. Ford, †S. C. Willis, J. B. D. Thompson, *M. M. Patel, D. W. Headley, N. W. Preston and T. N. Wren did not bat.

Bowling: Maclay 12–2–50–0; du Preez 10–1–41–0; Thomson 11–2–27–0; Malik 7–1–43–0; Wagh 7.3–1–29–0; Sutcliffe 2–0–8–0.

Umpires: G. I. Burgess and P. Willey.

KENT v DURHAM

At Maidstone, July 4, 5, 6, 8. Kent won by 83 runs. Kent 24 pts, Durham 6 pts. Toss: Kent.

Kent's fifth Championship win earned them maximum points and took them back to the top of the table with a five-point advantage over Yorkshire. Durham made them work hard for victory until they subsided quickly in the last hour, losing three wickets in 12 balls. McCague ended the match by uprooting Brown's leg stump. The two of them had shared the bowling honours: Brown's nine-wicket match return made him the first to reach 50 first-class wickets for the season, while McCague took seven, producing some lively hostile spells in the short stints he shared with Headley. After Kent had taken a first-innings lead of 94, Hooper's superb record at The Mote continued with his third Championship hundred there in his four seasons with Kent. That left Durham to chase 339, and they fell well short.

Close of play: First day, Durham 11-0 (S. L. Campbell 2*, S. Hutton 7*); Second day, Durham 217-6 (M. A. Roseberry 51*, M. M. Betts 21*); Third day, Durham 11-0 (S. L. Campbell 9*, S. Hutton 1*).

Kent

D. P. Fulton c Wood b Brown	64	– (9) c Ligertwood b Cox	5
M. V. Fleming lbw b Brown	0	– (1) c Ligertwood b Brown	12
T. R. Ward c Betts b Wood	50	– run out	60
C. L. Hooper c Bainbridge b Wood	66	– b Cox	105
G. R. Cowdrey c Ligertwood b Brown	9	– c Ligertwood b Brown	15
N. J. Llong hit wkt b Brown	64	– (2) lbw b Brown	0
*†S. A. Marsh c Campbell b Bainbridge	42	– (6) st Ligertwood b Cox	10
M. J. McCague c and b Bainbridge	0	– (7) c Ligertwood b Brown	1
D. W. Headley c Hutton b Wood	37	– (8) run out	21
N. W. Preston c Wood b Brown	2	– c Ligertwood b Wood	10
E. J. Stanford not out	10	– not out	2
L-b 14, w 1, n-b 4	19	B 2, l-b 1	3
1/1 2/109 3/156 4/187 5/213 6/306 7/310 8/312 9/315	363	1/9 2/16 3/170 4/185 5/200 6/204 7/209 8/224 9/239	244

Bonus points – Kent 4, Durham 4.

Bowling: *First Innings*—Brown 23–1–76–5; Betts 20–6–58–0; Wood 19.3–5–78–3; Bainbridge 18–3–54–2; Cox 15–1–83–0. *Second Innings*—Brown 18–1–58–4; Wood 17–2–78–1; Bainbridge 14–2–52–0; Cox 22.4–8–53–3.

Durham

S. L. Campbell b Headley	31	– c Preston b Llong	85
S. Hutton b McCague	8	– c Stanford b Hooper	35
J. E. Morris c Fulton b McCague	4	– b Stanford	18
D. A. Blenkiron c McCague b Headley	3	– c sub b Headley	5
*M. A. Roseberry c Marsh b McCague	60	– b McCague	17
P. Bainbridge b Fleming	71	– c Marsh b McCague	47
†D. G. C. Ligertwood c Llong b Hooper	11	– lbw b Headley	8
M. M. Betts lbw b McCague	32	– b Headley	0
S. J. E. Brown c Marsh b Preston	13	– b McCague	8
D. M. Cox not out	15	– c sub b Llong	3
J. Wood c Hooper b Preston	0	– not out	0
B 1, l-b 4, n-b 16	21	B 5, l-b 8, n-b 16	29
1/23 2/31 3/52 4/59 5/148 6/168 7/230 8/239 9/267	269	1/72 2/112 3/139 4/173 5/187 6/221 7/225 8/250 9/255	255

Bonus points – Durham 2, Kent 4.

Bowling: *First Innings*—McCague 26–7–69–4; Headley 27–4–86–2; Preston 16.1–4–42–2; Fleming 14–3–37–1; Hooper 9–2–24–1; Stanford 3–1–6–0. *Second Innings*—McCague 21.1–4–60–3; Headley 26.2–5–77–3; Preston 6–2–15–0; Hooper 23–8–46–1; Stanford 10–5–26–1; Llong 8–1–18–2.

Umpires: R. Palmer and N. T. Plews.

At Canterbury, July 20, 21, 22. KENT lost to PAKISTANIS by eight wickets. (See Pakistani tour section).

At Derby, July 25, 26, 27, 29. KENT drew with DERBYSHIRE.

KENT v WORCESTERSHIRE

At Canterbury, August 1, 2, 3, 5. Worcestershire won by 192 runs. Worcestershire 24 pts, Kent 6 pts. Toss: Worcestershire.

A sunny and well-attended Canterbury week ended badly for Kent, when they collapsed ignominiously to their first Championship defeat of the season. Chasing 301, they fell for just 108 to Lampitt and Sheriyar. With Marsh injured, Hooper was captain, and his resources were stretched after Ealham suffered a strained rib muscle. Kent also had to endure Hick's customary response to his impending banishment from the Test team. He made 148 in the first innings, putting on 160 with Spiring, and setting Worcestershire on the road to a declaration. Kent trailed by 93 and then suffered more punishment from Hick, although Headley delighted the crowd with his second hat-trick in consecutive first-class matches, a feat achieved only four times before in cricket history, by G. Freeman of Yorkshire in 1868, S. J. Pegler of the touring South Africans in 1912, J. S. Rao of Indian Services in 1963-64 and Mike Procter of Gloucestershire in 1979. Headley dismissed Moody at the end of one over, and Spiring and Solanki at the start of the next. Kent had no joy at all when they batted again and Lampitt finished off the innings to complete a match of 121 runs and seven wickets.

Close of play: First day, Worcestershire 311-6 (S. J. Rhodes 12*, S. R. Lampitt 16*); Second day, Kent 213-3 (C. L. Hooper 58*, N. J. Llong 15*); Third day, Worcestershire 146-6 (S. J. Rhodes 17*, S. R. Lampitt 8*).

Worcestershire

T. S. Curtis c Fulton b McCague	6	– c Willis b Headley	19
W. P. C. Weston c Hooper b Headley	19	– c Fulton b McCague	0
G. A. Hick run out	148	– b McCague	86
*T. M. Moody c Fulton b Ealham	11	– b Headley	2
K. R. Spiring b Ealham	71	– c Hooper b Headley	0
V. S. Solanki c Fulton b Patel	1	– b Headley	0
†S. J. Rhodes c Llong b Fleming	68	– not out	41
S. R. Lampitt c Hooper b Headley	88	– not out	33
R. K. Illingworth b Fleming	10		
S. W. K. Ellis not out	0		
B 9, l-b 8, n-b 20	37	B 12, l-b 10, n-b 4	26
1/22 2/59 3/106 4/266 5/278 6/284 7/443 8/459 9/459	(9 wkts dec.) 459	1/1 2/78 3/82 4/86 5/86 6/131	(6 wkts dec.) 207

A. Sheriyar did not bat.

Bonus points – Worcestershire 4, Kent 2 (Score at 120 overs: 375-6).

Bowling: *First Innings*—McCague 27–3–93–1; Headley 35.1–3–139–2; Ealham 23–10–39–2; Fleming 18–2–53–2; Patel 39–9–82–1; Hooper 8–1–28–0; Llong 1–0–8–0. *Second Innings*—McCague 11–1–49–2; Headley 17.3–1–81–4; Patel 22–9–49–0; Hooper 4–1–6–0.

Kent

D. P. Fulton lbw b Lampitt	28	– run out	1
M. J. Walker c Solanki b Moody	57	– c Rhodes b Moody	15
T. R. Ward b Lampitt	41	– c Ellis b Sheriyar	16
*C. L. Hooper b Illingworth	76	– lbw b Sheriyar	8
N. J. Llong c Lampitt b Ellis	49	– b Sheriyar	0
M. V. Fleming b Lampitt	37	– c Curtis b Sheriyar	31
†S. C. Willis lbw b Illingworth	29	– not out	21
M. J. McCague b Lampitt	0	– b Lampitt	4
D. W. Headley c Rhodes b Moody	10	– b Lampitt	5
M. M. Patel not out	15	– b Lampitt	0
M. A. Ealham b Illingworth	0	– absent hurt	
B 6, l-b 2, w 2, n-b 14	24	L-b 3, w 2, n-b 2	7
1/51 2/124 3/150 4/258 5/292 6/321 7/321 8/348 9/366	366	1/18 2/18 3/34 4/34 5/53 6/79 7/94 8/108 9/108	108

Bonus points – Kent 4, Worcestershire 4.

Bowling: *First Innings*—Sheriyar 20–3–83–0; Ellis 9–0–55–1; Lampitt 28–7–92–4; Moody 24–8–67–2; Illingworth 33.3–10–61–3. *Second Innings*—Sheriyar 16–6–58–4; Moody 7–2–22–1; Lampitt 8.4–3–25–3.

Umpires: H. D. Bird and J. W. Holder.

At Northampton, August 8, 9, 10. KENT beat NORTHAMPTONSHIRE by ten wickets.

KENT v SOMERSET

At Canterbury, August 15, 16, 17, 19. Kent won by 62 runs. Kent 21 pts, Somerset 5 pts. Toss: Kent.

This was Matthew Walker's match. He was on the field throughout and scored 275 not out, the highest innings ever made for Kent at Canterbury, beating Frank Woolley's 270 against Middlesex in 1923. It was Kent's fourth-highest at any venue, behind Bill Ashdown's two triple-hundreds and 295 by Les Ames. Walker batted for 565 minutes and hit 41 fours in 439 balls – a marvellous performance from an uncapped player making his third Championship appearance of the season. He mixed flamboyant strokeplay with a ruthless determination to make the most of the opportunity provided by an extremely weak Somerset attack. For a moment Walker thought he had missed the record when Ward declared, 13 overs after lunch on the second day – during the interval, he had heard that Woolley's score was 277. The Tannoy soon confirmed his achievement, however, to the delight of the crowd. Kent's hopes of bowling Somerset out twice were thwarted by a century from Harden and a career-best 94 from Ecclestone. But Bowler agreed to declare 227 behind on the final morning and fed Kent runs to set up a target of 320 in 88 overs. Somerset were all out with seven overs remaining.

Close of play: First day, Kent 413-4 (M. J. Walker 176*, M. V. Fleming 23*); Second day, Somerset 119-3 (R. J. Harden 36*, S. C. Ecclestone 19*); Third day, Somerset 389-8 (P. D. Bowler 48*, J. I. D. Kerr 1*).

Kent

D. P. Fulton c Turner b Kerr	29	– c and b Harden	9
M. J. Walker not out	275	– not out	43
*T. R. Ward c Turner b Kerr	57	– c Turner b Bowler	24
C. L. Hooper c and b Batty	76	– not out	16
N. J. Llong c Trescothick b Batty	26		
M. V. Fleming c Harden b Rose	26		
†S. C. Willis lbw b Rose	1		
M. M. Patel b Lee	14		
D. W. Headley not out	63		
B 9, l-b 14, n-b 26	49		
1/57 2/158 3/313 4/361 5/424 6/436 7/479 (7 wkts dec.)	616	1/18 2/61 (2 wkts dec.)	92

M. J. McCague and T. N. Wren did not bat.

Bonus points – Kent 4, Somerset 3 (Score at 120 overs: 492-7).

Bowling: *First Innings*—Rose 27–5–92–2; Lee 35–3–159–1; Kerr 27–3–143–2; Batty 41.3–11–122–2; Parsons 12–2–40–0; Trescothick 9–1–37–0. *Second Innings*—Harden 7–0–39–1; Bowler 6–0–53–1.

Somerset

M. N. Lathwell c Fulton b Headley	43	– b Headley	81
M. E. Trescothick lbw b Headley	8	– c Llong b Headley	0
K. A. Parsons c Willis b Headley	2	– (5) c Ward b McCague	30
R. J. Harden c McCague b Llong	136	– c Fulton b Llong	29
S. C. Ecclestone lbw b Wren	94	– (7) c Headley b Patel	56
*P. D. Bowler not out	48	– (3) c Fulton b Hooper	32
S. Lee c Patel b Hooper	1	– (6) lbw b Headley	0
†R. J. Turner c Willis b Hooper	11	– lbw b McCague	1
G. D. Rose b McCague	6	– b McCague	7
J. I. D. Kerr not out	1	– b McCague	0
J. D. Batty (did not bat)		– not out	7
B 10, l-b 10, w 11, n-b 8	39	B 4, l-b 8, n-b 2	14
1/22 2/28 3/90 4/262 5/345 6/350 7/375 8/388 (8 wkts dec.)	389	1/1 2/85 3/143 4/154 5/154 6/229 7/235 8/243 9/244	257

Bonus points – Somerset 2, Kent 1 (Score at 120 overs: 276-4).

Bowling: *First Innings*—McCague 23–6–69–1; Headley 29–10–60–3; Wren 20–7–53–1; Patel 43–18–94–0; Hooper 31–10–49–2; Fleming 4–1–12–0; Llong 15–5–32–1. *Second Innings*—Headley 13–4–39–3; McCague 10.3–3–21–4; Wren 7–1–29–0; Patel 29–8–81–1; Hooper 15–7–38–1; Llong 6–1–37–1.

Umpires: A. Clarkson and B. Leadbeater.

At Cardiff, August 22, 23, 24, 26. KENT drew with GLAMORGAN.

KENT v NOTTINGHAMSHIRE

At Tunbridge Wells, August 29, 30, 31, September 2. Kent won by seven wickets. Kent 21 pts, Nottinghamshire 5 pts. Toss: Kent.

Kent broke tradition by returning to the Nevill Ground for a second visit long after the rhododendrons had faded, and secured their eighth Championship win of the season, to go one point clear at the top of the table with two matches left. Their progress was threatened by the weather, which permitted only ten overs on the opening day, and the loss of Phillips, who was carried off after damaging his ankle as he attempted to begin the second over. Kent earned only a 30-run advantage on first innings, but Ealham then broke through, with four quick wickets, and Nottinghamshire were in danger of a three-day defeat before Tolley and Evans staged a recovery. McCague ended their defiance on the final morning and Kent's target was 213. While Ward played watchfully and responsibly, Hooper scored a rapid 86 off 80 balls – responding to a painful blow on the thumb from Bowen by hitting the next two balls for four and six. Llong, striking six fours and a six through the pavilion window, completed Kent's victory.

Close of play: First day, Nottinghamshire 40-3 (P. Johnson 20*, M. P. Dowman 0*); Second day, Kent 108-3 (C. L. Hooper 41*, N. J. Llong 1*); Third day, Nottinghamshire 167-6 (C. M. Tolley 64*, K. P. Evans 20*).

Nottinghamshire

R. T. Robinson c Marsh b McCague	10	– c Hooper b Ealham	12
A. A. Metcalfe lbw b Ealham	9	– c sub b Ealham	10
G. F. Archer b McCague	0	– b Hooper	34
*P. Johnson b Fleming	84	– lbw b Ealham	5
M. P. Dowman c Marsh b Fleming	37	– c Walker b Ealham	0
C. L. Cairns c Wren b Hooper	11	– (7) c Llong b McCague	9
C. M. Tolley c Fulton b Fleming	3	– (6) c Marsh b McCague	67
K. P. Evans c sub b McCague	4	– c Llong b McCague	54
†W. M. Noon c Hooper b McCague	19	– c Marsh b Ealham	2
M. N. Bowen b Ealham	22	– b McCague	19
J. A. Afford not out	0	– not out	0
B 5, l-b 7, w 1, n-b 2	15	B 8, l-b 13, w 7, n-b 2	30
1/14 2/14 3/40 4/112 5/148 6/161 7/164 8/166 9/214	214	1/18 2/29 3/47 4/50 5/73 6/105 7/170 8/183 9/232	242

Bonus points – Nottinghamshire 1, Kent 4.

Bowling: *First Innings*—McCague 20–4–55–4; Ealham 20.1–7–58–2; Wren 8–0–44–0; Fleming 14–3–34–3; Hooper 5–0–11–1. *Second Innings*—McCague 26.4–4–80–4; Ealham 28–11–52–5; Fleming 15–3–46–0; Hooper 6–1–17–1; Wren 10–1–26–0.

Kent

D. P. Fulton c Tolley b Cairns	0	– c Archer b Tolley	26
M. J. Walker c Noon b Tolley	49	– lbw b Bowen	10
T. R. Ward lbw b Evans	10	– not out	54
C. L. Hooper c sub b Evans	58	– c Noon b Bowen	86
N. J. Llong c Archer b Tolley	22	– not out	34
M. A. Ealham c Dowman b Evans	25		
M. V. Fleming c Archer b Bowen	39		
*†S. A. Marsh c and b Evans	23		
M. J. McCague c sub b Tolley	0		
B. J. Phillips c Noon b Tolley	2		
T. N. Wren not out	0		
B 1, l-b 6, w 1, n-b 8	16	B 4, l-b 1	5
1/0 2/23 3/107 4/139 5/159 6/214 7/222 8/226 9/244	244	1/36 2/47 3/163	(3 wkts) 215

Bonus points – Kent 1, Nottinghamshire 4.

Bowling: *First Innings*—Cairns 4–3–9–1; Evans 24–8–71–4; Bowen 21–3–75–1; Tolley 25–6–68–4; Afford 2–0–14–0. *Second Innings*—Evans 12–3–36–0; Bowen 14.5–2–78–2; Tolley 7–1–36–1; Afford 20–6–60–0.

Umpires: J. D. Bond and J. H. Harris.

KENT v HAMPSHIRE

At Canterbury, September 12, 13, 14, 16. Kent won by 148 runs. Kent 24 pts, Hampshire 5 pts. Toss: Kent.

At four minutes to two on Monday, Hampshire were in control of this match: needing 299, they were 143 for one. By 2.38 p.m., Kent had taken eight wickets for seven runs, with Stephenson unable to bat. The home club's president, Robin Baker White, ran on to greet them. Headley and

McCague both took hat-tricks. Headley's came on the third day, as he wrapped up Hampshire's first innings, and was his third of the season, equalling the world record of Charlie Parker in 1924 and J. S. Rao in 1963-64. McCague took his during a match-winning spell of five for three in 17 balls. Once considered prone to give in too quickly, he was inspired by the prospect of defeat to what his captain, Marsh, called "the best spell of fast bowling I have ever seen". Marsh said he was obliged to stand four yards further back because McCague started bowling so fast. Fleming finished Hampshire off with three for nought in six balls. Kent had led by 87 on first innings, after Llong scored a career-best 130 and Laney replied with his second hundred in successive games. But Kent's disappointing second innings left Hampshire a full day to pursue their target. The win put Kent 15 points behind Championship leaders Leicestershire, still just about chasing the title as they entered the final round.

Close of play: First day, Kent 376-4 (N. J. Llong 105*, M. A. Ealham 54*); Second day, Hampshire 249-5 (J. P. Stephenson 6*); Third day, Kent 211.

Kent

D. P. Fulton c Kendall b Stephenson	15	– c Kendall b Mascarenhas	8
M. J. Walker lbw b Mascarenhas	30	– lbw b Renshaw	6
T. R. Ward c and b Maru	79	– b Bovill	44
C. L. Hooper c Maru b Mascarenhas	84	– b Stephenson	14
N. J. Llong c Kendall b Stephenson	130	– c and b Stephenson	3
M. A. Ealham c White b Mascarenhas	74	– c Kendall b Mascarenhas	22
M. V. Fleming c Aymes b Stephenson	7	– c Kendall b Mascarenhas	7
*†S. A. Marsh lbw b Stephenson	1	– c Maru b Renshaw	55
D. W. Headley c Aymes b Mascarenhas	0	– (11) not out	1
M. M. Patel b Stephenson	9	– (9) lbw b Renshaw	32
M. J. McCague not out	4	– (10) lbw b Renshaw	5
L-b 5, w 1, n-b 6	12	B 1, l-b 7, n-b 6	14
1/37 2/50 3/187 4/249 5/422 6/422 7/424 8/425 9/431	445	1/12 2/30 3/74 4/74 5/77 6/91 7/125 8/175 9/210	211

Bonus points – Kent 4, Hampshire 1 (Score at 120 overs: 422-4).

Bowling: *First Innings*—Mascarenhas 28–7–101–4; Renshaw 26–7–94–0; Bovill 24–7–91–0; Stephenson 36–8–104–5; Maru 12–3–29–1; Whitaker 4–1–21–0. *Second Innings*—Mascarenhas 16–4–46–3; Renshaw 14.5–0–75–4; Stephenson 16–2–49–2; Bovill 11–0–33–1.

Hampshire

G. W. White c Patel b McCague	6	– c Hooper b Fleming	66
J. S. Laney c Marsh b Ealham	105	– lbw b McCague	14
P. R. Whitaker c Hooper b Ealham	18	– b McCague	53
W. S. Kendall lbw b Headley	34	– (5) c Hooper b McCague	3
R. A. Smith b Ealham	60	– (4) c Marsh b McCague	1
*J. P. Stephenson c Ealham b Headley	28	– absent hurt	
†A. N. Aymes hit wkt b Headley	52	– (6) c Patel b McCague	0
A. D. Mascarenhas b Ealham	14	– (7) lbw b McCague	0
R. J. Maru not out	10	– (8) b Fleming	1
J. N. B. Bovill lbw b Headley	0	– (9) b Fleming	0
S. J. Renshaw lbw b Headley	0	– (10) not out	0
L-b 29, n-b 2	31	B 6, l-b 6	12
1/10 2/74 3/155 4/226 5/249 6/338 7/338 8/358 9/358	358	1/25 2/143 3/145 4/149 5/149 6/149 7/149 8/149 9/150	150

Bonus points – Hampshire 4, Kent 4.

In the first innings J. P. Stephenson, when 22, retired hurt at 295 and resumed at 338-6.

Bowling: *First Innings*—McCague 32–6–99–1; Headley 32.3–6–83–5; Ealham 33–11–73–4; Patel 11–1–22–0; Hooper 3–1–16–0; Fleming 7–0–36–0. *Second Innings*—McCague 17–4–51–6; Headley 10–1–29–0; Ealham 11–1–41–0; Patel 4–0–10–0; Hooper 1–0–1–0; Fleming 4.2–2–6–3.

Umpires: R. Julian and G. Sharp.

At Bristol, September 19, 20, 21. KENT lost to GLOUCESTERSHIRE by ten wickets.

LANCASHIRE

Jason Gallian

Patron: HM The Queen
President: J. B. Statham
Chairman: R. Bennett
Chairman, Cricket Committee: G. Ogden
Chief Executive: J. M. Bower
Cricket Secretary: D. M. R. Edmundson
Captain: M. Watkinson
Head Coach: D. F. Whatmore
Head Groundsman: P. Marron
Scorer: W. Davies

A poll of Lancashire supporters on their impressions of the season would produce a mixed bag. For those who go for the one-day game and its quick cricket, this was a great year, with Lancashire striking the golden double of winning two Lord's finals for the second time. For the out-and-out traditionalist, the abject performance in the County Championship made this a wreck of a summer. In between, there are the loyalists who despair of winning the Championship but draw grudging comfort from the one-day successes. But there are four trophies on offer, and to win two of them – even the two easiest – twice in seven years is something of a triumph. Even the dyed-in-the-wools would have to admit 1996 was a thrilling, entertaining season.

The quarter-finals and semi-finals of both tournaments were staged at Old Trafford in front of huge crowds. Both semis were against Yorkshire and both were thrillers, particularly the game in the Benson and Hedges Cup, which Lancashire took by one wicket when Peter Martin drove the last ball for two to win. Martin gave Lancashire another one-wicket victory, over Northamptonshire, in the second round of the NatWest Trophy, while the quarter-final, against Derbyshire, went to the last ball before Lancashire won by two runs. It was all heady stuff, the sort of cricket that makes the Championship look like a donkey race in comparison with the Derby. Northamptonshire, like Yorkshire, suffered at Lancashire's hands in both competitions, losing the Benson and Hedges final three days after their NatWest defeat. Lancashire won both finals quite easily, in contrast to the closeness of the earlier rounds; even after losing the toss, traditionally decisive in the NatWest, and being held to 186, they demolished Essex in 27.2 overs for only 57 runs.

What was surprising was that Lancashire, with a membership of around 14,000, could not sell their allocation of 4,500 tickets for the NatWest final and returned 300. Maybe the cost – one person worked it out at nearly £150 – was too much to bear for a second final, after five knockout matches at Old Trafford. Maybe Lancashire had got it wrong in limiting members to one ticket each, or perhaps the supporters were just getting blasé. "What? Not *another* final?"

Their one-day form was not evident in the Sunday League, where Lancashire finished ninth only by winning their last three matches. Before then, they lacked consistency and there is little doubt that the success and excitement in the other two tournaments took the edge off their efforts on Sundays, as it did on most weekdays.

Lancashire's form in the Championship was desperately disappointing after their challenge for the title and final position of fourth in 1995. Fifteenth place was their worst finish for ten years and their number of wins – two, against Durham and Sussex – their lowest since 1984. Not all the blame could be placed on lifeless Old Trafford pitches. The wicket for the last home game, against Middlesex, was far from dead, taking spin lavishly from the first morning. When the game ended before lunch on the third day, with Middlesex winning a fascinating match, Lancashire were warned that, if another pitch was assessed as "poor" in the next 12 months, they would be fined ten points.

There were two major changes from the successful set-up of 1995. At the start of the season, county coach David Lloyd had been recruited by England, forming a Lancastrian partnership with Test captain Mike Atherton. But much of Lancashire's failure was attributed to the absence of Wasim Akram, who had taken 81 Championship wickets the previous season. His stand-in, South African Steve Elworthy, took only 26 – at 41.38 – in 11 matches. To be fair, he was not signed to replace Wasim, but as back-up for Martin and Glen Chapple. Even so, it was sad to see him struggling, failing to get into either Lord's final and being released before the season ended. On the other hand, there was much to admire in the lively pace bowling of 20-year-old Richard Green, all the way from Warrington rather than Pretoria.

Mike Watkinson, in his benefit year, was below his very best, though rumours that he might not keep the captaincy were denied. But Ian Austin had a good all-round year; he actually headed the Championship batting averages and won two match awards, one of them in the Benson and Hedges final. Jason Gallian and Graham Lloyd looked like being the only batsmen to score 1,000 runs until Neil Fairbrother swept past with a double-century in his final innings. Gallian scored 312 against Derbyshire, the highest ever innings at Old Trafford, but finished on the losing side; Lloyd made a career-best 241 at Chelmsford, which included the fastest hundred of the season in 70 balls. He joined England's one-day squad against Pakistan. Gallian, along with wicket-keeper Warren Hegg and Chapple, was chosen for the England A tour of Australia, while Atherton and John Crawley were in the Test squad for Zimbabwe and New Zealand.

Atherton, preoccupied with the game's most demanding job, had a mediocre season for Lancashire. In fact, he played on the winning side in only two first-class matches, over ten days in June, when England beat India in the opening Test and Lancashire beat Durham. Steve Titchard played only when a more senior batsman was absent but responded with an outstanding 939 in 13 matches. Lancashire decided to allow Nick Speak to move to another county where he could have more prospect of first-team cricket; he signed for Durham in November.

Less kindly, the club also dispensed with acting head coach John Stanworth. He had taken over when David Lloyd was released for England duties but learned he was to be stripped of the job shortly after helping Lancashire to their second cup final. The club had chosen to seek a coach with a high profile. They were turned down by Dennis Lillee, and were linked to several others, before announcing that they had signed Dav Whatmore, the Australian who had supervised Sri Lanka's World Cup triumph. – BRIAN BEARSHAW.

LANCASHIRE 1996

[*Bill Smith*

Back row: N. T. Wood, C. Brown, R. J. Green, J. J. Haynes, P. C. McKeown, D. J. Thompson, P. M. Ridgway, M. E. Harvey, L. J. Marland, M. J. Chilton. *Middle row:* W. Davies (*First Eleven scorer*), L. Brown (*physiotherapist*), G. Keedy, N. J. Speak, S. P. Titchard, S. Elworthy, G. Chapple, G. Yates, A. Flintoff, D. J. Shadford, P. R. Sleep (*Second Eleven captain/coach*). *Front row:* G. D. Lloyd, J. E. R. Gallian, P. J. Martin, N. H. Fairbrother, M. Watkinson (*captain*), M. A. Atherton, J. P. Crawley, I. D. Austin. *Inset:* W. K. Hegg.

LANCASHIRE RESULTS

All first-class matches – Played 18: Won 2, Lost 6, Drawn 10.

County Championship matches – Played 17: Won 2, Lost 6, Drawn 9.

Competition placings – Britannic Assurance County Championship, 15th; NatWest Trophy, winners; Benson and Hedges Cup, winners; AXA Equity & Law League, 9th.

COUNTY CHAMPIONSHIP AVERAGES

BATTING

Cap		*M*	*I*	*NO*	*R*	*HS*	*100s*	*50s*	*Avge*	*Ct/St*
1990	I. D. Austin†	9	11	3	433	95*	0	3	54.12	4
1985	N. H. Fairbrother†	12	20	0	1,068	204	2	8	53.40	10
1994	J. P. Crawley	12	20	3	904	112*	2	7	53.17	3
1992	G. D. Lloyd†	14	24	1	1,161	241	3	4	50.47	6
1994	J. E. R. Gallian	14	27	3	1,136	312	3	3	47.33	10
1995	S. P. Titchard†	12	22	2	935	163	2	5	46.75	11
1989	W. K. Hegg†	16	24	6	686	134	1	3	38.11	45/5
1989	M. A. Atherton†	8	14	0	519	98	0	5	37.07	3
1992	N. J. Speak†	11	19	3	559	138*	1	3	34.93	10
1987	M. Watkinson†	16	26	1	610	64	0	2	24.40	11
1994	P. J. Martin†	12	16	4	251	42	0	0	20.91	1
1994	G. Chapple	15	21	6	313	37*	0	0	20.86	1
	S. Elworthy§	11	15	2	200	45	0	0	15.38	5
	R. J. Green†	6	9	3	77	25*	0	0	12.83	2
	G. Keedy	13	13	7	65	26	0	0	10.83	7

Also batted: J. J. Haynes (1 match) 16, 10 (1 st); P. C. McKeown† (2 matches) 9, 64 (1 ct); N. T. Wood (1 match) 1; G. Yates† (2 matches) 16, 0, 0 (1 ct).

** Signifies not out.* *† Born in Lancashire.* *§ Overseas player.*

BOWLING

	O	*M*	*R*	*W*	*BB*	*5W/i*	*Avge*
P. J. Martin	393.4	96	1,091	43	7-50	1	25.37
I. D. Austin	200.4	51	602	21	5-116	1	28.66
J. E. R. Gallian	143.4	28	552	16	6-115	1	34.50
R. J. Green	170.5	32	558	16	4-78	0	34.87
G. Chapple	448.1	90	1,572	45	5-64	1	34.93
M. Watkinson	428	75	1,489	37	5-15	1	40.24
S. Elworthy	284.1	40	1,076	26	4-80	0	41.38
G. Keedy	457.1	123	1,183	23	3-45	0	51.43

Also bowled: M. A. Atherton 5–1–15–0; G. D. Lloyd 2–0–4–1; N. J. Speak 6–0–27–0; S. P. Titchard 35–7–110–1; G. Yates 83.2–16–313–5.

COUNTY RECORDS

Highest score for:	424	A. C. MacLaren v Somerset at Taunton	1895
Highest score against:	315*	T. W. Hayward (Surrey) at The Oval	1898
Best bowling for:	10-46	W. Hickton v Hampshire at Manchester	1870
Best bowling against:	10-40	G. O. B. Allen (Middlesex) at Lord's	1929
Highest total for:	863	v Surrey at The Oval	1990
Highest total against:	707-9 dec.	by Surrey at The Oval	1990
Lowest total for:	25	v Derbyshire at Manchester	1871
Lowest total against:	22	by Glamorgan at Liverpool	1924

LANCASHIRE v YORKSHIRE

Non-Championship Match

At Manchester, April 18, 19, 20. Drawn. Toss: Yorkshire. First-class debuts: I. D. Fisher, C. J. Schofield.

Only 21.1 overs were possible on the opening day; the match had already been reduced from four to three days after four players from each side were required for England A v The Rest, but the TCCB agreed that it should retain first-class status. Elworthy, a South African seamer signed as a one-season replacement for Wasim Akram, showed his prowess as a batsman with the top score in the match, falling 12 short of a maiden hundred. There were also encouraging performances from several young players. Green, Lancashire's highly promising 20-year-old medium-pacer, took a career-best six for 41, while, for Yorkshire, Wharf, Kettleborough and Morris all recorded personal bests. Though Austin bowled 9.3 overs before conceding a run, Yorkshire took a slender lead through a run-a-minute stand of 138 between Kettleborough and Morris. Rain set in again as Lancashire began their second innings.

Close of play: First day, Lancashire 59-3 (N. J. Speak 11*, A. Flintoff 0*); Second day, Yorkshire 64-3 (D. Byas 28*, R. A. Kettleborough 5*).

Lancashire

S. P. Titchard c Byas b Wharf	4		
*M. A. Atherton c Blakey b Wharf	3	– (1) lbw b Hamilton	16
N. J. Speak c Blakey b Morris	12	– (2) not out	8
G. D. Lloyd c Gough b Hamilton	33		
A. Flintoff c Morris b Gough	2		
†W. K. Hegg c Blakey b White	27		
I. D. Austin b Wharf	4		
S. Elworthy c Wharf b Vaughan	88		
G. Yates c White b Wharf	5	– (3) not out	0
R. J. Green st Blakey b Fisher	14		
G. Keedy not out	8		
B 1, l-b 7, n-b 4	12		
1/7 2/14 3/59 4/63 5/63 6/67 7/103 8/122 9/186	212	1/24	(1 wkt) 24

Bowling: *First Innings*—Gough 18–7–37–1; Wharf 19–10–29–4; Hamilton 15–0–53–1; Fisher 9–2–29–1; White 13–3–43–1; Morris 5–1–11–1; Vaughan 1–0–2–1. *Second Innings*—Hamilton 3–0–11–1; Wharf 2.4–0–13–0.

Yorkshire

C. J. Schofield c Yates b Green	25
M. P. Vaughan b Austin	5
*D. Byas c Hegg b Elworthy	32
C. White c Hegg b Green	0
R. A. Kettleborough c Hegg b Green	85
†R. J. Blakey c Flintoff b Elworthy	7
A. C. Morris c Hegg b Green	60
D. Gough c Hegg b Green	7
G. M. Hamilton b Green	0
A. G. Wharf not out	8
I. D. Fisher not out	0
B 1, l-b 5, n-b 2	8
1/14 2/50 3/50 4/69 5/79 6/217 7/227 8/227 9/236	(9 wkts dec.) 237

Bowling: Elworthy 24–3–89–2; Austin 23–13–43–1; Green 17–4–41–6; Keedy 18–8–32–0; Yates 10–4–12–0; Titchard 2–0–14–0.

Umpires: G. I. Burgess and R. Palmer.

At Canterbury, May 2, 3, 4, 6. LANCASHIRE lost to KENT by 64 runs.

LANCASHIRE v LEICESTERSHIRE

At Manchester, May 9, 10, 11, 13. Drawn. Lancashire 9 pts, Leicestershire 8 pts. Toss: Lancashire.

A slow-moving game in which only 42 overs were lost to rain had died by noon on Monday, when Leicestershire had avoided the follow-on and insufficient time remained to contrive a finish. Lancashire seemed to be in total command by the end of the second day, after piling up 495 and reducing their visitors to 98 for five. But Leicestershire, led by Nixon, dug in. They lost only two more wickets on the third day, when Millns and Nixon began a stand of 172. By the time it ended, they had set an eighth-wicket record for the county, beating the 164 by Maurice Hallam and Terry Spencer against Essex in 1964, and ensured their hosts would bat again. The Lancashire wicket-keeper, Hegg, had also scored a hundred. His 134 was his fourth and highest century in an 11-year career and he was well supported by Martin in a ninth-wicket century stand.

Close of play: First day, Lancashire 296-5 (G. D. Lloyd 58*, W. K. Hegg 25*); Second day, Leicestershire 98-5 (B. F. Smith 33*, A. Habib 0*); Third day, Leicestershire 308-7 (P. A. Nixon 74*, D. J. Millns 51*).

Lancashire

J. E. R. Gallian st Nixon b Pierson	24	– b Brimson	63
M. A. Atherton lbw b Brimson	87	– b Brimson	29
J. P. Crawley c Nixon b Millns	27	– b Brimson	61
N. J. Speak c and b Maddy	55	– not out	17
G. D. Lloyd c Brimson b Millns	65	– not out	12
*M. Watkinson c Simmons b Maddy	1		
†W. K. Hegg c Mullally b Pierson	134		
I. D. Austin lbw b Simmons	16		
S. Elworthy b Pierson	18		
P. J. Martin not out	34		
G. Keedy c Habib b Pierson	4		
B 2, l-b 20, w 4, n-b 4	30	B 1, l-b 3, w 1, n-b 4	9
1/51 2/100 3/191 4/234 5/240 6/313 7/341 8/380 9/486	495	1/97 2/98 3/177 (3 wkts dec.)	191

Bonus points – Lancashire 3, Leicestershire 2 (Score at 120 overs: 330-6).

Bowling: *First Innings*—Millns 24–9–62–2; Mullally 32–9–94–0; Simmons 17–2–48–1; Pierson 34.5–7–100–4; Wells 11–2–53–0; Brimson 31–4–95–1; Maddy 11–4–21–2. *Second Innings*—Mullally 7–2–7–0; Simmons 7–4–8–0; Pierson 20–3–72–0; Wells 4–0–16–0; Brimson 25.2–8–55–3; Maddy 7–2–29–0.

Leicestershire

V. J. Wells c Hegg b Martin	4
D. L. Maddy st Hegg b Watkinson	10
B. F. Smith lbw b Elworthy	81
P. V. Simmons lbw b Elworthy	25
*J. J. Whitaker c Hegg b Watkinson	18
A. R. K. Pierson c Hegg b Watkinson	0
A. Habib lbw b Watkinson	17
†P. A. Nixon b Keedy	106
D. J. Millns b Keedy	73
A. D. Mullally not out	7
M. T. Brimson lbw b Elworthy	0
B 10, l-b 6, n-b 20	36
1/12 2/22 3/64 4/98 5/98 6/142 7/185 8/357 9/374	377

Bonus points – Leicestershire 3, Lancashire 3 (Score at 120 overs: 319-7).

Bowling: Martin 28–7–57–1; Austin 22–6–35–0; Watkinson 34–12–71–4; Elworthy 24.4–0–133–3; Keedy 26–10–59–2; Gallian 3–0–6–0.

Umpires: H. D. Bird and R. A. White.

At Nottingham, May 16, 17, 18, 20. LANCASHIRE drew with NOTTINGHAMSHIRE.

LANCASHIRE v GLOUCESTERSHIRE

At Manchester, May 30, 31, June 1, 3. Drawn. Lancashire 10 pts, Gloucestershire 9 pts. Toss: Gloucestershire.

The weather determined the course of this game, which was abandoned at lunch on the final day. Only Friday came close to a full day's play, with 92 overs bowled. Gloucestershire were flagging at 98 for five on the opening day, before Russell and Alleyne revived them with a partnership of 138. Later, Atherton and Crawley compiled half-centuries for Lancashire. By Monday, the two teams had been playing each other for seven consecutive days, starting with the Benson and Hedges Cup quarter-final, which went to a second day, and including the Sunday match.

Close of play: First day, Gloucestershire 157-5 (M. W. Alleyne 49*, R. C. Russell 29*); Second day, Lancashire 134-1 (M. A. Atherton 65*, J. P. Crawley 21*); Third day, Lancashire 282-7 (S. Elworthy 5*, G. Chapple 5*).

Gloucestershire

A. J. Wright lbw b Chapple	1
N. J. Trainor c Hegg b Elworthy	9
R. J. Cunliffe b Chapple	10
T. H. C. Hancock c Lloyd b Martin	13
A. Symonds c Hegg b Chapple	38
M. W. Alleyne c Hegg b Elworthy	96
†R. C. Russell c Hegg b Martin	60
R. P. Davis c Hegg b Martin	0
M. C. J. Ball c and b Elworthy	11
A. M. Smith b Elworthy	2
*C. A. Walsh not out	15
B 3, l-b 10, n-b 2	15
1/1 2/13 3/35 4/35 5/98 6/236 7/237 8/248 9/251	270

Bonus points – Gloucestershire 2, Lancashire 4.

Bowling: Martin 26–8–45–3; Chapple 25–8–55–3; Elworthy 26–6–80–4; Watkinson 18–3–44–0; Keedy 22–9–33–0.

Lancashire

M. A. Atherton b Davis	80
N. J. Speak lbw b Alleyne	44
J. P. Crawley st Russell b Davis	70
N. H. Fairbrother c Alleyne b Davis	6
G. D. Lloyd c Symonds b Davis	43
*M. Watkinson c Cunliffe b Walsh	15
†W. K. Hegg c Alleyne b Ball	5
S. Elworthy not out	21
G. Chapple c Davis b Walsh	9
P. J. Martin c Symonds b Smith	22
G. Keedy not out	6
B 5, l-b 3, n-b 6	14
1/76 2/185 3/191 4/246 5/255 6/260 7/275 8/287 9/314	(9 wkts) 335

Bonus points – Lancashire 3, Gloucestershire 4 (Score at 120 overs: 319-9).

Bowling: Walsh 31–10–59–2; Smith 26–7–93–1; Alleyne 14–6–24–1; Ball 19–5–54–1; Davis 35–12–93–4; Trainor 1–0–4–0.

Umpires: D. J. Constant and K. J. Lyons.

At Chelmsford, June 6, 7, 8, 10. LANCASHIRE drew with ESSEX.

At Chester-le-Street, June 13, 14, 15. LANCASHIRE beat DURHAM by 345 runs.

LANCASHIRE v SOMERSET

At Manchester, June 27, 28, 29, July 1. Drawn. Lancashire 8 pts, Somerset 5 pts. Toss: Lancashire. First-class debut: P. C. McKeown.

Three declarations set up an interesting target for Somerset – 351 on the final day in a minimum of 96 overs. But it was not to be: rain, which had restricted play to two overs on the second day and 46 on the third, wiped out the fourth completely. Lancashire's innings contained two very different centuries from Titchard, who batted unbeaten through the entire 115 overs for 121, and Fairbrother, who hit 144, his sixth century against Somerset, in 162 balls, with six sixes and 16 fours.

Close of play: First day, Lancashire 373-5 (S. P. Titchard 116*, M. Watkinson 47*); Second day, Lancashire 380-5 (S. P. Titchard 121*, M. Watkinson 49*); Third day, Lancashire 45-0 dec.

Lancashire

S. P. Titchard not out	121	– (2) not out	21
J. E. R. Gallian c Turner b Batty	14	– (1) not out	22
S. Elworthy b Batty	13		
N. H. Fairbrother c Caddick b Trump	144		
G. D. Lloyd lbw b Hayhurst	11		
P. C. McKeown c and b Lee	9		
*M. Watkinson not out	49		
B 4, l-b 5, n-b 10	19	B 1, l-b 1	2
1/29 2/55 3/258 4/276 5/295 (5 wkts dec.)	380	(no wkt dec.)	45

†W. K. Hegg, I. D. Austin, G. Chapple and G. Keedy did not bat.

Bonus points – Lancashire 4, Somerset 2.

Bowling: *First Innings*—Caddick 18–7–28–0; Rose 18–5–53–0; Batty 38–5–127–2; Lee 18–1–74–1; Trump 18–3–81–1; Hayhurst 5–2–8–1. *Second Innings*—Hayhurst 4–1–6–0; Batty 7–0–19–0; Bowler 3.3–0–15–0; Turner 1–0–3–0.

Somerset

M. N. Lathwell not out	37
P. D. Bowler c Hegg b Elworthy	6
M. E. Trescothick c McKeown b Watkinson	9
S. C. Ecclestone b Keedy	16
B 1, n-b 6	7
1/18 2/36 3/75 (3 wkts dec.)	75

*A. N. Hayhurst, S. Lee, †R. J. Turner, G. D. Rose, J. D. Batty, A. R. Caddick and H. R. J. Trump did not bat.

Bonus point – Lancashire 1.

Bowling: Chapple 6–3–14–0; Elworthy 5–1–18–1; Watkinson 10–5–12–1; Austin 7–1–20–0; Keedy 2.1–0–10–1.

Umpires: T. E. Jesty and A. G. T. Whitehead.

LANCASHIRE v WORCESTERSHIRE

At Manchester, July 4, 5, 6, 8. Drawn. Lancashire 8 pts, Worcestershire 11 pts. Toss: Worcestershire.

More rain and an excess of caution produced Old Trafford's fourth successive Championship draw. Only 5.4 overs were possible on the opening day. Gallian, in his second match since breaking a finger in May, batted six and a half hours for his first century of the season, though he was dropped twice. But Worcestershire replied confidently. Weston hit 25 fours and three sixes in a career-best 171, spread over nearly five and a half hours, and put on 224 with Moody, whose century was his third in succession against Lancashire. Both teams delayed their declarations and a promising fourth morning, in which Lloyd hit four sixes to reach 72 in 50 balls, gave way to a dull draw. Lancashire had hopes when Worcestershire were 53 for four, but Moody and Solanki added 118 without being parted. It was an encouraging performance by Solanki, in his tenth first-class match. His off-breaks claimed five in an innings for the first time and he doubled that for a match return of ten.

Close of play: First day, Lancashire 17-0 (J. E. R. Gallian 12*, S. P. Titchard 5*); Second day, Lancashire 392; Third day, Lancashire 26-2 (S. P. Titchard 15*, G. Chapple 0*).

Lancashire

J. E. R. Gallian c Solanki b Illingworth	140	– (2) c Church b Ellis	0
S. P. Titchard c Rhodes b Ellis	8	– (1) st Rhodes b Solanki	20
N. J. Speak c Rhodes b Sheriyar	5	– st Rhodes b Solanki	11
N. H. Fairbrother b Lampitt	46	– (5) b Illingworth	53
G. D. Lloyd st Rhodes b Solanki	59	– (6) c Weston b Solanki	72
*M. Watkinson c Ellis b Solanki	2	– (7) c Curtis b Solanki	9
†W. K. Hegg c Rhodes b Solanki	1	– (8) not out	30
I. D. Austin c Lampitt b Solanki	47	– (9) not out	37
S. Elworthy c Weston b Solanki	45		
G. Chapple c Lampitt b Illingworth	18	– (4) c Illingworth b Solanki	19
G. Keedy not out	0		
B 4, l-b 3, w 2, n-b 12	21	B 4, l-b 1	5
1/24 2/37 3/103 4/189 5/191 6/193 7/283 8/371 9/392	392	1/8 2/26 3/31 4/98 5/108 6/139 7/204 (7 wkts dec.)	256

Bonus points – Lancashire 4, Worcestershire 4.

Bowling: *First Innings*—Sheriyar 18–4–47–1; Ellis 14–1–58–1; Moody 5–0–19–0; Lampitt 14–4–43–1; Illingworth 35–12–86–2; Solanki 25.2–3–116–5; Church 4–0–16–0. *Second Innings*—Sheriyar 4–0–11–0; Ellis 5–3–7–1; Illingworth 28–9–93–1; Solanki 27–3–140–5.

Worcestershire

W. P. C. Weston not out	171	– c Hegg b Chapple	11
M. J. Church run out	28	– c Austin b Elworthy	4
T. S. Curtis b Watkinson	29	– c Hegg b Chapple	0
*T. M. Moody c Titchard b Keedy	108	– (6) not out	67
K. R. Spiring not out	0	– (4) b Watkinson	21
V. S. Solanki (did not bat)		– (5) not out	62
B 11, w 1, n-b 2	14	L-b 6	6
1/70 2/105 3/329 (3 wkts dec.)	350	1/10 2/10 3/19 4/53 (4 wkts)	171

S. R. Lampitt, †S. J. Rhodes, R. K. Illingworth, S. W. K. Ellis and A. Sheriyar did not bat.

Bonus points – Worcestershire 4, Lancashire 1.

Bowling: *First Innings*—Chapple 12–1–61–0; Elworthy 10.2–2–42–0; Watkinson 23–4–82–1; Austin 17–5–52–0; Keedy 27–7–67–1; Gallian 6–0–35–0. *Second Innings*—Chapple 7–1–19–2; Elworthy 11–1–38–1; Watkinson 11–2–62–1; Keedy 10–3–27–0; Austin 3–0–13–0; Gallian 3–1–6–0.

Umpires: H. D. Bird and A. A. Jones.

LANCASHIRE v DERBYSHIRE

At Manchester, July 18, 19, 20, 22. Derbyshire won by two wickets. Derbyshire 21 pts, Lancashire 7 pts. Toss: Lancashire.

Jason Gallian finished on the losing side after scoring 312, the highest innings ever played at Old Trafford in its 139 years. Only Percy Perrin of Essex, 92 years earlier, had ever scored a triple-century for a losing side in England – also against Derbyshire. Gallian's innings, the longest in Championship history, occupied 11 hours 10 minutes and 583 balls; he hit 33 fours and four sixes. He beat Bobby Simpson's 311 for Australia in the Old Trafford Test of 1964 and his score was the fourth-highest for Lancashire. It was not an innings that will be remembered for its glittering strokeplay, but Gallian's batting was almost entirely blameless – he gave just one hard chance, when he was past 200 – and he played every ball on its merits right from the start. Of his team-mates, Titchard just missed his hundred after sharing a stand of 244; Crawley reached 48 in fours and passed 50 with a three that was stopped just short of the boundary; and Atherton failed to score at all. Lancashire's command seemed complete on the third afternoon when Derbyshire were 253 for seven, still needing 185 to avoid the follow-on. But Krikken and Cork turned the game round by adding 198. Krikken reached a maiden century with his third six, which

HIGHEST SCORES FOR LOSING SIDE

343*	P. A. Perrin, Essex v Derbyshire at Chesterfield	1904
338*	R. C. Blunt, Otago v Canterbury at Christchurch	1931-32
312	**J. E. R. Gallian, Lancashire v Derbyshire at Manchester**	**1996**
309	V. S. Hazare, The Rest v Hindus at Bombay	1943-44
280*	C. P. Mead, Hampshire v Nottinghamshire at Southampton	1921
273*	C. G. Greenidge, D. H. Robins' XI v Pakistanis at Eastbourne	1974
271	C. E. Pellew, South Australia v Victoria at Adelaide	1919-20
270	F. E. Woolley, Kent v Middlesex at Canterbury	1923

LONGEST COUNTY CHAMPIONSHIP INNINGS

Minutes			
670	**312**	**J. E. R. Gallian, Lancashire v Derbyshire at Manchester**	**1996**
638	235*	D. J. Bicknell, Surrey v Nottinghamshire at Nottingham	1994
615	267	A. Shrewsbury, Nottinghamshire v Middlesex at Nottingham	1887
606	277*	R. G. Twose, Warwickshire v Glamorgan at Birmingham	1994
598	248	T. S. Curtis, Worcestershire v Somerset at Worcester	1991
592	228*	D. J. Bicknell, Surrey v Nottinghamshire at Guildford	1995
585	285	P. Holmes, Yorkshire v Nottinghamshire at Nottingham	1929
582	192	R. R. Montgomerie, Northamptonshire v Kent at Canterbury	1995
570	228*	T. S. Curtis, Worcestershire v Derbyshire at Derby	1992
566	300	R. Subba Row, Northamptonshire v Surrey at The Oval	1958
565	**275***	**M. J. Walker, Kent v Somerset at Canterbury**	**1996**
562	203*	A. J. Moles, Warwickshire v Surrey at Guildford	1994
555	216*	A. A. Metcalfe, Yorkshire v Middlesex at Leeds	1988
555	281*	J. P. Crawley, Lancashire v Somerset at Southport	1994
553	405*	G. A. Hick, Worcestershire v Somerset at Taunton	1988
540	204*	D. Brookes, Northamptonshire v Essex at Northampton	1952
540	221	T. C. Middleton, Hampshire v Surrey at Southampton	1992
540	200*	A. S. Rollins, Derbyshire v Gloucestershire at Bristol	1995

Research: Robert Brooke

simultaneously saved the follow-on and established a county eighth-wicket record, overtaking 182 by A. H. M. Jackson and W. Carter in 1922. Derbyshire declared 114 behind and Watkinson gave them two sessions to score 289. Jones's third Championship century of the season and a stand of 198 with Barnett made that look simple. But when five wickets fell for 20, it needed a breezy 34 in 16 balls from Cork to bring victory with three balls to spare.

Close of play: First day, Lancashire 334-2 (J. E. R. Gallian 178*, S. P. Titchard 92*); Second day, Derbyshire 78-2 (C. J. Adams 37*, D. M. Jones 17*); Third day, Derbyshire 473-8 (D. G. Cork 83*, M. J. Vandrau 10*).

Lancashire

M. A. Atherton c Adams b Cork	0		
J. E. R. Gallian c Rollins b Vandrau	312	– (1) st Krikken b Jones	11
J. P. Crawley c DeFreitas b Wells	54	– not out	97
S. P. Titchard c Krikken b Harris	96	– (2) b DeFreitas	15
G. D. Lloyd run out	7	– (4) run out	46
*M. Watkinson c Cork b Barnett	46		
†W. K. Hegg lbw b Vandrau	2		
S. Elworthy c Krikken b Barnett	13		
G. Chapple c Jones b Wells	32		
P. J. Martin not out	1		
B 8, l-b 6, w 2, n-b 8	24	B 4, l-b 1	5
1/15 2/100 3/344 4/359 5/429 6/446 7/488 8/574 9/587 (9 wkts dec.)	587	1/24 2/30 3/174 (3 wkts dec.)	174

G. Keedy did not bat.

Bonus points – Lancashire 4, Derbyshire 1 (Score at 120 overs: 359-3).

Bowling: *First Innings*—Cork 26–11–62–1; Harris 29–4–91–1; DeFreitas 30–4–120–0; Vandrau 42–5–134–2; Wells 34–7–67–2; Jones 5–1–26–0; Barnett 23–0–73–2. *Second Innings*—Harris 2–0–3–0; DeFreitas 11–1–41–1; Jones 16–2–79–1; Barnett 2–0–17–0; Adams 9–1–29–0.

Derbyshire

K. J. Barnett lbw b Chapple	12	– c Hegg b Chapple	92
A. S. Rollins c Lloyd b Chapple	7	– c Hegg b Martin	4
C. J. Adams c Watkinson b Chapple	119	– c Keedy b Chapple	1
*D. M. Jones c Hegg b Watkinson	28	– c Titchard b Keedy	107
T. J. G. O'Gorman b Elworthy	28	– (6) b Keedy	6
C. M. Wells c Gallian b Watkinson	35	– (7) st Hegg b Keedy	1
P. A. J. DeFreitas c Watkinson b Chapple	1	– (5) c Titchard b Chapple	4
†K. M. Krikken c Crawley b Martin	104	– run out	12
D. G. Cork not out	83	– not out	34
M. J. Vandrau not out	10	– not out	1
B 20, l-b 14, w 2, n-b 10	46	B 11, l-b 12, w 2, n-b 2	27
1/20 2/35 3/102 4/162 5/237 6/240 7/253 8/451	(8 wkts dec.) 473	1/14 2/22 3/220 4/227 5/230 6/233 7/240 8/287	(8 wkts) 289

A. J. Harris did not bat.

Bonus points – Derbyshire 4, Lancashire 3 (Score at 120 overs: 456-8).

Bowling: *First Innings*—Chapple 23–7–83–4; Elworthy 21–4–92–1; Watkinson 28–1–108–2; Martin 22–3–69–1; Keedy 21–6–67–0; Gallian 5–0–12–0; Titchard 6–2–8–0. *Second Innings*—Chapple 15–0–55–3; Martin 8–1–15–1; Keedy 21–1–91–3; Watkinson 12.3–0–70–0; Elworthy 8–0–35–0.

Umpires: G. I. Burgess and A. Clarkson.

At Cardiff, July 25, 26, 27, 29. LANCASHIRE lost to GLAMORGAN by 48 runs.

LANCASHIRE v SURREY

At Southport, August 7, 8, 9. Surrey won by 140 runs. Surrey 21 pts, Lancashire 4 pts. Toss: Lancashire.

Surrey's fourth consecutive win put them on top of the table. After 15 wickets fell on the opening day, the TCCB Inspector of Pitches, Harry Brind, was summoned. But he must have wondered if his journey was necessary when he saw Surrey score 366 for six; Julian hit a maiden first-class century, with seven sixes and 14 fours. He had looked to be out on 66 when Speak held a mighty hit on the boundary before tossing the ball to Titchard as he felt himself about to cross the rope. Umpire John Holder ruled not out and gave Julian a single, although Law 32.3(b) states that a catch may be made in these circumstances. Gallian removed Julian at the start of the third day on his way to a career-best six for 115, and Lancashire had 181 overs to score 509. No side had ever made so much to win a first-class match and Julian, taking five wickets, finished them off with a day to spare.

Close of play: First day, Lancashire 128-5 (M. Watkinson 23*, W. K. Hegg 21*); Second day, Surrey 366-6 (B. P. Julian 119*, G. J. Kersey 22*).

Surrey

D. J. Bicknell b Chapple	12	– b Elworthy	42
M. A. Butcher b Martin	10	– c Titchard b Chapple	66
J. D. Ratcliffe lbw b Austin	20	– c Watkinson b Gallian	8
N. Shahid lbw b Martin	32	– c Hegg b Gallian	66
A. D. Brown b Austin	0	– b Gallian	1
*A. J. Hollioake c Hegg b Austin	20	– c Titchard b Chapple	22
B. P. Julian c Hegg b Elworthy	41	– b Gallian	119
†G. J. Kersey c Hegg b Martin	3	– c Hegg b Gallian	24
M. P. Bicknell b Austin	23	– c and b Gallian	23
R. M. Pearson not out	15	– c Hegg b Elworthy	13
J. E. Benjamin c Elworthy b Martin	6	– not out	38
L-b 10, n-b 19	29	B 4, l-b 8, n-b 8	20
1/30 2/36 3/57 4/57 5/105 6/107 7/129 8/158 9/192	211	1/96 2/123 3/123 4/124 5/159 6/249 7/366 8/371 9/396	442

Bonus points – Surrey 1, Lancashire 4.

Bowling: *First Innings*—Chapple 12–3–37–1; Martin 16.4–2–59–4; Austin 16–4–46–4; Elworthy 11–0–59–1. *Second Innings*—Martin 3–1–27–0; Austin 8–1–44–0; Elworthy 24.1–4–88–2; Chapple 15–2–93–2; Gallian 24–4–115–6; Watkinson 10–2–39–0; Titchard 5–0–24–0.

Lancashire

J. E. R. Gallian c Brown b M. P. Bicknell	3	– c Brown b M. P. Bicknell	57
S. P. Titchard b M. P. Bicknell	17	– b Benjamin	54
N. J. Speak b M. P. Bicknell	34	– b Benjamin	39
N. H. Fairbrother lbw b M. P. Bicknell	0	– b M. P. Bicknell	1
G. D. Lloyd c Kersey b Julian	19	– c Kersey b Julian	46
*M. Watkinson c Kersey b M. P. Bicknell	27	– c Kersey b Julian	53
†W. K. Hegg c Shahid b Benjamin	32	– b Julian	0
I. D. Austin b Benjamin	0	– st Kersey b Pearson	40
G. Chapple c Kersey b Benjamin	1	– not out	12
S. Elworthy c Butcher b Benjamin	0	– c Ratcliffe b Julian	17
P. J. Martin not out	1	– b Julian	0
L-b 1, w 2, n-b 8	11	B 10, l-b 4, w 4, n-b 31	49
1/14 2/42 3/42 4/75 5/89 6/132 7/133 8/135 9/136	145	1/96 2/174 3/180 4/180 5/245 6/261 7/329 8/335 9/368	368

Bonus points – Surrey 4.

Bowling: *First Innings*—M. P. Bicknell 17–2–48–5; Benjamin 15.3–4–38–4; Julian 8–0–42–1; Hollioake 2–0–16–0. *Second Innings*—M. P. Bicknell 23–7–83–2; Benjamin 21–5–80–2; Julian 20.3–3–99–5; Ratcliffe 9–2–30–0; Pearson 9–1–44–1; Hollioake 2–0–18–0.

Umpires: J. W. Holder and K. J. Lyons.

LANCASHIRE v HAMPSHIRE

At Manchester, August 15, 16, 17, 19. Drawn. Lancashire 10 pts, Hampshire 8 pts. Toss: Lancashire. Championship debut: S. J. Renshaw.

Despite leaving themselves 109 overs to bowl out Hampshire, Lancashire were unable to force their second victory of 1996 on a low, flat pitch. Crawley scored his first century of the season on the third day, to enable Watkinson to leave a target of 415. But both sides' ambitions faded during the final afternoon. Whitaker was dismissed in the first innings when a fierce cut rebounded from Watkinson's chest at gully to be caught by Atherton. Watkinson fell to the ground but continued after treatment. The pavilion had to be cleared during lunch on Thursday when an alarm in the kitchens was set off by a particularly fiery flambé, but play restarted on time.

Close of play: First day, Lancashire 303-8 (W. K. Hegg 42*, P. J. Martin 13*); Second day, Hampshire 228-7 (M. Keech 56*, M. J. Thursfield 4*); Third day, Hampshire 21-1 (P. R. Whitaker 15*, R. J. Maru 0*).

Lancashire

J. E. R. Gallian c Maru b Udal	41	– b Maru	44
M. A. Atherton c Aymes b Maru	63	– c and b Udal	50
J. P. Crawley c Kendall b Stephenson	4	– (4) not out	100
N. H. Fairbrother c White b Renshaw	54	– (3) c Maru b Whitaker	36
G. D. Lloyd c Whitaker b Udal	21	– lbw b Whitaker	19
*M. Watkinson b Renshaw	44	– c White b Stephenson	33
†W. K. Hegg c Maru b Renshaw	48	– not out	6
G. Chapple lbw b Udal	1		
R. J. Green lbw b Stephenson	9		
P. J. Martin c and b Stephenson	37		
G. Keedy not out	8		
L-b 7, w 1, n-b 4	12	B 5, l-b 9, n-b 4	18
1/77 2/86 3/133 4/162 5/235 6/242 7/243 8/278 9/319	342	1/96 2/116 3/190 4/234 5/288 (5 wkts dec.)	306

Bonus points – Lancashire 3, Hampshire 4 (Score at 120 overs: 327-9).

Bowling: *First Innings*—Thursfield 11–1–45–0; Renshaw 19–5–42–3; Stephenson 23–8–64–3; Udal 41–8–105–3; Maru 24–10–61–1; Whitaker 9–3–18–0. *Second Innings*—Renshaw 9–2–36–0; Thursfield 4–0–18–0; Udal 18–1–69–1; Stephenson 13–2–56–1; Maru 27–7–49–1; Whitaker 11–0–64–2.

Hampshire

*J. P. Stephenson c Hegg b Martin	7	– (7) not out	25
G. W. White lbw b Chapple	58	– (1) lbw b Chapple	4
P. R. Whitaker c Atherton b Chapple	10	– (2) run out	37
R. A. Smith b Martin	17	– (5) b Keedy	77
W. S. Kendall c Keedy b Watkinson	53	– (6) c Hegg b Green	75
M. Keech not out	60	– (4) st Hegg b Keedy	42
†A. N. Aymes b Watkinson	0	– (8) not out	7
S. D. Udal c Hegg b Gallian	10		
M. J. Thursfield b Chapple	4		
R. J. Maru c Gallian b Martin	1	– (3) lbw b Watkinson	21
S. J. Renshaw lbw b Chapple	1		
B 2, l-b 9, n-b 2	13	L-b 7, w 5, n-b 4	16
1/16 2/29 3/48 4/143 5/167 6/169 7/217 8/228 9/233	234	1/16 2/55 3/70 4/133 5/226 6/283 (6 wkts)	304

Bonus points – Hampshire 1, Lancashire 4.

Bowling: *First Innings*—Martin 19–10–26–3; Chapple 18–7–43–4; Watkinson 18–2–71–2; Keedy 21–6–44–0; Green 11–1–22–0; Atherton 2–0–7–0; Gallian 4–1–10–1. *Second Innings*—Martin 25–8–64–0; Chapple 19–7–48–1; Green 11–0–54–1; Watkinson 20–5–62–1; Keedy 27–10–49–2; Gallian 2–0–12–0; Atherton 3–1–8–0.

Umpires: J. D. Bond and B. Dudleston.

At Leeds, August 22, 23, 24, 26. LANCASHIRE drew with YORKSHIRE.

At Hove, August 29, 30, 31, September 2. LANCASHIRE beat SUSSEX by five wickets.

LANCASHIRE v MIDDLESEX

At Manchester, September 3, 4, 5. Middlesex won by 23 runs. Middlesex 20 pts, Lancashire 6 pts. Toss: Middlesex. First-class debut: J. J. Haynes.

Tufnell's match return of 13 wickets carried Middlesex to victory by lunch on the third day. But they looked likelier to give Lancashire their first home win of the season at 60 for four in their second innings, still needing 42 to avoid an innings defeat. The pitch took a generous amount of spin – too much, the TCCB's pitch inspectors said later – from the first morning: 17 wickets fell on the opening day, 16 on the second. Lancashire took a commanding first-innings lead of 102, but Brown, whose 83 was the best score of the match, helped Middlesex leave a target of 130. There was time for four overs on the second evening; Middlesex seized the initiative with three wickets. Two went to Tufnell, who bowled superbly throughout the innings. Lancashire were warned that if another pitch was assessed as "poor" in the next 12 months they would be fined ten points. Coincidentally, they had been docked 25 for a substandard pitch on Middlesex's previous visit in 1994.

Close of play: First day, Lancashire 175-7 (S. P. Titchard 47*); Second day, Lancashire 2-3 (M. Watkinson 2*).

Middlesex

P. N. Weekes c Titchard b Martin	26	– c Atherton b Watkinson	12
J. C. Pooley lbw b Elworthy	12	– b Martin	4
M. R. Ramprakash b Martin	24	– c Titchard b Watkinson	10
*M. W. Gatting st Haynes b Watkinson	40	– lbw b Watkinson	50
J. D. Carr c Martin b Watkinson	37	– b Watkinson	13
†K. R. Brown lbw b Watkinson	1	– b Elworthy	83
O. A. Shah c Keedy b Martin	5	– b Keedy	13
R. L. Johnson b Watkinson	0	– b Martin	9
R. A. Fay b Watkinson	0	– (11) b Elworthy	2
A. R. C. Fraser c Lloyd b Martin	2	– not out	2
P. C. R. Tufnell not out	0	– (9) c Watkinson b Keedy	22
B 8, l-b 3, n-b 2	13	L-b 6, w 1, n-b 4	11
1/16 2/65 3/66 4/139 5/143 6/152 7/154 8/154 9/160	160	1/6 2/27 3/30 4/60 5/119 6/155 7/186 8/227 9/227	231

Bonus points – Lancashire 4.

Bowling: *First Innings*—Martin 14–5–31–4; Elworthy 10–1–48–1; Green 15–3–42–0; Gallian 3–0–9–0; Keedy 2–1–4–0; Watkinson 9.4–1–15–5. *Second Innings*—Martin 15–2–37–2; Elworthy 9.1–2–15–2; Watkinson 25–2–104–4; Keedy 27–6–55–2; Green 4–0–14–0.

Lancashire

J. E. R. Gallian b Weekes	26	– (3) lbw b Tufnell	0
S. P. Titchard c Pooley b Ramprakash	67	– lbw b Johnson	0
J. P. Crawley lbw b Tufnell	36	– (4) c Ramprakash b Tufnell	0
M. A. Atherton lbw b Weekes	14	– (5) lbw b Tufnell	10
G. D. Lloyd c Pooley b Tufnell	5	– (6) b Johnson	42
*M. Watkinson c Gatting b Tufnell	0	– (1) c Brown b Tufnell	13
S. Elworthy b Tufnell	3	– c Ramprakash b Johnson	1
R. J. Green run out	20	– b Tufnell	2
P. J. Martin lbw b Tufnell	42	– c Pooley b Tufnell	21
†J. J. Haynes c Gatting b Tufnell	16	– c Carr b Tufnell	10
G. Keedy not out	1	– not out	2
B 19, l-b 5, n-b 8	32	L-b 3, n-b 2	5
1/45 2/106 3/125 4/130 5/130 6/138 7/175 8/231 9/253	262	1/1 2/2 3/2 4/13 5/42 6/57 7/72 8/72 9/103	106

Bonus points – Lancashire 2, Middlesex 4.

Bowling: *First Innings*—Fraser 6–1–17–0; Fay 3–0–6–0; Weekes 36–7–119–2; Johnson 2–0–7–0; Tufnell 38.1–11–74–6; Ramprakash 7–0–15–1. *Second Innings*—Johnson 15–3–37–3; Tufnell 20.1–4–49–7; Fraser 3–0–7–0; Weekes 3–0–10–0.

Umpires: J. W. Holder and G. Sharp.

At Northampton, September 12, 13, 14, 16. LANCASHIRE lost to NORTHAMPTONSHIRE by nine wickets.

At Birmingham, September 19, 20, 21, 22. LANCASHIRE drew with WARWICKSHIRE.

Vince Wells

LEICESTERSHIRE

President: B. A. F. Smith
Chairman: J. M. Josephs
Chairman, Cricket Committee: P. R. Haywood
Chief Executive: A. O. Norman
Captain: J. J. Whitaker
Cricket Manager: J. Birkenshaw
Head Groundsman: L. Spence
Scorer: G. A. York

One day David Coleman may ask the participants on the TV programme *A Question of Sport*: "Which county, in what year, were acclaimed county champions over a cuppa?" The answer will be "Leicestershire, 1996". An extraordinary year was crowned in extraordinary fashion when news came through during the penultimate tea interval of the season that Surrey had forfeited their first innings against Worcestershire and thus conceded the title to Grace Road.

Leicestershire's second Championship had several things in common with the first. Both teams lost only one match, to Surrey at The Oval. Both had a strong Yorkshire influence: in 1975 Jack Birkenshaw and Chris Balderstone were both important figures in Ray Illingworth's team; in 1996 Birkenshaw was the manager and James Whitaker the captain.

Illingworth's team never went into a huddle after the fall of each wicket, though, and did not have the pleasure of taking the title at home. More than 3,000 people were able to enjoy the tea party to end all tea parties, culminating in Paul Nixon leading a conga of fans on to the field singing "Cricket's coming home".

In the end, Surrey's capitulation was irrelevant: Leicestershire, despite the mother of all hangovers, beat Middlesex next morning to win the title by 27 points. It was their tenth victory. With the Second Eleven winning the limited-overs Bain Hogg Trophy for the third time in four years, the county with little money and a "dowdy ground" had every reason to celebrate. They had played some wonderful, positive cricket. Even against Surrey they had a chance of winning. Most of the rest they blew away. They won six games by an innings and three inside two days and, with a bit more luck, or nous, they might have won three more. Despite losing most of two days to rain, they had Warwickshire eight down at the close in May; in successive games in August, Glamorgan and Hampshire were both nine down.

If Leicestershire's win at Derby in their opening game was important, the thrashing of the then leaders Yorkshire by an innings in June was doubly so. It lifted them from seventh to fourth, sparking a run of four successive wins. Although they stumbled slightly, with three draws after that, they finished in style by winning their last four.

How did Leicestershire get it so right and the bookies, who had quoted them at odds of up to 40 to 1, get it so wrong? Firstly, cricket's betting fraternity, perhaps a touch prejudiced against the smaller counties, ignored the fact that Leicestershire had finished runners-up in 1994 and, despite a mid-season injury crisis, seventh in 1995. Secondly, no one could have foreseen what an outstanding captain Whitaker would be in his first season. With no disrespect to his predecessor, Nigel Briers, Leicestershire would probably not have won without him.

Whitaker, as Birkenshaw said, "took a good side and added an extra quality" – self-belief. Already, last winter, Whitaker was telling anyone who would listen that Leicestershire would win, and accepted bets from anyone who would take him on.

Tim Boon, his former team-mate, summed it up: "Jimmy goes into a bubble in the cricket season, and somehow he managed to get the others in there with him." That single-mindedness and infectious confidence were summed up by an early-season encounter with opener Darren Maddy. "How are you, Dazzer?" asked Whitaker. "Oh, all right," Maddy replied. "No, Dazzer, you're on fire," said Whitaker.

No one lit up Grace Road more than Whitaker's first lieutenant, West Indies all-rounder Phil Simmons, who was named Cricketer of the Year not only by Leicestershire but also by his peers nationally. He was also one of the *Wisden* five, only the fifth player since the war – after David Gower, Jonathan Agnew, Briers and Whitaker – to be picked for his feats while with Leicestershire. Dropping from opener to the middle order, Simmons scored 1,186 Championship runs, including four centuries, at 56.47, and took 33 catches at slip. But his 56 wickets at 18.23 were the biggest single factor. When Alan Mullally's form finally earned him Test status, Simmons moved up several gears, often bowling as fast as David Millns, who had a cracking season with 67 Championship wickets and a maiden first-class century.

There are so many variables in cricket that luck plays a significant part. Leicestershire had some: they won some important tosses and suffered so few injuries that only 13 players were used. Aftab Habib made an immediate impact with a double-hundred in his third Championship match since moving from Middlesex in 1995. Even the loss of Briers, following a knee operation, was turned into a plus: Vince Wells was promoted to open and scored 1,172 Championship runs at 46.88. Even Whitaker, who describes Wells as "one of the best timers of a ball I've played with", could hardly have predicted that he would come within three runs of three double-hundreds in 17 days in all cricket.

Things did not go so well in the one-day competitions. They failed to get past the Benson and Hedges group stage, lost to Sussex in the NatWest second round and fell away in the Sunday League.

None the less, the future looks bright. Money from new sponsors Midland Mainline, a privatised rail company, helped finance a contract keeping Mullally at Grace Road for another three years, and will also be used to improve wages. The 13 players shared something like £120,000 in the end, which would have been much more had they emulated the Warwickshire committee two years earlier and placed a large bet on themselves at the start of the season. At the end, Whitaker was taking bets for 1997: this time, no one was prepared to accept the risk. – CHRIS GODDARD.

LEICESTERSHIRE 1996

[*Bill Smith*

Back row: T. J. Mason, A. Habib, J. Ormond, S. Bartle, C. D. Crowe, D. I. Stevens, P. E. Robinson, D. Williamson. *Middle row:* C. Mortimer (*physiotherapist*), B. F. Smith, C. C. Remy, M. T. Brimson, V. J. Wells, A. R. K. Pierson, G. I. Macmillan, J. M. Dakin, V. P. Clarke, D. L. Maddy, G. A. York (*scorer*). *Front row:* A. D. Mullally, P. Whitticase, N. E. Briers, J. M. Josephs (*chairman*), J. Birkenshaw (*cricket manager*), B. A. F. Smith (*president*), J. J. Whitaker (*captain*), A. O. Norman (*chief executive*), G. J. Parsons, P. A. Nixon, D. J. Millns. *Inset:* P. V. Simmons.

LEICESTERSHIRE RESULTS

All first-class matches – Played 20: Won 10, Lost 2, Drawn 8.

County Championship matches – Played 17: Won 10, Lost 1, Drawn 6.

Competition placings – Britannic Assurance County Championship, winners; NatWest Trophy, 2nd round; Benson and Hedges Cup, 3rd in Group A; AXA Equity & Law League, 12th.

COUNTY CHAMPIONSHIP AVERAGES

BATTING

Cap		*M*	*I*	*NO*	*R*	*HS*	*100s*	*50s*	*Avge*	*Ct/St*
1986	J. J. Whitaker	15	21	3	1,046	218	4	2	58.11	2
1994	P. V. Simmons§	16	23	2	1,186	171	4	6	56.47	33
1994	V. J. Wells	17	25	0	1,172	204	4	1	46.88	19
1995	B. F. Smith	17	25	2	1,068	190	2	4	46.43	3
1994	P. A. Nixon	17	23	3	729	106	2	4	36.45	50/4
	A. Habib	14	21	2	652	215	1	1	34.31	10
1996	D. L. Maddy†	17	25	1	815	101*	1	3	33.95	18
1993	A. D. Mullally	9	8	1	195	75	0	2	27.85	1
1991	D. J. Millns	16	18	1	389	103	1	1	22.88	5
1995	A. R. K. Pierson	17	21	10	248	44	0	0	22.54	11
	G. I. Macmillan	6	10	1	176	41	0	0	19.55	0
1984	G. J. Parsons	16	20	4	266	53	0	2	16.62	20
	M. T. Brimson	10	10	4	37	13*	0	0	6.16	2

* *Signifies not out.* † *Born in Leicestershire.* § *Overseas player.*

BOWLING

	O	*M*	*R*	*W*	*BB*	*5W/i*	*Avge*
P. V. Simmons	364.4	87	1,021	56	6-14	3	18.23
A. D. Mullally	316.4	86	987	47	6-47	3	21.00
D. J. Millns	466.1	119	1,437	67	6-54	2	21.44
V. J. Wells	234.1	65	688	24	4-44	0	28.66
M. T. Brimson	288.2	62	849	29	5-12	2	29.27
A. R. K. Pierson	444.2	93	1,333	42	6-158	2	31.73
G. J. Parsons	488	148	1,352	40	4-21	0	33.80

Also bowled: G. I. Macmillan 14–2–58–2; D. L. Maddy 25–9–60–2.

COUNTY RECORDS

Highest score for:	261	P. V. Simmons v Northants at Leicester	1994
Highest score against:	341	G. H. Hirst (Yorkshire) at Leicester	1905
Best bowling for:	10-18	G. Geary v Glamorgan at Pontypridd	1929
Best bowling against:	10-32	H. Pickett (Essex) at Leyton	1895
Highest total for:	701-4 dec.	v Worcestershire at Worcester	1906
Highest total against:	761-6 dec.	by Essex at Chelmsford	1990
Lowest total for:	25	v Kent at Leicester	1912
Lowest total against:	24	by Glamorgan at Leicester	1971
	24	by Oxford University at Oxford	1985

At Oxford, April 13, 14, 15. LEICESTERSHIRE drew with OXFORD UNIVERSITY.

At Derby, May 2, 3, 4, 6. LEICESTERSHIRE beat DERBYSHIRE by six wickets.

At Manchester, May 9, 10, 11, 13. LEICESTERSHIRE drew with LANCASHIRE.

LEICESTERSHIRE v WORCESTERSHIRE

At Leicester, May 16, 17, 18. Leicestershire won by an innings and 130 runs. Leicestershire 24 pts, Worcestershire 2 pts. Toss: Leicestershire. Championship debut: K. R. Spiring.

On a pitch described by Whitaker as Grace Road's best for ten years, Leicestershire rewrote their record books and rose to the top of the Championship table. A total of 638 for eight was their highest ever at home, and second only to 701 for four at Worcester in 1906. Whitaker and Habib put on 320 for the fifth wicket, easily beating the county record of 233, by Nigel Briers and Roger Tolchard against Somerset in 1979. Whitaker scored 168 while Habib made 215 in his third Championship match since moving from Middlesex the previous year. Habib, born in Reading and educated at Millfield, lasted 375 minutes and 322 balls, hitting two sixes and 32 fours. Having scored briskly, Leicestershire had plenty of time to bowl out Worcestershire. Millns and Mullally dismissed them 483 behind and they had already lost another wicket following on before the second-day close. Moody scored a spirited century, but could not prevent Leicestershire winning with a day to spare.

Close of play: First day, Leicestershire 481-4 (J. J. Whitaker 145*, A. Habib 143*); Second day, Worcestershire 8-1 (W. P. C. Weston 3*, R. K. Illingworth 0*).

Leicestershire

V. J. Wells b Lampitt	35
D. L. Maddy c Rhodes b Moody	63
B. F. Smith c Weston b Lampitt	25
P. V. Simmons c Rhodes b Thomas	51
*J. J. Whitaker c Rhodes b Moody	168
A. Habib run out	215
†P. A. Nixon c Curtis b Moody	0
D. J. Millns c Weston b Thomas	4
G. J. Parsons not out	46
A. R. K. Pierson not out	8
L-b 6, w 1, n-b 16	23
1/49 2/81 3/174 4/200 5/520 6/524 7/537 8/622 (8 wkts dec.)	638

A. D. Mullally did not bat.

Bonus points – Leicestershire 4, Worcestershire 2 (Score at 120 overs: 520-5).

Bowling: Thomas 20–1–119–2; Sheriyar 32–5–110–0; Lampitt 20–3–105–2; Illingworth 38–4–129–0; Leatherdale 6–0–40–0; Moody 27–4–112–3; Hick 8–1–17–0.

Worcestershire

T. S. Curtis lbw b Millns	9	– c Smith b Mullally	5
W. P. C. Weston b Mullally	15	– b Wells	69
G. A. Hick c Habib b Mullally	1	– (4) c Simmons b Millns	4
*T. M. Moody b Millns	8	– (5) b Mullally	104
D. A. Leatherdale c Habib b Parsons	27	– (6) c Nixon b Parsons	27
K. R. Spiring c Simmons b Millns	8	– (7) c Nixon b Simmons	51
†S. J. Rhodes lbw b Wells	23	– (8) c Nixon b Simmons	36
S. R. Lampitt c Maddy b Simmons	23	– (9) b Wells	2
R. K. Illingworth b Mullally	31	– (3) c Nixon b Millns	4
P. A. Thomas c Simmons b Millns	5	– b Mullally	11
A. Sheriyar not out	0	– not out	12
L-b 4, w 1	5	B 11, l-b 13, w 2, n-b 2	28
1/20 2/21 3/30 4/56 5/73 6/73 7/108 8/134 9/155	155	1/5 2/16 3/36 4/157 5/226 6/230 7/324 8/328 9/328	353

Bonus points – Leicestershire 4.

Bowling: *First Innings*—Millns 14.1–4–37–4; Mullally 9–3–35–3; Parsons 12–3–35–1; Simmons 7–1–16–1; Pierson 5–2–7–0; Wells 5–2–21–1. *Second Innings*—Millns 22–4–67–2; Mullally 22.5–4–101–3; Pierson 10–1–32–0; Parsons 14–3–47–1; Wells 16–1–64–2; Simmons 7–2–18–2.

Umpires: A. Clarkson and P. Willey.

At Birmingham, May 23, 24, 25, 27. LEICESTERSHIRE drew with WARWICKSHIRE.

At Leicester, June 1, 2, 3. LEICESTERSHIRE drew with INDIANS (See Indian tour section).

LEICESTERSHIRE v KENT

At Leicester, June 5, 6, 7, 8. Drawn. Leicestershire 11 pts, Kent 9 pts. Toss: Kent.

This match ended tamely after a hard-fought encounter. Replying to Kent's 324, built around 90 from Ward, Leicestershire flourished while Simmons was hitting a sparkling 82 from 75 balls. At 298 for seven, however, they looked like conceding the advantage. But Smith, grinding out a career-best 174 not out lasting eight hours 40 minutes, led them to 431 and a lead of 107. Some awful bowling on the third afternoon then let Kent off the hook. Openers Fulton and Fleming, who hit successive sixes off Brimson to bring up his fifty, both scored Championship bests at they put on 195. Though Brimson recovered on the final day, taking five wickets for the first time, Kent were able to set a target of 245 from 48 overs. At 120 for one, it was on the cards; but wickets began to tumble and Leicestershire shut up shop.

Close of play: First day, Kent 318-8 (N. W. Preston 7*, B. J. Phillips 1*); Second day, Leicestershire 321-7 (B. F. Smith 117*, G. J. Parsons 7*); Third day, Kent 185-0 (D. P. Fulton 62*, M. V. Fleming 111*).

Kent

D. P. Fulton c Nixon b Simmons	34	– c Parsons b Brimson	88
M. V. Fleming c Nixon b Parsons	5	– c Maddy b Pierson	114
T. R. Ward c Maddy b Simmons	90	– c Maddy b Brimson	44
C. L. Hooper b Pierson	26	– c Habib b Brimson	22
G. R. Cowdrey c Simmons b Millns	71	– b Pierson	28
M. A. Ealham c Nixon b Parsons	14	– st Nixon b Brimson	6
*†S. A. Marsh lbw b Simmons	51	– c Parsons b Brimson	2
M. J. McCague c Habib b Millns	0	– not out	24
N. W. Preston b Parsons	12	– c Maddy b Pierson	3
B. J. Phillips lbw b Millns	1		
E. J. Stanford not out	0		
B 2, l-b 6, w 4, n-b 8	20	B 11, l-b 3, w 4, n-b 2	20
1/6 2/100 3/155 4/167 5/225 6/310 7/310 8/310 9/318	324	1/195 2/259 3/266 4/287 5/297 6/301 7/345 8/351 (8 wkts dec.)	351

Bonus points – Kent 3, Leicestershire 4.

Bowling: *First Innings*—Millns 21–9–43–3; Parsons 21–5–56–3; Wells 8–1–22–0; Pierson 22–5–70–1; Simmons 18–3–43–3; Brimson 24–5–82–0. *Second Innings*—Millns 8–2–21–0; Parsons 20–8–57–0; Pierson 35.4–5–133–3; Simmons 9–1–29–0; Brimson 26–5–97–5.

Leicestershire

V. J. Wells c Marsh b McCague	44	– (2) c Marsh b McCague	57
D. L. Maddy c Phillips b McCague	16	– (6) run out	2
B. F. Smith not out	174	– c Ealham b Hooper	60
P. V. Simmons lbw b Hooper	82	– st Marsh b Hooper	22
*J. J. Whitaker c Preston b Stanford	15	– (1) c Fulton b McCague	6
A. Habib st Marsh b Stanford	20	– (5) not out	9
†P. A. Nixon b Stanford	8	– b Stanford	7
D. J. Millns b Hooper	0		
G. J. Parsons c Fulton b McCague	14		
A. R. K. Pierson c and b Fleming	44	– (8) not out	0
M. T. Brimson b Fleming	0		
B 8, l-b 4, n-b 2	14	B 7, l-b 2, w 1	10
1/35 2/85 3/186 4/226 5/267 6/291 7/298 8/342 9/431	431	1/14 2/120 3/142 4/156 5/159 6/170	(6 wkts) 173

Bonus points – Leicestershire 4, Kent 3 (Score at 120 overs: 358-8).

Bowling: *First Innings*—McCague 25–5–79–3; Phillips 14–4–53–0; Preston 8–1–27–0; Ealham 29–10–82–0; Fleming 11–3–26–2; Hooper 33–8–68–2; Stanford 38–12–84–3. *Second Innings*—McCague 9–0–53–2; Ealham 3–1–13–0; Stanford 16.3–4–42–1; Hooper 19–3–56–2.

Umpires: J. D. Bond and D. J. Constant.

At The Oval, June 13, 14, 15, 17. LEICESTERSHIRE lost to SURREY by 108 runs.

At Bradford, June 20, 21, 22, 24. LEICESTERSHIRE beat YORKSHIRE by an innings and 151 runs.

LEICESTERSHIRE v ESSEX

At Leicester, July 4, 5, 6, 8. Leicestershire won by an innings and 44 runs. Leicestershire 24 pts, Essex 3 pts. Toss: Leicestershire.

Leicestershire won their second successive innings victory thanks to a superb two-man show from Millns and Wells. Millns became the fourth player to take ten wickets and score a century for Leicestershire in the same match. The three previous instances were by A. D. Pougher in 1894, F. Geeson in 1901 and V. E. Jackson in 1954. Thanks to Millns's four for 74, allied to four for 21 from Parsons, Essex were shot out for 163. Then Wells, still thriving on his promotion to open, took over. He fell just short of his third double-hundred in four innings in all cricket, after batting 407 minutes, and hit 31 fours in 346 balls. Millns joined him to add 187 for the seventh wicket and advanced to a maiden hundred in nearly four hours. Essex reached 193 for four by the third-day close but Millns finished them off in 66 minutes of hostile bowling on Monday morning, when he took six for 20 in 7.4 overs, including three in six balls.

Close of play: First day, Leicestershire 113-0 (V. J. Wells 58*, D. L. Maddy 34*); Second day, Leicestershire 304-6 (V. J. Wells 150*, D. J. Millns 51*); Third day, Essex 193-4 (P. J. Prichard 19*, P. M. Such 1*).

Essex

G. A. Gooch lbw b Simmons	30 – b Parsons	72
D. D. J. Robinson b Millns	13 – lbw b Simmons	15
A. P. Grayson c Simmons b Millns	11 – lbw b Simmons	35
S. G. Law b Wells	21 – c Pierson b Brimson	41
*P. J. Prichard b Parsons	1 – lbw b Millns	28
R. C. Irani c Nixon b Parsons	0 – (7) lbw b Millns	0
†R. J. Rollins c Simmons b Parsons	38 – (8) c Nixon b Millns	0
N. F. Williams b Millns	8 – (9) c Habib b Millns	17
A. P. Cowan c Simmons b Millns	25 – (10) b Millns	4
S. J. W. Andrew b Parsons	6 – (11) not out	4
P. M. Such not out	0 – (6) c Pierson b Millns	13
B 1, l-b 5, n-b 4	10 B 5, l-b 7, n-b 6	18
1/23 2/41 3/65 4/66 5/66 6/94 7/123 8/142 9/157	163 1/44 2/104 3/164 4/190 5/213 6/213 7/213 8/234 9/239	247

Bonus points – Leicestershire 4.

Bowling: *First Innings*—Millns 20–3–74–4; Parsons 16–8–21–4; Simmons 13–4–14–1; Wells 7–3–19–1; Pierson 8–2–29–0. *Second Innings*—Millns 13.4–2–54–6; Parsons 20–5–40–1; Simmons 15–2–65–2; Pierson 19–6–44–0; Wells 4–1–16–0; Brimson 7–1–16–1.

Leicestershire

V. J. Wells b Andrew	197
D. L. Maddy c Law b Irani	35
B. F. Smith c Rollins b Williams	18
P. V. Simmons c Gooch b Andrew	4
*J. J. Whitaker c Law b Andrew	4
A. Habib lbw b Irani	1
†P. A. Nixon b Irani	0
D. J. Millns lbw b Grayson	103
G. J. Parsons st Rollins b Grayson	8
A. R. K. Pierson not out	11
M. T. Brimson not out	13
B 1, l-b 22, w 3, n-b 34	60
1/116 2/177 3/195 4/203 5/204 6/204 7/391 8/425 9/430	(9 wkts dec.) 454

Bonus points – Leicestershire 4, Essex 3 (Score at 120 overs: 415-7).

Bowling: Cowan 16–2–82–0; Williams 30–6–79–1; Andrew 22–5–67–3; Irani 25–4–100–3; Law 14–4–38–0; Such 13–3–31–0; Grayson 13–2–34–2.

Umpires: J. H. Hampshire and J. W. Holder.

At Cheltenham, July 18, 19. LEICESTERSHIRE beat GLOUCESTERSHIRE by 102 runs.

LEICESTERSHIRE v SUSSEX

At Leicester, July 25, 26, 27, 29. Leicestershire won by 58 runs. Leicestershire 22 pts, Sussex 6 pts. Toss: Leicestershire.

Despite a typically slow and uneven Grace Road pitch, the two sides produced a thrilling contest, which ended in Leicestershire's fourth win on the trot. There were some marvellous individual performances, from Sussex left-arm seamer Lewry, for instance, who returned 11 wickets. But the most dynamic cricket came from Simmons, who took nine wickets, and left-arm spinner Brimson, who demolished Sussex's second innings with a career-best five for 12. Simmons also led in the field, after Whitaker suffered a calf strain, and rescued his team on Friday. Millns was off injured and Sussex, on 240 for five, were heading for a big lead, but Simmons bowled a lightning-fast spell to take the last five for 29 in 11.4 overs. The following evening, with Sussex chasing 213 to win, he blasted out three of the top order. Brimson did the rest on a turning pitch, completing victory just before lunch on Monday.

Close of play: First day, Leicestershire 258-9 (J. J. Whitaker 53*, P. A. Nixon 71*); Second day, Sussex 294; Third day, Sussex 76-4 (J. W. Hall 31*, C. W. J. Athey 9*).

Leicestershire

V. J. Wells b Lewry	7	– b Giddins	28
D. L. Maddy c Moores b Lewry	18	– c Moores b Lewry	68
B. F. Smith c Athey b Jarvis	22	– c Athey b Drakes	45
P. V. Simmons b Giddins	13	– c Moores b Lewry	36
*J. J. Whitaker not out	58	– (9) c sub b Lewry	3
A. Habib b Lewry	30	– (5) b Lewry	16
†P. A. Nixon c Moores b Lewry	74	– (6) lbw b Drakes	14
D. J. Millns c Moores b Giddins	23	– (7) lbw b Lewry	0
G. J. Parsons c Moores b Lewry	2	– (8) c Hall b Drakes	17
A. R. K. Pierson b Giddins	9	– not out	1
M. T. Brimson c Athey b Lenham	3	– lbw b Lewry	0
L-b 4, w 1, n-b 2	7	B 9, l-b 1, n-b 2	12
1/16 2/43 3/57 4/86 5/131 6/168 7/177 8/198 9/225	266	1/40 2/145 3/171 4/190 5/205 6/205 7/232 8/238 9/240	240

Bonus points – Leicestershire 2, Sussex 4.

In the first innings J. J. Whitaker, when 30, retired hurt at 117 and resumed at 225.

Bowling: *First Innings*—Lewry 30.2–6–74–5; Jarvis 8–1–23–1; Giddins 24.5–9–60–3; Drakes 30–9–79–0; Lenham 11.1–3–22–1; Greenfield 3–1–4–0. *Second Innings*—Drakes 32–9–108–3; Lewry 27.4–6–73–6; Lenham 7–0–29–0; Giddins 7–1–16–1; Greenfield 1–0–4–0.

Sussex

C. W. J. Athey c Nixon b Millns	0	– (6) c and b Simmons	35
J. W. Hall c Simmons b Millns	16	– c Pierson b Brimson	52
*A. P. Wells c Simmons b Parsons	7	– (1) c Maddy b Parsons	15
K. Greenfield c Nixon b Wells	69	– (3) b Simmons	9
N. J. Lenham c Simmons b Millns	27	– (4) c Wells b Simmons	2
M. P. Speight lbw b Simmons	68	– (5) c Nixon b Simmons	2
†P. Moores c Pierson b Simmons	47	– not out	14
V. C. Drakes c Nixon b Simmons	16	– lbw b Brimson	5
P. W. Jarvis not out	28	– c Maddy b Brimson	0
J. D. Lewry c Wells b Simmons	0	– c Simmons b Brimson	2
E. S. H. Giddins c Nixon b Simmons	7	– c Maddy b Brimson	2
B 2, l-b 7	9	B 2, l-b 6, n-b 8	16
1/0 2/19 3/27 4/93 5/157 6/240 7/243 8/260 9/284	294	1/30 2/41 3/49 4/57 5/127 6/127 7/132 8/132 9/150	154

Bonus points – Sussex 2, Leicestershire 4.

Bowling: *First Innings*—Millns 13.5–5–30–3; Parsons 29–6–85–1; Simmons 20.4–6–58–5; Brimson 23–5–48–0; Wells 10.1–3–28–1; Pierson 10–2–36–0. *Second Innings*—Parsons 17–5–45–1; Simmons 24–8–70–4; Wells 6–4–9–0; Brimson 10.3–3–12–5; Millns 3–0–10–0.

Umpires: J. H. Harris and K. J. Lyons. N. Dearman deputised for J. H. Harris on the 4th day.

LEICESTERSHIRE v NORTHAMPTONSHIRE

At Leicester, August 1, 2, 3, 5. Drawn. Leicestershire 9 pts, Northamptonshire 11 pts. Toss: Northamptonshire.

Leicestershire could not take full advantage of their game in hand over joint leaders Surrey, failing to beat an injury-hit Northamptonshire. Wells scored his second Championship double-hundred of the season, his third in all cricket, to set up a formidable total after Northamptonshire's stand-in captain, Fordham, had misjudged a green wicket and chosen to field. The visitors struggled to 114 for four but, against some poor bowling, Curran decided the best way out of a crisis was to hit out. He smacked a career-best 150 and shared a 226-run stand with Penberthy, which saved the follow-on and enabled his side to take a three-run lead. Simmons sentimentally delayed his second-innings declaration until 20 minutes after lunch on the final day to allow Maddy to complete a maiden Championship century and, although off-spinner Pierson took four wickets on a turning pitch, they ran out of time.

Close of play: First day, Leicestershire 364-7 (V. J. Wells 202*, A. R. K. Pierson 0*); Second day, Northamptonshire 301-4 (K. M. Curran 110*, A. L. Penberthy 79*); Third day, Leicestershire 176-4 (D. L. Maddy 61*, P. A. Nixon 14*).

Leicestershire

V. J. Wells c Fordham b Capel	204	– c Ripley b Ambrose	4
D. L. Maddy c Ambrose b Curran	23	– not out	101
B. F. Smith c Ripley b Curran	9	– (7) run out	41
A. Habib c Curran b Ambrose	19	– lbw b Ambrose	1
*P. V. Simmons b Snape	75	– b Snape	72
G. I. Macmillan c Ambrose b Snape	2	– (3) lbw b Taylor	12
†P. A. Nixon c Fordham b Emburey	18	– (6) run out	33
G. J. Parsons lbw b Snape	5	– b Emburey	8
A. R. K. Pierson c Penberthy b Snape	16	– not out	8
A. D. Mullally c Loye b Curran	29		
M. T. Brimson not out	2		
B 1, l-b 14, w 1, n-b 4	20	B 1, l-b 12, w 1, n-b 4	18
1/56 2/96 3/137 4/289 5/291 6/348 7/361 8/371 9/408	422	1/8 2/26 3/31 4/143 5/206 6/267 7/288	(7 wkts dec.) 298

Bonus points – Leicestershire 4, Northamptonshire 4 (Score at 120 overs: 410-9).

Bowling: *First Innings*—Ambrose 22–6–59–1; Taylor 15–1–66–0; Curran 16–2–75–3; Capel 16–3–58–1; Emburey 24–5–58–1; Penberthy 14–3–33–0; Walton 3–0–16–0; Snape 12.1–0–42–4. *Second Innings*—Ambrose 13–1–34–2; Taylor 11–0–36–1; Snape 38–13–93–1; Emburey 33.5–6–99–1; Penberthy 8–2–23–0.

Northamptonshire

*A. Fordham b Brimson	9	– c Parsons b Mullally	19
M. B. Loye c Nixon b Wells	4	– lbw b Pierson	69
T. C. Walton c Nixon b Simmons	51	– lbw b Pierson	38
D. J. Capel c Parsons b Simmons	29	– lbw b Pierson	14
K. M. Curran b Mullally	150	– not out	62
A. L. Penberthy c Parsons b Mullally	87	– c Simmons b Pierson	0
J. N. Snape lbw b Brimson	37	– not out	0
†D. Ripley b Pierson	9		
J. E. Emburey not out	6		
C. E. L. Ambrose c Nixon b Mullally	5		
J. P. Taylor c sub b Mullally	5		
B 13, l-b 9, w 2, n-b 9	33	B 1, l-b 1, n-b 8	10
1/7 2/32 3/85 4/114 5/340 6/371 7/404 8/404 9/411	425	1/45 2/99 3/123 4/165 5/197	(5 wkts) 212

Bonus points – Northamptonshire 4, Leicestershire 2 (Score at 120 overs: 398-6).

Bowling: *First Innings*—Mullally 38.2–10–112–4; Parsons 19–5–49–0; Wells 10–3–37–1; Brimson 19–5–65–2; Simmons 14–2–50–2; Pierson 32–4–85–1; Macmillan 1–0–5–0. *Second Innings*—Mullally 14–4–85–1; Parsons 21–8–56–0; Brimson 5–1–11–0; Pierson 18–5–49–4; Macmillan 1–0–9–0.

Umpires: J. D. Bond and R. Julian.

At Swansea, August 8, 9, 10, 12. LEICESTERSHIRE drew with GLAMORGAN.

At Leicester, August 14, 15, 16. LEICESTERSHIRE lost to PAKISTANIS by 101 runs (See Pakistani tour section).

LEICESTERSHIRE v HAMPSHIRE

At Leicester, August 22, 23, 24, 26. Drawn. Leicestershire 11 pts, Hampshire 7 pts. Toss: Leicestershire.

Leicestershire's captain, Whitaker, said the disappointment in the dressing-room at the end of this match was "impossible to describe". A third successive draw was a blow to their title hopes and it was the more frustrating because the opposition's final pair thwarted them for the second successive game. One day was lost to rain and further interruptions on Monday helped to wreck their efforts. Hampshire began the day on 81 for seven and followed on, but Parsons had dropped a catch off Udal, who went on to make 43, costing vital minutes. Even so, Hampshire looked beaten on 98 for seven in their second innings before rain wiped out 45 minutes; another shower intervened at 111 for nine. Play resumed for the last time at 5.45, but Bovill and Renshaw held out for six overs. Leicestershire had always been on top; on the opening day, Simmons had scored 108 in 117 balls, and later Parsons returned to form with a devastating spell of three for nought in nine balls.

Close of play: First day, Leicestershire 343-8 (P. A. Nixon 67*, A. R. K. Pierson 9*); Second day, No play; Third day, Hampshire 81-7 (A. N. Aymes 11*, S. D. Udal 7*).

Leicestershire

V. J. Wells c Aymes b Renshaw	24
D. L. Maddy lbw b James	11
*J. J. Whitaker b Bovill	48
B. F. Smith c Udal b Renshaw	34
P. V. Simmons c Smith b Renshaw	108
A. Habib c Aymes b Renshaw	4
†P. A. Nixon lbw b Bovill	67
D. J. Millns c James b Stephenson	17
G. J. Parsons c Stephenson b Bovill	0
A. R. K. Pierson not out	9
M. T. Brimson b Bovill	10
B 9, l-b 3, w 1, n-b 8	21
1/33 2/60 3/122 4/144 5/167 6/276 7/321 8/322 9/343	353

Bonus points – Leicestershire 4, Hampshire 4.

Bowling: Bovill 29–3–102–4; Renshaw 24–9–56–4; Stephenson 17–6–53–1; James 24–1–89–1; Udal 10–2–33–0; Keech 5–1–8–0.

Hampshire

G. W. White c Simmons b Millns	8	lbw b Wells	13
P. R. Whitaker b Millns	14	c Parsons b Millns	0
K. D. James c Simmons b Wells	5	b Parsons	23
R. A. Smith b Parsons	17	b Wells	14
W. S. Kendall c Simmons b Wells	14	c Parsons b Pierson	11
M. Keech lbw b Parsons	0	c Nixon b Wells	13
*J. P. Stephenson c Nixon b Parsons	0	c and b Brimson	11
†A. N. Aymes b Simmons	21	lbw b Brimson	4
S. D. Udal b Simmons	43	b Pierson	0
J. N. B. Bovill b Parsons	0	not out	17
S. J. Renshaw not out	0	not out	9
B 4, l-b 3, w 2, n-b 6	15	B 10, l-b 6, w 4	20
1/14 2/20 3/44 4/52 5/52 6/52 7/73 8/102 9/119	137	1/3 2/39 3/63 4/70 5/88 6/91 7/98 8/101 9/105	(9 wkts) 135

Bonus points – Leicestershire 4.

Bowling: *First Innings*—Millns 17–10–28–2; Parsons 16–9–36–4; Pierson 1–1–0–0; Simmons 10.2–3–32–2; Wells 10–2–34–2. *Second Innings*—Millns 12–2–28–1; Parsons 9–4–15–1; Simmons 13–3–26–0; Brimson 8–2–18–2; Pierson 6–2–9–2; Wells 9–2–23–3.

Umpires: G. I. Burgess and R. Palmer.

LEICESTERSHIRE v SOMERSET

At Leicester, August 29, 30. Leicestershire won by an innings and 39 runs. Leicestershire 22 pts, Somerset 4 pts. Toss: Leicestershire.

Leicestershire destroyed Somerset in two days thanks to an extraordinary bowling performance. They put the visitors in on a greenish pitch, and their four seamers skittled them for 83 inside 42 overs, the third-lowest Championship score of the season. Millns led the way with four for 35. Although the ball moved around, Somerset did not blame the pitch, admitting they had batted badly while Leicestershire had just done enough with the ball. It was a pitch on which 250 would have been par and, though not one Leicestershire player reached 50 – Smith's 48 was the top score of the match – a total of 296 gave them a significant advantage. When Somerset resumed, Simmons, who had been taking on more responsibility with the ball in Mullally's absences with England, did the damage with four for 38; Somerset collapsed from 135 for four to 174 all out.

Close of play: First day, Leicestershire 202-5 (P. A. Nixon 12*, A. R. K. Pierson 0*).

Somerset

M. N. Lathwell c Nixon b Parsons	0	– b Wells	13
M. E. Trescothick c Nixon b Millns	4	– lbw b Brimson	34
*P. D. Bowler c Parsons b Simmons	13	– (4) c Parsons b Pierson	14
R. J. Harden lbw b Millns	5	– (3) b Simmons	30
S. C. Ecclestone lbw b Simmons	5	– c Simmons b Pierson	5
S. Lee c Nixon b Parsons	7	– c Parsons b Simmons	43
†R. J. Turner not out	20	– b Simmons	0
G. D. Rose c Parsons b Wells	0	– lbw b Millns	0
J. D. Batty c Nixon b Wells	7	– c Pierson b Simmons	13
A. R. Caddick b Millns	9	– not out	8
A. P. van Troost c Simmons b Millns	11	– b Millns	1
L-b 2	2	L-b 5, n-b 8	13
1/4 2/4 3/14 4/27 5/30 6/42 7/46 8/54 9/67	83	1/46 2/68 3/87 4/93 5/135 6/135 7/142 8/152 9/169	174

Bonus points – Leicestershire 4.

Bowling: *First Innings*—Parsons 16–8–22–2; Millns 12.2–3–35–4; Simmons 8–2–19–2; Wells 5–3–5–2. *Second Innings*—Parsons 14–7–22–0; Millns 12.3–1–43–2; Simmons 18–6–38–4; Wells 8–3–17–1; Brimson 16–5–31–1; Pierson 6–1–18–2.

Leicestershire

V. J. Wells b Lee	9
D. L. Maddy lbw b Caddick	47
G. I. Macmillan c Turner b Rose	37
B. F. Smith lbw b Caddick	48
P. V. Simmons c Caddick b Lee	27
†P. A. Nixon c Lathwell b Caddick	23
A. R. K. Pierson c Turner b Rose	29
*J. J. Whitaker c Turner b Lee	33
D. J. Millns lbw b Batty	5
G. J. Parsons c Turner b Batty	5
M. T. Brimson not out	1
B 1, l-b 7, n-b 24	32
1/19 2/74 3/159 4/176 5/202 6/234 7/281 8/290 9/290	296

Bonus points – Leicestershire 2, Somerset 4.

Bowling: Caddick 31–8–83–3; Rose 19–3–50–2; Lee 21–5–78–3; van Troost 10–0–39–0; Batty 14.4–3–38–2.

Umpires: V. A. Holder and K. E. Palmer.

At Nottingham, September 3, 4, 5, 6. LEICESTERSHIRE beat NOTTINGHAMSHIRE by six wickets.

At Chester-le-Street, September, 12, 13. LEICESTERSHIRE beat DURHAM by an innings and 251 runs.

LEICESTERSHIRE v MIDDLESEX

At Leicester, September 19, 20, 21, 22. Leicestershire won by an innings and 74 runs. Leicestershire 24 pts, Middlesex 4 pts. Toss: Middlesex.

Leicestershire clinched the second Championship title in their history over a pot of tea and ham sandwiches on the penultimate day of the season. The tea interval had just started when supporters tuning into radios heard that Surrey had forfeited their first innings against Worcestershire, and thus could not get the maximum points they needed to take the title. Within minutes, 3,000 jubilant fans had gathered under the players' balcony. Ultimately, Leicestershire did not need Surrey's capitulation; they crushed Middlesex for their tenth victory of the season and their fourth in succession – three of them by an innings. Only Ramprakash, who made a couple of seventies, offered any resistance. Despite losing the toss, Leicestershire bowled Middlesex out on a quickish pitch for 190, Mullally taking four for 53, before rattling up 512, a club record against these opponents. Whitaker and Simmons provided the backbone of the innings but later the performance moved to inspired heights: Mullally scored a career-best 75 in 57 minutes during a last-wicket stand of 112 in just 13 overs with Simmons. Middlesex finished the third day five down and next morning Millns wrapped things up with four for 21 off 5.3 overs.

Close of play: First day, Leicestershire 36-1 (D. L. Maddy 17*, B. F. Smith 14*); Second day, Leicestershire 381-8 (P. V. Simmons 95*, A. R. K. Pierson 1*); Third day, Middlesex 194-5 (K. R. Brown 2*, K. P. Dutch 4*).

Middlesex

P. N. Weekes c Wells b Millns	5	– c Whitaker b Mullally	1
P. E. Wellings b Mullally	18	– lbw b Simmons	42
M. R. Ramprakash c and b Parsons	71	– b Pierson	78
*M. W. Gatting c Nixon b Mullally	7	– b Mullally	24
O. A. Shah lbw b Mullally	2	– st Nixon b Mullally	7
†K. R. Brown c Simmons b Wells	4	– lbw b Millns	21
K. P. Dutch lbw b Wells	0	– b Pierson	8
R. L. Johnson c Wells b Simmons	27	– b Millns	16
A. R. C. Fraser not out	8	– c Nixon b Millns	1
P. C. R. Tufnell c Wells b Mullally	16	– b Millns	0
R. A. Fay b Millns	0	– not out	10
L-b 10, n-b 22	32	B 4, l-b 6, n-b 30	40
1/16 2/50 3/60 4/66 5/76 6/76 7/156 8/166 9/183	190	1/1 2/106 3/150 4/182 5/190 6/208 7/225 8/231 9/231	248

Bonus points – Leicestershire 4.

Bowling: *First Innings*—Millns 12.4–5–42–2; Mullally 18–6–53–4; Simmons 5.4–2–14–1; Parsons 13.2–2–54–1; Wells 7–2–17–2. *Second Innings*—Millns 18.3–6–48–4; Mullally 14–5–40–3; Parsons 8–3–15–0; Pierson 23–4–83–2; Wells 2–1–7–0; Simmons 12–2–45–1.

Leicestershire

V. J. Wells c Brown b Fay	5
D. L. Maddy lbw b Fay	30
B. F. Smith lbw b Johnson	14
*J. J. Whitaker hit wkt b Tufnell	89
A. Habib c Brown b Johnson	49
P. V. Simmons not out	142
†P. A. Nixon c Brown b Fraser	2
D. J. Millns b Fay	40
G. J. Parsons b Weekes	6
A. R. K. Pierson c Brown b Fay	3
A. D. Mullally b Fraser	75
B 16, l-b 25, w 2, n-b 14	57
1/11 2/36 3/66 4/204 5/242 6/253 7/343 8/380 9/400	512

Bonus points – Leicestershire 4, Middlesex 4 (Score at 120 overs: 486-9).

Bowling: Fraser 31.5–5–119–2; Fay 34–5–140–4; Tufnell 26–4–89–1; Johnson 26–3–113–2; Weekes 5–1–10–1.

Umpires: B. Leadbeater and P. Willey.

Phil Tufnell

MIDDLESEX

Patron: HRH The Duke of Edinburgh
President: D. C. S. Compton
Chairman: A. E. Moss
Chairman, Cricket Committee: R. A. Gale
Secretary: J. Hardstaff
Captain: M. W. Gatting
Coach: D. Bennett
Scorer: M. J. Smith

It was all or nothing at all for Middlesex in 1996. Seven wins and six defeats indicate a lack of consistency and it was impossible to know which Middlesex you might see on any two consecutive days, let alone in consecutive matches. Injuries were a factor; the county coach, Don Bennett, said that he could not recall a season like it. While Leicestershire used only 13 players in winning the County Championship, Middlesex used 20 to finish ninth, down seven places.

Among the one-game players was overseas all-rounder Dion Nash, who missed the beginning of the season because of New Zealand's tour of the West Indies, though a back condition kept him out of the Tests. It was still a problem when he reached Lord's. He played against Sussex, bowling ten overs and taking one for 44. His back was still painful and he did not appear again. The county could not have done much more in trying to discover exactly what the problem was. Untold scans and X-rays failed to reveal anything specific; in June, it was decided to terminate his contract, and Nash returned to New Zealand.

In addition, Richard Johnson, who had spent the close season recovering from the back injury that kept him out of England's tour of South Africa, strained a shoulder during a pre-season game and played only one of the first seven Championship matches. This gave an opportunity to several inexperienced seamers, the most successful of whom was David Follett, who in four games took 23 wickets at 19.91, including a devastating eight for 22 against Durham. Then he, too, was injured and did not play again. In the winter he moved to Northamptonshire for "domestic reasons". Of the rest, Ricky Fay looked the most promising, while Jamie Hewitt also bowled well, as well as showing himself a useful lower-middle-order batsman.

Of the established bowlers, Philip Tufnell was by far the best, with 72 Championship wickets – and was recalled for England's winter tour. Meanwhile Angus Fraser was his usual loyal and reliable self, although he managed only 49. John Emburey, gone to Northamptonshire, proved difficult to replace; Paul Weekes's 25 wickets cost 37.92, in spite of a career-best eight for 39 against Glamorgan. Keith Dutch, the next off-spinner in line, played three Championship matches and bowled in only one of them, against Somerset at Uxbridge, but he claimed three for 25 there and invariably took wickets when given the chance in the Sunday League. In the Second Eleven Championship, he was the leading player in the country. Perhaps another county might give him more opportunity.

Ironically, although the bowling was most affected by injury, it was the batting that repeatedly let the side down. Maximum batting points were achieved on only five occasions; in six matches, Middlesex were bowled out in their first innings for under 200 and thus gained none. Only Durham and Gloucestershire scored fewer centuries than Middlesex's ten (Mark Ramprakash made ten on his own in 1995) and only Weekes and Ramprakash could look back on their records with any satisfaction.

Mike Gatting had a dreadful summer, although it started well. His 171 against Durham was his 90th first-class century and completed his set against each of the other 17 counties. But he finished with a disappointing 761 Championship runs and 901 in all. He missed three matches, two because of surgery to his right knee, which may have been troubling him throughout the season. It was the first year since 1980 that he had failed to reach 1,000.

In contrast, Weekes passed 1,000 for the first time and it was not his fault that the county rarely made a good start. Poor Jason Pooley lost his form and confidence as the year went on so that, all too often, Ramprakash was making his way to the middle in the first few overs of the innings. Ramprakash himself, while unable to capture his golden form of 1995, nevertheless made more than 1,400 runs and, towards the end of the season, began to dominate the bowling as only he can. He also became Gatting's heir apparent when John Carr announced, at the start of August, that he would be retiring to become cricket operations manager at the new ECB. He had had a disappointing year, scoring only four fifties, but his runs and slip catching, often breathtaking, will be sorely missed.

There were one or two saving graces to 1996, particularly the abundant promise shown by 17-year-old Owais Shah. When school commitments allowed, he made five Championship appearances, with two fifties, and was taken to Australia by England A. Though Peter Wellings seemed a little old at 26 to be making his first-class debut, he looked to have a sound method. As an experiment, he opened with Weekes at Leicester, where he made 42, suggesting a possible solution for 1997. And then there was Keith Brown – not the most stylish of wicket-keepers, but he missed little and his batting turned several matches. Only Ramprakash and Weekes were above him in the Championship batting averages and he was quite rightly named Middlesex's Player of the Year.

Once again, Middlesex performed poorly in the limited-overs competitions, beating just British Universities in the Benson and Hedges Cup and Cumberland in the NatWest Trophy. They lost only one of their first eight Sunday League matches, but then the slump set in; they won only three more and lost six. As in the first-class game, it was usually the batting that let them down.

So what of the future? Australian Greg Blewett was lined up to strengthen the batting in 1997, subject to him not being selected for the Ashes tour (with Michael Slater as a possible alternative), and Middlesex must hope that Gatting will bounce back. It could be his last season before moving into coaching – he took over England A when Graham Gooch withdrew for family reasons – so that will be another crucial place to fill. There are several youngsters knocking on the door, notably the young wicket-keeper, David Nash, and there surely cannot be another year with so many bowlers struck down by long-term injury. – NORMAN DE MESQUITA.

MIDDLESEX 1996

[*Bill Smith*

Back row: D. Follett, S. P. Moffat, P. E. Wellings, K. P. Dutch, O. A. Shah, A. A. Khan, D. C. Nash. *Middle row:* S. Shepard (*physiotherapist*), D. Bennett (*coach*), R. L. Johnson, I. N. Blanchett, M. R. Evans, R. A. Fay, J. C. Harrison, D. J. Goodchild, J. P. Hewitt, U. B. A. Rashid, M. A. Feltham, A. Jones (*Second Eleven scorer*), I. J. Gould (*assistant coach*). *Front row:* P. C. R. Tufnell, M. R. Ramprakash, J. D. Carr, M. W. Gatting (*captain*), A. R. C. Fraser, K. R. Brown, P. N. Weekes, J. C. Pooley. *Inset:* M. J. Smith (*First Eleven scorer*).

MIDDLESEX RESULTS

All first-class matches – Played 19: Won 7, Lost 6, Drawn 6.

County Championship matches – Played 17: Won 7, Lost 6, Drawn 4.

Competition placings – Britannic Assurance County Championship, 9th; NatWest Trophy, 2nd round; Benson and Hedges Cup, 5th in Group C; AXA Equity & Law League, 7th.

COUNTY CHAMPIONSHIP AVERAGES

BATTING

Cap		*M*	*I*	*NO*	*R*	*HS*	*100s*	*50s*	*Avge*	*Ct/St*
1990	M. R. Ramprakash	16	29	2	1,406	169	4	8	52.07	7
1993	P. N. Weekes	17	32	2	1,191	171*	4	4	39.70	10
1990	K. R. Brown†	17	30	5	884	83	0	8	35.36	59/1
	P. E. Wellings	4	8	1	237	48	0	0	33.85	1
1977	M. W. Gatting†	14	23	0	761	171	1	6	33.08	9
1987	J. D. Carr†	15	26	1	706	94	0	4	28.24	27
	O. A. Shah	5	9	1	212	75	0	2	26.50	2
1995	J. C. Pooley†	16	30	0	695	111	1	4	23.16	22
	D. Follett	4	6	5	22	17	0	0	22.00	2
	J. P. Hewitt	8	12	2	209	45	0	0	20.90	5
1990	P. C. R. Tufnell	16	26	10	290	67*	0	1	18.12	7
	J. C. Harrison	5	10	1	151	40	0	0	16.77	7
1995	R. L. Johnson	11	20	1	243	37*	0	0	12.78	1
1988	A. R. C. Fraser	17	28	6	238	33	0	0	10.81	3
	K. P. Dutch†	3	4	0	39	27	0	0	9.75	2
	R. A. Fay†	14	24	2	163	26	0	0	7.40	3
1995	M. A. Feltham†	2	4	0	1	1	0	0	0.25	0

Also batted: D. J. Goodchild† (1 match) 4, 0; (cap 1995) D. J. Nash§ (1 match) 1 (1 ct); U. B. A. Rashid (1 match) 9, 6.

* *Signifies not out.* † *Born in Middlesex.* § *Overseas player.*

BOWLING

	O	*M*	*R*	*W*	*BB*	*5W/i*	*Avge*
D. Follett	115.2	21	458	23	8-22	3	19.91
P. C. R. Tufnell	780.4	259	1,568	72	7-49	5	21.77
J. P. Hewitt	167.3	35	647	21	3-27	0	30.80
A. R. C. Fraser	592.4	138	1,636	49	5-55	2	33.38
R. L. Johnson	242.5	36	878	25	5-29	1	35.12
R. A. Fay	350	82	1,088	30	4-53	0	36.26
P. N. Weekes	322	63	948	25	8-39	1	37.92

Also bowled: K. P. Dutch 23–4–85–3; M. A. Feltham 57–14–185–4; M. W. Gatting 4–0–25–0; D. J. Goodchild 4.5–0–26–0; D. J. Nash 10–1–44–1; J. C. Pooley 4–0–42–0; M. R. Ramprakash 31–4–121–3; U. B. A. Rashid 6–1–17–0; O. A. Shah 5–0–24–1.

COUNTY RECORDS

Highest score for:	331*	J. D. Robertson v Worcestershire at Worcester	1949
Highest score against:	316*	J. B. Hobbs (Surrey) at Lord's	1926
Best bowling for:	10-40	G. O. B. Allen v Lancashire at Lord's	1929
Best bowling against:	9-38	R. C. Robertson-Glasgow (Somerset) at Lord's	1924
Highest total for:	642-3 dec.	v Hampshire at Southampton	1923
Highest total against:	665	by West Indians at Lord's	1939
Lowest total for:	20	v MCC at Lord's	1864
Lowest total against:	31	by Gloucestershire at Bristol	1924

At Oxford, April 20, 22, 23. MIDDLESEX drew with OXFORD UNIVERSITY.

MIDDLESEX v GLOUCESTERSHIRE

At Lord's, May 2, 3, 4. Gloucestershire won by five wickets. Gloucestershire 21 pts, Middlesex 5 pts. Toss: Middlesex. First-class debuts: D. J. Goodchild, U. B. A. Rashid. Championship debut: J. P. Hewitt.

Middlesex have rarely fielded such an inexperienced attack. With Johnson and Feltham injured, Nash still in the West Indies, Tufnell suffering from tonsillitis and Emburey gone to Northamptonshire, Fraser was the only seasoned bowler. Follett had played once in 1995; Rashid, Goodchild and Hewitt had yet to bowl in a first-class game. But Hewitt took a wicket with his opening first-class delivery. This feat was last achieved in England by Jason Gallian of Lancashire in 1990 and in the Championship by Chris Lethbridge of Warwickshire in 1981. Hewitt took another with his first ball next day, when Follett completed a five-wicket haul. Batting was never easy and 14 wickets fell on the first day. But a last-wicket stand of 48 between Davis and Smith gave Gloucestershire a narrow lead. Smith then worked through Middlesex's second innings for eight wickets, a personal best; their last six fell for 25 runs. Wright steered Gloucestershire to their target inside 61 overs, to win with more than a day to spare. It was their first Championship victory at Lord's since 1975.

Close of play: First day, Gloucestershire 94-4 (A. Symonds 42*, M. W. Alleyne 15*); Second day, Middlesex 207-4 (M. W. Gatting 46*, M. R. Ramprakash 15*).

Middlesex

P. N. Weekes lbw b Alleyne	34	– c Davis b Smith	50
J. C. Pooley b Cooper	3	– b Cooper	73
M. R. Ramprakash c Davis b Cooper	7	– (6) c Davis b Smith	34
*M. W. Gatting b Lewis	23	– (3) b Smith	54
J. D. Carr c Russell b Alleyne	48	– (4) b Smith	14
†K. R. Brown c Russell b Cooper	44	– (5) c Hancock b Smith	1
D. J. Goodchild c Davis b Cooper	4	– lbw b Smith	0
J. P. Hewitt lbw b Lewis	15	– b Smith	4
U. B. A. Rashid c Russell b Smith	9	– c Wright b Lewis	6
A. R. C. Fraser c Alleyne b Smith	7	– b Smith	1
D. Follett not out	0	– not out	0
L-b 2, w 2, n-b 2	6	B 1, l-b 4, w 1, n-b 4	10
1/9 2/23 3/66 4/80 5/149 6/163 7/168 8/191 9/197	200	1/124 2/124 3/148 4/150 5/222 6/222 7/228 8/239 9/246	247

Bonus points – Middlesex 1, Gloucestershire 4.

Bowling: *First Innings*—Smith 16.4–1–45–2; Cooper 22–5–54–4; Alleyne 17–3–46–2; Lewis 11–0–53–2. *Second Innings*—Smith 32–10–73–8; Cooper 17–7–28–1; Lewis 25–4–74–1; Alleyne 10–3–21–0; Davis 7–0–39–0; Hancock 2–1–2–0; Symonds 2–0–5–0.

Gloucestershire

A. J. Wright c Weekes b Fraser	0	– c sub b Hewitt	106
R. I. Dawson lbw b Hewitt	7	– c Carr b Fraser	11
R. J. Cunliffe c Brown b Follett	0	– c Brown b Follett	51
T. H. C. Hancock c Brown b Fraser	27	– b Weekes	13
A. Symonds c Carr b Hewitt	42	– c Follett b Hewitt	31
M. W. Alleyne lbw b Fraser	39	– not out	6
*†R. C. Russell c Weekes b Follett	26	– not out	3
R. P. Davis not out	27		
J. Lewis c Carr b Follett	6		
K. E. Cooper b Follett	5		
A. M. Smith b Follett	32		
L-b 3, n-b 4	7	L-b 7, w 1, n-b 2	10
1/0 2/5 3/24 4/50 5/96 6/136 7/150 8/160 9/170	218	1/19 2/127 3/160 4/220 5/223	(5 wkts) 231

Bonus points – Gloucestershire 1, Middlesex 4.

Bowling: *First Innings*—Fraser 17–7–33–3; Follett 18–3–94–5; Hewitt 17–4–77–2; Goodchild 2–0–11–0. *Second Innings*—Fraser 22–4–73–1; Follett 11–1–47–1; Hewitt 13–0–53–2; Rashid 6–1–17–0; Weekes 6–0–19–1; Goodchild 2.5–0–15–0.

Umpires: J. W. Holder and M. J. Kitchen.

MIDDLESEX v DURHAM

At Lord's, May 9, 10, 11, 13. Middlesex won by 306 runs. Middlesex 20 pts, Durham 5 pts. Toss: Middlesex.

David Follett, in his third Championship match, claimed eight for 22, the best figures at Lord's for 20 years, to dismiss Durham for 67, the county's lowest total in their five first-class seasons. He bowled with hostility and accuracy: two middle stumps went cartwheeling and his two lbws included Roseberry with his first delivery of the innings. On the opening day, when 16 wickets fell, another Middlesex seamer, Fay, playing his second first-class game because of Nash's bad back, had taken three in his second over, helping to make up for his team's poor batting. But Roseberry, returning to Lord's for the first time since leaving Middlesex, and Scott enabled Durham to take an 18-run lead. When the home side resumed, however, Weekes and Gatting shared the only three-figure stand of the match, and Gatting reached his 90th hundred, completing his set of centuries against the other 17 first-class counties. Durham's target was 374; thanks to Follett, they fell more than 300 short.

Close of play: First day, Durham 114-6 (M. J. Foster 9*, C. W. Scott 1*); Second day, Middlesex 167-3 (M. W. Gatting 54*, R. A. Fay 5*); Third day, Middlesex 391.

Middlesex

P. N. Weekes lbw b Brown	19	– c Scott b Foster	73
J. C. Pooley b Betts	1	– c Campbell b Brown	23
M. R. Ramprakash c Scott b Betts	6	– b Foster	9
*M. W. Gatting run out	74	– b Betts	171
J. D. Carr c Collingwood b Foster	16	– (6) lbw b Collingwood	23
†K. R. Brown lbw b Foster	32	– (7) lbw b Betts	1
R. L. Johnson b Betts	9	– (8) c Daley b Betts	35
A. R. C. Fraser c Roseberry b Foster	10	– (9) lbw b Brown	2
R. A. Fay c Campbell b Foster	0	– (5) run out	18
P. C. R. Tufnell c Campbell b Brown	2	– c Scott b Betts	11
D. Follett not out	0	– not out	5
L-b 10, n-b 12	22	B 6, l-b 7, w 3, n-b 4	20
1/2 2/20 3/34 4/94 5/156 6/169 7/186 8/186 9/191	191	1/27 2/52 3/153 4/229 5/296 6/297 7/365 8/374 9/374	391

Bonus points – Durham 4.

Bowling: *First Innings*—Brown 14–2–53–2; Betts 20–5–78–3; Foster 10.3–4–21–4; Collingwood 3–1–9–0; Boiling 8–2–20–0. *Second Innings*—Brown 42–8–115–2; Betts 28.1–5–101–4; Foster 30–5–117–2; Boiling 11–3–23–0; Collingwood 10–1–22–1.

Durham

*M. A. Roseberry lbw b Follett	43	– (2) lbw b Follett	5
S. L. Campbell c Ramprakash b Fay	13	– (1) b Follett	23
S. Hutton lbw b Fay	0	– c Carr b Follett	7
J. E. Morris c Carr b Fay	0	– c Gatting b Tufnell	3
P. D. Collingwood lbw b Fraser	7	– lbw b Follett	0
J. A. Daley b Johnson	34	– c Brown b Follett	3
M. J. Foster b Fraser	9	– b Follett	3
†C. W. Scott c Pooley b Fraser	59	– c Weekes b Follett	9
J. Boiling c Carr b Johnson	14	– b Fraser	6
S. J. E. Brown b Follett	15	– not out	0
M. M. Betts not out	8	– c Brown b Follett	1
L-b 5, n-b 2	7	L-b 5, n-b 2	7
1/30 2/30 3/30 4/41 5/88 6/109 7/114 8/148 9/177	209	1/19 2/36 3/41 4/41 5/41 6/46 7/49 8/62 9/66	67

Bonus points – Durham 1, Middlesex 4.

Bowling: *First Innings*—Fraser 23.2–5–47–3; Johnson 11–3–47–2; Fay 16–4–33–3; Follett 14–2–65–2; Weekes 6–4–10–0; Tufnell 4–3–2–0. *Second Innings*—Fraser 10–3–20–1; Fay 8–2–12–0; Follett 12.2–3–22–8; Tufnell 6–1–8–1.

Umpires: A. Clarkson and J. H. Harris.

At Cambridge, May 16, 17, 18. MIDDLESEX drew with CAMBRIDGE UNIVERSITY.

At Lord's, May 19. MIDDLESEX lost to INDIANS on scoring-rate (See Indian tour section).

At Horsham, May 22, 23, 24, 25. MIDDLESEX lost to SUSSEX by 234 runs.

MIDDLESEX v YORKSHIRE

At Lord's, May 30, 31, June 1, 3. Middlesex won by 21 runs. Middlesex 24 pts, Yorkshire 4 pts. Toss: Middlesex. Championship debut: J. C. Harrison.

Yorkshire struggled for two days, rallied on the third and looked like winning on the fourth; victory would have made them Championship leaders. But they lost their last six wickets in 34 balls. A persevering Fraser and an aggressive Tufnell struck home, a direct hit from Ramprakash at cover point ran out last man Stemp, and Middlesex won with ten balls to spare. If Bevan, who made a superb 107, had remained, or if rain had not robbed Yorkshire of three vital overs in the late afternoon, it might have been different. In the first innings, Ramprakash finally rediscovered his form of 1995, scoring his first century of the season, Carr just missed his, and last pair Follett and Tufnell hit 45 in 49 balls. At the second-day close, Yorkshire were 262 behind and nine down – five of them to Follett. But Hartley and Stemp survived another 100 minutes on Saturday morning, taking their stand to 113. Gatting waived the follow-on and gave Yorkshire just over a day to make 344; at times, that looked too generous.

Close of play: First day, Middlesex 322-5 (J. D. Carr 58*, K. R. Brown 33*); Second day, Yorkshire 185-9 (P. J. Hartley 34*, R. D. Stemp 2*); Third day, Yorkshire 14-0 (A. McGrath 12*, M. P. Vaughan 2*).

Middlesex

P. N. Weekes c Blakey b Hartley	1	– c Byas b Silverwood	15
J. C. Pooley b Gough	28	– c McGrath b Silverwood	9
J. C. Harrison c Blakey b White	37	– c Blakey b Stemp	17
M. R. Ramprakash b Hartley	134	– not out	60
*M. W. Gatting b Silverwood	17		
J. D. Carr c Morris b White	94	– (5) c Blakey b Stemp	0
†K. R. Brown c Blakey b Silverwood	49	– (6) not out	60
R. A. Fay c Blakey b Hartley	1		
D. Follett c Blakey b Silverwood	17		
A. R. C. Fraser lbw b White	15		
P. C. R. Tufnell not out	30		
L-b 8, n-b 16	24	B 5, l-b 3, n-b 2	10
1/5 2/35 3/135 4/182 5/265 6/348 7/379 8/379 9/402	447	1/16 2/25 3/52 4/54	(4 wkts dec.) 171

Bonus points – Middlesex 4, Yorkshire 2 (Score at 120 overs: 365-6).

Bowling: *First Innings*—Gough 32–7–81–1; Hartley 26–9–63–3; Silverwood 25.4–7–91–3; White 25–3–111–3; Morris 8–2–30–0; Stemp 21–6–53–0; Bevan 2–0–10–0. *Second Innings*—Gough 12–5–11–0; Hartley 10–0–36–0; Stemp 25.1–6–68–2; Silverwood 12–1–34–2; White 4–0–14–0.

Yorkshire

A. McGrath c Harrison b Follett	27	– lbw b Fay	12
M. P. Vaughan c Brown b Follett	0	– b Tufnell	67
*D. Byas c Brown b Fay	30	– b Follett	33
M. G. Bevan c Carr b Tufnell	31	– c Brown b Fraser	107
C. White b Tufnell	29	– c Harrison b Fraser	39
†R. J. Blakey c Tufnell b Follett	8	– c Pooley b Tufnell	19
A. C. Morris c Brown b Follett	0	– (9) b Tufnell	3
D. Gough b Follett	9	– c Pooley b Fraser	10
P. J. Hartley not out	88	– (7) c Ramprakash b Tufnell	12
C. E. W. Silverwood b Tufnell	1	– not out	0
R. D. Stemp c and b Fay	22	– run out	0
B 2, l-b 11, w 1, n-b 16	30	B 3, l-b 13, n-b 4	20
1/2 2/51 3/78 4/106 5/134 6/134 7/136 8/151 9/162	275	1/14 2/71 3/165 4/260 5/294 6/294 7/310 8/322 9/322	322

Bonus points – Yorkshire 2, Middlesex 4.

Bowling: *First Innings*—Fraser 20–6–50–0; Follett 26–4–99–5; Tufnell 29–9–73–3; Fay 16–1–40–2. *Second Innings*—Fraser 29.2–7–92–3; Follett 10–2–32–1; Fay 11–2–51–1; Tufnell 43–13–106–4; Weekes 6–2–25–0.

Umpires: J. C. Balderstone and A. A. Jones.

MIDDLESEX v GLAMORGAN

At Lord's, June 6, 7, 8. Middlesex won by nine wickets. Middlesex 23 pts, Glamorgan 5 pts. Toss: Glamorgan. Championship debut: A. W. Evans.

Weekes won the match with a dazzling all-round performance on the third day. First, he took a career-best eight for 39 with his off-spin, ending in a spell of five for seven in 34 balls as Glamorgan crashed from 119 for four to 141 all out. Then, with Middlesex needing 45 to win, he smashed 40 off 30 balls, completing victory half an hour after tea with his second six. It was the seamers who did the damage in Glamorgan's first innings: with Follett injured, Fay and Hewitt showed their worth as support for Fraser. Butcher made Glamorgan's only significant contribution, scoring his fifth half-century in as many matches. Middlesex looked uncertain at 92 for four. Then Ramprakash showed his stubborn streak, occupying the crease for nearly four and a half hours. Another off-spinner, Croft, claimed six, but a last-wicket stand of 47 on Saturday morning gave the home side a lead of 97 before Weekes's *tour de force*.

Close of play: First day, Middlesex 25-2 (R. A. Fay 5*, J. C. Harrison 0*); Second day, Middlesex 288-9 (A. R. C. Fraser 3*).

Glamorgan

S. P. James c Weekes b Hewitt	16	– lbw b Tufnell	33
A. W. Evans c Weekes b Fay	12	– c Brown b Weekes	27
G. P. Butcher c Brown b Fay	63	– b Weekes	8
*M. P. Maynard c Brown b Hewitt	11	– c Carr b Weekes	2
P. A. Cottey c Brown b Fay	7	– c Brown b Weekes	22
R. D. B. Croft c Brown b Fraser	28	– c Carr b Weekes	19
†A. D. Shaw c Brown b Fraser	38	– not out	9
S. D. Thomas c Weekes b Fay	48	– b Weekes	4
N. M. Kendrick c Pooley b Fraser	0	– c Brown b Weekes	0
S. L. Watkin not out	3	– b Weekes	0
S. R. Barwick c Gatting b Hewitt	1	– c Hewitt b Tufnell	6
L-b 6, w 1, n-b 4	11	B 2, l-b 9	11
1/26 2/38 3/58 4/68 5/128 6/143 7/229 8/229 9/237	238	1/60 2/64 3/69 4/84 5/119 6/120 7/124 8/126 9/130	141

Bonus points – Glamorgan 1, Middlesex 4.

Bowling: *First Innings*—Fraser 24–9–60–3; Fay 18–5–53–4; Hewitt 11.1–0–56–3; Tufnell 28–9–49–0; Weekes 10–5–14–0. *Second Innings*—Fraser 11–4–26–0; Fay 4–1–15–0; Hewitt 2–0–11–0; Tufnell 25.2–7–39–2; Weekes 20–5–39–8.

Middlesex

P. N. Weekes b Croft	15	– not out	40
J. C. Pooley c James b Thomas	1	– c Barwick b Croft	0
R. A. Fay c Cottey b Butcher	26		
J. C. Harrison c Maynard b Croft	35	– (3) not out	3
M. R. Ramprakash c Shaw b Watkin	97		
*M. W. Gatting c Shaw b Watkin	19		
J. D. Carr st Shaw b Croft	49		
†K. R. Brown c Cottey b Croft	25		
J. P. Hewitt lbw b Croft	4		
A. R. C. Fraser c Kendrick b Croft	33		
P. C. R. Tufnell not out	16		
L-b 12, w 1, n-b 2	15	L-b 1, w 1	2
1/11 2/25 3/67 4/92 5/119 6/248 7/266 8/281 9/288	335	1/13	(1 wkt) 45

Bonus points – Middlesex 3, Glamorgan 4 (Score at 120 overs: 304-9).

Bowling: *First Innings*—Watkin 33–9–89–2; Thomas 21–4–43–1; Croft 31.2–5–88–6; Barwick 20–5–47–0; Butcher 12–6–27–1; Kendrick 8–1–29–0. *Second Innings*—Thomas 3–0–16–0; Croft 5–2–8–1; Kendrick 2.3–0–20–0.

Umpires: J. H. Hampshire and K. E. Palmer.

At Canterbury, June 13, 14, 15, 17. MIDDLESEX drew with KENT.

At Derby, June 20, 21, 22, 24. MIDDLESEX lost to DERBYSHIRE by 363 runs.

MIDDLESEX v WARWICKSHIRE

At Lord's, June 27, 28, 29, July 1. Drawn. Middlesex 8 pts, Warwickshire 10 pts. Toss: Middlesex. First-class debut: M. D. Edmond.

Warwickshire had lost their last two Championship matches, and their approach to this game made it clear they did not intend to lose a third. In any case, frequent showers on the second and fourth days increased the difficulty of engineering a result on an easy-paced pitch. A mid-innings slump slowed Middlesex, but Ramprakash batted for over six and a half hours, hitting a six and 17 fours, before falling to Ostler's fourth excellent catch at second slip. Pollock, in his first match at Lord's, took six for 56, his best Championship performance yet. It highlighted Middlesex's misfortune with their own overseas player, Nash, who was released the day before this match, having played only two games all season because of a bad back. Acting-captain Moles outdid Ramprakash by occupying the crease for nearly seven and a half hours and added 235 with Penney. He declared 32 ahead on the final morning, too late to make much difference.

Close of play: First day, Middlesex 311-5 (M. R. Ramprakash 164*, K. R. Brown 60*); Second day, Warwickshire 76-1 (A. J. Moles 35*, W. G. Khan 4*); Third day, Warwickshire 388-5 (D. R. Brown 7*, S. M. Pollock 4*).

Middlesex

P. N. Weekes c Ostler b Pollock	42	– lbw b Edmond	42
J. C. Harrison lbw b Pollock	5	– lbw b Small	0
M. R. Ramprakash c Ostler b Pollock	169	– (4) not out	22
*M. W. Gatting c Ostler b Pollock	1		
J. D. Carr c Penney b Pollock	2		
J. C. Pooley c Ostler b P. A. Smith	5	– (3) b Small	12
†K. R. Brown c Burns b Brown	79		
R. L. Johnson lbw b Brown	15	– (5) not out	37
R. A. Fay not out	25		
A. R. C. Fraser c Burns b Brown	17		
P. C. R. Tufnell b Pollock	8		
B 5, l-b 24, w 4, n-b 12	45	B 5, l-b 1, w 1, n-b 2	9
1/13 2/94 3/114 4/124 5/138 6/322 7/351 8/376 9/398	413	1/0 2/56 3/63 (3 wkts)	122

Bonus points – Middlesex 4, Warwickshire 3 (Score at 120 overs: 370-7).

Bowling: *First Innings*—Pollock 28.4–9–56–6; Small 26–6–72–0; Edmond 16–1–73–0; Brown 33–7–93–3; P. A. Smith 20–3–58–1; N. M. K. Smith 8–1–32–0. *Second Innings*—Pollock 8–2–13–0; Small 7–0–37–2; N. M. K. Smith 7.1–2–33–0; Brown 10–2–26–0; Edmond 0.5–0–6–1; Khan 2–1–1–0.

Warwickshire

*A. J. Moles c Brown b Tufnell	176
N. M. K. Smith lbw b Tufnell	31
W. G. Khan c Harrison b Tufnell	17
D. P. Ostler lbw b Tufnell	17
T. L. Penney b Johnson	101
D. R. Brown b Fay	14
S. M. Pollock c Brown b Fraser	10
†M. Burns c Fraser b Tufnell	11
P. A. Smith c Tufnell b Fraser	21
M. D. Edmond not out	8
G. C. Small not out	2
B 1, l-b 24, n-b 12	37
1/60 2/96 3/142 4/377 5/377 6/401 7/401 8/432 9/437 (9 wkts dec.)	445

Bonus points – Warwickshire 4, Middlesex 1 (Score at 120 overs: 361-3).

Bowling: Fraser 30.2–6–109–2; Fay 29–8–86–1; Johnson 23–2–109–1; Tufnell 46–17–71–5; Ramprakash 1–0–2–0; Weekes 11–2–43–0.

Umpires: J. C. Balderstone and B. J. Meyer.

At The Oval, July 4, 5, 6, 8. MIDDLESEX lost to SURREY by seven wickets.

At Northampton, July 18, 19, 20, 22. MIDDLESEX beat NORTHAMPTONSHIRE by 26 runs.

MIDDLESEX v ESSEX

At Lord's, August 1, 2, 3. Essex won by an innings and 51 runs. Essex 24 pts, Middlesex 5 pts. Toss: Middlesex.

The fragility of the Middlesex batting was cruelly exposed, particularly by Ilott, who dismissed Weekes and Ramprakash without a run on the board in both innings; the two batsmen faced a total of 17 deliveries in the match. Although there was some kind of recovery in the first innings, there was no coming back in the second, when only Wellings – whose method and concentration looked promising – and Hewitt reached 20. Gooch batted magnificently and the only surprise was that he fell eight short of his century; in three hours, he had struck two sixes and 13 fours and, when 22, he overtook Keith Fletcher as Essex's leading run-scorer. He ended the match on 29,505. Grayson did reach his hundred, a career-best 140. Cowan also improved on his previous best with the ball in both innings, to back up Ilott and complete victory with a day to spare. Middlesex's acting-captain, Carr, announced on the opening day that he would retire at the end of the season to become cricket operations manager for the TCCB's successor body, the ECB.

Close of play: First day, Essex 32-0 (G. A. Gooch 11*, A. P. Grayson 15*); Second day, Essex 385-5 (P. J. Prichard 67*, R. J. Rollins 1*).

Middlesex

P. N. Weekes c Rollins b Ilott	0	– c Gooch b Ilott	0
J. C. Pooley c Gooch b Irani	50	– b Williams	15
M. R. Ramprakash lbw b Ilott	0	– lbw b Ilott	0
*J. D. Carr c Gooch b Cowan	66	– c Rollins b Cowan	17
P. E. Wellings c Grayson b Williams	19	– c Williams b Cowan	23
†K. R. Brown not out	64	– lbw b Irani	6
J. P. Hewitt c Law b Cowan	27	– b Cowan	27
R. L. Johnson c Rollins b Cowan	5	– c Such b Irani	5
R. A. Fay c Such b Cowan	2	– (11) c Rollins b Cowan	0
A. R. C. Fraser c Prichard b Ilott	3	– (9) c Prichard b Irani	4
P. C. R. Tufnell c Such b Ilott	6	– (10) not out	16
L-b 6, n-b 16	22	L-b 2, n-b 6	8
1/0 2/0 3/106 4/136 5/184 6/212 7/234 8/242 9/258	264	1/0 2/0 3/20 4/48 5/63 6/74 7/88 8/92 9/105	121

Bonus points – Middlesex 2, Essex 4.

In the first innings P. E. Wellings, when 4, retired hurt at 123 and resumed at 184.

Bowling: *First Innings*—Ilott 22.4–11–47–4; Williams 20–4–78–1; Irani 15–5–34–1; Cowan 21–2–76–4; Law 14–9–14–0; Such 2–0–9–0. *Second Innings*—Ilott 7–2–16–2; Williams 6–1–39–1; Irani 13–4–29–3; Cowan 12.3–2–35–4.

Essex

G. A. Gooch c Brown b Weekes	92
A. P. Grayson c Brown b Fraser	140
N. Hussain c Hewitt b Tufnell	35
S. G. Law c sub b Fraser	9
*P. J. Prichard c Brown b Johnson	67
R. C. Irani lbw b Fraser	9
†R. J. Rollins c Weekes b Johnson	10
M. C. Ilott c Brown b Fraser	1
N. F. Williams c Ramprakash b Tufnell	13
A. P. Cowan c and b Tufnell	24
P. M. Such not out	1
L-b 20, w 1, n-b 14	35
1/171 2/222 3/243 4/358 5/380 6/385 7/396 8/396 9/433	436

Bonus points – Essex 4, Middlesex 3 (Score at 120 overs: 419-8).

Bowling: Fraser 40–6–122–4; Johnson 23–3–96–2; Hewitt 17–3–101–0; Tufnell 39.4–21–53–3; Weekes 8–0–44–1.

Umpires: B. Leadbeater and B. J. Meyer.

At Nottingham, August 8, 9, 10. MIDDLESEX beat NOTTINGHAMSHIRE by an innings and seven runs.

MIDDLESEX v WORCESTERSHIRE

At Lord's, August 15, 16, 17, 19. Drawn. Middlesex 9 pts, Worcestershire 11 pts. Toss: Middlesex.

For three of the four days, this was Championship cricket at its best; two teams playing positively and the game tilting one way and then the other. It ended with Middlesex needing nine runs and Worcestershire one wicket for victory. Unfortunately, the second day seemed like something out of another game, with only 208 scored off 105 overs. At its close, Middlesex were 202 behind with four wickets left and risked following on. But next morning Tufnell made 67 not out, his maiden half-century, with 15 fours. He and Carr added an unbroken 101 – only the second century last-wicket partnership for Middlesex since the war. That enabled Gatting to declare 17 behind. Curtis then scored a five-and-a-half-hour hundred and Middlesex were left to get 251 in 49 overs, which could have been more had Worcestershire not slowed things down. When they realised they might win, the over-rate suddenly improved, too late; Hewitt survived the loss of four partners to earn the draw.

Close of play: First day, Worcestershire 328-7 (S. R. Lampitt 17*, R. K. Illingworth 0*); Second day, Middlesex 167-6 (J. D. Carr 14*, R. L. Johnson 0*); Third day, Worcestershire 89-4 (T. S. Curtis 43*, S. W. K. Ellis 3*).

Worcestershire

T. S. Curtis lbw b Fay	14	– c Fraser b Weekes	118
W. P. C. Weston c Brown b Fraser	59	– c Gatting b Tufnell	12
G. A. Hick lbw b Fay	0	– c Brown b Tufnell	7
*T. M. Moody c Pooley b Hewitt	124	– b Hewitt	1
K. R. Spiring c Fay b Tufnell	19	– c Pooley b Weekes	12
V. S. Solanki c Brown b Fraser	69	– (7) c Fraser b Tufnell	26
†S. J. Rhodes lbw b Tufnell	15	– (8) c Pooley b Weekes	1
S. R. Lampitt lbw b Hewitt	30	– (9) not out	22
R. K. Illingworth c Carr b Fraser	12	– (10) not out	2
S. W. K. Ellis b Hewitt	10	– (6) c Pooley b Tufnell	15
A. Sheriyar not out	2		
L-b 11, n-b 4	15	B 2, l-b 7, n-b 8	17
1/19 2/19 3/113 4/150 5/281 6/300 7/328 8/345 9/365	369	1/28 2/40 3/47 4/85 5/118 6/164 7/179 8/224 (8 wkts dec.)	233

Bonus points – Worcestershire 4, Middlesex 3 (Score at 120 overs: 355-8).

Bowling: *First Innings*—Fraser 33.5–8–69–3; Fay 27–7–70–2; Johnson 11–0–70–0; Hewitt 23–5–73–3; Tufnell 26–11–48–2; Weekes 6–0–28–0. *Second Innings*—Fraser 8–3–11–0; Fay 3–0–9–0; Tufnell 47–17–72–4; Hewitt 8–4–17–1; Johnson 5–2–12–0; Weekes 29–2–103–3.

Middlesex

P. N. Weekes c Hick b Sheriyar	0	– b Hick	37
J. C. Pooley c Weston b Illingworth	45	– lbw b Solanki	87
M. R. Ramprakash c Hick b Illingworth	64	– b Solanki	10
*M. W. Gatting b Lampitt	25	– b Solanki	0
J. D. Carr not out	66	– (6) run out	14
†K. R. Brown c Spiring b Lampitt	0	– (5) c Lampitt b Solanki	30
J. P. Hewitt lbw b Illingworth	10	– not out	14
R. L. Johnson c Weston b Illingworth	9	– c Curtis b Illingworth	28
R. A. Fay c Weston b Illingworth	14	– (10) run out	3
A. R. C. Fraser c Illingworth b Ellis	29	– (9) st Rhodes b Solanki	3
P. C. R. Tufnell not out	67	– not out	1
B 2, l-b 14, w 5, n-b 2	23	B 5, l-b 2, w 2, n-b 6	15
1/0 2/83 3/133 4/142 5/142 6/167 7/185 8/211 9/251 (9 wkts dec.)	352	1/100 2/134 3/134 4/155 5/185 6/192 7/225 8/238 9/241 (9 wkts)	242

Bonus points – Middlesex 3, Worcestershire 4 (Score at 120 overs: 302-9).

Bowling: *First Innings*—Sheriyar 24–4–53–1; Ellis 11–1–39–1; Moody 12–0–52–0; Lampitt 31.4–7–87–2; Illingworth 47–15–85–5; Solanki 11–4–20–0. *Second Innings*—Sheriyar 6–0–19–0; Ellis 3–0–17–0; Illingworth 14–0–57–1; Lampitt 8–0–42–0; Hick 7–1–31–1; Solanki 11–1–69–5.

Umpires: J. H. Harris and R. Julian.

At Portsmouth, August 28, 29, 30, 31. MIDDLESEX beat HAMPSHIRE by 188 runs.

At Manchester, September 3, 4, 5. MIDDLESEX beat LANCASHIRE by 23 runs.

MIDDLESEX v SOMERSET

At Uxbridge, September 12, 13, 14, 16. Drawn. Middlesex 9 pts, Somerset 7 pts. Toss: Somerset.

This match boiled up to an excellent climax, but the first three days were ruined by a pitch that made batting far too easy. As Angus Fraser grumbled: "If 15 wickets fall in a day, the pitch is reported. If only five fall, nothing is said. It definitely is a batsman's game." Despite the favourable conditions, Somerset scored at less than three an over on the first day and Holloway took eight and a half hours over his 168. The match fell so far behind schedule that Somerset were using occasional bowlers on the third day to get Middlesex towards maximum batting points so they could declare behind. That set up a fine finish after the captains agreed Middlesex should chase 394 in 84 overs. Weekes seemed unstoppable, making 331 in the match before being out, and Ramprakash also reached a hundred. At 297 for one Middlesex looked like winning, but the middle order were too impatient, and in the end Somerset were on the attack.

Close of play: First day, Somerset 289-5 (P. C. L. Holloway 109*, A. C. Cottam 3*); Second day, Middlesex 113-2 (P. N. Weekes 51*, O. A. Shah 27*); Third day, Somerset 211-3 (P. C. L. Holloway 68*, K. A. Parsons 59*).

Somerset

*P. D. Bowler c Shah b Fraser	12	lbw b Tufnell	22
M. E. Trescothick c Brown b Tufnell	27	b Tufnell	44
P. C. L. Holloway c Tufnell b Johnson	168	not out	90
R. J. Harden c Brown b Hewitt	20	c Dutch b Shah	12
K. A. Parsons c Dutch b Johnson	72	not out	83
S. Lee b Dutch	44		
A. C. Cottam c Brown b Johnson	3		
†R. J. Turner c and b Hewitt	75		
J. I. D. Kerr not out	32		
A. R. Caddick c Tufnell b Dutch	26		
K. J. Shine b Dutch	0		
B 2, l-b 4	6	L-b 5, n-b 2	7
1/26 2/42 3/77 4/207 5/283 6/289 7/416 8/432 9/485	485	1/55 2/84 3/112 (3 wkts dec.)	258

Bonus points – Somerset 3, Middlesex 2 (Score at 120 overs: 334-6).

Bowling: *First Innings*—Fraser 29–4–96–1; Johnson 30–5–89–3; Hewitt 33–8–118–2; Tufnell 45–19–86–1; Weekes 28–4–65–0; Dutch 7–2–25–3. *Second Innings*—Fraser 4–2–11–0; Johnson 3–1–8–0; Tufnell 18–5–46–2; Dutch 16–2–60–0; Ramprakash 11–0–62–0; Shah 5–0–24–1; Pooley 4–0–42–0.

Middlesex

P. N. Weekes not out	171	b Caddick	160
J. C. Pooley c Turner b Shine	0	st Turner b Cottam	41
M. R. Ramprakash c and b Shine	26	c Turner b Kerr	110
O. A. Shah c Caddick b Lee	75	(6) c Trescothick b Cottam	2
†K. R. Brown not out	56	c Lee b Kerr	11
*M. W. Gatting (did not bat)		(4) run out	5
K. P. Dutch (did not bat)		b Caddick	4
R. L. Johnson (did not bat)		run out	2
A. R. C. Fraser (did not bat)		not out	4
P. C. R. Tufnell (did not bat)		not out	0
B 2, l-b 9, w 1, n-b 10	22	B 1, l-b 14, w 1, n-b 2	18
1/8 2/62 3/206 (3 wkts dec.)	350	1/100 2/297 3/314 4/332 5/335 6/343 7/349 8/357 (8 wkts)	357

J. P. Hewitt did not bat.

Bonus points – Middlesex 4, Somerset 1.

Bowling: *First Innings*—Caddick 18–3–72–0; Shine 16–8–36–2; Kerr 11–2–37–0; Cottam 27–10–61–0; Lee 12–1–35–1; Bowler 6–0–42–0; Trescothick 5–0–20–0; Parsons 2–0–12–0; Holloway 2.2–0–21–0; Harden 1–0–3–0. *Second Innings*—Caddick 15–4–49–2; Shine 11–0–59–0; Cottam 29–1–127–2; Lee 14–1–62–0; Kerr 15–2–45–2.

Umpires: H. D. Bird and K. J. Lyons.

At Leicester, September 19, 20, 21, 22. MIDDLESEX lost to LEICESTERSHIRE by an innings and 74 runs.

David Sales

NORTHAMPTONSHIRE

Patrons: The Earl of Dalkeith and
The Earl Spencer
President: A. P. Arnold
Chairman: L. A. Wilson
Chairman, Cricket Committee: R. Wills
Chief Executive: S. P. Coverdale
Captain: R. J. Bailey
Coach: J. E. Emburey
Cricket Development Officer: B. L. Reynolds
Head Groundsman: D. Bates
Scorer: A. C. Kingston

For Northamptonshire, adjusting to Life After Lamb, another "not quite" season in the limited-overs competitions demonstrated that the retirement of the former captain had not changed everything at Wantage Road. Altogether less familiar, though, was the county's "nowhere near" showing in the County Championship, following four successive top five finishes.

The new leadership team of Rob Bailey and chief coach John Emburey saw all their hopes of success at Lord's disappear in the space of four days, Lancashire inflicting a one-wicket defeat in the NatWest Trophy second round at Old Trafford and then a more emphatic one at Lord's in the final of the Benson and Hedges Cup. That left the Sunday League, in which Northamptonshire won their first six matches. They led the table by two points after beating Leicestershire on August 4, but lost three of the remaining five games, including the crucial one against eventual winners Surrey on the penultimate Sunday, and finished sixth, out of the prize money.

The Championship campaign, in contrast, was depressing almost throughout. Just three victories, all at Northampton, left the side 16th, Northamptonshire's lowest placing for 18 years. Particularly frustrating for Bailey, who missed six matches in the second half with a damaged wrist, was the encouraging way in which they ended the programme. Lancashire were well beaten, and Yorkshire denied a likely win by an opening partnership of 372 between Richard Montgomerie and Mal Loye, who set a county first-wicket record when they followed on. The captain was left to reflect sorrowfully on what might have been, had they performed to that level in May and June.

No fewer than 24 players appeared for Northamptonshire in the Championship, the most since Robert Nelson called on 25 in 1938 when the county took the wooden spoon for the fifth year running. From the second match onwards, at least one team change was made for each succeeding fixture – often two or three, and once as many as six. Only two men, Tony Penberthy and Paul Taylor, were ever-present. With this lack of continuity, the disappointing results were hardly a surprise. Injuries, illness and England Under-19 calls on David Roberts, David Sales and Alec Swann, a trio of highly talented batsmen, were partly to blame. It was, however, difficult to escape the conclusion that Bailey and Emburey, both still developing their day-to-day management skills, were unclear about what Northamptonshire's first-choice side should be.

The season was just about summed up by the way the form of Kevin Curran, the club's undisputed player of the year, complicated the selection process further. Curran held the batting together, scoring 1,242 runs and enjoying a remarkably consistent spell from mid-June to late August when, in 15 Championship innings, he was not dismissed for less than 40. But his bowling deteriorated to such an extent that he could be picked only as a specialist batsman. That meant rethinking yet again the balance of the attack and, therefore, of the side.

Allan Lamb had announced his decision to retire at the end of March, a year earlier than planned, thus avoiding TCCB censorship of his forthcoming book, which discussed the sensitive topic of the Pakistanis' previous tour. The news reached the players on their pre-season trip to Johannesburg. The loss of Lamb and Anil Kumble, the principal architects of the county's spectacular season in 1995, was always likely to create a void in the short term. Curran apart, no one approached Lamb's ability to score runs in bulk and quickly, although Sales made the grandest of entrances with a double-century on first-class debut and, aged 18, looked a player who would excite crowds for many years to come.

Loye had more reason than most to feel aggrieved at his treatment, particularly on losing his place to vice-captain Alan Fordham – who endured a wretched season – for the Benson and Hedges final. A tougher individual than he is sometimes given credit for, Loye bounced back strongly, and gave a timely reminder of his class during the long, match-saving stand with Montgomerie against Yorkshire. Russell Warren began well, with an unbeaten 201 off Glamorgan, but lost form when obliged to take over the wicket-keeping from David Ripley in June, and then had his season curtailed by a fractured thumb. Montgomerie's Championship return fell short of expectations, although he blossomed in the shorter game and played several important limited-overs innings, proving his adaptability.

When it came to dismissing the opposition, much depended on Curtly Ambrose on his return from the West Indies. In nine matches, he claimed 43 wickets at a healthy strike rate of one every 40 balls, and he headed the national averages. But fitness problems greatly reduced his overall value to the club. Although they considered giving him another contract, it was no shock when Pakistan's Mohammad Akram – Ambrose's junior by eleven years – was signed for 1997.

Taylor was obliged to bear a heavy workload and did so admirably, sending down more than 750 overs in all competitions and securing 64 Championship wickets. No one else passed 50. Penberthy, who enhanced his reputation with bat and ball, and David Capel lent useful support, and Kevin Innes made the most of his opportunity at the end of the season, producing an impressive all-round display against Lancashire. David Follett, signed from Middlesex, should provide an extra option in 1997. In the spin department, Emburey struggled to combine his twin roles as player and coach, and was more effective in one-day than four-day cricket. Jeremy Snape did not develop as fast as he might have done, and the leg-spinner Andy Roberts was released at the end of the year, but much was hoped of slow left-armer Michael Davies who, after joining the county in July, helped the Second Eleven clinch runners-up spot in their Championship for the second season in a row, taking 28 wickets in six games.

In another significant personnel change, 24-year-old David Bates from Harrogate replaced Ray Bailey as head groundsman in October, Bailey stepping down after 11 years in the post. So the process of renewal at Northampton, both on and off the field, continues. – ANDREW RADD.

NORTHAMPTONSHIRE 1996

[*Bill Smith*

Back row: J. N. Snape, J. A. North, S. A. J. Boswell, T. C. Walton, J. F. Brown, K. J. Innes, A. R. Roberts. *Middle row:* N. A. Foster (*development coach*), A. L. Penberthy, J. G. Hughes, R. J. Warren, K. M. Curran, J. P. Taylor, M. B. Loye, R. R. Montgomerie, K. Russell (*physiotherapist*). *Front row:* N. A. Mallender, D. J. Capel, A. Fordham, R. J. Bailey (*captain*), J. E. Emburey (*player/coach*), N. G. B. Cook, D. Ripley. *Inset:* C. E. L. Ambrose.

NORTHAMPTONSHIRE RESULTS

All first-class matches – Played 19: Won 3, Lost 8, Drawn 8.

County Championship matches – Played 17: Won 3, Lost 8, Drawn 6.

Competition placings – Britannic Assurance County Championship, 16th; NatWest Trophy, 2nd round; Benson and Hedges Cup, finalists; AXA Equity & Law League, 6th.

COUNTY CHAMPIONSHIP AVERAGES

BATTING

Cap		*M*	*I*	*NO*	*R*	*HS*	*100s*	*50s*	*Avge*	*Ct/St*
1992	K. M. Curran	15	28	7	1,242	150	2	8	59.14	14
1987	D. Ripley	9	14	6	412	88*	0	3	51.50	22
1994	M. B. Loye†	12	22	1	974	205	2	4	46.38	4
	D. J. Sales	4	8	1	280	210*	1	0	40.00	4
1985	R. J. Bailey	11	20	2	686	163	1	3	38.11	7
	D. J. Roberts	3	6	0	182	73	0	1	30.33	0
1995	R. J. Warren†	10	17	1	485	201*	1	1	30.31	18/1
1995	R. R. Montgomerie	15	29	3	774	127	2	4	29.76	12
1986	D. J. Capel†	15	28	1	803	103	1	4	29.74	12
	T. C. Walton	5	9	0	247	58	0	3	27.44	2
1994	A. L. Penberthy	17	28	4	628	87	0	3	26.16	9
1990	A. Fordham	9	16	2	321	53	0	2	22.92	8
	J. E. Emburey	11	13	4	200	67*	0	1	22.22	6
	K. J. Innes†	4	5	0	108	63	0	1	21.60	3
	J. N. Snape	8	13	2	201	37	0	0	18.27	3
	A. R. Roberts†	5	8	0	141	39	0	0	17.62	1
1992	J. P. Taylor	17	23	9	242	57	0	1	17.28	3
1990	C. E. L. Ambrose§	9	13	2	116	25*	0	0	10.54	11
	A. J. Swann†	2	4	0	24	14	0	0	6.00	0

Also batted: T. M. B. Bailey† (2 matches) 31*, 2 (4 ct); S. A. J. Boswell (1 match) 1, 2*; J. F. Brown (1 match) 0* (1 ct); J. G. Hughes† (1 match) 8 (1 ct); N. A. Mallender (1 match) 13, 11 (1 ct).

* *Signifies not out.* † *Born in Northamptonshire.* § *Overseas player.*

BOWLING

	O	*M*	*R*	*W*	*BB*	*5W/i*	*Avge*
C. E. L. Ambrose	284.4	80	717	43	6-26	5	16.67
J. P. Taylor	549.2	116	1,766	64	7-88	3	27.59
A. L. Penberthy	352.2	68	1,077	34	5-92	1	31.67
D. J. Capel	324	55	1,087	30	3-31	0	36.23
J. E. Emburey	396.2	94	1,042	27	4-48	0	38.59
J. N. Snape	257.1	50	841	19	4-42	0	44.26
K. M. Curran	180	34	641	11	3-75	0	58.27

Also bowled: R. J. Bailey 48.3–6–145–1; S. A. J. Boswell 23.4–4–67–1; J. F. Brown 22–6–64–0; J. G. Hughes 24–4–93–2; K. J. Innes 59–7–193–8; N. A. Mallender 24–5–90–0; A. R. Roberts 142.5–33–470–7; T. C. Walton 19–1–71–2.

COUNTY RECORDS

Highest score for:	300	R. Subba Row v Surrey at The Oval	1958
Highest score against:	333	K. S. Duleepsinhji (Sussex) at Hove	1930
Best bowling for:	10-127	V. W. C. Jupp v Kent at Tunbridge Wells	1932
Best bowling against:	10-30	C. Blythe (Kent) at Northampton	1907
Highest total for:	781-7 dec.	v Nottinghamshire at Northampton	1995
Highest total against:	670-9 dec.	by Sussex at Hove	1921
Lowest total for:	12	v Gloucestershire at Gloucester	1907
Lowest total against:	33	by Lancashire at Northampton	1977

At Chester-le-Street, May 2, 3, 4, 6. NORTHAMPTONSHIRE drew with DURHAM.

NORTHAMPTONSHIRE v GLAMORGAN

At Northampton, May 9, 10, 11, 13. Glamorgan won by five wickets. Glamorgan 22 pts, Northamptonshire 7 pts. Toss: Northamptonshire.

A match of three declarations produced a generous offer to Glamorgan to get 279 to win in 64 overs; they reached their target with one ball to spare. This was thanks largely to Dale, who dominated the innings with 120 and found a willing partner in Cottey. Dale's bowling had set the early pattern of the match: he removed Northamptonshire's top three for one run in nine balls. But then Warren converted his second first-class century into an unbeaten 201; he faced 307 balls in five hours and 40 minutes, hitting two sixes and 27 fours, giving one chance, to James in the gully, on 199. His partnership with Capel realised 239 in 60 overs. Rain caused four stoppages on the second day, 40 overs being lost, but Glamorgan replied strongly, with Butcher scoring a maiden first-class fifty before Maynard declared 100 behind. The pitch was still playing well when Bailey declared again, and Glamorgan seized their chance gratefully.

Close of play: First day, Northamptonshire 332-4 (R. J. Warren 128*, D. J. Capel 51*); Second day, Glamorgan 101-2 (S. P. James 50*, M. P. Maynard 23*); Third day, Northamptonshire 22-0 (R. R. Montgomerie 12*, A. Fordham 8*).

Northamptonshire

R. R. Montgomerie c Watkin b Dale	51	– c Kendrick b Croft	53
A. Fordham c Metson b Dale	52	– retired hurt	29
*R. J. Bailey c Thomas b Dale	0	– c Maynard b Kendrick	34
M. B. Loye b Watkin	36	– c Butcher b Kendrick	28
R. J. Warren not out	201		
D. J. Capel c Maynard b Watkin	83	– (5) c Butcher b Croft	10
K. M. Curran lbw b Watkin	0	– (6) not out	5
A. L. Penberthy not out	7	– (7) st Metson b Croft	5
†D. Ripley (did not bat)		– (8) not out	5
B 4, l-b 8, w 1, n-b 8	21	B 3, l-b 6	9
1/105 2/105 3/110 4/186 5/425 6/430 (6 wkts dec.)	451	1/117 2/135 3/153 4/162 5/169 (5 wkts dec.)	178

J. E. Emburey and J. P. Taylor did not bat.

Bonus points – Northamptonshire 4, Glamorgan 2 (Score at 120 overs: 446-6).

In the second innings A. Fordham retired hurt at 47.

Bowling: *First Innings*—Watkin 35–6–110–3; Thomas 27–3–118–0; Dale 21–4–68–3; Croft 21–2–69–0; Kendrick 16–6–55–0; Butcher 2–0–19–0. *Second Innings*—Watkin 5–2–8–0; Thomas 8–0–34–0; Croft 12–2–52–3; Kendrick 11–0–49–2; Butcher 7–0–26–0.

Glamorgan

S. P. James c Warren b Penberthy	76	– lbw b Curran	9
H. Morris b Capel	20	– b Emburey	38
A. Dale b Curran	5	– c and b Emburey	120
*M. P. Maynard c Ripley b Taylor	52	– c Capel b Taylor	27
P. A. Cottey lbw b Capel	48	– not out	65
G. P. Butcher b Emburey	89	– (7) not out	8
R. D. B. Croft c Ripley b Emburey	25	– (6) b Taylor	0
N. M. Kendrick not out	16		
S. D. Thomas not out	2		
L-b 4, w 4, n-b 10	18	B 1, l-b 4, w 1, n-b 6	12
1/33 2/48 3/150 4/173 5/264 6/321 7/347 (7 wkts dec.)	351	1/21 2/91 3/139 4/256 5/263 (5 wkts)	279

†C. P. Metson and S. L. Watkin did not bat.

Bonus points – Glamorgan 4, Northamptonshire 3.

Bowling: *First Innings*—Taylor 15–4–46–1; Curran 20–5–77–1; Capel 20.2–4–74–2; Emburey 29–5–76–2; Penberthy 17–1–59–1; Bailey 5–2–15–0. *Second Innings*—Taylor 16–3–45–2; Curran 10–1–39–1; Emburey 19.5–2–85–2; Capel 5–0–40–0; Bailey 4–0–15–0; Penberthy 9–0–50–0.

Umpires: G. I. Burgess and M. J. Kitchen.

At Oxford, May 16, 17, 18. NORTHAMPTONSHIRE drew with OXFORD UNIVERSITY.

At Luton, May 21. NORTHAMPTONSHIRE beat INDIANS by five wickets (See Indian tour section).

At Taunton, May 23, 24, 25, 27. NORTHAMPTONSHIRE lost to SOMERSET by four wickets.

NORTHAMPTONSHIRE v WARWICKSHIRE

At Northampton, May 30, 31, June 1, 3. Warwickshire won by nine wickets. Warwickshire 24 pts, Northamptonshire 5 pts. Toss: Warwickshire.

Outstanding performances from Moles and Pollock set up Warwickshire's victory. For a time on the first day, the match threatened to boil over. Pollock was warned for bowling two bouncers in an over during a hostile spell, and the umpires intervened following a heated exchange of words which ended with Capel waving his bat at Piper, the wicket-keeper, and Reeve. Umpire Jesty described the incident as "a bit of hot air". Northamptonshire were in a strong position when they reduced Warwickshire to 118 for five, still needing 47 to avoid the follow-on. But Moles dug in for seven and threequarter hours. He added 194 with Pollock, who completed a maiden first-class century, to pull level, and then useful runs from the lower order boosted Warwickshire's lead to 133. Northamptonshire collapsed to 89 for seven on the third afternoon; Penberthy and Ripley offered just enough resistance to take the match into Monday.

Close of play: First day, Warwickshire 34-2 (A. J. Moles 11*, K. J. Piper 2*); Second day, Warwickshire 360-6 (A. J. Moles 160*, D. A. Reeve 20*); Third day, Northamptonshire 148-7 (A. L. Penberthy 36*, D. Ripley 22*).

Northamptonshire

R. R. Montgomerie c Reeve b Pollock	7	– c Piper b Pollock	12
R. J. Warren b Pollock	76	– c Khan b Small	0
*R. J. Bailey c Moles b Reeve	25	– run out	16
M. B. Loye c Small b Pollock	39	– c Ostler b Welch	7
D. J. Capel c Ostler b Welch	57	– lbw b Welch	0
K. M. Curran c Piper b Reeve	55	– (7) b Brown	16
A. L. Penberthy c Piper b Reeve	10	– (6) c Piper b Pollock	43
A. R. Roberts lbw b Reeve	0	– b Smith	19
†D. Ripley c Ostler b Reeve	20	– not out	35
C. E. L. Ambrose c Ostler b Smith	6	– c Penney b Smith	3
J. P. Taylor not out	1	– b Pollock	3
B 4, l-b 4, n-b 10	18	B 5, l-b 1, n-b 14	20
1/20 2/66 3/148 4/157 5/254 6/276 7/276 8/306 9/307	314	1/2 2/16 3/33 4/33 5/41 6/67 7/89 8/159 9/166	174

Bonus points – Northamptonshire 3, Warwickshire 4.

Bowling: *First Innings*—Pollock 20–3–78–3; Small 8–2–22–0; Welch 15–1–78–1; Reeve 19–4–37–5; Smith 16–5–57–1; Brown 10–1–34–0. *Second Innings*—Pollock 22.1–4–49–3; Small 2–0–3–1; Welch 15–4–46–2; Reeve 7–2–21–0; Brown 8–2–29–1; Smith 12–4–20–2.

Warwickshire

A. J. Moles c Penberthy b Ambrose	164	– c Montgomerie b Bailey	5
W. G. Khan c Warren b Ambrose	0	– not out	32
D. P. Ostler c Warren b Ambrose	15	– not out	6
†K. J. Piper lbw b Ambrose	8		
T. L. Penney c Ambrose b Roberts	20		
D. R. Brown b Taylor	8		
S. M. Pollock b Ambrose	107		
*D. A. Reeve lbw b Capel	36		
N. M. K. Smith c Capel b Penberthy	34		
G. Welch lbw b Roberts	19		
G. C. Small not out	12		
B 5, l-b 7, n-b 12	24	B 1	1
1/1 2/28 3/48 4/105 5/118 6/312 7/367 8/412 9/416	447	1/19	(1 wkt) 44

Bonus points – Warwickshire 4, Northamptonshire 2 (Score at 120 overs: 365-6).

Bowling: *First Innings*—Ambrose 28–6–62–5; Taylor 26–1–106–1; Capel 24–4–66–1; Curran 14–4–35–0; Penberthy 23–2–70–1; Roberts 24.5–3–64–2; Bailey 11–0–32–0. *Second Innings*—Ambrose 1–0–6–0; Taylor 2–0–8–0; Roberts 2–0–19–0; Bailey 1.5–0–10–1.

Umpires: A. Clarkson and T. E. Jesty.

At Nottingham, June 6, 7, 8, 10. NORTHAMPTONSHIRE drew with NOTTINGHAMSHIRE.

At Chelmsford, June 13, 14, 15, 17. NORTHAMPTONSHIRE drew with ESSEX.

At Basingstoke, June 19, 20, 21. NORTHAMPTONSHIRE lost to HAMPSHIRE by an innings and 72 runs.

NORTHAMPTONSHIRE v DERBYSHIRE

At Northampton, June 27, 28, 29. Northamptonshire won by four wickets. Northamptonshire 21 pts, Derbyshire 4 pts. Toss: Derbyshire.

Northamptonshire's fifth successive victory over Derbyshire – none of the matches had gone into a fourth day – came after 20 wickets fell on the opening day and Harry Brind, the TCCB's inspector of pitches, was summoned to the ground. However, his room for manoeuvre was somewhat restricted when he learned that Donald Carr, chairman of the pitches committee, had been to the ground before the game and advised that the match should be switched to this strip. Also, the umpires marked the pitch "above average" despite the inconsistent bounce. All 36 wickets fell to Test match bowlers. Derbyshire lost eight wickets before lunch on the opening day, shaping poorly against Ambrose, and were all out inside 36 overs. By the close, Northamptonshire had built a 112-run lead through the diligence of Bailey and a typical flourish from Curran. Ambrose tormented Derbyshire again in their second innings, returning match figures of 11 for 70, although Adams counter-attacked magnificently. Northamptonshire endured some anxious moments before passing a modest target; even 128 was not easy against Cork, Malcolm and DeFreitas, and Northamptonshire slipped to 77 for five. But Curran blended caution and aggression, and finished the game with a six. This was Northamptonshire's first Championship win of the season and lifted them off the bottom of the table.

Close of play: First day, Derbyshire 7-0 (K. J. Barnett 5*, A. S. Rollins 2*); Second day, Derbyshire 210-7 (K. M. Krikken 42*, D. G. Cork 5*).

Derbyshire

K. J. Barnett c Warren b Taylor	5	– c Capel b Taylor	27
A. S. Rollins c Capel b Ambrose	0	– c Curran b Ambrose	7
C. J. Adams b Ambrose	3	– b Ambrose	68
*D. M. Jones b Capel	6	– c Montgomerie b Emburey	17
J. E. Owen c Emburey b Ambrose	17	– b Ambrose	0
T. J. G. O'Gorman c Bailey b Capel	7	– b Ambrose	3
P. A. J. DeFreitas c Warren b Ambrose	14	– lbw b Emburey	22
†K. M. Krikken c Curran b Ambrose	9	– c Emburey b Capel	44
D. G. Cork b Capel	0	– b Ambrose	21
M. J. Vandrau not out	16	– not out	9
D. E. Malcolm c Curran b Taylor	5	– b Ambrose	0
B 8, l-b 7, w 1	16	B 6, l-b 9, n-b 6	21
1/5 2/10 3/18 4/33 5/45 6/64 7/64 8/67 9/93	98	1/24 2/44 3/136 4/136 5/139 6/144 7/186 8/214 9/239	239

Bonus points – Northamptonshire 4.

Bowling: *First Innings*—Ambrose 11–4–15–5; Taylor 8.3–3–19–2; Penberthy 7–1–16–0; Capel 8–2–31–3; Emburey 1–0–2–0. *Second Innings*—Ambrose 18.4–3–55–6; Taylor 19–3–68–1; Emburey 18–7–29–2; Capel 10–1–34–1; Penberthy 5–1–12–0; Curran 3–0–26–0.

Northamptonshire

D. J. Roberts lbw b Cork	3	– c Jones b Cork	13
R. R. Montgomerie lbw b DeFreitas	7	– c Krikken b Malcolm	18
*R. J. Bailey c Adams b DeFreitas	68	– c Krikken b Malcolm	13
M. B. Loye lbw b Cork	23	– c Barnett b DeFreitas	13
†R. J. Warren c Adams b Cork	4	– b DeFreitas	17
D. J. Capel c Adams b Cork	9	– lbw b Cork	0
K. M. Curran c Krikken b Malcolm	47	– not out	29
A. L. Penberthy c Krikken b Malcolm	17	– not out	7
J. E. Emburey c Vandrau b Malcolm	5		
C. E. L. Ambrose b Malcolm	3		
J. P. Taylor not out	3		
B 4, l-b 3, n-b 14	21	L-b 14, n-b 6	20
1/3 2/15 3/67 4/71 5/128 6/130 7/163 8/173 9/183	210	1/24 2/53 3/56 4/72 5/77 6/101	(6 wkts) 130

Bonus points – Northamptonshire 1, Derbyshire 4.

Bowling: *First Innings*—Malcolm 19.2–5–59–4; Cork 18–2–63–4; DeFreitas 21–3–64–2; Vandrau 2–0–17–0. *Second Innings*—Cork 14–1–49–2; Malcolm 11–3–28–2; DeFreitas 20.2–9–39–2.

Umpires: J. W. Holder and A. A. Jones.

At Northampton, July 6, 7, 8. NORTHAMPTONSHIRE drew with PAKISTANIS (See Pakistani tour section).

NORTHAMPTONSHIRE v MIDDLESEX

At Northampton, July 18, 19, 20, 22. Middlesex won by 26 runs. Middlesex 20 pts, Northamptonshire 4 pts. Toss: Middlesex. Championship debut: S. A. J. Boswell.

Middlesex spinners Weekes and Tufnell captured the home side's last six wickets in an hour on the final morning. But former Middlesex spinner John Emburey, now with Northamptonshire, also played a key role – chiefly through his absence. He was called to the High Court on the first day to give evidence for Ian Botham and ex-Northamptonshire captain Allan Lamb in their libel case against Imran Khan, then returned in time to take two wickets and batted at No. 3 rather than risk missing his turn while back in court next day. Bailey bitterly regretted not having him to bowl full-time on a dry pitch which turned from the start. After 15 wickets fell on the opening day, TCCB inspector Harry Brind arrived to inspect it, but no penalty was imposed. Weekes played the key innings of the match with 140 in five hours, his highest Championship score. By the time he figured in Taylor's career-best haul of 11 for 104, he had set up a target of 288. It looked well out of reach at 102 for four, but Capel and Curran doubled that before the close. Curran fell to Weekes's fourth ball on Monday morning, leaving Capel unsupported; his skilful innings ended after four and a half hours.

Close of play: First day, Northamptonshire 92-5 (A. L. Penberthy 24*, K. M. Curran 18*); Second day, Middlesex 232-3 (P. N. Weekes 133*, P. E. Wellings 31*); Third day, Northamptonshire 211-4 (D. J. Capel 70*, K. M. Curran 62*).

Middlesex

P. N. Weekes lbw b Taylor	8	– c Fordham b Taylor	140
J. C. Pooley lbw b Taylor	8	– c Fordham b Taylor	3
*M. W. Gatting c Warren b Taylor	0	– c Fordham b Taylor	1
J. D. Carr lbw b Capel	6	– c Capel b Emburey	57
P. E. Wellings c Montgomerie b Capel	4	– lbw b Capel	42
†K. R. Brown c Capel b Emburey	54	– not out	18
J. P. Hewitt b Taylor	45	– c Montgomerie b Penberthy	11
R. L. Johnson c Curran b Taylor	6	– b Taylor	6
R. A. Fay c Curran b Penberthy	11	– c Capel b Taylor	0
A. R. C. Fraser not out	8	– c Fordham b Taylor	0
P. C. R. Tufnell c Montgomerie b Emburey	0	– b Boswell	8
B 5, l-b 2	7	B 5, l-b 2, w 1, n-b 8	16
1/8 2/12 3/23 4/27 5/28 6/95 7/109 8/145 9/155	157	1/17 2/21 3/141 4/251 5/253 6/273 7/291 8/291 9/293	302

Bonus points – Northamptonshire 4.

Bowling: *First Innings*—Taylor 22–9–36–5; Boswell 14–2–44–0; Capel 12–1–30–2; Curran 8–1–25–0; Penberthy 7–1–8–1; Emburey 4.1–2–7–2. *Second Innings*—Taylor 26–7–68–6; Boswell 9.4–2–23–1; Capel 11–4–34–1; Curran 5–1–16–0; Snape 13–4–37–0; Bailey 8–0–31–0; Penberthy 15–5–27–1; Emburey 20–3–59–1.

Northamptonshire

R. R. Montgomerie c Carr b Fraser	4	– c Carr b Hewitt	26
A. Fordham c Brown b Fay	2	– b Hewitt	29
J. E. Emburey c and b Hewitt	11	– (8) c Pooley b Weekes	0
*R. J. Bailey c Brown b Johnson	6	– (3) c Brown b Tufnell	9
A. L. Penberthy c Weekes b Tufnell	25	– (4) lbw b Hewitt	0
D. J. Capel c Gatting b Fay	19	– (5) lbw b Weekes	95
K. M. Curran not out	55	– (6) c and b Weekes	62
J. N. Snape c Tufnell b Fraser	29	– (7) c Pooley b Weekes	8
J. P. Taylor c Brown b Fraser	4	– c Wellings b Tufnell	2
S. A. J. Boswell c Brown b Fraser	1	– (11) not out	2
†R. J. Warren c Brown b Hewitt	6	– (10) c Brown b Tufnell	11
L-b 5, w 1, n-b 4	10	B 1, l-b 5, w 1, n-b 10	17
1/4 2/10 3/21 4/25 5/53 6/94 7/143 8/147 9/155	172	1/48 2/63 3/63 4/102 5/216 6/238 7/238 8/245 9/253	261

Bonus points – Middlesex 4.

Bowling: *First Innings*—Fraser 17–6–28–4; Fay 15–4–45–2; Johnson 6–0–20–1; Hewitt 9–3–20–2; Weekes 11–4–18–0; Tufnell 8–1–36–1. *Second Innings*—Fraser 14–1–41–0; Fay 10–1–47–0; Tufnell 36.4–9–79–3; Hewitt 10–1–27–3; Weekes 20–1–61–4.

Umpires: M. J. Kitchen and K. J. Lyons.

At Kidderminster, July 24, 25, 26, 27. NORTHAMPTONSHIRE drew with WORCESTERSHIRE.

At Leicester, August 1, 2, 3, 5. NORTHAMPTONSHIRE drew with LEICESTERSHIRE.

NORTHAMPTONSHIRE v KENT

At Northampton, August 8, 9, 10. Kent won by ten wickets. Kent 23 pts, Northamptonshire 4 pts. Toss: Kent.

Led by Trevor Ward, their fourth acting-captain of the season in Benson's absence, Kent gained a comprehensive victory an hour after lunch on the third day, despite the loss of a couple of hours to the weather on the second. Fielding lapses proved costly for Northamptonshire. They enabled Kent to rally from 146 for five, through Willis, who was dropped twice, and Patel. Then McCague, generating hostile pace, troubled the home batsmen. Only Fordham and Curran showed much fight before the last seven wickets fell for 41. Kent enforced the follow-on, and Wren caused the early damage second time around, although Montgomerie grafted for four hours and Curran again counter-attacked boldly, until a bouncer from Headley split his batting helmet and caused him to retire dazed. He returned briefly but Hooper hastened the end with a spell of four for two in 26 balls.

Close of play: First day, Northamptonshire 3-0 (R. R. Montgomerie 2*, A. Fordham 1*); Second day, Northamptonshire 91-3 (R. R. Montgomerie 30*, K. M. Curran 29*).

Kent

D. P. Fulton b Snape	39	– not out	6
M. J. Walker lbw b Capel	40	– not out	11
*T. R. Ward c Curran b Capel	0		
C. L. Hooper c Capel b Taylor	41		
N. J. Llong c Ripley b Penberthy	7		
M. V. Fleming b Ambrose	40		
†S. C. Willis c Walton b Curran	78		
D. W. Headley c Ripley b Walton	19		
M. M. Patel c Fordham b Taylor	31		
M. J. McCague not out	1		
T. N. Wren lbw b Taylor	0		
B 4, l-b 12, n-b 4	20		
1/77 2/77 3/112 4/131 5/146 6/211 7/259 8/309 9/316	316	(no wkt)	17

Bonus points – Kent 3, Northamptonshire 4.

Bowling: *First Innings*—Ambrose 17–6–45–1; Taylor 17.4–4–68–3; Curran 11–1–30–1; Capel 13–1–40–2; Penberthy 10–1–28–1; Snape 16–2–63–1; Walton 7–0–26–1. *Second Innings*—Snape 1.5–0–10–0; Penberthy 1–0–7–0.

Northamptonshire

R. R. Montgomerie c Patel b McCague	8	– c Willis b Hooper	57
*A. Fordham c Llong b McCague	53	– lbw b Wren	1
D. J. Sales b McCague	0	– c Ward b Wren	25
D. J. Capel c Hooper b Wren	1	– c Ward b Wren	0
K. M. Curran c Ward b Headley	45	– b Hooper	49
T. C. Walton b Patel	0	– b Wren	15
A. L. Penberthy c Fulton b Patel	14	– b Wren	3
J. N. Snape c Willis b McCague	0	– c Walker b Hooper	16
†D. Ripley c Willis b McCague	5	– b McCague	0
C. E. L. Ambrose c Hooper b Patel	2	– c Fulton b Hooper	1
J. P. Taylor not out	0	– not out	0
L-b 5	5	B 10, l-b 9, n-b 10	29
1/12 2/12 3/23 4/92 5/97 6/109 7/117 8/129 9/131	133	1/4 2/34 3/34 4/143 5/155 6/179 7/180 8/191 9/193	196

Bonus points – Kent 4.

In the second innings K. M. Curran, when 45, retired hurt at 115 and resumed at 180.

Bowling: *First Innings*—McCague 13–5–21–5; Headley 13–1–41–1; Wren 3–1–20–1; Patel 13.4–2–46–3; Hooper 1–1–0–0. *Second Innings*—McCague 15–2–44–1; Wren 16–3–49–5; Headley 14–2–37–0; Patel 13–4–26–0; Fleming 3–0–14–0; Hooper 6.2–2–7–4.

Umpires: V. A. Holder and B. J. Meyer.

NORTHAMPTONSHIRE v SUSSEX

At Northampton, August 22, 23, 24, 26. Northamptonshire won by six wickets. Northamptonshire 24 pts, Sussex 8 pts. Toss: Sussex.

Ambrose decided the match with a destructive burst either side of tea on the third day, capturing four for four in 11 balls – all bowled. Needing only 141, Northamptonshire lost three wickets before the close, but comfortably completed their second Championship win of the season on Monday morning. Lenham, returning after a three-week absence with a broken finger, had led Sussex's first innings for 250 minutes, scoring 145 in 226 balls with 22 fours. He added 149 with Wells then, after a flurry of wickets, Drakes and Phillips shared a robust eighth-wicket stand of 80. Northamptonshire slipped to 22 for three but recovered through Curran, whose century included a six and 15 fours, before Ripley marshalled the tail to such good effect that the last two wickets realised 125 and three extra batting points. That gave them a psychological advantage which Ambrose ruthlessly pressed home, finishing with six for 26.

Close of play: First day, Sussex 368-7 (V. C. Drakes 59*, N. C. Phillips 23*); Second day, Northamptonshire 160-4 (K. M. Curran 79*, J. P. Taylor 4*); Third day, Northamptonshire 42-3 (D. J. Capel 12*, D. Ripley 8*).

Sussex

N. J. Lenham c Ripley b Penberthy	145	– c Penberthy b Ambrose	0
C. W. J. Athey lbw b Taylor	13	– c Ripley b Taylor	2
K. Greenfield c Ripley b Penberthy	22	– c Ripley b Taylor	9
*A. P. Wells b Penberthy	51	– b Ambrose	40
M. P. Speight c Ambrose b Emburey	12	– b Capel	6
D. R. Law lbw b Penberthy	11	– b Ambrose	13
†P. Moores b Emburey	2	– b Ambrose	8
V. C. Drakes lbw b Taylor	59	– run out	6
N. C. Phillips not out	30	– b Ambrose	0
J. D. Lewry b Emburey	14	– not out	11
R. J. Kirtley c Ripley b Taylor	0	– c Taylor b Ambrose	3
B 6, l-b 13, w 1, n-b 10	30	B 1, l-b 7, w 2, n-b 4	14
1/45 2/95 3/244 4/261 5/277 6/280 7/289 8/369 9/388	389	1/1 2/12 3/32 4/53 5/80 6/81 7/88 8/88 9/100	112

Bonus points – Sussex 4, Northamptonshire 4.

Bowling: *First Innings*—Ambrose 20–7–46–0; Taylor 21.1–2–104–3; Capel 15–1–58–0; Emburey 31–8–77–3; Snape 15–2–49–0; Penberthy 15–4–36–4. *Second Innings*—Ambrose 10.5–2–26–6; Taylor 5–1–21–2; Capel 6–1–38–1; Curran 4–0–19–0.

Northamptonshire

R. R. Montgomerie b Drakes	6	– b Lewry	14
*A. Fordham c Moores b Lewry	4	– lbw b Lewry	3
D. J. Capel c Speight b Drakes	0	– not out	39
K. M. Curran b Kirtley	117	– (6) not out	30
A. L. Penberthy c Moores b Drakes	42		
J. P. Taylor b Phillips	7	– (4) b Drakes	1
K. J. Innes c and b Phillips	20		
J. N. Snape lbw b Kirtley	0		
†D. Ripley not out	66	– (5) c Moores b Drakes	30
J. E. Emburey c Athey b Law	30		
C. E. L. Ambrose b Law	23		
B 1, l-b 8, w 3, n-b 34	46	B 8, l-b 4, w 1, n-b 12	25
1/8 2/12 3/22 4/146 5/178 6/226 7/226 8/236 9/319	361	1/10 2/23 3/24 4/87	(4 wkts) 142

Bonus points – Northamptonshire 4, Sussex 4.

Bowling: *First Innings*—Drakes 24–1–103–3; Lewry 17–5–53–1; Kirtley 17–5–63–2; Law 14.4–0–47–2; Phillips 22–2–76–2; Lenham 3–0–10–0. *Second Innings*—Drakes 13–2–56–2; Lewry 6–0–20–2; Law 7–0–35–0; Kirtley 5.2–2–19–0.

Umpires: A. Clarkson and J. W. Holder.

At Bristol, August 29, 30, 31, September 2. NORTHAMPTONSHIRE lost to GLOUCESTERSHIRE by 15 runs.

At The Oval, September 3, 4, 5, 6. NORTHAMPTONSHIRE lost to SURREY by 225 runs.

NORTHAMPTONSHIRE v LANCASHIRE

At Northampton, September 12, 13, 14, 16. Northamptonshire won by nine wickets. Northamptonshire 24 pts, Lancashire 7 pts. Toss: Lancashire. First-class debut: T. M. B. Bailey.

Loye and Rob Bailey guided Northamptonshire home against a stale-looking Lancashire side with an undefeated partnership of 163 in 35 overs, after Warren had fallen first ball. Gallian had been Lancashire's mainstay on the opening day, hitting a five-hour century; he received attractive rather than substantial support from Crawley and Watkinson. Northamptonshire's strong reply was built around Loye, Curran and Innes, who followed his four wickets with a maiden fifty, while Walton scored a spectacular 32-ball 52. Lancashire's arrears of 115 were cleared by Crawley and Lloyd, but Snape dismissed them both; Crawley perished to an impressive catch by debutant wicket-keeper Toby Bailey – who had caught Titchard off the second ball of the match. Taylor demolished the tail with four for 19 in 49 deliveries to leave Northamptonshire a straightforward target of 161 in 75 overs. Rob Bailey, making his first Championship appearance for seven weeks after injury, wrapped it up in style with 92 from just 99 balls.

Close of play: First day, Lancashire 337-8 (G. Yates 16*, R. J. Green 8*); Second day, Northamptonshire 357-5 (K. M. Curran 85*, K. J. Innes 13*); Third day, Lancashire 226-5 (M. Watkinson 34*, P. J. Martin 6*).

Lancashire

S. P. Titchard c T. M. B. Bailey b Taylor	0	– (2) b Snape	26
J. E. R. Gallian b Taylor	113	– (1) lbw b Hughes	1
J. P. Crawley c Loye b Innes	46	– (4) c T. M. B. Bailey b Snape	58
N. H. Fairbrother c T. M. B. Bailey b Taylor	9	– (3) c Taylor b Hughes	17
G. D. Lloyd b Penberthy	17	– c Hughes b Snape	70
*M. Watkinson c Curran b Snape	46	– c Innes b Taylor	39
†W. K. Hegg b Innes	28	– (8) c R. J. Bailey b Taylor	7
G. Chapple lbw b Innes	30	– (9) c Curran b Taylor	20
G. Yates c Warren b Innes	16	– (10) c Penberthy b Snape	0
R. J. Green not out	25	– (11) not out	5
P. J. Martin c Warren b Taylor	2	– (7) lbw b Taylor	18
B 9, l-b 9, w 2, n-b 4	24	B 2, l-b 5, n-b 7	14
1/0 2/88 3/110 4/143 5/222 6/266 7/303 8/316 9/337	356	1/1 2/27 3/85 4/162 5/203 6/238 7/243 8/252 9/253	275

Bonus points – Lancashire 4, Northamptonshire 4.

Bowling: *First Innings*—Taylor 27.1–6–73–4; Hughes 18–3–72–0; Penberthy 14–4–49–1; Snape 26–6–75–1; Innes 22–3–61–4; R. J. Bailey 3–0–8–0. *Second Innings*—Taylor 21.5–6–72–4; Hughes 6–1–21–2; Innes 7–1–36–0; Snape 31–5–102–4; R. J. Bailey 3–1–4–0; Penberthy 7–1–33–0.

Northamptonshire

R. J. Warren lbw b Green	31	– c Watkinson b Martin	0
M. B. Loye c Gallian b Watkinson	90	– not out	67
*R. J. Bailey lbw b Green	41	– not out	92
K. M. Curran c Hegg b Martin	93		
T. C. Walton c Fairbrother b Yates	52		
A. L. Penberthy c Fairbrother b Martin	29		
K. J. Innes lbw b Green	63		
J. N. Snape b Yates	12		
†T. M. B. Bailey not out	31		
J. G. Hughes c Watkinson b Yates	8		
J. P. Taylor b Green	1		
B 4, l-b 16	20	B 1, l-b 3	4
1/73 2/143 3/199 4/258 5/311 6/373 7/419 8/429 9/470	471	1/0	(1 wkt) 163

Bonus points – Northamptonshire 4, Lancashire 3 (Score at 120 overs: 423-7).

Bowling: *First Innings*—Martin 30–4–92–2; Chapple 26–6–94–0; Green 25.5–7–78–4; Yates 31–10–91–3; Gallian 11–3–33–0; Watkinson 18–2–63–1. *Second Innings*—Martin 9–1–25–1; Chapple 4–0–14–0; Watkinson 10–0–47–0; Green 4–0–20–0; Yates 8.2–0–53–0.

Umpires: V. A. Holder and K. E. Palmer.

NORTHAMPTONSHIRE v YORKSHIRE

At Northampton, September 19, 20, 21, 22. Drawn. Northamptonshire 6 pts, Yorkshire 11 pts. Toss: Yorkshire. First-class debut: J. F. Brown.

Northamptonshire's opening pair, Montgomerie and Loye, returned to the crease at 2.40 p.m. on the third day as the home side followed on 256 adrift. They were to defy Yorkshire's bowlers for six hours, finally being separated at 372. By then, they had broken not only the first-wicket record for Northamptonshire, surpassing the 361 by Norman Oldfield and Vince Broderick against Scotland at Peterborough in 1953, but also the record opening stand against Yorkshire – 346 by Somerset's Lionel Palairet and Herbert Hewett at Taunton in 1892. Loye scored a maiden double-hundred in 361 minutes and 306 balls, with 28 fours, playing with flair and confidence, while Montgomerie – whose aim, he later admitted, was to "bore them to death" – proved the perfect foil, facing two balls more than his partner and hitting half as many boundaries. Yorkshire's

HIGHEST CHAMPIONSHIP FIRST-WICKET PARTNERSHIPS

555	P. Holmes and H. Sutcliffe	Yorkshire v Essex at Leyton	1932
554	J. T. Brown and J. Tunnicliffe	Yorkshire v Derbyshire at Chesterfield	1898
490	E. H. Bowley and J. G. Langridge	Sussex v Middlesex at Hove	1933
391	A. O. Jones and A. Shrewsbury	Nottinghamshire v Gloucestershire at Bristol	1899
390	B. Dudleston and J. F. Steele	Leicestershire v Derbyshire at Leicester	1979
380	C. J. B. Wood and H. Whitehead	Leicestershire v Worcestershire at Worcester	1906
379	R. Abel and W. Brockwell	Surrey v Hampshire at The Oval	1897
378	J. T. Brown and J. Tunnicliffe	Yorkshire v Sussex at Sheffield	1897
377*	N. F. Horner and Khalid Ibadulla	Warwickshire v Surrey at The Oval	1960
372	**R. R. Montgomerie and M. B. Loye**	**Northamptonshire v Yorkshire at Northampton**	**1996**
368	A. C. MacLaren and R. H. Spooner	Lancashire v Gloucestershire at Liverpool	1903
368	E. H. Bowley and J. H. Parks	Sussex v Gloucestershire at Hove	1929
367*	G. D. Barlow and W. N. Slack	Middlesex v Kent at Lord's	1981
364	R. Abel and D. L. A. Jephson	Surrey v Derbyshire at The Oval	1900
362	A. J. Wright and G. D. Hodgson	Gloucestershire v Nottinghamshire at Bristol	1995
362	**M. D. Moxon and M. P. Vaughan**	**Yorkshire v Glamorgan at Cardiff**	**1996**
361	D. L. Haynes and I. J. F. Hutchinson	Middlesex v Kent at Uxbridge	1989
352	T. W. Hayward and J. B. Hobbs	Surrey v Warwickshire at The Oval	1909
351	G. Boycott and M. D. Moxon	Yorkshire v Worcestershire at Worcester	1985
350*	C. Washbrook and W. Place	Lancashire v Sussex at Manchester	1947

Vaughan had also batted for six hours, over the first two days. He equalled his previous best of 183, hitting one six and 27 fours. Northamptonshire's reply was a sorry affair, six wickets tumbling for 27 in 15 overs in mid-innings, but the magnificent fightback from Montgomerie and Loye more than made amends.

Close of play: First day, Yorkshire 213-3 (M. P. Vaughan 95*, R. A. Kettleborough 5*); Second day, Northamptonshire 83-2 (R. J. Bailey 8*, K. M. Curran 14*); Third day, Northamptonshire 157-0 (R. R. Montgomerie 36*, M. B. Loye 106*).

Yorkshire

M. D. Moxon c T. M. B. Bailey b Penberthy	57
M. P. Vaughan b Innes	183
*D. Byas c Brown b Taylor	21
A. McGrath c Curran b Innes	27
R. A. Kettleborough b Innes	32
C. White b Walton	66
†R. J. Blakey b Penberthy	33
D. Gough c R. J. Bailey b Penberthy	18
G. M. Hamilton b Penberthy	0
C. E. W. Silverwood c Emburey b Penberthy	12
R. D. Stemp not out	0
B 9, l-b 15, w 1, n-b 4	29
1/112 2/144 3/206 4/271 5/376 6/445 7/449 8/457 9/478	478

Bonus points – Yorkshire 4, Northamptonshire 2 (Score at 120 overs: 414-5).

Bowling: Taylor 27–3–96–1; Innes 25–3–79–3; Emburey 26–7–94–0; Penberthy 23.4–6–92–5; Brown 22–6–64–0; Walton 9–1–29–1.

Northamptonshire

R. R. Montgomerie c Blakey b Gough	10	– c Silverwood b Gough 127
M. B. Loye lbw b Hamilton	29	– c Byas b Gough 205
*R. J. Bailey c Blakey b Silverwood	28	– not out 61
K. M. Curran c Gough b Stemp	48	– c Kettleborough b Vaughan 29
T. C. Walton b Silverwood	6	– c White b Vaughan 58
A. L. Penberthy c Byas b Gough	6	– not out 2
K. J. Innes c White b Stemp	2	
†T. M. B. Bailey c Kettleborough b Gough	2	
J. E. Emburey lbw b White	15	
J. P. Taylor c McGrath b Stemp	36	
J. F. Brown not out	0	
B 9, l-b 7, n-b 24	40	B 5, l-b 11, n-b 33 49
1/50 2/54 3/140 4/149 5/154 6/159 7/166 8/167 9/222	222	1/372 2/375 3/436 4/526 (4 wkts) 531

Bonus points – Northamptonshire 1, Yorkshire 4.

Bowling: *First Innings*—Gough 22–5–62–3; Silverwood 17–1–61–2; Hamilton 17–4–33–1; Stemp 16.2–3–49–3; White 3–2–1–1. *Second Innings*—White 20–2–102–0; Silverwood 12–1–48–0; Hamilton 26–4–82–0; Gough 13–2–42–2; Stemp 25–7–51–0; Vaughan 32–1–147–2; Kettleborough 2–0–14–0; McGrath 6–0–29–0.

Umpires: B. Dudleston and A. G. T. Whitehead.

BIGGEST FALLS IN THE COUNTY CHAMPIONSHIP

15 places	Gloucestershire	second to 17th	1970
	Glamorgan	third to 18th	1994
14 places	Glamorgan	second to 16th	1971
	Middlesex	first to 15th	1991
13 places	Middlesex	first equal to 14th	1950
	Leicestershire	third equal to 16th	1954
	Kent	second to 15th	1989
	Worcestershire	second to 15th	1994
	Northamptonshire	third to 16th	1996

Paul Johnson

NOTTINGHAMSHIRE

President: C. W. Gillott
Chairman: A. Wheelhouse
Chairman, Cricket Committee: S. Foster
Secretary/General Manager: B. Robson
Captain: P. Johnson
Cricket Manager: J. A. Ormrod
Head Groundsman: S. Birks
Scorer: G. Stringfellow

Nottinghamshire's near miss in the Sunday League title race could not paper over ever-widening cracks during 1996, especially in the catastrophic second half of the Championship campaign. The fact that Surrey pipped them for the Sunday prize only on superior run-rate seemed pretty hollow when surrounded by so much gloom and despondency. As well as making the earliest possible exits from the two knockout competitions – they lost by a humiliating 205 runs to Yorkshire in the first round of the NatWest Trophy – Nottinghamshire suffered eight defeats in their last ten Championship matches, after their sole win in June. That left them languishing one place off the bottom of the table, their worst finish for 19 years.

Some discontented members tried to instigate an extraordinary general meeting. Their concern was justified, since the slump followed a similar capitulation in 1995, which featured heavy losses in each of the last six Championship games. Nottinghamshire officials, however, remained defiant, insisting that too much upheaval at the top in the early 1990s had contributed to the decline in fortunes and that only a period of continuity, with Alan Ormrod consolidating as cricket manager following his promotion from senior coach in late 1995, would ultimately lead to happier times. Some action was taken to address the shortcomings on the bowling side. Former Nottinghamshire and England off-spinner Eddie Hemmings returned to Trent Bridge as a specialist bowling coach and the club actively sought to sign a top-class fast bowler during the winter.

It was the remarkable success enjoyed by Nottinghamshire on Sundays, though, which did most to extract the sting from the situation. Opponents were stunned by the metamorphosis which seemed to take place some time between the close of Saturday's play in the first-class match and the start of the Sunday game. In an uncanny reversal of their disastrous Championship run, Nottinghamshire won eight of their last nine Sunday games, the one that got away being a crucial head-to-head with Surrey that was abandoned without a ball bowled. The presence of explosive hitters like Paul Johnson and Chris Cairns made them confident in the 40-overs game, but a key factor in stringing together such a prolific run was that they functioned effectively as a unit.

In his first full season as captain, Johnson's form was symptomatic of the side's fortunes. He led by example in the Sunday League to underline his reputation as a destructive one-day batsman, but looked a pale shadow of himself in the Championship. For the second successive year, he failed to reach 1,000 first-class runs, a shortfall he admitted was "pretty awful" for a batsman of his experience and ability. He was not alone: the failures of a seemingly strong batting line-up were as responsible for the Championship slump as the glaring weaknesses in the bowling. The only batsman who did pass 1,000, predictably enough, was Johnson's predecessor as captain, Tim Robinson. Even he found it hard to hold together a team that was forever on the back foot in the second half of the summer.

New Zealand all-rounder Cairns was another who seemed to save his best for Sundays in the closing stages. The previous season, he had passed 1,000 runs and 50 first-class wickets; this time he fell short on both sides, and his 37 wickets, at 39.48, cost twice as much as in 1995. But by tying him to a new two-year contract, Nottinghamshire demonstrated their conviction that he can spearhead an upturn in their fortunes, especially given better support as a strike bowler. Of the other front-line batsmen, Ashley Metcalfe could be satisfied with the way he found his feet again after three years in the wilderness at Yorkshire. But only a late flourish gave Graeme Archer's first season as a capped player a look of respectability – and an average over 40. The uncertainty surrounding Paul Pollard's future seemed to affect his form profoundly.

With promising signs shown by Usman Afzaal in his conversion from England Under-19 spinner to batsman and Mathew Dowman indicating that he may be about to fulfil his potential, Nottinghamshire's failings in the batting department may be rectified sooner rather than later. However, there is nowhere near as much optimism on the bowling front, where fears about their lack of penetration were confirmed. Left-arm spinner Jimmy Hindson's loss of form was a bitter blow, even though that enabled Andy Afford to seize the chance to resurrect his career. He was the county's leading wicket-taker with 51 in all first-class games. The appointment of Hemmings is seen as a way of getting the best out of Nottinghamshire's resources, particularly in a case like Hindson's, and they will be anxious to bring on the younger generation of seam bowlers following the release of David Pennett, Mark Broadhurst, Greg Mike and Bobby Chapman. The emergence of England Under-17 captain Paul Franks, who dismissed Tom Moody and Graeme Hick with successive balls in his first spell in first-team cricket – admittedly only a one-day festival match at Scarborough – was encouraging. But there is undoubtedly a need to develop greater strength in depth.

There was one non-playing victim of Nottinghamshire's disappointing season. After a year in the job, Frank Dalling decided that he was not cut out to succeed Ron Allsopp as head groundsman and asked to be restored to the position of number two. He had received a lot of complaints that his pitches were too flat. This criticism was unfairly directed at Dalling; many of the wickets he inherited were old and lifeless, which officials recognised in agreeing to press ahead with his recommendation of a pitch-relaying programme. Steve Birks moved over from Derby to replace him. Breathing new life into the pitches is not the only thing needed to improve Nottinghamshire's fortunes. Still, they hope that they can emulate Kent, who enjoyed a far better season after winning the Sunday League and finishing bottom of the Championship in 1995; perhaps the confidence generated by their own Sunday success can have a knock-on effect. – NICK LUCY.

NOTTINGHAMSHIRE 1996

[*Bill Smith*

Back row: G. E. Welton, P. J. Franks, L. N. P. Walker, N. A. Gie, U. Afzaal, J. R. Wileman, J. P. Hart, M. N. Bowen, M. Broadhurst, M. P. Dowman. *Middle row:* G. F. Archer, D. B. Pennett, R. J. Chapman, R. T. Bates, G. W. Mike, S. Ball (*physiotherapist*), J. E. Hindson, C. M. Tolley, A. A. Metcalfe, W. M. Noon. *Front row:* J. A. Afford, K. P. Evans, R. T. Robinson, J. A. Ormrod (*cricket manager*), P. Johnson (*captain*), R. A. Pick, P. R. Pollard, M. Newell. *Inset:* C. L. Cairns.

NOTTINGHAMSHIRE RESULTS

All first-class matches – Played 19: Won 1, Lost 9, Drawn 9.

County Championship matches – Played 17: Won 1, Lost 9, Drawn 7.

Competition placings – Britannic Assurance County Championship, 17th; NatWest Trophy, 1st round; Benson and Hedges Cup, 3rd in Group B; AXA Equity & Law League, 2nd.

COUNTY CHAMPIONSHIP AVERAGES

BATTING

Cap		*M*	*I*	*NO*	*R*	*HS*	*100s*	*50s*	*Avge*	*Ct/St*
1983	R. T. Robinson†	17	31	2	1,302	184	3	6	44.89	8
1995	G. F. Archer	12	22	2	819	143	2	4	40.95	15
1993	C. L. Cairns§	16	29	5	946	114	1	6	39.41	10
	A. A. Metcalfe	12	22	0	771	128	1	3	35.04	4
1990	K. P. Evans†	13	18	3	482	71	0	4	32.13	3
1986	P. Johnson†	17	32	2	954	109	2	6	31.80	10
1992	P. R. Pollard†	12	23	1	631	86	0	5	28.68	9
	U. Afzaal	4	8	1	191	67*	0	2	27.28	1
	M. P. Dowman	7	12	0	288	107	1	0	24.00	4
	C. M. Tolley	8	12	1	263	67	0	1	23.90	2
	L. N. P. Walker	4	6	1	93	36	0	0	18.60	14/2
1995	W. M. Noon	13	21	3	332	57	0	1	18.44	30/3
	R. T. Bates	10	14	1	214	34	0	0	16.46	7
	M. N. Bowen	12	18	2	173	22	0	0	10.81	3
1987	R. A. Pick†	6	8	0	66	32	0	0	8.25	1
	D. B. Pennett	3	4	0	27	10	0	0	6.75	1
1990	J. A. Afford	17	23	14	34	11*	0	0	3.77	7
	G. W. Mike†	2	4	0	12	7	0	0	3.00	0

Also batted: J. P. Hart (1 match) 18*, 0*. P. J. Franks† (1 match) did not bat.

* *Signifies not out.* † *Born in Nottinghamshire.* § *Overseas player.*

BOWLING

	O	*M*	*R*	*W*	*BB*	*5W/i*	*Avge*
J. A. Afford	543.5	155	1,382	47	6-51	2	29.40
M. N. Bowen	356.2	60	1,263	32	5-53	2	39.46
C. L. Cairns	427.3	73	1,461	37	6-110	1	39.48
K. P. Evans	404.1	99	1,179	29	5-30	2	40.65
R. T. Bates	255.2	41	895	19	3-42	0	47.10
C. M. Tolley	193	34	709	13	4-68	0	54.53

Also bowled: U. Afzaal 24–1–117–2; G. F. Archer 27–5–98–3; M. P. Dowman 32–9–108–2; P. J. Franks 41–14–102–3; J. P. Hart 18–7–51–0; P. Johnson 12–2–51–1; G. W. Mike 39–5–172–2; W. M. Noon 4–1–22–0; D. B. Pennett 91–15–376–7; R. A. Pick 155.1–31–483–7; R. T. Robinson 1–0–4–0.

COUNTY RECORDS

Highest score for:	312*	W. W. Keeton v Middlesex at The Oval	1939
Highest score against:	345	C. G. Macartney (Australians) at Nottingham	1921
Best bowling for:	10-66	K. Smales v Gloucestershire at Stroud	1956
Best bowling against:	10-10	H. Verity (Yorkshire) at Leeds	1932
Highest total for:	739-7 dec.	v Leicestershire at Nottingham	1903
Highest total against:	781-7 dec.	by Northamptonshire at Northampton	1995
Lowest total for:	13	v Yorkshire at Nottingham	1901
Lowest total against:	16	by Derbyshire at Nottingham	1879
	16	by Surrey at The Oval	1880

NOTTINGHAMSHIRE v SUSSEX

At Nottingham, May 2, 3, 4, 6. Drawn. Nottinghamshire 8 pts, Sussex 8 pts. Toss: Sussex. Championship debut: V. C. Drakes.

After the Nottinghamshire batsmen gave his bowlers a hammering both on Saturday and in the Sunday League match, Wells was reluctant to risk further punishment on Monday. He delayed his declaration until there were only 31 overs left for Nottinghamshire to chase 327, condemning the game to a tame draw. Even so, the home team might have been able to force a result had they been able to shift the Sussex tail. After the first-day washout, they reduced the visitors to 170 for seven, but the tailenders, especially Phillips, hung around to see Lenham to an unbeaten hundred. In the second innings, Nottinghamshire had Sussex at 202 for eight; this time, Phillips survived for two hours, gradually killing off the possibility of a successful run-chase. The most exciting passage of play was on Saturday, when Johnson, keen to move the match on, scored 90 from 77 balls, with 13 fours and a six, before declaring 48 behind.

Close of play: First day, No play; Second day, Sussex 279-8 (N. J. Lenham 90*, P. W. Jarvis 5*); Third day, Sussex 77-3 (A. P. Wells 9*, N. J. Lenham 8*).

Sussex

C. W. J. Athey b Pennett	43	– lbw b Bates	27
J. W. Hall c Noon b Pennett	34	– lbw b Cairns	0
M. P. Speight b Afford	16	– c Cairns b Bates	29
*A. P. Wells st Noon b Afford	24	– c Noon b Afford	38
N. J. Lenham not out	100	– b Afford	43
†P. Moores lbw b Evans	2	– c Pollard b Cairns	18
I. D. K. Salisbury lbw b Tolley	14	– c Noon b Cairns	2
V. C. Drakes c Cairns b Tolley	4	– c Afford b Bates	14
N. C. Phillips c Robinson b Pennett	20	– c Bates b Cairns	45
P. W. Jarvis not out	19	– not out	26
L-b 14, w 1, n-b 12	27	B 4, l-b 16, w 2, n-b 14	36
1/86 2/89 3/132 4/133 5/138 6/166 7/170 8/239 (8 wkts dec.)	303	1/3 2/59 3/60 4/142 5/159 6/174 7/179 8/202 9/278 (9 wkts dec.)	278

E. S. H. Giddins did not bat.

Bonus points – Sussex 3, Nottinghamshire 3.

Bowling: *First Innings*—Cairns 19–5–56–0; Pennett 22–5–61–3; Evans 23.3–7–67–1; Tolley 13–3–36–2; Bates 14–1–40–0; Afford 20–9–29–2. *Second Innings*—Cairns 22.4–4–70–4; Evans 14–3–38–0; Pennett 19–5–57–0; Afford 25–15–22–2; Bates 14–4–42–3; Robinson 1–0–4–0; Tolley 9–3–25–0.

Nottinghamshire

P. R. Pollard lbw b Salisbury	63	– c Speight b Jarvis	24
R. T. Robinson c Athey b Jarvis	22	– not out	14
A. A. Metcalfe c Speight b Giddins	1	– c sub b Giddins	16
*P. Johnson c Wells b Drakes	90	– not out	6
C. L. Cairns c Hall b Salisbury	33		
C. M. Tolley not out	13		
L-b 12, w 5, n-b 16	33	N-b 8	8
1/53 2/74 3/144 4/225 5/255 (5 wkts dec.)	255	1/29 2/58 (2 wkts)	68

R. T. Bates, K. P. Evans, †W. M. Noon, D. B. Pennett and J. A. Afford did not bat.

Bonus points – Nottinghamshire 2, Sussex 2.

Bowling: *First Innings*—Drakes 12.1–0–52–1; Giddins 11–1–44–1; Jarvis 16–4–47–1; Salisbury 14–2–60–2; Phillips 4–0–40–0. *Second Innings*—Drakes 7–2–24–0; Jarvis 6–1–29–1; Phillips 6–3–10–0; Giddins 5–2–5–1.

Umpires: H. D. Bird and G. I. Burgess.

At Taunton, May 9, 10, 11. NOTTINGHAMSHIRE lost to SOMERSET by ten wickets.

NOTTINGHAMSHIRE v LANCASHIRE

At Nottingham, May 16, 17, 18, 20. Drawn. Nottinghamshire 11 pts, Lancashire 9 pts. Toss: Nottinghamshire.

Gallian, his right arm in plaster after he broke a finger trying to take a catch, blocked out the final four deliveries from Afford as the fielders crowded round the bat. The real last man, Keedy, survived ten overs before that; had he gone sooner, Gallian would not have been risked and Nottinghamshire would have won. Lancashire needed 294 from 72 overs and were 172 for three, with Fairbrother in fine form. But a career-best six for 51 from Afford, whose left-arm spin seemed rejuvenated, plunged them into trouble. Earlier, Martin also returned career-best figures, seven for 50, to disrupt Nottinghamshire's attempt to leave Lancashire a bigger target and set up the compelling finish. On a chilly opening day, Robinson batted steadily for 326 minutes to score 122, the backbone of a substantial total of 452. Lancashire's reply was almost as solid; they declared behind after Gallian, Crawley and Fairbrother had all fallen in sight of their centuries. Umpire Hampshire protected himself against the cold by wearing gloves and a tea-cosy.

Close of play: First day, Nottinghamshire 320-4 (P. Johnson 31*, C. L. Cairns 21*); Second day, Lancashire 237-3 (N. H. Fairbrother 44*, G. Chapple 2*); Third day, Nottinghamshire 187-4 (P. Johnson 85*, C. L. Cairns 4*).

Nottinghamshire

P. R. Pollard c Watkinson b Elworthy	47	– lbw b Martin	2
R. T. Robinson run out	122	– b Elworthy	31
G. F. Archer c Speak b Martin	48	– lbw b Elworthy	14
A. A. Metcalfe c Speak b Chapple	31	– c Fairbrother b Gallian	41
*P. Johnson c Fairbrother b Gallian	63	– c Keedy b Martin	88
C. L. Cairns lbw b Elworthy	65	– lbw b Martin	8
†W. M. Noon b Elworthy	20	– c Hegg b Martin	7
R. T. Bates b Martin	18	– not out	25
R. A. Pick c Keedy b Gallian	5	– lbw b Martin	3
D. B. Pennett lbw b Elworthy	10	– lbw b Martin	2
J. A. Afford not out	0	– c sub b Martin	4
B 6, l-b 7, w 2, n-b 8	23	L-b 7, w 2, n-b 4	13
1/106 2/212 3/258 4/270 5/384 6/410 7/417 8/426 9/452	452	1/2 2/45 3/63 4/182 5/192 6/203 7/204 8/208 9/220	238

Bonus points – Nottinghamshire 4, Lancashire 2 (Score at 120 overs: 396-5).

Bowling: *First Innings*—Martin 25–5–83–2; Chapple 24–2–88–1; Watkinson 18–2–46–0; Elworthy 30.5–8–91–4; Keedy 23–4–71–0; Gallian 14–2–60–2. *Second Innings*—Martin 20–5–50–7; Chapple 5–0–19–0; Elworthy 20–3–52–2; Keedy 13–2–47–0; Watkinson 11–3–43–0; Gallian 4–2–20–1.

Lancashire

M. A. Atherton c Noon b Cairns	11	– lbw b Cairns	13
J. E. R. Gallian c Pennett b Bates	94	– (11) not out	0
J. P. Crawley c Noon b Pick	77	– c Archer b Bates	11
N. H. Fairbrother c Metcalfe b Afford	80	– c Noon b Afford	59
G. Chapple c Noon b Afford	2	– (8) c Pollard b Afford	1
N. J. Speak lbw b Cairns	1	– (5) not out	74
*M. Watkinson c Bates b Afford	6	– (2) lbw b Afford	39
†W. K. Hegg not out	65	– (6) b Bates	9
S. Elworthy c Noon b Pick	20	– (7) c Johnson b Afford	0
P. J. Martin lbw b Pick	0	– (9) b Afford	0
G. Keedy not out	17	– (10) c Robinson b Afford	0
B 5, l-b 9, n-b 10	24	B 4, l-b 7, n-b 8	19
1/20 2/162 3/233 4/239 5/256 6/277 7/286 8/347 9/347	(9 wkts dec.) 397	1/34 2/55 3/95 4/172 5/189 6/190 7/201 8/201 9/225	(9 wkts) 225

Bonus points – Lancashire 4, Nottinghamshire 4 (Score at 120 overs: 375-9).

Bowling: *First Innings*—Cairns 30–7–95–2; Pennett 20–2–76–0; Pick 20.4–4–74–3; Afford 44–15–83–3; Bates 17–5–55–1. *Second Innings*—Cairns 19–2–77–1; Pennett 4–0–21–0; Bates 17–3–42–2; Pick 7–1–23–0; Afford 25–8–51–6.

Umpires: J. H. Hampshire and J. H. Harris.

At Oxford, May 23, 24, 25. NOTTINGHAMSHIRE drew with OXFORD UNIVERSITY.

NOTTINGHAMSHIRE v DURHAM

At Nottingham, May 30, 31, June 1, 3. Drawn. Nottinghamshire 7 pts, Durham 11 pts. Toss: Nottinghamshire.

Both counties were yet to win in the Championship but Durham seemed well placed after two days. They had amassed 455 and Nottinghamshire were seven down and trailing by 261. The game began to turn when Evans and Pick put on 63 for the ninth wicket. Although the home side followed on, they lost no more wickets on Saturday, as Robinson scored his 60th first-class hundred and put on 211 with Pollard, and only three before rain ended play at tea on Monday. On the opening day, Campbell cut and drove fiercely for his maiden county hundred, after a miserable start at Durham – he had not reached 30 in any competition and his best in the previous five innings was nine. Equally encouraging was Blenkiron's second century of the week; he batted five hours and hit 19 fours. When Nottinghamshire replied, left-armer Brown, the country's leading wicket-taker, took another five. Unfortunately, England coach David Lloyd, who had come to watch him, had already gone.

Close of play: First day, Durham 333-5 (P. D. Collingwood 43*, M. M. Betts 1*); Second day, Nottinghamshire 194-7 (K. P. Evans 7*, M. N. Bowen 0*); Third day, Nottinghamshire 211-0 (P. R. Pollard 63*, R. T. Robinson 125*).

Durham

S. L. Campbell c Noon b Cairns	118
*M. A. Roseberry c Afford b Evans	9
J. E. Morris c Johnson b Evans	1
D. A. Blenkiron run out	130
P. Bainbridge b Pick	8
P. D. Collingwood lbw b Evans	46
M. M. Betts c Noon b Bowen	46
†C. W. Scott lbw b Evans	12
J. Boiling not out	31
J. Wood lbw b Afford	2
S. J. E. Brown c Bowen b Pick	19
L-b 27, n-b 6	33
1/42 2/64 3/206 4/214 5/332 6/338 7/382 8/425 9/428	455

Bonus points – Durham 4, Nottinghamshire 2 (Score at 120 overs: 376-6).

Bowling: Cairns 26–2–88–1; Pick 23.1–2–71–2; Evans 29–9–68–4; Bowen 23–5–67–1; Tolley 20–5–60–0; Afford 30–8–68–1; Archer 2–0–6–0.

Nottinghamshire

P. R. Pollard c Blenkiron b Brown	30	– b Brown	64
R. T. Robinson b Wood	14	– c Campbell b Boiling	184
G. F. Archer c Boiling b Betts	2	– not out	85
*P. Johnson c Scott b Brown	34	– c Collingwood b Boiling	7
C. L. Cairns c Morris b Brown	42	– not out	34
C. M. Tolley lbw b Wood	31		
†W. M. Noon c Bainbridge b Boiling	17		
K. P. Evans not out	40		
M. N. Bowen c Brown b Wood	5		
R. A. Pick c Boiling b Brown	32		
J. A. Afford c Bainbridge b Brown	1		
L-b 3, n-b 18	21	B 3, l-b 13, n-b 18	34
1/36 2/41 3/63 4/120 5/151 6/186 7/190 8/204 9/267	269	1/214 2/294 3/316	(3 wkts) 408

Bonus points – Nottinghamshire 2, Durham 4.

Bowling: *First Innings*—Brown 19.2–4–70–5; Wood 21–3–66–3; Betts 14–2–70–1; Collingwood 3–0–16–0; Boiling 21–7–44–1. *Second Innings*—Brown 24–4–71–1; Betts 15–0–79–0; Wood 21–4–67–0; Boiling 33–6–81–2; Collingwood 23–3–76–0; Bainbridge 4–0–18–0.

Umpires: R. Julian and B. J. Meyer.

NOTTINGHAMSHIRE v NORTHAMPTONSHIRE

At Nottingham, June 6, 7, 8, 10. Drawn. Nottinghamshire 8 pts, Northamptonshire 10 pts. Toss: Northamptonshire. Championship debut: L. N. P. Walker.

Like Durham the previous week, Northamptonshire arrived at Trent Bridge looking for their first Championship win but failed to press home their advantage after enforcing the follow-on. When these teams met in 1995, Northamptonshire scored 781 for seven; this time they contented themselves with 601, batting for five sessions. Tolley dropped both Loye and Bailey early on in their stand of 191 for the third wicket. Bailey survived for nearly eight hours, compiling 163, with back-up from most of his colleagues: Emburey scored 67 in 58 balls, his maiden fifty for his new county. Despite a three-hour century from Johnson, which helped to ensure full batting points, Nottinghamshire were made to follow on 242 behind. But the loss of most of the final morning to rain was a setback for the visitors. Though Emburey caused a tremor in the home camp with three wickets, Cairns and Lyndsay Walker, the Australian-born wicket-keeper now qualified as an Englishman, saw them to safety.

Close of play: First day, Northamptonshire 269-3 (R. J. Bailey 111*, J. P. Taylor 2*); Second day, Nottinghamshire 95-2 (P. R. Pollard 29*, P. Johnson 38*); Third day, Nottinghamshire 29-0 (P. R. Pollard 7*, R. T. Robinson 14*).

Northamptonshire

R. R. Montgomerie c Walker b Cairns	31
A. Fordham c Bates b Evans	2
*R. J. Bailey c Pollard b Afford	163
M. B. Loye c Archer b Evans	98
J. P. Taylor c Pick b Tolley	57
†R. J. Warren c Pollard b Afford	22
D. J. Capel c Walker b Tolley	3
A. L. Penberthy c Walker b Tolley	54
A. R. Roberts b Tolley	34
J. E. Emburey not out	67
C. E. L. Ambrose not out	25
B 14, l-b 17, n-b 14	45
1/24 2/73 3/264 4/365 5/389 6/400 7/410 8/481 9/524	(9 wkts dec.) 601

Bonus points – Northamptonshire 3, Nottinghamshire 1 (Score at 120 overs: 322-3).

Bowling: Cairns 27–4–75–1; Evans 35–12–71–2; Pick 28–7–71–0; Afford 38–9–106–2; Bates 30–5–140–0; Tolley 26–3–107–4.

Nottinghamshire

P. R. Pollard c Emburey b Ambrose	58	– b Emburey	40
R. T. Robinson c Ambrose b Taylor	9	– c Montgomerie b Emburey	44
G. F. Archer b Ambrose	7	– c Ambrose b Emburey	6
*P. Johnson lbw b Taylor	103	– b Roberts	24
†L. N. P. Walker c Montgomerie b Ambrose	36	– not out	17
C. L. Cairns c Penberthy b Emburey	62	– not out	22
C. M. Tolley c Montgomerie b Emburey	4		
K. P. Evans b Ambrose	46		
R. T. Bates c Loye b Ambrose	0		
R. A. Pick lbw b Ambrose	4		
J. A. Afford not out	1		
B 7, l-b 6, n-b 16	29	B 8, l-b 9, n-b 6	23
1/18 2/41 3/193 4/195 5/282 6/295 7/316 8/330 9/338	359	1/81 2/93 3/120 4/138	(4 wkts) 176

Bonus points – Nottinghamshire 4, Northamptonshire 4.

Bowling: *First Innings*—Ambrose 22.5–6–91–6; Taylor 27–6–84–2; Emburey 24–6–69–2; Penberthy 10–2–26–0; Roberts 22–7–58–0; Capel 8–1–18–0. *Second Innings*—Ambrose 7–5–5–0; Taylor 11–6–15–0; Capel 11–3–17–0; Penberthy 8–3–13–0; Emburey 26–7–43–3; Roberts 24–8–61–1; Bailey 5–3–5–0.

Umpires: J. C. Balderstone and N. T. Plews.

At Worcester, June 13, 14, 15, 17. NOTTINGHAMSHIRE drew with WORCESTERSHIRE.

NOTTINGHAMSHIRE v GLOUCESTERSHIRE

At Nottingham, June 20, 21, 22. Nottinghamshire won by an innings and three runs. Nottinghamshire 24 pts, Gloucestershire 3 pts. Toss: Nottinghamshire.

After playing 12 matches – seven defeats and five draws – since their last Championship victory, in July 1995, Nottinghamshire returned to form with an innings win inside three days. Robinson and Metcalfe laid the foundations in an opening stand of 155, then Cairns hit his first hundred of the season, breaking a dressing-room window with one of his three straight sixes. Having followed on in the previous two home games, Nottinghamshire turned the tables by dismissing Gloucestershire 270 behind (Davis was absent due to bereavement). Bowen underlined his emergence with three wickets, while Walker equalled the county record of six dismissals. Gloucestershire gave the home team some anxious moments on the third day, when Symonds celebrated an early let-off by blazing his way to a hundred. But Evans, who had dropped him and split the webbing on his left hand, returned from hospital to wrap the innings up with a spell of five for five in 33 balls.

Close of play: First day, Nottinghamshire 332-5 (C. L. Cairns 80*, L. N. P. Walker 20*); Second day, Gloucestershire 32-0 (A. J. Wright 17*, N. J. Trainor 14*).

Nottinghamshire

R. T. Robinson b Davis	84
A. A. Metcalfe lbw b Walsh	78
G. F. Archer lbw b Lewis	5
*P. Johnson c Lewis b Symonds	36
M. P. Dowman c Wright b Smith	9
C. L. Cairns c Williams b Alleyne	114
†L. N. P. Walker c sub b Walsh	20
K. P. Evans b Smith	33
R. T. Bates c Alleyne b Symonds	28
M. N. Bowen c Williams b Walsh	22
J. A. Afford not out	5
B 5, l-b 8, w 1, n-b 12	26
1/155 2/172 3/208 4/218 5/298 6/332 7/401 8/401 9/446	460

Bonus points – Nottinghamshire 4, Gloucestershire 3 (Score at 120 overs: 404-8).

Bowling: Walsh 28.3–9–80–3; Smith 26–4–110–2; Lewis 23–3–90–1; Alleyne 21–3–62–1; Davis 24–6–58–1; Symonds 14–2–47–2.

Gloucestershire

A. J. Wright c Walker b Cairns	0	b Cairns 19
N. J. Trainor lbw b Cairns	3	c Walker b Cairns 20
R. J. Cunliffe st Walker b Bates	40	b Evans 7
T. H. C. Hancock c Walker b Bowen	11	c Dowman b Bowen 36
A. Symonds st Walker b Bates	57	c Archer b Evans 117
M. W. Alleyne c Walker b Afford	0	c Cairns b Bowen 0
†R. C. J. Williams c Walker b Afford	0	c Archer b Afford 40
A. M. Smith not out	55	(9) c Archer b Evans 4
J. Lewis c Bates b Bowen	17	(10) c Robinson b Evans 9
*C. A. Walsh b Bowen	1	(11) not out 2
R. P. Davis absent		(8) lbw b Evans 0
L-b 2, n-b 4	6	B 4, l-b 5, n-b 4 13
1/0 2/7 3/36 4/97 5/116 6/116 7/125 8/186 9/190	190	1/40 2/45 3/147 4/147 5/229 6/248 7/248 8/251 9/262 267

Bonus points – Nottinghamshire 4.

In the second innings R. J. Cunliffe, when 5, retired hurt at 58 and resumed at 229.

Bowling: *First Innings*—Cairns 17–3–56–2; Evans 9–1–48–0; Bowen 9.1–2–31–3; Bates 13–5–45–2; Afford 5–3–8–2. *Second Innings*—Cairns 20–1–62–2; Bowen 13–5–41–2; Evans 18.4–8–30–5; Bates 16–2–63–0; Afford 19–4–62–1.

Umpires: A. Clarkson and D. R. Shepherd.

At Birmingham, July 4, 5, 6, 8. NOTTINGHAMSHIRE lost to WARWICKSHIRE by 85 runs.

At Chelmsford, July 18, 19, 20, 22. NOTTINGHAMSHIRE lost to ESSEX by six wickets.

At Nottingham, July 26, 27, 28, 29. NOTTINGHAMSHIRE drew with SOUTH AFRICA A (See South Africa A tour section).

NOTTINGHAMSHIRE v GLAMORGAN

At Worksop, August 1, 2, 3, 5. Glamorgan won by eight wickets. Glamorgan 23 pts, Nottinghamshire 6 pts. Toss: Nottinghamshire.

Winning the toss is generally supposed to win the match at Worksop, and Metcalfe took the opportunity to score his first century since joining Nottinghamshire from Yorkshire. He batted for five hours, hitting 18 fours and a straight six into the canal. But James seized the initiative for Glamorgan during a marathon innings lasting eight hours and 18 minutes. By the time he was ninth out, for 235, he had struck 32 fours from 397 balls, broken the ground record – 223 by Walter Keeton in 1934 – and passed his own previous best of 230. Good support from Gibson and Croft ensured a lead of 118. Still, Nottinghamshire looked capable of setting a testing target as Cairns raced to 70 in 67 balls on the final morning. But he gave a return catch first ball after lunch to Gibson, who followed up to produce a collapse of five for nine. Morris saw Glamorgan almost all the way home in pursuit of 124 from 46 overs.

Close of play: First day, Nottinghamshire 268-5 (A. A. Metcalfe 91*, M. N. Bowen 7*); Second day, Glamorgan 231-2 (S. P. James 130*, C. P. Metson 0*); Third day, Nottinghamshire 105-2 (R. T. Robinson 52*, A. A. Metcalfe 20*).

Nottinghamshire

P. R. Pollard b Watkin	34	– c James b Croft	24
R. T. Robinson c Maynard b Watkin	43	– c Gibson b Croft	61
†W. M. Noon c Metson b Croft	26	– lbw b Watkin	0
A. A. Metcalfe c Maynard b Kendrick	128	– c Cottey b Kendrick	41
*P. Johnson lbw b Gibson	7	– b Croft	4
C. L. Cairns b Gibson	38	– c and b Gibson	70
M. N. Bowen c Croft b Watkin	12	– (10) c Croft b Gibson	1
K. P. Evans c Metson b Croft	15	– (7) c and b Kendrick	24
R. T. Bates c Croft b Kendrick	21	– (8) c Cottey b Gibson	0
G. W. Mike c James b Gibson	7	– (9) c Morris b Kendrick	0
J. A. Afford not out	11	– not out	1
L-b 15, w 1, n-b 13	29	B 6, l-b 4, w 1, n-b 4	15
1/78 2/97 3/132 4/162 5/259 6/294 7/325 8/348 9/353	371	1/68 2/69 3/119 4/127 5/189 6/232 7/238 8/238 9/238	241

Bonus points – Nottinghamshire 3, Glamorgan 3 (Score at 120 overs: 325-7).

Bowling: *First Innings*—Watkin 33–16–74–3; Gibson 30.1–8–83–3; Croft 36–19–66–2; Butcher 17–2–74–0; Kendrick 23–8–59–2. *Second Innings*—Watkin 11–3–23–1; Gibson 28.3–7–67–3; Croft 35–8–92–3; Kendrick 13–5–31–3; Butcher 3–0–18–0.

Glamorgan

S. P. James c Noon b Bates	235	– b Bowen	0
H. Morris c Noon b Mike	69	– c Noon b Bates	71
A. W. Evans st Noon b Afford	21	– not out	48
†C. P. Metson c Pollard b Afford	11		
*M. P. Maynard c Noon b Cairns	38	– (4) not out	4
P. A. Cottey b Mike	11		
G. P. Butcher b Cairns	1		
O. D. Gibson c Noon b Evans	30		
R. D. B. Croft c Afford b Bates	56		
N. M. Kendrick not out	1		
S. L. Watkin c Cairns b Bates	0		
B 6, l-b 4, n-b 6	16	L-b 3	3
1/152 2/214 3/255 4/317 5/334 6/335 7/383 8/488 9/489	489	1/19 2/122	(2 wkts) 126

Bonus points – Glamorgan 4, Nottinghamshire 3 (Score at 120 overs: 401-7).

Bowling: *First Innings*—Evans 25–4–89–1; Mike 23–4–104–2; Bowen 20–7–64–0; Bates 23.5–4–72–3; Afford 35–10–90–2; Cairns 15–2–60–2. *Second Innings*—Cairns 7–3–14–0; Bowen 4–0–21–1; Afford 15–6–39–0; Evans 3–1–10–0; Bates 10.3–0–39–1.

Umpires: B. Dudleston and K. J. Lyons.

NOTTINGHAMSHIRE v MIDDLESEX

At Nottingham, August 8, 9, 10. Middlesex won by an innings and seven runs. Middlesex 24 pts, Nottinghamshire 6 pts. Toss: Nottinghamshire. First-class debut: O. A. Shah.

Ramprakash made a fine start as acting-captain, having become Gatting's new heir presumptive when Carr announced his imminent retirement. He led Middlesex to victory in three days and set a fine example with the bat, scoring 71 with 11 fours. It was also a promising beginning for 17-year-old Owais Shah, who came to his first-class debut with a big reputation, and enhanced it by stroking seven fours in his 53. All the visitors' front-line batsmen made useful contributions, in contrast to Nottinghamshire's. They were in trouble from the first morning, slumping to 82 for four, and only a maiden fifty by Afzaal lifted them to the respectability of 257. Facing a first-innings deficit of 170, they collapsed again, to 15 for three. Johnson finished them off with his first five-wicket haul of the season, confirming his return to fitness.

Close of play: First day, Nottinghamshire 257; Second day, Middlesex 407-9 (K. R. Brown 63*, P. C. R. Tufnell 4*).

Nottinghamshire

P. R. Pollard c Ramprakash b Fraser	0	– c Carr b Fay	2
R. T. Robinson b Johnson	23	– c Carr b Johnson	11
A. A. Metcalfe c Brown b Johnson	17	– lbw b Weekes	37
*P. Johnson c Brown b Fraser	18	– lbw b Johnson	0
U. Afzaal b Weekes	51	– b Tufnell	39
C. L. Cairns c Pooley b Tufnell	46	– c Carr b Tufnell	32
K. P. Evans c Shah b Tufnell	23	– b Weekes	0
†W. M. Noon not out	43	– c Brown b Johnson	21
G. W. Mike b Fraser	5	– c Brown b Johnson	0
M. N. Bowen b Tufnell	3	– c Brown b Johnson	2
J. A. Afford lbw b Tufnell	4	– not out	1
B 8, l-b 10, n-b 6	24	B 11, l-b 7	18
1/0 2/40 3/41 4/82 5/153 6/173 7/211 8/228 9/243	257	1/13 2/15 3/15 4/86 5/106 6/106 7/156 8/160 9/162	163

Bonus points – Nottinghamshire 2, Middlesex 4.

Bowling: *First Innings*—Fraser 23–7–73–3; Fay 11–3–31–0; Johnson 19–2–66–2; Tufnell 38–15–41–4; Weekes 12–1–28–1. *Second Innings*—Fraser 12–3–18–0; Fay 12–3–22–1; Johnson 19.5–6–29–5; Tufnell 33–13–45–2; Weekes 14–4–31–2.

Middlesex

P. N. Weekes c and b Cairns	58	R. A. Fay b Evans	14
J. C. Pooley lbw b Cairns	21	A. R. C. Fraser b Evans	9
*M. R. Ramprakash run out	71	P. C. R. Tufnell not out	13
J. D. Carr c and b Afford	49		
O. A. Shah c Noon b Afzaal	53	B 4, l-b 6, w 1, n-b 16	27
†K. R. Brown c Noon b Cairns	70		
K. P. Dutch b Afford	27	1/45 2/159 3/164 4/262 5/276	427
R. L. Johnson c and b Afford	15	6/326 7/357 8/382 9/402	

Bonus points – Middlesex 4, Nottinghamshire 4.

Bowling: Cairns 21.4–2–79–3; Mike 16–1–68–0; Evans 17–3–68–2; Bowen 16–0–60–0; Afford 30–1–87–3; Afzaal 12–0–55–1.

Umpires: H. D. Bird and N. T. Plews.

At Derby, August 15, 16, 17, 19. NOTTINGHAMSHIRE lost to DERBYSHIRE by 303 runs.

NOTTINGHAMSHIRE v SURREY

At Nottingham, August 22, 23, 24, 26. Drawn. Nottinghamshire 8 pts, Surrey 7 pts. Toss: Nottinghamshire.

Bad weather frustrated both sides, washing out the entire second day, half the third and most of the fourth. After five successive defeats, Nottinghamshire were wobbling again at 98 for three. But Archer and Dowman, both recalled after spells out of the first team, responded with a stylish stand of 187 in 38 overs. Dowman scored a maiden Championship century in 110 balls and Archer batted nearly five hours for 143. When play resumed on Saturday, Surrey struggled to 88 for four before Brown blasted a fifty, only his third in the 1996 Championship. Then rain forced contrivance on the final morning. A declaration and a forfeiture set Surrey 319 in 59 overs; they set off boldly but only 13 overs were possible.

Close of play: First day, Nottinghamshire 392-6 (G. F. Archer 143*, W. M. Noon 21*); Second day, No play; Third day, Surrey 128-4 (A. D. Brown 56*, A. J. Hollioake 7*).

Nottinghamshire

R. T. Robinson c Ratcliffe b Benjamin	34	R. T. Bates lbw b Julian	13
A. A. Metcalfe c Butcher b Julian	21	M. N. Bowen not out	1
G. F. Archer b Julian	143		
*P. Johnson c Julian b Pearson	13	B 8, l-b 11, w 6, n-b 22	47
M. P. Dowman c and b D. J. Bicknell	107		
C. L. Cairns c and b Pearson	4	1/64 2/83 3/98 (9 wkts dec.)	446
K. P. Evans c Kersey b D. J. Bicknell	6	4/285 5/290 6/309	
†W. M. Noon c Hollioake b Julian	57	7/399 8/445 9/446	

J. A. Afford did not bat.

Bonus points – Nottinghamshire 4, Surrey 4.

Bowling: M. P. Bicknell 17–2–56–0; Benjamin 16–2–59–1; Julian 21–2–104–4; Hollioake 12–3–43–0; Pearson 29–4–87–2; Shahid 4–0–27–0; D. J. Bicknell 15–0–51–2.

Nottinghamshire forfeited their second innings.

Surrey

D. J. Bicknell c Evans b Cairns	11 – not out	30
M. A. Butcher c Noon b Bowen	6 – not out	14
J. D. Ratcliffe lbw b Afford	23	
N. Shahid c Archer b Evans	20	
A. D. Brown not out	56	
*A. J. Hollioake not out	7	
L-b 2, w 1, n-b 2	5	L-b 3, n-b 6 ... 9
1/19 2/21 3/52 4/88	(4 wkts dec.) 128	(no wkt) 53

†G. J. Kersey, R. M. Pearson, B. P. Julian, M. P. Bicknell and J. E. Benjamin did not bat.

Bonus point – Nottinghamshire 1.

Bowling: *First Innings*—Cairns 7–0–25–1; Bowen 11–3–29–1; Evans 11–3–33–1; Afford 5.3–1–32–1; Bates 2–1–7–0. *Second Innings*—Cairns 4–1–7–0; Bowen 5.5–0–31–0; Evans 3–1–12–0.

Umpires: T. E. Jesty and A. A. Jones.

At Tunbridge Wells, August 29, 30, 31, September 2. NOTTINGHAMSHIRE lost to KENT by seven wickets.

NOTTINGHAMSHIRE v LEICESTERSHIRE

At Nottingham, September 3, 4, 5, 6. Leicestershire won by six wickets. Leicestershire 24 pts, Nottinghamshire 6 pts. Toss: Nottinghamshire.

Leicestershire's victory was rarely in doubt and put them back on top of the table. But Evans and Tolley offered some spirited resistance on the opening day, more than doubling Nottinghamshire's feeble start of 111 for five. However, Wells and Whitaker then took control in a second-wicket stand of 167. Each scored his fourth century of the summer; Wells continued his prolific form, spicing his 119 with 19 fours, while Whitaker played a captain's innings lasting 316 minutes and including 17 fours. Leicestershire led by 115 and looked like winning in three days as Nottinghamshire lost five for 24 in a mid-order collapse. Tolley again dug in, and dragged the game into the fourth day, when Millns quickly finished off his former county to complete a five-wicket haul. Fittingly, it was Whitaker who hit the winning runs before lunch.

Close of play: First day, Nottinghamshire 320-9 (W. M. Noon 38*, J. A. Afford 1*); Second day, Leicestershire 341-5 (J. J. Whitaker 116*, P. A. Nixon 5*); Third day, Nottinghamshire 189-8 (C. M. Tolley 45*, M. N. Bowen 11*).

Nottinghamshire

P. R. Pollard c Parsons b Millns	5 – b Millns	5
R. T. Robinson c Nixon b Simmons	18 – lbw b Millns	50
G. F. Archer c Millns b Simmons	32 – b Simmons	31
*P. Johnson run out	27 – c Maddy b Pierson	10
M. P. Dowman c Whitaker b Brimson	19 – c Parsons b Pierson	3
C. M. Tolley b Pierson	40 – lbw b Millns	46
K. P. Evans lbw b Pierson	71 – c Maddy b Millns	1
†W. M. Noon lbw b Parsons	42 – c Maddy b Pierson	1
R. T. Bates c Simmons b Pierson	31 – lbw b Simmons	8
M. N. Bowen c Nixon b Simmons	14 – b Millns	15
J. A. Afford not out	1 – not out	0
B 1, l-b 6, w 1, n-b 16	24	B 6, l-b 10, w 2, n-b 8 ... 26
1/6 2/64 3/64 4/111 5/111 6/228 7/231 8/287 9/304	324	1/10 2/65 3/98 4/108 5/110 6/116 7/122 8/147 9/195 ... 196

Bonus points – Nottinghamshire 3, Leicestershire 4.

Bowling: *First Innings*—Millns 20–4–69–1; Parsons 24.3–6–78–1; Simmons 26–7–64–3; Wells 10–4–23–0; Brimson 15–3–52–1; Pierson 14–2–31–3. *Second Innings*—Millns 18.1–6–31–5; Parsons 16–5–54–0; Simmons 18–4–46–2; Pierson 15–3–43–3; Brimson 3–1–6–0.

Leicestershire

V. J. Wells c Bates b Dowman	119	– lbw b Bowen	13
D. L. Maddy c Archer b Bates	28	– c and b Bowen	5
*J. J. Whitaker b Tolley	129	– (4) not out	30
B. F. Smith c and b Dowman	24	– (3) c Pollard b Bowen	11
P. V. Simmons b Bowen	0	– lbw b Bates	11
G. I. Macmillan b Afford	28	– not out	7
†P. A. Nixon b Afford	18		
D. J. Millns c Bates b Tolley	0		
G. J. Parsons c Robinson b Bates	53		
A. R. K. Pierson c Noon b Bowen	12		
M. T. Brimson not out	4		
B 8, l-b 4, n-b 12	24	L-b 1, n-b 4	5
1/61 2/228 3/262 4/267 5/327 6/357 7/357 8/387 9/429	439	1/7 2/25 3/40 4/59	(4 wkts) 82

Bonus points – Leicestershire 4, Nottinghamshire 3 (Score at 120 overs: 386-7).

Bowling: *First Innings*—Evans 12–4–23–0; Bowen 32.3–5–97–2; Tolley 25–6–93–2; Bates 25–2–88–2; Afford 33–7–83–2; Dowman 14–3–43–2. *Second Innings*—Bowen 8–0–29–3; Tolley 2–0–10–0; Dowman 2–0–8–0; Bates 5–0–21–1; Afford 1.3–0–13–0.

Umpires: B. J. Meyer and A. G. T. Whitehead.

At Scarborough, September 12, 13. NOTTINGHAMSHIRE lost to YORKSHIRE by an innings and six runs.

At Southampton, September 19, 20, 21, 22. NOTTINGHAMSHIRE drew with HAMPSHIRE.

THE WHYTE & MACKAY RANKINGS

Graham Gooch of Essex and Darren Gough of Yorkshire won £10,000 each after finishing top in the second year of the Whyte & Mackay Rankings.

Players were given a mark for their performance in each match, adjusted to take account of the strength of the opposition and the nature of the pitch. Prizes down to £1,000 were given to the top 20 in both batting and bowling. In addition, Alec Stewart of Surrey won £5,000 as Cricketer of the Year, while Ronnie Irani of Essex and Jack Russell of Gloucestershire took £3,500 each as Best All-Rounder and Best Wicket-Keeper/Batsman respectively. Only England-qualified players were eligible, but special £1,000 awards were made to the leading overseas batsman and bowler.

Batting: 1 G. A. Gooch 525 pts; **2** G. P. Thorpe 471; **3** C. J. Adams 460; **4** N. Hussain 459; **5** M. P. Maynard 447; **6** = M. R. Ramprakash, K. J. Barnett 443; **8** K. M. Curran 442; **9** M. A. Butcher 430; **10** A. J. Stewart 427. **Overseas award:** D. M. Jones 482.

Bowling: 1 D. Gough 526 pts; **2** R. D. B. Croft 510; **3** A. D. Mullally 485; **4** A. R. Caddick 481; **5** M. P. Bicknell 479; **6** S. J. E. Brown 469; **7** J. P. Taylor 468; **8** P. M. Such 455; **9** M. J. McCague 449; **10** D. G. Cork 448. **Overseas award:** C. A. Walsh 513.

SOMERSET

Shane Lee

President: J. Luff
Chairman: R. Parsons
Chairman, Cricket Committee: B. C. Rose
Chief Executive: P. W. Anderson
Captain: 1996 – A. N. Hayhurst
1997 – P. D. Bowler
Coach: D. A. Reeve
Head Groundsman: P. Frost
Scorer: D. A. Oldam

On the field, Somerset had a better year than many expected, given the absence of their Pakistani leg-spinner Mushtaq Ahmed, the unknown quality of his stand-in, 22-year-old Australian Shane Lee, and the fitness doubts surrounding Andrew Caddick. However, the last weeks of the season were darkened by the whiff of intrigue, and especially by the clumsiness the club showed in dumping the captain, Andy Hayhurst.

Hayhurst evidently felt his days were numbered: during the winter, he had applied (unsuccessfully) for an administrative post at his native county, Lancashire. But he and the vice-captain, Peter Bowler, were given exclusive responsibility for the first team. Hayhurst did make some useful one-day contributions, but his first-class form was poor and he was regularly criticised – losing captains often are – especially after the side's unsatisfactory performance in the NatWest quarter-final at The Oval. Back at Taunton next day, he was dropped before the Championship match against Hampshire and told to regain his form in the Second Eleven. He did make plenty of runs there, but was not picked for the first team again and he was then released. Somerset agreed to send him on a cricket-orientated business course organised by the TCCB, but it was a humiliating way to treat an amiable and loyal player. He left to take charge of Derbyshire's Second Eleven – while Colin Wells, let go by Derbyshire, moved to do that job at Somerset.

From August, the team was run by acting-captain Bowler, cricket committee chairman Brian Rose and Bob Cottam, director of cricket. But in early September, Cottam left ''by mutual consent'', with a year of his contract to run. Ironically, his son Andy, the left-arm spinner released in 1993, was hastily summoned to play in the two matches which followed the announcement. Dermot Reeve, whose inspirational reign as Warwickshire captain had ended after an unsuccessful hip operation, was soon linked to the Somerset coaching job and his appointment was then confirmed, with Bowler being handed the captaincy.

Somerset's achievements in 1996 did offer something for Reeve to build on. Five convincing Championship victories, including their first in Yorkshire since 1981, took them to 11th, a slight drop, but ten victories in the Sunday League – their most since 1983 – suggested a significant and rather surprising advance. The best point in the knockout competitions was the NatWest victory over Gloucestershire at Taunton, which featured a hat-trick from Caddick and was wrapped up before four o'clock.

The great playing bonus came from Lee. Members will remember his season fondly; his classical driving and general competence often rescued the batting, always lifted the scoring-rate and several times completely turned a match. A matter of 1,300 Championship runs at 65.00 and, after a rather expensive start, 36 wickets at 47.36, keen fielding and numerous important one-day efforts made him the Player of the Season. Graham Rose, although slow to find batting form, had one of his best years for bowling, with 50 wickets, while Caddick's recovery from his shin problems was remarkable. He bowled 525 overs – more than anyone else at Somerset – in 13 Championship matches, took 65 wickets at 26.81 and won a Test recall and a winter tour. It was a great tribute to his tenacity and drive to succeed.

The other main wicket-takers were Kevin Shine, signed from Middlesex, and off-spinner Jeremy Batty, though he was not re-engaged. Batty had also served some useful stints as night-watchman, while he and Shine bravely saved the match at Bristol by holding out for 46 minutes against a rampaging Courtney Walsh, who had just smashed Richard Harden's finger and sent Bowler to hospital for stitches to a horrid wound near his left eye. To Bowler's credit, he was ready to resume, but happily he was not needed. In the very next match, though, he made important runs opening the innings against Curtly Ambrose.

He and Mark Lathwell had a pretty satisfactory season, both averaging over 40, while Harden came back well after two finger fractures. But it was a variable year for Marcus Trescothick, who played only two significant innings, though those helped to beat Hampshire and Northamptonshire. Rob Turner batted in a much more attacking vein than previously and behind the stumps produced the two fielding moments of the season: a 40-yard sprint and full-length dive to catch Reeve, in the Sunday game with Warwickshire, and the stumping of Mark Butcher off a leg-side wide, at The Oval in the NatWest Trophy. Piran Holloway struggled at first, and spent a long time in the Second Eleven, but ended with a long, patient 168 against Middlesex. After an early injury, Keith Parsons made some good contributions with bat and ball, while Jason Kerr played match-saving innings against South Africa A and Derbyshire. Andre van Troost made little progress and Harvey Trump played only three Championship games, though he was a vital member of the one-day attack. Simon Ecclestone began superbly, with two centuries, 92 and 62 in his first five one-day innings, but never quite recaptured that brilliance after a knee injury.

The manoeuvrings surrounding Hayhurst and Cottam were not the only worries off the field. Talk of Caddick changing counties (he decided to stay) kept the rumours seething unpleasantly. It was announced that the Weston-super-Mare festival would be abandoned, after its main sponsor, who had kept it going since 1968, withdrew. Meanwhile, a member who paid a visit to the local planning department discovered that the club's plans to move from the County Ground at Taunton had progressed further than generally supposed. However, the membership are only just beginning to digest the implications of such an idea. It remains no more than a long-term committee objective, and there could be a lot of argument before it happens.

Most members will remember far worse discord in the not-too-distant past, but they were also reminded of happier times when the Pakistanis came to Taunton in July. During the match, Mushtaq signed a new contract for 1997 and 1998, before bowling Somerset to defeat, and there was also the opportunity to renew acquaintance with the tour manager Yawar Saeed – a well-liked, capable and enthusiastic Somerset player of the mid-1950s. – ERIC HILL.

SOMERSET 1996

[*Bill Smith*

Back row: P. C. L. Holloway, K. J. Shine, S. C. Ecclestone, G. D. Rose, J. I. D. Kerr, M. Dimond. *Middle row:* R. J. Turner, J. D. Batty, A. P. van Troost, J. C. Hallett, M. E. Trescothick, K. A. Parsons, I. E. Bishop, H. R. J. Trump. *Front row:* M. N. Lathwell, P. D. Bowler, A. N. Hayhurst (*captain*), R. Parsons (*chairman*), R. M. H. Cottam (*director of cricket*), R. J. Harden, A. R. Caddick. *Inset:* S. Lee.

SOMERSET RESULTS

All first-class matches – Played 19: Won 5, Lost 7, Drawn 7.

County Championship matches – Played 17: Won 5, Lost 6, Drawn 6.

Competition placings – Britannic Assurance County Championship, 11th; NatWest Trophy, q-f; Benson and Hedges Cup, 4th in Group C; AXA Equity & Law League, 5th.

COUNTY CHAMPIONSHIP AVERAGES

BATTING

Cap		*M*	*I*	*NO*	*R*	*HS*	*100s*	*50s*	*Avge*	*Ct/St*
1996	S. Lee§	16	23	3	1,300	167*	5	5	65.00	14
1992	M. N. Lathwell	16	28	4	1,059	109	1	7	44.12	10
1995	P. D. Bowler	17	30	4	1,075	207	2	5	41.34	5
	P. C. L. Holloway	9	14	1	482	168	1	3	37.07	6
1989	R. J. Harden†	12	20	1	676	136	1	5	35.57	11
1994	R. J. Turner	17	25	6	645	100*	1	3	33.94	61/3
	K. A. Parsons†	6	11	1	332	83*	0	3	33.20	2
	S. C. Ecclestone	6	9	1	237	94	0	2	29.62	2
	J. I. D. Kerr	5	7	3	116	68*	0	1	29.00	0
	M. E. Trescothick†	13	22	0	628	178	1	1	28.54	11
1988	G. D. Rose	14	19	4	338	93*	0	1	22.53	8
1990	A. N. Hayhurst	9	13	1	224	96	0	2	18.66	2
	J. D. Batty	14	20	4	276	44	0	0	17.25	4
1992	A. R. Caddick	13	17	4	187	38	0	0	14.38	7
	K. J. Shine	10	12	2	91	40	0	0	9.10	4
	A. P. van Troost	5	6	1	22	11	0	0	4.40	0

Also batted: A. C. Cottam (2 matches) 3, 12; H. R. J. Trump† (3 matches) 0*, 0 (3 ct).

* *Signifies not out.* † *Born in Somerset.* § *Overseas player.*

BOWLING

	O	*M*	*R*	*W*	*BB*	*5W/i*	*Avge*
G. D. Rose	382.2	96	1,171	50	7-47	3	23.42
A. R. Caddick	524.5	120	1,743	65	7-83	6	26.81
K. J. Shine	238.3	43	1,007	32	6-95	2	31.46
J. D. Batty	411.5	88	1,298	29	5-85	1	44.75
S. Lee	397.3	62	1,705	36	4-52	0	47.36
J. I. D. Kerr	116	14	512	10	3-108	0	51.20

Also bowled: P. D. Bowler 31.3–2–177–3; A. C. Cottam 89–22–248–3; R. J. Harden 8–0–42–1; A. N. Hayhurst 25–5–91–1; P. C. L. Holloway 4.4–1–34–0; K. A. Parsons 29–7–102–1; M. E. Trescothick 23–1–97–0; H. R. J. Trump 43–10–179–4; R. J. Turner 1–0–3–0; A. P. van Troost 92.3–12–409–9.

COUNTY RECORDS

Highest score for:	322	I. V. A. Richards v Warwickshire at Taunton	1985
Highest score against:	424	A. C. MacLaren (Lancashire) at Taunton	1895
Best bowling for:	10-49	E. J. Tyler v Surrey at Taunton	1895
Best bowling against:	10-35	A. Drake (Yorkshire) at Weston-super-Mare	1914
Highest total for:	675-9 dec.	v Hampshire at Bath	1924
Highest total against:	811	by Surrey at The Oval	1899
Lowest total for:	25	v Gloucestershire at Bristol	1947
Lowest total against:	22	by Gloucestershire at Bristol	1920

SOMERSET v SURREY

At Taunton, May 2, 3, 4, 6. Drawn. Somerset 11 pts, Surrey 9 pts. Toss: Somerset. Championship debuts: S. Lee; B. P. Julian.

Somerset had hopes of winning on the final day, after taking a lead of 191, but Surrey's runs came rapidly and only four wickets fell. Hollioake reached his second hundred of the game in 79 balls – the first Surrey batsman to score twin centuries since Alan Butcher in 1984 – and put on 196 in the final 31 overs with Thorpe. They also shared a 99-run stand in the first innings, when Thorpe resumed after being hit on the forearm by van Troost on the truncated opening day. Shine, like Lewis appearing for his third county, took six. When the home side replied, Lathwell went third ball, but Bowler and Hayhurst added 248 and next day Bowler reached 207, his best yet for Somerset. He batted for 381 minutes and 349 balls and hit 29 fours. Lee attacked delightfully in a run-a-ball 87 and Shine swung effectively for 40 from 24 balls, while Extras contributed 79. But there was too little time to achieve a result.

Close of play: First day, Surrey 34-2 (A. J. Stewart 10*, A. D. Brown 0*); Second day, Somerset 117-1 (P. D. Bowler 59*, A. N. Hayhurst 29*); Third day, Somerset 558.

Surrey

D. J. Bicknell c Lee b Shine	4	– c Lee b Rose	58
M. A. Butcher b Shine	13	– c sub b Shine	52
*A. J. Stewart b Shine	21	– c Turner b van Troost	33
G. P. Thorpe c Turner b Shine	52	– not out	100
A. D. Brown lbw b Shine	7	– b Lee	20
A. J. Hollioake b Lee	128	– not out	117
C. C. Lewis c Turner b Shine	42		
B. P. Julian b van Troost	50		
†G. J. Kersey lbw b van Troost	3		
M. P. Bicknell b Lee	19		
R. M. Pearson not out	8		
L-b 7, w 3, n-b 10	20	B 4, l-b 7, w 1, n-b 18	30
1/15 2/20 3/52 4/55 5/154 6/281 7/281 8/317 9/348	367	1/104 2/153 3/165 4/214	(4 wkts) 410

Bonus points – Surrey 4, Somerset 4.

In the first innings G. P. Thorpe, when 5, retired hurt at 27 and resumed at 52.

Bowling: *First Innings*—Shine 24–5–95–6; van Troost 22–2–109–2; Lee 19.2–1–88–2; Rose 15–3–68–0. *Second Innings*—Shine 22–6–101–1; van Troost 15–2–86–1; Rose 18–4–79–1; Lee 16–2–95–1; Hayhurst 5–1–29–0; Bowler 2–0–4–0; Holloway 2–1–5–0.

Somerset

M. N. Lathwell lbw b M. P. Bicknell	0
P. D. Bowler c Kersey b M. P. Bicknell	207
*A. N. Hayhurst c Lewis b Julian	69
R. J. Harden c Kersey b Lewis	3
P. C. L. Holloway b M. P. Bicknell	54
S. Lee not out	87
†R. J. Turner c Thorpe b Hollioake	6
G. D. Rose lbw b Hollioake	1
S. C. Ecclestone c D. J. Bicknell b Hollioake	6
K. J. Shine b Lewis	40
A. P. van Troost c Stewart b Lewis	6
B 5, l-b 16, w 4, n-b 54	79
1/0 2/248 3/253 4/377 5/444 6/471 7/473 8/487 9/544	558

Bonus points – Somerset 4, Surrey 2 (Score at 120 overs: 448-5).

Bowling: M. P. Bicknell 32–5–105–3; Lewis 28–3–125–3; Julian 24–2–98–1; Hollioake 17–1–80–3; Pearson 12–0–53–0; Butcher 16–3–50–0; Thorpe 8–2–26–0.

Umpires: D. J. Constant and K. E. Palmer.

SOMERSET v NOTTINGHAMSHIRE

At Taunton, May 9, 10, 11. Somerset won by ten wickets. Somerset 23 pts, Nottinghamshire 5 pts. Toss: Somerset.

Somerset won at 12.35 on Saturday, thanks largely to Rose. He made ideal use of the conditions – cold, cloudy weather and a pitch showing occasional life – to match his previous best analysis, six for 41 on debut for Middlesex back in 1985. Next day, he took another six, and he needed only two balls on the third day to lift his career-best to seven for 47. He claimed 13 for 88 in the match, never having taken ten before. Nottinghamshire collapsed from 144 for three to 200 on the opening day, but then reduced Somerset to 57 for three plus one retired; Cairns hit Hayhurst on the collar-bone, though he resumed on Friday. However, Lee played brilliantly for 82 in 77 balls, supported by Holloway, who scored a patient three-hour 50, while night-watchman Batty struck ten fours in his 44. The visitors' batting produced a little more the second time, but a target of 130 took Lathwell and Bowler just 22 overs.

Close of play: First day, Somerset 187-4 (P. C. L. Holloway 36*, J. D. Batty 8*); Second day, Nottinghamshire 236-9 (D. B. Pennett 7*, J. A. Afford 0*).

Nottinghamshire

R. T. Robinson lbw b Rose	34	– lbw b Caddick	37
A. A. Metcalfe c Turner b Shine	9	– c Holloway b Rose	47
G. F. Archer lbw b Lee	83	– b Shine	36
*P. Johnson lbw b Rose	0	– lbw b Rose	0
M. P. Dowman c Turner b Caddick	22	– b Lee	6
C. L. Cairns c Lee b Rose	15	– c Turner b Rose	48
C. M. Tolley c Turner b Rose	9	– c sub b Rose	12
†W. M. Noon c Turner b Rose	6	– lbw b Rose	18
R. A. Pick b Rose	0	– b Rose	10
D. B. Pennett c and b Lee	8	– c Lee b Rose	7
J. A. Afford not out	0	– not out	2
L-b 6, w 3, n-b 5	14	L-b 10, w 1, n-b 4	15
1/24 2/84 3/92 4/144 5/170 6/170 7/183 8/191 9/196	200	1/75 2/93 3/93 4/124 5/153 6/195 7/202 8/224 9/229	238

Bonus points – Nottinghamshire 1, Somerset 4.

Bowling: *First Innings*—Caddick 14–4–35–1; Shine 15–3–50–1; Lee 15–2–68–2; Rose 19–9–41–6. *Second Innings*—Caddick 21–8–70–1; Shine 11–2–53–1; Rose 20.2–8–47–7; Lee 10–2–30–1; Batty 11–3–28–0.

Somerset

M. N. Lathwell run out	40	– not out	66
P. D. Bowler lbw b Pennett	7	– not out	57
*A. N. Hayhurst not out	5		
R. J. Harden lbw b Cairns	0		
P. C. L. Holloway c Metcalfe b Pennett	50		
S. Lee c Metcalfe b Afford	82		
J. D. Batty b Pennett	44		
†R. J. Turner lbw b Pennett	4		
G. D. Rose c Dowman b Cairns	29		
A. R. Caddick c Johnson b Afford	7		
K. J. Shine c Archer b Afford	19		
B 1, l-b 5, w 2, n-b 14	22	L-b 3, n-b 4	7
1/36 2/47 3/57 4/175 5/238 6/244 7/255 8/267 9/303	309	(no wkt)	130

Bonus points – Somerset 3, Nottinghamshire 4.

In the first innings A. N. Hayhurst, when 0, retired hurt at 39 and resumed at 303.

Bowling: *First Innings*—Cairns 18.3–2–81–2; Pennett 20–2–116–4; Pick 11–2–41–0; Tolley 5–0–27–0; Dowman 3–1–12–0; Afford 13–4–26–3. *Second Innings*—Cairns 7–1–26–0; Pennett 6–1–45–0; Pick 5–0–37–0; Tolley 4–0–19–0.

Umpires: B. Leadbeater and R. Palmer.

At Bristol, May 16, 17, 18, 20. SOMERSET drew with GLOUCESTERSHIRE.

SOMERSET v NORTHAMPTONSHIRE

At Taunton, May 23, 24, 25, 27. Somerset won by four wickets. Somerset 20 pts, Northamptonshire 4 pts. Toss: Somerset.

Rain effectively reduced this match to two innings, with an exchange of declarations leaving Somerset to get 330 from 89 overs. They achieved it with nine balls to spare. The hostile Ambrose removed Lathwell first ball, but Bowler and Trescothick restored the innings before Lee joined Trescothick to put on 152 in 33 overs. Lee scored his maiden century for Somerset, an ebullient career-best 113 not out, from 135 balls, with two sixes and 11 fours. Northamptonshire had lost both openers cheaply in the 21 overs possible on the first day. But, after the second-day washout, Loye overcame some early troubles on a juicy surface to score his first hundred since June 1994, hitting 20 fours and a six. Then Capel, who struck three sixes and nine fours, and Penberthy put on 108 at six an over for the seventh wicket, before the bartering began.

Close of play: First day, Northamptonshire 62-2 (R. J. Bailey 26*, M. B. Loye 23*); Second day, No play; Third day, Somerset 88-0 (M. N. Lathwell 44*, P. D. Bowler 34*).

Northamptonshire

R. R. Montgomerie c Rose b Caddick	5	– not out	19
A. Fordham c Turner b Shine	4	– not out	14
*R. J. Bailey lbw b Rose	34		
M. B. Loye b Batty	114		
†R. J. Warren lbw b Rose	28		
D. J. Capel lbw b Shine	68		
K. M. Curran c Trescothick b Rose	5		
A. L. Penberthy c Bowler b Shine	45		
J. E. Emburey c Rose b Batty	12		
C. E. L. Ambrose not out	21		
J. P. Taylor not out	18		
B 5, l-b 10, w 6, n-b 8	29	W 1	1
1/8 2/14 3/86 4/187 5/201 6/206 7/314 8/321 9/343 (9 wkts dec.)	383	(no wkt dec.)	34

Bonus points – Northamptonshire 4, Somerset 4.

Bowling: *First Innings*—Caddick 23–5–56–1; Shine 22–4–95–3; Rose 22–7–47–3; Lee 11–2–78–0; Hayhurst 3–0–20–0; Batty 18–0–72–2. *Second Innings*—Trescothick 3–0–18–0; Hayhurst 2–0–8–0; Holloway 0.2–0–8–0.

Somerset

M. N. Lathwell not out	44	– c Curran b Ambrose	0
P. D. Bowler not out	34	– b Capel	66
*A. N. Hayhurst (did not bat)		– c Capel b Ambrose	15
M. E. Trescothick (did not bat)		– run out	83
P. C. L. Holloway (did not bat)		– c Emburey b Taylor	5
S. Lee (did not bat)		– not out	113
†R. J. Turner (did not bat)		– c Ambrose b Penberthy	15
G. D. Rose (did not bat)		– not out	9
L-b 6, n-b 4	10	B 5, l-b 4, w 1, n-b 14	24
(no wkt dec.)	88	1/0 2/36 3/101 4/114 5/266 6/308 (6 wkts)	330

J. D. Batty, A. R. Caddick and K. J. Shine did not bat.

Bowling: *First Innings*—Ambrose 6–1–12–0; Taylor 7–2–31–0; Capel 5–2–7–0; Curran 7–1–26–0; Emburey 3–1–6–0. *Second Innings*—Ambrose 21–2–61–2; Taylor 15–2–67–1; Emburey 19.3–0–70–0; Curran 6–1–34–0; Penberthy 15–0–52–1; Capel 7–1–23–1; Bailey 4–0–14–0.

Umpires: J. H. Hampshire and G. Sharp.

SOMERSET v WARWICKSHIRE

At Taunton, June 6, 7, 8, 10. Warwickshire won by 99 runs. Warwickshire 22 pts, Somerset 5 pts. Toss: Somerset. First-class debut: D. A. Altree.

Warwickshire won in the final session of a match made fascinating by the variations of the weather. A hot Thursday brought swing and movement off a grassy pitch, and Caddick bowled superbly. Penney repeatedly played and missed, but with luck and determination scored 77. When Somerset replied, in easier conditions, the only significant stand came from Lee and Trescothick, with 95 for the fifth wicket. Warwickshire's second innings was interrupted by a storm on Friday afternoon but, puzzlingly, Caddick was used at the wrong end next morning and could not exploit the dampest part of the wicket. The batsmen seized the advantage before Rose broke through and Caddick, finally switching ends, took four for three to complete ten in the match. Somerset's final target was 339 in 109 overs. But, from 79 for five, only Holloway and Lee showed much fight as the ball began to turn significantly.

Close of play: First day, Somerset 106-4 (M. E. Trescothick 18*, S. Lee 17*); Second day, Warwickshire 58-1 (A. J. Moles 27*, D. P. Ostler 0*); Third day, Somerset 18-1 (P. D. Bowler 14*, J. D. Batty 2*).

Warwickshire

*A. J. Moles lbw b Rose	17	– lbw b Rose	75
W. G. Khan b Caddick	1	– c Lathwell b Caddick	15
D. P. Ostler c Rose b Caddick	2	– c Turner b Rose	66
T. L. Penney run out	77	– c Turner b Caddick	52
D. R. Brown c Lathwell b Caddick	34	– c Hayhurst b Caddick	11
S. M. Pollock c Holloway b Lee	43	– c Turner b Caddick	0
†K. J. Piper lbw b Caddick	18	– c Turner b Caddick	8
G. Welch c Lee b Caddick	9	– c Caddick b Lee	31
N. M. K. Smith c Turner b Rose	28	– b Batty	37
A. F. Giles b Lee	5	– st Turner b Batty	3
D. A. Altree not out	0	– not out	0
B 2, l-b 3, w 6, n-b 10	21	B 4, l-b 12, w 1, n-b 10	27
1/3 2/7 3/46 4/124 5/159 6/202 7/214 8/219 9/240	255	1/58 2/159 3/206 4/237 5/237 6/248 7/253 8/322 9/322	325

Bonus points – Warwickshire 2, Somerset 4.

Bowling: *First Innings*—Caddick 23–6–76–5; Shine 11–1–33–0; Rose 13.1–4–37–2; Lee 19–5–85–2; Batty 7–3–19–0. *Second Innings*—Caddick 25–7–85–5; Shine 13–1–52–0; Lee 15–2–42–1; Rose 19–5–58–2; Batty 24.2–6–72–2.

Somerset

M. N. Lathwell lbw b Pollock	18	– c Moles b Pollock	1
P. D. Bowler c Penney b Brown	30	– c Piper b Pollock	16
*A. N. Hayhurst lbw b Pollock	11	– (4) run out	5
M. E. Trescothick run out	34	– (5) c and b Giles	20
P. C. L. Holloway b Brown	0	– (6) b Giles	42
S. Lee c Brown b Welch	65	– (7) c Smith b Giles	61
†R. J. Turner not out	24	– (8) c Giles b Pollock	14
G. D. Rose c Moles b Welch	0	– (9) not out	13
J. D. Batty c Piper b Altree	8	– (3) lbw b Smith	21
A. R. Caddick c Altree b Brown	10	– c Giles b Smith	11
K. J. Shine c Smith b Welch	9	– c Penney b Giles	0
B 6, l-b 8, w 11, n-b 8	33	B 5, l-b 13, w 1, n-b 16	35
1/35 2/63 3/78 4/80 5/175 6/193 7/193 8/204 9/232	242	1/12 2/22 3/40 4/61 5/79 6/175 7/211 8/215 9/236	239

Bonus points – Somerset 1, Warwickshire 4.

Bowling: *First Innings*—Pollock 21–8–35–2; Altree 13–2–68–1; Welch 15–1–64–3; Brown 20–6–61–3; Smith 1–1–0–0. *Second Innings*—Pollock 22–8–37–3; Brown 9–5–15–0; Smith 29–10–57–2; Welch 8–1–31–0; Altree 3–0–12–0; Giles 28.2–10–69–4.

Umpires: R. Julian and R. Palmer.

At Swansea, June 13, 14, 15, 17. SOMERSET lost to GLAMORGAN by 173 runs.

SOMERSET v WORCESTERSHIRE

At Bath, June 19, 20, 21, 22. Worcestershire won by one wicket. Worcestershire 20 pts, Somerset 6 pts. Toss: Somerset.

A memorable last day saw bottom-placed Worcestershire win by one wicket with three balls to spare. Their target of 446 equalled the second-highest fourth-innings total ever made to win a Championship match, and two men were run out on 445 before last man Sheriyar cover-drove his first ball for four. It was a captivating match of collapse and recovery. On the opening day, Bowler steered Somerset to 203 for two, before Illingworth stepped in with five wickets. After rain next morning, Caddick, who bowled throughout Worcestershire's innings, instigated a collapse to 91 for six, but Rhodes and Lampitt added a brave 75 before he took his haul to seven. Then it was Somerset's turn to fold, until Lee, who scored a personal best of 167 not out from 227 balls, with 25 fours and a six, and Turner added 278. They beat the county's seventh-wicket record of 240, set by Sammy Woods and Vernon Hill against Kent in 1898. Hayhurst's declaration gave his bowlers just over a day to dismiss Worcestershire, but the visitors were soon on the attack. There were tactical shortcomings, but also wonderful batting. Eventually, Solanki, with a lovely maiden fifty, and Rhodes, who survived a chance on 43 and went on to 92, played the decisive innings.

Close of play: First day, Worcestershire 8-0 (T. S. Curtis 0*, W. P. C. Weston 4*); Second day, Somerset 53-3 (P. C. L. Holloway 4*, M. E. Trescothick 0*); Third day, Worcestershire 44-0 (T. S. Curtis 28*, W. P. C. Weston 13*).

Somerset

M. N. Lathwell b Lampitt	37	– c Weston b Newport	18
P. D. Bowler c Spiring b Sheriyar	112	– c Curtis b Sheriyar	22
P. C. L. Holloway lbw b Leatherdale	11	– (4) b Illingworth	11
M. E. Trescothick st Rhodes b Illingworth	27	– (5) lbw b Newport	16
*A. N. Hayhurst c Rhodes b Illingworth	4	– (6) c Weston b Illingworth	10
S. Lee c Leatherdale b Illingworth	4	– (7) not out	167
†R. J. Turner c Solanki b Illingworth	12	– (8) not out	100
G. D. Rose c Illingworth b Newport	6		
J. D. Batty c Leatherdale b Newport	5	– (3) c Weston b Sheriyar	0
A. R. Caddick b Illingworth	4		
H. R. J. Trump not out	0		
B 8, l-b 1, n-b 32	41	L-b 16, w 2, n-b 14	32
1/126 2/170 3/203 4/213 5/221 6/235 7/254 8/254 9/259	263	1/38 2/39 3/52 4/81 5/87 6/98	(6 wkts dec.) 376

Bonus points – Somerset 2, Worcestershire 4.

Bowling: *First Innings*—Newport 20.5–5–54–2; Sheriyar 13–2–62–1; Leatherdale 14–5–28–1; Lampitt 23–6–70–1; Illingworth 29–10–40–5. *Second Innings*—Newport 19–3–53–2; Sheriyar 25.1–1–107–2; Lampitt 14–2–70–0; Illingworth 31–7–69–2; Moody 4–1–14–0; Solanki 11–2–47–0.

Worcestershire

T. S. Curtis c Trescothick b Caddick	7	– lbw b Rose	85
W. P. C. Weston c Trescothick b Caddick	15	– c Turner b Caddick	34
K. R. Spiring c Turner b Caddick	14	– lbw b Caddick	1
*T. M. Moody b Lee	20	– b Batty	54
D. A. Leatherdale c Turner b Lee	12	– (10) run out	0
V. S. Solanki c Batty b Caddick	13	– (5) c Hayhurst b Caddick	71
†S. J. Rhodes lbw b Rose	47	– (6) not out	92
S. R. Lampitt b Caddick	30	– (7) c Rose b Caddick	32
P. J. Newport c Trescothick b Caddick	18	– (8) c Holloway b Lee	23
R. K. Illingworth c Trump b Caddick	0	– (9) run out	32
A. Sheriyar not out	0	– not out	4
L-b 16, n-b 2	18	B 8, l-b 8, w 1, n-b 4	21
1/23 2/31 3/60 4/62 5/84 6/91 7/166 8/194 9/194	194	1/105 2/107 3/166 4/202 5/276 6/334 7/392 8/445 9/445	(9 wkts) 449

Bonus points – Somerset 4.

Bowling: *First Innings*—Caddick 27.4–10–83–7; Rose 8–2–20–1; Lee 19–3–75–2. *Second Innings*—Caddick 36.3–5–151–4; Rose 25–6–80–1; Batty 26–5–79–1; Lee 11–0–65–1; Trump 12–1–55–0; Hayhurst 2–0–3–0.

Umpires: J. D. Bond and N. T. Plews.

At Manchester, June 27, 28, 29, July 1. SOMERSET drew with LANCASHIRE.

At Taunton, July 3, 4, 5. SOMERSET lost to PAKISTANIS by 105 runs (See Pakistani tour section).

At Taunton, July 20, 21, 22. SOMERSET drew with SOUTH AFRICA A (See South Africa A tour section).

At Scarborough, July 24, 25, 26, 27. SOMERSET beat YORKSHIRE by 197 runs.

SOMERSET v HAMPSHIRE

At Taunton, August 1, 2, 3. Somerset won by an innings and 151 runs. Somerset 24 pts, Hampshire 3 pts. Toss: Hampshire. Championship debut: W. S. Kendall.

An hour before play began, Somerset's cricket chairman, Brian Rose, informed the captain, Andy Hayhurst, that he was being dropped because of poor form. He did not return to the first team and was released in the autumn. Bowler took charge while Trescothick replaced Hayhurst in the batting line-up. Bowler was out for a duck, but finished the game with three catches at deepish mid-on and led Somerset to victory before lunch on the third day. Meanwhile, Trescothick scored a career-best 178, with 32 fours. Harden helped him add 154 while Graham Rose made an unbeaten 93 out of a commanding 541. Then Caddick exploited cloud cover to take four for eight in 19 balls. Though Somerset had lost Shine, who damaged his ankle ligaments in practice on the second day, the decisive seam assault forced Hampshire to follow on 382 behind. They fared little better, though conditions had eased and Keech batted positively. Batty finished the match by taking five wickets, his best return for Somerset. The game marked the end of another career besides Hayhurst's: it was to be Terry's final appearance before leaving Hampshire.

Close of play: First day, Somerset 412-6 (R. J. Turner 29*, G. D. Rose 55*); Second day, Hampshire 103-5 (A. N. Aymes 3*, M. Keech 4*).

Somerset

M. N. Lathwell c Aymes b Bovill	13
M. E. Trescothick c Keech b Bovill	178
*P. D. Bowler c Aymes b Milburn	0
R. J. Harden c Keech b Udal	54
K. A. Parsons c Aymes b Stephenson	30
S. Lee c Kendall b Stephenson	26
†R. J. Turner lbw b Bovill	57
G. D. Rose not out	93
J. D. Batty c Terry b James	21
A. R. Caddick c Aymes b Bovill	38
K. J. Shine absent hurt	
B 2, l-b 8, w 3, n-b 18	31
1/22 2/39 3/193 4/244 5/310 6/324 7/468 8/491 9/541	541

Bonus points – Somerset 4, Hampshire 3 (Score at 120 overs: 494-8).

Bowling: Bovill 32.3–5–140–4; Milburn 27–1–127–1; James 23–2–101–1; Stephenson 23–2–97–2; Udal 23–6–63–1; Laney 2–0–3–0.

Hampshire

*J. P. Stephenson c Turner b Caddick	5	– c sub b Parsons	21
J. S. Laney lbw b Caddick	50	– c Turner b Caddick	32
K. D. James c Harden b Lee	12	– run out	19
R. A. Smith b Rose	8	– c Rose b Batty	3
V. P. Terry lbw b Caddick	13	– c Lathwell b Batty	20
M. Keech b Caddick	0	– (7) c Bowler b Batty	61
W. S. Kendall c Trescothick b Caddick	6	– (8) lbw b Rose	19
†A. N. Aymes not out	24	– (6) c Turner b Caddick	12
S. D. Udal lbw b Rose	0	– not out	25
S. M. Milburn c Turner b Rose	7	– c Bowler b Batty	4
J. N. B. Bovill c Parsons b Batty	17	– c Bowler b Batty	1
L-b 12, w 1, n-b 4	17	L-b 6, n-b 8	14
1/6 2/43 3/60 4/86 5/90 6/103 7/104 8/107 9/125	159	1/35 2/65 3/68 4/96 5/96 6/126 7/186 8/212 9/225	231

Bonus points – Somerset 4.

Bowling: *First Innings*—Caddick 14–1–46–5; Lee 9–2–36–1; Rose 13–3–49–3; Batty 3.4–0–16–1. *Second Innings*—Caddick 20–8–44–2; Lee 2–0–25–0; Rose 16–6–46–1; Parsons 7–2–25–1; Batty 24.4–4–85–5.

Umpires: A. A. Jones and M. J. Kitchen.

SOMERSET v ESSEX

At Taunton, August 8, 9, 10. Essex won by an innings and 11 runs. Essex 24 pts, Somerset 5 pts. Toss: Essex. Championship debut: S. D. Peters.

The visitors' three-day win was set up by Gooch's tenth double-hundred for Essex, while Such completed it with match figures of 12 for 135, on a dry pitch which turned from an early stage. Gooch batted throughout the first day, when he offered one sharp chance on 108, and was seventh out at 442 after batting six and a half hours, striking four sixes and 33 fours from 287 balls. He was supported by Law, who hit 63 in 65 balls, and Irani, who helped him add 170 for the sixth wicket. Led by Bowler, Somerset replied bravely to reach 195 for three. But their last seven fell to Such and Irani for 51. Following on, they slumped to 69 for five in 39 careworn overs. There was a minor recovery, but they were defeated by 5.20 p.m. on Saturday.

Close of play: First day, Essex 417-6 (G. A. Gooch 186*, M. C. Ilott 1*); Second day, Somerset 7-0 (M. N. Lathwell 7*, M. E. Trescothick 0*).

Essex

G. A. Gooch c Trescothick b Rose	201
A. P. Grayson b Kerr	14
*P. J. Prichard c and b Batty	23
S. G. Law c Harden b van Troost	63
S. D. Peters c Parsons b van Troost	4
†R. J. Rollins b Batty	10
R. C. Irani c Harden b Kerr	87
M. C. Ilott b van Troost	13
N. F. Williams c Harden b van Troost	11
A. P. Cowan c Turner b Rose	4
P. M. Such not out	5
L-b 10, n-b 20	30
1/52 2/118 3/219 4/229 5/244 6/414 7/442 8/452 9/457	465

Bonus points – Essex 4, Somerset 4.

Bowling: van Troost 20–2–90–4; Rose 26–5–100–2; Lee 20–2–74–0; Kerr 17–3–64–2; Batty 23–2–115–2; Parsons 2–0–12–0.

Somerset

M. N. Lathwell lbw b Williams	12	– c Gooch b Grayson	15
M. E. Trescothick lbw b Such	31	– c Prichard b Such	9
*P. D. Bowler c Law b Such	88	– c Peters b Such	16
R. J. Harden b Cowan	41	– b Grayson	18
K. A. Parsons lbw b Such	24	– b Grayson	5
S. Lee c Prichard b Such	18	– c Law b Such	36
†R. J. Turner b Such	0	– not out	44
G. D. Rose c Gooch b Irani	12	– run out	46
J. I. D. Kerr b Irani	0	– b Such	0
J. D. Batty not out	0	– c Peters b Such	10
A. P. van Troost b Such	4	– b Such	0
B 5, l-b 2, w 1, n-b 8	16	B 5, l-b 3, w 1	9
1/38 2/59 3/132 4/195 5/221 6/221 7/240 8/240 9/242	246	1/24 2/24 3/58 4/58 5/69 6/105 7/186 8/188 9/208	208

Bonus points – Somerset 1, Essex 4.

Bowling: *First Innings*—Ilott 17–5–59–0; Williams 13–3–59–1; Cowan 10–5–31–1; Such 31.2–10–63–6; Grayson 4–1–8–0; Law 4–2–4–0; Irani 8–1–15–2. *Second Innings*—Ilott 5–1–19–0; Such 42.3–17–72–6; Grayson 30–12–56–3; Law 12–2–39–0; Irani 4–0–14–0.

Umpires: G. I. Burgess and T. E. Jesty.

At Canterbury, August 15, 16, 17, 19. SOMERSET lost to KENT by 62 runs.

SOMERSET v DURHAM

At Weston-super-Mare, August 21, 22, 23, 24. Drawn. Somerset 9 pts, Durham 8 pts. Toss: Somerset.

Rain, which permitted only 80 overs during the last three days of the match, ruined all hopes of a result after an interesting beginning. It was a sad end to what really did appear to be the final year of the long-threatened Weston festival. Campbell, who hit two sixes and eight fours, got Durham off to a rapid start. But, from 145 for one, Rose reduced them to 170 for six, swinging the ball astutely in a spell of five for 15 in 31 balls. The damage was handsomely repaired by Cox, in a bristling innings of much character, 95 from 114 balls; Cox added Trescothick's wicket that evening and Somerset slipped to 96 for three. But Lathwell and Harden provided their reply with some backbone before the weather closed in.

Close of play: First day, Somerset 71-1 (M. N. Lathwell 29*, J. D. Batty 4*); Second day, Somerset 236-4 (R. J. Harden 38*, S. Lee 10*); Third day, Somerset 298-6 (S. C. Ecclestone 34*, R. J. Turner 4*).

Durham

S. L. Campbell b Rose	69	S. J. E. Brown b Lee	18
S. Hutton c Ecclestone b Lee	37	N. Killeen b Rose	2
J. A. Daley c Turner b Rose	22	M. J. Saggers lbw b Rose	18
P. Bainbridge c Lee b Rose	11		
*M. A. Roseberry lbw b Rose	0	B 1, l-b 7, w 6, n-b 24	38
R. M. S. Weston c Turner b Rose	2		
†D. G. C. Ligertwood b Lee	14	1/103 2/145 3/161 4/161 5/163	326
D. M. Cox not out	95	6/170 7/223 8/277 9/292	

Bonus points – Durham 3, Somerset 4.

Bowling: van Troost 17–6–45–0; Rose 26.5–6–73–7; Lee 24–2–101–3; Kerr 13–1–73–0; Batty 3–0–19–0; Bowler 2–0–7–0.

Somerset

M. N. Lathwell c Hutton b Killeen	85	S. Lee run out	40
M. E. Trescothick lbw b Cox	33	†R. J. Turner not out	4
J. D. Batty b Brown	8	B 1, l-b 18, w 1	20
*P. D. Bowler c Ligertwood b Brown	9		
R. J. Harden c Roseberry b Saggers	65	1/60 2/76 3/96	(6 wkts) 298
S. C. Ecclestone not out	34	4/154 5/294 6/294	

G. D. Rose, J. I. D. Kerr and A. P. van Troost did not bat.

Bonus points – Somerset 2, Durham 2.

S. C. Ecclestone, when 34, retired hurt at 217 and resumed at 294 for five.

Bowling: Brown 27–9–91–2; Saggers 21.4–3–67–1; Cox 30–11–76–1; Killeen 10–2–34–1; Bainbridge 8–5–11–0.

Umpires: H. D. Bird and R. A. White.

At Leicester, August 29, 30. SOMERSET lost to LEICESTERSHIRE by an innings and 39 runs.

SOMERSET v DERBYSHIRE

At Taunton, September 3, 4, 5, 6. Drawn. Somerset 10 pts, Derbyshire 10 pts. Toss: Derbyshire. First-class debut: G. M. Roberts.

Derbyshire's quest for the Championship was thwarted by a perfect pitch. After failing to take a decisive first-innings lead, they challenged Somerset to score 383 in 78 overs, and Lathwell launched the attack with 54 from 62 balls. Defensive tactics – debutant slow left-armer Glen Roberts bowled into the rough while the seamers spread their fields – slowed them down, and the third wicket added only 14 in 16 overs before Cork claimed three in 28 deliveries. When Bowler was sixth out, brilliantly stumped down the leg side by Krikken, standing up to DeFreitas, Derbyshire's hopes rose. DeFreitas clean bowled Kerr with his next ball, only for umpire Clarkson to rule that the batsman had not been ready. Kerr went on to a maiden Championship fifty, putting on 75 with Turner against an all-seam attack and seeing his side to safety. Derbyshire had scored 524, their best total against Somerset, with a century from Rollins backed up by several lower-order fifties – Roberts made 52 on his first outing. But Somerset were just as positive, thanks to hundreds from Lathwell and Lee. Batting conditions were still excellent as Barnett and Jones set up the final equation.

Close of play: First day, Derbyshire 389-7 (K. M. Krikken 30*, G. M. Roberts 9*); Second day, Somerset 238-4 (R. J. Harden 23*, J. D. Batty 2*); Third day, Derbyshire 221-2 (K. J. Barnett 120*, D. M. Jones 53*).

Derbyshire

K. J. Barnett c Ecclestone b van Troost	27	– c and b Caddick 141
A. S. Rollins c Turner b Lee	127	– lbw b Caddick 0
C. J. Adams c Harden b Caddick	7	– c Turner b Kerr 32
*D. M. Jones c Harden b van Troost	11	– st Turner b Bowler 74
T. J. G. O'Gorman c Turner b Caddick	10	– (6) not out 18
D. G. Cork c Turner b Lee	77	– (8) not out 12
†K. M. Krikken lbw b Kerr	89	– b Caddick 12
P. A. J. DeFreitas c Turner b Kerr	60	– (5) c Harden b Bowler 11
G. M. Roberts c Batty b Kerr	52	
A. J. Harris b Caddick	15	
D. E. Malcolm not out	6	
B 4, l-b 15, n-b 24	43	L-b 7, w 1, n-b 14 22
1/41 2/60 3/116 4/132 5/267 6/286 7/369 8/487 9/518	524	1/17 2/79 3/266 4/276 5/279 6/309 (6 wkts dec.) 322

Bonus points – Derbyshire 4, Somerset 3 (Score at 120 overs: 463-7).

Bowling: *First Innings*—Caddick 37.4–3–140–3; van Troost 8.3–0–40–2; Kerr 25–2–108–3; Lee 24–5–121–2; Batty 34–11–94–0; Bowler 4–2–2–0. *Second Innings*—Caddick 20–1–104–3; Kerr 8–1–42–1; Batty 21–3–73–0; Lee 4–1–20–0; Trescothick 6–0–22–0; Bowler 8–0–54–2.

Somerset

M. N. Lathwell b Malcolm	109	– c Adams b DeFreitas 54
M. E. Trescothick c Krikken b Cork	42	– b DeFreitas 8
*P. D. Bowler lbw b Harris	37	– st Krikken b DeFreitas 60
R. J. Harden run out	43	– b Cork 3
S. C. Ecclestone lbw b Roberts	13	– lbw b Cork 8
J. D. Batty c Roberts b Harris	27	– (9) lbw b Cork 14
S. Lee c sub b Harris	110	– (6) c O'Gorman b Cork 14
†R. J. Turner lbw b Malcolm	21	– (7) c Krikken b Malcolm 49
J. I. D. Kerr c Krikken b Malcolm	15	– (8) not out 68
A. R. Caddick b Harris	21	– not out 1
A. P. van Troost not out	0	
B 5, l-b 7, n-b 14	26	L-b 7, n-b 10 17
1/76 2/194 3/198 4/231 5/272 6/329 7/396 8/430 9/464	464	1/12 2/91 3/105 4/115 5/141 6/177 7/252 8/295 (8 wkts) 296

Bonus points – Somerset 4, Derbyshire 3 (Score at 120 overs: 419-7).

Bowling: *First Innings*—Malcolm 34–5–146–3; DeFreitas 22–3–90–0; Cork 14–5–48–1; Harris 23.4–5–95–4; Roberts 25–11–55–1; Barnett 9–0–18–0. *Second Innings*—Malcolm 18–1–108–1; DeFreitas 20–3–60–3; Harris 10–1–48–0; Roberts 11–7–18–0; Cork 19–3–55–4.

Umpires: A. Clarkson and P. Willey.

At Uxbridge, September 12, 13, 14, 16. SOMERSET drew with MIDDLESEX.

At Hove, September 19, 20, 21. SOMERSET beat SUSSEX by eight wickets.

Brendon Julian

SURREY

Patron: HM The Queen
President: Mrs B. Surridge
Chairman: M. J. Soper
Chief Executive: P. J. S. Sheldon
Captain: A. J. Stewart
Cricket Manager: D. R. Gilbert
Director of Cricket Development: M. J. Edwards
Head Groundsman: P. D. Brind
Scorer: K. R. Booth

For the first time since 1982, there was a glint of silver in The Oval trophy cupboard, after Surrey won their first Sunday League title. But, as 1997 began, cricketing success was put into perspective by the death – after a car crash in Australia – of wicket-keeper Graham Kersey, the most popular player on the staff.

The news left everyone at Surrey stunned. Back in mid-August, the mood at The Oval had been more buoyant than for many years: the county had been on course to complete a treble by collecting the Championship and NatWest Trophy as well. But the disappointment of their semi-final capitulation to Essex, despite Alec Stewart's unbeaten hundred, was a foretaste of further failure. The Championship slipped from their grasp, first with a draw in the rain at Trent Bridge, then with a dusty share of the spoils at Cardiff, where Surrey's need for a top-class spinner was starkly revealed. The rain-soaked final match against Worcestershire was reduced to a money-chase; second place was the best they could hope for and, despite a brave effort, they ended up third. At least Surrey had rid themselves of the monkey that had clung to their backs for the last 14 years, in which they won nothing but criticism for unfulfilled potential. They ended the season with the belief that the Sunday League should be the first of many trophies for this talented team, but Kersey's death will make 1997 much harder.

The contribution of Australian bite to Surrey's summer cannot be underestimated. The shrewdest signing was that of former Test fast bowler David Gilbert in the role of manager-cum-coach. He began by ordering the demolition of the wall between the capped and non-capped players' dressing-rooms. Having taken that first, dramatic step towards uniting his squad, Gilbert saw the players respond swiftly to his canny man-management skills. Another key figure was Australian all-rounder Brendon Julian, who overcame an alarming propensity to bowl no-balls and wides and completed an impressive double by passing 500 runs and 50 wickets. Meanwhile, Australian-born Adam Hollioake began the season at Taunton with a century in each innings – the 12th Surrey batsman to achieve the feat – and, while Stewart was on England duty, led Surrey to four of their eight Championship victories and five Sunday League wins. He was rewarded by being named captain of England A's winter tour – to Australia.

Surrey had an unpleasant five weeks before getting things right. They drew their first four Championship matches and lost the fifth, to the team who were already their *bête noire* for the season – Yorkshire. They also lost their Sunday game with Yorkshire and, less than a fortnight earlier, had been outbatted, outbowled and outplayed by them in the Benson and Hedges quarter-finals. In mid-June, they stood 13th in the Championship. After that, they finally woke up to their capabilities.

The batting was led by Hollioake and the prolific Mark Butcher – both scored over 1,500 Championship runs and Butcher also earned an England A call-up – as well as Graham Thorpe, when England could spare him. But their strength was in the bowling. They took 64 bowling points, more than any other county, and a maximum of four in 14 of their 17 matches. This was despite the unenviable landmark of conceding more than 1,000 extras, believed to be a first for any county, and the lack of a first-rate spinner: Richard Pearson toiled, but lacked the penetration required at this level.

Martin Bicknell, remarkably, stayed injury-free and was back to his best, with 66 wickets at 24.74. Joey Benjamin, ageless as ever, provided some superb support and Darren Bicknell compensated for missing out on 1,000 runs by revealing himself as an orthodox slow left-arm bowler who should not be taken lightly. His 16 wickets will have been all the sweeter because, coming at 23.00, they beat his brother into second place in the averages. Chris Lewis, transferred from Nottinghamshire, produced enough magic moments to convince everyone he has plenty more to offer. His rehabilitation was helped by an England recall, though, when that backfired, he captained the county to victory over Warwickshire.

Adam Hollioake's 18-year-old brother, Ben, made a big impact in his first season, with 13 Sunday League wickets; but for England Under-19 calls, it could have been a lot more. Irish seamer Mark Patterson was another addition to the young squad. Inevitably, there were departures, most notably that of beneficiary David Ward, a long-time favourite of Oval crowds. He still managed to leave his mark, with hundreds in Sunday victories over Kent and Durham, and will be sorely missed – as much for his sense of fun as for his big hitting. His buddy Alistair Brown had a spring to remember but a summer to forget. A century for England in the one-day series with India was followed by precious little for his county: he hit an unprecedented run of poor form, with just three fifties in the Championship. He admitted that being dropped late in the season came as a relief.

After all that, an unseasonably warm autumn buzzed with rumours. The most persistent said that leg-spinner Ian Salisbury was going to tread a well-worn path from Sussex to The Oval; in November, that turned out to be true, and could solve Surrey's most serious shortcoming. Another rumour claimed that the captaincy was once more an issue, with the cricket committee apparently in favour of Adam Hollioake succeeding Stewart. There was certainly a case for Hollioake taking over: apart from his impressive record when left in charge, there is the matter of continuity – Stewart's reign has always been interrupted by England calls. In 1997, though, Hollioake could also become a regular in the Test squad, in which case he would be away just as often.

Then, of course, there was the question of the overseas player. Julian was a treasure but he could continue for Surrey only if Australia ignored him in their Ashes party. Whether Gilbert can be persuaded to remain when his two-year contract expires is another matter. It is understood that he sees his long-term future in his native Australia; on the evidence of his first summer with Surrey, he should prosper wherever he goes.

What Surrey did not expect was to have to worry about the wicket-keeping. Over the past two years Kersey had emerged as a quality player – agile, unfussy and safe behind the stumps, gritty with the bat. Though Stewart kept him out of the one-day matches, in the longer game he was improving match by match. But it was Kersey's impact off the field that was perhaps more significant. He may not have been a household name, but no one who knew him could fail to be touched by his genial and gentle nature. Surrey will not find it easy to regroup for the new season without him. – DAVID LLEWELLYN.

SURREY 1996

[*Bill Smith*

Back row: N. Shahid, B. C. Hollioake, G. J. Kennis, A. J. Tudor, J. M. de la Pena, J. D. Ratcliffe, C. C. Lewis, R. M. Pearson, R. W. Nowell. *Middle row:* A. C. S. Pigott (*Second Eleven captain/coach*), G. J. Kersey, A. W. Smith, M. A. Butcher, S. G. Kenlock, N. F. Sargeant, J. A. Knott, D. R. Gilbert (*cricket manager*). *Front row:* A. D. Brown, J. E. Benjamin, M. P. Bicknell, A. J. Stewart (*captain*), A. J. Hollioake (*vice-captain*), D. M. Ward, D. J. Bicknell. *Insets:* G. P. Thorpe, B. P. Julian.

SURREY RESULTS

All first-class matches – Played 18: Won 8, Lost 3, Drawn 7.

County Championship matches – Played 17: Won 8, Lost 2, Drawn 7.

Competition placings – Britannic Assurance County Championship, 3rd; NatWest Trophy, s-f; Benson and Hedges Cup, q-f; AXA Equity & Law League, winners.

COUNTY CHAMPIONSHIP AVERAGES

BATTING

Cap		*M*	*I*	*NO*	*R*	*HS*	*100s*	*50s*	*Avge*	*Ct/St*
1991	G. P. Thorpe†	9	17	2	1,044	185	5	4	69.60	10
1995	A. J. Hollioake	16	28	6	1,521	129	5	8	69.13	18
1996	M. A. Butcher†	17	32	3	1,540	160	3	13	53.10	21
	C. C. Lewis	8	13	1	442	94	0	3	36.83	13
1996	B. P. Julian§	16	23	2	759	119	2	3	36.14	9
1990	D. J. Bicknell†	17	31	3	969	129*	2	3	34.60	9
	N. Shahid	10	17	3	448	101	1	3	32.00	5
	J. D. Ratcliffe	8	14	1	403	68*	0	3	31.00	5
1985	A. J. Stewart†	9	16	1	434	80	0	3	28.93	10
	R. M. Pearson	14	14	9	142	37	0	0	28.40	3
1990	D. M. Ward†	2	4	1	81	64*	0	1	27.00	2
1989	M. P. Bicknell†	16	18	5	333	59*	0	1	25.61	2
1996	G. J. Kersey	15	20	4	402	68*	0	3	25.12	45/1
1994	A. D. Brown	14	22	2	361	57	0	3	18.05	14
1993	J. E. Benjamin	13	14	6	141	38*	0	0	17.62	1
	B. C. Hollioake	3	4	0	63	46	0	0	15.75	3

* *Signifies not out.* † *Born in Surrey.* § *Overseas player.*

BOWLING

	O	*M*	*R*	*W*	*BB*	*5W/i*	*Avge*
D. J. Bicknell	124.2	21	368	16	3-7	0	23.00
M. P. Bicknell	568.1	146	1,633	66	5-17	3	24.74
B. C. Hollioake	65	12	252	10	4-74	0	25.20
B. P. Julian	447.4	86	1,762	61	6-37	3	28.88
J. E. Benjamin	375.3	83	1,217	39	4-17	0	31.20
C. C. Lewis	260.4	50	889	27	5-25	1	32.92
R. M. Pearson	475	101	1,509	31	5-142	1	48.67
A. J. Hollioake	226	44	764	12	3-80	0	63.66

Also bowled: A. D. Brown 6–2–8–0; M. A. Butcher 52–7–233–7; J. D. Ratcliffe 19–3–75–3; N. Shahid 52–11–170–3; A. J. Stewart 2–0–24–0; G. P. Thorpe 23–8–64–2.

COUNTY RECORDS

Highest score for:	357*	R. Abel v Somerset at The Oval	1899
Highest score against:	366	N. H. Fairbrother (Lancashire) at The Oval	1990
Best bowling for:	10-43	T. Rushby v Somerset at Taunton	1921
Best bowling against:	10-28	W. P. Howell (Australians) at The Oval	1899
Highest total for:	811	v Somerset at The Oval	1899
Highest total against:	863	by Lancashire at The Oval	1990
Lowest total for:	14	v Essex at Chelmsford	1983
Lowest total against:	16	by MCC at Lord's	1872

At Taunton, May 2, 3, 4, 6. SURREY drew with SOMERSET.

SURREY v KENT

At The Oval, May 9, 10, 11, 13. Drawn. Surrey 11 pts, Kent 8 pts. Toss: Kent.

A fine all-round performance on the last day by McCague made victory for Kent a distinct possibility. When he came in, their lead was only 107, with seven down. But his unbeaten, career-best 63 frustrated Surrey for three hours. Eventually, they needed 227 in 50 overs. Then, McCague whipped out the cream of the home batting in seven overs. But Butcher, though handicapped by a suspected hernia, batted on. Both sides had their ups and downs on a wicket with more bounce than most recent Oval pitches. All the pacier bowlers flourished, as did off-spinner Pearson. Martin Bicknell took two wickets in the very first over, when Kent's insistence on opening with Fleming seemed mistaken; but in the second innings Fleming thrashed some profligate bowling, pitched short to invite his pulls and cuts, and scored 56 in 60 balls. Surrey had taken a 135-run lead after Butcher just missed his hundred, Lewis scored his first fifty for the county and Julian his second in successive Championship innings. Thompson took five wickets for the first time.

Close of play: First day, Surrey 88-3 (M. A. Butcher 40*, A. D. Brown 18*); Second day, Surrey 360; Third day, Kent 241-6 (G. R. Cowdrey 41*, J. B. D. Thompson 7*).

Kent

D. P. Fulton c Brown b Lewis	28	– c Kersey b Julian	59
M. V. Fleming c Julian b M. P. Bicknell	0	– c Julian b Lewis	56
T. R. Ward c Kersey b M. P. Bicknell	0	– c Lewis b M. P. Bicknell	14
C. L. Hooper b Lewis	7	– c Thorpe b Pearson	23
G. R. Cowdrey b Pearson	45	– lbw b M. P. Bicknell	41
M. A. Ealham b Pearson	51	– c Stewart b Pearson	0
*†S. A. Marsh c Brown b Butcher	29	– lbw b Lewis	26
J. B. D. Thompson b Julian	16	– c Kersey b M. P. Bicknell	8
M. J. McCague c D. J. Bicknell b Pearson	14	– not out	63
M. M. Patel c Lewis b Julian	13	– c Kersey b Lewis	26
T. N. Wren not out	1	– c Brown b Pearson	6
L-b 4, w 1, n-b 16	21	B 5, l-b 12, w 6, n-b 16	39
1/1 2/1 3/13 4/88 5/92 6/176 7/180 8/210 9/214	225	1/93 2/115 3/161 4/161 5/161 6/230 7/242 8/261 9/350	361

Bonus points – Kent 1, Surrey 4.

Bowling: *First Innings*—M. P. Bicknell 17–6–52–2; Lewis 20–4–57–2; Julian 14.4–3–36–2; Butcher 13–3–41–1; Pearson 13–5–35–3. *Second Innings*—M. P. Bicknell 35–12–79–3; Lewis 27–3–81–3; Julian 22–5–82–1; Hollioake 6–1–18–0; Pearson 32.1–8–84–3.

Surrey

D. J. Bicknell c Cowdrey b McCague	8	– lbw b McCague	3
M. A. Butcher b Thompson	94	– (7) not out	35
*A. J. Stewart c Hooper b Ealham	6	– c Hooper b McCague	22
G. P. Thorpe b Ealham	8	– b McCague	0
A. D. Brown c Marsh b McCague	27	– (2) c Ealham b McCague	2
A. J. Hollioake c Wren b Thompson	40	– (5) b Hooper	42
C. C. Lewis c McCague b Hooper	61	– (6) b Patel	10
B. P. Julian c Patel b Thompson	74	– not out	41
†G. J. Kersey lbw b Thompson	5		
M. P. Bicknell c Cowdrey b Thompson	13		
R. M. Pearson not out	0		
B 4, l-b 17, w 1, n-b 2	24	B 3, l-b 2	5
1/18 2/35 3/47 4/104 5/180 6/206 7/295 8/339 9/350	360	1/3 2/12 3/16 4/53 5/81 6/81	(6 wkts) 160

Bonus points – Surrey 4, Kent 4.

Bowling: *First Innings*—McCague 28–9–76–2; Thompson 24.1–2–72–5; Ealham 17–1–64–2; Wren 7–0–44–0; Patel 11–1–34–0; Fleming 9–3–22–0; Hooper 13–4–27–1. *Second Innings*—McCague 10–2–33–4; Thompson 5–1–18–0; Ealham 5–0–23–0; Patel 15–5–36–1; Hooper 15–3–45–1.

Umpires: K. J. Lyons and B. J. Meyer.

At Gloucester, May 23, 24, 25, 27. SURREY drew with GLOUCESTERSHIRE.

SURREY v DERBYSHIRE

At The Oval, May 30, 31, June 1, 3. Drawn. Surrey 10 pts, Derbyshire 10 pts. Toss: Derbyshire.

By tea on the final day, victory was there for the taking, or rather Derbyshire's last two wickets were. But Surrey let them wriggle off the hook. They were not helped by the loss of Martin Bicknell, who suffered a groin strain while knocking over five wickets, including a burst of four in ten deliveries. With so little to do, it seemed reasonable for him to rest after tea. But Surrey reckoned without Cork. He swung the bat while Wells, requiring a runner after a severe foot injury, lasted half an hour and Aldred, with a damaged wrist, 87 minutes. The bat ruled for most of the match: Thorpe made 185, Butcher scored fifties in both innings, and Stewart was within touching distance of joining him but had to retire before the final day's play because his wife had gone into hospital. This was considered an "unavoidable cause" for retirement under Law 2.9, and he was ruled not out. Barnett dominated Derbyshire's best total against Surrey; he fell on 94, but became the county's highest scorer when 52, passing Denis Smith on 20,516. Wells was too badly hurt to hobble back to the pavilion at tea on the final day, so ground staff took a deckchair and a cup of tea to the middle for him, and Cork stayed to keep him company.

Close of play: First day, Surrey 382-7 (G. P. Thorpe 158*, G. J. Kersey 4*); Second day, Derbyshire 286-3 (D. M. Jones 61*, J. E. Owen 54*); Third day, Surrey 199-2 (A. J. Stewart 47*, G. P. Thorpe 56*).

Surrey

D. J. Bicknell c Harris b Cork	3	– c Adams b Cork	39
M. A. Butcher lbw b Cork	52	– b Barnett	57
*A. J. Stewart c Aldred b Wells	53	– retired not out	47
G. P. Thorpe c and b Harris	185	– lbw b Barnett	68
A. D. Brown c Krikken b Wells	3	– not out	56
A. J. Hollioake c Krikken b Aldred	72	– not out	71
C. C. Lewis c Rollins b Cork	5		
B. P. Julian b Malcolm	7		
†G. J. Kersey c Barnett b Harris	37		
M. P. Bicknell run out	28		
R. M. Pearson not out	7		
L-b 10, w 3, n-b 12	25	B 4, l-b 1, n-b 2	7
1/11 2/97 3/147 4/171 5/322 6/341 7/372 8/431 9/454	477	1/92 2/100 3/213 (3 wkts dec.)	345

Bonus points – Surrey 4, Derbyshire 3 (Score at 120 overs: 446-8).

In the second innings A. J. Stewart retired not out at 199.

Bowling: *First Innings*—Malcolm 31–4–121–1; Cork 30–7–94–3; Harris 21–5–79–2; Aldred 18.1–2–81–1; Wells 20–3–65–2; Jones 6–0–27–0. *Second Innings*—Malcolm 11–2–39–0; Cork 10–1–40–1; Harris 14–2–68–0; Barnett 17–0–99–2; Aldred 4.4–0–43–0; Jones 6.5–0–23–0; Rollins 2–0–25–0; Adams 1–0–3–0.

Derbyshire

K. J. Barnett b Pearson	94 – c Brown b M. P. Bicknell	0
A. S. Rollins c Thorpe b Julian	28 – lbw b Pearson	21
C. J. Adams c Julian b Lewis	24 – c Butcher b Julian	42
*D. M. Jones c Butcher b Julian	76 – lbw b Julian	10
J. E. Owen c Julian b M. P. Bicknell	54 – c Butcher b M. P. Bicknell	11
C. M. Wells c Hollioake b Thorpe	82 – (10) c Hollioake b Julian	28
†K. M. Krikken run out	20 – (6) b M. P. Bicknell	9
D. G. Cork c Stewart b Lewis	10 – (7) not out	82
P. Aldred lbw b Thorpe	33 – (11) not out	7
A. J. Harris not out	3 – (8) b M. P. Bicknell	0
D. E. Malcolm c Stewart b Pearson	4 – (9) c Butcher b M. P. Bicknell	4
B 2, l-b 10, w 3, n-b 26	41 L-b 5, w 1, n-b 26	32
1/71 2/121 3/179 4/287 5/335 6/373 7/400 8/455 9/464	469 1/0 2/57 3/81 4/86 5/107 6/110 7/110 8/124 9/172	(9 wkts) 246

Bonus points – Derbyshire 4, Surrey 3 (Score at 120 overs: 426-7).

Bowling: *First Innings*—M. P. Bicknell 31–9–101–1; Lewis 28–6–98–2; Pearson 26.5–6–75–2; Julian 23–5–100–2; Hollioake 17–2–70–0; Thorpe 6–2–13–2. *Second Innings*—M. P. Bicknell 9–3–17–5; Lewis 15–3–61–0; Pearson 15–5–41–1; Julian 18–5–93–3; Hollioake 6–0–25–0; D. J. Bicknell 1–0–4–0; Thorpe 1–1–0–0.

Umpires: N. T. Plews and P. Willey.

At Middlesbrough, June 6, 7, 8, 10. SURREY lost to YORKSHIRE by 221 runs.

SURREY v LEICESTERSHIRE

At The Oval, June 13, 14, 15, 17. Surrey won by 108 runs. Surrey 24 pts, Leicestershire 5 pts. Toss: Surrey.

Butcher, in awesome form, hit his second hundred of 1996 and the incomparable Thorpe his fourth. Their form and some high quality fast bowling from the rejuvenated Lewis helped Surrey record their first win of the campaign. It also papered over their lack of an effective spin bowler: Pierson took six for Leicestershire but Surrey's Pearson just one. Another worry was that the home attack again allowed the lower order to have a thrash. Needing 303 to avoid the follow-on, Leicestershire were 65 for five before Habib and Nixon put on 157. The last five wickets added 346, Mullally making his maiden first-class fifty. Had they shown the same fight on the final day, Leicestershire would have been able to shut up shop and leave Surrey queuing outside for nothing. But Lewis caught the dangerous Simmons at slip and then produced his first five-wicket haul for Surrey, including three for 13 in ten balls, to show his colleagues how to finish off sides.

Close of play: First day, Surrey 340-6 (G. P. Thorpe 94*, G. J. Kersey 8*); Second day, Leicestershire 222-6 (A. Habib 77*); Third day, Surrey 106-5 (C. C. Lewis 14*, G. J. Kersey 0*).

Surrey

D. J. Bicknell lbw b Parsons	34 – c Wells b Simmons	6
M. A. Butcher c Maddy b Pierson	120 – c Habib b Parsons	66
*A. J. Stewart c Maddy b Pierson	33 – b Millns	3
G. P. Thorpe c Nixon b Pierson	154 – c Nixon b Simmons	2
A. D. Brown c and b Pierson	7 – lbw b Simmons	0
A. J. Hollioake run out	7 – (8) not out	37
C. C. Lewis c Maddy b Pierson	20 – (6) c Wells b Simmons	36
†G. J. Kersey lbw b Pierson	28 – (7) not out	59
M. P. Bicknell c Habib b Parsons	15	
R. M. Pearson not out	8	
J. E. Benjamin b Parsons	9	
B 5, l-b 6, w 4, n-b 2	17 B 6, l-b 6, w 2, n-b 19	33
1/65 2/180 3/227 4/234 5/256 6/320 7/416 8/423 9/439	452 1/34 2/51 3/54 4/54 5/102 6/139	(6 wkts dec.) 242

Bonus points – Surrey 4, Leicestershire 2 (Score at 120 overs: 411-6).

Bowling: *First Innings*—Millns 18–5–58–0; Mullally 24–6–61–0; Wells 17–2–67–0; Parsons 23.3–4–81–3; Pierson 46–7–158–6; Simmons 7–2–16–0. *Second Innings*—Millns 17–6–36–1; Mullally 10–2–48–0; Simmons 18–2–56–4; Pierson 15–2–52–0; Parsons 9–3–36–1; Wells 4–2–2–0.

Leicestershire

V. J. Wells c and b Benjamin	41	– lbw b M. P. Bicknell	0
D. L. Maddy c Lewis b M. P. Bicknell	7	– c Kersey b M. P. Bicknell	43
B. F. Smith c Butcher b Benjamin	7	– c Lewis b M. P. Bicknell	17
P. V. Simmons c Butcher b Benjamin	0	– c Lewis b Pearson	9
*J. J. Whitaker c Thorpe b Benjamin	7	– c Kersey b Lewis	32
A. Habib c and b D. J. Bicknell	79	– c Brown b Lewis	16
†P. A. Nixon c Brown b D. J. Bicknell	66	– c Brown b D. J. Bicknell	5
D. J. Millns b Lewis	23	– not out	26
G. J. Parsons c Brown b M. P. Bicknell	51	– b Lewis	0
A. R. K. Pierson not out	33	– b Lewis	0
A. D. Mullally b D. J. Bicknell	68	– b Lewis	13
B 3, l-b 5, w 5, n-b 16	29	B 4, l-b 1, w 3, n-b 6	14
1/23 2/44 3/44 4/62 5/65 6/222 7/227 8/302 9/306	411	1/2 2/20 3/49 4/91 5/119 6/131 7/150 8/159 9/159	175

Bonus points – Leicestershire 3, Surrey 4 (Score at 120 overs: 344-9).

Bowling: *First Innings*—M. P. Bicknell 24–6–92–2; Lewis 23–6–77–1; Benjamin 21–4–74–4; Hollioake 15–5–25–0; Pearson 34–13–60–0; Butcher 1–0–12–0; Thorpe 6–3–13–0; D. J. Bicknell 19.4–5–50–3. *Second Innings*—M. P. Bicknell 12–0–58–3; Lewis 11.2–4–25–5; Hollioake 3–2–4–0; Benjamin 7–2–15–0; Pearson 9–2–50–1; D. J. Bicknell 8–2–18–1.

Umpires: R. Julian and M. J. Kitchen.

At Stockton-on-Tees, June 20, 21, 22, 24. SURREY beat DURHAM by eight wickets.

At Southend, June 27, 28, 29, July 1. SURREY drew with ESSEX.

SURREY v MIDDLESEX

At The Oval, July 4, 5, 6, 8. Surrey won by seven wickets. Surrey 24 pts, Middlesex 5 pts. Toss: Middlesex.

Surrey's victory, their first for nine years against Middlesex, owed as much to abject batting as to high-class swing and seam bowling. Martin Bicknell and Julian won the game but, Ramprakash and Gatting apart, the Middlesex batsmen put up little fight. Bicknell's first-innings five for 54 was his 25th haul of five or more. Tufnell worked hard to keep Middlesex in the match, taking five on the third day as the seamers struggled. Surrey, however, sailed serenely to a 134-run lead, with Hollioake scoring 84, the highest innings of the game, before giving Carr his 250th first-class catch. Middlesex put up even less resistance on resuming. Despite the absence of Test players Stewart, Thorpe and Lewis, and the loss of 98 overs to weather, Surrey fashioned a commendable win, with maximum points to boot.

Close of play: First day, Middlesex 227-6 (J. P. Hewitt 17*); Second day, Surrey 136-3 (J. D. Ratcliffe 14*, A. D. Brown 4*); Third day, Middlesex 43-2 (M. R. Ramprakash 22*, M. W. Gatting 9*).

Middlesex

P. N. Weekes b Julian	5	– lbw b Benjamin	3
J. C. Pooley c Brown b M. P. Bicknell	2	– b Benjamin	3
M. R. Ramprakash c Kersey b M. P. Bicknell	80	– c Ratcliffe b Julian	28
*M. W. Gatting b Hollioake	52	– b M. P. Bicknell	53
J. D. Carr c Brown b Julian	20	– b Julian	0
†K. R. Brown c Hollioake b M. P. Bicknell	4	– c Kersey b M. P. Bicknell	5
J. P. Hewitt b M. P. Bicknell	19	– not out	29
R. L. Johnson lbw b Julian	0	– lbw b Julian	3
R. A. Fay c Hollioake b M. P. Bicknell	2	– c Hollioake b M. P. Bicknell	14
A. R. C. Fraser c Butcher b Julian	1	– c and b M. P. Bicknell	2
P. C. R. Tufnell not out	0	– c Kersey b Hollioake	3
B 1, l-b 2, w 2, n-b 42	47	B 8, l-b 3, w 6, n-b 34	51
1/14 2/16 3/142 4/192 5/200 6/227 7/227 8/229 9/232	232	1/3 2/16 3/71 4/75 5/120 6/131 7/150 8/177 9/185	194

Bonus points – Middlesex 1, Surrey 4.

Bowling: *First Innings*—M. P. Bicknell 24–6–54–5; Julian 15.2–4–63–4; Benjamin 20–5–69–0; Hollioake 15–6–30–1; Pearson 1–0–13–0. *Second Innings*—M. P. Bicknell 25–5–57–4; Benjamin 22–10–50–2; Julian 21–6–54–3; Hollioake 5–0–22–1.

Surrey

D. J. Bicknell c Pooley b Hewitt	48		
M. A. Butcher c Pooley b Weekes	42	– (1) c Carr b Johnson	26
J. D. Ratcliffe c Pooley b Tufnell	37	– (2) b Tufnell	8
N. Shahid c Carr b Hewitt	13	– (3) not out	17
A. D. Brown lbw b Fraser	57	– (4) c sub b Johnson	2
*A. J. Hollioake c Carr b Tufnell	84	– (5) not out	6
B. P. Julian c Gatting b Johnson	9		
†G. J. Kersey b Tufnell	3		
M. P. Bicknell c Brown b Tufnell	25		
R. M. Pearson not out	14		
J. E. Benjamin c Hewitt b Tufnell	1		
B 2, l-b 11, w 4, n-b 16	33	N-b 2	2
1/85 2/118 3/132 4/206 5/296 6/315 7/320 8/320 9/364	366	1/28 2/40 3/48	(3 wkts) 61

Bonus points – Surrey 4, Middlesex 4.

Bowling: *First Innings*—Fraser 22–5–59–1; Fay 29–9–95–0; Johnson 17–0–70–1; Tufnell 25.3–6–56–5; Weekes 11–4–29–1; Hewitt 12–4–44–2. *Second Innings*—Fraser 5–2–19–0; Tufnell 12–5–17–1; Johnson 6–1–18–2; Hewitt 1.2–0–7–0.

Umpires: J. D. Bond and A. G. T. Whitehead.

SURREY v SUSSEX

At Guildford, July 17, 18, 19, 20. Surrey won by 135 runs. Surrey 24 pts, Sussex 6 pts. Toss: Surrey.

A new groundsman had shorn Woodbridge Road's outfield of the grass which used to slow down the ball and, seeing a flat track, the batsmen were licking their lips. But disciplined bowling and, perhaps, over-confidence left several of them disappointed. Thorpe showed his class; he missed a century first time but returned to score his sixth of the season and 25th in all. But the only other hundred came from Moores. He made a Championship-best 119 not out, after coming in at 95 for five in the second innings when Sussex, chasing 451, were already on the way to defeat. Two run-outs destroyed their last hopes of saving the game. Julian had given Surrey the edge when he reduced Sussex's first innings from 163 for three to 175 for seven. Then Darren

Bicknell, an occasional slow left-arm bowler, produced the figures of his life, 3–1–7–3, and almost forced the follow-on. He went on to complete the win with another three wickets, compensating for the loss of Lewis to a thigh strain. Jarvis took eight wickets for Sussex but had little support.

Close of play: First day, Surrey 317-8 (G. J. Kersey 13*, M. P. Bicknell 12*); Second day, Sussex 260-9 (I. D. K. Salisbury 58*); Third day, Sussex 60-1 (C. W. J. Athey 25*, A. P. Wells 14*).

Surrey

D. J. Bicknell c Moores b Law	48	– lbw b Jarvis	2
M. A. Butcher c Wells b Jarvis	57	– b Jarvis	0
*A. J. Stewart c Moores b Law	74	– c Speight b Law	80
G. P. Thorpe c Moores b Jarvis	66	– c Wells b Jarvis	130
A. D. Brown lbw b Jarvis	0		
A. J. Hollioake c Athey b Lewry	20	– (5) b Salisbury	27
C. C. Lewis c Athey b Salisbury	7	– (6) not out	29
B. P. Julian c Moores b Lewry	5	– (7) c Moores b Jarvis	0
†G. J. Kersey not out	68	– (8) not out	18
M. P. Bicknell b Jarvis	13		
R. M. Pearson b Salisbury	37		
B 4, l-b 6, w 2, n-b 4	16	B 1, l-b 14, w 1, n-b 2	18
1/99 2/123 3/251 4/251 5/270 6/285 7/285 8/300 9/320	411	1/1 2/22 3/185 4/241 5/277 6/277	(6 wkts dec.) 304

Bonus points – Surrey 4, Sussex 4 (Score at 120 overs: 355-9).

Bowling: *First Innings*—Jarvis 28–7–82–4; Lewry 22–3–64–2; Law 26–5–85–2; Giddins 14–2–55–0; Lenham 4–1–17–0; Salisbury 32.2–10–85–2; Greenfield 6–2–13–0. *Second Innings*—Jarvis 14.3–0–60–4; Lewry 23–2–79–0; Law 10–2–37–1; Giddins 4–1–9–0; Salisbury 20–1–89–1; Greenfield 5–0–15–0.

Sussex

C. W. J. Athey lbw b M. P. Bicknell	1	– b D. J. Bicknell	91
N. J. Lenham c Lewis b M. P. Bicknell	51	– c Thorpe b M. P. Bicknell	9
*A. P. Wells lbw b Julian	81	– b Pearson	27
K. Greenfield b Hollioake	11	– c Kersey b Julian	5
M. P. Speight c Kersey b Julian	8	– c Thorpe b Hollioake	0
D. R. Law b Julian	0	– c D. J. Bicknell b Pearson	1
†P. Moores c Butcher b Julian	2	– not out	119
I. D. K. Salisbury c sub b D. J. Bicknell	62	– run out	12
P. W. Jarvis b D. J. Bicknell	21	– run out	1
J. D. Lewry b D. J. Bicknell	0	– c Thorpe b D. J. Bicknell	16
E. S. H. Giddins not out	1	– lbw b D. J. Bicknell	0
B 5, l-b 10, n-b 12	27	B 13, l-b 3, w 6, n-b 12	34
1/1 2/124 3/150 4/163 5/169 6/170 7/175 8/258 9/260	265	1/38 2/80 3/89 4/94 5/95 6/259 7/289 8/292 9/313	315

Bonus points – Sussex 2, Surrey 4.

Bowling: *First Innings*—Lewis 17–4–57–0; M. P. Bicknell 17–4–45–2; Julian 13–0–41–4; Hollioake 15–1–48–1; Pearson 9–1–52–0; D. J. Bicknell 3–1–7–3. *Second Innings*—M. P. Bicknell 17–9–22–1; Julian 18–4–81–1; Pearson 31–10–73–2; D. J. Bicknell 18.5–5–41–3; Hollioake 10–3–30–1; Butcher 5–0–52–0.

Umpires: B. Leadbeater and R. Palmer.

At Southampton, July 25, 26, 27, 29. SURREY beat HAMPSHIRE by five wickets.

At The Oval, August 1, 2, 3, 4. SURREY lost to SOUTH AFRICA A by 157 runs (See South Africa A tour section).

At Southport, August 7, 8, 9. SURREY beat LANCASHIRE by 140 runs.

At Nottingham, August 22, 23, 24, 26. SURREY drew with NOTTINGHAMSHIRE.

SURREY v WARWICKSHIRE

At The Oval, August 29, 30, 31. Surrey won by an innings and 164 runs. Surrey 24 pts, Warwickshire 2 pts. Toss: Surrey.

The TCCB tried to persuade Surrey to omit Lewis after England had dropped him for arriving late during the Oval Test. The club's response was to make him captain instead: Stewart, Adam Hollioake and Thorpe were all still away in England's one-day squad. During the match, *The Times* published a letter in which Lewis defended his disciplinary record. He defended the rest of his reputation by taking four wickets, scoring 94, the highest innings of the match, and leading his team to victory and maximum points in three days. His side were helped by a dismal batting display from Warwickshire. They were nought for two in no time and 85 for six at lunch on the first day; they never got into the game. In the second innings, Benjamin got the ball to cut away late and lift; seizing three in 12 balls, he finished with four for 17 from eight overs.

Close of play: First day, Surrey 82-0 (D. J. Bicknell 35*, M. A. Butcher 44*); Second day, Surrey 429-7 (C. C. Lewis 80*, M. P. Bicknell 1*).

Warwickshire

A. J. Moles lbw b M. P. Bicknell	0	– b Benjamin	23
W. G. Khan c Brown b Lewis	0	– b Benjamin	14
M. J. Powell c Lewis b Benjamin	9	– c Kersey b Benjamin	2
D. P. Ostler c Kersey b Lewis	7	– c Lewis b Benjamin	2
T. L. Penney c Kersey b Lewis	38	– b M. P. Bicknell	27
D. R. Brown c Hollioake b Julian	11	– b Hollioake	11
†K. J. Piper b Lewis	45	– c Kersey b M. P. Bicknell	0
A. F. Giles c D. J. Bicknell b Julian	50	– c Butcher b Hollioake	7
G. Welch not out	4	– b M. P. Bicknell	5
*T. A. Munton b Julian	2	– not out	4
D. A. Altree b Julian	0	– b M. P. Bicknell	0
L-b 8, w 1, n-b 20	29	B 2, l-b 4, n-b 8	14
1/0 2/0 3/9 4/27 5/62 6/85 7/186 8/192 9/195	195	1/32 2/38 3/42 4/67 5/92 6/92 7/99 8/101 9/109	109

Bonus points – Surrey 4.

Bowling: *First Innings*—M. P. Bicknell 12–4–29–1; Lewis 14–3–45–4; Julian 12–1–66–4; Benjamin 9–4–22–1; Hollioake 2–0–19–0; D. J. Bicknell 1–0–6–0. *Second Innings*—M. P. Bicknell 15.3–3–38–4; Lewis 5–2–6–0; Julian 10–4–20–0; Benjamin 8–2–17–4; Hollioake 8–2–22–2.

Surrey

D. J. Bicknell c Ostler b Welch	55
M. A. Butcher lbw b Giles	70
J. D. Ratcliffe lbw b Brown	63
N. Shahid st Piper b Giles	18
†G. J. Kersey c Ostler b Powell	63
B. C. Hollioake lbw b Giles	46
*C. C. Lewis lbw b Munton	94
B. P. Julian b Welch	11
M. P. Bicknell c Ostler b Munton	17
A. D. Brown b Welch	3
J. E. Benjamin not out	2
B 12, l-b 9, w 1, n-b 4	26
1/135 2/153 3/180 4/272 5/289 6/400 7/417 8/455 9/462	468

Bonus points – Surrey 4, Warwickshire 2 (Score at 120 overs: 354-5).

Bowling: Altree 24–6–74–0; Munton 36–8–100–2; Brown 21–4–98–1; Giles 36–14–82–3; Welch 31.3–7–75–3; Powell 4–0–18–1.

Umpires: G. I. Burgess and J. H. Hampshire.

SURREY v NORTHAMPTONSHIRE

At The Oval, September 3, 4, 5, 6. Surrey won by 225 runs. Surrey 24 pts, Northamptonshire 5 pts. Toss: Northamptonshire.

If anyone had questioned Surrey's last-minute overseas signing, Julian dispelled their doubts now. He followed his second century of the summer – and his career – with his best bowling analysis, six for 37. With Hollioake, he had demolished the bowling to put on 181 for the seventh wicket, a county record against these opponents, after coming in at an uncertain 147 for six. Hollioake treated the fearsome Ambrose with contempt, striking him for 19 in one over to force him out of the attack. It was Julian's fellow-seamers who struck the early blows at Northamptonshire, reducing them to 27 for three, but he forestalled any recovery, proving almost unplayable. Stewart waived the follow-on before leaving to attend the birth of his second child, while Hollioake supervised the rest of the game. He just missed his second century of the match in going for quick runs and set an intimidating target of 459. Victory put Surrey one point behind Championship leaders Leicestershire with two rounds to go.

Close of play: First day, Surrey 378-9 (M. P. Bicknell 8*, J. E. Benjamin 0*); Second day, Surrey 82-1 (D. J. Bicknell 28*, G. J. Kersey 4*); Third day, Northamptonshire 173-6 (D. J. Capel 27*, D. Ripley 2*).

Surrey

D. J. Bicknell c Snape b Capel	5	– c Ripley b Taylor	29
M. A. Butcher lbw b Capel	26	– c and b Ambrose	37
*A. J. Stewart lbw b Ambrose	15		
G. P. Thorpe run out	25	– c and b Ambrose	2
N. Shahid b Taylor	1	– c Curran b Ambrose	2
A. J. Hollioake b Penberthy	129	– lbw b Snape	98
C. C. Lewis lbw b Taylor	10	– c Snape b Ambrose	31
B. P. Julian c Ripley b Taylor	117	– c Sales b Snape	20
†G. J. Kersey c Sales b Penberthy	11	– (3) c Ripley b Capel	21
M. P. Bicknell not out	18	– (9) lbw b Penberthy	19
J. E. Benjamin c Sales b Taylor	7	– (10) not out	4
B 2, l-b 13, n-b 16	31	B 4, l-b 15, w 2, n-b 14	35
1/34 2/47 3/66 4/81 5/104 6/147 7/328 8/354 9/374	395	1/78 2/88 3/97 4/101 5/127 6/178 7/248 8/288 9/298 (9 wkts dec.)	298

Bonus points – Surrey 4, Northamptonshire 4.

Bowling: *First Innings*—Ambrose 23–6–76–1; Taylor 23.5–5–87–4; Capel 19–4–74–2; Penberthy 17–4–57–2; Curran 5–0–27–0; Snape 14–1–59–0. *Second Innings*—Ambrose 25–12–55–4; Taylor 15–7–19–1; Capel 16–4–67–1; Penberthy 18–2–71–1; Snape 17.3–2–67–2.

Northamptonshire

R. R. Montgomerie c Shahid b M. P. Bicknell	4	– lbw b Benjamin	38
A. J. Swann b M. P. Bicknell	6	– lbw b M. P. Bicknell	2
M. B. Loye c Butcher b Lewis	9	– b Lewis	45
D. J. Sales c Thorpe b Julian	33	– lbw b Lewis	0
*K. M. Curran b Julian	17	– c Kersey b Lewis	1
D. J. Capel c Lewis b Julian	12	– c Kersey b Julian	48
A. L. Penberthy c Thorpe b Lewis	28	– c Butcher b M. P. Bicknell	26
†D. Ripley c Kersey b Julian	55	– retired hurt	9
J. N. Snape not out	36	– lbw b Julian	20
C. E. L. Ambrose c Kersey b Julian	3	– c Kersey b Benjamin	2
J. P. Taylor lbw b Julian	0	– not out	0
L-b 10, n-b 22	32	B 12, l-b 11, w 5, n-b 14	42
1/4 2/21 3/27 4/64 5/88 6/95 7/144 8/231 9/235	235	1/12 2/104 3/105 4/111 5/112 6/162 7/224 8/233 9/233	233

Bonus points – Northamptonshire 1, Surrey 4.

In the second innings D. Ripley retired hurt at 191.

Bowling: *First Innings*—M. P. Bicknell 14–2–58–2; Lewis 15–1–60–2; Benjamin 14–1–48–0; Julian 13–5–37–6; Hollioake 5–0–22–0; D. J. Bicknell 1–1–0–0. *Second Innings*—M. P. Bicknell 22–11–38–2; Lewis 22–5–65–3; Benjamin 13.3–3–57–2; Julian 11–3–43–2; D. J. Bicknell 2–1–7–0.

Umpires: J. D. Bond and V. A. Holder.

At Cardiff, September 12, 13, 14, 16. SURREY drew with GLAMORGAN.

SURREY v WORCESTERSHIRE

At The Oval, September 19, 20, 21, 22. Worcestershire won by 124 runs. Worcestershire 20 pts, Surrey 4 pts. Toss: Surrey.

Surrey finally conceded the title race at tea on the third day, when Stewart decided to forfeit their first innings; it cost them any chance of the maximum points needed to overtake Leicestershire, but, when Leicestershire won anyway, the matter became academic. The weather, which reduced the match to two days and one session, had forced Stewart to take the pragmatic option, which was to go flat out for second place. In fact, they were flattened themselves, but they still left the field with heads held high and third place, their best position for ten years. Not even Darren Bicknell's second hundred of the season (his first at The Oval since 1993) could take them to 424 at roughly four an over. He was the first Surrey player to carry his bat in a county game since he himself did it in 1991. But his colleagues slipped to 108 for seven before Julian smacked a cheery 80 and helped him add 141, a county eighth-wicket record against Worcestershire. The visitors' middle order had overcome a shaky start when rain finally permitted play; Solanki came close to a maiden hundred. The Bicknell and Hollioake brothers all appeared for Surrey, the first time two sets of brothers had played together for any county in a Championship match since the Bedsers and Pratts turned out for Surrey against Essex in July 1956.

Close of play: First day, No play; Second day, Worcestershire 134-3 (T. M. Moody 60*, K. R. Spiring 30*); Third day, Surrey 15-1 (D. J. Bicknell 6*, M. P. Bicknell 5*).

Worcestershire

T. S. Curtis lbw b M. P. Bicknell	16	– (2) not out	28
W. P. C. Weston b Benjamin	2	– (3) not out	22
G. A. Hick c M. P. Bicknell b Julian	13		
*T. M. Moody b M. P. Bicknell	60		
K. R. Spiring c Butcher b B. C. Hollioake	63		
V. S. Solanki lbw b Benjamin	90		
D. A. Leatherdale c Stewart b B. C. Hollioake	0		
†S. J. Rhodes c B. C. Hollioake b A. J. Hollioake	6	– (1) b M. P. Bicknell	0
S. R. Lampitt c A. J. Hollioake b Benjamin	29		
R. K. Illingworth not out	39		
P. A. Thomas b B. C. Hollioake	9		
L-b 9, n-b 26	35	B 1, l-b 6, n-b 4	11
1/6 2/32 3/32 4/134 5/218 6/226 7/246 8/290 9/321	362	1/8 (1 wkt dec.)	61

Bonus points – Worcestershire 4, Surrey 4.

Bowling: *First Innings*—M. P. Bicknell 29–9–75–2; Benjamin 26–5–76–3; Julian 18–5–72–1; A. J. Hollioake 15–3–52–1; B. C. Hollioake 18–3–78–3. *Second Innings*—M. P. Bicknell 3–1–5–1; B. C. Hollioake 3–1–11–0; Shahid 11–5–11–0; D. J. Bicknell 6–2–7–0; Brown 6–2–8–0; Thorpe 2–0–12–0.

Surrey

Surrey forfeited their first innings.

D. J. Bicknell not out	129
M. A. Butcher c Rhodes b Moody	2
M. P. Bicknell b Thomas	23
*†A. J. Stewart lbw b Moody	0
G. P. Thorpe c Moody b Lampitt	11
N. Shahid lbw b Lampitt	2
A. J. Hollioake c Leatherdale b Illingworth	14
A. D. Brown b Illingworth	0
B. P. Julian c Spiring b Solanki	80
B. C. Hollioake c Illingworth b Solanki	7
J. E. Benjamin c Lampitt b Solanki	14
L-b 7, n-b 10	17
1/3 2/40 3/45 4/79 5/81 6/98 7/108 8/249 9/268	299

Bowling: Moody 21–6–56–2; Thomas 15–3–67–1; Illingworth 27–9–78–2; Lampitt 14–1–60–2; Solanki 7.1–0–31–3.

Umpires: K. E. Palmer and G. Sharp.

Peter Moores

SUSSEX

President: The Duke of Richmond and Gordon
Chairman: A. M. Caffyn
Secretary: N. Bett
Captain: 1996 – A. P. Wells
1997 – P. Moores
Coaches: D. L. Haynes and C. E. Waller
Head Groundsman: P. Eaton
Scorer: L. V. Chandler

A year which started with renewed optimism under new coach Desmond Haynes ended with the team threatened by disintegration. In October, Alan Wells returned from a benefit tour in the Caribbean to learn that the captaincy had been given to his deputy, wicket-keeper Peter Moores. Wells had been a model of batting consistency over his 16 years at the club, passing 1,000 runs ten times. But his five seasons as captain attracted increasing criticism. At times he lacked imagination, and he was said to be unwilling to listen to experienced colleagues. Wells felt he had been less pig-headed in 1996, but the committee, concerned by lack of success on the field and tensions in the dressing-room, opted for change.

It did not prevent a general rush to the exit. In November, the long-running rumour that leg-spinner Ian Salisbury was planning to leave for Surrey was confirmed, though Sussex were so keen to keep him that they had offered him a five-year contract with the promise of a benefit. A day later, all-rounder Danny Law signed for Essex. Sussex had already released pace bowler Ed Giddins, after the TCCB banned him for 18 months for failing a random drugs test (he will play for Warwickshire in 1998). Wells himself signed for Kent, while swashbuckling batsman Martin Speight took his case to Lord's. He wanted to move to a county where he could keep wicket – which was out of the question at Hove with Moores as captain. It appeared that Sussex might have trouble fielding a team at all in 1997, never mind a team with ambitions, which is what some of the departing players coveted.

Yet 1996 was not a terrible year. After a slow start, three consecutive Championship victories in June and a thrilling win over Yorkshire in early August had suggested a rise in Sussex's fortunes. But a poor run-in saw them dip again: they lost five of their last six games and finished 12th, a modest three places higher than in 1995. "Our final position did not reflect the way we played," said Haynes. "It was disappointing we did not finish in the top six or seven." Their one-day record was also one of under-achievement. They fared poorly in the Benson and Hedges Cup, dropped four places to 14th in the Sunday League and their interest in the NatWest Trophy ended in the quarter-finals.

Inconsistent batting was once more Sussex's big problem. The county managed only 36 batting points and, for the second year running, only Wells reached 1,000 Championship runs, though Bill Athey passed the mark in all first-class games, with Neil Lenham and Keith Greenfield not far behind. Speight had a frustrating summer, after missing the whole of the previous season with post-viral fatigue syndrome; he hit 349 Championship runs at an average below 22 and then missed the final four games after twisting his ankle during a training run. Sussex gave a two-year contract to former Middlesex batsman Toby Radford early in the season and the promising Toby Peirce was due back in 1997, having thought better of his unexpected retirement the previous year to take up a job in the City. After the exodus, 37-year-old Neil Taylor was signed from Kent. But opener Jamie Hall was released.

Until the TCCB's verdict, Giddins was Sussex's leading wicket-taker, with 40. After failing the drugs test at the end of May, during the match against Kent, he performed unstintingly; he took 33 wickets at 24.18 in the following eight games, including a career-best six for 47 against Yorkshire. But in August, the TCCB's disciplinary committee found him guilty of using a prohibited substance, cocaine, and bringing the game into disrepute. They rejected Giddins's contention that he had ingested the cocaine inadvertently. Taking into account the fact that cocaine was a Class A illegal drug, the most serious category (though it seemed unlikely that it would have enhanced his performance), they banned him from professional cricket until April 1, 1998, stating that "cricket, its players and administrators will not tolerate in its ranks those who indulge in the use of a prohibited drug." Two days later, Sussex announced that they would not re-register Giddins when his ban expired. They insisted that this should not be regarded as a disciplinary measure, but as an opportunity for him to make a new start elsewhere, which he did.

After Giddins's season was cut short, the new overseas player, West Indian Vasbert Drakes, completed a modern all-rounder's double of 50 wickets and 500 runs. He had started slowly in his first county season, but gained in confidence in what Haynes described as "a learning process". The rest of Sussex's highly regarded bowling attack was handicapped by injury, with only Law unscathed. Paul Jarvis followed eight Championship matches in 1995 with seven this time; he was out for the last two months with a stress fracture in his ankle. Jason Lewry, who missed the first four Championship games and was ruled out of five of the final six, still claimed 36 wickets at 22.66 to head the averages. Haynes was disappointed by the absence of Sussex players from both England's winter touring parties and felt Lewry was especially unfortunate. He rated him one of the best swing bowlers in the country. "Jason has come on in leaps and bounds," he said. "He bowls long spells and, even when things aren't going his way, he hangs in there and fights, which are qualities you need to be a Test cricketer."

James Kirtley came to public attention in unexpected ways, with eight wickets when he was a late replacement for the TCCB XI against South Africa A and, in December, five for 53 for Mashonaland when they beat England in Harare, an unusual but perhaps effective way of getting noticed by selectors. Salisbury did earn selection for England, after an absence of two years, and took 44 wickets for the county. He finished on a high note, with a career-best eight for 75 to beat Essex, but that proved to be his penultimate game for Sussex.

The new captain, Moores, tried to persuade Salisbury and the others to stay, but stressed that he wanted it to be their own decision. He knew a change of mood was essential. "The club has become frustrated by a lack of success," he said. "We simply haven't played up to our potential. My aim is not only for us to enjoy our cricket, but also to be more consistent. Team harmony is vital and hopefully a different voice and perspective will pull us together." – ANDY ARLIDGE.

Jack Arlidge, Wisden's *Sussex correspondent for 21 years, has retired. He has long been one of the most popular of all cricket writers amongst his colleagues, and we wish him a very happy retirement. He is succeeded by his son Andy.*

SUSSEX 1996

[*Bill Smith*

Back row: R. J. Kirtley, N. C. Phillips, J. D. Lewry, D. R. Law, R. S. C. Martin-Jenkins, M. Newell, J. J. Bates, R. K. Rao. *Middle row:* S. Humphries, K. Newell, P. W. Jarvis, J. W. Hall, E. S. H. Giddins, M. P. Speight, K. Greenfield, A. D. Edwards, S. M. B. Robertson (*physiotherapist*). *Front row:* L. V. Chandler (*scorer*), I. D. K. Salisbury, C. W. J. Athey, D. L. Haynes (*First Eleven coach*), A. P. Wells (*captain*), C. E. Waller (*coach*), P. Moores (*vice-captain*), N. J. Lenham, J. Hartridge (*scorer*). *Inset:* V. C. Drakes.

SUSSEX RESULTS

All first-class matches – Played 19: Won 6, Lost 9, Drawn 4.

County Championship matches – Played 17: Won 6, Lost 9, Drawn 2.

Competition placings – Britannic Assurance County Championship, 12th; NatWest Trophy, q-f; Benson and Hedges Cup, 4th in Group D; AXA Equity & Law League, 14th.

COUNTY CHAMPIONSHIP AVERAGES

BATTING

Cap		*M*	*I*	*NO*	*R*	*HS*	*100s*	*50s*	*Avge*	*Ct/St*
	N. C. Phillips	6	12	7	223	45	0	0	44.60	4
1990	N. J. Lenham†	15	27	2	895	145	2	5	35.80	3
1986	A. P. Wells†	17	31	0	1,072	122	2	5	34.58	12
1996	K. Greenfield†	13	24	3	710	154*	2	2	33.80	8
1993	C. W. J. Athey	17	31	0	980	111	3	4	31.61	15
1996	V. C. Drakes§	15	27	3	649	145*	2	4	27.04	1
	P. W. Jarvis	7	11	4	164	35	0	0	23.42	3
1996	D. R. Law	15	27	0	609	97	0	3	22.55	6
1989	P. Moores	17	31	4	597	119*	1	1	22.11	49/1
1991	M. P. Speight	9	17	1	349	122*	1	1	21.81	7
1991	I. D. K. Salisbury	14	24	2	473	83	0	3	21.50	7
1992	J. W. Hall†	6	11	0	208	57	0	2	18.90	5
	K. Newell†	4	8	0	129	31	0	0	16.12	1
1996	J. D. Lewry†	8	13	3	138	28*	0	0	13.80	0
	T. A. Radford	4	6	0	30	14	0	0	5.00	1
1994	E. S. H. Giddins†	12	15	5	46	11	0	0	4.60	0
	R. J. Kirtley†	6	11	3	15	7	0	0	1.87	4

Also batted: M. Newell† (1 match) 0, 0 (1 ct); R. K. Rao (1 match) 17, 38.

* *Signifies not out.* † *Born in Sussex.* § *Overseas player.*

BOWLING

	O	*M*	*R*	*W*	*BB*	*5W/i*	*Avge*
J. D. Lewry	264	46	816	36	6-44	4	22.66
E. S. H. Giddins	312.4	55	1,012	40	6-47	2	25.30
I. D. K. Salisbury	391.2	93	1,136	44	8-75	3	25.81
D. R. Law	281.4	42	1,027	37	5-33	2	27.75
P. W. Jarvis	147	25	510	18	4-60	0	28.33
R. J. Kirtley	137.4	22	535	16	4-94	0	33.43
V. C. Drakes	454.3	79	1,675	50	5-47	2	33.50
N. C. Phillips	182	35	626	10	2-54	0	62.60

Also bowled: K. Greenfield 23–6–52–0; N. J. Lenham 56.1–9–146–3; K. Newell 3–0–16–0.

COUNTY RECORDS

Highest score for:	333	K. S. Duleepsinhji v Northamptonshire at Hove	1930
Highest score against:	322	E. Paynter (Lancashire) at Hove	1937
Best bowling for:	10-48	C. H. G. Bland v Kent at Tonbridge	1899
Best bowling against:	9-11	A. P. Freeman (Kent) at Hove	1922
Highest total for:	705-8 dec.	v Surrey at Hastings	1902
Highest total against:	726	by Nottinghamshire at Nottingham	1895
Lowest total for:	19	v Surrey at Godalming	1830
	19	v Nottinghamshire at Hove	1873
Lowest total against:	18	by Kent at Gravesend	1867

At Nottingham, May 2, 3, 4, 6. SUSSEX drew with NOTTINGHAMSHIRE.

SUSSEX v WARWICKSHIRE

At Hove, May 9, 10, 11, 13. Warwickshire won by an innings and 139 runs. Warwickshire 24 pts, Sussex 2 pts. Toss: Warwickshire. Championship debut: S. M. Pollock.

Sussex's new coach, Desmond Haynes, conducted an hour-long inquiry in the dressing-room after their sixth defeat in eight games in 1996. Champions Warwickshire comprehensively outplayed them, scoring 645, the highest total in the fixture's history. All five Sussex bowlers conceded over 100; the variety of Salisbury, who had a sore back, was badly missed. Knight starred on the opening day, making 115 not out by lunch. When he was bowled for 132, his third century in consecutive matches for Warwickshire, he had hit 23 fours and two sixes in 113 balls. Penney followed him to three figures and Reeve got his first Championship century since 1990 early next morning. All unfurled some magnificent attacking strokes – unlike Sussex. Athey pottered around for 98 minutes and 73 balls to make six. Only Law, with a maiden fifty, offered much resistance. When they followed on, half-centuries from Hall and Wells forced the match into the final morning – but only for 65 minutes.

Close of play: First day, Warwickshire 494-3 (T. L. Penney 129*, D. A. Reeve 97*); Second day, Sussex 136-5 (D. R. Law 38*, P. Moores 10*); Third day, Sussex 187-6 (P. Moores 6*, V. C. Drakes 4*).

Warwickshire

N. V. Knight b Drakes	132
W. G. Khan b Phillips	19
D. P. Ostler c Athey b Phillips	90
T. L. Penney b Jarvis	134
*D. A. Reeve not out	168
S. M. Pollock c Hall b Law	24
D. R. Brown c Athey b Law	0
N. M. K. Smith c Wells b Giddins	28
†K. J. Piper not out	11
B 1, l-b 9, w 1, n-b 28	39
1/68 2/209 3/291 4/505 5/547 6/547 7/591 (7 wkts dec.)	645

G. Welch and A. F. Giles did not bat.

Bonus points – Warwickshire 4, Sussex 1 (Score at 120 overs: 529-4).

Bowling: Giddins 29–3–113–1; Drakes 28–4–143–1; Jarvis 23–2–102–1; Phillips 33–2–145–2; Law 29.4–2–132–2.

Sussex

C. W. J. Athey c Ostler b Welch	6	– c Piper b Brown	14
J. W. Hall c Ostler b Reeve	3	– b Pollock	57
M. P. Speight c Reeve b Pollock	11	– lbw b Giles	13
*A. P. Wells lbw b Reeve	8	– lbw b Giles	51
N. J. Lenham c Piper b Giles	41	– c and b Giles	13
D. R. Law c Penney b Pollock	53	– c Khan b Brown	18
†P. Moores c Reeve b Giles	39	– c Reeve b Pollock	13
V. C. Drakes c Reeve b Welch	21	– c Knight b Smith	41
N. C. Phillips not out	6	– not out	29
P. W. Jarvis c Knight b Welch	5	– st Piper b Smith	23
E. S. H. Giddins c Pollock b Welch	0	– st Piper b Smith	0
B 4, l-b 2, w 1, n-b 22	29	B 4, l-b 2, n-b 6	12
1/4 2/17 3/26 4/62 5/111 6/151 7/207 8/211 9/216	222	1/41 2/68 3/93 4/152 5/167 6/181 7/206 8/247 9/280	284

Bonus points – Sussex 1, Warwickshire 4.

Bowling: *First Innings*—Pollock 20–5–56–2; Reeve 7–2–7–2; Smith 11–3–31–0; Welch 16.3–4–50–4; Giles 21–10–40–2; Brown 9–1–32–0. *Second Innings*—Pollock 26–4–76–2; Reeve 4–2–8–0; Brown 17–5–46–2; Welch 6–2–23–0; Giles 39–14–86–3; Smith 8.1–1–39–3.

Umpires: J. W. Holder and V. A. Holder.

At Hove, May 16, 17, 18. SUSSEX drew with INDIANS (See Indian tour section).

SUSSEX v MIDDLESEX

At Horsham, May 22, 23, 24, 25. Sussex won by 234 runs. Sussex 19 pts, Middlesex 3 pts. Toss: Middlesex.

Not for the first time, the Horsham festival coincided with wet weather; two days were lost and only 62.3 overs bowled on Thursday. But Sussex completed their first win over county opposition in 1996 by 3 p.m. on the final day, when their seamers dismissed Middlesex for 85 inside two hours. Wells scored a brilliant 92 out of 152 in 40 overs with Athey on the second day. However, he seemed to have come off worse in the negotiations. A double forfeit set Middlesex 320 in 72 overs on a quick-scoring ground. But Drakes, who deserved more than one wicket, and Jarvis bowled with great hostility to reduce them to 32 for four. Ramprakash and Brown briefly suggested they could save the match, before Law and Giddins joined in with three apiece. The last four tumbled in 14 balls.

Close of play: First day, No play; Second day, Sussex 216-3 (C. W. J. Athey 70*, N. J. Lenham 6*); Third day, No play.

Sussex

C. W. J. Athey run out	77
J. W. Hall c Carr b Hewitt	4
M. P. Speight c Brown b Nash	24
*A. P. Wells c Nash b Follett	92
N. J. Lenham c Follett b Ramprakash	40
D. R. Law lbw b Fraser	3
†P. Moores st Brown b Ramprakash	36
I. D. K. Salisbury not out	10
V. C. Drakes not out	3
L-b 7, w 1, n-b 22	30
1/6 2/57 3/209 4/262 5/266 6/280 7/310 (7 wkts dec.)	319

P. W. Jarvis and E. S. H. Giddins did not bat.

Bonus points – Sussex 3, Middlesex 3.

Bowling: Fraser 24–6–56–1; Hewitt 11–3–43–1; Nash 10–1–44–1; Follett 24–6–99–1; Tufnell 11–2–42–0; Weekes 1–0–2–0; Ramprakash 4–0–26–2.

Sussex forfeited their second innings.

Middlesex

Middlesex forfeited their first innings.

P. N. Weekes c Moores b Jarvis	1
J. C. Pooley c Moores b Drakes	5
M. R. Ramprakash b Law	24
*M. W. Gatting c and b Jarvis	1
J. D. Carr lbw b Jarvis	1
†K. R. Brown c Moores b Giddins	28
D. J. Nash c Moores b Giddins	1
J. P. Hewitt c Speight b Law	4
A. R. C. Fraser b Law	2
P. C. R. Tufnell b Giddins	0
D. Follett not out	0
L-b 3, w 1, n-b 14	18
1/7 2/17 3/20 4/32 5/63 6/64 7/81 8/83 9/85	85

Bowling: Drakes 9–0–36–1; Jarvis 8–4–26–3; Law 4–0–14–3; Giddins 3.2–1–6–3.

Umpires: B. Dudleston and B. J. Meyer.

At Tunbridge Wells, May 30, 31. SUSSEX lost to KENT by ten wickets.

SUSSEX v DURHAM

At Hove, June 6, 7, 8, 10. Sussex won by an innings and 67 runs. Sussex 24 pts, Durham 1 pt. Toss: Sussex. County debut: T. A. Radford.

Sussex made the most of a belting pitch in their fifth successive win against Durham. For the second season running, their innings contained three hundreds: the stoical Athey made his fourth century against Durham in four years (he missed the inaugural game); Wells scored 113 with effortless ease until Campbell took a stunning low catch at slip; and Greenfield, who was wrongly listed in the morning papers as out for 38, scored a patient, Championship-best 124. He was awarded his cap in his tenth season. Salisbury then bamboozled Durham with five for nought in 15 balls and, when they followed on 393 behind, Law matched him by taking the first five for nought in 25. From 50 for five, Campbell and Scott batted sensibly to add 129, and later Betts and Cox hit maiden fifties in an entertaining stand of 103, a Durham tenth-wicket record. They even survived into a fourth day, albeit for just seven balls.

Close of play: First day, Sussex 302-4 (K. Greenfield 37*); Second day, Durham 159; Third day, Durham 324-9 (M. M. Betts 56*, D. M. Cox 66*).

Sussex

C. W. J. Athey lbw b Birbeck	102
T. A. Radford b Brown	1
*A. P. Wells c Campbell b Birbeck	113
K. Greenfield not out	124
N. J. Lenham lbw b Brown	10
D. R. Law run out	35
†P. Moores c Boiling b Birbeck	4
I. D. K. Salisbury c Betts b Cox	22
V. C. Drakes c Scott b Cox	56
J. D. Lewry not out	28
B 1, l-b 15, w 3, n-b 38	57
1/15 2/211 3/288 4/302 5/369 6/373 7/411 8/515	(8 wkts dec.) 552

E. S. H. Giddins did not bat.

Bonus points – Sussex 4, Durham 1 (Score at 120 overs: 368-4).

Bowling: Brown 35–10–96–2; Betts 22–1–148–0; Birbeck 31–9–88–3; Boiling 34–10–74–0; Cox 40–10–116–2; Blenkiron 1.5–0–14–0.

Durham

S. L. Campbell c Greenfield b Giddins	45	– lbw b Drakes	87
*M. A. Roseberry b Giddins	34	– c and b Law	11
J. E. Morris c Wells b Salisbury	12	– lbw b Law	0
D. A. Blenkiron st Moores b Salisbury	22	– lbw b Law	3
P. D. Collingwood c Moores b Salisbury	16	– c Moores b Law	5
S. D. Birbeck lbw b Salisbury	0	– c and b Law	8
†C. W. Scott c Moores b Salisbury	0	– c Wells b Drakes	52
M. M. Betts c Drakes b Salisbury	0	– not out	57
J. Boiling c Salisbury b Drakes	4	– b Salisbury	1
S. J. E. Brown c Greenfield b Drakes	12	– c Moores b Salisbury	16
D. M. Cox not out	4	– b Giddins	67
B 2, l-b 2, n-b 6	10	B 1, l-b 6, w 1, n-b 11	19
1/71 2/99 3/119 4/132 5/132 6/136 7/136 8/139 9/152	159	1/24 2/24 3/28 4/40 5/50 6/179 7/180 8/185 9/223	326

Bonus points – Sussex 4.

Bowling: *First Innings*—Drakes 11.1–3–46–2; Lewry 8–0–28–0; Law 4–0–30–0; Salisbury 11–6–15–6; Giddins 10–1–36–2. *Second Innings*—Drakes 15–2–84–2; Giddins 12.1–2–56–1; Law 12–4–33–5; Lewry 10–0–57–0; Salisbury 26–5–84–2; Greenfield 3–2–5–0.

Umpires: T. E. Jesty and M. J. Kitchen.

At Bristol, June 13, 14, 15. SUSSEX beat GLOUCESTERSHIRE by three runs.

SUSSEX v GLAMORGAN

At Hove, June 20, 21, 22, 24. Sussex won by an innings and seven runs. Sussex 24 pts, Glamorgan 3 pts. Toss: Sussex.

Sussex completed three Championship wins in succession – for the first time since 1984 – after lunch on the final day, prompting Wells to hail his seam attack as the equal of any in England. After a first-day washout, he had put Glamorgan in on a green-tinged pitch that had sweated under the covers. It soon paid off as they folded inside 44 overs, with left-armer Lewry taking six for

44. Sussex equalled Glamorgan's 133 with two wickets down, only to lose their next three for one run. But Greenfield steadied the ship with his third century of the season, a career-best 154, playing some fine shots against Croft's off-spin. He put on 172 for the seventh wicket with Salisbury, who made 83, his biggest score in England. When Glamorgan resumed 273 behind, their last hope of the draw lay in Maynard. He also scored his third hundred of 1996, and put on 141 with Cottey, but defeat quickly followed his dismissal. The victory was overshadowed by the news that a Sussex player, at that stage unnamed, had failed a drugs test taken during the Tunbridge Wells match three weeks earlier.

Close of play: First day, No play; Second day, Sussex 162-5 (K. Greenfield 39*, P. Moores 22*); Third day, Glamorgan 122-3 (M. P. Maynard 45*, P. A. Cottey 33*).

Glamorgan

S. P. James b Law	9	– b Lewry	8
H. Morris lbw b Lewry	7	– lbw b Lewry	19
A. Dale b Lewry	4	– lbw b Giddins	5
*M. P. Maynard b Lewry	7	– c Greenfield b Salisbury	112
P. A. Cottey lbw b Law	23	– lbw b Drakes	57
G. P. Butcher b Law	15	– b Giddins	20
R. D. B. Croft lbw b Lewry	0	– b Giddins	4
S. D. Thomas c Wells b Lewry	12	– run out	6
†C. P. Metson not out	18	– b Giddins	6
S. L. Watkin b Lewry	16	– c Moores b Salisbury	5
O. T. Parkin b Drakes	0	– not out	0
B 1, l-b 6, w 1, n-b 14	22	B 4, l-b 11, w 1, n-b 8	24
1/16 2/22 3/36 4/44 5/77 6/80 7/80 8/96 9/132	133	1/23 2/36 3/38 4/179 5/211 6/225 7/244 8/256 9/266	266

Bonus points – Sussex 4.

Bowling: *First Innings*—Drakes 7.3–1–25–1; Lewry 16–4–44–6; Giddins 12–2–29–0; Law 8–2–28–3. *Second Innings*—Drakes 16–3–63–1; Lewry 16–4–56–2; Giddins 19.3–1–65–4; Salisbury 24–4–49–2; Law 3–0–18–0.

Sussex

C. W. J. Athey c Metson b Thomas	11
T. A. Radford c Maynard b Parkin	1
*A. P. Wells c Maynard b Thomas	78
K. Greenfield not out	154
N. J. Lenham b Thomas	0
D. R. Law c Metson b Watkin	0
†P. Moores lbw b Watkin	23
I. D. K. Salisbury c Butcher b Croft	83
V. C. Drakes c Metson b Parkin	9
J. D. Lewry b Thomas	28
E. S. H. Giddins c Metson b Thomas	5
L-b 7, w 3, n-b 4	14
1/4 2/31 3/133 4/133 5/134 6/164 7/336 8/358 9/400	406

Bonus points – Sussex 4, Glamorgan 3 (Score at 120 overs: 358-8).

Bowling: Watkin 31–7–78–2; Parkin 29–8–84–2; Thomas 28.2–4–121–5; Croft 32–4–75–1; Butcher 9–1–41–0.

Umpires: A. A. Jones and P. Willey.

SUSSEX v CAMBRIDGE UNIVERSITY

At Hove, June 29, 30, July 1. Drawn. Toss: Sussex. First-class debuts: R. K. Rao; R. W. Tennent.

A featherbed pitch, one short boundary and a Sussex attack without capped bowlers destined this match for stalemate. Only 12 wickets fell, though in the second innings Cambridge looked shaky at 42 for three before heavy showers swept in to give the game a quiet death in front of a single-figure crowd. The first batsman out, Radford, fell to the South African postgraduate Rob Tennent, who became the third player in 1996 – after Hewitt of Middlesex and Collingwood of Durham – to take a wicket with his first ball in first-class cricket. Sussex acting-captain Moores enjoyed himself with 185, easily his best, adding 246 with Newell, who dismantled the students' attack. But Cambridge replied in kind. Smith and Singh both scored their second centuries of the season, and Singh, on Warwickshire's books, reached 157, giving a little support to coach Derek Randall's prediction that he could make a hundred hundreds. Another solid innings from Sussex left the University a target of 322 before rain intervened.

Close of play: First day, Cambridge University 64-1 (E. T. Smith 30*, A. Singh 32*); Second day, Sussex 132-0 (T. A. Radford 51*, J. W. Hall 81*).

Sussex

T. A. Radford c Jones b Tennent	14	– b Tennent	53
J. W. Hall lbw b Tennent	29	– c Birks b Tennent	93
*P. Moores b Deakin	185		
M. P. Speight c House b Deakin	50	– not out	64
K. Newell not out	105		
R. K. Rao (did not bat)		– (3) not out	32
B 5, l-b 4, w 1, n-b 6	16	W 1	1
1/42 2/51 3/153 4/399 (4 wkts dec.)	399	1/140 2/152 (2 wkts dec.)	243

†S. Humphries, R. S. C. Martin-Jenkins, N. C. Phillips, A. D. Edwards and R. J. Kirtley did not bat.

Bowling: *First Innings*—Haste 20–4–95–0; Moffat 12–2–65–0; Whittall 18–4–66–0; Tennent 13–2–38–2; Jones 7–1–40–0; House 8–1–69–0; Deakin 4.4–1–17–2. *Second Innings*—Haste 6–0–23–0; Moffat 11–1–43–0; Tennent 10–0–34–2; Whittall 13–2–58–0; Deakin 5–0–24–0; Jones 9–2–43–0; House 5–0–18–0.

Cambridge University

R. O. Jones c Humphries b Kirtley	0	– (2) lbw b Kirtley	0
E. T. Smith c Radford b Newell	100		
A. Singh c Hall b Phillips	157	– b Martin-Jenkins	23
*R. Q. Cake not out	36	– (1) c Phillips b Kirtley	5
W. J. House not out	12	– not out	20
P. J. Deakin (did not bat)		– (4) not out	21
L-b 12, n-b 4	16	B 4	4
1/0 2/240 3/295 (3 wkts dec.)	321	1/3 2/18 3/42 (3 wkts)	73

A. R. Whittall, N. J. Haste, G. R. Moffat, R. W. Tennent and †M. J. Birks did not bat.

Bowling: *First Innings*—Kirtley 17–3–91–1; Edwards 13–2–64–0; Phillips 28–11–70–1; Martin-Jenkins 8–0–39–0; Newell 14–4–38–1; Rao 5–3–7–0. *Second Innings*—Kirtley 8–1–31–2; Martin-Jenkins 9–1–26–1; Newell 2–0–12–0.

Umpires: N. T. Plews and M. K. Reed.

SUSSEX v HAMPSHIRE

At Arundel, July 3, 4, 5, 6. Drawn. Sussex 7 pts, Hampshire 9 pts. Toss: Sussex.

Sussex were never in the hunt for a fourth successive Championship win on a typically slow Arundel wicket, where attacking shots were a rarity. Two sessions were lost on the first day, when a lively opening burst by Giddins and Jarvis had Hampshire 39 for four. But batting was easier when the sun came out and Keech, battling for his future, led Hampshire to respectability with a maiden hundred in four and a half hours. A surface on which runs had to be garnered with the utmost care seemed tailor-made for Athey but, though he dropped anchor for 39 in 28 overs, Stephenson ripped through Sussex to establish a lead of 77. Laney, demonstrating genuine potential, and James added 108 before the declaration set Sussex 316. Hampshire sniffed victory at 98 for five with 17 overs left before another heavy shower sent the players off for a fourth time.

Close of play: First day, Hampshire 82-4 (V. P. Terry 15*, M. Keech 30*); Second day, Sussex 82-3 (A. P. Wells 38*, P. W. Jarvis 2*); Third day, Hampshire 190-3 (K. D. James 60*, M. Keech 10*).

Hampshire

*J. P. Stephenson c Jarvis b Giddins	5	– (6) not out	9
J. S. Laney lbw b Jarvis	8	– (1) lbw b Lewry	83
K. D. James lbw b Giddins	3	– b Lewry	72
R. A. Smith lbw b Jarvis	21	– b Lewry	28
V. P. Terry lbw b Lenham	52	– (2) lbw b Lewry	4
M. Keech c Moores b Giddins	104	– (5) b Lewry	19
†A. N. Aymes c Moores b Law	29	– not out	11
S. D. Udal lbw b Lewry	18		
S. M. Milburn b Lewry	0		
C. A. Connor c Radford b Law	8		
J. N. B. Bovill not out	1		
B 12, l-b 8, w 1	21	L-b 11, w 1	12
1/13 2/13 3/27 4/39 5/175 6/231 7/257 8/257 9/261	270	1/21 2/129 3/173 4/216 5/217	(5 wkts dec.) 238

Bonus points – Hampshire 2, Sussex 4.

Bowling: *First Innings*—Lewry 17–3–46–2; Giddins 26–5–56–3; Jarvis 23–5–58–2; Law 13.3–3–39–2; Salisbury 14–2–33–0; Lenham 13–1–18–1. *Second Innings*—Giddins 16–2–49–0; Lewry 19–4–73–5; Law 13–2–28–0; Jarvis 4–0–10–0; Salisbury 16–2–56–0; Lenham 5–1–11–0.

Sussex

C. W. J. Athey c Terry b Stephenson	39	– c Terry b James	24
T. A. Radford b Connor	1	– lbw b Connor	2
*A. P. Wells c Aymes b Connor	43	– c Aymes b Milburn	8
K. Greenfield c Udal b Stephenson	0	– lbw b Stephenson	6
P. W. Jarvis b Connor	35		
N. J. Lenham c Aymes b Stephenson	14	– (5) not out	55
D. R. Law c Terry b Stephenson	17	– (6) lbw b Stephenson	13
†P. Moores c Terry b Stephenson	8	– (7) not out	7
I. D. K. Salisbury not out	19		
J. D. Lewry b Stephenson	0		
E. S. H. Giddins b Connor	11		
L-b 4, w 2	6	B 4, l-b 9	13
1/1 2/75 3/79 4/87 5/134 6/136 7/155 8/166 9/166	193	1/7 2/22 3/34 4/58 5/81	(5 wkts) 128

Bonus points – Hampshire 4.

Bowling: *First Innings*—Connor 20.5–5–57–4; Milburn 15–3–43–0; Bovill 6–2–17–0; Stephenson 20–7–48–6; James 7–2–24–0. *Second Innings*—Connor 11–2–33–1; Milburn 10–2–29–1; Stephenson 16–7–30–2; James 7–3–23–1.

Umpires: J. C. Balderstone and A. Clarkson.

At Guildford, July 17, 18, 19, 20. SUSSEX lost to SURREY by 135 runs.

At Leicester, July 25, 26, 27, 29. SUSSEX lost to LEICESTERSHIRE by 58 runs.

SUSSEX v YORKSHIRE

At Eastbourne, August 1, 2, 3. Sussex won by two wickets. Sussex 22 pts, Yorkshire 7 pts. Toss: Sussex.

Sussex's batting displayed some backbone for once to hit back after being reduced to 114 for seven chasing 226. Moores and Drakes, who were both dropped, added 104 to secure an unexpected win which prevented Yorkshire from topping the Championship. It was a match to remember for Giddins. After news broke that he must face the TCCB's disciplinary committee over drug-taking allegations, he claimed a career-best six for 47 in a masterly display of swing bowling that hustled out Yorkshire for 133 in their second innings. Drakes had also returned his best figures for the county, five for 99, on the opening day. Yorkshire were 150 for seven before some aggressive strokeplay from Blakey and Hartley added 151 at six an over. Athey ground out another century against his old county but Sussex trailed by 92 after losing their last five for 11 in 13 balls. They began their chase on the second evening but Gough bowled with great venom on a pitch which had flattened out under the baking sun, and Hartley completed ten in the match. Then Moores dug in while Drakes scored a match-winning fifty.

Close of play: First day, Sussex 33-2 (C. W. J. Athey 13*); Second day, Sussex 7-0 (C. W. J. Athey 6*, J. W. Hall 0*).

Yorkshire

M. D. Moxon b Lewry	2	– lbw b Lewry	10
M. P. Vaughan b Lewry	1	– c Moores b Drakes	6
*D. Byas b Drakes	5	– not out	72
M. G. Bevan hit wkt b Giddins	24	– b Drakes	1
A. McGrath c Salisbury b Drakes	41	– c Hall b Giddins	9
C. White c Speight b Drakes	47	– b Giddins	7
†R. J. Blakey not out	80	– lbw b Giddins	2
D. Gough lbw b Drakes	4	– b Giddins	5
P. J. Hartley c Speight b Drakes	89	– c Hall b Drakes	4
C. E. W. Silverwood b Salisbury	12	– b Giddins	0
R. D. Stemp b Giddins	5	– b Giddins	10
B 1, l-b 12, w 1, n-b 21	35	L-b 3, n-b 4	7
1/3 2/12 3/22 4/55 5/145 6/146 7/150 8/301 9/327	345	1/12 2/22 3/29 4/68 5/78 6/98 7/104 8/111 9/115	133

Bonus points – Yorkshire 3, Sussex 4.

Bowling: *First Innings*—Lewry 17–4–54–2; Drakes 27–5–99–5; Giddins 19–2–76–2; Law 9–0–61–0; Salisbury 17–11–42–1. *Second Innings*—Lewry 11–3–28–1; Drakes 14–1–36–3; Giddins 16.3–4–47–6; Law 5–1–19–0.

Sussex

C. W. J. Athey lbw b Hartley	100	– lbw b Hartley	47
J. W. Hall c Stemp b Hartley	6	– b Gough	3
J. D. Lewry lbw b Hartley	13	– (10) not out	6
*A. P. Wells c Blakey b Hartley	31	– (3) lbw b Gough	0
K. Greenfield lbw b White	15	– (4) b Hartley	12
M. P. Speight c Byas b Gough	22	– (5) c Stemp b Hartley	0
D. R. Law c Bevan b Hartley	39	– (6) c Blakey b Gough	43
†P. Moores c Byas b White	0	– (7) not out	39
I. D. K. Salisbury lbw b White	2	– (8) c Bevan b Hartley	0
V. C. Drakes not out	0	– (9) c and b Silverwood	59
E. S. H. Giddins c Stemp b Hartley	0		
B 4, l-b 3, w 2, n-b 16	25	B 2, l-b 5, n-b 10	17
1/19 2/33 3/87 4/135 5/187 6/242 7/251 8/253 9/253	253	1/24 2/24 3/47 4/47 5/111 6/114 7/114 8/218	(8 wkts) 226

Bonus points – Sussex 2, Yorkshire 4.

Bowling: *First Innings*—Gough 15–3–51–1; Silverwood 15–2–64–0; Hartley 16.5–2–67–6; White 12–2–50–3; Stemp 6–2–14–0. *Second Innings*—Hartley 22–4–86–4; Gough 19–6–59–3; White 4–2–11–0; Silverwood 8–0–32–1; Stemp 9–6–17–0; Bevan 3–0–14–0.

Umpires: V. A. Holder and T. E. Jesty.

SUSSEX v DERBYSHIRE

At Hove, August 8, 9, 10, 12. Derbyshire won by 47 runs. Derbyshire 23 pts, Sussex 6 pts. Toss: Derbyshire.

A decisive burst of pace on the final morning swung the game Derbyshire's way. On the first day, Salisbury got to work minutes after arriving at half past three, having been released from the Leeds Test, by taking Derbyshire's last three wickets. Speight then delighted his admirers with his first hundred since May 1994, to prop up Sussex's reply. In the second innings, the visitors took their lead to 174 with three wickets down before Drakes, bowling as quickly as he had done all season, swept away the middle order for a county-best five for 47. Derbyshire were saved by Rollins's defiance. He carried his bat for 78 and Malcolm bludgeoned 21 in a last-wicket partnership of 55 that ultimately made the difference. While Greenfield was scoring 51, Sussex hoped to win. But they lost three wickets in three overs on the final morning as DeFreitas and Malcolm – who took ten in the match – revelled. Moores hit 56 in 41 balls but the rest came quietly.

Close of play: First day, Sussex 88-5 (M. P. Speight 28*); Second day, Sussex 212-7 (M. P. Speight 92*, P. Moores 8*); Third day, Sussex 91-2 (I. D. K. Salisbury 9*, A. P. Wells 2*).

Derbyshire

K. J. Barnett b Law	55	– lbw b Giddins	17
A. S. Rollins c Wells b Drakes	1	– not out	78
C. J. Adams c Athey b Law	43	– c Moores b Drakes	1
*D. M. Jones lbw b Drakes	17	– c Athey b Law	30
T. J. G. O'Gorman c Moores b Kirtley	54	– c Salisbury b Drakes	22
C. M. Wells c Law b Kirtley	11	– (9) b Giddins	13
†K. M. Krikken c Kirtley b Salisbury	48	– (6) c Moores b Salisbury	1
P. A. J. DeFreitas lbw b Giddins	14	– (7) b Drakes	7
M. J. Vandrau c Greenfield b Salisbury	29	– (8) lbw b Drakes	0
K. J. Dean b Salisbury	3	– c Moores b Drakes	1
D. E. Malcolm not out	4	– b Kirtley	21
B 2, l-b 18, w 1, n-b 20	41	B 4, l-b 6, w 3, n-b 16	29
1/11 2/102 3/123 4/159 5/212 6/221 7/236 8/287 9/315	320	1/33 2/35 3/76 4/119 5/122 6/129 7/133 8/164 9/165	220

Bonus points – Derbyshire 3, Sussex 4.

Bowling: *First Innings*—Drakes 19–5–73–2; Kirtley 16–2–61–2; Giddins 17–1–78–1; Law 17–2–78–2; Salisbury 8–5–10–3. *Second Innings*—Drakes 21–5–47–5; Kirtley 7.5–0–33–1; Giddins 17–3–68–2; Law 5–0–29–1; Salisbury 11–2–33–1.

Sussex

C. W. J. Athey c Jones b Malcolm	6	– lbw b Vandrau	19
K. Greenfield c Rollins b Malcolm	12	– c Jones b Malcolm	51
*A. P. Wells c Adams b DeFreitas	35	– (4) c O'Gorman b DeFreitas	2
M. P. Speight not out	122	– (5) b Malcolm	1
R. J. Kirtley b Malcolm	0	– (10) b Malcolm	7
E. S. H. Giddins b Malcolm	1	– (11) not out	3
K. Newell c Rollins b Wells	30	– (6) lbw b Dean	31
D. R. Law lbw b Wells	8	– (7) c Vandrau b Malcolm	32
†P. Moores b Malcolm	8	– (8) c Barnett b Malcolm	56
I. D. K. Salisbury lbw b Dean	20	– (3) c Vandrau b DeFreitas	13
V. C. Drakes c Adams b DeFreitas	0	– (9) c Krikken b DeFreitas	2
L-b 17, n-b 6	23	B 4, l-b 1, n-b 6	11
1/18 2/21 3/85 4/86 5/88 6/177 7/191 8/212 9/264	265	1/75 2/81 3/91 4/92 5/96 6/144 7/208 8/211 9/223	228

Bonus points – Sussex 2, Derbyshire 4.

Bowling: *First Innings*—Malcolm 21–2–119–5; DeFreitas 38–10–87–2; Dean 8–2–22–1; Wells 17–7–20–2. *Second Innings*—Malcolm 25–6–96–5; DeFreitas 17–1–59–3; Dean 15–3–57–1; Vandrau 8–2–11–1.

Umpires: B. Dudleston and R. Palmer.

At Northampton, August 22, 23, 24, 26. SUSSEX lost to NORTHAMPTONSHIRE by six wickets.

SUSSEX v LANCASHIRE

At Hove, August 29, 30, 31, September 2. Lancashire won by five wickets. Lancashire 21 pts, Sussex 8 pts. Toss: Sussex.

Crawley shook off the effects of flu to lead Lancashire to only their second Championship win in 1996. An unbeaten 112, his third century in as many matches including the Oval Test, was the crucial difference. Athey had ground out a hundred and Drakes made a breezy fifty in Sussex's first innings, though Austin applied the brake with his naggingly accurate seamers. Lancashire were faltering at 85 for five. But Hegg and Chapple, whose eighth-wicket stand of 46 was the highest of the innings, enabled them to save the follow-on and they counter-attacked strongly on the third day. Green, enjoying himself down the slope, took three for eight in six overs as Sussex's brittle top order folded. Lancashire's target was 290 and Crawley and Fairbrother steered them most of the way home in a stand of 150. Fairbrother took a particular liking to Salisbury, hitting him for six fours and a six before becoming his first victim in a spell of three for nought in 19 balls, a belated act of defiance. Umpire Bird's reputation for finding improbable trouble was enhanced when a catering van reversed into his (unsponsored) BMW in the car park, causing considerable damage.

Close of play: First day, Sussex 285-6 (V. C. Drakes 24*, D. R. Law 2*); Second day, Lancashire 197-8 (G. Chapple 26*, R. J. Green 0*); Third day, Lancashire 53-0 (S. P. Titchard 26*, J. E. R. Gallian 24*).

Sussex

N. J. Lenham c Speak b Green	37	– c Hegg b Green	17
C. W. J. Athey c Hegg b Watkinson	111	– c Hegg b Chapple	8
K. Greenfield c Speak b Austin	24	– lbw b Watkinson	7
*A. P. Wells c Titchard b Gallian	21	– c Titchard b Keedy	29
K. Newell c and b Austin	31	– c Hegg b Green	2
V. C. Drakes b Austin	52	– c Gallian b Green	0
†P. Moores c Watkinson b Austin	22	– run out	8
D. R. Law b Chapple	3	– b Keedy	9
I. D. K. Salisbury lbw b Chapple	40	– lbw b Gallian	27
N. C. Phillips b Green	4	– c and b Gallian	24
R. J. Kirtley not out	0	– not out	1
B 7, l-b 8, w 1, n-b 2	18	B 4, l-b 6, n-b 2	12
1/68 2/111 3/147 4/217 5/238 6/276 7/314 8/314 9/331	363	1/21 2/34 3/34 4/54 5/54 6/76 7/81 8/99 9/129	144

Bonus points – Sussex 4, Lancashire 4.

Bowling: *First Innings*—Chapple 29.3–2–118–2; Green 25–6–101–2; Austin 27–12–37–4; Watkinson 20–6–55–1; Gallian 8–3–17–1; Keedy 8–2–20–0. *Second Innings*—Chapple 16–5–38–1; Green 14–7–20–3; Watkinson 9–5–22–1; Keedy 13–2–34–2; Gallian 4.4–0–20–2.

Lancashire

J. E. R. Gallian b Drakes	20	– (2) b Salisbury	37
S. P. Titchard b Phillips	41	– (1) c Moores b Law	30
J. P. Crawley c Moores b Law	1	– not out	112
N. H. Fairbrother b Kirtley	15	– c Kirtley b Salisbury	79
N. J. Speak b Kirtley	0	– b Salisbury	1
*M. Watkinson c Lenham b Salisbury	9	– c Wells b Salisbury	1
†W. K. Hegg c Athey b Lenham	54	– not out	10
I. D. Austin b Salisbury	18		
G. Chapple not out	37		
R. J. Green c Moores b Drakes	9		
G. Keedy c Moores b Kirtley	0		
B 1, l-b 5, w 2, n-b 6	14	B 4, l-b 9, w 1, n-b 6	20
1/35 2/40 3/64 4/68 5/85 6/119 7/150 8/196 9/217	218	1/63 2/97 3/247 4/249 5/253	(5 wkts) 290

Bonus points – Lancashire 1, Sussex 4.

Bowling: *First Innings*—Drakes 20–3–45–2; Kirtley 14.5–0–30–3; Phillips 31–13–49–1; Law 7–1–18–1; Salisbury 33–12–67–2; Lenham 3–2–3–1. *Second Innings*—Drakes 18–2–58–0; Kirtley 6.4–0–33–0; Phillips 10–1–44–0; Law 9–3–25–1; Salisbury 26–6–100–4; Lenham 3–0–17–0.

Umpires: H. D. Bird and D. J. Constant.

At Worcester, September 3, 4, 5. SUSSEX lost to WORCESTERSHIRE by an innings and 14 runs.

At Chelmsford, September 12, 13, 14, 16. SUSSEX beat ESSEX by 137 runs.

SUSSEX v SOMERSET

At Hove, September 19, 20, 21. Somerset won by eight wickets. Somerset 24 pts, Sussex 4 pts. Toss: Sussex. Championship debut: R. K. Rao.

Another season of underachievement by Sussex ended with their fifth defeat in six games. Caddick, who went on to claim his third ten-wicket haul of the season, had ripped through Sussex's top order on the first morning. Lee supported him with his best figures for Somerset and followed up with his fifth century of the season, batting his side into a strong position on the second day as he added 208 with Harden. Salisbury, one of the few Sussex players who finished the season well, collected five wickets, and they looked to be making a fight of it when Lenham and Athey began their second innings with a stand of 102. Rao showed remarkable concentration on his Championship debut, and was ninth out, but Sussex lost seven wickets for 77; Caddick troubled everyone with his extra bounce, change of pace and exemplary line. Needing only 58, Somerset completed a comfortable win with more than a day to spare.

Close of play: First day, Somerset 45-1 (M. N. Lathwell 28*, P. D. Bowler 13*); Second day, Sussex 63-0 (N. J. Lenham 41*, C. W. J. Athey 21*).

Sussex

N. J. Lenham c Holloway b Caddick	18	– c Turner b Caddick	64
C. W. J. Athey lbw b Lee	7	– c Turner b Shine	57
R. K. Rao c Harden b Caddick	17	– c and b Trump	38
*A. P. Wells c Trescothick b Caddick	1	– b Cottam	1
K. Greenfield c Lathwell b Lee	11	– c Harden b Caddick	22
V. C. Drakes c Trump b Caddick	2	– lbw b Caddick	0
†P. Moores c and b Shine	33	– b Trump	4
I. D. K. Salisbury lbw b Caddick	6	– c Turner b Trump	6
D. R. Law b Lee	32	– lbw b Caddick	39
N. C. Phillips not out	1	– not out	9
R. J. Kirtley lbw b Lee	3	– lbw b Caddick	0
L-b 3, n-b 7	10	L-b 4, w 4, n-b 22	30
1/20 2/42 3/44 4/44 5/53 6/63 7/70 8/133 9/137	141	1/102 2/143 3/144 4/193 5/193 6/198 7/204 8/253 9/269	270

Bonus points – Somerset 4.

Bowling: *First Innings*—Caddick 15–2–58–5; Shine 10–3–28–1; Lee 18.1–5–52–4. *Second Innings*—Caddick 31–8–122–5; Shine 3.2–0–16–1; Cottam 33–11–60–1; Trump 13–6–43–3; Lee 8–4–25–0.

Somerset

M. N. Lathwell c Moores b Drakes	56	– not out	38
M. E. Trescothick c Moores b Drakes	1	– c Athey b Kirtley	0
*P. D. Bowler lbw b Salisbury	20	– lbw b Kirtley	0
R. J. Harden c Wells b Salisbury	78	– not out	16
P. C. L. Holloway c Moores b Drakes	0		
S. Lee c Moores b Phillips	126		
†R. J. Turner not out	27		
A. R. Caddick c Greenfield b Salisbury	10		
H. R. J. Trump c Athey b Salisbury	0		
K. J. Shine b Phillips	1		
A. C. Cottam c Phillips b Salisbury	12		
B 4, l-b 10, w 1, n-b 8	23	B 5, l-b 1	6
1/23 2/75 3/87 4/87 5/295 6/305 7/330 8/330 9/331	354	1/21 2/23	(2 wkts) 60

Bonus points – Somerset 4, Sussex 4.

Bowling: *First Innings*—Drakes 18–0–88–3; Law 9–0–32–0; Salisbury 31.1–6–91–5; Phillips 21–2–92–2; Kirtley 9–1–37–0; Lenham 1–1–0–0. *Second Innings*—Kirtley 5–2–31–2; Salisbury 4.4–0–23–0.

Umpires: J. D. Bond and J. H. Hampshire.

THE CHAMPIONS

The dates on which the County Championship has been settled since 1979 are as follows:

			Final margin
1979	Essex	August 21	77 pts
1980	Middlesex	September 2	13 pts
1981	Nottinghamshire	September 14	2 pts
1982	Middlesex	September 11	39 pts
1983	Essex	September 13	16 pts
1984	Essex	September 11	14 pts
1985	Middlesex	September 17	18 pts
1986	Essex	September 10	28 pts
1987	Nottinghamshire	September 14	4 pts
1988	Worcestershire	September 16	1 pt
1989	Worcestershire	August 31	6 pts
1990	Middlesex	September 20	31 pts
1991	Essex	September 19	13 pts
1992	Essex	September 3	41 pts
1993	Middlesex	August 30	36 pts
1994	Warwickshire	September 2	42 pts
1995	Warwickshire	September 16	32 pts
1996	Leicestershire	September 21	27 pts

Note: The earliest date on which the Championship has been won since it was expanded in 1895 was August 12, 1910, by Kent.

Trevor Penney

WARWICKSHIRE

President: The Earl of Aylesford
Chairman: M. J. K. Smith
Chairman, Cricket Committee: J. Whitehouse
Chief Executive: D. L. Amiss
Captain: 1996 – D. A. Reeve
1997 – T. A. Munton
Director of Coaching: P. A. Neale
Head Groundsman: S. J. Rouse
Scorer: A. E. Davis

For the first time in four years, Warwickshire finished empty-handed in 1996. Objectively, though, they did well to sustain their challenges as long as they did, given a daunting run of injuries and changes of personnel that would have put most sides completely out of contention.

They had known they would be without Roger Twose, who had moved to New Zealand, and Allan Donald. Then in July captain Dermot Reeve, who had won two Championships and four one-day trophies since his appointment in 1993, was forced to retire because of a chronic hip injury. That was bad enough. A broken left wrist meant that vice-captain Tim Munton was absent for the first six Championship games, Gladstone Small played in only seven, Nick Knight missed half the programme through injury and international calls and Andy Moles and Keith Piper were also kept out by injuries. It was hardly surprising that Warwickshire could not dominate the county scene as gloriously as in the two previous seasons.

It is difficult to quantify, but Twose was probably missed more than anyone. With the exception of 1994, Brian Lara's year, the side has been short of a high-class batsman. But in previous seasons, the others scored enough to enable the bowlers to win matches. Not in 1996, when only Knight, Penney and Moles of the top order averaged above 30. Knight had a fine season, but was available for only eight Championship matches. With Knight and Moles absent, the batting was exposed. Only Trevor Penney did himself justice – or reached 1,000 for the county. The only ever-present apart from Dougie Brown, he anchored the batting with three hundreds and seven fifties, and his fielding was as brilliant as ever. He is one of a couple of dozen England-qualified batsmen with a career average over 40 – Moles is another – a significant statistic now that he has played more than 150 innings.

Dominic Ostler and Wasim Khan regressed. Both averaged under 30, compared with well over 40 in 1995. Ostler was handicapped by a knee injury and needed a second operation. Despite two hundreds, Khan managed only 579 at 23.16, just above youngsters Michael Powell and the highly regarded Anurag Singh. Too often for comfort, the side was rescued by the middle-lower order, where Ashley Giles and Neil Smith were outstanding. Giles reset his career-best score three times, crowning his season with a splendid maiden first-class hundred, against Lancashire, in his final innings. Another blow was Piper's finger injury, which kept him out for two months. Michael Burns deputised and did well enough with the bat to be selected as a specialist batsman in the last two matches. The arrival of David Hemp from Glamorgan should allow a little more flexibility in 1997.

The level of expectation surrounding Shaun Pollock, Donald's stand-in and fellow South African, was misplaced. He took time to adjust to the different length required on English pitches. He started sensationally, with four wickets in four balls in the opening Benson and Hedges match against Leicestershire, but a return of 42 first-class wickets in 13 matches did not suggest a match-winning pace bowler. Pollock's batting was that of a genuine all-rounder, however. His first two first-class hundreds, against Northamptonshire and Glamorgan, underpinned two of Warwickshire's seven Championship wins. But he had to return home in mid-August for ankle surgery.

The leading wicket-taker was Giles, whose emergence as a left-arm spinner good enough to take 55 Championship wickets was the most encouraging feature of an otherwise disappointing season for the bowlers. It also earned him a tour of Australia with England A. But the wickets taken by Munton, Neil Smith and Brown all cost well over 35 apiece, and off-spinner Smith tailed off after his appearances for England in the 1996 World Cup and in the one-day series against India. Graeme Welch made an encouraging return after missing nearly all of 1995, although he under-achieved with the bat, and Darren Altree looked a promising left-arm pace bowler.

It will take another outstanding season from Donald to carry Warwickshire to the title in 1997. As he is expected to tour England with South Africa and play in the World Cup in the following two years, this might well be his last season in county cricket.

Even with all their difficulties, Warwickshire remained on the fringe of the challengers for the Championship, until a rain-ruined draw against Worcestershire followed by heavy defeats by Surrey and Essex left them with too much to do; they had to settle for eighth, which they would have considered highly respectable in the old days. They did better in the Sunday League, finishing fourth, after losing their last match but two to eventual winners Surrey in disappointing fashion. Acting-captain Munton spread the field, allowing Surrey to pick off runs in the closing overs, instead of trying to exert pressure. Then, more than in any other game, Reeve's inspirational leadership was missed. Even Reeve, however, had not been able to prevent Northamptonshire from pulling off an improbable win in the Benson and Hedges semi-final. It was Surrey, again, who ended Warwickshire's run of three successive NatWest finals by inflicting a second-round home defeat with surprising ease.

Munton was appointed captain for 1997 with Knight, an influential figure on the field when he was around, as his vice-captain. They will not be able to call on Paul Smith, who retired, aged 32, before the end of the season, frustrated by lack of first-team cricket. So ended a 15-year career in which he played 221 games, scored 8,173 runs and took 283 wickets – as well as playing a leading part in the club's one-day successes. The period of transition that follows a run of success is always difficult, and six trophies between September 1993 and September 1995 may have made Warwickshire supporters more impatient than they used to be. – JACK BANNISTER.

WARWICKSHIRE 1996

[*Bill Smith*

Back row: T. Frost, S. McDonald, M. J. Powell, M. D. Edmond, D. A. Altree. *Middle row:* D. L. Amiss (*chief executive*), T. L. Penney, W. G. Khan, D. R. Brown, N. V. Knight, M. A. V. Bell, A. F. Giles, M. Burns, G. Welch, K. J. Piper, S. Nottingham (*physiotherapist*). *Front row:* R. N. Abberley (*head coach*), A. J. Moles, N. M. K. Smith, A. A. Donald (*bowling and fitness coach*), T. A. Munton (*vice-captain*), M. J. K. Smith (*chairman*), D. A. Reeve (*captain*), P. A. Neale (*director of coaching*), G. C. Small, D. P. Ostler, P. A. Smith. *Insets:* A. Singh, S. M. Pollock, M. A. Wagh.

WARWICKSHIRE RESULTS

All first-class matches – Played 19: Won 9, Lost 6, Drawn 4.

County Championship matches – Played 17: Won 7, Lost 6, Drawn 4.

Competition placings – Britannic Assurance County Championship, 8th; NatWest Trophy, 2nd round; Benson and Hedges Cup, s-f; AXA Equity & Law League, 4th.

COUNTY CHAMPIONSHIP AVERAGES

BATTING

Cap		*M*	*I*	*NO*	*R*	*HS*	*100s*	*50s*	*Avge*	*Ct/St*
1989	D. A. Reeve	5	8	1	351	168*	1	0	50.14	7
1994	T. L. Penney	17	30	3	1,221	134	3	7	45.22	13
1995	N. V. Knight	8	15	0	665	132	2	3	44.33	9
1987	A. J. Moles†	13	25	0	903	176	2	4	36.12	7
1996	A. F. Giles	15	25	9	555	106*	1	4	34.68	11
1996	S. M. Pollock§	13	21	1	606	150*	2	1	30.30	5
1993	N. M. K. Smith†	14	25	4	583	74	0	3	27.76	10
1991	D. P. Ostler†	15	27	1	712	90	0	7	27.38	28
	M. Burns	7	13	1	305	81	0	3	25.41	12/1
1989	T. A. Munton	9	13	8	118	54*	0	1	23.60	2
	W. G. Khan†	14	26	1	579	130	2	1	23.16	7
	M. J. Powell	4	8	0	182	39	0	0	22.75	2
1992	K. J. Piper	12	21	2	423	82	0	1	22.26	21/6
	A. Singh	2	4	1	66	23*	0	0	22.00	3
1995	D. R. Brown	17	29	1	540	55	0	2	19.28	12
1982	G. C. Small	7	9	5	55	23*	0	0	13.75	2
	G. Welch	11	15	1	166	45	0	0	11.85	6
	D. A. Altree†	2	4	2	0	0*	0	0	0.00	1

Also batted: M. D. Edmond (1 match) 8*; (cap 1986) P. A. Smith (1 match) 21.

* *Signifies not out.* † *Born in Warwickshire.* § *Overseas player.*

BOWLING

	O	*M*	*R*	*W*	*BB*	*5W/i*	*Avge*
A. F. Giles	584.3	168	1,530	55	6-45	3	27.81
S. M. Pollock	446.4	115	1,183	42	6-56	1	28.16
G. C. Small	164	35	536	19	4-41	0	28.21
G. Welch	245.4	40	887	27	4-50	0	32.85
N. M. K. Smith	436.4	102	1,268	36	5-76	3	35.22
T. A. Munton	315	84	897	25	3-29	0	35.88
D. R. Brown	365.2	71	1,257	34	6-52	2	36.97

Also bowled: D. A. Altree 40–8–154–1; M. Burns 3–0–13–0; M. D. Edmond 16.5–1–79–1; W. G. Khan 2.1–1–2–0; M. J. Powell 4–0–18–1; D. A. Reeve 103–32–195–9; P. A. Smith 20–3–58–1.

COUNTY RECORDS

Highest score for:	501*	B. C. Lara v Durham at Birmingham	1994
Highest score against:	322	I. V. A. Richards (Somerset) at Taunton	1985
Best bowling for:	10-41	J. D. Bannister v Combined Services at Birmingham	1959
Best bowling against:	10-36	H. Verity (Yorkshire) at Leeds	1931
Highest total for:	810-4 dec.	v Durham at Birmingham	1994
Highest total against:	887	by Yorkshire at Birmingham	1896
Lowest total for:	16	v Kent at Tonbridge	1913
Lowest total against:	15	by Hampshire at Birmingham	1922

At Cambridge, May 3, 4, 5. WARWICKSHIRE beat CAMBRIDGE UNIVERSITY by 218 runs.

At Hove, May 9, 10, 11, 13. WARWICKSHIRE beat SUSSEX by an innings and 139 runs.

WARWICKSHIRE v HAMPSHIRE

At Birmingham, May 16, 17, 18, 20. Hampshire won by 122 runs. Hampshire 22 pts, Warwickshire 4 pts. Toss: Hampshire.

Warwickshire were surprisingly outplayed by Hampshire, who were well led by Maru after the first acting-captain, Smith, injured his finger. Their first-innings 274 was unpromising, with only Laney getting past the twenties. But Connor and James then bowled out the champions 82 behind. James went on to make an unbeaten 118 and Hampshire's declaration set the home side 359 in what became 100 overs. When Benjamin, who had struck two early blows, was injured just after lunch, Warwickshire looked capable of saving the game. But the last six wickets fell in 29 overs. Connor wrapped it up with his eighth wicket of the match, taken with nine balls remaining. Hampshire's triumph was overshadowed, however, by the controversy surrounding Reeve's batting tactics on the final afternoon. He decided to counter Maru's left-arm spin from over the wicket by throwing his bat away, to avoid being caught off lifting deliveries. Reeve did this 15 times as he scored 22 from 89 balls, and argued that it was within the Laws. But MCC later ruled that an umpire could "seriously consider" giving a batsman out for obstruction in these circumstances, because the action is likely to impede the close catchers.

Close of play: First day, Hampshire 242-7 (A. N. Aymes 22*, R. J. Maru 16*); Second day, Warwickshire 192; Third day, Warwickshire 9-0 (N. V. Knight 4*, W. G. Khan 3*).

Hampshire

R. S. M. Morris c Ostler b Pollock	7	– b Welch	9
J. S. Laney c Piper b Reeve	73	– c Khan b Smith	40
K. D. James lbw b Welch	28	– not out	118
*R. A. Smith c Piper b Reeve	20		
G. W. White lbw b Smith	21	– (4) b Giles	24
P. R. Whitaker c Ostler b Giles	21	– (5) c Reeve b Giles	37
†A. N. Aymes c Knight b Pollock	28	– not out	22
W. K. M. Benjamin lbw b Giles	16	– (6) run out	2
R. J. Maru not out	28		
C. A. Connor c and b Giles	0		
S. M. Milburn b Pollock	9		
B 9, l-b 8, n-b 6	23	B 7, l-b 17	24
1/24 2/70 3/117 4/154 5/158 6/178 7/213 8/252 9/253	274	1/36 2/87 3/140 4/219 5/221 (5 wkts dec.)	276

Bonus points – Hampshire 2, Warwickshire 4.

Bowling: *First Innings*—Pollock 31–9–78–3; Brown 12–4–39–0; Welch 16–5–39–1; Giles 31–14–49–3; Reeve 18–8–20–2; Smith 11–5–32–1. *Second Innings*—Pollock 16–5–42–0; Brown 9.2–1–36–0; Reeve 21–7–42–0; Welch 11–2–29–1; Giles 25–8–62–2; Smith 19–4–41–1.

Warwickshire

N. V. Knight lbw b Connor	5	– b Milburn	60
W. G. Khan lbw b Maru	13	– b Benjamin	3
D. P. Ostler b Connor	0	– c Aymes b Benjamin	3
T. L. Penney b Connor	48	– b Connor	73
*D. A. Reeve lbw b Connor	41	– (6) c Aymes b James	22
S. M. Pollock c Benjamin b James	45	– (5) c James b Maru	6
D. R. Brown c Laney b Maru	11	– c Aymes b Connor	33
N. M. K. Smith c White b Connor	2	– b Connor	0
†K. J. Piper c Aymes b James	13	– c White b Milburn	19
G. Welch lbw b James	9	– lbw b Milburn	0
A. F. Giles not out	1	– not out	2
L-b 4	4	B 10, l-b 5	15
1/7 2/7 3/50 4/74 5/154 6/165 7/169 8/169 9/187	192	1/10 2/22 3/95 4/111 5/173 6/187 7/187 8/215 9/215	236

Bonus points – Hampshire 4.

Bowling: *First Innings*—Benjamin 12–2–25–0; Connor 24–6–57–5; Milburn 8–0–28–0; Maru 25–8–49–2; James 13.5–3–17–3; Whitaker 6–3–12–0. *Second Innings*—Connor 23.3–9–56–3; Maru 23–9–37–1; Benjamin 8.2–0–17–2; James 20–3–51–1; Milburn 19.4–4–47–3; Whitaker 4–0–13–0.

Umpires: K. J. Lyons and R. A. White.

WARWICKSHIRE v LEICESTERSHIRE

At Birmingham, May 23, 24, 25, 27. Drawn. Warwickshire 6 pts, Leicestershire 11 pts. Toss: Leicestershire.

Rain permitted only 55 overs' play during the first two days, so Championship leaders Leicestershire did well to come so close to winning. Penetrative seam bowling from Mullally, Millns and Parsons bowled Warwickshire out for 164 and then a glorious unbeaten 143 from the West Indian Simmons gave Leicestershire a lead of 189. Warwickshire had to survive 81 overs on the final day for a draw. Despite a solid 55 from Brown, five wickets for the off-spinner, Pierson, reduced his former county to 196 for eight, just seven ahead with 14 overs left. But after Maddy dropped Giles in Pierson's next over, the game drifted out of Leicestershire's reach.

Close of play: First day, Warwickshire 60-0 (A. J. Moles 24*, N. V. Knight 34*); Second day, Warwickshire 138-6 (D. A. Reeve 16*, K. J. Piper 3*); Third day, Leicestershire 289-6 (P. V. Simmons 100*, D. J. Millns 17*).

Warwickshire

A. J. Moles run out	45	– c Simmons b Parsons	21
N. V. Knight b Mullally	34	– c Wells b Pierson	23
D. P. Ostler c Nixon b Parsons	9	– lbw b Pierson	25
T. L. Penney c Wells b Millns	6	– c Simmons b Pierson	3
*D. A. Reeve c Nixon b Mullally	26	– (7) c Nixon b Pierson	29
S. M. Pollock lbw b Wells	8	– c and b Millns	22
D. R. Brown c Simmons b Millns	1	– (5) c Wells b Mullally	55
†K. J. Piper c Parsons b Mullally	15	– not out	28
G. Welch c Nixon b Mullally	4	– c Maddy b Pierson	0
A. F. Giles lbw b Parsons	0	– not out	21
G. C. Small not out	0		
B 9, l-b 6, w 1	16	B 6, l-b 5, w 1, n-b 2	14
1/60 2/86 3/103 4/105 5/120 6/121 7/154 8/163 9/164	164	1/44 2/54 3/57 4/100 5/139 6/188 7/196 8/196	(8 wkts) 241

Bonus points – Leicestershire 4.

Bowling: *First Innings*—Millns 20–6–51–2; Mullally 22.3–8–53–4; Parsons 20–4–37–2; Wells 5–1–8–1. *Second Innings*—Millns 14–3–48–1; Mullally 16–2–56–1; Parsons 13–2–41–1; Pierson 30.5–12–68–5; Simmons 6–4–7–0; Wells 1–0–10–0.

Leicestershire

V. J. Wells lbw b Small	21
D. L. Maddy lbw b Welch	36
B. F. Smith c Piper b Small	45
P. V. Simmons not out	143
*J. J. Whitaker b Brown	15
A. Habib c Piper b Welch	24
†P. A. Nixon c Piper b Welch	1
D. J. Millns run out	28
G. J. Parsons c Knight b Welch	1
A. R. K. Pierson not out	2
B 8, l-b 13, n-b 16	37
1/29 2/93 3/160 4/202 5/251 6/259 7/315 8/322 (8 wkts dec.)	353

A. D. Mullally did not bat.

Bonus points – Leicestershire 4, Warwickshire 3.

Bowling: Pollock 21–3–64–0; Small 12–0–55–2; Brown 10.5–0–49–1; Giles 15–4–38–0; Reeve 23–6–43–0; Welch 19–3–83–4.

Umpires: G. I. Burgess and D. R. Shepherd.

At Northampton, May 30, 31, June 1, 3. WARWICKSHIRE beat NORTHAMPTONSHIRE by nine wickets.

At Taunton, June 6, 7, 8, 10. WARWICKSHIRE beat SOMERSET by 99 runs.

At Leeds, June 13, 14, 15, 17. WARWICKSHIRE lost to YORKSHIRE by ten wickets.

WARWICKSHIRE v KENT

At Birmingham, June 20, 21, 22. Kent won by 32 runs. Kent 22 pts, Warwickshire 4 pts. Toss: Kent.

Warwickshire's third defeat in seven Championship matches – they had lost only three over the previous two seasons – took Kent back to the top of the table. The visitors won in three days on a dry, cracked pitch with variable bounce which received a low mark. Two seamers took ten wickets in a match for the first time: for Warwickshire, Brown improved on his previous best in both innings and finished with 11; but Ealham played the decisive role with eight for 36, to set up Kent's lead of 121. That was to be conclusive, despite a second-innings collapse, which enabled Moles to give Warwickshire a faint hope of what would have been an astounding victory. Warwickshire were 139 for eight chasing 286 when he resumed, after damaging his thumb. He hit 24 in one over from Headley and put on 92 in ten overs with Giles. Moles finally fell for 76 from 45 balls; appropriately, Ealham got him.

Close of play: First day, Warwickshire 42-4 (T. L. Penney 6*, D. R. Brown 4*); Second day, Warwickshire 58-2 (D. P. Ostler 17*, T. L. Penney 8*).

Kent

T. R. Ward b Pollock	0	– b Brown	25
M. V. Fleming c Welch b Pollock	61	– c Khan b Pollock	5
N. J. Llong c Brown b Pollock	20	– c Ostler b Pollock	53
C. L. Hooper lbw b Brown	12	– c Smith b Brown	20
G. R. Cowdrey c Burns b Brown	26	– c Ostler b Brown	11
M. A. Ealham c Welch b Brown	24	– c Giles b Brown	5
*†S. A. Marsh lbw b Brown	14	– c Giles b Welch	6
M. J. McCague c Penney b Pollock	36	– not out	8
M. M. Patel lbw b Brown	15	– c Burns b Welch	2
D. W. Headley c Pollock b Munton	15	– c Ostler b Brown	4
N. W. Preston not out	6	– c Burns b Brown	2
B 4, l-b 5, w 4, n-b 16	29	B 6, l-b 8, w 1, n-b 8	23
1/0 2/44 3/98 4/121 5/151 6/176 7/186 8/220 9/240	258	1/14 2/59 3/114 4/122 5/132 6/143 7/148 8/150 9/158	164

Bonus points – Kent 2, Warwickshire 4.

In the first innings C. L. Hooper, when 0, retired hurt at 46 and resumed at 151.

Bowling: *First Innings*—Pollock 23–6–60–4; Munton 19.1–7–35–1; Welch 14–0–79–0; Brown 20–3–68–5; Smith 2–0–7–0. *Second Innings*—Pollock 18–3–57–2; Brown 21.3–5–52–6; Welch 13–2–31–2; Giles 3–1–10–0.

Warwickshire

A. J. Moles lbw b Headley	2	– c Marsh b Ealham	76
W. G. Khan b Ealham	13	– (3) b McCague	4
D. P. Ostler c Llong b Ealham	8	– (4) c Marsh b McCague	17
T. L. Penney b Ealham	33	– (5) b Headley	20
A. F. Giles c Marsh b Ealham	0	– (10) c Hooper b Fleming	65
D. R. Brown c Hooper b Ealham	6	– c Marsh b Headley	0
S. M. Pollock c Marsh b Headley	14	– lbw b Ealham	6
†M. Burns c McCague b Ealham	27	– c Headley b McCague	21
G. Welch lbw b Ealham	6	– c Fleming b McCague	12
N. M. K. Smith not out	9	– (2) c Hooper b McCague	15
*T. A. Munton c Marsh b Ealham	3	– not out	0
B 1, l-b 6, w 1, n-b 8	16	B 10, l-b 2, w 1, n-b 4	17
1/11 2/31 3/34 4/38 5/48 6/73 7/107 8/124 9/124	137	1/25 2/39 3/60 4/61 5/78 6/96 7/108 8/139 9/231	253

Bonus points – Kent 4.

In the second innings A. J. Moles, when 10, retired hurt at 25-1 and resumed at 139.

Bowling: *First Innings*—McCague 9–3–22–0; Headley 12–1–43–2; Preston 13–3–29–0; Ealham 20–8–36–8. *Second Innings*—McCague 21–3–101–5; Headley 19–3–73–2; Ealham 15–6–38–2; Preston 10–3–29–0; Fleming 0.4–0–0–1.

Umpires: B. Dudleston and R. A. White.

At Lord's, June 27, 28, 29, July 1. WARWICKSHIRE drew with MIDDLESEX.

WARWICKSHIRE v NOTTINGHAMSHIRE

At Birmingham, July 4, 5, 6, 8. Warwickshire won by 85 runs. Warwickshire 21 pts, Nottinghamshire 4 pts. Toss: Warwickshire.

A decision not to use the Brumbrella cover because of its long-term adverse effects on the square cost 132 overs in the first three days and meant that a result was only possible with three declarations. Warwickshire won their first home Championship match in 1996 at their fourth attempt and also gained their first home batting point. That was due to their deputy wicket-keeper, Burns, who scored a career-best 81 and shared Edgbaston's first century stand of the summer with Penney. But a mid-innings wobble left them 221 for six and it was the tail, adding another 129, who earned the extra three points. Nottinghamshire declared 138 behind and, after Burns's second half-century, Moles set a target of 297 in 81 overs. He was rewarded when Giles and Pollock bowled Nottinghamshire out with 14 overs to spare.

Close of play: First day, Warwickshire 148-3 (M. Burns 44*, T. L. Penney 14*); Second day, Warwickshire 251-6 (T. L. Penney 52*, N. M. K. Smith 23*); Third day, Warwickshire 34-0 (A. J. Moles 25*, N. V. Knight 5*).

Warwickshire

*A. J. Moles c Pollard b Afford	27	– c Walker b Evans	25
N. V. Knight c Cairns b Bowen	33	– c Archer b Afford	46
†M. Burns c Archer b Cairns	81	– not out	65
D. P. Ostler c Pollard b Cairns	9		
T. L. Penney lbw b Bowen	60		
D. R. Brown c Walker b Cairns	4		
S. M. Pollock b Pick	1		
N. M. K. Smith c Walker b Bowen	54	– (4) not out	5
A. F. Giles not out	31		
G. C. Small not out	23		
B 2, l-b 5, w 2, n-b 18	27	B 4, l-b 3, n-b 10	17
1/57 2/67 3/108 4/216 5/220 6/221 7/293 8/304	(8 wkts dec.) 350	1/34 2/133	(2 wkts dec.) 158

G. Welch did not bat.

Bonus points – Warwickshire 4, Nottinghamshire 3.

Bowling: *First Innings*—Cairns 26–4–84–3; Evans 33–5–101–0; Pick 16–4–35–1; Bowen 22.5–5–80–3; Afford 13–4–43–1. *Second Innings*—Pick 4–3–4–0; Bowen 9–1–54–0; Evans 5–0–34–1; Afford 4–0–27–1; Archer 3–0–32–0.

Nottinghamshire

P. R. Pollard c Burns b Pollock	0	– c Moles b Giles	57
R. T. Robinson c Moles b Pollock	5	– lbw b Pollock	0
G. F. Archer retired hurt	35	– (5) b Pollock	1
A. A. Metcalfe c Penney b Smith	91	– (3) c Burns b Giles	44
*P. Johnson b Pollock	6	– (4) c Smith b Giles	2
C. L. Cairns not out	66	– b Small	24
K. P. Evans (did not bat)		– c Smith b Pollock	60
†L. N. P. Walker (did not bat)		– b Giles	1
M. N. Bowen (did not bat)		– b Small	2
R. A. Pick (did not bat)		– c Brown b Giles	2
J. A. Afford (did not bat)		– not out	0
B 4, w 1, n-b 4	9	B 10, l-b 8	18
1/0 2/5 3/72 4/212	(4 wkts dec.) 212	1/5 2/96 3/104 4/110 5/116 6/158 7/173 8/176 9/203	211

Bonus points – Nottinghamshire 1, Warwickshire 1.

In the first innings G. F. Archer retired hurt at 57.

Bowling: *First Innings*—Pollock 10–1–31–3; Small 11–4–24–0; Smith 16.2–4–52–1; Brown 9–1–53–0; Giles 12–0–48–0. *Second Innings*—Pollock 10.5–4–19–3; Small 13–2–52–2; Giles 26–7–70–5; Welch 5–2–7–0; Smith 7–0–29–0; Brown 5–0–16–0.

Umpires: M. J. Kitchen and K. E. Palmer.

At Birmingham, July 17, 18, 19. WARWICKSHIRE beat PAKISTANIS by seven wickets (See Pakistani tour section).

At Cheltenham, July 25, 26, 27. WARWICKSHIRE lost to GLOUCESTERSHIRE by an innings and 116 runs.

WARWICKSHIRE v DURHAM

At Birmingham, August 8, 9, 10, 12. Warwickshire won by 282 runs. Warwickshire 23 pts, Durham 6 pts. Toss: Warwickshire. First-class debut: M. J. Powell.

Durham sank to their ninth defeat in 13 matches after two collapses. On the first day, however, Brown and Cox had had Warwickshire struggling at 200 for seven. Ostler prevented a rout, before Smith hit 64 to take them past 300. Durham then collapsed from a promising 188 for three to Smith and Munton. When Warwickshire resumed, Khan established their ascendancy by scoring 130, after his previous 13 innings in the 1996 Championship had produced only 158. Though Cox finished with ten for 236 – a happy contrast to his none for 163 two years earlier, when Lara scored his 501 – Durham faced an unlikely target of 413. Their fragile batting survived only 55 overs, with Giles taking a career-best six for 45.

Close of play: First day, Durham 8-0 (S. L. Campbell 3*, S. Hutton 5*); Second day, Warwickshire 63-0 (A. J. Moles 40*, M. J. Powell 21*); Third day, Durham 24-2 (S. Hutton 5*, P. Bainbridge 0*).

Warwickshire

A. J. Moles c Cox b Brown	26	– b Cox	74
M. J. Powell lbw b Brown	26	– b Brown	32
W. G. Khan b Brown	0	– st Ligertwood b Cox	130
D. P. Ostler b Cox	86	– b Cox	6
T. L. Penney c Daley b Cox	3	– c Ligertwood b Wood	2
S. M. Pollock c Campbell b Cox	26	– run out	30
D. R. Brown hit wkt b Wood	31	– b Killeen	51
†M. Burns c Weston b Cox	6	– st Ligertwood b Cox	6
N. M. K. Smith st Ligertwood b Cox	64	– b Cox	0
A. F. Giles c Campbell b Killeen	13	– not out	6
*T. A. Munton not out	3		
L-b 3, w 1, n-b 18	22	L-b 10, n-b 14	24
1/60 2/60 3/69 4/92 5/181 6/182 7/200 8/238 9/280	306	1/81 2/133 3/157 4/188 5/263 6/337 7/345 8/345 9/361 (9 wkts dec.)	361

Bonus points – Warwickshire 3, Durham 4.

Bowling: *First Innings*—Brown 22–4–71–3; Wood 13–0–83–1; Killeen 18–4–52–1; Cox 42.1–14–97–5. *Second Innings*—Brown 18–0–70–1; Wood 15–5–64–1; Cox 44–11–139–5; Weston 1–1–0–0; Killeen 14.5–2–78–1.

Durham

S. L. Campbell c Ostler b Smith	64	– lbw b Munton	15
S. Hutton lbw b Smith	27	– c Brown b Munton	16
J. A. Daley lbw b Smith	23	– c Ostler b Giles	2
P. Bainbridge lbw b Munton	54	– lbw b Munton	7
*M. A. Roseberry c Ostler b Munton	18	– c Brown b Giles	16
R. M. S. Weston lbw b Munton	3	– c Brown b Giles	9
†D. G. C. Ligertwood not out	3	– not out	22
D. M. Cox c Munton b Giles	45	– b Giles	10
J. Wood c Ostler b Smith	1	– b Smith	5
S. J. E. Brown b Giles	0	– c Pollock b Giles	22
N. Killeen lbw b Smith	6	– c Penney b Giles	0
B 4, l-b 5, n-b 2	11	B 1, l-b 1, n-b 4	6
1/72 2/107 3/154 4/188 5/196 6/197 7/244 8/245 9/248	255	1/21 2/24 3/32 4/49 5/67 6/76 7/92 8/101 9/126	130

Bonus points – Durham 2, Warwickshire 4.

Bowling: *First Innings*—Pollock 19–6–64–0; Munton 16–4–53–3; Smith 41–14–76–5; Giles 29–7–53–2. *Second Innings*—Pollock 9–3–29–0; Munton 10–2–29–3; Giles 18–5–45–6; Smith 18–4–25–1.

Umpires: J. D. Bond and G. Sharp.

WARWICKSHIRE v GLAMORGAN

At Birmingham, August 15, 16, 17, 19. Warwickshire won by two wickets. Warwickshire 24 pts, Glamorgan 5 pts. Toss: Warwickshire.

Warwickshire won with maximum points, as had looked likely all along, but what might have been a rout turned into a tingling finish. Having forced Glamorgan to follow on 284 behind, they needed only 136 to win, but nervy batting almost cost them the match. Eight wickets went for 113 before Brown and Giles nudged them home. Warwickshire's dominance had started with Pollock's second first-class hundred, which enabled them to recover from 212 for six to 498. He hit 16 fours and a six in his unbeaten 150, and put on 180 with Piper – back after two months out through injury – in only 33 overs. Glamorgan lost their last eight wickets for 55, with Giles taking his second successive haul of six. But James and Maynard, Glamorgan's top two scorers in both innings, forced Warwickshire to bat again, and almost did enough to secure a remarkable victory.

Close of play: First day, Warwickshire 412-7 (S. M. Pollock 104*, N. M. K. Smith 4*); Second day, Glamorgan 35-1 (S. P. James 14*, D. L. Hemp 13*); Third day, Warwickshire 11-0 (N. V. Knight 6*, M. J. Powell 5*).

Warwickshire

N. V. Knight c Parkin b Croft	63	– b Gibson	12
M. J. Powell c Maynard b Watkin	0	– c and b Gibson	39
W. G. Khan lbw b Gibson	0	– b Watkin	8
D. P. Ostler lbw b Gibson	65	– lbw b Watkin	2
T. L. Penney c James b Croft	37	– lbw b Watkin	0
S. M. Pollock not out	150	– c Morris b Gibson	8
D. R. Brown b Croft	20	– not out	26
†K. J. Piper c Cottey b Parkin	82	– lbw b Croft	17
N. M. K. Smith c Metson b Watkin	26	– c James b Croft	6
A. F. Giles c Maynard b Watkin	1	– not out	10
*T. A. Munton b Gibson	14		
B 10, l-b 13, w 1, n-b 16	40	B 4, l-b 4	8
1/11 2/12 3/120 4/186 5/186 6/212 7/392 8/460 9/464	498	1/19 2/38 3/62 4/62 5/71 6/82 7/105 8/113	(8 wkts) 136

Bonus points – Warwickshire 4, Glamorgan 4 (Score at 120 overs: 472-9).

Bowling: *First Innings*—Watkin 34–7–136–3; Gibson 26.4–2–122–3; Parkin 15–3–56–1; Dale 11–2–39–0; Croft 36–7–110–3; Hemp 2–0–11–0; Maynard 1–0–1–0. *Second Innings*—Watkin 16–4–38–3; Croft 16–5–47–2; Gibson 8–0–43–3.

Glamorgan

S. P. James c Powell b Smith	90	– b Smith	148
H. Morris c Ostler b Giles	7	– c Ostler b Munton	0
D. L. Hemp c Piper b Munton	11	– c Brown b Smith	29
*M. P. Maynard st Piper b Giles	69	– c Smith b Giles	95
P. A. Cottey c Penney b Giles	1	– c Penney b Giles	22
A. Dale c Ostler b Smith	4	– c Brown b Smith	20
O. D. Gibson lbw b Giles	4	– c Smith b Giles	0
R. D. B. Croft c Ostler b Smith	0	– c Khan b Munton	78
†C. P. Metson b Giles	0	– c Brown b Smith	0
S. L. Watkin not out	5	– b Smith	0
O. T. Parkin b Giles	14	– not out	4
B 4, l-b 3, n-b 2	9	B 5, l-b 2, n-b 16	23
1/32 2/45 3/159 4/173 5/184 6/189 7/190 8/195 9/195	214	1/10 2/68 3/263 4/302 5/324 6/325 7/334 8/340 9/342	419

Bonus points – Glamorgan 1, Warwickshire 4.

Bowling: *First Innings*—Pollock 10–3–38–0; Munton 12–2–54–1; Giles 28.2–8–63–6; Smith 18–3–52–3. *Second Innings*—Pollock 20–4–57–0; Munton 17.5–2–62–2; Giles 34–4–118–3; Smith 49–13–166–5; Brown 1–0–9–0.

Umpires: J. C. Balderstone and V. A. Holder.

At Worcester, August 22, 23, 24, 26. WARWICKSHIRE drew with WORCESTERSHIRE.

At The Oval, August 29, 30, 31. WARWICKSHIRE lost to SURREY by an innings and 164 runs.

WARWICKSHIRE v ESSEX

At Birmingham, September 3, 4, 5, 6. Essex won by 170 runs. Essex 21 pts, Warwickshire 6 pts. Toss: Essex.

Essex's eighth win kept alive the possibility that they might succeed Warwickshire as champions, but the match was mainly notable for Gooch's 127th first-class hundred, which took him past W. G. Grace and into ninth place in the all-time list. He also became the first batsman to score 30,000 runs for Essex. Though he gave three chances, it took a fluke to get him out: on 147, he was run out by a deflection off the bowler, Brown, at the non-striker's end. The match had been evenly balanced until Gooch's innings. The ball seamed around on the opening day, and Small was most effective. A century by Khan earned Warwickshire a slender lead. But after scoring a hundred himself, Prichard was able to declare the Essex second innings on the third evening, and set Warwickshire 436. They lost three wickets for 36 before the close and could not recover.

Close of play: First day, Warwickshire 14-3 (W. G. Khan 4*, D. P. Ostler 1*); Second day, Essex 113-1 (G. A. Gooch 58*, N. Hussain 21*); Third day, Warwickshire 65-3 (D. P. Ostler 10*, T. L. Penney 19*).

Essex

G. A. Gooch c Ostler b Small	5	– run out	147
A. P. Grayson lbw b Small	4	– c Piper b Brown	30
N. Hussain c Piper b Small	26	– c Piper b Giles	39
*P. J. Prichard c Moles b Brown	26	– st Piper b Giles	108
R. C. Irani c Small b Brown	69	– not out	82
J. J. B. Lewis lbw b Small	0	– (8) not out	8
†R. J. Rollins c Knight b Brown	20	– (6) c Khan b Giles	2
M. C. Ilott c and b Giles	43	– (7) c Smith b Munton	4
N. F. Williams b Munton	9		
A. P. Cowan c Knight b Smith	2		
P. M. Such not out	11		
B 9, l-b 10, w 2, n-b 2	23	B 14, l-b 10, w 2, n-b 4	30
1/6 2/18 3/56 4/75 5/87 6/153 7/160 8/201 9/208	238	1/77 2/166 3/277 4/416 5/420 6/425 (6 wkts dec.)	450

Bonus points – Essex 1, Warwickshire 4.

Bowling: *First Innings*—Small 20–8–41–4; Munton 32–14–70–1; Brown 18–2–62–3; Giles 12.4–4–32–1; Smith 9–2–14–1. *Second Innings*—Small 11–1–62–0; Munton 24–2–78–1; Brown 15–2–50–1; Smith 27–1–117–0; Giles 41–9–119–3.

Warwickshire

N. V. Knight lbw b Williams	2	– lbw b Such	24
A. J. Moles c Rollins b Williams	2	– c sub b Williams	9
W. G. Khan c Rollins b Cowan	126	– lbw b Williams	0
A. F. Giles lbw b Ilott	0	– (9) c Such b Cowan	49
D. P. Ostler c Rollins b Williams	1	– (4) lbw b Williams	11
T. L. Penney c Gooch b Cowan	15	– (5) c Rollins b Cowan	70
D. R. Brown c Grayson b Cowan	31	– (6) c Cowan b Williams	4
†K. J. Piper c Irani b Such	27	– (7) b Such	13
N. M. K. Smith c Grayson b Irani	15	– (8) c Ilott b Such	46
G. C. Small c Hussain b Such	6	– st Rollins b Such	10
*T. A. Munton not out	1	– not out	0
B 1, l-b 12, n-b 14	27	B 5, l-b 12, n-b 12	29
1/5 2/10 3/11 4/14 5/65 6/125 7/180 8/202 9/231	253	1/36 2/36 3/36 4/82 5/92 6/136 7/174 8/236 9/257	265

Bonus points – Warwickshire 2, Essex 4.

Bowling: *First Innings*—Ilott 19–5–42–1; Williams 20–1–70–3; Irani 17–4–36–1; Cowan 16.4–4–37–3; Gooch 2–1–12–0; Such 16–4–43–2. *Second Innings*—Ilott 8–1–35–0; Williams 13–2–57–4; Such 24–2–114–4; Grayson 3–0–8–0; Cowan 8.4–1–34–2.

Umpires: A. A. Jones and N. T. Plews.

At Derby, September 12, 13, 14. WARWICKSHIRE beat DERBYSHIRE by four wickets.

WARWICKSHIRE v LANCASHIRE

At Birmingham, September 19, 20, 21, 22. Drawn. Warwickshire 9 pts, Lancashire 11 pts. Toss: Warwickshire.

A slow, low pitch produced four hundreds, including a double by Fairbrother, and only 26 wickets. The fast-improving Giles scored a maiden century, including 16 fours and a six. Coming in at 196 for seven, he added 163 with Smith and almost doubled the total. Fairbrother replied by hitting 24 fours and four sixes as he moved to 204 in 380 minutes, sharing in a fourth-wicket stand of 230 with Lloyd. Crawley, acting-captain while Watkinson was leading England in the Hong Kong Sixes and Atherton was resting, let Lancashire bat on to their biggest total against Warwickshire, which gave them a lead of 211; after that, the home side could only play for a draw. Knight reached his first Championship hundred since the opening match, courtesy of four overthrows, while Penney scored 70 for his best-ever aggregate, 1,295 runs. He was the only batsman to reach four figures for Warwickshire in a disappointing season.

Close of play: First day, Warwickshire 233-7 (N. M. K. Smith 28*, A. F. Giles 11*); Second day, Lancashire 281-3 (N. H. Fairbrother 55*, G. D. Lloyd 63*); Third day, Warwickshire 58-0 (N. V. Knight 35*, A. J. Moles 19*).

Warwickshire

N. V. Knight lbw b Chapple	33	– c and b Green	103
A. J. Moles c Keedy b Gallian	11	– b Green	59
W. G. Khan lbw b Green	6	– c Hegg b Yates	32
M. Burns c Lloyd b Keedy	61	– lbw b Chapple	24
T. L. Penney c and b Titchard	23	– not out	70
D. R. Brown c Fairbrother b Chapple	14	– c Yates b Keedy	25
†K. J. Piper c Lloyd b Yates	17	– st Hegg b Lloyd	28
N. M. K. Smith c Gallian b Chapple	74	– not out	2
A. F. Giles not out	106		
G. Welch c and b Green	4		
*T. A. Munton c Crawley b Chapple	5		
B 5, l-b 7, w 2, n-b 18	32	L-b 11, w 1, n-b 4	16
1/50 2/58 3/61 4/100 5/137 6/188 7/196 8/359 9/365	386	1/166 2/179 3/229 4/231 5/311 6/355	(6 wkts) 359

Bonus points – Warwickshire 4, Lancashire 4.

Bowling: *First Innings*—Chapple 28.3–6–85–4; Green 18–1–67–2; Gallian 14–2–56–1; Titchard 15–3–51–1; Keedy 15–4–50–1; Yates 16–0–65–1. *Second Innings*—Chapple 21–2–50–1; Green 16–2–52–2; Yates 28–6–104–1; Keedy 28–7–93–1; Titchard 9–2–27–0; Gallian 2–0–18–0; Lloyd 2–0–4–1.

Lancashire

S. P. Titchard b Giles	48
J. E. R. Gallian b Munton	3
*J. P. Crawley b Smith	73
N. H. Fairbrother st Burns b Giles	204
G. D. Lloyd b Welch	113
P. C. McKeown c Welch b Munton	64
†W. K. Hegg c Knight b Smith	14
G. Chapple b Giles	10
G. Yates c Penney b Smith	0
R. J. Green lbw b Giles	0
G. Keedy not out	1
B 34, l-b 15, w 2, n-b 16	67
1/7 2/143 3/143 4/373 5/505 6/548 7/574 8/581 9/584	597

Bonus points – Lancashire 4, Warwickshire 2 (Score at 120 overs: 520-5).

Bowling: Munton 29–6–92–2; Welch 17–2–93–1; Giles 48.4–13–165–4; Brown 20–0–106–0; Smith 32–10–92–3.

Umpires: A. Clarkson and N. T. Plews.

Tom Moody

WORCESTERSHIRE

Patron: The Duke of Westminster
President: T. W. Graveney
Chairman: C. D. Fearnley
Chairman, Cricket Committee: J. E. Chadd
Secretary: The Rev. M. D. Vockins
Captain: T. M. Moody
Coach: D. L. Houghton
Head Groundsman: R. McLaren
Scorer: J. W. Sewter

The 1996 season saw Worcestershire continuing to rebuild after the successes of the late 1980s and early 1990s. Several key players from that era had departed or were slowly losing their potency, while the county suffered an injury list described by coach David Houghton as the worst he had encountered in 20 years in the game.

Yet Worcestershire still managed to finish seventh in the County Championship, three places up on 1995, thanks to a final hat-trick of wins. They also challenged strongly in the Sunday League until three successive defeats in August and September ended their interest. An early exit from the Benson and Hedges Cup, and a second-round mauling in the NatWest Trophy by Hampshire, after Worcestershire's worst bowling performance of the summer, were the only major disappointments.

More significantly, they will look back on the emergence and establishment of several young cricketers who have a key role to play if the glory years of Ian Botham and Graham Dilley are to return. Of the county's young brigade of talent, opener Phil Weston, middle-order batsman Reuben Spiring and all-rounder Vikram Solanki all made considerable strides forward. Weston, who has a wise head on young shoulders, had passed 1,000 runs the previous season but now added consistency and a greater responsibility to his game. His reward was 1,389 runs, with four centuries, in 20 first-class matches, and he also blossomed as a clean-hitting limited-overs batsman. "He is now one of our big-time players," commented Houghton.

Spiring and Solanki were helped to emerge partly by the injury crisis and partly through captain Tom Moody following Australian custom and giving youth its head if the promise was there. Gavin Haynes damaged his knee ligaments while fielding on a pre-season tour of Barbados, which kept him out of action all season, but this provided Spiring, son of former Liverpool footballer Peter, with an opening he seized with both hands. He batted with maturity and composure to pass 1,000 first-class runs with three centuries. Solanki, the former England Under-19 player, had to wait longer. But his chance came when David Leatherdale broke a knuckle against Somerset in mid-June. He felt most at home as a No. 6 batsman, with his off-spin merely a secondary string, rather than being considered, as he had been, a fully-fledged member of the attack. More than 800 runs and three five-wicket hauls demonstrated his worth.

If ever a captain can be said to have led from the front, then it was Moody, in his first full season in charge after replacing Tim Curtis midway through 1995. Moody believed that "too many players get away with just doing enough" in county cricket, and was at pains to impress the need for greater competitiveness in the squad. This policy was sometimes difficult to implement, because of the injury problems, but he tried hard to compensate with his own sterling all-round efforts. Seldom has anyone more deserved the county's Player of the Year award.

Moody scored 1,427 runs, and also took on a far greater share of the bowling workload than was healthy for someone with a back problem, to finish with 37 first-class wickets. He headed the county's Championship averages for both batting and bowling. Sending down more than 70 overs for a career-best 13 wickets in the penultimate match of a gruelling season, against Gloucestershire, was an effort of near Herculean proportions.

For all his disappointments of the summer with England, Graeme Hick reinforced his outstanding value at county level with 1,202 runs at 54.63. He will be looking to re-establish himself as an international force in 1997 after a winter's rest from cricket – only his second long break in ten years. Wicket-keeper Steve Rhodes was able to enjoy that rare combination of a benefit season and a successful time on the field. He narrowly missed scoring 1,000 first-class runs for the second year running.

Phil Newport's Achilles tendon injury wiped out two-thirds of his season, which put a tremendous strain on the only other experienced seam bowler, Stuart Lampitt. The county had already released Neal Radford at the end of the previous year, and had then been stunned by the sudden death of young Parvaz Mirza. But Lampitt responded uncomplainingly to the challenge and the extra overs demanded of him with 54 wickets – and matched that with 658 runs, batting mostly at No. 8. Left-arm spinner Richard Illingworth drifted out of the international scene, despite having finished second in the Test averages during the winter tour of South Africa. But he put his disappointment to one side and emulated Lampitt in shouldering the responsibility of carrying an otherwise raw attack with 48 first-class wickets for the county. He was also as effective as ever in the one-day games, and was given a deserved benefit in 1997.

Worcestershire's main concern is to find a genuine strike bowler – something they have lacked since the days of Graham Dilley and then, more briefly, Kenny Benjamin. Paul Thomas might have fulfilled that role but failed to build on his initial promise of 1995, encountering run-up problems and then the kind of injury setbacks which also handicapped newcomer Ben Preece. However, left-armer Alamgir Sheriyar, recruited in the winter from Leicestershire, overcame a difficult start to his first full season of county cricket, finished strongly and hinted at better things to come.

In the meantime, the New Road faithful, so accustomed to success, were appeased for the lack of silverware by the emergence of Spiring, Solanki and co. Whether Worcestershire can add that cutting edge to their attack will decide if the trophy cabinet needs to be re-opened sooner rather than later. – JOHN CURTIS.

WORCESTERSHIRE 1996

[*Bill Smith*

Back row: M. Amjad, M. Diwan, V. S. Solanki, M. J. Rawnsley, I. Dawood, J. T. Ralph. *Middle row:* J. Smith (*physiotherapist*), K. R. Spiring, P. A. Thomas, M. J. Church, D. A. Leatherdale, W. P. C. Weston, G. R. Haynes, A. Sheriyar, J. E. Brinkley, B. E. A. Preece. *Front row:* D. B. D'Oliveira, S. R. Lampitt, R. K. Illingworth, T. S. Curtis, T. M. Moody (*captain*), S. J. Rhodes, G. A. Hick, P. J. Newport, D. L. Houghton (*coach*).

WORCESTERSHIRE RESULTS

All first-class matches – Played 20: Won 6, Lost 5, Drawn 9.

County Championship matches – Played 17: Won 6, Lost 4, Drawn 7.

Competition placings – Britannic Assurance County Championship, 7th; NatWest Trophy, 2nd round; Benson and Hedges Cup, 4th in Group B; AXA Equity & Law League, 8th.

COUNTY CHAMPIONSHIP AVERAGES

BATTING

Cap		*M*	*I*	*NO*	*R*	*HS*	*100s*	*50s*	*Avge*	*Ct/St*
1991	T. M. Moody§	17	30	2	1,361	212	7	3	48.60	11
1986	G. A. Hick	12	22	1	987	150	4	3	47.00	16
	V. S. Solanki	12	20	3	734	90	0	6	43.17	8
	K. R. Spiring	15	27	5	912	144	3	6	41.45	4
1995	W. P. C. Weston	17	33	5	1,147	171*	3	6	40.96	19
1986	S. J. Rhodes	17	26	5	835	110	1	6	39.76	33/8
1994	D. A. Leatherdale	9	15	2	436	122	1	3	33.53	5
1984	T. S. Curtis	16	30	2	933	118	2	5	33.32	8
1986	R. K. Illingworth	16	20	8	388	66*	0	1	32.33	10
1989	S. R. Lampitt	17	24	3	572	88	0	2	27.23	13
1986	P. J. Newport	5	6	0	142	68	0	1	23.66	1
	M. J. Church	4	8	0	97	29	0	0	12.12	3
	S. W. K. Ellis	8	8	4	46	15	0	0	11.50	6
	P. A. Thomas	3	5	0	37	11	0	0	7.40	0
	A. Sheriyar	15	15	9	38	13	0	0	6.33	4

Also batted: B. E. A. Preece (1 match) 0, 2 (1 ct); M. J. Rawnsley (3 matches) 4* (1 ct).

* *Signifies not out.* *No player was born in Worcestershire.* § *Overseas player.*

BOWLING

	O	*M*	*R*	*W*	*BB*	*5W/i*	*Avge*
T. M. Moody	295.4	83	892	34	7-92	3	26.23
V. S. Solanki	197.2	32	815	26	5-69	3	31.34
P. J. Newport	170.3	39	643	19	6-100	1	33.84
S. R. Lampitt	485.5	92	1,801	52	5-58	2	34.63
R. K. Illingworth	636	195	1,471	42	5-40	2	35.02
A. Sheriyar	432	74	1,576	34	6-99	1	46.35
S. W. K. Ellis	159	26	630	13	3-29	0	48.46

Also bowled: M. J. Church 24.1–3–98–4; T. S. Curtis 4.3–0–18–2; G. A. Hick 70–17–203–4; D. A. Leatherdale 62.5–16–185–6; B. E. A. Preece 20–0–131–1; M. J. Rawnsley 41–12–132–3; P. A. Thomas 52–4–296–4; W. P. C. Weston 1–0–1–0.

COUNTY RECORDS

Highest score for:	405*	G. A. Hick v Somerset at Taunton	1988
Highest score against:	331*	J. D. Robertson (Middlesex) at Worcester	1949
Best bowling for:	9-23	C. F. Root v Lancashire at Worcester	1931
Best bowling against:	10-51	J. Mercer (Glamorgan) at Worcester	1936
Highest total for:	670-7 dec.	v Somerset at Worcester	1995
Highest total against:	701-4 dec.	by Leicestershire at Worcester	1906
Lowest total for:	24	v Yorkshire at Huddersfield	1903
Lowest total against:	30	by Hampshire at Worcester	1903

WORCESTERSHIRE v ESSEX

At Worcester, May 2, 3, 4, 6. Essex won by five wickets. Essex 24 pts, Worcestershire 5 pts. Toss: Essex. Championship debut: S. G. Law.

Essex won in a thrilling finish. On the third afternoon, Worcestershire were 79 behind with five second-innings wickets remaining. But Leatherdale and Lampitt took them to a 17-run lead by the close and then Newport and Illingworth added 100. A home win was suddenly on the cards when Essex, pursuing an apparently straightforward 187 in 43 overs, slumped to 32 for five. But Irani took a significant step towards an England call-up by scoring 110 off 86 balls. His unbroken stand of 158 in 29 overs with Grayson secured Essex victory, with Irani's fifth six ending proceedings. After the first day was restricted to 32 overs, and Prichard wore a balaclava against the cold, Essex dismissed Worcestershire for 201 and then made up for lost time by scoring at 5.34 an over. Stuart Law scored 93 on his first-class debut for Essex, and Ilott, with a county-best 58, supervised the addition of 106 for the last two wickets.

Close of play: First day, Worcestershire 78-4 (D. A. Leatherdale 10*, S. J. Rhodes 2*); Second day, Essex 285-5 (S. G. Law 64*); Third day, Worcestershire 246-5 (D. A. Leatherdale 69*, S. R. Lampitt 39*).

Worcestershire

T. S. Curtis c Gooch b Williams	2	– c Rollins b Irani	32
W. P. C. Weston c Grayson b Ilott	13	– c Rollins b Ilott	7
G. A. Hick lbw b Ilott	18	– c Gooch b Law	36
*T. M. Moody lbw b Ilott	20	– b Ilott	33
D. A. Leatherdale c Prichard b Williams	50	– c Rollins b Ilott	69
†S. J. Rhodes c Rollins b Cowan	9	– lbw b Ilott	2
S. R. Lampitt c Grayson b Williams	46	– lbw b Ilott	45
P. J. Newport c Gooch b Irani	0	– lbw b Williams	68
R. K. Illingworth c Rollins b Williams	17	– not out	66
P. A. Thomas b Williams	1	– c Ilott b Cowan	11
A. Sheriyar not out	1	– c Rollins b Cowan	0
B 2, l-b 12, w 2, n-b 8	24	B 5, l-b 11, n-b 30	46
1/14 2/38 3/39 4/76 5/96 6/147 7/148 8/198 9/200	201	1/27 2/60 3/104 4/148 5/150 6/253 7/256 8/356 9/415	415

Bonus points – Worcestershire 1, Essex 4.

Bowling: *First Innings*—Ilott 32–7–82–3; Williams 22.2–6–57–5; Cowan 17–9–32–1; Irani 8–3–16–1. *Second Innings*—Ilott 43–9–105–5; Williams 30–6–107–1; Cowan 15.5–0–64–2; Irani 26–7–93–1; Law 11–5–30–1; Grayson 1–1–0–0.

Essex

G. A. Gooch lbw b Lampitt	85	– lbw b Newport	10
D. D. J. Robinson b Lampitt	61	– lbw b Sheriyar	0
N. Hussain c Rhodes b Lampitt	2	– c Moody b Newport	1
S. G. Law c Rhodes b Lampitt	93	– run out	1
*P. J. Prichard lbw b Thomas	20	– lbw b Sheriyar	9
R. C. Irani c and b Illingworth	14	– not out	110
A. P. Grayson c Hick b Lampitt	6	– not out	46
†R. J. Rollins b Newport	2		
M. C. Ilott c Lampitt b Illingworth	58		
N. F. Williams c Newport b Sheriyar	39		
A. P. Cowan not out	3		
B 11, l-b 14, w 2, n-b 20	47	B 1, l-b 6, n-b 6	13
1/158 2/162 3/203 4/256 5/285 6/301 7/324 8/324 9/400	430	1/6 2/10 3/12 4/20 5/32	(5 wkts) 190

Bonus points – Essex 4, Worcestershire 4.

Bowling: *First Innings*—Newport 18–4–87–1; Sheriyar 14–1–86–1; Lampitt 24–3–116–5; Thomas 11–0–84–1; Illingworth 11.3–3–23–2; Leatherdale 2–0–9–0. *Second Innings*—Newport 11.2–4–49–2; Sheriyar 9–3–32–2; Lampitt 10–1–57–0; Thomas 6–0–26–0; Illingworth 4–0–19–0.

Umpires: T. E. Jesty and R. A. White.

At Worcester, May 8, 9, 10. WORCESTERSHIRE drew with INDIANS (See Indian tour section).

At Leicester, May 16, 17, 18. WORCESTERSHIRE lost to LEICESTERSHIRE by an innings and 130 runs.

At Abergavenny, May 23, 24, 25, 27. WORCESTERSHIRE drew with GLAMORGAN.

WORCESTERSHIRE v HAMPSHIRE

At Worcester, May 30, 31, June 1, 3. Drawn. Worcestershire 9 pts, Hampshire 9 pts. Toss: Hampshire.

Worcestershire, and especially Hick, showed great application in recovering from six for two on a damp pitch. Hick scored one of his slowest centuries, taking five and a half hours, while Reuben Spiring, son of former Liverpool footballer Peter, made his maiden hundred in his third Championship match. Their eventual total was 431, and Hampshire risked following on at 168 for six. But Aymes batted for nearly four hours – extending his time at the crease since his last dismissal to nine hours – and century stands with White and Udal eventually secured four batting points. Hampshire reduced the chances of a positive result, however, by delaying the declaration until after tea, so that Aymes could complete his hundred. The home side took their lead to 271 at lunch on the fourth day, but rain then intervened. Moody opted to bat out time, reaching his century and adding 159 with Spiring, who looked capable of a second hundred until he was run out.

Close of play: First day, Worcestershire 254-5 (K. R. Spiring 78*, S. J. Rhodes 9*); Second day, Hampshire 152-4 (J. P. Stephenson 68*, J. N. B. Bovill 4*); Third day, Worcestershire 75-2 (G. A. Hick 26*, T. M. Moody 35*).

Worcestershire

T. S. Curtis b Connor	4	– lbw b Connor	6
W. P. C. Weston c White b Milburn	0	– c sub b Connor	1
G. A. Hick c Laney b Udal	123	– c White b Connor	44
*T. M. Moody c Aymes b Bovill	33	– not out	138
K. R. Spiring c Aymes b Connor	144	– run out	82
D. A. Leatherdale c Udal b James	0	– not out	3
†S. J. Rhodes lbw b James	47		
S. R. Lampitt c sub b Connor	14		
P. J. Newport c sub b Bovill	33		
R. K. Illingworth not out	20		
A. Sheriyar lbw b Bovill	0		
L-b 11, w 2	13	B 6, l-b 4, w 2, n-b 2	14
1/4 2/6 3/70 4/229 5/230 6/338 7/375 8/378 9/431	431	1/5 2/26 3/122 4/281 (4 wkts dec.)	288

Bonus points – Worcestershire 3, Hampshire 2 (Score at 120 overs: 309-5).

Bowling: *First Innings*—Connor 35–11–84–3; Milburn 23–11–41–1; Stephenson 20–5–53–0; Bovill 22.3–4–68–3; Udal 26–2–106–1; James 29–8–55–2; Whitaker 4–0–13–0. *Second Innings*—Connor 16–3–48–3; Bovill 15–2–59–0; James 5–0–21–0; Stephenson 11–4–35–0; Udal 23–5–67–0; Whitaker 15–2–48–0.

Hampshire

*J. P. Stephenson c and b Lampitt	74
J. S. Laney b Newport	39
K. D. James run out	7
R. A. Smith c Hick b Lampitt	8
P. R. Whitaker c Rhodes b Hick	22
J. N. B. Bovill c Illingworth b Newport	10
G. W. White c Rhodes b Hick	66
†A. N. Aymes not out	100
S. D. Udal not out	50
L-b 7, n-b 10	17
1/71 2/91 3/99 4/142 5/160 6/168 7/273 (7 wkts dec.)	393

C. A. Connor and S. M. Milburn did not bat.

Bonus points – Hampshire 4, Worcestershire 3.

Bowling: Newport 25.2–5–120–2; Sheriyar 24–5–71–0; Illingworth 17–4–49–0; Lampitt 28–6–103–2; Hick 20–6–43–2; Moody 2–2–0–0.

Umpires: B. Dudleston and M. J. Kitchen.

At Oxford, June 6, 7, 8. WORCESTERSHIRE drew with OXFORD UNIVERSITY.

WORCESTERSHIRE v NOTTINGHAMSHIRE

At Worcester, June 13, 14, 15, 17. Drawn. Worcestershire 10 pts, Nottinghamshire 10 pts. Toss: Worcestershire.

The pitch was recycled from the previous game with Hampshire, and both teams played three spinners. But it turned more slowly than expected and the game ended in stalemate; neither side had yet managed a Championship win. Moody set up an imposing first-innings total with 212, his highest score in England, and added 199 with the impressive Spiring. Nottinghamshire's attack was weakened when Pick crashed into the boundary, and pace bowler Cairns was obliged to send down 26 overs before tea on the first day. After Lampitt and Illingworth put on 116 for the ninth wicket, the visitors needed 344 to save the follow-on. Metcalfe's first Championship half-century since leaving Yorkshire helped to do that, though they still trailed by 101. Worcestershire then set what they considered a generous target of 296 in 69 overs and were exasperated when Nottinghamshire did not pursue it. Robinson, who batted throughout, seemed the perfect foil for the other batsmen, but Walker was sent in to survive 27 overs for five runs, ahead of potential match-winner Cairns.

Close of play: First day, Worcestershire 342-3 (T. M. Moody 194*, K. R. Spiring 55*); Second day, Nottinghamshire 172-2 (G. F. Archer 60*, R. T. Bates 0*); Third day, Worcestershire 108-1 (W. P. C. Weston 50*, G. A. Hick 49*).

Worcestershire

T. S. Curtis c Walker b Afford	46		
W. P. C. Weston c Bates b Cairns	21	– run out	54
G. A. Hick c Walker b Evans	17	– run out	85
*T. M. Moody b Cairns	212	– b Afford	17
K. R. Spiring c Robinson b Evans	64	– not out	20
D. A. Leatherdale lbw b Evans	0	– not out	7
†S. J. Rhodes c Walker b Evans	0	– (1) lbw b Cairns	4
S. R. Lampitt c Johnson b Pick	59		
P. J. Newport lbw b Evans	0		
R. K. Illingworth not out	41		
B 11, l-b 20, n-b 2	33	L-b 1, n-b 6	7
1/35 2/64 3/166 4/365 5/366 6/366 7/377 8/377 9/493 (9 wkts dec.)	493	1/4 2/118 3/165 4/166 (4 wkts dec.)	194

M. J. Rawnsley did not bat.

Bonus points – Worcestershire 4, Nottinghamshire 3 (Score at 120 overs: 386-8).

Bowling: *First Innings*—Cairns 39–8–124–2; Pick 25.2–6–69–1; Evans 47–12–116–5; Afford 22–6–55–1; Bates 20–2–77–0; Archer 7–1–21–0. *Second Innings*—Cairns 7–1–33–1; Pick 15–2–58–0; Afford 18–5–55–1; Bates 2–0–7–0; Evans 8–1–40–0.

Nottinghamshire

P. R. Pollard lbw b Newport	4		
R. T. Robinson c and b Moody	83	– (1) not out	111
G. F. Archer c Rhodes b Illingworth	70	– c Moody b Newport	3
R. T. Bates c Hick b Newport	34		
A. A. Metcalfe c Weston b Lampitt	80	– (2) c Leatherdale b Hick	1
*P. Johnson c Moody b Newport	22	– (4) c Curtis b Lampitt	15
C. L. Cairns c Spiring b Rawnsley	18	– (6) not out	1
†L. N. P. Walker c Weston b Lampitt	14	– (5) c Leatherdale b Illingworth	5
K. P. Evans not out	18		
R. A. Pick lbw b Leatherdale	10		
J. A. Afford c Hick b Leatherdale	2		
B 5, l-b 8, w 2, n-b 22	37	B 12, l-b 1, n-b 10	23
1/10 2/170 3/209 4/219 5/247 6/287 7/318 8/366 9/388	392	1/14 2/33 3/77 4/140 (4 wkts)	159

Bonus points – Nottinghamshire 4, Worcestershire 3 (Score at 120 overs: 380-8).

Bowling: *First Innings*—Newport 24–5–98–3; Moody 5–3–5–1; Illingworth 34–12–64–1; Lampitt 23–6–97–2; Hick 19–3–60–0; Rawnsley 17–5–52–1; Weston 1–0–1–0; Leatherdale 1.5–1–2–2. *Second Innings*—Newport 15–2–41–1; Lampitt 11–2–30–1; Hick 12–4–37–1; Illingworth 14–8–14–1; Rawnsley 7–4–11–0; Moody 4–1–13–0.

Umpires: R. Palmer and G. Sharp.

At Bath, June 19, 20, 21, 22. WORCESTERSHIRE beat SOMERSET by one wicket.

WORCESTERSHIRE v YORKSHIRE

At Worcester, June 27, 28, 29, July 1. Yorkshire won by 111 runs. Yorkshire 23 pts, Worcestershire 8 pts. Toss: Yorkshire. Championship debut: S. W. K. Ellis.

Fiery bowling on a seaming pitch enabled Yorkshire to move 19 points clear at the top of the table. Worcestershire had been set 233 in three and a half hours. Despite late defiance from Solanki, the contest was effectively settled when they were 28 for five. The decision to rest Hick, who had complained of mental and physical exhaustion between Tests, had prompted grumbling among members and an outspoken attack from club president Tom Graveney. But it was forgotten during a chanceless century from Spiring. Adding 176 with Curtis, he earned Worcestershire a 34-run advantage after McGrath had held Yorkshire's first innings together with 60 spread over 55 overs. On resuming, Yorkshire were wobbling at 130 for four. But a fourth successive half-century from Bevan and his partnership of 93 with White set up the declaration. Low bounce accounted for many of the 15 lbw decisions in the game; Worcestershire were on the receiving end of 12 of them.

Close of play: First day, Yorkshire 312-7 (D. Gough 26*, P. J. Hartley 27*); Second day, Worcestershire 147-3 (T. S. Curtis 30*, K. R. Spiring 58*); Third day, Yorkshire 88-0 (M. D. Moxon 36*, M. P. Vaughan 48*).

Yorkshire

M. D. Moxon c Lampitt b Moody	36	– lbw b Solanki	42
M. P. Vaughan c Rhodes b Ellis	9	– c Moody b Illingworth	60
*D. Byas lbw b Lampitt	14	– b Solanki	0
M. G. Bevan b Ellis	61	– c Weston b Church	57
A. McGrath lbw b Sheriyar	60	– c Church b Illingworth	6
C. White c Rhodes b Lampitt	53	– c Sheriyar b Solanki	65
†R. J. Blakey c Weston b Lampitt	14	– c sub b Church	22
D. Gough c Solanki b Ellis	26	– not out	1
P. J. Hartley not out	28		
C. E. W. Silverwood b Lampitt	8		
R. D. Stemp b Lampitt	0		
B 4, l-b 1, w 3, n-b 4	12	B 5, l-b 7, w 1	13
1/24 2/60 3/72 4/150 5/224 6/253 7/262 8/312 9/321	321	1/106 2/106 3/108 (7 wkts dec.) 4/130 5/223 6/253 7/266	266

Bonus points – Yorkshire 3, Worcestershire 4.

Bowling: *First Innings*—Sheriyar 23–4–77–1; Ellis 19–1–80–3; Moody 16–6–41–1; Lampitt 23–6–58–5; Illingworth 24–12–33–0; Solanki 6–1–27–0. *Second Innings*—Sheriyar 9–2–27–0; Ellis 6–2–20–0; Illingworth 28–10–41–2; Lampitt 4–0–10–0; Solanki 25.5–2–111–3; Moody 3–0–18–0; Church 6–0–27–2.

Worcestershire

W. P. C. Weston lbw b Gough	18	– c Byas b Silverwood	12
M. J. Church lbw b Silverwood	29	– lbw b Gough	5
T. S. Curtis lbw b Stemp	72	– c Blakey b Gough	0
*T. M. Moody b Silverwood	0	– lbw b Stemp	3
K. R. Spiring lbw b Vaughan	109	– lbw b Silverwood	6
V. S. Solanki lbw b Silverwood	32	– c Bevan b Vaughan	40
†S. J. Rhodes lbw b Hartley	51	– lbw b Stemp	16
S. R. Lampitt b Silverwood	0	– lbw b Gough	17
R. K. Illingworth b Silverwood	18	– (10) not out	4
S. W. K. Ellis not out	0	– (9) c Bevan b Stemp	0
A. Sheriyar not out	0	– lbw b Gough	0
B 4, l-b 6, n-b 16	26	B 6, l-b 5, w 1, n-b 6	18
1/38 2/58 3/58 4/234 5/244 6/317 7/317 8/355 9/355 (9 wkts dec.)	355	1/7 2/13 3/21 4/21 5/28 6/82 7/102 8/115 9/117	121

Bonus points – Worcestershire 4, Yorkshire 4 (Score at 120 overs: 355-9).

Bowling: *First Innings*—Gough 29–7–68–1; Hartley 19–6–52–1; Silverwood 23–5–72–5; White 3–0–25–0; Stemp 25–11–59–1; Bevan 6–1–18–0; Vaughan 16–4–51–1. *Second Innings*—Gough 14–9–27–4; Silverwood 13–7–16–2; Stemp 21–7–32–3; Vaughan 7–1–19–1; Hartley 2–0–12–0; Bevan 1–0–4–0.

Umpires: R. Julian and D. R. Shepherd.

At Manchester, July 4, 5, 6, 8. WORCESTERSHIRE drew with LANCASHIRE.

WORCESTERSHIRE v DURHAM

At Worcester, July 18, 19, 20. Worcestershire won by nine wickets. Worcestershire 23 pts, Durham 5 pts. Toss: Durham.

The frailty of Durham's batting and an over-reliance on Brown as their bowling spearhead was graphically illustrated as they went from total command to nine-wicket defeat inside four sessions. Bainbridge led Durham to 240 on the opening day, a challenging total on a grassy pitch. Then Brown reduced Worcestershire to 11 for four that evening. But Hick held firm and next morning recaptured his place in the supporters' affections after resting during the previous home game. He scored a superb 150, with five sixes and 20 fours, which completed his set of Championship centuries against every other county. Bowling splendidly, Brown finished with six for 77, but received little support as Worcestershire eventually led by 62. Then a typical Durham collapse to 38 for five condemned the visitors to their seventh defeat. Exploiting the conditions, Sheriyar and Ellis gave a glimpse of the role Worcestershire hoped they would play in the future, and victory was completed 15 minutes before lunch on the third day.

Close of play: First day, Worcestershire 39-4 (G. A. Hick 15*, V. S. Solanki 8*); Second day, Durham 132-8 (D. G. C. Ligertwood 33*).

Durham

S. L. Campbell c Moody b Lampitt	43	– b Lampitt	32
S. Hutton lbw b Moody	24	– lbw b Ellis	0
J. E. Morris b Illingworth	10	– c Hick b Ellis	0
P. D. Collingwood lbw b Lampitt	1	– b Sheriyar	8
*M. A. Roseberry c Solanki b Moody	7	– lbw b Sheriyar	1
P. Bainbridge c Sheriyar b Illingworth	67	– c Weston b Lampitt	9
†D. G. C. Ligertwood lbw b Lampitt	10	– not out	35
M. M. Betts c Rhodes b Moody	31	– run out	26
S. J. E. Brown b Church	1	– lbw b Sheriyar	1
D. M. Cox not out	16	– b Ellis	9
J. Wood c Hick b Lampitt	3	– b Sheriyar	9
L-b 3, w 2, n-b 22	27	L-b 3, w 1, n-b 18	22
1/61 2/79 3/91 4/91 5/116 6/186 7/188 8/193 9/233	240	1/10 2/10 3/24 4/26 5/38 6/73 7/116 8/132 9/143	152

Bonus points – Durham 1, Worcestershire 4.

Bowling: *First Innings*—Sheriyar 11–3–46–0; Ellis 12–0–38–0; Moody 20–6–39–3; Lampitt 18.2–1–57–4; Illingworth 16–5–39–2; Solanki 1–0–2–0; Church 6–3–16–1. *Second Innings*—Sheriyar 14.3–4–46–4; Ellis 12–2–29–3; Lampitt 8–0–45–2; Moody 10–4–29–0.

Worcestershire

W. P. C. Weston lbw b Brown	6	– not out	40
M. J. Church b Betts	2	– b Cox	23
G. A. Hick c Ligertwood b Betts	150	– not out	25
*T. M. Moody c Ligertwood b Brown	3		
K. R. Spiring lbw b Brown	0		
V. S. Solanki b Brown	16		
†S. J. Rhodes lbw b Cox	29		
S. R. Lampitt lbw b Brown	24		
R. K. Illingworth c Cox b Brown	23		
S. W. K. Ellis not out	14		
A. Sheriyar b Betts	4		
B 3, l-b 12, n-b 16	31	L-b 1, n-b 4	5
1/8 2/8 3/11 4/11 5/59 6/140 7/209 8/275 9/293	302	1/54	(1 wkt) 93

Bonus points – Worcestershire 3, Durham 4.

Bowling: *First Innings*—Brown 27–9–77–6; Betts 19.3–4–85–3; Wood 18–3–73–0; Bainbridge 3–0–14–0; Cox 14–5–38–1. *Second Innings*—Betts 6–2–16–0; Wood 6–0–43–0; Cox 10–5–17–1; Campbell 6.2–1–16–0.

Umpires: B. J. Meyer and R. A. White.

WORCESTERSHIRE v NORTHAMPTONSHIRE

At Kidderminster, July 24, 25, 26, 27. Drawn. Worcestershire 11 pts, Northamptonshire 9 pts. Toss: Northamptonshire. First-class debut: D. J. Sales.

This otherwise unmemorable high-scoring draw will achieve lasting fame thanks to the performance of 18-year-old David Sales. After a third-ball duck in the first innings, he scored an unbeaten 210, the first double-century ever scored by someone making his first-class debut in a Championship match. Sales became the youngest double-centurion in Britain since W. G. Grace in 1866, and the eighth-youngest worldwide; all 13 players who had previously scored 200 before their 19th birthday went on to play Test cricket. Sales certainly showed the temperament as well as the endurance to advance in the game: he finished the third day on 191, then moved, apparently nervelessly, to his landmark in just five balls next morning. His entire innings only took four and a half hours, and he hit three sixes and 28 fours in 226 balls, sharing a stand of 243 with Capel. It is fair to note that, once the shine was off the ball, batting was easy for just about

YOUNGEST PLAYERS TO SCORE 200 IN FIRST-CLASS CRICKET

Years	*Days*				
16	96	Ijaz Ahmed, sen.	201*	PACO v Karachi at Karachi	1984-85
17	205	I. D. Craig	213*	NSW v South Africans at Sydney	1952-53
17	312	Javed Miandad	311	Karachi Whites v National Bank at Karachi	1974-75
17	317	Taslim Arif	205	Karachi Blues v Hyderabad at Karachi	1971-72
17	324	Hanif Mohammad	203*	Pakistanis v Bombay at Bombay	1952-53
18	2	Mushtaq Mohammad	229*	Karachi Whites v East Pakistan at Karachi	1961-62
18	12	W. G. Grace	224*	England XI v Surrey at The Oval	1866
18	**237**	**D. J. Sales**	**210***	**Northants v Worcs at Kidderminster**	**1996**
18	267	G. A. Headley	211	Jamaica v Hon. L. H. Tennyson's XI at Kingston	1927-28
18	273	G. R. Viswanath	230	Mysore v Andhra at Vijayawada	1967-68
18	301	G. A. Greenidge	205	Barbados v Jamaica at Bridgetown	1966-67
18	303	Mohsin Khan	229	Universities v Sind at Lahore	1973-74
18	317	Inzamam-ul-Haq	201*	United Bank v PNSC at Karachi	1988-89
18	348	C. Hill	206*	South Australia v NSW at Sydney	1895-96

Research: Robert Brooke

everyone. Northamptonshire struggled on the first day, but that was mainly due to poor batting and good control from Illingworth. Ripley rescued them with his highest Championship score for four years. Worcestershire declared their first innings on the third morning and were eventually set 425 in 91 overs. Moody and Curtis surpassed the Capel–Sales stand, with Moody scoring his second century of the match and his third in succession at Chester Road. But three wickets fell on 302 and the chase was called off.

Close of play: First day, Northamptonshire 294-9 (D. Ripley 71*, J. P. Taylor 30*); Second day, Worcestershire 313-4 (T. M. Moody 100*, V. S. Solanki 65*); Third day, Northamptonshire 417-3 (D. J. Sales 191*, K. M. Curran 34*).

Northamptonshire

R. R. Montgomerie lbw b Sheriyar	34	– retired hurt	17
*A. Fordham c Ellis b Lampitt	29	– c Rhodes b Lampitt	31
T. C. Walton c Moody b Illingworth	0	– c Rhodes b Lampitt	27
K. M. Curran lbw b Lampitt	40	– (6) not out	42
D. J. Sales c Church b Illingworth	0	– not out	210
D. J. Capel c Lampitt b Illingworth	32	– (4) c Weston b Solanki	103
A. L. Penberthy c Lampitt b Illingworth	2		
J. N. Snape lbw b Lampitt	1		
A. R. Roberts b Solanki	39		
†D. Ripley not out	88		
J. P. Taylor lbw b Church	36		
L-b 16, w 3, n-b 8	27	B 4, l-b 3, w 1, n-b 8	16
1/53 2/55 3/82 4/83 5/137 6/144 7/145 8/145 9/233	328	1/44 2/80 3/323 (3 wkts dec.)	446

Bonus points – Northamptonshire 3, Worcestershire 4 (Score at 120 overs: 323-9).

In the second innings R. R. Montgomerie retired hurt at 61.

Bowling: *First Innings*—Sheriyar 27–4–81–1; Ellis 15–3–51–0; Lampitt 25–6–47–3; Illingworth 43–12–89–4; Moody 4–0–17–0; Solanki 6–1–21–1; Church 2.1–0–6–1. *Second Innings*—Sheriyar 10–1–39–0; Ellis 13–0–73–0; Lampitt 18–4–84–2; Solanki 22–1–103–1; Illingworth 16–4–57–0; Church 6–0–33–0; Moody 10–0–50–0.

Worcestershire

W. P. C. Weston c Fordham b Snape	68	– c and b Capel	7
M. J. Church b Capel	2	– c Penberthy b Capel	4
T. S. Curtis c Montgomerie b Roberts	65	– c Penberthy b Taylor	107
*T. M. Moody b Curran	106	– b Taylor	169
K. R. Spiring hit wkt b Snape	0	– c Ripley b Taylor	9
V. S. Solanki c Ripley b Snape	68	– c Snape b Curran	0
†S. J. Rhodes not out	12	– not out	53
S. R. Lampitt run out	0	– c Walton b Snape	28
R. K. Illingworth not out	16	– not out	5
L-b 5, n-b 8	13	L-b 4, n-b 2	6
1/28 2/118 3/185 4/186 5/318 6/322 7/323 (7 wkts dec.)	350	1/11 2/12 3/281 4/302 5/302 6/302 7/367 (7 wkts)	388

S. W. K. Ellis and A. Sheriyar did not bat.

Bonus points – Worcestershire 4, Northamptonshire 3.

Bowling: *First Innings*—Taylor 22–3–67–0; Capel 12–5–46–1; Roberts 10–1–41–1; Snape 32–8–98–3; Curran 19–5–58–1; Penberthy 7–1–35–0. *Second Innings*—Taylor 15–4–53–3; Capel 15–3–48–2; Curran 11–0–41–1; Roberts 23–2–119–0; Snape 26.4–2–123–1.

Umpires: G. I. Burgess and D. J. Constant.

At Canterbury, August 1, 2, 3, 5. WORCESTERSHIRE beat KENT by 192 runs.

At Worcester, August 9, 10, 11, 12. WORCESTERSHIRE lost to SOUTH AFRICA A by 172 runs (See South Africa A tour section).

At Lord's, August 15, 16, 17, 19. WORCESTERSHIRE drew with MIDDLESEX.

WORCESTERSHIRE v WARWICKSHIRE

At Worcester, August 22, 23, 24, 26. Drawn. Worcestershire 8 pts, Warwickshire 10 pts. Toss: Warwickshire.

For the second match running, Worcestershire were on the receiving end of a century last-wicket stand: this time, Giles and Munton put on 141. Both scored Championship bests and they broke the county's 66-year-old tenth-wicket record, set by F. R. Santall and W. Sanders against Yorkshire. Warwickshire openers Khan and Powell had plundered 92 in 64 minutes but then nine wickets fell for 77 to some excellent bowling from Illingworth and Lampitt. After the last-wicket heroics, Pollock brought down the curtain on his season – he was returning to South Africa for an ankle operation – with a spell of three for two in 25 balls. But a battling half-century from Spiring allayed Worcestershire's fears of having to follow on, and the loss of a day and a half to rain meant Warwickshire lost the advantage. Warwickshire were desperate for victory to preserve their last, slender, hopes of retaining the title and, after mutual declarations, Worcestershire had to make a very plausible 268 at five an over to win. The openers put on 100 but, after four quick wickets, the chase was abandoned.

Close of play: First day, Warwickshire 255-9 (A. F. Giles 57*, T. A. Munton 30*); Second day, Worcestershire 10-0 (T. S. Curtis 2*, W. P. C. Weston 8*); Third day, Worcestershire 205-9 (S. W. K. Ellis 0*, A. Sheriyar 0*).

Warwickshire

W. G. Khan c Hick b Lampitt	52	– c Curtis b Solanki	44
M. J. Powell lbw b Lampitt	36	– c Hick b Solanki	38
D. P. Ostler c Rhodes b Illingworth	0	– (4) c Ellis b Curtis	10
A. Singh c Curtis b Lampitt	20	– (5) not out	23
T. L. Penney c Rhodes b Illingworth	14	– (6) not out	31
S. M. Pollock c Rhodes b Lampitt	15		
D. R. Brown c Hick b Illingworth	0		
†K. J. Piper c Ellis b Illingworth	6		
N. M. K. Smith lbw b Sheriyar	9	– (3) st Rhodes b Illingworth	12
A. F. Giles b Sheriyar	83		
*T. A. Munton not out	54		
L-b 5, w 4, n-b 12	21	L-b 4	4
1/92 2/93 3/99 4/128 5/142 6/149 7/149 8/161 9/169	310	1/79 2/92 3/96 4/116 (4 wkts dec.)	162

Bonus points – Warwickshire 3, Worcestershire 4.

Bowling: *First Innings*—Sheriyar 15.2–3–61–2; Ellis 10–2–51–0; Moody 9–1–34–0; Lampitt 30–7–90–4; Illingworth 38–17–54–4; Hick 4–2–15–0. *Second Innings*—Sheriyar 7–0–29–0; Ellis 7–1–40–0; Illingworth 4–0–31–1; Solanki 8–0–41–2; Curtis 4–0–17–1.

Worcestershire

T. S. Curtis b Pollock	16	– b Smith	44
W. P. C. Weston c Giles b Munton	20	– c Powell b Giles	52
G. A. Hick c and b Pollock	15	– c Brown b Pollock	15
*T. M. Moody b Pollock	3	– c Khan b Smith	7
K. R. Spiring c Ostler b Munton	52	– not out	8
V. S. Solanki b Giles	45	– not out	25
†S. J. Rhodes c Giles b Munton	27		
S. R. Lampitt c Singh b Giles	7		
R. K. Illingworth b Giles	4		
S. W. K. Ellis not out	0		
A. Sheriyar not out	0		
B 8, l-b 3, w 1, n-b 4	16	B 8, l-b 3, n-b 2	13
1/37 2/37 3/47 4/62 5/134 6/183 7/200 8/204 9/205 (9 wkts dec.)	205	1/100 2/108 3/116 4/122 (4 wkts)	164

Bonus points – Worcestershire 1, Warwickshire 4.

Bowling: *First Innings*—Pollock 23–6–58–3; Munton 24–8–58–3; Brown 10–3–24–0; Smith 15–1–42–0; Giles 8–4–12–3. *Second Innings*—Pollock 10–3–26–1; Munton 10–3–45–0; Smith 13–1–50–2; Giles 13–5–32–1.

Umpires: A. G. T. Whitehead and P. Willey.

At Chesterfield, August 29, 30, 31. WORCESTERSHIRE lost to DERBYSHIRE by nine wickets.

WORCESTERSHIRE v SUSSEX

At Worcester, September 3, 4, 5. Worcestershire won by an innings and 14 runs. Worcestershire 24 pts, Sussex 4 pts. Toss: Sussex. First-class debut: M. Newell.

Sussex sank to their fourth successive defeat. They had run into trouble as the ball seamed and swung on a gloomy first morning, before being rescued from 64 for five by a maiden Championship century from Drakes. When Worcestershire replied, Curtis passed 20,000 first-class runs, but the contest was evenly balanced when they stood on 152 for five, still 67 in arrears. However, Leatherdale, called up from a Second Eleven match when Spiring fell ill, and Rhodes swung the game with a stand of 219. Leatherdale scored his first century since 1994 and Rhodes his first in the Championship since 1993. Sheriyar then returned a county-best six for 99, backed up by some brilliant fielding, to hurry Sussex towards defeat. They lost their first eight wickets inside 17 overs; Law hit a rapid 75 but only delayed the end, which arrived on the third afternoon.

Close of play: First day, Worcestershire 109-2 (T. S. Curtis 46*, T. M. Moody 12*); Second day, Sussex 21-0 (N. J. Lenham 12*, C. W. J. Athey 5*).

Sussex

N. J. Lenham b Ellis	1	– lbw b Lampitt	14
C. W. J. Athey c Weston b Sheriyar	0	– lbw b Lampitt	6
K. Greenfield lbw b Lampitt	26	– not out	36
*A. P. Wells c Weston b Moody	16	– c Ellis b Sheriyar	5
K. Newell c Hick b Sheriyar	22	– run out	2
M. Newell c Rhodes b Moody	0	– run out	0
V. C. Drakes c Lampitt b Leatherdale	103	– c Solanki b Sheriyar	1
†P. Moores c Moody b Ellis	11	– b Sheriyar	6
I. D. K. Salisbury b Ellis	4	– lbw b Sheriyar	9
D. R. Law c Sheriyar b Rawnsley	18	– c Solanki b Sheriyar	75
R. J. Kirtley not out	0	– lbw b Sheriyar	0
B 1, l-b 8, w 1, n-b 8	18	B 8, l-b 6, w 4, n-b 8	26
1/1 2/1 3/45 4/55 5/64 6/93 7/147 8/155 9/215	219	1/27 2/44 3/49 4/54 5/54 6/56 7/62 8/72 9/179	180

Bonus points – Sussex 1, Worcestershire 4.

Bowling: *First Innings*—Sheriyar 13–3–50–2; Ellis 17–6–58–3; Moody 17–5–36–2; Lampitt 16–2–57–1; Leatherdale 3–1–5–1; Rawnsley 1–0–4–1. *Second Innings*—Sheriyar 24–7–99–6; Ellis 6–4–14–0; Leatherdale 1–0–1–0; Lampitt 10–1–23–2; Moody 7–2–27–0; Solanki 1–0–2–0.

Worcestershire

T. S. Curtis c M. Newell b Salisbury	61
W. P. C. Weston c Kirtley b Law	42
G. A. Hick c Moores b Law	1
*T. M. Moody c Moores b Kirtley	30
V. S. Solanki c Moores b Kirtley	0
D. A. Leatherdale lbw b Drakes	122
†S. J. Rhodes lbw b Salisbury	110
S. R. Lampitt b Drakes	5
S. W. K. Ellis c Salisbury b Drakes	7
M. J. Rawnsley not out	4
B 2, l-b 9, w 4, n-b 16	31
1/51 2/61 3/152 4/152 5/152 6/371 7/383 8/409 9/413 (9 wkts dec.)	413

A. Sheriyar did not bat.

Bonus points – Worcestershire 4, Sussex 3 (Score at 120 overs: 398-7).

Bowling: Drakes 37–9–123–3; Kirtley 30–7–112–2; Law 21–4–67–2; K. Newell 3–0–16–0; Salisbury 24.1–6–60–2; Greenfield 5–1–11–0; Lenham 4–0–13–0.

Umpires: J. C. Balderstone and K. E. Palmer.

WORCESTERSHIRE v GLOUCESTERSHIRE

At Worcester, September 12, 13, 14, 16. Worcestershire won by five wickets. Worcestershire 23 pts, Gloucestershire 7 pts. Toss: Gloucestershire.

Worcestershire were taken to victory by the usual pairing of Moody and Hick, but this time Moody made his contribution as a bowler. With injuries decimating the attack, he defied a bad back and finished with match figures of 13 for 159. He and Sheriyar, who later suffered a side strain, caused trouble from the start. Gloucestershire recovered thanks to Alleyne's first Championship hundred of 1996 and an aggressive 70 from Lynch, and Walsh's bowling gave them the edge before Leatherdale and Illingworth put on 96 for the ninth wicket. Gloucestershire's second innings resembled their first: more early wickets to Moody before Alleyne and Lynch restored the balance. That left Worcestershire 308 to get, and Hick, out of sorts since England dropped him, returned to his best, blazing form. His 90th hundred included 18 fours and a six and he added 201 with Weston to ensure victory.

Close of play: First day, Gloucestershire 326-9 (M. C. J. Ball 0*); Second day, Worcestershire 313-8 (D. A. Leatherdale 66*, R. K. Illingworth 43*); Third day, Gloucestershire 236-8 (R. C. Russell 35*, M. C. J. Ball 5*).

Gloucestershire

D. R. Hewson c Rhodes b Moody	5	lbw b Leatherdale	9
M. G. N. Windows b Sheriyar	0	c Rhodes b Moody	6
A. Symonds lbw b Sheriyar	11	c Rhodes b Moody	6
R. I. Dawson c Hick b Moody	0	b Lampitt	16
M. A. Lynch c Rhodes b Moody	70	lbw b Moody	72
M. W. Alleyne lbw b Leatherdale	149	lbw b Moody	44
†R. C. Russell c Lampitt b Moody	29	not out	50
R. P. Davis st Rhodes b Solanki	7	c Weston b Moody	16
A. M. Smith c Hick b Moody	30	c Rhodes b Illingworth	5
M. C. J. Ball not out	5	c Hick b Moody	46
*C. A. Walsh c Illingworth b Moody	0	b Moody	0
B 4, l-b 6, n-b 18	28	B 6, l-b 9, w 1, n-b 6	22
1/5 2/11 3/13 4/37 5/119 6/189 7/237 8/326 9/326	334	1/12 2/22 3/22 4/85 5/160 6/163 7/204 8/221 9/292	292

Bonus points – Gloucestershire 3, Worcestershire 4.

Bowling: *First Innings*—Sheriyar 13–1–52–2; Moody 35–16–67–6; Lampitt 22–4–83–0; Leatherdale 12–3–47–1; Illingworth 19–6–52–0; Solanki 12–7–23–1. *Second Innings*—Moody 36.5–13–92–7; Leatherdale 23–6–53–1; Illingworth 23–5–57–1; Lampitt 12–3–40–1; Solanki 14–4–35–0.

Worcestershire

T. S. Curtis lbw b Smith	20	b Walsh	10
W. P. C. Weston lbw b Alleyne	28	c Lynch b Walsh	89
G. A. Hick c Windows b Walsh	54	b Walsh	106
V. S. Solanki b Walsh	41	not out	46
D. A. Leatherdale c Davis b Alleyne	70	b Symonds	19
*T. M. Moody b Walsh	0	b Smith	11
K. R. Spiring run out	12	not out	4
†S. J. Rhodes b Walsh	12		
S. R. Lampitt b Walsh	5		
R. K. Illingworth c Russell b Alleyne	44		
A. Sheriyar not out	0		
B 2, l-b 14, w 1, n-b 16	33	B 12, l-b 4, n-b 10	26
1/34 2/60 3/154 4/165 5/165 6/194 7/216 8/222 9/318	319	1/12 2/213 3/226 4/273 5/294	(5 wkts) 311

Bonus points – Worcestershire 3, Gloucestershire 4.

Bowling: *First Innings*—Walsh 24–6–64–5; Smith 12–4–32–1; Alleyne 27.1–6–73–3; Davis 20–7–47–0; Ball 11–4–40–0; Symonds 17–3–47–0. *Second Innings*—Walsh 19–2–85–3; Smith 20–5–81–1; Symonds 13–2–44–1; Alleyne 7–1–38–0; Davis 14–3–43–0; Dawson 0.2–0–4–0.

Umpires: J. H. Hampshire and R. Palmer.

At The Oval, September 19, 20, 21, 22. WORCESTERSHIRE beat SURREY by 124 runs.

Michael Bevan

YORKSHIRE

Patron: HRH The Duchess of Kent

President and Chairman: Sir Lawrence Byford

Chairman of Cricket: R. K. Platt

Chief Executive: C. D. Hassell

Captain: D. Byas

Head Groundsman: A. W. Fogarty

Scorer: J. T. Potter

In one sense, Yorkshire enjoyed their best season since 1972, when the county game was expanded to take in a fourth major competition, for they challenged strongly on all fronts. They failed, however, to win on any of them, and seemed to have the makings of a good side while remaining no more than a useful one. The fact that under their new captain, David Byas, they enjoyed some bursts of excellent form understandably encouraged high hopes among the members. In the final analysis, however, the improvement on 1995 was marginal.

Much was made of their success in reaching the semi-finals of both knockout competitions – despite the disappointment of losing both times to Lancashire, of all teams. But they had done almost as well in 1995. And in winning eight matches instead of seven, they climbed only two places to sixth in the Championship. So the significant progress came in the Sunday League, where they moved up from 12th to third, their best effort since winning the title in 1983.

Byas was able to retain an unchanged side for most of the season, as Yorkshire escaped serious injuries and avoided the attention of the Test selectors, despite the widespread perception elsewhere that chairman Ray Illingworth was predisposed in Yorkshire's favour. The only real setback was the departure of vice-captain Michael Bevan in mid-August, called up by Australia for a one-day tournament. Even then, Yorkshire hardly suffered heavily: they won three out of four Sunday League matches after he left and two out of five in the Championship, drawing two others largely owing to the weather and bowling limitations. Byas himself blamed poor catching for Yorkshire's failure to make the most of their opportunities. They also remained vulnerable to pressure and found it difficult to recover when things went badly.

On occasions, the batting creaked a little, leaving Bevan to shoulder a heavy responsibility. He scored consistently and at a reasonable pace, while Richard Blakey rediscovered form and confidence. Bevan and Michael Vaughan were the only batsmen to top 1,000 runs, however, and Byas himself had a patchy season. Anthony McGrath did well enough for a player in his first full season and was only one short of 1,000 in all first-class cricket. Craig White worked his way through a very lean spell: after 14 innings in the first eight Championship matches he averaged just 16.61, so raising this to an eventual 32.29 represented something of a triumph. He also bowled with genuine hostility at times, sustaining the theory that he has real all-round potential. Though sometimes expensive, White filled an important role in one-day cricket, particularly as Yorkshire often relied on only five bowlers. Eventually, Byas allowed Bevan's unorthodox left-arm spin more scope and was rewarded with a number of useful spells.

Darren Gough, emerging from a cloud of uncertainty, proved the most effective bowler, with 67 first-class wickets adding up to his best total yet. He needed time to find his rhythm, after injury worries, but rounded off the summer in style, taking 22 wickets at 12.13 in his last three games. By then, he was ready to go through an extensive repertoire of variations where earlier he had looked dispirited and short of ideas. Peter Hartley soldiered on with his usual sturdy reliability, to collect 54 wickets, though he showed understandable signs of wear and tear after a demanding game at Eastbourne, where he claimed ten in the defeat by Sussex.

The emergence of Chris Silverwood as a quick bowler of obvious ability was a godsend. Often given the new ball, he did well enough to be chosen, with Gough, for the senior England tour of Zimbabwe and New Zealand. He operated with unfailing enthusiasm although, like Hartley, his energies drained in late August and September. With Gavin Hamilton waiting in the wings, Yorkshire's seam bowling possessed reasonable strength in depth.

The slow bowling was less convincing. The county revived an almost forgotten tradition by capping left-arm spinner Stemp (and, later, Silverwood) between overs, but he failed to produce the expected control and his reluctance to flight the ball also made him predictable on flat pitches. He probably did not bowl enough; in one mid-season period, he was rationed to 63 overs in seven innings. Question-marks against Vaughan's off-spin also had much to do with his lack of opportunity. He found it almost impossible to build confidence as an occasional member of the attack – the more so as, when called upon, he was generally under pressure to take wickets on supposedly helpful surfaces. Along with McGrath and White, he was picked for England A's tour of Australia, and White then moved up to the main tour as a reinforcement.

Richard Kettleborough was promoted only after his fellow left-hander Bevan went, but he responded with a match-winning century against Essex. Hamilton and England Under-19 captain Alex Morris will also demand consideration. Yorkshire might find themselves mildly embarrassed by their riches in 1997.

Discussion of who will play for Yorkshire, and even how they will play, was rather muted over the winter compared to the subject of where they will play. In October, Yorkshire announced plans to move out of Headingley to a green field site near Wakefield, where they hoped to build a £50 million complex for the new millennium. Their present landlords, the Leeds Cricket, Football and Athletic Company, then began trying to persuade the club to change its mind. Yorkshire had already decided to abandon all their out-grounds except Scarborough from 1997. So, in the short run anyway, there will be more county cricket played at Headingley than ever before. – JOHN CALLAGHAN.

YORKSHIRE 1996

[*David Munden*

Back row: C. J. Schofield, C. A. Chapman, G. J. Batty, M. J. Hoggard, A. G. Wharf, A. C. Morris, R. J. Sidebottom, P. M. Hutchison, I. D. Fisher, M. J. Wood. *Middle row:* D. E. V. Padgett (*coach*), W. P. Morton (*physiotherapist*), B. Parker, R. D. Stemp, C. E. W. Silverwood, G. M. Hamilton, A. McGrath, R. A. Kettleborough, A. Sidebottom (*Academy coach*), S. Oldham (*cricket development manager*). *Front row:* D. Gough, R. J. Blakey, C. White, M. G. Bevan, D. Byas (*captain*), M. D. Moxon, P. J. Hartley, M. A. Robinson, M. P. Vaughan.

YORKSHIRE RESULTS

All first-class matches – Played 19: Won 8, Lost 5, Drawn 6.

County Championship matches – Played 17: Won 8, Lost 5, Drawn 4.

Competition placings – Britannic Assurance County Championship, 6th; NatWest Trophy, s-f; Benson and Hedges Cup, s-f; AXA Equity & Law League, 3rd.

COUNTY CHAMPIONSHIP AVERAGES

BATTING

Cap		*M*	*I*	*NO*	*R*	*HS*	*100s*	*50s*	*Avge*	*Ct/St*
1995	M. G. Bevan§	12	22	3	1,225	160*	3	8	64.47	6
1984	M. D. Moxon†	13	23	3	961	213	2	5	48.05	5
1995	M. P. Vaughan	17	31	2	1,156	183	3	6	39.86	4
1987	R. J. Blakey†	17	28	6	768	109*	1	4	34.90	36/1
	A. McGrath†	17	29	1	909	137	2	4	32.46	10
1993	C. White†	17	28	1	872	181	1	6	32.29	12
	R. A. Kettleborough†	5	7	0	222	108	1	0	31.71	6
1991	D. Byas†	17	29	1	858	138	1	5	30.64	29
1993	D. Gough†	15	24	3	494	121	1	2	23.52	5
1987	P. J. Hartley†	16	24	3	476	89	0	3	22.66	6
1996	R. D. Stemp	17	22	8	230	65	0	2	16.42	8
	A. C. Morris†	4	7	0	96	40	0	0	13.71	4
1996	C. E. W. Silverwood†	16	24	6	198	45*	0	0	11.00	6

Also batted: G. M. Hamilton (2 matches) 9*, 61, 0 (1 ct); A. G. Wharf† (2 matches) 62, 41.

* *Signifies not out.* † *Born in Yorkshire.* § *Overseas player.*

BOWLING

	O	*M*	*R*	*W*	*BB*	*5W/i*	*Avge*
D. Gough	555.3	135	1,498	66	6-36	2	22.69
C. White	282.2	47	1,035	36	4-15	0	28.75
P. J. Hartley	459.2	96	1,602	54	6-67	2	29.66
C. E. W. Silverwood	404.3	79	1,442	47	5-72	2	30.68
R. D. Stemp	530.4	156	1,442	37	5-38	1	38.97
M. P. Vaughan	186.3	28	726	16	4-62	0	45.37

Also bowled: M. G. Bevan 86.3–8–369–4; G. M. Hamilton 68.4–9–194–4; R. A. Kettleborough 12–1–40–2; A. McGrath 7–0–41–0; A. C. Morris 21–4–81–2; A. G. Wharf 31–5–166–1.

COUNTY RECORDS

Highest score for:	341	G. H. Hirst v Leicestershire at Leicester	1905
Highest score against:	318*	W. G. Grace (Gloucestershire) at Cheltenham	1876
Best bowling for:	10-10	H. Verity v Nottinghamshire at Leeds	1932
Best bowling against:	10-37	C. V. Grimmett (Australians) at Sheffield	1930
Highest total for:	887	v Warwickshire at Birmingham	1896
Highest total against:	681-7 dec.	by Leicestershire at Bradford	1996
Lowest total for:	23	v Hampshire at Middlesbrough	1965
Lowest total against:	13	by Nottinghamshire at Nottingham	1901

At Manchester, April 18, 19, 20. YORKSHIRE drew with LANCASHIRE (Non-Championship fixture).

At Cardiff, May 2, 3, 4, 6. YORKSHIRE beat GLAMORGAN by 43 runs.

YORKSHIRE v DERBYSHIRE

At Sheffield, May 9, 10, 11, 13. Drawn. Yorkshire 8 pts, Derbyshire 10 pts. Toss: Yorkshire.

Batsmen dominated on an easy-paced pitch until the last hour, when Derbyshire lost six wickets for 33, but they avoided defeat. Misled by early bounce, Cork and Malcolm had bowled too short, allowing Bevan to score almost at will, while McGrath fell just short of his first Championship hundred. Yorkshire took their total to 561, their highest at home against Derbyshire, who scored steadily in turn. An error by Stemp, who completely missed a fast slip chance offered by Owen on nine, proved costly; Owen hit his maiden century and added 278 with Jones – a county all-wicket record against Yorkshire. Jones, who turned his first hundred for Derbyshire into a double, batted into the last day to save the follow-on after interruptions from rain. Byas, however, opened up the game, setting a target of 288 in 50 overs. Attacking fields allowed Derbyshire to reach 201 for two. But when White snatched four for three in 11 balls, they found themselves defending grimly through the last seven overs. On the third day, a deer – believed to be a roebuck – found its way from adjoining woods on to the field, briefly stopping play before it panicked and managed to escape a rather dreary day's cricket.

Close of play: First day, Yorkshire 486-5 (C. White 47*, R. J. Blakey 5*); Second day, Derbyshire 128-3 (D. M. Jones 52*, J. E. Owen 2*); Third day, Derbyshire 386-4 (D. M. Jones 204*, C. M. Wells 0*).

Yorkshire

M. D. Moxon c Krikken b Cork	59	– not out	74
M. P. Vaughan c Adams b Malcolm	41	– b Malcolm	0
*D. Byas c Vandrau b Malcolm	79	– lbw b Malcolm	0
M. G. Bevan c Owen b Cork	136	– c Krikken b Aldred	26
A. McGrath c Adams b Cork	91	– not out	30
C. White c Cork b Malcolm	61		
†R. J. Blakey not out	32		
D. Gough c Jones b Wells	4		
P. J. Hartley b Wells	5		
C. E. W. Silverwood lbw b Malcolm	0		
R. D. Stemp c Owen b Aldred	20		
B 5, l-b 14, w 2, n-b 12	33	L-b 5, w 1, n-b 2	8
1/73 2/132 3/235 4/399 5/471 6/519 7/524 8/535 9/536	561	1/5 2/5 3/80 (3 wkts dec.)	138

Bonus points – Yorkshire 4, Derbyshire 3 (Score at 120 overs: 535-8).

Bowling: *First Innings*—Malcolm 25–5–109–4; Cork 37–7–148–3; Aldred 18.5–1–79–1; Vandrau 25–1–108–0; Wells 10–1–53–2; Barnett 8–0–45–0. *Second Innings*—Malcolm 9–0–30–2; Aldred 13–3–50–1; Wells 7–2–24–0; Vandrau 9–2–29–0.

Derbyshire

K. J. Barnett c Moxon b Silverwood	11 – c Vaughan b Stemp	51
A. S. Rollins c Byas b Silverwood	20 – run out	36
C. J. Adams c Bevan b Gough	37 – (4) c Silverwood b Gough	66
*D. M. Jones not out	214 – (5) c Blakey b White	10
J. E. Owen b White	101 – (7) c Moxon b White	6
C. M. Wells not out	12 – not out	19
†K. M. Krikken (did not bat)	– (3) run out	47
D. G. Cork (did not bat)	– b White	0
M. J. Vandrau (did not bat)	– lbw b White	0
P. Aldred (did not bat)	– not out	5
L-b 5, n-b 12	17 B 2, l-b 6	8
1/25 2/38 3/108 4/386 (4 wkts dec.)	412 1/69 2/94 3/201 4/201 5/220 6/234 7/234 8/234 (8 wkts)	248

D. E. Malcolm did not bat.

Bonus points – Derbyshire 4, Yorkshire 1.

Bowling: *First Innings*—Gough 23–2–82–1; Hartley 17–3–78–0; Silverwood 25.1–5–99–2; Stemp 15–3–50–0; White 13–2–60–1; Vaughan 7–1–38–0. *Second Innings*—Gough 12–2–51–1; Hartley 5–2–17–0; Silverwood 4–0–26–0; Stemp 11–1–42–1; Vaughan 8–1–52–0; Bevan 3–0–37–0; White 7–2–15–4.

Umpires: J. H. Hampshire and N. T. Plews.

At Chester-le-Street, May 16, 17, 18. YORKSHIRE beat DURHAM by 144 runs.

At Canterbury, May 23, 24, 25, 27. YORKSHIRE drew with KENT.

At Lord's, May 30, 31, June 1, 3. YORKSHIRE lost to MIDDLESEX by 21 runs.

YORKSHIRE v SURREY

At Middlesbrough, June 6, 7, 8, 10. Yorkshire won by 221 runs. Yorkshire 23 pts, Surrey 4 pts. Toss: Yorkshire. First-class debut: B. C. Hollioake.

Surrey surrendered the initiative on the second day when they imagined all sorts of problems in a pitch allowing some slow turn. The match belonged mainly to Vaughan, who exploited their uncertainty with his off-spin, linking with Stemp to earn a lead of 108. He had already batted with impressive authority to hold together Yorkshire's first innings in the face of some lively bowling by Ben Hollioake, the acting-captain's brother, who took four on his first-class debut. Vaughan was within nine runs of completing a century in each innings when he pulled a long hop from occasional seamer Ratcliffe to mid-wicket. But Bevan scored an unbeaten 160, his best score yet for Yorkshire. Surrey needed 496 in five sessions and Butcher, despite being dropped at first slip when six, at least prevented a second capitulation. His determination carried the contest into Monday, when Gough ended a lean spell by taking three for 17 in six very hostile overs; Surrey's last five fell in 70 minutes. Victory put Yorkshire on top of the Championship table for the first time since 1987.

Close of play: First day, Surrey 76-2 (D. J. Bicknell 37*, J. D. Ratcliffe 2*); Second day, Yorkshire 236-5 (M. G. Bevan 88*, R. J. Blakey 7*); Third day, Surrey 232-5 (A. D. Brown 31*, B. P. Julian 0*).

Yorkshire

A. McGrath c Kersey b Julian	41	– c Ward b Julian	13
M. P. Vaughan c Butcher b Benjamin	135	– c A. J. Hollioake b Ratcliffe	91
*D. Byas c A. J. Hollioake b Pearson	8	– lbw b B. C. Hollioake	5
M. G. Bevan c Bicknell b B. C. Hollioake	38	– not out	160
C. White b B. C. Hollioake	0	– c Ward b Pearson	0
†R. J. Blakey b B. C. Hollioake	3	– (7) c A. J. Hollioake b Butcher	45
A. C. Morris c Bicknell b A. J. Hollioake	21	– (8) c B. C. Hollioake b Butcher	5
D. Gough c A. J. Hollioake b Benjamin	28	– (9) c Butcher b Bicknell	16
P. J. Hartley c Kersey b B. C. Hollioake	3	– (10) c A. J. Hollioake b Butcher	5
C. E. W. Silverwood c Kersey b Benjamin	0	– (6) c and b Ratcliffe	0
R. D. Stemp not out	4	– c Kersey b Bicknell	3
L-b 4, w 2, n-b 18	24	B 4, l-b 15, w 3, n-b 22	44
1/63 2/86 3/161 4/167 5/207 6/266 7/270 8/301 9/301	305	1/36 2/41 3/211 4/219 5/222 6/326 7/334 8/359 9/378	387

Bonus points – Yorkshire 3, Surrey 4.

Bowling: *First Innings*—Julian 17–2–60–1; Benjamin 18.3–4–75–3; B. C. Hollioake 21–5–74–4; Pearson 15–3–68–1; A. J. Hollioake 6–2–24–1. *Second Innings*—Julian 9–1–44–1; B. C. Hollioake 13–1–48–1; A. J. Hollioake 7–2–25–0; Benjamin 12–2–67–0; Pearson 24–3–80–1; Bicknell 10.5–1–29–2; Ratcliffe 6–0–26–2; Butcher 11–1–49–3.

Surrey

D. J. Bicknell lbw b Vaughan	52	– c and b Vaughan	20
M. A. Butcher c Blakey b Stemp	29	– c Silverwood b Hartley	112
†G. J. Kersey c Blakey b Gough	1	– (8) lbw b Vaughan	10
J. D. Ratcliffe st Blakey b Vaughan	20	– (3) c Byas b Silverwood	26
*A. J. Hollioake lbw b Stemp	11	– (4) c Blakey b Hartley	30
A. D. Brown c Bevan b Stemp	10	– (5) lbw b Gough	31
D. M. Ward c Byas b Stemp	15	– (6) c Byas b Gough	2
B. P. Julian b Vaughan	0	– (7) c Blakey b Gough	20
B. C. Hollioake c Hartley b Vaughan	8	– b Gough	2
R. M. Pearson not out	16	– c Vaughan b Gough	8
J. E. Benjamin run out	23	– not out	2
L-b 3, w 1, n-b 8	12	L-b 1, n-b 10	11
1/59 2/66 3/104 4/115 5/133 6/133 7/134 8/148 9/156	197	1/46 2/109 3/169 4/202 5/216 6/233 7/254 8/256 9/266	274

Bonus points – Yorkshire 4.

Bowling: *First Innings*—Gough 14–4–37–1; Silverwood 6–1–30–0; Hartley 3–0–13–0; Stemp 25.5–11–44–4; Bevan 1–0–8–0; Vaughan 17–3–62–4. *Second Innings*—Gough 24–9–36–5; Hartley 12–3–34–2; Vaughan 17.3–6–39–2; Stemp 27–7–83–0; Bevan 9–2–35–0; McGrath 1–0–12–0; Silverwood 6–1–34–1.

Umpires: B. Dudleston and B. Leadbeater.

YORKSHIRE v WARWICKSHIRE

At Leeds, June 13, 14, 15, 17. Yorkshire won by ten wickets. Yorkshire 22 pts, Warwickshire 5 pts. Toss: Warwickshire.

On another easy-paced Headingley pitch, Yorkshire ground their way to victory on the final morning, ending a run of six successive defeats by Warwickshire. The visitors were rescued from ten for two by Ostler and Penney, who took a painful blow on the left arm from Gough and was then missed at silly point, but proceeded to a determined century. Yorkshire were less interested in bonus points than in building a big lead, and Moxon plodded to 131, passing 20,000 first-class runs on the way. Their caution could not prevent them from losing five wickets for 75. But Gough struck back with his first century in county cricket. Mixing sound defence with robust hitting, he collected four sixes and 11 fours. Warwickshire faced a 202-run deficit and their second innings was undone by Bevan's sharp left-arm wrist-spin; Yorkshire needed only 28 to win. Warwickshire will remember the match as Reeve's last Championship appearance before his hip injury forced him to announce his retirement.

Close of play: First day, Yorkshire 7-0 (M. D. Moxon 3*, M. P. Vaughan 4*); Second day, Yorkshire 293-4 (A. McGrath 55*, C. White 9*); Third day, Warwickshire 126-4 (D. R. Brown 20*, S. M. Pollock 23*).

Warwickshire

A. J. Moles b Gough	0	– b Hartley	7
W. G. Khan b Hartley	6	– c Moxon b Bevan	35
D. P. Ostler c and b Silverwood	85	– c Gough b Hartley	7
T. L. Penney lbw b White	125	– c McGrath b Bevan	18
D. R. Brown b Gough	32	– lbw b Bevan	31
S. M. Pollock lbw b Gough	0	– c McGrath b Stemp	34
*D. A. Reeve c Byas b Stemp	24	– lbw b Hartley	5
†K. J. Piper c Byas b Gough	6	– lbw b Stemp	14
G. Welch b White	5	– b Gough	13
N. M. K. Smith b White	9	– not out	22
A. F. Giles not out	0	– b Gough	2
B 1, l-b 11, n-b 2	14	B 13, l-b 10, n-b 18	41
1/10 2/10 3/126 4/173 5/173 6/246 7/265 8/296 9/297	306	1/13 2/33 3/75 4/82 5/144 6/161 7/163 8/196 9/212	229

Bonus points – Warwickshire 3, Yorkshire 4.

In the second innings K. J. Piper, when 6, retired hurt at 179 and resumed at 212.

Bowling: *First Innings*—Gough 23–5–66–4; Hartley 11–1–45–1; Silverwood 11–3–40–1; White 18.3–9–31–3; Stemp 23–8–65–1; Bevan 15–1–47–0. *Second Innings*—Gough 22–4–60–2; Hartley 18–5–51–3; Stemp 23.4–10–44–2; White 4–1–7–0; Bevan 10–2–36–3; Silverwood 5–2–8–0.

Yorkshire

M. D. Moxon c Moles b Brown	131	– not out	22
M. P. Vaughan b Pollock	18	– not out	6
*D. Byas b Smith	13		
M. G. Bevan c Piper b Giles	43		
A. McGrath c Welch b Smith	65		
C. White lbw b Smith	12		
†R. J. Blakey c Reeve b Smith	9		
D. Gough c and b Giles	121		
P. J. Hartley c Welch b Smith	5		
C. E. W. Silverwood c Smith b Brown	37		
R. D. Stemp not out	27		
B 7, l-b 9, w 1, n-b 10	27		
1/35 2/58 3/159 4/271 5/297 6/309 7/324 8/346 9/418	508	(no wkt)	28

Bonus points – Yorkshire 2, Warwickshire 2 (Score at 120 overs: 297-5).

Bowling: *First Innings*—Pollock 29–9–89–1; Brown 23–6–47–2; Welch 7–0–38–0; Reeve 4–1–17–0; Smith 49–11–127–5; Giles 68.3–17–174–2. *Second Innings*—Giles 2–0–12–0; Smith 2–0–15–0; Khan 0.1–0–1–0.

Umpires: D. J. Constant and A. G. T. Whitehead.

YORKSHIRE v LEICESTERSHIRE

At Bradford, June 20, 21, 22, 24. Leicestershire won by an innings and 151 runs. Leicestershire 24 pts, Yorkshire 4 pts. Toss: Leicestershire.

Yorkshire appeared to lose heart on having to field first on a batsman's pitch. Collectively, they bowled much too short and dropped seven catches as Leicestershire reached 681, the highest score ever conceded by Yorkshire. Wells reached a maiden double-hundred with 33 fours and two sixes in 301 balls, after being badly missed at short cover when 24; Whitaker, who had had only two hours' sleep because his hotel was so noisy, recorded a career-best 218, with two sixes and 26 fours in 324 balls and six hours. It was his fifth century against his native county, surpassing Bill Athey's record as a Yorkshire exile. His 218 was also believed to be the highest score by a Yorkshireman against Yorkshire, beating the 203 by Geoff Cook for Northamptonshire in 1988.

HIGHEST TOTALS AGAINST YORKSHIRE

681-7 dec.	**by Leicestershire at Bradford**	**1996**
630	by Somerset at Leeds	1901
592	by Somerset at Taunton	1892
592	by Jamaica at Kingston	1935-36
574	by Gloucestershire at Cheltenham	1990
566	by Sussex at Sheffield	1937
560-5 dec.	by Sussex at Hove	1901
560-6 dec.	by Surrey at The Oval	1933

Undoubtedly, there was increasing assistance for the bowlers when Yorkshire batted, but Millns and Parsons, in particular, operated with greater enthusiasm than any home bowler. Bevan, inevitably, provided some backbone and, when he passed 49 in the second innings, he became the first batsman to 1,000 runs for the summer in his 15th innings. But Leicestershire never relaxed their grip. Parsons took three for none in 32 balls to earn victory before lunch on the fourth day.

Close of play: First day, Leicestershire 461-4 (J. J. Whitaker 119*, A. R. K. Pierson 1*); Second day, Yorkshire 143-4 (M. G. Bevan 52*, C. White 15*); Third day, Yorkshire 160-5 (M. G. Bevan 45*, C. White 4*).

Leicestershire

V. J. Wells c Blakey b Gough	200
D. L. Maddy c Byas b Silverwood	18
B. F. Smith c Byas b Silverwood	23
P. V. Simmons c McGrath b Hartley	69
*J. J. Whitaker c White b Stemp	218
A. R. K. Pierson c Blakey b White	14
A. Habib c Vaughan b Stemp	17
†P. A. Nixon not out	77
G. J. Parsons not out	0
B 10, l-b 15, n-b 20	45
1/50 2/76 3/229 4/447 5/503 6/547 7/673 (7 wkts dec.)	681

D. J. Millns and M. T. Brimson did not bat.

Bonus points – Leicestershire 4, Yorkshire 1 (Score at 120 overs: 501-4).

Bowling: Gough 26–5–96–1; Hartley 27–4–113–1; Silverwood 25–4–110–2; White 26–2–111–1; Stemp 43–12–123–2; Bevan 2–0–15–0; Vaughan 23–2–88–0.

Yorkshire

M. D. Moxon b Parsons	0	lbw b Millns	18
M. P. Vaughan lbw b Parsons	0	b Pierson	54
*D. Byas c Parsons b Millns	42	c Simmons b Millns	0
M. G. Bevan c Pierson b Millns	82	not out	65
A. McGrath c Nixon b Wells	24	b Pierson	32
C. White c Pierson b Parsons	15	(7) c Nixon b Parsons	5
†R. J. Blakey c Pierson b Parsons	4	(8) c Wells b Parsons	0
D. Gough c Smith b Brimson	50	(9) lbw b Parsons	0
P. J. Hartley c Simmons b Brimson	3	(10) b Millns	4
C. E. W. Silverwood c Parsons b Brimson	44	(6) c Maddy b Brimson	0
R. D. Stemp not out	51	b Millns	0
B 4, l-b 3, n-b 20	27	B 3, l-b 2, w 3, n-b 2	10
1/0 2/15 3/61 4/117 5/150 6/154 7/229 8/234 9/263	342	1/45 2/47 3/79 4/149 5/152 6/162 7/168 8/172 9/188	188

Bonus points – Yorkshire 3, Leicestershire 4.

Bowling: *First Innings*—Millns 20–4–95–2; Parsons 21–7–83–4; Wells 16–9–27–1; Simmons 15–2–73–0; Brimson 14.3–2–57–3. *Second Innings*—Millns 20–4–67–4; Parsons 21–13–40–3; Pierson 18–6–30–2; Wells 8–2–26–0; Brimson 4–0–20–1.

Umpires: B. J. Meyer and K. E. Palmer.

At Worcester, June 27, 28, 29, July 1. YORKSHIRE beat WORCESTERSHIRE by 111 runs.

At Leeds, July 3, 4, 5. YORKSHIRE drew with SOUTH AFRICA A (See South Africa A tour section).

YORKSHIRE v HAMPSHIRE

At Harrogate, July 18, 19, 20. Yorkshire won by ten wickets. Yorkshire 24 pts, Hampshire 6 pts. Toss: Hampshire.

The contest turned on a forceful partnership of 272 between Byas and McGrath – the highest for Yorkshire's fourth wicket since 1921. They took command on a good cricket wicket which offered pace and bounce for seamers operating to a full length. But Hampshire's bowlers lost any sense of purpose as McGrath completed his century with a straight six off Udal, matching his captain stride for stride. Although Bovill's late flourish with the new ball saw the last seven wickets tumble for 34 in nine overs, Yorkshire's lead of 161 proved decisive. Hampshire's batting was also fallible. Keech, their most resolute batsman, twice ran himself out by rashly challenging the fielder at deep square leg. James was the only other batsman to reach 50 although Smith, after dashing to London when summoned to give evidence in the High Court case involving Botham, Lamb and Imran, hit nine boundaries in a brisk 44. Vaughan hurried to victory late on the third day. The win put Yorkshire 15 points clear at the head of the table.

Close of play: First day, Yorkshire 76-0 (M. D. Moxon 34*, M. P. Vaughan 39*); Second day, Hampshire 19-0 (J. P. Stephenson 1*, J. S. Laney 15*).

Hampshire

*J. P. Stephenson b Stemp	39	– c Byas b Gough	5
J. S. Laney lbw b Silverwood	5	– b Stemp	37
K. D. James c Blakey b Silverwood	71	– c Gough b Hartley	6
R. A. Smith lbw b White	0	– b Gough	44
V. P. Terry c Hartley b Silverwood	23	– c Blakey b Hartley	26
M. Keech run out	63	– run out	87
†A. N. Aymes not out	9	– c Stemp b Hartley	4
S. D. Udal b Gough	6	– b Hartley	0
S. M. Milburn c Stemp b Hartley	2	– c Byas b Silverwood	25
C. A. Connor b Hartley	0	– not out	4
J. N. B. Bovill lbw b Gough	5	– lbw b Hartley	0
B 7, l-b 9, w 9, n-b 18	43	B 4, l-b 2, w 3, n-b 2	11
1/22 2/75 3/76 4/118 5/228 6/241 7/253 8/258 9/259	266	1/29 2/51 3/59 4/102 5/185 6/193 7/195 8/244 9/249	249

Bonus points – Hampshire 2, Yorkshire 4.

Bowling: *First Innings*—Gough 20.3–8–50–2; Hartley 19–4–66–2; Silverwood 20–3–62–3; Stemp 11–4–27–1; White 10–2–20–1; Bevan 9–0–25–0. *Second Innings*—Gough 18–5–39–2; Silverwood 11–3–36–1; Hartley 19.5–5–57–5; Stemp 12–5–21–1; White 8–1–41–0; Bevan 4–0–16–0; Vaughan 9–1–33–0.

Yorkshire

M. D. Moxon b Connor	38	– not out	26
M. P. Vaughan c sub b Bovill	49	– not out	61
*D. Byas lbw b Bovill	138		
M. G. Bevan lbw b Stephenson	18		
A. McGrath lbw b Bovill	137		
C. White c Terry b Connor	5		
†R. J. Blakey c James b Bovill	2		
D. Gough b Connor	0		
P. J. Hartley b Bovill	1		
C. E. W. Silverwood b Connor	14		
R. D. Stemp not out	0		
B 7, l-b 7, w 1, n-b 10	25	L-b 2	2
1/91 2/93 3/121 4/393 5/402 6/408 7/410 8/411 9/420	427		(no wkt) 89

Bonus points – Yorkshire 4, Hampshire 4.

Bowling: *First Innings*—Connor 23.5–4–97–4; Milburn 9–0–56–0; James 16–2–67–0; Udal 26–8–77–0; Bovill 17–4–58–5; Stephenson 18–3–58–1. *Second Innings*—Connor 5–0–33–0; Bovill 8.3–2–27–0; Udal 7–1–27–0.

Umpires: H. D. Bird and J. H. Harris.

YORKSHIRE v SOMERSET

At Scarborough, July 24, 25, 26, 27. Somerset won by 197 runs. Somerset 23 pts, Yorkshire 6 pts. Toss: Yorkshire.

For the first time since 1981, 40 wickets fell in a Championship match at North Marine Road, suggesting the attempts to create a more even contest between bat and ball had succeeded. Unfortunately for Yorkshire, it was Somerset who took most advantage. Despite falling 17 behind on first innings, Yorkshire appeared to be taking control as Somerset then subsided to 121 for five. But Lee counter-attacked, hitting 134 in 113 minutes and 109 balls. The Yorkshire bowlers, Gough in particular, bowled much too short and Somerset were able to leave a target of 413. Shine, who had been withdrawn in the first innings after five overs cost him 37, now claimed three for four in seven balls. Nevertheless, Caddick stood out as Somerset's most accomplished bowler; his figures did no justice to the number of times he beat the hesitant defensive push. Hartley's unbeaten fifty from 47 deliveries just pushed the game into a fourth day.

Close of play: First day, Yorkshire 0-0 (M. D. Moxon 0*, M. P. Vaughan 0*); Second day, Somerset 69-3 (M. N. Lathwell 37*, J. D. Batty 5*); Third day, Yorkshire 160-7 (D. Gough 42*, P. J. Hartley 26*).

Somerset

M. N. Lathwell lbw b Hartley	43	– c Byas b Hartley	80
P. D. Bowler lbw b Hartley	30	– lbw b Gough	6
K. A. Parsons c McGrath b Gough	62	– b Hartley	4
R. J. Harden c Byas b Silverwood	54	– c Blakey b Gough	8
*A. N. Hayhurst lbw b Gough	0	– (6) lbw b White	2
S. Lee c McGrath b Silverwood	22	– (7) c White b Stemp	134
†R. J. Turner lbw b Silverwood	13	– (8) c White b Bevan	42
G. D. Rose not out	34	– (9) c White b Silverwood	29
J. D. Batty lbw b Silverwood	4	– (5) b Hartley	26
A. R. Caddick b Gough	0	– c White b Silverwood	23
K. J. Shine c McGrath b Hartley	7	– not out	3
B 4, l-b 6, n-b 30	40	B 12, l-b 12, n-b 14	38
1/86 2/91 3/213 4/217 5/238 6/247 7/264 8/276 9/298	309	1/23 2/29 3/62 4/106 5/121 6/201 7/296 8/347 9/383	395

Bonus points – Somerset 3, Yorkshire 4.

Bowling: *First Innings*—Gough 21–3–74–3; Silverwood 21–5–53–4; White 13–1–52–0; Hartley 19.4–7–66–3; Stemp 7–2–24–0; Vaughan 3–0–7–0; Bevan 5–0–23–0. *Second Innings*—Gough 25–6–71–2; Silverwood 20–6–77–2; Hartley 26–3–100–3; White 7–0–44–1; Stemp 11–0–50–1; Bevan 6.3–0–29–1.

Yorkshire

M. D. Moxon hit wkt b Shine	24	– c Lathwell b Rose	7
M. P. Vaughan c Turner b Rose	8	– c Turner b Caddick	12
*D. Byas b Caddick	88	– c Turner b Shine	4
M. G. Bevan c Rose b Batty	19	– c Lee b Caddick	29
A. McGrath c Lee b Batty	0	– c Lee b Shine	0
C. White c Turner b Lee	28	– c Turner b Shine	1
†R. J. Blakey c Turner b Caddick	21	– b Lee	25
D. Gough c Rose b Shine	51	– c Turner b Shine	47
P. J. Hartley b Rose	10	– not out	57
C. E. W. Silverwood c Turner b Shine	15	– c Lathwell b Caddick	7
R. D. Stemp not out	0	– c Turner b Shine	2
L-b 1, w 6, n-b 21	28	B 6, l-b 5, w 1, n-b 12	24
1/8 2/58 3/87 4/87 5/144 6/200 7/215 8/244 9/292	292	1/17 2/31 3/33 4/33 5/46 6/84 7/106 8/175 9/196	215

Bonus points – Yorkshire 2, Somerset 4.

Bowling: *First Innings*—Caddick 24–5–81–2; Rose 15–5–53–2; Shine 7.3–1–55–3; Lee 17–4–49–1; Batty 15–2–53–2. *Second Innings*—Caddick 19–3–72–3; Rose 6–0–29–1; Shine 11–1–48–5; Lee 7–0–54–1; Batty 1–0–1–0.

Umpires: G. Sharp and R. A. White.

At Eastbourne, August 1, 2, 3. YORKSHIRE lost to SUSSEX by two wickets.

At Bristol, August 15, 16. YORKSHIRE lost to GLOUCESTERSHIRE by ten wickets.

YORKSHIRE v LANCASHIRE

At Leeds, August 22, 23, 24, 26. Drawn. Yorkshire 11 pts, Lancashire 8 pts. Toss: Yorkshire.

Yorkshire dominated the Roses match but rain, which allowed only 13 overs on the final day, denied them the chance to regain some momentum after three successive defeats. Their rivals, strangely subdued throughout, were only 25 ahead with three wickets standing when play was abandoned. Earlier, White had punished some wayward bowling to reach a career-best 181, driving fluently off both the back and front foot. His partnership of 252 with Blakey, who completed his first century for four years, was Yorkshire's second-best for the sixth wicket. Fairbrother, missed on nine and 80, chanced his arm to great effect during Lancashire's hectic reply, which ended abruptly as Gough claimed three for one in 17 balls. Following on, Lancashire continued to bat casually, although Speak showed some signs of permanence. Gough continued to cause problems with his in-swinging yorker, before the weather closed in. Right at the end, he was denied a hat-trick by Green, who had already kept out Vaughan's hat-trick ball in the first innings.

Close of play: First day, Yorkshire 305-5 (C. White 66*, R. J. Blakey 10*); Second day, Lancashire 162-4 (N. H. Fairbrother 53*, G. Chapple 2*); Third day, Lancashire 210-5 (N. J. Speak 65*, W. K. Hegg 16*).

Yorkshire

M. D. Moxon c Lloyd b Keedy	66	P. J. Hartley c Hegg b Watkinson	1
M. P. Vaughan c Hegg b Keedy	57	C. E. W. Silverwood not out	1
*D. Byas c Watkinson b Green	45		
A. McGrath lbw b Green	15	B 7, l-b 5, n-b 8	20
R. A. Kettleborough b Gallian	34		
C. White b Watkinson	181	1/110 2/131 3/182 (8 wkts dec.)	529
†R. J. Blakey not out	109	4/187 5/273 6/525	
D. Gough c Hegg b Martin	0	7/526 8/527	

R. D. Stemp did not bat.

Bonus points – Yorkshire 4, Lancashire 2 (Score at 120 overs: 397-5).

Bowling: Martin 26–6–98–1; Chapple 16–2–81–0; Green 27–5–88–2; Keedy 44–10–122–2; Watkinson 19–4–73–2; Gallian 13–2–55–1.

Lancashire

J. E. R. Gallian c Kettleborough b White	27 – (2) c McGrath b Silverwood	12
S. P. Titchard b Silverwood	9 – (1) lbw b Hartley	18
N. J. Speak c Blakey b Gough	4 – b Gough	77
N. H. Fairbrother b Stemp	86 – c McGrath b Vaughan	55
G. D. Lloyd c White b Stemp	36 – lbw b Gough	19
G. Chapple c Stemp b Vaughan	23 – (8) b Gough	0
*M. Watkinson lbw b Gough	64 – (6) lbw b Gough	6
†W. K. Hegg c Byas b Vaughan	0 – (7) not out	24
R. J. Green b Gough	6 – not out	1
P. J. Martin not out	19	
G. Keedy b Gough	0	
B 4, l-b 19, n-b 26	49 B 4, l-b 1, n-b 14	19
1/26 2/41 3/74 4/147 5/208 6/259 7/259 8/298 9/303	323 1/14 2/48 3/127 4/155 5/167 6/230 7/230 (7 wkts)	231

Bonus points – Lancashire 3, Yorkshire 4.

Bowling: *First Innings*—Gough 21.3–6–53–4; Silverwood 8–1–33–1; Hartley 8–1–52–0; White 5–0–32–1; Stemp 26–10–85–2; Vaughan 9–3–45–2. *Second Innings*—Gough 19–3–48–4; Silverwood 13–4–37–1; Hartley 15–5–40–1; White 5–2–14–0; Stemp 14–3–50–0; Vaughan 10–1–37–1.

Umpires: J. H. Harris and V. A. Holder.

YORKSHIRE v ESSEX

At Leeds, August 29, 30, 31, September 2. Yorkshire won by 98 runs. Yorkshire 22 pts, Essex 8 pts. Toss: Yorkshire.

Essex, heading for a sixth successive victory and top place in the Championship, saw all their hopes crumble away on a dramatic Saturday, when a maiden century by Kettleborough transformed the game. His team were only nine ahead when they lost their fifth second-innings wicket. But Kettleborough first frustrated Essex and then destroyed their confidence. He batted for six hours and 20 minutes, showing admirable temperament as he shared in two crucial partnerships – 102 with Blakey and 93 with Hamilton, making his first Championship appearance of the season. Although Such had impressive figures, eight for 118, he did not make enough of some sharp turn in the later stages; Stemp did rather better, achieving his best Championship figures for two years to dismiss Essex as they chased 248. On the first day, Yorkshire had failed to make the most of reasonable batting conditions. Then Hussain put Essex very much on top. He was badly missed by Stemp when he lofted Vaughan to deep mid-off on 98, but otherwise exerted easy control on his way to 158. Byas, Yorkshire's captain, said he had never seen the team produce a better rearguard action; Headingley may not have seen a more startling turnaround since the ground's most famous game of all 15 years earlier.

Close of play: First day, Essex 79-2 (N. Hussain 35*, P. J. Prichard 13*); Second day, Yorkshire 119-5 (R. A. Kettleborough 35*, R. J. Blakey 10*); Third day, Essex 100-5 (S. D. Peters 3*, P. M. Such 0*).

Yorkshire

M. D. Moxon c Hussain b Williams	59	– b Such	23
M. P. Vaughan c Gooch b Williams	3	– lbw b Such	10
*D. Byas c Hussain b Gooch	23	– c Grayson b Such	4
A. McGrath c Lewis b Such	16	– c Lewis b Such	18
R. A. Kettleborough b Williams	28	– lbw b Such	108
C. White c Rollins b Grayson	76	– b Grayson	10
†R. J. Blakey c Grayson b Ilott	57	– c Rollins b Ilott	44
P. J. Hartley c Prichard b Grayson	2	– c Lewis b Such	20
G. M. Hamilton not out	9	– b Such	61
C. E. W. Silverwood c Rollins b Ilott	0	– c Lewis b Such	1
R. D. Stemp c Lewis b Ilott	0	– not out	1
B 4, l-b 9, n-b 4	17	B 7, l-b 16, n-b 6	29
1/4 2/51 3/99 4/127 5/141 6/256 7/264 8/286 9/286	290	1/18 2/26 3/43 4/66 5/91 6/193 7/224 8/317 9/326	329

Bonus points – Yorkshire 2, Essex 4.

Bowling: *First Innings*—Ilott 15.1–0–63–3; Williams 15–3–52–3; Cowan 13–1–74–0; Gooch 13–5–20–1; Such 19–6–47–1; Grayson 9–4–21–2. *Second Innings*—Ilott 13–3–43–1; Williams 19–2–44–0; Such 46.2–7–118–8; Cowan 11–1–39–0; Grayson 22–1–62–1.

Essex

G. A. Gooch c Blakey b Hartley	15	– b White	30
A. P. Grayson c Byas b Silverwood	9	– b Hartley	15
N. Hussain b White	158	– c Silverwood b Vaughan	38
*P. J. Prichard b White	71	– c Kettleborough b Stemp	2
J. J. B. Lewis lbw b Hamilton	33	– run out	2
S. D. Peters c Blakey b Vaughan	0	– lbw b Stemp	11
†R. J. Rollins c Byas b Stemp	18	– (8) c White b Vaughan	23
M. C. Ilott c Blakey b Hamilton	26	– (9) lbw b Stemp	6
N. F. Williams c White b Hamilton	15	– (10) c Hamilton b Stemp	1
A. P. Cowan b White	0	– (11) not out	0
P. M. Such not out	0	– (7) c Byas b Stemp	0
B 8, l-b 5, n-b 14	27	B 9, l-b 4, n-b 8	21
1/19 2/54 3/189 4/257 5/264 6/300 7/342 8/367 9/372	372	1/39 2/74 3/81 4/84 5/98 6/100 7/131 8/143 9/146	149

Bonus points – Essex 4, Yorkshire 4.

Bowling: *First Innings*—Silverwood 12–1–60–1; Hamilton 19.4–1–65–3; Hartley 19–2–73–1; White 15–0–45–3; Stemp 13–1–60–1; Vaughan 8–0–56–1. *Second Innings*—Silverwood 5–0–17–0; Hamilton 6–0–14–0; Hartley 8–1–20–1; Stemp 24–7–38–5; White 9–0–33–1; Vaughan 8–1–14–2.

Umpires: J. C. Balderstone and K. J. Lyons.

YORKSHIRE v NOTTINGHAMSHIRE

At Scarborough, September 12, 13. Yorkshire won by an innings and six runs. Yorkshire 23 pts, Nottinghamshire 4 pts. Toss: Yorkshire. First-class debut: J. P. Hart.

Yorkshire completed their first two-day victory since four-day Championship cricket was introduced in 1988, against a visiting side totally lacking in commitment. There was nothing in the easy-paced pitch to account for Nottinghamshire's miserable aggregate of 304; their wickets fell to a series of casual strokes. Only Dowman threatened prolonged occupation on the first day, but he took a nasty blow on the inside of his knee from Silverwood and departed soon afterwards. Gough, sensing the opportunity to boost his average, suddenly found an extra yard of pace in the second innings; he claimed six for 18 in 57 deliveries to finish with a match analysis of nine for 62. In between, Yorkshire's batting proved adequate rather than inspired: their last seven wickets yielded a mere 62, giving Cairns his best figures of the season.

Close of play: First day, Yorkshire 163-2 (D. Byas 23*, A. McGrath 29*).

Nottinghamshire

P. R. Pollard c Blakey b Hartley	26	– b Stemp	30
R. T. Robinson lbw b Silverwood	23	– lbw b White	27
G. F. Archer c Blakey b Silverwood	0	– lbw b White	1
*P. Johnson c White b Kettleborough	16	– c White b Gough	14
M. P. Dowman c Stemp b Silverwood	44	– b Gough	0
C. L. Cairns b Kettleborough	5	– b Gough	4
†W. M. Noon c Blakey b Gough	6	– b Gough	4
R. T. Bates lbw b Hartley	11	– st Blakey b Stemp	8
J. P. Hart not out	18	– (10) not out	0
M. N. Bowen b Gough	15	– (9) b Gough	7
J. A. Afford lbw b Gough	0	– c Blakey b Gough	0
B 3, l-b 8, n-b 12	23	B 4, l-b 10, n-b 8	22
1/43 2/43 3/53 4/76 5/82 6/115 7/150 8/154 9/187	187	1/53 2/61 3/83 4/84 5/91 6/92 7/97 8/117 9/117	117

Bonus points – Yorkshire 4.

Bowling: *First Innings*—Gough 11.5–3–26–3; Silverwood 13–1–55–3; Hartley 17–3–65–2; Kettleborough 10–1–26–2; Stemp 1–0–4–0. *Second Innings*—Gough 16.3–4–36–6; Silverwood 7–1–14–0; Hartley 9–3–15–0; Stemp 16–5–23–2; White 6–1–15–2.

Yorkshire

M. D. Moxon b Cairns	42
M. P. Vaughan c Johnson b Cairns	37
*D. Byas b Bates	56
A. McGrath c Archer b Bowen	63
R. A. Kettleborough c Robinson b Afford	11
C. White c Robinson b Cairns	23
†R. J. Blakey c Noon b Cairns	15
D. Gough c and b Cairns	4
P. J. Hartley b Afford	14
C. E. W. Silverwood not out	0
R. D. Stemp b Cairns	4
B 3, l-b 6, n-b 32	41
1/96 2/113 3/209 4/248 5/248 6/285 7/289 8/306 9/306	310

Bonus points – Yorkshire 3, Nottinghamshire 4.

Bowling: Cairns 22.4–2–110–6; Bowen 17–2–66–1; Hart 18–7–51–0; Bates 12–5–33–1; Dowman 2–1–8–0; Afford 11–1–33–2.

Umpires: J. W. Holder and P. Willey.

At Northampton, September 19, 20, 21, 22. YORKSHIRE drew with NORTHAMPTONSHIRE.

WOMBWELL CRICKET LOVERS' SOCIETY AWARDS, 1996

Michael Bevan of Yorkshire was voted Cricketer of the Year by members of the Wombwell Cricket Lovers' Society. Other award-winners were: Young Cricketer of the Year – Chris Silverwood; County Captain of the Year – James Whitaker; Cricket Writer of the Year – David Foot; Cricket Commentator of the Year – Richie Benaud.

PROFESSIONALS' AWARDS, 1996

The Cricketers' Association chose Phil Simmons of Leicestershire as the winner of the Reg Hayter Award for Player of the Year in 1996. The John Arlott Award for Young Player of the Year went to Chris Silverwood of Yorkshire.

Without the
right help
David Gower
might
have ended up
in court.
Well, that's where David Gower was heading as a law
student until somebody spotted a spark of talent.
By supporting the Development of Excellence programme,
NatWest is helping to identify, coach and develop
today's bright young hopefuls, giving them the same
chance to shine. Great news for English cricket, not
so good for the opposition.
NatWest
More than just a bank
National Westminster Bank Plc.

NATWEST TROPHY, 1996

Glen Chapple

Lancashire equalled their own achievement of 1990 by winning both the year's cup finals. Not only did they win the NatWest Trophy but they also overturned years of accumulated wisdom in blistering fashion: they became the first team in 11 years to win the final batting first, and did so by bowling Essex out for just 57. After their initial delight that they had won the toss – the usual prelude to victory – and restricted Lancashire to 186, the Essex batting, on a substandard pitch, collapsed around the solid but increasingly horror-struck figure of Graham Gooch. The Lancashire fast bowler Glen Chapple finished the match with figures of six for 18.

This was an even easier victory than their initial win over Oxfordshire, and far more comfortable than the intervening games. Lancashire were drawn at home three times running, but they scraped in by just one wicket against Northamptonshire and two runs against Derbyshire. For the second time in the summer, they were then given a home semi-final against Yorkshire (to the particular delight of the beneficiary, Mike Watkinson, who had a bumper collection), which they won by a comparatively straightforward 19 runs.

Essex's prolific Australian, Stuart Law, led them into the final, scoring well against Durham, Hampshire and Surrey. But he was obliged to miss Lord's because he was on national team duty and, with Lancashire having lost interest in their South African, Steve Elworthy, it was a final without overseas players.

The non-Championship teams again made minimal impact, failing to worry most of their opponents, let alone beat them. The ease with which Durham beat Scotland suggested that the gap between even the weakest of the first-class counties and the rest was enormous.

Prize money

£42,500 for winners: LANCASHIRE.
£21,000 for runners-up: ESSEX.
£10,500 for losing semi-finalists: SURREY and YORKSHIRE.
£5,250 for losing quarter-finalists: DERBYSHIRE, HAMPSHIRE, SOMERSET and SUSSEX.

Man of the Match award winners received £1,000 in the final, £425 in the semi-finals, £375 in the quarter-finals, £325 in the second round and £250 in the first round. The prize money was increased from £95,350 in the 1995 tournament to £115,450.

FIRST ROUND

CAMBRIDGESHIRE v KENT

At March, June 25. Kent won by 93 runs. Toss: Kent.

Kent were floundering at 27 for three after 12 overs, but Llong's first one-day century provided a lifeline. Llong went on to take three wickets with his off-breaks and made one catch; he dismissed both Giles Ecclestone (brother of Somerset's Simon) and Donelan, the only Cambridgeshire players to reach double figures, after their sixth-wicket stand of 86.

Man of the Match: N. J. Llong.

Kent

T. R. Ward c Ecclestone b Akhtar 14
M. V. Fleming c Williams b Masters 4
G. R. Cowdrey c Ecclestone b Masters . . . 3
N. J. Llong not out 115
M. A. Ealham b N. Mohammed 51
C. L. Hooper c Adams b Donelan 26
M. J. Walker not out 41
B 1, l-b 4, w 14, n-b 2 21

1/13 2/26 3/27 4/131 5/179 (5 wkts, 60 overs) 275

*†S. A. Marsh, M. M. Patel, D. W. Headley and N. W. Preston did not bat.

Bowling: Masters 12–4–52–2; Akhtar 10–3–35–1; Ralfs 10–0–61–0; Ecclestone 6–1–20–0; Donelan 12–0–58–1; N. Mohammed 10–0–44–1.

Cambridgeshire

*N. T. Gadsby c Llong b Ealham 1
S. Mohammed c Marsh b Headley 0
G. W. Ecclestone c Patel b Llong 92
S. A. Kellett c Marsh b Headley 3
N. J. Adams c Fleming b Ealham 8
N. Mohammed c and b Patel 5
B. T. P. Donelan c Ealham b Llong 29
†S. L. Williams c Patel b Llong 9
A. Akhtar st Marsh b Ward 2
D. F. Ralfs c Preston b Marsh 6
K. D. Masters not out 3
L-b 6, w 14, n-b 4 24

1/3 2/3 3/8 4/19 5/45 6/131 7/153 8/169 9/179 (58.3 overs) 182

Bowling: Headley 6–0–19–2; Ealham 8–2–11–2; Preston 6–2–6–0; Patel 12–2–26–1; Hooper 12–0–47–0; Llong 9–1–36–3; Ward 5–0–28–1; Marsh 0.3–0–3–1.

Umpires: D. J. Constant and M. J. Kitchen.

CORNWALL v WARWICKSHIRE

At St Austell, June 25. Warwickshire won by 133 runs. Toss: Warwickshire.

David Angove took three early wickets as Warwickshire stumbled to 76 for four, but Penney and Brown then put together a 101-run fifth-wicket stand. Chris Lovell finished with 12–0–107–2, the most expensive analysis in the competition's history, beating the two for 106 by Dave Gallop of Oxfordshire, also against Warwickshire, in 1984.

Man of the Match: D. J. Angove.

Warwickshire

*A. J. Moles c Williams b Angove 4
N. M. K. Smith b Willcock 30
P. A. Smith c Lovell b Angove 1
D. P. Ostler b Angove 20
T. L. Penney c Willcock b Lovell 90
D. R. Brown c Lello b Kent 67
S. M. Pollock b Lovell 17
†M. Burns not out 37
G. Welch c Hands b Angove 14
M. D. Edmond run out 0
G. C. Small not out 5
B 1, l-b 10, w 11, n-b 4 26

1/4 2/21 3/59 4/76 5/177 6/227 7/268 8/294 9/294 (9 wkts, 60 overs) 311

Bowling: Angove 12–0–65–4; Lovell 12–0–107–2; Willcock 12–1–43–1; Kent 12–3–23–1; Hands 5–0–33–0; Furse 6–0–17–0; Lello 1–0–12–0.

Cornwall

S. M. Williams b N. M. K. Smith	52	J. M. Hands lbw b Small	0
G. M. Thomas b Welch	44	†A. M. Snell not out	10
R. C. Driver run out	0	D. J. Angove c Brown b Small	6
C. P. Lello c sub b Edmond	20	L-b 3, w 1, n-b 12	16
J. P. Kent c Ostler b N. M. K. Smith	3		
K. J. Willcock c Ostler b P. A. Smith	25	1/72 2/77 3/113 (50.5 overs)	178
*G. R. Furse c Ostler b N. M. K. Smith	1	4/126 5/157 6/159	
C. C. Lovell lbw b P. A. Smith	1	7/159 8/160 9/162	

Bowling: Pollock 5–0–25–0; Small 8.5–1–26–2; Brown 7–1–19–0; Welch 5–2–11–1; N. M. K. Smith 12–3–40–3; Edmond 8–1–24–1; P. A. Smith 5–0–30–2.

Umpires: R. Dennis and R. Palmer.

CUMBERLAND v MIDDLESEX

At Carlisle, June 25. Middlesex won by 102 runs. Toss: Cumberland.

Cumberland's hero was opening bowler Mike Scothern, who returned the excellent figures of 11–4–29–3. Two of his wickets came at the end of the Middlesex innings, as they slumped from 235 for four to 270 for eight. But the part-timers were no match for Middlesex's powerful bowling attack. Gatting's match award was his seventh in this tournament.

Man of the Match: M. W. Gatting.

Middlesex

P. N. Weekes b Scothern	2	R. L. Johnson lbw b Scothern	1
M. R. Ramprakash c Knox b Fielding	30	A. R. C. Fraser c Ingham b Scothern	16
*M. W. Gatting b Wilson	71	B 4, l-b 7, w 7, n-b 11	29
J. C. Pooley c Pearson b Beech	36		
J. D. Carr c Dutton b O'Shaughnessy	62	1/3 2/110 3/110 (8 wkts, 60 overs)	270
†K. R. Brown b O'Shaughnessy	14	4/198 5/235 6/246	
P. E. Wellings not out	9	7/247 8/270	

R. A. Fay and P. C. R. Tufnell did not bat.

Bowling: Sharp 8–3–22–0; Scothern 11–4–29–3; O'Shaughnessy 11–1–74–2; Beech 11–0–60–1; Fielding 11–3–52–1; Wilson 8–2–22–1.

Cumberland

A. D. Mawson c Tufnell b Fay	41	A. G. Wilson c Fay b Weekes	10
D. J. Pearson c Carr b Fraser	1	M. G. Scothern c Pooley b Weekes	0
M. J. Ingham c Carr b Johnson	13	M. A. Sharp not out	3
S. T. Knox st Brown b Wellings	8	L-b 9, w 12, n-b 24	45
S. J. O'Shaughnessy c Brown b Tufnell	0		
*†S. M. Dutton c Carr b Tufnell	4	1/5 2/39 3/80 (49.5 overs)	168
P. Beech b Weekes	42	4/81 5/97 6/124	
J. M. Fielding lbw b Fay	1	7/138 8/158 9/163	

Bowling: Fraser 3–1–8–1; Fay 12–0–43–2; Johnson 8–1–29–1; Tufnell 12–3–22–2; Wellings 6–1–20–1; Weekes 7.5–0–35–3; Ramprakash 1–0–2–0.

Umpires: V. A. Holder and G. Sharp.

DURHAM v SCOTLAND

At Chester-le-Street, June 25. Durham won by 98 runs. Toss: Scotland.

Morris survived a dropped catch on 41 to reach his century – one of only two he scored in 1996, both in limited-overs games. Scotland's Barbadian professional, George Reifer, replied in kind, but the loss of three early wickets put the Scots well behind the required run-rate.

Man of the Match: J. E. Morris.

Durham

S. L. Campbell b Reifer	27
S. Hutton b Cowan	13
*J. E. Morris c Tennant b Thomson	109
D. A. Blenkiron c Davies b Cowan	25
P. Bainbridge b Williamson	21
P. D. Collingwood c Smith b Blain	26
S. J. E. Brown c and b Blain	1
†D. G. C. Ligertwood not out	30
M. M. Betts not out	1
L-b 6, w 29, n-b 12	47
1/45 2/103 3/163 4/215 5/245 6/250 7/289 (7 wkts, 60 overs)	300

N. Killeen and J. Boiling did not bat.

Bowling: Thomson 11–1–55–1; Blain 11–0–56–2; Cowan 9–1–52–2; Williamson 11–1–51–1; Reifer 11–0–53–1; Tennant 6–0–23–0; Smith 1–0–4–0.

Scotland

B. M. W. Patterson c Campbell b Betts	1
I. L. Philip c Ligertwood b Brown	7
G. N. Reifer not out	103
M. J. Smith c Killeen b Bainbridge	14
*G. Salmond c Boiling b Betts	52
J. G. Williamson b Betts	0
†A. G. Davies c Brown b Killeen	3
D. Cowan not out	0
B 2, l-b 5, w 9, n-b 6	22
1/5 2/11 3/37 4/122 5/128 6/160 (6 wkts, 60 overs)	202

J. A. R. Blain, A. M. Tennant and K. Thomson did not bat.

Bowling: Brown 7–2–19–1; Betts 12–4–33–3; Bainbridge 12–3–21–1; Killeen 12–0–46–1; Boiling 12–4–28–0; Blenkiron 4–0–31–0; Campbell 1–0–17–0.

Umpires: M. A. Johnson and K. E. Palmer.

ESSEX v DEVON

At Chelmsford, June 25. Essex won by 119 runs. Toss: Essex.

Both sides fielded well; Andy Pugh held fine catches at cover to dismiss Gooch, Law and Irani, three of Essex's most dangerous hitters. But Hussain remained, to score a century. Devon began well, with an opening stand of 66, but then lost three wickets to run-outs – all direct hits from long range – and two of their players could not bat after injuries in the field.

Man of the Match: N. Hussain.

Essex

G. A. Gooch c Pugh b Horrell	50
D. D. J. Robinson c Townsend b Rhodes	6
N. Hussain c Roebuck b Donohue	105
S. G. Law c Pugh b Donohue	31
R. C. Irani c Pugh b Donohue	50
*P. J. Prichard not out	31
†R. J. Rollins not out	1
B 1, l-b 11, w 16, n-b 10	38
1/23 2/117 3/179 4/272 5/283 (5 wkts, 60 overs)	312

A. P. Grayson, A. P. Cowan, M. C. Ilott and P. M. Such did not bat.

Bowling: Donohue 12–1–41–3; Rhodes 11–0–64–1; Le Fleming 7–0–58–0; Roebuck 12–0–53–0; Horrell 7–0–37–1; Cottam 11–0–47–0.

Devon

H. J. Morgan run out	34	R. Horrell not out	25
†C. M. W. Read run out	37	A. C. Cottam absent hurt	
N. A. Folland c Robinson b Law	64	J. Rhodes absent hurt	
G. T. J. Townsend run out	10	B 1, l-b 9, w 3, n-b 2	15
*P. M. Roebuck b Cowan	0		—
A. J. Pugh lbw b Such	8	1/66 2/85 3/116 (46.3 overs)	193
A. O. F. Le Fleming b Such	0	4/119 5/148 6/148	
K. Donohue b Law	0	7/152 8/193	

Bowling: Ilott 6–1–19–0; Cowan 8–1–44–1; Irani 7–0–17–0; Grayson 7–0–19–0; Such 12–0–48–2; Law 6.3–0–36–2.

Umpires: A. A. Jones and M. K. Reed.

GLAMORGAN v WORCESTERSHIRE

At Cardiff, June 25. Worcestershire won by 43 runs. Toss: Worcestershire. County debut: S. W. K. Ellis.

The first half of Worcestershire's innings was most unprofitable, taking them to 76 for four in the 31st over. Parkin had claimed three of those and finished with figures of 12–1–23–3. But Moody wrested the initiative back with 123 in 129 balls, and two early run-outs stymied Glamorgan's reply.

Man of the Match: T. M. Moody.

Worcestershire

T. S. Curtis c Cottey b Parkin	12	R. K. Illingworth run out	2
W. P. C. Weston c and b Parkin	6	P. J. Newport not out	4
G. A. Hick c Dale b Parkin	13	S. W. K. Ellis not out	0
*T. M. Moody c Cottey b Butcher	123	L-b 4, w 2	6
K. R. Spiring c Metson b Croft	16		—
V. S. Solanki c Parkin b Watkin	50	1/16 2/28 3/35 (9 wkts, 60 overs)	253
S. R. Lampitt c Cottey b Watkin	13	4/76 5/182 6/217	
†S. J. Rhodes c Croft b Dale	8	7/232 8/248 9/250	

Bowling: Watkin 12–3–46–2; Parkin 12–1–23–3; Croft 12–1–33–1; Barwick 12–0–63–0; Dale 6–0–34–1; Butcher 6–1–50–1.

Glamorgan

S. P. James run out	28	S. L. Watkin b Ellis	13
H. Morris c Rhodes b Illingworth	32	S. R. Barwick c sub b Ellis	1
A. Dale c Moody b Hick	40	O. T. Parkin not out	1
*M. P. Maynard c Hick b Lampitt	4	L-b 6, w 10	16
P. A. Cottey run out	17		—
G. P. Butcher st Rhodes b Hick	48	1/53 2/68 3/75 (57 overs)	210
R. D. B. Croft b Lampitt	9	4/111 5/153 6/182	
†C. P. Metson b Lampitt	1	7/184 8/203 9/209	

Bowling: Moody 12–1–34–0; Newport 8–0–36–0; Lampitt 11–1–35–3; Illingworth 10–2–28–1; Ellis 7–0–34–2; Hick 9–0–37–2.

Umpires: J. D. Bond and B. Leadbeater.

HAMPSHIRE v NORFOLK

At Southampton, June 25. Hampshire won by 99 runs. Toss: Hampshire.

Stephenson and Laney, who scored a century before lunch, compiled 269, the highest first-wicket partnership in the competition's history, surpassing Durham's 255 against Herefordshire a year earlier. Laney was making his NatWest debut. Eleven men of Norfolk failed to match their stand.

Man of the Match: J. S. Laney.

Hampshire

*J. P. Stephenson b Goldsmith 107	P. R. Whitaker not out 0
J. S. Laney run out 153	
R. A. Smith c and b Goldsmith 23	L-b 6, w 15, n-b 4............ 25
W. K. M. Benjamin c Boon b Goldsmith . 8	—
V. P. Terry c Goldsmith b Boon 5	1/269 2/285 3/305 (6 wkts, 60 overs) 322
S. D. Udal b Goldsmith................ 1	4/315 5/319 6/322

†A. N. Aymes, K. D. James, M. J. Thursfield and C. A. Connor did not bat.

Bowling: Newman 10–1–36–0; Saggers 10–1–56–0; Goldsmith 12–2–64–4; M. W. Thomas 6–0–39–0; Powell 8–0–43–0; D. R. Thomas 3–0–15–0; Boon 11–0–63–1.

Norfolk

T. J. Boon c Terry b Thursfield 8	M. W. Thomas b Connor 0
C. J. Rogers c Benjamin b Connor....... 0	M. J. Saggers run out 0
S. C. Goldsmith b James................ 43	†S. C. Crowley lbw b Connor 2
D. R. Thomas lbw b Udal.............. 41	L-b 8, w 12 20
M. J. P. Ward lbw b Stephenson 0	—
N. Fox b James 68	1/2 2/18 3/70 (54.4 overs) 223
M. G. Powell c and b James............ 37	4/78 5/116 6/215
*P. G. Newman not out................ 4	7/216 8/217 9/219

Bowling: Stephenson 7–0–27–1; Thursfield 10–2–34–1; Connor 11.4–2–39–3; James 12–1–46–3; Udal 9–1–35–1; Whitaker 5–1–34–0.

Umpires: J. H. Harris and P. Willey (A. R. Bundy deputised for J. H. Harris).

IRELAND v SUSSEX

At Belfast, June 25, 26. Sussex won by 304 runs. Toss: Ireland.

Rain stopped play on the first day with Sussex 323 for seven, thanks to a century from Wells; next morning, they added 61 in the final five overs to reach their highest limited-overs total. Then Jarvis and Giddins shot out Ireland for 80 to complete the second-biggest victory in the tournament's history.

Man of the Match: A. P. Wells.

Close of play: Sussex 323-7 (55 overs) (I. D. K. Salisbury 14*, V. C. Drakes 0*).

Sussex

C. W. J. Athey c and b Benson 57	V. C. Drakes not out.................. 30
K. Greenfield c Rutherford b Heasley 32	P. W. Jarvis c sub b Heasley 2
*A. P. Wells c Moore b Heasley 113	E. S. H. Giddins not out.............. 10
M. P. Speight c Harrison b McCrum 41	L-b 7, w 13, n-b 10........... 30
N. J. Lenham c Rutherford b McCrum ... 11	—
D. R. Law c Dunlop b Heasley 18	1/96 2/151 3/219 (9 wkts, 60 overs) 384
†P. Moores b M. W. Patterson 7	4/243 5/297 6/307
I. D. K. Salisbury c sub b Eagleson...... 33	7/311 8/353 9/359

Bowling: M. W. Patterson 11–1–88–1; Eagleson 11–0–74–1; McCrum 12–0–61–2; Heasley 11–0–66–4; Harrison 12–0–68–0; Benson 3–0–20–1.

Ireland

*J. D. R. Benson c Greenfield b Jarvis ... 0	R. L. Eagleson not out 15
W. K. McCallan lbw b Drakes 17	M. W. Patterson c Moores b Giddins..... 2
A. D. Patterson lbw b Jarvis 2	P. McCrum c sub b Law.............. 1
A. R. Dunlop b Jarvis 0	B 2, l-b 2, w 5, n-b 10 19
D. M. P. Moore b Giddins 5	—
D. Heasley c Speight b Drakes.......... 5	1/0 2/14 3/16 (33.3 overs) 80
†A. T. Rutherford b Giddins............ 2	4/26 5/38 6/39
G. D. Harrison c Jarvis b Salisbury 12	7/49 8/56 9/72

Bowling: Jarvis 8–1–22–3; Drakes 10–1–19–2; Giddins 9–1–24–3; Salisbury 5–1–9–1; Law 1.3–0–2–1.

Umpires: J. W. Lloyds and N. T. Plews.

LEICESTERSHIRE v BERKSHIRE

At Leicester, June 25. Leicestershire won by 106 runs. Toss: Leicestershire.

Wells's second double-century in six days was only the second scored in the competition's 34 years, following Alvin Kallicharran's 206 for Warwickshire against Oxfordshire in 1984. It helped Leicestershire to 406 for five, the second-highest total in the tournament. But Berkshire responded bravely with 300 for six, including their first NatWest century, from the Finchampstead player Harry Hall. He added 152 for the fourth wicket with Myles.

Man of the Match: V. J. Wells.

Leicestershire

V. J. Wells c H. M. Hall b Govett 201
D. L. Maddy c Lane b Oxley 9
A. Habib c H. M. Hall b Govett 35
P. V. Simmons run out 82
J. M. Dakin c T. L. Hall b Govett 26
†P. A. Nixon not out 38
C. C. Remy not out 0
L-b 6, w 5, n-b 4 15

1/14 2/91 3/293 4/359 5/387 (5 wkts, 60 overs) 406

*J. J. Whitaker, D. J. Millns, G. J. Parsons and A. R. K. Pierson did not bat.

Bowling: Barrow 12–2–62–0; Oxley 12–0–86–1; Myles 3–0–22–0; Barnett 12–0–54–0; Govett 12–0–103–3; Hartley 5–0–42–0; H. M. Hall 4–0–31–0.

Berkshire

*G. E. Loveday c Nixon b Dakin 38
R. Soza c Nixon b Parsons 10
T. L. Hall c Nixon b Simmons 8
S. D. Myles st Nixon b Maddy 81
H. M. Hall run out 108
A. A. Barnett b Maddy 22
P. J. Oxley not out.................... 4
†M. G. Lane not out 1
L-b 11, w 11, n-b 6 28

1/18 2/46 3/90 4/242 5/286 6/299 (6 wkts, 60 overs) 300

J. P. Govett, J. K. Barrow and D. J. B. Hartley did not bat.

Bowling: Parsons 6–3–5–1; Millns 6–0–32–0; Remy 12–1–65–0; Simmons 5–0–20–1; Dakin 12–1–63–1; Pierson 12–2–48–0; Maddy 7–0–56–2.

Umpires: T. E. Jesty and D. R. Shepherd.

LINCOLNSHIRE v GLOUCESTERSHIRE

At Sleaford, June 25. Gloucestershire won by 87 runs. Toss: Gloucestershire.

A lively pitch helped Lincolnshire rattle through the visitors' batting, with one notable exception: Symonds plundered 87 off 83 balls, hitting nine fours and four sixes. Walsh and Smith then made good use of the conditions to reduce Lincolnshire to 18 for four early in their innings.

Man of the Match: A. Symonds.

Gloucestershire

A. J. Wright b Gill 5
R. I. Dawson c Wilson b Gill........... 0
N. J. Trainor c Gill b Bradford.......... 14
A. Symonds st Wilson b Bradford 87
M. W. Alleyne b Towse 4
†R. C. Russell c Gouldstone b Armstrong . 27
T. H. C. Hancock st Wilson b Fell 10
M. C. J. Ball c Gillett b Gill 31
*C. A. Walsh c Wilson b Gill 0
A. M. Smith not out 12
J. Lewis run out 1
B 8, l-b 2, w 19, n-b 2 31

1/5 2/13 3/107 4/121 5/130 6/157 7/191 8/196 9/219 (59.5 overs) 222

Bowling: Oakes 9–1–19–0; Gill 11.5–0–44–4; Towse 12–1–47–1; Bradford 12–2–52–2; Fell 8–3–24–1; Armstrong 7–2–26–1.

Lincolnshire

R. J. Evans c Ball b Smith	3	S. Oakes c Russell b Lewis	21
D. E. Gillett lbw b Smith	1	N. J. Armstrong not out	6
M. R. Gouldstone b Walsh	12	†G. B. Wilson lbw b Alleyne	1
P. A. Rawden c Russell b Smith	0	L-b 4, w 7, n-b 8	19
*M. A. Fell c Ball b Alleyne	31		
S. A. Bradford b Symonds	11	1/4 2/13 3/14 (47.3 overs)	135
N. S. Gill c Hancock b Ball	0	4/18 5/62 6/66	
A. D. Towse c Ball b Lewis	30	7/78 8/127 9/134	

Bowling: Walsh 6–1–23–1; Smith 6–1–21–3; Lewis 9–2–19–2; Alleyne 9.3–3–26–2; Ball 9–3–24–1; Symonds 8–4–18–1.

Umpires: M. J. Harris and A. G. T. Whitehead.

NORTHAMPTONSHIRE v CHESHIRE

At Northampton, June 25. Northamptonshire won by nine wickets. Toss: Northamptonshire.

Hignett helped to raise Cheshire's innings from its nadir of 56 for five, only for Emburey to wrap it up with a hat-trick – the ninth recorded in the competition. Northamptonshire won with more than half their overs to spare; the whole match lasted 75.3 overs of a possible 120.

Man of the Match: R. G. Hignett.

Cheshire

P. R. J. Bryson b Ambrose	0	E. S. Garnett not out	0
J. D. Bean c Warren b Ambrose	13	A. D. Greasley c Bailey b Emburey	0
T. J. Bostock c Warren b Taylor	0	N. D. Peel lbw b Emburey	0
M. Saxelby c Capel b Penberthy	23	L-b 3, w 9	12
*I. Cockbain lbw b Capel	8		
R. G. Hignett b Taylor	52	1/0 2/1 3/27 (50.3 overs)	135
†S. Bramhall run out	23	4/52 5/56 6/127	
S. J. Renshaw c Ambrose b Emburey	4	7/135 8/135 9/135	

Bowling: Ambrose 10–4–18–2; Taylor 11–1–40–2; Capel 6–0–16–1; Penberthy 7–3–17–1; Curran 4–1–14–0; Emburey 8.3–3–14–3; Bailey 4–1–13–0.

Northamptonshire

D. J. Capel b Peel	35
R. R. Montgomerie not out	69
*R. J. Bailey not out	26
L-b 6, w 3	9
1/86 (1 wkt, 25 overs)	139

M. B. Loye, K. M. Curran, †R. J. Warren, T. C. Walton, A. L. Penberthy, J. E. Emburey, C. E. L. Ambrose and J. P. Taylor did not bat.

Bowling: Peel 7–1–37–1; Renshaw 5–0–25–0; Garnett 3–0–25–0; Greasley 7–0–19–0; Bostock 2–0–19–0; Hignett 1–0–8–0.

Umpires: P. Adams and R. Julian.

OXFORDSHIRE v LANCASHIRE

At Aston Rowant, June 25. Lancashire won by 109 runs. Toss: Oxfordshire.

Atherton moved straight from a Test match at Lord's to a village ground, where he built an opening stand of 147 with Watkinson and found himself introduced by the public address system as a composite: Mike Atkinson. Oxfordshire's reply was unthreatening, but honourable.

Man of the Match: M. A. Atherton.

Lancashire

M. A. Atherton c Arnold b Evans 79
*M. Watkinson c Knightley b Ellison 62
N. J. Speak b Joyner 83
N. H. Fairbrother c Evans b Ellison 46
G. D. Lloyd c Joyner b Ellison 2
†W. K. Hegg lbw b Arnold 8
I. D. Austin not out 2
S. Elworthy not out 5
L-b 5, w 18 23

1/147 2/159 3/252 4/260 5/293 6/303 (6 wkts, 60 overs) 310

G. Yates, G. Chapple and P. J. Martin did not bat.

Bowling: Arnold 11–1–57–1; Joyner 10–0–48–1; Laudat 10–0–44–0; Curtis 3–0–23–0; Jones 4–0–34–0; Evans 10–1–46–1; Ellison 12–0–53–3.

Oxfordshire

†J. N. Batty b Austin 1
K. R. Mustow b Austin 10
S. V. Laudat b Yates 57
R. J. Williams c Hegg b Elworthy 3
B. C. A. Ellison c and b Fairbrother 42
C. S. Knightley not out 61
S. G. Joyner c Hegg b Lloyd 11
A. Jones not out 5
L-b 7, w 2, n-b 2 11

1/1 2/16 3/33 4/101 5/157 6/180 (6 wkts, 60 overs) 201

*R. A. Evans, K. A. Arnold and I. J. Curtis did not bat.

Bowling: Martin 7–4–8–0; Austin 7–1–24–2; Elworthy 6–2–10–1; Chapple 4–0–18–0; Yates 12–5–20–1; Watkinson 12–0–32–0; Speak 4–0–31–0; Fairbrother 5–0–28–1; Lloyd 3–0–23–1.

Umpires: A. Clarkson and C. T. Spencer.

SOMERSET v SUFFOLK

At Taunton, June 25. Somerset won by 62 runs. Toss: Somerset.

Suffolk squandered a rare opportunity when they dropped Lee with his score on 38 and the total standing at 127 for four. Lee went on to make 104 from 103 balls; Suffolk's own success with the bat only served to emphasise the importance of his innings.

Man of the Match: S. Lee.

Somerset

M. N. Lathwell b Steel 7
P. D. Bowler run out 45
S. C. Ecclestone c Brown b Golding 17
M. E. Trescothick b Miller 15
S. Lee run out 104
*A. N. Hayhurst c and b Miller 21
K. A. Parsons b Graham 51
†R. J. Turner c Randall b Graham 40
G. D. Rose not out 12
A. R. Caddick not out 5
B 2, l-b 3, w 9, n-b 2 16

1/16 2/46 3/72 4/127 5/186 6/248 7/315 8/316 (8 wkts, 60 overs) 333

H. R. J. Trump did not bat.

Bowling: Graham 12–0–75–2; Steel 10–1–62–1; Miller 12–1–61–2; Golding 12–1–38–1; Caley 12–0–77–0; Wijesuriya 2–0–15–0.

Suffolk

D. W. Randall c Lathwell b Parsons 39
S. M. Clements c Turner b Caddick 11
K. M. Wijesuriya c Lee b Trump 62
R. J. Catley b Parsons 15
*P. J. Caley not out 88
I. D. Graham b Caddick 5
A. J. Squire c Trescothick b Rose 9
C. A. Miller not out 3
B 1, l-b 9, w 21, n-b 8 39

1/25 2/93 3/118 4/192 5/214 6/232 (6 wkts, 60 overs) 271

†A. D. Brown, A. K. Golding and S. A. Steel did not bat.

Bowling: Caddick 12–0–46–2; Rose 12–2–44–1; Trump 12–0–51–1; Lee 8–0–35–0; Parsons 10–0–46–2; Hayhurst 3–0–11–0; Trescothick 3–0–28–0.

Umpires: J. H. Hampshire and J. F. Steele.

STAFFORDSHIRE v DERBYSHIRE

At Stone, June 25. Derbyshire won by eight wickets. Toss: Staffordshire.

At 70 for one, Staffordshire seemed to have established a solid platform, but Kevin Dean and DeFreitas combined to blow away the middle order, leaving them at 89 for seven. Jones took the last two wickets with his only two deliveries. A minor recovery lifted the target to 179, and gave O'Gorman and Adams the chance to compile an unbeaten third-wicket stand of 131 in 17 overs.

Man of the Match: P. A. J. DeFreitas.

Staffordshire

*S. J. Dean run out	20
P. F. Shaw c Krikken b DeFreitas	22
J. A. Waterhouse lbw b Dean	20
L. Potter lbw b DeFreitas	3
K. N. Patel lbw b DeFreitas	0
A. J. Dutton c Jones b Dean	4
†M. I. Humphries c Krikken b Dean	0
C. G. Feltham b Vandrau	18
P. F. Ridgway not out	47
D. J. Brock b Jones	19
A. Richardson c and b Jones	0
L-b 7, w 18	25
1/33 2/70 3/78 4/78 5/78 6/78 7/89 8/126 9/178 (55.2 overs)	178

Bowling: Malcolm 10–1–49–0; Harris 9–4–19–0; DeFreitas 12–3–31–3; Dean 12–1–52–3; Vandrau 12–7–20–1; Jones 0.2–0–0–2.

Derbyshire

K. J. Barnett b Ridgway	34
J. E. Owen c Humphries b Brock	7
T. J. G. O'Gorman not out	62
C. J. Adams not out	68
L-b 8, w 1	9
1/31 2/49 (2 wkts, 26.5 overs)	180

*D. M. Jones, P. A. J. DeFreitas, †K. M. Krikken, M. J. Vandrau, A. J. Harris, K. J. Dean and D. E. Malcolm did not bat.

Bowling: Brock 6–1–33–1; Richardson 7–0–42–0; Ridgway 8–1–41–1; Potter 3–0–22–0; Dutton 1.5–0–27–0; Feltham 1–0–7–0.

Umpires: B. Dudleston and K. J. Lyons.

SURREY v HOLLAND

At The Oval, June 25. Surrey won by 159 runs. Toss: Surrey.

Holland's new captain, Tim de Leede, used eight bowlers, including New Zealand Test player Chris Pringle, and made 23 bowling changes, but failed to put Surrey off their stride. Brown's 72 in 61 balls provided acceleration in the middle order. Van Dijk did take four wickets at the end, preventing Surrey from passing their previous best of 350, but no Dutch batsman was able to pass 27 in reply.

Man of the Match: S. van Dijk.

Surrey

D. J. Bicknell c van Noortwijk b Zulfiqar	49
M. A. Butcher c Cantrell b Zulfiqar	60
*†A. J. Stewart lbw b Cantrell	50
A. D. Brown b Bakker	72
A. J. Hollioake c Zulfiqar b Cantrell	29
D. M. Ward b Boerstra	7
B. P. Julian b van Dijk	23
I. J. Ward c van Noortwijk b van Dijk	14
A. C. S. Pigott not out	12
J. E. Benjamin c Zuiderent b van Dijk	4
R. M. Pearson c de Leede b van Dijk	11
L-b 9, w 6	15
1/108 2/135 3/217 4/258 5/277 6/281 7/313 8/318 9/322 (60 overs)	346

Bowling: Pringle 12–2–41–0; Bakker 11–0–56–1; Boerstra 7–0–45–1; van Dijk 8–0–57–4; Cantrell 12–0–59–2; de Leede 1–0–11–0; Zulfiqar 7–0–53–2; Zuiderent 2–0–15–0.

Holland

P. E. Cantrell c Stewart b Benjamin	25
E. Gouka run out	9
*T. B. M. de Leede b Hollioake	19
B. Zuiderent st Stewart b Pearson	20
K. J. van Noortwijk lbw b Hollioake	12
A. Zulfiqar b Julian	27
†M. Schewe c Stewart b Pigott	21
H. Boerstra lbw b Julian	1
C. Pringle c and b Pigott	3
S. van Dijk b Julian	5
P. J. Bakker not out	0
L-b 19, w 14, n-b 12	45
1/43 2/56 3/71 4/90 5/116 6/169 7/170 8/171 9/181 (42.4 overs)	187

Bowling: Julian 9.4–0–48–3; Benjamin 7–2–24–1; Pigott 9–1–22–2; Hollioake 8–0–35–2; Pearson 9–1–39–1.

Umpires: J. C. Balderstone and R. A. White.

YORKSHIRE v NOTTINGHAMSHIRE

At Leeds, June 25. Yorkshire won by 205 runs. Toss: Nottinghamshire.

Yorkshire's mammoth 345 was built around Moxon's solid century, but it was Bevan's extraordinary 69 from 42 balls that caught the eye. No side had ever chased more than 321 successfully in the 60-over competition and Nottinghamshire collapsed, mainly to Stemp, who was capped during the match. The eventual 205-run margin has been exceeded only once between first-class sides.

Man of the Match: M. D. Moxon.

Yorkshire

M. D. Moxon c Pick b Tolley	137
M. P. Vaughan c Metcalfe b Evans	64
*D. Byas c Robinson b Pick	26
M. G. Bevan b Cairns	69
A. McGrath c Bowen b Evans	9
C. White not out	11
†R. J. Blakey not out	1
B 5, l-b 12, w 5, n-b 6	28
1/143 2/220 3/286 4/308 5/343 (5 wkts, 60 overs)	345

D. Gough, P. J. Hartley, C. E. W. Silverwood and R. D. Stemp did not bat.

Bowling: Evans 12–1–57–2; Cairns 12–1–76–1; Bowen 6–0–42–0; Bates 11–0–56–0; Pick 10–0–42–1; Tolley 9–0–55–1.

Nottinghamshire

P. R. Pollard b Hartley	23
R. T. Robinson c Vaughan b White	35
A. A. Metcalfe c Vaughan b Stemp	28
*P. Johnson b Stemp	6
C. L. Cairns c Blakey b Gough	5
C. M. Tolley c Silverwood b Stemp	16
†L. N. P. Walker lbw b Stemp	1
R. T. Bates lbw b Hartley	1
K. P. Evans b White	10
M. N. Bowen not out	0
R. A. Pick b Gough	1
L-b 5, w 7, n-b 2	14
1/55 2/76 3/91 4/98 5/114 6/116 7/121 8/131 9/138 (43.3 overs)	140

Bowling: Gough 9.3–2–24–2; Silverwood 6–0–21–0; White 8–1–23–2; Hartley 8–1–22–2; Stemp 12–2–45–4.

Umpires: G. I. Burgess and J. W. Holder.

SECOND ROUND

DERBYSHIRE v KENT

At Derby, July 10. Derbyshire won by two wickets. Toss: Derbyshire.

Jones twisted an ankle while warming up and was forced to withdraw. DeFreitas took over the captaincy and won his second match award of the season after doing everything right, from winning the toss through a fine bowling spell to an important innings as Derbyshire won with four balls to spare. Kent were never on top but an excellent half-century by Walker, his first in the competition, took them to a demanding total. Cork, Adams and Krikken set Derbyshire off enterprisingly. At 210 for four in the 51st over, a comfortable victory was in sight. McCague changed that by taking three wickets in ten balls, before DeFreitas and Harris batted through determinedly.

Man of the Match: P. A. J. DeFreitas.

Kent

T. R. Ward c and b Harris	30
M. V. Fleming c Owen b Harris	3
C. L. Hooper c and b DeFreitas	2
G. R. Cowdrey c Cork b Wells	41
N. J. Llong c O'Gorman b Wells	37
M. A. Ealham b Wells	10
M. J. Walker run out	51
*†S. A. Marsh lbw b Harris	26
M. J. McCague not out	25
M. M. Patel not out	5
L-b 8, w 9, n-b 4	21
1/21 2/38 3/42 4/104 5/124 6/148 7/206 8/236 (8 wkts, 60 overs)	251

D. W. Headley did not bat.

Bowling: Cork 12–2–40–0; Harris 12–0–58–3; DeFreitas 12–4–28–1; Dean 5–0–37–0; Wells 12–1–41–3; Vandrau 2–0–14–0; Barnett 5–0–25–0.

Derbyshire

K. J. Barnett run out	6
D. G. Cork c Llong b Patel	61
C. J. Adams b Ealham	37
†K. M. Krikken b Headley	55
T. J. G. O'Gorman b McCague	27
C. M. Wells c Marsh b McCague	10
J. E. Owen c Marsh b McCague	3
*P. A. J. DeFreitas not out	23
M. J. Vandrau run out	4
A. J. Harris not out	11
L-b 9, w 4, n-b 4	17
1/9 2/80 3/144 4/188 5/210 6/211 7/219 8/228 (8 wkts, 59.2 overs)	254

K. J. Dean did not bat.

Bowling: Headley 12–1–45–1; McCague 12–1–49–3; Ealham 12–1–35–1; Hooper 12–0–52–0; Cowdrey 1–0–6–0; Fleming 6–0–24–0; Patel 4.2–0–34–1.

Umpires: H. D. Bird and V. A. Holder.

ESSEX v DURHAM

At Chelmsford, July 10. Essex won by 67 runs. Toss: Essex.

Having captured three wickets for 43 in the opening 12 overs, including Gooch's for nought, Durham nursed hopes of an upset victory. These disappeared rapidly as Law and Irani treated their bowling with contempt. Law scored a century from 115 deliveries – his ninth of the season in all competitions – while Irani made 124 in 99. Rollins finished off with a quick unbeaten 54, which took Essex to their highest NatWest total against a first-class county. Roseberry batted with great purpose for Durham and was ninth out for his only competitive hundred of the season. But with his best support coming from Boiling at No. 10, the visitors never posed much threat.

Man of the Match: S. G. Law.

Essex

G. A. Gooch c Hutton b Brown	0
D. D. J. Robinson b Walker	15
A. P. Grayson lbw b Betts	9
S. G. Law c Ligertwood b Betts	100
*P. J. Prichard c Boiling b Walker	25
R. C. Irani c Roseberry b Brown	124
†R. J. Rollins not out	54
J. J. B. Lewis run out	12
M. C. Ilott not out	0
L-b 9, w 7, n-b 6	22
1/1 2/14 3/43 4/107 5/228 6/333 7/354 (7 wkts, 60 overs)	361

P. M. Such and S. J. W. Andrew did not bat.

Bowling: Brown 12–1–49–2; Betts 10–1–87–2; Walker 12–2–58–2; Bainbridge 12–1–73–0; Boiling 12–0–65–0; Collingwood 2–0–20–0.

Durham

S. L. Campbell b Law	39	M. M. Betts c Gooch b Ilott	11
S. Hutton b Andrew	5	J. Boiling not out	46
J. E. Morris c Rollins b Such	24	A. Walker b Andrew	5
P. Bainbridge c Rollins b Irani	14	L-b 7, w 3	10
*M. A. Roseberry c Ilott b Grayson	100		—
P. D. Collingwood b Law	28	1/9 2/55 3/74 (56.3 overs)	294
†D. G. C. Ligertwood b Such	12	4/109 5/157 6/208	
S. J. E. Brown c Irani b Such	0	7/208 8/226 9/265	

Bowling: Ilott 11–1–63–1; Andrew 7.3–0–52–2; Irani 6–1–19–1; Such 12–1–56–3; Grayson 12–0–60–1; Law 8–0–37–2.

Umpires: J. H. Harris and P. Willey.

LANCASHIRE v NORTHAMPTONSHIRE

At Manchester, July 10. Lancashire won by one wicket. Toss: Lancashire.

Lancashire completed the first leg of a week of triumphs against Northamptonshire – three days later they beat them in the Benson and Hedges final. The victory was achieved amid great tension when last man Martin drove the first ball he received for four, echoing his batting success in an even more dramatic situation at the end of the Benson and Hedges semi-final a month earlier. Martin had put Northamptonshire on the back foot at the start when he took their first four wickets with the new ball. They limped from 29 for four to 96 for seven, before Penberthy and Emburey, in a tournament record eighth-wicket stand of 112, fought back so effectively that they might have snatched a dramatic win. At 212 for seven, with 12 wanted from three overs, Lancashire looked home and dry. But an attack of the jitters cost them two wickets, so that they needed three from the last nine balls when Martin came in.

Man of the Match: P. J. Martin.

Northamptonshire

R. R. Montgomerie c Fairbrother b Martin	8	J. E. Emburey b Elworthy	46
A. Fordham c Hegg b Elworthy	27	C. E. L. Ambrose c Fairbrother b Elworthy	7
*R. J. Bailey b Martin	1	J. P. Taylor not out	1
M. B. Loye c Watkinson b Martin	2	L-b 7, w 2	9
D. J. Capel c Hegg b Martin	4		—
K. M. Curran c Gallian b Elworthy	26	1/15 2/19 3/21 (59.2 overs)	223
†R. J. Warren c Atherton b Watkinson	13	4/29 5/72 6/73	
A. L. Penberthy b Austin	79	7/96 8/208 9/216	

Bowling: Martin 12–2–36–4; Austin 11.2–2–32–1; Watkinson 12–1–42–1; Elworthy 12–2–40–4; Yates 12–1–66–0.

Lancashire

M. A. Atherton c Warren b Curran	29	S. Elworthy c Bailey b Curran	8
J. E. R. Gallian c Bailey b Ambrose	35	G. Yates not out	2
J. P. Crawley lbw b Emburey	4	P. J. Martin not out	4
N. H. Fairbrother c Warren b Capel	37	L-b 6, w 6	12
G. D. Lloyd c Montgomerie b Emburey	41		—
*M. Watkinson c Montgomerie b Emburey	26	1/68 2/68 3/86 (9 wkts, 58.4 overs)	225
†W. K. Hegg c Fordham b Capel	18	4/132 5/174 6/182	
I. D. Austin b Curran	9	7/198 8/217 9/221	

Bowling: Ambrose 12–2–21–1; Taylor 11–0–44–0; Capel 8.4–0–45–2; Curran 12–2–44–3; Emburey 12–1–38–3; Penberthy 3–0–27–0.

Umpires: J. C. Balderstone and D. J. Constant.

LEICESTERSHIRE v SUSSEX

At Leicester, July 10. Sussex won by 32 runs. Toss: Sussex.

Leicestershire's gamble of playing Sutcliffe, just back from Oxford University, instead of Habib, failed; he had a nightmare of a game, dropping two catches and then spending 24 overs making 15 on a slow pitch. Sussex had been in trouble at 129 for six. But a stand of 43 between Lenham and Salisbury gave them something to bowl at, while Leicestershire presented them with 42 extras – the highest score of the innings. In reply, they slumped to five for two after two overs, which became 78 for five against some tight bowling, especially from the sometimes erratic Salisbury, who conceded just 23 in 12 overs of leg-spin. A half-century from Whitaker kept the home side's hopes alive but, once he was dismissed, the last five tumbled for just 50.

Man of the Match: I. D. K. Salisbury.

Sussex

C. W. J. Athey b Mullally 18
K. Greenfield b Mullally 0
*A. P. Wells b Simmons 22
M. P. Speight c Simmons b Wells 33
N. J. Lenham b Parsons 36
†P. Moores c Nixon b Simmons 1
D. R. Law b Brimson 7
I. D. K. Salisbury b Wells 30
V. C. Drakes b Brimson 24
J. D. Lewry not out 5
E. S. H. Giddins st Nixon b Brimson 2
B 2, l-b 10, w 20, n-b 10 42

1/5 2/35 3/89 (57.4 overs) 220
4/100 5/103 6/129
7/172 8/209 9/214

Bowling: Mullally 11–2–40–2; Millns 10–0–37–0; Parsons 12–1–41–1; Simmons 8–0–34–2; Wells 6–0–22–2; Brimson 10.4–1–34–3.

Leicestershire

V. J. Wells lbw b Lewry 0
I. J. Sutcliffe c Salisbury b Lenham 15
B. F. Smith c Wells b Drakes 5
P. V. Simmons c Greenfield b Giddins . . . 27
*J. J. Whitaker c Law b Lewry 54
D. L. Maddy b Salisbury 4
†P. A. Nixon lbw b Drakes 39
D. J. Millns b Salisbury 4
G. J. Parsons run out 4
A. D. Mullally not out 8
M. T. Brimson c Greenfield b Lewry 9
B 2, l-b 5, w 10, n-b 2 19

1/0 2/5 3/40 (57 overs) 188
4/67 5/78 6/138
7/147 8/164 9/166

Bowling: Lewry 12–0–45–3; Drakes 12–4–35–2; Giddins 10–0–34–1; Law 1–0–10–0; Lenham 7–0–18–1; Salisbury 12–2–23–2; Greenfield 3–0–16–0.

Umpires: J. D. Bond and R. Palmer.

SOMERSET v GLOUCESTERSHIRE

At Taunton, July 10. Somerset won by five wickets. Toss: Gloucestershire.

Despite perfect weather and a good pitch, this remarkable match ended at 3.50 p.m. Rose began the visitors' troubles with two early wickets. But then, against some untidy bowling, Cunliffe and Lynch added 57 in seven overs. The innings swung swiftly round again when Caddick took Somerset's first hat-trick in the competition: Lynch snicked a wide long-hop, Symonds edged a good delivery and, in his next over, Cunliffe steered to gully. Caddick's first 34 deliveries cost 37 runs; his last 24 brought four wickets for two. Then Trump's spell of three for 15 in 11 overs completed Gloucestershire's collapse. A brilliant catch by Hancock and two wickets to successive balls from Lewis kept Somerset on edge but Ecclestone and Parsons did the necessary.

Man of the Match: H. R. J. Trump.

Gloucestershire

A. J. Wright lbw b Rose 7
R. J. Cunliffe c Trump b Caddick 37
T. H. C. Hancock b Rose 0
M. A. Lynch c Turner b Caddick 22
A. Symonds c Turner b Caddick 0
M. W. Alleyne c Turner b Trump 13
†R. C. Russell c Turner b Rose 3
M. C. J. Ball c Harden b Trump 4
A. M. Smith b Caddick 13
*C. A. Walsh c Parsons b Trump 0
J. Lewis not out 6
L-b 3, w 4, n-b 6 13

1/9 2/17 3/74 (32.4 overs) 118
4/74 5/75 6/87
7/95 8/104 9/104

Bowling: Caddick 9.4–1–39–4; Rose 12–2–61–3; Trump 11–2–15–3.

Somerset

M. N. Lathwell c Hancock b Smith 17
P. D. Bowler c Russell b Lewis 18
S. C. Ecclestone lbw b Lewis 37
R. J. Harden c Russell b Lewis 0
S. Lee lbw b Smith 14
K. A. Parsons not out 17
G. D. Rose not out 1
L-b 1, w 5, n-b 12 18

1/23 2/63 3/63 4/92 5/103 (5 wkts, 32.2 overs) 122

*A. N. Hayhurst, †R. J. Turner, A. R. Caddick and H. R. J. Trump did not bat.

Bowling: Walsh 10–2–41–0; Smith 10–1–28–2; Lewis 7.2–2–27–3; Ball 5–0–25–0.

Umpires: A. Clarkson and A. A. Jones.

WARWICKSHIRE v SURREY

At Birmingham, July 10. Surrey won by 88 runs. Toss: Warwickshire.

Warwickshire's attempt to reach a record fourth successive 60-over final was ended by in-form Surrey. Thorpe hit 96 to break the early stranglehold established by Pollock and Munton, as Warwickshire bowled six maiden overs in the first 17. Spinners Smith and Giles were heavily punished, yielding 94 from a combined 16 overs, as Hollioake struck 57 from 53 balls. A target of 292 was too much for Warwickshire's batsmen, who had not played well as a unit for most of the season. Knight continued his excellent form but, as the run-rate escalated, the last seven wickets fell for 45. The home side were bowled out with more than eight overs to spare.

Man of the Match: G. P. Thorpe.

Surrey

M. A. Butcher c Knight b Small 33
*†A. J. Stewart c Ostler b Pollock 10
G. P. Thorpe lbw b Giles 96
A. D. Brown lbw b Small 34
A. J. Hollioake c Small b Pollock 57
D. M. Ward c Moles b Pollock 20
C. C. Lewis c Small b Pollock 4
B. P. Julian not out 8
M. P. Bicknell not out 0
B 1, l-b 17, w 9, n-b 2 29

1/20 2/79 3/152 4/244 5/274 6/283 7/283 (7 wkts, 60 overs) 291

J. E. Benjamin and R. M. Pearson did not bat.

Bowling: Pollock 12–2–37–4; Munton 10–3–28–0; Brown 10–1–53–0; Small 12–2–61–2; Smith 9–0–50–0; Giles 7–0–44–1.

Warwickshire

N. V. Knight c and b Bicknell 68
N. M. K. Smith b Lewis 14
A. J. Moles c Lewis b Hollioake 30
D. P. Ostler c Benjamin b Hollioake 11
T. L. Penney c Stewart b Lewis 30
S. M. Pollock c Stewart b Julian 23
†M. Burns b Lewis 0
D. R. Brown c Hollioake b Benjamin 2
A. F. Giles c Ward b Julian 3
G. C. Small c Bicknell b Benjamin 9
*T. A. Munton not out 2
L-b 7, w 2, n-b 2 11

1/34 2/81 3/99 4/158 5/176 6/176 7/179 8/187 9/198 (51.3 overs) 203

Bowling: Bicknell 8–0–44–1; Lewis 10–1–33–3; Julian 9–0–23–2; Benjamin 10.3–0–38–2; Hollioake 8–0–28–2; Pearson 6–0–30–0.

Umpires: G. I. Burgess and K. J. Lyons.

WORCESTERSHIRE v HAMPSHIRE

At Worcester, July 10. Hampshire won by 125 runs. Toss: Worcestershire.

An innings of awesome power from Smith and undisciplined home bowling enabled Hampshire to saunter into the quarter-finals. Moody soon regretted putting the visitors in as Smith and Laney enjoyed a second-wicket stand of 179. Initially, Smith played the support role, but he accelerated to 158 off 151 balls – his fifth century in the competition – striking 21 fours and two sixes. Worcestershire's worst bowling performance of the season included 22 wides – 13 by Sheriyar. Any hopes of pursuing a total of 328 for six were effectively ended by James. He removed the top three, including Hick – who had needed treatment after colliding with Solanki in the field – for nought. Connor ensured that Hampshire kept their grip, despite some late-order hitting by Illingworth.

Man of the Match: R. A. Smith.

Hampshire

*J. P. Stephenson c Lampitt b Newport	20
J. S. Laney lbw b Lampitt	82
R. A. Smith c Solanki b Moody	158
W. K. M. Benjamin lbw b Lampitt	0
V. P. Terry c Newport b Illingworth	9
P. R. Whitaker c Rhodes b Lampitt	8
S. D. Udal not out	8
K. D. James not out	0
L-b 15, w 22, n-b 6	43
1/34 2/213 3/222 4/258 5/289 6/325 (6 wkts, 60 overs)	328

†A. N. Aymes, S. M. Milburn and C. A. Connor did not bat.

Bowling: Newport 12–3–60–1; Moody 11–0–57–1; Sheriyar 5–0–35–0; Lampitt 12–0–56–3; Illingworth 9–0–44–1; Hick 6–0–27–0; Church 5–0–34–0.

Worcestershire

T. S. Curtis c Aymes b James	15
M. J. Church b James	35
G. A. Hick lbw b James	0
*T. M. Moody c Aymes b Connor	44
K. R. Spiring c Aymes b Udal	25
V. S. Solanki c Aymes b Connor	9
S. R. Lampitt c Connor b Udal	5
†S. J. Rhodes run out	7
P. J. Newport c Connor b James	11
R. K. Illingworth not out	29
A. Sheriyar c Benjamin b Connor	10
B 2, l-b 4, w 7	13
1/47 2/53 3/56 4/108 5/136 6/137 7/146 8/156 9/165 (52.4 overs)	203

Bowling: Connor 9.4–2–17–3; Milburn 10–0–50–0; James 12–2–42–4; Stephenson 9–0–42–0; Udal 12–1–46–2.

Umpires: J. H. Hampshire and K. E. Palmer.

YORKSHIRE v MIDDLESEX

At Leeds, July 10. Yorkshire won by seven wickets. Toss: Middlesex.

Gatting's decision to bat first proved disastrous as Middlesex struggled on a seaming and bouncy pitch. Silverwood's opening spell of 6–3–10–1 set the tone for Yorkshire's work in the field and the visitors limped to 77 for four in 31 overs. Although Weekes prevented a complete collapse, he used up 214 balls and most of the 60 overs in scoring 104. Byas, with only his second half-century in 19 innings in all competitions, and Bevan made sure that Middlesex did not retrieve their fortunes; their third-wicket stand worth 91 in 17 overs effectively settled the issue as batting conditions improved.

Man of the Match: P. N. Weekes.

Middlesex

P. N. Weekes c Blakey b White	104	A. R. C. Fraser not out	2
M. R. Ramprakash lbw b Silverwood	1	R. A. Fay run out	0
*M. W. Gatting run out	6		
J. D. Carr c White b Stemp	2	B 5, l-b 6, w 3, n-b 20	34
J. C. Pooley b Hartley	1		
†K. R. Brown c Hartley b Silverwood	22	1/4 2/50 3/76 (9 wkts, 60 overs)	199
O. A. Shah c White b Silverwood	11	4/77 5/130 6/162	
R. L. Johnson b Gough	16	7/191 8/197 9/199	

P. C. R. Tufnell did not bat.

Bowling: Gough 12–1–42–1; Silverwood 12–5–45–3; White 12–3–26–1; Hartley 12–4–42–1; Stemp 12–0–33–1.

Yorkshire

M. D. Moxon b Johnson	22	A. McGrath not out	32
M. P. Vaughan c Brown b Fay	7	L-b 4, w 5, n-b 16	25
*D. Byas not out	73		
M. G. Bevan c Fay b Fraser	41	1/15 2/36 3/127 (3 wkts, 44 overs)	200

C. White, †R. J. Blakey, D. Gough, P. J. Hartley, C. E. W. Silverwood and R. D. Stemp did not bat.

Bowling: Fraser 11–0–39–1; Fay 5–0–20–1; Johnson 10–0–63–1; Tufnell 12–2–44–0; Weekes 6–0–30–0.

Umpires: B. Dudleston and T. E. Jesty.

QUARTER-FINALS

HAMPSHIRE v ESSEX

At Southampton, July 30. Essex won by 100 runs. Toss: Essex.

Law scored his second hundred in successive NatWest matches, and his third in three games against Hampshire in 1996. He had also taken 134 off them for Young Australia the previous season. Law hit three sixes and nine fours from 81 balls, and his stand of 127 in 18 overs with Rollins not only doubled the score from a shaky 127 for five but set a tournament record for the sixth wicket. Hampshire needed a comparable innings in reply; Benjamin, in what proved to be his final appearance before a premature retirement, reached 41 before Law caught him, while Smith, who had injured his right hand when he caught Gooch and had to leave the field, managed only seven. Essex won with more than 11 overs to spare.

Man of the Match: S. G. Law.

Essex

G. A. Gooch c Smith b James	20	M. C. Ilott run out	2
D. D. J. Robinson lbw b Udal	39	N. F. Williams not out	6
N. Hussain lbw b James	7	P. M. Such b Connor	0
S. G. Law c Laney b Whitaker	107	B 2, l-b 8, w 6	16
*P. J. Prichard c Aymes b Stephenson	15		
R. C. Irani c Aymes b Stephenson	9	1/56 2/72 3/76 (59.2 overs)	286
†R. J. Rollins c Udal b Whitaker	53	4/113 5/127 6/254	
A. P. Grayson c Udal b Whitaker	12	7/270 8/279 9/285	

Bowling: Connor 11.2–2–47–1; Milburn 10–0–58–0; Udal 12–0–38–1; James 10–0–36–2; Stephenson 7–0–49–2; Whitaker 9–0–48–3.

Hampshire

*J. P. Stephenson c Law b Williams 15
J. S. Laney c Such b Grayson 30
R. A. Smith lbw b Ilott 7
W. K. M. Benjamin c Law b Such 41
V. P. Terry c Ilott b Grayson 14
K. D. James run out 3
P. R. Whitaker run out 2
†A. N. Aymes run out.................. 10
S. D. Udal c and b Irani 18
S. M. Milburn c Ilott b Grayson......... 27
C. A. Connor not out.................. 3
L-b 4, w 4, n-b 8............ 16

1/21 2/46 3/93 4/117 5/123 6/125 7/127 8/155 9/160 (48.3 overs) 186

Bowling: Ilott 10–0–45–1; Williams 8–0–37–1; Irani 11–1–46–1; Such 9–1–23–1; Grayson 10.3–0–31–3.

Umpires: J. H. Harris and M. J. Kitchen.

LANCASHIRE v DERBYSHIRE

At Manchester, July 30. Lancashire won by two runs. Toss: Lancashire.

Lancashire held their nerve yet again to win a cup-tie on the last ball. Derbyshire went into the final over, bowled by Chapple, wanting ten, which became four from the last ball, to level the scores; as both sides had lost nine wickets, Derbyshire would have won because they had a higher score after 30 overs. Jones managed two, which at least brought him his century. In the previous over, he had hit Austin to the boundary where Fairbrother, jumping high with his feet inside the ropes, palmed the ball back into play to save five runs. Lancashire's innings also came to an unusual close; after Barnett took three wickets in the penultimate over, Dean had Yates and Martin caught on the boundary, but no-ball was called each time because they were full tosses above waist height. Atherton batted 58 overs for his century while Lloyd provided the impetus with 61 off 59 balls.

Man of the Match: M. A. Atherton.

Lancashire

J. E. R. Gallian c Cork b Dean 27
M. A. Atherton c O'Gorman b Dean 115
J. P. Crawley c Krikken b Wells 9
N. H. Fairbrother c Dean b Vandrau 11
G. D. Lloyd c Cork b Barnett........... 61
*M. Watkinson c Jones b Barnett........ 17
†W. K. Hegg c Khan b Barnett 18
I. D. Austin c Jones b Barnett 0
G. Chapple lbw b Barnett 0
G. Yates not out...................... 8
P. J. Martin not out 2
L-b 4, w 3, n-b 14............ 21

1/57 2/86 3/109 4/210 5/234 6/267 7/273 8/273 9/273 (9 wkts, 60 overs) 289

Bowling: Cork 12–0–61–0; DeFreitas 12–2–37–0; Wells 12–0–40–1; Dean 11–0–76–2; Vandrau 7–0–39–1; Barnett 6–1–32–5.

Derbyshire

K. J. Barnett c Fairbrother b Martin...... 38
D. G. Cork run out 59
*D. M. Jones not out..................100
C. J. Adams b Yates 13
T. J. G. O'Gorman c Lloyd b Yates 15
P. A. J. DeFreitas c Lloyd b Martin...... 17
†K. M. Krikken lbw b Watkinson 14
G. A. Khan c Watkinson b Chapple...... 15
C. M. Wells b Chapple 3
M. J. Vandrau run out................. 3
K. J. Dean not out 0
L-b 7, w 3 10

1/92 2/103 3/147 4/173 5/212 6/250 7/272 8/281 9/285 (9 wkts, 60 overs) 287

Bowling: Austin 12–2–56–0; Martin 12–2–50–2; Yates 12–1–42–2; Chapple 12–0–63–2; Watkinson 12–0–69–1.

Umpires: G. Sharp and R. A. White.

SURREY v SOMERSET

At The Oval, July 30, 31. Surrey won by five wickets. Toss: Surrey.

Butcher missed out on a maiden NatWest century but maintained Surrey's momentum on three fronts. They contained Somerset to 225 – it had been 180 for four with ten overs to go – through some fine fielding, notably by Ben Hollioake, standing in for the injured Lewis, and some excellent bowling. But they almost lost it: their first two wickets fell with just five runs on the board. By the time bad light drove everyone off at 126 for four, much rested on Butcher and the fact that the rejuvenated Caddick had only two overs left. Caddick failed to cause mayhem next morning, although his earlier performance probably cemented his England recall. Instead, Adam Hollioake and Butcher did their stuff and Surrey knocked off the remaining 100 runs in just over an hour.

Man of the Match: M. A. Butcher.

Close of play: Surrey 126-4 (35 overs) (M. A. Butcher 52*, A. J. Hollioake 2*).

Somerset

M. N. Lathwell c Stewart b Benjamin	9
P. D. Bowler c Thorpe b Benjamin	52
S. C. Ecclestone c A. J. Hollioake b M. P. Bicknell	52
R. J. Harden b Julian	34
S. Lee c A. J. Hollioake b M. P. Bicknell	4
K. A. Parsons c B. C. Hollioake b Julian	8
†R. J. Turner not out	21
*A. N. Hayhurst st Stewart b Pearson	4
G. D. Rose c B. C. Hollioake b A. J. Hollioake	8
A. R. Caddick c M. P. Bicknell b Julian	4
H. R. J. Trump b Julian	3
L-b 3, w 21, n-b 2	26
1/20 2/117 3/141 4/156 5/180 6/181 7/192 8/208 9/216 (59.1 overs)	225

Bowling: M. P. Bicknell 12–1–38–2; Benjamin 12–2–35–2; B. C. Hollioake 4–0–25–0; Julian 11.1–1–46–4; A. J. Hollioake 8–0–36–1; Pearson 12–0–42–1.

Surrey

D. J. Bicknell lbw b Caddick	4
M. A. Butcher st Turner b Parsons	91
*†A. J. Stewart run out	0
G. P. Thorpe c Turner b Caddick	13
A. D. Brown c Turner b Caddick	41
A. J. Hollioake not out	45
B. P. Julian not out	6
L-b 11, w 13, n-b 2	26
1/4 2/5 3/34 4/117 5/204 (5 wkts, 52.5 overs)	226

B. C. Hollioake, M. P. Bicknell, R. M. Pearson and J. E. Benjamin did not bat.

Bowling: Caddick 12–2–34–3; Rose 12–1–46–0; Trump 12–2–38–0; Hayhurst 5–0–30–0; Lee 8.5–0–48–0; Parsons 3–0–19–1.

Umpires: H. D. Bird and B. Leadbeater.

SUSSEX v YORKSHIRE

At Hove, July 30. Yorkshire won by five wickets. Toss: Sussex.

A dramatic post-lunch collapse – five men falling for nine in six overs – effectively strangled Sussex's hopes, frustrating the majority of a full house. The county had, for once, managed a stable start: Athey, who was to remain the top scorer with 54, and Hall opened with 85 in 26 overs. But then Gough tumbled backwards for a brilliant one-handed catch to remove Athey just before lunch, and afterwards he got Greenfield and Wells in the space of four balls. Drakes and Jarvis revived the innings with 56 in 11 overs. But a target of 213 on a pitch that had flattened out presented little difficulty. Moxon and Byas did much of the work with 99 in 19 overs. Though Sussex's fielding, typified by a direct hit from Lewry to remove Bevan, was exemplary and their bowling tight, they simply did not have enough runs on the board.

Man of the Match: D. Gough.

Sussex

C. W. J. Athey c Gough b White	54	V. C. Drakes c Blakey b Hartley	35
J. W. Hall lbw b Stemp	38	P. W. Jarvis not out	34
M. P. Speight b White	3	J. D. Lewry not out	3
*A. P. Wells lbw b Gough	10	L-b 4, w 8, n-b 6	18
K. Greenfield b Gough	10		
†P. Moores run out	6	1/85 2/102 3/111 (9 wkts, 60 overs)	212
I. D. K. Salisbury c Silverwood b Stemp	1	4/130 5/131 6/136	
D. R. Law b Hartley	0	7/138 8/139 9/195	

Bowling: Gough 12–2–34–2; Silverwood 12–1–42–0; Hartley 12–2–47–2; White 12–0–42–2; Stemp 12–0–43–2.

Yorkshire

M. D. Moxon c Moores b Lewry	76	†R. J. Blakey not out	15
M. P. Vaughan c Moores b Drakes	2		
*D. Byas b Salisbury	52	L-b 4, w 5, n-b 8	17
M. G. Bevan run out	27		
A. McGrath c Salisbury b Drakes	5	1/16 2/115 3/156 (5 wkts, 47.3 overs)	215
C. White not out	21	4/170 5/176	

D. Gough, P. J. Hartley, C. E. W. Silverwood and R. D. Stemp did not bat.

Bowling: Lewry 12–0–42–1; Drakes 8.3–0–48–2; Jarvis 6–0–31–0; Law 8–1–50–0; Salisbury 12–1–33–1; Greenfield 1–0–7–0.

Umpires: J. W. Holder and A. G. T. Whitehead.

SEMI-FINALS

LANCASHIRE v YORKSHIRE

At Manchester, August 13. Lancashire won by 19 runs. Toss: Lancashire.

Lancashire's second successive semi-final win over their old rivals at Old Trafford was more comfortable than the last-ball, one-wicket, victory in the Benson and Hedges Cup. Yorkshire's hopes faded when Bevan was out for 85, one of three victims in nine balls for Austin; White fell next ball to a brilliant mid-wicket catch by Yates, and the 50th over ended with Yorkshire 199 for six. Though Gough hit 42 from 33 balls, they could not catch up. Yorkshire dropped four chances in a Lancashire innings dominated by a stand of 145 between Crawley and Lloyd, whose 81 came off 90 balls. Immediately the game was over, Bevan flew by helicopter to Heathrow to return to Australia, where his team-mates were preparing to tour Sri Lanka. Despite his disappointment, he could look back on one moment of light relief, when a ball he struck flew into two pieces; its leather cover, ripped by a fielder's boot, fell off as he hit it, prompting speculation about what might have happened had either section been caught.

Man of the Match: I. D. Austin.

Lancashire

J. E. R. Gallian run out	19	G. Chapple not out	0
M. A. Atherton c Blakey b Stemp	18	G. Yates b Gough	0
J. P. Crawley c McGrath b Bevan	62		
N. H. Fairbrother c McGrath b Stemp	0	B 2, l-b 15, w 10, n-b 6	33
G. D. Lloyd c Silverwood b Bevan	81		
*M. Watkinson c Gough b Hartley	35	1/26 2/52 3/52 (9 wkts, 60 overs)	293
†W. K. Hegg c McGrath b Gough	35	4/197 5/209 6/262	
I. D. Austin c Byas b Gough	10	7/289 8/293 9/293	

P. J. Martin did not bat.

Bowling: Gough 12–3–47–3; Silverwood 6–0–23–0; White 10–0–38–0; Hartley 10–0–66–1; Stemp 12–1–55–2; Bevan 10–1–47–2.

Yorkshire

M. D. Moxon lbw b Yates	12
M. P. Vaughan c Gallian b Martin	14
*D. Byas c Gallian b Watkinson	39
M. G. Bevan c Chapple b Austin	85
A. McGrath b Austin	34
C. White c Yates b Austin	4
†R. J. Blakey c Lloyd b Martin	33
D. Gough c Chapple b Martin	42
P. J. Hartley not out	1
C. E. W. Silverwood not out	0
L-b 4, w 4, n-b 2	10
1/28 2/34 3/110 4/190 5/197 6/197 7/272 8/274 (8 wkts, 60 overs)	274

R. D. Stemp did not bat.

Bowling: Martin 12–2–53–3; Austin 12–1–47–3; Yates 12–0–55–1; Chapple 12–0–59–0; Watkinson 12–1–56–1.

Umpires: R. Julian and N. T. Plews.

SURREY v ESSEX

At The Oval, August 13. Essex won by four wickets. Toss: Essex.

Surrey paid heavily for their profligacy with extras. It cost them 47 unnecessary runs – 23 of them wides – and a £4,620 fine for their execrable over-rate. On top of that, their bowling was of two lengths, both hittable, in contrast to Essex's steadiness; and their batsmen scored too slowly, just 43 in the first hour. Although Stewart's unbeaten hundred was vital, no one else hurried things along; promoting Shahid ahead of Thorpe, Brown and Hollioake made little sense. Only Lewis showed the necessary urgency, with 45 in 29 balls. In contrast, Law wasted little time getting Essex going. He smacked 53 off 44 balls while Gooch scored a solid half-century. Law, like Yorkshire's Bevan, had to catch a flight to Brisbane to join the Australian squad; he was already in a taxi when he heard that a late flurry from Irani had ensured their team's place in the final. For Surrey, defeat ended dreams of the treble.

Man of the Match: A. J. Stewart.

Surrey

M. A. Butcher run out	27
*†A. J. Stewart not out	125
N. Shahid c Prichard b Williams	25
G. P. Thorpe c Robinson b Ilott	8
A. D. Brown st Rollins b Grayson	11
A. J. Hollioake c Law b Grayson	9
C. C. Lewis not out	45
L-b 6, w 13, n-b 6	25
1/81 2/151 3/163 4/193 5/214 (5 wkts, 60 overs)	275

J. E. Benjamin, B. P. Julian, M. P. Bicknell and R. M. Pearson did not bat.

Bowling: Ilott 11–2–59–1; Williams 12–0–43–1; Irani 8–2–33–0; Law 9–1–37–0; Such 12–0–50–0; Grayson 8–0–47–2.

Essex

G. A. Gooch b Lewis	50
A. P. Grayson lbw b Bicknell	4
N. Hussain c Julian b Lewis	12
S. G. Law c Julian b Benjamin	53
*P. J. Prichard b Julian	33
R. C. Irani not out	52
D. D. J. Robinson c Stewart b Julian	1
†R. J. Rollins not out	26
B 1, l-b 8, w 23, n-b 15	47
1/10 2/32 3/128 4/175 5/207 6/213 (6 wkts, 56.4 overs)	278

M. C. Ilott, N. F. Williams and P. M. Such did not bat.

Bowling: Bicknell 12–1–33–1; Lewis 12–0–71–2; Julian 7–0–41–2; Benjamin 12–1–62–1; Hollioake 6.4–0–32–0; Pearson 7–0–30–0.

Umpires: B. J. Meyer and R. Palmer.

FINAL

ESSEX v LANCASHIRE

At Lord's, September 7. Lancashire won by 129 runs. Toss: Essex.

The toss of the coin before the final of the premier one-day competition has become a matter of such perceived importance that the successful captain is sometimes feted by team-mates as if he has actually won the game. In the ten previous finals, the team batting second had won, hours after the morning dew had evaporated in the autumn sunshine. So when the toss was won by the Essex captain, Paul Prichard, and he invited the favourites Lancashire to bat, Ladbrokes adjusted their odds dramatically.

The conditions did indeed favour the Essex seamers, in particular Ilott and Irani, but they continued to assist bowlers throughout. Chasing a modest target, Essex were routed, cutting the record for the lowest total in the competition's 34 finals – 118 by Lancashire against Kent in 1974 – by more than half. They were all out for 57, not merely beaten but humiliated. Gooch, who had batted like an emperor throughout the season, was denied the valediction he craved in what was presumed to be his last major appearance at Lord's.

As a game, it was not a complete disaster. There was a good innings by Crawley, later viewed as outstanding in the context of those who floundered around him, some fine fielding and outstanding bowling from both sides. In the one-day game, however, crass cricket is often forgiven provided it produces a close finish. This match was over a little after tea with more than a quarter of the scheduled 120 overs still to bowl.

The pitch was poor, particularly for such a showpiece, with uneven bounce and exaggerated seam movement. But the Dukes balls also swung all day and both teams possessed the skill to exploit the difficult conditions fully. It was a kick in the teeth for those batsmen who think they own the over-limit game. Atherton had scored only four when he was bowled by an in-swinger from Ilott. Gallian, having attacked Williams with relish, was lbw to Irani, who showed great heart as he added Fairbrother and Lloyd for figures of three for 25. Crawley, who might have been given out lbw to his first ball, had by now embarked on an innings of patient skill. His 66 was three times the next-highest score of the match, and he survived into the 50th over. Lancashire could not dominate either the conditions or the bowlers, but showed their professionalism as well as the county's experience of 14 Lord's finals as they batted through to the last delivery of the 60th over.

Essex, needing a modest 187, thought the game was won, a notion not immediately dispelled when Grayson, Hussain and Prichard fell cheaply to Martin. Gooch was still there. But he was a helpless bystander as Irani, Robinson and Rollins – whose off stump was knocked back by a ball pitching on leg – succumbed to Chapple. Then, at 33, Gooch was seventh out for a tortuous ten scored in 20 overs and Essex knew their day was in ruins. They were bowled out in 27.2 overs. Nos 9 and 10, Williams and Cowan, were joint top scorers.

Chapple and Martin had bowled even better than Ilott and Irani: Chapple's figures of six for 18 replaced Joel Garner's six for 29, for Somerset in 1979, as the best in a September final. The Sunday newspaperman who had started his mid-afternoon first-edition report by writing, "Ronnie Irani was the only happy Lancastrian at Lord's yesterday," turned pale, lit a cigarette, and rewrote frantically. – PAUL WEAVER.

Man of the Match: G. Chapple. *Attendance:* 25,433; *receipts* £718,828.

Lancashire

J. E. R. Gallian lbw b Irani	21
M. A. Atherton b Ilott	4
J. P. Crawley st Rollins b Such	66
N. H. Fairbrother b Irani	9
G. D. Lloyd c Gooch b Irani	1
*M. Watkinson b Such	18
†W. K. Hegg b Grayson	15
I. D. Austin c Cowan b Grayson	18
G. Chapple c Cowan b Grayson	4
G. Yates run out	9
P. J. Martin not out	5
B 4, l-b 3, w 5, n-b 4	16
1/16 (2) 2/48 (1) 3/86 (4) 4/88 (5) 5/122 (6) 6/139 (3) 7/157 (7) 8/168 (8) 9/175 (9) 10/186 (10)	(60 overs) 186

Bowling: Ilott 12–2–29–1; Williams 7.4–0–39–0; Irani 12–5–25–3; Cowan 12–2–33–0; Such 12–1–29–2; Grayson 4.2–0–24–3.

Essex

G. A. Gooch lbw b Gallian	10	A. P. Cowan b Chapple	11
A. P. Grayson c Hegg b Martin	6	P. M. Such b Chapple	0
N. Hussain c Hegg b Martin	2		
*P. J. Prichard c Fairbrother b Martin	6	L-b 1, w 3	4
R. C. Irani b Chapple	5		—
D. D. J. Robinson c Fairbrother b Chapple	2	1/13 (2) 2/17 (3) 3/25 (4) (27.2 overs)	57
†R. J. Rollins b Chapple	0	4/31 (5) 5/33 (6) 6/33 (7)	
M. C. Ilott lbw b Chapple	0	7/33 (1) 8/34 (8)	
N. F. Williams not out	11	9/57 (10) 10/57 (11)	

Bowling: Martin 10–2–17–3; Austin 7–3–10–0; Chapple 6.2–1–18–6; Gallian 4–0–11–1.

Umpires: D. R. Shepherd and P. Willey.

NATWEST TROPHY RECORDS

(Including Gillette Cup, 1963-80)

Batting

Highest individual scores: 206, A. I. Kallicharran, Warwickshire v Oxfordshire, Birmingham, 1984; 201, V. J. Wells, Leicestershire v Berkshire, Leicester, 1996; 180*, T. M. Moody, Worcestershire v Surrey, The Oval, 1994; 177, C. G. Greenidge, Hampshire v Glamorgan, Southampton, 1975; 172*, G. A. Hick, Worcestershire v Devon, Worcester, 1987; 165*, V. P. Terry, Hampshire v Berkshire, Southampton, 1985; 162*, C. J. Tavaré, Somerset v Devon, Torquay, 1990; 162*, I. V. A. Richards, Glamorgan v Oxfordshire, Swansea, 1993; 159, C. L. Smith, Hampshire v Cheshire, Chester, 1989; 158, Zaheer Abbas, Gloucestershire v Leicestershire, Leicester, 1983; 158, G. D. Barlow, Middlesex v Lancashire, Lord's, 1984; 158, R. A. Smith, Hampshire v Worcestershire, Worcester, 1996; 156, D. I. Gower, Leicestershire v Derbyshire, Leicester, 1984; 155, J. J. Whitaker, Leicestershire v Wiltshire, Swindon, 1984; 154*, H. Morris, Glamorgan v Staffordshire, Cardiff, 1989; 154, P. Willey, Leicestershire v Hampshire, Leicester, 1987; 153, A. Hill, Derbyshire v Cornwall, Derby, 1986; 153, J. S. Laney, Hampshire v Norfolk, Southampton, 1996; 151*, M. P. Maynard, Glamorgan v Durham, Darlington, 1991; 151, N. V. Knight, Warwickshire v Somerset, Birmingham, 1995. *In the final:* 146, G. Boycott, Yorkshire v Surrey, 1965. (93 hundreds were scored in the Gillette Cup; 194 hundreds have been scored in the NatWest Bank Trophy.)

Most runs: 2,547, G. A. Gooch; 2,083, M. W. Gatting; 1,998, A. J. Lamb; 1,950, D. L. Amiss.

Fastest hundred: G. D. Rose off 36 balls, Somerset v Devon, Torquay, 1990.

Most hundreds: 7, C. L. Smith; 6, G. A. Gooch; 5, D. I. Gower, I. V. A. Richards, R. A. Smith and G. M. Turner.

Highest totals (off 60 overs)**:** 413 for four, Somerset v Devon, Torquay, 1990; 406 for five, Leicestershire v Berkshire, Leicester, 1996; 404 for three, Worcestershire v Devon, Worcester, 1987; 392 for five, Warwickshire v Oxfordshire, Birmingham, 1984; 386 for five, Essex v Wiltshire, Chelmsford, 1988; 384 for six, Kent v Berkshire, Finchampstead, 1994; 384 for nine, Sussex v Ireland, Belfast, 1996; 372 for five, Lancashire v Gloucestershire, Manchester, 1990; 371 for four, Hampshire v Glamorgan, Southampton, 1975; 365 for three, Derbyshire v Cornwall, Derby, 1986; 361 for eight, Essex v Cumberland, Chelmsford, 1992; 361 for eight, Warwickshire v Bedfordshire, Birmingham, 1994; 361 for seven, Essex v Durham, Chelmsford, 1996; 360 for two, Northamptonshire v Staffordshire, Northampton, 1990. *In the final:* 322 for five, Warwickshire v Sussex, Lord's, 1993.

Highest total by a minor county: 305 for nine, Durham v Glamorgan, Darlington, 1991.

Highest total by a side batting first and losing: 321 for six (60 overs), Sussex v Warwickshire, Lord's, 1993 (*in the final*).

Highest totals by a side batting second: 350 (59.5 overs), Surrey lost to Worcestershire, The Oval, 1994; 339 for nine (60 overs), Somerset lost to Warwickshire, Birmingham, 1995; 326 for nine (60 overs), Hampshire lost to Leicestershire, Leicester, 1987; 322 for five (60 overs), Warwickshire beat Sussex, Lord's, 1993 (*in the final*for nine (59.5 overs), Essex beat Lancashire, Chelmsford, 1992; 314 for eight (60 overs), Nottinghamshire lost to Northamptonshire, Nottingham, 1995; 307 for five (60 overs), Hampshire beat Essex, Chelmsford, 1990; 306 for six (59.3 overs), Gloucestershire beat Leicestershire, Leicester, 1983; 305 for nine (60 overs), Durham lost to Glamorgan, Darlington, 1991; 300 for six (60 overs), Berkshire lost to Leicestershire, Leicester, 1996.

Lowest completed totals: 39 (26.4 overs), Ireland v Sussex, Hove, 1985; 41 (20 overs), Cambridgeshire v Buckinghamshire, Cambridge, 1972; 41 (19.4 overs), Middlesex v Essex, Westcliff, 1972; 41 (36.1 overs), Shropshire v Essex, Wellington, 1974. *In the final:* 57 (27.2 overs), Essex v Lancashire, 1996.

Lowest total by a side batting first and winning: 98 (56.2 overs), Worcestershire v Durham, Chester-le-Street, 1968.

Shortest innings: 10.1 overs (60 for one), Worcestershire v Lancashire, Worcester, 1963.

Matches re-arranged on a reduced number of overs are excluded from the above.

Record partnerships for each wicket

269	for 1st	J. P. Stephenson and J. S. Laney, Hampshire v Norfolk at Southampton .	1996
286	for 2nd	I. S. Anderson and A. Hill, Derbyshire v Cornwall at Derby	1986
309*	for 3rd	T. S. Curtis and T. M. Moody, Worcestershire v Surrey at The Oval	1994
234*	for 4th	D. Lloyd and C. H. Lloyd, Lancashire v Gloucestershire at Manchester ..	1978
166	for 5th	M. A. Lynch and G. R. J. Roope, Surrey v Durham at The Oval	1982
127	for 6th	S. G. Law and R. J. Rollins, Essex v Hampshire at Southampton	1996
160*	for 7th	C. J. Richards and I. R. Payne, Surrey v Lincolnshire at Sleaford	1983
112	for 8th	A. L. Penberthy and J. E. Emburey, Northamptonshire v Lancashire at Manchester	1996
87	for 9th	M. A. Nash and A. E. Cordle, Glamorgan v Lincolnshire at Swansea ...	1974
81	for 10th	S. Turner and R. E. East, Essex v Yorkshire at Leeds	1982

Bowling

Most wickets: 81, G. G. Arnold; 79, J. Simmons.

Best bowling (12 overs unless stated)**:** eight for 21 (10.1 overs), M. A. Holding, Derbyshire v Sussex, Hove, 1988; eight for 31 (11.1 overs), D. L. Underwood, Kent v Scotland, Edinburgh, 1987; seven for 15, A. L. Dixon, Kent v Surrey, The Oval, 1967; seven for 15 (9.3 overs), R. P. Lefebvre, Somerset v Devon, Torquay, 1990; seven for 19, N. V. Radford, Worcestershire v Bedfordshire, Bedford, 1991; seven for 30, P. J. Sainsbury, Hampshire v Norfolk, Southampton, 1965; seven for 32, S. P. Davis, Durham v Lancashire, Chester-le-Street, 1983; seven for 33, R. D. Jackman, Surrey v Yorkshire, Harrogate, 1970; seven for 37, N. A. Mallender, Northamptonshire v Worcestershire, Northampton, 1984. *In the final:* six for 18 (6.2 overs), G. Chapple, Lancashire v Essex, 1996.

Most economical analysis: 12–9–3–1, J. Simmons, Lancashire v Suffolk, Bury St Edmunds, 1985.

Most expensive analysis: 12–0–107–2, C. C. Lovell, Cornwall v Warwickshire, St Austell, 1996.

Hat-tricks (10)**:** J. D. F. Larter, Northamptonshire v Sussex, Northampton, 1963; D. A. D. Sydenham, Surrey v Cheshire, Hoylake, 1964; R. N. S. Hobbs, Essex v Middlesex, Lord's, 1968; N. M. McVicker, Warwickshire v Lincolnshire, Birmingham, 1971; G. S. le Roux, Sussex v Ireland, Hove, 1985; M. Jean-Jacques, Derbyshire v Nottinghamshire, Derby, 1987; J. F. M. O'Brien, Cheshire v Derbyshire, Chester, 1988; R. A. Pick, Nottinghamshire v Scotland, Nottingham, 1995; J. E. Emburey, Northamptonshire v Cheshire, Northampton, 1996; A. R. Caddick, Somerset v Gloucestershire, Taunton, 1996.

Four wickets in five balls: D. A. D. Sydenham, Surrey v Cheshire, Hoylake, 1964.

Wicket-keeping and Fielding

Most dismissals: 66 (58 ct, 8 st), R. W. Taylor; 65 (59 ct, 6 st), A. P. E. Knott.

Most dismissals in an innings: 7 (all ct), A. J. Stewart, Surrey v Glamorgan, Swansea, 1994.

Most catches by a fielder: 27, J. Simmons; 26, G. A. Gooch; 25, G. Cook; 24, M. W. Gatting and P. J. Sharpe.

Most catches by a fielder in an innings: 4 – A. S. Brown, Gloucestershire v Middlesex, Bristol, 1963; G. Cook, Northamptonshire v Glamorgan, Northampton, 1972; C. G. Greenidge, Hampshire v Cheshire, Southampton, 1981; D. C. Jackson, Durham v Northamptonshire, Darlington, 1984; T. S. Smith, Hertfordshire v Somerset, St Albans, 1984; H. Morris, Glamorgan v Scotland, Edinburgh, 1988; C. C. Lewis, Nottinghamshire v Worcestershire, Nottingham, 1992.

Results

Largest victories in runs: Somerset by 346 runs v Devon, Torquay, 1990; Sussex by 304 runs v Ireland, Belfast, 1996; Worcestershire by 299 runs v Devon, Worcester, 1987; Essex by 291 runs v Wiltshire, Chelmsford, 1988; Sussex by 244 runs v Ireland, Hove, 1985; Lancashire by 241 runs v Gloucestershire, Manchester, 1990; Nottinghamshire by 228 runs v Northumberland, Jesmond, 1994; Warwickshire by 227 runs v Oxfordshire, Birmingham, 1984; Essex by 226 runs v Oxfordshire, Chelmsford, 1985; Durham by 207 runs v Herefordshire, Chester-le-Street, 1995; Yorkshire by 205 runs v Nottinghamshire, Leeds, 1996.

Victories by ten wickets (13)**:** By Glamorgan, Hampshire (twice), Middlesex, Northamptonshire, Surrey, Sussex, Warwickshire (twice), Yorkshire (four times).

Earliest finishes: both at 2.20 p.m. Worcestershire beat Lancashire by nine wickets at Worcester, 1963; Essex beat Middlesex by eight wickets at Westcliff, 1972.

Scores level (10)**:** Nottinghamshire 215, Somerset 215 for nine at Taunton, 1964; Surrey 196, Sussex 196 for eight at The Oval, 1970; Somerset 287 for six, Essex 287 at Taunton, 1978; Surrey 195 for seven, Essex 195 at Chelmsford, 1980; Essex 149, Derbyshire 149 for eight at Derby, 1981; Northamptonshire 235 for nine, Derbyshire 235 for six at Lord's, 1981 (*in the final*); Middlesex 222 for nine, Somerset 222 for eight at Lord's, 1983; Hampshire 224 for eight, Essex 224 for seven at Southampton, 1985; Essex 307 for six, Hampshire 307 for five at Chelmsford, 1990; Hampshire 204 for nine, Leicestershire 204 for nine at Leicester, 1995.
Note: Under the rules the side which lost fewer wickets won; at Leicester in 1995, Leicestershire won by virtue of their higher total after 30 overs.

Match Awards

Most awards: 9, G. A. Gooch; 8, C. H. Lloyd and C. L. Smith.

WINNERS 1963-96

Gillette Cup

		Man of the Match
1963	SUSSEX* beat Worcestershire by 14 runs.	N. Gifford†
1964	SUSSEX beat Warwickshire* by eight wickets.	N. I. Thomson
1965	YORKSHIRE beat Surrey* by 175 runs.	G. Boycott
1966	WARWICKSHIRE* beat Worcestershire by five wickets.	R. W. Barber
1967	KENT* beat Somerset by 32 runs.	M. H. Denness
1968	WARWICKSHIRE beat Sussex* by four wickets.	A. C. Smith
1969	YORKSHIRE beat Derbyshire* by 69 runs.	B. Leadbeater

		Man of the Match
1970	LANCASHIRE* beat Sussex by six wickets.	H. Pilling
1971	LANCASHIRE* beat Kent by 24 runs.	Asif Iqbal†
1972	LANCASHIRE* beat Warwickshire by four wickets.	C. H. Lloyd
1973	GLOUCESTERSHIRE* beat Sussex by 40 runs.	A. S. Brown
1974	KENT* beat Lancashire by four wickets.	A. P. E. Knott
1975	LANCASHIRE* beat Middlesex by seven wickets.	C. H. Lloyd
1976	NORTHAMPTONSHIRE* beat Lancashire by four wickets.	P. Willey
1977	MIDDLESEX* beat Glamorgan by five wickets.	C. T. Radley
1978	SUSSEX* beat Somerset by five wickets.	P. W. G. Parker
1979	SOMERSET beat Northamptonshire* by 45 runs.	I. V. A. Richards
1980	MIDDLESEX* beat Surrey by seven wickets.	J. M. Brearley

NatWest Bank Trophy

1981	DERBYSHIRE* beat Northamptonshire by losing fewer wickets with the scores level.	G. Cook†
1982	SURREY* beat Warwickshire by nine wickets.	D. J. Thomas
1983	SOMERSET beat Kent* by 24 runs.	V. J. Marks
1984	MIDDLESEX beat Kent* by four wickets.	C. T. Radley
1985	ESSEX beat Nottinghamshire* by one run.	B. R. Hardie
1986	SUSSEX* beat Lancashire by seven wickets.	D. A. Reeve
1987	NOTTINGHAMSHIRE* beat Northamptonshire by three wickets.	R. J. Hadlee
1988	MIDDLESEX* beat Worcestershire by three wickets.	M. R. Ramprakash
1989	WARWICKSHIRE beat Middlesex* by four wickets.	D. A. Reeve
1990	LANCASHIRE* beat Northamptonshire by seven wickets.	P. A. J. DeFreitas
1991	HAMPSHIRE* beat Surrey by four wickets.	R. A. Smith
1992	NORTHAMPTONSHIRE* beat Leicestershire by eight wickets.	A. Fordham
1993	WARWICKSHIRE* beat Sussex by five wickets.	Asif Din
1994	WORCESTERSHIRE* beat Warwickshire by eight wickets.	T. M. Moody
1995	WARWICKSHIRE beat Northamptonshire* by four wickets.	D. A. Reeve
1996	LANCASHIRE beat Essex* by 129 runs.	G. Chapple

* *Won toss.* † *On losing side.*

TEAM RECORDS 1963-96

	Rounds reached				*Matches*		
	W	*F*	*SF*	*QF*	*P*	*W*	*L*
Derbyshire	1	2	3	11	67*	34	33
Durham	0	0	0	1	38	12	26
Essex	1	2	5	14	74	41	33
Glamorgan	0	1	3	13	70	36	34
Gloucestershire	1	1	5	14	70	37	33
Hampshire	1	1	8	20	86	53	33
Kent	2	5	7	14	79	47	32
Lancashire	6	9	14	19	96	68	28
Leicestershire	0	1	3	14	69	35	34
Middlesex	4	6	13	18	92	62	30
Northamptonshire	2	7	10	19	88	56	32
Nottinghamshire	1	2	3	11	70	37	33
Somerset	2	4	9	17	82	50	32
Surrey	1	4	10	20	86*	53	33
Sussex	4	8	12	18	88	58	30
Warwickshire	5	9	15	19	96	67	29
Worcestershire	1	4	10	14	78	45	33
Yorkshire	2	2	6	15	72	40	32

* Derbyshire and Surrey totals each include a bowling contest after their first-round matches were abandoned in 1991; Derbyshire lost to Hertfordshire and Surrey beat Oxfordshire.

MINOR COUNTY RECORDS

From 1964 to 1979 the previous season's top five Minor Counties were invited to take part in the competition. In 1980 these were joined by Ireland, and in 1983 the competition was expanded to embrace 13 Minor Counties, Ireland and Scotland. The number of Minor Counties dropped to 12 in 1992 when Durham attained first-class status, and 11 in 1995 when Holland were admitted to the competition.

Between 1964 and 1991 Durham qualified 21 times, including 15 years in succession from 1977-91. They reached the second round a record six times.

Including the 1997 tournament, Staffordshire have qualified most among the remaining Minor Counties, 19 times, followed by Devon, Hertfordshire and Oxfordshire 18, Berkshire and Cambridgeshire 17, Buckinghamshire, Cheshire, Norfolk and Suffolk 16, Shropshire 13, Lincolnshire and Wiltshire 12, Bedfordshire, Cumberland and Dorset 11, Northumberland 8, Cornwall 7, Herefordshire and Wales Minor Counties twice.

Only Hertfordshire have reached the quarter-finals, beating Berkshire and then Essex in 1976.

Wins by a minor county over a first-class county (8): Durham v Yorkshire (by five wickets), Harrogate, 1973; Lincolnshire v Glamorgan (by six wickets), Swansea, 1974; Hertfordshire v Essex (by 33 runs), 2nd round, Hitchin, 1976; Shropshire v Yorkshire (by 37 runs), Telford, 1984; Durham v Derbyshire (by seven wickets), Derby, 1985; Buckinghamshire v Somerset (by seven runs), High Wycombe, 1987; Cheshire v Northamptonshire (by one wicket), Chester, 1988; Hertfordshire v Derbyshire (2-1 in a bowling contest after the match was abandoned), Bishop's Stortford, 1991.

THE DUCKWORTH/LEWIS METHOD

In 1997, the ECB's three domestic limited-overs competitions will use a new method to revise targets when play is interrupted, devised by Frank Duckworth of the Royal Statistical Society and Tony Lewis of the University of the West of England. Their system aims to preserve any advantage that one team has established before the interruption. It does so by taking into account the run-scoring resources available to the team batting – the number of overs and wickets they have left – and also the stage of the innings at which the overs are lost.

After analysing hundreds of recent one-day matches, Duckworth and Lewis have drawn up tables for innings of all lengths. The table for a 50-over match has 50 rows, representing the number of overs remaining, and ten columns, from nought to nine wickets down. Each figure in the table gives the percentage of the total runs in an innings that would, on average, be scored with a certain number of overs left and wickets lost.

If overs are lost, the tables are used to calculate the percentage of runs the team would be expected to score in those overs. This is obtained by reading off the figure for the number of overs left and wickets down when play stops and subtracting from it the corresponding figure for the number of overs remaining when it resumes.

If the first innings is complete and the second innings is interrupted, the target to be beaten is reduced by the percentage of the innings lost. If the suspension occurs between innings, as happened when the Duckworth/Lewis method was used in the one-day international between Zimbabwe and England at Harare on January 1, 1997, only one figure is required: the percentage of the innings remaining for the reduced number of overs with no wicket lost. Zimbabwe were all out for 200 and rain restricted England to 42 overs. The table showed that, on average, 42 overs should yield 92.5 per cent of a 50-over total. England needed to beat 185 (92.5 per cent of 200). Further modifications cover interruptions to the first innings, multiple interruptions and innings terminated by rain.

BENSON AND HEDGES CUP, 1996

Ian Austin

Lancashire re-established their claim to be the dominant force in knockout cricket when they swept through the tournament to take the Benson and Hedges Cup for the second successive year, a feat previously achieved only by Somerset 14 years earlier. Once again, they were unbeaten in the zonal matches. But they nearly went out in an epic semi-final against their ancient rivals, Yorkshire. One of the greatest matches in the 25-year history of this tournament ended in Lancashire's favour by a solitary wicket when their No. 11, Peter Martin, hit the last available ball for two.

In comparison, the final was an anticlimax. Northamptonshire, losers as they were in the NatWest final the previous September, never quite looked like chasing Lancashire's total of 245 and were undone by two bursts, early and late, from Ian Austin.

This was the first Benson and Hedges Cup played under the new standard regulations for one-day internationals, with each side batting for 50 overs – instead of the 55 that had been the norm since the competition began – extra restrictions on field placings for the first 15 overs, and a break only between innings instead of for lunch and tea.

Since the tournament started barely a month after the World Cup final in Lahore, much of the strategy was influenced by the fashions paraded in the subcontinent. The most obvious of these was "pinch-hitting", the practice of elevating lower-order hitters to go in first and give the innings a flying start. This worked less reliably on spring mornings in England, with the new ball darting about, than it did on brown pitches further south. But there were some spectacular examples none the less: these included Martin Speight hitting 64 off 26 balls for Sussex against Ireland, while his opening partner Bill Athey made two. Sussex, like Surrey against Gloucestershire, scored 134 off the first 15 overs.

Although the number of overs available diminished, high scoring became more common. There were five totals above 320, compared to 12 in the competition's previous history, and five match aggregates above 600, against seven in the past quarter-century. The most dynamic individual performance, however, came from a bowler: Shaun Pollock, Warwickshire's South African, took four wickets in four balls in the fourth over of his first match for the county. Not surprisingly, his season went downhill from there.

Prize money

£40,000 for winners: LANCASHIRE.
£20,000 for runners-up: NORTHAMPTONSHIRE.
£10,000 for losing semi-finalists: WARWICKSHIRE and YORKSHIRE.
£5,000 for losing quarter-finalists: GLAMORGAN, GLOUCESTERSHIRE, KENT and SURREY.

There was also £800 each for the winners of group matches. Gold Award winners received £850 in the final, £400 in the semi-finals, £350 in the quarter-finals, £225 in the group matches. The prize money was increased from £137,650 in the 1995 tournament to £154,300; the total sponsorship rose from £641,307 to £800,000.

FINAL GROUP TABLE

	Played	*Won*	*Lost*	*No result*	*Points*	*Net run-rate*
Group A						
LANCASHIRE	5	5	0	0	10	11.57
WARWICKSHIRE	5	3	1	1	7	39.57
Leicestershire	5	3	2	0	6	−3.92
Derbyshire	5	2	3	0	4	−4.78
Durham	5	1	3	1	3	−6.83
Minor Counties	5	0	5	0	0	−26.53
Group B						
NORTHAMPTONSHIRE	4	4	0	0	8	11.05
YORKSHIRE	4	3	1	0	6	15.25
Nottinghamshire	4	2	2	0	4	4.55
Worcestershire	4	1	3	0	2	2.28
Scotland	4	0	4	0	0	−36.25
Group C						
GLAMORGAN	5	4	1	0	8	8.73
KENT	5	4	1	0	8	4.07
Essex	5	3	2	0	6	11.24
Somerset	5	3	2	0	6	4.76
Middlesex	5	1	4	0	2	−11.46
British Universities	5	0	5	0	0	−17.94
Group D						
SURREY	4	4	0	0	8	18.97
GLOUCESTERSHIRE	4	3	1	0	6	17.85
Hampshire	4	2	2	0	4	12.38
Sussex	4	1	3	0	2	−1.28
Ireland	4	0	4	0	0	−49.52

Net run-rate was calculated by subtracting runs conceded per 100 balls from runs scored per 100 balls, revising figures in shortened matches and discounting those not played to a result.

GROUP A

The Minor Counties' squad for the competition was: I. Cockbain (Cheshire) (*captain*), J. N. Batty (Oxfordshire), S. J. Dean (Staffordshire), R. J. Evans (Lincolnshire), M. A. Fell (Lincolnshire), R. G. Hignett (Cheshire), S. V. Laudat (Oxfordshire), M. J. Marvell (Shropshire), S. D. Myles (Berkshire), L. Potter (Staffordshire), M. G. Powell (Norfolk), M. F. Robinson (Herefordshire), M. J. Saggers (Norfolk), K. Sharp (Shropshire), M. A. Sharp (Cumberland), Z. A. Sher (Bedfordshire), J. P. J. Sylvester (Wales), G. T. J. Townsend (Devon).

DERBYSHIRE v DURHAM

At Chesterfield, April 26. Derbyshire won by 104 runs. Toss: Durham. County debut: M. J. Foster.

Adams and Jones, leading Derbyshire against his former county, Durham, put on 135 in 19 overs, with Adams reaching his first century in the competition in 93 balls. Then Derbyshire's Test bowlers – Malcolm, Cork and DeFreitas – all found good form, and Durham subsided meekly.

Gold Award: C. J. Adams.

Derbyshire

K. J. Barnett b Foster	28	D. G. Cork not out	0
A. S. Rollins c sub b Boiling	42	B 1, l-b 11, w 14	26
C. J. Adams not out	100		—
*D. M. Jones c Morris b Killeen	67	1/54 2/98 (4 wkts, 50 overs)	266
P. A. J. DeFreitas c Collingwood b Foster	3	3/233 4/264	

T. A. Tweats, C. M. Wells, †K. M. Krikken, F. A. Griffith and D. E. Malcolm did not bat.

Bowling: Brown 10–1–43–0; Killeen 9–1–53–1; Birbeck 8–0–46–0; Foster 10–1–52–2; Boiling 5–0–18–1; Collingwood 8–0–42–0.

Durham

*M. A. Roseberry c Krikken b Malcolm	11	J. Boiling c Krikken b Malcolm	15
M. J. Foster run out	4	N. Killeen b Malcolm	0
S. Hutton b Griffith	36	S. J. E. Brown c Cork b Barnett	0
J. E. Morris c Cork b Griffith	26	L-b 2, w 7, n-b 18	27
J. A. Daley lbw b DeFreitas	6		—
P. D. Collingwood c Malcolm b DeFreitas	5	1/6 2/23 3/85 (40.4 overs)	162
S. D. Birbeck b Griffith	5	4/88 5/103 6/106	
†C. W. Scott not out	27	7/116 8/156 9/156	

Bowling: Malcolm 10–0–36–3; Cork 9–3–27–0; Griffith 10–0–63–3; DeFreitas 8–3–20–2; Wells 3–1–13–0; Barnett 0.4–0–1–1.

Umpires: V. A. Holder and A. A. Jones.

LANCASHIRE v MINOR COUNTIES

At Manchester, April 26. Lancashire won by 25 runs. Toss: Minor Counties.

Sharp catching from Minor Counties (who held all eight of their chances) almost embarrassed title-holders Lancashire, who were 102 for five before Watkinson and then Austin led a recovery. Gallian's three wickets were instrumental in limiting the Counties' reply, which never quite threatened to produce a shock.

Gold Award: M. Watkinson.

Lancashire

M. A. Atherton c Batty b Saggers	6	S. Elworthy c Dean b M. A. Sharp	1
J. E. R. Gallian run out	18	G. Yates c Potter b Hignett	7
†J. P. Crawley c Robinson b Myles	34	G. Chapple not out	0
N. H. Fairbrother c K. Sharp b Robinson	21	B 1, l-b 3, w 7, n-b 4	15
G. D. Lloyd b Hignett	7		—
N. J. Speak c and b Potter	28	1/17 2/29 3/59 (49.4 overs)	232
*M. Watkinson c Saggers b Myles	56	4/70 5/102 6/154	
I. D. Austin c Dean b Hignett	39	7/202 8/217 9/228	

Bowling: Saggers 9–0–47–1; M. A. Sharp 10–1–36–1; Robinson 8–0–36–1; Hignett 4.4–1–25–3; Potter 10–1–30–1; Myles 8–0–54–2.

Minor Counties

S. J. Dean b Chapple	34
K. Sharp b Gallian	31
L. Potter c Watkinson b Austin	26
M. A. Fell lbw b Gallian	0
*I. Cockbain lbw b Gallian	6
S. D. Myles not out	56
R. G. Hignett lbw b Chapple	19
†J. N. Batty c Fairbrother b Chapple	1
M. F. Robinson b Yates	7
M. J. Saggers c Fairbrother b Yates	10
M. A. Sharp not out	2
B 1, l-b 8, w 4, n-b 2	15
1/53 2/83 3/85 4/101 5/109 6/155 7/157 8/173 9/201 (9 wkts, 50 overs)	207

Bowling: Elworthy 10–0–49–0; Austin 10–4–25–1; Yates 8–0–43–2; Chapple 10–1–31–3; Gallian 9–2–30–3; Watkinson 3–0–20–0.

Umpires: T. E. Jesty and K. E. Palmer.

WARWICKSHIRE v LEICESTERSHIRE

At Birmingham, April 26. Warwickshire won by seven wickets. Toss: Warwickshire. County debut: S. M. Pollock.

Pollock made an extraordinary debut for his new club, becoming the first man to take four wickets in four balls in this competition. In his fourth over, he had Macmillan caught at first slip, Whitaker bowled off his pad, Robinson caught at short leg and Maddy caught at third slip. He finished the over with figures of 4–3–1–5; Leicestershire were nine for five. Smith did well to steer them to 182, but Ostler and Penney's unbroken stand of 127 settled the issue with 15 overs to spare. Pollock was presented with the Gold Award and his county cap to go with his final figures of 10–5–21–6.

Gold Award: S. M. Pollock.

Leicestershire

V. J. Wells c Ostler b Pollock	0
G. I. Macmillan c Reeve b Pollock	4
B. F. Smith c Reeve b Munton	61
*J. J. Whitaker b Pollock	0
P. E. Robinson c Moles b Pollock	0
D. L. Maddy c Ostler b Pollock	0
†P. A. Nixon c Moles b Pollock	14
G. J. Parsons lbw b Munton	19
D. J. Millns not out	39
T. J. Mason lbw b N. M. K. Smith	19
A. D. Mullally not out	1
L-b 7, w 12, n-b 6	25
1/2 2/9 3/9 4/9 5/9 6/33 7/114 8/122 9/181 (9 wkts, 50 overs)	182

Bowling: Pollock 10–5–21–6; Brown 10–1–36–0; Munton 10–2–31–2; Reeve 10–1–25–0; P. A. Smith 9–0–57–0; N. M. K. Smith 1–0–5–1.

Warwickshire

N. V. Knight c Smith b Mullally	0
N. M. K. Smith b Mullally	22
P. A. Smith c Mason b Parsons	32
D. P. Ostler not out	68
T. L. Penney not out	50
B 2, l-b 6, w 3	11
1/0 2/54 3/56 (3 wkts, 34.2 overs)	183

A. J. Moles, *D. A. Reeve, S. M. Pollock, D. R. Brown, †K. J. Piper and T. A. Munton did not bat.

Bowling: Mullally 10–0–44–2; Parsons 8–1–23–1; Millns 6.2–0–45–0; Mason 3–0–22–0; Wells 6–0–28–0; Maddy 1–0–13–0.

Umpires: A. Clarkson and B. J. Meyer.

LANCASHIRE v DURHAM

At Manchester, April 28, 29. Lancashire won by seven wickets. Toss: Lancashire.

On a rain-interrupted first day, only Durham's trialist Michael Foster (formerly with Yorkshire and Northamptonshire) could find any fluency against a miserly attack. Atherton's third century in the competition – and his highest one-day score for Lancashire – saw his side home on the reserve day.

Gold Award: M. A. Atherton.

Close of play: Lancashire 82-2 (24 overs) (M. A. Atherton 24*, J. P. Crawley 31*).

Durham

M. J. Foster b Watkinson 2
*M. A. Roseberry c Atherton b Austin . . . 7
J. A. Daley st Hegg b Yates 33
J. E. Morris c Atherton b Watkinson 30
J. I. Longley run out 29
P. D. Collingwood b Elworthy 17
S. D. Birbeck c Hegg b Austin 4
†C. W. Scott c Watkinson b Elworthy 9
N. Killeen b Austin 4
J. Boiling not out 7
S. J. E. Brown not out 2
B 1, l-b 9, w 6, n-b 4 20

1/19 2/95 3/131 (9 wkts, 50 overs) 214
4/140 5/178 6/187
7/190 8/204 9/206

Bowling: Austin 10–2–25–3; Chapple 8–0–30–0; Elworthy 10–0–59–2; Gallian 2–0–22–0; Yates 10–0–29–1; Watkinson 10–1–39–2.

Lancashire

J. E. R. Gallian lbw b Brown 10
M. A. Atherton not out 121
S. Elworthy c Brown b Killeen 13
J. P. Crawley c Morris b Brown 45
N. H. Fairbrother not out 23
L-b 2, w 3 5

1/14 2/28 3/133 (3 wkts, 47.1 overs) 217

G. D. Lloyd, *M. Watkinson, †W. K. Hegg, I. D. Austin, G. Chapple and G. Yates did not bat.

Bowling: Brown 10–1–28–2; Killeen 10–2–46–1; Foster 10–0–44–0; Birbeck 7–0–40–0; Boiling 6–0–28–0; Collingwood 4.1–0–29–0.

Umpires: J. H. Hampshire and V. A. Holder.

LEICESTERSHIRE v DERBYSHIRE

At Leicester, April 28. Leicestershire won by four runs. Toss: Leicestershire. First-team debut: D. Williamson.

When Leicestershire reduced their opponents to 238 for seven at the end of the 46th over the game seemed as good as won. Krikken and Griffith, however, struck 27 off the next two overs, and it took two wickets in the last over, bowled by Maddy, to wrap the innings up.

Gold Award: J. J. Whitaker.

Leicestershire

V. J. Wells run out 60
G. I. Macmillan lbw b Cork 0
B. F. Smith b Vandrau 53
*J. J. Whitaker c Jones b DeFreitas 70
P. E. Robinson b Malcolm 5
D. L. Maddy c Barnett b DeFreitas 38
†P. A. Nixon c Vandrau b Wells 14
G. J. Parsons lbw b Wells 5
T. J. Mason not out 7
D. Williamson run out 6
L-b 16, w 4, n-b 4 24

1/5 2/113 3/127 (9 wkts, 50 overs) 282
4/132 5/225 6/250
7/263 8/274 9/282

A. D. Mullally did not bat.

Bowling: Cork 10–4–25–1; Malcolm 10–0–64–1; DeFreitas 10–0–60–2; Wells 6–0–37–2; Vandrau 10–0–53–1; Griffith 4–0–27–0.

Derbyshire

K. J. Barnett c Nixon b Parsons 5
A. S. Rollins c Nixon b Wells 19
C. J. Adams b Parsons 72
*D. M. Jones st Nixon b Mason 24
C. M. Wells b Maddy 56
P. A. J. DeFreitas c Smith b Williamson . . 22
D. G. Cork c Wells b Mullally 14
†K. M. Krikken run out 27
F. A. Griffith b Maddy 24
M. J. Vandrau b Maddy 0
D. E. Malcolm not out 1
B 1, l-b 9, w 4 14

1/10 2/60 3/103 (50 overs) 278
4/141 5/181 6/209
7/230 8/269 9/277

Bowling: Mullally 10–0–42–1; Parsons 8–0–33–2; Williamson 10–0–64–1; Wells 7–0–57–1; Mason 10–0–40–1; Maddy 5–1–32–3.

Umpires: T. E. Jesty and B. Leadbeater.

MINOR COUNTIES v WARWICKSHIRE

At Jesmond, April 28. Warwickshire won by 195 runs. Toss: Minor Counties.

The pitch was attacked by vandals overnight, but emergency repairs allowed Knight to score 104 from 99 balls, sharing a stand of 159 with Ostler. One of Ostler's sixes smashed a window. Warwickshire scored 369, the second-highest total by any team in this competition, behind Essex's 388 for seven against Scotland at Chelmsford in 1992, when they had 55 overs, five more than the new standard.

Gold Award: N. V. Knight.

Warwickshire

N. V. Knight c M. A. Sharp b Myles	104	†K. J. Piper c Cockbain b Robinson	0
N. M. K. Smith c Hignett b Saggers	25	T. A. Munton not out	6
P. A. Smith c Dean b Hignett	28		
D. P. Ostler c Myles b Potter	86	L-b 6, w 19, n-b 2	27
T. L. Penney c Saggers b Potter	35		
*D. A. Reeve c Dean b Robinson	22	1/29 2/87 3/246 (8 wkts, 50 overs)	369
S. M. Pollock not out	28	4/273 5/310 6/328	
D. R. Brown c Myles b Robinson	8	7/344 8/345	

G. C. Small did not bat.

Bowling: Saggers 10–1–64–1; M. A. Sharp 10–0–49–0; Hignett 2.3–0–37–1; Robinson 10–0–75–3; Potter 8.3–0–72–2; Myles 9–0–66–1.

Minor Counties

S. J. Dean run out	21	R. G. Hignett c Reeve b P. A. Smith	6
K. Sharp lbw b Brown	5	M. A. Sharp not out	10
L. Potter c Piper b Reeve	47		
S. D. Myles c Piper b Reeve	29	L-b 3, w 5, n-b 8	16
*I. Cockbain c Piper b Reeve	9		
†J. N. Batty not out	26	1/32 2/37 3/96 (8 wkts, 50 overs)	174
M. F. Robinson c Pollock b Reeve	0	4/117 5/122 6/122	
M. J. Saggers c and b N. M. K. Smith	5	7/140 8/153	

M. A. Fell did not bat.

Bowling: Pollock 8–2–28–0; Brown 10–3–22–1; N. M. K. Smith 10–0–44–1; Reeve 10–2–23–4; Munton 7–0–33–0; P. A. Smith 5–0–21–1.

Umpires: N. T. Plews and G. Sharp.

DERBYSHIRE v LANCASHIRE

At Chesterfield, April 30, May 1. Lancashire won by three wickets. Toss: Derbyshire.

Cork returned to his exuberant form of 1995, coming in at 76 for six to share a stand of 29, Derbyshire's largest, with DeFreitas, and then taking five excellent wickets to leave Lancashire 70 for six in turn. The regulations, however, worked in Lancashire's favour. Rain forced the game into a second day and reduced the target to 121 from 44 overs. When more bad light interrupted the innings at 25 overs, the minimum necessary for a result, Lancashire had 107 for seven, enough to win had there been no further play. But, on resuming, Hegg and Austin finished the job in nine balls anyway.

Gold Award: D. G. Cork.

Close of play: Lancashire 70-6 (14 overs) (N. H. Fairbrother 14*, W. K. Hegg 0*).

Derbyshire

K. J. Barnett b Austin . . . 11	M. J. Vandrau not out . . . 12
T. A. Tweats c Watkinson b Austin . . . 10	F. A. Griffith c Watkinson b Gallian . . . 6
C. J. Adams c Hegg b Watkinson . . . 29	D. E. Malcolm b Austin . . . 12
*D. M. Jones c Martin b Chapple . . . 5	L-b 5, w 8 . . . 13
C. M. Wells c Lloyd b Watkinson . . . 0	—
P. A. J. DeFreitas c Hegg b Watkinson . . . 23	1/19 2/33 3/50 (33.3 overs) 137
†K. M. Krikken c Gallian b Watkinson . . . 2	4/54 5/64 6/76
D. G. Cork c Atherton b Watkinson . . . 14	7/105 8/111 9/118

Bowling: Martin 7–0–30–0; Austin 7.3–2–12–3; Chapple 7–0–37–1; Watkinson 9–0–44–5; Gallian 3–0–9–1.

Lancashire

J. E. R. Gallian lbw b Cork . . . 9	†W. K. Hegg not out . . . 28
M. A. Atherton lbw b Cork . . . 24	I. D. Austin not out . . . 8
G. Yates c Jones b Cork . . . 0	L-b 4, w 6, n-b 6 . . . 16
J. P. Crawley c Jones b Cork . . . 0	—
N. H. Fairbrother b Griffith . . . 25	1/27 2/29 3/35 (7 wkts, 26.3 overs) 124
G. D. Lloyd b Malcolm . . . 4	4/41 5/48
*M. Watkinson c Adams b Cork . . . 10	6/70 7/105

P. J. Martin and G. Chapple did not bat.

Bowling: Malcolm 10–1–38–1; Cork 10–1–49–5; DeFreitas 3.3–0–21–0; Griffith 3–0–12–1.

Umpires: T. E. Jesty and K. E. Palmer.

DURHAM v WARWICKSHIRE

At Chester-le-Street, April 30, May 1. No result. Toss: Warwickshire.

Frustratingly for Durham's struggling captain, Roseberry, his side were in a promising position, with his own score standing at 55, when the rain came down. No further play was possible, even on the reserve day.

Durham

M. J. Foster b Brown . . . 37	P. Bainbridge not out . . . 0
*M. A. Roseberry not out . . . 55	B 1, l-b 7, w 1, n-b 12 . . . 21
J. A. Daley c Piper b Munton . . . 8	—
J. E. Morris c Ostler b Brown . . . 7	1/52 2/69 (4 wkts, 34.2 overs) 143
J. I. Longley c Brown b Welch . . . 15	3/86 4/142

P. D. Collingwood, †C. W. Scott, N. Killeen, S. J. E. Brown and M. M. Betts did not bat.

Bowling: Pollock 6.2–0–32–0; Brown 10–2–26–2; N. M. K. Smith 1–0–14–0; Munton 10–1–38–1; Reeve 6–0–22–0; Welch 1–0–3–1.

Warwickshire

N. V. Knight, N. M. K. Smith, P. A. Smith, D. P. Ostler, T. L. Penney, *D. A. Reeve, S. M. Pollock, D. R. Brown, †K. J. Piper, G. Welch and T. A. Munton.

Umpires: G. I. Burgess and N. T. Plews.

MINOR COUNTIES v LEICESTERSHIRE

At Jesmond, April 30, May 1. Leicestershire won on scoring-rate. Toss: Minor Counties.

An unbeaten stand of 56 between Maddy and Nixon was taking Leicestershire towards a somewhat unconvincing victory when rain stopped play on the first day. No more cricket was possible, but Leicestershire won with a run-rate of 4.94 to the Minor Counties' 4.12.

Gold Award: D. L. Maddy.

Minor Counties

*S. J. Dean b Mullally 40
R. J. Evans b Mason 34
K. Sharp b Wells 15
S. D. Myles c Macmillan b Wells 13
G. T. J. Townsend b Mason 10
S. V. Laudat c Nixon b Parsons 14
†J. N. Batty run out 9
M. F. Robinson run out 7
M. J. Marvell c Macmillan b Maddy 10
M. J. Saggers not out 34
M. A. Sharp not out 1
B 1, l-b 9, w 9 19

1/46 2/83 3/109 4/110 5/138 6/140 7/155 8/155 9/192 (9 wkts, 50 overs) 206

Bowling: Parsons 10–1–43–1; Mullally 10–1–27–1; Williamson 4–0–27–0; Wells 10–1–39–2; Mason 10–0–35–2; Maddy 6–1–25–1.

Leicestershire

V. J. Wells b M. A. Sharp 17
G. I. Macmillan b Marvell 40
B. F. Smith b Laudat 2
P. E. Robinson c sub b Robinson 40
*J. J. Whitaker b Laudat 5
D. L. Maddy not out 33
†P. A. Nixon not out 26
L-b 3, w 7 10

1/38 2/52 3/101 4/112 5/117 (5 wkts, 35 overs) 173

G. J. Parsons, T. J. Mason, A. D. Mullally and D. Williamson did not bat.

Bowling: Saggers 8–1–44–0; M. A. Sharp 8–1–26–1; Laudat 10–1–40–2; Marvell 5–0–38–1; Robinson 4–0–22–1.

Umpires: V. A. Holder and K. J. Lyons.

DURHAM v MINOR COUNTIES

At Chester-le-Street, May 7. Durham won by five wickets. Toss: Minor Counties. County debut: S. L. Campbell.

Campbell made his county debut after completing his Test duties against New Zealand in the Caribbean. It was a far cry from his double-hundred in Bridgetown as he grafted for 90 minutes for 27 runs on a surface weighted against the batsmen. Longley's 38 not out off 60 balls was the most attacking innings of the day and ensured Durham's first win of the season.

Gold Award: J. I. Longley.

Minor Counties

*S. J. Dean b Brown 8
R. J. Evans c Scott b Betts 12
K. Sharp b Boiling 18
G. T. J. Townsend lbw b Boiling 2
J. P. J. Sylvester c Morris b Bainbridge . . 30
S. V. Laudat c Roseberry b Collingwood . 15
†J. N. Batty c Scott b Collingwood 7
M. G. Powell c Campbell b Collingwood . 11
M. J. Marvell c and b Betts 14
M. J. Saggers not out 8
M. A. Sharp c Scott b Foster 1
L-b 12, w 15, n-b 4 31

1/18 2/24 3/32 4/61 5/109 6/115 7/118 8/131 9/156 (48.2 overs) 157

Bowling: Brown 10–4–16–1; Betts 9–2–36–2; Boiling 8–0–22–2; Foster 9.2–0–28–1; Collingwood 10–1–28–3; Bainbridge 2–0–15–1.

Durham

*M. A. Roseberry c Batty b Saggers 0
S. L. Campbell c Batty b Saggers 27
J. E. Morris c Evans b Laudat 27
P. D. Collingwood run out 5
P. Bainbridge c M. A. Sharp b Marvell . . . 39
J. I. Longley not out 38
M. J. Foster not out 12
L-b 5, w 5 10

1/0 2/48 3/53 4/91 5/139 (5 wkts, 40.3 overs) 158

†C. W. Scott, J. Boiling, S. J. E. Brown and M. M. Betts did not bat.

Bowling: Saggers 10–0–49–2; M. A. Sharp 9–4–24–0; Laudat 8–0–30–1; Powell 7.3–0–29–0; Marvell 6–0–21–1.

Umpires: J. C. Balderstone and J. H. Hampshire.

LEICESTERSHIRE v LANCASHIRE

At Leicester, May 7. Lancashire won by eight wickets. Toss: Lancashire.

Lancashire's opening bowlers supplied a generous diet of long-hops, but Leicestershire were equally profligate with their wickets, the last six falling for 34. Lancashire's innings began nervously and they lost both openers for eight, though Speak and Fairbrother were more secure as they compiled an unbroken partnership of 169.

Gold Award: N. J. Speak.

Leicestershire

V. J. Wells b Elworthy	18
J. M. Dakin c Fairbrother b Martin	20
B. F. Smith c Hegg b Elworthy	11
P. V. Simmons c Martin b Elworthy	11
*J. J. Whitaker lbw b Watkinson	45
D. L. Maddy c Hegg b Martin	31
†P. A. Nixon c and b Watkinson	12
G. J. Parsons c Austin b Watkinson	8
D. J. Millns b Austin	1
A. R. K. Pierson not out	2
A. D. Mullally b Martin	5
L-b 6, w 6	12
1/32 2/49 3/52 4/83 5/142 6/144 7/165 8/167 9/170 (44 overs)	176

Bowling: Martin 9–1–43–3; Austin 8–1–26–1; Elworthy 7–0–30–3; Yates 10–3–30–0; Watkinson 10–1–41–3.

Lancashire

J. E. R. Gallian c Simmons b Mullally	0
M. A. Atherton lbw b Millns	4
N. J. Speak not out	79
N. H. Fairbrother not out	77
L-b 6, w 9, n-b 2	17
1/1 2/8 (2 wkts, 45 overs)	177

G. D. Lloyd, †W. K. Hegg, *M. Watkinson, I. D. Austin, S. Elworthy, P. J. Martin and G. Yates did not bat.

Bowling: Mullally 10–2–17–1; Millns 10–2–26–1; Parsons 10–0–37–0; Pierson 9–0–57–0; Simmons 3–0–13–0; Maddy 1–0–11–0; Wells 2–0–10–0.

Umpires: M. J. Kitchen and B. J. Meyer.

WARWICKSHIRE v DERBYSHIRE

At Birmingham, May 7. Warwickshire won by eight wickets. Toss: Derbyshire.

Pollock was Derbyshire's chief tormentor as they struggled to reach a defensible total. Only a stand of 105 between Jones and Owen gave them any hope. But Knight and Smith opened with 162 in just 19 overs, the biggest partnership in Warwickshire's Benson and Hedges history. Warwickshire needed less than half their allocation of overs to ensure their place in the quarter-finals.

Gold Award: N. M. K. Smith.

Derbyshire

*D. M. Jones lbw b Reeve	64
K. J. Barnett c Piper b Pollock	5
C. J. Adams c Piper b Pollock	1
J. E. Owen b N. M. K. Smith	49
C. M. Wells c Khan b Reeve	6
P. A. J. DeFreitas c sub b Pollock	20
†K. M. Krikken lbw b N. M. K. Smith	2
D. G. Cork lbw b Pollock	16
F. A. Griffith run out	3
P. Aldred c Giles b Pollock	7
D. E. Malcolm not out	1
L-b 12, w 3, n-b 4	19
1/5 2/27 3/132 4/142 5/144 6/148 7/174 8/184 9/190 (48.4 overs)	193

Bowling: Pollock 9.4–1–38–5; Brown 10–2–26–0; Giles 6–0–33–0; Munton 5–0–23–0; Reeve 9–1–24–2; N. M. K. Smith 9–0–37–2.

Warwickshire

N. V. Knight c Malcolm b Aldred	91
N. M. K. Smith b Aldred	80
P. A. Smith not out	12
W. G. Khan not out	0
L-b 2, w 5, n-b 4	11
1/162 2/187 (2 wkts, 23.3 overs)	194

T. L. Penney, *D. A. Reeve, S. M. Pollock, D. R. Brown, †K. J. Piper, A. F. Giles and T. A. Munton did not bat.

Bowling: Malcolm 5–0–54–0; Cork 4–0–22–0; Aldred 5–0–35–2; Jones 2–0–18–0; Wells 1–0–7–0; Griffith 4–0–42–0; Barnett 2.3–0–14–0.

Umpires: K. E. Palmer and R. A. White.

DERBYSHIRE v MINOR COUNTIES

At Derby, May 14. Derbyshire won by six wickets. Toss: Derbyshire.

Former Yorkshire batsman Kevin Sharp made 71 as Minor Counties notched up 232, their biggest total of the campaign. But Jones replied with 142 in 101 balls, the highest score for Derbyshire in the competition, and put on 196 with Barnett, which took only 29 overs.

Gold Award: D. M. Jones.

Minor Counties

*S. J. Dean st Krikken b Vandrau	32
K. Sharp run out	71
L. Potter c Krikken b Harris	20
S. D. Myles c Jones b Wells	57
J. P. J. Sylvester lbw b Wells	11
S. V. Laudat b Wells	17
†J. N. Batty run out	0
Z. A. Sher run out	14
M. G. Powell lbw b Wells	0
M. J. Saggers not out	1
M. A. Sharp c Harris b DeFreitas	1
L-b 2, w 6	8
1/49 2/91 3/177 4/196 5/197 6/197 7/208 8/227 9/230 (48.3 overs)	232

Bowling: Malcolm 6–0–41–0; Harris 7–0–34–1; Vandrau 10–1–59–1; DeFreitas 8.3–0–34–1; Aldred 4–0–18–0; Wells 10–1–36–4; Barnett 3–0–8–0.

Derbyshire

*D. M. Jones c Potter b Sher	142
K. J. Barnett c Batty b Sher	48
J. E. Owen lbw b Saggers	21
M. J. Vandrau c Potter b Sher	11
C. M. Wells not out	0
†K. M. Krikken not out	4
L-b 5, w 4	9
1/196 2/197 3/231 4/231 (4 wkts, 36.5 overs)	235

C. J. Adams, P. A. J. DeFreitas, P. Aldred, A. J. Harris and D. E. Malcolm did not bat.

Bowling: Saggers 4–0–43–1; M. A. Sharp 8–0–42–0; Laudat 4–0–36–0; Potter 7–1–18–0; Myles 3–0–32–0; Powell 6–0–39–0; Sher 4.5–1–20–3.

Umpires: H. D. Bird and B. J. Meyer.

LANCASHIRE v WARWICKSHIRE

At Manchester, May 14. Lancashire won by one wicket. Toss: Warwickshire.

The holders of the Benson and Hedges Cup met the holders of the NatWest Trophy and both sets of batsmen showed why they are so successful in the one-day format. The biggest partnerships in a match aggregate of 628 for 15 were from Knight and Smith (97 for Warwickshire's first wicket) and Gallian and Crawley (95 for Lancashire's fourth). But it was the 98 runs that Lloyd put on with the doughty tailenders that won Lancashire's fifth successive qualifier after they slipped to 218 for six. Lloyd hit 63 in 40 balls.

Gold Award: G. D. Lloyd.

Warwickshire

N. V. Knight c Fairbrother b Martin 47
N. M. K. Smith c Atherton b Yates 51
P. A. Smith c Gallian b Chapple 17
D. P. Ostler c Atherton b Yates 21
T. L. Penney c and b Martin 34
*D. A. Reeve st Hegg b Yates 27
S. M. Pollock not out 59
D. R. Brown not out 33
L-b 11, w 4, n-b 8 23

1/97 2/112 3/132 4/168 5/208 6/230 (6 wkts, 50 overs) 312

†K. J. Piper, G. Welch and A. F. Giles did not bat.

Bowling: Martin 10–0–57–2; Austin 10–1–62–0; Chapple 10–0–61–1; Yates 10–0–65–3; Watkinson 10–0–56–0.

Lancashire

M. A. Atherton lbw b Giles 15
*M. Watkinson c Reeve b Pollock 37
J. E. R. Gallian c Brown b Welch 61
I. D. Austin b N. M. K. Smith 16
J. P. Crawley c Reeve b Welch 47
N. H. Fairbrother c Reeve b N. M. K. Smith . 12
G. D. Lloyd not out 63
†W. K. Hegg b Reeve 10
G. Yates st Piper b Reeve 13
G. Chapple c P. A. Smith b Reeve 8
P. J. Martin not out 5
B 2, l-b 8, w 15, n-b 4 29

1/55 2/66 3/98 4/193 5/203 6/218 7/241 8/274 9/292 (9 wkts, 49.5 overs) 316

Bowling: Pollock 10–0–66–1; Brown 3–0–27–0; Giles 10–1–49–1; N. M. K. Smith 9–1–47–2; Reeve 8.5–0–55–3; P. A. Smith 2–0–19–0; Welch 7–0–43–2.

Umpires: G. I. Burgess and N. T. Plews.

LEICESTERSHIRE v DURHAM

At Leicester, May 14. Leicestershire won by four wickets. Toss: Durham.

Durham came tantalisingly close to their first victory against first-class opposition in 1996. Morris's 145 and a total of 287 were both county records for the tournament, and Leicestershire were 128 for four in reply. But uncapped batsmen Dakin and Maddy blocked Durham's progress, their fifth-wicket stand realising 153 and a maiden one-day hundred for Dakin. With two balls remaining, he hit the winning four off Killeen.

Gold Award: J. M. Dakin.

Durham

S. L. Campbell c Wells b Mullally 0
*M. A. Roseberry c Smith b Brimson 57
J. E. Morris c Whitaker b Parsons 145
J. I. Longley c Whitaker b Parsons 37
P. D. Collingwood not out 15
J. A. Daley run out 8
M. J. Foster not out 0
B 2, l-b 9, w 10, n-b 4 25

1/1 2/168 3/260 4/261 5/285 (5 wkts, 50 overs) 287

†D. G. C. Ligertwood, J. Boiling, S. J. E. Brown and N. Killeen did not bat.

Bowling: Mullally 10–1–56–1; Parsons 10–1–51–2; Simmons 9–0–50–0; Wells 8–1–34–0; Brimson 10–0–56–1; Remy 3–0–29–0.

Leicestershire

P. V. Simmons c Killeen b Brown 4
V. J. Wells c Roseberry b Collingwood... 40
B. F. Smith c Boiling b Collingwood 34
*J. J. Whitaker c Ligertwood b Foster 23
J. M. Dakin not out 108
D. L. Maddy b Boiling 61
†P. A. Nixon st Ligertwood b Boiling 1
C. C. Remy not out 1
L-b 4, w 11, n-b 2 17

1/4 2/81 3/94 4/128 5/281 6/283 (6 wkts, 49.4 overs) 289

G. J. Parsons, M. T. Brimson and A. D. Mullally did not bat.

Bowling: Brown 10–0–60–1; Killeen 9.4–0–54–0; Foster 10–0–59–1; Collingwood 8–0–61–2; Boiling 10–0–32–2; Daley 2–0–19–0.

Umpires: J. H. Hampshire and A. A. Jones.

GROUP B

WORCESTERSHIRE v NORTHAMPTONSHIRE

At Worcester, April 26. Northamptonshire won by four wickets. Toss: Worcestershire. County debuts: A. Sheriyar; J. E. Emburey.

There was little to choose between these teams. Both had top scores of 66, from Leatherdale and Loye, and important contributions from left-arm seamers, Taylor and Sheriyar, who had moved to Worcester from Leicestershire. Taylor removed Hick and Moody for a combined total of four runs, and his four wickets proved decisive.

Gold Award: J. P. Taylor.

Worcestershire

T. S. Curtis b Penberthy	49
W. P. C. Weston c Loye b Taylor	19
G. A. Hick b Taylor	4
*T. M. Moody lbw b Taylor	0
D. A. Leatherdale c Loye b Emburey	66
K. R. Spiring c Curran b Emburey	33
S. R. Lampitt not out	25
†S. J. Rhodes c Fordham b Taylor	8
R. K. Illingworth not out	2
L-b 4, w 7	11
1/35 2/49 3/54 4/114 5/169 6/192 7/212 (7 wkts, 50 overs)	217

J. E. Brinkley and A. Sheriyar did not bat.

Bowling: Taylor 10–1–32–4; Mallender 7–1–33–0; Curran 7–1–31–0; Capel 5–0–25–0; Penberthy 9–0–36–1; Emburey 10–0–45–2; Bailey 2–0–11–0.

Northamptonshire

D. J. Capel c Weston b Brinkley	43
A. Fordham c Curtis b Sheriyar	14
*R. J. Bailey c Leatherdale b Sheriyar	8
M. B. Loye c Spiring b Brinkley	66
†R. J. Warren c Leatherdale b Moody	2
K. M. Curran c Curtis b Sheriyar	32
R. R. Montgomerie not out	23
A. L. Penberthy not out	18
B 2, l-b 2, w 6, n-b 2	12
1/47 2/64 3/85 4/88 5/152 6/189 (6 wkts, 49 overs)	218

J. E. Emburey, J. P. Taylor and N. A. Mallender did not bat.

Bowling: Brinkley 9–1–44–2; Moody 10–5–37–1; Sheriyar 9–0–40–3; Lampitt 10–0–36–0; Illingworth 10–0–43–0; Hick 1–0–14–0.

Umpires: H. D. Bird and B. Leadbeater.

YORKSHIRE v NOTTINGHAMSHIRE

At Leeds, April 26. Yorkshire won by 69 runs. Toss: Yorkshire. County debuts: A. A. Metcalfe, C. M. Tolley.

Byas was dropped three times but reached 81, while White's heavily-improvised 57 from 49 balls caught the eye. Alex Wharf, 20, something of a surprise selection, bowled his seamers well for four wickets.

Gold Award: C. White.

Yorkshire

*D. Byas lbw b Tolley	81
M. D. Moxon c Bates b Pennett	20
M. P. Vaughan c Pennett b Bates	22
M. G. Bevan c Metcalfe b Mike	1
A. McGrath c Metcalfe b Dowman	29
C. White not out	57
†R. J. Blakey c Bates b Pennett	20
D. Gough run out	0
B 3, l-b 6, w 6, n-b 2	17
1/35 2/84 3/99 4/164 5/180 6/246 7/247 (7 wkts, 50 overs)	247

P. J. Hartley, A. G. Wharf and R. D. Stemp did not bat.

Bowling: Evans 8–0–34–0; Pennett 9–0–57–2; Tolley 8–0–39–1; Mike 8–3–33–1; Bates 10–1–38–1; Dowman 7–0–37–1.

Nottinghamshire

P. R. Pollard lbw b Wharf	3	R. T. Bates b Wharf	27
R. T. Robinson c Hartley b Wharf	8	G. W. Mike not out	1
A. A. Metcalfe c Vaughan b White	66	D. B. Pennett lbw b Gough	1
*P. Johnson c Byas b Hartley	18	L-b 11, w 4, n-b 6	21
M. P. Dowman b Stemp	14		—
C. M. Tolley c Gough b Stemp	10	1/9 2/16 3/51 (43.1 overs)	178
†W. M. Noon b White	1	4/94 5/116 6/123	
K. P. Evans b Wharf	8	7/136 8/169 9/176	

Bowling: Gough 7.1–2–20–1; Wharf 9–0–29–4; White 10–0–58–2; Hartley 7–1–27–1; Stemp 10–0–33–2.

Umpires: J. W. Holder and G. Sharp.

NOTTINGHAMSHIRE v SCOTLAND

At Nottingham, April 28. Nottinghamshire won by seven wickets. Toss: Nottinghamshire.

Philip gave Scotland a promising start, but Afford then took three wickets to restrict them. The only question after that was whether Nottinghamshire could win before the weather closed in. Johnson made sure with an unbeaten 54 off 28 balls.

Gold Award: J. A. Afford.

Scotland

B. M. W. Patterson lbw b Evans	12	I. R. Beven c Bates b Tolley	12
I. L. Philip lbw b Afford	47	J. A. R. Blain not out	10
G. N. Reifer c and b Dowman	11	K. Thomson not out	16
M. J. Smith c Metcalfe b Bates	8	L-b 8, w 8, n-b 4	20
*G. Salmond st Noon b Afford	18		—
J. G. Williamson st Noon b Bates	8	1/35 2/80 3/82 (9 wkts, 50 overs)	172
†A. G. Davies lbw b Afford	1	4/93 5/115 6/118	
I. M. Stanger b Bates	9	7/121 8/135 9/147	

Bowling: Evans 10–0–29–1; Pennett 8–0–39–0; Tolley 6–0–29–1; Dowman 6–0–28–1; Afford 10–3–18–3; Bates 10–0–21–3.

Nottinghamshire

R. T. Robinson c Davies b Thomson	27	*P. Johnson not out	54
C. M. Tolley b Reifer	66	W 3, n-b 2	5
A. A. Metcalfe c Davies b Reifer	6		—
P. R. Pollard not out	16	1/85 2/99 3/110 (3 wkts, 28.1 overs)	174

M. P. Dowman, †W. M. Noon, K. P. Evans, D. B. Pennett, R. T. Bates and J. A. Afford did not bat.

Bowling: Blain 3–0–21–0; Thomson 7.1–1–42–1; Stanger 4–0–34–0; Beven 10–2–57–0; Reifer 4–1–20–2.

Umpires: A. A. Jones and K. E. Palmer.

WORCESTERSHIRE v YORKSHIRE

At Worcester, April 28. Yorkshire won by six wickets. Toss: Worcestershire.

Yorkshire made the chase look easy on a batsman's day at Worcester, where Byas, out first ball, was the only man on either side to fail completely. Moxon and Vaughan added 100 for Yorkshire's second wicket, and Bevan paced his innings of 80 in 75 balls expertly.

Gold Award: M. G. Bevan.

Worcestershire

T. S. Curtis st Blakey b Stemp	67	D. A. Leatherdale not out	22
W. P. C. Weston c Moxon b Hartley	20	L-b 4, w 1	5
G. A. Hick c Vaughan b Wharf	95		—
*T. M. Moody not out	80	1/63 2/135 3/219 (3 wkts, 50 overs)	289

K. R. Spiring, S. R. Lampitt, †S. J. Rhodes, R. K. Illingworth, J. E. Brinkley and A. Sheriyar did not bat.

Bowling: Gough 10–1–51–0; Wharf 10–0–60–1; Hartley 10–0–52–1; Stemp 10–1–60–1; White 10–0–62–0.

Yorkshire

*D. Byas c Moody b Brinkley	0	C. White not out	26
M. D. Moxon c Rhodes b Lampitt	67	B 1, l-b 2, w 13	16
M. P. Vaughan b Lampitt	60		—
M. G. Bevan not out	80	1/0 2/100 (4 wkts, 49.1 overs)	292
A. McGrath b Illingworth	43	3/170 4/245	

†R. J. Blakey, D. Gough, P. J. Hartley, A. G. Wharf and R. D. Stemp did not bat.

Bowling: Brinkley 7–0–61–1; Moody 6–1–31–0; Hick 7–0–47–0; Lampitt 10–0–48–2; Sheriyar 9.1–1–40–0; Illingworth 10–0–62–1.

Umpires: H. D. Bird and A. Clarkson.

NOTTINGHAMSHIRE v WORCESTERSHIRE

At Nottingham, April 30. Nottinghamshire won by five wickets. Toss: Nottinghamshire.

With Worcestershire reaching 120 for one by the 23rd over, Hick and Curtis looked sure to set a big target. Instead, once Hick holed out to off-spinner Bates, the innings self-destructed, nine wickets falling for 68. Nottinghamshire made hard work of their reply, but Johnson's determination brought them a second successive victory.

Gold Award: R. T. Bates.

Worcestershire

T. S. Curtis b Afford	61	R. K. Illingworth c Johnson b Dowman	8
W. P. C. Weston c Bates b Evans	11	P. A. Thomas run out	3
G. A. Hick c Pollard b Bates	40	A. Sheriyar not out	1
*T. M. Moody run out	2	B 5, l-b 7, w 7, n-b 4	23
D. A. Leatherdale run out	1		—
S. R. Lampitt c Noon b Dowman	19	1/49 2/120 3/123 (48.2 overs)	188
†S. J. Rhodes c Pennett b Bates	4	4/124 5/133 6/138	
P. J. Newport b Dowman	15	7/166 8/175 9/181	

Bowling: Pennett 4–0–30–0; Evans 9–2–34–1; Tolley 9–0–48–0; Dowman 6.2–1–21–3; Afford 10–2–22–1; Bates 10–3–21–2.

Nottinghamshire

R. T. Robinson run out	52	M. P. Dowman not out	19
C. M. Tolley b Sheriyar	11		
R. T. Bates c Hick b Sheriyar	0	B 4, l-b 6, w 7, n-b 8	25
A. A. Metcalfe c Lampitt b Illingworth	31		—
P. R. Pollard c Weston b Lampitt	14	1/53 2/57 3/89 (5 wkts, 42.4 overs)	190
*P. Johnson not out	38	4/127 5/137	

†W. M. Noon, K. P. Evans, D. B. Pennett and J. A. Afford did not bat.

Bowling: Newport 10–0–39–0; Thomas 8.4–0–51–0; Sheriyar 7–2–28–2; Lampitt 8–0–27–1; Illingworth 9–1–35–1.

Umpires: J. H. Hampshire and A. G. T. Whitehead.

SCOTLAND v NORTHAMPTONSHIRE

At Forfar, April 30. Northamptonshire won by five wickets. Toss: Northamptonshire.

Opening batsman Iain Philip made a record-equalling 90th appearance for Scotland, and his 69 was the highest score of the match. But Bailey's 66 was made at a more bustling pace – in 70 balls – and Scotland's three late wickets were only a consolation.

Gold Award: R. J. Bailey.

Scotland

B. M. W. Patterson b Curran	29	M. J. D. Allingham not out	6
I. L. Philip run out	69	L-b 8, w 8	16
J. G. Williamson not out	51		—
M. J. Smith b Taylor	3	1/75 2/150 (4 wkts, 50 overs)	174
*G. Salmond c Capel b Mallender	0	3/156 4/159	

G. N. Reifer, †A. G. Davies, S. Gourlay, I. R. Beven and K. Thomson did not bat.

Bowling: Taylor 10–1–29–1; Mallender 10–0–30–1; Penberthy 6–1–26–0; Curran 10–2–20–1; Snape 9–0–38–0; Bailey 5–0–23–0.

Northamptonshire

D. J. Capel lbw b Beven	45	R. R. Montgomerie not out	3
A. Fordham c Beven b Thomson	9		
*R. J. Bailey c sub b Beven	66	L-b 6, w 6, n-b 8	20
M. B. Loye not out	31		—
†R. J. Warren c Davies b Beven	1	1/17 2/118 3/161 (5 wkts, 31.4 overs)	175
K. M. Curran c Allingham b Thomson	0	4/166 5/170	

A. L. Penberthy, J. N. Snape, N. A. Mallender and J. P. Taylor did not bat.

Bowling: Thomson 7.4–1–24–2; Williamson 6–2–25–0; Allingham 4–0–45–0; Reifer 5–0–28–0; Gourlay 3–0–13–0; Beven 6–0–34–3.

Umpires: B. J. Meyer and G. Sharp.

NORTHAMPTONSHIRE v NOTTINGHAMSHIRE

At Northampton, May 7. Northamptonshire won by six wickets. Toss: Northamptonshire.

Ambrose returned from the West Indies for his first game for Northamptonshire since 1994, yet it was his opening partner Taylor who returned figures of five for 45, his best in one-day cricket. Nottinghamshire's innings was built around a stand of 95 between Pollard and Metcalfe. But Bailey, with his third Benson and Hedges century, and Curran were still more successful, putting on a conclusive 119 for the fourth wicket. Defeat ended Nottinghamshire's chances of qualifying.

Gold Award: R. J. Bailey.

Nottinghamshire

R. T. Robinson c Warren b Taylor	1	R. A. Pick b Taylor	7
C. M. Tolley lbw b Taylor	3	D. B. Pennett not out	4
P. R. Pollard c Emburey b Penberthy	79	J. A. Afford not out	1
*P. Johnson c Montgomerie b Ambrose	4	B 1, l-b 12, w 11, n-b 2	26
A. A. Metcalfe c Loye b Penberthy	58		—
C. L. Cairns c Fordham b Taylor	21	1/8 2/13 3/46 (9 wkts, 50 overs)	232
†W. M. Noon c Montgomerie b Penberthy	10	4/141 5/183 6/184	
R. T. Bates b Taylor	18	7/202 8/227 9/228	

Bowling: Ambrose 10–0–32–1; Taylor 9–2–45–5; Penberthy 10–1–38–3; Curran 10–0–53–0; Emburey 10–0–42–0; Bailey 1–0–9–0.

Northamptonshire

D. J. Capel c Noon b Pick	14	†R. J. Warren not out	14
A. Fordham b Pick	2	L-b 11, w 2, n-b 4	17
*R. J. Bailey not out	115		
M. B. Loye lbw b Bates	24	1/16 2/32 (4 wkts, 48 overs)	236
K. M. Curran c Pennett b Cairns	50	3/91 4/210	

R. R. Montgomerie, A. L. Penberthy, J. E. Emburey, J. P. Taylor and C. E. L. Ambrose did not bat.

Bowling: Cairns 10–0–50–1; Pick 9–1–29–2; Pennett 9–1–49–0; Afford 8–0–33–0; Bates 7–0–48–1; Tolley 5–0–16–0.

Umpires: V. A. Holder and D. R. Shepherd.

YORKSHIRE v SCOTLAND

At Leeds, May 7. Yorkshire won by 128 runs. Toss: Yorkshire.

The best phase of the game for Scotland came early on, as they reduced Yorkshire to 170 for six in the 39th over. But Bevan and Gough, who hit 48 in 32 balls, helped Yorkshire to add another 100, and Silverwood then took four Scottish wickets for 13 in his first 27 balls.

Gold Award: C. E. W. Silverwood.

Yorkshire

*D. Byas c Reifer b Blain	40	D. Gough not out	48
M. D. Moxon c Tennant b Williamson	0	P. J. Hartley not out	17
M. P. Vaughan c Salmond b Tennant	50	L-b 5, w 6, n-b 10	21
M. G. Bevan c Gourlay b Williamson	75		
A. McGrath c Davies b Reifer	4	1/4 2/86 3/120 (7 wkts, 50 overs)	270
C. White c Davies b Reifer	4	4/137 5/151	
†R. J. Blakey c and b Tennant	11	6/170 7/228	

C. E. W. Silverwood and R. D. Stemp did not bat.

Bowling: Williamson 9–1–54–2; Stanger 6–0–62–0; Gourlay 10–0–39–0; Blain 6–0–37–1; Tennant 10–1–29–2; Reifer 9–0–44–2.

Scotland

I. L. Philip c Blakey b Silverwood	3	I. M. Stanger b McGrath	13
M. J. Smith b Silverwood	11	J. A. R. Blain b Silverwood	4
J. G. Williamson b Silverwood	2	A. M. Tennant not out	2
G. N. Reifer lbw b Silverwood	2	L-b 8, w 4, n-b 4	16
*G. Salmond c Moxon b Stemp	26		
†A. G. Davies b White	15	1/11 2/15 3/20 (41.4 overs)	142
M. J. D. Allingham b Vaughan	30	4/31 5/64 6/78	
S. Gourlay lbw b McGrath	18	7/117 8/131 9/140	

Bowling: Gough 7–0–22–0; Silverwood 7.4–0–28–5; Hartley 5–1–9–0; White 5–0–17–1; Stemp 10–2–26–1; Vaughan 5–1–22–1; McGrath 2–0–10–2.

Umpires: G. I. Burgess and A. G. T. Whitehead.

NORTHAMPTONSHIRE v YORKSHIRE

At Northampton, May 14. Northamptonshire won by seven wickets. Toss: Yorkshire.

Both sides entered the match unbeaten and assured of their places in the quarter-finals, but Northamptonshire were always favourites to complete a clean sweep. Yorkshire's innings was limited by an injury to Moxon's thumb, struck by Ambrose when he had made just six, and four run-outs. Capel and Bailey put on 148, though Capel was dropped three times before Hartley held on – too late – to a skier. Bailey won his third Gold Award in successive matches.

Gold Award: R. J. Bailey.

Yorkshire

*D. Byas b Taylor	8	P. J. Hartley not out	8
M. D. Moxon not out	11	C. E. W. Silverwood run out	1
M. P. Vaughan b Penberthy	28	R. D. Stemp c Ambrose b Curran	1
M. G. Bevan run out	81	B 6, l-b 3, w 2, n-b 8	19
A. McGrath run out	30		—
C. White c Bailey b Penberthy	3	1/15 2/70 3/137 (9 wkts, 50 overs)	205
†R. J. Blakey c Bailey b Penberthy	10	4/152 5/178 6/180	
D. Gough run out	5	7/191 8/194 9/198	

M. D. Moxon, when 6, retired hurt at 27 and resumed at 198.

Bowling: Ambrose 10–2–30–0; Taylor 10–1–40–1; Curran 8–0–36–1; Emburey 10–1–22–0; Penberthy 9–0–48–3; Bailey 3–0–20–0.

Northamptonshire

D. J. Capel c Hartley b Bevan	82	K. M. Curran not out	8
R. R. Montgomerie lbw b White	17	B 5, l-b 14, n-b 2	21
*R. J. Bailey not out	75		—
M. B. Loye lbw b Silverwood	3	1/33 2/181 3/187 (3 wkts, 45.1 overs)	206

†R. J. Warren, T. C. Walton, A. L. Penberthy, J. E. Emburey, C. E. L. Ambrose and J. P. Taylor did not bat.

Bowling: Gough 7–2–14–0; Hartley 8–2–33–0; White 4–0–17–1; Silverwood 10–1–49–1; Stemp 8–0–37–0; Vaughan 3–0–12–0; Bevan 5.1–0–25–1.

Umpires: D. R. Shepherd and R. A. White.

SCOTLAND v WORCESTERSHIRE

At Grange CC, Edinburgh, May 14. Worcestershire won by eight wickets. Toss: Scotland.

Scotland started brightly with a first-wicket stand of 96, but Lampitt's four wickets helped bring about a rapid late-order collapse, the last seven going down for 15 runs. For Worcestershire, Hick's dominant 67 contained eight fours and one six. It took him to precisely 2,500 runs in Benson and Hedges cricket – he was the seventh player to reach the landmark – and earned him his 11th Gold Award. This was Worcestershire's only win of the qualifying rounds.

Gold Award: G. A. Hick.

Scotland

B. M. W. Patterson run out	50	S. Gourlay not out	2
I. L. Philip c Moody b Illingworth	54	I. R. Beven lbw b Lampitt	0
M. J. Smith c Hick b Lampitt	33	K. Thomson c Rhodes b Lampitt	1
M. J. D. Allingham b Thomas	1	B 1, l-b 1, w 2	4
J. G. Williamson c Spiring b Moody	12		—
*G. Salmond c Rhodes b Lampitt	0	1/96 2/119 3/122 (48.2 overs)	159
G. N. Reifer run out	2	4/144 5/148 6/155	
†A. G. Davies lbw b Brinkley	0	7/155 8/155 9/155	

Bowling: Thomas 10–2–34–1; Brinkley 9–1–31–1; Lampitt 9.2–1–29–4; Moody 5–0–22–1; Illingworth 10–2–18–1; Leatherdale 5–0–23–0.

Worcestershire

*T. M. Moody lbw b Gourlay	17
T. S. Curtis c Beven b Thomson	61
G. A. Hick not out	67
D. A. Leatherdale not out	10
B 2, l-b 3, w 1	6
	—
1/58 2/136 (2 wkts, 34.2 overs)	161

K. R. Spiring, †S. J. Rhodes, W. P. C. Weston, R. K. Illingworth, S. R. Lampitt, J. E. Brinkley and P. A. Thomas did not bat.

Bowling: Thomson 8–1–34–1; Williamson 7–0–42–0; Reifer 6–1–17–0; Gourlay 4.2–2–21–1; Allingham 4–0–15–0; Beven 5–0–27–0.

Umpires: D. J. Constant and B. Dudleston.

GROUP C

The British Universities' squad for the competition was: R. Q. Cake (Cambridge) (*captain*), J. Bahl (Brighton), S. A. J. Boswell (Wolverhampton), S. W. K. Ellis (Warwick), M. R. Evans (Loughborough), C. M. Gupte (Oxford), M. E. Harvey (Loughborough), W. J. House (Cambridge), G. A. Khan (Oxford), K. Marc (St Martin's, London), R. S. C. Martin-Jenkins (Durham), U. B. A. Rashid (South Bank), A. C. Ridley (Oxford), A. Singh (Cambridge), M. A. Wagh (Oxford), A. R. Whittall (Cambridge).

R. R. Dibden (Loughborough) withdrew through injury.

BRITISH UNIVERSITIES v KENT

At Oxford, April 26. Kent won by 84 runs. Toss: British Universities.

After umpire Whitehead recovered from a blow from opening bowler Scott Boswell's elbow during the first over of the match, Kent openers Ward and Fleming took advantage of the new fielding restrictions to reach 109 in 15 overs. But once they had gone, only Ealham, with 75 in 59 balls, could manage double figures. Anurag Singh, previously a stalwart of England Under-19s, batted impressively for the Universities (now known as British, rather than Combined, signifying their allegiance to the British Universities Sports Association).

Gold Award: M. A. Ealham.

Kent

T. R. Ward c Ridley b Rashid	46	M. J. McCague c Evans b Whittall	3
M. V. Fleming c Khan b Evans	72	M. M. Patel not out	6
C. L. Hooper b Martin-Jenkins	1	T. N. Wren run out	0
G. R. Cowdrey c Bahl b Martin-Jenkins	5	L-b 1, w 11, n-b 10	22
M. J. Walker c and b Evans	7		—
M. A. Ealham c Cake b Whittall	75	1/109 2/112 3/120 (47.4 overs)	250
N. J. Llong lbw b Evans	5	4/139 5/150 6/161	
*†S. A. Marsh b Martin-Jenkins	8	7/195 8/198 9/249	

Bowling: Boswell 10–0–55–0; Evans 10–1–64–3; Whittall 8.4–1–52–2; Rashid 10–3–32–1; Martin-Jenkins 9–0–46–3.

British Universities

G. A. Khan c Marsh b Wren	1	M. R. Evans c Hooper b Fleming	8
A. C. Ridley st Marsh b Patel	26	S. A. J. Boswell b McCague	3
A. Singh c McCague b Ealham	72	†J. Bahl not out	1
*R. Q. Cake c Wren b Llong	22	B 1, l-b 6, w 9	16
M. E. Harvey run out	5		—
R. S. C. Martin-Jenkins c Walker b Llong	2	1/13 2/55 3/124 (48.4 overs)	166
U. B. A. Rashid b McCague	10	4/135 5/138 6/139	
A. R. Whittall b Ealham	0	7/145 8/159 9/161	

Bowling: McCague 7.4–1–30–2; Wren 2–0–21–1; Hooper 10–0–26–0; Patel 10–2–20–1; Llong 10–0–38–2; Ealham 7–0–22–2; Fleming 2–0–2–1.

Umpires: R. A. White and A. G. T. Whitehead.

GLAMORGAN v ESSEX

At Cardiff, April 26. Glamorgan won by four wickets. Toss: Essex. County debuts: A. P. Grayson, S. G. Law.

Thomas made an immediate impact, plucking out Essex's powerful top three in his first five overs. His work was followed up by Croft to keep Essex to a feeble 151. Then, as Glamorgan's innings faltered at 110 for six, Thomas scored an aggressive, run-a-ball 27 to ensure victory.

Gold Award: S. D. Thomas.

Essex

G. A. Gooch c Metson b Thomas	16	M. C. Ilott c James b Thomas	12
*P. J. Prichard c Metson b Thomas	8	P. M. Such not out	10
N. Hussain c Metson b Thomas	0	D. M. Cousins b Barwick	10
S. G. Law run out	17	L-b 3, w 7	10
R. C. Irani c Cottey b Croft	28		—
D. D. J. Robinson c Maynard b Croft	36	1/9 2/9 3/37 (47.3 overs)	151
A. P. Grayson c Cottey b Croft	1	4/44 5/105 6/107	
†R. J. Rollins b Croft	3	7/111 8/128 9/128	

Bowling: Watkin 10–2–23–0; Thomas 10–0–51–4; Barwick 8.3–1–23–1; Dale 9–2–21–0; Croft 10–3–30–4.

Glamorgan

R. D. B. Croft c Hussain b Ilott	12	A. Dale not out	18
H. Morris b Such	33	S. D. Thomas not out	27
S. P. James lbw b Cousins	4	L-b 8, w 8	16
D. L. Hemp b Irani	33		—
*M. P. Maynard b Irani	12	1/19 2/28 3/69 (6 wkts, 47.4 overs)	155
P. A. Cottey c Prichard b Irani	0	4/100 5/102 6/110	

†C. P. Metson, S. L. Watkin and S. R. Barwick did not bat.

Bowling: Ilott 10–2–27–1; Cousins 8.4–0–33–1; Irani 10–1–43–3; Such 10–2–16–1; Grayson 9–2–28–0.

Umpires: G. I. Burgess and K. J. Lyons.

MIDDLESEX v SOMERSET

At Lord's, April 26. Somerset won by 152 runs. Toss: Somerset. County debuts: S. Lee, K. J. Shine.

Somerset beat their previous highest total in the competition by one run after Lathwell and Ecclestone, who scored his first century in any first-team game for Somerset, added 188 for the second wicket. Turner maintained their progress with 45 off 23 balls. Middlesex only got going briefly, when Ramprakash and Carr put together a stand of 82.

Gold Award: S. C. Ecclestone.

Somerset

M. N. Lathwell c Feltham b Johnson	121	S. Lee not out	0
P. D. Bowler c and b Feltham	21	L-b 14, w 5, n-b 4	23
S. C. Ecclestone not out	112		—
†R. J. Turner run out	45	1/57 2/245 (4 wkts, 50 overs)	322
G. D. Rose run out	0	3/320 4/321	

R. J. Harden, *A. N. Hayhurst, K. A. Parsons, K. J. Shine and H. R. J. Trump did not bat.

Bowling: Follett 10–1–49–0; Fraser 10–2–55–0; Feltham 10–0–63–1; Johnson 9–1–66–1; Ramprakash 5–0–30–0; Weekes 6–0–45–0.

Middlesex

P. N. Weekes c Turner b Shine	7	R. L. Johnson c Lee b Trump	8
J. C. Pooley b Shine	8	A. R. C. Fraser not out	2
M. R. Ramprakash c Turner b Hayhurst	50	D. Follett run out	0
*M. W. Gatting b Rose	12	L-b 5, w 2, n-b 4	11
J. D. Carr b Hayhurst	51		—
O. A. Shah lbw b Trump	6	1/11 2/28 3/45 (42.2 overs)	170
†K. R. Brown c Lee b Hayhurst	3	4/127 5/138 6/142	
M. A. Feltham c Lathwell b Trump	12	7/150 8/163 9/170	

Bowling: Shine 8–2–57–2; Rose 10–3–30–1; Lee 6.2–1–21–0; Trump 10–1–28–3; Hayhurst 8–1–29–3.

Umpires: B. Dudleston and J. H. Harris.

BRITISH UNIVERSITIES v GLAMORGAN

At Cambridge, April 28. Glamorgan won by eight wickets. Toss: British Universities.

In a high-scoring match, the Universities reached 300 for the first time, and to beat them Glamorgan had to make their own biggest total in this competition. The students' innings was dominated by a magnificent 147 off 131 balls by Gul Khan, studying at Oxford after Essex dispensed with his services. Indirectly, he also disposed of Hemp, who broke two ribs after colliding with Morris in an attempt to catch him; Hemp missed most of the season. But Maynard struck back with a 58-ball century, the fastest in Glamorgan's one-day history. He hit five sixes and seven fours and his partnership of 184 in 20 overs with James turned the match.

Gold Award: M. P. Maynard.

British Universities

G. A. Khan b Croft	147
A. C. Ridley c Morris b Cottey	58
A. Singh c Metson b Dale	34
*R. Q. Cake run out	28
M. E. Harvey b Thomas	1
R. S. C. Martin-Jenkins c Dale b Barwick	12
U. B. A. Rashid not out	17
K. Marc c Thomas b Watkin	6
A. R. Whittall lbw b Watkin	0
S. A. J. Boswell not out	0
B 1, l-b 6, w 2	9
1/127 2/209 3/265 4/272 5/279 6/290 7/295 8/300 (8 wkts, 50 overs)	312

†J. Bahl did not bat.

Bowling: Watkin 8–1–66–2; Thomas 8–0–46–1; Dale 4–0–35–1; Barwick 10–1–69–1; Croft 10–0–40–1; Cottey 10–0–49–1.

Glamorgan

S. P. James not out	121
H. Morris c Harvey b Whittall	32
A. Dale c Ridley b Marc	23
*M. P. Maynard not out	110
B 4, l-b 2, w 10, n-b 12	28
1/92 2/130 (2 wkts, 46.4 overs)	314

P. A. Cottey, D. L. Hemp, R. D. B. Croft, S. D. Thomas, †C. P. Metson, S. L. Watkin and S. R. Barwick did not bat.

Bowling: Boswell 10–1–54–0; Marc 9–0–70–1; Whittall 9–0–60–1; Martin-Jenkins 8.4–0–52–0; Rashid 5–0–33–0; Ridley 5–0–39–0.

Umpires: M. J. Kitchen and D. R. Shepherd.

ESSEX v MIDDLESEX

At Chelmsford, April 28. Essex won by five wickets. Toss: Essex.

For the second match running, Ramprakash and Carr were the only Middlesex batsmen to apply themselves, putting together a cautious stand of 91 in 23 overs after a slump to 33 for three. But Hussain's unbeaten 67 was more than enough to overtake their modest total.

Gold Award: N. Hussain.

Middlesex

P. N. Weekes c Gooch b Irani	12
J. C. Pooley c Gooch b Ilott	6
M. R. Ramprakash c Hussain b Such	56
*M. W. Gatting b Law	0
J. D. Carr c Gooch b Such	51
†K. R. Brown c and b Ilott	5
R. L. Johnson c Robinson b Ilott	1
R. A. Fay b Ilott	1
A. R. C. Fraser not out	10
P. C. R. Tufnell not out	3
B 1, l-b 2, w 2	5
1/13 2/32 3/33 4/124 5/132 6/136 7/136 8/143 (8 wkts, 50 overs)	150

D. Follett did not bat.

Bowling: Ilott 10–3–17–4; Cousins 6–4–8–0; Irani 10–0–40–1; Law 10–0–35–1; Such 10–0–32–2; Grayson 4–0–15–0.

Essex

G. A. Gooch c Weekes b Fraser	15	A. P. Grayson not out	12
*P. J. Prichard c Brown b Fay	5		
N. Hussain not out	67	B 1, l-b 7, w 1	9
S. G. Law c Pooley b Weekes	39		—
R. C. Irani b Tufnell	1	1/21 2/27 3/101	(5 wkts, 43 overs) 151
D. D. J. Robinson c and b Tufnell	3	4/103 5/111	

†R. J. Rollins, M. C. Ilott, P. M. Such and D. M. Cousins did not bat.

Bowling: Fraser 7–3–10–1; Fay 7–2–13–1; Johnson 8–0–35–0; Follett 4–1–20–0; Tufnell 10–1–31–2; Weekes 7–0–34–1.

Umpires: R. Palmer and A. G. T. Whitehead.

KENT v SOMERSET

At Maidstone, April 28. Kent won by 45 runs. Toss: Kent.

Some crucial dropped catches helped Kent to their highest total in the competition. Hooper scored most, with 98 in 94 balls, but Ealham's innings was the more dramatic: he made 72 off 39 balls including five sixes. Of Kent's batsmen, only Cowdrey failed, but he later took two particularly fine catches in the deep, one to prevent Ecclestone from reaching a second century in three days; his 92 took 63 balls. The match aggregate of 631 runs for 15 wickets was the biggest in Benson and Hedges cricket, even though there were now only 100 overs available, rather than 110.

Gold Award: M. A. Ealham.

Kent

T. R. Ward c Rose b Parsons	58	N. J. Llong not out	12
M. V. Fleming run out	41	*†S. A. Marsh not out	4
C. L. Hooper c Hayhurst b Parsons	98	B 1, l-b 5, w 2, n-b 4	12
G. R. Cowdrey c Trump b Hayhurst	0		—
M. J. Walker c Turner b Rose	41	1/62 2/193 3/193	(6 wkts, 50 overs) 338
M. A. Ealham lbw b Rose	72	4/210 5/321 6/322	

M. J. McCague, M. M. Patel and T. N. Wren did not bat.

Bowling: Shine 5–0–57–0; Rose 9–1–42–2; Lee 10–1–73–0; Trump 10–0–72–0; Hayhurst 10–3–28–1; Parsons 6–0–60–2.

Somerset

M. N. Lathwell c Marsh b Patel	29	K. A. Parsons c Marsh b Ealham	3
G. D. Rose c Marsh b Ealham	37	H. R. J. Trump c Marsh b Ealham	10
P. D. Bowler b Hooper	2	K. J. Shine not out	38
S. C. Ecclestone c Cowdrey b Fleming	92	L-b 4, w 3, n-b 2	9
R. J. Harden c Cowdrey b Patel	8		—
S. Lee c and b Fleming	13	1/46 2/54 3/101	(9 wkts, 50 overs) 293
†R. J. Turner c Cowdrey b Ealham	28	4/155 5/176 6/209	
*A. N. Hayhurst not out	24	7/217 8/222 9/245	

Bowling: McCague 10–1–36–0; Wren 3–0–32–0; Ealham 10–0–50–4; Hooper 7–0–44–1; Patel 10–0–74–2; Fleming 10–1–53–2.

Umpires: J. C. Balderstone and J. H. Harris.

ESSEX v BRITISH UNIVERSITIES

At Chelmsford, April 30. Essex won by 107 runs. Toss: British Universities.

Gooch, far and away the most prolific batsman in the competition's history, scored his 15th century and passed 5,000 runs in his 108th innings, while his nearest rival, Gatting, was still below 3,000. Gooch scored 100 in 104 balls and his opening stand with Prichard raised 200. Nevertheless, Irani deprived him of his 23rd Gold Award by hitting 62 off 28 balls and then taking four wickets.

Gold Award: R. C. Irani.

Essex

G. A. Gooch run out	100
*P. J. Prichard lbw b Rashid	82
N. Hussain c Singh b Boswell	21
S. G. Law c Boswell b Rashid	20
R. C. Irani not out	62
D. D. J. Robinson c Cake b Martin-Jenkins	10
A. P. Grayson not out	10
L-b 8, w 10, n-b 8	26
1/200 2/203 3/233 4/243 5/264 (5 wkts, 50 overs)	331

†R. J. Rollins, M. C. Ilott, P. M. Such and N. F. Williams did not bat.

Bowling: Boswell 10–0–95–1; Marc 10–0–60–0; Martin-Jenkins 10–0–38–1; Evans 10–0–73–0; Rashid 10–0–57–2.

British Universities

G. A. Khan lbw b Irani	33
A. C. Ridley c Gooch b Law	33
A. Singh c Gooch b Ilott	12
*R. Q. Cake c Rollins b Irani	14
C. M. Gupte not out	54
R. S. C. Martin-Jenkins c Rollins b Irani	2
K. Marc c Grayson b Irani	13
U. B. A. Rashid b Williams	25
M. R. Evans lbw b Williams	2
S. A. J. Boswell c Ilott b Grayson	14
†J. Bahl not out	0
L-b 14, w 6, n-b 2	22
1/54 2/77 3/91 4/110 5/120 6/138 7/180 8/190 9/223 (9 wkts, 50 overs)	224

Bowling: Ilott 7–0–29–1; Williams 10–0–67–2; Law 5–1–25–1; Irani 10–1–30–4; Such 10–3–31–0; Grayson 8–1–28–1.

Umpires: J. C. Balderstone and R. Julian.

GLAMORGAN v SOMERSET

At Cardiff, April 30, May 1. Somerset won on scoring-rate. Toss: Glamorgan.

Somerset were 69 for five before Hayhurst and Turner built a sixth-wicket stand of 113. In reply, Maynard and Dale seemed to have matters in hand at 108 for two, but rain necessitated a second day's play, and then returned to reduce the target to 173 from 36 overs. Glamorgan could not re-adjust their sights, and two late wickets from Lee sealed the visitors' victory.

Gold Award: R. J. Turner.

Close of play: Glamorgan 108-2 (27 overs) (A. Dale 32*, M. P. Maynard 31*).

Somerset

M. N. Lathwell lbw b Watkin	1
P. D. Bowler c Metson b Watkin	23
S. C. Ecclestone c Metson b Thomas	4
R. J. Harden b Dale	11
S. Lee c and b Barwick	19
*A. N. Hayhurst not out	67
†R. J. Turner lbw b Croft	70
G. D. Rose run out	1
J. D. Batty c Thomas b Watkin	14
A. R. Caddick not out	7
L-b 6, w 16	22
1/10 2/28 3/32 4/69 5/69 6/182 7/194 8/231 (8 wkts, 50 overs)	239

H. R. J. Trump did not bat.

Bowling: Watkin 10–3–51–3; Thomas 9–0–53–1; Dale 5–0–18–1; Barwick 10–1–49–1; Butcher 6–0–27–0; Croft 10–0–35–1.

Glamorgan

S. P. James c Trump b Caddick	1	S. D. Thomas c Ecclestone b Lee	0
H. Morris c Turner b Caddick	34	G. P. Butcher not out	3
A. Dale c Trump b Rose	46	L-b 6, w 8	14
*M. P. Maynard b Hayhurst	37		—
P. A. Cottey not out	24	1/16 2/50 3/121 (6 wkts, 36 overs)	161
R. D. B. Croft c Trump b Lee	2	4/140 5/143 6/146	

†C. P. Metson, S. L. Watkin and S. R. Barwick did not bat.

Bowling: Caddick 10–3–42–2; Rose 8–1–33–1; Lee 7–0–36–2; Ecclestone 8–0–31–0; Hayhurst 3–0–13–1.

Umpires: B. Dudleston and J. W. Holder.

KENT v MIDDLESEX

At Canterbury, April 30. Kent won by six wickets. Toss: Middlesex.

Middlesex lost their third consecutive match in the competition after their batting – apart from Carr, with his third successive fifty – disappointed again. Thompson, the doctor who dismissed Brian Lara for a pair in 1995, did most of the damage. As Hooper and Ealham continued their prolific form, Middlesex's only consolation came from the 17-year-old Owais Shah, who hit McCague for a straight six during his unbeaten 42.

Gold Award: J. B. D. Thompson.

Middlesex

P. N. Weekes b Thompson	5	O. A. Shah not out	42
J. C. Pooley c Walker b Thompson	1	A. R. C. Fraser not out	10
M. R. Ramprakash c Marsh b Fleming	26	L-b 5, w 6, n-b 8	19
*M. W. Gatting c Marsh b Thompson	18		—
J. D. Carr run out	55	1/12 2/12 3/44 (6 wkts, 50 overs)	219
†K. R. Brown b McCague	43	4/79 5/138 6/197	

D. Follett, P. C. R. Tufnell and R. A. Fay did not bat.

Bowling: McCague 10–1–53–1; Thompson 10–2–29–3; Fleming 9–1–30–1; Ealham 10–0–56–0; Hooper 7–0–31–0; Patel 4–0–15–0.

Kent

T. R. Ward c Gatting b Follett	46	M. A. Ealham not out	21
M. V. Fleming c Pooley b Fay	12	B 1, l-b 5, w 12, n-b 2	20
C. L. Hooper c Ramprakash b Weekes	62		—
G. R. Cowdrey c Ramprakash b Weekes	31	1/20 2/105 (4 wkts, 47.2 overs)	220
M. J. Walker not out	28	3/167 4/171	

N. J. Llong, *†S. A. Marsh, M. J. McCague, J. B. D. Thompson and M. M. Patel did not bat.

Bowling: Fay 10–0–38–1; Fraser 6–1–27–0; Follett 10–0–53–1; Carr 9–1–31–0; Weekes 7.2–0–39–2; Tufnell 5–0–26–0.

Umpires: B. Leadbeater and D. R. Shepherd.

ESSEX v KENT

At Chelmsford, May 7. Kent won by one wicket. Toss: Essex.

Thompson again showed his knack for taking the big wicket by having Gooch caught behind for 12. Patel's left-arm spin was treated with contempt by Hussain and Law, who took 34 off his four overs, but he had his revenge in the last over of the game when he took a four and a two off Law's medium-pace to complete Kent's fourth straight win.

Man of the Match: J. B. D. Thompson.

Essex

G. A. Gooch c Marsh b Thompson 12
*P. J. Prichard b Thompson 24
N. Hussain b Hooper 82
S. G. Law c Fleming b Hooper 33
R. C. Irani c Marsh b McCague 43
D. D. J. Robinson not out 10
A. P. Grayson run out 12
†R. J. Rollins not out 0
L-b 7, w 2 9

1/29 2/36 3/102 4/188 5/205 6/224 (6 wkts, 50 overs) 225

M. C. Ilott, P. M. Such and A. P. Cowan did not bat.

Bowling: McCague 8–1–35–1; Thompson 10–2–26–2; Fleming 10–0–44–0; Patel 4–0–34–0; Hooper 10–0–36–2; Ealham 8–0–43–0.

Kent

T. R. Ward b Such 51
M. V. Fleming c Rollins b Ilott 22
C. L. Hooper c Irani b Cowan 45
G. R. Cowdrey c Rollins b Ilott 31
M. J. Walker lbw b Grayson 33
M. A. Ealham c Hussain b Ilott 6
N. J. Llong lbw b Grayson 0
*†S. A. Marsh b Grayson 17
M. J. McCague run out 1
J. B. D. Thompson not out 4
M. M. Patel not out 6
L-b 7, w 1, n-b 2 10

1/29 2/95 3/143 4/162 5/172 6/173 7/207 8/214 9/218 (9 wkts, 49.4 overs) 226

Bowling: Ilott 10–3–32–3; Law 8.4–0–66–0; Cowan 9–0–38–1; Such 10–0–33–1; Irani 3–0–20–0; Grayson 9–1–30–3.

Umpires: J. H. Harris and J. W. Holder.

MIDDLESEX v GLAMORGAN

At Lord's, May 7. Glamorgan won by six wickets. Toss: Middlesex.

Middlesex continued their dismal form, allowing Maynard to run up the highest score by a Glamorgan batsman in the competition. His 151 took just 119 balls, with five sixes and 11 fours, and he shared in a stand of 137 with Dale, who had earlier ripped out Middlesex's middle order with five for 41.

Gold Award: M. P. Maynard.

Middlesex

P. N. Weekes lbw b Watkin 37
J. C. Harrison run out 24
*M. W. Gatting c Metson b Dale 45
J. C. Pooley c Morris b Dale 50
J. D. Carr c Metson b Dale 22
†K. R. Brown c James b Dale 18
K. P. Dutch b Croft 13
P. E. Wellings not out 14
R. L. Johnson c Cottey b Dale 9
A. R. C. Fraser run out 1
R. A. Fay lbw b Barwick 0
L-b 14, w 12, n-b 4 30

1/71 2/93 3/162 4/192 5/205 6/235 7/241 8/256 9/262 (49.2 overs) 263

Bowling: Gibson 8–1–37–0; Watkin 10–1–40–1; Thomas 6–1–35–0; Barwick 9.2–0–40–1; Croft 9–0–56–1; Dale 7–0–41–5.

Glamorgan

S. P. James c Brown b Fraser........... 11
H. Morris c Wellings b Fay 12
A. Dale c Gatting b Wellings 42
*M. P. Maynard not out 151
P. A. Cottey c Johnson b Weekes 29
R. D. B. Croft not out 9
L-b 3, w 3, n-b 5 11

1/25 2/25 3/162 4/243 (4 wkts, 48.5 overs) 265

O. D. Gibson, S. D. Thomas, †C. P. Metson, S. L. Watkin and S. R. Barwick did not bat.

Bowling: Fraser 10–2–30–1; Fay 10–1–43–1; Johnson 10–1–63–0; Dutch 5–0–33–0; Weekes 8–0–48–1; Wellings 5.5–0–45–1.

Umpires: A. A. Jones and R. Palmer.

SOMERSET v BRITISH UNIVERSITIES

At Taunton, May 7. Somerset won by three wickets. Toss: British Universities.

Not for the first time, the Universities came very close to upsetting Somerset, who were floundering at 209 for seven in the 41st over, still needing 63. But strong batting down the order from Turner and Parsons, a better batsman than his No. 9 position might suggest, saw them to safety with seven balls to spare. Earlier, Singh's stylish 123 was taken from 133 balls, and included 13 fours and a six.

Gold Award: A. Singh.

British Universities

G. A. Khan lbw b Caddick	25	M. R. Evans not out	8
A. C. Ridley run out	35	S. A. J. Boswell lbw b Caddick	1
A. Singh c Parsons b Lee	123	†J. Bahl b Caddick	0
*R. Q. Cake c Parsons b Lee	24	L-b 14, w 8, n-b 2	24
C. M. Gupte c and b Rose	21		—
M. A. Wagh b Caddick	6	1/34 2/98 3/171 (49 overs)	271
K. Marc b Caddick	0	4/213 5/239 6/241	
S. W. K. Ellis b Lee	4	7/253 8/263 9/271	

Bowling: Caddick 10–1–51–5; Rose 10–1–39–1; Lee 9–0–60–3; Trump 10–0–44–0; Hayhurst 3–0–26–0; Parsons 7–0–37–0.

Somerset

M. N. Lathwell c Bahl b Marc	76	G. D. Rose lbw b Evans	1
P. D. Bowler b Boswell	2	K. A. Parsons not out	33
S. C. Ecclestone c Marc b Wagh	62	L-b 1, w 8, n-b 2	11
R. J. Harden run out	0		—
S. Lee run out	23	1/5 2/143 3/143 (7 wkts, 48.5 overs)	272
*A. N. Hayhurst lbw b Ellis	25	4/162 5/177	
†R. J. Turner not out	39	6/206 7/209	

A. R. Caddick and H. R. J. Trump did not bat.

Bowling: Boswell 9.5–0–61–1; Marc 10–0–54–1; Ellis 9–0–50–1; Evans 8–0–55–1; Wagh 10–1–41–1; Ridley 2–0–10–0.

Umpires: J. D. Bond and T. E. Jesty.

BRITISH UNIVERSITIES v MIDDLESEX

At Cambridge, May 14. Middlesex won by five wickets. Toss: Middlesex.

Middlesex finally won in their fifth and last group game, against their only non-first-class opposition. In an odd match, their best bowling figures were returned by Ramprakash. They then made heavy weather of chasing 185; the fact that they had eight overs to spare owed much to the fact that the students donated a tournament record of 45 extras.

Gold Award: P. N. Weekes.

British Universities

C. M. Gupte lbw b Fraser	1	M. R. Evans not out	16
G. A. Khan b Follett	26	S. A. J. Boswell st Brown b Tufnell	3
A. Singh c Carr b Fraser	19	†J. Bahl st Brown b Tufnell	0
*R. Q. Cake run out	23	B 3, l-b 7, w 12	22
W. J. House c Fay b Ramprakash	22		—
M. A. Wagh c Gatting b Ramprakash	23	1/2 2/42 3/67 (49.5 overs)	184
U. B. A. Rashid c Carr b Ramprakash	29	4/101 5/114 6/148	
K. Marc c Gatting b Weekes	0	7/149 8/166 9/183	

Bowling: Fraser 10–3–27–2; Fay 7–1–29–0; Tufnell 7.5–1–33–2; Follett 5–1–11–1; Weekes 10–0–39–1; Ramprakash 10–1–35–3.

Middlesex

P. N. Weekes b Evans	52	†K. R. Brown not out	13
M. R. Ramprakash lbw b Marc	11		
O. A. Shah lbw b Marc	4	L-b 2, w 19, n-b 24	45
*M. W. Gatting c Rashid b Evans	8		—
J. C. Pooley c House b Wagh	12	1/53 2/74 3/97 (5 wkts, 41.3 overs)	185
J. D. Carr not out	40	4/121 5/125	

R. A. Fay, A. R. C. Fraser, D. Follett and P. C. R. Tufnell did not bat.

Bowling: Boswell 10–1–37–0; Evans 7–0–53–2; Rashid 9.3–0–24–0; Marc 5–0–30–2; Wagh 10–1–39–1.

Umpires: V. A. Holder and K. J. Lyons.

KENT v GLAMORGAN

At Canterbury, May 14. Glamorgan won by eight wickets. Toss: Kent.

Glamorgan's victory brought them level on points with Kent and, by establishing a better net run-rate, they earned home advantage in the quarter-finals. Kent suffered a collapse to 35 for five, engineered by Watkin, and Glamorgan were left needing 209. They calculated that they had to do it in 38.4 overs to top the group; in fact they took less than 33, after James and Morris shared a county record opening stand of 181 and Morris brought up his hundred in just 68 balls. He hit a six and 21 fours and Maynard called it the best innings he had ever seen.

Gold Award: S. L. Watkin.

Kent

T. R. Ward b Watkin	1	M. J. McCague c Metson b Gibson	17
M. V. Fleming c Dale b Watkin	16	M. M. Patel not out	18
C. L. Hooper c Maynard b Croft	62	J. B. D. Thompson not out	12
G. R. Cowdrey c James b Watkin	0	L-b 10, w 7	17
M. J. Walker c Metson b Watkin	0		—
M. A. Ealham c Maynard b Thomas	5	1/14 2/26 3/26 (9 wkts, 50 overs)	208
N. J. Llong lbw b Croft	31	4/26 5/35 6/102	
*†S. A. Marsh run out	29	7/133 8/176 9/177	

Bowling: Watkin 10–3–31–4; Gibson 8–2–33–1; Thomas 7–0–31–1; Barwick 10–0–47–0; Croft 10–1–41–2; Dale 5–1–15–0.

Glamorgan

S. P. James c Patel b Ealham	60
H. Morris not out	136
A. Dale c Ward b Ealham	1
*M. P. Maynard not out	11
W 2	2
	—
1/181 2/183 (2 wkts, 32.4 overs)	210

P. A. Cottey, R. D. B. Croft, O. D. Gibson, S. D. Thomas, †C. P. Metson, S. L. Watkin and S. R. Barwick did not bat.

Bowling: McCague 8–0–55–0; Thompson 4–0–21–0; Ealham 6–0–27–2; Fleming 6.4–1–47–0; Patel 3–0–28–0; Hooper 5–0–32–0.

Umpires: A. Clarkson and J. W. Holder.

SOMERSET v ESSEX

At Taunton, May 14. Essex won by eight wickets. Toss: Somerset.

Both sides were still fighting to reach the quarter-finals and could have done it on net run-rate, though Essex depended on Glamorgan losing at Canterbury; news of events there ended their hopes and Law's destructive century, which took 73 balls and contained 18 fours and two sixes, was thus in vain.

Gold Award: S. G. Law.

Somerset

M. N. Lathwell b Grayson	51
*P. D. Bowler run out	26
G. D. Rose c Grayson b Irani	11
R. J. Harden lbw b Law	38
S. Lee lbw b Law	8
†R. J. Turner not out	42
M. E. Trescothick not out	57
B 2, l-b 10, w 5	17
1/65 2/83 3/108 4/132 5/151 (5 wkts, 50 overs)	250

M. Dimond, A. R. Caddick, H. R. J. Trump and K. J. Shine did not bat.

Bowling: Cowan 10–2–28–0; Ilott 9–0–46–0; Law 8–0–57–2; Such 6–0–29–0; Irani 7–1–23–1; Grayson 10–0–55–1.

Essex

D. D. J. Robinson c Bowler b Lee	34
S. G. Law lbw b Trump	116
N. Hussain not out	68
G. A. Gooch not out	29
L-b 3, w 3	6
1/69 2/201 (2 wkts, 41.3 overs)	253

*P. J. Prichard, R. C. Irani, †R. J. Rollins, A. P. Grayson, M. C. Ilott, P. M. Such and A. P. Cowan did not bat.

Bowling: Caddick 7–2–31–0; Rose 7–0–39–0; Lee 8–0–55–1; Trump 10–0–47–1; Dimond 3–0–26–0; Shine 6–0–48–0; Bowler 0.3–0–4–0.

Umpires: R. Julian and A. G. T. Whitehead.

GROUP D

GLOUCESTERSHIRE v SUSSEX

At Bristol, April 26. Gloucestershire won by five wickets. Toss: Sussex. County debuts: R. P. Davis; V. C. Drakes.

After Lenham, who had rescued Sussex from 98 for five, ran himself out, Sussex struggled to produce a match-winning total on a firm pitch. Gloucestershire's reply began unconvincingly, but Symonds was as pugnacious as ever in his 59-ball 67, sharing a partnership of 108 with Hancock.

Gold Award: A. Symonds.

Sussex

C. W. J. Athey b Davis	22
M. P. Speight c Symonds b Cooper	20
*A. P. Wells lbw b Alleyne	22
K. Greenfield c Ball b Alleyne	4
N. J. Lenham run out	61
†P. Moores lbw b Davis	10
K. Newell c Wright b Smith	46
I. D. K. Salisbury lbw b Cooper	7
V. C. Drakes not out	11
P. W. Jarvis not out	10
B 3, l-b 10, w 5	18
1/24 2/64 3/70 4/70 5/98 6/186 7/198 8/207 (8 wkts, 50 overs)	231

E. S. H. Giddins did not bat.

Bowling: Smith 10–1–37–1; Cooper 10–1–48–2; Alleyne 9–0–47–2; Davis 10–1–26–2; Ball 10–0–54–0; Hancock 1–0–6–0.

Gloucestershire

A. J. Wright lbw b Drakes	15	M. W. Alleyne not out	19
R. I. Dawson lbw b Salisbury	28		
R. J. Cunliffe b Salisbury	26	L-b 3, w 3	6
M. C. J. Ball b Jarvis	0		—
T. H. C. Hancock not out	71	1/19 2/53 3/57 (5 wkts, 44.4 overs)	232
A. Symonds run out	67	4/87 5/195	

*†R. C. Russell, K. E. Cooper, A. M. Smith and R. P. Davis did not bat.

Bowling: Giddins 9.4–0–61–0; Drakes 9–1–37–1; Jarvis 7–0–23–1; Salisbury 10–0–55–2; Lenham 1–0–12–0; Greenfield 5–0–28–0; Newell 3–0–13–0.

Umpires: J. D. Bond and D. R. Shepherd.

HAMPSHIRE v IRELAND

At Southampton, April 26. Hampshire won by 166 runs. Toss: Hampshire. County debut: S. M. Milburn.

Stephenson, Hampshire's new captain, batted throughout their innings for his first one-day century for the county, adding 100 with Benjamin in a brutal assault during the last nine overs. None of Ireland's batsmen could pass 18, though the last three wickets doubled the score to reach three figures.

Gold Award: J. P. Stephenson.

Hampshire

*J. P. Stephenson not out	124	W. K. M. Benjamin not out	58
J. S. Laney c Benson b McCrum	26		
R. A. Smith c Benson b McCrum	0	L-b 4, w 11	15
G. W. White c McCrum b Harrison	30		—
M. Keech c Lewis b Benson	0	1/53 2/53 3/143 (5 wkts, 50 overs)	268
P. R. Whitaker c Rutherford b Harrison	15	4/145 5/168	

†A. N. Aymes, M. J. Thursfield, C. A. Connor and S. M. Milburn did not bat.

Bowling: Eagleson 6–0–61–0; Patterson 8–1–50–0; McCrum 10–4–10–2; Graham 8–0–41–0; Harrison 9–0–50–2; Benson 8–0–41–1; Lewis 1–0–11–0.

Ireland

S. J. S. Warke c Aymes b Milburn	3	†A. T. Rutherford not out	18
M. P. Rea c Keech b Benjamin	0	P. McCrum b Whitaker	9
S. G. Smyth run out	4	M. W. Patterson lbw b Milburn	3
*D. A. Lewis c Keech b Connor	4	L-b 16, w 2	18
J. D. R. Benson c Aymes b Benjamin	0		—
G. D. Harrison c Keech b Thursfield	12	1/7 2/11 3/11 (41.1 overs)	102
S. Graham lbw b Connor	18	4/12 5/30 6/32	
R. L. Eagleson c Milburn b Stephenson	13	7/50 8/71 9/91	

Bowling: Benjamin 6–2–13–2; Milburn 8.1–5–7–2; Thursfield 8–1–16–1; Connor 6–0–22–2; Stephenson 6–2–10–1; Whitaker 7–1–18–1.

Umpires: D. J. Constant and R. Palmer.

SURREY v HAMPSHIRE

At The Oval, April 28. Surrey won by 59 runs. Toss: Hampshire. County debuts: B. P. Julian, C. C. Lewis, R. M. Pearson.

Two England batsmen, struggling to re-establish their credentials, dominated the match. Stewart scored 160 in 151 balls, seven short of his own county record for the competition, but the total beat Surrey's previous best, also against Hampshire at The Oval, by two runs. His stand of 132 with Butcher was a sixth-wicket record for any side in the competition – though it stood for only a month. In response, Smith's admirable 123, his fifth Benson and Hedges hundred, came off 114 balls, but none of the other middle-order batsmen could manage a run.

Gold Award: A. J. Stewart.

Surrey

D. M. Ward c Aymes b Benjamin 24
A. D. Brown c Smith b Thursfield 51
*†A. J. Stewart b Benjamin 160
G. P. Thorpe b Whitaker 25
A. J. Hollioake c Benjamin b Stephenson . 3
D. J. Bicknell b Whitaker 4
M. A. Butcher not out 42
C. C. Lewis not out 7
L-b 3, w 7, n-b 7 17

1/40 2/128 3/169 (6 wkts, 50 overs) 333
4/174 5/188 6/320

R. M. Pearson, B. P. Julian and M. P. Bicknell did not bat.

Bowling: Benjamin 10–0–68–2; Milburn 6–1–54–0; Connor 10–0–73–0; Thursfield 10–0–74–1; Whitaker 10–0–33–2; Stephenson 4–0–28–1.

Hampshire

*J. P. Stephenson b M. P. Bicknell 17
J. S. Laney lbw b Hollioake 41
R. S. M. Morris lbw b M. P. Bicknell 0
R. A. Smith b Hollioake 123
G. W. White c Stewart b Hollioake 0
P. R. Whitaker c Stewart b Julian 0
W. K. M. Benjamin c Lewis b Hollioake . 5
†A. N. Aymes b Lewis 38
M. J. Thursfield c Thorpe b Lewis 19
S. M. Milburn lbw b Lewis 2
C. A. Connor not out 0
B 3, l-b 10, w 6, n-b 10 29

1/32 2/38 3/82 (48 overs) 274
4/84 5/90 6/105
7/224 8/260 9/274

Bowling: M. P. Bicknell 10–0–66–2; Lewis 9–1–32–3; Julian 10–0–55–1; Hollioake 7–1–34–4; Butcher 3–0–26–0; Pearson 9–0–48–0.

Umpires: J. D. Bond and B. Dudleston.

SUSSEX v IRELAND

At Hove, April 28. Sussex won by eight wickets. Toss: Ireland.

Speight careered to 64 from 26 balls in the same time it took the phlegmatic Athey to make two, and Sussex were 134 for two when the fielding restrictions were relaxed after 15 overs. The pace of Drakes had earlier removed both Irish openers for ten and he returned to interrupt a promising recovery.

Gold Award: M. P. Speight.

Ireland

S. J. S. Warke c Salisbury b Drakes 4
G. D. Harrison lbw b Drakes 4
S. G. Smyth c Giddins b Newell 32
*D. A. Lewis lbw b Jarvis 11
J. D. R. Benson c Salisbury b Drakes 35
A. R. Dunlop lbw b Salisbury 50
S. Graham b Drakes 13
R. L. Eagleson c Salisbury b Drakes 5
†A. T. Rutherford not out 6
P. McCrum not out 2

L-b 15, w 13 28

1/9 2/10 3/46 (8 wkts, 50 overs) 190
4/57 5/141 6/176
7/179 8/185

M. W. Patterson did not bat.

Bowling: Drakes 10–3–19–5; Giddins 10–1–19–0; Jarvis 10–1–45–1; Newell 7–1–25–1; Salisbury 10–1–47–1; Greenfield 3–0–20–0.

Sussex

C. W. J. Athey c Rutherford b Patterson . . 3
M. P. Speight c Eagleson b Patterson 64
*A. P. Wells not out 53
K. Greenfield not out 51
L-b 8, w 7, n-b 8 23

1/79 2/90 (2 wkts, 20 overs) 194

N. J. Lenham, †P. Moores, K. Newell, I. D. K. Salisbury, V. C. Drakes, P. W. Jarvis and E. S. H. Giddins did not bat.

Bowling: Eagleson 4–0–47–0; Patterson 6–1–66–2; Graham 3–0–24–0; McCrum 4–0–28–0; Lewis 1–0–8–0; Harrison 2–0–13–0.

Umpires: R. Julian and R. A. White.

HAMPSHIRE v SUSSEX

At Southampton, April 30. Hampshire won by 67 runs. Toss: Hampshire.

Athey made the top score of the match, but took 33 overs over his 55, while Benjamin and Connor made inroads at the other end. Whitaker was one of the few batsmen to look comfortable on a bowler's pitch and his 66-ball 53 gave Hampshire's innings its substance.

Gold Award: P. R. Whitaker.

Hampshire

*J. P. Stephenson c Moores b Jarvis	37	S. D. Udal run out	10
J. S. Laney b Giddins	8	M. J. Thursfield not out	1
R. S. M. Morris c Moores b Jarvis	32	C. A. Connor not out	4
R. A. Smith c Wells b Salisbury	41	W 10, n-b 8	18
G. W. White c Moores b Law	2		—
P. R. Whitaker b Drakes	53	1/17 2/68 3/87 (9 wkts, 50 overs)	235
W. K. M. Benjamin st Moores b Salisbury	13	4/108 5/174 6/196	
†A. N. Aymes c Greenfield b Jarvis	16	7/219 8/219 9/231	

Bowling: Giddins 10–1–42–1; Drakes 10–1–51–1; Salisbury 10–0–50–2; Jarvis 10–0–48–3; Law 10–0–44–1.

Sussex

C. W. J. Athey lbw b Stephenson	55	V. C. Drakes c Smith b Stephenson	18
M. P. Speight lbw b Benjamin	0	P. W. Jarvis c Benjamin b Thursfield	3
*A. P. Wells c Morris b Connor	2	E. S. H. Giddins not out	0
K. Greenfield c Morris b Thursfield	34		
N. J. Lenham c Aymes b Connor	14	L-b 2, w 6	8
†P. Moores c Aymes b Benjamin	7		—
D. R. Law c Stephenson b Benjamin	8	1/1 2/4 3/68 (43.1 overs)	168
I. D. K. Salisbury c Thursfield b Stephenson	19	4/110 5/110 6/126 7/128 8/162 9/167	

Bowling: Benjamin 8–2–26–3; Connor 8–0–30–2; Stephenson 7.1–0–33–3; Thursfield 10–1–33–2; Udal 10–0–44–0.

Umpires: J. D. Bond and M. J. Kitchen.

SURREY v GLOUCESTERSHIRE

At The Oval, April 30. Surrey won by three wickets. Toss: Gloucestershire.

Cunliffe's 137, off 143 balls, was his first century against professional opposition. His partnership with Wright realised 161 and Gloucestershire reached their biggest total in this competition. But Surrey's reply gained irresistible momentum from Brown's spectacular hitting: he moved from 31 to 81 in just 17 balls, despatching one ball into the street by the gas-holders. After 15 overs of field restrictions, Surrey were 134 for one. Brown ran himself out soon afterwards, but Surrey's batting line-up had enough depth to capitalise.

Gold Award: R. J. Cunliffe.

Gloucestershire

A. J. Wright c Julian b Pearson 63
R. I. Dawson b Lewis 7
R. J. Cunliffe not out 137
A. Symonds c and b Julian 5
T. H. C. Hancock c Butcher b M. P. Bicknell . 43
M. W. Alleyne not out 17
B 1, l-b 9, w 15, n-b 10 35

1/13 2/174 3/183 4/263 (4 wkts, 50 overs) 307

*†R. C. Russell, R. P. Davis, K. E. Cooper, A. M. Smith and M. J. Cawdron did not bat.

Bowling: Lewis 10–1–40–1; M. P. Bicknell 10–0–51–1; Hollioake 6–0–47–0; Julian 10–0–73–1; Butcher 4–0–23–0; Pearson 10–0–63–1.

Surrey

D. M. Ward b Cawdron 32
A. D. Brown run out 82
*†A. J. Stewart c Smith b Davis 11
G. P. Thorpe b Alleyne 34
A. J. Hollioake c Alleyne b Cawdron 45
D. J. Bicknell b Smith 46
B. P. Julian c Symonds b Davis 27
M. A. Butcher not out 6
C. C. Lewis not out 3
L-b 9, w 3, n-b 10 22

1/73 2/136 3/153 4/185 5/254 6/296 7/297 (7 wkts, 48.5 overs) 308

R. M. Pearson and M. P. Bicknell did not bat.

Bowling: Smith 9.5–0–73–1; Cooper 9–0–61–0; Cawdron 6–0–48–2; Davis 10–0–64–2; Alleyne 10–0–30–1; Symonds 4–0–23–0.

Umpires: R. A. White and P. Willey.

IRELAND v GLOUCESTERSHIRE

At Clontarf, Dublin, May 7. Gloucestershire won by 168 runs. Toss: Gloucestershire.

Cunliffe made another unbeaten hundred and Gloucestershire bettered their highest total for the second time in successive games. Wright also reached his century – his first in this competition, in which he made his debut in 1984 – and his stand of 221 with Cunliffe was an all-wicket county record for the tournament.

Gold Award: A. J. Wright.

Gloucestershire

A. J. Wright run out 123
R. I. Dawson c Doak b Patterson 5
R. J. Cunliffe not out 116
A. Symonds b Patterson 9
T. H. C. Hancock not out 20
B 4, l-b 10, w 13, n-b 8 35

1/26 2/247 3/257 (3 wkts, 50 overs) 308

M. W. Alleyne, *†R. C. Russell, R. P. Davis, A. M. Smith, J. Lewis and K. E. Cooper did not bat.

Bowling: Patterson 10–0–55–2; McCrum 10–0–63–0; Moore 2–0–11–0; Gillespie 5–0–17–0; Harrison 9–0–42–0; Benson 7–0–47–0; Doak 3–0–20–0; Lewis 4–0–39–0.

Ireland

S. J. S. Warke lbw b Cooper 0
G. D. Harrison lbw b Smith 6
D. Moore c and b Smith 10
*D. A. Lewis c and b Alleyne 61
J. D. R. Benson run out 29
A. R. Dunlop lbw b Lewis 0
N. G. Doak c Russell b Lewis 1
P. G. Gillespie lbw b Smith 0
P. McCrum b Lewis 0
†A. T. Rutherford st Russell b Davis 10
M. W. Patterson not out 8
B 1, l-b 9, w 3, n-b 2 15

1/0 2/16 3/29 4/71 5/71 6/76 7/85 8/86 9/132 (40.1 overs) 140

Bowling: Cooper 10–1–26–1; Smith 10–3–23–3; Lewis 10–1–31–3; Davis 5.1–0–20–1; Alleyne 5–0–30–1.

Umpires: B. Dudleston and G. Sharp.

SUSSEX v SURREY

At Hove, May 7. Surrey won by nine wickets. Toss: Sussex.

Another exciting innings from Brown helped Surrey to pass a small total with almost 14 overs to spare. His maiden hundred in the competition took 105 balls; he hit 11 fours and five sixes and put on 151 with Stewart. Sussex would have lost by an even greater margin but for Jarvis's big hitting; he took 20 off Pearson's last over before holing out.

Gold Award: A. D. Brown.

Sussex

C. W. J. Athey run out	18
M. P. Speight b Lewis	4
K. Greenfield c Stewart b Lewis	0
*A. P. Wells b Pearson	69
K. Newell lbw b Julian	0
†P. Moores c D. J. Bicknell b Julian	17
D. R. Law c Thorpe b Julian	0
V. C. Drakes c Julian b Pearson	26
N. C. Phillips c Ward b Lewis	10
P. W. Jarvis c Brown b Pearson	38
J. D. Lewry not out	8
L-b 7, w 7, n-b 4	18
1/7 2/15 3/38 4/43 5/72 6/76 7/144 8/161 9/162 (49.5 overs)	208

Bowling: Lewis 10–2–29–3; M. P. Bicknell 8–1–33–0; Julian 10–3–28–3; Hollioake 7–0–26–0; Pearson 9.5–0–60–3; Butcher 5–0–25–0.

Surrey

D. M. Ward c Athey b Jarvis	17
A. D. Brown not out	117
*†A. J. Stewart not out	61
B 2, l-b 7, w 3, n-b 2	14
1/58 (1 wkt, 36.1 overs)	209

G. P. Thorpe, A. J. Hollioake, D. J. Bicknell, M. A. Butcher, C. C. Lewis, B. P. Julian, M. P. Bicknell and R. M. Pearson did not bat.

Bowling: Drakes 6–1–36–0; Lewry 6–0–22–0; Jarvis 10–1–42–1; Phillips 5–0–49–0; Law 6–0–32–0; Newell 3.1–0–19–0.

Umpires: A. Clarkson and R. Julian.

GLOUCESTERSHIRE v HAMPSHIRE

At Bristol, May 14. Gloucestershire won by 21 runs. Toss: Hampshire.

Both counties needed to win to join Surrey in the quarter-finals. Cunliffe continued his good form with an excellent 73, and the 113 he put on with Alleyne for the sixth wicket was ultimately decisive. Hampshire should have got closer from a platform of 186 for four, but Hancock's occasional seamers encouraged a terminal rush of blood from Benjamin, and then removed Stephenson (batting down the order after injuring a finger) and Whitaker as well.

Gold Award: M. W. Alleyne.

Gloucestershire

A. J. Wright lbw b James	31
R. I. Dawson c Benjamin b Maru	33
R. J. Cunliffe b Benjamin	73
T. H. C. Hancock run out	10
A. Symonds c Morris b Maru	26
*C. A. Walsh c James b Whitaker	6
M. W. Alleyne lbw b Connor	75
†R. C. Russell run out	8
R. P. Davis b Connor	2
A. M. Smith not out	0
L-b 3, w 3, n-b 2	8
1/65 2/69 3/88 4/128 5/145 6/258 7/270 8/272 9/272 (9 wkts, 50 overs)	272

K. E. Cooper did not bat.

Bowling: Benjamin 10–2–58–1; Connor 6–0–46–2; James 4–0–24–1; Maru 10–0–43–2; Udal 10–0–57–0; Whitaker 10–0–41–1.

Hampshire

R. S. M. Morris st Russell b Davis	39	S. D. Udal c Symonds b Smith	32
J. S. Laney c Walsh b Cooper	34	C. A. Connor c Davis b Walsh	1
K. D. James run out	56	R. J. Maru not out	6
R. A. Smith c Alleyne b Davis	1	L-b 3, w 6	9
W. K. M. Benjamin c Smith b Hancock	43		—
*J. P. Stephenson c Wright b Hancock	7	1/47 2/113 3/115 (49.2 overs)	251
P. R. Whitaker c Davis b Hancock	6	4/162 5/186 6/186	
†A. N. Aymes run out	17	7/195 8/231 9/237	

Bowling: Cooper 8–0–48–1; Smith 8.2–0–50–1; Alleyne 9–0–46–0; Walsh 10–0–41–1; Davis 10–0–50–2; Hancock 4–0–13–3.

Umpires: J. H. Harris and B. Leadbeater.

IRELAND v SURREY

At Eglinton, May 14. Surrey won by five wickets. Toss: Ireland.

Surrey scored their fourth successive victory, and left Ireland still looking for a win after 25 matches in the NatWest and Benson and Hedges tournaments. After collapsing to 17 for five, they recovered to 196, thanks to a responsible 84 not out from Neil Doak, their highest individual innings in this competition. Against Surrey, the dominant force in this group, it was an honourable performance.

Gold Award: N. G. Doak.

Ireland

J. D. R. Benson c D. J. Bicknell b Lewis	0	R. L. Eagleson c Thorpe b B. C. Hollioake	13
D. Moore c Brown b M. P. Bicknell	0	†A. T. Rutherford c Stewart b Julian	26
G. D. Harrison c Stewart b Lewis	4		
*D. A. Lewis c D. J. Bicknell b M. P. Bicknell	8	B 3, l-b 8, w 9, n-b 4	24
N. G. Doak not out	84		—
A. R. Dunlop c Julian b M. P. Bicknell	1	1/0 2/1 3/15 (8 wkts, 50 overs)	196
D. Heasley lbw b Julian	36	4/16 5/17 6/62	
		7/126 8/196	

P. McCrum and M. W. Patterson did not bat.

Bowling: Lewis 10–2–35–2; M. P. Bicknell 10–5–19–3; A. J. Hollioake 3–1–18–0; Pearson 10–1–43–0; Julian 10–0–45–2; B. C. Hollioake 7–1–25–1.

Surrey

D. M. Ward c Heasley b Eagleson	9	C. C. Lewis not out	30
A. D. Brown c McCrum b Patterson	24		
*†A. J. Stewart c Benson b Harrison	63	L-b 2, w 3, n-b 2	7
G. P. Thorpe c Rutherford b Heasley	30		—
A. J. Hollioake b Harrison	1	1/9 2/46 3/132 (5 wkts, 37.5 overs)	198
D. J. Bicknell not out	34	4/132 5/145	

B. C. Hollioake, R. M. Pearson, B. P. Julian and M. P. Bicknell did not bat.

Bowling: Patterson 6–0–37–1; Eagleson 5.5–0–51–1; McCrum 6–0–33–0; Heasley 7–0–32–1; Harrison 10–0–30–2; Doak 3–1–13–0.

Umpires: J. C. Balderstone and J. D. Bond.

QUARTER-FINALS

GLAMORGAN v WARWICKSHIRE

At Cardiff, May 28. Warwickshire won by 12 runs. Toss: Glamorgan.

Glamorgan lost their last five wickets for 11 runs in 23 balls after Maynard and Gibson had shared what was then a tournament record of 136 in 22 overs for the sixth wicket. They had slumped to 80 for five, but that stand had brought them in sight of victory, requiring only 24 from five overs, when Gibson was dismissed by Pollock. Small then took two wickets in an over before Brown claimed the last two in successive deliveries. Ostler scored a responsible 85 for Warwickshire, while Brown made an effective 44. Both were hit on the fingers, as was Knight, who suffered a fracture, batting on the uncertain pitch. Maynard was later fined by his county for publicly criticising the umpires over several decisions, including the one that gave him leg-before to Small.

Gold Award: D. P. Ostler.

Warwickshire

N. V. Knight b Watkin	10	A. F. Giles c Watkin b Croft	9
N. M. K. Smith c Thomas b Watkin	3	†K. J. Piper not out	5
D. R. Brown b Butcher	44	G. C. Small run out	1
D. P. Ostler b Croft	85	L-b 13, w 6, n-b 6	25
T. L. Penney c James b Butcher	3		—
*D. A. Reeve st Metson b Barwick	26	1/5 2/32 3/68 (48.5 overs)	239
S. M. Pollock run out	4	4/81 5/143 6/151	
G. Welch c Thomas b Barwick	24	7/218 8/229 9/238	

Bowling: Watkin 10–2–35–2; Gibson 9–0–56–0; Thomas 6–0–28–0; Butcher 6–0–21–2; Croft 7.5–0–37–2; Barwick 10–0–49–2.

Glamorgan

S. P. James c Piper b Pollock	11	†C. P. Metson c Piper b Brown	4
H. Morris c Piper b Reeve	38	S. L. Watkin not out	2
G. P. Butcher lbw b Small	9	S. R. Barwick b Brown	0
*M. P. Maynard lbw b Small	75	L-b 1, w 10, n-b 6	17
P. A. Cottey c and b Reeve	2		—
R. D. B. Croft c Piper b Reeve	1	1/31 2/60 3/67 (48.3 overs)	227
O. D. Gibson c Ostler b Pollock	68	4/78 5/80 6/216	
S. D. Thomas c Ostler b Small	0	7/220 8/221 9/227	

Bowling: Pollock 10–0–51–2; Brown 6.3–1–27–2; Reeve 10–1–39–3; Small 9–0–25–3; Welch 9–0–48–0; Giles 3–0–23–0; Smith 1–0–13–0.

Umpires: T. E. Jesty and A. A. Jones.

LANCASHIRE v GLOUCESTERSHIRE

At Manchester, May 28, 29. Lancashire won by five wickets. Toss: Lancashire.

Lancashire overcame the loss of their first three wickets in six overs on the first evening to charge to victory with ten overs to spare. Conditions had favoured the bowlers, especially Elworthy, who had one of his best days for Lancashire with four for 14, and Gloucestershire were 119 for nine before an encouraging last-wicket stand of 39. Lancashire's own crisis was compounded when Speak went quickly the following morning, but that opened the way for Crawley and Fairbrother to end the bowlers' supremacy. They shared a partnership of 110 in 22 overs, Fairbrother scoring an unbeaten 80 in 80 balls to win his eighth Gold Award.

Gold Award: N. H. Fairbrother.

Close of play: Lancashire 12-3 (6 overs) (N. J. Speak 0*, J. P. Crawley 0*).

Gloucestershire

A. J. Wright b Elworthy	26	R. P. Davis run out	10
N. J. Trainor c Hegg b Austin	25	M. C. J. Ball c Hegg b Watkinson	25
A. M. Smith c Watkinson b Elworthy	7	*C. A. Walsh not out	21
R. J. Cunliffe b Watkinson	1	W 7, n-b 2	9
T. H. C. Hancock c Hegg b Elworthy	6		—
†R. C. Russell c Hegg b Austin	24	1/52 2/52 3/59 (46.5 overs)	158
A. Symonds lbw b Elworthy	4	4/66 5/69 6/75	
M. W. Alleyne c Hegg b Watkinson	0	7/82 8/98 9/119	

Bowling: Austin 10–0–41–2; Martin 10–2–49–0; Elworthy 10–4–14–4; Watkinson 9.5–0–33–3; Yates 7–1–21–0.

Lancashire

M. A. Atherton c Russell b Walsh	3	G. D. Lloyd not out	10
*M. Watkinson c Cunliffe b Smith	4		
I. D. Austin c Ball b Smith	2	L-b 1, w 6, n-b 2	9
N. J. Speak c Russell b Hancock	6		—
J. P. Crawley b Ball	48	1/9 2/12 3/12 (5 wkts, 39.4 overs)	162
N. H. Fairbrother not out	80	4/32 5/142	

†W. K. Hegg, S. Elworthy, P. J. Martin and G. Yates did not bat.

Bowling: Walsh 8.4–2–33–1; Smith 9–3–30–2; Hancock 8–1–32–1; Alleyne 2–0–15–0; Davis 6–0–34–0; Ball 6–1–17–1.

Umpires: B. Dudleston and V. A. Holder.

NORTHAMPTONSHIRE v KENT

At Northampton, May 28, 29. Northamptonshire won by 23 runs. Toss: Kent.

Kent squandered a winning position, undone by impatience and the skill of Emburey, who took his seventh Gold Award at the age of 43. He first ran out Ealham with an accurate throw from long-off, and then, when Kent needed 57 from nine overs with Ward and Walker well set, he returned to dismiss both of them, plus McCague, in seven balls. Marsh holed out to give Emburey his fourth wicket, and Ambrose returned to dismiss Thompson. Northamptonshire owed much to Bailey, who scored 105 in 129 balls, despite changing his bat three times, after Capel's initial assault brought 63 from 45 deliveries. Fleming was even more spectacular – 40 from 23 – until Ambrose bowled him. The rain was already falling by then, and three more wickets fell that evening before play was finally abandoned; the next day belonged to Emburey.

Gold Award: J. E. Emburey.

Close of play: Kent 108-4 (20.5 overs) (T. R. Ward 31*, M. A. Ealham 16*).

Northamptonshire

D. J. Capel c Patel b Ealham	63	A. L. Penberthy c Cowdrey b Fleming	24
A. Fordham c Marsh b Thompson	0	J. E. Emburey not out	9
*R. J. Bailey not out	105	L-b 1, w 8	9
M. B. Loye lbw b Patel	43		—
K. M. Curran b Ealham	15	1/11 2/76 3/163 (7 wkts, 50 overs)	293
†R. J. Warren run out	0	4/184 5/185	
R. R. Montgomerie run out	25	6/230 7/270	

C. E. L. Ambrose and J. P. Taylor did not bat.

Bowling: McCague 7–0–58–0; Thompson 6–0–38–1; Ealham 10–0–38–2; Fleming 10–0–58–1; Hooper 4–0–28–0; Patel 5–0–27–1; Cowdrey 8–0–45–0.

Kent

T. R. Ward lbw b Emburey	98	M. J. McCague c Penberthy b Emburey	1
M. V. Fleming b Ambrose	40	M. M. Patel not out	8
C. L. Hooper c Emburey b Penberthy	9	J. B. D. Thompson c Warren b Ambrose	1
G. R. Cowdrey c Warren b Penberthy	0	B 1, l-b 15, w 8, n-b 4	28
N. J. Llong b Curran	0		—
M. A. Ealham run out	32	1/56 2/79 3/79 (47.2 overs)	270
M. J. Walker c Ambrose b Emburey	30	4/80 5/157 6/237	
*†S. A. Marsh c Capel b Emburey	23	7/238 8/242 9/264	

Bowling: Taylor 6–0–53–0; Ambrose 9.2–0–40–2; Curran 10–1–41–1; Penberthy 10–2–50–2; Capel 7–0–46–0; Emburey 5–0–24–4.

Umpires: J. D. Bond and G. I. Burgess.

SURREY v YORKSHIRE

At The Oval, May 28. Yorkshire won by nine wickets. Toss: Yorkshire.

A stunning unbeaten century from Byas, regarded by many witnesses as the best one-day innings they had seen, helped Yorkshire inflict a hefty defeat on Surrey, who began the match as hot favourites. Byas hit 116 in 103 balls with 18 fours, his highest one-day score, to earn his first Gold Award in 12 seasons of Cup cricket. He and Bevan put on an unbroken 136 for the second wicket. Surrey's batting had been shackled by exemplary Yorkshire bowling; their attack was ripped to shreds and they succumbed with more than a dozen overs remaining.

Gold Award: D. Byas.

Surrey

D. M. Ward c Morris b Hartley	23
A. D. Brown c Vaughan b White	40
*†A. J. Stewart b Silverwood	2
G. P. Thorpe b Stemp	41
A. J. Hollioake lbw b Stemp	12
D. J. Bicknell c and b Silverwood	24
C. C. Lewis c Blakey b Gough	32
B. P. Julian c and b Silverwood	2
M. P. Bicknell c Blakey b White	22
R. M. Pearson not out	12
J. E. Benjamin c Byas b Gough	3
L-b 7, w 5, n-b 4	16
1/47 2/60 3/84 4/115 5/148 6/157 7/166 8/208 9/222 (49.5 overs)	229

Bowling: Gough 9.5–0–44–2; Hartley 10–2–32–1; Silverwood 10–2–41–3; White 10–0–56–2; Stemp 9–0–45–2; Morris 1–0–4–0.

Yorkshire

*D. Byas not out	116
M. P. Vaughan c Lewis b Benjamin	36
M. G. Bevan not out	65
L-b 3, w 2, n-b 8	13
1/94 (1 wkt, 37.1 overs)	230

A. McGrath, C. White, †R. J. Blakey, A. C. Morris, D. Gough, P. J. Hartley, C. E. W. Silverwood and R. D. Stemp did not bat.

Bowling: M. P. Bicknell 4–0–29–0; Lewis 8–0–59–0; Julian 6.1–0–31–0; Hollioake 6–0–37–0; Benjamin 10–2–53–1; Pearson 3–0–18–0.

Umpires: K. J. Lyons and P. Willey.

SEMI-FINALS

LANCASHIRE v YORKSHIRE

At Manchester, June 11, 12. Lancashire won by one wicket. Toss: Lancashire.

The draw turned up the most resonant of all county fixtures in the heightened atmosphere of a semi-final, and the contest went to the last ball. It will stand as not only one of the great modern Roses matches but as a contender for any list of best-ever limited-overs matches. Lancashire won through to the final for the fifth time in seven years when their No. 11, Martin, drove the final ball of the 50th over for the two runs that were needed. Unfortunately, the match had been delayed by rain, and the 16,000 who thronged Old Trafford expectantly at the start had dwindled to less than half that by the time the climax came on the second afternoon. The match twisted and turned throughout. Play did not begin until 4.30 on the opening day, and Yorkshire quickly crumpled to 83 for five. However, Bevan and Blakey had brought about a striking recovery even before the day was out, and in the four overs Lancashire still had to bowl next day they took their stand from 115 to 167, raising the tournament's sixth-wicket record for the third time in 1996. Bevan hit 95 off 75 balls and Blakey 80 off 94. Lancashire also lost half their wickets for less than 100 and initially the stand between Fairbrother and Hegg seemed a touch panic-stricken. Yorkshire were still favourites with three wickets standing and 77 wanted off eight overs. But

Hegg had stronger nerves than most of the spectators. He stayed until 11 were wanted off 13 balls, but only three came off the penultimate over, from Gough, leaving eight to get from the last, to be bowled by White. Chapple hit four off the first ball, and there was a wide and a single before Martin missed the fourth and fifth to set up the breathless finale. Martin, who was brought up in Yorkshire, had to beat a throw from Vaughan, born in Manchester. Like many features of this remarkable game, this would not have been possible in an old-fashioned Roses fixture.

Gold Award: W. K. Hegg.

Close of play: Yorkshire 198-5 (46 overs) (M. G. Bevan 73*, R. J. Blakey 50*).

Yorkshire

*D. Byas c Hegg b Martin	22
M. D. Moxon c Atherton b Watkinson	25
M. P. Vaughan c Atherton b Chapple	15
M. G. Bevan not out	95
A. McGrath c Hegg b Elworthy	0
C. White c Hegg b Watkinson	4
†R. J. Blakey not out	80
L-b 6, w 3	9
1/29 2/66 3/77 4/78 5/83 (5 wkts, 50 overs)	250

D. Gough, P. J. Hartley, C. E. W. Silverwood and R. D. Stemp did not bat.

Bowling: Austin 10–0–54–0; Martin 10–0–62–1; Chapple 10–0–46–1; Elworthy 10–0–52–1; Watkinson 10–1–30–2.

Lancashire

M. A. Atherton c Byas b Gough	0
*M. Watkinson run out	6
N. J. Speak run out	34
S. Elworthy c Gough b Silverwood	12
N. H. Fairbrother run out	59
G. D. Lloyd c Blakey b Silverwood	9
†W. K. Hegg b White	81
I. D. Austin c and b Gough	5
G. Yates run out	26
G. Chapple not out	6
P. J. Martin not out	2
L-b 4, w 1, n-b 6	11
1/2 2/21 3/36 4/79 5/97 6/161 7/174 8/240 9/243 (9 wkts, 50 overs)	251

Bowling: Gough 10–1–39–2; Silverwood 10–2–40–2; Hartley 10–1–47–0; White 10–1–74–1; Stemp 10–0–47–0.

Umpires: D. J. Constant and K. E. Palmer.

NORTHAMPTONSHIRE v WARWICKSHIRE

At Northampton, June 11, 12. Northamptonshire won by 27 runs. Toss: Warwickshire.

Tim Walton emerged from obscurity in his sixth year on the Northamptonshire staff to upstage everyone and take his county to their first Benson and Hedges final since 1987. Walton hit an unbeaten 70 off 73 balls, the top score of the match. And he was still touched with magic after the rain came and the players had to come back the following day: he ran out both Penney and Paul Smith with direct throws from deep mid-wicket and backward point. For most of the match, Northamptonshire's position – as in their quarter-final – seemed unpromising. Only Montgomerie, of their top-order batsmen, managed to get a start against Warwickshire's seamers; at 88 for six, respectability appeared the main objective. However, Walton and Penberthy counter-attacked with 108 in 17 overs – a county record for the seventh wicket in any limited-overs competition. Northamptonshire then removed three wickets before the weather halted play for the fifth time. Next day, Warwickshire were well-placed on 147 for four, before Walton's dead-eye throws. With Reeve still there, anything seemed possible, especially in the minds of Northamptonshire supporters still haunted by the NatWest final nine months earlier. However, Warwickshire suddenly seemed more impotent than invincible; Ambrose's sharp fielding accounted for Piper and Giles, and Reeve could do nothing.

Gold Award: T. C. Walton.

Close of play: Warwickshire 91-3 (23.2 overs) (D. P. Ostler 18*, P. A. Smith 18*).

Northamptonshire

D. J. Capel c Piper b Brown	7	A. L. Penberthy c Brown b Pollock	41
R. R. Montgomerie c Giles b P. A. Smith	49	J. E. Emburey not out	2
*R. J. Bailey b Welch	10	L-b 8, w 11, n-b 8	27
M. B. Loye run out	1		—
K. M. Curran b Reeve	3	1/15 2/42 3/58 (7 wkts, 50 overs)	220
†R. J. Warren c Piper b P. A. Smith	10	4/69 5/83	
T. C. Walton not out	70	6/88 7/196	

C. E. L. Ambrose and J. P. Taylor did not bat.

Bowling: Pollock 10–2–41–1; Brown 10–1–46–1; Welch 10–1–32–1; Reeve 10–2–30–1; P. A. Smith 9–0–56–2; N. M. K. Smith 1–0–7–0.

Warwickshire

A. J. Moles c Penberthy b Curran	33	G. Welch lbw b Emburey	1
N. M. K. Smith c Ambrose b Taylor	15	†K. J. Piper run out	7
D. R. Brown b Taylor	0	A. F. Giles run out	8
D. P. Ostler b Ambrose	33	L-b 7, w 2	9
P. A. Smith run out	45		—
T. L. Penney run out	14	1/34 2/36 3/61 (47.5 overs)	193
S. M. Pollock c Loye b Capel	7	4/118 5/147 6/151	
*D. A. Reeve not out	21	7/157 8/159 9/172	

Bowling: Ambrose 9–0–39–1; Taylor 10–1–25–2; Capel 10–0–29–1; Curran 6–0–32–1; Penberthy 4–0–30–0; Emburey 8.5–1–31–1.

Umpires: J. C. Balderstone and J. H. Hampshire.

FINAL

NORTHAMPTONSHIRE v LANCASHIRE

At Lord's, July 13. Lancashire won by 31 runs. Toss: Lancashire.

A match in which half the men taking part were Test players was decided by perhaps the least charismatic man on the field. Ian Austin, who looks, in Mike Selvey's words, like "a stoker on a merchant steamer", broke through the Northamptonshire batting at both the start and finish to settle the final in Lancashire's favour. The result was what everyone expected, given the teams' records. This was Northamptonshire's tenth Lord's final and their seventh defeat. It was Lancashire's ninth win in 14. The victory also continued their extraordinary recent record in this competition: excluding one washout, they have won 15 consecutive matches.

The switch of this competition to the now standard format for one-day internationals made very little difference. Both the makeshift openers (Capel in particular is known to dislike being called a pinch-hitter) went quickly, and the early batsmen had too much of a battle against the new ball to think about smashing it through the gaps. The change in rules had more effect on the crowd: the lunch interval, shifted from its normal time to take place between innings, played havoc with the day's social arrangements. However, the most aggrieved figure of all was Elworthy, the Lancashire overseas player, who was dropped from the team and temporarily left the ground in despair.

The Englishmen he left behind had an early slice of luck when Elworthy's Northamptonshire counterpart, Ambrose, pulled a hamstring in his opening spell. This released some of the pressure on the batsmen, but no one played a big, dominating innings. Both Atherton and Crawley got out just as they seemed ready to assume command. And it was left to Fairbrother to play one of his most bustling innings – Bob Willis called him "the manic midget" at the awards ceremony – to take Lancashire to 245 for nine.

This might have been within Northamptonshire's reach. But during the belated lunch interval the sun went in, and Austin had cloud cover to help him through a beautifully crafted opening spell of two for seven in seven overs. Bailey and Montgomerie kept the game open, but both went in rapid succession in mid-innings. The decisive moments came when Warren smacked successive balls from Watkinson to the Grand Stand boundary. Crawley grasped the first, but the momentum carried him over the ropes. Next ball, Warren pushed his luck and this time Crawley held it magnificently.

Austin came back to finish things off, and bowled both Penberthy and Emburey, who was representing his new county in what was expected to be his last match at Lord's, and certainly his last big one. – MATTHEW ENGEL.

Gold Award: I. D. Austin. *Attendance:* 24,793; *receipts* £723,932.

Lancashire

M. A. Atherton c Bailey b Emburey	48	G. Chapple not out	6
*M. Watkinson c Emburey b Taylor	7	P. J. Martin not out	1
J. E. R. Gallian run out	17	W 10, n-b 8	18
J. P. Crawley c Warren b Penberthy	34		—
N. H. Fairbrother b Capel	63	1/18 (2) 2/52 (3) (9 wkts, 50 overs)	245
G. D. Lloyd b Taylor	26	3/105 (4) 4/131 (1)	
†W. K. Hegg run out	11	5/180 (6) 6/203 (7)	
I. D. Austin c and b Ambrose	14	7/236 (5) 8/236 (9)	
G. Yates c Penberthy b Capel	0	9/243 (8)	

Bowling: Ambrose 10–2–35–1; Taylor 9–0–55–2; Curran 7–0–48–0; Capel 8–1–37–2; Penberthy 6–0–31–1; Emburey 10–1–39–1.

Northamptonshire

D. J. Capel c Hegg b Austin	0	C. E. L. Ambrose run out	10
A. Fordham b Austin	4	J. P. Taylor not out	0
*R. J. Bailey c Hegg b Chapple	46	L-b 10, w 12, n-b 2	24
R. R. Montgomerie c Hegg b Yates	42		—
K. M. Curran c Crawley b Chapple	35	1/1 (1) 2/10 (2) (48.3 overs)	214
†R. J. Warren c Crawley b Watkinson	11	3/97 (3) 4/111 (4)	
T. C. Walton st Hegg b Watkinson	28	5/132 (6) 6/184 (7)	
A. L. Penberthy b Austin	8	7/186 (5) 8/194 (9)	
J. E. Emburey b Austin	6	9/214 (10) 10/214 (8)	

Bowling: Austin 9.3–2–21–4; Martin 9–2–32–0; Chapple 10–1–51–2; Watkinson 10–0–66–2; Yates 10–0–34–1.

Umpires: M. J. Kitchen and G. Sharp.

BENSON AND HEDGES CUP RECORDS

55 overs available in all games 1972-95, 50 overs in 1996.

Batting

Highest individual scores: 198*, G. A. Gooch, Essex v Sussex, Hove, 1982; 177, S. J. Cook, Somerset v Sussex, Hove, 1990; 173*, C. G. Greenidge, Hampshire v Minor Counties (South), Amersham, 1973; 167*, A. J. Stewart, Surrey v Somerset, The Oval, 1994; 160, A. J. Stewart, Surrey v Hampshire, The Oval, 1996; 158*, B. F. Davison, Leicestershire v Warwickshire, Coventry, 1972; 158, W. J. Cronje, Leicestershire v Lancashire, Manchester, 1995; 155*, M. D. Crowe, Somerset v Hampshire, Southampton, 1987; 155*, R. A. Smith, Hampshire v Glamorgan, Southampton, 1989; 154*, M. J. Procter, Gloucestershire v Somerset, Taunton, 1972; 154*, C. L. Smith, Hampshire v Combined Universities, Southampton, 1990; 151*, M. P. Maynard, Glamorgan v Middlesex, Lord's, 1996. *In the final:* 132*, I. V. A. Richards, Somerset v Surrey, 1981. (283 hundreds have been scored in the competition. The most hundreds in one season is 26 in 1996.)

Most runs: 5,106, G. A. Gooch; 2,859, M. W. Gatting; 2,761, C. J. Tavaré; 2,663, D. W. Randall; 2,660, W. Larkins; 2,636, A. J. Lamb; 2,500, G. A. Hick.

Fastest hundred: M. A. Nash in 62 minutes, Glamorgan v Hampshire at Swansea, 1976.

Most hundreds: 15, G. A. Gooch; 7, G. A. Hick and W. Larkins; 5, C. G. Greenidge, A. J. Lamb, R. A. Smith and N. R. Taylor.

Highest totals: 388 for seven, Essex v Scotland, Chelmsford, 1992; 369 for eight, Warwickshire v Minor Counties, Jesmond, 1996; 366 for four, Derbyshire v Combined Universities, Oxford, 1991; 353 for seven, Lancashire v Nottinghamshire, Manchester, 1995; 350 for three, Essex v Oxford & Cambridge Univs, Chelmsford, 1979; 338 for six, Kent v Somerset, Maidstone, 1996; 333 for four, Essex v Oxford & Cambridge Univs, Chelmsford, 1985; 333 for six, Surrey v Hampshire, The Oval, 1996; 331 for five, Surrey v Hampshire, The Oval, 1990; 331 for five, Essex v British Univs, Chelmsford, 1996; 330 for four, Lancashire v Sussex, Manchester, 1991. *In the final:* 290 for six, Essex v Surrey, 1979.

Highest total by a side batting second and winning: 318 for five (54.3 overs), Lancashire v Leicestershire (312 for five), Manchester, 1995. *In the final:* 244 for six (55 overs), Yorkshire v Northamptonshire (244 for seven), 1987; 244 for seven (55 overs), Nottinghamshire v Essex (243 for seven), 1989.

Highest total by a side batting second and losing: 303 for seven (55 overs), Derbyshire v Somerset (310 for three), Taunton, 1990. *In the final:* 255 (51.4 overs), Surrey v Essex (290 for six), 1979.

Highest match aggregates: 631 for 15 wickets, Kent (338 for six) v Somerset (293 for nine), Maidstone, 1996; 630 for ten wickets, Leicestershire (312 for five) v Lancashire (318 for five), Manchester, 1995; 629 for 14 wickets, Lancashire (353 for seven) v Nottinghamshire (276 for seven), Manchester, 1995; 628 for 15 wickets, Warwickshire (312 for six) v Lancashire (316 for nine), Manchester, 1996; 626 for ten wickets, British Univs (312 for eight) v Glamorgan (314 for two), Cambridge, 1996; 615 for 11 wickets, Gloucestershire (307 for four) v Surrey (308 for seven), The Oval, 1996; 613 for ten wickets, Somerset (310 for three) v Derbyshire (303 for seven), Taunton, 1990; 610 for eight wickets, Sussex (303 for six) v Kent (307 for two), Hove, 1995.

Lowest totals: 50 in 27.2 overs, Hampshire v Yorkshire, Leeds, 1991; 56 in 26.2 overs, Leicestershire v Minor Counties, Wellington, 1982; 59 in 34 overs, Oxford & Cambridge Univs v Glamorgan, Cambridge, 1983; 60 in 26 overs, Sussex v Middlesex, Hove, 1978; 61 in 25.3 overs, Essex v Lancashire, Chelmsford, 1992; 62 in 26.5 overs, Gloucestershire v Hampshire, Bristol, 1975. *In the final:* 117 in 46.3 overs, Derbyshire v Hampshire, 1988.

Shortest completed innings: 21.4 overs (156), Surrey v Sussex, Hove, 1988.

Record partnership for each wicket

252	for 1st	V. P. Terry and C. L. Smith, Hampshire v Combined Universities at Southampton	1990
285*	for 2nd	C. G. Greenidge and D. R. Turner, Hampshire v Minor Counties (South) at Amersham	1973
269*	for 3rd	P. M. Roebuck and M. D. Crowe, Somerset v Hampshire at Southampton	1987
184*	for 4th	D. Lloyd and B. W. Reidy, Lancashire v Derbyshire at Chesterfield	1980
160	for 5th	A. J. Lamb and D. J. Capel, Northamptonshire v Leicestershire at Northampton	1986
167*	for 6th	M. G. Bevan and R. J. Blakey, Yorkshire v Lancashire at Manchester	1996
149*	for 7th	J. D. Love and C. M. Old, Yorkshire v Scotland at Bradford	1981
109	for 8th	R. E. East and N. Smith, Essex v Northamptonshire at Chelmsford	1977
83	for 9th	P. G. Newman and M. A. Holding, Derbyshire v Nottinghamshire at Nottingham	1985
80*	for 10th	D. L. Bairstow and M. Johnson, Yorkshire v Derbyshire at Derby	1981

Bowling

Most wickets: 149, J. K. Lever; 132, I. T. Botham.

Best bowling: seven for 12, W. W. Daniel, Middlesex v Minor Counties (East), Ipswich, 1978; seven for 22, J. R. Thomson, Middlesex v Hampshire, Lord's, 1981; seven for 32, R. G. D. Willis, Warwickshire v Yorkshire, Birmingham, 1981. *In the final:* five for 13, S. T. Jefferies, Hampshire v Derbyshire, 1988.

Hat-tricks (11): G. D. McKenzie, Leicestershire v Worcestershire, Worcester, 1972; K. Higgs, Leicestershire v Surrey in the final, Lord's, 1974; A. A. Jones, Middlesex v Essex,

Lord's, 1977; M. J. Procter, Gloucestershire v Hampshire, Southampton, 1977; W. Larkins, Northamptonshire v Oxford & Cambridge Univs, Northampton, 1980; E. A. Moseley, Glamorgan v Kent, Cardiff, 1981; G. C. Small, Warwickshire v Leicestershire, Leicester, 1984; N. A. Mallender, Somerset v Combined Universities, Taunton, 1987; W. K. M. Benjamin, Leicestershire v Nottinghamshire, Leicester, 1987; A. R. C. Fraser, Middlesex v Sussex, Lord's, 1988; S. M. Pollock (four in four balls), Warwickshire v Leicestershire, Birmingham, 1996.

Wicket-keeping and Fielding

Most dismissals: 122 (117 ct, 5 st), D. L. Bairstow.

Most dismissals in an innings: 8 (all ct), D. J. S. Taylor, Somerset v Oxford & Cambridge Univs, Taunton, 1982.

Most catches by a fielder: 68, G. A. Gooch; 55, C. J. Tavaré; 53, I. T. Botham.

Most catches by a fielder in an innings: 5, V. J. Marks, Oxford & Cambridge Univs v Kent, Oxford, 1976.

Results

Largest victories in runs: Essex by 272 runs v Scotland, Chelmsford, 1992; Somerset by 233 runs v Ireland, Eglinton, 1995; Glamorgan by 217 runs v Combined Universities, Cardiff, 1995; Essex by 214 runs v Oxford & Cambridge Univs, Chelmsford, 1979; Derbyshire by 206 runs v Combined Universities, Oxford, 1991; Warwickshire by 195 runs v Minor Counties, Jesmond, 1996.

Victories by ten wickets (19): By Derbyshire, Essex (twice), Glamorgan, Hampshire, Kent (twice), Lancashire, Leicestershire (twice), Middlesex, Northamptonshire, Somerset, Warwickshire, Worcestershire (twice), Yorkshire (three times).

Gold Awards

Most awards: 22, G. A. Gooch; 11, M. W. Gatting, G. A. Hick, T. E. Jesty and B. Wood.

WINNERS 1972-96

		Gold Award
1972	LEICESTERSHIRE* beat Yorkshire by five wickets.	J. C. Balderstone
1973	KENT* beat Worcestershire by 39 runs.	Asif Iqbal
1974	SURREY* beat Leicestershire by 27 runs.	J. H. Edrich
1975	LEICESTERSHIRE beat Middlesex* by five wickets.	N. M. McVicker
1976	KENT* beat Worcestershire by 43 runs.	G. W. Johnson
1977	GLOUCESTERSHIRE* beat Kent by 64 runs.	A. W. Stovold
1978	KENT beat Derbyshire* by six wickets.	R. A. Woolmer
1979	ESSEX beat Surrey* by 35 runs.	G. A. Gooch
1980	NORTHAMPTONSHIRE* beat Essex by six runs.	A. J. Lamb
1981	SOMERSET* beat Surrey by seven wickets.	I. V. A. Richards
1982	SOMERSET* beat Nottinghamshire by nine wickets.	V. J. Marks
1983	MIDDLESEX beat Essex* by four runs.	C. T. Radley
1984	LANCASHIRE* beat Warwickshire by six wickets.	J. Abrahams
1985	LEICESTERSHIRE* beat Essex by five wickets.	P. Willey
1986	MIDDLESEX beat Kent* by two runs.	J. E. Emburey
1987	YORKSHIRE* beat Northamptonshire, having taken more wickets with the scores tied.	J. D. Love
1988	HAMPSHIRE* beat Derbyshire by seven wickets.	S. T. Jefferies
1989	NOTTINGHAMSHIRE beat Essex* by three wickets.	R. T. Robinson
1990	LANCASHIRE beat Worcestershire* by 69 runs.	M. Watkinson
1991	WORCESTERSHIRE beat Lancashire* by 65 runs.	G. A. Hick
1992	HAMPSHIRE beat Kent* by 41 runs.	R. A. Smith
1993	DERBYSHIRE beat Lancashire* by six runs.	D. G. Cork
1994	WARWICKSHIRE* beat Worcestershire by six wickets.	P. A. Smith
1995	LANCASHIRE beat Kent* by 35 runs.	P. A. de Silva†
1996	LANCASHIRE* beat Northamptonshire by 31 runs.	I. D. Austin

* *Won toss.* † *On losing side.*

WINS BY NON-CHAMPIONSHIP TEAMS

1973	OXFORD beat Northamptonshire at Northampton by two wickets.
1975	OXFORD & CAMBRIDGE beat Worcestershire at Cambridge by 66 runs.
	OXFORD & CAMBRIDGE beat Northamptonshire at Oxford by three wickets.
1976	OXFORD & CAMBRIDGE beat Yorkshire at Barnsley by seven wickets.
1980	MINOR COUNTIES beat Gloucestershire at Chippenham by three runs.
1981	MINOR COUNTIES beat Hampshire at Southampton by three runs.
1982	MINOR COUNTIES beat Leicestershire at Wellington by 131 runs.
1984	OXFORD & CAMBRIDGE beat Gloucestershire at Bristol by 27 runs.
1986	SCOTLAND beat Lancashire at Perth by three runs.
1987	MINOR COUNTIES beat Glamorgan at Oxford (Christ Church) by seven wickets.
1989	COMBINED UNIVERSITIES beat Surrey at Cambridge by nine runs.
	COMBINED UNIVERSITIES beat Worcestershire at Worcester by five wickets.
1990	COMBINED UNIVERSITIES beat Yorkshire at Leeds by two wickets.
	SCOTLAND beat Northamptonshire at Northampton by two runs.
1992	MINOR COUNTIES beat Sussex at Marlow by 19 runs.
1995	MINOR COUNTIES beat Leicestershire at Leicester by 26 runs.

TEAM RECORDS 1972-96

	Rounds reached				*Matches*			
	W	*F*	*SF*	*QF*	*P*	*W*	*L*	*NR*
Derbyshire	1	3	4	9	112	59	45	8
Durham	0	0	0	0	17	6	9	2
Essex	1	5	8	14	124	76	46	2
Glamorgan	0	0	1	8	106	47	55	4
Gloucestershire	1	1	2	7	106	52	51	3
Hampshire	2	2	5	12	115	60	50	5
Kent	3	7	12	17	131	84	45	2
Lancashire	4	6	10	16	129	83	39	7
Leicestershire	3	4	6	9	117	63	47	7
Middlesex	2	3	5	14	120	63	49	8
Northamptonshire	1	3	5	10	112	53	51	8
Nottinghamshire	1	2	5	13	116	68	42	6
Somerset	2	2	8	12	117	64	51	2
Surrey	1	3	7	11	117	64	49	4
Sussex	0	0	1	9	106	52	53	1
Warwickshire	1	2	7	13	118	65	46	7
Worcestershire	1	5	8	15	122	64	54	4
Yorkshire	1	2	6	10	112	59	46	7
Cambridge University	0	0	0	0	8	0	8	0
Oxford University	0	0	0	0	4	1	3	0
Oxford & Cambridge Universities	0	0	0	0	48	4	42	2
Combined/British Universities	0	0	0	1	37	3	33	1
Minor Counties	0	0	0	0	65	6	55	4
Minor Counties (North)	0	0	0	0	20	0	20	0
Minor Counties (South)	0	0	0	0	20	0	19	1
Minor Counties (East)	0	0	0	0	12	0	12	0
Minor Counties (West)	0	0	0	0	12	0	12	0
Scotland	0	0	0	0	62	2	57	3
Ireland	0	0	0	0	9	0	9	0

Middlesex beat Gloucestershire on the toss of a coin in their quarter-final in 1983. Derbyshire, Kent, Somerset and Warwickshire totals each include a bowling contest; Derbyshire beat Somerset and Warwickshire beat Kent when their quarter-finals, in 1993 and 1994 respectively, were abandoned.

AXA EQUITY & LAW LEAGUE, 1996

Adam Hollioake

In the 28th season of Sunday League cricket, Surrey became the 15th team to win the title, after a close contest – more muddled than tense – which half the counties threatened to win at one stage or another. The race went to the wire, and Surrey had to win in Cardiff on the final Sunday to make sure. But although Nottinghamshire finished level on both points and wins, Surrey's net run-rate was far superior. Only a slip-up against Glamorgan could have cost them the title, and they coasted home by seven wickets.

As it did for two of the previous three winners, Glamorgan and Kent, this often-abused competition gave a taste of success to a club that was beginning to starve: Surrey had not won anything since 1982. It also fortified them for disappointment the following week when they failed to win the County Championship.

The campaign was a personal triumph for Surrey's 25-year-old vice-captain, Adam Hollioake, who led the side in five of their wins and smashed the record of wickets in a season. This had stood at 34 since being set by Bob Clapp of Somerset in 1974, although it was equalled by Clive Rice in 1986. Hollioake took 39. No one else reached 30 in 1996, and only 19 players got to 20. Hollioake's success was founded on constant variations, in a form of cricket which can easily become stereotyped; among his tricks was a slow "knuckleball", based on baseball technique.

He was occasionally upstaged, as when a junior team-mate bowled out Derbyshire with the extraordinary figures of 8–1–10–5. But the player in question was his younger brother Ben, so the Hollioake household was contented enough. Surrey's victories included an astonishing win over the eventual county champions Leicestershire, who were bowled out for 48 and lost in less than two hours, creating mixed feelings among spectators at The Oval hoping for an afternoon watching cricket.

Surrey lost only once after June, and played with growing authority, their Sunday form mirroring their strong weekday performances. In contrast, their closest rivals were looking for compensation for seasons that had otherwise turned sour. Nottinghamshire, who had a terrible year in the other competitions, lost four of their first eight Sunday games as well. But they won eight of the last nine, missing out only when Surrey came to Trent Bridge on August 25 and the teams were unable to start because of rain.

The early pacemakers, Northamptonshire, won their first six but, as so often, faded away and eventually came sixth. They now rank with Gloucestershire and Durham as the only teams never to win the League. Yorkshire, who played consistently well, came third without ever quite looking like winners. Warwickshire came fourth, a disappointment by their recent standards. They ran into form after mid-June and looked to be timing their run perfectly until they went to The Oval on September 1, got into a tactical mess, and lost by two wickets.

As usual, nearly all the teams were capable of beating anyone else when things went right and they were paying attention: Essex, for instance, conquered Surrey at Southend before embarking on a sequence of nine successive defeats. There was, however, one great exception: Durham managed only one win – over Essex – and one washout all summer, giving them just six points, and easily the worst season in the League's history.

The previous worst was Warwickshire, with two wins and one washout for ten points in 1979; the following year they were champions. Glamorgan also took only ten points in 1972, but at that time there was only one point for an abandonment. Durham's two points were gained at Portsmouth; the north-eastern weather failed to be helpful in a year when the team could have done with some sympathetic rainfall.

AXA EQUITY & LAW LEAGUE

	M	*W*	*L*	*T*	*NR*	*Pts*	*Net run-rate*
1 – Surrey (9)	17	12	4	0	1	50	16.31
2 – Nottinghamshire (11)	17	12	4	0	1	50	9.20
3 – Yorkshire (12)	17	11	6	0	0	44	11.47
4 – Warwickshire (2)	17	10	6	0	1	42	4.88
5 – Somerset (14)	17	10	6	0	1	42	1.14
6 – Northamptonshire (13)	17	10	6	0	1	42	0.42
7 – Middlesex (17)	17	9	7	0	1	38	−0.92
8 – Worcestershire (3)	17	8	6	0	3	38	1.88
9 – Lancashire (4)	17	9	8	0	0	36	−0.16
10 – Kent (1)	17	8	8	1	0	34	−7.65
11 – Derbyshire (8)	17	7	7	1	2	34	4.35
12 – Leicestershire (7)	17	7	7	0	3	34	0.10
13 – Glamorgan (6)	17	7	8	0	2	32	2.73
14 – Sussex (10)	17	6	9	0	2	28	−11.67
15 – Hampshire (18)	17	4	10	0	3	22	−6.22
16 – Gloucestershire (15)	17	4	10	0	3	22	−8.19
17 – Essex (5)	17	4	12	0	1	18	−3.57
18 – Durham (16)	17	1	15	0	1	6	−15.37

1995 positions are shown in brackets.

When two or more counties finish with an equal number of points, the positions are decided by a) most wins, b) higher net run-rate (runs scored per 100 balls minus runs conceded per 100 balls).

No play was possible in the following seven matches: May 19 – Glamorgan v Derbyshire at Cardiff; Gloucestershire v Somerset at Bristol; Leicestershire v Worcestershire at Leicester; May 26 – Hampshire v Durham at Portsmouth; Sussex v Middlesex at Horsham; August 11 – Hampshire v Gloucestershire at Southampton; August 25 – Nottinghamshire v Surrey at Nottingham.

Leading run-scorers: P. V. Simmons 815 (£3,000 individual award), D. M. Jones 749 (£1,500), T. M. Moody 680, K. J. Barnett 649, P. Johnson 645, R. T. Robinson 602, C. L. Hooper 579, R. A. Smith 551.

Leading wicket-takers: A. J. Hollioake 39 (£3,000 individual award), M. V. Fleming 29 (£1,500), C. L. Cairns, P. J. Hartley, S. Lee and S. M. Pollock 25, J. P. Taylor 24, A. R. Caddick and H. R. J. Trump 23, A. F. Giles 22.

Most economical bowlers: (runs per over, minimum 100 overs): C. E. L. Ambrose 3.39, S. M. Pollock 3.71, S. L. Watkin 3.98, J. E. Emburey 4.10, K. P. Evans 4.16, S. R. Barwick 4.30, R. K. Illingworth 4.36.

Leading wicket-keepers: S. J. Rhodes 19 (14 ct, 5 st) (£1,500 individual award), A. N. Aymes 18 (12 ct, 6 st), K. R. Brown 17 (12 ct, 5 st), K. M. Krikken 17 (12 ct, 5 st), R. M. Turner 17 (14 ct, 3 st).

Leading fielders: A. Symonds 12, R. J. Bailey, M. P. Maynard and J. P. Stephenson 10.

Prize money

£40,000 for winners: SURREY.
£20,000 for runners-up: NOTTINGHAMSHIRE.
£10,000 for third place: YORKSHIRE.
£5,000 for fourth place: WARWICKSHIRE.
£475 for the winners of each match, shared if tied or no result.

SUMMARY OF RESULTS, 1996

	Derbyshire	Durham	Essex	Glamorgan	Gloucestershire	Hampshire	Kent	Lancashire	Leicestershire	Middlesex	Northamptonshire	Nottinghamshire	Somerset	Surrey	Sussex	Warwickshire	Worcestershire	Yorkshire
Derbyshire	—	**W**	**N**	*N*	**W**	*L*	**T**	*W*	**W**	**L**	*W*	**L**	*L*	*L*	*L*	**W**	**W**	*L*
Durham	*L*	—	**W**	**L**	**L**	*N*	*L*	**L**	**L**	*L*	**L**	*L*	*L*	**L**	*L*	*L*	*L*	**L**
Essex	*N*	*L*	—	**L**	**L**	*W*	**L**	**W**	*L*	*L*	**L**	**L**	*L*	**W**	**W**	*L*	*L*	*L*
Glamorgan	**N**	*W*	*W*	—	*W*	*W*	**W**	**L**	**L**	*L*	*L*	*L*	**L**	**L**	*W*	*L*	**N**	**W**
Gloucestershire	*L*	*W*	*W*	**L**	—	*N*	**W**	*L*	**L**	*L*	**L**	*W*	**N**	**L**	**L**	**N**	*L*	**L**
Hampshire	**W**	**N**	**L**	**L**	**N**	—	*L*	*L*	*N*	**L**	**W**	**L**	*W*	**L**	*W*	*L*	*L*	*L*
Kent	*T*	**W**	*W*	*L*	*L*	**W**	—	**L**	*W*	**W**	*W*	**L**	**L**	*L*	**W**	*L*	**L**	**W**
Lancashire	**L**	*W*	*L*	*W*	**W**	**W**	*W*	—	**L**	**W**	*W*	*W*	**L**	**L**	*W*	*L*	**L**	*L*
Leicestershire	*L*	*W*	**W**	*W*	*W*	**N**	**L**	*W*	—	**W**	**L**	*L*	**L**	*L*	**N**	*W*	**N**	*L*
Middlesex	*W*	**W**	**W**	**W**	**W**	*W*	*L*	*L*	*L*	—	*L*	*L*	**W**	*L*	*N*	**W**	**L**	**W**
Northamptonshire	**L**	*W*	*W*	**W**	*W*	*L*	**L**	**L**	*W*	**W**	—	*W*	*W*	*L*	**W**	**W**	*N*	**L**
Nottinghamshire	*W*	**W**	*W*	**W**	**L**	*W*	*W*	**L**	**W**	**W**	**L**	—	*W*	**N**	**W**	*L*	*W*	*W*
Somerset	**W**	**W**	**W**	*W*	*N*	**L**	*W*	*W*	*W*	*L*	**L**	**L**	—	**W**	*L*	**W**	**L**	*W*
Surrey	**W**	*W*	*L*	*W*	*W*	*W*	**W**	*W*	**W**	**W**	**W**	*N*	*L*	—	**L**	**W**	**W**	*L*
Sussex	**W**	**W**	*L*	**L**	*W*	**L**	*L*	**L**	*N*	**N**	*L*	*L*	**W**	*W*	—	**L**	*W*	**L**
Warwickshire	*L*	**W**	**W**	**W**	*N*	**W**	**W**	**W**	**L**	*L*	*L*	**W**	*L*	*L*	*W*	—	**W**	*W*
Worcestershire	*L*	**W**	**W**	*N*	**W**	**W**	*W*	*W*	*N*	*W*	**N**	**L**	*W*	*L*	**L**	*L*	—	**L**
Yorkshire	**W**	*W*	**W**	*L*	*W*	**W**	*L*	**W**	**W**	*L*	*W*	**L**	**L**	**W**	*W*	**L**	*W*	—

Home games in bold, away games in italics. W = Won, L = Lost, T = Tied, N = No result.

DERBYSHIRE

DERBYSHIRE v LEICESTERSHIRE

At Derby, May 5. Derbyshire won by four wickets. Toss: Derbyshire.

Derbyshire's new captain, Jones, and his predecessor, Barnett, set up victory with a century opening partnership. At the fall of Barnett's wicket, a bogus batsman in Derbyshire replica kit made his way to the crease, along with a startled Adams. The intruder was allowed to face a joke delivery before being hustled away. Jones went on to make an unbeaten 103 from 108 balls; he had also scored a hundred on his Sunday debut for Durham four years earlier.

Leicestershire

V. J. Wells c Wells b Cork	21
G. I. Macmillan c Owen b Harris	17
B. F. Smith c Wells b Griffith	37
P. V. Simmons c Wells b Griffith	10
*J. J. Whitaker b Aldred	60
D. L. Maddy b Aldred	19
†P. A. Nixon not out	32
C. C. Remy c Barnett b Aldred	8
T. J. Mason lbw b Aldred	7
G. J. Parsons c Aldred b Harris	8
A. D. Mullally not out	0
L-b 1, w 5	6
1/33 2/39 3/78 4/92 5/151 6/178 7/199 8/212 9/225 (9 wkts, 40 overs)	225

Bowling: Cork 8–0–41–1; DeFreitas 3–0–21–0; Harris 7–1–39–2; Griffith 8–0–36–2; Jones 5–0–28–0; Aldred 6–0–41–4; Wells 3–0–18–0.

Derbyshire

*D. M. Jones not out	103
K. J. Barnett c and b Remy	47
C. J. Adams b Remy	12
C. M. Wells run out	8
J. E. Owen b Wells	0
P. A. J. DeFreitas st Nixon b Simmons	26
†K. M. Krikken c Macmillan b Mullally	1
D. G. Cork not out	0
B 1, l-b 16, w 15	32
1/117 2/151 3/164 4/164 5/217 6/220 (6 wkts, 39.2 overs)	229

A. J. Harris, P. Aldred and F. A. Griffith did not bat.

Bowling: Mullally 7–0–43–1; Parsons 8–0–38–0; Simmons 7.2–0–34–1; Mason 4–0–29–0; Remy 8–0–42–2; Wells 5–0–26–1.

Umpires: J. C. Balderstone and R. Palmer.

At Sheffield, May 12. DERBYSHIRE lost to YORKSHIRE by 45 runs.

At Cardiff, May 19. GLAMORGAN v DERBYSHIRE. No result (abandoned).

DERBYSHIRE v ESSEX

At Derby, May 26. No result. Toss: Derbyshire.

Jones was out to the first ball of Derbyshire's reply, but rain after five overs prevented a result.

Essex

D. D. J. Robinson c Rollins b Base	12
S. G. Law c Harris b Barnett	46
N. Hussain c and b Vandrau	41
*P. J. Prichard c Krikken b Wells	42
G. A. Gooch c Adams b Vandrau	7
†R. J. Rollins c Owen b Barnett	19
M. C. Ilott run out	14
A. P. Grayson not out	5
A. P. Cowan not out	7
B 2, l-b 10, w 2	14
1/40 2/78 3/134 4/152 5/168 6/189 7/199 (7 wkts, 40 overs)	207

S. J. W. Andrew and P. M. Such did not bat.

Bowling: Base 6–0–34–1; Harris 6–1–16–0; Wells 7–0–37–1; Vandrau 8–0–36–2; Barnett 7–0–36–2; Aldred 6–0–36–0.

Derbyshire

*D. M. Jones lbw b Ilott	0
K. J. Barnett not out	8
C. J. Adams not out	7
L-b 1, w 1	2
1/0 (1 wkt, 5 overs)	17

A. S. Rollins, J. E. Owen, C. M. Wells, †K. M. Krikken, M. J. Vandrau, P. Aldred, A. J. Harris and S. J. Base did not bat.

Bowling: Ilott 3–0–10–1; Cowan 2–0–6–0.

Umpires: J. D. Bond and K. J. Lyons.

At The Oval, June 2. DERBYSHIRE lost to SURREY by 50 runs.

At Southampton, June 9. DERBYSHIRE lost to HAMPSHIRE by five wickets.

DERBYSHIRE v MIDDLESEX

At Derby, June 23. Middlesex won by eight runs. Toss: Middlesex.

Ramprakash scored 122 in 113 balls with a six and 11 fours, helping Middlesex to score 115 off their last ten overs. With Jones reaching his third Sunday hundred of the season, Derbyshire mounted a spirited reply, but fell just short of the seven an over required.

Middlesex

P. N. Weekes c Barnett b Jones	52
M. R. Ramprakash c Dean b Aldred	122
J. C. Pooley c DeFreitas b Barnett	17
*M. W. Gatting run out	41
J. D. Carr not out	23
†K. R. Brown not out	0
B 2, l-b 4, w 13, n-b 4	23
1/136 2/163 3/226 4/269 (4 wkts, 40 overs)	278

P. E. Wellings, R. L. Johnson, A. R. C. Fraser, R. A. Fay and U. B. A. Rashid did not bat.

Bowling: Base 6–0–38–0; Dean 8–0–50–0; Aldred 8–0–55–1; Griffith 6–0–45–0; Jones 6–0–35–1; Barnett 6–0–49–1.

Derbyshire

K. J. Barnett c Johnson b Rashid	64
A. S. Rollins c Weekes b Fraser	4
*D. M. Jones c Weekes b Johnson	118
P. A. J. DeFreitas c Pooley b Weekes	15
J. E. Owen b Weekes	11
†K. M. Krikken c Weekes b Ramprakash	22
T. J. G. O'Gorman not out	17
F. A. Griffith not out	6
B 1, l-b 10, w 2	13
1/6 2/139 3/158 4/193 5/225 6/262 (6 wkts, 40 overs)	270

P. Aldred, S. J. Base and K. J. Dean did not bat.

Bowling: Fay 4–0–19–0; Fraser 8–0–47–1; Johnson 5–0–37–1; Carr 6–0–43–0; Rashid 7–0–60–1; Weekes 8–0–32–2; Ramprakash 2–0–21–1.

Umpires: D. J. Constant and R. Julian.

At Northampton, June 30. DERBYSHIRE beat NORTHAMPTONSHIRE by 90 runs.

DERBYSHIRE v DURHAM

At Derby, July 14. Derbyshire won by 60 runs. Toss: Derbyshire.

An opening partnership of 83 between Jones and Barnett was enough to put the match beyond Durham's reach. An undefeated, but laboured, innings from Roseberry was the only significant contribution to an undistinguished reply; he took 25 overs to make 45, whereas Jones took 44 off 50 balls.

Derbyshire

*D. M. Jones c Ligertwood b Walker	44	D. G. Cork c Hutton b Brown	3
K. J. Barnett c Longley b Brown	69	M. J. Vandrau not out	21
C. J. Adams c Hutton b Boiling	6	L-b 14, w 5, n-b 4	23
†K. M. Krikken c Roseberry b Boiling	5		
T. J. G. O'Gorman c Boiling b Wood	40	1/83 2/104 3/115 (7 wkts, 40 overs)	240
P. A. J. DeFreitas b Wood	7	4/151 5/184	
C. M. Wells not out	22	6/195 7/201	

A. J. Harris and K. J. Dean did not bat.

Bowling: Brown 8–0–32–2; Bainbridge 8–1–36–0; Wood 8–0–68–2; Walker 8–0–45–1; Boiling 8–1–45–2.

Durham

S. L. Campbell lbw b Cork	14	S. J. E. Brown c Harris b Wells	18
S. Hutton c O'Gorman b Dean	24	J. Wood not out	6
P. D. Collingwood b DeFreitas	12		
P. Bainbridge b Dean	11	L-b 10, n-b 4	14
*M. A. Roseberry not out	45		
J. I. Longley c Harris b Vandrau	12	1/30 2/54 3/63 (7 wkts, 40 overs)	180
†D. G. C. Ligertwood st Krikken b Vandrau	24	4/77 5/103 6/148 7/173	

A. Walker and J. Boiling did not bat.

Bowling: Cork 5–0–16–1; Harris 6–0–32–0; Dean 8–0–35–2; DeFreitas 8–2–19–1; Vandrau 6–0–36–2; Wells 7–0–32–1.

Umpires: H. D. Bird and P. Willey.

At Manchester, July 21. DERBYSHIRE beat LANCASHIRE by five wickets.

DERBYSHIRE v KENT

At Derby, July 28. Tied. Toss: Kent. County debut: W. J. House.

DeFreitas continued his Sunday batting form with his third unbeaten fifty in four matches. His career-best 72 not out included five sixes from only 37 balls in a match shortened by rain. However, Kent opener Fleming was almost as effective and DeFreitas found it harder with the ball; he conceded 44 from four overs, including 11 off the last, when he resorted to off-spin. The Cambridge batsman, Will House, needed three off the final ball to win his first match for Kent; two secured the tie.

Derbyshire

K. J. Barnett c House b McCague	16	C. M. Wells c Willis b Headley	1
C. J. Adams c Willis b Headley	8	G. A. Khan not out	1
*D. M. Jones b McCague	32	L-b 5, w 6, n-b 2	13
T. J. G. O'Gorman c Ward b Hooper	26		
P. A. J. DeFreitas not out	72	1/24 2/46 3/90 (6 wkts, 25 overs)	183
†K. M. Krikken c Hooper b Fleming	14	4/95 5/152 6/164	

P. Aldred, M. J. Vandrau and K. J. Dean did not bat.

Bowling: Headley 5–0–31–2; Wren 5–0–34–0; McCague 5–0–34–2; Hooper 5–0–30–1; Fleming 4–0–36–1; Llong 1–0–13–0.

Kent

T. R. Ward c Jones b Aldred 4
M. V. Fleming c Adams b Vandrau 65
*C. L. Hooper c Dean b Wells 25
M. J. Walker c Jones b Wells 4
N. J. Llong st Krikken b DeFreitas 15
D. P. Fulton st Krikken b Barnett 18
W. J. House not out 19
†S. C. Willis st Krikken b Barnett 16
M. J. McCague run out 8
D. W. Headley not out 0
B 2, l-b 3, w 4 9

1/7 2/92 3/97 4/101 5/127 6/140 7/158 8/177 (8 wkts, 25 overs) 183

T. N. Wren did not bat.

Bowling: Aldred 5–0–25–1; Vandrau 5–0–26–1; Wells 5–0–35–2; Dean 2–0–22–0; Barnett 4–0–26–2; DeFreitas 4–0–44–1.

Umpires: J. H. Hampshire and M. J. Kitchen.

DERBYSHIRE v GLOUCESTERSHIRE

At Derby, August 4. Derbyshire won by eight wickets. Toss: Gloucestershire.

Gloucestershire lost their captain, Walsh, to a leg injury in the 14th over of Derbyshire's innings; meanwhile, they lost the match to the bowling of Dean, who took five for 32, and the batting of Jones, whose undefeated century was his fourth of the season in the Sunday League, equalling Tom Moody's record in 1991.

Gloucestershire

R. I. Dawson c Krikken b Dean 68
M. G. N. Windows c Cork b DeFreitas ... 1
M. W. Alleyne lbw b Cork 0
M. A. Lynch b Dean 47
A. Symonds c Krikken b Dean 0
†R. C. Russell lbw b Dean 5
M. J. Cawdron not out 32
M. C. J. Ball c DeFreitas b Dean 1
R. P. Davis st Krikken b Barnett 0
*C. A. Walsh b Barnett 38
J. Lewis not out 5
L-b 3, w 6, n-b 2 11

1/4 2/5 3/110 4/110 5/124 6/133 7/135 8/137 9/201 (9 wkts, 40 overs) 208

Bowling: Cork 8–1–23–1; DeFreitas 8–1–43–1; Aldred 2–0–18–0; Vandrau 2–0–21–0; Wells 8–0–34–0; Dean 8–1–32–5; Barnett 4–0–34–2.

Derbyshire

*D. M. Jones not out 101
K. J. Barnett run out 33
G. A. Khan c Davis b Cawdron 27
C. M. Wells not out 39
L-b 10, w 2 12

1/69 2/126 (2 wkts, 36.5 overs) 212

D. G. Cork, T. J. G. O'Gorman, P. A. J. DeFreitas, †K. M. Krikken, M. J. Vandrau, P. Aldred and K. J. Dean did not bat.

Bowling: Walsh 5–1–10–0; Lewis 8–0–45–0; Alleyne 7.5–0–47–0; Ball 7–0–35–0; Davis 6–0–37–0; Cawdron 3–0–28–1.

Umpires: J. H. Harris and G. Sharp.

At Hove, August 11. DERBYSHIRE lost to SUSSEX on scoring-rate.

DERBYSHIRE v NOTTINGHAMSHIRE

At Derby, August 18. Nottinghamshire won by eight wickets. Toss: Derbyshire. First-team debut: G. M. Roberts.

With Barnett missing what would have been his first League century for six years by a single run, Derbyshire failed to use a good opportunity to set a demanding target. Robinson and then Johnson saw Nottinghamshire to their ninth win of the season with little difficulty.

Derbyshire

*D. M. Jones lbw b Bates	20
K. J. Barnett b Cairns	99
C. J. Adams c Dowman b Bates	42
G. A. Khan c Dowman b Bowen	14
P. A. J. DeFreitas c Bowen b Tolley	6
T. J. G. O'Gorman c Noon b Tolley	0
†K. M. Krikken not out	26
G. M. Roberts not out	6
B 4, l-b 9, w 3	16
1/45 2/117 3/171 4/179 5/180 6/217 (6 wkts, 40 overs)	229

P. Aldred, A. J. Harris and K. J. Dean did not bat.

Bowling: Evans 8–0–40–0; Bowen 8–0–35–1; Tolley 7–0–43–2; Bates 8–0–39–2; Cairns 8–0–47–1; Dowman 1–0–12–0.

Nottinghamshire

R. T. Robinson b Harris	90
M. P. Dowman c Aldred b Harris	29
*P. Johnson not out	71
C. L. Cairns not out	27
L-b 6, w 3, n-b 6	15
1/87 2/174 (2 wkts, 36.5 overs)	232

G. F. Archer, A. A. Metcalfe, C. M. Tolley, K. P. Evans, †W. M. Noon, R. T. Bates and M. N. Bowen did not bat.

Bowling: DeFreitas 6–0–35–0; Dean 6–0–27–0; Harris 8–0–47–2; Roberts 6–0–33–0; Barnett 3–0–19–0; Aldred 6.5–0–57–0; Jones 1–0–8–0.

Umpires: K. E. Palmer and R. A. White.

DERBYSHIRE v WORCESTERSHIRE

At Chesterfield, September 1. Derbyshire won by six wickets. Toss: Worcestershire.

Worcestershire recovered slightly from 120 for eight but never stretched Derbyshire. The home side's only serious mistake was that they took the field with 12 players. A breakdown in communications was blamed. After hasty consultations with club captain Jones, who was injured and on the balcony, Wells was withdrawn, to sympathetic applause. Barnett's 50th run was his 7,000th in the Sunday League, in his 253rd match; he was the sixth batsman to achieve the landmark.

Worcestershire

*T. M. Moody c Krikken b Harris	44
W. P. C. Weston c Adams b Dean	3
G. A. Hick c Cork b Dean	1
K. R. Spiring b Harris	16
V. S. Solanki c Krikken b Cork	7
D. A. Leatherdale c O'Gorman b Barnett	14
S. R. Lampitt c Krikken b Barnett	29
†S. J. Rhodes b Roberts	7
M. J. Rawnsley c Khan b Roberts	2
A. Sheriyar c Roberts b Barnett	19
B. E. A. Preece not out	1
L-b 5, w 6, n-b 4	15
1/19 2/31 3/53 4/73 5/94 6/105 7/115 8/120 9/151 (36.3 overs)	158

Bowling: Cork 8–0–28–1; Dean 6–0–37–2; Harris 8–0–34–2; Roberts 8–0–28–2; Barnett 6.3–0–26–3.

Derbyshire

D. G. Cork c Spiring b Solanki	35	†K. M. Krikken not out	2
K. J. Barnett c Lampitt b Preece	51	W 16, n-b 2	18
G. A. Khan b Sheriyar	25		—
T. J. G. O'Gorman lbw b Leatherdale	0	1/48 2/118 (4 wkts, 32.5 overs)	159
*P. A. J. DeFreitas not out	28	3/120 4/143	

A. S. Rollins, C. J. Adams, K. J. Dean, A. J. Harris and G. M. Roberts did not bat.

Bowling: Moody 6–1–20–0; Solanki 8–0–41–1; Lampitt 4–0–20–0; Rawnsley 5.5–1–31–0; Leatherdale 4–0–11–1; Sheriyar 3–0–26–1; Preece 2–0–10–1.

Umpires: B. Dudleston and T. E. Jesty.

At Taunton, September 8. DERBYSHIRE lost to SOMERSET by 12 runs.

DERBYSHIRE v WARWICKSHIRE

At Derby, September 15. Derbyshire won by eight wickets. Toss: Derbyshire.

Asked to bat on a slow pitch, Warwickshire could not recover from 72 for six, despite late flurries from Knight and Giles. An opening stand of 70 in reply ensured that Derbyshire would not face the same difficulties.

Warwickshire

N. V. Knight run out	44	G. Welch not out	16
N. M. K. Smith c Aldred b Harris	4	G. C. Small run out	4
W. G. Khan lbw b Harris	0	*T. A. Munton not out	3
D. R. Brown c Khan b Aldred	5	L-b 17, w 6, n-b 2	25
T. L. Penney run out	8		—
M. Burns c Barnett b Wells	4	1/22 2/22 3/33 (9 wkts, 40 overs)	156
†K. J. Piper b Roberts	7	4/53 5/61 6/72	
A. F. Giles c Jones b Barnett	36	7/113 8/146 9/152	

Bowling: Harris 5–0–21–2; Aldred 8–2–16–1; Wells 8–1–16–1; Barnett 4–0–23–1; Roberts 8–1–30–1; DeFreitas 7–1–33–0.

Derbyshire

*D. M. Jones st Piper b Giles	41
K. J. Barnett not out	57
C. J. Adams b Giles	6
T. J. G. O'Gorman not out	40
L-b 6, w 8, n-b 2	16
	—
1/70 2/92 (2 wkts, 30.4 overs)	160

G. A. Khan, C. M. Wells, P. A. J. DeFreitas, †K. M. Krikken, A. J. Harris, G. M. Roberts and P. Aldred did not bat.

Bowling: Munton 6–1–19–0; Brown 2–0–17–0; Welch 6.4–0–51–0; Giles 8–0–25–2; Smith 6–0–31–0; Small 2–0–11–0.

Umpires: M. J. Kitchen and B. Leadbeater.

DURHAM

DURHAM v NORTHAMPTONSHIRE

At Chester-le-Street, May 5. Northamptonshire won by eight wickets. Toss: Durham.

In a one-sided contest, Collingwood alone offered resistance with a maiden one-day fifty. Despite the early loss of Loye, Northamptonshire were never seriously troubled.

Durham

M. J. Foster c Curran b Taylor	10	N. Killeen lbw b Emburey	0
*M. A. Roseberry b Taylor	3	S. J. E. Brown c Bailey b Taylor	9
S. Hutton c Bailey b Mallender	17	M. M. Betts not out	0
J. E. Morris c Capel b Mallender	6	B 1, l-b 6, w 3, n-b 4	14
P. D. Collingwood not out	54		—
J. I. Longley c Penberthy b Curran	11	1/11 2/28 3/35 (9 wkts, 40 overs)	141
†C. W. Scott b Curran	9	4/50 5/70 6/85	
J. Boiling c Bailey b Emburey	8	7/113 8/113 9/130	

Bowling: Taylor 8–1–37–3; Mallender 8–2–20–2; Emburey 8–0–18–2; Curran 8–0–25–2; Penberthy 8–0–34–0.

Northamptonshire

A. Fordham c Collingwood b Killeen	43
M. B. Loye c Collingwood b Killeen	7
*R. J. Bailey not out	62
K. M. Curran not out	11
B 4, l-b 3, w 8, n-b 4	19
	—
1/37 2/105 (2 wkts, 35.3 overs)	142

D. J. Capel, †R. J. Warren, A. L. Penberthy, J. N. Snape, J. E. Emburey, N. A. Mallender and J. P. Taylor did not bat.

Bowling: Brown 7–1–19–0; Betts 8–0–31–0; Foster 6–1–14–0; Killeen 5.3–0–25–2; Boiling 7–0–36–0; Collingwood 2–0–10–0.

Umpires: K. J. Lyons and A. G. T. Whitehead.

At Lord's, May 12. DURHAM lost to MIDDLESEX by 17 runs.

DURHAM v YORKSHIRE

At Chester-le-Street, May 19. Yorkshire won by 63 runs. Toss: Durham.

An unbroken sixth-wicket stand worth 93 in 11 overs between Blakey and Morris took the match beyond Durham's reach. Silverwood took three for 11 in his opening six-over spell and went on to a one-day best four for 26 to confirm Yorkshire's superiority.

Yorkshire

*D. Byas c Ligertwood b Betts	12	A. C. Morris not out	48
M. P. Vaughan lbw b Betts	7		
M. G. Bevan c Roseberry b Birbeck	46	L-b 4, w 8, n-b 2	14
A. McGrath c Collingwood b Betts	3		—
C. White c Ligertwood b Foster	8	1/19 2/38 3/46 (5 wkts, 40 overs)	199
†R. J. Blakey not out	61	4/61 5/106	

D. Gough, P. J. Hartley, C. E. W. Silverwood and R. D. Stemp did not bat.

Bowling: Betts 8–0–26–3; Wood 8–0–41–0; Killeen 8–0–30–0; Foster 8–0–48–1; Birbeck 8–0–50–1.

Durham

S. L. Campbell lbw b Silverwood	7	N. Killeen c Blakey b Gough	0
*M. A. Roseberry b Silverwood	1	J. Wood b Morris	2
J. E. Morris c Bevan b Silverwood	9	M. M. Betts not out	1
J. I. Longley c Blakey b Morris	21	B 7, l-b 13, w 8	28
P. D. Collingwood c Bevan b Hartley	9		—
S. D. Birbeck run out	7	1/5 2/27 3/31 (32 overs)	136
M. J. Foster c Morris b Silverwood	36	4/56 5/75 6/83	
†D. G. C. Ligertwood lbw b Gough	15	7/123 8/125 9/134	

Bowling: Gough 6–1–16–2; Silverwood 8–0–26–4; Hartley 6–0–18–1; Stemp 7–0–37–0; Morris 5–0–19–2.

Umpires: D. J. Constant and T. E. Jesty.

At Portsmouth, May 26. HAMPSHIRE v DURHAM. No result (abandoned).

At Nottingham, June 2. DURHAM lost to NOTTINGHAMSHIRE by 39 runs.

At Hove, June 9. DURHAM lost to SUSSEX by six runs.

DURHAM v LANCASHIRE

At Chester-le-Street, June 16. Lancashire won by eight wickets. Toss: Durham.

Despite needing lengthy treatment after a blow on his finger from Brown, Atherton remained to score an unbeaten 91 and steer Lancashire to a comfortable victory.

Durham

S. L. Campbell hit wkt b Martin	1
S. Hutton c Hegg b Martin	10
*J. E. Morris c Watkinson b Martin	10
D. A. Blenkiron run out	34
P. Bainbridge c Fairbrother b Chapple	14
P. D. Collingwood c Yates b Watkinson	28
†D. G. C. Ligertwood not out	36
N. Killeen run out	7
S. J. E. Brown lbw b Watkinson	16
J. Boiling not out	11
L-b 2, w 2, n-b 2	6
1/1 2/20 3/25 4/57 5/98 6/108 7/119 8/137 (8 wkts, 40 overs)	173

A. Walker did not bat.

Bowling: Austin 8–0–29–0; Martin 7–0–29–3; Chapple 5–0–16–1; Elworthy 5–0–23–0; Watkinson 7–1–41–2; Yates 8–0–33–0.

Lancashire

M. A. Atherton not out	91
*M. Watkinson b Walker	26
S. Elworthy st Ligertwood b Bainbridge	10
N. J. Speak not out	39
L-b 1, w 7	8
1/33 2/48 (2 wkts, 35.3 overs)	174

N. H. Fairbrother, G. D. Lloyd, I. D. Austin, †W. K. Hegg, G. Chapple, G. Yates and P. J. Martin did not bat.

Bowling: Brown 8–4–17–0; Killeen 7–0–42–0; Walker 6.3–0–39–1; Boiling 8–0–36–0; Bainbridge 4–0–24–1; Blenkiron 2–0–15–0.

Umpires: J. C. Balderstone and B. Leadbeater.

DURHAM v SURREY

At Stockton-on-Tees, June 23. Surrey won by 59 runs. Toss: Durham. First-team debut: C. L. Campbell.

Ward hit eight sixes in 14 balls to reach a 55-ball century, with his second fifty coming from only 13 deliveries. Bainbridge went for four sixes in consecutive balls. Durham could not match that scoring-rate and went meekly to their seventh Sunday defeat of the season.

Surrey

D. J. Bicknell c Ligertwood b Wood 3
A. D. Brown c Morris b Killeen 30
J. D. Ratcliffe c Ligertwood b Walker 42
N. Shahid c Hutton b C. L. Campbell 20
D. M. Ward c sub b Killeen 108
*A. J. Hollioake c S. L. Campbell b Killeen . 33
B. P. Julian run out 2
†G. J. Kersey b Walker 4
M. P. Bicknell not out 1
B 4, l-b 9, w 6, n-b 6 25

1/25 2/54 3/97 4/138 5/261 6/261 7/267 8/268 (8 wkts, 40 overs) 268

R. M. Pearson and J. E. Benjamin did not bat.

Bowling: Wood 8–1–45–1; C. L. Campbell 8–0–44–1; Killeen 8–0–45–3; Walker 8–0–57–2; Bainbridge 8–0–64–0.

Durham

S. L. Campbell b Hollioake 49
*J. E. Morris b Benjamin 30
P. D. Collingwood b Hollioake 26
S. Hutton c Ward b Julian 27
D. A. Blenkiron c Ward b Hollioake 0
P. Bainbridge c Shahid b M. P. Bicknell . . 15
†D. G. C. Ligertwood c Ward b M. P. Bicknell . 8
J. Wood not out 19
N. Killeen run out 5
A. Walker run out 1
C. L. Campbell run out 0
L-b 9, w 8, n-b 12 29

1/56 2/93 3/146 4/148 5/149 6/164 7/178 8/200 9/205 (35.4 overs) 209

Bowling: Benjamin 8–1–33–1; M. P. Bicknell 8–0–50–2; Pearson 8–0–44–0; Hollioake 6–0–30–3; Julian 5.4–0–43–1.

Umpires: G. I. Burgess and G. Sharp.

DURHAM v GLOUCESTERSHIRE

At Chester-le-Street, June 30. Gloucestershire won by four runs. Toss: Durham.

By restricting Gloucestershire to 180, Durham gave themselves every chance of beating a first-class county for the first time in 1996. However, their batting lacked conviction in the face of a disciplined attack.

Gloucestershire

A. J. Wright b C. L. Campbell 1
R. I. Dawson c Ligertwood b C. L. Campbell . 67
M. W. Alleyne lbw b Betts 0
A. Symonds c Ligertwood b Killeen 7
T. H. C. Hancock b Bainbridge 31
*†R. C. Russell b Bainbridge 1
M. G. N. Windows not out 31
M. J. Cawdron c Blenkiron b Killeen 7
M. C. J. Ball not out 24
L-b 4, w 7 11

1/6 2/11 3/33 4/100 5/102 6/122 7/150 (7 wkts, 40 overs) 180

A. M. Smith and J. Lewis did not bat.

Bowling: Betts 8–0–44–1; C. L. Campbell 8–0–45–2; Killeen 8–0–36–2; Boiling 8–1–25–0; Bainbridge 8–0–26–2.

Durham

S. L. Campbell b Smith 57
S. Hutton c Symonds b Smith 0
*J. E. Morris c Alleyne b Symonds 46
P. Bainbridge c Ball b Symonds 12
P. D. Collingwood b Ball 9
D. A. Blenkiron b Symonds 11
†D. G. C. Ligertwood c Symonds b Lewis 9
M. M. Betts not out 7
J. Boiling c Ball b Smith 9
N. Killeen not out 3
L-b 4, w 5, n-b 4 13

1/1 2/81 3/97 4/115 5/136 6/152 7/158 8/172 (8 wkts, 40 overs) 176

C. L. Campbell did not bat.

Bowling: Smith 8–0–29–3; Lewis 5–0–27–1; Cawdron 3–0–20–0; Alleyne 8–0–28–0; Ball 8–0–29–1; Symonds 8–0–39–3.

Umpires: B. Dudleston and V. A. Holder.

At Maidstone, July 7. DURHAM lost to KENT by six wickets.

At Derby, July 14. DURHAM lost to DERBYSHIRE by 60 runs.

At Worcester, July 21. DURHAM lost to WORCESTERSHIRE by nine wickets.

DURHAM v ESSEX

At Hartlepool, July 28. Durham won by eight wickets. Toss: Essex.

Durham finally pulled off their first win against a first-class county in 29 starts during 1996 (excluding the Costcutter Cup earlier in July). It was also their first Sunday League win since August 6 the previous year; since then, they had lost 14, with three washed out. Saggers, bowling tightly for his one for 19 off eight overs in his first League match, and Campbell, with a Sunday-best 77 from 83 balls, saw Durham home with more than eight overs in hand.

Essex

D. D. J. Robinson c Roseberry b Cox	16
S. G. Law c Cox b Wood	3
*P. J. Prichard lbw b Cox	19
R. C. Irani c Daley b Killeen	11
†R. J. Rollins lbw b Saggers	23
J. J. B. Lewis lbw b Wood	28
A. P. Grayson st Ligertwood b Boiling	33
M. C. Ilott c Roseberry b Killeen	2
N. F. Williams c Daley b Killeen	12
S. J. W. Andrew c Killeen b Boiling	0
P. M. Such not out	1
B 2, l-b 3, w 10, n-b 2	17
1/8 2/44 3/45 4/76 5/89 6/137 7/151 8/164 9/164 (39.2 overs)	165

Bowling: Wood 8–1–36–2; Killeen 8–0–46–3; Cox 8–0–34–2; Saggers 8–0–19–1; Boiling 7.2–0–25–2.

Durham

S. L. Campbell run out	77
S. Hutton not out	47
P. D. Collingwood b Grayson	0
J. A. Daley not out	17
B 4, l-b 10, w 8, n-b 6	28
1/147 2/147 (2 wkts, 31.3 overs)	169

*M. A. Roseberry, D. M. Cox, †D. G. C. Ligertwood, N. Killeen, J. Boiling, J. Wood and M. J. Saggers did not bat.

Bowling: Ilott 4–0–16–0; Andrew 7–2–38–0; Irani 4–0–23–0; Such 7–0–30–0; Williams 4–0–15–0; Grayson 5.3–0–33–1.

Umpires: B. Dudleston and D. R. Shepherd.

At Birmingham, August 11. DURHAM lost to WARWICKSHIRE by 88 runs.

At Weston-super-Mare, August 25. DURHAM lost to SOMERSET by seven wickets.

DURHAM v GLAMORGAN

At Chester-le-Street, September 1. Glamorgan won on scoring-rate. Toss: Glamorgan.

Defeat ensured that Durham would occupy last place in the final League table. Once again, their batting failed to produce an adequate total and, when rain stopped play, Glamorgan were well ahead of the required rate.

Durham

S. L. Campbell c Butcher b Parkin 14
S. Hutton b Gibson 37
J. A. Daley b Gibson 4
P. D. Collingwood c Cottey b Butcher . . . 12
M. A. Roseberry not out 34
D. A. Blenkiron lbw b Butcher 1
†D. G. C. Ligertwood run out 24
M. M. Betts st Shaw b Dale 2
*S. J. E. Brown not out 9
B 2, l-b 15, w 15, n-b 4 36

1/35 2/55 3/79 4/93 5/96 6/134 7/154 (7 wkts, 40 overs) 173

M. J. Saggers and A. Walker did not bat.

Bowling: Watkin 8–0–33–0; Parkin 8–1–26–1; Gibson 8–0–31–2; Barwick 4–0–15–0; Dale 6–0–23–1; Butcher 6–1–28–2.

Glamorgan

S. P. James c Ligertwood b Betts 22
A. Dale not out 43
D. L. Hemp c Collingwood b Betts 3
†A. D. Shaw not out 24
L-b 8, w 2, n-b 10 20

1/36 2/44 (2 wkts, 21 overs) 112

H. Morris, *P. A. Cottey, G. P. Butcher, O. D. Gibson, S. R. Barwick, S. L. Watkin and O. T. Parkin did not bat.

Bowling: Brown 4–0–22–0; Betts 6–0–31–2; Walker 4–0–17–0; Saggers 4–0–16–0; Blenkiron 3–0–18–0.

Umpires: B. J. Meyer and N. T. Plews.

DURHAM v LEICESTERSHIRE

At Chester-le-Street, September 15. Leicestershire won by 130 runs. Toss: Durham.

Leicestershire's total was the third-highest in the history of the competition, yet included only one six. Simmons hit 115 from 95 balls, while Maddy's maiden one-day hundred was the fastest century of the season, coming from just 54. Durham's final showing of one win and six points was the worst by any county in the Sunday League.

Leicestershire

P. V. Simmons c Killeen b Brown 115
V. J. Wells st Ligertwood b Boiling 23
*J. J. Whitaker c Roseberry b Walker 2
B. F. Smith b Killeen 21
D. L. Maddy not out 106
A. Habib not out 50
B 3, l-b 12, w 1, n-b 11 27

1/82 2/85 3/133 4/204 (4 wkts, 40 overs) 344

G. I. Macmillan, †P. A. Nixon, G. J. Parsons, D. Williamson and A. R. K. Pierson did not bat.

Bowling: Brown 8–0–69–1; Betts 6–0–79–0; Boiling 8–0–33–1; Walker 8–0–55–1; Killeen 7–0–70–1; Blenkiron 3–0–23–0.

Durham

S. L. Campbell lbw b Wells 22
S. Hutton c Whitaker b Simmons 81
†D. G. C. Ligertwood st Nixon b Pierson . 54
J. A. Daley not out 29
M. A. Roseberry not out 11
B 3, l-b 3, w 3, n-b 8 17

1/56 2/158 3/184 (3 wkts, 40 overs) 214

D. A. Blenkiron, M. M. Betts, J. Boiling, *S. J. E. Brown, N. Killeen and A. Walker did not bat.

Bowling: Parsons 8–0–32–0; Williamson 8–0–44–0; Wells 5–0–34–1; Pierson 8–0–31–1; Maddy 6–0–35–0; Simmons 4–0–26–1; Macmillan 1–0–6–0.

Umpires: D. J. Constant and A. A. Jones.

WORST SEASONAL RECORDS IN THE SUNDAY LEAGUE

	P	*W*	*L*	*NR*	*Pts*	*Season*
Durham	**17**	**1**	**15**	**1**	**6**	**1996**
Warwickshire	16	2	13	1	10	1979
Glamorgan	16	2	12	2	10	1972
Glamorgan	16	2	12	2	12	1989
Gloucestershire	16	3	13	0	12	1989
Nottinghamshire	16	3	13	0	12	1974
Somerset	17	2	12	3	14	1993
Hampshire	16	3	12	1	14	1991
Northamptonshire	16	3	12	1	14	1990
Sussex	16	3	11	2	14	1969
Sussex	16	3	10	3	15	1970

Until 1974 only one point was awarded for a no result.

ESSEX

At Worcester, May 5. ESSEX lost to WORCESTERSHIRE by four wickets.

At Southampton, May 12. ESSEX beat HAMPSHIRE by ten wickets.

ESSEX v KENT

At Ilford, May 19. Kent won by five runs. Toss: Essex.

Defending champions Kent registered their first win of the season thanks to a fine all-round performance from Fleming. His 112 – a maiden one-day century – came from only 91 balls and included five sixes; Law recorded the most expensive League figures ever by an Essex bowler. Fleming then added three wickets, restricting Essex to three runs off the last over when they needed nine. Essex suffered four run-outs in the last two overs. The penultimate was the first bowled by Preston in the competition. He only came on because Marsh had miscalculated, and conceded 15.

Kent

T. R. Ward c Irani b Law 19
M. V. Fleming c Irani b Law 112
N. J. Llong c Law b Irani 16
C. L. Hooper c Law b Grayson 73
G. R. Cowdrey c Robinson b Grayson 2
M. A. Ealham not out 25
M. J. Walker c Hussain b Ilott 9
*†S. A. Marsh not out 0
L-b 5, w 9, n-b 2 16

1/49 2/101 3/192 (6 wkts, 40 overs) 272
4/194 5/251 6/271

M. J. McCague, N. W. Preston and T. N. Wren did not bat.

Bowling: Ilott 8–0–29–1; Cowan 8–0–34–0; Law 8–1–81–2; Irani 6–0–42–1; Such 3–0–24–0; Grayson 7–0–57–2.

Essex

D. D. J. Robinson b McCague	54	M. C. Ilott c Walker b Fleming	0
S. G. Law c Marsh b Wren	6	A. P. Cowan run out	0
N. Hussain b Fleming	45	P. M. Such not out	1
R. C. Irani run out	80	B 4, l-b 12, w 9	25
G. A. Gooch b Fleming	32		—
*P. J. Prichard run out	13	1/18 2/94 3/148 (9 wkts, 40 overs)	267
†R. J. Rollins not out	10	4/224 5/249 6/263	
A. P. Grayson run out	1	7/264 8/264 9/266	

Bowling: Ealham 8–1–34–0; Wren 8–0–50–1; McCague 8–0–63–1; Hooper 8–0–39–0; Fleming 7–0–50–3; Preston 1–0–15–0.

Umpires: V. A. Holder and B. Leadbeater.

At Derby, May 26. DERBYSHIRE v ESSEX. No result.

ESSEX v LANCASHIRE

At Chelmsford, June 9. Essex won by 17 runs. Toss: Essex.

Lancashire's challenge ended when Watkinson, who had hit five sixes, was out with 12 overs remaining and 89 required. A fourth-wicket partnership worth 123 in 16 overs between Gooch and Prichard in the later stages of the Essex innings proved decisive.

Essex

D. D. J. Robinson b Elworthy	48	A. P. Grayson not out	0
S. G. Law lbw b Chapple	28		
†R. J. Rollins run out	13	B 1, l-b 8, w 12	21
G. A. Gooch b Martin	87		—
*P. J. Prichard b Martin	50	1/59 2/86 3/112 (6 wkts, 40 overs)	249
M. C. Ilott run out	2	4/235 5/247 6/249	

S. J. W. Andrew, J. J. B. Lewis, P. M. Such and A. P. Cowan did not bat.

Bowling: Austin 8–0–49–0; Martin 8–0–55–2; Chapple 7–1–45–1; Elworthy 8–0–36–1; Yates 5–0–27–0; Watkinson 4–0–28–0.

Lancashire

S. P. Titchard run out	1	G. Yates c Such b Andrew	38
*M. Watkinson c and b Grayson	88	G. Chapple lbw b Ilott	2
J. P. Crawley c Such b Andrew	23	P. J. Martin not out	10
G. D. Lloyd c Cowan b Grayson	12	L-b 6, w 11, n-b 2	19
N. H. Fairbrother c Ilott b Grayson	18		—
†W. K. Hegg c Gooch b Grayson	4	1/6 2/68 3/105 (39 overs)	232
I. D. Austin b Law	16	4/146 5/161 6/180	
S. Elworthy run out	1	7/181 8/181 9/192	

Bowling: Cowan 4–0–36–0; Ilott 7–0–39–1; Andrew 8–0–47–2; Such 4–0–24–0; Grayson 8–0–46–4; Law 8–0–34–1.

Umpires: R. A. White and P. Willey.

ESSEX v NORTHAMPTONSHIRE

At Chelmsford, June 16. Northamptonshire won by eight wickets. Toss: Essex.

After a thoroughly disciplined performance in the field, where they were challenged only by Hussain, Northamptonshire moved easily towards their 12th consecutive win of the season in one-day competitions. Gooch held the 99th catch of his Sunday League career in the first over of their reply, but then dropped Bailey when his 100th might have affected the result.

Essex

*P. J. Prichard hit wkt b Ambrose	9	A. P. Cowan c Curran b Capel	1
S. G. Law c Warren b Taylor	2	S. J. W. Andrew c Emburey b Ambrose	13
N. Hussain c Warren b Taylor	70	P. M. Such b Ambrose	1
R. C. Irani run out	17	L-b 1, w 3	4
G. A. Gooch c Bailey b Penberthy	18		
†R. J. Rollins c Ambrose b Taylor	27	1/13 2/15 3/44 (39 overs)	178
A. P. Grayson c Warren b Emburey	0	4/100 5/146 6/146	
J. J. B. Lewis not out	16	7/148 8/151 9/171	

Bowling: Ambrose 8–1–19–3; Taylor 8–2–22–3; Capel 8–0–32–1; Curran 6–0–33–0; Penberthy 3–0–29–1; Emburey 6–0–42–1.

Northamptonshire

R. R. Montgomerie c Gooch b Andrew	0
*R. J. Bailey c Prichard b Andrew	70
K. M. Curran not out	70
M. B. Loye not out	25
L-b 5, w 9	14
1/0 2/147 (2 wkts, 33 overs)	179

†R. J. Warren, D. J. Capel, A. L. Penberthy, T. C. Walton, J. E. Emburey, C. E. L. Ambrose and J. P. Taylor did not bat.

Bowling: Andrew 8–1–27–2; Cowan 5–1–22–0; Irani 6–0–35–0; Law 6–0–34–0; Such 3–0–21–0; Grayson 5–0–35–0.

Umpires: G. I. Burgess and B. J. Meyer.

ESSEX v SURREY

At Southend, June 30. Essex won by 27 runs. Toss: Essex.

Law's second century in two days, and his eighth in all cricket since arriving at Essex, was the basis for a formidable target. He hit 110 in 95 balls and put on 203 for the first wicket with Robinson. Surrey threatened a total of 278 but could not overtake it.

Essex

D. D. J. Robinson c Brown b Pearson	80	J. J. B. Lewis b Lewis	2
S. G. Law c I. J. Ward b Pearson	110	M. C. Ilott not out	1
N. Hussain b Hollioake	31	B 4, l-b 8, w 12, n-b 10	34
R. C. Irani c Stewart b Julian	4		
*P. J. Prichard c D. M. Ward b Hollioake	5	1/203 2/221 3/239 (8 wkts, 40 overs)	278
†R. J. Rollins run out	0	4/255 5/258 6/271	
A. P. Grayson b Lewis	11	7/277 8/278	

P. M. Such and S. J. W. Andrew did not bat.

Bowling: M. P. Bicknell 8–0–44–0; Lewis 8–1–28–2; Hollioake 7–0–43–2; Julian 8–0–66–1; Pearson 7–0–58–2; I. J. Ward 2–0–27–0.

Surrey

D. J. Bicknell c Grayson b Law	46	B. P. Julian c Grayson b Andrew	2
A. D. Brown c Rollins b Grayson	41	I. J. Ward not out	1
*†A. J. Stewart c Law b Such	12	L-b 9, w 9	18
A. J. Hollioake c Ilott b Such	17		
D. M. Ward lbw b Such	33	1/66 2/109 3/112 (7 wkts, 40 overs)	251
N. Shahid c Grayson b Ilott	37	4/134 5/177	
C. C. Lewis not out	44	6/230 7/240	

M. P. Bicknell and R. M. Pearson did not bat.

Bowling: Andrew 4–0–30–1; Ilott 8–0–52–1; Grayson 8–0–50–1; Irani 4–0–22–0; Such 8–0–53–3; Law 8–0–35–1.

Umpires: A. Clarkson and D. J. Constant.

At Leicester, July 7. ESSEX lost to LEICESTERSHIRE by nine runs.

ESSEX v GLAMORGAN

At Chelmsford, July 14. Glamorgan won by four runs. Toss: Essex.

A second-wicket partnership of 174 in 23 overs between Morris and Maynard built a substantial total for Glamorgan. Morris batted throughout the innings for his unbeaten hundred and Maynard scored 87 from 68 balls with three sixes and nine fours. Prichard also made a century, and added 104 in 16 overs with Irani, but could not quite keep Essex up with the required rate. When Gooch caught Gibson for a duck, it was his 100th catch in this competition.

Glamorgan

S. P. James b Ilott	9
H. Morris not out	101
*M. P. Maynard c Grayson b Such	87
O. D. Gibson c Gooch b Such	0
P. A. Cottey c Lewis b Grayson	11
D. L. Hemp b Grayson	18
A. W. Evans not out	3
B 4, l-b 5, w 12, n-b 5	26
1/21 2/195 3/195 4/212 5/250 (5 wkts, 40 overs)	255

O. T. Parkin, †A. D. Shaw, S. L. Watkin and S. R. Barwick did not bat.

Bowling: Ilott 8–0–26–1; Andrew 8–1–40–0; Irani 6–0–57–0; Law 2–0–25–0; Grayson 8–0–51–2; Such 8–1–47–2.

Essex

D. D. J. Robinson c Cottey b Gibson	1
S. G. Law c Watkin b Barwick	37
*P. J. Prichard lbw b Watkin	102
R. C. Irani c Evans b Cottey	42
G. A. Gooch c and b Cottey	2
†R. J. Rollins c Maynard b Cottey	7
J. J. B. Lewis c Evans b Cottey	10
M. C. Ilott not out	24
A. P. Grayson not out	17
L-b 6, w 3	9
1/10 2/64 3/168 4/176 5/192 6/202 7/210 (7 wkts, 40 overs)	251

P. M. Such and S. J. W. Andrew did not bat.

Bowling: Gibson 8–0–45–1; Watkin 8–1–41–1; Parkin 6–0–45–0; Barwick 8–0–41–1; Cottey 8–0–56–4; Hemp 2–0–17–0.

Umpires: K. E. Palmer and A. G. T. Whitehead.

ESSEX v NOTTINGHAMSHIRE

At Chelmsford, July 21. Nottinghamshire won by five wickets. Toss: Nottinghamshire.

A notable spell of three wickets in 22 balls from Bowen kept Essex's total within bounds on a green, bouncy pitch. Nottinghamshire struggled in turn, and needed 61 from the last seven overs. But Cairns, who hit 66 from 47 balls, saw them through with three balls to spare.

Essex

D. D. J. Robinson c Tolley b Bates	39
S. G. Law lbw b Bowen	16
*P. J. Prichard c Noon b Bowen	3
R. C. Irani c Noon b Bowen	2
†R. J. Rollins b Pennett	32
J. J. B. Lewis run out	61
A. P. Grayson c Pollard b Pennett	14
M. C. Ilott c Noon b Evans	4
A. J. E. Hibbert run out	0
S. J. W. Andrew not out	13
P. M. Such not out	4
L-b 6, w 17, n-b 8	31
1/38 2/55 3/64 4/94 5/129 6/192 7/195 8/198 9/212 (9 wkts, 40 overs)	219

Bowling: Pennett 7–0–48–2; Evans 8–0–39–1; Bowen 8–0–28–3; Tolley 7–0–42–0; Bates 8–0–39–1; Dowman 2–0–17–0.

Nottinghamshire

R. T. Robinson c Prichard b Irani	24	C. M. Tolley not out	9
M. P. Dowman c Hibbert b Law	27		
*P. Johnson b Irani	26	B 4, l-b 5, w 7	16
P. R. Pollard lbw b Such	47		—
C. L. Cairns not out	66	1/47 2/57 3/103 (5 wkts, 39.3 overs)	222
R. T. Bates b Grayson	7	4/140 5/157	

K. P. Evans, †W. M. Noon, M. N. Bowen and D. B. Pennett did not bat.

Bowling: Andrew 6–1–30–0; Ilott 8–0–50–0; Irani 8–0–38–2; Law 5–0–21–1; Such 8–1–38–1; Grayson 4.3–0–36–1.

Umpires: D. J. Constant and G. Sharp.

At Hartlepool, July 28. ESSEX lost to DURHAM by eight wickets.

At Lord's, August 4. ESSEX lost to MIDDLESEX by five runs.

At Taunton, August 11. ESSEX lost to SOMERSET by eight wickets.

ESSEX v GLOUCESTERSHIRE

At Colchester, August 25. Gloucestershire won by four wickets. Toss: Gloucestershire. First-team debut: T. P. Hodgson.

An inadequate Essex total began to appear more substantial than it was when Gloucestershire were 39 for two in the 13th over. Symonds then hit 70 from 42 balls to win the match, including six sixes, three of them in one over from Such. Two of his shots cleared an eight-foot fence some 20 yards beyond the extra cover boundary to go out of the ground.

Essex

A. P. Grayson lbw b Symonds	34	M. C. Ilott lbw b Smith	4
A. J. E. Hibbert b Averis	25	S. J. W. Andrew not out	2
*P. J. Prichard c Symonds b Averis	31	P. M. Such not out	2
R. C. Irani c and b Ball	8	L-b 3, w 4, n-b 4	11
†R. J. Rollins c Lewis b Symonds	19		—
J. J. B. Lewis c Lewis b Symonds	12	1/55 2/91 3/105 (9 wkts, 40 overs)	176
T. P. Hodgson b Alleyne	21	4/105 5/125 6/139	
D. G. Wilson c Symonds b Ball	7	7/165 8/172 9/172	

Bowling: Smith 6–0–27–1; Lewis 3–0–9–0; Averis 8–0–35–2; Alleyne 7–1–31–1; Symonds 8–1–34–3; Ball 8–1–37–2.

Gloucestershire

R. I. Dawson c Such b Andrew	10	M. C. J. Ball c Ilott b Grayson	0
M. G. N. Windows run out	21	*†R. C. Russell not out	20
R. J. Cunliffe lbw b Irani	3	L-b 7, w 10	17
A. Symonds c Such b Grayson	70		—
M. A. Lynch not out	32	1/25 2/39 3/43 (6 wkts, 33.3 overs)	178
M. W. Alleyne c Irani b Grayson	5	4/147 5/155 6/155	

J. M. M. Averis, A. M. Smith and J. Lewis did not bat.

Bowling: Ilott 7–1–15–0; Andrew 8–1–28–1; Irani 6–0–36–1; Such 6–0–50–0; Grayson 6.3–0–42–3.

Umpires: J. D. Bond and K. E. Palmer.

At Leeds, September 1. ESSEX lost to YORKSHIRE by six wickets.

At Birmingham, September 10. ESSEX lost to WARWICKSHIRE by six wickets.

ESSEX v SUSSEX

At Chelmsford, September 15. Essex won by seven wickets. Toss: Essex. First-team debuts: J. C. Powell; J. J. Bates.

Law ended a run of nine successive League defeats for Essex with 120 from 82 balls. It was his third Sunday century and his 12th in all cricket for the county. With the help of Hussain, Law put on 167 for the second wicket. Essex won with 12.4 overs in hand, but it was not enough to prevent them from finishing next to bottom in the table.

Sussex

R. K. Rao c Rollins b Wilson	13
K. Greenfield c Rollins b Irani	11
K. Newell c Wilson b Powell	32
*A. P. Wells c Rollins b Irani	12
M. Newell lbw b Wilson	0
†P. Moores b Andrew	55
D. R. Law c Hussain b Powell	21
N. C. Phillips not out	38
J. J. Bates b Wilson	8
M. R. Strong not out	2
B 9, l-b 4, w 6, n-b 4	23
1/26 2/32 3/46 4/47 5/129 6/149 7/178 8/195 (8 wkts, 40 overs)	215

R. J. Kirtley did not bat.

Bowling: Andrew 7–0–33–1; Irani 8–1–23–2; Wilson 8–0–40–3; Law 4–1–17–0; Grayson 5–1–27–0; Powell 8–0–62–2.

Essex

D. D. J. Robinson c M. Newell b Law	2
S. G. Law c Bates b Law	120
*N. Hussain c K. Newell b Law	71
R. C. Irani not out	4
†R. J. Rollins not out	2
L-b 5, w 7, n-b 6	18
1/20 2/187 3/210 (3 wkts, 27.2 overs)	217

A. P. Grayson, T. P. Hodgson, J. J. B. Lewis, D. G. Wilson, S. J. W. Andrew and J. C. Powell did not bat.

Bowling: Law 7–0–36–3; Strong 4.2–0–45–0; Phillips 4–0–26–0; Kirtley 5–0–27–0; Rao 2–0–17–0; K. Newell 2–0–15–0; Bates 3–0–46–0.

Umpires: J. H. Harris and A. G. T. Whitehead.

GLAMORGAN

GLAMORGAN v YORKSHIRE

At Cardiff, May 5. Glamorgan won by four wickets. Toss: Glamorgan.

With Croft and Barwick conceding only 42 runs from 16 overs, Glamorgan bowled themselves into a good position. However, Croft was needed again in a fifth-wicket partnership of 80 with Dale, who finally scampered a single off the last ball for victory.

Yorkshire

*D. Byas lbw b Croft	44
M. D. Moxon b Croft	23
M. P. Vaughan lbw b Croft	20
A. McGrath c Maynard b Cottey	4
C. White c Maynard b Dale	31
†R. J. Blakey c James b Dale	2
A. C. Morris run out	23
D. Gough not out	6
P. J. Hartley not out	1
B 1, l-b 7, w 5	13
1/60 2/94 3/95 4/105 5/110 6/156 7/166 (7 wkts, 40 overs)	167

A. G. Wharf and R. D. Stemp did not bat.

Bowling: Watkin 8–0–33–0; Thomas 5–0–36–0; Croft 8–0–21–3; Barwick 8–0–21–0; Cottey 5–1–16–1; Dale 6–0–32–2.

Glamorgan

S. P. James c Blakey b White	16	G. P. Butcher run out	3
H. Morris lbw b Hartley	26	S. D. Thomas not out	1
*M. P. Maynard run out	4	B 4, l-b 9, w 2, n-b 2	17
P. A. Cottey b Hartley	8		—
A. Dale not out	53	1/40 2/44 3/48 (6 wkts, 40 overs)	168
R. D. B. Croft c Morris b Gough	40	4/74 5/154 6/158	

†C. P. Metson, S. L. Watkin and S. R. Barwick did not bat.

Bowling: Gough 8–0–40–1; Wharf 3–1–14–0; White 8–1–24–1; Hartley 8–1–20–2; Stemp 8–2–22–0; Morris 5–0–35–0.

Umpires: J. D. Bond and P. Willey.

At Northampton, May 12. GLAMORGAN lost to NORTHAMPTONSHIRE by four wickets.

GLAMORGAN v DERBYSHIRE

At Cardiff, May 19. No result (abandoned).

GLAMORGAN v WORCESTERSHIRE

At Ebbw Vale, May 26. No result. Toss: Worcestershire.

Rain reduced the match to 21 overs a side. Worcestershire's openers were making good progress chasing 115 when further rain ended play for the day. Earlier, Rhodes became the first keeper to make 50 Sunday League stumpings.

Glamorgan

S. P. James c Solanki b Moody	4	G. P. Butcher not out	0
H. Morris c Lampitt b Illingworth	27		
O. D. Gibson lbw b Moody	8	L-b 1, w 7	8
*P. A. Cottey not out	44		—
A. Dale st Rhodes b Illingworth	3	1/10 2/27 3/66 (5 wkts, 21 overs)	114
R. D. B. Croft c Spiring b Lampitt	20	4/72 5/110	

S. D. Thomas, †C. P. Metson, S. L. Watkin and S. R. Barwick did not bat.

Bowling: Moody 6–1–26–2; Newport 5–0–16–0; Lampitt 4–0–30–1; Illingworth 4–0–18–2; Sheriyar 2–0–23–0.

Worcestershire

*T. M. Moody not out	10
T. S. Curtis not out	23
L-b 1	1
	—
(no wkt, 5.3 overs)	34

W. P. C. Weston, D. A. Leatherdale, K. R. Spiring, S. R. Lampitt, †S. J. Rhodes, V. S. Solanki, P. J. Newport, R. K. Illingworth and A. Sheriyar did not bat.

Bowling: Watkin 3–0–13–0; Barwick 2.3–0–20–0.

Umpires: V. A. Holder and N. T. Plews.

At Lord's, June 9. GLAMORGAN lost to MIDDLESEX by eight wickets.

GLAMORGAN v SOMERSET

At Swansea, June 16. Somerset won by 24 runs. Toss: Somerset.

Glamorgan lost four top-order wickets for 20 as Trump exploited a pitch offering help to the spinners. He held a stunning caught-and-bowled to remove Maynard, and the batsmen lost their way. A Somerset total of 217 was built around a fine contribution from Lee.

Somerset

M. N. Lathwell c Maynard b Barwick	26	*A. N. Hayhurst not out	4
P. D. Bowler run out	32		
S. C. Ecclestone run out	26	B 2, l-b 4, w 9	15
S. Lee not out	71		—
M. E. Trescothick c Maynard b Dale	36	1/52 2/84 3/98 (5 wkts, 40 overs)	217
G. D. Rose c Metson b Watkin	7	4/171 5/193	

†R. J. Turner, K. A. Parsons, A. R. Caddick and H. R. J. Trump did not bat.

Bowling: Watkin 8–0–32–1; Thomas 4–0–31–0; Butcher 3–0–14–0; Barwick 8–0–23–1; Croft 8–0–43–0; Dale 6–0–43–1; Cottey 3–0–25–0.

Glamorgan

S. P. James b Trump	24	†C. P. Metson c Lee b Caddick	0
H. Morris c Trump b Lee	59	S. L. Watkin not out	9
*M. P. Maynard c and b Trump	27	S. R. Barwick not out	1
P. A. Cottey c Parsons b Trump	1	B 1, l-b 5, w 4	10
A. Dale b Hayhurst	12		—
G. P. Butcher b Lee	13	1/48 2/110 3/112 (9 wkts, 40 overs)	193
R. D. B. Croft c Lathwell b Caddick	35	4/126 5/130 6/161	
S. D. Thomas b Caddick	2	7/164 8/164 9/190	

Bowling: Caddick 8–0–44–3; Rose 8–0–37–0; Trump 8–1–28–3; Parsons 3–0–22–0; Hayhurst 6–0–26–1; Lee 7–0–30–2.

Umpires: J. W. Holder and K. J. Lyons.

At Hove, June 23. GLAMORGAN beat SUSSEX by 124 runs.

At Bristol, July 7. GLAMORGAN beat GLOUCESTERSHIRE by 94 runs.

At Chelmsford, July 14. GLAMORGAN beat ESSEX by four runs.

GLAMORGAN v LANCASHIRE

At Swansea, July 28. Lancashire won on scoring-rate. Toss: Glamorgan.

Lancashire's seven-an-over scoring owed much to Lloyd's Sunday-best 116 from 82 balls. Maynard and Cottey did match the rate in a third-wicket partnership of 71 but, when they had gone, the task of scoring a revised target of 198 in 28 overs proved beyond Glamorgan.

Lancashire

*M. Watkinson c Croft b Watkin	9	I. D. Austin not out	1
J. E. R. Gallian run out	48		
J. P. Crawley lbw b Watkin	4	L-b 9, w 6	15
G. D. Lloyd lbw b Barwick	116		—
N. H. Fairbrother c Barwick b Dale	7	1/22 2/29 3/129 (5 wkts, 31 overs)	219
†W. K. Hegg not out	19	4/165 5/208	

S. Elworthy, G. Yates, G. Chapple and P. J. Martin did not bat.

Bowling: Watkin 7–0–36–2; Gibson 6–0–28–0; Dale 6–0–34–1; Barwick 7–0–62–1; Croft 5–0–50–0.

Glamorgan

H. Morris c Hegg b Martin	7	R. D. B. Croft not out	17
D. L. Hemp c Fairbrother b Martin	4	†A. D. Shaw not out	16
*M. P. Maynard b Watkinson	43	L-b 4, w 4, n-b 4	12
P. A. Cottey c Crawley b Watkinson	39		—
A. Dale run out	12	1/7 2/14 3/85 (7 wkts, 28 overs)	185
A. W. Evans c Chapple b Martin	19	4/104 5/118	
O. D. Gibson c Fairbrother b Elworthy	16	6/139 7/158	

S. L. Watkin and S. R. Barwick did not bat.

Bowling: Austin 7–0–31–0; Martin 6–0–52–3; Chapple 2–0–17–0; Elworthy 7–0–39–1; Watkinson 6–0–42–2.

Umpires: B. J. Meyer and R. Palmer.

At Nottingham, August 4. GLAMORGAN lost to NOTTINGHAMSHIRE by nine wickets.

GLAMORGAN v LEICESTERSHIRE

At Swansea, August 11. Leicestershire won by 60 runs. Toss: Leicestershire.

Smith and Maddy put on 91 in 11 overs on a turning pitch to give substance to Leicestershire's innings. Glamorgan's batsmen did not cope as well with the conditions; Brimson and Macmillan, who had previously taken two wickets between them in the League, dismissed five of the middle order.

Leicestershire

*P. V. Simmons c Hemp b Cosker	27	G. J. Parsons not out	23
V. J. Wells b Watkin	11	D. Williamson not out	0
B. F. Smith b Hemp	80	L-b 5, w 12, n-b 3	20
G. I. Macmillan c Gibson b Dale	4		—
A. Habib st Shaw b Cosker	1	1/26 2/68 3/92 (7 wkts, 35 overs)	218
D. L. Maddy c Maynard b Gibson	51	4/99 5/190	
†P. A. Nixon c Hemp b Gibson	1	6/193 7/196	

J. Ormond and M. T. Brimson did not bat.

Bowling: Watkin 8–1–43–1; Gibson 7–0–44–2; Dale 6–0–31–1; Cosker 8–0–38–2; Cottey 4–0–43–0; Hemp 2–0–14–1.

Glamorgan

A. W. Evans b Ormond	7	†A. D. Shaw c Simmons b Parsons	5
H. Morris c Habib b Macmillan	28	D. A. Cosker b Wells	4
*M. P. Maynard c Simmons b Macmillan	31	S. L. Watkin lbw b Wells	0
P. A. Cottey lbw b Brimson	1	L-b 5, w 8, n-b 13	26
D. L. Hemp c Habib b Brimson	5		—
A. Dale lbw b Wells	26	1/25 2/79 3/84 (33.5 overs)	158
O. D. Gibson st Nixon b Brimson	13	4/86 5/96 6/125	
S. P. James not out	12	7/142 8/153 9/158	

Bowling: Parsons 7–0–34–1; Ormond 6–0–32–1; Macmillan 8–0–37–2; Brimson 8–0–23–3; Simmons 2–0–8–0; Wells 2.5–0–19–3.

Umpires: A. A. Jones and R. A. White.

At Birmingham, August 18. GLAMORGAN lost to WARWICKSHIRE by seven wickets.

GLAMORGAN v KENT

At Cardiff, August 25. Glamorgan won by eight wickets. Toss: Glamorgan.

To reach 147 after slipping to 94 for eight – Parkin took three wickets in four balls – represented some sort of recovery for Kent. But, once Glamorgan's openers had put on 85, the issue was never in doubt; they won with eight overs in hand.

Kent

M. V. Fleming c Dale b Watkin	5
M. J. Walker c Cottey b Parkin	19
C. L. Hooper b Parkin	1
T. R. Ward c Shaw b Watkin	11
M. A. Ealham c Maynard b Parkin	0
G. R. Cowdrey st Shaw b Barwick	18
N. J. Llong c and b Gibson	5
*†S. A. Marsh b Gibson	17
J. B. D. Thompson c Hemp b Barwick	30
B. J. Phillips c Maynard b Barwick	29
T. N. Wren not out	0
L-b 8, w 2, n-b 2	12
1/19 2/29 3/29 4/29 5/41 6/62 7/64 8/94 9/145 (39.3 overs)	147

Bowling: Watkin 8–3–12–2; Parkin 8–3–32–3; Gibson 8–2–18–2; Barwick 7.3–0–26–3; Butcher 4–0–33–0; Dale 4–0–18–0.

Glamorgan

S. P. James lbw b Fleming	50
A. Dale not out	65
*M. P. Maynard c Marsh b Fleming	5
P. A. Cottey not out	20
B 1, l-b 1, w 3, n-b 4	9
1/85 2/92 (2 wkts, 31.5 overs)	149

D. L. Hemp, O. T. Parkin, G. P. Butcher, O. D. Gibson, †A. D. Shaw, S. L. Watkin and S. R. Barwick did not bat.

Bowling: Ealham 8–0–34–0; Wren 5–1–24–0; Thompson 4–0–22–0; Hooper 7–0–23–0; Fleming 4–0–17–2; Phillips 3.5–0–27–0.

Umpires: B. Dudleston and G. Sharp.

At Chester-le-Street, September 1. GLAMORGAN beat DURHAM on scoring-rate.

At Southampton, September 8. GLAMORGAN beat HAMPSHIRE by seven wickets.

GLAMORGAN v SURREY

At Cardiff, September 15. Surrey won by seven wickets. Toss: Surrey.

Surrey's victory brought them their first domestic title since 1982 and their first ever success in the Sunday League. Another three wickets for Hollioake extended his total for the season, already a record, to 39, leaving Glamorgan to defend an inadequate four an over. After a rapid start, Surrey's progress slowed but was never halted, as victory and the title became a formality; Nottinghamshire also won, to stay level on points, but Surrey's net run-rate was 16.31 to their 9.20. The boundary rope had to be relaid around a TV cameraman who refused to move from his position, which had been authorised by the TCCB, even though it was inside the original boundary.

Glamorgan

S. P. James b Pearson	43	†A. D. Shaw c Benjamin b Lewis	6
A. Dale c Benjamin b Bicknell	6	S. L. Watkin not out	7
D. L. Hemp run out	8	S. R. Barwick not out	1
A. J. Dalton c Thorpe b Benjamin	6	B 1, l-b 4, w 4, n-b 4	13
P. A. Cottey b Hollioake	41		—
*M. P. Maynard c and b Pearson	8	1/11 2/29 3/47 (9 wkts, 40 overs)	159
O. D. Gibson lbw b Hollioake	4	4/96 5/112 6/121	
R. D. B. Croft c Julian b Hollioake	16	7/128 8/143 9/156	

Bowling: Bicknell 8–0–29–1; Lewis 5–0–15–1; Benjamin 6–0–25–1; Julian 5–0–24–0; Pearson 8–0–33–2; Hollioake 8–0–28–3.

Surrey

M. A. Butcher lbw b Croft	30	N. Shahid not out	4
A. D. Brown b Barwick	41	L-b 9, w 2, n-b 6	17
*†A. J. Stewart not out	41		—
G. P. Thorpe c Gibson b Cottey	28	1/82 2/90 3/157 (3 wkts, 32.5 overs)	161

A. J. Hollioake, C. C. Lewis, B. P. Julian, M. P. Bicknell, R. M. Pearson and J. E. Benjamin did not bat.

Bowling: Watkin 8–0–43–0; Gibson 4–0–29–0; Barwick 8–0–32–1; Croft 8–0–28–1; Dale 4–0–16–0; Cottey 0.5–0–4–1.

Umpires: J. C. Balderstone and A. Clarkson.

GLOUCESTERSHIRE

At Lord's, May 5. GLOUCESTERSHIRE lost to MIDDLESEX by 31 runs.

GLOUCESTERSHIRE v SOMERSET

At Bristol, May 19. No result (abandoned).

GLOUCESTERSHIRE v SURREY

At Gloucester, May 26. Surrey won by 72 runs. Toss: Gloucestershire.

Given that rain had restricted the match to 15 overs a side, Surrey's 138 was a formidable total. Gloucestershire lost two wickets in the first over of their reply, and Julian took three of the last four wickets for five runs in eight balls to dismiss them for 66.

Surrey

D. M. Ward run out	4	B. C. Hollioake not out	8
D. J. Bicknell lbw b Ball	51		
*A. J. Hollioake run out	4	L-b 3, w 5, n-b 6	14
B. P. Julian c Symonds b Lewis	1		—
N. Shahid c Alleyne b Ball	38	1/15 2/19 3/23 (5 wkts, 15 overs)	138
J. D. Ratcliffe not out	18	4/106 5/106	

†G. J. Kersey, M. P. Bicknell, I. J. Ward and J. E. Benjamin did not bat.

Bowling: Smith 3–0–8–0; Lewis 3–0–13–1; Alleyne 3–0–39–0; Walsh 3–0–51–0; Ball 2–0–16–2; Dawson 1–0–8–0.

Gloucestershire

A. J. Wright b Julian	29
R. I. Dawson c Kersey b M. P. Bicknell	0
A. Symonds c Shahid b M. P. Bicknell	0
T. H. C. Hancock c D. M. Ward b Benjamin	3
M. A. Lynch c Kersey b Benjamin	1
M. W. Alleyne c Ratcliffe b B. C. Hollioake	5
†R. C. Russell c D. J. Bicknell b A. J. Hollioake	14
*C. A. Walsh b Julian	0
M. C. J. Ball b A. J. Hollioake	3
J. Lewis not out	0
A. M. Smith b Julian	0
B 1, l-b 5, w 5	11
1/1 2/1 3/11 4/23 5/41 6/59 7/59 8/64 9/64 (12.2 overs)	66

Bowling: M. P. Bicknell 3–0–13–2; Benjamin 3–0–11–2; B. C. Hollioake 3–0–14–1; A. J. Hollioake 2–0–17–2; Julian 1.2–0–5–3.

Umpires: H. D. Bird and T. E. Jesty.

At Manchester, June 2. GLOUCESTERSHIRE lost to LANCASHIRE by seven runs.

GLOUCESTERSHIRE v SUSSEX

At Bristol, June 16. Sussex won by 14 runs. Toss: Sussex.

Having lost Symonds before the start, when he sustained an injury during the warm-up, Gloucestershire inflicted further damage on their own cause by bowling 11 wides. Despite 96 from Wright, his highest Sunday score, Sussex did a good containing job.

Sussex

R. K. Rao b Ball	91
J. W. Hall c Cunliffe b Smith	10
K. Greenfield b Smith	0
*A. P. Wells c Cunliffe b Ball	48
C. W. J. Athey c Ball b Walsh	18
D. R. Law c Wright b Smith	11
†P. Moores not out	29
V. C. Drakes c and b Walsh	10
I. D. K. Salisbury not out	0
L-b 8, w 11	19
1/19 2/19 3/117 4/173 5/189 6/195 7/213 (7 wkts, 40 overs)	236

J. D. Lewry and P. W. Jarvis did not bat.

Bowling: Walsh 8–0–28–2; Smith 8–1–55–3; Alleyne 8–0–42–0; Lewis 8–0–44–0; Ball 8–0–59–2.

Gloucestershire

A. J. Wright c Jarvis b Lewry	96
R. I. Dawson b Salisbury	37
R. J. Cunliffe b Jarvis	16
M. A. Lynch b Law	14
†R. C. Russell b Drakes	2
M. W. Alleyne b Law	17
T. H. C. Hancock c Wells b Lewry	19
M. C. J. Ball b Jarvis	0
*C. A. Walsh not out	2
A. M. Smith not out	0
B 1, l-b 10, w 6, n-b 2	19
1/59 2/92 3/125 4/133 5/200 6/209 7/212 8/222 (8 wkts, 40 overs)	222

J. Lewis did not bat.

Bowling: Drakes 8–0–28–1; Lewry 8–0–55–2; Law 8–0–54–2; Jarvis 8–0–36–2; Salisbury 8–0–38–1.

Umpires: J. H. Hampshire and R. A. White.

At Nottingham, June 23. GLOUCESTERSHIRE beat NOTTINGHAMSHIRE by 119 runs.

At Chester-le-Street, June 30. GLOUCESTERSHIRE beat DURHAM by four runs.

GLOUCESTERSHIRE v GLAMORGAN

At Bristol, July 7. Glamorgan won by 94 runs. Toss: Gloucestershire.

Glamorgan fought back from 56 for six, having lost four wickets in ten balls, thanks largely to Alun Evans, who scored an unbeaten fifty on his League debut. He put on 91 for the seventh wicket with Gibson, a county record, before Shaw took 14 off the final over. Gloucestershire's early batting also failed, but there was to be no recovery for them.

Glamorgan

S. P. James run out	6
H. Morris c Williams b Walsh	13
R. D. B. Croft lbw b Smith	2
*M. P. Maynard c Smith b Lewis	13
P. A. Cottey lbw b Smith	2
G. P. Butcher c Williams b Alleyne	14
A. W. Evans not out	50
O. D. Gibson b Lewis	43
†A. D. Shaw not out	36
B 2, l-b 8, w 7	17
1/21 2/23 3/23 4/25 5/51 6/56 7/147 (7 wkts, 40 overs)	196

S. L. Watkin and S. R. Barwick did not bat.

Bowling: Walsh 8–3–20–1; Smith 8–0–39–2; Lewis 8–1–37–2; Alleyne 7–0–32–1; Symonds 4–0–22–0; Ball 5–0–36–0.

Gloucestershire

A. J. Wright lbw b Butcher	16
R. I. Dawson lbw b Gibson	0
M. W. Alleyne b Watkin	8
A. M. Smith c Shaw b Watkin	0
T. H. C. Hancock run out	1
A. Symonds b Croft	30
M. G. N. Windows c Shaw b Butcher	23
†R. C. J. Williams c Morris b Butcher	11
M. C. J. Ball c Gibson b Butcher	0
*C. A. Walsh c Watkin b Croft	0
J. Lewis not out	0
L-b 8, w 5	13
1/6 2/27 3/27 4/29 5/38 6/81 7/95 8/100 9/101 (29.2 overs)	102

Bowling: Watkin 6–2–9–2; Gibson 6–1–17–1; Butcher 6.2–0–32–4; Barwick 6–1–18–0; Croft 5–0–18–2.

Umpires: G. I. Burgess and J. H. Harris.

GLOUCESTERSHIRE v KENT

At Moreton-in-Marsh, July 14. Gloucestershire won by 22 runs. Toss: Gloucestershire.

Both teams batted badly on a slow, low pitch. Alleyne did much to help Gloucestershire recover from 54 for five, scoring 67 not out in a match where no one else reached 30. Ealham's figures of three for 21 were superseded by Smith's three for 16, which gave the home team an unlikely win. Despite a large crowd, the ground was not given a fixture in 1997.

Gloucestershire

A. J. Wright c Marsh b Thompson	0
R. I. Dawson lbw b Ealham	12
M. W. Alleyne not out	67
M. A. Lynch b Ealham	2
A. Symonds c McCague b Ealham	8
M. G. N. Windows c Marsh b Hooper	0
†R. C. Russell c Hooper b Llong	10
M. C. J. Ball c Walker b Headley	18
A. M. Smith not out	26
B 4, l-b 9, w 9	22
1/0 2/34 3/38 4/54 5/54 6/82 7/116 (7 wkts, 40 overs)	165

J. Lewis and *C. A. Walsh did not bat.

Bowling: Thompson 3–0–19–1; Headley 7–2–29–1; Hooper 8–2–14–1; Ealham 8–0–21–3; Llong 6–0–29–1; Fleming 8–0–40–0.

Kent

T. R. Ward c Russell b Lewis	28	M. J. McCague run out	0
M. V. Fleming b Smith	6	D. W. Headley not out	29
C. L. Hooper c Walsh b Smith	0	J. B. D. Thompson b Walsh	0
G. R. Cowdrey c Russell b Lewis	1	L-b 4, w 4, n-b 2	10
M. A. Ealham c Smith b Alleyne	9		—
N. J. Llong c and b Ball	28	1/12 2/12 3/23 (36.2 overs)	143
M. J. Walker c Russell b Ball	7	4/45 5/50 6/72	
*†S. A. Marsh lbw b Smith	25	7/99 8/104 9/142	

Bowling: Walsh 6.2–0–19–1; Smith 7–2–16–3; Lewis 7–1–30–2; Alleyne 8–0–44–1; Ball 8–0–30–2.

Umpires: J. H. Hampshire and T. E. Jesty.

GLOUCESTERSHIRE v LEICESTERSHIRE

At Cheltenham, July 21. Leicestershire won by six wickets. Toss: Leicestershire.

Gloucestershire reached their highest total in the competition and yet were still defeated with 16 balls to spare. Mullally had helped their cause by bowling away-swingers without slips or a gully; his first over went for 16. Alleyne scored a 95-ball century and, when Leicestershire replied, Habib was undefeated on 99 from 75 balls when Walsh bowled a no-ball, which gave them victory but denied him a hundred.

Gloucestershire

A. J. Wright c Nixon b Millns	7	†R. C. Russell not out	8
R. I. Dawson c Nixon b Millns	48	L-b 4, w 7, n-b 12	23
M. W. Alleyne not out	100		—
M. A. Lynch c Smith b Williamson	38	1/35 2/116 (4 wkts, 40 overs)	284
A. Symonds c Millns b Simmons	60	3/178 4/265	

M. G. N. Windows, M. C. J. Ball, A. M. Smith, J. Lewis and *C. A. Walsh did not bat.

Bowling: Mullally 8–2–52–0; Millns 8–1–37–2; Williamson 8–0–55–1; Wells 8–0–81–0; Simmons 8–0–55–1.

Leicestershire

P. V. Simmons b Ball	51	*J. J. Whitaker not out	5
V. J. Wells c Wright b Lewis	41	B 4, l-b 4, w 9, n-b 14	31
B. F. Smith run out	1		—
A. Habib not out	99	1/90 2/91 (4 wkts, 37.2 overs)	286
G. I. Macmillan run out	58	3/121 4/264	

D. L. Maddy, †P. A. Nixon, D. J. Millns, D. Williamson and A. D. Mullally did not bat.

Bowling: Walsh 7.2–0–47–0; Smith 7–0–54–0; Lewis 6–0–49–1; Ball 8–0–46–1; Alleyne 7–0–64–0; Symonds 2–0–18–0.

Umpires: B. Dudleston and N. T. Plews.

GLOUCESTERSHIRE v WARWICKSHIRE

At Cheltenham, July 28. No result. Toss: Gloucestershire.

Warwickshire's useful total, built around an innings of 75 not out from Penney, counted for nothing when rain ended play after ten overs of Gloucestershire's reply.

Warwickshire

A. J. Moles st Williams b Ball	17	A. F. Giles c Symonds b Ball	9
N. M. K. Smith c Walsh b Alleyne	36	G. C. Small not out	9
D. P. Ostler st Williams b Davis	31		
A. Singh c Ball b Alleyne	2	B 8, l-b 6, w 2, n-b 2	18
T. L. Penney not out	75		
S. M. Pollock c Lynch b Hancock	5	1/65 2/70 3/76 (8 wkts, 40 overs)	235
†M. Burns c Windows b Davis	17	4/120 5/137 6/175	
D. R. Brown b Davis	16	7/196 8/208	

*T. A. Munton did not bat.

Bowling: Walsh 8–1–37–0; Smith 6–0–33–0; Ball 8–0–55–2; Alleyne 8–1–39–2; Davis 8–0–42–3; Hancock 2–0–15–1.

Gloucestershire

R. I. Dawson not out	12
M. G. N. Windows b Munton	13
M. W. Alleyne not out	9
L-b 1, w 3	4
1/25 (1 wkt, 10 overs)	38

T. H. C. Hancock, M. A. Lynch, A. Symonds, †R. C. J. Williams, M. C. J. Ball, A. M. Smith, R. P. Davis and *C. A. Walsh did not bat.

Bowling: Pollock 5–1–12–0; Munton 4–0–20–1; Smith 1–0–5–0.

Umpires: H. D. Bird and B. Leadbeater.

At Derby, August 4. GLOUCESTERSHIRE lost to DERBYSHIRE by eight wickets.

At Southampton, August 11. HAMPSHIRE v GLOUCESTERSHIRE. No result (abandoned).

GLOUCESTERSHIRE v YORKSHIRE

At Bristol, August 18. Yorkshire won by 133 runs. Toss: Yorkshire.

An inept display by Gloucestershire surrendered the match to a Yorkshire side in positive mood. Even Walsh could not stem the flow of runs, while Symonds began with two wides and a wicket before being hammered by Hartley, whose 52 came off 29 balls. The visiting attack then dismissed Gloucestershire with nearly 11 overs in hand.

Yorkshire

*D. Byas b Walsh	56	A. McGrath b Ball	4
M. D. Moxon c Russell b Alleyne	41	R. A. Kettleborough not out	12
M. P. Vaughan lbw b Lewis	44	B 1, l-b 3, w 7, n-b 8	19
C. White b Symonds	8		
D. Gough run out	4	1/94 2/110 3/146 (7 wkts, 40 overs)	262
P. J. Hartley b Smith	52	4/159 5/182	
†R. J. Blakey not out	22	6/230 7/237	

C. E. W. Silverwood and R. D. Stemp did not bat.

Bowling: Smith 7–0–41–1; Lewis 8–0–59–1; Alleyne 8–1–29–1; Walsh 7–0–43–1; Ball 6–0–47–1; Symonds 4–0–39–1.

Gloucestershire

R. I. Dawson b White	15	*C. A. Walsh b Stemp	9
M. G. N. Windows run out	8	A. M. Smith not out	11
M. W. Alleyne b White	5	J. Lewis b Gough	7
A. Symonds lbw b White	19	B 4, l-b 2, w 3	9
M. A. Lynch c Moxon b Stemp	23		—
†R. C. Russell lbw b Stemp	13	1/24 2/24 3/39 (29.1 overs)	129
T. H. C. Hancock b Stemp	9	4/53 5/89 6/101	
M. C. J. Ball lbw b Gough	1	7/102 8/102 9/116	

Bowling: Gough 7.1–1–34–2; Silverwood 5–0–22–0; White 6–1–23–3; Hartley 5–1–19–0; Stemp 6–0–25–4.

Umpires: G. I. Burgess and A. A. Jones.

At Colchester, August 25. GLOUCESTERSHIRE beat ESSEX by four wickets.

GLOUCESTERSHIRE v NORTHAMPTONSHIRE

At Bristol, September 1. Northamptonshire won by five wickets. Toss: Northamptonshire.

Northamptonshire held back their main strike bowler, Ambrose, to curb the middle-order menace of Symonds; in fact, Ambrose caught him, rather than bowling him. Gloucestershire could not accelerate and the visitors' batsmen encountered few problems.

Gloucestershire

R. I. Dawson c Montgomerie b Penberthy	13	A. M. Smith b Curran	1
M. G. N. Windows c Ripley b Penberthy	4	J. Lewis not out	5
*M. W. Alleyne lbw b Capel	38	J. M. M. Averis not out	1
A. Symonds c Ambrose b Taylor	18	B 4, l-b 5, w 5, n-b 4	18
M. A. Lynch lbw b Curran	35		—
†R. C. Russell c Ripley b Capel	7	1/6 2/30 3/56 (9 wkts, 40 overs)	175
A. J. Wright b Curran	23	4/110 5/123 6/126	
M. C. J. Ball c and b Emburey	12	7/158 8/168 9/170	

Bowling: Penberthy 4–0–21–2; Taylor 8–0–26–1; Ambrose 8–1–38–0; Capel 8–1–32–2; Emburey 8–2–33–1; Curran 4–0–16–3.

Northamptonshire

R. R. Montgomerie c Symonds b Alleyne	42	A. L. Penberthy not out	24
M. B. Loye b Smith	7		
K. M. Curran b Averis	39	W 5	5
D. J. Capel c Wright b Averis	22		—
*R. J. Bailey b Symonds	9	1/21 2/62 3/113 (5 wkts, 39.2 overs)	179
T. C. Walton not out	31	4/122 5/124	

J. E. Emburey, †D. Ripley, C. E. L. Ambrose and J. P. Taylor did not bat.

Bowling: Smith 8–0–31–1; Lewis 6–0–25–0; Ball 8–1–27–0; Alleyne 7.2–0–34–1; Averis 6–0–43–2; Symonds 4–0–19–1.

Umpires: B. Leadbeater and R. A. White.

At Worcester, September 15. GLOUCESTERSHIRE lost to WORCESTERSHIRE by 14 runs.

HAMPSHIRE

HAMPSHIRE v ESSEX

At Southampton, May 12. Essex won by ten wickets. Toss: Essex.

A solo effort from Stephenson, who batted through the innings for a Sunday-best 110 against his old county, could not lift his side into a winning position. Essex openers Robinson and Law, with his second century in two days against Hampshire, completed a ten-wicket victory with 7.4 overs to spare.

Hampshire

*J. P. Stephenson not out	110	W. K. M. Benjamin not out	11
J. S. Laney c Law b Cowan	16		
R. A. Smith c Rollins b Cowan	0	L-b 9, w 6	15
P. R. Whitaker c Grayson b Irani	7		—
R. S. M. Morris c Rollins b Irani	18	1/52 2/54 3/80 (5 wkts, 40 overs)	187
G. W. White c Grayson b Ilott	10	4/134 5/163	

†A. N. Aymes, S. D. Udal, M. J. Thursfield and C. A. Connor did not bat.

Bowling: Ilott 6–0–34–1; Cowan 8–3–17–2; Law 6–0–20–0; Such 8–0–46–0; Irani 8–0–32–2; Grayson 4–0–29–0.

Essex

D. D. J. Robinson not out	76
S. G. Law not out	108
L-b 3, w 3	6
	—
(no wkt, 32.2 overs)	190

J. J. B. Lewis, *N. Hussain, G. A. Gooch, R. C. Irani, A. P. Grayson, †R. J. Rollins, M. C. Ilott, P. M. Such and A. P. Cowan did not bat.

Bowling: Benjamin 6–0–20–0; Connor 8–1–40–0; Thursfield 5–0–51–0; Stephenson 3–0–23–0; Udal 8–0–34–0; Whitaker 2.2–0–19–0.

Umpires: A. A. Jones and D. R. Shepherd.

At Birmingham, May 19. HAMPSHIRE lost to WARWICKSHIRE on scoring-rate.

HAMPSHIRE v DURHAM

At Portsmouth, May 26. No result (abandoned).

At Worcester, June 2. HAMPSHIRE lost to WORCESTERSHIRE by 36 runs.

HAMPSHIRE v DERBYSHIRE

At Southampton, June 9. Hampshire won by five wickets. Toss: Derbyshire.

Hampshire's first Sunday win in 1996 depended on a powerful run-a-ball 91 from Smith, which countered a century from the visiting captain, Jones.

Derbyshire

K. J. Barnett lbw b Connor	9	T. A. Tweats run out	0
A. S. Rollins lbw b Stephenson	0		
*D. M. Jones not out	101	B 2, l-b 8, w 3, n-b 2	15
C. J. Adams c Aymes b Stephenson	1		—
J. E. Owen c White b Whitaker	40	1/1 2/40 3/45 (7 wkts, 40 overs)	226
P. A. J. DeFreitas c and b Udal	46	4/140 5/201	
†K. M. Krikken c James b Udal	14	6/224 7/226	

S. J. Base, A. J. Harris and K. J. Dean did not bat.

Bowling: Stephenson 8–0–27–2; Thursfield 2–0–18–0; Connor 8–0–41–1; Udal 8–0–56–2; James 8–0–34–0; Whitaker 6–0–40–1.

Hampshire

*J. P. Stephenson c Base b Jones	31	S. D. Udal not out	2
J. S. Laney c and b Base	23		
R. A. Smith b Harris	91	B 4, l-b 8, w 10	22
W. K. M. Benjamin c Adams b Base	40		—
†A. N. Aymes c Krikken b Harris	12	1/48 2/105 3/184 (5 wkts, 39.1 overs)	227
P. R. Whitaker not out	6	4/218 5/225	

G. W. White, K. D. James, M. J. Thursfield and C. A. Connor did not bat.

Bowling: Dean 8–0–34–0; Base 8–0–34–2; Harris 7–1–28–2; DeFreitas 3–0–38–0; Jones 7.1–0–47–1; Barnett 6–0–34–0.

Umpires: B. J. Meyer and G. Sharp.

HAMPSHIRE v NORTHAMPTONSHIRE

At Basingstoke, June 23. Hampshire won by seven wickets. Toss: Northamptonshire.

Northamptonshire suffered their first defeat in a Sunday League game in 1996, on a pitch their batsmen distrusted. Connor exploited that fear and the conditions to take five wickets for the first time in limited-overs cricket. Then both Hampshire openers fell at six before Benjamin hit a 71-ball century, his last fifty coming from 20 balls. Northamptonshire's unbeaten run in all one-day cricket had lasted 16 games since they lost the NatWest final to Warwickshire on September 3, 1995.

Northamptonshire

R. R. Montgomerie lbw b Stephenson	4	J. E. Emburey run out	3
*R. J. Bailey c Connor b James	24	C. E. L. Ambrose not out	3
K. M. Curran c Stephenson b Connor	32	J. P. Taylor run out	1
T. C. Walton c Stephenson b Connor	4	B 4, l-b 14, w 2, n-b 2	22
M. B. Loye c James b Connor	7		—
D. J. Capel c Stephenson b Connor	35	1/10 2/63 3/70 (40 overs)	169
†R. J. Warren b Connor	0	4/83 5/89 6/89	
A. L. Penberthy c Laney b James	34	7/159 8/164 9/164	

Bowling: Stephenson 8–2–23–1; Thursfield 8–0–43–0; James 8–0–29–2; Connor 8–1–25–5; Udal 8–0–31–0.

Hampshire

*J. P. Stephenson c Emburey b Taylor	0	†A. N. Aymes not out	23
J. S. Laney lbw b Taylor	5	B 2, l-b 4, w 2	8
R. A. Smith c Bailey b Curran	30		—
W. K. M. Benjamin not out	104	1/6 2/6 3/68 (3 wkts, 32.3 overs)	170

P. R. Whitaker, G. W. White, S. D. Udal, K. D. James, M. J. Thursfield and C. A. Connor did not bat.

Bowling: Ambrose 7.3–2–22–0; Taylor 8–1–45–2; Capel 4–0–14–0; Emburey 5–0–22–0; Curran 5–1–23–1; Penberthy 3–0–38–0.

Umpires: J. H. Harris and N. T. Plews.

At Arundel, July 7. HAMPSHIRE beat SUSSEX by 40 runs.

HAMPSHIRE v NOTTINGHAMSHIRE

At Southampton, July 14. Nottinghamshire won by 82 runs. Toss: Hampshire.

Nottinghamshire relied heavily on a partnership of 135 for the third wicket between Robinson and Pollard. Both fell to James, who recorded a career-best six for 35, but fellow left-arm medium-pacer Tolley was equally effective with five for 16, also a career-best, to leave Hampshire some way off the pace.

Nottinghamshire

R. T. Robinson c Aymes b James	76
A. A. Metcalfe c and b Stephenson	6
*P. Johnson b Milburn	1
P. R. Pollard c Stephenson b James	58
M. P. Dowman c Aymes b Connor	1
C. M. Tolley c Udal b James	14
K. P. Evans lbw b James	5
R. T. Bates b Connor	16
†W. M. Noon c and b James	1
M. N. Bowen not out	7
R. A. Pick b James	0
L-b 14, w 10	24
1/16 2/19 3/154 4/156 5/177 6/177 7/200 8/202 9/209 (37 overs)	209

Bowling: Stephenson 8–0–32–1; Milburn 8–0–50–1; Connor 8–0–41–2; Udal 5–0–37–0; James 8–0–35–6.

Hampshire

*J. P. Stephenson c Noon b Pick	8
J. S. Laney c Metcalfe b Pick	9
R. A. Smith c Dowman b Tolley	45
W. K. M. Benjamin lbw b Bowen	18
M. Keech c Pick b Tolley	32
P. R. Whitaker c Noon b Tolley	2
K. D. James c Evans b Bates	2
S. D. Udal c Pollard b Tolley	0
†A. N. Aymes lbw b Bowen	3
S. M. Milburn not out	1
C. A. Connor c Pick b Tolley	0
L-b 2, w 3, n-b 2	7
1/16 2/21 3/61 4/108 5/111 6/114 7/116 8/126 9/126 (28 overs)	127

Bowling: Evans 5–1–15–0; Pick 6–0–31–2; Bates 8–0–36–1; Bowen 4–0–27–2; Tolley 5–0–16–5.

Umpires: A. A. Jones and B. Leadbeater.

At Leeds, July 21. HAMPSHIRE lost to YORKSHIRE by seven wickets.

HAMPSHIRE v SURREY

At Southampton, July 28. Surrey won by 23 runs. Toss: Hampshire.

An efficient Surrey side strengthened their position at the top of the table. Hampshire had a chance when Surrey captain Adam Hollioake brought Shahid's leg-breaks into the attack, hoping to tempt Benjamin into an indiscretion, but he took 18 off that over on his way to 30 off 24 balls. It was Hollioake himself who got Benjamin when he skied another attempted six-hit, and Hampshire's batting then fell away.

Surrey

M. A. Butcher lbw b James	57
A. D. Brown st Aymes b Whitaker	51
N. Shahid c Benjamin b Milburn	19
*A. J. Hollioake c Aymes b Stephenson	14
D. J. Bicknell lbw b Stephenson	6
D. M. Ward b Whitaker	12
†G. J. Kersey c Milburn b Whitaker	11
B. C. Hollioake c Stephenson b James	13
M. P. Bicknell c Keech b Stephenson	15
R. M. Pearson not out	9
J. E. Benjamin not out	0
L-b 10, w 3, n-b 2	15
1/84 2/130 3/136 4/153 5/160 6/182 7/182 8/202 9/221 (9 wkts, 40 overs)	222

Bowling: Stephenson 8–0–44–3; Milburn 8–1–43–1; Maru 8–1–36–0; James 8–0–45–2; Whitaker 8–0–44–3.

Hampshire

M. Keech b Pearson 25
J. S. Laney b Benjamin 14
R. A. Smith b A. J. Hollioake 30
W. K. M. Benjamin c D. J. Bicknell
b A. J. Hollioake . 30
W. S. Kendall run out 0
*J. P. Stephenson c Kersey
b M. P. Bicknell . 14
P. R. Whitaker c Kersey b B. C. Hollioake. 9
K. D. James b Benjamin 37
†A. N. Aymes c B. C. Hollioake
b A. J. Hollioake . 20
S. M. Milburn c Shahid b A. J. Hollioake . 8
R. J. Maru not out 1
L-b 2, w 9 11

1/33 2/61 3/101 (39.3 overs) 199
4/101 5/112 6/130
7/130 8/185 9/195

Bowling: M. P. Bicknell 8–0–38–1; Benjamin 7–0–28–2; Pearson 8–0–36–1; Shahid 1–0–18–0; A. J. Hollioake 7.3–0–38–4; B. C. Hollioake 8–0–39–1.

Umpires: V. A. Holder and A. G. T. Whitehead.

At Taunton, August 4. HAMPSHIRE beat SOMERSET by 44 runs.

HAMPSHIRE v GLOUCESTERSHIRE

At Southampton, August 11. No result (abandoned).

At Manchester, August 18. HAMPSHIRE lost to LANCASHIRE by one run.

At Leicester, August 25. LEICESTERSHIRE v HAMPSHIRE. No result.

HAMPSHIRE v MIDDLESEX

At Portsmouth, September 1. Middlesex won by seven wickets. Toss: Middlesex.

An unbroken partnership of 110 for the fourth wicket between Ramprakash and Gatting ensured Middlesex a comfortable victory against a Hampshire side containing only three capped players.

Hampshire

G. W. White run out 24
P. R. Whitaker c Dutch b Hewitt 21
*R. A. Smith c Brown b Johnson........ 10
M. Keech c Shah b Hewitt 4
W. S. Kendall lbw b Hewitt 0
L. J. Botham c Brown b Fraser 1
†A. N. Aymes lbw b Fay 31
D. A. Mascarenhas lbw b Fraser 0
S. D. Udal c Weekes b Fay 54
S. J. Renshaw not out 1
J. N. B. Bovill not out................. 6
L-b 11, w 6, n-b 15........... 32

1/57 2/63 3/73 (9 wkts, 40 overs) 184
4/73 5/76 6/76
7/76 8/169 9/173

Bowling: Fay 6–0–56–2; Hewitt 8–3–26–3; Fraser 8–1–20–2; Johnson 8–0–21–1; Weekes 6–0–31–0; Dutch 4–0–19–0.

Middlesex

P. N. Weekes c Aymes b Mascarenhas ... 42
K. P. Dutch c Mascarenhas b Renshaw ... 12
M. R. Ramprakash not out 54
J. C. Pooley lbw b Mascarenhas......... 0
*M. W. Gatting not out................ 55
L-b 5, w 7, n-b 10............ 22

1/33 2/75 3/75 (3 wkts, 30.4 overs) 185

†K. R. Brown, O. A. Shah, R. L. Johnson, J. P. Hewitt, R. A. Fay and A. R. C. Fraser did not bat.

Bowling: Bovill 6–0–40–0; Renshaw 7–0–36–1; Mascarenhas 8–0–42–2; Botham 4–0–33–0; Udal 4–0–21–0; Keech 1.4–0–8–0.

Umpires: G. Sharp and P. Willey.

HAMPSHIRE v GLAMORGAN

At Southampton, September 8. Glamorgan won by seven wickets. Toss: Hampshire.

A second-wicket partnership worth 136 between James and Hemp allowed Glamorgan to overtake Hampshire's total with seven wickets and seven balls in hand. Earlier, Barwick had taken his 200th League wicket; nine days later, he learned that his 16-year career with Glamorgan was over.

Hampshire

G. W. White c Hemp b Croft	55	D. A. Mascarenhas not out	7
J. S. Laney c Maynard b Gibson	23	S. D. Udal not out	0
P. R. Whitaker b Dale	47	B 1, l-b 2, w 5, n-b 2	10
R. A. Smith c Maynard b Croft	23		——
W. S. Kendall st Shaw b Dale	13	1/52 2/124 3/138 (7 wkts, 40 overs)	220
*J. P. Stephenson c Cottey b Barwick	37	4/170 5/172	
†A. N. Aymes c Croft b Barwick	5	6/197 7/219	

R. J. Maru and S. J. Renshaw did not bat.

Bowling: Gibson 8–0–33–1; Parkin 8–0–42–0; Barwick 8–0–45–2; Dale 8–0–47–2; Croft 8–1–50–2.

Glamorgan

S. P. James c and b Stephenson	91	P. A. Cottey not out	9
A. Dale c Aymes b Stephenson	25	B 4, l-b 7, w 5	16
D. L. Hemp not out	64		——
A. J. Dalton st Aymes b Mascarenhas	19	1/39 2/175 3/212 (3 wkts, 38.5 overs)	224

*M. P. Maynard, R. D. B. Croft, O. D. Gibson, †A. D. Shaw, S. R. Barwick and O. T. Parkin did not bat.

Bowling: Stephenson 8–0–49–2; Renshaw 4–0–20–0; Mascarenhas 7.5–0–48–1; Udal 8–0–40–0; Maru 8–0–41–0; Whitaker 3–0–15–0.

Umpires: D. J. Constant and N. T. Plews.

At Canterbury, September 15. HAMPSHIRE lost to KENT by one run.

KENT

KENT v LANCASHIRE

At Canterbury, May 5. Lancashire won by nine wickets. Toss: Kent.

After scoring a meagre 184 themselves, defending Sunday champions Kent bowled their two opening bowlers unchanged for the first 16 overs. Atherton and Gallian survived a difficult examination, then accelerated, putting on 159 for the first wicket on their way to a comfortable victory.

Kent

T. R. Ward b Martin	18	M. J. McCague c and b Austin	1
M. V. Fleming run out	8	J. B. D. Thompson run out	1
C. L. Hooper c Austin b Watkinson	15	T. N. Wren not out	0
G. R. Cowdrey b Watkinson	23	B 1, l-b 5, w 8, n-b 6	20
M. A. Ealham c Gallian b Yates	53		——
M. J. Walker b Elworthy	2	1/21 2/37 3/60 (9 wkts, 40 overs)	184
N. J. Llong c Speak b Martin	20	4/97 5/101 6/149	
*†S. A. Marsh not out	23	7/157 8/165 9/172	

Bowling: Martin 8–1–24–2; Austin 8–0–32–1; Watkinson 8–0–29–2; Elworthy 8–1–51–1; Yates 8–0–42–1.

Lancashire

J. E. R. Gallian c Hooper b Llong	85
M. A. Atherton not out	79
N. H. Fairbrother not out	11
L-b 1, w 5, n-b 4	10
1/159 (1 wkt, 35 overs)	185

G. D. Lloyd, N. J. Speak, *M. Watkinson, †W. K. Hegg, I. D. Austin, S. Elworthy, G. Yates and P. J. Martin did not bat.

Bowling: Wren 8–0–28–0; Thompson 8–0–28–0; McCague 6–0–40–0; Ealham 4–0–32–0; Fleming 4–0–24–0; Hooper 4–0–22–0; Llong 1–0–10–1.

Umpires: A. A. Jones and R. Julian.

At The Oval, May 12. KENT lost to SURREY by 150 runs.

At Ilford, May 19. KENT beat ESSEX by five runs.

KENT v YORKSHIRE

At Canterbury, May 26. Kent won by ten wickets. Toss: Kent.

A ten-overs-a-side match, beginning just before six o'clock, was all that was possible due to rain, but it allowed Kent to record their first ten-wicket win in the League. As at Ilford the previous week, Fleming was the star. He took a career-best four for 13 before hitting 63 not out with seven sixes and three fours. Fleming faced only 20 balls and failed to score off just three of them; by reaching fifty in 16 balls, he equalled Graham Rose's Sunday League record, set in 1990.

Yorkshire

M. G. Bevan c McCague b Fleming	28
†R. J. Blakey c Marsh b Thompson	9
C. White c Wren b Fleming	27
*D. Byas not out	6
A. McGrath c Llong b Fleming	0
M. P. Vaughan c Llong b Fleming	8
A. G. Wharf not out	2
L-b 3, w 4	7
1/22 2/66 3/66 4/69 5/84 (5 wkts, 10 overs)	87

A. C. Morris, C. E. W. Silverwood, P. J. Hartley and G. M. Hamilton did not bat.

Bowling: McCague 2–0–16–0; Thompson 2–0–9–1; Preston 2–0–19–0; Wren 1–0–22–0; Fleming 2–0–13–4; Hooper 1–0–5–0.

Kent

T. R. Ward not out	25
M. V. Fleming not out	63
N-b 2	2
(no wkt, 5.5 overs)	90

C. L. Hooper, G. R. Cowdrey, M. J. Walker, N. J. Llong, *†S. A. Marsh, M. J. McCague, J. B. D. Thompson, N. W. Preston and T. N. Wren did not bat.

Bowling: Hartley 1–0–8–0; Silverwood 2–0–30–0; Hamilton 2–0–33–0; White 0.5–0–19–0.

Umpires: A. Clarkson and R. Palmer.

KENT v SUSSEX

At Tunbridge Wells, June 2. Kent won by 35 runs. Toss: Sussex.

Both sides reached 53 for four after 17 overs of their respective innings. But Kent's lower order consolidated their position, whereas, with the honourable exception of Law, Sussex subsided.

Kent

T. R. Ward c Moores b Drakes	12
M. V. Fleming b Law	14
C. L. Hooper c Jarvis b Law	1
G. R. Cowdrey b Giddins	44
M. A. Ealham b Drakes	0
N. J. Llong c Speight b Jarvis	70
M. J. Walker run out	27
*†S. A. Marsh not out	32
M. J. McCague b Jarvis	0
J. B. D. Thompson b Jarvis	0
B. J. Phillips not out	2
L-b 7, w 10, n-b 2	19
1/24 2/27 3/32 4/33 5/115 6/180 7/195 8/197 9/218 (9 wkts, 40 overs)	221

Bowling: Drakes 8–0–50–2; Law 8–1–36–2; Giddins 8–1–49–1; Jarvis 8–1–35–3; Salisbury 8–0–44–0.

Sussex

K. Greenfield c Llong b Thompson	3
J. W. Hall run out	0
M. P. Speight c Hooper b Thompson	16
*A. P. Wells c Cowdrey b Thompson	3
N. J. Lenham c Ealham b Fleming	43
†P. Moores c Llong b Phillips	18
D. R. Law not out	79
V. C. Drakes run out	4
I. D. K. Salisbury c Phillips b Fleming	1
P. W. Jarvis b Fleming	6
E. S. H. Giddins b Fleming	0
B 1, l-b 5, w 5, n-b 2	13
1/7 2/11 3/26 4/31 5/61 6/127 7/148 8/150 9/186 (39.2 overs)	186

Bowling: Thompson 8–1–26–3; Ealham 8–0–20–0; Phillips 5–0–23–1; McCague 4–0–17–0; Fleming 7.2–0–33–4; Hooper 7–0–61–0.

Umpires: G. I. Burgess and K. E. Palmer.

At Leicester, June 9. KENT beat LEICESTERSHIRE by four wickets.

KENT v MIDDLESEX

At Canterbury, June 16. Kent won by 92 runs. Toss: Kent.

Middlesex suffered their first Sunday defeat of the season. Kent mounted a formidable batting display, in which Ealham was outstanding, with 89 not out from 51 balls. Brown apart, the Middlesex batsmen showed no signs of matching them.

Kent

T. R. Ward c Ramprakash b Feltham	65
M. V. Fleming lbw b Fraser	26
C. L. Hooper c Weekes b Ramprakash	31
G. R. Cowdrey c Pooley b Fay	68
M. A. Ealham not out	89
N. J. Llong run out	2
M. J. Walker not out	12
B 1, l-b 5, w 4	10
1/70 2/107 3/159 4/223 5/228 (5 wkts, 40 overs)	303

*†S. A. Marsh, M. J. McCague, J. B. D. Thompson and T. N. Wren did not bat.

Bowling: Fraser 8–0–64–1; Fay 8–0–82–1; Weekes 8–0–36–0; Feltham 8–0–51–1; Ramprakash 6–0–43–1; Carr 2–0–21–0.

Middlesex

P. N. Weekes c Hooper b Wren	7	M. A. Feltham run out	8
M. R. Ramprakash b McCague	45	A. R. C. Fraser c McCague b Hooper	14
J. C. Pooley b Ealham	15	R. A. Fay not out	1
*J. D. Carr c Ward b McCague	17	L-b 6, w 6	12
†K. R. Brown c Walker b Fleming	74		—
O. A. Shah b Thompson	13	1/15 2/43 3/83 (38.4 overs)	211
P. E. Wellings b Fleming	5	4/94 5/126 6/137	
U. B. A. Rashid lbw b Fleming	0	7/137 8/163 9/202	

Bowling: Wren 8–0–25–1; Ealham 8–1–37–1; McCague 4–0–34–2; Thompson 6–0–36–1; Fleming 7.4–0–41–3; Hooper 5–0–32–1.

Umpires: T. E. Jesty and N. T. Plews.

At Birmingham, June 23. KENT lost to WARWICKSHIRE by eight runs.

KENT v DURHAM

At Maidstone, July 7. Kent won by six wickets. Toss: Kent.

Durham, still looking for their first Sunday win, could only score 207, and a third-wicket partnership of 120 in 19 overs between Hooper and Cowdrey effectively settled the issue.

Durham

S. L. Campbell c Llong b Hooper	33	N. Killeen b McCague	0
S. Hutton st Marsh b Hooper	58	J. Wood not out	13
P. D. Collingwood not out	61		
S. J. E. Brown st Marsh b Hooper	3		
P. Bainbridge run out	4	B 1, l-b 5, w 3	9
*M. A. Roseberry b Fleming	19		—
D. A. Blenkiron lbw b McCague	0	1/86 2/113 3/120 (8 wkts, 40 overs)	207
†D. G. C. Ligertwood c Cowdrey b Fleming	7	4/129 5/162 6/163	
		7/186 8/187	

J. Boiling did not bat.

Bowling: Wren 6–1–31–0; Thompson 8–0–42–0; McCague 8–0–42–2; Hooper 8–1–21–3; Fleming 8–0–53–2; Llong 2–0–12–0.

Kent

T. R. Ward b Killeen	30	M. J. Walker not out	13
M. V. Fleming c Collingwood b Brown	27	L-b 5, w 1	6
C. L. Hooper not out	76		—
G. R. Cowdrey lbw b Boiling	59	1/48 2/62 (4 wkts, 35.1 overs)	211
N. J. Llong c Hutton b Boiling	0	3/182 4/182	

*†S. A. Marsh, M. J. McCague, J. B. D. Thompson, N. W. Preston and T. N. Wren did not bat.

Bowling: Wood 8–0–47–0; Brown 6–0–45–1; Bainbridge 7.1–0–34–0; Killeen 6–0–38–1; Boiling 8–0–42–2.

Umpires: R. Palmer and N. T. Plews.

At Moreton-in-Marsh, July 14. KENT lost to GLOUCESTERSHIRE by 22 runs.

At Derby, July 28. KENT tied with DERBYSHIRE.

KENT v WORCESTERSHIRE

At Canterbury, August 4. Worcestershire won by ten wickets. Toss: Kent.

Kent made a partial recovery from 62 for seven but still fell woefully short of setting a challenging target. Moody and Weston scored 92 of the 136 required in boundaries, and it was a six by Weston off Llong which concluded the win inside 18 overs. This was Worcestershire's sixth ten-wicket victory in the League; no other county has had more than four.

Kent

M. V. Fleming b Ellis	9	M. J. McCague c Sheriyar b Hick	11
M. J. Walker c Hick b Moody	2	D. W. Headley b Hick	9
T. R. Ward c Solanki b Ellis	6	T. N. Wren run out	7
*C. L. Hooper c Rhodes b Moody	6	B 2, l-b 7, w 11, n-b 10	30
N. J. Llong run out	18		
G. R. Cowdrey c Hick b Lampitt	2	1/15 2/15 3/26 (36.3 overs)	135
W. J. House c Rhodes b Lampitt	4	4/36 5/58 6/62	
†S. C. Willis not out	31	7/62 8/97 9/117	

Bowling: Moody 8–0–19–2; Ellis 8–0–35–2; Illingworth 7.3–1–22–0; Lampitt 6–0–18–2; Sheriyar 3–0–19–0; Hick 4–0–13–2.

Worcestershire

*T. M. Moody not out	53
W. P. C. Weston not out	78
B 1, l-b 2, w 1, n-b 4	8
(no wkt, 17.1 overs)	139

G. A. Hick, K. R. Spiring, A. Sheriyar, V. S. Solanki, D. A. Leatherdale, †S. J. Rhodes, S. R. Lampitt, R. K. Illingworth and S. W. K. Ellis did not bat.

Bowling: Wren 4–1–29–0; Headley 5–0–28–0; McCague 5–0–34–0; Fleming 2–0–25–0; Llong 1.1–0–20–0.

Umpires: H. D. Bird and J. W. Holder.

At Northampton, August 11. KENT beat NORTHAMPTONSHIRE by four wickets.

KENT v SOMERSET

At Canterbury, August 18. Somerset won by three wickets. Toss: Kent.

Lee hit 62 not out off 46 balls, including 14 off the last over, to give Somerset victory with one ball to spare. Earlier, Kent had lost seven wickets for 56 in 13 overs after reaching a promising 137 for two.

Kent

M. V. Fleming c Ecclestone b Trescothick	33	D. W. Headley not out	12
M. J. Walker b Rose	4	B. J. Phillips c and b Lee	2
C. L. Hooper c Caddick b Parsons	50	T. N. Wren not out	7
*T. R. Ward c Rose b Trump	52	B 4, l-b 14, w 3	21
N. J. Llong c Turner b Parsons	7		
G. R. Cowdrey c Trescothick b Rose	9	1/21 2/72 3/137 (9 wkts, 40 overs)	206
W. J. House c Ecclestone b Lee	6	4/156 5/167 6/173	
†S. C. Willis c Turner b Rose	3	7/180 8/184 9/193	

Bowling: Caddick 8–0–27–0; Rose 8–0–33–3; Trescothick 4–0–27–1; Lee 8–0–38–2; Trump 8–0–44–1; Parsons 4–0–19–2.

Somerset

M. N. Lathwell c Cowdrey b Hooper	45	†R. J. Turner c Phillips b Fleming	9
*P. D. Bowler c Willis b Wren	3	G. D. Rose not out	2
S. C. Ecclestone c Willis b Headley	12	L-b 3, w 8	11
R. J. Harden c Cowdrey b Phillips	56		
S. Lee not out	62	1/15 2/36 3/110 (7 wkts, 39.5 overs)	210
M. E. Trescothick c Willis b Phillips	4	4/140 5/152	
K. A. Parsons b Headley	6	6/171 7/185	

A. R. Caddick and H. R. J. Trump did not bat.

Bowling: Wren 8–0–38–1; Headley 8–0–34–2; Hooper 8–0–37–1; Phillips 8–0–42–2; Fleming 7.5–0–56–1.

Umpires: A. Clarkson and B. Leadbeater.

At Cardiff, August 25. KENT lost to GLAMORGAN by eight wickets.

KENT v NOTTINGHAMSHIRE

At Tunbridge Wells, September 1. Nottinghamshire won by seven wickets. Toss: Kent.

This was a dismal performance from the defending champions. Kent's batsmen never came to terms with a keen Nottinghamshire attack in which Cairns, with four wickets, was outstanding; they struggled from 34 for six to 99 all out. Kent's bowlers fared little better, as the visitors beat them with 17 overs to spare.

Kent

M. V. Fleming lbw b Bowen	8	J. B. D. Thompson b Cairns	1
D. P. Fulton c Noon b Evans	0	N. W. Preston not out	7
C. L. Hooper lbw b Bowen	1	T. N. Wren c Noon b Dowman	0
T. R. Ward c Noon b Tolley	15	B 3, l-b 2, w 5, n-b 2	12
M. A. Ealham c Metcalfe b Tolley	1		
G. R. Cowdrey lbw b Cairns	38	1/1 2/6 3/23 (27.5 overs)	99
N. J. Llong hit wkt b Cairns	1	4/26 5/31 6/34	
*†S. A. Marsh c Pollard b Cairns	15	7/71 8/79 9/90	

Bowling: Evans 6–1–11–1; Bowen 6–0–22–2; Tolley 4–0–9–2; Cairns 8–1–26–4; Bates 3–0–21–0; Dowman 0.5–0–5–1.

Nottinghamshire

R. T. Robinson c Fulton b Wren	35	P. R. Pollard not out	2
M. P. Dowman c Hooper b Thompson	12	W 5, n-b 4	9
A. A. Metcalfe not out	43		
*P. Johnson c Fleming b Wren	2	1/18 2/72 3/80 (3 wkts, 23.1 overs)	103

C. L. Cairns, C. M. Tolley, K. P. Evans, †W. M. Noon, R. T. Bates and M. N. Bowen did not bat.

Bowling: Ealham 4–0–19–0; Thompson 5–1–15–1; Wren 8–0–32–2; Preston 2–0–17–0; Fleming 4.1–0–20–0.

Umpires: J. D. Bond and J. H. Harris.

KENT v HAMPSHIRE

At Canterbury, September 15. Kent won by one run. Toss: Kent.

Hampshire needed only 43 from seven overs, with nine wickets in hand, but an inexperienced batting line-up could not complete what older hands would regard as a routine task after White and Laney had put on 118. Smith came in with 22 wanted off 26 balls, but he was suffering from flu and could not prevent an embarrassing defeat. He had the minor satisfaction of scoring his 5,000th League run. White ran one short in the first over of the innings; but for this Hampshire would have tied. Kent's total relied heavily on a 109-run stand between Hooper and Ward.

Kent

M. V. Fleming c and b Maru 1
M. J. Walker c Laney b Maru 9
C. L. Hooper lbw b Bovill 70
T. R. Ward b Bovill 51
M. A. Ealham lbw b Whitaker 4
G. R. Cowdrey lbw b Bovill............ 11
N. J. Llong b Udal.................... 0
*†S. A. Marsh b Mascarenhas 8
J. B. D. Thompson not out 4
B. J. Phillips st Aymes b Udal 0
N. W. Preston c Smith b Mascarenhas.... 4
L-b 1, w 5, n-b 4............. 10

1/2 2/23 3/132 (39.3 overs) 172
4/143 5/149 6/155
7/159 8/166 9/167

Bowling: Maru 8–1–25–2; Renshaw 6–0–20–0; Bovill 8–0–45–3; Udal 8–1–24–2; Mascarenhas 5.3–0–34–2; Whitaker 4–0–23–1.

Hampshire

G. W. White run out 56
J. S. Laney c Phillips b Llong 57
P. R. Whitaker c and b Hooper 17
W. S. Kendall c and b Llong 9
*R. A. Smith not out.................. 11
†A. N. Aymes not out................. 7
L-b 7, w 3, n-b 4............. 14

1/118 2/130 (4 wkts, 40 overs) 171
3/151 4/154

J. N. B. Bovill, D. A. Mascarenhas, S. D. Udal, R. J. Maru and S. J. Renshaw did not bat.

Bowling: Phillips 4–0–20–0; Ealham 5–1–19–0; Fleming 8–0–25–0; Hooper 8–0–33–1; Preston 8–0–32–0; Llong 7–0–35–2.

Umpires: R. Julian and G. Sharp.

LANCASHIRE

At Canterbury, May 5. LANCASHIRE beat KENT by nine wickets.

LANCASHIRE v LEICESTERSHIRE

At Manchester, May 12. Leicestershire won by one run. Toss: Lancashire.

Fairbrother came close to bringing his side victory, after two escapes. First, umpire Bird turned down an appeal for caught behind, to the annoyance of the Leicestershire fielders; then the disappointed bowler, Pierson, tried to run him out backing up at the non-striker's end. He was given out by Bird, but eventually the Leicestershire captain, Whitaker, called him back, and he continued to 93 from 77 balls. There was further confusion right at the end, when the umpires changed their minds twice over whether Austin was run out off the final ball. Finally he was reprieved, but it was an academic debate – Lancashire were still one short.

Leicestershire

P. V. Simmons b Yates 91
V. J. Wells c Gallian b Yates........... 45
B. F. Smith c Atherton b Watkinson 26
J. M. Dakin c Fairbrother b Martin 0
*J. J. Whitaker b Watkinson............ 27
†P. A. Nixon not out.................. 28
D. L. Maddy st Hegg b Gallian 16
C. C. Remy c Elworthy b Gallian 4
G. J. Parsons not out 2
B 1, l-b 4, w 8............... 13

1/107 2/159 3/160 (7 wkts, 40 overs) 252
4/187 5/206
6/235 7/241

A. R. K. Pierson and A. D. Mullally did not bat.

Bowling: Martin 8–0–45–1; Austin 8–0–33–0; Elworthy 4–0–36–0; Yates 8–0–49–2; Watkinson 7–0–50–2; Gallian 5–0–34–2.

Lancashire

J. E. R. Gallian c Remy b Mullally	23	†W. K. Hegg not out	47
M. A. Atherton c Whitaker b Parsons	14	I. D. Austin not out	3
J. P. Crawley c Simmons b Parsons	3	B 6, l-b 5, w 1, n-b 4	16
N. H. Fairbrother c Nixon b Mullally	93		
G. D. Lloyd c and b Simmons	51	1/36 2/40 3/42	(6 wkts, 40 overs) 251
*M. Watkinson c Dakin b Pierson	1	4/149 5/160 6/230	

S. Elworthy, G. Yates and P. J. Martin did not bat.

Bowling: Mullally 8–1–27–2; Parsons 8–0–33–2; Remy 5–0–31–0; Wells 3–0–31–0; Pierson 7–0–64–1; Simmons 8–0–40–1; Maddy 1–0–14–0.

Umpires: H. D. Bird and R. A. White.

At Nottingham, May 19. LANCASHIRE beat NOTTINGHAMSHIRE by seven wickets.

LANCASHIRE v GLOUCESTERSHIRE

At Manchester, June 2. Lancashire won by seven runs. Toss: Gloucestershire.

Lancashire recovered from three for two in the second over to reach 187, thanks to a run-a-ball innings from Watkinson. It still looked a modest total. However, no Gloucestershire batsman played the substantial innings which would almost certainly have given them their first Sunday win of the season. Lynch managed just five, but that was enough to take him past 5,000 runs in the League.

Lancashire

M. A. Atherton lbw b Walsh	0	G. Yates not out	0
*M. Watkinson c Wright b Hancock	79	G. Chapple b Walsh	6
N. J. Speak b Smith	0	P. J. Martin not out	2
J. P. Crawley c Symonds b Lewis	21	L-b 5, n-b 6	11
G. D. Lloyd b Ball	18		
†W. K. Hegg c Hancock b Smith	27	1/2 2/3 3/38	(9 wkts, 40 overs) 187
I. D. Austin st Russell b Ball	8	4/108 5/140 6/150	
S. Elworthy run out	15	7/171 8/179 9/185	

Bowling: Walsh 7–2–25–2; Smith 6–1–26–2; Lewis 6–0–33–1; Alleyne 6–0–30–0; Ball 8–0–27–2; Hancock 7–0–41–1.

Gloucestershire

A. J. Wright c Crawley b Watkinson	34	M. C. J. Ball not out	7
R. I. Dawson b Yates	26	J. Lewis not out	0
M. A. Lynch lbw b Yates	5		
T. H. C. Hancock c Speak b Watkinson	21	B 2, l-b 3, w 3	8
A. Symonds c Lloyd b Martin	34		
M. W. Alleyne c Watkinson b Austin	23	1/47 2/53 3/88	(8 wkts, 40 overs) 180
†R. C. Russell c Crawley b Chapple	19	4/95 5/141 6/154	
*C. A. Walsh b Elworthy	3	7/166 8/179	

A. M. Smith did not bat.

Bowling: Austin 8–0–31–1; Martin 8–2–28–1; Yates 8–0–25–2; Chapple 7–1–35–1; Watkinson 5–0–28–2; Elworthy 4–0–28–1.

Umpires: D. J. Constant and K. J. Lyons.

At Chelmsford, June 9. LANCASHIRE lost to ESSEX by 17 runs.

At Chester-le-Street, June 16. LANCASHIRE beat DURHAM by eight wickets.

LANCASHIRE v SOMERSET

At Manchester, June 30. Somerset won by one run. Toss: Lancashire.

Good bowling by Caddick and Rose made Lancashire struggle and set up another exciting last-ball finish and their second one-run defeat of the season. Chapple – who had earlier bowled six overs for six runs – hit two fours, a six and a three off Lee's final over, leaving Yates to score three off the last ball. He missed, and a bye left Somerset with the narrowest of victories.

Somerset

M. N. Lathwell lbw b Chapple	17
P. D. Bowler lbw b Chapple	20
S. C. Ecclestone c Speak b Yates	30
S. Lee lbw b Elworthy	10
M. E. Trescothick c Atherton b Yates	10
†R. J. Turner c Chapple b Yates	12
*A. N. Hayhurst not out	42
G. D. Rose c Yates b Martin	2
K. A. Parsons not out	12
B 1, l-b 14, w 1, n-b 4	20
1/37 2/50 3/74 4/101 5/105 6/123 7/142 (7 wkts, 40 overs)	175

A. R. Caddick and H. R. J. Trump did not bat.

Bowling: Austin 8–0–44–0; Martin 8–2–36–1; Chapple 6–3–6–2; Elworthy 8–0–33–1; Watkinson 6–0–23–0; Yates 4–0–18–3.

Lancashire

M. A. Atherton c Ecclestone b Trump	18
*M. Watkinson b Caddick	6
S. Elworthy c Turner b Caddick	0
N. J. Speak run out	21
N. H. Fairbrother c Parsons b Trump	14
G. D. Lloyd b Caddick	41
†W. K. Hegg c Rose b Lee	16
I. D. Austin c Bowler b Parsons	4
G. Yates not out	22
G. Chapple not out	20
B 2, l-b 5, w 3, n-b 2	12
1/23 2/25 3/34 4/58 5/98 6/123 7/127 8/132 (8 wkts, 40 overs)	174

P. J. Martin did not bat.

Bowling: Caddick 8–1–21–3; Rose 8–0–23–0; Trump 8–1–20–2; Hayhurst 8–0–32–0; Lee 6–0–49–1; Parsons 2–0–22–1.

Umpires: T. E. Jesty and A. G. T. Whitehead.

LANCASHIRE v WORCESTERSHIRE

At Manchester, July 7. Worcestershire won by four runs. Toss: Lancashire.

This match was Sunday League cricket at its best, with the all-round talent of Moody just enough to give his side victory. Worcestershire's captain hit 104 from 86 balls, including 28 off one over from Yates, and then took four wickets and a catch. Lancashire were 175 for nine, but Chapple and Martin put on 82 for the last wicket – a League record – and were only five short of an astonishing win when Chapple was run out off the penultimate ball.

Worcestershire

*T. M. Moody b Watkinson	104
T. S. Curtis c Gallian b Watkinson	40
K. R. Spiring not out	47
W. P. C. Weston c Austin b Elworthy	40
V. S. Solanki not out	9
L-b 10, w 9, n-b 2	21
1/136 2/168 3/244 (3 wkts, 40 overs)	261

D. A. Leatherdale, †S. J. Rhodes, S. R. Lampitt, R. K. Illingworth, A. Sheriyar and S. W. K. Ellis did not bat.

Bowling: Austin 8–0–32–0; Martin 8–0–43–0; Chapple 8–0–62–0; Elworthy 8–0–40–1; Yates 2–0–30–0; Watkinson 6–0–44–2.

Lancashire

J. E. R. Gallian c Rhodes b Moody 18	G. Yates c Illingworth b Ellis 5
*M. Watkinson c Leatherdale b Moody . . . 25	G. Chapple run out 43
N. H. Fairbrother run out 25	P. J. Martin not out 35
G. D. Lloyd c Moody b Lampitt 6	B 2, l-b 6, w 6, n-b 2 16
N. J. Speak c Ellis b Moody 20	—
†W. K. Hegg c Curtis b Moody 25	1/43 2/51 3/64 (39.5 overs) 257
I. D. Austin b Sheriyar 31	4/83 5/125 6/127
S. Elworthy c Lampitt b Ellis 8	7/143 8/167 9/175

Bowling: Moody 8–0–46–4; Ellis 8–0–46–2; Lampitt 8–0–41–1; Sheriyar 8–0–49–1; Illingworth 7.5–0–67–0.

Umpires: H. D. Bird and A. A. Jones.

At Birmingham, July 16. LANCASHIRE lost to WARWICKSHIRE by 13 runs.

LANCASHIRE v DERBYSHIRE

At Manchester, July 21. Derbyshire won by five wickets. Toss: Lancashire.

Lancashire were again unable to translate their cup-tie form into League cricket and were bowled out with three and a half overs to spare. But Derbyshire appeared to be in trouble until DeFreitas struck an undefeated 50 from 29 balls, with four sixes and four fours.

Lancashire

*M. Watkinson b Harris 28	G. Yates c Krikken b Wells 0
J. E. R. Gallian c Jones b Harris 1	G. Chapple c Harris b Wells 9
J. P. Crawley c Krikken b Harris 14	P. J. Martin not out 3
G. D. Lloyd c Jones b Vandrau 29	L-b 1, w 10, n-b 2 13
N. J. Speak run out 36	—
†W. K. Hegg c and b Vandrau 42	1/5 2/45 3/46 (36.3 overs) 188
I. D. Austin b Wells 12	4/92 5/159 6/165
S. Elworthy c Barnett b Wells 1	7/169 8/174 9/183

Bowling: Cork 7–0–31–0; Harris 8–0–41–3; DeFreitas 7–0–31–0; Dean 2–0–15–0; Vandrau 7–0–49–2; Wells 5.3–0–20–4.

Derbyshire

*D. M. Jones c Watkinson b Austin 15	P. A. J. DeFreitas not out 50
K. J. Barnett c Hegg b Elworthy 42	
C. J. Adams c Hegg b Austin 7	L-b 9, w 8, n-b 2 19
T. J. G. O'Gorman not out 43	—
†K. M. Krikken c Elworthy b Yates 10	1/42 2/63 3/84 (5 wkts, 35.5 overs) 191
C. M. Wells c Chapple b Watkinson 5	4/114 5/127

D. G. Cork, M. J. Vandrau, A. J. Harris and K. J. Dean did not bat.

Bowling: Martin 5–0–22–0; Chapple 4–0–27–0; Austin 7.5–1–44–2; Elworthy 6–1–17–1; Yates 8–0–40–1; Watkinson 5–0–32–1.

Umpires: G. I. Burgess and A. Clarkson.

At Swansea, July 28. LANCASHIRE beat GLAMORGAN on scoring-rate.

LANCASHIRE v SURREY

At Manchester, August 11. Surrey won on scoring-rate. Toss: Surrey.

Surrey's in-form attack secured the win after an indifferent batting performance. Chasing only 203, Lancashire fell to 41 for three, before a shower gave them a revised target of 182 from 36 overs. Tight bowling meant they never threatened.

Surrey

M. A. Butcher b Chapple ... 1
A. D. Brown b Chapple ... 35
D. J. Bicknell run out ... 19
N. Shahid c Fairbrother b Yates ... 58
*A. J. Hollioake b Green ... 26
B. P. Julian c Fairbrother b Elworthy ... 22
B. C. Hollioake not out ... 22
†G. J. Kersey c Hegg b Chapple ... 4
M. P. Bicknell not out ... 1
L-b 8, w 4, n-b 2 ... 14

1/3 2/45 3/69 (7 wkts, 40 overs) 202
4/125 5/174
6/180 7/188

R. M. Pearson and J. E. Benjamin did not bat.

Bowling: Elworthy 8–0–45–1; Chapple 8–0–29–3; Green 8–0–30–1; Yates 8–0–39–1; Watkinson 8–0–51–0.

Lancashire

J. E. R. Gallian run out ... 3
*M. Watkinson lbw b Benjamin ... 21
N. H. Fairbrother lbw b Benjamin ... 6
G. D. Lloyd c Shahid b M. P. Bicknell ... 24
N. J. Speak b B. C. Hollioake ... 33
P. C. McKeown c A. J. Hollioake b M. P. Bicknell ... 1
†W. K. Hegg b Julian ... 2
G. Chapple c D. J. Bicknell b M. P. Bicknell ... 7
G. Yates c Julian b A. J. Hollioake ... 8
S. Elworthy c Julian b A. J. Hollioake ... 15
R. J. Green not out ... 0
L-b 6, w 2 ... 8

1/7 2/26 3/41 (31.3 overs) 128
4/69 5/71 6/85
7/94 8/109 9/119

Bowling: Benjamin 8–1–22–2; M. P. Bicknell 8–1–25–3; Pearson 5–0–23–0; Julian 5–0–22–1; B. C. Hollioake 3–0–17–1; A. J. Hollioake 2.3–0–13–2.

Umpires: M. J. Kitchen and K. J. Lyons.

LANCASHIRE v HAMPSHIRE

At Manchester, August 18. Lancashire won by one run. Toss: Lancashire.

For the third time in 1996, Old Trafford saw a Sunday game settled by one run; this time it was in the home side's favour. But Hampshire appeared to have their first Sunday win over Lancashire since 1986 in their sights while Smith was in full flow. They reached the last over needing 14, and the last ball needing a boundary. But Renshaw could manage only two.

Lancashire

*M. Watkinson c Kendall b James ... 21
M. A. Atherton c Stephenson b Udal ... 53
J. P. Crawley c Maru b Keech ... 19
N. H. Fairbrother c Kendall b Stephenson ... 55
G. D. Lloyd c Maru b Udal ... 23
J. E. R. Gallian st Aymes b Udal ... 17
†W. K. Hegg c Aymes b James ... 6
I. D. Austin not out ... 8
G. Yates st Aymes b James ... 5
S. Elworthy not out ... 2
B 2, l-b 6, w 6 ... 14

1/42 2/89 3/113 (8 wkts, 40 overs) 223
4/145 5/184 6/201
7/210 8/215

R. J. Green did not bat.

Bowling: Stephenson 8–0–42–1; Renshaw 1–0–15–0; James 8–1–43–3; Maru 8–0–32–0; Keech 4–0–26–1; Whitaker 3–0–21–0; Udal 8–0–36–3.

Hampshire

M. Keech c Atherton b Austin	11	S. D. Udal not out	12
P. R. Whitaker c Watkinson b Austin	2	R. J. Maru c Watkinson b Yates	11
R. A. Smith c Hegg b Gallian	77	S. J. Renshaw not out	6
W. S. Kendall c Yates b Green	11	L-b 8, w 5, n-b 6	19
G. W. White lbw b Austin	44		—
*J. P. Stephenson b Elworthy	17	1/6 2/27 3/76 (9 wkts, 40 overs)	222
K. D. James b Watkinson	6	4/135 5/167 6/187	
†A. N. Aymes lbw b Yates	6	7/189 8/196 9/216	

Bowling: Austin 8–1–39–3; Elworthy 6–0–36–1; Green 8–0–39–1; Yates 7–0–39–2; Watkinson 8–0–38–1; Gallian 3–0–23–1.

Umpires: J. D. Bond and B. Dudleston.

At Leeds, August 25. LANCASHIRE lost to YORKSHIRE by six wickets.

At Hove, September 1. LANCASHIRE beat SUSSEX by four wickets.

LANCASHIRE v MIDDLESEX

At Manchester, September 10. Lancashire won by six wickets. Toss: Middlesex.

Chapple began with a wide but took a wicket with his second legal delivery to set the pattern for the match, which was staged on Tuesday because of Lancashire's appearance in the NatWest final. Only Ramprakash played an innings of substance as Middlesex set a target which was always within Lancashire's reach.

Middlesex

P. N. Weekes c McKeown b Green	23	R. L. Johnson run out	1
K. P. Dutch c Fairbrother b Chapple	0		
M. R. Ramprakash st Hegg b Watkinson	74	L-b 3, w 13	16
J. C. Pooley c Gallian b Green	10		—
*M. W. Gatting b Yates	10	1/1 2/50 3/74 (7 wkts, 40 overs)	165
†K. R. Brown b Watkinson	21	4/87 5/138	
O. A. Shah not out	10	6/163 7/165	

J. P. Hewitt, R. A. Fay and A. R. C. Fraser did not bat.

Bowling: Chapple 7–1–19–1; Martin 6–2–18–0; Gallian 5–1–27–0; Green 6–0–23–2; Yates 8–0–31–1; Watkinson 8–0–44–2.

Lancashire

J. E. R. Gallian c Brown b Hewitt	9	*M. Watkinson not out	5
P. C. McKeown c Fay b Hewitt	17	L-b 5, w 9	14
J. P. Crawley b Hewitt	46		—
G. D. Lloyd b Weekes	58	1/15 2/34 (4 wkts, 37.5 overs)	166
N. H. Fairbrother not out	17	3/137 4/153	

†W. K. Hegg, G. Yates, P. J. Martin, G. Chapple and R. J. Green did not bat.

Bowling: Fraser 8–1–25–0; Hewitt 8–0–28–3; Johnson 8–0–36–0; Fay 4–1–13–0; Dutch 4–0–31–0; Weekes 5.5–0–28–1.

Umpires: V. A. Holder and R. A. White.

At Northampton, September 15. LANCASHIRE beat NORTHAMPTONSHIRE by seven wickets.

LEICESTERSHIRE

At Derby, May 5. LEICESTERSHIRE lost to DERBYSHIRE by four wickets.

At Manchester, May 12. LEICESTERSHIRE beat LANCASHIRE by one run.

LEICESTERSHIRE v WORCESTERSHIRE

At Leicester, May 19. No result (abandoned).

At Birmingham, May 26. LEICESTERSHIRE beat WARWICKSHIRE on scoring-rate.

LEICESTERSHIRE v KENT

At Leicester, June 9. Kent won by four wickets. Toss: Leicestershire.

Two West Indian batsmen dominated the match. Simmons, who put on 228 with Wells, scored 139 from 105 balls to help Leicestershire to 311 for four, then their highest total in the competition, and set Kent a target never achieved by any side batting second over 40 overs. Taking up the challenge, Hooper started comparatively slowly – his first fifty came from 59 balls with only one boundary – but paced his innings to perfection. The remaining 95 runs came from 51 balls with three sixes and another 11 fours, and Kent won with ten balls to spare.

Leicestershire

P. V. Simmons lbw b Cowdrey	139
V. J. Wells b Fleming	84
B. F. Smith run out	23
*J. J. Whitaker not out	25
D. L. Maddy c Llong b Fleming	20
†P. A. Nixon not out	0
B 5, l-b 11, w 2, n-b 2	20
1/228 2/259 3/269 4/307 (4 wkts, 40 overs)	311

A. Habib, G. J. Parsons, C. C. Remy, A. R. K. Pierson and D. J. Millns did not bat.

Bowling: Thompson 4–0–23–0; Ealham 7–0–57–0; Headley 6–0–51–0; Hooper 4–0–29–0; Fleming 7–0–56–2; McCague 6–0–35–0; Cowdrey 6–0–44–1.

Kent

T. R. Ward b Parsons	43
M. V. Fleming c Remy b Millns	10
C. L. Hooper b Millns	145
G. R. Cowdrey c Nixon b Simmons	17
M. A. Ealham c Maddy b Remy	56
N. J. Llong b Remy	3
M. J. Walker not out	18
*†S. A. Marsh not out	4
B 1, l-b 7, w 10	18
1/19 2/63 3/96 4/200 5/218 6/309 (6 wkts, 38.2 overs)	314

M. J. McCague, D. W. Headley and J. B. D. Thompson did not bat.

Bowling: Parsons 8–0–46–1; Millns 6–0–47–2; Simmons 7.2–0–52–1; Wells 6–0–50–0; Pierson 6–0–57–0; Remy 4–0–41–2; Maddy 1–0–13–0.

Umpires: H. D. Bird and J. H. Harris.

At The Oval, June 16. LEICESTERSHIRE lost to SURREY by ten wickets.

At Bradford, June 23. LEICESTERSHIRE lost to YORKSHIRE by 36 runs.

LEICESTERSHIRE v ESSEX

At Leicester, July 7. Leicestershire won by nine runs. Toss: Essex.

Leicestershire's innings centred on a run-a-ball 71 by Simmons, during which he scored his 1,000th League run in his 24th innings, equalling Tom Moody's achievement in 1991. Maddy was the next-highest scorer, and later his medium-pace enlivened the match when he bowled the last over, with Essex needing 30 to win. Hibbert took a single off the first ball, and then Lewis hit three straight sixes. But Maddy beat the bat with his fifth ball, a yorker, and conceded only one off the final delivery.

Leicestershire

P. V. Simmons b Such	71
*J. J. Whitaker lbw b Andrew	17
B. F. Smith c Lewis b Irani	18
V. J. Wells b Williams	28
G. I. Macmillan c Cowan b Williams	19
D. L. Maddy b Andrew	49
†P. A. Nixon run out	16
C. C. Remy b Grayson	5
D. Williamson not out	3
J. Ormond not out	2
L-b 15, w 3, n-b 14	32
1/55 2/119 3/121 4/172 5/180 6/248 7/250 8/258 (8 wkts, 40 overs)	260

M. T. Brimson did not bat.

Bowling: Andrew 8–0–42–2; Cowan 2–0–19–0; Grayson 7.5–0–43–1; Irani 8–0–61–1; Such 7.1–0–24–1; Williams 7–0–56–2.

Essex

D. D. J. Robinson st Nixon b Brimson	31
*P. J. Prichard c Macmillan b Williamson	38
A. P. Grayson c Whitaker b Wells	10
R. C. Irani c Maddy b Simmons	60
†R. J. Rollins c Williamson b Remy	32
J. J. B. Lewis not out	53
A. J. E. Hibbert not out	6
B 4, l-b 5, w 12	21
1/60 2/86 3/92 4/152 5/215 (5 wkts, 40 overs)	251

A. P. Cowan, N. F. Williams, P. M. Such and S. J. W. Andrew did not bat.

Bowling: Remy 8–0–59–1; Simmons 8–0–37–1; Wells 6–0–23–1; Williamson 4–0–26–1; Brimson 8–0–37–1; Ormond 3–0–27–0; Maddy 3–0–33–0.

Umpires: J. H. Hampshire and J. W. Holder.

LEICESTERSHIRE v MIDDLESEX

At Leicester, July 14. Leicestershire won by seven wickets. Toss: Middlesex.

Simmons's best bowling figures in one-day county cricket of five for 37, followed by an unbeaten 92 in as many balls, were enough to defeat a Middlesex side which performed as poorly as the slow and unreliable pitch. Leicestershire's batsmen had fewer problems and got home with six overs in hand.

Middlesex

P. N. Weekes b Simmons	12
M. R. Ramprakash c Whitaker b Williamson	44
*M. W. Gatting c and b Simmons	1
J. C. Pooley b Simmons	0
J. D. Carr c Smith b Williamson	39
†K. R. Brown b Simmons	15
P. E. Wellings run out	5
R. L. Johnson not out	19
A. R. C. Fraser c Smith b Simmons	9
L-b 7, w 20, n-b 9	36
1/27 2/44 3/44 4/109 5/131 6/144 7/160 8/180 (8 wkts, 40 overs)	180

R. A. Fay and P. C. R. Tufnell did not bat.

Bowling: Mullally 8–0–31–0; Simmons 8–0–37–5; Wells 8–0–41–0; Remy 8–0–26–0; Williamson 8–0–38–2.

Leicestershire

P. V. Simmons not out	92	G. I. Macmillan not out	34
V. J. Wells c Pooley b Fraser	9	L-b 4, w 2	6
B. F. Smith c Ramprakash b Fay	5		—
*J. J. Whitaker c Johnson b Carr	35	1/23 2/43 3/107 (3 wkts, 34 overs)	181

D. L. Maddy, †P. A. Nixon, C. C. Remy, C. D. Crowe, D. Williamson and A. D. Mullally did not bat.

Bowling: Fraser 8–0–28–1; Fay 8–1–27–1; Tufnell 5–0–28–0; Weekes 3–0–23–0; Johnson 4–0–31–0; Carr 3–0–14–1; Wellings 3–0–26–0.

Umpires: G. I. Burgess and R. A. White.

At Cheltenham, July 21. LEICESTERSHIRE beat GLOUCESTERSHIRE by six wickets.

LEICESTERSHIRE v SUSSEX

At Leicester, July 28. No result. Toss: Sussex.

Leicestershire exceeded eight runs an over during their rain-shortened innings, but further rain washed away Sussex's reply after four overs.

Leicestershire

V. J. Wells c Greenfield b Law	15	A. Habib not out	7
V. P. Clarke lbw b Lewry	1	D. Williamson not out	2
*P. V. Simmons st Moores b Greenfield	83		
D. L. Maddy b Drakes	24	B 1, l-b 9, w 4, n-b 4	18
G. I. Macmillan c Lewry b Greenfield	10		—
B. F. Smith c sub b Newell	14	1/11 2/34 3/95 (8 wkts, 24 overs)	199
†P. A. Nixon run out	20	4/117 5/147 6/164	
C. C. Remy b Giddins	5	7/175 8/192	

J. Ormond did not bat.

Bowling: Law 5–0–37–1; Lewry 5–1–24–1; Giddins 5–0–23–1; Drakes 4–0–51–1; Greenfield 4–0–42–2; Newell 1–0–12–1.

Sussex

R. K. Rao not out	3
K. Greenfield not out	6
L-b 5, w 2	7
	—
(no wkt, 4 overs)	16

M. P. Speight, K. Newell, *A. P. Wells, N. J. Lenham, D. R. Law, †P. Moores, V. C. Drakes, E. S. H. Giddins and J. D. Lewry did not bat.

Bowling: Ormond 2–0–4–0; Simmons 2–0–7–0.

Umpires: J. H. Harris and K. J. Lyons.

LEICESTERSHIRE v NORTHAMPTONSHIRE

At Leicester, August 4. Northamptonshire won by six wickets. Toss: Northamptonshire.

Both sides fielded weakened line-ups, but Northamptonshire coped far better. Three run-outs in the middle of Leicestershire's innings did nothing to help their cause and the visitors reached their target with nearly 12 overs in hand.

Leicestershire

*P. V. Simmons lbw b Capel	26	A. R. K. Pierson lbw b Snape	11
V. J. Wells c Capel b Ambrose	8	D. Williamson lbw b Ambrose	5
G. I. Macmillan c Taylor b Curran	17	M. T. Brimson not out	4
A. Habib run out	23	L-b 7, w 7	14
D. L. Maddy run out	1		—
V. P. Clarke run out	1	1/24 2/60 3/62 (34.1 overs)	133
†P. A. Nixon c Ambrose b Emburey	19	4/73 5/75 6/97	
C. C. Remy b Snape	4	7/103 8/117 9/122	

Bowling: Ambrose 5.1–1–13–2; Taylor 5–0–28–0; Capel 6–0–17–1; Curran 4–0–18–1; Emburey 8–0–32–1; Snape 6–1–18–2.

Northamptonshire

R. R. Montgomerie c Pierson b Wells	4	A. L. Penberthy not out	19
M. B. Loye c Pierson b Remy	34	L-b 6, w 7	13
K. M. Curran not out	57		—
T. C. Walton lbw b Clarke	0	1/19 2/80 (4 wkts, 28.1 overs)	136
D. J. Capel lbw b Remy	9	3/85 4/100	

J. N. Snape, *J. E. Emburey, †D. Ripley, C. E. L. Ambrose and J. P. Taylor did not bat.

Bowling: Wells 5–0–28–1; Simmons 3–0–15–0; Brimson 5–0–20–0; Clarke 6–0–36–1; Remy 4–0–9–2; Pierson 2–0–15–0; Williamson 2–0–3–0; Macmillan 1–1–0–0; Habib 0.1–0–4–0.

Umpires: J. D. Bond and R. Julian.

At Swansea, August 11. LEICESTERSHIRE beat GLAMORGAN by 60 runs.

LEICESTERSHIRE v HAMPSHIRE

At Leicester, August 25. No result. Toss: Leicestershire.

Despite weather interruptions, Hampshire managed a defensible total before further rain ended Leicestershire's reply.

Hampshire

P. R. Whitaker b Brimson	54	†A. N. Aymes not out	25
G. W. White c Nixon b Simmons	11		
*R. A. Smith c Nixon b Remy	20	L-b 6, w 12	18
M. Keech run out	19		—
W. S. Kendall not out	38	1/24 2/61 3/111 (5 wkts, 38 overs)	199
K. D. James c Williamson b Remy	14	4/117 5/163	

J. N. B. Bovill, S. D. Udal, R. J. Maru and S. J. Renshaw did not bat.

Bowling: Simmons 8–0–37–1; Williamson 6–1–28–0; Wells 8–0–49–0; Remy 8–1–34–2; Brimson 8–0–45–1.

Leicestershire

P. V. Simmons lbw b Renshaw	12	G. I. Macmillan not out	0
V. J. Wells c Smith b Renshaw	2	L-b 1, w 2	3
†P. A. Nixon c Udal b Bovill	10		—
B. F. Smith not out	11	1/5 2/16 3/38 (3 wkts, 9.2 overs)	38

*J. J. Whitaker, A. Habib, D. L. Maddy, M. T. Brimson, C. C. Remy and D. Williamson did not bat.

Bowling: Renshaw 5–0–18–2; Maru 3–0–14–0; Bovill 1.2–0–5–1.

Umpires: G. I. Burgess and R. Palmer.

LEICESTERSHIRE v SOMERSET

At Leicester, September 1. Somerset won by seven wickets. Toss: Somerset.

With only Maddy answering the Somerset attack, Leicestershire scarcely stretched the visitors, whose victory was never in doubt once Bowler and Lathwell had put on 133 for the first wicket.

Leicestershire

P. V. Simmons c Harden b Kerr	18	C. C. Remy not out	17
V. J. Wells b Parsons	18	D. Williamson not out	4
B. F. Smith c Bowler b Parsons	31		
*J. J. Whitaker run out	6	L-b 3, w 6, n-b 6	15
G. I. Macmillan lbw b Caddick	21		—
J. M. Dakin c Bowler b Parsons	0	1/28 2/51 3/70 (8 wkts, 40 overs)	194
D. L. Maddy run out	57	4/85 5/85 6/118	
†P. A. Nixon c Bowler b Lee	7	7/148 8/189	

M. T. Brimson did not bat.

Bowling: Caddick 8–1–30–1; Kerr 8–0–55–1; Parsons 8–0–36–3; Lee 8–0–35–1; Trump 8–0–35–0.

Somerset

M. N. Lathwell c Smith b Macmillan	63	S. Lee not out	8
*P. D. Bowler run out	76	B 5, l-b 11, w 5, n-b 6	27
S. C. Ecclestone run out	7		—
R. J. Harden not out	14	1/133 2/155 3/182 (3 wkts, 37.5 overs)	195

M. E. Trescothick, K. A. Parsons, †R. J. Turner, J. I. D. Kerr, A. R. Caddick and H. R. J. Trump did not bat.

Bowling: Simmons 7–0–32–0; Williamson 5.5–0–22–0; Wells 5–0–18–0; Brimson 4–0–29–0; Dakin 2–0–16–0; Remy 8–1–29–0; Macmillan 6–0–33–1.

Umpires: V. A. Holder and K. E. Palmer.

At Nottingham, September 8. LEICESTERSHIRE lost to NOTTINGHAMSHIRE by six wickets.

At Chester-le-Street, September 15. LEICESTERSHIRE beat DURHAM by 130 runs.

MIDDLESEX

MIDDLESEX v GLOUCESTERSHIRE

At Lord's, May 5. Middlesex won by 31 runs. Toss: Gloucestershire. First-team debuts: P. E. Wellings; D. R. Hewson.

Carr's second fifty came from only 19 balls as Middlesex scored 173 from their final 20 overs. Russell and Cawdron added 94 for the eighth wicket, a Gloucestershire record, but not even that could put them into serious contention.

Middlesex

P. N. Weekes c Russell b Alleyne	13	K. P. Dutch not out	9
M. A. Feltham c Hancock b Cawdron	10	P. E. Wellings not out	1
*M. W. Gatting c Symonds b Davis	46	L-b 9, w 10, n-b 2	21
J. D. Carr c Cawdron b Alleyne	106		—
J. C. Pooley c Lewis b Davis	32	1/31 2/32 3/100 (6 wkts, 40 overs)	255
†K. R. Brown b Alleyne	17	4/159 5/243 6/243	

R. L. Johnson, J. P. Hewitt and A. R. C. Fraser did not bat.

Bowling: Lewis 7–0–51–0; Smith 8–1–25–0; Cawdron 7–0–43–1; Alleyne 8–0–52–3; Hancock 4–0–30–0; Davis 6–0–45–2.

Gloucestershire

M. W. Alleyne c Dutch b Feltham	2	*†R. C. Russell c Johnson b Wellings	59
R. I. Dawson b Feltham	4	J. Lewis not out	9
R. J. Cunliffe b Weekes	52	R. P. Davis b Weekes	0
T. H. C. Hancock c Brown b Feltham	6	B 4, l-b 5, w 6, n-b 6	21
A. Symonds c Brown b Johnson	6		—
A. M. Smith b Fraser	25	1/7 2/8 3/25 (38.2 overs)	224
D. R. Hewson st Brown b Weekes	3	4/35 5/109 6/109	
M. J. Cawdron b Weekes	37	7/114 8/208 9/216	

Bowling: Feltham 8–2–30–3; Johnson 8–0–40–1; Fraser 8–0–59–1; Weekes 5.2–0–29–4; Dutch 7–0–35–0; Wellings 2–0–22–1.

Umpires: J. W. Holder and M. J. Kitchen.

MIDDLESEX v DURHAM

At Lord's, May 12. Middlesex won by 17 runs. Toss: Middlesex.

Middlesex appeared to have the match already won when Durham were 116 for seven in the 30th over. Then Bainbridge rallied the tail to take Durham to within 18 runs of their objective.

Middlesex

P. N. Weekes lbw b Collingwood	57	O. A. Shah not out	23
M. R. Ramprakash lbw b Brown	4		
*M. W. Gatting b Killeen	39	B 4, l-b 6, w 2, n-b 2	14
J. D. Carr st Scott b Bainbridge	13		—
J. C. Pooley c Collingwood b Brown	30	1/6 2/80 3/113 (5 wkts, 40 overs)	208
†K. R. Brown not out	28	4/129 5/162	

K. P. Dutch, A. R. C. Fraser, R. A. Fay and D. Follett did not bat.

Bowling: Betts 5–0–32–0; Brown 8–0–35–2; Foster 6–0–27–0; Killeen 8–0–37–1; Collingwood 8–0–37–1; Bainbridge 5–0–30–1.

Durham

S. L. Campbell st Brown b Weekes	29	N. Killeen st Brown b Dutch	32
M. J. Foster c Pooley b Fraser	6	S. J. E. Brown not out	14
S. Hutton c Gatting b Carr	7	M. M. Betts c Follett b Dutch	11
J. E. Morris c Carr b Follett	12	B 2, l-b 5, w 5	12
*M. A. Roseberry lbw b Carr	12		—
P. Bainbridge c Ramprakash b Weekes	34	1/12 2/28 3/44 (39.1 overs)	191
P. D. Collingwood st Brown b Weekes	5	4/67 5/77 6/99	
†C. W. Scott c Weekes b Dutch	17	7/116 8/159 9/165	

Bowling: Fay 8–1–34–0; Fraser 8–1–38–1; Follett 8–0–48–1; Carr 5–0–25–2; Weekes 8–0–29–3; Dutch 2.1–0–10–3.

Umpires: A. Clarkson and J. H. Harris.

At Horsham, May 26. SUSSEX v MIDDLESEX. No result (abandoned).

MIDDLESEX v YORKSHIRE

At Lord's, June 2. Middlesex won by six wickets. Toss: Yorkshire.

Weekes, dropped before scoring in the first over of the Middlesex innings, went on to compile the only fifty of a low-scoring encounter. The top five Yorkshire batsmen were all bowled – by different bowlers – while only one Middlesex wicket fell that way, when a ball deflected off Gatting's elbow.

Yorkshire

*D. Byas b Fay	11	P. J. Hartley not out	7
M. P. Vaughan b Hewitt	21	C. E. W. Silverwood not out	1
M. G. Bevan b Fraser	10		
A. McGrath b Follett	9	L-b 11, w 6	17
C. White b Carr	38		—
†R. J. Blakey st Brown b Weekes	35	1/14 2/47 3/47 (8 wkts, 40 overs)	167
A. C. Morris c Carr b Follett	2	4/81 5/117 6/124	
D. Gough c Shah b Weekes	16	7/150 8/164	

R. D. Stemp did not bat.

Bowling: Fay 6–2–20–1; Fraser 8–1–19–1; Hewitt 5–1–16–1; Weekes 6–0–32–2; Carr 7–1–22–1; Follett 8–0–47–2.

Middlesex

P. N. Weekes c Blakey b Morris	50	†K. R. Brown not out	31
M. R. Ramprakash c Stemp b Gough	0	B 1, l-b 3, w 5, n-b 2	11
*M. W. Gatting b Silverwood	4		—
J. D. Carr lbw b Morris	37	1/1 2/9 (4 wkts, 35.5 overs)	170
J. C. Pooley not out	37	3/94 4/103	

O. A. Shah, J. P. Hewitt, R. A. Fay, A. R. C. Fraser and D. Follett did not bat.

Bowling: Gough 7–0–19–1; Silverwood 8–1–29–1; Hartley 8–0–41–0; White 5.5–0–26–0; Stemp 3–0–24–0; Morris 4–0–27–2.

Umpires: J. C. Balderstone and A. A. Jones.

MIDDLESEX v GLAMORGAN

At Lord's, June 9. Middlesex won by eight wickets. Toss: Middlesex.

Weekes, who scored a maiden Sunday League century, and Gatting put on 203 in 30 overs to level the scores; the winning run came with more than four overs to spare. Earlier, Morris had become the first Glamorgan batsman to reach 5,000 runs in the competition, and Croft hit left-arm spinner Rashid for four sixes.

Glamorgan

S. P. James c Gatting b Fraser	3	R. D. B. Croft not out	45
H. Morris c Brown b Carr	55	S. D. Thomas not out	7
*M. P. Maynard c Carr b Rashid	44	L-b 4, w 3	7
P. A. Cottey c Pooley b Weekes	32		—
A. Dale c Pooley b Weekes	23	1/3 2/65 3/137 (6 wkts, 40 overs)	221
G. P. Butcher c Weekes b Rashid	5	4/138 5/160 6/174	

†C. P. Metson, S. L. Watkin and S. R. Barwick did not bat.

Bowling: Fay 6–0–26–0; Fraser 8–1–38–1; Rashid 7–0–57–2; Hewitt 4–0–25–0; Carr 7–0–34–1; Weekes 8–0–37–2.

Middlesex

P. N. Weekes not out	119
M. R. Ramprakash run out	5
*M. W. Gatting run out	90
J. D. Carr not out	0
L-b 3, w 5	8
	—
1/18 2/221 (2 wkts, 35.4 overs)	222

J. C. Pooley, †K. R. Brown, O. A. Shah, J. P. Hewitt, R. A. Fay, A. R. C. Fraser and U. B. A. Rashid did not bat.

Bowling: Thomas 7.4–0–52–0; Watkin 8–2–26–0; Butcher 4–0–23–0; Barwick 7–0–45–0; Croft 6–0–42–0; Dale 3–0–31–0.

Umpires: J. H. Hampshire and K. E. Palmer.

At Canterbury, June 16. MIDDLESEX lost to KENT by 92 runs.

At Derby, June 23. MIDDLESEX beat DERBYSHIRE by eight runs.

MIDDLESEX v WARWICKSHIRE

At Lord's, June 30. Middlesex won by 57 runs. Toss: Warwickshire.

A brisk century opening stand between Weekes and Ramprakash and solid batting to follow helped speed up the Middlesex innings, which was more than the bowlers did; Warwickshire took a full ten minutes more than the allotted time to complete their 40 overs but were unpenalised. Their batsmen never came to terms with the task in hand and Middlesex moved to the top of the table.

Middlesex

P. N. Weekes c Knight b Smith	52	R. L. Johnson c Burns b Pollock	0
M. R. Ramprakash c Burns b Edmond	37	A. R. C. Fraser b Giles	2
J. C. Pooley b Giles	33	R. A. Fay not out	1
*M. W. Gatting c Burns b Brown	47	L-b 12, w 15, n-b 6	33
J. D. Carr b Giles	9		—
†K. R. Brown b Giles	3	1/101 2/101 3/195	(40 overs) 241
P. E. Wellings run out	12	4/199 5/212 6/213	
M. A. Feltham c Brown b Pollock	12	7/236 8/237 9/240	

Bowling: Brown 8–0–36–1; Pollock 7–0–29–2; Small 6–0–44–0; Smith 8–0–60–1; Edmond 5–0–26–1; Giles 6–0–34–4.

Warwickshire

N. V. Knight c Ramprakash b Fay	20	A. F. Giles b Johnson	31
D. P. Ostler c Brown b Fraser	26	M. D. Edmond c Fay b Weekes	4
P. A. Smith c Carr b Fay	10	G. C. Small not out	15
D. R. Brown b Fay	11	B 4, l-b 6, w 4	14
T. L. Penney b Johnson	0		—
S. M. Pollock c Weekes b Feltham	18	1/47 2/63 3/75	(34.5 overs) 184
*A. J. Moles c Brown b Fay	0	4/76 5/82 6/82	
†M. Burns lbw b Feltham	35	7/117 8/150 9/157	

Bowling: Feltham 8–1–49–2; Fraser 8–1–24–1; Fay 8–0–33–4; Johnson 6.5–0–28–2; Weekes 4–0–40–1.

Umpires: J. C. Balderstone and B. J. Meyer.

At The Oval, July 7. MIDDLESEX lost to SURREY by eight wickets.

At Leicester, July 14. MIDDLESEX lost to LEICESTERSHIRE by seven wickets.

At Northampton, July 21. MIDDLESEX lost to NORTHAMPTONSHIRE by six wickets.

MIDDLESEX v ESSEX

At Lord's, August 4. Middlesex won by five runs. Toss: Middlesex.

Both sides managed to reach 197 for six in the 37th over of their respective innings, but Middlesex built on that position while Essex fell back. Earlier, a six by Pooley broke the window in the office of MCC's assistant secretary for cricket, John Jameson, some 30 feet up in the pavilion annexe.

Middlesex

P. N. Weekes c Andrew b Law	17	P. E. Wellings b Grayson	1
M. R. Ramprakash lbw b Such	14	J. P. Hewitt not out	16
J. C. Pooley lbw b Law	68	B 1, l-b 15, w 5, n-b 2	23
*J. D. Carr c Hussain b Law	43		——
K. P. Dutch c Rollins b Law	1	1/28 2/41 3/137 (6 wkts, 40 overs)	220
†K. R. Brown not out	37	4/139 5/162 6/165	

R. L. Johnson, R. A. Fay and A. R. C. Fraser did not bat.

Bowling: Andrew 8–0–38–0; Ilott 8–2–34–0; Law 8–0–40–4; Such 8–1–33–1; Grayson 8–0–59–1.

Essex

D. D. J. Robinson c Dutch b Weekes	31	M. C. Ilott not out	5
A. J. E. Hibbert c Brown b Fay	6	S. J. W. Andrew b Weekes	0
N. Hussain b Dutch	77	P. M. Such not out	4
S. G. Law c Hewitt b Weekes	6	L-b 12, w 13, n-b 2	27
*P. J. Prichard c Brown b Fay	19		——
†R. J. Rollins b Dutch	6	1/22 2/76 3/92 (9 wkts, 40 overs)	215
J. J. B. Lewis c Carr b Johnson	17	4/151 5/168 6/175	
A. P. Grayson c Fraser b Weekes	17	7/197 8/211 9/211	

Bowling: Hewitt 4–0–23–0; Fay 8–1–33–2; Fraser 8–0–55–0; Johnson 8–1–40–1; Weekes 7–0–29–4; Dutch 5–0–23–2.

Umpires: B. Leadbeater and B. J. Meyer.

At Nottingham, August 11. MIDDLESEX lost to NOTTINGHAMSHIRE by nine wickets.

MIDDLESEX v WORCESTERSHIRE

At Lord's, August 18. Worcestershire won by two runs. Toss: Middlesex.

Middlesex were all out trying to get the winning runs off the penultimate ball; they had only 39 overs available because they had bowled their own too slowly. Leatherdale hit four of just five boundaries in Worcestershire's innings as he recorded his first League fifty for eight years. Then, bowling for the first time in the competition this season, he registered a career-best four for 31, which ended Middlesex's last hopes of keeping up with the leaders.

Worcestershire

*T. M. Moody lbw b Fraser	40	†S. J. Rhodes not out	27
W. P. C. Weston c Brown b Fay	0	R. K. Illingworth not out	4
G. A. Hick run out	2	B 2, l-b 2, w 6, n-b 2	12
K. R. Spiring c Hewitt b Johnson	16		——
V. S. Solanki c Hewitt b Weekes	7	1/3 2/9 3/61 (7 wkts, 40 overs)	173
D. A. Leatherdale c Shah b Weekes	50	4/66 5/82	
S. R. Lampitt c Hewitt b Dutch	15	6/135 7/157	

S. W. K. Ellis and A. Sheriyar did not bat.

Bowling: Fay 8–0–27–1; Hewitt 6–0–20–0; Johnson 8–0–42–1; Fraser 8–1–28–1; Weekes 8–0–40–2; Dutch 2–0–12–1.

Middlesex

P. N. Weekes b Lampitt	24	R. L. Johnson b Leatherdale	29
*M. R. Ramprakash run out	25	A. R. C. Fraser c Ellis b Leatherdale	5
J. D. Carr lbw b Leatherdale	7	R. A. Fay not out	0
J. C. Pooley c Spiring b Illingworth	10	L-b 2, w 9, n-b 4	15
O. A. Shah run out	23		——
†K. R. Brown c Lampitt b Leatherdale	14	1/52 2/66 3/70 (38.5 overs)	171
K. P. Dutch c Hick b Illingworth	8	4/96 5/108 6/118	
J. P. Hewitt run out	11	7/135 8/146 9/171	

Bowling: Ellis 3–0–17–0; Moody 8–0–23–0; Lampitt 8–0–45–1; Sheriyar 4–0–30–0; Leatherdale 7.5–0–31–4; Illingworth 8–1–23–2.

Umpires: J. H. Harris and R. Julian.

At Portsmouth, September 1. MIDDLESEX beat HAMPSHIRE by seven wickets.

At Manchester, September 10. MIDDLESEX lost to LANCASHIRE by six wickets.

MIDDLESEX v SOMERSET

At Uxbridge, September 15. Middlesex won by four wickets. Toss: Somerset.

A carefully paced 80 from Ramprakash and a more explosive 42 in 48 balls from Wellings allowed Middlesex to overtake Somerset, who were bowled out with nine balls of their 40 overs remaining.

Somerset

M. N. Lathwell c Wellings b Fay	0	J. I. D. Kerr b Hewitt	8
*P. D. Bowler c Weekes b Fay	15	A. R. Caddick not out	4
S. Lee c Dutch b Johnson	24	H. R. J. Trump b Hewitt	7
R. J. Harden lbw b Dutch	46	L-b 14, w 9, n-b 2	25
M. E. Trescothick b Fay	0		
K. A. Parsons lbw b Johnson	0	1/1 2/17 3/51 (38.3 overs)	194
†R. J. Turner c Wellings b Fraser	11	4/52 5/55 6/92	
G. D. Rose run out	54	7/171 8/176 9/184	

Bowling: Fay 8–2–22–3; Hewitt 7.3–0–45–2; Johnson 8–0–24–2; Fraser 8–0–35–1; Weekes 5–0–35–0; Dutch 2–0–19–1.

Middlesex

P. N. Weekes c Lee b Caddick	7	P. E. Wellings c and b Lee	42
K. P. Dutch c Turner b Caddick	0	R. L. Johnson not out	3
M. R. Ramprakash not out	80	B 1, l-b 7, w 20, n-b 2	30
O. A. Shah c Trescothick b Trump	22		
*M. W. Gatting run out	7	1/3 2/17 3/66 (6 wkts, 38.5 overs)	195
†K. R. Brown c Lee b Trump	4	4/80 5/90 6/188	

J. P. Hewitt, R. A. Fay and A. R. C. Fraser did not bat.

Bowling: Caddick 8–2–24–2; Rose 8–0–42–0; Kerr 7–0–39–0; Lee 7.5–0–40–1; Trump 8–0–42–2.

Umpires: H. D. Bird and K. J. Lyons.

NORTHAMPTONSHIRE

At Chester-le-Street, May 5. NORTHAMPTONSHIRE beat DURHAM by eight wickets.

NORTHAMPTONSHIRE v GLAMORGAN

At Northampton, May 12. Northamptonshire won by four wickets. Toss: Northamptonshire.

Gibson hit four sixes, one of which cleared the indoor school and landed in the car park – a rare achievement on this ground – as he and Croft rescued Glamorgan from 72 for five. Northamptonshire needed five an over; they were never far in front of the requirement and finished the game with only two balls to spare.

Glamorgan

S. P. James c Ripley b Ambrose	0	O. D. Gibson not out	47
H. Morris b Capel	17	S. D. Thomas not out	20
*M. P. Maynard c Bailey b Ambrose	9	B 1, l-b 9, w 4, n-b 2	16
P. A. Cottey c Ripley b Ambrose	1		—
A. Dale c Ambrose b Curran	21	1/0 2/13 3/17 (6 wkts, 40 overs)	199
R. D. B. Croft run out	68	4/34 5/72 6/147	

†C. P. Metson, S. L. Watkin and S. R. Barwick did not bat.

Bowling: Ambrose 8–3–14–3; Mallender 8–1–29–0; Capel 8–1–29–1; Emburey 8–1–44–0; Curran 5–0–41–1; Penberthy 3–0–32–0.

Northamptonshire

R. R. Montgomerie c Metson b Barwick	32	A. L. Penberthy not out	30
A. Fordham c Morris b Gibson	13	†D. Ripley not out	0
*R. J. Bailey b Barwick	8	L-b 10, w 6, n-b 6	22
K. M. Curran c Metson b Barwick	4		—
M. B. Loye c Cottey b Barwick	58	1/26 2/46 3/56 (6 wkts, 39.4 overs)	200
D. J. Capel lbw b Dale	33	4/79 5/149 6/192	

J. E. Emburey, C. E. L. Ambrose and N. A. Mallender did not bat.

Bowling: Gibson 7.4–1–26–1; Watkin 8–1–36–0; Barwick 8–0–34–4; Croft 8–1–43–0; Dale 6–0–34–1; Thomas 2–0–17–0.

Umpires: G. I. Burgess and M. J. Kitchen.

At Taunton, May 26. NORTHAMPTONSHIRE beat SOMERSET by one wicket.

NORTHAMPTONSHIRE v WARWICKSHIRE

At Northampton, June 2. Northamptonshire won by three wickets. Toss: Warwickshire.

For the second week in succession, Ambrose won the match with the bat in the final over, though it was Capel, scoring 81 from 82 balls, who really turned the game Northamptonshire's way. Both wicket-keepers, Piper and Warren, claimed four victims.

Warwickshire

N. V. Knight c Warren b Taylor	10	P. A. Smith not out	12
N. M. K. Smith run out	11	†K. J. Piper not out	2
D. R. Brown c Fordham b Ambrose	24		
D. P. Ostler c Warren b Ambrose	21	L-b 6, w 6	12
T. L. Penney st Warren b Emburey	8		—
S. M. Pollock run out	28	1/14 2/40 3/58 (8 wkts, 40 overs)	184
*D. A. Reeve st Warren b Emburey	2	4/83 5/83 6/85	
G. Welch c Fordham b Taylor	54	7/142 8/181	

A. F. Giles did not bat.

Bowling: Mallender 8–1–42–0; Taylor 8–2–40–2; Ambrose 8–1–21–2; Emburey 8–2–25–2; Capel 6–0–27–0; Bailey 2–0–23–0.

Northamptonshire

A. Fordham c Piper b Reeve	0	J. E. Emburey not out	0
M. B. Loye c P. A. Smith b N. M. K. Smith	32	C. E. L. Ambrose not out	4
*R. J. Bailey c Piper b P. A. Smith	8	B 4, l-b 4, w 6, n-b 10	24
K. M. Curran c Piper b P. A. Smith	3		—
D. J. Capel c Pollock b Reeve	81	1/0 2/31 3/40 (7 wkts, 39.4 overs)	188
†R. J. Warren c Piper b Pollock	17	4/103 5/136	
T. C. Walton lbw b P. A. Smith	19	6/181 7/182	

N. A. Mallender and J. P. Taylor did not bat.

Bowling: Reeve 7–2–22–2; Pollock 8–1–17–1; P. A. Smith 4.4–0–27–3; Welch 5–0–28–0; Giles 2–0–15–0; Brown 5–0–28–0; N. M. K. Smith 8–0–43–1.

Umpires: A. Clarkson and T. E. Jesty.

At Nottingham, June 9. NORTHAMPTONSHIRE beat NOTTINGHAMSHIRE by five wickets.

At Chelmsford, June 16. NORTHAMPTONSHIRE beat ESSEX by eight wickets.

At Basingstoke, June 23. NORTHAMPTONSHIRE lost to HAMPSHIRE by seven wickets.

NORTHAMPTONSHIRE v DERBYSHIRE

At Northampton, June 30. Derbyshire won by 90 runs. Toss: Northamptonshire.

Derbyshire were reduced to 146 for six. However, DeFreitas, with 61 from 33 balls – his maiden League half-century – and Cork put on 76 in the last 43 balls to leave a target of 223. That proved far too much for Northamptonshire. DeFreitas picked up three wickets bowling off-breaks in harness with the regular off-spinner, Vandrau. Mallender reached 200 Sunday League wickets; Barnett reached 10,000 runs in the three one-day competitions.

Derbyshire

K. J. Barnett c and b Taylor	14
J. E. Owen c Emburey b Mallender	32
*D. M. Jones c Warren b Mallender	14
C. J. Adams c Loye b Ambrose	26
T. J. G. O'Gorman b Emburey	21
P. A. J. DeFreitas not out	61
†K. M. Krikken b Emburey	2
D. G. Cork not out	17
B 1, l-b 15, w 13, n-b 6	35
1/32 2/70 3/78 4/134 5/137 6/146 (6 wkts, 40 overs)	222

K. J. Dean, M. J. Vandrau and D. E. Malcolm did not bat.

Bowling: Ambrose 8–0–41–1; Taylor 8–0–35–1; Emburey 8–0–15–2; Mallender 8–0–42–2; Bailey 6–1–47–0; Capel 2–0–26–0.

Northamptonshire

†R. J. Warren c Krikken b Dean	10
*R. J. Bailey c Cork b Vandrau	30
K. M. Curran c O'Gorman b Dean	14
M. B. Loye b Vandrau	3
D. J. Capel c Vandrau b DeFreitas	34
T. C. Walton b Vandrau	11
D. J. Sales b DeFreitas	6
J. E. Emburey b DeFreitas	2
C. E. L. Ambrose c Cork b Jones	8
N. A. Mallender c Adams b Jones	5
J. P. Taylor not out	3
L-b 2, w 4	6
1/19 2/45 3/61 4/66 5/80 6/97 7/105 8/118 9/128 (31.4 overs)	132

Bowling: Cork 4–0–17–0; Dean 8–0–30–2; Vandrau 8–1–30–3; DeFreitas 7.4–0–38–3; Jones 4–0–15–2.

Umpires: J. W. Holder and A. A. Jones.

NORTHAMPTONSHIRE v YORKSHIRE

At Northampton, July 16. Yorkshire won by two wickets. Toss: Yorkshire.

The match was put back to Tuesday because Northamptonshire had been in the Benson and Hedges Cup final. But they were unable to make up for their failure at Lord's. Moxon and McGrath received just enough support to overcome a respectable Northamptonshire total, founded on the contributions of Curran and Montgomerie.

Northamptonshire

R. R. Montgomerie lbw b Silverwood	69	D. J. Capel not out	20
A. Fordham c Blakey b Gough	3	L-b 11, w 8, n-b 8	27
K. M. Curran not out	92		—
A. L. Penberthy c White b Bevan	20	1/20 2/126 (4 wkts, 40 overs)	236
*R. J. Bailey b Hartley	5	3/158 4/195	

†R. J. Warren, T. C. Walton, J. E. Emburey, J. P. Taylor and N. A. Mallender did not bat.

Bowling: Gough 8–1–32–1; Silverwood 8–0–55–1; Hartley 8–0–38–1; White 8–0–36–0; Stemp 4–0–33–0; Bevan 4–0–31–1.

Yorkshire

M. D. Moxon c Taylor b Curran	72	P. J. Hartley c Taylor b Mallender	2
M. P. Vaughan b Taylor	6	C. E. W. Silverwood not out	14
M. G. Bevan c Bailey b Taylor	12		
*D. Byas b Taylor	7	L-b 5, w 5, n-b 6	16
C. White c Curran b Emburey	2		—
A. McGrath lbw b Emburey	69	1/15 2/31 3/39 (8 wkts, 40 overs)	240
†R. J. Blakey not out	35	4/47 5/158 6/199	
D. Gough c Emburey b Capel	5	7/213 8/216	

R. D. Stemp did not bat.

Bowling: Mallender 5–0–25–1; Taylor 8–0–41–3; Capel 8–0–50–1; Emburey 8–0–34–2; Curran 8–0–57–1; Penberthy 3–0–28–0.

Umpires: J. C. Balderstone and N. T. Plews.

NORTHAMPTONSHIRE v MIDDLESEX

At Northampton, July 21. Northamptonshire won by six wickets. Toss: Northamptonshire.

Emburey helped to defeat the county he served for 23 years, with two wickets, which took him to 350 in his Sunday League career. The Middlesex total of 181 never appeared adequate, especially when Montgomerie established early superiority, first with Bailey, who was forced to retire hurt after a blow on the wrist, and then with Curran. Shah, who had played several Sunday games without bowling, dismissed Capel with his first ball.

Middlesex

P. N. Weekes b Curran	54	J. P. Hewitt b Taylor	12
†K. R. Brown c Capel b Penberthy	15	A. R. C. Fraser not out	16
*M. W. Gatting c Snape b Emburey	17		
J. C. Pooley c Sales b Emburey	1	L-b 8, w 4	12
J. D. Carr not out	37		—
P. E. Wellings b Curran	4	1/45 2/89 3/93 (8 wkts, 40 overs)	181
O. A. Shah lbw b Capel	12	4/101 5/113 6/139	
K. P. Dutch b Snape	1	7/140 8/165	

R. A. Fay did not bat.

Bowling: Taylor 8–0–44–1; Penberthy 6–0–24–1; Capel 7–0–31–1; Curran 8–0–34–2; Emburey 8–0–30–2; Snape 3–1–10–1.

Northamptonshire

R. R. Montgomerie lbw b Fay	69	D. J. Sales not out	0
*R. J. Bailey retired hurt	15		
K. M. Curran c Brown b Hewitt	36	L-b 8, w 7, n-b 6	21
T. C. Walton not out	23		—
D. J. Capel c Wellings b Shah	17	1/133 2/136 (4 wkts, 35.1 overs)	182
A. L. Penberthy c Fraser b Wellings	1	3/177 4/181	

†D. Ripley, J. E. Emburey, J. P. Taylor and J. N. Snape did not bat.

R. J. Bailey retired hurt at 57.

Bowling: Fay 8–0–23–1; Fraser 8–1–28–0; Hewitt 8–0–52–1; Weekes 6–0–34–0; Carr 2–0–9–0; Wellings 2–0–24–1; Shah 1.1–0–4–1.

Umpires: M. J. Kitchen and K. J. Lyons.

At Worcester, July 28. WORCESTERSHIRE v NORTHAMPTONSHIRE. No result.

At Leicester, August 4. NORTHAMPTONSHIRE beat LEICESTERSHIRE by six wickets.

NORTHAMPTONSHIRE v KENT

At Northampton, August 11. Kent won by four wickets. Toss: Kent.

Northamptonshire's defeat knocked them off the top of the table. Kent needed 95 to win from the final 11 overs with six wickets in hand when Cowdrey came in and hit an undefeated 52 from 36 balls to secure victory. Fleming had opened the batting to good effect, as Montgomerie had done for Northamptonshire earlier in the day; Penberthy's 70 came from 55 balls.

Northamptonshire

R. R. Montgomerie lbw b Hooper	66
M. B. Loye c Headley b Fleming	24
K. M. Curran c Headley b Hooper	8
A. L. Penberthy c Llong b Headley	70
D. J. Capel run out	13
T. C. Walton c Ward b Fleming	40
J. N. Snape b Fleming	0
*J. E. Emburey not out	5
W 5, n-b 4	9
1/64 2/93 3/109 4/123 5/211 6/213 7/235 (7 wkts, 40 overs)	235

†D. Ripley, C. E. L. Ambrose and J. P. Taylor did not bat.

Bowling: Headley 8–0–40–1; Wren 8–0–35–0; McCague 8–0–64–0; Fleming 8–0–55–3; Hooper 8–0–41–2.

Kent

M. V. Fleming b Capel	72
M. J. Walker b Emburey	21
C. L. Hooper lbw b Capel	11
*T. R. Ward b Capel	13
N. J. Llong c Ripley b Capel	21
G. R. Cowdrey not out	52
W. J. House c Ripley b Ambrose	17
†S. C. Willis not out	5
B 1, l-b 7, w 6, n-b 10	24
1/58 2/106 3/128 4/141 5/162 6/218 (6 wkts, 38.4 overs)	236

M. J. McCague, D. W. Headley and T. N. Wren did not bat.

Bowling: Ambrose 7.4–0–28–1; Taylor 8–0–67–0; Emburey 8–1–37–1; Curran 2–0–24–0; Capel 8–1–44–4; Snape 5–0–28–0.

Umpires: V. A. Holder and B. J. Meyer.

NORTHAMPTONSHIRE v SUSSEX

At Northampton, August 25. Northamptonshire won by five wickets. Toss: Northamptonshire.

With Northamptonshire's innings reduced to first 26 overs and then 21, their batsmen had to adjust the scoring-rate throughout. They reached the revised target with seven balls to spare. Earlier, Sussex had recovered well from 58 for four, after Capel took three wickets in 12 balls.

Sussex

V. C. Drakes c Snape b Capel 20
K. Greenfield c Ripley b Ambrose 10
M. P. Speight c Ripley b Capel 14
K. Newell b Capel 2
*A. P. Wells c Snape b Emburey 41
M. Newell c Capel b Taylor 69
†P. Moores b Taylor 42
D. R. Law b Penberthy 5
N. C. Phillips not out 2
L-b 4, w 8, n-b 12 24

1/25 2/52 3/52 4/58 5/130 6/202 7/207 8/229 (8 wkts, 38.5 overs) 229

J. D. Lewry and R. J. Kirtley did not bat.

Bowling: Penberthy 6–0–48–1; Ambrose 8–0–46–1; Capel 8–0–32–3; Emburey 8–0–29–1; Snape 2–0–11–0; Taylor 6.5–0–59–2.

Northamptonshire

R. R. Montgomerie c Moores b Drakes ... 0
J. N. Snape b Drakes 6
K. M. Curran c Speight b Law 19
D. J. Capel c K. Newell b Kirtley 26
T. C. Walton c Moores b Lewry 9
A. L. Penberthy not out 31
*R. J. Bailey not out 12
B 2, l-b 12, w 10 24

1/1 2/35 3/41 4/70 5/89 (5 wkts, 19.5 overs) 127

†D. Ripley, J. E. Emburey, J. P. Taylor and C. E. L. Ambrose did not bat.

Bowling: Drakes 6–0–29–2; Lewry 3–0–26–1; Law 7–0–31–1; Kirtley 3–0–19–1; Phillips 0.5–0–8–0.

Umpires: A. Clarkson and J. W. Holder.

At Bristol, September 1. NORTHAMPTONSHIRE beat GLOUCESTERSHIRE by five wickets.

At The Oval, September 8. NORTHAMPTONSHIRE lost to SURREY by two wickets.

NORTHAMPTONSHIRE v LANCASHIRE

At Northampton, September 15. Lancashire won by seven wickets. Toss: Northamptonshire.

McKeown helped Lancashire towards a comfortable win with 69 in 73 balls, sharing an opening partnership of 125 with Gallian. A century stand between Penberthy and Bailey had enabled Northamptonshire to pass 200.

Northamptonshire

R. R. Montgomerie c Lloyd b Martin 0
M. B. Loye c Fairbrother b Green 7
K. M. Curran c Haynes b Green 16
T. C. Walton c McKeown b Yates 18
A. L. Penberthy c Gallian b Martin 80
*R. J. Bailey not out 57
†R. J. Warren not out 13
L-b 4, w 5, n-b 2 11

1/0 2/21 3/30 4/59 5/174 (5 wkts, 40 overs) 202

J. N. Snape, K. J. Innes, C. E. L. Ambrose and J. P. Taylor did not bat.

Bowling: Martin 8–1–32–2; Austin 8–0–31–0; Green 8–1–44–2; Elworthy 8–2–27–0; Yates 4–0–24–1; Gallian 4–0–40–0.

Lancashire

J. E. R. Gallian lbw b Innes 70
P. C. McKeown c Bailey b Penberthy 69
*J. P. Crawley c Innes b Snape 4
N. H. Fairbrother not out 42
G. D. Lloyd not out 3
L-b 9, w 2, n-b 4 15

1/125 2/133 3/174 (3 wkts, 37.4 overs) 203

I. D. Austin, S. Elworthy, †J. J. Haynes, G. Yates, P. J. Martin and R. J. Green did not bat.

Bowling: Ambrose 8–2–12–0; Taylor 8–1–45–0; Innes 6.4–0–57–1; Snape 8–0–41–1; Penberthy 7–1–39–1.

Umpires: V. A. Holder and K. E. Palmer.

NOTTINGHAMSHIRE

NOTTINGHAMSHIRE v SUSSEX

At Nottingham, May 5. Nottinghamshire won by 129 runs. Toss: Sussex.

Nottinghamshire could thank Pollard, who hit 118 from 108 balls, and Johnson, with 97 not out from 78, for reaching the county's highest 40-over total – they had passed 300 twice in 1993, when the Sunday League ran to 50 overs. Sussex never even began to challenge.

Nottinghamshire

P. R. Pollard c Salisbury b Giddins	118
R. T. Robinson b Jarvis	32
*P. Johnson not out	97
C. L. Cairns not out	23
L-b 4, w 14, n-b 4	22
1/89 2/254 (2 wkts, 40 overs)	292

C. M. Tolley, A. A. Metcalfe, R. T. Bates, K. P. Evans, †W. M. Noon, D. B. Pennett and R. A. Pick did not bat.

Bowling: Giddins 8–0–62–1; Drakes 8–0–62–0; Law 6–0–43–0; Jarvis 8–0–62–1; Salisbury 8–0–42–0; Lenham 2–0–17–0.

Sussex

K. Greenfield c Noon b Pennett	7
J. W. Hall c Johnson b Pennett	26
M. P. Speight c Noon b Pick	20
†P. Moores lbw b Pick	2
*A. P. Wells c and b Bates	5
V. C. Drakes c Tolley b Bates	22
D. R. Law c Robinson b Bates	31
I. D. K. Salisbury c Pick b Evans	39
P. W. Jarvis run out	0
E. S. H. Giddins not out	1
N. J. Lenham absent hurt	
L-b 3, w 7	10
1/34 2/57 3/59 4/65 5/67 6/97 7/133 8/159 9/163 (31.5 overs)	163

Bowling: Evans 5.5–0–36–1; Pennett 6–0–22–2; Pick 4–0–20–2; Bates 8–0–42–3; Tolley 6–0–24–0; Cairns 2–0–16–0.

Umpires: H. D. Bird and G. I. Burgess.

At Taunton, May 12. NOTTINGHAMSHIRE beat SOMERSET by six wickets.

NOTTINGHAMSHIRE v LANCASHIRE

At Nottingham, May 19. Lancashire won by seven wickets. Toss: Lancashire.

Watkinson opened the batting for the first time in the Sunday League and proved to be an instant success with 121 from 75 balls, including seven sixes and 11 fours – his maiden century in the one-day competitions. He and Atherton put on 145 in 19 overs and set the pace for his team to overtake Nottinghamshire with nearly seven overs to go.

Nottinghamshire

P. R. Pollard b Austin	10
A. A. Metcalfe lbw b Austin	12
G. F. Archer lbw b Watkinson	14
*P. Johnson b Chapple	48
C. L. Cairns c Lloyd b Gallian	53
M. P. Dowman b Gallian	24
C. M. Tolley c Atherton b Martin	18
†W. M. Noon not out	7
R. T. Bates not out	9
L-b 7, w 7	14
1/23 2/28 3/59 4/111 5/167 6/179 7/196 (7 wkts, 38 overs)	209

R. A. Pick and D. B. Pennett did not bat.

Bowling: Austin 8–2–17–2; Martin 8–0–38–1; Watkinson 6–0–49–1; Chapple 8–0–54–1; Gallian 8–0–44–2.

Lancashire

M. A. Atherton lbw b Dowman	47	N. H. Fairbrother not out	4
*M. Watkinson c Bates b Pennett	121	L-b 4, w 1	5
J. E. R. Gallian not out	35		—
J. P. Crawley lbw b Pennett	0	1/145 2/185 3/185 (3 wkts, 31.1 overs)	212

G. D. Lloyd, I. D. Austin, †W. K. Hegg, G. Yates, G. Chapple and P. J. Martin did not bat.

Bowling: Pennett 8–0–47–2; Pick 6–0–41–0; Cairns 4–0–32–0; Tolley 5–0–28–0; Dowman 5.1–0–53–1; Archer 3–0–7–0.

Umpires: J. H. Hampshire and J. H. Harris.

NOTTINGHAMSHIRE v DURHAM

At Nottingham, June 2. Nottinghamshire won by 39 runs. Toss: Durham.

Johnson's undefeated 99 from 68 balls was the feature of a solid batting display by Nottinghamshire. Several batsmen threatened to play a major innings for Durham but the home bowlers, especially Cairns, with three for 15 in his eight overs, ensured the challenge did not materialise.

Nottinghamshire

P. R. Pollard c Scott b Foster	44	K. P. Evans not out	2
R. T. Robinson c Scott b Birbeck	47		
G. F. Archer b Foster	8	B 1, l-b 4, w 6, n-b 7	18
*P. Johnson not out	99		—
C. L. Cairns c Collingwood b Killeen	33	1/85 2/99 3/124 (5 wkts, 40 overs)	267
C. M. Tolley b Wood	16	4/210 5/264	

†W. M. Noon, R. T. Bates, M. N. Bowen and D. B. Pennett did not bat.

Bowling: Wood 8–0–57–1; Betts 5–0–39–0; Killeen 8–0–44–1; Foster 8–0–57–2; Boiling 8–0–44–0; Birbeck 3–0–21–1.

Durham

S. L. Campbell c Evans b Pennett	56	N. Killeen b Evans	4
D. A. Blenkiron b Cairns	14	M. M. Betts not out	5
*J. E. Morris c Noon b Evans	1	J. Boiling c Tolley b Pennett	0
P. D. Collingwood c Pennett b Tolley	40	B 1, l-b 9, w 9	19
M. J. Foster c Evans b Pennett	44		—
S. D. Birbeck c Bates b Cairns	24	1/33 2/34 3/115 (40 overs)	228
†C. W. Scott c Pollard b Cairns	0	4/133 5/185 6/191	
J. Wood b Evans	21	7/191 8/220 9/223	

Bowling: Evans 8–1–38–3; Pennett 8–0–49–3; Cairns 8–1–15–3; Bowen 6–0–41–0; Bates 6–0–35–0; Tolley 4–0–40–1.

Umpires: R. Julian and B. J. Meyer.

NOTTINGHAMSHIRE v NORTHAMPTONSHIRE

At Nottingham, June 9. Northamptonshire won by five wickets. Toss: Northamptonshire.

With the League's leading scorer, Johnson, failing for once, Nottinghamshire had no batsman capable of playing a substantial innings. Montgomerie and Curran eased Northamptonshire towards their fifth successive win.

Nottinghamshire

P. R. Pollard c Loye b Ambrose	2	R. T. Bates c Warren b Penberthy	13
R. T. Robinson retired hurt	7	R. A. Pick not out	32
G. F. Archer b Taylor	12	M. N. Bowen not out	23
*P. Johnson c Bailey b Ambrose	0	L-b 5, w 9, n-b 4	18
C. L. Cairns c Warren b Capel	24		——
C. M. Tolley c Ambrose b Emburey	11	1/12 2/26 3/27 (8 wkts, 40 overs)	157
K. P. Evans c and b Capel	3	4/66 5/67 6/74	
†W. M. Noon lbw b Bailey	12	7/93 8/107	

R. T. Robinson retired hurt at 22.

Bowling: Ambrose 8–3–19–2; Taylor 8–0–39–1; Capel 6–0–24–2; Emburey 7–0–30–1; Bailey 5–0–17–1; Penberthy 6–0–23–1.

Northamptonshire

R. R. Montgomerie c Bates b Pick	77	T. C. Walton not out	4
M. B. Loye c Noon b Pick	0		
*R. J. Bailey c sub b Bowen	8	L-b 3, w 2	5
K. M. Curran b Pick	46		——
D. J. Capel lbw b Bates	11	1/8 2/24 3/125 (5 wkts, 38.1 overs)	158
†R. J. Warren not out	7	4/142 5/148	

J. E. Emburey, C. E. L. Ambrose, A. L. Penberthy and J. P. Taylor did not bat.

Bowling: Evans 6–1–17–0; Pick 8–1–31–3; Cairns 7.1–1–31–0; Bowen 6–0–24–1; Bates 8–0–34–1; Tolley 3–0–18–0.

Umpires: J. C. Balderstone and N. T. Plews.

At Worcester, June 16. NOTTINGHAMSHIRE beat WORCESTERSHIRE by six wickets.

NOTTINGHAMSHIRE v GLOUCESTERSHIRE

At Nottingham, June 23. Gloucestershire won by 119 runs. Toss: Nottinghamshire.

Despite an unremarkable total, which depended mainly on Symonds and Dawson, Gloucestershire recorded their first Sunday win of the season in their sixth match. A highly efficient seam attack only just allowed Nottinghamshire to reach three figures as they succumbed inside 27 overs.

Gloucestershire

A. J. Wright run out	2	A. M. Smith not out	16
R. I. Dawson lbw b Evans	61	J. Lewis not out	0
M. W. Alleyne lbw b Bowen	13		
A. Symonds b Evans	76	B 1, l-b 11, w 2, n-b 2	16
T. H. C. Hancock st Noon b Tolley	3		——
N. J. Trainor c Tolley b Pick	20	1/4 2/33 3/143 (8 wkts, 40 overs)	220
M. C. J. Ball c Johnson b Cairns	11	4/159 5/166 6/194	
†R. C. J. Williams b Pick	2	7/196 8/216	

*C. A. Walsh did not bat.

Bowling: Evans 8–1–23–2; Pick 8–0–40–2; Bowen 5–0–45–1; Tolley 8–0–34–1; Cairns 8–0–43–1; Bates 3–0–23–0.

Nottinghamshire

P. R. Pollard c Alleyne b Smith	4	M. N. Bowen c and b Hancock	15
R. T. Robinson b Walsh	0	R. A. Pick not out	22
A. A. Metcalfe lbw b Walsh	18	K. P. Evans c Symonds b Hancock	4
*P. Johnson c Symonds b Smith	2	L-b 2, w 5	7
C. L. Cairns c Wright b Alleyne	17		—
C. M. Tolley c Williams b Lewis	10	1/1 2/16 3/20 (26.5 overs)	101
†W. M. Noon c Williams b Alleyne	0	4/38 5/46 6/51	
R. T. Bates b Lewis	2	7/56 8/60 9/90	

Bowling: Walsh 6–1–17–2; Smith 6–0–26–2; Alleyne 6–0–22–2; Lewis 7–0–28–2; Hancock 1.5–0–6–2.

Umpires: A. Clarkson and D. R. Shepherd.

At Birmingham, July 7. NOTTINGHAMSHIRE lost to WARWICKSHIRE by 18 runs.

At Southampton, July 14. NOTTINGHAMSHIRE beat HAMPSHIRE by 82 runs.

At Chelmsford, July 21. NOTTINGHAMSHIRE beat ESSEX by five wickets.

NOTTINGHAMSHIRE v GLAMORGAN

At Nottingham, August 4. Nottinghamshire won by nine wickets. Toss: Glamorgan.

Once Maynard had fallen to Bates's first ball, Glamorgan struggled to reach a defensible total against keen bowling and fielding. When Nottinghamshire replied, Robinson passed 6,000 runs in the League; he fell at 111, but his team still won comfortably.

Glamorgan

S. P. James c Tolley b Evans	2	†A. D. Shaw b Cairns	10
A. W. Evans c Tolley b Cairns	14	S. L. Watkin run out	1
*M. P. Maynard lbw b Bates	31	S. R. Barwick not out	1
P. A. Cottey b Bates	25	B 4, l-b 8, w 5, n-b 2	19
A. Dale c and b Bowen	22		—
G. P. Butcher b Bates	4	1/3 2/41 3/63 (9 wkts, 40 overs)	157
O. D. Gibson c Metcalfe b Evans	3	4/102 5/110 6/112	
R. D. B. Croft not out	25	7/121 8/147 9/150	

Bowling: Evans 8–0–25–2; Bowen 8–0–38–1; Cairns 8–1–26–2; Tolley 4–0–14–0; Bates 8–1–30–3; Dowman 4–1–12–0.

Nottinghamshire

R. T. Robinson b Barwick	55
M. P. Dowman not out	74
A. A. Metcalfe not out	16
W 7, n-b 6	13
	—
1/111 (1 wkt, 32.2 overs)	158

P. R. Pollard, *P. Johnson, C. L. Cairns, C. M. Tolley, K. P. Evans, †W. M. Noon, R. T. Bates and M. N. Bowen did not bat.

Bowling: Watkin 6–0–28–0; Gibson 6–0–36–0; Dale 4–0–18–0; Butcher 2–0–12–0; Barwick 6–0–30–1; Croft 8–0–32–0; Maynard 0.2–0–2–0.

Umpires: B. Dudleston and K. J. Lyons.

NOTTINGHAMSHIRE v MIDDLESEX

At Nottingham, August 11. Nottinghamshire won by nine wickets. Toss: Nottinghamshire.

Middlesex could not survive for even the 32 overs that rain allowed each side; Nottinghamshire reached their meagre target with nearly seven overs to spare.

Middlesex

P. N. Weekes b Evans	5
*M. R. Ramprakash run out	4
J. C. Pooley c Bates b Bowen	14
J. D. Carr c Bowen b Cairns	20
O. A. Shah run out	38
†K. R. Brown b Evans	25
K. P. Dutch c Evans b Tolley	3
J. P. Hewitt lbw b Cairns	6
R. L. Johnson not out	2
A. R. C. Fraser b Cairns	8
R. A. Fay c Bates b Cairns	0
L-b 7, w 3, n-b 2	12
1/10 2/20 3/31 4/70 5/108 6/116 7/127 8/127 9/137 (31.4 overs)	137

Bowling: Evans 8–0–34–2; Bowen 8–1–34–1; Tolley 8–1–25–1; Cairns 5.4–0–22–4; Dowman 2–0–15–0.

Nottinghamshire

R. T. Robinson not out	66
M. P. Dowman c Shah b Fraser	33
*P. Johnson not out	19
L-b 6, w 9, n-b 6	21
1/83 (1 wkt, 25.1 overs)	139

P. R. Pollard, A. A. Metcalfe, C. M. Tolley, C. L. Cairns, K. P. Evans, †W. M. Noon, R. T. Bates and M. N. Bowen did not bat.

Bowling: Fay 8–0–36–0; Johnson 5–0–27–0; Fraser 6–0–31–1; Weekes 2–0–21–0; Hewitt 4–1–14–0; Ramprakash 0.1–0–4–0.

Umpires: H. D. Bird and N. T. Plews.

At Derby, August 18. NOTTINGHAMSHIRE beat DERBYSHIRE by eight wickets.

NOTTINGHAMSHIRE v SURREY

At Nottingham, August 25. No result (abandoned).

At Tunbridge Wells, September 1. NOTTINGHAMSHIRE beat KENT by seven wickets.

NOTTINGHAMSHIRE v LEICESTERSHIRE

At Nottingham, September 8. Nottinghamshire won by six wickets. Toss: Nottinghamshire.

Leicestershire's innings, interrupted three times by squally showers, began well but fell away towards its premature end. With one eye on the weather, Johnson struck out, hitting three sixes and six fours in an unbeaten 85 from 61 balls to ensure a win that put Nottinghamshire level with Surrey on 46 points at the top of the table.

Leicestershire

*P. V. Simmons b Cairns	35	C. C. Remy c Robinson b Tolley	14
V. J. Wells c Tolley b Evans	38	G. J. Parsons not out	2
B. F. Smith c Tolley b Bates	26	L-b 4, w 4, n-b 8	16
G. I. Macmillan c and b Bates	6		—
A. Habib lbw b Cairns	1	1/65 2/110 3/115 (7 wkts, 33 overs)	194
D. L. Maddy not out	33	4/119 5/123	
†P. A. Nixon c Noon b Bates	23	6/163 7/191	

D. Williamson and A. R. K. Pierson did not bat.

Bowling: Evans 7–0–26–1; Bowen 5–0–49–0; Tolley 7–0–51–1; Cairns 6–0–21–2; Bates 8–0–43–3.

Nottinghamshire

R. T. Robinson c Simmons b Pierson	48	G. F. Archer not out	4
M. P. Dowman b Parsons	10	L-b 6, w 1	7
*P. Johnson not out	85		—
C. L. Cairns c Wells b Pierson	38	1/23 2/124 (4 wkts, 30.2 overs)	198
P. R. Pollard c Macmillan b Pierson	6	3/182 4/193	

C. M. Tolley, K. P. Evans, †W. M. Noon, R. T. Bates and M. N. Bowen did not bat.

Bowling: Parsons 6–0–40–1; Simmons 6–0–28–0; Williamson 8–0–50–0; Pierson 7–1–21–3; Remy 2–0–40–0; Maddy 1.2–0–13–0.

Umpires: A. Clarkson and M. J. Kitchen.

At Scarborough, September 15. NOTTINGHAMSHIRE beat YORKSHIRE by 24 runs.

SOMERSET

SOMERSET v SURREY

At Taunton, May 5. Somerset won by 53 runs. Toss: Surrey. First-team debut: B. C. Hollioake.

A Somerset League record second-wicket partnership of 183 between Bowler and Ecclestone took their side to a formidable total. Ecclestone scored 130, his second one-day hundred in ten days, off 112 balls with 11 fours and five sixes. Stewart replied with a century for Surrey, but had too little support.

Somerset

P. D. Bowler lbw b Julian	66	R. J. Harden not out	15
S. Lee c Stewart b Lewis	0	L-b 13, w 14, n-b 2	29
S. C. Ecclestone lbw b A. J. Hollioake	130		—
†R. J. Turner c Bicknell b A. J. Hollioake	26	1/0 2/183 (4 wkts, 40 overs)	285
G. D. Rose not out	19	3/228 4/267	

*A. N. Hayhurst, K. A. Parsons, A. R. Caddick, H. R. J. Trump and K. J. Shine did not bat.

Bowling: Bicknell 8–2–51–0; Lewis 4–0–15–1; Julian 8–0–59–1; A. J. Hollioake 8–0–62–2; Pearson 8–0–51–0; B. C. Hollioake 4–0–34–0.

Surrey

D. M. Ward b Caddick	3	B. C. Hollioake run out	3
A. D. Brown b Caddick	13	M. P. Bicknell c and b Lee	5
*†A. J. Stewart c Harden b Lee	101	R. M. Pearson not out	1
G. P. Thorpe c Harden b Rose	34	L-b 4, w 6, n-b 2	12
A. J. Hollioake c Parsons b Hayhurst	41		—
B. P. Julian b Hayhurst	5	1/20 2/21 3/103 (36.5 overs)	232
M. A. Butcher st Turner b Hayhurst	6	4/181 5/195 6/213	
C. C. Lewis run out	8	7/217 8/222 9/230	

Bowling: Caddick 6–0–44–2; Shine 5–0–26–0; Trump 8–0–53–0; Rose 6–0–41–1; Lee 6.5–0–43–2; Hayhurst 5–0–21–3.

Umpires: D. J. Constant and K. E. Palmer.

SOMERSET v NOTTINGHAMSHIRE

At Taunton, May 12. Nottinghamshire won by six wickets. Toss: Nottinghamshire.

With Cairns hitting three leg-side sixes, two of them out of the ground, and Johnson taking 42 off 30 balls, Nottinghamshire overtook Somerset's respectable total with time to spare.

Somerset

M. N. Lathwell c Metcalfe b Tolley	28	M. E. Trescothick run out	10
*P. D. Bowler c Pick b Bates	24	P. C. L. Holloway not out	3
S. C. Ecclestone c Pollard b Tolley	18	L-b 2, w 4	6
R. J. Harden c Johnson b Cairns	66		—
S. Lee c Johnson b Pick	68	1/41 2/69 3/76 (8 wkts, 40 overs)	232
†R. J. Turner b Pick	3	4/208 5/212 6/213	
G. D. Rose b Cairns	6	7/222 8/232	

A. R. Caddick and H. R. J. Trump did not bat.

Bowling: Pennett 8–0–44–0; Pick 8–0–39–2; Tolley 8–0–50–2; Cairns 8–1–42–2; Bates 6–0–43–1; Archer 2–0–12–0.

Nottinghamshire

P. R. Pollard lbw b Trump	48	C. L. Cairns not out	31
R. T. Robinson b Ecclestone	19	L-b 4, w 7, n-b 2	13
G. F. Archer c Holloway b Trump	47		—
*P. Johnson c Caddick b Trump	42	1/54 2/85 (4 wkts, 36.3 overs)	234
A. A. Metcalfe not out	34	3/151 4/175	

C. M. Tolley, †W. M. Noon, R. T. Bates, R. A. Pick and D. B. Pennett did not bat.

Bowling: Caddick 6.3–0–35–0; Rose 8–1–58–0; Ecclestone 8–1–49–1; Lee 6–0–44–0; Trump 8–0–44–3.

Umpires: B. Leadbeater and R. Palmer.

At Bristol, May 19. GLOUCESTERSHIRE v SOMERSET. No result (abandoned).

SOMERSET v NORTHAMPTONSHIRE

At Taunton, May 26. Northamptonshire won by one wicket. Toss: Northamptonshire.

At 7.40 p.m., Ambrose got an inside edge to the fine-leg boundary and Northamptonshire won in the dark by one wicket with one ball to spare; he and last man Taylor had put on 18 in eight balls. Rain reduced the match to 28 overs a side; Somerset would not even have been in contention but for Hayhurst and Turner, who put on 86 in 12 overs after they collapsed to 40 for five. Victory gave Northamptonshire sole possession of the top of the table.

Somerset

M. N. Lathwell c Curran b Taylor	9	†R. J. Turner c Warren b Ambrose	39
P. D. Bowler lbw b Taylor	5	J. I. D. Kerr not out	4
M. E. Trescothick lbw b Curran	5	B 1, l-b 2, w 6, n-b 2	11
S. Lee c Fordham b Taylor	2		—
G. D. Rose c Ambrose b Curran	6	1/13 2/25 3/25 (6 wkts, 28 overs)	141
*A. N. Hayhurst not out	60	4/31 5/40 6/126	

K. J. Shine, A. R. Caddick and H. R. J. Trump did not bat.

Bowling: Ambrose 6–1–28–1; Taylor 6–0–22–3; Curran 6–0–33–2; Penberthy 5–0–27–0; Capel 5–0–28–0.

Northamptonshire

R. R. Montgomerie c Shine b Rose	6	J. E. Emburey b Caddick	5
A. Fordham lbw b Caddick	12	C. E. L. Ambrose not out	11
*R. J. Bailey c Trump b Shine	28	J. P. Taylor not out	9
M. B. Loye c Turner b Caddick	8	L-b 12, w 5	17
D. J. Capel b Shine	29		
K. M. Curran c Caddick b Shine	9	1/14 2/22 3/32 (9 wkts, 27.5 overs)	145
†R. J. Warren c Turner b Shine	2	4/86 5/95 6/103	
A. L. Penberthy b Lee	9	7/110 8/123 9/127	

Bowling: Caddick 5–1–25–3; Rose 6–0–26–1; Lee 4.5–0–33–1; Shine 6–0–31–4; Trump 6–0–18–0.

Umpires: J. H. Hampshire and G. Sharp.

SOMERSET v WARWICKSHIRE

At Taunton, June 9. Somerset won by 26 runs. Toss: Warwickshire.

Australian Shane Lee's all-round performance was the difference between the sides in Richard Harden's benefit match. Injury prevented Harden from playing, but Lee, with 71 in 65 balls, and Lathwell put on a county-best fourth-wicket stand of 156. Lee then took three wickets as Warwickshire's reply fell away after a rousing opening from Neil Smith. Turner's brilliant catch to dismiss Reeve was a special highlight.

Somerset

M. N. Lathwell c Giles b Welch	93	*A. N. Hayhurst not out	15
P. D. Bowler st Piper b Reeve	1	K. A. Parsons not out	2
S. C. Ecclestone c Piper b Pollock	12	L-b 4, w 15	19
M. E. Trescothick b N. M. K. Smith	18		
S. Lee c Reeve b Pollock	71	1/6 2/19 3/56 (7 wkts, 40 overs)	249
G. D. Rose c and b Brown	3	4/212 5/213	
†R. J. Turner b Brown	15	6/222 7/247	

A. R. Caddick and H. R. J. Trump did not bat.

Bowling: Reeve 8–0–36–1; Pollock 8–0–36–2; Welch 6–0–54–1; N. M. K. Smith 8–0–32–1; Giles 2–0–22–0; P. A. Smith 4–0–22–0; Brown 4–0–43–2.

Warwickshire

A. J. Moles c Lathwell b Rose	3	P. A. Smith c sub b Parsons	8
N. M. K. Smith c Parsons b Trump	89	A. F. Giles not out	6
D. R. Brown c Caddick b Lee	32	†K. J. Piper c Caddick b Hayhurst	0
D. P. Ostler c Ecclestone b Trump	9	L-b 9, w 6	15
T. L. Penney c Parsons b Hayhurst	44		
S. M. Pollock b Lee	17	1/12 2/86 3/117 (39.3 overs)	223
*D. A. Reeve c Turner b Hayhurst	0	4/156 5/185 6/186	
G. Welch lbw b Lee	0	7/192 8/208 9/222	

Bowling: Caddick 8–0–36–0; Rose 7–0–37–1; Lee 8–0–37–3; Trump 8–0–53–2; Hayhurst 7.3–0–38–3; Parsons 1–0–13–1.

Umpires: R. Julian and R. Palmer.

At Swansea, June 16. SOMERSET beat GLAMORGAN by 24 runs.

SOMERSET v WORCESTERSHIRE

At Bath, June 23. Worcestershire won by seven wickets. Toss: Worcestershire.

Worcestershire captain Moody was the major influence in his side's comfortable victory. He opened the bowling and dismissed Somerset's top three; only some spirited defiance from the tail gave them any sort of total. Moody then opened the batting as well and laid the foundations of the Worcestershire innings with 50.

Somerset

M. N. Lathwell c Rhodes b Moody	6	J. D. Batty lbw b Illingworth	6
M. E. Trescothick c Sheriyar b Moody	22	A. R. Caddick lbw b Lampitt	25
S. C. Ecclestone c Curtis b Moody	1	H. R. J. Trump not out	14
S. Lee c Rhodes b Newport	1	L-b 4, w 10, n-b 9	23
*A. N. Hayhurst c Rhodes b Newport	1		—
G. D. Rose b Illingworth	32	1/7 2/12 3/23 (39 overs)	150
†R. J. Turner c Rhodes b Lampitt	4	4/25 5/48 6/65	
K. A. Parsons c Lampitt b Newport	15	7/87 8/97 9/121	

Bowling: Newport 8–2–21–3; Moody 8–1–27–3; Lampitt 8–1–24–2; Sheriyar 7–0–43–0; Illingworth 8–0–31–2.

Worcestershire

*T. M. Moody b Trump	50	V. S. Solanki not out	11
T. S. Curtis c Turner b Rose	18	B 2, l-b 13, w 2, n-b 2	19
K. R. Spiring not out	31		—
W. P. C. Weston c Parsons b Lee	23	1/59 2/93 3/134 (3 wkts, 34 overs)	152

M. J. Church, †S. J. Rhodes, P. J. Newport, R. K. Illingworth, S. R. Lampitt and A. Sheriyar did not bat.

Bowling: Caddick 6–0–23–0; Rose 8–2–24–1; Lee 7–0–27–1; Hayhurst 7–0–34–0; Trump 6–1–29–1.

Umpires: J. C. Balderstone and V. A. Holder.

At Manchester, June 30. SOMERSET beat LANCASHIRE by one run.

At Hove, July 14. SOMERSET lost to SUSSEX by 12 runs.

At Scarborough, July 28. SOMERSET beat YORKSHIRE by two runs.

SOMERSET v HAMPSHIRE

At Taunton, August 4. Hampshire won by 44 runs. Toss: Hampshire.

Smith's ninth League hundred – with 18 fours, two sixes and a second 50 from only 37 balls – almost alone gave Hampshire a reasonable total. Then Stephenson bowled an economical spell, including three valuable wickets, to eliminate Somerset's challenge.

Hampshire

J. S. Laney lbw b Caddick	25	K. D. James not out	4
M. Keech c Trump b Rose	6		
R. A. Smith not out	122	L-b 2, w 4, n-b 2	8
P. R. Whitaker c Turner b Lee	18		—
W. S. Kendall c Turner b Caddick	28	1/32 2/32 3/89 (5 wkts, 40 overs)	229
*J. P. Stephenson lbw b Lee	18	4/190 5/225	

†A. N. Aymes, S. D. Udal, S. M. Milburn and J. N. B. Bovill did not bat.

Bowling: Caddick 8–0–48–2; Rose 8–1–34–1; Parsons 6–0–34–0; Trescothick 2–0–15–0; Lee 8–0–49–2; Trump 8–0–47–0.

Somerset

M. N. Lathwell c Keech b Stephenson ... 49
M. E. Trescothick c Aymes b Milburn ... 5
S. C. Ecclestone b James ... 21
S. Lee run out ... 14
R. J. Harden b Whitaker ... 16
*P. D. Bowler lbw b Stephenson ... 1
K. A. Parsons lbw b Whitaker ... 1
†R. J. Turner c Laney b Stephenson ... 1
G. D. Rose c Stephenson b Udal ... 16
A. R. Caddick c Smith b Udal ... 39
H. R. J. Trump not out ... 8
L-b 7, w 3, n-b 4 ... 14

1/10 2/62 3/78 4/108 5/112 6/115 7/120 8/122 9/160 (36.5 overs) 185

Bowling: Stephenson 8–0–23–3; Milburn 8–0–39–1; James 8–0–53–1; Udal 5.5–0–33–2; Bovill 2–0–10–0; Whitaker 5–0–20–2.

Umpires: A. A. Jones and M. J. Kitchen.

SOMERSET v ESSEX

At Taunton, August 11. Somerset won by eight wickets. Toss: Somerset.

Despite reaching 77 for one at the half-way stage of their innings, shortened by the weather to 32 overs, Essex capitulated against the medium-pace of Kerr and Lee. Once the Somerset openers had put on 90, there was little doubt about the result.

Essex

D. D. J. Robinson c Kerr b Trescothick .. 28
A. J. E. Hibbert retired hurt ... 8
R. C. Irani c Rose b Kerr ... 58
S. G. Law c Trescothick b Trump ... 15
*P. J. Prichard b Kerr ... 16
†R. J. Rollins b Lee ... 1
J. J. B. Lewis b Kerr ... 4
M. C. Ilott b Lee ... 3
A. P. Grayson c Trump b Lee ... 4
S. J. W. Andrew not out ... 0
L-b 3, w 8 ... 11

1/42 2/92 3/120 4/121 5/140 6/141 7/148 8/148 (8 wkts, 32 overs) 148

P. M. Such did not bat.

A. J. E. Hibbert retired hurt at 30.

Bowling: Rose 6–0–20–0; Kerr 6–0–27–3; Parsons 3–0–18–0; Trescothick 3–0–13–1; Trump 7–0–39–1; Lee 7–1–28–3.

Somerset

M. N. Lathwell st Rollins b Grayson ... 51
*P. D. Bowler not out ... 68
S. C. Ecclestone run out ... 1
R. J. Harden not out ... 27
L-b 2, w 3 ... 5

1/90 2/95 (2 wkts, 30.5 overs) 152

M. E. Trescothick, S. Lee, K. A. Parsons, †R. J. Turner, G. D. Rose, J. I. D. Kerr and H. R. J. Trump did not bat.

Bowling: Andrew 4–0–16–0; Ilott 6–0–22–0; Such 7–0–30–0; Irani 2–0–16–0; Grayson 7–0–37–1; Law 4.5–0–29–0.

Umpires: G. I. Burgess and T. E. Jesty.

At Canterbury, August 18. SOMERSET beat KENT by three wickets.

SOMERSET v DURHAM

At Weston-super-Mare, August 25. Somerset won by seven wickets. Toss: Durham.

Caddick's fifth over started a spell of three wickets in 12 balls that reduced Durham to 51 for three. A 107-run partnership between Roseberry and Daley halted the slide, but half-centuries from Ecclestone and Bowler took Somerset most of the way home.

Durham

S. L. Campbell c Turner b Caddick	15	†D. G. C. Ligertwood not out	1
S. Hutton c Turner b Caddick	22		
D. M. Cox c Trump b Caddick	7	L-b 7, w 4, n-b 2	13
J. A. Daley b Rose	47		—
*M. A. Roseberry b Lee	63	1/32 2/46 3/51 (5 wkts, 40 overs)	183
D. A. Blenkiron not out	15	4/158 5/182	

J. Boiling, S. J. E. Brown, N. Killeen and A. Walker did not bat.

Bowling: Caddick 8–0–41–3; Rose 8–0–28–1; Parsons 8–1–38–0; Lee 8–1–27–1; Trump 8–1–42–0.

Somerset

M. N. Lathwell b Brown	4	S. Lee not out	25
*P. D. Bowler c Campbell b Walker	62	L-b 2, w 2, n-b 2	6
S. C. Ecclestone c Ligertwood b Brown	75		—
R. J. Harden not out	15	1/4 2/140 3/154 (3 wkts, 37.1 overs)	187

M. E. Trescothick, K. A. Parsons, †R. J. Turner, G. D. Rose, A. R. Caddick and H. R. J. Trump did not bat.

Bowling: Brown 8–0–36–2; Walker 7–0–26–1; Killeen 8–0–46–0; Cox 8–0–44–0; Boiling 6–0–29–0; Daley 0.1–0–4–0.

Umpires: K. J. Lyons and R. A. White.

At Leicester, September 1. SOMERSET beat LEICESTERSHIRE by seven wickets.

SOMERSET v DERBYSHIRE

At Taunton, September 8. Somerset won by 12 runs. Toss: Derbyshire.

Trescothick was dropped down the order and came in at No. 6 with a powerful innings to lift the Somerset total. Derbyshire were well set at 152 for one, with Jones seemingly in command, but then lost seven wickets for 54.

Somerset

M. N. Lathwell lbw b Cork	2	†R. J. Turner not out	20
*P. D. Bowler c Barnett b DeFreitas	40		
S. Lee c Barnett b Harris	30	L-b 7, w 3, n-b 2	12
R. J. Harden c Jones b DeFreitas	40		—
G. D. Rose c Dean b Roberts	16	1/4 2/52 3/115 (5 wkts, 40 overs)	221
M. E. Trescothick not out	61	4/115 5/162	

K. A. Parsons, J. I. D. Kerr, A. R. Caddick and H. R. J. Trump did not bat.

Bowling: Cork 8–0–41–1; Dean 5–1–24–0; Wells 7–0–34–0; Harris 8–0–33–1; Roberts 8–0–58–1; DeFreitas 4–0–24–2.

Derbyshire

*D. M. Jones st Turner b Kerr	81
K. J. Barnett c Parsons b Trump	34
C. J. Adams c Trescothick b Trump	28
G. A. Khan b Kerr	7
D. G. Cork lbw b Trump	7
C. M. Wells c Lathwell b Lee	11
P. A. J. DeFreitas run out	16
†K. M. Krikken b Caddick	0
G. M. Roberts not out	0
A. J. Harris not out	0
B 3, l-b 16, w 6	25
1/102 2/152 3/157 4/171 5/173 6/199 7/205 8/206 (8 wkts, 40 overs)	209

K. J. Dean did not bat.

Bowling: Caddick 8–0–36–1; Rose 6–0–30–0; Kerr 7–0–23–2; Parsons 3–0–16–0; Trump 8–0–41–3; Lee 8–0–44–1.

Umpires: J. D. Bond and R. Julian.

At Uxbridge, September 15. SOMERSET lost to MIDDLESEX by four wickets.

SURREY

At Taunton, May 5. SURREY lost to SOMERSET by 53 runs.

SURREY v KENT

At The Oval, May 12. Surrey won by 150 runs. Toss: Surrey.

Surrey quickly moved to an unassailable 307, after Ward and Brown opened with 127 in 18 overs; Ward hit five sixes and Brown four. Kent began brightly but a steady fall of wickets halted their momentum. Surrey fielded two sets of brothers, the Bicknells and the Hollioakes. It was the first time any county had done this since Surrey themselves played both the Bedsers, Alec and Eric, and the Pratts, Derek and Ron, against Oxford in 1957.

Surrey

D. M. Ward run out	112
A. D. Brown b Ealham	84
A. J. Hollioake c Llong b Fleming	25
C. C. Lewis c Walker b Fleming	27
B. P. Julian not out	34
B. C. Hollioake lbw b Fleming	0
D. J. Bicknell not out	2
B 6, l-b 10, w 5, n-b 2	23
1/127 2/198 3/251 4/296 5/305 (5 wkts, 40 overs)	307

*†A. J. Stewart, G. P. Thorpe, M. P. Bicknell and R. M. Pearson did not bat.

Bowling: Wren 6–0–43–0; Thompson 3–0–30–0; Hooper 8–0–50–0; McCague 8–0–43–0; Ealham 7–0–63–1; Fleming 7–0–46–3; Llong 1–0–16–0.

Kent

T. R. Ward c Stewart b M. P. Bicknell	24
M. V. Fleming c Julian b M. P. Bicknell	4
C. L. Hooper c Stewart b Julian	43
G. R. Cowdrey c Brown b Julian	10
M. A. Ealham c Thorpe b A. J. Hollioake	10
M. J. Walker run out	8
N. J. Llong c Stewart b Julian	5
*†S. A. Marsh lbw b A. J. Hollioake	10
M. J. McCague c Ward b A. J. Hollioake	16
J. B. D. Thompson not out	6
T. N. Wren b A. J. Hollioake	5
L-b 2, w 8, n-b 6	16
1/6 2/49 3/69 4/91 5/111 6/111 7/120 8/132 9/150 (26.5 overs)	157

Bowling: M. P. Bicknell 6–0–39–2; Lewis 4–0–24–0; Julian 6–0–38–3; A. J. Hollioake 7.5–0–34–4; B. C. Hollioake 3–0–20–0.

Umpires: K. J. Lyons and B. J. Meyer.

At Gloucester, May 26. SURREY beat GLOUCESTERSHIRE by 72 runs.

SURREY v DERBYSHIRE

At The Oval, June 2. Surrey won by 50 runs. Toss: Derbyshire. First-team debut: K. J. Dean.

Surrey recovered from 16 for four, thanks to a century from Stewart and valuable contributions from Shahid and Julian. An inspired spell from the younger of the Hollioake brothers, Ben, gave him five for ten as seven Derbyshire wickets fell for 23. Hollioake's bowling was fast as well as straight, and Stewart, who had been behind the stumps, said he hit the gloves harder than any of the established quick bowlers. Jones was run out at the non-striker's end, backing up, when the ball was deflected on to the stumps as Adam Hollioake dropped a difficult caught and bowled chance. The game ended with an unavailing last-wicket stand of 60 between Dean and Malcolm, a League record which stood for only five weeks until it was beaten by Chapple and Martin of Lancashire.

Surrey

D. M. Ward c Krikken b Cork	0
A. D. Brown run out	0
*†A. J. Stewart not out	112
A. J. Hollioake b Dean	0
D. J. Bicknell lbw b Cork	7
N. Shahid c Cork b Barnett	47
B. P. Julian c Jones b Malcolm	41
L-b 4, w 10	14
1/0 2/4 3/6 4/16 5/134 6/221 (6 wkts, 40 overs)	221

B. C. Hollioake, M. P. Bicknell, R. M. Pearson and J. E. Benjamin did not bat.

Bowling: Cork 8–1–19–2; Dean 8–0–19–1; Harris 7–0–44–0; Malcolm 8–0–64–1; Jones 3–0–22–0; Barnett 4–0–33–1; Aldred 2–0–16–0.

Derbyshire

*D. M. Jones run out	26
K. J. Barnett c Stewart b M. P. Bicknell	15
C. J. Adams c A. J. Hollioake b B. C. Hollioake	25
J. E. Owen b B. C. Hollioake	12
A. S. Rollins c and b A. J. Hollioake	2
†K. M. Krikken b A. J. Hollioake	4
D. G. Cork lbw b B. C. Hollioake	2
P. Aldred c Ward b B. C. Hollioake	9
A. J. Harris b B. C. Hollioake	0
K. J. Dean not out	8
D. E. Malcolm b Pearson	42
B 4, l-b 18, w 2, n-b 2	26
1/45 2/61 3/88 4/92 5/97 6/98 7/100 8/100 9/111 (36.5 overs)	171

Bowling: M. P. Bicknell 8–0–34–1; Benjamin 7–0–41–0; Julian 4–0–15–0; A. J. Hollioake 8–0–34–2; B. C. Hollioake 8–1–10–5; Pearson 1.5–0–15–1.

Umpires: N. T. Plews and P. Willey.

At Leeds, June 9. SURREY lost to YORKSHIRE by eight wickets.

SURREY v LEICESTERSHIRE

At The Oval, June 16. Surrey won by ten wickets. Toss: Leicestershire.

The shortest Sunday League match on record was completed in 26.3 overs and one hour 53 minutes, 20 minutes quicker than Essex v Northamptonshire at Ilford in 1971. Leicestershire were all out for 48, having scored 311 (and still lost) in 40 overs the previous week. The innings plunged to disaster after Wells was brilliantly caught by Brown at third man in the second over. There was just one boundary and only Extras reached double figures. Darren Bicknell and Brown then blazed to victory in just 27 balls.

Leicestershire

P. V. Simmons c Thorpe b M. P. Bicknell	0	G. J. Parsons b Julian	2
V. J. Wells c Brown b Lewis	0	D. Williamson not out	2
B. F. Smith c Stewart b Lewis	8	A. R. K. Pierson b Benjamin	0
*J. J. Whitaker b Lewis	3	B 1, l-b 1, w 6, n-b 4	12
J. M. Dakin c Stewart b M. P. Bicknell	8		
D. L. Maddy c Thorpe b M. P. Bicknell	1	1/0 2/0 3/12 (22 overs)	48
†P. A. Nixon lbw b Benjamin	4	4/15 5/23 6/26	
C. C. Remy b Julian	8	7/33 8/37 9/47	

Bowling: M. P. Bicknell 8–2–16–3; Lewis 6–0–13–3; Benjamin 5–0–10–2; Julian 3–0–7–2.

Surrey

D. J. Bicknell not out	15
A. D. Brown not out	30
W 3, n-b 2	5
(no wkt, 4.3 overs)	50

N. Shahid, *†A. J. Stewart, G. P. Thorpe, A. J. Hollioake, C. C. Lewis, B. P. Julian, M. P. Bicknell, R. M. Pearson and J. E. Benjamin did not bat.

Bowling: Simmons 2–0–10–0; Parsons 2–0–24–0; Dakin 0.3–0–16–0.

Umpires: R. Julian and M. J. Kitchen.

At Stockton-on-Tees, June 23. SURREY beat DURHAM by 59 runs.

At Southend, June 30. SURREY lost to ESSEX by 27 runs.

SURREY v MIDDLESEX

At The Oval, July 7. Surrey won by eight wickets. Toss: Surrey.

Middlesex, the League leaders, were bowled out for 131, which would have been even more humiliating but for 28 extras – 21 of which were wides as heavy cloud cover induced the ball to swing alarmingly. After ten overs of Surrey's reply, the sun appeared to ease conditions and their batsmen moved to a comfortable success; they now trailed Middlesex by only two points.

Middlesex

P. N. Weekes c Kersey b M. P. Bicknell	1	R. L. Johnson c B. C. Hollioake b A. J. Hollioake	10
M. R. Ramprakash c B. C. Hollioake b M. P. Bicknell	7	M. A. Feltham run out	2
*M. W. Gatting b Benjamin	18	A. R. C. Fraser not out	0
J. C. Pooley run out	16	L-b 7, w 21	28
J. D. Carr c Kersey b B. C. Hollioake	17		
†K. R. Brown b B. C. Hollioake	11	1/2 2/15 3/43 (33.2 overs)	131
O. A. Shah c Ward b B. C. Hollioake	20	4/54 5/82 6/100	
J. P. Hewitt b Pearson	1	7/112 8/118 9/129	

Bowling: M. P. Bicknell 8–1–29–2; Benjamin 8–0–27–1; Julian 2–0–10–0; B. C. Hollioake 8–0–42–3; A. J. Hollioake 3.2–0–7–1; Pearson 4–0–9–1.

Surrey

D. J. Bicknell not out	52
A. D. Brown c Hewitt b Fraser	23
N. Shahid c sub b Carr	18
D. M. Ward not out	22
B 1, l-b 5, w 7, n-b 4	17
1/57 2/95 (2 wkts, 28.4 overs)	132

B. C. Hollioake, *A. J. Hollioake, B. P. Julian, †G. J. Kersey, M. P. Bicknell, R. M. Pearson and J. E. Benjamin did not bat.

Bowling: Fraser 8–1–30–1; Feltham 3–1–8–0; Johnson 7–0–43–0; Carr 6–2–16–1; Weekes 4–1–21–0; Ramprakash 0.4–0–8–0.

Umpires: J. D. Bond and A. G. T. Whitehead.

SURREY v WORCESTERSHIRE

At The Oval, July 14. Surrey won by eight wickets. Toss: Surrey.

Tight bowling dismissed Worcestershire for 175 – though Surrey were fined £660 for bowling only 38 overs in the time specified for 40. Then rain meant that their reply was reduced to 34 overs. At first, their revised target was 149. But Worcestershire's twelfth man, Matthew Rawnsley, was sent out to show the umpires the regulation indicating that the calculation should be made on the basis of 38 overs, not 40. The target was then raised to 157; it made no difference. Brown scored 55 from 39 balls; though he became Illingworth's 200th League victim, he had already made sure the task would present no problems. Surrey won with ten overs left and went top of the League table.

Worcestershire

*T. M. Moody b Bicknell	20
M. J. Church c Thorpe b Bicknell	11
G. A. Hick b Julian	21
K. R. Spiring b B. C. Hollioake	20
V. S. Solanki c Stewart b A. J. Hollioake	23
D. A. Leatherdale c Ward b A. J. Hollioake	13
S. R. Lampitt c Thorpe b Julian	14
†S. J. Rhodes c Lewis b A. J. Hollioake	8
R. K. Illingworth lbw b Lewis	12
S. W. K. Ellis run out	1
A. Sheriyar not out	11
L-b 9, w 12	21
1/25 2/44 3/64 4/105 5/105 6/139 7/142 8/153 9/156 (39.5 overs)	175

Bowling: Bicknell 6–0–28–2; Lewis 6.5–0–23–1; Julian 8–0–28–2; Benjamin 6–0–26–0; B. C. Hollioake 5–1–21–1; A. J. Hollioake 8–0–40–3.

Surrey

*†A. J. Stewart c Rhodes b Lampitt	7
A. D. Brown c Solanki b Illingworth	55
G. P. Thorpe not out	36
A. J. Hollioake not out	47
B 2, l-b 5, w 8, n-b 2	17
1/38 2/90 (2 wkts, 24 overs)	162

B. C. Hollioake, D. M. Ward, C. C. Lewis, B. P. Julian, M. P. Bicknell, R. M. Pearson and J. E. Benjamin did not bat.

Bowling: Ellis 3–1–21–0; Moody 6–0–35–0; Lampitt 6–1–32–1; Illingworth 5–0–23–1; Sheriyar 3–1–32–0; Church 1–0–12–0.

Umpires: J. H. Harris and R. Palmer.

SURREY v SUSSEX

At Guildford, July 21. Sussex won by 75 runs. Toss: Sussex.

Sussex were 71 for five when two batsmen emerged from different parts of the pavilion to join Speight in the middle. Salisbury reached the crease ahead of Drakes, and proceeded to add 137 in 19 overs with centurion Speight, a tournament record for the sixth wicket. Adam Hollioake took five wickets and was then Surrey's main contributor with the bat, scoring 74 from 50 balls in a lost cause.

Sussex

K. Newell b Benjamin	6
R. K. Rao run out	11
M. P. Speight b Pearson	117
K. Greenfield c B. C. Hollioake b Benjamin	0
*†P. Moores c Julian b A. J. Hollioake	0
D. R. Law c Thorpe b A. J. Hollioake	12
I. D. K. Salisbury c Benjamin b M. P. Bicknell	42
V. C. Drakes c Thorpe b A. J. Hollioake	18
P. W. Jarvis c Pearson b A. J. Hollioake	43
R. S. C. Martin-Jenkins b A. J. Hollioake	0
J. D. Lewry not out	0
L-b 23, w 7, n-b 2	32
1/7 2/41 3/47 4/53 5/71 6/208 7/223 8/259 9/260 (40 overs)	281

Bowling: M. P. Bicknell 8–0–63–1; Benjamin 7–0–26–2; A. J. Hollioake 8–0–44–5; Julian 5–0–31–0; B. C. Hollioake 4–0–34–0; Pearson 8–0–60–1.

Surrey

D. J. Bicknell b Jarvis	36
A. D. Brown c Salisbury b Law	8
*†A. J. Stewart c Rao b Lewry	2
G. P. Thorpe b Drakes	22
A. J. Hollioake b Drakes	74
D. M. Ward b Jarvis	5
B. P. Julian c Moores b Salisbury	21
B. C. Hollioake c Speight b Salisbury	12
M. P. Bicknell not out	1
J. E. Benjamin b Drakes	0
R. M. Pearson b Drakes	1
L-b 13, w 7, n-b 4	24
1/10 2/15 3/59 4/111 5/123 6/160 7/197 8/202 9/204 (32 overs)	206

Bowling: Lewry 4–0–19–1; Law 8–1–45–1; Drakes 8–0–50–4; Jarvis 5–0–36–2; Martin-Jenkins 1–0–6–0; Salisbury 6–0–37–2.

Umpires: J. H. Hampshire and P. Willey.

At Southampton, July 28. SURREY beat HAMPSHIRE by 23 runs.

At Manchester, August 11. SURREY beat LANCASHIRE on scoring-rate.

At Nottingham, August 25. NOTTINGHAMSHIRE v SURREY. No result (abandoned).

SURREY v WARWICKSHIRE

At The Oval, September 1. Surrey won by two wickets. Toss: Warwickshire.

Victory in a tight finish was instrumental in knocking Warwickshire out of contention, and sending Surrey towards the title. But the game deserves to be remembered for the 36 wides: 15 of them were gifted by Surrey to Warwickshire, who then proceeded to bowl 21. Not surprisingly, Surrey could not bowl 40 overs in the allotted time. They were fined £1,320 and were allowed only 37 overs to score the 186 they needed. Left with three to win from the final over with three wickets to fall, Surrey were helped by Munton's decision to spread the field and they were able to pick out the spaces for victory. Warwickshire's Brown had an excellent all-round game.

Warwickshire

W. G. Khan c Butcher b Lewis	9	G. Welch not out	9
N. M. K. Smith c Kersey b Julian	12	G. C. Small c D. J. Bicknell b Lewis	3
D. P. Ostler c Kersey b Benjamin	6	*T. A. Munton b Hollioake	3
D. R. Brown c Lewis b Benjamin	66	L-b 10, w 15, n-b 2	27
T. L. Penney c Butcher b Benjamin	0		
M. Burns b Pearson	29	1/19 2/37 3/43 (39.4 overs)	185
†K. J. Piper b Pearson	12	4/43 5/123 6/156	
A. F. Giles c Butcher b Pearson	9	7/165 8/170 9/175	

Bowling: M. P. Bicknell 6–0–22–0; Lewis 8–1–25–2; Julian 7–1–41–1; Benjamin 8–0–33–3; Hollioake 4.4–1–21–1; Pearson 6–0–33–3.

Surrey

M. A. Butcher c Piper b Small	48	M. P. Bicknell not out	5
A. D. Brown c Piper b Brown	6	R. M. Pearson not out	0
D. J. Bicknell b Small	21		
N. Shahid run out	43	L-b 9, w 21	30
†G. J. Kersey lbw b Giles	0		
*C. C. Lewis c Brown b Munton	26	1/14 2/79 3/121 (8 wkts, 36.4 overs)	186
B. P. Julian c Giles b Brown	7	4/122 5/169 6/173	
B. C. Hollioake c Burns b Brown	0	7/173 8/184	

J. E. Benjamin did not bat.

Bowling: Munton 8–0–52–1; Brown 6.4–1–28–3; Welch 8–0–40–0; Small 8–0–29–2; Giles 6–0–28–1.

Umpires: G. I. Burgess and J. H. Hampshire.

SURREY v NORTHAMPTONSHIRE

At The Oval, September 8. Surrey won by two wickets. Toss: Surrey.

Martin Bicknell prompted a pitch invasion when, in sepulchral gloom, he hit the last ball to the boundary to give Surrey a narrow victory; with one match to go, they were level on points with Nottinghamshire but had a far superior net run-rate. Capel's 112 for Northamptonshire had taken 88 balls, but he suffered an injured hand and then conceded 25 off two overs as Surrey began their charge from 100 for five. Hollioake's five wickets took him to 36 for the season, two past the old Sunday League record.

Northamptonshire

R. R. Montgomerie b Lewis	2	J. E. Emburey not out	8
M. B. Loye c Lewis b Hollioake	53	C. E. L. Ambrose b Hollioake	0
K. M. Curran c Stewart b Benjamin	0	J. P. Taylor not out	1
D. J. Capel run out	112	B 1, l-b 10, w 8, n-b 2	21
A. L. Penberthy c Stewart b Hollioake	25		
T. C. Walton c Bicknell b Hollioake	8	1/4 2/18 3/101 (9 wkts, 40 overs)	234
*R. J. Bailey c Lewis b Pearson	1	4/191 5/204 6/205	
†R. J. Warren lbw b Hollioake	3	7/215 8/233 9/233	

Bowling: Bicknell 8–0–37–0; Lewis 4.2–0–20–1; Butcher 0.4–0–0–0; Benjamin 8–1–32–1; Julian 7–0–49–0; Hollioake 8–0–58–5; Pearson 4–0–27–1.

Surrey

M. A. Butcher lbw b Penberthy	3	M. P. Bicknell not out	19
*†A. J. Stewart b Penberthy	21	R. M. Pearson not out	1
G. P. Thorpe c Walton b Taylor	2		
A. D. Brown c Warren b Ambrose	49	B 1, l-b 6, w 5, n-b 2	14
A. J. Hollioake c Curran b Penberthy	8		
N. Shahid lbw b Emburey	41	1/18 2/25 3/38 (8 wkts, 40 overs)	237
C. C. Lewis c Bailey b Curran	63	4/78 5/100 6/159	
B. P. Julian c Warren b Taylor	16	7/189 8/230	

J. E. Benjamin did not bat.

Bowling: Ambrose 8–1–37–1; Taylor 8–3–25–2; Penberthy 8–0–44–3; Emburey 8–1–47–1; Capel 2–0–25–0; Curran 6–0–52–1.

Umpires: J. H. Harris and T. E. Jesty.

At Cardiff, September 15. SURREY beat GLAMORGAN by seven wickets.

MOST WICKETS IN A SUNDAY LEAGUE SEASON

	Matches	*O*	*M*	*R*	*W*	*Avge*	*4W/i*	*Runs per over*	*Season*
A. J. Hollioake	**15**	**91.1**	**1**	**474**	**39**	**12.15**	**4**	**5.19**	**1996**
R. J. Clapp	13	92.4	5	448	34	13.17	3	4.83	1974
C. E. B. Rice	15	109.1	4	539	34	15.85	5	4.93	1986
D. L. Williams	16	93.3	4	409	33	12.39	3	4.37	1971
K. D. Boyce	16	121.4	16	419	33	12.69	3	3.44	1971
A. M. Ferreira	14	108	6	554	33	16.78	4	5.12	1981
V. A. Holder	16	116.1	10	390	32	12.18	2	3.35	1971
D. L. Williams	15	106.1	16	434	32	13.56	2	4.08	1974
N. Phillip	16	105.5	8	448	32	14.00	2	4.23	1982
S. L. Watkin	16	125.1	10	508	32	15.87	3	4.05	1995
R. A. Woolmer	16	121.1	7	540	32	16.87	1	4.45	1970

SUSSEX

At Nottingham, May 5. SUSSEX lost to NOTTINGHAMSHIRE by 129 runs.

SUSSEX v WARWICKSHIRE

At Hove, May 12. Warwickshire won by eight wickets. Toss: Sussex.

The match was settled by an all-wicket record partnership for Warwickshire in the Sunday League. Neil Smith, with a maiden League century from 88 balls, and Ostler put on an unbroken 214 for the third wicket after two early wickets for Drakes had given Sussex an apparent edge.

Sussex

K. Greenfield run out	72
J. W. Hall c Knight b N. M. K. Smith	33
M. P. Speight c N. M. K. Smith b Welch	39
*A. P. Wells run out	33
†P. Moores run out	16
D. R. Law c Ostler b Pollock	16
K. Newell not out	8
V. C. Drakes not out	3
B 1, l-b 7, w 7, n-b 6	21
1/67 2/124 3/192 4/194 5/221 6/232 (6 wkts, 40 overs)	241

N. C. Phillips, P. W. Jarvis and E. S. H. Giddins did not bat.

Bowling: Reeve 8–0–35–0; Brown 5–0–25–0; Pollock 8–0–50–1; N. M. K. Smith 8–0–41–1; P. A. Smith 4–0–27–0; Welch 6–0–44–1; Giles 1–0–11–0.

Warwickshire

N. V. Knight c Wells b Drakes	10
N. M. K. Smith not out	111
P. A. Smith c and b Drakes	10
D. P. Ostler not out	91
B 1, l-b 15, w 7	23
1/18 2/31 (2 wkts, 34.1 overs)	245

T. L. Penney, *D. A. Reeve, S. M. Pollock, D. R. Brown, †K. J. Piper, A. F. Giles and G. Welch did not bat.

Bowling: Drakes 8–0–41–2; Jarvis 6–0–30–0; Law 4.1–0–41–0; Giddins 8–0–43–0; Newell 2–0–23–0; Phillips 6–0–51–0.

Umpires: J. W. Holder and V. A. Holder.

SUSSEX v MIDDLESEX

At Horsham, May 26. No result (abandoned).

At Tunbridge Wells, June 2. SUSSEX lost to KENT by 35 runs.

SUSSEX v DURHAM

At Hove, June 9. Sussex won by six runs. Toss: Sussex. First-team debut: R. K. Rao.

Sussex recorded their first Sunday win of the season just when it appeared that Durham were on course for theirs. Durham were 165 for two chasing 218 in the 31st over, but when Roseberry was out, their younger batsmen were unable to complete the task. The Sussex innings ended with a blast of 47 from 25 balls by Law.

Sussex

R. K. Rao c Ligertwood b Walker	21
K. Greenfield c Campbell b Boiling	49
*A. P. Wells c Betts b Boiling	17
M. P. Speight b Killeen	37
N. J. Lenham c Ligertwood b Walker	8
†P. Moores c Campbell b Walker	3
D. R. Law not out	47
V. C. Drakes c Morris b Boiling	6
I. D. K. Salisbury not out	11
B 4, l-b 4, w 4, n-b 6	18
1/50 2/90 3/122 4/144 5/146 6/157 7/169 (7 wkts, 40 overs)	217

J. D. Lewry and P. W. Jarvis did not bat.

Bowling: Brown 8–0–42–0; Killeen 8–0–37–1; Betts 8–0–34–0; Walker 8–0–31–3; Boiling 8–0–65–3.

Durham

S. L. Campbell run out	31
*M. A. Roseberry b Greenfield	65
J. E. Morris c Greenfield b Salisbury	28
D. A. Blenkiron b Lewry	32
P. D. Collingwood b Jarvis	10
†D. G. C. Ligertwood run out	5
N. Killeen b Law	1
S. J. E. Brown not out	7
M. M. Betts not out	2
B 4, l-b 12, w 8, n-b 6	30
1/67 2/126 3/165 4/180 5/198 6/200 7/207 (7 wkts, 40 overs)	211

J. Boiling and A. Walker did not bat.

Bowling: Drakes 8–0–34–0; Lewry 6–0–30–1; Law 4–0–33–1; Jarvis 8–0–36–1; Salisbury 8–1–32–1; Greenfield 6–0–30–1.

Umpires: M. J. Kitchen and T. E. Jesty.

At Bristol, June 16. SUSSEX beat GLOUCESTERSHIRE by 14 runs.

SUSSEX v GLAMORGAN

At Hove, June 23. Glamorgan won by 124 runs. Toss: Glamorgan.

A late change of pitch, after the first one was judged to be too close to the boundary, proved fatal for Sussex. They crashed for 59, their lowest total in 28 years of Sunday League cricket; only Athey managed double figures. Their chief destroyer was Owen Parkin, who took five for 28 on his first appearance in the competition, while Barwick and Croft conceded a mere 13 runs in 12 overs. Metson made his 200th League dismissal.

Glamorgan

S. P. James lbw b Lewry	13	S. L. Watkin b Lewry	7
H. Morris b Greenfield	39	S. R. Barwick not out	3
R. D. B. Croft b Jarvis	11		
*M. P. Maynard c Greenfield b Lewry	52	B 4, l-b 10, w 5	19
P. A. Cottey c Moores b Salisbury	1		
A. Dale b Jarvis	18	1/26 2/62 3/75 (8 wkts, 40 overs)	183
G. P. Butcher not out	20	4/76 5/143 6/153	
†C. P. Metson lbw b Jarvis	0	7/153 8/170	

O. T. Parkin did not bat.

Bowling: Drakes 8–2–44–0; Lewry 8–0–22–3; Jarvis 8–1–29–3; Law 2–0–17–0; Salisbury 8–0–30–1; Greenfield 6–0–27–1.

Sussex

R. K. Rao lbw b Watkin	0	I. D. K. Salisbury c Metson b Croft	5
†P. Moores b Parkin	1	P. W. Jarvis not out	1
K. Greenfield c Morris b Parkin	7	J. D. Lewry st Metson b Croft	0
*A. P. Wells b Parkin	2	L-b 1, w 6	7
N. J. Lenham lbw b Watkin	6		
C. W. J. Athey lbw b Barwick	17	1/0 2/4 3/12 (26 overs)	59
D. R. Law b Parkin	5	4/17 5/26 6/32	
V. C. Drakes b Parkin	8	7/50 8/58 9/58	

Bowling: Watkin 6–0–17–2; Parkin 8–1–28–5; Barwick 7–4–5–1; Croft 5–2–8–2.

Umpires: A. A. Jones and P. Willey.

SUSSEX v HAMPSHIRE

At Arundel, July 7. Hampshire won by 40 runs. Toss: Sussex.

On a surface not conducive to fast scoring, Hampshire struggled to get past the 200 mark, with Stephenson taking 13 overs for his eight runs. Even this proved too much for Sussex, who slumped to 58 for seven, though some big hitting from the lower order reduced the margin of defeat. One six from Drakes carried an estimated 110 yards to the roof of a tent.

Hampshire

*J. P. Stephenson run out	8	S. D. Udal not out	8
J. S. Laney c Law b Jarvis	43	K. D. James not out	1
R. A. Smith lbw b Lenham	47	B 5, l-b 5, w 12	22
W. K. M. Benjamin c Law b Lenham	17		
M. Keech run out	28	1/42 2/64 3/111 (7 wkts, 39 overs)	208
P. R. Whitaker c Greenfield b Lewry	31	4/144 5/188	
†A. N. Aymes b Drakes	3	6/197 7/199	

S. M. Milburn and C. A. Connor did not bat.

Bowling: Lewry 8–0–32–1; Drakes 8–1–32–1; Law 5–0–24–0; Jarvis 4–0–43–1; Lenham 8–1–32–2; Salisbury 6–0–35–0.

Sussex

R. K. Rao lbw b Stephenson	2	I. D. K. Salisbury c Stephenson b James	28
K. Greenfield c Aymes b Stephenson	16	P. W. Jarvis not out	29
M. P. Speight c Aymes b Milburn	2	J. D. Lewry c James b Udal	4
*A. P. Wells c Aymes b Stephenson	4	B 3, l-b 8, w 7, n-b 2	20
N. J. Lenham b James	9		——
D. R. Law c Keech b James	6	1/7 2/18 3/24 (36 overs)	168
†P. Moores c Keech b Connor	11	4/33 5/39 6/51	
V. C. Drakes c Aymes b Milburn	37	7/58 8/113 9/134	

Bowling: Stephenson 8–1–22–3; Milburn 8–0–18–2; James 8–0–28–3; Connor 6–0–38–1; Udal 6–0–51–1.

Umpires: J. C. Balderstone and D. R. Shepherd.

SUSSEX v SOMERSET

At Hove, July 14. Sussex won by 12 runs. Toss: Somerset.

Sussex rediscovered their Sunday form in an excellent batting display, which put the match just out of Somerset's reach. Lee took four wickets, but his failure with the bat left too much for Harden and Parsons to do.

Sussex

N. J. Lenham b Caddick	12	V. C. Drakes not out	14
K. Greenfield b Lee	23	I. D. K. Salisbury c Lee b Caddick	9
†M. P. Speight c Caddick b Shine	62	J. D. Lewry c Turner b Lee	0
*A. P. Wells c Parsons b Lee	56	L-b 7, w 10, n-b 6	23
K. Newell c Rose b Trump	11		——
P. W. Jarvis c Rose b Trump	11	1/15 2/71 3/123 (39.2 overs)	263
R. K. Rao st Turner b Trump	6	4/152 5/177 6/186	
D. R. Law b Lee	36	7/236 8/237 9/250	

Bowling: Caddick 8–0–58–2; Rose 8–0–64–0; Lee 7.2–0–40–4; Shine 8–0–46–1; Trump 8–0–48–3.

Somerset

M. N. Lathwell b Drakes	2	A. R. Caddick lbw b Jarvis	0
*P. D. Bowler lbw b Law	31	H. R. J. Trump run out	1
S. C. Ecclestone c Speight b Lewry	13	K. J. Shine not out	1
R. J. Harden c Salisbury b Law	90	B 2, l-b 17, w 10, n-b 2	31
S. Lee c Rao b Law	4		——
K. A. Parsons lbw b Drakes	56	1/6 2/51 3/64 (9 wkts, 40 overs)	251
†R. J. Turner c Rao b Jarvis	9	4/69 5/214 6/224	
G. D. Rose not out	13	7/243 8/243 9/250	

Bowling: Drakes 8–0–45–2; Lewry 8–0–37–1; Jarvis 8–0–33–2; Law 6–0–49–3; Salisbury 8–0–49–0; Newell 2–0–19–0.

Umpires: D. J. Constant and B. J. Meyer.

At Guildford, July 21. SUSSEX beat SURREY by 75 runs.

At Leicester, July 28. LEICESTERSHIRE v SUSSEX. No result.

SUSSEX v YORKSHIRE

At Eastbourne, August 4. Yorkshire won by eight wickets. Toss: Yorkshire.

The Sussex openers had put on 108 when Bevan, who came on in the 20th over, separated them and proceeded to take a career-best five for 29 with his slow left-arm unorthodox deliveries. His success with the ball meant that he was not required to bat, as Vaughan and Byas made half-centuries.

Sussex

R. K. Rao st Blakey b Bevan	64
K. Greenfield lbw b Bevan	47
M. P. Speight c Stemp b Bevan	2
*A. P. Wells c Moxon b Hartley	41
D. R. Law c Stemp b Bevan	13
V. C. Drakes lbw b Bevan	2
†P. Moores b Hartley	2
C. W. J. Athey b Hartley	3
I. D. K. Salisbury run out	1
E. S. H. Giddins c Blakey b Gough	2
R. J. Kirtley not out	1
B 3, l-b 10, w 9, n-b 6	28
1/108 2/114 3/141 4/161 5/173 6/179 7/194 8/196 9/198 (39.3 overs)	206

Bowling: Gough 7–0–33–1; Silverwood 4–0–25–0; White 6–0–35–0; Hartley 7.3–1–30–3; Stemp 7–0–41–0; Bevan 8–1–29–5.

Yorkshire

*D. Byas c Salisbury b Greenfield	61
M. D. Moxon b Kirtley	3
M. P. Vaughan not out	71
A. McGrath not out	49
L-b 10, w 9, n-b 4	23
1/24 2/138 (2 wkts, 35.4 overs)	207

M. G. Bevan, C. White, †R. J. Blakey, D. Gough, P. J. Hartley, C. E. W. Silverwood and R. D. Stemp did not bat.

Bowling: Kirtley 6–0–20–1; Law 4.4–0–33–0; Drakes 6–0–33–0; Giddins 6–0–42–0; Salisbury 8–0–49–0; Greenfield 5–0–20–1.

Umpires: V. A. Holder and T. E. Jesty.

SUSSEX v DERBYSHIRE

At Hove, August 11. Sussex won on scoring-rate. Toss: Derbyshire. First-team debuts: G. R. Haywood, M. Newell; D. R. Womble.

After Derbyshire's batsmen had done a good job in reaching 232, rain intervened to finish play early; Sussex were just three runs ahead of the required run-rate. Debutant Mark Newell, younger brother of Keith, scored 48 in 42 balls.

Derbyshire

*D. M. Jones c Moores b Giddins	30
K. J. Barnett b Law	39
C. J. Adams not out	88
G. A. Khan b Salisbury	7
T. J. G. O'Gorman b Salisbury	14
P. A. J. DeFreitas c Moores b Kirtley	3
†K. M. Krikken not out	27
B 1, l-b 9, w 12, n-b 2	24
1/66 2/96 3/107 4/147 5/154 (5 wkts, 40 overs)	232

G. M. Roberts, M. J. Vandrau, D. R. Womble and K. J. Dean did not bat.

Bowling: Drakes 8–0–43–0; Kirtley 8–0–51–1; Giddins 8–1–49–1; Law 8–0–41–1; Salisbury 8–1–38–2.

Sussex

K. Greenfield c and b Roberts	60	D. R. Law not out	27
K. Newell c Adams b DeFreitas	10	L-b 6, w 3, n-b 4	13
G. R. Haywood c O'Gorman b Dean	4		—
*A. P. Wells c Dean b Roberts	38	1/17 2/31 3/104 (5 wkts, 33.5 overs)	200
M. Newell b Barnett	48	4/143 5/200	

†P. Moores, I. D. K. Salisbury, V. C. Drakes, E. S. H. Giddins and R. J. Kirtley did not bat.

Bowling: DeFreitas 8–1–34–1; Dean 8–0–34–1; Vandrau 4–0–27–0; Roberts 8–0–49–2; Barnett 2.5–0–21–1; Womble 3–0–29–0.

Umpires: B. Dudleston and R. Palmer.

At Northampton, August 25. SUSSEX lost to NORTHAMPTONSHIRE by five wickets.

SUSSEX v LANCASHIRE

At Hove, September 1. Lancashire won by four wickets. Toss: Sussex.

Both sides had an experimental look, but Lancashire won through a polished innings from one of their old hands, Fairbrother. He made 93 at a run a ball, including nine fours and a six, to steer them to success, despite tight bowling from Law, who conceded just 12 in eight overs.

Sussex

V. C. Drakes c Hegg b Elworthy	21	I. D. K. Salisbury b Chapple	2
K. Greenfield c Hegg b Elworthy	25	N. C. Phillips not out	0
R. K. Rao c McKeown b Green	23		
*A. P. Wells run out	20	L-b 7, w 7, n-b 4	18
M. Newell not out	35		—
K. Newell c Gallian b Yates	3	1/53 2/56 3/97 (8 wkts, 40 overs)	204
†P. Moores c Elworthy b Green	38	4/101 5/108 6/173	
D. R. Law c Gallian b Chapple	19	7/199 8/204	

R. J. Kirtley did not bat.

Bowling: Elworthy 8–1–33–2; Chapple 8–0–42–2; Gallian 4–0–15–0; Green 8–0–57–2; Yates 8–0–29–1; Watkinson 4–0–21–0.

Lancashire

*M. Watkinson c Moores b Law	5	†W. K. Hegg not out	8
S. P. Titchard b Drakes	40	G. Chapple not out	0
J. E. R. Gallian c Greenfield b Law	3	B 3, l-b 14, w 12, n-b 8	37
N. H. Fairbrother c Drakes b Phillips	93		—
N. J. Speak c Phillips b Salisbury	9	1/7 2/15 3/121 (6 wkts, 39.2 overs)	207
P. C. McKeown b Drakes	12	4/158 5/190 6/204	

R. J. Green, G. Yates and S. Elworthy did not bat.

Bowling: Drakes 7.2–0–38–2; Law 8–1–12–2; Kirtley 8–0–43–0; Phillips 8–0–58–1; Salisbury 8–0–39–1.

Umpires: H. D. Bird and D. J. Constant.

At Worcester, September 8. SUSSEX beat WORCESTERSHIRE by 29 runs.

At Chelmsford, September 15. SUSSEX lost to ESSEX by seven wickets.

WARWICKSHIRE

At Hove, May 12. WARWICKSHIRE beat SUSSEX by eight wickets.

WARWICKSHIRE v HAMPSHIRE

At Birmingham, May 19. Warwickshire won on scoring-rate. Toss: Hampshire.

Knight's maiden League century, 134 from 104 balls, was the highest score for Warwickshire in the competition. Warwickshire's innings had been reduced to 35 overs by rain which then reduced Hampshire's target to 226 off 30. They never threatened to come to terms with that and were all out inside 26 overs.

Warwickshire

N. V. Knight c James b Connor 134
N. M. K. Smith st Aymes b Thursfield ... 30
D. P. Ostler c Whitaker b Udal 53
T. L. Penney c Thursfield b Udal 3
S. M. Pollock not out 35
*D. A. Reeve not out 3
L-b 2, w 3 5

1/73 2/176 3/191 4/245 (4 wkts, 35 overs) 263

P. A. Smith, D. R. Brown, †K. J. Piper, G. Welch and A. F. Giles did not bat.

Bowling: Benjamin 7–0–48–0; James 6–0–41–0; Thursfield 4–0–38–1; Connor 6–0–47–1; Udal 8–0–44–2; Maru 4–0–43–0.

Hampshire

R. S. M. Morris b Pollock 21
J. S. Laney b Pollock 25
M. Keech c Giles b Pollock 16
W. K. M. Benjamin c N. M. K. Smith b Brown . 22
P. R. Whitaker b Giles 4
K. D. James b Reeve 29
†A. N. Aymes b Brown 4
S. D. Udal c Piper b Brown 4
M. J. Thursfield c Giles b Brown 3
C. A. Connor c Giles b Reeve 0
*R. J. Maru not out 0
L-b 9, w 6, n-b 2 17

1/48 2/59 3/85 4/103 5/103 6/115 7/137 8/143 9/145 (25.3 overs) 145

Bowling: Reeve 5.3–0–23–2; Pollock 8–0–36–3; Welch 3.1–0–19–0; Brown 6.5–0–47–4; Giles 2–0–11–1.

Umpires: K. J. Lyons and R. A. White.

WARWICKSHIRE v LEICESTERSHIRE

At Birmingham, May 26. Leicestershire won on scoring-rate. Toss: Warwickshire.

Set a revised target of 134 in 36 overs, Warwickshire subsided to Mullally, who returned career-best League figures of five for 15, while wicket-keeper Nixon took five catches. They perished for 95. Leicestershire's innings had been accompanied by music from the neighbouring park, which was staging the Lord Mayor's Show.

Leicestershire

P. V. Simmons lbw b Reeve 1
V. J. Wells c Reeve b Small............ 33
B. F. Smith lbw b Reeve 12
*J. J. Whitaker b Small 10
D. L. Maddy c Penney b Pollock 55
A. Habib b Small 2
†P. A. Nixon b Giles 12
C. C. Remy c Burns b Brown 1
G. J. Parsons b Giles 0
D. Williamson c Penney b Reeve 9
A. D. Mullally not out.................. 0
B 1, l-b 8, w 4............... 13

1/1 2/19 3/53 4/73 5/87 6/109 7/112 8/113 9/148 (37.1 overs) 148

Bowling: Pollock 7–0–32–1; Reeve 6.1–0–22–3; Small 8–1–24–3; Welch 6–0–24–0; Giles 6–2–15–2; Brown 4–0–22–1.

Warwickshire

N. V. Knight c Nixon b Mullally	0	†M. Burns not out	11
P. A. Smith c Nixon b Mullally	6	A. F. Giles run out	9
D. P. Ostler c Nixon b Mullally	12	G. C. Small b Simmons	1
D. R. Brown b Mullally	8	L-b 1, w 1, n-b 4	6
T. L. Penney c Nixon b Mullally	0		
S. M. Pollock c Nixon b Simmons	19	1/1 2/12 3/28 (26.3 overs)	95
*D. A. Reeve c Habib b Wells	5	4/28 5/31 6/52	
G. Welch c Williamson b Wells	18	7/54 8/78 9/93	

Bowling: Mullally 8–2–15–5; Parsons 7–0–32–0; Wells 6–0–27–2; Simmons 5.3–0–20–2.

Umpires: G. I. Burgess and D. R. Shepherd.

At Northampton, June 2. WARWICKSHIRE lost to NORTHAMPTONSHIRE by three wickets.

At Taunton, June 9. WARWICKSHIRE lost to SOMERSET by 26 runs.

At Leeds, June 16. WARWICKSHIRE beat YORKSHIRE by five runs.

WARWICKSHIRE v KENT

At Birmingham, June 23. Warwickshire won by eight runs. Toss: Warwickshire.

Warwickshire's bowlers and fielders remained calm when Kent needed 21 off their last three overs with four wickets in hand. Pollock, top scorer in the match with 57 from 38 balls, bowled two of those overs, conceded only ten and took the wicket of the dangerous Ealham.

Warwickshire

N. M. K. Smith run out	40	*A. J. Moles not out	16
D. P. Ostler c Hooper b Wren	32	†M. Burns not out	1
D. R. Brown c Hooper b McCague	17	L-b 1, w 3	4
P. A. Smith c Thompson b McCague	25		
T. L. Penney c Cowdrey b Llong	30	1/73 2/73 3/108 (6 wkts, 40 overs)	222
S. M. Pollock c Cowdrey b Fleming	57	4/125 5/174 6/217	

G. Welch, M. D. Edmond and G. C. Small did not bat.

Bowling: Wren 8–0–38–1; Ealham 5–0–27–0; Fleming 8–0–60–1; Hooper 8–0–30–0; McCague 7–0–35–2; Llong 4–0–31–1.

Kent

T. R. Ward c Penney b Pollock	8	M. J. McCague b Edmond	1
M. V. Fleming c Welch b Brown	33	J. B. D. Thompson not out	2
C. L. Hooper c Moles b Small	31		
G. R. Cowdrey run out	6	L-b 10, w 6, n-b 6	22
M. A. Ealham c Edmond b Pollock	56		
N. J. Llong run out	20	1/41 2/59 3/75 (8 wkts, 40 overs)	214
M. J. Walker c Small b N. M. K. Smith	14	4/96 5/147 6/175	
*†S. A. Marsh not out	21	7/202 8/208	

T. N. Wren did not bat.

Bowling: Welch 4–0–27–0; Pollock 8–0–33–2; Small 8–0–43–1; Brown 8–0–33–1; Edmond 8–1–34–1; N. M. K. Smith 4–0–34–1.

Umpires: B. Dudleston and R. A. White.

At Lord's, June 30. WARWICKSHIRE lost to MIDDLESEX by 57 runs.

WARWICKSHIRE v NOTTINGHAMSHIRE

At Birmingham, July 7. Warwickshire won by 18 runs. Toss: Nottinghamshire.

Keen fielding and tight bowling enabled Warwickshire to defend a modest target with some ease. Only 20 boundaries were scored in the match and Nottinghamshire's challenge faded once Robinson departed in the 32nd over.

Warwickshire

N. V. Knight b Dowman	1
N. M. K. Smith b Dowman	4
D. P. Ostler lbw b Bates	27
A. J. Moles run out	36
T. L. Penney not out	62
S. M. Pollock c Pollard b Bates	1
†M. Burns b Evans	37
D. R. Brown not out	15
B 2, l-b 6, w 6	14
1/2 2/5 3/57 4/78 5/82 6/172 (6 wkts, 40 overs)	197

A. F. Giles, *T. A. Munton and G. C. Small did not bat.

Bowling: Dowman 8–0–34–2; Evans 8–0–40–1; Bowen 8–0–40–0; Pick 8–0–41–0; Bates 8–0–34–2.

Nottinghamshire

P. R. Pollard c Burns b Pollock	10
R. T. Robinson b Giles	52
C. L. Cairns c Pollock b Smith	23
*P. Johnson c Giles b Pollock	43
A. A. Metcalfe c Penney b Munton	16
M. P. Dowman lbw b Giles	8
R. T. Bates not out	11
†W. M. Noon not out	7
L-b 8, w 1	9
1/25 2/67 3/129 4/144 5/161 6/161 (6 wkts, 40 overs)	179

M. N. Bowen, R. A. Pick and K. P. Evans did not bat.

Bowling: Munton 8–1–38–1; Pollock 8–1–21–2; Small 8–1–33–0; Smith 6–0–19–1; Giles 8–0–41–2; Brown 2–0–19–0.

Umpires: M. J. Kitchen and K. E. Palmer.

WARWICKSHIRE v LANCASHIRE

At Birmingham, July 16. Warwickshire won by 13 runs. Toss: Warwickshire.

The match was postponed to the Tuesday after Lancashire's Benson and Hedges Cup triumph, but the same set of players failed to maintain their form. Warwickshire relied heavily on the performance of their opener, Smith; Lancashire lost too many early wickets to sustain a challenge.

Warwickshire

N. V. Knight b Yates	32
N. M. K. Smith c Martin b Austin	76
D. P. Ostler lbw b Watkinson	11
A. J. Moles b Chapple	15
T. L. Penney run out	21
S. M. Pollock not out	21
†M. Burns lbw b Yates	1
D. R. Brown not out	17
B 4, l-b 11, w 3	18
1/66 2/93 3/133 4/161 5/170 6/173 (6 wkts, 40 overs)	212

A. F. Giles, G. C. Small and *T. A. Munton did not bat.

Bowling: Martin 7–0–28–0; Austin 8–0–52–1; Yates 8–0–32–2; Watkinson 8–0–32–1; Lloyd 2–0–18–0; Chapple 7–0–35–1.

Lancashire

*M. Watkinson b Munton 5
M. A. Atherton c Ostler b Brown 33
J. E. R. Gallian run out 14
J. P. Crawley c Penney b Pollock 52
G. D. Lloyd run out 7
†W. K. Hegg c Ostler b Munton 34
N. H. Fairbrother c Penney b Giles 4
I. D. Austin lbw b Pollock 30
G. Yates st Burns b Munton 2
G. Chapple not out 3
P. J. Martin not out 3
L-b 9, w 3 12

1/6 2/30 3/71 (9 wkts, 40 overs) 199
4/108 5/124 6/133
7/189 8/192 9/192

Bowling: Munton 8–1–35–3; Pollock 8–0–33–2; Small 6–0–33–0; Brown 4–0–19–1; Smith 6–0–29–0; Giles 8–0–41–1.

Umpires: J. W. Holder and D. R. Shepherd.

At Cheltenham, July 28. GLOUCESTERSHIRE v WARWICKSHIRE. No result.

WARWICKSHIRE v DURHAM

At Birmingham, August 11. Warwickshire won by 88 runs. Toss: Durham.

Brown took charge of Durham for the first time and they responded well, reducing Warwickshire to 118 for six. But Pollock led a recovery and then bowled too venomously for a side with no batting confidence. Small also had outstanding figures – four for 14 – as Durham were bowled out for 99, their lowest total in the League.

Warwickshire

A. J. Moles b Saggers 7
N. M. K. Smith c Walker b Brown 8
D. P. Ostler b Boiling 27
D. R. Brown lbw b Boiling 17
T. L. Penney lbw b Killeen 22
S. M. Pollock c Collingwood b Brown . . . 56
W. G. Khan b Saggers 5
†M. Burns c Killeen b Brown 20
A. F. Giles not out 3
G. C. Small not out 5
B 3, l-b 7, w 5, n-b 2 17

1/18 2/19 3/67 (8 wkts, 40 overs) 187
4/85 5/109 6/118
7/176 8/180

*T. A. Munton did not bat.

Bowling: Brown 8–0–50–3; Saggers 8–0–24–2; Killeen 8–0–41–1; Boiling 8–1–25–2; Walker 8–0–37–0.

Durham

S. L. Campbell run out 10
S. Hutton c Penney b Pollock 1
J. Boiling c Burns b Small 27
J. A. Daley c Burns b Small 7
P. D. Collingwood b Smith 0
R. M. S. Weston b Small 13
†D. G. C. Ligertwood b Small 0
M. J. Saggers b Pollock 13
N. Killeen run out 3
*S. J. E. Brown not out 0
A. Walker b Giles 3
B 8, l-b 8, w 4, n-b 2 22

1/7 2/23 3/45 (32.4 overs) 99
4/46 5/58 6/58
7/80 8/88 9/88

Bowling: Pollock 6–1–17–2; Munton 6–0–20–0; Smith 8–0–21–1; Small 8–3–14–4; Giles 4.4–1–11–1.

Umpires: J. D. Bond and G. Sharp.

WARWICKSHIRE v GLAMORGAN

At Birmingham, August 18. Warwickshire won by seven wickets. Toss: Glamorgan.

Once Glamorgan had been reduced to 33 for five in the 17th over on a slow pitch, they had little chance. Despite the efforts of Croft, who bowled his eight overs for 15, Knight steered Warwickshire home with few alarms.

Glamorgan

A. W. Evans c Knight b Munton	6	†A. D. Shaw b Giles	8
H. Morris c Brown b Munton	0	S. L. Watkin b Pollock	1
*M. P. Maynard c Small b Munton	9	S. R. Barwick not out	1
P. A. Cottey c Brown b Small	8	L-b 6, w 9	15
D. L. Hemp c Piper b Small	6		—
A. Dale st Piper b Giles	29	1/4 2/14 3/19 (39.2 overs)	128
O. D. Gibson c Brown b Smith	22	4/29 5/33 6/76	
R. D. B. Croft b Pollock	23	7/115 8/119 9/122	

Bowling: Pollock 8–2–14–2; Munton 8–2–17–3; Small 8–0–30–2; Smith 8–1–23–1; Giles 5.2–0–26–2; Brown 2–0–12–0.

Warwickshire

N. V. Knight not out	73	T. L. Penney not out	5
N. M. K. Smith b Watkin	0	B 2, l-b 2, w 2, n-b 2	8
D. P. Ostler lbw b Watkin	8		—
D. R. Brown lbw b Croft	37	1/1 2/21 3/102 (3 wkts, 37.5 overs)	131

M. Burns, S. M. Pollock, †K. J. Piper, A. F. Giles, G. C. Small and *T. A. Munton did not bat.

Bowling: Watkin 8–0–28–2; Gibson 8–1–32–0; Barwick 6.5–0–20–0; Dale 5–0–21–0; Croft 8–0–15–1; Hemp 2–0–11–0.

Umpires: J. C. Balderstone and V. A. Holder.

WARWICKSHIRE v WORCESTERSHIRE

At Birmingham, August 25. Warwickshire won by seven wickets. Toss: Warwickshire.

A career-best return of five for 36 from Giles, followed by an unbeaten 62 from Smith, enabled Warwickshire to reach a reduced target of 109 from 26 overs with something to spare against their neighbours. The result effectively knocked Worcestershire out of contention. Pollock also bowled well in his last appearance at Edgbaston before returning to South Africa with an injury. The match was a benefit for Dermot Reeve, the Warwickshire captain, who had retired after an unsuccessful hip operation in July; he contributed by winning the toss on behalf of his deputy, Munton.

Worcestershire

*T. M. Moody c Pollock b Giles	26	R. K. Illingworth lbw b Pollock	6
W. P. C. Weston c Ostler b Giles	43	M. J. Rawnsley b Pollock	2
G. A. Hick b Giles	0	A. Sheriyar not out	1
K. R. Spiring c and b Giles	13	L-b 9, w 8	17
V. S. Solanki b Small	5		—
D. A. Leatherdale b Giles	2	1/67 2/69 3/82 (36.3 overs)	154
S. R. Lampitt b Pollock	30	4/89 5/92 6/104	
†S. J. Rhodes c Khan b Brown	9	7/126 8/145 9/153	

Bowling: Pollock 7.3–0–27–3; Munton 6–0–30–0; Small 8–1–21–1; Giles 8–0–36–5; Brown 3–0–15–1; Smith 4–0–16–0.

Warwickshire

W. G. Khan c and b Hick	2	T. L. Penney not out	1
N. M. K. Smith not out	62	B 4, l-b 3, w 3	10
D. P. Ostler c Leatherdale b Illingworth	22		—
D. R. Brown b Illingworth	12	1/9 2/77 3/103 (3 wkts, 23.5 overs)	109

M. Burns, S. M. Pollock, †K. J. Piper, A. F. Giles, G. C. Small and *T. A. Munton did not bat.

Bowling: Hick 6–0–23–1; Moody 4–0–20–0; Illingworth 7–0–23–2; Rawnsley 2–0–12–0; Lampitt 4.5–0–24–0.

Umpires: A. G. T. Whitehead and P. Willey.

At The Oval, September 1. WARWICKSHIRE lost to SURREY by two wickets.

WARWICKSHIRE v ESSEX

At Birmingham, September 10. Warwickshire won by six wickets. Toss: Warwickshire.

The match featured an outstanding display of fielding from Penney, who took two catches at backward point and twice threw down the wicket for run-outs. Essex slid to 76 for seven, three days after their 57 all out in the NatWest final, before being rallied by Lewis and Cowan. But it was not enough to challenge Warwickshire. It was Essex's ninth successive League defeat.

Essex

D. D. J. Robinson lbw b Brown	0	M. C. Ilott c Penney b Small	1
A. P. Grayson run out	7	A. P. Cowan not out	22
N. Hussain b Giles	40	B 1, l-b 3, w 1	5
*P. J. Prichard c Munton b Welch	17		
T. P. Hodgson c Penney b Small	0	1/1 2/12 3/44 (7 wkts, 40 overs)	138
J. J. B. Lewis not out	46	4/56 5/74	
†B. J. Hyam run out	0	6/75 7/76	

S. J. W. Andrew and P. M. Such did not bat.

Bowling: Munton 8–3–28–0; Brown 8–3–22–1; Welch 5–0–16–1; Small 8–0–30–2; Giles 8–1–19–1; Smith 3–1–19–0.

Warwickshire

W. G. Khan c Hussain b Ilott	8	†K. J. Piper not out	7
N. M. K. Smith c Ilott b Grayson	49	L-b 4, w 4	8
M. Burns c Ilott b Cowan	24		
D. R. Brown c and b Cowan	8	1/28 2/71 (4 wkts, 34.2 overs)	142
T. L. Penney not out	38	3/85 4/117	

N. V. Knight, G. Welch, A. F. Giles, G. C. Small and *T. A. Munton did not bat.

Bowling: Ilott 6–0–26–1; Andrew 6–0–26–0; Such 8–0–31–0; Cowan 8–0–36–2; Grayson 6–0–15–1; Lewis 0.2–0–4–0.

Umpires: K. E. Palmer and G. Sharp.

At Derby, September 15. WARWICKSHIRE lost to DERBYSHIRE by eight wickets.

WORCESTERSHIRE

WORCESTERSHIRE v ESSEX

At Worcester, May 5. Worcestershire won by four wickets. Toss: Worcestershire.

Moody, whose three wickets included two return catches off successive balls, restricted Essex to 159, though Worcestershire had a hard time overtaking it. They were aided by two nine-ball overs from Cowan, who had Rhodes caught off a no-ball.

Essex

*P. J. Prichard lbw b Newport	10	M. C. Ilott c and b Moody	0
S. G. Law c Hick b Newport	4	A. P. Cowan c Rhodes b Lampitt	18
N. Hussain c Weston b Moody	8	P. M. Such not out	4
G. A. Gooch b Illingworth	40	L-b 4, w 5, n-b 4	13
R. C. Irani c Rhodes b Lampitt	25		
D. D. J. Robinson c and b Moody	14	1/11 2/15 3/33 (38.5 overs)	159
A. P. Grayson c and b Illingworth	10	4/94 5/94 6/121	
†R. J. Rollins run out	13	7/121 8/121 9/147	

Bowling: Newport 6–0–24–2; Moody 8–1–27–3; Sheriyar 7–0–32–0; Lampitt 7.5–0–32–2; Illingworth 8–0–30–2; Hick 2–0–10–0.

Worcestershire

*T. M. Moody c Irani b Such	32
T. S. Curtis c Rollins b Irani	22
G. A. Hick c Gooch b Ilott	43
D. A. Leatherdale c Rollins b Irani	6
W. P. C. Weston b Such	7
K. R. Spiring not out	20
S. R. Lampitt lbw b Ilott	6
†S. J. Rhodes not out	8
L-b 1, w 12, n-b 4	17
1/54 2/57 3/65 4/101 5/131 6/140 (6 wkts, 38.2 overs)	161

P. J. Newport, R. K. Illingworth and A. Sheriyar did not bat.

Bowling: Law 7–1–26–0; Ilott 8–1–37–2; Irani 8–1–32–2; Such 8–0–24–2; Cowan 5.2–0–33–0; Grayson 2–0–8–0.

Umpires: T. E. Jesty and R. A. White.

At Leicester, May 19. LEICESTERSHIRE v WORCESTERSHIRE. No result (abandoned).

At Ebbw Vale, May 26. GLAMORGAN v WORCESTERSHIRE. No result.

WORCESTERSHIRE v HAMPSHIRE

At Worcester, June 2. Worcestershire won by 36 runs. Toss: Hampshire.

For the first time since July 1994, the New Road pitch produced a Sunday League innings in excess of 200. Hick was at the heart of Worcestershire's effort; Hampshire's reply was uninspired.

Worcestershire

*T. M. Moody b Stephenson	45
T. S. Curtis b Stephenson	12
G. A. Hick c Laney b James	61
K. R. Spiring c Connor b Stephenson	48
W. P. C. Weston c White b James	20
D. A. Leatherdale b James	9
S. R. Lampitt not out	2
†S. J. Rhodes not out	10
B 2, l-b 5, w 4, n-b 2	13
1/55 2/67 3/173 4/194 5/207 6/209 (6 wkts, 40 overs)	220

P. J. Newport, R. K. Illingworth and J. E. Brinkley did not bat.

Bowling: James 8–0–50–3; Connor 8–0–44–0; Thursfield 8–0–24–0; Stephenson 8–0–35–3; Maru 4–0–32–0; Udal 4–0–28–0.

Hampshire

*J. P. Stephenson c Spiring b Moody	8
J. S. Laney c Rhodes b Lampitt	19
R. A. Smith c Hick b Brinkley	35
M. Keech c Leatherdale b Hick	23
G. W. White lbw b Brinkley	7
K. D. James c Moody b Lampitt	24
†A. N. Aymes b Moody	9
S. D. Udal c Leatherdale b Lampitt	20
M. J. Thursfield c Moody b Lampitt	0
C. A. Connor not out	14
R. J. Maru not out	6
L-b 4, w 9, n-b 6	19
1/23 2/64 3/79 4/95 5/111 6/124 7/163 8/163 9/172 (9 wkts, 40 overs)	184

Bowling: Newport 8–0–36–0; Moody 8–0–39–2; Illingworth 8–1–29–0; Lampitt 8–1–40–4; Brinkley 4–0–26–2; Hick 4–0–10–1.

Umpires: B. Dudleston and M. J. Kitchen.

WORCESTERSHIRE v NOTTINGHAMSHIRE

At Worcester, June 16. Nottinghamshire won by six wickets. Toss: Nottinghamshire.

Worcestershire suffered their first Sunday League defeat since July 1995 – they had won seven, with three no-results and one abandoned – on a desperately slow pitch which defied fast scoring. A total of 213 appeared enough in these conditions, but Metcalfe and Johnson dispelled that notion.

Worcestershire

*T. M. Moody st Noon b Tolley	43	D. A. Leatherdale not out	26
W. P. C. Weston b Tolley	44	B 2, l-b 4, w 11	17
G. A. Hick not out	63		—
K. R. Spiring c Evans b Cairns	20	1/89 2/105 3/140 (3 wkts, 40 overs)	213

V. S. Solanki, †S. J. Rhodes, S. R. Lampitt, P. J. Newport, R. K. Illingworth and A. Sheriyar did not bat.

Bowling: Pick 8–0–40–0; Evans 8–2–42–0; Bowen 8–0–41–0; Tolley 8–0–37–2; Cairns 8–0–47–1.

Nottinghamshire

A. A. Metcalfe lbw b Moody	65	C. M. Tolley not out	20
M. P. Dowman b Lampitt	10	L-b 3, w 7	10
G. F. Archer b Illingworth	12		—
*P. Johnson c Weston b Moody	58	1/31 2/57 (4 wkts, 39.1 overs)	216
C. L. Cairns not out	41	3/142 4/158	

K. P. Evans, †W. M. Noon, R. T. Bates, R. A. Pick and M. N. Bowen did not bat.

Bowling: Moody 8–0–59–2; Newport 8–0–35–0; Lampitt 8–1–51–1; Sheriyar 7.1–1–26–0; Illingworth 8–0–42–1.

Umpires: R. Palmer and G. Sharp.

At Bath, June 23. WORCESTERSHIRE beat SOMERSET by seven wickets.

WORCESTERSHIRE v YORKSHIRE

At Worcester, June 30. Yorkshire won by five wickets. Toss: Yorkshire.

Maiden League half-centuries from Vaughan (who had an unexpected opening partner in Gough) and Solanki cancelled one another out, but Yorkshire's greater depth of batting carried them through. Rhodes and Illingworth, both born in Bradford but playing for Worcestershire, combined to help Illingworth to three wickets in 11 balls.

Worcestershire

*T. M. Moody c Vaughan b Stemp	41	R. K. Illingworth not out	27
T. S. Curtis c Byas b Silverwood	5	J. E. Brinkley b Hartley	0
G. A. Hick c Blakey b Hartley	10	A. Sheriyar not out	1
K. R. Spiring b White	2	L-b 5, n-b 6	11
W. P. C. Weston c White b Stemp	16		—
V. S. Solanki b Hartley	55	1/6 2/38 3/49 (9 wkts, 40 overs)	175
S. R. Lampitt b Silverwood	6	4/73 5/93 6/106	
†S. J. Rhodes c Vaughan b White	1	7/108 8/174 9/174	

Bowling: Gough 8–1–26–0; Silverwood 8–0–44–2; Hartley 8–0–47–3; White 8–0–24–2; Stemp 8–0–29–2.

Yorkshire

D. Gough b Brinkley	22	†R. J. Blakey not out	4
M. P. Vaughan st Rhodes b Illingworth	53		
M. G. Bevan lbw b Illingworth	33	L-b 2, w 3	5
A. McGrath st Rhodes b Illingworth	12		—
*D. Byas not out	27	1/38 2/113 3/114 (5 wkts, 38.5 overs)	177
C. White b Sheriyar	21	4/129 5/173	

P. J. Hartley, A. C. Morris, C. E. W. Silverwood and R. D. Stemp did not bat.

Bowling: Brinkley 8–1–30–1; Moody 8–1–44–0; Sheriyar 7.5–1–33–1; Lampitt 7–0–34–0; Illingworth 8–0–34–3.

Umpires: R. Julian and D. R. Shepherd.

At Manchester, July 7. WORCESTERSHIRE beat LANCASHIRE by four runs.

At The Oval, July 14. WORCESTERSHIRE lost to SURREY by eight wickets.

WORCESTERSHIRE v DURHAM

At Worcester, July 21. Worcestershire won by nine wickets. Toss: Durham.

An efficient performance from Worcestershire left Durham winless for the 17th successive Sunday match, dating back to August 1995. To add to their problems, Bainbridge dropped Weston off the bowling of Walker when he had only eight; in the process he bit through his lip and was taken to hospital for stitches. Walker later pulled up with an ankle injury, while Weston scored an unbeaten 80.

Durham

S. L. Campbell b Hick 40
S. Hutton run out 38
J. E. Morris b Lampitt 12
P. D. Collingwood c Rhodes b Lampitt . . . 2
*M. A. Roseberry b Sheriyar 19
P. Bainbridge c Hick b Sheriyar 21
†D. G. C. Ligertwood lbw b Sheriyar 22
J. Boiling not out 7
D. M. Cox b Sheriyar 0
N. Killeen not out 1
L-b 5, w 5 10

1/55 2/77 3/83 4/97 5/130 6/150 7/169 8/169 (8 wkts, 40 overs) 172

A. Walker did not bat.

Bowling: Ellis 4–0–22–0; Moody 6–0–26–0; Illingworth 8–0–21–0; Lampitt 6–0–26–2; Hick 8–0–45–1; Sheriyar 8–0–27–4.

Worcestershire

*T. M. Moody c Killeen b Boiling 35
W. P. C. Weston not out 80
G. A. Hick not out 54
L-b 1, w 3, n-b 2 6

1/65 (1 wkt, 35.3 overs) 175

K. R. Spiring, D. A. Leatherdale, V. S. Solanki, S. R. Lampitt, †S. J. Rhodes, R. K. Illingworth, A. Sheriyar and S. W. K. Ellis did not bat.

Bowling: Killeen 6–1–33–0; Walker 2–0–10–0; Cox 8–0–28–0; Boiling 8–0–40–1; Campbell 5.3–0–34–0; Bainbridge 4–0–23–0; Collingwood 2–0–6–0.

Umpires: B. J. Meyer and R. A. White.

WORCESTERSHIRE v NORTHAMPTONSHIRE

At Worcester, July 28. No result. Toss: Northamptonshire.

This was Worcestershire's fifth match without a result in 13 Sunday fixtures going back to September 1995.

Worcestershire

*T. M. Moody c Fordham b Curran 31
W. P. C. Weston not out 36
K. R. Spiring not out 12
L-b 1 1

1/49 (1 wkt, 17 overs) 80

M. J. Church, V. S. Solanki, D. A. Leatherdale, †S. J. Rhodes, S. R. Lampitt, R. K. Illingworth, P. J. Newport and A. Sheriyar did not bat.

Bowling: Ambrose 4–1–9–0; Taylor 3–0–24–0; Curran 4–0–25–1; Capel 5–0–20–0; Emburey 1–0–1–0.

Northamptonshire

M. B. Loye, *A. Fordham, K. M. Curran, T. C. Walton, D. J. Capel, A. L. Penberthy, D. J. Sales, †D. Ripley, J. E. Emburey, J. P. Taylor and C. E. L. Ambrose.

Umpires: A. Clarkson and K. E. Palmer.

At Canterbury, August 4. WORCESTERSHIRE beat KENT by ten wickets.

At Lord's, August 18. WORCESTERSHIRE beat MIDDLESEX by two runs.

At Birmingham, August 25. WORCESTERSHIRE lost to WARWICKSHIRE by seven wickets.

At Chesterfield, September 1. WORCESTERSHIRE lost to DERBYSHIRE by six wickets.

WORCESTERSHIRE v SUSSEX

At Worcester, September 8. Sussex won by 29 runs. Toss: Sussex. First-team debut: M. R. Strong.

Sussex opener Rao was their top scorer with 59 and then had Hick caught off a full toss with only his second delivery in the competition. That prompted a collapse: seven wickets fell for 76 runs and Rao finished with three for 31.

Sussex

R. K. Rao run out	59	N. C. Phillips c Solanki b Lampitt	15
K. Greenfield c Rhodes b Sheriyar	7	M. R. Strong b Illingworth	1
K. Newell c Rhodes b Lampitt	8	R. J. Kirtley not out	0
*A. P. Wells run out	5	L-b 13, w 2	15
M. Newell b Solanki	13		——
†P. Moores not out	51	1/15 2/51 3/62 (9 wkts, 40 overs)	216
D. R. Law c Solanki b Sheriyar	42	4/104 5/105 6/173	
I. D. K. Salisbury c Leatherdale b Moody	0	7/173 8/202 9/216	

Bowling: Moody 8–0–36–1; Sheriyar 5–0–33–2; Lampitt 8–0–34–2; Illingworth 7–0–31–1; Leatherdale 2–0–12–0; Rawnsley 5–0–26–0; Solanki 5–0–31–1.

Worcestershire

*T. M. Moody c Moores b Law	4	M. J. Rawnsley run out	7
W. P. C. Weston run out	22	A. Sheriyar not out	3
G. A. Hick c M. Newell b Rao	56	R. K. Illingworth not out	1
K. R. Spiring c Phillips b Rao	31	B 5, l-b 9, w 8	22
V. S. Solanki lbw b Kirtley	7		——
D. A. Leatherdale c and b Rao	2	1/18 2/46 3/109 (9 wkts, 40 overs)	187
S. R. Lampitt c Wells b Law	27	4/121 5/126 6/148	
†S. J. Rhodes c M. Newell b Law	5	7/160 8/175 9/185	

Bowling: Law 8–0–34–3; Strong 8–2–29–0; Phillips 3–0–19–0; Salisbury 8–0–35–0; Kirtley 6–0–25–1; Rao 7–0–31–3.

Umpires: J. W. Holder and B. J. Meyer.

WORCESTERSHIRE v GLOUCESTERSHIRE

At Worcester, September 15. Worcestershire won by 14 runs. Toss: Gloucestershire.

Moody and Curtis opened with 169. Then Hick, whose half-century came from 27 balls with two fours and four sixes, saw Worcestershire to a substantial total. But Gloucestershire were serious contenders until the loss of Dawson.

Worcestershire

*T. M. Moody b Symonds	102
T. S. Curtis c Symonds b Ball	77
G. A. Hick not out	57
W. P. C. Weston not out	4
L-b 5, w 12	17
1/169 2/219 (2 wkts, 40 overs)	257

V. S. Solanki, D. A. Leatherdale, S. R. Lampitt, †S. J. Rhodes, R. K. Illingworth, P. A. Thomas and S. W. K. Ellis did not bat.

Bowling: Smith 8–2–36–0; Lewis 8–0–46–0; Ball 8–0–69–1; Symonds 8–0–46–1; Davis 8–0–55–0.

Gloucestershire

R. I. Dawson c Illingworth b Solanki	85
M. G. N. Windows b Illingworth	37
A. Symonds b Leatherdale	37
*†M. W. Alleyne b Leatherdale	3
M. A. Lynch c Leatherdale b Moody	45
A. J. Wright st Rhodes b Illingworth	21
T. H. C. Hancock st Rhodes b Illingworth	2
M. C. J. Ball not out	2
R. P. Davis not out	2
L-b 3, w 2, n-b 4	9
1/98 2/149 3/159 4/188 5/235 6/238 7/241 (7 wkts, 40 overs)	243

A. M. Smith and J. Lewis did not bat.

Bowling: Thomas 6–0–30–0; Moody 8–0–49–1; Lampitt 8–0–49–0; Illingworth 8–0–52–3; Leatherdale 8–0–41–2; Solanki 2–0–19–1.

Umpires: J. H. Hampshire and R. Palmer.

YORKSHIRE

At Cardiff, May 5. YORKSHIRE lost to GLAMORGAN by four wickets.

YORKSHIRE v DERBYSHIRE

At Sheffield, May 12. Yorkshire won by 45 runs. Toss: Derbyshire.

No white ball was available for this match, Yorkshire's supply having been left at Headingley. A special dispensation to use a red ball was given by Lord's. The actual cricket gave Yorkshire few problems.

Yorkshire

*D. Byas c Jones b Harris	31
M. P. Vaughan b Cork	24
M. G. Bevan run out	5
A. McGrath c Krikken b Griffith	16
C. White c DeFreitas b Aldred	45
†R. J. Blakey c Adams b Wells	36
D. Gough c DeFreitas b Cork	20
A. C. Morris run out	14
P. J. Hartley c Wells b Cork	2
C. E. W. Silverwood not out	1
L-b 4, w 4, n-b 8	16
1/58 2/68 3/87 4/87 5/171 6/173 7/202 8/207 9/210 (9 wkts, 40 overs)	210

R. D. Stemp did not bat.

Bowling: Cork 8–0–41–3; DeFreitas 6–0–46–0; Griffith 8–0–30–1; Harris 6–1–23–1; Wells 6–0–26–1; Jones 1–0–5–0; Aldred 5–0–35–1.

Derbyshire

K. J. Barnett lbw b Silverwood	52	F. A. Griffith run out	0
*D. M. Jones c Byas b Stemp	23	P. Aldred not out	7
C. J. Adams b Gough	39	A. J. Harris b White	1
J. E. Owen c and b Stemp	0	B 1, l-b 8, w 2, n-b 2	13
C. M. Wells c and b Stemp	8		—
P. A. J. DeFreitas lbw b White	12	1/80 2/81 3/82 (37.3 overs)	165
†K. M. Krikken lbw b Gough	0	4/103 5/138 6/139	
D. G. Cork run out	10	7/148 8/149 9/162	

Bowling: Hartley 7–0–30–0; Gough 8–0–38–2; Silverwood 8–0–26–1; White 6.3–0–30–2; Stemp 8–0–32–3.

Umpires: J. H. Hampshire and N. T. Plews.

At Chester-le-Street, May 19. YORKSHIRE beat DURHAM by 63 runs.

At Canterbury, May 26. YORKSHIRE lost to KENT by ten wickets.

At Lord's, June 2. YORKSHIRE lost to MIDDLESEX by six wickets.

YORKSHIRE v SURREY

At Leeds, June 9. Yorkshire won by eight wickets. Toss: Surrey.

The Yorkshire bowlers were in miserly mood, none more so than Hartley, who bowled eight overs for nine runs. Surrey were bowled out for 90, their lowest total against Yorkshire in this competition. Yorkshire survived the loss of two early wickets to make serene progress to their target in the 26th over.

Surrey

D. M. Ward c Bevan b Silverwood	2	†G. J. Kersey not out	22
A. D. Brown b Silverwood	5	M. P. Bicknell c Hartley b Silverwood	0
D. J. Bicknell run out	22	J. E. Benjamin lbw b Gough	0
N. Shahid c Blakey b White	2	L-b 3, w 3	6
*A. J. Hollioake b White	2		—
B. P. Julian lbw b Hartley	16	1/7 2/8 3/22 (32.4 overs)	90
I. J. Ward lbw b Hartley	1	4/30 5/40 6/50	
B. C. Hollioake lbw b Stemp	12	7/57 8/72 9/73	

Bowling: Gough 5.4–1–12–1; Silverwood 8–1–28–3; White 5–0–14–2; Hartley 8–2–9–2; Stemp 6–0–24–1.

Yorkshire

*D. Byas c B. C. Hollioake b M. P. Bicknell	8	M. G. Bevan not out	37
M. D. Moxon c M. P. Bicknell b A. J. Hollioake	16	L-b 1, w 4, n-b 2	7
			—
M. P. Vaughan not out	25	1/10 2/29 (2 wkts, 25.5 overs)	93

C. White, †R. J. Blakey, A. C. Morris, D. Gough, P. J. Hartley, C. E. W. Silverwood and R. D. Stemp did not bat.

Bowling: M. P. Bicknell 6–2–17–1; B. C. Hollioake 8–1–16–0; A. J. Hollioake 7–1–26–1; Julian 2–0–11–0; Benjamin 1–0–8–0; I. J. Ward 1.5–0–14–0.

Umpires: B. Dudleston and B. Leadbeater.

YORKSHIRE v WARWICKSHIRE

At Leeds, June 16. Warwickshire won by five runs. Toss: Yorkshire. First-team debut: M. D. Edmond.

Needing 27 to win with eight wickets in hand, Yorkshire lost six in 20 balls and, with them, the match. Byas and Bevan had set up an apparently impregnable position with a second-wicket partnership of 140, but Warwickshire's bowlers and fielders stuck at their task.

Warwickshire

N. M. K. Smith b Silverwood	1
D. P. Ostler b Hartley	86
D. R. Brown st Blakey b Stemp	29
P. A. Smith run out	1
T. L. Penney c Vaughan b Bevan	12
S. M. Pollock c White b Bevan	16
*A. J. Moles b Gough	16
G. Welch not out	19
†K. J. Piper b Gough	4
A. F. Giles b Gough	7
M. D. Edmond not out	5
B 4, l-b 4, w 1	9
1/5 2/65 3/66 4/84 5/131 6/163 7/181 8/187 9/197 (9 wkts, 40 overs)	205

Bowling: Gough 7–0–31–3; Silverwood 5–0–30–1; White 5–0–23–0; Stemp 8–0–33–1; Bevan 8–0–39–2; Vaughan 1–0–13–0; Hartley 6–0–28–1.

Yorkshire

*D. Byas b Edmond	77
M. P. Vaughan b Pollock	0
M. G. Bevan st Piper b Welch	89
A. McGrath run out	14
C. White lbw b Pollock	3
†R. J. Blakey c sub b Welch	2
D. Gough run out	5
P. J. Hartley not out	2
A. C. Morris c Piper b Welch	0
C. E. W. Silverwood not out	0
L-b 1, w 1, n-b 6	8
1/4 2/144 3/179 4/190 5/190 6/197 7/197 8/198 (8 wkts, 40 overs)	200

R. D. Stemp did not bat.

Bowling: Welch 7–0–37–3; Pollock 8–0–30–2; Giles 4–0–18–0; P. A. Smith 3–0–27–0; N. M. K. Smith 2–0–25–0; Edmond 8–1–27–1; Brown 8–0–35–0.

Umpires: D. J. Constant and A. G. T. Whitehead.

YORKSHIRE v LEICESTERSHIRE

At Bradford, June 23. Yorkshire won by 36 runs. Toss: Yorkshire.

On a pitch more suited to Championship than one-day cricket, Yorkshire successfully defended 181. Only Maddy and Simmons reached double figures for Leicestershire as Stemp spun Yorkshire to victory.

Yorkshire

*D. Byas c Whitaker b Parsons	6
M. P. Vaughan c Simmons b Wells	20
M. G. Bevan run out	13
A. McGrath c Simmons b Williamson	41
C. White b Remy	1
†R. J. Blakey c Parsons b Remy	9
A. C. Morris st Nixon b Williamson	12
D. Gough b Williamson	21
P. J. Hartley not out	22
C. E. W. Silverwood b Parsons	8
R. D. Stemp c Smith b Parsons	7
L-b 10, w 7, n-b 4	21
1/15 2/41 3/58 4/61 5/90 6/109 7/122 8/144 9/168 (40 overs)	181

Bowling: Simmons 8–0–42–0; Parsons 8–0–37–3; Remy 8–0–20–2; Wells 8–1–31–1; Williamson 6–0–29–3; Maddy 2–0–12–0.

Leicestershire

P. V. Simmons c Stemp b Hartley	44	G. J. Parsons not out	2
V. J. Wells c Byas b Silverwood	6	D. Williamson b Stemp	0
B. F. Smith lbw b Gough	7	A. R. K. Pierson b Hartley	9
D. L. Maddy c McGrath b Bevan	54	B 1, l-b 1, w 4, n-b 2	8
*J. J. Whitaker b Hartley	2		—
J. M. Dakin c Gough b Stemp	7	1/24 2/34 3/76 (34.3 overs)	145
†P. A. Nixon run out	5	4/85 5/114 6/128	
C. C. Remy b Stemp	1	7/130 8/130 9/130	

Bowling: Gough 6–1–25–1; Silverwood 4–0–27–1; Hartley 7.3–0–27–3; White 4–0–26–0; Stemp 8–1–17–3; Bevan 5–1–21–1.

Umpires: B. J. Meyer and K. E. Palmer.

At Worcester, June 30. YORKSHIRE beat WORCESTERSHIRE by five wickets.

At Northampton, July 16. YORKSHIRE beat NORTHAMPTONSHIRE by two wickets.

YORKSHIRE v HAMPSHIRE

At Leeds, July 21. Yorkshire won by seven wickets. Toss: Yorkshire.

After picking up two wickets, Bevan reverted to his more usual role of batsman to score an undefeated 98 from 96 balls. In the process he passed 1,000 League runs in only 26 innings. Yorkshire objected to a substitute fielder coming on for Benjamin, whom they suspected of being injured before the game. Benjamin then returned.

Hampshire

R. A. Smith b Gough	10	†A. N. Aymes b White	0
J. S. Laney b White	29	S. D. Udal not out	0
M. Keech c Blakey b Bevan	37	B 1, l-b 4, w 4, n-b 2	11
W. K. M. Benjamin c Stemp b Bevan	62		—
W. S. Kendall b Gough	31	1/27 2/48 3/136 (8 wkts, 40 overs)	211
*J. P. Stephenson c Byas b White	28	4/143 5/204 6/209	
K. D. James run out	3	7/210 8/211	

S. M. Milburn and C. A. Connor did not bat.

Bowling: Gough 8–0–43–2; Silverwood 8–2–28–0; White 8–1–41–3; Hartley 8–0–41–0; Stemp 4–0–27–0; Bevan 4–0–26–2.

Yorkshire

M. D. Moxon c Benjamin b Udal	46	A. McGrath not out	24
M. P. Vaughan c Milburn b James	19	L-b 4, w 2, n-b 2	8
M. G. Bevan not out	98		—
C. White c Kendall b Stephenson	18	1/41 2/111 3/158 (3 wkts, 38 overs)	213

*D. Byas, †R. J. Blakey, D. Gough, P. J. Hartley, C. E. W. Silverwood and R. D. Stemp did not bat.

Bowling: Stephenson 8–0–29–1; Milburn 8–0–49–0; James 7–0–46–1; Connor 7–0–44–0; Udal 8–0–41–1.

Umpires: H. D. Bird and J. H. Harris.

YORKSHIRE v SOMERSET

At Scarborough, July 28. Somerset won by two runs. Toss: Somerset.

After his opening spell, Caddick returned to concede only six runs from two overs near the end of Yorkshire's innings to secure his side's narrow victory. In his last over, he also bowled top-scorer Blakey, who had controlled the reply to a competent batting display by Somerset.

Somerset

M. N. Lathwell c Blakey b Hartley	19
P. D. Bowler b Gough	53
S. C. Ecclestone c Blakey b Hartley	1
R. J. Harden b White	57
S. Lee c Bevan b Hartley	52
†R. J. Turner not out	23
G. D. Rose not out	7
B 2, l-b 6, w 6, n-b 6	20
1/57 2/59 3/117 4/176 5/223 (5 wkts, 40 overs)	232

*A. N. Hayhurst, K. A. Parsons, H. R. J. Trump and A. R. Caddick did not bat.

Bowling: Silverwood 8–1–34–0; Gough 8–0–56–1; Stemp 8–1–36–0; Hartley 8–0–45–3; White 6–0–34–1; Bevan 2–0–19–0.

Yorkshire

M. D. Moxon c and b Rose	8
M. P. Vaughan c Trump b Rose	31
M. G. Bevan c Turner b Trump	33
C. White lbw b Hayhurst	26
*D. Byas lbw b Trump	17
A. McGrath lbw b Hayhurst	1
†R. J. Blakey b Caddick	49
D. Gough c Caddick b Hayhurst	21
P. J. Hartley not out	22
C. E. W. Silverwood not out	9
L-b 2, w 3, n-b 8	13
1/17 2/80 3/85 4/117 5/118 6/137 7/171 8/215 (8 wkts, 40 overs)	230

R. D. Stemp did not bat.

Bowling: Caddick 8–0–38–1; Rose 8–0–38–2; Lee 8–0–54–0; Trump 8–0–51–2; Hayhurst 8–1–47–3.

Umpires: G. Sharp and R. A. White.

At Eastbourne, August 4. YORKSHIRE beat SUSSEX by eight wickets.

At Bristol, August 18. YORKSHIRE beat GLOUCESTERSHIRE by 133 runs.

YORKSHIRE v LANCASHIRE

At Leeds, August 25. Yorkshire won by six wickets. Toss: Yorkshire.

A crowd of 6,500 saw Yorkshire's first home League win over Lancashire since 1983. After the visitors' powerful batting line-up had been restricted to 205, Byas guided Yorkshire home with 111 not out in 100 balls and eight overs to spare. Victory put Yorkshire in sole possession of top place in the table, though their rivals had games in hand. When he dismissed Vaughan, Watkinson took his 200th Sunday League wicket.

Lancashire

J. E. R. Gallian c Kettleborough b White	7
*M. Watkinson c Byas b White	46
P. C. McKeown c Blakey b Hartley	18
G. D. Lloyd c McGrath b Stemp	46
N. H. Fairbrother c Byas b Stemp	19
A. Flintoff c Kettleborough b Gough	2
†W. K. Hegg b Hartley	16
I. D. Austin c Kettleborough b Hartley	7
G. Yates not out	12
S. Elworthy not out	7
B 1, l-b 19, w 1, n-b 4	25
1/56 2/56 3/101 4/138 5/145 6/158 7/180 8/187 (8 wkts, 40 overs)	205

P. J. Martin did not bat.

Bowling: Gough 8–0–55–1; Silverwood 8–1–33–0; White 8–2–18–2; Hartley 8–0–43–3; Stemp 8–0–36–2.

Yorkshire

*D. Byas not out 111
M. D. Moxon c Watkinson b Yates 7
M. P. Vaughan lbw b Watkinson 21
D. Gough b Watkinson 2
P. J. Hartley c Elworthy b Watkinson 38
C. White not out 5
B 2, l-b 9, w 5, n-b 6 22

1/44 2/108 3/112 4/172 (4 wkts, 32.1 overs) 206

A. McGrath, R. A. Kettleborough, †R. J. Blakey, C. E. W. Silverwood and R. D. Stemp did not bat.

Bowling: Austin 8–0–32–0; Martin 5–0–52–0; Yates 5–0–34–1; Elworthy 6–0–33–0; Watkinson 8–0–40–3; Gallian 0.1–0–4–0.

Umpires: J. H. Harris and V. A. Holder.

YORKSHIRE v ESSEX

At Leeds, September 1. Yorkshire won by six wickets. Toss: Yorkshire.

After a disastrous performance the previous day that was to cost them their chance of the Championship, Essex returned to the scene of the crime to perform predictably badly in a competition about which they cared little. A depleted team slumped to an eighth successive League defeat, while Yorkshire won their eighth out of nine to stay top of the table though, having played more than their rivals, they knew they were unlikely to be champions. White's four wickets came in 16 balls.

Essex

*N. Hussain b Silverwood.............. 6
A. P. Grayson c Blakey b Silverwood 15
†R. J. Rollins lbw b Hamilton 0
J. J. B. Lewis lbw b Stemp............. 21
T. P. Hodgson c Moxon b White 6
A. J. E. Hibbert b White............... 0
S. D. Peters b White 1
M. C. Ilott c McGrath b White.......... 2
A. P. Cowan b Hartley 0
S. J. W. Andrew c Vaughan b Stemp 32
P. M. Such not out 9
B 4, l-b 5, w 1, n-b 6 16

1/19 2/22 3/30 4/46 5/46 6/50 7/54 8/56 9/73 (37.3 overs) 108

Bowling: Hamilton 8–2–26–1; Silverwood 8–3–16–2; White 8–1–21–4; Hartley 7–1–23–1; Stemp 6.3–1–13–2.

Yorkshire

*D. Byas not out 40
M. D. Moxon lbw b Ilott 10
M. P. Vaughan run out 21
P. J. Hartley b Andrew 12
C. White st Rollins b Grayson 11
A. McGrath not out 6
L-b 3, w 4, n-b 2............. 9

1/27 2/78 3/92 4/103 (4 wkts, 24.2 overs) 109

R. A. Kettleborough, †R. J. Blakey, G. M. Hamilton, C. E. W. Silverwood and R. D. Stemp did not bat.

Bowling: Andrew 5.2–0–28–1; Ilott 6–2–12–1; Cowan 5–0–14–0; Such 4–0–19–0; Grayson 4–0–33–1.

Umpires: J. C. Balderstone and K. J. Lyons.

YORKSHIRE v NOTTINGHAMSHIRE

At Scarborough, September 15. Nottinghamshire won by 24 runs. Toss: Yorkshire.

If Nottinghamshire were to take the title, they needed to win while Surrey slipped up; Yorkshire had to win to secure second place. To the disappointment of most of an 8,000 crowd, Nottinghamshire were the victors, but had to be content with being runners-up as Surrey took the trophy on net run-rate. Cairns hit his first ball for six, thrashed 38 off 16 balls, and then took five wickets.

Nottinghamshire

R. T. Robinson c Gough b Silverwood	51	C. M. Tolley not out	14
M. P. Dowman c Kettleborough b Hartley	26		
A. A. Metcalfe c Gough b Stemp	15	L-b 8, w 2, n-b 10	20
*P. Johnson lbw b Gough	52		—
P. R. Pollard b Hartley	35	1/50 2/102 3/108 (5 wkts, 40 overs)	251
C. L. Cairns not out	38	4/189 5/216	

K. P. Evans, †W. M. Noon, R. T. Bates and M. N. Bowen did not bat.

Bowling: Gough 8–0–41–1; Silverwood 8–0–32–1; White 8–0–49–0; Hartley 8–0–66–2; Stemp 8–0–55–1.

Yorkshire

*D. Byas lbw b Evans	9	R. A. Kettleborough not out	11
M. D. Moxon c Bates b Cairns	45	C. E. W. Silverwood b Cairns	2
M. P. Vaughan b Dowman	48	R. D. Stemp c Bates b Cairns	11
C. White b Cairns	5	L-b 4, w 2	6
A. McGrath c Evans b Cairns	3		—
P. J. Hartley c Bowen b Tolley	28	1/18 2/78 3/86 (39 overs)	227
†R. J. Blakey b Tolley	29	4/90 5/139 6/155	
D. Gough c Pollard b Bowen	30	7/196 8/206 9/211	

Bowling: Evans 7–0–33–1; Bowen 8–0–47–1; Tolley 8–0–45–2; Cairns 8–1–41–5; Bates 4–0–33–0; Dowman 4–0–24–1.

Umpires: J. W. Holder and P. Willey.

SUNDAY LEAGUE RECORDS

Batting

Highest individual score: 176, G. A. Gooch, Essex v Glamorgan, Southend, 1983.

Most runs: 8,545, G. A. Gooch; 7,499, W. Larkins; 7,252, C. W. J. Athey; 7,092, K. J. Barnett; 7,062, D. W. Randall; 7,040, D. L. Amiss; 6,650, C. T. Radley; 6,639, D. R. Turner; 6,507, M. W. Gatting; 6,506, P. Willey. **In a season:** 917, T. M. Moody, Worcestershire, 1991.

Most hundreds: 14, W. Larkins; 12, G. A. Gooch; 11, C. G. Greenidge; 9, K. S. McEwan, T. M. Moody, B. A. Richards and R. A. Smith. 552 hundreds have been scored in the League. The most in one season is 40 in 1990.

Most sixes in an innings: 13, I. T. Botham, Somerset v Northamptonshire, Wellingborough School, 1986. **By a team in an innings:** 18, Derbyshire v Worcestershire, Knypersley, 1985, and Surrey v Yorkshire, Scarborough, 1994. **In a season:** 26, I. V. A. Richards, Somerset, 1977.

Highest total: 375 for four, Surrey v Yorkshire, Scarborough, 1994. **By a side batting second:** 317 for six, Surrey v Nottinghamshire, The Oval, 1993 (50-overs match).

Highest match aggregate: 631 for 13 wickets, Nottinghamshire (314 for seven) v Surrey (317 for six), The Oval, 1993 (50-overs match).

Lowest total: 23 (19.4 overs), Middlesex v Yorkshire, Leeds, 1974.

Shortest completed innings: 16 overs (59), Northamptonshire v Middlesex, Tring, 1974.

Record partnerships for each wicket

239	for 1st	G. A. Gooch and B. R. Hardie, Essex v Nottinghamshire at Nottingham	1985
273	for 2nd	G. A. Gooch and K. S. McEwan, Essex v Nottinghamshire at Nottingham	1983
223	for 3rd	S. J. Cook and G. D. Rose, Somerset v Glamorgan at Neath	1990
219	for 4th	C. G. Greenidge and C. L. Smith, Hampshire v Surrey at Southampton	1987
190	for 5th	R. J. Blakey and M. J. Foster, Yorkshire v Leicestershire at Leicester	1993
137	for 6th	M. P. Speight and I. D. K. Salisbury, Sussex v Surrey at Guildford	1996
132	for 7th	K. R. Brown and N. F. Williams, Middlesex v Somerset at Lord's	1988
110*	for 8th	C. L. Cairns and B. N. French, Nottinghamshire v Surrey at The Oval	1993
105	for 9th	D. G. Moir and R. W. Taylor, Derbyshire v Kent at Derby	1984
82	for 10th	G. Chapple and P. J. Martin, Lancashire v Worcestershire at Manchester	1996

Bowling

Most wickets: 386, J. K. Lever; 355, J. E. Emburey; 346, D. L. Underwood; 307, J. Simmons; 303, S. Turner; 284, N. Gifford; 281, E. E. Hemmings; 267, J. N. Shepherd; 260, A. C. S. Pigott; 256, I. T. Botham; 249, T. E. Jesty; 234, R. D. Jackman and P. Willey. **In a season:** 39, A. J. Hollioake, Surrey, 1996.

Best bowling: eight for 26, K. D. Boyce, Essex v Lancashire, Manchester, 1971; seven for 15, R. A. Hutton, Yorkshire v Worcestershire, Leeds, 1969; seven for 39, A. Hodgson, Northamptonshire v Somerset, Northampton, 1976; seven for 41, A. N. Jones, Sussex v Nottinghamshire, Nottingham, 1986; six for six, R. W. Hooker, Middlesex v Surrey, Lord's, 1969; six for seven, M. Hendrick, Derbyshire v Nottinghamshire, Nottingham, 1972; six for nine, N. G. Cowans, Middlesex v Lancashire, Lord's, 1991.

Most economical analysis: 8–8–0–0, B. A. Langford, Somerset v Essex, Yeovil, 1969.

Most expensive analyses: 8–0–96–1, D. G. Cork, Derbyshire v Nottinghamshire, Nottingham, 1993; 8–0–94–2, P. N. Weekes, Middlesex v Leicestershire, Leicester, 1994; 7.5–0–89–3, G. Miller, Derbyshire v Gloucestershire, Gloucester, 1984; 8–0–88–1, E. E. Hemmings, Nottinghamshire v Somerset, Nottingham, 1983.

Hat-tricks: There have been 24 hat-tricks, four of them for Glamorgan.

Four wickets in four balls: A. Ward, Derbyshire v Sussex, Derby, 1970.

Wicket-keeping and Fielding

Most dismissals: 257 (234 ct, 23 st), D. L. Bairstow; 240 (186 ct, 54 st), S. J. Rhodes; 236 (187 ct, 49 st), R. W. Taylor; 223 (184 ct, 39 st), E. W. Jones. **In a season:** 29 (26 ct, 3 st), S. J. Rhodes, Worcestershire, 1988. **In an innings:** 7 (6 ct, 1 st), R. W. Taylor, Derbyshire v Lancashire, Manchester, 1975.

Most catches in an innings: 6, K. Goodwin, Lancashire v Worcestershire, Worcester, 1969; R. W. Taylor, Derbyshire v Lancashire, Manchester, 1975; K. M. Krikken, Derbyshire v Hampshire, Southampton, 1994; and P. A. Nixon, Leicestershire v Essex, Leicester, 1994.

Most stumpings in an innings: 4, S. J. Rhodes, Worcestershire v Warwickshire, Birmingham, 1986 and N. D. Burns, Somerset v Kent, Taunton, 1991.

Most catches by a fielder: 103, V. P. Terry; 101, J. F. Steele; 100, G. A. Gooch; 97, D. P. Hughes; 95, C. W. J. Athey†; 94, G. Cook and P. W. G. Parker. **In a season:** 16, J. M. Rice, Hampshire, 1978. **In an innings:** 5, J. M. Rice, Hampshire v Warwickshire, Southampton, 1978.

† C. W. J. Athey has also taken two catches as a wicket-keeper.

Results

Largest victory in runs: Somerset by 220 runs v Glamorgan, Neath, 1990.

Victories by ten wickets (32)**:** By Derbyshire, Durham, Essex (four times), Glamorgan (twice), Hampshire (twice), Kent, Leicestershire (twice), Middlesex (twice), Northamptonshire, Nottinghamshire, Somerset (twice), Surrey (three times), Warwickshire, Worcestershire (six times) and Yorkshire (three times). This does not include those matches in which the side batting second was set a reduced target but does include matches where both sides faced a reduced number of overs.

Ties: There have been 43 tied matches. Worcestershire have tied nine times.

Shortest match: 1 hr 53 min (26.3 overs), Surrey v Leicestershire, The Oval, 1996.

CHAMPIONS 1969-96

John Player's County League
1969 Lancashire
John Player League
1970 Lancashire
1971 Worcestershire
1972 Kent
1973 Kent
1974 Leicestershire
1975 Hampshire
1976 Kent
1977 Leicestershire
1978 Hampshire
1979 Somerset
1980 Warwickshire
1981 Essex
1982 Sussex
1983 Yorkshire
John Player Special League
1984 Essex
1985 Essex
1986 Hampshire
Refuge Assurance League
1987 Worcestershire
1988 Worcestershire
1989 Lancashire
1990 Derbyshire
1991 Nottinghamshire
Sunday League
1992 Middlesex
AXA Equity & Law League
1993 Glamorgan
1994 Warwickshire
1995 Kent
1996 Surrey

MATCH RESULTS 1969-96

	Matches					*League positions*		
	P	*W*	*L*	*T*	*NR*	*1st*	*2nd*	*3rd*
Derbyshire	453	194	210	4	45	1	0	1
Durham	85	26	45	2	12	0	0	0
Essex	453	234	174	7	38	3	5*	3
Glamorgan	453	161	239	4	49	1	0	0
Gloucestershire	453	154	242	4	53	0	1	1
Hampshire	453	218	189	7	39	3	1	3
Kent	453	244	161	6	42	4	3	4
Lancashire	453	229	167	8	49	3	2	2
Leicestershire	453	193	201	2	57	2	2*	2
Middlesex	453	207	193	6	47	1	1	3
Northamptonshire	453	176	226	5	46	0	0	1
Nottinghamshire	453	192	218	3	40	1	3	1
Somerset	453	213	193	2	45	1	6*	0
Surrey	453	203	198	4	48	1	0	1
Sussex	453	196	204	5	48	1	2*	1
Warwickshire	453	189	209	6	49	2	1	1
Worcestershire	453	222	182	9	40	3	3	2
Yorkshire	453	202	202	2	47	1	1	1

* *Includes one shared 2nd place in 1976.*

THE UNIVERSITIES IN 1996

OXFORD

President: C. A. Fry (Trinity)
Hon. Treasurer: Dr S. R. Porter (St Cross College)

Captain: C. M. Gupte (John Lyon and Pembroke)
Secretary: D. P. Mather (Wirral GS and St Hugh's)

Captain for 1997: M. A. Wagh (King Edward's, Birmingham, and Keble)
Secretary: B. W. Byrne (Western Australia U. and Balliol)

A record-breaking batting display in the Varsity match at Lord's was the highlight of Oxford University's campaign. They were unbeaten in their ten first-class matches, but the programme was once again sabotaged by wet and cold conditions. The die was cast when the curtain-raiser with Leicestershire was delayed until mid-afternoon on the opening day of the season as the ground recovered from an overnight blizzard. By the time the Nottinghamshire fixture was washed out, five of the opening 18 days had been completely swallowed up by bad weather.

When the sun did finally shine, the Oxford batsmen performed with distinction, as they consolidated their improvement under coach Les Lenham. Five topped 400 first-class runs, with captain Chinmay Gupte crowning his sixth and final season by scoring 606 runs, including two centuries, with his text-book technique. Gul Khan, a post-graduate from Swansea University released by Essex at the end of 1995, revealed himself as a natural strokeplayer, and his arrival injected much adventure into the middle order. After several near-misses, he fashioned a maiden first-class century against Kent at Canterbury, which followed a brilliant 147 for the British Universities against Glamorgan in the Benson and Hedges Cup. He joined Derbyshire in July. Iain Sutcliffe, already on Leicestershire's books, Will Kendall, signed up with Hampshire, and Andrew Ridley, the Bradman Scholar, also played several notable innings, not least in the Varsity match. There, Oxford took revenge for their defeat in the second limited-overs Varsity game, played in May, by scoring 513 for six, the highest total in the history of a fixture dating back to 1827. Kendall, who played no first-class cricket before June because of exams, and Ridley both made big hundreds. Ridley's maiden first-class century in the opening match against Leicestershire had given Oxford a glimpse of what could have been a famous victory. Jonathan Batty, a wicket-keeper/batsman who played for the Minor Counties in the Benson and Hedges Cup, also enhanced Oxford's reputation as a breeding ground for batsmen.

Again, the University's shortcomings were in the bowling. Their lack of new-ball penetration was always evident on featherbed wickets offering little encouragement to seamers, though they toiled manfully for their meagre rewards. In eight first-class games in The Parks, the South African left-armer Pierre du Preez, a rugby Blue, mustered just three victims (for 482 runs). Both Russell Thomson and David Mather struggled, although Mather could count himself a touch unfortunate to be omitted from the Varsity team. Off-spinners Mark Wagh and Hasnain Malik did more to catch the eye on pitches that turned more than in previous years. Wagh, a freshman on the Warwickshire staff and an England Under-19 player, takes over as captain from Gupte in 1997, when Oxford will also have a new coach. Les Lenham stepped down after seven seasons and Andy Flower, the Zimbabwean Test player, was named as his successor. But with most of the players departing – some after completing one-year courses – only two Blues, Wagh himself and Mather, are expected to be in residence. The portents are for a demanding baptism. – MIKE BERRY.

OXFORD UNIVERSITY RESULTS

First-class matches – Played 10: Drawn 10.

FIRST-CLASS AVERAGES

BATTING AND FIELDING

	Birthplace	*M*	*I*	*NO*	*R*	*HS*	*Avge*	*Ct/St*
W. S. Kendall	*Wimbledon*	4	7	2	444	145*	88.80	2
G. A. Khan	*Gujrat, Pakistan*	9	11	2	517	101*	57.44	3
C. M. Gupte	*Poona, India*	10	13	1	606	132	50.50	1
A. C. Ridley.........	*Sydney, Australia*	7	9	0	417	155	46.33	1
I. J. Sutcliffe.........	*Leeds*	6	9	0	408	83	45.33	1
J. N. Batty	*Chesterfield*	10	13	3	302	56	30.20	9/2
H. S. Malik	*Sargodha, Pakistan*	10	13	3	240	61	24.00	7
M. E. D. Jarrett	*London*	7	6	2	82	50*	20.50	4
M. A. Wagh.........	*Birmingham*	10	12	3	169	43	18.77	1
C. G. R. Lightfoot	*Amersham*	4	4	1	15	9	5.00	0
R. B. Thomson	*Johannesburg, SA*	10	6	6	34	14*	–	1

Also batted: J. J. Bull (*Leicester*) (2 matches) 4; S. P. du Preez (*Port Elizabeth, SA*) (10 matches) 1*, 9 (3 ct); A. W. Maclay (*Salisbury*) (2 matches) 1*; D. P. Mather (*Bebington*) (8 matches) 2, 0; G. J. Wright (*Holmfirth*) (1 match) did not bat.

* *Signifies not out.*

The following played a total of seven three-figure innings for Oxford University – C. M. Gupte 2, W. S. Kendall 2, A. C. Ridley 2, G. A. Khan 1.

BOWLING

	O	*M*	*R*	*W*	*BB*	*5W/i*	*Avge*
M. A. Wagh	155.3	27	469	9	3-82	0	52.11
R. B. Thomson ...	183.4	36	527	9	2-24	0	58.55
D. P. Mather	137.4	19	536	9	3-31	0	59.55
H. S. Malik	197	23	826	10	3-119	0	82.60
S. P. du Preez	168	24	634	5	2-44	0	126.80

Also bowled: C. M. Gupte 2–0–10–0; M. E. D. Jarrett 2–0–5–0; W. S. Kendall 5–0–35–0; G. A. Khan 25–0–151–3; C. G. R. Lightfoot 27.5–5–129–2; A. W. Maclay 31–3–147–1; A. C. Ridley 5–1–19–0; I. J. Sutcliffe 12–1–47–2; G. J. Wright 9–0–33–0.

Note: Matches in this section which were not first-class are signified by a dagger.

†At Oxford, April 12. Oxford University v Northamptonshire. Abandoned.

OXFORD UNIVERSITY 1996

[*Bill Smith*

Back row: L. J. Lenham (*coach*), G. A. Khan, M. E. D. Jarrett, S. P. du Preez, A. W. Maclay, M. A. Wagh, R. B. Thomson, W. S. Kendall, J. N. Batty, G. S. Gordon (*scorer*). *Front row:* H. S. Malik, I. J. Sutcliffe, C. M. Gupte (*captain*), A. C. Ridley, D. P. Mather.

OXFORD UNIVERSITY v LEICESTERSHIRE

At Oxford, April 13, 15, 16. Drawn. Toss: Leicestershire. First-class debuts: S. P. du Preez, G. A. Khan, R. B. Thomson, M. A. Wagh. Oxford debut: J. N. Batty. County debut: C. C. Remy.

Oxford, set a sporting target of 238 in 42 overs, gave Leicestershire a run for their money. Ridley inspired the chase with his maiden first-class century, from 108 balls with four sixes and eight fours. The university entered the last 20 overs on 80 for one and clubbed 40 off the next four. With ten overs left, they needed 86; then Ridley departed, Khan perished second ball and three run-outs saw the match fizzle out. No play had been possible until 3 p.m. on the opening day. That evening Smith, who scored a career-best 123, and Nixon began a forceful fifth-wicket stand of 176. Khan just missed a century on debut, scoring an entertaining 94 off 123 balls, and he hit Millns for six with an audacious hook over a 90-yard boundary.

Close of play: First day, Leicestershire 139-4 (B. F. Smith 58*, P. A. Nixon 10*); Second day, Oxford University 133-4 (G. A. Khan 56*, H. S. Malik 6*).

Leicestershire

G. I. Macmillan b du Preez	8	– (2) c Jarrett b Mather	17
V. J. Wells run out	57	– (3) c Ridley b Malik	33
B. F. Smith not out	123		
D. L. Maddy c du Preez b Malik	2	– not out	33
*J. J. Whitaker lbw b Thomson	0	– (1) b Malik	47
†P. A. Nixon not out	100		
G. J. Parsons (did not bat)		– (5) not out	14
L-b 6, w 3	9	W 1	1
1/14 2/115 3/121 4/123	(4 wkts dec.) 299	1/38 2/84 3/105	(3 wkts dec.) 145

A. D. Mullally, C. C. Remy, A. R. K. Pierson and D. J. Millns did not bat.

Bowling: *First Innings*—du Preez 18–0–60–1; Thomson 19–6–46–1; Wagh 7–0–29–0; Mather 19.4–2–81–0; Malik 20–3–65–1; Khan 2–0–12–0. *Second Innings*—Mather 11–1–56–1; du Preez 5–0–20–0; Malik 11–0–46–2; Wagh 4–0–18–0; Khan 1–0–5–0.

Oxford University

*C. M. Gupte c Parsons b Pierson	29	– c Pierson b Millns	5
I. J. Sutcliffe c Wells b Parsons	16	– c Pierson b Parsons	65
A. C. Ridley c Nixon b Mullally	15	– c Pierson b Maddy	104
G. A. Khan c Nixon b Millns	94	– lbw b Maddy	0
M. A. Wagh c Millns b Wells	0	– run out	13
H. S. Malik c Nixon b Millns	15	– not out	11
M. E. D. Jarrett not out	8	– run out	0
†J. N. Batty not out	16	– run out	1
R. B. Thomson (did not bat)		– not out	0
B 4, l-b 10	14	L-b 11, n-b 2	13
1/30 2/45 3/113 4/114 5/176 6/187	(6 wkts dec.) 207	1/5 2/152 3/157 4/177 5/202 6/210 7/212	(7 wkts) 212

D. P. Mather and S. P. du Preez did not bat.

Bowling: *First Innings*—Millns 18–6–59–2; Mullally 15–2–53–1; Parsons 13–3–37–1; Pierson 13–2–33–1; Wells 4–0–9–1; Maddy 2–1–1–0; Macmillan 2–1–1–0. *Second Innings*—Mullally 9.4–2–31–0; Millns 6–1–21–1; Parsons 10–2–43–1; Pierson 9–0–58–0; Wells 2–0–20–0; Maddy 5–0–28–2.

Umpires: N. G. Cowley and A. G. T. Whitehead.

OXFORD UNIVERSITY v DURHAM

At Oxford, April 17, 18, 19. Drawn. Toss: Durham.

Hutton and Roseberry rewrote Durham's record books with an unbroken opening stand of 334. It overhauled their all-wicket record of 222, set by openers Paul Parker and John Glendenen in the county's very first first-class match, also against Oxford in The Parks, in 1992; it also bettered

Durham's all-time best of 251, set in the Minor Counties Championship in 1935. Hutton, who hit 23 fours in a career-best 172, and Roseberry, scoring his maiden hundred for Durham, batted throughout the first day. Oxford's openers then responded with 145 until Sutcliffe became the first batsman dismissed, after nine hours and 16 minutes, 146 overs and 479 runs. Gupte stood firm with a polished 113 not out, his fourth first-class century. He declared 107 in arrears, but the final day was abandoned without a ball bowled.

Close of play: First day, Durham 334-0 (S. Hutton 172*, M. A. Roseberry 145*); Second day, Durham 20-0 (J. A. Daley 12*, J. E. Morris 7*).

Durham

S. Hutton not out	172		
*M. A. Roseberry not out	145		
J. A. Daley (did not bat)	–	(1) not out	12
J. E. Morris (did not bat)	–	(2) not out	7
B 9, l-b 7, w 1	17	W 1	1
	(no wkt dec.) 334		(no wkt) 20

J. I. Longley, S. D. Birbeck, †C. W. Scott, N. Killeen, J. Boiling, S. J. E. Brown and M. M. Betts did not bat.

Bowling: *First Innings*—du Preez 15–1–53–0; Thomson 18–3–47–0; Malik 18–1–83–0; Mather 14–1–65–0; Wagh 21–7–41–0; Khan 3–0–19–0; Sutcliffe 4–0–10–0. *Second Innings*—du Preez 3–0–12–0; Thomson 3–1–8–0.

Oxford University

*C. M. Gupte not out	113
I. J. Sutcliffe c Scott b Brown	65
A. C. Ridley c Brown b Birbeck	3
G. A. Khan b Boiling	33
M. A. Wagh b Killeen	2
H. S. Malik not out	1
L-b 8, n-b 2	10
1/145 2/160 3/212 4/225	(4 wkts dec.) 227

M. E. D. Jarrett, †J. N. Batty, R. B. Thomson, D. P. Mather and S. P. du Preez did not bat.

Bowling: Brown 15–5–26–1; Betts 14–0–45–0; Birbeck 11–0–56–1; Boiling 26–8–50–1; Killeen 13–1–42–1.

Umpires: N. G. Cowley and A. G. T. Whitehead.

OXFORD UNIVERSITY v MIDDLESEX

At Oxford, April 20, 22, 23. Drawn. Toss: Middlesex. First-class debuts: G. J. Wright; J. P. Hewitt, S. P. Moffat.

Rain shortened the first day and then claimed both the final two. The only real excitement occurred when Oxford snapped up three wickets in successive overs with the Middlesex total on 168. Du Preez collected Gatting and debutant Scott Moffat in three balls and Thomson added Carr, a former Oxford Blue. Ian Gould, who had played for Middlesex in the 1970s, moved to Sussex for ten years and then returned to Middlesex to captain the Second Eleven, played his first first-class match since 1990, though he never appeared on the field.

Close of play: First day, Middlesex 197-5 (M. A. Feltham 13*, J. P. Hewitt 16*); Second day, No play.

Middlesex

P. N. Weekes c Batty b Thomson	8
J. C. Harrison c Batty b Mather	38
*M. W. Gatting c Wagh b du Preez	63
J. D. Carr c Batty b Thomson	43
S. P. Moffat lbw b du Preez	0
M. A. Feltham not out	13
J. P. Hewitt not out	16
L-b 6, w 10	16
1/25 2/90 3/168 4/168 5/168	(5 wkts) 197

†I. J. Gould, A. R. C. Fraser, D. Follett and P. C. R. Tufnell did not bat.

Bowling: du Preez 20–6–44–2; Thomson 19.4–5–51–2; Wright 9–0–33–0; Mather 11–0–45–1; Malik 2–0–18–0.

Oxford University

*C. M. Gupte, G. J. Wright, A. C. Ridley, G. A. Khan, M. A. Wagh, H. S. Malik, M. E. D. Jarrett, †J. N. Batty, R. B. Thomson, S. P. du Preez and D. P. Mather.

Umpires: M. K. Reed and D. R. Shepherd.

OXFORD UNIVERSITY v HAMPSHIRE

At Oxford, May 2, 3, 4. Drawn. Toss: Oxford University. County debut: S. M. Milburn.

An uninspiring match, played in bitterly cold and gloomy conditions, ended in stalemate following Oxford's perplexing decision to extend their first innings into the final afternoon. The declaration eventually came with the students five runs behind. Smith enlivened a meaningless session with nine fours in a bright 46 from 62 balls. On the first day, Laney batted solidly for five hours to reach his maiden first-class century, hitting a six and 15 fours. But the county failed to dominate a persevering attack and left-arm seamer Mather triggered a middle-order collapse. Oxford's search for parity was bolstered by Gupte and Ridley, who added 139 in 53 overs, before Malik and Wagh shared an aggressive fifth-wicket stand of 95.

Close of play: First day, Hampshire 264-7 (A. N. Aymes 11*, M. J. Thursfield 3*); Second day, Oxford University 204-4 (M. A. Wagh 10*, H. S. Malik 5*).

Hampshire

*J. P. Stephenson b Wagh	47		
J. S. Laney st Batty b Wagh	112		
R. S. M. Morris lbw b Mather	28	(2) c and b Khan	11
R. A. Smith c Malik b Mather	2	(1) st Batty b Khan	46
G. W. White c Jarrett b Mather	10	(3) not out	29
P. R. Whitaker b Malik	38	(4) lbw b Mather	20
S. D. Udal c Khan b Malik	1	(5) not out	5
†A. N. Aymes c Batty b Malik	30		
M. J. Thursfield not out	30		
S. M. Milburn not out	17		
B 6, l-b 4, w 2	12	B 2, l-b 1, w 1, n-b 4	8
1/91 2/151 3/163 4/182 5/229 6/234 7/251 8/292 (8 wkts dec.)	327	1/31 2/60 3/107 (3 wkts)	119

C. A. Connor did not bat.

Bowling: *First Innings*—du Preez 11–2–44–0; Thomson 13–3–37–0; Wagh 30–7–86–2; Malik 43–14–119–3; Mather 17–5–31–3. *Second Innings*—du Preez 7–1–20–0; Thomson 9–5–16–0; Khan 9–0–48–2; Mather 10–3–27–1; Jarrett 2–0–5–0.

Oxford University

*C. M. Gupte st Aymes b Whitaker	75
I. J. Sutcliffe c Aymes b Connor	5
A. C. Ridley c Aymes b Whitaker	70
G. A. Khan lbw b Thursfield	37
M. A. Wagh lbw b Whitaker	43
H. S. Malik c Aymes b Udal	61
M. E. D. Jarrett lbw b Thursfield	10
†J. N. Batty c Laney b Thursfield	8
R. B. Thomson not out	7
L-b 6	6
1/6 2/145 3/160 4/194 5/289 6/301 7/307 8/322 (8 wkts dec.)	322

S. P. du Preez and D. P. Mather did not bat.

Bowling: Milburn 23–3–76–0; Connor 20–8–38–1; Udal 28.4–5–80–1; Stephenson 18–5–41–0; Thursfield 19.3–6–45–3; Whitaker 20.2–6–36–3.

Umpires: B. Leadbeater and J. W. Lloyds.

†At Oxford, May 9. Oxford University won by six wickets. Toss: Oxfordshire. Oxfordshire 206 for five (46.5 overs) (A. G. Sabin 40, B. C. A. Ellison 42, C. S. Knightley 60); Oxford University 207 for four (47 overs) (H. S. Malik 41, W. S. Kendall 30, J. N. Batty 52 not out, G. A. Khan 41 not out).

†At Oxford, May 11. Cambridge University won by 103 runs. Toss: Cambridge University. Cambridge University 321 for six (50 overs) (R. T. Ragnauth 58, A. Singh 108, R. Q. Cake 74; A. C. Ridley four for 68); Oxford University 218 (42.5 overs) (C. M. Gupte 47, M. E. D. Jarrett 36; A. N. Janisch three for 60).

OXFORD UNIVERSITY v NORTHAMPTONSHIRE

At Oxford, May 16, 17, 18. Drawn. Toss: Oxford University. First-class debuts: J. J. Bull, C. G. R. Lightfoot; D. J. Roberts, A. J. Swann, R. D. Wild.

Rain at lunchtime on the third day removed the possibility of an interesting afternoon's cricket. Northamptonshire, boosted by a fluent 76 from Swann on his first-class debut, led by 251 and intended to leave a challenging target. On the first day, former Oxford captain Montgomerie and another debutant, Cornishman David Roberts, shared an opening stand of 147 in 42 overs, then Loye and Walton enjoyed some batting practice. Oxford's reply was built around Khan, who hit 15 fours and looked set for a stylish maiden century until he fell to Andy Roberts's leg-spin, and Batty, who scored his first fifty. They batted on until Jarrett had completed his own first fifty for Oxford – he made one for Cambridge in 1993.

Close of play: First day, Oxford University 25-1 (J. N. Batty 6*, G. A. Khan 14*); Second day, Northamptonshire 21-0 (A. L. Penberthy 7*, A. J. Swann 14*).

Northamptonshire

D. J. Roberts c du Preez b Wagh	72		
R. R. Montgomerie c and b Malik	126		
M. B. Loye not out	67		
T. C. Walton not out	55		
A. L. Penberthy (did not bat)	–	(1) b Thomson	7
A. J. Swann (did not bat)	–	(2) not out	76
J. N. Snape (did not bat)	–	(3) c Jarrett b Malik	64
*†D. Ripley (did not bat)	–	(4) not out	23
B 13, l-b 1, w 1	15	B 2, l-b 1, w 1	4
1/147 2/253 (2 wkts dec.)	335	1/21 2/131 (2 wkts)	174

A. R. Roberts, N. A. Mallender and R. D. Wild did not bat.

Bowling: *First Innings*—Wagh 13–0–46–1; du Preez 9–2–35–0; Thomson 17–4–53–0; Malik 23–1–85–1; Mather 18–1–75–0; Khan 2–0–17–0; Lightfoot 1–0–10–0. *Second Innings*—du Preez 10–2–29–0; Thomson 10–2–33–1; Malik 9–0–67–1; Mather 7–0–27–0; Khan 2–0–15–0.

Oxford University

*C. M. Gupte lbw b Mallender	4
†J. N. Batty run out	56
G. A. Khan lbw b A. R. Roberts	96
H. S. Malik b Wild	1
M. A. Wagh c Swann b A. R. Roberts	27
M. E. D. Jarrett not out	50
C. G. R. Lightfoot b A. R. Roberts	9
J. J. Bull run out	4
R. B. Thomson not out	2
L-b 9	9
1/4 2/147 3/157 4/168 5/204 6/226 7/250 (7 wkts dec.)	258

S. P. du Preez and D. P. Mather did not bat.

Bowling: Mallender 15–7–27–1; Wild 14–4–62–1; A. R. Roberts 30–11–57–3; Walton 10–1–42–0; Snape 24.2–5–46–0; Swann 5–1–15–0.

Umpires: R. Julian and K. E. Palmer.

†At Arundel, May 21. Drawn. Toss: Oxford University. Oxford University 257 for four dec. (C. M. Gupte 72 retired hurt, G. A. Khan 30, M. A. Wagh 94); Earl of Arundel's XI 179 for seven (J. Wright 34, F. R. McLachlan 35, D. Banks 51; M. A. Wagh four for 20).

OXFORD UNIVERSITY v NOTTINGHAMSHIRE

At Oxford, May 23, 24, 25. Drawn. Toss: Oxford University. County debuts: M. N. Bowen, M. Broadhurst.

The onset of two and a half days of dismal weather frustrated Khan's hopes of a maiden first-class hundred yet again. Having been dismissed for 94 and 96 in earlier games, he reached his fifty in 54 balls and was homing in on his target at 72 not out when the players were forced off the field on the first afternoon. They were never to return. Nottinghamshire's makeshift attack showed willing industry on a flat pitch, but Batty's studious defence and stylish driving laid the foundation for Khan to punish some overpitching from Broadhurst, who conceded 37 runs in three overs.

Close of play: First day, Oxford University 178-3 (G. A. Khan 72*, M. A. Wagh 5*); Second day, No play.

Oxford University

C. M. Gupte c Afzaal b Evans	18
J. N. Batty lbw b Bowen	31
G. A. Khan not out	72
*H. S. Malik c Broadhurst b Chapman	38
M. A. Wagh not out	5
L-b 2, n-b 12	14
1/44 2/66 3/164	(3 wkts) 178

M. E. D. Jarrett, R. B. Thomson, S. P. du Preez, †D. P. Mather, C. G. R. Lightfoot and J. J. Bull did not bat.

Bowling: Bowen 10–4–18–1; Chapman 13–1–50–1; Evans 8.3–0–38–1; Broadhurst 7–0–60–0; Hindson 3–1–7–0; Afzaal 1–0–3–0.

Nottinghamshire

J. R. Wileman, M. P. Dowman, *P. Johnson, N. A. Gie, K. P. Evans, M. N. Bowen, †L. N. P. Walker, U. Afzaal, M. Broadhurst, R. J. Chapman and J. E. Hindson.

Umpires: B. Leadbeater and J. F. Steele.

†At Oxford, May 27. Oxford University won by 93 runs. Toss: Oxford University. Oxford University 321 for eight (50 overs) (J. N. Batty 156, M. E. D. Jarrett 82; R. H. Wade three for 49); Wiltshire 228 for six (50 overs) (N. Stoddard 68, R. H. Wade 71).

†At Oxford, May 28, 29, 30. MCC won by six wickets. Toss: Oxford University. Oxford University 194 for nine dec. (J. N. Batty 80, C. G. R. Lightfoot 35; G. A. R. Harris four for 48) and 193 (J. N. Batty 36, J. J. Bull 31); MCC 231 (M. P. W. Jeh 71; R. B. Thomson three for 30) and 157 for four (J. E. M. Nicholson 43, G. Miller 37, D. A. Banks 33 not out, M. P. W. Jeh 31 not out).

†At Oxford, May 31. Drawn. Toss: Oxford University. Oxford University 224 for eight dec. (J. Haynes 51, J. J. Bull 61; S. D. Weale four for 66); Harlequins 156 for five (D. A. Thorne 42, J. M. Attfield 31, A. D. MacRobert 39; M. A. Wagh three for 56).

OXFORD UNIVERSITY v GLAMORGAN

At Oxford, June 1, 3, 4. Drawn. Toss: Glamorgan. First-class debut: A. W. Evans.

Twenty-year-old Alun Evans marked his debut with two unbeaten half-centuries, playing some classic drives after Butcher and Croft launched Glamorgan with a third-wicket stand of 128. Oxford finished the second day on 196 for five, with Gupte 97 not out. His decision to bat on in search of three extra runs ended in embarrassment: the scores were unchanged when he was bowled by Croft in the fifth over of the final day. Evans's second innings – 71 from 80 balls – enabled Glamorgan to leave a target of 273 in 58 overs. Gupte and Malik helped them to 137 for four going into the final 20 overs, but they were always behind the asking-rate. Kendall, returning to the side after exams, weighed in with an unbeaten 73.

Close of play: First day, Oxford University 26-0 (J. N. Batty 8*, C. M. Gupte 15*); Second day, Oxford University 196-5 (C. M. Gupte 97*, M. A. Wagh 2*).

Glamorgan

*P. A. Cottey c Batty b Mather	27	– (4) c and b Malik	0
R. D. B. Croft c Kendall b Khan	71		
A. Dale c Batty b Wagh	0	– (1) c du Preez b Lightfoot	55
G. P. Butcher lbw b Wagh	83		
A. W. Evans not out	66	– not out	71
A. J. Dalton b Wagh	17	– (3) c Thomson b Lightfoot	15
†A. D. Shaw c Jarrett b Mather	7	– (2) run out	7
S. D. Thomas not out	9	– (6) c Batty b Malik	6
N. M. Kendrick (did not bat)		– (7) not out	1
B 2, l-b 3, w 1, n-b 18	24	W 1, n-b 8	9
1/60 2/61 3/189 4/199 5/242 6/265 (6 wkts dec.)	304	1/16 2/50 3/53 4/115 5/149 (5 wkts dec.)	164

A. P. Davies and O. T. Parkin did not bat.

Bowling: *First Innings*—du Preez 13–2–52–0; Thomson 15–2–50–0; Mather 13–3–46–2; Wagh 30–5–82–3; Malik 11–0–49–0; Khan 4–0–20–1. *Second Innings*—du Preez 7–1–19–0; Thomson 7–0–23–0; Lightfoot 13.5–3–65–2; Malik 13–2–57–2.

Oxford University

†J. N. Batty c Shaw b Kendrick	51	– lbw b Parkin	8
*C. M. Gupte b Croft	97	– lbw b Kendrick	40
G. A. Khan b Butcher	11	– lbw b Davies	5
H. S. Malik c Cottey b Croft	19	– c Cottey b Croft	37
M. E. D. Jarrett c Kendrick b Croft	1	– c Evans b Croft	13
W. S. Kendall c Shaw b Kendrick	4	– not out	73
M. A. Wagh not out	2	– c Parkin b Kendrick	22
C. G. R. Lightfoot (did not bat)		– not out	4
L-b 3, n-b 8	11	B 7, l-b 1, n-b 6	14
1/107 2/122 3/159 4/165 5/194 6/196 (6 wkts dec.)	196	1/12 2/17 3/91 4/101 5/145 6/194 (6 wkts)	216

R. B. Thomson, S. P. du Preez and D. P. Mather did not bat.

Bowling: *First Innings*—Thomas 20–2–49–0; Parkin 8–1–30–0; Kendrick 18–7–45–2; Davies 6–3–18–0; Butcher 5–1–16–1; Croft 17.1–7–32–3; Dale 2–0–3–0. *Second Innings*—Parkin 6–0–33–1; Davies 5–0–25–1; Butcher 4–1–20–0; Kendrick 20–3–79–2; Croft 19–4–48–2; Thomas 3–1–3–0.

Umpires: J. D. Bond and J. F. Steele.

†At Wormsley, June 2. Drawn. Toss: Oxford University. Oxford University 208 (J. Parker 39, G. A. Khan 59, C. G. R. Lightfoot 31; D. R. Doshi six for 38); J. Paul Getty's XI 167 for eight (P. R. Shaw 59, G. J. Toogood 32; M. A. Wagh four for 58).

OXFORD UNIVERSITY v WORCESTERSHIRE

At Oxford, June 6, 7, 8. Drawn. Toss: Worcestershire. First-class debut: B. E. A. Preece. County debut: I. Dawood.

A collapse inspired by Illingworth on the final afternoon left Oxford blocking to preserve their unbeaten first-class record in their last home match. But the batsmen were on top for most of the game. On a brutal first day for the bowlers, Church scored a scorching run-a-ball 152, with 13 fours and seven sixes, and Weston a career-best 124 with 13 fours and four sixes. Their partnership raced from 200 to 250 in 7.3 overs before a freak breakthrough, when Wagh deflected a drive on to the stumps to run out the non-striker. Oxford's reply was dominated by Gupte's limpet-like marathon. He occupied the crease for 323 minutes for his fifth and highest century, which was ended only by a tired dragged shot to square leg. Worcestershire left Oxford 264 to win in 65 overs, but Illingworth's six wickets almost finished them. On the final day journalist Ralph Dellor fielded as 12th man for Oxford and his son Tim was on as substitute for Worcestershire.

Close of play: First day, Oxford University 55-0 (C. M. Gupte 29*, I. J. Sutcliffe 12*); Second day, Worcestershire 46-0 (V. S. Solanki 29*, S. R. Lampitt 17*).

Worcestershire

W. P. C. Weston run out	124		
M. J. Church c Malik b Wagh	152		
K. R. Spiring b Wagh	12	– not out	78
*T. M. Moody not out	66		
V. S. Solanki c Sutcliffe b Thomson	22	– (1) c Batty b Mather	29
S. R. Lampitt not out	16	– (2) c Malik b Thomson	70
†I. Dawood (did not bat)		– (4) c Gupte b Thomson	1
R. K. Illingworth (did not bat)		– (5) not out	17
B 3, l-b 2, n-b 6	11	B 1, l-b 2	3
1/255 2/276 3/297 4/363 (4 wkts dec.)	403	1/46 2/126 3/128 (3 wkts dec.)	198

P. J. Newport, M. J. Rawnsley and B. E. A. Preece did not bat.

Bowling: *First Innings*—du Preez 8–0–63–0; Thomson 12–0–40–1; Mather 10–0–64–0; Malik 20–1–121–0; Wagh 20–4–71–2; Lightfoot 7–1–31–0; Sutcliffe 1–0–8–0. *Second Innings*—du Preez 9–1–31–0; Kendall 5–0–35–0; Mather 7–3–19–1; Thomson 10–3–24–2; Wagh 8–3–18–0; Lightfoot 6–1–23–0; Malik 6–0–23–0; Gupte 1–0–6–0; Ridley 4–1–16–0.

Oxford University

*C. M. Gupte c Solanki b Moody	132	– b Rawnsley	20
I. J. Sutcliffe c Dawood b Rawnsley	24	– c Dawood b Illingworth	78
A. C. Ridley lbw b Lampitt	32	– b Illingworth	14
†J. N. Batty c Spiring b Preece	1	– b Illingworth	48
W. S. Kendall c Dawood b Church	52	– c Illingworth b Moody	8
H. S. Malik b Church	8	– c Lampitt b Solanki	8
M. A. Wagh c Lampitt b Church	33	– c Church b Illingworth	14
C. G. R. Lightfoot lbw b Church	0	– b Illingworth	2
R. B. Thomson not out	14	– not out	0
D. P. Mather run out	2	– c Moody b Illingworth	0
S. P. du Preez (did not bat)		– not out	1
B 8, l-b 13, w 1, n-b 18	40	L-b 2	2
1/79 2/140 3/144 4/254 5/268 6/292 7/309 8/324 9/338 (9 wkts dec.)	338	1/48 2/77 3/147 4/168 5/172 6/181 7/189 8/194 9/194 (9 wkts)	195

Bowling: *First Innings*—Newport 11–5–13–0; Preece 19–1–77–1; Rawnsley 19–3–44–1; Illingworth 15–0–55–0; Lampitt 5–1–18–1; Solanki 11–3–35–0; Church 11–1–50–4; Moody 8.1–1–25–1. *Second Innings*—Newport 6–0–14–0; Preece 6–1–21–0; Rawnsley 16–3–43–1; Illingworth 24–4–75–6; Moody 10–0–34–1; Solanki 3–1–6–1.

Umpires: V. A. Holder and J. Lloyds.

†At Oxford, June 10. Drawn. Toss: Royal Navy. Royal Navy 230 for eight dec. (A. Falconer 65, B. Harrison 43; C. Battersby three for 58, C. G. R. Lightfoot four for 85); Oxford University 175 for eight (I. J. Sutcliffe 44, J. Haynes 69; A. Hurry four for 26).

†At Oxford, June 11. Drawn. Toss: Oxford University. Oxford University 305 for five dec. (I. J. Sutcliffe 139, W. S. Kendall 59, J. N. Batty 57 not out); Midlands Club Cricket Conference 228 for six (P. F. Shaw 80, N. A. French 38, J. S. Hartley 45).

†At Oxford, June 12, 13, 14. Oxford University v Durham University. Called off.

†At Oxford, June 15. Drawn. Toss: Oxford University. Oxford University 296 for six dec. (H. S. Malik 88, A. P. Scrini 59, S. P. du Preez 30, W. S. Kendall 55 not out; J. D. Ricketts three for 91); Free Foresters 200 for seven (C. Rowe 95, Hon. P. Fitzherbert 65; H. S. Malik four for 77).

†At Oxford, June 18. Oxford University won by four wickets. Toss: Hertfordshire. Hertfordshire 257 for four (50 overs) (T. Rafton 58, N. Gilbert 74, I. Fletcher 60); Oxford University 260 for six (49.5 overs) (I. J. Sutcliffe 112, W. S. Kendall 63; C. N. Spinks three for 89).

†At Oxford, June 19. Berkshire won by 64 runs. Toss: Berkshire. Berkshire 182 (49 overs) (A. Spink 44, A. A. Barnett 33; H. S. Malik seven for 50); Oxford University 118 (29.5 overs) (A. C. Ridley 44; A. A. Barnett four for 16, C. West four for 41).

†At Oxford, June 25, 26, 27. Drawn. Toss: Oxford University. Oxford University 230 for seven dec. (W. S. Kendall 96, C. G. R. Lightfoot 49, H. S. Malik 35) and 344 for five dec. (W. S. Kendall 206 not out, A. C. Ridley 45 not out, C. G. R. Lightfoot 42); Combined Services 405 for four dec. (SAC M. Bray 161, Sgt G. S. Lumb 170, Cpl A. Pick 40) and 145 for eight (SAC M. Bray 32; A. W. Maclay four for 44).

In Combined Services' first innings, Bray and Lumb put on 329 for the first wicket.

At Canterbury, June 29, 30, July 1. OXFORD UNIVERSITY drew with KENT.

At Lord's, July 2, 3, 4. OXFORD UNIVERSITY drew with CAMBRIDGE UNIVERSITY.

CAMBRIDGE

President: Professor A. D. Buckingham (Pembroke)

Captain: R. Q. Cake (KCS, Wimbledon, and St John's)
Secretary: D. R. H. Churton (Wellington College and St Catharine's)

Captain for 1997: A. Singh (King Edward's, Birmingham, and Gonville & Caius)
Secretary: W. J. House (Sevenoaks and Gonville & Caius)

Cambridge will be hoping that 1996 proves to be a watershed in their fortunes: the statistics suggested that the decline in the quality of both the student cricketers and the Fenner's pitches has been arrested. One-day successes against other universities – Loughborough, Durham and Oxford were all comprehensively beaten – and the early performances against the counties promised much, though this form tailed off towards the end.

Four batsmen scored seven centuries between them against county opposition. The fact that the three who scored two centuries each were undergraduate freshmen was all the more satisfying. The seventh came from the captain, Russell Cake. In his fourth year, he proved that excellence as a sportsman and as an academic can go side by side. Yet Cake left Cambridge for a career in industry with one regret; he had played eight Varsity Matches (four as a hockey Blue) against Oxford without a single win. His team's performance at Lord's, where they conceded a record total of 513 for six, was hugely disappointing. But until the break for examinations, Cambridge had played their cricket positively and with few hints of inferiority against the counties. Apart from the players available, there were two major factors contributing to this upturn. The first was the vastly improved quality of the pitches after the Fenner's square was completely relaid. Only the three pitches done in autumn 1994 were available to groundsman John Moden and, first time round, they produced pace and evenness of bounce not evident for years. Unfortunately, a cold spring meant they were slow to recover. None played as well on their second use and two late matches had to be played on pitches relaid only nine months earlier. Not surprisingly, the quality suffered. During the summer, the sad recent history of the Fenner's pitches was aired in the national press when Moden's predecessor, Tony Pocock, tried unsuccessfully to pursue a case of constructive dismissal against the university.

The second factor in the upturn was the eleventh-hour appointment of former England batsman Derek Randall as coach, in succession to Graham Saville, who was concentrating on his duties with the England Under-19 squad. Randall's zest for the game quickly rubbed off on his new charges.

He was fortunate that in Edward Smith and Will House, two Kent-registered batsmen, and Warwickshire's Anurag Singh he had three outstanding recruits. Smith, an 18-year-old straight from Tonbridge School, scored a century on debut against Glamorgan, while the left-handed House, a product of Sevenoaks School, completed a century before lunch on the second day of the Derbyshire match, against an attack including Devon Malcolm and Dominic Cork. Singh, an England Under-19 batsman from King Edward's School in Birmingham, took a little longer to blossom in three-day cricket, though he scored 123 for the British Universities in the Benson and Hedges Cup.

Yet again, Cambridge's bowling was disappointing, particularly that of Nick Haste and former captain Andrew Whittall, the two most experienced seniors. They bowled more than 440 overs between them but took only 18 wickets. Whittall was overshadowed by two fellow off-spinners formerly at Durham University: Peter Deakin, who, although under-used, topped the averages with nine wickets at 27.66, and Robin Jones. Rob Tennent, a South African graduate ruled out by injury in 1995, again missed much of the term, but made his debut against Sussex in the penultimate game and took a wicket with his first ball. But Cambridge must recruit some bowlers to go with their undoubted batting talent if they are to maintain, let alone improve upon, the progress made in 1996. – DAVID HALLETT.

CAMBRIDGE UNIVERSITY RESULTS

First-class matches – Played 8: Lost 3, Drawn 5.

FIRST-CLASS AVERAGES

BATTING AND FIELDING

	Birthplace	*M*	*I*	*NO*	*R*	*HS*	*Avge*	*Ct/St*
W. J. House	*Sheffield*	8	15	5	526	136	52.60	2
E. T. Smith	*Pembury*	6	10	0	519	101	51.90	1
A. Singh	*Kanpur, India*	8	15	1	590	157	42.14	2
R. Q. Cake	*Chertsey*	8	15	3	407	102*	33.91	3
A. R. Whittall	*Mutare, Zimbabwe*	7	6	1	127	36	25.40	4
N. J. Haste	*Northampton*	6	6	2	101	51*	25.25	1
J. Ratledge	*Preston*	2	4	0	89	30	22.25	0
P. J. Deakin	*Liverpool*	6	9	4	100	24*	20.00	0
R. O. Jones	*Crewe*	8	13	1	205	61	17.08	4
R. T. Ragnauth	*Cambridge*	6	11	1	121	29	12.10	1
G. R. Moffat	*Morecambe*	8	8	3	45	27	9.00	4
D. R. H. Churton	*Salisbury*	7	7	0	34	20	4.85	7/3

Also batted: M. J. Birks (*Keighley*) (1 match) did not bat (1 ct); E. J. How (*Amersham*) (2 matches) 0*, 7*; A. N. Janisch (*Hammersmith*) (3 matches) 0, 25, 4*; R. W. Tennent (*Ficksburg, SA*) (2 matches) did not bat.

* *Signifies not out.*

The following played a total of seven three-figure innings for Cambridge University – W. J. House 2, A. Singh 2, E. T. Smith 2, R. Q. Cake 1.

BOWLING

	O	*M*	*R*	*W*	*BB*	*5W/i*	*Avge*
P. J. Deakin	71.1	9	249	9	2-17	0	27.66
R. W. Tennent	38	5	136	4	2-34	0	34.00
A. N. Janisch	70	12	263	4	2-23	0	65.75
R. O. Jones	185.4	29	660	9	2-45	0	73.33
N. J. Haste	165.5	16	673	8	3-51	0	84.12
A. R. Whittall	274.3	56	932	10	3-103	0	93.20
G. R. Moffat	185	28	788	8	2-50	0	98.50

Also bowled: W. J. House 89–8–412–2; E. J. How 27–5–161–0; A. Singh 3–0–13–0.

CAMBRIDGE UNIVERSITY 1996

[*Bill Smith*

Back row: D. W. Randall (*coach*), A. Singh, P. J. Deakin, G. R. Moffat, M. J. Birks, E. T. Smith, R. W. Tennent, W. J. House, R. O. Jones, A. R. May (*scorer*). *Front row:* D. R. H. Churton, A. R. Whittall, R. Q. Cake (*captain*), N. J. Haste, J. Ratledge.

Note: Matches in this section which were not first-class are signified by a dagger.

†At Cambridge, April 11. Cambridge University won by 62 runs. Toss: Cambridge University. Cambridge University 222 for nine (50 overs) (R. Q. Cake 35, R. O. Jones 63 not out); Loughborough Students 160 for nine (50 overs) (T. M. B. Bailey 55 not out; G. R. Moffat three for 29).

†At Cambridge, April 12. Cambridge University v Loughborough Students. Abandoned.

†At Cambridge, April 13. Cambridge University won by 16 runs. Toss: Cambridge University. Cambridge University 235 for eight (50 overs) (R. T. Ragnauth 44, A. Singh 62, J. Ratledge 32, W. J. House 37; M. J. Chilton three for 23); Durham University 219 for five (50 overs) (T. P. Hodgson 57, M. Gillison 48, M. J. Chilton 32).

†At Cambridge, April 14. Cambridge University won by 114 runs. Toss: Cambridge University. Cambridge University 264 for five (50 overs) (E. T. Smith 65, A. Singh 43, R. Q. Cake 30, W. J. House 60 not out, R. O. Jones 34); Durham University 150 (38.3 overs) (T. P. Hodgson 85).

CAMBRIDGE UNIVERSITY v GLAMORGAN

At Cambridge, April 17, 18, 19. Drawn. Toss: Cambridge University. First-class debuts: W. J. House, R. O. Jones, G. R. Moffat, E. T. Smith. Cambridge debut: A. Singh.

Five players launched their seasons with centuries on a newly relaid, batsman-friendly pitch. Four belonged to Glamorgan, but the University were delighted by a hundred on debut from 18-year-old Edward Smith, the first Cambridge batsman to achieve the feat for 42 years. Supported by a pleasant fifty from Singh, who was like him an undergraduate freshman, Smith hit 13 fours in an innings of considerable application, modelled on the century made by Morris the previous day. Morris rarely put a foot wrong, playing straight and waiting for the all-too-frequent bad ball. He shared a 247-run stand with Hemp, who also made a watchful hundred, before Morris's successor as captain, Maynard, declared, unaware that they were only three short of breaking Glamorgan's second-wicket record. James and Maynard added centuries on the final day after rain, which wiped out the morning session, prevented a meaningful conclusion. The unluckiest participant was Watkin who had his wallet stolen. He asked a member of the press to cancel his credit cards for him while he was in the field, leading to the unusual shout of "Bowler's mother's maiden name".

Close of play: First day, Cambridge University 19-0 (R. T. Ragnauth 4*, E. T. Smith 13*); Second day, Glamorgan 105-0 (S. P. James 29*, M. P. Maynard 66*).

Glamorgan

S. P. James c Singh b Haste	12	– not out	102
H. Morris not out	126		
D. L. Hemp not out	103		
*M. P. Maynard (did not bat)		– (2) retired hurt	100
P. A. Cottey (did not bat)		– (3) c House b Jones	21
R. D. B. Croft (did not bat)		– (4) not out	6
B 4, l-b 4, w 1, n-b 12	21	L-b 5, w 2, n-b 12	19
1/15 (1 wkt dec.)	262	1/224 (1 wkt dec.)	248

A. Dale, S. D. Thomas, †C. P. Metson, S. L. Watkin and S. R. Barwick did not bat.

In the second innings M. P. Maynard retired hurt at 162.

Bowling: *First Innings*—Haste 15–0–47–1; Moffat 14–6–31–0; Whittall 32–16–61–0; How 10–3–44–0; Jones 21.4–10–36–0; House 7–1–35–0. *Second Innings*—Haste 13–1–62–0; Moffat 13–2–64–0; Whittall 7–0–30–0; How 5–1–46–0; House 6–0–29–0; Jones 7–1–12–1.

Cambridge University

R. T. Ragnauth c Barwick b Watkin	8	– lbw b Thomas	4
E. T. Smith c Metson b Thomas	101	– c Metson b Hemp	8
*R. Q. Cake c Watkin b Barwick	39	– (4) not out	0
A. Singh not out	52	– (3) c sub b Watkin	16
W. J. House not out	14	– not out	3
L-b 3, n-b 8	11	L-b 1	1
1/36 2/138 3/177 (3 wkts dec.)	225	1/7 2/26 3/29 (3 wkts)	32

R. O. Jones, †D. R. H. Churton, N. J. Haste, A. R. Whittall, G. R. Moffat and E. J. How did not bat.

Bowling: *First Innings*—Watkin 17–6–43–1; Thomas 18–4–73–1; Croft 17–3–54–0; Barwick 22–11–24–1; Dale 2–1–1–0; Hemp 3–0–27–0. *Second Innings*—Watkin 4–1–10–1; Thomas 3–0–16–1; Croft 4–3–2–0; Hemp 3–1–3–1.

Umpires: J. W. Lloyds and R. A. White.

CAMBRIDGE UNIVERSITY v DERBYSHIRE

At Cambridge, April 20, 21, 22. Drawn. Toss: Cambridge University. First-class debut: P. J. Deakin. County debut: D. M. Jones.

Another undergraduate freshman took centre stage, when left-hander Will House scored 136 from 123 balls in only his second first-class match. He came in on the second morning in a crisis; five students had fallen for 115 the previous evening, after Derbyshire's new captain, Jones, made a challenging teatime declaration. But House reached his century in 102 balls and was 117 not out by lunch. Particularly severe on Malcolm, who conceded 80 in 16 overs, he hit 20 fours and two sixes as he added 193 in 134 minutes with his captain, Cake, who compiled an unbeaten hundred from 176 balls. Their efforts secured Cambridge an unexpected lead of 42. Rollins and Cork replied with centuries for Derbyshire, who set a target of 286 in two sessions, only for rain to intervene.

Close of play: First day, Cambridge University 115-5 (R. Q. Cake 37*); Second day, Derbyshire 249-1 (A. S. Rollins 100*, M. J. Vandrau 1*).

Derbyshire

K. J. Barnett c and b Whittall	20		
A. S. Rollins b Janisch	2	– (1) c Jones b Deakin	112
C. J. Adams c Ragnauth b Whittall	54	– (5) not out	31
*D. M. Jones c Cake b Moffat	71		
T. A. Tweats not out	89		
C. M. Wells not out	36		
†K. M. Krikken (did not bat)		– (2) run out	36
D. G. Cork (did not bat)		– (3) retired hurt	101
M. J. Vandrau (did not bat)		– (4) not out	34
B 5, l-b 3, w 1, n-b 6	15	B 3, l-b 4, n-b 6	13
1/6 2/54 3/92 4/214 (4 wkts dec.)	287	1/55 2/269 (2 wkts dec.)	327

A. E. Warner and D. E. Malcolm did not bat.

In the second innings D. G. Cork retired hurt at 238.

Bowling: *First Innings*—Moffat 14–1–73–1; Janisch 13–0–45–1; Whittall 27–6–92–2; Jones 10–1–53–0; House 3–0–7–0; Deakin 2–1–9–0. *Second Innings*—Moffat 20–3–82–0; Janisch 17–3–72–0; Jones 10–0–44–0; Whittall 20–4–60–0; House 6–0–36–0; Deakin 8–0–26–1.

Cambridge University

R. T. Ragnauth c Jones b Malcolm	7	R. O. Jones b Vandrau	6
E. T. Smith lbw b Barnett	54	P. J. Deakin not out	0
A. Singh c Barnett b Warner	13	L-b 6, n-b 4	10
*R. Q. Cake not out	102		—
†D. R. H. Churton lbw b Vandrau	0	1/10 2/38 3/105 (7 wkts dec.)	329
G. R. Moffat lbw b Barnett	1	4/106 5/115	
W. J. House b Vandrau	136	6/308 7/324	

A. R. Whittall and A. N. Janisch did not bat.

Bowling: Malcolm 16–1–80–1; Cork 14–2–49–0; Warner 8–0–41–1; Vandrau 24–3–90–3; Barnett 13–4–49–2; Tweats 3–0–14–0.

Umpires: J. W. Lloyds and R. A. White.

CAMBRIDGE UNIVERSITY v WARWICKSHIRE

At Cambridge, May 3, 4, 5. Warwickshire won by 218 runs. Toss: Warwickshire.

Knight and Khan struck polished centuries in an opening partnership of 228, which was broken only when Cake ran out Khan with a direct hit from cover. But the county's progress remained untroubled and they were able to declare late on the first evening. Smith passed 50 for the third time in his first four innings, but the students' best batting came from Jones, who bolstered the tail with a maiden half-century. Warwickshire waived the follow-on and their revised line-up slipped to 107 for seven before Khan, batting at No. 8 this time, rallied the innings, enabling Munton to declare 350 ahead and leave himself 275 minutes to bowl out Cambridge. They achieved victory with more than an hour to spare. It was Cambridge's first home defeat since May 2, 1994.

Close of play: First day, Cambridge University 20-1 (E. T. Smith 12*, A. Singh 6*); Second day, Warwickshire 107-7 (W. G. Khan 0*).

Warwickshire

N. V. Knight c Churton b Moffat	128	– (10) not out	1
W. G. Khan run out	108	– (8) c Jones b Janisch	51
D. P. Ostler not out	81	– (9) not out	31
T. L. Penney b Haste	0	– b Janisch	1
D. R. Brown not out	38	– (7) c Cake b Jones	17
†K. J. Piper (did not bat)		– (1) c Churton b Haste	6
N. M. K. Smith (did not bat)		– (2) lbw b Haste	20
P. A. Smith (did not bat)		– (3) c Moffat b Haste	2
G. Welch (did not bat)		– (5) b Moffat	35
A. F. Giles (did not bat)		– (6) c Churton b Moffat	17
L-b 6, w 1, n-b 6	13	B 1, l-b 7, w 1	9
	—		—
1/228 2/268 3/270 (3 wkts dec.)	368	1/22 2/26 3/31 (8 wkts dec.) 4/43 5/78 6/101 7/107 8/187	190

*T. A. Munton did not bat.

Bowling: *First Innings*—Haste 17–2–74–1; Janisch 17–3–95–0; Moffat 16–1–50–1; Jones 12–1–72–0; How 12–1–71–0. *Second Innings*—Haste 18–3–51–3; Janisch 11–4–23–2; Moffat 10–3–50–2; Jones 9–1–55–1; House 1–0–3–0.

Cambridge University

R. T. Ragnauth c Ostler b Munton	2	– (6) retired hurt	27
E. T. Smith lbw b Brown	55	– lbw b Munton	20
A. Singh c Khan b N. M. K. Smith	26	– c Welch b Brown	16
*R. Q. Cake c Khan b N. M. K. Smith	14	– c Penney b Welch	11
W. J. House c P. A. Smith b N. M. K. Smith	6	– lbw b Brown	0
R. O. Jones c Ostler b Giles	61	– (1) lbw b Munton	0
†D. R. H. Churton c and b N. M. K. Smith	0	– c Brown b Welch	7
N. J. Haste lbw b P. A. Smith	2	– c Ostler b Giles	5
G. R. Moffat c Khan b Welch	27	– c and b Welch	0
A. N. Janisch c Ostler b Giles	0	– c Khan b Giles	25
E. J. How not out	0	– not out	7
B 1, l-b 2, w 4, n-b 8	15	B 4, l-b 2, n-b 8	14
1/10 2/65 3/101 4/111 5/111 6/112 7/123 8/200 9/200	208	1/0 2/37 3/37 4/40 5/60 6/74 7/91 8/95 9/132	132

In the second innings R. T. Ragnauth retired hurt at 91-6.

Bowling: *First Innings*—Munton 13–6–18–1; Brown 10–3–31–1; Giles 10.4–5–34–2; Welch 7.3–0–61–1; N. M. K. Smith 22–7–49–4; P. A. Smith 6.2–2–12–1. *Second Innings*—Munton 11–6–19–2; Brown 11–3–36–2; Welch 8–0–29–3; Giles 8.2–2–10–2; N. M. K. Smith 5–1–14–0; P. A. Smith 6–2–18–0.

Umpires: B. Dudleston and J. H. Hampshire.

†At Cambridge, May 9. Cambridge University won by four wickets. Toss: Cambridge University. Cambridgeshire 247 for seven (50 overs) (G. W. Ecclestone 103 not out, R. J. Doel 32; N. J. Haste three for 69); Cambridge University 249 for six (45.4 overs) (W. J. House 121 not out, R. O. Jones 85).

At Oxford, May 11. CAMBRIDGE UNIVERSITY beat OXFORD UNIVERSITY by 103 runs.

†At Cambridge, May 12. Drawn. Toss: Cryptics. Cryptics 226 for eight dec. (J. A. Claughton 42, W. J. Dean 51, S. J. Ball 35; R. W. Tennent three for 41); Cambridge University 226 for nine (M. W. Dawson 95, S. J. Elcock 34).

†At King's College, Cambridge, May 13. Cambridge University won by three wickets. Toss: Hertfordshire. Hertfordshire 149 (45.3 overs) (A. Pickett 30; R. O. Jones three for 32, J. A. Seddon three for 30); Cambridge University 153 for seven (49.3 overs) (P. J. Deakin 39 not out, M. W. Dawson 38; D. Surridge three for 29).

CAMBRIDGE UNIVERSITY v MIDDLESEX

At Cambridge, May 16, 17, 18. Drawn. Toss: Cambridge University.

House scored his second century in only his fourth first-class match and shared a 114-run partnership with Jones, enabling Cambridge to declare at 300 and capture their first Middlesex wicket in six overs that night. But next morning, night-watchman Hewitt supported Pooley in a stand of 188. Pooley scored a career-best 138, Hewitt a maiden fifty, and Gatting declared 57 behind. Smith, with another half-century, and Singh took Cambridge to 133 for one before they lost nine for 64 against spinners Tufnell and Weekes. Left to score 255 in 57 overs, Middlesex were on course at 146 for one. But Gatting was caught by Derek Randall, the Cambridge coach acting as substitute, as five wickets fell in quick succession. Brown, the Middlesex wicket-keeper, had been hit on the nose by the first delivery of the match; Gatting kept wicket until lunch when Ian Gould, summoned from the second team, arrived to take over for the rest of the innings.

Close of play: First day, Middlesex 21-1 (J. C. Pooley 4*, J. P. Hewitt 1*); Second day, Cambridge University 99-1 (E. T. Smith 47*, A. Singh 22*).

Cambridge University

R. T. Ragnauth lbw b Fay	29	– (6) b Weekes	0
E. T. Smith c Weekes b Hewitt	15	– b Tufnell	76
A. Singh c Carr b Tufnell	42	– c Fay b Tufnell	41
*R. Q. Cake b Weekes	1	– c Harrison b Weekes	1
W. J. House lbw b Hewitt	127	– c Harrison b Tufnell	11
R. O. Jones c Gatting b Weekes	43	– (1) lbw b Weekes	18
P. J. Deakin not out	24	– c Harrison b Weekes	7
†D. R. H. Churton c Fay b Hewitt	3	– b Tufnell	1
G. R. Moffat not out	1	– lbw b Weekes	2
A. R. Whittall (did not bat)		– c Brown b Tufnell	16
A. N. Janisch (did not bat)		– not out	4
L-b 9, n-b 6	15	B 6, l-b 6, n-b 8	20
1/32 2/80 3/88 4/92 5/206 6/280 7/294 (7 wkts dec.)	300	1/52 2/133 3/145 4/163 5/164 6/168 7/169 8/174 9/189	197

Bowling: *First Innings*—Follett 21–4–77–0; Hewitt 12–3–34–3; Fay 4–1–19–1; Tufnell 30–3–88–1; Weekes 25–6–73–2. *Second Innings*—Follett 11–1–54–0; Fay 6–1–14–0; Tufnell 28.3–11–56–5; Weekes 24–6–61–5.

Middlesex

P. N. Weekes c Churton b Moffat	14	– run out	5
J. C. Pooley not out	138	– (6) st Churton b Whittall	10
J. P. Hewitt c Moffat b Deakin	72	– (8) not out	15
J. C. Harrison b Jones	3	– (7) not out	7
D. J. Nash not out	8	– b Whittall	6
*M. W. Gatting (did not bat)		– (2) c sub b Whittall	77
J. D. Carr (did not bat)		– (3) c Churton b Janisch	34
†K. R. Brown (did not bat)		– (4) c Smith b Jones	33
B 4, l-b 2, n-b 2	8	B 7, l-b 4, w 1, n-b 12	24
1/20 2/208 3/225 (3 wkts dec.)	243	1/59 2/146 3/165 4/178 5/183 6/187 (6 wkts)	211

P. C. R. Tufnell, R. A. Fay and D. Follett did not bat.

Bowling: *First Innings*—Moffat 16–1–70–1; Whittall 21–3–79–0; Janisch 7–2–9–0; Jones 17–2–31–1; House 8–1–20–0; Deakin 9–1–28–1. *Second Innings*—Moffat 5–1–22–0; Whittall 27.3–1–103–3; Janisch 5–0–19–1; Jones 19–2–56–1.

Umpires: R. Palmer and J. F. Steele.

†At Cambridge, May 19. Cambridge University won by five wickets. Toss: Free Foresters. Free Foresters 188 for five dec. (R. M. F. Cox 41, R. C. W. Mason 59 not out); Cambridge University 189 for five (R. Q. Cake 71 not out, P. J. Deakin 36; J. Ashworth four for 64).

†At Cambridge, June 6. Cambridge University won by 172 runs. Toss: Cambridge University. Cambridge University 290 for seven (50 overs) (S. J. Elcock 39, R. Q. Cake 141 not out, W. J. House 66; C. Notton five for 95); Middlesex League Select XI 118 (40.5 overs) (G. Notton 31; W. J. House four for eight).

†At Cambridge, June 9. Drawn. Toss: Cambridge University. Cambridge University 210 for four dec. (R. T. Ragnauth 115 not out, E. T. Smith 34); Quidnuncs 89 for eight (P. J. Deakin four for 23).

†At Arundel, June 10. Cambridge University won by 36 runs. Toss: Earl of Arundel's XI. Cambridge University 249 for two dec. (J. Ratledge 47, R. O. Jones 81, A. Singh 74 not out, R. Q. Cake 34 not out); Earl of Arundel's XI 213 (J. Robinson 41, J. P. Arscott 106; P. J. Deakin three for 43, W. J. House five for 32).

†At Cambridge, June 11, 12, 13. Drawn. Toss: Cambridge University. Cambridge University 239 (R. Q. Cake 61, R. O. Jones 71; M. Warden five for 69) and 326 for nine dec. (W. J. House 94, R. Q. Cake 88 not out, R. O. Jones 75; P. A. Strang five for 115); MCC 323 for four dec. (A. M. Brown 121, T. Patel 59, R. J. Greatorex 63 not out) and 226 for eight (A. D. Hobson 63, J. L. P. Meadows 58, R. J. Greatorex 33 not out; P. J. Deakin four for 76).

CAMBRIDGE UNIVERSITY v HAMPSHIRE

At Cambridge, June 14, 15, 16. Hampshire won by 114 runs. Toss: Hampshire. First-class debut: M. Garaway. County debut: S. J. Renshaw.

Challenged to score 267 from 65 overs, Cambridge collapsed to 74 for seven. A brisk stand of 64 from tailenders Whittall and Haste spared them humiliation but could not avert defeat. For Hampshire, Morris made a slow century on the first day, taking 248 balls, and added 183 for the second wicket with Keech, who missed his maiden hundred by two runs. Next day, Singh became the third of Cambridge's freshman undergraduates to score a maiden first-class century in 1996. He hit 17 fours in 127 balls. There was solid support and Cambridge were confident enough to declare 56 behind. Promoted to No. 4 in a revised batting order, Udal scored a 42-ball half-century and then added four wickets to earn his county victory.

Close of play: First day, Cambridge University 2-0 (J. Ratledge 0*, R. O. Jones 0*); Second day, Hampshire 33-1 (G. W. White 16*, M. Garaway 0*).

Hampshire

R. S. M. Morris c Moffat b Jones	112		
J. S. Laney c Churton b Haste	4	– st Churton b Whittall	15
M. Keech c Singh b Deakin	98	– (8) not out	15
P. R. Whitaker not out	50	– (7) not out	23
*V. P. Terry not out	49	– (6) c Jones b Deakin	9
G. W. White (did not bat)		– (1) lbw b House	34
†M. Garaway (did not bat)		– (3) b Jones	44
S. D. Udal (did not bat)		– (4) c Whittall b Jones	58
M. J. Thursfield (did not bat)		– (5) c Cake b Deakin	0
B 7, l-b 5, w 1, n-b 16	29	L-b 6, n-b 6	12
1/7 2/190 3/272 (3 wkts dec.)	342	1/29 2/63 3/150 4/151 5/163 6/183 (6 wkts dec.)	210

J. N. B. Bovill and S. J. Renshaw did not bat.

Bowling: *First Innings*—Haste 12–1–39–1; Moffat 16–1–64–0; House 11–1–37–0; Whittall 23–2–101–0; Deakin 11–1–38–1; Jones 16–4–51–1. *Second Innings*—Moffat 2–0–11–0; House 11–0–61–1; Whittall 12–0–52–1; Jones 12–0–45–2; Deakin 9.4–2–35–2.

Cambridge University

J. Ratledge c Laney b Bovill	30	– c Morris b Whitaker	26
R. O. Jones c Garaway b Whitaker	35	– (6) lbw b Whitaker	7
A. Singh c Garaway b Thursfield	101	– c Morris b Bovill	15
*R. Q. Cake lbw b Udal	37	– c Laney b Whitaker	17
W. J. House c Garaway b Renshaw	5	– c Terry b Udal	1
R. T. Ragnauth b Udal	27	– (2) lbw b Bovill	2
P. J. Deakin c Morris b Udal	13	– st Garaway b Udal	2
A. R. Whittall not out	22	– c Garaway b Thursfield	33
N. J. Haste (did not bat)		– c and b Udal	34
†D. R. H. Churton (did not bat)		– c Laney b Udal	3
G. R. Moffat (did not bat)		– not out	5
B 4, l-b 4, n-b 8	16	B 6, l-b 1	7
1/73 2/89 3/168 4/179 5/235 6/253 7/286 (7 wkts dec.)	286	1/7 2/27 3/59 4/60 5/68 6/70 7/74 8/138 9/142	152

Bowling: *First Innings*—Bovill 17–5–60–1; Thursfield 22–6–59–1; Renshaw 14–3–54–1; Udal 25.5–7–80–3; Whitaker 4–0–25–1. *Second Innings*—Bovill 8–2–26–2; Thursfield 9–5–13–1; Udal 20.2–4–55–4; Whitaker 13–6–51–3.

Umpires: H. D. Bird and M. K. Reed.

†At Queens' College, Cambridge, June 17, 18, 19. Cambridge University won by 45 runs. Toss: Cambridge University. Cambridge University 214 (G. R. Moffat 45, M. E. Thomas 31; Marine A. Proctor five for 70) and 350 for eight dec. (R. T. Ragnauth 77, W. J. House 98, M. J. Birks 34, G. R. Moffat 60); Combined Services 212 (Sgt N. Palmer 32, Lt C. H. G. St George 55, L/Cpl M. Hutton 39; R. W. Tennent three for 62) and 307 (SAC M. Bray 103, Cpl A. Pick 69, Sgt N. Palmer 44, Extras 33; R. W. Tennent seven for 57, A. Singh three for 62).

CAMBRIDGE UNIVERSITY v ESSEX

At Cambridge, June 21, 22, 23. Essex won by 122 runs. Toss: Essex. First-class debut: S. D. Peters.

Cambridge's final home game saw their third defeat. This time, the precocious batsman scoring his maiden first-class hundred was playing for their opponents; 17-year-old Stephen Peters became the fourth and much the youngest Essex cricketer to make a century on debut. His 110 was an innings of considerable maturity. He hit 12 fours and a six from 195 balls and batted for 222 minutes. The wiles of Such, Essex's acting-captain, on an uneven pitch proved too much for Cambridge; only 50 from Cake helped them to limp past the follow-on target. In the county's second innings, Robinson just missed out on a century. A second declaration left the University the whole of the final day to chase 341. Although House led stern middle-order resistance they were bowled out by the spin of Such and Childs.

Close of play: First day, Cambridge University 35-1 (J. Ratledge 9*, D. R. H. Churton 10*); Second day, Essex 197-4 (A. J. E. Hibbert 9*, S. D. Peters 12*).

Essex

D. D. J. Robinson b House	11	– b Jones	97
A. J. E. Hibbert st Churton b Deakin	85	– (5) not out	9
J. J. B. Lewis lbw b Moffat	29	– (2) b Moffat	5
S. D. Peters c Moffat b Deakin	110	– (6) not out	12
R. J. Rollins c and b Whittall	48	– (3) b Jones	51
†B. J. Hyam run out	5	– (4) c sub b Haste	11
S. J. W. Andrew not out	3		
B 9, l-b 6, w 3, n-b 4	22	B 4, l-b 3, w 1, n-b 4	12
1/13 2/66 3/189 4/283 5/301 6/313 (6 wkts dec.)	313	1/18 2/147 3/176 4/176 (4 wkts dec.)	197

M. C. Ilott, *P. M. Such, N. A. Derbyshire and J. H. Childs did not bat.

Bowling: *First Innings*—Haste 12–0–55–0; House 13–2–44–1; Moffat 16–4–63–1; Whittall 28–9–75–1; Jones 7–1–20–0; Deakin 14.5–2–41–2. *Second Innings*—Haste 16–1–51–1; Moffat 6–2–18–1; House 5–1–20–0; Whittall 6–0–32–0; Jones 13–0–53–2; Deakin 2–0–16–0.

Cambridge University

J. Ratledge lbw b Ilott	19	– (3) c Robinson b Childs	14
R. O. Jones c Hyam b Andrew	16	– c Peters b Ilott	0
†D. R. H. Churton c Hyam b Andrew	20	– absent ill	
A. Singh lbw b Ilott	0	– (7) c Lewis b Childs	7
*R. Q. Cake lbw b Such	50	– (4) b Such	38
W. J. House c and b Such	26	– (5) b Such	64
R. T. Ragnauth c Derbyshire b Such	2	– (1) c and b Derbyshire	13
P. J. Deakin b Such	0	– (6) c Peters b Childs	19
G. R. Moffat st Hyam b Childs	1	– (10) not out	8
A. R. Whittall b Such	19	– (8) c Rollins b Such	36
N. J. Haste not out	7	– (9) c Peters b Such	2
B 8, l-b 2	10	B 5, l-b 6, n-b 6	17
1/17 2/55 3/55 4/56 5/131 6/133 7/143 8/144 9/148	170	1/0 2/18 3/71 4/85 5/133 6/141 7/183 8/199 9/218	218

Bowling: *First Innings*—Andrew 9–1–42–2; Ilott 11–3–26–2; Derbyshire 6–0–20–0; Childs 14–6–38–1; Such 11–2–34–5. *Second Innings*—Andrew 5–4–1–0; Ilott 12–4–30–1; Derbyshire 14–2–67–1; Such 24.4–6–55–4; Childs 25–9–54–3.

Umpires: M. J. Kitchen and M. K. Reed.

At Hove, June 29, 30, July 1. CAMBRIDGE UNIVERSITY drew with SUSSEX.

THE UNIVERSITY MATCH, 1996

OXFORD UNIVERSITY v CAMBRIDGE UNIVERSITY

At Lord's, July 2, 3, 4. Drawn. Toss: Cambridge University.

Oxford's total of 513 for six, a record for the Varsity Match, was the game's most notable feature. But when that score was combined with the loss of three hours to rain on the second day, the draw, always a favourite given two teams stronger on batting than bowling, became near-inevitable. Curiously, Cake put Oxford in, giving them a licence to amass 390 in 106 overs on the first day. Gupte and Sutcliffe opened with 107 and were only separated by a run-out. Then Ridley made 155, his highest score, from 217 balls, with 17 fours and seven sixes. Next day, Kendall also reached a career-best, an unbeaten 145 from 217 balls; he hit 16 fours and one six. Oxford added 123 in 18 overs on the second morning, passing the previous Varsity record, their own 503 in 1900, through a six from Wagh. But Cambridge replied by scoring at six an over in the time permitted by the weather; House smashed 47 from 30 balls. After negotiations between the teams, they declared at their overnight score and Oxford knocked up 63 in half an hour, leaving a target of 413 from 86 overs. That seemed unlikely even before more rain wiped out another 13 overs, though Cambridge's top order all contributed. Sutcliffe raised Oxford's hopes when his very occasional spin removed two in six balls. They needed another four wickets in the final hour, but they lacked the resources to press home their advantage. Haste, with a maiden fifty, and Deakin batted safely to the close.

Close of play: First day, Oxford University 390-4 (W. S. Kendall 79*, J. N. Batty 1*); Second day, Cambridge University 164-3 (R. O. Jones 11*, W. J. House 47*).

Oxford University

*C. M. Gupte (*John Lyon and Pembroke*) run out	60		
I. J. Sutcliffe (*Leeds GS and Queen's*) c Churton b Whittall	55		
A. C. Ridley (*St Aloysius C., Sydney, Sydney U. and Exeter*) c and b Haste	155		
G. A. Khan (*Ipswich S., Swansea U. and Keble*) c Whittall b Moffat	34		
W. S. Kendall (*Bradfield C. and Keble*) not out	145		
†J. N. Batty (*Repton, Durham U. and Keble*) b Whittall	27	(1) not out	30
H. S. Malik (*KCS, Wimbledon, and Keble*) lbw b Whittall	12	(2) not out	19
M. A. Wagh (*King Edward's, Birmingham, and Keble*) not out	8		
L-b 11, w 6	17	B 7, l-b 3, n-b 4	14
1/107 2/140 3/230 4/379 5/478 6/500 (6 wkts dec.)	513	(no wkt dec.)	63

R. B. Thomson (*St Stithian's, Cape Town U. and Keble*), S. P. du Preez (*Diocesan C., Cape Town, Stellenbosch U. and Keble*) and A. W. Maclay (*Winchester and St Edmund Hall*) did not bat.

Bowling: *First Innings*—Haste 31–4–141–1; Moffat 14–0–82–1; Whittall 38–8–118–3; Tennent 15–3–64–0; Deakin 5–1–15–0; House 5–1–33–0; Jones 16–3–49–0. *Second Innings*—Haste 5.5–0–35–0; Singh 3–0–13–0; Whittall 2–1–5–0.

Cambridge University

	First innings		Second innings	
*R. Q. Cake (*KCS, Wimbledon, and St John's*)	c Kendall b du Preez	23	run out	33
E. T. Smith (*Tonbridge and Peterhouse*)	c Batty b du Preez	40	lbw b Thomson	50
A. Singh (*King Edward's, Birmingham, and Gonville & Caius*)	lbw b Maclay	36	c Malik b Thomson	45
R. O. Jones (*Millfield, Durham U. and Homerton*)	not out	11	(6) lbw b Sutcliffe	8
W. J. House (*Sevenoaks and Gonville & Caius*)	not out	47	(4) c Khan b Sutcliffe	54
A. R. Whittall (*Falcon, Zimbabwe, and Trinity*)	(did not bat)		(5) c Malik b Wagh	1
P. J. Deakin (*Chorley St Michael's HS, Durham U. and Hughes Hall*)	(did not bat)		not out	14
N. J. Haste (*Wellingborough and Pembroke*)	(did not bat)		not out	51
	L-b 3, n-b 4	7	B 6, l-b 4, w 5	15
	1/34 2/79 3/111 (3 wkts dec.)	164	1/86 2/87 3/172 4/173 5/198 6/203 (6 wkts)	271

†D. R. H. Churton (*Wellington C. and St Catharine's*), G. R. Moffat (*RGS, Lancaster, Durham U. and Homerton*) and R. W. Tennent (*St Andrew's, Bloemfontein, Natal U. and St John's*) did not bat.

Bowling: *First Innings*—du Preez 13–2–78–2; Maclay 11–0–67–1; Wagh 2–0–12–0; Thomson 1–0–4–0. *Second Innings*—Maclay 8–1–30–0; du Preez 10–3–33–0; Malik 14–0–50–0; Thomson 19–0–68–2; Wagh 13–0–37–1; Sutcliffe 5–1–21–2; Khan 2–0–15–0; Ridley 1–0–3–0; Gupte 1–0–4–0.

Umpires: R. Julian and K. J. Lyons.

OXFORD v CAMBRIDGE, NOTES

The University Match dates back to 1827. Altogether there have been 151 official matches, Cambridge winning 55 and Oxford 48, with 48 drawn. Since the war Cambridge have won nine times (1949, 1953, 1957, 1958, 1972, 1979, 1982, 1986 and 1992) and Oxford nine (1946, 1948, 1951, 1959, 1966, 1976, 1984, 1993 and 1995). All other matches have been drawn; the 1988 fixture was abandoned without a ball being bowled.

One hundred and two three-figure innings have been played in the University matches, 55 for Oxford and 47 for Cambridge. For the fullest lists see the 1940 and 1993 *Wisdens*. There have been three double-centuries for Cambridge (211 by G. Goonesena in 1957, 201 by A. Ratcliffe in 1931 and 200 by Majid Khan in 1970) and two for Oxford (238* by Nawab of Pataudi, sen. in 1931 and 201* by M. J. K. Smith in 1954). Ratcliffe's score was a record for the match for only one day, before being beaten by Pataudi's. M. J. K. Smith and R. J. Boyd-Moss (Cambridge) are the only players to score three hundreds.

The highest totals in the fixture are 513 for six in 1996, 503 in 1900, 457 in 1947, 453 for eight in 1931 and 453 for nine in 1994, all by Oxford. Cambridge's highest is 432 for nine in 1936. The lowest totals are 32 by Oxford in 1878 and 39 by Cambridge in 1858.

F. C. Cobden, in the Oxford v Cambridge match in 1870, performed the hat-trick by taking the last three wickets and won an extraordinary game for Cambridge by two runs. Other hat-tricks, all for Cambridge, have been achieved by A. G. Steel (1879), P. H. Morton (1880), J. F. Ireland (1911) and R. G. H. Lowe (1926). S. E. Butler, in the 1871 match, took all ten wickets in the Cambridge first innings.

D. W. Jarrett (Oxford 1975, Cambridge 1976), S. M. Wookey (Cambridge 1975-76, Oxford 1978) and G. Pathmanathan (Oxford 1975-78, Cambridge 1983) gained Blues for both Universities.

A full list of Blues from 1837 may be found in Wisdens *published between 1923 and 1939. The lists thereafter were curtailed:* Wisdens *from 1948 to 1972 list Blues since 1880; from 1973 to 1983 since 1919; from 1984 to 1992 since 1946.*

THE VASELINE BUSA CHAMPIONSHIP, 1996

By GRENVILLE HOLLAND

The long overdue reform of university cricket got under way in 1996. The British Universities Sports Association (BUSA) had inherited the competition from the Universities Athletic Union (UAU) only the previous year, but it was immediately obvious that its format was both unwieldy and unfair. The handful of universities which had taken part in the early tournaments of the 1920s had swollen to a high point of 110 in 1993, all scrambling to reach the final within the confines of a short summer term beset by examinations. Too often results would depend on the vagaries of weather or term schedules rather than actual playing ability.

BUSA observed this system at work for one year, and then resolved to remedy matters. From 1997, a two-level championship is to come into operation. The top tier of 24 universities, selected on historical grounds, will play in four regional leagues of six teams, and those finishing in first and second places will go into the quarter-finals of the championship. A second tier, containing the remaining universities, will be divided into about 12 regional leagues, playing in a separate competition for the BUSA Shield. An extra incentive will be provided by promotion and relegation between the tiers.

But while these plans were being developed, another breathless season of university "It's a Knock-Out" went ahead. In countless regional mini-leagues across the country, participants undertook the uneven task of reaching the last 32 – the first round of sudden death. Not that all of these 16 matches were destined to take place: Nottingham Trent never turned up at Durham, and West London Institute failed to appear at Exeter. Elsewhere, the weather intervened, to the detriment of two leading contenders – Manchester, who lost on the toss of a coin to Northumberland, and Swansea, whose match with East Anglia was rearranged because of rain to a date which left them fatally weakened by exams.

Most of the other heavyweights passed this first test with little difficulty, but 1995 quarter-finalists Brighton were knocked out by an extraordinary individual performance. Bowling first against Reading, they disposed of the entire team for just 93 (on a treacherous pitch, admittedly), only to be confounded by the medium-pace of George Hosier. He produced figures of 7.5–3–8–9 as Brighton crashed to 58 all out.

Reading had an easier passage in the second round, when they travelled to Warwick, found the umpires missing and were awarded the game. But their batting failed again in the next match against Luton (all out for 111 this time) and even Hosier couldn't save them. Luton won by nine wickets, and reached the semi-final stage for the first time in their short history as a university.

Another new university making unexpected progress was Staffordshire, who eliminated Scottish champions Edinburgh in the second round. Chasing a modest target of 162 in 60 overs, Staffordshire won with 18 overs to spare, thanks largely to 86 not out from their prolific opener Tony Hurdley. The tables were soon turned, however, when they met a powerful all-round side from Midlands neighbours Loughborough. Staffordshire were held to 148 all out, with left-arm spinner Mike Davies taking four for 34, and Loughborough went into the semi-final with a ten-wicket win.

Their opponents were to be holders Durham, who had not failed to reach the final since 1983, and had already brushed aside Oxford and Northumbria with routine ease. Invited to bat first, Loughborough took advantage of an excellent Chesterfield wicket to build a daunting total of 294 for nine, founded on a third-wicket partnership of 169 between captain Will Hearsey and Neeraj Prabhu. Durham's openers, Tim Hodgson and Matt Windows, promised much with a century opening stand, but momentum drained away after Windows mistimed a pull and was well caught by Prabhu. Loughborough held their nerve, maintaining a high standard of outfielding, and deservedly won through by 22 runs.

In the other semi-final, Luton were drawn against Bristol, whose spinners Andy James and Harry Duberley had taken all ten wickets between them in their quarter-final against Exeter. Bristol batted first and made uncertain progress before lunching at 87 for five. After the interval, however, Anthony Cutler and James Smallridge boosted the total to 202 for eight, and then James took six wickets and Duberley four for the second match in succession. Luton's impressive campaign came off the rails at last as they were bowled out for 143.

SEMI-FINALS

At Chesterfield, June 17. Loughborough won by 22 runs. Toss: Durham. Loughborough 294 for nine (60 overs) (W. J. Hearsey 110, N. V. Prabhu 97, S. Catterall 32; M. J. Chilton four for 60); Durham 272 (58.2 overs) (T. P. Hodgson 72, M. G. N. Windows 35, Extras 33).

At Radlett, June 17. Bristol won by 59 runs. Toss: Bristol. Bristol 202 for eight (A. J. Cutler 53, J. M. Smallridge 44); Luton 143 (A. M. James six for 48, H. G. Duberley four for 64).

FINAL

BRISTOL v LOUGHBOROUGH

At Wardown Park, Luton, June 24. Loughborough won by four wickets. Toss: Bristol.

A flat track, a fast outfield and a clear day all contributed to the decision by Bristol's captain, Andy Walker, to bat first. Unfortunately for him, his batsmen never took advantage of the helpful conditions, and neither did they come to terms with Loughborough's steady rather than penetrating attack. Half the team were back in the pavilion by the time the score had reached 58, and a total of 139 did not look enough. To their credit, Bristol fought back defiantly; Smallridge removed Hearsey in his first over and, with the score on ten, Taylor trapped Reynolds in front. For a moment it appeared that Loughborough too might get stuck in the doldrums. But Mike Fletcher made 61, comfortably the highest score of the match, and though he fell with the score on 101, Stuart Catterall was on hand to see his side home. It was Loughborough's first title for seven years.

Bristol

B. W. Griffiths b Jones 8	*†A. C. Walker c Catterall b Evans 22
J. F. A. Poulet c T. M. B. Bailey b Jones . 6	A. M. James not out 8
H. St J. R. Foster c T. M. B. Bailey b Evans . 13	N. C. F. Taylor st T. M. B. Bailey b M. K. Davies . 0
J. M. Smallridge b C. D. J. Bailey 4	B 7, l-b 5, n-b 5 17
A. J. Lomas b Jones 20	——
A. J. Cutler c P. Davies b M. K. Davies . . 4	1/8 2/23 3/30 (55.2 overs) 139
T. Sherman run out 18	4/32 5/58 6/81
H. G. Duberley b Evans 19	7/90 8/115 9/137

Bowling: Jones 15–5–31–3; Lang 9–2–19–0; C. D. J. Bailey 6–1–8–1; Evans 10–1–24–3; M. K. Davies 15.2–5–45–2.

Loughborough

J. Reynolds lbw b Taylor	4	C. D. J. Bailey c Lomas b Smallridge	7
*W. J. Hearsey c Foster b Smallridge	0	S. Jones not out	5
M. Fletcher lbw b James	61	L-b 3, n-b 1	4
P. Davies lbw b James	22		
†T. M. B. Bailey c James b Duberley	10	1/0 2/10 3/80 (6 wkts, 52.5 overs)	141
S. Catterall not out	28	4/99 5/101 6/121	

M. K. Davies, M. R. Evans and A. Lang did not bat.

Bowling: Taylor 12.5–5–23–1; Smallridge 9–0–27–2; Griffiths 5–0–22–0; James 17–4–38–2; Duberley 9–2–28–1.

Umpires: K. Hopley and R. Wallis.

WINNERS 1927-96

The UAU Championship was replaced by the BUSA Championship after 1994.

1927	Manchester	1955	Birmingham	1975	Loughborough Colls.
1928	Manchester	1956	Null and void	1976	Loughborough
1929	Nottingham	1957	Loughborough Colls.	1977	Durham
1930	Sheffield	1958	Null and void	1978	Manchester
1931	Liverpool	1959	Liverpool	1979	Manchester
1932	Manchester	1960	Loughborough Colls.	1980	Exeter
1933	Manchester	1961	Loughborough Colls.	1981	Durham
1934	Leeds	1962	Manchester	1982	Exeter
1935	Sheffield	1963	Loughborough Colls.	1983	Exeter
1936	Sheffield	1964	Loughborough Colls.	1984	Bristol
1937	Nottingham	1965	Hull	1985	Birmingham
1938	Durham	1966	Newcastle	1986	Durham
1939	Durham		Southampton	1987	Durham
1946	Not completed	1967	Manchester	1988	Swansea
1947	Sheffield	1968	Southampton	1989	Loughborough
1948	Leeds	1969	Southampton	1990	Durham
1949	Leeds	1970	Southampton	1991	Durham
1950	Manchester	1971	Loughborough Colls.	1992	Durham
1951	Manchester	1972	Durham	1993	Durham
1952	Loughborough Colls.	1973	Leicester	1994	Swansea
1953	Durham		Loughborough Colls.	1995	Durham
1954	Manchester	1974	Durham	1996	Loughborough

OTHER FIRST-CLASS MATCHES, 1996

ENGLAND A v THE REST

At Chelmsford, April 20, 21, 22. England A won by eight wickets. Toss: The Rest.

The traditional season-opener underwent another transformation: the England selectors invited a scratch team, The Rest, rather than county champions Warwickshire, to face England A (who had replaced MCC in this fixture in 1992). The successful ethos established by Hussain during the winter – all of his team, apart from his Essex colleague Rollins, had been on the A tour of Pakistan – secured victory with a day to spare, even though The Rest had the game's outstanding batsman in Thorpe. He was the only man to reach 20 in their first innings, which lasted just 49 overs as Giddins and Munton exploited an uneven pitch. Despite losing Knight first ball, England A already led by 33 when bad light ended the first day. A maiden fifty from No. 9 Munton extended that to 194, though the lively Chapple took five wickets. Thorpe then scored an unbeaten 141 out of 222 in nearly five hours at the crease, hitting 19 fours and a six. But he had little support. England A reached a target of 60 in the 12th over.

Close of play: First day, England A 156-5 (R. C. Irani 26*, R. J. Rollins 0*); Second day, The Rest 128-4 (G. P. Thorpe 73*, R. C. Russell 2*).

The Rest

M. D. Moxon c Knight b Munton	0	– lbw b Giddins	0
J. E. R. Gallian c Rollins b Irani	8	– lbw b Giddins	12
J. P. Crawley c McGrath b Munton	4	– b Munton	16
M. R. Ramprakash b Giddins	18	– c Rollins b Salisbury	17
G. P. Thorpe c Hussain b Munton	32	– not out	141
*†R. C. Russell c Knight b Giddins	9	– c Salisbury b Munton	2
M. Watkinson lbw b Giddins	0	– c and b Irani	35
G. Chapple c Hussain b Irani	15	– c Rollins b Irani	1
R. K. Illingworth not out	12	– c Knight b Munton	3
P. M. Hutchison c McGrath b Munton	0	– lbw b Giddins	0
J. D. Lewry c Rollins b Irani	0	– c Irani b Giddins	0
B 2, l-b 4, w 1, n-b 18	25	B 13, l-b 7, n-b 6	26
1/5 2/20 3/34 4/50 5/79 6/79 7/95 8/119 9/120	123	1/2 2/29 3/31 4/110 5/128 6/223 7/225 8/244 9/245	253

Bowling: *First Innings*—Giddins 17–4–52–3; Munton 21–8–41–4; Irani 10.5–3–24–3. *Second Innings*—Giddins 21–6–60–4; Munton 21–5–54–3; Stemp 10–2–26–0; Irani 15–2–53–2; Salisbury 18–4–40–1.

England A

N. V. Knight c Watkinson b Lewry	0	– not out	36
A. McGrath c Hutchison b Illingworth	28	– c Chapple b Lewry	9
*N. Hussain b Chapple	41	– b Hutchison	13
J. C. Pooley c Crawley b Lewry	38	– not out	0
D. P. Ostler b Chapple	13		
R. C. Irani c Crawley b Chapple	40		
†R. J. Rollins b Chapple	31		
I. D. K. Salisbury st Russell b Illingworth	38		
T. A. Munton c Watkinson b Illingworth	54		
R. D. Stemp c Thorpe b Chapple	8		
E. S. H. Giddins not out	9		
B 1, l-b 8, n-b 8	17	L-b 2	2
1/0 2/71 3/71 4/99 5/156 6/176 7/222 8/268 9/283	317	1/15 2/58	(2 wkts) 60

Bowling: *First Innings*—Lewry 21–9–60–2; Hutchison 17–1–84–0; Chapple 29–4–99–5; Illingworth 15.1–4–31–3; Gallian 7–0–22–0; Watkinson 5–3–12–0. *Second Innings*—Lewry 5–1–18–1; Hutchison 5.1–0–39–1; Thorpe 1–0–1–0.

Umpires: J. H. Hampshire and N. T. Plews.

SCOTLAND v IRELAND

At Boghall CC, Linlithgow, August 17, 18, 19. Drawn. Toss: Scotland. First-class debuts: M. J. D. Allingham, J. A. R. Blain, G. E. Gardner, D. R. Lockhart, B. G. Lockie, A. M. Tennant; O. F. X. Butler, R. L. Eagleson, P. G. Gillespie, W. K. McCallan, G. L. Molins, D. M. P. Moore, A. D. Patterson, A. T. Rutherford.

Two inexperienced sides scored an aggregate of 1,265 for 24 wickets, a record for this fixture. But the match ended in disappointment for Ireland. Chasing 319 in 70 overs, they had rallied after early losses, and Eagleson and Harrison added 92 brisk runs in drizzle before the umpires decided the rain was too heavy for them to continue. They were only 18 short of victory, with five overs and four wickets in hand. Home captain Salmond dominated the opening day with 181; only the Rev. James Aitchison had surpassed that for either side in these games, with 190 not out for Scotland in 1959. After the Irish declared in arrears, for a healthy 323, Philip took over, becoming the first batsman to score 4,000 runs for Scotland during his tenth hundred. The third declaration of the match set up Ireland's run-chase, which came to such a tantalising conclusion.

Close of play: First day, Ireland 25-0 (W. K. McCallan 9*, D. A. Lewis 8*); Second day, Scotland 97-3 (I. L. Philip 50*, A. G. Davies 14*).

Scotland

I. L. Philip c Rutherford b Eagleson	2	– c Eagleson b Molins	110
B. G. Lockie c Harrison b Gillespie	32	– lbw b Eagleson	6
D. R. Lockhart c Lewis b Gillespie	36	– c Eagleson b Gillespie	4
*G. Salmond c Lewis b Gillespie	181	– c Rutherford b Gillespie	0
J. G. Williamson c Moore b Molins	55	– (6) c Dunlop b Molins	49
M. J. D. Allingham not out	50	– (7) not out	36
†A. G. Davies not out	5	– (5) c Rutherford b Eagleson	24
J. W. Govan (did not bat)		– c Lewis b Molins	5
G. E. Gardner (did not bat)		– not out	2
L-b 4, w 5, n-b 10	19	B 4, l-b 3, w 2, n-b 16	25
1/3 2/61 3/91 4/256 5/370 (5 wkts dec.)	380	1/26 2/49 3/51 4/128 5/205 6/236 7/243 (7 wkts dec.)	261

J. A. R. Blain and A. M. Tennant did not bat.

Bowling: *First Innings*—Eagleson 17.1–2–99–1; Butler 9–0–31–0; Gillespie 18–3–93–3; Molins 20–5–57–1; Harrison 14–3–47–0; Moore 3–1–14–0; McCallan 9–1–35–0. *Second Innings*—Gillespie 12–2–43–2; Eagleson 14–0–50–2; Moore 3–0–23–0; Harrison 9–0–47–0; Molins 12.5–0–62–3; McCallan 6–0–29–0.

Ireland

W. K. McCallan c Philip b Gardner	51	– c Davies b Allingham	11
*D. A. Lewis b Allingham	28	– c Lockhart b Allingham	71
D. M. P. Moore c Blain b Govan	51	– c Davies b Allingham	17
A. R. Dunlop c Allingham b Tennant	57	– lbw b Williamson	1
A. D. Patterson st Davies b Tennant	16	– c Lockie b Gardner	29
P. G. Gillespie st Davies b Tennant	0	– c Davies b Williamson	53
R. L. Eagleson not out	50	– not out	41
G. D. Harrison not out	31	– not out	46
B 2, l-b 8, w 3, n-b 26	39	B 12, l-b 8, w 2, n-b 10	32
1/72 2/125 3/191 4/213 5/221 6/242 (6 wkts dec.)	323	1/26 2/50 3/53 4/86 5/198 6/209 (6 wkts)	301

†A. T. Rutherford, O. F. X. Butler and G. L. Molins did not bat.

Bowling: *First Innings*—Blain 17–5–67–0; Williamson 17.2–3–72–0; Govan 15–1–65–1; Tennant 12–7–28–3; Allingham 10–1–45–1; Gardner 9–1–36–1. *Second Innings*—Williamson 16–6–51–2; Blain 5–0–36–0; Allingham 12–3–53–3; Gardner 7–1–38–1; Tennant 20–6–94–0; Govan 5–2–9–0.

Umpires: J. Breslin and L. Redford.

MCC MATCHES IN 1996

MCC played a first-class match in 1996 for the first time since 1991, when the traditional MCC v Champion County fixture was discontinued, and the club also broke new ground by staging the match, against South Africa A, at Shenley Park in Hertfordshire. Lord's was not available because of the Benson and Hedges Cup final that coming weekend, on the Sunday of which MCC also played a limited-overs game against Wasim Akram's Pakistani touring team at Shenley.

For MCC members and others more accustomed to St John's Wood, Shenley offered the rural attraction of first-class cricketers knee-deep in ripening wheat, searching for the ball, as the West Indian Test player, Keith Arthurton, and the young South African, Herschelle Gibbs, literally hit the bowling out of the ground. Such is the nature of MCC cricket that a fortnight earlier Arthurton had been rattling the tiles in Buckinghamshire with an explosive 136 not out against Royal Grammar School, High Wycombe. MCC's 242 for one declared did not daunt the boys, however, and in the final over, begun with 11 needed, their captain, Geoff Watts, struck Arthurton's penultimate ball for six over mid-wicket to gain a memorable two-wicket win.

Schools provided 232 of MCC's 366 opponents in their 1996 scheduled matches, of which 142 were won, 114 drawn, 70 lost and 40 abandoned either during play or without a ball being bowled. Among many highlights were the seven stumpings by the former Scotland wicket-keeper, Hamish More, in the win over Hutcheson's Grammar School. Members also played four MCC inter-regional matches.

In keeping with its declared missionary role of developing cricket abroad, MCC sent sides to Bangladesh, Belgium, The Netherlands and Malta. The team to Bangladesh, captained by Alan Fordham and containing six first-class county players, managed only one win against five defeats and found themselves confined to their hotel for two days because of a somewhat volatile election. An incident of slightly less serious import happened to the Over-40s side which visited The Netherlands as part of CTC de Flamingo's 75th anniversary celebrations. They and their opponents returned from tea to discover that the local groundsman, thinking the game over, had rolled up the mat and stored it away. Clearly this missionary work has some way to go. – GRAEME WRIGHT.

Note: With the exception of the game against South Africa A, matches in this section were not first-class.

At Lord's, May 1. MCC Young Cricketers won by three wickets. Toss: MCC. MCC 210 for three dec. (P. Bedford 64, M. A. Crawley 100); MCC Young Cricketers 211 for seven (P. R. Shaw 61, P. G. Hudson 68).

At Lord's, May 21. Club Cricket Conference won by three wickets. Toss: MCC. MCC 236 for nine dec. (G. J. Whittall 53, A. J. Hollioake 69, R. M. Wight 33, R. D. V. Knight 30; D. Carter four for 39); Club Cricket Conference 237 for seven (R. Falconer 118; A. J. Hollioake four for 66).

At Lord's, May 22. MCC v Midlands Club Cricket Conference. Abandoned.

At Oxford, May 28, 29, 30. MCC beat OXFORD UNIVERSITY by six wickets (See The Universities in 1996).

At Durham, June 10, 11. Drawn. Toss: MCC. MCC 228 for five dec. (P. W. Romaines 48, G. J. Lord 46, J. L. Prentis 32, K. C. Williams 56 not out; M. Cooper four for 81) and 168 (T. S. Smith 55 not out; J. Chaplin four for 48); Durham University 198 for one dec. (J. A. Ford 108 not out, M. J. Chilton 52 retired hurt) and 191 for nine (J. A. Ford 37, A. Strauss 66; T. S. Smith four for 53, R. A. Hawthorne five for 42).

At Cambridge, June 11, 12, 13. MCC drew with CAMBRIDGE UNIVERSITY (See The Universities in 1996).

At Malahide CC, June 15, 16, 17. MCC won by three wickets. Toss: Ireland. Ireland 243 (W. K. McCallan 100, D. Heasley 73; A. I. C. Dodemaide three for 49, G. A. R. Harris three for 55) and 335 for seven dec. (A. D. Patterson 73, A. R. Dunlop 148, D. Heasley 34; G. A. R. Harris three for 55); MCC 307 (D. A. Thorne 65, A. I. C. Dodemaide 94, G. J. Toogood 38; P. McCrum five for 52) and 272 for seven (P. W. G. Parker 129, T. S. Smith 36 not out; P. McCrum three for 56, D. Heasley three for 32).

At Arundel, June 16. MCC won by four wickets. Toss: Earl of Arundel's XI. Earl of Arundel's XI 259 for six dec. (T. W. Harrison 108, S. Munday 54, I. Gray 31; C. J. Hollins three for 98); MCC 263 for six (D. A. Stewart 95, L. Potter 54, C. J. Hollins 31; D. G. Shufflebotham three for 62).

At Beaconsfield, July 8. National Association of Young Cricketers won by three wickets. Toss: MCC. MCC 234 for five dec. (D. R. Thomas 59, N. R. C. MacLaurin 81 not out); National Association of Young Cricketers 235 for seven (M. Swarbrick 117, D. A. Ellis 52; B. S. Phelps four for 106).

At Shenley Park, July 10, 11, 12. MCC drew with SOUTH AFRICA A (See South Africa A tour section).

At Shenley Park, July 14. MCC lost to PAKISTANIS on scoring-rate (See Pakistani tour section).

At Lord's, July 16. MCC lost to MCC SCHOOLS by three wickets (See Schools Cricket in 1996).

At RAF Vine Lane, Uxbridge, July 16. MCC won by five wickets. Toss: Combined Services. Combined Services 213 (Lt C. H. G. St George 114 not out, Sgt N. Palmer 33; L. Potter five for 33); MCC 215 for five (R. J. Greatorex 47, S. D. Welch 60, S. J. Cooper 36 not out).

At Sherborne School, July 19. Drawn. Toss: MCC. MCC 259 for four dec. (N. A. Folland 51, J. E. M. Nicolson 71, W. S. Kendall 36 not out, J. D. Ricketts 52 not out); Dorset 221 for nine (M. Swarbrick 60, J. Cassell 50; J. D. Ricketts five for 94, C. K. Bullen three for 38).

At Wormsley, July 21. J. Paul Getty's XI won by four wickets. Toss: J. Paul Getty's XI. MCC 216 for eight dec. (C. M. Gupte 64, R. J. Robinson 52; S. Martin three for 30); J. Paul Getty's XI 217 for six (R. Boon 38, C. T. Radley 80, B. W. Byrne 31; R. J. Robinson three for 94, N. G. B. Cook three for 58).

At Lord's, August 7, 8. Scotland won by seven wickets. Toss: Scotland. MCC 210 for eight dec. (J. N. Batty 50, K. C. Williams 59; K. Thomson three for 39) and 196 for seven dec. (A. G. Lawson 33, G. D. Hodgson 40; I. R. Beven three for 55); Scotland 191 for four dec. (B. G. Lockie 74, D. R. Lockhart 39, G. N. Reifer 52 not out) and 216 for three (I. L. Philip 64, D. R. Lockhart 60, G. N. Reifer 63 not out).

At Swansea, August 27, 28, 29. MCC won by 156 runs. Toss: MCC. MCC 309 for eight dec. (J. L. P. Meadows 34, R. Smith 79, I. Gompertz 44, N. A. Folland 63 not out, M. P. W. Jeh 32; A. Davies three for 64) and 174 for two dec. (I. Gompertz 68 not out, R. Smith 63 not out); Wales 174 for seven dec. (M. Tamplin 39, M. Powell 45, A. Davies 46; M. P. W. Jeh three for 37) and 153 (K. C. Williams four for 24, M. P. W. Jeh three for 53).

At Lord's, September 10. MCC won by 33 runs. Toss: de Flamingo's. MCC 337 for three dec. (J. R. Wood 83, T. J. G. O'Gorman 134, A. J. Hollioake 88 not out); de Flamingo's 304 (T. B. M. de Leede 167, M. Nota 34; R. M. O. Cooke seven for 123).

OTHER MATCHES, 1996

Note: Matches in this section were not first-class.

At Southampton, April 15, 16, 17, 18. Drawn. Toss: Hampshire Second XI. Hampshire Second XI 450 (G. R. Treagus 38, M. Garaway 38, M. Keech 66, K. D. James 106, R. J. Maru 73, Extras 86; G. J. Batty three for 54) and 264 for four dec. (M. Garaway 54, M. Keech 96, K. D. James 57); England Under-19 343 (A. J. Swann 114, D. J. Sales 55, L. D. Sutton 38, C. L. Campbell 31 not out; J. N. B. Bovill four for 50) and 305 for six (D. J. Roberts 169, D. J. Sales 60, L. D. Sutton 45).

In the first innings England Under-19 conceded 17 byes, 22 leg-byes, nine wides and 38 no-balls in 122.5 overs.

At Manchester, April 21. Lancashire won by five wickets. Toss: Lancashire. Yorkshire 152 for nine (40 overs) (P. J. Martin three for 44); Lancashire 154 for five (36.2 overs) (A. Flintoff 50 not out).

At Manchester, April 22. Lancashire won by six wickets. Toss: Yorkshire. Yorkshire 145 (48.5 overs) (R. J. Blakey 30; R. J. Green four for 22, S. P. Titchard three for 29); Lancashire 146 for four (35.2 overs) (S. P. Titchard 30, N. J. Speak 44 not out, G. D. Lloyd 31 not out).

At Oxford, April 24. Warwickshire won by 168 runs. Toss: Warwickshire. Warwickshire 355 for seven (50 overs) (N. V. Knight 128, P. A. Smith 51, D. P. Ostler 63, D. A. Reeve 30 not out, Extras 46); British Universities 187 for eight (50 overs) (A. Singh 40, M. E. Harvey 63 not out).

Knight scored his 128 from 134 balls.

HARROGATE FESTIVAL

Costcutter Cup

A 55-over competition contested by Yorkshire and three other invited counties.

At Harrogate, July 15. Gloucestershire won by 89 runs. Toss: Gloucestershire. Gloucestershire 297 for six (55 overs) (M. G. N. Windows 47, A. J. Wright 43, T. H. C. Hancock 56, M. A. Lynch 68, A. Symonds 35 not out, Extras 34); Yorkshire 208 (46.1 overs) (M. G. Bevan 51, A. McGrath 44; J. Lewis four for 24, M. W. Alleyne three for 47).

At Harrogate, July 16. Durham won by seven wickets. Toss: Leicestershire. Leicestershire 211 for nine (55 overs) (D. L. Maddy 36, B. F. Smith 65, J. J. Whitaker 36; N. Killeen three for 47); Durham 215 for three (46 overs) (S. L. Campbell 99, S. Hutton 87).

Durham's first win of the season over a first-class county. Campbell and Hutton shared an opening stand of 196.

At Harrogate, July 17. **Final:** Durham won by four wickets. Toss: Gloucestershire. Gloucestershire 249 for seven (55 overs) (M. G. N. Windows 72, A. J. Wright 36, M. A. Lynch 63 not out; M. M. Betts three for 47); Durham 252 for six (53.2 overs) (S. L. Campbell 56, S. Hutton 105 not out).

DERMOT REEVE BENEFIT MATCH

At Birmingham, August 3. Warwickshire won by four wickets. Toss: Warwickshire. World XI 215 for nine (50 overs) (P. A. de Silva 34, R. G. Twose 52, B. M. McMillan 36; T. A. Munton three for 15); Warwickshire 217 for six (46.1 overs) (S. M. Pollock 72, D. R. Brown 79 not out).

SCARBOROUGH FESTIVAL

At Scarborough, September 6. Yorkshire won by three wickets. Toss: Yorkshire. Tesco International XI 249 for six (50 overs) (D. W. Randall 34, T. B. M. de Leede 44, C. Z. Harris 89 not out, J. C. Adams 43); Yorkshire 253 for seven (48.2 overs) (M. D. Moxon 71, M. P. Vaughan 36, A. McGrath 79; C. Z. Harris four for 39).

At Scarborough, September 7 (Northern Electric Trophy). Yorkshire won by 45 runs. Toss: Durham. Yorkshire 337 for eight (50 overs) (M. D. Moxon 38, M. P. Vaughan 85, D. Byas 43, A. McGrath 54, C. White 48); Durham 292 for seven (50 overs) (S. Hutton 31, J. E. Morris 92, J. A. Daley 54, D. G. C. Ligertwood 45 not out).

At Scarborough, September 8 (McCain Challenge). Holland won by three wickets. Toss: Holland. Yorkshire 204 (48.4 overs) (M. P. Vaughan 41; T. B. M. de Leede three for 49); Holland 206 for seven (47.5 overs) (L. van Troost 38, P. E. Cantrell 33, K. J. van Noortwijk 33 not out; G. M. Hamilton three for 44).

Tetley Bitter Festival Trophy

A 50-over competition contested by Yorkshire and three other invited counties.

At Scarborough, September 9. Yorkshire won by 123 runs. Toss: Durham. Yorkshire 366 for nine (48 overs) (D. Byas 113, M. P. Vaughan 118, Extras 30; J. Wood four for 92); Durham 243 (44.2 overs) (S. Hutton 35, J. A. Daley 40, M. A. Roseberry 66, M. M. Betts 49; G. M. Hamilton four for 63).

At Scarborough, September 10. Worcestershire won by 13 runs. Toss: Worcestershire. Worcestershire 202 for nine (47 overs) (T. S. Curtis 91; J. P. Hart three for 38, M. P. Dowman three for 23); Nottinghamshire 189 (46 overs) (P. R. Pollard 82 not out; R. J. Chapman three for 32, V. S. Solanki three for 37).

At Scarborough, September 11. **Final:** Yorkshire won by five wickets. Toss: Worcestershire. Worcestershire 196 (49.1 overs) (G. A. Hick 41, I. Dawood 39); Yorkshire 198 for five (44 overs) (D. Byas 106 not out, R. J. Blakey 47).

TRIPLE CROWN TOURNAMENT

At Ynysygerwn, July 2. England NCA XI won by nine wickets. Toss: England NCA XI. Scotland 218 for six (50 overs) (I. L. Philip 59, J. G. Williamson 37); England NCA XI 222 for one (38.5 overs) (S. Foster 81 not out, M. J. Roberts 98).

At Pontarddulais, July 2. Ireland won by five wickets. Toss: Ireland. Wales 199 for eight (50 overs) (S. Jenkins 58, K. M. Bell 40, M. Davies 33); Ireland 203 for five (41.5 overs) (D. J. Curry 69, J. D. R. Benson 44, A. R. Dunlop 52 not out).

At Ynysygerwn, July 3. Scotland won by seven wickets. Toss: Scotland. Ireland 245 for six (40 overs) (A. D. Patterson 30, J. D. R. Benson 34, A. R. Dunlop 35, N. G. Doak 42 not out, D. Heasley 45); Scotland 246 for three (37 overs) (I. L. Philip 121, B. G. Lockie 70; R. L. Eagleson three for 34).

At Swansea, July 3. England NCA XI won by 16 runs. Toss: Wales. England NCA XI 166 for four (32 overs) (S. Foster 30, M. J. Roberts 54; M. Davies three for 16); Wales 150 for six (32 overs) (M. J. Newbold 38 not out).

At Pontarddulais, July 4. Ireland won by seven wickets. Toss: Ireland. England NCA XI 152 (45 overs) (D. Snellgrove 34 not out, S. N. V. Waterton 30 not out; M. W. Patterson three for 16); Ireland 153 for three (30.2 overs) (D. J. Curry 44, A. D. Patterson 41, J. D. R. Benson 45 not out).

At Swansea, July 4. Wales won by four wickets. Toss: Wales. Scotland 198 for eight (50 overs) (G. Salmond 74, M. J. D. Allingham 32); Wales 200 for six (49.1 overs) (S. Jenkins 34, G. Davies 45 not out).

Final table

	Played	*Won*	*Lost*	*Points*	*Avge*
Ireland	3	2	1	4	1.138
England NCA XI	3	2	1	4	0.801
Scotland	3	1	2	2	0.659
Wales	3	1	2	2	0.628

The average was obtained by dividing teams' scoring-rate (runs scored divided by wickets lost) by their strike-rate (balls bowled divided by wickets taken).

THE MINOR COUNTIES IN 1996

By MICHAEL BERRY and ROBERT BROOKE

Devon's dominance of Minor Counties cricket brought them a fourth Western Division title in the space of five years, and their third consecutive outright title. They became only the third county in history to achieve a Championship hat-trick, following in the footsteps of Worcestershire (1896 to 1898) and Staffordshire (1991 to 1993). But Peter Roebuck's side did things the hard way in 1996, losing three of their nine Western Division games and using 22 players during the season.

They also had six different wicket-keepers, including stand-in Nick Folland who took over the gloves when Chris Read was injured in the Championship final against Norfolk. Folland played a more orthodox role with the bat, scoring 1,055 runs, the seventh-best aggregate in the 90 seasons of the competition. In a summer governed by batsmen, Wayne Larkins scored 1,024 Championship runs for Bedfordshire, who were beaten by Cheshire in the final of the MCC Trophy at Lord's. It was only the second time that two players had reached 1,000 Championship runs in the same season.

Folland and Peter Roebuck were the stars of **Devon's** title-winning campaign. Left-hander Folland's runs came at an average of 95.90 to win him the Wilfred Rhodes Trophy for the second successive season, and the third time in five years. Skipper Roebuck, an inspirational leader, was pipped by Bedfordshire's Richard Dalton for the Frank Edwards Trophy for bowling, but finished as the Championship's leading wicket-taker. His all-sorts claimed 47 Championship scalps at a cost of just 15.63, and included a match return of 11 for 60 in the win over Berkshire. Nick Gaywood scored 816 runs and Haydn Morgan 629; both Gaywood and Folland completed 100 Championship appearances and passed 6,000 Championship runs during the year.

Continued over

MINOR COUNTIES CHAMPIONSHIP, 1996

Eastern Division	*M*	*W*	*L*	*D*	*NR*	*Bonus Points Batting*	*Bonus Points Bowling*	*Total Points*
Norfolk^NW	9	4	1	4	0	23	20	107
Cambridgeshire^NW	9	3	2	4	0	19	30	97
Buckinghamshire^NW	9	3	4	2	0	21	27	96
Staffordshire^NW	9	3	1	5	0	13	29	90
Cumberland^NW	9	3	1	5	0	18	20	86
Bedfordshire^NW	9	2	4	3	0	23	29	84
Lincolnshire^NW	9	2	1	5	1	24	22	83
Suffolk	9	2	1	6	0	20	23	75
Hertfordshire	9	1	3	4	1	12	21	62
Northumberland	9	0	5	4	0	24	14	38

Western Division	*M*	*W*	*L*	*D*	*NR*	*Bonus Points Batting*	*Bonus Points Bowling*	*Total Points*
Devon^NW	9	5	3	1	0	26	18	124
Herefordshire^NW	9	5	1	3	0	21	23	124
Shropshire^NW	9	3	1	4	1	26	24	103
Berkshire^NW	9	3	4	1	1	15	24	92
Cornwall	9	2	2	4	1	24	21	82
Cheshire	9	2	3	4	0	27	20	79
Oxfordshire	9	2	0	7	0	17	18	75
Dorset	9	2	2	5	0	16	15	63
Wales	9	1	5	3	0	16	18	50
Wiltshire	9	0	4	4	1	21	14	40

Devon won the Western Division title by virtue of a higher net batting average.

The totals for Hertfordshire and Oxfordshire include eight points for batting second in a match drawn with the scores level.

Win = 16 pts. No result = 5 pts.

NW *Denotes qualified for NatWest Trophy in 1997.*

The signing of Neal Radford and Kevin Cooper gave **Herefordshire's** bowling a match-winning spearhead. They combined to share 57 victims (Radford 30, Cooper 27) but the Herefordshire batting, apart from a couple of exceptions (notably a new record total of 380 for four against Cornwall) was less prolific than in previous seasons. Harshad Patel, who scored 1,093 runs in 1995, was hampered by a back problem and made only 165 in five appearances. Richard Skyrme, their captain, also missed the early part of the season after knee surgery. Steve Brogan maintained his good form with 511, but the season ended in a bitter last-match defeat against Wales, who denied Herefordshire the four points they needed for the regional title by a controversial first-innings declaration.

Asif Din, the new **Shropshire** professional, was a resounding success with bat and ball. The former Warwickshire player managed 890 runs and 21 wickets in his first season, and was a motivational presence in the dressing-room. Shropshire prospered by equalling their best-ever Western Division placing of third, and looked to be an emerging force. Slow left-armer Adam Byram took 24 wickets, while Kevin Sharp, as well as scoring 439 runs, confirmed his ability as a slip fielder with 17 catches.

Gary Loveday's first season as captain of **Berkshire** produced a personal tally of 575 runs to take him past 6,000 in his career. Simon Myles confirmed his ranking as the best all-rounder in the Championship with 425 runs and 27 wickets, while 46-year-old Peter Lewington, who came out of retirement in search of the extra 35 wickets needed to become the county's top wicket-taker of all time, added another seven to his total. Berkshire (who had undertaken a ten-match centenary tour of South Africa during the winter) escaped the ignominy of recording the lowest ever total in Championship history – currently 14 – against Cheshire when they recovered from an incredible four for seven to 96 all out.

The **Cornwall** opening pairing of Gary Thomas and Steve Williams were again among the runs. Their combined tally of 1,611 was boosted by an unbroken stand of 258 against Wiltshire, followed by a partnership of 176 in the next game against Shropshire. Ryan Driver, a teenaged newcomer to the batting line-up, scored 374, while David Angove, the promising young quick bowler, was leading wicket-taker with 21 victims. He also won the match award against Warwickshire in the NatWest Trophy. Kevin Willcock, son of former Cornwall captain Eric, captured the best Championship bowling figures of the summer with eight for 83 against Berkshire.

Despite their success in the one-day competition, **Cheshire** were inconsistent in the Championship. An early-season eye injury to Ian Cockbain, the captain, proved disruptive, even though Jon Bean scored 756 runs, and three different bowlers broke the 20-wicket barrier: Nigel Peel, one-time Surrey seamer Tony Murphy and Andy Greasley.

Bruce Ellison (508 runs) and Keith Mustow (544) emerged as **Oxfordshire's** top batsmen, and left-hander Charlie Knightley was an impressive newcomer with 359. All three scored freely, while Keith Arnold (29 wickets) and skipper Rupert Evans (20) led the bowling. But Oxfordshire were hit by the unavailability of Jon Batty, the Oxford University wicket-keeper/batsman, and Stewart Laudat. They were the only county not to suffer a Championship defeat, but still missed the cut for the 1997 NatWest Trophy.

New captain Jon Hardy (560) was the only **Dorset** batsman to reach 500 runs, although Richard Scott was close with 480 and their former skipper Giles Reynolds had 227 to his name from three matches before ending his season early to embark on a holiday in India. Julian Shackleton was the most successful bowler, with 22 wickets. Dorset celebrated their centenary season with a cricket week at Sherborne School, the highlight of which was a drawn game with MCC.

Jamie Sylvester set a new individual record for **Wales** with 856 runs, bettering his own total of 773 in 1995. In the game against Cheshire, Wales amassed their biggest ever Minor Counties total, 331 for six, and Sylvester and Andrew Jones then shared an unbroken opening stand of 263 in the second innings. Jones finished with 582 runs and the industrious Adrian Griffiths took 27 wickets. Wales also broke their duck in the one-day competition, reaching the semi-finals after no wins in their previous eight years.

Wiltshire, who recruited the former Hampshire slow left-armer Darren Flint, finished at the foot of the Western Division after failing to win a single match. But a transitional season was not without individual highs. Skipper David Mercer (610 runs, taking him past 7,000 in his career) saved them from defeat at Shropshire with a marathon career-best 147, Dwain Winter made 509 runs and Richard Turnell, son of racehorse trainer Andy, burst on to the scene with 21 wickets. Billy Taylor, who took 20 Championship scalps, was another newcomer with potential.

Paul Newman, having moved from Staffordshire, guided **Norfolk** to the Eastern Division title in his first season as captain, and his 29 wickets were a key factor in their success. Tim Boon (902 runs) and Steve Goldsmith (618) were prime contributors; Boon scored four centuries. Goldsmith also took 21 wickets while Mark Thomas returned a decisive five for six in the ten-wicket thrashing of Northumberland. Norfolk lost the services of fast bowler Martin Saggers midway through the campaign when he signed a two-year contract with Durham.

Former Yorkshire batsman Simon Kellett's first season with **Cambridgeshire** brought 813 runs, and Giles Ecclestone's greater availability yielded 559. Off-spinner Brad Donelan collected 36 wickets and seamer Dominic Ralfs 26. Cambridgeshire, who scored their best ever one-day total of 313 for five against Suffolk at Copdock, could have stolen the Eastern Division title from Norfolk if they had won their last game against Hertfordshire. In the event, the match was a draw with the scores level.

Buckinghamshire, who led the Eastern Division for much of the season, unearthed one of the most impressive newcomers of the year in Anatole Thomas, a Hammersmith-born fast bowler of West Indian origin. His 35 Championship wickets were matched by leg-spinner Andy Clarke, while both Malcolm Roberts (699) and the influential Neil Burns (693) scored freely. Roberts made two centuries in the same game against Northumberland at Jesmond (the 36th instance in the Championship) and his unbeaten 177 was the highest total of the Championship year. Buckinghamshire began 1996 with a 13-match tour of South Africa.

Staffordshire's first year under the captaincy of Steve Dean was similar to the last under the long-serving Nick Archer. For the second year running, only a last-match victory salvaged their proud record of having qualified for the NatWest Trophy every year since the introduction of geographical divisions in 1983, and the expanded entry for Minor Counties sides that went with it. Dean top-scored with 699 runs while Alan Richardson's return from Derbyshire yielded 39 wickets to help fill the void left by Paul Newman's departure to Norfolk.

David Pearson (539 runs) and Grahame Clarke (450) were **Cumberland's** top batsmen, and Marcus Sharp, who bowled eight overs for just 22 runs in the representative fixture against the Pakistanis at Stone, finished with 31 Championship wickets. Jonathan Fielding took 24 in his debut season and Mike Scothern 23. An up-and-down season saw Cumberland, like Staffordshire and Lincolnshire, qualify for the NatWest Trophy by winning their last game.

Bedfordshire's improved form was largely attributable to the arrival of Wayne Larkins. The former England Test batsman crowned his first season with his native county by finishing with a record Bedfordshire aggregate and seven centuries (six in the Championship). Richard Dalton and Bobby Sher both claimed 23 wickets, Dalton's at a cost of just 15.56 apiece to win him the Frank Edwards Trophy for finishing at the top of the Minor Counties national bowling averages. He also scored a century in the MCC Trophy final at Lord's.

Lincolnshire new boy Simon Oakes, an opening bowler, caught the eye with 23 wickets, the same as slow left-armer Steve Bradford. But Lincolnshire struggled to live up to their mantle as the reigning Eastern Division champions. Steve Plumb, recruited from Norfolk, had a below-par summer by his high standards, and skipper Mark Fell's 501 runs lacked support. He will be expecting better things in 1997, his Testimonial year.

Former England batsman Derek Randall had another rewarding season with **Suffolk**. His 822 runs were solidly backed up by Russell Catley (568) and Glucka Wijesuriya (540), while the experienced Simon Clements inched to a career total of 9,059 runs. Suffolk's bowling resources were stretched by injury and unavailability, but Andrew Golding, the slow left-armer, was as dependable as ever with 39 wickets, and Phil Caley, the captain, took crucial wickets in the two Championship wins over Northumberland and Norfolk.

Hertfordshire's David Surridge and Alan Garofall both scaled the career milestone of 300 Championship wickets during the season, coincidentally in the same match against Norfolk. Garofall, called into action again at the age of 50, played only two games, but took nine wickets. Freshman quick bowler Paul O'Reilly enjoyed a fruitful baptism with 20 wickets, but no batsman managed to score 400 runs. Ian Fletcher led the way with 396 and Andrew Griffin produced one of the highlights of the season with an unbeaten 146 against Norfolk.

Northumberland failed to win in the Eastern Division, losing five of their nine games to finish with a disappointing record in their centenary year. Consolation came in the form of Tim Adcock's best season to date, which realised a creditable 716 runs, while skipper Graeme Morris reached the career landmark of 5,000 runs and pace bowler Craig Stanley took 24 wickets. But generally Northumberland were ill-equipped and Morris stood down as captain at the end of the season after four years in charge.

LEADING AVERAGES, 1996

BATTING

(Qualification: 8 innings, average 30.00)

	M	*I*	*NO*	*R*	*HS*	*100s*	*Avge*
N. A. Folland (*Devon*)	10	18	7	1,055	127	3	95.90
W. Larkins (*Bedfordshire*)	9	18	4	1,024	155*	6	73.14
J. P. J. Sylvester (*Wales*)	8	15	3	856	143*	2	71.33
H. J. Morgan (*Devon*)	5	10	1	629	144	1	69.88
S. R. Bevins (*Herefordshire*)	8	12	6	417	74*	0	69.50
Asif Din (*Shropshire*)	9	15	2	890	175	3	68.46
T. J. Boon (*Norfolk*)	10	18	4	902	116*	4	64.42
M. J. Roberts (*Buckinghamshire*)	7	14	3	699	177*	3	63.54
S. A. Kellett (*Cambridgeshire*)	9	18	5	813	126*	1	62.53
P. M. Roebuck (*Devon*)	10	10	4	374	79	0	62.33
I. Cockbain (*Cheshire*)	8	13	6	436	70	0	62.28
G. W. Ecclestone (*Cambridgeshire*)	6	12	3	559	126*	2	62.11
G. M. Thomas (*Cornwall*)	9	17	2	832	148*	2	55.46
D. W. Randall (*Suffolk*)	8	15	0	822	121	1	54.80
N. D. Burns (*Buckinghamshire*)	9	18	5	693	100*	1	53.30
I. R. Payne (*Shropshire*)	9	10	4	314	73*	0	52.33
S. M. Williams (*Cornwall*)	9	17	2	779	106*	2	51.93
M. R. Davies (*Shropshire*)	9	12	4	412	67	0	51.50
T. W. Adcock (*Northumberland*)	9	16	2	716	150*	2	51.14
N. R. Gaywood (*Devon*)	9	17	1	816	134	1	51.00
J. D. Bean (*Cheshire*)	9	17	2	756	102	1	50.40
G. R. Morris (*Northumberland*)	7	12	3	433	69*	0	48.11
C. K. Bullen (*Bedfordshire*)	6	9	2	336	128*	1	48.00
S. M. Brogan (*Herefordshire*)	7	12	1	511	87	0	46.45
M. P. Briers (*Cornwall*)	6	9	2	320	95*	0	45.71
A. C. H. Seymour (*Cornwall*)	5	8	1	316	94	0	45.14
C. S. Knightley (*Oxfordshire*)	6	10	2	359	98*	0	44.87
A. J. Jones (*Wales*)	8	15	2	582	105*	1	44.76
M. I. Humphries (*Staffordshire*)	9	10	4	267	102*	1	44.50
R. Hall (*Herefordshire*)	8	13	4	398	93*	0	44.22
R. J. Scott (*Dorset*)	9	15	4	480	71*	0	43.63
D. J. M. Mercer (*Wiltshire*)	9	17	3	610	147	1	43.57
O. S. Youll (*Northumberland*)	6	8	1	302	101*	1	43.14
D. A. Winter (*Wiltshire*)	7	13	1	509	104*	1	42.41
B. C. A. Ellison (*Oxfordshire*)	8	14	2	508	90	0	42.33
S. J. Dean (*Staffordshire*)	9	18	1	699	173*	1	41.11
P. J. Caley (*Suffolk*)	9	14	5	366	60	0	40.66
A. M. Small (*Devon*)	7	9	2	284	54*	0	40.57

	M	*I*	*NO*	*R*	*HS*	*100s*	*Avge*
A. N. Johnson (*Shropshire*)	8	9	4	200	71	0	40.00
K. Sharp (*Shropshire*)	8	14	3	439	156*	2	39.90
G. T. J. Townsend (*Devon*)	10	16	3	518	60	0	39.84
S. C. Goldsmith (*Norfolk*)	10	18	2	618	81	0	38.62
S. M. Perrin (*Wiltshire*)	9	16	6	386	78*	0	38.60
K. M. Wijesuriya (*Suffolk*)	9	17	3	540	96	0	38.57
M. A. Fell (*Lincolnshire*)	9	13	0	501	65	0	38.53
D. J. Pearson (*Cumberland*)	9	17	3	539	90*	0	38.50
G. E. Loveday (*Berkshire*)	9	17	2	575	113*	1	38.33
R. N. Dalton (*Bedfordshire*)	8	13	2	418	101*	1	38.00
M. R. Gouldstone (*Lincolnshire*)	5	9	2	264	61	0	37.71
G. J. Clarke (*Cumberland*)	6	12	0	450	92	0	37.50
J. J. E. Hardy (*Dorset*)	9	17	2	560	107	1	37.33
K. Donohue (*Devon*)	9	8	4	148	78*	0	37.00
J. L. Taylor (*Wiltshire*)	5	10	0	369	109	1	36.90
L. Potter (*Staffordshire*)	6	11	3	295	70*	0	36.87
I. Fletcher (*Hertfordshire*)	7	11	0	396	131	1	36.00
B. T. P. Donelan (*Cambridgeshire*)	9	17	3	498	93*	0	35.57
R. G. Hignett (*Cheshire*)	9	15	2	462	75	0	35.53
R. J. Catley (*Suffolk*)	9	17	1	568	86	0	35.50
A. J. Dutton (*Staffordshire*)	6	10	4	212	59	0	35.33
M. Saxelby (*Cheshire*)	6	9	0	315	65	0	35.00
R. J. Williams (*Oxfordshire*)	7	13	2	382	91*	0	34.72
K. R. Mustow (*Oxfordshire*)	9	18	2	544	128	2	34.00
A. J. Squire (*Suffolk*)	8	13	3	340	91*	0	34.00
A. Roseberry (*Northumberland*)	8	14	1	439	76*	0	33.76
G. P. Swann (*Bedfordshire*)	5	9	0	301	86	0	33.44
R. C. Williams (*Bedfordshire*)	7	9	3	196	60	0	32.66
A. J. Pugh (*Devon*)	9	14	2	391	80	0	32.58
S. T. Knox (*Cumberland*)	7	14	1	419	113	1	32.23
S. J. Musgrove (*Lincolnshire*)	4	8	0	257	55	0	32.12
S. G. Plumb (*Lincolnshire*)	7	13	1	385	69	0	32.08
H. M. Hall (*Berkshire*)	8	13	3	320	44*	0	32.00
K. M. Bell (*Wales*)	9	16	1	475	89	0	31.66
A. D. Griffin (*Hertfordshire*)	8	14	4	316	146*	1	31.60
N. V. Radford (*Herefordshire*)	8	12	6	189	43*	0	31.50
C. N. Spinks (*Hertfordshire*)	9	13	1	377	64	0	31.41
N. W. Pitcher (*Berkshire*)	6	11	0	341	100	1	31.00
D. K. Pashley (*Staffordshire*)	7	14	2	372	87	0	31.00
G. Davies (*Wales*)	5	8	2	186	99	0	31.00
S. M. Dutton (*Cumberland*)	9	14	4	306	50*	0	30.60
S. W. D. Rintoul (*Dorset*)	9	17	3	427	70*	0	30.50
S. D. Myles (*Berkshire*)	9	17	3	425	112*	1	30.35
I. A. Hawtin (*Oxfordshire*)	9	14	5	272	93	0	30.22
P. R. J. Bryson (*Cheshire*)	9	17	2	453	127*	1	30.20
D. A. J. Wise (*Oxfordshire*)	7	13	1	361	105*	1	30.08

* *Signifies not out.*

BOWLING

(Qualification: 10 wickets, average 30.00)

	O	*M*	*R*	*W*	*BB*	*5W/i*	*Avge*
A. J. Dutton (*Staffordshire*)	76	16	242	18	4-58	0	13.44
R. N. Dalton (*Bedfordshire*)	121.4	33	358	23	5-39	1	15.56
P. M. Roebuck (*Devon*)	329	85	735	47	6-33	4	15.63
G. J. Byram (*Shropshire*)	61	9	195	12	4-36	0	16.25
L. Potter (*Staffordshire*)	87.3	23	278	17	5-40	2	16.35
K. E. Cooper (*Herefordshire*)	194.2	50	467	27	5-25	2	17.29

	O	M	R	W	BB	5W/i	Avge
N. V. Radford (*Herefordshire*)	207.2	61	545	30	6-28	1	18.16
S. D. Myles (*Berkshire*)	153.5	33	501	27	6-43	1	18.55
M. R. White (*Bedfordshire*)	111.5	23	298	16	3-24	0	18.62
N. Sajjad (*Staffordshire*)	99.3	23	302	16	5-50	1	18.87
S. Oakes (*Lincolnshire*)	135	21	435	23	5-41	1	18.91
T. S. Smith (*Cambridgeshire*)	86.5	15	284	15	5-61	2	18.93
P. J. O'Reilly (*Hertfordshire*)	122	30	393	20	5-60	1	19.65
P. J. Caley (*Suffolk*)	104.4	11	361	18	6-29	2	20.05
D. F. Ralfs (*Cambridgeshire*)	158.3	26	530	26	5-44	1	20.38
D. M. Owen (*Buckinghamshire*)	104.1	20	319	15	4-21	0	21.26
M. J. Bailey (*Herefordshire*)	165	50	455	21	5-56	1	21.66
D. R. Thomas (*Norfolk*)	119	27	330	15	5-27	1	22.00
M. A. Sharp (*Cumberland*)	244.2	67	684	31	4-30	0	22.06
A. Richardson (*Staffordshire*)	279.4	67	903	39	6-60	2	23.15
G. P. Swann (*Bedfordshire*)	69.5	13	256	11	4-33	0	23.27
S. C. Goldsmith (*Norfolk*)	162.1	28	490	21	3-25	0	23.33
M. J. Parkinson (*Cumberland*)	64.3	8	263	11	5-87	1	23.90
M. G. Scothern (*Cumberland*)	152.5	32	551	23	4-43	0	23.95
D. S. Small (*Wiltshire*)	108	28	312	13	3-53	0	24.00
M. W. Thomas (*Norfolk*)	94.5	28	264	11	5-6	1	24.00
D. Surridge (*Hertfordshire*)	128	30	337	14	4-58	0	24.07
K. A. Arnold (*Oxfordshire*)	205	40	701	29	6-101	1	24.17
K. G. Shaw (*Suffolk*)	118.3	22	351	14	3-29	0	25.07
K. J. Willcock (*Cornwall*)	115.1	13	434	17	8-83	2	25.52
G. P. Savin (*Oxfordshire*)	84	23	281	11	3-32	0	25.54
C. E. Sketchley (*Hertfordshire*)	75	19	283	11	3-21	0	25.72
A. W. Thomas (*Buckinghamshire*)	259.2	39	903	35	4-37	0	25.80
A. R. Clarke (*Buckinghamshire*)	300.1	73	908	35	5-15	2	25.94
T. J. A. Scriven (*Buckinghamshire*) ...	138.5	36	473	18	5-49	2	26.27
J. M. Fielding (*Cumberland*)	164.1	25	632	24	5-22	1	26.33
Asif Din (*Shropshire*)	170.4	40	559	21	4-8	0	26.61
A. Barr (*Wales*)	102	16	321	12	3-60	0	26.75
G. L. Machin (*Cambridgeshire*)	69	9	295	11	3-44	0	26.81
B. T. P. Donelan (*Cambridgeshire*)....	275	36	966	36	4-87	0	26.83
M. P. Briers (*Cornwall*)	132.5	21	511	19	6-131	2	26.89
I. R. Payne (*Shropshire*)	119	37	302	11	5-53	1	27.45
A. K. Golding (*Suffolk*)	348.4	64	1,088	39	6-75	1	27.89
A. D. Greasley (*Cheshire*)	195.1	63	563	20	5-77	1	28.15
D. J. Brock (*Staffordshire*)	151.5	29	511	18	5-54	1	28.38
E. P. M. Holland (*Herefordshire*)	106.3	22	313	11	3-52	0	28.45
P. Beech (*Cumberland*)	90	16	342	12	2-17	0	28.50
A. J. Murphy (*Cheshire*)	196.2	43	658	23	4-20	0	28.60
A. D. Towse (*Lincolnshire*)	106.5	25	348	12	4-76	0	29.00
C. A. Miller (*Suffolk*)	72.3	7	355	12	4-77	0	29.58
P. G. Newman (*Norfolk*)	292.3	74	859	29	5-69	1	29.62
J. H. Shackleton (*Dorset*)	221.1	59	653	22	4-40	0	29.68
A. B. Byram (*Shropshire*)	195	42	720	24	6-70	2	30.00

Eastern Division

At Sleaford, May 26, 27. Drawn. Bedfordshire 201 for five dec. and 269 for four dec. (W. Larkins 124); Lincolnshire 213 for seven dec. and 243 for six. *Lincolnshire 5 pts, Bedfordshire 6 pts.*

At Jesmond, May 26, 27. Drawn. Hertfordshire 220 for seven dec. and 76 for one; Northumberland 225 for two dec. (T. W. Adcock 133*). *Northumberland 7 pts, Hertfordshire 3 pts.*

At Beaconsfield, May 28, 29. Buckinghamshire won by six wickets. Suffolk 94 and 293 for nine dec.; Buckinghamshire 173 (I. D. Graham five for 51) and 218 for four. *Buckinghamshire 21 pts, Suffolk 4 pts.*

At Carlisle, May 28, 29. Drawn. Cumberland 228 for six dec. and forfeited second innings; Hertfordshire forfeited first innings and 200 for eight. *Cumberland 1 pt, Hertfordshire 2 pts.*

At Bishop's Stortford, June 2, 3. Drawn. Suffolk 206 for eight dec. and 273 for two dec.; Hertfordshire 206 for eight dec. and 181 for six. *Hertfordshire 6 pts, Suffolk 6 pts.*

At Bourne, June 2, 3. Drawn. Staffordshire 213 for seven dec. and 309 for one dec. (S. J. Dean 173*, J. A. Waterhouse 121*); Lincolnshire 231 for six dec. and 126 for three. *Lincolnshire 7 pts, Staffordshire 3 pts.*

At Jesmond, June 2, 3. Drawn. Buckinghamshire 307 for seven dec. (M. J. Roberts 177*) and 172 for one (M. J. Roberts 101*); Northumberland 286 for two dec. (T. W. Adcock 150*). *Northumberland 7 pts, Buckinghamshire 4 pts.*

At Barrow, June 4, 5. Cumberland won by five wickets. Buckinghamshire 178 for six dec. and 125; Cumberland 177 (A. R. Clarke five for 40) and 128 for five. *Cumberland 20 pts, Buckinghamshire 6 pts.*

At Millom, June 10, 11. Drawn. Cumberland 203 for nine dec. and 238 for one dec. (S. T. Knox 113); Norfolk 202 for five dec. and 108 for seven. *Cumberland 2 pts, Norfolk 7 pts.*

At Wisbech, June 12, 13. Drawn. Suffolk 169 for nine dec. (D. F. Ralfs five for 44) and 252 for five dec. (D. W. Randall 121); Cambridgeshire 197 for five dec. and 141 for seven. *Cambridgeshire 6 pts, Suffolk 3 pts.*

At Cannock, June 12, 13. Drawn. Norfolk 195 for nine dec. (A. Richardson six for 60) and 187 for eight dec.; Staffordshire 160 for five dec. and 118 for four. *Staffordshire 4 pts, Norfolk 2 pts.*

At Shenley Park, June 16, 17. Buckinghamshire won by 165 runs. Buckinghamshire 206 (P. J. O'Reilly five for 60) and 284 for one dec. (M. J. Roberts 119*, N. D. Burns 100*); Hertfordshire 159 (A. R. Clarke five for 15) and 166. *Buckinghamshire 23 pts, Hertfordshire 5 pts.*

At Grimsby, June 16, 17. Drawn. Northumberland 212 for eight dec. and 269 for nine dec.; Lincolnshire 225 for six dec. and 242 for nine. *Lincolnshire 7 pts, Northumberland 5 pts.*

At Ransome's, Ipswich, June 16, 17. Drawn. Suffolk 227 for four dec. and 336 for nine dec.; Bedfordshire 225 for one dec. (W. Larkins 101*) and 233 for nine (A. K. Golding six for 75). *Suffolk 4 pts, Bedfordshire 5 pts.*

At Saffron Walden, June 18, 19. Cambridgeshire won by six wickets. Northumberland 246 for seven dec. (O. S. Youll 101*) and 277 for six dec.; Cambridgeshire 233 for three dec. (G. W. Ecclestone 126*) and 294 for four. *Cambridgeshire 23 pts, Northumberland 3 pts.*

At Bedford, June 23, 24. Hertfordshire won by 116 runs. Hertfordshire 207 for eight dec. and 231; Bedfordshire 200 for five dec. (R. N. Dalton 101*) and 122. *Hertfordshire 20 pts, Bedfordshire 6 pts.*

At Fenner's, Cambridge, July 3, 4. Staffordshire won by three wickets. Cambridgeshire 196 for eight dec. (L. Potter five for 40) and 194 for eight dec.; Staffordshire 180 for six dec. and 213 for seven. *Staffordshire 21 pts, Cambridgeshire 4 pts.*

At Henlow, July 7, 8. Bedfordshire won by four wickets. Northumberland 217 and 271; Bedfordshire 253 for two dec. (W. Larkins 118*) and 238 for six. *Bedfordshire 24 pts, Northumberland 3 pts.*

At Lincoln, July 7, 8. Cambridgeshire won by 94 runs. Cambridgeshire 177 for nine dec. (S. A. Bradford five for 47) and 243 for three dec. (G. W. Ecclestone 113*); Lincolnshire 169 (T. S. Smith five for 61) and 157. *Cambridgeshire 21 pts, Lincolnshire 5 pts.*

At Old Hill, July 9, 10. Buckinghamshire won by five wickets. Staffordshire 149 and 197 (T. J. A. Scriven five for 52); Buckinghamshire 165 and 182 for five (L. Potter five for 73). *Buckinghamshire 21 pts, Staffordshire 4 pts.*

At Southill Park, July 14, 15. Norfolk won by five wickets. Bedfordshire 200 for six dec. and 301 for three dec. (C. K. Bullen 128*); Norfolk 227 for six dec. (T. J. Boon 101*) and 275 for five (C. J. Rogers 104). *Norfolk 21 pts, Bedfordshire 5 pts.*

At Grantham, July 15, 16. Lincolnshire won by 21 runs. Lincolnshire 204 for nine dec. and 239 (M. J. Parkinson five for 87); Cumberland 209 for six dec. and 213 (S. Oakes five for 41) *Lincolnshire 20 pts, Cumberland 7 pts.*

At High Wycombe, July 16, 17. Norfolk won by nine wickets. Buckinghamshire 243 for six dec. and 146 (D. R. Thomas five for 27); Norfolk 243 for one dec. (T. J. Boon 100*) and 147 for one. *Norfolk 22 pts, Buckinghamshire 3 pts.*

At Fenner's, Cambridge, July 17, 18. Cumberland won by 114 runs. Cumberland 280 for eight dec. (T. S. Smith five for 92) and 208 for seven dec.; Cambridgeshire 235 and 139 (J. M. Fielding five for 22). *Cumberland 23 pts, Cambridgeshire 5 pts.*

At Jesmond, July 22, 23. Drawn. Staffordshire 232 for five dec. and 264 for eight dec.; Northumberland 222 for seven dec. and 219 for seven. *Northumberland 5 pts, Staffordshire 5 pts.*

At Kimbolton, July 24, 25. Drawn. Cambridgeshire 136 (T. J. A. Scriven five for 49) and 342 for four dec. (S. A. Kellett 126*); Buckinghamshire 198 for five dec. (R. B. Hurd 105*) and 239 for seven. *Cambridgeshire 2 pts, Buckinghamshire 6 pts.*

At Askam, July 24, 25. Drawn. Cumberland 240 and 197 (N. Sajjad five for 50); Staffordshire 222 for six dec. and 119 for five. *Cumberland 4 pts, Staffordshire 6 pts.*

At Slough, July 28, 29. Bedfordshire won by five wickets. Buckinghamshire 229 and 187 for five dec.; Bedfordshire 144 and 274 for five (W. Larkins 155*). *Bedfordshire 20 pts, Buckinghamshire 6 pts.*

At Lakenham, July 28, 29. Drawn. Lincolnshire 192 for six dec. and 91 for three; Norfolk 203 for five dec. *Norfolk 5 pts, Lincolnshire 4 pts.*

At Ipswich School, July 28, 29. Suffolk won by 36 runs. Suffolk 233 for four dec. and 220 for two dec.; Northumberland 188 and 229 (P. J. Caley five for 78). *Suffolk 24 pts, Northumberland 2 pts.*

At Longton, July 29, 30. Staffordshire won by seven wickets. Hertfordshire 147 (A. Richardson five for 87) and 167; Staffordshire 210 for seven dec. and 105 for three. *Staffordshire 22 pts, Hertfordshire 3 pts.*

At Lakenham, July 30, 31. Norfolk won by ten wickets. Norfolk 225 for two dec. (T. J. Boon 116*) and eight for no wkt; Northumberland 100 (M. W. Thomas five for six) and 130. *Norfolk 24 pts.*

At Lakenham, August 1, 2. Drawn. Norfolk 176 and 266 for seven dec.; Cambridgeshire 179 for three dec. and 112 for eight. *Norfolk 2 pts, Cambridgeshire 6 pts.*

At Lakenham, August 5, 6. Norfolk won by one wicket. Hertfordshire 261 for four dec. (A. D. Griffin 146*) and 174 for eight dec.; Norfolk 192 (A. R. Garofall five for 91) and 244 for nine (T. J. Boon 115). *Norfolk 19 pts, Hertfordshire 6 pts.*

At Bury St Edmund's, August 5, 6. Drawn. Lincolnshire 238 for five dec. and 209 for six dec.; Suffolk 197 (S. A. Bradford five for 60) and 213 for eight. *Suffolk 2 pts, Lincolnshire 8 pts.*

At Luton, August 6, 7. Cambridgeshire won by 145 runs. Cambridgeshire 227 (Z. A. Sher five for 52) and 261 for two dec.; Bedfordshire 209 (W. Larkins 109) and 134. *Cambridgeshire 23 pts, Bedfordshire 6 pts.*

At Dunstable, August 11, 12. Drawn. Bedfordshire 237 for two dec. (W. Larkins 101*) and 148 for five dec.; Cumberland 139 for nine dec. and 89 for two. *Bedfordshire 8 pts.*

At Balls Park, Hertford, August 11, 12. Drawn (no result). Hertfordshire 243 for four dec. (I. Fletcher 131); Lincolnshire 43 for two. *Hertfordshire 5 pts, Lincolnshire 5 pts.*

At Netherfield, August 13, 14. Drawn. Cumberland 200 for seven dec. and 206 for eight dec.; Suffolk 165 and 240 for nine. *Cumberland 7 pts, Suffolk 4 pts.*

At Stone, August 15, 16. Drawn. Staffordshire 249 for four dec. and 284 for eight dec. (M. I. Humphries 102*); Suffolk 226 for four dec. and 82 for three. *Staffordshire 5 pts, Suffolk 5 pts.*

At Marlow, August 20, 21. Lincolnshire won by six wickets. Buckinghamshire 227 for six dec. and 190; Lincolnshire 233 for eight dec. and 188 for four. *Lincolnshire 22 pts, Buckinghamshire 6 pts.*

At Long Marston, August 20, 21. Drawn with the scores level. Cambridgeshire 207 for eight dec. and 232 for five dec.; Hertfordshire 178 (Ajaz Akhtar five for 50) and 261 for nine. *Hertfordshire 12 pts, Cambridgeshire 7 pts.*

At Jesmond, August 20, 21. Cumberland won by 45 runs. Cumberland 225 for five dec. and 295 for seven dec.; Northumberland 229 for five dec. and 246. *Cumberland 22 pts, Northumberland 6 pts.*

At Brewood, August 20, 21. Staffordshire won by eight wickets. Bedfordshire 166 (D. J. Brock five for 54) and 110; Staffordshire 141 (R. N. Dalton five for 39) and 136 for two. *Staffordshire 20 pts, Bedfordshire 4 pts.*

At Mildenhall, August 20, 21. Suffolk won by ten runs. Suffolk 220 for six dec. and 246 for three dec.; Norfolk 215 for nine dec. and 241 (P. J. Caley six for 29). *Suffolk 23 pts, Norfolk 5 pts.*

Western Division

At Budleigh Salterton, May 26, 27. Devon won by six wickets in a match reduced by the weather to one innings per side. Dorset 295 for eight dec.; Devon 299 for four (N. A. Folland 108). *Devon 16 pts.*

At Bridgnorth, May 26, 27. Drawn. Herefordshire 241 for six dec. and 130 for seven dec.; Shropshire 19 for two dec. and 279 for seven. *Shropshire 2 pts, Herefordshire 4 pts.*

At Colwall, June 2, 3. Drawn. Herefordshire 218 for five dec. and 221 for three dec.; Dorset 201 for seven dec. and 66 for five. *Herefordshire 6 pts, Dorset 5 pts.*

At Shrewsbury, June 2, 3. Drawn. Oxfordshire 202 for six dec. and 11 for no wkt; Shropshire 209 for three dec. *Shropshire 5 pts, Oxfordshire 3 pts.*

At Neston, June 4, 5. Oxfordshire won by six wickets. Cheshire 194 for five dec. and 163; Oxfordshire 228 for five dec. and 133 for four. *Oxfordshire 22 pts, Cheshire 2 pts.*

At Falkland, June 16, 17. Herefordshire won by eight wickets. Berkshire 155 and 149 (M. J. Bailey five for 56); Herefordshire 211 and 96 for two. *Herefordshire 22 pts, Berkshire 4 pts.*

At Challow & Childrey, June 16, 17. Drawn with the scores level. Wales 201 for eight dec. and 214 for four dec. (J. P. J. Sylvester 109*); Oxfordshire 196 for nine dec. (A. D. Griffiths six for 52) and 219 for five. *Oxfordshire 12 pts, Wales 5 pts.*

At Wellington, June 16, 17. Drawn. Shropshire 290 for six dec. (K. Sharp 156*) and 40 for two; Wiltshire 113 and 325 (D. J. M. Mercer 147; I. R. Payne five for 53). *Shropshire 8 pts, Wiltshire 2 pts.*

At Falmouth, June 17, 18. Drawn. Cheshire 225 for nine dec. (K. J. Willcock five for 73) and 308 for eight dec.; Cornwall 281 (A. D. Greasley five for 77) and 214 for eight. *Cornwall 8 pts, Cheshire 8 pts.*

At Torquay, June 19, 20. Drawn. Devon 297 for two dec. (H. J. Morgan 144) and 263 for four dec.; Cheshire 279 for six dec. and 30 for no wkt. *Devon 6 pts, Cheshire 4 pts.*

At Hurst, June 23, 24. Berkshire won by 26 runs. Berkshire 261 for four dec. and 164 for eight dec.; Wales 121 and 278. *Berkshire 24 pts, Wales 1 pt.*

At Reading, July 7, 8. Cornwall won by six wickets. Berkshire 203 for six dec. and 220 (K. J. Willcock eight for 83); Cornwall 238 for five dec. (S. M. Williams 103*) and 186 for four *Cornwall 22 pts, Berkshire 3 pts.*

At Hereford, July 7, 8. Herefordshire won by three wickets. Devon 162 and 212 for five dec.; Herefordshire 156 for five dec. and 220 for seven. *Herefordshire 21 pts, Devon 3 pts.*

At Pontypridd, July 7, 8. Shropshire won by ten wickets. Wales 141 and 176; Shropshire 239 for four dec. (Asif Din 127*) and 82 for no wkt. *Shropshire 24 pts, Wales 1 pt.*

At South Wiltshire, July 7, 8. Drawn. Oxfordshire 223 for five dec. and 219 for eight dec.; Wiltshire 201 for two dec. and 238 for five (J. L. Taylor 109). *Wiltshire 5 pts.*

At Thame, July 9, 10. Drawn. Oxfordshire 225 for six dec. (K. R. Mustow 115*) and 271 for seven dec.; Cornwall 223 for six dec. and 175 for seven. *Oxfordshire 6 pts, Cornwall 5 pts.*

At Bowdon, July 14, 15. Cheshire won by eight wickets. Berkshire 229 for three dec. and 96; Cheshire 228 for seven dec. and 99 for two. *Cheshire 21 pts, Berkshire 6 pts.*

At Truro, July 14, 15. Drawn. Dorset 277 for eight dec. and 201 for five dec.; Cornwall 173 (A. D. Mascarenhas seven for 64) and 191 for five. *Cornwall 4 pts, Dorset 7 pts.*

At Brockhampton, July 14, 15. Herefordshire won by one wicket. Wiltshire 223 for five dec. and 270; Herefordshire 264 for five dec. and 230 for nine (R. Turnell seven for 111). *Herefordshire 22 pts, Wiltshire 5 pts.*

At Oswestry, July 16, 17. Berkshire won by eight wickets. Shropshire 306 for five dec. (Asif Din 129) and 196 (S. D. Myles six for 43); Berkshire 249 and 254 for two (G. E. Loveday 113*, N. W. Pitcher 100). *Berkshire 21 pts, Shropshire 8 pts.*

At Colwyn Bay, July 22, 23. Devon won by nine wickets. Wales 206 for five dec. and 242; Devon 225 for three dec. and 224 for one. *Devon 22 pts, Wales 4 pts.*

At Weymouth, July 28, 29. Drawn. Dorset 204 for nine dec. and 282 for five dec. (G. D. Reynolds 121); Shropshire 224 for six dec. and 189 for seven. *Dorset 3 pts, Shropshire 7 pts.*

At Thame, July 28, 29. Oxfordshire won by 31 runs. Oxfordshire 219 for four dec. and 234 for four dec.; Devon 201 for one dec. (N. A. Folland 116*) and 221 (K. A. Arnold six for 101). *Oxfordshire 18 pts, Devon 4 pts.*

At Pontarddulais, July 28, 29. Cornwall won by 59 runs. Cornwall 227 for seven dec. and 223 for seven dec.; Wales 227 for seven dec. and 164 (M. P. Briers five for 36). *Cornwall 23 pts, Wales 7 pts.*

At Westbury, July 28, 29. Cheshire won by 62 runs. Cheshire 229 for five dec. and 165 for two dec.; Wiltshire 93 for four dec. and 239. *Cheshire 21 pts, Wiltshire 2 pts.*

At Reading, July 30, 31. Devon won by 136 runs. Devon 253 for eight dec. and 167 for two dec.; Berkshire 179 (P. M. Roebuck six for 33) and 105 (P. M. Roebuck five for 27). *Devon 22 pts, Berkshire 3 pts.*

At Dorchester, July 30, 31. Drawn. Dorset 121 (N. D. Peel five for 42) and 167 for seven; Cheshire 314. *Dorset 4 pts, Cheshire 5 pts.*

At Dale's, Leominster, July 30, 31. Herefordshire won by an innings and 121 runs. Cornwall 167 for nine dec. (K. E. Cooper five for 51) and 92 (K. E. Cooper five for 25); Herefordshire 380 for four dec. (R. G. R. Barlow 103). *Herefordshire 24 pts, Cornwall 1 pt.*

At Boughton Hall, Chester, August 4, 5. Drawn. Wales 331 for six dec. and 263 for no wkt dec. (J. P. J. Sylvester 143*, A. J. Jones 105*); Cheshire 230 for four dec. (J. D. Bean 102) and 299 for eight (M. Davies six for 101). *Cheshire 6 pts, Wales 5 pts.*

At Camborne, August 4, 5. Drawn. Cornwall 275 for four dec. and 258 for no wkt dec. (S. M. Williams 106*, G. M. Thomas 118*); Wiltshire 230 for five dec. (K. J. Parsons 111) and 171 for seven. *Cornwall 6 pts, Wiltshire 5 pts.*

At Exmouth, August 4, 5. Shropshire won by 54 runs. Shropshire 317 for three dec. (Asif Din 175) and 230 for seven dec.; Devon 266 for seven dec. and 227 (A. B. Byram five for 82). *Shropshire 23 pts, Devon 5 pts.*

At Dean Park, Bournemouth, August 4, 5. Drawn. Dorset 312 for seven dec. and 242 for eight dec.; Oxfordshire 229 for two dec. (K. R. Mustow 128) and 272 for seven (D. A. J. Wise 105*). *Dorset 1 pt, Oxfordshire 7 pts.*

At St Austell, August 6, 7. Drawn (no result). Cornwall 324 for one dec. (G. M. Thomas 148*); Shropshire 111 for five. *Cornwall 5 pts, Shropshire 5 pts.*

At Bovey Tracey, August 6, 7. Devon won by 127 runs. Devon 270 for four dec. (N. A. Folland 127) and 260 for four dec.; Wiltshire 239 for five dec. and 164 (P. M. Roebuck six for 44). *Devon 22 pts, Wiltshire 5 pts.*

At Rover, Cowley, August 11, 12. Drawn. Oxfordshire 76 (N. V. Radford six for 28) and 90 for six; Herefordshire 135 for eight dec. *Oxfordshire 3 pts, Herefordshire 4 pts.*

At St Fagan's, August 11, 12. Dorset won by 38 runs. Dorset 192 for nine dec. and 90 for four dec.; Wales forfeited first innings and 244 (R. A. Pyman six for 65). *Dorset 17 pts, Wales 4 pts.*

At Marlborough, August 11, 12. Drawn (no result). Wiltshire 251 for three dec. (D. A. Winter 104*); Berkshire 126 for three. *Wiltshire 5 pts, Berkshire 5 pts.*

At New Brighton, August 18, 19. Herefordshire won by seven wickets. Cheshire 224 for six dec. and 224 for four dec. (P. R. J. Bryson 127*); Herefordshire 118 (N. D. Peel seven for 67) and 332 for three. *Herefordshire 18 pts, Cheshire 7 pts.*

At Dean Park, Bournemouth, August 18, 19. Berkshire won by five wickets. Dorset 234 for five dec. (J. J. E. Hardy 107) and 241 for nine dec.; Berkshire 248 for six dec. (S. D. Myles 112*) and 228 for five. *Berkshire 22 pts, Dorset 6 pts.*

At Trowbridge, August 18, 19. Drawn. Wales 185 for six dec. and 238 (R. Turnell six for 78); Wiltshire 227 for four dec. and 163 for eight. *Wiltshire 6 pts, Wales 3 pts.*

At Kidmore End, August 20, 21. Drawn. Oxfordshire 108 (T. Bloomfield five for 39) and 265 for eight dec.; Berkshire 178 (I. J. Curtis five for 66) and 121 for five. *Berkshire 4 pts, Oxfordshire 4 pts.*

At Toft, August 20, 21. Shropshire won by 86 runs. Shropshire 249 for six dec. and 231 for five dec. (K. Sharp 117); Cheshire 204 for three dec. and 190 (A. B. Byram six for 70). *Shropshire 21 pts, Cheshire 5 pts.*

At Truro, August 20, 21. Devon won by 64 runs. Devon 365 for nine dec. (M. P. Briers six for 131) and 244 for two dec.; Cornwall 272 for nine dec. and 273 (P. M. Roebuck five for 63). *Devon 24 pts, Cornwall 8 pts.*

At Kington, August 20, 21. Wales won by three wickets. Herefordshire 210 for six dec. and 281 for five dec.; Wales 184 for two dec. and 308 for seven. *Wales 20 pts, Herefordshire 3 pts.*

At Trowbridge, August 20, 21. Dorset won by five wickets. Wiltshire 202 for four dec. and 162 (S. R. Walbridge five for 53); Dorset 203 for five dec. and 162 for five. *Dorset 20 pts, Wiltshire 5 pts.*

FINAL

DEVON v NORFOLK

At Exmouth, September 8, 9. Devon won by 168 runs. Toss: Norfolk.

Nick Gaywood's penchant for high-profile centuries put Devon in the driving seat. A near-chanceless 134 (153 balls, two sixes, 13 fours) enabled Devon to lay the foundations for a first-innings lead of 94 in the compulsory 50 overs. Norfolk then collapsed to 77 for five as Roebuck exploited a turning wicket, and it needed the efforts of Newman and Fox to restore respectability. On day two, Devon extended their advantage to 345 as Folland stretched his own seasonal tally to 1,055, despite Newman bowling his heart out. Norfolk were left a mountainous task and, although Boon showed admirable adhesive qualities, they never recovered from 15 for three. It was left to spinners Roebuck and Horrell to perform the last rites.

Devon

N. R. Gaywood c Newman b Powell	134	– st Crowley b Powell	40
H. J. Morgan c and b D. R. Thomas	19	– lbw b Newman	49
N. A. Folland c M. W. Thomas b D. R. Thomas	17	– c Boon b Newman	49
G. T. J. Townsend st Crowley b Powell	38	– b Newman	0
*P. M. Roebuck c Fox b Powell	30	– not out	43
A. J. Pugh not out	2	– b Newman	44
†C. M. W. Read not out	4	– c Rogers b Newman	6
K. Donohue (did not bat)		– not out	5
B 4, l-b 4, w 3, n-b 4	15	B 5, l-b 8, n-b 2	15
1/64 2/112 3/184 4/253 5/254 (5 wkts, 50 overs)	259	1/61 2/133 3/135 4/164 5/217 6/223 (6 wkts dec.)	251

M. C. Theedom, I. A. Bond and R. Horrell did not bat.

Bowling: *First Innings*—Newman 13–0–73–0; D. R. Thomas 15–0–62–2; Fox 9–0–43–0; Powell 11–1–56–3; Boon 2–0–17–0. *Second Innings*—Goldsmith 3–0–10–0; Newman 23–2–69–5; Bradshaw 2–0–12–0; Powell 20–3–83–1; Fox 3–1–7–0; M. W. Thomas 5–0–21–0; D. R. Thomas 10–1–36–0.

Norfolk

T. J. Boon c Read b Roebuck	18	– c Horrell b Roebuck	55
C. J. Rogers b Roebuck	25	– c Read b Theedom	0
S. C. Goldsmith lbw b Roebuck	8	– c Pugh b Donohue	2
C. Amos run out	14	– c Donohue b Theedom	0
M. G. Powell c Pugh b Horrell	4	– (6) c Morgan b Roebuck	20
D. R. Thomas run out	2	– (5) run out	33
*P. G. Newman not out	41	– c Townsend b Horrell	5
N. Fox b Bond	29	– st Folland b Horrell	6
M. W. Thomas not out	1	– b Roebuck	29
P. J. Bradshaw (did not bat)		– c Theedom b Horrell	1
†S. C. Crowley (did not bat)		– not out	5
B 14, l-b 8, w 1	23	B 14, l-b 6, w 1	21
1/35 2/49 3/65 4/75 5/77 6/101 7/162 (7 wkts, 50 overs)	165	1/8 2/12 3/15 4/96 5/103 6/117 7/139 8/149 9/151	177

Bowling: *First Innings*—Donohue 4–0–27–0; Bond 5–0–27–1; Roebuck 23–6–49–3; Horrell 17–4–37–1; Pugh 1–0–3–0. *Second Innings*—Donohue 6–1–23–1; Theedom 10–3–26–2; Pugh 5–0–14–0; Roebuck 19.3–4–38–3; Horrell 17–5–45–3; Morgan 1–0–11–0.

Umpires: P. Adams and M. K. Reed.

THE MINOR COUNTIES CHAMPIONS

1895	Norfolk	1927	Staffordshire	1965	Somerset II
	Durham	1928	Berkshire	1966	Lincolnshire
	Worcestershire	1929	Oxfordshire	1967	Cheshire
1896	Worcestershire	1930	Durham	1968	Yorkshire II
1897	Worcestershire	1931	Leicestershire II	1969	Buckinghamshire
1898	Worcestershire	1932	Buckinghamshire	1970	Bedfordshire
1899	Northamptonshire	1933	Undecided	1971	Yorkshire II
	Buckinghamshire	1934	Lancashire II	1972	Bedfordshire
1900	Glamorgan	1935	Middlesex II	1973	Shropshire
	Durham	1936	Hertfordshire	1974	Oxfordshire
	Northamptonshire	1937	Lancashire II	1975	Hertfordshire
1901	Durham	1938	Buckinghamshire	1976	Durham
1902	Wiltshire	1939	Surrey II	1977	Suffolk
1903	Northamptonshire	1946	Suffolk	1978	Devon
1904	Northamptonshire	1947	Yorkshire II	1979	Suffolk
1905	Norfolk	1948	Lancashire II	1980	Durham
1906	Staffordshire	1949	Lancashire II	1981	Durham
1907	Lancashire II	1950	Surrey II	1982	Oxfordshire
1908	Staffordshire	1951	Kent II	1983	Hertfordshire
1909	Wiltshire	1952	Buckinghamshire	1984	Durham
1910	Norfolk	1953	Berkshire	1985	Cheshire
1911	Staffordshire	1954	Surrey II	1986	Cumberland
1912	In abeyance	1955	Surrey II	1987	Buckinghamshire
1913	Norfolk	1956	Kent II	1988	Cheshire
1914	Staffordshire†	1957	Yorkshire II	1989	Oxfordshire
1920	Staffordshire	1958	Yorkshire II	1990	Hertfordshire
1921	Staffordshire	1959	Warwickshire II	1991	Staffordshire
1922	Buckinghamshire	1960	Lancashire II	1992	Staffordshire
1923	Buckinghamshire	1961	Somerset II	1993	Staffordshire
1924	Berkshire	1962	Warwickshire II	1994	Devon
1925	Buckinghamshire	1963	Cambridgeshire	1995	Devon
1926	Durham	1964	Lancashire II	1996	Devon

† *Disputed. Some sources claim the Championship was never decided.*

MCC TROPHY FINAL

BEDFORDSHIRE v CHESHIRE

At Lord's, August 28. Cheshire won by six wickets. Toss: Cheshire.

Cheshire became the first county to win the Minor Counties knockout title for a third time. The previous occasions had been in 1983 (when they won the inaugural final) and 1987, in both cases before the competition was allocated a Lord's final. Paul Bryson was their star turn, overshadowing Bedfordshire century-maker Dalton with a match-winning display. Bryson, an occasional slow-medium bowler, took over the final five balls of the 16th over when Bostock split the webbing of a hand taking a return catch from Larkins. He made a diving caught-and-bowled to dismiss Stanley with his second ball, later ran out Dalton for 103 (117 balls, four sixes, nine fours) with a direct hit from mid-wicket and made a vital 74 as Bedfordshire had cause to regret a couple of costly missed catches.

Bedfordshire

W. Larkins c and b Bostock	15	R. C. Williams not out	10
R. N. Dalton run out	103	Z. A. Sher not out	6
N. A. Stanley c and b Bryson	0	L-b 14, w 18, n-b 4	36
D. R. Clarke b Peel	55		——
C. K. Bullen lbw b Greasley	7	1/70 2/71 3/170 (7 wkts, 55 overs)	253
A. J. Trott c Bean b Greasley	17	4/197 5/218	
*P. D. B. Hoare lbw b Lamb	4	6/223 7/237	

†G. D. Sandford and M. R. White did not bat.

Bowling: Peel 11–0–48–1; Lamb 11–1–41–1; Greasley 11–0–44–2; Bostock 9.1–0–59–1; Bryson 0.5–0–3–1; Cross 11–0–26–0; Hignett 1–0–18–0.

Cheshire

P. R. J. Bryson b White	74	N. D. Cross not out	18
J. D. Bean c Larkins b Sher	43	B 1, l-b 7, w 20, n-b 10	38
M. Saxelby b Williams	44		——
*I. Cockbain not out	27	1/70 2/185 (4 wkts, 54 overs)	254
R. G. Hignett c Sandford b Williams	10	3/200 4/214	

T. J. Bostock, †S. Bramhall, C. Lamb, A. D. Greasley and N. D. Peel did not bat.

Bowling: Williams 11–1–56–2; White 11–0–53–1; Bullen 9–2–30–0; Sher 11–0–44–1; Dalton 10–0–51–0; Trott 2–0–12–0.

Umpires: D. L. Burden and C. Stone.

WINNERS 1983-96

1983	Cheshire	1988	Dorset	1993	Staffordshire
1984	Hertfordshire	1989	Cumberland	1994	Devon
1985	Durham	1990	Buckinghamshire	1995	Cambridgeshire
1986	Norfolk	1991	Staffordshire	1996	Cheshire
1987	Cheshire	1992	Devon		

I ZINGARI RESULTS, 1996

Matches 22: Won 11, Lost 9, Drawn 2. Abandoned 3.

April 23	Eton College	Abandoned
May 12	Hampshire Hogs	Won by six wickets
May 18	Eton Ramblers	Abandoned
May 19	Staff College	Won by 170 runs
May 30	Harrow School	Lost by nine wickets
June 1	Royal Armoured Corps	Won by 67 runs
June 9	Earl of Carnarvon's XI	Won by four wickets
June 9	Bradfield Waifs	Lost by seven wickets
June 15	Charterhouse School	Lost by seven wickets
June 16	Sandhurst Wanderers	Lost by five wickets
June 22	Guards CC	Won by 152 runs
June 30	J. Paul Getty's XI	Won by five wickets
July 2	Winchester College	Lost by eight wickets
July 7	Hagley CC	Won by two wickets
July 13	Green Jackets Club	Won by six wickets
July 14	Rickling Green CC	Lost by two wickets
July 21	Earl of Arundel's XI	Drawn
July 21	Sir John Starkey's XI	Won by three wickets
July 27	Hurlingham CC	Won by two wickets
August 4	Band of Brothers	Lost by seven wickets
August 10	South Wales Hunts XI	Drawn
August 11	South Wales Hunts XI	Abandoned
August 18	Royal Navy CC	Lost by eight wickets
September 1	Willow Warblers	Won by six runs
September 8	J. H. Pawle's XI	Lost by four wickets

SECOND ELEVEN CHAMPIONSHIP, 1996

Warwickshire, who failed to win a major trophy for the first time in four years, gained both consolation and hope for the future by dominating the Second Eleven Championship. Ten wins in a season when the competition was blighted by draws was a fine achievement, and left them 50 points clear of the rest. For the second year running, Northamptonshire finished second and collected more bonus points than any other team, while Middlesex's third place owed a great deal to the excellence of Keith Dutch, the competition's leading all-rounder.

Dutch's season amounted to a sustained assault on the record books. In one match against Somerset he made the highest ever individual score for Middlesex, and fourth-highest in the competition, as well as sharing in the county's highest sixth-wicket stand. His 63 wickets were also the most in the competition this year, so it was no surprise when he became the first man to be awarded the Player of the Year title twice (he had previously won it in 1993).

Elsewhere, Bradley Parker of Yorkshire scored the most runs (1,481) and Neil Taylor concluded a highly distinguished career at Kent with six hundreds – the highest number since Jason Gallian's seven in 1992. Fourteen batsmen passed 1,000 runs, three more than the previous record of 11 in 1994. Parker's came at the best average (67.31), while two players scored 500 runs at a three-figure average, David Sales averaging 123.20 for Northamptonshire and Darren Robinson 100.20 for Essex. There were nine double-centuries, of which Dutch's 261 was the biggest.

In second place among the bowlers was Darren Altree, whose 62 wickets in only 316.3 overs were a major contribution to Warwickshire's success. The menace of Altree's left-arm pace was shown in the match against Hampshire, when he took eight for 58 including a hat-trick of lbws (Liam Botham, Dimitri Mascarenhas and Derek Kenway). As umpire Alan Bundy said: "They were all very straight balls."

Still more dangerous was the batting of Somerset's Keith Parsons, who made more of an impression on the umpire than he did on the scorebook in the match against Gloucestershire at Bristol. A powerful straight drive struck Judith West, one of the country's leading women umpires, as she stood at the bowler's end, fracturing her skull and rupturing her eardrum. She said later: "It was 6 p.m. after a hot day and I suppose my reactions were just a bit slow," but said that she would not be retiring from the circuit.

Yorkshire, meanwhile, showed the other counties the way when it came to blooding new talent. At 14 years old, wicket-keeper Matthew Thewlis (just 4 ft 8 in) became the youngest Second Eleven player ever. He served notice of his ability with five catches in his one match, when Durham were defeated by 119 runs.

Continued over

SECOND ELEVEN CHAMPIONSHIP, 1996

					Bonus points		
Win = 16 points	*M*	*W*	*L*	*D*	*Batting*	*Bowling*	*Points*
1 – Warwickshire (6)	17	10	4	3	47	56	263
2 – Northamptonshire (2)	17	6	2	9	58	59	213
3 – Middlesex (10)	17	7	2	8	46	43	201
4 – Yorkshire (5)	17	6	3	8	45	42	183
5 – Lancashire (13)	17	6	1	10	37	48	181
6 – Kent (4)	17	4	3	10	55	55	174
7 – Leicestershire (12)	17	5	5	7	40	53	173
8 – Durham (3)	17	4	5	8	53	48	165
9 – Derbyshire (16)	17	3	4	10	49	45	150
10 – Worcestershire (8)	17	3	4	10	42	55	145
11 – Nottinghamshire (11)	17	3	2	12	53	40	141
12 – Gloucestershire (14)	17	2	0	15	45	53	130
13 – Glamorgan (18)	17	2	5	10	47	48	127
14 – Somerset (15)	17	2	6	9	45	46	123
15 – Hampshire (1)	17	2	6	9	40	50	122
16 – Sussex (9)	17	2	3	12	41	48	121
17 – Surrey (7)	17	1	8	8	47	56	119
18 – Essex (17)	17	1	6	10	45	46	107

1995 positions are shown in brackets.

The total for Derbyshire includes 8 points for batting second in a match drawn with the scores level.

Derbyshire contributed the most exciting finish of the season when they played Middlesex in August. Chasing a target of 266 in 54 overs in the second innings, they were just 28 runs short with five overs to go, but wicket-keeper Steven Griffiths was run out off the last ball of the match, leaving the scores level. Ninth place represented an improvement: they had finished in the bottom three for the previous three years.

Durham saved their best cricket for the Bain Hogg Trophy, where they reached the final. Unfortunately, they came up against Leicestershire, now a crack limited-overs outfit after four consecutive finals, and lost by 46 runs. Meanwhile, left-arm spinner David Cox bowled well enough to gain a chance in the first team, where he enjoyed unexpected success with the bat, finishing 34th in the national averages at 48.22. Second-team coach Martin Robinson remained unconvinced: "Let's just say you wouldn't ask him to bat for your life."

Essex slipped from the previous year's 17th position to bottom of the heap. The seam bowlers were particularly ineffective, with only Duncan Ayres taking more than 15 wickets. The 17-year-old off-spinner Jonathan Powell took 30, if expensively, but it was Paul Grayson who made a dramatic impact in his only appearance, against Derbyshire. His first spell of left-arm spin lasted 17 overs and brought him figures of five for five, and he took four for 24 in the second innings, thus finishing the season with nine wickets at an average of 3.22. In his only innings he made a comparatively mundane 137.

Alun Evans brightened a dull year for **Glamorgan** with a county record tally of 1,070 runs in only 12 matches, but the best individual performance – and another Glamorgan record – came from off-spinner Chris Sketchley. On trial against Somerset in May, he made a clear statement with figures of nine for 90 in the second innings of a tight match. The season ended on an embarrassing note, however, after the county announced the release of Steve Barwick, Alistair Dalton and Neil Kendrick during the final match. All three failed to turn up for the third day's play, leaving Worcestershire to complete a devalued victory against eight men.

Gloucestershire distinguished themselves in two ways. They were the only county to complete an unbeaten season, but they also set an unenviable all-time record for number of draws with 15. By August, their captain Robert Dawson was so concerned about the situation that he declared at 63 for two in the first innings against Kent. Gloucestershire went on to win by three wickets.

A remodelled batting line-up was responsible for **Hampshire's** freefall from champions to 15th place in the table. Without Tony Middleton (who had retired), Jason Laney and Matthew Keech (both promoted to the first team), only six centuries were scored in the Championship, in contrast to the 15 last year. All-rounder Liam Botham struggled to live up to high expectations in his first full season.

In his last season at **Kent**, Neil Taylor led from the front with six centuries – including 211 against Hampshire at Canterbury, the ground on which he has scored a record 14 first-class hundreds. At the other end of the scale of experience was 17-year-old Londoner Robert Key, who made a maiden century against Essex. With another score of 96 against Lancashire and an average of 37, Key did enough to earn a cricket scholarship to South Africa in the winter.

Lancashire were delighted by the progress made by Paddy McKeown and Nathan Wood. McKeown was one of nine players in 1996 to appear in all his county's matches and scored 1,437 runs, smashing Nick Speak's seven-year-old record by 150. He and Wood put on 361 for the first wicket against Kent at Canterbury, eclipsing the Lancashire record of 266 set by John Abrahams and Nathan's father, Barry, in 1975. The bowling was equally strong, with 43 wickets contributed by Gary Keedy's left-arm spin. Regular first-teamer Ian Austin made a notable cameo appearance in May; his five for 15 helped bowl Leicestershire out for 51 in their second innings, giving Lancashire an unlikely victory by an innings and nine runs.

Leicestershire were once again unstoppable in the Bain Hogg Trophy, winning it for the third time in four years (in 1994 they were only runners-up). Highly rated left-hander Iain Sutcliffe scored 61 from 74 balls in the final against Durham. In an earlier round, Leicestershire had humiliated Middlesex, as Jon Dakin scored 193 out of a 55-over total of 385 for eight. Victory was completed by a margin of 162 runs.

Keith Dutch was the outstanding player in the **Middlesex** side, and in the whole Championship for that matter. Against Somerset at Uxbridge he scored 261 from 182 balls, with 38 fours and six sixes, and his partnership for the sixth wicket with England Under-19 wicket-keeper David Nash realised 249. Dutch also took ten wickets in the same match with his off-breaks, becoming only the ninth player in the history of the Championship to complete the match double. Against Leicestershire at Hinckley he claimed figures of eight for 36 and seven for 121; the match return (15 for 157) was the fifth-best in Second Eleven history. Less successful was Jason Pooley, who had toured with England A in the winter, but was dismissed for a pair in his only appearance against Gloucestershire. This came right on the heels of another duck for the first team in the Sunday League.

Northamptonshire had an embarrassment of riches as far as talented teenage batsmen go, with three members of England's Under-19 squad on their books. David Roberts and Alec Swann scored five hundreds each, and shared a county record stand of 330 for the first wicket against Somerset, while David Sales matched his first-class 210 not out with 211 against Derbyshire in the final game of the season, sharing a second-wicket stand of 309 with Richard Montgomerie, another record. With Andy Roberts, Jason Brown and John Hughes each taking 41 wickets, Northamptonshire were well clear of the field on both batting and bowling points, and maintained their position near the top of the table.

With **Nottinghamshire's** first team enduring a miserable summer, there was plenty of traffic between the squads. Graeme Archer made the best use of his opportunities, averaging 41 in the Championship for the firsts and 66 for the seconds, but Mathew Dowman, Chris Tolley and Richard Bates could not quite translate good second-team form into first-class success. Left-arm spinner James Hindson must have felt unlucky not to have been promoted; his 50 wickets included five-wicket hauls in two of Nottinghamshire's three victories, and he scored a century into the bargain.

Somerset had recorded two good wins by the end of May, but failed to score another. The reason for this was an exceptionally toothless bowling attack; among the regulars, only Andre van Troost averaged under 35. Somerset were on the wrong end of three double-hundreds during the season. Although Haydn Morgan made one himself in a first-innings total of 417 for one against Glamorgan, Somerset went on to lose by two wickets.

The **Surrey** team never settled, partly as a consequence of the injury that forced premature retirement upon their coach and captain Tony Pigott, and they managed to avoid the wooden spoon only by defeating Glamorgan in the last match of the season. A particular disappointment was the lack of progress shown by England Under-19 spearhead Alex Tudor, whose fast bowling was affected by a problem described by Surrey's physiotherapist as a discrepancy of leg length. Tudor's best contribution was made with the bat, when he scored 134 against Worcestershire at Kidderminster.

Sussex won only two matches, but could take some consolation from the performance of their batsmen. Toby Peirce, who had departed at the end of the 1995 season to seek employment in the City, returned to the fold in August and finished on top of the averages, but the highlight of the season was the fourth-wicket stand of 256 between brothers Keith and Mark Newell against Surrey at Cheam.

Warwickshire took their first title since 1979 with something to spare. Several players excelled themselves: Michael Powell's 1,103 runs included 210 out of a total of 524 for five against the hapless Somerset attack, while Darren Altree became the first man to take two hat-tricks in a Second Eleven season. Overall, Altree's left-arm fast bowling brought him 62 wickets (one every 31 balls). Mike Edmond, an English-born all-rounder talent-spotted while playing for Australia's indoor team, was almost as effective with the ball, collecting match figures of ten for 77 in the innings victory over Sussex. In an intriguing sub-plot, Mark Wagh and Anurag Singh, captains-elect of Oxford and Cambridge Universities respectively, both finished the season with 562 runs.

Winless at the beginning of August, **Worcestershire** emulated their first team by staging a late rally. But one of their three victories came against an eight-man Glamorgan side (see above), and there was a general lack of inspirational individual performances. Two of the batting mainstays, Matthew Church and James Ralph, were released at the end of the summer.

Under the influence of the club's successful Cricket Academy, **Yorkshire's** side continued to grow ever younger. For most of the season it included seven or eight teenagers and, at 23, captain Richard Kettleborough looked a veteran by comparison. Kettleborough and 26-year-old Bradley Parker provided a steady foundation for the batting, however, and but for an injury to leading wicket-taker Ian Fisher, Yorkshire might have managed even better than their fourth place.

DERBYSHIRE SECOND ELEVEN

Matches 17: Won - Glamorgan, Surrey, Warwickshire. Lost - Essex, Kent, Northamptonshire, Somerset. Drawn - Durham, Gloucestershire, Hampshire, Lancashire, Leicestershire, Middlesex, Nottinghamshire, Sussex, Worcestershire, Yorkshire.

Batting Averages

	M	*I*	*NO*	*R*	*HS*	*100s*	*Avge*
T. J. G. O'Gorman	4	6	1	417	150*	1	83.40
*T. A. Tweats	11	18	2	822	134	2	51.37
M. R. May	15	27	3	1,054	147*	3	43.91
M. J. Vandrau	4	6	0	216	110	1	36.00
G. A. Khan	6	10	2	284	126*	1	35.50
J. E. Owen	10	16	2	469	119*	1	33.50
T. M. Smith	6	7	5	67	28*	0	33.50
M. E. Cassar	13	22	2	651	125	2	32.55
J. D. Cokayne	4	6	2	121	62	0	30.25
F. A. Griffith	4	6	1	135	38	0	27.00
B. L. Spendlove	7	13	2	273	50*	0	24.81
I. D. Blackwell	9	13	1	293	132*	1	24.41
G. M. Roberts	7	8	0	180	57	0	22.50
*P. Aldred	12	15	4	244	43	0	22.18
†S. P. Griffiths	15	19	4	239	39	0	15.93
A. E. Warner	4	5	1	63	47*	0	15.75
R. C. Driver	3	6	1	73	41*	0	14.60
K. J. Dean	8	6	2	57	25	0	14.25
S. J. Lacey	7	8	1	66	25	0	9.42
S. J. Base	4	5	1	33	15	0	8.25

Played in four matches: D. R. Womble 28*, 75, 21*. Played in three matches: C. M. Wells 38, 34, 0, 8. Played in two matches: N. Aslam 1*; A. J. Harris 0, 2; †W. Ritzema 5, 51; D. Smit 0*, 5, 5, 12; S. A. Twigg 61, 27, 37. Played in one match: P. J. G. Appleton 48*; C. Beaumont 0, 23; P. Blakemore 30, 7; V. P. Clarke 70, 62; C. E. Dagnall 25*; D. Dalton 11; M. Deane 8; C. Entwhistle 38, 19; J. Fielding 1, 0; M. Fletcher 19, 9; B. Meaney 4*, 19; S. A. Moore 2; S. O. Moore 7*; I. C. Parkin 0; D. B. Pennett 12, 18; †D. J. Pipe 67, 27; A. J. Thompson 2, 17; A. Worthy 8; N. Brett did not bat.

Note: In the match v Kent at Chesterfield G. A. Khan and P. Aldred, called up for a first-team match, were replaced by S. J. Lacey and B. L. Spendlove.

Bowling Averages

	O	*M*	*R*	*W*	*BB*	*Avge*
M. Deane	32.3	13	43	4	3-20	10.75
C. E. Dagnall	46	16	97	7	4-51	13.85
C. Entwhistle	30	7	65	4	2-22	16.25
K. J. Dean	193.5	48	495	23	5-32	21.52
P. Aldred	315.1	59	886	40	8-40	22.15
N. Aslam	62.3	13	212	9	3-78	23.55
M. J. Vandrau	156.2	35	349	14	5-28	24.92
F. A. Griffith	107.2	27	339	13	5-71	26.07
A. E. Warner	90	40	169	6	3-31	28.16

	O	*M*	*R*	*W*	*BB*	*Avge*
N. Brett	28.1	4	114	4	3-64	28.50
G. M. Roberts	192.1	51	581	16	3-39	36.31
I. D. Blackwell	301	84	895	24	5-47	37.29
T. M. Smith	107.1	16	414	10	3-48	41.40
S. J. Lacey	134	33	402	5	2-54	80.40
M. E. Cassar	157.1	25	597	6	1-19	99.50

Also bowled: P. J. G. Appleton 15–5–51–0; S. J. Base 67.3–18–203–1; V. P. Clarke 23–1–118–1; D. Dalton 15–1–46–1; R. C. Driver 4–2–3–0; J. Fielding 27–8–86–3; A. J. Harris 40–10–145–3; G. A. Khan 1–0–5–0; S. A. Moore 19–3–67–2; S. O. Moore 18–8–37–1; J. E. Owen 13–3–37–0; I. C. Parkin 4–1–3–0; D. B. Pennett 25–3–136–1; T. A. Tweats 25–5–60–2; C. M. Wells 30–8–74–1; D. R. Womble 47.3–9–211–2; A. Worthy 25–4–94–1.

DURHAM SECOND ELEVEN

Matches 17: Won – Kent, Middlesex, Northamptonshire, Surrey. Lost – Gloucestershire, Hampshire, Leicestershire, Warwickshire, Yorkshire. Drawn – Derbyshire, Essex, Glamorgan, Lancashire, Nottinghamshire, Somerset, Sussex, Worcestershire.

Batting Averages

	M	*I*	*NO*	*R*	*HS*	*100s*	*Avge*
J. A. Daley	3	6	2	296	128*	1	74.00
M. J. Foster	4	7	0	371	71	0	53.00
S. Hutton	5	9	1	393	133	2	49.12
R. M. S. Weston	9	14	1	612	126*	2	47.07
*J. I. Longley	12	21	3	836	141	3	46.44
†D. G. C. Ligertwood	5	8	1	321	90	0	45.85
P. D. Collingwood	5	7	1	259	148	1	43.16
D. A. Blenkiron	9	16	1	528	92	0	35.20
C. Clark	10	16	1	486	103	1	32.40
J. E. Morris	3	4	0	126	64	0	31.50
J. Wood	4	6	1	142	103*	1	28.40
†A. Pratt	13	21	6	423	69*	0	28.20
Q. J. Hughes	8	13	1	326	90	0	27.16
D. M. Cox	7	8	3	135	31	0	27.00
I. Jones	10	12	0	216	87	0	18.00
A. Walker	9	11	3	138	36	0	17.25
†C. W. Scott	5	8	0	126	39	0	15.75
S. D. Birbeck	6	10	0	157	43	0	15.70
*J. Boiling	6	8	1	96	40	0	13.71
N. Killeen	8	11	2	122	33	0	13.55
M. A. J. Gough	3	5	0	42	33	0	8.40
C. L. Campbell	7	8	1	26	12*	0	3.71
J. P. Searle	14	16	6	18	13	0	1.80

Played in four matches: M. J. Saggers 6, 3*, 6. Played in three matches: J. A. Graham 16, 53*, 21, 6*, 91, 89*; S. J. Harmison 2*, 0*, 0; S. Lugsden 0, 11*; M. J. Robinson 25, 87*, 43, 68*. Played in two matches: M. M. Betts 10, 1, 70. Played in one match: P. Bainbridge 8, 43; S. J. Birtwisle 1, 0; S. E. Brinkley 53; P. L. Carlin 7, 37; M. A. Roseberry 4; I. H. Shah 0*; D. J. Rutherford did not bat.

Note: Owing to first-team calls N. Killeen was replaced by D. J. Rutherford in the match v Essex at Darlington, A. Walker was replaced by I. Jones in the match v Yorkshire at Shildon and R. M. S. Weston was replaced by M. J. Robinson in the match v Kent at Eltham.

Bowling Averages

	O	*M*	*R*	*W*	*BB*	*Avge*
I. H. Shah	36.5	11	112	7	7-39	16.00
D. M. Cox	273.3	117	501	27	6-56	18.55
S. J. Harmison	64.2	12	216	11	3-17	19.63
S. Lugsden	68	20	157	7	3-38	22.42
M. J. Saggers	67	16	187	8	4-31	23.37
P. D. Collingwood	33	8	102	4	2-10	25.50
A. Walker	275.4	66	691	26	4-25	26.57
J. Boiling	181.5	44	570	20	6-85	28.50
S. D. Birbeck	96.5	29	295	10	3-32	29.50
C. Clark	56	20	140	4	1-15	35.00
N. Killeen	207	58	603	17	3-27	35.47
J. P. Searle	430	104	1,401	37	4-57	37.86
C. L. Campbell	160.4	35	543	14	6-78	38.78
I. Jones	200.5	40	680	13	3-63	52.30
J. Wood	75.5	11	279	5	2-58	55.80

Also bowled: P. Bainbridge 8–1–41–0; M. M. Betts 24–6–88–3; S. J. Birtwisle 2–0–8–0; D. A. Blenkiron 44–10–150–3; S. E. Brinkley 10–1–42–0; M. A. J. Gough 14–1–51–0; Q. J. Hughes 25–5–100–2; J. E. Morris 3–0–20–1; D. J. Rutherford 8–1–41–0; R. M. S. Weston 48–2–51–0.

ESSEX SECOND ELEVEN

Matches 17: Won – Derbyshire. Lost – Lancashire, Leicestershire, Nottinghamshire, Warwickshire, Worcestershire, Yorkshire. Drawn – Durham, Glamorgan, Gloucestershire, Hampshire, Kent, Middlesex, Northamptonshire, Somerset, Surrey, Sussex.

Batting Averages

	M	*I*	*NO*	*R*	*HS*	*100s*	*Avge*
D. D. J. Robinson	3	5	0	501	224	2	100.20
E. J. Wilson	8	14	3	626	127*	2	56.90
S. D. Peters	14	24	3	1,101	112*	2	52.42
N. F. Williams	4	5	1	199	89	0	49.75
A. J. E. Hibbert	12	21	3	770	231*	1	42.77
*A. R. Butcher	10	12	4	310	82	0	38.75
J. J. B. Lewis	10	18	2	603	113	2	37.68
T. P. Hodgson	10	18	3	551	112*	2	36.73
P. R. Shaw	8	13	1	421	118	1	35.08
I. N. Flanagan	6	12	0	366	139	1	30.50
A. P. Cole	3	5	2	80	32*	0	26.66
†B. J. Hyam	16	24	2	543	94	0	24.68
D. G. Wilson	5	8	1	166	54	0	23.71
N. A. Derbyshire	10	12	4	131	27*	0	16.37
J. C. Powell	12	13	1	133	40	0	11.08
D. W. Ayres	12	17	3	154	32*	0	11.00
M. Ismael	2	4	0	41	23	0	10.25
S. J. W. Andrew	5	5	0	50	22	0	10.00
G. J. A. Goodwin	13	13	4	36	11	0	4.00

Played in five matches: J. H. Childs 2*, 1, 11, 5*, 2*. Played in four matches: J. O. Grove 5*, 0, 0, 0*. Played in two matches: D. J. Angove 1, 0; S. O. Moore 8, 9*. Played in one match: A. Anderson 16*; P. J. Bradshaw 6, 26; A. J. Clarke 15, 23; A. P. Cowan 43; A. P. Grayson 137; T. E. Hemmings 11*; G. P. McMillan 37; T. J. Phillips 3; A. Richardson 2*; C. Warn 9, 21; H. Sana did not bat.

Bowling Averages

	O	*M*	*R*	*W*	*BB*	*Avge*
A. P. Grayson	35	22	29	9	5-5	3.22
A. R. Butcher	15.1	4	48	4	1-0	12.00
H. Sana	49	14	146	11	6-52	13.27
D. J. Angove	42	7	157	5	2-60	31.40
D. G. Wilson	103	18	354	11	2-39	32.18
N. F. Williams	82	12	307	9	3-52	34.11
A. J. E. Hibbert	53	17	140	4	2-19	35.00
D. W. Ayres	250.2	48	908	25	5-40	36.32
S. J. W. Andrew	101.1	23	238	6	4-43	39.66
J. H. Childs	160	50	437	10	4-94	43.70
J. C. Powell	405.2	91	1,339	30	4-103	44.63
S. O. Moore	56.5	16	201	4	2-32	50.25
G. J. A. Goodwin	305.4	69	1,099	21	4-58	52.33
A. P. Cole	63	11	277	5	4-68	55.40
N. A. Derbyshire	219.3	36	833	13	3-35	64.07

Also bowled: A. Anderson 28–7–119–1; P. J. Bradshaw 13–0–50–2; A. J. Clarke 14–3–53–1; A. P. Cowan 32–2–143–3; J. O. Grove 59–11–223–2; T. E. Hemmings 10–2–41–2; T. P. Hodgson 5.2–0–16–0; M. Ismael 34–9–99–2; G. P. McMillan 18–1–69–0; T. J. Phillips 14–7–32–0; A. Richardson 29–7–70–3; E. J. Wilson 1–0–2–0.

GLAMORGAN SECOND ELEVEN

Matches 17: Won – Somerset, Warwickshire. Lost – Derbyshire, Middlesex, Northamptonshire, Surrey, Worcestershire. Drawn – Durham, Essex, Gloucestershire, Hampshire, Kent, Lancashire, Leicestershire, Nottinghamshire, Sussex, Yorkshire.

Batting Averages

	M	*I*	*NO*	*R*	*HS*	*100s*	*Avge*
A. D. Shaw	6	10	4	485	173*	1	80.83
A. W. Evans	12	22	0	1,070	156	2	48.63
†R. E. Evans	2	4	2	93	63*	0	46.50
W. L. Law	8	13	4	364	80*	0	40.44
G. P. Butcher	4	6	1	201	68	0	40.20
A. J. Dalton	16	28	1	925	132	2	34.25
D. L. Hemp	7	12	1	373	152*	1	33.90
A. Dale	3	4	0	128	78	0	32.00
*J. R. A. Williams	17	30	1	869	106	1	29.96
S. D. Thomas	8	12	1	291	95	0	26.45
†C. P. Metson	7	12	2	255	58	0	25.50
N. M. Kendrick	9	12	3	229	61*	0	25.44
I. Gompertz	11	20	2	450	90	0	25.00
M. J. Powell	7	12	3	179	41	0	19.88
R. V. Almond	4	7	1	105	54*	0	17.50
A. P. Davies	14	17	4	223	55*	0	17.15
S. R. Barwick	7	8	3	65	18*	0	13.00
B. W. Gannon	2	4	1	22	12*	0	7.33
O. T. Parkin	8	7	3	28	7*	0	7.00
C. E. Sketchley	3	6	0	41	31	0	6.83
T. J. Hemp	2	4	0	14	9	0	3.50

Played in six matches: G. J. M. Edwards 0, 0, 2*. Played in four matches: B. M. Morgan 10*, 0. Played in three matches: D. A. Cosker 59, 0, 0; M. D. O'Leary 9*, 0*, 0*. Played in two matches: P. S. Jones 9, 0, 5; S. O. Moore 6, 2; M. A. Payne 4, 6. Played in one match: J. A. Clutterbuck 2, 18*; R. L. Eagleson 2, 17; S. P. Jones 0*; D. J. Lovell 49, 29; P. Melville 4, 1; T. A. Radford 27; G. A. Rollins and M. J. Selleck did not bat.

Bowling Averages

	O	*M*	*R*	*W*	*BB*	*Avge*
O. T. Parkin	183.4	44	514	22	4-34	23.36
S. D. Thomas	211.5	37	631	26	5-29	24.26
S. R. Barwick	241	74	548	22	6-54	24.90
C. E. Sketchley	102.3	17	356	14	9-90	25.42
P. S. Jones	47	7	154	5	3-17	30.80
A. P. Davies	329.3	59	1,218	35	4-41	34.80
S. O. Moore	58	11	187	5	2-64	37.40
B. W. Gannon	34	2	210	4	2-70	52.50
N. M. Kendrick	211.4	44	740	14	3-30	52.85
D. A. Cosker	124.4	41	281	5	2-52	56.20
G. J. M. Edwards	182.3	43	584	10	3-28	58.40
I. Gompertz	72.3	7	374	5	2-26	74.80
B. M. Morgan	78.5	6	333	4	2-53	83.25

Also bowled: G. P. Butcher 33–2–167–2; J. A. Clutterbuck 12–4–49–2; A. Dale 20–2–62–1; A. J. Dalton 57.1–6–236–3; R. L. Eagleson 15–2–81–2; A. W. Evans 4.4–1–25–0; D. L. Hemp 54–16–177–3; S. P. Jones 12–2–54–0; W. L. Law 2–0–8–0; P. Melville 28–7–85–1; M. D. O'Leary 29–5–109–2; M. J. Powell 11–0–77–0; G. A. Rollins 14–3–86–0; M. J. Selleck 11–3–39–2; J. R. A. Williams 17.4–2–150–3.

GLOUCESTERSHIRE SECOND ELEVEN

Matches 17: Won – Durham, Kent. Drawn – Derbyshire, Essex, Glamorgan, Hampshire, Lancashire, Leicestershire, Middlesex, Northamptonshire, Nottinghamshire, Somerset, Surrey, Sussex, Warwickshire, Worcestershire, Yorkshire.

Batting Averages

	M	*I*	*NO*	*R*	*HS*	*100s*	*Avge*
M. G. N. Windows	4	8	1	448	104	1	64.00
N. J. Trainor	12	20	2	1,045	172*	4	58.05
*R. I. Dawson	9	15	1	647	213	3	46.21
A. J. Wright	2	4	0	178	83	0	44.50
D. R. Hewson	12	20	2	784	184	3	43.55
†C. M. W. Read	7	11	3	325	119*	1	40.62
R. J. Cunliffe	7	11	1	390	81	0	39.00
M. P. Hunt	7	12	3	338	70*	0	37.55
M. J. Cawdron	12	19	5	500	94*	0	35.71
†R. C. J. Williams	10	14	2	419	129	1	34.91
K. P. Sheeraz	13	16	7	276	53	0	30.66
C. G. Taylor	4	6	1	128	46	0	25.60
M. A. Lynch	6	9	0	224	68	0	24.88
J. M. M. Averis	8	9	5	97	31*	0	24.25
P. S. Lazenbury	6	10	0	195	82	0	19.50
S. Patel	6	10	0	189	76	0	18.90
D. J. P. Boden	11	14	2	202	36	0	16.83
B. L. Worrad	3	5	0	63	44	0	12.60
J. G. Whitby-Coles	15	6	4	11	4*	0	5.50

Played in four matches: J. Lewis 7, 4; R. Turnell 0, 4, 0. Played in three matches: R. P. Davis 32*, 36*, 23; A. M. James 21*, 13*. Played in two matches: M. C. J. Ball 14, 0; T. H. C. Hancock 38*, 26, 18, 2; A. M. Smith 1. Played in one match: M. W. Alleyne 13; I. M. Collins 0, 9; L. P. Collins 7; D. J. Cowley 103*, 34; M. A. Hardinges 8, 27*; †J. H. Langworth 15*, 7; †P. J. Nicholson 3, 0*; P. A. Spence 2; A. W. Stovold 18*; A. Symonds 43, 9*; M. J. Whitney 9, 0; J. F. Cotterell and M. J. Marvell did not bat.

Bowling Averages

	O	M	R	W	BB	Avge
M. W. Alleyne	17	5	65	4	3-31	16.25
A. M. Smith	43	16	83	5	3-8	16.60
R. I. Dawson	36	11	114	5	2-12	22.80
R. P. Davis	101.1	27	347	15	5-49	23.13
M. J. Cawdron	261	70	731	27	4-40	27.07
K. P. Sheeraz	271.3	54	939	33	6-80	28.45
J. Lewis	145.2	32	498	16	3-30	31.12
M. C. J. Ball	64	13	159	5	2-52	31.80
J. M. M. Averis	152.3	23	619	17	4-60	36.41
R. Turnell	88	16	276	7	2-34	39.42
D. J. P. Boden	292.4	48	1,081	25	3-45	43.24
N. J. Trainor	127.2	30	454	8	2-58	56.75
A. M. James	75.2	6	295	5	2-107	59.00
J. G. Whitby-Coles	250.5	57	749	10	2-32	74.90

Also bowled: L. P. Collins 11–2–46–0; D. J. Cowley 29–8–68–1; R. J. Cunliffe 2–0–29–0; T. H. C. Hancock 15–2–53–1; M. A. Hardinges 7–0–31–0; D. R. Hewson 9–4–34–1; M. P. Hunt 58–7–258–3; M. J. Marvell 12–1–62–0; S. Patel 28–4–108–2; P. A. Spence 6–0–48–0; A. Symonds 6–0–28–0; C. G. Taylor 6–0–34–0; R. C. J. Williams 2–0–34–0; M. G. N. Windows 1–0–11–1.

HAMPSHIRE SECOND ELEVEN

Matches 17: Won – Durham, Worcestershire. Lost – Lancashire, Leicestershire, Nottinghamshire, Somerset, Warwickshire, Yorkshire. Drawn – Derbyshire, Essex, Glamorgan, Gloucestershire, Kent, Middlesex, Northamptonshire, Surrey, Sussex.

Batting Averages

	M	I	NO	R	HS	100s	Avge
R. S. M. Morris	7	12	3	545	110*	3	60.55
G. W. White	9	16	2	633	152	1	45.21
W. S. Kendall	4	7	1	270	100	1	45.00
P. R. Whitaker	4	7	1	268	86	0	44.66
R. J. Maru	4	5	1	136	69*	0	34.00
M. J. Thursfield	9	13	2	366	73	0	33.27
G. R. Treagus	16	30	3	890	79*	0	32.96
L. J. Botham	16	27	1	807	68	0	31.03
D. A. Kenway	5	9	1	245	56	0	30.62
A. D. Mascarenhas	13	20	4	482	76*	0	30.12
M. Keech	6	12	1	317	67	0	28.81
M. Swarbrick	9	16	2	391	92	0	27.92
S. D. Udal	3	5	0	129	56	0	25.80
*†M. Garaway	16	27	3	602	48	0	25.08
J. N. B. Bovill	5	8	3	120	40*	0	24.00
D. M. Lane	3	4	0	72	46	0	18.00
R. R. Dibden	11	13	4	141	48*	0	15.66
L. Savident	6	11	0	156	39	0	14.18
D. M. Thomas	10	14	0	167	31	0	11.92
S. J. Renshaw	13	18	9	100	31	0	11.11
S. R. G. Francis	3	4	2	13	7*	0	6.50
M. Dillon	5	6	0	15	13	0	2.50
B. S. Phelps	2	4	0	7	5	0	1.75

Played in two matches: R. S. G. Anderson did not bat. Played in one match: A. P. Cole 4, 5*; T. A. Edwards 4, 9; K. D. James 100, 23; V. P. Terry 10; N. J. Thurgood 9, 13; J. S. Laney did not bat.

Bowling Averages

	O	M	R	W	BB	Avge
S. D. Udal	107.3	32	285	17	5-15	16.76
R. J. Maru	189.3	63	446	22	4-49	20.27
M. Dillon	155	26	526	23	5-85	22.86
A. D. Mascarenhas	245.5	49	884	34	5-60	26.00
M. J. Thursfield	198.2	59	560	20	3-17	28.00
S. J. Renshaw	291.5	67	835	25	5-23	33.40
J. N. B. Bovill	148	30	445	13	2-39	34.23
R. R. Dibden	331.5	69	1,114	29	5-135	38.41
D. M. Thomas	179.5	30	687	17	3-42	40.41
L. J. Botham	160.4	21	730	16	3-77	45.62
S. R. G. Francis	58	14	200	4	2-56	50.00
P. R. Whitaker	71.4	11	238	4	2-58	59.50

Also bowled: R. S. G. Anderson 25–4–103–2; A. P. Cole 19–2–84–1; K. D. James 20–6–57–1; D. M. Lane 44–12–132–1; B. S. Phelps 50.2–14–167–3; L. Savident 24.4–4–105–1; G. R. Treagus 30.4–6–96–3; G. W. White 2–0–14–0.

KENT SECOND ELEVEN

Matches 17: Won – Derbyshire, Leicestershire, Surrey, Warwickshire. Lost – Durham, Gloucestershire, Middlesex. Drawn – Essex, Glamorgan, Hampshire, Lancashire, Northamptonshire, Nottinghamshire, Somerset, Sussex, Worcestershire, Yorkshire.

Batting Averages

	M	I	NO	R	HS	100s	Avge
D. P. Fulton	2	4	0	270	230	1	67.50
*N. R. Taylor	15	23	5	1,204	211	6	66.88
D. J. Spencer	7	9	2	411	89	0	58.71
J. B. D. Thompson	9	16	5	557	150*	1	50.63
G. R. Cowdrey	5	10	2	367	80	0	45.87
M. J. Walker	5	8	0	348	95	0	43.50
W. J. House	7	14	0	540	110	1	38.57
R. Key	10	16	2	519	146*	1	37.07
†S. C. Willis	12	20	3	625	60	0	36.76
N. W. Preston	9	10	3	234	73	0	33.42
E. J. Stanford	16	16	8	258	52	0	32.25
B. J. Phillips	12	15	5	260	57*	0	26.00
C. D. Walsh	8	16	0	332	65	0	20.75
E. T. Smith	3	6	0	115	29	0	19.16
A. P. Igglesden	6	6	1	90	25	0	18.00
D. A. Scott	9	5	4	18	9*	0	18.00
J. A. Ford	9	18	0	322	67	0	17.88
J. H. Baldock	8	10	0	171	80	0	17.10
G. M. Stephens	11	15	6	153	59*	0	17.00
T. N. Wren	7	8	2	38	16	0	6.33

Played in five matches: †J. S. Bond 21, 1, 0, 5*. Played in three matches: N. D. Gowers 29, 8, 7, 3*. Played in two matches: J. B. Hockley 0, 20, 11; N. J. Llong 29, 8, 192. Played in one match: M. A. Ealham 8, 0; D. W. Headley 0; M. M. Patel 19, 37; T. V. Smith 0; S. J. Taylor 39; D. M. Cook did not bat.

Note: In the match v Warwickshire at Coventry, T. N. Wren, called up for a first-team match, was replaced by N. W. Preston.

Bowling Averages

	O	M	R	W	BB	Avge
D. W. Headley	33	14	48	5	3-27	9.60
M. A. Ealham	25	7	74	4	3-64	18.50
N. J. Llong	53.3	11	113	5	3-30	22.60
N. W. Preston	230	51	666	29	6-61	22.96
J. A. Ford	92.3	28	242	10	2-24	24.20
T. N. Wren	230	62	613	25	5-60	24.52
J. B. D. Thompson	270.2	56	893	35	5-46	25.51
E. J. Stanford	607.5	164	1,579	51	5-81	30.96
G. M. Stephens	79	18	277	7	3-75	39.57
B. J. Phillips	276.3	52	985	24	3-49	41.04
A. P. Igglesden	117.1	19	389	9	4-69	43.22
D. A. Scott	232.4	44	774	16	5-23	48.37

Also bowled: J. H. Baldock 10–3–37–0; D. M. Cook 1–0–5–0; G. R. Cowdrey 7–1–32–0; J. B. Hockley 7–1–28–0; W. J. House 36–5–148–3; R. Key 1.5–0–26–0; M. M. Patel 45–7–142–2; T. V. Smith 14.3–2–68–0; N. R. Taylor 45.4–7–126–1; M. J. Walker 3–0–21–0; C. D. Walsh 5–1–28–0.

LANCASHIRE SECOND ELEVEN

Matches 17: Won – Essex, Hampshire, Leicestershire, Surrey, Warwickshire, Yorkshire. Lost – Middlesex. Drawn – Derbyshire, Durham, Glamorgan, Gloucestershire, Kent, Northamptonshire, Nottinghamshire, Somerset, Sussex, Worcestershire.

Batting Averages

	M	I	NO	R	HS	100s	Avge
*P. R. Sleep	15	19	10	586	121*	1	65.11
P. C. McKeown	17	30	1	1,437	175	5	49.55
N. T. Wood	16	29	7	1,067	140	2	48.50
I. D. Austin	2	3	0	140	78	0	46.66
M. J. Chilton	8	12	1	389	113	2	35.36
R. J. Green	12	17	5	395	63	0	32.91
S. P. Titchard	6	9	1	236	60*	0	29.50
D. J. Shadford	12	17	4	368	101*	1	28.30
L. J. Marland	5	10	0	271	71	0	27.10
A. Flintoff	12	19	1	486	103	1	27.00
†J. J. Haynes	17	21	6	363	66*	0	24.20
G. A. Knowles	4	6	0	126	41	0	21.00
G. Keedy	7	9	1	132	45	0	16.50
P. M. Ridgway	15	16	2	184	28	0	13.14
D. J. Pipe	2	3	0	39	29	0	13.00
C. Brown	15	13	5	78	32	0	9.75
M. E. Harvey	9	15	0	140	23	0	9.33
G. Yates	3	4	0	36	20	0	9.00
D. J. Thompson	6	5	0	17	7	0	3.40

Played in one match: A. D. Bairstow 0; M. P. Smethurst 7*; N. J. Speak 2, 9*; P. J. G. Appleton did not bat.

Bowling Averages

	O	M	R	W	BB	Avge
I. D. Austin	56	17	122	12	5-15	10.16
M. J. Chilton	94.3	21	299	14	6-33	21.35
S. P. Titchard	48	17	107	5	2-9	21.40
R. J. Green	299.4	92	821	37	5-55	22.18
G. Keedy	422.2	129	999	43	6-70	23.23

	O	M	R	W	BB	Avge
G. Yates	91	29	267	8	6-65	33.37
P. M. Ridgway	302	46	1,152	34	4-53	33.88
C. Brown	497	142	1,445	33	5-47	43.78
P. R. Sleep	102	32	280	6	2-37	46.66
D. J. Shadford	214.3	37	843	17	5-58	49.58
D. J. Thompson	117	21	372	6	2-26	62.00

Also bowled; P. J. G. Appleton 20–3–82–1; A. D. Bairstow 1–0–3–0; A. Flintoff 4–1–10–0; G. A. Knowles 1–0–13–0; P. C. McKeown 1–0–7–0; L. J. Marland 2–0–7–1; D. J. Pipe 2–0–16–0; M. P. Smethurst 15–4–43–1; N. J. Speak 1.2–0–8–1.

LEICESTERSHIRE SECOND ELEVEN

Matches 17: Won – Durham, Essex, Hampshire, Surrey, Sussex. Lost – Kent, Lancashire, Middlesex, Northamptonshire, Warwickshire. Drawn – Derbyshire, Glamorgan, Gloucestershire, Nottinghamshire, Somerset, Worcestershire, Yorkshire.

Batting Averages

	M	I	NO	R	HS	100s	Avge
†I. J. Sutcliffe	6	9	3	411	127	1	68.50
†P. Whitticase	9	10	2	425	132	1	53.12
J. D. Hanger	2	4	1	156	100	1	52.00
V. P. Clarke	13	19	2	879	189	3	51.70
C. C. Remy	10	13	1	489	128	2	40.75
J. M. Dakin	7	9	0	352	115	1	39.11
S. Ahmed	4	6	1	165	92*	0	33.00
D. I. Stevens	16	25	0	786	96	0	31.44
G. I. Macmillan	8	15	2	407	105*	1	31.30
T. J. Mason	13	18	6	342	50*	0	28.50
*†P. E. Robinson	11	14	5	250	43	0	27.77
D. Williamson	13	17	5	328	69	0	27.33
C. D. Crowe	16	23	1	574	59	0	26.09
†M. D. R. Sutliff	6	10	1	226	52	0	25.11
J. Ormond	8	9	3	146	34	0	24.33
S. A. Richardson	5	8	1	163	78	0	23.28
A. Habib	2	4	1	65	39	0	21.66
†N. C. Price	3	3	2	16	10	0	16.00
S. Bartle	5	10	1	131	38	0	14.55
M. T. Brimson	4	4	0	44	16	0	11.00

Played in three matches: A. Thomas 16. Played in two matches: S. Kirby 0, 0*; G. P. McMillan 0. Played in one match: S. R. Bowman 0, 0*; A. S. Christmas 1, 1; C. E. Dagnall 7; N. B. Francis 40, 31*; N. S. Gill 4; K. G. Howarth 13*, 1; D. L. Maddy 36, 16; R. A. E. Martin 2, 0; D. J. Millns 11; A. D. Mullally 5; P. A. Nixon 11, 5; G. J. Parsons 16*, 0; †D. J. Pipe 8*, 3; B. F. Smith 91; J. I. M. Smith 13, 12; S. A. Twigg 82, 66; V. J. Wells 11, 5; K. Adams and M. K. Davies did not bat.

Bowling Averages

	O	M	R	W	BB	Avge
J. M. Dakin	66	25	153	10	4-36	15.30
J. Ormond	193.2	48	561	30	4-21	18.70
M. T. Brimson	93	27	221	10	5-63	22.10
A. Thomas	81.3	16	264	11	5-44	24.00
D. Williamson	302.2	82	846	33	5-80	25.63
T. J. Mason	318.1	92	853	32	5-86	26.65

	O	*M*	*R*	*W*	*BB*	*Avge*
V. P. Clarke	230.5	41	793	23	4-31	34.47
C. D. Crowe	356	101	1,001	29	3-50	34.51
C. C. Remy	146.3	34	441	10	3-41	44.10
G. P. McMillan	55	10	185	4	2-31	46.25

Also bowled: K. Adams 9–2–27–0; S. Ahmed 38–5–192–2; S. R. Bowman 24.5–4–163–1; A. S. Christmas 8–1–31–0; C. E. Dagnall 28–10–113–0; M. K. Davies 12.2–0–82–1; N. B. Francis 31–1–129–2; N. S. Gill 25–6–89–2; K. G. Howarth 27–4–119–2; S. Kirby 19–5–50–1; G. I. Macmillan 18–4–42–0; D. J. Millns 14–3–29–3; A. D. Mullally 13–2–34–1; G. J. Parsons 13–6–26–1; P. E. Robinson 5–0–28–0; J. I. M. Smith 12–1–43–1; D. I. Stevens 1–0–7–0; I. J. Sutcliffe 6.4–0–34–3; V. J. Wells 10–2–36–0; P. Whitticase 4–3–1–1.

MIDDLESEX SECOND ELEVEN

Matches 17: Won – Glamorgan, Kent, Lancashire, Leicestershire, Northamptonshire, Somerset, Worcestershire. Lost – Durham, Nottinghamshire. Drawn – Derbyshire, Essex, Gloucestershire, Hampshire, Surrey, Sussex, Warwickshire, Yorkshire.

Batting Averages

	M	*I*	*NO*	*R*	*HS*	*100s*	*Avge*
*K. P. Dutch	15	24	7	1,043	261	2	61.35
J. P. Hewitt	8	14	6	407	76*	0	50.87
P. E. Wellings	14	25	5	1,004	178*	2	50.20
J. C. Harrison	9	15	1	624	129	2	44.57
O. A. Shah	3	4	0	156	97	0	39.00
S. P. Moffat	7	13	0	481	94	0	37.00
A. J. Strauss	4	7	1	218	98	0	36.33
D. J. Goodchild	12	20	2	626	100*	1	34.77
†G. M. Pooley	5	10	0	345	129	1	34.50
M. R. Evans	8	8	5	101	44*	0	33.66
*†I. J. Gould	10	9	5	122	52*	0	30.50
†J. N. Batty	5	9	0	225	80	0	25.00
R. P. Lane	8	12	0	291	62	0	24.25
N. B. Francis	2	4	0	89	47	0	22.25
M. A. Feltham	6	9	2	144	54*	0	20.57
A. A. Khan	7	6	2	50	15*	0	12.50
U. B. A. Rashid	11	12	1	130	20	0	11.81
A. W. Laraman	2	4	0	45	40	0	11.25
I. N. Blanchett	10	11	4	69	15	0	9.85
A. G. Norman	5	8	2	55	26*	0	9.16
N. D. Martin	9	4	1	15	6*	0	5.00

Played in five matches: †D. C. Nash 51, 74*, 3, 100*, 49, 16*. Played in three matches: C. J. Batt 5, 4, 5, 5*; †N. D. J. Cartmell 0, 11, 18*, 0. Played in two matches: C. M. Gupte 61, 16, 1; R. L. Johnson 26, 49, 15*; Ali Khan 0; J. S. Norman 9, 13, 26*. Played in one match: †J. Bahl 9*; J. R. Carpenter 10, 1; J. D. Carr 34, 21; B. David 5, 23*; C. P. Lowndes 27, 22; D. F. Lye 1; D. J. Nash 47, 8; M. T. E. Peirce 10, 10; J. C. Pooley 0, 0; S. A. Selwood 0, 10.

Note: Owing to first-team calls, J. C. Harrison was replaced by A. G. Norman in the match v Essex at Southgate and J. P. Hewitt was replaced by I. J. Gould in the match v Surrey at Uxbridge.

Bowling Averages

	O	*M*	*R*	*W*	*BB*	*Avge*
M. A. Feltham	73	19	211	12	4-25	17.58
J. P. Hewitt	182.3	33	575	28	5-59	20.53
N. B. Francis	28.5	5	140	6	5-28	23.33
K. P. Dutch	543.2	109	1,641	63	8-36	26.04
R. L. Johnson	42	9	106	4	2-38	26.50
U. B. A. Rashid	331.3	94	861	31	4-48	27.77
I. N. Blanchett	233.2	36	811	24	4-56	33.79

	O	M	R	W	BB	Avge
P. E. Wellings	110.3	19	423	11	3-29	38.45
M. R. Evans	85	15	385	9	4-31	42.77
R. P. Lane	57	14	175	4	2-35	43.75
N. D. Martin	174	38	579	13	4-26	44.53
A. A. Khan	114	32	336	5	3-110	67.20

Also bowled: C. J. Batt 37–3–188–1; B. David 14–2–41–1; D. J. Goodchild 24–5–71–0; I. J. Gould 30.4–6–68–3; J. C. Harrison 2–1–2–0; Ali Khan 37–3–149–2; A. W. Laraman 5–3–8–2; D. J. Nash 4–1–14–0.

NORTHAMPTONSHIRE SECOND ELEVEN

Matches 17: Won – Derbyshire, Glamorgan, Leicestershire, Somerset, Surrey, Sussex. Lost – Durham, Middlesex. Drawn – Essex, Gloucestershire, Hampshire, Kent, Lancashire, Nottinghamshire, Warwickshire, Worcestershire, Yorkshire.

Batting Averages

	M	I	NO	R	HS	100s	Avge
D. J. Sales	6	8	3	616	211	1	123.20
M. B. Loye	3	6	2	410	126	2	102.50
*A. Fordham	5	9	1	499	159	2	62.37
D. J. Roberts	9	16	2	852	172	5	60.85
T. C. Walton	10	14	1	766	101	1	58.92
A. J. Swann	11	19	2	991	174	5	58.29
A. R. Roberts	13	17	2	666	102	1	44.40
J. G. Hughes	16	20	5	446	53*	0	29.73
†T. M. B. Bailey	10	15	3	355	80	0	29.58
K. J. Innes	13	22	3	552	106	1	29.05
J. A. North	4	6	1	129	63	0	25.80
M. V. Steele	7	9	5	101	24*	0	25.25
†W. Ritzema	4	5	1	80	39	0	20.00
S. A. J. Boswell	9	6	1	62	25	0	12.40
†D. Ripley	7	9	1	98	37	0	12.25
J. N. Snape	8	13	0	141	31	0	10.84
J. F. Brown	15	10	4	44	15	0	7.33
R. D. Wild	12	10	1	56	16	0	6.22
*N. G. B. Cook	10	5	2	11	7	0	3.66

Played in six matches: M. K. Davies 0, 6. Played in three matches: P. A. Spence 0*. Played in two matches: G. P. Swann 3, 19*; R. J. Warren 0, 42*, 35, 98. Played in one match: R. R. Montgomerie 113, 46; A. R. Oram 17; P. A. Sogbodjor 0, 10*; †A. Romaine did not bat.

Note: Owing to first-team calls, N. G. B. Cook replaced T. C. Walton in the match v Worcestershire at Worcester and M. V. Steele replaced T. C. Walton in the match v Lancashire at Bedford School.

Bowling Averages

	O	M	R	W	BB	Avge
G. P. Swann	36.2	11	85	6	3-20	14.16
M. K. Davies	182.4	55	476	28	6-46	17.00
A. R. Roberts	338.1	97	937	41	7-85	22.85
M. V. Steele	62.5	11	230	10	4-31	23.00
J. N. Snape	241	63	662	26	5-21	25.46
P. A. Spence	45	12	159	6	3-30	26.50
K. J. Innes	111.5	26	379	14	5-64	27.07
J. F. Brown	473.2	161	1,130	41	5-44	27.56
J. G. Hughes	424.2	77	1,431	41	5-63	34.90
S. A. J. Boswell	227	35	892	23	5-107	38.78
T. C. Walton	100	27	342	7	2-25	48.85
R. D. Wild	220	45	818	16	3-35	51.12

Also bowled: J. A. North 21–2–80–2; A. R. Oram 8–3–22–1; A. J. Swann 3–0–10–0.

NOTTINGHAMSHIRE SECOND ELEVEN

Matches 17: Won – Essex, Hampshire, Middlesex. Lost – Warwickshire, Yorkshire. Drawn – Derbyshire, Durham, Glamorgan, Gloucestershire, Kent, Lancashire, Leicestershire, Northamptonshire, Somerset, Surrey, Sussex, Worcestershire.

Batting Averages

	M	*I*	*NO*	*R*	*HS*	*100s*	*Avge*
G. F. Archer	8	12	1	729	147*	3	66.27
C. M. Tolley	8	12	1	675	119*	4	61.36
U. Afzaal	10	14	2	728	182	2	60.66
†L. N. P. Walker	8	9	3	318	127*	1	53.00
M. N. Bowen	3	3	1	90	46	0	45.00
D. B. Pennett	7	8	4	178	44*	0	44.50
R. T. Bates	5	8	0	351	112	1	43.87
*M. Newell	10	8	3	200	51	0	40.00
J. R. Wileman	10	15	2	481	132	2	37.00
N. A. Gie	15	23	3	710	90	0	35.50
M. P. Dowman	12	17	0	591	108	2	34.76
G. E. Welton	13	19	3	515	112*	1	32.18
J. E. Hindson	16	16	3	417	102	1	32.07
†W. M. Noon	5	8	0	199	82	0	24.87
G. L. Brophy	5	7	1	125	44	0	20.83
R. J. Chapman	9	9	4	78	17*	0	15.60
J. P. Hart	11	9	3	88	32	0	14.66
M. Broadhurst	8	4	2	10	6	0	5.00

Played in four matches: P. J. Franks 1*, 0; I. Riches 0, 1. Played in two matches: K. Afzaal 26, 0; G. W. Mike 0, 46; J. I. M. Smith 7; D. C. Lucas did not bat. Played in one match: A. Crozier 2; K. P. Evans 39*, 0; R. W. J. Howitt 56, 22; P. Johnson 0, 78; R. A. Pick 24; P. R. Pollard 133, 6; J. Hemmings and S. J. Musgrove did not bat.

Bowling Averages

	O	*M*	*R*	*W*	*BB*	*Avge*
R. T. Bates	279.1	77	732	32	7-76	22.87
M. P. Dowman	56.2	12	186	8	2-1	23.25
R. J. Chapman	151	18	587	19	5-45	30.89
J. E. Hindson	485.5	78	1,681	50	5-65	33.62
I. Riches	72.4	15	271	8	2-31	33.87
J. P. Hart	259	71	702	20	3-66	35.10
J. I. M. Smith	56	10	186	5	2-53	37.20
U. Afzaal	206	43	606	15	4-54	40.40
M. Broadhurst	116	20	443	10	3-36	44.30
P. J. Franks	103.5	17	371	8	4-56	46.37
M. N. Bowen	82.3	22	235	5	2-54	47.00
C. M. Tolley	146.2	27	445	9	2-36	49.44
G. W. Mike	59	13	206	4	2-36	51.50
D. B. Pennett	138.3	33	490	4	1-24	122.50

Also bowled: G. F. Archer 4–0–20–0; K. P. Evans 22–8–39–2; J. Hemmings 20–3–64–0; D. C. Lucas 40–4–177–2; R. A. Pick 8–1–24–1.

SOMERSET SECOND ELEVEN

Matches 17: Won – Derbyshire, Hampshire. Lost – Glamorgan, Middlesex, Northamptonshire, Sussex, Warwickshire, Yorkshire. Drawn – Durham, Essex, Gloucestershire, Kent, Lancashire, Leicestershire, Nottinghamshire, Surrey, Worcestershire.

Batting Averages

	M	I	NO	R	HS	100s	Avge
*A. N. Hayhurst	4	7	3	380	160*	1	95.00
†J. N. Batty	2	4	0	293	140	1	73.25
P. C. L. Holloway	14	20	6	979	131*	3	69.92
H. J. Morgan	6	11	2	585	200*	2	65.00
M. J. Church	2	4	0	216	142	1	54.00
M. E. Trescothick	7	12	1	537	144	1	48.81
J. C. Hallett	11	18	1	748	144	2	44.00
K. A. Parsons	6	10	2	341	91*	0	42.62
L. D. Sutton	9	14	1	407	96	0	31.30
B. R. F. Staunton	3	5	0	155	58	0	31.00
J. I. D. Kerr	12	17	2	461	115	1	30.73
S. C. Ecclestone	5	7	0	180	89	0	25.71
S. M. Trego	12	16	1	383	78	0	25.53
H. R. J. Trump	8	11	3	197	44	0	24.62
C. J. Barker	2	4	0	61	51	0	15.25
A. P. van Troost	8	6	1	70	37*	0	14.00
M. Dimond	14	16	8	105	24	0	13.12
I. E. Bishop	14	13	2	51	17	0	4.63
D. F. Lye	4	5	0	21	10	0	4.20
J. D. Batty	4	4	0	16	8	0	4.00

Played in three matches: A. Botha 9, 5, 56*, 30*. Played in two matches: P. J. G. Appleton 0, 2*; P. M. Roebuck 47*, 10*; K. J. Shine 0, 4*, 0, 13; J. Tucker 10*; P. M. Warren 11*, 16, 0; M. E. Watson 33*, 23; G. J. Williams 19, 23*, 30*, 15; P. J. Witherley did not bat. Played in one match: S. Ali 29, 0; A. D. Bairstow 6, 63; K. A. O. Barrett 8; N. R. Boulton 2, 2; N. A. Brett 0, 7; A. R. Caddick 0; B. L. Crosdale 38; J. R. Dalwood 11*, 7; R. C. Driver 0, 1; A. N. Edwards 12, 0; A. J. Fear 0, 22; R. Horrell 1, 48; M. J. M. Humphrey 2, 0*; A. J. Marsh 0, 0*; A. J. Pugh 28, 17; J. M. Smallridge 12; B. M. Wellington 2; J. G. Wyatt 38, 0; S. Lee, A. Sellek and R. J. Turner did not bat.

Bowling Averages

	O	M	R	W	BB	Avge
N. A. Brett	34	8	105	7	6-53	15.00
A. P. van Troost	155.1	33	479	23	5-25	20.82
P. J. Witherley	23	4	104	4	4-74	26.00
K. A. Parsons	59	18	147	5	3-34	29.40
K. J. Shine	49	5	245	7	5-132	35.00
H. R. J. Trump	262.4	77	792	22	4-14	36.00
I. E. Bishop	276.2	43	1,133	31	5-55	36.54
J. I. D. Kerr	192.5	27	753	19	4-51	39.63
J. D. Batty	137	32	369	8	3-68	46.12
S. M. Trego	116.4	21	419	9	3-32	46.55
M. Dimond	249	44	1,042	20	3-35	52.10

Also bowled: S. Ali 9–1–42–0; P. J. G. Appleton 41.5–13–98–2; K. A. O. Barrett 2–0–16–0; A. Botha 38–6–155–2; A. R. Caddick 18–5–49–3; M. J. Church 3–0–20–0; J. R. Dalwood 51–13–145–2; R. C. Driver 7–1–31–0; S. C. Ecclestone 13–2–46–2; A. N. Hayhurst 46.2–9–186–1; R. Horrell 17–3–125–1; M. J. M. Humphrey 12–1–61–1; S. Lee 17–5–50–1; D. F. Lye 3–0–12–0; H. J. Morgan 5–0–26–0; P. M. Roebuck 16–6–27–1; A. Sellek 14–2–57–0; J. M. Smallridge 5–1–26–0; B. R. F. Staunton 24–0–50–0; L. D. Sutton 6–0–31–0; M. E. Trescothick 30–8–86–1; J. Tucker 20–1–111–1; P. M. Warren 31–1–165–1; B. M. Wellington 14–1–47–2; G. J. Williams 3–1–4–0.

SURREY SECOND ELEVEN

Matches 17: Won – Glamorgan. Lost – Derbyshire, Durham, Kent, Lancashire, Leicestershire, Northamptonshire, Warwickshire, Yorkshire. Drawn – Essex, Gloucestershire, Hampshire, Middlesex, Nottinghamshire, Somerset, Sussex, Worcestershire.

Batting Averages

	M	I	NO	R	HS	100s	Avge
I. J. Ward	13	21	3	956	164*	2	53.11
G. J. Kennis	17	29	1	1,107	189	1	39.53
J. D. Ratcliffe	9	17	1	616	110	2	38.50
†J. A. Knott	17	29	6	827	89	0	35.95
A. W. Smith	10	17	2	523	114*	1	34.86
B. C. Hollioake	10	16	0	525	135	2	32.81
N. Shahid	7	12	0	380	136	1	31.66
D. M. Ward	6	7	0	192	78	0	27.42
†N. F. Sargeant	11	16	2	355	86	0	25.35
J. A. North	6	11	0	264	82	0	24.00
A. J. Tudor	14	18	1	406	134	1	23.88
A. Saleem	9	11	4	147	33	0	21.00
†S. N. de Silva	3	5	0	103	48	0	20.60
R. W. Nowell	16	25	7	325	49	0	18.05
*A. C. S. Pigott	5	7	3	61	18	0	15.25
S. G. Kenlock	5	7	0	89	28	0	12.71
J. M. de la Pena	13	14	6	82	26*	0	10.25
M. W. Patterson	6	6	2	20	16	0	5.00

Played in two matches: N. A. Brett 7, 2; A. D. Brown 57, 0, 43, 118*; G. Puckle 3*, 1, 4. Played in one match: †J. N. Batty 0, 46; J. E. Benjamin 9, 0; S. Carter 0*; A. Down 0; J. Powell 27, 16; M. R. Powell 21*; P. Skuse 52, 14; A. F. Haye did not bat.

Note: Owing to first-team calls, J. E. Benjamin was replaced by B. C. Hollioake in the match v Durham at The Oval, D. M. Ward and I. J. Ward were replaced by J. D. Ratcliffe and N. Shahid in the match v Sussex at Cheam and D. M. Ward was replaced by A. J. Tudor in the match v Essex at Saffron Walden.

Bowling Averages

	O	M	R	W	BB	Avge
J. E. Benjamin	10.3	2	28	5	5-28	5.60
J. D. Ratcliffe	82	22	280	16	4-14	17.50
N. Shahid	72	23	236	9	4-25	26.22
R. W. Nowell	531	146	1,476	53	5-44	27.84
J. A. North	60	5	307	11	4-44	27.90
G. J. Kennis	144.5	43	372	12	4-41	31.00
A. Saleem	194.1	32	778	22	4-48	35.36
A. W. Smith	175.2	34	603	17	4-49	35.47
B. C. Hollioake	149	42	466	13	3-48	35.84
M. W. Patterson	123.2	19	479	12	3-63	39.91
A. J. Tudor	150.3	26	504	12	3-39	42.00
I. J. Ward	107	27	314	7	2-33	44.85
S. G. Kenlock	77	14	299	6	3-85	49.83
J. M. de la Pena	233.5	31	1,068	21	5-92	50.85

Also bowled: N. A. Brett 21.4–5–75–0; A. D. Brown 1–0–1–0; S. Carter 15–3–87–1; A. F. Haye 8–1–42–0; J. A. Knott 68–10–299–3; A. C. S. Pigott 57.4–11–181–3; M. R. Powell 22–4–53–1; G. Puckle 40–8–100–2; P. Skuse 8–1–24–0; D. M. Ward 4–1–9–0.

SUSSEX SECOND ELEVEN

Matches 17: Won – Somerset, Worcestershire. Lost – Leicestershire, Northamptonshire, Warwickshire. Drawn – Derbyshire, Durham, Essex, Glamorgan, Gloucestershire, Hampshire, Kent, Lancashire, Middlesex, Nottinghamshire, Surrey, Yorkshire.

Batting Averages

	M	*I*	*NO*	*R*	*HS*	*100s*	*Avge*
M. T. E. Peirce	5	10	1	449	90*	0	49.88
K. Newell	7	12	1	522	168	1	47.45
T. A. Radford	14	26	4	1,038	136*	4	47.18
*J. W. Hall	7	14	1	569	136	2	43.76
M. Newell	16	29	2	825	138	1	30.55
R. K. Rao	13	23	0	611	108	1	26.56
R. G. Halsall	3	5	0	128	76	0	25.60
A. D. Edwards	13	19	3	387	71	0	24.18
*†S. Humphries	17	28	4	553	71	0	23.04
J. J. Bates	16	22	7	286	51*	0	19.06
R. S. C. Martin-Jenkins	3	6	1	93	28*	0	18.60
J. P. Pyemont	2	4	0	65	19	0	16.25
K. Greenfield	3	5	0	72	61	0	14.40
*N. C. Phillips	11	18	1	231	83	0	13.58
G. B. Horan	5	6	0	79	36	0	13.16
R. J. Kirtley	11	13	6	76	24*	0	10.85
J. D. Lewry	2	3	0	23	12	0	7.66
G. R. Haywood	3	6	0	45	13	0	7.50
A. Cole	2	4	2	15	9*	0	7.50

Played in five matches: M. R. Strong 6. Played in three matches: T. Bloomfield 0, 11, 12*; C. E. Waller 13, 0; G. P. McMillan did not bat. Played in two matches: D. A. Alderman 15*, 9*, 7*; S. Ali 2, 8, 53*; P. G. Hudson 27, 11*, 16, 11*; N. J. Lenham 37, 1, 151*, 9; M. J. O'Sullivan 9*, 8*; R. C. Thelwell 53, 3, 10; N. J. Wilton 0, 0. Played in one match: J. D. Chaplin 7; J. C. Forrest 9; E. S. H. Giddins 2*; B. J. Kempster 13; J. R. Morgan 2; J. M. Palmer 10*; D. J. Thompson 0, 6*.

Note: In the match v Essex at Eastbourne E. S. H. Giddins, called up for a first-team match, was replaced by K. Newell.

Bowling Averages

	O	*M*	*R*	*W*	*BB*	*Avge*
J. D. Chaplin	21	6	61	4	3-47	15.25
J. D. Lewry	63.2	12	153	7	5-34	21.85
R. J. Kirtley	316.4	39	884	38	5-65	23.26
K. Newell	96.4	26	219	9	2-9	24.33
M. R. Strong	133	23	473	19	7-68	24.89
J. J. Bates	468	117	1,309	46	5-14	28.45
R. S. C. Martin-Jenkins	64.5	10	173	6	3-55	28.83
N. C. Phillips	409.5	138	936	32	5-58	29.25
A. D. Edwards	290.4	60	968	26	7-83	37.23
R. K. Rao	112.4	29	424	6	1-18	70.66

Also bowled: D. A. Alderman 45–15–120–3; S. Ali 28–3–127–1; T. Bloomfield 40–1–155–1; A. Cole 27–6–89–2; E. S. H. Giddins 18–2–48–1; R. G. Halsall 15–0–104–0; G. R. Haywood 27–7–81–2; G. B. Horan 32–4–132–2; P. G. Hudson 2–0–14–1; B. J. Kempster 11.5–1–61–0; N. J. Lenham 15–2–42–1; G. P. McMillan 42–4–229–1; J. R. Morgan 12–2–45–0; M. J. O'Sullivan 35–9–128–1; J. M. Palmer 9–0–38–2; M. T. E. Peirce 25–6–77–1; R. C. Thelwell 10–0–42–0; D. J. Thompson 24–7–78–2.

WARWICKSHIRE SECOND ELEVEN

Matches 17: Won – Durham, Essex, Hampshire, Leicestershire, Nottinghamshire, Somerset, Surrey, Sussex, Worcestershire, Yorkshire. Lost – Derbyshire, Glamorgan, Kent, Lancashire. Drawn – Gloucestershire, Middlesex, Northamptonshire.

Batting Averages

	M	I	NO	R	HS	100s	Avge
*M. J. Powell	14	24	3	1,103	210	4	52.52
*W. G. Khan	7	12	1	552	179	2	50.18
D. J. Lovell	4	5	1	185	105*	1	46.25
M. A. Wagh	9	16	3	562	115*	1	43.23
M. D. Edmond	13	18	6	468	72*	0	39.00
†T. Frost	17	25	8	661	100	1	38.88
A. Singh	9	16	1	562	80	0	37.46
M. Burns	8	13	0	461	127	1	35.46
M. A. Sheikh	16	25	2	678	102	1	29.47
C. R. Howell	5	8	0	181	83	0	22.62
N. V. Prabhu	11	16	3	284	65	0	21.84
*G. Welch	9	13	1	256	71	0	21.33
S. McDonald	16	18	5	191	50*	0	14.69
D. A. T. Dalton	5	5	1	48	19	0	12.00
D. A. Altree	11	11	1	40	10	0	4.00

Played in eight matches: R. N. Abberley 0*, 11*, 12, 0, 22*. Played in three matches: A. Hafeez 52*, 46*, 22, 5, 15*; P. A. Smith 0, 43, 4; G. R. Thorpe 1; S. Vestergaard 6. Played in two matches: D. J. Angove 3, 0*; T. E. Hemmings 9, 7; K. Shah 0, 11, 2*. Played in one match: M. A. V. Bell 53, 2*; R. G. East 0; A. F. Giles 0; M. V. Humphrey 24, 32; D. R. Maynard 27*; D. P. Ostler 92; M. T. Pidgeon 6; K. J. Piper 99; J. Troughton 22; T. A. Munton and G. J. Williams did not bat.

Note; Owing to first-team calls, W. G. Khan was replaced by P. A. Smith in the match v Sussex at Stratford-upon-Avon, T. A. Munton was replaced by R. N. Abberley in the match v Durham at Chester-le-Street, and A. Singh and G. Welch were replaced by R. N. Abberley and N. V. Prabhu in the match v Northamptonshire at Northampton.

Bowling Averages

	O	M	R	W	BB	Avge
P. A. Smith	56.3	15	154	15	6-28	10.26
D. A. Altree	316.3	80	943	62	8-58	15.20
M. D. Edmond	288.3	70	974	53	6-21	18.37
S. Vestergaard	51	8	141	7	2-16	20.14
G. J. Williams	32.5	11	100	4	3-70	25.00
W. G. Khan	29	6	103	4	2-42	25.75
G. Welch	209.1	46	817	30	5-26	27.23
S. McDonald	326.5	77	1,012	26	5-115	38.92
M. A. Sheikh	239.3	77	697	17	2-29	41.00
D. A. T. Dalton	65	13	213	5	3-40	42.60
M. A. Wagh	109.1	14	429	10	3-19	42.90

Also bowled: D. J. Angove 23–3–106–1; M. A. V. Bell 31.5–6–112–2; M. Burns 28.3–2–120–1; R. G. East 24–5–88–1; A. F. Giles 19–4–32–0; T. E. Hemmings 34.1–1–147–3; C. R. Howell 4–0–23–0; D. J. Lovell 4–0–29–0; D. R. Maynard 14–5–37–3; T. A. Munton 18–5–58–1; M. T. Pidgeon 10–2–29–0; M. J. Powell 42–14–136–3; N. V. Prabhu 26–6–97–3; K. Shah 17–1–165–3; A. Singh 1–0–2–1; G. R. Thorpe 16–1–55–0; J. Troughton 8–1–23–0.

WORCESTERSHIRE SECOND ELEVEN

Matches 17: Won – Essex, Glamorgan, Yorkshire. Lost – Hampshire, Middlesex, Sussex, Warwickshire. Drawn – Derbyshire, Durham, Gloucestershire, Kent, Lancashire, Leicestershire, Northamptonshire, Nottinghamshire, Somerset, Surrey.

Batting Averages

	M	*I*	*NO*	*R*	*HS*	*100s*	*Avge*
V. S. Solanki	6	11	1	584	156	2	58.40
P. P. Luxon	3	6	1	216	100	1	43.20
†I. Dawood	17	27	4	854	143*	1	37.13
*D. A. Leatherdale	7	12	1	381	62	0	34.63
M. J. Church	11	20	0	650	124	2	32.50
P. A. Thomas	12	16	6	294	41	0	29.40
J. T. Ralph	13	21	0	604	100	1	28.76
*D. B. D'Oliveira	14	16	4	345	62	0	28.75
M. Diwan	14	26	3	540	64*	0	23.47
R. J. Chapman	4	4	0	87	27	0	21.75
J. E. Brinkley	6	9	2	122	55*	0	17.42
M. Amjad	13	19	6	218	30	0	16.76
S. J. Price	5	9	0	141	41	0	15.66
M. M. Mirza	5	5	3	31	24*	0	15.50
M. J. Rawnsley	15	19	4	218	42*	0	14.53
S. W. K. Ellis	3	5	1	56	21	0	14.00
C. P. Harrison	7	14	1	181	55	0	13.92
B. E. A. Preece	10	14	3	59	26*	0	5.36

Played in three matches: K. Marc 0, 2*, 0, 16. Played in two matches: G. D. Franklin 11, 44*; C. J. Schofield 54*, 28*, 76, 25; Z. A. Sher 1, 0; E. J. Wilson 91, 52, 86, 96*; N. D. Slade did not bat. Played in one match: J. A. Carruthers 0, 0; G. R. Haynes 109, 42; D. M. Lane 0, 24; C. G. Mason 1, 27; Ravi Nagra 12, 15; S. Patel 45, 51*; S. A. Richardson 14, 2; A. Sheriyar 2, 5; C. E. Shreck 1, 1; S. A. Twigg 11, 27*; R. C. Williams 8, 17; D. L. Worrad 7*.

Note: Owing to first-team calls, P. A. Thomas was replaced by J. E. Brinkley in the match v Middlesex at Uxbridge and D. A. Leatherdale and S. W. K. Ellis were replaced by C. J. Schofield and Z. A. Sher in the match v Essex at Chelmsford.

Bowling Averages

	O	*M*	*R*	*W*	*BB*	*Avge*
C. G. Mason	34	14	54	5	4-37	10.80
Z. A. Sher	44	7	135	6	3-36	22.50
R. J. Chapman	92.2	17	319	14	3-49	22.78
D. A. Leatherdale	88	22	252	11	5-23	22.90
J. T. Ralph	26.1	4	147	6	4-56	24.50
S. W. K. Ellis	54.5	10	224	9	4-110	24.88
M. J. Church	43	7	161	6	4-34	26.83
M. J. Rawnsley	396.2	91	1,136	42	7-56	27.04
K. Marc	77.4	12	279	10	3-26	27.90
M. Amjad	196.5	30	714	24	7-71	29.75
J. E. Brinkley	112.4	19	360	12	5-37	30.00
M. M. Mirza	143.1	27	529	15	4-85	35.26
B. E. A. Preece	234.3	42	923	24	5-59	38.45
V. S. Solanki	63.3	12	222	4	1-4	55.50
P. A. Thomas	222	41	794	13	4-64	61.07

Also bowled: J. A. Carruthers 30–6–131–2; D. M. Lane 10–3–37–0; S. Patel 15–3–43–1; A. Sheriyar 20–1–83–3; C. E. Shreck 17–6–53–1; N. D. Slade 34–17–53–1; R. C. Williams 24–1–126–3; D. L. Worrad 13–1–68–1.

YORKSHIRE SECOND ELEVEN

Matches 17: Won – Durham, Essex, Hampshire, Nottinghamshire, Somerset, Surrey. Lost – Lancashire, Warwickshire, Worcestershire. Drawn – Derbyshire, Glamorgan, Gloucestershire, Kent, Leicestershire, Middlesex, Northamptonshire, Sussex.

Batting Averages

	M	*I*	*NO*	*R*	*HS*	*100s*	*Avge*
B. Parker	17	31	9	1,481	173	3	67.31
R. Robinson	8	15	4	585	122	2	53.18
*R. A. Kettleborough	12	22	2	1,001	192*	2	50.05
N. G. Russell	4	7	2	169	64*	0	33.80
M. J. Wood	13	23	2	701	144*	2	33.38
†C. A. Chapman	15	27	1	851	88	0	32.73
C. J. Schofield	13	23	2	636	74	0	30.28
A. G. Wharf	10	15	1	391	127	1	27.92
A. C. Morris	5	9	0	250	58	0	27.77
I. D. Fisher	14	16	7	194	50	0	21.55
G. J. Batty	12	16	1	277	51	0	18.46
J. W. Hood	10	16	2	233	41	0	16.64
M. J. Hoggard	12	12	9	49	14*	0	16.33
J. D. Middlebrook	6	9	0	138	39	0	15.33
G. M. Hamilton	10	13	1	154	45	0	12.83
M. A. Robinson	13	9	2	20	11	0	2.85

Played in four matches: R. J. Sidebottom 1*, 8, 0, 1. Played in three matches: P. M. Hutchison 4, 3, 0. Played in one match: C. D. J. Bailey 20*; A. McGrath 0, 81; Z. C. Morris 1; R. Wilkinson 21*, 44; †S. Guy, †M. Thewlis and R. C. Towler did not bat.

Note: In the match v Hampshire at Marske-by-Sea M. J. Hoggard, called up for an Under-19 unofficial Test, was replaced by R. J. Sidebottom.

Bowling Averages

	O	*M*	*R*	*W*	*BB*	*Avge*
A. G. Wharf	201.4	34	800	27	5-67	29.62
G. M. Hamilton	255.1	55	839	26	4-47	32.26
M. A. Robinson	259.5	57	840	26	4-60	32.30
J. D. Middlebrook	159	28	513	15	5-63	34.20
R. J. Sidebottom	53	13	179	5	3-63	35.80
I. D. Fisher	349.5	73	1,165	31	6-99	37.58
G. J. Batty	312.3	62	1,041	27	4-22	38.55
J. W. Hood	66	11	247	6	3-45	41.16
M. J. Hoggard	220.5	33	908	17	4-42	53.41

Also bowled: C. D. J. Bailey 16–3–40–2; P. M. Hutchison 23–4–75–2; R. A. Kettleborough 4–1–18–0; A. McGrath 9–2–37–0; A. C. Morris 32–9–121–3; Z. C. Morris 23–7–63–1; N. G. Russell 5–1–5–1; C. J. Schofield 10–1–22–1; R. C. Towler 24–4–58–3; R. Wilkinson 9–1–40–0.

SECOND ELEVEN CHAMPIONS

1959	Gloucestershire	1972	Nottinghamshire	1985	Nottinghamshire
1960	Northamptonshire	1973	Essex	1986	Lancashire
1961	Kent	1974	Middlesex	1987	Kent / Yorkshire
1962	Worcestershire	1975	Surrey	1988	Surrey
1963	Worcestershire	1976	Kent	1989	Middlesex
1964	Lancashire	1977	Yorkshire	1990	Sussex
1965	Glamorgan	1978	Sussex	1991	Yorkshire
1966	Surrey	1979	Warwickshire	1992	Surrey
1967	Hampshire	1980	Glamorgan	1993	Middlesex
1968	Surrey	1981	Hampshire	1994	Somerset
1969	Kent	1982	Worcestershire	1995	Hampshire
1970	Kent	1983	Leicestershire	1996	Warwickshire
1971	Hampshire	1984	Yorkshire		

BAIN HOGG TROPHY, 1996

Counties are restricted to players qualified for England and for competitive county cricket, only two of whom may be capped players. The matches are of 55 overs per side.

North Zone	*P*	*W*	*L*	*NR*	*Points*	*Net run-rate*
Durham	8	6	2	0	12	16.88
Yorkshire	8	5	3	0	10	6.22
Nottinghamshire	8	4	4	0	8	2.81
Lancashire	8	3	5	0	6	−14.16
Derbyshire	8	2	6	0	4	−12.85

Central Zone	*P*	*W*	*L*	*NR*	*Points*	*Net run-rate*
Leicestershire	8	5	2	1	11	17.11
Northamptonshire	8	5	3	0	10	6.29
Middlesex	8	4	4	0	8	−17.50
Warwickshire	8	3	4	1	7	−0.70
Minor Counties	8	1	5	2	4	−7.03

South-West Zone	*P*	*W*	*L*	*NR*	*Points*	*Net run-rate*
Worcestershire	8	5	2	1	11	4.19
Hampshire	8	5	2	1	11	2.59
Gloucestershire	8	4	3	1	9	1.34
Glamorgan	8	3	4	1	7	3.23
Somerset	8	1	7	0	2	−10.59

South-East Zone	*P*	*W*	*L*	*NR*	*Points*	*Net run-rate*
Kent	8	6	1	1	13	11.17
Surrey	8	5	3	0	10	15.89
Essex	8	4	4	0	8	−5.87
Sussex	8	4	4	0	8	−8.66
MCC Young Cricketers	8	0	7	1	1	−11.67

SEMI-FINALS

At Hinckley, August 15. Leicestershire won by 155 runs. Toss: Worcestershire. Leicestershire 305 for seven (55 overs) (D. I. Stevens 31, P. E. Robinson 91 not out, C. C. Remy 53, G. I. Macmillan 39, D. Williamson 38 not out; B. E. A. Preece three for 83); Worcestershire 150 (37.2 overs) (D. A. Leatherdale 43, I. Dawood 30).

At Darlington, August 16. Durham won by one wicket. Toss: Kent. Kent 211 (54 overs) (N. R. Taylor 72; N. Killeen three for 28); Durham 213 for nine (54.5 overs) (D. A. Blenkiron 58, J. Boiling 34; B. J. Phillips five for 32).

FINAL

LEICESTERSHIRE v DURHAM

At Leicester, September 9. Leicestershire won by 46 runs. Toss: Leicestershire.
Man of the Match: I. J. Sutcliffe.

Leicestershire

D. I. Stevens b Cox	41	T. J. Mason not out	16
I. J. Sutcliffe c Longley b Boiling	61	D. Williamson run out	14
J. M. Dakin c Collingwood b Blenkiron	33	J. Ormond b Walker	0
G. I. Macmillan c Cox b Blenkiron	9	L-b 6, w 5	11
C. C. Remy c Killeen b Blenkiron	18		—
V. P. Clarke c and b Cox	21	1/96 2/122 3/147 (53.3 overs)	238
*P. E. Robinson c Hughes b Blenkiron	3	4/158 5/186 6/193	
†P. Whitticase b Walker	11	7/197 8/216 9/237	

Bowling: Killeen 9–0–41–0; Campbell 2–0–13–0; Walker 10.3–1–35–2; Boiling 11–0–42–1; Cox 11–1–57–2; Blenkiron 9–0–40–4; Hughes 1–0–4–0.

Durham

*J. I. Longley lbw b Dakin	8	J. Boiling run out	3
R. M. S. Weston c Dakin b Ormond	78	A. Walker not out	5
P. D. Collingwood b Ormond	4	C. L. Campbell b Ormond	0
D. A. Blenkiron b Mason	32	B 1, l-b 9, w 7	17
Q. J. Hughes b Ormond	24		—
†C. W. Scott c and b Macmillan	4	1/10 2/22 3/87 (52 overs)	192
D. M. Cox b Macmillan	2	4/115 5/119 6/155	
N. Killeen c Ormond b Macmillan	15	7/169 8/174 9/192	

Bowling: Ormond 9–0–20–4; Dakin 6–1–23–1; Mason 11–1–27–1; Williamson 6–2–18–0; Macmillan 11–0–49–3; Remy 9–0–45–0.

Umpires: H. D. Bird and G. I. Burgess.

WINNERS 1986-96

1986	Northamptonshire	1990	Lancashire	1994	Yorkshire
1987	Derbyshire	1991	Nottinghamshire	1995	Leicestershire
1988	Yorkshire	1992	Surrey	1996	Leicestershire
1989	Middlesex	1993	Leicestershire		

UMPIRES FOR 1997

FIRST-CLASS UMPIRES

J. C. Balderstone, H. D. Bird, J. D. Bond, G. I. Burgess, A. Clarkson, D. J. Constant, B. Dudleston, J. H. Hampshire, J. H. Harris, J. W. Holder, V. A. Holder, T. E. Jesty, A. A. Jones, R. Julian, M. J. Kitchen, B. Leadbeater, B. J. Meyer, K. E. Palmer, R. Palmer, N. T. Plews, G. Sharp, D. R. Shepherd, J. F. Steele, R. A. White, A. G. T. Whitehead and P. Willey. *Reserves:* P. Adams, N. G. Cowley, M. J. Harris, J. W. Lloyds, K. J. Lyons and M. K. Reed.

MINOR COUNTIES UMPIRES

P. Adams, K. Bray, P. Brown, A. R. Bundy, D. L. Burden, K. Coburn, M. A. Johnson, C. S. Kelly, S. W. Kuhlmann, R. E. Lawson, D. Lea, G. Lowden, G. I. McLean, M. P. Moran, D. Norton, C. T. Puckett, G. P. Randall-Johnson, J. G. Reed, M. K. Reed, K. S. Shenton, W. E. Smith, C. Stone, J. M. Tythcott, B. H. Willey, T. G. Wilson and R. Wood. *Reserves:* N. Bainton, S. F. Bishopp, S. P. Chitty, P. D. Clubb, D. R. M. Crowson, M. Dixon, C. J. Edwards, J. H. Evans, A. J. Hardy, J. Ilott, J. H. James, P. W. Kingston-Davey, T. R. Riley, G. Ripley, R. M. Sutton, K. J. Timpson and D. J. Warnford.

CAREER FIGURES

Players not expected to appear in county cricket in 1997

BATTING

	M	I	NO	R	HS	100s	Avge	1,000r/ season
M. Amjad	1	2	0	8	7	0	4.00	0
P. Bainbridge	324	539	73	15,707	169	24	33.70	9
S. R. Barwick	212	203	74	873	30	0	6.76	0
S. J. Base	133	170	35	1,526	58	0	11.30	0
J. D. Batty	84	97	25	1,149	51	0	15.95	0
W. K. M. Benjamin	171	213	36	3,985	117	2	22.51	0
M. R. Benson	292	491	34	18,387	257	48	40.23	11
S. D. Birbeck	7	9	2	120	75*	0	17.14	0
D. J. P. Boden	8	5	0	13	5	0	2.60	0
L. J. Botham	3	3	0	31	30	0	10.33	0
N. E. Briers	381	628	61	18,726	201*	31	33.02	11
M. Broadhurst	6	3	0	7	6	0	2.33	0
J. D. Carr	212	331	51	10,895	261*	24	38.91	5
R. J. Chapman	14	16	3	114	25	0	8.76	0
J. H. Childs	381	359	173	1,690	43	0	9.08	0
M. J. Church	14	25	1	471	152	1	19.62	0
A. J. Dalton	13	23	3	426	51*	0	21.30	0
J. M. de la Pena	6	7	5	10	7*	0	5.00	0
N. A. Derbyshire	5	5	1	52	17	0	13.00	0
M. A. Feltham	160	197	48	3,199	101	1	21.46	0
F. A. Griffith	43	63	9	1,087	81	0	20.12	0
J. W. Hall	97	175	10	4,997	140*	6	30.28	2
J. C. Hallett	18	19	4	349	111*	1	23.26	0
A. N. Hayhurst	164	263	34	7,819	172*	14	34.14	3
A. P. Igglesden	145	158	59	862	41	0	8.70	0
N. M. Kendrick	81	106	30	1,206	59	0	15,86	0
†G. J. Kersey	53	82	14	1,578	83	0	23.20	0
A. J. Lamb	467	772	108	32,502	294	89	48.94	13
R. P. Lefebvre	77	89	16	1,494	100	1	20.46	0
J. I. Longley	35	62	3	1,381	110	2	23.40	0
N. A. Mallender	345	396	122	4,709	100*	1	17.18	0
G. W. Mike	43	66	12	1,019	66*	0	18.87	0
R. S. M. Morris	37	67	4	1,830	174	3	29.04	0
D. B. Pennett	31	31	11	196	50	0	9.80	0
A. C. S. Pigott	260	317	66	4,841	104*	1	19.28	0
J. T. Ralph	1	2	0	0	0	0	0.00	0
D. A. Reeve	241	322	77	8,541	202*	7	34.86	2
C. C. Remy	22	29	3	480	60	0	18.46	0
A. R. Roberts	61	83	18	1,173	62	0	18.04	0
M. A. Robinson	155	161	68	312	23	0	3.35	0
N. F. Sargeant	52	67	11	786	49	0	14.03	0
C. J. Schofield	1	1	0	25	25	0	25.00	0
C. W. Scott	129	176	31	3,228	108	2	22.26	0
A. W. Smith	38	59	7	1,379	202*	1	26.51	0
P. A. Smith	221	351	42	8,173	140	4	26.44	2
V. P. Terry	292	493	45	16,427	190	38	36.66	11
D. M. Ward	155	244	34	8,078	294*	16	38.46	2
A. E. Warner	200	272	52	3,763	95*	0	17.10	0
C. M. Wells	318	510	78	14,289	203	24	33.07	6
R. D. Wild	1	–	–	–	–	–	–	–
J. R. Wileman	12	21	6	447	109	1	29.80	0
J. R. A. Williams	1	2	0	6	6	0	3.00	0

* *Signifies not out.* † *Died January 1, 1997.*

BOWLING AND FIELDING

	R	*W*	*BB*	*Avge*	*5W/i*	*10W/m*	*Ct/St*
M. Amjad	25	0	–	–	–	–	0
P. Bainbridge	13,094	349	8-53	37.51	10	0	149
S. R. Barwick	16,186	456	8-42	35.49	10	1	47
S. J. Base	11,363	388	7-60	29.28	16	1	60
J. D. Batty	7,441	179	6-48	41.56	4	0	32
W. K. M. Benjamin	12,358	476	7-54	25.96	23	2	95
M. R. Benson	493	5	2-55	98.60	–	–	140
S. D. Birbeck	428	10	3-88	42.80	–	–	2
D. J. P. Boden	611	15	4-11	40.73	–	–	5
L. J. Botham	268	8	5-67	33.50	1	0	2
N. E. Briers	988	32	4-29	30.87	–	–	152
M. Broadhurst	291	7	3-61	41.57	–	–	1
J. D. Carr	2,939	68	6-61	43.22	3	0	260
R. J. Chapman	1,224	23	4-109	53.21	–	–	3
J. H. Childs	30,600	1,028	9-56	29.76	52	8	116
M. J. Church	163	9	4-50	18.11	–	–	8
A. J. Dalton	–	–	–	–	–	–	9
J. M. de la Pena	502	13	4-77	38.61	–	–	0
N. A. Derbyshire	303	5	1-18	60.60	–	–	2
M. A. Feltham	12,279	388	6-41	31.64	8	0	67
F. A. Griffith	2,571	73	4-33	35.21	–	–	28
J. W. Hall	14	0	–	–	–	–	47
J. C. Hallett	1,342	31	4-59	43.29	–	–	7
A. Hayhurst	4,961	109	4-27	45.51	–	–	53
A. P. Igglesden	12,748	483	7-28	26.39	23	4	37
N. M. Kendrick	6,891	179	7-115	38.49	6	1	58
G. J. Kersey	–	–	–	–	–	–	169/12
A. J. Lamb	199	8	2-29	24.87	–	–	371
R. P. Lefebvre	5,399	149	6-45	36.23	3	0	36
J. I. Longley	47	0	–	–	–	–	18
N. A. Mallender	24,654	937	7-27	26.31	36	5	111
G. W. Mike	3,420	87	5-44	39.31	2	0	13
R. S. M. Morris	1	0	–	–	–	–	43
D. B. Pennett	2,697	60	5-36	44.95	1	0	7
A. C. S. Pigott	20,831	672	7-74	30.99	26	2	121
J. T. Ralph	–	–	–	–	–	–	1
D. A. Reeve	12,232	456	7-37	26.82	8	0	200
C. C. Remy	1,051	19	4-63	55.31	–	–	7
A. R. Roberts	4,829	107	6-72	45.13	1	0	23
M. A. Robinson	12,059	369	9-37	32.68	7	2	31
N. F. Sargeant	88	1	1-88	88.00	–	–	120/16
C. J. Schofield	–	–	–	–	–	–	0
C. W. Scott	40	0	–	–	–	–	283/17
A. W. Smith	2,435	43	5-103	56.62	1	0	12
P. A. Smith	10,109	283	6-91	35.72	7	0	60
V. P. Terry	58	0	–	–	–	–	332
D. M. Ward	113	2	2-66	56.50	–	–	120/3
A. E. Warner	13,399	426	6-21	31.45	8	1	46
C. M. Wells	14,748	428	7-42	34.45	7	0	111
R. D. Wild	62	1	1-62	62.00	–	–	0
J. R. Wileman	217	4	2-33	54.25	–	–	9
J. R. A. Williams	–	–	–	–	–	–	0

THE LANCASHIRE LEAGUES, 1996

By CHRIS ASPIN

Electrifying performances by Allan Donald, the South African fast bowler, dominated the Lancashire League in 1996 and, in a season decided on the final afternoon, he helped Rishton retain their title, a point ahead of East Lancashire.

If the ground was slippery, Donald bowled within himself, but when conditions were right, he was unplayable. One return of seven for three helped to demolish Accrington for 18 (nine extras; six ducks), and in another fearsome spell, he claimed seven Haslingden wickets for 18 in 6.3 overs, hitting the stumps every time. Haslingden made 31, including nine extras.

Donald finished the season with 106 wickets at 10.75, yet he did not have it all his own way. Against Bacup, he met his match in their West Indian professional Roger Harper, who hammered an unbeaten 162. Donald might also remember the return fixture with Haslingden, who batted first and made 104. The game seemed to be finished when Rishton reached 92 for two, but eight wickets then fell for 11 runs, the last five without addition to the total. Michael Tracy did the hat-trick and Haslingden's own pro, Brad McNamara, took seven for 25.

Among the batsmen, two major records were broken by the Colne pro, Ben Johnson of South Australia. He amassed 1,718 runs at 78.09 to beat the 1,621 for Rishton by Peter Sleep in 1991, and was the first man to hit eight centuries. Graham Knowles, Haslingden's 22-year-old opening batsman, scored an unbeaten 183, containing seven sixes and 18 fours, at Rawtenstall, the highest individual innings since the league adopted the limited-overs game in 1971. Haslingden reached 301 for one, with Knowles sharing 150-run partnerships with Michael Ingham and McNamara. The previous best was 179 by Collis King, the West Indian, for Colne against Todmorden in 1982.

Ramsbottom's New Zealand professional Chris Harris, who had topped both sets of averages in 1995, made his presence felt again with four wickets in four balls (all close catches) against Enfield. And in the Jennings Worsley Cup Final at Bacup, Harris turned the match by taking a spectacular diving catch in the deep to dismiss Harper. Ramsbottom, who had scored only 160 themselves, scraped home by 12 runs for their first cup win since 1957.

Batsmen had a fruitful season in the Central Lancashire League, with ten professionals and three amateurs each scoring over 1,000. The bowlers, on the other hand, had to toil for their wickets, and only the South African Alan Badenhorst (Heywood) and the Queenslander Michael Warden (Stand) topped 100. Littleborough, with a 12-point lead over Norden, won the championship for the 16th time, and Milnrow beat Middleton to achieve their first Lees Wood Cup success since 1989.

Most unusually, two amateurs – David Lees of Werneth and Dominic Ball of Ashton – achieved the best bowling averages, with 45 wickets at 12.86 and 73 at 13.94 respectively. Oldham's 43-year-old off-spinner Ian Shaw produced the best single performance, however, in a 103-run victory over Royton. Going for a return catch early on in his spell, Shaw broke the little finger of his bowling hand, but the injury did not stop him from taking all ten wickets for 20 in 12.5 overs. After 27 seasons of competing in the CLL, he richly deserved his success.

Gus Logie, the former Test player, left Unsworth at the end of June in order to coach the West Indies Under-19 side. This upset the league management committee, who found the reason for his departure unacceptable and refused to allow the club to engage another pro for the rest of the season. They also banned Logie for three years for breaking his contract.

On a more positive note, both league committees got together and laid out the schedule for a new knockout competition that will involve all 30 clubs in 1997. But the comprehensive overhaul of the whole Lancashire League system, recommended in 1995 by the authorities at Old Trafford, went on hold. Stern opposition from local clubs has already forced the proposed ban on professionals to be dropped; other sticking points included plans for the removal of Sunday matches from the calendar and the abolition of the Lancashire League rule insisting that the amateurs have some local connection. The Lancashire Premier League was still scheduled to start in 1998; many clubs were torn between tradition and ambition, and remained uncertain whether to join or not.

MARSDEN LANCASHIRE LEAGUE

	P	*W*	*L*	*NR*	*Bonus Pts*	*Pts*	*Professional*	*Runs*	*Avge*	*Wkts*	*Avge*
Rishton	26	17	7	2	15	87	A. A. Donald	389	27.78	106	10.75
East Lancs.	26	18	7	1	12	86	W. F. Stelling	589	26.77	75	14.54
Ramsbottom	26	17	7	2	10	82	C. Z. Harris	686	57.16	61	18.36
Haslingden	26	14	9	2	8	70*	B. E. McNamara	1,081	63.58	73	15.83
Colne	26	15	11	0	9	69	B. A. Johnson	1,718	78.09	62	22.08
Lowerhouse	26	14	10	2	8	68	S. L. Flegler	838	39.90	55	19.10
Todmorden	26	14	11	1	9	67	D. J. Marsh	1,000	58.82	68	15.66
Nelson	26	13	12	1	7	61	J. C. Scuderi	1,175	58.75	55	16.23
Bacup	26	12	12	2	5	57	R. A. Harper	996	55.33	67	17.83
Enfield	26	10	13	2	7	53*	F. A. Rose	503	20.95	87	16.40
Church	26	10	16	0	6	46	M. P. Mott	1,097	57.73	43	23.32
Burnley	26	7	17	2	3	35	R. P. Singh	586	30.84	40	25.52
Rawtenstall	26	6	19	1	5	31	‡G. J. Whittall	635	37.35	51	24.45
Accrington	26	5	21	0	3	23	C. Grainger	828	34.50	38	24.97

Notes: Four points awarded for a win; two points for a no-result; one point for bowling out the opposition in a completed match.

* Includes two points for a tie.
‡ Did not play full season.

CENTRAL LANCASHIRE LEAGUE

	P	*OW*	*LW*	*L*	*D*	*Pts*	*Professional*	*Runs*	*Avge*	*Wkts*	*Avge*
Littleborough	30	9	12	5	4	103†	H. A. G. Anthony	732	31.82	78	17.47
Norden	30	11	7	8	4	91	R. P. Snell	1,302	68.52	41	28.82
Walsden	30	13	2	8	7	89†	P. M. Hutchison	1,225	51.04	85	14.29
Milnrow	30	10	7	12	1	80	J. D. Fitton	1,727	61.67	59	23.27
Oldham	30	9	6	11	4	79†	J. Sylvester	775	26.72	49	20.32
Werneth	30	8	7	10	5	79*	‡C. Stuart	59	6.55	43	19.23
Middleton	30	8	6	13	3	70	K. Williams	1,162	43.03	55	19.74
Rochdale	30	8	6	14	2	68	M. J. R. Rindel	1,028	42.83	67	15.56
Stand	30	7	5	13	5	67†	M. Warden	862	37.47	103	14.55
Stockport	30	7	6	14	3	65	Mujahid Jamshed	1,049	47.68	23	21.26
Ashton	30	11	1	16	2	63	A. G. Lawson	1,046	41.84	1	111.00
Radcliffe	30	3	10	15	2	60*	R. C. Haynes	1,550	59.61	73	29.34
Unsworth	30	4	7	14	5	59*	‡A. L. Logie	1,016	59.76	37	21.13
Royton	30	8	2	17	3	55*	R. P. Campbell	1,437	47.90	53	26.00
Heywood	30	6	2	19	3	44	A. Badenhorst	683	22.76	105	17.03
Crompton	30	1	3	23	3	23	Zafar Iqbal	802	33.41	54	31.03

Notes: Five points awarded for an outright win; four points for a limited win; two points for a draw. A team achieves an outright win by bowling out the opposition. CLL averages include cup games.

* Includes three points for a tie.
† Includes six points for two ties.
‡ Did not play full season.

LEAGUE CRICKET IN ENGLAND AND WALES IN 1996

By GEOFFREY DEAN

After bitter disappointment at the end of the 1995 season – when they were almost certainly deprived of the Birmingham League title by the umpires' decision to come off for bad light – Walsall had a year to end all years. Their victory at Lord's in the Abbot Ale Club Championship final was followed the next day by another that gave them a League and Cup double. No Birmingham League side had ever managed such a feat, and their second and third teams won their divisions too. Walsall lost their first game – to local rivals and runners-up Wolverhampton – but remained unbeaten for the rest of the season.

It was Walsall's experienced players who were instrumental in making them the outstanding club side in the country. Nick Archer was a wily old fox of a captain, as well as a useful run-maker, but, above all, it was the England NCA players, Steve Dean and Keith Arnold, who ensured success. Dean, a stocky and powerful opener with a lot of shots and the confidence to play them, was just three short of 1,000 runs, a milestone which has been reached only ten times before in the League's history, once by Dean himself. Arnold's seam and swing brought him 77 league wickets in 22 games, a club record. Nine of these wickets came in one game against Stourbridge, when Arnold was denied the chance to take all ten because an opponent's car had broken down. Stourbridge's Australian all-rounder Byron Byrne arrived at Walsall with his side's innings already closed at 42 after 23 overs.

The batsman left not out that day was 60-year-old spinner Gordon Smith. At the end of the season he finally decided to retire after 47 years of Birmingham League cricket. Smith had joined Stourbridge in 1982 from Dudley when their ground disappeared owing to subsidence. His last first-team appearance brought him six for 71 against Wolverhampton and a standing ovation. Another stalwart retiring from this League was Colin Price of Aston Unity, who did not miss a first-team match between 1964 and 1995.

If Walsall were the team of the year, the individual star may well have been Lesroy Weekes, Rotherham's Montserrat-born professional. Weekes made one – undistinguished – appearance for Yorkshire, against the 1994 New Zealanders, when he was being considered as a possible overseas signing. He made his presence felt round the Yorkshire League, however, taking a League record 88 wickets at an average of 10.77. Weekes was far too quick for most of the batsmen, and formed a devastating new-ball partnership with Mark Smallman, which took Rotherham to the title in fine style.

Elsewhere, overseas players dominated many Leagues, as usual: Stockton's Indian leg-spinner Sairaj Bahutule became the first player in the 103-year history of the North Yorkshire & South Durham League to do the double of 1,000 runs and 100 wickets. But Guisborough won the League: their professional, the Rhodesian-born Western Australian Murray Goodwin, passed 1,700 runs. Philo Wallace, Sunderland's Barbadian, set a Durham Senior League record of 1,667. And in the Bolton League the Victorian Brad Hodge broke the batting record with 1,760 runs for Farnworth.

But English players had their successes too. In the Lancashire County League, Steve O'Shaughnessy did the double for Denton, and in the North Staffs & South Cheshire League one of Sir Garfield Sobers's lesser-known records fell twice. His total of 97 wickets in a season was beaten by the former Sussex leg-spinner Andy Clarke, who took 103 for Longton. However, the Tamil Nadu left-arm spinner Sunil Subramaniam also passed the old mark, and his 101 wickets guided Stone to their first title in 15 years. Both players, it should be noted, played 26 matches compared to 19 by Sobers.

Perhaps the most glorious finale to the season was produced by a 17-year-old schoolboy, Charles Shreck, in the Cornwall League. Earlier in the season, he had taken eight for 39 against St Buryan. He came to the crease with Truro nine down and needing six runs to beat Callington and win the League. He calmly hit a four and a two. There was an equally tense – if more confusing – climax in the Thames Valley League. Wokingham needed only to win to be champions, but lost. Finchampstead overtook them by trouncing Old Merchant Taylors' by eight wickets. But League rules give only 20 points for a win by a team batting second, and 25 for a win batting first. This enabled Basingstoke to leapfrog them both, by bowling out Marlow with two overs to go.

There was bitterness in the Surrey Championship where four clubs – Sunbury, Wimbledon, Old Whitgiftians and Old Emanuel – went to the High Court to try to overturn a decision to penalise them for playing unregistered overseas players. They claimed the rule had never been applied before, but eventually withdrew their action "in the interests of cricket" before it was heard. Wimbledon, the 1995 champions, slumped to 15th, though the penalty was only a minor factor in this. Esher were the decisive winners.

As in 1995, the Essex league threw up one of the season's more bizarre controversies. In a Division Two match in May, Buckhurst Hill, visiting Billericay, declared on 41 for six after 22 overs. Two of their batsmen had suffered broken hands and several blows on the body from former Essex fast bowler Ian Pont, who took all six wickets. Billericay knocked off the runs in nine overs to win by nine wickets, whereupon Buckhurst Hill captain Noel Gibbons denounced the pitch as "definitely unfit to play cricket on. It was something worse than dangerous – to be honest, I should have declared earlier."

Gibbons complained to the League, who sent representatives to inspect the pitch. No action was taken against Billericay, who said TCCB grounds advisor Harry Brind had provided the specifications for the square at the new Blunt Wall Road ground. Pont said that Buckhurst Hill could not cope with the pace of the pitch. "It was very, very quick for a club wicket and their batsmen weren't used to it. It was bouncy but you had to bowl a fullish length to profit rather than halfway down as their bowlers did." Billericay felt obliged to water the square heavily for the rest of the season.

The former England bowler, Neal Radford, was found guilty of racial abuse during a Cherwell League match in August. The League's disciplinary committee deducted ten points from Radford's club, Banbury, for the start of the 1997 season. Radford was said to have insulted the black Oxfordshire captain, Rupert Evans, despite having received a warning earlier in the season for similar language. Cherwell League chairman Derek Primett said: "We cannot tolerate this sort of behaviour. It is distinctly distressing that it has come from a player who has achieved the highest honours."

In various parts of the country, there were moves to bring in regional premier leagues playing two-day cricket on the Australian model. Discussions were held in both Yorkshire and London, where 11 clubs from five different existing Leagues met to consider the formation of a London League. However, the idea of playing 100-overs-a-side matches, so appealing to those anxious for success at Test level, seemed less attractive to many weekend players without ambitions. Progress was slow.

LEAGUE WINNERS, 1996

League	*Winners*	*League*	*Winners*
Airedale & Wharfedale	Rawdon	**Midland Combined Counties**	Old Edwardians
Bassetlaw	Retford	**Norfolk Alliance**	Swardeston
Birmingham	Walsall	**Northants County**	Peterborough
Bolton	Tonge	**Northern**	St Anne's
Bradford	East Bierley	**North Staffs & South Cheshire**	Stone
Central	Lutterworth	**Northumberland County**	Benwell Hill
Central Yorkshire	Gomersal	**North Wales**	Brymbo
Cheshire County	Bowdon	**North Yorks & South Durham**	Guisborough
Cornwall	Truro	**Notts Alliance**	Kimberley Institute
Derbyshire County	Langley Mill	**Ribblesdale**	Earby
Devon	Torquay	**Saddleworth**	Hollinwood
Durham County	Tudhoe	**Shropshire**	St Georges
Durham Senior	Burnmoor	**Somerset**	Ilminster
Essex	Saffron Walden	**Southern**	Bournemouth
Hertfordshire	Radlett	**South Wales Association**	Swansea
Huddersfield	Meltham	**Surrey Championship**	Esher
Kent	Bexley	**Sussex**	Three Bridges
Lancashire County	Denton West	**Thames Valley**	Basingstoke
Leeds	Carlton	**Three Counties**	Hereford
Lincolnshire	Belton	**Two Counties (Suffolk/Essex)**	Clacton
Liverpool Competition	Southport	**Tyneside Senior**	Annfield Plain
Manchester Association	Ashton on Mersey	**Western**	Optimists
Middlesex	Teddington	**West Wales Club Conference**	Llanybydder
Midland Club Championship	Harborne	**Yorkshire**	Rotherham Town

Note: To avoid confusion, traditional League names have been given in this list and sponsors' names omitted.

FIFTY YEARS AGO

From WISDEN CRICKETERS' ALMANACK 1947

NOTES BY THE EDITOR: "Although handicapped by execrable weather, both wet and cold, the resumption of first-class cricket showed in every way how ready players and public were to welcome their favourite pastime. . . . Teams generally put zest into the game; spectators gave such splendid support that the counties fared well financially and the touring team paid their way. Record attendances came to many grounds and club membership mounted new heights, notably in Hampshire and Somerset."

FIVE CRICKETERS OF THE YEAR – A. V. BEDSER: "Many experts have compared Alec with Maurice Tate, whose style and action he closely resembles, but Alec says he never saw Tate in his prime, and did not model himself on any bowler. For a pace bowler he takes a comparatively short run of eight paces and imparts all his energy at the moment of delivery. Immensely strong, he can keep bowling for long spells and when at the top of his form he rarely sends down a loose ball."

SOUTH AFRICA AND ENGLAND by R. C. Robertson-Glasgow: ". . . We would do well to forget the Tests played in South Africa during 1938-39; not their social delights and friendships, but their cricket; that thirty-runs-an-hour crawl, and that grand climacteric of the ten-day Test when the home-bound ship foreclosed on the battle between eight and a half whole Englishmen and seven and threequarter South Africans still erect on their legs."

NATIONAL CLUB CHAMPIONSHIP, 1996

Chorley's remarkable unbeaten run in the National Club Championship, which stretched back to 1993, came to an end. Their bid for a third consecutive Abbot Ale Cup was running smoothly until they lost in the final to Walsall, who completed an *annus mirabilis* by claiming the Birmingham League title the very next day. Victory was all the sweeter because the competition was at full strength again after the Club Cricket Conference boycott in 1995, ensuring that the Midlands could feel they had seen off the south.

Chorley's route to the final involved Chesterfield, Birkenhead Park (who were beaten by just four runs) and a semi-final in Blackpool, where they easily reached a target of 182 and won by seven wickets. For their part, Walsall repelled a strong challenge from Finchampstead of Berkshire in the sixth round by 14 runs, and then beat Wanstead by four wickets in the semi-final. This was their first National Club title, although they were runners-up to Teddington in 1991.

Perhaps the unluckiest club was Scarborough – still the only side to have won the competition five times. In the third round they were well on top against Sheffield Colliery, who batted first and were 106 for nine when rain intervened. The match was decided by a bowling contest, which Scarborough lost 6-5.

FINAL

CHORLEY v WALSALL

At Lord's, August 30. Walsall won by 25 runs. Toss: Walsall.

Despite an assiduous 40 from Dave Clarke, Walsall's 152 looked distinctly inadequate at the halfway point. But Chorley's experienced batting line-up was stifled by determined bowling. The 45-year-old left-arm medium-pacer Terry Rawlinson, promoted from the second team, sent down nine overs for just 15 runs and two wickets – and that after his first two balls had produced a four and a wide. The unpredictability of the pitch compounded Chorley's difficulties, and the ninth-wicket partnership of 31 between Critchley and Purnell was the highest of their innings; by then their fate was more or less sealed.

Walsall

S. J. Dean c Senior b Walmsley	14
P. R. Oliver c Horridge b Lee	11
D. R. Clarke c Horridge b Catterall	40
†J. N. Batty c Senior b Lee	6
M. J. Marvell c Senior b Eccleshare	11
*N. J. Archer c Fazackerley b Critchley	21
M. F. D. Robinson lbw b Lee	6
P. Wicker not out	27
J. D. Mayer not out	1
L-b 6, w 7, n-b 2	15
1/22 2/27 3/46 4/83 5/87 6/102 7/141 (7 wkts, 45 overs)	152

K. A. Arnold and T. Rawlinson did not bat.

Bowling: Walmsley 9–1–40–1; Purnell 9–0–21–0; Lee 9–1–38–3; Eccleshare 9–1–17–1; Catterall 4–0–15–1; Critchley 5–0–15–1.

Chorley

N. D. R. Bannister b Arnold	6
J. E. A. Fazackerley b Marvell	30
*R. E. W. G. Horridge c Batty b Robinson	0
N. J. Heaton c Archer b Rawlinson	9
†N. A. Senior c Clarke b Rawlinson	6
G. E. Lee b Robinson	26
D. A. Catterall c Dean b Arnold	1
N. Walmsley b Mayer	6
M. J. Critchley not out	13
R. A. B. Purnell b Mayer	18
K. Eccleshare b Robinson	2
B 6, w 3, n-b 1	10
1/8 2/10 3/26 4/45 5/65 6/76 7/89 8/93 9/124 (42.4 overs)	127

Bowling: Arnold 9–2–24–2; Robinson 7.4–0–25–3; Rawlinson 9–5–15–2; Mayer 8–1–21–2; Marvell 7–1–21–1; Wicker 2–0–15–0.

Umpires: T. H. Duckett and C. D. B. Lucas.

WINNERS 1969-96

1969	Hampstead	1979	Scarborough	1989	Teddington
1970	Cheltenham	1980	Moseley	1990	Blackpool
1971	Blackheath	1981	Scarborough	1991	Teddington
1972	Scarborough	1982	Scarborough	1992	Optimists
1973	Wolverhampton	1983	Shrewsbury	1993	Old Hill
1974	Sunbury	1984	Old Hill	1994	Chorley
1975	York	1985	Old Hill	1995	Chorley
1976	Scarborough	1986	Stourbridge	1996	Walsall
1977	Southgate	1987	Old Hill		
1978	Cheltenham	1988	Enfield		

NATIONAL VILLAGE CRICKET CHAMPIONSHIP, 1996

Caldy, a community on the Wirral close to Ian Botham's birthplace at Heswall, won the 25th National Village Championship, organised by *The Cricketer* and sponsored by Alliance & Leicester Giro. Caldy repelled the perennial Scottish challenge of Freuchie in the semi-final, to meet Langleybury of Hertfordshire, who conquered their jitters – they had lost in the semis five times – and this time got to Lord's, where they went down by six runs.

Langleybury had a remarkable quarter-final win in Kent, against Linton Park, who needed six off the last over, with Paul Gibson 71 not out. But he was stranded at the wrong end and three run-outs settled the issue. The last time Langleybury had played there, 17 years earlier, they also won off the last ball.

Fate toyed with them in the semi-final too. Their opponents, Uphill Castle from Somerset, were 181 for six, chasing 209, but then lost three wickets in one over. Still the last pair kept fighting. With 26 needed off two overs, 13 came off the 39th and a six was hit off the first ball of the 40th. Then Simon Baldwin uprooted the middle stump.

Marcus Steed of Rushton in Northamptonshire scored 200, with 21 sixes, off 82 balls against Winterton-on-Sea of Norfolk. Mark Schofield of Bilton in Yorkshire made 206 against Staveley. Steve Cole, of the Essex club Horndon on the Hill, put his team in the last 16 by making 176 against Little Waltham – having been hit on the head first ball.

Woodmancote, winners of the Sussex group, were asked to leave the competition after 60 villages complained that they were recruiting players from too far afield. – Andrew Tong.

FINAL

CALDY v LANGLEYBURY

At Lord's, September 1. Caldy won by six runs. Toss: Caldy.

The innocuous-looking wobblers of Brett Saunders took four wickets in a thrilling finish to give Caldy victory. Caldy had looked favourites from an early stage when Saunders and Phil Eymond had put on 124 for the first wicket. But the combative seam bowling of Baldwin and Javed Khan put Langleybury back in the game. They were still set 223, the third-highest target in the 25 finals, but captain Paul Reynolds led by example, breaking two bats as he hit flamboyantly over the infield. Javed Khan's enthusiasm helped propel his partner, Simon Palmer, through a stand of 49 in six overs, and he took 12 off the penultimate over. But Saunders kept cool and won the game.

Caldy

B. M. Saunders c Reid b Baldwin	76	P. I. Macdonald not out	3
P. M. Eymond c Fry b Baldwin	57		
C. J. Findlay c and b J. Khan	11	B 1, l-b 12, w 7, n-b 5	25
*C. M. Ruddock c Beesley b J. Khan	15		—
B. L. Cooper not out	21	1/124 2/162 3/167 (5 wkts, 40 overs)	222
K. G. Findlay c A. Khan b J. Khan	14	4/184 5/215	

D. A. Aston, M. Dean, †M. Rowan and P. W. Urwin did not bat.

Bowling: Beesley 8–0–35–0; S. N. Palmer 9–2–19–0; Rice 7–0–34–0; Dunstone 6–0–45–0; S. M. Palmer 1–0–12–0; Baldwin 4–0–32–2; J. Khan 5–0–32–3.

Langleybury

G. S. Reid st Rowan b Dean	10	M. C. Dunstone not out	1
*P. K. Reynolds run out	73	T. Beesley b Saunders	2
M. Fry b Dean	28	S. N. Palmer c K. G. Findlay b Saunders	0
I. T. C. Rice c C. J. Findlay b Urwin	13	B 3, l-b 12, w 7	22
†A. Khan c K. G. Findlay b Urwin	2		—
J. Khan st Rowan b Saunders	34	1/32 2/113 3/139 (40 overs)	216
S. M. Palmer c Cooper b Saunders	31	4/143 5/149 6/198	
S. P. J. Baldwin run out	0	7/203 8/214 9/216	

Bowling: K. G. Findlay 9–1–51–0; Urwin 9–1–23–2; Dean 9–1–46–2; Aston 4–0–28–0; Saunders 9–0–53–4.

Umpires: G. Bullock and D. Pye.

WINNERS 1972-96

1972 Troon (Cornwall)
1973 Troon (Cornwall)
1974 Bomarsund (Northumberland)
1975 Gowerton (Glamorgan)
1976 Troon (Cornwall)
1977 Cookley (Worcestershire)
1978 Linton Park (Kent)
1979 East Bierley (Yorkshire)
1980 Marchwiel (Clwyd)
1981 St Fagans (Glamorgan)
1982 St Fagans (Glamorgan)
1983 Quarndon (Derbyshire)
1984 Marchwiel (Clwyd)
1985 Freuchie (Fife)
1986 Forge Valley (Yorkshire)
1987 Longparish (Hampshire)
1988 Goatacre (Wiltshire)
1989 Toft (Cheshire)
1990 Goatacre (Wiltshire)
1991 St Fagans (Glamorgan)
1992 Hursley Park (Hampshire)
1993 Kington (Herefordshire)
1994 Elvaston (Derbyshire)
1995 Woodhouse Grange (Yorkshire)
1996 Caldy (Cheshire)

IRISH CRICKET IN 1996

By DEREK SCOTT

The achievements of the Irish team in 1996 owed much to the continued hard work of national coach Mike Hendrick, who was ably assisted in his second year by the former Indian Test batsman M. V. Narasimha Rao. Under their expert guidance Ireland succeeded in winning their first Triple Crown (at the fourth attempt) and, two weeks later, claimed first place in the inaugural European Tournament in Denmark.

This purple patch brought victories against Wales and England in the Triple Crown, despite a loss to Scotland that left the trophy to be decided on run-rate, and against Italy, Denmark and Gibraltar in the group stage of the European Tournament. In a close-fought final, Ireland overhauled Holland's total of 223 with three wickets intact, while Justin Benson took the Man of the Match award for his 79. Benson had taken over the captaincy earlier in the season as a temporary replacement for Alan Lewis, but these two cup wins confirmed his tenure for the foreseeable future.

Ireland's traditional batting strength was maintained throughout the season by the prolific form of Benson, Angus Dunlop and Desmond Curry, although a sad farewell was bid to Stephen Warke, who retired after 15 years, 114 matches, and 4,275 runs. But it was in the bowling department that Hendrick's inspiration had been most urgently required, and here there was a major improvement. The fast-medium bowler Mark Patterson's 24 wickets earned him a trial at Surrey, where he went on to record the best figures on debut in the club's history, six for 80, playing against South Africa A. Off-spinner Neil Doak and the seamer Paul McCrum were also instrumental in what was Ireland's most economical attack in recent years.

It was still too much to expect parity in the English one-day competitions. Ireland finished their five matches with the expected five losses, the lowlight being a 304-run massacre at the hands of Sussex in the first round of the NatWest Trophy. In their three-day matches, they were thwarted only by heavy rain against Scotland, but lost to MCC and drew a slow-scoring game with Wales, in the course of which debutant Kyle McCallan took a wicket with his first ball – the first instance of such a feat being recorded for Ireland.

On the domestic scene, Brigade finally secured their first Royal Liver All Ireland Cup, having been on the losing side in three previous finals. The holders did well in the other provincial competitions: Cork County won their second consecutive League/Cup double in Munster, while Limavady retained the North-West title, Clontarf the Leinster League, and Northern Union holders Cliftonville shared their league with Lisburn. The Interprovincial Tournament was revamped, with each of the four unions entering one team and a fifth being found in the shape of an Irish Development XI. To their surprise and delight, the youngsters won all four of their matches, two of which were reduced to ten overs per side by poor weather, and finished on top.

The Development XI also managed to contribute seven players to the full Irish side during the season, and five of them were selected in the squad for the 1997 ICC Trophy in Malaysia.

SCOTTISH CRICKET IN 1996

By J. WATSON BLAIR

It was a year of landmarks for Iain Philip, Scotland's most durable batsman. During the match against Ireland he became the first man to score 4,000 runs for Scotland, and his final score of 110 was his tenth hundred for his country. He had already broken the record for appearances, winning his 91st cap in the Benson and Hedges match against Yorkshire in May. Philip won the Famous Grouse Batsman Award for 1996, despite strong competition from his captain, George Salmond, whose magnificent 181 in the same match against Ireland was the second-highest score in the history of the fixture.

But, for the team as a whole, 1996 failed to live up to expectations. Two defeats against England – one in the Triple Crown tournament, one in the European Championship – dashed any hopes of taking those titles, and even though Scotland won the rest of their matches in the European competition, the rules worked against them, and they finished in fifth place out of eight.

There was little encouragement for Scotland in the English limited-overs competitions either. All five matches in the Benson and Hedges and NatWest tournaments showed the gulf in expertise and practice facilities between the weekend amateurs and the professionals. Indeed, Scotland's only century in these games was scored by their own professional, the Barbadian George Reifer, during the NatWest tie with Durham.

A youthful Pakistani side came to Edinburgh in August for an exciting 50-overs game, watched by a bumper crowd, and recorded a 108-run victory, but Scotland fared better on their visit to Lord's six days later, when they beat MCC convincingly by seven wickets. The positive effects of the busy national schedule were in evidence here, but the downside was that many players felt unable to participate in all the matches, and a total of 20 men represented Scotland during the season.

Meanwhile, the league system was radically reconstituted, with the long-awaited National League finally seeing the light of day. It was sponsored by Caledonian Breweries, and comprised two divisions, each including eight clubs drawn from the East League and the disbanded County Championship. The East League will henceforth function as a feeder system, with the winner of its First Division gaining promotion to the Second Division of the National League each year. However, there was a breakaway led by the Western Union (the oldest of the Scottish federations, founded in 1893) which refused to integrate with the new order. Its 1996 winners, Ayr, who also won in 1994, decided to apply independently for admission to the National League, and were accepted as members of Division Two.

The first national title went to Aberdeenshire, who underlined their superiority – and thus enhanced the new league's credibility – by also winning the Whyte & Mackay Scottish Cup, a competition for all-comers.

Winners of other Scottish Leagues and Cups:

SCU Trophy: Ayr; **West League Cup:** Ferguslie; **Border League:** Gala; **Small Clubs' Cup:** Manderston; **Rowan Cup:** Clydesdale; **Scottish Counties Cup:** Aberdeenshire.

NEW ZEALAND UNDER-19 IN ENGLAND, 1996

By GERALD HOWAT

The adult New Zealand Test team has been going through a lean patch, but this might not go on for too long. The country has a well-established youth structure, leading towards an Under-19 side that did well in Australia early in 1996 and came to England full of confidence. It was not misplaced.

Their manager, former New Zealand captain John Reid, said he believed the strength of his side lay in its teamwork, while the coach, Test off-spinner John Bracewell, said they had come "to win the series and enjoy their cricket". Both aims were fulfilled and Reid's conviction was demonstrated. In a collective performance, only left-arm pace bowler David Sewell stood far above the pack.

As usual for Under-19 visitors, the tour opened at Wellington College, where the New Zealanders beat an English Schools' Cricket Association XI but lost to a National Cricket Association XI. Thereafter, their only defeat was in the first one-day international when they lost to England in a high-scoring game. High scoring was a feature of their play in several of the matches – 512 against a Development of Excellence XI, 492 against the Midlands and 298 for two against England Under-18.

New Zealand and England were finely balanced in the First and Third unofficial Tests. Had England declared earlier at Old Trafford, they might just have forced a win on the last afternoon. At Hove, both sides batted too slowly. But in the middle game, at Worcester, New Zealand established a mastery through their bowling, and earned the win which secured them the series.

Neither country had strong opening partnerships; 39 by New Zealand at Old Trafford was the highest in any of the three matches. Matthew Bell, however, got fifties in both innings at Worcester, made two other centuries and showed himself to be an especially strong player on the off side. His partner, Matthew Walker, demonstrated his concentration with several half-centuries. Neal Parlane reserved his best efforts for the Tests, in which he averaged 46.20, but had the ability to shape his innings to the occasion. That nine of the side passed 40 in a Test innings testifies both to the depth of competent batting and to the all-round qualities of several who were primarily bowlers.

Among these were the medium-paced Stephen Cunis, son of the former Test player, and the left-arm spinner Daniel Vettori. At 17, Vettori was the second-youngest tourist and he performed well throughout, flighting the ball deceptively. In the Tests he secured 12 wickets at 24.08, and dismissed England's two best batsmen, David Sales and Owais Shah, three times and twice respectively. But the left-armer Sewell was voted New Zealand's Player of the Series. A student of the Lincoln University Cricket Academy, who had already appeared in first-class cricket for Otago, Sewell was consistently fast and hostile, and his ten wickets for 98 in the Second Test, where he exploited some uneven bounce, effectively settled the series.

Gareth Hopkins kept wicket capably and played three responsible late-order innings in the Tests to finish with an impressive average of 45.33. The side was imaginatively captained by Craig McMillan, another Academy member, whose 150 not out against England Under-18 was the second-highest individual score of the tour, behind only the 159 from 16-year-old Jarrod Englefield against a Development of Excellence XI.

England Under-19, in a less than vintage year, were handicapped by the absence through injury of several of their bowlers, as well as their captain and all-rounder, Alex Morris, during the first two Tests. They still remained without a Test win against New Zealand at Under-19 level, having lost four out of nine with five drawn.

NEW ZEALAND UNDER-19 TOURING PARTY

C. D. McMillan (Canterbury) (*captain*), M. D. Bell (Northern Districts), R. D. Burson (Canterbury), S. J. Cunis (Northern Districts), J. I. Englefield (Central Districts), G. J. Hopkins (Northern Districts), G. A. Howell (Canterbury), N. D. Morland (Otago), J. D. P. Oram (Central Districts), N. R. Parlane (Northern Districts), D. G. Sewell (Otago), D. L. Vettori (Northern Districts), M. D. J. Walker (Central Districts), D. J. Wilson (Central Districts), J. A. Yovich (Northern Districts).

Manager: J. R. Reid. *Coach:* J. G. Bracewell.

RESULTS

Matches – Played 14: Won 6, Lost 2, Drawn 6.

Note: Matches in this section were not first-class.

At Wellington College, July 9. New Zealand Under-19 won by four wickets. Toss: ESCA. ESCA 143 (48.2 overs) (C. G. Taylor 37); New Zealand Under-19 147 for six (49 overs) (J. A. Yovich 35 not out, S. J. Cunis 34).

At Wellington College July 10. England NCA won by five wickets. Toss: New Zealand Under-19. New Zealand Under-19 214 for six (50 overs) (M. D. Bell 47, M. D. J. Walker 71, N. R. Parlane 48; M. Wight three for 53); England NCA 215 for five (48.1 overs) (S. Luckhurst 60, M. Hussain 47).

At Eton College, July 11. New Zealand Under-19 won by 90 runs. Toss: New Zealand Under-19. New Zealand Under-19 292 for four (50 overs) (M. D. J. Walker 85, N. R. Parlane 88, J. I. Englefield 30, C. D. McMillan 70 not out); Hampshire Second XI 202 (46.5 overs) (G. R. Treagus 41, L. J. Botham 40, R. R. Dibden 33 not out; D. J. Wilson three for 44, N. D. Morland three for 33).

At Cambridge, July 13, 14, 15. Drawn. Toss: England South Under-19. England South Under-19 355 for four dec. (E. T. Smith 68, S. D. Peters 57, U. Afzaal 89 not out, G. R. Haywood 89, Extras 35) and 218 (E. T. Smith 30, R. Key 52, U. Afzaal 40, Extras 40; S. J. Cunis three for 36, D. J. Wilson four for 37); New Zealand Under-19 339 for nine dec. (M. D. Bell 97, D. L. Vettori 51 not out, Extras 58; U. Afzaal three for 78, S. Randall three for 104) and 98 for no wkt (M. D. J. Walker 60 not out, J. I. Englefield 32 not out).

At Leeds, July 16. New Zealand Under-19 won by one wicket. Toss: Yorkshire Second XI. Yorkshire Second XI 198 for seven (50 overs) (R. A. Kettleborough 74, R. Robinson 44; R. D. Burson three for 39); New Zealand Under-19 202 for nine (50 overs) (M. D. Bell 62, C. D. McMillan 36; M. A. Robinson three for 39, I. D. Fisher three for 36).

At Chester-le-Street, July 18. First unofficial one-day international: England Under-19 won by two wickets. Toss: England Under-19. New Zealand Under-19 265 for seven (50 overs) (M. D. J. Walker 60, N. R. Parlane 34, C. D. McMillan 57, S. J. Cunis 38; B. C. Hollioake three for 35); England Under-19 268 for eight (49 overs) (A. J. Swann 42, O. A. Shah 31, A. C. Morris 76, A. Flintoff 30, B. C. Hollioake 40).

At Nottingham, July 20. Second unofficial one-day international: New Zealand Under-19 won by 29 runs. Toss: England Under-19. New Zealand Under-19 228 for seven (50 overs) (M. D. Bell 32, N. R. Parlane 44); England Under-19 199 (46.1 overs) (D. L. Vettori three for 40).

At West Bromwich Dartmouth, Birmingham, July 22, 23, 24. Drawn. Toss: Midlands Under-19 XI. Midlands Under-19 XI 187 (G. E. Welton 63, B. E. A. Preece 32, Extras 46; D. G. Sewell six for 79) and 400 for seven (T. W. Roberts 150, B. Spendlove 32, M. A. Wagh 123, G. P. Swann 57 not out; N. D. Morland three for 98); New Zealand Under-19 492 (M. D. Bell 119 retired ill, J. D. P. Oram 46, N. R. Parlane 38, J. A. Yovich 32, D. J. Wilson 74, R. D. Burson 63, Extras 53).

At Chester, July 26, 27, 28. Drawn. Toss: England North Under-19. England North Under-19 275 (M. J. Chilton 99, J. D. Middlebrook 83; N. D. Morland six for 54) and 47 for two; New Zealand Under-19 395 (J. A. Yovich 38, N. R. Parlane 51, S. J. Cunis 74, D. L. Vettori 70, N. D. Morland 33, R. D. Burson 54 not out; J. W. Hood three for 41, R. Wilkinson four for 69).

ENGLAND UNDER-19 v NEW ZEALAND UNDER-19

First Unofficial Test

At Manchester, August 1, 2, 3, 4. Drawn. Toss: England Under-19.

England batted on for 50 minutes, adding 52, on the fourth morning, leaving New Zealand 323 to get in a little over two sessions. On a worn pitch which prompted complaints from both managers, the spinners Cosker and Batty bowled 64 overs – to add to their 68 in the first innings. Although they took five wickets between them, and thus 12 in the match, a draw already seemed the likeliest outcome when New Zealand were 171 for four at tea. On the first day, Sales, fresh from his double-century on Championship debut for Northamptonshire, batted fluently with support from Hollioake. He led the way again in the second innings, this time with Shah's backing. New Zealand's off-spinner, Morland, and 17-year-old left-armer Vettori who bowled with accuracy and flight, also had much work to do. Their top eight batsmen all contributed in one innings or the other, with Parlane restraining his attacking instincts to secure the draw on the final day.

Close of play: First day, England Under-19 203-6 (D. J. Sales 57*, D. C. Nash 3*); Second day, New Zealand Under-19 224-7 (J. A. Yovich 53*, D. G. Sewell 2*); Third day, England Under-19 259-6 (O. A. Shah 60*, D. C. Nash 2*).

England Under-19

D. J. Roberts run out	22	– c Bell b Sewell	13
E. T. Smith c Walker b McMillan	28	– c Morland b Vettori	20
A. J. Swann c Walker b Vettori	19	– lbw b McMillan	18
D. J. Sales c and b Vettori	66	– c Oram b Sewell	77
O. A. Shah c Parlane b Vettori	13	– c Cunis b Morland	77
B. C. Hollioake c and b Morland	55	– lbw b Morland	41
*G. J. Batty lbw b Morland	0	– c and b McMillan	2
†D. C. Nash run out	12	– not out	26
D. A. Cosker c Parlane b Morland	2	– st Hopkins b Morland	0
C. L. Campbell not out	8		
J. Ormond b Sewell	29	– (10) not out	5
B 4, l-b 3, n-b 2	9	B 19, l-b 7, n-b 6	32
1/38 2/72 3/72 4/92 5/193 6/193 7/217 8/224 9/226	263	1/26 2/43 3/99 4/159 5/237 6/244 7/290 8/303 (8 wkts dec.)	311

Bowling: *First Innings*—Sewell 15.5–4–33–1; Yovich 4–0–25–0; Cunis 12–2–39–0; Vettori 30–11–75–3; McMillan 8–2–14–1; Morland 33–11–70–3. *Second Innings*—Sewell 9–2–39–2; Cunis 4–1–9–0; Morland 40–15–90–3; McMillan 29–11–79–2; Vettori 23–8–54–1; Parlane 1–0–14–0.

New Zealand Under-19

M. D. Bell c Roberts b Batty	13	– b Cosker	21
M. D. J. Walker c Nash b Hollioake	21	– c Hollioake b Cosker	22
N. R. Parlane run out	35	– c Smith b Campbell	61
*C. D. McMillan lbw b Cosker	16	– c Nash b Batty	54
J. D. P. Oram c Hollioake b Cosker	59	– c Nash b Hollioake	12
J. A. Yovich st Nash b Cosker	57	– lbw b Cosker	6
S. J. Cunis c Smith b Hollioake	4	– not out	42
†G. J. Hopkins c and b Cosker	0	– hit wkt b Batty	20
D. G. Sewell not out	11		
D. L. Vettori c Hollioake b Batty	7	– (9) not out	0
N. D. Morland lbw b Batty	4		
B 14, l-b 9, n-b 2	25	B 12, l-b 12, w 1	25
1/39 2/53 3/82 4/106 5/210 6/219 7/222 8/233 9/242	252	1/30 2/52 3/132 4/155 5/180 6/200 7/252 (7 wkts)	263

Bowling: *First Innings*—Campbell 7–0–27–0; Hollioake 13–4–25–2; Cosker 37–6–87–4; Ormond 8–4–18–0; Batty 30.5–12–72–3. *Second Innings*—Campbell 8–1–37–1; Hollioake 13–2–46–1; Ormond 5–3–5–0; Batty 29–11–69–2; Cosker 35–12–82–3.

Umpires: R. Palmer and D. R. Shepherd.

At Old Hill, August 8. New Zealand Under-19 won by eight wickets. Toss: England Under-18. England Under-18 297 for nine (55 overs) (T. W. Roberts 41, S. Widdup 71, C. Reed 46); New Zealand Under-19 298 for two (45.5 overs) (M. D. Bell 100 not out, C. D. McMillan 150 not out).

At Kimbolton, August 10, 11, 12. Drawn. Toss: New Zealand Under-19. New Zealand Under-19 512 (J. I. Englefield 159, C. D. McMillan 101, G. A. Howell 54, S. J. Cunis 47) and 110 for three (J. A. Yovich 83 not out); Development of Excellence XI 385 for nine dec. (R. Key 61, J. P. Pyemont 87, R. Wilkinson 110).

ENGLAND UNDER-19 v NEW ZEALAND UNDER-19

Second Unofficial Test

At Worcester, August 15, 16, 17. New Zealand Under-19 won by eight wickets. Toss: England Under-19.

New Zealand set their mark on this match from the third over when left-arm seamer Sewell had Roberts caught hooking. Swinging the ball well and getting considerable bounce, Sewell took three for 18 in his first seven overs and dismissed England with his sixth wicket, half an hour before tea. Shah, despite one chance, made the only significant score; he drove and pulled superbly to reach a half-century in 89 balls. In reply, the tourists were 162 for seven, still 14 behind with only three wickets left. But they were allowed to establish a 153-run lead through an eighth-wicket partnership of 115 between Hopkins and Vettori, not to mention the donation of 50 extras. Despite a recovery in their second innings, led by the pugnacious Swann and Hollioake, England finished only 85 ahead. Sewell's match analysis was ten for 98. New Zealand reached their target in 20 overs, with eight wickets and a day to spare.

Close of play: First day, New Zealand Under-19 128-3 (M. D. Bell 64*); Second day, England Under-19 110-4 (A. J. Swann 40*, D. A. Cosker 1*).

England Under-19

D. J. Roberts c Burson b Sewell	4	– c Hopkins b Sewell	17
E. T. Smith run out	26	– c Oram b Burson	26
A. J. Swann c Bell b Sewell	15	– b Burson	66
D. J. Sales lbw b Sewell	6	– lbw b Vettori	13
O. A. Shah c and b Burson	69	– c Walker b Vettori	4
B. C. Hollioake c Bell b Walker	3	– (7) lbw b Sewell	44
*G. J. Batty c McMillan b Sewell	8	– (8) c Hopkins b Sewell	22
†D. C. Nash c Burson b Vettori	12	– (9) not out	3
D. A. Cosker lbw b Sewell	9	– (6) c Englefield b Vettori	23
J. Ormond c Hopkins b Sewell	2	– b Sewell	1
M. J. Hoggard not out	0	– c Hopkins b Vettori	0
B 4, l-b 5, w 1, n-b 12	22	B 5, l-b 3, w 1, n-b 10	19
1/4 2/32 3/38 4/70 5/85 6/111 7/156 8/170 9/174	176	1/38 2/53 3/88 4/94 5/160 6/198 7/229 8/232 9/237	238

Bowling: *First Innings*—Sewell 13.2–3–47–6; Burson 19–8–47–1; Cunis 13–1–48–0; Walker 9–3–19–1; Vettori 5–3–2–1; McMillan 1–0–4–0. *Second Innings*—Sewell 21–3–51–4; Burson 17–3–65–2; Cunis 12–4–49–0; Vettori 26.4–8–64–4; McMillan 1–0–1–0.

New Zealand Under-19

M. D. Bell c Nash b Hoggard	66	– not out	53
J. I. Englefield b Hollioake	6		
M. D. J. Walker c Sales b Cosker	34	– (2) lbw b Ormond	9
*C. D. McMillan lbw b Hoggard	11		
J. D. P. Oram lbw b Hoggard	0	– (4) not out	1
N. R. Parlane c Swann b Hollioake	11	– (3) c Hollioake b Cosker	10
S. J. Cunis c Hollioake b Hoggard	4		
†G. J. Hopkins b Sales	79		
D. L. Vettori c and b Hoggard	42		
R. D. Burson not out	24		
D. G. Sewell c Nash b Hollioake	2		
B 9, l-b 13, w 8, n-b 20	50	B 9, w 2, n-b 4	15
1/19 2/99 3/128 4/128 5/143 6/143 7/162 8/277 9/303	329	1/36 2/47	(2 wkts) 88

Bowling: *First Innings*—Hollioake 34.1–6–103–3; Ormond 20–3–73–0; Hoggard 30–6–85–5; Cosker 13–6–19–1; Batty 11–3–22–0; Sales 2–0–5–1. *Second Innings*—Hoggard 6–1–30–0; Hollioake 3–0–14–0; Ormond 6–2–22–1; Cosker 4.3–1–13–1.

Umpires: T. E. Jesty and B. J. Meyer.

ENGLAND UNDER-19 v NEW ZEALAND UNDER-19

Third Unofficial Test

At Hove, August 22, 23, 24, 25. Drawn. Toss: England Under-19.

England had just opened their second innings when a brief but heavy shower at noon on the fourth day ended the match. Had there been any prospect of a result, there might have been an incentive to play again on what proved to be a hot afternoon. England made amends for their defeat at Worcester with a first-innings total of 400. Sales, driving strongly to reach his century, and Shah shared a third-wicket partnership of 139 and Morris had brief hopes of enforcing the follow-on: Cosker had taken three wickets, reducing New Zealand to 143 for four. But Parlane amassed a century, the tourists' late order backed him up, and the moment passed. Only seven overs were bowled on the last day: New Zealand's innings ended when Morland was hit on the head and had to go to hospital. With the management more concerned about whether he would be fit enough to fly home next day than about the cricket, the series fizzled out.

Close of play: First day, England Under-19 345-7 (D. C. Nash 19*, D. A. Cosker 0*); Second day, New Zealand Under-19 132-2 (N. R. Parlane 59*, D. G. Sewell 1*); Third day, New Zealand Under-19 341-9 (G. J. Hopkins 37*).

England Under-19

E. T. Smith lbw b Sewell	2	– not out 4
A. J. Swann lbw b Cunis	25	– not out 5
O. A. Shah lbw b Sewell	91	
D. J. Sales c McMillan b Vettori	135	
*A. C. Morris b Sewell	0	
U. Afzaal b Vettori	12	
M. A. Wagh c Parlane b Cunis	38	
†D. C. Nash not out	49	
D. A. Cosker c Hopkins b Vettori	14	
C. L. Campbell b Morland	5	
M. J. Hoggard c Oram b Sewell	2	
B 10, l-b 3, n-b 14	27	
1/10 2/50 3/189 4/190 5/239 6/310 7/343 8/376 9/385	400	(no wkt) 9

Bowling: *First Innings*—Sewell 27–2–96–4; Cunis 19–1–73–2; Walker 8–1–40–0; Vettori 39–10–94–3; McMillan 10–3–22–0; Morland 28–8–62–1. *Second Innings*—Sewell 2–0–7–0; Cunis 1.4–0–2–0.

New Zealand Under-19

M. D. Bell b Campbell	1
M. D. J. Walker lbw b Cosker	51
N. R. Parlane c Morris b Shah	114
D. G. Sewell c Swann b Cosker	2
*C. D. McMillan b Cosker	6
J. D. P. Oram b Cosker	43
J. I. Englefield lbw b Cosker	17
†G. J. Hopkins not out	37
S. J. Cunis c and b Shah	12
D. L. Vettori lbw b Shah	22
N. D. Morland retired hurt	0
B 19, l-b 20, w 2, n-b 2	43
1/1 2/129 3/137 4/143 5/213 6/265 7/269 8/291 9/341	348

N. D. Morland retired hurt at 348.

Bowling: Hoggard 13.3–5–31–0; Campbell 15–5–32–1; Wagh 23–6–66–0; Morris 7–0–21–0; Cosker 39–8–110–5; Afzaal 6–0–17–0; Shah 17–5–32–3.

Umpires: D. J. Constant and B. Leadbeater.

CRICKET SOCIETY AWARDS, 1996

Owais Shah of Middlesex won the Cricket Society's Most Promising Young Cricketer of the Year Award. The A. A. Thomson Fielding Prize, for the best schoolboy fieldsman, went to Timothy Roberts, now at Durham University. The Sir John Hobbs Memorial Prize, for the outstanding Under-16 schoolboy, was won by John Francis of King Edward VI School, Southampton. Cricket Society awards under the Wetherell bequest went to Phil Simmons as the outstanding all-rounder in the first-class game, and to Steven Tomlinson of The Oratory School, who was the outstanding all-rounder in schools cricket.

NAYC UNDER-19 COUNTY FESTIVALS, 1996

By PHILIP HOARE

Warwickshire emulated Kent's 1995 achievement by doing the Under-19 double in 1996. They beat Staffordshire in the overall final of the Oxford and Cambridge festivals, and then went on to win the Hilda Overy Championship, which is awarded on results across the entire county season.

This was a deserved reward for Warwickshire's impressive youth programme, developed under the aegis of a dedicated committee and implemented by coach Richard Cox. At Cambridge, his side held the advantage against Staffordshire for most of the day, and came out with an 84-run victory which marked the end of the festivals in their familiar form. It was perhaps fitting that a first-class county should meet one of the minor counties in the last final, as the two have competed side by side since the Cambridge and Oxford festivals began in 1974.

Warwickshire had comfortably eliminated holders Kent the day before on a batsman's wicket at Clare College. Neeraj Prabhu, David Young and skipper Chris Howell all scored freely as Warwickshire ran up 302 for seven in their 55 overs, and the eventual margin of victory was 89 runs. For their part, Staffordshire had endured a nail-biting climax to the final of the Oxford division after setting Worcestershire a target of 211. Nigel Davenport and Richard Hall scored fifties in reply before the Staffordshire bowlers regrouped and squeezed out an eight-run win. However, they were handicapped in the grand final next day by the absence of star seamer David Womble, who had earlier played for Derbyshire in the Sunday League, and they soon became the third successive county to lose the final to opponents with "home advantage".

The festivals' outstanding individuals were representing other teams, however. At Oxford, where Worcestershire were the only first-class county taking part, Charles Hodgson of Berkshire scored the two largest centuries of the festivals, 127 against West of Scotland and 118 against Wiltshire. Nemesh Patel of Leicestershire came close to matching him with 106 against Kent and 101 not out against Yorkshire at Cambridge. The best bowling figures belonged to Leicestershire's Neil Widdowson, who took six for 11 against Cambridgeshire.

The NAYC have announced a new format for Under-19 competitions in 1997. The festivals will be replaced by a competition based on regional centres – Taunton, Guildford, Oxford and Northampton/Cambridge – while the Hilda Overy Championship will continue and an increasing amount of two-day cricket will be introduced. It was hoped the first-class counties who have been absent from the festivals over the past two years would support the new plans, but only Surrey and Derbyshire rushed back in, which still left seven absentees: Essex, Glamorgan, Gloucestershire, Hampshire, Middlesex, Somerset and Sussex.

AREA FINALS

At Clare College, Cambridge, August 16. Warwickshire won by 89 runs. Toss: Warwickshire. Warwickshire 302 for seven (55 overs) (D. J. Young 65, I. Mohammed 38, C. R. Howell 54, N. V. Prabhu 70 not out, M. A. Wagh 38; S. Evans three for 47); Kent 213 for nine (55 overs) (J. H. Baldock 32, R. Champion 32).

At Christ Church, Oxford, August 16. Staffordshire won by eight runs. Toss: Staffordshire. Staffordshire 210 for five (55 overs) (A. Sharma 54, G. D. Franklin 43 not out); Worcestershire 202 for nine (55 overs) (N. J. Davenport 59, R. J. Hall 55; R. Logan three for 42, D. R. Womble four for 38).

FINAL

WARWICKSHIRE v STAFFORDSHIRE

At Fenner's, Cambridge, August 17. Warwickshire won by 84 runs. Toss: Warwickshire.

Warwickshire's spinners, Raoul East and Jim Troughton, teamed up to end Staffordshire's hopes after tea, when the last five wickets fell for 11 runs. But the damage had been done earlier, when Warwickshire had been allowed to reach 211 on a relaid Fenner's wicket which offered variable bounce and an unusual degree of help for the bowlers. Howell and Abdul Hafeez shared an invaluable century partnership for the third wicket, and the momentum was sustained by Prabhu's 40. When their turn came, Staffordshire managed only one stand of consequence – 59 for the fifth wicket between captain Gavin Franklin and Paul Goodwin – before the spinners wrapped things up. Three wickets fell with the score on 116 and East finished with remarkable figures of four for six from 37 balls.

Warwickshire

D. J. Young c Dhillon b Logan	10
I. Mohammed lbw b Clowes	0
*C. R. Howell st Dhillon b Farrington	42
A. Hafeez run out	64
N. V. Prabhu c Finney b Clowes	40
J. Troughton b Franklin	6
M. A. Wagh b Clowes	17
R. G. East c Dhillon b Clowes	4
J. Webster not out	12
K. Shah run out	0
†S. Eustace not out	1
B 2, l-b 5, w 8	15
	—
1/4 2/12 3/112 4/126 5/136 6/173 7/183 8/210 9/210 (9 wkts, 55 overs)	211

Bowling: Clowes 11–1–27–4; Logan 11–0–44–1; Farrington 11–3–32–1; Franklin 11–0–48–1; Finney 11–0–53–0.

Staffordshire

C. Tranter c Prabhu b Webster	18
A. Sharma lbw b Shah	0
N. Finney lbw b Webster	7
*G. D. Franklin c Young b East	28
D. Proffitt c Troughton b Prabhu	6
P. Goodwin b East	35
R. Jervis run out	2
R. Logan lbw b Troughton	0
D. J. Clowes b East	4
L. Farrington c sub b East	2
†J. Dhillon not out	1
B 6, l-b 5, w 9, n-b 4	24
	—
1/2 2/34 3/37 4/50 5/109 6/116 7/116 8/116 9/125 (47.1 overs)	127

Bowling: Shah 8–0–29–1; Webster 11–2–26–2; Prabhu 7–2–10–1; Wagh 7–1–24–0; Troughton 8–0–21–1; East 6.1–2–6–4.

Umpires: D. J. Constant and J. W. Holder.

PAST WINNERS

1986	Lancashire	1990	Essex	1994	Yorkshire
1987	Yorkshire	1991	Middlesex	1995	Kent
1988	Warwickshire	1992	Yorkshire	1996	Warwickshire
1989	Warwickshire	1993	Lancashire		

LOMBARD WORLD UNDER-15 CHALLENGE

By IVO TENNANT

The inaugural under-15 World Cup culminated in a final at Lord's that will be remembered less for the cricket than for several pitch invasions, the inadequacy of MCC's stewarding and for the police frog-marching one so-called supporter to custody through the Long Room. He was not even wearing a tie. None of these unseemly occurrences, though, could mar the overall success of a competition that the organisers intend, sponsorship permitting, to repeat every three or four years.

India were the winners. The fact that they were contesting the final against their traditional rivals Pakistan should have alerted MCC to the possibility of crowd trouble. They were warned by the organisers, English Schools' Cricket Association, that the attendance could be as big as 10,000, since admission would be free. The police were called by a schoolmaster and arrived through the Grace Gate with sirens at full blast. But it is an indication of the problems faced by ground authorities all over the world that the first person arrested was not some over-enthusiastic teenager, but a man who had been led away during the England-Pakistan Test at Lord's earlier in the summer.

The competition had been dreamed up by ESCA and David English, the cricket enthusiast and creator of the Bunbury cartoon books. Ten countries took part, playing 55 overs a side but otherwise participating under ICC rules. The semi-finals, as well as the final, were played on Test grounds and shown on satellite TV. If there was a concern, it was whether boys of 15 years and under were sufficiently mature to participate in international cricket and cope with the media. Pleasingly, they were.

The standard was remarkably high – at least it was among the eight Test-playing nations (New Zealand did not attend). Neither Canada nor Holland, alas, looked the part and were eliminated from the group stages all too easily. The likes of Ian Botham, who volunteered to commentate, and Bob Woolmer, who interrupted his holiday and who soon came to the conclusion that South Africa's next generation of fast bowlers would come from this age group, were mightily impressed. "We demand academic excellence at this age," said Ken Lake, the long-standing general secretary of ESCA, "so why not sporting excellence?"

It was soon evident – as if this had not been known already – that boys were reaching cricketing maturity more quickly on the subcontinent than in Europe. No matter that 15-year-olds from India knew little of English pitches and still less of life beyond their country. Their party consisted not merely of small, guileful spinners but strapping boys, who bowled more quickly than their years suggested they could and who struck the ball handsomely off the front foot without being too bothered about playing themselves in. "You could find a Tendulkar among them," said Sarkar Telwar, their coach, and he was not speaking lightly.

The Pakistani team was captained by Faisal Iqbal, the nephew of Javed Miandad, and included Bazid Khan and Imran Qadir, the sons of Majid Khan and Abdul Qadir – in other words, the immediate family of three of Pakistan's greatest cricketers. Imran, who was named, it need scarcely be said, after his father's former captain, bowled leg-breaks and googlies with an action and a skip in his run-up that were instantly recognisable. In the semi-final against

England at Headingley, several batsmen could not read him. His command of line and length in the 11 overs he was permitted had much to do with Pakistan winning by 90 runs.

For England, who reached the semi-finals by beating West Indies in their final group match, Alex Loudon captained and batted with composure, and James Adams and John Francis, who made an unbeaten century against Zimbabwe, made runs consistently. That Australia failed to reach the knockout stages was something of a surprise, if only for the emphasis they put on the development of young cricketers. South Africa's team was beaten by India in the semi-final at Trent Bridge. Woolmer said he was worried about the alternative attraction of basketball in the townships.

So to the final, staged on an August day when there was no other cricket. For India to beat Pakistan, even at under-15 level, is cause for over-exuberance of a kind few other countries comprehend. Regrettably, this also resulted in three pitch invasions followed by further trouble when India's four-wicket victory was completed. Stumps were uprooted and cans thrown on to the outfield. When six runs were required, the Indian batsmen, Ratinder Sodhi, the captain, who made a match-winning unbeaten 82, and his partner, Vivek Mahajan, sought refuge in the pavilion. Men as well as boys were running on to the square. The police, seemingly concerned that the pavilion would be stormed, formed a protective barrier in front of aghast MCC members.

Roger Knight, MCC's secretary, admitted the following day that the club was simply not expecting such trouble at a match between schoolboys. Nobody was seriously injured and, once the presentations had been made amid the sanctuary of the balcony, the trouble-makers dispersed. The cricket itself had been enjoyable. Much had depended on whether Shoaib Malik and Imran Qadir, the Pakistan spinners, could restrict India's middle order. When Pardeep Chawla and Mohammad Kaif were out in quick succession, the former deceived by a googly, it appeared as if they could. Yet they were unable to rid themselves of Sodhi.

The likelihood is that the tournament, which overall was well-received and might lead to under-15 internationals on a regular basis, will continue to be staged in England.

FINAL GROUP TABLES

Group A

	P	*W*	*L*	*NR*	*Pts*
India	4	4	0	0	8
England	4	3	1	0	6
West Indies	4	2	2	0	4
Zimbabwe	4	1	3	0	2
Canada	4	0	4	0	0

Group B

	P	*W*	*L*	*NR*	*Pts*
Pakistan	4	4	0	0	8
South Africa	4	3	1	0	6
Sri Lanka	4	2	2	0	4
Australia	4	1	3	0	2
Holland	4	0	4	0	0

SEMI-FINALS

At Nottingham, August 15. India won by five wickets. Toss: South Africa. South Africa 262 for seven (55 overs) (D. Makalima 52, R. Sierra 90, M. Otto 60); India 263 for five (52 overs) (R. S. Sodhi 67, P. Chawla 63, M. Kaif 54 not out, B. Chander 43).

At Leeds, August 17. Pakistan won by 90 runs. Toss: Pakistan. Pakistan 208 (50.4 overs) (Taufeeq Umar 87, Bazid Khan 32, Yasir Arafat 37); England 118 (44.2 overs) (A. Loudon 44).

FINAL

INDIA v PAKISTAN

At Lord's, August 20. India won by four wickets. Toss: India.

Pakistan

Taufeeq Umar lbw b Sodhi	29
Hassan Raza c Mahajan b Ganda	80
Bazid Khan c Chawla b Jolly	6
*Faisal Iqbal b Ganda	16
Jan Nisar Khan st Chawla b Ganda	24
Yasir Arafat c R. Singh b Sodhi	16
†Kamran Akmal b Sodhi	4
Imran Qadir not out	9
Shoaib Malik not out	19
B 3, l-b 6, w 9, n-b 1	19
	—
1/57 2/78 3/134 4/161 5/178 6/191 7/199 (7 wkts, 55 overs)	222

Kashif Mehmood and Shahzad Nazir did not bat.

Bowling: Gulza Inder Singh 5–0–30–0; Jha 6–1–24–0; Sodhi 11–3–34–3; Mahajan 10–1–38–0; Ganda 11–0–58–3; Jolly 11–2–25–1; Kaif 1–0–4–0.

India

Gagan Inder Singh b Shahzad Nazir	0
R. Singh lbw b Kashif Mehmood	7
†P. Chawla c Faisal Iqbal b Imran Qadir	34
*R. S. Sodhi not out	82
M. Kaif st Kamran Akmal b Shoaib Malik	8
B. Chander b Yasir Arafat	27
I. Ganda lbw b Yasir Arafat	8
V. Mahajan not out	19
L-b 5, w 28, n-b 5	38
	—
1/12 2/19 3/105 4/118 5/165 6/178 (6 wkts, 52.4 overs)	223

R. Jolly, Gulza Inder Singh and R. R. Jha did not bat.

Bowling: Kashif Mehmood 9.4–0–40–1; Shahzad Nazir 7–0–17–1; Jan Nisar Khan 7–0–39–0; Yasir Arafat 7–0–41–2; Shoaib Malik 11–0–28–1; Imran Qadir 10–0–45–1; Hassan Raza 1–0–8–0.

Umpires: J. W. Holder and T. E. Jesty.

SCHOOLS CRICKET IN 1996

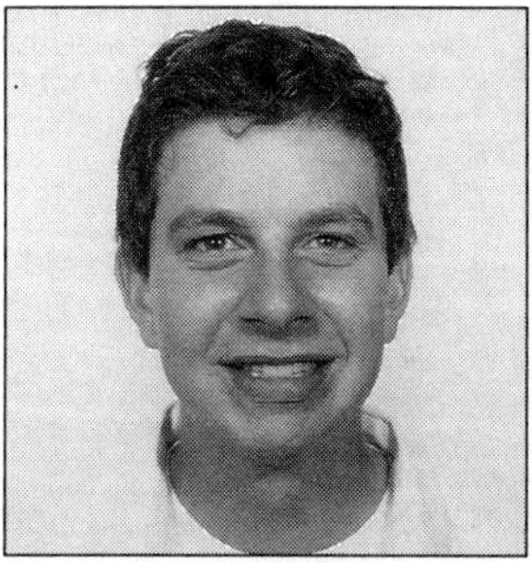

James Pyemont of Tonbridge School (left) and Warwick School's David Young both scored centuries in the MCC Schools Festival at Oxford.

The 13th MCC Schools Festival, held in fine weather at Oxford from July 12-15, featured some of the best schoolboy cricketers in teams chosen separately by the Headmasters' Conference (HMC) and the English Schools Cricket Association (ESCA). Although some of the older boys are unavailable these days, owing to the increasing representative opportunities elsewhere, this does give younger boys a chance of making their mark. And many do.

The following were selected to play at the Festival:

HMC: N. R. Boulton (King's, Taunton), E. D. C. Craig (Winchester), A. Cruttenden (Judd), R. K. Dawson (Batley GS), S. N. de Silva (Trinity), Z. R. Feather (Birkenhead), J. A. G. Fulton (Eton), T. E. Goodworth (Tonbridge), D. P. Hemmings (Loughborough GS), C. P. R. Hodgson (Wellington C.), E. J. Lyons (Ipswich), I. J. W. McCarter (Shrewsbury), R. A. E. Martin (Oakham), J. M. Milton (Oundle), S. C. A. Pickstone (Batley GS), G. S. Peddy (St Edward's, Oxford), J. P. Pyemont (Tonbridge), S. A. Richardson (Manchester GS), S. M. Sheikh (King's College School, Wimbledon), D. J. H. Walder (Oundle), R. Wilkinson (Worksop), D. J. Young (Warwick).

ESCA: M. Bishop (St Ambrose; Cheshire), C. Budd (Ridings HS; Glos), L. M. Chronnell (Poynton County HS; Cheshire), L. Collins (Cheltenham SFC; Glos), A. J. Crozier (Bridgewater County HS; Cheshire), N. J. Davenport (King Edward's, Stourbridge; Worcs), J. Dhillon (Highfield; Warwicks), A. N. Edwards (Millfield; Somerset), A. Hafeez (Handsworth GS; Warwicks), R. J. Hall (Royal GS, Worcester; Worcs), J. B. Hockley (Kelsey Park; Kent), C. Jack (St Joseph's C.; Suffolk), P. Lindsay (Tynemouth C.; Durham), A. Long (St Peter's, Bournemouth; Dorset), A. J. Marsh (Abbotsholme; Derbys), G. Reynolds (St Francis Xavier; Lancs), T. W. Roberts (Bishop Stopford; Northants), J. G. C. Rowe (Tonbridge; Kent), G. P. Swann (Sponne S.; Northants), C. G. Taylor (Colston's; Glos), J. Webster (Handsworth GS; Warwicks), P. J. Witherley (Stowupland HS; Suffolk).

At the end of the four days at Oxford, the following 16 boys were selected to play at Lord's: Anthony Crozier, Nigel Davenport, Shehan de Silva, Jagbir Dhillon, James Fulton, Charles Hodgson, James Pyemont, Scott Richardson, Tim Roberts, Graeme Swann, Chris Taylor, David Walder, Jay Webster, Richard Wilkinson, Paul Witherley, David Young.

HMC SOUTHERN SCHOOLS v HMC NORTHERN SCHOOLS

At Wadham College, July 12, 13. HMC Northern Schools won by eight wickets.

It was a match for batsmen, with four reaching three figures and no bowler taking more than two wickets. Southern Schools dominated the first day, on which Pyemont scored an excellent century before lunch. A century from Hodgson on the second day enabled Fulton to set a target of 291, whereupon an imposing partnership between the game's other centurions, Young and Richardson, settled matters decisively with time to spare.

HMC Southern Schools

J. P. Pyemont c Feather b Walder	104		
C. P. R. Hodgson c Richardson b Walder	49	– retired hurt	110
*J. A. G. Fulton st Lyons b Young	74		
E. D. C. Craig c Walder b Dawson	72	– run out	4
G. S. Peddy not out	2	– not out	25
R. Wilkinson b Young	2	– (3) c Young b Milton	22
†S. N. de Silva (did not bat)		– (1) lbw b Milton	12
S. M. Sheikh (did not bat)		– (6) not out	10
Extras	18	Extras	9
1/147 2/172 3/315 4/317 5/321 (5 wkts dec.)	321	1/43 2/97 3/176 (3 wkts dec.)	192

D. P. Hemmings, T. E. Goodworth and A. Cruttenden did not bat.

Bowling: *First Innings*—Pickstone 13–1–68–0; McCarter 8–1–31–0; Feather 9–1–50–0; Dawson 12–0–70–1; Milton 6–0–52–0; Walder 8–1–36–2; Young 2.1–0–10–2. *Second Innings*—Pickstone 9–2–33–0; Feather 8–0–43–0; Dawson 10–1–39–0; Milton 13–4–32–2; Walder 6–1–16–0; Young 2–0–23–0.

HMC Northern Schools

S. A. Richardson run out	84	– retired hurt	102
N. R. Boulton c Hodgson b Cruttenden	27	– c Pyemont b Cruttenden	26
D. J. Young c Hodgson b Wilkinson	13	– retired hurt	101
R. A. E. Martin lbw b Peddy	18	– c Hodgson b Goodworth	6
R. K. Dawson c de Silva b Hemmings	25	– not out	30
Z. R. Feather c de Silva b Hemmings	0		
*D. J. H. Walder b Sheikh	20		
I. J. W. McCarter not out	15	– (6) not out	15
J. M. Milton not out	11		
Extras	10	Extras	11
1/40 2/63 3/114 4/153 5/153 6/186 7/188 (7 wkts dec.)	223	1/50 2/240 (2 wkts)	291

†E. J. Lyons and S. C. A. Pickstone did not bat.

Bowling: *First Innings*—Sheikh 13–2–68–1; Hemmings 11–1–50–2; Goodworth 14–4–44–0; Cruttenden 6–0–26–1; Wilkinson 9–4–16–1; Peddy 7–1–17–1. *Second Innings*—Sheikh 4–0–23–0; Hemmings 14–1–55–0; Goodworth 11–0–61–1; Cruttenden 3–0–11–1; Wilkinson 19–3–61–0; Peddy 9–0–39–0; Hodgson 11–3–33–0.

ESCA NORTH v ESCA SOUTH

At St Edward's School, July 12, 13. Drawn.

The South never quite looked capable of reaching their target of 215 and the game finished in a fairly even draw. On a wicket giving some help to the bowlers, only two fifties were scored, with Crozier and Taylor looking the most accomplished batsmen. Jack was the quickest of the bowlers, while slow left-armer Hall also performed well and Swann conceded only 20 runs in 12 overs in the second innings.

ESCA North

T. W. Roberts st Dhillon b Hockley	41	– c Long b Jack	20
A. Hafeez b Jack	7	– b Budd	0
*A. J. Crozier c Edwards b Witherley	54	– c Taylor b Jack	4
†M. Bishop lbw b Hockley	14	– c and b Swann	38
A. J. Marsh c Dhillon b Budd	20	– c Hockley b Swann	44
R. J. Hall c Dhillon b Jack	34	– b Hockley	25
J. Webster c Edwards b Long	21	– b Witherley	9
N. J. Davenport b Jack	4	– c Dhillon b Witherley	0
G. Reynolds not out	15	– lbw b Budd	9
L. M. Chronnell c Hockley b Jack	1	– not out	0
P. Lindsay not out	0	– c Swann b Long	7
Extras	6	Extras	26
1/25 2/66 3/94 4/122 5/152 6/192 7/198 8/199 9/203 (9 wkts dec.)	217	1/7 2/46 3/58 4/88 5/119 6/127 7/133 8/163 9/167	182

Bowling: *First Innings*—Witherley 12–1–35–1; Jack 10–1–44–4; Long 13–2–58–1; Hockley 8–3–22–2; Collins 8–3–19–0; Budd 3–0–19–1; Swann 6–0–17–0. *Second Innings*—Witherley 9.1–0–28–2; Jack 7–3–39–2; Long 10–4–24–1; Hockley 8–2–28–1; Collins 6–0–19–0; Budd 6–3–3–2; Swann 12–7–20–2.

ESCA South

*C. G. Taylor c Crozier b Lindsay	43	– c Marsh b Hall	49
C. Budd lbw b Roberts	35	– c Lindsay b Crozier	14
A. N. Edwards run out	0	– b Webster	18
J. G. C. Rowe st Bishop b Crozier	28	– c Reynolds b Crozier	60
G. P. Swann c Davenport b Roberts	13	– c Hall b Webster	11
J. B. Hockley b Hall	15	– c Crozier b Hall	16
†J. Dhillon not out	23	– not out	17
L. Collins not out	3		
P. J. Witherley (did not bat)		– not out	3
A. Long (did not bat)		– st Bishop b Hall	0
Extras	25	Extras	13
1/71 2/78 3/102 4/116 5/117 6/173 (6 wkts dec.)	185	1/33 2/35 3/138 4/165 5/165 6/168 7/187 (7 wkts)	201

C. Jack did not bat.

Bowling: *First Innings*—Davenport 8–2–27–0; Webster 7–3–13–0; Lindsay 10–5–20–1; Hall 22–11–53–1; Roberts 4–0–21–2; Reynolds 5–1–17–0; Crozier 4–0–13–1. *Second Innings*—Davenport 4–0–17–0; Webster 8–0–38–2; Lindsay 6–1–27–0; Hall 18–4–41–3; Reynolds 5–1–17–0; Crozier 9–0–40–2; Chronnell 4–1–18–0.

At St Edward's School, July 14. D. J. H. Walder's XI won by two wickets. C. G. Taylor's XI 176 for seven dec. (S. A. Richardson 31 retired hurt, R. A. E. Martin 31, A. J. Marsh 40 not out; R. J. Hall three for 43); D. J. H. Walder's XI 180 for eight (D. J. Young 59; N. A. Denning three for 26).

At St John's College, July 14. Drawn. J. A. G. Fulton's XI 220 (J. A. G. Fulton 63, N. J. Davenport 60; A. Long three for 47, L. Collins three for 50); A. J. Crozier's XI 155 for four (A. J. Crozier 53, J. G. C. Rowe 35).

At Christ Church, July 15. Drawn. MCC Schools East 209 for five dec. (T. W. Roberts 49, C. P. R. Hodgson 54 not out); MCC Schools West 183 for eight (D. J. Young 53, Z. R. Feather 31; J. M. Milton three for 70).

MCC v MCC SCHOOLS

At Lord's, July 16. MCC Schools won by three wickets. Toss: MCC.

A second-wicket partnership of 105 between Lawson and Warrington provided the backbone of MCC's innings, before Trestrail added some much needed impetus. The Schools' opening bowler, Webster, had a hand in all five wickets to fall, with four for 75 and a catch. In reply, Young and Crozier continued their fine form at Oxford with invaluable fifties, before Wilkinson and Webster's unbroken stand of 51 saw the Schools to victory with three balls to spare.

MCC

A. G. Lawson c Taylor b Webster	70
C. H. Forward c Dhillon b Webster	2
A. G. Warrington c Webster b Wilkinson	50
G. J. Rickman c Dhillon b Webster	7
*N. J. L. Trestrail not out	44
M. Warden lbw b Webster	7
K. C. Williams not out	8
B 11, l-b 6, w 10, n-b 1	28
1/3 2/108 3/132 4/157 5/192	(5 wkts dec.) 216

K. G. Sedgbeer, P. A. W. Heseltine, †M. S. L. Rollinson and P. A. Veness did not bat.

Bowling: Webster 19–2–75–4; Witherley 4–2–9–0; Swann 17–6–38–0; Walder 5–0–18–0; Wilkinson 15–3–54–1; Hodgson 2–0–5–0.

MCC Schools

T. W. Roberts c Warrington b Veness	20
C. G. Taylor b Williams	4
D. J. Young c Trestrail b Sedgbeer	53
A. J. Crozier c Warden b Trestrail	61
C. P. R. Hodgson b Sedgbeer	16
G. P. Swann lbw b Williams	3
*D. J. H. Walder lbw b Williams	1
R. Wilkinson not out	26
J. Webster not out	25
L-b 4, w 4, n-b 3	11
1/14 2/38 3/111 4/152 5/155 6/167 7/169	(7 wkts) 220

†J. Dhillon and P. J. Witherley did not bat.

Bowling: Warden 17–0–55–0; Williams 12–1–43–3; Heseltine 6–2–26–0; Veness 8–2–30–1; Sedgbeer 10.3–2–55–2; Trestrail 1–0–7–1.

Umpires: K. Bray and C. T. Puckett.

MCC SCHOOLS v NATIONAL ASSOCIATION OF YOUNG CRICKETERS

At Lord's, July 17. Drawn. Toss: MCC Schools.

MCC Schools had much the better of the match, in which neither side did themselves justice. After the pace of Smith had reduced MCC Schools to 58 for four, a fifth-wicket partnership of 83 between Richardson and Swann and a rapid 24 from Walder enabled them to declare at 217. NAYC also lost early wickets and could never really get going. Ellis batted defensively for three hours, but with 141 still needed from the last 20 overs, they could only hold on for the draw.

MCC Schools

J. P. Pyemont c Swarbrick b Smith	8
S. A. Richardson c Davies b Christmas	39
T. W. Roberts c Clarke b Smith	10
A. J. Crozier c Swarbrick b Smith	0
J. A. G. Fulton c Davies b Womble	11
G. P. Swann lbw b Womble	79
R. Wilkinson c Christmas b Womble	7
*D. J. H. Walder c Davies b Lamb	24
J. Webster c Davies b Womble	5
N. J. Davenport not out	7
†S. N. de Silva not out	8
B 1, l-b 9, w 7, n-b 2	19
1/13 2/34 3/34 4/58 5/141 6/160 7/186 8/194 9/202	(9 wkts dec.) 217

Bowling: Christmas 11–1–39–1; Smith 10–2–32–3; Womble 17–2–54–4; Lewis 17–5–38–0; Woosey 6–0–27–0; Lamb 3–0–17–1.

National Association of Young Cricketers

*M. Swarbrick b Davenport	5	A. S. Christmas not out	0
T. C. Z. Lamb run out	18	T. M. Smith not out	0
D. A. Ellis lbw b Wilkinson	62	B 1, w 1, n-b 2	4
J. Clarke b Wilkinson	0		
P. S. Lazenbury run out	18	1/12 2/36 3/46	(7 wkts) 129
†P. G. T. Davies st de Silva b Wilkinson	5	4/76 5/90	
D. R. Womble c Richardson b Wilkinson	17	6/116 7/129	

D. J. Lewis and J. I. T. Woosey did not bat.

Bowling: Webster 10–1–32–0; Davenport 7–2–22–1; Wilkinson 19–11–31–4; Walder 3–0–19–0; Swann 7–3–24–0.

Umpires: K. T. Bailey and N. L. Bainton.

The National Cricket Association selected the following to play for NCA Young Cricketers against Combined Services: A. S. Christmas (Leics), J. Clarke (Lincs), S. N. de Silva (Surrey), D. A. Ellis (Yorks), J. A. G. Fulton (Devon), D. J. Lewis (Salop), A. Long (Dorset), S. A. Richardson (Lancs), M. Swarbrick (Hants), D. J. H. Walder (Northumb) and J. I. T. Woosey (Lancs).

At Lord's, July 18. Combined Services won by six wickets. Toss: Combined Services. NCA Young Cricketers 191 for six (55 overs) (S. A. Richardson 55, D. A. Ellis 67); Combined Services 195 for four (45.2 overs) (SAC M. Bray 75, Sgt N. Palmer 60).

ETON v HARROW

At Lord's, June 25. Drawn. Toss: Eton.

Eton won the toss, but could not take advantage of it. Having asked Harrow to bat, they made them fight for their runs at first; Maydon took 50 minutes over his three. After lunch, however, Harrow's batsmen accelerated. Norris hit nine fours and a six in his half-century, and put on 85 in an hour with Gillions. Then he was caught behind, the first victim of medium-pacer Bailey's spell of four for 12 in five overs. Harrow declared at 238, giving their bowlers two hours and 40 minutes to bowl Eton out. At tea, they were hopeful: they had dismissed the top three for 31 in 15 overs. But the final session saw Lea and Bailey take their partnership to 87 in as many minutes. Only one more wicket fell, that of Lea, whose 57 was the highest score of the match. With only half an hour to the close, he had already ensured Eton's safety.

Harrow

*E. G. L. Maydon c and b Barnett	3	C. R. C. Parker c Dixon b Bailey	9
†R. G. MacAndrew b Barnett	32	E. G. Henson not out	0
A. N. L. Cox c Loudon b Bailey	37		
J. R. W. Norris c Horne b Bailey	56	B 4, l-b 18, w 12, n-b 9	43
S. D. G. Engelen lbw b R. W. J. Bruce	10		
W. A. T. Gillions c Fulton b Bailey	28	1/32 2/88 3/90	(8 wkts dec.) 238
D. C. L. Tregoning c J. T. A. Bruce b Bailey	20	4/117 5/202 6/209	
		7/238 8/238	

E. W. Nicol and J. W. B. Neame did not bat.

Bowling: Barnett 18–5–48–2; R. W. J. Bruce 9–1–36–1; J. T. A. Bruce 14–4–39–0; Jowett 9–2–49–0; Bailey 13.3–2–44–5.

Eton

H. H. Dixon b Parker	6	D. C. Kay-Shuttleworth not out	15
H. J. H. Loudon c Cox b Engelen	7		
*J. A. G. Fulton c and b Engelen	0	B 7, l-b 5, w 6	18
A. M. Lea c MacAndrew b Neame	57		—
N. A. Bailey not out	36	1/14 2/20 3/23 4/110 (4 wkts)	139

R. W. J. Bruce, J. T. A. Bruce, O. L. Barnett, †R. F. Horne and C. R. J. Jowett did not bat.

Bowling: Gillions 11–3–24–0; Parker 8–1–12–1; Engelen 14–3–38–2; Neame 13–6–26–1; Nicol 6–3–10–0; Maydon 3–2–9–0; Norris 1–0–4–0; Cox 1–0–4–0.

Umpires: J. Bugden and J. A. Carter.

Of the 161 matches between the two schools since 1805, Eton have won 52, Harrow 44 and 65 have been drawn. Matches during the two world wars are excluded from the reckoning. The fixture was reduced from a two-day, two-innings-a-side match to one day in 1982. Forty-nine centuries have been scored, the highest being 183 by D. C. Boles of Eton in 1904; M. C. Bird of Harrow is the only batsman to have made two hundreds in a match, in 1907. The highest score since the First World War is 161 not out by M. K. Fosh of Harrow in 1975, Harrow's last victory. Since then Eton have won in 1977, 1985, 1990 and 1991; all other games have been drawn. A full list of centuries since 1918 and results from 1950 can be found in Wisdens *prior to 1994.*

HIGHLIGHTS FROM THE SCHOOLS

Although it was not a vintage year, some memorable moments and notable performances were reported by the schools. Seven batsmen passed 1,000 runs, four doing so in less than 20 innings. The most prolific were R. Wilkinson of Worksop, who scored 1,161 runs at 82.92 in 17 innings, and M. A. Truman of Framlingham, who made the same number, but in 22 innings at an average of 64.50. Close behind them was S. J. Birtwisle of Durham, whose 1,107 came at the best average of 110.70. J. P. Pyemont of Tonbridge had 1,098 at 64.58, followed by D. C. Nash of Malvern (1,093 at 68.31), E. D. C. Craig of Winchester (1,061 at 55.84) and D. P. Reddyhough of Loughborough GS (1,041 at 65.06). Of those passing 400 runs, three-figure averages were also recorded by N. Millar of Fettes, with 668 at the season's best of 111.33, and C. G. Taylor of Colston's Collegiate, who scored 410 in only four innings at an average of 102.50. D. J. Young of Warwick School and A. Major of Canford both scored double-centuries, and there were five innings of 175 or more. Two scored five hundreds: B. J. Thompson of Magdalen College School collected his at a rate of one every 3.6 innings.

The bowlers fared rather better than in 1995. Two passed 60 wickets. J. M. Milton of Oundle had by far the most, with 75 at 17.44, although he bowled a phenomenal 433 overs; T. W. Briggs of Reigate GS bowled 148 fewer overs for his 67 at 13.86. The others to take 50 or more were G. R. Saxton of Bradford GS (55 at 13.18), P. R. Elsley of Framlingham (53 at 16.20), P. W. Anderson of Kingston GS (51 at only 8.66), I. Azam of Christ's College, Finchley (51 at 10.74), T. J. Phillips of Felsted (51 at 14.01) and N. G. Hatch of Barnard Castle (50 at 13.26). Single-figure averages were also achieved by G. S. Sodhi of Ellesmere, who was the most economical of all with 49 at 8.28, and S. C. B. Tomlinson of the Oratory School, whose 43 cost 8.81 apiece.

The outstanding analysis was Azam's ten for 37 against Gents of Hertfordshire, followed by nine for 27 by S. A. Musk of Royal GS, High Wycombe. No one else took nine in an innings. E. Smallman of Ardingly took four wickets in four balls, and there were eight other hat-tricks – from Hatch, D. Finch of St Edmund's, Canterbury, H. Fitch of Bryanston, M. Lloyd of South Craven, R. P. F. Montagu-Williams and R. Robinson of Solihull, G. L. Walters of Monmouth and P. Young of St Edmund's, Ware.

In terms of quantity, the leading all-rounders were Sodhi, who scored 747 runs at 49.80 in addition to his 49 wickets, Tomlinson, with 759 runs at 75.90 to set alongside his 43 wickets, D. J. H. Walder of Oundle with 682 runs at 52.46 and 49 wickets at 14.59, G. D. Franklin of Malvern (541 runs and 45 wickets), D. Bell of Dauntsey's (516 runs and 42 wickets) and E. Sellwood of Royal GS, Worcester (546 runs and 43 wickets). In terms of averages, the best among those with 500 runs and 30 wickets was Tomlinson, winner of the Cricket Society's Wetherell Award, followed by Sodhi and Worksop's Wilkinson, who took 33 wickets at 14.33 in addition to his 1,161 runs.

Imran Azam (left) took ten wickets in an innings for Christ's College, Finchley, and Ben Thompson made five hundreds for Magdalen College School in 1996.

Of the 40 schools who won more than half their matches, Bangor GS recorded the best winning percentage of 86, while Campbell College and Durham both won 83 per cent and Taunton 82 per cent. The six unbeaten sides were Langley Park, Merchant Taylors', Northwood, Eton and King Edward VI, Southampton – all of whom won more than half their matches – plus Fettes and Trinity. Dover College and Llandovery College were the only sides to win none at all.

Although a surprising number managed at least to start all their fixtures, nine schools, from all parts of the country, reported as many as five completely abandoned, while Gordonstoun, Llandovery, King Edward VI, Stourbridge, South Craven and St Lawrence, Ramsgate all lost a third of their fixtures. In contrast, Brighton College lost only one hour all season and wondered whether that was a record in Britain. Many schools played a variety of types of game – declaration, limited overs or "proportional limited overs" (in which the side batting first faces 50 overs, their opponents face 45 and a draw is possible).

The five British schools who participated in the Sir Garfield Sobers Schools Cricket Festival in Barbados were Ashville, City of London Freemen's School, Gresham's, Merchiston Castle and Uppingham. Gresham's, who had also played in the inaugural festival in 1987, achieved the highest placing of sixth, with only a dropped catch preventing them from heading their group. The tournament was won jointly by Transvaal Schools and Dominican Schools after the final was rained off.

Details of records broken, other outstanding performances and interesting features of the season may be found in the returns from the schools which follow.

THE SCHOOLS

(Qualification: Batting 150 runs; Bowling 15 wickets)

* *On name indicates captain.* * *On figures indicates not out.*

Note: The line for batting reads Innings–Not Outs–Runs–Highest Score–100s–Average; that for bowling reads Overs–Maidens–Runs–Wickets–Best Bowling–Average.

ABINGDON SCHOOL *Played 17: W 5, L 6, D 6*

Master i/c: A. M. Broadbent

Batting—J. R. C. Horton 16–2–559–89*–0–39.92; E. J. K. Ryder 15–2–425–69–0–32.69; H. R. W. Whalen 17–2–462–88*–0–30.80; H. E. Dorling 11–4–195–72*–0–27.85; *G. A. O. Jones 15–1–253–102*–1–18.07.

Bowling—R. A. Pike 179.1–27–634–32–6/63–19.81; T. W. Jones 85.2–7–355–17–6/37–20.88; S. E. Watts 179.1–23–860–34–7/64–25.29.

ALDENHAM SCHOOL *Played 11: W 3, L 2, D 6*

Master i/c: S. Thomas

Batting—K. Habib 11–3–384–83–0–48.00; J. Allen 11–0–335–98–0–30.45; M. Bell 11–4–207–65–0–29.57; A. Meara 11–0–298–45–0–27.09; K. Worsnop 9–2–157–45–0–22.42; A. Thrussell 10–1–169–60–0–18.77.

Bowling—T. Smith 137–24–380–18–3/28–21.11.

ALLEYN'S SCHOOL *Played 15: W 6, L 7, D 2*

Master i/c: D. Tickner Professional: P. Edwards

Simon Payne headed both batting and bowling and broke the school record with an innings of 183 not out against Emanuel. Also prominent were the Allen twins, who were both playing their fourth full season in the eleven: Tom captained the side and James hit a century against Westminster.

Batting—S. Payne 15–1–487–183*–1–34.78; J. L. Allen 13–1–396–103–1–33.00; P. J. Mitchener 13–3–270–36*–0–27.00; *T. J. Allen 14–1–239–44–0–18.38.

Bowling—S. Payne 97.3–10–368–21–4/51–17.52; J. L. Allen 127.4–20–479–17–3/2–28.17.

AMPLEFORTH COLLEGE *Played 16: W 4, L 5, D 7. A 2*

Master i/c: G. Thurman Professional: D. Wilson

Batting—P. Field 17–1–457–94–0–28.56; A. Jenkins 15–3–284–63–0–23.66; J. Melling 14–2–254–46–0–21.16; *M. Hirst 14–3–214–41*–0–19.45; G. Denny 17–1–292–79–0–18.25; R. Simpson 17–0–286–73–0–16.82; P. Cartwright-Tayor 10–0–156–51–0–15.60.

Bowling—T. Pinsent 210.1–42–591–33–6/28–17.90; N. Zoltowski 156.4–19–644–23–5/39–28.00; C. Shillington 137.5–17–654–23–5/36–28.43; M. Hirst 140–26–496–16–4/12–31.00.

ARDINGLY COLLEGE *Played 22: W 5, L 11, D 6. A 2*

Master i/c: G. Hart Professional: S. Sawant

Edward Smallman took four wickets in four balls against Brighton College in the quarter-final of the Langdale Cup. Bowling left-arm medium pace, he had the first caught at square leg and bowled the next three with leg-stump yorkers.

Batting—M. Turner 17–3–799–100*–1–57.07; J. Fairbrother 19–2–654–109*–1–38.47; *A. Spencer 21–2–501–151*–1–26.36; J. Andrews 10–1–210–77*–0–23.33; N. Strugnell 18–0–375–47–0–20.83; N. Holloway 16–1–234–52*–0–15.60; J. Dower 13–2–159–31–0–14.45; J. Lindsten 17–1–193–47*–0–12.06.

Bowling—R. Iqbal 92.3–21–325–19–5/26–17.10; E. Smallman 140.2–24–501–29–5/29–17.27; D. Macaulay 115.3–27–390–21–4/40–18.57; J. Dower 125–17–465–20–4/55–23.25; A. Toomey 140.2–20–642–17–4/66–37.76.

ARNOLD SCHOOL *Played 19: W 7, L 5, D 7*

Master i/c: D. Grimshaw Professional: K. Higgs

For the success of their centenary season, which featured a first win over MCC, Arnold owed much to the all-round contribution of Jonathan Ashworth, as well as the determination and emerging talent of Alexander Rawlinson. David Fielding, the captain, completed a record fifth year in the eleven.

Batting—A. Rawlinson 19–2–513–100*–1–30.17; *D. Fielding 19–2–507–73–0–29.82; M. Wallwork 16–1–446–115–1–29.73; J. Ashworth 19–4–413–92–0–27.53; T. Wyles 13–0–157–47–0–12.07.

Bowling—J. Ashworth 243.1–58–738–42–4/14–17.57; M. Wand 121.1–22–445–15–4/29–29.66.

ASHVILLE COLLEGE *Played 16: W 2, L 4, D 10. A 2*

Master i/c: S. Herrington

Batting—B. Quick 14–1–566–102–1–43.53; R. Rawlings 15–2–538–101–1–41.38; J. Cartwright 15–2–466–71–0–35.84.

Bowling—B. Quick 143–24–542–32–8/62–16.93; A. Hughes 135–26–399–20–5/33–19.95.

BABLAKE SCHOOL *Played 12: W 1, L 6, D 5*

Master i/c: B. J. Sutton Professional: C. Patel

Highlights were Stephen Byng's hundred against King Edward's, Birmingham, and a visit from Bishop's School, Cape Town. Byng was the England Under-15 vice-captain in the Lombard World Challenge.

Batting—S. P. Byng 9–2–256–105*–1–36.57; H. W. Ayers 10–2–243–84*–0–30.37; A. C. Smyth 8–0–178–62–0–22.25.

Bowling—S. P. Byng 58.5–7–176–16–4/19–11.00; A. C. Smyth 85–16–255–16–3/17–15.93.

BANCROFT'S SCHOOL *Played 16: W 3, L 7, D 6. A 1*

Master i/c: J. G. Bromfield Professional: J. K. Lever

An inexperienced side developed confidence under the positive captaincy of James Davey. One highlight was a century in the victory over J. G. Bromfield's XI by Matthew Cole, a forceful opening bat and useful leg-break bowler. Left-armer Andy Duff was an inspiration in the field.

Batting—A. Duff 12–5–337–96–0–48.14; M. Cole 14–2–345–134*–1–28.75; R. Glassberg 12–2–272–54*–0–27.20; J. E. C. Hull 10–3–157–41–0–22.42; S. J. Harston 16–0–272–85–0–17.00; R. Gevertz 15–1–222–46–0–15.85; *J. R. Davey 16–0–211–45–0–13.18.

Bowling—A. Duff 142.2–30–442–27–4/29–16.37; M. Cole 100.2–13–483–18–4/45–26.83; J. R. Davey 166.3–20–701–21–4/27–33.38.

BANGOR GRAMMAR SCHOOL *Played 21: W 18, L 1, D 2. A 1*

Master i/c: C. C. J. Harte

The season was preceded by a memorable winter trip to the Sydney Youth Cricket Festival. The team spirit fostered during that tour produced perhaps the side's best season. Mark English took his career total above 2,000 runs, second only to the 2,654 recorded by M. P. Rea. Bryn Cunningham – like his elder brother Jan a double schoolboy international in cricket and rugby – improved on Rea's career average of 34.92 by finishing with 1,773 runs at 39.40.

Batting—B. J. Cunningham 13–6–481–95–0–68.71; M. McBride 16–5–400–69–0–36.36; *M. T. C. English 18–1–518–80–0–30.47; G. J. Campbell 16–1–265–49–0–17.66; M. C. W. Harte 19–7–206–39–0–17.16; M. K. Hutchinson 15–2–215–58–0–16.53; K. P. Macauley 15–0–213–39–0–14.20.

Bowling—R. J. Coghlin 94.2–12–347–32–5/11–10.84; J. C. W. Harte 153–40–386–35–5/19–11.02; R. J. Irwin 106.4–25–282–22–3/17–12.81; K. P. Macauley 86.1–14–289–19–4/21–15.21; P. B. Neill 143–29–410–20–3/31–20.50; M. K. Hutchinson 126.4–18–420–19–5/5–22.10.

BARNARD CASTLE SCHOOL *Played 17: W 3, L 6, D 8. A 2*

Master i/c: C. P. Johnson

Nick Hatch's 50 wickets included a hat-trick in his seven for 36 against University College School.

Batting—L. A. J. Haslam 10–2–275–85*–0–34.37; S. N. Whitehead 18–1–449–85–0–26.41; S. C. Davies 17–1–299–61–0–18.68; N. G. Hatch 18–0–316–49–0–17.55; T. J. Wilks 17–2–218–48–0–14.53; *D. M. Cook 14–2–150–24–0–12.50.

Bowling—N. G. Hatch 251.2–62–663–50–7/36–13.26; S. C. Davies 98.3–9–499–21–7/72–23.76; D. M. Cook 104.1–16–387–15–4/93–25.80.

BEDFORD SCHOOL *Played 15: W 3, L 7, D 5. A 2*

Master i/c: D. W. Jarrett Professional: R. G. Caple

The side consistently under-performed, resulting in even more of an anticlimax than had been expected after the success of 1995. Although there were three good hundreds from Marc Snell, in his fifth year with the eleven, he could not produce his best form against quality opposition and the side as a whole lacked the character to stave off seven defeats.

Batting—*M. E. Snell 17–3–768–141*–3–54.85; S. R. W. Lincoln 16–1–359–100–1–23.93; G. D. Graham 17–0–376–94–0–22.11; T. W. J. Chapman 15–5–208–67*–0–20.80; S. Sims 12–1–222–39–0–20.18; D. R. Pointer 14–0–173–42–0–12.35.

Bowling—G. D. Graham 89–16–298–15–3/22–19.86; A. Gulzar 220–46–702–31–6/77–22.64; T. W. J. Chapman 202–29–734–29–6/42–25.31; J. A. G. Neale 160–28–543–19–5/47–28.57.

BEDFORD MODERN SCHOOL *Played 21: W 3, L 5, D 13*

Master i/c: N. J. Chinneck

In a strong batting side, Oliver Clayson included three hundreds and a 99 in his 904 runs. However, a lack of fast bowlers was a handicap. Gentlemen of Bedfordshire were beaten by one wicket off the last ball.

Batting—K. J. Locke 15–5–521–80–0–52.10; O. J. Clayson 19–1–904–141–3–50.22; K. Patel 9–3–249–77–0–41.50; *I. R. Chadwick 19–1–611–126–2–33.94; C. A. Ferguson 16–1–435–85–0–29.00; A. J. Whitehead 14–5–213–43–0–23.66; P. E. Timewell 17–2–209–45–0–13.93.

Bowling—J. A. Dilleigh 124–25–326–18–3/18–18.11; A. J. Whitehead 177.3–44–579–26–4/18–22.26; O. J. Clayson 213–45–771–24–5/53–32.12.

BEECHEN CLIFF SCHOOL *Played 9: W 6, L 1, D 2. A 1*

Master i/c: K. J. L. Mabe Professional: G. Sheppard

Hard work in the nets was rewarded with five straight wins and impressive individual performances. David Burton was the leading batsman and set a superb example in the field. Other commitments restricted the appearances of both Mark Thorburn and Ben Staunton, the latter with Somerset Second Eleven and Under-19.

Batting—*M. Thorburn 7–3–199–92*–0–49.75; D. A. Burton 9–1–395–77–0–49.37.

Bowling—M. Thorburn 78.3–23–239–22–6/19–10.86; N. D. Wrigley 51.3–10–181–15–3/19–12.06; M. J. Trim 62–10–200–15–3/15–13.33.

BERKHAMSTED SCHOOL *Played 17: W 4, L 7, D 6. A 1*

Master i/c: J. G. Tolchard Professional: M. R. Herring

Batting—P. S. Davey 7–2–221–89–0–44.20; *G. A. S. McHugh 17–2–636–93*–0–42.40; M. A. Bartholomew 16–3–421–77–0–32.38; C. W. Read 11–0–239–78–0–21.72; M. L. A. Davis 14–0–267–61–0–19.07; L. N. H. Brightman 10–2–152–37–0–19.00.

Bowling—E. N. Clark 148–19–489–24–6/24–20.37; M. A. Bartholomew 133.2–20–525–17–4/29–30.88.

BETHANY SCHOOL *Played 11: W 2, L 4, D 5. A 5*

Master i/c: K. R. Daniel

Batting—R. J. Clark 11–0–326–107–1–29.63; T. B. Playfoot 11–3–232–51*–0–29.00; J. M. Frape 11–2–236–55–0–26.22; *N. C. W. Pontifex 11–1–262–60–0–26.20.

Bowling—R. J. Clark 141–29–477–23–4/26–20.73.

BIRKENHEAD SCHOOL *Played 15: W 7, L 1, D 7*

Master i/c: P. A. Whittel

Zack Feather participated in the MCC Schools Festival at Oxford and went on to play for English Schools.

Batting—M. R. Smathers 10–5–208–73*–0–41.60; Z. R. Feather 12–0–496–107–1–41.33; W. P. L. Roberts 14–2–430–100*–1–35.83; O. J. Rule 15–3–330–79*–0–27.50;*R. S. Whalley 12–2–151–32–0–15.10.

Bowling—M. R. Smathers 72–9–279–16–3/23–17.43; O. J. Rule 125–23–406–21–3/20–19.33; Z. R. Feather 128–33–371–16–3/11–23.18; Z. A. Smith 122–15–435–16–4/46–27.18.

BISHOP'S STORTFORD COLLEGE *Played 22: W 9, L 6, D 7*

Master i/c: D. Hopper Professional: C. Bannister

Inspired by the positive captaincy of Luke Westell, the side equalled the school record of nine wins – only to be frustrated by narrow defeats against Monkton Combe (one run) and Hereford Cathedral School (three runs) in the last two matches. They fielded superbly, with Andrew Hill and Jeremy Thompson outstanding; Andrew Bruce passed 40 wickets for the third successive season.

Batting—J. J. Mew 20–2–588–102*–1–32.66; D. O'Donnell 22–1–654–125–1–31.14; J. R. Addison 8–2–164–52*–0–27.33; S. R. Mason 20–4–382–75*–0–23.87; *L. P. Westell 21–2–449–52–0–23.63; P. J. H. Fishpool 18–1–387–70–0–22.76.

Bowling—J. F. Beatty 92–22–260–18–4/10–14.44; A. D. Hill 220–52–654–42–7/28–15.57; A. J. Bruce 269–52–876–45–7/63–19.46; D. O'Donnell 101–14–370–15–3/24–24.66; L. P. Westell 195–43–674–23–5/44–29.30.

BLOXHAM SCHOOL *Played 15: W 5, L 4, D 6. A 1*

Master i/c: C. N. Boyns

Batting—M. Palmer 13–2–343–74–0–31.18; I. de Weymarn 13–2–329–60*–0–29.90; T. Palmer 12–2–229–49–0–22.90.

Bowling—T. Palmer 64–13–184–16–4/5–11.50; S. Covington 114–31–320–17–4/43–18.82; S. Jones 123.4–9–488–22–5/62–22.18.

BLUNDELL'S SCHOOL *Played 16: W 5, L 8, D 3. A 2*

Master i/c: N. A. Folland

The young side, headed by Paul Warren, varied between playing excellent and undistinguished cricket. Warren and Quenton Miller both passed 500 runs, while Austin Smith developed well as an all-rounder.

Batting—*P. M. Warren 15–1–540–124*–1–38.57; Q. H. Miller 16–1–542–132–1–36.13; G. M. C. Vaughan 15–2–381–85*–0–29.30; T. J. Hooper 15–2–233–51–0–17.92; A. C. Smith 14–3–178–52*–0–16.18; P. J. Stormonth 14–1–180–45–0–13.84.

Bowling—P. M. Warren 166.5–41–403–30–4/16–13.43; A. C. Smith 116.3–17–452–16–2/14–28.25.

BRADFIELD COLLEGE *Played 18: W 2, L 5, D 11*

Master i/c: D. R. Evans Professional: J. F. Harvey

Batting—J. R. Perkins 16–2–632–100*–1–45.14; *R. J. Holland 14–0–387–126–1–27.64; N. A. Denning 14–4–266–51–0–26.60; T. A. M. Campbell 15–2–229–39–0–17.61; R. D. Nevin 16–1–182–60–0–12.13.

Bowling—N. A. Denning 238.5–54–651–40–5/29–16.27; C. A. K. Carpenter 186.3–35–579–22–4/28–26.31; M. C. Giles 129.1–35–722–23–5/37–31.39.

BRADFORD GRAMMAR SCHOOL *Played 18: W 7, L 5, D 6. A 5*

Master i/c: A. G. Smith

A record of only one win before half term and six afterwards paints a fair picture of the season of rebuilding. Seam bowler Guy Saxton was outstanding, his 55 wickets being the most this century.

Batting—*A. J. Myers 15–0–543–83–0–36.20; R. E. Walker 17–3–419–74–0–29.92; A. J. Modgill 17–0–448–77–0–26.35; G. R. Saxton 15–5–193–43*–0–19.30; B. D. Cocker 18–1–314–72–0–18.47; A. Pathmanathan 16–0–231–68–0–14.43; C. H. Harper 18–4–201–40*–0–14.35.

Bowling—G. R. Saxton 241.1–65–725–55–6/49–13.18; K. D. A. Howes 182.3–37–672–25–3/20–26.88; R. E. Walker 125.4–22–516–19–4/48–27.15.

BRENTWOOD SCHOOL *Played 20: W 6, L 11, D 3*

Master i/c: B. R. Hardie

Batting—G. R. Boyce 12–6–252–95*–0–42.00; J. R. Stanton 17–1–531–111*–2–33.18; R. J. Wybrow 15–1–389–65–0–27.78; D. J. Ox 18–1–464–57–0–27.29; *A. W. Pratt 9–2–151–35*–0–21.57; B. G. L. Rylah 12–2–188–65–0–18.80; A. S. Taker 17–2–260–55–0–17.33; J. D. T. Watkins 15–0–233–53–0–15.53; E. Kirby 13–1–184–27–0–15.33.

Bowling—R. A. J. Wybrow 222–33–901–38–8/89–23.71; I. T. Belchamber 174–24–695–18–3/41–38.61.

BRIGHTON COLLEGE *Played 21: W 5, L 8, D 8*

Master i/c: J. Spencer Professional: J. D. Morley

Only one hour was lost to the weather in a season which saw the side overcome a disappointing start to record five victories, thanks largely to the fast bowling of A. J. Pope. The side included twins, Chris and James Sell, who each dislocated a shoulder in the same match – against the Old Brightonians.

Batting—A. J. Nichol 19–3–544–100*–1–34.00; J. B. James 18–1–536–104–1–31.52; J. L. Crown 21–1–541–128–1–27.05; T. P. Gayton 21–2–438–62–0–23.05; P. J. S. Spencer 14–1–247–38–0–19.00; R. W. Ainsworth 14–1–197–47–0–15.15.

Bowling—A. J. Pope 263.4–62–751–40–6/25–18.77; J. A. Potter 118–29–393–16–2/16–24.56; M. S. Wilson 127.3–13–576–20–5/12–28.80; P. J. S. Spencer 144–22–527–15–3/41–35.13; R. W. Ainsworth 147–19–620–16–4/48–38.75.

BRISTOL GRAMMAR SCHOOL *Played 16: W 7, L 3, D 6*

Masters i/c: D. M. Crawford and K. Blackburn

Batting—N. Miller 11–2–313–85*–0–34.77; A. Richardson 16–2–408–84–0–29.14; R. Dallimore 10–2–221–82–0–27.62; *J. Reed 15–1–360–79*–0–25.71; J. Tyler 13–1–291–54–0–24.25; M. Bolton 11–1–157–70*–0–15.70.

Bowling—M. Bolton 78–9–304–21–4/14–14.47; J. Reed 91–17–284–18–3/7–15.77; T. Pring 81–10–350–19–6/27–18.42; K. Hudswell 134–23–479–24–4/21–19.95.

BROMSGROVE SCHOOL *Played 18: W 6, L 4, D 8*

Master i/c: P. Newman

Batting—A. N. Brown 16–4–524–107*–2–43.66; J. V. A. Robertson 10–4–254–102*–1–42.33; P. J. Goodrem 15–4–367–83–0–33.36; B. R. Steer 9–2–227–58–0–32.42; E. H. Binham 12–0–335–72–0–27.91; J. R. France 15–1–361–58–0–25.78; A. D. Langlands 10–3–162–36*–0–23.14; N. W. Reade 13–2–238–59*–0–21.63; J. H. M. Beddall 10–1–186–46–0–20.66; S. M. Eustace 15–4–227–46–0–20.63.

Bowling—M. J. Gough 68–15–208–17–4/13–12.23; A. D. Langlands 132.5–17–446–21–3/26–21.23.

BRYANSTON SCHOOL *Played 15: W 4, L 7, D 4*

Master i/c: T. J. Hill

An inexperienced team owed much to the captain, Philip Chapman, who inspired three of the four victories with 103 not out against Dorset Rangers, five slip catches at Monkton Combe and eight wickets against the Old Boys. The fourth win – over Caulfield – featured a hat-trick by Henry Fitch.

Batting—A. H. D. McArthur 15–0–302–52–0–20.13; *P. G. P. Chapman 15–1–218–103*–1–15.57; S. P. Nugent 12–1–170–42*–0–15.45; M. L. M. Davies 15–0–154–39–0–10.26.

Bowling—P. G. P. Chapman 114.2–13–429–28–8/25–15.32; S. J. Denning 140.3–38–390–22–5/26–17.72.

CAMPBELL COLLEGE *Played 12: W 10, L 2, D 0*

Master i/c: B. Robinson Professional: M. Horne

Batting—R. K. Long 9–2–193–71–0–27.57; J. D. Rodgers 11–0–294–76–0–26.72; R. J. Wallace 9–1–188–100–1–23.50; W. R. Clements 12–1–187–34–0–17.00.

Bowling—J. D. Rodgers 65.3–10–189–23–4/10–8.21; R. K. Long 80–15–228–24–5/20–9.50; R. J. M. Miller 49.4–4–199–17–4/24–11.70; R. M. Heasley 65.5–5–238–18–4/19–13.22.

CANFORD SCHOOL *Played 16: W 5, L 6, D 5*

Master i/c: A. R. Hobbs Professional: J. J. E. Hardy

Batting—N. Makin 13–3–733–117*–1–73.30; A. Major 12–4–522–225*–1–65.25; W. McLaren-Clarke 7–2–212–91–0–42.40; P. Stapleton 8–1–250–74–0–35.71; P. Young 10–1–193–45–0–21.44.

Bowling—A. Major 66–8–292–15–4/71–19.46.

CATERHAM SCHOOL *Played 15: W 8, L 4, D 3. A 2*

Master i/c: A. G. Tapp Professional: Wasim Raja

Another successful season was dominated by fifth-former Richard Jackson, who headed both the averages.

Batting—R. Jackson 16–2–769–154*–2–54.92; R. Connelly 15–1–263–47–0–18.78; G. Goodwin 16–1–245–67–0–16.33; T. Slade 15–2–185–40–0–14.23; *B. Barton 13–1–156–48–0–13.00.

Bowling—R. Jackson 162.2–47–461–28–5/49–16.46; T. Slade 265.2–77–699–33–5/55–21.18; B. Barton 197.2–46–624–27–5/46–23.11.

CHARTERHOUSE *Played 19: W 9, L 5, D 5. A 1*

Master i/c: A. S. Morrison Professional: R. V. Lewis

The opener and Surrey Under-16 captain, A. P. Hollingsworth, hit an outstanding 197 against a strong Old Boys' side. It ended when he ran himself out going for quick runs and enabled Charterhouse to declare at 346 for seven after following on.

Batting—A. P. Hollingsworth 18–1–830–197–3–48.82; A. J. M. Burrows 19–1–501–101–2–27.83; E. A. J. Breeze 19–1–436–93–0–24.22; B. M. J. Warburton 17–4–281–59–0–21.61; J. R. C. Hamblin 16–2–266–59–0–19.00; A. D. W. Smith 18–2–284–62–0–17.75.

Bowling—J. R. C. Hamblin 161–32–470–28–4/42–16.78; A. D. W. Smith 102–21–347–16–3/37–21.68; B. J. O. Lewis 167–39–528–19–3/36–27.78; *C. T. Allen 171–44–421–15–4/35–28.06.

CHELTENHAM COLLEGE *Played 15: W 7, L 3, D 5. A 2*

Master i/c: M. W. Stovold Professional: M. P. Briers

Batting—S. T. J. Cowley 16–3–751–108–2–57.76; *T. E. Lacey 13–4–421–100*–1–46.77; T. A. O. Hughes 16–1–572–107–1–38.13; W. F. A. Chambers 12–3–321–58*–0–35.66; S. A. A. Block 6–1–176–73–0–35.20; T. F. G. Richardson 10–3–223–60*–0–31.85.

Bowling—R. L. Dredge 157.3–12–645–28–5/66–23.03; T. O. B. Morris 115–18–418–17–3/26–24.58; M. A. Hopkins 139–34–486–15–3/32–32.40.

CHIGWELL SCHOOL *Played 18: W 10, L 3, D 5*

Master i/c: D. N. Morrison Professional: F. Griffiths

Positive cricket and an excellent team effort brought a record of ten wins and only one defeat in schools matches, the best for more than 20 years. Mussam Ali, outstanding with 718 runs and 30 wickets, was runner-up for the Lord's Taverners Under-19 Cricketer of the Year award.

Batting—M. Ali 17–5–718–88*–0–59.83; L. Mines 7–3–153–47–0–38.25; R. Chauhan 14–1–370–77–0–28.46; T. Jolly 15–1–354–66–0–25.28; G. Calder 10–1–194–53–0–21.55; S. Spindlow 13–1–198–48–0–16.50; N. Timpson 14–4–164–37–0–16.40; A. Mandrekar 14–2–166–72–0–13.83.

Bowling—P. Landsman 90–23–319–19–8/58–16.78; M. Ali 132–28–537–30–5/46–17.90; N. Timpson 108–18–324–18–4/6–18.00; R. Chauhan 121–24–336–18–4/24–18.66; D. Sharma 110–38–342–15–7/36–22.80.

CHRIST COLLEGE, BRECON *Played 16: W 7, L 5, D 4. A 4*

Master i/c: C. W. Kleiser Professionals: R. P. Lefebvre and T. W. Higginson

In the best season for many years, the side boasted a strong attack, backed by good fielding, and attributed their five defeats to batting failures. In a remarkable match, Monmouth were bowled out for 107, only for Christ College to collapse to 89 for nine; however, Chris Davenport hit an unbeaten 48 at No. 7 and won the contest with his third consecutive four.

Batting—R. J. Chilman 14–1–572–157–2–44.00; C. M. P. Davenport 11–5–189–48*–0–31.50; R. J. W. Fish 12–2–225–44–0–22.50; B. G. John 13–2–201–88*–0–18.27; *T. Harbottle 13–0–213–79–0–16.38.

Bowling—K. Dias 149.1–34–427–25–5/13–17.08; C. M. P. Davenport 156.4–37–434–21–4/26–20.66; R. Jones 174.3–25–586–25–5/41–23.44.

CHRIST'S COLLEGE, FINCHLEY *Played 21: W 13, L 6, D 2*

Master i/c: S. S. Goldsmith

A season of entertaining cricket was highlighted by the performance of opening bowler Imran Azam. His 51 wickets included ten for 37 against Gents of Hertfordshire – the first time anyone had taken all ten for the first team – and he also played some explosive innings.

Batting—C. Spanos 10–4–215–47–0–35.83; C. R. Depala 17–1–390–94–0–24.37; R. Johnstone 13–0–287–52–0–22.07; I. Azam 18–3–277–75*–0–18.46; *R. R. Persad 15–1–209–42–0–14.92; Z. L. Anwari 14–1–167–52–0–12.84.

Bowling—I. Azam 197.1–48–548–51–10/37–10.74; R. Depala 73.3–8–329–23–6/37–14.30; C. R. Depala 95–18–314–20–3/1–15.70; R. R. Persad 66–13–243–15–4/23–16.20.

CHRIST'S HOSPITAL *Played 17: W 6, L 6, D 5. A 1*

Master i/c: H. P. Holdsworth Professionals: K. G. Suttle and P. J. Graves

With three spinners regularly operating, James Gladding equalled the wicket-keeping record of 32 dismissals in a season with 16 caught and 16 stumped. A highlight was the match against Toowoomba GS, Australia, who were beaten by one wicket off the last ball.

Batting—T. Pickhaver 16–2–424–70–0–30.28; *P. J. Wilkins 17–0–470–73–0–27.64; F. M. Thomas 17–1–424–86–0–26.50; J. A. Cordery 16–1–336–102–1–22.40; D. F. Morley 15–4–189–31–0–17.18; J. J. Kingsbury 12–1–166–52–0–15.09.

Bowling—S. J. Peters 115–17–437–25–6/21–17.48; E. G. Young 158–38–530–30–5/34–17.66; J. A. Cordery 171–30–538–27–5/47–19.92; D. F. Morley 103–19–371–16–3/77–23.18; R. O. Stringfellow 104–20–386–15–4/30–25.73.

CLAYESMORE SCHOOL *Played 15: W 5, L 5, D 5*

Masters i/c: R. J. Hammond and R. J. Denning

Adam Philp and Tom Denning both completed four years in the eleven.

Batting—*A. M. Philp 12–3–471–81–0–52.33; M. D. Senior 13–3–269–68–0–26.90; T. J. Denning 14–0–303–60–0–21.64.

Bowling—A. M. Philp 138–35–350–24–8/31–14.58; G. S. Tew 123–26–416–22–5/31–18.90; T. J. Sharpe 108–24–409–18–4/40–22.72; R. J. S. Lack 171–33–547–23–4/24–23.78.

CLIFTON COLLEGE *Played 16: W 4, L 8, D 4*

Master i/c: D. C. Henderson Professional: F. J. Andrew

Batting—*D. R. Grewcock 9–4–279–92–0–55.80; J. D. Walters 16–1–392–85–0–26.13; J. A. England 16–1–391–74–0–26.06; E. H. Kenworthy 14–2–298–78–0–24.83; J. D. Biddle 11–0–218–44–0–19.81; M. H. R. Bowden 13–1–171–47–0–14.25.

Bowling—A. G. S. Lawson 124.3–22–402–17–4/8–23.64.

COLFE'S SCHOOL *Played 11: W 2, L 3, D 6. A 2*

Master i/c: P. Clegg Professional: A. Reid-Smith

The batting was headed by the Under-14 player, Richard Clinton, son of Grahame, formerly of Kent and Surrey.

Batting—R. Clinton 9–1–437–90*–0–54.62; P. Rogers 9–1–270–73–0–33.75; *O. Chapman 10–1–289–75–0–32.11; T. Allen 10–1–188–62–0–20.88.

Bowling—No bowler took 15 wickets. The leading bowler was J. Gaston 44–8–146–9–3/49–16.22.

COLSTON'S COLLEGIATE SCHOOL *Played 18: W 7, L 8, D 3. A 1*

Master i/c: M. P. B. Tayler

Although Christopher Taylor played only four innings, he scored two centuries in totalling 410 runs at an average of 102.50. He played for MCC Schools and captained English Schools.

Batting—C. G. Taylor 4–0–410–183–2–102.50; J. P. Tucker 9–2–377–85*–0–53.85; *J. A. Ewens 16–1–400–108–1–26.66; M. P. Barrow 9–1–192–86–0–24.00; S. J. Clapp 17–5–283–72*–0–23.58; A. M. Holloway 13–0–280–101–1–21.53; K. S. Gozra 17–0–262–40–0–15.41.

Bowling—S. J. Clapp 131.1–20–458–19–4/38–24.10; J. A. Ewens 220.3–23–499–20–4/51–24.95.

CRANBROOK SCHOOL *Played 16: W 8, L 3, D 5. A 1*

Master i/c: A. J. Presnell

Dan Furnival's 175 against Kent College came in 29 overs and was a record for the school, as was wicket-keeper James Harfoot's tally of 47 victims to date.

Batting—*D. Furnival 16–4–671–175–2–55.91; M. Knight 14–3–303–62*–0–27.54; T. Hinchliffe 16–8–207–103*–1–25.87; O. Furnival 10–2–184–51–0–23.00; J. Harfoot 14–2–267–83–0–22.25.

Bowling—J. Frape 56.2–10–203–16–4/21–12.68; T. Hinchliffe 143.2–32–415–27–5/22–15.37; W. Chuter 93–17–264–17–5/33–15.52; P. Wicken 98.3–15–354–18–4/34–19.66; N. Green 128–37–370–15–4/42–24.66.

CRANLEIGH SCHOOL *Played 16: W 6, L 5, D 5. A 1*

Master i/c: D. C. Williams

The strongest side for many years boasted depth in both batting and bowling, supported by enthusiastic fielding. Ed Copleston and Abeed Janmohamed headed the batting, while Andy Hillier was the leading bowler, taking 43 wickets with commendable accuracy.

Batting—A. M. T. Janmohamed 16–5–464–99–0–42.18; *D. E. M. G. Copleston 17–1–502–76–0–31.37; J. Bennett 17–0–363–60–0–21.35; I. D. Houston 13–3–166–35–0–16.60; J. C. D. Wright 13–0–171–90–0–13.15; L. E. Moorby 17–1–174–55–0–10.87.

Bowling—A. G. Hillier 161.2–29–560–43–5/29–13.02; I. D. Houston 146.1–42–457–24–3/17–19.04; L. E. Moorby 130.1–29–411–20–5/36–20.55; M. J. Hillier 177.2–44–542–20–3/12–27.10.

CULFORD SCHOOL *Played 16: W 4, L 5, D 7*

Master i/c: R. P. Shepperson

The first five matches brought two maiden centuries and four wins, including a first ever over MCC. However, despite much positive cricket, the other matches were all lost or drawn, including that against Gresham's, in which Culford's 257 for five in pursuit of 289 was a school record.

Batting—S. F. Ornbo 12–3–386–107*–1–42.88; R. J. R. Evans 12–4–339–64–0–42.37; D. S. Holliday 14–1–489–102–1–37.61; *M. J. L. Grinham 14–2–431–70–0–35.91; N. C. M. Sawyer 13–1–306–56–0–25.50; G. N. Lindley 14–2–214–67–0–17.83.

Bowling—S. F. Ornbo 93–15–325–18–4/44–18.05; P. R. Hamshere 145–23–578–23–5/49–25.13; B. J. Unwin 160–27–604–19–4/20–31.78.

DARTFORD GRAMMAR SCHOOL *Played 15: W 8, L 1, D 6*

Master i/c: C. J. Plummer Professional: M. M. Patel

In a successful season with eight wins and only one defeat, Edward Tyler shared stands of 216 with Martin Pask against Royal Hospital School and 160 with Gary Cook against Chislehurst and Sidcup GS.

Batting—E. C. Tyler 9–3–407–98–0–67.83; G. Siveyer 6–1–206–86*–0–41.20; *M. J. L. Pask 8–1–264–103*–1–37.71; G. J. Cook 8–2–212–53–0–35.33; K. C. Newman 10–1–297–100–1–33.00; S. D. L. Henderson 13–2–178–44–0–16.18.

Bowling—M. J. L. Pask 71.5–11–218–21–6/18–10.38; D. W. Ring 93.1–19–280–18–5/17–15.55.

DAUNTSEY'S SCHOOL *Played 22: W 10, L 7, D 5. A 1*

Master i/c: D. C. R. Baker Professional: P. Knowles

After winning the first three matches, the side lost their way before finishing on a high note. Particularly satisfying was the match at Dean Close, where the side performed abysmally in the field, conceding 258, but went on to win the match by five wickets. The season finished with a successful tour of Canada – the first time the school had undertaken a major tour for any sport.

Batting—D. Bell 19–2–516–108–1–30.35; J. Hope 18–0–505–74–0–28.05; B. Darbyshire 16–3–361–101*–1–27.76; *S. Gaiger 18–2–290–80–0–18.12; N. Paget 19–6–227–46–0–17.46; N. Gough 19–3–229–36–0–14.31; R. Gater 14–1–163–39–0–12.53.

Bowling—J. Stafford-Wood 35–4–103–18–6/5–5.72; D. Bell 192.5–23–616–42–4/29–14.66; N. Paget 66.1–11–256–15–3/7–17.06; A. Houchin 177–32–551–31–4/19–17.77; J. Somerville 72–7–287–15–5/27–19.13; J. Reynolds 124–13–483–25–5/52–19.32.

DEAN CLOSE SCHOOL *Played 16: W 5, L 6, D 5*

Master i/c: C. M. Kenyon Professional: S. Hansford

Batting—*A. J. Thompson 12–1–562–148–3–51.09; W. M. Kinder 16–2–400–98–0–28.57; G. D. M. Lane 13–4–245–48–0–27.22; D. T. Gilroy 8–0–179–63–0–22.37; J. Mears 14–1–231–39–0–17.76; J. R. T. Sidebottom 11–2–151–48–0–16.77; S. J. Gilbert 15–0–210–55–0–14.00.

Bowling—W. M. Kinder 150.3–21–571–26–5/56–21.96; O. E. Bretherton 98.3–10–408–15–3/18–27.20; N. G. E. Ball 114.3–11–502–18–3/21–27.88; A. J. Thompson 119–12–504–16–4/45–31.50.

DENSTONE COLLEGE *Played 16: W 1, L 2, D 13. A 4*

Master i/c: A. N. James

A young side struggled to complete victory from strong positions. W. J. L. Bagshawe and P. M. Cheadle shared century partnerships for the first and fifth wickets, their opening stand of 174 against King Edward's, Birmingham, being the season's highlight.

Batting—P. M. Cheadle 14–1–550–125–2–42.30; W. J. L. Bagshawe 16–2–507–65*–0–36.21; J. A. Blackwell 9–2–216–62*–0–30.85; B. J. Brookes 12–2–167–30–0–16.70.

Bowling—W. E. Nicholls 182–47–607–24–4/20–25.29; B. S. Johal 165–35–610–24–6/61–25.41.

DOVER COLLEGE *Played 13: W 0, L 8, D 5. A 1*

Master i/c: D. C. Butler

A consolation in a disappointing season with no wins was a maiden century by Alex Bradley, a colt. Coming in at 22 for four against Sutton Valence, he was unbeaten on 100 from 131 balls at the declaration on 176 for eight.

Batting—*C. D. G. Crofton-Martin 13–0–280–54–0–21.53; A. K. Bradley 12–1–223–100*–1–20.27; J. R. Telford 12–1–202–52–0–18.36.

Bowling—A. W. Barrow 125.2–14–495–25–4/39–19.80; J. R. Telford 145.3–33–423–21–6/33–20.14.

DOWNSIDE SCHOOL *Played 14: W 2, L 11, D 1. A 1*

Master i/c: K. J. Burke Professional: J. Bird

Batting—*J. P. Taylor 14–0–402–58–0–28.71; J. P. Acheson 13–1–237–48*–0–19.75; D. M. Reeve-Tucker 14–2–207–40*–0–17.25; I. W. Kirkpatrick 11–0–184–68–0–16.72.

Bowling—F. S. H. Perkins 100.5–20–306–17–5/32–18.00; D. J. Northwood 142.2–18–522–20–5/52–26.10; I. W. Kirkpatrick 133–15–547–15–5/63–36.46.

DUKE OF YORK'S ROYAL MILITARY SCHOOL *Played 12: W 5, L 1, D 6. A 2*

Master i/c: S. Salisbury Professionals: C. Penn and J. H. Dawes

The successful side, undefeated by schools, included two sets of twins – Stephan and Michael Hayward, who shared the bulk of the bowling, and all-rounders Edward and Paul Thompson – as well as the Morris brothers.

Batting—T. C. L. Davies 11–5–312–74*–0–52.00; M. Bassett 7–0–208–62–0–29.71; E. J. D. Thompson 8–1–172–45–0–24.57; G. B. Morris 8–1–153–80–0–21.85; *T. O. G. Hickson 10–0–193–51–0–19.30.

Bowling—S. Hayward 106–25–275–23–5/6–11.95; P. de M. Thompson 71–14–186–15–5/61–12.40.

DULWICH COLLEGE *Played 15: W 5, L 6, D 4*

Master i/c: S. R. Northcote-Green Professional: A. Ransom

Batting—O. J. Farley 11–2–324–62–0–36.00; N. A. Bhatti 14–0–439–99–0–31.35; N. Martin 10–1–222–63–0–24.66; R. Barry 13–0–294–81–0–22.61; R. Amlot 9–0–185–56–0–20.55; V. Kumar 12–1–212–45–0–19.27; F. Hutton-Mills 13–4–150–30–0–16.66.

Bowling—A. Patel 130–21–444–25–4/23–17.76; F. Hutton-Mills 157–30–480–16–4/22–30.00.

DURHAM SCHOOL *Played 12: W 10, L 1, D 1. A 5*

Master i/c: M. E. Hirsch

The Christmas tour to Australia stood the side in good stead when they faced adult opponents and they won ten of their 12 matches. Simon Birtwisle was the outstanding batsman with 1,107 runs at 110.70; the last 808 came in nine innings at an average of 269. His four unbeaten centuries included 176 against Barnard Castle and two in the match against Old Dunelmians. Adrian Hedley also scored two hundreds and the captain, Ross McLaren, returned after a back injury to finish the season with an innings of 159 not out in a three-day game against Christ Church GS from Perth, Australia. Birtwisle played for Durham Second Eleven and joined the newly formed Durham Cricket Academy.

Batting—S. J. Birtwisle 17–7–1,107–176*–4–110.70; *R. D. McLaren 8–2–402–159*–1–67.00; A. J. Hedley 14–4–575–123*–2–57.50; A. G. Greig 10–4–257–72–0–42.83; D. F. Watts 16–1–473–79–0–31.53; I. Laidler 8–3–157–48–0–31.40; R. J. Windows 15–1–328–80–0–23.42.

Bowling—W. Bishop 104–21–324–17–4/12–19.05; I. J. Mosey 108–12–404–20–4/40–20.20; R. J. Windows 89–15–312–15–4/30–20.80; S. J. Birtwisle 129–31–358–17–5/50–21.05; N. D. Howe 130–32–399–16–3/9–24.93.

EASTBOURNE COLLEGE *Played 19: W 9, L 2, D 8. A 2*

Masters i/c: N. L. Wheeler and D. A. Stewart Professional: J. N. Shepherd

Left-arm spinner S. J. W. Whitton took a hat-trick against The Lodge School on a tour of Barbados in March and went on to collect 45 wickets during the season. R. F. S. Hill, at medium pace, took six in an innings on consecutive Saturdays against Cranleigh, Hurstpierpoint and Epsom. Sixteen-year-old M. J. Lock, in his third season, batted with great consistency, as well as taking 23 wickets.

Batting—M. J. Lock 15–4–536–68*–0–48.72; C. P. C. Williams 11–6–206–60*–0–41.20; S. J. W. Whitton 12–4–289–64*–0–36.12; A. J. Fyfe 16–1–523–86–0–34.86; H. F. G. Southwell 15–2–437–86*–0–33.61; A. D. Simcox 16–2–399–75–0–28.50; D. J. M. Garner 14–1–259–103*–1–19.92; *R. F. Marchant 15–3–213–82–0–17.75.

Bowling—S. J. W. Whitton 195.1–49–544–45–6/27–12.08; M. J. Kemp 73–16–220–16–3/1–13.75; R. F. S. Hill 155.1–32–500–31–6/37–16.12; M. J. Lock 157.2–39–406–23–4/25–17.65.

THE EDINBURGH ACADEMY *Played 15: W 4, L 6, D 5. A 2*

Master i/c: G. R. Bowe

Batting—J. P. L. Boyd 15–2–490–90–0–37.69; R. N. Gray 14–1–387–125–1–29.76; N. J. Hillyard 14–3–275–64*–0–25.00; M. J. Bruce 13–3–232–63–0–23.20; M. Martin 12–0–266–88–0–22.16.

Bowling—M. Martin 142–41–295–20–5/23–14.75; A. J. Cowie 139–30–424–27–5/10–15.70; R. N. Gray 98–23–353–17–4/12–20.76.

ELIZABETH COLLEGE, GUERNSEY *Played 21: W 10, L 5, D 6. A 2*

Master i/c: M. E. Kinder

Inspired by the positive captaincy of Kevin Graham, the side recorded ten wins. In scoring 198 for five in 41 overs to beat Victoria College, Jersey, T. J. Ozanne hit 62 off 40 balls, and Old Elizabethans were beaten off the last ball when, with nine wickets down, debutant leg-spinner D. Walder hit the winning runs.

Batting—M. Brehaut 19–5–585–77*–0–41.78; C. J. Colclough 13–6–178–28*–0–25.42; S. D. Wilson 14–3–241–102–1–21.90; A. L. Peacegood 19–1–351–73–0–19.50; A. I. Alford 14–4–175–62–0–17.50; T. J. Ozanne 19–1–306–62–0–17.00; *K. R. Graham 17–0–282–50–0–16.58.

Bowling—J. A. Barrett 94–20–346–25–4/25–13.84; S. D. Wilson 75–19–259–15–3/21–17.26; J. L. Winn 158–40–439–23–4/10–19.08; A. I. Alford 113.5–14–366–18–4/27–20.33.

ELLESMERE COLLEGE *Played 15: W 7, L 3, D 5. A 1*

Master i/c: E. Marsh Professional: R. G. Mapp

Gurtek Singh Sodhi, a newcomer to the sixth form, made a big impact on the side. A fast away-swing bowler with an effective yorker, he took a college record 49 wickets and scored three centuries in his 747 runs.

Batting—G. S. Sodhi 15–0–747–127–3–49.80; *O. J. Pughe 12–1–305–69–0–27.72; T. H. Pearson 9–3–162–41*–0–27.00; G. T. Edwards 13–5–201–56–0–25.12; P. J. Furniss 15–0–359–73–0–23.93; H. A. Murphy 14–0–242–63–0–17.28.

Bowling—G. S. Sodhi 178–71–406–49–7/21–8.28; T. H. Pearson 106–31–281–26–5/19–10.80.

ELTHAM COLLEGE *Played 16: W 4, L 5, D 7. A 1*

Masters i/c: P. C. McCartney and B. M. Withecombe Professional: R. W. Hills

The side developed as the season progressed, although the lack of a penetrative attack was always a handicap. The opening batsmen, S. J. Whitehead and M. N. Roche, scored consistently, while the captain, P. J. Fenn, made a useful all-round contribution.

Batting—S. J. Whitehead 16–4–541–99–0–45.08; M. N. Roche 14–2–431–105–1–35.91; *P. J. Fenn 15–2–329–52*–0–25.30; A. J. Branchflower 13–3–236–75*–0–23.60; T. J. Willis 12–0–216–95–0–18.00.

Bowling—P. S. Attreed 131.2–18–503–23–5/25–21.86; P. J. Fenn 166.5–33–649–25–5/30–25.96.

ENFIELD GRAMMAR SCHOOL *Played 19: W 4, L 7, D 8*

Master i/c: M. Alder

Batting—M. Wright 18–1–646–106–1–38.00; M. Kapadia 18–1–534–94–0–31.41; B. Lyons 11–4–151–48–0–21.57; M. Bowen 18–1–329–50–0–19.35; O. Edwards 12–3–157–42*–0–17.44; G. Mohammed 16–1–240–32–0–16.00; M. Marston 12–1–152–45–0–13.81.

Bowling—M. Bowen 134–25–403–20–4/48–20.15; M. Wright 108–15–397–19–5/62–20.89; N. Meggison 137–32–547–19–3/43–28.78; J. Marston 141–34–531–15–3/36–35.40.

EPSOM COLLEGE *Played 15: W 4, L 6, D 5. A 1*

Master i/c: G. A. Jones Professional: A. Flower

Batting—M. P. Snow 16–1–473–141*–1–31.53; G. E. Fowler 16–2–440–79–0–31.42; A. J. Hunt 15–0–447–81–0–29.80; J. R. Gill 14–0–344–92–0–24.57; J. E. Felton 15–1–284–58–0–20.28; C. J. Valentine 16–2–264–70*–0–18.85.

Bowling—H. P. E. Kingham 109–12–397–16–7/40–24.81; A. J. Hunt 149–16–632–23–4/76–27.47; L. J. Webster 213–42–810–26–7/57–31.15.

ETON COLLEGE *Played 14: W 9, L 0, D 5. A 3*

Master i/c: J. A. Claughton Professional: J. M. Rice

Excellently captained by James Fulton, Eton were unbeaten and equalled the record of nine wins, including three in the Silk Trophy over Knox GS from Sydney, Shrewsbury and Scotch College, Melbourne. They attributed their success to the penetrative fast bowling of Oliver Barnett and Robert Bruce. The batting was dominated by Hugo Loudon and his opening partner, Henry Dixon, who has scored 1,490 runs with five centuries in two seasons. The pair shared three century partnerships, of which the highest was 236 against King Edward's, Birmingham. Alex Loudon, Hugo's younger brother and England Under-15 captain, joined the side later in the season.

Batting—H. J. H. Loudon 14–3–615–106*–2–55.90; A. M. Lea 12–6–321–57–0–53.50; H. H. Dixon 14–0–703–121–3–50.21; *J. A. G. Fulton 13–3–379–98–0–37.90.

Bowling—O. L. Barnett 171–43–357–31–8/37–11.51; R. W. J. Bruce 152.2–32–407–31–5/32–13.12; C. R. J. Jowett 131.4–43–349–15–3/26–23.26.

EXETER SCHOOL *Played 18: W 9, L 3, D 6. A 2*

Master i/c: M. C. Wilcock

The Devon Under-16 captain, Ian Gamble, topped the batting averages in his first full season. While the ground fielding was consistently good, with Patrick Drought outstanding, it took until half term for the bowling to become consistent, whereupon six of the last eight matches were won.

Batting—I. P. Gamble 15–3–721–100*–1–60.08; M. C. Scoble 7–4–157–102–1–52.33; *W. C. Cruft 16–3–636–93–0–48.92; J. D. E. Boase 15–1–394–88–0–28.14; P. J. Drought 17–5–325–59*–0–27.08; J. D. Retter 12–4–212–102–1–26.50; B. P. Keylock 9–1–211–59–0–26.37; J. P. Cruft 13–2–281–67–0–25.54; M. W. Goode 9–1–198–74*–0–24.75.

Bowling—J. W. Porter 70–17–176–15–4/16–11.73; J. J. Youngs 156–55–494–29–7/52–17.03; J. D. Retter 178–36–593–30–5/43–19.76; I. P. Gamble 112–19–419–16–4/41–26.18; M. W. Goode 151–34–549–19–3/42–28.89.

FELSTED SCHOOL *Played 15: W 7, L 1, D 7*

Master i/c: F. C. Hayes

Fifteen-year-old Timothy Phillips took 51 wickets, including a return of eight for 48 against Framlingham. That match was also memorable for a third century of the season from the Essex Under-19 captain, Richard Hayes, son of former England player Frank Hayes, the school's cricket master.

Batting—*R. F. C. Hayes 16–4–709–110*–3–59.08; R. T. Wright 12–2–356–74–0–35.60; L. M. G. Cooper 11–3–279–85*–0–34.87; B. J. Tabor 9–4–158–63*–0–31.60; R. R. S. King 16–2–345–91–0–24.64; A. G. Tabor 15–2–305–69–0–23.46; T. J. Phillips 12–1–222–58*–0–20.18.

Bowling—T. J. Phillips 284–99–715–51–8/48–14.01; C. P. Homer 95–20–326–16–4/16–20.37; E. H. Ekins 203–25–708–26–6/41–27.23.

FETTES COLLEGE *Played 9: W 4, L 0, D 5. A 1*

Master i/c: J. G. A. Frost Professional: J. van Geloven

Unbeaten for the first time since 1981, the side owed much to the batting of the 15-year-old Scotland Under-19 representative, Neil Millar, whose 11 innings featured a fine century against Edinburgh Academy and eight more fifties.

Batting—N. Millar 11–5–668–104–1–111.33.

Bowling—*F. M. Mair 107.5–25–311–16–3/34–19.43; T. J. D. Strahan 116.1–26–320–15–4/26–21.33.

FOREST SCHOOL *Played 17: W 7, L 2, D 8. A 1*

Master i/c: S. Turner

Batting—R. Marshall 10–0–370–98–0–37.00; *S. Kuru 15–2–313–56*–0–24.07; T. Cartwright 13–3–236–49–0–23.60; J. Foster 13–0–248–53–0–19.07; R. Perry 14–3–203–51*–0–18.45; G. Heaton 15–3–214–35–0–17.83; S. Woolmer 14–0–216–42–0–15.42.

Bowling—C. White 179.4–31–496–35–6/30–14.17; T. Cartwright 136–23–554–30–7/21–18.46; M. Orchard-Lisle 165.3–36–534–21–6/52–25.42; R. Smith 157–22–680–24–7/39–28.33.

FOYLE AND LONDONDERRY COLLEGE *Played 15: W 8, L 6, D 1*

Masters i/c: G. R. McCarter and I. McCracken

Batting—*K. Dunn 14–2–271–63*–0–22.58; G. King 14–1–226–71–0–17.38; D. Wallace 13–2–171–34–0–15.54; S. Bratton 12–2–152–50*–0–15.20.

Bowling—S. Hanna 78–21–142–15–4/16–9.46; A. Fleming 115.2–24–328–29–6/28–11.31; G. Moore 107.1–29–263–20–4/19–13.15.

FRAMLINGHAM COLLEGE *Played 22: W 13, L 4, D 4, Tied 1*

Master i/c: A. S. Griffiths Professional: C. Rutterford

Batting—M. A. Truman 22–4–1,161–115–3–64.50; C. J. Goodfellow 20–2–596–88–0–33.11; M. A. A. Low 14–5–288–68*–0–32.00; C. J. Clementson 17–1–385–103*–1–24.06; P. J. Pineo 14–3–207–33*–0–18.81; M. A. H. Rodwell 20–4–291–43–0–18.18.

Bowling—P. R. Elsley 271.3–62–859–53–6/13–16.20; P. J. Pineo 249.4–34–790–36–4/32–21.94; A. J. Tucker 128.5–28–384–17–3/38–22.58; I. Lancaster 186–28–647–22–3/40–29.40.

GIGGLESWICK SCHOOL *Played 12: W 6, L 4, D 2. A 3*

Master i/c: C. Green Professional: A. G. Lawson

Batting—C. R. Woolsey 9–4–196–40*–0–39.20; *O. R. J. Cruse 12–2–216–47*–0–21.60.

Bowling—C. R. Woolsey 90.2–23–196–15–4/22–13.06; E. W. M. Smith 141–34–353–24–7/24–14.70.

GLENALMOND *Played 13: W 3, L 3, D 7. A 1*

Master i/c: J. D. Bassett

The side's inexperience showed in their frequent failure to force victory. On slow wickets which inhibited attacking strokeplay, the fragile batting depended much on Tom Stevenson, who performed better early on. Alisdair Sim played some valuable innings at No. 6 and headed both averages, although his off-spin could be erratic. Henry Smuts-Muller and Harry Monro both showed potential as fast bowlers.

Batting—A. Sim 9–3–182–48*–0–30.33; T. Stevenson 13–2–323–64–0–29.36; *G. Christie 13–2–259–70–0–23.54; W. McCarter 12–2–209–31*–0–20.90.

Bowling—A. Sim 77.5–24–171–20–6/19–8.55; H. Smuts-Muller 157–55–395–25–4/39–15.80; J. Hamilton 110.2–16–307–18–3/32–17.05; H. Monro 195.1–56–464–25–5/34–18.56.

GORDONSTOUN SCHOOL *Played 7: W 5, L 2, D 0. A 4*

Master i/c: C. J. Barton

The wettest summer for 15 years severely curtailed the season.

Batting—J. Rae 5–1–315–122–2–78.75; A. H. B. Fraser-Tytler 7–1–331–91–0–55.16; M. C. Hepburn 7–2–152–41–0–30.40.

Bowling—T. H. Illingworth 38–14–113–16–3/24–7.06; M. C. Hepburn 61–17–155–15–5/16–10.33.

GRENVILLE COLLEGE *Played 10: W 3, L 4, D 3. A 2*

Master i/c: C. R. Beechey

Batting—B. Moore 9–0–263–95–0–29.22; J. Kirkham-Brown 8–0–204–57–0–25.50; A. Bott 9–0–216–52–0–24.00; *J. Morris 10–0–196–68–0–19.60.

Bowling—N. Lenihan 33–2–164–15–5/44–10.93; J. Morris 87.4–4–331–15–3/29–22.06.

GRESHAM'S SCHOOL *Played 18: W 9, L 4, D 5. A 1*

Master i/c: A. M. Ponder

A fine team effort resulted in the best season to date, with victory in eight out of ten schools matches. The most satisfying were those over Oundle and Melbourne HS from Australia, both of whom were otherwise unbeaten. The total of 305 for eight against the Drones was a school record, as was Jonathan Wyatt's aggregate of 787, which included a century against MCC.

Batting—D. L. Roper 15–5–498–105*–1–49.80; J. P. Wyatt 17–1–787–109–1–49.18; *D. P. Copas 9–2–262–115–1–37.42; O. W. Morgan 16–3–471–103*–1–36.23; O. B. Jackson 9–3–203–52–0–33.83; R. M. C. Oakley 11–2–236–52–0–26.22; J. O. Hughes 9–2–180–53–0–25.71; J. N. Worby 12–2–213–59–0–21.30; T. J. Hood 18–0–305–62–0–16.94.

Bowling—R. P. Macnair 108–20–335–21–4/25–15.95; J. G. Woodwark 186.3–39–558–32–6/37–17.43; M. P. Lintott 80–4–358–16–2/11–22.37; R. M. C. Oakley 144–19–487–21–7/59–23.19.

HABERDASHERS' ASKE'S SCHOOL *Played 20: W 4, L 3, D 13. A 1*

Masters i/c: S. D. Charlwood and D. I. Yeabsley

A young side lost only once to schools opposition, but their inexperience in capitalising on winning positions resulted in too many draws. A highlight was an excellent win over Exeter CC during the annual tour to Devon.

Batting—S. L. Bloom 20–1–612–72*–0–32.21; D. B. Wilson 19–1–535–101*–1–29.72; C. C. K. Brown 14–4–291–57*–0–29.10; M. J. Tang 16–4–278–46–0–23.16; A. M. Reid 17–1–273–43–0–17.06; K. Pandit 12–1–173–37–0–15.72; D. M. Williams 18–2–222–48–0–13.87.

Bowling—S. A. Merchant 114–12–430–21–6/66–20.47; A. K. Notaney 176–29–683–31–7/68–22.03; N. Rooban 242.4–43–839–31–4/53–27.06.

HAILEYBURY *Played 16: W 5, L 4, D 7. A 1*

Master i/c: M. S. Seymour Professionals: G. D. Barlow and J. W. Lloyds

Batting—*N. D. Hughes 16–3–605–103*–2–46.53; R. J. Palmer 16–4–511–90–0–42.58; D. Fitzgerald 11–3–249–53–0–31.12; J. S. Rixson 15–0–428–85–0–28.53; M. H. Bradford 12–2–243–64–0–24.30; T. J. Pearman 13–3–211–48*–0–21.10; J. E. Collyer 13–1–218–64–0–18.16.

Bowling—S. D. Roy 224–45–700–34–4/35–20.58; C. J. Box 135–28–415–18–3/22–23.05; D. Fitzgerald 144–23–419–15–4/46–27.93; A. W. R. E. Okines 107–16–447–15–3/42–29.80.

HAMPTON SCHOOL *Played 19: W 6, L 7, D 6. A 2*

Master i/c: A. J. Cook Professional: P. Farbrace

By the end of the season, the team regularly featured three Under-15 players, all of whom were in the side that won the Holmwood's six-a-side competition in July.

Batting—*B. C. A. Mott 18–3–778–113–3–51.86; P. J. Frost 17–4–556–100*–1–42.76; S. B. Powell 17–2–506–99–0–33.73; P. C. K. Wood 13–3–267–95–0–26.70; D. N. Battey 16–2–252–50–0–18.00; R. T. H. Gaines 13–0–200–75–0–15.38.

Bowling—P. J. Frost 106–26–278–19–5/36–14.63; B. C. A. Mott 114–24–379–22–6/35–17.22; J. E. Cudd 143.3–31–441–23–4/12–19.17; A. J. Evans 131.4–37–408–20–7/50–20.40; P. C. K. Wood 118–23–380–16–5/45–23.75; N. Critchley 134.1–26–501–15–3/39–33.40.

HARROW SCHOOL *Played 19: W 7, L 3, D 9. A 1*

Master i/c: C. M. B. Williams Professional: R. K. Sethi

In another successful season three batsmen passed 500 runs and shared six hundreds. Andrew Cox batted aggressively, scoring centuries against Dulwich, Wellington College and MCC, while the wicket-keeper Robin MacAndrew, a left-hander, made two, James Norris one and Simon Engelen was close behind with 472 runs, including a 99. A fine all-rounder, Engelen also took 49 wickets with his left-arm in-swing, including five or more five times. Otherwise the attack was limited and struggled to bring off victory from strong positions.

Batting—A. N. L. Cox 18–2–672–115*–3–42.00; J. R. W. Norris 16–3–502–104–1–38.61; R. G. MacAndrew 18–2–585–100*–2–36.56; S. D. G. Engelen 16–1–472–99–0–31.46; C. R. C. Parker 10–1–167–35–0–18.55; W. A. T. Gillions 14–3–202–74*–0–18.36; D. C. L. Tregoning 13–2–201–58–0–18.27; *E. G. L. Maydon 18–3–251–69*–0–16.73.

Bowling—S. D. G. Engelen 289.1–89–762–49–7/22–15.55; E. G. L. Maydon 114–26–400–15–4/43–26.66; E. W. Nicol 195.5–37–599–16–4/7–37.43; W. A. T. Gillions 200.3–50–574–15–4/29–38.26.

THE HARVEY GRAMMAR SCHOOL *Played 17: W 9, L 4, D 4*

Master i/c: P. J. Harding

Batting—*L. Fletcher 12–5–283–95*–0–40.42; N. Jackson 12–2–302–72–0–30.20; J. Reene 13–1–324–76–0–27.00; N. Brandon 12–2–230–51–0–23.00; K. Temple 12–0–243–51–0–20.25; N. Hazledene 10–1–180–75–0–20.00.

Bowling—L. Fletcher 138.5–31–361–31–5/23–11.64; M. Ritchie 131–28–368–26–4/26–14.15; T. Keel 78–15–252–16–4/20–15.75.

HEREFORD CATHEDRAL SCHOOL *Played 17: W 8, L 5, D 4. A 2*

Master i/c: A. H. Connop

Stephen Price's aggregate of 763 runs was 17 more than the record set in 1992 by Edward Symonds.

Batting—*S. J. Price 13–2–763–136–3–69.36; M. S. Tomlinson 14–2–292–89–0–24.33; D. C. Jennings 13–3–236–71–0–23.60; A. J. Last 16–4–257–51–0–21.41; O. D. R. Hewlett 16–1–305–69–0–20.33; P. M. Whittal 12–0–221–77–0–18.41; R. D. J. Edwards 14–0–234–54–0–16.71.

Bowling—J. E. A. Layton 238.4–59–695–36–7/44–19.30; N. R. Brown 176.1–39–549–25–3/14–21.96; M. S. Tomlinson 178.3–29–594–21–6/15–28.28.

HIGHGATE SCHOOL *Played 14: W 5, L 2, D 7*

Master i/c: R. G. W. Marsh Professional: R. E. Jones

Batting—R. A. Swann 13–3–580–107*–2–58.00; D. J. L. Walters 9–1–349–101*–1–43.62; R. H. Beenstock 11–3–342–82–0–42.75; M. A. P. O'Brien 9–0–342–89–0–38.00; D. J. Miller 7–1–176–71–0–29.33; D. C. Cohen 12–1–230–58–0–20.90.

Bowling—D. C. Cohen 136.2–16–566–18–3/38–31.44.

HURSTPIERPOINT COLLEGE *Played 17: W 9, L 5, D 3. A 1*

Master i/c: M. J. Mance Professional: D. J. Semmence

Ably led by Simon Warrender, an inexperienced eleven enjoyed a better season than expected, including victory over a strong MCC side. R. K. H. Redford made a significant all-round contribution with 530 runs and 36 wickets.

Batting—J. N. Cation 18–4–593–82–0–42.35; R. K. H. Redford 18–4–530–103–1–37.85; M. J. E. Imber 16–4–381–73–0–31.75; D. N. Rodbourne 13–4–267–65–0–29.66; A. N. Rayner 11–2–243–70–0–27.00; *S. J. Warrender 18–0–423–77–0–23.50.

Bowling—R. K. H. Redford 183–45–505–36–6/29–14.02; T. R. Brewer 158–26–505–26–6/27–19.42; D. G. Burstow 146.2–14–566–22–3/59–25.72; M. T. Harrison 155–29–577–21–4/53–27.47.

IPSWICH SCHOOL *Played 18: W 7, L 5, D 6. A 1*

Master i/c: A. K. Golding Professional: R. E. East

Batting—G. McCartney 19–6–910–132*–2–70.00; T. Green 18–5–590–122*–2–45.38; D. Sim 9–2–227–68–0–32.42; E. J. Lyons 14–0–265–50–0–18.92; T. Jervis 12–3–161–75–0–17.88; J. Collins 14–1–216–60*–0–16.61; J. East 12–1–166–46–0–15.09; J. Achar 14–0–183–39–0–13.07.

Bowling—J. East 269–51–882–38–5/56–23.21; J. Collins 147–20–497–18–4/17–27.61; J. Bell 176–33–589–21–6/71–28.04; W. Douglas 161–22–636–18–5/46–35.33.

THE JOHN LYON SCHOOL *Played 17: W 7, L 4, D 6*

Master i/c: I. Parker

Opening batsman Manoraj Navratnarajah scored five consecutive fifties, while Kashir Maan took his wickets at an average of 8.94 in his first season. The season was followed by an enjoyable tour of Barbados.

Batting—M. Navratnarajah 15–5–591–88*–0–59.10; *K. Merali 13–3–355–78–0–35.50; N. Goh 14–3–361–74–0–32.81.

Bowling—K. Maan 76.1–22–152–17–4/25–8.94; K. Merali 156.2–31–445–29–4/14–15.34; D. Mehta 67–8–263–16–4/23–16.43; R. Mehta 151.2–33–453–22–4/34–20.59; N. Goh 172–35–570–24–5/56–23.75.

KELLY COLLEGE *Played 13: W 7, L 2, D 4. A 1*

Master i/c: G. C. L. Cooper

A young eleven exceeded all expectations in achieving the most victories since 1985.

Batting—R. G. Goldring 13–2–467–82–0–42.45; S. W. James 7–3–150–38–0–37.50; R. P. C. Jones 13–2–278–46*–0–25.27; M. R. Anderson 11–4–162–33–0–23.14; *R. H. Harrison 12–2–221–37–0–22.10.

Bowling—C. C. W. Procter 113–27–343–23–6/11–14.91; D. A. Nicholls 53–5–304–17–5/54–17.88; R. G. Goldring 157–18–527–28–6/59–18.82.

KIMBOLTON SCHOOL *Played 18: W 5, L 7, D 6. A 3*

Master i/c: R. P. Merriman Professional: M. E. Latham

William Follett's 146 against the visiting Ermolo HS, South Africa, was a school record, as was the side's total of 330 in 54.4 overs. Follett dominated both batting and bowling, although the batting averages were headed by the captain, Mark Klein, whose younger brother, Ben, took 20 wickets with his leg-spin.

Batting—*M. Klein 18–3–619–109*–1–41.26; W. Follett 18–0–654–146–2–36.33; J. Caswell 17–3–396–78*–0–28.28; G. Woods 18–2–397–75–0–24.81; J. Pepperman 17–0–396–44–0–23.29; M. Hatfield 14–1–193–42–0–14.84; B. Klein 13–2–159–28–0–14.45.

Bowling—W. Follett 171–32–670–29–4/37–23.10; B. Klein 120–13–540–20–4/21–27.00; G. Woods 227–45–707–25–4/49–28.28.

KING EDWARD VI COLLEGE, STOURBRIDGE *Played 9: W 2, L 4, D 3. A 5*

Master i/c: R. A. Williams

Nigel Davenport's 155 not out in 25.1 overs against Wyggeston & Queen Elizabeth I College equalled the record set by G. R. Haynes in 1988. He then equalled Haynes's 1987 record of two centuries in a season when he made 147 against Hagley RC School, completing a fine match with a return of five for 17. He went on to play for MCC Schools, English Schools and Worcestershire Under-19.

Batting—N. J. Davenport 8–1–470–155*–2–67.14; R. J. Perkins 8–1–242–100*–1–34.57.

Bowling—L. Ashton 60.4–10–264–17–6/49–15.52; N. J. Davenport 86–9–323–18–5/17–17.94.

KING EDWARD VI SCHOOL, SOUTHAMPTON *Played 20: W 12, L 0, D 8. A 3*

Master i/c: R. J. Putt

The captain, John Claughton, again dominated the batting with 967 runs as the young side recorded the school's highest percentage of wins, including a first over MCC. The all-rounder John Francis played for England Under-15 in the Lombard World Challenge.

Batting—*J. A. Claughton 20–4–967–115–3–60.43; B. W. Craft 13–5–421–65*–0–52.62; J. D. Francis 11–2–294–65–0–32.66; A. J. Hart 19–2–477–106–1–28.05; M. H. Tarry 17–1–382–77*–0–23.87; L. D. Sully 12–3–212–47*–0–23.55; N. P. Evans 11–0–176–64–0–16.00.

Bowling—L. D. Sully 250–56–774–43–5/32–18.00; P. S. Eyers 137–26–523–26–4/23–20.11; N. S. J. Bedford 140–25–477–18–5/13–26.50; G. C. Douglas 106–20–422–15–6/23–28.13.

KING EDWARD VII SCHOOL, LYTHAM *Played 20: W 11, L 5, D 4*

Master i/c: A. M. Weston Professional: E. A. E. Baptiste

The batting was headed by the captain, R. M. Moore, and the powerful opener, L. M. Hilton, who hit two centuries and five fifties. Impressive contributions from Lancashire Under-15 players G. Evans (opening bat and leg-spin bowler), the left-handed B. Godfrey and opening bowler M. Wilkinson promised much for the future.

Batting—*R. M. Moore 19–4–741–112*–1–49.40; L. M. Hilton 20–2–738–111*–2–41.00; G. Evans 16–2–465–75–0–33.21; J. B. Kok 15–2–312–72*–0–24.00; B. Godfrey 13–3–214–70*–0–21.40; S. T. Long 19–3–335–81–0–20.93; M. J. Crook 14–2–246–59–0–20.50.

Bowling—G. Evans 153.3–34–521–24–4/30–21.70; M. Wilkinson 201.5–40–653–29–5/21–22.51; T. K. Brown 238.5–49–722–31–5/28–23.29.

KING EDWARD'S SCHOOL, BIRMINGHAM *Played 24: W 7, L 9, D 8. A 1*

Master i/c: M. D. Stead Professional: J. Huband

Batting—A. C. G. Brindley 8–1–205–98–0–29.28; A. D. Treharne 22–1–518–98*–0–24.66; R. J. McGuire 22–1–509–77*–0–24.23; J. J. Child 22–4–420–100*–1–23.33; *A. J. Martin 15–0–333–60–0–22.20; A. M. Purdon 24–0–502–83–0–20.91.

Bowling—R. J. McGuire 85.3–7–412–19–5/39–21.68; M. A. Robertson 103–14–385–17–4/66–22.64; A. D. Treharne 236–61–701–28–4/29–25.03; J. H. Allen 193–31–713–28–4/37–25.46; J. S. Ross 226–50–721–25–4/44–28.84.

KING HENRY VIII SCHOOL *Played 15: W 5, L 6, D 4. A 2*

Master i/c: A. M. Parker

Batting—A. J. Goode 13–1–397–83–0–33.08; J. S. Grindal 10–1–242–65–0–26.88; G. R. Long 13–2–283–89–0–25.72; R. T. Martin 15–0–367–89–0–24.46; N. A. Phelps 12–4–177–50–0–22.12; M. R. Goode 13–1–258–49–0–21.50.

Bowling—A. J. Goode 111–19–390–21–7/22–18.57; M. J. Burrows 108–4–540–16–4/94–33.75.

KING WILLIAM'S COLLEGE *Played 11: W 2, L 4, D 5*

Master i/c: A. Maree Professional: D. Mark

Batting—G. Peacock 9–1–450–121–1–56.25; H. Tyson 10–2–351–74*–0–43.87; J. Manuja 11–1–232–63*–0–23.20; E. Zuiderent 11–1–223–39–0–22.30.

Bowling—J. Manuja 114–25–395–24–3/46–16.45; G. Peacock 139–37–345–18–2/48–19.16.

KING'S COLLEGE, TAUNTON *Played 14: W 8, L 4, D 2*

Master i/c: R. J. R. Yeates Professional: D. Breakwell

Nicholas Boulton, the left-handed opener who claimed the innings and season's aggregate records in 1995, improved on his own record average for a season with 82.40. With two more years to come in the eleven, he has already accumulated the highest career total and average (2,275 at 63.19) and most hundreds (eight). Sam Diment, at fast-medium, headed the bowling with 32 economical wickets, taking his career tally to a record 136. Both played for Somerset Second Eleven.

Batting—N. R. Boulton 14–4–824–145–3–82.40; *S. H. Diment 11–4–264–65*–0–37.71; T. C. Gardiner 11–2–280–62–0–31.11; G. Armstrong 9–3–162–42–0–27.00; C. P. Bostock 11–1–241–68*–0–24.10.

Bowling—S. H. Diment 132.3–19–384–32–7/29–12.00; N. R. Boulton 99–15–306–16–4/17–19.12.

KING'S COLLEGE SCHOOL, WIMBLEDON *Played 17: W 9, L 2, D 6*

Master i/c: G. C. McGinn Professional: G. S. Clinton

Reputations were enhanced as the young side won more than half their matches, including a nine-wicket defeat of local rivals St Paul's. The captain, Luke Whitaker, led by example with the bat, although it was his prolific opening partner, Andrew Sleigh, who topped the averages again. Samir Sheikh was particularly impressive in capturing 47 wickets with his quick, accurate deliveries.

Batting—A. P. Sleigh 17–1–616–141–1–38.50; *L. A. Whitaker 17–3–525–102–1–37.50; D. A. P. Bowen 14–6–220–69*–0–27.50; R. W. Codd 14–3–281–58–0–25.54; C. P. Elliott 11–4–171–51*–0–24.42; S. M. Sheikh 13–2–264–42–0–24.00; I. S. Pay 13–0–230–52–0–17.69; B. E. Davies 12–0–180–27–0–15.00.

Bowling—S. M. Sheikh 213–45–576–47–6/20–12.25; D. A. P. Bowen 177–41–507–31–5/33–16.35; J. C. Walsh 177.5–29–542–31–6/46–17.48.

KING'S SCHOOL, BRUTON *Played 16: W 6, L 6, D 4*

Master i/c: P. Platts-Martin Professional: N. J. Lockhart

Batting—D. P. Weir 16–2–465–70*–0–33.21; K. J. Pike 9–2–207–58*–0–29.57; R. C. Whyte 13–4–266–39*–0–29.55; S. Pollok 15–1–360–92–0–25.71; *L. C. Crofts 13–2–262–41–0–23.81; T. P. K. Rooke 15–0–295–71–0–19.66; N. A. B. Price 10–1–172–42–0–19.11.

Bowling—D. Wyatt 167–36–525–31–7/61–16.93; N. A. B. Price 132.4–26–416–22–4/23–18.90; L. C. Crofts 145.3–41–425–22–7/36–19.31.

THE KING'S SCHOOL, CANTERBURY *Played 13: W 7, L 1, D 5. A 1*

Master i/c: A. W. Dyer Professional: A. G. E. Ealham

Having lost their first match to Epsom College, the side were undefeated thereafter, the most notable win being that by seven wickets over King's College School, Wimbledon. Both Chris North and Marcus Pyke averaged over 50; the last time two batsmen did so was 1970, when the two were Charles Rowe and the South African Bruce Weedon.

Batting—*C. M. North 11–4–506–119*–1–72.28; M. J. A. Pyke 12–5–436–65*–0–62.28; T. J. Palmer 10–3–224–40*–0–32.00; Q. Wiseman 12–1–314–82–0–28.54; W. R. Bax 14–2–313–60–0–26.08.

Bowling—A. Sonaike 149.4–36–427–27–5/29–15.81; U. S. Shariff 117.3–27–320–18–4/40–17.77; C. M. Mounsey-Thear 179.1–36–511–26–6/31–19.65.

THE KING'S SCHOOL, CHESTER *Played 15: W 6, L 8, D 1. A 2*

Master i/c: S. Neal

Once again much depended on Robert Falconer and Kieron Ollier, who shared the captaincy. Falconer was particularly successful with the ball, taking seven for 18 against Rydal (all bowled), and lifted his career batting aggregate to 1,629. Ollier hit hundreds against strong attacks at Stockport GS and William Hulme's GS to take his career total to 1,339. Other highlights included slow left-armer Nigel Bellamy's eight for 30 against King William's College at the Liverpool College Festival.

Batting—*K. J. Ollier 15–1–577–101–2–41.21; *R. J. Falconer 13–0–325–75–0–25.00; D. Z. Testi 14–3–229–57*–0–20.81; D. J. Reeves 15–3–242–54*–0–20.16.

Bowling—R. J. Falconer 110.3–23–374–28–7/18–13.35; N. J. Bellamy 128.3–20–478–23–8/30–20.78; D. J. Reeves 98.3–14–468–15–5/30–31.20.

THE KING'S SCHOOL, ELY *Played 16: W 4, L 5, D 7. A 1*

Masters i/c: C. J. Limb and W. J. Marshall

Although results were slightly disappointing in a season of rebuilding, the side won the Solway (Cambridgeshire Schools) Cup for a record fourth successive year. In the final, against Hills Road College, they compiled a record total of 328 for eight.

Batting—M. C. Parker 14–2–555–158–1–46.25; I. P. N. Haigh 15–0–561–109–2–37.40; D. M. Donaldson 13–3–335–106*–1–33.50; T. E. Mitzman 14–1–388–94–0–29.84; F. C. Thorogood 13–1–236–74–0–19.66.

Bowling—I. P. N. Haigh 115–30–391–23–6/68–17.00; M. C. Parker 146–35–581–24–6/20–24.20.

THE KING'S SCHOOL, MACCLESFIELD *Played 20: W 11, L 3, D 6. A 1*

Master i/c: D. M. Harbord Professional: S. Moores

The side finished on a high note by winning nine of their last 12 matches, including the last seven. Andrew Bones's aggregate of 972 was the third-highest for the school.

Batting—*A. S. Bones 20–2–972–126–2–54.00; C. J. Buckley 18–4–561–118–2–40.07; A. J. Wheeler 14–4–250–40*–0–25.00; T. A. Jenkins 17–4–324–83–0–24.92; M. J. Patterson 15–3–249–48–0–20.75; N. M. Mason 18–2–308–105*–1–19.25.

Bowling—G. A. Emmett 208–56–567–33–4/33–17.18; S. O. Jones 177–32–549–27–5/28–20.33; N. M. Mason 149–23–545–23–4/17–23.69; A. J. Wheeler 168–26–644–22–3/44–29.27.

KING'S SCHOOL, ROCHESTER *Played 16: W 3, L 7, D 6. A 2*

Master i/c: G. R. Williams

Batting—G. E. Davies 16–2–694–92–0–49.57; G. J. E. Hunt 14–3–374–95*–0–34.00; S. P. A. Nicholls 14–1–399–70–0–30.69; S. D. R. Lapthorn 16–3–378–54*–0–29.07; J. W. H. Dunn 12–0–171–46–0–14.25.

Bowling—S. D. R. Lapthorn 154.3–33–441–20–5/27–22.05; M. A. Maurice 134–24–491–21–5/20–23.38; M. P. Saunders 150.5–27–591–20–3/28–29.55.

KING'S SCHOOL, WORCESTER *Played 24: W 10, L 8, D 6*

Master i/c: D. P. Iddon

Recovering from a poor start, the side played more to their potential to finish with ten wins. Edward Oliver scored ten fifties, but could not go on to a century and narrowly missed his thousand runs. Toby Heyes was the leading bowler and took eight for 20 against Reigate during the end-of-season tour of Jersey.

Batting—E. M. Oliver 24–4–968–86–0–48.40; T. A. Morris 19–2–777–107–1–45.70; D. A. Cullen 17–5–480–88*–0–40.00; *S. R. Thomas 20–2–465–65*–0–25.83; J. E. Harris 18–0–377–102–1–20.94; L. A. Hinton 18–2–276–61–0–17.25; T. S. Heyes 16–6–168–30–0–16.80.

Bowling—T. S. Heyes 236.5–37–836–45–8/20–18.57; A. T. C. Phillips 119.2–22–462–21–4/14–22.00; J. Riaz 222.4–41–758–31–4/27–24.45.

KINGSTON GRAMMAR SCHOOL *Played 16: W 7, L 3, D 6. A 3*

Master i/c: J. A. Royce Professional: C. Mutucumarana

A well-balanced attack, which proved too strong for many school teams, was headed by the economical slow left-armer Philip Anderson. Batting performances were less convincing and depended too much on the wicket-keeper and captain, Luke Garrard.

Batting—*L. D. Garrard 15–2–616–86*–0–47.38; D. J. Spenceley 9–2–190–54–0–27.14; P. W. Anderson 14–3–280–65*–0–25.45; A. D. Evans 11–2–202–40–0–22.44.

Bowling—P. W. Anderson 175.3–45–442–51–7/20–8.66; D. J. Spenceley 117.2–37–261–20–4/18–13.05; E. G. R. Thorne 95.3–18–310–17–4/29–18.23.

KINGSWOOD SCHOOL *Played 8: W 1, L 7, D 0*

Master i/c: G. D. Opie

Batting—J. Davies-Yandle 8–0–159–36–0–19.87.

Bowling—No bowler took 15 wickets. The leading bowler was D. Booth 66–2–252–10–4/32–25.20.

LANCING COLLEGE *Played 17: W 9, L 4, D 4*

Master i/c: M. P. Bentley Professional: R. Davies

Giles Haywood played for England Under-17.

Batting—D. Clapp 16–2–506–81*–0–36.14; G. R. Haywood 14–2–404–51–0–33.66; *G. R. M. Campbell 17–0–570–150–1–33.52; G. D. Price 15–1–424–74*–0–30.28; H. N. E. Campbell 13–1–187–40–0–15.58; M. J. D. Stewart 13–2–169–39*–0–15.36.

Bowling—G. R. Haywood 148–47–324–18–3/48–18.00; M. J. D. Stewart 139–34–461–24–6/25–19.20.

LANGLEY PARK SCHOOL *Played 13: W 10, L 0, D 3*

Master i/c: C. H. Williams

In what was probably their best season ever, the side were unbeaten with ten victories. They won the Lemon (Kent Under-18 County) Cup for the first time in five years, beating Rochester Maths in the final by one wicket with a six off the penultimate ball. Robert Key played for the Development of Excellence XI and Kent Second Eleven.

Batting—R. Key 4–1–183–88–0–61.00; B. Simpson 7–0–344–109–2–49.14; D. Evans 11–2–269–44*–0–29.88; *A. Shepherd 10–2–163–45–0–20.37.

Bowling—N. Codling 112–23–282–22–5/32–12.81; D. Martin 129.5–24–422–29–6/7–14.55.

LEEDS GRAMMAR SCHOOL *Played 15: W 4, L 3, D 8*

Master i/c: R. Hill

Adam Walton, brother of Northamptonshire's Tim Walton, headed both averages and was a member of the England Under-14 squad.

Batting—A. N. Walton 13–0–414–85–0–31.84; A. P. Wood 11–4–195–60–0–27.85; J. R. Wyn-Griffiths 15–0–417–56–0–27.80; *T. J. N. Golby 15–4–303–61*–0–27.54; A. N. Brown 15–4–257–47–0–23.36; C. M. Du Pré 13–2–222–40–0–20.18; L. W. B. Kendall 12–0–237–47–0–19.75.

Bowling—A. N. Walton 114–19–404–18–4/28–22.44; S. D. Kershaw 174.3–37–557–22–3/12–25.31; T. J. N. Golby 140–22–516–20–4/37–25.80; L. W. B. Kendall 101–14–415–16–4/14–25.93.

LEIGHTON PARK SCHOOL *Played 13: W 6, L 2, D 5*

Master i/c: M. L. Simmons Professional: S. D. Myles

Tom Rose, the captain and opening bat, scored 151 not out against Reading School. The leading all-rounder was Ross Stewart, a hard-hitting middle-order batsman and opening bowler.

Batting—*T. W. M. Rose 9–3–548–151*–1–91.33; R. I. Stewart 8–3–377–117*–2–75.40; R. Sharma 4–0–150–69–0–37.50.

Bowling—R. I. Stewart 74.2–13–229–20–7/41–11.45; M. E. Bloxham 65.2–17–288–15–4/46–19.20.

THE LEYS SCHOOL *Played 17: W 5, L 6, D 6*

Master i/c: T. Firth Professional: B. T. P. Donelan

Batting—A. Newman 18–1–519–67–0–30.52; N. Barber 16–1–407–111–1–27.13; W. Graham 18–3–390–76–0–26.00; W. Spriggs 18–3–363–55–0–24.20; R. Bentley 18–0–347–56–0–19.27; J. Welch 17–1–199–49–0–12.43.

Bowling—T. Nix 84–20–246–19–4/22–12.94; J. Welch 116–24–381–25–4/14–15.24; W. Spriggs 146–39–417–25–6/15–16.68; T. Biddle 140–25–489–25–3/32–19.56.

LIVERPOOL COLLEGE *Played 13: W 2, L 5, D 6*

Master i/c: A. Fox

Batting—A. S. Rogers 13–0–597–124–2–45.92; N. D. Robinson 13–0–167–40–0–12.84.

Bowling—*M. Rastogi 112–30–419–19–5/72–22.05; D. N. Wilkie Harris 152–3–524–21–5/78–24.95.

LLANDOVERY COLLEGE *Played 8: W 0, L 5, D 3. A 5*

Master i/c: T. G. Marks

A difficult season was severely disrupted by the weather. Aled Leyshon, a fast and accurate bowler and powerful batsman, was selected for Welsh Independent Schools.

Batting—*C. H. Rees 7–1–164–55–0–27.33.

Bowling—A. L. Leyshon 103–15–486–16–3/47–30.37.

LORD WANDSWORTH COLLEGE *Played 19: W 7, L 4, D 8. A 1*

Master i/c: M. C. Russell

This was the strongest side in the college's history. Facing an increasingly challenging fixture list, they grew in confidence. The excellent results stemmed from a fine team effort, with Jonny Wilkinson outstanding. Guy Hicks played for England Under-15.

Batting—K. P. Clinker 14–2–402–88–0–33.50; T. C. Hicks 13–2–368–111*–2–33.45; *C. J. Walker 17–2–463–99*–0–30.86; J. P. Wilkinson 15–2–398–87–0–30.61; D. I. Holman 18–3–432–93–0–28.80; I. J. Leek 15–0–302–82–0–20.13.

Bowling—T. C. Hicks 142.3–24–457–26–7/55–17.57; J. P. Wilkinson 234.1–55–680–38–5/41–17.89; G. D. Hicks 141.1–29–440–21–5/29–20.95.

LORD WILLIAMS'S SCHOOL *Played 15: W 9, L 1, D 5*

Master i/c: J. E. Fulkes

Excellently led by Alex Wilson, the side enjoyed their best season for 15 years, winning nine and losing only to MCC on a drying track. The outstanding innings was Alan Cawston's 138 against Dr Challoner's, while the attack boasted genuine pace from left-armer Andrew Millington and Chris Eaton.

Batting—A. Eason 10–6–276–101*–1–69.00; E. Barnett 7–2–208–68–0–41.60; A. Cawston 11–1–330–138–1–33.00; M. Kelloway 8–1–218–63–0–31.14; A. Bartlett 12–0–201–55–0–16.75; *A. Wilson 11–1–164–50–0–16.40.

Bowling—A. Millington 81.4–14–252–22–5/32–11.45; C. Eaton 112.4–14–388–19–5/77–20.42.

LORETTO SCHOOL *Played 15: W 8, L 3, D 4. A 3*

Master i/c: R. P. Whait

Batting—*A. G. Fleming-Brown 14–1–389–102*–1–29.92; M. B. McCreath 11–5–156–42*–0–26.00; J. T. Boon 13–2–272–41*–0–24.72; S. J. S. Smith 13–3–245–45–0–24.50; W. A. Nicholson 13–1–279–55–0–23.25; M. J. Ritchie 15–2–250–89*–0–19.23; W. A. D. Oliver 15–0–204–68–0–13.60.

Bowling—H. Balfour-Melville 220.5–76–492–40–7/16–12.30; M. B. McCreath 230.2–68–572–40–7/47–14.30; J. T. Boon 151–47–453–26–4/30–17.42.

LOUGHBOROUGH GRAMMAR SCHOOL *Played 17: W 10, L 3, D 4*

Master i/c: J. S. Weitzel Professional: H. T. Tunnicliffe

Daniel Reddyhough's 1,041 runs passed Richard Merriman's 19-year-old record, while Richard Widdowson completed his career in the eleven with 2,341 runs and six centuries. Both scored hundreds in a stand of 226 against Ermolo HS from South Africa, while a record total of 344 for six against the touring Antipodeans from Australia contributed to a record match aggregate of 607.

Batting—D. P. Reddyhough 19–3–1,041–119*–4–65.06; R. G. H. Widdowson 19–2–841–135–3–49.47; C. B. Keast 16–5–338–36–0–30.72; E. O. Woodcock 7–1–182–96–0–30.33; M. J. Hayes 10–3–208–128*–1–29.71; S. Morgan 10–0–183–46–0–18.30; R. J. Peregrine 17–3–229–68–0–16.35.

Bowling—M. J. Hayes 132.2–21–443–27–3/23–16.40; D. P. Hemmings 169–25–550–24–4/25–22.91; R. J. Peregrine 99.1–17–425–17–4/59–25.00; M. P. Kavanagh 157–26–615–22–3/34–27.95.

MAGDALEN COLLEGE SCHOOL *Played 16: W 4, L 5, D 7. A 5*

Master i/c: P. Askew

Both Ben Thompson (936) and Christopher Rees-Gay (886) passed the previous record aggregate. Thompson, who hit five hundreds, played for Oxfordshire and South of England Under-15.

Batting—B. J. Thompson 18–5–936–133–5–72.00; *C. J. Rees-Gay 20–3–886–131–3–52.11; D. Matheson 12–0–270–72–0–22.50; J. Ellis 10–1–201–60–0–22.33.

Bowling—B. Bradshaw 135.3–35–361–20–4/18–18.05; A. Hirtenstein 198.1–38–673–28–5/63–24.03.

MALVERN COLLEGE *Played 22: W 14, L 1, D 7. A 2*

Master i/c: P. Goode Professional: R. W. Tolchard

In another excellent season, the side comfortably broke its own record in schools matches and retained the Chesterton Cup. A highlight among the 14 wins was that over Millfield. David Nash was again outstanding; his 1,093 runs, 23 dismissals and 13 stumpings in 17 matches were all records. Mark Hardinges was also prolific, and Gavin Franklin led the side by example. Nash again played for England Under-19 and Middlesex, while Hardinges represented Gloucestershire Second Eleven.

Batting—D. C. Nash 21–5–1,093–137–3–68.31; M. A. Hardinges 20–2–905–112–2–50.27; *G. D. Franklin 20–4–541–60*–0–33.81; D. G. Walker 15–6–264–75*–0–29.33; N. D. Harrison 14–5–245–55*–0–27.22; J. B. Horton 16–2–268–50*–0–19.14.

Bowling—G. D. Franklin 275.5–73–749–45–5/20–16.64; G. D. Simons 98.5–19–388–23–6/17–16.86; S. J. Morgan 157.2–29–404–23–4/17–17.56; W. R. F. Harrison 140.1–33–380–21–3/7–18.09; M. A. Hardinges 154.4–29–524–25–5/40–20.96.

MANCHESTER GRAMMAR SCHOOL *Played 19: W 7, L 5, D 7. A 2*

Master i/c: D. Moss

In an improved attack, 72 wickets were shared between pace bowlers Richard Seddon, Neil Lomax and Ben Twemlow, although none played in much more than half the games. Scott Richardson (102 not out) and Jonathan Lee (95 not out) put on 193 unbroken for the second wicket to defeat MCC. Richardson played his best innings early in the season, while Lee's form improved to bring him 893 runs and four centuries. Richardson played for MCC Schools and NCA Young Cricketers at Lord's.

Batting—*S. A. Richardson 13–1–672–132–2–56.00; J. R. Lee 17–1–893–109–4–55.81; P. Dhir 13–4–396–151*–1–44.00; R. P. J. Seddon 13–5–260–58–0–32.50; C. J. Garner 14–2–380–96–0–31.66; N. D. Garner 17–3–327–84*–0–23.35.

Bowling—R. P. J. Seddon 129.3–28–375–28–5/18–13.39; N. R. Lomax 126–27–377–22–4/50–17.13; B. J. Twemlow 111.4–18–405–22–4/55–18.40; A. J. E. King 88–7–417–16–6/80–26.06; G. M. Lee 177.3–50–482–16–4/21–30.12.

MARLBOROUGH COLLEGE *Played 15: W 3, L 5, D 7. A 1*

Master i/c: R. B. Pick Professional: R. M. Ratcliffe

Will Caldwell, who held the batting together, scored a match-winning century against Free Foresters. The introduction of colts Hugh Dobie and Tom Burne provided the attack with much-needed pace and consistency.

Batting—W. O. Caldwell 15–1–570–118–1–40.71; D. J. F. Miller 12–2–228–107*–1–22.80; C. G. Ingham 14–2–258–60*–0–21.50; T. E. F. Burne 9–1–168–40*–0–21.00; A. J. R. Bird 14–2–188–65–0–15.66.

Bowling—T. E. F. Burne 85.1–12–267–15–4/29–17.80.

MERCHANT TAYLORS' SCHOOL, CROSBY *Played 15: W 7, L 3, D 5*

Master i/c: Rev. D. A. Smith Professional: G. W. Flower

Stephen Howard was the outstanding batsman; his innings of 172 not out against St Mary's College, Crosby, beat the previous record of 169 by L. B. P. Adams in 1934; his partnership of 186 with R. S. Holden in the same match was a fifth-wicket record; and his 828 runs were the most since W. Snowden's 1,108 in 1971.

Batting—*S. B. Howard 14–2–828–172*–3–69.00; C. J. Cheetham 14–3–321–62*–0–29.18; G. A. McMillan 14–2–210–56–0–17.50.

Bowling—J. N. C. Rees 121.4–20–362–24–6/26–15.08; D. R. Ball 121.3–24–464–24–5/25–19.33.

MERCHANT TAYLORS' SCHOOL, NORTHWOOD *Played 21: W 15, L 0, D 6*

Master i/c: H. C. Latchman

All-round strength in depth brought the school an unbeaten season, with 15 wins, including all four games at the Loretto Festival. Of the seven batsmen to pass 200 runs, Andrew Thorpe was the most prolific, but Daniel Grundy made the only century – against St Paul's. Although seam bowler Niraj Sapra was the leading wicket-taker with 42, most of the bowling was in the hands of the four spinners, notably Jawwad Rasheed, who took eight for 31 against Felsted. The captain, Edward Lamb, was the leading all-rounder.

Batting—A. C. Thorpe 15–5–513–79–0–51.30; D. J. Grundy 13–2–478–110–1–43.45; *E. N. Lamb 12–3–301–57*–0–33.44; M. A. Howard 9–2–222–73*–0–31.71; P. D. C. Wise 15–1–437–61–0–31.21; K. G. W. Fowler 19–3–488–81–0–30.50; A. Latchman 15–5–231–55*–0–23.10.

Bowling—E. N. Lamb 108.4–16–322–25–5/35–12.88; N. P. Sapra 230.4–53–592–42–5/1–14.09; J. Rasheed 174.3–41–488–34–8/31–14.35; A. Latchman 71–15–234–16–4/13–14.62; B. Knowles 149.2–37–354–22–7/27–16.09; M. A. Howard 131.2–35–298–17–4/22–17.52; S. J. Boardley 105–22–328–15–3/18–21.86.

MERCHISTON CASTLE SCHOOL *Played 16: W 6, L 4, D 6. A 4*

Master i/c: C. W. Swan

Three batsmen shared a record four centuries, of which J. N. Mackley's 141 and A. P. Paterson's 100 not out both came in the first innings of the two-day game against Fettes. It was the first instance of two in an innings in the school's 163-year history.

Batting—A. P. Paterson 13–5–374–100*–1–46.75; *J. N. Mackley 11–1–389–141–2–38.90; R. A. Swan 15–4–287–66*–0–26.09; G. M. English 10–2–206–100*–1–25.75; J. A. C. Easton 11–2–195–66*–0–21.66; C. M. R. Tulloch 15–1–286–46–0–20.42.

Bowling—C. M. R. Tulloch 214–76–487–41–6/7–11.87; E. A. T. Algie 83–19–323–21–7/11–15.38; A. P. Paterson 159–31–461–24–4/29–19.20; A. R. Evans 184–42–556–28–6/20–19.85.

MILLFIELD SCHOOL *Played 21: W 10, L 6, D 5. A 3*

Master i/c: R. M. Ellison Professional: G. C. Wilson

Batting—*D. A. Cosker 13–5–332–111*–1–41.50; A. N. Edwards 18–1–698–127*–1–41.05; W. T. A. Simmons 16–6–386–74*–0–38.60; C. A. Sayers 9–0–271–45–0–30.11; R. Dorey 10–1–271–71–0–30.11; E. J. S. Newton 18–4–418–59*–0–29.85; M. T. Byrne 10–1–198–38–0–22.00; D. A. J. White 15–3–241–37–0–20.08.

Bowling—D. A. Cosker 247–77–692–36–7/35–19.22; E. J. S. Newton 129.5–24–486–19–5/36–25.57.

MILL HILL SCHOOL *Played 17: W 4, L 6, D 7. A 1*

Master i/c: P. H. Edwards Professional: I. Hutchinson

Batting—S. A. Selwood 17–1–729–133*–2–45.56; S. Mohamed 16–0–405–89–0–25.31; *M. Dweck 16–1–325–72–0–21.66; M. P. Brandon 16–1–323–75*–0–21.53; P. Martin 16–3–175–31–0–13.46.

Bowling—J. G. Graves 124–30–340–16–4/26–21.25; M. P. Brandon 127–42–352–16–3/29–22.00; S. Mohamed 188–37–601–26–4/81–23.11; S. A. Selwood 115–17–461–15–4/68–30.73.

MILTON ABBEY SCHOOL *Played 11: W 5, L 1, D 5. A 4*

Master i/c: P. W. Wood

Batting—*F. Gibson 11–2–461–107*–1–51.22; C. Gold 10–0–232–56–0–23.20; T. Godsal 9–0–185–62–0–20.55; G. Fox 11–1–201–50–0–20.10.

Bowling—F. Gibson 64–12–218–20–5/27–10.90; C. Gold 122.3–33–380–29–5/48–13.10; G. Fox 65.5–7–234–15–4/29–15.60.

MONKTON COMBE SCHOOL *Played 12: W 4, L 5, D 3*

Master i/c: N. D. Botton

Batting—*J. S. Wheeler 12–2–359–108*–1–35.90; J. I. Solly 11–0–256–59–0–23.27; E. F. D. Halden 11–1–182–63–0–18.20; J. C. I. Hooton 11–2–159–59*–0–17.66; C. D. T. Bickers 9–0–158–48–0–17.55.

Bowling—D. P. W. Smith 151–34–411–26–5/39–15.80; M. E. K. Rooke 118–23–392–18–4/50–21.77.

MONMOUTH SCHOOL *Played 20: W 9, L 9, D 2. A 2*

Master i/c: D. H. Messenger Professional: G. I. Burgess

A positive approach resulted in only two drawn games and some unexpected last-minute victories. The batting tended to revolve around the captain, Michael Brogan, whose 130 against Kimbolton was a highlight. He also held 13 catches, passing the record set by Steve James in 1983. Greg Walters, a medium-pace in-swing bowler, took a hat-trick against King's, Worcester, in the first match, and leg-spinner Glen Scrivener collected 33 wickets. He also shared a record seventh-wicket partnership with Edward Barlow.

Batting—*M. M. Brogan 19–0–613–130–1–32.26; N. Jorgensen 18–1–536–92–0–31.52; E. T. Barlow 12–2–281–73–0–28.10; T. J. Allan 17–1–335–89–0–20.93; J. G. Scrivener 18–7–229–33–0–20.81; T. J. J. Ricks 18–1–342–80*–0–20.11; M. S. J. Dunn 13–0–215–45–0–16.53; A. S. Narula 17–0–276–61–0–16.23.

Bowling—G. L. Walters 179.5–29–659–33–6/64–19.96; M. M. Brogan 95.2–10–339–15–4/31–22.60; J. G. Scrivener 208.1–30–852–33–5/45–25.81; J. C. M. Roberts 186.1–32–697–25–4/18–27.88; N. Jorgensen 158–38–494–17–4/27–29.05.

NEWCASTLE-UNDER-LYME SCHOOL *Played 13: W 3, L 3, D 7. A 3*

Master i/c: S. A. Robson Professional: A. J. Dutton

Under the imaginative captaincy of wicket-keeper and leg-spinner M. D. Turner, the side remained competitive and undaunted throughout. Most exciting was their recovery at Denstone from 13 for three to 214 for nine to win off the last ball. Team efforts from the batsmen brought a record five totals of 200 or more from the last six matches and B. R. Oakden became only the sixth centurion in the school's history.

Batting—B. R. Oakden 13–0–356–102–1–27.38; V. S. C. Handley 13–1–251–59*–0–20.91; N. R. Allchin 13–0–263–58–0–20.23; J. Rodgers 12–2–192–38–0–19.20; L. J. Norcup 9–0–151–37–0–16.77; R. M. Wheat 12–0–195–43–0–16.25; R. C. Overstall 11–0–152–28–0–13.81.

Bowling—R. M. Wheat 163–37–505–23–5/68–21.95; R. C. Overstall 131–26–533–24–5/51–22.20.

NOTTINGHAM HIGH SCHOOL *Played 17: W 8, L 5, D 4. A 1*

Master i/c: J. Lamb

Batting—J. L. Rayner 4–2–204–105*–1–102.00; K. S. Tate 15–5–674–133*–3–67.40; A. J. Hunt 15–2–575–102*–2–44.23; A. S. Parker 14–3–407–72–0–37.00; R. A. Nicholson 16–2–501–65–0–35.78; *M. A. Fletcher 13–4–190–66*–0–21.11; P. J. Harrison 9–0–166–57–0–18.44.

Bowling—A. R. Phillips 80.4–15–338–15–2/8–22.53; A. J. Hunt 119–21–418–16–3/20–26.12; R. Kitching 120–19–490–17–3/33–28.82.

OAKHAM SCHOOL *Played 17: W 8, L 2, D 7. A 2*

Master i/c: J. Wills Professional: D. S. Steele

Richard Martin's four centuries were a school record. He and Robert Duck, the captain, shared five century partnerships, including a first-wicket record of 232 against Worksop.

Batting—R. A. E. Martin 15–1–679–123*–4–48.50; *R. M. Duck 14–2–470–105–1–39.16; O. J. C. Marshall 12–5–274–78–0–39.14; N. M. Schanschieff 14–4–340–85–0–34.00; M. R. K. Bailey 12–2–297–100*–1–29.70; W. H. J. M. Greaves 10–3–191–77*–0–27.28.

Bowling—R. M. Duck 169.1–34–481–31–6/17–15.51; W. H. J. M. Greaves 155.3–29–503–18–4/50–27.94.

THE ORATORY SCHOOL *Played 19: W 13, L 2, D 4. A 3*

Master i/c: P. L. Tomlinson Professional: J. B. K. Howell

In another excellent season, the outstanding player was again Steven Tomlinson, the British Under-18 real tennis champion, who is on Glamorgan's books. A fine captain, he headed both batting and bowling as he took his career record to date to 2,616 runs at 72.66 and 140 wickets at 10.74.

Batting—*S. C. B. Tomlinson 19–9–759–96–0–75.90; D. J. Allaway 19–2–791–91*–0–46.52; S. Bird 7–1–206–98–0–34.33; C. J. Clayton 19–4–451–79*–0–30.06; N. J. Davison 19–0–307–62–0–16.15.

Bowling—S. C. B. Tomlinson 146–41–379–43–6/17–8.81; E. W. Orchard 179–47–425–34–6/57–12.50; T. C. Wigley 92.5–25–343–21–4/33–16.33; R. O. Waldron 80–11–290–16–5/9–18.12; J. G. Taylor 115–30–420–22–3/36–19.09.

OUNDLE SCHOOL *Played 21: W 13, L 1, D 7. A 1*

Master i/c: J. R. Wake Professional: T. Howorth

The side equalled their 1995 record of 13 wins and lost only once in their best season yet. They owed much to the outstanding leadership of David Walder, who also scored 682 runs and took 49 wickets, bowling medium-fast out-swing. He went on to captain MCC Schools and English Schools. Leg-spinner Jake Milton bowled a phenomenal 433 overs in taking a record 75 wickets.

Batting—R. Samworth 9–5–233–81*–0–58.25; *D. J. H. Walder 20–7–682–103–1–52.46; D. Lowe 21–2–924–100*–1–48.63; W. Jefferson 16–3–425–94–0–32.69; J. Cope 15–7–219–57*–0–27.37; S. Cates 15–6–214–78*–0–23.77; S. Lowe 13–2–250–76–0–22.72; J. M. Milton 15–3–192–55*–0–16.00; M. Mountain 19–2–262–75–0–15.41.

Bowling—D. J. H. Walder 261.2–54–715–49–6/36–14.59; J. M. Milton 433–98–1,308–75–8/67–17.44; H. Bryers 154–36–429–24–4/34–17.87; O. Hallam 112.4–26–299–15–4/29–19.93; W. Jefferson 206–39–568–27–4/25–21.03.

THE PERSE SCHOOL *Played 14: W 4, L 4, D 6. A 1*

Master i/c: A. C. Porter Professional: D. C. Collard

Batting—*D. Colquhoun 13–1–416–87–0–34.66; M. Lorimer 12–1–345–78–0–31.36; J. Salmon 15–1–347–111–2–24.78; M. Mayer 14–1–224–52–0–17.23.

Bowling—C. Rodger 170–31–520–25–4/32–20.80; M. Lorimer 106.4–20–401–16–4/41–25.06; J. Garner 106–15–419–15–4/25–27.93; D. Robinson 114–12–487–15–3/28–32.46.

Two prominent players from Oundle School: Jake Milton (left), who took 75 wickets in 1996, and the captain David Walder, one of the season's leading all-rounders who also captained MCC Schools and English Schools.

PLYMOUTH COLLEGE *Played 12: W 2, L 5, D 5. A 5*

Master i/c: T. J. Stevens

Batting—N. Pope 11–0–289–79–0–26.27; J. Newnham 12–1–279–62–0–25.36; *D. Saunders 12–1–250–60*–0–22.72; R. Moist 12–0–258–50–0–21.50.

Bowling—W. Andrews 89–24–345–24–4/18–14.37.

POCKLINGTON SCHOOL *Played 21: W 5, L 9, D 7. A 1*

Master i/c: R. Smith

The Mouncey brothers, Stephen and Paul, shared 1,032 runs and 49 wickets, although it was the captain, Matthew Stacey, who headed the batting averages.

Batting—*M. B. Stacey 19–5–628–96–0–44.85; P. R. Mouncey 21–4–709–90–0–41.70; G. J. T. Stewart 21–0–485–76–0–23.09; G. Johnson 10–2–183–69–0–22.87; N. G. Hadfield 21–0–463–104–1–22.04; S. D. Mouncey 18–3–323–77–0–21.53; C. R. Rook 15–1–295–68–0–21.07.

Bowling—S. D. Mouncey 194.5–33–668–27–5/67–24.74; P. R. Mouncey 187.5–34–594–22–4/39–27.00; N. G. Hadfield 135–27–541–18–6/51–30.05; G. J. T. Stewart 189.1–36–732–23–5/29–31.82.

PORTSMOUTH GRAMMAR SCHOOL *Played 12: W 7, L 1, D 4. A 5*

Master i/c: G. D. Payne Professional: R. J. Parks

Unbeaten until the last over of the season – against Portsmouth CC – the side were well captained by Andrew Ainsley, who showed tactical awareness and a willingness to attack. James Moon, again the dominant batsman, was joined in the side by his younger brothers, Chris and Simon.

Batting—J. C. E. Moon 12–1–442–112–1–40.18; C. Moon 12–2–309–62–0–30.90; S. Hamilton 12–1–318–67–0–28.90; J. Gannon 12–2–284–64*–0–28.40; S. R. Foulger 9–0–159–64–0–17.66.

Bowling—J. R. M. Tod 69–13–203–16–3/7–12.68; S. Hamilton 107–30–294–22–5/17–13.36; M. Slater 126.2–33–353–24–5/37–14.70.

PRIOR PARK COLLEGE *Played 18: W 9, L 6, D 3*

Master i/c: D. R. Holland Professional: R. Chambers

Lee Dokic set new records with 49 wickets and a return of eight for 26 against Clayesmore, while the 447 runs scored by Tony Atkins, grandson of former Hampshire wicket-keeper Leo Harrison, were the most for eight years. Other successes included a first victory over Bryanston and a record total of 297 for nine against King Edward's, Bath.

Batting—A. Atkins 16–0–447–122–1–27.93; A. Owen 15–1–319–101*–1–22.78; S. Phillips 14–2–273–43–0–22.75; L. Dokic 14–1–237–69–0–18.23; S. Brandon 13–2–194–54–0–17.63.

Bowling—L. Dokic 199–48–535–49–8/26–10.91; D. Gadsden 65–13–183–16–4/13–11.43; A. Atkins 73–17–191–15–4/22–12.73; S. Phillips 165–36–485–33–6/64–14.69.

QUEEN ELIZABETH GS, WAKEFIELD *Played 14: W 4, L 5, D 5. A 2*

Master i/c: T. Barker

David Bousfield, a left-handed opener, scored more runs than anyone else in the 27 years in which records have been kept.

Batting—D. Bousfield 14–3–620–125–1–56.36; J. Lowe 13–2–532–101–1–48.36; B. Sykes 13–1–267–79–0–22.25.

Bowling—J. Lowe 100.5–18–309–17–3/15–18.17; A. Sharma 92–17–344–16–4/46–21.50; D. Cleave 131.2–9–579–24–4/57–24.12.

QUEEN ELIZABETH'S HOSPITAL *Played 15: W 5, L 6, D 4*

Master i/c: M. S. E. Broadley

Batting—G. Parker-Jones 14–1–517–108–1–39.76; *A. Brenner 15–1–477–121*–1–34.07; P. Ross 8–1–158–64–0–22.57; A. Hollingdale 14–1–240–67–0–18.46; N. Varshney 14–0–186–92–0–13.28.

Bowling—D. Chard 122.4–23–411–30–7/72–13.70; W. Nash 135.1–30–428–26–4/25–16.46; P. Nice 133.1–22–447–22–4/26–20.31; M. Popham 131–21–512–21–4/38–24.38.

QUEEN'S COLLEGE, TAUNTON *Played 16: W 9, L 3, D 4. A 1*

Master i/c: A. S. Free

The batting was dominated by the Bailey brothers, Alex and Grant, who scored 1,050 runs between them and a century apiece.

Batting—A. W. Bailey 16–3–512–104–1–39.38; G. C. Bailey 16–2–538–132*–1–38.42; D. E. Bell 12–2–248–67–0–24.80; T. J. Jones 12–5–167–60–0–23.85; W. R. Handel 16–1–330–69–0–22.00; *P. M. Burke 15–1–272–58–0–19.42; J. C. Stotesbury 11–2–150–41–0–16.66.

Bowling—A. W. Bailey 79.1–6–244–16–4/19–15.25; S. J. Pratt 167.2–40–516–33–6/34–15.63; P. M. Burke 138–20–492–23–7/26–21.39.

RADLEY COLLEGE *Played 14: W 3, L 1, D 10. A 1*

Master i/c: W. J. Wesson Professionals: A. G. Robinson and A. R. Wagner

Batting—J. Johnson 14–2–563–104*–1–46.91; O. R. Hutton 12–1–459–75–0–41.72; E. A. N. Jennings 12–6–180–47*–0–30.00; *C. R. N. Jennings 9–2–190–44–0–27.14; B. C. A. Hawkins 7–1–154–73*–0–25.66; C. E. Pragnell 10–1–195–37*–0–21.66.

Bowling—C. G. van der Gucht 202.2–60–489–29–5/33–16.86; J. A. J. Harris 82.3–16–283–15–6/40–18.86; C. E. Pragnell 121–28–290–15–3/21–19.33; C. F. E. Hughes 128.4–34–377–15–4/35–25.13; J. B. Scott 143–31–437–17–3/16–25.70.

RATCLIFFE COLLEGE *Played 16: W 8, L 3, D 5*

Master i/c: R. Hughes Professional: B. Benkenstein

Elliot Hill was the outstanding batsman with 923 runs, 109 of which came in the convincing defeat of The Oratory; competing in the inaugural Emeriti Trophy for Catholic HMC Schools, Ratcliffe made 307 for five before dismissing The Oratory for 140.

Batting—*E. V. Hill 15–3–923–136*–3–76.91; J. Hart 15–3–539–79–0–44.91; K. B. Smith 12–3–283–51*–0–31.44; B. R. Stephens 13–2–206–59*–0–18.72; W. J. Birchall 13–2–168–53–0–15.27.

Bowling—K. B. Smith 167.3–30–463–28–6/23–16.53; J. Hart 136–22–523–22–6/40–23.77; W. J. Birchall 151.5–26–502–19–4/20–26.42.

READING SCHOOL *Played 13: W 1, L 7, D 5*

Master i/c: S. A. Stevenson

Batting—*I. Azuike 11–3–362–109*–1–45.25; D. Lowe 11–2–288–100*–1–32.00; J. Taylor 10–0–163–37–0–16.30; J. Eatherley 12–0–155–63–0–12.91.

Bowling—O. Mann 107–14–433–16–6/42–27.06; J. Eatherley 117.5–21–502–16–6/41–31.37.

REIGATE GRAMMAR SCHOOL *Played 24: W 7, L 9, D 8*

Master i/c: D. E. R. Jones Professional: H. Newton

Going into their last Saturday fixture, the side had won six, drawn six and lost only once; thereafter they won only once more and lost eight out of 11 festival and tour fixtures. The captain, James Hylton, scored more than half his 823 runs in the first seven innings, finishing his career in the eleven with 2,077 runs, 91 wickets and a record 40 catches. Outshining everything else was the quick away-swing of Toby Briggs, whose 67 wickets passed Dan Sainsbury's 1992 record of 61. Mark Bowden, who held 22 catches, fielded brilliantly at slip.

Batting—*J. J. Hylton 24–1–823–113–1–35.78; M. R. Bowden 23–2–482–96–0–22.95; P. W. Sainsbury 18–5–282–56*–0–21.69; O. Bate 17–3–300–54–0–21.42; T. W. Briggs 22–2–350–64–0–17.50; R. C. G. Young 23–2–353–84*–0–16.80; O. J. Jago 18–1–257–51–0–15.11; I. N. Bezodis 20–0–212–46–0–10.60.

Bowling—T. W. Briggs 284.5–52–929–67–8/36–13.86; P. W. Sainsbury 125.5–29–439–24–5/18–18.29; R. C. G. Young 192.5–28–689–27–6/53–25.51; J. J. Hylton 260.1–50–874–31–4/45–28.19.

RENDCOMB COLLEGE *Played 12: W 3, L 6, D 3. A 2*

Master i/c: J. P. Watson

Batting—F. W. Newcombe 10–1–381–78–0–42.33; *J. C. G. Fairbank 10–2–195–52–0–24.37; C. P. E. Barton 9–1–151–43–0–18.87.

Bowling—A. J. Taylor 105–36–375–28–7/24–13.39; H. E. J. Davies 70–13–284–15–4/21–18.93.

REPTON SCHOOL *Played 14: W 3, L 3, D 8. A 1*

Master i/c: M. Stones Professional: M. K. Kettle

Batting—*D. J. O'Gram 15–3–664–110–3–55.33; M. R. Lakin 14–3–451–110–1–41.00; T. A. Swerling 15–1–318–70–0–22.71; A. E. Kington 12–3–187–40*–0–20.77; A. J. Currie 12–2–180–65–0–18.00; J. O. Henry 13–0–196–39–0–15.07.

Bowling—M. Gillespie 164.5–16–431–31–6/31–13.90; C. H. M. Standage 74–11–262–15–4/37–17.46; M. R. Lakin 176–30–609–29–6/35–21.00; R. D. J. Probert 127–19–500–18–4/41–27.77.

RICHARD HUISH COLLEGE *Played 12: W 7, L 3, D 2*

Master i/c: J. L. N. Grace

Batting—S. P. Jenkins 7–2–423–114*–2–84.60; B. Jeffery 7–0–150–44–0–21.42.

Bowling—*P. Lacy 59.3–9–167–16–7/55–10.43; E. Warren 52–8–218–15–6/37–14.53.

ROSSALL SCHOOL *Played 12: W 1, L 7, D 4*

Master i/c: T. Todd Professional: K. Higgs

A highlight was a record opening partnership of 136 against Stonyhurst between James Atkins (68) and Stuart Fraser-Cattanach (82).

Batting—*J. R. Atkins 12–0–391–102–1–32.58; M. Clapp 8–2–166–40*–0–27.66; S. Fraser-Cattanach 9–0–201–82–0–22.33.

Bowling—M. J. Dewhurst 123–29–368–23–7/52–16.00.

THE ROYAL GRAMMAR SCHOOL, COLCHESTER *Played 24: W 6, L 14, D 4. A 1*

Master i/c: R. Bayes

Batting—J. Oxborrow 24–2–653–99–0–29.68; M. Tyler 14–4–284–72–0–28.40; *A. Stephen 24–1–620–84–0–26.95; G. Gorringe 23–2–526–73*–0–25.04; P. Sadler 21–1–388–68–0–19.40; G. Gwyn-Jones 16–3–242–48*–0–18.61; R. Burt 9–0–151–42–0–16.77; G. Wilson 17–0–258–38–0–15.17; W. Peacock 16–3–164–47–0–12.61.

Bowling—M. Tyler 191.3–41–649–35–7/32–18.54; A. Stephen 107.2–12–444–22–5/24–20.18; W. Peacock 219.3–25–939–36–5/72–26.08; C. Norfolk 158.2–28–571–21–4/24–27.19; P. Sadler 203.3–20–922–23–4/57–40.08.

THE ROYAL GRAMMAR SCHOOL, GUILDFORD *Played 15: W 2, L 8, D 5*

Master i/c: S. B. R. Shore

Batting—A. R. Hemmingway 14–2–309–53*–0–25.75; R. C. Kitzinger 14–0–339–87–0–24.21; M. B. Copsey 9–2–159–41–0–22.71; G. W. G. Donne 13–2–226–54*–0–20.54; C. J. Heath 11–2–165–53–0–18.33; *D. L. Tompsett 12–0–199–68–0–16.58; G. G. Thomas 10–0–164–57–0–16.40.

Bowling—T. D. Lackey 165.5–40–451–28–6/53–16.10; J. A. Mitchell 188.1–45–620–29–5/25–21.37; C. A. G. Cooper 136.4–31–493–20–4/39–24.65.

ROYAL GRAMMAR SCHOOL, HIGH WYCOMBE *Played 15: W 9, L 3, D 3. A 1*

Master i/c: M. Davies

The most successful season for many years featured a two-wicket win over MCC and victory in all their matches in the Royal Grammar Schools Festival for the first time. The batting was always a team effort, with opener Andrew Bentall dominating the early season and the fluent strokeplay of Kaushik Guha blossoming on the drier wickets.

Batting—K. Guha 14–1–381–64–0–29.30; A. J. Bentall 16–1–408–82–0–27.20; A. W. Pembroke 15–5–268–56*–0–26.80; D. J. Moore 15–0–357–58–0–23.80; D. P. Wilson 15–4–246–55–0–22.36; C. J. Dark 11–1–220–41–0–22.00; R. A. Royce 17–1–310–59–0–19.37.

Bowling—D. J. Moore 154.3–27–446–31–6/10–14.38; *G. F. Watts 199.4–48–604–34–6/22–17.76; S. A. Musk 172.3–35–539–29–9/27–18.58; A. R. Moore 116–18–420–18–4/35–23.33.

THE ROYAL GRAMMAR SCHOOL, NEWCASTLE *Played 17: W 7, L 4, D 6*

Master i/c: D. W. Smith Professional: C. Craven

Nicky Peng, a member of the England Under-13 squad, became the youngest player to represent the school's first team.

Batting—A. Kahn 16–1–434–93*–0–28.93; R. Smalley 14–4–280–55*–0–28.00; *I. Park 17–1–322–69–0–20.12; J. Park 12–3–175–55–0–19.44; C. Robson 14–1–237–48–0–18.23; M. Robinson 14–3–176–48*–0–16.00; N. Peng 10–0–158–35–0–15.80.

Bowling—J. McKenna 190.5–44–540–40–6/15–13.50; R. Munro 132.4–27–431–24–4/31–17.95; J. Harte 168.5–31–508–27–5/23–18.81.

THE ROYAL GRAMMAR SCHOOL, WORCESTER *Played 23: W 17, L 5, D 1. A 3*

Master i/c: B. M. Rees Professional: M. J. Horton

Seventeen wins from 23 matches was a school record. The team owed much to the all-round excellence of Richard Hall, who headed the batting, bowling and fielding and went on to play for English Schools and Worcestershire Under-19.

Batting—R. J. Hall 21–4–966–142*–3–56.82; J. E. K. Schofield 6–0–270–87–0–45.00; J. R. J. Cockrell 19–2–619–115*–1–36.41; N. S. A. Cockrell 6–1–155–53–0–31.00; M. W. J. Wilkinson 19–1–536–118*–1–29.77; *E. Sellwood 23–2–546–109*–1–26.00; T. M. Betts 12–3–173–65*–0–19.22; D. B. Rees 18–5–234–45–0–18.00.

Bowling—R. J. Hall 224.4–54–614–36–6/28–17.05; A. J. Stephens 147–21–558–32–4/6–17.43; E. Sellwood 228.1–32–788–43–4/67–18.32; M. R. Blackbourn 133.3–15–490–16–4/35–30.62.

RUGBY SCHOOL *Played 16: W 5, L 5, D 6*

Master i/c: P. J. Rosser Professional: L. Tennant

There were victories against strong Radley and Cheltenham sides, as well as in the two-day game against Marlborough. This was the first positive result in the fixture since 1984 and Rugby's first win since 1979. Against Malvern, the No. 10 and 11 batsmen, Benedict Williams and Christopher Wilkinson, hung on through the last 20 overs to save the match.

Batting—*A. R. Davies 15–6–325–52–0–36.11; D. J. Howe 15–4–386–82–0–35.09; S. J. G. Beazley 17–1–460–88–0–28.75; J. R. Walton 11–2–251–107*–1–27.88; O. G. Taylor 16–0–421–100–1–26.31; T. J. T. Barton-Knott 14–1–317–46*–0–24.38; A. N. G. Beazley 16–2–294–65–0–21.00.

Bowling—B. H. B. Williams 200–26–661–25–4/25–26.44; J. R. Corbett 165–30–555–18–5/41–30.83; T. J. T. Barton-Knott 138.3–11–564–18–4/27–31.33; A. R. Davies 179–21–671–21–4/53–31.95.

RYDAL SCHOOL *Played 9: W 1, L 4, D 4*

Master i/c: M. T. Leach Professional: R. W. C. Pitman

As he did in 1995, David Hanlon scored two centuries, hitting 156 not out against Cheadle Hulme and 141 against Coleraine AI. James Griffiths, a competent wicket-keeper/batsman, played for Welsh Schools Under-16.

Batting—J. B. Griffiths 3–1–166–74–0–83.00; *D. S. Hanlon 10–1–421–156*–2–46.77; R. W. Williams 10–1–244–60–0–27.11; B. Kamya 8–1–178–71*–0–25.42.

Bowling—R. J. Binks 105.2–26–286–28–6/7–10.21.

ST ALBANS SCHOOL *Played 17: W 4, L 6, D 7. A 2*

Master i/c: I. P. Jordan

Jon Freedman was unable to recapture his excellent form of the previous three years and finished his career 70 short of the 90-year-old record, on 2,283 runs.

Batting—B. J. Collins 10–4–460–117*–1–76.66; J. A. Freedman 13–1–400–80–0–33.33; S. J. O'Reilly 14–2–336–50–0–28.00; D. C. Jacobs 12–3–171–51–0–19.00; P. P. Culverhouse 11–1–172–48*–0–17.20.

Bowling—T. C. Shuttleworth 76.1–18–269–16–6/36–16.81; A. S. Khan 155.4–32–488–24–5/38–20.33; D. C. Jacobs 106.2–15–434–18–5/45–24.11; S. J. O'Reilly 134.3–20–445–17–4/39–26.17.

ST DUNSTAN'S COLLEGE *Played 16: W 6, L 3, D 7*

Master i/c: O. T. Price Professionals: R. Chowdhary and G. S. Clinton

Batting was the side's strength in a successful season. A century from John Welch helped save the game against MCC, while two more came from the captain, Ian Pressney. A highlight was the successful pursuit of 240 in 36 overs against Christ Church GS from Australia.

Batting—D. G. Darroch 12–5–371–85*–0–53.00; *I. Pressney 16–3–530–118*–2–40.76; J. C. Welch 13–2–405–109–1–36.81; N. V. Kirby 16–2–515–76*–0–36.78; J. M. Scott 14–3–229–63–0–20.81; A. Ryle 13–2–216–63*–0–19.63.

Bowling—J. C. Welch 126.2–20–478–26–4/19–18.38; M. Z. Chowdhry 158.1–22–557–28–5/19–19.89; D. Augustine 92–12–406–16–3/39–25.37; D. K. Farley 168.1–26–620–19–4/49–32.63.

ST EDMUND'S COLLEGE, WARE *Played 13: W 6, L 3, D 4*

Master i/c: J. D. T. Faithfull

Batting in depth, the side accumulated 14 individual fifties, as well as Johnathan Hilliard's century against Bishop's Stortford HS. There were several successful run-chases, the most notable being at Christ's Hospital, where 157 were scored in the last 20 overs. The best bowling performance was a hat-trick against Old Edmundians by Peter Young.

Batting—*J. Hilliard 13–2–577–102*–1–52.45; M. McGovern 11–3–279–64*–0–34.87; R. Gillham 11–1–336–64–0–33.60; A. Bilimoria 11–0–247–63–0–22.45; P. Adshead 9–1–177–61*–0–22.12; M. Sharp 12–0–198–55–0–16.50.

Bowling—J. Hilliard 105.3–14–460–18–3/25–25.55; A. Dowling 109–18–414–15–6/42–27.60; A. Logue 95–7–426–15–5/45–28.40.

ST EDMUND'S SCHOOL, CANTERBURY *Played 10: W 4, L 1, D 5. A 1*

Master i/c: P. M. Evans

A potentially strong attack was eclipsed by some enterprising batting, which brought several healthy totals and a satisfying win over the XL Club. Although the bowling was tight and the leading all-rounder David Finch took a hat-trick against Dover College, there were some frustrating finishes when they were unable to prise out the last batsmen.

Batting—G. Rees 9–2–236–86–0–33.71; D. Thorne 10–2–262–88–0–32.75; D. Finch 10–1–214–47–0–23.77.

Bowling—D. Finch 99–17–329–26–8/47–12.65; M. Harlow 130.2–41–290–15–3/22–19.33.

ST EDWARD'S SCHOOL, OXFORD *Played 15: W 2, L 6, D 7*

Master i/c: D. Drake-Brockman Professional: G. V. Palmer

Batting—R. W. Tootill 14–3–489–111*–2–44.45; G. S. Peddy 14–2–479–88–0–39.91; S. J. Perks 14–0–399–63–0–28.50; M. S. Cannon 10–1–196–58–0–21.77.

Bowling—O. M. Wills 145–25–482–15–4/7–32.13; G. S. Peddy 201–65–575–17–4/14–33.82.

ST GEORGE'S COLLEGE, WEYBRIDGE *Played 20: W 7, L 8, D 5. A 1*

Master i/c: D. G. Ottley

Batting—R. Wilson 20–4–601–85*–0–37.56; *J. Turner 18–1–607–101–1–35.70; N. Carlino 15–4–322–87*–0–29.27; A. Neill 20–1–518–78–0–27.26; M. Lawson 21–0–568–60–0–27.04; T. Clouston 19–4–255–35–0–17.00; A. Collin 20–1–278–40–0–14.63; A. Crow 17–1–218–62–0–13.62; C. Neill 18–1–192–38–0–11.29.

Bowling—A. Neill 229–48–747–34–5/28–21.97; T. Clouston 124–19–549–22–4/32–24.95; J. Knox 210.5–33–845–27–5/60–31.29; N. Carlino 185.5–42–628–19–3/48–33.05.

ST JOHN'S SCHOOL, LEATHERHEAD *Played 17: W 5, L 5, D 7. A 1*

Master i/c: A. B. Gale Professional: E. Shepperd

Batting—J. J. Porter 15–0–667–111–1–44.46; J. M. A. Cook 16–1–419–122*–1–27.93; *R. B. Vosser 16–0–376–69–0–23.50; N. B. Diacon 16–1–219–35–0–14.60; N. Keeley 16–2–167–56–0–11.92.

Bowling—M. T. Morton 217.1–67–647–39–6/71–16.58; H. C. R. Harris 174–29–601–36–4/48–16.69; J. S. Harvey 64–18–285–16–4/22–17.81; N. B. Diacon 178.5–20–625–21–4/44–29.76.

ST JOSEPH'S COLLEGE, IPSWICH *Played 17: W 8, L 4, D 5*

Master i/c: K. Brooks

C. Jack, the leading bowler, went on to play for South of England. Considered the quickest bowler at the MCC Schools Festival at Oxford, he was prevented from taking his place for MCC Schools at Lord's because of a school rugby tour.

Batting—*N. Rider 13–1–603–109*–1–50.25; P. King 16–4–522–102*–1–43.50; J. Townrow 13–3–273–67*–0–27.30; C. Townrow 15–4–290–83–0–26.36; R. Daynes 12–1–243–52–0–22.09; J. Debenham 16–2–262–34*–0–18.71; C. Jack 10–1–152–43–0–16.88; J. Regan 11–1–159–45–0–15.90; J. Eaglesham 14–1–183–36–0–14.07.

Bowling—C. Jack 141–33–426–31–5/31–13.74; J. Townrow 112–13–474–26–5/17–18.23; J. Regan 98–19–341–17–4/22–20.05; P. King 141–27–503–18–5/41–27.94.

ST LAWRENCE COLLEGE, RAMSGATE *Played 10: W 5, L 3, D 2. A 5*

Master i/c: N. O. S. Jones Professional: A. P. E. Knott

Ben Swindells, opening bat, wicket-keeper and captain for the last three seasons, fell five short of a century in his last innings after five years in the eleven. A third of the fixtures were cancelled because of bad weather.

Batting—*B. Swindells 10–1–357–95–0–39.66; G. J. Cook 10–0–188–41–0–18.80; G. A. P. Grinsted 9–0–155–52–0–17.22.

Bowling—G. J. Cook 140.5–56–268–32–7/28–8.37.

ST PAUL'S SCHOOL *Played 16: W 4, L 2, D 10. A 1*

Master i/c: G. Hughes Professional: M. Heath

Batting—*S. W. Peters 13–1–523–98–0–43.58; J. A. C. Matthews 14–2–521–101*–1–43.41; T. E. B. Etherton 13–0–292–63–0–22.46; O. J. R. Corner 12–3–201–50*–0–22.33; S. A. Hyman 10–1–168–53*–0–18.66; P. de Villiers 11–2–167–79*–0–18.55.

Bowling—P. de Villiers 136–19–473–21–5/41–22.52; D. J. McGaughey 185–63–490–21–5/41–23.33; J. A. C. Matthews 137–26–500–17–4/51–29.41.

ST PETER'S SCHOOL, YORK *Played 19: W 8, L 3, D 8*

Master i/c: D. Kirby Professional: K. F. Mohan

The Kay brothers both made significant contributions. Andrew, the elder, captained the side and opened the batting to head the averages, followed by Nick, who batted at No. 4. They scored 113 not out and 66 respectively in a stand of 137 at Ampleforth. Nick also opened the bowling and took 38 wickets at a brisk medium pace.

Batting—*A. L. T. Kay 18–3–793–138*–3–52.86; N. J. C. Kay 17–1–601–115–1–37.56; J. E. Reynolds 17–3–360–59–0–25.71; J. A. M. Duggin 16–3–305–52–0–23.46; R. O. Rastall 9–0–177–63–0–19.66; S. J. Leveson 14–2–153–22*–0–12.75.

Bowling—N. J. C. Kay 215.4–51–554–38–6/21–14.57; N. D. Riggall 204–50–569–27–5/7–21.07; D. Joshi 202–32–670–28–5/56–23.92.

SEDBERGH SCHOOL *Played 16: W 5, L 3, D 8. A 2*

Master i/c: N. A. Rollings Professional: J. Potter

Putting behind them a poor start, with three defeats before half term, Sedbergh did not lose again. Particularly satisfying were the wins over Royal GS, Lancaster (off the penultimate ball), and Pocklington (with 110 taken from the last ten overs). Simon Farnsworth opened the batting to good effect, scoring centuries against Rossall and Glenalmond, while slow left-armer Mark Chapman was again the leading wicket-taker.

Batting—S. P. Farnsworth 16–3–563–130*–2–43.30; *C. E. Heap 17–4–367–54–0–28.23; C. M. Jameson 14–1–274–44–0–21.07; J. C. M. Lofthouse 13–5–158–38*–0–19.75; D. R. Scargill 14–2–229–42–0–19.08.

Bowling—B. R. Biker 193–71–467–27–5/59–17.29; J. M. Chapman 184–43–544–28–6/32–19.42; S. P. Farnsworth 195–56–496–24–4/52–20.66; J. Jameson 155–38–428–20–4/20–21.40.

SEVENOAKS SCHOOL *Played 16: W 3, L 4, D 9. A 2*

Master i/c: I. J. B. Walker

Batting—*N. A. Shirreff 15–3–606–117*–1–50.50; M. J. Wesley 15–4–518–74*–0–47.09; H. S. Snuggs 14–2–299–79*–0–24.91; M. T. Wilson 12–0–278–56–0–23.16; M. A. Soulsby 11–3–171–47–0–21.37; C. D. Young-Wootton 13–2–197–84–0–17.90.

Bowling—N. A. Shirreff 72.5–16–286–16–6/24–17.87; M. T. Wilson 112.3–28–350–19–5/30–18.42; Paraag Amin 94–15–382–15–3/3–25.46.

SHEBBEAR COLLEGE *Played 15: W 1, L 6, D 8*

Master i/c: A. Bryan

Batting—R. Knapman 12–2–365–55–0–36.50; A. Lewis 14–2–315–84–0–26.25; G. Spencer 11–2–184–38–0–20.44; R. Bryan 14–0–250–63–0–17.85; *N. Laws 14–3–192–52*–0–17.45; G. Carleton 12–0–157–64–0–13.08.

Bowling—R. Bryan 112.2–24–332–19–3/17–17.47; N. Laws 107–20–389–20–3/17–19.45.

SHERBORNE SCHOOL *Played 13: W 9, L 2, D 2. A 4*

Master i/c: M. D. Nurton Professional: A. Willows

Batting—A. N. P. Searson 13–4–381–91*–0–42.33; C. C. M. Warren 13–2–454–101–1–41.27; M. Shearer 8–0–257–103–1–32.12.

Bowling—J. Cheung 68.3–4–236–22–4/14–10.72; J. M. A. Fradgley 111.1–13–300–23–5/16–13.04; A. N. P. Searson 102–23–336–18–3/35–18.66.

SHREWSBURY SCHOOL *Played 18: W 7, L 7, D 4*

Master i/c: S. M. Holroyd Professional: A. P. Pridgeon

Batting—B. J. Chesters 19–2–558–106–1–32.82; B. R. Tonge 16–3–373–87*–0–28.69; I. J. W. McCarter 15–4–308–74*–0–28.00; B. J. Champkin 17–4–362–56–0–27.84; A. S. Umpleby 14–3–257–59*–0–23.36; *J. D. W. Cox 18–1–244–73–0–14.35.

Bowling—I. J. W. McCarter 151–32–383–30–4/12–12.76; A. P. Ligertwood 133–36–319–24–5/26–13.29; A. S. Umpleby 129–20–424–25–4/26–16.96; W. M. Lilley 149–26–488–22–4/37–22.18; B. J. Champkin 194–49–551–24–3/15–22.95.

SIMON LANGTON GRAMMAR SCHOOL *Played 17: W 6, L 4, D 7. A 2*

Master i/c: R. H. Green

Having bowled out the opposition each time to win their first six matches, the side won no more, and had too many boring draws. The most disappointing defeat was that by Rochester Maths in the play-off final of the Kent SCA Under-19 League.

Batting—D. Mathews 12–3–429–86–0–47.66; *E. Roberts 15–2–594–129–1–45.69; S. Fletcher 12–0–521–106–1–43.41; D. Patching 17–5–419–79*–0–34.91; D. Lloyd-James 14–4–293–101*–1–29.30.

Bowling—D. Brazier 93.4–25–291–28–6/38–10.39; O. Lloyd-James 90.1–17–351–19–3/6–18.47; R. Murray 124.1–24–379–20–6/43–18.95.

SIR ROGER MANWOOD'S SCHOOL *Played 12: W 2, L 4, D 6. A 1*

Master i/c: I. Mellor

Batting—T. Birch 10–3–309–107*–2–44.14; *S. Judd 9–1–206–73–0–25.75; M. Birkett 9–1–194–48–0–24.25; R. Graeme 12–0–247–67–0–20.58; A. Crisp 10–0–196–82–0–19.60; *A. Mellor 9–0–175–61–0–19.44.

Bowling—No bowler took 15 wickets.

SOLIHULL SCHOOL *Played 15: W 6, L 6, D 3*

Master i/c: S. A. Morgan Professional: K. Patel

Some substantial totals were compiled during a successful season in which the side won the Warwickshire Under-19 Trophy. They made 303 for six, with hundreds from James Parks and James Spires, against Nottingham High School, and hung on for a draw with 293 for nine in reply to Warwick School's 317 for two. Both Robert Montagu-Williams and Richard Robinson took hat-tricks, against King Edward's, Birmingham, and King Edward's, Aston, respectively.

Batting—J. C. Parks 15–2–706–133–3–54.30; J. A. Spires 12–1–363–100*–1–33.00; J. M. S. Hawkins 12–2–193–47–0–19.30; L. O. R. Davis 15–0–231–58–0–15.40; M. S. Travis 13–1–174–51*–0–14.50.

Bowling—*R. P. F. Montagu-Williams 119–15–544–29–6/17–18.75; J. A. Spires 153–20–609–25–5/15–24.36.

SOUTH CRAVEN SCHOOL *Played 8: W 6, L 1, D 1. A 4*

Master i/c: D. M. Birks

In a rain-hit season, the side won a record six matches, including a first victory over MCC. Fifteen-year-old Matthew Lloyd made a spectacular debut against Bingley GS, taking eight for 18, including a hat-trick in a spell of eight for four in four overs. Adrian Emmott, the captain, became the leading wicket-taker with a total of 45 in three seasons.

Batting—No batsman scored 150 runs. The leading batsman was L. Gordon 7–0–148–48–0–21.14.

Bowling—*A. Emmott 73–23–212–17–6/27–12.47.

STAMFORD SCHOOL *Played 16: W 2, L 10, D 4. A 2*

Master i/c: J. M. H. Beale

Batting—*D. J. Scott 16–2–459–107*–1–32.78; D. H. Precey 16–0–321–64–0–20.06; H. P. Wickham 16–1–281–48–0–18.73; D. McDonald 16–2–255–62–0–18.21; N. J. Doggett 13–0–216–62–0–16.61; J. Fuller 16–1–222–50*–0–14.80.

Bowling—No bowler took 15 wickets. The leading bowler was B. J. E. Tate 126.4–23–438–13–3/43–33.69.

STOCKPORT GRAMMAR SCHOOL *Played 14: W 2, L 2, D 10*

Master i/c: A. Brett Professional: D. J. Makinson

Batting—C. Pimlott 13–3–379–80–0–37.90; J. Bale 11–0–344–71–0–31.27; P. Handler 11–4–203–56*–0–29.00; T. Pritchard 11–3–191–35*–0–23.87; C. Jones 8–1–158–72*–0–22.57; A. Massey 9–1–170–60*–0–21.25; R. Jones 11–1–159–35–0–15.90.

Bowling—C. Pimlott 143–30–402–25–5/46–16.08; R. Jones 86–8–278–15–4/51–18.53; G. Coglan 97–20–299–16–5/17–18.68.

STOWE SCHOOL *Played 14: W 4, L 4, D 6. A 1*

Master i/c: M. J. Harris

Two all-rounders were pre-eminent, Robert White and Richard Harris, son of M. J. Harris, sharing 986 runs and 81 wickets between them.

Batting—R. A. White 16–2–607–119–2–43.35; R. A. Harris 16–2–379–68*–0–27.07; R. T. D. Searle 14–0–319–57–0–22.78; C. E. D. Saunders 16–2–289–57*–0–20.64; J. R. W. McDonagh 16–0–320–71–0–20.00.

Bowling—R. A. Harris 286.3–50–724–47–7/68–15.40; R. A. White 196–44–608–34–5/34–17.88; T. R. Stables 122–18–535–16–3/70–33.43.

STRATHALLAN SCHOOL *Played 14: W 3, L 5, D 6. A 2*

Master i/c: R. J. W. Proctor Professional: I. L. Philip

Batting—H. J. Hensman 13–3–320–87*–0–32.00; R. J. D. Barr 12–1–317–80–0–28.81; J. J. Ward 7–0–179–90–0–25.57; *K. R. Parker 10–1–179–32–0–19.88; E. A. M. MacKay 15–3–180–36–0–15.00.

Bowling—M. S. Elder 147–33–416–27–8/35–15.40; I. Stewart 127–39–355–22–5/25–16.13; A. A. Chapman 142.2–37–391–16–4/43–24.43; R. J. D. Barr 160.5–44–458–18–2/16–25.44.

SUTTON VALENCE SCHOOL *Played 15: W 4, L 2, D 9*

Master i/c: J. H. Kittermaster Professional: A. R. Day

The best results for four years were enjoyed by a young side.

Batting—M. Wooderson 13–5–473–111*–1–59.12; M. Day 13–1–342–100*–1–28.50; T. Watts 12–3–244–90*–0–27.11; G. Horton 13–1–286–90–0–23.83; F. Debney 12–0–179–37–0–14.91.

Bowling—J. Vincent 128.4–16–474–21–5/54–22.57.

TAUNTON SCHOOL *Played 17: W 14, L 2, D 1. A 2*

Master i/c: D. Baty Professional: A. Kennedy

Concentration on limited-overs cricket, plus all-round ability and strength in depth, brought Taunton their best season to date with 14 wins out of 17 and ten sides bowled out.

Batting—S. Rose 14–7–385–76*–0–55.00; R. Selway 16–8–423–65*–0–52.87; L. Cooper 15–1–579–84–0–41.35; *D. Cooper 9–2–238–70*–0–34.00; D. Law 9–2–233–72–0–33.28; H. Tarr 12–0–349–76–0–29.08; S. Bail 11–1–239–67*–0–23.90.

Bowling—R. Selway 140–30–409–28–3/19–14.60; T. Bradnock 195.1–54–527–35–6/52–15.05; M. Bulbeck 118–30–337–17–3/28–19.82.

TIFFIN SCHOOL *Played 16: W 1, L 7, D 8. A 2*

Master i/c: M. J. Williams

Although it was not a vintage year, with only one match won, some good cricket was played – often in adversity.

Batting—B. W. O'Connell 15–0–478–109–2–31.86; *M. C. Anstey 16–1–403–108*–1–26.86; D. A. Urquhart 15–0–254–74–0–16.93; C. D. O'Connell 16–0–263–97–0–16.43; D. J. Procter 16–1–244–42–0–16.26; I. J. Lulham 16–1–172–38–0–11.46.

Bowling—B. W. O'Connell 224.4–45–756–32–4/6–23.62; A. J. Pitts 105–21–412–15–3/40–27.46; C. D. O'Connell 148.2–21–580–16–4/37–36.25.

TONBRIDGE SCHOOL *Played 19: W 14, L 2, D 3*

Master i/c: P. B. Taylor Professional: C. Stone

Victory in the first nine matches, none of which was a limited-overs contest, set the tone for a record tally of 14 in all. James Pyemont was the first for ten years to pass 1,000 runs and his 167 against Epsom College was the highest since Colin Cowdrey's 175 not out in 1950. He made a hundred before lunch at the MCC Schools Festival at Oxford, was named the *Cricketer's* Schoolboy Cricketer of the Year and played for Sussex Second Eleven. He was superbly supported by Matthew Banes, a colt, who scored 919 runs.

Batting—J. P. Pyemont 19–2–1,098–167–2–64.58; M. J. Banes 20–2–919–143*–2–51.05; D. D. Cherry 12–6–262–68–0–43.66; J. J. McCulley 19–2–650–78–0–38.23; *A. D. Bolot 19–7–403–73*–0–33.58; J. G. C. Rowe 16–6–278–59*–0–27.80.

Bowling—T. J. E. Reed 133–32–310–19–3/22–16.31; R. P. T. Langdon 204–43–616–31–7/50–19.87; T. E. Goodworth 215.4–40–687–34–5/31–20.20; A. T. Hunter 133–26–354–17–3/16–20.82; D. D. Cherry 181–32–634–30–4/11–21.13.

TRENT COLLEGE *Played 19: W 4, L 3, D 12*

Master i/c: Dr T. P. Woods Professional: G. Miller

Although the results were less spectacular than in 1995, much positive and exciting cricket was played. Tom Hancock had an outstanding all-round season and went on to play for Derbyshire Second Eleven. A slow left-armer, he was also asked to bowl to both the Indian and England teams prior to the Third Test at Trent Bridge.

Batting—A. P. Siddall 13–5–377–65*–0–47.12; *T. W. Hancock 18–6–491–122*–2–40.91; D. I. Jordison 17–3–535–122–2–38.21; N. J. Brown 14–3–348–69*–0–31.63; A. C. Garratt 17–5–356–53*–0–29.66; D. J. Eckersley 18–0–363–78–0–20.16; O. C. K. Henshell 14–2–205–33–0–17.08; F. L. Larke 15–2–174–53–0–13.38.

Bowling—T. W. Hancock 239.2–64–599–40–6/49–14.97; D. I. Jordison 188.2–39–473–22–3/23–21.50; A. C. Garratt 136–20–513–21–5/48–24.42; A. P. Siddall 167–29–603–21–5/25–28.71.

TRINITY SCHOOL *Played 19: W 7, L 0, D 12. A 1*

Masters i/c: I. W. Cheyne and B. Widger

The third unbeaten season in five years none the less featured a disappointing proportion of draws. Shehan de Silva led from the front to finish his career with 2,655 runs, second only to Richard Nowell's 4,250. He went on to play for MCC Schools, NCA Young Cricketers, English Schools and Surrey Second Eleven. The Under-15 captain, Robert Mutucumarana, made an immediate impression when he joined the side in the second half of the season, taking seven for 45 at King's, Canterbury, and batting with maturity.

Batting—R. S. A. Mutucumarana 7–5–176–71–0–88.00; S. A. Newman 7–1–395–146–2–65.83; *S. N. de Silva 17–5–782–108*–1–65.16; M. G. Macaskill 17–1–516–98–0–32.25; B. D. Cox 8–2–189–100*–1–31.50; R. J. Duke 13–2–184–66–0–16.72; D. O. Robinson 11–1–167–49–0–16.70; A. J. C. Mutucumarana 14–3–159–30*–0–14.45.

Bowling—R. S. A. Mutucumarana 114–32–295–25–7/45–11.80; A. R. Blackmore 195–41–543–35–5/66–15.51; C. M. Donovan 140.2–27–396–23–5/21–17.21.

TRURO SCHOOL *Played 14: W 6, L 4, D 3, Tied 1. A 2*

Master i/c: D. M. Phillips

Batting—*T. Sharp 11–1–447–108–1–44.70; B. Price 6–0–173–89–0–28.83; C. Penhaligon 8–0–189–42–0–23.62; J. Price 13–1–274–86*–0–22.83; R. Harmer 9–1–176–43*–0–22.00; M. Barry 11–1–194–75*–0–19.40; N. Willcocks 13–3–176–59–0–17.60.

Bowling—T. Sharp 69.2–8–256–21–5/35–12.19; C. Shreck 123.1–27–360–26–4/66–13.84.

UNIVERSITY COLLEGE SCHOOL *Played 18: W 5, L 8, D 5*

Master i/c: S. M. Bloomfield Professional: W. G. Jones

Batting—D. Beary 17–4–657–102*–2–50.53; M. Floyd 12–1–403–71–0–36.63; P. Durban 18–1–498–102*–1–29.29; *T. Gladstone 17–0–424–84–0–24.94; J. Craig 15–5–191–32–0–19.10.

Bowling—J. Rose 84–11–380–20–6/30–19.00; A. Renton 126–32–336–17–5/38–19.76; D. Sanders 110.5–28–574–15–3/61–38.26.

UPPINGHAM SCHOOL *Played 17: W 3, L 6, D 8. A 1*

Master i/c: I. E. W. Sanders Professional: M. R. Hallam

Maurice Hallam's 19th and final season as coach was followed by a tour to Barbados in July.

Batting—*C. D. Gent 18–2–587–121*–1–36.68; R. E. C. Watts 17–2–414–135*–1–27.60; A. S. B. Lees 17–0–309–66–0–18.17; H. J. G. Waite 17–5–208–35–0–17.33; P. A. S. Moser 14–0–171–40–0–12.21.

Bowling—J. A. Brydon 135.3–21–543–25–5/19–21.72; C. A. P. Freestone 155–22–562–21–6/33–26.76; C. D. Gent 235.2–45–821–30–7/48–27.36.

VICTORIA COLLEGE, JERSEY *Played 24: W 8, L 10, D 6*

Master i/c: D. A. R. Ferguson

A record one-day total of 303 for five was amassed against Reigate GS, who were then dismissed for 226.

Batting—I. J. D. R. MacEachern 16–5–574–86*–0–52.18; D. Mills 17–7–394–67*–0–39.40; R. D. Minty 21–4–609–77*–0–35.82; R. O. Thompson 19–3–442–72*–0–27.62; A. M. B. Thomas 20–5–395–74–0–26.33; J. E. Mashiter 22–1–552–95–0–26.28; *C. D. Mullin 21–2–393–100*–1–20.68; F. D. McInnes 18–3–215–34–0–14.33.

Bowling—R. O. Thompson 238–39–826–40–5/23–20.65; N. S. Broughton 163–18–641–27–4/58–23.74; M. J. Billington 172–34–561–20–3/46–28.05; F. D. McInnes 129–8–609–17–3/30–35.82.

WARWICK SCHOOL *Played 13: W 5, L 3, D 5. A 2*

Master i/c: G. A. Tedstone

David Young, whose 200 not out against Solihull was a school record, scored a century and two fifties in the MCC Schools Festival at Oxford and played for Warwickshire Under-19.

Batting—*D. J. Young 13–1–838–200*–3–69.83; J. M. Moffatt 13–1–434–82*–0–36.16; A. J. Preece 12–5–201–56*–0–28.71; A. M. Deverill-Smith 13–0–359–89–0–27.61; A. J. Hume 13–0–183–45–0–14.07.

Bowling—No bowler took 15 wickets. The leading bowler was D. J. Young 104–13–367–13–4/45–28.23.

WATFORD GRAMMAR SCHOOL *Played 13: W 6, L 4, D 3. A 1*

Master i/c: R. W. Panter

J. C. K. Phang scored the side's only century, hitting 111 not out against Enfield.

Batting—*J. C. K. Phang 13–3–451–111*–1–45.10; K. T. Farrell 12–3–273–50*–0–30.33; S. J. Farrell 12–1–276–97–0–25.09; F. Samadi 11–4–175–38*–0–25.00; J. A. Rylett 12–0–292–97–0–24.33.

Bowling—R. L. Hodgkinson 149.3–31–526–22–5/78–23.90; J. A. Rylett 108.5–10–474–16–5/41–29.62.

WELLINGBOROUGH SCHOOL *Played 17: W 2, L 4, D 11. A 1*

Master i/c: M. H. Askham — Professional: J. C. J. Dye

Batting—K. M. C. Saville 15–4–286–59–0–26.00; J. P. Phipps 14–5–223–30–0–24.77; J. E. Bannard 17–3–336–68*–0–24.00; *T. N. Mason 16–1–297–52–0–19.80; L. L. Jones 15–1–277–44*–0–19.78; J. Lower 16–2–177–35–0–12.64.

Bowling—R. Johnson 233.1–45–843–39–5/21–21.61; K. M. C. Saville 244–59–829–38–6/85–21.81; J. P. Phipps 158–17–618–22–5/32–28.09.

WELLINGTON COLLEGE *Played 17: W 6, L 4, D 7. A 1*

Masters i/c: C. M. St G. Potter and R. I. H. B. Dyer — Professional: P. J. Lewington

Charles Hodgson, who went on to play for MCC Schools, took his tally of hundreds for the eleven to eight in two years. Adrian Northey's aggregate of 968 was second only to Hodgson's own record in 1995.

Batting—A. C. Northey 18–1–968–114–3–56.94; *C. P. R. Hodgson 18–0–616–116–2–34.22; A. J. Ash 17–1–416–66–0–26.00; M. P. Chicken 18–2–219–44*–0–13.68.

Bowling—A. T. Gowar 125.3–20–392–21–4/21–18.66; C. P. R. Hodgson 186–43–541–28–5/16–19.32; P. C. Melville 172.5–32–558–26–3/26–21.46; S. F. Streatfeild 127–18–434–15–2/17–28.93; T. P. D. Squires 199–31–685–15–3/83–45.66.

WELLINGTON SCHOOL *Played 15: W 5, L 5, D 5. A 3*

Master i/c: P. M. Pearce

The captain, Robert Urwin, became the first player to score four hundreds in a season.

Batting—*R. J. Urwin 14–4–744–115*–4–74.40; J. P. Derbyshire 14–3–388–81*–0–35.27; L. J. Greany 12–3–160–63*–0–17.77; J. B. Copp 14–0–246–60–0–17.57; S. M. Gallagher 14–0–223–69–0–15.92.

Bowling—B. A. House 111–19–392–20–6/34–19.60; S. A. Sheldon 78–12–370–18–3/2–20.55; J. P. Derbyshire 98.1–18–437–16–5/17–27.31; S. Cooper 143.2–30–521–16–3/25–32.56.

WELLS CATHEDRAL SCHOOL *Played 13: W 4, L 9, D 0*

Master i/c: M. Stringer

Batting—B. Clements 12–2–239–61*–0–23.90; M. Shercliffe 12–1–161–30–0–14.63.

Bowling—B. Clements 112–30–341–26–4/15–13.11; H. Parkinson 103.3–25–316–23–3/15–13.73.

WESTMINSTER SCHOOL *Played 11: W 1, L 5, D 5. A 1*

Master i/c: G. Brown Professional: R. O. Butcher

Batting—B. Gordon 9–2–283–99–0–40.42; R. Korgoankar 7–2–182–89*–0–36.40; K. Raghuveer 6–0–154–117–1–25.66; R. McHugh 10–0–241–75–0–24.10.

Bowling—No bowler took 15 wickets. The leading bowler was *A. Jones 106.5–15–394–14–4/29–28.14.

WHITGIFT SCHOOL *Played 19: W 7, L 2, D 10*

Master i/c: P. C. Fladgate Professionals: M. A. Butcher and G. S. Clinton

In an encouraging season, James Furner was the leading scorer with two hundreds in his 658 runs, while one each came from the captain, Nick Jarvis, and the young Nishal Patel, who played several match-winning innings. Medium-pace bowlers Darren Ashby and Brian Smith shared 67 wickets. Smith and Giles Coffey put on 44 for the last wicket against Reigate GS to win the match.

Batting—J. P. Furner 13–2–658–127*–2–59.81; N. A. Patel 17–6–547–114*–1–49.72; A. E. Courtenay 11–3–263–55*–0–32.87; *N. D. A. Jarvis 14–2–378–103*–1–31.50; T. Clarke 16–2–416–98*–0–29.71; T. N. J. L. Platts 19–1–396–53–0–22.00.

Bowling—D. P. R. Ashby 222.4–51–702–33–4/30–21.27; K. Patel 115.2–31–335–15–3/29–22.33; B. P. Smith 268–65–819–34–5/28–24.08.

WINCHESTER COLLEGE *Played 20: W 6, L 4, D 10. A 1*

Master i/c: C. J. Good Professional: I. C. D. Stuart

Ed Craig passed a thousand runs for the second successive season. His 1,061 were second only to the 1,068 scored by the Nawab of Pataudi in 1959 and his nine hundreds in the first team were one more than the previous record – also set by the Nawab of Pataudi.

Batting—*E. D. C. Craig 20–1–1,061–129–5–55.84; T. Powell-Jackson 19–1–739–100–1–41.05; R. O'Keeffe 19–4–337–59–0–22.46; C. Awdry 13–3–206–47–0–20.60; T. V. Hanson 17–2–289–63–0–19.26; J. Curtis 13–0–190–42–0–14.61.

Bowling—W. Close-Brooks 95–11–311–17–4/23–18.29; C. Foster 149–27–543–23–6/46–23.60; C. Awdry 155–38–501–17–4/27–29.47; G. Warren 132–13–480–15–3/51–32.00.

WOODBRIDGE SCHOOL *Played 13: W 2, L 8, D 3. A 1*

Master i/c: Rev. M. E. Percival

Batting—T. E. Percival 13–0–340–93–0–26.15; M. P. Johnston 13–0–276–57–0–21.23; A. Charlton 13–0–160–49–0–12.30.

Bowling—M. P. Johnston 135.5–32–399–23–6/48–17.34; T. E. Percival 132.1–36–318–15–3/2–21.20.

WOODHOUSE GROVE SCHOOL *Played 17: W 3, L 3, D 11. A 1*

Master i/c: R. I. Frost Professional: F. H. Tyson

Putting behind them three early defeats, the side lost no more and won three. Andrew Brimacombe scored 133 against Arnold, and Guy Bennett hit 101 against Old Grovians, as well as taking the most wickets with his leg-spin. He played for HMC North Under-15, while Stephen Brimacombe and Nick Verity both represented Yorkshire Under-15.

Batting—N. Smith 17–4–413–63*–0–31.76; S. Brimacombe 17–0–441–93–0–25.94; A. Brimacombe 17–0–413–133–1–24.29; G. Bennett 14–1–283–101–1–21.76; *D. Brier 12–1–229–82–0–20.81; C. Dibb 11–1–196–41–0–19.60; T. Hope 15–5–181–36*–0–18.10; N. Verity 15–4–196–55*–0–17.81.

Bowling—G. Bennett 161.1–27–626–31–6/51–20.19; B. Rhodes 108.4–19–335–16–4/37–20.93; S. Brimacombe 134–25–357–17–4/37–21.00.

WORKSOP COLLEGE *Played 18: W 4, L 4, D 10. A 2*

Master i/c: C. P. Paton Professional: A. Kettleborough

Richard Wilkinson was pre-eminent, scoring 1,161 runs, with four centuries, as well as heading the bowling with his off-spin. He played for MCC Schools, England North Under-19 and the Development of Excellence XI.

Batting—*R. Wilkinson 17–3–1,161–141–4–82.92; G. Harvey 14–2–625–83–0–52.08; J. Pearson 17–4–433–60–0–33.30; R. Turner 18–2–441–74–0–27.56.

Bowling—R. Wilkinson 210.3–55–473–33–5/20–14.33; G. Harvey 159–35–448–29–4/26–15.44.

WREKIN COLLEGE *Played 12: W 3, L 2, D 7*

Master i/c: M. de Weymarn Professional: D. A. Banks

Dan Thornburn and James Horwood compiled two consecutive century opening stands of 144 against Oswestry and 128 against Denstone. Stuart Ingram kept wicket, batted No. 3 and captained the side for the second year, while promise was shown by the Under-15 player, Patrick Snodgrass.

Batting—V. Padhaal 9–3–283–66*–0–47.16; P. Snodgrass 8–1–271–76–0–38.71; D. Thornburn 10–1–249–74–0–27.66; *S. Ingram 9–1–209–55–0–26.12; J. Horwood 10–2–196–53–0–24.50.

Bowling—J. Turner 75–16–264–15–4/54–17.60; R. Boyes 121–16–420–23–5/60–18.26; C. Rice 100–20–309–15–5/24–20.60.

WYCLIFFE COLLEGE *Played 13: W 3, L 5, D 5*

Master i/c: C. R. C. Tetley Professional: N. Martin

Batting—L. Bowery 13–1–385–71*–0–32.08; M. Arnold 12–0–357–83–0–29.75; J. Skinner 12–1–268–56–0–24.36; G. Williams 13–0–279–78–0–21.46; A. Drury 12–2–206–59–0–20.60.

Bowling—J. Wilkinson 57–4–205–15–6/21–13.66; G. Williams 118.1–21–403–24–5/51–16.79; L. Bowery 106–14–394–15–3/28–26.26.

WYGGESTON & QUEEN ELIZABETH I COLLEGE *Played 10: W 6, L 1, D 3*

Master i/c: G. G. Wells

Batting—*S. Patel 8–5–340–130*–2–113.33; J. Mason 7–1–404–116*–1–67.33.

Bowling—A. Khoda 70–13–284–15–5/28–18.93.

GIRLS' SCHOOL

ROEDEAN SCHOOL *Played 12: W 5, L 5, D 2*

Staff i/c: A. S. England and A. F. Romanov

Tamsyn Kelson played for Sussex Under-21 and South of England Under-17.

Batting—T. J. Kelson 10–1–218–48–0–24.22.

Bowling—No bowler took 15 wickets. The leading bowler was N. M. Chinai 34–1–148–11–4/12–13.45.

YOUTH CRICKET, 1996

UNDER-16 CRICKET

The Lord's Taverners launched a new initiative in 1996 in the form of the Britvic Inner Cities Cup. Schoolboys from "neglected areas" were targeted for the competition, which brought teams from Birmingham, Bristol, Cardiff, Lambeth, Manchester, Nottingham, Sheffield and Sunderland down to Arundel for three days of cricket. John Barclay, England's tour manager, supervised coaching sessions, and after the 30-overs group matches had been concluded, Cardiff met Nottingham in a 40-overs final. Cardiff won by eight wickets, finishing with a six.

UNDER-15 CRICKET

It was difficult to separate the four regional under-15 teams that took part in the Bunbury ESCA Festival at Oxford. Both the North and the West won two games and lost one, but the West were proclaimed overall victors by virtue of their earlier six-wicket win over the North. The Midlands and the South won one match each. Chris Taylor of Yorkshire was awarded the Neil Lloyd Trophy for the top batsman of the festival. In the Sun Life of Canada Under-15 Club Championship, Horsham of Sussex held their nerve after the scheduled final was interrupted by a downpour. A replay was arranged for the following day, and Horsham's 106 for three from 20 overs was too good for Wolverhampton, who were all out for 77. James Clark took five for 15. Millfield tightened their grip on the Lord's Taverners/*Cricketer* Colts Trophy for Schools, winning their second consecutive title and their seventh in 11 years. In the final, Shrewsbury set them a target of 128, and Millfield were in trouble at 76 for six before they were rescued by 54 not out from Jason Gilbey. The Army Careers/ESCA Under-15 County Championship went to Sussex, who knocked out the holders and favourites Yorkshire by a 93-run margin in the semi-final. Sussex captain Mark Nash took five wickets in that match, and six in the final, against Hampshire.

UNDER-13 CRICKET

It was all change at the Under-13 Club Championship, which this year had a new sponsor, Subaru, and a new venue, Oakham School. Harrold of Bedfordshire entered the competition for the first time, and wound up as winners of the Ken Barrington Trophy.

Nearly 1,400 teams took part in the competition's qualifying stage. Eight teams made it to the finals, held over the course of a week, and they finished in the following order: Harrold, Leamington (Warwickshire), Tynemouth (Northumberland), Old Leodiensians (Yorkshire), Send (Surrey), Weston-super-Mare (Somerset), Diss (Norfolk) and Perkins (Shropshire). Each team consists of eight players, who bat in pairs for five overs each, starting with a base score of 200 and conceding eight runs each time they lose a wicket. Harrold, who won every match they played, were captained by Will Smith, and the squad also included Robert Adkin, Eddie Billson, Ollie Chinneck, Peter Heady, Will Skinner, James Stedman, Robert Ward and Robin Wycherley.

UNDER-11 CRICKET

The annual Wrigley Softball Cricket Tournament was held at Edgbaston on July 12. Its founder, Trevor Bailey, said that the overall standard was the highest he has seen in the competition's 16 years. Three thousand primary schools from all over Britain had participated in the qualifying rounds, but Headfield Junior School from Dewsbury, the winners for the last two years, were not among the 16 who went through to the finals. Their crown was taken by St Mary's of Shenfield – the first side from Essex to win the tournament. The squad comprised Robert Rayner, David Burgess, Chris Keogh, David Hammond, Jonathan Coppin, William Mew, Bobby Bull, Nishant Varma, Jamie Walton and Philip Prior. Among the school's other pupils are Megan and Sally Gooch, whose father Graham was, coincidentally, the guest of honour. This led to some disappointment among the parents, who felt a bit let down that the trophy was presented by someone they saw every week outside the school gates.

On the finals day of the ESCA/Red Fox Hardball Competition, Queen Elizabeth Grammar School from Wakefield claimed first place, winning all four of their matches comfortably, while Millfield School were runners up. Both of these competitions follow an eight-a-side format, in which the teams begin with 200 runs and lose six of them every time a wicket falls, but the batsman stays in.

WOMEN'S CRICKET, 1996

By CAROL SALMON

NEW ZEALAND WOMEN IN ENGLAND, 1996

New Zealand's last visit to England, for the World Cup in 1993, had ended in defeat by their hosts in the Lord's final. But they had gained considerable ground since then, and they ended their 1996 tour head and shoulders the better side, winning the one-day series 3-0. All the Tests were drawn – as on their previous tours of England, in 1966 and 1984 – but this time it was England who were desperately hanging on. Their ninth-wicket pair had to hold out for 95 minutes in the final Test to deny New Zealand their first victory over England in 22 attempts.

Debbie Hockley had an outstanding tour, scoring 682 at 75.77 in all matches. She averaged nearly 95 in the Tests and her one-day form was phenomenal – 54 in 60 balls, 75 in 69 and 117 in 127. Kirsty Flavell (née Bond), her Canterbury team-mate, became the first woman to score a double-hundred in a Test. With batting form like that, New Zealand were bowled out only once, in their opening game. Like England, though, their attack could not find a consistent cutting edge on some fine batting pitches. Off-spinner Catherine Campbell was their leading wicket-taker, with 24 at 19.66, despite arriving with chicken-pox.

England had set great store by their evergreen opener Janette Brittin, who needed 172 to equal Rachael Heyhoe-Flint's world record of 1,594 Test runs. But she suffered a serious eye injury beforehand and broke a finger during the one-day series. She returned for the Second Test and scored a fifty in the Third, but finished still 109 short. There were encouraging performances from vice-captain Barbara Daniels and leg-spinning all-rounder Kathryn Leng: both scored Test centuries at Scarborough. All were overshadowed, however, by the selection of 16-year-old Charlotte Edwards, England's youngest Test player of either sex.

England's preparations were not helped by the sudden resignation of coach John Bown, for health reasons, after their winter tour of India. Former international Megan Lear stepped in. They were also handicapped by having to return to work between matches. By contrast, the tourists had the financial backing of New Zealand Cricket; for the first time, they were travelling under the aegis of the men's board and there was even bonus money at stake.

NEW ZEALAND WOMEN TOURING PARTY

S. L. Illingworth (Canterbury) (*captain*), M. A. M. Lewis (Wellington) (*vice-captain*), H. R. Bastion (Northern Districts), K. D. Brown (Auckland), C. A. Campbell (Canterbury), E. C. Drumm (Auckland), K. E. Flavell (Canterbury), S. Fruin (Auckland), J. A. Fryer (Wellington), J. E. Harris (Wellington), D. A. Hockley (Canterbury), K. Le Comber (Canterbury), C. M. Nicholson (Auckland), A. M. O'Leary (Wellington), K. M. Withers (Canterbury).

Le Comber replaced L. Astle, also of Canterbury, who withdrew before the tour.

Manager: K. Gilray. *Coach:* A. McKenna.

Note: Matches in this section were not first-class.

At Lord's, June 13. First one-day international: New Zealand won by eight wickets. Toss: England. England 139 for six (50 overs); New Zealand 140 for two (33.3 overs) (S. Fruin 41, D. A. Hockley 54).

For the first time, MCC admitted women guests to the Lord's pavilion during play.

At Leicester, June 16. Second one-day international: New Zealand won by 56 runs. Toss: New Zealand. New Zealand 201 for nine (50 overs) (D. A. Hockley 75, M. A. M. Lewis 33 not out; M. Reynard three for 41); England 145 (42.1 overs) (D. Stock 46; K. M. Withers three for 17).

At Chester-le-Street, June 18. Third one-day international: New Zealand won by 25 runs. Toss: England. New Zealand 237 for seven (50 overs) (S. Fruin 51, D. A. Hockley 117; K. Smithies three for 40); England 212 (49.3 overs) (H. C. Plimmer 53, B. A. Daniels 66; K. M. Withers three for 45).

ENGLAND v NEW ZEALAND

First Test Match

At Scarborough, June 24, 25, 26, 27. Drawn. Toss: England. Test debuts: S-J. Cook, R. Lupton; H. R. Bastion, K. D. Brown.

A docile pitch produced several records, but the most notable was that achieved by Kirsty Flavell. She survived chances on nine and 166 to score the first double-century in any women's Test, beating Denise Annetts's 193 for Australia against England in 1987. Several other healthy contributions helped New Zealand reach 517 for eight, second only to Australia's 525 against India in 1983-84. England had also found batting easy. Barbara Daniels and Kathryn Leng, the Yorkshire leg-spinner, scored maiden Test hundreds and added 132, a sixth-wicket record.

Close of play: First day, England 300-7 (K. Leng 90*, M. Reynard 8*); Second day, New Zealand 139-1 (S. Fruin 46*, K. E. Flavell 21*); Third day, New Zealand 281-3 (K. E. Flavell 113*, C. M. Nicholson 6*).

England

H. C. Plimmer c Brown b Harris	16
R. Lupton c Brown b Harris	0
B. A. Daniels c Flavell b Harris	160
S. Metcalfe run out	11
*K. Smithies b Campbell	5
†J. Smit c Hockley b Campbell	7
K. Leng st Illingworth b Campbell	144
D. Stock c Hockley b Harris	1
M. Reynard not out	60
C. E. Taylor run out	5
S-J. Cook c Hockley b Campbell	2
L-b 1, w 1, n-b 1	3
1/3 2/52 3/84 4/105 5/133 6/265 7/279 8/393 9/408	414

Bowling: Harris 40–7–119–4; Brown 20–5–40–0; Bastion 16–3–59–0; Campbell 34.5–7–94–4; Fryer 20–1–76–0; Nicholson 10–1–25–0.

New Zealand

S. Fruin c Lupton b Stock	80
D. A. Hockley b Leng	63
K. E. Flavell b Leng	204
M. A. M. Lewis c Plimmer b Smithies	1
C. M. Nicholson c Smit b Taylor	46
*†S. L. Illingworth c Smit b Reynard	27
C. A. Campbell c Metcalfe b Leng	8
J. E. Harris c Plimmer b Daniels	0
K. D. Brown not out	50
J. A. Fryer not out	7
B 2, l-b 18, w 10, n-b 1	31
1/91 2/237 3/264 4/353 5/434 6/454 7/455 8/457	(8 wkts) 517

H. R. Bastion did not bat.

Bowling: Taylor 34–13–89–1; Cook 28–3–98–0; Stock 39–13–102–1; Leng 46–15–112–3; Smithies 33–19–32–1; Reynard 30–16–49–1; Daniels 5–1–15–1.

Umpires: J. Hayes and A. L. Roberts.

ENGLAND v NEW ZEALAND

Second Test Match

At Worcester, July 4, 5, 6, 7. Drawn. Toss: England. Test debut: A. M. O'Leary.

Like the First Test, the Second never reached its third innings; rain badly affected the second and third days. Jan Brittin, returning after injuring her hand in the one-day game at Leicester, gained a record 23rd cap the day before turning 37. England elected to bat, but seamer Katrina Withers had them in trouble at 37 for four before Sue Metcalfe and Jane Smit scored sixties. Debbie Hockley replied with her fourth Test hundred and New Zealand easily took the lead before the game ended.

Close of play: First day, England 146-5 (S. Metcalfe 57*, J. Smit 23*); Second day, New Zealand 92-2 (D. A. Hockley 49*, A. M. O'Leary 0*); Third day, New Zealand 150-2 (D. A. Hockley 86*, A. M. O'Leary 19*).

England

H. C. Plimmer b Withers	11
J. A. Brittin c Illingworth b Withers	3
B. A. Daniels c Brown b Withers	12
S. Metcalfe lbw b Withers	66
J. Godman b Brown	2
*K. Smithies c Lewis b Brown	27
†J. Smit c Fruin b Withers	69
K. Leng c O'Leary b Brown	22
M. Reynard c Campbell b Withers	8
S. Redfern c Withers b Harris	30
C. E. Taylor not out	10
B 5, l-b 7, w 4	16
1/6 2/22 3/31 4/37 5/90 6/159 7/190 8/200 9/255	276

Bowling: Withers 40.3–19–73–6; Harris 34–11–74–1; Brown 22–4–66–3; Campbell 34–15–41–0; Nicholson 8–2–10–0.

New Zealand

S. Fruin c Smit b Taylor	6
D. A. Hockley c Redfern b Leng	115
K. E. Flavell c Smithies b Redfern	34
A. M. O'Leary st Smit b Leng	27
M. A. M. Lewis c Redfern b Taylor	65
C. M. Nicholson b Reynard	28
*†S. L. Illingworth not out	6
K. M. Withers not out	3
B 2, l-b 5, w 2, n-b 3	12
1/11 2/90 3/172 4/211 5/281 6/287	(6 wkts dec.) 296

C. A. Campbell, J. E. Harris and K. D. Brown did not bat.

Bowling: Taylor 32–14–64–2; Redfern 32–10–82–1; Leng 26–12–74–2; Smithies 9–4–17–0; Reynard 15–4–44–1; Daniels 2–0–8–0.

Umpires: A. Fox and V. A. Williams.

ENGLAND v NEW ZEALAND

Third Test Match

At Guildford, July 12, 13, 14, 15. Drawn. Toss: New Zealand. Test debuts: C. Edwards, L. Pearson.

The 99th women's Test provided an exciting climax to the series: England's ninth-wicket pair narrowly averted their first ever defeat by New Zealand. The home side had lost sight of a target of 311 by the time they were 66 for four, just after lunch. It was 160 for eight when Clare Taylor joined Suzanne Redfern, but they held out for 95 minutes, mostly against the new ball, with up to eight fielders clustered around the bat. The tourists took the initiative on the opening day, when openers Shelley Fruin and Debbie Hockley put on 150 and then Kirsty Flavell and Emily Drumm added 106 for the third wicket, both New Zealand records. In reply, Jan Brittin scored her only international fifty of the summer. But England drew hope for the future from her opening partner, Charlotte Edwards, who became their youngest Test player at the age of 16, and suggested a great talent as she scored 34 and 31.

Close of play: First day, New Zealand 362-5 (S. L. Illingworth 0*, K. D. Brown 2*); Second day, England 242-8 (S. Redfern 19*, C. E. Taylor 9*); Third day, New Zealand 219-4 dec.

New Zealand

S. Fruin run out	80	– b Leng	13
D. A. Hockley c Smit b Taylor	65	– (6) not out	41
K. E. Flavell c Taylor b Smithies	97	– (2) lbw b Taylor	5
E. C. Drumm c Taylor b Redfern	62	– (3) not out	112
M. A. M. Lewis b Daniels	36	– (4) c sub (M. Reynard) b Leng	0
*†S. L. Illingworth not out	0	– (5) c Pearson b Stock	39
K. D. Brown not out	2		
B 2, l-b 13, w 3, n-b 2	20	B 4, l-b 2, w 2, n-b 1	9
1/150 2/167 3/273 4/351 5/357 (5 wkts dec.)	362	1/7 2/33 3/37 4/125 (4 wkts dec.)	219

C. A. Campbell, J. E. Harris, K. M. Withers and J. A. Fryer did not bat.

Bowling: *First Innings*—Taylor 26–3–92–1; Redfern 21–6–50–1; Leng 17–6–53–0; Pearson 11–1–35–0; Smithies 12–3–48–1; Stock 10–1–39–0; Daniels 3–0–30–1. *Second Innings*—Taylor 19–5–58–1; Redfern 11–3–25–0; Leng 10–2–26–2; Pearson 13–5–27–0; Smithies 8–0–37–0; Stock 8–0–32–1; Daniels 2–0–8–0.

England

J. A. Brittin c Fryer b Campbell	57	– c Illingworth b Withers	3
C. Edwards lbw b Brown	34	– c Illingworth b Brown	31
B. A. Daniels st Illingworth b Campbell	22	– c Campbell b Withers	4
S. Metcalfe lbw b Brown	22	– b Campbell	63
*K. Smithies st Illingworth b Fryer	23	– c Brown b Drumm	15
†J. Smit b Fryer	15	– b Campbell	27
K. Leng lbw b Brown	31	– c sub (C. M. Nicholson) b Fryer	10
D. Stock c Harris b Fryer	2	– c Fruin b Campbell	5
S. Redfern not out	29	– not out	26
C. E. Taylor st Illingworth b Fryer	24	– not out	38
L. Pearson lbw b Harris	0		
B 2, l-b 7, w 2, n-b 1	12	B 1, l-b 1, w 1	3
1/63 2/108 3/133 4/141 5/178 6/179 7/185 8/225 9/270	271	1/18 2/32 3/39 4/66 5/129 6/140 7/157 8/160 (8 wkts)	225

Bowling: *First Innings*—Withers 19–9–33–0; Harris 15.3–3–51–1; Brown 25–8–47–3; Drumm 20–9–34–0; Campbell 31–12–60–2; Fryer 13–3–37–4. *Second Innings*—Withers 16–4–41–2; Harris 13–6–24–0; Brown 6–3–7–1; Drumm 12–4–24–1; Campbell 32–7–86–3; Fryer 27–12–41–1.

Umpires: K. Taylor and V. A. Williams.

ENGLISH WOMEN'S CRICKET, 1996

The Women's Cricket Association had high hopes for the game, following the advent of the England and Wales Cricket Board in 1997. Administrative links with the former Test and County Cricket Board had grown closer in recent years and, in 1996, the New Zealand tourists provided a clear example of how the women's game can link positively with the men's. Their amalgamation into New Zealand Cricket has been accompanied by a significant improvement on the field, a higher profile, and increased numbers taking up the sport.

Their English counterparts hoped that the support of the new Board would help to provide similar benefits and consolidate the surge of interest after the World Cup win in 1993. There has already been an increase in the number of women's clubs integrating into men's, and closer ties are being established with county cricket boards. Membership of the WCA – whose new executive director, Barbara Daniels, is also the England vice-captain – continued to rise. Sky TV broadcast two one-day internationals as part of a three-year contract, and is likely to show two matches when South Africa tour in 1997, while the premier domestic competition, the National Knockout Cup, found a sponsor in the stockbrokers Tilney.

Wakefield easily won the Knockout Cup and almost completed a domestic double; in the National League final against Invicta of Kent, they were all out to the final ball of the match with the scores level. Invicta won on fewer wickets lost. At Cambridge in July, Yorkshire won the area championship for the fifth year in a row; they also took the Under-21 and Under-17 competitions. Yorkshire won all their five matches, as did Kent, who were relegated in 1995 but won an immediate return to Division One. Unexpectedly, the East Midlands tumbled out of the top flight, despite fielding England captain Karen Smithies and three other international players. In 1997, the area championship is to be split into three divisions. The Second Elevens of Yorkshire and Surrey will play off for the last place in Division Two, with the losers joining Hampshire, Derbyshire and a fourth team in Division Three. There will also be an Under-15 area championship.

South Africa's visit should provide a pointer for the World Cup, scheduled for India in December 1997. England and South Africa are in the same pool and face each other in the opening match. Twelve teams are expected, the biggest number yet, and first-time entrants include Pakistan, Canada and Japan – as well as South Africa. But the financial insecurity of the women's game was underlined when the England Under-23 tour of Australia had to be cancelled for lack of funding, after the players had trained as a squad throughout the summer.

Note: Matches in this section were not first-class.

AREA CHAMPIONSHIP

Division One

	Played	*Won*	*Lost*	*Points*
Yorkshire	5	5	0	104
West Midlands	5	4	1	83.5
Surrey	5	3	2	72
East Anglia	5	2	3	55
The West	5	1	4	37
East Midlands	5	0	5	29.5

Division Two

	Played	*Won*	*Lost*	*Points*
Kent	5	5	0	97
Thames Valley	5	4	1	86.5
Yorkshire Second XI	5	2	3	55.5
Middlesex	5	2	3	54.5
Sussex	5	1	4	41
Lancashire & Cheshire	5	1	4	40.5

TILNEY NATIONAL CLUB KNOCKOUT FINAL

At Christ Church, Oxford, August 31. Wakefield won by eight wickets. Toss: Redoubtables. Redoubtables 109 (39.4 overs) (J. Tedstone four for 13); Wakefield 111 for two (34.3 overs) (K. Leng 39, M-P. Moore 35 not out).

NATIONAL LEAGUE FINAL

At Campbell Park, Milton Keynes, September 8. Invicta won by virtue of losing fewer wickets. Toss: Wakefield. Invicta 163 for six (50 overs) (B. A. Daniels 43, A. Bainbridge 32; S. Gill four for 23); Wakefield 163 (50 overs) (K. Leng 34, M-P. Moore 34; B. A. Daniels three for 30).

PART FIVE: OVERSEAS CRICKET IN 1995-96

FEATURES OF 1995-96

Double-Hundreds (43)

303*	S. Chanderpaul	Guyana v Jamaica at Kingston.
283	M. H. Parmar	Gujarat v Maharashtra at Ahmedabad.
259*	N. S. Sidhu	Punjab v Himachal Pradesh at Jalandhar.
253*	M. S. Atapattu§	Sinhalese SC v Galle CC at Colombo.
250*	D. P. Samaraweera	Colts CC v Colombo CC at Colombo.
244	G. Kirsten	Western Province v Border at East London.
237*	V. B. Chandrasekhar	Goa v Kerala at Panaji.
237	S. I. de Saram	Tamil Union C and AC v Kurunegala Youth CC at Colombo.
234	M. L. Hayden	Queensland v Tasmania at Brisbane.
229	G. F. J. Liebenberg	Free State v Natal at Bloemfontein.
227	S. S. Bhave	Maharashtra v Baroda at Pune.
226*	L. J. Wilkinson	Free State v Boland at Bloemfontein.
225†	Aamer Hanif	Allied Bank v Bahawalpur at Karachi.
223*	P. Dharmani	Punjab v Delhi at Amritsar.
220*	D. F. Hills	Tasmania v Queensland at Hobart.
219	M. J. Slater	Australia v Sri Lanka (First Test) at Perth.
217*	R. P. Arnold	Nondescripts CC v Moors CC at Colombo.
215*	Azam Khan	Karachi Whites v Lahore City at Lahore.
214*	M. S. Atapattu§	Sinhalese SC v Singha SC at Colombo.
213	D. Gandhi	Bengal v Tripura at Agartala.
212*	N. Ranatunga	Colts CC v Moors SC at Colombo.
209*†	A. Pandey	Madhya Pradesh v Uttar Pradesh at Bhilai.
209	A. V. Kale	Maharashtra v Gujarat at Ahmedabad.
209	A. A. Muzumdar	West Zone v North Zone at Indore.
208*	J. C. Adams	West Indies v New Zealand (Second Test) at St John's.
208	S. L. Campbell	West Indies v New Zealand (First Test) at Bridgetown.
207*	E. L. R. Stewart	Natal B v Border B at Durban.
204*	S. Sharath	Tamil Nadu v Goa at Madras.
203*	V. V. S. Laxman	Hyderabad v Karnataka at Bangalore.
203*	D. R. Martyn	Western Australia v Tasmania at Perth.
203	M. T. G. Elliott§	Victoria v Tasmania at Melbourne.
202*	L. J. Koen	Eastern Province v Boland at Port Elizabeth.
202	M. J. Greatbatch	Central Districts v Northern Districts at Rotorua.
202	Mansoor Akhtar	United Bank v Pakistan Railways at Lahore.
202†	C. S. Pandit	Madhya Pradesh v Uttar Pradesh at Bhilai.
201*	S. Dogra	Delhi v Services at Delhi.
201*	Sanjeewa Silva	Sebastianites C and AC v Moratuwa SC at Moratuwa.
200*	S. S. Karim	East Zone v West Zone at Nagpur.
200*	C. Mendis	Colts CC v Singha SC at Colombo.
200*	R. V. Sapru	Uttar Pradesh v Vidarbha at Kanpur.
200	M. T. G. Elliott§	Victoria v South Australia at Melbourne.
200	R. A. Lawson	Otago v Central Districts at Napier.
200†	Mohammad Nawaz, sen.	Allied Bank v Bahawalpur at Karachi.

† A. Pandey and C. S. Pandit scored double-hundreds in the same innings, as did Mohammad Nawaz and Aamer Hanif.

§ M. S. Atapattu and M. T. G. Elliott both scored two double-hundreds.

Hundred on First-Class Debut

209*	A. Pandey	Madhya Pradesh v Uttar Pradesh at Bhilai.
174	K. Sriram	Karnataka v Tamil Nadu at Bhadravati.
160	S. Gunasekera	Sinhalese SC v Colts CC at Colombo.

160	D. P. M. Jayawardene	President's XI v South Africa Under-24 at Colombo.
132	S. Ramesh	Tamil Nadu v Hyderabad at Madras.
122	R. R. Kanade	Maharashtra v Saurashtra at Pune.
115	J. M. Oates	Mashonaland Country Districts v Matabeleland at Bulawayo.
102*	C. Jayasinghe	Tamil Union C and AC v Singha SC at Colombo.
100*	R. Paul	Tamil Nadu v Goa at Madras.

Three Hundreds in Successive Innings

M. J. Greatbatch (Central Districts)	115 v Canterbury at Christchurch
	202 v Northern Districts at Rotorua
	162* v Auckland at Auckland.
M. H. Parmar (Gujarat)	174 and 101 v Saurashtra at Rajkot
	283 v Maharashtra at Ahmedabad.
M. V. Sridhar (Hyderabad)	105 and 123 v Kerala at Thiruvananthapuram
	137 v Goa at Margao.

Hundred in Each Innings of a Match

Basit Ali	137	101*	Pakistanis v South Australia at Adelaide.
P. B. du Plessis	101	104*	Border B v Western Province B at East London.
M. T. G. Elliott	104*	135	Victoria v Western Australia at Perth.
Ijaz Ahmed, jun.	127*	106	Allied Bank v PNSC at Rawalpindi.
C. Mendis	111	200*	Colts CC v Singha SC at Colombo.
M. H. Parmar	174	101	Gujarat v Saurashtra at Rajkot.
R. T. Ponting	118*	100*	Tasmania v Queensland at Hobart.
Ajay Sharma	136	182	Delhi v Railways at Delhi.
M. V. Sridhar	105	123	Hyderabad v Kerala at Thiruvananthapuram.

Hundred Before Lunch

R. Paul	100*†	Tamil Nadu v Goa at Madras (3rd day).
N. S. Sidhu	152* to 259*	Punjab v Himachal Pradesh at Jalandhar (2nd day).
P. A. Wallace	100*	Barbados v Trinidad & Tobago at Pointe-à-Pierre (1st day).

† *On first-class debut.*

Carrying Bat Through Completed Innings

Akhtar Sarfraz	134*	Peshawar (242) v Bahawalpur at Bahawalpur.
V. B. Chandrasekhar	237*	Goa (384) v Kerala at Panaji.
M. H. Dekker	162*	Zimbabwe A (312) v Transvaal at Johannesburg.
P. Dharmani	223*	Punjab (415) v Delhi at Amritsar.
M. T. G. Elliott	104*	Victoria (215) v Western Australia at Perth.
Kamran Haider	69*	PNSC (144) v United Bank at Karachi.
Kashif Ahmed	111*	Karachi Whites (201) v Rawalpindi A at Rawalpindi.
Mohammad Ramzan	121*	Combined XI (223) v England A at Karachi.
W. A. M. P. Perera	64*	Antonians SC (201) v Colombo CC at Colombo.
Shakeel Ahmed	81*	Rawalpindi B (135) v Bahawalpur at Bahawalpur.
Sunil Kumar	74*	Bihar (133) v Assam at Jamshedpur.
D. J. Watson	103*	Natal B (246) v Free State B at Durban.
B. M. White	159*	Transvaal (365) v Boland at Johannesburg.

First-Wicket Partnerships of 100 in Each Innings

125	125	D. F. Hills/J. Cox, Tasmania v Victoria at Melbourne
133	122	S. Somasunder/A. Vaidya, Karnataka v Tamil Nadu at Madras.

Notable Partnerships

First Wicket
380 Mohammad Nawaz, sen./Aamer Hanif, Allied Bank v Bahawalpur at Karachi.
329 K. Srinath/S. Ramesh, Tamil Nadu v Kerala at Tirunelveli.
327 A. Verma/D. Gandhi, Bengal v Tripura at Agartala.
305 R. A. Lawson/M. G. Croy, Otago v Central Districts at Napier.
301 N. S. Sidhu/V. Rathore, Punjab v Himachal Pradesh at Jalandhar.
301 Shahid Anwar/Sajid Ali, National Bank v PNSC at Lahore.

Second Wicket
368* M. L. Hayden/M. L. Love, Queensland v Tasmania at Hobart.
365 M. L. Hayden/M. L. Love, Queensland v Tasmania at Brisbane.
338 P. G. Amm/L. J. Koen, Eastern Province v Boland at Port Elizabeth.

Third Wicket
315† S. T. Perera/R. S. Kalpage, Bloomfield C and AC v Antonians SC at Colombo.
270 S. S. Bhave/H. H. Kanitkar, Maharashtra v Baroda at Pune.
262 R. Vijay/R. Dravid, Karnataka v Tamil Nadu at Madras.
256 M. I. Gidley/P. H. Barnard, Griqualand West v Natal B at Durban.

Fourth Wicket
328 A. Pandey/C. S. Pandit, Madhya Pradesh v Uttar Pradesh at Bhilai.
305 S. Chanderpaul/R. A. Harper, Guyana v Jamaica at Kingston.
295 S. S. More/S. K. Kulkarni, Bombay v Saurashtra at Thane.
255 Azam Khan/Sohail Jaffer, Karachi Whites v Hyderabad at Rahimyarkhan.
250 Sourav C. Ganguly/S. S. Karim, East Zone v West Zone at Nagpur.

Fifth Wicket
391† A. Malhotra/S. Dogra, Delhi v Services at Delhi.
285 A. A. Muzumdar/A. V. Kale, West Zone v North Zone at Indore.

Sixth Wicket
283 S. S. Karim/S. J. Kalyani, Bengal v Bihar at Patna.
247 A. V. Kale/S. M. Kondhalkar, Maharashtra v Gujarat at Ahmedabad.

Seventh Wicket
265 Aamer Hanif/Raj Hans, Allied Bank v National Bank at Sahiwal.

Eighth Wicket
195 Wasim Haider/Javed Qadeer, PIA v Pakistan Railways at Rawalpindi.
185 L. J. Wilkinson/H. C. Bakkes, Free State v Boland at Bloemfontein.
168 A. C. Gilchrist/G. B. Hogg, Western Australia v South Australia at Adelaide.

Ninth Wicket
185 Asif Mujtaba/Athar Laeeq, Karachi Blues v Islamabad at Karachi.
184 Mansoor Rana/Sabih Azhar, ADBP v PNSC at Rawalpindi.
169* R. C. Russell/R. K. Illingworth, England XI v Boland at Paarl.

* *Unbroken partnership.* † *National record for that wicket.*

Thirteen or More Wickets in a Match (4)

16-167	R. Dhanraj	Trinidad & Tobago v Leeward Islands at Charlestown.
13-161	S. C. de Silva	Sebastianites C and AC v Singha SC at Moratuwa.
13-172	B. de Silva	Bloomfield C and AC v Colts CC at Colombo.
13-240	Naeem Tayyab	Karachi Whites v Lahore City at Lahore.

Eight or More Wickets in an Innings (15)

10-28	Naeem Akhtar	Rawalpindi B v Peshawar at Peshawar.
9-54	Murtaza Hussain	Bahawalpur v Islamabad at Bahawalpur.
9-76	S. G. Peall	Zimbabwe Board XI v Boland B at Paarl.
9-97	R. Dhanraj	Trinidad & Tobago v Leeward Islands at Charlestown.
8-34	L. Klusener	Natal v Western Province at Durban.
8-38	L. Hannibal	Nondescripts CC v Moors SC at Colombo.
8-49	D. A. Freedman	New South Wales v West Indians at Newcastle.
8-56	Ata-ur-Rehman	Allied Bank v PNSC at Rawalpindi.
8-71	A. A. Donald	South Africa v Zimbabwe (Only Test) at Harare.
8-79	B. de Silva	Bloomfield C and AC v Colts CC at Colombo.
8-83	S. V. Mudkavi	Goa v Andhra at Kakinada.
8-85	R. Priyadarshana	Singha SC v Police SC at Colombo.
8-102	D. Hettiarachchi	Colts CC v Bloomfield C and AC at Colombo.
8-112	Naeem Tayyab	Karachi Whites v Lahore City at Lahore.
8-182	S. V. Mudkavi	Goa v Karnataka at Bangalore.

Hat-Tricks

R. L. Hayes	Northern Districts v Central Districts at Rotorua (all lbw).
M. W. Pringle	South African Invitation XI v England XI at Soweto.
M. Suresh Kumar	Railways v Rajasthan at Delhi.

Outstanding Match Analysis

21.3–14–16–11†	P. Acharjee	Bengal v Tripura at Agartala.

† *On first-class debut.*

Outstanding Innings Analysis

9–5–6–7†	P. Acharjee	Bengal v Tripura at Agartala.

† *On first-class debut.*

Most Overs Bowled in a Match

108–29–222–5	P. Thakur	Haryana v Vidarbha at Nagpur.

Ten or More Wicket-Keeping Dismissals in a Match

11 ct, 2 st†	W. R. James	Matabeleland v Mashonaland Country Districts at Bulawayo.
11 ct	D. S. Berry	Victoria v Pakistanis at Melbourne.
11 ct	R. C. Russell	England v South Africa (Second Test) at Johannesburg.
10 ct, 1 st	W. A. Seccombe	Queensland v Western Australia at Brisbane.
10 ct‡	J. Burger	Griqualand West v Northern Transvaal B at Kimberley.
6 ct, 4 st‡	S. S. Dighe	West Zone v Central Zone at Bikaner.
10 ct‡	M. O. Johnston	Transvaal B v Boland B at Randjesfontein.
10 ct‡	C. J. Nevin	Wellington v Otago at Dunedin.
10 ct	Rafaqat Ali	Allied Bank v United Bank at Rawalpindi.
10 ct	P. J. Roach	Victoria v South Australia at Melbourne.

† *World record.* ‡ *National record.*

Six or More Wicket-Keeping Dismissals in an Innings

7 ct, 2 st†	W. R. James	Matabeleland v Mashonaland Country Districts at Bulawayo.
7 ct	D. J. R. Campbell	Mashonaland Country Districts v Matabeleland at Bulawayo.
7 ct‡	H. H. Devapriya	Colts CC v Sinhalese SC at Colombo.
7 ct	A. C. Gilchrist	Western Australia v South Australia at Perth.
6 ct	D. S. Berry	Victoria v Pakistanis at Melbourne.
5 ct, 1 st	S. S. Dighe	West Zone v Central Zone at Bikaner.
6 ct	M. O. Johnston	Transvaal B v Boland B at Randjesfontein.
5 ct, 1 st	C. J. Nevin	Wellington v Central Districts at Nelson.
6 ct	Rafaqat Ali	Allied Bank v United Bank at Rawalpindi.
6 ct	Rafaqat Ali	Allied Bank v National Bank at Sahiwal.
6 ct	P. J. Roach	Victoria v South Australia at Melbourne.
5 ct, 1 st	B. I. Robinson	Zimbabwe Board XI v Griqualand West at Harare.
6 ct	R. C. Russell	England v South Africa (Second Test) at Johannesburg.
6 ct	W. A. Seccombe	Queensland v Western Australia at Brisbane.
5 ct, 1 st	Tahir Rashid	Habib Bank v Pakistan Railways at Sialkot.

† *World record.* ‡ *National record.*

Seven Catches in a Match in the Field

M. A. Taylor .... New South Wales v Victoria at Melbourne.

Six Catches in an Innings in the Field

C. M. Wickremasinghe† ... Sebastianites C and AC v Police SC at Colombo.

† *National record.*

Match Double (100 Runs and 10 Wickets)

S. B. Joshi	118; 7-60, 4-66	Karnataka v Hyderabad at Secunderabad.
W. N. M. Soysa	28, 101*; 4-32, 6-60	Police SC v Singha SC at Colombo.

Wicket-Keeper's Match Double (100 Runs and 10 Dismissals)

W. R. James .... 99, 99*; 7 ct 2 st, 4 ct Matabeleland v Mashonaland Country Districts at Bulawayo.

No Byes Conceded in Total of 500 or More

R. Paul .... Tamil Nadu v Karnataka (716) at Bhadravati.
L. K. Germon .... New Zealand v West Indies (548-7 dec.) (Second Test) at St John's.
M. N. Atkinson .... Tasmania v Queensland (533-6 dec.) at Brisbane.
T. J. Nielsen .... South Australia v Western Australia (520-9 dec.) at Adelaide.
R. S. Kaluwitharana ... Sri Lanka v Australia (500-6 dec.) (Second Test) at Melbourne.

Highest Innings Totals

716 .... Karnataka v Tamil Nadu at Bhadravati.
640 .... Gujarat v Maharashtra at Ahmedabad.
627-9 dec. .... Karachi Blues v Islamabad at Karachi.
620-8 dec. .... Karnataka v Tamil Nadu at Madras.
620 .... Hyderabad v Vidarbha at Secunderabad.
617-5 dec. .... Australia v Sri Lanka (First Test) at Perth.

Highest Fourth-Innings Totals

453-8 .... Northern Districts v Wellington at Wellington (set 453).
402-6 .... Tasmania v Western Australia at Perth (set 402).

Lowest Innings Totals

41 .... Andhra v Karnataka at Eluru.
42 .... Panadura SC v Sinhalese SC at Panadura.
42 .... Tripura v Bengal (2nd innings) at Agartala.
53 .... Tripura v Bengal (1st innings) at Agartala.
55† .... Moratuwa SC v Tamil Union C and AC at Moratuwa.
59 .... Police SC v Sinhalese SC at Colombo.
59 .... Western Transvaal v Natal B at Durban.
65 .... Central Districts v Wellington at Nelson.
66† .... Police SC v Panadura SC at Colombo.
67 .... Central Zone v North Zone at Bhilwara.
68 .... PNSC v ADBP at Rawalpindi.
70 .... Tripura v Bihar at Agartala.
71 .... Eastern Province v Natal at Durban.
72 .... Hyderabad v Peshawar at Peshawar.

† *One man absent.*

50 Extras in an Innings

	b	*l-b*	*w*	*n-b*	
53	6	12	2	33	Jamaica (377) v Barbados at Bridgetown.
51	24	19	0	8	Sebastianites C and AC (492-6 dec.) v Moratuwa SC at Moratuwa.

THE WILLS WORLD CUP, 1996

There were some good, uplifting aspects to the sixth cricket World Cup, not least the style and smiles of its unsuspected winners, Sri Lanka, but overall this was not a tournament to linger fondly in the memory. Wounded by events beyond its control even before its opening, the competition proceeded to frustrate and bewilder through an interminable and largely irrelevant saga of group games in India, Pakistan and Sri Lanka before hastening frantically through its knockout games in little more than a week.

The event was poorly conceived in its format and its logistics and suffered throughout from the threat – and ultimately the reality – of crowd disorder. The abandonment of the semi-final at Eden Gardens, Calcutta, following bottle-throwing and fire-lighting on the terraces, was a shameful reflection on standards of sportsmanship in an area until recently renowned for its appreciation of all things good in the game of cricket.

Perhaps, however, we should not be too harsh on the individuals responsible for the riot in Calcutta. They were merely responding to the seductions created for them by the promoters of the Wills World Cup, an event that plainly, disastrously, put money making above all the fundamentals of organising a global sporting competition. As the glamorising of the Indian and Pakistani cricketers reached new and absurd heights, so too did the unshakeable belief of the masses in their invincibility. Defeat, of the kind that came to India that night in Calcutta, was popularly unimaginable, with consequences for which many must share the blame.

It was all markedly at odds with the 1987 World Cup, also co-hosted by India and Pakistan and widely judged to be an organisational triumph. Players and observers alike enjoyed that competition far more than the 1996 event. Yet the paradox is that, when the accounts were complete, they showed a negligible profit. Within a decade, the profile of the game had altered substantially; so too, it transpired, had the methods and ambitions of those charged with running the tournament. Suddenly, it was deemed more important to register a company as supplier of "official chewing gum" – and take its money – than to pay proper attention to the welfare of the competing teams. Of course, it is possible to become too nannyish about professional sportsmen, who by and large lead a pretty pampered existence, but the wearisome travel schedules, illogical playing itineraries and inadequate practice facilities inflicted on most of the visiting teams would have caused a serious rebellion had this been a football championship.

In fact, such elementary flaws should have been dealt with at source, long before they became a millstone around the event. The reason they were not – the handing over by the International Cricket Council of all responsibility for the tournament to the World Cup committee, Pilcom – reflects poorly on all those responsible. What function does ICC perform if it is not to be a vigilant monitor of events like this? Cricket must never permit such complacency again.

ICC must also take the blame for the format. The expansion of the field to 12, from nine in 1992, was quite right. By embracing three of ICC's Associate Members, the non-Test countries, the World Cup was fulfilling its missionary aim (though whether the Associates, wooed by financial guarantees, had too much say in the venue is another serious matter for ICC to consider). The problem arose when the extra teams were accommodated by a complete change from the successful 1992 system, a round-robin producing four semi-finalists.

Instead, the teams were divided into two groups of six, from which not four but eight sides would proceed to the knockout rounds. The effect of this, obvious in advance, was to reduce virtually a month of cricket to the status of little more than practice games: duly, almost inevitably, the three Associate nations and the junior Test-playing team, Zimbabwe, were eliminated.

All this could have been avoided, and a genuinely competitive group programme installed, by discarding the idea of quarter-finals and going straight to a last four. Presumably, the attraction of four big crowds, four big television games, was too great, but this was a decision taken on flawed grounds. The people were not all fooled; the group games in Pakistan, particularly, drew very small crowds.

The logistical chaos of the competition stemmed largely from the decision, laudable in theory but utterly unrealistic, to spread the tournament to virtually every corner of the vast country of India. The 17 games scheduled for the country were all staged in different cities and insufficient attention had been paid to the practicalities of moving teams (let alone television crews and media people) between games. Travel in India is problematical at best; a few specific alterations were made to airline schedules to oblige the competition organisers but nowhere near enough to surmount the problem, the size of which became clear during the first, eventful weekend. The teams were all due to gather in Calcutta for a variety of briefing meetings before the much-vaunted opening ceremony, a celebration of technology for which the organisers had outlaid considerable capital.

As it transpired, however, the weekend was dominated by the issue of two teams, Australia and West Indies, adamantly refusing to play their scheduled group games in Colombo. The bomb blast in the city, a fortnight earlier, was the clinching factor, but Australia's players were already uncomfortable about visiting Sri Lanka, with whom they had just played an acrimonious Test series. In truth, they were reluctant to participate in the Cup at all, the backwash of their bribery allegations against Salim Malik having brought threats of an unpleasant nature from a number of fanatics around Pakistan. West Indies had far less reason for prudence on the Colombo issue, but the condemnatory tone of the organisers against the two defectors gave the episode an unwarranted tone, intensified by a press conference that touched heights of incoherent rancour. It was even suggested that Australia and West Indies were indulging in a vendetta against the Third World, until it was gently pointed out, by ICC's chairman, Sir Clyde Walcott, that the Caribbean forms part of the Third World.

Positions being entrenched, the matches were forfeited, though it was a commentary on the cosiness of the format that Australia and West Indies could make such a sacrifice without seriously endangering their progress to the business end of the tournament. Sri Lanka were both winners and losers – winners because they received four points, and a comfortable passage to the last eight, without playing, but losers because their lovely island was deprived of its two biggest matches at a time when the public was most in need of rousing diversions. For them, however, the grandest of compensations awaited.

The opening ceremony was attended by more than 100,000 people, most of whom must have left wondering what on earth they had been watching. The laser show malfunctioned, the compère was embarrassing and the grand launch was a complete flop – so much so that there were subsequent calls at Calcuttan government level for the arrest of the Pilcom convenor, Jagmohan Dalmiya, on a charge of wasting public money.

At 4 a.m. the following morning, four teams gathered blearily in the lobby of Calcutta's Oberoi hotel. They were all slated for the 6 a.m. flight to Delhi (India's internal flights tend to run before dawn and after dusk), whereafter they were required to wait many hours before connecting to flights for their various first-game destinations. Had no one thought of organising a charter flight at a civilised hour? Apparently not.

Given this, the choice of the unlovely city of Ahmedabad, and the teams of England and New Zealand, for the opening game of the tournament, should perhaps not seem curious. It was, however, a deflating start, and not just for England, whose obsolete one-day tactics and lack of specific preparation for the only limited-overs event that matters were exposed from the beginning. England were destined to win only two games in the competition, both against "non-league" opposition, and one of those, against Holland, by an unflatteringly narrow margin. Their players had come to the event tired and unfocused, which was not entirely their fault, but the need for a progressive team manager to replace Raymond Illingworth became ever clearer as their ill-fated campaign continued. England once dictated the terms in one-day cricket; unnoticed by them, other countries have caught up and left them behind, developing new and innovative ways of overcoming the essentially negative restrictions of the overs game.

The use of "pinch-hitters" was one such method, much discussed and granted more significance than it merited, but it was certainly the case that the successful teams no longer looked to accrue the majority of their runs in the closing overs of their innings. Instead of settling for 60 or 70 runs from the initial 15 overs, when fielding restrictions applied, teams were now looking to pass the 100 mark. On the blissful batting pitches encountered here, it was seldom impossible. Sri Lanka, through their fearless openers, Sanath Jayasuriya – later to be named the Most Valued Player of the Tournament – and Romesh Kaluwitharana, were the trendsetters and, as the outcome proved, nobody did it better. Jayasuriya's assault on England's bowling in the quarter-final at Faisalabad was authentic, aggressive batting without insult to the coaching manual.

There were some memorable images from the over-long group stages. Mark Taylor's sportsmanship, in refusing to claim a slip catch at a pivotal stage against West Indies, was one; the imperious batting of Mark Waugh and Sachin Tendulkar provided more. But the majority involved the minnow nations. The best of them was the catch by Kenya's portly, bespectacled and none-too-nimble wicket-keeper, Tariq Iqbal, to dismiss Brian Lara. That it led to a Kenyan victory by 73 runs was part of the romance; here was the greatest upset the World Cup has known and, perhaps, a salutary lesson to a West Indies team that had become surly and unattractive. Kenya played their cricket as the West Indians once loved to do, without inhibition; defeat paradoxically restored pride to West Indies. They not only rallied to reach the last eight – roused by 93 not out from their beleaguered captain, Richie Richardson, against Australia – but, there, beat the team that had hitherto looked the slickest in the event, South Africa.

The two main host nations predictably reached the quarter-finals but it was not in the preferred script that they should meet each other so soon. Bangalore had the dubious honour of staging the game and this beautiful, bustling city has never known such an event. The fact that India won it, before an intensely partisan crowd, perhaps averted the kind of disgraceful scenes witnessed four days later in Calcutta, where Sri Lanka utterly outplayed the Indians. In the other semi-final, Australia recovered from an apparently hopeless position to beat West Indies, whose collective nerve crumbled.

Thus was created a meeting, in the final, between two teams who were prevented by politics and expediency from playing each other earlier. Sri Lanka's victory was to the great approval and acclaim of much of the cricketing world. It was also a result that, to some degree, rescued this World Cup from an abiding image of bungling mediocrity.

The tournament achieved one aim in increasing the profile of cricket, through television coverage on an impressive but largely uncritical scale, and undoubtedly it satisfied the organisers in the amount of money accrued. But the impression was that the cricket was secondary to the commercialism. Even in a game newly awakened to its financial opportunities, that cannot be right. – ALAN LEE.

Note: Matches in this section were not first-class.

GROUP A

WEST INDIES v ZIMBABWE

At Hyderabad, February 16 (day/night). West Indies won by six wickets. Toss: Zimbabwe.

Lara returned to the West Indian team after refusing to join the trip to Australia and was quickly back in the limelight. He hit a six over mid-off to complete a comfortable victory with more than 20 overs to spare. Strang's leg-spin had troubled the West Indian batsmen, claiming all the four wickets that fell – three of them in seven balls – while he had Lara dropped in the slips by Campbell. But a good start from the openers ensured that West Indies would overtake a feeble target of 152 with ease. The Zimbabweans had been hesitant against the pace of Ambrose and his colleagues, with Grant Flower their most fluent player. Their three run-outs included one freakish dismissal – Whittall went when he tripped over the heel of Bishop, the bowler, who was watching the ball being fielded.

Man of the Match: C. E. L. Ambrose.

Zimbabwe

*†A. Flower c Browne b Ambrose	3
G. W. Flower c and b Gibson	31
G. J. Whittall run out	14
A. D. R. Campbell run out	0
A. C. Waller st Browne b Harper	21
C. N. Evans c Browne b Ambrose	21
S. G. Davies run out	9
H. H. Streak lbw b Walsh	7
P. A. Strang not out	22
E. A. Brandes c Chanderpaul b Ambrose	7
A. C. I. Lock not out	1
L-b 10, w 4, n-b 1	15
(9 wkts, 50 overs)	151

1/11 (1) 2/53 (2) 3/56 (4) 4/59 (3) 5/91 (6) 6/103 (5) 7/115 (7) 8/125 (8) 9/142 (10)

Score at 15 overs: 40-1

Bowling: Ambrose 10–2–28–3; Walsh 10–3–27–1; Gibson 9–1–27–1; Bishop 10–3–18–0; Harper 10–1–30–1; Arthurton 1–0–11–0.

West Indies

S. L. Campbell b Strang	47
*R. B. Richardson c Campbell b Strang	32
B. C. Lara not out	43
S. Chanderpaul b Strang	8
K. L. T. Arthurton c Campbell b Strang	1
R. A. Harper not out	5
B 5, l-b 3, w 10, n-b 1	19
(4 wkts, 29.3 overs)	155

1/78 (2) 2/115 (1) 3/123 (4) 4/136 (5)

Score at 15 overs: 63-0

†C. O. Browne, O. D. Gibson, I. R. Bishop, C. E. L. Ambrose and C. A. Walsh did not bat.

Bowling: Streak 7–0–34–0; Lock 6–0–23–0; Brandes 7–0–42–0; Whittall 2–0–8–0; Strang 7.3–1–40–4.

Umpires: R. S. Dunne and S. Venkataraghavan. Referee: R. Subba Row.

SRI LANKA v AUSTRALIA

At R. Premadasa Stadium, Colombo, February 17. Sri Lanka awarded match by default after Australia failed to turn up.

Australia had made it clear that they would not travel to Colombo because of fears for the safety of their team. Nevertheless, the Sri Lankan team arrived at the stadium to be formally awarded the game, although the walkover did not please them. "We'd rather play and lose than get forfeited points," said manager Duleep Mendis.

INDIA v KENYA

At Cuttack, February 18. India won by seven wickets. Toss: India. International debuts: Kenya (all).

Kenya's batsmen gave them a satisfactory launch into senior international cricket, but had to give way to one of the world's best, Tendulkar. The first part of the day belonged to Steve Tikolo, however. He scored 65 in 83 balls, hit a six and six fours and put on 96 with his captain, Maurice Odumbe. Then the middle order rashly tried to hit out against Kumble, who took three wickets in four overs. India needed only 200, and Jadeja and Tendulkar began with 100 in 20 overs, putting on 163 – India's highest for any wicket in the World Cup – before Jadeja, who had just begun to show signs of cramp, was caught on the boundary in the 33rd over. Tendulkar was then 98 and he was stuck on 99 for nine balls before completing his fifth hundred in one-day internationals. The tension seemed to be transmitted to his team-mates, Sidhu and Kambli; both struggled to get going before hitting out to find catchers in the deep. But by then Tendulkar had resumed his surge onwards, finishing on 127 from 134 balls, with 15 fours and a six. It was Mongia who hit the winning four; Azharuddin, who had just become the seventh player to appear in 200 limited-overs internationals, did not need to bat.

Man of the Match: S. R. Tendulkar.

Kenya

D. Chudasama c Mongia b Prasad	29
†K. Otieno c Mongia b Raju	27
S. Tikolo c Kumble b Raju	65
*M. Odumbe st Mongia b Kumble	26
Hitesh Modi c Jadeja b Kumble	2
T. Odoyo c Prabhakar b Kumble	8
E. Odumbe not out	15
Asif Karim not out	6
B 2, l-b 11, w 7, n-b 1	21
1/41 (1) 2/65 (2) 3/161 (4) 4/161 (3) 5/165 (5) 6/184 (6) — (6 wkts, 50 overs)	199
Score at 15 overs: 43-1	

D. Tikolo, M. Suji and Rajab Ali did not bat.

Bowling: Prabhakar 5–1–19–0; Srinath 10–0–38–0; Prasad 10–0–41–1; Kumble 10–0–28–3; Raju 10–2–34–2; Tendulkar 5–0–26–0.

India

A. Jadeja c Rajab Ali b Asif Karim	53
S. R. Tendulkar not out	127
N. S. Sidhu c Suji b S. Tikolo	1
V. G. Kambli c D. Tikolo b M. Odumbe	2
†N. R. Mongia not out	8
L-b 5, w 6, n-b 1	12
1/163 (1) 2/167 (3) 3/182 (4) — (3 wkts, 41.5 overs)	203
Score at 15 overs: 74-0	

*M. Azharuddin, M. Prabhakar, A. Kumble, J. Srinath, B. K. V. Prasad and S. L. V. Raju did not bat.

Bowling: Rajab Ali 5–0–25–0; E. Odumbe 3–0–18–0; Suji 5–0–20–0; Odoyo 3–0–22–0; Asif Karim 10–1–27–1; D. Tikolo 3–0–21–0; M. Odumbe 9.5–1–39–1; S. Tikolo 3–0–26–1.

Umpires: K. T. Francis and D. R. Shepherd. Referee: C. H. Lloyd.

SRI LANKA v ZIMBABWE

At Sinhalese Sports Club, Colombo, February 21. Sri Lanka won by six wickets. Toss: Zimbabwe.

Colombo, delighted to welcome visitors after being shunned by the Australians and West Indies, offered Zimbabwe a warm welcome and the sort of security normally provided for visiting heads of state. It was not only the players who required reassurance; New Zealand umpire Steve Dunne hesitated about travelling to Sri Lanka. But he duly stood, though several of his decisions were criticised, notably when he sent back Andy Flower without calling for the TV replay, which suggested Flower had made his ground. The Zimbabweans were easily outclassed, though their popularity grew further when they agreed to stay on the field in drizzle as Sri Lanka reached their target with 13 overs in hand. Despite a shaky start when Kaluwitharana – suffering from cramp after keeping throughout Zimbabwe's innings – and Jayasuriya fell to Streak in the first five overs, Gurusinha and de Silva scored at more than a run a ball. Their stand of 172 in 27 overs was Sri Lanka's best for any wicket in one-day internationals; de Silva's 91, from 86 balls, was his country's highest World Cup innings to date and Gurusinha hit six sixes to equal the World Cup record shared by Viv Richards and Kapil Dev. Zimbabwe had also lost their openers cheaply, both run out; interest in their innings was maintained by Whittall and especially Campbell, who made 75.

Man of the Match: P. A. de Silva.

Zimbabwe

*†A. Flower run out	8
G. W. Flower run out	15
G. J. Whittall c Jayasuriya b Muralitharan	35
A. D. R. Campbell c Muralitharan b Vaas	75
A. C. Waller b Jayasuriya	19
C. N. Evans not out	39
H. H. Streak c de Silva b Vaas	15
P. A. Strang not out	0
B 1, l-b 16, w 4, n-b 1	22
1/19 (1) 2/51 (2) 3/92 (3) 4/160 (5) 5/194 (4) 6/227 (7) — (6 wkts, 50 overs)	228
Score at 15 overs: 57-2	

S. G. Peall, E. A. Brandes and A. C. I. Lock did not bat.

Bowling: Vaas 10–0–30–2; Wickremasinghe 8–0–36–0; Ranatunga 2–0–14–0; Dharmasena 10–1–50–0; Muralitharan 10–0–37–1; Jayasuriya 10–0–44–1.

Sri Lanka

S. T. Jayasuriya b Streak	6
†R. S. Kaluwitharana c Peall b Streak	0
A. P. Gurusinha run out	87
P. A. de Silva lbw b Streak	91
*A. Ranatunga not out	13
H. P. Tillekeratne not out	7
L-b 5, w 17, n-b 3	25
1/5 (2) 2/23 (1) 3/195 (3) 4/209 (4) — (4 wkts, 37 overs)	229
Score at 15 overs: 90-2	

R. S. Mahanama, W. P. U. J. C. Vaas, H. D. P. K. Dharmasena, G. P. Wickremasinghe and M. Muralitharan did not bat.

Bowling: Streak 10–0–60–3; Lock 4–0–17–0; Brandes 8–0–35–0; Peall 3–0–23–0; Strang 5–0–43–0; Whittall 2–0–20–0; G. W. Flower 5–1–26–0.

Umpires: R. S. Dunne and Mahboob Shah. Referee: Nasim-ul-Ghani.

INDIA v WEST INDIES

At Gwalior, February 21 (day/night). India won by five wickets. Toss: West Indies.

This match was the first real test for both teams and India won it hands down. First, they dismissed the West Indians for 173 – less than they conceded to Kenya – on a decent pitch; then, inspired again by Tendulkar, they knocked off the runs inside 40 overs. In fact, both innings followed the same pattern up to the halfway mark: two early wickets falling to the strike bowler, then a recovery checked by the loss of the captain, caught in the deep, with the total in the early nineties. But whereas Richardson's departure sparked the first of two West Indian collapses – curiously, both of three wickets for eight in 12 balls – India steamed on. The key moments of the match came when Lara was given caught behind fifth ball, apparently off his pad, and later when Browne dropped a skier off Tendulkar, then 22. Tendulkar advanced to 70 from 91 balls, earning his second successive match award, before he was run out in a mix-up with Kambli, who then took charge of the closing stages. Despite some tight bowling by Walsh, West Indies' task had become hopeless. A crowd of 30,000 lit torches and firecrackers, and the smoke drifted through the floodlights as they celebrated a home victory.

Man of the Match: S. R. Tendulkar.

West Indies

S. L. Campbell b Srinath	5	C. E. L. Ambrose c Kumble b Prabhakar	8
*R. B. Richardson c Kambli b Prabhakar	47	C. A. Walsh not out	9
B. C. Lara c Mongia b Srinath	2		
S. Chanderpaul c Azharuddin b Kapoor	38	L-b 2, w 5, n-b 1	8
R. I. C. Holder b Kumble	0		
R. A. Harper b Kumble	23	1/16 (1) 2/24 (3) 3/91 (2) (50 overs)	173
†C. O. Browne b Prabhakar	18	4/99 (5) 5/99 (4) 6/141 (6)	
O. D. Gibson b Kumble	6	7/141 (7) 8/149 (8)	
I. R. Bishop run out	9	9/162 (10) 10/173 (9) Score at 15 overs: 53-2	

Bowling: Prabhakar 10–0–39–3; Srinath 10–0–22–2; Kumble 10–0–35–3; Prasad 10–0–34–0; Kapoor 10–2–41–1.

India

A. Jadeja b Ambrose	1	†N. R. Mongia not out	24
S. R. Tendulkar run out	70	L-b 3, w 1, n-b 8	12
N. S. Sidhu b Ambrose	1		
*M. Azharuddin c Walsh b Harper	32	1/2 (1) 2/15 (3) (5 wkts, 39.4 overs)	174
V. G. Kambli not out	33	3/94 (4) 4/125 (2)	
M. Prabhakar c and b Harper	1	5/127 (6) Score at 15 overs: 55-2	

A. R. Kapoor, A. Kumble, J. Srinath and B. K. V. Prasad did not bat.

Bowling: Ambrose 8–1–41–2; Walsh 9–3–18–0; Bishop 5–0–28–0; Gibson 8.4–0–50–0; Harper 9–1–34–2.

Umpires: Khizar Hayat and I. D. Robinson. Referee: R. Subba Row.

AUSTRALIA v KENYA

At Vishakhapatnam, February 23. Australia won by 97 runs. Toss: Kenya.

Australia finally opened their campaign and Kenya provided them with a valuable workout. Backed up by tight fielding, their opening bowlers dismissed Taylor and Ponting inside eight overs. But the Waugh twins gradually flowered to add 207 in 32 overs – the first double-century partnership in World Cup history. Mark scored 130 from 128 balls, striking 14 fours and a six; in support, Steve hit 82 in 88. Australia's 304 did not scare Kenya, however. Though they also lost two early wickets, including star batsman Steve Tikolo, Otieno and Maurice Odumbe put on 102. Over for over, they kept ahead up to the halfway mark. Odumbe made 50 in 53 balls and Otieno might have reached a century but for cramp. After 50 overs keeping wicket and another 35 batting, he limped off, collapsing on the boundary. Later, Otieno resumed with a runner, but McGrath yorked him for 85, which featured a six and eight fours. Australia had a more worrying casualty: McDermott's recurrent calf injury forced him off after five overs and he soon flew home.

Man of the Match: M. E. Waugh.

Australia

*M. A. Taylor c Hitesh Modi b Suji	6	S. K. Warne not out	0
M. E. Waugh c Suji b Rajab Ali	130		
R. T. Ponting c Otieno b Rajab Ali	6	B 1, w 10, n-b 2	13
S. R. Waugh c and b Suji	82		—
S. G. Law run out	35	1/10 (1) 2/26 (3)	(7 wkts, 50 overs) 304
M. G. Bevan b Rajab Ali	12	3/233 (2) 4/237 (4)	
†I. A. Healy c E. Odumbe b Asif Karim	17	5/261 (6) 6/301 (7)	
P. R. Reiffel not out	3	7/301 (5)	Score at 15 overs: 52-2

C. J. McDermott and G. D. McGrath did not bat.

Bowling: Suji 10–1–55–2; Rajab Ali 10–0–45–3; Odoyo 8–0–58–0; E. Odumbe 4–0–21–0; Asif Karim 10–1–54–1; M. Odumbe 4–0–35–0; D. Tikolo 3–0–21–0; S. Tikolo 1–0–14–0.

Kenya

†K. Otieno b McGrath	85	M. Suji not out	1
D. Chudasama c Healy b McDermott	5		
S. Tikolo c Ponting b Reiffel	6	L-b 7, w 6, n-b 2	15
*M. Odumbe c Reiffel b Bevan	50		—
Hitesh Modi b Bevan	10	1/12 (2) 2/30 (3)	(7 wkts, 50 overs) 207
E. Odumbe c Bevan b Reiffel	14	3/132 (4) 4/167 (5)	
D. Tikolo not out	11	5/188 (6) 6/195 (1)	
T. Odoyo st Healy b Warne	10	7/206 (8)	Score at 15 overs: 74-2

Asif Karim and Rajab Ali did not bat.

K. Otieno, when 82, retired hurt at 166 and resumed at 188.

Bowling: McDermott 3–0–12–1; Reiffel 7–1–18–2; McGrath 10–0–44–1; S. R. Waugh 7–0–43–0; Warne 10–0–25–1; M. E. Waugh 5–0–23–0; Bevan 8–0–35–2.

Umpires: C. J. Mitchley and D. R. Shepherd. Referee: C. H. Lloyd.

SRI LANKA v WEST INDIES

At R. Premadasa Stadium, Colombo, February 25. Sri Lanka awarded match by default after West Indies failed to turn up.

West Indies followed Australia's example in boycotting Colombo because of the dangers of terrorist bombs, giving Sri Lanka another two points which put them at the top of the table. The home team remained anxious about their shortage of match practice – eight days were to elapse between their games against Zimbabwe and India.

KENYA v ZIMBABWE

At Patna, February 26. No result. Toss: Zimbabwe. International debut: Tariq Iqbal.

Before rain washed out play on the day scheduled for the match, this seemed to be Kenya's best chance of an unexpected triumph. Andy Flower chose to bat in cloudy conditions but Zimbabwe had lost three wickets, with Edward Odumbe having a hand in all of them, when the weather intervened. All chance of resumption that day was lost when a helicopter, supposed to be helping to dry the ground, instead blew off the covers so that water spilled over the pitch. The same cast – and the crowd of 30,000 – returned the following day for a completely new game. Under a 1996 ICC ruling, matches which are abandoned and then replayed still count as full one-day internationals.

Zimbabwe

G. W. Flower not out	25
A. C. Waller c E. Odumbe b Rajab Ali	3
G. J. Whittall c M. Odumbe b E. Odumbe	12
A. D. R. Campbell lbw b E. Odumbe	0
*†A. Flower not out	0
L-b 2, w 3	5
	—
1/8 (2) 2/44 (3) 3/45 (4)	(3 wkts, 15.5 overs) 45

C. N. Evans, H. H. Streak, P. A. Strang, B. C. Strang, S. G. Peall and A. C. I. Lock did not bat.

Bowling: Suji 5–1–11–0; Rajab Ali 5–0–14–1; Odoyo 3–0–10–0; E. Odumbe 2.5–0–8–2.

Kenya

D. Chudasama, †Tariq Iqbal, K. Otieno, S. Tikolo, *M. Odumbe, Hitesh Modi, E. Odumbe, T. Odoyo, Asif Karim, M. Suji and Rajab Ali.

Umpires: Khizar Hayat and C. J. Mitchley. Referee: Mansur Ali Khan.

KENYA v ZIMBABWE

At Patna, February 27. Zimbabwe won by five wickets. Toss: Zimbabwe.

In the second match Flower asked Kenya to bat and dismissed them for a mere 134 as they unsuccessfully tried to hit out. Leg-spinner Paul Strang, continuing to enjoy the turn and bounce of Indian pitches, finished them off with five for 21, the best return for his country in a limited-overs international, while his brother Bryan took two. The Zimbabwean openers got off to a brisk start, with 59 in 13 overs. Though the middle order stumbled against Rajab Ali, Grant Flower made easily the highest score of the match and Zimbabwe were home with nearly eight overs to spare. It was to be Zimbabwe's only win of the tournament.

Man of the Match: P. A. Strang.

Kenya

D. Chudasama run out	34
†Tariq Iqbal b Lock	1
K. Otieno b Peall	19
S. Tikolo st A. Flower b B. C. Strang	0
*M. Odumbe c B. C. Strang b P. A. Strang	30
Hitesh Modi b B. C. Strang	3
E. Odumbe c Campbell b P. A. Strang	20
T. Odoyo c G. W. Flower b P. A. Strang	0
Asif Karim lbw b P. A. Strang	0
M. Suji c G. W. Flower b P. A. Strang	15
Rajab Ali not out	0
L-b 3, w 8, n-b 1	12
1/7 (2) 2/60 (3) 3/61 (4) 4/63 (1) 5/67 (6) 6/109 (7) 7/109 (8) 8/109 (9) 9/134 (5) 10/134 (10) — (49.4 overs)	134

Score at 15 overs: 40-1

Bowling: Streak 7–2–23–0; Lock 8–2–19–1; Whittall 5–0–21–0; Peall 10–1–23–1; B. C. Strang 10–0–24–2; P. A. Strang 9.4–1–21–5.

Zimbabwe

A. C. Waller c Tikolo b M. Odumbe	30
G. W. Flower b Rajab Ali	45
A. D. R. Campbell c Tikolo b M. Odumbe	6
G. J. Whittall c E. Odumbe b Rajab Ali	6
*†A. Flower lbw b Rajab Ali	5
C. N. Evans not out	8
H. H. Streak not out	15
B 3, l-b 4, w 12, n-b 3	22
1/59 (1) 2/79 (3) 3/104 (2) 4/108 (4) 5/113 (5) — (5 wkts, 42.2 overs)	137

Score at 15 overs: 60-1

P. A. Strang, B. C. Strang, S. G. Peall and A. C. I. Lock did not bat.

Bowling: Suji 9.2–0–37–0; Rajab Ali 8–1–22–3; E. Odumbe 2–0–14–0; Odoyo 2–0–7–0; Asif Karim 10–1–21–0; M. Odumbe 10–2–24–2; Tikolo 1–0–5–0.

Umpires: Khizar Hayat and C. J. Mitchley (Shakeel Khan deputised for Khizar Hayat).
Referee: Mansur Ali Khan.

INDIA v AUSTRALIA

At Bombay, February 27 (day/night). Australia won by 16 runs. Toss: Australia.

The first floodlit international in Bombay was also illuminated by some thrilling batting. Mark Waugh became the first man to score consecutive World Cup centuries, and Tendulkar treated his home crowd to an explosive 90. At first, Waugh was overshadowed by Taylor, who galloped to 59 as they opened with 103 at five an over; Australia looked capable of topping 300. But once Taylor was caught on the boundary, the spinners Raju and Kumble thwarted such ambitions. Waugh eventually went for 126 from 135 balls, having hit three sixes and eight fours, and the last seven wickets fell for 26 – four of them in the final over, which yielded only two runs. After six overs, India had lost two wickets to Fleming, while McGrath had bowled three maidens. But Tendulkar hit three fours off McGrath's fifth over, and blazed from 12 to 56 in 25 balls, with seven fours and one six. When Fleming bowled Azharuddin, Tendulkar steadied himself slightly, then raced to 90 from 84 balls, with 14 fours and a six. He was finally stumped off a wide – delivered by his rival, Mark Waugh, trying his hand at off-spin. Until then, no one could write off India, and, though Warne bowled tightly, Manjrekar and Mongia kept them in the hunt. They were always a couple of wickets adrift, however, and Fleming ended the innings by bowling Kumble, his fifth victim, with two overs to go.

Man of the Match: M. E. Waugh.

Australia

M. E. Waugh run out	126	D. W. Fleming run out	0
*M. A. Taylor c Srinath b Raju	59	G. D. McGrath not out	0
R. T. Ponting c Manjrekar b Raju	12		
S. R. Waugh run out	7	L-b 8, w 2, n-b 2	12
S. G. Law c and b Kumble	21		——
M. G. Bevan run out	6	1/103 (2) 2/140 (3) 3/157 (4) (50 overs)	258
S. Lee run out	9	4/232 (1) 5/237 (5) 6/244 (6)	
†I. A. Healy c Kumble b Prasad	6	7/258 (7) 8/258 (9)	
S. K. Warne c Azharuddin b Prasad	0	9/258 (8) 10/258 (10) Score at 15 overs: 74-0	

Bowling: Prabhakar 10–0–55–0; Srinath 10–1–51–0; Prasad 10–0–49–2; Kumble 10–1–47–1; Raju 10–0–48–2.

India

A. Jadeja lbw b Fleming	1	B. K. V. Prasad c Bevan b S. R. Waugh	0
S. R. Tendulkar st Healy b M. E. Waugh	90	S. L. V. Raju not out	3
V. G. Kambli b Fleming	0		
*M. Azharuddin b Fleming	10	B 5, l-b 8, w 8, n-b 1	22
S. V. Manjrekar c Healy b S. R. Waugh	62		——
M. Prabhakar run out	3	1/7 (1) 2/7 (3) 3/70 (4) (48 overs)	242
†N. R. Mongia c Taylor b Warne	27	4/143 (2) 5/147 (6) 6/201 (7)	
A. Kumble b Fleming	17	7/205 (5) 8/224 (9)	
J. Srinath c Lee b Fleming	7	9/231 (10) 10/242 (8) Score at 15 overs: 73-3	

Bowling: McGrath 8–3–48–0; Fleming 9–0–36–5; Warne 10–1–28–1; Lee 3–0–23–0; M. E. Waugh 10–0–44–1; Bevan 5–0–28–0; S. R. Waugh 3–0–22–2.

Umpires: R. S. Dunne and D. R. Shepherd. Referee: C. H. Lloyd.

KENYA v WEST INDIES

At Pune, February 29. Kenya won by 73 runs. Toss: West Indies.

Kenya's victory was hailed as one of the biggest upsets in cricket history. It was the more extraordinary for being the work of their bowlers, rather than their highly rated batting. Captain Maurice Odumbe thought his team was done for when he lost the toss; once they were all out for 166, he was certain of it. But his amateur attack dismissed West Indies for 93, their lowest World Cup total and their second worst in any one-day international. Kenya had struggled to 81 for six after Walsh removed their top three. The last four, however, added 85, thanks to Hitesh Modi and the 17-year-old Thomas Odoyo, and survived into the final over, though the highest scorer was Extras, with 35. Part-time wicket-keeper Adams equalled the World Cup record of five dismissals. West Indies' nightmare began with Richardson being bowled leg stump by Rajab Ali. Three balls later, Campbell was also bowled, by Suji. The collapse became critical when Lara was caught behind by Tariq Iqbal, whose stout figure and village-standard juggling had hitherto caused much mirth. Only Chanderpaul and Harper reached double figures and both fell to the off-spin of Maurice Odumbe, whose figures of three for 15 in ten overs exactly mirrored those of his more famous counterpart, Harper. The last wicket went the same way as the first – Cuffy was bowled by Rajab Ali, who fell into his team-mates' arms. As the Kenyans ran an exuberant victory lap, cheered on by local spectators, West Indies realised that, level on points with Kenya and Zimbabwe, they could no longer be certain of reaching the quarter-finals. The future of their captain, Richardson, looked even bleaker.

Man of the Match: M. Odumbe.

Kenya

D. Chudasama c Lara b Walsh 8
†Tariq Iqbal c Cuffy b Walsh 16
K. Otieno c Adams b Walsh 2
S. Tikolo c Adams b Harper 29
*M. Odumbe hit wkt b Bishop 6
Hitesh Modi c Adams b Ambrose 28
M. Suji c Lara b Harper 0
T. Odoyo st Adams b Harper 24
E. Odumbe b Cuffy 1
Asif Karim c Adams b Ambrose 11
Rajab Ali not out 6

L-b 8, w 14, n-b 13 35

1/15 (1) 2/19 (3) 3/45 (2) (49.3 overs) 166
4/72 (5) 5/77 (4) 6/81 (7)
7/125 (8) 8/126 (9)
9/155 (6) 10/166 (10) Score at 15 overs: 62-3

Bowling: Ambrose 8.3–1–21–2; Walsh 9–0–46–3; Bishop 10–2–30–1; Cuffy 8–0–31–1; Harper 10–4–15–3; Arthurton 4–0–15–0.

West Indies

S. L. Campbell b Suji 4
*R. B. Richardson b Rajab Ali 5
B. C. Lara c Tariq Iqbal b Rajab Ali 8
S. Chanderpaul c Tikolo b M. Odumbe . . . 19
K. L. T. Arthurton run out 0
†J. C. Adams c Hitesh Modi b M. Odumbe 9
R. A. Harper c Tariq Iqbal b M. Odumbe . 17
I. R. Bishop not out 6
C. E. L. Ambrose run out 3
C. A. Walsh c Chudasama b Asif Karim . . 4
C. E. Cuffy b Rajab Ali 1

B 5, l-b 6, w 4, n-b 2 17

1/18 (2) 2/22 (1) 3/33 (3) (35.2 overs) 93
4/35 (5) 5/55 (4) 6/65 (6)
7/78 (7) 8/83 (9)
9/89 (10) 10/93 (11) Score at 15 overs: 46-4

Bowling: Suji 7–2–16–1; Rajab Ali 7.2–2–17–3; Asif Karim 8–1–19–1; M. Odumbe 10–3–15–3; Odoyo 3–0–15–0.

Umpires: Khizar Hayat and V. K. Ramaswamy. Referee: Mansur Ali Khan.

AUSTRALIA v ZIMBABWE

At Nagpur, March 1. Australia won by eight wickets. Toss: Zimbabwe.

A tiny crowd, perhaps kept down by memories of the accident in which nine spectators died at the ground in November, saw a one-sided game. Zimbabwe's single victory over Australia in seven limited-overs internationals had come in the 1983 World Cup, their debut in senior cricket, but they were swept aside here. Only Waller reached 20 after they took first use of the pitch; he went on to 67 from 109 balls before hesitating too long over a second run. A total of 154 was 70 short of what they had hoped for; Warne's fourth wicket wrapped up the tail with four and a half overs to go. Another leg-spinner, Paul Strang, was again Zimbabwe's best bowler, taking both wickets after Streak opened with three maidens. But Australia soon accelerated to five an over. Mark Waugh might well have scored his third successive hundred had the target been a little higher; he and his brother knocked off the runs in the 36th over.

Man of the Match: S. K. Warne.

Zimbabwe

A. C. Waller run out 67
G. W. Flower b McGrath 4
G. J. Whittall c and b S. R. Waugh 6
A. D. R. Campbell c M. E. Waugh b S. R. Waugh . 5
*†A. Flower st Healy b Warne 7
C. N. Evans c Healy b Warne 18
H. H. Streak c S. R. Waugh b Fleming . . . 13
P. A. Strang not out 16
B. C. Strang b Fleming 0
S. G. Peall c Healy b Warne 0
A. C. I. Lock b Warne 5

L-b 8, w 3, n-b 2 13

1/21 (2) 2/41 (3) 3/55 (4) (45.3 overs) 154
4/68 (5) 5/106 (6)
6/126 (1) 7/140 (7)
8/140 (9) 9/145 (10)
10/154 (11) Score at 15 overs: 48-2

Bowling: McGrath 8–2–12–1; Fleming 9–1–30–2; Lee 4–2–8–0; S. R. Waugh 7–2–22–2; Warne 9.3–1–34–4; M. E. Waugh 5–0–30–0; Law 3–0–10–0.

Australia

*M. A. Taylor c B. C. Strang b P. A. Strang	34
M. E. Waugh not out	76
R. T. Ponting c and b P. A. Strang	33
S. R. Waugh not out	5
B 6, l-b 2, w 1, n-b 1	10
1/92 (1) 2/150 (3) (2 wkts, 36 overs)	158
Score at 15 overs: 74-0	

S. G. Law, M. G. Bevan, †I. A. Healy, S. Lee, S. K. Warne, D. W. Fleming and G. D. McGrath did not bat.

Bowling: Streak 10–3–29–0; Lock 4–0–25–0; B. C. Strang 3–0–20–0; Whittall 2–0–11–0; P. A. Strang 10–2–33–2; Peall 4–0–20–0; G. W. Flower 3–0–12–0.

Umpires: R. S. Dunne and D. R. Shepherd. Referee: C. H. Lloyd.

INDIA v SRI LANKA

At Delhi, March 2. Sri Lanka won by six wickets. Toss: Sri Lanka.

A devastating assault by their openers ensured Sri Lanka first place in the group. They made 272 look a simple target, though Kumble made the middle order work hard for it. Victory by half-time seemed possible when Jayasuriya and Kaluwitharana smashed 42 in their first three overs – Prabhakar conceded 11 and 22 – and they had shot past 50 in five when Kaluwitharana, looking for his seventh four, gave Kumble a diving catch. Jayasuriya charged on, though his final statistics of 79 in 76 balls, with nine fours and two sixes, seemed sedate after his initial rampage. Having set off at twice the required rate, Sri Lanka gradually fell behind, as spinners Kumble and Tendulkar bowled 12 overs in harness for 48. Kumble instigated a mini-collapse as he completed the run-out of Gurusinha and then, in his next two overs, dismissed Jayasuriya and de Silva. With another slow bowler – they had opted for a four-man seam attack, while Sri Lanka augmented their spin – India might have suffocated the innings. But Ranatunga and Tillekeratne restarted the ignition in a stand of 131, winning with eight balls to spare. India paid for their slow progress in the morning. They began batting in light mist, after play was delayed 15 minutes by dew on the outfield, and took 25 overs to score 100. After a short rain-break, the final 11 overs brought 105, thanks to Tendulkar. His run-a-ball 137, with five sixes and eight fours, was his second century of the tournament and he added 175 with Azharuddin, an all-wicket World Cup record for India. Pushpakumara's last over cost 23 – but that only prefigured the carnage to come.

Man of the Match: S. T. Jayasuriya.

India

M. Prabhakar c Gurusinha b Pushpakumara	7
S. R. Tendulkar run out	137
S. V. Manjrekar c Kaluwitharana b Dharmasena	32
*M. Azharuddin not out	72
V. G. Kambli not out	1
B 4, l-b 7, w 11	22
1/27 (1) 2/93 (3) 3/268 (2) (3 wkts, 50 overs)	271
Score at 15 overs: 47-1	

A. Jadeja, †N. R. Mongia, A. Kumble, J. Srinath, S. A. Ankola and B. K. V. Prasad did not bat.

Bowling: Vaas 9–3–37–0; Pushpakumara 8–0–53–1; Muralitharan 10–1–42–0; Dharmasena 9–0–53–1; Jayasuriya 10–0–52–0; Ranatunga 4–0–23–0.

Sri Lanka

S. T. Jayasuriya c Prabhakar b Kumble	79
†R. S. Kaluwitharana c Kumble b Prasad	26
A. P. Gurusinha run out	25
P. A. de Silva st Mongia b Kumble	8
*A. Ranatunga not out	46
H. P. Tillekeratne not out	70
B 4, l-b 9, w 3, n-b 2	18
1/53 (2) 2/129 (3) 3/137 (1) 4/141 (4) (4 wkts, 48.4 overs)	272
Score at 15 overs: 117-1	

R. S. Mahanama, H. D. P. K. Dharmasena, W. P. U. J. C. Vaas, K. R. Pushpakumara and M. Muralitharan did not bat.

Bowling: Prabhakar 4–0–47–0; Srinath 9.4–0–51–0; Prasad 10–1–53–1; Ankola 5–0–28–0; Kumble 10–1–39–2; Tendulkar 10–0–41–0.

Umpires: C. J. Mitchley and I. D. Robinson. Referee: J. R. Reid.

AUSTRALIA v WEST INDIES

At Jaipur, March 4. West Indies won by four wickets. Toss: Australia.

Four days after their humiliation by Kenya, West Indies fought back to inflict the first proper defeat of the tournament on the strongly fancied Australians. The revival was embodied by their captain, Richardson, who had 93 at the finish. He had repaired the damage to his dignity and, most importantly, salvaged the World Cup campaign. Nevertheless, he announced next day that he would retire from international cricket – saying he had made his mind up after the 1995 tour of England – and manager Wes Hall and coach Andy Roberts subsequently departed. Back in India, a lengthy meeting had focused the West Indians on their mission and they imposed themselves from the start. After Taylor chose to bat on an uneven pitch, Ambrose and Walsh bowled six maidens and conceded just eight between them in the first nine overs. But they did not convert their dominance into wickets and Australia were able to accelerate – their last 20 overs brought 135. Ponting surged to 102 in 112 balls, surviving a run-out appeal on 96. West Indies' pursuit of 230 started badly, with Campbell edging to Healy in the second over. They were 26 for two when Richardson joined Lara, whom, it had emerged, he would have preferred not to bring to the World Cup. But the pair combined effectively to add 87 and Lara scored 60 in 70 balls, his first fifty of the tournament. Then Richardson took charge, hitting ten fours and a six, which Ponting carried over the boundary. He might have reached his century, but Adams scored successive fours for victory, and Richardson did not seem to notice as he accepted the emotional embraces of his team-mates.

Man of the Match: R. B. Richardson.

Australia

M. E. Waugh st Browne b Harper	30
*M. A. Taylor c Browne b Walsh	9
R. T. Ponting run out	102
S. R. Waugh b Walsh	57
M. G. Bevan run out	2
S. G. Law not out	12
†I. A. Healy run out	3
P. R. Reiffel not out	4
L-b 3, w 6, n-b 1	10
1/22 (2) 2/84 (1) 3/194 (4) 4/200 (5) 5/216 (3) 6/224 (7) (6 wkts, 50 overs)	229

Score at 15 overs: 35-1

S. K. Warne, D. W. Fleming and G. D. McGrath did not bat.

Bowling: Ambrose 10–4–25–0; Walsh 9–2–35–2; Bishop 9–0–52–0; Harper 10–0–46–1; Arthurton 9–0–53–0; Adams 3–0–15–0.

West Indies

S. L. Campbell c Healy b Fleming	1
†C. O. Browne run out	10
B. C. Lara c McGrath b M. E. Waugh	60
*R. B. Richardson not out	93
S. Chanderpaul b M. E. Waugh	10
R. A. Harper lbw b Reiffel	22
K. L. T. Arthurton lbw b M. E. Waugh	0
J. C. Adams not out	17
L-b 12, w 5, n-b 2	19
1/1 (1) 2/26 (2) 3/113 (3) 4/146 (5) 5/194 (6) 6/196 (7) (6 wkts, 48.5 overs)	232

Score at 15 overs: 68-2

I. R. Bishop, C. E. L. Ambrose and C. A. Walsh did not bat.

Bowling: Reiffel 10–2–45–1; Fleming 7.5–1–44–1; McGrath 9–0–46–0; Warne 10–1–30–0; M. E. Waugh 10–1–38–3; Bevan 2–0–17–0.

Umpires: Mahboob Shah and D. R. Shepherd. Referee: R. Subba Row.

INDIA v ZIMBABWE

At Kanpur, March 6. India won by 40 runs. Toss: Zimbabwe.

Putting India in on a firm, flat pitch looked inspired when the Zimbabwean seamers reduced them to 32 for three by the 13th over. Streak scattered Tendulkar's stumps while Manjrekar and Azharuddin drove straight to Campbell at mid-wicket. But the apparent calamity was a blessing for Sidhu and Kambli, overshadowed in earlier games. They added 142 in 29 overs. Kambli beat Sidhu to his fifty by one ball, despite giving him a 22-run start; dropped twice, he advanced to 106 in 110 balls, with 11 fours, before being caught on the boundary. With Jadeja taking 19 off Lock's last over, India set a target of 248. Grant Flower and Waller bounded to 50 in the 11th, but the advent of the spinners swiftly turned the match. Flower was dismissed in Raju's first over and Waller in Kumble's second. At the halfway mark, Zimbabwe were 92 for two, to India's 85 for three, but the next three wickets, in consecutive overs, all but ended their World Cup campaign. The last rites were delayed only by a brief pitch invasion by a dog determined to complete its own lap of honour.

Man of the Match: A. Jadeja.

India

S. R. Tendulkar b Streak	3	†N. R. Mongia not out	6
N. S. Sidhu c Streak b P. A. Strang	80	L-b 1, w 3	4
S. V. Manjrekar c Campbell b Lock	2		—
*M. Azharuddin c Campbell b B. C. Strang	2	1/5 (1) 2/25 (3)	(5 wkts, 50 overs) 247
V. G. Kambli c G. W. Flower b Lock	106	3/32 (4) 4/174 (2)	
A. Jadeja not out	44	5/219 (5)	Score at 15 overs: 44-3

A. Kumble, J. Srinath, B. K. V. Prasad and S. L. V. Raju did not bat.

Bowling: Streak 10–3–29–1; Lock 10–1–57–2; B. C. Strang 5–1–22–1; P. A. Strang 10–0–55–1; Peall 6–0–35–0; Whittall 3–0–19–0; G. W. Flower 3–0–16–0; Campbell 3–0–13–0.

Zimbabwe

A. C. Waller c Tendulkar b Kumble	22	S. G. Peall c Raju b Kumble	9
G. W. Flower c Azharuddin b Raju	30	A. C. I. Lock not out	2
G. J. Whittall run out	10	B 4, l-b 9, w 11, n-b 1	25
A. D. R. Campbell c and b Jadeja	28		—
*†A. Flower b Raju	28	1/59 (2) 2/59 (1) 3/96 (4)	(49.4 overs) 207
C. N. Evans c Srinath b Jadeja	6	4/99 (3) 5/105 (6)	
H. H. Streak lbw b Raju	30	6/168 (7) 7/173 (5)	
P. A. Strang b Srinath	14	8/193 (8) 9/195 (9)	
B. C. Strang lbw b Srinath	3	10/207 (10)	Score at 15 overs: 61-2

Bowling: Srinath 10–1–36–2; Prasad 7–0–40–0; Kumble 9.4–1–33–2; Raju 10–2–30–3; Tendulkar 6–0–23–0; Jadeja 7–0–32–2.

Umpires: S. A. Bucknor and C. J. Mitchley. Referee: J. R. Reid.

SRI LANKA v KENYA

At Kandy, March 6. Sri Lanka won by 144 runs. Toss: Kenya. International debut: L. Onyango.

Kenya swiftly returned to earth after their apotheosis against West Indies, while Sri Lanka were heading for the stratosphere. Determined to show that they would have scored maximum points even if Australia and West Indies had come to Colombo, they bagged a clutch of records. Most notably, their 398 for five was a world record for any one-day international, comfortably leaving behind England's 363 for seven against Pakistan in 1992 – and that total occupied 55 overs, not 50. The star batsman was de Silva, who scored his country's maiden World Cup century and went on to 145, a Sri Lankan record in all limited-overs internationals. He needed only 115 balls, hitting 14 fours and five sixes. Ranatunga, his captain, might have scored an even faster hundred; he made 75 not out in just 40 balls, with 13 fours and a six, having reached 50 in 29 balls, another World Cup record. Both de Silva and Ranatunga passed 5,000 one-day international runs – the first Sri Lankans to do so. The tone had been set right from the start, when Jayasuriya and Kaluwitharana raced to 83 in a mere 40 balls, paving the way for de Silva and Gurusinha to add

184 in 182 balls, Sri Lanka's best for any wicket in limited-overs internationals. Kenya had opted to chase, but they could hardly have reckoned on chasing eight an over. They rose gallantly to the occasion, however; their 254 for seven was the third-highest total by a non-Test side, after Zimbabwe's 312 against Sri Lanka in the 1992 World Cup and Sri Lanka's 276 for five against Australia in 1975. Steve Tikolo was yorked four short of Kenya's first century at senior level – he hit eight fours and four sixes in 95 balls – after adding 137 for the fourth wicket with Hitesh Modi. That helped to set up a combined match total of 652 for 12, only ten behind the world record of 662 for 17 set by Sri Lanka and West Indies at Sharjah in October 1995.

Man of the Match: P. A. de Silva.

Sri Lanka

S. T. Jayasuriya c D. Tikolo b E. Odumbe	44
†R. S. Kaluwitharana b E. Odumbe	33
A. P. Gurusinha c Onyango b Asif Karim	84
P. A. de Silva c Hitesh Modi b Suji	145
*A. Ranatunga not out	75
H. P. Tillekeratne run out	0
R. S. Mahanama not out	0
B 1, l-b 5, w 11	17
1/83 (1) 2/88 (2) 3/272 (3) 4/378 (4) 5/384 (6) — (5 wkts, 50 overs)	398

Score at 15 overs: 123-2

H. D. P. K. Dharmasena, W. P. U. J. C. Vaas, K. R. Pushpakumara and M. Muralitharan did not bat.

Bowling: Suji 9–0–85–1; Rajab Ali 6–0–67–0; Onyango 4–0–31–0; E. Odumbe 5–0–34–2; Asif Karim 10–0–50–1; D. Tikolo 2–0–13–0; M. Odumbe 9–0–74–0; S. Tikolo 5–0–38–0.

Kenya

D. Chudasama b Muralitharan	27
†K. Otieno b Vaas	14
S. Tikolo b Dharmasena	96
*M. Odumbe st Kaluwitharana b Muralitharan	0
Hitesh Modi run out	41
D. Tikolo not out	25
E. Odumbe c Muralitharan b Ranatunga	4
L. Onyango c sub (M. S. Atapattu) b Ranatunga	23
M. Suji not out	2
B 1, l-b 9, w 7, n-b 5	22
1/47 (2) 2/51 (1) 3/51 (4) 4/188 (5) 5/196 (3) 6/215 (7) 7/246 (8) — (7 wkts, 50 overs)	254

Score at 15 overs: 84-3

Asif Karim and Rajab Ali did not bat.

Bowling: Pushpakumara 7–0–46–0; Vaas 10–0–44–1; Muralitharan 10–1–40–2; Dharmasena 10–0–45–1; Jayasuriya 7–0–34–0; Ranatunga 5–0–31–2; Tillekeratne 1–0–4–0.

Umpires: R. S. Dunne and V. K. Ramaswamy. Referee: Mansur Ali Khan.

GROUP A FINAL TABLE

	Played	*Won*	*Lost*	*Points*	*Net run-rate*
SRI LANKA	5	5	0	10	1.60
AUSTRALIA	5	3	2	6	0.90
INDIA	5	3	2	6	0.45
WEST INDIES	5	2	3	4	−0.13
Zimbabwe	5	1	4	2	−0.93
Kenya	5	1	4	2	−1.00

Where teams finished with an equal number of points, the winner of their head-to-head game was placed higher. Net run-rate, calculated by subtracting runs conceded per over from runs scored per over, would have been used had three or more teams tied on this method.

GROUP B

ENGLAND v NEW ZEALAND

At Ahmedabad, February 14. New Zealand won by 11 runs. Toss: England.

New Zealand hit form just in time for the tournament; England were still struggling to find it. Atherton attributed defeat to scrappy fielding, which contrasted with their opponents' keen approach. He himself was responsible for one of four missed catches, but Thorpe, who dropped both openers at slip, made the most costly error. Reprieved on one, Astle went on to 101 from 132 balls, with eight fours and two sixes – his third century in his last ten one-day internationals. Cairns also hit out, with four fours and a six, but after his dismissal England restricted New Zealand to just 43 in the final ten overs. That left them to chase 240, a target which seemed bigger when Atherton was bowled in the second over. But Hick, despite a hamstring strain, finally began to look the part of England's premier batsman. He hit 85 in 101 balls, including nine fours, before Twose, New Zealand's English-born recruit, ran out his runner, Atherton. The result was all but certain once Cork, who had slogged two fours and a six in 11 balls, was caught behind in the 47th over.

Man of the Match: N. J. Astle.

New Zealand

C. M. Spearman c and b Cork	5	*†L. K. Germon not out	13
N. J. Astle c Hick b Martin	101		
S. P. Fleming c Thorpe b Hick	28	B 4, l-b 2, w 4, n-b 2	12
R. G. Twose c Thorpe b Hick	17		——
C. L. Cairns c Cork b Illingworth	36	1/12 (1) 2/108 (3) (6 wkts, 50 overs)	239
C. Z. Harris run out	10	3/141 (4) 4/196 (5)	
S. A. Thomson not out	17	5/204 (2) 6/212 (6) Score at 15 overs: 64-1	

D. J. Nash, G. R. Larsen and D. K. Morrison did not bat.

Bowling: Cork 10–1–36–1; Martin 6–0–37–1; Gough 10–0–63–0; Illingworth 10–1–31–1; Hick 9–0–45–2; White 5–0–21–0.

England

*M. A. Atherton b Nash	1	P. J. Martin c Cairns b Nash	3
A. J. Stewart c and b Harris	34	R. K. Illingworth not out	3
G. A. Hick run out	85	B 1, l-b 4, w 1, n-b 2	8
G. P. Thorpe b Larsen	9		——
N. H. Fairbrother b Morrison	36	1/1 (1) 2/100 (2) (9 wkts, 50 overs)	228
†R. C. Russell c Morrison b Larsen	2	3/123 (4) 4/144 (3)	
C. White c Cairns b Thomson	13	5/151 (6) 6/180 (7)	
D. G. Cork c Germon b Nash	19	7/185 (5) 8/210 (8)	
D. Gough not out	15	9/222 (10) Score at 15 overs: 55-1	

Bowling: Morrison 8–0–38–1; Nash 7–1–26–3; Cairns 4–0–24–0; Larsen 10–1–33–2; Thomson 10–0–51–1; Harris 9–0–45–1; Astle 2–0–6–0.

Umpires: B. C. Cooray and S. G. Randell. Referee: Mansur Ali Khan.

SOUTH AFRICA v UNITED ARAB EMIRATES

At Rawalpindi, February 15, 16. South Africa won by 169 runs. Toss: United Arab Emirates. International debuts: S. Dukanwala, Mohammad Aslam, G. Mylvaganam, Shahzad Altaf.

The first day was washed out and, as the covers had been on for four days out of six, the pitch was expected to offer something to bowlers. Unfortunately for Sultan Zarawani, his bowlers could not find it. The South Africans piled up 321 for two, their biggest total in limited-overs internationals, and Kirsten smashed 188 not out, the highest score in World Cup history, passing Viv Richards's 181 against Sri Lanka at Karachi in 1987-88. He was only one short of the all-time one-day international record, Richards's unbeaten 189 against England at Manchester in 1984. It was South Africa's first World Cup century. Kirsten batted throughout the innings, hitting four sixes and 13 fours in 159 balls. He added 116 with Cronje and 145 with Cullinan in the final 20 overs. The Emirates' openers were commendably aggressive and their ninth-wicket pair solid in defence, but in between they lost eight for 48. Donald hit Zarawani on the head first ball – he had emerged in a floppy hat rather than a helmet, and was taken to hospital for a check-up when he was out seven balls later. But South Africa then dropped a gear and allowed Arshad Laiq and Dukanwala to bat out the last 22 overs, more than doubling the score.

Man of the Match: G. Kirsten.

South Africa

A. C. Hudson b Samarasekera	27
G. Kirsten not out	188
*W. J. Cronje st Imtiaz Abbasi b Zarawani	57
D. J. Cullinan not out	41
B 1, l-b 1, w 3, n-b 3	8
1/60 (1) 2/176 (3) (2 wkts, 50 overs)	321
Score at 15 overs: 82-1	

J. H. Kallis, J. N. Rhodes, B. M. McMillan, S. M. Pollock, †S. J. Palframan, C. R. Matthews and A. A. Donald did not bat.

Bowling: Samarasekera 9–2–39–1; Shahzad Altaf 3–0–22–0; Arshad Laiq 6–0–52–0; Dukanwala 10–0–64–0; Azhar Saeed 7–0–41–0; Zarawani 10–0–69–1; Mazhar Hussain 5–0–32–0.

United Arab Emirates

Azhar Saeed c McMillan b Pollock	11
G. Mylvaganam c Palframan b Donald	23
Mazhar Hussain b Donald	14
V. Mehra run out	2
Mohammad Aslam b McMillan	9
Arshad Laiq not out	43
J. A. Samarasekera c Hudson b Donald	4
*Sultan M. Zarawani c Cronje b McMillan	0
†Imtiaz Abbasi c Palframan b McMillan	1
S. Dukanwala not out	40
W 3, n-b 2	5
1/24 (1) 2/42 (2) 3/46 (4) 4/60 (5) 5/62 (3) 6/68 (7) 7/70 (8) 8/72 (9) (8 wkts, 50 overs)	152
Score at 15 overs: 46-2	

Shahzad Altaf did not bat.

Bowling: Pollock 9–2–28–1; Matthews 10–0–39–0; Donald 10–0–21–3; Cronje 4–0–17–0; McMillan 8–1–11–3; Kallis 6–0–27–0; Kirsten 3–1–9–0.

Umpires: S. A. Bucknor and V. K. Ramaswamy. Referee: R. S. Madugalle.

HOLLAND v NEW ZEALAND

At Baroda, February 17. New Zealand won by 119 runs. Toss: New Zealand. International debuts: Holland (all).

Holland were comprehensively beaten on their first senior appearance, but played with winning determination and enthusiasm. Their opponents, New Zealand, were not all strangers: Astle had played for Dutch club VOC and Germon had coached in Holland. In fact Astle, a century-maker against England, was one of the few New Zealand batsmen not to contribute – he was run out in the second over. Spearman and Fleming erased any anxiety with 116 in the next 19, until Spearman, having scored 68 from 59 balls, gave Zuiderent a skied catch off Lubbers's fifth delivery; Fleming fell the same way soon afterwards. A steady run-rate of six an over was one Holland could hardly hope to match. Their West Indian opener, Clarke, the oldest man in the tournament at 47, went early, but his Australian partner, Cantrell, batted for 30 overs; he and Lefebvre, who had played first-class cricket in England and New Zealand, were the top scorers. Van Noortwijk's 36 not out suggested promise for the future, but the seamers had no difficulty keeping the total below four an over.

Man of the Match: C. M. Spearman.

New Zealand

C. M. Spearman c Zuiderent b Lubbers	68
N. J. Astle run out	0
S. P. Fleming c Zuiderent b Lubbers	66
R. G. Twose st Schewe b Lubbers	25
C. L. Cairns b Cantrell	52
A. C. Parore c Clarke b Aponso	55
C. Z. Harris c Schewe b Bakker	8
*†L. K. Germon not out	14
D. N. Patel c Schewe b Bakker	11
D. K. Morrison not out	0
L-b 7, w 1	8
1/1 (2) 2/117 (1) 3/155 (3) 4/165 (4) 5/253 (5) 6/279 (6) 7/292 (7) 8/306 (9) (8 wkts, 50 overs)	307

Score at 15 overs: 92-1

R. J. Kennedy did not bat.

Bowling: Lefebvre 10–0–48–0; Bakker 10–0–51–2; de Leede 7–0–58–0; Aponso 10–0–60–1; Lubbers 9–0–48–3; Cantrell 4–0–35–1.

Holland

N. E. Clarke b Kennedy	14
P. E. Cantrell c Astle b Harris	45
G. J. A. F. Aponso c Astle b Harris	11
*S. W. Lubbers run out	5
R. P. Lefebvre b Kennedy	45
T. B. M. de Leede lbw b Harris	1
K. J. van Noortwijk not out	36
†M. Schewe st Germon b Fleming	12
B. Zuiderent not out	1
B 3, l-b 5, w 8, n-b 2	18
1/18 (1) 2/52 (3) 3/66 (4) 4/100 (2) 5/102 (6) 6/147 (5) 7/181 (8) (7 wkts, 50 overs)	188

Score at 15 overs: 52-1

E. Gouka and P. J. Bakker did not bat.

Bowling: Morrison 4–1–11–0; Kennedy 10–2–36–2; Cairns 7–1–24–0; Harris 10–1–24–3; Patel 10–0–42–0; Astle 5–0–19–0; Fleming 2–0–8–1; Twose 2–0–16–0.

Umpires: Khizar Hayat and I. D. Robinson. Referee: Mansur Ali Khan.

ENGLAND v UNITED ARAB EMIRATES

At Peshawar, February 18. England won by eight wickets. Toss: United Arab Emirates.

England beat the Emirates with 15 overs in hand, but felt little more than relief at avoiding embarrassment. Meanwhile, they lost White for the rest of the tournament when he strained an intercostal muscle – as he had done in Australia a year earlier. England's man of the match, Neil Smith, also made an enforced departure from the field. He was violently sick after being promoted to open, his customary role in Warwickshire's Sunday side, and scoring 27 in 31 balls. That slowed down England's reply a little, but Thorpe finished the job. The result had never been in doubt. Though Zarawani chose to bat on a cracked, dry pitch, his batsmen made little headway – apart from Hussain, who hit six fours. DeFreitas, recalled on his 30th birthday, claimed two for 11 in his first eight-over spell and, after the restrictions on deep fielders during the first 15 overs were removed, the Emirates took 11 overs to limp from 44 for two to 50 for five. Those three wickets fell to Smith's off-spin. He had Mehra caught behind and bowled Hussain and Arshad Laiq, all in the space of eight balls. Despite his accident against Donald, Zarawani continued to spurn a helmet.

Man of the Match: N. M. K. Smith.

United Arab Emirates

Azhar Saeed lbw b DeFreitas	9
G. Mylvaganam c Fairbrother b DeFreitas	0
Mazhar Hussain b Smith	33
V. Mehra c Russell b Smith	1
Mohammad Aslam b Gough	23
Arshad Laiq b Smith	0
Saleem Raza b Cork	10
J. A. Samarasekera run out	29
*Sultan M. Zarawani b Cork	2
S. Dukanwala lbw b Illingworth	15
†Imtiaz Abbasi not out	1
B 4, l-b 4, w 4, n-b 1	13
1/3 (2) 2/32 (1) 3/48 (4) 4/49 (3) 5/49 (6) 6/80 (5) 7/88 (7) 8/100 (9) 9/135 (10) 10/136 (8) (48.3 overs)	136

Score at 15 overs: 44-2

Bowling: Cork 10–1–33–2; DeFreitas 9.3–3–16–2; Gough 8–3–23–1; White 1.3–1–2–0; Smith 9.3–2–29–3; Illingworth 10–2–25–1.

England

A. J. Stewart c Mylvaganam b Arshad Laiq	23
N. M. K. Smith retired ill	27
G. P. Thorpe not out	44
*M. A. Atherton b Azhar Saeed	20
N. H. Fairbrother not out	12
B 4, l-b 2, w 2, n-b 6	14
1/52 (1) 2/109 (4) (2 wkts, 35 overs)	140
Score at 15 overs: 61-1	

†R. C. Russell, C. White, D. G. Cork, P. A. J. DeFreitas, D. Gough and R. K. Illingworth did not bat.

N. M. K. Smith retired ill at 57.

Bowling: Samarasekera 7–1–35–0; Arshad Laiq 7–0–25–1; Saleem Raza 5–1–20–0; Azhar Saeed 10–1–26–1; Zarawani 6–0–28–0.

Umpires: B. C. Cooray and V. K. Ramaswamy. Referee: J. R. Reid.

NEW ZEALAND v SOUTH AFRICA

At Faisalabad, February 20. South Africa won by five wickets. Toss: New Zealand.

South Africa cruised to victory with 12.3 overs to spare after superlative out-cricket restricted New Zealand to 177 on a good pitch. The South Africans' fielding had been famous since their return to international cricket four years before, but coach Bob Woolmer described this display as "close to awesome – the best since I've been in charge". They pulled off three run-outs (two thanks to Kirsten), though the first was slightly suspect, as it was given on the basis of an inadequate TV replay. There was no square-leg camera and the third umpire had to give his verdict on a distant view from behind the bowler's arm. It was the second time in four days that Astle had been run out in the second over. In contrast, New Zealand gave both South African openers lives in the first three overs of their reply. When Morrison did make the breakthrough, by bowling Palframan, it brought in Cronje, who stormed to 78 in 64 balls, striking three sixes and 11 fours. By the time he went, the result was inevitable and Germon's meagre consolation was that New Zealand conceded no extras.

Man of the Match: W. J. Cronje.

New Zealand

C. M. Spearman c Palframan b Matthews	14
N. J. Astle run out	1
S. P. Fleming b McMillan	33
R. G. Twose c McMillan b Pollock	13
C. L. Cairns b Donald	9
A. C. Parore run out	27
C. Z. Harris run out	8
S. A. Thomson c Cronje b Donald	29
*†L. K. Germon not out	31
G. R. Larsen c Cullinan b Donald	1
D. K. Morrison not out	5
L-b 4, n-b 2	6
1/7 (2) 2/17 (1) 3/36 (4) 4/54 (5) 5/85 (3) 6/103 (7) 7/116 (6) 8/158 (8) 9/165 (10) (9 wkts, 50 overs)	177
Score at 15 overs: 52-3	

Bowling: Pollock 10–1–45–1; Matthews 10–2–30–1; Donald 10–0–34–3; Cronje 3–0–13–0; Symcox 10–1–25–0; McMillan 7–1–26–1.

South Africa

G. Kirsten lbw b Harris	35
†S. J. Palframan b Morrison	16
*W. J. Cronje c Fleming b Astle	78
D. J. Cullinan c Thomson b Astle	27
J. H. Kallis not out	11
J. N. Rhodes c and b Larsen	9
B. M. McMillan not out	2
1/41 (2) 2/87 (1) 3/146 (3) 4/159 (4) 5/170 (6) (5 wkts, 37.3 overs)	178
Score at 15 overs: 83-1	

S. M. Pollock, P. L. Symcox, C. R. Matthews and A. A. Donald did not bat.

Bowling: Morrison 8–0–44–1; Cairns 6–0–24–0; Larsen 8–1–41–1; Harris 4–0–25–1; Thomson 8.3–0–34–0; Astle 3–1–10–2.

Umpires: S. G. Randell and S. Venkataraghavan. Referee: R. S. Madugalle.

ENGLAND v HOLLAND

At Peshawar, February 22. England won by 49 runs. Toss: England. International debut: F. Jansen.

Hick, restored after resting an injured hamstring, insured England against an upset with a century. He completed it in the final over with his second six, and also struck six fours in 133 balls. Thorpe had been the dominant partner as they added 143 in 25 overs; he scored 89 in 82 balls before being trapped by Lefebvre, who was barely fit but bowled heroically. The rest of England's line-up still looked experimental. Stewart and Neil Smith opened again – and Smith did his job, with 31 in 33 balls – while Atherton remained down the order. But a total of 279 was disappointing and, later, sharp Dutch running re-emphasised the raggedness of the English fielding. England had planned to use three spinners on a dead pitch, until Illingworth was taken ill, and the seam bowlers had mixed fortunes: Cork, troubled by his knee injury, was expensive, though DeFreitas, bowling ten overs off the reel, claimed a creditable three for 31. Van Noortwijk and the 18-year-old Zuiderent scored Holland's first fifties at this level, adding 114 in 27 overs. But England's nerves were settled once van Noortwijk, trying for a third six, was caught in the deep.

Man of the Match: G. A. Hick.

England

A. J. Stewart b Bakker	5	N. H. Fairbrother not out	24
N. M. K. Smith c Clarke b Jansen	31	L-b 12, w 4	16
G. A. Hick not out	104		——
G. P. Thorpe lbw b Lefebvre	89	1/11 (1) 2/42 (2) (4 wkts, 50 overs)	279
*M. A. Atherton b Lubbers	10	3/185 (4) 4/212 (5) Score at 15 overs: 58-2	

†R. C. Russell, D. G. Cork, P. A. J. DeFreitas, D. Gough and P. J. Martin did not bat.

Bowling: Lefebvre 10–1–40–1; Bakker 8–0–46–1; Jansen 7–0–40–1; Aponso 8–0–55–0; Lubbers 10–0–51–1; de Leede 2–0–9–0; Cantrell 5–0–26–0.

Holland

N. E. Clarke lbw b Cork	0	†M. Schewe not out	11
P. E. Cantrell lbw b DeFreitas	28		
T. B. M. de Leede lbw b DeFreitas	41	L-b 4, w 6, n-b 2	12
*S. W. Lubbers c Russell b DeFreitas	9		——
K. J. van Noortwijk c Gough b Martin	64	1/1 (1) 2/46 (2) (6 wkts, 50 overs)	230
B. Zuiderent c Thorpe b Martin	54	3/70 (4) 4/81 (3)	
R. P. Lefebvre not out	11	5/195 (5) 6/208 (6) Score at 15 overs: 69-2	

G. J. A. F. Aponso, F. Jansen and P. J. Bakker did not bat.

Bowling: Cork 8–0–52–1; DeFreitas 10–3–31–3; Smith 8–0–27–0; Gough 3–0–23–0; Martin 10–1–42–2; Hick 5–0–23–0; Thorpe 6–0–28–0.

Umpires: S. A. Bucknor and K. T. Francis. Referee: J. R. Reid.

PAKISTAN v UNITED ARAB EMIRATES

At Gujranwala, February 24. Pakistan won by nine wickets. Toss: Pakistan.

Pakistan made a late entry into the tournament, delayed by the fasting month of Ramadan. They were further held up by overnight rain, which left the outfield waterlogged and reduced the match to 33 overs a side. But they needed only 18 overs to overtake the United Arab Emirates' 109; Javed Miandad, now the sole surviving player from the first World Cup in 1975, was not required to bat. After the loss of Aamir Sohail in the first over, Saeed Anwar and Ijaz Ahmed knocked off their target at a run a ball – assisted by 12 wides. Batting first while the ball was moving in the damp atmosphere, the Emirates made another aggressive start. Saleem Raza, who dashed to 22 in 20 balls, hit Wasim Akram over square leg for a huge six. But once he skied a catch to Miandad they struggled. Mushtaq Ahmed took three wickets in ten balls; the first was his 100th wicket in limited-overs internationals, in his 91st match.

Man of the Match: Mushtaq Ahmed.

United Arab Emirates

G. Mylvaganam b Mushtaq Ahmed 13
Saleem Raza c Javed Miandad b Aqib Javed . 22
Azhar Saeed run out 1
Mazhar Hussain c Waqar Younis b Mushtaq Ahmed . 7
Mohammad Aslam b Mushtaq Ahmed 5
Mohammad Ishaq b Wasim Akram 12
Arshad Laiq c Ijaz Ahmed b Aqib Javed . 9
J. A. Samarasekera b Waqar Younis 10
S. Dukanwala not out 21
*Sultan M. Zarawani b Wasim Akram 1
†Imtiaz Abbasi not out 0
L-b 1, w 5, n-b 2 8

1/27 (2) 2/40 (3) 3/47 (1) 4/53 (5) 5/54 (4) 6/70 (7) 7/80 (6) 8/108 (8) 9/109 (10) — (9 wkts, 33 overs) 109

Score at 9 overs: 34-1

Bowling: Wasim Akram 7–1–25–2; Waqar Younis 7–0–33–1; Aqib Javed 6–0–18–2; Mushtaq Ahmed 7–0–16–3; Aamir Sohail 6–1–16–0.

Pakistan

Aamir Sohail b Samarasekera 5
Saeed Anwar not out 40
Ijaz Ahmed, sen. not out 50
L-b 1, w 12, n-b 4 17

1/7 (1) — (1 wkt, 18 overs) 112

Score at 9 overs: 47-1

Inzamam-ul-Haq, Javed Miandad, Salim Malik, *Wasim Akram, †Rashid Latif, Mushtaq Ahmed, Waqar Younis and Aqib Javed did not bat.

Bowling: Samarasekera 3–0–17–1; Arshad Laiq 4–0–24–0; Dukanwala 3–1–14–0; Saleem Raza 3–0–17–0; Zarawani 3–0–23–0; Azhar Saeed 2–0–16–0.

Umpires: B. C. Cooray and S. Venkataraghavan. Referee: R. S. Madugalle.

ENGLAND v SOUTH AFRICA

At Rawalpindi, February 25. South Africa won by 78 runs. Toss: South Africa.

South Africa maintained the dominance they established over England in their one-day series in January. Though no one played a major innings, they compiled a decent score of 230, briefly interrupted by rain at 133 for three. England's fielding did improve a little, on a better surface than Peshawar, but they could hardly expect to outshine the South Africans in that department. Their carelessness contributed to their own downfall, however – Stewart was run out when he would have been home in comfort had he taken the elementary precaution of running his bat in ahead of him; later, DeFreitas remembered to extend his bat, but forgot to ground it and was also run out. The innings looked shaky from its fourth ball, when Atherton, resuming the opener's job, edged to the keeper. England struggled to get the ball away and, despite 46 from Thorpe, the top score of the match, were bowled out inside 45 overs for 152. It was exactly the same total as that made by the United Arab Emirates against South Africa nine days earlier. At the press conference, Atherton added to England's local unpopularity by referring to a Pakistani journalist as a buffoon. He apologised next day.

Man of the Match: J. N. Rhodes.

South Africa

G. Kirsten run out 38
†S. J. Palframan c Russell b Martin 28
*W. J. Cronje c Russell b Gough 15
D. J. Cullinan b DeFreitas 34
J. H. Kallis c Russell b Cork 26
J. N. Rhodes b Martin 37
B. M. McMillan b Smith 11
S. M. Pollock c Fairbrother b Cork 12
P. L. Symcox c Thorpe b Martin 1
C. R. Matthews not out 9
P. S. de Villiers c Smith b Gough 12
L-b 1, w 5, n-b 1 7

1/56 (2) 2/85 (1) 3/88 (3) 4/137 (4) 5/163 (5) 6/195 (6) 7/199 (7) 8/202 (9) 9/213 (8) 10/230 (11) — (50 overs) 230

Score at 15 overs: 63-1

Bowling: Cork 10–0–36–2; DeFreitas 10–0–55–1; Gough 10–0–48–2; Martin 10–0–33–3; Smith 8–0–40–1; Thorpe 2–0–17–0.

England

*M. A. Atherton c Palframan b Pollock . . 0
N. M. K. Smith b de Villiers 11
G. A. Hick c McMillan b de Villiers 14
G. P. Thorpe c Palframan b Symcox 46
A. J. Stewart run out 7
N. H. Fairbrother c Palframan b Symcox . 3
†R. C. Russell c Rhodes b Pollock 12
D. G. Cork b Matthews 17
P. A. J. DeFreitas run out 22
D. Gough b Matthews 11
P. J. Martin not out 1
L-b 7, w 1 8

1/0 (1) 2/22 (3) 3/33 (2) 4/52 (5) 5/62 (6) 6/97 (4) 7/97 (7) 8/139 (9) 9/141 (8) 10/152 (10) — (44.3 overs) 152

Score at 15 overs: 38-3

Bowling: Pollock 8–1–16–2; de Villiers 7–1–27–2; Matthews 9.3–0–30–2; McMillan 6–0–17–0; Symcox 10–0–38–2; Cronje 4–0–17–0.

Umpires: S. G. Randell and I. D. Robinson. Referee: J. R. Reid.

PAKISTAN v HOLLAND

At Lahore, February 26. Pakistan won by eight wickets. Toss: Holland.

Pakistan sailed past their target with nearly 20 overs to spare when Saeed Anwar hit his third six. Their only concern was that the middle order was still waiting for batting practice. But the bowling was in fine shape, especially Waqar Younis, who rediscovered his rhythm after a slow recovery from back injury. His pace and swing claimed four wickets, the first two in one over, which reduced Holland to 29 for three. In the closing stages, he also bowled Aponso, who had accumulated 58, and Lefebvre, acting-captain because Lubbers had damaged his knee. Aponso and van Noortwijk had resisted bravely during a stand of 73 in 27 overs, and both hit sixes off Mushtaq Ahmed, but it was merely a holding operation. Though Pakistan started slowly, and lost Aamir Sohail cheaply again, Anwar accelerated to 83 in 75 balls to complete an early win. By then the morning's small crowd had grown to 16,000.

Man of the Match: Waqar Younis.

Holland

N. E. Clarke c Rashid Latif b Aqib Javed . 4
P. E. Cantrell c Ijaz Ahmed b Waqar Younis . 17
T. B. M. de Leede c Rashid Latif b Waqar Younis . 0
K. J. van Noortwijk c Mushtaq Ahmed b Aqib Javed . 33
G. J. A. F. Aponso b Waqar Younis 58
*R. P. Lefebvre b Waqar Younis 10
B. Zuiderent run out 6
E. Gouka not out 0
L-b 7, w 4, n-b 6 17

1/16 (1) 2/28 (2) 3/29 (3) 4/102 (4) 5/130 (5) 6/143 (6) 7/145 (7) — (7 wkts, 50 overs) 145

Score at 15 overs: 30-3

†M. Schewe, F. Jansen and P. J. Bakker did not bat.

Bowling: Wasim Akram 10–1–30–0; Waqar Younis 10–0–26–4; Aqib Javed 9–2–25–2; Mushtaq Ahmed 10–2–27–0; Aamir Sohail 9–0–21–0; Salim Malik 2–0–9–0.

Pakistan

Aamir Sohail c Jansen b Lefebvre 9
Saeed Anwar not out 83
Ijaz Ahmed, sen. c Lefebvre b Cantrell . . . 39
Inzamam-ul-Haq not out 18
L-b 1, w 1 2

1/10 (1) 2/104 (3) — (2 wkts, 30.4 overs) 151

Score at 15 overs: 48-1

Javed Miandad, Salim Malik, *Wasim Akram, †Rashid Latif, Mushtaq Ahmed, Waqar Younis and Aqib Javed did not bat.

Bowling: Lefebvre 7–1–20–1; Bakker 7–1–13–0; Jansen 2–0–22–0; de Leede 4–0–20–0; Aponso 5–0–38–0; Cantrell 4–0–18–1; Gouka 1.4–0–19–0.

Umpires: S. A. Bucknor and K. T. Francis. Referee: R. Subba Row.

NEW ZEALAND v UNITED ARAB EMIRATES

At Faisalabad, February 27. New Zealand won by 109 runs. Toss: United Arab Emirates.

Fog held up the start and trimmed each innings by three overs – the fact that both sides were dressed in grey could not have improved their visibility. But the teams were clearly differentiated once the game got under way, with the Emirates hopelessly outclassed again. They did make two early breakthroughs, as Astle's poor run continued, but Spearman, with ten fours in a run-a-ball 78, and Twose added 120 in 21 overs. Twose batted on to fall eight short of a maiden international hundred and New Zealand's total challenged the Emirates to score nearly six an over. With the middle order collapsing again, the innings was given respectability only by Samarasekera, who came in at 92 for seven and hit 47 from 59 balls.

Man of the Match: R. G. Twose.

New Zealand

C. M. Spearman b Saleem Raza	78	D. J. Nash lbw b Azhar Saeed	8
N. J. Astle b Samarasekera	2	D. K. Morrison not out	10
S. P. Fleming c and b Dukanwala	16		
R. G. Twose c Mazhar Hussain b Azhar Saeed	92	B 2, l-b 12, n-b 1	15
C. L. Cairns c Imtiaz Abbasi b Zarawani	6	1/11 (2) 2/42 (3) (8 wkts, 47 overs)	276
A. C. Parore c Azhar Saeed b Zarawani	15	3/162 (1) 4/173 (5)	
S. A. Thomson not out	31	5/210 (6) 6/228 (4)	
*†L. K. Germon b Azhar Saeed	3	7/239 (8) 8/266 (9) Score at 14 overs: 86-2	

R. J. Kennedy did not bat.

Bowling: Samarasekera 6–0–30–1; Arshad Laiq 2–0–16–0; Dukanwala 10–0–46–1; Mazhar Hussain 3–0–28–0; Azhar Saeed 7–0–45–3; Saleem Raza 9–0–48–1; Zarawani 10–0–49–2.

United Arab Emirates

Azhar Saeed c Fleming b Nash	5	*Sultan M. Zarawani c Thomson b Nash	13
Saleem Raza c Kennedy b Morrison	21	†Imtiaz Abbasi not out	2
Mazhar Hussain c Cairns b Thomson	29	L-b 2, w 3, n-b 2	7
V. Mehra c Cairns b Thomson	12		
Mohammad Ishaq c Fleming b Kennedy	8	1/23 (1) 2/29 (2) (9 wkts, 47 overs)	167
Mohammad Aslam c Twose b Thomson	1	3/63 (4) 4/70 (3)	
S. Dukanwala c and b Cairns	8	5/81 (5) 6/88 (6)	
Arshad Laiq run out	14	7/92 (7) 8/124 (8)	
J. A. Samarasekera not out	47	9/162 (10) Score at 14 overs: 53-2	

Bowling: Morrison 7–0–37–1; Nash 9–1–34–2; Cairns 10–2–31–1; Kennedy 6–0–20–1; Thomson 10–2–20–3; Astle 5–0–23–0.

Umpires: B. C. Cooray and S. Venkataraghavan. Referee: R. S. Madugalle.

PAKISTAN v SOUTH AFRICA

At Karachi, February 29. South Africa won by five wickets. Toss: Pakistan.

South Africa's efficient performance earned their fourth straight win and ensured that they would head Group B. Pakistan gambled by dropping their third seamer to play six batsmen (but not Javed Miandad, who was said to have back problems). They entrusted the attack to two pace bowlers, two specialist spinners and slow left-armer Aamir Sohail as back-up. The gamble failed, while the South Africans' policy of sweeping the spinners paid off. Mushtaq Ahmed had a particularly bad day. Off-spinner Saqlain Mushtaq emerged with most credit - his two wickets in successive overs briefly looked to have taken the wind out of the batsmen's sails. But a scoring-rate of seven an over during the first 15 had given South Africa such a substantial advantage that they could complete their task at a comparatively relaxed pace. As ever, their strategy was carefully planned: Cronje promoted McMillan in the order and held himself back to bolster the later stages. Earlier in the day, Aamir Sohail dominated Pakistan's innings with 111 from 139 balls. The pitch offered little to the South African bowlers – including Adams, appearing for the first time in the tournament – apart from the medium-paced Cronje, who claimed two wickets in his first over.

Man of the Match: W. J. Cronje.

Pakistan

Aamir Sohail c Cronje b Pollock 111
Saeed Anwar c McMillan b Cronje 25
Ijaz Ahmed, sen. lbw b Cronje 0
Inzamam-ul-Haq run out 23
Salim Malik c Palframan b Adams 40
*Wasim Akram not out 32
†Rashid Latif lbw b Matthews 0
Ramiz Raja not out 2
B 1, l-b 2, w 4, n-b 2 9

1/52 (2) 2/52 (3) 3/112 (4) 4/189 (5) 5/233 (1) 6/235 (7) — (6 wkts, 50 overs) 242

Score at 15 overs: 64-2

Mushtaq Ahmed, Waqar Younis and Saqlain Mushtaq did not bat.

Bowling: Pollock 9–0–49–1; Matthews 10–0–47–1; Cronje 5–0–20–2; Donald 8–0–50–0; Adams 10–0–42–1; McMillan 8–0–31–0.

South Africa

A. C. Hudson b Waqar Younis 33
G. Kirsten b Saqlain Mushtaq 44
B. M. McMillan lbw b Waqar Younis 1
D. J. Cullinan b Waqar Younis 65
J. H. Kallis c and b Saqlain Mushtaq 9
*W. J. Cronje not out 45
S. M. Pollock not out 20
B 8, l-b 4, w 6, n-b 8 26

1/51 (1) 2/53 (3) 3/111 (2) 4/125 (5) 5/203 (4) — (5 wkts, 44.2 overs) 243

Score at 15 overs: 105-2

†S. J. Palframan, C. R. Matthews, A. A. Donald and P. R. Adams did not bat.

Bowling: Wasim Akram 9.2–0–49–0; Waqar Younis 8–0–50–3; Mushtaq Ahmed 10–0–54–0; Aamir Sohail 6–0–35–0; Saqlain Mushtaq 10–1–38–2; Salim Malik 1–0–5–0.

Umpires: S. A. Bucknor and K. T. Francis. Referee: R. Subba Row.

HOLLAND v UNITED ARAB EMIRATES

At Lahore, March 1. United Arab Emirates won by seven wickets. Toss: United Arab Emirates. International debuts: R. F. van Oosterom; Saeed-al-Saffar.

On form, Holland were strong favourites in the tournament's only meeting between ICC Associate Members. Instead, the United Arab Emirates finally played like ICC Trophy champions, with tight bowling and exhilarating batting. Just as in their previous encounter, the Trophy semi-final two years before, Zarawani put Holland in. The batsmen struggled as the ball moved around and only Aponso looked comfortable; Cantrell batted 41 overs for 47 before becoming one of six men out in the final ten overs, trying to force the pace. Off-spinner Dukanwala took five for 29, including four in his last 11 balls, while bespectacled seamer Shahzad Altaf conceded just 15 in ten overs. Chasing 217, the Emirates scored a stunning 94 in the opening 15 overs, thanks to Saleem Raza, a native of Lahore. There were six sixes – equalling the World Cup record – and seven fours in his 84 from 68 balls before he was caught, inevitably, on the boundary. His team-mates stuck at it and Mohammad Ishaq hit successive fours to win in the 45th over.

Men of the Match: S. Dukanwala and Saleem Raza.

Holland

N. E. Clarke c Mehra b Shahzad Altaf . . . 0
P. E. Cantrell c Imtiaz Abbasi b Azhar Saeed . 47
G. J. A. F. Aponso c and b Dukanwala . . . 45
T. B. M. de Leede c and b Azhar Saeed . . 36
K. J. van Noortwijk c Zarawani b Dukanwala . 26
*S. W. Lubbers c Saeed-al-Saffar b Zarawani . 8
R. P. Lefebvre c Mohammad Ishaq b Dukanwala . 12
B. Zuiderent st Imtiaz Abbasi b Dukanwala 3
†M. Schewe b Dukanwala 6
R. F. van Oosterom not out 2
P. J. Bakker not out 1
B 4, l-b 15, w 11 30

1/3 (1) 2/77 (3) 3/148 (4) 4/153 (2) 5/168 (6) 6/200 (5) 7/200 (7) 8/209 (8) 9/210 (9) — (9 wkts, 50 overs) 216

Score at 15 overs: 38-1

Bowling: Shahzad Altaf 10–3–15–1; Samarasekera 9–1–36–0; Saeed-al-Saffar 3–0–25–0; Dukanwala 10–0–29–5; Zarawani 8–0–40–1; Saleem Raza 5–0–23–0; Azhar Saeed 5–0–29–2.

United Arab Emirates

Azhar Saeed run out	32
Saleem Raza c Zuiderent b Lubbers	84
Mazhar Hussain c Clarke b Lefebvre	16
V. Mehra not out	29
Mohammad Ishaq not out	51
L-b 7, w 1	8
1/117 (2) 2/135 (3) 3/138 (1) — (3 wkts, 44.2 overs)	220
Score at 15 overs: 94-0	

J. A. Samarasekera, S. Dukanwala, *Sultan M. Zarawani, Saeed-al-Saffar, †Imtiaz Abbasi and Shahzad Altaf did not bat.

Bowling: Lefebvre 8–0–24–1; Bakker 8–0–41–0; de Leede 4–0–33–0; Aponso 7.2–0–47–0; Lubbers 9–0–38–1; Cantrell 8–0–30–0.

Umpires: Mahboob Shah and S. G. Randell. Referee: Nasim-ul-Ghani.

PAKISTAN v ENGLAND

At Karachi, March 3. Pakistan won by seven wickets. Toss: England.

This was England's third successive defeat in the tournament against Test opponents; only victories over the two Associates guaranteed them a quarter-final place. Briefly, it did look as if their luck had changed. Atherton batted on a flat pitch (already used by Pakistan against South Africa) and finally rediscovered his form. Together with his third opening partner, Robin Smith, now recovered from a groin strain, he ran up 147 in 28 overs, England's best for any wicket against Pakistan in limited-overs internationals. But once Smith lofted a catch to long-off, they went into decline: Hick and Atherton followed in the next three overs and no one offered real support to Thorpe. Pakistan's strike bowlers, expensive under the opening assault, returned with a vengeance after Aamir Sohail and Salim Malik had broken through; Mushtaq Ahmed claimed three in successive overs. The final target was a round 250. Openers Sohail and Saeed Anwar were soon up with the rate, raising 81 in 16 overs, but all the home batsmen made healthy contributions. Most warmly received was 38-year-old Javed Miandad, opening his account in his sixth World Cup; earlier, he had led the team out in what was expected to be his last big game before his own Karachi crowd.

Man of the Match: Aamir Sohail.

England

R. A. Smith c Waqar Younis b Salim Malik	75
*M. A. Atherton b Aamir Sohail	66
G. A. Hick st Rashid Latif b Aamir Sohail	1
G. P. Thorpe not out	52
N. H. Fairbrother c Wasim Akram b Mushtaq Ahmed	13
†R. C. Russell c and b Mushtaq Ahmed	4
D. A. Reeve b Mushtaq Ahmed	3
D. G. Cork lbw b Waqar Younis	0
D. Gough b Wasim Akram	14
P. J. Martin run out	2
R. K. Illingworth not out	1
L-b 11, w 4, n-b 3	18
1/147 (1) 2/151 (3) 3/156 (2) 4/194 (5) 5/204 (6) 6/212 (7) 7/217 (8) 8/241 (9) 9/247 (10) — (9 wkts, 50 overs)	249
Score at 15 overs: 69-0	

Bowling: Wasim Akram 7–1–31–1; Waqar Younis 10–1–45–1; Aqib Javed 7–0–34–0; Mushtaq Ahmed 10–0–53–3; Aamir Sohail 10–0–48–2; Salim Malik 6–1–27–1.

Pakistan

Aamir Sohail c Thorpe b Illingworth	42
Saeed Anwar c Russell b Cork	71
Ijaz Ahmed, sen. c Russell b Cork	70
Inzamam-ul-Haq not out	53
Javed Miandad not out	11
L-b 1, w 2	3
1/81 (1) 2/139 (2) 3/214 (3) (3 wkts, 47.4 overs)	250
Score at 15 overs: 77-0	

Salim Malik, *Wasim Akram, †Rashid Latif, Mushtaq Ahmed, Waqar Younis and Aqib Javed did not bat.

Bowling: Cork 10–0–59–2; Martin 9–0–45–0; Gough 10–0–45–0; Illingworth 10–0–46–1; Reeve 6.4–0–37–0; Hick 2–0–17–0.

Umpires: B. C. Cooray and S. Venkataraghavan. Referee: R. S. Madugalle.

HOLLAND v SOUTH AFRICA

At Rawalpindi, March 5. South Africa won by 160 runs. Toss: South Africa.

South Africa completed their group programme with maximum points. Their total of 328 beat their previous best, against the Emirates 18 days earlier, by seven, while Kirsten and Hudson set a World Cup first-wicket record with a stand of 186. Hudson went on to 161 in 132 balls, with four sixes and 13 fours, and was finally caught on the boundary seeking a third straight six. Holland's best bowler, Lefebvre, had surrendered to his groin strain and their captain, the off-spinner Lubbers, shared the new ball in what he said would be his last international. The Dutch batsmen got halfway to their target; the West Indian veteran, Clarke, was their top scorer, with 32 in 46 balls, and brought up the fifty with a six off Pollock. It was the only innings in which Clarke provided a glimpse of the power that had helped Holland into the World Cup. His poor form was one reason why they were the only team to lose every match. The South Africans won all theirs, and their previous run at home to England made this their tenth successive one-day victory. Some critics, however, thought Cronje should have dropped down the order, to allow some of the later batsmen a little more time in the middle.

Man of the Match: A. C. Hudson.

South Africa

G. Kirsten c Zuiderent b Aponso	83
A. C. Hudson c van Oosterom b Gouka	161
*W. J. Cronje c Lubbers b Cantrell	41
D. J. Cullinan not out	19
J. H. Kallis not out	17
L-b 5, w 2	7
1/186 (1) 2/274 (2) 3/301 (3) (3 wkts, 50 overs)	328
Score at 15 overs: 84-0	

B. M. McMillan, S. M. Pollock, †S. J. Palframan, P. L. Symcox, C. R. Matthews and A. A. Donald did not bat.

Bowling: Bakker 10–1–64–0; Lubbers 8–0–50–0; de Leede 10–0–59–0; Aponso 10–0–57–1; Cantrell 10–0–61–1; Gouka 2–0–32–1.

Holland

N. E. Clarke c Pollock b Donald	32
P. E. Cantrell c and b Matthews	23
T. B. M. de Leede b Donald	12
K. J. van Noortwijk c Palframan b Symcox	9
G. J. A. F. Aponso c Kirsten b Symcox	6
B. Zuiderent run out	27
†M. Schewe b Matthews	20
E. Gouka c Kallis b Pollock	19
R. F. van Oosterom not out	5
*S. W. Lubbers not out	2
L-b 7, w 5, n-b 1	13
1/56 (2) 2/70 (1) 3/81 (3) 4/86 (4) 5/97 (5) 6/126 (6) 7/158 (8) 8/163 (7) (8 wkts, 50 overs)	168
Score at 15 overs: 69-1	

P. J. Bakker did not bat.

Bowling: Pollock 8–0–35–1; Matthews 10–0–38–2; Donald 6–0–21–2; Cronje 3–1–3–0; Symcox 10–1–22–2; McMillan 4–2–5–0; Kallis 7–0–30–0; Cullinan 2–0–7–0.

Umpires: Khizar Hayat and S. G. Randell. Referee: Nasim-ul-Ghani.

PAKISTAN v NEW ZEALAND

At Lahore, March 6. Pakistan won by 46 runs. Toss: New Zealand.

This game – like Holland v United Arab Emirates – was originally scheduled as a day/night match, a dress rehearsal for the final at the Gaddafi Stadium. But with workmen still perched on the floodlights, it was played in daytime. The match's real significance was its impact on the teams' prospects for the quarter-finals; Pakistan's victory took them to Bangalore to meet India, while New Zealand drew Australia. Both sides lost key players on the way. Morrison struggled for rhythm, conceding 17 in two overs before yielding to a groin injury, while Wasim Akram, who started with a dislocated thumb, strained his side batting; he could not take the field and Aamir Sohail deputised as captain. Sohail had scored 50 out of 70 in Pakistan's first 15 overs before he was brilliantly caught by Thomson – leaping, falling and just reaching the ball with his left hand. Saeed Anwar and Inzamam-ul-Haq (both wearing shirts saying their name was "Younis") kept on course, but it was Salim Malik who inspired the final assault of 83 in ten overs. New Zealand – whose captain, Germon, boldly promoted himself to No. 3 and made 41 – never quite lost sight of their target until their final ten, needing 87; they managed only 40, punctuated by three wickets. Rashid Latif defied a hand injury to make five dismissals, equalling the World Cup record.

Man of the Match: Salim Malik.

Pakistan

Aamir Sohail c Thomson b Kennedy	50	*Wasim Akram not out	28
Saeed Anwar run out	62	L-b 5, w 5, n-b 6	16
Ijaz Ahmed, sen. c Spearman b Cairns	26		—
Inzamam-ul-Haq run out	39	1/70 (1) 2/139 (2) (5 wkts, 50 overs)	281
Javed Miandad run out	5	3/155 (3) 4/173 (5)	
Salim Malik not out	55	5/201 (4) Score at 15 overs: 73-1	

†Rashid Latif, Mushtaq Ahmed, Waqar Younis and Aqib Javed did not bat.

Bowling: Morrison 2–0–17–0; Nash 10–1–49–0; Cairns 10–1–53–1; Kennedy 5–0–32–1; Astle 9–0–50–0; Thomson 6–0–35–0; Twose 8–0–40–0.

New Zealand

C. M. Spearman c Rashid Latif b Aqib Javed	14	S. A. Thomson c Rashid Latif b Waqar Younis	13
N. J. Astle c Rashid Latif b Waqar Younis	6	D. J. Nash not out	5
*†L. K. Germon c sub (Ata-ur-Rehman) b Mushtaq Ahmed	41	R. J. Kennedy b Aqib Javed	2
S. P. Fleming st Rashid Latif b Salim Malik	42	D. K. Morrison absent hurt	
		B 4, l-b 9, w 6, n-b 1	20
			—
R. G. Twose c Salim Malik b Mushtaq Ahmed	24	1/23 (2) 2/23 (1) (47.3 overs)	235
C. L. Cairns c Rashid Latif b Aamir Sohail	32	3/83 (4) 4/132 (3) 5/138 (5) 6/182 (6)	
A. C. Parore c Mushtaq Ahmed b Salim Malik	36	7/221 (7) 8/228 (8) 9/235 (10) Score at 15 overs: 74-2	

Bowling: Waqar Younis 9–2–32–2; Aqib Javed 7.3–0–45–2; Mushtaq Ahmed 10–0–32–2; Salim Malik 7–0–41–2; Ijaz Ahmed 4–0–21–0; Aamir Sohail 10–0–51–1.

Umpires: K. T. Francis and I. D. Robinson. Referee: C. H. Lloyd.

GROUP B FINAL TABLE

	Played	*Won*	*Lost*	*Points*	*Net run-rate*
SOUTH AFRICA	5	5	0	10	2.04
PAKISTAN	5	4	1	8	0.96
NEW ZEALAND	5	3	2	6	0.55
ENGLAND	5	2	3	4	0.08
United Arab Emirates	5	1	4	2	−1.83
Holland	5	0	5	0	−1.92

If two teams had finished with an equal number of points, the winner of their head-to-head game would have been placed higher. Net run-rate, calculated by subtracting runs conceded per over from runs scored per over, would have been used had three or more teams tied on this method.

QUARTER-FINALS

ENGLAND v SRI LANKA

At Faisalabad, March 9. Sri Lanka won by five wickets. Toss: England.

Sri Lanka continued their glorious ascent, while England sank ignominiously; they had never been knocked out before the semi-finals in the five previous World Cups. They were all but dead by the time Jayasuriya departed at 113 for one, virtually halfway to Sri Lanka's target of 236, in their 13th over. Jayasuriya had thumped 82 off 44 balls, with three sixes and 13 fours. He was most savage on the left-arm spin of Illingworth, whom he hit for four successive fours, and the seam of DeFreitas, whose second over went for 22. DeFreitas was withdrawn, having conceded 32 in 12 balls; later, he bowled some tidy off-spin, but by then there was nothing to play for. England's only real breakthrough came in the second over when Illingworth, opening the attack in an attempt to surprise the Sri Lankans, got Kaluwitharana third ball – he had hit the first two for fours. Jayasuriya's spree was finally ended when the third umpire gave him out stumped, one delivery after Reeve bowled him with a no-ball. De Silva and the rest could not keep up his momentum, but still won with nine overs in hand. Atherton had elected to bat, hoping for 300, though even that might not have withstood the Sri Lankan assault. As it was, only DeFreitas, promoted to No. 5, managed the sustained aggression necessary. He hit 67 from 64 balls, his maiden one-day fifty for England, with two big sixes and five fours, and looked a little unlucky to be out lbw to Jayasuriya. The run-out of Smith – also by the ubiquitous Jayasuriya, with a direct hit – was still more controversial, even after the third umpire's judgment. With the middle order crumbling, only a 62-run stand by Reeve and Gough took England past 200.

Man of the Match: S. T. Jayasuriya.

England

R. A. Smith run out	25
*M. A. Atherton c Kaluwitharana b Vaas	22
G. A. Hick c Ranatunga b Muralitharan	8
G. P. Thorpe b Dharmasena	14
P. A. J. DeFreitas lbw b Jayasuriya	67
A. J. Stewart b Muralitharan	17
†R. C. Russell b Dharmasena	9
D. A. Reeve b Jayasuriya	35
D. Gough not out	26
P. J. Martin not out	0
L-b 8, w 4	12
1/31 (2) 2/58 (3) 3/66 (1) 4/94 (4) 5/145 (6) 6/171 (7) 7/173 (5) 8/235 (8) — (8 wkts, 50 overs)	235

Score at 15 overs: 59-2

R. K. Illingworth did not bat.

Bowling: Wickremasinghe 7–0–43–0; Vaas 8–1–29–1; Muralitharan 10–1–37–2; Dharmasena 10–0–30–2; Jayasuriya 9–0–46–2; de Silva 6–0–42–0.

Sri Lanka

S. T. Jayasuriya st Russell b Reeve 82	R. S. Mahanama not out 22
†R. S. Kaluwitharana b Illingworth 8	L-b 1, w 2, n-b 1 4
A. P. Gurusinha run out 45	——
P. A. de Silva c Smith b Hick 31	1/12 (2) 2/113 (1) (5 wkts, 40.4 overs) 236
*A. Ranatunga lbw b Gough 25	3/165 (4) 4/194 (5)
H. P. Tillekeratne not out 19	5/198 (3) Score at 15 overs: 121-2

H. D. P. K. Dharmasena, W. P. U. J. C. Vaas, G. P. Wickremasinghe and M. Muralitharan did not bat.

Bowling: Martin 9–1–41–0; Illingworth 10–1–72–1; Gough 10–1–36–1; DeFreitas 3.4–0–38–0; Reeve 4–1–14–1; Hick 4–0–34–1.

Umpires: Mahboob Shah and I. D. Robinson. Referee: Nasim-ul-Ghani.

INDIA v PAKISTAN

At Bangalore, March 9 (day/night). India won by 39 runs. Toss: India.

This encounter inspired high passions which boiled over back in Pakistan after India won. One fan reportedly shot his television and then himself, while captain Wasim Akram was burned in effigy. Wasim was not even playing, having ruptured his side muscles, but conspiracy theorists, fuelled by the previous year's allegations of bribery, speculated that he might have withdrawn deliberately, a charge he indignantly denied. In fact, the game looked keenly contested and turned into a thriller. India chose to bat but, though the bowlers made no gains until the 22nd over, their top batsmen never quite took control either. Tendulkar's 31 was a trifle by his standards. Sidhu, seven short of his century when Mushtaq Ahmed's flipper deceived him, steered India to an impressive-sounding 168 for two, but the scoring-rate was barely four and a half an over. It was Jadeja who played the decisive role, scoring 45 from 25 balls (four fours and two sixes), coupled with a tremendous onslaught from the tail. They smashed 51 off the last three overs. Waqar bowled two of those overs for 40 runs, after his first eight had cost just 27; when he got Jadeja he became the fourth player to take 200 wickets in one-day internationals. Meanwhile, a slow over-rate was punished by the deduction of an over from Pakistan's reply, the only such penalty in the tournament. Even so, their openers seized the initiative. Saeed Anwar had scored 48 from 32 balls, including two sixes, when he skied to Kumble; stand-in captain Aamir Sohail was 55 from 46, with one six, when he slashed wildly at Prasad. Pakistan made 113 for two from the vital first 15 overs, putting them way ahead of India. But Prasad grabbed two more wickets and, gradually, the scoring-rate faltered. Rashid Latif, with two big sixes in a run-a-ball 26, kept Pakistan going, but his stumping sparked a collapse to Kumble. The run-out of Javed Miandad signalled the end of Pakistan's reign as one-day champions and, apparently, of a career spanning three decades. With characteristic rancour, he used the announcement of his retirement to denounce the team management for ignoring his batting and strategic expertise.

Man of the Match: N. S. Sidhu.

India

N. S. Sidhu b Mushtaq Ahmed 93	A. Kumble c Javed Miandad b Aqib Javed 10
S. R. Tendulkar b Ata-ur-Rehman 31	J. Srinath not out 12
S. V. Manjrekar c Javed Miandad b Aamir Sohail . 20	B. K. V. Prasad not out 0
*M. Azharuddin c Rashid Latif b Waqar Younis . 27	L-b 3, w 15, n-b 4 22
	——
V. G. Kambli b Mushtaq Ahmed 24	1/90 (2) 2/138 (3) (8 wkts, 50 overs) 287
A. Jadeja c Aamir Sohail b Waqar Younis 45	3/168 (1) 4/200 (4)
†N. R. Mongia run out 3	5/226 (5) 6/236 (7)
	7/260 (8) 8/279 (6) Score at 15 overs: 67-0

S. L. V. Raju did not bat.

Bowling: Waqar Younis 10–1–67–2; Aqib Javed 10–2–67–1; Ata-ur-Rehman 10–0–40–1; Mushtaq Ahmed 10–0–56–2; Aamir Sohail 5–0–29–1; Salim Malik 5–0–25–0.

Pakistan

*Aamir Sohail b Prasad	55	Ata-ur-Rehman lbw b Kumble	0
Saeed Anwar c Kumble b Srinath	48	Aqib Javed not out	6
Ijaz Ahmed, sen. c Srinath b Prasad	12	B 1, l-b 3, w 5	9
Inzamam-ul-Haq c Mongia b Prasad	12		—
Salim Malik lbw b Kumble	38	1/84 (2) 2/113 (1) (9 wkts, 49 overs)	248
Javed Miandad run out	38	3/122 (3) 4/132 (4)	
†Rashid Latif st Mongia b Raju	26	5/184 (5) 6/231 (7)	
Mushtaq Ahmed c and b Kumble	0	7/232 (8) 8/239 (6)	
Waqar Younis not out	4	9/239 (10) Score at 15 overs: 113-2	

Bowling: Srinath 9–0–61–1; Prasad 10–0–45–3; Kumble 10–0–48–3; Raju 10–0–46–1; Tendulkar 5–0–25–0; Jadeja 5–0–19–0.

Umpires: S. A. Bucknor and D. R. Shepherd. Referee: R. Subba Row.

SOUTH AFRICA v WEST INDIES

At Karachi, March 11. West Indies won by 19 runs. Toss: West Indies.

West Indies' stubborn fightback after crashing against Kenya carried them through against favourites South Africa. A century from Lara – 111 in 94 balls – set up their victory and it was completed by the spin of Jimmy Adams and Harper, who turned the game with three wickets in the first over of his second spell. At the start, though, the spinners in the news were the South Africans, Symcox and Paul Adams: uncharacteristically, South Africa played both, omitting Donald from their pace attack. But Lara, gaining confidence after a wary start, thrived on spin. Five of his 16 fours came from one over by Symcox, and a second-wicket stand with Chanderpaul of 138 from 25 overs promised a big total. However, after Symcox returned for his belated revenge – finding Lara's top edge as he tried to sweep – the later order struggled. The final ten overs brought only 48 runs, 16 off the last one, bowled by Adams. South Africa were also propelled by their second-wicket pair: Hudson and Cullinan, who struck three sixes, had taken the score to 118 for one at the halfway mark. It was slow left-armer Jimmy Adams, not normally a frontline bowler, who made the breakthrough, removing both of them in 15 balls and dismissing Cronje, for a hard-hitting 40, in his final over. Harper then replaced him and with his first delivery had Rhodes caught by Adams on the mid-wicket boundary. His next ball trapped McMillan lbw and, three balls later, he dived to take a left-handed return catch from Palframan. Symcox attempted to rescue South Africa's campaign with two sixes. Harper was the bowler but he had the last laugh, making Pollock his fourth victim and then catching Symcox in the very next over.

Man of the Match: B. C. Lara.

West Indies

S. Chanderpaul c Cullinan b McMillan	56	I. R. Bishop b Adams	17
†C. O. Browne c Cullinan b Matthews	26	C. E. L. Ambrose not out	0
B. C. Lara c Pollock b Symcox	111	B 2, l-b 11, w 2, n-b 1	16
*R. B. Richardson c Kirsten b Symcox	10		—
R. A. Harper lbw b McMillan	9	1/42 (2) 2/180 (1) (8 wkts, 50 overs)	264
R. I. C. Holder run out	5	3/210 (4) 4/214 (3)	
K. L. T. Arthurton c Hudson b Adams	1	5/227 (5) 6/230 (7)	
J. C. Adams not out	13	7/230 (6) 8/254 (9) Score at 15 overs: 74-1	

C. A. Walsh did not bat.

Bowling: Pollock 9–0–46–0; Matthews 10–0–42–1; Cronje 3–0–17–0; McMillan 10–1–37–2; Symcox 10–0–64–2; Adams 8–0–45–2.

South Africa

A. C. Hudson c Walsh b Adams	54
G. Kirsten hit wkt b Ambrose	3
D. J. Cullinan c Bishop b Adams	69
*W. J. Cronje c Arthurton b Adams	40
J. N. Rhodes c Adams b Harper	13
B. M. McMillan lbw b Harper	6
S. M. Pollock c Adams b Harper	6
†S. J. Palframan c and b Harper	1
P. L. Symcox c Harper b Arthurton	24
C. R. Matthews not out	8
P. R. Adams b Walsh	10
B 1, l-b 4, w 2, n-b 4	11
	—
1/21 (2) 2/118 (1) 3/140 (3) 4/186 (4) 5/196 (5) 6/196 (6) 7/198 (8) 8/227 (7) 9/228 (9) 10/245 (11)	(49.3 overs) 245

Score at 15 overs: 69-1

Bowling: Ambrose 10–0–29–1; Walsh 8.3–0–51–1; Bishop 5–0–31–0; Harper 10–0–47–4; Adams 10–0–53–3; Arthurton 6–0–29–1.

Umpires: K. T. Francis and S. G. Randell. Referee: R. S. Madugalle.

AUSTRALIA v NEW ZEALAND

At Madras, March 11 (day/night). Australia won by six wickets. Toss: New Zealand.

The Waughs relentlessly steered Australia into the semi-finals as Mark became the first batsman to score three hundreds in one World Cup. New Zealand must have been delighted with their total of 286 – it was their highest in 63 one-day games against Australia, and more than any team had chased successfully in this tournament. Their heroes were Germon, who continued to bat at No. 3, and Harris, recalled after scoring only 26 in the opening three matches. Together, they put on 168 – a fourth-wicket record for New Zealand and the World Cup – at more than six an over. Germon scored 89 from 96 balls, his maiden international fifty, and Harris his first century for New Zealand. He was finally caught, one-handed by Reiffel on the boundary, in the penultimate over, for 130 from 124 balls with four sixes and 13 fours. With Morrison injured, Germon reverted to New Zealand's surprise tactic of the last World Cup – giving off-spinner Patel the new ball. It had unsettled Australia in 1992, and he did have Taylor caught behind in the sixth over. But Mark Waugh was soon into his stride, with some unexpected support: Warne was promoted to No. 4 as the latest pinch-hitter, and smashed two sixes in 24 from 14 balls. It was Waugh's more familiar partner, his twin Steve, who saw him past his hundred. Mark made 110 from 112 balls with two sixes, five fours and a lot of running, before he grew tired and slightly misjudged a shot to the boundary which found Parore. However, Steve supervised the closing stages. Australia's victory, with 13 balls to spare, meant that all four semi-finalists came from Group A; their counterparts from Group B – by coincidence, the four semi-finalists of 1992 – had been wiped out.

Man of the Match: M. E. Waugh.

New Zealand

C. M. Spearman c Healy b Reiffel	12
N. J. Astle c Healy b Fleming	1
*†L. K. Germon c Fleming b McGrath	89
S. P. Fleming c S. R. Waugh b McGrath	8
C. Z. Harris c Reiffel b Warne	130
R. G. Twose b Bevan	4
C. L. Cairns c Reiffel b M. E. Waugh	4
A. C. Parore lbw b Warne	11
S. A. Thomson run out	11
D. N. Patel not out	3
L-b 6, w 3, n-b 4	13
	—
1/15 (2) 2/16 (1) 3/44 (4) 4/212 (3) 5/227 (6) 6/240 (7) 7/259 (8) 8/282 (5) 9/286 (9)	(9 wkts, 50 overs) 286

Score at 15 overs: 95-3

D. J. Nash did not bat.

Bowling: Reiffel 4–0–38–1; Fleming 5–1–20–1; McGrath 9–2–50–2; M. E. Waugh 8–0–43–1; Warne 10–0–52–2; Bevan 10–0–52–1; S. R. Waugh 4–0–25–0.

Australia

*M. A. Taylor c Germon b Patel	10	S. G. Law not out	42
M. E. Waugh c Parore b Nash	110		
R. T. Ponting c sub (R. J. Kennedy) b Thomson	31	B 1, l-b 6, w 3, n-b 3	13
S. K. Warne lbw b Astle	24	1/19 (1) 2/84 (3) (4 wkts, 47.5 overs)	289
S. R. Waugh not out	59	3/127 (4) 4/213 (2) Score at 15 overs: 63-1	

M. G. Bevan, †I. A. Healy, P. R. Reiffel, D. W. Fleming and G. D. McGrath did not bat.

Bowling: Nash 9–1–44–1; Patel 8–0–45–1; Cairns 6.5–0–51–0; Harris 10–0–41–0; Thomson 8–0–57–1; Astle 3–0–21–1; Twose 3–0–23–0.

Umpires: C. J. Mitchley and S. Venkataraghavan. Referee: Mansur Ali Khan.

SEMI-FINALS

INDIA v SRI LANKA

At Calcutta, March 13 (day/night). Sri Lanka won by default after a crowd riot. Toss: India.

Sri Lanka played brilliantly after a disastrous first over to achieve an unbeatable advantage. But the headlines were devoted to the riot which ended the match. Enraged by an Indian collapse of seven wickets for 22, some home supporters threw bottles on to the outfield and set fire to the seating. Referee Clive Lloyd took the teams off for 15 minutes, attempted a restart and then awarded Sri Lanka the game by default. Nobody questioned the result; India needed a near-impossible 132 from 15.5 overs, with only two wickets standing. But the Indian board smarted at the word "default" and asked for Sri Lanka to be declared winners on run-rate. The authorities – and many home fans – were intensely embarrassed by the trouble. Even as the match was abandoned, one Indian raised a banner reading "Congratulation [sic] Sri Lanka – we are sorry". Some took out apologetic advertisements in the Sri Lankan press. But, like the Pakistani fans four days before, others raged against their unsuccessful players and a guard was put on captain Azharuddin's house. Azharuddin took much criticism for fielding first. He knew Sri Lanka preferred to chase, as they did to beat India in Delhi, but critics argued that he should play to his team's strengths, not his opponents' weaknesses. There were few objections, however, when Kaluwitharana and Jayasuriya, Sri Lanka's celebrated pinch-hitters, both hit straight to third man in the first four balls of the game. Gurusinha soon followed, but de Silva determinedly stuck to the strategy of scoring as heavily as possible early on: he hit 22 off Prasad's first two overs. Though he was bowled in the 15th over, de Silva had scored 66, with 14 fours, off 47 balls, and Sri Lanka already had 85. Ranatunga and Mahanama (who eventually succumbed to cramp) kept up a steady five an over. A target of 252 was not necessarily beyond India's batting heroes, however. Tendulkar, their tidiest bowler earlier, and Manjrekar advanced confidently to 98 for one. But when Tendulkar was stumped and, seven balls later, Azharuddin gave Dharmasena a return catch, the 100,000 crowd was stunned into silence. That did not last, as the collapse fuelled their fury, and no play was possible after the loss of Kapoor to de Silva's running catch in the deep. Yet the presentation ceremony went ahead as if nothing untoward had occurred, and, against the smoking backdrop, Tony Greig conducted post-match interviews so normal they were bizarre. A day later, Jayasuriya was named Most Valued Player of the Tournament, an award clinched by his three for 12 in seven overs, in addition to two catches and a run-out.

Man of the Match: P. A. de Silva.

Sri Lanka

S. T. Jayasuriya c Prasad b Srinath	1	W. P. U. J. C. Vaas run out	23
†R. S. Kaluwitharana c Manjrekar b Srinath	0	G. P. Wickremasinghe not out	4
A. P. Gurusinha c Kumble b Srinath	1	M. Muralitharan not out	5
P. A. de Silva b Kumble	66	B 1, l-b 10, w 4, n-b 2	17
R. S. Mahanama retired hurt	58	1/1 (2) 2/1 (1) (8 wkts, 50 overs)	251
*A. Ranatunga lbw b Tendulkar	35	3/35 (3) 4/85 (4)	
H. P. Tillekeratne c Tendulkar b Prasad	32	5/168 (6) 6/206 (8)	
H. D. P. K. Dharmasena b Tendulkar	9	7/236 (7) 8/244 (9) Score at 15 overs: 86-4	

R. S. Mahanama retired hurt at 182.

Bowling: Srinath 7–1–34–3; Kumble 10–0–51–1; Prasad 8–0–50–1; Kapoor 10–0–40–0; Jadeja 5–0–31–0; Tendulkar 10–1–34–2.

India

S. R. Tendulkar st Kaluwitharana b Jayasuriya	65	A. R. Kapoor c de Silva b Muralitharan	0
N. S. Sidhu c Jayasuriya b Vaas	3	A. Kumble not out	0
S. V. Manjrekar b Jayasuriya	25	L-b 5, w 5	10
*M. Azharuddin c and b Dharmasena	0		
V. G. Kambli not out	10	1/8 (2) 2/98 (1) (8 wkts, 34.1 overs)	120
J. Srinath run out	6	3/99 (4) 4/101 (3)	
A. Jadeja b Jayasuriya	0	5/110 (6) 6/115 (7)	
†N. R. Mongia c Jayasuriya b de Silva	1	7/120 (8) 8/120 (9) Score at 15 overs: 63-1	

B. K. V. Prasad did not bat.

Bowling: Wickremasinghe 5–0–24–0; Vaas 6–1–23–1; Muralitharan 7.1–0–29–1; Dharmasena 7–0–24–1; Jayasuriya 7–1–12–3; de Silva 2–0–3–1.

Umpires: R. S. Dunne and C. J. Mitchley. Referee: C. H. Lloyd.

AUSTRALIA v WEST INDIES

At Mohali, March 14 (day/night). Australia won by five runs. Toss: Australia.

West Indies pulled off an extraordinary defeat, losing eight wickets in the final 50 minutes. After 41 overs, they were 165 for two, needing 43 from the last nine; Lara had gone for a run-a-ball 45, but Chanderpaul was heading for a century and Richardson for a glorious conclusion to his captaincy. Once Chanderpaul – hampered by cramp – fell, however, the innings swerved out of control. Big hitters Harper and Gibson were promoted in the order but their wickets, in quick succession, placed more pressure on the recognised batsmen, Adams and the out-of-form Arthurton, who soon followed. Australia were on top for the first time in the game and a devastating three-over spell from Warne culled three for six. But Richardson was still there to face the last over, from Fleming. When he struck the first delivery for four, West Indies required six from five balls, with two wickets left, and victory was in his grasp. The final fatal misjudgment was to set off for a single, for even if Ambrose had got home, it was Richardson who needed the strike. In fact, Ambrose was given out on a TV replay. Last man Walsh heaved at his first ball and was bowled. Taylor had controlled the closing stages perfectly but said afterwards that West Indies had won 95 per cent of the match. The game had seemed dead after 40 minutes, when Australia, electing to bat on one of the grassier pitches of the tournament, were 15 for four. Ambrose and Bishop had fired out both Waughs, Ponting, who scored 102 in their last meeting, and Taylor himself for a combined four runs, and a rout threatened. But Law and Bevan batted with determination and growing confidence to add 138 in 32 overs and the later order pushed the total past 200. Though Warne dismissed Browne with his first ball, West Indies seemed to have the task well in hand until panic overtook them.

Man of the Match: S. K. Warne.

Australia

M. E. Waugh lbw b Ambrose	0	S. K. Warne not out	6
*M. A. Taylor b Bishop	1		
R. T. Ponting lbw b Ambrose	0	L-b 11, w 5, n-b 2	18
S. R. Waugh b Bishop	3		
S. G. Law run out	72	1/0 (1) 2/7 (2) (8 wkts, 50 overs)	207
M. G. Bevan c Richardson b Harper	69	3/8 (3) 4/15 (4)	
†I. A. Healy run out	31	5/153 (5) 6/171 (6)	
P. R. Reiffel run out	7	7/186 (8) 8/207 (7) Score at 15 overs: 29-4	

D. W. Fleming and G. D. McGrath did not bat.

Bowling: Ambrose 10–1–26–2; Bishop 10–1–35–2; Walsh 10–1–33–0; Gibson 2–0–13–0; Harper 9–0–47–1; Adams 9–0–42–0.

West Indies

S. Chanderpaul c Fleming b McGrath	80
†C. O. Browne c and b Warne	10
B. C. Lara b S. R. Waugh	45
*R. B. Richardson not out	49
R. A. Harper lbw b McGrath	2
O. D. Gibson c Healy b Warne	1
J. C. Adams lbw b Warne	2
K. L. T. Arthurton c Healy b Fleming	0
I. R. Bishop lbw b Warne	3
C. E. L. Ambrose run out	2
C. A. Walsh b Fleming	0
L-b 4, w 2, n-b 2	8
1/25 (2) 2/93 (3) 3/165 (1) 4/173 (5) 5/178 (6) 6/183 (7) 7/187 (8) 8/194 (9) 9/202 (10) 10/202 (11) (49.3 overs)	202

Score at 15 overs: 60-1

Bowling: McGrath 10–2–30–2; Fleming 8.3–0–48–2; Warne 9–0–36–4; M. E. Waugh 4–0–16–0; S. R. Waugh 7–0–30–1; Reiffel 5–0–13–0; Bevan 4–1–12–0; Law 2–0–13–0.

Umpires: B. C. Cooray and S. Venkataraghavan. Referee: J. R. Reid.

FINAL

AUSTRALIA v SRI LANKA

At Lahore, March 17. Sri Lanka won by seven wickets. Toss: Sri Lanka.

Contrary to most expectations, Sri Lanka controlled their first World Cup final after the initial stages. Their batting was vastly more proficient against spin than Australia's; their catching was flawless whereas the Australians held one chance out of five; their ground-fielding was sure while the Australians frequently fumbled; and their spinners obtained enough turn on what was otherwise a batsman's pitch to stifle the Australians after their confident start. Only in pace bowling were the Sri Lankans the lesser side on the day, and their two opening bowlers did not feature again after their first 13 overs had cost 72 runs.

The first day/night international in Pakistan was played in cool conditions, and there was no sun even in daytime. Storms the previous night were followed by rain just as Prime Minister Benazir Bhutto presented the Wills World Cup to Arjuna Ranatunga, one of the longest survivors among contemporary Test cricketers. In spite of the dampness, the Australians would have batted first in any event, but Ranatunga chose to field first in the hope of some early wickets for his seamers, and because his batsmen had shown exceptional maturity of temperament in their earlier run-chases. If his plan did not work out exactly – the hitherto impressive Vaas pitching too short – his seamers did succeed in removing Australia's best player of spin, Mark Waugh, who clipped a half-volley to square leg. But the significance of his dismissal was not apparent while Taylor and Ponting took the score to 137 by the 27th over. Then Taylor was caught sweeping at de Silva, who began his various contributions with a spell of five overs for two wickets and 19 runs.

Four overs later Ponting missed his cut at an off-break, which left Australia without a settled batsman to take on the four spinners as they tightened their grip. The balance shifted, and Australia's incoming batsmen were unable to work the ball through the gaps in the infield often enough, let alone score boundaries. After 20 overs their score was 110 for one, after 40 overs 178 for five. From the 24th over to their 49th, they did not reach the boundary except for a pulled six by Law. Whereas Taylor hit eight fours and a six, his team-mates mustered just five fours between them, as Ranatunga shrewdly kept his three off-spinners and Jayasuriya going until the end.

Given the excellence of Sri Lanka's batting, the Australians had to take early wickets and catch everything. By the sixth over they did have two wickets, Jayasuriya run out by the narrowest of margins on a TV replay, and Kaluwitharana mispulling to square leg. That, however, was the extent of Australia's catching: Law dropped Gurusinha when 53 off a straightforward pull to deep mid-wicket, and three half-chances were not taken. Considerable dew made the ball slippery, especially for the spinners Warne and Mark Waugh, and the Australians seemed to have little left in their tank for their third high-intensity game in seven days.

Gurusinha flat-batted Warne for four to long-on and for six over long-off from consecutive balls, and provided steadily accelerating support for de Silva, who began with a model on-drive for three first ball, and whipped Fleming's straight slower ball in front of square to give Sri Lanka's innings a momentum it never lost. In mid-innings he was content to push the spinners around and hit only the bad ball hard, and he made sure of his wicket, after Gurusinha was out to a wild swing and while Ranatunga was playing himself in. Just as the required rate was climbing towards a run a ball, Mark Waugh conceded 12 runs from an over, so Sri Lanka needed just 51 off their last ten overs, which became a mere ten from five. De Silva went on to score the third hundred in a World Cup final (after Clive Lloyd and Viv Richards), and finished with 107 from 124 balls, including 13 fours, a remarkable strike-rate given his certainty of application. It was the first time in six attempts that a side batting second had won the World Cup final.

While a light-hearted crowd favoured Sri Lanka throughout, no malice was directed towards the Australians, worried though they had been about repercussions from the Salim Malik affair. A well-lit and well-staged match was enjoyed by considerably more than the official capacity of 23,826 spectators. – SCYLD BERRY.

Man of the Match: P. A. de Silva. *Most Valued Player of the Tournament:* S. T. Jayasuriya.

Australia

*M. A. Taylor c Jayasuriya b de Silva	74
M. E. Waugh c Jayasuriya b Vaas	12
R. T. Ponting b de Silva	45
S. R. Waugh c de Silva b Dharmasena	13
S. K. Warne st Kaluwitharana b Muralitharan	2
S. G. Law c de Silva b Jayasuriya	22
M. G. Bevan not out	36
†I. A. Healy b de Silva	2
P. R. Reiffel not out	13
L-b 10, w 11, n-b 1	22
1/36 (2) 2/137 (1) 3/152 (3) 4/156 (5) 5/170 (4) 6/202 (6) 7/205 (8) (7 wkts, 50 overs)	241
Score at 15 overs: 82-1	

D. W. Fleming and G. D. McGrath did not bat.

Bowling: Wickremasinghe 7–0–38–0; Vaas 6–1–30–1; Muralitharan 10–0–31–1; Dharmasena 10–0–47–1; Jayasuriya 8–0–43–1; de Silva 9–0–42–3.

Sri Lanka

S. T. Jayasuriya run out	9
†R. S. Kaluwitharana c Bevan b Fleming	6
A. P. Gurusinha b Reiffel	65
P. A. de Silva not out	107
*A. Ranatunga not out	47
B 1, l-b 4, w 5, n-b 1	11
1/12 (1) 2/23 (2) 3/148 (3) (3 wkts, 46.2 overs)	245
Score at 15 overs: 71-2	

R. S. Mahanama, H. P. Tillekeratne, H. D. P. K. Dharmasena, W. P. U. J. C. Vaas, G. P. Wickremasinghe and M. Muralitharan did not bat.

Bowling: McGrath 8.2–1–28–0; Fleming 6–0–43–1; Warne 10–0–58–0; Reiffel 10–0–49–1; M. E. Waugh 6–0–35–0; S. R. Waugh 3–0–15–0; Bevan 3–0–12–0.

Umpires: S. A. Bucknor and D. R. Shepherd. Referee: C. H. Lloyd.

Leading run-scorers: S. R. Tendulkar 523; M. E. Waugh 484; P. A. de Silva 448; G. Kirsten 391; Saeed Anwar 329; A. P. Gurusinha 307; W. J. Cronje 276; A. C. Hudson 275.

Leading wicket-takers: A. Kumble 15; Waqar Younis 13; D. W. Fleming, R. A. Harper, P. A. Strang and S. K. Warne 12; C. E. L. Ambrose and Mushtaq Ahmed 10; Rajab Ali 9.

Most economical bowlers (runs per over, minimum 40 overs): B. M. McMillan 2.95; C. E. L. Ambrose 3.00; Asif Karim 3.56; P. L. Symcox 3.72; R. A. Harper and M. Muralitharan 3.77; C. A. Walsh 3.78; C. R. Matthews 3.79; S. K. Warne 3.83.

Leading wicket-keepers: I. A. Healy 12 (9 ct, 3 st); Rashid Latif 9 (7 ct, 2 st); S. J. Palframan 8 (all ct); R. C. Russell 8 (7 ct, 1 st); N. R. Mongia 7 (4 ct, 3 st). (J. C. Adams made four catches and one stumping as a wicket-keeper and added two catches in the field.)

Leading fielders: A. Kumble 8; C. L. Cairns, A. D. R. Campbell, S. T. Jayasuriya and G. P. Thorpe 5.

ENGLAND IN SOUTH AFRICA, 1995-96

It was another long and losing tour by England, their fourth in a row, and third under Mike Atherton's captaincy. But it was the first of those three in which they had gone with a fair chance of winning the Test series, which ultimately made their defeat more disappointing than the preceding reverses in the West Indies and Australia. Following their excellent summer, when they held West Indies to 2-2, England would have moved into the upper half of the unofficial table of Test-playing countries if they had beaten South Africa. As it was, they competed on more or less equal terms for the first four Tests, only to disintegrate and lose the series 1-0 and the subsequent one-day internationals 6-1.

The correlation between the length of the tour and the losing made for some debate. The United Cricket Board of South Africa had initially proposed four Tests, and nine internationals to pay the bills. The nine would have been far too many, but the extra Test was a mistake for England. Without it, their players could have had a longer rest after the most demanding home series of recent times, followed by more preparation, and need not have left until November. Instead, the TCCB successfully argued in favour of five Tests and the players left in mid-October, only to run out of steam in the second of the back-to-back Tests, at Cape Town. The South Africans, apart from Hansie Cronje, Daryll Cullinan and Allan Donald, who had been engaged in county cricket, were fresh after a six-month respite from playing, and had prepared in camps organised by their coach Bob Woolmer, with the help of numerous specialists.

The summer was the wettest in South African memory, and the series so curtailed that there were only 17 and a bit days of Test cricket out of the 25 scheduled (however, the total attendance of 249,000 was only 26,000 less than the UCBSA had budgeted for). Another consequence of the rain was that England could not keep all of their original 16 players in match practice, or sometimes even 11. This was most serious when they sent South Africa in to bat in the Second Test: only Dominic Cork was in a condition to justify a decision that went in the face of all precedent at the Wanderers. Cork was outstanding in the series as England's penetrator, always swinging the new ball away and sometimes reverse-swinging the old one in. So intense, though, were the demands on his bowling that he could not make the runs of which he was capable.

After the First Test at Centurion Park had been washed out (an unfortunate debut for the world's 76th Test ground), the dominant feature of the series was South Africa's pace bowling, which might not have matched the West Indians' for technical skill but had a vigour and often a passion of its own. Although Fanie de Villiers had a complicated hamstring injury which ruled him out for the whole Test series, and Brett Schultz broke down, having started the First Test unfit, the South Africans still had an array of high-quality quick bowlers. They enjoyed fine slip-catching support from Cullinan at first slip, Brian McMillan at second, and Andrew Hudson, who was flawless at third slip or gully. South African bowlers hit the stumps 12 times in the series, while England's bowlers did it twice, and they were Donald's stumps on both occasions. When the pitch was lifeless, and Cronje set defensive fields, his bowlers were more difficult to get away: overall England scored at 2.40 per over to the home side's 2.77.

For his bowling, Donald was chosen as Man of the Series, by a short head from several rivals. His last-wicket stand at Durban was significant too, for Atherton had secured the upper hand for England by his great innings at

Johannesburg, in the previous Test, and South Africa were wilting at 153 for nine when Donald joined his partner. That partner, 22-year-old Shaun Pollock, was the find of the series. From his debut in the First Test he immediately looked the part, and his cricket combined some of the best features of both his famous relatives, uncle Graeme and father Peter. He regularly shored up the later order with cool thirties, and bowled close to the stumps with a springy bounce and sharp pace. He bowled straight, whereas Donald, from a shortened run, bowled from wider in the crease, and angled the ball in. On the four occasions that Donald dismissed Atherton in his opening spell, England did not get beyond 200. But of all the South African players, England were most envious of McMillan, not only for the balance he gave the side but for his competitiveness.

None of these three, though, could shift Atherton and Jack Russell on the last day at Johannesburg, when their 277-minute partnership went straight into the game's folklore. Russell also set a new Test record of 11 dismissals in this match, on his way to an England record of 27 dismissals in the series (effectively, for him, four Tests); but he kept even better at Port Elizabeth. There, England had their one real chance of winning, when South Africa were 69 for six in their second innings and Cork was still inspired as he neared the end of a 20-over spell. England had continually to be aware of bowling him into the ground, but at that moment it was a risk worth taking.

Unfortunately for England, when Russell was promoted to No. 6 for the deciding Test, and for once five bowlers were selected, it was the one time he and Atherton failed with the bat in both innings – and another South African last-wicket stand prospered. Dave Richardson, who maintained his record of taking part in all of South Africa's Tests since re-admission, and Paul Adams, half his age, ended in an hour the equilibrium which had hitherto prevailed. Although Devon Malcolm was made the scapegoat for bowling too gently at Adams, England's other bowlers – and the fielders – also wilted at the crucial moment. None the less, this marked the terminal breakdown in relations between Malcolm, who believed he was being treated unfairly, and the England management, who believed he had been carrying an injury when the party was selected, and would not listen to technical advice. The slanging between Malcolm and the manager, Ray Illingworth, continued in print and led to both being hauled up before the TCCB: Malcolm was reprimanded and Illingworth fined £2,000, later rescinded. The whole business apparently hastened the departure from Test cricket of both of them.

England's batsmen arrived to much fanfare, but only Graeme Hick got on top of South Africa's bowling, and then only once, in the washed-out Test at Centurion Park. Three times England were dismissed in fewer than 70 overs, while South Africa – thin though their batting looked on paper – were never bowled out in under 100. The sides suffered from similar deficiencies, such as an opening batsman who never got going (i.e. Hudson and Alec Stewart, whose footwork became minimal); and neither had a consistent No. 3. There Cronje, like Hudson, failed against England for the second series running, not entirely at home against the short ball and perhaps – under the pressure of captaincy – too intense, like his counterpart in the first two Tests, Mark Ramprakash. It was a major mistake by England's selectors to have expected the Middlesex player, his Test average 17 after as many games, simultaneously to establish himself in the side *and* to fill the No. 3 position, when only six hundreds had been made there for England, by six different batsmen, since 1987. Adding to England's weakness at the top of the order, Graham Thorpe had to go home for a week because of his wife's ill health and never got going until Cape Town.

When John Crawley pulled a hamstring in the Third Test, Jason Gallian was flown in from the England A tour in Pakistan to try the No. 3 position, and offered studious defence. An injury which worked in England's favour occurred before the tour began, when Richard Johnson had to withdraw with back trouble. He was replaced by Peter Martin, who added a pinch of pace to his out-swing and was England's most improved player. Darren Gough, disturbed by a leg injury, never found his rhythm until the one-day internationals.

While Illingworth would have preferred warm-up matches against the stronger provincial sides on the Test grounds, the party recognised the political desirability of playing in Soweto on a new pitch, and carried out other requests by the United Cricket Board without fuss. Indeed it was a cheerful England squad, at least until the last month. The contrasting combination of the forthright Illingworth and the emollient assistant manager, John Barclay, worked very well. The mood changed even before the party was chopped around for the one-day internationals, when the wives and families flew in for Christmas and the party grew to more than 60. Illingworth believed this was highly disruptive and it was a factor in his growing disenchantment with his responsibilities. Among the 60 were the first doctor England had taken on a Test tour, the conscientious Philip Bell, and the BBC scorer Malcolm Ashton, who was controversially chosen by Illingworth ahead of any county scorer but fitted in well.

The appearance of Adams for the Fourth and Fifth Tests, and the disappearance of rain, were the sparks which the series wanted. At 18 years and 340 days, and after five first-class games, in which he had taken 32 wickets, Adams became South Africa's youngest Test player, and he was not overawed. Bending his head before delivery so that he looked down at the ground, and without any follow-through, he put enormous strain on his right knee, but his impact on the imagination was also profound. He was not only a left-arm wrist-spinner who rapidly extended his range from a stock googly to a quicker chinaman; he also heightened the interest in cricket which had traditionally existed in the Cape Coloured community, as it had among the Indians of Natal. To create from scratch an interest among the African population was the next challenge awaiting the energetic South African board. – SCYLD BERRY.

ENGLAND TOURING PARTY

M. A. Atherton (Lancashire) (*captain*), A. J. Stewart (Surrey) (*vice-captain*), D. G. Cork (Derbyshire), J. P. Crawley (Lancashire), A. R. C. Fraser (Middlesex), D. Gough (Yorkshire), G. A. Hick (Worcestershire), R. K. Illingworth (Worcestershire), M. C. Ilott (Essex), D. E. Malcolm (Derbyshire), P. J. Martin (Lancashire), M. R. Ramprakash (Middlesex), R. C. Russell (Gloucestershire), R. A. Smith (Hampshire), G. P. Thorpe (Surrey), M. Watkinson (Lancashire).

R. L. Johnson (Middlesex) withdrew through injury before the tour and was replaced by Martin. J. E. R. Gallian (Lancashire) joined the party from England A's tour of Pakistan. P. A. J. DeFreitas (Derbyshire), N. H. Fairbrother (Lancashire), D. A. Reeve (Warwickshire), N. M. K. Smith (Warwickshire) and C. White (Yorkshire) joined for the one-day internationals. Crawley and Ilott, who were injured, Fraser, Gallian and Malcolm flew home.

Tour manager: R. Illingworth. *Assistant manager:* J. R. T. Barclay. *Scorer:* M. N. Ashton. *Physiotherapist:* W. P. Morton (Yorkshire). *Doctor:* P. A. Bell.

ENGLAND TOUR RESULTS

Test matches – Played 5: Lost 1, Drawn 4.
First-class matches – Played 11: Won 1, Lost 2, Drawn 8.
Win – Border.
Losses – South Africa, South Africa A.
Draws – South Africa (4), South African Invitation XI, Free State, Boland, South African Students' XI.
One-day internationals – Played 7: Won 1, Lost 6.
Other non-first-class matches – Played 5: Won 4, Lost 1. *Wins* – N. F. Oppenheimer's XI, Easterns, Free State, Boland. *Loss* – Western Province.

TEST MATCH AVERAGES

SOUTH AFRICA – BATTING

	T	*I*	*NO*	*R*	*HS*	*100s*	*Avge*	*Ct*
D. J. Cullinan	5	6	0	307	91	0	51.16	5
G. Kirsten	5	7	1	303	110	1	50.50	2
B. M. McMillan	5	6	1	224	100*	1	44.80	5
D. J. Richardson	5	6	1	168	84	0	33.60	8
J. N. Rhodes	5	6	0	165	57	0	27.50	3
S. M. Pollock	5	6	1	133	36*	0	26.60	2
A. A. Donald	5	6	3	68	32	0	22.66	1
A. C. Hudson	5	7	1	124	45	0	20.66	7
W. J. Cronje	5	6	0	113	48	0	18.83	0
P. R. Adams	2	3	1	29	29	0	14.50	2
C. R. Matthews	3	3	0	20	15	0	6.66	2

Played in two Tests: J. H. Kallis 1, 7 (1 ct). Played in one Test: C. E. Eksteen 13, 2 (1 ct); M. W. Pringle 10*, 2; B. N. Schultz did not bat.

* *Signifies not out.*

BOWLING

	O	*M*	*R*	*W*	*BB*	*5W/i*	*Avge*
S. M. Pollock	149.5	44	377	16	5-32	1	23.56
A. A. Donald	173.5	45	497	19	5-46	1	26.15
P. R. Adams	107.1	37	231	8	3-75	0	28.87
C. E. Eksteen	63	25	88	3	3-12	0	29.33
B. M. McMillan	111.3	30	247	8	3-50	0	30.87
C. R. Matthews	81	35	165	4	3-31	0	41.25

Also bowled: W. J. Cronje 16–11–16–0; J. H. Kallis 4–2–2–0; G. Kirsten 6–4–2–0; M. W. Pringle 40–9–98–2; B. N. Schultz 16–5–47–1.

ENGLAND – BATTING

	T	*I*	*NO*	*R*	*HS*	*100s*	*Avge*	*Ct/St*
M. A. Atherton	5	8	1	390	185*	1	55.71	2
G. A. Hick	5	8	2	293	141	1	48.83	4
R. A. Smith	5	7	0	254	66	0	36.28	4
A. J. Stewart	5	8	0	235	81	0	29.37	1
R. C. Russell	5	7	2	140	50*	0	28.00	25/2
G. P. Thorpe	5	8	1	184	59	0	26.28	1
D. G. Cork	5	6	1	69	23*	0	13.80	1

	T	I	NO	R	HS	100s	Avge	Ct
A. R. C. Fraser	3	4	2	10	5*	0	5.00	0
M. R. Ramprakash	2	3	0	13	9	0	4.33	1
P. J. Martin	3	3	0	13	9	0	4.33	1
D. E. Malcolm	2	3	2	1	1	0	1.00	0

Played in three Tests: R. K. Illingworth 0, 28 (2 ct). Played in two Tests: D. Gough 0, 2 (1 ct); M. C. Ilott 0*. Played in one Test: J. E. R. Gallian 14, 28; M. Watkinson 11, 0; J. P. Crawley did not bat (1 ct).

* *Signifies not out.*

BOWLING

	O	M	R	W	BB	5W/i	Avge
P. J. Martin	105	37	218	11	4-60	0	19.81
R. K. Illingworth	90.5	27	187	9	3-37	0	20.77
D. G. Cork	189.2	48	485	19	5-84	1	25.52
D. E. Malcolm	57	13	195	6	4-62	0	32.50
M. C. Ilott	44.4	10	130	4	3-48	0	32.50
A. R. C. Fraser	66	21	187	4	3-84	0	46.75

Also bowled: J. E. R. Gallian 2–0–6–0; D. Gough 27–4–112–0; G. A. Hick 45.4–6–117–1; M. R. Ramprakash 4–0–19–0; M. Watkinson 19–3–59–2.

ENGLAND TOUR AVERAGES – FIRST-CLASS MATCHES

BATTING

	M	I	NO	R	HS	100s	Avge	Ct/St
J. P. Crawley	5	7	2	336	108	1	67.20	6
R. C. Russell	10	13	4	520	129*	1	57.77	39/5
A. J. Stewart	11	16	2	769	110	2	54.92	5
M. A. Atherton	9	15	2	587	185*	1	45.15	3
G. P. Thorpe	9	14	4	415	131*	1	41.50	3
G. A. Hick	10	14	2	456	141	1	38.00	8
D. E. Malcolm	5	6	4	62	48*	0	31.00	0
D. G. Cork	7	8	2	179	67*	0	29.83	2
R. K. Illingworth	8	6	2	112	57*	0	28.00	3
R. A. Smith	11	16	0	401	66	0	25.06	10
M. R. Ramprakash	5	8	0	183	70	0	22.87	1
M. Watkinson	5	7	0	65	26	0	9.28	2
M. C. Ilott	7	5	3	15	8	0	7.50	0
A. R. C. Fraser	5	7	2	36	15	0	7.20	1
D. Gough	5	6	0	42	26	0	7.00	1
P. J. Martin	7	6	1	34	13*	0	6.80	1

Played in two matches: J. E. R. Gallian 3, 14, 28.

* *Signifies not out.*

BOWLING

	O	M	R	W	BB	5W/i	Avge
M. C. Ilott	149.3	41	427	22	6-89	2	19.40
D. G. Cork	237.5	54	627	29	5-48	2	21.62
R. K. Illingworth	239	71	524	21	6-76	1	24.95
P. J. Martin	167.2	55	407	16	4-60	0	25.43
D. Gough	88.4	18	283	9	3-30	0	31.44
M. Watkinson	143	38	406	11	3-38	0	36.90
A. R. C. Fraser	119	32	330	8	3-49	0	41.25
D. E. Malcolm	129	24	451	9	4-62	0	50.11

Also bowled: J. E. R. Gallian 7–0–25–0; G. A. Hick 65.4–9–165–3; M. R. Ramprakash 16–3–44–1; G. P. Thorpe 4–1–15–0.

Note: Matches in this section which were not first-class are signified by a dagger.

†At NFO Ground, Randjesfontein, October 24. England XI won by 112 runs. England XI batted first by agreement. England XI 242 for five dec. (M. A. Atherton 34, A. J. Stewart 74 retired hurt, M. R. Ramprakash 48, R. C. Russell 35 not out); N. F. Oppenheimer's XI 130 (R. K. Illingworth five for 48).

†At Springs, October 25 (day/night). England XI won by five wickets. Toss: Easterns. Easterns 261 for five (50 overs) (W. R. Radford 92, M. J. Mitchley 42, C. R. Norris 32, C. Grainger 58); England XI 264 for five (49 overs) (M. A. Atherton 33, G. A. Hick 34, R. A. Smith 33, M. R. Ramprakash 89 not out).

SOUTH AFRICAN INVITATION XI v ENGLAND XI

At Soweto, October 27, 28, 29, 30. Drawn. Toss: England XI.

Following their two warm-up wins, England would probably have added a third victory if rain had not washed out the fourth day. The home side then required 380 more runs and the ball was turning a lot, though not bouncing, on a ground being used for the first time for a first-class match. On the opening day, 3,000 school-children were bused in and President Mandela arrived by helicopter during an opening stand of 163 by Atherton and Stewart. After 20 emotional minutes of introductions, Stewart went on driving until caught at long-off, but he reached a century in his second innings after spending 22 balls on 91. Crawley, brought in only when Ramprakash went down with stomach trouble, also excelled by grafting for almost five hours, in defiance of Pringle, who took a hat-trick with full-length balls. But Malcolm, remembered in South Africa for his nine for 57 at The Oval and greeted as "the Destroyer" by the President, was taken out of the match on the third morning for extra work on his action in the nets at Centurion Park. Of the township players, Masikazana made the best impression with his neat keeping and brisk hitting.

Close of play: First day, England XI 285-7 (J. P. Crawley 56*, R. K. Illingworth 11*); Second day, South African Invitation XI 209-9 (L. Masikazana 44*, H. S. Williams 1*); Third day, South African Invitation XI 25-1 (P. G. Amm 10*, M. W. Pringle 0*).

England XI

*M. A. Atherton c Rhodes b Strydom	59	– retired hurt	22
A. J. Stewart c Cronje b Strydom	94	– not out	101
J. P. Crawley c Rhodes b Davis	85	– c Rhodes b Davis	1
R. A. Smith st Masikazana b Davis	4	– c Masikazana b Pringle	0
G. A. Hick c Williams b Strydom	15	– c Masikazana b Williams	55
†R. C. Russell lbw b Pringle	11	– c Toyana b Cronje	43
M. Watkinson lbw b Pringle	0	– b Williams	26
M. C. Ilott b Pringle	0	– not out	6
R. K. Illingworth c Rhodes b Davis	19		
A. R. C. Fraser st Masikazana b Davis	6		
D. E. Malcolm not out	0		
B 9, l-b 14, n-b 16	39	B 9, l-b 5, w 1, n-b 13	28
1/163 2/170 3/179 4/210 5/250 6/250 7/250 8/312 9/325	332	1/48 2/56 3/165 4/230 5/269	(5 wkts dec.) 282

In the second innings M. A. Atherton retired hurt at 38.

Bowling: *First Innings*—Pringle 26–4–75–3; Snell 13–6–30–0; Williams 29–9–73–0; Cronje 8–3–17–0; Davis 21.4–8–68–4; Strydom 34–14–46–3. *Second Innings*—Pringle 17–2–87–1; Williams 22–5–77–2; Davis 25–8–66–1; Strydom 4–0–17–0; Cronje 12–3–21–1.

South African Invitation XI

J. M. Arthur c Russell b Ilott	1	– b Watkinson	12
P. G. Amm c Crawley b Illingworth	30	– not out	10
*W. J. Cronje b Watkinson	56		
J. N. Rhodes c Russell b Illingworth	1		
G. Toyana st Russell b Watkinson	3		
P. C. Strydom c Crawley b Watkinson	11		
R. P. Snell c Hick b Illingworth	14		
†L. Masikazana b Illingworth	44		
M. J. G. Davis c Russell b Illingworth	1		
M. W. Pringle st Russell b Illingworth	36	– (3) not out	0
H. S. Williams not out	1		
L-b 9, n-b 3	12	L-b 1, n-b 2	3
1/2 2/53 3/63 4/92 5/97 6/118 7/128 8/138 9/207	210	1/25	(1 wkt) 25

Bowling: *First Innings*—Malcolm 14–4–32–0; Ilott 14–6–41–1; Fraser 9–2–14–0; Illingworth 25.1–10–76–6; Watkinson 16–5–38–3. *Second Innings*—Malcolm 5–1–18–0; Fraser 4–2–2–0; Watkinson 3–1–4–1; Illingworth 2–2–0–0.

Umpires: M. Bagus and W. A. Diedricks.

BORDER v ENGLAND XI

At East London, November 2, 3, 4, 5. England XI won by an innings and 53 runs. Toss: England XI.

In spite of the loss of the first session and the second day to rain, England won by tea on the fourth under Stewart's captaincy – their first innings win abroad since the Christchurch Test in New Zealand in January 1992. Border's batting was minor county standard apart from two former Derbyshire players, Kirsten and Cullinan, while England's pace bowlers both swung and reverse-swung the ball on a pitch of minimal bounce. Only Ramprakash and Russell, who also kept outstandingly, batted with any fluency, but Crawley made his first hundred for the senior England team in almost six hours of disciplined shot selection. Ilott, brought in only because Thorpe had flown home to visit his wife in hospital, was the pick of the bowlers along with Cork. For Border, the slightly-built 18-year-old, Makhaya Ntini, made an impressive first-class debut by maintaining nippy speed with great heart.

Close of play: First day, England XI 218-4 (J. P. Crawley 87*, R. C. Russell 16*); Second day, No play; Third day, Border 153-6 (D. J. Cullinan 15*, I. L. Howell 5*).

England XI

J. P. Crawley lbw b Fourie	108
*A. J. Stewart c Kirsten b Ntini	11
M. R. Ramprakash c Cullinan b Fourie	70
R. A. Smith lbw b Fourie	0
G. A. Hick c Palframan b Cronje	18
†R. C. Russell c Palframan b Howell	64
D. G. Cork c and b Howell	43
D. Gough c Emslie b Ntini	7
P. J. Martin c Botha b Howell	5
R. K. Illingworth b Fourie	3
M. C. Ilott not out	1
B 1, l-b 6, w 2, n-b 12	21
1/23 2/143 3/145 4/184 5/280 6/306 7/315 8/330 9/347	351

Bowling: Fourie 30–7–75–4; Ntini 32–5–84–2; Botha 14–1–42–0; Emslie 11–2–39–0; Howell 29.1–9–58–3; Cronje 13–2–31–1; Pope 3–0–15–0; Strydom 1–1–0–0.

Border

F. J. C. Cronje c Cork b Gough	24	– lbw b Ilott	13
P. J. Botha c Russell b Cork	1	– c Smith b Cork	21
*P. N. Kirsten lbw b Ilott	53	– c Russell b Ilott	6
D. J. Cullinan lbw b Cork	20	– b Gough	55
P. C. Strydom run out	10	– lbw b Cork	3
†S. J. Palframan b Cork	21	– b Cork	10
S. C. Pope c Illingworth b Cork	1	– b Ilott	8
I. L. Howell c Russell b Gough	11	– not out	5
B. C. Fourie not out	0	– c Russell b Ilott	0
P. A. N. Emslie lbw b Gough	0	– lbw b Gough	0
M. Ntini b Cork	1	– lbw b Ilott	0
B 8, l-b 6, w 1, n-b 9	24	L-b 10, n-b 1	11
1/8 2/81 3/90 4/111 5/141 6/144 7/164 8/164 9/164	166	1/18 2/34 3/55 4/63 5/92 6/127 7/127 8/128 9/129	132

Bowling: *First Innings*—Ilott 14–4–34–1; Cork 16.3–2–48–5; Gough 12–4–30–3; Martin 7–2–23–0; Illingworth 9–4–17–0. *Second Innings*—Ilott 13.5–3–36–5; Martin 5–2–11–0; Gough 9–3–9–2; Cork 12–0–33–3; Illingworth 12–1–33–0.

Umpires: R. A. Noble and D. L. Orchard.

SOUTH AFRICA A v ENGLAND XI

At Kimberley, November 9, 10, 11, 12. South Africa A won by six wickets. Toss: South Africa A.

England's collapse to 59 for four in reply to a methodically compiled home total, and a bold decision to enforce the follow-on in extreme heat, effectively decided a hard-fought contest. The collapse was prompted by Paul Adams, an 18-year-old in his third first-class match: his second ball, to Stewart, recalled Warne's first ball in the Old Trafford Test of 1993, pitching on middle-and-leg and hitting off-stump. In his fourth over, Thorpe was caught at silly point and Hick drove back a full toss. As the novelty of left-arm googlies from around the wicket wore off, Russell hit 18 fours and got England back in the game. They still had to follow on, 162 behind, and needed some mighty hitting from Malcolm – six sixes off 45 balls – to set 148 off 43 overs. Led by their captain, Commins, with a fifty, South Africa A won with 4.1 overs to spare on an excellent pitch prepared by former Derbyshire spinner Fred Swarbrook. In the first innings, Adam Bacher – Ali's nephew – had made his second first-class hundred during a stay of 307 minutes, as he and Kallis added 181 for the second wicket.

Close of play: First day, South Africa A 325-5 (L. Klusener 19*, S. J. Palframan 12*); Second day, England XI 127-4 (M. A. Atherton 49*, R. A. Smith 31*); Third day, England XI 136-4 (G. A. Hick 23*).

South Africa A

P. J. R. Steyn c Thorpe b Gough	17	– c Hick b Fraser	16
A. M. Bacher c Watkinson b Gough	116	– c Russell b Fraser	39
J. H. Kallis b Hick	93	– c Russell b Gough	1
*J. B. Commins c Russell b Fraser	27	– c and b Fraser	54
L. J. Wilkinson c Thorpe b Malcolm	16	– not out	18
L. Klusener lbw b Gough	61	– not out	16
†S. J. Palframan c Hick b Watkinson	30		
N. Boje c Stewart b Hick	22		
S. D. Jack b Watkinson	44		
R. Telemachus not out	9		
B 16, l-b 6, w 2, n-b 11	35	W 1, n-b 3	4
1/33 2/214 3/261 4/290 5/294 6/362 7/395 8/418 9/470	(9 wkts dec.) 470	1/39 2/40 3/106 4/115	(4 wkts) 148

P. R. Adams did not bat.

Bowling: *First Innings*—Malcolm 22–3–88–1; Gough 29–6–85–3; Fraser 25–3–78–1; Watkinson 42–8–137–2; Thorpe 4–1–15–0; Hick 14–3–34–2; Ramprakash 6–1–11–0. *Second Innings*—Fraser 15–4–49–3; Malcolm 7–0–27–0; Gough 8–0–33–1; Watkinson 7.5–0–32–0; Hick 1–0–7–0.

England XI

*M. A. Atherton lbw b Klusener	53	– lbw b Jack	0
A. J. Stewart b Adams	34	– c Commins b Adams	56
M. R. Ramprakash c Palframan b Kallis	1	– lbw b Adams	42
G. P. Thorpe c Klusener b Adams	1	– st Palframan b Adams	3
G. A. Hick c and b Adams	0	– c Wilkinson b Kallis	43
R. A. Smith c Palframan b Kallis	48	– c Palframan b Telemachus	28
†R. C. Russell not out	93	– c Bacher b Boje	40
M. Watkinson b Boje	2	– lbw b Adams	2
D. Gough st Palframan b Boje	26	– c Palframan b Jack	4
A. R. C. Fraser lbw b Kallis	5	– c Wilkinson b Adams	15
D. E. Malcolm b Adams	13	– not out	48
B 14, l-b 9, w 9	32	B 10, l-b 7, w 9, n-b 2	28
1/55 2/58 3/59 4/59 5/135 6/179 7/197 8/245 9/262	308	1/2 2/97 3/101 4/136 5/183 6/210 7/217 8/233 9/250	309

Bowling: *First Innings*—Jack 10–4–31–0; Telemachus 11–2–41–0; Klusener 21–3–67–1; Kallis 15–4–32–3; Adams 28.3–9–65–4; Boje 21–7–49–2. *Second Innings*—Jack 8–0–38–2; Telemachus 7–2–20–1; Klusener 15–2–55–0; Adams 38.4–7–116–5; Kallis 17–6–25–1; Boje 28–12–38–1.

Umpires: R. E. Koertzen and D. L. Orchard.

SOUTH AFRICA v ENGLAND

First Test Match

At Centurion, November 16, 17, 18, 19, 20. Drawn. Toss: South Africa. Test debut: S. M. Pollock.

At 3.30 on the second afternoon a huge thunderstorm flooded the ground at Centurion Park, a routine occurrence in a Highveld summer, normally followed by a return to sunshine and cricket with a rapidity that astonishes those accustomed to English weather. On this occasion there was no return. It carried on drizzling, raining and sometimes pouring for the next three days. Thus England's first Test in South Africa for more than 30 years and Centurion Park's debut as Test cricket's 76th ground will be remembered unkindly. The rain delighted locals, whose primary concern was the harvest rather than the cricket, but it cost the Northern Transvaal Cricket Union an expected R500,000 profit.

The ten hours' cricket that was played did change initial perceptions of the series as England, who went into the Test as underdogs, had the better of the limited exchanges. South Africa packed their side with pace bowlers, leaving the spinner Eksteen out of their twelve, and put England in. England would have batted anyway; they thought the pitch might break up. South Africa bowled so poorly that they did not prove their strategy conclusively wrong. One of their strike bowlers, Schultz, went into the match with a buttock injury and was in pain in his first over. After the match, officials criticised everyone involved in letting him play: the player, the management team and the physiotherapist, Craig Smith, who was instructed by Ali Bacher, managing director of the United Cricket Board and a doctor himself, to concentrate on treating injuries in future and rely on specialists for diagnoses. Donald also struggled for rhythm, and the bowler of the match was the debutant Shaun Pollock, whose father Peter was convenor of selectors, and the man who had been bowling when England's previous Test in South Africa had been rained off more than 30 years earlier. The latest sprig of South Africa's most famous cricketing family belied his innocent looks and manner with the sharpness of his bowling, mostly fast in-swing, including some very well-aimed bouncers.

South Africa did have some early successes, which included Richardson's 100th Test dismissal. At 64 for three, England were in a familiar position of struggle. But Atherton played one of his most typical innings: taking all the blows, physical and otherwise, waiting for the bad ball and hitting it hard – then, having averted the crisis, getting out short of his century. Unusually, his companion in this exercise was Hick. Most of South Africa's attempts at bowling short were far less effective than Pollock's bouncer, and Hick treated them all with contempt. He hit 20 fours, several of them hooked, before reaching his fourth Test century in brilliant style.

On the second day, however, South Africa bowled more effectively and Hick was more introspective at a time when England needed him to turn control into complete command. There were only five further fours and 157 of his 392 minutes at the crease were spent adding 36 to his overnight 105. Smith, previously out of touch, batted confidently and well, and England were saved from further collapse by Russell, who played a highly effective innings. He was so determined that, even as the storm gathered and gloom descended, he was anxious to bat on, until umpire Mitchley insisted that the lightning made conditions unsafe. No one had an inkling that the game would never resume. But there was no hope at all until 2 p.m. on the last day when, after a couple of bright hours, play was about to restart. England knew they could not win, but hoped they could embarrass the home batsmen on a sweaty pitch. Just before the umpires were due to appear, it rained again and the match was abandoned. – MATTHEW ENGEL.

Attendance: 12,800.

Close of play: First day, England 221-4 (G. A. Hick 105*, R. A. Smith 1*); Second day, England 381-9 (R. C. Russell 50*, A. R. C. Fraser 4*); Third day, No play; Fourth day, No play.

England

*M. A. Atherton c Donald b Pollock	78
A. J. Stewart c Matthews b Schultz	6
M. R. Ramprakash c Richardson b Donald	9
G. P. Thorpe c Richardson b Pollock	13
G. A. Hick lbw b Pollock	141
R. A. Smith b McMillan	43
†R. C. Russell not out	50
D. G. Cork c Matthews b McMillan	13
D. Gough b McMillan	0
R. K. Illingworth b Donald	0
A. R. C. Fraser not out	4
L-b 16, w 1, n-b 7	24
1/14 (2) 2/36 (3) 3/64 (4) 4/206 (1) 5/290 (6) 6/320 (5) 7/350 (8) 8/358 (9) 9/359 (10) (9 wkts dec.)	381

Bowling: Donald 33–10–92–2; Schultz 16–5–47–1; Matthews 30–13–63–0; Pollock 29–7–98–3; McMillan 25–10–50–3; Cronje 8–5–14–0; Kirsten 2–1–1–0.

South Africa

A. C. Hudson, G. Kirsten, *W. J. Cronje, D. J. Cullinan, J. N. Rhodes, B. M. McMillan, †D. J. Richardson, S. M. Pollock, C. R. Matthews, A. A. Donald and B. N. Schultz.

Umpires: S. Venkataraghavan (India) and C. J. Mitchley. Referee: C. H. Lloyd (West Indies).

FREE STATE v ENGLAND XI

At Bloemfontein, November 23, 24, 25. Drawn. Toss: England XI.

As England had not bowled in the First Test, the tour management requested a three-day and a one-day match instead of the original four-day fixture, so that all their players could have a game. The Springbok Park pitch, however, was too true for a three-day match after it dried out. Atherton received the one ball to misbehave. Then Stewart peeled off 21 fours with pulls and drives, while Thorpe found his touch in a stay of 262 minutes. The youngest of the seven Grey College alumni in the Free State team, Hendrik Dippenaar, pulled Malcolm for six on his first-class debut, before Crawley again batted handsomely to launch England's second innings. But on the third morning they could add only 60 and let the game drift. By the time England had set the home side 311 to win, only 55 overs remained.

Close of play: First day, Free State 36-0 (D. Jordaan 20*, G. F. J. Liebenberg 12*); Second day, England XI 121-1 (J. P. Crawley 69*, M. R. Ramprakash 37*).

England XI

*M. A. Atherton c Wilkinson b Pretorius	0	– (2) c Cronje b Craven	13
†A. J. Stewart lbw b Boje	110		
M. R. Ramprakash b Craven	15	– lbw b Pretorius	42
G. P. Thorpe not out	131		
R. A. Smith c Radley b Bakkes	27	– (4) b Pretorius	0
J. P. Crawley not out	28	– (1) c Radley b Craven	90
D. G. Cork (did not bat)		– (5) not out	67
R. K. Illingworth (did not bat)		– (6) retired hurt	5
P. J. Martin (did not bat)		– (7) not out	13
L-b 2, w 2, n-b 1	5	B 3, l-b 2, w 1, n-b 3	9
1/4 2/45 3/186 4/240 (4 wkts dec.)	316	1/44 2/134 3/144 4/163 (4 wkts dec.)	239

M. C. Ilott and D. E. Malcolm did not bat.

In the second innings R. K. Illingworth retired hurt at 181.

Bowling: *First Innings*—Pretorius 17–3–79–1; Bakkes 16–3–42–1; Boje 34.5–14–91–1; Craven 15–5–51–1; Cronje 6–0–31–0; Venter 9–1–20–0. *Second Innings*—Pretorius 26–3–75–2; Bakkes 21–5–50–0; Craven 13–5–25–2; Cronje 2–0–14–0; Boje 11–3–43–0; Venter 11–3–22–0; Jordaan 1–0–5–0.

Free State

D. Jordaan c Stewart b Malcolm	52	– lbw b Ilott	3
G. F. J. Liebenberg c Crawley b Martin	30	– lbw b Malcolm	18
*W. J. Cronje b Cork	30		
L. J. Wilkinson c Stewart b Ilott	19	– lbw b Ramprakash	23
J. F. Venter lbw b Cork	4	– not out	2
H. H. Dippenaar c Stewart b Illingworth	46		
C. F. Craven c Crawley b Martin	5	– (3) not out	60
N. Boje lbw b Illingworth	45		
H. C. Bakkes not out	3		
†P. J. L. Radley lbw b Illingworth	0		
L-b 7, w 1, n-b 3	11	L-b 2, n-b 2	4
1/74 2/112 3/122 4/129 5/159 6/176 7/232 8/245 9/245 (9 wkts dec.)	245	1/9 2/29 3/106 (3 wkts)	110

N. W. Pretorius did not bat.

Bowling: *First Innings*—Malcolm 15–2–59–1; Ilott 10–1–37–1; Cork 13–2–40–2; Illingworth 19–6–50–3; Martin 12–3–45–2; Ramprakash 3–1–7–0. *Second Innings*—Malcolm 9–1–32–1; Ilott 7–3–12–1; Cork 7–2–21–0; Martin 6–0–29–0; Illingworth 7–2–7–0; Ramprakash 3–1–7–1.

Umpires: S. B. Lambson and C. J. Mitchley.

†At Bloemfontein, November 26. England XI won by seven wickets. Toss: Free State. Free State 201 for eight (50 overs) (D. Jordaan 54, N. Boje 31 not out; M. Watkinson three for 40); England XI 202 for three (41 overs) (M. A. Atherton 60, A. J. Stewart 81, G. A. Hick 31).

SOUTH AFRICA v ENGLAND

Second Test Match

At Johannesburg, November 30, December 1, 2, 3, 4. Drawn. Toss: England.

"One of the great innings of all time", in the opinion of Ray Illingworth, saved England from going 1-0 down. Others acclaimed Atherton's innings as the finest by any England captain, as he had no particular partner until Russell joined him for the last 277 minutes, whereas Peter May had Colin Cowdrey to help repulse Sonny Ramadhin at Edgbaston in 1957. Possibly only the 262 not out by Dennis Amiss at Kingston in 1973-74 was a greater match-saving innings for England.

Atherton, resolutely single-minded in any event, became even more so when he saw his decision to play four fast bowlers and send South Africa in fail badly. This was his bowlers' fault as much as his. Only Cork fired until Malcolm, who had replaced Richard Illingworth, clicked with the second new ball. Gough never got going at all and while Fraser eventually did it was not until the second innings; in the first, Kirsten had frequently clipped him off his legs, and square-cut and square-driven his maiden Test hundred. Kirsten also set an example by taking quick singles with Cronje to set South Africa going, whereas England were rudderless in their first innings once Atherton shouldered arms to a ball which just brushed his off stump. He later described his team's disintegration – to a sequence of soft dismissals in the face of some passionate and often short-pitched bowling – as "fairly unforgivable", although Thorpe did receive one of several debated decisions made by Karl Liebenberg. South African coach Bob Woolmer publicly criticised the umpiring, for which he was censured by Clive Lloyd, the referee.

England's bowlers, and Cork especially, kept a fuller length than the South Africans. This enabled Russell to take the world record for dismissals in a Test from Bob Taylor, who was at the ground. Russell took 11 catches out of 13 possible chances, all but one standing back. South Africa, in their second innings, scored so freely against defensive fields – Cullinan's dashing strokeplay was reminiscent of Kim Hughes – that they had a lead of 400 well before the third-day close. England's mood brightened a little when they realised they would not have to bat that evening, with the ball still seaming.

South Africa indeed were so cautious that they came off for light that was not unplayably bad when 428 ahead, and with 7.3 overs remaining. Shortly beforehand, McMillan had hooked consecutive balls from Malcolm for six, four and six. Next morning, they went on for 92 more minutes to add 50 superfluous runs – and it was their bowlers who had to do the batting – just so that McMillan could complete his second Test hundred, made with three sixes in all off 168 balls.

England therefore had to survive for four overs and five sessions, not two whole days, or more. They had drawn their three previous Tests, but only after batting first and banking large totals. Atherton and Stewart, in his 50th Test, were aspiring to new heights when they set out to save the game – a target of 479 was theoretical. Only a shower was forecast, and that did not materialise. What did help was that the one lively pitch of the series went to sleep once it had fully dried, and

LONGEST INNINGS FOR ENGLAND

L. Hutton	364 in 797 minutes v Australia at The Oval	1938
K. F. Barrington	256 in 683 minutes v Australia at Old Trafford	1964
C. T. Radley	158 in 648 minutes v New Zealand at Auckland	1977-78
M. A. Atherton	**185* in 643 minutes v South Africa at Johannesburg**	**1995-96**
G. Boycott	191 in 629 minutes v Australia at Leeds	1977

its numerous cracks never became influential: fortunately for England, it had been moved half a pitch width in the week before the Test to avoid the worst of them. A full house of 30,000 on the fourth day waited for England to capitulate, and by the close Atherton had lost four partners. Twice in three balls, McMillan hit the stumps with yorkers – Ramprakash beaten in an uncontrolled drive for the second time – and yet they were not scathed again in the next nine hours.

On the fifth morning Atherton took a while to return to his groove, until his feet began moving again. On 99, he forced off his body into Kirsten's hands at short-leg, and straight out again. He hooked his next ball from Donald to bring up his ninth hundred and 4,000 runs in Tests, and celebrated with rare animation, exchanging hugs with Smith. Soon after, Smith's slash was caught at third man and Russell offered a return catch to Pringle when five, which was missed. A draw was still only the faintest of hopes.

Gradually that hope grew stronger. Back home, England's supporters hung on to television and radio commentaries, if not quite as grimly as Atherton and Russell. The captain's tempo was perfect, as he did not try an uncontrolled shot, and restricted his scoring arc to his favourite areas square of the wicket, yet he put away the bad ball to the boundary 28 times to stop the bowlers getting on top. Russell took more than his share of the strike and kept reminding his captain of England's collapse in the Barbados Test of 1989-90.

Cronje made little effort to disturb the batsmen's rhythm by varying his bowlers and fields. Donald had nothing left when the third ball was taken – and certainly no time to exploit it, owing to the timing of the delayed declaration. Atherton batted for 643 minutes in all – the fourth longest innings for England – and 492 balls, Russell for 277 minutes and 235 balls. – SCYLD BERRY.

Men of the Match: M. A. Atherton and R. C. Russell. *Attendance:* 87,100.

Close of play: First day, South Africa 278-7 (S. M. Pollock 3*); Second day, South Africa 5-0 (A. C. Hudson 5*, G. Kirsten 0*); Third day, South Africa 296-6 (B. M. McMillan 76*, S. M. Pollock 0*); Fourth day, England 167-4 (M. A. Atherton 82*, R. A. Smith 11*).

South Africa

A. C. Hudson c Stewart b Cork	0	– c Russell b Fraser	17
G. Kirsten c Russell b Malcolm	110	– c Russell b Malcolm	1
*W. J. Cronje c Russell b Cork	35	– c Russell b Cork	48
D. J. Cullinan c Russell b Hick	69	– c Gough b Cork	61
J. N. Rhodes c Russell b Cork	5	– c Russell b Fraser	57
B. M. McMillan lbw b Cork	35	– not out	100
†D. J. Richardson c Russell b Malcolm	0	– c Ramprakash b Malcolm	23
S. M. Pollock c Smith b Malcolm	33	– lbw b Cork	5
C. E. Eksteen c Russell b Cork	13	– c Russell b Cork	2
M. W. Pringle not out	10	– c Hick b Fraser	2
A. A. Donald b Malcolm	0	– not out	9
B 1, l-b 14, w 2, n-b 5	22	B 5, l-b 12, w 1, n-b 3	21
1/3 (1) 2/74 (3) 3/211 (4) 4/221 (5) 5/260 (2) 6/260 (7) 7/278 (6) 8/314 (8) 9/331 (9) 10/332 (11)	332	1/7 (2) 2/29 (1) 3/116 (4) 4/145 (3) 5/244 (5) 6/296 (7) 7/304 (8) 8/311 (9) 9/314 (10)	(9 wkts dec.) 346

Bowling: *First Innings*—Cork 32–7–84–5; Malcolm 22–5–62–4; Fraser 20–5–69–0; Gough 15–2–64–0; Hick 15–1–38–1. *Second Innings*—Cork 31.3–6–78–4; Malcolm 13–2–65–2; Fraser 29–6–84–3; Gough 12–2–48–0; Hick 15–3–35–0; Ramprakash 4–0–19–0.

England

*M. A. Atherton b Donald	9	– not out	185
A. J. Stewart c Kirsten b Pringle	45	– b McMillan	38
M. R. Ramprakash b Donald	4	– b McMillan	0
G. P. Thorpe c Kirsten b Eksteen	34	– lbw b Pringle	17
G. A. Hick c and b Eksteen	6	– c Richardson b Donald	4
R. A. Smith c and b McMillan	52	– c Pollock b Donald	44
†R. C. Russell c Rhodes b Eksteen	12	– not out	29
D. G. Cork c Cullinan b Pollock	8		
D. Gough c and b Pollock	2		
A. R. C. Fraser lbw b Pollock	0		
D. E. Malcolm not out	0		
B 6, l-b 1, n-b 21	28	B 4, l-b 7, n-b 23	34
1/10 (1) 2/45 (3) 3/109 (4) 4/116 (2) 5/125 (5) 6/147 (7) 7/178 (8) 8/193 (9) 9/200 (10) 10/200 (6)	200	1/75 (2) 2/75 (3) 3/134 (4) 4/145 (5) 5/232 (6)	(5 wkts) 351

Bowling: *First Innings*—Donald 15–3–49–2; Pringle 17–4–46–1; Pollock 15–2–44–3; McMillan 10.3–0–42–1; Eksteen 11–5–12–3. *Second Innings*—Donald 35–9–95–2; Pringle 23–5–52–1; Pollock 29–11–65–0; McMillan 21–0–50–2; Eksteen 52–20–76–0; Cronje 3–1–2–0; Kirsten 2–2–0–0.

Umpires: D. B. Hair (Australia) and K. E. Liebenberg. Referee: C. H. Lloyd (West Indies).

BOLAND v ENGLAND XI

At Paarl, December 7, 8, 9. Drawn. Toss: England XI.

Russell completed an eventful week by making the highest score of his first-class career and briefly taking over the captaincy from Stewart. But apart from his unbroken ninth-wicket stand of 169 with Illingworth, which lasted until after lunch on the second day, it was such an uneventful game on a slowly turning but otherwise lifeless pitch that both teams agreed to abandon the fourth scheduled day and play a one-day match instead. The home batting was even more sluggish than

England's in the intense heat, apart from a bright fifty by DeFreitas, who had bowled eight consecutive maidens on the first day and would join the touring party a month later. Boland's innings culminated in a ninth-wicket stand which took 25 overs to make 37 runs to avert the follow-on. Hence the extraordinary yet justifiable decision of euthanasia.

Close of play: First day, England XI 263-8 (R. C. Russell 45*, R. K. Illingworth 7*); Second day, Boland 129-4 (A. P. Kuiper 2*, W. F. Stelling 0*).

England XI

R. A. Smith b Stelling	39	– (2) c sub b Willoughby	1
*A. J. Stewart b Stelling	39		
J. P. Crawley st Germishuys b Drew	6	– (1) not out	18
G. P. Thorpe c Germishuys b Drew	56	– not out	3
G. A. Hick b Henderson	32		
†R. C. Russell not out	129		
M. Watkinson c Stelling b Henderson	24		
D. Gough b Willoughby	3		
P. J. Martin c Germishuys b DeFreitas	3		
R. K. Illingworth not out	57		
M. C. Ilott (did not bat)		– (3) c Lazard b Henderson	8
L-b 8, w 3, n-b 3	14	W 3	3
1/54 2/74 3/113 4/160 5/180 6/217 7/224 8/233 (8 wkts dec.)	402	1/3 2/27 (2 wkts)	33

Bowling: *First Innings*—DeFreitas 18–10–21–1; Willoughby 21–2–78–1; Stelling 19–5–47–2; Henderson 49–17–88–2; Drew 39–4–128–2; Jackson 6–0–25–0; Kuiper 0.5–0–7–0. *Second Innings*—Willoughby 6–2–7–1; Stelling 3.3–0–18–0; Henderson 3–0–8–1.

Boland

B. C. Baguley c Watkinson b Martin	21
L. D. Ferreira b Illingworth	35
T. N. Lazard st Russell b Illingworth	37
K. C. Jackson c Crawley b Watkinson	29
*A. P. Kuiper c Hick b Illingworth	5
W. F. Stelling c Smith b Watkinson	20
P. A. J. DeFreitas c Smith b Martin	54
†L-M. Germishuys b Ilott	7
C. W. Henderson c Russell b Ilott	31
B. J. Drew not out	30
C. M. Willoughby b Ilott	11
B 5, l-b 2, n-b 1	8
1/46 2/78 3/127 4/129 5/141 6/181 7/198 8/216 9/267	288

Bowling: Gough 3.4–1–14–0; Ilott 22–8–48–3; Martin 21.2–6–48–2; Illingworth 50–16–89–3; Watkinson 38–17–82–2.

Umpires: M. Bagus and R. Brooks.

†At Paarl, December 10. England XI won by 74 runs. Toss: England XI. England XI 244 (49.4 overs) (J. P. Crawley 48, M. A. Atherton 77); Boland 170 (42.4 overs) (A. P. Kuiper 54; P. J. Martin four for 35).

SOUTH AFRICA v ENGLAND

Third Test Match

At Durban, December 14, 15, 16, 17, 18. Drawn. Toss: South Africa. Test debut: J. H. Kallis.

A promising match was ruined by a sustained cold front which brought first relief and then flooding to an area threatened by drought, but financial disappointment to the Natal Cricket Union, whose expected profit was reduced by R225,000. The pity was greater for the loss of momentum in the series following the rousing match at Johannesburg. When rain intervened for the final time after two brief sessions on the third day, England, 73 behind South Africa's 225 with five wickets in hand, held a small advantage, if only because Hick was batting with an authority no one else had managed on a true surface.

The pitch, prepared by Phil Russell, had plenty of grass, but it was dry and brown, so Cronje clearly took the right course in batting first against a completely reshaped England attack. With rare decisiveness, Ray Illingworth and Atherton decided that the ball must swing in the strong sea-breezes and humid atmosphere. Malcolm and Fraser were left out, despite having taken nine of South Africa's 19 wickets at the Wanderers between them, and so was the injured Gough. They were replaced by Ilott and Martin, and slow left-armer Richard Illingworth. Crawley was lined up at No. 3 instead of Ramprakash, but pulled a hamstring in the field, an injury serious enough to prevent him batting and to persuade the management to send for Jason Gallian. South Africa played an extra batsman, the 20-year-old Kallis, instead of the spinner Eksteen, and swapped one seamer, Matthews, for another, Pringle.

Martin's tendency to overpitch his away-swingers, a lesser evil than bowling long hops, enabled Hudson to get a flying start with flowing off-drives and cover-drives. Illingworth immediately dampened the fire when Atherton brought him on in the 16th over: he first gained, then retained the initiative through his accuracy and nice variations of flight. Switched to the Old Fort End, Martin had Kirsten caught high to the left of second slip, the first indication that the ball would bounce quite steeply off a good length. The subsequent low scoring was due chiefly to batsmen ignoring this danger and choosing the wrong balls to hit. Hudson, caught next over off a glove at silly point, was an exception, but Cronje drove to mid-on, Cullinan hit a wide out-swinger to cover, and Martin produced an especially good ball to find Kallis's outside edge. South Africa had lost half their wickets in the space of 35 runs; McMillan and Rhodes stopped the rot but, when bad light ended the first day after 64 overs, they were only 139 for five.

They were 153 for nine in the 12th over next morning, Ilott, in turn, finding some late swing to take three in six balls. But Pollock and Donald batted with the freedom of men from whom little is expected, in a forthright and attractive last-wicket stand of 72 lasting 103 minutes. Donald followed up with an admirable spell of out-and-out fast bowling to a full length, having Atherton caught low in the gully off his sixth ball and Thorpe at first slip four overs later. Stewart and Smith had to battle to get England out of the mire but two more sharp close catches off the accurate and hostile Matthews, and a typical diving effort at cover by Rhodes, reduced them to 123 for five by the close. As rain drenched the match and all who sailed in her, the referee, Clive Lloyd, was obliged to study television film of Matthews and Pollock after a newspaper report suggested they had tampered with the ball. They were rapidly exonerated. – CHRISTOPHER MARTIN-JENKINS.

Attendance: 33,600.

Close of play: First day, South Africa 139-5 (J. N. Rhodes 36*, B. M. McMillan 26*); Second day, England 123-5 (G. A. Hick 16*, D. G. Cork 10*); Third day, England 152-5 (G. A. Hick 31*, D. G. Cork 23*); Fourth day, No play.

South Africa

G. Kirsten c Hick b Martin	8	S. M. Pollock not out	36
A. C. Hudson c Crawley b Illingworth	45	C. R. Matthews lbw b Ilott	0
*W. J. Cronje c Martin b Illingworth	8	A. A. Donald b Illingworth	32
D. J. Cullinan c Smith b Martin	10	L-b 11, n-b 1	12
J. N. Rhodes lbw b Ilott	38		—
J. H. Kallis c Russell b Martin	1	1/54 (1) 2/56 (2) 3/73 (3) 4/85 (4)	225
B. M. McMillan c Russell b Martin	28	5/89 (6) 6/141 (7) 7/152 (5)	
†D. J. Richardson c Russell b Ilott	7	8/153 (8) 9/153 (10) 10/225 (11)	

Bowling: Cork 27–12–64–0; Ilott 15–3–48–3; Martin 27–9–60–4; Illingworth 29–12–37–3; Hick 2–0–5–0.

England

*M. A. Atherton c Hudson b Donald	2	D. G. Cork not out	23
A. J. Stewart c Hudson b Matthews	41		
G. P. Thorpe c Cullinan b Donald	2	L-b 4, n-b 7	11
R. A. Smith c McMillan b Matthews	34		—
G. A. Hick not out	31	1/2 (1) 2/13 (3) 3/83 (4)	(5 wkts) 152
†R. C. Russell c Rhodes b Matthews	8	4/93 (2) 5/109 (6)	

J. P. Crawley, R. K. Illingworth, P. J. Martin and M. C. Ilott did not bat.

Bowling: Donald 12.1–1–57–2; Pollock 15–2–39–0; Matthews 12–5–31–3; McMillan 9–3–21–0.

Umpires: S. A. Bucknor (West Indies) and D. L. Orchard. Referee: C. H. Lloyd (West Indies).

SOUTH AFRICAN STUDENTS' XI v ENGLAND XI

At Pietermaritzburg, December 20, 21, 22. Drawn. Toss: South African Students' XI.

After England's coach from Durban had broken down, delaying the start by 30 minutes, Ilott took four early wickets, leaving the students 23 for five. They were revived by Pothas, with an impressive maiden century, aided by Davis, who later conceded one boundary in 31 overs of off-breaks, and Boje. On the ever slower pitch Stewart was unusually patient for four hours and ten minutes, and Crawley's replacement, Gallian, who had arrived from Pakistan the day before the game, lasted for ten overs before cutting to cover. Rain resumed three overs after tea on the second day, and became torrential. Within the week more than 150 people had drowned in a township on the outskirts of Pietermaritzburg.

Close of play: First day, South African Students' XI 253-6 (N. Pothas 141*, N. Boje 42*); Second day, England XI 186-2 (A. J. Stewart 89*, G. P. Thorpe 37*).

South African Students' XI

A. Wessels c Smith b Ilott	6
*G. F. J. Liebenberg c Russell b Martin	12
M. van Jaarsveld b Ilott	2
N. Adams c Russell b Ilott	0
†N. Pothas c Smith b Watkinson	147
V. Wandrag c Smith b Ilott	0
M. J. G. Davis c Russell b Ilott	44
N. Boje c Atherton b Ilott	51
B. P. Horan not out	1
L-b 2, w 1, n-b 3	6
1/6 2/19 3/23 4/23 5/23 6/108 7/265 8/269 (8 wkts dec.)	269

J. D. Albanie and J. September did not bat.

Bowling: Ilott 24–6–89–6; Martin 11–5–33–1; Gallian 5–0–19–0; Watkinson 17.1–4–54–1; Illingworth 24–3–65–0; Hick 5–0–7–0.

England XI

*M. A. Atherton c Liebenberg b Boje	50
A. J. Stewart not out	89
J. E. R. Gallian c Wessels b Albanie	3
G. P. Thorpe not out	37
B 4, w 1, n-b 2	7
1/86 2/104 (2 wkts)	186

G. A. Hick, R. A. Smith, †R. C. Russell, M. Watkinson, P. J. Martin, R. K. Illingworth and M. C. Ilott did not bat.

Bowling: Albanie 9–2–32–1; September 12–2–29–0; Davis 31–8–43–0; Horan 4–0–11–0; Boje 13–1–45–1; Wandrag 9–2–22–0.

Umpires: S. F. Marais and R. B. Shah.

SOUTH AFRICA v ENGLAND

Fourth Test Match

At Port Elizabeth, December 26, 27, 28, 29, 30. Drawn. Toss: South Africa. Test debut: P. R. Adams.

At 18 years and 340 days, the left-arm wrist-spinner Paul Adams became South Africa's youngest Test player, after an extraordinary rise. He had taken 32 wickets in five first-class matches, including nine for South Africa A against England, with his highly unorthodox and contorted action, the left-armer's googly being his stock delivery. He was also only the second non-white to represent South Africa, following Omar Henry, and his presence delighted the most racially mixed crowd of the series, which included the St George's brass band, who played loud and lively music throughout the match.

The game itself, though not without incident, was slow, and by the end it appeared both captains considered the risk of losing outweighed the potential rewards. Afterwards, the South African press attacked England for their negativity; it was their sixth successive draw. South Africa took first possession of a pitch of slow but even bounce, better grassed than usual for Port Elizabeth. Their openers started confidently until Hudson pushed at an away-swinger from Cork and was caught behind. Cronje managed just one scoring stroke in 27 balls before lofting a drive to short cover, where Atherton took a superb catch, and when Kirsten, who hit nine fours in his fifty, edged tamely to first slip, South Africa were 89 for three. As in Durban, a good start had evaporated.

Cullinan, in excellent form, and the more cautious Rhodes stabilised the innings. Gradually accelerating, Rhodes hooked Cork for six before pulling hard and low to Smith, the only fielder covering a vast area at mid-wicket. Cullinan was heading for a century until he cut at Cork's first ball next morning, which was wide of his off stump. But McMillan and Richardson, batting fluently in front of his home crowd, continued to build a good total. Richardson's was a fluke dismissal: the ball popped off his pads and tangled in his gloves long enough for Russell to scamper in front of the stumps and take it. The England bowlers, despite losing Ilott to a thigh strain, stuck to their task, but the fielding was patchy. Six catches went down (none especially expensive), with three in one over from Illingworth.

When England replied, Pollock started with a wide, was hit for four by Stewart and then had him caught behind next ball. Gallian, who had arrived from Pakistan a week before, never looked settled and Thorpe, typically, started aggressively, then presented Adams with his first Test victim by pulling a short ball to mid-wicket. Although less of a mystery to the batsmen than he was in Kimberley, Adams bowled accurately and turned the ball enough to merit respect and gain three wickets. One of them was Atherton, who looked immovable for five hours until he was given caught behind by umpire Mitchley. Replays suggested the ball had come off the pad; Atherton looked astonished and left the crease reluctantly. Some questioned Mitchley again when he gave Hick lbw to Donald. But a sound partnership between Russell and Illingworth took England's innings into the fourth day.

Although it had taken longer than they would have liked, South Africa had a useful lead of 165. Their second innings started disastrously, however, with six tumbling for 69, despite bowling tactics seemingly geared to containment rather than penetration. Martin's first spell, seven maiden overs and two wickets, was a fine effort and Cork was magnificent, bowling 20 overs unchanged either side of lunch and eventually claiming three for nought in 17 balls. But after tea he bowled so many deliveries outside leg stump that Mitchley called a wide, arguing that the batsmen could not reach the ball. Kirsten held the innings together with his second half-century of the match, batting for 288 minutes and facing 176 balls. His partnership with Pollock, who played his normal attacking game, almost doubled the total and enabled South Africa to set a challenging target of 328 in a minimum of 99 overs.

Closing on 20 without loss, Atherton and Stewart set the scene for a promising final day. In the first hour of the morning, they advanced by 42 in 13 overs, at which point the required run-rate was 3.45. But neither side would go all out for an exciting finish. Cronje set defensive fields and England added only 18 in the next hour. After Atherton broke a long spell of slow cricket by hooking Matthews for four, he was lbw when the next delivery cut back and kept low. Stewart and Gallian continued to bat cautiously for more than two hours. It was Stewart's only substantial innings of the series, but he cut Donald to gully at the start of the final hour, just 19 short of his hundred. – COLIN BRYDEN.

Man of the Match: G. Kirsten. *Attendance:* 58,900.

Close of play: First day, South Africa 230-4 (D. J. Cullinan 83*, B. M. McMillan 3*); Second day, England 40-1 (M. A. Atherton 15*, J. E. R. Gallian 14*); Third day, England 250-7 (R. C. Russell 26*, R. K. Illingworth 25*); Fourth day, England 20-0 (M. A. Atherton 9*, A. J. Stewart 8*).

South Africa

A. C. Hudson c Russell b Cork	31	– c Russell b Martin	4
G. Kirsten c Thorpe b Ilott	51	– c Illingworth b Martin	69
*W. J. Cronje c Atherton b Martin	4	– c Russell b Martin	6
D. J. Cullinan c Russell b Cork	91	– st Russell b Illingworth	14
J. N. Rhodes c Smith b Cork	49	– lbw b Cork	0
B. M. McMillan c Russell b Illingworth	49	– c Hick b Cork	1
†D. J. Richardson c Russell b Illingworth	84	– c Russell b Cork	0
S. M. Pollock lbw b Cork	23	– c Cork b Illingworth	32
C. R. Matthews st Russell b Illingworth	15	– c and b Illingworth	5
A. A. Donald not out	12	– not out	12
P. R. Adams run out	0	– not out	0
L-b 11, n-b 8	19	B 8, l-b 7, w 1, n-b 3	19
1/57 (1) 2/85 (3) 3/89 (2) 4/207 (5) 5/251 (4) 6/326 (6) 7/379 (8) 8/408 (7) 9/426 (9) 10/428 (11)	428	1/6 (1) 2/18 (3) 3/60 (4) 4/65 (5) 5/69 (6) 6/69 (7) 7/135 (8) 8/146 (9) 9/160 (2) (9 wkts dec.)	162

[*Patrick Eagar*

Likened to a "frog in a blender" for his unorthodox action, left-arm wrist-spinner Paul Adams became South Africa's youngest Test player when he made his debut at Port Elizabeth in only his sixth first-class game.

Bowling: *First Innings*—Cork 43.2–12–113–4; Ilott 29.4–7–82–1; Martin 33–9–79–1; Illingworth 39.5–8–105–3; Hick 12–2–32–0; Gallian 2–0–6–0. *Second Innings*—Cork 26.3–5–63–3; Martin 17–8–39–3; Illingworth 22–7–45–3.

England

*M. A. Atherton c Richardson b Adams	72	– lbw b Matthews	34
A. J. Stewart c Richardson b Pollock	4	– c Hudson b Donald	81
J. E. R. Gallian c Cullinan b Pollock	14	– lbw b Adams	28
G. P. Thorpe c Rhodes b Adams	27	– not out	12
G. A. Hick lbw b Donald	62	– not out	11
R. A. Smith lbw b McMillan	2		
†R. C. Russell c Cullinan b Donald	30		
D. G. Cork c Richardson b Pollock	1		
R. K. Illingworth c Hudson b Donald	28		
P. J. Martin b Adams	4		
M. C. Ilott not out	0		
L-b 9, w 1, n-b 9	19	B 9, l-b 8, w 1, n-b 5	23
1/7 (2) 2/50 (3) 3/88 (4) 4/163 (1) 5/168 (6) 6/199 (5) 7/200 (8) 8/258 (9) 9/263 (10) 10/263 (7)	263	1/84 (1) 2/157 (3) 3/167 (2)	(3 wkts) 189

Bowling: *First Innings*—Donald 25.4–7–49–3; Pollock 22–8–58–3; Adams 37–13–75–3; Matthews 20–7–42–0; McMillan 15–6–30–1; Cronje 1–1–0–0. *Second Innings*—Pollock 10–4–15–0; Donald 19–4–60–1; Adams 28–13–51–1; McMillan 14–6–16–0; Matthews 19–10–29–1; Kirsten 2–1–1–0.

Umpires: S. A. Bucknor (West Indies) and C. J. Mitchley. Referee: C. H. Lloyd (West Indies).

SOUTH AFRICA v ENGLAND

Fifth Test Match

At Cape Town, January 2, 3, 4. South Africa won by ten wickets. Toss: England.

After clinging tenaciously on to equality with South Africa through the first four Tests, England finally fell off the precipice at Newlands, where they were beaten inside three days with what later seemed like historical inevitability. The series was won and lost on the second afternoon when 18-year-old Adams, in his second Test, shared a last-wicket stand of 73 with Richardson to turn a low-scoring match.

Adams came to the crease when South Africa were 171 for nine, just 18 ahead on a pitch that no one trusted. He had faced only 16 balls in his entire first-class career, and was up against an experienced England attack armed with the new ball. But it was England whose nerve cracked.

After a tentative beginning, helped by four overthrows, eight leg-byes and a Chinese cut, Adams was soon playing impetuously, and then imperiously. Malcolm, the man who had destroyed South Africa in the final Test of the teams' previous series, performed ineptly and appeared to bowl himself out of Test cricket. The consequences of this one hour's play were immense. England's morale fell to pieces: they were slaughtered in the one-day international series that followed, and had a dreadful World Cup; the nation went into crisis mode about the state of its cricket and Ray Illingworth got into trouble for his remarks about Malcolm and ceased to be manager. In contrast, South Africa rejoiced and began to sense it had a Test team which could be ranked near the top of the world.

Adams's involvement gave the situation added piquancy. The match had started with a special presentation to Basil D'Oliveira, the man whose exclusion from South Africa when England picked him had precipitated South Africa's long exile. And D'Oliveira was able to watch a young man from his own Coloured community and his old club, St Augustine's, become the hero of the people who would once have spurned him just because he was not white.

The pitch, prepared by the former Edgbaston groundsman Andy Atkinson, caused endless discussion and, since the game went nowhere near the distance, it remained enigmatic to the end. It was much faster than anything seen before in the series and though England chose to bat first, believing it would deteriorate, they were in trouble from the start when Atherton failed (out in the seventh over without a run on the board) and his team-mates followed.

England went into the game with their attack reshaped yet again, and a batsman light: Malcolm, Watkinson and Fraser replaced Gallian and the injured Ilott and Illingworth. South Africa went in the other direction and had only four front-line bowlers, having preferred Kallis to Matthews. Encouraged by the surface, a packed house and fielding that lived up to South Africa's best traditions, Donald was at his most formidable. The only substantial resistance came from Smith, who batted more than four hours, defying the demons that afflict him whenever he is confronted by a top-class spinner, in this case Adams.

Cork gave England a little hope with two wickets before the close and next day they hauled themselves back into the match. After Kirsten and Cullinan had put on 60, South Africa lost seven wickets for 92. Their middle order all got established but never gained control against bowlers – Martin to the fore – who used the pitch's vagaries with the traditional skills of English seamers. Then, when the teenager came to the crease, their professionalism fell to pieces.

For England, there could be no recovery from that. Second time round, Pollock was the main destroyer, but England were so shot mentally they might have been blown down with a feather. The main resistance came from Thorpe, whose innings ended in extraordinary circumstances. He attempted a single off Adams but Hudson hit the stumps with a direct throw from backward square leg. Umpire Dave Orchard turned down the appeal. But the spectators in the hospitality boxes, who all had access to TV sets, watched the replay, which suggested Thorpe should have been given out, and began baying for Orchard to change his mind.

The South African captain Cronje approached Orchard, who consulted his colleague Steve Randell and then called for the TV replay, which confirmed the majority view. In a narrow, technical sense, justice was done, but this was perilously close to mob rule. Orchard, who was not a member of the international panel and standing in only his second Test, was later quoted as saying he had momentarily forgotten the replay was available. The referee, Clive Lloyd, fined Cronje half his match fee for appealing to the replay, against ICC regulations. But he was not over-censorious and, like the South African coach, Bob Woolmer, said he thought TV decisions should be extended.

The incident can have made no difference to the result: South Africa's openers knocked off the runs with ease, leaving the huge contingent of English spectators more than two days to enjoy the beaches and a grumble. Some of the grumbling was not only about England's performance, but about the cramped and unshaded seats they were given. The main loser was probably Russell, who finished with 27 dismissals in the series and, given a full second innings, would presumably have overhauled Rod Marsh's world record of 28. – MATTHEW ENGEL.

Man of the Match: A. A. Donald. *Man of the Series:* A. A. Donald.

Attendance: 56,300.

Close of play: First day, South Africa 44-2 (G. Kirsten 15*, D. J. Cullinan 7*); Second day, England 17-1 (A. J. Stewart 4*, A. R. C. Fraser 0*).

England

*M. A. Atherton c Hudson b Donald	0	– c Richardson b Donald	10
A. J. Stewart b McMillan	13	– c Cullinan b Pollock	7
R. A. Smith b Adams	66	– (4) c Richardson b Adams	13
G. P. Thorpe c McMillan b Donald	20	– (5) run out	59
G. A. Hick c McMillan b Donald	2	– (6) lbw b Pollock	36
†R. C. Russell c McMillan b Pollock	9	– (7) c Hudson b Pollock	2
M. Watkinson lbw b Pollock	11	– (8) lbw b Adams	0
D. G. Cork b Donald	16	– (9) c Kallis b Pollock	8
P. J. Martin c Hudson b Donald	0	– (10) c Adams b Pollock	9
A. R. C. Fraser not out	5	– (3) c Adams b Donald	1
D. E. Malcolm b Adams	1	– not out	0
B 4, l-b 1, w 1, n-b 4	10	B 2, l-b 5, n-b 5	12
1/0 (1) 2/24 (2) 3/58 (4) 4/60 (5) 5/103 (6) 6/115 (7) 7/141 (8) 8/147 (9) 9/151 (3) 10/153 (11)	153	1/16 (1) 2/22 (2) 3/22 (3) 4/66 (4) 5/138 (6) 6/140 (7) 7/140 (5) 8/140 (8) 9/150 (9) 10/157 (10)	157

Bowling: *First Innings*—Donald 16–5–46–5; Pollock 14–6–26–2; McMillan 10–2–22–1; Adams 20.1–5–52–2; Kallis 4–2–2–0; Cronje 4–4–0–0. *Second Innings*—Donald 18–6–49–2; Pollock 15.5–4–32–5; Adams 22–6–53–2; McMillan 7–3–16–0.

South Africa

G. Kirsten c Atherton b Watkinson	23	– not out	41
A. C. Hudson lbw b Cork	0	– not out	27
*W. J. Cronje c Russell b Cork	12		
D. J. Cullinan c Russell b Martin	62		
J. N. Rhodes c Russell b Fraser	16		
B. M. McMillan run out	11		
J. H. Kallis lbw b Martin	7		
†D. J. Richardson not out	54		
S. M. Pollock c Smith b Watkinson	4		
A. A. Donald c Russell b Cork	3		
P. R. Adams c Hick b Martin	29		
L-b 22, n-b 1	23	L-b 1, n-b 1	2
1/1 (2) 2/19 (3) 3/79 (1) 4/125 (4) 5/125 (5) 6/144 (6) 7/154 (7) 8/163 (9) 9/171 (10) 10/244 (11)	244		(no wkt) 70

Bowling: *First Innings*—Cork 25–6–60–3; Malcolm 20–6–56–0; Martin 24–9–37–3; Fraser 17–10–34–1; Watkinson 15–3–35–2. *Second Innings*—Cork 4–0–23–0; Malcolm 2–0–12–0; Martin 4–2–3–0; Watkinson 4–0–24–0; Hick 1.4–0–7–0.

Umpires: S. G. Randell (Australia) and D. L. Orchard. Referee: C. H. Lloyd (West Indies).

†At Cape Town, January 6 (day/night). Western Province won by three wickets. Toss: England XI. England XI 196 (49.5 overs) (N. H. Fairbrother 46, C. White 46; M. W. Pringle four for 34); Western Province 200 for seven (49 overs) (F. Davids 55 not out, P. Kirsten 32 not out).

The match was arranged after the Fifth Test ended in three days.

†SOUTH AFRICA v ENGLAND

First One-Day International

At Cape Town, January 9 (day/night). South Africa won by six runs. Toss: South Africa. International debut: N. M. K. Smith.

England suffered their third defeat at Newlands in the space of a week following their three-day loss in the Fifth Test and the day/night reverse at the hands of Western Province. South Africa's win owed much to the all-round brilliance of Pollock, who first produced a run-a-ball 66 to rescue his side from 107 for six in the 31st over and then, in company with the hostile Donald, bowled nervelessly at the death. But England contributed to their own downfall, dropping Pollock on 30 and later panicking badly, losing their last seven wickets for 50. Thorpe kept the visitors' hopes alive but, when his 96-ball innings was ended by a brilliant catch in the 48th over, South Africa could start to celebrate their first ever one-day win over England, at the fifth attempt.

Man of the Match: S. M. Pollock. *Attendance:* 21,300.

South Africa

G. Kirsten lbw b Cork	8
†D. J. Richardson c Stewart b Martin	11
B. M. McMillan c Stewart b Martin	4
D. J. Cullinan c Stewart b Reeve	17
J. N. Rhodes c Stewart b White	16
*W. J. Cronje run out	24
J. H. Kallis c Thorpe b White	38
S. M. Pollock not out	66
C. R. Matthews c Reeve b Cork	10
B 1, l-b 6, w 4, n-b 6	17
1/12 (1) 2/20 (3) 3/44 (2) 4/57 (4) 5/77 (5) 6/107 (6) 7/152 (7) 8/211 (9)	(8 wkts, 50 overs) 211

A. A. Donald and P. R. Adams did not bat.

Bowling: Cork 10–0–51–2; Martin 10–1–34–2; Gough 9–0–39–0; Reeve 9–1–40–1; White 10–1–31–2; Smith 2–0–9–0.

England

*M. A. Atherton b Donald	35	D. Gough b Pollock	3
†A. J. Stewart lbw b Donald	23	P. J. Martin not out	4
G. A. Hick lbw b Donald	21	L-b 6, w 4, n-b 2	12
G. P. Thorpe c Matthews b McMillan	62		
N. H. Fairbrother c Adams b Pollock	28	1/59 (2) 2/64 (1) (49.5 overs)	205
C. White c and b Pollock	5	3/95 (3) 4/155 (5)	
D. A. Reeve c Richardson b Matthews	2	5/161 (6) 6/166 (7)	
D. G. Cork run out	7	7/177 (8) 8/189 (9)	
N. M. K. Smith c McMillan b Pollock	3	9/199 (4) 10/205 (10)	

Bowling: Matthews 10–1–39–1; Pollock 9.5–0–34–4; Donald 10–0–38–3; McMillan 10–0–38–1; Adams 2–0–18–0; Cronje 5–0–18–0; Kallis 3–0–14–0.

Umpires: K. E. Liebenberg and D. L. Orchard.

†SOUTH AFRICA v ENGLAND

Second One-Day International

At Bloemfontein, January 11 (day/night). England won by five wickets. Toss: South Africa.

Although Atherton won the match award for a well-paced 85, it was Hick's blazing half-century which set England on the road to a series-levelling win. Both sides used lower-order players – Snell and DeFreitas – to open, in the role becoming known by the baseball term "pinch-hitter" to try and hit out while the field was restricted in the first 15 overs. But Hick showed what class players could do in the circumstances, hitting Donald's first three balls for four on the way to 50 in just 33 deliveries, and easing the pressure on those who followed. England's task should have been tougher after Hudson and Snell opened with 116 in 23 overs, but containing off-spin from Hick and Smith and a later spell of three for seven from Cork meant they lost their way. In the 24th over, England's innings was halted for 45 minutes due to floodlight failure; when play resumed, Thorpe, who faced 85 balls for 72, saw his side home with ten balls to spare.

Man of the Match: M. A. Atherton. *Attendance:* 15,700.

South Africa

A. C. Hudson c Stewart b Hick	64	†D. J. Richardson not out	13
R. P. Snell c Fairbrother b Hick	63	N. Boje not out	2
B. M. McMillan b Martin	44	B 6, l-b 4, w 7	17
J. H. Kallis c Hick b Smith	29		
*W. J. Cronje b Cork	19	1/116 (2) 2/164 (1) (8 wkts, 50 overs)	262
J. N. Rhodes b Cork	4	3/197 (3) 4/226 (5)	
G. Kirsten c Fairbrother b Cork	2	5/228 (4) 6/236 (7)	
S. M. Pollock c Ramprakash b Smith	5	7/237 (6) 8/248 (8)	

A. A. Donald did not bat.

Bowling: Cork 10–0–44–3; DeFreitas 6–0–30–0; White 6–0–37–0; Martin 6–0–43–1; Smith 10–0–46–2; Hick 10–0–38–2; Ramprakash 2–0–14–0.

England

P. A. J. DeFreitas c Rhodes b Pollock	17	†A. J. Stewart not out	13
*M. A. Atherton c Cronje b Pollock	85	L-b 4, w 5, n-b 1	10
G. A. Hick lbw b Cronje	55		
G. P. Thorpe not out	72	1/37 (1) 2/108 (3) (5 wkts, 48.2 overs)	265
M. R. Ramprakash run out	1	3/198 (2) 4/200 (5)	
N. H. Fairbrother c Rhodes b McMillan	12	5/223 (6)	

C. White, D. G. Cork, N. M. K. Smith and P. J. Martin did not bat.

Bowling: Pollock 9.2–0–48–2; Snell 6–0–39–0; McMillan 7–0–46–1; Donald 10–1–44–0; Cronje 7–0–32–1; Kallis 5–0–27–0; Boje 4–0–25–0.

Umpires: W. A. Diedricks and R. E. Koertzen.

†SOUTH AFRICA v ENGLAND

Third One-Day International

At Johannesburg, January 13. South Africa won by three wickets. Toss: England.

South Africa regained the lead with a victory which was more straightforward than the margin might suggest. England were always struggling after Pollock's opening burst of three for seven in six overs, including Atherton – at the scene of his heroic Test century less than two months earlier – first ball. It took a dogged 92-ball fifty from Fairbrother, with support from Ramprakash, White and Russell, playing his first one-day international since May 1991, to usher them to respectability. DeFreitas and Gough impressed with the ball as South Africa then stuttered to 73 for four, but responsible innings from Rhodes and McMillan revived them and Pollock secured the win, along with his second match award.

Man of the Match: S. M. Pollock. *Attendance:* 28,800.

England

P. A. J. DeFreitas c Donald b Pollock	13	†R. C. Russell c Cronje b Snell	18
*M. A. Atherton c McMillan b Pollock	0		
R. A. Smith lbw b Pollock	9	L-b 7, w 7, n-b 2	16
G. A. Hick b Donald	14		—
M. R. Ramprakash c Richardson b Cronje	27	1/1 (2) 2/23 (1) (8 wkts, 50 overs)	198
N. H. Fairbrother not out	57	3/25 (3) 4/53 (4)	
C. White c Cronje b McMillan	34	5/88 (5) 6/139 (7)	
D. A. Reeve c Richardson b Donald	10	7/168 (8) 8/198 (9)	

M. Watkinson and D. Gough did not bat.

Bowling: Pollock 10–2–31–3; Matthews 8–0–34–0; Donald 10–0–53–2; McMillan 10–0–27–1; Snell 6–1–29–1; Cronje 6–0–17–1.

South Africa

A. C. Hudson b Gough	17	†D. J. Richardson not out	10
R. P. Snell c Fairbrother b DeFreitas	8		
*W. J. Cronje c Russell b DeFreitas	7	B 1, l-b 7, w 8, n-b 3	19
D. J. Cullinan c Russell b Gough	25		—
J. H. Kallis run out	16	1/19 (2) 2/29 (3) (7 wkts, 48.1 overs)	199
J. N. Rhodes c Russell b Gough	44	3/63 (1) 4/73 (4)	
B. M. McMillan c Smith b White	35	5/114 (5) 6/157 (6)	
S. M. Pollock not out	18	7/180 (7)	

C. R. Matthews and A. A. Donald did not bat.

Bowling: Gough 10–2–31–3; DeFreitas 8–0–35–2; Reeve 10–0–43–0; Hick 3–0–13–0; Watkinson 9–0–43–0; White 8.1–1–26–1.

Umpires: R. E. Koertzen and D. L. Orchard.

†SOUTH AFRICA v ENGLAND

Fourth One-Day International

At Centurion, January 14. South Africa won by seven wickets. Toss: England.

Kirsten's century, the only one of the series, ensured a comfortable win for South Africa after England failed to exploit an excellent start. With Atherton resting, stand-in captain Stewart and Robin Smith opened with 103 in 23 overs, which should have set up a massive total. But both failed to go on, and, with the middle order well shackled by Pollock and Symcox, it took a remarkable 19-ball innings from Russell, with six fours, to achieve a competitive 272. Openers Kirsten and Hudson responded with 156 in 29 overs, a South African all-wicket record against England; Kirsten, who passed 1,000 runs in his 32nd one-day international, hit 11 fours in 125 balls. Cronje, with two sixes and three fours in 46 balls, made sure of the win against an attack now looking distinctly jaded – though Thorpe had his revenge for the Cape Town run-out when he caught him on the boundary, and suggested to the umpire, who thought it was six, that he consult the TV replay. Surprisingly, he was not fined.

Man of the Match: G. Kirsten. *Attendance:* 15,900.

England

*A. J. Stewart c Cullinan b Symcox 64
R. A. Smith c Symcox b Donald 63
G. A. Hick b Cronje 21
G. P. Thorpe c Pollock b Symcox 15
M. R. Ramprakash c Kallis b Donald 32
C. White c Donald b Cronje 19
†R. C. Russell not out 39
D. G. Cork c Richardson b Matthews 0
P. A. J. DeFreitas c Cullinan b Donald . . . 2
D. Gough not out 1
L-b 5, w 10, n-b 1 16

1/103 (1) 2/139 (3) 3/168 (4) 4/174 (2) 5/216 (6) 6/245 (5) 7/249 (8) 8/260 (9) (8 wkts, 50 overs) 272

R. K. Illingworth did not bat.

Bowling: Matthews 10–0–48–1; Pollock 10–1–36–0; Cronje 10–0–57–2; Donald 9–0–72–3; Symcox 10–1–48–2; Kirsten 1–0–6–0.

South Africa

A. C. Hudson lbw b Gough 72
G. Kirsten b Cork .116
*W. J. Cronje c Thorpe b Illingworth 47
D. J. Cullinan not out 25
J. H. Kallis not out 14
W 2 2

1/156 (1) 2/223 (2) 3/247 (3) (3 wkts, 48 overs) 276

J. N. Rhodes, S. M. Pollock, †D. J. Richardson, P. L. Symcox, C. R. Matthews and A. A. Donald did not bat.

Bowling: Cork 10–0–65–1; DeFreitas 10–0–46–0; Gough 10–1–41–1; Hick 3–0–17–0; Illingworth 9–0–65–1; White 6–0–42–0.

Umpires: W. A. Diedricks and K. E. Liebenberg.

†SOUTH AFRICA v ENGLAND

Fifth One-Day International

At Durban, January 17 (day/night). South Africa won by five wickets. Toss: South Africa.

South Africa secured the series with two matches in hand, producing a superbly disciplined all-round display. In humid, overcast conditions, Donald's burst of four for 19 in 27 balls unhinged England's top order and, although Thorpe once again played fluently during a 74-ball half-century, the home side's attack, including de Villiers – recalled after a long-term hamstring injury – allowed just 12 boundaries in the innings and only 38 runs from the last 9.5 overs. Cork gave England a glimmer of hope, at nine for two, but they were made to pay for dropping both Cronje (three times) and Kallis, as the pair responded with a third-wicket stand of 118. Kallis recorded his first fifty at international level.

Man of the Match: A. A. Donald. *Attendance:* 23,300.

England

*M. A. Atherton c Richardson b Donald . . 17
A. J. Stewart b Donald 31
R. A. Smith c Richardson b Donald 8
G. A. Hick c Richardson b Donald 6
G. P. Thorpe b Matthews 63
C. White b Pollock 16
†R. C. Russell run out 21
D. G. Cork b Matthews 1
P. A. J. DeFreitas b Pollock 3
D. Gough b de Villiers 3
P. J. Martin not out 2
B 1, l-b 6, w 6 13

1/51 (1) 2/52 (2) 3/61 (4) 4/78 (3) 5/132 (6) 6/164 (5) 7/170 (8) 8/177 (7) 9/178 (9) 10/184 (10) (49.5 overs) 184

Bowling: Pollock 10–1–31–2; Matthews 10–1–37–2; de Villiers 9.5–0–35–1; Donald 10–0–41–4; McMillan 8–0–25–0; Cronje 2–0–8–0.

South Africa

A. C. Hudson lbw b Cork	5	S. M. Pollock not out	1
G. Kirsten c Russell b Cork	0	L-b 1, w 3, n-b 4	8
*W. J. Cronje b White	78		—
J. H. Kallis c Hick b DeFreitas	67	1/1 (2) 2/9 (1) (5 wkts, 48.2 overs)	185
B. M. McMillan c Hick b DeFreitas	14	3/127 (4) 4/150 (5)	
J. N. Rhodes not out	12	5/183 (3)	

†D. J. Richardson, P. S. de Villiers, C. R. Matthews and A. A. Donald did not bat.

Bowling: Martin 10–2–34–0; Cork 9.2–3–29–2; DeFreitas 9–0–41–2; Gough 10–0–32–0; White 8–1–40–1; Hick 2–0–8–0.

Umpires: W. A. Diedricks and D. L. Orchard.

†SOUTH AFRICA v ENGLAND

Sixth One-Day International

At East London, January 19 (day/night). South Africa won by 14 runs. Toss: South Africa. International debut: L. Klusener.

South Africa's growing self-belief, set against England's increasing lack of it, saw the home side defend a modest 129 on a sub-standard pitch. The ground authority, Border, was later fined R5,000 (£914) by the United Cricket Board. At 75 for three, Atherton's men looked on course for victory against a team which had rested Donald and lost Rhodes and Richardson through injury; Richardson's broken left index finger kept him out of the World Cup. But when Adams removed Hick – through a doubtful catch by substitute keeper Kirsten – and, after a wide, Thorpe, England self-destructed, losing their last seven for 40 in 16 overs. Earlier, McMillan's 92-ball innings showed once again why the tourists regarded him so highly, and his partnership with de Villiers proved crucial. For England, Gough exploited the low, seaming conditions expertly, giving Natal's Klusener, who was out third ball, a debut to forget.

Man of the Match: P. R. Adams. *Attendance:* 14,400.

South Africa

G. Kirsten c Smith b Cork	17	P. S. de Villiers b White	15
R. P. Snell c Atherton b Martin	8	P. R. Adams b Cork	0
*W. J. Cronje b White	13		
J. H. Kallis lbw b Martin	0	B 1, l-b 11, w 1, n-b 2	15
B. M. McMillan not out	45		—
J. N. Rhodes c Gough b Illingworth	10	1/25 (1) 2/29 (2) 3/29 (4) (41.4 overs)	129
L. Klusener lbw b Gough	0	4/54 (3) 5/89 (6) 6/89 (7)	
S. M. Pollock b Gough	6	7/98 (8) 8/98 (9)	
†D. J. Richardson lbw b Gough	0	9/128 (10) 10/129 (11)	

Bowling: Cork 8.4–1–22–2; Martin 7–0–23–2; Gough 10–1–25–3; White 7–1–18–2; Illingworth 9–1–29–1.

England

*M. A. Atherton c Richardson b de Villiers	6	D. Gough lbw b Snell	4
C. White c Richardson b de Villiers	6	P. J. Martin not out	5
R. A. Smith b Pollock	0		
G. A. Hick c Kirsten b Adams	39	B 1, l-b 13, w 12, n-b 1	27
†R. C. Russell run out	12		—
G. P. Thorpe b Adams	0	1/10 (2) 2/11 (3) 3/19 (1) (43.4 overs)	115
N. H. Fairbrother b Snell	13	4/75 (4) 5/76 (6) 6/78 (5)	
D. G. Cork b Adams	2	7/88 (8) 8/95 (9)	
R. K. Illingworth run out	1	9/104 (10) 10/115 (7)	

Bowling: Pollock 10–3–15–1; de Villiers 8–1–10–2; Klusener 4–0–19–0; Snell 9.4–2–22–2; Kallis 3–0–9–0; Adams 9–1–26–3.

Umpires: C. J. Mitchley and D. L. Orchard.

†SOUTH AFRICA v ENGLAND

Seventh One-Day International

At Port Elizabeth, January 21. South Africa won by 64 runs. Toss: South Africa. International debut: S. J. Palframan.

South Africa completed a 6-1 series victory with a win which illustrated England's collective loss of batting form. Facing a modest total, this time on a good pitch, and with Donald still resting, they were never in touch. Led by de Villiers and Symcox, South Africa bowled with their usual commendable discipline. Cronje and Hudson had given them the ideal launch pad for a large score, but Gough – on a hat-trick in his last over and once again England's outstanding bowler – and White pegged them back and they made just 49 in their last ten overs. It required 61 in 65 balls from Kuiper, much of it with a runner after he strained a hamstring in his only game of the series, to get them to 218. This eventually proved more than enough.

Man of the Match: A. P. Kuiper. *Man of the Series:* S. M. Pollock. *Attendance:* 17,300.

South Africa

A. C. Hudson c Thorpe b White	44
†S. J. Palframan c Russell b Martin	10
G. Kirsten c Russell b Gough	17
*W. J. Cronje c Hick b Martin	60
A. P. Kuiper not out	61
J. H. Kallis run out	2
B. M. McMillan b White	4
S. M. Pollock c Thorpe b Gough	0
P. L. Symcox b Gough	7
P. S. de Villiers b Gough	0
P. R. Adams not out	0
B 1, l-b 7, w 5	13
1/30 (2) 2/61 (3) 3/123 (1) 4/167 (4) 5/172 (6) 6/195 (7) 7/196 (8) 8/206 (9) 9/206 (10)	(9 wkts, 50 overs) 218

Bowling: Cork 10–0–53–0; Martin 9–0–47–2; Gough 10–0–33–4; Illingworth 10–1–31–0; Hick 4–0–19–0; White 7–0–27–2.

England

*M. A. Atherton c McMillan b Pollock	3
C. White c sub (A. A. Donald) b de Villiers	20
R. A. Smith c Palframan b McMillan	21
G. A. Hick b Symcox	43
N. H. Fairbrother b McMillan	0
G. P. Thorpe b Adams	21
†R. C. Russell c McMillan b Symcox	3
D. G. Cork lbw b de Villiers	21
P. J. Martin c Symcox b de Villiers	6
D. Gough b de Villiers	4
R. K. Illingworth not out	2
B 1, l-b 5, w 2, n-b 2	10
1/5 (1) 2/35 (2) 3/70 (3) 4/70 (5) 5/113 (4) 6/118 (6) 7/124 (7) 8/147 (9) 9/151 (8) 10/154 (10)	(46.1 overs) 154

Bowling: de Villiers 9.1–1–32–4; Pollock 6–1–17–1; Cronje 4–0–17–0; McMillan 8–0–29–2; Symcox 10–0–31–2; Adams 9–1–22–1.

Umpires: R. E. Koertzen and C. J. Mitchley. Series referee: C. W. Smith (West Indies).

ENGLAND A IN PAKISTAN, 1995-96

By MARK BALDWIN

A young and energetic side, under Nasser Hussain, built on England A's growing reputation overseas with a 1-0 victory in the unofficial Test series against Pakistan A, and a 2-1 win in the one-day international series which concluded a two-month tour. Their success followed a 3-0 Test win in India the previous winter; on their last three tours, England A teams have lost just one first-class match – against Natal in January 1994.

England's last Test tour to Pakistan was the infamous 1987-88 trip, which descended into chaos and acrimony, epitomised by the captain Mike Gatting's unseemly clash with Pakistani umpire Shakoor Rana. England A had previously visited in January 1991, but were forced to switch to Sri Lanka after a fortnight because of the outbreak of the Gulf War, though the Under-19 side toured safely the following year. Bridge-building was thus an important object, and a great deal of good was done – the English team were looked after well and both countries benefited from a welcome lack of on-field controversy.

John Emburey, on his first tour in charge, made himself a respected and popular cricket manager. It was a crash course in organisational skills and man-management, and he learned fast. Hussain and Jason Gallian, who was later summoned by the Test side, took the batting honours; Nick Knight did his own international ambitions no harm in foreign conditions which forced all the Englishmen to adapt and learn. Leg-spinner Ian Salisbury, like those three a Test player already, showed his growing maturity, with 20 first-class wickets at 20 runs apiece, but it was Kent seamer Dean Headley, a late addition to the tour party, who grabbed top billing in Emburey's final report.

Headley, who was called up only when Peter Martin replaced the injured Richard Johnson on the senior trip to South Africa, grabbed his chance with a mixture of delight and "I'll show 'em" determination. Mike Smith's early-tour rib injury gave him an even clearer run and Headley became a willing focal point of Hussain's strategy in the field – to starve Pakistan's strokemakers of scoring opportunities and wait for them to make mistakes on predominantly slow, low pitches. Hussain needed bowlers with consistency of line and length, good temperament, and the ability to keep going for long spells. In all three areas Headley was outstanding. He kept a tight off-stump line for over after over, moving the ball occasionally both ways and often hurrying the batsman with the deceptive pace his natural athleticism and rhythm generated. In four first-class games Headley delivered 176.2 overs, 42 of them maidens, and took 25 wickets at only 15.36. After Salisbury had destroyed Pakistan A's first innings at Multan, it was Headley and slow left-arm spinner Richard Stemp who combined to finish them off second time around and give England the victory which eventually clinched the series. But Headley was even more impressive in the Second and Third unofficial Tests, taking six for 73 at Rawalpindi and five for 109 at Peshawar to underline his sudden emergence, at the age of 25, as a fast bowler of class.

Other highlights for the tourists included Anthony McGrath's maiden first-class hundred in Lahore, a century of character from Jason Pooley, which ended a poor trot, and the previously underemployed Dominic Ostler's invaluable 68 in the Peshawar Test.

The experienced Asif Mujtaba apart, the young Pakistani batsmen seemed largely unable to cope with the extra know-how and professionalism of the England bowlers. Hussain's insistence on a disciplined, aggressive and committed approach in the field also built pressure – but the home batsmen were not short of strokeplaying talent, and they will also have learned much. Teenage seamer Shahid Nazir ended the series strongly, while all-rounder Azhar Mahmood, not picked until the one-day games, displayed promise. Left-arm pace bowler Kabir Khan was rated highly by England – and the general quality of the cricket played makes Pakistan a tough test for any visiting side.

Yet, behind the welcome success of the tour both on and off the field, there was a major flaw which made it one of the least useful of the seven England A ventures since 1990. Too many players returned complaining, with ample justification, of too little cricket. This side of the tour was summed up on the fourth day of the Rawalpindi Test; Salisbury made a fine 86 as night-watchman in a partnership with Gallian that lasted 74 overs – yet most of his batting team-mates were cursing, because of the lack of opportunity that it left them.

When Hussain's squad set out, their itinerary promised 32 days' cricket out of 55 on the tour, which was hardly enough; in the end they lost about a third of that. Winning in just over three days in Multan did not help, of course, but the problems were foreseeable. Bad light and rain plagued the second month of the tour, but only because the players headed ever further north as winter approached. Ideally, the team should have warmed up in Islamabad and then played their later, most important, matches in the south. The result of this inactivity, for England, was too much time in hotel rooms and not enough on the field. Hampshire off-spinner Shaun Udal, for instance, bowled only 66 first-class overs on tour – 39 of them in the first match. Several other players had similar frustrations. Future A tours must pack in as much cricket as possible. Rest days have to feature in any itinerary, but these players were young, fit, enthusiastic and hungry for cricket. It is up to the administrators not to sell them short.

ENGLAND A TOURING PARTY

N. Hussain (Essex) (*captain*), J. E. R. Gallian (Lancashire), E. S. H. Giddins (Sussex), D. W. Headley (Kent), R. C. Irani (Essex), N. V. Knight (Warwickshire), A. McGrath (Yorkshire), D. P. Ostler (Warwickshire), K. J. Piper (Warwickshire), J. C. Pooley (Middlesex), I. D. K. Salisbury (Sussex), A. M. Smith (Gloucestershire), R. D. Stemp (Yorkshire), S. D. Udal (Hampshire), C. White (Yorkshire).

Pooley was included after A. Symonds (Gloucestershire) declined to tour and Headley after P. J. Martin (Lancashire) was promoted to the England tour of South Africa. T. A. Munton (Warwickshire) replaced Smith, who flew home injured.

Tour manager: The Rev. M. D. Vockins (Worcestershire). *Cricket manager:* J. E. Emburey (Middlesex). *Physiotherapist:* D. O. Conway (Glamorgan).

ENGLAND A TOUR RESULTS

First-class matches – Played 6: Won 3, Drawn 3.
Wins – Combined XI, PCB Combined XI, Pakistan A.
Draws – PCB Patron's XI, Pakistan A (2).
Other non-first-class matches – Played 5: Won 4, Lost 1. *Wins* – Pakistan Cricket Board XI (2), Pakistan A (2). *Loss* – Pakistan A.

ENGLAND A AVERAGES – FIRST-CLASS MATCHES

BATTING

	M	*I*	*NO*	*R*	*HS*	*100s*	*Avge*	*Ct*
J. E. R. Gallian	5	7	0	376	153	1	53.71	5
N. Hussain	6	8	1	370	89	0	52.85	5
N. V. Knight	6	9	1	350	107	1	43.75	8
J. C. Pooley	5	8	3	182	100*	1	36.40	1
R. C. Irani	4	6	1	170	58	0	34.00	3
C. White	4	6	2	105	37*	0	26.25	1
I. D. K. Salisbury	5	6	0	152	86	0	25.33	5
A. McGrath	5	8	1	163	103	1	23.28	7
S. D. Udal	3	5	1	91	50	0	22.75	2
D. P. Ostler	3	6	0	106	68	0	17.66	5
K. J. Piper	5	7	1	104	46	0	17.33	20
D. W. Headley	4	4	2	25	13	0	12.50	0
E. S. H. Giddins	3	3	2	5	5*	0	5.00	0

Played in four matches: R. D. Stemp 14*, 1 (2 ct). Played in two matches: A. M. Smith 0; T. A. Munton did not bat.

** Signifies not out.*

BOWLING

	O	*M*	*R*	*W*	*BB*	*5W/i*	*Avge*
T. A. Munton	67.5	25	116	9	5-54	1	12.88
R. C. Irani	50.5	12	111	8	5-19	1	13.87
D. W. Headley	176	42	384	25	6-73	4	15.36
I. D. K. Salisbury	140.1	21	413	20	6-39	1	20.65
R. D. Stemp	95.5	29	230	11	5-64	1	20.90
E. S. H. Giddins	102	25	223	10	5-104	1	22.30
C. White	63.3	11	215	7	3-74	0	30.71

Also bowled: J. E. R. Gallian 15–5–32–0; A. McGrath 7–1–14–0; A. M. Smith 22.1–7–68–0; S. D. Udal 66–12–179–3.

Note: Matches in this section which were not first-class are signified by a dagger.

†At Karachi (Defence Stadium), November 1. England A won by six wickets. Toss: England A. Pakistan Cricket Board XI 191 for nine (50 overs) (Shahid Anwar 84 not out, Manzoor Akhtar 42; C. White three for 36); England A 192 for four (50 overs) (N. V. Knight 78, N. Hussain 60).

Transferred to the Defence Stadium from the National Stadium in Karachi because of political unrest and World Cup preparations. White fractured his right thumb attempting a catch. England A won off the final ball.

†At Thatta, November 3. England A won by seven runs. Toss: Pakistan Cricket Board XI. England A 168 (44.3 overs) (A. McGrath 34, N. Hussain 64; Kabir Khan four for 20); Pakistan Cricket Board XI 161 (43.4 overs) (Mohammad Ramzan 34).

Reduced to 45 overs because the pitch was damp. Kabir Khan finished England A's innings with four wickets in six balls.

COMBINED XI v ENGLAND A

At Karachi (Defence Stadium), November 5, 6, 7, 8. England A won by six wickets. Toss: Combined XI.

Eight wickets from Salisbury kicked off his fourth A tour in style, but it was Irani's third-day spell of five for 14 which finally swung the match England's way. Even then, they wobbled. Opener Mohammad Ramzan had carried his bat for more than six hours in a dedicated and defiant 121, enabling the home team to leave a target of 116, which looked trickier at 18 for three. Knight's unbeaten 71 soothed the nerves and, with McGrath, he completed the job. Knight and McGrath also launched England's first innings with a solid opening stand. That was followed up by a classy 89 from Hussain and a determined 50 from Udal, who dominated a useful last-wicket stand of 36 with Giddins. Giddins had enjoyed a good opening day, with three wickets, but his new-ball partner Smith only managed 37 deliveries in the match after suffering a side strain.

Close of play: First day, England A 47-0 (N. V. Knight 20*, A. McGrath 25*); Second day, England A 279-9 (S. D. Udal 26*, E. S. H. Giddins 0*); Third day, Combined XI 211-9 (Mohammad Ramzan 111*, Taufiq Badar 4*).

Combined XI

Mohammad Ramzan b Giddins	3	– not out	121
Shahid Anwar c Pooley b Salisbury	15	– c Ostler b Udal	34
*Shoaib Mohammad c Piper b Giddins	40	– c Ostler b Salisbury	7
Azam Khan c Knight b Udal	55	– (5) c Piper b Irani	15
Sohail Jaffer c McGrath b Irani	19	– (4) lbw b Salisbury	0
Mahmood Hamid c Knight b Salisbury	30	– lbw b Irani	20
†Wasim Yousufi c Salisbury b Giddins	1	– lbw b Irani	1
Nadeem Khan c Piper b Irani	10	– (9) c Piper b Irani	0
Shahid Afridi c Irani b Salisbury	11	– (10) b Salisbury	1
Athar Laeeq not out	4	– (8) c Piper b Irani	0
Taufiq Badar c and b Salisbury	0	– c Ostler b Salisbury	5
B 2, l-b 10, n-b 4	16	B 11, l-b 4, w 2, n-b 2	19
1/17 2/25 3/108 4/140 5/146 6/165 7/188 8/188 9/201	204	1/53 2/89 3/89 4/135 5/171 6/175 7/179 8/183 9/195	223

Bowling: *First Innings*—Giddins 15–6–27–3; Smith 3.1–1–7–0; Irani 10.5–1–43–2; Salisbury 23–3–72–4; Udal 14–4–38–1; McGrath 2–0–5–0. *Second Innings*—Giddins 22–7–34–0; Smith 3–0–11–0; Udal 25–4–70–1; Salisbury 23–3–74–4; Irani 14–3–19–5.

England A

N. V. Knight c Mahmood Hamid b Shahid Afridi	36	– not out	71
A. McGrath c Wasim Yousufi b Nadeem Khan	30	– (6) not out	21
*N. Hussain lbw b Shahid Afridi	89		
D. P. Ostler lbw b Shahid Afridi	0	– (3) lbw b Athar Laeeq	1
J. C. Pooley b Athar Laeeq	19	– (2) c Wasim Yousufi b Athar Laeeq	2
R. C. Irani lbw b Shahid Afridi	22	– (5) c Shahid Afridi b Nadeem Khan	14
†K. J. Piper c Sohail Jaffer b Shoaib Mohammad	6	– (4) lbw b Nadeem Khan	3
I. D. K. Salisbury b Taufiq Badar	27		
S. D. Udal c Shahid Anwar b Nadeem Khan	50		
A. M. Smith c and b Taufiq Badar	0		
E. S. H. Giddins not out	5		
B 10, l-b 7, w 4, n-b 7	28	B 1, l-b 2, n-b 1	4
1/67 2/103 3/103 4/141 5/188 6/199 7/227 8/272 9/276	312	1/9 2/13 3/18 4/56	(4 wkts) 116

Bowling: *First Innings*—Athar Laeeq 31–10–68–1; Taufiq Badar 16–4–41–2; Shahid Afridi 30–8–72–4; Nadeem Khan 41.2–12–95–2; Shoaib Mohammad 8–0–19–1. *Second Innings*—Athar Laeeq 9–3–18–2; Shahid Anwar 4–1–6–0; Nadeem Khan 17.4–2–52–2; Shoaib Mohammad 2–0–9–0; Shahid Afridi 12–2–28–0.

Umpires: Islam Khan and Salim Badar.

PCB COMBINED XI v ENGLAND A

At Lahore (Bagh-i-Jinnah), November 11, 12, 13, 14. England A won by eight wickets. Toss: PCB Combined XI.

England's bowlers had to work hard on the first day, when watchful fifties from Adil Nisar and Shadab Kabir were followed by a powerful hundred from Saeed Azad, with 19 fours and a six. Headley had struck in each of his first three spells and next morning combined with White to blitz the lower order. England's reply was based on fine batting by Gallian and Hussain and sustained by a maiden century of distinction from 20-year-old McGrath, in only his seventh first-class match. McGrath displayed good temperament as well as ability. He was 56 when the ninth wicket fell, but accelerated excitingly to reach 103, with two sixes and 11 fours. His Yorkshire colleague Stemp supported him gamely in a last-wicket stand which put on 64 to earn a 54-run lead. After some early wickets from Headley, Stemp and Salisbury wrapped up the home side for 153 and a belligerent 53 off 63 balls from Irani took England A to their target.

Close of play: First day, PCB Combined XI 259-4 (Saeed Azad 96*, Wajahatullah Wasti 20*); Second day, England A 199-5 (A. McGrath 26*, C. White 1*); Third day, PCB Combined XI 67-4 (Adil Nisar 29*).

PCB Combined XI

Javed Sami c Gallian b Headley	11	– c Knight b Headley	3
Adil Nisar c Piper b Headley	57	– c sub (D. P. Ostler) b Headley	29
Shadab Kabir c Knight b Headley	61	– c Knight b Headley	2
Saeed Azad c Piper b Headley	117	– b Stemp	21
*Aamer Hanif c Stemp b Irani	0	– c Hussain b Salisbury	10
Wajahatullah Wasti c Stemp b Headley	27	– c Piper b Stemp	22
†Majid Inayat c Irani b White	6	– c Hussain b Stemp	16
Iftikhar Asghar c Knight b White	6	– b Salisbury	35
Fahad Khan c Piper b White	0	– not out	4
Shoaib Akhtar run out	0	– b Stemp	0
Mubashir Nazir not out	0	– lbw b Salisbury	1
B 8, l-b 3, n-b 5	16	L-b 8, n-b 2	10
1/22 2/109 3/198 4/205 5/272 6/279 7/289 8/289 9/301	301	1/4 2/6 3/40 4/67 5/72 6/99 7/148 8/148 9/148	153

Bowling: *First Innings*—Headley 27.2–6–68–5; White 19–2–74–3; Stemp 27–5–76–0; Irani 11–2–26–1; Salisbury 7–1–37–0; McGrath 5–1–9–0. *Second Innings*—Headley 12–1–33–3; White 8–1–30–0; Stemp 17–6–46–4; Irani 2–1–5–0; Salisbury 11.4–3–31–3.

England A

N. V. Knight c Wajahatullah Wasti b Shoaib Akhtar	1	– b Fahad Khan	19
J. E. R. Gallian c Shoaib Akhtar b Fahad Khan	67		
*N. Hussain c Iftikhar Asghar b Mubashir Nazir	83		
A. McGrath b Aamer Hanif	103		
J. C. Pooley b Mubashir Nazir	0	– (2) c Adil Nisar b Mubashir Nazir	2
R. C. Irani lbw b Iftikhar Asghar	12	– (3) not out	53
C. White lbw b Fahad Khan	21	– (4) not out	15
†K. J. Piper c Iftikhar Asghar b Fahad Khan	14		
I. D. K. Salisbury c Aamer Hanif b Mubashir Nazir	18		
D. W. Headley b Mubashir Nazir	0		
R. D. Stemp not out	14		
B 5, l-b 7, n-b 10	22	B 1, l-b 4, n-b 6	11
1/8 2/125 3/168 4/168 5/190 6/233 7/257 8/291 9/291	355	1/5 2/46	(2 wkts) 100

Bowling: *First Innings*—Shoaib Akhtar 17–0–92–1; Mubashir Nazir 20.5–7–51–4; Fahad Khan 37–4–111–3; Iftikhar Asghar 39.1–11–82–1; Wajahatullah Wasti 1–0–5–0; Aamer Hanif 4.5–3–2–1. *Second Innings*—Mubashir Nazir 6–2–13–1; Shoaib Akhtar 5–1–20–0; Aamer Hanif 1–0–8–0; Fahad Khan 6.4–0–37–1; Iftikhar Asghar 6–1–17–0.

Umpires: Azhar Hassan and Mohammad Iqbal.

PAKISTAN v ENGLAND A

First Unofficial Test

At Multan, November 17, 18, 19, 20. England A won by an innings and 43 runs. Toss: Pakistan A.

A young and largely inexperienced home side could not live with a determined England A, led uncompromisingly by Hussain. They succumbed by an innings with more than five sessions to spare. Salisbury ripped apart Pakistan A's first innings with an impressive spell of attacking leg-spin. He took six for 39 as they tumbled to 137 all out soon after tea, though credit was due too to Headley and Giddins for hostile and stiflingly accurate seam bowling in largely unhelpful conditions. Positive innings from the tourists' upper order – especially Irani, who struck two sixes and eight fours, and a valuable 46 from Piper – ensured a winning total of 327. Pakistan A needed 190 to make the English bat again and, by the close of the third day, were down and out at 115 for five. Only their captain, Asif Mujtaba, showed the necessary willpower to resist. He was last out after nearly four and a half hours. Headley's final figures of five for 34 from 26 overs, despite a stomach upset, testified to his control; the other five went to Stemp, whose competitive nature meant the Pakistanis were never let off the hook.

Close of play: First day, England A 15-0 (N. V. Knight 10*, J. E. R. Gallian 5*); Second day, England A 285-6 (K. J. Piper 23*, I. D. K. Salisbury 4*); Third day, Pakistan A 115-5 (Asif Mujtaba 36*, Akram Raza 15*).

Pakistan A

Mohammad Ramzan lbw b Giddins	4	– c Piper b Headley	12
Shahid Anwar c White b Salisbury	50	– lbw b Stemp	30
Shadab Kabir c McGrath b Giddins	0	– lbw b Headley	1
*Asif Mujtaba c McGrath b Salisbury	29	– c Salisbury b Stemp	57
Saeed Azad c McGrath b Salisbury	16	– b Headley	10
Naveed Rana run out	11	– c Piper b Stemp	3
Akram Raza b Headley	5	– c Gallian b Stemp	17
†Wasim Yousufi c Irani b Salisbury	7	– c Piper b Stemp	3
Nadeem Khan c and b Salisbury	0	– lbw b Headley	0
Kabir Khan c Knight b Salisbury	5	– c Hussain b Headley	0
Mohammad Zahid not out	1	– not out	2
B 4, l-b 2, n-b 3	9	B 6, l-b 4, n-b 2	12
1/16 (1) 2/16 (3) 3/63 (4) 4/84 (5) 5/104 (6) 6/117 (7) 7/120 (2) 8/120 (9) 9/126 (10) 10/137 (8)	137	1/18 (1) 2/26 (3) 3/64 (2) 4/82 (5) 5/98 (6) 6/130 (7) 7/136 (8) 8/137 (9) 9/137 (10) 10/147 (4)	147

Bowling: *First Innings*—Headley 22–9–29–1; Giddins 16–4–43–2; White 4–3–14–0; Irani 3–2–2–0; Salisbury 17.3–4–39–6; Stemp 2–0–4–0. *Second Innings*—Headley 26–11–34–5; Giddins 10–3–15–0; Salisbury 8–0–17–0; Stemp 26.5–8–64–5; Irani 5–2–7–0.

England A

N. V. Knight c Wasim Yousufi b Asif Mujtaba	46
J. E. R. Gallian b Asif Mujtaba	62
*N. Hussain c Akram Raza b Naveed Rana	52
A. McGrath c Wasim Yousufi b Akram Raza	0
R. C. Irani b Mohammad Zahid	58
C. White lbw b Kabir Khan	19
†K. J. Piper c Shadab Kabir b Mohammad Zahid	46
I. D. K. Salisbury b Mohammad Zahid	8
R. D. Stemp b Kabir Khan	1
D. W. Headley b Mohammad Zahid	13
E. S. H. Giddins not out	0
B 2, l-b 6, n-b 14	22
1/119 (2) 2/120 (1) 3/121 (4) 4/213 (3) 5/234 (5) 6/274 (6) 7/291 (8) 8/292 (9) 9/324 (7) 10/327 (10)	327

Bowling: Kabir Khan 23–7–72–2; Mohammad Zahid 22.2–1–67–4; Naveed Rana 15–6–48–1; Nadeem Khan 18–3–59–0; Akram Raza 24–6–51–1; Asif Mujtaba 12–3–22–2.

Umpires: Mian Aslam and Shakeel Khan.

PCB PATRON'S XI v ENGLAND A

At Lahore (Bagh-i-Jinnah), November 25, 26, 27. Drawn. Toss: England A.

The opening day was divided between two left-handers, who completed centuries against keen bowling. Knight dominated the first half and was especially fluent backward of square on the off side, partly thanks to some pre-tour coaching from John Edrich. But leg-spinner Anwar Ali, barely known even to Pakistan's selectors, finally came on in mid-afternoon and quickly took three for 30 in a bewitching ten-over spell. However, Pooley countered Ali aggressively and sped to a 123-ball hundred. Munton, just arrived as cover for the struggling Smith (who played this game but then went home), took four wickets in 13 balls to leave the Patron's XI at 48 for six next morning. But Azhar Mahmood and Shahid Nazir resisted bravely and had added 51 for the last wicket when the home team declared, 111 behind. The same pair then bowled incisively, reducing England to 53 for four. What could have been a fine contest, given the fourth day which had originally been scheduled, then subsided into a draw.

Close of play: First day, England A 298-6 (J. C. Pooley 100*, S. D. Udal 14*); Second day, England A 10-2 (S. D. Udal 8*, D. P. Ostler 1*).

England A

N. V. Knight lbw b Anwar Ali	107		
J. E. R. Gallian c Anwar Ali b Aamer Wasim	19	– lbw b Shahid Nazir	1
*N. Hussain b Azhar Mahmood	23	– (5) not out	42
†D. P. Ostler c Javed Qadir b Anwar Ali	9	– c Javed Qadir b Shahid Nazir	23
J. C. Pooley not out	100		
A. McGrath c Javed Qadir b Anwar Ali	2	– (1) c Javed Qadir b Shahid Nazir	0
C. White b Shahid Nazir	12	– (6) not out	37
S. D. Udal not out	14	– (3) c Javed Qadir b Azhar Mahmood	21
B 4, l-b 4, n-b 4	12	B 5, n-b 1	6
1/62 2/136 3/160 4/165 5/191 6/243 (6 wkts dec.)	298	1/0 2/9 3/37 4/53 (4 wkts dec.)	130

T. A. Munton, R. D. Stemp and A. M. Smith did not bat.

Bowling: *First Innings*—Azhar Mahmood 11–2–21–1; Mohammad Ali 9–0–53–0; Shahid Nazir 11–2–31–1; Aamer Wasim 12–2–46–1; Manzoor Akhtar 10–1–36–0; Akram Raza 13.2–3–37–0; Anwar Ali 21–5–66–3. *Second Innings*—Shahid Nazir 11–2–35–3; Azhar Mahmood 10–2–23–1; Mohammad Ali 3–0–13–0; Anwar Ali 8–3–21–0; Aamer Wasim 8–2–27–0; Manzoor Akhtar 3–1–6–0.

PCB Patron's XI

Shakeel Ahmed run out	18	– b Udal	8
Nadeem Younis b White	19	– c Udal b Munton	4
Atif Rauf c Hussain b Munton	1	– c McGrath b Munton	1
Manzoor Akhtar c McGrath b Munton	0	– not out	35
†Javed Qadir c McGrath b Munton	2		
*Akram Raza b Munton	0	– (5) not out	29
Azhar Mahmood not out	63		
Aamer Wasim c Knight b Stemp	28		
Mohammad Ali lbw b Munton	9		
Anwar Ali b White	3		
Shahid Nazir not out	28		
B 4, l-b 9, n-b 3	16	B 2, l-b 9	11
1/34 2/44 3/44 4/44 5/47 6/48 7/114 8/129 9/136 (9 wkts dec.)	187	1/10 2/14 3/18 (3 wkts)	88

Bowling: *First Innings*—Munton 22–7–54–5; Smith 12–4–43–0; White 15–3–46–2; Stemp 13–6–27–1; Udal 2–1–4–0. *Second Innings*—Munton 11–5–13–2; Smith 4–2–7–0; Udal 13–1–36–1; Gallian 6–0–21–0; Stemp 1–1–0–0.

Umpires: Ikram Rabbani and Mian Aslam.

PAKISTAN A v ENGLAND A

Second Unofficial Test

At Rawalpindi (KRL Ground), November 30, December 1, 2, 3, 4. Drawn. Toss: England A.

Heavy rain on the day before the match, exacerbated by the lack of top-quality covering on a ground rarely used for major matches, wiped out the first four and a half sessions. Hussain then won the toss and gleefully put Pakistan A in. But the helpful conditions he expected did not materialise. With a much strengthened home team 73 for one at the close of the second day, the game was already heading for a draw. A magnificently sustained afternoon spell from Headley, well supported by Salisbury, breathed some life into the contest; he finished with six for 73. And the fourth day was dominated by a 197-run second-wicket stand between Gallian and night-watchman Salisbury. Gallian, whose 153 stretched across three days, displayed all his virtues of dependability and selective strokeplay, while Salisbury, playing sensibly within his limitations, was often just as sound. Quick runs on the final morning enabled Hussain to declare 118 ahead, and when Pakistan A were 46 for two the tourists had hopes. But Shakeel Ahmed and Asif Mujtaba would not budge on a surface which had become sluggish. White eventually removed them both in a spirited last fling, but it came too late, with bad light again closing in.

Close of play: First day, No play; Second day, Pakistan A 73-1 (Shakeel Ahmed 39*, Saeed Azad 10*); Third day, England A 8-1 (J. E. R. Gallian 5*, I. D. K. Salisbury 2*); Fourth day, England A 281-2 (J. E. R. Gallian 146*, N. Hussain 40*).

Pakistan A

Shakeel Ahmed c Gallian b Headley	62	– c Gallian b White	73
Shahid Anwar c Piper b Salisbury	13	– b Stemp	15
Saeed Azad c and b Salisbury	10	– b Munton	1
*Asif Mujtaba c Piper b Headley	24	– c Piper b White	26
Manzoor Akhtar c Gallian b Headley	13	– not out	9
Mazhar Qayyum lbw b Headley	17	– not out	14
†Wasim Yousufi c Piper b Headley	9		
Athar Laeeq c Hussain b Salisbury	0		
Anwar Ali b Headley	20		
Salman Fazal c Piper b Munton	17		
Mohammad Zahid not out	10		
B 2, l-b 6, n-b 11	19	B 8, l-b 4, n-b 4	16
1/45 (2) 2/75 (3) 3/114 (1) 4/132 (4) 5/139 (5) 6/158 (6) 7/159 (8) 8/165 (7) 9/185 (9) 10/214 (10)	214	1/45 (2) 2/46 (3) 3/120 (1) 4/127 (4)	(4 wkts) 154

Bowling: *First Innings*—Headley 32–6–73–6; Munton 22.5–9–25–1; White 8–1–29–0; Salisbury 31–6–76–3; Stemp 2–0–3–0. *Second Innings*—Headley 12–1–38–0; Munton 12–4–24–1; Salisbury 13–1–39–0; Stemp 7–3–10–1; Irani 5–1–9–0; White 9.3–1–22–2.

England A

N. V. Knight lbw b Athar Laeeq	0
J. E. R. Gallian c Athar Laeeq b Mohammad Zahid	153
I. D. K. Salisbury c Anwar Ali b Mohammad Zahid	86
*N. Hussain c Wasim Yousufi b Athar Laeeq	43
J. C. Pooley not out	15
R. C. Irani c sub (Javed Sami) b Athar Laeeq	11
C. White c Asif Mujtaba b Mohammad Zahid	1
†K. J. Piper not out	14
B 3, l-b 4, w 1, n-b 1	9
1/2 (1) 2/199 (3) 3/291 (2) 4/291 (4) 5/303 (6) 6/313 (7)	(6 wkts dec.) 332

D. W. Headley, T. A. Munton and R. D. Stemp did not bat.

Bowling: Athar Laeeq 27–4–84–3; Mohammad Zahid 23–3–91–3; Anwar Ali 11–0–55–0; Salman Fazal 23–7–37–0; Asif Mujtaba 3–0–9–0; Manzoor Akhtar 18–3–49–0.

Umpires: Mahboob Shah and Siddiq Khan.

PAKISTAN A v ENGLAND A

Third Unofficial Test

At Peshawar, December 8, 9, 10, 11, 12. Drawn. Toss: Pakistan A.

This match was also hit by the weather, with a day and a half lost in all. England's cricketers took the covers off themselves on the first morning, in an effort to start on time, but local officials insisted on waiting 90 minutes, citing overnight dew. As it turned out, a shortened opening day suited the tourists better. They struggled to 102 for four in 50 overs before bad light intervened, and were eventually bowled out for 199. Only Knight and Ostler made much mark as Shahid Nazir, just 18, consistently reverse-swung the old ball to take six for 64. Pakistan A's reply turned on a dropped catch in a remarkable opening over from Headley. He was on a hat-trick when Asif Mujtaba edged the fifth ball of the innings to second slip, where Knight could not cling on. When Giddins struck in his first over, the score was one for three. But Mujtaba put all his experience and courage into a superb fightback. Conditions did not suit the spinners and, by the time Headley and Giddins had worked through the late order, Mujtaba had batted eight and a half hours for 147 not out and Pakistan A were in charge with a lead of 101. By the close England were two down. But a farcical start to the final day held up the home attack. Bemused players watched the ground staff using hot coals in metal bowls to dry out a damp patch after the dew-covered sheets were removed. Despite the 100-minute delay, Pakistan had one last chance to level the series, when a mid-afternoon collapse left England on 126 for seven, only 25 ahead. But Pooley remained calm. He was never afraid to play his shots, taking the runs-time ratio away from Pakistan, while Headley survived 50 minutes before bad light ended play for good. England were 1-0 series winners, but had nearly wrecked all their hard work in one careless session.

Close of play: First day, England A 102-4 (D. P. Ostler 13*, J. C. Pooley 6*); Second day, Pakistan A 97-4 (Asif Mujtaba 33*, Shahid Javed 40*); Third day, Pakistan A 207-6 (Asif Mujtaba 103*, Akram Raza 25*); Fourth day, England A 62-2 (J. E. R. Gallian 42*, S. D. Udal 1*).

England A

N. V. Knight lbw b Shahid Nazir	55	– lbw b Shahid Nazir	15
J. E. R. Gallian c and b Akram Raza	16	– lbw b Salman Fazal	58
*N. Hussain lbw b Shahid Nazir	9	– (5) run out	29
A. McGrath lbw b Athar Laeeq	0	– (6) c Wasim Yousufi b Athar Laeeq	7
D. P. Ostler b Shahid Nazir	68	– (7) b Salman Fazal	5
J. C. Pooley c Salman Fazal b Athar Laeeq	6	– (8) not out	38
†K. J. Piper b Shahid Nazir	11	– (9) c Wasim Yousufi b Salman Fazal	10
I. D. K. Salisbury c Akram Raza b Salman Fazal	11	– (3) c Javed Sami b Akram Raza	2
S. D. Udal lbw b Shahid Nazir	4	– (4) c Javed Sami b Shahid Nazir	2
D. W. Headley not out	8	– not out	4
E. S. H. Giddins b Shahid Nazir	0		
B 1, l-b 10	11	B 9, l-b 12	21
1/42 (2) 2/70 (3) 3/71 (4) 4/87 (1) 5/102 (6) 6/137 (7) 7/163 (8) 8/184 (9) 9/199 (5) 10/199 (11)	199	1/56 (1) 2/61 (3) 3/80 (4) 4/97 (2) 5/109 (5) 6/126 (7) 7/126 (6) 8/142 (9)	(8 wkts) 191

Bowling: *First Innings*—Athar Laeeq 29–15–34–2; Shahid Nazir 27.5–9–64–6; Asif Mujtaba 3–0–3–0; Akram Raza 13–1–37–1; Salman Fazal 17–3–50–1. *Second Innings*—Athar Laeeq 16–4–47–1; Shahid Nazir 22–6–55–2; Shahid Anwar 2–1–3–0; Akram Raza 15.1–1–33–1; Salman Fazal 16–8–20–3; Asif Mujtaba 1–0–5–0; Babar Zaman 2–0–6–0; Shahid Javed 1–0–1–0.

Pakistan A

Shakeel Ahmed c Ostler b Giddins	1
Shahid Anwar b Headley	0
Babar Zaman b Headley	0
*Asif Mujtaba not out	147
Javed Sami lbw b Giddins	6
Shahid Javed c Piper b Headley	40
†Wasim Yousufi c Piper b Headley	5
Akram Raza b Giddins	40
Salman Fazal c Ostler b Giddins	5
Athar Laeeq c Udal b Giddins	19
Shahid Nazir c Piper b Headley	4
B 6, l-b 11, n-b 16	33
1/1 (2) 2/1 (3) 3/1 (1) 4/22 (5) 5/97 (6) 6/112 (7) 7/250 (8) 8/258 (9) 9/285 (10) 10/300 (11)	300

Bowling: Headley 44.4–8–109–5; Giddins 39–5–104–5; Salisbury 6–0–28–0; Udal 12–2–31–0; Gallian 9–5–11–0.

Umpires: Feroz Butt and Iftikhar Malik.

†At Peshawar, December 15. First unofficial one-day international: England A won by one run. Toss: England A. England A 225 for five (40 overs) (N. V. Knight 35, N. Hussain 100 not out, C. White 39 not out); Pakistan A 224 for six (40 overs) (Shahid Anwar 100 not out).

Hussain scored his 100 from 99 balls. Pakistan A needed five off the final over, bowled by White, but managed only three.

†At Faisalabad, December 18. Second unofficial one-day international: England A won by seven wickets. Toss: England A. Pakistan A 186 for six (40 overs) (Shahid Anwar 87 not out, Asif Mujtaba 42); England A 190 for three (38.3 overs) (N. V. Knight 90 not out, N. Hussain 50).

†At Sheikhupura, December 20. Third unofficial one-day international: Pakistan A won by 133 runs. Toss: England A. Pakistan A 248 for five (40 overs) (Sajid Ali 38, Shakeel Ahmed 69, Asif Mujtaba 62); England A 115 (23.4 overs) (Sajid Shah six for 43).

England A suffered their only defeat of the tour, but took the one-day series 2-1. Cricket manager John Emburey acted as twelfth man because of injuries to several of the party. Sajid Shah took England A's first six wickets in one eight-over spell.

ENGLAND'S INTERNATIONAL SCHEDULE

Home

1997	Tests and one-day internationals v Australia
1998	Tests and one-day internationals v South Africa and Sri Lanka
1999	WORLD CUP Tests v New Zealand
2000	Tests and one-day internationals v West Indies
2001	Tests and one-day internationals v Australia

Away

1997-98	One-day internationals in Sharjah
1997-98	Tests and one-day internationals in West Indies
1998-99	Tests and one-day internationals in Australia
1999-2000	Tests and one-day internationals in South Africa and Zimbabwe
2000-01	Tests and one-day internationals in Pakistan and Sri Lanka

All fixtures subject to confirmation.

THE SRI LANKANS IN PAKISTAN, 1995-96

By QAMAR AHMED

Arjuna Ranatunga's Sri Lankans created history by winning a Test series against Pakistan for the first time in six attempts. Their triumph was the more remarkable for the fact that they had lost the First Test by an innings in four days. Over the next fortnight, they came back strongly to level the rubber at Faisalabad and then crush Pakistan at Sialkot. Curiously, they were the third team to come from behind to win a three-Test series in 1995, following South Africa against New Zealand in January, and Pakistan in Zimbabwe a month later; the only previous instance had been England against Australia in 1888. The pattern was repeated in the ensuing one-day series, where Sri Lanka bounced back from a nine-wicket defeat for another 2-1 win. They had never won any series in Pakistan before, Test or limited-overs, but their success followed straight on from their first ever Test win overseas, against New Zealand the previous March. Deservedly, they returned home to a tumultuous welcome, and were driven through the streets of Colombo in a cavalcade.

For Pakistan, however, their first home series defeat since 1980-81, when they lost to Clive Lloyd's West Indians, added to a sense of crisis. Their former captain, Salim Malik, had been suspended in March after three Australian players accused him of attempted bribery; investigations were continuing and he was not considered for selection, despite an attempt to secure reinstatement through the law-courts.

The home team's new captain was Ramiz Raja, who started with the resounding victory at Peshawar but then saw his team's form slide. Pakistan were weakened by the absence of Malik and his brother-in-law Ijaz Ahmed, also under the cloud of disciplinary charges. Javed Miandad had declared himself unfit and Pakistan's famous pace duo, Wasim Akram and Waqar Younis, did not last the series. Waqar, who had left the tour of South Africa with a back injury, looked rusty and unfit; he withdrew after the First Test to seek full match fitness in domestic cricket. Wasim played the key role in Pakistan's victory at Peshawar but was then forced out by a damaged shoulder, which prevented him from bowling after the first innings of the Second Test. After that, Aqib Javed took over as the spearhead, taking 16 wickets at 19.56 apiece, and there were promising Test debuts for off-spinner Saqlain Mushtaq and seamer Mohammad Akram. A teenaged opening batsman, Salim Elahi, scored 102 in a dazzling one-day debut. But the other Ijaz Ahmed (five months younger than his unrelated namesake), who had a reputation as a prolific batsman for Faisalabad and Allied Bank, failed to make much impression and was dropped by the final Test. In both defeats, it was the wicket-keeper, Moin Khan, who saved Pakistan from complete embarrassment, particularly in the final innings at Sialkot, where he came in at 15 for five and scored an unbeaten 117.

The tourists' most reliable batsman was Hashan Tillekeratne, who played magnificently in all the Tests and averaged 56.20. He made 115 out of a meagre first-innings 223 to keep Sri Lanka in the game at Faisalabad; Aravinda de Silva scored the century that put them in control in the second innings, but it was one of the few occasions when he came to terms with conditions in Pakistan after his season in English county cricket. Chandika Hathurusinghe was almost as steady as Tillekeratne, and Ranatunga played some fine innings in both series. The most successful bowler was off-spinner Muttiah Muralitharan, with 15 wickets at

27.33, who became Sri Lanka's leading wicket-taker during the tour; left-arm medium-pacer Chaminda Vaas was close behind, with 13 at 19.53. But, after their initial defeat, the Sri Lankans played better cricket all round: they bowled better, fielded better and, in a generally low-scoring series, batted with greater consistency.

SRI LANKAN TOURING PARTY

A. Ranatunga (Sinhalese SC) (*captain*), R. S. Mahanama (Bloomfield C and AC) (*vice-captain*), P. A. de Silva (Nondescripts CC), H. D. P. K. Dharmasena (Bloomfield C and AC), C. I. Dunusinghe (Antonians SC), A. P. Gurusinha (Sinhalese SC), U. C. Hathurusinghe (Tamil Union), S. T. Jayasuriya (Bloomfield C and AC), M. Muralitharan (Tamil Union), K. R. Pushpakumara (Nondescripts CC), S. Ranatunga (Nondescripts CC), D. P. Samaraweera (Colts CC), K. J. Silva (Sinhalese SC), H. P. Tillekeratne (Nondescripts CC), W. P. U. J. C. Vaas (Colts CC), G. P. Wickremasinghe (Sinhalese SC).

M. Munasinghe (Sinhalese SC) withdrew through injury before the tour and was replaced by Dharmasena. R. S. Kalpage (Bloomfield C and AC), R. S. Kaluwitharana (Galle CC) and E. A. Upashantha (Colts CC) joined the party for the one-day internationals.

Manager: L. R. D. Mendis. *Coach:* D. F. Whatmore.

SRI LANKAN TOUR RESULTS

Test matches – Played 3: Won 2, Lost 1.
First-class matches – Played 5: Won 2, Lost 2, Drawn 1.
Wins – Pakistan (2).
Losses – Pakistan, PCB Patron's XI.
Draw – Pakistan Cricket Board XI.
One-day internationals – Played 3: Won 2, Lost 1.

TEST MATCH AVERAGES

PAKISTAN – BATTING

	T	*I*	*NO*	*R*	*HS*	*100s*	*Avge*	*Ct/St*
Moin Khan	3	5	1	274	117*	1	68.50	6/1
Saeed Anwar	2	3	0	154	54	0	51.33	3
Ramiz Raja	3	5	0	208	78	0	41.60	4
Inzamam-ul-Haq	3	5	0	192	95	0	38.40	7
Saqlain Mushtaq	2	3	1	49	34	0	24.50	2
Wasim Akram	2	3	0	64	36	0	21.33	2
Aqib Javed	3	5	2	62	28*	0	20.66	0
Aamir Sohail	3	5	0	101	48	0	20.20	2
Shoaib Mohammad	3	5	0	83	57	0	16.60	1
Ijaz Ahmed, jun.	2	3	0	29	16	0	9.66	3
Mohammad Akram	2	4	1	7	5	0	2.33	2

Played in one Test: Aamir Nazir 5*; 11; Ata-ur-Rehman 9, 4; Basit Ali 4, 27; Waqar Younis 0; Zahid Fazal 23, 1.

* *Signifies not out.*

BOWLING

	O	*M*	*R*	*W*	*BB*	*5W/i*	*Avge*
Wasim Akram	43	12	110	9	5-55	1	12.22
Aqib Javed	113.1	22	313	16	5-84	1	19.56
Mohammad Akram	78	19	196	7	3-39	0	28.00
Saqlain Mushtaq	100	28	265	9	3-74	0	29.44
Aamir Nazir	36	8	101	3	2-46	0	33.66
Aamir Sohail	116.3	29	270	7	4-54	0	38.57

Also bowled: Ata-ur-Rehman 42–11–108–2; Ijaz Ahmed, jun. 4–0–6–0; Shoaib Mohammad 19–7–40–0; Waqar Younis 20–3–86–1.

SRI LANKA – BATTING

	T	*I*	*NO*	*R*	*HS*	*100s*	*Avge*	*Ct/St*
H. P. Tillekeratne	3	6	1	281	115	1	56.20	2
U. C. Hathurusinghe	3	6	0	291	83	0	48.50	2
H. D. P. K. Dharmasena	2	4	1	118	62*	0	39.33	2
A. Ranatunga	3	6	0	197	87	0	32.83	3
P. A. de Silva	2	4	0	113	105	1	28.25	1
A. P. Gurusinha	3	6	0	118	45	0	19.66	2
W. P. U. J. C. Vaas	3	6	0	112	40	0	18.66	1
R. S. Mahanama	3	6	0	82	29	0	13.66	7
M. Muralitharan	3	6	3	30	10*	0	10.00	3
C. I. Dunusinghe	3	6	0	47	27	0	7.83	5/2
G. P. Wickremasinghe	3	5	0	10	6	0	2.00	0

Played in one Test: K. R. Pushpakumara 1, 0* (1 ct); S. Ranatunga 33, 18.

* *Signifies not out.*

BOWLING

	O	*M*	*R*	*W*	*BB*	*5W/i*	*Avge*
W. P. U. J. C. Vaas	96	18	254	13	5-99	1	19.53
P. A. de Silva	31.3	6	88	4	2-29	0	22.00
M. Muralitharan	137.4	26	410	15	5-68	1	27.33
G. P. Wickremasinghe	97	18	258	8	4-55	0	32.25
H. D. P. K. Dharmasena	78.1	17	178	5	3-43	0	35.60

Also bowled: A. P. Gurusinha 17–2–57–2; U. C. Hathurusinghe 24–11–39–0; K. R. Pushpakumara 17–2–89–0.

Note: Matches in this section which were not first-class are signified by a dagger.

At Karachi, August 30, 31, September 1. Drawn. Toss: Sri Lankans. Sri Lankans 286 for eight dec. (U. C. Hathurusinghe 39, A. P. Gurusinha 32, S. Ranatunga 58, S. T. Jayasuriya 55, H. P. Tillekeratne 33; Haaris Khan three for 77) and 148 for four (R. S. Mahanama 48 not out, A. P. Gurusinha 82; Haaris Khan three for 50); Pakistan Cricket Board XI 244 for eight dec. (Aamir Sohail 80, Zahid Fazal 40, Javed Sami 44).

At Rawalpindi, September 4, 5. PCB Patron's XI won by an innings and six runs. Toss: Sri Lankans. Sri Lankans 104 (Nadeem Iqbal three for 36, Saqlain Mushtaq three for ten) and 171 (H. P. Tillekeratne 38; Mohammad Akram three for 18, Saqlain Mushtaq four for 67); PCB Patron's XI 281 for nine dec. (Shahid Anwar 38, Shoaib Mohammad 73, Saeed Azad 81, Inzamam-ul-Haq 49; M. Muralitharan three for 68).

PAKISTAN v SRI LANKA

First Test Match

At Peshawar, September 8, 9, 10, 11. Pakistan won by an innings and 40 runs. Toss: Pakistan. Test debuts: Ijaz Ahmed, jun., Saqlain Mushtaq.

Pakistan's emphatic win, by an innings and 40 runs inside four days, was an encouraging start for their latest captain, Ramiz Raja, who led by example. He had taken over the job after the dismissal of Salim Malik, under investigation because of Australian allegations of attempted bribery. Ramiz had not played Test cricket since 1993; neither had Shoaib Mohammad, and, as well as two debutants, Pakistan welcomed back Waqar Younis, absent since pulling out of the Johannesburg Test in January with a stress fracture. The city of Peshawar was also making a Test comeback after a rather longer gap; it had staged one Test, with India the visitors, in 1955 at the Services Ground. This match was played at the Arbab Niaz Stadium, Test cricket's 75th venue. It was not a trouble-free debut. On the first day, tea was taken early, when some of the crowd threw glass at the Sri Lankan fielders, and on the fourth a firecracker was thrown at Wasim Akram.

Wasim was to be the Sri Lankans' chief tormentor. Bowling with sustained accuracy, he pulverised their first innings with five for 55: they collapsed in 62 overs. But Pakistan had dominated from the opening day, when they scored 235 for three before bad light stopped play. Ramiz had just mishooked Vaas, in the fading hours of the day, after adding 132 with Inzamam-ul-Haq. Inzamam was unlucky to miss his century next morning, falling leg-before to Vaas after five hours. Shoaib scored another fifty, then Wasim and Moin Khan put on 82 in even time to take Pakistan past 400. Ramiz declared an hour after tea on the second day at 459 for nine.

Sri Lanka lost no wickets that evening, but by the third-day close they were 86 for two in their second innings, having followed on 273 behind, and staring defeat in the face. They had reached lunch at a respectable 102 for four – with wickets for Saqlain Mushtaq, the 18-year-old off-spinner, in his second and third overs in Test cricket. But they lost their next four for 41 as Wasim scythed down the middle order. Only the ninth-wicket stand of 41 between Tillekeratne and Muralitharan provided some respectability; Tillekeratne defied the bowlers for 145 minutes in a vain attempt to avert the follow-on.

Sri Lanka began the fourth day needing 187 to make Pakistan bat again. They lost their overnight batsmen with just three runs added but their captain, Arjuna Ranatunga, and Tillekeratne then put on 125 for the fifth wicket. Once Ranatunga was caught at first slip off Aamir Sohail, however, the last six wickets fell for only 19. Sohail, with his best return for Pakistan, Saqlain and Wasim hastened Sri Lanka's demise.

Man of the Match: Wasim Akram.

Close of play: First day, Pakistan 235-3 (Inzamam-ul-Haq 65*, Shoaib Mohammad 1*); Second day, Sri Lanka 23-0 (R. S. Mahanama 18*, U. C. Hathurusinghe 5*); Third day, Sri Lanka 86-2 (U. C. Hathurusinghe 53*, S. Ranatunga 17*).

Pakistan

Saeed Anwar c A. Ranatunga b Muralitharan	50
Aamir Sohail c Dunusinghe b Vaas	28
*Ramiz Raja c Pushpakumara b Vaas	78
Inzamam-ul-Haq lbw b Vaas	95
Shoaib Mohammad c A. Ranatunga b Vaas	57
Ijaz Ahmed, jun. c Gurusinha b Muralitharan	5
Wasim Akram c and b Muralitharan	36
†Moin Khan c Hathurusinghe b Vaas	51
Waqar Younis c Mahanama b Muralitharan	0
Aqib Javed not out	28
Saqlain Mushtaq not out	8
B 1, l-b 4, w 1, n-b 17	23
1/59 (2) 2/102 (1) 3/234 (3) 4/285 (4) 5/318 (6) 6/340 (5) 7/422 (7) 8/422 (8) 9/425 (9) (9 wkts dec.)	459

Bowling: Wickremasinghe 32–5–98–0; Vaas 29–3–99–5; Pushpakumara 17–2–89–0; Muralitharan 50–9–134–4; Hathurusinghe 18–10–29–0; Gurusinha 3–1–5–0.

Sri Lanka

R. S. Mahanama c Moin Khan b Waqar Younis	29	lbw b Aqib Javed	2
U. C. Hathurusinghe c Inzamam-ul-Haq b Saqlain Mushtaq	23	c Saeed Anwar b Wasim Akram	53
A. P. Gurusinha c Wasim Akram b Saqlain Mushtaq	24	c Saeed Anwar b Aamir Sohail	10
S. Ranatunga lbw b Wasim Akram	33	c Moin Khan b Aqib Javed	18
*A. Ranatunga lbw b Aqib Javed	8	c Inzamam-ul-Haq b Aamir Sohail	76
H. P. Tillekeratne not out	44	c Ramiz Raja b Wasim Akram	48
†C. I. Dunusinghe lbw b Wasim Akram	0	c Inzamam-ul-Haq b Aamir Sohail	0
W. P. U. J. C. Vaas b Wasim Akram	4	c Ramiz Raja b Saqlain Mushtaq	4
G. P. Wickremasinghe b Wasim Akram	0	c Ramiz Raja b Saqlain Mushtaq	6
M. Muralitharan c Saqlain Mushtaq b Wasim Akram	8	st Moin Khan b Aamir Sohail	0
K. R. Pushpakumara run out	1	not out	0
B 1, l-b 6, n-b 5	12	B 1, l-b 6, n-b 9	16
1/39 (1) 2/76 (2) 3/83 (3) 4/101 (5) 5/132 (4) 6/134 (7) 7/142 (8) 8/143 (9) 9/184 (10) 10/186 (11)	186	1/8 (1) 2/36 (3) 3/86 (2) 4/89 (4) 5/214 (5) 6/222 (6) 7/222 (7) 8/232 (8) 9/233 (10) 10/233 (9)	233

Bowling: *First Innings*—Wasim Akram 20–3–55–5; Waqar Younis 11–2–47–1; Saqlain Mushtaq 18–4–49–2; Aqib Javed 11.1–2–27–1; Aamir Sohail 2–1–1–0. *Second Innings*—Waqar Younis 9–1–39–0; Aqib Javed 13–1–50–2; Saqlain Mushtaq 26–10–58–2; Aamir Sohail 21–4–54–4; Ijaz Ahmed 1–0–1–0; Wasim Akram 10–3–24–2.

Umpires: B. L. Aldridge (New Zealand) and Mahboob Shah.
Referee: P. L. van der Merwe (South Africa).

PAKISTAN v SRI LANKA

Second Test Match

At Faisalabad, September 15, 16, 17, 18, 19. Sri Lanka won by 42 runs. Toss: Pakistan. Test debut: Mohammad Akram.

Sri Lanka levelled the series with their first Test win on Pakistani soil, a victory which underlined the rise in their fortunes: it was only six months since their first overseas win, against New Zealand in Napier. They were strengthened by de Silva, who flew in from England after spending a season with Kent and scored what proved a match-winning century. Pakistan, on the other hand, lost another experienced player when Waqar Younis withdrew, saying he needed longer to regain his fitness, and suffered a further heavy blow when a shoulder injury prevented Wasim Akram from bowling in Sri Lanka's second innings.

At first, however, Pakistan looked likely to take the series. Sri Lanka lost Mahanama in the opening over and were 33 for four when Saqlain Mushtaq dismissed de Silva and Ranatunga with successive balls. Tillekeratne averted the hat-trick and batted sensibly to reach 115, his third Test century. But his only real support came from Hathurusinghe and Vaas. In reply, Pakistan took the lead with only four wickets down and captain Ramiz Raja continued his successful comeback with another seventy. Their luck began to change when Inzamam-ul-Haq was hit on the helmet by Wickremasinghe: dizziness kept him out of the game for the next two days. Just before the second-day close, Pakistan lost three wickets for three to the second new ball.

Still, they took a 110-run lead next morning and quickly reduced Sri Lanka to 24 for two. It was Hathurusinghe and de Silva who turned the game in a stand of 176, a Sri Lankan third-wicket record. Hathurusinghe scored 83, his best in internationals, while de Silva batted more than six and a half hours for 105, his eighth Test hundred, which included 11 fours; he also became the second Sri Lankan to reach 3,000 Test runs, following Ranatunga. Sri Lanka led by 130 when he fell at last but the last four wickets added another 121. Aqib Javed finally saw them off on the fourth evening to complete his first five-wicket haul in Tests.

That left Pakistan to score 252: they were already two down by stumps, with Ramiz out in the final over. On the fifth day, Saeed Anwar advanced to his third fifty in as many innings, but the home batsmen then lost their way against the pace of Vaas and the off-spin of Muralitharan and

Dharmasena. Inzamam, allowed to bat at No. 4 despite his absence in the field, still seemed shaky and gave Muralitharan a return catch just before lunch. That wicket, Muralitharan's seventh in the match, made him Sri Lanka's leading Test wicket-taker, overtaking Rumesh Ratnayake with 73. A fighting fifty from Moin Khan, backed up by the injured Wasim, could not deny Sri Lanka their historic victory.

Man of the Match: M. Muralitharan.

Close of play: First day, Pakistan 43-1 (Saeed Anwar 21*, Saqlain Mushtaq 0*); Second day, Pakistan 294-8 (Moin Khan 2*, Aqib Javed 1*); Third day, Sri Lanka 174-2 (U. C. Hathurusinghe 67*, P. A. de Silva 78*); Fourth day, Pakistan 58-2 (Saeed Anwar 30*, Inzamam-ul-Haq 0*).

Sri Lanka

R. S. Mahanama lbw b Wasim Akram	0	– lbw b Mohammad Akram	10
U. C. Hathurusinghe c Saeed Anwar b Mohammad Akram	47	– c Ijaz Ahmed b Aqib Javed	83
A. P. Gurusinha c Wasim Akram b Aqib Javed	9	– lbw b Aqib Javed	12
P. A. de Silva c and b Saqlain Mushtaq	0	– lbw b Saqlain Mushtaq	105
*A. Ranatunga c Ijaz Ahmed b Saqlain Mushtaq	0	– (6) c and b Aamir Sohail	2
H. P. Tillekeratne c Moin Khan b Saqlain Mushtaq	115	– (5) lbw b Aqib Javed	0
H. D. P. K. Dharmasena run out	0	– c Moin Khan b Mohammad Akram	49
†C. I. Dunusinghe lbw b Wasim Akram	12	– c Mohammad Akram b Saqlain Mushtaq	27
W. P. U. J. C. Vaas c Ijaz Ahmed b Aqib Javed	21	– b Aqib Javed	40
G. P. Wickremasinghe c Moin Khan b Aqib Javed	1	– (11) b Aqib Javed	2
M. Muralitharan not out	8	– (10) not out	10
B 3, l-b 1, n-b 6	10	B 4, l-b 10, n-b 7	21
1/0 (1) 2/32 (3) 3/33 (4) 4/33 (5) 5/117 (2) 6/117 (7) 7/149 (8) 8/213 (9) 9/213 (6) 10/223 (10)	223	1/11 (1) 2/24 (3) 3/200 (2) 4/212 (5) 5/225 (6) 6/240 (4) 7/279 (8) 8/344 (9) 9/354 (7) 10/361 (11)	361

Bowling: *First Innings*—Wasim Akram 13–6–31–2; Mohammad Akram 14–4–42–1; Aqib Javed 13–5–34–3; Saqlain Mushtaq 20–3–74–3; Aamir Sohail 7–2–28–0; Shoaib Mohammad 3–2–10–0. *Second Innings*—Aqib Javed 32.3–6–84–5; Mohammad Akram 27–5–78–2; Aamir Sohail 44–12–87–1; Saqlain Mushtaq 36–11–84–2; Ijaz Ahmed 3–0–5–0; Shoaib Mohammad 4–2–9–0.

Pakistan

Saeed Anwar c de Silva b Muralitharan	54	– b Dharmasena	50
Aamir Sohail b Muralitharan	20	– lbw b Vaas	0
Saqlain Mushtaq c Mahanama b Muralitharan	34	– (9) c Ranatunga b Vaas	7
*Ramiz Raja c sub (D. P. Samaraweera) b de Silva	75	– (3) c Tillekeratne b Muralitharan	25
Inzamam-ul-Haq b Gurusinha	50	– (4) c and b Muralitharan	26
Shoaib Mohammad run out	12	– (5) lbw b Wickremasinghe	5
Ijaz Ahmed, jun. c Dunusinghe b Wickremasinghe	16	– (6) c Dharmasena b Vaas	8
Wasim Akram c Mahanama b Gurusinha	2	– b Dharmasena	26
†Moin Khan st Dunusinghe b Muralitharan	30	– (7) c Muralitharan b Vaas	50
Aqib Javed b Muralitharan	8	– not out	1
Mohammad Akram not out	0	– c Mahanama b Dharmasena	0
B 4, l-b 15, n-b 13	32	N-b 11	11
1/42 (2) 2/109 (1) 3/168 (3) 4/213 (4) 5/248 (6) 6/288 (7) 7/288 (5) 8/291 (8) 9/324 (10) 10/333 (9)	333	1/6 (2) 2/58 (3) 3/99(1) 4/108 (5) 5/119 (4) 6/129 (6) 7/175 (8) 8/206 (7) 9/209 (9) 10/209 (11)	209

Bowling: *First Innings*—Wickremasinghe 23–6–53–1; Vaas 14–4–35–0; Gurusinha 8–1–30–2; Dharmasena 30–4–79–0; Muralitharan 23.3–6–68–5; Hathurusinghe 6–1–10–0; de Silva 13.3–3–39–1. *Second Innings*—Wickremasinghe 11–1–23–1; Vaas 15–2–45–4; Muralitharan 20–2–83–2; Dharmasena 22.1–6–43–3; de Silva 4–0–15–0.

Umpires: N. T. Plews (England) and Khizar Hayat.
Referee: P. L. van der Merwe (South Africa).

PAKISTAN v SRI LANKA

Third Test Match

At Sialkot, September 22, 23, 24, 25, 26. Sri Lanka won by 144 runs. Toss: Sri Lanka.

Sri Lanka's triumph gave them their first series win over Pakistan, and their second series win overseas, following swiftly on the first, over New Zealand in March. It was Ranatunga's fifth Test win in his 32nd Test in charge, making him easily Sri Lanka's most successful captain. But it was the beginning of the end of Ramiz Raja's brief reign: Pakistan had not lost a home series since the West Indians toured in 1980-81.

The tide seemed to have turned in Sri Lanka's favour after their victory in Faisalabad; they were able to field an unchanged team and won the toss for the first time, while Pakistan had to make three changes because of injury and dropped the disappointing Ijaz Ahmed junior. Still, the inexperienced home attack, led by Aqib Javed, bowled well in the first innings to keep Sri Lanka down to 232. Gurusinha and Ranatunga began the recovery from 41 for three, but the only batsman to reach fifty was Dharmasena. Coming in at No. 7, he remained unbeaten on 62 after three and a half hours. Pakistan were batting in the first hour of the second morning but ran into trouble after lunch, when they slid from 72 for one to 122 for five. Muralitharan had claimed three men lbw and, backed up by fellow off-spinners Dharmasena and de Silva, finished the innings off for 214 early next morning.

Sri Lanka were to convert a marginal lead of 18 into a strong position in their second innings. Hathurusinghe batted solidly for most of the day, falling just before bad light ended play three overs early, and the forceful Ranatunga continued throughout the fourth morning to score 87. Pakistan took the new ball in the second over of the day but, missing the strike force of Wasim Akram and Waqar Younis, were unable to prevent the tourists from plundering runs. Though a spectacular slip catch by Inzamam-ul-Haq finally removed Ranatunga, a valuable half-century from Tillekeratne gave Sri Lanka the confidence to declare before tea, leaving a target of 357 in four sessions.

Total humiliation for Pakistan was on the cards when Vaas and Wickremasinghe, the sometimes overlooked Sri Lankan seamers, ripped out three wickets with the score on seven and quickly added two more to leave them 15 for five. That brought in Moin Khan to join Basit Ali: they began a desperate struggle to stop the rot by adding 64 for the sixth wicket. They steered Pakistan safely past their lowest score in Tests, 62 against Australia in 1981-82, but, when Basit fell before the close, Moin must have known survival was out of the question. Nevertheless, he batted on into the final afternoon for 117 not out, his second Test hundred, thanks to last man Aamir Nazir, who held out for 75 minutes.

Man of the Match: A. Ranatunga.

Men of the Series: Pakistan – Moin Khan; Sri Lanka – H. P. Tillekeratne.

Close of play: First day, Sri Lanka 216-7 (H. D. P. K. Dharmasena 52*, W. P. U. J. C. Vaas 16*); Second day, Pakistan 199-8 (Aqib Javed 14*, Mohammad Akram 1*); Third day, Sri Lanka 176-4 (A. Ranatunga 33*, C. I. Dunusinghe 1*); Fourth day, Pakistan 99-6 (Moin Khan 46*, Aqib Javed 5*).

Sri Lanka

R. S. Mahanama c Mohammad Akram b Aqib Javed	21	– lbw b Aqib Javed	20
U. C. Hathurusinghe c Inzamam-ul-Haq b Aamir Nazir	12	– c Moin Khan b Aqib Javed	73
A. P. Gurusinha run out	45	– c Ramiz Raja b Ata-ur-Rehman	18
P. A. de Silva c Shoaib Mohammad b Ata-ur-Rehman	0	– lbw b Aamir Nazir	8
*A. Ranatunga b Aamir Sohail	24	– c Inzamam-ul-Haq b Mohammad Akram	87
H. P. Tillekeratne c Inzamam-ul-Haq b Mohammad Akram	24	– (7) b Aamir Sohail	50
H. D. P. K. Dharmasena not out	62	– (8) c Inzamam-ul-Haq b Mohammad Akram	7
†C. I. Dunusinghe lbw b Aqib Javed	1	– (6) b Mohammad Akram	7
W. P. U. J. C. Vaas b Aqib Javed	16	– run out	27
M. Muralitharan c Aamir Sohail b Aamir Nazir	4	– not out	0
G. P. Wickremasinghe run out	1		
B 1, l-b 12, n-b 9	22	B 23, l-b 10, n-b 8	41
1/32 (1) 2/36 (2) 3/41 (4) 4/108 (5) 5/118 (3) 6/158 (6) 7/171 (8) 8/216 (9) 9/225 (10) 10/232 (11)	232	1/37 (1) 2/71 (3) 3/97 (4) 4/175 (2) 5/208 (6) 6/265 (5) 7/279 (8) 8/338 (7) 9/338 (9)	(9 wkts dec.) 338

Bowling: *First Innings*—Aqib Javed 19.3–6–47–3; Mohammad Akram 17–4–37–1; Aamir Nazir 19–6–46–2; Ata-ur-Rehman 19–6–42–1; Aamir Sohail 17–3–45–1; Shoaib Mohammad 1–0–2–0. *Second Innings*—Aqib Javed 24–2–71–2; Ata-ur-Rehman 23–5–66–1; Mohammad Akram 20–6–39–3; Aamir Nazir 17–2–55–1; Shoaib Mohammad 11–3–19–0; Aamir Sohail 25.3–7–55–1.

Pakistan

Aamir Sohail b Dharmasena	48	c Hathurusinghe b Wickremasinghe	5
Shoaib Mohammad lbw b Muralitharan	8	c and b Vaas	1
*Ramiz Raja lbw b Muralitharan	26	c Mahanama b Wickremasinghe	4
Inzamam-ul-Haq b Wickremasinghe	21	c Mahanama b Vaas	0
Basit Ali lbw b Muralitharan	4	c Dharmasena b Vaas	27
Zahid Fazal st Dunusinghe b de Silva	23	c Gurusinha b Vaas	1
†Moin Khan c Dunusinghe b Wickremasinghe	26	not out	117
Aqib Javed c Dunusinghe b Dharmasena	19	run out	6
Ata-ur-Rehman c Mahanama b de Silva	9	c Dunusinghe b Wickremasinghe	4
Mohammad Akram b Muralitharan	5	b Wickremasinghe	2
Aamir Nazir not out	5	c Tillekeratne b de Silva	11
B 3, l-b 4, n-b 13	20	B 13, l-b 10, n-b 11	34
1/39 (2) 2/72 (1) 3/111 (4) 4/119 (3) 5/122 (5) 6/173 (6) 7/173 (7) 8/196 (9) 9/204 (8) 10/214 (10)	214	1/7 (1) 2/7 (2) 3/7 (4) 4/13 (3) 5/15 (6) 6/79 (5) 7/108 (8) 8/132 (9) 9/147 (10) 10/212 (11)	212

Bowling: *First Innings*—Wickremasinghe 13–2–29–2; Vaas 14–0–38–0; Gurusinha 3–0–6–0; Muralitharan 27.1–6–72–4; de Silva 10–1–29–2; Dharmasena 16–5–33–2. *Second Innings*—Wickremasinghe 18–4–55–4; Vaas 24–9–37–4; Gurusinha 3–0–16–0; Dharmasena 10–2–23–0; Muralitharan 17–3–53–0; de Silva 4–2–5–1.

Umpires: B. L. Aldridge (New Zealand) and Shakeel Khan.
Referee: P. L. van der Merwe (South Africa).

†PAKISTAN v SRI LANKA

First One-Day International

At Gujranwala, September 29. Pakistan won by nine wickets. Toss: Pakistan. International debut: Salim Elahi.

Nineteen-year-old Salim Elahi, brother of the Test player Manzoor, had a sensational debut, winning the game with an unbeaten 102. Only three other players – Dennis Amiss, Desmond Haynes and Andy Flower – had scored a century in their first limited-overs international. And, astonishingly, Elahi had never even appeared in a first-class match. He reached three figures with a straight six off Wickremasinghe and also hit seven fours in 134 balls. He put on 156 in 34 overs with Aamir Sohail, then 78 in ten with Ramiz Raja, to complete victory with six overs to spare. Earlier, Sri Lanka were put in and looked vulnerable at 48 for three. But Ranatunga joined Gurusinha to rescue the innings with a stand of 137. Ranatunga scored 102 not out – the same as Elahi, though slightly quicker, hitting ten fours in 114 balls.

Man of the Match: Salim Elahi.

Sri Lanka

R. S. Mahanama run out	12
S. T. Jayasuriya c Basit Ali b Ata-ur-Rehman	25
A. P. Gurusinha c Saqlain Mushtaq b Mohammad Akram	57
P. A. de Silva c Saqlain Mushtaq b Ata-ur-Rehman	1
*A. Ranatunga not out	102
†R. S. Kaluwitharana run out	6
H. P. Tillekeratne not out	11
B 1, l-b 8, w 6, n-b 4	19
1/32 2/39 3/48 4/185 5/206 (5 wkts, 50 overs)	233

R. S. Kalpage, H. D. P. K. Dharmasena, G. P. Wickremasinghe and K. R. Pushpakumara did not bat.

Bowling: Aqib Javed 9–1–43–0; Mohammad Akram 10–1–43–1; Ata-ur-Rehman 10–0–46–2; Aamer Hanif 10–0–38–0; Saqlain Mushtaq 5–0–27–0; Aamir Sohail 6–0–27–0.

Pakistan

Aamir Sohail c sub (M. Muralitharan) b Jayasuriya	77
Salim Elahi not out	102
*Ramiz Raja not out	44
B 1, l-b 1, w 7, n-b 2	11
1/156 (1 wkt, 44 overs)	234

Inzamam-ul-Haq, Basit Ali, †Moin Khan, Aamer Hanif, Saqlain Mushtaq, Aqib Javed, Ata-ur-Rehman and Mohammad Akram did not bat.

Bowling: Wickremasinghe 7–0–41–0; Pushpakumara 7–0–47–0; Dharmasena 7–1–35–0; Ranatunga 2–0–14–0; Kalpage 6–0–32–0; Jayasuriya 10–0–43–1; de Silva 5–0–20–0.

Umpires: Ikram Rabbani and Mian Aslam.

†PAKISTAN v SRI LANKA

Second One-Day International

At Faisalabad, October 1. Sri Lanka won by 49 runs. Toss: Pakistan.

Sri Lanka turned the tables on their hosts, pulling level on the back of a highly respectable total of 257. But Pakistan's run-chase was well on its way while Ramiz Raja and Salim Elahi were adding 79 for the second wicket. The loss of both, within three runs, put the brakes on: wickets then tumbled and the target slipped out of reach. Needing 97 from the final ten overs, Pakistan managed less than half that. The tourists' top four had given them a sound start. Opener Jayasuriya scored a brisk fifty and Gurusinha, sharing a 109-run stand with de Silva, made 66 from 73 balls, which took him past 3,000 runs in one-day internationals.

Man of the Match: S. T. Jayasuriya.

Sri Lanka

R. S. Mahanama lbw b Ata-ur-Rehman	30
S. T. Jayasuriya c Aqib Javed b Ata-ur-Rehman	51
A. P. Gurusinha st Moin Khan b Arshad Khan	66
P. A. de Silva run out	47
*A. Ranatunga b Mohammad Akram	15
H. P. Tillekeratne b Mohammad Akram	14
†R. S. Kaluwitharana run out	11
W. P. U. J. C. Vaas not out	0
H. D. P. K. Dharmasena not out	1
L-b 14, w 5, n-b 3	22
1/75 2/100 3/209 4/222 5/232 6/256 7/256 (7 wkts, 50 overs)	257

G. P. Wickremasinghe and M. Muralitharan did not bat.

Bowling: Aqib Javed 8–1–34–0; Mohammad Akram 10–0–48–2; Ata-ur-Rehman 10–0–46–2; Aamer Hanif 2–0–21–0; Arshad Khan 10–0–32–1; Aamir Sohail 10–0–62–0.

Pakistan

Aamir Sohail c Muralitharan b Vaas	9
Salim Elahi run out	47
*Ramiz Raja c Jayasuriya b Dharmasena	33
Inzamam-ul-Haq c Gurusinha b Jayasuriya	14
†Moin Khan c sub (R. S. Kalpage) b Muralitharan	31
Basit Ali b Jayasuriya	16
Aamer Hanif b de Silva	19
Aqib Javed b de Silva	21
Ata-ur-Rehman not out	6
Arshad Khan not out	4
L-b 5, w 1, n-b 2	8
1/10 2/89 3/92 4/116 5/154 6/160 7/195 8/200 (8 wkts, 50 overs)	208

Mohammad Akram did not bat.

Bowling: Wickremasinghe 7–0–36–0; Vaas 2–0–17–1; de Silva 10–0–33–2; Dharmasena 10–0–38–1; Muralitharan 10–2–37–1; Jayasuriya 10–0–38–2; Ranatunga 1–0–4–0.

Umpires: Salim Badar and Siddiq Khan.

†PAKISTAN v SRI LANKA

Third One-Day International

At Rawalpindi, October 3. Sri Lanka won by four wickets. Toss: Sri Lanka. International debuts: Saeed Azad; E. A. Upashantha.

The limited-overs series mirrored the Tests perfectly as Sri Lanka came from behind to win 2-1. They overhauled Pakistan's total of 183 with two balls to spare. Rain leaked through the covers and delayed play for three hours, reducing the game to 38 overs a side. Pakistan began well enough, but again the loss of Salim Elahi signalled disaster: off-spinners Dharmasena and de Silva grabbed three wickets each in a collapse from 55 without loss to 134 for six. Sri Lanka, in contrast, were a shaky 63 for three after 15 overs. Then de Silva and Ranatunga united to put on 75, and their colleagues managed the final requirement of 32 from five overs without much fuss.

Man of the Match: A. Ranatunga.

Pakistan

Aamir Sohail st Kaluwitharana b Dharmasena	26
Salim Elahi c Kalpage b Dharmasena	30
*Ramiz Raja st Kaluwitharana b Dharmasena	4
Inzamam-ul-Haq c Jayasuriya b de Silva	25
Saeed Azad c Wickremasinghe b de Silva	19
Aamer Hanif not out	36
†Moin Khan c Kaluwitharana b de Silva	0
Zafar Iqbal run out	13
Aqib Javed c Gurusinha b Kalpage	11
Arshad Khan run out	2
Mohammad Akram not out	0
L-b 7, w 6, n-b 4	17
1/55 2/65 3/80 4/104 5/134 6/134 7/158 8/176 9/180 (9 wkts, 38 overs)	183

Bowling: Wickremasinghe 5–0–11–0; Upashantha 5–0–36–0; Dharmasena 8–0–30–3; Gurusinha 1–0–6–0; Kalpage 4–0–26–1; Jayasuriya 8–0–31–0; de Silva 7–0–36–3.

Sri Lanka

R. S. Mahanama b Zafar Iqbal	23
S. T. Jayasuriya c Inzamam-ul-Haq b Aqib Javed	19
A. P. Gurusinha b Zafar Iqbal	10
P. A. de Silva lbw b Aamer Hanif	32
*A. Ranatunga lbw b Aamer Hanif	42
†R. S. Kaluwitharana c Saeed Azad b Aamer Hanif	12
H. P. Tillekeratne not out	13
R. S. Kalpage not out	10
L-b 12, w 11	23
1/45 2/60 3/63 4/138 5/151 6/165 (6 wkts, 37.4 overs)	184

H. D. P. K. Dharmasena, G. P. Wickremasinghe and E. A. Upashantha did not bat.

Bowling: Aqib Javed 7.4–0–28–1; Mohammad Akram 8–0–38–0; Zafar Iqbal 8–0–37–2; Arshad Khan 7–1–26–0; Aamer Hanif 6–0–36–3; Aamir Sohail 1–0–7–0.

Umpires: Islam Khan and Shakeel Khan. Series referee: P. L. van der Merwe (South Africa).

THE NEW ZEALANDERS IN INDIA, 1995-96

By R. MOHAN

Whoever thought up the idea of this Test series, played during the monsoon months, must have regretted it. Meant to fill a gap before the World Cup, it proved such a damp squib that the Indian cricket board was forced to rethink its future scheduling of international cricket. The choice of Test venues – Bangalore, Madras and Cuttack – was questionable because all three are susceptible to the north-east monsoon which sweeps the southern half of the Indian peninsula in October and November. India's three-day victory in the First Test at Bangalore was a blessing; it rained heavily the day after. The Madras game suffered the dubious distinction of becoming the shortest Test in terms of overs bowled – 71 – in Indian history. Cuttack was not much better.

India's win at Bangalore was thus decisive and preserved their record of not losing a Test series at home since 1986-87, when they were beaten at the same venue by Imran Khan's Pakistan. Their captain, Mohammad Azharuddin, played a key role with a classy 87 in the first innings, further consolidating his position; he had already won more Tests than any of his predecessors. Jadeja, whose three previous Tests were all in South Africa in 1992-93, staked his claim to the opener's spot with two forceful half-centuries. Of the bowlers, seamer Javagal Srinath and spinner Anil Kumble, both fresh from stints in the English County Championship, were the chief destroyers. With his very first wicket, Kumble had touched the landmark of 100 Test wickets in his 21st game, while his fellow wrist-spinner, Narendra Hirwani, livened up the final day of the series with an enticing spell of six for 59. His successful come-back, after five years, furthered the growing international fashion for leg-spin.

The Kiwis had a new coach, Glenn Turner, and a new captain, wicket-keeper Lee Germon, appointed when Ken Rutherford became one of the many scape-goats for New Zealand's dismal centenary season. Germon had played only one limited-overs international and no Tests but provided most of his team's resistance with the bat at Bangalore. Despite that disappointing start, the New Zealanders did show a positive attitude to the tour until a busy one-day schedule of six matches in 15 days took its toll on fitness and discipline. One plus was the batting of Nathan Astle, who blossomed with confidence in those games. But the tour was to mark the end of the international career of Martin Crowe, New Zealand's batting star for the past decade. After a final hundred in the one-day series, he flew home before the last match saying that his knee, which had hampered him for the past few years, would take no more.

After the fiasco of the Tests, the one-day international series proved more popular, especially since New Zealand began with a win and were level before the sixth and final scheduled match (the third was abandoned, due to more rain). By then, they were weakened by the loss of Crowe, and India comfortably extended their unbeaten run in home one-day tournaments to five years. But the penultimate game at Nagpur was marred by tragedy, when a wall collapsed in the lunch interval; nine spectators died and 50 were injured.

NEW ZEALAND TOURING PARTY

L. K. Germon (Canterbury) (*captain*), C. L. Cairns (Canterbury), M. D. Crowe (Wellington), S. B. Doull (Northern Districts), S. P. Fleming (Canterbury), A. J. Gale (Otago), M. J. Greatbatch (Central Districts), M. N. Hart (Northern Districts), M. J. Haslam (Auckland), D. K. Morrison (Auckland), D. J. Nash (Northern Districts), A. C. Parore (Northern Districts), S. A. Thomson (Northern Districts), R. G. Twose (Wellington), B. A. Young (Northern Districts).

Haslam replaced D. N. Patel (Auckland) who withdrew with an Achilles tendon injury. N. J. Astle (Canterbury) and G. R. Larsen (Wellington) replaced Gale and Hart for the one-day internationals.

Manager: G. D. Alabaster. *Coach:* G. M. Turner.

NEW ZEALAND TOUR RESULTS

Test matches – Played 3: Lost 1, Drawn 2.
First-class matches – Played 6: Lost 1, Drawn 5.
Loss – India.
Draws – India (2); Board President's XI, Bombay, Indian Colts XI.
One-day internationals – Played 5: Won 2, Lost 3. Abandoned 1.

TEST MATCH AVERAGES

INDIA – BATTING

	T	*I*	*NO*	*R*	*HS*	*100s*	*Avge*	*Ct*
M. Azharuddin	3	2	0	122	87	0	61.00	1
N. R. Mongia	3	2	1	46	45*	0	46.00	4
A. Jadeja	3	4	0	180	73	0	45.00	2
S. V. Manjrekar	1	2	1	44	29*	0	44.00	1
N. S. Sidhu	2	2	0	74	41	0	37.00	0
M. Prabhakar	3	4	1	110	43	0	36.66	1
S. R. Tendulkar	3	4	2	58	52*	0	29.00	3
V. G. Kambli	3	2	0	55	28	0	27.50	1
J. Srinath	3	2	1	21	21*	0	21.00	1
A. Kumble	3	2	1	8	6*	0	8.00	2

Played in two Tests: R. K. Chauhan 1; S. L. V. Raju 0. Played in one Test: A. R. Kapoor 42; N. D. Hirwani did not bat.

* *Signifies not out.*

BOWLING

	O	*M*	*R*	*W*	*BB*	*5W/i*	*Avge*
N. D. Hirwani	31	10	59	6	6-59	1	9.83
A. Kumble	72.2	21	152	10	5-81	1	15.20
J. Srinath	37	14	81	5	3-24	0	16.20
S. L. V. Raju	30	8	90	3	2-47	0	30.00

Also bowled: R. K. Chauhan 20–8–38–1; A. R. Kapoor 17–3–32–0; M. Prabhakar 19–5–48–2.

NEW ZEALAND – BATTING

	T	*I*	*NO*	*R*	*HS*	*100s*	*Avge*	*Ct/St*
L. K. Germon	3	3	0	91	48	0	30.33	2/1
S. P. Fleming	3	2	0	57	41	0	28.50	1
M. J. Greatbatch	3	3	0	76	50	0	25.33	2
M. N. Hart	2	3	1	36	27*	0	18.00	2
C. L. Cairns	3	3	0	51	23	0	17.00	0
M. D. Crowe.......	3	3	0	50	24	0	16.66	1
D. J. Nash	3	3	1	27	17	0	13.50	0
S. A. Thomson	2	2	0	23	17	0	11.50	0
B. A. Young	1	2	0	22	14	0	11.00	3
A. C. Parore	3	3	0	17	12	0	5.66	2
D. K. Morrison	3	3	1	10	9	0	5.00	0

Played in two Tests: M. J. Haslam 1*; R. G. Twose 36 (1 ct).

* *Signifies not out.*

BOWLING

	O	*M*	*R*	*W*	*BB*	*5W/i*	*Avge*
D. J. Nash	67	11	160	8	4-62	0	20.00
C. L. Cairns	66.3	17	170	8	4-44	0	21.25
D. K. Morrison	52	9	181	3	3-61	0	60.33

Also bowled: M. N. Hart 21.5–4–92–2; M. J. Haslam 32.1–5–92–1; S. A. Thomson 32–4–97–0; R. G. Twose 1–0–5–0.

Note: Matches in this section which were not first-class are signified by a dagger.

At Rajkot, October 7, 8, 9. Drawn. Toss: New Zealanders. New Zealanders 366 for five dec. (M. J. Greatbatch 138, B. A. Young 52, A. C. Parore 79; A. R. Kapoor three for 137) and 251 for five dec. (M. D. Crowe 101 not out, S. P. Fleming 72; A. R. Kapoor three for 82); Board President's XI 399 for six dec. (A. Jadeja 40, R. Dravid 145 not out, M. Azharuddin 100, Robin Singh 50) and 69 for one (V. Rathore 39).

At Bombay, October 12, 13, 14. Drawn. Toss: Bombay. New Zealanders 217 for eight dec. (M. J. Greatbatch 100; P. L. Mhambrey four for 79) and 192 for three (A. C. Parore 64, S. P. Fleming 79 not out, S. A. Thomson 45 not out); Bombay 360 (S. V. Manjrekar 79, S. R. Tendulkar 39, V. G. Kambli 104, A. A. Muzumdar 53; D. K. Morrison three for 48).

Greatbatch scored his second hundred in successive matches.

INDIA v NEW ZEALAND

First Test Match

At Bangalore, October 18, 19, 20. India won by eight wickets. Toss: New Zealand. Test debut: L. K. Germon.

Lee Germon became the first cricketer to captain an established Test country on debut since Tony Lewis of England at Delhi 23 years earlier. Despite winning the toss, he could not end New Zealand's disastrous run of form; they lost their sixth Test out of eight with two days to spare, while India's most successful captain, Azharuddin, celebrated his 11th Test win.

Batting first on a pitch still to shed its residual moisture was not a blessing, as the pace of Srinath and Kumble's leg-spin sent New Zealand reeling. Kumble's first wicket, Crowe, was his 100th in his 21st Test; he was to take nine in the match in front of his home crowd. The only resistance came from Germon himself, in his first international innings (he had not batted in his only previous game for New Zealand, a one-day match against Sri Lanka in South Africa). Coming in at 71 for six, he scored a fine 48 with a technical correctness none of his colleagues had displayed – no one else reached 20. Next, he took his first Test catch ten minutes into India's reply. The pitch was still lively enough for New Zealand to pick up three wickets, including Tendulkar, in 28 overs before stumps.

But the overnight pair, Jadeja and Azharuddin, took India past the tourists' total of 145, with Jadeja scoring an adventurous maiden Test fifty. He had been recalled as opener for only his fourth Test, and his first since January 1993, because Sidhu was injured. Azharuddin went on to 87 in 222 minutes, by far the biggest as well as the longest innings of the match, but was finally undone by Cairns's changes of pace, which claimed four for eight in a 22-ball burst. This sent India tumbling from 211 for four to 228 all out and restricted their lead to just 83.

A clever opening spell from Prabhakar then quickly removed both openers, and New Zealand were 58 for four when Crowe was given lbw, pulling a short ball from Kumble – a decision which became the talking point of the day, as he was hit well above the pads. Fleming and Cairns dragged the fight into the third day but were dismissed early in the morning. That left Germon, who had positioned himself at a humble No. 8, as the lone resister, with his second forty of the match. India's target of 151 could have been a teasing one, but Jadeja smoothed their passage with some sparkling strokes. He dominated a century stand for the opening wicket with a well-made 73 off 92 balls; Azharuddin, who received the match award for his batting in the first innings, graciously said that Jadeja was the more deserving candidate.

Man of the Match: M. Azharuddin.

Close of play: First day, India 81-3 (A. Jadeja 30*, M. Azharuddin 21*); Second day, New Zealand 125-5 (S. P. Fleming 33*, C. L. Cairns 23*).

New Zealand

B. A. Young c Tendulkar b Raju	14	(2) lbw b Prabhakar	8
M. J. Greatbatch b Srinath	10	(1) b Prabhakar	16
A. C. Parore lbw b Srinath	2	lbw b Srinath	3
M. D. Crowe c Tendulkar b Kumble	11	lbw b Kumble	24
S. P. Fleming c Mongia b Srinath	16	c and b Kumble	41
S. A. Thomson c Mongia b Chauhan	17	c Mongia b Kumble	6
C. L. Cairns c Manjrekar b Raju	15	b Srinath	23
*†L. K. Germon c Tendulkar b Kumble	48	lbw b Kumble	41
D. J. Nash lbw b Kumble	0	c Kumble b Raju	17
M. N. Hart c Prabhakar b Kumble	1	not out	27
D. K. Morrison not out	1	c Azharuddin b Kumble	9
B 4, l-b 5, n-b 1	10	B 8, l-b 10	18
1/14 (2) 2/22 (3) 3/30 (1) 4/44 (4) 5/71 (5) 6/71 (6) 7/116 (7) 8/116 (9) 9/144 (10) 10/145 (8)	145	1/19 (2) 2/32 (1) 3/36 (3) 4/58 (4) 5/80 (6) 6/130 (7) 7/134 (5) 8/173 (9) 9/210 (8) 10/233 (11)	233

Bowling: *First Innings*—Prabhakar 6–0–15–0; Srinath 14–5–24–3; Raju 16–6–47–2; Kumble 18–5–39–4; Chauhan 11–7–11–1. *Second Innings*—Prabhakar 8–3–23–2; Srinath 15–6–41–2; Kumble 27.2–4–81–5; Chauhan 9–1–27–0; Raju 14–2–43–1.

India

M. Prabhakar c Germon b Morrison	4	– c Greatbatch b Hart	43
A. Jadeja c Young b Morrison	59	– c Parore b Hart	73
S. V. Manjrekar lbw b Nash	15	– not out	29
S. R. Tendulkar c Young b Nash	4	– not out	0
*M. Azharuddin b Cairns	87		
V. G. Kambli c Parore b Nash	27		
†N. R. Mongia lbw b Cairns	1		
A. Kumble not out	6		
J. Srinath b Cairns	0		
R. K. Chauhan c Young b Morrison	1		
S. L. V. Raju c Hart b Cairns	0		
L-b 8, w 4, n-b 12	24	L-b 3, n-b 3	6
1/11 (1) 2/45 (3) 3/54 (4) 4/149 (2) 5/211 (6) 6/214 (7) 7/220 (5) 8/220 (9) 9/227 (10) 10/228 (11)	228	1/101 (2) 2/145 (1)	(2 wkts) 151

Bowling: *First Innings*—Morrison 18–5–61–3; Cairns 17.4–5–44–4; Nash 16–3–50–3; Hart 7–1–28–0; Thomson 12–3–37–0. *Second Innings*—Nash 7–1–26–0; Morrison 7–1–34–0; Cairns 6–1–13–0; Thomson 11–1–41–0; Hart 9.5–3–34–2.

Umpires: M. J. Kitchen (England) and S. K. Bansal. Referee: P. J. Burge (Australia).

INDIA v NEW ZEALAND

Second Test Match

At Madras, October 25, 26, 27, 28, 29. Drawn. Toss: India. Test debut: R. G. Twose.

This Test came two days after a total eclipse of the sun, which had brought the country to a halt. It was the more mundane phenomenon of monsoon rain that ruined the match. At only 71.1 overs, it was the shortest Test in terms of actual playing time ever staged in India; doubts were surfacing about the Indian board's wisdom in picking the city of Madras, on the Coromandel Coast, which is more susceptible than most to monsoons at this time of the year. But it was the relaid outfield, even more than the rain, which was the villain of the piece. It just did not allow the water to run away into the drains. After the first day, when play began at 2.30 p.m., there was no further play until the fourth day, although the sun shone brightly on the second. The teams suggested calling off the Test and playing a limited-overs match on the final day, but the host association scotched these thoughts, citing its legal obligations to those who bought season tickets for a five-day game. In fact the fifth day was abandoned too.

In the play possible after 3 p.m. on the fourth day, Tendulkar had time to make an unbeaten fifty, before bad light and showers drove the players off the ground for the last time. Prabhakar batted throughout the 304 minutes of play to score 41, one of the slower innings in the history of the game.

Man of the Match: S. R. Tendulkar.

Close of play: First day, India 54-1 (M. Prabhakar 19*, N. S. Sidhu 18*); Second day, No play; Third day, No play; Fourth day, India 144-2 (M. Prabhakar 41*, S. R. Tendulkar 52*).

India

M. Prabhakar not out	41
A. Jadeja b Nash	3
N. S. Sidhu c Twose b Cairns	33
S. R. Tendulkar not out	52
L-b 1, w 1, n-b 13	15
1/18 (2) 2/73 (3)	(2 wkts) 144

*M. Azharuddin, V. G. Kambli, †N. R. Mongia, A. Kumble, J. Srinath, R. K. Chauhan and S. L. V. Raju did not bat.

Bowling: Morrison 14–3–34–0; Cairns 16–7–18–1; Nash 15–3–22–1; Haslam 17.1–4–50–0; Thomson 9–0–19–0.

New Zealand

M. J. Greatbatch, R. G. Twose, A. C. Parore, M. D. Crowe, S. P. Fleming, S. A. Thomson, C. L. Cairns, *†L. K. Germon, D. J. Nash, D. K. Morrison and M. J. Haslam.

Umpires: K. T. Francis (Sri Lanka) and S. Venkataraghavan. Referee: P. J. Burge (Australia).

At Hyderabad, November 2, 3, 4. Drawn. Toss: New Zealanders. New Zealanders 454 for four dec. (R. G. Twose 119 retired ill, A. C. Parore 33, M. D. Crowe 110, S. P. Fleming 65, C. L. Cairns 75 not out) and 276 for two (M. J. Greatbatch 36, A. C. Parore 96, S. P. Fleming 100 not out, C. L. Cairns 31 not out); Indian Colts XI 180 (Jyoti P. Yadav 59, R. Morris 39; M. N. Hart six for 73).

Crowe scored his 71st and last first-class hundred before he announced his retirement in January – and also captained the side, though Germon played after a last-minute change. Hart's figures were his best in first-class cricket.

INDIA v NEW ZEALAND

Third Test Match

At Cuttack, November 8, 9, 10, 11, 12. Drawn. Toss: India.

The folly of the tour schedule became clear when the Third Test, like the Second, was hit by the monsoon rains, which swept in off the Bay of Bengal. Two days were completely lost, though play should have been possible on the third day. But groundsmen discovered that the pitch had been drenched by water seeping through holes in the multi-layered plastic covers, prompting a row about whether the local association or the Indian board was responsible. Proceedings in the match itself could only be of academic interest, but the drudgery was reduced by the tubby leg-spinner Hirwani, making a comeback in his first Test since he bowled against Sri Lanka at Chandigarh five years before. Hirwani took six wickets on the final day in a teasing exhibition of orthodox leg-breaks mixed liberally with googlies.

Play had begun on time on the opening morning. Cairns, bowling what were virtually off-breaks, was among the wickets again on a pitch which had aroused the tourists' misgivings. But drizzle on the first afternoon became a deluge as the storm blew in next day. It was a relief for the bored cricketers to resume on the fourth day, though a result was near-impossible. Cairns and Nash continued to trouble the Indian batsmen, who were in some disarray at 188 for six before Mongia and Kapoor joined forces. They showed how well the pitch was holding up, despite all the moisture. On the fifth morning the English-born Twose finally got to the batting crease, 18 days after his debut in Madras, and he batted for 204 minutes to make 36 before falling victim to Hirwani, while Greatbatch recovered the form with which he had begun the tour.

The draw gave India a 1-0 series win; it was now nine years since their last series defeat on home soil, by Imran Khan's Pakistan in 1986-87.

Man of the Match: N. D. Hirwani.

Close of play: First day, India 120-3 (N. S. Sidhu 20*, M. Azharuddin 23*); Second day, No play; Third day, No play; Fourth day, India 296-8 dec.

India

M. Prabhakar c Crowe b Nash	22
A. Jadeja c Hart b Cairns	45
N. S. Sidhu c Fleming b Nash	41
S. R. Tendulkar b Cairns	2
*M. Azharuddin lbw b Cairns	35
V. G. Kambli c Germon b Nash	28
†N. R. Mongia not out	45
A. R. Kapoor st Germon b Haslam	42
A. Kumble c Greatbatch b Nash	2
J. Srinath not out	21
L-b 10, n-b 3	13
1/69 (1) 2/75 (2) 3/77 (4) 4/143 (5) 5/172 (3) 6/188 (6) 7/254 (8) 8/267 (9) (8 wkts dec.)	296

N. D. Hirwani did not bat.

Bowling: Morrison 13–0–52–0; Cairns 26.5–4–95–3; Nash 29–4–62–4; Twose 1–0–5–0; Haslam 15–1–42–1; Hart 5–0–30–0.

New Zealand

M. J. Greatbatch c Jadeja b Hirwani	50	D. K. Morrison lbw b Kumble	0
R. G. Twose lbw b Hirwani	36	M. J. Haslam not out	1
A. C. Parore c Mongia b Hirwani	12	B 7, l-b 19, n-b 2	28
M. D. Crowe c Kambli b Hirwani	15		
C. L. Cairns c Jadeja b Hirwani	13	1/86 (1) 2/109 (2)	(8 wkts) 175
*†L. K. Germon run out	2	3/130 (3) 4/139 (4)	
M. N. Hart c Srinath b Hirwani	8	5/151 (6) 6/155 (5)	
D. J. Nash not out	10	7/166 (7) 8/166 (9)	

S. P. Fleming did not bat.

Bowling: Prabhakar 5–2–10–0; Srinath 8–3–16–0; Kapoor 17–3–32–0; Kumble 27–12–32–1; Hirwani 31–10–59–6.

Umpires: I. D. Robinson (Zimbabwe) and V. K. Ramaswamy. Referee: P. J. Burge (Australia).

†INDIA v NEW ZEALAND

First One-Day International

At Jamshedpur, November 15. New Zealand won by eight wickets. Toss: New Zealand.

New Zealand beat their hosts for the first time in a one-day international on Indian soil. It confirmed the Keenan Stadium's reputation as unlucky for India, who have won none of their five games there. Crowe dominated the match, though the fielders gave him three lives between 27 and 50. He went on to 107 not out from 129 balls, his fourth and highest century in a limited-overs international. With Fleming, he shared an unbroken stand of 171 which guided the team home by the 47th over. India's total of 236 had not been enough on a good pitch with a fast outfield. Tendulkar gave them the usual brisk start, but the middle order was checked by New Zealand's seamers.

Man of the Match: M. D. Crowe.

India

M. Prabhakar c Astle b Larsen	83	J. Srinath not out	17
S. R. Tendulkar c Greatbatch b Morrison	30	U. Chatterjee run out	3
N. S. Sidhu c Nash b Larsen	12	B. K. V. Prasad b Cairns	1
*M. Azharuddin b Cairns	32	L-b 6, w 7	13
V. G. Kambli b Nash	15		
A. Jadeja c and b Thomson	0	1/45 2/94 3/159	(49.1 overs) 236
†N. R. Mongia b Morrison	26	4/177 5/178 6/194	
A. Kumble b Nash	4	7/204 8/222 9/234	

Bowling: Morrison 9–0–49–2; Nash 10–0–56–2; Cairns 9.1–1–33–2; Larsen 10–0–40–2; Astle 3–0–17–0; Thomson 8–0–35–1.

New Zealand

M. J. Greatbatch b Prasad	31
N. J. Astle lbw b Prabhakar	7
M. D. Crowe not out	107
S. P. Fleming not out	78
L-b 9, w 3, n-b 2	14
1/18 2/66 (2 wkts, 46.5 overs)	237

R. G. Twose, C. L. Cairns, S. A. Thomson, *†L. K. Germon, G. R. Larsen, D. J. Nash and D. K. Morrison did not bat.

Bowling: Prabhakar 7–0–36–1; Srinath 8–1–30–0; Prasad 10–0–50–1; Kumble 10–0–40–0; Chatterjee 8.5–0–54–0; Tendulkar 3–0–18–0.

Umpires: K. S. Giridharan and C. K. Sathe.

†INDIA v NEW ZEALAND

Second One-Day International

At Amritsar, November 18. India won by six wickets. Toss: India.

Astutely exploiting the colder conditions of the north, where the ball often moves around, Prabhakar picked up only his second bag of five wickets in 122 one-day internationals. He kept New Zealand down to 145, despite a fifty from opener Astle; it was left to Morrison, not renowned as a defensive batsman, to deny him a hat-trick. But the target might have proved a bit of a test on a pitch not conducive to strokeplay. India lost their top four with just 72 on the board, before Manjrekar and Jadeja levelled the series with an unbroken stand which more than doubled the score.

Man of the Match: M. Prabhakar.

New Zealand

M. J. Greatbatch c Tendulkar b Prabhakar	2
N. J. Astle lbw b Tendulkar	59
M. D. Crowe lbw b Prabhakar	2
S. P. Fleming c Mongia b Srinath	3
R. G. Twose b Prasad	5
C. L. Cairns b Kumble	4
S. A. Thomson c Srinath b Prabhakar	14
*†L. K. Germon c Mongia b Prabhakar	9
G. R. Larsen c Mongia b Srinath	20
D. J. Nash lbw b Prabhakar	0
D. K. Morrison not out	2
B 2, l-b 12, w 8, n-b 3	25
1/12 2/22 3/37 4/57 5/69 6/96 7/112 8/123 9/123 (44.1 overs)	145

Bowling: Prabhakar 10–0–33–5; Srinath 8.1–1–26–2; Prasad 6–0–14–1; Kumble 6–0–16–1; Kapoor 10–1–27–0; Tendulkar 4–0–15–1.

India

M. Prabhakar lbw b Nash	1
S. R. Tendulkar c Germon b Thomson	39
N. S. Sidhu c Fleming b Cairns	8
*M. Azharuddin run out	17
S. V. Manjrekar not out	44
A. Jadeja not out	26
B 2, l-b 1, w 4, n-b 4	11
1/2 2/25 3/65 4/72 (4 wkts, 43.4 overs)	146

†N. R. Mongia, J. Srinath, A. R. Kapoor, A. Kumble and B. K. V. Prasad did not bat.

Bowling: Morrison 6–0–20–0; Nash 6–1–17–1; Cairns 7–0–33–1; Larsen 10–3–23–0; Thomson 10–1–38–1; Astle 4–0–9–0; Twose 0.4–0–3–0.

Umpires: S. K. Porel and S. K. Sharma.

†INDIA v NEW ZEALAND

Third One-Day International

At Goa, November 21. Abandoned.

The rain began early in the day and not even the helicopters brought in to dry wet patches on the outfield could get the ground ready in time for play to begin. It was only the second one-day international in India to be abandoned without a ball bowled.

†INDIA v NEW ZEALAND

Fourth One-Day International

At Pune, November 24. India won by five wickets. Toss: India.

Despite a brilliant all-round performance from Cairns, India pulled ahead for the first time in the series. Cairns scored 103 from 87 balls, with four sixes and ten fours, his first century for New Zealand. But, though he added 147 with Twose to pull New Zealand well past the 200 mark, it was too late to recover fully from 75 for four. Strokeplay became ever easier in the afternoon and the Indians made steady progress to their target. Brisk progress by Kambli and Azharuddin was backed up by a quick 36 from Mongia and Manjrekar's more sedate 47. Cairns picked up three wickets, but the match was in India's bag.

Man of the Match: C. L. Cairns.

New Zealand

M. J. Greatbatch c Mongia b Srinath	13	S. A. Thomson not out	7
N. J. Astle run out	11		
M. D. Crowe lbw b Kapoor	15	L-b 7, w 5, n-b 2	14
S. P. Fleming c and b Tendulkar	26		—
R. G. Twose c Mongia b Prasad	46	1/28 2/31 3/68 (6 wkts, 50 overs)	235
C. L. Cairns st Mongia b Tendulkar	103	4/75 5/222 6/235	

*†L. K. Germon, G. R. Larsen, D. J. Nash and D. K. Morrison did not bat.

Bowling: Prabhakar 8–0–31–0; Srinath 10–1–42–1; Prasad 8–1–45–1; Kumble 8–0–35–0; Kapoor 7–0–26–1; Tendulkar 9–0–49–2.

India

M. Prabhakar c Twose b Cairns	20	†N. R. Mongia not out	36
S. R. Tendulkar c Larsen b Morrison	7		
V. G. Kambli run out	42	L-b 3, w 8, n-b 3	14
*M. Azharuddin lbw b Cairns	58		—
S. V. Manjrekar not out	47	1/20 2/56 3/127 (5 wkts, 45.5 overs)	236
A. Jadeja b Cairns	12	4/158 5/179	

J. Srinath, A. R. Kapoor, A. Kumble and B. K. V. Prasad did not bat.

Bowling: Morrison 9–0–62–1; Nash 8–0–48–0; Cairns 10–1–37–3; Larsen 8.5–0–42–0; Thomson 4–0–17–0; Twose 3–0–16–0; Astle 3–0–11–0.

Umpires: S. Chowdhury and K. A. Parthasarathy.

†INDIA v NEW ZEALAND

Fifth One-Day International

At Nagpur, November 26. New Zealand won by 99 runs. Toss: India.

The match was overshadowed by the terrible tragedy that occurred when the parapet wall of a newly-built extension to a stand collapsed during the lunch interval. Nine spectators were confirmed dead and at least 50 injured; some youngsters fell 70 feet to their deaths (See *Wisden* 1996, page 50). Officials did not dare to call off play, for fear of crowd reaction. Before the disaster, New Zealand had amassed 348 for eight, the third highest total in any limited-overs international. Astle led the way on a run-filled pitch with a fine maiden hundred for his country, though he benefited from dropped catches. It was Crowe, however, who took the initiative. His 63 was to be his last innings for New Zealand; he pulled out of the final game with his long-running knee injury and announced his retirement soon afterwards. Fleming made a fluent 60, but the innings ran into controversy when Twose angrily disputed a boundary catch which dismissed Cairns; he was later fined half his match fee. India had little hope of scoring 349, but made the attempt. The players were unaware of the deaths.

Man of the Match: N. J. Astle.

New Zealand

M. J. Greatbatch b Kapoor	38	G. R. Larsen not out	5
N. J. Astle c Azharuddin b Prasad	114	D. J. Nash not out	4
M. D. Crowe st Mongia b Kapoor	63		
S. P. Fleming c Azharuddin b Prasad	60	L-b 20, w 3, n-b 2	25
C. L. Cairns c Manjrekar b Kumble	14		—
R. G. Twose run out	9	1/62 2/190 3/288 (8 wkts, 50 overs)	348
S. A. Thomson lbw b Kumble	15	4/306 5/317 6/325	
*†L. K. Germon b Srinath	1	7/337 8/343	

D. K. Morrison did not bat.

Bowling: Prabhakar 8–0–55–0; Srinath 9–0–42–1; Kapoor 7–0–48–2; Kumble 10–0–48–2; Prasad 8–0–62–2; Tendulkar 6–0–54–0; Jadeja 2–0–19–0.

India

M. Prabhakar run out	9	A. R. Kapoor lbw b Larsen	6
S. R. Tendulkar run out	65	A. Kumble c sub (B. A. Young) b Thomson	12
V. G. Kambli c Crowe b Cairns	16	B. K. V. Prasad not out	0
*M. Azharuddin b Cairns	1	L-b 5, n-b 4	9
S. V. Manjrekar c sub (B. A. Young) b Astle	44		
A. Jadeja st Germon b Larsen	61	1/23 2/71 3/77 4/123 5/150 6/202 7/211 8/218 9/241	(39.3 overs) 249
†N. R. Mongia c sub (B. A. Young) b Thomson	20		
J. Srinath c Nash b Thomson	6		

Bowling: Morrison 4–0–25–0; Nash 5–0–35–0; Cairns 7–0–32–2; Larsen 9–0–58–2; Astle 5–0–31–1; Thomson 9.3–0–63–3.

Umpires: N. Menon and S. Shastri.

†INDIA v NEW ZEALAND

Sixth One-Day International

At Brabourne Stadium, Bombay, November 29. India won by six wickets. Toss: India.

Victory secured the tournament for India and preserved Azharuddin's record of never having lost a series, Test or limited-overs, on home ground since he took up the captaincy in 1990. It was the ninth one-day competition he had won in India, with one draw against England. The New Zealanders found themselves in desperate straits on a pitch which allowed the ball to seam around in the morning. They had lost Crowe and Cairns to injuries and, after the early blows struck by Srinath, the middle order could not handle the crisis; spinners Kumble and Kapoor teased them into surrender. While Prabhakar anchored the Indian reply, Kambli's assault on Doull helped him to 48 in 34 balls and hastened the end. The match, watched by 35,000, was designated a benefit for former Test wicket-keeper Syed Kirmani.

Man of the Match: J. Srinath. *Man of the Series:* M. Prabhakar.

New Zealand

M. J. Greatbatch c Manjrekar b Srinath	4	D. J. Nash c Prasad b Kumble	11
N. J. Astle c Prasad b Prabhakar	9	S. B. Doull c Prasad b Kumble	2
S. P. Fleming c and b Srinath	8	D. K. Morrison not out	1
A. C. Parore run out	14	L-b 3, w 2, n-b 3	8
R. G. Twose st Mongia b Kapoor	14		
S. A. Thomson run out	20	1/7 2/20 3/38 4/38 5/64 6/88 7/97 8/113 9/125	(35 overs) 126
*†L. K. Germon b Kumble	29		
G. R. Larsen c Srinath b Kapoor	6		

Bowling: Prabhakar 5–0–29–1; Srinath 6–0–22–2; Prasad 6–0–22–0; Kapoor 10–0–33–2; Kumble 8–0–17–3.

India

M. Prabhakar not out	32	A. Jadeja not out	35
S. R. Tendulkar b Morrison	1	L-b 2, w 6	8
V. G. Kambli c Greatbatch b Doull	48		
*M. Azharuddin c Germon b Doull	4	1/7 2/71 3/75 4/75	(4 wkts, 32 overs) 128
S. V. Manjrekar c Thomson b Doull	0		

†N. R. Mongia, J. Srinath, A. R. Kapoor, A. Kumble and B. K. V. Prasad did not bat.

Bowling: Morrison 9–2–32–1; Nash 8–1–25–0; Doull 6–0–42–3; Larsen 9–1–27–0.

Umpires: A. V. Jayaprakash and I. Shivram. Series referee: P. J. Burge (Australia).

THE SOUTH AFRICANS IN ZIMBABWE, 1995-96

By PETER ROBINSON

South Africa warmed up for a crowded summer with a quick and highly successful trip north of the Limpopo River. Their inaugural Test with Zimbabwe and two one-day internationals were all played at the picturesque Harare Sports Club before good crowds – an estimated 7,000 turned up on both the Saturday and Sunday of the Test, outstripping anything achieved before in Zimbabwe, outside one-day cricket. However, the visiting team was never seriously challenged.

Zimbabwe's great handicap, as captain Andy Flower was quick to acknowledge, is a shortage of competitive cricket, both at Test and first-class level. Despite Zimbabwe's unexpected win against Pakistan in February, the country's cricketers get most of their practice playing against each other in inter-district competitions.

The contrast between the sociable amateurism of the Zimbabweans and the professionalism of the South Africans, driven by their coach, Bob Woolmer, was apparent throughout. It was difficult to see how Zimbabwe could develop their game without extending their existing participation in South Africa's domestic competitions.

SOUTH AFRICAN TOURING PARTY

W. J. Cronje (Free State) (*captain*), D. J. Cullinan (Transvaal), P. S. de Villiers (Northern Transvaal), A. A. Donald (Free State), A. C. Hudson (Natal), G. Kirsten (Western Province), B. M. McMillan (Western Province), C. R. Matthews (Western Province), J. N. Rhodes (Natal), D. J. Richardson (Eastern Province), P. J. R. Steyn (Free State), P. L. Symcox (Natal).

B. N. Schultz (Eastern Province) joined the party as cover for de Villiers, who was injured. N. Boje (Free State), A. P. Kuiper (Western Province) and G. F. J. Liebenberg (Free State) joined for the one-day internationals.

Manager: Mustafa Khan. *Coach:* R. A. Woolmer.

SOUTH AFRICAN TOUR RESULTS

Test match – Played 1: Won 1.
One-day internationals – Played 2: Won 2.
Other non-first-class match – Won v Zimbabwe Country Districts.

Note: Matches in this section which were not first-class are signified by a dagger.

ZIMBABWE v SOUTH AFRICA

Inaugural Test Match

At Harare, October 13, 14, 15, 16. South Africa won by seven wickets. Toss: Zimbabwe. Test debuts: A. C. I. Lock, C. B. Wishart.

South Africa's first Test against their immediate neighbours was notable mostly for some wonderful fast bowling from Donald as Zimbabwe were beaten inside four days. Coming in off a shortened run but with little noticeable loss of pace, Donald was simply too quick and too controlled for the Zimbabweans in their second innings. Taking full advantage of a slight ridge, he claimed eight for 71 – the best Test analysis by any South African since their return to international cricket – to leave Zimbabwe at least 100 short of a defensible target.

The Zimbabweans did play with great spirit, none more so than Streak, who bowled and batted with gusto. Their shortage of meaningful competition showed, however, and South Africa had few moments of real anxiety. The return of Donald's new-ball partner, Schultz, attracted keen interest, particularly in view of England's imminent tour. He had been out of Test cricket for two years with a bad knee and was called up here only because de Villiers was injured. Schultz was perhaps over-anxious to do well. He fell in his delivery stride three times and was spoken to by umpire Shepherd and warned by referee Jarman after an "unsportsmanlike gesture" when he had Houghton caught behind. That was one of three early wickets he claimed as Zimbabwe slipped to 23 for four. Although Streak fashioned a lusty fifty to take the total to 170, South Africa had gained the early initiative.

They seemed to have lost it, though, in a nervous start against Streak and the left-arm seamer Bryan Strang. Early on the second morning, they were 85 for four. But Hudson, who had returned to open after being dropped the previous summer, batted beautifully for more than five hours. He scored his third Test century and shared a partnership of 101 with McMillan to take South Africa well into the lead. After he fell, McMillan increased that lead to a handsome 176, mainly with the help of Donald, before he was stranded two short of his century.

Most of the Zimbabweans got themselves in in the second innings before Donald got them out. Of the recognised batsmen, only Grant Flower failed to reach 20, but only his brother Andy pressed on for a half-century.

With most of two days remaining to chase 108 for victory, the South Africans again began edgily, losing three for 48. The Zimbabweans, however, seemed torn between sticking with Streak and Lock, who had made the breakthrough, and leg-spinner Paul Strang, their only realistic hope of snatching something from the game. In the event, Strang was not called up until Cronje had played himself in, and the match ended shortly after lunch. The Zimbabweans were forced to wait before buying their opponents a post-match drink, as South Africa immediately embarked upon a lengthy fielding practice.

Man of the Match: A. A. Donald.

Close of play: First day, South Africa 74-3 (A. C. Hudson 45*, C. R. Matthews 10*); Second day, Zimbabwe 13-0 (M. H. Dekker 2*, G. W. Flower 5*); Third day, Zimbabwe 272-8 (P. A. Strang 34*, B. C. Strang 18*).

Zimbabwe

M. H. Dekker c Hudson b Donald	1	– c Hudson b Schultz	24
G. W. Flower c Richardson b Donald	24	– c McMillan b Donald	5
*†A. Flower b Schultz	7	– (5) c Richardson b Donald	63
D. L. Houghton c Richardson b Schultz	5	– c Matthews b Donald	30
A. D. R. Campbell c Richardson b Schultz	0	– (3) c Schultz b McMillan	28
G. J. Whittall c Richardson b Matthews	29	– lbw b Donald	38
C. B. Wishart c Kirsten b Symcox	24	– b Donald	13
P. A. Strang b Matthews	0	– c Richardson b Donald	37
H. H. Streak c McMillan b Donald	53	– c Cronje b Donald	0
B. C. Strang lbw b Schultz	0	– not out	25
A. C. I. Lock not out	8	– b Donald	0
L-b 10, w 5, n-b 4	19	L-b 10, w 1, n-b 9	20
1/3 (1) 2/12 (3) 3/22 (4) 4/23 (5) 5/71 (2) 6/84 (6) 7/84 (8) 8/127 (7) 9/128 (10) 10/170 (9)	170	1/13 (2) 2/64 (3) 3/70 (1) 4/102 (4) 5/199 (6) 6/206 (5) 7/231 (7) 8/231 (9) 9/279 (8) 10/283 (11)	283

Bowling: *First Innings*—Donald 17.1–3–42–3; Schultz 21–7–54–4; Matthews 13–5–30–2; McMillan 3–0–13–0; Symcox 11–5–21–1. *Second Innings*—Donald 33–12–71–8; Schultz 24–7–72–1; Symcox 11–3–22–0; Matthews 20–7–52–0; McMillan 15–3–53–1; Cronje 1–0–3–0.

South Africa

A. C. Hudson b B. C. Strang	135	– (2) c B. C. Strang b Lock	4
G. Kirsten lbw b Streak	1	– (1) c A. Flower b Lock	13
*W. J. Cronje c Houghton b Streak	5	– not out	56
D. J. Cullinan c Whittall b Lock	11		
C. R. Matthews c G. W. Flower b B. C. Strang	10		
J. N. Rhodes c A. Flower b B. C. Strang	15	– (4) b Streak	6
B. M. McMillan not out	98	– (5) not out	25
†D. J. Richardson c B. C. Strang b Lock	13		
P. L. Symcox c Houghton b Lock	4		
A. A. Donald b B. C. Strang	33		
B. N. Schultz lbw b B. C. Strang	0		
B 9, l-b 6, w 3, n-b 3	21	L-b 2, w 2	4
1/1 (2) 2/24 (3) 3/59 (4) 4/85 (5) 5/145 (6) 6/246 (1) 7/261 (8) 8/265 (9) 9/344 (10) 10/346 (11)	346	1/6 (2) 2/36 (1) 3/48 (4)	(3 wkts) 108

Bowling: *First Innings*—Streak 26–6–79–2; Lock 17–4–68–3; B. C. Strang 32–4–101–5; P. A. Strang 23–2–58–0; Whittall 2–0–11–0; G. W. Flower 3–1–14–0. *Second Innings*—Streak 9–2–24–1; Lock 13–1–37–2; B. C. Strang 12–6–18–0; P. A. Strang 4–0–27–0.

Umpires: D. R. Shepherd (England) and R. B. Tiffin. Referee: B. N. Jarman (Australia).

†At Harare South Country Club, Harare, October 19. South Africans won by 151 runs. Toss: South Africans. South Africans 354 for six (50 overs) (B. M. McMillan 135, P. J. R. Steyn 98, G. Kirsten 32, W. J. Cronje 51 not out); Zimbabwe Country Districts 203 for nine (50 overs) (A. C. Waller 77; B. N. Schultz four for 25).

†ZIMBABWE v SOUTH AFRICA

First One-Day International

At Harare, October 21. South Africa won by 134 runs. Toss: Zimbabwe. International debut: N. Boje.

South Africa reshuffled their batting order, promoting McMillan to No. 3. He responded with a brutal century, his first in one-day internationals, as they amassed a total of 303. McMillan had missed out on a hundred by two runs in the Test, but made amends in no uncertain fashion as he weighed into the bowling. He hit 14 fours and three sixes in his 127 from 122 balls. Campbell made a watchful half-century, but Zimbabwe were never in the hunt after losing their first five wickets for 44. Though they lost only two more – Paul Strang becoming Richardson's 100th one-day international victim – South Africa achieved victory with ease.

Man of the Match: B. M. McMillan.

South Africa

A. C. Hudson run out	36
†D. J. Richardson c A. Flower b Olonga	5
B. M. McMillan c A. Flower b Streak	127
*W. J. Cronje c Campbell b P. A. Strang	33
J. N. Rhodes c A. Flower b Streak	25
G. Kirsten not out	36
A. P. Kuiper not out	14
B 4, l-b 15, w 6, n-b 2	27
1/7 2/66 3/152 4/192 5/284 (5 wkts, 50 overs)	303

N. Boje, C. R. Matthews, P. S. de Villiers and A. A. Donald did not bat.

Bowling: Streak 10–2–54–2; Olonga 10–1–59–1; B. C. Strang 9–0–51–0; Whittall 7–0–48–0; P. A. Strang 10–0–51–1; G. W. Flower 4–0–21–0.

Zimbabwe

*†A. Flower c Richardson b Matthews	2	P. A. Strang c Richardson b Cronje	24
G. W. Flower c Richardson b McMillan	19	H. H. Streak not out	23
A. C. Waller run out	0	L-b 6, w 4	10
D. L. Houghton c Cronje b Matthews	9		—
A. D. R. Campbell not out	68	1/11 2/14 3/30 (7 wkts, 50 overs)	169
G. J. Whittall c Richardson b McMillan	6	4/30 5/44	
C. N. Evans c Richardson b Donald	8	6/68 7/119	

B. C. Strang and H. K. Olonga did not bat.

Bowling: de Villiers 10–2–34–0; Matthews 10–1–42–2; McMillan 5–0–13–2; Donald 10–2–28–1; Boje 10–1–29–0; Cronje 5–0–17–1.

Umpires: Q. J. Goosen and I. D. Robinson.

†ZIMBABWE v SOUTH AFRICA

Second One-Day International

At Harare, October 22. South Africa won by 112 runs. Toss: South Africa. International debut: G. F. J. Liebenberg.

South Africa's all-round strength again proved too much for Zimbabwe as they completed their tour with a 100 per cent record. Kuiper held their innings together with 50 and Rhodes chipped in with a sprightly 53 off 47 balls, though Zimbabwe did dismiss South Africa in the 50th over. Streak bowled intelligently to claim four for 25. But their batsmen were unable to put together a meaningful response. Cronje also took four and they were all out with seven overs to spare; de Villiers opened what became the final over by bowling a paper cup.

Man of the Match: H. H. Streak. *Man of the Series:* B. M. McMillan.

South Africa

†D. J. Richardson hit wkt b Streak	0	C. R. Matthews c A. Flower b Streak	6
G. F. J. Liebenberg c A. Flower b Streak	12	P. S. de Villiers c A. Flower b Whittall	5
P. J. R. Steyn c A. Flower b Streak	4	A. A. Donald not out	5
A. P. Kuiper lbw b Campbell	50	L-b 7, w 14, n-b 3	24
G. Kirsten run out	38		—
J. N. Rhodes c Houghton b Campbell	53	1/1 2/18 3/28 (49.2 overs)	239
*W. J. Cronje c A. Flower b Whittall	7	4/87 5/171 6/180	
P. L. Symcox c Houghton b Brandes	35	7/184 8/203 9/217	

Bowling: Streak 10–1–25–4; Olonga 4–0–32–0; Brain 5–1–28–0; Brandes 4.2–0–23–1; Strang 5–0–30–0; G. W. Flower 5–0–25–0; Whittall 10–0–47–2; Campbell 6–1–22–2.

Zimbabwe

*†A. Flower c Richardson b Matthews	2	D. H. Brain not out	12
G. W. Flower c Richardson b Donald	21	E. A. Brandes c Matthews b Cronje	5
A. C. Waller c Richardson b Cronje	15	H. K. Olonga c Symcox b de Villiers	6
D. L. Houghton c de Villiers b Symcox	25	L-b 6, w 1, n-b 1	8
A. D. R. Campbell c Matthews b Cronje	5		—
G. J. Whittall run out	0	1/3 2/35 3/48 (42.5 overs)	127
P. A. Strang b Matthews	15	4/53 5/55 6/82	
H. H. Streak c Richardson b Cronje	13	7/92 8/113 9/119	

Bowling: de Villiers 8.5–2–30–1; Matthews 8–2–19–2; Cronje 10–0–33–4; Donald 8–0–21–1; Symcox 8–1–18–1.

Umpires: I. D. Robinson and R. B. Tiffin. Series referee: B. N. Jarman (Australia).

THE PAKISTANIS IN AUSTRALIA AND NEW ZEALAND, 1995-96

By DAVID HOPPS and QAMAR AHMED

Pakistan's tour of Australia was widely expected to be one of the most quarrelsome and unsavoury series in Test history. It took place in the aftermath of Australian bribery allegations against the former Pakistani captain, Salim Malik, an affair which had been unsatisfactorily concluded because of ICC's inability – or unwillingness – to hold its own investigation (see *Wisden* 1996, page 17).

But the three-Test series passed off relatively peacefully, which was testimony to superb leadership on both sides. Mark Taylor had already established himself as a highly principled Australian captain and his authority was emphasised as his players' behaviour remained exemplary, despite their resentment that a Pakistani judge had proclaimed Malik's innocence and effectively called the Australians liars. Taylor said merely: "I think the players feel a little let down." Wasim Akram, reinstated as captain in place of Ramiz Raja, deserved equal commendation for his handling of the Pakistani squad. They had been riven by conflict and mistrust over the allegations of bribery and betting scams but, in trying circumstances, they generally maintained a cordial and dignified air.

Malik himself often cut a peripheral figure, his prevailing mood summed up on the eve of the First Test when he stated: "I hate Australia; it's hell. I just stay in my room all day watching TV." When he required six stitches in a hand wound on the first day of the series, it precipitated the arrival of his brother-in-law Ijaz Ahmed, who not only strengthened the batting, carving a stubborn hundred in the final Test in Sydney, but provided Malik with some much needed succour.

On the field, Pakistan were far from impressive, going 2-0 down within eight days before gaining a consoling victory in Sydney when Australia eased off with the series already won, just as they had against England the previous summer. Pakistan's fielding was at times inept, one hapless practice session after their defeat in Brisbane being turned into an *It'll Be Alright On The Night* comic sequence by Australian TV. It gave Australia the chance to wipe away their draining experience in Pakistan a year earlier, when they dominated all three Tests, but lost the series 1-0; Taylor had likened that to having his heart torn out.

Pakistan rarely considered the Test series in isolation, instead constantly referring to its importance in terms of World Cup preparations. Never had limited-overs cricket been afforded so much significance when measured against the traditional format. To regard a competitive Test series as something akin to a training ground for a one-day tournament seemed psychologically flawed, even to the greatest enthusiast for the limited-overs game. Malik had played little cricket while the bribery investigation was pending, but his selection was justified on the basis of World Cup planning. Pakistan's desperation to retain their title in front of their own supporters was also illustrated by the bowling of Waqar Younis, who had missed their previous World Cup victory (and the adulation and rewards which followed) because of injury. With his history of back trouble, Waqar chose to ease himself through the series. He gradually rediscovered his in-swinging yorker, but rarely approached his old hostility until the final stages of the Third Test in Sydney. Arguably, his most aggressive over was bowled in the nets during a match against Victoria at the MCG; Aamir Sohail, who was batting without a helmet, received three bouncers in a row, the third of which hit him in the face and demanded five stitches above his top lip. ''Accidents happen,'' said Wasim.

Commercial pressures in modern Test cricket were underlined in the First Test in Brisbane when the Australian Cricket Board agreed to a Sunday rest day (the only rest day in a six-Test summer) because Channel 9 had a commitment to cover the Adelaide Grand Prix. Traditionalists bemoaned the fact that Queensland's cricket followers were denied a Sunday at the Test, but the TV company's demands held sway.

Leg-spinner Shane Warne, Malik's principal accuser, had received lengthy counselling before the Brisbane Test, and he was beset by other off-field problems. A picture of him smoking during a press conference was used by one newspaper to whip up a health storm, and he also started court action over the publication of private wedding pictures. Warne did not look his usual exuberant self, but such impressions were misleading – his match figures of 11 for 77 at the Gabba were the best by an Australian against Pakistan and no one played him comfortably.

In building their reputation as the best Test team in the world, Australia had had one nagging doubt in the back of their minds. Since he was dropped after his first four undistinguished Tests, Warne's leg-spin had brought 183 wickets at 21.47 each. What would happen if he was missing? They discovered the answer, briefly at least, in the Second Test at the Bellerive Oval when Warne broke a toe while batting on the first day. Warne's big toe became the talk of Australia, but a national crisis was averted; Hobart's chilly, overcast conditions meant a three-man attack could cope. Craig McDermott fell well below his usual standards for much of the series, inviting the suspicion that his best years were behind him, but Paul Reiffel bowled soundly, and Glenn McGrath took over as the leader of Australia's pace attack.

Australians were initially much taken by Pakistan's 18-year-old off-spinner, Saqlain Mushtaq, who hinted at an ability to turn an occasional ball away from the right-hander, much in the manner of John Gleeson a generation before. As the series progressed, they warmed instead to the prankish leg-spin of Mushtaq Ahmed, who bowled with a perpetual smile and regularly appealed more through enthusiasm than sense. But his nine wickets in the Second Test in Hobart represented the best return by any overseas spinner in Australia since Bhagwat Chandrasekhar took 12 in a match for India 18 years earlier, and he took nine again at Sydney.

At Somerset, Mushtaq's tendency to bowl many more googlies than leg-breaks had encouraged the belief that he could be played predominantly as an off-spinner. The Australians had barely begun to chew over that theory when he began to turn his leg-break appreciably and often. Left out of the First Test, he finished with 18 wickets at 21.33, although even that was overshadowed by Warne, who also bowled in only two Tests, but took 19 wickets at 10.42.

After their success at Sydney, Pakistan crossed over to New Zealand for their third visit in four seasons, where their revival continued with another Test win at Christchurch. Again, Mushtaq was the key figure, taking seven wickets in the second innings and ten in the match. Four one-day internationals followed, giving both teams further practice for the World Cup; honours were shared, as Pakistan twice took the lead and New Zealand twice drew level. – D.H.

PAKISTANI TOURING PARTY

Wasim Akram (PIA) (*captain*), Aamir Sohail (Lahore/Allied Bank) (*vice-captain*), Aamir Nazir (Allied Bank), Aqib Javed (Allied Bank), Ata-ur-Rehman (Lahore/Allied Bank), Basit Ali (United Bank), Inzamam-ul-Haq (United Bank), Mohammad Akram (Rawalpindi/Allied Bank), Moin Khan (Karachi/PIA), Mushtaq Ahmed (Islamabad/United Bank), Ramiz Raja (Allied Bank), Rashid Latif (Karachi/United Bank), Salim Elahi (Lahore/United Bank), Salim Malik (Habib Bank), Saqlain Mushtaq (Islamabad/PIA), Waqar Younis (United Bank).

Saeed Anwar (ADBP) was selected but withdrew because of illness. Ijaz Ahmed, sen. (Lahore/Habib Bank) joined the party after Salim Malik was injured.

Tour manager: Intikhab Alam.

PAKISTANI TOUR RESULTS

Test matches – Played 4: Won 2, Lost 2.
First-class matches – Played 7: Won 2, Lost 3, Drawn 2.
Wins – Australia, New Zealand.
Losses – Australia (2), Victoria.
Draws – Western Australia, South Australia.
One-day internationals – Played 4: Won 2, Lost 2. *Wins* – New Zealand (2). *Losses* – New Zealand (2).
Other first-class match – Won v ACB Chairman's XI.

TEST MATCH AVERAGES – AUSTRALIA v PAKISTAN

AUSTRALIA – BATTING

	T	*I*	*NO*	*R*	*HS*	*100s*	*Avge*	*Ct/St*
M. A. Taylor	3	5	0	338	123	1	67.60	5
M. E. Waugh	3	5	0	300	116	1	60.00	4
S. R. Waugh	3	5	1	200	112*	1	50.00	1
M. J. Slater	3	5	0	139	73	0	27.80	3
D. C. Boon	3	5	0	110	54	0	22.00	3
I. A. Healy	3	5	0	92	37	0	18.40	7/1
G. S. Blewett	3	5	0	87	57	0	17.40	3
S. K. Warne	3	4	1	39	27*	0	13.00	0
P. R. Reiffel	3	5	2	35	14	0	11.66	1
C. J. McDermott	3	5	0	28	20	0	5.60	4
G. D. McGrath	3	5	1	10	5	0	2.50	2

* *Signifies not out.*

BOWLING

	O	*M*	*R*	*W*	*BB*	*5W/i*	*Avge*
S. K. Warne	115	52	198	19	7-23	1	10.42
G. D. McGrath	121.5	25	342	15	5-61	1	22.80
P. R. Reiffel	75.2	20	213	8	4-38	0	26.62
C. J. McDermott	92.3	19	300	11	5-49	1	27.27

Also bowled: G. S. Blewett 16–8–31–2; M. E. Waugh 49–12–97–2; S. R. Waugh 16–2–40–1.

PAKISTAN – BATTING

	T	*I*	*NO*	*R*	*HS*	*100s*	*Avge*	*Ct/St*
Ijaz Ahmed, sen.	2	4	1	190	137	1	63.33	0
Aamir Sohail	3	6	0	233	99	0	38.83	0
Inzamam-ul-Haq	3	6	0	232	62	0	38.66	2
Ramiz Raja	3	6	0	180	59	0	30.00	1
Salim Malik	2	3	0	81	45	0	27.00	1
Wasim Akram	3	6	0	68	33	0	11.33	2
Waqar Younis	3	6	3	34	19*	0	11.33	1
Basit Ali	3	6	0	65	26	0	10.83	2
Salim Elahi	2	4	0	43	17	0	10.75	1
Moin Khan	2	4	0	41	16	0	10.25	3/1
Mushtaq Ahmed	2	4	0	10	8	0	2.50	1
Saqlain Mushtaq	2	4	1	4	2*	0	1.33	1
Mohammad Akram	2	4	1	1	1	0	0.33	2

Played in one Test: Rashid Latif 1, 3 (6 ct, 2 st).

* *Signifies not out.*

BOWLING

	O	*M*	*R*	*W*	*BB*	*5W/i*	*Avge*
Wasim Akram	122.4	32	273	14	4-50	0	19.50
Mushtaq Ahmed	134.2	26	384	18	5-95	2	21.33
Waqar Younis	84	20	263	8	3-15	0	32.87
Saqlain Mushtaq	79	19	227	4	2-130	0	56.75

Also bowled: Aamir Sohail 33.5–5–80–2; Mohammad Akram 53.1–6–196–2.

Note: Matches in this section which were not first-class are signified by a dagger.

†At Lilac Hill, October 26. Pakistanis won by three runs. Toss: ACB Chairman's XI. Pakistanis 210 (50 overs) (Aamir Sohail 74, Ramiz Raja 106; J. Angel five for 40); ACB Chairman's XI 207 (49.5 overs) (J. L. Langer 85).

At Perth, October 28, 29, 30, 31. Drawn. Toss: Western Australia. Western Australia 402 for five dec. (M. E. Hussey 146, T. M. Moody 42, G. B. Hogg 101 not out, A. C. Gilchrist 58 not out; Mushtaq Ahmed three for 114) and 189 for seven dec. (M. P. Lavender 49, J. L. Langer 40; Saqlain Mushtaq five for 39); Pakistanis 164 (Salim Elahi 54, Inzamam-ul-Haq 34, Moin Khan 56; J. Angel three for 42, B. P. Julian three for 32, B. J. Oldroyd three for 45) and 226 for eight (Salim Elahi 40, Ramiz Raja 84, Basit Ali 69 not out; J. Angel three for 61).

Hussey and Hogg scored their maiden first-class centuries.

At Adelaide, November 2, 3, 4, 5. Drawn. Toss: South Australia. South Australia 392 for eight dec. (B. A. Johnson 54, D. S. Lehmann 138, T. J. Nielsen 57, J. A. Brayshaw 40 not out, Extras 35; Saqlain Mushtaq three for 128) and 249 for five dec. (G. S. Blewett 103 not out, J. D. Siddons 125; Wasim Akram four for 43); Pakistanis 276 (Aamir Sohail 34, Ramiz Raja 33, Inzamam-ul-Haq 39, Basit Ali 137; M. A. Harrity four for 90, J. N. Gillespie four for 82) and 298 for five (Inzamam-ul-Haq 96, Basit Ali 101 not out, Moin Khan 38 not out).

Basit Ali scored his second century of the match on the final afternoon. Salim Malik, who had arrived two days earlier, was stumped off Tim May, one of the three Australians who had accused him of attempted bribery, in the second innings.

AUSTRALIA v PAKISTAN

First Test Match

At Brisbane, November 9, 10, 11, 13. Australia won by an innings and 126 runs. Toss: Australia. Test debut: Salim Elahi.

After Warne's match-rigging allegations against Salim Malik, dramatic necessity dictated that the pair should confront each other at the Gabba. Warne dismissed Malik for nought, fourth ball, which was as satisfying in itself for Australia as the entire lop-sided result, achieved with more than five sessions to spare. On the first day Malik had made a splendid diving catch at mid-wicket to dismiss Australia's captain, Taylor, and had needed six stitches in split webbing on his left hand. By the time he walked out to bat at No. 8 in Pakistan's second innings, to sporadic abuse, with overwhelming defeat beckoning and his hand heavily strapped, all Australia had cast Warne in the role of avenging angel. Malik offered a hesitant leading edge against a slightly turning top-spinner and McDermott plunged to hold a low catch at mid-off.

The fielders' temperate reaction was testimony to Taylor's positive influence, but Warne, understandably, could not resist commenting after the match. "It showed that there is justice in the game," he said. Warne's match figures of 44–19–77–11 took his record in three Tests at the Gabba, a traditional haven for seam bowling, to 30 wickets at 10.40. Brisbane's extra bounce enabled him to make full use of flight and dip as well as turn. At times, by his own high standards, he did not bowl uncommonly well, but he did not need to, such was his psychological hold over the batsmen.

Australia spent the best part of two days making 463. Their batsmen were not at their smoothest and Pakistan bowled assiduously in enervating heat, none more so than the two youngsters, Mohammad Akram, a rangy out-swing bowler, and the 18-year-old off-spinner Saqlain Mushtaq. Wasim Akram, as ever, bowled with great craft and Waqar Younis showed signs of rediscovering his in-swinger, even if, as one Australian batsman said, it was two yards slower. Steve Waugh scored an unbeaten six-hour 112, characterised by his singular method against short balls, jumping up and nudging where others would prefer to hook or avoid. He himself called it an ugly innings and he was missed twice in the eighties off Aamir Sohail's left-arm spin.

Pakistan, 40 for three on the second evening, capitulated to 97 all out, with Warne's morning's work amounting to six for 16 in 12.1 overs. Though temporarily denied Malik, his dominance was otherwise complete. Sohail – the only one to reach 20 – was stumped trying to sweep; Basit Ali was deceived by flight, Wasim by bounce; Moin misguidedly heaved to leg. The greatest culprit was Inzamam, who seemed more settled than most, but scooped suicidally to short mid-wicket as he sought to lift Warne out of the ground.

Sohail's indignation fuelled a dynamic 99 when Pakistan followed on, and they had regained some respect at 217 for three on the fourth morning. Then Mark Waugh, brought on simply to allow Warne to switch ends, tempted Inzamam to spoon him to mid-off, and Pakistan's last seven wickets – Malik among them – duly fell for 23, with Australia securing victory after only 88 minutes cricket.

Man of the Match: S. K. Warne. *Attendance:* 23,639.

Close of play: First day, Australia 262-4 (S. R. Waugh 24*, G. S. Blewett 0*); Second day, Pakistan 40-3 (Aamir Sohail 17*); Third day, Pakistan 197-3 (Inzamam-ul-Haq 56*, Basit Ali 11*).

Australia

*M. A. Taylor c Salim Malik b Saqlain Mushtaq	69
M. J. Slater c Mohammad Akram b Wasim Akram	42
D. C. Boon c Inzamam-ul-Haq b Wasim Akram	54
M. E. Waugh c Salim Elahi b Saqlain Mushtaq	59
S. R. Waugh not out	112
G. S. Blewett lbw b Waqar Younis	57
†I. A. Healy c sub (Mushtaq Ahmed) b Mohammad Akram	18
P. R. Reiffel lbw b Waqar Younis	9
S. K. Warne c Moin Khan b Aamir Sohail	5
C. J. McDermott b Waqar Younis	8
G. D. McGrath st Moin Khan b Aamir Sohail	5
B 2, l-b 6, w 4, n-b 13	25
1/107 (1) 2/119 (2) 3/213 (4) 4/250 (3) 5/385 (6) 6/411 (7) 7/434 (8) 8/441 (9) 9/452 (10) 10/463 (11)	463

Bowling: Wasim Akram 38–9–84–2; Waqar Younis 29.5–7–101–3; Mohammad Akram 33.1–4–97–1; Saqlain Mushtaq 44–12–130–2; Aamir Sohail 16.5–2–43–2.

Pakistan

Aamir Sohail st Healy b Warne	32	– b McGrath 99
Salim Elahi c Taylor b McDermott	11	– c Healy b McGrath 2
Ramiz Raja c Taylor b Warne	8	– c Healy b McGrath 16
Saqlain Mushtaq lbw b McGrath	0	– (9) not out 2
Inzamam-ul-Haq c S. R. Waugh b Warne	5	– (4) c McDermott b M. E. Waugh 62
Basit Ali c Taylor b Warne	1	– (5) lbw b McGrath 26
†Moin Khan c McDermott b Warne	4	– (6) c Healy b Reiffel 9
*Wasim Akram c Boon b Warne	1	– (7) c Slater b Warne 6
Waqar Younis not out	19	– (10) lbw b Warne 0
Mohammad Akram c Blewett b Warne	1	– (11) lbw b Warne 0
Salim Malik absent hurt		– (8) c McDermott b Warne 0
B 4, l-b 5, n-b 6	15	B 7, n-b 11 18
1/20 (2) 2/37 (3) 3/40 (4) 4/62 (1) 5/66 (5) 6/70 (7) 7/70 (6) 8/80 (8) 9/97 (10)	97	1/30 (2) 2/88 (3) 3/167 (1) 4/217 (4) 5/218 (5) 6/233 (7) 7/233 (8) 8/239 (6) 9/240 (10) 10/240 (11) 240

Bowling: *First Innings*—McDermott 11–4–32–1; McGrath 14–3–33–1; Warne 16.1–9–23–7. *Second Innings*—McDermott 11–0–47–0; Reiffel 15–4–47–1; McGrath 25–7–76–4; Warne 27.5–10–54–4; S. R. Waugh 2–1–3–0; M. E. Waugh 5–2–6–1.

Umpires: K. E. Liebenberg (South Africa) and S. G. Randell. Referee: R. Subba Row (England).

AUSTRALIA v PAKISTAN

Second Test Match

At Hobart, November 17, 18, 19, 20. Australia won by 155 runs. Toss: Australia.

Australian fears that they were over-reliant upon Warne's leg-spin were eased at the Bellerive Oval. Warne broke a toe on the first evening – always a possibility against Waqar Younis's in-swinging yorker – leaving Australia with only three specialist bowlers, all seamers. Even so, they achieved their second win inside four days. Taylor resourcefully bowled McGrath, Reiffel and McDermott downwind as much as possible, to conserve their energy, while using bit-part bowlers into the jabbing Tasmanian squalls. The bleak weather also ensured that three seamers would be sufficient. Even if the snow forecast for the third day never quite materialised, the Pakistanis could hardly have imagined more inhospitable conditions.

Australia's batsmen also struggled. Their first-innings 267 owed much to Mark Waugh, who failed to add to his record of eight centuries in 50 Tests, but undoubtedly deserved to. His first fifty was blessed with his usual grace and freedom of expression, despite shooting pains in his right leg. The regular fall of wickets drew a more cautious approach, but Healy astutely lofted Mushtaq Ahmed into the leg-side gaps. Mushtaq had his revenge on both, with Waugh falling when Ramiz Raja unexpectedly conjured up an excellent running catch over his shoulder at mid-wicket.

Pakistan mustered 198 in reply as Reiffel and McGrath maintained a consistent length on a rain-touched pitch. Ramiz emerged with most credit, even if his persistent fifty mixed mis-judgments with buoyant drives and pulls, and he was unfortunate to chip back a return catch as Reiffel made one pop.

A lead of 69 would not have been secure if Australia had stumbled on the second evening. But Taylor and Slater batted brilliantly, their positive outlook in mind-numbing cold reaping 107 in 24 overs. In that brief period, the outcome was settled; next day, Taylor made certain by proceeding to 123. But otherwise it was Australia's turn to flounder against leg-spin. Mushtaq Ahmed finished with nine for 198 in the match, bowling with a childlike sense of fun and, in his appealing, occasionally a childlike absence of logic.

A target of 376 to win a Test had been achieved only twice. But once Sohail, who had retired overnight when McDermott struck him on the thigh, resumed, his captivating off-side driving helped Pakistan make a decent start at 132 for two. Then their last eight fell for 88, a sequence beginning with Blewett's first Test wicket. At the betting booth on the ground, Blewett had been offered at 500 to 1 (odds with enormous resonance for Australian cricket since Headingley 1981) to take the next wicket. An ice-cream seller, spotting him loosening up, could not resist this. So when Sohail chipped his third ball, delivered at innocuous medium-pace, to mid-wicket, it was debatable whether the bookmaker or the batsman was the more peeved. Sohail rehearsed the shot with such vehemence as he strode off that he dropped the bat, an incident he paid for heavily when referee Raman Subba Row fined him half his fee and added a two-match suspended sentence. Pakistan's final downfall was engineered by McGrath, who had Wasim Akram athletically caught by Blewett at mid-on before making quick work of the tail with the new ball.

Man of the Match: M. A. Taylor. *Attendance:* 18,068.

Close of play: First day, Pakistan 33-2 (Aamir Sohail 15*, Ramiz Raja 4*); Second day, Australia 107-0 (M. A. Taylor 42*, M. J. Slater 62*); Third day, Pakistan 15-0 (Salim Elahi 7*, Ramiz Raja 6*).

Australia

M. J. Slater lbw b Wasim Akram	0	(2) lbw b Mushtaq Ahmed	73
*M. A. Taylor b Wasim Akram	40	(1) b Waqar Younis	123
D. C. Boon run out	34	c Waqar Younis b Mushtaq Ahmed	0
M. E. Waugh c Ramiz Raja b Mushtaq Ahmed	88	b Wasim Akram	3
S. R. Waugh c Moin Khan b Mushtaq Ahmed	7	c Moin Khan b Mohammad Akram	29
G. S. Blewett b Mushtaq Ahmed	0	c Basit Ali b Wasim Akram	11
†I. A. Healy c Basit Ali b Mushtaq Ahmed	37	c Inzamam-ul-Haq b Wasim Akram	24
P. R. Reiffel c Mohammad Akram b Mushtaq Ahmed	14	b Mushtaq Ahmed	0
S. K. Warne not out	27	absent hurt	
C. J. McDermott b Waqar Younis	0	(9) c Wasim Akram b Mushtaq Ahmed	20
G. D. McGrath b Wasim Akram	3	(10) not out	2
B 3, l-b 9, n-b 5	17	B 6, l-b 5, w 1, n-b 9	21
1/0 (1) 2/68 (3) 3/111 (2) 4/156 (5) 5/156 (6) 6/209 (7) 7/235 (8) 8/238 (4) 9/244 (10) 10/267 (11)	267	1/120 (2) 2/125 (3) 3/132 (4) 4/189 (5) 5/233 (6) 6/255 (1) 7/256 (8) 8/296 (9) 9/306 (7)	306

Bowling: *First Innings*—Wasim Akram 18.3–7–42–3; Waqar Younis 17–3–54–1; Mohammad Akram 10–1–41–0; Mushtaq Ahmed 30–5–115–5; Aamir Sohail 3–1–3–0. *Second Innings*—Wasim Akram 26.1–7–72–3; Waqar Younis 20–4–67–1; Mohammad Akram 10–1–58–1; Mushtaq Ahmed 38–8–83–4; Aamir Sohail 8–2–15–0.

Pakistan

Aamir Sohail c Healy b Reiffel	32	c sub (B. P. Julian) b Blewett	57
Salim Elahi b McGrath	13	c Boon b McGrath	17
Mushtaq Ahmed lbw b McGrath	0	(9) b McGrath	8
Ramiz Raja c and b Reiffel	59	(3) lbw b Reiffel	25
Inzamam-ul-Haq c Healy b S. R. Waugh	27	(4) lbw b Reiffel	40
Ijaz Ahmed, sen. not out	34	(5) lbw b Blewett	4
Basit Ali lbw b McGrath	2	(6) b Reiffel	5
†Moin Khan b McDermott	12	(7) c M. E. Waugh b McGrath	16
*Wasim Akram c Taylor b McDermott	2	(8) c Blewett b McGrath	33
Waqar Younis c sub (B. P. Julian) b Reiffel	10	c Blewett b McGrath	4
Mohammad Akram lbw b Reiffel	0	not out	0
L-b 1, n-b 6	7	L-b 11	11
1/24 (2) 2/24 (3) 3/79 (1) 4/126 (4) 5/150 (5) 6/155 (7) 7/173 (8) 8/183 (9) 9/198 (10) 10/198 (11)	198	1/27 (2) 2/62 (3) 3/132 (1) 4/142 (5) 5/152 (4) 6/157 (6) 7/205 (8) 8/210 (7) 9/220 (10) 10/220 (9)	220

In the second innings Aamir Sohail, when 0, retired hurt at 6 and resumed at 27.

Bowling: *First Innings*—McDermott 18–2–72–2; McGrath 19–4–46–3; Reiffel 15.5–3–38–4; M. E. Waugh 8–0–23–0; S. R. Waugh 6–0–18–1. *Second Innings*—McDermott 16–7–38–0; McGrath 24.3–7–61–5; Reiffel 14–6–42–3; M. E. Waugh 12–2–24–0; S. R. Waugh 8–1–19–0; Blewett 10–4–25–2.

Umpires: H. D. Bird (England) and D. B. Hair. Referee: R. Subba Row (England).

At Melbourne, November 24, 25, 26. Victoria won by eight wickets. Toss: Pakistanis. Pakistanis 154 (Basit Ali 46; B. A. Williams three for 57, D. J. Saker three for 35) and 279 (Ijaz Ahmed, sen. 39, Inzamam-ul-Haq 132, Basit Ali 32; D. W. Fleming four for 64); Victoria 362 (D. M. Jones 127, J. R. Bakker 31, B. A. Williams 35 not out, Extras 49; Ata-ur-Rehman three for 101, Saqlain Mushtaq five for 107) and 72 for two (G. R. Vimpani 32 not out).

Victorian wicket-keeper Darren Berry made 11 dismissals in the match, a state record; all were caught, equalling the world record.

AUSTRALIA v PAKISTAN

Third Test Match

At Sydney, November 30, December 1, 2, 3, 4. Pakistan won by 74 runs. Toss: Pakistan.

The series won, Australia's high standards slipped. Pakistan's victory, inspired by another excellent display of leg-spin by Mushtaq Ahmed, allowed them to leave for New Zealand in good heart. Mushtaq's quick, skiddy style proved well suited to the SCG's slow turner and he returned nine for the second time running. As at Hobart, the Australians faced him with great discomfort; his leg-break turned threateningly throughout.

Improbably, Pakistan's first-innings 299 was the highest total of the match. The mainstay was Ijaz Ahmed, who batted nearly seven and a half hours for his third Test century – all against Australia. It was born of earnest defence interspersed with occasional drives or cuts. He progressed from 89 to 97 with edges through the slips and reached three figures in the last over of the first day, cutting McDermott over point. Finally, on 137, he slapped a knee-high full toss from Warne straight to McGrath at deep backward square. People talk about Warne's mystique; this owed everything to luck.

Salim Malik had come out to a raucous Sydney welcome. He raised his bat in mock celebration as he got off the mark to boos and cat-calls. The next time his bat was raised it was to respectful applause after a skilful and bloody-minded 36, which included three successive cover drives against McGrath. When he was fourth out at 210, Pakistan envisaged at least 400, but the opportunity was wasted, despite Wasim Akram hitting four boundaries in five balls from McDermott.

Australia also seemed handily placed at 151 for three by the close of the second day. But Mushtaq was at his most ebullient next morning, supported by wicket-keeper Rashid Latif. The most impressive of his five wickets was the one that drew Steve Waugh from his crease, not an easy task; the most telling the gently floating in-swinger that accounted for Blewett. Australia were all out 42 behind, and the only batsman with cause for pleasure was Mark Waugh, whose four-and-a-half-hour 116 was his first Test century on his home ground.

If one player could lift Australia's spirits, it was Warne, on his much-trumpeted return from injury, and he did so with the last ball on Saturday. Believing that Basit Ali was temperamentally vulnerable, he broke his concentration with a prolonged mid-pitch discussion with Healy, and then bowled him through his legs trying to pad the ball away. The next day, Pakistan lost their last six for 103, suffering four lbw decisions, three keenly debated. Two went to McDermott, rousing himself with four for 11 in 36 balls, easily his most hostile spell of the series, and extra valuable as Australia had lost Reiffel to a torn hamstring.

That left Australia needing 247 and, when they resumed on the final day at 121 for three, their chances seemed even. But when Taylor unexpectedly charged at Mushtaq and was stumped for an otherwise discriminating 59, their cause was forlorn. Waqar, a fast bowler with the World Cup on his mind, for once slipped himself to make short shrift of the tail and Pakistan won before lunch.

Man of the Match: Mushtaq Ahmed. *Man of the Series:* S. K. Warne.

Attendance: 61,733.

Close of play: First day, Pakistan 231-4 (Ijaz Ahmed 101*, Basit Ali 8*); Second day, Australia 151-3 (M. E. Waugh 54*, S. R. Waugh 26*); Third day, Pakistan 101-4 (Salim Malik 21*); Fourth day, Australia 121-3 (M. A. Taylor 49*, I. A. Healy 4*).

Pakistan

Aamir Sohail c M. E. Waugh b McDermott	4	– c Boon b McDermott	9
Ramiz Raja c Slater c Warne	33	– c M. E. Waugh b Warne	39
Ijaz Ahmed, sen. c McGrath b Warne	137	– lbw b Warne	15
Inzamam-ul-Haq c Healy b Warne	39	– (6) c Taylor b McDermott	59
Salim Malik lbw b McGrath	36	– (4) lbw b M. E. Waugh	45
Basit Ali c Slater b McDermott	17	– (5) b Warne	14
†Rashid Latif c Healy b McDermott	1	– (8) lbw b Warne	3
*Wasim Akram c and b McGrath	21	– (7) lbw b McDermott	5
Saqlain Mushtaq run out	0	– c M. E. Waugh b McDermott	2
Mushtaq Ahmed c McDermott b Warne	0	– lbw b McDermott	2
Waqar Younis not out	0	– not out	1
L-b 3, w 2, n-b 6	11	B 1, l-b 5, n-b 4	10
1/4 (1) 2/64 (2) 3/141 (4) 4/210 (5) 5/263 (6) 6/269 (7) 7/297 (3) 8/299 (9) 9/299 (10) 10/299 (8)	299	1/18 (1) 2/58 (3) 3/82 (2) 4/101 (5) 5/163 (4) 6/185 (7) 7/188 (8) 8/198 (6) 9/203 (9) 10/204 (10)	204

Bowling: *First Innings*—McDermott 21–6–62–3; McGrath 22.2–1–79–2; Reiffel 22–5–71–0; Warne 34–20–55–4; M. E. Waugh 10–4–23–0; Blewett 4–2–6–0. *Second Innings*—McDermott 15.3–0–49–5; McGrath 17–3–47–0; Warne 37–13–66–4; Reiffel 8.3–2–15–0; M. E. Waugh 14–4–21–1; Blewett 2–2–0–0.

Australia

M. J. Slater b Wasim Akram	1	– (2) lbw b Mushtaq Ahmed	23
*M. A. Taylor c Rashid Latif b Saqlain Mushtaq	47	– (1) st Rashid Latif b Mushtaq Ahmed	59
D. C. Boon c Rashid Latif b Mushtaq Ahmed	16	– c sub (Moin Khan) b Saqlain Mushtaq	6
M. E. Waugh c Mushtaq Ahmed b Wasim Akram	116	– c Rashid Latif b Wasim Akram	34
S. R. Waugh st Rashid Latif b Mushtaq Ahmed	38	– (6) b Mushtaq Ahmed	14
G. S. Blewett b Mushtaq Ahmed	5	– (7) b Waqar Younis	14
†I. A. Healy c Rashid Latif b Mushtaq Ahmed	6	– (5) c Rashid Latif b Wasim Akram	7
P. R. Reiffel not out	10	– (10) not out	2
S. K. Warne c Rashid Latif b Wasim Akram	2	– (8) c Saqlain Mushtaq b Mushtaq Ahmed	5
C. J. McDermott b Wasim Akram	0	– (9) b Waqar Younis	0
G. D. McGrath c Wasim Akram b Mushtaq Ahmed	0	– b Waqar Younis	0
L-b 6, n-b 10	16	L-b 5, n-b 3	8
1/2 (1) 2/44 (3) 3/91 (2) 4/174 (5) 5/182 (6) 6/226 (7) 7/240 (4) 8/249 (9) 9/249 (10) 10/257 (11)	257	1/42 (2) 2/69 (3) 3/117 (4) 4/126 (5) 5/146 (6) 6/152 (1) 7/170 (7) 8/170 (9) 9/172 (8) 10/172 (11)	172

Bowling: *First Innings*—Wasim Akram 24–4–50–4; Waqar Younis 11–4–26–0; Mushtaq Ahmed 36.2–7–95–5; Saqlain Mushtaq 22–2–62–1; Aamir Sohail 5–0–18–0. *Second Innings*—Wasim Akram 16–5–25–2; Waqar Younis 6.1–2–15–3; Mushtaq Ahmed 30–6–91–4; Saqlain Mushtaq 13–5–35–1; Aamir Sohail 1–0–1–0.

Umpires: H. D. Bird (England) and S. G. Randell. Referee: R. Subba Row (England).

NEW ZEALAND v PAKISTAN

Test Match

At Christchurch, December 8, 9, 10, 11, 12. Pakistan won by 161 runs. Toss: New Zealand. Test debut: C. M. Spearman.

Eight days after their consolation win over Australia, Pakistan won again in New Zealand. As at Sydney, their heroes were Mushtaq Ahmed, who took ten wickets in a Test for the first time, and Ijaz Ahmed, with his second hundred in successive games.

The tourists had thrown away a strong position on the first day, when Aamir Sohail and Ramiz Raja shared an opening stand of 135, only for all ten wickets to crash for 73. Cairns started the slide with three for three in 21 balls. Sohail fell for 88 from 94 balls when he lost his balance and dislodged the bails; some thought Cairns was unlucky not to have had him hit wicket earlier, on 29. In New Zealand's reply, debutant Craig Spearman made a promising 40, hitting five fours and a six off Mushtaq before he was deceived by a top-spinner. The home side closed on 98 for three, but lost only Fleming next morning. Ramiz Raja missed a sitter at mid-on when Cairns was 30; Pakistan suffered for it when Cairns made 76, adding 102 with Twose. But once Wasim Akram had separated them, there was little resistance. The last six wickets fell for 65 and Wasim picked up five for 14 in ten overs.

New Zealand had a useful lead of 78, but this time the Pakistani batsmen applied themselves. By the second-day close, they were 60 runs in credit with only one wicket down, though Ramiz had temporarily retired after a blow to the wrist. They batted throughout the third day, extending their lead to 291. Ijaz and Inzamam-ul-Haq had taken their second-wicket stand to 140 before Inzamam was caught at slip; Ijaz escaped on 81, when Parore dropped him off Morrison's bowling, but after lunch surged from 89 to his fourth Test hundred with three fours. In all, he hit 13 fours and two sixes and batted for almost five hours. He was supported by Salim Malik and then Ramiz, who returned to make another half-century. Pakistan were finally out for 434 an hour into the fourth morning, after Waqar Younis and Mushtaq had put on a brisk 41 for the ninth wicket.

Chasing an unlikely 357, Spearman and Young gave New Zealand another respectable start, with 50, but once Mushtaq broke through they collapsed to 75 for five. When the captain, Germon, was run out at 101 for six, it looked as if the match might be over in four days. Twose rallied the lower order and reached his second fifty of the game, but Pakistan needed little more than an hour to complete victory on the final morning. Mushtaq took seven for 56, his best Test figures, which gave him a total of 28 in his last three Tests; Waqar Younis claimed his 200th Test wicket in his 38th match by bowling Nash. Last man Morrison postponed creating a new landmark when he scored a single before falling to Mushtaq; in the first innings, he had equalled the Test record of 23 ducks by India's Bhagwat Chandrasekhar.

Man of the Match: Mushtaq Ahmed.

Close of play: First day, New Zealand 98-3 (S. P. Fleming 16*, R. G. Twose 11*); Second day, Pakistan 138-1 (Ijaz Ahmed 54*, Inzamam-ul-Haq 52*); Third day, Pakistan 369-7 (Wasim Akram 11*, Mushtaq Ahmed 1*); Fourth day, New Zealand 158-7 (R. G. Twose 44*, G. R. Larsen 8*).

Pakistan

Aamir Sohail hit wkt b Cairns	88	– b Patel	30
Ramiz Raja lbw b Cairns	54	– lbw b Morrison	62
Ijaz Ahmed, sen. c Morrison b Larsen	30	– c Germon b Nash	103
Inzamam-ul-Haq lbw b Cairns	0	– c Fleming b Nash	82
Salim Malik c Germon b Nash	0	– c Germon b Morrison	21
Basit Ali c Germon b Larsen	5	– lbw b Cairns	0
†Rashid Latif c Spearman b Morrison	2	– c Germon b Cairns	39
*Wasim Akram c Young b Morrison	2	– c Fleming b Cairns	19
Mushtaq Ahmed lbw b Nash	5	– c Germon b Larsen	24
Waqar Younis not out	12	– lbw b Larsen	34
Ata-ur-Rehman c and b Cairns	5	– not out	0
L-b 1, w 1, n-b 3	5	B 5, l-b 6, w 4, n-b 5	20
1/135 (2) 2/146 (1) 3/148 (4) 4/149 (5) 5/177 (6) 6/184 (3) 7/184 (7) 8/187 (8) 9/203 (9) 10/208 (11)	208	1/55 (1) 2/195 (4) 3/224 (5) 4/260 (3) 5/265 (6) 6/339 (2) 7/363 (7) 8/384 (8) 9/425 (9) 10/434 (10)	434

In the second innings Ramiz Raja, when 1, retired hurt at 2 and resumed at 224.

Bowling: *First Innings*—Morrison 14–0–57–2; Cairns 11.1–2–51–4; Larsen 15–2–44–2; Nash 11–3–43–2; Patel 3–1–12–0. *Second Innings*—Morrison 27–5–99–2; Nash 30–6–91–2; Cairns 35–6–114–3; Patel 24–8–61–1; Larsen 29–10–58–2.

New Zealand

B. A. Young c Rashid Latif b Ata-ur-Rehman	16	– c Rashid Latif b Mushtaq Ahmed . 18
C. M. Spearman b Mushtaq Ahmed	40	– c Aamir Sohail b Mushtaq Ahmed. 33
A. C. Parore c Rashid Latif b Ata-ur-Rehman	9	– lbw b Mushtaq Ahmed . 5
S. P. Fleming st Rashid Latif b Mushtaq Ahmed	25	– lbw b Ata-ur-Rehman . 0
R. G. Twose lbw b Wasim Akram	59	– not out . 51
C. L. Cairns b Wasim Akram	76	– c Salim Malik b Mushtaq Ahmed . 8
*†L. K. Germon c Rashid Latif b Wasim Akram	21	– run out . 12
D. N. Patel c Aamir Sohail b Wasim Akram	3	– b Mushtaq Ahmed . 15
G. R. Larsen not out	5	– c Aamir Sohail b Mushtaq Ahmed. 13
D. J. Nash c Rashid Latif b Wasim Akram	11	– b Waqar Younis . 22
D. K. Morrison b Mushtaq Ahmed	0	– c Salim Malik b Mushtaq Ahmed . 1
L-b 4, n-b 17	21	B 3, l-b 9, w 1, n-b 4 . 17
1/48 (1) 2/65 (2) 3/73 (3) 4/119 (4) 5/221 (5) 6/262 (7) 7/265 (6) 8/269 (8) 9/283 (10) 10/286 (11)	286	1/50 (1) 2/57 (3) 3/60 (4) 4/60 (2) 5/75 (6) 6/101 (7) 7/131 (8) 8/163 (9) 9/192 (10) 10/195 (11) 195

Bowling: *First Innings*—Wasim Akram 24.5–4–53–5; Waqar Younis 16–2–60–0; Ata-ur-Rehman 17.1–4–47–2; Mushtaq Ahmed 30.4–4–115–3; Aamir Sohail 3–0–7–0. *Second Innings*—Wasim Akram 11–3–31–0; Waqar Younis 26–6–73–1; Mushtaq Ahmed 34.4–13–56–7; Ata-ur-Rehman 9–1–23–1.

Umpires: B. C. Cooray (Sri Lanka) and R. S. Dunne. Referee: R. S. Madugalle (Sri Lanka).

†NEW ZEALAND v PAKISTAN

First One-Day International

At Dunedin, December 15. Pakistan won by 20 runs. Toss: Pakistan.

Pakistan kicked off the one-day series with a comfortable win, despite a disappointing total of 189. None of their batsmen reached 40 and wickets fell at regular intervals. But New Zealand lost both openers cheaply and then Waqar Younis joined the demolition act by removing Young, Fleming and Parore in nine balls. There was little chance of a home recovery from 50 for five. Although Twose continued his Test form with a fine 59 and Larsen hit out towards the end, Wasim Akram finished them off in the 48th over.

Man of the Match: Waqar Younis.

Pakistan

Ramiz Raja b Cairns	35
Aamir Sohail c Spearman b Patel	17
Ijaz Ahmed, sen. lbw b Larsen	9
Inzamam-ul-Haq c Patel b Astle	32
Salim Malik c Twose b Astle	13
Basit Ali run out	19
*Wasim Akram run out	16
†Rashid Latif not out	26
Mushtaq Ahmed c Twose b Cairns	5
Waqar Younis b Morrison	0
Aqib Javed not out	8
L-b 6, w 3	9
1/31 2/52 3/82 4/101 5/123 6/138 7/158 8/173 9/175 (9 wkts, 50 overs)	189

Bowling: Patel 7–0–21–1; Morrison 9–0–39–1; Larsen 10–0–29–1; Cairns 9–1–42–2; Astle 10–0–34–2; Twose 5–0–18–0.

New Zealand

C. M. Spearman c Ijaz Ahmed b Aqib Javed	5
N. J. Astle c and b Wasim Akram	5
B. A. Young b Waqar Younis	17
S. P. Fleming lbw b Waqar Younis	15
A. C. Parore b Waqar Younis	2
R. G. Twose b Wasim Akram	59
C. L. Cairns c Rashid Latif b Mushtaq Ahmed	18
*†L. K. Germon c Wasim Akram b Mushtaq Ahmed	1
D. N. Patel c Basit Ali b Salim Malik	9
G. R. Larsen c Ijaz Ahmed b Wasim Akram	23
D. K. Morrison not out	0
L-b 9, w 5, n-b 1	15
1/5 2/16 3/43 4/46 5/50 6/92 7/94 8/114 9/164 (47.4 overs)	169

Bowling: Wasim Akram 9.4–1–18–3; Aqib Javed 9–0–38–1; Waqar Younis 9–0–38–3; Mushtaq Ahmed 10–1–31–2; Aamir Sohail 9–0–30–0; Salim Malik 1–0–5–1.

Umpires: R. S. Dunne and C. E. King.

†NEW ZEALAND v PAKISTAN

Second One-Day International

At Christchurch, December 17. New Zealand won by one wicket. Toss: Pakistan.

A thrilling climax saw New Zealand win with one ball to spare. Their pursuit of 233 had reached a healthy 204 for four when Wasim Akram and Waqar Younis struck five deadly blows – Waqar picked up three wickets in an over. Morrison joined Larsen at 221 for nine, with 12 still needed, but a couple of no-balls in Wasim's final over helped Larsen see his team through. Pakistan's innings had been dominated by a blistering 80, in 95 balls, from Inzamam-ul-Haq. With Salim Malik, he put on 114 for the fourth wicket. But Morrison took four wickets in the closing stages, helping him to five for 46, his best analysis in limited-overs internationals, including his 100th wicket at this level.

Man of the Match: Inzamam-ul-Haq.

Pakistan

Ramiz Raja b Morrison	14
Aamir Sohail c Spearman b Patel	10
Ijaz Ahmed, sen. lbw b Cairns	14
Inzamam-ul-Haq b Larsen	80
Salim Malik c sub (G. R. Loveridge) b Twose	58
*Wasim Akram b Morrison	10
Basit Ali b Morrison	23
†Rashid Latif c Astle b Morrison	11
Waqar Younis b Morrison	0
Mushtaq Ahmed not out	0
B 5, l-b 5, w 2	12
1/25 2/27 3/61 4/175 5/185 6/202 7/230 8/231 9/232 (9 wkts, 50 overs)	232

Aqib Javed did not bat.

Bowling: Patel 10–0–41–1; Morrison 10–0–46–5; Larsen 10–0–49–1; Cairns 10–1–42–1; Astle 8–0–32–0; Twose 2–0–12–1.

New Zealand

C. M. Spearman c Rashid Latif b Aqib Javed	8
N. J. Astle c Rashid Latif b Aqib Javed	5
B. A. Young c Wasim Akram b Aamir Sohail	34
S. P. Fleming b Aamir Sohail	48
A. C. Parore c Basit Ali b Wasim Akram	45
C. L. Cairns c Ramiz Raja b Wasim Akram	54
R. G. Twose c Mushtaq Ahmed b Waqar Younis	10
*†L. K. Germon c Basit Ali b Waqar Younis	5
D. N. Patel c Ijaz Ahmed b Waqar Younis	0
G. R. Larsen not out	14
D. K. Morrison not out	0
L-b 5, w 5, n-b 3	13
1/13 2/21 3/98 4/107 5/204 6/214 7/220 8/221 9/221 (9 wkts, 49.5 overs)	236

Bowling: Aqib Javed 10–0–53–2; Wasim Akram 9.5–0–41–2; Waqar Younis 10–0–55–3; Mushtaq Ahmed 6–0–30–0; Aamir Sohail 10–0–39–2; Salim Malik 4–0–13–0.

Umpires: C. E. King and D. M. Quested.

†NEW ZEALAND v PAKISTAN

Third One-Day International

At Wellington, December 20. Pakistan won by 54 runs. Toss: New Zealand.

Pakistan regained the lead in the series after a convincing performance by their batsmen. Aamir Sohail shared fifty stands with Ramiz Raja and Ijaz Ahmed, before Inzamam-ul-Haq scored his second successive half-century. But Wasim Akram was the most spectacular, smashing 36 in 15 balls, with two sixes and three fours. He continued to dominate the game by taking three wickets, backed up by Aqib Javed. New Zealand lost their ninth wicket at 174, still 87 behind, but Germon and Morrison edged them past 200. Referee Ranjan Madugalle fined two Pakistani players; Aqib lost half his match fee for an exchange with Parore when he had him lbw, and Mushtaq Ahmed paid up ten per cent for his reaction when umpire Watkin turned down a caught-and-bowled appeal against Germon.

Man of the Match: Wasim Akram.

Pakistan

Aamir Sohail b Larsen	58	*Wasim Akram not out	36
Ramiz Raja run out	21	B 2, l-b 5, w 1	8
Ijaz Ahmed, sen. c Cairns b Twose	42		—
Inzamam-ul-Haq b Twose	54	1/51 2/107 (4 wkts, 50 overs)	261
Salim Malik not out	42	3/138 4/217	

Basit Ali, †Rashid Latif, Mushtaq Ahmed, Waqar Younis and Aqib Javed did not bat.

Bowling: Morrison 10–0–59–0; Patel 10–2–43–0; Cairns 10–1–62–0; Larsen 10–0–37–1; Twose 7–0–31–2; Astle 3–0–22–0.

New Zealand

N. J. Astle c Ramiz Raja b Aqib Javed	9	D. N. Patel run out	13
C. M. Spearman c Aamir Sohail b Wasim Akram	33	G. R. Larsen c sub (Moin Khan) b Aqib Javed	2
B. A. Young lbw b Wasim Akram	0	D. K. Morrison not out	11
S. P. Fleming c Basit Ali b Mushtaq Ahmed	35	L-b 13, w 3	16
A. C. Parore lbw b Aqib Javed	4		—
R. G. Twose b Aamir Sohail	37	1/48 2/48 3/48 (44.5 overs)	207
C. L. Cairns run out	7	4/60 5/107 6/119	
*†L. K. Germon b Wasim Akram	40	7/143 8/166 9/174	

Bowling: Aqib Javed 10–1–51–3; Wasim Akram 7.5–0–31–3; Waqar Younis 4–0–22–0; Mushtaq Ahmed 10–2–26–1; Salim Malik 3–0–17–0; Aamir Sohail 10–0–47–1.

Umpires: R. S. Dunne and E. A. Watkin.

†NEW ZEALAND v PAKISTAN

Fourth One-Day International

At Auckland, December 23. New Zealand won by 32 runs. Toss: Pakistan.

New Zealand bounced back to level the series by bowling out Pakistan with 20 balls in hand. Rain had delayed the start and reduced the game to 45 overs a side, but New Zealand made 244, their biggest total of the series, helped by some poor fielding. Waqar Younis conceded 70 in his nine overs and there were 20 extras. Most of the top order contributed, and Astle scored 20 in 14 balls, including three fours in Waqar's final over. He was later responsible for three wickets, plus a catch and two run-outs. Pakistan were a forlorn 146 for seven by the 32nd over, but Salim Malik hit an impressive 58, with three sixes, and took them to 188 with Mushtaq Ahmed's help. Once he fell, Pakistan had no chance.

Man of the Match: N. J. Astle.

New Zealand

C. M. Spearman c Basit Ali b Mushtaq Ahmed . 48
B. A. Young c Rashid Latif b Aqib Javed . 15
S. P. Fleming c Wasim Akram b Aamir Sohail . 38
A. C. Parore b Waqar Younis 42
C. L. Cairns c Wasim Akram b Aamir Sohail . 11
R. G. Twose b Waqar Younis 41
N. J. Astle not out 20
*†L. K. Germon b Wasim Akram 5
D. N. Patel b Waqar Younis 1
G. R. Larsen not out 3
L-b 11, w 6, n-b 3 20

1/28 2/88 3/132 4/148 5/207 6/214 7/222 8/223 (8 wkts, 45 overs) 244

D. K. Morrison did not bat.

Bowling: Wasim Akram 9–0–27–1; Aqib Javed 6–0–28–1; Waqar Younis 9–0–70–3; Mushtaq Ahmed 7–0–39–1; Aamir Sohail 9–0–42–2; Salim Malik 5–0–27–0.

Pakistan

Aamir Sohail c Patel b Cairns 37
Ramiz Raja c Cairns b Astle 46
Salim Elahi run out 7
Inzamam-ul-Haq c sub (G. R. Loveridge) b Astle . 17
Salim Malik lbw b Astle 58
Basit Ali run out 0
*Wasim Akram c Astle b Morrison 4
†Rashid Latif b Larsen 3
Mushtaq Ahmed b Larsen 16
Waqar Younis c Young b Twose 5
Aqib Javed not out 12
L-b 5, w 2 7

1/56 2/89 3/109 4/117 5/118 6/125 7/146 8/188 9/196 (41.4 overs) 212

Bowling: Morrison 6–0–22–1; Patel 4–0–26–0; Cairns 7–0–38–1; Larsen 9–0–42–2; Twose 7.4–0–37–1; Astle 8–0–42–3.

Umpires: B. F. Bowden and D. B. Cowie. Series referee: R. S. Madugalle (Sri Lanka).

WEST INDIES YOUTH IN PAKISTAN, 1995-96

At Iqbal Stadium, Faisalabad, October 17, 18, 19. West Indies Youth won by five wickets. Pakistan Juniors* 116 (Zeeshan Pervez 39; R. D. King five for 37, M. V. Nagamootoo three for 34) and 132 (Adil Nisar 34, Shahid Afridi 30; M. V. Nagamootoo five for 29, D. St D. McKenzie three for 24); West Indies Youth 132 (M. V. Nagamootoo 40, Extras 38; Mohammad Zahid six for 48, Naved-ul-Hasan three for 54) and 119 for five (Naved-ul-Hasan three for 36).

At KRL Cricket Ground, Rawalpindi, October 24, 25, 26, 27. Drawn. West Indies Youth 187 (N. A. De Groot 31, G. R. Breese 38, M. V. Nagamootoo 54; Mohammad Zahid four for 46, Naved-ul-Hasan five for 48) and 257 for six (W. W. Hinds 47, G. R. Breese 64, M. V. Nagamootoo 37 not out, Extras 41); Pakistan Juniors* 388 (Adil Nisar 60, Shadab Kabir 52, Zeeshan Pervez 33, Majid Inayat 95, Mohammad Riaz 83 not out; O. R. Richards three for 85).

At Railways Stadium, Lahore, November 1, 2, 3, 4. West Indies Youth won by 14 runs. West Indies Youth* 147 (G. R. Breese 40; Shahid Afridi four for 53) and 183 (S. M. Clarke 30, W. W. Hinds 45; Naved-ul-Hasan three for 47, Salman Fazal five for 44); Pakistan Juniors 141 (Salman Fazal 31, Zeeshan Pervez 48; O. R. Richards three for 16, M. V. Nagamootoo three for 68) and 175 (Fahad Usman 40, Shadab Kabir 61 not out; O. R. Richards four for 33, M. V. Nagamootoo three for 66).

THE SRI LANKANS IN AUSTRALIA, 1995-96

By TRENT BOUTS

Sri Lanka arrived in November to provide the second and, according to most forecasts, the subsidiary act of the Australian summer, following Pakistan and the reincarnated Salim Malik. On their departure ten weeks later, Arjuna Ranatunga's men were so much the main event that the two countries' political leaders were forced to take note.

Sadly, government interest had less to do with the cricket than with the drama it generated. The three Tests barely qualified as contests. Mark Taylor's Australians were both professional and ruthless, winning by an innings and 36 runs in Perth, ten wickets in Melbourne and then by 148 runs in Adelaide. They landed another sweep, although Sri Lanka would argue just how clean it was, in the finals of the one-day World Series, which they won 2-0. But Sri Lanka's very presence in the finals was significant; West Indies, minus Brian Lara, failed to qualify.

Despite the lop-sided scorelines, public interest remained high and ultimately exceeded expectations. In Melbourne, the 55,239 who attended on Boxing Day bettered the equivalent crowd for England 12 months earlier, and a staggering 72,614 watched the first World Series final. The incendiary nature of the summer may have helped: there was certainly no lack of publicity, although it was overwhelmingly at Sri Lanka's expense. They were briefly convicted of doctoring the ball in the First Test, had their leading wicket-taker branded a chucker in the Second and played the Third under a thinly veiled threat to behave if Australia were not to pull out of their upcoming World Cup match in Colombo.

All the while, the Sri Lankans and their supporters, including a significant expatriate population, simmered over umpiring. The players' patience ran out in the one-day decider at Sydney in January, though by then they may have been itching for a dust-up. Several verbal and physical brushes, and probably the disappointment of defeat in a rain-shortened affair, led many Sri Lankans to snub Taylor's outstretched hand at the presentation in full public view. Although competition was stiff, it was probably the least savoury incident of the summer. Earlier that day, Shane Warne had talked about his fears as one of several Australians who had received a death threat. Craig McDermott was told to expect a "diet of hand-grenades" when he arrived in Colombo. Small wonder the Australian Cricket Board sought advice from the Department of Foreign Affairs and that Sri Lanka mobilised diplomatic resources in an attempt to quell Australian alarm. Though it was a terrorist bomb unconnected with cricket that eventually persuaded the Australians not to go to Colombo, many players were pretty happy to have found an excuse.

Remarkably, up to and after the Sydney final, relations between the players on both sides were no more strained than in most international competition. But as the series wore on, the home team found themselves subject to increasing criticism from their own public. This was partly due to Australians' traditional support for the underdog, though Taylor, a staunch advocate of improved on-field behaviour, was hurt by the backlash. While his players were by no means perfect – Glenn McGrath, for one, needed to calm down a little – the street-smart Ranatunga was no angel either. Still, the players had less to answer for than some officers of the game.

The officials got things seriously wrong in the Perth Test. Umpires Khizar Hayat of Pakistan and Peter Parker of Queensland failed to impound the ball when they suspected interference and referee Graham Dowling, the former New Zealand captain, gave the impression that he had made his mind up that the Sri Lankans were guilty even before the post-match hearing began. ICC overturned his verdict.

When Muttiah Muralitharan was called for throwing by Australian umpire Darrell Hair on the first day of the Melbourne Test, both had a right to ask why the bowler had been able to negotiate 22 Tests, indeed his entire first-class career, in safety until then. Either Hair was wrong or some, if not all, of those who had not called Muralitharan in the past six years were. ICC divulged that umpires, via match referees, had expressed doubts about his legitimacy for more than two years. But Sri Lanka produced an array of doctors and biomechanists who declared the off-spinner in the clear. None said Muralitharan could not throw, but they argued that the elbow he had been unable to straighten completely since birth could create the "visual illusion" of a throw, a contention lost on most observers. It was certainly lost on Ross Emerson who, umpiring his first international ten days later, also no-balled Muralitharan repeatedly, even after the distraught bowler resorted to leg-spin. Instead of the intended celebration of the 25th anniversary of one-day internationals, the first such match under lights in Brisbane provided one of the short game's darkest hours. The umpires were booed from the field under police escort and Muralitharan did not play again on tour.

Not surprisingly, the cricket ran a distant second to the trouble all too often. The seeds that would grow into Sri Lanka's historic World Cup triumph within weeks were sown almost without notice. Romesh Kaluwitharana's blazing approach at the top of the one-day order offered some welcome relief but few thought it could last, let alone be embellished by Sanath Jayasuriya, although Jayasuriya's maiden Test century in Adelaide was a glorious thrash. Like the other two Sri Lankan centuries in the series, Jayasuriya's came in the second innings when the match was already all but lost. By contrast, each of Australia's five centuries came in the first innings, as did two 96s in Perth. The Sri Lankans simply could not bowl the Australians out, even before Muralitharan's demise. While the home side declared in every innings, losing 26 wickets in total at an average return of 72.11, Sri Lanka lost all 60 on offer at 28.16.

David Boon, who had played 107 Tests over 12 years, bid the international arena an emotional farewell in Adelaide after a fighting century in Melbourne, and Steve Waugh maintained his remarkable rate of ascent, scoring 362 for once out. McGrath pressed his case as a world-class pace bowler with 21 wickets at 20.85 each. Of course, Sri Lanka's best paled by comparison. Hashan Tillekeratne and Asanka Gurusinha were the leading run-scorers – both passed 240 at just over 40 – while rising fast bowler Chaminda Vaas, who took time to regain confidence and top pace after a back injury, finally managed nine wickets at 41.22.

SRI LANKAN TOURING PARTY

A. Ranatunga (Sinhalese SC) (*captain*), P. A. de Silva (Nondescripts CC) (*vice-captain*), H. D. P. K. Dharmasena (Bloomfield C and AC), C. I. Dunusinghe (Antonians SC), A. P. Gurusinha (Sinhalese SC), U. C. Hathurusinghe (Tamil Union), S. T. Jayasuriya (Bloomfield C and AC), R. S. Kaluwitharana (Galle CC), R. S. Mahanama (Bloomfield C and AC),

M. Munasinghe (Sinhalese SC), M. Muralitharan (Tamil Union), K. R. Pushpakumara (Nondescripts CC), S. Ranatunga (Nondescripts CC), K. J. Silva (Sinhalese SC), H. P. Tillekeratne (Nondescripts CC), E. A. Upashantha (Colts CC), W. P. U. J. C. Vaas (Colts CC), G. P. Wickremasinghe (Sinhalese SC).

R. S. Kalpage (Bloomfield C and AC) joined the party after Muralitharan was no-balled for throwing.

Manager: L. R. D. Mendis. *Coach:* D. F. Whatmore.

SRI LANKAN TOUR RESULTS

Test matches – Played 3: Lost 3.
First-class matches – Played 5: Lost 4, Drawn 1.
Losses – Australia (3), Queensland.
Draw – Tasmania.
One-day internationals – Played 10: Won 4, Lost 6. *Wins* – Australia (2), West Indies (2). *Losses* – Australia (4), West Indies (2).
Other non-first-class matches – Played 2: Won 1, Lost 1. *Win* – Tasmania. *Loss* – Queensland.

TEST MATCH AVERAGES

AUSTRALIA – BATTING

	T	*I*	*NO*	*R*	*HS*	*100s*	*Avge*	*Ct/St*
S. R. Waugh	2	3	2	362	170	2	362.00	1
M. J. Slater	3	5	1	309	219	1	77.25	1
P. R. Reiffel	2	3	2	74	56	0	74.00	2
M. E. Waugh	3	4	0	255	111	1	63.75	2
I. A. Healy	3	3	0	154	70	0	51.33	17/2
D. C. Boon	3	4	0	201	110	1	50.25	2
R. T. Ponting	3	4	0	193	96	0	48.25	4
M. A. Taylor	3	5	1	159	96	0	39.75	7

Played in three Tests: C. J. McDermott 15*; S. K. Warne 33 (5 ct); G. D. McGrath did not bat. Played in one Test: S. G. Law 54* (1 ct); B. P. Julian did not bat (1 ct).

** Signifies not out.*

BOWLING

	O	*M*	*R*	*W*	*BB*	*5W/i*	*Avge*
S. R. Waugh	19	8	34	4	4-34	0	8.50
G. D. McGrath	154.5	35	438	21	5-40	1	20.85
P. R. Reiffel	74.1	16	218	9	5-39	1	24.22
C. J. McDermott	107.4	25	335	10	3-44	0	33.50
S. K. Warne	164.4	43	433	12	4-71	0	36.08

Also bowled: B. P. Julian 30–12–72–1; S. G. Law 3–1–9–0; R. T. Ponting 4–2–8–1; M. E. Waugh 25–5–73–2.

SRI LANKA – BATTING

	T	*I*	*NO*	*R*	*HS*	*100s*	*Avge*	*Ct*
A. Ranatunga	2	4	1	140	51	0	46.66	0
H. P. Tillekeratne	3	6	0	245	119	1	40.83	1
A. P. Gurusinha	3	6	0	242	143	1	40.33	2
R. S. Kaluwitharana	3	6	0	173	50	0	28.83	6

	T	*I*	*NO*	*R*	*HS*	*100s*	*Avge*	*Ct*
U. C. Hathurusinghe	3	6	0	129	39	0	21.50	2
R. S. Mahanama	2	4	0	69	48	0	17.25	0
P. A. de Silva	3	6	0	98	28	0	16.33	0
H. D. P. K. Dharmasena	2	4	0	50	30	0	12.50	0
G. P. Wickremasinghe	3	6	0	71	28	0	11.83	1
W. P. U. J. C. Vaas	3	6	0	48	26	0	8.00	0
M. Muralitharan	2	4	2	14	11	0	7.00	3

Played in one Test: S. T. Jayasuriya 48, 112; K. R. Pushpakumara 2*, 3* (3 ct); S. Ranatunga 60, 65; K. J. Silva 6*, 0.

* *Signifies not out.*

BOWLING

	O	*M*	*R*	*W*	*BB*	*5W/i*	*Avge*
W. P. U. J. C. Vaas	137.4	33	371	9	3-44	0	41.22
K. R. Pushpakumara	51	6	189	4	2-63	0	47.25
G. P. Wickremasinghe	113.5	20	359	6	3-120	0	59.83
M. Muralitharan	92	10	348	3	2-224	0	116.00

Also bowled: P. A. de Silva 29–1–93–2; H. D. P. K. Dharmasena 78–9–231–1; A. P. Gurusinha 5–1–14–0; U. C. Hathurusinghe 22–3–69–0; S. T. Jayasuriya 13–2–41–0; K. J. Silva 35–5–120–1; H. P. Tillekeratne 0.4–0–5–0.

Note: Matches in this section which were not first-class are signified by a dagger.

†At Cairns, November 19. Queensland won by 46 runs. Toss: Sri Lankans. Queensland 208 (49.3 overs) (M. L. Hayden 53, S. A. Prestwidge 30); Sri Lankans 162 (45.1 overs) (R. S. Mahanama 58, A. P. Gurusinha 50; S. G. Law five for 26).

At Mackay, November 22, 23, 24, 25. Queensland won by 273 runs. Toss: Queensland. Queensland 305 (J. P. Maher 50, A. Symonds 73, A. R. Border 48, Extras 31; G. P. Wickremasinghe four for 49, K. R. Pushpakumara four for 114) and 255 (T. J. Barsby 51, M. L. Hayden 36, A. R. Border 31, W. A. Seccombe 38 not out; M. Muralitharan five for 87, K. J. Silva five for 96); Sri Lankans 178 (A. Ranatunga 77; M. S. Kasprowicz seven for 64, A. J. Bichel three for 43) and 109 (A. Ranatunga 37; M. S. Kasprowicz five for 31, D. Tazelaar three for 36).

In their second innings, the Sri Lankans were 87 for three before they lost seven wickets for 22 runs.

†At Devonport, November 29. Sri Lankans won on scoring-rate when rain ended play. Toss: Sri Lankans. Tasmania 230 for five (50 overs) (D. F. Hills 33, R. T. Ponting 99, S. Young 76); Sri Lankans 220 for five (45.2 overs) (P. A. de Silva 67, A. Ranatunga 46 not out).

At Launceston, December 1, 2, 3, 4. Drawn. Toss: Tasmania. Tasmania 335 for four dec. (A. J. Daly 70, R. T. Ponting 131 not out, R. J. Tucker 54 not out, Extras 32) and 273 for five dec. (J. Cox 34, M. N. Atkinson 42, A. J. Daly 62 not out, R. J. Tucker 60 not out; W. P. U. J. C. Vaas three for 22); Sri Lankans 369 (U. C. Hathurusinghe 73, A. Ranatunga 145; M. A. Hatton three for 87) and 160 for two (U. C. Hathurusinghe 61 not out, S. T. Jayasuriya 31, R. S. Kaluwitharana 53).

Ranatunga scored his 145 from 158 balls, with 20 fours and a six.

AUSTRALIA v SRI LANKA

First Test Match

At Perth, December 8, 9, 10, 11. Australia won by an innings and 36 runs. Toss: Sri Lanka. Test debuts: S. G. Law, R. T. Ponting.

Australia won inside four days for the fifth time in eight Tests. But the controversy that dogged the series began on the second morning, when the umpires decided someone in Sri Lanka's attack had doctored the seam of the ball. The tourists protested vehemently. The umpires failed to impound the ball, so that any evidence was lost, while referee Graham Dowling seemed assured of their guilt before hearing the Sri Lankans' story. They became the first team convicted of ball-tampering in Test cricket, but ICC reversed the finding a fortnight later.

On a flat opening day, eight Sri Lankan batsmen reached double figures, but only Kaluwitharana managed 50. Warne's reputation, rather than his spin, spurred de Silva into suicide-by-bravado right on lunch. When Australia replied, the Sri Lankan attack looked below par; strike bowler Vaas was toying with his run and his confidence after back problems. Muralitharan's action attracted plenty of attention; Khizar Hayat spent an over or two watching closely from square leg, but appeared more satisfied than some television commentators, who nearly burned out their slow-motion replay. Taylor and Slater ran up 228, their second-highest opening stand in Tests, before Taylor became the first of two Australians lbw on 96. But Slater slept on a career-best 189 and completed his maiden double-hundred in the morning. Mark Waugh's tenth Test century, an imperious 111 off 223 balls, was so smooth it almost slipped by without notice. One section of the crowd even ragged him for not having a go. Debutant Ricky Ponting, nine days short of his 21st birthday, was cruelly denied a hundred. Hayat ruled him leg-before when replays showed the ball heading over the stumps. Ponting soon lent a sober perspective. He'd been lucky to survive an outside edge first ball, he said, and besides, he would "gladly cop 96 each hit".

Taylor declared as soon as Ponting was out, with the other newcomer, Stuart Law, unbeaten on 54. Australia led by 366 and, after 12 hours hunting leather, Sri Lanka slumped to 105 for four in the next two. A century from Tillekeratne could not stave off defeat but suggested that the remaining Tests might be less one-sided. His 119 from 206 balls outpaced Waugh's and, though he became Warne's 201st Test wicket when he was last out, Warne found him as elusive as any along the way in his 42 Tests. Indeed, he conceded more than four an over while Tillekeratne and his fellow left-hander Ranatunga were together. Tillekeratne used his long reach and soft hands to good effect; his captain was more ungainly but equally threatening – and turned to the umpires after colliding with McDermott, one of a string of incidents that came to irritate the Australians. Ranatunga finally fell, for 46 in 64 balls, to a yorker from round the wicket – a calculated piece of bowling by McGrath. Taylor claimed the extra half-hour to complete the game on the fourth evening.

Man of the Match: M. J. Slater. *Attendance:* 28,883.

Close of play: First day, Sri Lanka 251; Second day, Australia 358-2 (M. J. Slater 189*, M. E. Waugh 36*); Third day, Sri Lanka 13-0 (R. S. Mahanama 2*, U. C. Hathurusinghe 7*).

Sri Lanka

R. S. Mahanama c Warne b McDermott	15	– b McGrath	48
U. C. Hathurusinghe c Law b McGrath	14	– c Healy b McGrath	11
A. P. Gurusinha b McGrath	46	– c Healy b McDermott	7
P. A. de Silva c and b Warne	10	– c Ponting b Warne	20
*A. Ranatunga c Healy b McGrath	32	– b McGrath	46
H. P. Tillekeratne lbw b McDermott	6	– c Ponting b Warne	119
†R. S. Kaluwitharana c Taylor b Warne	50	– c Ponting b Julian	40
H. D. P. K. Dharmasena b McDermott	30	– lbw b McDermott	18
W. P. U. J. C. Vaas c Healy b Warne	4	– c Healy b Warne	4
G. P. Wickremasinghe c Julian b McGrath	28	– c Warne b McDermott	0
M. Muralitharan not out	0	– not out	3
B 4, l-b 9, n-b 3	16	L-b 4, n-b 10	14
1/25 (2) 2/38 (1) 3/54 (4) 4/129 (3) 5/132 (5) 6/172 (6) 7/193 (7) 8/205 (9) 9/251 (10) 10/251 (8)	251	1/35 (2) 2/56 (3) 3/87 (4) 4/105 (1) 5/193 (5) 6/258 (7) 7/310 (8) 8/318 (9) 9/319 (10) 10/330 (6)	330

Bowling: *First Innings*—McDermott 18.4–5–44–3; McGrath 24–3–81–4; Julian 17–8–32–0; Warne 27–7–75–3; Waugh 3–1–6–0. *Second Innings*—McGrath 24–7–86–3; McDermott 20–3–73–3; Warne 29.4–6–96–3; Julian 13–4–40–1; Waugh 4–0–22–0; Law 3–1–9–0.

Australia

M. J. Slater c and b Muralitharan	219	S. G. Law not out	54
*M. A. Taylor lbw b de Silva	96	B 4, l-b 6, n-b 18	28
D. C. Boon c Hathurusinghe b Muralitharan	13	1/228 (2) 2/266 (3) (5 wkts dec.)	617
M. E. Waugh c Kaluwitharana b Vaas	111	3/422 (1) 4/496 (4)	
R. T. Ponting lbw b Vaas	96	5/617 (5)	

†I. A. Healy, B. P. Julian, S. K. Warne, C. J. McDermott and G. D. McGrath did not bat.

Bowling: Wickremasinghe 31–3–123–0; Vaas 31–5–103–2; Muralitharan 54–3–224–2; Hathurusinghe 9–3–31–0; Dharmasena 31–5–84–0; de Silva 18–1–42–1.

Umpires: Khizar Hayat (Pakistan) and P. D. Parker. Referee: G. T. Dowling (New Zealand).

Sri Lanka's matches v Australia and West Indies in the Benson and Hedges World Series (December 15–December 21) may be found in that section.

AUSTRALIA v SRI LANKA

Second Test Match

At Melbourne, December 26, 27, 28, 29, 30. Australia won by ten wickets. Toss: Sri Lanka. Test debut: K. J. Silva.

Ranatunga gambled by sending Australia in on a fine pitch. But that soon paled against the drama on the first afternoon, when umpire Hair called Muralitharan seven times in three overs for throwing. Unusually, he made his judgment from the bowler's end, and several minutes passed before the crowd realised that Muralitharan's elbow, rather than his foot, was at fault. Many were unimpressed. Ian Meckiff, who retired after being called in Brisbane in 1963, was so affected that he went home. Muralitharan switched ends and bowled until tea on the second day. Then Hair told the Sri Lankans he was ready to call him from square leg.

As Muralitharan's career was set adrift, Boon was fighting for his. Since his 20th Test hundred, against England 12 months earlier, he had averaged under 18 in 18 innings. Retained on an unwritten loyalty clause, he ground out 100 in 363 minutes, the slowest of eight centuries in this series by an hour and a half. Steve Waugh was two and a half hours quicker reaching three figures and Ponting again seemed destined for a maiden hundred until he fell to debutant left-arm spinner Jayantha Silva, for 71 from 94 balls. Taylor declared on 500 and had time to take his 100th Test catch before stumps.

Sri Lanka's malaise deepened next day. The dressing-room's attention was divided between Muralitharan's plight and a procession of batsmen, which began when Taylor's punt on the medium-pace of Ponting removed Gurusinha. It was typical of Taylor's refreshing approach, mixing two parts instinct with an ounce of nous: Ponting had troubled him at net practice. Ranatunga stood his ground for 141 minutes and Kaluwitharana cut, hooked and drove a bright fifty off 59 balls. That prompted his promotion to open in one-day games, a move with far-reaching consequences in the World Cup. But de Silva disappointed again and Tillekeratne was struck four times in one over as McGrath exploited his instinctive push forward. McGrath topped and tailed the innings, as well as drilling the middle, to finish with five for 40, and 50 wickets in the calendar year; Warne was to pass 50 for the third year running in the second innings.

Sri Lanka followed on 267 behind and their chances of making Australia bat again seemed distant. But Gurusinha, respected as a good bloke by his opponents, achieved a minor moral victory. He scored 143 – the other ten managed 144 between them – to force a fifth day and ensure that Australia would indeed bat again. It was a brave effort: a painful blow from McGrath meant he could see several balls through watering eyes as he approached his century.

The Victorian Cricket Association threw the gates open on the final morning. An estimated 15,000 watched McGrath and Warne capture the last four wickets for 23 before the Australian openers knocked off 41 in eight overs.

Man of the Match: G. D. McGrath. *Attendance:* 105,388.

Close of play: First day, Australia 234-3 (D. C. Boon 93*, S. R. Waugh 2*); Second day, Sri Lanka 29-1 (U. C. Hathurusinghe 16*, A. P. Gurusinha 10*); Third day, Sri Lanka 33-1 (U. C. Hathurusinghe 20*, A. P. Gurusinha 8*); Fourth day, Sri Lanka 284-6 (A. Ranatunga 6*, W. P. U. J. C. Vaas 5*).

Australia

M. J. Slater c Wickremasinghe b Vaas	62	– (2) not out	13
*M. A. Taylor b Wickremasinghe	7	– (1) not out	25
D. C. Boon c Muralitharan b Wickremasinghe	110		
M. E. Waugh b Muralitharan	61		
S. R. Waugh not out	131		
R. T. Ponting c Gurusinha b Silva	71		
†I. A. Healy c Muralitharan b de Silva	41		
P. R. Reiffel not out	4		
L-b 8, w 2, n-b 3	13	L-b 1, n-b 2	3
1/14 (2) 2/116 (1) 3/219 (4) 4/280 (3) 5/395 (6) 6/488 (7)	(6 wkts dec.) 500		(no wkt) 41

S. K. Warne, C. J. McDermott and G. D. McGrath did not bat.

Bowling: *First Innings*—Wickremasinghe 30.2–9–77–2; Vaas 40.4–11–93–1; Hathurusinghe 9–0–23–0; Gurusinha 2–0–8–0; Muralitharan 38–7–124–1; Silva 35–5–120–1; de Silva 10–0–47–1. *Second Innings*—Vaas 3–0–25–0; Gurusinha 3–1–6–0; de Silva 1–0–4–0; Tillekeratne 0.4–0–5–0.

Sri Lanka

R. S. Mahanama c Taylor b McGrath	3	– c Warne b Reiffel	3
U. C. Hathurusinghe lbw b McGrath	23	– lbw b Warne	39
A. P. Gurusinha c Healy b Ponting	27	– lbw b Reiffel	143
P. A. de Silva c Reiffel b McGrath	18	– c Healy b McDermott	28
*A. Ranatunga c Warne b McDermott	51	– (7) not out	11
H. P. Tillekeratne c Taylor b Warne	14	– c Ponting b M. E. Waugh	38
†R. S. Kaluwitharana c Boon b McDermott	50	– (5) st Healy b Warne	2
W. P. U. J. C. Vaas c Healy b Reiffel	0	– c Boon b McGrath	6
G. P. Wickremasinghe c Healy b McGrath	10	– st Healy b Warne	17
M. Muralitharan c Slater b McGrath	11	– c Taylor b Warne	0
K. J. Silva not out	6	– b McGrath	0
B 6, l-b 7, n-b 7	20	B 7, l-b 5, n-b 8	20
1/3 (1) 2/64 (3) 3/68 (2) 4/128 (4) 5/140 (5) 6/182 (6) 7/183 (8) 8/213 (9) 9/221 (7) 10/233 (10)	233	1/11 (1) 2/97 (2) 3/168 (4) 4/172 (5) 5/255 (3) 6/273 (6) 7/285 (8) 8/306 (9) 9/306 (10) 10/307 (11)	307

Bowling: *First Innings*—McDermott 23–8–63–2; McGrath 23.4–9–40–5; Reiffel 20–5–60–1; Ponting 4–2–8–1; Warne 18–5–49–1. *Second Innings*—McGrath 33.5–6–92–2; McDermott 17–1–54–1; Reiffel 20–7–59–2; Warne 37–10–71–4; M. E. Waugh 9–1–19–1.

Umpires: R. S. Dunne (New Zealand) and D. B. Hair. Referee: G. T. Dowling (New Zealand).

Sri Lanka's matches v Australia and West Indies in the Benson and Hedges World Series (January 3–January 20) may be found in that section.

AUSTRALIA v SRI LANKA

Third Test Match

At Adelaide, January 25, 26, 27, 28, 29. Australia won by 148 runs. Toss: Australia.

Australia completed a 3-0 series win in a match which the nation turned into a tribute to David Boon. The day before, Boon had announced that his 107th Test would be his last; only Allan Border had played more for Australia, or scored more than Boon's 7,422 runs. There was to be no farewell century and he did not take the one catch which would have lifted him to 100. But Man of the Match Steve Waugh presented him with the ball and Taylor hailed him as "a great Australian, a great person and a great personality".

The passing of Boon doubled as a distraction from the sour events preceding the Test, notably the acrimonious one-day final the weekend before. The conduct of the match was thought critical to Australia's willingness to play World Cup games in Sri Lanka but there was no hint of trouble. Given the pre-match posturing between Arjuna Ranatunga and Australian officials, Ranatunga's unavailability because of a hand injury might have helped.

Under siege all summer, Sri Lanka fought back with their best performance of the series, but once again every run was about catching up. During the first two days, Steve Waugh had scored 170 – only once in 11 Test hundreds has he been dismissed for under 164. Mark Waugh's 71 was a delightful cameo, while Healy and Reiffel contributed half-centuries. Taylor declared at 502 and Australia appeared primed to steamroll the tourists again. But the boyish Jayasuriya thought otherwise. Recalled for his first Test in 15 months, he cover-drove McGrath for six, plundered 13 off one over from McDermott and finished the second day on 47 – from 44 balls. Though he and Hathurusinghe fell to Reiffel in the fourth over next morning, Sanjeeva Ranatunga, Arjuna's younger brother and stand-in, and Tillekeratne enabled Sri Lanka to reach 317, their best first-innings offering of the series. It was still 185 shy.

Australia wanted quick runs, but Slater's decline since his double-hundred at Perth continued; as in his first-ball duck three days earlier, he fell to a ball passing between bat and pad. That brought in Boon, amid thunderous applause. Perhaps overcome, he appeared to edge his first ball from Vaas to the keeper but umpire Barker spared him. Later, Boon joked that he could not even match Bradman by being out for nought in his last innings. Steve Waugh notched up 61 not out – and, in doing so, passed 5,000 Test runs and became the proud owner of an average over 50 before Taylor made his fourth declaration in five innings.

Waugh had more work to do to wrap up the match. Jayasuriya broke loose again with a maiden Test hundred – he scored 112 in four and a half hours and 188 balls, with 14 fours and two sixes – and the first three hours of the final day produced only one wicket. At 195 for two, the draw was in sight. Though reduced to short spells by an increasingly reluctant body, Waugh imposed his will, bending one away from Jayasuriya and another in to the dangerous Kaluwitharana two balls later. He finished with four for 34 as the last eight wickets fell in two hours.

Man of the Match: S. R. Waugh. *Man of the Series:* S. R. Waugh.

Attendance: 63,478.

Close of play: First day, Australia 239-5 (S. R. Waugh 70*, I. A. Healy 21*); Second day, Sri Lanka 80-0 (U. C. Hathurusinghe 24*, S. T. Jayasuriya 47*); Third day, Australia 16-0 (M. J. Slater 7*, M. A. Taylor 9*); Fourth day, Sri Lanka 69-1 (S. T. Jayasuriya 50*, A. P. Gurusinha 2*).

Australia

*M. A. Taylor c Kaluwitharana b Vaas	21	– (2) b Pushpakumara	10
M. J. Slater c Kaluwitharana b Vaas	0	– (1) b Wickremasinghe	15
D. C. Boon b Pushpakumara	43	– c Kaluwitharana b Vaas	35
M. E. Waugh c Pushpakumara b Wickremasinghe	71	– c Tillekeratne b Vaas	12
S. R. Waugh b Pushpakumara	170	– not out	61
R. T. Ponting c Kaluwitharana b Vaas	6	– c Kaluwitharana b Vaas	20
†I. A. Healy c Pushpakumara b Dharmasena	70	– c Hathurusinghe b Pushpakumara	43
P. R. Reiffel c Gurusinha b Wickremasinghe	56	– not out	14
S. K. Warne c Pushpakumara b Wickremasinghe	33		
C. J. McDermott not out	15		
B 5, l-b 9, w 1, n-b 2	17	B 1, l-b 1, n-b 3	5
1/1 (2) 2/36 (1) 3/96 (3) 4/181 (4) 5/196 (6) 6/326 (7) 7/443 (5) 8/467 (8) 9/502 (9)	(9 wkts dec.) 502	1/22 (2) 2/36 (1) 3/70 (4) 4/75 (3) 5/122 (6) 6/186 (7)	(6 wkts dec.) 215

G. D. McGrath did not bat.

Bowling: *First Innings*—Vaas 42–11–106–3; Pushpakumara 34–4–126–2; Wickremasinghe 39.3–7–120–3; Hathurusinghe 4–0–15–0; Dharmasena 25–3–80–1; Jayasuriya 13–2–41–0. *Second Innings*—Vaas 21–6–44–3; Pushpakumara 17–2–63–2; Wickremasinghe 13–1–39–1; Dharmasena 22–1–67–0.

Sri Lanka

U. C. Hathurusinghe c M. E. Waugh b Reiffel	28 – (2) c Healy b McGrath	14
S. T. Jayasuriya c Healy b Reiffel	48 – (1) c Healy b S. R. Waugh	112
A. P. Gurusinha c Reiffel b McGrath	17 – b Reiffel	2
S. Ranatunga c S. R. Waugh b McDermott	60 – c Healy b S. R. Waugh	65
†R. S. Kaluwitharana lbw b Reiffel	31 – b S. R. Waugh	0
H. P. Tillekeratne c Healy b McGrath	65 – c Healy b McGrath	3
*P. A. de Silva c Taylor b McGrath	19 – c Taylor b M. E. Waugh	3
H. D. P. K. Dharmasena c Healy b McGrath	0 – c Taylor b S. R. Waugh	2
W. P. U. J. C. Vaas c M. E. Waugh b Reiffel	8 – c Healy b McGrath	26
G. P. Wickremasinghe b Reiffel	10 – b Warne	6
K. R. Pushpakumara not out	2 – not out	3
B 8, l-b 13, w 1, n-b 7	29 B 1, l-b 6, n-b 9	16
1/86 (2) 2/89 (1) 3/129 (3) 4/171 (5) 5/237 (4) 6/290 (7) 7/290 (8) 8/299 (9) 9/309 (6) 10/317 (10)	317 1/51 (2) 2/70 (3) 3/195 (1) 4/195 (5) 5/199 (6) 6/208 (7) 7/216 (4) 8/225 (8) 9/232 (10) 10/252 (9)	252

Bowling: *First Innings*—McDermott 20–5–81–1; McGrath 27–4–91–4; Warne 26–4–74–0; Reiffel 19.1–4–39–5; M. E. Waugh 5–2–11–0. *Second Innings*—McGrath 22.2–6–48–3; Reiffel 15–0–60–1; S. R. Waugh 19–8–34–4; Warne 27–11–68–1; McDermott 9–3–20–0; M. E. Waugh 4–1–15–1.

Umpires: L. H. Barker (West Indies) and S. G. Randell. Referee: G. T. Dowling (New Zealand).

THE WEST INDIANS IN AUSTRALIA, 1995-96

As the West Indian party set off to take part in the one-day World Series with Australia and Sri Lanka, their best-known player, Brian Lara, contacted the Board to announce that he would not be coming. A few days earlier, a disciplinary committee had fined him ten per cent of his earnings for the 1995 tour of England. Consequently, the trip to Australia was overshadowed by speculation about Lara's future, especially whether he would take part in the World Cup.

They played six warm-up matches before the World Series and the strain on team morale showed in their results. After drawing their opening first-class match, they lost five one-day games on the trot – starting with the giant-killers of the Australian Cricket Academy. They rallied a little in the New Year, with three straight wins in the World Series, but the tour ended in despondency as they were kept out of the finals by the rising stars of Sri Lanka.

WEST INDIAN TOURING PARTY

R. B. Richardson (Leeward Islands) (*captain*), C. A. Walsh (Jamaica) (*vice-captain*), J. C. Adams (Jamaica), C. E. L. Ambrose (Leeward Islands), I. R. Bishop (Trinidad & Tobago), C. O. Browne (Barbados), S. L. Campbell (Barbados), S. Chanderpaul (Guyana), A. C. Cummins (Barbados), O. D. Gibson (Barbados), R. A. Harper (Guyana), R. I. C. Holder (Barbados), C. L. Hooper (Guyana), P. V. Simmons (Trinidad & Tobago), S. C. Williams (Leeward Islands).

Holder was selected after B. C. Lara (Trinidad & Tobago) declined to tour.

Manager: W. W. Hall. *Coach:* A. M. E. Roberts.

WEST INDIAN TOUR RESULTS

First-class matches – Played 2: Drawn 2.
Draws – New South Wales, Australian XI.
One-day internationals – Played 8: Won 3, Lost 5. *Wins:* Australia, Sri Lanka (2). *Losses:* Australia (3), Sri Lanka (2).
Other non-first-class matches – Played 4: Won 1, Lost 3. Abandoned 1. *Win* – Queensland XI. *Losses* – Australian Cricket Academy, Queensland, Australia A. *Abandoned:* Prime Minister's XI.

Note: Matches in this section which were not first-class are signified by a dagger.

†At Canberra, December 5. Prime Minister's XI v West Indians. Abandoned.

At Newcastle, December 7, 8, 9, 10. Drawn. Toss: West Indians. West Indians 246 (S. L. Campbell 53, C. L. Hooper 63, S. Chanderpaul 36; D. A. Freedman eight for 49) and 160 (S. C. Williams 34, J. C. Adams 32; N. D. Maxwell three for 25, G. R. J. Matthews five for 43); New South Wales 318 (M. G. Bevan 86, R. Chee Quee 105, Extras 32; C. A. Walsh four for 63) and 77 for two (R. J. Davidson 30 not out).

†At Wollongong, December 12. Australian Cricket Academy won by eight wickets. Toss: Australian Cricket Academy. West Indians 92 (33.5 overs) (R. B. Richardson 30; M. A. Harrity three for 23); Australian Cricket Academy 96 for two (28.4 overs).

West Indies' matches v Australia and Sri Lanka in the Benson and Hedges World Series (December 15–December 19) may be found in that section.

At Brisbane, December 22, 23, 24. Drawn. Toss: West Indians. Australian XI 323 for seven dec. (M. T. G. Elliott 76, G. S. Blewett 115, B. P. Julian 35 not out; O. D. Gibson three for 68) and 17 for no wkt; West Indians 325 (P. V. Simmons 35, S. C. Williams 47, C. L. Hooper 48, J. C. Adams 47, C. O. Browne 32, A. C. Cummins 34; G. S. Blewett four for 59).
There was no play on the second day.

†At Brisbane, December 26 (day/night). Queensland won by four wickets. Toss: West Indians. West Indians 206 for eight (50 overs) (R. B. Richardson 37, R. A. Harper 46 not out; A. C. Dale three for 31); Queensland 207 for six (47.1 overs) (M. P. Mott 30, S. G. Law 70).

†At Toowoomba, December 29. West Indians won by seven wickets. Toss: West Indians. Queensland XI 237 for eight (50 overs) (T. J. Dixon 51, G. I. Foley 42, B. N. Creevey 38, Extras 46; C. L. Hooper four for 28); West Indians 241 for three (48.1 overs) (P. V. Simmons 91, R. B. Richardson 75 not out).

West Indies' matches v Australia and Sri Lanka in the Benson and Hedges World Series (January 1–January 14) may be found in that section.

†At Sydney, January 10 (day/night). Australia A won by six wickets. Toss: West Indians. West Indians 243 for five (50 overs) (S. C. Williams 57, R. I. C. Holder 80 not out, S. Chanderpaul 37); Australia A 245 for four (40.4 overs) (G. S. Blewett 85, D. M. Jones 30, S. R. Waugh 56, D. S. Lehmann 35).

THE ZIMBABWEANS IN NEW ZEALAND, 1995-96

By TERRY POWER

The Zimbabweans opened their first Test tour of New Zealand on New Year's Day and departed a month later with honours fairly even. They shared the Test series, which was drawn 0-0, but had a chance of a win at Hamilton, thanks to an unusually sporting declaration from Lee Germon; though they lost the one-day games 2-1, they finished on a victorious note at Napier. The limited-overs series was one of New Zealand Cricket's better pieces of timing. They were the last one-day internationals played before the World Cup and gave both countries useful match preparation before their departure; New Zealand showed how useful by beating England in the Cup's opening game at Ahmedabad 11 days later. But, at the time, the Zimbabweans had more reason for satisfaction, despite the lack of wins; they had made the most of their limited resources.

They had one world-class performer with the bat and one with the ball. What a reputation and what figures Dave Houghton might have had by now, either if Zimbabwe had won Test status a dozen years earlier or if he had "done a Hick" and, as a youngster, sought his fortune in another country! His fourth Test century at Eden Park, where he broke his foot in the fifties, was marvellously brave and, given the circumstances, fluent. Unfortunately for Zimbabwe, the fracture kept him out of the World Cup. On the bowling side, Heath Streak had speed, stamina and strength but not much support. At the other end of the scale there were a few tourists who, on this showing, might have had their work cut out securing regular places in New Zealand's better provincial elevens. But Paul Strang was a courageous young leg-spinner possessing reasonable control and considerable ability to turn the ball. His figures were ravaged during Chris Cairns's blazing maiden Test century and did him little justice. Strang looked the likeliest slow bowler on either side, however, and at least as good a long-term bet as his left-arm trundler brother Bryan.

There had been Test wicket-keeper/captains before, as far back as Billy Murdoch at Sydney in February 1882, but never had two opposed each other until Andy Flower and Germon met at Hamilton in January 1996. Neither looked a top international keeper, which was understandable; it is hard to maintain the level of concentration needed to combine the job with on-field decision-making, especially for teams of limited resources. Flower had more batting to do in this series. He was punchy or cautious as the situation demanded, without having Houghton's masterful strokes. Zimbabwe's fielding reached its low point in New Zealand's second innings at Auckland, when Cairns and Adam Parore put on 166 in 171 balls, and its zenith at Napier, in the one-day win that was the tourists' chief success.

New Zealand had more talent available, but never fielded their best eleven. There were a few irritating injuries, and more zip in pitches might have helped, but the tameness of the bowling at Eden Park arose mainly from bad selection. Morrison, Doull, Thomson and Priest, who had repeatedly shown their wicket-taking ability, were all excluded.

The itinerary was not only short for the main attraction of the New Zealand summer but also regressive. New Zealand Cricket abandoned the Arundel-type festival opening match which Northern Districts had striven to establish and, having rekindled local interest in the warm-up games the previous year by reinstating matches against provincial opposition, went back to conglomerate teams, which attracted little support. The theory is that budding internationals will thrust forward by heroic deeds against overseas opposition. Allott and Kennedy were suddenly promoted after playing in these games, but neither was the right answer.

Zimbabwe's first Test tour of New Zealand – the only earlier visit was for the 1992 World Cup, with two Northern Districts games thrown in – was harmonious by 1990s standards. Denis Streak, Heath's father and a pace bowler who once played at Bulawayo army barracks against a sanctions-busting private New Zealand team, the Tuis, in 1974, renewed friendships and managed the side capably.

ZIMBABWEAN TOURING PARTY

A. Flower (Mashonaland) (*captain*), D. L. Houghton (Mashonaland) (*vice-captain*), E. A. Brandes (Mashonaland Country Districts), A. D. R. Campbell (Mashonaland Country Districts), S. V. Carlisle (Mashonaland), S. G. Davies (Mashonaland), G. W. Flower (Young Mashonaland), A. C. I. Lock (Mashonaland Country Districts), H. K. Olonga (Matabeleland), S. G. Peall (Mashonaland Country Districts), B. C. Strang (Mashonaland Country Districts), P. A. Strang (Mashonaland Country Districts), H. H. Streak (Matabeleland), G. J. Whittall (Matabeleland), C. B. Wishart (Young Mashonaland).

C. N. Evans (Mashonaland Country Districts) joined the party after Houghton returned home injured.

Manager: D. H. Streak. *Coach:* J. H. Hampshire.

ZIMBABWEAN TOUR RESULTS

Test matches – Played 2: Drawn 2.
First-class matches – Played 4: Won 1, Drawn 3.
Win – New Zealand XI.
Draws – New Zealand (2), New Zealand Academy XI.
One-day internationals – Played 3: Won 1, Lost 2.
Other non-first-class matches – Won v Wanganui. Abandoned v Central Districts.

TEST MATCH AVERAGES

NEW ZEALAND – BATTING

	T	*I*	*NO*	*R*	*HS*	*100s*	*Avge*	*Ct*
A. C. Parore	2	4	2	176	84*	0	88.00	1
C. L. Cairns	2	4	0	191	120	1	47.75	0
C. M. Spearman	2	4	0	181	112	1	45.25	2
R. G. Twose	2	4	0	162	94	0	40.50	0
S. P. Fleming	2	4	0	157	84	0	39.25	2
L. K. Germon	2	4	2	72	25	0	36.00	8
N. J. Astle	2	4	0	77	32	0	19.25	4

Played in two Tests: G. I. Allott 0*, 0; R. J. Kennedy 2*, 0 (2 ct); D. N. Patel 31, 7*. Played in one Test: G. R. Larsen 0; G. R. Loveridge 4*.

* *Signifies not out.*

BOWLING

	O	*M*	*R*	*W*	*BB*	*5W/i*	*Avge*
R. G. Twose	21	2	55	3	2-36	0	18.33
D. N. Patel	76.5	16	221	8	2-44	0	27.62
C. L. Cairns	93	29	240	8	4-56	0	30.00
R. J. Kennedy	59	10	181	5	3-28	0	36.20
G. I. Allott	66	15	209	4	3-56	0	52.25

Also bowled: N. J. Astle 4–1–7–0; G. R. Larsen 26–11–38–1.

ZIMBABWE - BATTING

	T	*I*	*NO*	*R*	*HS*	*100s*	*Avge*	*Ct*
D. L. Houghton	2	3	1	166	104*	1	83.00	0
A. Flower	2	4	2	144	58*	0	72.00	8
P. A. Strang	2	3	1	93	49	0	46.50	1
G. W. Flower	2	4	0	140	71	0	35.00	1
G. J. Whittall	2	4	0	111	54	0	27.75	0
S. V. Carlisle	2	4	0	93	58	0	23.25	3
A. D. R. Campbell	2	4	0	59	34	0	14.75	1
H. H. Streak	2	3	0	32	24	0	10.66	1

Played in two Tests: E. A. Brandes 3*, 39 (1 ct); B. C. Strang 4, 14* (1 ct). Played in one Test: H. K. Olonga 0 (3 ct); C. B. Wishart 7, 12* (1 ct).

** Signifies not out.*

BOWLING

	O	*M*	*R*	*W*	*BB*	*5W/i*	*Avge*
H. H. Streak	99	27	268	12	4-52	0	22.33
E. A. Brandes	64	13	208	5	2-69	0	41.60
B. C. Strang	87.3	28	198	4	3-64	0	49.50
P. A. Strang	81	17	229	3	1-1	0	76.33

Also bowled: A. D. R. Campbell 2–0–3–0; G. W. Flower 8–1–27–0; H. K. Olonga 17–3–85–1; G. J. Whittall 25–8–76–1.

Note: Matches in this section which were not first-class are signified by a dagger.

†At Wanganui, January 1. Zimbabweans won by 122 runs. Toss: Zimbabweans. Zimbabweans 284 for seven (50 overs) (G. W. Flower 79, A. Flower 72, S. V. Carlisle 34 not out; C. Fraser three for 46); Wanganui 162 (47.1 overs) (C. Fraser 40 not out; B. C. Strang four for 15).

At Wanganui, January 2, 3, 4. Zimbabweans won by seven wickets. Toss: New Zealand XI. New Zealand XI 111 (S. M. Lynch 30; B. C. Strang six for 20) and 212 (L. G. Howell 51, R. G. Hart 31, G. R. Loveridge 31; B. C. Strang six for 39); Zimbabweans 172 (H. K. Olonga 41; R. J. Kennedy four for 22, M. J. Haslam three for 17) and 154 for three (G. W. Flower 89, S. V. Carlisle 30).

Strang's first-innings six for 20 included five for two in 29 balls.

At Whangarei, January 6, 7, 8. Drawn. Toss: New Zealand Academy XI. Zimbabweans 274 for seven dec. (D. L. Houghton 86, A. Flower 73, A. D. R. Campbell 38 not out, G. J. Whittall 40; G. I. Allott four for 32) and 207 for four dec. (G. W. Flower 53, A. D. R. Campbell 59 not out, D. L. Houghton 34 not out); New Zealand Academy XI 213 for one dec. (R. A. Lawson 113 not out, M. D. Bell 83) and 109 for one (J. M. Aiken 51, L. G. Howell 39 not out).

NEW ZEALAND v ZIMBABWE

First Test Match

At Hamilton, January 13, 14, 15, 16, 17. Drawn. Toss: Zimbabwe. Test debuts: G. I. Allott, N. J. Astle, R. J. Kennedy, G. R. Loveridge.

With that rarity in modern Test cricket – a declaration setting a realistic target – Germon tried to produce a result from a rain-ravaged match. Challenged to score 257 in two sessions, Zimbabwe might have pulled it off, too; they were 143 for three from 39 overs before three decisions went against them. Andy Flower, who saw them all from the bowler's end, said afterwards: "I wish I was allowed to comment. I think I would get into a lot of trouble if I did . . . Those hiccups in the middle destroyed our momentum."

Houghton, who had just become the first batsman to score 1,000 Test runs for Zimbabwe, in his 15th game, was given lbw to one that could easily have missed leg stump. Campbell was caught behind off his forearm sleeve, while Cairns secured a dubious lbw against Streak. Flower then gave up the chase, though he reached his fifty by taking safe boundaries against close fields and loose bowling. Zimbabwe ended 49 short with four wickets left.

Rain and inadequate drainage limited play to 110 overs during the first three days and New Zealand's first declaration came at the third lunch interval. As so often, Fleming cut himself off in his prime. He had struck nine fours, the best of them impeccable off and straight drives, when he tapped what he hoped would be his 50th run, to Olonga at mid-off, and was thrown out by metres. Next ball, Twose, on 12, seemed absolutely plumb but survived. On the third morning, leg-spinner Greg Loveridge marked his 21st birthday by straight-driving Olonga to the boundary, but the following delivery fractured his knuckle. The injury ended Loveridge's season but he did not retire until Patel was out, which meant that his fellow-debutants, Kennedy and Allott, made their first entry into the game together. Streak was easily the best Zimbabwean bowler; his four for 52 made him their first to reach 50 Test wickets, in 11 matches.

Conditions were equally favourable to New Zealand's No. 1 bowler, Cairns, and Zimbabwe were struggling to recover from 56 for five before lightning ended the day. Kennedy, who seemed out of his depth for much of the international season, had his best spell on the fourth afternoon, when he ended a dogged 91-run stand between Whittall and Paul Strang. It was largely due to them that New Zealand's first-innings advantage was kept to just 34. New Zealand needed quick runs to build a target but, after Twose's foolish run-out, they scored only 2.8 an over until the close. Parore gradually cast off restraint and developed easily the best innings of the match, an unbeaten 84 with some especially attractive cuts and cover drives, to help make his captain's second declaration possible.

Man of the Match: C. L. Cairns.

Close of play: First day, New Zealand 68-2 (R. G. Twose 13*, A. C. Parore 0*); Second day, New Zealand 154-4 (N. J. Astle 16*, C. L. Cairns 7*); Third day, Zimbabwe 82-5 (G. J. Whittall 9*, H. H. Streak 15*); Fourth day, New Zealand 129-4 (A. C. Parore 23*, C. L. Cairns 6*).

New Zealand

C. M. Spearman c A. Flower b Streak	0	– lbw b Streak	27
R. G. Twose b Brandes	42	– run out	8
S. P. Fleming run out	49	– c A. Flower b P. A. Strang	21
A. C. Parore c A. Flower b Streak	16	– not out	84
N. J. Astle lbw b Streak	18	– c Olonga b B. C. Strang	32
C. L. Cairns c A. Flower b Streak	7	– c Olonga b Brandes	7
*†L. K. Germon c Carlisle b Olonga	24	– not out	22
D. N. Patel c Olonga b P. A. Strang	31		
G. R. Loveridge retired hurt	4		
R. J. Kennedy not out	2		
G. I. Allott not out	0		
B 4, l-b 11, w 1, n-b 21	37	B 4, l-b 7, w 4, n-b 6	21
1/0 (1) 2/67 (3) 3/115 (4) 4/143 (2) 5/160 (6) 6/164 (5) 7/216 (7) 8/226 (8) (8 wkts dec.)	230	1/36 (1) 2/63 (3) 3/64 (2) 4/121 (5) 5/140 (6) (5 wkts dec.)	222

In the first innings G. R. Loveridge retired hurt at 226-8.

Bowling: *First Innings*—Streak 25–7–52–4; B. C. Strang 24–11–51–0; Brandes 15–3–46–1; Olonga 14–2–65–1; P. A. Strang 2–1–1–1. *Second Innings*—Streak 22–4–56–1; Brandes 18–4–52–1; B. C. Strang 5–1–19–1; P. A. Strang 24–7–57–1; G. W. Flower 3–1–7–0; Olonga 3–1–20–0.

Zimbabwe

G. W. Flower b Cairns	5	– c Germon b Cairns	59
S. V. Carlisle c Germon b Cairns	4	– c Fleming b Patel	19
A. D. R. Campbell c Astle b Allott	5	– (6) c Germon b Patel	3
D. L. Houghton lbw b Cairns	31	– lbw b Twose	31
*†A. Flower c Spearman b Kennedy	6	– not out	58
G. J. Whittall c Germon b Kennedy	54	– (3) c Kennedy b Twose	20
H. H. Streak c Spearman b Cairns	24	– lbw b Cairns	6
P. A. Strang b Patel	49	– not out	0
H. K. Olonga c Germon b Kennedy	0		
E. A. Brandes not out	3		
B. C. Strang c Astle b Patel	4		
L-b 3, w 2, n-b 6	11	L-b 4, w 1, n-b 7	12
1/8 (2) 2/13 (3) 3/21 (1) 4/41 (5) 5/56 (4) 6/98 (7) 7/189 (6) 8/189 (8) 9/191 (9) 10/196 (11)	196	1/56 (2) 2/99 (3) 3/125 (1) 4/143 (4) 5/151 (6) 6/177 (7)	(6 wkts) 208

Bowling: *First Innings*—Cairns 24–7–56–4; Allott 17–5–51–1; Kennedy 12–4–28–3; Twose 5–1–14–0; Patel 16.5–4–44–2. *Second Innings*—Cairns 15–4–43–2; Allott 7–0–49–0; Kennedy 5–0–19–0; Patel 21–6–57–2; Twose 13–0–36–2.

Umpires: L. H. Barker (West Indies) and D. M. Quested. Referee: Nasim-ul-Ghani (Pakistan).

NEW ZEALAND v ZIMBABWE

Second Test Match

At Auckland, January 20, 21, 22, 23, 24. Drawn. Toss: New Zealand.

This series never looked so much like the battle for the international wooden spoon as in the early stages here. New Zealand selected a wholly inadequate attack, and not this time because of injuries. Morrison and Doull, their best strike bowlers, were fit again; somehow Kennedy and Allott were preferred, while Patel played ahead of Thomson and the proven Canterbury spinner Mark Priest. Cairns was a clear-cut choice – and provided some batting fireworks in his maiden Test hundred – but stock bowler Larsen could not be expected to make the breakthrough and Germon gave him just five overs in the second innings. In a match quite unscathed by the weather, in which New Zealand won the toss and had much the better fielding side, they managed only 13 wickets at 44 each against below Test-strength batting. They did not even have to dismiss Zimbabwe's best batsman, Houghton, whose left foot was broken by Kennedy when he was 55 in the first innings. He battled on until stumps to score the first and bravest of three hundreds in the game; then his season was over.

Cairns was later criticised for saying Zimbabwe played within their limitations. It was the plain truth but, with New Zealand all out 27 balls into the second morning, on an easy pitch, they also succeeded. The tourists pressed home that advantage to gain a lead of 75. Houghton and Andy Flower – who joined him in passing 1,000 Test runs, taking one more match – laid the groundwork and Houghton gallantly continued after his fracture, protecting more technically fragile partners. He was in plaster, not pads, next morning, but Brandes and Paul Strang added another 79 without difficulty.

So often, New Zealand have folded instead of fighting: what happened next was a welcome change. Spearman used his long reach effectively and dug in with the less fluent but dogged Twose for a double-century opening stand – New Zealand's third in Test cricket. Starting two overs before lunch, they persevered throughout the third afternoon, though late on Twose played a ball on to his stumps without disturbing the bails. Next morning he gave a straightforward return catch and Spearman soon followed for a responsible maiden Test century – though he reached three figures when he was dropped by Streak at square leg. Their batting, and Parore's, provided the platform for an epic blitz by Cairns. He hit nine sixes, one short of Hammond's Test record on the same ground in 1932-33. Once, he stepped well outside leg stump and lifted Paul Strang over cover on to the roof of the North Stand; then he pulled the replacement ball into the top deck of the South Stand. He reached 100 in 86 balls and hit 120 from 96, with ten fours as well as the sixes. New Zealand shot from 350 to 400 in 26 balls.

Germon's declaration on the fourth evening set Zimbabwe 367 in 109 overs; they never seriously attempted it, even though Carlisle and Grant Flower batted devotedly into the final afternoon for 120, Zimbabwe's biggest opening stand to date.

Man of the Match: C. L. Cairns.

Close of play: First day, New Zealand 246-8 (D. N. Patel 2*); Second day, Zimbabwe 231-7 (D. L. Houghton 104*, P. A. Strang 5*); Third day, New Zealand 138-0 (C. M. Spearman 71*, R. G. Twose 57*); Fourth day, Zimbabwe 39-0 (G. W. Flower 22*, S. V. Carlisle 14*).

New Zealand

C. M. Spearman c G. W. Flower b B. C. Strang	42	– c Carlisle b Streak	112
R. G. Twose c A. Flower b Brandes	18	– c and b Streak	94
S. P. Fleming c Carlisle b Whittall	84	– c Wishart b Streak	3
A. C. Parore c A. Flower b B. C. Strang	0	– not out	76
N. J. Astle c and b Brandes	14	– c A. Flower b Brandes	13
C. L. Cairns c and b P. A. Strang	57	– b Streak	120
*†L. K. Germon c A. Flower b Streak	25	– not out	1
D. N. Patel not out	7		
G. R. Larsen lbw b Streak	0		
R. J. Kennedy c Campbell b Streak	0		
G. I. Allott c and b B. C. Strang	0		
L-b 3, n-b 1	4	B 6, l-b 15, n-b 1	22
1/50 (2) 2/78 (1) 3/86 (4) 4/117 (5) 5/216 (3) 6/232 (6) 7/244 (7) 8/246 (9) 9/246 (10) 10/251 (11)	251	1/214 (2) 2/217 (1) 3/221 (3) 4/261 (5) 5/427 (6)	(5 wkts dec.) 441

Bowling: *First Innings*—Streak 22–9–50–3; Brandes 18–3–69–2; B. C. Strang 31.3–8–64–3; P. A. Strang 12–2–29–1; Whittall 12–4–36–1. *Second Innings*—Streak 30–7–110–4; Brandes 13–3–41–1; B. C. Strang 27–8–64–0; Whittall 13–4–40–0; P. A. Strang 43–7–142–0; Campbell 2–0–3–0; G. W. Flower 5–0–20–0.

Zimbabwe

G. W. Flower lbw b Allott	5	– c Kennedy b Patel	71
S. V. Carlisle c Astle b Kennedy	12	– c Fleming b Kennedy	58
G. J. Whittall c Germon b Cairns	27	– c Germon b Patel	10
D. L. Houghton retired hurt	104		
*†A. Flower lbw b Allott	35	– (4) not out	45
A. D. R. Campbell lbw b Allott	17	– (5) c Germon b Twose	34
C. B. Wishart b Larsen	7	– (6) not out	12
H. H. Streak b Cairns	2		
P. A. Strang c Parore b Patel	44		
E. A. Brandes c Astle b Patel	39		
B. C. Strang not out	14		
B 1, l-b 11, w 2, n-b 6	20	L-b 6, w 2, n-b 8	16
1/5 (1) 2/38 (2) 3/50 (3) 4/138 (5) 5/196 (6) 6/217 (7) 7/222 (8) 8/310 (10) 9/326 (9)	326	1/120 (2) 2/144 (3) 3/145 (1) 4/225 (5)	(4 wkts) 246

In the first innings D. L. Houghton retired hurt at 231.

Bowling: *First Innings*—Cairns 31–12–92–2; Allott 23–7–56–3; Kennedy 20–3–73–1; Larsen 21–8–30–1; Patel 12–0–60–2; Astle 3–1–3–0. *Second Innings*—Allott 19–3–53–0; Cairns 23–6–49–0; Kennedy 22–3–61–1; Patel 27–6–60–2; Larsen 5–3–8–0; Twose 3–1–5–1; Astle 1–0–4–0.

Umpires: Mahboob Shah (Pakistan) and D. B. Cowie. Referee: Nasim-ul-Ghani (Pakistan).

†At Napier, January 26. Central Districts v Zimbabweans. Abandoned.

†NEW ZEALAND v ZIMBABWE

First One-Day International

At Auckland, January 28. New Zealand won by 74 runs. Toss: New Zealand. International debut: S. G. Davies.

Restored to open, Astle scored 120 from 137 deliveries, with 13 fours and a six, though he was helped when in full flow by a generous supply of over-pitched deliveries. Only Glenn Turner, now the team coach, had scored more for New Zealand in a one-day international (twice). In reply, Grant Flower and Whittall gave Zimbabwe the faster early run-rate but, once brilliant catches by Parore and Larsen removed the Flower brothers, their chance of success soon ended. The best crowd of the summer – 23,000 – turned up despite New Zealand Cricket's gaffe in advertising the match for Saturday instead of Sunday – and then opening so few entrances that queues persisted deep into the New Zealand innings.

Man of the Match: N. J. Astle.

New Zealand

C. M. Spearman c Whittall b Streak	22
N. J. Astle c Campbell b Peall	120
S. P. Fleming run out	2
R. G. Twose c Brandes b P. A. Strang	53
C. L. Cairns run out	23
A. C. Parore not out	26
S. A. Thomson not out	11
L-b 6, w 14, n-b 1	21
1/40 2/61 3/196 4/232 5/252 (5 wkts, 50 overs)	278

*†L. K. Germon, D. N. Patel, G. R. Larsen and D. K. Morrison did not bat.

Bowling: Streak 10–0–32–1; Brandes 6–0–58–0; B. C. Strang 7–0–34–0; Whittall 10–0–58–0; Peall 7–0–48–1; P. A. Strang 10–0–42–1.

Zimbabwe

G. W. Flower c Parore b Larsen	46
C. N. Evans lbw b Morrison	1
G. J. Whittall run out	70
*†A. Flower c Larsen b Thomson	21
A. D. R. Campbell c sub (D. J. Nash) b Thomson	23
S. G. Davies c Fleming b Thomson	3
H. H. Streak c Spearman b Larsen	17
P. A. Strang c Thomson b Larsen	11
E. A. Brandes b Morrison	1
S. G. Peall c Patel b Morrison	0
B. C. Strang not out	0
L-b 2, w 4, n-b 5	11
1/6 2/91 3/117 4/158 5/170 6/171 7/193 8/200 9/200 (43.5 overs)	204

Bowling: Morrison 6.5–0–34–3; Patel 10–0–44–0; Larsen 8–0–42–3; Astle 5–0–28–0; Thomson 10–1–32–3; Twose 4–0–22–0.

Umpires: B. F. Bowden and R. S. Dunne.

†NEW ZEALAND v ZIMBABWE

Second One-Day International

At Wellington, January 31. New Zealand won by six wickets. Toss: Zimbabwe.

Thomson and Twose both hit the stumps from narrow angles to remove Grant Flower (when he looked likely to make a big score) and Whittall, and there were two more run-outs in Zimbabwe's innings, by Morrison and Kennedy off their own bowling. To cap a fine home effort in the field, Nash took three for 30, his best limited-overs international figures, and Larsen conceded just 1.4 an over. Andy Flower concluded too late that batting first was an error; Fleming led an easy chase to win with ten overs to spare and New Zealand took the series 2-0. Afterwards, the press were excited by reports that two New Zealanders and a Zimbabwean had been found smoking an unidentified substance. They scented a repeat of the previous year's cannabis incident. Officials from both teams stated firmly that the exotic cigarettes were merely Turkish ones.

Man of the Match: S. P. Fleming.

Zimbabwe

G. W. Flower run out 48
C. N. Evans c Fleming b Morrison 2
G. J. Whittall run out 9
*†A. Flower lbw b Nash 10
A. D. R. Campbell lbw b Nash 2
S. G. Davies b Larsen 10
S. V. Carlisle run out 28
H. H. Streak b Nash 15
P. A. Strang not out 28
B. C. Strang run out 3
B 1, l-b 14, w 8, n-b 3 26

1/10 2/33 3/55 4/65 5/98 6/98 7/132 8/171 9/181 (9 wkts, 50 overs) 181

A. C. I. Lock did not bat.

Bowling: Morrison 10–2–37–1; Kennedy 10–0–57–0; Nash 10–0–30–3; Larsen 10–5–14–1; Astle 10–0–28–0.

New Zealand

C. M. Spearman c G. W. Flower b Streak. 1
N. J. Astle b Whittall 18
S. P. Fleming b Streak 70
R. G. Twose c G. W. Flower b Evans 41
A. C. Parore not out 25
S. A. Thomson not out 4
B 1, l-b 7, w 15, n-b 2 25

1/6 2/56 3/143 4/169 (4 wkts, 39.3 overs) 184

*†L. K. Germon, G. R. Larsen, D. J. Nash, D. K. Morrison and R. J. Kennedy did not bat.

Bowling: Streak 10–0–44–2; Lock 8–1–34–0; Whittall 5–0–22–1; B. C. Strang 9.3–0–50–0; P. A. Strang 5–0–20–0; Evans 2–1–6–1.

Umpires: D. B. Cowie and C. E. King.

†NEW ZEALAND v ZIMBABWE

Third One-Day International

At Napier, February 3 (day/night). Zimbabwe won by 21 runs. Toss: New Zealand.

Charlie Lock, without a wicket or a run on the tour, had his 15 minutes of fame right at the end, with the first five-wicket analysis by a Zimbabwean in one-day internationals. Single-handedly, he removed the last five for five in 11 balls, to give his team their first ever win over New Zealand. "I just bowled straight," he said. That was in sharp contrast to Kennedy, who bowled six wides in one over during Zimbabwe's innings. Morrison had taken three early wickets, but Andy Flower led the recovery, then Streak and Paul Strang added 54 in 40 balls. Chasing 268, Fleming and Twose seemed to have the task under control. Lock, and some fine Zimbabwean fielding, checked their assault. New Zealand's first international day/night game avoided rain, often a curse at Napier, roused high enthusiasm and was a financial success. The downside was ticketing trouble, lighting problems in the outfield, excessive beer-selling and resultant yobbery.

Man of the Match: A. Flower.

Zimbabwe

G. W. Flower c Astle b Morrison 7
C. N. Evans c Fleming b Morrison 0
G. J. Whittall c Harris b Morrison 12
*†A. Flower lbw b Patel 57
A. D. R. Campbell c Germon b Nash 26
S. G. Davies run out 45
S. V. Carlisle run out 25
H. H. Streak not out 36
P. A. Strang not out 24
B 1, l-b 11, w 19, n-b 4 35

1/6 2/18 3/38 4/93 5/133 6/199 7/213 (7 wkts, 50 overs) 267

E. A. Brandes and A. C. I. Lock did not bat.

Bowling: Morrison 10–2–39–3; Kennedy 9–0–67–0; Patel 10–0–49–1; Nash 10–2–39–1; Astle 6–1–36–0; Harris 5–0–25–0.

New Zealand

C. M. Spearman lbw b Brandes	28
N. J. Astle c A. Flower b Brandes	30
S. P. Fleming lbw b Strang	50
R. G. Twose lbw b Lock	60
A. C. Parore c Streak b G. W. Flower	3
C. Z. Harris c A. Flower b Strang	22
*†L. K. Germon b Lock	7
D. N. Patel c and b Lock	4
D. J. Nash b Lock	4
D. K. Morrison lbw b Lock	1
R. J. Kennedy not out	8
L-b 11, w 14, n-b 4	29
1/65 2/72 3/164 4/169 5/201 6/228 7/229 8/233 9/235 (48.1 overs)	246

Bowling: Streak 9–0–45–0; Lock 8.1–0–44–5; Brandes 8–1–37–2; Strang 10–0–44–2; Whittall 9–0–49–0; G. W. Flower 4–0–16–1.

ERRATA

WISDEN, 1986

Page 73 A. P. E. Knott played 19 first-class matches in 1985, and 511 in his career: his highest score was 156.

WISDEN, 1991

Page 979 In the one-day international between West Indies and England at Georgetown on March 15, A. J. Lamb was caught by C. A. Best, not R. B. Richardson.

Page 1087 In the second World Series final between Australia and Pakistan, Border bowled 7–0–34–0 and Pakistan's innings lasted 45 overs.

WISDEN, 1993

Page 1268 The first Bengali to represent India in Test cricket was P. Sen.

WISDEN, 1995

Page 633 In the match between Warwickshire and Durham, the pre-lunch session on the final day, in which B. C. Lara scored 174, was 120 minutes.

Page 1404 South Africa's 324-run victory over Pakistan at Johannesburg in 1994-95 was their biggest home win by runs; they had beaten England by 356 runs at Lord's in 1994. See also correction for *Wisden* 1996 p. 1086.

WISDEN, 1996

Page 445 In Essex's first innings, G. A. Gooch was caught by S. P. Griffiths, not T. W. Harrison.

Page 560 Before Nottinghamshire's 527, the highest score by a team losing by an innings in the County Championship was 439 by Sussex v Gloucestershire in 1936 as listed.

Page 676 In Worcestershire's innings against Cumberland, N. V. Radford was run out for 0 and P. J. Newport was 19 not out.

Page 868 After a change to the scorecard, Dorset's total against Buckinghamshire in the Minor Counties knockout cup was revised from 49 to 46.

Page 1077 In the Zimbabweans' one-day game at Launceston, Tasmania scored 160 for three in 35 overs and Boon made 30 not out. In their three-day match at Devonport, Peall bowled 5–0–27–1 and Butchart 3–0–17–0 in Tasmania's second innings.

Page 1086 South Africa's 324-run victory over Pakistan at Johannesburg in 1994-95 was their biggest home win by runs; they had beaten Australia by an innings and 129 runs at Durban in 1969-70, which offers no direct comparison.

THE NEW ZEALANDERS IN THE WEST INDIES, 1995-96

By D. J. CAMERON

Both teams were looking for credibility rather than earth-shattering performances when New Zealand made their third tour of the Caribbean – which featured five one-day internationals and only two Tests. West Indies' previous home series ended in their historic defeat by Australia. Since then, they had under-performed generally and lost traumatically to Kenya in the World Cup; captain Richie Richardson had resigned, and the management team of Wes Hall and Andy Roberts been replaced; and Brian Lara was too often in the headlines for the wrong reasons. More disasters at home were unthinkable.

Fortunately for West Indies, the New Zealanders were in modest form – no Hadlee, no Crowe and the whole mechanism of the team dismantled ten months beforehand, when an old coach, Glenn Turner, and a new captain, Lee Germon, were charged with retuning the motor. They had recovered somewhat from their disastrous centenary season in 1994-95, however, and had just fought a boisterous World Cup campaign.

After the tour, both sides would have counted more pluses than minuses. West Indies seemed more solid, with Clive Lloyd in command off the field and Courtney Walsh on it. The search to replace the golden Greenidge–Haynes opening combination made encouraging progress when Sherwin Campbell scored a cultured double-century in the First Test, and Robert Samuels a powerful maiden Test hundred in the Second. Meanwhile, Jimmy Adams rediscovered his magical touch, batting solidly throughout and scoring a flowing double-hundred in Antigua.

There may be problems ahead: Curtly Ambrose and Walsh are a year closer to the resting paddock, and Patterson Thompson will take time to add accuracy and control to his raw speed. But West Indies strengthened their team, showed they could win with modest input from Lara, had satisfactory gates and signed another six-year sponsorship deal with Cable & Wireless.

New Zealand were also reasonably contented. They had brought Turner-inspired vitality to their one-day game; West Indies got home 3-2, but the series was so closely fought that no one would have complained had it gone the other way. Yet, as so often on tour, they played badly in the First Test, losing in four days by ten wickets. A lively, boundary-studded second-innings century from Nathan Astle provided their only warm memory. They started just as badly in the Second Test, putting West Indies in and watching them score 548 for seven. But another, more sober Astle century led New Zealand past the follow-on and a late burst by Danny Morrison even had West Indies looking anxious. New Zealand did not have the bowling resources to force the win, but nor did West Indies look like dismissing New Zealand again on a flat pitch.

Though New Zealand seemed to have made some progress on the batting front, the bowling was less satisfactory. Dion Nash was never properly fit, Shane Thomson's off-spin was hampered by a damaged shoulder, and Chris Cairns's precarious international status suffered another setback when damaged ribs ended his tour prematurely. He departed for Nottinghamshire, which ended his unhappy relationship with Turner. As Cairns left under a cloud and the team returned with its reputation enhanced, it appeared that Turner was ahead in the popularity stakes. But the ambush awaited at home and he was sacked as coach in July.

NEW ZEALAND TOURING PARTY

L. K. Germon (Canterbury) (*captain*), N. J. Astle (Canterbury), C. L. Cairns (Canterbury), S. P. Fleming (Canterbury), C. Z. Harris (Canterbury), R. J. Kennedy (Otago), G. R. Larsen (Wellington), D. K. Morrison (Auckland), D. J. Nash (Northern Districts), A. C. Parore (Northern Districts), D. N. Patel (Auckland), C. M. Spearman (Auckland), S. A. Thomson (Northern Districts), R. G. Twose (Wellington).

M. D. Bailey (Northern Districts), M. J. Haslam (Auckland) and J. T. C. Vaughan (Auckland) joined the party as replacements for the injured Cairns, Nash and Thomson.

Manager: G. D. Alabaster. *Coach:* G. M. Turner.

NEW ZEALAND TOUR RESULTS

Test matches – Played 2: Lost 1, Drawn 1.
First-class matches – Played 4: Won 1, Lost 2, Drawn 1.
Win – West Indies Board XI.
Losses – West Indies, President's XI.
Draw – West Indies.
One-day internationals – Played 5: Won 2, Lost 3.
Other non-first-class match – Won v University of West Indies Vice-Chancellor's XI.

TEST MATCH AVERAGES

WEST INDIES – BATTING

	T	*I*	*NO*	*R*	*HS*	*100s*	*Avge*	*Ct/St*
J. C. Adams	2	3	1	235	208*	1	117.50	3
S. L. Campbell	2	4	1	286	208	1	95.33	2
B. C. Lara	2	3	0	149	74	0	49.66	3
R. G. Samuels	2	4	1	141	125	1	47.00	4
S. Chanderpaul	2	3	0	131	82	0	43.66	2
P. V. Simmons	2	3	0	81	59	0	27.00	2
I. R. Bishop	2	3	0	54	31	0	18.00	1
C. E. L. Ambrose	2	3	1	35	21*	0	17.50	0
C. O. Browne	2	3	0	43	20	0	14.33	9/1

Played in two Tests: C. A. Walsh 12*, 17*. Played in one Test: R. Dhanraj 9 (1 ct); P. I. C. Thompson 1.

* *Signifies not out.*

BOWLING

	O	*M*	*R*	*W*	*BB*	*5W/i*	*Avge*
C. E. L. Ambrose	75	25	164	8	5-68	1	20.50
J. C. Adams	30	7	114	5	5-17	1	22.80
C. A. Walsh	82	19	204	8	4-72	0	25.50
I. R. Bishop	62.3	11	218	7	4-67	0	31.14
P. I. C. Thompson	22	1	135	4	2-58	0	33.75

Also bowled: S. Chanderpaul 7–1–28–0; R. Dhanraj 56–15–165–2; P. V. Simmons 13–6–23–1.

NEW ZEALAND – BATTING

	T	*I*	*NO*	*R*	*HS*	*100s*	*Avge*	*Ct*
N. J. Astle	2	4	0	290	125	2	72.50	2
S. P. Fleming	2	4	1	118	56*	0	39.33	3
J. T. C. Vaughan	2	4	0	126	44	0	31.50	2
D. K. Morrison	2	3	2	30	26*	0	30.00	0
C. M. Spearman	2	4	0	98	54	0	24.50	1
L. K. Germon	2	4	1	72	49	0	24.00	5
G. R. Larsen	2	3	1	35	17*	0	17.50	0
C. Z. Harris	2	4	0	44	40	0	11.00	1
R. J. Kennedy	2	3	0	26	22	0	8.66	0
R. G. Twose	2	4	0	6	2	0	1.50	0

Played in one match: A. C. Parore 59, 1; D. N. Patel 78.

* *Signifies not out.*

BOWLING

	O	*M*	*R*	*W*	*BB*	*5W/i*	*Avge*
G. R. Larsen	76	27	172	5	3-76	0	34.40
J. T. C. Vaughan	79.3	23	190	5	3-30	0	38.00
C. Z. Harris	73	22	192	5	2-75	0	38.40
D. K. Morrison	77.3	12	313	7	5-61	1	44.71

Also bowled: N. J. Astle 1–0–3–0; R. J. Kennedy 47–7–199–1; D. N. Patel 38–6–131–2; R. G. Twose 4–0–20–0.

Note: Matches in this section which were not first-class are signified by a dagger.

†At Kingston, March 23. New Zealanders won by 207 runs. Toss: New Zealanders. New Zealanders 348 for six (50 overs) (C. M. Spearman 42, S. P. Fleming 89, C. L. Cairns 107); University of West Indies Vice-Chancellor's XI 141 (35 overs) (S. Chanderpaul 30, I. V. A. Richards 41).

†WEST INDIES v NEW ZEALAND

First One-Day International

At Kingston, March 26. West Indies won by one wicket. Toss: West Indies. International debut: R. D. Jacobs.

Sent in on the fastest pitch they were to meet in the Caribbean, New Zealand started nervously and lost wickets regularly to eager bowling from Ambrose, and Harper's brilliant fielding. It took a dashing 111-run stand for the seventh wicket by Parore and Patel, who hit three sixes in 71 from 58 balls, to lift them to 243, their biggest one-day total against West Indies. Though Williams and Chanderpaul started boldly with 126 in 26 overs, New Zealand struck back and, at 197 for eight, many of the crowd were leaving. Ambrose regained the impetus with 17 from ten balls, leaving the last-wicket pair, Harper and Walsh, to get 23 from 14. Harper scored 15 from Nash's final over and two no-balls from Morrison ensured a home win.

Man of the Match: D. N. Patel.

New Zealand

C. M. Spearman c Holder b Ambrose	11	G. R. Larsen b Ambrose	9
N. J. Astle c Adams b Ambrose	41	D. J. Nash b Walsh	2
*†L. K. Germon run out	0	D. K. Morrison not out	1
S. P. Fleming b Walsh	8	L-b 4, w 8, n-b 4	16
C. Z. Harris c Lara b Ambrose	2		—
C. L. Cairns c and b Harper	21	1/22 2/24 3/51 (49.1 overs)	243
A. C. Parore c Harper b Walsh	61	4/70 5/70 6/113	
D. N. Patel c and b Simmons	71	7/224 8/238 9/241	

Bowling: Ambrose 10–0–36–4; Bishop 10–0–56–0; Walsh 9.1–1–30–3; Harper 10–0–63–1; Simmons 7–0–38–1; Adams 3–0–16–0.

West Indies

S. C. Williams b Harris	62	I. R. Bishop lbw b Larsen	0
S. Chanderpaul c and b Harris	61	C. E. L. Ambrose b Morrison	17
B. C. Lara lbw b Harris	12	*C. A. Walsh not out	5
P. V. Simmons b Larsen	28	B 1, l-b 6, w 5, n-b 3	15
J. C. Adams c Fleming b Morrison	2		—
R. I. C. Holder c Germon b Cairns	16	1/126 2/133 3/142 (9 wkts, 49.1 overs)	247
†R. D. Jacobs c Spearman b Astle	3	4/147 5/179 6/184	
R. A. Harper not out	26	7/197 8/197 9/221	

Bowling: Nash 6–0–46–0; Morrison 5.1–0–38–2; Harris 10–0–45–3; Patel 5–0–28–0; Astle 6–0–28–1; Cairns 7–1–26–1; Larsen 10–3–29–2.

Umpires: L. H. Barker and S. A. Bucknor.

†WEST INDIES v NEW ZEALAND

Second One-Day International

At Port-of-Spain, March 29. New Zealand won by four wickets. Toss: New Zealand.

New Zealand got home with a ball to spare for their first ever victory over West Indies in the Caribbean. Trading on the slow, lifeless pitch, they left out Morrison and relied on the pop-gun bowlers – Larsen, Harris, Patel and Astle – to confuse the West Indians. This they did admirably, reducing the home side to 42 for three, before Adams led the recovery to 238 for seven; Holder struck 65 from 48 balls. Then Fleming played a steady hand for 106 not out from 108 balls, his maiden international century, hitting Ambrose's penultimate ball for two to level the series.

Man of the Match: S. P. Fleming.

West Indies

S. C. Williams c Cairns b Patel	20	†R. D. Jacobs c Thomson b Larsen	10
S. Chanderpaul b Nash	6	I. R. Bishop not out	12
B. C. Lara c Astle b Harris	11	B 1, l-b 2, w 3, n-b 2	8
P. V. Simmons c Fleming b Larsen	45		—
J. C. Adams not out	59	1/15 2/32 3/42 (7 wkts, 50 overs)	238
R. I. C. Holder b Astle	65	4/119 5/210	
R. A. Harper c and b Astle	2	6/212 7/225	

C. E. L. Ambrose and *C. A. Walsh did not bat.

Bowling: Nash 6–0–29–1; Larsen 10–1–42–2; Harris 10–3–45–1; Patel 8–0–30–1; Astle 9–1–32–2; Thomson 5–0–36–0; Cairns 2–0–21–0.

New Zealand

C. M. Spearman c Simmons b Harper	37
N. J. Astle c Harper b Ambrose	2
*†L. K. Germon c Simmons b Walsh	6
S. P. Fleming not out	106
A. C. Parore c Adams b Walsh	0
C. L. Cairns b Adams	41
C. Z. Harris b Ambrose	32
D. N. Patel not out	4
L-b 7, w 3, n-b 1	11
1/16 2/35 3/71 4/71 5/163 6/230 (6 wkts, 49.5 overs)	239

S. A. Thomson, G. R. Larsen and D. J. Nash did not bat.

Bowling: Ambrose 9.5–1–42–2; Bishop 5–0–37–0; Walsh 10–0–51–2; Harper 10–2–28–1; Simmons 10–0–50–0; Adams 5–0–24–1.

Umpires: L. H. Barker and S. A. Bucknor.

†WEST INDIES v NEW ZEALAND

Third One-Day International

At Port-of-Spain, March 30. West Indies won by seven wickets. Toss: New Zealand. International debut: L. R. Williams.

The New Zealanders had feared, and the crowd expected, something special from Lara on his home ground. He obliged with his eighth century in limited-overs internationals, an incredible 146 not out from 134 balls, with 12 fours and three sixes, the last of which won the game. Lara shared hundred partnerships with Simmons and Adams; New Zealand, overjoyed when Larsen removed both West Indies openers for six, could only stand and watch the master at work. Earlier, Twose and Astle had lifted New Zealand to 104 for one in the 27th over. But erratic batting and unwise running – West Indies pulled off three run-outs – prevented the tourists from building on that start.

Man of the Match: B. C. Lara.

New Zealand

C. M. Spearman b Ambrose	7
R. G. Twose c and b Harper	48
N. J. Astle run out	43
S. P. Fleming c Walsh b Simmons	4
C. L. Cairns st Jacobs b Harper	38
A. C. Parore c Harper b Adams	33
C. Z. Harris run out	10
*†L. K. Germon not out	13
S. A. Thomson run out	6
D. N. Patel not out	3
B 1, l-b 6, w 6, n-b 1	14
1/10 2/104 3/105 4/113 5/178 6/197 7/205 8/215 (8 wkts, 50 overs)	219

G. R. Larsen did not bat.

Bowling: Ambrose 10–0–33–1; Walsh 9–2–37–0; Simmons 10–1–35–1; L. R. Williams 2–0–18–0; Adams 9–0–44–1; Harper 10–0–45–2.

West Indies

S. C. Williams c Fleming b Larsen	4
S. Chanderpaul lbw b Larsen	1
B. C. Lara not out	146
P. V. Simmons lbw b Larsen	47
J. C. Adams not out	24
L-b 3	3
1/5 2/6 3/116 (3 wkts, 45.4 overs)	225

R. I. C. Holder, R. A. Harper, †R. D. Jacobs, L. R. Williams, C. E. L. Ambrose and *C. A. Walsh did not bat.

Bowling: Patel 10–0–45–0; Larsen 8.4–3–26–3; Astle 8–0–43–0; Harris 8–1–37–0; Thomson 4–0–24–0; Twose 3–0–19–0; Cairns 4–0–28–0.

Umpires: L. H. Barker and S. A. Bucknor.

†WEST INDIES v NEW ZEALAND

Fourth One-Day International

At Georgetown, April 3. New Zealand won by four runs. Toss: West Indies.

On the slowest imaginable pitch, New Zealand started at breakneck speed: they were 90 for three after only 13.2 overs. Rather than curb their scoring-rate and save wickets, they charged on – to apparent disaster, all out for 158 with 14 overs unused. Simmons was later fined for intimidatory appealing. West Indies needed only 3.2 an over, but again slow-medium New Zealand bowling, backed by inspired fielding, steadily cut through the batting. Even so, Holder looked capable of steering them through. But with only five runs needed and one over left, Cairns bowled Walsh to complete an astonishing four-run victory. Adjudicator Basil Butcher pronounced it a team performance and declined to pick out any individual.

Men of the Match: New Zealand team.

New Zealand

C. M. Spearman b Ambrose	41
N. J. Astle lbw b Ambrose	20
*†L. K. Germon run out	19
S. P. Fleming c Harper b Simmons	9
C. Z. Harris c Harper b Simmons	8
R. G. Twose run out	8
C. L. Cairns c and b L. R. Williams	29
S. A. Thomson c Harper b L. R. Williams	6
D. N. Patel c Jacobs b Walsh	2
J. T. C. Vaughan not out	4
G. R. Larsen hit wkt b L. R. Williams	1
L-b 7, w 3, n-b 1	11
1/55 2/77 3/90 4/100 5/113 6/113 7/138 8/145 9/154 (35.5 overs)	158

Bowling: Ambrose 7–1–33–2; Walsh 6–0–38–1; Simmons 10–0–42–2; Harper 8–1–22–0; L. R. Williams 4.5–0–16–3.

West Indies

S. C. Williams lbw b Larsen	6
S. Chanderpaul c Harris b Patel	11
B. C. Lara c Astle b Larsen	17
P. V. Simmons c Harris b Vaughan	11
J. C. Adams run out	23
R. I. C. Holder not out	49
†R. D. Jacobs c Germon b Cairns	0
R. A. Harper b Harris	5
L. R. Williams c Twose b Astle	1
C. E. L. Ambrose lbw b Vaughan	16
*C. A. Walsh b Cairns	1
B 1, l-b 8, w 5	14
1/21 2/35 3/39 4/68 5/104 6/111 7/116 8/120 9/152 (49.1 overs)	154

Bowling: Patel 10–2–35–1; Larsen 10–1–18–2; Harris 10–1–23–1; Vaughan 7–0–26–2; Astle 7–1–26–1; Cairns 5.1–0–17–2.

Umpires: C. R. Duncan and E. Nicholls.

†WEST INDIES v NEW ZEALAND

Fifth One-Day International

At St Vincent, April 6. West Indies won by seven wickets. Toss: West Indies.

The lovely Arnos Vale ground, by the blue Caribbean, brought out the best in the West Indians, who gained a convincing one-day win to secure the series. Again, a century from Lara played a decisive role, but this time Simmons matched him. Fleming and Germon, batting spiritedly at No. 3, rescued New Zealand from ten for two with a solid stand of 120. New Zealand hopes were high when West Indies were 31 for two, but then they were blown out of sight as Lara and Simmons put on 186 in 31 overs. Lara's second hundred of the series occupied 103 balls, and he hit ten fours and a six; Simmons followed him with 103 from 125 balls, ten fours and two sixes. His tenth four brought up his century and West Indies' victory with nine balls to spare.

Man of the Match: P. V. Simmons.

New Zealand

C. M. Spearman c Browne b Walsh	4	D. N. Patel run out	2
N. J. Astle c Simmons b Ambrose	4	J. T. C. Vaughan not out	13
*†L. K. Germon c and b Adams	50		
S. P. Fleming c Simmons b Adams	75	B 2, l-b 2, w 6, n-b 1	11
R. G. Twose c Browne b Chanderpaul	6		—
C. L. Cairns c and b Adams	11	1/10 2/10 3/130 (8 wkts, 50 overs)	241
A. C. Parore b Williams	23	4/137 5/154 6/167	
C. Z. Harris not out	42	7/189 8/197	

G. R. Larsen did not bat.

Bowling: Ambrose 7–0–32–1; Walsh 9–0–38–1; Simmons 3–0–25–0; Harper 10–0–48–0; Adams 10–0–50–3; Chanderpaul 8–0–35–1; Williams 3–0–9–1.

West Indies

P. A. Wallace c Fleming b Patel	0	R. I. C. Holder not out	13
S. Chanderpaul c Twose b Harris	13	L-b 2, w 6, n-b 1	9
B. C. Lara c Patel b Cairns	104		—
P. V. Simmons not out	103	1/0 2/31 3/217 (3 wkts, 48.3 overs)	242

J. C. Adams, R. A. Harper, †C. O. Browne, L. R. Williams, C. E. L. Ambrose and *C. A. Walsh did not bat.

Bowling: Patel 10–1–46–1; Larsen 8–2–31–0; Harris 8–0–48–1; Vaughan 10–0–37–0; Cairns 8.3–0–49–1; Astle 2–0–14–0; Fleming 2–0–15–0.

Umpires: L. H. Barker and B. Morgan. Series referee: M. H. Denness (England).

At St Vincent, April 8, 9, 10. New Zealanders won by 156 runs. Toss: New Zealanders. New Zealanders 319 for nine dec. (S. P. Fleming 61, N. J. Astle 55, A. C. Parore 59, C. Z. Harris 32, Extras 31; C. E. L. Stuart three for 43, A. Samaroo three for 62) and 204 for seven dec. (A. C. Parore 39, C. Z. Harris 55 not out, J. T. C. Vaughan 32; C. E. L. Stuart three for 54); West Indies Board XI 158 (S. L. Campbell 81; C. L. Cairns five for 29) and 209 (M. D. Ventura 51, M. V. Nagamootoo 38, H. A. G. Anthony 42; D. K. Morrison three for 35, C. L. Cairns three for 23, R. J. Kennedy three for 70).

The first first-class win by a New Zealand team in three tours of the West Indies.

At St George's, Grenada, April 12, 13, 14. President's XI won by an innings and 49 runs. Toss: New Zealanders. President's XI 454 (R. G. Samuels 124, T. O. Powell 53, D. R. E. Joseph 30, F. L. Reifer 130, N. A. M. McLean 49 not out; C. L. Cairns four for 66); New Zealanders 113 (C. E. Cuffy three for 35, N. A. M. McLean four for 32) and 292 (C. M. Spearman 32, A. C. Parore 46, N. J. Astle 40, C. L. Cairns 94; N. A. M. McLean three for 52, C. E. Cuffy three for 44).

New Zealanders lost with a day to spare. Lee Germon retired hurt after being hit on the toe in the first innings and did not bat in the second.

WEST INDIES v NEW ZEALAND

First Test Match

At Bridgetown, April 19, 20, 21, 23. West Indies won by ten wickets. Toss: West Indies. Test debuts: R. G. Samuels, P. I. C. Thompson.

With Cairns injured two days before and Nash already out with a back injury, the New Zealanders needed all the luck – including the toss – in a match played on a surprisingly green Kensington Oval pitch.

The good luck instead was with West Indies, who won in four days. Walsh sent New Zealand in and reduced them to a calamitous six for three within the first half-hour. Two decisions in that innings raised doubts: Spearman appeared to be caught off his pad, and later Bucknor gave Patterson Thompson his second Test wicket when Harris seemed to be caught off his arm-guard. It was a rare break for Thompson, who struggled to live up to West Indian fast bowling standards, conceding 25 in his first two overs and being no-balled 26 times in the match.

Parore and Vaughan were just starting to build an interesting sixth-wicket stand when Adams, a reluctant Test bowler, was persuaded to try his slow left-armers. His first ball bounced so crazily that Parore jerked a close catch to Simmons. In a bizarre form of suicide, New Zealand lost five wickets to Adams in nine overs – a career-best for him. They were all out for 195; Campbell and Lara had already knocked off half of that by stumps.

Lara was quickly taken in the morning, but Campbell worked on to reach his maiden Test hundred in six hours. By the end of the day, he and Chanderpaul had New Zealand under the thumb at 334 for four. New Zealand's bowlers had allowed only 236 more runs but never looked like breaking Campbell's grip. On the third morning, he went mercilessly on to his 200 in 648 minutes, joining the pantheon of West Indians (Denis Atkinson, Garry Sobers, Rohan Kanhai, Seymour Nurse, Lawrence Rowe, Faoud Bacchus and Brian Lara) whose maiden Test centuries were doubles. He was finally eighth out, having batted 15 minutes over 11 hours; he had hit 30 fours in 497 balls.

New Zealand resumed 277 behind and, at the close of the third day, they were four down, still needing 126 to make West Indies bat again. But Astle, picked for his one-day big hitting, was attacking cheerfully. He had reached his fifty in 56 balls, to follow a 48-ball 54 in the first innings, and rushed headlong to his maiden Test century, in his third match. He and Vaughan put on 144 – a New Zealand record for the fifth wicket against West Indies – of which Vaughan scored only 24. When Astle fell, at 215 for six, his 125 had taken only 204 minutes and 154 balls. It contained precisely 100 in boundaries: 22 fours and two sixes.

The tail postponed the inevitable, and Morrison and Kennedy had a tenth-wicket stand of 45, another New Zealand–West Indies record. But Campbell blithely hit all the 29 runs needed for victory in four overs.

Man of the Match: S. L. Campbell.

Close of play: First day, West Indies 98-1 (S. L. Campbell 47*, B. C. Lara 32*); Second day, West Indies 334-4 (S. L. Campbell 149*, S. Chanderpaul 81*); Third day, New Zealand 151-4 (N. J. Astle 82*, J. T. C. Vaughan 10*).

New Zealand

C. M. Spearman c Browne b Ambrose	0	– c Lara b Thompson	20
R. G. Twose c Samuels b Walsh	2	– c Lara b Walsh	0
S. P. Fleming c Chanderpaul b Walsh	1	– c Samuels b Bishop	22
A. C. Parore c Simmons b Adams	59	– (7) c Campbell b Bishop	1
N. J. Astle c Browne b Thompson	54	– (4) c Campbell b Thompson	125
C. Z. Harris c Lara b Thompson	0	– (5) c Samuels b Bishop	0
J. T. C. Vaughan c Bishop b Adams	44	– (6) lbw b Bishop	24
*†L. K. Germon c Chanderpaul b Adams	0	– lbw b Walsh	23
G. R. Larsen st Browne b Adams	12	– lbw b Walsh	6
D. K. Morrison not out	4	– not out	26
R. J. Kennedy c Browne b Adams	0	– c Adams b Walsh	22
L-b 1, w 1, n-b 17	19	L-b 7, n-b 29	36
1/2 (1) 2/2 (2) 3/6 (3) 4/86 (5) 5/87 (6) 6/154 (4) 7/157 (8) 8/186 (9) 9/193 (7) 10/195 (11)	195	1/14 (2) 2/28 (1) 3/48 (3) 4/57 (5) 5/201 (6) 6/215 (4) 7/219 (7) 8/254 (9) 9/260 (8) 10/305 (11)	305

Bowling: *First Innings*—Ambrose 13–4–33–1; Walsh 17–6–30–2; Bishop 10–3–36–0; Thompson 8–0–58–2; Simmons 3–0–11–0; Adams 9–4–17–5; Chanderpaul 2–0–9–0. *Second Innings*—Ambrose 18–6–41–0; Walsh 22–3–72–4; Thompson 14–1–77–2; Bishop 19–1–67–4; Adams 6–1–32–0; Chanderpaul 3–1–9–0.

West Indies

S. L. Campbell b Harris	208	– not out	29
R. G. Samuels lbw b Larsen	12	– not out	0
B. C. Lara c Spearman b Larsen	35		
P. V. Simmons lbw b Larsen	22		
J. C. Adams c Germon b Vaughan	21		
S. Chanderpaul c Harris b Morrison	82		
†C. O. Browne c Astle b Kennedy	20		
I. R. Bishop c Germon b Harris	31		
C. E. L. Ambrose c Germon b Vaughan	8		
*C. A. Walsh not out	12		
P. I. C. Thompson lbw b Morrison	1		
L-b 8, n-b 12	20		
1/46 (2) 2/103 (3) 3/129 (4) 4/182 (5) 5/337 (6) 6/386 (7) 7/445 (8) 8/458 (1) 9/466 (9) 10/472 (11)	472		(no wkt) 29

Bowling: *First Innings*—Morrison 29.3–4–120–2; Kennedy 22–3–89–1; Larsen 40–15–76–3; Vaughan 34–10–81–2; Harris 34–11–75–2; Twose 4–0–20–0; Astle 1–0–3–0. *Second Innings*—Morrison 2–0–8–0; Kennedy 2–0–21–0.

Umpires: P. Willey (England) and S. A. Bucknor. Referee: M. H. Denness (England).

WEST INDIES v NEW ZEALAND

Second Test Match

At St John's, April 27, 28, 29, May 1, 2. Drawn. Toss: New Zealand.

Hoping that the pitch would turn, West Indies brought in leg-spinner Dhanraj and New Zealand recalled off-spinner Patel. The Antiguan Andy Roberts said the pitch would be low, slow and favour batsmen prepared to get on the front foot and work for their runs over the razor-sharp outfield.

Germon, however, felt New Zealand's best chance was to snatch four or five wickets before lunch on the first day. He had 166 overs to consider his folly: an attack relying heavily on two trundlers, Larsen and Vaughan, made little impression on the West Indian batting.

Samuels, who had picked up an easy 124 when the President's XI thrashed the New Zealanders in Grenada, was even more impressive here, with 125 in five and a half hours. He faced 219 balls and hit 15 fours and three sixes, completing his first Test century – in his second game – with a straight six off Patel. West Indies strolled amiably to stumps at 302 for four. Referee Denness fined Morrison for dissent over a rejected appeal against Lara. Adams, 50 overnight, completed his hundred just before lunch, skipped to 150 and reached his maiden double-century in 427 minutes; his last 100 had taken only 112 balls. In all, he faced 334 balls and struck 31 fours and a six before Walsh declared on 548.

In the 12 overs New Zealand faced on the second evening, Morrison, a sacrificial night-watchman, fell for his 24th Test duck, beating the record of Bhagwat Chandrasekhar of India. He promised a commemorative tie for his benefit.

New Zealand faced another dismal defeat; however, they made a brave show. After a rally from Spearman and Fleming, the astonishing Astle had the New Zealand flag fluttering bravely for most of the third day. His second successive century was rather more subdued than the first, but he still managed 12 fours and a six. Though Astle was whisked away by Ambrose with the second new ball, Patel's biggest Test innings for nearly five years took New Zealand to 346 for seven at stumps, needing only three more to save the follow-on.

A final total of 437 had them out of jail, only 111 behind. Suddenly, Morrison found some movement in the pitch and some strength in his right shoulder. Campbell started briskly with 36 and Lara batted with all the control of a tipsy sailor but still scored 74. The others fell like skittles and, at 147 for seven, the home side's lead was only 258 and a New Zealand victory looked possible.

But it took them another 70 minutes to end the innings, which left a target of 296 from 73 overs. Twose scored his regulation two – his four Test innings were 2, 0, 2 and 2 – and, once the third wicket fell at 39, Fleming had the duty of scoring a patient four-hour 56 to make sure of the draw.

Man of the Match: J. C. Adams. *Man of the Series:* J. C. Adams.

Close of play: First day, West Indies 302-4 (J. C. Adams 50*, S. Chanderpaul 6*); Second day, New Zealand 21-2 (C. M. Spearman 14*, S. P. Fleming 5*); Third day, New Zealand 346-7 (L. K. Germon 25*, D. N. Patel 37*); Fourth day, West Indies 147-7 (C. O. Browne 3*, C. E. L. Ambrose 0*).

West Indies

S. L. Campbell run out	13	– c Fleming b Vaughan	36
R. G. Samuels b Harris	125	– lbw b Morrison	4
B. C. Lara c Germon b Patel	40	– c Fleming b Morrison	74
P. V. Simmons b Harris	59	– c Vaughan b Harris	0
J. C. Adams not out	208	– c and b Vaughan	6
S. Chanderpaul c Astle b Patel	41	– b Morrison	8
†C. O. Browne run out	18	– lbw b Larsen	5
I. R. Bishop c Fleming b Larsen	14	– c Germon b Morrison	9
C. E. L. Ambrose not out	21	– lbw b Morrison	6
*C. A. Walsh (did not bat)		– not out	17
R. Dhanraj (did not bat)		– b Vaughan	9
L-b 3, n-b 6	9	L-b 2, n-b 8	10
1/35 (1) 2/96 (3) 3/193 (4) 4/280 (2) 5/405 (6) 6/448 (7) 7/495 (8)	(7 wkts dec.) 548	1/5 (2) 2/89 (1) 3/94 (4) 4/119 (5) 5/128 (6) 6/133 (3) 7/147 (8) 8/155 (7) 9/158 (9) 10/184 (11)	184

Bowling: *First Innings*—Morrison 26–6–124–0; Larsen 25–9–69–1; Vaughan 29–8–79–0; Patel 38–6–131–2; Kennedy 13–2–59–0; Harris 35–11–83–2. *Second Innings*—Morrison 20–2–61–5; Larsen 11–3–27–1; Kennedy 10–2–30–0; Vaughan 16.3–5–30–3; Harris 4–0–34–1.

New Zealand

C. M. Spearman c Browne b Walsh	54	– c Browne b Ambrose	24
R. G. Twose b Ambrose	2	– c Samuels b Ambrose	2
D. K. Morrison lbw b Ambrose	0		
S. P. Fleming c Browne b Bishop	39	– (3) not out	56
N. J. Astle c Simmons b Ambrose	103	– (4) c Adams b Simmons	8
J. T. C. Vaughan b Dhanraj	26	– (5) lbw b Walsh	32
C. Z. Harris c Adams b Ambrose	40	– (6) c and b Dhanraj	4
*†L. K. Germon c Browne b Ambrose	49	– (7) not out	0
D. N. Patel c Browne b Bishop	78		
G. R. Larsen not out	17		
R. J. Kennedy c Browne b Bishop	4		
L-b 7, n-b 18	25	L-b 1, w 2, n-b 1	4
1/9 (2) 2/9 (3) 3/98 (4) 4/108 (1) 5/202 (6) 6/276 (7) 7/281 (5) 8/391 (8) 9/425 (9) 10/437 (11)	437	1/19 (2) 2/30 (1) 3/39 (4) 4/96 (5) 5/127 (6)	(5 wkts) 130

Bowling: *First Innings*—Ambrose 32–12–68–5; Walsh 27–5–70–1; Dhanraj 38–9–132–1; Bishop 26.3–6–90–3; Adams 13–1–60–0; Chanderpaul 2–0–10–0. *Second Innings*—Ambrose 12–3–22–2; Walsh 16–5–32–1; Simmons 10–6–12–1; Dhanraj 18–6–33–1; Bishop 7–1–25–0; Adams 2–1–5–0.

Umpires: C. J. Mitchley (South Africa) and L. H. Barker. Referee: M. H. Denness (England).

THE SRI LANKANS IN THE WEST INDIES, 1995-96

By TONY COZIER

Less than a month after their victory in the World Cup final in Lahore, Sri Lanka made their first appearance in the Caribbean an impressive and triumphant one. They were fulfilling an arrangement with the Queen's Park Cricket Club, agreed several months earlier, to play two matches to mark the 100th anniversary of the club's Test ground. They comfortably won both, defeating a West Indies Masters Invitation XI, comprising mostly players from the great teams of the 1980s, one day, and the full West Indies team in a one-day international the next.

SRI LANKAN TOURING PARTY

A. Ranatunga (Sinhalese SC) (*captain*), P. A. de Silva (Nondescripts CC) (*vice-captain*), M. S. Atapattu (Sinhalese SC), U. U. Chandana (Tamil Union), H. D. P. K. Dharmasena (Bloomfield C and AC), A. P. Gurusinha (Sinhalese SC), S. T. Jayasuriya (Bloomfield C and AC), R. S. Kaluwitharana (Galle CC), R. S. Mahanama (Bloomfield C and AC), M. Muralitharan (Tamil Union), K. R. Pushpakumara (Nondescripts CC), H. P. Tillekeratne (Nondescripts CC), W. P. U. J. C. Vaas (Colts CC), G. P. Wickremasinghe (Sinhalese SC).

Manager: L. R. D. Mendis. *Coach:* D. F. Whatmore.

SRI LANKAN TOUR RESULTS

One-day international – Played 1: Won 1.
Other non-first-class match – Won v West Indies Masters Invitation XI.

Note: Matches in this section were not first-class.

At Port-of-Spain, April 12. Sri Lankans won by 141 runs. Toss: West Indies Masters Invitation XI. Sri Lankans 309 for five (50 overs) (R. S. Kaluwitharana 86, A. P. Gurusinha 99, M. S. Atapattu 72 not out); West Indies Masters Invitation XI 168 (40 overs) (C. L. Hooper 34, C. L. King 35; M. Muralitharan three for 21).

WEST INDIES v SRI LANKA

One-Day International

At Port-of-Spain, April 13. Sri Lanka won by 35 runs. Toss: Sri Lanka.

The appeal of the new world champions attracted the biggest crowd of the season, estimated at 20,000, to Queen's Park. They were disappointed by a limp West Indian batting performance, on a pitch that encouraged the spinners, but not by the confident all-round cricket of the Sri Lankans, who batted with flair and whose fielders and wicket-keeper supported their bowlers with athletic efficiency. As they did so frequently in the World Cup, Jayasuriya and Kaluwitharana began with a withering assault on the fast bowling, scoring 67 in just 6.2 overs. The West Indian spinners separated them and checked the scoring-rate, but 251 was a challenging total. A third-wicket stand of 116 between Lara and Simmons regained some ground after the early loss of both openers but, after Dharmasena dismissed Lara, West Indies never looked like making it.

Man of the Match: H. D. P. K. Dharmasena.

Sri Lanka

S. T. Jayasuriya c Wallace b Walsh	46
†R. S. Kaluwitharana c Adams b Harper	25
A. P. Gurusinha c Lara b Adams	59
P. A. de Silva c and b Williams	25
*A. Ranatunga c Wallace b Adams	15
H. P. Tillekeratne c and b Chanderpaul	22
W. P. U. J. C. Vaas b Bishop	12
R. S. Mahanama c Chanderpaul b Walsh	14
U. U. Chandana c Adams b Harper	7
H. D. P. K. Dharmasena not out	3
M. Muralitharan c Adams b Harper	4
L-b 8, w 8, n-b 3	19
1/67 2/88 3/137 4/168 5/200 6/217 7/219 8/243 9/246 (48.3 overs)	251

Bowling: Bishop 5–0–49–1; Walsh 8–1–40–2; Harper 9.3–1–34–3; Williams 8–0–42–1; Adams 10–0–42–2; Chanderpaul 8–0–36–1.

West Indies

S. Chanderpaul run out	3
P. A. Wallace c Muralitharan b Vaas	3
B. C. Lara c Jayasuriya b Dharmasena	71
P. V. Simmons c Dharmasena b Muralitharan	45
J. C. Adams not out	37
R. I. C. Holder b Dharmasena	1
R. A. Harper c Kaluwitharana b Chandana	0
L. R. Williams b Muralitharan	5
†C. O. Browne c and b Jayasuriya	9
I. R. Bishop c Ranatunga b Tillekeratne	22
L-b 8, w 10, n-b 2	20
1/8 2/15 3/131 4/134 5/140 6/141 7/156 8/180 9/216 (9 wkts, 50 overs)	216

*C. A. Walsh did not bat.

Bowling: Vaas 6–1–19–1; de Silva 9–1–42–0; Muralitharan 10–1–37–2; Dharmasena 9–1–33–2; Chandana 10–0–40–1; Jayasuriya 5–0–32–1; Tillekeratne 1–0–5–1.

Umpires: C. E. Cumberbatch and E. Nicholls. Referee: M. H. Denness (England).

INTERNATIONAL SCHEDULE, 1997-98

The following tours were arranged as at January 1997.

1997

August–September	India to Sri Lanka
October–November	South Africa, West Indies and Sri Lanka to Pakistan
November–December	Sri Lanka to India
November–January 1998	New Zealand to Australia
December–January 1998	South Africa to Australia

1998

January–February	Zimbabwe to Sri Lanka
January–April	England to the West Indies
February	Australia to New Zealand
February–March	Sri Lanka to New Zealand
February–April	Pakistan to South Africa and Zimbabwe
March–April	Sri Lanka to South Africa
March–April	Australia to India
May–June	New Zealand to Sri Lanka

All fixtures subject to alteration.

SINGER CHAMPIONS TROPHY, 1995-96

Sri Lanka's growing pre-World Cup confidence was boosted by this triumph in Sharjah, their first victory in a limited-overs tournament involving more than two Test countries. They collected the valued scalps of Pakistan and West Indies after their batsmen, especially Roshan Mahanama, who averaged 96, found the consistency they had often lacked in the past; one of their most remarkable achievements came in a match they lost, when they managed 329 chasing West Indies' 333. They went home $US30,000 richer and captain Arjuna Ranatunga was already talking confidently about reaching the World Cup semi-finals.

Pakistan had beaten both Sri Lanka and West Indies in their opening two games and were expected to sail into the final. But with several batsmen injured they crashed in their last two matches; all three teams tied on four points and Pakistan went out on run-rate. Their home board promptly organised an inquiry, amid the usual rumours of dressing-room quarrels. Ramiz Raja's brief reign as captain was terminated and managers Majid Khan and Mushtaq Mohammad were sacked. Wasim Akram, who missed the tournament with a bad shoulder, was appointed to lead the team in Australia.

West Indies were also missing several key players: after the England tour, they offered some a rest, including bowlers Curtly Ambrose and Courtney Walsh. They recovered from two defeats to head the qualifying table on run-rate, significantly after Brian Lara's only two major batting contributions, but Richie Richardson's captaincy continued to attract criticism.

Note: Matches in this section were not first-class.

SRI LANKA v WEST INDIES

At Sharjah, October 11. Sri Lanka won by six runs. Toss: West Indies. International debut: H. A. G. Anthony.

Opener Mahanama batted into the final over, though cramp meant that he needed a runner to complete his century. He also owed much to the inspiration of Ranatunga, who scored 58 in 54 balls and raised the tempo as they added 126 in 20 overs. Richardson had chosen to bowl, hoping to find something in the pitch early on. But he had only one class bowler, Bishop, and the most successful West Indian was a fielder, Simmons, with four catches. West Indies were still on course at 165 for two, needing another 70 from 11 overs. However, Campbell was caught on the mid-wicket boundary and then six fell for 34 runs.

Man of the Match: R. S. Mahanama.

Sri Lanka

R. S. Mahanama c Simmons b Bishop	101
S. T. Jayasuriya c Simmons b Bishop	1
A. P. Gurusinha c Harper b Simmons	18
P. A. de Silva c Simmons b Chanderpaul	9
*A. Ranatunga c Browne b Gibson	58
†R. S. Kaluwitharana run out	11
H. P. Tillekeratne c Simmons b Bishop	7
R. S. Kalpage not out	1
H. D. P. K. Dharmasena not out	1
L-b 7, w 20	27
1/8 2/59 3/84 4/210 5/222 6/228 7/232 (7 wkts, 50 overs)	234

M. Muralitharan and G. P. Wickremasinghe did not bat.

Bowling: Bishop 10–1–42–3; Gibson 10–1–40–1; Anthony 8–0–49–0; Simmons 8–1–29–1; Harper 10–0–49–0; Chanderpaul 4–0–18–1.

West Indies

P. V. Simmons c de Silva b Wickremasinghe	5
S. L. Campbell c Dharmasena b Muralitharan	86
B. C. Lara run out	19
*R. B. Richardson st Kaluwitharana b Jayasuriya	67
R. I. C. Holder not out	26
R. A. Harper c and b Jayasuriya	1
S. Chanderpaul c de Silva b Dharmasena	11
O. D. Gibson lbw b Dharmasena	0
H. A. G. Anthony c Muralitharan b de Silva	2
†C. O. Browne st Kaluwitharana b Dharmasena	2
I. R. Bishop not out	1
L-b 6, w 1, n-b 1	8
1/13 2/69 3/165 4/192 5/194 6/211 7/211 8/218 9/226 (9 wkts, 50 overs)	228

Bowling: Wickremasinghe 7–0–27–1; de Silva 10–0–38–1; Dharmasena 9–0–49–3; Muralitharan 10–1–35–1; Jayasuriya 10–0–48–2; Kalpage 4–0–25–0.

Umpires: R. S. Dunne and D. B. Hair.

PAKISTAN v SRI LANKA

At Sharjah, October 12. Pakistan won by 82 runs. Toss: Pakistan.

Pakistan gained revenge for their home defeat by Sri Lanka with a crushing win. It could have been even more crushing but for tailenders Kalpage and Dharmasena, who put on 60 after combining at 114 for seven. Aamir Sohail had taken four of those; earlier, he made 85 and shared an opening stand of 107 with Salim Elahi, whose average after four one-day internationals stood at 76. Inzamam-ul-Haq scored a dashing 69 in 59 balls, hitting three sixes. Sri Lanka's only pace bowler, Wickremasinghe, was their most expensive, going for nearly eight an over.

Man of the Match: Aamir Sohail.

Pakistan

Aamir Sohail c Kaluwitharana b Muralitharan	85
Salim Elahi c Wickremasinghe b de Silva	50
*Ramiz Raja c Hathurusinghe b Muralitharan	12
Inzamam-ul-Haq c Jayasuriya b Dharmasena	69
Saeed Anwar st Kaluwitharana b Jayasuriya	14
†Moin Khan c Ranatunga b Wickremasinghe	5
Zafar Iqbal c Gurusinha b Dharmasena	2
Mushtaq Ahmed not out	9
Waqar Younis not out	9
B 2, l-b 1, w 6	9
1/107 2/138 3/162 4/213 5/232 6/244 7/246 (7 wkts, 50 overs)	264

Aqib Javed and Saqlain Mushtaq did not bat.

Bowling: Wickremasinghe 7–1–54–1; Hathurusinghe 10–0–39–0; Dharmasena 10–0–43–2; Muralitharan 10–0–51–2; Jayasuriya 8–0–51–1; de Silva 5–0–23–1.

Sri Lanka

U. C. Hathurusinghe lbw b Aqib Javed	11
S. T. Jayasuriya c sub (Basit Ali) b Saqlain Mushtaq	24
A. P. Gurusinha b Aamir Sohail	19
P. A. de Silva c and b Saqlain Mushtaq	3
*A. Ranatunga c Ramiz Raja b Aamir Sohail	14
H. P. Tillekeratne c Moin Khan b Aamir Sohail	15
†R. S. Kaluwitharana b Aamir Sohail	19
R. S. Kalpage b Saeed Anwar	22
H. D. P. K. Dharmasena not out	30
M. Muralitharan not out	7
L-b 10, w 3, n-b 5	18
1/33 2/44 3/51 4/67 5/82 6/106 7/114 8/174 (8 wkts, 50 overs)	182

G. P. Wickremasinghe did not bat.

Bowling: Waqar Younis 7–0–29–0; Aqib Javed 8–1–31–1; Zafar Iqbal 5–1–12–0; Saqlain Mushtaq 10–1–30–2; Aamir Sohail 8–0–22–4; Mushtaq Ahmed 10–0–39–0; Saeed Anwar 2–0–9–1.

Umpires: R. S. Dunne and N. T. Plews.

PAKISTAN v WEST INDIES

At Sharjah, October 13. Pakistan won by 15 runs. Toss: Pakistan.

Pakistan started slowly, and Ramiz Raja scored three in his first 31 balls. But his next 101 runs took only 103, and he put on 141 in 29 overs with Basit Ali. The tour de force came from Moin Khan: he smashed 27 in ten balls and hit the last three balls of the innings for six. Bishop went for 27 in that final over, equalling the record conceded by Muralitharan to Pakistan in Colombo 14 months before. Several West Indian batsmen made good starts, but they threw away a promising halfway position of 124 for three. Pakistan's second straight victory was West Indies' second defeat and seemed to settle the identity of the finalists.

Man of the Match: Ramiz Raja.

Pakistan

Aamir Sohail c Browne b Bishop	10
Salim Elahi c Harper b Cummins	9
*Ramiz Raja not out	104
Saeed Anwar c Browne b Anthony	18
Basit Ali c Harper b Cummins	64
†Moin Khan not out	27
L-b 1, w 8, n-b 1	10
1/16 2/24 3/49 4/190 (4 wkts, 50 overs)	242

Zafar Iqbal, Mushtaq Ahmed, Waqar Younis, Aqib Javed and Saqlain Mushtaq did not bat.

Bowling: Bishop 10–0–78–1; Cummins 10–0–31–2; Anthony 10–0–47–1; Simmons 9–0–40–0; Harper 10–0–38–0; Chanderpaul 1–0–7–0.

West Indies

P. V. Simmons lbw b Waqar Younis	4
S. L. Campbell lbw b Aamir Sohail	42
B. C. Lara c Aqib Javed b Saqlain Mushtaq	21
*R. B. Richardson b Aqib Javed	34
S. Chanderpaul c Salim Elahi b Waqar Younis	36
R. I. C. Holder st Moin Khan b Saqlain Mushtaq	11
R. A. Harper not out	43
†C. O. Browne st Moin Khan b Saqlain Mushtaq	12
A. C. Cummins c Moin Khan b Saqlain Mushtaq	4
H. A. G. Anthony run out	0
I. R. Bishop st Moin Khan b Mushtaq Ahmed	7
L-b 8, w 3, n-b 2	13
1/5 2/51 3/74 4/124 5/154 6/156 7/189 8/197 9/198 (49 overs)	227

Bowling: Aqib Javed 9–0–30–1; Waqar Younis 9–0–51–2; Zafar Iqbal 1–0–13–0; Saqlain Mushtaq 10–1–47–4; Aamir Sohail 10–1–40–1; Mushtaq Ahmed 10–1–38–1.

Umpires: D. B. Hair and N. T. Plews.

PAKISTAN v WEST INDIES

At Sharjah, October 15. West Indies won by four wickets. Toss: West Indies.

Two days later, West Indies turned the tables on Pakistan, producing their first victory since the Birmingham Test in July. Pakistan were weakened by injuries but Salim Elahi steered them to 148 for two in 37 overs before becoming the first of three run-outs in 16 balls; the last seven wickets added just 46. To maintain their interest in the tournament, West Indies wanted to reach their target of 195 as quickly as possible. They did it in style, led by Williams, in his first match at Sharjah. He scored 57 in 63 balls, while Lara contributed 52 in 58; West Indies were home with nearly 11 overs to spare.

Man of the Match: S. C. Williams.

Pakistan

Salim Elahi run out 66
*Ramiz Raja b Simmons 20
Inzamam-ul-Haq c sub (R. I. C. Holder) b Harper . 34
Basit Ali c Lara b Bishop 25
†Moin Khan run out 1
Zafar Iqbal run out 0
Mushtaq Ahmed c Browne b Gibson 4
Waqar Younis lbw b Gibson 6
Aqib Javed not out 8
Saqlain Mushtaq run out 0
Mohammad Akram not out 7
L-b 5, w 17, n-b 1 23

1/74 2/139 3/148 4/150 5/150 6/168 7/177 8/180 9/181 (9 wkts, 50 overs) 194

Bowling: Bishop 8–0–29–1; Cummins 9–0–31–0; Gibson 9–1–47–2; Simmons 10–1–31–1; Chanderpaul 5–0–25–0; Harper 9–1–26–1.

West Indies

S. C. Williams c Zafar Iqbal b Saqlain Mushtaq . 57
S. L. Campbell c Basit Ali b Mohammad Akram . 20
B. C. Lara c Basit Ali b Mushtaq Ahmed . 52
*R. B. Richardson b Saqlain Mushtaq 34
P. V. Simmons lbw b Mohammad Akram . 1
S. Chanderpaul c Moin Khan b Aqib Javed 11
R. A. Harper not out 5
†C. O. Browne not out 2
L-b 3, w 9, n-b 1 13

1/44 2/109 3/147 4/151 5/183 6/189 (6 wkts, 39.1 overs) 195

O. D. Gibson, A. C. Cummins and I. R. Bishop did not bat.

Bowling: Aqib Javed 8.1–0–41–1; Waqar Younis 4–0–30–0; Mushtaq Ahmed 10–1–43–1; Mohammad Akram 7–0–36–2; Saqlain Mushtaq 10–1–42–2.

Umpires: R. S. Dunne and D. B. Hair.

SRI LANKA v WEST INDIES

At Sharjah, October 16. West Indies won by four runs. Toss: West Indies.

For once, Richardson chose to bat, and his team piled up 333 runs. But Sri Lanka almost trumped them with 329, their biggest limited-overs total yet. They were all out in the final over when Tillekeratne swung Cummins's third ball to mid-wicket, seeking the six which would have won the match; instead, he found Williams just inside the fence. The match aggregate of 662 for 17 was a world record, easily beating 626 for 14 in a 60-over World Cup game between Pakistan and Sri Lanka in 1983. Lara scored 169 from 129 balls; he fell 21 short of beating Viv Richards's one-day international best of 189 and adding that record to the Test and first-class ones he gained in 1994. He hit 15 fours and four sixes and made nearly two-thirds of the runs added as West Indies ascended from six to 282. Chanderpaul dominated the closing stages with 62 from 45 balls. Sri Lanka set off at a terrific rate, scoring 46 for two in the first five overs. Mahanama, with a run-a-ball 76, and Kaluwitharana put on another 55 in six, but three wickets in nine balls set them back. Tillekeratne then took centre stage, reaching his hundred, which took 106 balls, just before the dramatic climax.

Man of the Match: B. C. Lara.

West Indies

S. C. Williams lbw b Wickremasinghe . . . 2
S. L. Campbell c de Silva b Wickremasinghe . 10
B. C. Lara b Dharmasena 169
*R. B. Richardson b Muralitharan 29
P. V. Simmons b Hathurusinghe 30
S. Chanderpaul not out 62
O. D. Gibson c Mahanama b Hathurusinghe . 10
R. A. Harper run out 1
A. C. Cummins not out 0
L-b 3, w 12, n-b 5 20

1/6 2/37 3/133 4/193 5/282 6/315 7/319 (7 wkts, 50 overs) 333

†C. O. Browne and I. R. Bishop did not bat.

Bowling: Wickremasinghe 10–0–58–2; Hathurusinghe 10–0–67–2; de Silva 6–0–51–0; Dharmasena 10–0–72–1; Muralitharan 10–0–52–1; Jayasuriya 4–0–30–0.

Sri Lanka

R. S. Mahanama c and b Simmons	76
S. T. Jayasuriya c Richardson b Gibson	5
P. A. de Silva lbw b Bishop	20
†R. S. Kaluwitharana c Simmons b Cummins	31
A. P. Gurusinha b Harper	1
*A. Ranatunga run out	0
H. P. Tillekeratne c Williams b Cummins	100
U. C. Hathurusinghe c Chanderpaul b Gibson	45
H. D. P. K. Dharmasena run out	24
M. Muralitharan run out	2
G. P. Wickremasinghe not out	5
L-b 4, w 15, n-b 1	20
1/21 2/46 3/101 4/103 5/103 6/171 7/257 8/306 9/316 (49.3 overs)	329

Bowling: Cummins 9.3–0–61–2; Gibson 8–0–74–2; Bishop 8–0–63–1; Harper 10–0–38–1; Simmons 10–0–53–1; Chanderpaul 4–0–36–0.

Umpires: R. S. Dunne and N. T. Plews.

PAKISTAN v SRI LANKA

At Sharjah, October 17. Sri Lanka won by eight wickets. Toss: Pakistan.

Pakistan's hopes of reaching the final were shattered when their inexperienced top six were dismissed for 82 by the 29th over. Only tailenders Mushtaq Ahmed and Saqlain Mushtaq made some amends, adding 52 for the seventh wicket. Ranatunga, who removed Basit Ali with his first ball, and Dharmasena were particularly economical, with combined figures of 20–4–37–5. A day earlier, the Sri Lankans had fallen just short of a target of 334; now they needed only 144 to go through, and cruised home in the 27th over when de Silva hit his second six off Saqlain.

Man of the Match: A. Ranatunga.

Pakistan

Salim Elahi c Kaluwitharana b Hathurusinghe	0
*Ramiz Raja c Kaluwitharana b Wickremasinghe	9
Basit Ali c Mahanama b Ranatunga	21
Aamer Hanif run out	17
†Moin Khan c and b Dharmasena	16
Zafar Iqbal c Mahanama b Ranatunga	2
Mushtaq Ahmed b Jayasuriya	26
Saqlain Mushtaq c Wickremasinghe b Dharmasena	30
Waqar Younis lbw b Dharmasena	3
Aqib Javed not out	3
Mohammad Akram c Ranatunga b Jayasuriya	1
L-b 1, w 11, n-b 3	15
1/11 2/25 3/52 4/63 5/68 6/82 7/134 8/137 9/140 (48.3 overs)	143

Bowling: Wickremasinghe 7–1–19–1; Hathurusinghe 10–1–33–1; Muralitharan 9–0–43–0; Ranatunga 10–1–21–2; Dharmasena 10–3–16–3; Jayasuriya 2.3–0–10–2.

Sri Lanka

R. S. Mahanama not out	45
S. T. Jayasuriya c Moin Khan b Mohammad Akram	25
A. P. Gurusinha c Salim Elahi b Mushtaq Ahmed	31
P. A. de Silva not out	35
L-b 7, w 2, n-b 4	13
1/35 2/94 (2 wkts, 26.5 overs)	149

*A. Ranatunga, H. P. Tillekeratne, †R. S. Kaluwitharana, U. C. Hathurusinghe, H. D. P. K. Dharmasena, M. Muralitharan and G. P. Wickremasinghe did not bat.

Bowling: Aqib Javed 5–0–25–0; Mohammad Akram 5–0–24–1; Saqlain Mushtaq 4.5–0–27–0; Zafar Iqbal 1–0–8–0; Mushtaq Ahmed 8–0–35–1; Waqar Younis 3–0–23–0.

Umpires: D. B. Hair and N. T. Plews.

QUALIFYING TABLE

	Played	*Won*	*Lost*	*Points*	*Run-rate*
West Indies	4	2	2	4	5.19
Sri Lanka	4	2	2	4	5.05
Pakistan	4	2	2	4	4.21

FINAL

SRI LANKA v WEST INDIES

At Sharjah, October 20. Sri Lanka won by 50 runs. Toss: West Indies.

Richardson repeated his gamble of the opening game when he asked Sri Lanka to bat. It failed then, and this time, with the Sri Lankans in prime form, it proved fatal. The top three made half-centuries, de Silva's coming from just 35 balls. By the 34th over they were 157 for one. Wickets began to fall after that, but the batsmen remained aggressive, and successive short blasts raised Sri Lanka to 273. They had taken lunch at 262 from 48 overs, because of the West Indian bowlers' slow rate, but, after the interval, referee Raman Subba Row decided the innings should be completed after all. It made little difference to West Indies, who were a sorry 88 for five at the halfway mark; Upashantha, in his second international, removed Williams and Lara by the 11th over. The match was settled at 177 for nine, though the last pair, Gibson and Anthony, put on 46 in 32 balls to delay Sri Lanka's celebrations.

Man of the Match: A. Ranatunga. *Man of the Series:* R. S. Mahanama.

Sri Lanka

R. S. Mahanama b Cummins 66
S. T. Jayasuriya c Gibson b Simmons 57
P. A. de Silva c Chanderpaul b Anthony 50
*A. Ranatunga c Cummins b Anthony 17
H. P. Tillekeratne c Browne b Gibson 32
†R. S. Kaluwitharana b Cummins 15
A. P. Gurusinha c Browne b Gibson 12
U. C. Hathurusinghe b Gibson 0
H. D. P. K. Dharmasena c Campbell b Gibson 4
E. A. Upashantha run out 3
M. Muralitharan not out 0
L-b 8, w 7, n-b 2 17

1/111 2/157 3/196 4/215 5/234 6/259 7/259 8/269 9/273 (49.5 overs) 273

Bowling: Cummins 9–1–50–2; Gibson 5.5–0–35–4; Anthony 8–0–47–2; Simmons 7–1–44–1; Harper 10–1–36–0; Chanderpaul 10–0–53–0.

West Indies

S. C. Williams c Muralitharan b Upashantha 5
S. L. Campbell b Muralitharan 38
B. C. Lara c and b Upashantha 8
*R. B. Richardson run out 10
P. V. Simmons run out 7
S. Chanderpaul c Muralitharan b Dharmasena 27
R. A. Harper c sub (R. S. Kalpage) b Muralitharan 31
†C. O. Browne c and b Jayasuriya 18
A. C. Cummins c Ranatunga b Muralitharan 0
O. D. Gibson not out 33
H. A. G. Anthony c de Silva b Dharmasena 21
L-b 15, w 7, n-b 3 25

1/28 2/41 3/59 4/74 5/88 6/141 7/156 8/157 9/177 (47.3 overs) 223

Bowling: Upashantha 8–1–24–2; Hathurusinghe 8–0–30–0; Muralitharan 10–0–31–3; Ranatunga 7–0–25–0; Dharmasena 8.3–1–58–2; Jayasuriya 6–0–40–1.

Umpires: R. S. Dunne and D. B. Hair. Series referee: R. Subba Row.

BENSON AND HEDGES WORLD SERIES, 1995-96

By TRENT BOUTS

Australia won their third successive World Series, as expected, but the tournament did not quite follow the expected script. Their opponents in the finals were Sri Lanka, not West Indies. No one suspected this was a pointer to the course of the World Cup. But Sri Lanka had arrived fresh from success in Sharjah, were invigorated by an experimental opener, Romesh Kaluwitharana, and enjoyed a form of cricket in which they could get by without having to bowl their opponents out. They fought back after early difficulties and pressed Australia hard in the two finals, though they could not force a third.

Relations between the two sides, already tense after allegations of ball tampering and throwing in the Test series, deteriorated further, with Muttiah Muralitharan dropping out of the team after being called again for throwing. Peace talks were held at the Australian Cricket Board, where umpire Darrell Hair denied that he made racist remarks to the Sri Lankans and explained that he had addressed them as "you blokes". It was a season of crossed wires as much as crossed swords and the rancour continued into the last match at Sydney.

The problems seemed to harden the Sri Lankans, but distractions told against the West Indians. Brian Lara had refused to join the tour and they were as busy coping with enquiries over him as they were with the cricket. They did well to recover from four straight defeats, but losing their last match to Sri Lanka saw them out of the tournament.

Australia's plans for the World Cup began to take shape as the series progressed: they did not use David Boon at all and eventually dropped Michael Slater; Mark Waugh took over the opener's job with great success. Meanwhile, players wore numbers for the first time in this competition, but another initiative, the use of retractable light towers for day/night games at Adelaide, was postponed because of engineering difficulties.

Note: Matches in this section were not first-class.

SRI LANKA v WEST INDIES

At Adelaide, December 15. Sri Lanka won by four wickets. Toss: Sri Lanka.

Eight weeks before, Sri Lanka had beaten West Indies in the Champions' final in Sharjah, and they maintained their advantage here. The West Indians were tentative and appeared low on confidence. Sent in on a slow pitch, they never lifted above a crawl and still managed to stumble regularly. Opener Campbell top-scored with 47, but needed all of 40 overs to make them. Though Ambrose and Bishop each claimed first-ball wickets, de Silva's rapid-fire 46 left his team-mates time to ease home without undue risk.

Man of the Match: A. Ranatunga. *Attendance:* 5,669.

West Indies

P. V. Simmons c Mahanama b Ranatunga	18
S. L. Campbell lbw b Muralitharan	47
*R. B. Richardson c Kaluwitharana b Ranatunga	5
S. Chanderpaul run out	1
C. L. Hooper c Tillekeratne b Muralitharan	23
J. C. Adams c Muralitharan b Dharmasena	11
R. A. Harper c Jayasuriya b Vaas	23
†C. O. Browne run out	6
I. R. Bishop not out	8
C. E. L. Ambrose not out	0
L-b 10, w 6, n-b 2	18
1/40 2/50 3/56 4/101 5/122 6/122 7/136 8/160 (8 wkts, 50 overs)	160

C. A. Walsh did not bat.

Bowling: Wickremasinghe 7–0–22–0; Vaas 7–1–17–1; Gurusinha 8–0–25–0; Ranatunga 10–1–24–2; Muralitharan 10–0–35–2; Dharmasena 8–0–27–1.

Sri Lanka

R. S. Mahanama c Campbell b Ambrose	0	†R. S. Kaluwitharana c Browne b Bishop	8
S. T. Jayasuriya c Bishop b Walsh	28	H. D. P. K. Dharmasena not out	5
A. P. Gurusinha b Bishop	15	B 1, l-b 5, w 2, n-b 7	15
P. A. de Silva c Browne b Hooper	46		—
*A. Ranatunga c Campbell b Bishop	27	1/0 2/24 3/54 (6 wkts, 45 overs)	161
H. P. Tillekeratne not out	17	4/113 5/130 6/152	

W. P. U. J. C. Vaas, G. P. Wickremasinghe and M. Muralitharan did not bat.

Bowling: Ambrose 7–0–29–1; Walsh 10–5–23–1; Bishop 10–1–38–3; Simmons 3–0–17–0; Harper 5–0–25–0; Hooper 10–1–23–1.

Umpires: D. J. Harper and T. A. Prue.

AUSTRALIA v WEST INDIES

At Adelaide, December 17. Australia won by 121 runs. Toss: West Indies. International debut: S. Lee.

Australia's comprehensive victory was also the heaviest defeat ever suffered by West Indies in their 305 one-day internationals to date. Debutant Shane Lee crashed 39 off 27 balls to turn a sound Australian start, built around a brisk fifty from Waugh, into a stunning finish, on 242 for six after three of their 50 overs were lost to rain. Lee also dismissed Adams, but it was McDermott who was mainly responsible for West Indies' demise, reducing them to 17 for four, effecting a run-out to go with his single spell of 7–2–8–2.

Man of the Match: M. E. Waugh. *Attendance:* 22,189.

Australia

*M. A. Taylor b Harper	47	S. Lee st Browne b Hooper	39
M. J. Slater b Bishop	32	†I. A. Healy not out	0
M. E. Waugh c Hooper b Harper	53	B 1, l-b 7, w 7	15
R. T. Ponting st Browne b Harper	11		—
S. G. Law c Hooper b Harper	13	1/60 2/108 3/142 (6 wkts, 47 overs)	242
M. G. Bevan not out	32	4/166 5/169 6/232	

S. K. Warne, C. J. McDermott and G. D. McGrath did not bat.

Bowling: Ambrose 9–0–43–0; Walsh 10–1–46–0; Bishop 8–0–33–1; Simmons 2–0–17–0; Hooper 8–0–49–1; Harper 10–0–46–4.

West Indies

P. V. Simmons c Waugh b McGrath	7	R. A. Harper not out	31
S. L. Campbell run out	4	†C. O. Browne not out	11
*R. B. Richardson c Healy b McDermott	4	L-b 2, w 3	5
C. L. Hooper lbw b McDermott	0		—
S. Chanderpaul c Taylor b Waugh	39	1/8 2/16 3/16 (6 wkts, 47 overs)	121
J. C. Adams c Law b Lee	20	4/17 5/54 6/97	

I. R. Bishop, C. E. L. Ambrose and C. A. Walsh did not bat.

Bowling: McDermott 7–2–8–2; McGrath 5–1–13–1; Law 7–1–23–0; Lee 7–0–20–1; Waugh 10–0–26–1; Warne 7–1–22–0; Bevan 3–0–7–0; Slater 1–1–0–0.

Umpires: A. J. McQuillan and T. A. Prue.

AUSTRALIA v WEST INDIES

At Melbourne, December 19 (day/night). Australia won by 24 runs. Toss: Australia. International debut: M. S. Kasprowicz.

The most remarkable aspect of this match was that it went ahead at all; after days of rain, Melbourne produced one of its coldest summer evenings on record. Law enhanced his World Cup claims with 74 after West Indies had reduced Australia to 46 for three in the 15th over, while Bevan was simply brilliant with an unbeaten 44 off 41 balls. Australia's 249 for six appeared insurmountable and so it proved, despite the first signs of fight from a fractured West Indies camp. Chanderpaul's 73 included one six off McDermott of which many larger men would have been proud.

Man of the Match: M. G. Bevan. *Attendance:* 43,350.

Australia

M. J. Slater c Richardson b Ambrose	2	S. Lee c Chanderpaul b Ambrose	3
*M. A. Taylor c Hooper b Simmons	63	†I. A. Healy not out	34
M. E. Waugh run out	15	L-b 4, w 2, n-b 2	8
R. T. Ponting c Browne b Walsh	6		—
S. G. Law st Browne b Hooper	74	1/6 2/39 3/46 (6 wkts, 50 overs)	249
M. G. Bevan not out	44	4/164 5/172 6/181	

S. K. Warne, C. J. McDermott and M. S. Kasprowicz did not bat.

Bowling: Ambrose 10–1–36–2; Walsh 9–0–32–1; Cummins 6–0–40–0; Harper 10–1–46–0; Hooper 9–0–60–1; Simmons 6–0–31–1.

West Indies

S. C. Williams lbw b Lee	44	†C. O. Browne run out	2
S. L. Campbell c Ponting b Kasprowicz	2	C. E. L. Ambrose b McDermott	1
S. Chanderpaul c and b Bevan	73	C. A. Walsh c Healy b Warne	1
P. V. Simmons c McDermott b Waugh	24	L-b 9, w 1, n-b 2	12
C. L. Hooper c Healy b Bevan	10		—
*R. B. Richardson c Law b McDermott	15	1/5 2/84 3/125 (49.1 overs)	225
R. A. Harper st Healy b Warne	15	4/147 5/166 6/177	
A. C. Cummins not out	26	7/209 8/213 9/224	

Bowling: McDermott 10–0–40–2; Kasprowicz 6–0–32–1; Lee 10–1–40–1; Warne 9.1–1–41–2; Waugh 6–0–32–1; Bevan 8–0–31–2.

Umpires: P. D. Parker and S. G. Randell.

AUSTRALIA v SRI LANKA

At Sydney, December 21 (day/night). Australia won by five wickets. Toss: Sri Lanka.

Sri Lanka reached 255 thanks to a superb 75 by de Silva and a clear error by umpire Harper, which denied Mark Waugh a catch and gave Tillekeratne an early second chance en route to 62. Slater failed again in the chase but Taylor looked set for his first century in the short game until he was beaten by Muralitharan's throw on 90. Sri Lanka used eight bowlers but none of them could prevent Bevan steering Australia home with two balls' breathing space.

Man of the Match: M. A. Taylor. *Attendance:* 28,301.

Sri Lanka

R. S. Mahanama run out	5	W. P. U. J. C. Vaas run out	14
S. T. Jayasuriya c Healy b McGrath	24	G. P. Wickremasinghe not out	4
A. P. Gurusinha c Waugh b Bevan	38	M. Muralitharan not out	0
P. A. de Silva c and b Lee	75	B 2, l-b 11, w 5, n-b 1	19
*A. Ranatunga run out	7		—
H. P. Tillekeratne c Lee b McGrath	62	1/7 2/32 3/111 (9 wkts, 50 overs)	255
†R. S. Kaluwitharana b Kasprowicz	0	4/134 5/173 6/175	
H. D. P. K. Dharmasena run out	7	7/203 8/239 9/253	

Bowling: McGrath 10–1–47–2; Kasprowicz 10–0–51–1; Lee 10–0–40–1; Warne 10–1–53–0; Waugh 6–0–31–0; Bevan 4–0–20–1.

Australia

*M. A. Taylor run out . . . 90
M. J. Slater c Kaluwitharana b Vaas . . . 10
M. E. Waugh run out . . . 55
R. T. Ponting c Muralitharan b Dharmasena . 56
S. G. Law run out . . . 7
M. G. Bevan not out . . . 18
S. Lee not out . . . 4
L-b 13, w 4 . . . 17

1/23 2/131 3/192 4/212 5/239 (5 wkts, 49.4 overs) 257

†I. A. Healy, S. K. Warne, M. S. Kasprowicz and G. D. McGrath did not bat.

Bowling: Wickremasinghe 7–0–24–0; Vaas 9–0–50–1; Gurusinha 2–0–12–0; Ranatunga 1–0–12–0; Muralitharan 10–0–52–0; Dharmasena 8.4–0–41–1; Jayasuriya 8–0–35–0; de Silva 4–0–18–0.

Umpires: D. B. Hair and D. J. Harper.

AUSTRALIA v WEST INDIES

At Sydney, January 1 (day/night). Australia won by one wicket. Toss: West Indies.

The tournament resumed after Christmas with its most thrilling game yet. With the last man in, Bevan lofted the final ball straight to the boundary to extend Australia's winning streak to four, while West Indies completed their fourth straight defeat. The bowler, Harper, shared a high-five with Bevan; given that he had claimed a catch against him earlier, which the umpires correctly decreed had hit the ground, it was pleasant to see them dispel any tension. Bevan had scored 78 from 89 balls to rescue Australia from 38 for six, and Bobby Simpson, who had witnessed most of his country's 337 one-day internationals as player, commentator or coach, called it the best chasing innings he had seen. Hooper's role was not dissimilar in rallying West Indies from 54 for five. It was Reiffel, however, who took the match award, having helped Bevan to double the score in a critical eighth-wicket stand after bagging four for 29.

Man of the Match: P. R. Reiffel. *Attendance:* 37,562.

West Indies

S. C. Williams c Healy b Reiffel . . . 5
S. L. Campbell lbw b Warne . . . 15
P. V. Simmons c Warne b Reiffel . . . 4
S. Chanderpaul c Taylor b Reiffel . . . 3
C. L. Hooper not out . . . 93
J. C. Adams c Waugh b Warne . . . 0
R. A. Harper run out . . . 28
O. D. Gibson b McGrath . . . 4
†C. O. Browne c Warne b Reiffel . . . 2
C. E. L. Ambrose b Warne . . . 0
*C. A. Walsh not out . . . 3
L-b 6, w 7, n-b 2 . . . 15

1/13 2/21 3/28 4/54 5/54 6/135 7/150 8/164 9/168 (9 wkts, 43 overs) 172

Bowling: McGrath 9–2–22–1; Reiffel 9–2–29–4; Law 6–0–34–0; Lee 6–0–20–0; Warne 9–2–30–3; Bevan 4–0–31–0.

Australia

M. J. Slater c Simmons b Ambrose . . . 5
*M. A. Taylor run out . . . 1
M. E. Waugh c Harper b Gibson . . . 16
R. T. Ponting b Ambrose . . . 0
S. G. Law c Browne b Ambrose . . . 10
M. G. Bevan not out . . . 78
S. Lee c Browne b Gibson . . . 0
†I. A. Healy b Harper . . . 16
P. R. Reiffel c Hooper b Simmons . . . 34
S. K. Warne run out . . . 3
G. D. McGrath not out . . . 1
L-b 2, w 3, n-b 4 . . . 9

1/4 2/15 3/15 4/32 5/38 6/38 7/74 8/157 9/167 (9 wkts, 43 overs) 173

Bowling: Ambrose 9–3–20–3; Walsh 9–2–22–0; Gibson 9–2–40–2; Harper 8–0–38–1; Simmons 5–0–31–1; Hooper 3–0–20–0.

Umpires: A. J. McQuillan and P. D. Parker.

SRI LANKA v WEST INDIES

At Hobart, January 3. West Indies won by 70 runs. Toss: Sri Lanka.

Though West Indies arrived in Hobart still looking for their first win, their reputation was not the only one at stake; Sri Lankan off-spinner Muralitharan had been called for throwing in the Melbourne Test eight days earlier. Umpires Prue and Davis admitted paying attention to his action, but neither saw anything so out of the ordinary as to be unfair. Muralitharan managed two wickets, including that of the diminutive Chanderpaul, who blamed his over-sized pads for an attack of cramp but still scored 77. The exuberant Gibson made sure that was enough, taking five for 42 at a lively pace.

Man of the Match: S. Chanderpaul. *Attendance:* 6,048.

West Indies

P. V. Simmons c Kaluwitharana b Vaas	0
S. L. Campbell c Kaluwitharana b Hathurusinghe	38
S. Chanderpaul c Vaas b Muralitharan	77
*R. B. Richardson c Gurusinha b Dharmasena	18
C. L. Hooper c de Silva b Vaas	36
R. A. Harper b Muralitharan	1
O. D. Gibson c de Silva b Hathurusinghe	6
†C. O. Browne not out	4
I. R. Bishop run out	3
C. E. L. Ambrose c Tillekeratne b Vaas	0
C. A. Walsh b Munasinghe	1
L-b 3, w 7	10
1/0 2/83 3/125 4/161 5/168 6/179 7/187 8/193 9/193 (48.2 overs)	194

Bowling: Vaas 9–2–21–3; Munasinghe 8.2–1–21–1; Hathurusinghe 10–1–50–2; Gurusinha 3–0–14–0; Muralitharan 10–0–46–2; Dharmasena 6–0–30–1; Jayasuriya 2–0–9–0.

Sri Lanka

R. S. Mahanama c Campbell b Gibson	10
S. T. Jayasuriya c Ambrose b Walsh	3
A. P. Gurusinha run out	48
*P. A. de Silva c Campbell b Gibson	6
H. P. Tillekeratne c Browne b Gibson	5
†R. S. Kaluwitharana run out	8
U. C. Hathurusinghe c Richardson b Bishop	3
H. D. P. K. Dharmasena c Browne b Gibson	12
W. P. U. J. C. Vaas c Campbell b Harper	10
M. Munasinghe c Simmons b Gibson	0
M. Muralitharan not out	2
L-b 2, w 5, n-b 10	17
1/4 2/39 3/47 4/74 5/89 6/94 7/100 8/121 9/121 (37.4 overs)	124

Bowling: Ambrose 6–0–13–0; Walsh 8–1–22–1; Bishop 8–1–28–1; Gibson 8.4–0–42–5; Harper 7–0–17–1.

Umpires: S. J. Davis and T. A. Prue.

SRI LANKA v WEST INDIES

At Brisbane, January 5 (day/night). West Indies won by seven wickets. Toss: Sri Lanka.

Bad weather spoiled the first floodlit international in Brisbane, staged on the 25th anniversary of the original one-day game between Australia and England at Melbourne. The weather was not as damaging, however, as the controversy that re-erupted around Muralitharan. Sri Lanka deserved to lose after choosing to bat on a pitch as green and damp as the outfield. Dismissed for 102, after Ambrose wrecked the top order and Browne made a record-equalling five dismissals, they were over-run by the 27th over. But they were really overwhelmed when Muralitharan was no-balled repeatedly by umpire Emerson, standing in his first international. Muralitharan resorted to leg-spin; he was still no-balled. Acting-captain de Silva seemed ready to prolong the agony, until frantic calls from the dressing-room prompted the bowler's removal. The senior umpire, McQuillan, who signalled no-ball himself from square leg, shook hands with Emerson before leaving the field, surrounded by police, as the crowd booed.

Man of the Match: C. E. L. Ambrose. *Attendance:* 13,899.

Sri Lanka

U. C. Hathurusinghe c Browne b Ambrose.	0	M. Munasinghe c Browne b Simmons	8
S. T. Jayasuriya c Browne b Walsh	3	G. P. Wickremasinghe c Harper b Walsh	2
A. P. Gurusinha c Hooper b Ambrose	3	M. Muralitharan b Gibson	0
*P. A. de Silva c Gibson b Bishop	10	L-b 2, w 18, n-b 5	25
R. S. Mahanama c Browne b Ambrose	0		—
H. P. Tillekeratne not out	37	1/0 2/12 3/17 (45.2 overs)	102
†R. S. Kaluwitharana run out	0	4/19 5/33 6/34	
W. P. U. J. C. Vaas c Browne b Gibson	14	7/77 8/95 9/98	

Bowling: Ambrose 10–3–20–3; Walsh 9–2–19–2; Gibson 8.2–2–15–2; Bishop 7–1–18–1; Simmons 9–2–19–1; Harper 2–0–9–0.

West Indies

P. V. Simmons lbw b Vaas	6	C. L. Hooper not out	18
S. L. Campbell c Muralitharan b Vaas	34	L-b 2, w 8, n-b 7	17
S. Chanderpaul run out	10		—
*R. B. Richardson not out	19	1/6 2/46 3/68 (3 wkts, 26.1 overs)	104

R. A. Harper, O. D. Gibson, †C. O. Browne, I. R. Bishop, C. E. L. Ambrose and C. A. Walsh did not bat.

Bowling: Vaas 10–2–24–2; Munasinghe 7–1–34–0; Wickremasinghe 6–0–24–0; Muralitharan 3–0–16–0; Tillekeratne 0.1–0–4–0.

Umpires: R. A. Emerson and A. J. McQuillan.

AUSTRALIA v WEST INDIES

At Brisbane, January 7. West Indies won by 14 runs. Toss: Australia.

This was West Indies' third successive win, but they were under no illusions that their problems had been solved; nor were the Australians unduly perturbed. Richardson appeared to have shaken off his hamstring injury, scoring 81, but it was Gibson who provided the vital impetus with bat and ball. His 52 off 40 balls included four fours and two sixes, and later he ended Australia's last fighting chance when he removed Healy in the 48th over.

Man of the Match: O. D. Gibson. *Attendance:* 21,632.

West Indies

S. C. Williams c Healy b McGrath	0	I. R. Bishop run out	5
S. L. Campbell b McGrath	5	C. E. L. Ambrose not out	3
P. V. Simmons c Lee b Waugh	42	C. A. Walsh b McGrath	0
*R. B. Richardson c Bevan b Law	81	L-b 3, w 6, n-b 5	14
C. L. Hooper c Slater b Reiffel	18		—
R. A. Harper b Waugh	10	1/2 2/27 3/103 (49.3 overs)	231
†C. O. Browne run out	1	4/133 5/167 6/169	
O. D. Gibson b Lee	52	7/173 8/220 9/230	

Bowling: McGrath 9.3–1–47–3; Reiffel 7–1–50–1; McDermott 8–0–43–0; Waugh 10–0–30–2; Bevan 3–0–16–0; Lee 8–1–30–1; Law 4–1–12–1.

Australia

*M. A. Taylor c Browne b Bishop	14	P. R. Reiffel run out	14
M. J. Slater c Campbell b Ambrose	0	C. J. McDermott b Gibson	1
M. E. Waugh c Browne b Walsh	5	G. D. McGrath not out	0
R. T. Ponting c Harper b Bishop	61	L-b 6, w 7, n-b 9	22
S. G. Law c and b Simmons	62		—
M. G. Bevan run out	17	1/1 2/10 3/27 (47.4 overs)	217
S. Lee c Simmons b Walsh	6	4/142 5/179 6/180	
†I. A. Healy c Walsh b Gibson	15	7/187 8/216 9/217	

Bowling: Ambrose 9–2–20–1; Walsh 9–0–56–2; Bishop 10–0–49–2; Gibson 5.4–0–38–2; Harper 4–1–9–0; Simmons 10–0–39–1.

Umpires: D. B. Hair and P. D. Parker.

AUSTRALIA v SRI LANKA

At Melbourne, January 9 (day/night). Sri Lanka won by three wickets. Toss: Australia.

Acting-captain de Silva dedicated Sri Lanka's victory to the exiled spinner Muralitharan, who was not to be risked again following his disaster in Brisbane. A replacement, Kalpage, was flown out and played hours after arriving in Australia. Interest had shifted to two openers, however. The Australian, Slater, was dropped after his fifth successive low score; but for Sri Lanka, Kaluwitharana set the pattern of whirlwind starts that would represent the key to their World Cup success. Hitting through any line he could reach, he thrashed 77 off 79 balls. This left his middle order time to bat more conservatively, pacing their way to victory with 15 balls to spare. Ponting's maiden century for Australia was a gem lost beneath Kaluwitharana's avalanche; he shared a stand of 159 with Bevan, a world record for the fifth wicket in limited-overs internationals.

Man of the Match: R. S. Kaluwitharana. *Attendance:* 60,110.

Australia

M. J. Slater c Kaluwitharana b Munasinghe	2
*M. A. Taylor c Kaluwitharana b Munasinghe	9
M. E. Waugh b Munasinghe	0
R. T. Ponting run out	123
S. G. Law c Tillekeratne b Wickremasinghe	8
M. G. Bevan not out	65
L-b 2, w 2, n-b 2	6
1/8 2/10 3/33 4/54 5/213 (5 wkts, 50 overs)	213

S. Lee, †I. A. Healy, P. R. Reiffel, S. K. Warne and C. J. McDermott did not bat.

Bowling: Vaas 10–3–41–0; Munasinghe 10–1–30–3; Wickremasinghe 6–0–29–1; Dharmasena 10–0–31–0; Jayasuriya 10–0–56–0; Kalpage 4–0–24–0.

Sri Lanka

S. T. Jayasuriya c Lee b Reiffel	8
†R. S. Kaluwitharana run out	77
A. P. Gurusinha run out	0
*P. A. de Silva lbw b McDermott	35
R. S. Mahanama lbw b Bevan	51
H. P. Tillekeratne lbw b McDermott	0
R. S. Kalpage b Warne	1
H. D. P. K. Dharmasena not out	28
W. P. U. J. C. Vaas not out	0
L-b 7, w 5, n-b 2	14
1/17 2/39 3/127 4/144 5/144 6/147 7/209 (7 wkts, 47.3 overs)	214

M. Munasinghe and G. P. Wickremasinghe did not bat.

Bowling: McDermott 10–0–42–2; Reiffel 10–0–47–1; Lee 6–2–26–0; Warne 10–1–37–1; Waugh 6–0–31–0; Bevan 5.3–0–24–1.

Umpires: D. J. Harper and A. J. McQuillan.

AUSTRALIA v SRI LANKA

At Perth, January 12 (day/night). Australia won by 83 runs. Toss: Australia.

Mark Waugh, seizing the opener's spot with a career-best 130, and Taylor seemed to have put the result out of doubt with 189 for the first wicket. That was until rival openers Kaluwitharana and Jayasuriya flayed 54 off the first ten overs. Astutely, Taylor stole their momentum through Law's less-than-medium pace and four wickets tumbled as Sri Lanka sought to make up the difference. Plenty of heat remained in the match, however, and Gurusinha was reprimanded by referee Graham Dowling for a verbal clash with Steve Waugh. After that judgment was delivered, close to midnight, Sri Lankan manager Duleep Mendis could be seen through a committee-room window arguing with Dowling.

Man of the Match: M. E. Waugh. *Attendance:* 27,978.

Australia

*M. A. Taylor c sub (M. Muralitharan) b Jayasuriya . 85
M. E. Waugh run out 130
R. T. Ponting b Jayasuriya 11
S. R. Waugh b Vaas 11
S. G. Law run out 9
M. G. Bevan not out 1
†I. A. Healy c Jayasuriya b Vaas 0
L-b 8, w 9, n-b 2 19

1/189 2/209 3/251 4/259 5/266 6/266 (6 wkts, 50 overs) 266

P. R. Reiffel, S. K. Warne, C. J. McDermott and G. D. McGrath did not bat.

Bowling: Vaas 10–1–33–2; Pushpakumara 8–0–41–0; Wickremasinghe 9–0–60–0; Dharmasena 10–0–51–0; de Silva 1–0–7–0; Kalpage 2–0–18–0; Jayasuriya 10–0–48–2.

Sri Lanka

S. T. Jayasuriya c Healy b Law 27
†R. S. Kaluwitharana c Ponting b McGrath 20
A. P. Gurusinha b McDermott 45
*P. A. de Silva lbw b Law 0
R. S. Mahanama c Healy b Reiffel 3
H. P. Tillekeratne not out 58
R. S. Kalpage c Bevan b McDermott 1
H. D. P. K. Dharmasena run out 2
W. P. U. J. C. Vaas st Healy b Warne . . . 10
G. P. Wickremasinghe run out 2
K. R. Pushpakumara not out 1
L-b 8, w 5, n-b 1 14

1/56 2/56 3/56 4/67 5/138 6/142 7/151 8/172 9/175 (9 wkts, 50 overs) 183

Bowling: McDermott 10–0–39–2; McGrath 8–1–22–1; Law 10–0–30–2; Reiffel 9–2–25–1; Warne 10–0–45–1; S. R. Waugh 3–0–14–0.

Umpires: D. B. Hair and P. D. Parker.

SRI LANKA v WEST INDIES

At Perth, January 14. Sri Lanka won by 16 runs. Toss: West Indies.

A fourth straight win would have carried West Indies into the finals; instead, Sri Lanka pulled level again. Kaluwitharana scored another half-century in a breathtaking 55 balls. But Gibson, the least heralded but far and away the most effective of the West Indies pace quartet, took four wickets as Sri Lanka slid from 80 without loss to 92 for five. A final haul of five for 40 gave him 16 wickets in five appearances, a remarkable strike-rate in one-day cricket. Once again, though, West Indies could not find the runs to exploit his work. De Silva had failed with the bat but claimed three critical wickets, including Gibson's, with his part-time spin.

Man of the Match: R. S. Kaluwitharana. *Attendance:* 9,278.

Sri Lanka

S. T. Jayasuriya lbw b Gibson 28
†R. S. Kaluwitharana b Gibson 50
A. P. Gurusinha c Browne b Gibson 5
*P. A. de Silva run out 1
H. P. Tillekeratne c Browne b Gibson 0
R. S. Mahanama b Bishop 50
S. Ranatunga b Hooper 5
H. D. P. K. Dharmasena hit wkt b Walsh . 16
W. P. U. J. C. Vaas c Ambrose b Gibson . 21
E. A. Upashantha not out 8
K. R. Pushpakumara run out 5
L-b 4, w 4, n-b 5 13

1/80 2/89 3/90 4/91 5/92 6/121 7/161 8/176 9/193 (50 overs) 202

Bowling: Ambrose 8–2–32–0; Walsh 9–0–34–1; Bishop 10–2–46–1; Gibson 10–1–40–5; Hooper 10–0–33–1; Simmons 3–0–13–0.

West Indies

P. V. Simmons b Upashantha	5	I. R. Bishop run out	4
S. L. Campbell c Vaas b de Silva	20	C. E. L. Ambrose not out	8
S. Chanderpaul c Gurusinha b de Silva	44	C. A. Walsh not out	3
*R. B. Richardson run out	7		
C. L. Hooper c Gurusinha b Dharmasena	1	L-b 3, w 4, n-b 8	15
R. I. C. Holder c Kaluwitharana b Jayasuriya	38	1/18 2/51 3/65 (9 wkts, 50 overs)	186
†C. O. Browne c Pushpakumara b Vaas	22	4/67 5/114 6/131	
O. D. Gibson st Kaluwitharana b de Silva	19	7/160 8/171 9/176	

Bowling: Vaas 9–0–27–1; Pushpakumara 8–2–21–0; Upashantha 6–0–31–1; Dharmasena 7–2–22–1; de Silva 10–0–43–3; Jayasuriya 10–1–39–1.

Umpires: D. J. Harper and T. A. Prue.

AUSTRALIA v SRI LANKA

At Melbourne, January 16 (day/night). Sri Lanka won by three wickets. Toss: Australia.

Sri Lanka earned a place in the finals with their second win over Australia. Steve Waugh had missed the bulk of the World Series through injury but made up for lost time with his first century in his 187 one-day internationals. Meanwhile, Bevan pushed his series aggregate to 298 for once out. But Australia's 242 would prove insufficient. Again, Kaluwitharana was the wild card, or wild horse, bolting out of the gate with 74 off 69 balls and leaving McGrath with the worst figures by any Australian at this level – one for 76. Sri Lanka were able to glide home with minimal risk; Kaluwitharana won his third match award and, a few days later, was named the outstanding player of the preliminary rounds.

Man of the Match: R. S. Kaluwitharana. *Attendance:* 40,571.

Australia

M. E. Waugh c Mahanama b Vaas	6	S. G. Law c Ranatunga b Pushpakumara	47
*M. A. Taylor c Kaluwitharana b Wickremasinghe	32	M. G. Bevan not out	43
R. T. Ponting c Kaluwitharana b Wickremasinghe	5	L-b 3, w 2, n-b 2	7
S. R. Waugh not out	102	1/12 2/28 (4 wkts, 50 overs)	242
		3/54 4/156	

†I. A. Healy, P. R. Reiffel, S. K. Warne, C. J. McDermott and G. D. McGrath did not bat.

Bowling: Vaas 10–2–43–1; Pushpakumara 10–0–47–1; Wickremasinghe 8–0–33–2; Dharmasena 8–0–42–0; de Silva 6–0–30–0; Jayasuriya 8–0–44–0.

Sri Lanka

S. T. Jayasuriya c Healy b McGrath	3	H. D. P. K. Dharmasena not out	24
†R. S. Kaluwitharana c M. E. Waugh b Warne	74	W. P. U. J. C. Vaas not out	13
A. P. Gurusinha c Healy b Reiffel	17	B 1, l-b 18, w 2	21
H. P. Tillekeratne c Healy b Warne	0		
P. A. de Silva lbw b Bevan	45	1/35 2/96 3/107 (7 wkts, 49.4 overs)	246
R. S. Mahanama b Warne	31	4/108 5/180	
*A. Ranatunga run out	18	6/196 7/222	

G. P. Wickremasinghe and K. R. Pushpakumara did not bat.

Bowling: McDermott 10–3–27–0; McGrath 9.4–0–76–1; Reiffel 10–1–36–1; Warne 10–0–40–3; Law 6–0–28–0; M. E. Waugh 2–0–11–0; Bevan 2–0–9–1.

Umpires: D. B. Hair and S. G. Randell.

QUALIFYING TABLE

	Played	*Won*	*Lost*	*Points*	*Net run-rate*
Australia	8	5	3	10	0.51
Sri Lanka	8	4	4	8	−0.52
West Indies	8	3	5	6	−0.01

Net run-rate was calculated by subtracting runs conceded per over from runs scored per over.
Player of the Preliminaries: R. S. Kaluwitharana.

AUSTRALIA v SRI LANKA

First Final Match

At Melbourne, January 18 (day/night). Australia won by 18 runs. Toss: Sri Lanka.

A double breakthrough inside five overs by the rapidly improving Vaas helped restrict Australia to 201 in front of the largest crowd of the summer. Sri Lanka felt Steve Waugh was lucky to survive an lbw appeal and were positively peeved when the same umpire, Randell, gave Kaluwitharana out just as he was warming up, with three fours in nine balls. Even so, they ought to have won after reaching 107 for two in the 24th over. But Warne produced two wickets in that over and McDermott chimed in with a spell of three for 14, including one with an experimental delivery in which the ball slewed off his knuckles. During the game McDermott joined Wasim Akram and Kapil Dev as the only bowlers to take 200 wickets in one-day internationals. Mahanama resumed with a runner after tearing a hamstring and Ranatunga forged on despite an injured hand, but pluck alone could not repair the earlier damage.

Attendance: 72,614.

Australia

*M. A. Taylor c Kaluwitharana b Vaas	0
M. E. Waugh b Vaas	4
R. T. Ponting run out	51
S. R. Waugh c Gurusinha b Wickremasinghe	13
S. G. Law c Kaluwitharana b Pushpakumara	0
M. G. Bevan c Mahanama b Pushpakumara	59
†I. A. Healy not out	50
P. R. Reiffel b Vaas	15
S. K. Warne not out	3
L-b 3, w 2, n-b 1	6
1/0 2/9 3/39 4/39 5/100 6/155 7/192 (7 wkts, 50 overs)	201

C. J. McDermott and G. D. McGrath did not bat.

Bowling: Vaas 10–1–42–3; Pushpakumara 10–1–34–2; Wickremasinghe 8–0–30–1; Dharmasena 10–1–31–0; de Silva 5–0–24–0; Jayasuriya 7–0–37–0.

Sri Lanka

S. T. Jayasuriya c S. R. Waugh b McGrath	19
†R. S. Kaluwitharana lbw b McGrath	13
A. P. Gurusinha c Bevan b McDermott	47
P. A. de Silva c Taylor b Warne	34
H. P. Tillekeratne c Healy b Warne	1
R. S. Mahanama b M. E. Waugh	16
*A. Ranatunga b McGrath	31
H. D. P. K. Dharmasena b McDermott	4
W. P. U. J. C. Vaas c Healy b McDermott	2
G. P. Wickremasinghe c Taylor b Reiffel	0
K. R. Pushpakumara not out	8
L-b 5, w 2, n-b 1	8
1/17 2/46 3/107 4/110 5/120 6/129 7/131 8/132 9/152 (48.1 overs)	183

R. S. Mahanama, when 4, retired hurt at 124 and resumed at 132.

Bowling: McGrath 9.1–0–28–3; Reiffel 10–2–44–1; M. E. Waugh 6–0–23–1; McDermott 10–1–41–3; Warne 10–1–29–2; Law 3–0–13–0.

Umpires: D. B. Hair and S. G. Randell.

AUSTRALIA v SRI LANKA

Second Final Match

At Sydney, January 20 (day/night). Australia won by eight runs, Sri Lanka's target having been revised to 168 from 25 overs. Toss: Sri Lanka.

Australia's series victory was tainted by angry exchanges both in the middle and at the presentation ceremony. With few exceptions, the Sri Lankans refused to shake Taylor's hand and Healy passed remarks to opposing coach Dav Whatmore for which he later apologised. Mark Waugh continued to revel in opening; his 135-run stand with Taylor laid the base for Australia's 273, the best total of this tournament. Bevan was productive again and Healy's 40 off 28 balls was invaluable. Rain during the break reduced Sri Lanka's target to 168 and their batting time by half, thus pushing their required run-rate closer to seven than six. McGrath completed his revenge on Kaluwitharana when he had him lbw cheaply for the second match running. Still, Sri Lanka looked capable of winning at 135 for six with five overs remaining. But Warne produced two wickets on cue, as he had done in Melbourne, dismissing Ranatunga and Dharmasena in successive overs.

Players of the Finals: M. A. Taylor and S. K. Warne. *Attendance:* 39,223.

Australia

M. E. Waugh c and b Kalpage	73
*M. A. Taylor c Kaluwitharana b Kalpage	82
R. T. Ponting c Vaas b Dharmasena	17
S. R. Waugh c Kalpage b Dharmasena	2
S. G. Law b Vaas	21
M. G. Bevan not out	32
†I. A. Healy not out	40
L-b 5, w 1	6
1/135 2/170 3/176 4/184 5/210 (5 wkts, 50 overs)	273

P. R. Reiffel, S. K. Warne, C. J. McDermott and G. D. McGrath did not bat.

Bowling: Vaas 10–1–47–1; Pushpakumara 8–1–39–0; Munasinghe 4–0–33–0; Dharmasena 10–0–45–2; Kalpage 10–0–47–2; Jayasuriya 8–0–57–0.

Sri Lanka

S. T. Jayasuriya c McGrath b Warne	30
†R. S. Kaluwitharana lbw b McGrath	0
P. A. de Silva c Reiffel b M. E. Waugh	6
A. P. Gurusinha c Warne b Reiffel	24
*A. Ranatunga c Law b Warne	41
R. S. Kalpage c Taylor b McDermott	9
H. P. Tillekeratne run out	25
H. D. P. K. Dharmasena c S. R. Waugh b Warne	7
M. Munasinghe not out	3
W. P. U. J. C. Vaas not out	8
L-b 3, w 3	6
1/1 2/22 3/49 4/66 5/87 6/135 7/146 8/146 (8 wkts, 25 overs)	159

K. R. Pushpakumara did not bat.

Bowling: McGrath 5–0–36–1; M. E. Waugh 5–0–31–1; Warne 5–0–20–3; S. R. Waugh 1–0–14–0; Reiffel 4–0–22–1; McDermott 5–0–33–1.

Umpires: P. D. Parker and S. G. Randell. Series referee: G. T. Dowling (New Zealand).

SINGER CUP, 1995-96

By R. MOHAN

Pakistan triumphed under their acting-captain, Aamir Sohail, at the latest venue for official international cricket. The picturesque Padang in Singapore had a dramatic debut, with a spate of records being broken, mostly by Sanath Jayasuriya of Sri Lanka. He plundered the fastest century in one-day internationals, with a record 11 sixes, in the opening game, and the fastest fifty in the final. There was some speculation that the boundaries were too short for the games to be recorded as official internationals but ICC received assurances that minimum standards were met.

Only two strips were available; they lost pace after just a day's use and this led to huge fluctuations in the scoring-rate. The fortunes of the three teams, Sri Lanka, Pakistan and India, fluctuated too, and the finalists had to be selected on net run-rate. That eliminated India, to the disappointment of the home crowds, which were dominated by expatriate Indians; during the India–Pakistan game, the temporary stand for 5,000 failed to meet the demand, though attendances on other days were thin.

The final was a low-scoring game – Pakistan and Sri Lanka scored a combined 387, after a record 664 in their previous encounter – and the Pakistanis surprised the World Cup champions by crushing them after Jayasuriya took them to 96 for one in the ninth over. As well as winning $US30,000, Pakistan revived their morale and Sohail's reputation. Both had been damaged by the traumatic defeat in the World Cup quarter-final against India, when Sohail began his brief stint deputising as captain for the injured Wasim Akram.

Note: Matches in this section were not first-class.

PAKISTAN v SRI LANKA

At Singapore, April 1. No result. Toss: Sri Lanka.

The first scheduled day of official international cricket in Singapore lasted only ten overs. Ranatunga had made the most of winning the toss and Pakistan were three down when rain ended play. The match was abandoned and a new one started the following day. Under an ICC ruling, both matches are now deemed to count as internationals.

Pakistan

*Aamir Sohail c Kaluwitharana b Vaas	22
Saeed Anwar c Dharmasena b Vaas	3
Inzamam-ul-Haq c Vaas b Ranatunga	15
Ijaz Ahmed, sen. not out	6
Salim Malik not out	6
W 2	2
1/9 2/32 3/43 (3 wkts, 10 overs)	54

Basit Ali, †Rashid Latif, Waqar Younis, Saqlain Mushtaq, Aqib Javed and Mohammad Akram did not bat.

Bowling: Wickremasinghe 4–0–31–0; Vaas 3–1–11–2; Ranatunga 2–0–8–1; Dharmasena 1–0–4–0.

Sri Lanka

S. T. Jayasuriya, †R. S. Kaluwitharana, A. P. Gurusinha, P. A. de Silva, *A. Ranatunga, R. S. Mahanama, H. P. Tillekeratne, H. D. P. K. Dharmasena, W. P. U. J. C. Vaas, G. P. Wickremasinghe and M. Muralitharan.

Umpires: D. L. Orchard and R. B. Tiffin.

PAKISTAN v SRI LANKA

At Singapore, April 2. Sri Lanka won by 34 runs. Toss: Pakistan.

When Aamir Sohail asked Sri Lanka to bat in the second attempt at starting the game, Jayasuriya exploded into action with the quickest century in the history of limited-overs internationals. He rushed from a 32-ball 50 to a 48-ball hundred, with seven sixes and nine fours, easily beating Mohammad Azharuddin's 62 balls against New Zealand in 1988-89. Three balls later, he overtook Gordon Greenidge's record of eight sixes in a one-day international, set against India the same season. He had hit four successive sixes off Sohail in the most expensive over ever bowled at this level: it yielded 30 runs, 29 to Jayasuriya and one wide. Jayasuriya was eventually out for 134, out of 196 for two, from 65 balls, with 11 sixes and 11 fours (in fact, his last scoring stroke came off his 58th ball, before a final lull). A late fifty from Dharmasena lifted Sri Lanka to 349 and challenged Pakistan to score seven an over. Salim Malik and Inzamam-ul-Haq batted defiantly and Pakistan managed to finish in sight of the target. The match aggregate of 664 for 19 was one more record, beating the 662 for 17 scored by West Indies and Sri Lanka at Sharjah in October 1995.

Man of the Match: S. T. Jayasuriya.

Sri Lanka

S. T. Jayasuriya c Mohammad Akram b Saqlain Mushtaq	134
†R. S. Kaluwitharana c Saqlain Mushtaq b Waqar Younis	24
A. P. Gurusinha c Aamir Sohail b Saqlain Mushtaq	29
P. A. de Silva c and b Salim Malik	7
*A. Ranatunga c Inzamam-ul-Haq b Waqar Younis	14
H. P. Tillekeratne b Mohammad Akram	25
R. S. Mahanama c Waqar Younis b Mohammad Akram	35
H. D. P. K. Dharmasena b Waqar Younis	51
W. P. U. J. C. Vaas c Aamir Sohail b Waqar Younis	6
G. P. Wickremasinghe not out	7
M. Muralitharan not out	2
B 1, l-b 3, w 9, n-b 2	15
1/40 2/196 3/197 4/203 5/238 6/245 7/318 8/328 9/346 (9 wkts, 50 overs)	349

Bowling: Waqar Younis 10–0–62–4; Mohammad Akram 7–0–66–2; Saqlain Mushtaq 10–0–45–2; Aqib Javed 10–0–65–0; Aamir Sohail 8–0–73–0; Salim Malik 5–0–34–1.

Pakistan

*Aamir Sohail lbw b Dharmasena	46
Saeed Anwar c Kaluwitharana b Vaas	32
Ramiz Raja c and b de Silva	27
Salim Malik c Dharmasena b Muralitharan	68
Inzamam-ul-Haq b Vaas	67
Ijaz Ahmed, sen. st Kaluwitharana b Jayasuriya	32
Waqar Younis c Muralitharan b Dharmasena	1
†Rashid Latif c Dharmasena b Muralitharan	7
Saqlain Mushtaq run out	0
Aqib Javed c Muralitharan b Tillekeratne	20
Mohammad Akram not out	3
B 3, l-b 6, w 1, n-b 2	12
1/77 2/96 3/120 4/247 5/253 6/257 7/281 8/291 9/291 (49.4 overs)	315

Bowling: Wickremasinghe 5–0–46–0; Vaas 10–0–50–2; Muralitharan 10–0–59–2; Dharmasena 8–0–51–2; de Silva 4–0–22–1; Jayasuriya 10–0–45–1; Ranatunga 2–0–20–0; Tillekeratne 0.4–0–13–1.

Umpires: D. L. Orchard and R. B. Tiffin.

INDIA v SRI LANKA

At Singapore, April 3. India won by 12 runs. Toss: India. International debut: R. Dravid.

Both teams struggled on the same pitch which had seen so many runs flow the previous day, but India managed to defend a meagre 199. The pitch had lost its bounce and India took first innings in extreme heat and humidity. Sidhu, who batted for three hours, was later taken to hospital after suffering heatstroke. His patient 94 anchored India; of the rest, only Tendulkar and

Srinath reached double figures. The Sri Lankans bowled well, but they were in deep trouble when Srinath reduced them to 23 for four after Jayasuriya and Kaluwitharana, their unconventional openers, were caught in the circle by the third over. Mahanama and Tillekeratne added a disciplined 92 but, once they were dismissed by Raju, Sri Lanka were bowled out with 11 balls to spare.

Man of the Match: J. Srinath.

India

S. R. Tendulkar c Jayasuriya b Wickremasinghe	28
N. S. Sidhu b Vaas	94
*M. Azharuddin run out	9
R. Dravid c Kaluwitharana b Muralitharan	3
S. V. Manjrekar lbw b Muralitharan	7
A. Jadeja c Chandana b Jayasuriya	7
†N. R. Mongia c and b de Silva	4
A. Kumble c Atapattu b de Silva	4
J. Srinath not out	28
B. K. V. Prasad c Jayasuriya b Vaas	7
S. L. V. Raju c Kaluwitharana b Vaas	0
L-b 2, w 2, n-b 4	8
1/33 2/58 3/62 4/82 5/114 6/130 7/136 8/191 9/199 (45.4 overs)	199

Bowling: Wickremasinghe 8–0–39–1; Vaas 7.4–0–35–3; Muralitharan 8–0–25–2; Chandana 10–0–52–0; Jayasuriya 8–0–31–1; de Silva 4–0–15–2.

Sri Lanka

S. T. Jayasuriya c Manjrekar b Srinath	7
†R. S. Kaluwitharana c Azharuddin b Srinath	4
M. S. Atapattu lbw b Srinath	10
P. A. de Silva c Dravid b Prasad	1
R. S. Mahanama c Dravid b Raju	59
*A. Ranatunga c Azharuddin b Raju	13
H. P. Tillekeratne c Prasad b Raju	42
U. U. Chandana run out	11
W. P. U. J. C. Vaas b Srinath	6
M. Muralitharan not out	7
G. P. Wickremasinghe run out	11
L-b 8, w 7, n-b 1	16
1/5 2/12 3/13 4/23 5/53 6/145 7/163 8/169 9/169 (48.1 overs)	187

Bowling: Srinath 10–0–35–4; Prasad 10–2–39–1; Kumble 10–1–46–0; Raju 10–1–26–3; Tendulkar 5.1–0–19–0; Jadeja 3–0–14–0.

Umpires: G. Sharp and R. B. Tiffin.

INDIA v PAKISTAN

At Singapore, April 5. Pakistan won by eight wickets, their target having been revised to 187 from 33 overs. Toss: Pakistan.

Pakistan's win brought all three teams level on points, but they joined Sri Lanka in the final on net run-rate. The heavy rain which ended India's innings probably helped Pakistan; their revised target demanded a scoring-rate guaranteed to see them through, whereas before they needed to win with overs in hand. In fact, the aggressive Aamir Sohail and Saeed Anwar put on 144 in 20 overs, with Anwar scoring 74 from 49 balls, including three sixes off Raju, and Sohail steering his team home with five overs to spare. For India, Tendulkar led the way with a 111-ball century, his seventh in one-day internationals. But he got bogged down as he neared the landmark, and so did his side. Saqlain Mushtaq bowled impressively to choke them in the closing overs.

Man of the Match: Aamir Sohail.

India

N. S. Sidhu c Rashid Latif b Aqib Javed	14
S. R. Tendulkar st Rashid Latif b Saqlain Mushtaq	100
*M. Azharuddin c Rashid Latif b Aamir Sohail	29
R. Dravid run out	4
S. V. Manjrekar c Aqib Javed b Saqlain Mushtaq	41
A. Jadeja run out	5
†N. R. Mongia run out	3
A. Kumble not out	14
J. Srinath st Rashid Latif b Saqlain Mushtaq	0
B. K. V. Prasad not out	1
L-b 3, w 9, n-b 3	15
1/44 2/110 3/127 4/186 5/195 6/205 7/223 8/224 (8 wkts, 47.1 overs)	226

S. L. V. Raju did not bat.

Bowling: Waqar Younis 8–1–42–0; Aqib Javed 7.1–0–12–1; Inzamam-ul-Haq 1–0–10–0; Mushtaq Ahmed 9–0–58–0; Saqlain Mushtaq 10–0–38–3; Salim Malik 3–0–17–0; Aamir Sohail 9–0–46–1.

Pakistan

*Aamir Sohail not out	76
Saeed Anwar c Dravid b Raju	74
Ramiz Raja lbw b Kumble	5
Salim Malik not out	25
L-b 3, w 4, n-b 3	10
1/144 2/162 (2 wkts, 28 overs)	190

Inzamam-ul-Haq, Ijaz Ahmed, sen., †Rashid Latif, Waqar Younis, Saqlain Mushtaq, Mushtaq Ahmed and Aqib Javed did not bat.

Bowling: Srinath 7–0–34–0; Prasad 7–0–45–0; Kumble 7–1–39–1; Raju 5–0–51–1; Tendulkar 2–0–18–0.

Umpires: D. L. Orchard and G. Sharp.

QUALIFYING TABLE

	Played	*Won*	*Lost*	*Points*	*Net run-rate*
Pakistan	2	1	1	2	0.56
Sri Lanka	2	1	1	2	0.22
India	2	1	1	2	−0.46

Net run-rate was calculated by subtracting runs conceded per over from runs scored per over.

FINAL

PAKISTAN v SRI LANKA

At Singapore, April 7. Pakistan won by 43 runs. Toss: Sri Lanka.

Pakistan won comprehensively despite another astonishing innings by Jayasuriya. This time he reached fifty off his 17th ball, with a six over mid-wicket, to beat Simon O'Donnell's one-day international record of 18 balls, against Sri Lanka at Sharjah in 1989-90. When Kaluwitharana was bowled in the sixth over, for nought, Jayasuriya had 66. He eventually holed out for 76 from 28 balls, having hit eight fours and five sixes. With Sri Lanka 96 for two in nine overs, chasing 216, all seemed over bar the shouting. But once Jayasuriya went, the Pakistanis stepped up the pressure and seized three more quick wickets. Saqlain Mushtaq bowled admirably, but they were assisted by the fact that all the umpiring decisions seemed to go against Sri Lanka. Ata-ur-Rehman finished the game with three wickets in five balls, including Tillekeratne to a doubtful lbw just as he was getting the innings together again. Pakistan could not have dared to think of victory with 17 overs to spare after being put in and struggling against accurate off-spin. Only Ijaz Ahmed enabled them to reach 215.

Man of the Match: Saqlain Mushtaq. *Man of the Series:* S. T. Jayasuriya.

Pakistan

*Aamir Sohail b Vaas	18
Saeed Anwar c Muralitharan b Wickremasinghe	17
Ramiz Raja run out	37
Salim Malik c and b Muralitharan	27
Inzamam-ul-Haq c Tillekeratne b de Silva	24
Ijaz Ahmed, sen. b Jayasuriya	51
†Rashid Latif b Dharmasena	2
Aqib Javed c Mahanama b Muralitharan	11
Saqlain Mushtaq c Tillekeratne b Vaas	8
Waqar Younis run out	0
Ata-ur-Rehman not out	1
B 6, l-b 4, w 6, n-b 3	19
1/29 2/41 3/102 4/106 5/140 6/143 7/175 8/199 9/199 (48.3 overs)	215

Bowling: Wickremasinghe 8–1–30–1; Vaas 8–0–35–2; Muralitharan 10–0–42–2; Dharmasena 10–1–39–1; Jayasuriya 8.3–0–39–1; de Silva 4–0–20–1.

Sri Lanka

S. T. Jayasuriya c Saeed Anwar b Waqar Younis	76	H. D. P. K. Dharmasena c Inzamam-ul-Haq b Saqlain Mushtaq	5
†R. S. Kaluwitharana b Aqib Javed	0	W. P. U. J. C. Vaas not out	5
A. P. Gurusinha lbw b Aqib Javed	20	G. P. Wickremasinghe b Ata-ur-Rehman	0
P. A. de Silva c Rashid Latif b Saqlain Mushtaq	4	M. Muralitharan c Ramiz Raja b Ata-ur-Rehman	0
R. S. Mahanama lbw b Waqar Younis	14	L-b 5, w 7, n-b 3	15
*A. Ranatunga c Rashid Latif b Saqlain Mushtaq	0	1/70 2/96 3/100 4/106 5/106 6/146 7/164 8/172 9/172 (32.5 overs)	172
H. P. Tillekeratne lbw b Ata-ur-Rehman	33		

Bowling: Waqar Younis 7–0–38–2; Aqib Javed 7–0–32–2; Ata-ur-Rehman 3.5–0–27–3; Saqlain Mushtaq 7–0–46–3; Aamir Sohail 6–0–21–0; Salim Malik 2–0–3–0.

Umpires: G. Sharp and R. B. Tiffin. Series referee: H. Gardiner.

ICC CODE OF CONDUCT – BREACHES AND PENALTIES IN 1995-96

Aamir Sohail Pakistan v Australia, 2nd Test at Hobart.
Throwing bat on dismissal. Fined 50 per cent of match fee and given two-match ban suspended over six months by R. Subba Row.

A. Jadeja India v New Zealand, one-day international at Pune.
Dissent – making sign for TV replay. Fined 10 per cent of match fee by P. J. Burge.

R. G. Twose New Zealand v India, one-day international at Nagpur.
Verbal abuse of fielder who claimed disputed catch. Fined 50 per cent of match fee by P. J. Burge.

A. L. Wadekar
(Indian manager) India v New Zealand, one-day international at Nagpur.
Revealed contents of his report to referee. Reprimanded by P. J. Burge and referred to BCCI.

R. A. Woolmer
(South African manager) South Africa v England, 2nd Test at Johannesburg.
Criticised dismissals of three players. Severely reprimanded by C. H. Lloyd.

W. J. Cronje South Africa v England, 5th Test at Cape Town.
Asked umpire to consult TV replay after giving decision. Fined 50 per cent of match fee by C. H. Lloyd.

Aqib Javed Pakistan v New Zealand, one-day international at Wellington.
Offensive gesture to dismissed batsman. Fined 50 per cent of match fee by R. S. Madugalle.

Mushtaq Ahmed Pakistan v New Zealand, one-day international at Wellington.
Asked umpire to consult TV replay. Fined 10 per cent of match fee by R. S. Madugalle.

A. P. Gurusinha Australia v Sri Lanka, one-day international at Perth.
Comments to opposing player on field. Reprimanded by R. Subba Row.

A. C. Parore New Zealand v Zimbabwe, 2nd Test at Auckland.
Breach of advertising code. Fined 20 per cent of match fee by Nasim-ul-Ghani.

C. L. Cairns New Zealand v Zimbabwe, 2nd Test at Auckland.
Excessive appeal. Fined 10 per cent of match fee by Nasim-ul-Ghani.

P. V. Simmons West Indies v New Zealand, one-day international at Georgetown.
Attempted intimidation of umpire. Fined 10 per cent of match fee by M. H. Denness.

D. K. Morrison New Zealand v West Indies, 2nd Test at St John's.
Sank to knees and struck wicket after disallowed appeal. Fined 10 per cent of match fee by M. H. Denness.

PEPSI CUP, 1995-96

By COLIN BRYDEN

South Africa were impressive winners on their first visit to Sharjah, providing themselves with some compensation for the bitter disappointment of departing the World Cup at the first knockout stage after winning all their five round-robin matches by convincing margins. Here they were unbeaten and took their record for the 1995-96 season to 18 wins in 20 one-day internationals. They were a well-drilled side, whose bowling and fielding were several notches above those of their rivals, India and Pakistan. Their batting was consistent and enterprising and scored at an average of 62 runs per wicket and 5.6 an over.

India and Pakistan had just met in another triangular tournament in Singapore. There, Pakistan had triumphed; here, the balance tipped back towards India. Both were swept aside by South Africa, but they scored one win apiece against each other and India edged through to the final on net run-rate, thanks to a record-breaking total in their second encounter. It was the third time running that Pakistan failed to reach a final at Sharjah, where they once seemed near-invincible.

The start of the tournament was put back one day because of an official period of mourning for Sheikh Mohammed bin Khalid al-Qassimi, a member of Sharjah's ruling family. He had been hit by a stray firework while attending a local football match in March; he was transferred to a hospital in Scotland, but later died of his injuries.

Note: Matches in this section were not first-class.

INDIA v PAKISTAN

At Sharjah, April 12. Pakistan won by 38 runs. Toss: India.

Azharuddin's decision to send Pakistan in, on an excellent batting pitch in hot weather, was questionable. After Srinath beat Aamir Sohail with his first delivery and started the match with a maiden, the advantage lay almost entirely with Pakistan. Sohail advanced to his fifth century in limited-overs internationals and set India a target of nearly five and a half an over. They made a bad start: Tendulkar drove a wide ball to cover and Saqlain Mushtaq's off-spin and Mushtaq Ahmed's leg-spin reduced India to 95 for five. Mongia, who helped Manjrekar to add 116 for the sixth wicket, scored his maiden fifty at this level before he was last out.

Man of the Match: Aamir Sohail.

Pakistan

*Aamir Sohail c and b Kumble	105	†Rashid Latif not out	21
Saeed Anwar b Vaidya	44		
Ramiz Raja run out	17	L-b 6, w 4	10
Salim Malik run out	22		—
Inzamam-ul-Haq c Mongia b Tendulkar	9	1/77 2/115 3/156 (5 wkts, 50 overs)	271
Ijaz Ahmed, sen. not out	43	4/167 5/235	

Saqlain Mushtaq, Aqib Javed, Waqar Younis and Mushtaq Ahmed did not bat.

Bowling: Srinath 10–1–46–0; Vaidya 9–0–55–1; Kumble 10–0–50–1; Raju 9–0–57–0; Tendulkar 10–0–46–1; Azharuddin 2–0–11–0.

India

A. Jadeja c Saeed Anwar b Saqlain Mushtaq	43
S. R. Tendulkar c Saeed Anwar b Aqib Javed	1
N. S. Sidhu c and b Saqlain Mushtaq	31
*M. Azharuddin c Aqib Javed b Mushtaq Ahmed	7
R. Dravid c Rashid Latif b Mushtaq Ahmed	3
S. V. Manjrekar c Saeed Anwar b Waqar Younis	59
†N. R. Mongia b Mushtaq Ahmed	69
J. Srinath run out	0
A. Kumble c sub (Ata-ur-Rehman) b Mushtaq Ahmed	3
P. S. Vaidya b Waqar Younis	3
S. L. V. Raju not out	0
L-b 4, w 10	14
1/8 2/76 3/89 4/91 5/95 6/211 7/212 8/219 9/229 (47.2 overs)	233

Bowling: Waqar Younis 9–1–44–2; Aqib Javed 7–0–33–1; Saqlain Mushtaq 9–0–42–2; Mushtaq Ahmed 9.2–0–47–4; Aamir Sohail 6–0–28–0; Salim Malik 7–0–35–0.

Umpires: D. B. Cowie and M. J. Kitchen.

PAKISTAN v SOUTH AFRICA

At Sharjah, April 13. South Africa won by 143 runs. Toss: South Africa.

South Africa marked their Sharjah debut with a crushing win. Hudson and Kirsten gave them an ideal opening, with 115 in 17 overs; their strokeplay was sensible rather than extravagant, though Hudson pulled Waqar Younis for a remarkable six. Cullinan made capital with a maiden one-day international century, scoring 110 not out from 109 balls as South Africa equalled their biggest limited-overs total against a Test country. Pakistan started with a flurry but, once Aamir Sohail slashed to gully, dropped out of contention. A futile attempt to force the pace against accurate bowling and enthusiastic fielding saw five wickets fall in the first 15 overs. Aqib Javed scored a career-best 45 as he and Salim Malik played out time.

Man of the Match: D. J. Cullinan.

South Africa

A. C. Hudson c Aqib Javed b Waqar Younis	57
G. Kirsten b Aqib Javed	64
D. J. Cullinan not out	110
*W. J. Cronje c Inzamam-ul-Haq b Mushtaq Ahmed	26
J. N. Rhodes not out	47
L-b 7, w 3	10
1/115 2/157 3/222 (3 wkts, 50 overs)	314

B. M. McMillan, P. L. Symcox, S. M. Pollock, †D. J. Richardson, C. R. Matthews and P. S. de Villiers did not bat.

Bowling: Waqar Younis 10–1–56–1; Aqib Javed 9–0–59–1; Mushtaq Ahmed 10–0–63–1; Saqlain Mushtaq 9–1–55–0; Aamir Sohail 10–0–56–0; Salim Malik 2–0–18–0.

Pakistan

*Aamir Sohail c Hudson b de Villiers	11
Saeed Anwar c Cronje b de Villiers	33
Ramiz Raja c McMillan b Pollock	1
Salim Malik not out	64
Inzamam-ul-Haq run out	1
Ijaz Ahmed, sen. c Richardson b McMillan	1
†Rashid Latif c McMillan b Matthews	2
Saqlain Mushtaq lbw b Cronje	7
Aqib Javed not out	45
L-b 2, w 4	6
1/24 2/45 3/49 4/50 5/58 6/62 7/90 (7 wkts, 50 overs)	171

Waqar Younis and Mushtaq Ahmed did not bat.

Bowling: Pollock 10–1–44–1; de Villiers 10–0–40–2; McMillan 7–1–20–1; Matthews 8–1–21–1; Symcox 10–1–21–0; Cronje 5–0–23–1.

Umpires: B. C. Cooray and D. B. Cowie.

INDIA v SOUTH AFRICA

At Sharjah, April 14. South Africa won by 80 runs. Toss: South Africa.

South Africa shrugged off the setbacks of losing Hudson, caught at slip, to the second ball of the match, and then Cullinan and Symcox, who was promoted as a pinch-hitter, to successive deliveries in the tenth over. A century from Kirsten provided a sound anchor, while Cronje hit out for an aggressive 90 off 82 balls. They had added 154 in 25 overs when Cronje was sent back by Kirsten and run out. Chasing 289, India saw their chances vanish when the South African seamers reduced them to 62 for four in the 14th over. They settled for playing out the overs and trying to keep their net run-rate in sight of Pakistan's.

Man of the Match: W. J. Cronje.

South Africa

G. Kirsten b Raju	106
A. C. Hudson c Tendulkar b Srinath	0
D. J. Cullinan c Dravid b Kumble	28
P. L. Symcox b Kumble	0
*W. J. Cronje run out	90
J. N. Rhodes c Dravid b Raju	23
B. M. McMillan not out	14
S. M. Pollock not out	15
L-b 7, w 4, n-b 1	12
1/1 2/56 3/56 4/210 5/249 6/266 (6 wkts, 50 overs)	288

†D. J. Richardson, C. R. Matthews and P. S. de Villiers did not bat.

Bowling: Srinath 9–0–43–1; Vaidya 6–0–42–0; Kumble 10–0–45–2; Raju 10–0–67–2; Tendulkar 7–0–40–0; Jadeja 8–0–44–0.

India

A. Jadeja c Richardson b Matthews	42
S. R. Tendulkar c Kirsten b de Villiers	2
P. S. Vaidya lbw b Pollock	12
N. S. Sidhu c Kirsten b Pollock	1
S. V. Manjrekar c Cronje b Symcox	53
*M. Azharuddin c Hudson b Symcox	28
J. Srinath b de Villiers	35
R. Dravid c Rhodes b Pollock	11
†N. R. Mongia not out	9
A. Kumble not out	9
B 1, l-b 1, w 3, n-b 1	6
1/20 2/41 3/45 4/62 5/143 6/147 7/188 8/194 (8 wkts, 50 overs)	208

S. L. V. Raju did not bat.

Bowling: Pollock 10–0–42–3; de Villiers 10–0–54–2; McMillan 7–0–18–0; Matthews 10–0–26–1; Symcox 7–0–43–2; Cronje 6–0–23–0.

Umpires: B. C. Cooray and M. J. Kitchen.

INDIA v PAKISTAN

At Sharjah, April 15. India won by 28 runs. Toss: India. International debut: V. Rathore.

India passed 300 for the first time in one-day cricket to set up a satisfying win. It was rooted in a 231-run stand between Tendulkar and Sidhu, an Indian all-wicket record in limited-overs internationals. With Waqar Younis's line much improved and newcomer Rathore falling for two, India started slowly. Tendulkar was intent on building an innings after scoring just three in India's two defeats. The tempo rose as he put on a classical display, Sidhu punished the slow bowlers and both reached three figures. After they went, a frenzied assault plundered 60 in five overs: Azharuddin hit 24 off the last, from Ata-ur-Rehman. Pakistan had two overs deducted for their slow over-rate, but replied with spirit. They were 172 for two in the 26th over when Aamir Sohail, on 78 from 76 balls, was furious to be run out – by his runner, Rashid Latif. Earlier, Latif had hit fifty from 31 balls. But Sohail's dismissal, followed up by accurate bowling from Kumble, gave the upper hand to India again.

Man of the Match: S. R. Tendulkar.

India

V. Rathore c Inzamam-ul-Haq b Waqar Younis . 2
S. R. Tendulkar c Aamir Sohail b Waqar Younis . 118
N. S. Sidhu run out . . . 101
A. Jadeja c Rashid Latif b Waqar Younis . 17
J. Srinath c Aamir Sohail b Ata-ur-Rehman 16
*M. Azharuddin not out . . . 29
S. V. Manjrekar not out . . . 0
B 2, l-b 7, w 12, n-b 1 . . . 22

1/9 2/240 3/245 4/264 5/281 (5 wkts, 50 overs) 305

†N. R. Mongia, A. Kumble, A. R. Kapoor and B. K. V. Prasad did not bat.

Bowling: Waqar Younis 10–2–44–3; Aqib Javed 10–0–58–0; Ata-ur-Rehman 10–0–85–1; Saqlain Mushtaq 10–1–60–0; Aamir Sohail 10–0–49–0.

Pakistan

*Aamir Sohail run out . . . 78
Saeed Anwar c Mongia b Prasad . . . 2
†Rashid Latif c Azharuddin b Kumble . . . 50
Ijaz Ahmed, sen. b Srinath . . . 42
Salim Malik c Kapoor b Kumble . . . 42
Inzamam-ul-Haq c Azharuddin b Prasad . . 6
Basit Ali c Rathore b Tendulkar . . . 32
Aqib Javed c Rathore b Srinath . . . 5
Waqar Younis not out . . . 8
Ata-ur-Rehman c sub (R. Dravid) b Srinath 4
Saqlain Mushtaq lbw b Tendulkar . . . 0
L-b 4, w 4 . . . 8

1/16 2/88 3/172 4/190 5/199 6/246 7/260 8/271 9/277 (46.1 overs) 277

Bowling: Srinath 10–0–65–3; Prasad 9–0–64–2; Kumble 9–1–38–2; Kapoor 9–0–52–0; Tendulkar 7.1–0–40–2; Jadeja 2–0–14–0.

Umpires: D. B. Cowie and M. J. Kitchen.

PAKISTAN v SOUTH AFRICA

At Sharjah, April 16. South Africa won by eight wickets. Toss: Pakistan.

South Africa cruised to another easy win. Both de Villiers and Matthews bowled superbly, finding movement off a pitch which had yielded nothing in earlier matches. Then Kallis, given an outing with Crookes as South Africa rested Cullinan and McMillan, picked up his first wickets in international cricket – starting with Inzamam-ul-Haq, the only Pakistani batsman who threatened to take command. Pakistan scored 188, a small total for Sharjah, when it was essential to boost their run-rate. Defending it, Sohail surprisingly held back Waqar Younis until Hudson and Kirsten had made a flying start. Hudson finished unbeaten on 94 from 86 balls.

Man of the Match: C. R. Matthews.

Pakistan

*Aamir Sohail c Cronje b Matthews . . . 46
Saeed Anwar c Kirsten b Pollock . . . 10
Ramiz Raja c Matthews b de Villiers . . . 40
Inzamam-ul-Haq c Richardson b Kallis . . . 41
†Rashid Latif lbw b de Villiers . . . 7
Salim Malik c Crookes b Matthews . . . 10
Basit Ali c Crookes b Kallis . . . 8
Aqib Javed c Richardson b Matthews . . . 6
Waqar Younis not out . . . 8
Mushtaq Ahmed c Richardson b Kallis . . . 0
Mohammad Akram lbw b de Villiers . . . 0
B 2, l-b 4, w 6 . . . 12

1/22 2/84 3/145 4/151 5/162 6/169 7/177 8/185 9/185 (45 overs) 188

Bowling: de Villiers 10–1–28–3; Pollock 8–1–34–1; Matthews 8–1–19–3; Cronje 1–0–4–0; Symcox 7–0–38–0; Crookes 5–0–38–0; Kallis 6–1–21–3.

South Africa

A. C. Hudson not out . . . 94
G. Kirsten c Mohammad Akram b Waqar Younis . 32
P. L. Symcox lbw b Mohammad Akram . . 35
J. H. Kallis not out . . . 24
W 4 . . . 4

1/73 2/132 (2 wkts, 33.1 overs) 189

*W. J. Cronje, J. N. Rhodes, D. N. Crookes, S. M. Pollock, †D. J. Richardson, C. R. Matthews and P. S. de Villiers did not bat.

Bowling: Mohammad Akram 10–0–52–1; Aqib Javed 4–0–27–0; Mushtaq Ahmed 10–1–50–0; Aamir Sohail 1–0–12–0; Waqar Younis 7–0–44–1; Salim Malik 1.1–0–4–0.

Umpires: B. C. Cooray and D. B. Cowie.

INDIA v SOUTH AFRICA

At Sharjah, April 17. South Africa won by five wickets. Toss: India.

South Africa secured their fourth straight win while India preserved their run-rate advantage over Pakistan to reach the final. Even that modest objective was in doubt after a splendid opening spell by de Villiers. He took two for 11 in seven overs, and fooled Tendulkar for the second time in four days with a slower delivery. Adams then sowed confusion with his unorthodox left-arm spin. Rathore batted soundly and Jadeja brightly, but 215 was unlikely to be enough. Though South Africa's batting was not their most convincing, a solid 64 from Cullinan and a maiden international fifty by Crookes saw them home.

Man of the Match: P. R. Adams.

India

V. Rathore c Cronje b Adams	50
S. R. Tendulkar c Kirsten b de Villiers	17
N. S. Sidhu lbw b de Villiers	1
S. V. Manjrekar c Kirsten b Kallis	14
*M. Azharuddin st Richardson b Adams	4
A. Jadeja not out	71
†N. R. Mongia c Kirsten b Adams	13
A. Kumble run out	16
J. Srinath c sub (C. R. Matthews) b Pollock	15
B. K. V. Prasad not out	1
L-b 4, w 7, n-b 2	13
1/23 2/26 3/72 4/89 5/100 6/140 7/177 8/199 (8 wkts, 50 overs)	215

S. L. V. Raju did not bat.

Bowling: Pollock 8–0–39–1; de Villiers 10–2–28–2; McMillan 5–0–25–0; Kallis 7–0–34–1; Adams 10–0–30–3; Crookes 10–0–55–0.

South Africa

G. Kirsten c Mongia b Kumble	39
J. H. Kallis run out	22
D. J. Cullinan c Prasad b Raju	64
*W. J. Cronje b Raju	1
D. N. Crookes b Raju	54
S. M. Pollock not out	11
J. N. Rhodes not out	12
B 3, l-b 2, w 8	13
1/53 2/85 3/98 4/192 5/193 (5 wkts, 47.1 overs)	216

B. M. McMillan, †D. J. Richardson, P. S. de Villiers and P. R. Adams did not bat.

Bowling: Srinath 10–0–55–0; Prasad 10–0–43–0; Kumble 10–0–37–1; Raju 10–0–38–3; Jadeja 7–0–37–0; Sidhu 0.1–0–1–0.

Umpires: B. C. Cooray and M. J. Kitchen.

QUALIFYING TABLE

	Played	*Won*	*Lost*	*Points*	*Net run-rate*
South Africa	4	4	0	8	1.68
India	4	1	3	2	0.64
Pakistan	4	1	3	2	−1.15

Net run-rate was calculated by subtracting runs conceded per over from runs scored per over.

FINAL

INDIA v SOUTH AFRICA

At Sharjah, April 19. South Africa won by 38 runs. Toss: South Africa.

South Africa completed a clean sweep to take the Cup. They had looked unconvincing in the early morning, while the Indians were swinging the ball, but Kirsten displayed excellent temperament and concentration, batting throughout the innings for his second century of the tournament and his fourth in limited-overs internationals in the past six months. Meanwhile, Symcox clubbed 61 off 49 balls – his maiden one-day fifty for South Africa – while McMillan hit three huge sixes, two of them out of the ground. India needed 5.76 an over, but they seemed to have a chance as long as Tendulkar was at the crease. The decisive factor was South Africa's athletic fielding. Tendulkar was stranded when Pollock made a fast pick-up at mid-off, the second of four run-outs which made India's task impossible.

Man of the Match: G. Kirsten. *Man of the Series:* G. Kirsten.

South Africa

G. Kirsten not out	115
A. C. Hudson c Azharuddin b Srinath	0
D. J. Cullinan b Prasad	2
P. L. Symcox c Jadeja b Raju	61
*W. J. Cronje c Rathore b Kumble	25
D. N. Crookes c Rathore b Kumble	26
B. M. McMillan not out	37
L-b 5, w 16	21
1/5 2/20 3/115 4/175 5/227 (5 wkts, 50 overs)	287

S. M. Pollock, †D. J. Richardson, C. R. Matthews and P. S. de Villiers did not bat.

Bowling: Srinath 10–1–51–1; Prasad 10–0–50–1; Tendulkar 7–0–51–0; Kumble 10–0–42–2; Raju 9–0–70–1; Jadeja 4–0–18–0.

India

V. Rathore c Richardson b Matthews	23
S. R. Tendulkar run out	57
A. Kumble run out	10
N. S. Sidhu c Matthews b Cronje	26
S. V. Manjrekar run out	41
*M. Azharuddin run out	39
A. Jadeja c Cullinan b McMillan	2
J. Srinath c Richardson b de Villiers	10
†N. R. Mongia c and b Pollock	23
B. K. V. Prasad not out	5
S. L. V. Raju not out	0
L-b 10, w 1, n-b 2	13
1/59 2/78 3/112 4/130 5/204 6/208 7/209 8/243 9/249 (9 wkts, 50 overs)	249

Bowling: de Villiers 10–0–42–1; Pollock 10–0–57–1; McMillan 10–0–48–1; Matthews 10–1–46–1; Symcox 6–0–23–0; Cronje 4–0–23–1.

Umpires: B. C. Cooray and M. J. Kitchen. Series referee: R. S. Madugalle.

COCA-COLA CRICKET WEEK, 1995-96

South Africa's 53rd annual Cricket Week for the country's best young players, formerly known as Nuffield Week, was marred by wet weather, which prevented any play on the first two days. It was decided at the end of the week to end the experiment of Under-19 cricket and again concentrate on Under-18 players. The team selected at the end of the week, to play a Border Invitation XI, was restricted to players still at school and called the South African Schools XI. The team was: D. R. Gain (Natal, *captain*), A. G. Botha (Natal), R. Groom (Natal), M. Hayward (Eastern Province), P. Joubert (Eastern Province), J. P. Michau (S. A. Country), M. Morkel (Transvaal), T. Ngxoweni (Border), M. Ntini (Border), M. Street (Transvaal), W. Wingfield (Natal). Twelfth man H. H. Dippenaar (Free State).

ENGLAND UNDER-19 IN ZIMBABWE, 1995-96

By EDWARD BEVAN

England Under-19 toured Zimbabwe for the first time in January and February 1996. Although rain disrupted much of the tour, they won the three-match Test series 2-0, as well as the one-day international played at Bulawayo. The last two one-day internationals were completely washed out, while the first unofficial Test was restricted to only 75 overs. England confirmed their all-round superiority by winning both the other Tests by an innings with a day to spare. They played five other games, winning three and drawing two, and would probably have won the lot but for the weather. The captain, Alex Morris, led from the front with 145 runs at 48.33 in the Test series and 386 at 48.25 in all, while Noel Gie and Owais Shah both scored centuries in the final Test at Bulawayo. Morris's fellow Yorkshireman, left-arm seamer Paul Hutchison, claimed 15 victims at 8.66 – all the more impressive as he was able to bowl in only two Tests – and 34 at 9.41 altogether. Colin Campbell partnered him ably with the new ball.

ENGLAND UNDER-19 TOURING PARTY

A. C. Morris (Yorkshire) (*captain*), U. Afzaal (Nottinghamshire), G. J. Batty (Yorkshire), C. L. Campbell (Durham), G. J. M. Edwards (Glamorgan), A. Flintoff (Lancashire), N. A. Gie (Nottinghamshire), P. M. Hutchison (Yorkshire), D. C. Nash (Middlesex), J. Ormond (Leicestershire), D. J. Roberts (Northamptonshire), D. J. Sales (Northamptonshire), O. A. Shah (Middlesex), A. J. Tudor (Surrey), M. J. Wood (Yorkshire).

M. J. Hoggard (Yorkshire) replaced Ormond and Tudor, who returned home early because of injuries.

Manager: G. J. Saville (Essex). *Coach:* D. Lloyd (Lancashire). *Physiotherapist:* S. M. B. Robertson (Sussex).

RESULTS

Matches – Played 9: Won 6, Drawn 3. Abandoned 2.

Note: Matches in this section were not first-class.

At St John's College, Harare, January 2. England Under-19 won by two wickets. Toss: Zimbabwe Under-18. Zimbabwe Under-18 162 (46.2 overs) (K. J. Davies 51, Extras 32; P. M. Hutchison three for 26); England Under-19 165 for eight (48.2 overs) (M. J. Wood 38, A. C. Morris 30, N. A. Gie 41 not out; T. B. Manyimo three for 25).

At Harare South Country Club, Harare, January 3. England Under-19 won by 53 runs. Toss: England Under-19. England Under-19 238 (50 overs) (M. J. Wood 41, A. Flintoff 78, A. C. Morris 36; G. I. Thom four for 44); Mashonaland Districts 185 (48.2 overs) (D. P. Viljoen 30, K. B. Bennett 31; G. J. M. Edwards three for 24).

At Alexandra Sports Club, Harare, January 4, 5, 6. England Under-19 won by an innings and 153 runs. Toss: Zimbabwe Schools. Zimbabwe Schools 75 (P. M. Hutchison three for 18, C. L. Campbell three for 12) and 172 (D. J. Murphy 64, R. L. C. Smith 34; P. M. Hutchison five for 64, G. J. Batty three for 55); England Under-19 400 for seven dec. (N. A. Gie 50, D. J. Sales 74, A. C. Morris 126 not out, U. Afzaal 66 not out).

At Old Hararians Sports Club, Harare, January 8, 9, 10. Drawn. Toss: England Under-19. England Under-19 278 (M. J. Wood 62, D. J. Roberts 34, N. A. Gie 32, D. J. Sales 31, D. C. Nash 38; B. A. Murphy three for 42) and 204 for seven dec. (M. J. Wood 79, A. Flintoff 33, D. J. Sales 43); Mashonaland Under-21 143 (G. J. Rennie 78, B. A. Murphy 36; C. L. Campbell three for five, M. J. Hoggard three for 47) and 80 for four (G. J. Rennie 36).

ZIMBABWE UNDER-19 v ENGLAND UNDER-19

First Unofficial Test

At St George's College, Harare, January 13, 14, 15, 16. Drawn. Toss: England Under-19.

Rain prevented any play after the opening day; even then, the start was delayed two hours by a thunderstorm. After the loss of two early wickets, Flintoff and Morris both completed fifties to lay the foundations of a substantial first-innings total. Zimbabwe's seamers seemed preoccupied with bowling wide of the off stump and David Murphy, twin brother of their captain, Brian, was called for throwing twice in his five-over spell.

Close of play: First day, England Under-19 181-4 (D. J. Sales 23*, O. A. Shah 0*); Second day, No play; Third day, No play.

England Under-19

M. J. Wood c Viljoen b Madondo	16
A. Flintoff lbw b Viljoen	55
N. A. Gie c Marillier b Madondo	1
*A. C. Morris c Gilmour b Madondo	74
D. J. Sales not out	23
O. A. Shah not out	0
L-b 3, w 7, n-b 2	12
1/36 2/42 3/131 4/176 (4 wkts)	181

G. J. Batty, †D. C. Nash, U. Afzaal, P. M. Hutchison and C. L. Campbell did not bat.

Bowling: D. J. Murphy 5–1–9–0; Steyn 12–4–30–0; Hoffman 18–6–30–0; Madondo 19–7–44–3; B. A. Murphy 5–1–14–0; Viljoen 10–2–24–1; Ferreira 6–1–27–0.

Zimbabwe Under-19

D. J. Murphy, W. Gilmour, D. P. Viljoen, K. J. Davies, R. L. C. Smith, *B. A. Murphy, T. N. Madondo, †E. R. Marillier, G. D. Ferreira, A. G. Steyn and A. P. Hoffman.

Umpires: G. Evans and D. Kalan.

At Goromonzi Country Club, Goromonzi, January 19, 20, 21. Drawn. Toss: Mashonaland Districts. England Under-19 225 (N. A. Gie 36, O. A. Shah 62, D. J. Sales 55, Extras 33; C. Robertson three for 34); Mashonaland Districts 124 for eight (C. L. Campbell three for 35, P. M. Hutchison three for 49).

ZIMBABWE UNDER-19 v ENGLAND UNDER-19

Second Unofficial Test

At Harare Sports Club, Harare, January 23, 24, 25. England Under-19 won by an innings and 142 runs. Toss: England Under-19.

Zimbabwe could not cope with left-arm seamer Hutchison on a drying pitch; they collapsed for 47 in 29 overs, with only Davies reaching double figures. Hutchison took three wickets in his first seven-over spell and returned to finish the innings with two in two overs. Despite losing their openers cheaply, England already led by 73 at the first-day close and everybody contributed to extending their lead to 297 next day. Resuming, Hutchison soon had Zimbabwe at 12 for two, though they put up a little more resistance on the third day, when the Murphy twins shared a dour seventh-wicket stand of 42. But Hutchison took his match figures to eight for 43 while Campbell claimed five for 42 and England gained a comprehensive victory with an hour plus a day to spare.

Close of play: First day, England Under-19 120-4 (D. J. Sales 4*, O. A. Shah 4*); Second day, Zimbabwe Under-19 13-2 (D. P. Viljoen 3*, A. G. Steyn 0*).

Zimbabwe Under-19

D. J. Murphy c Sales b Hutchison	0	– (7) c Nash b Morris	26
K. J. Davies c Shah b Campbell	16	– (1) c Shah b Hutchison	0
B. M. Hutchings b Hutchison	2	– (5) c Gie b Batty	7
D. P. Viljoen c Nash b Hutchison	0	– (3) c Batty b Flintoff	25
T. N. Madondo run out	9	– (6) lbw b Morris	9
*B. A. Murphy lbw b Campbell	0	– (8) lbw b Hutchison	24
R. L. C. Smith run out	6	– (9) c Afzaal b Campbell	15
G. D. Ferreira not out	9	– (2) b Hutchison	9
†E. R. Marillier c Flintoff b Morris	0	– (10) not out	5
A. P. Hoffman c Nash b Hutchison	3	– (11) c Flintoff b Campbell	0
A. G. Steyn c Shah b Hutchison	0	– (4) c Nash b Campbell	20
L-b 1, w 1	2	B 2, l-b 9, w 3, n-b 1	15
1/4 2/13 3/19 4/22 5/24 6/29 7/35 8/40 9/47	47	1/0 2/12 3/58 4/71 5/73 6/85 7/127 8/140 9/153	155

Bowling: *First Innings*—Hutchison 9–5–11–5; Campbell 11–5–13–2; Morris 7–2–15–1; Batty 2–0–7–0. *Second Innings*—Hutchison 20–7–32–3; Campbell 15–4–29–3; Afzaal 18–8–28–0; Morris 15–9–18–2; Flintoff 6–1–10–1; Batty 18–10–23–1; Gie 3–1–4–0.

England Under-19

M. J. Wood lbw b Madondo	8
A. Flintoff c Marillier b Steyn	10
N. A. Gie c Davies b B. A. Murphy	31
*A. C. Morris c Hoffman b Steyn	51
D. J. Sales c Viljoen b B. A. Murphy	50
O. A. Shah c Hutchings b D. J. Murphy	45
†D. C. Nash not out	65
G. J. Batty c Steyn b Viljoen	35
U. Afzaal not out	19
B 1, l-b 3, w 23, n-b 3	30
1/11 2/33 3/77 4/113 5/197 6/221 7/284 (7 wkts dec.)	344

P. M. Hutchison and C. L. Campbell did not bat.

Bowling: Steyn 22–4–71–2; D. J. Murphy 20–3–50–1; Madondo 18–2–58–1; Hoffman 11–2–26–0; B. A. Murphy 41–13–79–2; Ferreira 21–8–29–0; Viljoen 10–1–27–1.

Umpires: Q. J. Goosen and I. D. Robinson.

ZIMBABWE UNDER-19 v ENGLAND UNDER-19

Third Unofficial Test

At Queens Sports Club, Bulawayo, January 31, February 1, 2. England Under-19 won by an innings and 44 runs. Toss: England Under-19.

England's second successive innings win secured the series. Again, Hutchison set up victory, taking six for 21 in just 17.4 overs on the first day. Though the England openers failed once more, Gie and Shah both made centuries. Shah batted for seven hours and shared stands of 131 with Gie and 139 with his Middlesex colleague, Nash. Zimbabwe needed 248 to make England bat again. This time the Glamorgan off-spinner, Edwards, did the damage, claiming four wickets as they struggled to 56 for five. Viljoen and Davies fought back with sixties but could not stave off defeat, though Zimbabwe managed to reach 200 for the first time in the series. Morris claimed the extra half-hour on the third evening and Campbell finished them off in the final over.

Close of play: First day, England Under-19 96-3 (N. A. Gie 44*, D. J. Sales 13*); Second day, England Under-19 335-5 (O. A. Shah 114*, D. C. Nash 34*).

Zimbabwe Under-19

D. J. Murphy run out	46	– b Edwards	14
†W. Gilmour b Hutchison	1	– lbw b Hutchison	1
D. P. Viljoen c Sales b Edwards	7	– lbw b Campbell	61
*B. A. Murphy c Shah b Batty	18	– lbw b Edwards	6
T. N. Madondo c Shah b Hutchison	5	– c Nash b Edwards	1
K. J. Davies c Campbell b Edwards	14	– (8) not out	63
B. M. Hutchings b Hutchison	7	– c Shah b Morris	15
C. B. McGaw b Hutchison	0	– (9) c Hutchison b Morris	14
G. D. Ferreira not out	15	– (6) lbw b Edwards	6
A. G. Steyn lbw b Hutchison	0	– b Campbell	1
A. P. Hoffman b Hutchison	3	– c Batty b Campbell	12
B 17, l-b 7, w 1, n-b 2	27	B 4, l-b 4, n-b 2	10
1/1 2/20 3/68 4/83 5/101 6/123 7/124 8/127 9/127	143	1/13 2/24 3/42 4/48 5/56 6/99 7/124 8/161 9/166	204

Bowling: *First Innings*—Hutchison 17.4–8–21–6; Campbell 11–6–9–0; Edwards 21–2–48–2; Batty 10–5–17–1; Morris 9–3–24–0. *Second Innings*—Hutchison 17–2–66–1; Campbell 21.1–7–42–3; Edwards 25–10–48–4; Batty 3–1–11–0; Morris 11–3–29–2.

England Under-19

M. J. Wood c Gilmour b Steyn	0
A. Flintoff c B. A. Murphy b D. J. Murphy	15
N. A. Gie c Madondo b Viljoen	118
*A. C. Morris st Gilmour b B. A. Murphy	20
D. J. Sales c Hutchings b Steyn	17
O. A. Shah run out	139
†D. C. Nash not out	55
C. L. Campbell c Gilmour b Madondo	2
G. J. Batty c McGaw b Ferreira	4
P. M. Hutchison not out	0
B 4, l-b 1, w 12, n-b 4	21
1/0 2/31 3/66 4/108 5/239 6/378 7/384 8/389 (8 wkts dec.)	391

G. J. M. Edwards did not bat.

Bowling: Steyn 22–5–58–2; D. J. Murphy 8–1–24–1; B. A. Murphy 21–8–70–1; Hoffman 10–3–33–0; Ferreira 16–4–43–1; Madondo 30–5–73–1; Viljoen 40–18–64–1; Davies 8–2–21–0.

Umpires: J. Fenwick and R. Strang.

At Queens Sports Club, Bulawayo, February 6. First unofficial one-day international: England Under-19 won by 25 runs. Toss: England Under-19. England Under-19 209 (48.4 overs) (N. A. Gie 36, A. C. Morris 32, D. J. Sales 30, U. Afzaal 30); Zimbabwe Under-19 184 (45.5 overs) (D. J. Murphy 58, B. A. Murphy 67; P. M. Hutchison five for 33, M. J. Hoggard three for 25).

At Queens Sports Club, Bulawayo, February 8. Second unofficial one-day international: No result (abandoned owing to rain).

At Alexandra Sports Club, Harare, February 10. Third unofficial one-day international: No result (abandoned owing to rain).

ENGLISH COUNTIES OVERSEAS, 1995-96

Scorecards of first-class matches, played by English counties on pre-season tours to other countries.

NORTHERN TRANSVAAL v GLAMORGAN

At Centurion, April 1, 2, 3. Northern Transvaal won by seven wickets. Toss: Glamorgan.

Close of play: First day, Northern Transvaal 24-1 (M. van Jaarsveld 13*, D. J. J. de Vos 3*); Second day, Glamorgan 104-5 (M. P. Maynard 45*, G. P. Butcher 2*).

Glamorgan

S. P. James b de Bruyn	2	– c Seymore b Davis	18
H. Morris b de Bruyn	77	– (9) retired hurt	0
D. L. Hemp c de Bruyn b Bryson	3	– (6) c Dros b van Noordwyk	11
*M. P. Maynard b Bryson	21	– c Martin b Bryson	65
P. A. Cottey c Martin b Davis	65	– c Seymore b Davis	0
A. Dale c Pistorius b Krug	7	– (3) c Davis b Bryson	21
R. D. B. Croft c Dros b de Bruyn	34	– (8) b Bryson	2
G. P. Butcher c van Jaarsveld b van Noordwyk	5	– (7) c Martin b Bryson	2
S. D. Thomas lbw b van Noordwyk	4	– (10) c Seymore b Davis	8
†C. P. Metson lbw b de Bruyn	13	– (2) c de Vos b van Noordwyk	3
S. L. Watkin not out	3	– not out	2
B 1, l-b 3, w 2, n-b 3	9	B 1, l-b 2, w 2, n-b 3	8
1/8 2/44 3/88 4/127 5/156 6/196 7/220 8/225 9/226	243	1/9 2/44 3/62 4/67 5/91 6/111 7/119 8/130 9/140	140

In the second innings H. Morris retired hurt at 119-7.

Bowling: *First Innings*—Bryson 19–11–20–2; van Noordwyk 20–8–47–2; de Bruyn 12.2–0–44–4; Martin 2–0–11–0; de Vos 10–3–33–0; Krug 10–1–34–1; Davis 18–5–50–1. *Second Innings*—Bryson 17–5–33–4; van Noordwyk 16–2–37–2; Davis 17.5–6–42–3; de Bruyn 6–1–25–0; de Vos 3–3–0–0; Krug 1–1–0–0.

Northern Transvaal

A. J. Seymore lbw b Watkin	6	– c James b Hemp	77
M. van Jaarsveld c Metson b Hemp	69	– c Metson b Watkin	0
D. J. J. de Vos c Cottey b Croft	29	– c Croft b Thomas	39
G. Dros c James b Thomas	15	– not out	31
†I. Pistorius run out	4	– not out	20
*M. J. G. Davis c Metson b Hemp	2		
N. Martin c Metson b Watkin	29		
P. de Bruyn c Metson b Thomas	19		
R. E. Bryson c Maynard b Thomas	16		
C. van Noordwyk c James b Thomas	0		
M. C. Krug not out	0		
L-b 4, w 4, n-b 4	12	B 1, l-b 9, w 7, n-b 3	20
1/10 2/99 3/117 4/124 5/126 6/164 7/183 8/196 9/201	201	1/1 2/91 3/151	(3 wkts) 187

Bowling: *First Innings*—Watkin 16–5–34–2; Thomas 15.3–3–46–4; Croft 23–8–48–1; Dale 4–0–11–0; Butcher 5–1–28–0; Hemp 7–1–30–2. *Second Innings*—Watkin 13–1–38–1; Thomas 15–3–54–1; Croft 15–4–38–0; Hemp 5–0–36–1; Maynard 0.4–0–11–0.

Umpires: J. Cloete and S. F. Marais.

MASHONALAND INVITATION XI v YORKSHIRE

At Harare Sports Club, Harare, April 1, 2, 3. Yorkshire won by 53 runs. Toss: Yorkshire. First-class debuts: P. M. Hutchison, I. D. Fisher.

Close of play: First day, Mashonaland Invitation XI 0-0 (D. P. Viljoen 0*, G. J. Rennie 0*); Second day, Yorkshire 45-1 (M. D. Moxon 22*, A. McGrath 5*).

Yorkshire

M. D. Moxon c Flower b Evans	9	– c Flower b Martin	22
M. P. Vaughan c Flower b Mbangwa	43	– c Shah b Mbangwa	17
*D. Byas not out	143	– (7) b Mbangwa	30
†R. J. Blakey lbw b Shah	8	– c Wishart b Martin	4
A. McGrath run out	48	– (3) c Mbangwa b Shah	43
B. Parker c Rennie b Shah	2	– (5) lbw b Campbell	16
A. C. Morris lbw b Mbangwa	1	– (6) c Davies b Shah	41
G. M. Hamilton not out	6	– not out	30
C. E. W. Silverwood (did not bat)		– not out	8
B 4, w 1, n-b 2	7	B 2, l-b 2	4
1/34 2/62 3/83 4/182 5/199 6/206 (6 wkts dec.)	267	1/33 2/47 3/67 4/88 5/123 6/163 7/189 (7 wkts dec.)	215

P. M. Hutchison and I. D. Fisher did not bat.

Bowling: *First Innings*—Mbangwa 17–4–43–2; Martin 16–4–50–0; Evans 15–4–43–1; Shah 21–11–28–2; Campbell 18–8–48–0; Rennie 14–3–25–0; Strang 5–0–26–0. *Second Innings*—Mbangwa 17–5–52–2; Martin 13–4–26–2; Shah 14–7–24–2; Wishart 3–1–7–0; Rennie 2–0–2–0; Strang 7–2–13–0; Evans 9–0–37–0; Campbell 13–2–50–1.

Mashonaland Invitation XI

D. P. Viljoen lbw b Hamilton	0	– (10) lbw b Hutchison	0
G. J. Rennie b Fisher	26	– c Blakey b Silverwood	15
*†G. W. Flower b Hamilton	3	– (1) b Fisher	45
C. N. Evans c sub (R. A. Kettleborough) b Silverwood	13	– c sub (R. A. Kettleborough) b Fisher	35
C. B. Wishart c sub (R. A. Kettleborough) b Morris	75	– (6) c Byas b Hutchison	12
A. D. R. Campbell c Byas b Vaughan	51	– (5) c Blakey b Hutchison	22
G. C. Martin lbw b Fisher	25	– c sub (R. A. Kettleborough) b Hutchison	8
S. G. Davies not out	42	– c McGrath b Fisher	5
A. H. Shah c Byas b Hutchison	31	– (3) c Silverwood b Fisher	10
B. C. Strang lbw b Hutchison	0	– (9) lbw b Fisher	0
M. Mbangwa (did not bat)		– not out	0
B 4, w 1, n-b 2	7	B 2, l-b 2	4
1/1 2/14 3/39 4/48 5/160 6/182 7/218 8/273 9/273 (9 wkts dec.)	273	1/45 2/70 3/73 4/126 5/142 6/143 7/152 8/152 9/153	156

Bowling: *First Innings*—Hutchison 15.3–3–63–2; Hamilton 17–4–44–2; Silverwood 14–5–30–1; Fisher 19–2–52–2; Vaughan 11–1–55–1; Morris 7–2–16–1; McGrath 3–0–9–0. *Second Innings*—Hutchison 9.5–2–23–4; Hamilton 7–0–46–0; Silverwood 5–0–16–1; Morris 2–0–14–0; Fisher 14–2–35–5; Vaughan 3–0–18–0.

Umpires: D. Kalan and K. Kanjee.

JAMAICA v LANCASHIRE

At Kingston, April 10, 11, 12. Drawn. Toss: Lancashire. County debut: S. Elworthy.

Close of play: First day, Jamaica 61-0 (W. E. Cuff 24*, W. W. Hinds 33*); Second day, Jamaica 324-8 (M. C. Gibbs 4*, O. R. Richards 0*).

Lancashire

J. E. R. Gallian c and b Perry	97		
M. A. Atherton c Richards b Taylor	27	– c Taylor b Murphy	117
J. P. Crawley c Richards b Perry	42	– c Cuff b Murphy	18
N. J. Speak c Cuff b Murphy	25	– b Murphy	8
G. D. Lloyd b Richards	58		
*M. Watkinson c Hinds b Gibbs	62		
†W. K. Hegg not out	21	– (1) c Burton b Taylor	15
I. D. Austin not out	7	– (6) not out	2
S. Elworthy (did not bat)		– (5) not out	57
B 5, w 3, n-b 3	11	B 4, w 3, n-b 4	11
1/78 2/171 3/184 4/218 5/293 6/325	(6 wkts dec.) 350	1/51 2/75 3/97 4/207	(4 wkts dec.) 228

G. Chapple and G. Keedy did not bat.

Bowling: *First Innings*—Richards 11–0–48–1; Burton 10–2–47–0; Taylor 10–0–65–1; Gibbs 17–2–71–1; Murphy 20–3–60–1; Perry 14–1–54–2. *Second Innings*—Burton 11–2–53–0; Taylor 7–0–35–1; Breese 7–0–25–0; Perry 11–4–37–0; Murphy 14.5–0–51–3; Gibbs 7–0–23–0.

Jamaica

W. E. Cuff c Hegg b Chapple	24	– c Speak b Elworthy	7
W. W. Hinds c Hegg b Austin	34	– c Speak b Chapple	2
D. B. Taylor c Elworthy b Watkinson	60	– c Chapple b Watkinson	20
G. R. Breese c Lloyd b Gallian	124	– not out	36
*D. S. Morgan c Austin b Keedy	17	– not out	20
N. O. Perry c Hegg b Chapple	1		
R. S. Murphy lbw b Keedy	47		
†A. N. Coley c Watkinson b Gallian	4		
M. C. Gibbs not out	4		
O. R. Richards not out	0		
B 2, l-b 1, w 3, n-b 3	9	B 5, w 1, n-b 2	8
1/62 2/62 3/177 4/217 5/224 6/298 7/308 8/324	(8 wkts dec.) 324	1/11 2/19 3/67	(3 wkts) 93

S. N. Burton did not bat.

Bowling: *First Innings*—Chapple 19–3–49–2; Elworthy 16–1–84–0; Austin 14–3–35–1; Watkinson 16–3–40–1; Keedy 28–8–73–2; Speak 2–0–7–0; Gallian 7–0–33–2. *Second Innings*—Chapple 6–0–16–1; Elworthy 8–1–33–1; Watkinson 7–1–19–1; Gallian 5–2–20–0.

Umpires: C. Fletcher and V. Johnson.

MATABELELAND SELECT XI v YORKSHIRE

At Bulawayo Athletic Club, Bulawayo, April 11, 12. Yorkshire won by an innings and 11 runs. Toss: Matabeleland Select XI.

Close of play: First day, Matabeleland Select XI 2-2 (G. Peck 0*).

Yorkshire

M. D. Moxon b Mbangwa	134
M. P. Vaughan c Rennie b Dekker	106
*D. Byas c Whittall b Mbangwa	8
†R. J. Blakey c James b Vaghmaria	28
A. McGrath c James b Vaghmaria	19
R. A. Kettleborough not out	9
A. C. Morris not out	13
L-b 8, n-b 4	12
1/203 2/227 3/266 4/306 5/307	(5 wkts dec.) 329

P. J. Hartley, G. M. Hamilton, P. M. Hutchison and I. D. Fisher did not bat.

Bowling: Streak 18–8–55–0; Mbangwa 22–7–53–2; Whittall 12–2–38–0; Rennie 8–1–29–0; Vaghmaria 17–1–67–2; Dekker 9–3–24–1; Manyimo 3–0–24–0; Peck 10–0–31–0.

Matabeleland Select XI

M. H. Dekker lbw b Hamilton	0	– (3) c Blakey b Hutchison	7
G. Peck b Hutchison	0	– (1) lbw b Hartley	13
G. J. Whittall b Hamilton	0	– (5) c McGrath b Hamilton	2
M. D. Abrams lbw b Hamilton	7	– lbw b Hutchison	0
*†W. R. James b Hutchison	23	– (6) b Hamilton b Hutchison	22
H. H. Streak c Blakey b Fisher	20	– (7) c Blakey b Hartley	101
J. A. Rennie c Morris b Hartley	5	– (8) c Blakey b Hartley	52
T. B. Manyimo c Blakey b Hartley	8	– (2) c Blakey b Hamilton	0
D. Vaghmaria not out	7	– not out	26
W. Wessels c Kettleborough b Fisher	0	– lbw b Fisher	0
M. Mbangwa c Moxon b Hartley	10	– lbw b Hartley	5
L-b 4	4	B 2, l-b 3, n-b 1	6
1/2 2/2 3/2 4/32 5/32 6/42 7/63 8/71 9/71	84	1/1 2/10 3/10 4/17 5/42 6/50 7/187 8/214 9/217	234

Bowling: *First Innings*—Hamilton 7–4–13–3; Hutchison 7–1–34–2; Fisher 7–2–20–2; Hartley 7.4–4–13–3. *Second Innings*—Hamilton 10–2–31–2; Hutchison 14–2–44–3; Hartley 13.5–3–54–4; Fisher 16–5–46–1; Morris 6–2–11–0; Vaughan 5–1–22–0; Kettleborough 2–0–21–0.

Umpires: C. Coventry and G. Evans.

ONE HUNDRED YEARS AGO

From JOHN WISDEN'S CRICKETERS' ALMANACK FOR 1897

MR. W. G. GRACE AND THE SURREY CLUB: "Various rumours having gained currency as to the amount of money allowed to Mr. Grace for expenses when playing for England at the Oval, the following official statement was made public on August 10 – the opening day of the third test match. 'The Committee of the Surrey County Cricket Club have observed paragraphs in the Press respecting amounts alleged to be paid, or promised to, Dr. W. G. Grace for playing in the match England v. Australia. The Committee desire to give the statements contained in the paragraphs the most unqualified contradiction. During many years, on the occasions of Dr. W. G. Grace playing at the Oval, at the request of the Surrey County Committee, in the matches Gentlemen v. Players and England v. Australia, Dr. Grace has received the sum of £10 a match to cover his expenses in coming to and remaining in London during the three days. Beyond this amount Dr. Grace has not received, directly or indirectly, one farthing for playing in a match at the Oval. Signed on behalf of the Committee, C. W. ALCOCK, August 10, 1896."

SOME CURRENT TOPICS By The Editor: "Nothing in connection with cricket has for some years past caused so much excitement as the so-called strike of the professionals, on the eve of the England and Australian match at the Oval. Happily the storm subsided almost as soon as it was raised, the players quickly withdrawing from the position which, without thoroughly weighing the consequences, they had taken up. I thought at the time, and I think still, that the players were right in principle, but that their action was ill-judged and inopportune."

PUBLIC SCHOOL CRICKET IN 1896 By W. J. Ford: ". . . This set me thinking whether it would be impossible for public school authorities to establish a sort of *kindergarten* for the young and promising, where good wickets would be provided as well as experienced teaching; for, to tell the truth, the ordinary professional bowler knows little or nothing about coaching. He bowls very well and is a very good fellow, but he has probably been bowling at the nets all his life, and has no practical knowledge of batting."

ENGLAND WOMEN IN INDIA, 1995-96

By CAROL SALMON

England's first full tour of India was packed with incident. Feted wherever they went, the 18-strong tour party were not prepared for the overwhelming hospitality – or for the security the hosts deemed necessary. It was five and a half weeks before any of the players was allowed out of sight of their armed guards. Media coverage was intense, and the matches were watched by large crowds, with 18,000 attending the third one-day international at Patna.

Honours were just about shared on the field. England took the Test series 1-0 after winning a nail-biter at Jamshedpur by two runs; the final Test at Hyderabad was even more tense, with England's last-wicket pair having to survive 110 minutes to save the match and prevent India from drawing level. In the five-match one-day series, England took a 2-1 lead. But the turning point was the fourth match at Lucknow, when the Indian selectors suddenly replaced the captain Purnima Rau (née Janardhan), who had recently been widowed, with Pramila Bhat. England scored a poor 131, losing five wickets to lbws, and were thrashed by nine wickets. India comfortably won the decider.

The tourists found the Indian cricketers much improved since they last met in the World Cup in 1993. They had won a triangular series with New Zealand and Australia earlier in the year and prepared in a three-month training camp before England arrived. Their spinners were superb, particularly 18-year-old left-armer Neetu David, who took eight for 53 in England's second innings at Jamshedpur. While the fielding was not up to the visitors' standards, they generally outbatted England and should do well when they host the 1997 World Cup.

England's shortcomings were underlined in the one-day game at Gauhati, when they were unable to better a meagre total of 85. Their lack of experience showed: six players made their Test debuts and Suzanne Redfern, at 18, became England's youngest Test player. Janette Brittin, England's most capped player, was easily the most prolific batsman, scoring 229 at 38.16 in the Tests. Spinner Debbie Stock led the bowlers, with 11 wickets at 15.54.

ENGLAND WOMEN TOURING PARTY

K. Smithies (East Midlands) (*captain*), B. A. Daniels (West Midlands) (*vice-captain*), J. A. Brittin (Surrey), J. M. Chamberlain (East Midlands), C. J. Connor (Sussex), K. Leng (Yorkshire), D. Maybury (Yorkshire), S. Metcalfe (Yorkshire), H. C. Plimmer (Yorkshire), S. Redfern (East Midlands), M. Reynard (Yorkshire), J. Smit (East Midlands), D. Stock (Thames Valley), C. E. Taylor (Yorkshire), A. Thorose (Thames Valley).

Manager: S. Taylor. *Coach:* J. Bown. *Physiotherapist:* J. Strickland.

Note: Matches in this section were not first-class.

At Delhi, November 11. First one-day international: England won by nine wickets. Toss: England. India 112 (45.5 overs) (Extras 33); England 113 for one (41.2 overs) (J. A. Brittin 40 not out, B. A. Daniels 40 not out).

At Gauhati, November 14. Second one-day international: India won by seven runs. Toss: England. India 85 (32.3 overs) (J. M. Chamberlain four for 18, K. Leng three for 27); England 78 (43.4 overs) (S. Metcalfe 32; K. S. P. Bhat three for nine, S. Dabir three for 13).

INDIA v ENGLAND

First Test Match

At Calcutta, November 17, 18, 19, 20. Drawn. Toss: India. Test debuts: A. Chopra, S. Shaw; B. A. Daniels, K. Leng, M. Reynard, C. E. Taylor.

Rain ruined the first Test, with ten hours lost. Asked to bat, Jan Brittin and Helen Plimmer gave England a sound start with 108, before left-arm spinner Sangeeta Dabir took three wickets in eight balls. But Sue Metcalfe and Jane Smit saw them out of trouble and, after a second-day washout, Karen Smithies declared on the third afternoon. Anju Jain, promoted to open, scored a maiden hundred in her second Test, batting for five and a half hours and hitting 11 fours. India took a first-innings lead of 105, but could not exploit their advantage in the hour remaining.

Close of play: First day, England 117-1 (J. A. Brittin 66*, B. A. Daniels 7*); Second day, No play; Third day, India 66-1 (A. Jain 35*, A. Chopra 8*).

England

J. A. Brittin c Chopra b Dabir	84	– c Chopra b Shaw	16
H. C. Plimmer b Bhat	42	– not out	11
B. A. Daniels lbw b Dabir	21	– c Dabir b Bhat	0
S. Metcalfe not out	33	– not out	0
*K. Smithies b Dabir	0		
†J. Smit st Jain b David	19		
J. M. Chamberlain not out	4		
B 3, l-b 2, w 1	6	W 1	1
1/108 2/150 3/151 4/151 5/194 (5 wkts dec.)	209	1/23 2/28 (2 wkts)	28

K. Leng, D. Stock, M. Reynard and C. E. Taylor did not bat.

Bowling: *First Innings*—Francis 17–3–43–0; Margaret 13–2–34–0; Chopra 4–0–7–0; David 13–3–26–1; Bhat 19–3–52–1; Dabir 12–5–8–3; Rau 11–4–17–0; Shaw 5–0–17–0. *Second Innings*—Francis 7–4–9–0; Chopra 3–0–13–0; Margaret 4–3–1–0; Shaw 3–2–4–1; Bhat 3–2–1–1.

India

S. Agarwal c Plimmer b Leng	17
†A. Jain run out	110
A. Chopra c and b Smithies	27
C. Aheer c Smit b Taylor	21
*P. Rau c Smit b Stock	33
K. S. P. Bhat c Taylor b Smithies	9
S. Dabir not out	50
S. Shaw not out	24
B 13, l-b 2, w 3, n-b 5	23
1/41 2/140 3/176 4/206 5/234 6/242 (6 wkts dec.)	314

L. Francis, R. Margaret and N. David did not bat.

Bowling: Chamberlain 24–7–48–0; Taylor 25–9–71–1; Stock 17–5–40–1; Smithies 21–5–52–2; Leng 19–9–41–1; Reynard 8–0–47–0.

Umpires: S. Banerjee and S. B. Nandi.

INDIA v ENGLAND

Second Test Match

At Jamshedpur, November 24, 25, 26, 27. England won by two runs. Toss: England. Test debut: S. Redfern.

A momentous finish transformed the game. India needed just 128 to win and recovered from a shaky 75 for five to 105 without further loss. Then Debbie Stock struck twice with successive balls and a run-out left them 106 for eight. Another run-out, when India were four short, brought in Neetu David, who must have thought she had won the match when she completed a Test record of eight wickets for 53 earlier in the day. She played the first ball of the penultimate over for a single; Laya Francis blocked the next delivery, but the third one hit her on the pads and ran to fine leg. The crowd shouted to the batsmen to run, England shouted to Metcalfe to throw the ball in, but Jo Chamberlain shouted an appeal to the umpire who, after what seemed an age, raised his finger. England had been under pressure throughout, having to recover from 75 for five on the opening day. India took a lead of 67, and then the left-arm spin of David, who found both bounce and turn in the pitch, seemed to have seen off England. But the final twist saw the tourists home with nine balls to spare.

Close of play: First day, England 194-9 (J. Smit 18*, S. Redfern 1*); Second day, India 169-6 (S. Dabir 55*, S. Shaw 0*); Third day, England 94-4 (K. Smithies 26*).

England

J. A. Brittin run out	44	– lbw b Margaret	1
H. C. Plimmer c Jain b Chopra	13	– c Jain b David	13
B. A. Daniels lbw b Dabir	15	– c Dabir b David	20
S. Metcalfe c Jain b Dabir	1	– c Chopra b David	21
*K. Smithies b Shaw	21	– c Dabir b David	30
D. Maybury b Dabir	0	– b David	6
J. M. Chamberlain c and b David	39	– c Dabir b David	14
†J. Smit not out	20	– not out	42
K. Leng lbw b Bhat	18	– c sub (M. Nadgoda) b Dabir	15
D. Stock b Dabir	17	– lbw b David	10
S. Redfern c Dabir b Bhat	1	– b David	7
B 1, l-b 6	7	B 5, l-b 10	15
1/32 2/67 3/73 4/74 5/75 6/115 7/144 8/169 9/191	196	1/7 2/39 3/44 4/94 5/101 6/104 7/123 8/152 9/171	194

Bowling: *First Innings*—Francis 12–3–17–0; Margaret 7–4–6–0; Chopra 6–3–9–1; David 14–2–37–1; Bhat 26.3–8–49–2; Dabir 21–5–36–4; Rau 15–5–25–0; Shaw 4–0–10–1. *Second Innings*—Francis 11–5–13–0; Margaret 8–2–14–1; David 31.3–12–53–8; Bhat 29–13–33–0; Rau 17–7–25–0; Dabir 22–11–27–1; Shaw 8–4–14–0.

India

†A. Jain b Chamberlain	42	– st Smit b Stock	7
A. Vaidya c Smit b Chamberlain	13	– (7) b Stock	15
A. Chopra c Maybury b Stock	5	– (2) c Stock b Leng	31
*P. Rau b Chamberlain	13	– (5) lbw b Redfern	9
C. Aheer lbw b Redfern	14	– (4) st Smit b Leng	12
S. Dabir c Plimmer b Stock	60	– run out	25
K. S. P. Bhat c Smit b Leng	18	– (8) c Smit b Stock	0
S. Shaw c Smithies b Leng	54	– (3) c Redfern b Stock	9
R. Margaret c Maybury b Leng	27	– run out	0
L. Francis c Smithies b Stock	1	– lbw b Chamberlain	4
N. David not out	1	– not out	1
B 3, l-b 9, w 1, n-b 2	15	B 5, l-b 6, n-b 1	12
1/19 2/42 3/75 4/76 5/121 6/168 7/188 8/250 9/259	263	1/7 2/38 3/57 4/75 5/75 6/105 7/105 8/106 9/124	125

Bowling: *First Innings*—Chamberlain 18–7–53–3; Smithies 28–14–47–0; Stock 27–14–44–3; Redfern 17–5–35–1; Leng 17–1–49–3; Maybury 5–0–14–0; Daniels 2–0–9–0. *Second Innings*—Chamberlain 6.3–3–13–1; Stock 12–2–32–4; Smithies 1–0–6–0; Redfern 11–4–29–1; Leng 8–1–34–2.

Umpires: R. Biswas and K. Chakraborty.

At Patna, December 1. Third one-day international: England won by 41 runs. Toss: India. England 194 for six (50 overs) (J. A. Brittin 81, H. C. Plimmer 34; P. Rau three for 43); India 153 for nine (46.4 overs) (A. Jain 42, A. Chopra 31; K. Smithies three for 20).

The umpires mistakenly allowed Rau to bowl 11 overs, rather than ten.

At Lucknow, December 5. Fourth one-day international: India won by nine wickets. Toss: India. England 131 for nine (50 overs) (K. Smithies 36 not out; K. S. P. Bhat four for 25); India 132 for one (41.3 overs) (A. Jain 65, A. Chopra 49 not out).

The Indian selectors replaced Purnima Rau as captain with Pramila Bhat.

INDIA v ENGLAND

Third Test Match

At Hyderabad, December 10, 11, 12, 13. Drawn. Toss: England. Test debut: C. J. Connor.

The final Test reached a climax no less nerve-racking than that at Jamshedpur. This time, India were sure they had won when they reduced England to 160 for nine with 110 minutes to go. But the last-wicket pair, Debbie Stock and Clare Taylor, hung on to draw the match and win the series. They survived for 38.4 overs – India packed 23 into the final hour. England had reduced India to 85 for seven on the first day, only for Shyama Shaw and Pramila Bhat to add 93 for the eighth wicket. Next, the tourists scored a dismal 98, conceding a deficit of 86. India extended their lead to 302 before declaring on the third evening, leaving themselves just over a day to bowl England out and level the series – and they so nearly did.

Close of play: First day, England 5-0 (J. A. Brittin 4*, H. C. Plimmer 0*); Second day, India 36-1 (A. Chopra 13*, C. Aheer 19*); Third day, England 38-1 (J. A. Brittin 27*, B. A. Daniels 10*).

India

†A. Jain c Smit b Taylor	15	– b Taylor	3
A. Chopra run out	17	– c Smit b Smithies	32
R. Mudgal c Smit b Taylor	2	– (8) c Brittin b Chamberlain	2
R. Venugopal b Taylor	0	– (6) c Brittin b Stock	5
P. Rau c Daniels b Chamberlain	17	– (4) c Daniels b Smithies	24
C. Aheer c Smit b Taylor	11	– (3) c Plimmer b Stock	67
S. Dabir c Plimmer b Chamberlain	20	– (5) b Chamberlain	39
S. Shaw run out	66	– (7) not out	31
*K. S. P. Bhat b Connor	28	– not out	6
R. Margaret not out	4		
L. Francis c Plimmer b Stock	1		
L-b 2, w 1	3	B 6, l-b 1	7
1/23 2/29 3/29 4/39 5/57 6/83 7/85 8/178 9/179	184	1/11 2/79 3/117 4/163 5/174 6/184 7/202 (7 wkts dec.)	216

Bowling: *First Innings*—Chamberlain 21–8–57–2; Taylor 24–14–38–4; Stock 14.4–8–15–1; Smithies 13–4–22–0; Leng 9–3–32–0; Connor 8–3–18–1. *Second Innings*—Chamberlain 28–8–64–2; Taylor 28–14–57–1; Stock 19–6–40–2; Smithies 18–8–36–2; Connor 4–0–12–0.

England

J. A. Brittin c Rau b Francis	16	– c Chopra b Rau	68
H. C. Plimmer lbw b Francis	3	– c Mudgal b Francis	0
B. A. Daniels c Chopra b Rau	19	– lbw b Rau	29
S. Metcalfe c Chopra b Shaw	23	– c Mudgal b Bhat	1
*K. Smithies c Rau b Dabir	0	– st Jain b Bhat	3
†J. Smit c Dabir b Shaw	3	– c Chopra b Francis	27
J. M. Chamberlain st Jain b Bhat	17	– st Jain b Bhat	10
K. Leng st Jain b Bhat	0	– c Mudgal b Rau	1
C. J. Connor not out	3	– c Shaw b Rau	13
D. Stock c Bhat b Shaw	3	– not out	9
C. E. Taylor lbw b Dabir	0	– not out	9
B 1, l-b 7, n-b 3	11	B 5, l-b 4, w 1, n-b 2	12
1/16 2/31 3/56 4/57 5/67 6/92 7/92 8/93 9/98	98	1/3 2/72 3/73 4/85 5/131 6/136 7/138 8/156 9/160 (9 wkts)	182

Bowling: *First Innings*—Francis 14–4–20–2; Margaret 1–0–1–0; Bhat 14–9–18–2; Chopra 9–3–11–0; Dabir 13.3–8–13–2; Rau 12–9–8–1; Shaw 14–7–19–3. *Second Innings*—Francis 16–6–20–2; Chopra 7–2–11–0; Bhat 35–19–42–3; Rau 54–26–51–4; Shaw 22–7–43–0; Venugopal 2–0–6–0; Mudgal 1–1–0–0.

Umpires: Rajan and V. K. Ramaswamy.

At Madras, December 15. Fifth one-day international: India won by seven wickets. Toss: India. England 146 for nine (50 overs) (K. Smithies 38, J. Smit 35 not out); India 147 for three (44.1 overs) (A. Chopra 53 not out, P. Rau 46 not out). *India took the series 3-2.*

CRICKET IN AUSTRALIA, 1995-96

By JOHN MACKINNON

Adelaide Advertiser

Jamie Siddons

There was a memorable climax to the Sheffield Shield season that brought spectators rushing to the Adelaide Oval as in the days when Bradman was batting. An eight-hour rearguard action by South Australia, who had to draw the match to win the Shield, ended in success when the last pair, Peter McIntyre and Shane George, held the Western Australian attack at bay for the last 59 balls.

Older spectators were reminded of Ken Mackay and Lindsay Kline saving the Test against West Indies on the same ground 35 years earlier. Those with shorter memories noted that just three months earlier the roles had been reversed when Western Australia's last pair held out in Perth. The upshot was that Western Australia narrowly failed to become the second team in 14 years of Shield finals to win the title from the runners-up position.

The thrilling final gave domestic cricket some encouragement after a season in which all the efforts of the marketing whizzkids failed to have an obvious impact on the Shield's diminished appeal. Shield attendances – about 207,000 in all – were about five per cent down on 1994-95 levels, though they were still slightly better than in the early 1990s. The states gave themselves new nicknames to keep pace with football and basketball. New South Wales remained the Blues, but they had to compete with the Queensland Bulls, the Victorian Bushrangers, the Western Warriors, the Tassie Tigers (predictably enough) and – after much soul-searching – the South Australian Redbacks, after the venomous spider. In one-day games, the players took to wearing numbers – any number, it seemed, as Shane Warne wore 23.

There were four day-night Shield matches – it would have been five if the Adelaide lights had worked in time. But the yellow ball became more or less invisible after a few overs, and many of the players objected, as much to the change in their daily routine as anything else. However, the Australian Cricket Board have now authorised the use of lights in daytime games when required.

The continued success of the national team meant these problems stayed in the background. But the insipid performances of the visiting teams meant that the summer's two Test series will be mostly remembered for their controversies, and nothing happened on the international scene to match South Australia's victory, a triumph made extra sweet for the team and their shaven-headed captain, Jamie Siddons, by the memories of their terrible flop in the final at Brisbane 12 months earlier.

The team was always attractive and their batsmen revelled on the Adelaide Oval – excellently prepared by curator Les Burdett – where they achieved four of their five outright wins. Siddons led by example, though he was eventually struck down by a nagging hip injury, which caused him to miss the penultimate game and to struggle in the final. But with Tim May and Greg Blewett out of international favour, the side was virtually always at full strength. Blewett and the powerful left-hander Darren Lehmann both had wonderful seasons. Each scored over 1,000 runs and hit five hundreds and, at 24 and 26 respectively, they both had time to resurrect their international careers. Jamie Brayshaw was not far behind. For the second year running, Paul Nobes adorned the final with one of his bustling, shuffling hundreds which have frustrated so many bowlers. No stylist, he was never short of courage, as he showed in Sydney where he received an awful blow to the head but returned to score an unfussy 70. Nobes's career may be near its end, but fast bowler Jason Gillespie was a real find in his first full season. At 20, he was summoned to replace Craig McDermott at the World Cup. His advance was timely because George disappeared with a rib injury, only to return for two matches in March, depriving the up-and-coming left-armer Mark Harrity of a place in the final. May and McIntyre are both over 30, but shared more than 80 wickets, which made them a potent spin combination, even if they were not the most athletic pair of cricketers in Australia. May announced his retirement in August. Tim Nielsen spent much of his time standing up to the stumps for the spinners; like most Australian keepers, he was always combative. The state's coach, Jeff Hammond, left for South Africa after their Shield triumph, and Siddons was appointed coach as well as captain.

Western Australia reached the final despite having their share of problems. After only three matches, Damien Martyn was relieved of the captaincy he took on 15 months earlier. His successor, Tom Moody, provided much-needed maturity and stability, with each ensuing match realising either outright or first-innings points. Martyn was lucky to keep his place; but for a double-century against Tasmania, he might have been dropped for the final. A great sadness was the retirement of 32-year-old Bruce Reid in February, when a side strain ended his career-long battle with injury. His form had been pretty good, but the physical demands on his spare frame proved too much. Though Reid's spasmodic presence will be missed, Western Australia have never lacked depth in pace bowling, and Jo Angel and Brendon Julian bore the major burden on their broad shoulders. Young Brad Hogg's left-arm wrist-spin marked him as an all-rounder of some promise. Moody remained the leading all-rounder, and the side also owed much to the batting form of Justin Langer and 20-year-old Mike Hussey. But it was wicket-keeper Adam Gilchrist who stood out as a young man on a mission. The previous year he had made 51 dismissals, a Shield record for Western Australia; this time his 50 catches and four stumpings were a Shield record for any state. He batted exuberantly and scored a run-a-ball 189 in the final. At 24, he looked a natural successor to Ian Healy.

Queensland's bid to retain their historic first title came to an inglorious end when their batting fell apart in their last match, against Victoria. Allan Border played his 625th and final innings in this game, a rather anonymous effort yielding 34 in 146 minutes. He took his career aggregate after 20 years to

27,131 at 51.38. Matthew Hayden made 401 of his 752 runs off the hapless Tasmanian bowlers. Martin Love, who shared two stands of over 360 with him against Tasmania, was the best of the other batsmen. But 20-year-old Andrew Symonds, Gloucestershire's six-hitting phenomenon, scored a mere 77 in five Shield matches and averaged less than ten. Mike Kasprowicz led a bowling attack based mostly on speed. Past heroes Carl Rackemann and Greg Rowell were picked for only a handful of games, and Rowell's action was officially designated as suspect, which led to a frantic search for a remedy from guru Dennis Lillee. On their day, and especially on the odd Brisbane green-top, Kasprowicz and his cohorts, usually Andy Bichel and Dirk Tazelaar, were quite deadly. Kasprowicz was Australia's leading wicket-taker of the season with 64, easily breaking Craig McDermott's state record of 54. That kept Wade Seccombe busy behind the stumps, and he caught almost everything that came his way. Queensland at least won the limited-overs Mercantile Mutual Cup; they barely qualified for the semi-finals, with only two wins from the five preliminary games, but beat Western Australia – disappointed finalists again – for the title.

In retrospect, New South Wales's season followed a predictable decline from three triumphant early wins; they took only four points from the last six games. Of course it was hard to replace seven players on call for Tests and the World Cup. But the New South Wales reserves, many of whom were no longer young hopefuls, generally did not measure up. Some encouragement came from Anthony Stuart, a 26-year-old fast-medium bowler built on the same lines as Glenn McGrath. He headed the national averages and added credibility to an attack that tended to lean on the spin of Greg Matthews and David Freedman. Phil Emery, who had captained the side for several years in the absence of Mark Taylor and Steve Waugh, asked to surrender that duty, but he kept wicket as well as ever. The captaincy eventually passed to Matthews. Geoff Lawson's job as coach seems to be a year-to-year proposition; the Cricket Association apparently wished to keep other options open. Steve Waugh endeared himself to his colleagues by depositing a drive on to the sponsor's sign at the WACA in a one-day game: the team were paid $A140,000 for the extra publicity, though the obliging bowler, Tom Moody, was left empty-handed.

Tasmania's batting was as strong as any in the competition. Though they lost Ricky Ponting to the Test side, they were eventually compensated by the return of David Boon, who had decided to retire from international cricket. The high point of the season was a successful run-chase in Perth, where Boon guided them to 402 for six in 124 overs. The pitch at Bellerive remained a paradise for batsmen and a graveyard for bowlers. While that equation continues, Tasmania will be well served by the likes of Dene Hills, Jamie Cox, Michael Di Venuto and Shaun Young, but the bowlers will break their hearts.

Victoria celebrated their Cricket Association's centenary but not much else. The coach, Les Stillman, and captain Dean Jones were embroiled in a simmering dispute with players and administrators, which boiled over when wicket-keeper Darren Berry was dropped, seemingly for reasons other than form. At club level, Jones was suspended for one match for bringing the game into disrepute. By the season's end, the Association decided it was time to seek new blood. Stillman and Jones set off for Derbyshire, who appreciated them more. The VCA appointed Shane Warne as captain, Tony Dodemaide as deputy and John Scholes as coach. Scholes's credentials were impeccable. He captained Victoria in the 1980s and, in spite of crippling injuries, was still doggedly playing first grade at the age of 46. On the playing side, Matthew Elliott managed to keep his head when many were losing theirs. Not only did he top the national batting averages, with 1,233 runs at 68.50, including two double-hundreds, but he won both the umpires' and the cricketers' Player of the Year awards. Though they finished bottom, Victoria won their last three games in Melbourne – against the three teams who came top – thanks largely to Elliott's command, the resurgence of Warren Ayres and the now traditional end-of-season haul of wickets by Dodemaide. They used no fewer than 27 players thanks to a wretched run of injuries. Brad Williams was one casualty but, as a fast and abrasive bowler, he should be one to watch.

Australian cricket moves on, as Bob Simpson discovered while on holiday in Italy, where he learned that his job as national coach had gone to Geoff Marsh. There was change, too, on the sponsorship front where the Benson and Hedges era of 22 summers came to an end, after years of struggle against tighter controls on tobacco advertising. Ansett Airlines were to sponsor the Tests from 1996-97 and the brewers Fosters the World Series. Meanwhile, the real groundwork for the future was being laid down by the new coach's namesake, the indomitable Rodney Marsh, at the Cricket Academy in Adelaide. He continued to feed new talent into the game and, following their triumph over England a year earlier, his charges added Richie Richardson's West Indians to their list of victims.

FIRST-CLASS AVERAGES, 1995-96

BATTING

(Qualification: 500 runs)

	M	*I*	*NO*	*R*	*HS*	*100s*	*Avge*
M. T. G. Elliott (*Vic*)	11	21	3	1,233	203	5	68.50
R. T. Ponting (*Tas*)	8	13	3	681	131*	3	68.10
M. G. Bevan (*NSW*)	8	15	4	721	119*	3	65.54
S. R. Waugh (*NSW*)	10	18	3	952	170	4	63.46
D. S. Lehmann (*SA*)	12	23	1	1,237	161	5	56.22
D. F. Hills (*Tas*)	10	19	2	914	220*	1	53.76
M. L. Hayden (*Qld*)	10	17	3	752	234	2	53.71
S. G. Law (*Qld*)	9	14	3	565	107*	1	51.36
D. M. Jones (*Vic*)	11	19	0	974	145	3	51.26
A. C. Gilchrist (*WA*)	13	22	5	859	189*	1	50.52
S. Young (*Tas*)	11	19	4	739	175*	2	49.26
M. A. Taylor (*NSW*)	11	20	1	931	126	2	49.00
M. J. Slater (*NSW*)	11	20	2	863	219	2	47.94
M. E. Waugh (*NSW*)	11	19	2	805	116	2	47.35
J. A. Brayshaw (*SA*)	12	22	3	865	141*	2	45.52
D. C. Boon (*Tas*)	15	25	0	1,134	152	4	45.36
G. S. Blewett (*SA*)	15	27	1	1,173	135	5	45.11
T. M. Moody (*WA*)	12	24	4	887	90	0	44.35
M. J. Di Venuto (*Tas*)	11	19	1	791	154	2	43.94
M. L. Love (*Qld*)	13	22	1	921	186	2	43.85
A. R. Border (*Qld*)	11	17	1	669	94	0	41.81
J. D. Siddons (*SA*)	11	20	1	790	130	3	41.57
J. L. Langer (*WA*)	12	24	1	950	161	4	41.30
M. E. Hussey (*WA*)	12	24	1	945	146	2	41.08
P. C. Nobes (*SA*)	12	23	0	840	121	2	36.52
D. R. Martyn (*WA*)	12	24	3	757	203*	1	36.04
J. P. Maher (*Qld*)	12	19	2	578	108	1	34.00
J. Cox (*Tas*)	11	22	1	670	94	0	31.90
T. J. Barsby (*Qld*)	11	21	1	616	133	1	30.80

* *Signifies not out.*

BOWLING

(Qualification: 20 wickets)

	O	*M*	*R*	*W*	*BB*	*5W/i*	*Avge*
A. M. Stuart (*NSW*)	119.2	36	335	25	4-22	0	13.40
A. I. C. Dodemaide (*Vic*)	157.2	40	374	22	6-67	2	17.00
M. S. Kasprowicz (*Qld*)	428.3	108	1,310	64	7-64	8	20.46
J. N. Gillespie (*SA*)	366.3	93	1,142	51	6-68	1	22.39
G. D. McGrath (*NSW*)	445.4	115	1,142	51	5-40	2	22.39
B. A. Reid (*WA*)	258.5	77	569	24	5-36	1	23.70
D. Tazelaar (*Qld*)	237.5	66	571	24	5-42	1	23.79
A. J. Bichel (*Qld*)	229.4	49	767	32	5-31	1	23.96
J. Angel (*WA*)	445	128	1,225	49	6-68	3	25.00
S. K. Warne (*Vic*)	449.5	131	1,057	42	7-23	2	25.16
D. J. Saker (*Vic*)	277.4	85	763	30	7-32	1	25.43
D. A. Freedman (*NSW*)	384.3	88	1,083	40	8-49	3	27.07
P. R. Reiffel (*Vic*)	284	75	772	28	5-39	1	27.57
G. R. J. Matthews (*NSW*)	499.5	140	1,236	43	5-43	2	28.74
B. P. Julian (*WA*)	442.5	120	1,327	46	5-41	4	28.84
C. J. McDermott (*Qld*)	343.1	83	1,083	34	5-49	2	31.85
N. D. Maxwell (*NSW*)	255	59	706	22	6-56	1	32.09
T. B. A. May (*SA*)	561.5	115	1,540	44	6-83	3	35.00
T. M. Moody (*WA*)	319	83	880	25	7-38	1	35.20
M. W. Ridgway (*Tas*)	327.5	57	1,152	32	5-64	1	36.00
M. A. Harrity (*SA*)	261.4	37	1,021	27	4-75	0	37.81
B. A. Williams (*Vic*)	219	38	770	20	6-98	1	38.50
P. E. McIntyre (*SA*)	476	84	1,502	39	6-133	1	38.51
J. P. Marquet (*Tas*)	336.3	70	1,140	28	5-94	1	40.71
G. B. Hogg (*WA*)	340.5	103	942	21	5-59	2	44.85

SHEFFIELD SHIELD, 1995-96

	Played	*Won*	*Lost*	*Drawn*	*1st-inns Points*	*Points*	*Quotient*
South Australia	10	5	3	2	4	34	1.002
Western Australia	10	3	3	4	12	30	1.085
Queensland	10	4	3	3	2	26	1.111
Tasmania	10	3	5	2	5*	23	0.773
New South Wales	10	3	3	4	4	22	1.103
Victoria	10	3	4	3	3.4§	21.4	0.933

Final: South Australia drew with Western Australia, but took the Sheffield Shield by virtue of heading the table.

* *One point for tie on first innings in outright loss.* § *0.6 points deducted for slow over-rates.*

Outright win = 6 pts; lead on first innings in a drawn or lost game = 2 pts.
Quotient = runs per wicket scored divided by runs per wicket conceded.

Under ACB playing conditions, two extras are scored for every no-ball bowled whether scored off or not. Any runs scored off the bat are credited to the batsman, while byes and leg-byes are counted as no-balls, in accordance with Law 24.9, in addition to the initial penalty.

*In the following scores, * by the name of a team indicates that they won the toss.*

At Perth, October 18, 19, 20, 21. Drawn. Western Australia* 351 for three dec. (M. P. Lavender 173 not out, M. E. Hussey 42, D. R. Martyn 45, T. M. Moody 57 not out) and 206 for four dec. (M. E. Hussey 81, M. P. Lavender 46, T. M. Moody 30 not out); New South Wales 211 for nine dec. (M. E. Waugh 48, G. R. J. Matthews 40, D. A. Freedman 37) and 243 for four (M. J. Slater 96, M. A. Taylor 38, S. R. Waugh 31, M. E. Waugh 33, M. G. Bevan 30 not out; B. J. Oldroyd three for 82). *Western Australia 2 pts.*

No play on the first day.

At Brisbane, October 19, 20, 21, 22. Drawn. Queensland* 361 for eight dec. (M. L. Hayden 64, S. G. Law 89, J. P. Maher 88, W. A. Seccombe 54 not out; S. K. Warne three for 111) and 246 for six (M. L. Love 40, S. G. Law 53, A. R. Border 70 not out); Victoria 482 (M. T. G. Elliott 138, R. P. Larkin 34, D. M. Jones 145, D. S. Berry 74, Extras 30; M. S. Kasprowicz three for 94, P. W. Jackson four for 158). *Victoria 1.7 pts.*

At Brisbane, October 25, 26, 27, 28. Queensland won by eight wickets. South Australia* 276 (J. D. Siddons 130, T. J. Nielsen 47; M. S. Kasprowicz six for 48) and 243 (G. S. Blewett 126, J. A. Brayshaw 64; C. J. McDermott five for 58, M. S. Kasprowicz three for 78); Queensland 356 for nine dec. (M. L. Love 62, J. P. Maher 108, A. R. Border 59; J. N. Gillespie four for 62) and 164 for two (M. L. Hayden 47 not out, T. J. Barsby 69, S. G. Law 38 not out). *Queensland 6 pts.*

In the first innings, Siddons was given out caught behind when 31; umpire Steve Randell reversed the decision and he went on to 130.

At Sydney, October 26, 27, 28, 29. New South Wales won by 218 runs. New South Wales* 457 for five dec. (M. A. Taylor 53, S. R. Waugh 107, M. E. Waugh 44, M. G. Bevan 103 not out, S. Lee 101 not out) and 188 for two dec. (M. J. Slater 100 not out, S. R. Waugh 54); Tasmania 262 (D. F. Hills 43, J. Cox 62, S. Young 35; G. D. McGrath three for 48, S. H. Cook three for 43) and 165 (D. C. Boon 57, R. T. Ponting 43; S. H. Cook four for 20, S. Lee four for 20). *New South Wales 6 pts.*

At Melbourne, November 1, 2, 3. New South Wales won by six wickets. Victoria* 158 (M. T. G. Elliott 53, J. R. Bakker 31; G. R. J. Matthews four for 52, D. A. Freedman three for 19) and 241 (M. T. G. Elliott 32, D. S. Berry 48, S. K. Warne 36, D. W. Fleming 30; G. D. McGrath three for 59, G. R. J. Matthews three for 101); New South Wales 344 (M. A. Taylor 126, S. R. Waugh 80, M. G. Bevan 44 not out; S. K. Warne five for 122) and 56 for four (P. R. Reiffel three for 19). *New South Wales 6 pts.*

Simon Cook fractured his tibia while bowling the second over of the match and took no further part; Fleming injured a hamstring in the fourth over of New South Wales's first innings and did not bowl again. Freedman took his three wickets in four balls. Taylor took seven catches.

At Hobart, November 2, 3, 4, 5. Drawn. Tasmania* 458 for two dec. (D. F. Hills 220 not out, D. C. Boon 88, R. T. Ponting 118 not out) and 290 for three dec. (J. Cox 39, D. C. Boon 56, R. T. Ponting 100 not out, S. Young 62 not out); Queensland 377 for one dec. (M. L. Hayden 152 not out, M. L. Love 185 not out, Extras 35) and 260 for five (T. J. Barsby 74, S. G. Law 107 not out; M. W. Ridgway three for 59). *Tasmania 2 pts.*

Hills's 220 not out, his maiden double-hundred, lasted 440 minutes and 323 balls and included 25 fours. Hayden and Love added 368 for Queensland's second wicket in 255 minutes, a state record. Only four wickets fell on the first three days for 923 runs (four hours were lost to rain). Ponting's second hundred came off 97 balls and Law scored 107 not out in 104 balls.

At Adelaide, November 24, 25, 26, 27. Western Australia won by 146 runs. Western Australia* 309 (M. E. Hussey 48, T. M. Moody 31, A. C. Gilchrist 99 not out, B. P. Julian 42; M. A. Harrity four for 75, T. B. A. May three for 83) and 376 for nine dec. (M. P. Lavender 32, J. L. Langer 153, D. R. Martyn 43, A. C. Gilchrist 68; J. N. Gillespie three for 94, T. B. A. May three for 65); South Australia 353 for nine dec. (P. C. Nobes 48, G. S. Blewett 44, D. S. Lehmann 116, J. D. Siddons 96; B. A. Reid four for 53, B. P. Julian five for 70) and 186 (B. A. Johnson 54, G. S. Blewett 66; B. A. Reid three for 40, G. B. Hogg five for 59). *Western Australia 6 pts, South Australia 2 pts.*

At Hobart, November 24, 25, 26, 27. New South Wales won by 109 runs. New South Wales 368 for nine dec. (M. J. Slater 55, G. R. J. Matthews 73, S. Lee 63, S. M. Thompson 40, N. D. Maxwell 46 not out; S. Young four for 74) and 270 for five dec. (M. A. Taylor 73, M. J. Slater

50, K. J. Roberts 62, G. R. J. Matthews 40 not out, S. Lee 33 not out); Tasmania* 263 (D. F. Hills 85, J. Cox 33, R. T. Ponting 46, R. J. Tucker 40 not out; S. M. Thompson three for 59, N. D. Maxwell six for 56) and 266 (D. F. Hills 32, J. Cox 42, S. Young 57, M. J. Di Venuto 46, M. N. Atkinson 31 not out; S. M. Thompson three for 65, G. R. J. Matthews four for 31). *New South Wales 6 pts.*

At Brisbane, November 30, December 1, 2. Queensland won by an innings and 11 runs. Western Australia* 110 (A. J. Bichel five for 31) and 241 (D. R. Martyn 37, T. M. Moody 82, A. C. Gilchrist 47; M. S. Kasprowicz five for 72); Queensland 362 (M. L. Hayden 32, T. J. Barsby 133, J. P. Maher 88, W. A. Seccombe 48 not out, M. S. Kasprowicz 31; J. Angel five for 90, B. J. Oldroyd three for 41). *Queensland 6 pts.*

Queensland wicket-keeper Seccombe made ten catches and one stumping in the match.

At Adelaide, November 30, December 1, 2, 3. South Australia won by six wickets. Victoria* 297 (G. R. Vimpani 79, R. P. Larkin 49, C. J. Peake 46; M. A. Harrity four for 84) and 237 (M. T. G. Elliott 35, D. M. Jones 85, C. J. Peake 43; T. B. A. May five for 70); South Australia 397 (P. C. Nobes 43, B. A. Johnson 61, D. S. Lehmann 103, J. A. Brayshaw 113; B. A. Williams six for 98) and 141 for four (D. S. Webber 45 not out, D. S. Lehmann 44 not out). *South Australia 6 pts, Victoria −0.1 pts.*

Scheduled as a day/night game, but the floodlights were not ready.

At Melbourne, December 13, 14, 15, 16. Tasmania won by four wickets. Victoria* 430 for six dec. (M. T. G. Elliott 203, G. R. Vimpani 71, D. M. Jones 45, P. J. Roach 62 not out) and 174 for seven dec. (G. R. Vimpani 51, D. M. Jones 37, G. B. Gardiner 31; M. A. Hatton four for 48); Tasmania 292 (D. F. Hills 54, J. Cox 99, D. C. Boon 45, S. Young 45, Extras 33; I. J. Harvey three for 46) and 313 for six (D. F. Hills 59, J. Cox 79, R. J. Tucker 95 not out, M. N. Atkinson 40; D. W. Fleming three for 72). *Tasmania 6 pts, Victoria 1.8 pts.*

Elliott's 203, his maiden double-hundred, lasted 481 minutes and 358 balls and included 17 fours and one six. Hills and Cox shared century opening stands in both innings.

At Adelaide, December 29, 30, 31, January 1. South Australia won by 141 runs. South Australia* 331 (G. S. Blewett 51, P. C. Nobes 56, D. S. Webber 50, D. S. Lehmann 32, T. B. A. May 30, Extras 32; G. J. Rowell three for 50) and 252 for nine dec. (D. S. Webber 42, D. S. Lehmann 71, J. A. Brayshaw 47; A. J. Bichel four for 58, G. J. Rowell three for 31); Queensland 200 (A. R. Border 79; T. B. A. May five for 88, P. E. McIntyre three for 46) and 242 (A. R. Border 94, A. J. Bichel 36; J. N. Gillespie four for 50, T. B. A. May six for 83). *South Australia 6 pts.*

At Perth, December 29, 30, 31, January 1. Drawn. Western Australia* 413 for seven dec. (M. E. Hussey 37, J. L. Langer 161, A. C. Gilchrist 82, G. B. Hogg 31) and 238 for eight (D. R. Martyn 30, J. L. Langer 56, T. M. Moody 59; T. F. Corbett three for 64); Victoria 215 (M. T. G. Elliott 104 not out, C. J. Peake 34; B. A. Reid five for 36) and 459 for nine dec. (M. T. G. Elliott 135, D. M. Jones 70, I. J. Harvey 55, P. J. Roach 84, B. A. Williams 41 not out; G. B. Hogg five for 126). *Western Australia 2 pts.*

Moody replaced Martyn as Western Australian captain. Elliott carried his bat for 317 minutes in the first innings and completed his second century of the match when Victoria followed on. Williams was unable to bowl in Western Australia's second innings; a stress fracture of the back ruled him out for the rest of the season.

At Perth, January 5, 6, 7, 8. Drawn. South Australia 235 (D. S. Lehmann 62, J. A. Brayshaw 60; B. A. Reid three for 54, J. Angel three for 53) and 390 (G. S. Blewett 96, D. S. Webber 37, D. S. Lehmann 161, J. D. Siddons 40; T. M. Moody four for 68, B. P. Julian three for 81); Western Australia* 377 (M. P. Lavender 34, M. E. Hussey 96, J. L. Langer 44, G. B. Hogg 66, B. J. Oldroyd 47; T. B. A. May four for 131) and 204 for nine (M. E. Hussey 38, M. P. Lavender 55, J. L. Langer 51 not out; J. N. Gillespie six for 68). *Western Australia 2 pts.*

Adam Gilchrist took seven catches in South Australia's second innings, a Western Australian record.

At Adelaide, January 12, 13, 14, 15. South Australia won by 122 runs. South Australia* 392 (P. C. Nobes 121, J. D. Siddons 110, J. N. Gillespie 35, Extras 40; A. M. Stuart three for 67) and 243 for eight dec. (P. C. Nobes 55, D. S. Webber 89); New South Wales 284 (K. J. Roberts 50, G. R. J. Matthews 55, P. A. Emery 60, S. M. Thompson 49 not out; J. N. Gillespie three for 71, P. E. McIntyre three for 70) and 229 (M. J. Slater 44, K. J. Roberts 39; J. N. Gillespie three for 39, T. B. A. May four for 72, P. E. McIntyre three for 59). *South Australia 6 pts.*

On the first day, South Australia were 54 for four; then Nobes and Siddons added 228 in 211 minutes.

At Hobart, January 12, 13, 14, 15. Tasmania won by ten wickets. Victoria* 275 (D. M. Jones 53, C. J. Peake 36, I. J. Harvey 85; J. P. Marquet four for 63, S. Young three for 51) and 206 (G. R. Vimpani 46, D. M. Jones 58; M. W. Ridgway three for 37, R. J. Tucker three for 33); Tasmania 455 for eight dec. (D. F. Hills 66, M. A. Hatton 35, D. C. Boon 108, M. J. Di Venuto 61, S. Young 100 not out, M. N. Atkinson 37; D. W. Fleming three for 112, D. J. Saker three for 105) and 27 for no wkt. *Tasmania 6 pts.*

Tasmania's third successive Shield win over Victoria.

At Brisbane, January 26, 27, 28, 29. Drawn. Queensland* 533 for six dec. (M. L. Hayden 234, M. L. Love 186, S. G. Law 53); Tasmania 336 (D. F. Hills 85, M. J. Di Venuto 89, S. Young 56, Extras 40; A. J. Bichel four for 87, S. G. Law five for 39) and 330 for eight (S. Young 175 not out, R. J. Tucker 42, C. R. Miller 30, Extras 32; G. J. Rowell three for 53). *Queensland 2 pts.*

Hayden's 234 lasted 503 minutes and 392 balls and included 29 fours and three sixes, but he suffered stress fractures to the vertebrae. He and Love added 365 for Queensland's second wicket in 334 minutes; in their previous match against Tasmania, in November, they shared a stand of 368. Following on, Tasmania were 42 for three, still 155 behind, at the start of the final day, but lost only five more wickets. Rowell bowled 17 no-balls (conceding 34) over two innings.

At Sydney, January 26, 27, 28, 29 (day/night). Drawn. Western Australia* 402 (M. E. Hussey 105, D. R. Martyn 41, G. B. Hogg 111 not out, B. P. Julian 43; N. D. Maxwell three for 75) and 193 for four dec. (M. E. Hussey 49, M. P. Lavender 73, D. R. Martyn 37; D. A. Freedman three for 71); New South Wales 259 (R. J. Davison 44, S. Lee 69, N. D. Maxwell 30, Extras 45; B. A. Reid three for 59, B. P. Julian five for 58) and 220 for five (C. J. Richards 46, M. G. Bevan 109). *Western Australia 2 pts.*

Hogg scored a maiden hundred after being dropped before scoring.

At Hobart, February 7, 8, 9, 10. South Australia won by six wickets. Tasmania 258 for eight dec. (D. F. Hills 47, D. C. Boon 31, M. N. Atkinson 59 not out, C. R. Miller 31; P. Wilson four for 50) and 21 for one dec.; South Australia* forfeited first innings and 280 for four (D. S. Webber 46, D. S. Lehmann 105, J. A. Brayshaw 80 not out). *South Australia 6 pts, Tasmania 2 pts.*

No play on the second and third days. Lehmann scored his fifth hundred of the season.

At Brisbane, February 7, 8, 9 (day/night). Queensland won by 12 runs. Queensland 150 (M. S. Kasprowicz 44, Extras 32; A. M. Stuart four for 48, N. D. Maxwell three for 17) and 181 (T. J. Barsby 43, W. A. Seccombe 36; A. M. Stuart four for 33, G. R. J. Matthews four for 34); New South Wales* 159 (R. Chee Quee 32; D. Tazelaar five for 42) and 160 (R. Chee Quee 32, B. E. McNamara 36; M. S. Kasprowicz three for 57, D. Tazelaar four for 29, C. G. Rackemann three for 40). *Queensland 6 pts, New South Wales 2 pts.*

On the first day, 19 wickets fell for 301.

At Melbourne, February 13, 14, 15, 16 (day/night). Victoria won by ten wickets. South Australia 309 (P. C. Nobes 86, T. J. Nielsen 115; D. J. Saker three for 82) and 229 (P. C. Nobes 74, D. S. Lehmann 64; D. J. Saker three for 66, I. J. Harvey three for 25, A. I. C. Dodemaide four for 49); Victoria* 519 for seven dec. (M. T. G. Elliott 200, W. G. Ayres 73, D. M. Jones 56, I. J. Harvey 136; J. N. Gillespie three for 105, P. E. McIntyre three for 171) and 20 for no wkt. *Victoria 6 pts.*

Elliott's 200, his fifth century of the season and his second double, lasted 480 minutes and 364 balls and included 18 fours and a six. Harvey's 136, his maiden hundred, lasted 122 minutes and 132 balls and included 15 fours and three sixes. Victorian wicket-keeper Peter Roach took ten catches in the match.

At Perth, February 13, 14, 15, 16 (day/night). Western Australia won by seven wickets. Queensland 154 (M. P. Mott 35; S. R. Cary three for 49) and 237 (M. L. Love 89, A. R. Border 45; J. Angel five for 45); Western Australia* 207 (T. M. Moody 59, A. C. Gilchrist 35; J. P. Maher three for 11) and 185 for three (M. E. Hussey 31, M. P. Lavender 77, J. L. Langer 32). *Western Australia 6 pts.*

Bruce Reid announced his retirement because of a side-strain.

At Sydney, March 8, 9, 10, 11. Drawn. New South Wales 319 for five dec. (J. L. Arnberger 47, M. T. Haywood 97, K. J. Roberts 72, G. R. J. Matthews 40 not out, P. A. Emery 31 not out); Victoria* 99 (B. P. Ricci 36; A. M. Stuart four for 22, G. R. J. Matthews four for 19) and 338 for eight (G. R. Vimpani 54, D. M. Jones 45, B. P. Ricci 55, I. J. Harvey 46, A. I. C. Dodemaide 49 not out, I. S. L. Hewett 34 not out; A. M. Stuart four for 48, G. R. J. Matthews three for 75). *New South Wales 2 pts.*

Eight hours were lost to rain.

At Perth, March 8, 9, 10, 11. Tasmania won by four wickets. Western Australia 224 (T. M. Moody 90; J. P. Marquet three for 50, M. W. Ridgway three for 57) and 361 for eight dec. (J. L. Langer 107, D. R. Martyn 203 not out; J. P. Marquet five for 94); Tasmania* 184 (M. J. Di Venuto 104; J. Angel six for 68, B. P. Julian three for 42) and 402 for six (J. Cox 96, M. J. Di Venuto 66, D. C. Boon 152, R. J. Tucker 37; J. Angel three for 64). *Tasmania 6 pts, Western Australia 2 pts.*

Ridgway lost nine kilograms in the heat of the first day. Martyn's 203 not out, his first century for 17 months, lasted 338 minutes and 271 balls and included 23 fours and one six. Challenged to score 402 in 125 overs, Tasmania completed their first win in Perth with seven balls to spare.

At Sydney, March 14, 15, 16. Queensland won by ten wickets. Queensland* 371 (T. J. Barsby 79, M. L. Hayden 44, M. L. Love 69, A. R. Border 78; G. R. J. Matthews five for 134, D. A. Freedman five for 91) and one for no wkt; New South Wales 193 (R. Chee Quee 59; A. J. Bichel three for 34, P. W. Jackson three for 39) and 178 (P. A. Emery 72; M. S. Kasprowicz five for 34). *Queensland 6 pts.*

Dean (D. P.) Waugh of New South Wales, brother of Steve and Mark, made his first-class debut.

At Adelaide, March 14, 15, 16, 17. South Australia won by 21 runs. South Australia* 507 for seven dec. (G. S. Blewett 135, D. S. Lehmann 89, J. A. Brayshaw 141 not out, J. D. Siddons 36, T. B. A. May 41; M. W. Ridgway four for 166) and 182 for nine dec. (D. S. Lehmann 50, J. A. Brayshaw 59; M. W. Ridgway five for 64, C. R. Miller three for 47); Tasmania 320 (D. F. Hills 70, D. C. Boon 117, S. Young 32; P. E. McIntyre four for 75) and 348 (D. F. Hills 30, M. J. Di Venuto 154, S. Young 38, C. R. Miller 34, Extras 35; T. B. A. May four for 106). *South Australia 6 pts.*

At Melbourne, March 14, 15, 16, 17. Victoria won by 76 runs. Victoria* 152 (W. G. Ayres 79, B. J. Hodge 43; J. Angel three for 41, B. P. Julian five for 41) and 456 for six dec. (M. T. G. Elliott 98, W. G. Ayres 140, D. M. Jones 107, I. J. Harvey 54); Western Australia 223 (R. M. Baker 46, T. M. Moody 60; A. I. C. Dodemaide six for 67) and 309 (M. E. Hussey 85, T. M. Moody 37, A. C. Gilchrist 59, B. P. Julian 31). *Victoria 6 pts, Western Australia 2 pts.*

Opener Ayres batted throughout Victoria's first innings.

At Sydney, March 23, 24, 25, 26. Drawn. South Australia* 383 (P. C. Nobes 70, G. S. Blewett 106, D. S. Lehmann 82, T. J. Nielsen 32, T. B. A. May 33; G. D. McGrath three for 70, S. Lee three for 53) and 234 (B. A. Johnson 90, P. C. Nobes 38, D. S. Lehmann 35; G. D. McGrath three for 39); New South Wales 267 (M. A. Taylor 38, M. E. Waugh 57, M. G. Bevan 87, G. R. J. Matthews 45; J. N. Gillespie four for 50, P. E. McIntyre four for 94) and 323 for nine (M. A. Taylor 32, S. R. Waugh 41, M. G. Bevan 57, P. A. Emery 36, D. A. Freedman 54 not out; P. E. McIntyre six for 133). *South Australia 2 pts.*

In South Australia's first innings, Nobes was hit on the head by McGrath when seven. Blewett scored his fifth century of the season. May did not bowl in either New South Wales innings because of bruised fingers, and Gillespie did not bowl in the second innings because of a bruised foot. Matthews played his 104th game for New South Wales, a state record.

At Hobart, March 23, 24, 25, 26. Western Australia won by five wickets. Tasmania* 357 for nine dec. (D. F. Hills 43, J. Cox 54, M. J. Di Venuto 93, D. C. Boon 91; J. Angel three for 79, S. R. Cary three for 82) and 183 (J. Cox 34, S. Young 51 not out; S. R. Cary three for 35, T. M. Moody seven for 38); Western Australia 357 (M. E. Hussey 47, J. L. Langer 120, R. M. Baker 32, D. R. Martyn 65; J. P. Marquet three for 83, M. W. Ridgway four for 89) and 184 for five (D. R. Martyn 62 not out, A. C. Gilchrist 41 not out; J. P. Marquet three for 45). *Western Australia 6 pts, Tasmania 1 pt.*

Tasmania earned one point for a tie on first innings.

At Melbourne, March 23, 24, 25, 26. Victoria won by five wickets. Queensland 142 (D. J. Saker seven for 32) and 338 (M. L. Hayden 33, M. L. Love 88, I. A. Healy 45, A. R. Border 34, A. J. Bichel 30, Extras 45; D. J. Saker four for 88, A. I. C. Dodemaide five for 70); Victoria* 255 (W. G. Ayres 68, D. M. Jones 69; M. S. Kasprowicz five for 74) and 226 for five (M. T. G. Elliott 54, W. G. Ayres 100, B. J. Hodge 33 not out; M. S. Kasprowicz five for 74). *Victoria 6 pts.*

In the second innings, his last before retirement, Border overtook Peter Burge as the second-highest run-scorer for Queensland; his 7,661 was second only to Sam Trimble's 9,465. In his 20-year first-class career, he had scored 27,131 runs in 385 matches at 51.38, including 70 hundreds. Among Australians, only Bradman, with 28,067 in 234 matches, has scored more.

FINAL

SOUTH AUSTRALIA v WESTERN AUSTRALIA

At Adelaide, March 30, 31, April 1, 2, 3. Drawn. Toss: Western Australia.

South Australia's last two batsmen, McIntyre and George, survived 59 balls to draw the match and thus win the Shield by dint of finishing top of the table. Needing an outright victory, Western Australia were forced to make the running. They recovered from an unpromising 71 for three, thanks to a tremendous innings by Gilchrist. He came in at 215 for five and helped to add another 305, hammering both pace and spin to all parts of the Oval. He went to his hundred with a pull off Gillespie for the second of his five sixes; his eighth-wicket partnership of 168 with Hogg took only 163 minutes. South Australia's batting was laborious by comparison, and Lehmann and Nobes took more than three hours to add 123. Several of the home players were carrying injuries, but Western Australia also had medical problems, and Angel needed pain-killers to bowl at all. However, Julian rose to the occasion and bowled superbly in both innings. South Australia, in no hurry, extended their first innings into the fourth day and kept the lead down to 173. A revised batting order did nothing for Western Australia's need for quick runs and only a steadying partnership of 101 between Moody and Hussey enabled Moody to declare with a day plus 100 minutes left. Apart from some lusty hits by Brayshaw, South Australia concentrated on survival. Blewett batted nearly five and a half hours for 72, Siddons 166 minutes for four and May 64 minutes for nought, while the last 54 overs yielded just 39. The end justified the means. People rushed from their offices to fill the ground for the last dramatic moments and the state's first Sheffield Shield for 14 years.

Close of play: First day, Western Australia 255-6 (A. C. Gilchrist 25*, J. Angel 0*); Second day, South Australia 100-2 (P. C. Nobes 57*, D. S. Lehmann 24*); Third day, South Australia 330-7 (J. A. Brayshaw 70*, J. N. Gillespie 10*); Fourth day, South Australia 57-2 (G. S. Blewett 22*, J. N. Gillespie 4*).

Western Australia

M. P. Lavender c Siddons b May	18	– c Nobes b Gillespie	6
M. E. Hussey lbw b Blewett	11	– (7) c Nielsen b Gillespie	32
J. L. Langer c Nielsen b Gillespie	30	– c Lehmann b May	28
R. M. Baker c Nielsen b George	83	– (5) c Nielsen b Gillespie	11
*T. M. Moody b Gillespie	68	– (6) c sub b Gillespie	72
D. R. Martyn run out	9	– (2) run out	2
†A. C. Gilchrist not out	189	– (4) run out	0
J. Angel c Nielsen b Gillespie	7		
G. B. Hogg lbw b George	61	– not out	1
B. P. Julian c George b May	25	– (8) c May b George	2
L-b 4, w 1, n-b 14	19	L-b 5, n-b 10	15
1/23 2/55 3/71 4/200 5/215 6/251 7/291 8/459 9/520	(9 wkts dec.) 520	1/12 2/12 3/18 4/36 5/64 6/165 7/167 8/169	(8 wkts dec.) 169

S. R. Cary did not bat.

Bowling: *First Innings*—Gillespie 30–10–96–3; George 30–4–102–2; Blewett 15–4–53–1; May 47.4–9–157–2; McIntyre 23–0–105–0; Lehmann 1–0–3–0. *Second Innings*—Gillespie 9–1–33–4; George 8.5–2–36–1; May 18–3–57–1; Blewett 6–1–16–0; McIntyre 8–1–22–0.

South Australia

G. S. Blewett lbw b Angel	5	– lbw b Julian	72
P. C. Nobes b Julian	103	– b Hogg	24
D. S. Webber c Langer b Angel	0	– c Gilchrist b Baker	5
D. S. Lehmann c Langer b Angel	43	– (5) lbw b Julian	0
*J. D. Siddons b Julian	38	– (7) c Langer b Hogg	4
J. A. Brayshaw run out	87	– c and b Hogg	66
†T. J. Nielsen c Langer b Julian	27	– (8) b Angel	4
T. B. A. May c Lavender b Martyn	5	– (9) b Julian	0
J. N. Gillespie c Gilchrist b Julian	10	– (4) c Moody b Julian	5
P. E. McIntyre b Julian	0	– not out	6
S. P. George not out	0	– not out	1
B 3, l-b 1, w 3, n-b 22	29	B 7, w 1, n-b 13	21
1/8 2/8 3/131 4/208 5/217 6/291 7/296 8/331 9/331	347	1/40 2/53 3/67 4/67 5/169 6/189 7/193 8/198 9/202	(9 wkts) 208

Bowling: *First Innings*—Angel 17.5–4–56–3; Cary 16–6–29–0; Moody 27–10–45–0; Julian 30.2–7–95–5; Baker 8–5–9–0; Hogg 34–10–89–0; Langer 5–2–8–0; Martyn 4–1–12–1. *Second Innings*—Julian 29–13–56–4; Angel 19–7–27–1; Hogg 36–25–42–3; Baker 11–3–26–1; Moody 19–9–24–0; Martyn 7–5–6–0; Cary 8–4–20–0.

Umpires: D. B. Hair and S. G. Randell.

SHEFFIELD SHIELD WINNERS

1892-93	Victoria
1893-94	South Australia
1894-95	Victoria
1895-96	New South Wales
1896-97	New South Wales
1897-98	Victoria
1898-99	Victoria
1899-1900	New South Wales
1900-01	Victoria
1901-02	New South Wales
1902-03	New South Wales
1903-04	New South Wales
1904-05	New South Wales
1905-06	New South Wales
1906-07	New South Wales
1907-08	Victoria
1908-09	New South Wales
1909-10	South Australia
1910-11	New South Wales
1911-12	New South Wales
1912-13	South Australia
1913-14	New South Wales
1914-15	Victoria
1915-19	No competition
1919-20	New South Wales
1920-21	New South Wales
1921-22	Victoria
1922-23	New South Wales
1923-24	Victoria
1924-25	Victoria
1925-26	New South Wales
1926-27	South Australia
1927-28	Victoria
1928-29	New South Wales
1929-30	Victoria
1930-31	Victoria
1931-32	New South Wales
1932-33	New South Wales
1933-34	Victoria
1934-35	Victoria
1935-36	South Australia
1936-37	Victoria
1937-38	New South Wales
1938-39	South Australia
1939-40	New South Wales
1940-46	No competition
1946-47	Victoria
1947-48	Western Australia
1948-49	New South Wales
1949-50	New South Wales
1950-51	Victoria
1951-52	New South Wales
1952-53	South Australia
1953-54	New South Wales
1954-55	New South Wales
1955-56	New South Wales
1956-57	New South Wales
1957-58	New South Wales
1958-59	New South Wales
1959-60	New South Wales
1960-61	New South Wales
1961-62	New South Wales
1962-63	Victoria
1963-64	South Australia
1964-65	New South Wales
1965-66	New South Wales
1966-67	Victoria
1967-68	Western Australia
1968-69	South Australia
1969-70	Victoria
1970-71	South Australia
1971-72	Western Australia
1972-73	Western Australia
1973-74	Victoria
1974-75	Western Australia
1975-76	South Australia
1976-77	Western Australia
1977-78	Western Australia
1978-79	Victoria
1979-80	Victoria
1980-81	Western Australia
1981-82	South Australia
1982-83	New South Wales
1983-84	Western Australia
1984-85	New South Wales
1985-86	New South Wales
1986-87	Western Australia
1987-88	Western Australia
1988-89	Western Australia
1989-90	New South Wales
1990-91	Victoria
1991-92	Western Australia
1992-93	New South Wales
1993-94	New South Wales
1994-95	Queensland
1995-96	South Australia

New South Wales have won the Shield 42 times, Victoria 25, South Australia and Western Australia 13, Queensland 1, Tasmania 0.

OTHER FIRST-CLASS MATCHES

At Brisbane, September 26, 27, 28. Queensland won by six wickets. Western Province* 112 (J. H. Kallis 58; M. S. Kasprowicz six for 17) and 478 for three dec. (G. Kirsten 130, J. H. Kallis 186 not out, J. B. Commins 120); Queensland 275 (T. J. Barsby 65, I. A. Healy 41, M. S. Kasprowicz 33; E. O. Simons three for 21) and 316 for four (T. J. Dixon 122, M. L. Love 60, S. G. Law 73, A. Symonds 31 not out).

At Hurstville Oval, Sydney, October 3, 4, 5. New South Wales won by 126 runs. New South Wales 244 for six dec. (M. G. Bevan 45, S. R. Waugh 47, S. Lee 84, P. A. Emery 36 not out; C. R. Matthews four for 46) and 202 for three dec. (M. G. Bevan 119 not out, S. Lee 67 not out); Western Province* 128 (P. Kirsten 32; A. M. Stuart three for 31) and 192 (S. G. Koenig 57, H. D. Ackerman 48; D. A. Freedman five for 75).

MERCANTILE MUTUAL INSURANCE CUP

Note: Matches in this section were not first-class.

At Brisbane, October 8. No result. Queensland* 173 for four (33.2 overs) (M. L. Hayden 62 not out, S. G. Law 77) v Victoria.

At North Sydney, October 15. New South Wales won by 11 runs. New South Wales* 273 for eight (50 overs) (M. J. Slater 77, M. A. Taylor 44, S. R. Waugh 49, M. G. Bevan 30; S. A. Prestwidge four for 56); Queensland 262 (49.4 overs) (M. L. Hayden 30, S. G. Law 32, M. L. Love 31, A. R. Border 50, C. J. McDermott 41).

At Perth, October 15. Western Australia won by three wickets. Tasmania* 204 for seven (50 overs) (M. J. Di Venuto 59, D. C. Boon 54, S. Young 45); Western Australia 207 for seven (49 overs) (M. P. Lavender 48, J. L. Langer 93, D. R. Martyn 36).

At Adelaide, October 21. Tasmania won by eight wickets. South Australia* 176 (48.5 overs) (D. S. Webber 38, T. J. Nielsen 40; M. W. Ridgway three for 47); Tasmania 177 for two (39.4 overs) (R. T. Ponting 87 not out, D. C. Boon 54 not out).

At Perth, October 22. New South Wales won by seven wickets. Western Australia* 200 for eight (50 overs) (M. P. Lavender 65, A. C. Gilchrist 64; G. D. McGrath three for 27, S. Lee four for 59); New South Wales 201 for three (46 overs) (M. A. Taylor 70, S. R. Waugh 90).

Steve Waugh hit a sponsor's sign and earned New South Wales a $A140,000 jackpot.

At Brisbane, October 29. Queensland won by 61 runs. Queensland 274 for seven (50 overs) (M. L. Hayden 51, S. G. Law 109, A. Symonds 42; B. N. Wigney three for 39); South Australia* 213 (47.4 overs) (J. D. Siddons 61, D. S. Webber 34, T. J. Nielsen 31; A. J. Bichel four for 45).

At Melbourne, November 5. New South Wales won on scoring-rate when rain ended play. Victoria 106 (38 overs) (N. D. Maxwell four for 15); New South Wales* 91 for three (26.2 overs) (M. E. Waugh 43 not out).

At Adelaide, December 10. South Australia won by six wickets. Western Australia 160 for eight (50 overs) (R. M. Baker 55); South Australia* 163 for four (46.1 overs) (D. S. Lehmann 52, P. C. Nobes 40, J. D. Siddons 41 not out).

Scheduled as a day/night game, but the floodlights were not ready.

At Hobart, December 10. Victoria won by 43 runs. Victoria 218 for four (50 overs) (D. M. Jones 121 not out, M. T. G. Elliott 64); Tasmania* 175 for eight (50 overs) (M. N. Atkinson 33, A. J. Daly 34 not out; T. F. Corbett three for 23).

At Melbourne, February 2 (day/night). Western Australia won by five wickets. Victoria* 180 (49.2 overs) (D. M. Jones 42, I. J. Harvey 36; T. M. Moody three for 37); Western Australia 181 for five (45.4 overs) (M. P. Lavender 72, J. L. Langer 58).

At Hobart, February 3. Tasmania won by 17 runs. Tasmania 175 (50 overs) (R. T. Ponting 37, M. W. Ridgway 32; M. S. Kasprowicz four for 21, S. A. Prestwidge three for 36); Queensland* 158 (49 overs) (J. P. Maher 36, I. A. Healy 48; J. P. Marquet five for 23).

At Sydney, February 4. South Australia won by three wickets. New South Wales* 248 for seven (50 overs) (K. J. Roberts 101, R. Chee Quee 80; J. N. Gillespie four for 46); South Australia 249 for seven (50 overs) (D. S. Lehmann 67, J. D. Siddons 58, J. A. Brayshaw 35, J. C. Scuderi 55 not out).

After the match ended, South Australia's total was increased by two because a no-ball had been missed in the 48th over. This transformed their one-run defeat into victory.

At Hobart, February 17. New South Wales won by 56 runs. New South Wales 207 for nine (50 overs) (M. W. Patterson 34, M. T. Haywood 57, G. R. J. Matthews 30; M. W. Ridgway three for 33); Tasmania* 151 (43.3 overs) (M. J. Di Venuto 43; A. M. Stuart three for 40).

At Melbourne, February 18. South Australia won by seven wickets. Victoria 186 (44.4 overs) (B. P. Ricci 42); South Australia* 187 for three (46 overs) (D. S. Lehmann 31, P. C. Nobes 45, G. S. Blewett 59 not out).

At Perth, February 18 (day/night). Queensland won by eight runs. Queensland* 237 (49.5 overs) (M. L. Love 47, A. Symonds 85; B. P. Julian four for 43); Western Australia 229 (49.4 overs) (D. R. Martyn 79, A. C. Gilchrist 59; A. C. Dale four for 26).

New South Wales 8 pts, South Australia 6 pts, Queensland 5 pts, Western Australia 4 pts, Tasmania 4 pts, Victoria 3 pts. Western Australia qualified for the semi-finals ahead of Tasmania on better net run-rate.

Semi-finals

At Adelaide, February 24. Queensland won by 91 runs. Queensland 230 for five (50 overs) (T. J. Barsby 48, J. P. Maher 62, A. Symonds 34, A. R. Border 36; J. N. Gillespie three for 33); South Australia* 139 (42.2 overs) (D. S. Lehmann 31, D. S. Webber 44; M. S. Kasprowicz three for 39, G. I. Foley four for 34).

At Sydney, February 25. Western Australia won by three wickets. New South Wales* 210 (48.2 overs) (M. T. Haywood 60, K. J. Roberts 32; B. P. Julian three for 44); Western Australia 211 for seven (47.2 overs) (A. C. Gilchrist 76 not out, B. P. Julian 48 not out).

Final

At Brisbane, March 3. Queensland won by four wickets. Western Australia* 166 (49.1 overs) (T. M. Moody 40, Extras 31; S. A. Prestwidge three for 39, G. I. Foley three for 34); Queensland 167 for six (44.5 overs) (T. J. Barsby 50; B. P. Julian three for 46).

SHEFFIELD SHIELD PLAYER OF THE YEAR

The Sheffield Shield Player of the Year Award for 1995-96 was won by Matthew Elliott of Victoria. The Award, instituted in 1975-76, is adjudicated by the umpires over the course of the season. Each of the two umpires standing in each of the 30 Sheffield Shield matches (excluding the final) allocated marks of 3, 2 and 1 to the three players who most impressed them during the game. Elliott earned 23 votes in his nine matches, eight ahead of Darren Lehmann of South Australia. He also won the Player of the Year award sponsored by Lord's Taverners and decided by his fellow players.

CRICKET IN SOUTH AFRICA, 1995-96

By COLIN BRYDEN and ANDREW SAMSON

Meyrick Pringle

With the national team performing exceptionally well, failing only in their quest to win the World Cup, South African cricket was in a healthy state at the end of the 1995-96 season. South Africa beat Zimbabwe and England in Tests and won 18 of their 20 limited-overs internationals. It was a record which prompted Peter Pollock, the convenor of selectors, to suggest that a five-year plan to make South Africa the top cricket nation had been successfully implemented a year ahead of schedule. Since their return from 22 years of international isolation, they had won series against all the Test countries except West Indies – to whom they lost their one-off comeback Test – and Australia, with whom they had shared two rubbers. Pollock sensibly added that it was rarely possible to identify one team as unquestionably the best, such as West Indies in the early 1980s. "You can very seldom say for sure who is number one, but what is beyond doubt is that we are up there with the giants."

In analysing the reasons for South Africa's success, Pollock paid tribute to the spirit of common purpose in the South African game, from administrators to players. Provincial interests have been put aside when necessary, although not always to the delight of the provinces. Natal were far from pleased when they were instructed to rest Shaun Pollock (Peter's son), their key strike bowler, for a crucial first-class match against Western Province. Pollock had come through his first Test and one-day series with flying colours and it was felt he needed a break before the World Cup. Western Province, at full strength, salvaged a draw after following on in a rain-affected game and went on to win the Castle Cup. Natal, having set the pace by winning five of their first six matches, also had their last match wrecked by rain and had to settle for third place; victory in either game would have secured the title.

As in the previous season, young talent blossomed, nowhere more spectacularly than in the Western Province, where Paul Adams, at 18, and Jacques Kallis, barely 20, won national colours. Adams was the find of the season. A left-arm bowler of chinamen and googlies with an extraordinary, contorted action, his emergence exceeded the wildest dreams of the game's promoters. In one shy yet resolute personage was a highly talented slow bowler and the first young non-white star to emerge since the formation of the United Cricket Board in 1991. The UCB's development programme could not take credit, however; Adams hailed from a middle-class Coloured family, came from a community in which cricket was long established and (like Kallis) attended Wynberg Boys' High, the school which produced Allan Lamb and Garth le Roux.

There were various changes to the names and make-up of the domestic tournaments. South African Breweries ended their 24-year association with provincial cricket, although they were continuing to support Test matches and the national team. It is one of the by-products of sponsorship that competitions undergo bewildering name changes. For just over a century, provinces competed for the Currie Cup, named after shipping magnate Sir Donald Currie. With the advent of the UCB, the old gold trophy was locked away and replaced by the Castle Cup. After just five seasons, that in turn was consigned to the vaults. The new sponsor was the M-Net pay television channel, which promised R20 million over five years, and from 1996-97 the premier first-class competition will be known as the Supersport Series. Meanwhile, on the one-day front, Benson and Hedges have ended their involvement in both the domestic competition and limited-overs internationals. The new sponsor was Standard Bank, which was to provide R50 million over five years. Both deals represented a considerable advance on previous sums and will further strengthen the financial structure of the game.

Amid the euphoria, however, there was some concern about future standards, especially when it was decided to expand the Supersport Series to nine teams in 1997-98 by including Griqualand West, who have already played in the senior one-day tournament. With international commitments preventing the best players from appearing in more than half their domestic fixtures, it is debatable whether there are enough players of genuine first-class standard to fill nine teams when the stars are away. For much of South Africa's isolation, only five provinces were deemed strong enough to play at top level. But Ali Bacher, the UCB's managing director, argued that Griquas' promotion would help to spread the base of the game. Another innovation was the decision that floodlights, now installed at all the main grounds, may be switched on if necessary during Supersport Series matches to reduce stoppages for bad light.

The Standard Bank limited-overs series was to be split into two competitions. As before, all 11 provinces will compete in a round-robin league, featuring day/night matches, and some daylight games on Sundays. A new knockout competition will be held later in the season, involving the top six from the league plus teams from Kenya and Mashonaland, the leading province in Zimbabwe.

There was a thrilling finish to the Castle Cup in its final season, with three teams separated by four points after winning five games apiece. Western Province won their last two matches to take the title by two points from Transvaal, who had been docked four points for preparing an unsuitable pitch against Northern Transvaal. Ironically, Transvaal lost not only the points but the game, inside two days. Natal were two points behind Transvaal.

Western Province triumphed despite losing Gary Kirsten, Brian McMillan, Craig Matthews, Jacques Kallis and Paul Adams to the national squad for extended periods. Kirsten, nevertheless, was the most prolific batsman, hitting

509 runs at 72.71 in only five matches. Hylton "H.D." Ackerman averaged more than 50 in the Castle Cup. Their player of the season, however, was the veteran swing bowler Meyrick Pringle, the leading wicket-taker in the competition with 41 at 15.29. He took five or more wickets in an innings on five occasions. Aubrey Martyn, the left-arm fast bowler who had missed a year with a back injury, made a pleasing recovery and took 20 wickets at 22.00. John Commins took over the captaincy from Eric Simons at the season's end.

Transvaal's rise owed much to the dynamic leadership of the former New Zealand captain, Ken Rutherford, the coaching of the former captain, Jimmy Cook, and the belated introduction of a youth policy. Rutherford, in the first season of a two-year contract, brought a spirit of adventure and enjoyment to the dressing-room. The pace and seam bowlers, Steven Jack, Richard Snell and Stefan Jacobs, all finished high in the Castle Cup averages, aided by lively pitches at the Wanderers. Opening batsman Brad White, who returned to the side in the second half of the season, was the most successful batsman, but two outstanding young prospects emerged in Neil McKenzie and Nick Pothas.

Natal, led by the former West Indian Test bowler Malcolm Marshall, in his final season of first-class cricket, seemed set to retain their title. Pollock was outstanding before international calls took him away, and headed the Castle Cup averages with 27 wickets at 11.37. As in 1994-95, Natal had a potent mixture of youthful all-rounders. Derek Crookes and Errol Stewart were the leading batsmen, while Lance Klusener and Ross Veenstra featured in the bowling averages. But Pollock's absence from the crucial match against Western Province and the washout of their final game at Centurion Park robbed Marshall of a fitting finale to his career.

There was a sizeable gap between these three and the rest. Free State lacked the depth to overcome the loss of national players Hansie Cronje and Allan Donald. Border's batting was prone to collapse, despite the efforts of Peter Kirsten. For Eastern Province the main batsmen, led by Louis Koen, scored heavily, but they were extraordinarily unlucky with injuries to all their front-line pace bowlers – Schultz, Botha and Baptiste. Northern Transvaal and Boland both had disappointing seasons. Western Province were on course for a double when they won all ten of their round-robin matches in the Benson and Hedges Series, an unprecedented feat, and finished seven points ahead of the field. But the other teams were strengthened by the return of the national players from the World Cup, and for the second successive season Western Province lost to Free State in the semi-finals. Boland shrugged off their poor first-class form to finish second in the one-day table, owing mainly to the batting of Kenny Jackson and their captain, Adrian Kuiper. Jackson hit a century and six fifties in nine round-robin games and added another half-century before Boland bowed out to Transvaal. He finished with 614 runs at 61.40, a tournament record. Despite having home advantage in the final, Transvaal were thrashed by Free State, who completed a hat-trick of one-day titles. After Franklyn Stephenson fell cheaply, Free State sent in a second "pinch-hitter", Bradley Player, at No. 3: he hit 83 off 50 deliveries, his team raced to 290 for six, a record for a 45-overs final, and Transvaal managed only 148 in reply. The total attendance for Benson and Hedges matches was 256,100, whereas only 81,500 paid to watch Castle Cup matches. The five Tests against England were watched by 248,700 spectators, while the attendance at the seven limited-overs internationals was 136,700.

In the three-day Bowl competition, title-holders Natal B easily headed their group but had to share the trophy with Griqualand West after they drew the final. Western Province B were one-day champions.

The anomaly of the Bowl's first-class status had yet to be fully resolved. Having initially indicated that matches involving provincial B teams would lose their first-class status, the UCB decided to split the Bowl into two divisions from 1996-97 and to seek ICC support for first-class status being awarded to the higher division. There would be automatic promotion and relegation between the divisions and Namibia would be invited to take part.

South Africa's Academy system underwent some modifications in its second year; it was felt there was too wide a spread of ability in 1995. The 24 youngsters, based at the Rand Afrikaans University in Johannesburg for four months, were mainly players who had made a mark at senior provincial level and three, Adams, Kallis and Gerhardus Liebenberg, had already represented South Africa. For the first time, the Academy included a player from Zimbabwe and one from Kenya. Women's cricket was revived during the season, with a four-team provincial tournament in Johannesburg. South Africa planned to send a team to the women's World Cup in India in 1997-98. – C.B.

Note: Orange Free State and Eastern Transvaal changed their names to Free State and Easterns before the 1995-96 season.

FIRST-CLASS AVERAGES, 1995-96

BATTING

(Qualification: 8 innings, average 40.00)

	M	*I*	*NO*	*R*	*HS*	*100s*	*Avge*
Z. de Bruyn (*Transvaal B*)	5	9	5	390	126*	1	97.50
E. L. R. Stewart (*Natal*)	7	8	2	568	207*	3	94.66
D. N. Crookes (*Natal*)	7	9	1	537	111*	1	67.12
B. M. White (*Transvaal*)	8	16	4	787	180*	3	65.58
G. Kirsten (*W. Province*)	10	16	3	812	244	3	62.46
D. J. Callaghan (*E. Province*)	9	16	4	739	133*	2	61.58
D. B. Rundle (*W. Province*)	7	9	3	324	103	1	54.00
L. J. Koen (*E. Province*)	9	16	1	804	202*	2	53.60
K. C. Wessels (*E. Province*)	9	16	1	803	173	2	53.53
H. C. Bakkes (*Free State*)	9	13	6	359	68	0	51.28
H. D. Ackerman (*W. Province*)	8	13	3	504	106*	1	50.40
L. J. Wilkinson (*Free State*)	9	17	4	605	226*	1	46.53
W. J. Cronje (*Free State*)	11	16	2	650	158	2	46.42
N. Martin (*N. Transvaal*)	6	10	3	318	89*	0	45.42
S. G. Koenig (*W. Province*)	6	10	1	401	89	0	44.55
L. P. Vorster (*N. Transvaal B*)	5	9	1	354	90*	0	44.25
P. N. Kirsten (*Border*)	9	16	0	699	147	2	43.68
S. M. Pollock (*Natal*)	10	11	3	348	74*	0	43.50
P. G. Amm (*E. Province*)	9	17	2	646	157	1	43.06
T. N. Lazard (*Boland*)	8	14	2	508	89*	0	42.33
B. M. McMillan (*W. Province*)	9	12	1	465	116	2	42.27
J. H. Kallis (*W. Province*)	8	12	0	506	146	1	42.16
W. M. Dry (*Griqualand W.*)	6	9	0	374	99	0	41.55
P. H. Barnard (*Griqualand W.*)	6	10	1	364	146	2	40.44

* *Signifies not out.*

BOWLING

(Qualification: 20 wickets)

	O	*M*	*R*	*W*	*BB*	*5W/i*	*Avge*
E. W. Kidwell (*Transvaal*)	174.3	39	477	31	6-23	2	15.38
S. M. Pollock (*Natal*)	340.1	94	798	51	7-33	5	15.64
K. G. Storey (*Natal*)	172	42	462	25	5-26	2	18.48
V. A. Walsh (*Griqualand W.*)	209	56	583	31	6-52	1	18.80
M. W. Pringle (*W. Province*)	300.4	53	887	47	6-32	5	18.87
A. Martyn (*W. Province*).........	252.1	54	685	35	6-22	3	19.57
S. Jacobs (*Transvaal*)	277.3	83	639	32	5-30	1	19.96
R. P. Snell (*Transvaal*)	194.5	41	589	28	5-64	2	21.03
R. E. Veenstra (*Natal*)	196.3	52	529	25	6-38	2	21.16
C. R. Matthews (*W. Province*)	235.3	85	508	23	5-43	1	22.08
A. C. Dawson (*W. Province*)	187.3	50	469	21	6-18	1	22.33
B. C. Fourie (*Border*)	316.5	88	739	33	6-76	2	22.39
S. D. Jack (*Transvaal*)	273.2	65	878	39	5-69	1	22.51
G. J. Smith (*N. Transvaal*)	212.5	54	616	26	5-32	1	23.69
B. N. Schultz (*E. Province*)	302.1	65	854	36	6-84	3	23.72
J. F. Venter (*Free State*)	189.1	52	504	21	4-52	0	24.00
L. Klusener (*Natal*)	191.5	30	653	27	8-34	2	24.18
A. A. Donald (*Free State*)	309.5	85	823	34	5-44	2	24.20
P. R. Adams (*W. Province*).......	415	116	1,065	43	6-101	3	24.76
S. Elworthy (*N. Transvaal*)	173	26	572	21	3-19	0	27.23
R. E. Bryson (*N. Transvaal*)	191.3	41	583	21	4-16	0	27.76
R. Telemachus (*Boland*)	272.5	50	780	28	5-72	2	27.85
C. W. Henderson (*Boland*)	405	91	1,075	36	4-33	0	29.86
F. D. Stephenson (*Free State*)	249.5	56	727	23	5-63	1	31.60
C. E. Eksteen (*Transvaal*)........	490.3	146	1,201	34	4-64	0	35.32
N. Boje (*Free State*)	406.5	113	973	27	4-39	0	36.03
T. G. Shaw (*E. Province*)	351.1	111	850	23	6-45	2	36.95
I. L. Howell (*Border*)	317.4	77	777	21	3-52	0	37.00
N. W. Pretorius (*Free State*)......	251	51	857	21	5-79	1	40.80

CASTLE CUP, 1995-96

					Bonus points		
	Played	*Won*	*Lost*	*Drawn*	*Batting*	*Bowling*	*Points*
Western Province	8	5	1	2	22	30	102
Transvaal	8	5	3	0	25	25	100†
Natal	8	5	1	2	23	25	98
Free State	8	2	2	4	24	29	73
Border	8	3	5	0	12	22	64
Eastern Province	8	2	2	4	20	21	61
Northern Transvaal	8	1	4	3	13	22	45
Boland	8	0	5	3	15	21	36

† *Transvaal had 4 points deducted for an unsatisfactory pitch.*

Outright win = 10 pts.

Bonus points are awarded for the first 100 overs of each team's first innings. One batting point is awarded for the first 150 runs and for every subsequent 50. One bowling point is awarded for the third wicket taken and for every subsequent two.

*In the following scores, * by the name of a team indicates that they won the toss.*

At Buffalo Park, East London, October 27, 28, 29, 30. Natal won by an innings and 80 runs. Natal* 448 (P. J. R. Steyn 79, N. C. Johnson 55, M. L. Bruyns 62, D. N. Crookes 83, L. Klusener 33, S. M. Pollock 53 not out; B. P. Horan three for 79, P. A. N. Emslie four for 83); Border 91 (P. J. Botha 32; S. M. Pollock seven for 33) and 277 (P. J. Botha 81, P. N. Kirsten 147; M. D. Marshall four for 48, D. N. Crookes five for 59). *Natal 17 pts, Border 2 pts.*

At Springbok Park, Bloemfontein, October 27, 28, 29, 30. Drawn. Free State* 451 for nine dec. (L. J. Wilkinson 226 not out, F. D. Stephenson 48, H. C. Bakkes 68; R. Telemachus five for 152); Boland 215 (T. N. Lazard 63, P. A. J. DeFreitas 44, L-M. Germishuys 31; N. Boje three for 37) and 226 for seven (K. C. Jackson 57, P. A. J. DeFreitas 53, L-M. Germishuys 40; F. D. Stephenson three for 68). *Free State 9 pts, Boland 5 pts.*

Wilkinson's 226 not out lasted 446 minutes and 308 balls and included 22 fours and one six. He added 185 for the eighth wicket with Bakkes.

At Centurion Park, Centurion, October 27, 28, 29, 30. Drawn. Northern Transvaal* 365 (B. J. Sommerville 45, M. J. R. Rindel 67, S. Elworthy 37, D. J. van Zyl 56, I. Pistorius 63 not out, G. J. Smith 35; B. N. Schultz six for 84) and 263 for eight dec. (A. J. Seymore 72, C. B. Lambert 108, R. F. Pienaar 35; T. G. Shaw five for 98); Eastern Province 331 for four dec. (G. C. Victor 88, L. J. Koen 82, K. C. Wessels 33, D. J. Callaghan 73 not out) and 150 for seven (K. C. Wessels 66 not out; M. C. Krug three for 32). *Northern Transvaal 4 pts, Eastern Province 6 pts.*

At Newlands, Cape Town, October 27, 28, 29, 30. Transvaal won by 79 runs. Transvaal 375 (K. R. Rutherford 134, D. R. Laing 72, N. D. McKenzie 67, S. Jacobs 35; C. R. Matthews four for 72) and 266 (N. Pothas 66, M. W. Rushmere 83, G. A. Pollock 52; C. R. Matthews five for 43); Western Province* 304 (G. Kirsten 53, J. H. Kallis 146; S. D. Jack three for 53, C. E. Eksteen three for 94) and 258 (D. L. Haynes 52, J. H. Kallis 49, J. B. Commins 37, B. M. McMillan 60; S. D. Jack four for 55, S. Jacobs three for 44). *Transvaal 19 pts, Western Province 7 pts.*

At St George's Park, Port Elizabeth, November 3, 4, 5, 6. Drawn. Eastern Province* 218 (P. G. Amm 89; A. A. Donald five for 44, F. D. Stephenson three for 35) and 458 (P. G. Amm 35, G. C. Victor 58, K. C. Wessels 173, D. J. Richardson 122; N. Boje three for 111, C. F. Craven four for 62); Free State 517 for nine dec. (D. Jordaan 88, G. F. J. Liebenberg 38, J. F. Venter 91, F. D. Stephenson 166, H. C. Bakkes 54 not out; B. N. Schultz three for 134, A. G. Huckle three for 130) and 136 for five (W. J. Cronje 70 not out; T. G. Shaw three for 41). *Eastern Province 4 pts, Free State 8 pts.*

Wessels and Richardson added 229 for the fifth wicket in Eastern Province's second innings.

At Kingsmead, Durban, November 3, 4, 5, 6. Natal won by 167 runs. Natal 297 (J. N. Rhodes 82 not out, D. N. Crookes 81, S. M. Pollock 43; S. D. Jack four for 83, R. P. Snell five for 67) and 253 (A. C. Hudson 93, M. L. Bruyns 52, S. M. Pollock 37; S. D. Jack three for 61, C. E. Eksteen four for 64); Transvaal* 259 (K. R. Rutherford 51, D. R. Laing 56, G. A. Pollock 37; R. E. Veenstra five for 77) and 124 (A. M. Bacher 53; R. E. Veenstra three for 14). *Natal 17 pts, Transvaal 7 pts.*

At Centurion Park, Centurion, November 4, 5, 6, 7. Western Province won by eight wickets. Northern Transvaal* 344 (A. J. Seymore 124, M. J. R. Rindel 42, G. J. Smith 68; C. R. Matthews three for 55) and 231 (R. F. Pienaar 38, S. Elworthy 32; P. R. Adams six for 101); Western Province 451 (D. L. Haynes 71, J. B. Commins 94, B. M. McMillan 116, H. D. Ackerman 30, E. O. Simons 54, D. B. Rundle 30; M. J. G. Davis three for 86) and 126 for two (D. L. Haynes 46 not out, J. H. Kallis 55). *Western Province 17 pts, Northern Transvaal 5 pts.*

Paul Adams had match figures of eight for 190 on Castle Cup debut.

At Boland Bank Park, Paarl, November 10, 11, 12, 13. Natal won by nine wickets. Boland* 255 (K. C. Jackson 69, A. P. Kuiper 87; S. M. Pollock four for 57) and 128 (R. E. Veenstra six for 38); Natal 363 (A. C. Hudson 67, M. L. Bruyns 36, E. L. R. Stewart 119, J. N. Rhodes 52, D. N. Crookes 51; P. A. J. DeFreitas three for 64, C. W. Henderson three for 72, B. J. Drew three for 108) and 22 for one. *Natal 13 pts, Boland 3 pts.*

Natal wicket-keeper Bruyns caught nine in the match.

At Springbok Park, Bloemfontein, November 10, 11, 12, 13. Free State won by four wickets. Northern Transvaal 259 (M. J. G. Davis 71, R. F. Pienaar 32, S. Elworthy 38, D. J. van Zyl 32; F. D. Stephenson four for 58, H. C. Bakkes three for 50) and 368 (C. B. Lambert 47, M. J. R. Rindel 174, D. J. van Zyl 57 not out; F. D. Stephenson five for 63, J. F. Venter three for 54); Free State* 239 (W. J. Cronje 54, H. C. Bakkes 41; S. Elworthy three for 73, R. E. Bryson three for 57) and 389 for six (W. J. Cronje 158, J. F. Venter 95, F. D. Stephenson 51, C. F. Craven 33 not out; S. Elworthy three for 72). *Free State 16 pts, Northern Transvaal 7 pts.*

At Wanderers Stadium, Johannesburg, November 10, 11, 12, 13. Transvaal won by nine wickets. Transvaal* 431 (B. M. White 85, M. W. Rushmere 133, K. R. Rutherford 51; B. C. Fourie three for 79, I. L. Howell three for 106) and 77 for one (N. Pothas 54 not out); Border 180 (P. J. Botha 35, P. N. Kirsten 62; C. E. Eksteen three for 40, S. Jacobs five for 30) and 324 (P. J. Botha 94, P. N. Kirsten 85, P. C. Strydom 36; T. C. Webster four for 113, S. Jacobs four for 45). *Transvaal 19 pts, Border 4 pts.*

At Newlands, Cape Town, November 10, 11, 12. Western Province won by seven wickets. Eastern Province 234 (G. C. Victor 39, L. J. Koen 37, D. J. Callaghan 58, T. G. Shaw 31 not out; A. Martyn four for 68, E. O. Simons four for 38) and 109 (M. W. Pringle six for 32); Western Province* 121 (S. G. Koenig 32, D. L. Haynes 37; A. Badenhorst five for 49, D. J. Callaghan four for 17) and 224 for three (S. G. Koenig 47, G. Kirsten 104 not out, H. D. Ackerman 50 not out). *Western Province 14 pts, Eastern Province 6 pts.*

At Boland Bank Park, Paarl, November 24, 25, 26, 27. Transvaal won by three wickets. Boland* 199 (B. C. Baguley 45, A. P. Kuiper 52, W. F. Stelling 34 not out; S. D. Jack four for 54, S. Jacobs three for 31) and 361 (L. D. Ferreira 50, K. C. Jackson 38, A. P. Kuiper 155, W. F. Stelling 39, C. W. Henderson 44; S. D. Jack five for 69, S. Jacobs three for 52); Transvaal 310 (A. M. Bacher 91, M. W. Rushmere 83, D. R. Laing 71; P. A. J. DeFreitas three for 42) and 251 for seven (K. R. Rutherford 50, D. R. Laing 107, N. D. McKenzie 31). *Transvaal 17 pts, Boland 5 pts.*

At Buffalo Park, East London, November 24, 25, 26, 27. Border won by an innings and 126 runs. Northern Transvaal* 183 (C. B. Lambert 39, M. J. R. Rindel 82; F. J. C. Cronje three for 12, I. L. Howell three for 56) and 118 (C. B. Lambert 37; B. C. Fourie three for 23, F. J. C. Cronje four for 16); Border 427 (P. J. Botha 71, S. J. Palframan 42, P. N. Kirsten 63, D. J. Cullinan 49, P. C. Strydom 47, S. Tikolo 64; S. Elworthy three for 55, M. C. Krug three for 99). *Border 16 pts, Northern Transvaal 2 pts.*

At Kingsmead, Durban, November 24, 25, 26, 27. Natal won by an innings and 159 runs. Eastern Province 71 (D. J. Richardson 30 not out; S. M. Pollock five for 19, L. Klusener three for 22) and 219 (L. J. Koen 31, K. C. Wessels 77, D. J. Callaghan 65 not out; S. M. Pollock five for 40); Natal* 449 for five dec. (A. C. Hudson 153, P. J. R. Steyn 108, D. N. Crookes 64, J. N. Rhodes 33, M. L. Bruyns 33). *Natal 19 pts, Eastern Province 1 pt.*

Hudson and Steyn put on 270 for Natal's first wicket.

At St George's Park, Port Elizabeth, December 1, 2, 3, 4. Drawn. Eastern Province* 452 for three dec. (P. G. Amm 157, L. J. Koen 202 not out, K. C. Wessels 57) and 139 for eight dec. (K. C. Wessels 51; C. W. Henderson four for 71); Boland 326 (L. D. Ferreira 46, T. N. Lazard 77, P. A. J. DeFreitas 42, R. Telemachus 46 not out; G. A. Roe three for 34, E. A. E. Baptiste four for 58) and 110 for four (P. A. J. DeFreitas 32, T. N. Lazard 34 not out). *Eastern Province 7 pts, Boland 2 pts.*

Koen's 202 not out lasted 550 minutes and 450 balls and included 20 fours and one six; he and Amm added 338, a Castle Cup second-wicket record.

At Buffalo Park, East London, December 8, 9, 10, 11. Western Province won by an innings and 21 runs. Border* 173 (S. Tikolo 37; M. W. Pringle four for 30, C. R. Matthews four for 46) and 306 (P. N. Kirsten 104, D. J. Cullinan 56, S. Tikolo 55; A. C. Dawson four for 25, P. R. Adams five for 128); Western Province 500 for five dec. (D. L. Haynes 52, G. Kirsten 244, J. H. Kallis 53, H. D. Ackerman 83 not out; I. L. Howell three for 114). *Western Province 18 pts, Border 1 pt.*

Gary Kirsten's 244 lasted 555 minutes and 399 balls and included 21 fours.

At Springbok Park, Bloemfontein, December 8, 9, 10, 11. Free State won by eight wickets. Free State* 532 for seven dec. (D. Jordaan 36, G. F. J. Liebenberg 229, W. J. Cronje 116, L. J. Wilkinson 61; D. N. Crookes five for 119) and 113 for two (G. F. J. Liebenberg 32, W. J. Cronje 30 not out); Natal 167 (A. C. Hudson 36, N. C. Johnson 75 not out; N. W. Pretorius four for 28) and 474 (P. J. R. Steyn 31, E. L. R. Stewart 131, M. L. Bruyns 46, D. N. Crookes 63, M. D. Marshall 99 not out, R. E. Veenstra 45; N. Boje four for 128, J. F. Venter four for 52). *Free State 18 pts, Natal 1 pt.*

Liebenberg's 229 lasted 561 minutes and 427 balls and included 23 fours and two sixes.

At Boland Bank Park, Paarl, December 15, 16, 17, 18. Border won by two wickets. Boland* 209 (B. C. Baguley 30, T. N. Lazard 89 not out, W. F. Stelling 30; B. C. Fourie five for 46) and 185 (L. D. Ferreira 34; P. J. Botha four for 31); Border 177 (P. N. Kirsten 31, S. C. Pope 44; R. Telemachus three for 53, C. W. Henderson four for 41) and 221 for eight (P. J. Botha 93, P. C. Strydom 69; R. Telemachus five for 72). *Border 15 pts, Boland 6 pts.*

At Wanderers Stadium, Johannesburg, December 15, 16. Northern Transvaal won by 109 runs. Northern Transvaal* 131 (R. F. Pienaar 37; S. D. Jack four for 24, E. W. Kidwell three for 47) and 191 (C. B. Lambert 69, C. van Noordwyk 34; R. P. Snell four for 43, S. Jacobs three for 26); Transvaal 130 (G. J. Smith three for 29, R. E. Bryson four for 16) and 83 (S. Elworthy three for 19, G. J. Smith five for 32). *Northern Transvaal 14 pts (Transvaal had their 4 bonus points deducted for preparing an unsatisfactory pitch).*

At Newlands, Cape Town, December 15, 16, 17, 18. Drawn. Free State 247 (D. Jordaan 33, H. H. Dippenaar 46, L. J. Wilkinson 48, H. C. Bakkes 43; M. W. Pringle five for 89) and 252 (D. Jordaan 41, F. D. Stephenson 104, N. Boje 31; M. W. Pringle four for 76); Western Province* 257 (S. G. Koenig 65, H. H. Gibbs 35, J. B. Commins 55; N. W. Pretorius five for 79, J. F. Venter four for 52) and 162 for four (S. G. Koenig 47, H. D. Ackerman 34, J. B. Commins 36 not out; N. Boje four for 39). *Western Province 7 pts, Free State 6 pts.*

At Boland Bank Park, Paarl, December 26, 27, 28, 29. Western Province won by an innings and 68 runs. Boland* 231 (K. C. Jackson 56; M. W. Pringle five for 67, A. Martyn three for 80) and 123 (T. N. Lazard 44, K. C. Jackson 35; M. W. Pringle six for 41, A. Martyn three for 32); Western Province 422 for nine dec. (D. L. Haynes 38, S. G. Koenig 35, H. H. Gibbs 112, H. D. Ackerman 84, J. B. Commins 57, D. B. Rundle 50; C. W. Henderson four for 147, M. Erasmus five for 87). *Western Province 18 pts, Boland 3 pts.*

At Buffalo Park, East London, December 26, 27, 28. Border won by ten wickets. Free State* 188 (G. F. J. Liebenberg 39, C. F. Craven 47, P. J. L. Radley 30; B. C. Fourie three for 25, M. Ntini three for 49) and 167 (D. Jordaan 45; S. C. Pope seven for 62); Border 301 (P. J. Botha 42, P. N. Kirsten 34, S. Tikolo 43, P. C. Strydom 58, F. J. C. Cronje 41; N. W. Pretorius three for 76, S. G. Cronje three for 59, J. F. Venter four for 65) and 55 for no wkt (P. J. Botha 31 not out). *Border 17 pts, Free State 3 pts.*

At Kingsmead, Durban, January 1, 2, 3. Natal won by an innings and 17 runs. Northern Transvaal 161 (R. F. Pienaar 30, M. J. R. Rindel 51; L. Klusener five for 57) and 191 (C. B. Lambert 95 not out; R. E. Veenstra three for 25, N. C. Johnson three for 25); Natal* 369 (P. J. R. Steyn 34, E. L. R. Stewart 75, N. C. Johnson 55, M. D. Marshall 38, R. E. Veenstra 34, P. L. Symcox 31 not out; G. J. Smith three for 87). *Natal 19 pts, Northern Transvaal 5 pts.*

At St George's Park, Port Elizabeth, January 4, 5, 6, 7. Eastern Province won by 19 runs. Eastern Province* 390 for six dec. (M. G. Beamish 47, K. C. Wessels 94, D. J. Callaghan 133 not out, T. G. Shaw 74 not out; R. P. Snell three for 72) and 241 for seven dec. (L. J. Koen 84, K. C. Wessels 41, D. J. Callaghan 39; S. D. Jack three for 55); Transvaal 331 for seven dec. (A. M. Bacher 38, B. M. White 40, M. W. Rushmere 31, N. D. McKenzie 150 not out, N. Pothas 37) and 281 (K. R. Rutherford 109, N. D. McKenzie 60; B. N. Schultz three for 66, E. A. E. Baptiste three for 49). *Eastern Province 14 pts, Transvaal 5 pts.*

At St George's Park, Port Elizabeth, January 26, 27, 28, 29. Eastern Province won by ten wickets. Border* 263 (P. J. Botha 48, P. N. Kirsten 30, P. C. Strydom 50; T. G. Shaw six for 45) and 181 (P. J. Botha 37, F. J. C. Cronje 31; B. N. Schultz three for 53); Eastern Province 409 (P. G. Amm 83, L. J. Koen 154, D. J. Callaghan 66; B. C. Fourie six for 76) and 37 for no wkt. *Eastern Province 16 pts, Border 3 pts.*

At Kingsmead, Durban, January 26, 27, 28, 29. Drawn. Natal 277 (N. C. Johnson 33, D. M. Benkenstein 34, D. N. Crookes 111 not out; B. M. McMillan three for 46, P. R. Adams three for 65); Western Province* 85 (L. Klusener eight for 34) and 273 for seven (G. Kirsten 76 not out, J. H. Kallis 31, B. M. McMillan 32, H. D. Ackerman 50). *Natal 7 pts, Western Province 4 pts.*
Natal rested Shaun Pollock on the orders of the UCB.

At Centurion Park, Centurion, January 26, 27, 28, 29. Drawn. Boland 256 (T. N. Lazard 42, K. C. Jackson 100, A. Wessels 65; P. S. de Villiers four for 53, R. E. Bryson three for 52); Northern Transvaal* 95 (R. F. Pienaar 34; R. Telemachus four for 25, C. W. Henderson four for 33) and 335 for eight (R. F. Pienaar 50, C. B. Lambert 42, M. J. R. Rindel 81, M. J. G. Davis 65, R. E. Bryson 35 not out; H. S. Williams four for 48). *Northern Transvaal 4 pts, Boland 7 pts.*

At Wanderers Stadium, Johannesburg, January 26, 27, 28, 29. Transvaal won by four runs. Transvaal 214 (B. M. White 31, M. W. Rushmere 62; A. A. Donald three for 59) and 294 for eight dec. (N. D. McKenzie 88, R. P. Snell 105; A. A. Donald three for 82); Free State* 203 for seven dec. (J. F. Venter 56 not out, H. C. Bakkes 51 not out; R. P. Snell three for 59) and 301 (L. J. Wilkinson 66, C. F. Craven 90; R. P. Snell three for 78, C. E. Eksteen three for 104). *Transvaal 15 pts, Free State 6 pts.*

At Springbok Park, Bloemfontein, February 9, 10, 11, 12. Drawn. Eastern Province* 391 (P. G. Amm 90, L. J. Koen 93, D. J. Callaghan 105, G. Morgan 38) and 275 for eight dec. (P. G. Amm 76, M. G. Beamish 52, D. J. Callaghan 55, G. Morgan 33; H. C. Bakkes three for 51); Free State 317 (G. F. J. Liebenberg 63, C. F. Craven 86, N. Boje 69; B. N. Schultz six for 90) and 172 for four (G. F. J. Liebenberg 65, H. H. Dippenaar 36). *Free State 7 pts, Eastern Province 7 pts.*

At Centurion Park, Centurion, February 9, 10, 11, 12. Drawn. Northern Transvaal* 213 (M. van Jaarsveld 36, S. Elworthy 51 not out); Natal 167 for six (D. M. Benkenstein 35, D. N. Crookes 74; G. J. Smith four for 49). *Northern Transvaal 4 pts, Natal 5 pts.*

At Wanderers Stadium, Johannesburg, February 9, 10, 11, 12. Transvaal won by nine wickets. Boland* 206 (L. D. Ferreira 31, A. P. Kuiper 44; R. P. Snell five for 64, E. W. Kidwell three for 57) and 182 (L. D. Ferreira 31, A. P. Kuiper 51, T. N. Lazard 37; R. P. Snell three for 53, E. W. Kidwell four for 36); Transvaal 365 (B. M. White 159 not out, K. R. Rutherford 54, C. E. Eksteen 34, N. Pothas 35, R. P. Snell 52; C. M. Willoughby four for 86, C. W. Henderson four for 87) and 27 for one. *Transvaal 18 pts, Boland 5 pts.*

At Newlands, Cape Town, February 9, 10, 11, 12. Western Province won by 92 runs. Western Province 266 (J. B. Commins 31, H. D. Ackerman 106 not out, E. O. Simons 71; P. C. Strydom three for 22) and 230 (S. G. Koenig 56, P. Kirsten 46, M. W. Pringle 43; B. P. Horan four for 43, I. L. Howell three for 52); Border* 206 (F. J. C. Cronje 35, W. Wiblin 32, M. V. Boucher 37, I. L. Howell 43; M. W. Pringle four for 73, A. Martyn five for 63) and 198 (P. C. Strydom 69, F. J. C. Cronje 48; M. W. Pringle five for 67). *Western Province 17 pts, Border 6 pts.*

CURRIE CUP AND CASTLE CUP WINNERS

The Currie Cup was replaced by the Castle Cup after the 1990-91 season.

1889-90	Transvaal
1890-91	Kimberley
1892-93	Western Province
1893-94	Western Province
1894-95	Transvaal
1896-97	Western Province
1897-98	Western Province
1902-03	Transvaal
1903-04	Transvaal
1904-05	Transvaal
1906-07	Transvaal
1908-09	Western Province
1910-11	Natal
1912-13	Natal
1920-21	Western Province
1921-22	Transvaal/Natal/W. Prov. (Tied)
1923-24	Transvaal
1925-26	Transvaal
1926-27	Transvaal
1929-30	Transvaal
1931-32	Western Province
1933-34	Natal
1934-35	Transvaal
1936-37	Natal
1937-38	Natal/Transvaal (Tied)
1946-47	Natal
1947-48	Natal
1950-51	Transvaal
1951-52	Natal
1952-53	Western Province
1954-55	Natal
1955-56	Western Province

1958-59	Transvaal
1960-61	Natal
1962-63	Natal
1963-64	Natal
1965-66	Natal/Transvaal (Tied)
1966-67	Natal
1967-68	Natal
1968-69	Transvaal
1969-70	Transvaal/W. Province (Tied)
1970-71	Transvaal
1971-72	Transvaal
1972-73	Transvaal
1973-74	Natal
1974-75	Western Province
1975-76	Natal
1976-77	Natal
1977-78	Western Province
1978-79	Transvaal
1979-80	Transvaal
1980-81	Natal
1981-82	Western Province
1982-83	Transvaal
1983-84	Transvaal
1984-85	Transvaal
1985-86	Western Province
1986-87	Transvaal
1987-88	Transvaal
1988-89	Eastern Province
1989-90	E. Province/W. Province (Shared)
1990-91	Western Province
1991-92	Eastern Province
1992-93	Orange Free State
1993-94	Orange Free State
1994-95	Natal
1995-96	Western Province

Transvaal have won the title outright 24 times, Natal 18, Western Province 15, Eastern Province and Orange Free State 2, Kimberley 1. The title has been shared five times as follows: Transvaal 4, Natal and Western Province 3, Eastern Province 1.

UCB BOWL, 1995-96

Section 1

					Bonus points		
	Played	*Won*	*Lost*	*Drawn*	*Batting*	*Bowling*	*Points*
Griqualand West	5	2	0	3	16	15	51
Northern Transvaal B	5	1	1	3	16	14	40
Transvaal B	5	1	0	4	14	12	36
Boland B	5	0	3	2	9	16	25
Eastern Province B	5	0	0	5	14	8	22
Zimbabwe Board XI	5	0	0	5	9	12	21

Section 2

					Bonus points		
	Played	*Won*	*Lost*	*Drawn*	*Batting*	*Bowling*	*Points*
Natal B	4	3	0	1	20	15	65
Western Province B	5	2	0	3	19	18	57
Free State B	5	1	2	2	11	17	38
Easterns	4	0	0	4	17	13	30
Border B	5	0	3	2	12	10	22
Western Transvaal	5	0	1	4	6	15	21

Final: Natal B drew with Griqualand West and shared the title.

The match between Easterns and Natal B was abandoned.

Outright win = 10 pts.

Bonus points are awarded for the first 85 overs of each team's first innings. One batting point is awarded for the first 100 runs and for every subsequent 50. One bowling point is awarded for the second wicket taken and for every subsequent two up to eight.

*In the following scores, * by the name of a team indicates that they won the toss.*

Section 1

At Boland Bank Park, Paarl, October 27, 28, 29. Drawn. Boland B* 238 (A. K. Volsteedt 61, M. S. Nackerdien 117; S. G. Peall nine for 76) and 226 for six dec. (B. C. Baguley 50, J. M. Villet 49; S. G. Peall three for 72); Zimbabwe Board XI 229 for nine dec. (C. B. Wishart 34, A. D. R. Campbell 64, S. G. Davies 50 not out; C. M. Willoughby four for 43, J. D. Albanie three for 40) and 176 for seven (A. D. R. Campbell 49, G. C. Martin 38 not out; J. D. Albanie three for 18). *Boland B 6 pts, Zimbabwe Board XI 6 pts.*

At St George's Park, Port Elizabeth, October 27, 28, 29. Drawn. Griqualand West* 392 for nine dec. (M. I. Gidley 106, W. M. Dry 99, H. A. Page 37, B. N. Benkenstein 31 not out; C. C. Wait three for 85) and 133 for seven (S. Abrahams three for 49); Eastern Province B 256 (M. G. Beamish 101, C. N. du Plessis 41; V. A. Walsh six for 52). *Eastern Province B 4 pts, Griqualand West 5 pts.*

At Wanderers Stadium, Johannesburg, October 27, 28, 29. Drawn. Transvaal B* 320 for six dec. (M. R. Benfield 96, B. M. White 43, H. A. Manack 94, N. R. Rhodes 32 not out) and 225 for three dec. (M. R. Benfield 52, B. M. White 102 not out, Z. de Bruyn 34 not out); Northern Transvaal B 301 for nine dec. (L. P. Vorster 88, G. Dros 56, D. J. Smith 36, P. Joubert 31 not out; M. J. Vandrau four for 93) and 180 for five (M. van Jaarsveld 64, L. P. Vorster 90 not out). *Transvaal B 7 pts, Northern Transvaal B 6 pts.*

At St George's Park, Port Elizabeth, November 24, 25, 26. Drawn. Transvaal B* 316 for six dec. (B. M. White 180 not out, M. J. Vandrau 48; W. E. Jamieson three for 70) and 214 for four dec. (M. R. Benfield 59, B. M. White 60, G. A. Pollock 50 not out, Z. de Bruyn 35); Eastern Province B 248 for nine dec. (M. G. Beamish 86, C. C. Wait 40, S. Abrahams 52; E. W. Kidwell four for 54) and 172 for three (M. C. Venter 70 not out, A. G. Prince 35; E. W. Kidwell three for 28). *Eastern Province B 5 pts, Transvaal B 7 pts.*

At Kimberley Country Club, Kimberley, November 24, 25, 26. Griqualand West won by one wicket. Boland B 215 (J. M. Villet 51, A. T. Holdstock 81; V. A. Walsh four for 65, J. E. Johnson four for 54) and 196 (A. T. Holdstock 55, M. Erasmus 45; C. V. English three for 41); Griqualand West* 283 (W. M. Dry 40, C. V. English 67 not out, J. E. Johnson 30, V. A. Walsh 51; C. M. Willoughby three for 73, J. D. Albanie three for 76) and 132 for nine (F. C. Brooker 50; B. J. Drew five for 79, M. Erasmus three for 26). *Griqualand West 17 pts, Boland B 7 pts.*

At Centurion Park, Centurion, November 24, 25, 26. Drawn. Northern Transvaal B* 339 (M. van Jaarsveld 81, L. P. Vorster 66, G. Dros 83 not out; B. C. Strang five for 69) and 244 for eight dec. (M. van Jaarsveld 93, D. J. J. de Vos 77, J. J. Strydom 33 not out; E. A. Brandes four for 46); Zimbabwe Board XI 334 for nine dec. (S. V. Carlisle 31, A. C. Waller 39, C. B. Wishart 39, A. D. R. Campbell 53, G. J. Whittall 85, E. A. Brandes 41; P. Joubert three for 73) and 131 for seven (C. B. Wishart 33; D. J. J. de Vos four for 34). *Northern Transvaal B 6 pts, Zimbabwe Board XI 6 pts.*

At NFO Ground, Randjesfontein, December 9, 10, 11. Transvaal B won by ten wickets. Boland B 108 (M. Erasmus 31; E. W. Kidwell six for 23, G. C. Yates three for 40) and 215 (A. K. Volsteedt 92, M. M. Brink 40; E. W. Kidwell six for 65, G. C. Yates three for 50); Transvaal B* 297 (H. A. Manack 32, Z. de Bruyn 78, M. J. Vandrau 38, G. C. Yates 50; Z. A. Abrahim three for 74, M. Erasmus five for 70) and 30 for no wkt. *Transvaal B 18 pts, Boland B 5 pts.*

Transvaal B wicket-keeper Mark Johnston caught ten in the match, equalling the South African domestic record.

At Harlequins, Pretoria, December 15, 16, 17. Drawn. Eastern Province B* 150 (G. C. Victor 73; G. J. Kruis five for 36, D. J. van Zyl three for 15) and 190 for four (M. C. Venter 107 not out, S. Abrahams 49); Northern Transvaal B 296 (M. van Jaarsveld 36, L. P. Vorster 77, D. J. van Zyl 69, G. Dros 36 not out; D. Rossouw five for 57). *Northern Transvaal B 8 pts, Eastern Province B 5 pts.*

At Harare South Country Club, Harare, December 15, 16, 17. Drawn. Griqualand West 290 for nine dec. (M. I. Gidley 105, W. M. Dry 93; H. K. Olonga four for 94, B. C. Strang three for 63) and 183 for nine dec. (W. M. Dry 43, F. C. Brooker 53, B. N. Benkenstein 35 not out; B. C. Strang three for 65, S. G. Peall three for 25); Zimbabwe Board XI* 153 (A. C. Waller 43; V. A. Walsh four for 37, C. V. English four for 47) and 258 for nine (S. V. Carlisle 54, A. C. Waller 74, B. C. Strang 44; B. N. Benkenstein three for 59). *Zimbabwe Board XI 5 pts, Griqualand West 8 pts.*

Zimbabwe Board wicket-keeper Bradley Robinson caught five and stumped one in Griquas' second innings.

At Boland Bank Park, Paarl, January 25, 26, 27. Northern Transvaal B won by 143 runs. Northern Transvaal B* 277 for nine dec. (B. J. Sommerville 138, M. van Jaarsveld 41, N. Martin 56; Z. A. Abrahim four for 49) and 203 for five dec. (D. J. J. de Vos 48 not out, N. Martin 89 not out); Boland B 201 (A. R. Wylie 48, J. M. Villet 37, L-M. Germishuys 47; G. J. Kruis three for 35) and 136 (L-M. Germishuys 32; P. de Bruyn six for 38). *Northern Transvaal B 17 pts, Boland B 5 pts.*

At Alexandra Sports Club, Harare, January 25, 26, 27. Drawn. Eastern Province B 297 for six (G. C. Victor 100, A. G. Lawson 49, A. G. Prince 35, C. C. Wait 36 not out, G. K. Miller 41) v Zimbabwe Board XI*. *Zimbabwe Board XI 2 pts, Eastern Province B 3 pts.*

At Kimberley Country Club, Kimberley, January 26, 27, 28. Drawn. Transvaal B* 357 for six dec. (N. R. Rhodes 98, H. A. Manack 51, Z. de Bruyn 126 not out; V. A. Walsh three for 83) and 74 for two (H. A. Manack 36 not out); Griqualand West 421 for eight dec. (J. M. Arthur 109, M. I. Gidley 91, W. E. Schonegevel 37, P. H. Barnard 108, F. C. Brooker 46; M. J. Vandrau four for 97). *Griqualand West 4 pts, Transvaal B 3 pts.*

At Boland Bank Park, Paarl, February 8, 9, 10. Drawn. Boland B* 217 for nine dec. (B. C. Baguley 45, E. Liebenberg 62, A. R. Wylie 50) and 263 for five (B. C. Baguley 32, A. R. Wylie 108 not out, M. Erasmus 42 not out); Eastern Province B 348 for six dec. (C. C. Bradfield 61, M. C. Venter 119, A. G. Prince 50, C. C. Wait 78). *Boland B 2 pts, Eastern Province B 5 pts.*

At Bulawayo Athletic Club, Bulawayo, February 8, 9, 10. Drawn. Transvaal B 119 for four dec. (Z. de Bruyn 60 not out) and 67 for two; Zimbabwe Board XI* nought for no wkt dec. *Zimbabwe Board XI 2 pts, Transvaal B 1 pt.*

At Kimberley Country Club, Kimberley, February 9, 10, 11. Griqualand West won by an innings and 58 runs. Northern Transvaal B 131 (N. Martin 64; V. A. Walsh four for 61, A. J. Swanepoel five for 35) and 156 (D. J. J. de Vos 42, N. Martin 32 not out; V. A. Walsh four for 44, A. J. Swanepoel five for 29); Griqualand West* 345 (M. I. Gidley 85, W. E. Schonegevel 55, W. M. Dry 48, F. C. Brooker 35; G. J. Kruis three for 72, P. de Bruyn four for 96). *Griqualand West 17 pts, Northern Transvaal B 3 pts.*

Griquas' wicket-keeper Jaco Burger caught ten in the match, equalling the South African domestic record.

Section 2

At PAM Brink Stadium, Springs, October 27, 28, 29. Drawn. Easterns* 391 for nine dec. (M. J. Mitchley 92, C. R. Norris 59, C. Grainger 119, T. Jamal 36; P. R. Adams three for 48) and 207 for six (B. Randall 43, M. J. Mitchley 58 not out; I. R. Solomon three for 53); Western Province B 360 for six dec. (S. G. Koenig 89, F. B. Touzel 102, F. Davids 46). *Easterns 7 pts, Western Province B 6 pts.*

At Kingsmead, Durban, October 27, 28. Natal B won by an innings and 172 runs. Border B 86 (G. T. Love 35; K. G. Storey five for 26) and 210 (D. J. Stephen 37, D. O. Nosworthy 94; K. G. Storey five for 38, R. K. McGlashan four for 83); Natal B* 468 for seven dec. (E. L. R. Stewart 207 not out, K. A. Forde 122, R. E. Veenstra 57, U. H. Goedeke 31; S. E. Fourie four for 117). *Natal B 22 pts, Border B 2 pts.*

Stewart's 207 not out lasted 284 minutes and 245 balls and included 18 fours and three sixes.

At Witrand Cricket Field, Potchefstroom, October 27, 28, 29. Drawn. Western Transvaal* 202 (J. S. Olivier 35, S. Nicolson 30, V. Wandrag 34; H. Botha three for 27) and 298 (H. M. de Vos 115, J. S. Olivier 41; S. G. Cronje four for 87, B. T. Player four for 73); Free State B 273 (F. P. Schoeman 103, C. C. van der Merwe 64; G. Radford five for 51) and 159 for three (H. L. M. Wessels 80 not out, C. C. van der Merwe 42 not out). *Western Transvaal 6 pts, Free State B 7 pts.*

At Newlands, Cape Town, November 16, 17, 18. Drawn. Natal B* 243 (D. M. Benkenstein 98, R. K. McGlashan 64; A. Martyn six for 67) and 417 (S. W. Broughton 31, K. A. Forde 40, M. S. Dada 34, U. H. Goedeke 137, A. G. Small 72; D. B. Rundle three for 49); Western Province B 350 (D. B. Rundle 103, M. T. Solomons 67; K. G. Storey four for 78, D. J. Pryke five for 92) and seven for no wkt. *Western Province B 8 pts, Natal B 6 pts.*

At PAM Brink Stadium, Springs, November 24, 25, 26. Drawn. Easterns* 228 (W. R. Radford 40, M. J. Mitchley 34, C. Grainger 71; B. P. Horan four for 48, S. C. Pope four for 54) and 307 for seven dec. (M. J. Mitchley 46, C. Grainger 65, G. P. Cooke 49, S. M. Skeete 61 not out); Border B 289 for nine dec. (D. O. Nosworthy 141 not out; J. R. Meyer three for 28) and 91 for two (L. M. Fuhri 34, Q. R. Still 33 not out). *Easterns 7 pts, Border B 7 pts.*

At Newlands, Cape Town, November 25, 26, 27. Western Province B won by nine wickets. Free State B 206 (H. L. M. Wessels 31, I. G. van Aswegen 46, C. Light 44, B. T. Player 44; A. Cilliers three for 53, F. Davids four for 24) and 124 (I. G. van Aswegen 32; A. C. Dawson six for 18); Western Province B* 289 (F. Davids 52, G. F. Gillett 65, A. C. Dawson 55; S. A. Cilliers three for 77, H. Botha three for 77) and 43 for one. *Western Province B 18 pts, Free State B 6 pts.*

At Kingsmead, Durban, December 1, 2. Natal B won by an innings and 83 runs. Natal B 401 for seven dec. (C. B. Sugden 91, D. M. Benkenstein 33, K. A. Forde 121, P. L. Symcox 65; G. Radford three for 89); Western Transvaal* 59 (D. J. Pryke six for 27, K. G. Storey four for 20) and 259 (J. S. Olivier 45, H. M. de Vos 38, A. J. van Deventer 38, M. Strydom 58; R. K. McGlashan five for 94, P. L. Symcox four for 61). *Natal B 20 pts, Western Transvaal 3 pts.*

At Sandringham CC, Queenstown, December 15, 16, 17. Drawn. Border B 86 for four (L. M. Fuhri 46; G. Radford three for 25) v Western Transvaal*. *Western Transvaal 2 pts.*

At Springbok Park, Bloemfontein, December 15, 16, 17. Drawn. Free State B* 199 (H. Linde 36, H. Botha 31; J. R. Meyer three for 52, L. C. R. Jordaan three for 25); Easterns 317 for six dec. (C. R. Norris 132 not out, C. Grainger 73; C. C. van der Merwe three for 43). *Free State B 5 pts, Easterns 9 pts.*

At PAM Brink Stadium, Springs, January 25, 26, 27. Easterns v Natal B. Abandoned.

At Fanie du Toit Stadium, Potchefstroom, January 25, 26, 27. Drawn. Western Transvaal 97 (A. Martyn six for 22, D. B. Rundle three for 26); Western Province B* 229 for nine (F. B. Touzel 90, T. Robertson 32, H. H. Gibbs 47; G. Radford six for 70). *Western Transvaal 4 pts, Western Province B 7 pts.*

At Springbok Park, Bloemfontein, January 26, 27, 28. Free State B won by four wickets. Border B* 301 for five dec. (C. R. Wilson 43, W. Wiblin 160, M. V. Boucher 47) and 91 for no wkt dec. (G. A. King 37 not out, I. Mitchell 42 not out); Free State B 100 for five dec. and 293 for six (H. L. M. Wessels 43, H. Linde 32, A. Moreby 79, C. C. van der Merwe 67; P. B. du Plessis three for 99, P. A. N. Emslie three for 46). *Free State B 13 pts, Border B 7 pts.*

At Buffalo Park, East London, February 8, 9, 10. Western Province B won by six wickets. Border B 242 (S. C. Pope 44, P. B. du Plessis 101; A. van Reenen five for 47) and 285 for five dec. (C. R. Wilson 47, S. C. Pope 71, P. B. du Plessis 104 not out; D. B. Rundle three for 37); Western Province B* 275 for six dec. (F. B. Touzel 40, M. C. de Villiers 88, T. J. Mitchell 40, D. B. Rundle 69 not out) and 256 for four (F. B. Touzel 75, M. C. de Villiers 86, T. J. Mitchell 50 not out; P. B. du Plessis three for 49). *Western Province B 18 pts, Border B 6 pts.*

At Kingsmead, Durban, February 8, 9. Natal B won by five wickets. Free State B* 201 (H. L. M. Wessels 58, H. Linde 43, B. T. Player 44, S. A. Cilliers 32 not out; G. M. Gilder five for 40) and 115 (A. Moreby 38; G. M. Gilder five for 20); Natal B 246 (D. J. Watson 103 not out, U. H. Goedeke 37; S. A. Cilliers three for 84, H. Botha four for 31) and 71 for five (S. A. Cilliers three for 26). *Natal B 17 pts, Free State B 7 pts.*

Watson carried his bat through Natal B's first innings.

At Fanie du Toit Stadium, Potchefstroom, February 8, 9, 10. Drawn. Western Transvaal* 240 (J. S. Olivier 101, S. Nicolson 45; L. C. R. Jordaan three for 88) and 352 for five dec. (A. J. van Deventer 57, L. Botes 38, S. Nicolson 117 not out, S. Kip 50 not out); Easterns 334 (J. S. Lerm 56, C. Grainger 51, T. A. Marsh 34, I. A. Hoffmann 40, B. Randall 68 not out; M. Strydom three for 70) and 123 for four (C. Grainger 30, C. R. Norris 38 not out; C. T. Enslin four for 46). *Western Transvaal 6 pts, Easterns 7 pts.*

Final

At Kingsmead, Durban, March 8, 9, 10. Drawn. Griqualand West 406 for seven dec. (M. I. Gidley 160, P. H. Barnard 146; A. G. Small three for 86) and 161 for two (J. M. Arthur 66 not out, M. I. Gidley 79); Natal B* 398 (D. J. Watson 86, M. L. Bruyns 55, K. A. Forde 129, C. B. Sugden 70; C. V. English three for 99, A. J. Swanepoel three for 53).

Gidley and Barnard added 256 for the third wicket in Griquas' first innings.

OTHER FIRST-CLASS MATCHES

Zimbabwe A in South Africa

At Wanderers Stadium, Johannesburg, September 21, 22, 23, 24. Transvaal won by nine wickets. Zimbabwe A 264 (G. K. Bruk-Jackson 65, A. H. Shah 85, W. R. James 41, D. N. Erasmus 42; G. C. Yates five for 69) and 312 (M. H. Dekker 162 not out; C. E. Eksteen four for 107); Transvaal* 509 (A. M. Bacher 48, N. Pothas 78, K. R. Rutherford 47, N. D. McKenzie 128, G. A. Pollock 95, C. E. Eksteen 58; E. A. Brandes three for 112, P. A. Strang five for 109) and 70 for one (H. A. Manack 36 not out).

Dekker carried his bat through Zimbabwe A's second innings.

At St George's Park, Port Elizabeth, September 28, 29, 30. Eastern Province won by an innings and 57 runs. Zimbabwe A 112 (D. N. Erasmus 37; B. N. Schultz five for 35, D. Rossouw four for 35) and 144 (G. K. Bruk-Jackson 32, C. N. Evans 31; B. N. Schultz three for 31, S. Abrahams five for 49); Eastern Province* 313 (K. C. Wessels 110, D. J. Callaghan 78; H. K. Olonga four for 57, B. C. Strang three for 57).

At Kingsmead, Durban, October 6, 7, 8, 9. Drawn. Zimbabwe A 221 (G. J. Whittall 62, W. R. James 39, P. A. Strang 36 not out; S. M. Pollock five for 66, R. Telemachus three for 51) and 256 for eight (C. N. Evans 74, W. R. James 64; S. M. Pollock three for 48); South Africa A* 310 (J. H. Kallis 57, N. C. Johnson 55, S. M. Pollock 74 not out, S. D. Jack 55; P. A. Strang five for 69).

The match between Northern Transvaal and Glamorgan on April 1, 2, 3 may be found in English Counties Overseas, 1995-96.

BENSON AND HEDGES SERIES, 1995-96

Note: Matches in this section were not first-class.

Semi-finals

At Wanderers Stadium, Johannesburg, March 15 (day/night). Transvaal won by four wickets. Boland* 280 for four (45 overs) (L. D. Ferreira 77, T. N. Lazard 90, A. P. Kuiper 64 not out); Transvaal 281 for six (44.5 overs) (A. M. Bacher 34, R. P. Snell 32, K. R. Rutherford 48, N. D. McKenzie 44, N. Pothas 51 not out).

At Boland Bank Park, Paarl, March 20 (day/night). Boland won by 81 runs. Boland* 247 for four (45 overs) (L. D. Ferreira 78, T. N. Lazard 32, K. C. Jackson 54, A. P. Kuiper 63 not out); Transvaal 166 (43 overs) (N. Pothas 52).

At Boland Bank Park, Paarl, March 22 (day/night). Transvaal won by 143 runs. Transvaal* 229 for six (45 overs) (R. P. Snell 96, N. Pothas 74 not out); Boland 86 (29.3 overs) (S. Jacobs three for 23, C. E. Eksteen five for 13).
Transvaal won 2-1.

At Springbok Park, Bloemfontein, March 15 (day/night). Free State won by five wickets. Western Province* 204 (45 overs) (G. Kirsten 48, B. M. McMillan 37, P. Kirsten 37; A. A. Donald three for 44); Free State 205 for five (39.5 overs) (F. D. Stephenson 36, C. F. Craven 59 not out; B. M. McMillan four for 36).

At Newlands, Cape Town, March 22 (day/night). Free State won by four wickets. Western Province* 160 for nine (45 overs) (B. M. McMillan 50; F. D. Stephenson four for 16, A. A. Donald three for 20); Free State 162 for six (42 overs) (F. D. Stephenson 40, W. J. Cronje 59 not out).
Free State won 2-0.

Final

At Wanderers Stadium, Johannesburg, March 29 (day/night). Free State won by 142 runs. Free State 290 for six (45 overs) (D. Jordaan 51, B. T. Player 83, G. F. J. Liebenberg 70, L. J. Wilkinson 39); Transvaal* 148 (37.4 overs) (B. T. Player three for 36, C. F. Craven three for nine).

CRICKET IN THE WEST INDIES, 1995-96

By TONY COZIER

Rajindra Dhanraj

West Indies cricket has never known a more tempestuous period. Dissension and indiscipline within the Test team, which had first surfaced in April 1995 as West Indies surrendered the Frank Worrell Trophy to Australia for the first time in 17 years, ultimately led to the resignation of the captain, Richie Richardson, and the replacement of the coach, Andy Roberts, both announced midway through the World Cup.

At virtually the same time, the president of the West Indies Cricket Board of Control, Peter Short, said he would not seek re-election and the team manager, Wes Hall, announced that he would no longer be available because of business commitments. That meant a complete change of the leadership on all fronts in the space of a few weeks.

Richardson, unfairly but not unexpectedly, took most of the blame for the upheavals within the team and for its erratic performances, the nadir being the World Cup loss to Kenya. The upheavals were compounded by the controversies surrounding Brian Lara, West Indies' most celebrated player, who had temporarily walked out of the 1995 tour of England, refused to join the subsequent trip to Australia, twice appeared before the board's disciplinary committee and twice issued public apologies for indiscretions that brought him a fine, a "written reprimand" and a warning about his future conduct.

Getting wind that the Board was about to remove him, Richardson pre-empted the decision. It was a distressing end to the career of one of the most exciting batsmen and genuine sportsmen of his time. He had led West Indies in 24 of his 86 Tests and played 224 one-day internationals, 87 as captain. His replacement was the 33-year-old fast bowler Courtney Walsh, who had already stood in when illness forced Richardson to rest a year earlier. This was a short-term choice. But Lara's persistent disciplinary troubles were delaying his elevation to the position for which he had been groomed since he was a teenager. His appointment as vice-captain for the 1996-97 tour of Australia clearly put him on probation. The Board's other refuge in its moment of crisis was Clive Lloyd, the most successful of West Indies captains and a universally respected figure. Having discarded him as manager, after the home series against England in 1989-90, and ignored him ever since, the administrators initially installed him to succeed Roberts as coach and then made him overall manager on a three-year contract. Malcolm Marshall, like Roberts a member of Lloyd's fearsome attack of the 1980s, was named coach for the same period.

The appointment of Lloyd and Marshall was one of several radical changes made by the board under its new president, Pat Rousseau. A 62-year-old Jamaican attorney and business executive, who described his own cricket as of "very modest" club standard, Rousseau earned his reputation heading the marketing committee, achieving substantial increases in sponsorship and television rights. At its first meeting under his direction, the Board dropped the word "Control", part of its title since its formation in 1927. It was not, it explained, "in keeping with the new dispensation and did not speak of the attitude which was being brought to its deliberations and decision-making". Seeking to improve relations with the players, the Board declared that representatives of the Players' Association would be invited to future annual meetings and that $US50,000 would be given to the Association to establish a permanent secretariat. It assembled several former players at a three-day meeting in Barbados to "draft a blueprint for the development of West Indies cricket" and staged a grand banquet in Kingston in September to which all 137 living West Indies Test cricketers, and their wives, were invited. Unrelated to all this, but adding to the sense of upheaval, the Board decided to shift its secretariat from Barbados to Antigua. The move took place in September. The Barbados Government was said not to have fully implemented tax and other concessions that had been promised.

The new Board's most far-reaching decision was to expand the Red Stripe Cup, the only annual first-class tournament, in 1996-97, so that each team would play every other twice, on a home-and-away basis, doubling the number of league matches from 15 to 30. This followed the introduction, in 1995-96, of a final between the two top teams. Meanwhile, Bermuda and Canada, two ICC associate members assigned to West Indies' "sphere of influence", were invited to take part in the limited-overs Shell/Sandals Trophy. At the same time, India and Sri Lanka were both due to visit in 1996-97, the first time West Indies had staged two Test series in the same season, so the programme would almost certainly extend into June. This would pose a dilemma for players contracted to English counties and league teams; they must be available for all Red Stripe Cup matches to be eligible for Test selection. It was planned to put about 20 of the leading players under retaining contracts to make it easier for them to avoid county cricket in future. All this was to be funded by the extra money being earned from TV rights and the big increase in sponsorship from Cable & Wireless, who are putting in $US12.6 million over six years, a fourfold increase.

The innovation of a five-day final in the Red Stripe Cup, following the example of the Sheffield Shield in Australia, prompted opposition from some officials, who contended that it was an unfair imposition on the team that topped the league table. Illustrating their arguments, Trinidad & Tobago won four of their five qualifying matches, only to lose the final to the Leeward Islands, who had trailed them by 16 points and whom they had soundly beaten by nine wickets two weeks earlier. Moreover, the fact that the final was contested with the leading players still on World Cup duty diminished public interest.

The Red Stripe Cup yielded contrary results and inconsistent performances, again due to the loss of the leading players, who had thoroughly dominated the first round. In theory, the way was open for newer contenders to advertise their worth. Very few did; the remaining rounds were heavily influenced by the established international reserves not needed in India. By the end of the season,

100 players had appeared in the tournament, but the disparity between those with international experience and the rest was evident throughout. In the only round for which he was available, Shivnarine Chanderpaul scored an unbeaten 303 for Guyana against Jamaica, becoming the 11th West Indian to score a triple-hundred and the first in a regional match since Jeffrey Stollmeyer in 1946-47. In the course of it, he shared a tournament record fourth-wicket partnership of 305 with Roger Harper, who followed his 124 with bowling figures of five for 38. But once Chanderpaul and Harper had gone, Guyana lost three of their last four matches and finished bottom of the table. Carl Hooper's illness ruled him out of the first-class season entirely, forcing them to rely on a very young, untested team which failed to pass 200 in six successive innings. For their last, rain-spoiled match, Guyana introduced all-rounder Ramnaresh Sarwan who, at 15 years and 245 days, became the youngest first-class cricketer in West Indian history, 31 days younger than the late Roy Marshall.

Stuart Williams of the Leewards and Phil Simmons of Trinidad & Tobago, the openers dropped after disappointing one-day tournaments in Sharjah and Australia, were two of only three batsmen who exceeded 500 runs in the Red Stripe Cup. Both earned reinstatement for the home internationals against New Zealand, but the third of the top-scorers, Adrian Griffith, a tall left-hander from Barbados who made three hundreds in five matches, eventually gained selection ahead of them for the tour of Australia starting in November. Simmons, who captained in Lara's absence, and the leg-spinner Rajindra Dhanraj, another Test player, were principally responsible for Trinidad & Tobago's best season since they last won the championship in 1984-85. Dhanraj reaped a record 40 wickets in the five qualifying matches, adding another eight in the final. His match return of 16 for 167 (nine for 97 and seven for 70) against the Leewards, on a helpful pitch in Nevis, eclipsed Derick Parry's 15 for 101 for the Combined Islands against Jamaica in 1979-80 as the best ever in inter-territorial cricket. It was enough to gain him a Test recall, but he bowled disappointingly against New Zealand and was dropped again.

Kenny Benjamin, suspended from the West Indies team for a year for indiscipline, was the tournament's leading fast bowler with 24 wickets at just over 20 for the Leewards. But, given the need to find replacements for the aging Walsh and Curtly Ambrose, the powerfully built 24-year-old, Patterson Thompson, attracted more attention, as he took 23 wickets for Barbados. Though his control was erratic and he was plagued by no-balls, notably in an unhappy Test debut against New Zealand, his pace and hostility were enough to get him on the tour to Australia.

Generally, spin was to the fore, most of it from young bowlers who, like Dhanraj, delivered from the back of the hand. Mahendra Nagamootoo, 20-year-old nephew of former Test captain Alvin Kallicharran, had 20 wickets for Guyana with his quickish leg-breaks and googlies, including seven in an innings against the Leewards. Avidesh Samaroo, an unorthodox schoolboy left-armer in his debut season for Trinidad & Tobago, took 19, as did 21-year-old leg-spinner Rawl Lewis for the Windwards. The second-highest wicket-taker after Dhanraj was the Dominican, Roy Marshall (unrelated to the former West Indies and Hampshire opener of the same name), who took 30 wickets at 17.20 for the Windwards with his orthodox left-arm variety and added a maiden century against Trinidad & Tobago. His all-round talent was obvious, but erratic; at 30, his chance of higher honours seemed to have passed.

The Shell/Sandals Trophy was staged, for the first time, quite separately from the Red Stripe Cup, in October and November. Underlining their reliance on the all-round input of their three international players, Chanderpaul, Harper and Hooper, Guyana advanced to the final against Trinidad & Tobago. Rain thwarted two attempts to complete the match and the championship had to be shared.

Guyana's Under-19s secured the annual Nortel championships for the fifth successive year in August 1996, after Jamaica won the inaugural Carib Cement Under-15 title in April. This was staged primarily as preparation for the Lombard World Challenge in England, which provided further international exposure for young players. West Indies Under-19s toured Pakistan and Bangladesh in October and November 1995, and hosted a return visit a year later. The downside of Under-19 cricket appeared when the Barbados team was reported for ball tampering during a match in the 1995 Nortel tournament. The Board disciplinary committee concluded there was "clear evidence" and docked their points. The Barbados Cricket Association protested that the players had not been given a proper hearing, but Clive Lloyd said, "If they are guilty, a strong signal should be sent to these youngsters who are hoping to play Test cricket."

FIRST-CLASS AVERAGES, 1995-96

BATTING

(Qualification: 200 runs)

	M	*I*	*NO*	*R*	*HS*	*100s*	*Avge*
S. Chanderpaul (*Guyana*)	3	4	1	434	303*	1	144.66
J. C. Adams (*Jamaica*)	3	5	1	357	208*	2	89.25
B. C. Lara (*T & T*)	3	5	0	345	119	1	69.00
G. R. Breese (*Jamaica*)	3	6	2	245	124	1	61.25
S. L. Campbell (*Barbados*)	4	8	1	423	208	1	60.42
A. F. G. Griffith (*Barbados*)	6	10	0	592	145	3	59.20
P. V. Simmons (*T & T*)	8	14	1	722	156	1	55.53
S. C. Williams (*Leeward I.*)	6	10	0	548	165	1	54.80
T. O. Powell (*Jamaica*)	6	10	1	452	125*	1	50.22
R. G. Samuels (*Jamaica*)	8	14	1	629	125	3	48.38
F. L. Reifer (*Barbados*)	6	10	2	387	130	1	48.37
R. D. Jacobs (*Leeward I.*)	6	10	3	299	89	0	42.71
P. A. Wallace (*Barbados*)	5	9	0	373	108	1	41.44
R. L. Hoyte (*Barbados*)	4	7	1	244	75	0	40.66
D. R. E. Joseph (*Leeward I.*)	7	11	0	409	118	1	37.18
M. Bodoe (*T & T*)	6	9	1	287	65	0	35.87
R. A. M. Smith (*T & T*)	4	7	1	201	99	0	33.50
A. R. Percival (*Guyana*)	5	7	0	223	78	0	31.85
D. A. Joseph (*Windward I.*)	4	7	0	220	78	0	31.42
D. S. Morgan (*Jamaica*)	6	11	2	274	67	0	30.44
D. Williams (*T & T*)	6	9	2	201	102*	1	28.71
R. A. Marshall (*Windward I.*)	5	10	0	280	112	1	28.00
S. G. B. Ford (*Jamaica*)	6	10	2	203	56*	0	25.37
M. D. Ventura (*Jamaica*)	6	11	0	279	102	1	25.36
J. R. Murray (*Windward I.*)	6	11	1	252	70	0	25.20
N. O. Perry (*Jamaica*)	6	9	1	201	74	0	25.12
S. Ragoonath (*T & T*)	6	11	0	267	85	0	24.27
L. A. Harrigan (*Leeward I.*)	6	11	0	261	67	0	23.72
U. Pope (*Windward I.*)	6	12	0	256	84	0	21.33
H. A. G. Anthony (*Leeward I.*)	7	12	1	217	53	0	19.72

* *Signifies not out.*

BOWLING

(Qualification: 15 wickets)

	O	M	R	W	BB	5W/i	Avge
R. A. Marshall (*Windward I.*)	220.5	37	516	30	7-99	2	17.20
L. R. Williams (*Jamaica*)	140	40	351	20	5-32	2	17.55
R. Dhanraj (*T & T*)	314.5	59	964	50	9-97	4	19.28
K. C. G. Benjamin (*Leeward I.*)	196.4	59	490	24	5-22	2	20.41
M. V. Nagamootoo (*Guyana*)	195.5	31	544	23	7-76	1	23.65
P. I. C. Thompson (*Barbados*)	154.2	15	649	27	5-105	1	24.03
A. Samaroo (*T & T*)	141.3	15	568	22	4-44	0	25.81
B. St A. Browne (*Guyana*)	128	24	393	15	5-48	1	26.20
L. C. Weekes (*Leeward I.*)	159	28	464	17	5-83	1	27.29
R. N. Lewis (*Windward I.*)	203.2	32	602	22	7-66	2	27.36
W. D. Phillip (*Leeward I.*)	219.3	51	598	20	5-37	1	29.90
B. S. Murphy (*Jamaica*)	200.3	30	633	21	5-35	2	30.14
H. A. G. Anthony (*Leeward I.*)	168	30	577	19	4-84	0	30.36
M. C. Gibbs (*Jamaica*)	196.1	52	461	15	4-35	0	30.73
N. O. Perry (*Jamaica*)	206.3	54	506	16	5-58	1	31.62

RED STRIPE CUP, 1995-96

	Played	Won	Lost	Drawn	1st-inns Points	Points
Trinidad & Tobago	5	4	1	0	0	64
Leeward Islands	5	3	2	0	0	48
Jamaica	5	2	1	2	4	44
Windward Islands	5	2	3	0	0	32
Barbados	5	1	2	2	5	29
Guyana	5	0	3	2	4	12

Final: Leeward Islands beat Trinidad & Tobago by 73 runs.

Win = 16 pts; draw = 4 pts; 1st-innings lead in a drawn match = 4 pts; 1st-innings lead in a lost match = 5 pts.

*In the following scores, * by the name of a team indicates that they won the toss.*

At Sabina Park, Kingston, January 26, 27, 28, 29. Drawn. Guyana* 559 for five dec. (S. Chanderpaul 303 not out, R. A. Harper 124, A. R. Percival 78; J. B. Grant three for 112); Jamaica 154 (N. O. Perry 56; R. A. Harper five for 38) and 370 for six (R. G. Samuels 52, J. C. Adams 120, T. O. Powell 56, N. O. Perry 56 not out; M. V. Nagamootoo three for 105). *Jamaica 4 pts, Guyana 8 pts.*

Chanderpaul's 303 not out, his maiden double and triple-century, lasted 632 minutes and 478 balls and included 38 fours. It was the highest score ever made in Shell Shield/Red Stripe Cup cricket, and the highest in inter-territorial cricket since 1947. He and Harper added 305 for Guyana's fourth wicket.

At Webster Park, The Valley (Anguilla), January 26, 27, 28. Leeward Islands won by an innings and seven runs. Leeward Islands 320 (S. C. Williams 77, R. B. Richardson 82, Extras 37; R. A. Marshall six for 71); Windward Islands* 159 (A. J. Pierre 40, J. R. Murray 40, N. A. M. McLean 31 not out; C. E. L. Ambrose three for 31, K. C. G. Benjamin four for 18, H. A. G. Anthony three for 54) and 154 (K. C. G. Benjamin three for 50, C. E. L. Ambrose three for 11). *Leeward Islands 16 pts.*

At Guaracara Park, Pointe-à-Pierre, January 26, 27, 28, 29. Trinidad & Tobago won by three wickets. Barbados* 337 (P. A. Wallace 108, R. I. C. Holder 138; R. Dhanraj three for 101, M. Bodoe three for 65, A. Samaroo three for 80) and 226 (F. L. Reifer 81 not out, V. C. Drakes 30; I. R. Bishop three for 72, A. Samaroo four for 74); Trinidad & Tobago 263 (P. V. Simmons 53, S. Ragoonath 32, B. C. Lara 77, Extras 47; O. D. Gibson four for 79, P. I. C. Thompson three for 59) and 301 for seven (S. Ragoonath 85, B. C. Lara 119, I. R. Bishop 30; P. I. C. Thompson four for 48). *Trinidad & Tobago 16 pts, Barbados 5 pts.*

Wallace reached his hundred in the final over before lunch on the first day; it took him 91 balls.

At Kensington Oval, Bridgetown, February 2, 3, 4, 5. Barbados won by four wickets. Windward Islands* 233 (K. K. Sylvester 77, I. B. A. Allen 35; W. E. Reid three for 32, H. R. Bryan three for 46) and 318 (D. A. Joseph 33, U. Pope 74, C. A. Davis 40, J. R. Murray 70, Extras 33; P. I. C. Thompson three for 66, W. E. Reid three for 66); Barbados 339 (P. A. Wallace 38, A. F. G. Griffith 101, F. L. Reifer 58, R. L. Hoyte 70; N. A. M. McLean three for 52) and 213 for six (P. A. Wallace 44, S. H. Armstrong 46; C. A. Davis three for 38). *Barbados 16 pts.*

At Jarrett Park, Montego Bay, February 2, 3, 4, 5. Jamaica won by an innings and 13 runs. Jamaica* 424 for seven dec. (D. S. Morgan 67, R. G. Samuels 125, T. O. Powell 51, N. O. Perry 74, S. G. B. Ford 45, Extras 34; H. A. G. Anthony four for 84); Leeward Islands 227 (S. C. Williams 75, R. D. Jacobs 54 not out; L. R. Williams three for 51, M. C. Gibbs four for 61) and 184 (L. A. Harrigan 46, R. D. Jacobs 34, J. E. S. Joseph 31; L. R. Williams three for 39, M. C. Gibbs four for 35). *Jamaica 16 pts.*

At Queen's Park Oval, Port-of-Spain, February 2, 3, 4, 5. Trinidad & Tobago won by eight wickets. Guyana 173 (R. E. Browne 35; R. Dhanraj four for 64, A. Samaroo three for 36) and 152 (N. A. De Groot 78; E. C. Antoine five for 47); Trinidad & Tobago* 238 (P. V. Simmons 80, K. Mason 67; B. St A. Browne five for 48) and 88 for two (P. V. Simmons 44). *Trinidad & Tobago 16 pts.*

At Kensington Oval, Bridgetown, February 9, 10, 11. Leeward Islands won by six wickets. Leeward Islands* 446 (S. C. Williams 165, C. M. Tuckett 63, D. R. E. Joseph 78, R. D. Jacobs 70 not out; V. C. Drakes three for 79, P. I. C. Thompson four for 115) and 84 for four (L. A. Harrigan 30); Barbados 185 (A. F. G. Griffith 59; W. D. Phillip five for 37) and 342 (A. F. G. Griffith 115, S. H. Armstrong 92, V. C. Drakes 50; L. C. Weekes four for 34, W. D. Phillip three for 118). *Leeward Islands 16 pts.*

At Guaracara Park, Pointe-à-Pierre, February 9, 10, 11. Trinidad & Tobago won by an innings and 94 runs. Trinidad & Tobago* 408 (P. V. Simmons 156, R. A. M. Smith 40, M. Bodoe 41, D. Williams 102 not out; L. R. Williams five for 76); Jamaica 172 (S. G. B. Ford 41; R. Dhanraj five for 50) and 142 (R. G. Samuels 34, L. R. Williams 53; E. C. Antoine three for 38, R. Dhanraj six for 48). *Trinidad & Tobago 16 pts.*

At Windsor Park, Roseau (Dominica), February 9, 10, 11, 12. Windward Islands won by 196 runs. Windward Islands 234 (R. A. Marshall 34, D. Thomas 70, C. A. Davis 32 not out; B. St A. Browne four for 32) and 278 (D. A. Joseph 67, R. A. Marshall 38, D. Thomas 49, R. N. Lewis 51 not out; B. St A. Browne three for 56, N. C. McGarrell three for 44); Guyana* 125 (A. R. Percival 42; C. A. Davis three for 35, D. Thomas three for eight) and 191 (N. A. De Groot 41, A. R. Percival 64; R. N. Lewis seven for 66, R. A. Marshall three for 41). *Windward Islands 16 pts.*

At Kensington Oval, Bridgetown, February 16, 17, 18, 19. Drawn. Barbados* 270 (A. F. G. Griffith 69, R. L. Hoyte 75, R. O. Hurley 47, Extras 31; L. R. Williams five for 32) and 355 for seven dec. (P. A. Wallace 44, A. F. G. Griffith 145, A. E. Proverbs 50, R. O. Hurley 36 not out; B. S. Murphy five for 125); Jamaica 377 (R. G. Samuels 53, M. D. Ventura 44, G. R. Breese 50, D. S. Morgan 63, S. G. B. Ford 56 not out, B. S. Murphy 35, Extras 53; P. I. C. Thompson five for 105) and 151 for four (T. O. Powell 58, L. R. Williams 33). *Barbados 4 pts, Jamaica 8 pts.*

At Bourda, Georgetown, February 16, 17, 18. Leeward Islands won by eight wickets. Guyana* 148 (Extras 33; K. C. G. Benjamin five for 22) and 147 (K. F. Semple 32; W. D. Phillip four for 31, H. A. G. Anthony three for 32); Leeward Islands 210 (S. C. Williams 40, L. A. Harrigan 39, C. M. Tuckett 34; M. V. Nagamootoo seven for 76) and 86 for two (L. C. Weekes 39 not out). *Leeward Islands 16 pts.*

At Queen's Park, St George's (Grenada), February 16, 17, 18, 19. Windward Islands won by seven wickets. Trinidad & Tobago* 279 (P. V. Simmons 55, R. A. M. Smith 43, M. Bodoe 59, D. Williams 33; R. N. Lewis three for 70) and 165 (P. V. Simmons 32, S. Ragoonath 53, L. A. Roberts 31; R. N. Lewis five for 49, R. A. Marshall four for 60); Windward Islands 376 (D. A. Joseph 78, U. Pope 84, R. A. Marshall 112; N. B. Francis three for 66, M. Bodoe three for 78) and 69 for three (J. A. R. Sylvester 35 not out; E. C. Antoine three for 31). *Windward Islands 16 pts.*

At Albion, Berbice, February 23, 24, 25, 26. Drawn. Barbados* 216 for six (P. A. Wallace 81, A. F. G. Griffith 56, F. L. Reifer 33 not out) v Guyana. *Guyana 4 pts, Barbados 4 pts.*

Leg-spinner Ramnaresh Sarwan of Guyana became the youngest first-class player in the history of West Indian cricket, making his debut at 15 years and 245 days. He returned figures of 10–4–9–1.

At Sabina Park, Kingston, February 23, 24, 25, 26. Jamaica won by 208 runs. Jamaica* 222 (T. O. Powell 125 not out; D. Thomas four for 42, R. A. Marshall three for 77) and 340 (R. G. Samuels 33, M. D. Ventura 102, T. O. Powell 69; R. A. Marshall seven for 99); Windward Islands 162 (K. K. Sylvester 34, J. A. R. Sylvester 52; N. O. Perry three for 52, B. S. Murphy five for 35) and 192 (A. J. Pierre 54, C. A. Davis 32; N. O. Perry five for 58). *Jamaica 16 pts.*

At Grove Park, Charlestown (Nevis), February 23, 24, 25, 26. Trinidad & Tobago won by nine wickets. Leeward Islands 295 (S. C. Williams 61, L. A. Harrigan 67, D. R. E. Joseph 43; R. Dhanraj nine for 97) and 175 (S. C. Williams 38, D. R. E. Joseph 62; R. Dhanraj seven for 70, D. Ramnarine three for 56); Trinidad & Tobago* 317 (A. Balliram 53, P. V. Simmons 97, M. Bodoe 32, E. C. Antoine 34 not out; K. C. G. Benjamin five for 82) and 156 for one (A. Balliram 70 not out, P. V. Simmons 64 not out). *Trinidad & Tobago 16 pts.*

Leg-spinners Dhanraj and Ramnarine took all 20 Leeward Islands wickets. Dhanraj's 16 wickets in the match was a record in Shell Shield/Red Stripe Cup cricket.

FINAL

TRINIDAD & TOBAGO v LEEWARD ISLANDS

At Guaracara Park, Pointe-à-Pierre, March 8, 9, 10, 11, 12. Leeward Islands won by 73 runs. Toss: Leeward Islands. First-class debut: R. M. Powell.

Trinidad & Tobago lost the inaugural Red Stripe Cup final, despite having led the table by 16 points from their successful challengers, Leeward Islands. Their captain, Simmons, leading the side because Brian Lara was at the World Cup, took it philosophically: "It was a new system, and everyone knew beforehand the conditions under which it was being played," he said. The Leewards completed victory on the fifth morning, but had held the advantage from the opening day, when they ran up 400. Joseph, their captain, and wicket-keeper Jacobs rescued them from a shaky 122 for four and Anthony smashed 53 off 40 balls. The home side looked positive at 264 for four, but off-spinner Ronald Powell, on his first-class debut, instigated a collapse of four wickets for 19, and they trailed by 70 runs. As the pitch began to turn, the Leewards struggled against Dhanraj's leg-spin; his eighth wicket of the match reduced them to 99 for five. But Powell rose to the occasion again, helping Cannonier set a target of 301. Trinidad & Tobago had just over two days to make the runs, but only Balliram, who batted more than six hours, showed the necessary staying power.

Man of the Match: D. R. E. Joseph.

Close of play: First day, Leeward Islands 400; Second day, Trinidad & Tobago 327-9 (R. Dhanraj 13*, N. B. Francis 12*); Third day, Trinidad & Tobago 10-0 (A. Balliram 4*, A. Lawrence 0*); Fourth day, Trinidad & Tobago 204-8 (R. Dhanraj 21*, E. C. Antoine 6*).

Leeward Islands

S. C. Williams b Francis	29	– c and b Dhanraj	24
L. A. Harrigan c Williams b Francis	9	– c Dhanraj b Lawrence	36
M. D. Liburd c Simmons b Dhanraj	25	– c Simmons b Dhanraj	13
*D. R. E. Joseph c Balliram b Antoine	118	– c Bodoe b Dhanraj	13
C. D. Cannonier c sub (K. Mason) b Dhanraj	8	– not out	41
†R. D. Jacobs lbw b Dhanraj	89	– c sub (K. Mason) b Dhanraj	1
R. M. Powell c Lawrence b Bodoe	14	– b Samaroo	43
H. A. G. Anthony lbw b Antoine	53	– b Samaroo	13
L. C. Weekes c Simmons b Dhanraj	21	– run out	9
K. C. G. Benjamin c Smith b Samaroo	16	– (11) c Smith b Samaroo	8
W. D. Phillip not out	8	– (10) c Bodoe b Samaroo	21
B 1, l-b 4, w 3, n-b 2	10	B 1, l-b 5, n-b 2	8
1/16 2/54 3/79 4/122 5/231 6/263 7/339 8/371 9/382	400	1/46 2/76 3/79 4/94 5/99 6/163 7/181 8/196 9/222	230

Bowling: *First Innings*—Antoine 22–2–88–2; Francis 10–0–42–2; Dhanraj 29–3–140–4; Samaroo 13–0–66–1; Bodoe 12–0–47–1; Simmons 4–0–12–0. *Second Innings*—Antoine 7–1–32–0; Simmons 3–0–16–0; Lawrence 12–4–28–1; Dhanraj 25–5–67–4; Bodoe 15–5–37–0; Samaroo 13.4–0–44–4.

Trinidad & Tobago

A. Balliram b Weekes	5	– c and b Phillip	57
A. Lawrence c Jacobs b Benjamin	44	– lbw b Benjamin	5
S. Ragoonath c Jacobs b Weekes	4	– c Jacobs b Anthony	7
*P. V. Simmons c Jacobs b Benjamin	36	– run out	24
R. A. M. Smith c Liburd b Powell	99	– c Williams b Phillip	10
M. Bodoe c Williams b Powell	65	– c Jacobs b Powell	19
†D. Williams c Williams b Powell	10	– b Phillip	12
A. Samaroo c Jacobs b Weekes	1	– c Powell b Anthony	19
R. Dhanraj not out	14	– b Benjamin	26
E. C. Antoine c Cannonier b Weekes	13	– b Anthony	19
N. B. Francis c Williams b Weekes	14	– not out	0
L-b 8, w 1, n-b 16	25	B 3, l-b 17, n-b 9	29
1/18 2/38 3/93 4/126 5/264 6/282 7/283 8/283 9/301	330	1/17 2/28 3/64 4/77 5/118 6/146 7/155 8/189 9/225	227

Bowling: *First Innings*—Benjamin 21–4–76–2; Weekes 23.2–4–83–5; Anthony 15–1–76–0; Phillip 3–1–19–0; Powell 29–5–68–3. *Second Innings*—Benjamin 33.3–15–38–2; Weekes 23–8–33–0; Anthony 20–2–52–3; Phillip 26–8–65–3; Powell 9–2–19–1.

Umpires: L. H. Barker and E. Nicholls
(C. E. Cumberbatch deputised for Barker on the 4th and 5th days).

SHELL SHIELD AND RED STRIPE CUP WINNERS

The Shell Shield was replaced by the Red Stripe Cup after the 1986-87 season.

1965-66	Barbados	1975-76	Trinidad / Barbados
1966-67	Barbados	1976-77	Barbados
1967-68	No competition	1977-78	Barbados
1968-69	Jamaica	1978-79	Barbados
1969-70	Trinidad	1979-80	Barbados
1970-71	Trinidad	1980-81	Combined Islands
1971-72	Barbados	1981-82	Barbados
1972-73	Guyana	1982-83	Guyana
1973-74	Barbados	1983-84	Barbados
1974-75	Guyana		

1984-85	Trinidad & Tobago	1990-91	Barbados
1985-86	Barbados	1991-92	Jamaica
1986-87	Guyana	1992-93	Guyana
1987-88	Jamaica	1993-94	Leeward Islands
1988-89	Jamaica	1994-95	Barbados
1989-90	Leeward Islands	1995-96	Leeward Islands

Barbados have won the title outright 13 times, Guyana 5, Jamaica 4, Leeward Islands and Trinidad/Trinidad & Tobago 3, Combined Islands 1. Barbados and Trinidad also shared the title once.

OTHER FIRST-CLASS MATCH

The match between Jamaica and Lancashire on April 10, 11, 12 may be found in English Counties Overseas, 1995-96.

SHELL/SANDALS TROPHY, 1995-96

Note: Matches in this section were not first-class.

Zone A

At Kensington Oval, Bridgetown, October 28. Barbados won by one wicket. Jamaica 230 (47.2 overs) (D. S. Morgan 56, M. D. Ventura 38, N. O. Perry 56, Extras 39; A. C. Cummins five for 37, O. D. Gibson three for 39); Barbados* 234 for nine (48.5 overs) (P. A. Wallace 53, O. D. Gibson 41 not out; J. C. Adams three for 44).

At Kensington Oval, Bridgetown, October 29. Barbados won by four wickets. Jamaica 236 (50 overs) (T. O. Powell 53, J. C. Adams 57, M. D. Ventura 50; A. C. Cummins three for 35); Barbados* 240 for six (46.3 overs) (S. L. Campbell 44, R. I. C. Holder 49, A. C. Cummins 43 not out).

At Kaiser Sports Ground, Discovery Bay, November 4. Jamaica won by seven wickets. Windward Islands 148 for eight (50 overs) (D. A. Joseph 30, J. R. Murray 40; R. C. Haynes four for 22); Jamaica* 151 for three (41.4 overs) (D. S. Morgan 52, T. O. Powell 41).

At Sabina Park, Kingston, November 5. Jamaica won by five wickets, their target having been revised to 148 from 44 overs. Windward Islands 160 for nine (50 overs) (D. A. Joseph 48; M. C. Gibbs three for 22); Jamaica* 150 for five (39.5 overs) (D. S. Morgan 32, J. C. Adams 56 not out).

At Mindoo Phillip Park, Castries (St Lucia), November 11. No result. Barbados 180 for three (37 overs) (P. A. Wallace 34, F. L. Reifer 38, R. I. C. Holder 76 not out) v Windward Islands*.

At Mindoo Phillip Park, Castries (St Lucia), November 12, 13. Windward Islands v Barbados. Abandoned.

A replay was planned on November 13 but was also abandoned because insufficient time was available to play 25 overs a side.

Barbados 6 pts, Jamaica 4 pts, Windward Islands 2 pts.

Zone B

At Bourda, Georgetown, October 28. Guyana won by 33 runs. Guyana* 264 for six (50 overs) (S. Chanderpaul 69, C. L. Hooper 79, R. A. Harper 31); Trinidad & Tobago 231 (49.3 overs) (P. V. Simmons 55, S. Ragoonath 41, R. J. Bishop 44; R. A. Harper four for 18).

At Hampton Court, Essequibo, October 29. Trinidad & Tobago won by 135 runs. Trinidad & Tobago 265 for nine (50 overs) (P. V. Simmons 59, S. Ragoonath 35, B. C. Lara 67, L. A. Roberts 55; S. Chanderpaul four for 22); Guyana* 130 for seven (50 overs) (R. A. Harper 38 not out).

At Albion, Berbice, November 4. Leeward Islands won by seven wickets. Guyana* 149 for eight (50 overs) (K. F. Semple 51 not out); Leeward Islands 150 for three (40.2 overs) (S. C. Williams 74).

At Blairmont, West Coast Berbice, November 5. Guyana won by 62 runs. Guyana 296 for five (50 overs) (R. E. Browne 54, S. Chanderpaul 51, C. L. Hooper 104, R. A. Harper 44 not out; K. C. G. Benjamin three for 55); Leeward Islands* 234 (48.2 overs) (M. D. Liburd 43, K. L. T. Arthurton 66, D. R. E. Joseph 34; S. Chanderpaul four for 45).

At Queen's Park Oval, Port-of-Spain, November 11. Trinidad & Tobago won by four wickets. Leeward Islands* 199 (47.2 overs) (R. B. Richardson 30, D. R. E. Joseph 64; I. R. Bishop three for 43, R. Dhanraj three for 47); Trinidad & Tobago 200 for six (44.5 overs) (B. C. Lara 109, L. A. Roberts 36).

At Queen's Park Oval, Port-of-Spain, November 12. No result. Trinidad & Tobago* 269 for seven (50 overs) (B. C. Lara 112, K. Mason 30 not out, I. R. Bishop 39) v Leeward Islands.

At Queen's Park Oval, Port-of-Spain, November 14. No result. Leeward Islands* 70 for two (20 overs) (S. C. Williams 43 not out) v Trinidad & Tobago.

The WICBC ordered a replay of the unfinished November 12 match against the ruling of match referee Ralph Gosein after a disagreement over playing regulations.

Trinidad & Tobago 5 pts, Guyana 4 pts, Leeward Islands 3 pts.

Semi-finals

At Kensington Oval, Bridgetown, November 18. Guyana won by 47 runs, Barbados's target having been revised to 243 from 39 overs. Guyana 289 for five (50 overs) (S. Chanderpaul 80, C. L. Hooper 99, R. A. Harper 30 not out); Barbados* 195 (34.4 overs) (S. L. Campbell 56, R. I. C. Holder 38, C. O. Browne 31; R. A. Harper four for 22, S. Chanderpaul three for 22).

At Queen's Park Oval, Port-of-Spain, November 18. Trinidad & Tobago won on scoring-rate when rain ended play. Trinidad & Tobago* 168 (48.3 overs) (P. V. Simmons 42, K. Mason 37; R. C. Haynes three for 31); Jamaica 95 for four (31.2 overs) (D. S. Morgan 34).

Final

At Queen's Park Oval, Port-of-Spain, November 25. No result. Trinidad & Tobago* 43 for one (7.3 overs) v Guyana.

(Replay of Final) At Queen's Park Oval, Port-of-Spain, November 26. No result. Guyana* 88 for three (18.2 overs) (N. E. F. Barry 36) v Trinidad & Tobago.

Trinidad & Tobago and Guyana were declared joint champions.

HONOURS' LIST, 1996-97

In 1996-97, the following were decorated for their services to cricket:

Queen's Birthday Honours, 1996: K. L. T. Arthurton (West Indies) MBE (St Kitts and Nevis list), T. E. E. Pratt (services to cricket in Wales) MBE, R. C. Russell (England) MBE, Rev. M. D. Vockins (Worcestershire secretary) OBE.

New Year's Honours, 1997: A. V. Bedser (England) Knight Bachelor, W. J. Orford (services to cricket in West Midlands) MBE, O. S. Wheatley (Warwickshire and Glamorgan; chairman of Sports Council for Wales and former TCCB cricket chairman) CBE.

CRICKET IN NEW ZEALAND, 1995-96

By TERRY POWER

Mark Greatbatch

One small mid-winter news item showed how much the last two domestic seasons had been maladministered by the board of New Zealand Cricket. The item was Adam Parore's announcement that he would be available for Auckland again in 1996-97 after spending two seasons with Northern Districts. Well, nominally. The programme had been so arranged that Parore had not played for Northern Districts in a single first-class match. Including Tests and tour games, the full first-class programme in 1995-96 totalled 21 matches, the lowest number since 1974-75 and an indication of how far back the first-class game was being dragged.

In its dying months before being replaced, the old board installed Glenn Turner as coach and convenor of selectors, for what proved to be a short term of office. Turner had most recently been a perceptive TV commentator, and his clear-headed, analytical approach to coaching was a considerable improvement on Geoff Howarth's methods. Nathan Astle especially appreciated Turner's help – he scored five hundreds in Tests and one-day internationals during the season. The results were actually a mixed bag. The Test record was even worse than in 1994-95, when New Zealand did beat South Africa once. There were three big losses and no wins in eight Tests, with no near-misses, even against Zimbabwe. The record in one-day internationals improved from four wins and 14 losses to 11 up and 12 down. Subjectively, it seemed there were more days, especially against Pakistan and in the Caribbean, when New Zealand looked able to beat anybody, and little abject surrender. However, the average standard of opposition (including Zimbabwe, the United Arab Emirates and Holland) was lower than the previous summer.

Turner inherited a team in which several key relationships were poor, and he did not improve matters. Indeed, his view of man-management – it was "quite trivial and I believe quite puerile almost to refer to it" – helped to explain why his second term as coach lasted just one season.

A significant decision was to choose Canterbury wicket-keeper/batsman Lee Germon as captain. This meant removing Ken Rutherford as skipper, for which there was an arguable case, and as batsman, for which there was no cricketing case at all, especially in a World Cup season. He and Parore were easily New Zealand's best limited-overs batsmen in 1994-95, yet, when the one-day series in

India started, neither was playing. But there was a view that Rutherford's flow of candid comment would be hard to stop, and could weaken a new, insecure leadership. He left New Zealand to captain Transvaal. Meanwhile, Simon Doull, the best Test bowler on the South African tour, was discarded for the raw, unready Robert Kennedy before the Zimbabwe series and said he had been "blatantly lied to" from within the selection panel. The off-with-their-heads policy, which also affected other established performers from Chris Pringle to Mark Greatbatch, was an approach which a country with playing resources as thin as New Zealand's could ill afford. Another unhappy feature of the new order was that it seemed to be moving away from the open society favoured by former NZC chairman Peter McDermott and Rutherford.

Other aspects of the old regime were not missed. The changeover came after years of dissatisfaction over alleged inefficiencies and mistakes. The board had invested unsuccessfully in both stocks and property. And New Zealand's increasing number of setbacks on the field had culminated in the disastrous 1994-95 centenary season and a public outcry. A committee led by John Hood was set up to review the game's administration, and the Hood Report was adopted in full. It put more emphasis on the role of chief executive, and reduced the board from 11 to eight, ending the system whereby each major association elected a representative, which was deemed to have caused excessive parochialism.

Graham Dowling was replaced as chief executive by Christopher Doig, a former club player, operatic singer and arts administrator. His increased power meant that the new, smaller board lost the spotlight. Its best-known member was Terry Jarvis, who established the New Zealand first-wicket record of 387 with Turner at Georgetown in 1971-72 and later, as a businessman, was responsible for New Zealand's vastly expanded sports coverage from Sky Television. Other important appointments included John F. Reid, the former Test batsman, as operations manager, while New South Wales player Neil Maxwell became marketing manager.

The season ended with another change in direction, however. Turner was originally offered a two-year contract, but had preferred one initially, and the board chose to advertise the coach's job internationally. From 17 applications, they picked Steve Rixon, the former Australian wicket-keeper who had coached New South Wales to three Sheffield Shield successes. This meant sacking Turner, who responded with a fierce attack on Doig's alleged dictatorial tendencies, and promised to keep the public informed about what was really going on. Turner also lost his other post as convenor of selectors to Ross Dykes, who immediately said he would consider all those left by the wayside the previous season, and retrieved several, including Greatbatch and Bryan Young, but discarded Shane Thomson and Matthew Hart. In August, 14 players were offered contracts for 1996-97, when England toured, but the list specifically excluded Chris Cairns and Parore, "as a result of breaches of the New Zealand Cricket code of conduct". This evidently referred to comments mildly critical of Turner's leadership which these two made after leaving the West Indies tour with injuries. Both were, however, included in a training squad of 26.

The new board had not taken office until November 1995, at an NZC annual meeting two months later than usual, so it could not be blamed for the bizarre planning for 1995-96, including the latest start to a peacetime domestic first-class season since 1890-91. There was no first-class cricket before the Pakistan Test in December and the Shell Trophy finally kicked off on January 17 – during the First Test against Zimbabwe. One of the most obvious problems of the national team was that they tended to take undue risks when they needed to get their heads down; while the players have to take final responsibility, the one-day oriented programme did them a disservice.

Aucklanders were rarely in the selectors' eyes, which largely accounts for their triumph in the Shell Trophy. Justin Vaughan combined intelligent captaincy with the best all-round cricket in the competition – 453 runs at over 50, and 19 wickets – before his belated recall to the national colours in the West Indies. Medium-pacer Pringle was frequently effective in both first-class and one-day cricket; left-arm spinner Mark Haslam at last became a regular and successful Auckland team member, bowling 300 overs for 28 wickets. Opener Craig Spearman did earn international recognition, scoring a maiden Test century against Zimbabwe on his home ground, Eden Park. Matt Horne, younger brother of former Test batsman Phil Horne, capped a fine club season by being picked for the last two matches, both against Wellington. He made 113 in the group match, where victory meant that Auckland led the table by one point, and 190 in the final. Both were memorable, stroke-filled innings which should lead on to a substantial first-class career.

When dropped by New Zealand, Greatbatch said he was told by Turner to go away and score runs. The opposition he faced was not always of the highest class, but he was easily the outstanding Shell Trophy batsman, with four centuries for Central Districts, three of them in successive innings, including a double, at an average of 155.75. Reselection still eluded him. Central Districts had three of the top four places in the averages. Behind Greatbatch was Llorne Howell, who led the two conglomerate elevens against the Zimbabweans. Left-handed opener Glen Sulzberger, a former New Zealand Youth player, made his first-class debut at nearly 23 and responded with two centuries. Central Districts were joint top with Wellington after three rounds. They then collapsed for 65 in the top-of-the-table match with Wellington and failed to reach the final. Greatbatch also denounced Auckland for using the same pitch (substandard, in his opinion) for successive matches, both of which they needed to win. "We have to play on first-class pitches," said Greatbatch. "You can't tell me Eden Park No. 2 [the Outer Oval] is that. It's a disgrace, to my mind." Auckland coach John Bracewell cracked back that this was "rather trivial and vindictive". Ethics aside, Eden Park pitches have attracted widespread criticism throughout the 1990s.

Wellington's counterpoint to Central Districts' batting was to have three seamers in the top five bowling averages. The 28 wickets secured by Dougie Brown, from Warwickshire, equalled Haslam's as the season's biggest haul and, at 15.71, were almost half the price. The fiery Richard Petrie startled some, first by being made captain and then with his effectiveness in the role; he also batted with useful vigour and took 18 economical wickets. Glen Jonas continued to improve as a stock medium-pacer. But the one genuinely fast bowler, Heath Davis, was less productive. The batting, led by opener John Aiken, proved inadequate when put to the test in the two crucial matches in Auckland, though Ian Billcliff, once an outstanding Dunedin schoolboy batsman, moved from Otago and suggested he was adjusting to the adult game at last.

Canterbury were second-last when it came to the first-class Shell Trophy, chiefly due to being shredded by national team requirements, but for the later stages of the Shell Cup they had the best one-day side in the 25-year history of inter-provincial limited-overs; they won all ten matches and romped through the semi-final and final, where they beat Northern Districts. An outstanding fielding side backed by big, keen crowds – there were over 17,000 at the cup final – the "Lancaster Bombers" had an attack which could both penetrate and contain, headed by Mark Priest and the miserly Chris Harris. A powerful batting line-up was led by Astle, who joined the Indian tour for the one-day internationals and returned to run up a record Shell Cup aggregate of 687 at 62.45.

The other team most affected by multiple international calls were the beaten cup finalists, Northern Districts. They also lost Doull, after their opening Shell

Trophy game, against Wellington; he suffered a foot injury during a match-winning ninth-wicket stand. Richard de Groen retired on a high note, with 11 wickets in his final match against Canterbury. The best batsman was Young, who had lost his international place after a mediocre Indian tour. Mark Bailey, promoted prematurely as a teenager, developed into a mature batsman and was a late reinforcement on the Caribbean tour. Robbie Hart – Matthew's younger brother – became the wicket-keeping heir apparent when he was the pick of a New Zealand Emerging Players team which toured Australia in March.

Otago fought doggedly but took no points at all. In the second season of his transformation from left-arm spinner into middle-order batsman, Mark Richardson showed his century against the West Indians a year before was no fluke with three more hundreds. Robbie Lawson followed his maiden century against the Zimbabweans with a double against Central Districts, justifying the selectors who stuck with him through lean times. Jeff Wilson returned from All Black travels to first-class cricket after missing the whole of 1994-95. A few bright performances prompted some watchers to suggest he should go to the World Cup. Off-spinner Paul Wiseman achieved a breakthrough, but the pace attack was less effective than recently.

Beyond major provincial cricket, there were several worthwhile steps forward. An inter-districts competition, which provides the early-season minor representative action, spread to involve Auckland and Wellington, thus covering the whole country except Christchurch and Dunedin. A national secondary schoolgirls' knockout, compliments of Yoplait Yoghurt, now accompanies the equivalent boys' Gillette Cup. The New Zealand cricket academy opened at Lincoln University, south of Christchurch, with Dayle Hadlee at the helm. The Under-19 and women's teams brightened the winter back home with bulletins from their successful tours of England.

After his retirement, Richard de Groen produced a report along with Northern Districts coach David White, based on a survey of provincial players. Its sensible proposals for the future of domestic first-class cricket showed yet again how far the New Zealand game had gone off the track in recent years.

FIRST-CLASS AVERAGES, 1995-96

BATTING

(Qualification: 5 innings, average 40.00)

	M	*I*	*NO*	*R*	*HS*	*100s*	*Avge*
M. J. Greatbatch (*C. Districts*)	5	6	2	623	202	4	155.75
L. G. Howell (*C. Districts*)	7	9	1	550	181	2	68.75
M. H. Richardson (*Otago*)	5	10	1	615	146	3	68.33
G. R. Sulzberger (*C. Districts*)	5	6	0	328	142	2	54.66
R. G. Twose (*New Zealand*)	3	6	1	272	94	0	54.40
R. A. Lawson (*Otago*)	5	9	1	414	200	2	51.75
J. T. C. Vaughan (*Auckland*)	6	10	1	453	127	1	50.33
H. T. Davis (*Wellington*)	5	8	5	143	38*	0	47.66
A. C. Parore (*New Zealand*)	3	6	2	190	84*	0	47.50
M. D. Bailey (*N. Districts*)	5	7	0	322	98	0	46.00
C. L. Cairns (*New Zealand*)	3	6	0	275	120	1	45.83
B. A. Young (*N. Districts*)	6	11	1	444	133	2	44.40
C. O. Findlay (*C. Districts*)	5	6	3	133	52	0	44.33
M. E. Parlane (*N. Districts*)	5	8	2	261	132*	1	43.50
C. M. Spearman (*New Zealand*)	3	6	0	254	112	1	42.33
J. M. Aiken (*Wellington*)	8	15	3	501	170*	1	41.75

* *Signifies not out.*

BOWLING

(Qualification: 15 wickets)

	O	*M*	*R*	*W*	*BB*	*5W/i*	*Avge*
D. R. Brown (*Wellington*)	166.1	43	440	28	5-39	2	15.71
R. G. Petrie (*Wellington*)	134.5	53	294	18	5-23	1	16.33
R. P. de Groen (*N. Districts*)	196.2	64	453	22	7-58	1	20.59
D. K. Morrison (*Auckland*)	116	27	376	18	5-43	1	20.88
G. R. Jonas (*Wellington*)	195.1	57	510	23	4-39	0	22.17
C. Pringle (*Auckland*)	222.5	62	606	25	5-198	1	24.24
G. I. Allott (*Canterbury*)	242.5	49	644	26	6-93	1	24.76
P. J. Wiseman (*Otago*)	268.5	78	587	23	7-50	2	25.52
W. A. Wisneski (*C. Districts*)	185.5	43	545	21	5-88	1	25.95
J. T. C. Vaughan (*Auckland*)	209.5	77	510	19	4-44	0	26.84
C. L. Cairns (*New Zealand*)	139.1	37	405	15	4-51	0	27.00
M. J. Haslam (*Auckland*)	299.4	102	822	28	4-60	0	29.35
H. T. Davis (*Wellington*)	127	26	482	16	5-32	1	30.12
S. J. Roberts (*Canterbury*)	170	41	523	16	4-113	0	32.68
S. B. O'Connor (*Otago*)	183.2	47	529	15	4-62	0	35.26
J. W. Wilson (*Otago*)	194	49	529	15	5-71	1	35.26
A. J. Penn (*C. Districts*)	193	36	626	17	4-53	0	36.82

SHELL TROPHY, 1995-96

	Played	*Won*	*Lost*	*Drawn*	*1st-inns Points*	*Points*
Auckland	5	4	1	0	12	44
Wellington	5	3	2	0	20	43†
Central Districts	5	2	1	2	16	32
Northern Districts	5	2	1	2	8	24
Canterbury	5	1	4	0	4	12
Otago	5	0	3	2	0	0

Final: Auckland beat Wellington by nine wickets.

Win = 8 pts; lead on first innings = 4 pts.
† One point deducted for slow over-rate.

Under New Zealand Cricket playing conditions, two extras are scored for every no-ball bowled whether scored off or not. Any runs scored off the bat are credited to the batsman, while byes and leg-byes are counted as no-balls, in accordance with Law 24.9, in addition to the initial penalty.

*In the following scores, * by the name of a team indicates that they won the toss.*

At Lancaster Park, Christchurch, January 17, 18, 19. Central Districts won by an innings and 148 runs. Canterbury* 128 (A. J. Penn four for 53, W. A. Wisneski three for 27) and 199 (C. D. Cumming 33, M. W. Priest 30, S. J. Roberts 34; C. J. M. Furlong three for 50); Central Districts 475 for nine dec. (L. G. Howell 181, M. J. Greatbatch 115, W. A. Wisneski 73; M. F. Sharpe three for 75). *Central Districts 12 pts.*

At Molyneux Park, Alexandra, January 17, 18, 19, 20. Auckland won by 148 runs. Auckland* 234 (S. J. Peterson 34, J. T. C. Vaughan 42; S. B. O'Connor four for 62, A. J. Gale three for 63) and 394 for six dec. (R. A. Jones 75, S. J. Peterson 37, S. M. Lynch 42, A. C. Barnes 100 not out, J. M. Mills 73 not out; A. J. Gale three for 92); Otago 127 (R. T. King 35, M. H. Richardson 36; D. K. Morrison five for 43) and 353 (R. A. Lawson 34, M. J. Lamont 92, M. H. Richardson 146; D. K. Morrison three for 98, C. Pringle four for 54). *Auckland 12 pts.*

At Basin Reserve, Wellington, January 17, 18, 19, 20. Northern Districts won by two wickets. Wellington 282 (J. M. Aiken 41, D. R. Brown 47, J. D. Wells 69; S. B. Doull three for 60, M. N. Hart three for 40) and 370 for eight dec. (P. J. B. Chandler 41, J. M. Aiken 170 not out, J. D. Wells 47; S. B. Doull three for 55, S. A. Thomson three for 65); Northern Districts* 200 (S. A. Thomson 35, M. N. Hart 31; D. R. Brown four for 35, R. G. Petrie four for 41) and 453 for eight (B. A. Pocock 50, M. D. Bell 74, M. D. Bailey 72, M. N. Hart 87 not out, S. B. Doull 67 not out, Extras 48; G. R. Jonas three for 100, J. D. Wells three for 116). *Northern Districts 8 pts, Wellington 4 pts.*

Northern Districts were 346 for eight chasing 453; Hart and Doull shared an unbroken stand of 107 to secure victory.

At Dudley Park, Rangiora, January 22, 23, 24, 25. Auckland won by ten wickets. Auckland* 517 for nine dec. (A. T. Reinholds 52, S. J. Peterson 53, S. M. Lynch 65, J. T. C. Vaughan 127, A. C. Barnes 44, J. M. Mills 42, C. Pringle 47, D. K. Morrison 40 not out, Extras 37; S. J. Roberts four for 113) and 46 for no wkt (A. T. Reinholds 31 not out); Canterbury 216 (B. R. Hartland 33, C. D. Cumming 41, M. W. Priest 53; D. K. Morrison three for 35, C. Pringle three for 59) and 345 (C. D. McMillan 34, R. M. Frew 125, M. W. Priest 41, M. E. L. Lane 52; D. K. Morrison three for 44, M. J. Haslam four for 94). *Auckland 12 pts.*

At Smallbone Park, Rotorua, January 22, 23, 24, 25. Drawn. Northern Districts* 382 (B. A. Young 125, M. E. Parlane 54, R. G. Hart 58, A. R. Tait 64; A. J. Penn three for 78, W. A. Wisneski three for 99) and 128 for one (B. A. Young 71 not out, B. A. Pocock 43); Central Districts 456 (L. G. Howell 92, M. J. Greatbatch 202, Extras 42; R. L. Hayes three for 121, including a hat-trick, A. R. Tait five for 109); *Central Districts 4 pts.*

Greatbatch's 202 lasted 452 minutes and 349 balls and included 25 fours. Hayes took a hat-trick of lbws, unique in first-class cricket in New Zealand; they were given by umpire M. B. Glennie.

At Carisbrook, Dunedin, January 22, 23, 24. Wellington won by 66 runs. Wellington 187 (D. R. Brown 40, C. J. Nevin 43 not out; S. B. O'Connor four for 77, J. W. Wilson five for 71) and 212 (P. J. B. Chandler 45, J. M. Aiken 68, R. G. Petrie 33; P. J. Wiseman seven for 50); Otago* 169 (M. H. Richardson 40, J. W. Wilson 49; G. R. Jonas three for 42, D. R. Brown five for 39) and 164 (J. W. Wilson 58; D. R. Brown five for 39, G. R. Jonas four for 40). *Wellington 12 pts.*

Wellington wicket-keeper Nevin caught ten in the match, a New Zealand record.

At Eden Park Outer Oval, Auckland, February 4, 5, 6, 7. Central Districts won by an innings and 90 runs. Central Districts 594 for eight dec. (G. R. Sulzberger 142, M. D. J. Walker 63, A. H. Jones 55, M. J. Greatbatch 162 not out, S. W. Duff 57, C. O. Findlay 52; C. Pringle five for 198); Auckland* 161 (A. T. Reinholds 37, J. I. Pamment 30, S. M. Lynch 31; S. W. Duff three for 47, G. R. Sulzberger four for 19) and 343 (A. T. Reinholds 41, R. A. Jones 42, S. J. Peterson 30, S. M. Lynch 63, J. T. C. Vaughan 62, J. M. Mills 36, M. J. Haslam 30 not out; A. J. Penn three for 94, S. W. Duff four for 41). *Central Districts 12 pts.*

Central Districts' total was their first over 500. Greatbatch scored his third century in successive innings.

At Trust Bank Park, Hamilton, February 4, 5, 6, 7. Drawn. Otago* 255 (M. J. Lamont 52, R. T. King 64, M. H. Richardson 45, S. A. Robinson 33; R. L. Hayes three for 50, G. E. Bradburn three for 63) and 358 for six (C. B. Gaffaney 56, M. J. Lamont 80, M. H. Richardson 105 not out, J. W. Wilson 59); Northern Districts 472 (B. A. Young 133, B. A. Pocock 53, M. D. Bell 49, M. D. Bailey 98, M. N. Hart 43, R. G. Hart 58; A. J. Gale three for 58, P. J. Wiseman four for 123). *Northern Districts 4 pts.*

Wiseman bowled 68 overs in Northern Districts' innings, a record for an Otago bowler.

At Basin Reserve, Wellington, February 4, 5. Wellington won by eight wickets. Canterbury* 147 (C. D. Cumming 43; G. R. Jonas three for 41, R. G. Petrie five for 23) and 141 (S. J. Pawson 48; H. T. Davis five for 32); Wellington 190 (J. M. Aiken 55) and 101 for two (M. H. Austen 68 not out). *Wellington 12 pts.*

At Eden Park Outer Oval, Auckland, February 9, 10, 11, 12. Auckland won by 70 runs. Auckland 189 (J. T. C. Vaughan 35, H. D. Barton 60 not out; R. P. de Groen three for 33, S. B. Styris four for 43) and 173 (R. A. Jones 34; S. B. Styris five for 52, M. N. Hart three for 15); Northern Districts* 150 (M. D. Bailey 63, R. G. Hart 30; J. T. C. Vaughan four for 44, M. J. Haslam three for 15) and 142 (M. D. Bailey 33; J. T. C. Vaughan three for 40, M. J. Haslam three for 17). *Auckland 12 pts.*

At Lancaster Park, Christchurch, February 9, 10, 11, 12. Canterbury won by five wickts. Otago 175 (S. A. Robinson 61; S. J. Roberts three for 48, G. I. Allott three for 37) and 334 (R. T. King 30, M. H. Richardson 66, J. W. Wilson 33, S. A. Robinson 93, Extras 33; S. J. Roberts three for 52, G. I. Allott six for 93); Canterbury* 176 (B. R. Hartland 56, C. D. Cumming 35, C. D. McMillan 37; J. W. Wilson four for 51, P. J. Wiseman five for 27) and 335 for five (B. R. Hartland 95, B. J. K. Doody 61, G. R. Stead 66, C. D. McMillan 51 not out, M. W. Priest 36 not out; P. J. Wiseman three for 126). *Canterbury 12 pts.*

At Trafalgar Park, Nelson, February 9, 10, 11. Wellington won by ten wickets. Central Districts* 65 (R. G. Petrie four for ten) and 247 (L. G. Howell 101, C. O. Findlay 37; G. R. Jonas four for 39, S. W. Weenink four for 69); Wellington 282 (M. H. Austen 44, D. R. Brown 40, C. J. Nevin 49; W. A. Wisneski five for 88) and 31 for no wkt. *Wellington 12 pts.*

Wellington wicket-keeper Nevin caught five and stumped one in Central Districts' second innings.

At Eden Park Outer Oval, Auckland, February 15, 16, 17, 18. Auckland won by five wickets. Wellington* 157 (P. J. B. Chandler 36, C. J. Nevin 34 not out; M. J. Haslam four for 60) and 230 (I. S. Billcliff 59, R. G. Petrie 65, D. R. Brown 35; M. J. Haslam three for 75); Auckland 143 (R. A. Jones 68; D. R. Brown three for 17, J. D. Wells four for 38) and 245 for five (A. T. Reinholds 43, M. J. Horne 113, J. T. C. Vaughan 49 not out; M. H. Austen four for 43). *Auckland 8 pts, Wellington 4 pts.*

At McLean Park, Napier, February 15, 16, 17, 18. Drawn. Otago* 280 (M. H. Richardson 104, P. J. Wiseman 77; W. A. Wisneski three for 60, C. J. M. Furlong three for 63) and 571 for eight (R. A. Lawson 200, M. G. Croy 104, R. T. King 117 not out, M. H. Richardson 39, J. W. Wilson 42; S. W. Duff three for 94); Central Districts 526 (G. R. Sulzberger 128, A. J. Penn 90, M. J. Greatbatch 126 not out, W. A. Wisneski 42; D. G. Sewell three for 93). *Central Districts 4 pts.*

Sulzberger and night-watchman Penn added 207 for Central Districts' fourth wicket. Lawson's 200, his maiden double-hundred, lasted 324 minutes and 260 balls and included 25 fours; he put on 305 with Croy for Otago's first wicket in the second innings.

At Trust Bank Park, Hamilton, February 15, 16, 17, 18. Northern Districts won by nine wickets. Northern Districts* 323 (M. D. Bell 48, M. D. Bailey 33, M. E. Parlane 132 not out, G. E. Bradburn 44; G. I. Allott three for 77) and 109 for one (B. A. Young 40, M. D. Bell 37 not out); Canterbury 98 (S. J. Roberts 34; R. P. de Groen seven for 58, R. L. Hayes three for 24) and 331 (B. R. Hartland 62, G. R. Stead 30, C. D. McMillan 35, R. M. Frew 84 not out; R. P. de Groen four for 71, G. E. Bradburn three for 81). *Northern Districts 12 pts.*

De Groen, who had announced this would be his final match, took 11 wickets, the first of which was his 200th in first-class cricket.

Final

At Eden Park Outer Oval, Auckland, February 29, March 1, 2, 3. Auckland won by nine wickets. Auckland 416 (M. J. Horne 190, S. J. Peterson 39, J. T. C. Vaughan 88; D. R. Brown four for 82, H. T. Davis three for 75) and 93 for one (A. T. Reinholds 52 not out); Wellington* 261 (J. M. Aiken 35, C. J. Nevin 86, H. T. Davis 38 not out; C. M. Brown four for 80, C. Pringle four for 46); and 247 (I. S. Billcliff 86, J. D. Wells 73; C. Pringle three for 56, J. T. C. Vaughan four for 68).

Horne scored the first two centuries of his career in successive innings against Wellington. In Auckland's second innings, Davis conceded 35 runs in his fifth over; the first five deliveries were no-balls.

PLUNKET SHIELD AND SHELL TROPHY WINNERS

The Plunket Shield was replaced by the Shell Trophy after the 1974-75 season.

1921-22	Auckland	1927-28	Wellington
1922-23	Canterbury	1928-29	Auckland
1923-24	Wellington	1929-30	Wellington
1924-25	Otago	1930-31	Canterbury
1925-26	Wellington	1931-32	Wellington
1926-27	Auckland	1932-33	Otago

1933-34	Auckland	1967-68	Central Districts
1934-35	Canterbury	1968-69	Auckland
1935-36	Wellington	1969-70	Otago
1936-37	Auckland	1970-71	Central Districts
1937-38	Auckland	1971-72	Otago
1938-39	Auckland	1972-73	Wellington
1939-40	Auckland	1973-74	Wellington
1940-45	No competition	1974-75	Otago
1945-46	Canterbury	1975-76	Canterbury
1946-47	Auckland	1976-77	Otago
1947-48	Otago	1977-78	Auckland
1948-49	Canterbury	1978-79	Otago
1949-50	Wellington	1979-80	Northern Districts
1950-51	Otago	1980-81	Auckland
1951-52	Canterbury	1981-82	Wellington
1952-53	Otago	1982-83	Wellington
1953-54	Central Districts	1983-84	Canterbury
1954-55	Wellington	1984-85	Wellington
1955-56	Canterbury	1985-86	Otago
1956-57	Wellington	1986-87	Central Districts
1957-58	Otago	1987-88	Otago
1958-59	Auckland	1988-89	Auckland
1959-60	Canterbury	1989-90	Wellington
1960-61	Wellington	1990-91	Auckland
1961-62	Wellington	1991-92	Central Districts
1962-63	Northern Districts		Northern Districts
1963-64	Auckland	1992-93	Northern Districts
1964-65	Canterbury	1993-94	Canterbury
1965-66	Wellington	1994-95	Auckland
1966-67	Central Districts	1995-96	Auckland

Auckland and Wellington have won the title outright 18 times, Otago 13, Canterbury 12, Central Districts 5, Northern Districts 3. Central Districts and Northern Districts also shared the title once.

SHELL CUP, 1995-96

Note: Matches in this section were not first-class.

Play-offs

At Basin Reserve, Wellington, January 6. Wellington won by 50 runs. Wellington* 287 for seven (50 overs) (M. H. Austen 62, P. J. B. Chandler 45, I. S. Billcliff 32, D. R. Brown 53, R. G. Petrie 61); Auckland 237 (46.2 overs) (C. M. Spearman 67, J. I. Pamment 66, A. C. Barnes 41; G. R. Larsen five for 30).

At Lancaster Park, Christchurch, January 6. Canterbury won by 131 runs. Canterbury* 245 for seven (42 overs) (N. J. Astle 96, S. P. Fleming 36, C. Z. Harris 43 not out); Northern Districts 114 (27.4 overs) (B. G. Cooper 30; C. L. Cairns four for 33).

At Trust Bank Park, Hamilton, January 8. Northern Districts won by 30 runs. Northern Districts* 220 for nine (50 overs) (M. E. Parlane 78, B. G. Cooper 37, S. A. Thomson 37; G. R. Jonas four for 52); Wellington 190 (47.4 overs) (R. G. Petrie 44; S. A. Thomson three for 28).

Final

At Lancaster Park, Christchurch, January 10. Canterbury won by 116 runs. Canterbury* 329 for five (50 overs) (N. J. Astle 129, C. D. McMillan 33, S. P. Fleming 102); Northern Districts 213 (44.4 overs) (M. E. Parlane 31, A. C. Parore 51, R. L. Hayes 33 not out; M. B. Owens three for 24, G. I. Allott three for 72)

Canterbury's 329 was the highest ever total in the Shell Cup. Astle scored the first century in a Shell Cup final.

CRICKET IN INDIA, 1995-96

By R. MOHAN and SUDHIR VAIDYA

Sunil Joshi

With the World Cup, the game's quadrennial showpiece, overshadowing the season, limited-overs cricket once again dominated the year. Between October and April, the Indian team played a mere three Tests, and those were severely shortened by rain, before embarking on a schedule of 20 one-day internationals – almost exactly the same imbalance as the previous season. But with no internationals at all between the end of November and mid-February, the cream of the country's talent were often available to play on the domestic circuit, where the longer game still holds sway. The Irani Cup, the Duleep Trophy and the knockout stages of the Ranji Trophy are all staged over five days, theoretically offering some preparation for Test cricket – when it comes.

In the year of their diamond jubilee, Karnataka won the Ranji Trophy for the fourth time in all, and the first time since 1982-83. They won six of their nine matches, four by an innings, and took first-innings lead in the other three. The reason for Karnataka's dominance was not hard to find. The possession of class bowlers in a varied and effective attack enabled them to beat the plumb batting conditions which can make the Indian first-class game tedious. They fielded Anil Kumble, Javagal Srinath and Venkatesh Prasad, the national team's front-line bowlers, supplemented by left-arm spinner Sunil Joshi, who toured England a few months later, and young Anglo-Indian seamer David Johnson, who might have been picked but for a motorcycle accident. Joshi had such an extraordinary run with bat and ball that he became the first man to complete the double of 500 runs and 50 wickets in the 62-year history of the Ranji competition. With his Duleep games thrown in, he took 65 wickets in the full first-class season; no one else managed 50. The prolific contributions of the promising Rahul Dravid and 20-year-old Raghvendrarao Vijay, as well as the seniors, ensured that there were always plenty of runs to bowl against. Dravid, who also captained the team in Kumble's absence, was the fifth Karnataka player to make the England tour: not since the heyday of Bombay had so many cricketers from one state appeared for their country. Their pride was further enhanced by the fact that they contributed so heavily to the bowling department, in which India have been somewhat deficient.

Karnataka's opponents in the Ranji final were Tamil Nadu. They benefited from the fact that they had no international calls during the knockout rounds, which clashed with the World Cup, and made the most of playing at home on turning tracks to record their first-ever wins over Bombay and Delhi. The semi-final with Delhi saw a curious row when the captains, Robin Singh and Ajay Sharma, both claimed they had won the toss: Tamil Nadu agreed to toss again, but Delhi held out until the first session had been lost. Tamil Nadu also hosted the final at Chepauk, Madras, but losing the toss on a good batting pitch was a blow from which they never recovered. Karnataka piled up 620 for eight before declaring on the third day; Tamil Nadu managed only 370 in their hunt for what was bound to be a decisive first-innings lead. Kumble, now back from the World Cup, did not bother to enforce the follow-on.

The Duleep Trophy offers the national selection committee a chance to view the best cricketers in the country in a five-team round-robin format, but it can provide a taxing schedule for the players. It is invariably held in non-traditional centres with poor basic facilities, linked by chaotic railway schedules, and this season the tournament was shunted to remote northern venues in the wintry months of October and November. Two teams, South Zone and East Zone, began their stay in Lucknow in a dormitory, moved on to a rat-infested hotel and then on to another hotel on the outskirts of the city on consecutive days. Living in such unsettled conditions and playing on under-prepared pitches of dubious bounce hardly helped the players to tackle a limited-overs Deodhar match, a one-day break and then the five-day Duleep fixture. South Zone were champions for the first time since 1989-90; Karnataka's Joshi and Dravid had a prominent role in South's success, as did Vangipurappu Laxman, the 21-year-old batsman from Hyderabad who made hundreds in successive matches and was one of three batsmen to pass 1,000 runs in the season; he and Ajay Sharma of Delhi and North Zone scored five centuries each as did Laxman's Hyderabad team-mate, Maruti Sridhar, who made 991; while Abhijit Kale of Maharashtra and West scored four hundreds in his 1,006. Central Zone, who needed a convincing win in their last match, against West Zone, to pull ahead of South on run quotient, lost it in just over two days. The Duleep title-holders for the past five seasons, North Zone, did not win until their final game and often lost well within the distance but had the consolation of winning the one-day Deodhar Trophy. A last-ball one-wicket win over Central early on stood them in good stead as they edged out East and West Zones.

The Wills Trophy, a one-day tournament staged between the Second and Third Tests against New Zealand, was won by the Wills XI, led by Sachin Tendulkar. They set a spate of records against Hyderabad at Rajkot, rampaging to 379 for three, the highest limited-overs total in India. Tendulkar, Sanjay Manjrekar and Gagan Khoda all scored centuries, another record. Hyderabad captain Mohammad Azharuddin was fined by the Board of Control for skipping this match, breaching the rule that Test players should make themselves available for all domestic matches unless on national duty or attending training camps. He helped to recoup his losses in the third one-day tournament, the Challenger Trophy; he led the Indian Seniors to victory over India A, led by Tendulkar, earning his team prize money of £5,000. That was much more than the winners of the first-class Duleep and Ranji competitions received. – R.M.

FIRST-CLASS AVERAGES, 1995-96

BATTING

(Qualification: 500 runs)

	M	*I*	*NO*	*R*	*HS*	*100s*	*Avge*
N. S. Sidhu (*Punjab*)	5	5	1	533	259*	2	133.25
A. V. Kale (*Maharashtra*)	8	12	1	1,006	209	4	91.45
M. Azharuddin (*Hyderabad*)	6	6	0	536	118	3	89.33
M. H. Parmar (*Gujarat*)	4	7	0	595	283	3	85.00
R. Dravid (*Karnataka*)	11	16	4	968	153	5	80.66
V. V. S. Laxman (*Hyderabad*)	11	17	2	1,170	203*	5	78.00
V. B. Chandrasekhar (*Goa*)	5	9	1	601	237*	2	75.12
S. Sharath (*Tamil Nadu*)	14	22	9	917	204*	2	70.53
Ajay Sharma (*Delhi*)	11	19	1	1,217	188	5	67.61
S. Dogra (*Delhi*)	7	11	3	515	201*	1	64.37
W. V. Raman (*Tamil Nadu*)	11	15	2	835	116*	2	64.23
P. Dharmani (*Punjab*)	9	13	3	641	223*	2	64.10
S. S. Karim (*Bengal*)	8	11	2	569	200*	2	63.22
S. Somasunder (*Karnataka*)	9	13	0	803	166	2	61.76
S. S. Bhave (*Maharashtra*)	10	16	1	894	227	2	59.60
M. V. Sridhar (*Hyderabad*)	11	19	2	991	137	5	58.29
S. B. Joshi (*Karnataka*)	12	15	4	600	118	1	54.54
Akash Malhotra (*Delhi*)	10	17	2	815	197	3	54.33
A. Pathak (*Andhra*)	5	10	0	540	132	3	54.00
A. A. Muzumdar (*Bombay*)	10	16	1	788	209	2	52.53
S. B. Bangar (*Railways*)	6	11	1	523	161	2	52.30
C. S. Pandit (*Madhya Pradesh*)	8	12	1	567	202	1	51.54
D. Gandhi (*Bengal*)	9	14	0	718	213	2	51.28
R. Vijay (*Karnataka*)	9	14	2	602	146	3	50.16
P. K. Amre (*Rajasthan*)	7	12	1	530	161	2	48.18
S. Ramesh (*Tamil Nadu*)	9	15	0	710	158	2	47.33
Rizwan Shamshad (*Uttar Pradesh*)	8	14	1	599	156	1	46.07
K. A. Jeshwant (*Karnataka*)	9	13	0	559	138	1	43.00
S. S. Das (*Orissa*)	10	15	1	591	178	1	42.21
V. Rathore (*Punjab*)	9	15	0	580	156	1	38.66

* *Signifies not out.*

BOWLING

(Qualification: 25 wickets)

	O	*M*	*R*	*W*	*BB*	*5W/i*	*Avge*
A. Kumble (*Karnataka*)	163.2	47	378	32	6-20	3	11.81
R. B. Biswal (*Orissa*)	228.2	82	535	35	5-44	5	15.28
R. A. Swarup (*Baroda*)	194.2	57	446	25	5-40	2	17.84
M. Suresh Kumar (*Railways*)	292.2	95	571	32	6-34	3	17.84
S. B. Joshi (*Karnataka*)	529.1	174	1,169	65	7-60	4	17.98
Avinash Kumar (*Bihar*)	360.4	115	739	39	7-111	3	18.94
H. Ramkishen (*Andhra*)	253.3	68	673	33	6-75	2	20.39
R. Sanghvi (*Delhi*)	220	44	718	35	7-42	3	20.51
N. D. Hirwani (*Madhya Pradesh*)	229.4	49	608	29	6-59	3	20.96
R. Sridhar (*Hyderabad*)	353.2	121	716	32	6-91	2	22.37
P. S. Vaidya (*Bengal*)	213	49	628	28	5-22	3	22.42
K. N. A. Padmanabhan (*Kerala*)	269.3	50	617	27	7-113	3	22.85
B. Vij (*Punjab*)	441	94	1,125	49	6-19	4	22.95

	O	*M*	*R*	*W*	*BB*	*5W/i*	*Avge*
Robin Singh (*Tamil Nadu*)	242.4	39	672	29	7-54	1	23.17
V. N. Buch (*Baroda*)	273	51	733	31	5-55	1	23.64
A. Kuruvilla (*Bombay*)	244.5	59	664	28	6-83	2	23.71
D. J. Johnson (*Karnataka*)	205.1	27	720	30	6-63	2	24.00
D. Vasu (*Tamil Nadu*)	415.2	110	886	35	5-36	2	25.31
R. K. Chauhan (*Madhya Pradesh*)	328	92	788	31	5-120	1	25.41
S. V. Mudkavi (*Goa*)	274.1	45	792	28	8-83	2	28.28
N. M. Kulkarni (*Bombay*)	319.4	96	743	26	6-37	1	28.57
S. Subramaniam (*Tamil Nadu*)	424.5	117	1,047	34	7-85	2	30.79
S. V. Bahutule (*Bombay*)	453.5	111	1,128	36	6-90	2	31.33
Kanwaljit Singh (*Hyderabad*)	408.2	99	923	29	5-53	1	31.82
W. D. Balaji Rao (*Tamil Nadu*)	305.3	53	890	26	5-53	1	34.23

*In the following scores, * by the name of a team indicates that they won the toss.*

Note: The names of some Indian cities have been changed by their state governments. Bombay is now officially Mumbai and Madras is Chennai. To avoid confusion, *Wisden* will retain the traditional names until such changes are generally accepted.

IRANI CUP, 1995-96

Ranji Trophy Champions (Bombay) v Rest of India

At Wankhede Stadium, Bombay, October 2, 3, 4. Bombay won by nine wickets. Rest of India* 99 (P. L. Mhambrey five for 20) and 186 (S. S. Bhave 44, Sourav C. Ganguly 40; P. L. Mhambrey three for 35); Bombay 266 (S. S. Dighe 35, V. G. Kambli 112, A. A. Muzumdar 35; B. K. V. Prasad four for 75, S. L. V. Raju three for 55) and 20 for one.

DULEEP TROPHY, 1995-96

	Played	*Won*	*Lost*	*Drawn*	*1st-innings Points*	*Points*	*Quotient*
South Zone	4	3	0	1	0	19	2.79
Central Zone	4	2	1	1	0	13	3.67
West Zone	4	2	2	0	0	12	2.95
East Zone	4	1	3	0	0	6	2.72
North Zone	4	1	3	0	0	6	3.08

Outright win = 6 pts; lead on first innings in a drawn or lost game = 2 pts; draw in which first innings not completed = 1 pt.

At Indira Gandhi Stadium, Alwar, October 11, 12, 13. Central Zone won by ten wickets. Central Zone* 356 (C. S. Pandit 85, P. K. Amre 152; Avinash Kumar six for 94) and 32 for no wkt; East Zone 154 (D. Gandhi 30, Sourav C. Ganguly 31; R. K. Chauhan three for 42, N. D. Hirwani five for 41) and 231 (S. S. Das 38, D. Gandhi 54, S. Raul 31, Chetan Sharma 35, Avinash Kumar 39 not out; R. K. Chauhan four for 35, N. D. Hirwani three for 111). *Central Zone 6 pts.*

At VCA Stadium, Nagpur, October 11, 12, 13, 14. South Zone won by an innings and 101 runs. North Zone* 200 (Bhupinder Singh, jun. 51, A. R. Kapoor 40; J. Srinath three for 24, A. Kumble three for 48) and 123 (M. Prabhakar 43; A. Kumble four for 35, S. L. V. Raju three for three); South Zone 424 (W. V. Raman 103, R. Dravid 75, V. V. S. Laxman 34, A. Kumble 111; A. R. Kapoor seven for 144). *South Zone 6 pts.*

At Jayanti Stadium, Bhilai, October 20, 21, 22, 23, 24. Drawn. Central Zone 373 for six dec. (G. K. Khoda 100, A. R. Khurasia 89, C. S. Pandit 90, Rizwan Shamshad 47); South Zone* 234 for four (M. V. Sridhar 53, V. V. S. Laxman 48, R. Dravid 69, S. Sharath 35 not out; Mohammad Aslam three for 54). *Central Zone 1 pt, South Zone 1 pt.*

At VCA Stadium, Nagpur, October 20, 21, 22, 23, 24. East Zone won by an innings and 178 runs. West Zone* 197 (S. S. Bhave 98, A. A. Muzumdar 32; P. S. Vaidya three for 20, S. T. Banerjee three for 41, U. Chatterjee three for 69) and 176 (S. V. Bahutule 61; U. Chatterjee three for 54); East Zone 551 for eight dec. (S. S. Das 62, Sourav C. Ganguly 171, S. S. Karim 200 not out, S. Raul 40, U. Chatterjee 38). *East Zone 6 pts.*

Karim's 200 not out lasted 492 minutes and 403 balls and included 16 fours and six sixes.

At Sukhadia Stadium, Bhilwara, November 10, 11, 12. Central Zone won by 100 runs. Central Zone* 404 (Abhay Sharma 63, A. R. Khurasia 46, Rizwan Shamshad 63, Y. T. Ghare 122, P. Krishnakumar 38; S. Subramaniam three for 117, B. Vij four for 121) and 67 (B. Vij six for 19); North Zone 259 (V. Rathore 64, Bhupinder Singh, jun. 42, Ajay Sharma 51, V. S. Yadav 32; R. K. Chauhan three for 89, Mohammad Aslam three for 43) and 112 (V. Rathore 33, F. Ghayas 38; R. K. Chauhan four for 41, Mohammad Aslam five for 42). *Central Zone 6 pts.*

At Indira Gandhi Stadium, Alwar, November 10, 11, 12, 13, 14. South Zone won by 143 runs. South Zone* 313 (M. V. Sridhar 33, V. V. S. Laxman 47, R. Dravid 49, S. Sharath 51, S. B. Joshi 40, Extras 43; S. V. Bahutule three for 77, H. J. Parsana three for 56) and 293 for three dec. (W. V. Raman 48, V. V. S. Laxman 121, R. Dravid 101 not out); West Zone 181 (S. S. Bhave 48, S. S. Sugwekar 32; S. B. Joshi three for 51, Kanwaljit Singh three for 58) and 282 (S. S. Bhave 65, S. S. Sugwekar 83 not out, S. A. Ankola 46; D. Vasu four for 36, Kanwaljit Singh three for 61). *South Zone 6 pts.*

At K. D. Singh "Babu" Stadium, Lucknow, November 19, 20, 21, 22. South Zone won by 219 runs. South Zone* 165 (W. V. Raman 31; P. S. Vaidya five for 50, K. V. P. Rao three for 14) and 360 (V. V. S. Laxman 137, R. Dravid 59, M. S. K. Prasad 33, Extras 33; P. S. Vaidya five for 76); East Zone 159 (S. B. Joshi three for 29) and 147 (S. S. Das 44; S. B. Joshi five for 26). *South Zone 6 pts.*

At Nehru Stadium, Indore, November 19, 20, 21, 22, 23. West Zone won by 247 runs. West Zone* 526 (A. A. Muzumdar 209, S. S. Dighe 41, A. V. Kale 144, J. J. Martin 37; F. Ghayas four for 103) and 298 (S. S. Bhave 57, M. V. Joglekar 79, S. V. Bahutule 30, A. V. Kale 47; B. Vij six for 87, Akash Malhotra three for 56); North Zone 371 (V. Rathore 53, Ajay Sharma 188, P. Dharmani 46, V. S. Yadav 53; S. A. Ankola five for 90, V. N. Buch four for 72) and 206 (Ajay Sharma 47, Akash Malhotra 31; S. A. Ankola three for 52). *West Zone 6 pts.*

Muzumdar's 209 lasted 509 minutes and 396 balls and included 19 fours.

At Railways Stadium, Bikaner, November 28, 29, 30. West Zone won by an innings and 45 runs. Central Zone* 127 (G. K. Khoda 58; N. M. Kulkarni three for 43, V. N. Buch four for five) and 180 (G. K. Pandey 71, R. K. Chauhan 34; S. A. Ankola four for 52, V. N. Buch five for 55); West Zone 352 (M. V. Joglekar 55, A. A. Muzumdar 48, J. J. Martin 115, H. J. Parsana 42; Iqbal Thakur four for 89, R. K. Chauhan five for 120). *West Zone 6 pts.*

West Zone wicket-keeper S. S. Dighe made six catches and four stumpings in the match, an Indian record.

At K. D. Singh "Babu" Stadium, Lucknow, November 28, 29, 30, December 1. North Zone won by eight wickets. East Zone* 184 (S. Raul 43; F. Ghayas four for 35, B. Vij four for 64) and 284 (D. Gandhi 81, Sourav C. Ganguly 55, S. J. Kalyani 37; F. Ghayas three for 90, B. Vij four for 95); North Zone 381 (P. Dharmani 65, Ajay Sharma 65, Bhupinder Singh, jun. 100, V. S. Yadav 66, Extras 32; Avinash Kumar three for 94) and 92 for two (P. Dharmani 56 not out). *North Zone 6 pts.*

DULEEP TROPHY WINNERS

1961-62	West Zone	1973-74	North Zone	1985-86	West Zone
1962-63	West Zone	1974-75	South Zone	1986-87	South Zone
1963-64	West Zone	1975-76	South Zone	1987-88	North Zone
1964-65	West Zone	1976-77	West Zone	1988-89	North Zone / West Zone
1965-66	South Zone	1977-78	West Zone		
1966-67	South Zone	1978-79	North Zone	1989-90	South Zone
1967-68	South Zone	1979-80	North Zone	1990-91	North Zone
1968-69	West Zone	1980-81	West Zone	1991-92	North Zone
1969-70	West Zone	1981-82	West Zone	1992-93	North Zone
1970-71	South Zone	1982-83	North Zone	1993-94	North Zone
1971-72	Central Zone	1983-84	North Zone	1994-95	North Zone
1972-73	West Zone	1984-85	South Zone	1995-96	South Zone

RANJI TROPHY, 1995-96

Central Zone

At Captain Roop Singh Stadium, Gwalior, December 10, 11, 12, 13. Drawn. Railways* 247 (R. Bora 47, Y. Gowda 42, A. Kapoor 68; H. S. Sodhi six for 55) and 299 for six (V. Z. Yadav 47, Abhay Sharma 48, Y. Gowda 79 not out, K. Bharathan 58 not out); Madhya Pradesh 380 (Jai P. Yadav 125, K. K. Patel 79, A. R. Khurasia 42, C. S. Pandit 42; M. Suresh Kumar five for 125, K. Bharathan five for 99). *Madhya Pradesh 2 pts.*

At Green Park, Kanpur, December 10, 11, 12, 13. Drawn. Uttar Pradesh* 442 (Rizwan Shamshad 61, R. V. Sapru 200 not out, G. K. Pandey 71, S. A. Shukla 41) and 113 for three; Vidarbha 349 (Y. T. Ghare 108, U. I. Ghani 45, P. K. Hedaoo 66, Extras 35; S. Kesarwani three for 67). *Uttar Pradesh 2 pts.*

R. V. Sapru's 200 not out lasted 526 minutes and 388 balls and included 18 fours and one six.

At M. B. College Ground, Udaipur, December 18, 19, 20, 21. Madhya Pradesh won by nine wickets. Madhya Pradesh* 516 (Jai P. Yadav 135, A. R. Khurasia 131, P. K. Dwevedi 35, C. S. Pandit 38, D. K. Nilosey 81, Extras 37; R. P. Rathore three for 65, P. Krishnakumar three for 93) and 30 for one; Rajasthan 228 (R. J. Kanwat 41, Mohammad Aslam 31; N. D. Hirwani four for 75) and 317 (G. K. Khoda 115, P. K. Amre 35, P. Krishnakumar 69; R. K. Chauhan three for 104). *Madhya Pradesh 6 pts.*

At VCA Stadium, Nagpur, December 18, 19, 20, 21. Drawn. Railways* 246 (P. S. Rawat 140 not out; P. B. Hingnikar five for 62) and 275 for one dec. (V. Z. Yadav 100 not out, S. B. Bangar 148); Vidarbha 341 (S. V. Wankhede 76, M. S. Doshi 52, S. G. Gujar 47, Y. T. Ghare 36, U. I. Ghani 43; Iqbal Thakur three for 71, M. Suresh Kumar three for 89) and 97 for four (Y. T. Ghare 39, P. K. Hedaoo 30 not out). *Vidarbha 2 pts.*

At Karnail Singh Stadium, Delhi, January 5, 6, 7, 8. Railways won by six wickets. Uttar Pradesh* 261 (Rizwan Shamshad 48, R. V. Sapru 68, M. Khalil 31; M. Suresh Kumar three for 40, P. Munnuswamy three for 74) and 164 (S. B. Yadav 50, Extras 39; M. Suresh Kumar six for 34); Railways 377 for seven dec. (S. B. Bangar 161, Z. Zuffri 43, P. S. Rawat 64, Extras 47; G. K. Pandey five for 74) and 49 for four. *Railways 6 pts.*

At Mansarovar Stadium, Jaipur, January 5, 6, 7, 8. Rajasthan won by 20 runs. Rajasthan* 244 (A. D. Sinha 111, P. K. Amre 43; P. B. Hingnikar four for 74) and 188 (G. K. Khoda 90, A. S. Parmar 50; P. B. Hingnikar four for 38, M. S. Doshi six for 42); Vidarbha 278 (P. B. Hingnikar 37, P. K. Hedaoo 38, M. S. Doshi 32, U. V. Gandhe 44 not out, Extras 30; P. Krishnakumar three for 90) and 134 (Mohammad Aslam four for 29, R. J. Kanwat three for 24). *Rajasthan 6 pts, Vidarbha 2 pts.*

At Jayanti Stadium, Bhilai, January 13, 14, 15, 16. Drawn. Madhya Pradesh* 536 for seven dec. (A. Pandey 209 not out, Jai P. Yadav 43, C. S. Pandit 202); Uttar Pradesh 292 (M. S. Mudgal 35, Jyoti P. Yadav 80, Rizwan Shamshad 68, Extras 33; H. S. Sodhi four for 102, S. S. Lahore five for 75) and 240 for four (M. S. Mudgal 62, Jyoti P. Yadav 51, Rizwan Shamshad 75; S. S. Lahore three for 73). *Madhya Pradesh 2 pts.*

Pandey became the tenth player to score a double-hundred on first-class debut. His 209 not out lasted 676 minutes and 545 balls and included 20 fours. He added 328 for the fourth wicket with Pandit, whose 202 lasted 391 minutes and 332 balls and included 25 fours.

At Karnail Singh Stadium, Delhi, January 13, 14, 15, 16. Drawn. Railways* 256 (V. Z. Yadav 36, Z. Zuffri 44, Abhay Sharma 43, M. Suresh Kumar 42; D. Pal Singh six for 58) and 149 for six dec. (V. Z. Yadav 34, K. Bharathan 31); Rajasthan 107 (P. K. Amre 52; M. Suresh Kumar three for 24, Javed Alam four for 29) and 60 for three. *Railways 2 pts.*

Suresh Kumar took a hat-trick in Rajasthan's first innings.

At K. D. Singh "Babu" Stadium, Lucknow, January 22, 23, 24, 25. Drawn. Uttar Pradesh 564 for four dec. (M. S. Mudgal 31, S. B. Yadav 79, Jyoti P. Yadav 146, Rizwan Shamshad 156, R. V. Sapru 101 not out) and 50 for two dec.; Rajasthan* 439 (G. K. Khoda 45, R. J. Kanwat 46, P. K. Amre 161, P. Krishnakumar 40, A. S. Parmar 50, Extras 40; A. Gera three for 93, Jasbir Singh six for 112) and 95 for eight (A. S. Parmar 34 not out). *Uttar Pradesh 2 pts.*

At VCA Ground, Nagpur, January 22, 23, 24, 25. Madhya Pradesh won by four wickets. Vidarbha* 240 (P. K. Hedaoo 47, U. V. Gandhe 64; D. V. Parmar three for 56) and 144 (S. V. Wankhede 31, U. I. Ghani 41; S. S. Lahore three for 69, M. Majithia four for 29); Madhya Pradesh 163 (Jai P. Yadav 41, M. Majithia 51; P. V. Gandhe seven for 62) and 222 for six (K. K. Patel 71, P. K. Dwevedi 37; P. V. Gandhe three for 85). *Madhya Pradesh 6 pts, Vidarbha 2 pts.*

Madhya Pradesh 16 pts, Railways 8 pts, Vidarbha 6 pts, Rajasthan 6 pts, Uttar Pradesh 4 pts. Madhya Pradesh, Railways and Vidarbha (on better quotient) qualified for the knockout stage.

East Zone

At Athletic Stadium, Baripada, December 11, 12, 13, 14. Drawn. Orissa* 402 (P. R. Mohapatra 100, S. S. Das 95, A. Khatua 89 not out; U. Chatterjee four for 91) and eight for no wkt; Bengal 299 (H. Ferojee 43, D. Gandhi 147; R. B. Biswal five for 82). *Orissa 2 pts.*

At Polytechnic Ground, Agartala, December 11, 12, 13, 14. Bihar won by an innings and 45 runs. Bihar* 247 (V. Khullar 50, Tariq-ur-Rehman 38, Adil Hussain 49; A. Das three for 50, S. Chowdhary five for 64); Tripura 70 (Avinash Kumar three for 17, Deepak Kumar three for 17) and 132 (Avinash Kumar four for 31, Sanjay Singh four for 30). *Bihar 6 pts.*

At North-Eastern Frontier Railway Stadium, Gauhati, December 20, 21, 22. Assam won by an innings and 188 runs. Tripura 111 (G. Banik 30; Javed Zaman three for 34) and 106 (R. Deb-Burman 44 not out; S. Limaye six for 35); Assam* 405 for nine dec. (Rajinder Singh 55, S. Sawant 121, S. Limaye 50, V. Samant 75, Extras 38; C. Dey five for 87). *Assam 6 pts.*

At Moin-ul-Haq Stadium, Patna, December 20, 21, 22. Bengal won by an innings and 190 runs. Bihar* 144 (V. Khullar 33, Sunil Kumar 34; A. Sarkar four for 63, U. Chatterjee five for 23) and 134 (V. Khullar 54; P. S. Vaidya five for 22); Bengal 468 for six dec. (D. Gandhi 35, A. Lahiri 58, S. S. Karim 199, S. J. Kalyani 117 not out). *Bengal 6 pts.*

At Keenan Stadium, Jamshedpur, January 6, 7, 8, 9. Drawn. Bihar 284 (Tariq-ur-Rehman 122, S. T. Banerjee 58; G. Dutta three for 55, S. Sawant three for 63) and 133 (Sunil Kumar 74 not out; G. Dutta three for 23, Rajinder Singh three for 24, S. Sawant four for 55); Assam* 205 (S. Saikia 56, S. Sawant 49, S. Limaye 51; Avinash Kumar five for 44, Anil Kumar five for 74) and 103 for five (K. V. P. Rao three for 26). *Bihar 2 pts.*

Sunil Kumar carried his bat through Bihar's second innings.

At Barabati Stadium, Cuttack, January 6, 7, 8, 9. Orissa won by an innings and 209 runs. Tripura 141 (S. Chowdhary 31, R. Deb-Burman 34; R. B. Biswal five for 54, S. Khan five for 42) and 171 (A. Poddar 41; S. Khan three for 35, P. Sushil Kumar three for 29); Orissa* 521 for six dec. (M. Bhatt 68, P. R. Mohapatra 105, S. S. Das 178, R. R. Parida 32, S. Raul 71, R. Seth 45 not out). *Orissa 6 pts.*

At Barabati Stadium, Cuttack, January 14, 15, 16, 17. Orissa won by an innings and 93 runs. Orissa* 411 (P. R. Mohapatra 72, S. S. Das 74, R. R. Parida 49, S. Raul 60, R. B. Biswal 69 not out, B. D. Mohanty 30, Extras 32; S. Limaye three for 78); Assam 112 (R. B. Biswal four for 29, P. Sushil Kumar five for nine) and 206 (Rajinder Singh 37, S. Limaye 44 not out; R. B. Biswal five for 73). *Orissa 6 pts.*

At Polytechnic Ground, Agartala, January 14, 15, 16, 17. Bengal won by an innings and 351 runs. Bengal* 446 for four dec. (A. Verma 141, D. Gandhi 213, M. Sengupta 65); Tripura 53 (A. Das three for 28, P. Acharjee seven for six) and 42 (P. Acharjee four for ten, S. P. Mukherjee five for 18). *Bengal 6 pts.*

Gandhi's 213 lasted 314 minutes and 244 balls and included 33 fours and two sixes. He and Verma put on 327 for Bengal's first wicket. Acharjee took 11 for 16 on first-class debut.

At Krishnanagar Stadium, Krishnanagar, January 22, 23, 24, 25. Bengal won by nine wickets. Assam 301 (D. Chakraborty 72, N. Bordoloi 59, G. Dutta 87; P. S. Vaidya three for 80, Sourav C. Ganguly four for 67) and 219 for seven dec. (S. Saikia 127, G. Dutta 34; Sourav C. Ganguly three for 51); Bengal* 258 (A. Verma 43, D. Gandhi 31, S. S. Karim 37, S. P. Mukherjee 58; A. Bhagwati six for 49) and 266 for one (A. Verma 106 not out, D. Gandhi 76, Sourav C. Ganguly 65 not out). *Bengal 6 pts, Assam 2 pts.*

At Permit Ground, Balasore, January 22, 23, 24, 25. Orissa won by eight wickets. Orissa* 471 (P. R. Mohapatra 64, S. S. Das 37, S. Raul 125, R. B. Biswal 73, B. D. Mohanty 31, R. Seth 37; Avinash Kumar seven for 111) and 62 for two; Bihar 293 (Sunil Kumar 55, Tarun Kumar 100, R. Raja 33, Avinash Kumar 49; R. B. Biswal five for 114, P. Sushil Kumar four for 90) and 237 (Tariq-ur-Rehman 105, R. Raja 42, Avinash Kumar 41; R. B. Biswal five for 44). *Orissa 6 pts.*

Orissa 20 pts, Bengal 18 pts, Assam 8 pts, Bihar 8 pts, Tripura 0 pt. Orissa, Bengal and Assam (on better quotient) qualified for the knockout stage.

North Zone

At Air Force Complex, Palam, Delhi, December 10, 11, 12. Delhi won by 145 runs. Delhi 262 (M. Prabhakar 111, Akash Malhotra 39; V. Jain three for 28) and 160 (S. Dogra 74; V. Jain five for 34, Dhanraj Singh three for 54); Haryana* 153 (A. Jadeja 42; Robin Singh seven for 53) and 124 (R. Puri 46, P. Thakur 39; Shakti Singh five for 24). *Delhi 6 pts.*

At PCA Stadium, Mohali, Chandigarh, December 10, 11, 12, 13. Drawn. Punjab 360 (Ajay Mehra 30, Sudhir Sharma 39, N. S. Sidhu 137, P. Dharmani 113 not out; J. P. Pandey four for 96) and 18 for one; Services* 246 (Chinmoy Sharma 123; Sandeep Sharma four for 26, B. Vij three for 58). *Punjab 2 pts.*

At Burlton Park, Jalandhar, December 17, 18, 19. Punjab won by an innings and 258 runs. Punjab* 507 for four dec. (V. Rathore 156, N. S. Sidhu 259 not out, Ajay Mehra 65); Himachal Pradesh 149 (N. Gaur 56; Sandeep Sharma four for 22, B. Vij five for 29) and 100 (Shambhu Sharma 46; B. Vij five for 31, A. R. Kapoor four for 50). *Punjab 6 pts.*

Sidhu's 259 not out lasted 510 minutes and 409 balls and included 14 fours and four sixes. He put on 301 with Rathore for Punjab's first wicket and went from 152 to 259 on the second morning.

At Air Force Complex, Palam, Delhi, December 17, 18, 19. Delhi won by an innings and 208 runs. Delhi* 519 for five dec. (M. Prabhakar 45, Akash Malhotra 197, S. Dogra 201 not out; S. Shirsat three for 128); Services 135 (Sarabjit Singh 50; R. Sanghvi seven for 42) and 176 (C. D. Thomson 32; R. Sanghvi four for 64, N. Chopra six for 91). *Delhi 6 pts.*

Dogra's 201 not out lasted 495 minutes and 381 balls and included 13 fours and one six. He and Malhotra added 391, an Indian fifth-wicket record.

At Paddal Stadium, Mandi, January 3, 4, 5, 6. Services won by ten wickets. Himachal Pradesh* 172 (Virender Sharma 63; J. P. Pandey three for 40, Arun Sharma five for 28) and 250 (R. Nayyar 134 not out; M. V. Rao three for 42, J. P. Pandey three for 79); Services 391 (Swapna Dutta 33, J. P. Pandey 38, Chinmoy Sharma 95, R. Mehta 103 not out, S. Subramaniam 39) and 32 for no wkt. *Services 6 pts.*

At Gandhi Ground, Amritsar, January 3, 4, 5, 6. Drawn. Delhi* 341 (A. Dani 32, Ajay Sharma 147, Akash Malhotra 72, A. S. Wassan 33; Sandeep Sharma four for 86) and 286 for five (A. Dani 141, Bantoo Singh 54, Ajay Sharma 51; B. Vij four for 75); Punjab 415 (P. Dharmani 223 not out, N. S. Sidhu 63, Bhupinder Singh, sen. 48; F. Ghayas three for 99, R. Sanghvi four for 157). *Punjab 2 pts.*

Dharmani carried his bat through Punjab's innings. His 223 not out lasted 565 minutes and 446 balls and included 25 fours and two sixes.

At Indira Stadium, Una, January 9, 10, 11. Delhi won by an innings and 51 runs. Himachal Pradesh* 125 (M. Prabhakar three for 35, R. Sanghvi six for 49) and 307 (N. Gaur 66, R. Nayyar 125, Virender Sharma 73; R. Sanghvi five for 137); Delhi 483 for six dec. (A. Dani 83, R. Chopra 95, Bantoo Singh 44, Ajay Sharma 30, M. Prabhakar 125, Akash Malhotra 65). *Delhi 6 pts.*

At Nahar Singh Stadium, Faridabad, January 11, 12, 13, 14. Haryana won by an innings and 54 runs. Haryana* 471 (A. Jadeja 189, Jitender Singh 37, A. S. Kaypee 110, R. Puri 73; J. P. Pandey three for 105, S. Subramaniam three for 148); Services 209 (Sarabjit Singh 32, S. Subramaniam 45, M. V. Rao 34; R. P. Singh three for 48, P. Jain four for 49) and 208 (Sarabjit Singh 35, K. M. Roshan 58; P. Jain four for 39, P. Thakur five for 66). *Haryana 6 pts.*

At Vishkarma School Ground, Rohtak, January 16, 17, 18, 19. Drawn. Himachal Pradesh 263 (R. Nayyar 114, Raj Kumar 52; P. Jain three for 34, Sonu Sharma three for 44); Haryana* 264 (R. Puri 71, A. S. Kaypee 49, V. S. Yadav 58; Jaswant Rai three for 68). *Haryana 2 pts.*

Nayyar's hundred was his third in successive matches.

At Nehru Stadium, Gurgaon, January 23, 24, 25, 26. Punjab won by four wickets. Haryana* 233 (Jitender Singh 32, R. Puri 39, P. Jain 40, Dhanraj Singh 33; B. Vij three for 49, Harvinder Singh three for 48) and 241 (Avtar Singh 53, V. S. Yadav 42, Dhanraj Singh 56; Harvinder Singh three for 33, G. Doel four for 67); Punjab 231 (P. Dharmani 47, V. Rathore 34, Amit Sharma 69; P. Thakur four for 38) and 244 for six (V. Rathore 91, Ajay Mehra 33, Bhupinder Singh, jun. 44 not out; P. Jain three for 94). *Punjab 6 pts, Haryana 2 pts.*

Delhi 18 pts, Punjab 16 pts, Haryana 10 pts, Services 6 pts, Himachal Pradesh 0 pt. Delhi, Punjab and Haryana qualified for the knockout stage.

Jammu and Kashmir did not turn up for any of their matches.

South Zone

At Alluri Seetharamaraju Stadium, Eluru, December 10, 11. Karnataka won by an innings and 109 runs. Karnataka* 247 (J. Arun Kumar 58, A. Kumble 63, A. Vaidya 40; H. Ramkishen six for 75); Andhra 41 (B. K. V. Prasad six for 23, D. Ganesh four for 12) and 97 (S. B. Joshi three for 19). *Karnataka 6 pts.*

The highest scorer in Andhra's first innings was debutant R. V. Prasad, with nine.

At Gymkhana Ground, Kampal, Panaji, December 10, 11, 12, 13. Drawn. Kerala* 166 (A. Kudva 39; S. Kamat four for 32, N. D. Kambli three for 60) and 307 for seven (A. Kudva 162 not out, S. Oasis 61, B. Ramaprakash 34; S. V. Mudkavi four for 78); Goa 384 (V. B. Chandrasekhar 237 not out, S. V. Mudkavi 32, M. Senthilnathan 60; K. N. A. Padmanabhan seven for 113). *Goa 2 pts.*

Chandrasekhar, who scored 61 per cent of Goa's total, carried his bat. His 237 not out lasted 727 minutes and 534 balls and included 16 fours and two sixes.

At M. A. Chidambaram Stadium, Madras, December 10, 11, 12, 13. Drawn. Tamil Nadu 245 (T. Karunamurthy 36, S. Ramesh 59, K. Srinath 43, J. Gokulkrishnan 38; R. Sridhar five for 48) and 241 for three dec. (T. Karunamurthy 35, S. Ramesh 132, D. Vasu 53); Hyderabad 292 (A. Nandakishore 56, M. V. Sridhar 104, V. Pratap 66 not out; Robin Singh three for 21) and 58 for two (G. A. Shetty 30 not out). *Hyderabad 2 pts.*

S. Ramesh scored 132 on first-class debut.

At Vizzy Stadium, Vishakhapatnam, December 19, 20, 21, 22. Tamil Nadu won by two wickets. Andhra* 277 (A. Pathak 132, B. S. Naik 41; S. Subramaniam seven for 85) and 219 (A. Pathak 30, R. V. Prasad 61; W. D. Balaji Rao four for 57, M. Venkataramana five for 65); Tamil Nadu 209 (S. Ramesh 75, D. Vasu 47; H. Ramkishen six for 89, K. Chakradhar Rao three for 45) and 288 for eight (S. Ramesh 48, T. Karunamurthy 57, S. Sharath 54, Robin Singh 71; H. Ramkishen three for 122, K. Chakradhar Rao three for 70). *Tamil Nadu 6 pts, Andhra 2 pts.*

At M. Chinnaswamy Stadium, Bangalore, December 19, 20, 21. Karnataka won by an innings and 237 runs. Goa* 132 (S. V. Mudkavi 51; J. Srinath three for 38, S. B. Joshi three for 47) and 97 (S. B. Joshi four for 48, A. Kumble six for 20); Karnataka 466 (S. Somasunder 114, J. Arun Kumar 39, R. Dravid 108, R. Vijay 49, A. Kumble 51; S. V. Mudkavi eight for 182). *Karnataka 6 pts.*

At Vellayani Agricultural College Ground, Thiruvananthapuram, December 19, 20, 21, 22. Hyderabad won by 125 runs. Hyderabad* 283 (M. V. Sridhar 105, M. Azharuddin 91; B. Ramaprakash five for 103, K. N. A. Padmanabhan four for 86) and 259 for six dec. (M. V. Sridhar 123, M. Azharuddin 105); Kerala 234 (S. Shankar 35, A. Kudva 30, K. N. A. Padmanabhan 36; S. L. V. Raju five for 89) and 183 (S. Shankar 54, B. Ramaprakash 30, K. N. A. Padmanabhan 51; S. L. V. Raju seven for 82). *Hyderabad 6 pts.*

At Arlem Breweries Ground, Margao, January 7, 8, 9. Hyderabad won by an innings and 182 runs. Hyderabad* 576 for five dec. (A. Nandakishore 132, Yuvraj Singh 46, M. V. Sridhar 137, V. V. S. Laxman 48, M. Azharuddin 118, V. Pratap 58 not out); Goa 182 (S. Kamat 53; Kanwaljit Singh five for 53, R. Sridhar three for 47) and 212 (Y. Barde 39, S. V. Mudkavi 63; Kanwaljit Singh three for 51, R. Sridhar four for 62). *Hyderabad 6 pts.*

M. V. Sridhar's hundred was his third in successive innings.

At Vellayani Agricultural College Ground, Thiruvananthapuram, January 7, 8, 9. Kerala won by eight wickets. Andhra* 206 (A. Pathak 73, V. Vinay Kumar 37; K. N. A. Padmanabhan five for 73) and 105 (Shreehari Rao 35, A. Pathak 34; S. Oasis three for 24, K. N. A. Padmanabhan six for 39); Kerala 227 (S. Oasis 58, P. G. Sunder 46; K. Chakradhar Rao five for 57) and 85 for two (K. N. Balasubramaniam 52 not out). *Kerala 6 pts.*

At Gymkhana Ground, Secunderabad, January 16, 17, 18, 19. Andhra won by nine wickets. Hyderabad* 223 (M. V. Sridhar 54, V. V. S. Laxman 32, N. David 55; H. Ramkishen three for 99, N. Madhukar five for 43) and 139 (H. Ramkishen four for 68, N. Madhukar three for 53); Andhra 332 (A. Pathak 116, B. S. Naik 46, M. S. K. Prasad 50; R. Sridhar six for 91) and 34 for one. *Andhra 6 pts.*

At RSI Stadium, Bangalore, January 18, 19, 20, 21. Karnataka won by three wickets. Kerala* 151 (Feroz Rashid 43; D. J. Johnson six for 63, D. Ganesh three for 46) and 346 (S. Shankar 57, S. Oasis 69, S. Manoj 37, Extras 42; D. J. Johnson four for 89, S. B. Joshi three for 105); Karnataka 244 (J. Arun Kumar 44, P. V. Shashikanth 103; B. Ramaprakash four for 73) and 254 for seven (S. Somasunder 51, K. A. Jeshwant 59, S. B. Joshi 59 not out; B. Ramaprakash five for 102). *Karnataka 6 pts.*

At Guru Nanak College Ground, Madras, January 18, 19, 20, 21. Tamil Nadu won by eight wickets. Goa* 312 (V. B. Chandrasekhar 168, B. Misquin 43; Robin Singh four for 27) and 315 (D. Patil 43, B. Misquin 107, S. Mahadevan 57; D. Vasu three for 39, Robin Singh three for 72); Tamil Nadu 509 for six dec. (W. V. Raman 88, S. Sharath 204 not out, K. Srinath 52, R. Paul 100 not out; Y. Barde four for 133) and 121 for two (W. V. Raman 86 not out). *Tamil Nadu 6 pts.*

Sharath's 204 not out lasted 467 minutes and 361 balls and included 20 fours. Paul scored 100 not out on first-class debut in 60 balls on the third morning and hit five sixes in an over from R. Naik.

At District Sports Stadium, Kakinada, January 28, 29, 30, 31. Andhra won by 79 runs. Andhra* 275 (V. Nagini Kumar 46, A. Pathak 114, V. Vinay Kumar 40, R. V. Prasad 34 not out; S. V. Mudkavi eight for 83) and 271 for six dec. (B. S. Naik 64, M. S. K. Prasad 100 not out, R. V. Prasad 38; S. V. Mudkavi three for 103); Goa 195 (V. B. Chandrasekhar 55, R. Naik 44; H. Ramkishen four for 57, K. Chakradhar Rao three for 42) and 272 (V. B. Chandrasekhar 95, M. Senthilnathan 35, S. V. Mudkavi 32, S. Mahadevan 30; H. Ramkishen four for 87, K. Chakradhar Rao four for 80). *Andhra 6 pts.*

Mudkavi took eight wickets in an innings for the second time in six weeks.

At Gymkhana Ground, Secunderabad, January 28, 29, 30, 31. Karnataka won by nine wickets. Karnataka* 398 (S. Somasunder 30, P. V. Shashikanth 75, S. B. Joshi 118, A. Vaidya 69, Extras 30; N. P. Singh three for 89, V. Pratap five for 100) and 19 for one; Hyderabad 191 (V. Pratap 69; S. B. Joshi seven for 60) and 222 (Yuvraj Singh 50, M. V. Sridhar 30, V. V. S. Laxman 79; S. B. Joshi four for 66, R. Ananth three for 61). *Karnataka 6 pts.*

At India Cement Ground, Tirunelveli, January 28, 29, 30. Tamil Nadu won by an innings and 165 runs. Tamil Nadu* 541 for five dec. (K. Srinath 159, S. Ramesh 158, S. Sharath 101 not out, Robin Singh 57, Extras 32; K. Rejith Kumar four for 133); Kerala 184 (A. Kudva 42, Feroz Rashid 49) and 192 (K. N. Balasubramaniam 52, S. Shankar 50, K. Rejith Kumar 33; S. Subramaniam six for 73, M. Venkataramana four for 66). *Tamil Nadu 6 pts.*

Srinath and Ramesh put on 329 for Tamil Nadu's first wicket.

At VISL Stadium, Bhadravati, February 4, 5, 6, 7. Drawn. Karnataka* 716 (S. Somasunder 166, R. Vijay 122, K. Sriram 174, K. A. Jeshwant 91, S. B. Joshi 61 not out, D. J. Johnson 39; S. Subramaniam four for 174) and 172 for three (S. Somasunder 62, R. Vijay 45 not out, K. A. Jeshwant 31); Tamil Nadu 366 (S. Ramesh 54, W. V. Raman 89, S. Sharath 37, Robin Singh 68, R. Paul 48; D. J. Johnson three for 121, S. B. Joshi four for 93). *Karnataka 2 pts.*

Sriram scored 174 on first-class debut. Tamil Nadu wicket-keeper Paul conceded no byes in a total of 716.

Karnataka 26 pts, Tamil Nadu 18 pts, Hyderabad 14 pts, Andhra 14 pts, Kerala 6 pts, Goa 2 pts. Karnataka, Tamil Nadu and Hyderabad (on better quotient) qualified for the knockout stage.

West Zone

At Sardar Patel Stadium, Valsad, December 13, 14, 15. Bombay won by an innings and 110 runs. Gujarat 215 (P. H. Patel 38, B. Mehta 71; A. Kuruvilla three for 68, A. Dani five for 40) and 105 (A. Kuruvilla five for 44, S. V. Bahutule four for 15); Bombay* 430 for eight dec. (M. V. Joglekar 32, S. S. More 53, S. V. Manjrekar 37, V. G. Kambli 138, S. R. Tendulkar 31, A. Dani 88; B. Mehta four for 119). *Bombay 6 pts.*

At Nehru Stadium, Pune, December 13, 14, 15, 16. Drawn. Baroda* 550 (N. R. Mongia 152, J. J. Martin 56, K. S. More 71, T. B. Arothe 142, M. S. Narula 60; M. S. Kulkarni five for 89); Maharashtra 562 for seven (S. Nadkarni 43, S. S. Bhave 227, H. H. Kanitkar 142, A. V. Kale 49; V. N. Buch four for 185). *Maharashtra 2 pts.*

Bhave's 227 lasted 556 minutes and 354 balls and included 22 fours and one six.

At GSFC Ground, Baroda, December 21, 22, 23, 24. Bombay won by five wickets. Baroda* 112 (K. S. Chavan 36; S. V. Bahutule three for 31, N. M. Kulkarni six for 37) and 211 (T. B. Arothe 50, V. N. Buch 53; N. M. Kulkarni four for 87); Bombay 238 (S. K. Kulkarni 49, V. G. Kambli 31, S. V. Bahutule 71; R. A. Swarup four for 52) and 87 for five (S. S. Hazare three for 31). *Bombay 6 pts.*

At Municipal Ground, Rajkot, December 21, 22, 23, 24. Drawn. Gujarat* 319 (M. H. Parmar 174, B. Mehta 30) and 241 for nine dec. (M. H. Parmar 101, H. D. Patel 41 not out; R. Pandit three for 54); Saurashtra 252 (B. M. Jadeja 107 not out; D. Patel three for 64, B. H. Patel three for 49) and 140 for five (S. S. Tanna 74; B. Mehta five for 28). *Gujarat 2 pts.*

Parmar scored a hundred in each innings for the third time in Ranji matches.

At Municipal Ground, Rajkot, January 9, 10, 11, 12. Drawn. Saurashtra* 258 (S. S. Tanna 78, N. R. Odedra 44, B. Dutta 31, H. J. Parsana 35; Sukhbir Singh three for 78, T. B. Arothe three for nine) and 214 (S. S. Tanna 57, N. R. Odedra 43, S. H. Kotak 43; R. A. Swarup four for 42, S. S. Hazare five for 81); Baroda 239 (N. R. Mongia 70, J. J. Martin 83; R. Pandit three for 68, H. J. Parsana five for 88) and 214 for eight (K. S. Chavan 33, N. R. Mongia 39, T. B. Arothe 47, K. S. More 32; R. Pandit four for 75, H. J. Parsana three for 59). *Saurashtra 2 pts.*

At Dadoji Konddeo Stadium, Thane, January 10, 11, 12, 13. Drawn. Bombay 427 (A. A. Muzumdar 165, S. R. Tendulkar 81, S. K. Kulkarni 96, S. A. Ankola 30; S. Inamdar four for 82, M. Sane four for 119) and 361 for three (S. S. More 110 not out, A. A. Muzumdar 55, S. R. Tendulkar 151); Maharashtra* 318 (S. S. Bhave 90, S. S. Sugwekar 85, A. V. Kale 90, Extras 31; S. V. Bahutule six for 90). *Bombay 2 pts.*

At Dadoji Konddeo Stadium, Thane, January 17, 18, 19, 20. Drawn. Saurashtra 244 (N. R. Odedra 68, S. H. Kotak 48, B. Dutta 47; A. Kuruvilla six for 83) and 264 for six (N. R. Odedra 58, B. Dutta 37, B. M. Jadeja 88, M. M. Parmar 30; S. V. Bahutule three for 71); Bombay* 495 for six dec. (S. S. More 184, M. D. Phadke 45, S. K. Kulkarni 161, S. S. Dighe 53). *Bombay 2 pts.*

At Sardar Patel Stadium, Ahmedabad, January 17, 18, 19, 20. Drawn. Gujarat 640 (A. Kotecha 33, M. H. Parmar 283, N. A. Patel 36, P. H. Patel 68, H. D. Patel 81, D. Patel 61; U. Gotkhindikar three for 103); Maharashtra* 449 for seven (A. V. Kale 209, S. M. Kondhalkar 121, S. Inamdar 34 not out). *Maharashtra 1 pt, Gujarat 1 pt.*

Parmar's 283 lasted 538 minutes and 446 balls and included 30 fours and one six. It was his third century in successive innings. Kale's 209 lasted 444 minutes and 387 balls and included 19 fours.

At Motibaug Palace Ground, Baroda, January 25, 26, 27. Baroda won by an innings and 25 runs. Gujarat* 146 (N. A. Patel 30, B. Mehta 36; R. A. Swarup five for 40) and 127 (N. S. Bakriwala 34; R. A. Swarup five for 51); Baroda 298 (T. B. Arothe 85, H. Jadhav 42; B. Mehta five for 107, H. D. Patel four for 94). *Baroda 6 pts.*

At Nehru Stadium, Pune, January 25, 26, 27, 28. Drawn. Maharashtra* 388 (A. V. Kale 77, S. S. Sugwekar 73, R. R. Kanade 122; C. C. Mankad four for 117, R. Pandit three for 59) and 373 for five (S. S. Bhave 103, A. V. Kale 119, H. H. Kanitkar 97); Saurashtra 274 (S. S. Tanna 53, M. M. Parmar 43, N. P. Rana 61; P. J. Kanade three for 84). *Maharashtra 2 pts.*

R. R. Kanade scored 122 on first-class debut.

Bombay 16 pts, Baroda 6 pts, Maharashtra 5 pts, Gujarat 3 pts, Saurashtra 2 pts. Bombay, Baroda and Maharashtra qualified for the knockout stage.

Pre-quarter-finals

At Air Force Complex, Palam, Delhi, February 12, 13, 14, 15, 16. Drawn. Delhi were declared winners by virtue of their first-innings lead. Maharashtra 345 (A. V. Kale 63, H. H. Kanitkar 104, S. S. Sugwekar 51, R. R. Kanade 36; A. S. Wassan five for 92) and 284 (S. S. Bhave 52, A. V. Kale 131, R. R. Kanade 36; S. Dogra three for 14); Delhi* 454 (A. Dani 42, R. Lamba 110, Ajay Sharma 187, Akash Malhotra 50; U. Gotkhindikar four for 86) and 123 for two (R. Lamba 46, Ajay Sharma 34 not out).

At Gymkhana Ground, Secunderabad, February 12, 13, 14, 15. Hyderabad won by ten wickets. Assam* 112 (S. Sawant 40; N. P. Singh six for 69, Pawan Kumar three for five) and 296 (D. Chakraborty 45, Rajinder Singh 35, S. Sawant 55, S. Limaye 43; N. P. Singh three for 80, R. Sridhar three for 64); Hyderabad 294 (A. Nandakishore 38, V. V. S. Laxman 130, M. V. Sridhar 42, N. David 56; G. Dutta four for 44) and 115 for no wkt (A. Nandakishore 39 not out, M. V. Sridhar 69 not out).

At RSI Ground, Bangalore, February 12, 13, 14. Karnataka won by an innings and 29 runs. Bengal* 153 (S. S. Karim 30, Chetan Sharma 59; D. J. Johnson four for 49) and 148 (A. Verma 36, S. S. Karim 40 not out; S. B. Joshi six for 47); Karnataka 330 (S. Somasunder 57, R. Vijay 43, K. A. Jeshwant 70, K. Sriram 32, S. B. Joshi 39 not out, Extras 30; Chetan Sharma three for 65, U. Chatterjee three for 97, A. Verma three for 42).

At Nehru Stadium, Indore, February 12, 13, 14. Tamil Nadu won by an innings and 11 runs. Tamil Nadu* 345 (K. Srinath 53, S. Ramesh 31, W. V. Raman 85, Robin Singh 48, T. Jabbar 33 not out, Extras 34; S. S. Lahore three for 67, N. D. Hirwani five for 88); Madhya Pradesh 134 (P. K. Dwevedi 35; D. Vasu three for 27, S. Subramaniam four for 52) and 200 (P. K. Dwevedi 82, D. Bundela 34, Extras 30; D. Vasu five for 36, W. D. Balaji Rao five for 53).

At PCA Stadium, Mohali, Chandigarh, February 12, 13, 14, 15, 16. Drawn. Baroda were declared winners by virtue of their first-innings lead. Baroda* 393 (H. Indulkar 50, C. Williams 69, T. B. Arothe 75, K. S. More 112, V. N. Buch 44; Sandeep Sharma three for 99, Chaman Lal three for 75) and 429 for seven (C. Williams 109, J. J. Martin 81, H. Jadhav 58, V. N. Buch 94, Extras 37); Punjab 314 for nine dec. (Ajay Mehra 95, Amit Sharma 36, Bhupinder Singh, sen. 37; V. N. Buch four for 65).

At Karnail Singh Stadium, Delhi, February 12, 13, 14. Railways won by nine wickets. Orissa* 178 (M. Bhatt 33, P. R. Mohapatra 59, R. B. Biswal 34; M. Suresh Kumar three for 44) and 92 (K. Bharathan six for 36); Railways 214 (S. B. Bangar 65; R. B. Biswal four for 67, P. Sushil Kumar four for 28) and 59 for one.

At VCA Stadium, Nagpur, February 12, 13, 14, 15, 16. Drawn. Vidarbha were declared winners by virtue of their first-innings lead. Vidarbha* 414 (Mohammad Sabir 87, U. I. Ghani 94, U. V. Gandhe 50, P. V. Gandhe 81; P. Thakur three for 150) and 269 for seven dec. (Mohammad Sabir 30, M. S. Doshi 89, P. K. Hedaoo 35, U. I. Ghani 66); Haryana 355 (Jitender Singh 79, R. Puri 55, V. S. Yadav 111; P. B. Hingnikar three for 96, P. V. Gandhe three for 107, M. S. Doshi three for 49) and 64 for two (P. Thakur 35).

Quarter-finals

At Air Force Complex, Palam, Delhi, February 26, 27, 28, 29, March 1. Drawn. Delhi were declared winners by virtue of their first-innings lead. Delhi* 431 (Ajay Sharma 136, Akash Malhotra 102, S. Dogra 86, V. Dahiya 44; Iqbal Thakur four for 101, M. Suresh Kumar five for 86) and 561 for nine. (A. Dani 64, Bantoo Singh 106, Ajay Sharma 182, Akash Malhotra 77, Shakti Singh 52 not out; Javed Alam three for 121); Railways 223 (V. Z. Yadav 75, Y. Gowda 33; A. S. Wassan six for 75, R. Sanghvi four for 62).

Ajay Sharma's two centuries were his fourth and fifth of the season.

At Gymkhana Ground, Secunderabad, February 26, 27, 28, 29, March 1. Drawn. Hyderabad were declared winners by virtue of their first-innings lead. Vidarbha* 409 (U. S. Phate 115, U. I. Ghani 32, U. V. Gandhe 97, P. V. Gandhe 60; N. P. Singh four for 120) and 32 for one; Hyderabad 620 (A. Nandakishore 90, V. V. S. Laxman 196, V. Pratap 45, M. V. Sridhar 101, N. David 64).

Sridhar's 101 was his fifth century of the season, all in the Ranji Trophy.

At RSI Ground, Bangalore, February 26, 27, 28, 29. Karnataka won by an innings and 79 runs. Karnataka 480 (S. Somasunder 35, R. Vijay 106, K. A. Jeshwant 138, K. Sriram 47, S. B. Joshi 56, A. Vaidya 36; R. A. Swarup four for 84); Baroda* 213 (R. A. Swarup 32, K. S. More 49, M. S. Narula 34, V. N. Buch 37; D. J. Johnson five for 91) and 188 (H. Indulkar 38, M. S. Narula 41 not out; R. Ananth four for 57, K. A. Jeshwant three for 40).

At India Cement Ground, Tirunelveli, February 26, 27, 28, 29, March 1. Tamil Nadu won by 153 runs. Tamil Nadu* 246 (S. Ramesh 52, S. Sharath 86, D. Vasu 44; S. V. Bahutule five for 91) and 250 (S. Sharath 90, D. Vasu 80; N. M. Kulkarni three for 67); Bombay 196 (A. A. Muzumdar 54, S. K. Kulkarni 84 not out; D. Vasu three for 41, W. D. Balaji Rao four for 46) and 147 (A. A. Muzumdar 58 not out, Extras 30; Robin Singh seven for 54).

Semi-finals

At M. Chinnaswamy Stadium, Bangalore, March 14, 15, 16, 17, 18. Drawn. Karnataka were declared winners by virtue of their first-innings lead. Karnataka* 423 (S. Somasunder 74, R. Dravid 153, K. Sriram 31, A. Vaidya 30, D. Ganesh 75 not out; M. Mohiuddin three for 101, R. Sridhar three for 128) and 312 (R. Vijay 57, R. Dravid 33, K. A. Jeshwant 85, A. Vaidya 31; R. Sridhar three for 58); Hyderabad 188 (V. V. S. Laxman 51, N. David 57; S. B. Joshi four for 58) and 363 for seven (V. V. S. Laxman 203 not out, V. Pratap 45; S. B. Joshi five for 126).

D. J. Johnson of Karnataka missed the match after injuring his hand in a road accident. Laxman's 203 not out lasted 514 minutes and 342 balls and included 19 fours. It was his fifth century of the season.

At M. A. Chidambaram Stadium, Madras, March 14, 15, 16, 17, 18. Tamil Nadu won by eight wickets. Delhi* 256 (Ajay Sharma 39, Akash Malhotra 117, R. Sanghvi 41; D. Vasu five for 71) and 232 (S. Dogra 97, A. S. Wassan 45; W. D. Balaji Rao three for 46); Tamil Nadu 272 (W. V. Raman 85, D. Vasu 57, S. Sharath 31, R. Paul 35; N. Chopra four for 122) and 220 for two (W. V. Raman 116 not out, S. Sharath 76 not out).

The first morning was lost after both captains claimed to have won the toss, owing to a dispute about which face of a recently introduced coin was "heads". The umpires ordered another toss, but Ajay Sharma of Delhi at first refused. After two hours he agreed and this time won without argument.

Final

At M. A. Chidambaram Stadium, Madras, March 27, 28, 29, 30, 31. Drawn. Karnataka were declared winners by virtue of their first-innings lead. Karnataka* 620 for eight dec.

(S. Somasunder 99, A. Vaidya 42, R. Vijay 146, R. Dravid 114, S. B. Joshi 86, K. Sriram 37, Extras 49; W. D. Balaji Rao three for 173) and 277 for six dec. (S. Somasunder 53, A. Vaidya 61, K. A. Jeshwant 46); Tamil Nadu 370 (K. Srinath 85, W. V. Raman 61, S. Sharath 37, Robin Singh 38, P. Rajesh 34; A. Kumble five for 95) and 31 for three.

Dravid's 114 was his fifth century of the season. Somasunder and Vaidya shared century opening stands in both innings.

RANJI TROPHY WINNERS

1934-35	Bombay	1955-56	Bombay	1976-77	Bombay
1935-36	Bombay	1956-57	Bombay	1977-78	Karnataka
1936-37	Nawanagar	1957-58	Baroda	1978-79	Delhi
1937-38	Hyderabad	1958-59	Bombay	1979-80	Delhi
1938-39	Bengal	1959-60	Bombay	1980-81	Bombay
1939-40	Maharashtra	1960-61	Bombay	1981-82	Delhi
1940-41	Maharashtra	1961-62	Bombay	1982-83	Karnataka
1941-42	Bombay	1962-63	Bombay	1983-84	Bombay
1942-43	Baroda	1963-64	Bombay	1984-85	Bombay
1943-44	Western India	1964-65	Bombay	1985-86	Delhi
1944-45	Bombay	1965-66	Bombay	1986-87	Hyderabad
1945-46	Holkar	1966-67	Bombay	1987-88	Tamil Nadu
1946-47	Baroda	1967-68	Bombay	1988-89	Delhi
1947-48	Holkar	1968-69	Bombay	1989-90	Bengal
1948-49	Bombay	1969-70	Bombay	1990-91	Haryana
1949-50	Baroda	1970-71	Bombay	1991-92	Delhi
1950-51	Holkar	1971-72	Bombay	1992-93	Punjab
1951-52	Bombay	1972-73	Bombay	1993-94	Bombay
1952-53	Holkar	1973-74	Karnataka	1994-95	Bombay
1953-54	Bombay	1974-75	Bombay	1995-96	Karnataka
1954-55	Madras	1975-76	Bombay		

Bombay have won the Ranji Trophy 32 times, Delhi 6, Baroda, Holkar and Karnataka 4, Bengal, Hyderabad and Maharashtra 2, Haryana, Madras, Nawanagar, Punjab, Tamil Nadu and Western India 1.

CEAT CRICKETER OF THE YEAR

The inaugural CEAT International Cricketer of the Year was Brian Lara of West Indies. CEAT Ltd, an Indian tyre company, created the award to identify the foremost world cricketer from May 1, 1995, to April 30, 1996. Judges Sunil Gavaskar, Clive Lloyd and Ian Chappell have devised a system awarding points for performances in Tests and limited-overs internationals. A player earns one point for a score of 50 and another for every 25 runs thereafter in that innings, with a three-point bonus for a hundred and a six-point bonus for a double-hundred. Two wickets in an innings earn one point, with another for every subsequent wicket in that innings, plus a three-point bonus for five in the innings and a six-point bonus for ten in the match. Every catch and every stumping is worth one point. The judges make monthly assessments and add the CEAT Efficiency Quotient. Lara scored 74 points, edging out Australians Mark Waugh (63) and Ian Healy (56). But immigration officials were reluctant to let him into India for the presentation in Bombay, because he did not have the relevant visa.

CRICKET IN PAKISTAN, 1995-96

By ABID ALI KAZI

Murtaza Hussain

The 1995-96 season was overshadowed by the World Cup, the optimistic belief that Pakistan would retain their title and the national trauma when they were knocked out in the quarter-finals. Looking at Pakistan's performances over the previous year, the mess created by the Salim Malik affair, changes in the captaincy and management and internal bickering, their chances of remaining champions were always slim. But the media falsely raised the hopes of the nation. After the anticlimax of defeat in the quarter-finals – the first serious hurdle – by neighbours and arch-rivals India, the mood of both media and people swung sharply from patriotic enthusiasm to wrath against the players. Allegations of bribery were made, resignations were demanded and some disheartened fans even stoned captain Wasim Akram's house in Lahore, forcing him to take refuge with his in-laws in Islamabad.

Wasim had returned to the captaincy after Ramiz Raja, a compromise choice, lost a home series to Sri Lanka and failed to reach the final of a one-day tournament in Sharjah. Majid Khan and Mushtaq Mohammad, the administration and cricket managers, were sacked along with Ramiz, and Majid resigned from the World Cup's Technical Committee in protest. But both were back by the end of the year. Majid Khan replaced Arif Ali Khan Abbasi as chief executive officer of the Pakistan Cricket Board in May, and he soon reinstated Mushtaq.

The fall-out from Australian allegations of attempted bribery kept former captain Salim Malik out of the side until he was cleared by a judicial inquiry, just in time to join the tour of Australia and New Zealand. Also back in favour for that trip, Pakistan's last before the World Cup, were Rashid Latif and Basit Ali, who had been fined for walking out of the previous year's tour of Zimbabwe after their own disagreements with Malik.

Besides helping to stage the World Cup, Pakistan hosted Sri Lanka for a three-Test series and welcomed an Australian Academy team, a West Indian Youth team and England A. The United Arab Emirates were invited to play in the one-day Wills King Cup to assist their own preparation for the World Cup: they won one of their four games.

There were exactly 100 first-class matches during the season – five in the Sri Lankan tour, six with England A, 31 in the PCB Patron's Trophy, 47 in the Quaid-e-Azam tournament and 11 in the Pentangular championship. Most of the domestic games were played without the international stars. Karachi Blues retained the Quaid-e-Azam Trophy. Whatever the result of the final, it would have been the 15th time this had gone to a Karachi side, as the Blues' opponents were Karachi Whites. In 1995-96, the Quaid-e-Azam was again contested by ten teams, Hyderabad replacing Sargodha, who were disqualified last year. This time, Lahore City were scratched, and all points scored for or against them cancelled after they conceded their match with Karachi Blues. They claimed the Karachi players had changed the ball in the drinks interval; the umpires and referee disagreed and asked them to get on with the game, but Lahore captain Aamer Malik refused.

Karachi's third string, the Greens, beat Lahore Division on first-innings lead in the Grade II final, but were not promoted to the first-class competition, because in 1996-97 the Trophy reverted to its earlier eight-team format. In addition, only one team from each association would be eligible to play, although Karachi, as in previous years, were allowed two. Lahore City retained their place – their decision to suspend Malik for four matches mollified the Board. Hyderabad were relegated and Rawalpindi were restricted to one team again.

ADBP won the PCB Patron's Trophy, despite finishing fourth at the league stage, by beating the league-leaders and reigning champions Allied Bank in the final. The same eight teams contested Grade I as in the previous year, because the board had ruled that promotions and relegations should take place at two-year intervals. The 1994-95 Grade II winners, Khan Research Laboratories, thus missed out, but Pakistan Customs, who beat Pakistan Steel in this season's final, will replace Pakistan Railways, who finished bottom for the second year.

The Pentangular Trophy, reintroduced in 1994-95, was expanded to include a final, in which United Bank beat Allied Bank. The tournament featured the top three teams from the Patron's league and the top two from the Quaid-e-Azam, though Karachi's two finalists combined forces to play alongside second-placed Bahawalpur. PIA won the national one-day competition, now called the Wills Kings Cup. The National Under-19 Junior Cup was won by Karachi Whites.

The national batting averages were headed by Asif Mujtaba of Karachi and PIA, with 1,367 runs at 68.35 in his 22 innings. He hit eight centuries, beating the Pakistan record of seven, set by Zaheer Abbas in 1982-83 and Ijaz Ahmed jun. in 1994-95. Mujtaba was also the leading fielder, with 19 catches from his 16 matches. His performance was enough to earn him a recall for the tour of England in 1996. Sohail Jaffer of Karachi Whites and PNSC was the leading run-scorer with 1,465 at 44.39 and a third Karachi player, Tahir Rashid, who also appeared for Habib Bank, was the most successful wicket-keeper, with 48 catches and eight stumpings in 15 games. Murtaza Hussain of Bahawalpur and PNSC took most wickets, 105 in 851 overs, falling just short of the record of 107 by Ijaz Faqih of Karachi in 1985-86. His Bahawalpur team-mate, Mohammad Altaf, headed the averages with 35 wickets at 11.65 apiece. But the individual performance of the season came from Naeem Akhtar of Rawalpindi B, who set an all-time national record with ten for 28 in an innings against Peshawar. He was only the third Pakistani to take ten in an innings, following Shahid Mahmood in 1969-70 and Imran Adil in 1989-90.

FIRST-CLASS AVERAGES, 1995-96

BATTING

(Qualification: 600 runs)

	M	*I*	*NO*	*R*	*HS*	*100s*	*Avge*
Asif Mujtaba (*Karachi Blues/Karachi/PIA*)	16	22	2	1,367	170	8	68.35
Mahmood Hamid (*Karachi Blues/Karachi/PIA*)	20	28	7	1,151	162	3	54.80
Sajid Ali (*National Bank*)	14	18	1	897	139	3	52.76
Saeed Azad (*Karachi Whites/Karachi/National Bank*)	16	26	2	1,189	117	3	49.54
Naseer Ahmed (*Rawalpindi A*)	9	15	2	612	161	2	47.07
Aamer Hanif (*Karachi Blues/Allied Bank*)	11	16	1	699	225	3	46.60
Mohammad Nawaz, sen. (*Faisalabad/Allied Bank*)	16	27	1	1,205	200	3	46.34
Sohail Jaffer (*Karachi Whites/PNSC*)	23	35	2	1,465	125	4	44.39
Azam Khan (*Karachi Whites/PNSC*)	20	31	2	1,281	215*	5	44.17
Zahoor Elahi (*Rawalpindi A/ADBP*)	10	16	0	668	178	3	41.75
Mohammad Ramzan (*Faisalabad/United Bank*)	16	23	2	867	141	3	41.28
Manzoor Akhtar (*Karachi Blues/Allied Bank*)	19	27	4	891	145	4	38.73
Shakeel Ahmed (*Rawalpindi B/Habib Bank*)	13	25	2	875	101	1	38.04
Javed Sami (*Karachi Whites/United Bank*)	16	25	4	794	141*	1	37.80
Shahid Nawaz (*Lahore City/Habib Bank*)	14	23	1	791	130	3	35.95
Nadeem Younis (*Rawalpindi A/ADBP*)	14	23	0	774	135	3	33.65
Moin-ul-Atiq (*Karachi Blues/Habib Bank*)	14	25	3	726	120	1	33.00
Mazhar Qayyum (*Peshawar/PNSC*)	17	27	3	781	129	2	32.54
Raj Hans (*Islamabad/Allied Bank*)	15	22	3	612	110*	2	32.21
Ijaz Ahmed, jun. (*Faisalabad/Allied Bank*)	14	22	2	644	127*	2	32.20
Sher Ali (*Peshawar/PNSC*)	13	22	1	673	113*	1	32.04
Majid Saeed (*Bahawalpur/Railways*)	12	22	1	659	90	0	31.38
Mohammad Javed (*Karachi Whites/Karachi/N. Bank*)	17	26	5	615	75	0	29.28
Iqbal Imam (*Karachi Whites/United Bank*)	16	22	0	622	100	1	28.27
Aaley Haider (*Islamabad/Allied Bank*)	22	33	0	922	105	1	27.93
Qayyum-ul-Hasan (*Bahawalpur/Railways*)	14	24	2	612	150*	2	27.81

* *Signifies not out.*

BOWLING

(Qualification: 30 wickets)

	O	*M*	*R*	*W*	*BB*	*5W/i*	*Avge*
Mohammad Altaf (*Bahawalpur*)	246.3	77	408	35	5-34	3	11.65
Bilal Rana (*Islamabad/Allied Bank*)	464.4	164	929	63	6-51	4	14.74
Shakeel Ahmed (*Rawalpindi A*)	251.4	58	597	39	6-77	2	15.30
Tauseef Ahmed (*United Bank*)	286	69	594	38	5-47	2	15.63
Aamer Hanif (*Karachi Blues/Allied Bank*)	217.3	51	617	36	6-55	3	17.13
Naeem Akhtar (*Rawalpindi B*)	202.3	42	596	34	10-28	3	17.52
Aqib Javed (*Allied Bank*)	189.2	34	572	32	5-13	2	17.87
Murtaza Hussain (*Bahawalpur/PNSC*)	851	277	1,882	105	9-54	7	17.92
Humayun Hussain (*Rawalpindi A/Allied Bank*)	232.2	48	646	35	5-64	2	18.45
Mohammad Hussain (*Lahore City/United Bank*)	671.4	206	1,500	78	7-80	4	19.23
Mohammad Asif (*Lahore City/ADBP*)	659.5	164	1,392	72	7-49	5	19.33
Manzoor Elahi (*Lahore City/ADBP*)	339.5	68	1,001	51	6-32	5	19.62
Shahid Hussain (*Peshawar/United Bank*)	333.1	88	753	38	6-77	3	19.81
Naeem Tayyab (*Karachi Whites/Karachi*)	522.3	102	1,401	69	8-112	5	20.30
Wasim-ur-Rehman (*Karachi Whites*)	290	80	675	33	5-41	1	20.45
Raj Hans (*Islamabad/Allied Bank*)	297.1	60	782	37	6-90	3	21.13

	O	*M*	*R*	*W*	*BB*	*5W/i*	*Avge*
Athar Laeeq (*Karachi Whites/Karachi/N. Bank*)	413.3	84	1,170	54	5-27	3	21.66
Mohammad Javed (*Kar. Whites/Kar./N. Bank*) .	418.3	70	1,329	61	6-62	5	21.78
Shahid Mahboob (*Islamabad/Allied Bank*)	402.4	79	1,232	56	7-101	4	22.00
Azhar Mahmood (*Islamabad/United Bank*)	307	78	839	38	6-40	2	22.07
Shehzad Butt (*Lahore City/United Bank*)......	211	27	752	34	5-127	1	22.11
Aamer Wasim (*Rawalpindi A/Railways*)	464.3	92	1,175	53	7-169	5	22.16
Ali Gauhar (*Karachi Blues/United Bank*)......	279.4	41	905	40	6-28	4	22.62
Nadeem Khan (*Karachi Blues/PIA*)	376.5	96	953	42	6-42	3	22.69
Mohammad Zahid (*Bahawalpur/Allied Bank*) ..	386	126	778	34	6-49	2	22.88
Sajid Shah (*Peshawar/PNSC*)	309	44	1,104	47	7-63	3	23.48
Azhar Shafiq (*Bahawalpur*)..................	244.1	41	854	36	7-93	4	23.72
Wasim Hussain (*Faisalabad*)	245.3	45	784	32	5-63	1	24.50
Lal Faraz (*Karachi Whites/Karachi*)	358.3	63	1,168	46	5-66	2	25.39
Arshad Khan (*Peshawar/Allied Bank*)	483.4	124	1,131	44	6-54	1	25.70
Mohammad Ali (*Rawalpindi A/ADBP*)	372.4	67	1,265	39	6-63	3	32.43
Sajjad Ali (*Lahore City/PNSC*)	292	36	1,143	32	5-47	1	35.71

QUAID-E-AZAM TROPHY, 1995-96

	Played	*Won*	*Lost*	*Drawn*	*1st-inns Points*	*Points*
Karachi Blues	9	6	1	2	10	60
Bahawalpur	9	5	4	0	10	60
Islamabad	8	4	0	4	10	50
Karachi Whites	9	5	1	3	6	46
Rawalpindi A	9	3	3	3	10	40
Peshawar	9	2	5	2	0	20
Faisalabad	9	1	4	4	8	18
Rawalpindi B	8	1	5	2	4	14
Hyderabad	9	0	7	2	0	0
Lahore City	9	5	2	2	0	0

Note: Lahore City were disqualified from the competition after they conceded their match against Karachi Blues; all points earned by them and against them were cancelled. The match between Rawalpindi B and Islamabad was abandoned.

Semi-finals: Karachi Blues beat Islamabad by an innings and 215 runs; Karachi Whites beat Bahawalpur by seven wickets.

Final: Karachi Blues beat Karachi Whites by 59 runs.

Outright win = 10 pts; lead on first innings in a won or drawn game = 2 pts.

*In the following scores, * by the name of a team indicates that they won the toss.*

At Bohranwala Ground, Faisalabad, November 2, 3, 4. Lahore City won by an innings and 64 runs. Lahore City* 398 (Zahid Umar 93, Zahid Fazal 36, Shahid Nawaz 91, Mohammad Hussain 56, Extras 30; Masood Anwar five for 100); Faisalabad 218 (Nadeem Arshad 37 retired hurt, Mohammad Ashraf 56, Nadeem Afzal 33; Mohammad Hussain three for 60, Akram Raza three for 65) and 116 (Ahmed Siddiq 45; Akram Raza five for 43). *Points cancelled.*

At Mahmood Stadium, Rahimyarkhan, November 2, 3, 4. Bahawalpur won by an innings and 11 runs. Bahawalpur* 309 (Saifullah 77, Nasir Jam 35, Majid Saeed 59, Pervez Shah 33; Sohail Qureshi four for 79, Iqbal Sheikh three for 50); Hyderabad 101 (Ahmed Ali Jafri 33; Mohammad Altaf four for 25, Murtaza Hussain four for 22) and 197 (Ahmed Ali Jafri 33, Abdul Waheed Rashid 75 not out; Mohammad Altaf five for 82, Murtaza Hussain three for 63). *Bahawalpur 12 pts.*

Mahmood Stadium became the 62nd first-class ground in Pakistan and Rahimyarkhan the 20th centre to stage first-class cricket.

At Asghar Ali Shah Stadium, Karachi, November 2, 3, 4, 5. Karachi Whites won by five wickets. Karachi Whites* 323 for six dec. (Faisal Qureshi 105, Sohail Jaffer 85) and 199 for five (Saeed Azad 106 not out, Iqbal Imam 60); Karachi Blues 168 (Munir-ul-Haq 57; Wasim-ur-Rehman three for 65, Iqbal Imam four for 42) and 353 (Manzoor Akhtar 114, Munir-ul-Haq 77, Wasim Arif 53, Irfanullah 56; Wasim-ur-Rehman four for 113). *Karachi Whites 12 pts.*

At KRL Cricket Ground, Rawalpindi, November 2, 3, 4. Rawalpindi A won by eight wickets. Rawalpindi B 177 (Naved Ashraf 30, Naeem Akhtar 46; Shakeel Ahmed five for 58) and 192 (Pervez Iqbal 76; Shakeel Ahmed four for 41); Rawalpindi A* 303 (Nadeem Younis 132, Mohammad Nadeem 65; Naeem Akhtar six for 80) and 68 for two (Naseer Ahmed 50 not out). *Rawalpindi A 12 pts.*

At Arbab Niaz Stadium, Peshawar, November 3, 4, 5. Islamabad won by an innings and 185 runs. Peshawar* 101 (Bilal Rana four for 11, Fahad Khan four for 14) and 76 (Azhar Mahmood three for 42, Bilal Rana four for ten); Islamabad 362 (Ehsan Butt 136, Raj Hans 83, Extras 35; Shahid Hussain three for 93, Arshad Khan four for 84). *Islamabad 12 pts.*

At Bohranwala Ground, Faisalabad, November 8, 9, 10, 11. Bahawalpur won by 11 runs. Bahawalpur 289 (Azhar Shafiq 77, Pervez Shah 87, Mohammad Altaf 38; Masood Anwar four for 52) and 157 (Majid Saeed 59; Wasim Hussain three for 34); Faisalabad* 256 (Fida Hussain 83, Saadat Gul 62; Azhar Shafiq three for 61) and 179 (Sami-ul-Haq 37, Javed Iqbal 34, Mohammad Ashraf 37; Azhar Shafiq three for 38, Murtaza Hussain five for 56). *Bahawalpur 12 pts.*

At Makli Cricket Ground, Thatta, November 8, 9, 10. Karachi Blues won by eight wickets. Hyderabad 172 (Imran Naseer 30; Ghulam Ali five for 43) and 190 (Tahir Mahmood 46; Imranullah three for 67, Ali Haider three for 68); Karachi Blues* 331 (Sajid Ali 64, Moin-ul-Atiq 84, Ghulam Ali 57, Munir-ul-Haq 47; Aamer Ali four for 99, Shahid Iqbal four for 75) and 33 for two. *Karachi Blues 12 pts.*

Makli Cricket Ground became the 63rd first-class ground in Pakistan and Thatta the 21st centre to stage first-class cricket.

At KCCA Stadium, Karachi, November 8, 9, 10, 11. Karachi Whites won by 152 runs. Karachi Whites* 185 (Mohammad Javed 58; Tauqeer Hussain five for 68) and 349 for eight dec. (Javed Sami 92, Saeed Azad 68, Iqbal Imam 54, Tahir Rashid 37, Wasim-ur-Rehman 34 not out; Tauqeer Hussain three for 90); Rawalpindi B 214 (Arif Butt 41, Tasawwar Hussain 61, Asif Mohammad 41; Naeem Tayyab seven for 66) and 168 (Shakeel Ahmed 75, Naved Ashraf 30; Wasim-ur-Rehman three for 41, Naeem Tayyab five for 67). *Karachi Whites 10 pts.*

Karachi City Cricket Association Stadium became the 64th first-class ground in Pakistan.

At Arbab Niaz Stadium, Peshawar, November 8, 9, 10, 11. Lahore City won by 34 runs. Lahore City* 293 (Shahid Saeed 43, Manzoor Elahi 72, Akram Raza 32, Mohammad Hussain 30; Kabir Khan four for 94, Arshad Khan three for 66) and 201 (Shahid Saeed 48, Aamer Malik 47; Shahid Hussain five for 55); Peshawar 168 (Sher Ali 63; Sajjad Ali three for 62, Mohammad Hussain four for 28) and 292 (Jahangir Khan, sen. 41, Aamer Bashir 76, Taimur Khan 57; Mohammad Hussain three for 56). *Points cancelled.*

At KRL Cricket Ground, Rawalpindi, November 8, 9, 10, 11. Islamabad won by 120 runs. Islamabad 213 (Aaley Haider 72, Raj Hans 93; Shakeel Ahmed three for 36) and 261 for nine dec. (Aaley Haider 69, Raj Hans 48, Bilal Rana 42, Extras 39; Shoaib Akhtar five for 97); Rawalpindi A* 263 (Shahid Javed 69, Naseer Ahmed 38, Mohammad Ali 54 not out; Bilal Rana three for 44, Raj Hans five for 46) and 91 (Azhar Mahmood six for 40, Bilal Rana three for 16). *Islamabad 10 pts.*

Rawalpindi A wicket-keeper Mohammad Nadeem made five catches in Islamabad's second innings.

At Bahawal Stadium, Bahawalpur, November 14, 15, 16, 17. Islamabad won by two runs. Islamabad* 155 (Murtaza Hussain nine for 54) and 189 (Ehsan Butt 36, Qaiser Mahmood 32, Azhar Mahmood 47 not out; Murtaza Hussain three for 100, Mohammad Zahid six for 49); Bahawalpur 142 (Bilal Rana six for 51, Raj Hans four for 72) and 200 (Qayyum-ul-Hasan 35; Bilal Rana four for 56, Raj Hans six for 90). *Islamabad 12 pts.*

At Asghar Ali Shah Stadium, Karachi, November 14, 15, 16, 17. Karachi Blues won by eight wickets. Rawalpindi B 288 (Shakeel Ahmed 33, Tasawwar Hussain 87, Sabih Azhar 35, Pervez Iqbal 33; Ali Rizvi three for 81, Manzoor Akhtar five for 38) and 215 (Shakeel Ahmed 42, Pervez Iqbal 32; Manzoor Akhtar six for 72); Karachi Blues* 427 for seven dec. (Moin-ul-Atiq 120, Mahmood Hamid 162, Munir-ul-Haq 40, Aamer Iqbal 34) and 77 for two (Sajid Ali 35). *Karachi Blues 12 pts.*

At LCCA Ground, Lahore, November 14, 15, 16, 17. Karachi Whites won by nine wickets. Karachi Whites* 488 (Kashif Ahmed 41, Azam Khan 215 not out, Sohail Jaffer 58, Iqbal Imam 45, Tahir Rashid 46; Mohammad Hussain four for 131, Mohammad Asif three for 146) and 78 for one (Kashif Ahmed 36 not out); Lahore City 272 (Idrees Baig 68, Tahir Shah 77, Aamer Malik 61; Naeem Tayyab eight for 112) and 290 (Idrees Baig 31, Tahir Shah 30, Shahid Nawaz 105, Kamran Khan 49; Naeem Tayyab five for 128, Wasim-ur-Rehman three for 66). *Points cancelled.*

Azam Khan's 215 not out lasted 393 minutes and 286 balls and included 25 fours. Naeem Tayyab took his bowling figures over four innings and ten days to 25 for 373.

At Arbab Niaz Stadium, Peshawar, November 14, 15, 16. Peshawar won by seven wickets. Hyderabad* 184 (Rizwan Umar 36, Tahir Mahmood 52; Farrukh Zaman four for 59) and 72 (Sajid Shah six for 29); Peshawar 91 (Shahid Iqbal four for 48, Aamer Ali three for 34) and 166 for three (Sher Ali 88; Anwar Ali three for 50). *Peshawar 10 pts.*

At KRL Cricket Ground, Rawalpindi, November 14, 15, 16, 17. Faisalabad won by four wickets. Rawalpindi A* 167 (Mohammad Wasim 57, Irfan Bhatti 35; Shahid Nazir five for 49) and 269 (Mohammad Nadeem 35, Naseer Ahmed 45, Shahid Javed 104; Shahid Nazir three for 79, Masood Anwar three for 86); Faisalabad 288 (Mohammad Nawaz, sen. 55, Masood Anwar 31, Shahid Nazir 60 not out; Shakeel Ahmed three for 64) and 149 for six (Sami-ul-Haq 63; Shahid Javed three for 52). *Faisalabad 12 pts.*

At Bahawal Stadium, Bahawalpur, November 20, 21, 22. Bahawalpur won by seven wickets. Rawalpindi B* 135 (Shakeel Ahmed 81 not out; Murtaza Hussain five for 34) and 189 (Iqbal Saleem 38; Murtaza Hussain four for 65, Mohammad Zahid four for 60); Bahawalpur 281 (Qayyum-ul-Hasan 102, Majid Saeed 64, Murtaza Hussain 47 not out; Tauqeer Hussain six for 87, Iftikhar Asghar three for 53) and 47 for three (Sabih Azhar three for eight). *Bahawalpur 12 pts.*

Shakeel Ahmed carried his bat through Rawalpindi B's first innings.

At Bohranwala Ground, Faisalabad, November 20, 21, 22, 23. Peshawar won by eight wickets. Faisalabad 177 (Saadat Gul 58 not out, Masood Anwar 35; Arshad Khan four for 69, Shahid Hussain five for 67) and 157 (Sami-ul-Haq 43, Saadat Gul 38; Arshad Khan six for 54); Peshawar* 127 (Masood Anwar five for 24) and 210 for two (Jahangir Khan, sen. 87, Sher Ali 113 not out). *Peshawar 10 pts.*

At Chaudhry Rehmat Ali Cricket Ground, Islamabad, November 20, 21, 22. Islamabad won by an innings and 57 runs. Hyderabad 161 (Sajid Asghar 30, Abdul Waheed Rashid 80; S. John three for 25, Raj Hans three for 24) and 242 (Sajid Asghar 35, Abdul Waheed Rashid 70, Anwar Ali 30; Azhar Mahmood three for 71, Bilal Rana four for 37); Islamabad* 460 for nine dec. (Ehsan Butt 50, Aaley Haider 105, Raj Hans 102, Fareed Ahmed 37, Bilal Rana 68, Extras 32; Anwar Ali three for 76, Mohtashim Rasheed four for 85). *Islamabad 12 pts.*

Chaudhry Rehmat Ali Ground became the 65th first-class ground in Pakistan.

At Defence Cricket Stadium, Karachi, November 20, 21, 22. Karachi Blues won by default after Lahore City conceded the match. Karachi Blues* 296 (Sajid Ali 98, Mahmood Hamid 40, Munir-ul-Haq 57; Mohammad Hussain five for 115, Mohammad Asif three for 98); Lahore City 141 (Mohammad Hussain 45; Aamer Hanif four for 49, Ali Rizvi three for 28) and 193 for four (Babar Zaman 65, Atif Malik 44, Idrees Baig 38). *Points cancelled.*

Lahore City captain Aamer Malik called back his batsmen, alleging that Karachi Blues had secretly replaced the ball during the drinks interval. The umpires and referee rejected the accusation, but Lahore City refused to continue.

At KRL Cricket Ground, Rawalpindi, November 20, 21, 22, 23. Drawn. Rawalpindi A 257 (Salman Ahmed 53, Shahid Javed 64, Shakeel Ahmed 35 not out; Naeem Tayyab four for 116, Salman Fazal five for 94) and 265 for six (Masroor Hussain 96, Shahid Javed 36, Naseer Ahmed 92; Salman Fazal three for 81, Naeem Tayyab three for 65); Karachi Whites* 201 (Kashif Ahmed 111 not out; Aamer Wasim three for 57, Raja Afaq five for 76). *Rawalpindi A 2 pts.*

Kashif Ahmed carried his bat.

At Bahawal Stadium, Bahawalpur, November 26, 27, 28. Lahore City won by 39 runs. Lahore City* 152 (Shahid Nawaz 43) and 173 (Inamullah Khan 67 not out; Murtaza Hussain four for 57); Bahawalpur 117 (Aamir Sohail 33; Mohammad Hussain four for 50, Mohammad Asif five for 29) and 169 (Pervez Shah 36; Mohammad Asif seven for 49). *Points cancelled.*

At Chaudhry Rehmat Ali Cricket Ground, Islamabad, November 26, 27, 28, 29. Drawn. Islamabad 176 (Zaheer Abbasi 35, Ehsan Butt 58, Aaley Haider 42; Lal Faraz four for 33); Karachi Whites* 354 for three (Javed Sami 141 not out, Zahid Ali 45, Sohail Jaffer 125). *Karachi Whites 2 pts.*

No play was possible on the last two days.

At Defence Cricket Stadium, Karachi, November 26, 27, 28, 29. Karachi Blues won by an innings and two runs. Faisalabad* 121 (Adnan Sana 32, Wasim Hussain 32; Zafar Iqbal three for 25, Aamer Hanif three for 34) and 232 (Naeem Hafeez 45, Mohammad Yousuf 36, Umar Tanvir 46, Wasim Hussain 30; Ali Rizvi six for 77); Karachi Blues 355 (Mahmood Hamid 106, Munir-ul-Haq 31, Aamer Iqbal 32, Nadeem Khan 41; Wasim Hussain four for 103, Hamid Iqbal three for 74). *Karachi Blues 12 pts.*

At KRL Cricket Ground, Rawalpindi, November 26, 27, 28, 29. Drawn. Peshawar* 106 (Jahangir Khan, sen. 36; Mohammad Riaz seven for 27); Rawalpindi A 299 for seven (Mohammad Wasim 38, Masroor Hussain 125 not out, Naseer Ahmed 42, Nadeem Abbasi 31; Shahid Hussain three for 70). *Rawalpindi A 2 pts.*

No play was possible on the last two days.

At Rawalpindi Cricket Stadium, Rawalpindi, November 26, 27, 28, 29. Drawn. Rawalpindi B 184 (Naved Ashraf 86, Arif Butt 43; Shahid Iqbal four for 60) and 42 for two; Hyderabad* 118 (Naeem Akhtar three for 36, Sabih Azhar five for 30). *Rawalpindi B 2 pts.*

No play was possible on the last two days.

At Chaudhry Rehmat Ali Cricket Ground, Islamabad, December 2, 3, 4, 5. Drawn. Karachi Blues 162 (Nadeem Khan 35; S. John seven for 51); Islamabad* 165 for four (Zaheer Abbasi 93 not out). *Islamabad 2 pts.*

The match did not start until 12.40 on the third day owing to a wet pitch.

At LCCA Ground, Lahore, December 2, 3, 4. Lahore City won by an innings and 102 runs. Lahore City* 372 (Mujahid Jamshed 134, Shahid Nawaz 116, Manzoor Elahi 32, Inamullah Khan 44; Shahid Iqbal six for 77); Hyderabad 144 (Iqbal Sheikh 45; Mohammad Asif five for 29) and 126 (Naumanullah 50; Ali Kamran five for 63, Mohammad Hussain three for 14). *Points cancelled.*

At Arbab Niaz Stadium, Peshawar, December 2, 3, 4. Rawalpindi B won by 121 runs. Rawalpindi B 230 (Naved Ashraf 76, Iqbal Saleem 50, Sabih Azhar 41; Sajid Shah three for 62, Ijaz Elahi four for 40) and 132 (Arif Butt 39; Sajid Shah five for 57); Peshawar* 92 (Naeem Akhtar ten for 28) and 149 (Jahangir Khan, sen. 67; Naeem Akhtar three for 60, Sabih Azhar five for 50). *Rawalpindi B 12 pts.*

Naeem Akhtar's ten for 28 in an innings was the all-time best analysis in first-class cricket in Pakistan. He became the third Pakistani to take ten in an innings after Shahid Mahmood (ten for 58 for Karachi Whites v Khairpur in 1969-70) and Imran Adil (ten for 92 for Bahawalpur v Faisalabad in 1989-90).

At Army Cricket Ground, Rawalpindi, December 2, 3, 4. Rawalpindi A won by 196 runs. Rawalpindi A 216 (Shahid Javed 43, Naseer Ahmed 100 not out; Aamir Sohail three for 22, Murtaza Hussain five for 79) and 150 (Naseer Ahmed 43; Mohammad Altaf five for 34, Mohammad Zahid three for 38); Bahawalpur* 76 (Aamir Sohail 34; Raja Afaq four for 41, Shakeel Ahmed four for seven) and 94 (Raja Afaq five for 42, Mohammad Aslam three for 20). *Rawalpindi A 12 pts.*

At Defence Cricket Stadium, Karachi, December 3, 4, 5, 6. Drawn. Karachi Whites 263 (Azam Khan 53, Tahir Rashid 85 not out, Naeem Tayyab 31; Wasim Hussain four for 87, Naved Nazir three for 46) and 237 for seven (Azam Khan 62, Sohail Jaffer 37, Mohammad Javed 60 not out; Wasim Hussain five for 63); Faisalabad* 326 (Mohammad Ramzan 141, Hamid Iqbal 37, Wasim Hussain 32, Extras 37; Shahid Afridi five for 93). *Faisalabad 2 pts.*

The first day's play was abandoned owing to a city-wide strike.

At Bahawal Stadium, Bahawalpur, December 8, 9, 10. Bahawalpur won by an innings and 44 runs. Karachi Whites* 101 (Murtaza Hussain six for 27) and 162 (Kashif Ahmed 45; Mohammad Altaf three for 26, Murtaza Hussain four for 73); Bahawalpur 307 (Saifullah 62, Aamir Sohail 43, Nasir Jam 53, Murtaza Hussain 31, Mohammad Zahid 38 not out; Wasim-ur-Rehman three for 53). *Bahawalpur 12 pts.*

At Bohranwala Ground, Faisalabad, December 8, 9, 10, 11. Drawn. Hyderabad* 234 (Naumanullah 44, Ijaz Shah 49, Abdul Waheed Rashid 71 not out; Hamid Iqbal four for 83) and 354 for seven (Naumanullah 86, Hanif-ur-Rehman 76, Ijaz Shah 90; Wasim Hussain three for 78); Faisalabad 487 for nine dec. (Mohammad Nawaz, sen. 171, Amjad Ali 57, Mohammad Ramzan 75, Naseer Shaukat 62 not out, Extras 37; Abdul Waheed Rashid three for 117, Iqbal Sheikh three for 129). *Faisalabad 2 pts.*

At LCCA Ground, Lahore, December 8, 9, 10, 11. Drawn. Lahore City 267 (Mujahid Jamshed 79, Shahid Nawaz 60, Manzoor Elahi 70; Mohammad Riaz four for 50) and 211 (Aamer Manzoor 42, Mujahid Jamshed 79; Shakeel Ahmed six for 77); Rawalpindi A* 261 (Abdul Basit 128, Mohammad Nadeem 30; Mohammad Asif six for 105, Mohammad Hussain four for 84) and 26 for one. *Points cancelled.*

At Gymkhana Club Ground, Peshawar, December 8, 9, 10, 11. Drawn. Karachi Blues 191 (Moin-ul-Atiq 33, Mahmood Hamid 85 not out; Sajid Shah seven for 63, Shahid Hussain three for 49) and 48 for two; Peshawar* 124 (Jahangir Khan, sen. 31; Umar Rasheed three for 49, Nadeem Khan five for 36). *Karachi Blues 2 pts.*

No play was possible on the first and fourth days.

At KRL Cricket Ground, Rawalpindi, December 8, 9, 10, 11. Rawalpindi B v Islamabad. Abandoned, owing to rain, which prevented any play.

At Bahawal Stadium, Bahawalpur, December 14, 15, 16. Bahawalpur won by seven wickets. Peshawar 106 (Murtaza Hussain five for 35) and 242 (Akhtar Sarfraz 134 not out; Mohammad Altaf five for 46, Murtaza Hussain three for 109); Bahawalpur* 224 (Tahir Gulzar 35, Saifullah 66; Arshad Khan three for 66, Shahid Hussain six for 77) and 125 for three (Qayyum-ul-Hasan 45 not out). *Bahawalpur 12 pts.*

Akhtar Sarfraz carried his bat through Peshawar's second innings.

At Bohranwala Ground, Faisalabad, December 14, 15, 16, 17. Drawn. Islamabad 275 (Zaheer Abbasi 84, Aaley Haider 76, Extras 31; Wasim Hussain four for 48, Saadat Gul three for 64) and 309 for seven dec. (Zaheer Abbasi 62, Bilal Asad 38, Ehsan Butt 34, Shahid Naqi 47, Qaiser Mahmood 31, Extras 30; Wasim Hussain four for 88); Faisalabad* 237 (Amjad Ali 45, Mohammad Nawaz, jun. 94; Rizwan Bhatti three for 43, Raj Hans five for 86) and 118 for eight (Rizwan Bhatti four for seven, Fahad Khan three for 49). *Islamabad 2 pts.*

At Mahmood Stadium, Rahimyarkhan, December 14, 15, 16, 17. Karachi Whites won by ten wickets. Hyderabad* 207 (Iqbal Sheikh 84; Naeem Tayyab three for 62, Wasim-ur-Rehman three for 42) and 224 (Abdul Waheed Rashid 36 not out, Javed Khan 34; Naeem Tayyab six for 82, Wasim-ur-Rehman three for 50); Karachi Whites 425 for five dec. (Azam Khan 174 not out, Sohail Jaffer 117, Mohammad Javed 34; Abdul Waheed Rashid four for 182) and seven for no wkt. *Karachi Whites 12 pts.*

Azam Khan and Sohail Jaffer added 255 for Karachi Whites' fourth wicket.

At National Stadium, Karachi, December 14, 15. Karachi Blues won by eight wickets. Rawalpindi A 84 (Imranullah five for 32, Aamer Hanif four for 15) and 135 (Saad Khan 34; Imranullah five for 45, Aamer Hanif three for 56); Karachi Blues* 173 (Shadab Kabir 30; Humayun Hussain four for 44, Yasir Ashfaq four for 63) and 47 for two. *Karachi Blues 12 pts.*

At LCCA Ground, Lahore, December 14, 15, 16. Lahore City won by ten wickets. Rawalpindi B* 212 (Sabih Azhar 71, Naeem Akhtar 51; Manzoor Elahi five for 40, Mohammad Hussain three for 43) and 221 (Arif Butt 32, Zahid Javed 35, Tasawwar Hussain 38; Mohammad Hussain seven for 80); Lahore City 419 (Aamer Manzoor 127, Kamran Khan 152, Mohammad Asif 70; Naeem Akhtar five for 111) and 17 for no wkt. *Points cancelled.*

At Mahmood Stadium, Rahimyarkhan, December 20, 21, 22. Rawalpindi A won by an innings and 189 runs. Hyderabad* 117 (Iqbal Sikandar 32; Irfan Bhatti four for 16, Zakaullah three for 43) and 100 (Mohammad Riaz three for 14, Shakeel Ahmed four for 37); Rawalpindi A 406 (Abdul Basit 69, Mohammad Wasim 35, Naseer Ahmed 161, Irfan Bhatti 35, Extras 35; Shahid Iqbal three for 112, Iqbal Sikandar five for 86). *Rawalpindi A 12 pts.*

At Makli Cricket Ground, Thatta, December 20, 21, 22. Karachi Blues won by 30 runs. Karachi Blues 101 (Azhar Shafiq six for 37, Murtaza Hussain three for 18) and 224 (Ameer-ud-Din 59, Irfanullah 37, Ishtiaq Ahmed 64 not out; Azhar Shafiq seven for 93); Bahawalpur* 144 (Aamir Sohail 52, Qayyum-ul-Hasan 31; Mohammad Hasnain three for 44, Aamer Hanif six for 56) and 151 (Azhar Shafiq 63; Mohammad Hasnain four for 62, Aamer Hanif six for 55). *Karachi Blues 10 pts.*

At KCCA Stadium, Karachi, December 20, 21, 22, 23. Karachi Whites won by six wickets. Peshawar* 260 (Akhtar Sarfraz 162; Naeem Tayyab four for 83) and 181 (Asmatullah 50, Jahangir Khan, sen. 30; Naeem Tayyab four for 66, Wasim-ur-Rehman five for 41); Karachi Whites 225 (Mansoor Khan 34, Faisal Qureshi 89; Farrukh Zaman three for 47) and 220 for four (Kashif Ahmed 59, Zeeshan Pervez 42 not out, Mohammad Javed 60 not out). *Karachi Whites 10 pts.*

At LCCA Ground, Lahore, December 20, 21, 22, 23. Drawn. Lahore City 513 for nine dec. (Aamer Manzoor 42, Mujahid Jamshed 125, Shahid Nawaz 130, Aamer Malik 117 not out; S. John three for 163, Raj Hans three for 108); Islamabad* 150 (Shahid Naqi 31, Rizwan Bhatti 32; Manzoor Elahi three for 34, Atif Dar five for 85) and 221 for three (Shahid Naqi 108, Ehsan Butt 51 not out). *Points cancelled.*

At KRL Cricket Ground, Rawalpindi, December 20, 21, 22, 23. Drawn. Rawalpindi B 252 (Arif Butt 111, Tasawwar Hussain 37; Wasim Hussain four for 92, Nadeem Ashraf five for 48) and 278 (Arif Butt 74, Maqsood Aslam 43, Sabih Azhar 62; Nadeem Ashraf five for 81, Naved Nazir three for 41); Faisalabad* 270 (Amjad Ali 44, Javed Iqbal 101; Pervez Iqbal three for 67, Raja Sarfraz four for 55) and 99 for four. *Faisalabad 2 pts.*

Semi-finals

At National Stadium, Karachi, March 29, 30, 31, April 1. Karachi Blues won by an innings and 215 runs. Islamabad* 215 (Asif Ali 33, Azhar Mahmood 31, Kamran Siddiqi 54, Fahad Khan 49; Athar Laeeq four for 44, Zafar Iqbal three for 37) and 197 (Ehsan Butt 30, Asif Ali 72; Aamer Hanif five for 58); Karachi Blues 627 for nine dec. (Sajid Ali 100, Shadab Kabir 88, Manzoor Akhtar 105, Mahmood Hamid 59, Asif Mujtaba 139 not out, Athar Laeeq 99, Extras 34; Shahid Mahboob four for 151).

Asif Mujtaba and Athar Laeeq added 185 for the ninth wicket.

At Makli Cricket Ground, Thatta, April 1, 2, 3, 4. Karachi Whites won by seven wickets. Bahawalpur 240 (Saifullah 33, Pervez Shah 50; Mohammad Javed five for 48) and 198 (Aamir Sohail 32, Saifullah 31; Lal Faraz four for 66); Karachi Whites* 267 (Iqbal Imam 44, Naeem Tayyab 71, Jahangir Bakhsh 51; Azhar Shafiq five for 82) and 172 for three (Saeed Azad 42, Sohail Jaffer 76 not out, Mohammad Javed 33 not out).

Final

At National Stadium, Karachi, April 6, 7, 8, 9. Karachi Blues won by 59 runs. Karachi Blues 181 (Zafar Iqbal 38, Athar Laeeq 46; Lal Faraz five for 66, Mohammad Javed four for 63) and 425 (Sajid Ali 46, Shadab Kabir 33, Mahmood Hamid 54, Asif Mujtaba 114, Zafar Iqbal 79; Lal Faraz three for 179, Mohammad Javed four for 125); Karachi Whites* 297 (Kashif Ahmed 38, Faisal Qureshi 85, Iqbal Imam 66, Tahir Rashid 48; Athar Laeeq three for 72, Zafar Iqbal five for 94) and 250 (Saeed Azad 76, Sohail Jaffer 30, Iqbal Imam 39; Athar Laeeq four for 59, Zafar Iqbal three for 70, Manzoor Akhtar three for 80).

Karachi Blues won the five-day final with a day to spare.

QUAID-E-AZAM TROPHY WINNERS

1953-54	Bahawalpur	1970-71	Karachi Blues	1984-85	United Bank
1954-55	Karachi	1972-73	Railways	1985-86	Karachi
1956-57	Punjab	1973-74	Railways	1986-87	National Bank
1957-58	Bahawalpur	1974-75	Punjab A	1987-88	PIA
1958-59	Karachi	1975-76	National Bank	1988-89	ADBP
1959-60	Karachi	1976-77	United Bank	1989-90	PIA
1961-62	Karachi Blues	1977-78	Habib Bank	1990-91	Karachi Whites
1962-63	Karachi A	1978-79	National Bank	1991-92	Karachi Whites
1963-64	Karachi Blues	1979-80	PIA	1992-93	Karachi Whites
1964-65	Karachi Blues	1980-81	United Bank	1993-94	Lahore City
1966-67	Karachi	1981-82	National Bank	1994-95	Karachi Blues
1968-69	Lahore	1982-83	United Bank	1995-96	Karachi Blues
1969-70	PIA	1983-84	National Bank		

PCB PATRON'S TROPHY, 1995-96

	Played	*Won*	*Lost*	*Drawn*	*1st-inns Points*	*Points*
Allied Bank	7	4	1	2	6	46
PNSC	7	3	1	3	10	40
United Bank	7	3	2	2	10	40
ADBP	7	2	1	4	10	30
PIA	7	2	0	5	8	28
National Bank	7	1	1	5	4	14
Habib Bank	7	0	5	2	4	4
Pakistan Railways	7	0	4	3	0	0

Semi-finals: Allied Bank beat United Bank by virtue of their first-innings lead; ADBP beat PNSC by an innings and 263 runs.

Final: ADBP beat Allied Bank by 212 runs.

Outright win = 10 pts; lead on first innings in a won or drawn game = 2 pts.

*In the following scores, * by the name of a team indicates that they won the toss.*

At Montgomery Biscuit Factory Ground, Sahiwal, September 9, 10, 11, 12. Drawn. ADBP* 284 (Nadeem Younis 31, Javed Hayat 79, Mohammad Ali 60 not out; Mohammad Zahid six for 103) and 291 for six dec. (Nadeem Younis 46, Zahoor Elahi 117, Ghaffar Kazmi 69; Mohammad Zahid four for 102); Allied Bank 192 (Aaley Haider 81; Mohammad Asif four for 82, Javed Hayat five for 44) and 165 for three (Iqbal Saleem 59, Wajahatullah Wasti 50 not out; Mohammad Asif three for 46). *ADBP 2 pts.*

At Defence Cricket Stadium, Karachi, September 9, 10, 11, 12. Drawn. Habib Bank* 348 (Sohail Miandad 45, Anwar Miandad 121, Naved Anjum 41, Asadullah Butt 61; Salman Fazal six for 110) and 112 for three (Shakeel Ahmed 58 not out); National Bank 258 (Saeed Azad 94, Mohammad Javed 31, Extras 32; Asadullah Butt four for 75, Nadeem Ghauri four for 89). *Habib Bank 2 pts.*

The second day's play was abandoned owing to a city-wide strike.

At KRL Cricket Ground, Rawalpindi, September 9, 10, 11, 12. Drawn. PIA 411 for eight dec. (Rizwan-uz-Zaman 37, Mahmood Hamid 44, Wasim Haider 184, Javed Qadeer 66 not out; Aamer Wasim four for 111); Pakistan Railways* 192 (Mohammad Nawaz, jun. 79, Majid Saeed 46; Nadeem Khan five for 78) and 27 for two. *PIA 2 pts.*

Wasim Haider and Javed Qadeer added 195 for PIA's eighth wicket.

At Rawalpindi Cricket Stadium, Rawalpindi, September 9, 10, 11, 12. United Bank won by nine wickets. PNSC 210 (Mazhar Qayyum 34, Tahir Mahmood 50, Sajjad Akbar 70; Umar Rasheed three for 50, Saleem Jaffer three for 29, Mohammad Hussain three for 26) and 188 (Sajjad Akbar 95 not out; Ali Gauhar six for 83); United Bank* 294 (Basit Ali 56, Aamer Bashir 93, Mohammad Hussain 58 not out; Tariq Hussain three for 74, Sajjad Akbar three for 53) and 108 for one (Javed Sami 55 not out, Mansoor Akhtar 33 not out). *United Bank 12 pts.*

At KRL Cricket Ground, Rawalpindi, September 15, 16, 17, 18. PNSC won by 45 runs. PNSC 272 (Nasir Wasti 70, Mazhar Qayyum 72, Sajjad Akbar 58 not out, Sajjad Ali 38; Ata-ur-Rehman three for 65, Bilal Rana four for 44) and 128 (Sher Ali 51; Ata-ur-Rehman eight for 56); Allied Bank* 244 (Mohammad Nawaz, sen. 69, Bilal Rana 62 not out, Ata-ur-Rehman 32; Mohsin Kamal four for 80) and 111 (Manzoor Akhtar 33; Mohsin Kamal five for 46, Sajjad Ali five for 47). *PNSC 12 pts.*

At Montgomery Biscuit Factory Ground, Sahiwal, September 15, 16, 17. PIA won by an innings and eight runs. PIA* 409 (Ghulam Ali 48, Rizwan-uz-Zaman 83, Asif Mujtaba 42, Sagheer Abbas 51, Mahmood Hamid 65, Zahid Ahmed 58, Nadeem Khan 32; Shahid Mahmood four for 196); Habib Bank 205 (Shahid Nawaz 75, Tahir Rashid 66; Mohammad Zahid five for 44, Nadeem Khan three for 65) and 196 (Shakeel Ahmed 34, Anwar Miandad 32, Tahir Rashid 47; Nadeem Khan three for 56, Asif Mujtaba three for 32). *PIA 12 pts.*

At LCCA Ground, Lahore, September 15, 16, 17. United Bank won by an innings and 164 runs. Pakistan Railways 155 (Iqbal Zahoor 32, Aamer Wasim 39 not out; Waqar Younis three for 44, Ali Gauhar six for 56) and 99 (Zahid Javed 32; Waqar Younis three for 60, Ali Gauhar six for 28); United Bank* 418 for six dec. (Mohammad Ramzan 80, Mansoor Akhtar 202, Umar Rasheed 57 not out; Aamer Wasim four for 149). *United Bank 12 pts.*

Mansoor Akhtar's 202 lasted 435 minutes and 328 balls and included 19 fours and two sixes.

At Zafar Ali Stadium, Sahiwal, September 16, 17, 18, 19. Drawn. ADBP* 458 (Zahoor Elahi 54, Atif Rauf 163, Mansoor Rana 71, Javed Hayat 45; Salman Fazal three for 128, Mohammad Javed three for 60); National Bank 303 (Sajid Ali 43, Ameer Akbar 33, Zafar Iqbal 99, Athar Laeeq 51; Manzoor Elahi five for 58) and 265 for three (Sajid Ali 106, Wasim Arif 50, Ameer Akbar 51 not out, Mohammad Javed 34 not out). *ADBP 2 pts.*

At Arbab Niaz Stadium, Peshawar, September 21, 22, 23. ADBP won by an innings and 28 runs. ADBP 354 (Mansoor Rana 75, Javed Hayat 75, Sabih Azhar 51 not out, Extras 35; Asif Malik four for 106); Habib Bank* 112 (Manzoor Elahi six for 38, Mohammad Ali four for 60) and 214 (Mujahid Jamshed 37, Idrees Baig 31, Tahir Rashid 32; Manzoor Elahi three for 75, Mohammad Ali five for 68). *ADBP 12 pts.*

At Montgomery Biscuit Factory Ground, Sahiwal, September 21, 22, 23, 24. Allied Bank won by an innings and 35 runs. National Bank* 307 (Wasim Arif 43, Ameer Akbar 128 not out, Zafar Iqbal 30, Athar Laeeq 31; Shahid Mahboob four for 63, Raj Hans three for 51) and 246 (Sajid Ali 98, Tahir Shah 48; Shahid Mahboob three for 116, Bilal Rana five for 58); Allied Bank 588 for seven dec. (Mohammad Nawaz, sen. 41, Manzoor Akhtar 145, Ijaz Ahmed, jun. 44, Aamer Hanif 179, Raj Hans 110 not out, Extras 33; Hafeez-ur-Rehman three for 187). *Allied Bank 12 pts.*

Allied Bank wicket-keeper Rafaqat Ali made six catches in National Bank's first innings. Aamer Hanif and Raj Hans added 265 for Allied Bank's seventh wicket.

At Qasim Bagh Stadium, Multan, September 21, 22, 23, 24. PNSC won by an innings and 87 runs. PNSC* 447 (Azam Khan 138, Sher Ali 40, Sohail Jaffer 58, Mazhar Qayyum 119 not out, Extras 31; Imran Adil three for 104, Aamer Wasim seven for 169); Pakistan Railways 165 (Majid Saeed 41; Murtaza Hussain four for 22) and 195 (Zahid Javed 46, Majid Saeed 90; Tariq Hussain four for 27, Murtaza Hussain four for 68). *PNSC 12 pts.*

At Defence Cricket Stadium, Karachi, September 21, 22, 23, 24. Drawn. PIA* 277 (Asif Mujtaba 33, Zahid Ahmed 57, Ayaz Jilani 77, Nadeem Khan 35; Umar Rasheed three for 19, Mohammad Hussain three for 84, Tauseef Ahmed three for 67) and 111 for one (Ghulam Ali 39 not out, Mahmood Hamid 66 not out); United Bank 355 (Mohammad Ramzan 127 retired not out, Raees Ahmed 30, Aamer Bashir 41, Ali Gauhar 30 retired not out, Mohammad Hussain 43; Ayaz Jilani four for 90). *United Bank 2 pts.*

The first day's play was abandoned owing to a city-wide strike. Mohammad Ramzan and Ali Gauhar had to retire at their overnight scores on the fourth morning as they were called to play for Pakistan A against the Australian Cricket Academy.

At KRL Cricket Ground, Rawalpindi, September 27, 28, 29. ADBP won by 22 runs. ADBP 83 (Mohammad Hussain six for 35, Tauseef Ahmed three for 27) and 129 (Manzoor Elahi 50; Mohammad Hussain three for 39, Tauseef Ahmed four for 50); United Bank* 97 (Mohammad Asif four for 23, Javed Hayat six for 41) and 93 (Raja Afaq three for 23, Javed Hayat three for 38). *ADBP 10 pts.*

At LCCA Ground, Lahore, September 27, 28, 29, 30. Allied Bank won by 116 runs. Allied Bank* 156 (Bilal Rana 39; Nadeem Ghauri four for 48) and 255 (Mohammad Nawaz, sen. 51, Kamran Khan 124; Nadeem Ghauri three for 59, Abdul Qadir three for 60); Habib Bank 163 (Anwar Miandad 30; Shahid Mahboob six for 80) and 132 (Humayun Hussain four for 43, Bilal Rana four for 40). *Allied Bank 10 pts.*

At Arbab Niaz Stadium, Peshawar, September 27, 28, 29. National Bank won by ten wickets. National Bank 247 (Wasim Arif 37, Saeed Azad 50, Tahir Shah 55, Athar Laeeq 35; Azhar Abbas four for 96, Kifayat Hussain three for 70) and 66 for no wkt (Sajid Ali 33 not out); Pakistan Railways* 94 (Zafar Iqbal three for 27, Athar Laeeq five for 27) and 218 (Mohammad Nawaz, jun. 46, Majid Saeed 89; Zafar Iqbal five for 49, Mohammad Javed three for 34). *National Bank 12 pts.*

At Montgomery Biscuit Factory Ground, Sahiwal, September 27, 28, 29, 30. Drawn. PIA* 498 for six dec. (Rizwan-uz-Zaman 105, Aamer Malik 39, Asif Mujtaba 170, Sagheer Abbas 50, Wasim Haider 69 not out); PNSC 502 for seven (Azam Khan 92, Aamer Ishaq 60, Sohail Jaffer 90, Mazhar Qayyum 58, Tahir Mahmood 82 not out, Sajjad Akbar 35; Asif Mujtaba three for 102). *PNSC 2 pts.*

At Jinnah Stadium, Sialkot, October 3, 4, 5, 6. PIA won by seven wickets. PIA 478 (Shoaib Mohammad 44, Rizwan-uz-Zaman 155, Asif Mujtaba 121, Mahmood Hamid 33, Wasim Haider 54, Extras 36; Mohammad Asif four for 100) and 51 for three (Mubashir Nazir three for 17); ADBP* 235 (Nadeem Younis 37, Mansoor Rana 31; Mohammad Zahid five for 76, Nadeem Khan three for 23) and 293 (Nadeem Younis 41, Zahoor Elahi 100, Javed Hayat 60, Extras 38; Nadeem Khan four for 90, Shoaib Mohammad three for 21). *PIA 12 pts.*

At Iqbal Stadium, Faisalabad, October 3, 4, 5. Allied Bank won by 47 runs. Allied Bank* 194 (Mohammad Nawaz, sen. 37, Masroor Hussain 37, Ijaz Ahmed, jun. 35, Aaley Haider 37; Aamer Wasim six for 74, Mohammad Nawaz, jun. four for 56) and 127 (Bilal Rana 36 not out; Aamer Wasim five for 56, Mohammad Nawaz, jun. four for 37); Pakistan Railways 166 (Tariq Mahmood 34, Babar Javed 33, Intikhab Alam 40 not out; Bilal Rana six for 64) and 108 (Javed Qayyum 34; Bilal Rana five for 32, Raj Hans three for 41). *Allied Bank 12 pts.*

Pakistan Railways' Babar Javed took five catches in the field in Allied Bank's first innings.

At Municipal Stadium, Gujranwala, October 3, 4, 5. United Bank won by an innings and 49 runs. Habib Bank* 144 (Shahid Nawaz 32, Shahid Mahmood 30; Ali Gauhar three for 29, Mushtaq Ahmed six for 56) and 199 (Shakeel Ahmed 96, Shahid Mahmood 32; Waqar Younis three for 52, Mushtaq Ahmed four for 78); United Bank 392 for seven dec. (Mohammad Ramzan 48, Javed Sami 63, Iqbal Imam 100, Umar Rasheed 36, Mohammad Hussain 58 not out, Waqar Younis 30; Asadullah Butt four for 102). *United Bank 12 pts.*

At LCCA Ground, Lahore, October 3, 4, 5, 6. Drawn. PNSC 594 (Azam Khan 122, Aamer Ishaq 43, Nasir Wasti 84, Mazhar Qayyum 31, Sohail Jaffer 98, Sajjad Ali 100, Extras 48; Salman Fazal three for 165, Mohammad Javed five for 119); National Bank* 508 (Shahid Anwar 195, Sajid Ali 139, Mohammad Javed 51, Wasim Arif 37, Extras 34; Tahir Mahmood three for 65). *PNSC 2 pts.*

Shahid Anwar and Sajid Ali put on 301 in 362 minutes for National Bank's first wicket.

At Bagh-i-Jinnah Ground, Lahore, October 8, 9, 10. Allied Bank won by nine wickets. Allied Bank 333 (Mohammad Nawaz, sen. 34, Kamran Khan 38, Manzoor Akhtar 97, Rafaqat Ali 62; Shehzad Butt four for 109, Ali Gauhar five for 86) and 11 for one; United Bank* 141 (Shahid Mahboob four for 60, Humayun Hussain five for 64) and 202 (Mohammad Ramzan 52, Javed Sami 67; Shahid Mahboob five for 72, Humayun Hussain three for 50). *Allied Bank 12 pts.*

At Qasim Bagh Stadium, Multan, October 9, 10, 11, 12. Drawn. Pakistan Railways* 193 (Mohammad Nawaz, jun. 54, Majid Saeed 53, Javed Qayyum 31, Asif Ali 32; Mohammad Ali three for 61, Raja Afaq five for 40) and 386 for nine dec. (Intikhab Alam 127, Qayyum-ul-Hasan 150 not out, Extras 41; Mohammad Asif four for 105); ADBP 203 (Zahoor Elahi 41, Sabih Azhar 40, Manzoor Elahi 32, Mohammad Nadeem 48; Aamer Wasim five for 80) and 345 for eight (Zahoor Elahi 178, Mohammad Nadeem 105; Aamer Wasim four for 149). *ADBP 2 pts.*

Intikhab Alam and Qayyum-ul-Hasan added 245 for the fifth wicket in Pakistan Railways' second innings. Zahoor Elahi and Mohammad Nadeem added 264 for the second wicket in ADBP's second innings.

At Zafar Ali Stadium, Sahiwal, October 9, 10, 11, 12. PNSC won by three wickets. Habib Bank* 389 (Moin-ul-Atiq 81, Shaukat Mirza 78, Shahid Javed 73, Sohail Fazal 87 not out; Sajjad Akbar seven for 103) and 230 (Shakeel Ahmed 50, Moin-ul-Atiq 47, Shahid Mahmood 32; Tariq Hussain four for 80, Murtaza Hussain three for 60); PNSC 405 (Sohail Jaffer 122, Mazhar Qayyum 129, Sajjad Akbar 46, Extras 41; Shakeel Khan three for 124, Shahid Mahmood three for 123) and 217 for seven (Azam Khan 57, Nasir Wasti 68; Shahid Mahmood three for 75). *PNSC 12 pts.*

At Municipal Stadium, Gujranwala, October 9, 10, 11, 12. Drawn. PIA 323 (Shoaib Mohammad 60, Asif Mujtaba 118, Zahid Fazal 34, Aamer Malik 36, Extras 41; Athar Laeeq four for 87, Mohammad Javed five for 88) and 204 for two (Rizwan-uz-Zaman 65, Shoaib Mohammad 102 not out); National Bank* 387 (Shahid Anwar 85, Sajid Ali 49, Saeed Azad 57, Ameer Akbar 56, Athar Laeeq 36, Extras 46; Nadeem Khan three for 98). *National Bank 2 pts.*

At LCCA Ground, Lahore, October 15, 16, 17, 18. Drawn. ADBP 483 for nine dec. (Zahoor Elahi 38, Nadeem Younis 135, Mohammad Nadeem 68, Mansoor Rana 113 not out, Manzoor Elahi 40, Extras 46); PNSC* 308 (Aamer Ishaq 54, Sohail Jaffer 78, Mazhar Qayyum 49, Extras 36; Sabih Azhar three for 46, Mohammad Asif five for 69) and 222 for four (Aamer Ishaq 35, Pervez-ul-Hasan 33, Sohail Jaffer 108 not out, Mazhar Qayyum 32 not out). *ADBP 2 pts.*

At Arbab Niaz Stadium, Peshawar, October 15, 16, 17, 18. Drawn. Allied Bank 154 (Kamran Khan 34, Ijaz Ahmed, jun. 60; Nadeem Khan six for 42); PIA* 157 for one (Rizwan-uz-Zaman 41, Shoaib Mohammad 71 not out, Aamer Malik 34 not out). *PIA 2 pts.*

No play was possible on the first two days.

At Jinnah Stadium, Sialkot, October 15, 16, 17, 18. Drawn. Pakistan Railways 267 (Mohammad Nawaz, jun. 71, Intikhab Alam 64; Kabir Khan four for 85, Shahid Nawaz three for 60) and 267 (Intikhab Alam 39, Qayyum-ul-Hasan 86, Kifayat Hussain 50, Extras 30; Kabir Khan four for 84, Abdul Qadir four for 104); Habib Bank* 377 (Moin-ul-Atiq 50, Shakeel Ahmed 101, Shaukat Mirza 96 not out, Sohail Fazal 33; Aamer Wasim six for 80) and 126 for seven (Moin-ul-Atiq 58; Aamer Wasim three for 33). *Habib Bank 2 pts.*

Habib Bank wicket-keeper Tahir Rashid made five catches and one stumping in Pakistan Railways' first innings.

At Rawalpindi Cricket Stadium, Rawalpindi, October 15, 16, 17, 18. Drawn. National Bank 133 (Saeed Azad 37; Umar Rasheed three for 44, Shehzad Butt four for 34); United Bank* 134 for eight (Iqbal Imam 40; Athar Laeeq three for 45, Mohammad Javed four for 40). *United Bank 2 pts.*

No play was possible on the first two days.

Semi-Finals

At Bagh-i-Jinnah Ground, Lahore, October 21, 22, 23, 24. Drawn. Allied Bank won on first-innings lead. Allied Bank 437 (Mohammad Nawaz, sen. 100, Aamer Hanif 117, Bilal Rana 116; Shehzad Butt five for 127, Ali Gauhar four for 132) and 136 for three (Mohammad Nawaz, sen. 72 not out, Aamer Hanif 30); United Bank* 251 (Javed Sami 83, Mansoor Akhtar 37, Mohammad Hussain 35; Shahid Mahboob seven for 101).

At Rawalpindi Cricket Stadium, Rawalpindi, October 23, 24, 25. ADBP won by an innings and 263 runs. PNSC 68 (Manzoor Elahi six for 32, Mohammad Ali four for 34) and 239 (Tahir Mahmood 35, Sohail Jaffer 83; Mohammad Ali six for 103); ADBP* 570 (Nadeem Younis 91, Mansoor Rana 188, Mohammad Asif 35, Javed Hayat 55, Sabih Azhar 91 not out, Extras 45; Sajid Shah three for 132, Sohail Jaffer three for 73).

Mansoor Rana and Sabih Azhar added 184 for ADBP's ninth wicket.

Final

At Arbab Niaz Stadium, Peshawar, October 29, 30, 31, November 1. ADBP won by 212 runs. ADBP 295 (Nadeem Younis 107, Atif Rauf 84; Humayun Hussain five for 76) and 273 (Zahoor Elahi 40, Mohammad Asif 45, Raja Afaq 56; Shahid Mahboob four for 120, Humayun Hussain four for 71); Allied Bank* 212 (Wajahatullah Wasti 35, Rafaqat Ali 49; Manzoor Elahi six for 68, Mohammad Asif three for 13) and 144 (Wajahatullah Wasti 35; Mohammad Ali six for 63).

ADBP won the five-day final with a day to spare.

AYUB TROPHY AND PCB (BCCP) PATRON'S TROPHY WINNERS

The Ayub Trophy was replaced by the BCCP Trophy after the 1969-70 season, by the BCCP Patron's Trophy after the 1971-72 season and by the PCB Patron's Trophy after the 1994-95 season.

1960-61	Railways-Quetta	1974-75	National Bank	1985-86	Karachi Whites
1961-62	Karachi	1975-76	National Bank	1986-87	National Bank
1962-63	Karachi	1976-77	Habib Bank	1987-88	Habib Bank
1964-65	Karachi	1977-78	Habib Bank	1988-89	Karachi
1965-66	Karachi Blues	1978-79	National Bank	1989-90	Karachi Whites
1967-68	Karachi Blues	†1979-80	IDBP	1990-91	ADBP
1969-70	PIA	†1980-81	Rawalpindi	1991-92	Habib Bank
1970-71	PIA	†1981-82	Allied Bank	1992-93	Habib Bank
1971-72	PIA	†1982-83	PACO	1993-94	ADBP
1972-73	Karachi Blues	1983-84	Karachi Blues	1994-95	Allied Bank
1973-74	Railways	1984-85	Karachi Whites	1995-96	ADBP

† *The competition was not first-class between 1979-80 and 1982-83, when it served as a qualifying competition for the Quaid-e-Azam Trophy.*

PENTANGULAR TROPHY, 1995-96

	Played	*Won*	*Lost*	*Drawn*	*1st-inns Points*	*Points*
United Bank	4	3	1	0	6	36
Allied Bank	4	2	1	1	6	26
PNSC	4	2	1	1	4	24
Karachi	4	2	2	0	4	24
Bahawalpur	4	0	4	0	0	0

Final: United Bank beat Allied Bank by five wickets.

Outright win = 10 pts; lead on first innings in a won or drawn game = 2 pts.

*In the following scores, * by the name of a team indicates that they won the toss.*

At Rawalpindi Cricket Stadium, Rawalpindi, April 12, 13, 14. Allied Bank won by 84 runs. Allied Bank 144 (Mohammad Nawaz, sen. 57; Hasnain Kazim three for 26, Azhar Mahmood three for 33, Tauseef Ahmed four for 22) and 160 (Mohammad Nawaz, sen. 35, Bilal Rana 35; Azhar Mahmood six for 45); United Bank* 109 (Aamir Nazir seven for 54, Shahid Mahboob three for 41) and 111 (Shahid Mahboob five for 51, Humayun Hussain three for ten). *Allied Bank 12 pts.*

Allied Bank wicket-keeper Rafaqat Ali made four catches in United Bank's first innings and six catches in the second.

At KRL Cricket Ground, Rawalpindi, April 12, 13, 14, 15. PNSC won by an innings and four runs. PNSC 417 for nine dec. (Kamran Haider 114, Sher Ali 75, Sajjad Akbar 100 not out; Aamir Sohail four for 64); Bahawalpur* 209 (Azhar Shafiq 70; Murtaza Hussain three for 34) and 204 (Bilal Moin 71, Aamir Sohail 39, Nasir Jam 30; Sajjad Ali three for 45, Tahir Mahmood four for 45). *PNSC 12 pts.*

At KRL Cricket Ground, Rawalpindi, April 17, 18, 19, 20. Drawn. Allied Bank 294 (Mohammad Nawaz, sen. 53, Ijaz Ahmed, jun. 127 not out; Murtaza Hussain five for 92) and 302 for six dec. (Mohammad Nawaz, sen. 33, Bilal Rana 68, Ijaz Ahmed, jun. 106, Aamer Hanif 43); PNSC* 280 (Azam Khan 34, Mazhar Qayyum 46, Zeeshan Siddiqi 81; Aamir Nazir three for 88, Shahid Mahboob four for 69). *Allied Bank 2 pts.*

Ijaz Ahmed, jun. scored a century in each innings, the only instance of the season.

At Rawalpindi Cricket Stadium, Rawalpindi, April 17, 18. Karachi won by an innings and 141 runs. Karachi 414 (Mahmood Hamid 118, Saeed Azad 99, Mohammad Javed 75; Azhar Shafiq five for 97); Bahawalpur* 153 (Sajid Rehmani 36; Mohammad Javed six for 62) and 120 (Mohammad Javed five for 44, Lal Faraz three for 31). *Karachi 12 pts.*

At KRL Cricket Ground, Rawalpindi, April 22, 23, 24, 25. United Bank won by an innings and 86 runs. Bahawalpur 190 (Azhar Shafiq 86, Kamran Hussain 35, Inam-ul-Haq 34; Mohammad Hussain three for 37) and 127 (Mohammad Hussain five for 44, Tauseef Ahmed four for 33); United Bank* 403 (Mohammad Ramzan 67, Aamer Bashir 95, Wasim Yousufi 49, Mohammad Hussain 63; Kamran Hussain three for 48, Wahid Bakhsh five for 101). *United Bank 12 pts.*

At Rawalpindi Cricket Stadium, Rawalpindi, April 22, 23, 24, 25. PNSC won by one wicket. Karachi 193 (Mahmood Hamid 66 not out, Extras 40; Mohsin Kamal three for 57) and 335 (Saeed Azad 56, Asif Mujtaba 115, Moin Khan 39, Extras 40; Sajid Shah three for 90, Sajjad Akbar four for 75); PNSC* 319 (Sher Ali 41, Azam Khan 100, Zeeshan Siddiqi 34, Mohsin Kamal 30 not out; Lal Faraz four for 68, Mohammad Javed three for 96) and 213 for nine (Sher Ali 37, Sohail Jaffer 70, Zeeshan Siddiqi 37; Mohammad Javed three for 60, Naeem Tayyab four for 58). *PNSC 12 pts.*

At National Stadium, Karachi, May 2, 3, 4. Allied Bank won by an innings and 180 runs. Bahawalpur 103 (Bilal Moin 50; Aqib Javed five for 13) and 193 (Sajid Rehmani 39, Bilal Moin 72; Aqib Javed four for 59, Aamir Nazir three for 42); Allied Bank* 476 for two dec. (Mohammad Nawaz, sen. 200, Aamer Hanif 225, Ijaz Ahmed, jun. 37 not out). *Allied Bank 12 pts.*

Mohammad Nawaz, sen.'s 200 lasted 324 minutes and 243 balls and included 26 fours; Aamer Hanif's 225 lasted 415 minutes and 304 balls and included 29 fours and a six. They shared an opening partnership of 380.

At UBL Sports Complex, Karachi, May 2, 3, 4, 5. United Bank won by 132 runs. United Bank 237 (Salim Elahi 78, Azhar Mahmood 45; Athar Laeeq five for 61) and 255 (Hasnain Kazim 37, Aamer Bashir 42, Basit Ali 55, Mansoor Akhtar 32, Azhar Mahmood 34; Athar Laeeq three for 77, Lal Faraz three for 100, Naeem Tayyab three for 59); Karachi* 209 (Shadab Kabir 39, Moin Khan 65; Hasnain Kazim four for 37, Shehzad Butt four for 41) and 151 (Saeed Azad 52, Asif Mujtaba 40, Athar Laeeq 31; Hasnain Kazim three for 47, Tauseef Ahmed four for 23). *United Bank 12 pts.*

At UBL Sports Complex, Karachi, May 7, 8, 9, 10. Karachi won by seven wickets. Karachi 295 (Asif Mujtaba 107; Aqib Javed four for 57, Arshad Khan three for 67) and 172 for three (Saeed Azad 103 not out, Mahmood Hamid 34 not out); Allied Bank* 110 (Aaley Haider 30; Athar Laeeq five for 36, Lal Faraz three for 34) and 355 (Aamir Sohail 104, Mohammad Nawaz, sen. 51, Manzoor Akhtar 30, Aaley Haider 90, Aqib Javed 34; Lal Faraz five for 105). *Karachi 12 pts.*

At National Stadium, Karachi, May 7, 8, 9. United Bank won by seven wickets. PNSC 144 (Kamran Haider 69 not out; Hasnain Kazim three for 27) and 164 (Sajjad Ali 40; Tauseef Ahmed five for 56, Azhar Mahmood three for 37); United Bank* 208 (Aamer Bashir 53, Basit Ali 64; Sajjad Ali three for 57, Murtaza Hussain four for 46) and 101 for three (Javed Sami 55 not out). *United Bank 12 pts.*

Kamran Haider carried his bat through PNSC's first innings.

Final

At National Stadium, Karachi, May 13, 14, 15, 16. United Bank won by five wickets. Allied Bank* 233 (Aamir Sohail 37, Ijaz Ahmed, jun. 52, Aaley Haider 43; Mohammad Hussain three for 57, Tauseef Ahmed five for 47) and 227 (Manzoor Akhtar 104; Shehzad Butt three for 34, Azhar Mahmood three for 36); United Bank 353 (Hasnain Kazim 31, Inzamam-ul-Haq 56, Basit Ali 155, Azhar Mahmood 55; Aamir Nazir three for 92, Aamir Sohail four for 49) and 110 for five.

Allied Bank wicket-keeper Rafaqat Ali made five catches in United Bank's first innings. United Bank won the five-day final with a day to spare.

PENTANGULAR TROPHY WINNERS

The competition was called the PACO Cup between 1980-81 and 1986-87, after sponsors Pakistan Automobile Corporation.

1973-74	PIA	1981-82	Habib Bank	1990-91	United Bank
1974-75	National Bank	1982-83	Habib Bank	1994-95	National Bank
1975-76	PIA	1984-85	United Bank	1995-96	United Bank
1976-77	PIA	1985-86	PACO		
1980-81	PIA	1986-87	PIA		

Note: Matches in the following sections were not first-class.

AUSTRALIAN CRICKET ACADEMY IN PAKISTAN, 1995-96

At Bagh-i-Jinnah Ground, Lahore, September 10, 11, 12, 13. Drawn. Pakistan A* 479 for seven dec. (Ghulam Ali 35, Shahid Anwar 74, Salim Elahi 42, Mohammad Nawaz 42, Manzoor Akhtar 117, Babar Zaman 86, Zafar Iqbal 39 not out) and 24 for two; Australian Cricket Academy 358 (C. J. Peake 80, E. M. C. Arnold 43, P. J. Roach 136 not out; Arshad Khan five for 111).

At KRL Cricket Ground, Rawalpindi, September 19, 20, 21, 22. Australian Cricket Academy won by 46 runs. Australian Cricket Academy* 297 (C. J. Richards 51, M. E. Hussey 69, M. P. Mott 51, I. S. Hewett 36; Haaris Khan three for 95) and 183 (M. E. Hussey 62, K. M. Harvey 64 not out; Haaris Khan four for 66, Shoaib Akhtar five for 55); Pakistan A 205 (Shahid Anwar 45, Salim Elahi 70, Babar Zaman 37 not out; I. S. Hewett five for 63, E. M. C. Arnold four for 33) and 229 (Wasim Yousufi 108, Javed Sami 40; M. J. Nicolson three for 46, E. M. C. Arnold three for 88).

At Iqbal Stadium, Faisalabad, September 24, 25, 26, 27. Pakistan A won by 208 runs. Pakistan A* 280 (Shahid Anwar 33, Manzoor Akhtar 40, Babar Zaman 41, Ali Gauhar 31; B. Lee three for 58, E. M. C. Arnold three for 39) and 298 (Manzoor Akhtar 172 not out; E. M. C. Arnold four for 94); Australian Cricket Academy 189 (C. T. Perren 71; Nadeem Khan five for 73, Arshad Khan three for 58) and 181 (C. J. Richards 60, M. P. Mott 33; Nadeem Khan five for 74, Arshad Khan three for 33).

WILLS KINGS CUP, 1995-96

Semi-finals

At Iqbal Stadium, Faisalabad, January 12. Rawalpindi A won by three wickets. ADBP 253 for four (44 overs) (Saeed Anwar 31, Zahoor Elahi 111 not out, Manzoor Elahi 30, Extras 33); Rawalpindi A* 254 for seven (43.2 overs) (Zubair Nadeem 78, Asif Mahmood 107 not out).

At Municipal Stadium, Sheikhupura, January 12. PIA won by three wickets. National Bank 134 (43.1 overs) (Shahid Anwar 56, Tahir Shah 31; Wasim Akram four for 13); PIA* 135 for seven (36.1 overs) (Extras 36; Athar Laeeq four for 38).

Final

At Municipal Stadium, Sheikhupura, January 19. PIA won by seven wickets. Rawalpindi A 124 (42.5 overs) (Zubair Nadeem 36; Wasim Akram four for 21); PIA* 125 for three (30.5 overs) (Ghulam Ali 52, Zahid Fazal 45).

CRICKET IN SRI LANKA, 1995-96

By GERRY VAIDYASEKERA and SA'ADI THAWFEEQ

Marvan Atapattu

Sri Lankan enthusiasm for cricket, even among those who have never handled a bat, reached a new peak as Arjuna Ranatunga led the nation to their World Cup triumph. The game boomed and, for one-day internationals, the island almost came to a standstill. It was a wonderful time for a country beset by internal strife and thirsting for recognition.

It was also an unexpectedly early success for the campaign to make Sri Lanka world champions by the end of the century. Nevertheless, the Sri Lankan board's president, Ana Punchihewa, who was closely identified with that campaign, was deposed shortly after the World Cup. His successor was another businessman, Upali Dharmadasa.

The excitement surrounding the national team's performance overshadowed domestic cricket in Sri Lanka, apart from the ever-popular big school matches. But the first-class programme continued to grow. Though there was no Inter-Provincial competition, the P. Saravanamuttu Trophy was revamped yet again. Segment A, the first-class section, featured 15 teams, down from 16, but instead of being divided into two groups with the group-winners proceeding to a final, they played in one round-robin league. This expanded the tournament to 104 matches, up from 57.

A severe drought during the season led to some high scoring. In one weekend in early December, five clubs made 400 or more in an innings and seven batsmen hit hundreds. No one took advantage more than 23-year-old Marvan Atapattu of Sinhalese. He scored centuries in each of his first three matches of the season – including 214 not out against Singha – to reach 552 at an average of 184.00 in four innings. By the time he was called up for World Cup duty, another double-century – 253 not out against Galle – had lifted him past 1,000 for the season; he returned to score a sixth hundred and finished on 1,223 at 111.18. Had he not missed five games, he would surely have set a record aggregate for a Sri Lankan season. But Russell Arnold of Nondescripts did: he scored 1,475 runs, in 16 matches to Atapattu's nine, to beat Aravinda de Silva's 1,308 in 1992-93.

Losing Atapattu may have cost Sinhalese the title; they lost by a fraction of a point to Colombo, a band of promising young cricketers led by Jerome Jayaratne. It was Colombo's first championship since the tournament was given first-class status in 1988-89. It must have helped that they had no international call-ups, whereas the next three in the table – Sinhalese, Nondescripts and Bloomfield – supplied the bulk of the Sri Lankan team for both the World Cup and the preceding tour of Australia. Colombo and Sinhalese were well ahead of the rest of the field, as each recorded seven outright wins and six on first innings. With hindsight, their meeting in January was crucial; Colombo forced Sinhalese to follow on for the first time in 20 years and claimed the six points for first-innings lead in a draw. But they did not secure the title until they beat Sebastianites in their final game in March.

Bloomfield batsmen Sampath Perera and Ruwan Kalpage provided one of the highlights of the season when they added 315 for the third wicket against Antonians, a national all-wicket record. In that match, Kalpage reached his hundred in 117 balls, but Perera later bettered him with a century in 96 balls against Moors. Suresh Gunasekera of Sinhalese, just out of school, was not far behind them, though, when he completed his maiden hundred in 119 balls, against Colts, on first-class debut. Another school captain, Chaminda Jayasinghe, scored 102 not out on debut for Tamil Union against Singha. Colts opener Chaminda Mendis became the first batsman to score a century in each innings in Sri Lankan cricket, against Singha, and made the record still more impressive by converting the second hundred into an unbeaten double.

In the non-first-class Segment B of the P. Saravanamuttu Trophy, which was contested by 16 teams, hard-hitting batsman Sathya Jayasuriya led Burgher Recreation Club to the title. They won 11 of their 13 matches. Outstation club Kalutara Town were runners-up; schoolboy Nilantha Tillekeratne, the captain of Kalutara Maha Vidyalala, scored three hundreds and six fifties for them.

Nondescripts, captained by Russell Hewage, won the GTE Yellow Pages Under-23 title for the second year running, with Moors runners-up. In limited-overs cricket, Division Three side Ragama Sports Club ran up a record total of 467 for eight in 50 overs to beat Ganemulla by 351 runs. Hambantota District won the Minor District tournament ahead of 1993-94 champions Puttalam-Chilaw. Overseas, Atapattu led Sri Lanka to victory over India in the final of a six-a-side tournament in Singapore.

In schools cricket, Dumitha Hunukumbara scored 279 to help Maliyadeva reach 505 for eight declared against Thurstan at Kurunegala. He was one of four schoolboy batsmen to reach 1,000 runs in the season, the others being Nilantha Tillekeratne of Kalutara Maha Vidyalala, Roshan Wimalesena of Sri Sumangala in Panadura and Anushka Polonovita of Royal College. Ranga Dias of Maris Stella took 16 for 110 – eight in each innings – against Gurukula at Negombo, and Nimesh Perera, the vice-captain of St Sebastian's College, broke his own record of 131 wickets in a season; this time he collected 134. His team shared the Inter-School limited-overs title with Nalanda after the final was ruined by rain. Indika Prasad, captain of Government Science College, Matale, Lenin Weerasinghe of De Mazenod and Sarath Ranaweera of Vidyartha each took nine wickets in an innings. Seminda Ratnayake of Dharmadutha had match figures of nine for five when he took three for two in the first innings and six for three in the second.

FIRST-CLASS AVERAGES, 1995-96

BATTING

(Qualification: 500 runs, average 35.00)

	M	*I*	*NO*	*R*	*HS*	*100s*	*Avge*
M. S. Atapattu (*Sinhalese SC*)	9	14	3	1,223	253*	6	111.18
R. P. Arnold (*Nondescripts CC*)	16	24	3	1,475	217*	5	70.23
V. S. K. Waragoda (*Colombo CC*)	13	18	2	1,036	170	4	64.75

	M	*I*	*NO*	*R*	*HS*	*100s*	*Avge*
R. S. Kalpage (*Bloomfield C and AC*)	9	14	2	739	139	4	61.58
C. Mendis (*Colts CC*)	13	20	3	1,043	200*	4	61.35
S. K. L. de Silva (*Kurunegala Youth CC*)	15	26	5	1,171	183*	3	55.76
Sanjeewa Silva (*Sebastianites C and AC*)	14	23	1	1,196	201*	3	54.36
D. P. Samaraweera (*Colts CC*)	14	24	2	1,149	250*	3	52.22
S. Wijesiri (*Tamil Union C and AC*)	9	14	2	595	127	1	49.58
U. U. Chandana (*Tamil Union C and AC*)	11	15	3	585	75	0	48.75
D. D. Wickremasinghe (*Galle CC*)	14	23	4	914	127*	2	48.10
A. M. de Silva (*Colombo CC*)	14	18	3	706	186	3	47.06
S. I. de Saram (*Tamil Union C and AC*)	17	26	2	1,116	237	3	46.50
R. Peiris (*Tamil Union C and AC*)	15	22	0	988	139	2	44.90
S. T. Perera (*Bloomfield C and AC*)	14	22	0	942	164	3	42.81
A. K. D. A. S. Kumara (*Panadura SC*)	13	20	1	812	110	2	42.73
M. T. Sampath (*Singha SC*)	14	23	3	849	190	2	42.45
S. K. Silva (*Sebastianites C and AC*)	13	21	0	862	144	1	41.04
N. Ranatunga (*Colts CC*)	14	20	2	738	212*	2	41.00
R. P. A. H. Wickremaratne (*Sinhalese SC*)	13	19	1	725	82	0	40.27
B. Ediriweera (*Colombo CC*)	13	19	0	761	106	1	40.05
A. C. Seneviratne (*Colombo CC*)	13	17	1	639	141	1	39.93
S. Kumara (*Panadura SC*)	14	23	2	818	116	1	38.95
H. Premasiri (*Singha SC*)	9	15	0	564	140	1	37.60
P. B. Dassanayake (*Bloomfield C and AC*)	13	20	1	712	111	1	37.47
S. Jayantha (*Singha SC*)	14	23	1	817	133	1	37.13
W. M. J. Kumudu (*Singha SC*)	13	22	0	816	146	2	37.09
W. A. M. P. Perera (*Antonians SC*)	11	20	2	645	92	0	35.83

* *Signifies not out.*

BOWLING

(Qualification: 20 wickets, average 25.00)

	O	*M*	*R*	*W*	*BB*	*5W/i*	*Avge*
E. A. R. de Silva (*Galle CC*)	202.2	59	414	30	6-48	1	13.80
K. J. Silva (*Sinhalese SC*)	220.2	51	554	40	6-7	5	13.85
S. Dodanwala (*Sinhalese SC*)	266.1	70	796	57	6-44	4	13.96
S. D. Anurasiri (*Panadura SC*)	477.5	187	837	50	6-19	5	16.74
W. N. M. Soysa (*Police SC*)	303.1	62	776	44	6-22	3	17.63
A. Dalugoda (*Colombo CC*)	216.1	73	463	25	5-45	1	18.52
P. K. Serasinghe (*Police SC*)	395.5	99	899	48	6-40	3	18.72
N. Dabare (*Colombo CC*)	205.5	52	564	30	7-61	2	18.80
B. de Silva (*Bloomfield C and AC*)	251.4	41	872	46	8-79	5	18.95
M. de Silva (*Galle CC*)	175.1	40	461	24	4-25	0	19.20
C. P. H. Ramanayake (*Tamil Union C and AC*)	390.2	94	1,123	58	7-24	2	19.36
S. C. de Silva (*Sebastianites C and AC*)	385.2	72	1,249	64	7-76	4	19.51
D. P. Samaraweera (*Colts CC*)	163.5	33	472	24	5-78	1	19.66
L. Hannibal (*Nondescripts CC*)	289.4	56	928	46	8-38	1	20.17
H. M. L. Sagara (*Colombo CC*)	210.2	55	496	24	5-38	1	20.66
N. Saranasekera (*Nondescripts CC*)	386.4	83	1,038	50	7-74	3	20.76
A. Rideegammana (*Galle CC*)	337.2	89	767	36	5-26	1	21.30
M. Jayasena (*Panadura SC*)	511.3	100	1,435	67	5-72	4	21.41
R. S. Kalpage (*Bloomfield C and AC*)	376.4	114	911	42	6-61	2	21.69
M. Villavarayan (*Colombo CC*)	380.1	87	1,067	48	5-43	2	22.22
S. H. S. M. K. Silva (*Sinhalese SC*)	350	65	1,115	48	6-82	1	23.22
P. W. Gunaratne (*Bloomfield C and AC*)	241	36	827	35	6-58	2	23.62
U. U. Chandana (*Tamil Union C and AC*)	290.1	64	798	33	5-47	2	24.18
R. P. Arnold (*Nondescripts CC*)	387	93	1,063	43	5-34	2	24.72
N. Bandaratilleke (*Tamil Union C and AC*)	386	93	1,090	44	5-22	2	24.77
S. Kumara (*Panadura SC*)	229.3	48	649	26	4-41	0	24.96

P. SARAVANAMUTTU TROPHY, 1995-96

	Played	*Won*	*Lost*	*Drawn*	*1st-inns Points*	*Bonus Points*	*Points*
Colombo CC	14	7	0	7	36	60.60	180.60
Sinhalese SC	14	7	0	7	36	59.80	179.80
Nondescripts CC	14	4	2	8	30	61.70	139.70
Bloomfield C and AC	14	3	1	10	30	59.00	125.00
Sebastianites C and AC	14	4	3	7	22	52.80	122.80
Tamil Union C and AC	14	3	1	10	24	61.70	121.70
Colts CC	14	3	1	10	36	47.10	119.10
Panadura SC	14	2	4	8	42	52.10	118.10
Galle SC	14	3	1	10	30	49.80	115.80
Police SC	14	3	4	7	6	47.90	89.90
Singha SC	14	2	5	7	6	46.80	76.80
Antonians SC	13	1	3	9	24	39.50	75.50
Kurunegala Youth CC	14	1	3	10	24	39.30	75.30
Moors SC	14	0	7	7	16	43.90	59.90
Moratuwa SC	13	0	8	5	0	27.60	27.60

The match between Antonians and Moratuwa was not played. The match between Galle and Tamil Union at Galle was stopped because of a dangerous pitch and replayed at Colombo four weeks later.

Outright win = 12 pts; 1st-innings lead in drawn match = 6 pts; 1st-innings lead in lost match = 4 pts.

*In the following scores, * by the name of a team indicates that they won the toss.*

At Reid Avenue, Colombo, November 17, 18, 19. Bloomfield C and AC won by 178 runs. Bloomfield C and AC 201 (I. Batuwitarachchi 39, S. K. Perera 66, S. T. Perera 32; R. Pushpakumara seven for 53) and 254 for three dec. (S. T. Perera 95, R. S. Kalpage 103 not out); Singha SC* 109 (S. Jayantha 60; P. W. Gunaratne six for 58, R. Palliyaguru three for 17) and 168 (M. T. Sampath 49, T. A. de Silva 35; R. S. Kalpage five for 22).

Bloomfield wicket-keeper P. B. Dassanayake took nine catches in the match.

At Maitland Crescent, Colombo (CCC), November 17, 18, 19. Drawn. Colombo CC* 262 (C. P. Handunettige 32, B. Ediriweera 68, V. S. K. Waragoda 68, A. Dalugoda 37 not out; N. Bandaratilleke four for 38) and 109 for eight (N. Bandaratilleke four for 45); Tamil Union C and AC 210 (W. T. de Silva 31, W. M. J. P. Weerasinghe 35 not out, Extras 38; W. Labrooy three for 70, A. Dalugoda five for 45).

At Braybrooke Place, Colombo, November 17, 18, 19. Drawn. Moratuwa SC 256 (D. Bodiyabaduge 78 not out; S. A. de Silva four for 37, T. Jeffry three for 77) and 258 for eight (W. A. A. Wasantha 35, S. Soysa 86; T. Jeffry three for 85); Moors SC* 290 (H. Wimalasekera 74, A. Hettiarachchi 34, T. Jeffry 61, Extras 34; C. de Silva three for 96).

At Maitland Place, Colombo (NCC), November 17, 18, 19. Nondescripts CC won by eight wickets. Colts CC* 124 (M. V. Perera 32; P. Hewage four for 56) and 181 (D. P. Samaraweera 30, N. Ranatunga 57, S. Alexander 31; N. Saranasekera five for 38); Nondescripts CC 136 (S. Alexander four for 56, N. Ranatunga three for 23) and 170 for two (S. Weerasinghe 50, D. Perera 65, R. V. Hewage 34 not out).

At Police Park, Colombo, November 17, 18, 19. Panadura SC won by an innings and 76 runs. Police SC* 176 (D. Gunawardene 30, P. K. Serasinghe 30 not out) and 66 (M. Jayasena three for 29, S. D. Anurasiri six for 19); Panadura SC 318 for eight dec. (D. Passawa 84, S. Kumara 45, A. K. D. A. S. Kumara 103; D. Gunawardene four for 72).

At Tyronne Fernando Stadium, Moratuwa, November 17, 18, 19. Sebastianites C and AC won by ten wickets. Sebastianites C and AC* 341 (G. J. A. F. Aponso 32, Sanjeewa Silva 129, C. M. Wickremasinghe 45, K. Anton 47, Extras 34; J. A. W. Kumara three for 52, U. Bandara three for 34) and 11 for no wkt; Kurunegala Youth CC 157 (S. K. L. de Silva 57; D. Samarasinghe three for 37, G. J. A. F. Aponso three for 16) and 192 (R. Jaymon 68, V. Samarawickrama 34, A. Balalla 30 not out).

At Maitland Place, Colombo (SSC), November 17, 18, 19. Drawn. Antonians SC 367 (W. A. M. P. Perera 71, P. Wanasinghe 136, K. Dharmasena 33, G. H. Perera 57; C. Boteju three for 71) and 72 for two (S. Jayawardene 36); Sinhalese SC* 402 for six dec. (D. Ranatunga 73, M. S. Atapattu 122, R. P. A. H. Wickremaratne 70, C. Ranasinghe 62 not out).

At Reid Avenue, Colombo, November 24, 25, 26. Drawn. Bloomfield C and AC* 407 for seven dec. (S. K. Perera 80, S. T. Perera 78, R. S. Kalpage 86, P. B. Dassanayake 52, R. Palliyaguru 50 not out; A. Dalugoda three for 107); Colombo CC 161 (C. P. Handunettige 36, V. S. K. Waragoda 31; H. Boteju four for 32, R. S. Kalpage three for 13) and 147 for three (B. Ediriweera 83, J. Jaymon 39; H. Boteju three for 24).

At Galle Esplanade, Galle, November 24, 25, 26. Drawn. Galle CC 379 (A. Rideegammana 90, E. A. R. de Silva 46, C. K. Hewamanna 85 not out, Extras 30; S. C. de Silva four for 56) and 109 for two dec. (S. M. Faumi 30 not out); Sebastianites C and AC* 232 (S. K. Silva 78, N. R. G. Perera 48, Extras 35; A. Rideegammana four for 59, E. A. R. de Silva three for 25) and 99 for four.

At Braybrooke Place, Colombo, November 24, 25, 26. Drawn. Police SC 170 (D. Gunawardene 52; S. H. U. Karnain three for 37) and 135 for seven (S. Rajapakse 33, W. N. M. Soysa 35); Moors SC* 166 (P. Abeygunasekera 40, M. H. O. Azeez 35; D. Gunawardene four for 82, A. Ranaweera three for 44).

At Tyronne Fernando Stadium, Moratuwa, November 24, 25, 26. Drawn. Kurunegala Youth CC* 409 for four dec. (S. K. L. de Silva 183 not out, A. Balalla 102 not out); Moratuwa SC 303 for eight (M. Narayanage 36, W. Abeywardene 30, W. A. A. Wasantha 55, C. Fernando 33, A. Bandara 60).

De Silva and Balalla added an unbroken 231 for Kurunegala's fifth wicket.

At Maitland Place, Colombo (NCC), November 24, 25, 26. Drawn. Nondescripts CC 350 for nine dec. (R. P. Arnold 109, R. V. Hewage 49, A. S. Pietersz 53, Extras 30; K. Dharmasena three for 58); Antonians SC* 163 (W. A. M. P. Perera 66; R. P. Arnold three for 38, C. P. Mapatuna five for 31) and 81 for eight (P. Hewage three for 15).

At Maitland Place, Colombo (SSC), November 24, 25, 26. Drawn. Singha SC 318 (H. Premasiri 40, S. Jayantha 52, M. T. Sampath 100, G. Sanjeewa 36; S. Dodanwela three for 62) and 197 for five (W. M. J. Kumudu 53, S. Jayantha 99 not out); Sinhalese SC* 401 for eight dec. (A. A. W. Gunawardene 87, M. S. Atapattu 214 not out, S. H. S. M. K. Silva 35; L. Pradeep three for 72, S. Jayantha three for 71).

At P. Saravanamuttu Stadium, Colombo, November 24, 25, 26. Drawn. Colts CC 115 (H. H. Devapriya 33; C. M. Hathurusinghe four for 15, N. Bandaratilleke five for 36) and 35 for no wkt; Tamil Union C and AC* 268 (M. Perera 39, S. I. de Saram 129, N. Bandaratilleke 34; S. Alexander four for 84).

At Reid Avenue, Colombo, December 1, 2, 3. Drawn. Sinhalese SC* 278 (M. S. Atapattu 66, C. Ranasinghe 38, U. N. K. Fernando 94 not out; R. Palliyaguru five for 47) and 350 for nine (A. A. W. Gunawardene 36, M. S. Atapattu 150, R. P. A. H. Wickremaratne 57, S. H. S. M. K. Silva 30; P. W. Gunaratne three for 29); Bloomfield C and AC 252 (I. Batuwitarachchi 31, S. K. Perera 35, R. Palliyaguru 50, H. Boteju 30; S. H. S. M. K. Silva six for 82).

At Maitland Crescent, Colombo (CCC), December 1, 2, 3. Drawn. Colts CC* 436 for eight dec. (D. P. Samaraweera 250 not out, C. Mendis 37, S. Alexander 36 not out, Extras 33; M. Villavarayan three for 104, A. Dalugoda three for 91); Colombo CC 440 for seven (C. P. Handunettige 172 not out, A. Perera 46, V. S. K. Waragoda 64, A. C. Seneviratne 78, Extras 47).

Samaraweera batted throughout Colts' 617-minute innings and Handunettige throughout Colombo's 566-minute innings. Handunettige shared successive century stands with Perera, Waragoda and Seneviratne.

At Galle Esplanade, Galle, December 1, 2, 3. Galle CC won by six wickets. Panadura SC* 208 (S. Kumara 32, M. V. Deshapriya 72; J. C. Gamage three for 67) and 177 (A. K. D. A. S. Kumara 71; S. M. Faumi six for 52); Galle CC 258 (C. K. Hewamanna 67, E. A. R. de Silva 76; B. Perera four for 58, M. Jayasena five for 72) and 129 for four (D. D. Wickremasinghe 48, D. Sudarshana 30; K. Silva three for 38).

At Maitland Place, Colombo (NCC), December 1, 2, 3. Drawn. Singha SC* 423 (H. Premasiri 36, W. M. J. Kumudu 132, M. T. Sampath 66, J. Nanda 76 not out, Extras 42) and 110 (L. Hannibal three for 39, C. D. U. S. Weerasinghe four for 31); Nondescripts CC 425 (R. P. Arnold 144, D. Perera 82, P. Dabare 82, C. D. U. S. Weerasinghe 56; R. Pushpakumara three for 79, H. M. N. C. Dhanasinghe three for 134) and 17 for two.

At Tyronne Fernando Stadium, Moratuwa, December 1, 2, 3. Sebastianites C and AC won by an innings and 89 runs. Sebastianites C and AC* 492 for six dec. (S. K. Silva 46, G. J. A. F. Aponso 37, Sanjeewa Silva 201 not out, C. M. Wickremasinghe 68, N. R. G. Perera 63, Extras 51); Moratuwa SC 293 (M. Narayanage 45, D. Bodiyabaduge 37, C. Fernando 33, W. A. A. Wasantha 57, S. de Mel 32) and 110 (W. Abeywardene 56; G. R. M. A. Perera three for eight, N. R. G. Perera five for 34).

At P. Saravanamuttu Stadium, Colombo, December 1, 2, 3. Drawn. Antonians SC* 370 (P. Wanasinghe 41, K. Dharmasena 33, A. Pathirana 71, M. Prasanga 65, Extras 40; C. P. H. Ramanayake four for 77) and 152 (P. Wanasinghe 70 not out; C. M. Hathurusinghe three for 24, U. U. Chandana five for 47); Tamil Union C and AC 304 (R. Peiris 94, D. N. Nadarajah 101, U. U. Chandana 61; P. M. Weragoda four for 78, K. Dharmasena three for 67) and 82 for three (U. U. Chandana 55 not out).

At Reid Avenue, Colombo, December 8, 9, 10. Drawn. Bloomfield C and AC* 324 (I. Batuwitarachchi 64, B. de Silva 76, R. Yasalal 37, P. K. Wijetunge 47; P. Hewage three for 52) and 235 (S. T. Perera 35, H. Boteju 58, B. de Silva 61 not out; L. Hannibal three for 35, N. Saranasekera four for 50); Nondescripts CC 238 for nine dec. (R. P. Arnold 44, D. Perera 48, P. Rajapakse 59, P. Hewage 39; B. de Silva five for 68) and 249 for seven (R. P. Arnold 60, S. Weerasinghe 45, P. Rajapakse 67 not out, P. Hewage 32; P. K. Wijetunge three for 81).

At Maitland Crescent, Colombo (CCC), December 8, 9, 10. Drawn. Colombo CC* 332 (B. Ediriweera 50, A. C. Seneviratne 141, H. M. L. Sagara 30 not out; P. M. Weragoda four for 102, K. Dharmasena three for 56) and 191 for six (C. P. Handunettige 61); Antonians SC 201 (W. A. M. P. Perera 64 not out; H. M. L. Sagara three for 84, N. Rajan four for 61).

Perera carried his bat through Antonians' innings.

At Galle Esplanade, Galle, December 8, 9, 10. Galle CC won by 166 runs. Galle CC 168 (A. Rideegammana 35, C. K. Hewamanna 44, E. A. R. de Silva 31; M. H. Ghaffoor four for 28, S. H. U. Karnain five for 53) and 232 (A. Rideegammana 40, D. D. Wickremasinghe 69, C. K. Hewamanna 39; R. Sridhar three for 86, T. Jeffry four for 29); Moors SC* 102 (S. H. U. Karnain 51 not out; S. M. Faumi four for 51, K. P. J. Warnaweera three for 20) and 132 (A. Hettiarachchi 40; M. de Silva four for 55).

At Panadura Esplanade, Panadura, December 8, 9, 10. Drawn. Moratuwa SC* 298 (M. Narayanage 39, W. Abeywardene 55, S. Soysa 33, M. de Alwis 33, S. de Mel 58; M. Jayasena three for 62, S. Kumara four for 67) and 287 (S. Soysa 65, A. Bandara 37, M. de Alwis 42, K. G. Perera 52, Extras 34; I. Gallage three for 58, M. V. Deshapriya four for 100); Panadura SC 425 (M. Silva 44, A. K. D. A. S. Kumara 49, M. V. Deshapriya 120, S. Liyanage 68, I. Gallage 33, K. Silva 37; K. G. Perera three for 150).

At Police Park, Colombo, December 8, 9, 10. Drawn. Sebastianites C and AC* 278 (S. K. Silva 69, M. Peiris 65, Anusha Perera 36; P. K. Serasinghe six for 40) and 116 for seven dec. (Anusha Perera 59); Police SC 173 (R. Wimalasiri 57, D. Gunawardene 38; S. C. de Silva three for 26, Primal Salgado three for 30) and 150 for five (C. Liyanage 91; S. C. de Silva four for 37).

C. M. Wickremasinghe took six catches in Police's first innings, a national record.

At Maitland Place, Colombo (SSC), December 8, 9, 10. Drawn. Sinhalese SC 461 (S. Gunasekera 160, E. F. M. U. Fernando 112, C. Ranasinghe 33, R. Jayawardene 76, S. H. S. M. K. Silva 35) and 162 for nine (S. Gunasekera 50, S. H. S. M. K. Silva 44; D. Hettiarachchi four for 53); Colts CC* 361 (S. Attanayake 41, M. V. Perera 61, J. Kulatunga 63, H. de Silva 56 not out, Extras 38; C. Boteju three for 61, R. Jayawardene three for 94).

Gunasekera scored 160 on first-class debut. Colts wicket-keeper H. H. Devapriya took seven catches in Sinhalese's first innings, a national record.

At P. Saravanamuttu Stadium, Colombo, December 8, 9, 10. Tamil Union C and AC won by an innings and 13 runs. Tamil Union C and AC* 501 for four dec. (R. Peiris 139, W. T. de Silva 60, S. I. de Saram 123, C. Jayasinghe 102 not out, W. M. J. P. Weerasinghe 52 not out; H. M. N. C. Dhanasinghe three for 104); Singha SC 243 (W. M. J. Kumudu 40, S. Jayantha 133, M. T. Sampath 30; M. Perera three for 72, S. de Silva three for 20) and 245 (W. M. J. Kumudu 53, T. A. de Silva 33; C. P. H. Ramanayake three for 56).

Jayasinghe scored 102 not out on first-class debut.

At Reid Avenue, Colombo, December 15, 16, 17. Drawn. Tamil Union C and AC* 259 (R. Peiris 60, W. T. de Silva 48, U. U. Chandana 55; B. de Silva seven for 38) and 356 for eight dec. (R. Peiris 89, S. I. de Saram 69, D. N. Nadarajah 62, U. U. Chandana 75; P. W. Gunaratne three for 87, R. Palliyaguru three for 22); Bloomfield C and AC 358 (I. Galagoda 52, R. S. Kalpage 138, B. de Silva 41, R. Palliyaguru 31, Extras 30; U. U. Chandana four for 135) and 32 for two.

At Maitland Crescent, Colombo (CCC), December 15, 16, 17. Colombo CC won by nine wickets. Singha SC* 266 (W. M. J. Kumudu 45, S. Jayantha 34, G. Sanjeewa 74 not out; W. Labrooy three for 47, M. Villavarayan three for 61) and 152 (W. M. J. Kumudu 40; N. Dabare seven for 61); Colombo CC 365 (C. P. Handunettige 54, A. M. de Silva 52, V. S. K. Waragoda 48, A. C. Seneviratne 73, W. Labrooy 50; R. Pushpakumara three for 95) and 56 for one.

At Havelock Park, Colombo (Colts), December 15, 16, 17. Drawn. Antonians SC* 355 (P. Wanasinghe 32, T. P. Kodikara 75, N. Devarajan 40, K. Dharmasena 99 not out, Extras 32; S. Alexander four for 119, N. Ranatunga four for 93) and 364 (V. S. Sittamige 44, S. Jayawardene 67, M. Prasanga 40, P. Wanasinghe 34, N. Devarajan 84, K. Dharmasena 36; D. Hettiarachchi four for 85, C. Mendis five for 155); Colts CC 326 (C. Mendis 78, S. Attanayake 42, D. Kanchana 43, J. Kulatunga 62, H. H. Devapriya 31; P. M. Weragoda four for 86, T. P. Kodikara three for 46).

At Welagedera Stadium, Kurunegala, December 15, 16, 17. Drawn. Galle CC 242 (N. Shiroman 39, S. M. Faumi 44, E. A. R. de Silva 55; R. K. B. Amunugama three for 39, V. Samarawickrama five for 47) and 204 for nine dec. (H. S. S. Fonseka 37, D. D. Wickremasinghe 30, E. A. R. de Silva 31; V. Samarawickrama four for 71); Kurunegala Youth CC* 116 (J. C. Gamage three for 30, S. M. Faumi three for 44) and 149 for eight (R. Jaymon 64, A. W. R. Madurasinghe 33 not out; S. M. Faumi four for 58).

At Panadura Esplanade, Panadura, December 15, 16, 17. Drawn. Panadura SC* 316 (B. Perera 62, N. Mendis 61, S. Kumara 59, A. K. D. A. S. Kumara 43, M. Jayasena 41 not out; R. Sridhar five for 69) and 219 for six dec. (B. Perera 42, M. Silva 96); Moors SC 213 (S. A. de Silva 48, S. H. U. Karnain 73; S. D. Anurasiri four for 79, S. Kumara four for 41) and 99 for six (M. H. M. Unais 34, T. Jeffry 36 not out; M. Jayasena four for 41).

At Maitland Place, Colombo (SSC), December 15, 16, 17. Sinhalese SC won by an innings and 121 runs. Nondescripts CC 108 (R. P. Arnold 37; C. Boteju four for 38, S. H. S. M. K. Silva three for 23) and 138 (S. Weerasinghe 44; S. Dodanwela six for 55); Sinhalese SC* 367 (D. Ranatunga 40, E. F. M. U. Fernando 31, M. S. Atapattu 133, R. P. A. H. Wickremaratne 80, S. H. S. M. K. Silva 34; A. P. Weerakkody three for 87, P. Hewage three for 83).

At Police Park, Colombo, December 16, 17, 18. Police SC won by an innings and 79 runs. Moratuwa SC 124 (M. de Alwis 46 not out; D. Gunawardene three for 25, V. Ranaweera four for 44, W. N. M. Soysa three for 23) and 148 (S. Soysa 42; W. N. M. Soysa six for 22); Police SC* 351 (S. Gunaratne 44, W. N. M. Soysa 170, G. Silva 42, M. Kudagodage 41 not out; K. G. Perera seven for 120).

At Reid Avenue, Colombo, January 5, 6, 7. Drawn. Antonians SC* 359 (S. Jayawardene 65, W. A. M. P. Perera 78, T. P. Kodikara 80, G. H. Perera 44; P. W. Gunaratne six for 79, R. S. Kalpage three for 95) and 100 for five (W. A. M. P. Perera 44; B. de Silva three for 18); Bloomfield C and AC 178 (I. Galagoda 89; P. M. Weragoda three for 23, P. Wanasinghe three for 43, P. L. A. W. N. Alwis three for 43) and 422 for eight dec. (S. T. Perera 164, R. S. Kalpage 139; P. L. A. W. N. Alwis three for 122).

Perera and Kalpage put on 315 for Bloomfield's third wicket in the second innings, a national all-wicket record.

At Havelock Park, Colombo (Colts), January 5, 6, 7. Drawn. Singha SC* 448 (S. Jayantha 59, M. T. Sampath 190, T. A. de Silva 82, J. Nanda 35; N. Ranatunga five for 97); Colts CC 246 (D. P. Samaraweera 39, C. Mendis 111, D. Kanchana 42; L. Ranasinghe six for 48) and 313 for five (C. Mendis 200 not out, J. Kulatunga 53).

Mendis was the first player to score a century in each innings in Sri Lankan first-class cricket.

At Braybrooke Place, Colombo, January 5, 6, 7. Drawn. Sebastianites C and AC 408 for nine dec. (S. K. Silva 69, C. M. Wickremasinghe 79, Primal Salgado 47, D. Samarasinghe 106 not out, Anura Perera 32, Extras 31) and 180 for five dec. (Anusha Perera 44, Sanjeewa Silva 30); Moors SC* 264 (A. Hettiarachchi 47, P. Abeygunasekera 85; M. Peiris three for 52, Primal Salgado four for 69) and 159 for six (N. de Silva 87, P. Abeygunasekera 31).

At Maitland Place, Colombo (NCC), January 5, 6, 7. Drawn. Colombo CC 288 (A. Perera 45, A. M. de Silva 108 not out, M. Villavarayan 33; A. P. Weerakkody three for 46, N. Saranasekera three for 47) and 252 for five dec. (V. S. K. Waragoda 105 not out, J. Jayaratne 57, A. C. Seneviratne 45); Nondescripts CC* 212 for nine dec. (R. P. Arnold 66, T. G. N. S. Warusamana 50; M. Villavarayan five for 56) and 180 for three (R. P. Arnold 39, S. Weerasinghe 58, D. Perera 51 not out).

At Panadura Esplanade, Panadura, January 5, 6, 7. Drawn. Panadura SC* 329 (S. Kumara 89, A. K. D. A. S. Kumara 68, M. V. Deshapriya 39, M. Jayasena 41, I. Gallage 40; J. A. W. Kumara three for 78, R. K. B. Amunugama five for 115); Kurunegala Youth CC 169 (S. K. L. de Silva 40; S. D. Anurasiri six for 43) and 232 (A. H. Bandaranayake 75, S. K. L. de Silva 41, H. Liyanage 49; S. D. Anurasiri six for 52, M. Jayasena three for 93).

At Police Park, Colombo, January 5, 6, 7. Galle CC won by 133 runs. Galle CC 311 (A. Rideegammana 54, N. Shiroman 45, D. D. Wickremasinghe 86; V. Ranaweera three for 56, P. K. Serasinghe four for 70) and 155 for nine dec. (D. D. Wickremasinghe 52 not out; P. K. Serasinghe six for 44); Police SC* 171 (S. Gunaratne 43; E. A. R. de Silva six for 48) and 162 (M. Kudagodage 32, D. Gunawardene 37).

At Maitland Place, Colombo (SSC), January 5, 6, 7. Sinhalese SC won by eight wickets. Tamil Union C and AC 112 (R. Peiris 75; C. Boteju four for 38, S. Dodanwela four for 33) and 144 (W. M. J. P. Weerasinghe 30, U. U. Chandana 31; S. Dodanwela six for 44, S. H. S. M. K. Silva four for 36); Sinhalese SC* 205 (A. A. W. Gunawardene 88, S. H. S. M. K. Silva 36; C. P. H. Ramanayake three for 49, C. M. Hathurusinghe three for 45) and 52 for two.

At Reid Avenue, Colombo, January 12, 13, 14. Drawn. Colts CC* 304 (D. P. Samaraweera 86, C. Mendis 58, J. Kulatunga 90 not out; B. de Silva five for 93) and 188 (D. P. Samaraweera 42, C. Mendis 30, N. Ranatunga 32; B. de Silva eight for 79); Bloomfield C and AC 285 (P. B. Dassanayake 111, I. Batuwitarachchi 53; D. Hettiarachchi eight for 102) and 65 for three (D. Hettiarachchi three for 36).

At Braybrooke Place, Colombo, January 12, 13, 14. Drawn. Moors SC* 288 (P. Abeygunasekera 39, A. Hettiarachchi 34, S. H. U. Karnain 45, I. Thahir 47; R. K. B. Amunugama five for 74, A. W. R. Madurasinghe three for 53) and 28 for one; Kurunegala Youth CC 400 for six dec. (R. Kariyawasam 177, S. K. L. de Silva 30, H. Liyanage 59, R. K. B. Amunugama 52 not out, Extras 34).

At Tyronne Fernando Stadium, Moratuwa, January 12, 13, 14. Drawn. Moratuwa SC 244 (M. Narayanage 43, D. Bodiyabaduge 80 not out; A. Rideegammana three for 29) and 99 for four (W. Abeywardene 42 not out, M. Narayanage 41); Galle CC* 404 for eight dec. (H. S. S. Fonseka 128, D. D. Wickremasinghe 127 not out, E. A. R. de Silva 43, H. Rajapakse 35; M. de Alwis three for 96).

At Panadura Esplanade, Panadura, January 12, 13, 14. Drawn. Sebastianites C and AC 208 (S. K. Silva 75, Sanjeewa Silva 96; M. Jayasena three for 49, S. D. Anurasiri three for 56) and 194 (Sanjeewa Silva 60, Anusha Perera 42, S. C. de Silva 31; M. Jayasena four for 84, S. Kumara four for 46); Panadura SC* 327 (M. Silva 49, S. Kumara 97, M. V. Deshapriya 36, M. Jayasena 69; S. C. de Silva six for 95, Primal Salgado three for 77) and 36 for two.

At Maitland Place, Colombo (SSC), January 12, 13, 14. Drawn. Colombo CC 376 (B. Ediriweera 106, V. S. K. Waragoda 94, A. C. Seneviratne 73; S. Dodanwela three for 79); Sinhalese SC* 226 (M. S. Atapattu 37, C. Ranasinghe 40, E. F. M. U. Fernando 49; W. Labrooy four for 78, J. Jayaratne three for 32) and 229 for six (A. A. W. Gunawardene 44, M. S. Atapattu 39, R. Jayawardene 59 not out; H. M. L. Sagara three for 54).

At P. Saravanamuttu Stadium, Colombo, January 12, 13, 14. Drawn. Tamil Union C and AC 514 (R. Peiris 127, S. Wijesiri 127, C. Jayasinghe 35, S. I. de Saram 59, C. P. H. Ramanayake 70; L. Hannibal three for 87, N. Saranasekera five for 132); Nondescripts CC* 325 for seven (R. P. Arnold 49, S. Weerasinghe 32, S. A. R. Silva 58, C. D. U. S. Weerasinghe 112 not out; U. U. Chandana four for 74).

At Braybrooke Place, Colombo, January 19, 20, 21. Panadura SC won by five wickets. Antonians SC* 131 (T. P. Kodikara 32; M. Jayasena four for 57, S. D. Anurasiri five for 35) and 213 (T. P. Kodikara 35, G. H. Perera 58; M. Jayasena four for 81, S. D. Anurasiri five for 69); Panadura SC 194 (M. Silva 30, S. Kumara 59; N. Samarawickrama three for 38, K. Dharmasena three for 24) and 155 for five (B. Perera 31, N. Mendis 63 not out).

At Maitland Crescent, Colombo (CCC), January 19, 20, 21. Colombo CC won by an innings and 78 runs. Kurunegala Youth CC 134 (S. K. L. de Silva 34; W. Labrooy four for 53, M. Villavarayan four for 50) and 204 (R. Kariyawasam 39, H. Liyanage 76, R. K. B. Amunugama 31; M. Villavarayan three for 43, H. M. L. Sagara five for 38); Colombo CC* 416 for nine dec. (B. Ediriweera 70, V. S. K. Waragoda 110, A. C. Seneviratne 35, A. M. de Silva 101 not out, H. M. L. Sagara 43; J. A. W. Kumara three for 121, A. H. Bandaranayake three for 92).

At Havelock Park, Colombo (Colts), January 19, 20, 21. Colts CC won by an innings and 23 runs. Colts CC 394 (N. Ranatunga 212 not out, S. Attanayake 75; S. A. de Silva three for 62, T. Jeffry four for 95); Moors SC* 201 (N. de Silva 37, T. B. Bongso 32, S. H. U. Karnain 43; D. Hettiarachchi four for 34, D. P. Samaraweera four for 45) and 170 (S. A. de Silva 45, T. Jeffry 44; D. Hettiarachchi four for 60, D. P. Samaraweera four for 48).

At Galle Esplanade, Galle, January 19, 20, 21. Drawn. Galle CC* 236 (N. Shiroman 34, S. M. Faumi 70; R. Priyadarshana three for 68, L. Ranasinghe three for 65) and 217 for five (S. Kodituwakku 69, D. D. Wickremasinghe 125 not out); Singha SC 221 (H. Premasiri 42, J. Nanda 40, P. Chandana 64 not out; E. A. R. de Silva four for 65, A. Rideegammana five for 26).

At Tyronne Fernando Stadium, Moratuwa, January 19, 20, 21. Drawn. Nondescripts CC* 306 (R. P. Arnold 44, D. Perera 114, Extras 33; D. Bodiyabaduge three for 38) and 205 for seven dec. (R. P. Arnold 100 not out; K. G. Perera four for 59); Moratuwa SC 229 (W. Abeywardene 74, S. Soysa 34, K. G. Perera 30; J. Bandara four for 44, R. P. Arnold three for 24) and 232 for nine (W. Abeywardene 62, S. Soysa 96; R. P. Arnold five for 38).

At Maitland Place, Colombo (SSC), January 19, 20, 21. Sinhalese SC won by 242 runs. Sinhalese SC 208 (C. Ranasinghe 88 not out; D. Gunawardene three for 56, A. Priyantha three for 43) and 248 for seven dec. (A. A. W. Gunawardene 44, E. F. M. U. Fernando 81, U. N. K. Fernando 74); Police SC* 155 (M. Perera three for 28, S. H. S. M. K. Silva four for 34) and 59 (C. Boteju three for 13, S. Dodanwela four for 11).

At P. Saravanamuttu Stadium, Colombo, January 19, 20, 21. Tamil Union C and AC won by six wickets. Sebastianites C and AC* 129 (S. K. Silva 63; C. P. H. Ramanayake seven for 24) and 303 (Sanjeewa Silva 87, K. Anton 52, Primal Salgado 52; U. U. Chandana three for 96); Tamil Union C and AC 268 for eight dec. (C. Jayasinghe 32, D. N. Nadarajah 59, S. I. de Saram 56, U. U. Chandana 48; D. Samarasinghe three for 68) and 167 for four (S. I. de Saram 35 not out, U. U. Chandana 61 not out).

At Havelock Park, Colombo (Colts), January 26, 27, 28. Drawn. Kurunegala Youth CC* 322 (A. H. Bandaranayake 83, R. Jaymon 85, Extras 36; N. Ranatunga three for 40, D. Hettiarachchi three for 89) and 27 for one; Colts CC 450 (C. Mendis 44, D. P. Samaraweera 73, N. Ranatunga 78, J. Kulatunga 36, D. K. Liyanage 59, H. Alles 50 not out).

At Galle Esplanade, Galle, January 26, 27, 28. Drawn. Colombo CC* 209 (B. Ediriweera 36, V. S. K. Waragoda 82, J. Jayaratne 37; E. A. R. de Silva three for 34) and 199 for five dec. (B. Ediriweera 69, D. Tissera 59); Galle CC 139 (S. M. Faumi 44; W. Labrooy three for 52, H. M. L. Sagara three for 21) and 106 for seven (N. Dabare three for 17).

At Braybrooke Place, Colombo, January 26, 27, 28. Antonians SC won by 109 runs. Antonians SC* 291 (M. Prasanga 109, K. Dharmasena 37; I. Thahir three for 83, T. Jeffry four for 64) and 235 for eight dec. (S. Jayawardene 69, W. A. M. P. Perera 38, P. Wanasinghe 41; T. Jeffry three for 59); Moors SC 309 (N. de Silva 36, T. Jeffry 35, M. H. M. Unais 38, I. Thahir 62 not out, A. Hettiarachchi 45; K. Dharmasena four for 74, M. Prasanga three for 35) and 108 (P. Abeygunasekera 32; K. Dharmasena three for 27, M. Prasanga three for two).

At Tyronne Fernando Stadium, Moratuwa, January 26, 27, 28. Tamil Union C and AC won by an innings and 49 runs. Moratuwa SC* 274 (D. Bodiyabaduge 45, D. Chandrasena 37 not out; U. U. Chandana five for 84) and 55 (C. P. H. Ramanayake three for 19, C. M. Hathurusinghe three for ten, U. U. Chandana three for 14); Tamil Union C and AC 378 for nine dec. (S. Wijesiri 84, C. Jayasinghe 67, S. I. de Saram 53, U. U. Chandana 63; K. G. Perera four for 110).

At Panadura Esplanade, Panadura, January 26, 27, 28. Drawn. Panadura SC* 233 (B. Perera 47, A. K. D. A. S. Kumara 44, M. Jayasena 58; R. Pushpakumara six for 45) and 217 (N. Mendis 45, A. K. D. A. S. Kumara 38; L. Ranasinghe four for 58, R. Pushpakumara three for 70); Singha SC 152 (W. M. J. Kumudu 54, S. Jayantha 32; S. D. Anurasiri four for 31).

At Police Park, Colombo, January 26, 27, 28. Drawn. Police SC* 268 (S. Gunaratne 36, G. Silva 72, M. Kudagodage 35, A. Priyantha 45) and 229 (S. Gunaratne 80, W. N. M. Soysa 54; R. P. Arnold three for 54); Nondescripts CC 300 (R. P. Arnold 140, S. Weerasinghe 49, A. G. D. Wickremasinghe 35 not out; R. Wimalasiri three for 71) and 72 for two (R. P. Arnold 34 not out).

At Reid Avenue, Colombo, January 27, 28, 29. Drawn. Bloomfield C and AC 347 (S. K. Perera 43, P. B. Dassanayake 92, S. T. Perera 67, I. Batuwitarachchi 33, A. Sudhantha 45, Extras 30; S. C. de Silva three for 48) and 248 for seven (P. B. Dassanayake 46, S. T. Perera 123, I. Batuwitarachchi 41); Sebastianites C and AC* 254 (Sanjeewa Silva 92, G. R. M. A. Perera 31 not out; B. de Silva six for 87).

At Reid Avenue, Colombo, February 2, 3, 4. Drawn. Bloomfield C and AC 226 (P. B. Dassanayake 37, A. Sudhantha 32, R. Yasalal 79, P. W. Gunaratne 34; I. Gallage four for 75, M. Jayasena four for 22) and 117 for three (S. K. Perera 31 not out); Panadura SC* 406 for nine dec. (S. Kumara 116, A. K. D. A. S. Kumara 34, M. V. Deshapriya 99, S. Liyanage 63 not out; R. Yasalal three for 59).

At Maitland Crescent, Colombo (CCC), February 2, 3, 4. Colombo CC won by an innings and 70 runs. Moratuwa SC 200 (M. de Alwis 33, C. de Silva 48; W. Labrooy five for 61, M. Villavarayan four for 69) and 138 (C. Perera 37, W. A. A. Wasantha 37; W. Labrooy three for 49, A. C. Seneviratne three for 16); Colombo CC* 408 for six dec. (B. Ediriweera 59, A. M. de Silva 76, V. S. K. Waragoda 140, D. Tissera 55; C. Perera three for 82).

At Braybrooke Place, Colombo, February 2, 3, 4. Drawn. Singha SC* 284 (H. Premasiri 52, W. M. J. Kumudu 54, R. Priyadarshana 34; T. Jeffry six for 78) and 175 for three (H. Premasiri 62, W. M. J. Kumudu 36, M. T. Sampath 41 not out); Moors SC 327 (N. de Silva 42, P. Abeygunasekera 44, A. Hettiarachchi 54, T. Jeffry 60, I. Thahir 50; R. Priyadarshana five for 100).

At Police Park, Colombo, February 2, 3, 4. Drawn. Tamil Union C and AC 326 (R. Peiris 45, S. Wijesiri 55, C. Jayasinghe 75, S. I. de Saram 36, U. U. Chandana 42; A. Priyantha three for 73); Police SC* 169 (R. Wimalasiri 52 not out, G. Silva 50; C. P. H. Ramanayake five for 52, C. M. Hathurusinghe three for 44) and 173 for five (S. Rajapakse 50).

At Tyronne Fernando Stadium, Moratuwa, February 2, 3, 4. Drawn. Colts CC* 344 (D. P. Samaraweera 32, C. Mendis 67, H. de Silva 43, S. Alexander 83, D. Hettiarachchi 35; S. C. de Silva three for 60, G. R. M. A. Perera five for 87) and 135 for three (D. P. Samaraweera 35, N. Ranatunga 80); Sebastianites C and AC 231 (S. K. Silva 38, Sanjeewa Silva 90; D. P. Samaraweera five for 78).

At Maitland Place, Colombo (SSC), February 2, 3, 4. Drawn. Sinhalese SC 428 for six dec. (M. S. Atapattu 253 not out, E. F. M. U. Fernando 79, Extras 32; J. C. Gamage four for 118); Galle CC* 172 (D. Sudarshana 30, D. D. Wickremasinghe 52; S. Dodanwela four for 46) and 161 for five (A. Rideegammana 56, H. Rajapakse 37 not out, D. D. Wickremasinghe 49; C. Boteju four for 33).

Atapattu's 253 not out lasted 357 minutes.

At Reid Avenue, Colombo, February 9, 10, 11. Bloomfield C and AC won by an innings and 60 runs. Bloomfield C and AC* 413 (I. Batuwitarachchi 51, P. B. Dassanayake 77, S. T. Perera 100, R. S. Kalpage 106 not out; T. Jeffry four for 141, M. H. O. Azeez three for 97); Moors SC 213 (N. de Silva 40, A. Hettiarachchi 58, I. Thahir 71 not out; R. S. Kalpage three for 63) and 140 (B. Rasanjana three for 38, R. S. Kalpage four for 40).

At Maitland Crescent, Colombo (CCC), February 9, 10, 11. Colombo CC won by an innings and one run. Colombo CC 322 (A. M. de Silva 62, D. Tissera 67, A. Dalugoda 52, W. Labrooy 35; V. Ranaweera three for 87, W. N. M. Soysa three for 79); Police SC* 121 (C. Silva 39; W. Labrooy four for 39, A. Dalugoda three for four) and 200 (S. Rajapakse 47, R. Wimalasiri 40, G. Silva 40; W. Labrooy five for 100).

At Galle Esplanade, Galle, February 9, 10, 11. Drawn. Galle CC* 200 (A. Rideegammana 56, E. A. R. de Silva 39; L. Hannibal four for 21, N. Saranasekera four for 64) and 150 for seven (A. Rideegammana 71 not out; R. P. Arnold three for 37); Nondescripts CC 273 (R. P. Arnold 93, D. Perera 30, C. D. U. S. Weerasinghe 49 not out; H. Rajapakse six for 90, E. A. R. de Silva four for 71).

At Welagedera Stadium, Kurunegala, February 9, 10, 11. Drawn. Singha SC 184 (H. Premasiri 34, G. Sanjeewa 56 not out; J. A. W. Kumara three for 38, R. K. B. Amunugama five for 85) and 268 (S. Jayantha 65, T. A. de Silva 57, G. Sanjeewa 42; J. A. W. Kumara three for 23, A. W. Ekanayake three for 63); Kurunegala Youth CC* 271 (S. K. L. de Silva 122, A. Balalla 31; R. Priyadarshana three for 52) and 102 for two (R. Kariyawasam 38, S. K. L. de Silva 57 not out).

At Panadura Esplanade, Panadura, February 9, 10, 11. Drawn. Colts CC* 391 (D. P. Samaraweera 106, C. Mendis 61, N. Ranatunga 47, S. Alexander 67, H. Alles 53 not out; S. D. Anurasiri three for 114, M. Jayasena five for 151); Panadura SC 205 (A. K. D. A. S. Kumara 82; S. Alexander five for 26) and 150 for six (M. Silva 59, S. Kumara 31; D. P. Samaraweera three for 22).

At Tyronne Fernando Stadium, Moratuwa, February 9, 10, 11. Drawn. Sebastianites C and AC* 245 (Sanjeewa Silva 92, D. Samarasinghe 80; S. Jayawardene five for 30) and 224 (Sanjeewa Silva 59, C. M. Wickremasinghe 36; N. Samarawickrama three for 60, P. M. Weragoda three for 64, P. L. A. W. N. Alwis three for 36); Antonians SC 226 (W. A. M. P. Perera 38, V. S. Sittamige 39, K. Dharmasena 37, G. H. Perera 41 not out; S. C. de Silva four for 65) and 121 for three (S. Jayawardene 56, W. A. M. P. Perera 53 not out).

At Maitland Place, Colombo (SSC), February 9, 10, 11. Sinhalese SC won by an innings and 66 runs. Sinhalese SC 302 for seven dec. (R. P. A. H. Wickremaratne 82, S. H. S. M. K. Silva 53 not out); Moratuwa SC* 145 (W. A. A. Wasantha 38; S. Dodanwela six for 50, R. Jayawardene four for 40) and 91 (S. Dodanwela three for 12, M. Perera six for 37).

At Welagedera Stadium, Kurunegala, February 23, 24, 25. Drawn. Police SC 223 (S. Rajapakse 53, C. Liyanage 42, R. Wimalasiri 82; A. W. Ekanayake five for 83, A. W. R. Madurasinghe three for 42) and 159 (S. Gunaratne 58; A. W. Ekanayake five for 54); Kurunegala Youth CC* 261 (A. H. Bandaranayake 56, R. Kariyawasam 37, S. K. L. de Silva 72, H. Liyanage 30; R. Wimalasiri three for 52, W. N. M. Soysa four for 27, C. Silva three for 39) and 71 for six (R. Jaymon 38).

At Maitland Crescent, Colombo (CCC), March 1, 2, 3. Colombo CC won by an innings and 19 runs. Moors SC 144 (W. Labrooy five for 58) and 238 (M. H. M. Unais 71, T. Jeffry 72 not out; W. Labrooy three for 71, A. Dalugoda three for 63); Colombo CC* 401 for six dec. (B. Ediriweera 38, A. M. de Silva 186, C. P. Handunettige 84).

At Galle Esplanade, Galle, March 1, 2, 3. Drawn. Antonians SC* 367 (S. Jayawardene 53, M. Prasanga 31, V. S. Sittamige 155, Extras 35; D. Sudarshana four for 30) and 27 for no wkt; Galle CC 303 (H. S. S. Fonseka 41, D. D. Wickremasinghe 42, A. Wewalwala 61, C. K. Hewamanna 49, Extras 31; T. P. Kodikara five for 78).

At Welagedera Stadium, Kurunegala, March 1, 2, 3. Drawn. Sinhalese SC 310 (A. A. W. Gunawardene 79, N. Adikaram 45, U. N. K. Fernando 88, E. F. M. U. Fernando 40; A. W. R. Madurasinghe six for 122) and 200 for five dec. (U. N. K. Fernando 54, R. P. A. H. Wickremaratne 78 not out, S. H. S. M. K. Silva 38); Kurunegala Youth CC* 236 (S. K. L. de Silva 90, S. S. Guruge 55, H. Liyanage 35; K. J. Silva six for 77) and 228 for two (R. Jaymon 47, S. K. L. de Silva 92 not out, S. S. Guruge 64 not out).

At Maitland Place, Colombo (NCC), March 1, 2, 3. Sebastianites C and AC won by four wickets. Nondescripts CC* 170 (C. P. Mapatuna 61, A. G. D. Wickremasinghe 35 not out; D. Samarasinghe five for 65, S. C. de Silva four for 75) and 193 (D. Perera 32, P. Rajapakse 37; S. C. de Silva four for 51, Piyal Salgado three for 53); Sebastianites C and AC 269 (M. Mendis 43, S. K. Silva 30, K. Anton 62, Primal Salgado 48; N. Saranasekera seven for 74) and 96 for six (N. Saranasekera three for 35).

At Panadura Esplanade, Panadura, March 1, 2, 3. Drawn. Tamil Union C and AC* 258 (W. M. J. P. Weerasinghe 120 not out, N. Bandaratilleke 31; I. Gallage three for 66, S. Kumara three for 69) and 241 for five (U. C. Hathurusinghe 38, R. Peiris 78, S. Wijesiri 69, S. I. de Saram 31; M. V. Deshapriya three for 65); Panadura SC 346 (B. Perera 35, A. K. D. A. S. Kumara 110, M. V. Deshapriya 31, M. Jayasena 50; C. P. H. Ramanayake four for 88).

At Police Park, Colombo, March 1, 2, 3. Drawn. Police SC 263 (R. Wimalasiri 80, S. Gunaratne 33, G. Silva 39) and 117 for four (C. Liyanage 51); Bloomfield C and AC* 295 (S. T. Perera 62, R. S. Kalpage 46, H. Boteju 74; W. N. M. Soysa four for 69).

Play was delayed for half an hour by a helicopter landing to transfer Kenya's World Cup team to Kandy.

At Reid Avenue, Colombo, March 8, 9, 10. Bloomfield C and AC won by an innings and 46 runs. Moratuwa SC* 146 (W. A. A. Wasantha 31, K. G. Perera 36; R. S. Kalpage six for 61) and 240 (C. Perera 38, W. A. A. Wasantha 42, C. Subasinghe 38; R. S. Kalpage four for 74, B. de Silva three for 43); Bloomfield C and AC 432 for six dec. (S. K. Perera 115, P. B. Dassanayake 77, B. de Silva 101 not out, R. Yasalal 91).

At Maitland Crescent, Colombo (CCC), March 8, 9, 10. Colombo CC won by an innings and 50 runs. Panadura SC 245 (M. Silva 54, A. K. D. A. S. Kumara 31, M. Jayasena 32; M. Villavarayan three for 78) and 126 (S. Kumara 44 retired hurt; W. Labrooy five for 65, M. Villavarayan four for 48); Colombo CC* 421 for seven dec. (B. Ediriweera 46, A. M. de Silva 38, V. S. K. Waragoda 170, C. P. Handunettige 67, A. C. Seneviratne 33; M. Jayasena five for 121).

At Galle Esplanade, Galle, March 8, 9, 10. Colts CC won by seven runs. Colts CC* 195 (E. A. Upashantha 56) and 136 (M. de Silva four for 25); Galle CC 99 (D. Hettiarachchi three for 29, N. Ranatunga four for 25) and 225 (H. S. S. Fonseka 52, E. A. R. de Silva 31, Extras 34; S. Alexander four for 44).

At Braybrooke Place, Colombo, March 8, 9, 10. Drawn. Tamil Union C and AC 280 (R. Peiris 83, S. Wijesiri 36, S. I. de Saram 34, C. Jayasinghe 37; D. Schafter four for 82, A. Hettiarachchi three for 55) and 247 for five dec. (U. C. Hathurusinghe 108 not out, W. M. J. P. Weerasinghe 51 not out; A. K. M. Rezvi three for 81); Moors SC* 195 (N. de Silva 59, S. Makewita 34; C. P. H. Ramanayake four for 55, N. Bandaratilleke four for 60) and 276 for seven (N. de Silva 124, A. Hettiarachchi 42, U. I. Weerawarna 57 not out; C. P. H. Ramanayake three for 93, N. Bandaratilleke three for 103).

At Maitland Place, Colombo (NCC), March 8, 9, 10. Nondescripts CC won by an innings and 108 runs. Kurunegala Youth CC 94 (L. Hannibal three for 30) and 203 (R. Kariyawasam 51, R. Jaymon 41, S. K. L. de Silva 64; R. P. Arnold four for 55, S. A. R. Silva three for 17); Nondescripts CC* 405 for nine dec. (R. P. Arnold 80, P. Rajapakse 108, S. Ranatunga 56, A. S. Pietersz 46, S. A. R. Silva 31 not out; A. W. Ekanayake three for 112, A. W. R. Madurasinghe four for 90).

At Police Park, Colombo, March 8, 9, 10. Police SC won by 191 runs. Police SC 208 (S. Rajapakse 36, R. Wimalasiri 41 not out, P. K. Serasinghe 43; R. Priyadarshana eight for 85) and 292 for two dec. (R. Janaka 44, C. Liyanage 115 not out, W. N. M. Soysa 101 not out); Singha SC* 146 (S. Jayantha 38, G. Sanjeewa 36 not out; W. N. M. Soysa four for 32) and 163 (H. Premasiri 38; P. K. Serasinghe four for 36, W. N. M. Soysa six for 60).

At Tyronne Fernando Stadium, Moratuwa, March 8, 9, 10. Sinhalese SC won by seven wickets. Sebastianites C and AC 253 (S. K. Silva 31, D. Samarasinghe 63, M. Peiris 57 not out; S. Dodanwela five for 39, K. J. Silva three for 75) and 132 (S. K. Silva 35; S. Dodanwela three for 43, K. J. Silva six for 49); Sinhalese SC* 223 (N. Adikaram 43, S. Gunasekera 42, R. Jayawardene 38; S. C. de Silva seven for 76, N. R. G. Perera three for 54) and 163 for three (N. Adikaram 55 not out, R. P. A. H. Wickremaratne 76).

At Havelock Park, Colombo (Colts), March 15, 16, 17. Colts CC won by nine wickets. Moratuwa SC* 174 for nine dec. (W. Abeywardene 39, K. Perera 33, W. A. A. Wasantha 46; S. I. Fernando three for 26) and 320 (C. Perera 56, W. Abeywardene 91, W. A. A. Wasantha 115; E. A. Upashantha four for 77, S. I. Fernando three for 62); Colts CC 437 for four dec. (D. P. Samaraweera 82, C. Mendis 134, S. I. Fernando 55, N. Ranatunga 100 not out, Extras 32) and 58 for one.

At Maitland Place, Colombo (NCC), March 15, 16, 17. Nondescripts CC won by an innings and 196 runs. Moors SC 108 (L. Hannibal three for 19, R. P. Arnold five for 34) and 188 (A. K. M. Rezvi 43, S. Makewita 34; L. Hannibal eight for 38); Nondescripts CC* 492 for four dec. (R. P. Arnold 217 not out, S. Weerasinghe 114, C. P. Mapatuna 129 not out).

Arnold's 217 not out lasted 370 minutes. He put on 232 for Nondescripts' first wicket with Weerasinghe – then, a national record – and 234 for the fifth wicket with Mapatuna.

At Panadura Esplanade, Panadura, March 15, 16, 17. Sinhalese SC won by nine wickets. Panadura SC* 145 (M. Silva 45, Extras 31; K. J. Silva five for 32) and 42 (K. J. Silva six for seven, S. H. S. M. K. Silva four for 14); Sinhalese SC 147 (R. P. A. H. Wickremaratne 41; S. D. Anurasiri four for 55, M. Jayasena five for 75) and 45 for one.

At Police Park, Colombo, March 15, 16, 17. Police SC won by nine wickets. Antonians SC* 111 (M. Prasanga 41, N. Samarawickrama 31; V. Ranaweera three for 37, P. K. Serasinghe four for 27) and 189 (W. A. M. P. Perera 92, S. Thithugoda 32; V. Ranaweera four for 42); Police SC 225 (C. Liyanage 77, G. Silva 34; N. Samarawickrama four for 82) and 76 for one (W. N. M. Soysa 36 not out).

At Reid Avenue, Colombo, March 22, 23, 24. Kurunegala Youth CC won by seven wickets. Bloomfield C and AC 196 (S. K. Perera 33, R. S. Kalpage 33, B. Rasanjana 46; A. W. R. Madurasinghe four for 42, A. W. Ekanayake three for 29) and 171 (I. Batuwitarachchi 64, B. Rasanjana 34; A. W. R. Madurasinghe three for 38, A. W. Ekanayake three for 40); Kurunegala Youth CC* 249 (R. Kariyawasam 87; R. S. Kalpage four for 71) and 122 for three (S. K. L. de Silva 71 not out).

At Havelock Park, Colombo (Colts), March 22, 23, 24. Drawn. Colts CC* 456 (D. P. Samaraweera 123, C. Mendis 151, S. I. Fernando 90, J. Kulatunga 30; V. Ranaweera three for 64, P. K. Serasinghe five for 88) and 262 for nine (D. P. Samaraweera 50, J. Kulatunga 55, E. A. Upashantha 32, H. de Silva 38; W. N. M. Soysa five for 52); Police SC 278 (C. Liyanage 44, C. Silva 48, D. Gunawardene 94; E. A. Upashantha three for 64, S. I. Fernando three for 59).

At Galle Esplanade, Galle, March 22, 23, 24. Drawn. Galle CC* 171 (E. A. R. de Silva 58; C. P. H. Ramanayake four for 48); Tamil Union C and AC 91 for one (U. C. Hathurusinghe 46 not out).

The match was stopped on the second day because of a dangerous pitch and replayed at P. Saravanamuttu Stadium, Colombo, on April 19, 20, 21.

At Braybrooke Place, Colombo, March 22, 23, 24. Sinhalese SC won by 180 runs. Sinhalese SC 280 (M. S. Atapattu 113, R. P. A. H. Wickremaratne 74; D. Schafter six for 58) and 238 for five dec. (N. Adikaram 41, U. N. K. Fernando 41, M. S. Atapattu 46, R. P. A. H. Wickremaratne 60; M. H. O. Azeez three for 48); Moors SC* 204 (N. de Silva 82, T. B. Bongso 41; K. J. Silva three for 63) and 134 (N. de Silva 42; K. J. Silva five for 42, R. Jayawardene five for 48).

At Maitland Place, Colombo (NCC), March 22, 23, 24. Nondescripts CC won by seven wickets. Panadura SC 224 (M. Silva 62, S. Kumara 43; M. J. H. Rushdie five for 77) and 284 (S. Kumara 35, A. K. D. A. S. Kumara 43, S. Liyanage 61, M. Jayasena 63; L. Hannibal four for 91, M. J. H. Rushdie three for 62); Nondescripts CC* 321 (R. P. Arnold 89, S. Weerasinghe 84, P. Dabare 30; I. Gallage four for 81, M. Jayasena four for 70) and 191 for three (S. Weerasinghe 60, C. P. Mapatuna 38 not out).

At Tyronne Fernando Stadium, Moratuwa, March 22, 23, 24. Sebastianites C and AC won by an innings and 90 runs. Singha SC 238 (G. Sanjeewa 88, M. T. Sampath 66; S. C. de Silva seven for 97) and 156 (H. Premasiri 41, W. M. J. Kumudu 37, G. Sanjeewa 34; S. C. de Silva six for 64, Piyal Salgado four for 25); Sebastianites C and AC* 484 (M. Mendis 35, S. K. Silva 144, Sanjeewa Silva 126, K. Anton 52, A. Fernando 40).

At Havelock Park, Colombo (BRC), March 29, 30, 31. Drawn. Bloomfield C and AC* 253 (S. K. Perera 63, S. T. Perera 66, R. S. Kalpage 35, R. Yasalal 32 not out; N. Shiroman four for 78, H. Rajapakse three for 45) and 321 (I. Batuwitarachchi 144, P. B. Dassanayake 61, B. de Silva 54; N. Shiroman three for 61, C. Mudalige five for 61); Galle CC 266 (D. Sudarshana 42, D. D. Wickremasinghe 87 not out; R. Yasalal three for 46, P. K. Wijetunge three for 73).

At Maitland Crescent, Colombo (CCC), March 29, 30, 31. Colombo CC won by 128 runs. Colombo CC 351 (V. S. K. Waragoda 68, Y. N. Tillekeratne 103, A. Dalugoda 59, W. Labrooy 34; S. C. de Silva three for 115) and 180 for four dec. (B. Ediriweera 31, D. Tissera 68 not out); Sebastianites C and AC* 128 (W. Labrooy three for 62, M. Villavarayan five for 43) and 275 (M. Mendis 48, Primal Salgado 64, Sanjeewa Silva 46; N. Dabare six for 85).

At P. Saravanamuttu Stadium, Colombo, March 29, 30, 31. Drawn. Tamil Union C and AC 502 (U. C. Hathurusinghe 71, S. Wijesiri 68, S. I. de Saram 237; A. W. Ekanayake four for 133, A. W. R. Madurasinghe four for 135) and 32 for three dec.; Kurunegala Youth CC* 150 (S. K. L. de Silva 62; N. Bandaratilleke five for 22) and 239 for five (S. K. L. de Silva 108, H. Liyanage 66; C. M. Hathurusinghe three for 57).

At P. Saravanamuttu Stadium, Colombo, April 19, 20, 21. Drawn. Tamil Union C and AC* 237 for nine dec. (U. C. Hathurusinghe 124, S. Wijesiri 30; A. Rideegammana four for 72, S. Weerakoon three for 68) and 208 for six (U. C. Hathurusinghe 92, S. Wijesiri 50; A. Rideegammana four for 101); Galle CC 214 (S. Weerakoon 31, A. Rideegammana 66, D. Sudarshana 48; C. P. H. Ramanayake four for 46).

At R. Premadasa Stadium, Colombo, April 26, 27, 28. Drawn. Antonians SC 157 (G. H. Perera 49; A. W. Ekanayake four for 60, A. W. R. Madurasinghe three for 43) and 177 for eight dec. (V. S. Sittamige 71, R. Peiris 36 not out, S. Algama 30; A. W. Ekanayake five for 71); Kurunegala Youth CC* 173 (R. Kariyawasam 42, A. W. Ekanayake 33, Extras 38; N. Samarawickrama three for 46) and 38 for one.

At Tyronne Fernando Stadium, Colombo, April 26, 27, 28. Singha SC won by an innings and 19 runs. Moratuwa SC* 231 (C. Perera 30, D. Bodiyabaduge 44, P. Fernando 41; M. T. Sampath four for 71, L. Ranasinghe three for 50) and 186 (C. Perera 38, D. Bodiyabaduge 51; L. Ranasinghe three for 47, P. Chandana three for 35); Singha SC 436 for four dec. (H. Premasiri 140, W. M. J. Kumudu 146, S. Jayantha 40, M. T. Sampath 65 not out, Extras 34).

Premasiri and Kumudu put on 255 for Singha's first wicket, a national record.

At P. Saravanamuttu Stadium, Colombo, May 24, 25, 26. Singha SC won by an innings and 51 runs. Antonians SC* 181 (C. Fernando 33, G. Ferdinansz 31, M. Prasanga 43; M. T. Sampath six for 51) and 121 (S. Thithugoda 54; C. Soysa three for 37, L. Ranasinghe five for 36); Singha SC 353 for six dec. (G. Sanjeewa 87, S. Jagath 71, M. T. Sampath 106 not out; R. Perera three for 62).

P. SARAVANAMUTTU TROPHY WINNERS

The competition was known as the Lakspray Trophy in 1988-89 and 1989-90.

1988-89	Nondescripts CC Sinhalese SC
1989-90	Sinhalese SC
1990-91	Sinhalese SC
1991-92	Colts CC
1992-93	Sinhalese SC
1993-94	Nondescripts CC
1994-95	Bloomfield C and AC Sinhalese SC
1995-96	Colombo CC

SOUTH AFRICA UNDER-24 IN SRI LANKA

At Reid Avenue, Colombo, August 6, 7, 8. Drawn. Sri Lankan Board President's XI* 300 (S. I. Fernando 50, D. P. M. Jayawardene 160, S. I. de Saram 42; R. Telemachus three for 41, L. Klusener three for 86) and 225 for four (S. I. Fernando 36, S. I. de Saram 70 not out, U. U. Chandana 54 not out); South Africa Under-24 451 for five dec. (A. M. Bacher 86, G. F. J. Liebenberg 123, D. M. Benkenstein 105 not out, M. L. Bruyns 85, Extras 31; S. H. S. M. K. Silva three for 110).

Jayawardene scored 160 on first-class debut.

At P. Saravanamuttu Stadium, Colombo, August 10, 11, 12, 13. First Unofficial Test: Drawn. Sri Lanka Under-24* 391 (D. P. Samaraweera 75, S. I. Fernando 70, T. G. N. S. Warusamana 117, E. F. M. U. Fernando 58, Extras 38; J. H. Kallis five for 96) and 95 for four (T. T. Samaraweera 37 not out); South Africa Under-24 410 (A. M. Bacher 33, G. F. J. Liebenberg 40, J. H. Kallis 80, D. M. Benkenstein 98, N. Boje 53, S. M. Pollock 37; K. R. Pushpakumara three for 81, N. R. G. Perera three for 84).

At Welagedera Stadium, Kurunegala, August 17, 18, 19, 20. Second Unofficial Test: South Africa Under-24 won by eight wickets. Sri Lanka Under-24* 196 (M. N. Nawaz 54; L. Klusener four for 72, N. Boje three for 16) and 174 (A. M. N. Munasinghe 31; S. M. Pollock three for 55, N. Boje four for 31); South Africa Under-24 338 (G. F. J. Liebenberg 168, D. M. Benkenstein 61, L. Masikazana 46; K. J. Silva four for 87) and 35 for two.

At Asgiriya Stadium, Kandy, August 24, 25, 26, 27. Third Unofficial Test: Drawn. Sri Lanka Under-24 127 for two (R. P. Arnold 30, S. I. Fernando 44, M. N. Nawaz 41 not out) v South Africa Under-24*.

PETER SMITH MEMORIAL AWARD, 1996

The Peter Smith Memorial Award, given by the Cricket Writers' Club in memory of its former chairman for services to the presentation of cricket to the public, was won in 1996 by the Sri Lankan World Cup squad for "a romantic victory in difficult circumstances and for refusing to betray their principles of attacking cricket despite all the competitive pressures". The Award was instituted in 1992. Previous winners were David Gower, John Woodcock, Brian Lara and Mark Taylor.

CRICKET IN ZIMBABWE, 1995-96

By JOHN WARD

Matabeleland

Cricket

Wayne James

After the exhilarating victory over Pakistan the previous season, Zimbabwe's Test side had to make do with consolidation. Only three Test matches were played, two of them in New Zealand, in contrast with the six home Tests of 1994-95. The home Test was part of a very brief visit by Zimbabwe's neighbours, South Africa, which aroused tremendous interest; for the first time, a tour to Zimbabwe made a handsome profit. Predictably, against such powerful opposition, Zimbabwe were beaten but, as in their previous 13 Tests, they were not overwhelmed.

An interesting and unexpected debutant in this match was the 33-year-old seamer Charlie Lock, whose last first-class season had been 1989-90. Since then, he had been working in England, but some notable performances on his return catapulted him into the Test team ahead of Henry Olonga or David Brain. After initial nervousness, he settled down and bowled well.

Zimbabwe had hopes of recording their first Test victory away from home in New Zealand, but had to be content with two well-fought draws. It was a matter of pride that three players – batsmen Andy Flower and Dave Houghton and pace bowler Heath Streak – continued to maintain Test match form comparable to the best in the world. While in New Zealand, Flower and Houghton passed 1,000 Test runs at averages of almost 50, while Streak passed 50 wickets at an average of 21.

At the end of the season, John Hampshire finished his four-year spell as the team's coach. He deserves great credit for his part in making Zimbabwe, with their limited resources, so competitive at Test level. Dave Houghton, also coach of Worcestershire, was appointed his successor for 1996-97, which may be his final year as a player. During the off-season, Andy Flower resigned as captain. For three years, he had carried a triple burden as captain, wicket-keeper and leading batsman, and inevitably the strain was taking its effect. Despite this, Flower's Test record in all three departments was most creditable. Of his 12 Tests as captain, he had won one, lost five and drawn six. With Houghton unavailable, the selectors appointed left-handed batsman Alistair Campbell to lead the tour of Sri Lanka in August and September 1996.

Zimbabwe's form was more disappointing in the one-day arena than in Test cricket. They played 11 matches but won only two, one in New Zealand and one against Kenya in the World Cup. Most of the defeats were clear-cut, and a new strategy is needed if this record is to be improved.

On the domestic scene, the Lonrho Logan Cup competition was won by Matabeleland, for the first time in over 20 years and the first time since it became first-class. They defeated Mashonaland Country Districts, who had topped the table, in a remarkable final, despite missing several regular players; Denis Streak joined his son Heath in the side, the first instance of father and son playing together in Zimbabwe. The elder Streak was by no means a passenger, as he is still turning in good all-round performances in national club cricket.

But the match was most notable for the unparalleled performance of the Matabele captain and wicket-keeper Wayne James. His nine dismissals (seven caught, two stumped) in the Districts' first innings equalled the world first-class record, while four more catches in the second innings beat the record for a match. Not content with this, he scored 99 runs in both innings, being stranded one short of his century second time round when Matabeleland completed victory by six wickets.

Unfortunately the Logan Cup again suffered from the lack of availability and commitment of many cricketers just below international level; all four teams were frequently forced to call in players below first-class standard to make up numbers. The Zimbabwe Cricket Union, concerned at this mockery of first-class status, announced that in 1996-97 only two domestic teams would be awarded first-class status, Matabeleland and Mashonaland (which would draw from the existing Mashonaland, Young Mashonaland and the Districts team). These two would play a best-of-three series for the Logan Cup.

Changes in South Africa's domestic competitions also reduced the amount of first-class cricket played by Zimbabweans. In 1995-96, a Zimbabwe Board XI again took part in South Africa's UCB Bowl, again with disappointing results (all five matches were drawn), although off-spinner Steve Peall took nine in an innings against Boland B. But in 1996-97, the Bowl will be split into divisions, with the Board XI initially assigned to the second, non-first-class, division.

The Zimbabwe Cricket Union continued its policy of apportioning a large part of its tight budget to coaching the underprivileged in the townships. Black talent is gradually coming through; close on the heels of Henry Olonga are two more promising pace bowlers, Mpumelelo Mbangwa of Matabeleland, and Bernard Pswarayi of Mashonaland. A number of other blacks have played Logan Cup cricket, but inevitably there is some way to go before they will form a majority of players.

Houghton's continued dominance of the Zimbabwean game in 1995-96 was reflected in the fact that he headed the batting averages with 599 runs, including three centuries, at 85.57. Only one batsman, Campbell, scored more, and he played in ten matches to Houghton's five. Bryan Strang was the leading wicket-taker, as he had been in his debut season the previous year; he took 43 at 22 in his eight games, almost 20 more than anyone else, and collected five or more in an innings four times.

FIRST-CLASS AVERAGES, 1995-96

BATTING

(Qualification: 200 runs)

	M	*I*	*NO*	*R*	*HS*	*100s*	*Avge*
D. L. Houghton (*Mashonaland*)	5	8	1	599	160	3	85.57
H. H. Streak (*Matabeleland*)	6	9	1	426	131	2	53.25
G. W. Flower (*Young Mashonaland*)	6	11	1	499	103*	1	49.90
W. R. James (*Matabeleland*)	5	10	1	391	99*	0	43.44
S. V. Carlisle (*Mashonaland*)	4	8	1	303	147	1	43.28
G. J. Whittall (*Matabeleland*)	6	12	1	470	139*	1	42.72
P. A. Strang (*Mashonaland Country Districts*)	4	7	1	244	63	0	40.66
G. C. Martin (*Mashonaland*)	6	9	1	322	113	1	40.25
A. D. R. Campbell (*Mashonaland Country Districts*)	10	19	1	708	114*	1	39.33
S. G. Davies (*Mashonaland*)	8	15	2	491	117	1	37.76
A. Flower (*Mashonaland*)	5	9	1	284	82	0	35.50
M. H. Dekker (*Matabeleland*)	8	13	2	344	73	0	31.27
A. C. Waller (*Mashonaland Country Districts*)	6	10	0	269	74	0	26.90
C. B. Wishart (*Young Mashonaland*)	10	19	1	480	75	0	26.66
C. N. Evans (*Mashonaland Country Districts*)	6	12	1	289	73	0	26.27
G. J. Rennie (*Young Mashonaland*)	7	10	0	223	63	0	22.30
B. C. Strang (*Mashonaland Country Districts*)	8	14	4	213	66	0	21.30

* *Signifies not out.*

BOWLING

(Qualification: 10 wickets)

	O	*M*	*R*	*W*	*BB*	*5W/i*	*Avge*
J. A. Rennie (*Matabeleland*)	99.4	25	291	16	6-42	1	18.18
A. C. I. Lock (*Mashonaland Country Districts*)	151.3	38	446	24	6-59	1	18.58
D. H. Brain (*Mashonaland*)	81.2	20	202	10	6-61	1	20.20
E. A. Brandes (*Mashonaland Country Districts*)	128	37	349	17	6-98	1	20.52
B. C. Strang (*Mashonaland Country Districts*)	322.4	78	946	43	6-96	4	22.00
S. G. Peall (*Mashonaland Country Districts*)	200	48	523	23	9-76	1	22.73
H. K. Olonga (*Matabeleland*)	131.1	24	442	19	5-80	1	23.26
H. H. Streak (*Matabeleland*)	190	46	511	20	7-69	1	25.55
G. J. Whittall (*Matabeleland*)	124.3	13	496	15	4-39	0	33.06
M. Mbangwa (*Matabeleland*)	217	51	671	18	2-26	0	37.27
G. C. Martin (*Mashonaland*)	186.2	52	512	13	3-65	0	39.38
C. B. Wishart (*Young Mashonaland*)	95.4	19	395	10	3-86	0	39.50

Note: These averages include performances for the Zimbabwe Board XI in the South African UCB Bowl.

LONRHO LOGAN CUP, 1995-96

					1st-inns	*Bonus points*		
	Played	*Won*	*Lost*	*Drawn*	*Points*	*Batting*	*Bowling*	*Points*
Mashonaland Country Districts	3	2	1	0	2	23.5	30	75§
Matabeleland	3	2	0	1	2	26	26	72.4§
Mashonaland	3	1	2	0	0	19.5	27.5	56.2§
Young Mashonaland	3	0	2	1	0	18	16.5	34.5

Final: Matabeleland beat Mashonaland Country Districts by six wickets.

§ *Points deducted for slow over-rates.*

Outright win = 10 pts; lead on first innings in a drawn or lost game = 2 pts.

Bonus points: One point is awarded for the first 100 runs in each innings and half a point for every subsequent 25 (restricted to the first 85 overs in the first innings). Half a point is awarded for every wicket taken throughout both innings.

*In the following scores, * by the name of a team indicates that they won the toss.*

At Harare Sports Club, Harare, September 15, 16, 17. Matabeleland won by 159 runs. Matabeleland* 305 (H. A. Price 53, G. J. Whittall 99, M. D. Abrams 71; S. A. Reid four for 52) and 300 for seven dec. (J. R. Craig 49, G. J. Whittall 64, W. R. James 66, M. D. Abrams 31); Mashonaland 219 (G. C. Martin 50, S. G. Davies 71, Extras 34; H. K. Olonga four for 50, G. J. Whittall three for 62) and 227 (S. G. Davies 63, U. Ranchod 43; J. A. Rennie four for 43). *Matabeleland 29.3 pts, Mashonaland 14.9 pts.*

At Alexandra Sports Club, Harare, September 15, 16, 17. Mashonaland Country Districts won by 223 runs. Mashonaland Country Districts 309 (A. D. R. Campbell 31, P. A. Strang 63, E. A. Brandes 65, S. G. Peall 38; S. D. Bean three for 50) and 264 for two dec. (T. G. Bartlett 52, A. D. R. Campbell 114 not out, C. N. Evans 66); Young Mashonaland* 182 (G. J. Rennie 41, A. J. Erasmus 39 not out, G. B. Brent 37; B. C. Strang three for 61, P. A. Strang three for 53) and 168 (D. N. Erasmus 42; A. C. I. Lock four for 23). *Mashonaland Country Districts 29 pts, Young Mashonaland 10.5 pts.*

Charlie Lock made his first appearance in first-class cricket since 1989-90, having returned from working overseas.

At Bulawayo Athletic Club, Bulawayo, November 3, 4, 5. Drawn. Matabeleland* 221 (M. H. Dekker 56, H. H. Streak 70, G. Peck 41 not out; G. B. Brent four for 51, A. J. Erasmus three for 31) and 370 for five dec. (J. S. Laney 67, K. Newell 52, G. J. Whittall 139 not out, W. R. James 61; D. Matambanadzo three for 57); Young Mashonaland 203 (G. W. Flower 42, G. J. Rennie 63; G. J. Whittall four for 63) and 202 for two (G. W. Flower 103 not out, C. B. Wishart 55 not out). *Matabeleland 17 pts, Young Mashonaland 13.5 pts.*

At Harare Sports Club, Harare, November 17, 18, 19. Mashonaland won by ten wickets. Young Mashonaland* 262 (G. W. Flower 66, C. B. Wishart 39, S. Cloete 34, A. J. Erasmus 41; D. H. Brain six for 61) and 250 (G. W. Flower 92, S. Cloete 41); Mashonaland 457 for six dec. (S. V. Carlisle 147, S. G. Davies 117, D. L. Houghton 127; E. Matambanadzo three for 71, C. B. Wishart three for 86) and 59 for no wkt (S. V. Carlisle 31 not out). *Mashonaland 25.5 pts, Young Mashonaland 10.5 pts.*

At Bulawayo Athletic Club, Bulawayo, November 17, 18, 19. Matabeleland won by four runs. Matabeleland* 152 (M. H. Dekker 50; B. C. Strang five for 41, E. A. Brandes four for 45) and 344 (M. H. Dekker 73, H. H. Streak 131, J. A. Rennie 35, M. J. Hammett 37; E. A. Brandes six for 98); Mashonaland Country Districts 209 (G. K. Bruk-Jackson 45, A. C. Waller 43; H. K. Olonga five for 80, G. J. Whittall four for 39) and 283 (R. G. Maggs 48, C. N. Evans 73, A. D. R. Campbell 78; H. H. Streak seven for 69). *Matabeleland 26.1 pts, Mashonaland Country Districts 19 pts.*

Districts wicket-keeper Donald Campbell caught seven in Matabeleland's first innings and nine in the match.

At Harare South Country Club, December 8, 9, 10. Mashonaland Country Districts won by two wickets. Mashonaland* 133 (D. L. Houghton 61; B. C. Strang three for 45, A. C. I. Lock three for 38, A. D. R. Campbell three for nought) and 352 (D. L. Houghton 160, G. C. Martin 113; B. C. Strang six for 96); Mashonaland Country Districts 279 (R. D. Brown 53, A. D. R. Campbell 47, P. A. Strang 61; B. W. S. Pswarayi three for 75, G. C. Martin three for 65, A. A. Brookes three for 37) and 207 for eight (R. D. Brown 37, P. A. Strang 56 not out; B. W. S. Pswarayi five for 72). *Mashonaland Country Districts 27 pts, Mashonaland 15.8 pts.*

This match was postponed from November 3, 4, 5, owing to the weather. Robin Brown reappeared in first-class cricket at the age of 44. The Strang brothers took Districts to victory with an unbroken ninth-wicket partnership of 56 in 57 minutes.

FINAL

MATABELELAND v MASHONALAND COUNTRY DISTRICTS

At Bulawayo Athletic Club, Bulawayo, April 19, 20, 21. Matabeleland won by six wickets. Toss: Mashonaland Country Districts. First-class debuts: G. D. Ferreira; J. M. Oates, K. R. Scott.

Home captain Wayne James dominated the match in a manner unprecedented in world cricket. He made nine dismissals in the Districts' first innings, to equal the world record of Tahir Rashid, who caught eight and stumped one for Habib Bank v PACO in 1992-93. In the second innings, he added four more to set a new record of 13 dismissals in a match, beating 12 by Edward Pooley for Surrey v Sussex in 1868, Don Tallon for Queensland v New South Wales in 1938-39 and Brian Taber for New South Wales v South Australia in 1968-69. He also scored 99 in both Matabele innings, though he might have reached his century in the second if the wicket-keeper had not conceded four byes to give the home side victory. Only one player is known to have scored two 99s in a first-class match, Amay Khurasia of Madhya Pradesh, against Vidarbha in 1991-92. He was also left stranded in the second innings – but did not break the world wicket-keeping record.

Matabeleland had home advantage, although the Districts headed the table and would have won the Cup on their first-innings lead in the event of a draw. But that was never likely in a match of sudden collapses. Chasing 174, the Matabeles were 15 for four early on the final morning, before James and Dekker began their match-winning stand of 161. Both sides had difficulty raising a full team. Jason Oates – who managed to elude James's gloves – became the third player to score a century for a Zimbabwean or Rhodesian team on first-class debut, while 46-year-old Denis Streak joined his son Heath in the Matabele line-up for his first first-class match since he toured England in 1985.

Close of play: First day, Matabeleland 73-4 (W. R. James 42*, H. H. Streak 7*); Second day, Matabeleland 15-3 (G. Peck 6*).

Mashonaland Country Districts

*R. D. Brown c James b Vaghmaria	18	– c James b Rennie	0
T. B. Stead c James b H. H. Streak	27	– lbw b H. H. Streak	2
J. M. Oates c Peck b Vaghmaria	115	– lbw b H. H. Streak	0
A. D. R. Campbell c James b H. H. Streak	0	– c James b Rennie	9
G. K. Bruk-Jackson st James b Vaghmaria	4	– c James b Rennie	6
C. N. Evans st James b Vaghmaria	7	– c H. H. Streak b Rennie	26
†D. J. R. Campbell c James b Rennie	9	– not out	35
R. G. Maggs c James b Rennie	0	– c Dube b Rennie	11
B. C. Strang c James b Dekker	66	– c James b Vaghmaria	19
K. R. Scott not out	9	– run out	2
S. G. Peall c James b Dekker	0	– c Ranchod b Rennie	5
B 5, l-b 1, w 1, n-b 3	10	L-b 10, n-b 3	13
1/43 2/47 3/47 4/56 5/73 6/108 7/114 8/251 9/263	265	1/3 2/3 3/17 4/17 5/35 6/53 7/69 8/103 9/119	128

Bowling: *First Innings*—H. H. Streak 20–5–48–2; Rennie 18–3–55–2; Vaghmaria 25–3–108–4; Peck 5–1–13–0; D. H. Streak 5–2–10–0; Dekker 12–3–25–2. *Second Innings*—H. H. Streak 18–3–57–2; Rennie 19.3–8–42–6; Vaghmaria 2–0–19–1.

Matabeleland

L. E. Dube c D. J. R. Campbell b A. D. R. Campbell	2	– lbw b Strang	0
G. D. Ferreira hit wkt b Strang	0	– lbw b Peall	6
T. B. Manyimo c D. J. R. Campbell b Strang	0		
M. H. Dekker c A. D. R. Campbell b Evans	18	– (5) not out	57
*†W. R. James c A. D. R. Campbell b Peall	99	– (6) not out	99
H. H. Streak c Brown b Evans	30		
J. A. Rennie lbw b Strang	4		
M. Ranchod lbw b Peall	40	– (3) b Stead	3
G. Peck run out	5	– (4) lbw b Stead	6
D. H. Streak c D. J. R. Campbell b Strang	3		
D. Vaghmaria not out	10		
L-b 5, n-b 4	9	B 4, n-b 1	5
1/1 2/1 3/15 4/39 5/125 6/141 7/166 8/177 9/197	220	1/0 2/5 3/15 4/15	(4 wkts) 176

Bowling: *First Innings*—Strang 26–8–69–4; A. D. R. Campbell 18–7–44–1; Evans 10–0–28–2; Peall 22.1–6–62–2; Scott 6–1–12–0. *Second Innings*—Strang 12–3–46–1; Stead 8–2–19–2; Peall 7–2–34–1; A. D. R. Campbell 7.2–0–37–0; Scott 4–1–15–0; Evans 5–0–20–0; Brown 1–0–1–0.

Umpires: G. Evans and J. Fenwick.

LONRHO LOGAN CUP WINNERS

1993-94	Mashonaland Under-24
1994-95	Mashonaland
1995-96	Matabeleland

OTHER FIRST-CLASS MATCHES

Tasmania in Zimbabwe

At Harare Sports Club, Harare, October 3, 4, 5. Drawn. Mashonaland XI* 293 (C. B. Wishart 60, S. G. Davies 42, D. H. Brain 45 not out; S. Young five for 68) and 296 for seven dec. (A. Flower 57, D. L. Houghton 77 not out, G. A. Briant 61; S. Young three for 38); Tasmania 311 for six dec. (D. F. Hills 73, D. C. Boon 81, S. Young 59 not out) and 162 for three (D. F. Hills 70, J. Cox 54).

At Bulawayo Athletic Club, Bulawayo, October 9, 10, 11. Drawn. Tasmania* 196 (J. Cox 47, R. T. Ponting 30, M. N. Atkinson 42; A. C. I. Lock six for 59) and 309 for four (D. F. Hills 94, J. Cox 130, D. C. Boon 40 not out); ZCU President's XI 403 for nine dec. (G. W. Flower 79, A. Flower 82, A. D. R. Campbell 68, D. L. Houghton 112; G. J. Denton four for 39, M. A. Hatton five for 113).

Mashonaland Invitation XI v Yorkshire (April 1, 2, 3) and Matabeleland Select XI v Yorkshire (April 11, 12) may be found in English Counties Overseas, 1995-96.

CRICKETERS IN ICC ASSOCIATE COUNTRIES

	Clubs			*Players*		
	Senior	*Junior*	*Total*	*Senior*	*Junior*	*Total*
Bangladesh	1,088	500	1,588	18,000	75,000	93,000
Canada	350	175	525	10,690	17,000	27,690
Scotland	154	165	319	11,000	6,500	17,500
Ireland	141	61	202	5,807	3,419	9,226
United States	400	10	410	7,000	130	7,130
The Netherlands	72	–	72	5,800	975	6,775
Papua New Guinea	112	36	148	2,000	1,600	3,600
Denmark	49	2	51	2,278	836	3,114
United Arab Emirates	16	125	141	288	2,250	2,538
Singapore	6	45	51	600	1,500	2,100
West Africa†	34	40	74	630	1,180	1,810
Fiji	52	38	90	750	550	1,300
Namibia	7	10	17	170	1,000	1,170
Kenya	26	28	54	640	500	1,140
Hong Kong	28	6	34	700	400	1,100
Malaysia	63	22	85	250	400	650
East and Central Africa	37	5	42	465	180	645
Israel	19	4	23	525	100	625
Bermuda	24	16	40	360	228	588
Gibraltar	16	10	26	240	180	420
Argentina	5	5	10	160	120	280
Italy	21	1	22	270	–	270

† *Nigeria only.*

Figures are latest available – either 1994 or 1995 – as provided by member countries to ICC.

CRICKET IN DENMARK, 1996

By PETER S. HARGREAVES

The season was dominated by the hosting of the first official European Cricket Championship in July, where Denmark gained a creditable third place. Drawn in Pool B alongside Italy, Gibraltar and Ireland (who had lost a warm-up match against Danish champions Svanholm), Denmark were slight favourites to go through to the final. But in the crucial tie against Ireland, the fielders were uncharacteristically fallible, and only Søren Vestergaard – the most impressive pace bowler of the tournament – kept to a steady line of attack.

Honour was restored in the third-place play-off, when England's amateur batsmen were humbled by a fine display of bowling, mustering only 97 runs between them. When Holland, who have lost both their meetings with Denmark in the last two years, opposed Ireland in the final, there was food for local thought as to what the result of a theoretical all-continental showdown might have been.

The domestic clubs began the season in the knowledge that the first division would be reduced from ten teams to eight in 1997. After everyone had played each other once, the top four clubs had a play-off series to decide the title, which soon came down to another contest between the 1995 winners, Svanholm, and runners-up, Glostrup. Glostrup had already beaten their arch-rivals on their way to winning the knockout competition, but on the final day of the season they were undone by the excellence of Vestergaard, who took six for 18 to leave his batsmen an easy target of 104.

At the foot of the table, Skanderborg and Nykøbing Mors suffered relegation, but neither of the two teams just above them, Herning and Esbjerg, had difficulty in staving off the challenges for promotion from Ishøj and Albertslund of the second division. Svanholm's second team had actually topped the table, not for the first time, but could not be promoted by the rules of the league.

For the second year running, Nørrebro's Pakistani batsman Aftab Ahmed headed the batting, with an average of nearly 56. Jan Jensen of Glostrup came in second, more than ten runs behind. The highest-placed member of the national side was the captain, Søren Henriksen, who was fifth, averaging just under 39.

Another Pakistani, Amjad Khan from KB, led the bowling averages, but bowled only 38 overs. Vestergaard was immediately behind him, with a superb haul of 35 wickets for just six runs apiece. He is certain to continue playing an important role in the plans of national coach Ole Mortensen.

CRICKET IN THE NETHERLANDS, 1996

By DAVID HARDY

When 25-year-old Klaas Jan van Noortwijk and Bas Zuiderent, not quite 19, were confidently compiling a partnership of 114 against England during their World Cup group match in Peshawar on February 22, it marked a moment when not only Dutch cricket but, more significantly, Dutch cricketers felt they had really arrived.

There could have been no greater testimony to the game's development in the Netherlands than these two products of the VOC club in Rotterdam. The performance against England not only of these two batsmen, but of the team as a whole, was the highlight of the tournament for Holland. It was a pity that the same level was not approached in the other group matches, the loss against the United Arab Emirates being particularly painful.

Unfortunately, the team was never at full strength and fitness, with wicket-keeper/batsman Reinout Scholte missing the whole tournament, and several key players less than 100 per cent fit. Van Noortwijk was easily the pick of the Dutch batsmen, scoring 168 runs at 42.00. In contrast, the older players, who had played vital roles in Holland's qualification for the World Cup, disappointed. Nolan Clarke managed only 50 runs in the five group matches, 32 of these in the last. In fact, for each of the over-forties (Clarke, captain Steven Lubbers and Flavian Aponso), the last group match against South Africa was his last for the national team.

In 172 internationals – easily a national record – Lubbers scored 3,302 runs and took 145 wickets. His international career spanned no fewer than 25 seasons, during which he played in every match Holland had ever played in the ICC Trophy, and also captained his country more times than anyone else. Barbadian Clarke's career was shorter (99 internationals) but extremely prolific, producing 3,379 runs, a Dutch record, at an average of more than 38. He was the dominant batsman from any country in both the 1990 and 1994 ICC Trophy tournaments. The Sri Lankan, Aponso, played in 60 internationals, contributing many useful innings and steady overs of off-spin.

The South Africa match was also the last for the coach-manager partnership of the New Zealander, David Trist, and John Wories, who were succeeded by Australian John Bell and Hans Mulder respectively. During the 1996 Dutch season, the backbone of the bowling attack – Floris Jansen (93 matches, 134 wickets) and Paul-Jan Bakker (51 matches, 80 wickets), both still in their thirties – also announced their retirements from the national team. So in one year a vast amount of experience had disappeared. An ideal opportunity now presented itself for more young Dutch players to come through. Twenty-eight-year-old Tim de Leede became the new captain and new names such as Marc Nota, Luc van Troost, Asim Khan, and Ahmed Zulfiqar were given extended runs in the team.

As might be expected after this upheaval, results were less than outstanding. The visiting Indian and Pakistani Test teams secured two victories each, while Holland surprisingly lost to Ireland (in the final) and Scotland in the inaugural European Championship staged in Denmark in July, having beaten the England amateur team and Israel. Even Devon managed to beat Holland, in a warm-up match prior to the country's second ever NatWest Trophy match, which they lost emphatically to Surrey by 159 runs, despite Steven van Dijk's four wickets which earned him the Man of the Match award. The season ended, however, on a high note with a win over Yorkshire at the Scarborough festival in September.

There was another reason why 1996 was a momentous year. On June 16, the first ever match in the Netherlands on a grass wicket was played at the Koninklijke UD club in Deventer, one of the outposts of the Dutch game. In August the VRA club in Amstelveen, at Dutch cricket's headquarters, became the second club to switch to grass. These were indeed historic events, but if Holland are ever to become a force in world cricket, then the whole of the premier league and all internationals must be played on grass. That is a long way off, but at least a start has been made.

The Premier League (*Hoofdklasse*) was dominated by the two clubs from the unfashionable town of Schiedam, near Rotterdam. Excelsior captured the title for the fourth time in six seasons, but needed a play-off against neighbours Hermes DVS to seal it. No fewer than four Excelsior bowlers – professional Mark Atkinson, Erik Dulfer, Sebastiaan Gokke and Luc van Troost – featured in the top nine of the averages. The leading performers in the league were all New Zealanders: Brad White (VOC, Rotterdam) was the only batsman to score more than 1,000 runs (1,250 at 62.50); Roger Bradley (Hermes DVS, Schiedam) topped the batting averages with 972 at 74.76; and Chris Pringle (HCC, The Hague) took 62 wickets at a very cheap 8.74. Koninklijke UD were relegated from the Premier League – thus depriving the premier league of half its grass wickets – losing a play-off in the last over to ACC, Amstelveen. They will be replaced in 1997 by promoted Gandhi CC of Amsterdam, one of the clubs involved in the disgraceful match-fixing incident of 1994.

THE EUROPEAN CHAMPIONSHIP, 1996

By PETER S. HARGREAVES

As cricket has grown in popularity amongst Britain's continental neighbours, the launch of an official European tournament has looked increasingly overdue. In 1996 it finally happened, prompted both by the entry of Ireland and Scotland into ICC as Associate Members, and by Denmark's eagerness to host the competition in honour of the centenary of the Danish Sports Federation.

The most surprising entrants were Israel, who were invited to play after the late withdrawal of Wales. This exchange allowed the original format of the competition (two pools of four, comprising seven ICC Associate Members and England's amateur NCA team) to be retained. Pool B became something of a two-horse race, with Denmark and Ireland enjoying easy matches against Gibraltar and Italy, before Ireland eventually came through a tense decider, defeating the hosts by four runs.

In Pool A, England, Scotland and Holland shared the honours with one win and one loss against one another, while Israel went down to three predictably conclusive defeats. Holland's demolition of England's bowling attack, which brought them 342 runs in their 50 overs, turned out to be crucial when the placings were decided on run-rate.

The final was another cliffhanger for Ireland, who paced their innings well – led by the former Leicestershire batsman Justin Benson – and eventually surpassed Holland's 223 for nine with less than four overs to spare. All the other teams were involved in play-off games, and in the tie for third place England were blown away by Denmark's bowlers, losing by six wickets after being bowled out for 97.

At Brondby, July 19. **Final:** Ireland won by three wickets. Toss: Ireland. Holland 223 for nine (50 overs) (R. Vos 35, T. B. M. de Leede 30, K. J. van Noortwijk 33, Extras 35; J. D. Curry three for 33); Ireland 225 for seven (46.2 overs) (J. D. Curry 55, J. D. R. Benson 79).

Other placings: 3 Denmark; 4 England; 5 Scotland; 6 Gibraltar; 7 Italy; 8 Israel.

CRICKET ROUND THE WORLD, 1996

AFGHANISTAN

The ravages of war have brought cricket to Afghanistan. More than 1.5 million refugees fled to Pakistan through the Khyber Pass; a small percentage picked up an enthusiasm for cricket during their exile and took it home with them. This has been especially evident in Nangarhar Province, east of Kabul, which has been comparatively peaceful and liberal in its attitudes. In April 1996 eight teams played a 50-over softball cricket tournament with finals in the provincial capital, Jalalabad, using a tennis ball covered in plastic adhesive tape to reduce the bounce. A crowd of 200 – almost entirely male, as usual at sporting events in Afghanistan – watched the final. Since then interest has grown and in 1997 there were due to be 18 school teams and two at the University of Nangarhar. The game is played on dusty, uneven grounds, often with war-damaged buildings in the background. The dust is swept from the wicket, and the game has to start in the late afternoon due to the intense summer heat. Players wear traditional Afghan dress, with the umpires in black or dark brown. In Nangarhar many people were able to watch the World Cup on TV and copied the style and even mannerisms of the stars. During the final in Jalalabad, the captain of the fielding team had a catch dropped off his bowling. When the ball was returned to him, he angrily hurled it to the ground, at which point the umpire correctly signalled "Dead ball" under Law 23. – Rajah M. Wickremesinhe (*former UN High Commissioner for Refugees' officer-in-charge, Jalalabad*).

ASIAN CRICKET COUNCIL TROPHY

Bangladesh beat United Arab Emirates in the final of the 1996-97 ACC Trophy in Kuala Lumpur, and thus qualified to play alongside the three main Asian cricketing countries in the Asia Cup in Colombo. The tournament involved ten other countries, Fiji and Papua New Guinea – the beaten semi-finalists – plus Brunei, Hong Kong, Japan, Malaysia, the Maldives, Nepal, Singapore and Thailand, playing under more stringent residential qualifications than were in use for the 1996 World Cup. The Japan team, for instance, consisted entirely of Japanese nationals. It achieved two remarkable and contrasting feats. Against Bangladesh, Tetsuo Fuji took two wickets in consecutive balls, the first bowled right-arm over, the second left-arm over. The bad news came against Fiji, who scored 469 in their 50 overs.

AUSTRIA

There was drama in the final of the Austrian Open League in September. Lord's CC triumphed over Pakistan CC thanks to A. Ajay, who took the first-ever recorded hat-trick in Austrian championship cricket. An English touring team visited Vienna in May, and formally opened Austria's first full-sized ground at nearby Seebarn. France then arrived to play the first two internationals there, but Austria won both matches – the first by just two runs after setting a target of 301. Another new cricket ground was inaugurated at Velden in September, becoming the third purpose-built venue in the country. Two of them are surrounded by breathtaking Alpine mountains, and the last – Seebarn – is in the centre of one of Austria's wine regions. – Andrew Simpson-Parker.

BAHRAIN

Cricket thrives in Bahrain. The island state has a population of 500,000 and boasts about 50 teams, playing most Fridays in temperatures that can approach 50°C. The vast majority of the players are from the Indian subcontinent, and those Bahrainis that take part are usually either naturalised immigrants or have been educated abroad. The game came to Bahrain with expatriate oil-workers in the 1930s when the first wells were spudded in. The oldest club is in the oil village of Awali, and it is an oasis of cricketing comfort, complete with cucumber sandwiches. This is the exception, however, as the facilities at the other grounds vary from the rudimentary to the non-existent. The outfields are desert; sometimes rolled, sometimes not; sometimes sandy, sometimes concrete-hard; but always unpredictable. The best wickets are concrete strips covered with coir; Awali use a green composite mat designed for use as a swimming-pool surround. There is not a blade of grass to be seen anywhere. Nevertheless, the best four or five teams among the 16 that make up the Bahrain Cricket Association include some very strong players – mostly from Pakistan. In recent years the BCA Select XI has beaten a touring PIA XI containing eight current or recent Pakistani Test players, and narrowly lost to a strong MCC side out to celebrate Awali CC's 60th season. Desert cricket is an unforgettable experience – and camels really do sometimes wander across the pitch. – Guy Parker.

BANGLADESH

Both the Damal Summer Tournament, the season's curtain-raiser, and the Dhaka Premier Division were won by Mohammedan Sporting Club. In 1995-96, West Indies Under-19 toured the country and lost all three matches they played against Bangladesh Under-19.

BERMUDA

In 1996, Cup Match – Bermuda's annual cricket festival and two-day public holiday – reached one of its most thrilling conclusions. St George's CC have generally held the advantage over Somerset CC in recent years, but this time Somerset, with three wickets standing, needed only three runs off the last two balls of their innings to win. St George's cracked under the pressure, conceding four runs via an overthrow. In the Open Championship's Premier League, now comprising only eight teams since the rest have been relegated to a First Division, Western Stars retained their title. They also achieved Bermuda's first double by winning the new limited-overs competition. The national side took part in the Shell/Sandals Tournament in October 1996, where it failed to win a match, but was the only team to score over 200 in an innings on three different occasions – a good enough performance to earn Bermuda an invitation to enter the Red Stripe competition in future years, although this is unlikely to happen before 1998-99. Bobby Simpson, the former Australian coach, has been recruited as a consultant to assist with the Shell/Sandals series and Bermuda's preparations for the 1997 ICC Trophy Competition. – Maurice F. Hankey.

BRUNEI

Just as in 1994, the league competition went down to the wire, ending in a tie between Manggis and Cavaliers. Meanwhile, Royal Brunei Yacht Club showed their taste for the knockout game, winning the Galfar Cup for the second year running. The final, against Cavaliers, was a low-scoring affair with several batsmen becoming the victims of their own nerves. – Derek Thursby.

CANADA

Big-time international cricket came to Canada for the first time in 1996 as the inaugural Sahara Cup was contested by India and Pakistan at the Toronto Cricket Club in September 1996. The Canadian team had no shortage of international commitments itself, hosting a visit from Bangladesh and taking part in two tournaments – the 1996-97 Shell/Sandals Trophy in Jamaica and the Caribbean-Atlantic Tournament in Barbados. The captain Ingleton Liburd batted superbly throughout. This came against a difficult domestic background of drastically reduced Government funding, which has affected all non-Olympic sports. Further cuts were expected, and Canada will have to find money from commercial sources to remain competitive. However, the number of cricketers throughout the country continues to increase: there are now more than 10,000 seniors and 17,000 juniors.

CHINA

The Peking Cricket Club began the 1996 season with a full complement of six teams after Bangladesh and Sri Lanka returned to the fold (the other four represent England, Australia, India and Pakistan). It was reinvigorated on other fronts as well: the Beijing Chaoyang stadium became the club's new ground. This offers a vast improvement on the hazardous conditions at the Beijing Physical Institute: it has more grass than dust, it is more centrally located, it has "facilities", and it provides shade for those wanting to sleep before they are called out to bat. Pakistan won both the PCC League and the Knock Out Cup. "Bruce" Wang, who plays for the Australia team, topped the batting averages, and became the first local Chinese to achieve this honour. The PCC went on its first ever tour, to Shanghai, where it just managed to better the Shanghai Cricket Club in 35-degree heat. History was made in the Third Beijing International Sixes Tournament when an all-Chinese team made its debut. Soon afterwards, government sports officials announced that they would make Beijing Sports University available for a cricket development scheme. – Tony Fisher.

COLOMBIA

Cricket is not endemic in the High Andes. Indeed, it is so alien to local culture that Colombian customs reputedly impounded a priceless shipment of bats and balls from Venezuela some years ago as "dangerous, possibly subversive material". Bogota is a challenge for the bowler. At 8,300 feet above sea level, anyone trying to bowl medium-fast soon runs out of puff, and the ball will not swing much in the thin, dry air. A spinner gets a little more help from our new

Astroturf than from the old matting we had until 1994, and the batsman does not have an easy time. The field is kikuyu grass: the ball will not skim the surface, and must be hit dangerously high to reach the boundary. Cricket's popularity in Colombia has ebbed and flowed depending on the numbers of expatriates. It was first regularly played by Shell employees in the mid-1950s. Since then English schoolmasters, Scottish accountants and Pakistani bankers have come and gone, and now oil – this time BP – again provides most of the players. However, it is difficult to get teams together more than once or twice a month. We would very much welcome any touring side with the ambition to do something different. Please write to the Cricket Secretary, Bogota Sports Club, PO Box 10286, Bogota or fax (57) 1-338 4579. – Anthony Letts.

CYPRUS

Within the Services community, cricket is a popular and flourishing sport. There is an island-wide league of six teams, who play 40-over games on Saturday between mid-April and early August, culminating in a Cup competition and the Army v RAF fixture. The 1996 league was won by Ayios Nikolaos Station and the Cup by the 1st Battalion The King's Regiment, both based near Larnaca. There are also three midweek leagues, involving 20 teams. Two or three native Cypriots play for Mouflons, a Limassol-based team, named after a wild sheep found in the Troodos Mountains. Mouflons also have the island's most gifted cricketer, Darren Stubbing, who is an Australian – they get everywhere. All the pitches are concrete with matting but at Happy Valley, built by HM Forces in the 1950s, the outfield is lush and green, and maintained in pristine condition. – S. J. Vickery.

ETHIOPIA

Cricket used to be played regularly in Addis Ababa at the General Wingate School, with British and Indian teachers. A 1967 guidebook advised cricket lovers simply to turn up at the school on Saturday mornings if they wanted a game. However, these teachers left during the rule of General Mengistu, and we are left with only a few scratch games involving staff, students and parents from the Sandford English Community School. They are played on the football field, which is composed of volcanic rock with a covering of soil and grass. The pitch is marked out by string, then the groundsman cuts it with his sickle, and the clippings are taken away in a sack to feed his donkey. The bigger rocks are pulled out by hand, but it is still imperative to use a soft ball. Few Ethiopians play, although we can always find some students to join in, and there is talent among the batsmen. We also had a wonderful fast bowler here, a young man from Sierra Leone called Sahr Komba, but he has now gone to an American university and plays basketball. – Stephen Spawls.

EUROPEAN CLUB CHAMPIONSHIP

An Italian side won the title for the second year running, as Cesena thrashed Germany's DSSC Berlin-Brandenburg in the final at Bologna. DSSC batted first and seemed well set at 116 for four, but the last six batsmen could manage only two runs off the bat, and the innings faded to 120 all out. Cesena knocked off the runs for the loss of only one wicket.

EUROPEAN NATIONS CUP

Former Essex wicket-keeper David East coached France to an unexpected yet convincing victory in the Nations Cup at Osnabrück. They won twice against the holders, Portugal, and their 16-year-old all-rounder Fabrice Bronard hit the winning runs in the final. Germany came joint third with Austria.

FIJI

The annual Crompton Cup competition, which involves local district teams as well as club sides from Australia and New Zealand, was won by Suva. They beat Moce, a team from Lau, in the final. Unfortunately, the holders Tubou (who also come from Lau) were unable to take part for financial reasons. Cricket is generally under siege from other sports – rugby league in particular – but the generosity of the Dubbo District Cricket Association of New South Wales has helped Fiji to fund its coaching programme.

FRANCE

France made a bright start to 1996 as the native-born team, wooden-spoonists in 1995, earned third place at the six-a-side European Cricket Federation Indoor Trophy at Lord's. This success convinced the selectors of the need to accelerate the introduction of French youngsters to the team – a policy that led to mixed results at first, but was soon vindicated by success in the ECF Nations Cup and by a first victory against an ICC Associate Member – away to Italy in Turin. At home, the French Championship was claimed by Paris Université and the Open Championship by Northern. France is now hoping for promotion from Affiliate to Associate status in 1998. – Simon Hewitt.

GERMANY

Mönchengladbach staged two limited-overs internationals against France in June. The series was tied at one each, but Germany pulled off an emphatic victory in the second match by 138 runs, having piled up 254 for five in their 40 overs. The German Championship, held in Berlin in September, was won by Pak Orient, Munich, who beat the holders DSSC Berlin-Brandenburg in a low-scoring but thrilling final. It was the first time that a team from South Germany had taken the title. A new regional league may be launched next season in the North West. – Brian Fell.

GIBRALTAR

The dominance established in 1995 by Gibraltar CC, the oldest club on the rock, was continued as it carried off three of the four major domestic titles. Curiously enough, they again failed to win Gibraltar's oldest trophy, the Murto Cup, which dates back to the early 1920s, a target which has eluded them since the war. Sixteen-year-old Daniel Johnson, one of our most promising youngsters, was sent to Lord's in August for a three-week coaching course. – T. J. Finlayson.

HONG KONG

As the handover of control from Britain to China grew ever closer, cricket in Hong Kong changed too. While the traditional centres, Kowloon Cricket Club and Hong Kong Cricket Club, with their magnificent facilities, continued to play a major role, a growing number of ethnic Asian players joined in. In particular, junior cricket has taken off and hundreds of young Chinese players have been introduced to the game. The Hong Kong Sixes, the colony's most famous event, moved from the Kowloon club to the huge Hong Kong Stadium in 1996. This caused much debate and the event lost some of its old flavour; but the move had to be made if the event was to grow in international stature. It was a big success, despite the effects of Typhoon Willy on the first day, and West Indies beat India in the final. We can now look forward to further big matches in the territory and, as a result of the interest shown in trips to China and Japan by Hong Kong coaches, growth throughout the region. We can foresee the day when the Hong Kong team is made up of Chinese cricketers, and China is a serious player within the game. – Russell Mawhinney.

ISRAEL

Israeli cricket took a step closer to finding a home. The National Athletics Stadium – where the facilities include floodlights and an electronic scoreboard – has agreed to lay down two Astroturf wickets. Another significant development was the appointment of the former Kent and Worcestershire player Steve Herzberg as national coach. He accompanied the team on its tour of Denmark in July, and quickly succeeded in instilling his players with a sense of purpose. At home, the season was rescheduled to run through from April to November, with a mid-season break to gain respite from August's 40-degree heat. Ashdod A won the league, edging out the 1995 champions Lions Lod by two wickets in the penultimate game of the season, with the hard-hitting Barbadian St Eval Neblett making a crucial century. However, Lions Lod took consolation in their victory over Neve Yonathan in the knockout final. Finally, this report must make reference to the refusal of the Pakistan government to allow the chairman of the Israel Cricket Association to attend the final of the 1996 World Cup. This decision was in breach of everything that cricket stands for. – Stanley Perlman.

ITALY

Italy's first full season as an Associate Member of ICC saw a hard but highly instructive tour to South Africa and Namibia in April, and a first outing for the national Under-21 side, which drew a two-game series with Austria. At club level, arch-rivals Pianoro and Cesena exchanged trophies. Cesena knocked Pianoro, the holders, out of the ECF Club Championship semi-final and went on to take the title, but Pianoro replied by winning the National Championship. Capanelle retained the Italian Cup by beating Grosseto in the final. – Simone Gambino.

JAPAN

Enthusiasm for cricket is high in Japan and the Gunma Cup, a two-day competition for Japanese men, enjoyed great popularity in its third year. Tokyo Bay CC won the cup for the second time. During the competition one of their players, Hiroki Minami, fell foul of a local rule which deducts five runs for a shot on to the nearby tennis court and was dismissed with a score of minus three. There are very few grounds we can use and if an innocent tennis player were injured it would cause serious problems. Two new Japanese university teams emerged and it was possible to send a team of 14 Japanese natives to the Asian Cricket Council Trophy in Malaysia. The foreign community contested the Kanto Cup, won by Lala CC, a team of Pakistanis. – Trevor Bayley.

KENYA

The centenary year of cricket in Kenya could hardly have been more memorable. In 1896 the first known cricket match in Kenya took place in Mombasa between a local team and *HMS Sparrow*. In February 1996 a young Kenyan team astonished the cricketing world with their World Cup victory over the mighty West Indians. This has had a tremendous effect. Test-playing countries at once showed a willingness to play Kenya, and later in the year Sri Lanka, Pakistan and South Africa took part in a four-nation tournament in Nairobi, given full one-day international status, which was a great popular success and will be remembered for Shahid Afridi's 37-ball century. The only disappointment was Kenya's own form: the leading batsmen all failed consistently, although the bowlers had Pakistan in trouble at 61 for five before they recovered. Inside the country there has been a surge of interest at every level, and cricket has perhaps replaced hockey as the third-most popular sport in the country – still a long way behind football and athletics. Nairobi Gymkhana won the League for the first time in many years – and did the double by winning the Uhuru Cup. The season was marred by the withdrawal, followed by expulsion, of Premier, one of the oldest clubs in Kenya. They were later reinstated but demoted to Division Two. Nationally, the emphasis has been on development with the aim of increasing the number of cricketers tenfold in the next five years. The immediate aim is to achieve full one-day international status. There is every chance of achieving this in 1997, provided the team does itself justice at the ICC Trophy in Malaysia early in the year. – Jasmer Singh.

KIRIBATI

Cricket in the Republic of Kiribati – 33 fragmented and isolated South Pacific atolls that used to be the Gilbert Islands – dates back to the arrival of the British in 1892. The game has now dwindled to two or three matches a year, between an Australian XI and the Rest of the World, on a ground of white coral sand with no shade from the burning sun, other than the odd passing frigate bird. The eccentricities of early cricket here were recorded in Arthur Grimble's *A Pattern of Islands*. The most dramatic event of recent years came when the Kiribati XI flew to play an away fixture against the Republic of Tuvalu, formerly the Ellice Islands. Batting second, Kiribati were down to the last pair and needed six to win off the last ball. Darkness was falling fast and pressure mounting in more ways than one – the plane for the return journey had to take off from a narrow strip of land, between the ocean and the lagoon, with no landing lights. The batsman on strike was a strapping player called Tapatulu, a man of fearsome strength renowned locally for having once been lost at sea in a canoe for three months. It was a good-length ball, Tapatulu took a step outside leg stump and, with the well-used "Len Hutton" team bat, despatched the ball over cow-shot corner for six. – David de Silva.

NAMIBIA

The Namibian senior side moved into regular cross-border competition in 1996, when it was admitted to the B section of South Africa's UCB Bowl. Junior teams began taking part in the South African Country Districts competition. TransNamib won the 1995-96 senior league.

ST HELENA

At the instigation of the Governor, David Smallman, MCC generously donated an artificial turf pitch. When it arrived by ship, a celebration match was played between the Governor's XI and the President's XI, which ended in a tie. – Fraser M. Simm.

SINGAPORE

The domestic league continued to grow in 1996. Already comprising 19 clubs and three divisions, it welcomed new members in the form of Singapore Airlines, the National University, and Nanyang Technological University. The country's real strength lies in the schools, however, and the junior national squads enjoyed a successful year. The Under-18s participated in the Tuanka Ja'afar Cup, where they won all their matches (against Malaysia, Hong Kong and Thailand).

SOUTH KOREA

Five teams participated in the spring and autumn competitions. A major difficulty arose in September when there were no decent balls left, but Qantas came to the rescue with a delivery hours before the start of the autumn competition. They were rewarded with victory for Australia, who twice scored over 200 in 20 overs, and convincingly won the final. Their opponents, All Stars, had beaten India to win the Spring Competition. – Olivier de Braekeleer.

SPAIN

The executive officers of the Spanish Cricket Association came up against frustrating financial constraints in 1996. The Spanish Government failed to approve all the sports federations' budgets, and an international in Portugal had to be cancelled. Domestically, it proved impossible to organise the planned regional matches. League and cup competitions did go ahead, however, with the help of sponsorship from Sun Alliance S. A. and Columbus Insurance. Javea completed the double – equalling the 1995 achievements of Barcelona. One positive step was the development of a fine new cricketing facility at L'Alfas del Pi, on the Costa Blanca. – Clive Woodbridge.

TRISTAN DA CUNHA

News travels slowly from this South Atlantic island, but the first match for ten years took place there in January 1995 through the initiative of a local official, Alan Waters. The coir matting once used as a surface had long since disappeared, and it was not safe to play with a cricket ball on the concrete, so a rounders ball was used. Some of the older islanders could still handle a bat but were no longer sufficiently co-ordinated to take catches. However, with 60 children among the 300 islanders, Waters saw his chance and ordered a Kwik Cricket set from England. He was also hoping to arrange matches against passing ships, but the cost of adult equipment is prohibitive. British missionaries originally helped the game thrive: among the Victorian pioneers was Edwin Dodgson, Lewis Carroll's brother. The game was also played regularly in the 1950s when the matting was laid at a spot called Hottentot Fence, but that era ended with the volcanic eruption of 1961 which forced the island to be evacuated. – Peter S. Hargreaves.

UNITED ARAB EMIRATES

Except for the victory over Holland, the UAE did not perform as well as expected in the World Cup. A total of 28 tournaments were conducted in 1995-96, of which six were under floodlights. Some were washed out, owing to unusual and incessant rains. The Pepsi Sharjah Cup in April 1996 included the 100th one-day international at the stadium, the most on any ground.

UNITED STATES

Cricket's sleeping giant showed some signs of awakening in 1996. A new body, the US Cricket Federation, was founded to challenge the traditional authority, the US Cricket Association, and a vote of no confidence ousted the Association's main officials. Following a meeting in New York with the chairman and chief executive of ICC, talks began to merge the two bodies in an attempt to forge a more dynamic future for American cricket. It was thought real progress could only come following success on the field, and the new formula for the ICC Trophy insisting that at least seven members had to have citizenship was expected to damage the chances of the US team, which is heavily dependent on expatriates. However, the Walt Disney Company showed enthusiasm for the idea of a cricket ground at a new sports complex it is developing at Disney World in Florida, and executives talked of promoting one-day internationals there. It was also said that Disney were contemplating a film on the exploits of the LA Kricketts, the group of homeless players who toured England in 1995.

WEST AFRICA

Cricket continues to struggle because of political difficulties and poor communications between the countries. The Quadrangular competition scheduled for Banjul in December 1995 was cancelled. Cricket is continuing within Nigeria and a national knockout cup began in 1995-96: the Image Technologies Trophy, won by Foundation CC of Lagos. The Jay-Jay League, centred on Lagos, continued with nine clubs, and Cosmopolitan CC were the winners.

PART SIX: ADMINISTRATION AND LAWS

INTERNATIONAL CRICKET COUNCIL

On June 15, 1909, representatives of cricket in England, Australia and South Africa met at Lord's and founded the Imperial Cricket Conference. Membership was confined to the governing bodies of cricket in countries within the British Commonwealth where Test cricket was played. India, New Zealand and West Indies were elected as members on May 31, 1926, Pakistan on July 28, 1952, Sri Lanka on July 21, 1981, and Zimbabwe on July 8, 1992. South Africa ceased to be a member of ICC on leaving the British Commonwealth in May, 1961, but was elected as a Full Member on July 10, 1991.

On July 15, 1965, the Conference was renamed the International Cricket Conference and new rules were adopted to permit the election of countries from outside the British Commonwealth. This led to the growth of the Conference, with the admission of Associate Members, who were each entitled to one vote, while the Foundation and Full Members were each entitled to two votes, on ICC resolutions. On July 12, 13, 1989, the Conference was renamed the International Cricket Council and revised rules were adopted.

On July 7, 1993, ICC ceased to be administered by MCC and became an independent organisation with its own chief executive, the headquarters remaining at Lord's. The category of Foundation Member, with its special rights, was abolished. On October 1, 1993, Sir Clyde Walcott became the first non-British chairman of ICC.

Officers

Chairman: Sir Clyde Walcott. *Chief Executive:* D. L. Richards. *Administration Officer:* C. D. Hitchcock.

Constitution

Chairman: Elected for a three-year term from the date of the Council's annual conference. Normally, a new chairman will be chosen at the conference a year before the previous Chairman's term expires. Sir Clyde Walcott's term ends in 1997.

Chief Executive: Appointed by the Council. D. L. Richards has been given a contract until 1998.

Membership

Full Members: Australia, England, India, New Zealand, Pakistan, South Africa, Sri Lanka, West Indies and Zimbabwe.

Associate Members*: Argentina (1974), Bangladesh (1977), Bermuda (1966), Canada (1968), Denmark (1966), East and Central Africa (1966), Fiji (1965), Gibraltar (1969), Hong Kong (1969), Ireland (1993), Israel (1974), Italy (1995), Kenya (1981), Malaysia (1967), Namibia (1992), Nepal (1996), Netherlands (1966), Papua New Guinea (1973), Scotland (1994), Singapore (1974), United Arab Emirates (1990), USA (1965) and West Africa (1976).

Affiliate Members*: Austria (1992), Bahamas (1987), Belgium (1991), Brunei (1992), France (1987), Germany (1991), Greece (1995), Japan (1989), Portugal (1996), Spain (1992), Switzerland (1985), Thailand (1995) and Vanuatu (1995).

* *Year of election shown in parentheses.*

The following governing bodies for cricket shall be eligible for election.

Full Members: The governing body for cricket recognised by ICC of a country, or countries associated for cricket purposes, or a geographical area, from which representative teams are qualified to play official Test matches.

Associate Members: The governing body for cricket recognised by ICC of a country, or countries associated for cricket purposes, or a geographical area, which does not qualify as a Full Member but where cricket is firmly established and organised.

Affiliate Members: The governing body for cricket recognised by ICC of a country, or countries associated for cricket purposes, or a geographical area (which is not part of one of those already constituted as a Full or Associate Member) where ICC recognises that cricket is played in accordance with the Laws of Cricket. Affiliate Members have no right to vote or to propose or second resolutions at ICC meetings.

ENGLAND AND WALES CRICKET BOARD

The England and Wales Cricket Board became responsible for the administration of all cricket – professional and recreational – on January 1, 1997. It took over the functions of the Cricket Council, the Test and County Cricket Board and the National Cricket Association which had run the game in England and Wales since 1968. The Management Committee is answerable to the First-Class Forum on matters concerning the first-class game and to the Recreational Forum on matters concerning the non-professional game. Each of the forums elects four members to the Management Committee.

Officers

Chairman: Lord MacLaurin of Knebworth. *Chief Executive:* T. M. Lamb.

Management Committee: Lord MacLaurin (*chairman*), D. L. Acfield, R. Bennett, A. J. Cross, B. G. K. Downing, P. J. Edwards, F. H. Elliott, P. W. Gooden, R. Jackson, R. D. V. Knight, F. D. Morgan, M. P. Murray, J. B. Pickup, A. Wheelhouse.

Chairmen of Committees: First-Class Forum: F. D. Morgan; *Recreational Forum:* J. B. Pickup; *Cricket Advisory Committee:* D. L. Acfield; *England Management Advisory Committee:* R. Bennett; *Finance Advisory Committee:* M. P. Murray; *Marketing Advisory Committee:* B. G. K. Downing; *Discipline Standing Committee:* G. Elias QC; *Registration Standing Committee:* A. Wheelhouse.

Deputy Chief Executive and Finance Director: C. A. Barker; *Marketing Director:* T. D. M. Blake; *Administration Manager:* A. S. Brown; *Corporate Affairs Manager:* R. E. Little; *Cricket Operations Manager:* J. D. Carr; *National Development Manager:* T. N. Bates; *Director of Coaching and Excellence:* M. J. Stewart.

THE MARYLEBONE CRICKET CLUB

The Marylebone Cricket Club evolved out of the White Conduit Club in 1787, when Thomas Lord laid out his first ground in Dorset Square. Its members revised the Laws in 1788 and gradually took responsibility for cricket throughout the world. However, it relinquished control of the game in the UK in 1968 and the International Cricket Council finally established its own secretariat in 1993. MCC still owns Lord's and remains the guardian of the Laws. It calls itself "a private club with a public function" and aims to support cricket everywhere, especially at grassroots level and in countries where the game is least developed.

Patron: HER MAJESTY THE QUEEN

Officers

President: 1996-98 – A. C. D. Ingleby-Mackenzie.

Treasurer: M. E. L. Melluish. *Chairman of Finance:* D. L. Hudd.

Trustees: Field Marshal The Rt Hon. The Lord Bramall, The Rt Hon. The Lord Griffiths, J. C. Woodcock.

Hon. Life Vice-Presidents: Sir Donald Bradman, D. G. Clark, Sir Colin Cowdrey, G. H. G. Doggart, D. J. Insole, F. G. Mann, C. H. Palmer, C. G. A. Paris, E. W. Swanton.

Secretary: R. D. V. Knight.

Assistant Secretaries: M. R. Blow (Finance), J. A. Jameson (Cricket), C. W. W. Rea (Marketing), J. R. Smith (Administration). *Personal Assistant to Secretary:* Miss S. A. Lawrence. *Curator:* S. E. A. Green.

MCC Committee, elected members 1996-97: The Rt Hon. The Lord Alexander, E. R. Dexter, C. A. Fry, D. A. Graveney, C. B. Howland, A. R. Lewis, D. R. Male, M. C. J. Nicholas, Sir Tim Rice, D. Rich, D. R. W. Silk, M. O. C. Sturt.

Chairmen of main sub-committees: Sir Colin Cowdrey (Cricket); B. M. Thornton (Estates); R. V. C. Robins (General Purposes). *Chairmen of specialist sub-committees:* J. R. T. Barclay (Indoor School Management); R. P. Hodson (Players and Fixtures); B. A. Sharp (Tennis and Squash); T. M. B. Sissons (Marketing); H. M. Wyndham (Arts and Libraries).

EUROPEAN CRICKET FEDERATION

The ECF was founded in Munich in 1989 by the national cricket associations of Austria, Germany, Italy and Switzerland to help promote and develop cricket in Europe. Spain became the 12th member country in 1995, joining the original four plus Belgium, France, Greece, Luxembourg, Malta, Portugal and Sweden.

President: R. D. V. Knight. *Administrator:* Miss D. H. Moore.

ADDRESSES

INTERNATIONAL CRICKET COUNCIL

D. L. Richards, The Clock Tower, Lord's Cricket Ground, London NW8 8QN (0171-266 1818; fax 0171-266 1777).

Full Members

AUSTRALIA: Australian Cricket Board, 90 Jolimont Street, Jolimont, Victoria 3002 (00 61 3 9653 9999; fax 00 61 3 9653 9911).
ENGLAND: England and Wales Cricket Board, T. M. Lamb, Lord's Ground, London NW8 8QZ (0171-286 4405; fax 0171-289 5619).
INDIA: Board of Control for Cricket in India, J. Dalmiya, Dr B. C. Roy Club House, Eden Gardens, Calcutta 700 021 (00 91 33 248 2447; fax 00 91 33 248 7555).
NEW ZEALAND: New Zealand Cricket Inc., C. Doig, PO Box 958, 109 Cambridge Terrace, Christchurch (00 64 3 366 2964; fax 00 64 3 365 7491).
PAKISTAN: Pakistan Cricket Board, Ghulam Mustafa Khan, Gaddafi Stadium, Lahore 54600 (00 92 42 877 817; fax 00 92 42 571 1860).
SOUTH AFRICA: United Cricket Board of South Africa, Dr A. Bacher, PO Box 55009, Northlands 2116, Transvaal (00 27 11 880 2810; fax 00 27 11 880 6578).
SRI LANKA: Board of Control for Cricket in Sri Lanka, D. Ranatunga, 35 Maitland Place, Colombo 7 (00 94 1 691439/689551; fax 00 94 1 697405).
WEST INDIES: West Indies Cricket Board, G. S. Camacho, Factory Road, PO Box 616 W, Woods Centre, St John's, Antigua (00 1 268 460 5462/5465; fax 00 1 268 460 5452/5453).
ZIMBABWE: Zimbabwe Cricket Union, D. Arnott, PO Box 2739, Harare (00 263 4 704616/704617/704618; fax 00 263 4 729370).

Associate and Affiliate Members

ARGENTINA: Argentine Cricket Association, B. C. Roberts, ACA Sede Central, J. M. Gutierrez 3829, 1425 Buenos Aires.
AUSTRIA: Austrian Cricket Association, A. Simpson-Parker, Benidikt-Schellingergasse 22/16, 1150 Vienna.

BAHAMAS: Bahamas Cricket Association, S. Deveaux, PO Box 1001, Nassau.

BANGLADESH: Bangladesh Cricket Control Board, M. Aminul Huq Moni, National Stadium, Dhaka 1000.

BELGIUM: Belgian Cricket Federation, C. Wolfe, Rue de l'Eglise St Martin 12, B-1390 BIEZ.

BERMUDA: Bermuda Cricket Board of Control, W. Smith, PO Box HM992, Hamilton HM DX.

BRUNEI: Brunei Darussalam National Cricket Association, c/o Panaga Club, Seria 7082, Brunei Darussalam via Singapore.

CANADA: Canadian Cricket Association, R. Jagoo, 1650 Abbey Road, Ottawa, Ontario, K1G 0H3.

DENMARK: Danish Cricket Association, J. Holmen, Idraettens Hus, 2605 Brøndby.

EAST AND CENTRAL AFRICA: East and Central African Cricket Conference, T. B. McCarthy, PO Box 34321, Lusaka 1010, Zambia.

FIJI: Fiji Cricket Association, P. I. Knight, PO Box 300, Suva.

FRANCE: Fédération Française du Cricket, O. Dubaut, 73 Rue Curial, 75019 Paris.

GERMANY: Deutscher Cricket Bund, B. Fell, Luragogasse 5, 94032 Passau.

GIBRALTAR: Gibraltar Cricket Association, T. J. Finlayson, 21 Sandpits House, Withams Road.

GREECE: Greek Cricket Association, Y. Arvanitakis, Sossikleous 16, 116 32 Athens.

HONG KONG: Hong Kong Cricket Association, J. A. Cribbin, Room 1019, Sports House, 1 Stadium Path, So Kon Po, Causeway Bay.

IRELAND: Irish Cricket Union, D. Scott, 45 Foxrock Park, Foxrock, Dublin 18.

ISRAEL: Israel Cricket Association, S. Perlman, PO Box 65085, Tel-Aviv 61650.

ITALY: Associazione Italiana Cricket, S. Gambino, Via S. Ignazio 9, 00186 Roma.

JAPAN: Japan Cricket Association, R. G. Martineau, c/o Office of Cricket Development and Promotion, Amagawa Oshima Machi 2-8-17, Maebashi City 379-21.

KENYA: Kenya Cricket Association, S. Sarkar, PO Box 45870, Nairobi.

MALAYSIA: Malaysian Cricket Association, C. Chelliah, 1st Floor, Wisma OCM, Jalan Hang Jebat, 50150 Kuala Lumpur.

NAMIBIA: Namibia Cricket Board, L. Pieters, PO Box 457, Windhoek 9000.

NEPAL: Cricket Association of Nepal, B. R. Pandey, Dasharath Stadium, PO Box 925, Kathmandu.

NETHERLANDS: Royal Netherlands Cricket Board, A. de la Mar, Neuiwe Kalfjeslaan 21-B, 1182 AA Amstelveen.

PAPUA NEW GUINEA: Papua New Guinea Cricket Board of Control, W. Satchell, PO Box 83, Konedobu.

PORTUGAL: Cricket Association of Portugal, J. Simonson, Vila D'Acia, Rua do Pinhal s/n, Bicese, 2765 Estoril.

SCOTLAND: Scottish Cricket Union, R. W. Barclay, Caledonia House, South Gyle, Edinburgh EH12 9DQ.

SINGAPORE: Singapore Cricket Association, A. Kalaver, c/o Drew & Napier, 20 Raffles Place, #17-01, Ocean Towers, Singapore 048620.

SPAIN: Asociacion Española de Cricket, C. E. Woodbridge, Apartado 269, 03730 Javea, Alicante.

SWITZERLAND: Swiss Cricket Association, P. Barnes, Spitzackerstrasse 32, 4103 Bottmingen.

THAILAND: Thailand Cricket League, T. Karnasuta, 17th Floor, Silom Complex Building, 191 Silom Road, Bangkok 10500.

UNITED ARAB EMIRATES: Emirates Cricket Board, M. Khan, Sharjah Cricket Stadium, PO Box 783, Sharjah.

USA: United States of America Cricket Association, A. Syed, 1689 Gilberto Avenue, Glendale Heights, Illinois 60139.

VANUATU: Vanuatu Cricket Association, M. Stafford, c/o Stafford and Associates, PO Box 734, Court Villa, Vanuatu.

WEST AFRICA: West Africa Cricket Conference, Mrs Tayo Oreweme, Tafawa Balewa Square, Surulere, Lagos, Nigeria.

UK ADDRESSES

ENGLAND AND WALES CRICKET BOARD: T. M. Lamb, Lord's Ground, London NW8 8QZ (0171-286 4405; fax 0171-289 5619).

MARYLEBONE CRICKET CLUB: R. D. V. Knight, Lord's Ground, London NW8 8QN (0171-289 1611; fax 0171-289 9100. Club office 0171-289 8979; fax 0171-266 3459).

First-Class Counties

DERBYSHIRE: County Ground, Nottingham Road, Derby DE21 6DA (01332-383211; fax 01332-290251).

DURHAM: County Ground, Riverside, Chester-le-Street, County Durham DH3 3QR (0191-387 1717; fax 0191-387 1616).

ESSEX: County Ground, New Writtle Street, Chelmsford CM2 0PG (01245-252420; fax 01245-491607).

GLAMORGAN: Sophia Gardens, Cardiff CF1 9XR (01222-343478; fax 01222-377044).

GLOUCESTERSHIRE: Phoenix County Ground, Nevil Road, Bristol BS7 9EJ (0117-924 5216; fax 0117-924 1193).

HAMPSHIRE: Northlands Road, Southampton SO9 2TY (01703-333788; fax 01703-330121).

KENT: St Lawrence Ground, Old Dover Road, Canterbury CT1 3NZ (01227-456886; fax 01227-762168).

LANCASHIRE: County Cricket Ground, Old Trafford, Manchester M16 0PX (0161-282 4000; fax 0161-282 4100).

LEICESTERSHIRE: County Ground, Grace Road, Leicester LE2 8AD (0116-283 1880/2128; fax 0116-244 0363).

MIDDLESEX: Lord's Cricket Ground, London NW8 8QN (0171-289 1300; fax 0171-289 5831).

NORTHAMPTONSHIRE: County Ground, Wantage Road, Northampton NN1 4TJ (01604-32917; fax 01604-232855).

NOTTINGHAMSHIRE: County Cricket Ground, Trent Bridge, Nottingham NG2 6AG (0115-982 1525; fax 0115-945 5730).

SOMERSET: County Ground, St James's Street, Taunton TA1 1JT (01823-272946; fax 01823-332395).

SURREY: The Oval, London SE11 5SS (0171-582 6660; fax 0171-735 7769).

SUSSEX: County Ground, Eaton Road, Hove BN3 3AN (01273-732161; fax 01273-771549).

WARWICKSHIRE: County Ground, Edgbaston, Birmingham B5 7QU (0121-446 4422; fax 0121-446 4544).

WORCESTERSHIRE: County Ground, New Road, Worcester WR2 4QQ (01905-748474; fax 01905-748005).

YORKSHIRE: Headingley Cricket Ground, Leeds LS6 3BU (0113-278 7394; fax 0113-278 4099).

Minor Counties

MINOR COUNTIES CRICKET ASSOCIATION: D. J. M. Armstrong, Thorpe Cottage, Mill Common, Ridlington, North Walsham NR28 9TY (01692-650563).

BEDFORDSHIRE: D. J. F. Hoare, 5 Brecon Way, Bedford MK41 8DF (01234-266648).

BERKSHIRE: C. M. S. Crombie, Orchard Cottage, Waltham St Lawrence, Reading, Berkshire RG10 0JH (01734-343387 home/fax).

BUCKINGHAMSHIRE: S. J. Tomlin, Orchardleigh Cottage, Bigfrith Lane, Cookham Dean, Berkshire SL6 9PH (01628-482202).

CAMBRIDGESHIRE: P. W. Gooden, The Redlands, Oakington Road, Cottenham, Cambridge CB4 4TW (01954-250429).

CHESHIRE: J. B. Pickup, 2 Castle Street, Northwich, Cheshire CW8 1AB (01606-74970 home, 01606-74301 business; fax 01606-871034).

CORNWALL: The Rev. Canon Kenneth Rogers, The Rectory, Priory Road, Bodmin, Cornwall PL31 2AB (01208-73867).

CUMBERLAND: D. Lamb, 42 Croft Road, Carlisle, Cumbria CA3 9AG (01228-23017).

DEVON: G. R. Evans, Blueberry Haven, 20 Boucher Road, Budleigh Salterton, Devon EX9 6JF (01395-445216 home, 01392-58406 business; fax 01392-411697).

DORSET: K. H. House, The Barn, Higher Farm, Bagber Common, Sturminster Newton, Dorset DT10 2HB (01258-473394).

HEREFORDSHIRE: P. Sykes, 5 Dale Drive, Holmer Grange, Hereford HR4 9RF (01432-264703 home, 01432-382684 business).

HERTFORDSHIRE: D. S. Dredge, "Trevellis", 38 Santers Lane, Potters Bar, Hertfordshire EN6 2BX (01707-658377 home, 0171-359 3579 business).

LINCOLNSHIRE: C. A. North, "Koorah", Whisby Road, Whisby Moor, Lincoln LN6 9BY (01522-681636).

NORFOLK: S. J. Skinner, 27 Colkett Drive, Old Catton, Norwich NR6 7ND (01603-485940 home – weekend, 01354-659026 – midweek, 01733-412152 business).

NORTHUMBERLAND: A. B. Stephenson, Northumberland County Cricket Club, Osborne Avenue, Jesmond, Newcastle-upon-Tyne NE2 1JS (0191-281 2738).

OXFORDSHIRE: A. W. Moss, 14 Croft Avenue, Kidlington, Oxford OX5 2HU (01865-372399, also fax).

SHROPSHIRE: N. H. Birch, 8 Port Hill Close, Shrewsbury, Shropshire SY3 8RR (01743-233650).

STAFFORDSHIRE: W. S. Bourne, 10 The Pavement, Brewood, Staffordshire ST19 9BZ (01902-850325 home, 01902-23038 business).

SUFFOLK: Toby Pound, 94 Henley Road, Ipswich IP1 4NJ (01473-213288 home, 01473-232121 business).

WALES MINOR COUNTIES: Bill Edwards, 59a King Edward Road, Swansea SA1 4LN (01792-462233).

WILTSHIRE: C. R. Sheppard, 45 Ipswich Street, Swindon SN2 1DB (01793-511811 home, 01793-530784 business, 0831-565866 mobile).

Other Bodies

ASSOCIATION OF CRICKET UMPIRES AND SCORERS: G. J. Bullock, PO Box 399, Camberley, Surrey GU16 5ZJ (01276-27962).

BRITISH UNIVERSITIES SPORTS ASSOCIATION: J. Ellis, 8 Union Street, London SE1 1SZ (0171-357 8555).

CLUB CRICKET CONFERENCE: D. Franklin, 361 West Barnes Lane, New Malden, Surrey KT3 6JF (0181-949 4001).

COMBINED SERVICES: Major R. Ross-Hurst, c/o Army Sports Control Board, Clayton Barracks, Aldershot, Hampshire GU11 2BG.

ENGLISH SCHOOLS' CRICKET ASSOCIATION: K. S. Lake, 38 Mill House, Woods Lane, Cottingham, Hull HU16 4HQ.

EUROPEAN CRICKET FEDERATION: Miss D. H. Moore, MCC, Lord's Ground, London NW8 8QN (0171-289 1611; fax 0171-289 9100).

LEAGUE CRICKET CONFERENCE: N. Edwards, 1 Longfield, Freshfield, Formby, Merseyside.

MIDLAND CLUB CRICKET CONFERENCE: D. R. Thomas, 4 Silverdale Gardens, Wordsley, Stourbridge, W. Midlands DY8 5NU.

SCARBOROUGH CRICKET FESTIVAL: Colin T. Adamson, Cricket Ground, North Marine Road, Scarborough, North Yorkshire YO12 7TJ.

WOMEN'S CRICKET ASSOCIATION: Warwickshire County Cricket Ground, Edgbaston Road, Birmingham B5 7QX (0121-440 0567; fax/answerphone 0121-440 0520).

INTERNATIONAL UMPIRES' PANEL

On December 21, 1993, the International Cricket Council announced the formation of an international umpires' panel, backed by £1.1 million sponsorship over three years from National Grid. Each Full Member of ICC was to nominate two officials – apart from England, who named four, because of their large number of professional umpires and the fact that most Tests take place during the English winter. A third-country member of the panel was to stand with a "home" umpire, not necessarily from the panel, in every Test staged from February 1994. Teams would have no right of objection to appointments.

The following umpires were on the panel from August 1996:

S. K. Bansal (India), L. H. Barker (West Indies), S. A. Bucknor (West Indies), B. C. Cooray (Sri Lanka), D. B. Cowie (New Zealand), R. S. Dunne (New Zealand), K. T. Francis (Sri Lanka), D. B. Hair (Australia), Khizar Hayat (Pakistan), M. J. Kitchen (England), Mahboob Shah (Pakistan), C. J. Mitchley (South Africa), D. L. Orchard (South Africa), S. G. Randell (Australia), I. D. Robinson (Zimbabwe), G. Sharp (England), D. R. Shepherd (England), R. B. Tiffin (Zimbabwe), S. Venkataraghavan (India), P. Willey (England).

Note: Compared with the 1995-96 list, S. K. Bansal has replaced V. K. Ramaswamy, D. B. Cowie has replaced B. L. Aldridge and D. L. Orchard has replaced K. E. Liebenberg.

THE LAWS OF CRICKET

(1980 CODE)

INDEX TO THE LAWS

Law 1. The Players ... 1310
Law 2. Substitutes and Runners: Batsman or Fieldsman Leaving the Field: Batsman Retiring: Batsman Commencing Innings ... 1310
Law 3. The Umpires ... 1311
Law 4. The Scorers ... 1313
Law 5. The Ball ... 1314
Law 6. The Bat ... 1314
Law 7. The Pitch ... 1314
Law 8. The Wickets ... 1315
Law 9. The Bowling, Popping and Return Creases ... 1315
Law 10. Rolling, Sweeping, Mowing, Watering the Pitch and Re-marking of Creases ... 1316
Law 11. Covering the Pitch ... 1317
Law 12. Innings ... 1317
Law 13. The Follow-on ... 1318
Law 14. Declarations ... 1318
Law 15. Start of Play ... 1318
Law 16. Intervals ... 1319
Law 17. Cessation of Play ... 1320
Law 18. Scoring ... 1321
Law 19. Boundaries ... 1322
Law 20. Lost Ball ... 1323
Law 21. The Result ... 1323
Law 22. The Over ... 1324
Law 23. Dead Ball ... 1325
Law 24. No-ball ... 1326
Law 25. Wide-ball ... 1327
Law 26. Bye and Leg-bye ... 1328
Law 27. Appeals ... 1328
Law 28. The Wicket is Down ... 1329
Law 29. Batsman Out of His Ground ... 1330
Law 30. Bowled ... 1330
Law 31. Timed Out ... 1330
Law 32. Caught ... 1331
Law 33. Handled the Ball ... 1331
Law 34. Hit the Ball Twice ... 1332
Law 35. Hit Wicket ... 1332
Law 36. Leg Before Wicket ... 1332
Law 37. Obstructing the Field ... 1333
Law 38. Run Out ... 1333
Law 39. Stumped ... 1334
Law 40. The Wicket-keeper ... 1334
Law 41. The Fieldsman ... 1334
Law 42. Unfair Play ... 1335
42.1. Responsibility of Captains ... 1335
42.2. Responsibility of Umpires ... 1335
42.3. Intervention by the Umpire ... 1335
42.4. Lifting the Seam ... 1335
42.5. Changing the Condition of the Ball ... 1335
42.6. Incommoding the Striker ... 1335

42.7. Obstruction of a Batsman in Running ... 1336
42.8. The Bowling of Fast Short-pitched Balls ... 1336
42.9. The Bowling of Fast High Full Pitches ... 1336
42.10. Time Wasting ... 1336
42.11. Players Damaging the Pitch ... 1337
42.12. Batsman Unfairly Stealing a Run ... 1337
42.13. Player's Conduct ... 1337

LAW 1. THE PLAYERS

1. Number of Players and Captain

A match is played between two sides each of 11 players, one of whom shall be captain. In the event of the captain not being available at any time, a deputy shall act for him.

2. Nomination of Players

Before the toss for innings, the captain shall nominate his players, who may not thereafter be changed without the consent of the opposing captain.

Note

(a) More or Less than 11 Players a Side
A match may be played by agreement between sides of more or less than 11 players, but not more than 11 players may field.

LAW 2. SUBSTITUTES AND RUNNERS: BATSMAN OR FIELDSMAN LEAVING THE FIELD: BATSMAN RETIRING: BATSMAN COMMENCING INNINGS

1. Substitutes

In normal circumstances, a substitute shall be allowed to field only for a player who satisfies the umpires that he has become injured or become ill during the match. However, in very exceptional circumstances, the umpires may use their discretion to allow a substitute for a player who has to leave the field for other wholly acceptable reasons, subject to consent being given by the opposing captain. If a player wishes to change his shirt, boots, etc., he may leave the field to do so (no changing on the field), but no substitute will be allowed.

2. Objection to Substitutes

The opposing captain shall have no right of objection to any player acting as substitute in the field, nor as to where he shall field; however, no substitute shall act as wicket-keeper.

3. Substitute not to Bat or Bowl

A substitute shall not be allowed to bat or bowl.

4. A Player for whom a Substitute has Acted

A player may bat, bowl or field even though a substitute has acted for him.

5. Runner

A runner shall be allowed for a batsman who, during the match, is incapacitated by illness or injury. The person acting as runner shall be a member of the batting side and shall, if possible, have already batted in that innings.

6. Runner's Equipment

The player acting as runner for an injured batsman shall wear the same external protective equipment as the injured batsman.

7. Transgression of the Laws by an Injured Batsman or Runner

An injured batsman may be out should his runner break any one of Laws 33 (Handled the Ball), 37 (Obstructing the Field) or 38 (Run Out). As striker he remains himself subject to the Laws. Furthermore, should he be out of his ground for any purpose and the wicket at the wicket-keeper's end be put down he shall be out under Law 38 (Run Out) or Law 39 (Stumped), irrespective of the position of the other batsman or the runner, and no runs shall be scored.

When not the striker, the injured batsman is out of the game and shall stand where he does not interfere with the play. Should he bring himself into the game in any way, then he shall suffer the penalties that any transgression of the Laws demands.

8. Fieldsman Leaving the Field

No fieldsman shall leave the field or return during a session of play without the consent of the umpire at the bowler's end. The umpire's consent is also necessary if a substitute is required for a fieldsman, when his side returns to the field after an interval. If a member of the fielding side leaves the field or fails to return after an interval and is absent from the field for longer than 15 minutes, he shall not be permitted to bowl after his return until he has been on the field for at least that length of playing time for which he was absent. This restriction shall not apply at the start of a new day's play.

9. Batsman Leaving the Field or Retiring

A batsman may leave the field or retire at any time owing to illness, injury or other unavoidable cause, having previously notified the umpire at the bowler's end. He may resume his innings at the fall of a wicket, which for the purposes of this Law shall include the retirement of another batsman.

If he leaves the field or retires for any other reason he may resume his innings only with the consent of the opposing captain.

When a batsman has left the field or retired and is unable to return owing to illness, injury or other unavoidable cause, his innings is to be recorded as "retired, not out". Otherwise it is to be recorded as "retired, out".

10. Commencement of a Batsman's Innings

A batsman shall be considered to have commenced his innings once he has stepped on to the field of play.

Note

(a) Substitutes and Runners

For the purpose of these Laws, allowable illnesses or injuries are those which occur at any time after the nomination by the captains of their teams.

LAW 3. THE UMPIRES

1. Appointment

Before the toss for innings, two umpires shall be appointed, one for each end, to control the game with absolute impartiality as required by the Laws.

2. Change of Umpires

No umpire shall be changed during a match without the consent of both captains.

3. Special Conditions

Before the toss for innings, the umpires shall agree with both captains on any special conditions affecting the conduct of the match.

4. The Wickets

The umpires shall satisfy themselves before the start of the match that the wickets are properly pitched.

5. Clock or Watch

The umpires shall agree between themselves and inform both captains before the start of the match on the watch or clock to be followed during the match.

6. Conduct and Implements

Before and during a match the umpires shall ensure that the conduct of the game and the implements used are strictly in accordance with the Laws.

7. Fair and Unfair Play

The umpires shall be the sole judges of fair and unfair play.

8. Fitness of Ground, Weather and Light

(a) The umpires shall be the sole judges of the fitness of the ground, weather and light for play.

(i) However, before deciding to suspend play, or not to start play, or not to resume play after an interval or stoppage, the umpires shall establish whether both captains (the batsmen at the wicket may deputise for their captain) wish to commence or to continue in the prevailing conditions; if so, their wishes shall be met.

(ii) In addition, if during play the umpires decide that the light is unfit, only the batting side shall have the option of continuing play. After agreeing to continue to play in unfit light conditions, the captain of the batting side (or a batsman at the wicket) may appeal against the light to the umpires, who shall uphold the appeal only if, in their opinion, the light has deteriorated since the agreement to continue was made.

(b) After any suspension of play, the umpires, unaccompanied by any of the players or officials, shall, on their own initiative, carry out an inspection immediately the conditions improve and shall continue to inspect at intervals. Immediately the umpires decide that play is possible they shall call upon the players to resume the game.

9. Exceptional Circumstances

In exceptional circumstances, other than those of weather, ground or light, the umpires may decide to suspend or abandon play. Before making such a decision the umpires shall establish, if the circumstances allow, whether both captains (the batsmen at the wicket may deputise for their captain) wish to continue in the prevailing conditions; if so, their wishes shall be met.

10. Position of Umpires

The umpires shall stand where they can best see any act upon which their decision may be required.

Subject to this over-riding consideration, the umpire at the bowler's end shall stand where he does not interfere with either the bowler's run-up or the striker's view.

The umpire at the striker's end may elect to stand on the off instead of the leg side of the pitch, provided he informs the captain of the fielding side and the striker of his intention to do so.

11. Umpires Changing Ends

The umpires shall change ends after each side has had one innings.

12. Disputes

All disputes shall be determined by the umpires, and if they disagree the actual state of things shall continue.

13. Signals

The following code of signals shall be used by umpires who will wait until a signal has been answered by a scorer before allowing the game to proceed.

Boundary	– by waving the arm from side to side.
Boundary 6	– by raising both arms above the head.
Bye	– by raising an open hand above the head.
Dead Ball	– by crossing and re-crossing the wrists below the waist.
Leg-bye	– by touching a raised knee with the hand.
No-ball	– by extending one arm horizontally.
Out	– by raising the index finger above the head. If not out, the umpire shall call "not out".
Short Run	– by bending the arm upwards and by touching the nearer shoulder with the tips of the fingers.
Wide	– by extending both arms horizontally.

14. Correctness of Scores

The umpires shall be responsible for satisfying themselves on the correctness of the scores throughout and at the conclusion of the match. See Law 21.6 (Correctness of Result).

Notes

(a) Attendance of Umpires
The umpires should be present on the ground and report to the ground executive or the equivalent at least 30 minutes before the start of a day's play.

(b) Consultation between Umpires and Scorers
Consultation between umpires and scorers over doubtful points is essential.

(c) Fitness of Ground
The umpires shall consider the ground as unfit for play when it is so wet or slippery as to deprive the bowlers of a reasonable foothold, the fieldsmen, other than the deep-fielders, of the power of free movement, or the batsmen of the ability to play their strokes or to run between the wickets. Play should not be suspended merely because the grass and the ball are wet and slippery.

(d) Fitness of Weather and Light
The umpires should suspend play only when they consider that the conditions are so bad that it is unreasonable or dangerous to continue.

LAW 4. THE SCORERS

1. Recording Runs

All runs scored shall be recorded by scorers appointed for the purpose. Where there are two scorers they shall frequently check to ensure that the score-sheets agree.

2. Acknowledging Signals

The scorers shall accept and immediately acknowledge all instructions and signals given to them by the umpires.

LAW 5. THE BALL

1. Weight and Size

The ball, when new, shall weigh not less than $5\frac{1}{2}$ ounces/155.9g, nor more than $5\frac{3}{4}$ ounces/163g; and shall measure not less than $8\frac{13}{16}$ inches/22.4cm, nor more than 9 inches/22.9cm in circumference.

2. Approval of Balls

All balls used in matches shall be approved by the umpires and captains before the start of the match.

3. New Ball

Subject to agreement to the contrary, having been made before the toss, either captain may demand a new ball at the start of each innings.

4. New Ball in Match of Three or More Days' Duration

In a match of three or more days' duration, the captain of the fielding side may demand a new ball after the prescribed number of overs has been bowled with the old one. The governing body for cricket in the country concerned shall decide the number of overs applicable in that country, which shall be not less than 75 six-ball overs (55 eight-ball overs).

5. Ball Lost or Becoming Unfit for Play

In the event of a ball during play being lost or, in the opinion of the umpires, becoming unfit for play, the umpires shall allow it to be replaced by one that in their opinion has had a similar amount of wear. If a ball is to be replaced, the umpires shall inform the batsman.

Note

(a) Specifications
The specifications, as described in 1 above, shall apply to top-grade balls only. The following degrees of tolerance will be acceptable for other grades of ball.

(i) *Men's Grades 2–4*
Weight: $5\frac{5}{16}$ ounces/150g to $5\frac{13}{16}$ ounces/165g.
Size: $8\frac{11}{16}$ inches/22.0cm to $9\frac{1}{16}$ inches/23.0cm.

(ii) *Women's*
Weight: $4\frac{15}{16}$ ounces/140g to $5\frac{5}{16}$ ounces/150g.
Size: $8\frac{1}{4}$ inches/21.0cm to $8\frac{7}{8}$ inches/22.5cm.

(iii) *Junior*
Weight: $4\frac{11}{16}$ ounces/133g to $5\frac{1}{16}$ ounces/143g.
Size: $8\frac{1}{16}$ inches/20.5cm to $8\frac{11}{16}$ inches/22.0cm.

LAW 6. THE BAT

1. Width and Length

The bat overall shall not be more than 38 inches/96.5cm in length; the blade of the bat shall be made of wood and shall not exceed $4\frac{1}{4}$ inches/10.8cm at the widest part.

Note

(a) The blade of the bat may be covered with material for protection, strengthening or repair. Such material shall not exceed $\frac{1}{16}$ inch/1.56mm in thickness.

LAW 7. THE PITCH

1. Area of Pitch

The pitch is the area between the bowling creases – see Law 9 (The Bowling and Popping Creases). It shall measure 5 feet/1.52m in width on either side of a line joining the centre of the middle stumps of the wickets – see Law 8 (The Wickets).

2. Selection and Preparation

Before the toss for innings, the executive of the ground shall be responsible for the selection and preparation of the pitch; thereafter the umpires shall control its use and maintenance.

3. Changing Pitch

The pitch shall not be changed during a match unless it becomes unfit for play; and then only with the consent of both captains.

4. Non-Turf Pitches

In the event of a non-turf pitch being used, the following shall apply:

(a) Length: That of the playing surface to a minimum of 58 feet/17.68m.

(b) Width: That of the playing surface to a minimum of 6 feet/1.83m.

See Law 10 (Rolling, Sweeping, Mowing, Watering the Pitch and Re-marking of Creases) Note (a).

LAW 8. THE WICKETS

1. Width and Pitching

Two sets of wickets, each 9 inches/22.86cm wide, and consisting of three wooden stumps with two wooden bails upon the top, shall be pitched opposite and parallel to each other at a distance of 22 yards/20.12m between the centres of the two middle stumps.

2. Size of Stumps

The stumps shall be of equal and sufficient size to prevent the ball from passing between them. Their tops shall be 28 inches/71.1cm above the ground, and shall be dome-shaped except for the bail grooves.

3. Size of Bails

The bails shall be each $4\frac{3}{8}$ inches/11.1cm in length and when in position on the top of the stumps shall not project more than $\frac{1}{2}$ inch/1.3cm above them.

Notes

(a) Dispensing with Bails
In a high wind the umpires may decide to dispense with the use of bails.

(b) Junior Cricket
For junior cricket, as defined by the local governing body, the following measurements for the wickets shall apply:

Width – 8 inches/20.32cm.
Pitched – 21 yards/19.20m.
Height – 27 inches/68.58cm.
Bails – each $3\frac{7}{8}$ inches/9.84cm in length and should not project more than $\frac{1}{2}$ inch/1.3cm above the stumps.

LAW 9. THE BOWLING, POPPING AND RETURN CREASES

1. The Bowling Crease

The bowling crease shall be marked in line with the stumps at each end and shall be 8 feet 8 inches/2.64m in length, with the stumps in the centre.

2. The Popping Crease

The popping crease, which is the back edge of the crease marking, shall be in front of and parallel with the bowling crease. It shall have the back edge of the crease marking 4 feet/1.22m from the centre of the stumps and shall extend to a minimum of 6 feet/1.83m on either side of the line of the wicket.

The popping crease shall be considered to be unlimited in length.

3. The Return Crease

The return crease marking, of which the inside edge is the crease, shall be at each end of the bowling crease and at right angles to it. The return crease shall be marked to a minimum of 4 feet/1.22m behind the wicket and shall be considered to be unlimited in length. A forward extension shall be marked to the popping crease.

LAW 10. ROLLING, SWEEPING, MOWING, WATERING THE PITCH AND RE-MARKING OF CREASES

1. Rolling

During the match the pitch may be rolled at the request of the captain of the batting side, for a period of not more than seven minutes before the start of each innings, other than the first innings of the match, and before the start of each day's play. In addition, if, after the toss and before the first innings of the match, the start is delayed, the captain of the batting side may request to have the pitch rolled for not more than seven minutes. However, if in the opinion of the umpires the delay has had no significant effect upon the state of the pitch, they shall refuse any request for the rolling of the pitch.

The pitch shall not otherwise be rolled during the match.

The seven minutes' rolling permitted before the start of a day's play shall take place not earlier than half an hour before the start of play and the captain of the batting side may delay such rolling until ten minutes before the start of play should he so desire.

If a captain declares an innings closed less than 15 minutes before the resumption of play, and the other captain is thereby prevented from exercising his option of seven minutes' rolling or if he is so prevented for any other reason, the time for rolling shall be taken out of the normal playing time.

2. Sweeping

Such sweeping of the pitch as is necessary during the match shall be done so that the seven minutes allowed for rolling the pitch, provided for in 1 above, is not affected.

3. Mowing

(a) Responsibilities of Ground Authority and of Umpires
All mowings which are carried out before the toss for innings shall be the responsibility of the ground authority; thereafter they shall be carried out under the supervision of the umpires. See Law 7.2 (Selection and Preparation).

(b) Initial Mowing
The pitch shall be mown before play begins on the day the match is scheduled to start, or in the case of a delayed start on the day the match is expected to start. See 3(a) above (Responsibilities of Ground Authority and of Umpires).

(c) Subsequent Mowings in a Match of Two or More Days' Duration
In a match of two or more days' duration, the pitch shall be mown daily before play begins. Should this mowing not take place because of weather conditions, rest days or other reasons, the pitch shall be mown on the first day on which the match is resumed.

(d) Mowing of the Outfield in a Match of Two or More Days' Duration
In order to ensure that conditions are as similar as possible for both sides, the outfield shall normally be mown before the commencement of play on each day of the match, if ground and weather conditions allow. See Note (b) to this Law.

4. Watering

The pitch shall not be watered during a match.

5. Re-marking Creases

Whenever possible the creases shall be re-marked.

6. Maintenance of Foot-holes

In wet weather, the umpires shall ensure that the holes made by the bowlers and batsmen are cleaned out and dried whenever necessary to facilitate play. In matches of two or more days' duration, the umpires shall allow, if necessary, the re-turfing of foot-holes made by the bowler in his delivery stride, or the use of quick-setting fillings for the same purpose, before the start of each day's play.

7. Securing of Footholds and Maintenance of Pitch

During play, the umpires shall allow either batsman to beat the pitch with his bat and players to secure their footholds by the use of sawdust, provided that no damage to the pitch is so caused, and Law 42 (Unfair Play) is not contravened.

Notes

(a) Non-turf Pitches
The above Law 10 applies to turf pitches.

The game is played on non-turf pitches in many countries at various levels. Whilst the conduct of the game on these surfaces should always be in accordance with the Laws of Cricket, it is recognised that it may sometimes be necessary for governing bodies to lay down special playing conditions to suit the type of non-turf pitch used in their country.

In matches played against touring teams, any special playing conditions should be agreed in advance by both parties.

(b) Mowing of the Outfield in a Match of Two or More Days' Duration
If, for reasons other than ground and weather conditions, daily and complete mowing is not possible, the ground authority shall notify the captains and umpires, before the toss for innings, of the procedure to be adopted for such mowing during the match.

(c) Choice of Roller
If there is more than one roller available, the captain of the batting side shall have a choice.

LAW 11. COVERING THE PITCH

1. Before the Start of a Match

Before the start of a match, complete covering of the pitch shall be allowed.

2. During a Match

The pitch shall not be completely covered during a match unless prior arrangement or regulations so provide.

3. Covering Bowlers' Run-up

Whenever possible, the bowlers' run-up shall be covered, but the covers so used shall not extend further than 4 feet/1.22m in front of the popping crease.

Note

(a) Removal of Covers
The covers should be removed as promptly as possible whenever the weather permits.

LAW 12. INNINGS

1. Number of Innings

A match shall be of one or two innings of each side according to agreement reached before the start of play.

2. Alternate Innings

In a two-innings match each side shall take their innings alternately except in the case provided for in Law 13 (The Follow-on).

3. The Toss

The captains shall toss for the choice of innings on the field of play not later than 15 minutes before the time scheduled for the match to start, or before the time agreed upon for play to start.

4. Choice of Innings

The winner of the toss shall notify his decision to bat or to field to the opposing captain not later than ten minutes before the time scheduled for the match to start, or before the time agreed upon for play to start. The decision shall not thereafter be altered.

5. Continuation after One Innings of Each Side

Despite the terms of 1 above, in a one-innings match, when a result has been reached on the first innings, the captains may agree to the continuation of play if, in their opinion, there is a prospect of carrying the game to a further issue in the time left. See Law 21 (Result).

Notes

(a) Limited Innings – One-innings Match
In a one-innings match, each innings may, by agreement, be limited by a number of overs or by a period of time.

(b) Limited Innings – Two-innings Match
In a two-innings match, the first innings of each side may, by agreement, be limited to a number of overs or by a period of time.

LAW 13. THE FOLLOW-ON

1. Lead on First Innings

In a two-innings match the side which bats first and leads by 200 runs in a match of five days or more, by 150 runs in a three-day or four-day match, by 100 runs in a two-day match, or by 75 runs in a one-day match, shall have the option of requiring the other side to follow their innings.

2. Day's Play Lost

If no play takes place on the first day of a match of two or more days' duration, 1 above shall apply in accordance with the number of days' play remaining from the actual start of the match.

LAW 14. DECLARATIONS

1. Time of Declaration

The captain of the batting side may declare an innings closed at any time during a match, irrespective of its duration.

2. Forfeiture of Second Innings

A captain may forfeit his second innings, provided his decision to do so is notified to the opposing captain and umpires in sufficient time to allow seven minutes' rolling of the pitch. See Law 10 (Rolling, Sweeping, Mowing, Watering the Pitch and Re-marking of Creases). The normal ten-minute interval between innings shall be applied.

LAW 15. START OF PLAY

1. Call of Play

At the start of each innings and of each day's play, and on the resumption of play after any interval or interruption, the umpire at the bowler's end shall call "play".

2. Practice on the Field

At no time on any day of the match shall there be any bowling or batting practice on the pitch.

No practice may take place on the field if, in the opinion of the umpires, it could result in a waste of time.

3. Trial Run-up

No bowler shall have a trial run-up after "play" has been called in any session of play, except at the fall of a wicket when an umpire may allow such a trial run-up if he is satisfied that it will not cause any waste of time.

LAW 16. INTERVALS

1. Length

The umpire shall allow such intervals as have been agreed upon for meals, and ten minutes between each innings.

2. Luncheon Interval – Innings Ending or Stoppage within Ten Minutes of Interval

If an innings ends or there is a stoppage caused by weather or bad light within ten minutes of the agreed time for the luncheon interval, the interval shall be taken immediately.

The time remaining in the session of play shall be added to the agreed length of the interval but no extra allowance shall be made for the ten-minute interval between innings.

3. Tea Interval – Innings Ending or Stoppage within 30 Minutes of Interval

If an innings ends or there is a stoppage caused by weather or bad light within 30 minutes of the agreed time for the tea interval, the interval shall be taken immediately.

The interval shall be of the agreed length and, if applicable, shall include the ten-minute interval between innings.

4. Tea Interval – Continuation of Play

If, at the agreed time for the tea interval, nine wickets are down, play shall continue for a period not exceeding 30 minutes or until the innings is concluded.

5. Tea Interval – Agreement to Forgo

At any time during the match, the captains may agree to forgo a tea interval.

6. Intervals for Drinks

If both captains agree before the start of a match that intervals for drinks may be taken, the option to take such intervals shall be available to either side. These intervals shall be restricted to one per session, shall be kept as short as possible, shall not be taken in the last hour of the match, and in any case shall not exceed five minutes.

The agreed times for these intervals shall be strictly adhered to, except that if a wicket falls within five minutes of the agreed time then drinks shall be taken out immediately.

If an innings ends or there is a stoppage caused by weather or bad light within 30 minutes of the agreed time for a drinks interval, there will be no interval for drinks in that session.

At any time during the match the captains may agree to forgo any such drinks interval.

Notes

(a) Tea Interval – One-day Match
In a one-day match, a specific time for the tea interval need not necessarily be arranged, and it may be agreed to take this interval between the innings of a one-innings match.

(b) Changing the Agreed Time of Intervals
In the event of the ground, weather or light conditions causing a suspension of play, the umpires, after consultation with the captains, may decide in the interests of time-saving to bring forward the time of the luncheon or tea interval.

LAW 17. CESSATION OF PLAY

1. Call of Time

The umpire at the bowler's end shall call "time" on the cessation of play before any interval or interruption of play, at the end of each day's play, and at the conclusion of the match. See Law 27 (Appeals).

2. Removal of Bails

After the call of "time", the umpires shall remove the bails from both wickets.

3. Starting a Last Over

The last over before an interval or the close of play shall be started provided the umpire, after walking at his normal pace, has arrived at his position behind the stumps at the bowler's end before time has been reached.

4. Completion of the Last Over of a Session

The last over before an interval or the close of play shall be completed unless a batsman is out or retires during that over within two minutes of the interval or the close of play or unless the players have occasion to leave the field.

5. Completion of the Last Over of a Match

An over in progress at the close of play on the final day of a match shall be completed at the request of either captain, even if a wicket falls after time has been reached.

If, during the last over, the players have occasion to leave the field, the umpires shall call "time" and there shall be no resumption of play and the match shall be at an end.

6. Last Hour of Match – Number of Overs

The umpires shall indicate when one hour of playing time of the match remains according to the agreed hours of play. The next over after that moment shall be the first of a minimum of 20 six-ball overs (15 eight-ball overs), provided a result is not reached earlier or there is no interval or interruption of play.

7. Last Hour of Match – Intervals between Innings and Interruptions of Play

If, at the commencement of the last hour of the match, an interval or interruption of play is in progress or if, during the last hour, there is an interval between innings or an interruption of play, the minimum number of overs to be bowled on the resumption of play shall be reduced in proportion to the duration, within the last hour of the match, of any such interval or interruption.

The minimum number of overs to be bowled after the resumption of play shall be calculated as follows:

(a) In the case of an interval or interruption of play being in progress at the commencement of the last hour of the match, or in the case of a first interval or interruption, a deduction shall be made from the minimum of 20 six-ball overs (or 15 eight-ball overs).

(b) If there is a later interval or interruption, a further deduction shall be made from the minimum number of overs which should have been bowled following the last resumption of play.

(c) These deductions shall be based on the following factors:

(i) The number of overs already bowled in the last hour of the match or, in the case of a later interval or interruption, in the last session of play.

(ii) The number of overs lost as a result of the interval or interruption allowing one six-ball over for every full three minutes (or one eight-ball over for every full four minutes) of interval or interruption.

(iii) Any over left uncompleted at the end of an innings to be excluded from these calculations.

(iv) Any over of the minimum number to be played which is left uncompleted at the start of an interruption of play to be completed when play is resumed and to count as one over bowled.

(v) An interval to start with the end of an innings and to end ten minutes later; an interruption to start on the call of "time" and to end on the call of "play".

(d) In the event of an innings being completed and a new innings commencing during the last hour of the match, the number of overs to be bowled in the new innings shall be calculated on the basis of one six-ball over for every three minutes or part thereof remaining for play (or one eight-ball over for every four minutes or part thereof remaining for play); or alternatively on the basis that sufficient overs be bowled to enable the full minimum quota of overs to be completed under circumstances governed by (a), (b) and (c) above. In all such cases the alternative which allows the greater number of overs shall be employed.

8. Bowler Unable to Complete an Over during Last Hour of the Match

If, for any reason, a bowler is unable to complete an over during the period of play referred to in 6 above, Law 22.7 (Bowler Incapacitated or Suspended during an Over) shall apply.

LAW 18. SCORING

1. A Run

The score shall be reckoned by runs. A run is scored:

(a) So often as the batsmen, after a hit or at any time while the ball is in play, shall have crossed and made good their ground from end to end.

(b) When a boundary is scored. See Law 19 (Boundaries).

(c) When penalty runs are awarded. See 6 below.

2. Short Runs

(a) If either batsman runs a short run, the umpire shall call and signal "one short" as soon as the ball becomes dead and that run shall not be scored. A run is short if a batsman fails to make good his ground on turning for a further run.

(b) Although a short run shortens the succeeding one, the latter, if completed, shall count.

(c) If either or both batsmen deliberately run short the umpire shall, as soon as he sees that the fielding side have no chance of dismissing either batsman, call and signal "dead ball" and disallow any runs attempted or previously scored. The batsmen shall return to their original ends.

(d) If both batsmen run short in one and the same run, only one run shall be deducted.

(e) Only if three or more runs are attempted can more than one be short and then, subject to (c) and (d) above, all runs so called shall be disallowed. If there has been more than one short run the umpires shall instruct the scorers as to the number of runs disallowed.

3. Striker Caught

If the striker is caught, no run shall be scored.

4. Batsman Run Out

If a batsman is run out, only that run which was being attempted shall not be scored. If, however, an injured striker himself is run out, no runs shall be scored. See Law 2.7 (Transgression of the Laws by an Injured Batsman or Runner).

5. Batsman Obstructing the Field

If a batsman is out Obstructing the Field, any runs completed before the obstruction occurs shall be scored unless such obstruction prevents a catch being made, in which case no runs shall be scored.

6. Runs Scored for Penalties

Runs shall be scored for penalties under Laws 20 (Lost Ball), 24 (No-ball), 25 (Wide-ball), 41.1 (Fielding the Ball) and for boundary allowances under Law 19 (Boundaries).

7. Batsman Returning to Wicket he has Left

If, while the ball is in play, the batsmen have crossed in running, neither shall return to the wicket he has left, even though a short run has been called or no run has been scored as in the case of a catch. Batsmen, however, shall return to the wickets they originally left in the cases of a boundary and of any disallowance of runs and of an injured batsman being, himself, run out. See Law 2.7 (Transgression by an Injured Batsman or Runner).

Note

(a) Short Run
A striker taking stance in front of his popping crease may run from that point without penalty.

LAW 19. BOUNDARIES

1. The Boundary of the Playing Area

Before the toss for innings, the umpires shall agree with both captains on the boundary of the playing area. The boundary shall, if possible, be marked by a white line, a rope laid on the ground, or a fence. If flags or posts only are used to mark a boundary, the imaginary line joining such points shall be regarded as the boundary. An obstacle, or person, within the playing area shall not be regarded as a boundary unless so decided by the umpires before the toss for innings. Sightscreens within, or partially within, the playing area shall be regarded as the boundary and when the ball strikes or passes within or under or directly over any part of the screen, a boundary shall be scored.

2. Runs Scored for Boundaries

Before the toss for innings, the umpires shall agree with both captains the runs to be allowed for boundaries, and in deciding the allowance for them, the umpires and captains shall be guided by the prevailing custom of the ground. The allowance for a boundary shall normally be four runs, and six runs for all hits pitching over and clear of the boundary line or fence, even though the ball has been previously touched by a fieldsman. Six runs shall also be scored if a fieldsman, after catching a ball, carries it over the boundary. See Law 32 (Caught) Note (a). Six runs shall not be scored when a ball struck by the striker hits a sightscreen full pitch if the screen is within, or partially within, the playing area, but if the ball is struck directly over a sightscreen so situated, six runs shall be scored.

3. A Boundary

A boundary shall be scored and signalled by the umpire at the bowler's end whenever, in his opinion:

(a) A ball in play touches or crosses the boundary, however marked.

(b) A fieldsman with ball in hand touches or grounds any part of his person on or over a boundary line.

(c) A fieldsman with ball in hand grounds any part of his person over a boundary fence or board. This allows the fieldsman to touch or lean on or over a boundary fence or board in preventing a boundary.

4. Runs Exceeding Boundary Allowance

The runs completed at the instant the ball reaches the boundary shall count if they exceed the boundary allowance.

5. Overthrows or Wilful Act of a Fieldsman

If the boundary results from an overthrow or from the wilful act of a fieldsman, any runs already completed and the allowance shall be added to the score. The run in progress shall count provided that the batsmen have crossed at the instant of the throw or act.

Note

(a) Position of Sightscreens
Sightscreens should, if possible, be positioned wholly outside the playing area, as near as possible to the boundary line.

LAW 20. LOST BALL

1. Runs Scored

If a ball in play cannot be found or recovered, any fieldsman may call "lost ball" when six runs shall be added to the score; but if more than six have been run before "lost ball" is called, as many runs as have been completed shall be scored. The run in progress shall count provided that the batsmen have crossed at the instant of the call of "lost ball".

2. How Scored

The runs shall be added to the score of the striker if the ball has been struck, but otherwise to the score of byes, leg-byes, no-balls or wides as the case may be.

LAW 21. THE RESULT

1. A Win – Two-innings Matches

The side which has scored a total of runs in excess of that scored by the opposing side in its two completed innings shall be the winner.

2. A Win – One-innings Matches

(a) One-innings matches, unless played out as in 1 above, shall be decided on the first innings, but see Law 12.5 (Continuation after One Innings of Each Side).

(b) If the captains agree to continue play after the completion of one innings of each side in accordance with Law 12.5 (Continuation after One Innings of Each Side) and a result is not achieved on the second innings, the first innings result shall stand.

3. Umpires Awarding a Match

(a) A match shall be lost by a side which, during the match, (i) refuses to play, or (ii) concedes defeat, and the umpires shall award the match to the other side.

(b) Should both batsmen at the wickets or the fielding side leave the field at any time without the agreement of the umpires, this shall constitute a refusal to play and, on appeal, the umpires shall award the match to the other side in accordance with (a) above.

4. A Tie

The result of a match shall be a tie when the scores are equal at the conclusion of play, but only if the side batting last has completed its innings.

If the scores of the completed first innings of a one-day match are equal, it shall be a tie but only if the match has not been played out to a further conclusion.

5. A Draw

A match not determined in any of the ways as in 1, 2, 3 and 4 above shall count as a draw.

6. Correctness of Result

Any decision as to the correctness of the scores shall be the responsibility of the umpires. See Law 3.14 (Correctness of Scores).

If, after the umpires and players have left the field in the belief that the match has been concluded, the umpires decide that a mistake in scoring has occurred, which affects the result, and provided time has not been reached, they shall order play to resume and to continue until the agreed finishing time unless a result is reached earlier.

If the umpires decide that a mistake has occurred and time has been reached, the umpires shall immediately inform both captains of the necessary corrections to the scores and, if applicable, to the result.

7. Acceptance of Result

In accepting the scores as notified by the scorers and agreed by the umpires, the captains of both sides thereby accept the result.

Notes

(a) Statement of Results

The result of a finished match is stated as a win by runs, except in the case of a win by the side batting last when it is by the number of wickets still then to fall.

(b) Winning Hit or Extras

As soon as the side has won, see 1 and 2 above, the umpire shall call "time", the match is finished, and nothing that happens thereafter other than as a result of a mistake in scoring (see 6 above) shall be regarded as part of the match.

However, if a boundary constitutes the winning hit – or extras – and the boundary allowance exceeds the number of runs required to win the match, such runs scored shall be credited to the side's total and, in the case of a hit, to the striker's score.

LAW 22. THE OVER

1. Number of Balls

The ball shall be bowled from each wicket alternately in overs of either six or eight balls according to agreement before the match.

2. Call of "Over"

When the agreed number of balls has been bowled, and as the ball becomes dead or when it becomes clear to the umpire at the bowler's end that both the fielding side and the batsmen at the wicket have ceased to regard the ball as in play, the umpire shall call "over" before leaving the wicket.

3. No-ball or Wide-ball

Neither a no-ball nor a wide-ball shall be reckoned as one of the over.

4. Umpire Miscounting

If an umpire miscounts the number of balls, the over as counted by the umpire shall stand.

5. Bowler Changing Ends

A bowler shall be allowed to change ends as often as desired, provided only that he does not bowl two overs consecutively in an innings.

6. The Bowler Finishing an Over

A bowler shall finish an over in progress unless he be incapacitated or be suspended under Law 42.8 (The Bowling of Fast Short-pitched Balls), 9 (The Bowling of Fast High Full Pitches), 10 (Time Wasting) and 11 (Players Damaging the Pitch). If an over is left incomplete for any reason at the start of an interval or interruption of play, it shall be finished on the resumption of play.

7. Bowler Incapacitated or Suspended during an Over

If, for any reason, a bowler is incapacitated while running up to bowl the first ball of an over, or is incapacitated or suspended during an over, the umpire shall call and signal "dead ball" and another bowler shall be allowed to bowl or complete the over from the same end, provided only that he shall not bowl two overs, or part thereof, consecutively in one innings.

8. Position of Non-striker

The batsman at the bowler's end shall normally stand on the opposite side of the wicket to that from which the ball is being delivered, unless a request to do otherwise is granted by the umpire.

LAW 23. DEAD BALL

1. The Ball Becomes Dead

When:

(a) It is finally settled in the hands of the wicket-keeper or the bowler.

(b) It reaches or pitches over the boundary.

(c) A batsman is out.

(d) Whether played or not, it lodges in the clothing or equipment of a batsman or the clothing of an umpire.

(e) A ball lodges in a protective helmet worn by a member of the fielding side.

(f) A penalty is awarded under Law 20 (Lost Ball) or Law 41.1 (Fielding the Ball).

(g) The umpire calls "over" or "time".

2. Either Umpire Shall Call and Signal "Dead Ball"

When:

(a) He intervenes in a case of unfair play.

(b) A serious injury to a player or umpire occurs.

(c) He is satisfied that, for an adequate reason, the striker is not ready to receive the ball and makes no attempt to play it.

(d) The bowler drops the ball accidentally before delivery, or the ball does not leave his hand for any reason other than in an attempt to run out the non-striker (See Law 24.5 – Bowler Attempting to Run Out Non-striker before Delivery).

(e) One or both bails fall from the striker's wicket before he receives delivery.

(f) He leaves his normal position for consultation.

(g) He is required to do so under Law 26.3 (Disallowance of Leg-byes), etc.

3. The Ball Ceases to be Dead

When:

(a) The bowler starts his run-up or bowling action.

4. The Ball is Not Dead

When:

(a) It strikes an umpire (unless it lodges in his dress).

(b) The wicket is broken or struck down (unless a batsman is out thereby).

(c) An unsuccessful appeal is made.

(d) The wicket is broken accidentally either by the bowler during his delivery or by a batsman in running.

(e) The umpire has called "no-ball" or "wide".

Notes

(a) Ball Finally Settled

Whether the ball is finally settled or not – see 1(a) above – must be a question for the umpires alone to decide.

(b) Action on Call of "Dead Ball"

(i) If "dead ball" is called prior to the striker receiving a delivery, the bowler shall be allowed an additional ball.

(ii) If "dead ball" is called after the striker receives a delivery, the bowler shall not be allowed an additional ball, unless a "no-ball" or "wide" has been called.

LAW 24. NO-BALL

1. Mode of Delivery

The umpire shall indicate to the striker whether the bowler intends to bowl over or round the wicket, overarm or underarm, right or left-handed. Failure on the part of the bowler to indicate in advance a change in his mode of delivery is unfair and the umpire shall call and signal "no-ball".

2. Fair Delivery – The Arm

For a delivery to be fair the ball must be bowled, not thrown – see Note (a) below. If either umpire is not entirely satisfied with the absolute fairness of a delivery in this respect he shall call and signal "no-ball" instantly upon delivery.

3. Fair Delivery – The Feet

The umpire at the bowler's wicket shall call and signal "no-ball" if he is not satisfied that in the delivery stride:

(a) The bowler's back foot has landed within and not touching the return crease or its forward extension; or

(b) Some part of the front foot whether grounded or raised was behind the popping crease.

4. Bowler Throwing at Striker's Wicket before Delivery

If the bowler, before delivering the ball, throws it at the striker's wicket in an attempt to run him out, the umpire shall call and signal "no-ball". See Law 42.12 (Batsman Unfairly Stealing a Run) and Law 38 (Run Out).

5. Bowler Attempting to Run Out Non-striker before Delivery

If the bowler, before delivering the ball, attempts to run out the non-striker, any runs which result shall be allowed and shall be scored as no-balls. Such an attempt shall not count as a ball in the over. The umpire shall not call "no-ball". See Law 42.12 (Batsman Unfairly Stealing a Run).

6. Infringement of Laws by a Wicket-keeper or a Fieldsman

The umpire shall call and signal "no-ball" in the event of the wicket-keeper infringing Law 40.1 (Position of Wicket-keeper) or a fieldsman infringing Law 41.2 (Limitation of On-side Fieldsmen) or Law 41.3 (Position of Fieldsmen).

7. Revoking a Call

An umpire shall revoke the call "no-ball" if the ball does not leave the bowler's hand for any reason. See Law 23.2 (Either Umpire Shall Call and Signal "Dead Ball").

8. Penalty

A penalty of one run for a no-ball shall be scored if no runs are made otherwise.

9. Runs from a No-ball

The striker may hit a no-ball and whatever runs result shall be added to his score. Runs made otherwise from a no-ball shall be scored no-balls.

10. Out from a No-ball

The striker shall be out from a no-ball if he breaks Law 34 (Hit the Ball Twice) and either batsman may be run out or shall be given out if either breaks Law 33 (Handled the Ball) or Law 37 (Obstructing the Field).

11. Batsman Given Out off a No-ball

Should a batsman be given out off a no-ball the penalty for bowling it shall stand unless runs are otherwise scored.

Notes

(a) Definition of a Throw
A ball shall be deemed to have been thrown if, in the opinion of either umpire, the process of straightening the bowling arm, whether it be partial or complete, takes place during that part of the delivery swing which directly precedes the ball leaving the hand. This definition shall not debar a bowler from the use of the wrist in the delivery swing.

(b) No-ball Not Counting in Over
A no-ball shall not be reckoned as one of the over. See Law 22.3 (No-ball or Wide-ball).

LAW 25. WIDE-BALL

1. Judging a Wide

If the bowler bowls the ball so high over or so wide of the wicket that, in the opinion of the umpire, it passes out of reach of the striker, standing in a normal guard position, the umpire shall call and signal "wide-ball" as soon as it has passed the line of the striker's wicket.

The umpire shall not adjudge a ball as being wide if:

(a) The striker, by moving from his guard position, causes the ball to pass out of his reach.

(b) The striker moves and thus brings the ball within his reach.

2. Penalty

A penalty of one run for a wide shall be scored if no runs are made otherwise.

3. Ball Coming to Rest in Front of the Striker

If a ball which the umpire considers to have been delivered comes to rest in front of the line of the striker's wicket, "wide" shall not be called. The striker has a right, without interference from the fielding side, to make one attempt to hit the ball. If the fielding side interfere, the umpire shall replace the ball where it came to rest and shall order the fieldsmen to resume the places they occupied in the field before the ball was delivered.

The umpire shall call and signal "dead ball" as soon as it is clear that the striker does not intend to hit the ball, or after the striker has made an unsuccessful attempt to hit the ball.

4. Revoking a Call

The umpire shall revoke the call if the striker hits a ball which has been called "wide".

5. Ball Not Dead

The ball does not become dead on the call of "wide-ball" – see Law 23.4 (The Ball is Not Dead).

6. Runs Resulting from a Wide

All runs which are run or result from a wide-ball which is not a no-ball shall be scored wide-balls, or if no runs are made one shall be scored.

7. Out from a Wide

The striker shall be out from a wide-ball if he breaks Law 35 (Hit Wicket), or Law 39 (Stumped). Either batsman may be run out and shall be out if he breaks Law 33 (Handled the Ball), or Law 37 (Obstructing the Field).

8. Batsman Given Out off a Wide

Should a batsman be given out off a wide, the penalty for bowling it shall stand unless runs are otherwise made.

Note

(a) Wide-ball Not Counting in Over
A wide-ball shall not be reckoned as one of the over – see Law 22.3 (No-ball or Wide-ball).

LAW 26. BYE AND LEG-BYE

1. Byes

If the ball, not having been called "wide" or "no-ball", passes the striker without touching his bat or person, and any runs are obtained, the umpire shall signal "bye" and the run or runs shall be credited as such to the batting side.

2. Leg-byes

If the ball, not having been called "wide" or "no-ball", is unintentionally deflected by the striker's dress or person, except a hand holding the bat, and any runs are obtained the umpire shall signal "leg-bye" and the run or runs so scored shall be credited as such to the batting side.

Such leg-byes shall be scored only if, in the opinion of the umpire, the striker has:

(a) Attempted to play the ball with his bat; or

(b) Tried to avoid being hit by the ball.

3. Disallowance of Leg-byes

In the case of a deflection by the striker's person, other than in 2(a) and (b) above, the umpire shall call and signal "dead ball" as soon as one run has been completed or when it is clear that a run is not being attempted, or the ball has reached the boundary.

On the call and signal of "dead ball" the batsmen shall return to their original ends and no runs shall be allowed.

LAW 27. APPEALS

1. Time of Appeals

The umpires shall not give a batsman out unless appealed to by the other side which shall be done prior to the bowler beginning his run-up or bowling action to deliver the next ball. Under Law 23.1 (g) (The Ball Becomes Dead), the ball is dead on "over" being called; this does not, however, invalidate an appeal made prior to the first ball of the following over provided "time" has not been called – see Law 17.1 (Call of Time).

2. An Appeal "How's That?"

An appeal "How's That?" shall cover all ways of being out.

3. Answering Appeals

The umpire at the bowler's wicket shall answer appeals before the other umpire in all cases except those arising out of Law 35 (Hit Wicket) or Law 39 (Stumped) or Law 38 (Run Out) when this occurs at the striker's wicket.

When either umpire has given a batsman not out, the other umpire shall, within his jurisdiction, answer the appeal or a further appeal, provided it is made in time in accordance with 1 above (Time of Appeals).

4. Consultation by Umpires

An umpire may consult with the other umpire on a point of fact which the latter may have been in a better position to see and shall then give his decision. If, after consultation, there is still doubt remaining the decision shall be in favour of the batsman.

5. Batsman Leaving his Wicket under a Misapprehension

The umpires shall intervene if satisfied that a batsman, not having been given out, has left his wicket under a misapprehension that he has been dismissed.

6. Umpire's Decision

The umpire's decision is final. He may alter his decision, provided that such alteration is made promptly.

7. Withdrawal of an Appeal

In exceptional circumstances the captain of the fielding side may seek permission of the umpire to withdraw an appeal provided the outgoing batsman has not left the playing area. If this is allowed, the umpire shall cancel his decision.

LAW 28. THE WICKET IS DOWN

1. Wicket Down

The wicket is down if:

(a) Either the ball or the striker's bat or person completely removes either bail from the top of the stumps. A disturbance of a bail, whether temporary or not, shall not constitute a complete removal, but the wicket is down if a bail in falling lodges between two of the stumps.

(b) Any player completely removes with his hand or arm a bail from the top of the stumps, provided that the ball is held in that hand or in the hand of the arm so used.

(c) When both bails are off, a stump is struck out of the ground by the ball, or a player strikes or pulls a stump out of the ground, providing that the ball is held in the hand(s) or in the hand of the arm so used.

2. One Bail Off

If one bail is off, it shall be sufficient for the purpose of putting the wicket down to remove the remaining bail, or to strike or pull any of the three stumps out of the ground in any of the ways stated in 1 above.

3. All the Stumps Out of the Ground

If all the stumps are out of the ground, the fielding side shall be allowed to put back one or more stumps in order to have an opportunity of putting the wicket down.

4. Dispensing with Bails

If, owing to the strength of the wind, it has been agreed to dispense with the bails in accordance with Law 8, Note (a) (Dispensing with Bails), the decision as to when the wicket is down is one for the umpires to decide on the facts before them. In such circumstances and if the umpires so decide, the wicket shall be held to be down even though a stump has not been struck out of the ground.

Note

(a) Remaking the Wicket
If the wicket is broken while the ball is in play, it is not the umpire's duty to remake the wicket until the ball has become dead – see Law 23 (Dead Ball). A member of the fielding side, however, may remake the wicket in such circumstances.

LAW 29. BATSMAN OUT OF HIS GROUND

1. When out of his Ground

A batsman shall be considered to be out of his ground unless some part of his bat in his hand or of his person is grounded behind the line of the popping crease.

LAW 30. BOWLED

1. Out Bowled

The striker shall be out *Bowled* if:

(a) His wicket is bowled down, even if the ball first touches his bat or person.

(b) He breaks his wicket by hitting or kicking the ball on to it before the completion of a stroke, or as a result of attempting to guard his wicket. See Law 34.1 (Out Hit the Ball Twice).

Note

(a) Out Bowled – Not lbw
The striker is out bowled if the ball is deflected on to his wicket even though a decision against him would be justified under Law 36 (lbw).

LAW 31. TIMED OUT

1. Out Timed Out

An incoming batsman shall be out *Timed Out* if he wilfully takes more than two minutes to come in – the two minutes being timed from the moment a wicket falls until the new batsman steps on to the field of play.

If this is not complied with and if the umpire is satisfied that the delay was wilful and if an appeal is made, the new batsman shall be given out by the umpire at the bowler's end.

2. Time to be Added

The time taken by the umpires to investigate the cause of the delay shall be added at the normal close of play.

Notes

(a) Entry in Scorebook
The correct entry in the scorebook when a batsman is given out under this Law is "timed out", and the bowler does not get credit for the wicket.

(b) Batsmen Crossing on the Field of Play
It is an essential duty of the captains to ensure that the in-going batsman passes the out-going one before the latter leaves the field of play.

LAW 32. CAUGHT

1. Out Caught

The striker shall be out *Caught* if the ball touches his bat or if it touches below the wrist his hand or glove, holding the bat, and is subsequently held by a fieldsman before it touches the ground.

2. A Fair Catch

A catch shall be considered to have been fairly made if:

(a) The fieldsman is within the field of play throughout the act of making the catch.

(i) The act of making the catch shall start from the time when the fieldsman first handles the ball and shall end when he both retains complete control over the further disposal of the ball and remains within the field of play.

(ii) In order to be within the field of play, the fieldsman may not touch or ground any part of his person on or over a boundary line. When the boundary is marked by a fence or board the fieldsman may not ground any part of his person over the boundary fence or board, but may touch or lean over the boundary fence or board in completing the catch.

(b) The ball is hugged to the body of the catcher or accidentally lodges in his dress or, in the case of the wicket-keeper, in his pads. However, a striker may not be caught if a ball lodges in a protective helmet worn by a fieldsman, in which case the umpire shall call and signal "dead ball". See Law 23 (Dead Ball).

(c) The ball does not touch the ground even though a hand holding it does so in effecting the catch.

(d) A fieldsman catches the ball, after it has been lawfully played a second time by the striker, but only if the ball has not touched the ground since being first struck.

(e) A fieldsman catches the ball after it has touched an umpire, another fieldsman or the other batsman. However, a striker may not be caught if a ball has touched a protective helmet worn by a fieldsman.

(f) The ball is caught off an obstruction within the boundary provided it has not previously been agreed to regard the obstruction as a boundary.

3. Scoring of Runs

If a striker is caught, no run shall be scored.

Notes

(a) Scoring from an Attempted Catch
When a fieldsman carrying the ball touches or grounds any part of his person on or over a boundary marked by a line, six runs shall be scored.

(b) Ball Still in Play
If a fieldsman releases the ball before he crosses the boundary, the ball will be considered to be still in play and it may be caught by another fieldsman. However, if the original fieldsman returns to the field of play and handles the ball, a catch may not be made.

LAW 33. HANDLED THE BALL

1. Out Handled the Ball

Either batsman on appeal shall be out *Handled the Ball* if he wilfully touches the ball while in play with the hand not holding the bat unless he does so with the consent of the opposite side.

Note

(a) Entry in Scorebook
The correct entry in the scorebook when a batsman is given out under this Law is "handled the ball', and the bowler does not get credit for the wicket.

LAW 34. HIT THE BALL TWICE

1. Out Hit the Ball Twice

The striker, on appeal, shall be out *Hit the Ball Twice* if, after the ball is struck or is stopped by any part of his person, he wilfully strikes it again with his bat or person except for the sole purpose of guarding his wicket: this he may do with his bat or any part of his person other than his hands, but see Law 37.2 (Obstructing a Ball From Being Caught).

For the purpose of this Law, a hand holding the bat shall be regarded as part of the bat.

2. Returning the Ball to a Fieldsman

The striker, on appeal, shall be out under this Law if, without the consent of the opposite side, he uses his bat or person to return the ball to any of the fielding side.

3. Runs from Ball Lawfully Struck Twice

No runs except those which result from an overthrow or penalty – see Law 41 (The Fieldsman) – shall be scored from a ball lawfully struck twice.

Notes

(a) Entry in Scorebook
The correct entry in the scorebook when the striker is given out under this Law is "hit the ball twice", and the bowler does not get credit for the wicket.

(b) Runs Credited to the Batsman
Any runs awarded under 3 above as a result of an overthrow or penalty shall be credited to the striker, provided the ball in the first instance has touched the bat, or, if otherwise, as extras.

LAW 35. HIT WICKET

1. Out Hit Wicket

The striker shall be out *Hit Wicket* if, while the ball is in play:

(a) His wicket is broken with any part of his person, dress, or equipment as a result of any action taken by him in preparing to receive or in receiving a delivery, or in setting off for his first run, immediately after playing, or playing at, the ball.

(b) He hits down his wicket whilst lawfully making a second stroke for the purpose of guarding his wicket within the provisions of Law 34.1 (Out Hit the Ball Twice).

Notes

(a) Not Out Hit Wicket
A batsman is not out under this Law should his wicket be broken in any of the ways referred to in 1(a) above if:

(i) It occurs while he is in the act of running, other than in setting off for his first run immediately after playing at the ball, or while he is avoiding being run out or stumped.

(ii) The bowler after starting his run-up or bowling action does not deliver the ball; in which case the umpire shall immediately call and signal "dead ball".

(iii) It occurs whilst he is avoiding a throw-in at any time.

LAW 36. LEG BEFORE WICKET

1. Out lbw

The striker shall be out *lbw* in the circumstances set out below:

(a) Striker Attempting to Play the Ball
The striker shall be out lbw if he first intercepts with any part of his person, dress or equipment a fair ball which would have hit the wicket and which has not previously touched his bat or a hand holding the bat, provided that:

(i) The ball pitched in a straight line between wicket and wicket or on the off side of the striker's wicket, or was intercepted full pitch; and

(ii) The point of impact is in a straight line between wicket and wicket, even if above the level of the bails.

(b) Striker Making No Attempt to Play the Ball
The striker shall be out lbw even if the ball is intercepted outside the line of the off stump if, in the opinion of the umpire, he has made no genuine attempt to play the ball with his bat, but has intercepted the ball with some part of his person and if the other circumstances set out in (a) above apply.

LAW 37. OBSTRUCTING THE FIELD

1. Wilful Obstruction

Either batsman, on appeal, shall be out *Obstructing the Field* if he wilfully obstructs the opposite side by word or action.

2. Obstructing a Ball From Being Caught

The striker, on appeal, shall be out should wilful obstruction by either batsman prevent a catch being made.

This shall apply even though the striker causes the obstruction in lawfully guarding his wicket under the provisions of Law 34. See Law 34.1 (Out Hit the Ball Twice).

Notes

(a) Accidental Obstruction
The umpires must decide whether the obstruction was wilful or not. The accidental interception of a throw-in by a batsman while running does not break this Law.

(b) Entry in Scorebook
The correct entry in the scorebook when a batsman is given out under this Law is "obstructing the field", and the bowler does not get credit for the wicket.

LAW 38. RUN OUT

1. Out Run Out

Either batsman shall be out *Run Out* if in running or at any time while the ball is in play – except in the circumstances described in Law 39 (Stumped) – he is out of his ground and his wicket is put down by the opposite side. If, however, a batsman in running makes good his ground he shall not be out run out if he subsequently leaves his ground, in order to avoid injury, and the wicket is put down.

2. "No-ball" Called

If a no-ball has been called, the striker shall not be given run out unless he attempts to run.

3. Which Batsman Is Out

If the batsmen have crossed in running, he who runs for the wicket which is put down shall be out; if they have not crossed, he who has left the wicket which is put down shall be out. If a batsman remains in his ground or returns to his ground and the other batsman joins him there, the latter shall be out if his wicket is put down.

4. Scoring of Runs

If a batsman is run out, only that run which is being attempted shall not be scored. If, however, an injured striker himself is run out, no runs shall be scored. See Law 2.7 (Transgression of the Laws by an Injured Batsman or Runner).

Notes

(a) Ball Played on to Opposite Wicket
If the ball is played on to the opposite wicket, neither batsman is liable to be run out unless the ball has been touched by a fieldsman before the wicket is broken.

(b) Entry in Scorebook
The correct entry in the scorebook when a batsman is given out under this Law is "run out", and the bowler does not get credit for the wicket.

(c) Run Out off a Fieldsman's Helmet
If, having been played by a batsman, or having come off his person, the ball rebounds directly from a fieldsman's helmet on to the stumps, with either batsman out of his ground, the batsman shall be "not out".

LAW 39. STUMPED

1. Out Stumped

The striker shall be out *Stumped* if, in receiving the ball, not being a no-ball, he is out of his ground otherwise than in attempting a run and the wicket is put down by the wicket-keeper without the intervention of another fieldsman.

2. Action by the Wicket-keeper

The wicket-keeper may take the ball in front of the wicket in an attempt to stump the striker only if the ball has touched the bat or person of the striker.

Note

(a) Ball Rebounding from Wicket-keeper's Person
The striker may be out stumped if, in the circumstances stated in 1 above, the wicket is broken by a ball rebounding from the wicket-keeper's person or equipment other than a protective helmet or is kicked or thrown by the wicket-keeper on to the wicket.

LAW 40. THE WICKET-KEEPER

1. Position of Wicket-keeper

The wicket-keeper shall remain wholly behind the wicket until a ball delivered by the bowler touches the bat or person of the striker, or passes the wicket, or until the striker attempts a run.

In the event of the wicket-keeper contravening this Law, the umpire at the striker's end shall call and signal "no-ball" at the instant of delivery or as soon as possible thereafter.

2. Restriction on Actions of the Wicket-keeper

If the wicket-keeper interferes with the striker's right to play the ball and to guard his wicket, the striker shall not be out except under Laws 33 (Handled the Ball), 34 (Hit the Ball Twice), 37 (Obstructing the Field) and 38 (Run Out).

3. Interference with the Wicket-keeper by the Striker

If, in the legitimate defence of his wicket, the striker interferes with the wicket-keeper, he shall not be out, except as provided for in Law 37.2 (Obstructing a Ball From Being Caught).

LAW 41. THE FIELDSMAN

1. Fielding the Ball

The fieldsman may stop the ball with any part of his person, but if he wilfully stops it otherwise, five runs shall be added to the run or runs already scored; if no run has been scored five penalty runs shall be awarded. The run in progress shall count provided that the batsmen have crossed at the instant of the act. If the ball has been struck, the penalty shall be added to the score of the striker, but otherwise to the score of byes, leg-byes, no-balls or wides as the case may be.

2. Limitation of On-side Fieldsmen

The number of on-side fieldsmen behind the popping crease at the instant of the bowler's delivery shall not exceed two. In the event of infringement by the fielding side the umpire at the striker's end shall call and signal "no-ball" at the instant of delivery or as soon as possible thereafter.

3. Position of Fieldsmen

Whilst the ball is in play and until the ball has made contact with the bat or the striker's person or has passed his bat, no fieldsman, other than the bowler, may stand on or have any part of his person extended over the pitch (measuring 22 yards/20.12m × 10 feet/3.05m). In the event of a fieldsman contravening this Law, the umpire at the bowler's end shall call and signal "no-ball" at the instant of delivery or as soon as possible thereafter. See Law 40.1 (Position of Wicket-keeper).

4. Fieldsmen's Protective Helmets

Protective helmets, when not in use by members of the fielding side, shall be placed, if above the surface, only on the ground behind the wicket-keeper. In the event of the ball, when in play, striking a helmet whilst in this position, five penalty runs shall be awarded as laid down in Law 41.1 and Note (a).

Note

(a) Batsmen Changing Ends
The five runs referred to in 1 and 4 above are a penalty and the batsmen do not change ends solely by reason of this penalty.

LAW 42. UNFAIR PLAY

1. Responsibility of Captains

The captains are responsible at all times for ensuring that play is conducted within the spirit of the game as well as within the Laws.

2. Responsibility of Umpires

The umpires are the sole judges of fair and unfair play.

3. Intervention by the Umpire

The umpires shall intervene without appeal by calling and signalling "dead ball" in the case of unfair play, but should not otherwise interfere with the progress of the game except as required to do so by the Laws.

4. Lifting the Seam

A player shall not lift the seam of the ball for any reason. Should this be done, the umpires shall change the ball for one of similar condition to that in use prior to the contravention. See Note (a).

5. Changing the Condition of the Ball

Any member of the fielding side may polish the ball provided that such polishing wastes no time and that no artificial substance is used. No one shall rub the ball on the ground or use any artificial substance or take any other action to alter the condition of the ball.

In the event of a contravention of this Law, the umpires, after consultation, shall change the ball for one of similar condition to that in use prior to the contravention.

This Law does not prevent a member of the fielding side from drying a wet ball, or removing mud from the ball. See Note (b).

6. Incommoding the Striker

An umpire is justified in intervening under this Law and shall call and signal "dead ball" if, in his opinion, any player of the fielding side incommodes the striker by any noise or action while he is receiving a ball.

7. Obstruction of a Batsman in Running

It shall be considered unfair if any fieldsman wilfully obstructs a batsman in running. In these circumstances the umpire shall call and signal "dead ball" and allow any completed runs and the run in progress, or alternatively any boundary scored.

8. The Bowling of Fast Short-pitched Balls

The bowling of fast short-pitched balls is unfair if, in the opinion of the umpire at the bowler's end, it constitutes an attempt to intimidate the striker. See Note (d).

Umpires shall consider intimidation to be the deliberate bowling of fast short-pitched balls which by their length, height and direction are intended or likely to inflict physical injury on the striker. The relative skill of the striker shall also be taken into consideration.

In the event of such unfair bowling, the umpire at the bowler's end shall adopt the following procedure:

(a) In the first instance the umpire shall call and signal "no-ball", caution the bowler and inform the other umpire, the captain of the fielding side and the batsmen of what has occurred.

(b) If this caution is ineffective, he shall repeat the above procedure and indicate to the bowler that this is a final warning.

(c) Both the above caution and final warning shall continue to apply even though the bowler may later change ends.

(d) Should the above warnings prove ineffective the umpire at the bowler's end shall:

- (i) At the first repetition call and signal "no-ball" and when the ball is dead direct the captain to take the bowler off forthwith and to complete the over with another bowler, provided that the bowler does not bowl two overs or part thereof consecutively. See Law 22.7 (Bowler Incapacitated or Suspended during an Over).
- (ii) Not allow the bowler, thus taken off, to bowl again in the same innings.
- (iii) Report the occurrence to the captain of the batting side as soon as the players leave the field for an interval.
- (iv) Report the occurrence to the executive of the fielding side and to any governing body responsible for the match, who shall take any further action which is considered to be appropriate against the bowler concerned.

9. The Bowling of Fast High Full Pitches

The bowling of fast high full pitches is unfair.

A fast high full-pitched ball is defined as a ball that passes, or would have passed, on the full above waist height of a batsman standing upright at the crease. Should a bowler bowl a fast high full-pitched ball, either umpire shall call and signal "no-ball" and adopt the procedure of caution, final warning, action against the bowler and reporting as set out in Law 42.8.

10. Time Wasting

Any form of time wasting is unfair.

(a) In the event of the captain of the fielding side wasting time or allowing any member of his side to waste time, the umpire at the bowler's end shall adopt the following procedure:

- (i) In the first instance he shall caution the captain of the fielding side and inform the other umpire of what has occurred.
- (ii) If this caution is ineffective he shall repeat the above procedure and indicate to the captain that this is a final warning.
- (iii) The umpire shall report the occurrence to the captain of the batting side as soon as the players leave the field for an interval.
- (iv) Should the above procedure prove ineffective the umpire shall report the occurrence to the executive of the fielding side and to any governing body responsible for that match, who shall take appropriate action against the captain and the players concerned.

(b) In the event of a bowler taking unnecessarily long to bowl an over the umpire at the bowler's end shall adopt the procedures, other than the calling of "no-ball", of caution, final warning, action against the bowler and reporting as set out in 8 above.

(c) In the event of a batsman wasting time (See Note (e)) other than in the manner described in Law 31 (Timed Out), the umpire at the bowler's end shall adopt the following procedure:

(i) In the first instance he shall caution the batsman and inform the other umpire at once, and the captain of the batting side, as soon as the players leave the field for an interval, of what has occurred.

(ii) If this proves ineffective, he shall repeat the caution, indicate to the batsman that this is a final warning and inform the other umpire.

(iii) The umpire shall report the occurrence to both captains as soon as the players leave the field for an interval.

(iv) Should the above procedure prove ineffective, the umpire shall report the occurrence to the executive of the batting side and to any governing body responsible for that match, who shall take appropriate action against the player concerned.

11. Players Damaging the Pitch

The umpires shall intervene and prevent players from causing damage to the pitch which may assist the bowlers of either side. See Note (c).

(a) In the event of any member of the fielding side damaging the pitch, the umpire shall follow the procedure of caution, final warning and reporting as set out in 10(a) above.

(b) In the event of a bowler contravening this Law by running down the pitch after delivering the ball, the umpire at the bowler's end shall first caution the bowler. If this caution is ineffective the umpire shall adopt the procedures, other than the calling of "no-ball", as set out in 8 above.

(c) In the event of a batsman damaging the pitch the umpire at the bowler's end shall follow the procedures of caution, final warning and reporting as set out in 10(c) above.

12. Batsman Unfairly Stealing a Run

Any attempt by the batsman to steal a run during the bowler's run-up is unfair. Unless the bowler attempts to run out either batsman – see Law 24.4 (Bowler Throwing at Striker's Wicket before Delivery) and Law 24.5 (Bowler Attempting to Run Out Non-striker before Delivery) – the umpire shall call and signal "dead ball" as soon as the batsmen cross in any such attempt to run. The batsmen shall then return to their original wickets.

13. Player's Conduct

In the event of a player failing to comply with the instructions of an umpire, criticising his decisions by word or action, or showing dissent, or generally behaving in a manner which might bring the game into disrepute, the umpire concerned shall, in the first place, report the matter to the other umpire and to the player's captain, requesting the latter to take action. If this proves ineffective, the umpire shall report the incident as soon as possible to the executive of the player's team and to any governing body responsible for the match, who shall take any further action which is considered appropriate against the player or players concerned.

Notes

(a) The Condition of the Ball
Umpires shall make frequent and irregular inspections of the condition of the ball.

(b) Drying of a Wet Ball
A wet ball may be dried on a towel or with sawdust.

(c) Danger Area
The danger area on the pitch, which must be protected from damage by a bowler, shall be regarded by the umpires as the area contained by an imaginary line 4 feet/1.22m from the popping crease, and parallel to it, and within two imaginary and parallel lines drawn down the pitch from points on that line 1 foot/30.48cm on either side of the middle stump.

(d) Fast Short-pitched Balls
As a guide, a fast short-pitched ball is one which pitches short and passes, or would have passed, above the shoulder height of the striker standing in a normal batting stance at the crease.

(e) Time Wasting by Batsmen
Other than in exceptional circumstances, the batsman should always be ready to take strike when the bowler is ready to start his run-up.

REGULATIONS OF THE INTERNATIONAL CRICKET COUNCIL

Extracts

1. Standard Playing Conditions

In July 1995, ICC Full Members adopted standard playing conditions to apply to all Tests and one-day internationals for an initial three-year period. These include the following:

Duration of Test Matches

Test matches shall be of five days' scheduled duration. The two participating countries may:

(a) Provide for a rest day during the match, and/or a reserve day after the scheduled days of play.

(b) Play on any scheduled rest day, conditions and circumstances permitting, should a full day's play be lost on any day prior to the rest day.

(c) Play on any scheduled reserve day, conditions and circumstances permitting, should a full day's play be lost on any day. Play shall not take place on more than five days.

(d) Make up time lost in excess of five minutes in each day's play owing to circumstances outside the game, other than acts of God.

Hours of Play and Minimum Overs in the Day in Test Matches

1. Start and cessation times shall be determined by the home board, subject to there being six hours scheduled for play per day (Pakistan a minimum of five and a half hours).

(a) Play shall continue on each day until the completion of a minimum number of overs or until the scheduled or rescheduled cessation time, whichever is the later. The minimum number of overs to be completed, unless an innings ends or an interruption occurs, shall be:

(i) on days other than the last day – a minimum of 90 overs.

(ii) on the last day – a minimum of 75 overs (or 15 overs per hour) for playing time other than the last hour when a minimum of 15 six-ball overs shall be bowled. All calculations with regard to suspensions of play or the start of a new innings shall be based on one over for each full four minutes. If, however, at any time after 30 minutes of the last hour have elapsed both captains (the batsmen at the wicket may act for their captain) accept that there is no prospect of a result to the match, they may agree to cease play at that time.

Subject to weather and light, except in the last hour of the match, in the event of play being suspended for any reason other than normal intervals, the playing time on that day shall be extended by the amount of time lost up to a maximum of one hour. The minimum number of overs to be bowled shall be in accordance with the provisions of this clause and the cessation time shall be rescheduled accordingly.

(b) When an innings ends, a minimum number of overs shall be bowled from the start of the new innings. The number of overs to be bowled shall be calculated at the rate of one over for each full four minutes to enable a minimum of 90 overs to be bowled in a day, and the time for close of play shall be rescheduled accordingly. The last hour of the match shall be excluded from this calculation (see (a) (ii)).

Where a change of innings occurs during a day's play in the event of the team bowling second being unable to complete its overs by the scheduled cessation time, play shall continue until the required number of overs have been completed.

2. Either captain may decide to play 30 minutes (a minimum eight overs) extra time at the end of any day other than the last day if, in their opinion, it would bring about a definite result on that day. If it is decided to play such extra time, the whole period shall be played out even though the possibility of finishing the match may have disappeared before the full period has expired. The time by which play is extended on any day shall be deducted from the total number of hours of play remaining and the match shall end earlier on the final day by that amount of time.

The Bowling of Fast, Short-Pitched Balls: Law 42.8. Experimental Regulation for Test matches only for three years with effect from October 1, 1994

1. A bowler shall be limited to two fast, short-pitched deliveries per over.
2. A fast, short-pitched ball is defined as a ball which passes or would have passed above the shoulder height of the batsman standing upright at the crease.
3. In the event of a bowler bowling more than two fast, short-pitched deliveries in an over, either umpire shall call and signal "no-ball" on each occasion.
4. The penalty for a fast, short-pitched no-ball shall be two runs, plus any runs scored from the delivery.
5. The umpire shall call and signal "no-ball" and then raise the other arm across the chest.

Where a bowler delivers a third fast, short-pitched ball in one over which is also a no-ball under Law 24, e.g. a front-foot no-ball, the penalty will be two runs plus any runs scored from that delivery, i.e. the greater penalty will apply. The umpire shall also adopt the procedures of caution, final warning, action against the bowler and reporting as set out in Law 42.8.

The above Regulation is not a substitute for Law 42.8 (as amended below), which umpires are able to apply at any time:

The bowling of fast, short-pitched balls is unfair if the umpire at the bowler's end considers that, by their repetition and taking into account their length, height and direction, they are likely to inflict physical injury on the striker, irrespective of the protective clothing and equipment he may be wearing. The relative skill of the striker shall also be taken into consideration.

The umpire at the bowler's end shall adopt the procedures of caution, final warning, action against the bowler and reporting as set out in Law 42.8.

New Ball: Law 5.4

The captain of the fielding side shall have the choice of taking a new ball any time after 80 overs have been bowled with the previous ball.

Ball Lost or Becoming Unfit for Play: Law 5.5

In the event of a ball during play being lost or, in the opinion of the umpires, being unfit for play through normal use, the umpires shall allow it to be replaced by one that in their opinion has had a similar amount of wear. If the ball is to be replaced, the umpires shall inform the batsmen.

Practice on the Field: Law 15.2

At no time on any day of the match shall there be any bowling or batting practice on the pitch or the square, except in official netted practice pitch areas. In addition there shall be no bowling or batting practice on any part of the square or the area immediately parallel to the match pitch after the commencement of play on any day. Any fielder contravening this Law may not bowl his next over.

No practice may take place on the field if, in the opinion of the umpires, it could result in a waste of time.

Fieldsman Leaving the Field: Law 2.8

No fieldsman shall leave the field or return during a session of play without the consent of the umpire at the bowler's end. The umpire's consent is also necessary if a substitute is required for a fieldsman at the start of play or when his side returns to the field after an interval.

If a member of the fielding side does not take the field at the start of play, leaves the field, or fails to return after an interval and is absent from the field longer than 15 minutes, he shall not be permitted to bowl in that innings after his return until he has been on the field for at least that length of playing time for which he was absent. In the event of a follow-on, this restriction will, if necessary, continue into the second innings. Nor shall he be permitted to bat unless or until, in the aggregate, he has returned to the field and/or his side's innings has been in progress for at least that length of playing time for which he has been absent or, if earlier, when his side has lost five wickets. The restrictions shall not apply if he has suffered an external blow (as opposed to an internal injury such as a pulled muscle) while participating earlier in the match and consequently been forced to leave the field, nor if he has been absent for exceptional and acceptable reasons (other than injury or illness) and consent for a substitute has been granted by the opposing captain.

2. Classification of First-Class Matches

1. Definitions

A match of three or more days' duration between two sides of 11 players officially adjudged first-class shall be regarded as a first-class fixture.

2. Rules

(a) Full Members of ICC shall decide the status of matches of three or more days' duration played in their countries.

(b) In matches of three or more days' duration played in countries which are not Full Members of ICC:

(i) If the visiting team comes from a country which is a Full Member of ICC, that country shall decide the status of matches.

(ii) If the visiting team does not come from a country which is a Full Member of ICC, or is a Commonwealth team composed of players from different countries, ICC shall decide the status of matches.

Notes

(a) Governing bodies agree that the interest of first-class cricket will be served by ensuring that first-class status is *not* accorded to any match in which one or other of the teams taking part cannot on a strict interpretation of the definition be adjudged first-class.

(b) In case of any disputes arising from these Rules, the Chief Executive of ICC shall refer the matter for decision to the Council, failing unanimous agreement by postal communication being reached.

3. First-Class Status

The following matches shall be regarded as first-class, subject to the provisions of 2.1 (Definitions) being complied with:

(a) **In Great Britain and Ireland:** (i) County Championship matches. (ii) Official representative tourist matches from Full Member countries unless specifically excluded. (iii) MCC v any first-class county. (iv) Oxford v Cambridge and either University against first-class counties. (v) Scotland v Ireland.

(b) **In Australia:** (i) Sheffield Shield matches. (ii) Matches played by teams representing states of the Commonwealth of Australia between each other or against opponents adjudged first-class.

(c) **In India:** (i) Ranji Trophy matches. (ii) Duleep Trophy matches. (iii) Irani Trophy matches. (iv) Matches played by teams representing state or regional associations affiliated to the Board of Control between each other or against opponents adjudged first-class. (v) All three-day matches played against representative visiting sides.

(d) **In New Zealand:** (i) Shell Trophy matches. (ii) Matches played by teams representing major associations of the North and South Islands, between each other or against opponents adjudged first-class.

(e) **In Pakistan:** (i) Matches played by teams representing divisional associations affiliated to the Pakistan Cricket Board, between each other or against teams adjudged first-class. (ii) Quaid-e-Azam Trophy matches. (iii) PCB Patron's Trophy matches. (iv) PCB Pentangular Trophy matches.

(f) **In South Africa:** (i) Supersport Series four-day matches between Boland, Border, Eastern Province, Free State, Griqualand West, Natal, Northern Transvaal, Transvaal, Western Province. (ii) The United Cricket Board Bowl competition three-day matches between Easterns, North West and the B teams of Eastern Province, Natal, Transvaal and Western Province.

(g) **In Sri Lanka:** (i) Matches of three days or more against touring sides adjudged first-class. (ii) Singer Inter-Provincial Cricket tournament matches played over four days for the President's Trophy. (iii) Inter-Club Division I tournament matches played over three days for the P. Saravanamuttu Trophy.

(h) **In West Indies:** Matches played by teams representing Barbados, Guyana, Jamaica, the Leeward Islands, Trinidad & Tobago and the Windward Islands, either for the Red Stripe Cup or against other opponents adjudged first-class.

(i) **In Zimbabwe:** (i) Matches of three days or more against touring sides adjudged first-class. (ii) Lonrho Logan Cup competition three-day matches between Mashonaland and Matabeleland.

(j) **In all Full Member countries represented on the Council:** (i) Test matches and matches against teams adjudged first-class played by official touring teams. (ii) Official Test Trial matches. (iii) Special matches between teams adjudged first-class by the governing body or bodies concerned.

3. Classification of One-Day International Matches

The following should be classified as one-day internationals:

(a) All matches played between the Full Member countries of ICC as part of an official tour itinerary.

(b) All matches played as part of an official tournament by Full Member countries. These need not necessarily be held in a Full Member country.

(c) All matches played in the official World Cup competition, including matches involving Associate Member countries.

(d) All matches played in the Asia Cup and Austral-Asia Cup competitions.

4. Qualification Rules for Test Matches and One-Day International Matches

Qualification by Birth

A cricketer is qualified to play in Tests, one-day internationals or any other representative cricket match for the country of his birth provided he has not played in Tests, one-day internationals or, after October 1, 1994, in any other representative cricket match for any other Member country during the two immediately preceding years.

Qualification by Residence

A cricketer is qualified to play in Tests, one-day internationals or in any other representative cricket match for any Full or Associate Member country in which he has resided for at least 183 days in each of the four immediately preceding years provided that he has not played in Tests, one-day internationals or, after October 1, 1994, in any other representative cricket match for any other Member country during that period of four years.

Notes: "Representative cricket match" means any cricket match in which a team representing a Member country at Under-19 level or above takes part, including Tests and one-day internationals.

The governing body for cricket of any Member country may impose more stringent qualification rules for that country.

ICC CODE OF CONDUCT

1. The captains are responsible at all times for ensuring that play is conducted within the spirit of the game as well as within the Laws.

2. Players and team officials shall not at any time engage in conduct unbecoming to an international player or team official which could bring them or the game into disrepute.

3. Players and team officials must at all times accept the umpire's decision. Players must not show dissent at the umpire's decision.

4. Players and team officials shall not intimidate, assault or attempt to intimidate or assault an umpire, another player or a spectator.

5. Players and team officials shall not use crude or abusive language (known as "sledging") nor make offensive gestures.

6. Players and team officials shall not use or in any way be concerned in the use or distribution of illegal drugs.

7. Players and team officials shall not disclose or comment upon any alleged breach of the Code or upon any hearing, report or decision arising from such breach.

8. Players and team officials shall not make any public pronouncement or media comment which is detrimental either to the game in general; or to a particular tour in which they are involved; or about any tour between other countries which is taking place; or to relations between the Boards of the competing teams.

9. Players and team officials shall not engage, directly or indirectly, in betting, gambling or any form of financial speculation on the outcome of any cricket match to which this Code applies and in which the player is a participant or with which a team official is associated or on any event which, in the opinion of the referee, shall be connected with any such cricket match the purpose (or pretended purpose) of which is to benefit such player or team official either directly or indirectly whether financially or otherwise. Players and team officials shall not accept any form of inducement which is considered by the referee to be likely to affect the performance of any player involved in any such cricket match adversely.

REGULATIONS FOR FIRST-CLASS MATCHES IN BRITAIN, 1996

Hours of Play

1st, 2nd, 3rd days.... 11.00 a.m. to 6.30 p.m.
4th day .... 11.00 a.m. to 6.00 p.m.

Non-Championship matches:

1st, 2nd days........ 11.30 a.m. to 6.30 p.m. (11.00 a.m. to 6.30 p.m. in tourist matches and Oxford v Cambridge)
3rd day .... 11.00 a.m. to 6.00 p.m.

Note: The hours of play, including intervals, are brought forward by half an hour for matches scheduled to start in September.

(i) (In Championship and tourist matches) Play shall continue on each day until the completion of a minimum number of overs or until the scheduled cessation time, whichever is the later. The minimum number of overs, unless an innings ends or an interruption occurs, shall be 104 on days other than the last day, and 80 on the last day before the last hour (98 and 75 respectively in tourist matches).

(ii) When an innings ends, a minimum number of overs shall be bowled from the start of the new innings. The number shall be calculated at the rate of one over for each full $3\frac{3}{4}$ minutes (4 in tourist matches) to enable a minimum of 104 (98) overs to be bowled (80 (75) on the last day before the last hour) and the time for close of play (on the last day, the start of the last hour) shall be rescheduled accordingly. Where there is a change of innings during the day (except during an interval or suspension of play), two overs will be deducted from the minimum number.

(iii) If interruptions for weather or light occur, other than in the last hour of the match, the minimum number of overs shall be reduced by one over for each full $3\frac{3}{4}$ minutes (4 in tourist matches) of the aggregate playing time lost.

(iv) On the last day, if any of the minimum of 80 overs (75 in tourist matches), or as recalculated, have not been bowled when one hour of scheduled playing time remains, the last hour of the match shall be the hour immediately following the completion of those overs.

(v) Law 17.6 and 17.7 will apply except that a minimum of 16 six-ball overs (15 in tourist matches) shall be bowled in the last hour, and *all* calculations with regard to suspensions of play or the start of a new innings shall be based on one over for each full $3\frac{3}{4}$ (4) minutes. If, however, at 5.30 p.m. both captains accept that there is no prospect of a result or of either side gaining any further first-innings bonus points, they may agree to cease play at that time or at any time after 5.30 p.m.

(vi) (In all matches) The captains may agree or, in the event of disagreement, the umpires may decide to play 30 minutes (a minimum eight overs in Championship and tourist matches, or ten in other domestic matches) extra time at the end of the first and/or second day's play (and/or the third day of four) if, in their opinion, it would bring about a definite result on that day. In the event of the possibility of a finish disappearing before the full period has expired, the whole period must be played out. The time by which play is extended on any day shall be deducted from the total number of hours remaining in the match, and the match shall end earlier on the last day by the actual amount of time by which play was extended.

(vii) (In Championship and tourist matches) Notwithstanding any other provision, there shall be no further play on any day, other than the last day, if a wicket falls or a batsman retires, or if the players leave the field during the last minimum over within two minutes of the scheduled cessation time or thereafter.

(viii) An over completed on resumption of a new day's play shall be disregarded in calculating minimum overs for that day.

(ix) Fractions are to be ignored in all calculations re the number of overs.

(x) The scoreboard shall show the total number of overs bowled with the ball in use and the minimum number remaining to be bowled in a day.

Intervals

Lunch: 1.15 p.m. to 1.55 p.m. (1st, 2nd [3rd] days) in Championship and tourist matches and Oxford v Cambridge, 1.30 p.m. to 2.10 p.m. in others
1.00 p.m. to 1.40 p.m. (final day)
In the event of lunch being taken early because an innings ends or because of a stoppage caused by weather or bad light (Law 16.2), the interval shall be limited to 40 minutes.

Tea: (Championship matches) A tea interval of 20 minutes shall normally be taken at 4.10 p.m. (3.40 p.m. on final day), or when 32 overs or less remain to be bowled (except on final day). The over in progress shall be completed unless a batsman is out or retires during that over within two minutes of the interval or the players have occasion to leave the field.

If an innings ends or there is a stoppage caused by weather within 30 minutes of the scheduled time, the tea interval shall be taken immediately. There will be no tea interval if the scheduled timing for the cessation of play is earlier than 5.30 p.m.

(Other matches) 4.10 p.m. to 4.30 p.m. (1st, 2nd [3rd] days), 3.40 p.m. to 4.00 p.m. (final day).

Substitutes

(Domestic matches only) Law 2.1 will apply, but in addition:

No substitute may take the field until the player for whom he is to substitute has been absent from the field for five consecutive complete overs, with the exception that if a fieldsman sustains an obvious, serious injury or is taken ill, a substitute shall be allowed immediately. In the event of any disagreement between the two sides as to the seriousness of an injury or illness, the umpires shall adjudicate. If a player leaves the field during an over, the remainder of that over shall not count in the calculation of the five complete overs.

A substitute shall be allowed by right immediately in the event of a cricketer currently playing in a Championship match being required to join the England team for a Test match (or one-day international). Such a substitute may be permitted to bat or bowl in that match, subject to the approval of the TCCB. The cricketer who is substituted shall take no further part in the match, even though he may not be required by England. If batting at the time, he shall retire "not out" and his substitute may be permitted to bat later in that innings subject to the approval of the TCCB.

Fieldsman Leaving the Field

ICC regulations apply (see pages 1339-1340) but without mention of the follow-on, except in tourist matches.

New Ball

The captain of the fielding side shall have the choice of taking the new ball after 100 overs (80 in tourist matches) have been bowled with the old one.

Covering of Pitches and Bowler's Run-up

(Domestic matches) The whole pitch shall be covered:

(*a*) The night before the match and, if necessary, until the first ball is bowled; and whenever necessary and possible at any time prior to that during the preparation of the pitch.

(*b*) On each night of the match and, if necessary, throughout any rest days.

(*c*) In the event of play being suspended on account of bad light or rain, during the specified hours of play.

The bowler's run-up shall be covered to a distance of at least ten yards, with a width of four yards, as will the areas ten feet either side of the length of the pitch.

Declarations

Law 14 will apply, but, in addition, a captain may also forfeit his first innings, subject to the provisions set out in Law 14.2. If, due to weather conditions, a County Championship match has not started when less than eight hours' playing time remains, the first innings of each side shall automatically be forfeited and a one-innings match played.

MEETINGS AND DECISIONS IN 1996

TCCB SPRING MEETING

At the spring meeting of the Test and County Cricket Board on March 5 and 6, David Acfield, chairman of the cricket committee, was asked to set up a working party to review by the end of the season "all aspects relating to the administration, selection and management of England teams at home and abroad". Ray Illingworth's two-year term as chairman of selectors was up on March 31; members were invited to submit nominations for the post (which could include Illingworth) by March 20, three days after the World Cup final in Lahore. Two decisions were made concerning the County Championship. As an experiment during 1996, three points would be awarded to each team for a draw. It was also confirmed that, in 1997 and 1998, 13 out of 20 rounds of Championship matches would be scheduled to start on Wednesday instead of Thursday. This move was intended to avoid the interruption of the Sunday League game, help clubs commercially by providing more opportunity for corporate hospitality, and encourage groundsmen to produce pitches which would last into the fourth day, to bring in the Saturday crowd. In domestic limited-overs games, the number of fieldsmen on the leg side was to be limited to five.

ENGLAND SELECTORS' ELECTION

Ray Illingworth faced one challenger, David Graveney, in the election for the chairman of selectors in March. But the day after the deadline for nominations, Graveney withdrew. His employers, the Cricketers' Association, told him he could not remain their general secretary if he were elected. Illingworth was thus returned unopposed, but stood down as team manager.

There was an election, however, for the two places as England selectors alongside Illingworth, the captain and the coach (David Lloyd, who was appointed at the end of March after John Emburey, the other favoured candidate, said he was not ready for the job). By the deadline at midnight on April 3, nine candidates had come forward: the incumbents, Graveney and Fred Titmus, plus Kim Barnett, Brian Bolus, Ian Botham, Chris Cowdrey, John Edrich, Graham Gooch and Geoff Miller. Titmus withdrew two days later, calling the election a "rat-race". After a postal ballot of the 20 TCCB members (the 18 first-class counties, MCC and the Minor Counties), Gooch and Graveney were elected. No voting figures were given. Botham alleged that he was the victim of a "dirty tricks" campaign; the TCCB had circulated a letter saying that media work could conflict with selection duties, but denied that it was intended to block Botham.

MCC MEETINGS

The 209th annual general meeting of the Marylebone Cricket Club was held on May 1. The President, Sir Oliver Popplewell, announced that his successor for two years from October 1 would be Colin Ingleby-Mackenzie. The annual report was adopted and resolutions regarding the names and composition of sub-committees and subscription increases for 1997 approved. Membership of the club on December 31, 1995, was 19,759, made up of 17,060 full members, 1,998 associate members, 595 honorary members and 106 senior members. There were 9,659 candidates awaiting election. In 1995, 374 vacancies arose.

On August 29, a special general meeting approved plans for the development of the new Grand Stand, to be completed during 1998. After the club had been denied assistance from public funds, the meeting accepted a scheme whereby people on the waiting list would be offered immediate membership in return for a £10,000 payment, and members would be able to purchase life membership.

A special general meeting on December 16 approved plans for a £3.5 million futuristic all-aluminium media centre, to be erected between the Compton and Edrich Stands at the Nursery End by 1998, in preparation for the World Cup final in 1999. It was proposed that the National Westminster Bank would provide a £2.6 million six-year sponsorship package.

TCCB CHIEF EXECUTIVE

On May 31, Tim Lamb, the cricket secretary of the Test and County Cricket Board, was named as its next chief executive, to succeed A. C. Smith on his retirement at the end of October and to take over its successor body when that started. The TCCB's executive committee preferred Lamb to Tony Cross, the vice-chairman of Warwickshire, an accountant and venture capitalist. Lamb said that he believed cricket should be "a business within a game rather than a game within a business". Both men had first-class experience: Lamb played for Oxford University, Middlesex and Northamptonshire (160 matches), and Cross for Cambridge and Warwickshire (six).

ICC ANNUAL CONFERENCE

The meeting of the International Cricket Council on July 10 and 11 failed to elect a chairman to succeed Sir Clyde Walcott in July 1997. None of the candidates – Jagmohan Dalmiya of India, Krish Mackerdhuj of South Africa and Malcolm Gray of Australia – could secure the necessary two-thirds majority among the nine Full (Test-playing) Members. Mackerdhuj withdrew, but that did not end the stalemate, though Dalmiya led Gray by 25 to 13 in the second ballot. He was supported by most of the 22 Associate Members (who had one vote each, to Full Members' two) but only three Full Members, whereas Gray had five Full Members (South Africa abstained). It was decided to restage the election at the 1997 conference.

ICC settled the format for the next World Cup, to be staged in England in 1999. The Test nations and the top three Associate teams from the 1997 ICC Trophy would be divided into two round-robin groups of six; the top three from each group would then play each of the top three from the other group to produce a league table to provide the four semi-finalists. England (who were seeded eighth), India, South Africa, Sri Lanka, Zimbabwe and the ICC Trophy runners-up were drawn in the first group, Australia, New Zealand, Pakistan, West Indies and the ICC winners and third-placed team in the second. The competition would feature coloured clothing and white balls.

ICC set up a development committee, chaired by Ali Bacher of South Africa and also including Julian Hunte (West Indies), Mackerdhuj, Ehsan Mani (Pakistan) and ICC chief executive David Richards, which was to report to the 1997 conference on how Test nations could do more to encourage the game in countries within their designated sphere of influence. Another sub-committee was to review the ICC constitution and rules, while a Full Members' executive committee was set up to support the chairman and chief executive. The system used by referees and captains to review international umpires' performances was simplified. A review panel would be set up to investigate bowlers suspected by umpires of throwing. The use of TV replays was extended to settling doubts about whether the ball had crossed the boundary. Nepal were promoted to associate membership, with Portugal becoming an affiliate member.

THE ACFIELD REPORT

The Acfield working party on the selection, management and coaching of England teams published its report on July 31. The working party consisted of David Acfield, Bob Bennett, Mike Gatting, David Gower, Micky Stewart and Tim Lamb. They consulted the boards of the other eight Test-playing countries, the 18 first-class counties, MCC and the Minor Counties, and recent England captains, managers, and players, journalists, umpires, county chairmen and captains.

The report said that responsibility for the England team was fragmented and recommended that one "specialist overseeing group" should take charge: the England Management Committee. This would have six core members: a chairman elected by the TCCB or ECB, the Board chairman, chief executive (non-voting), chairman of the cricket committee and two more elected members. The core members would appoint three more members, to chair the three sub-committees: Selection, Development of Excellence and International Affairs.

The Selection Sub-committee would consist of four members: a (salaried) chairman, appointed by the EMC core members for two years, the England captain and two others, appointed by the chairman of the sub-committee and the EMC core members. These should not be involved in the media but could be current county players. The chairman of the Selection Sub-committee and the two appointed selectors would appoint the captain; the chairman and the EMC core members would appoint the England coach, who would not be on the sub-committee but should be consulted and could be invited to attend. The Development of Excellence Sub-committee would have responsibility for England Under-19 and other youth teams, and should include representatives of the non-professional game. The International Affairs Sub-committee would replace the TCCB's International Committee.

The working party felt strongly that England cricketers were playing too much cricket, especially the bowlers. Over five years, they had played an average of 152 days a year; the only other team averaging more than 100 were the Australians, on 111. The report argued that they must be allowed to rest before, after and during the England season. It did not recommend full-time contracts but said that the chairman of the Selection Sub-committee should have the "right and power" to withdraw any player from any county match. The county should be compensated in line with payments when a player was absent playing for England. England tours were considered to be too long, and extraneous matches should be kept to a minimum.

It was recommended that England A should also play home internationals. These games, like England Under-19 matches, should take precedence over county cricket. The report recommended establishing Centres of Excellence in all or most first-class counties.

THE CRICKET FOUNDATION

On August 19, the Cricket Foundation announced awards totalling £2.38 million to the boards of the 38 first-class and minor counties, to promote development in the 12 to 17 age group. The money would be used to pay regional development officers and to train coaches. The TCCB had agreed the previous December that some of the profits from international cricket and TV revenue should be put into the Cricket Foundation, which could maximise them through its charity status before redistribution. The largest award – £132,121 – was made to the largest county, Yorkshire. An additional award of £45,000 was made to Durham University, which was to establish a Centre of Excellence.

TCCB SUMMER MEETING

The Test and County Cricket Board met on August 20 to consider the Acfield Report. It approved the establishment of the England Management Committee, as outlined in the report, to appoint the coach and selectors, including a salaried chairman of selectors. But county representatives again rejected the idea that the chairman of selectors should have the right to withdraw England players from domestic games. They promised that such requests would be listened to sympathetically. The cricket committee's proposal to ban overseas players in 1999 and 2000 was also turned down again, on the grounds that foreign stars added quality to the game. Sir Ian MacLaurin (later Lord MacLaurin), the retiring chairman of Tesco, was elected to succeed Dennis Silk as chairman of the TCCB in October, and thus to become the first chairman of the England and Wales Cricket Board in January. David Morgan presented a preliminary report on plans for the new board, to be discussed more fully in September. A working party was to review the domestic programme during the winter of 1996-97, a year earlier than planned, so that information about the planned format from 1999 or 2000 onwards would be available to sponsors and television companies. (In October, it was decided that this review would not take place until the summer of 1997, but that Tim Lamb, the new chief executive, and MacLaurin would visit the counties to canvass opinion.) It was agreed that there should be no rest days in the 1997 Test series with Australia, even on the Sunday coinciding with the men's tennis final at Wimbledon.

THE MORGAN REPORT

The Morgan working party on the establishment of the England and Wales Cricket Board, which was to replace the Test and County Cricket Board, the Cricket Council and the National Cricket Association, published its report on September 13. The working party, set up at the TCCB's meeting in December 1996, consisted of David Morgan, Stuart Anderson, Cliff Barker, John Bower, Steve Coverdale, Brian Ford, Don Robson, the Rev. Michael Vockins and Alan Wheelhouse.

The report agreed that cricket administration in England and Wales was fragmented and required co-ordination of effort and resources "from the playground to the Test arena" to maximise enjoyment and raise standards. But it argued that the TCCB executive committee's original proposals were "perhaps too great a one-off step" and suggested an evolutionary approach would be more likely to command support.

The working party said that the England and Wales Cricket Board (to be known as the ECB) should be a company limited by guarantee. Its members would be the 18 first-class county chairmen, the 20 minor counties chairmen and the treasurer of MCC. There should be a Management Board to implement policy, a First-Class Forum to consider cricketing and financial policy in the first-class game and a Recreational Forum to consider policy for the game in the non-first-class counties and in league, club and school cricket.

The report recommended a Management Board of 15: a chairman (initially elected by the TCCB, in future by the ECB from the FCF's nominations), four chairmen for cricket, finance, marketing and the England Management Committee, all elected by the FCF, four first-class county representatives elected by the FCF, four recreational representatives elected by the RF, an MCC representative and the ECB chief executive, a non-voting member. The Management Board would exercise its powers in regulating professional domestic and international cricket in England and Wales and the allocation of resources to the counties, subject to obtaining the approval of the FCF, and operate in similar manner in the non-first-class game with reference to the RF.

The First-Class Forum should consist of up to two representatives of each of the 18 first-class counties and MCC, who would meet at least twice a year. Its chairman would be the ECB's deputy chairman. The Recreational Forum would consist of representatives from the 38 County Boards, representing cricket at all levels in the 18 first-class and 20 minor counties, the Minor Counties Cricket Association, current associate members of the National Cricket Association and other representatives of the non-first-class game. But the Minor Counties Cricket Association would retain sole control of Minor Counties cricket. The working party recommended a management audit of the ECB within three years.

TCCB AUTUMN MEETING

The Test and County Cricket Board unanimously approved the Morgan working party's proposals for its successor body, the England and Wales Cricket Board (ECB), at its meeting on September 24. It was to come into being on January 1, 1997, run by a 15-strong Management Board which would refer all matters of significant cricketing and financial importance to the First-Class Forum, representing the 18 first-class counties. An amendment from Warwickshire proposing that written constitutions for the First-Class Forum and the Recreational Forum should be seen and approved was accepted. A special board meeting on November 12 approved the FCF and on November 28 the RF met and approved its constitution. The National Cricket Association met on October 16 and agreed to dissolve itself in order to become part of the ECB.

TCCB WINTER MEETING

The final meeting of the Test and County Cricket Board, to be superseded by the England and Wales Cricket Board in the New Year, was held on December 11 and 12. The board agreed to lift the proposed moratorium on signing new overseas players for 1999 and beyond, but ruled that no overseas player should be contracted for more than two years at a time, though rolling contracts would be allowed. Counties who rested England players at the chairman of selectors' request would be compensated £500 per match day. The cricket committee proposed that the penalty for wides should be two runs in all English first-class cricket (except Tests) in 1997, though not in limited-overs games, and that the wide rule should be interpreted more strictly to discourage negative bowling into the rough outside leg stump by left-arm spinners. Rules for revising targets in rain-affected limited-overs games were to be altered: a new table drawn up by Frank Duckworth of the Royal Statistical Society and Tony Lewis of the University of the West of England took into account the number of wickets fallen in an innings. In accordance with ICC regulations, under-arm bowling was declared illegal; the danger area for bowlers following through was increased from four feet from the popping crease to five; and, in addition to calling no-ball for thrown deliveries, umpires were to warn the bowler that he could be taken off. England were to choose the ball for home Tests, rather than tossing for choice. Philip Frost of Somerset was named groundsman of the year, with Steve Birks of Derbyshire runner-up.

PART SEVEN: MISCELLANEOUS

CHRONICLE OF 1996

JANUARY

11 Dickie Bird, the world's most experienced Test umpire, says he will retire from Tests in the summer. **15** Martin Crowe retires from international cricket. **24** David Boon announces retirement from international cricket. **31** Bomb in Colombo kills up to 90 people and throws plans for World Cup into turmoil.

FEBRUARY

5 Australia and West Indies pull out of their World Cup fixtures in Sri Lanka because of safety fears. **11** World Cup begins with opening ceremony in Calcutta. **12** Malcolm Marshall retires from first-class cricket. **29** Kenya beat West Indies by 73 runs in Pune, the biggest ever World Cup upset.

MARCH

5 West Indies captain Richie Richardson announces retirement from international cricket. **9** England beaten by Sri Lanka in Faisalabad and miss out on World Cup semi-finals for the first time. **13** Sri Lanka reach the World Cup final as India forfeit match in Calcutta due to riot. **17** Sri Lanka beat Australia by seven wickets in Lahore to win the World Cup. **26** Allan Border retires from first-class cricket; Ray Illingworth stands down as England manager but remains chairman of selectors. **29** David Lloyd appointed England coach.

APRIL

2 Sanath Jayasuriya of Sri Lanka scores the fastest century in a one-day international: 48 balls against Pakistan in Singapore. **20** Wayne James of Matabeleland breaks the world wicket-keeping record by making 13 dismissals in a match – he also scores 99 and 99 not out in the same game.

MAY

11 The bat used by Don Bradman to score 212 against England in the Adelaide Test of 1936-37 fetches £23,000 at auction in London. **17** Bobby Simpson replaced by Geoff Marsh as Australian coach after ten years. **31** Tim Lamb named as chief executive of the new England and Wales Cricket Board.

JUNE

18 Ray Illingworth fined £2,000 by TCCB for bringing the game into disrepute.

20 Dickie Bird begins umpiring his 66th and last Test match. **22** Ray Lindwall dies, aged 74. Soccer – the roar when England beat Spain in the European Championships – stops play in the Lord's Test. **27** Kirsty Flavell of New Zealand becomes the first woman to score a Test double-century, against England at Scarborough. **30** Kevan James of Hampshire becomes the first man to get a century and four wickets in four balls in the same match.

JULY

2 Andy Flower resigns as captain of Zimbabwe. **10** ICC annual conference fails to agree on new chairman. **27** David Sales of Northamptonshire scores a double-century on debut, a feat never before achieved in the County Championship. **31** High Court jury finds against Ian Botham and Allan Lamb in their libel case against Imran Khan.

AUGUST

9 Sachin Tendulkar appointed captain of India in place of Mohammad Azharuddin. **20** Sussex fast bowler Ed Giddins banned until April 1998 for using cocaine. Pitch invasion at Lord's as India beat Pakistan in Under-15 World Cup final. **26** Wasim Akram takes his 300th Test wicket as he leads Pakistan to victory over England at The Oval. **28** Liam Botham, son of Ian, takes five for 67 for Hampshire on his first-class debut.

SEPTEMBER

3 Ray Illingworth's fine overturned by Cricket Council Appeals Panel. **7** Essex bowled out for 57 by Lancashire in NatWest Trophy final, the lowest total in 62 major Lord's Cup finals; Lancashire emulate their 1990 feat of winning both domestic cups. **14** Dean Headley of Kent becomes the third man in history to take three hat-tricks in a season. **21** Leicestershire become county champions for the second time.

OCTOBER

4 Shahid Afridi, 18, scores 100 in 37 balls for Pakistan against Sri Lanka in Nairobi, breaking the one-day international record set by Jayasuriya in April. **7** Yorkshire announce plans to leave Headingley and move to a new stadium in Wakefield by 2000. **13** Australia lose their one-off Test against India by seven wickets in Delhi, putting South Africa on top of *Wisden's* new unofficial World Championship. **20** Wasim Akram hits 12 sixes in an innings, a Test record, scoring 257 not out for Pakistan against Zimbabwe at Sheikhupura; his stand of 313 with Saqlain Mushtaq breaks the Test eighth-wicket record. **24** Hassan Raza of Pakistan reportedly becomes the world's youngest Test player, at 14 years 227 days, though the Pakistan Board later insist he is already 15.

NOVEMBER

24 New Zealand win a Test in Pakistan for the first time in more than 27 years.

DECEMBER

1 Lance Klusener takes eight for 64 to win the Calcutta Test, South Africa's best Test bowling figures since 1961-62. Mohammad Zahid has match figures of 11 for 130, the best by a Pakistani on Test debut, as Pakistan beat New Zealand in Rawalpindi. **22** The inaugural Test between Zimbabwe and England in Bulawayo is the first to be drawn with the scores level. **28** West Indies beat Australia in Melbourne to reduce the series deficit to 2-1 and keep alive their hopes of regaining the Frank Worrell Trophy.

The following were also among items reported in the media during 1996:

Imran Khan won a poll among 25,000 British curry-eaters as the person with whom they would most like to have dinner. The Prime Minister, John Major, came bottom of the poll. (*The Guardian*, January 17)

John Major defeated 500 guests at a benefit dinner in a competition to choose the top post-war England team. The Major team (Hutton, Cowdrey, May, Compton, Barrington, Botham, Knott, Laker, Wardle, Trueman and Statham) coincided exactly with that of the judge, Fred Trueman, except that Trueman preferred Graveney to Barrington. After "whisperings at the top table", Mr Major withdrew his ballot paper and the prize went to a fellow-guest who had got nine correct. (*Daily Telegraph*, February 9)

Derek Pringle, the former England all-rounder and cricket correspondent of *The Independent*, hit six sixes in an over in a media match between the English and Pakistani Press in Karachi off the bowling of Muzzafar Ejaz of the *Urdu News*. (*The Times*, March 6)

Shane Warne, a four-year-old bay colt, beat 11 rivals to win the Pakistan Derby, the country's richest horse race, at Lahore. (*Dawn*, Karachi, March)

The Bat and Ball pub at Broadhalfpenny Down, home of the Hambledon club, has been restored to its original name after many protests during the two years in which it was known as Natterjacks. (*Daily Express*, March 21)

The Brolgas, playing the Emus in the Moree under-16s competition in rural New South Wales, levelled the scores with three wickets and three overs left, before the Emus' captain took a hat-trick and tied the match. (*Sunday Age*, Melbourne, March 24)

A 14-year-old schoolboy has been arrested and charged with murder after bashing another 14-year-old with a cricket bat at a playground in Kandivali, Bombay. (*Indian Express*, March 27)

A pair of shoes belonging to the Sri Lankan captain, Arjuna Ranatunga, went missing and were replaced by a brand new pair when he visited a former Sri Lankan president's house and left them outside as a mark of respect. Police discovered a woman fan had taken them as a souvenir, and had put the new pair down instead. Ranatunga did not press charges. (*Times of India*, March 31)

At least ten children have been treated at hospital in Chilaw, Sri Lanka, for eye injuries as cricket fever gripped the country after the national team's World Cup win. A doctor said cricket was being played on every available open space, often with pebbles or stones instead of a ball. Onlookers, mainly small children, were inevitable casualties, he said. (*Daily News*, Colombo, April 25)

Imran Khan announced plans for a new political organisation, the Movement for Justice, saying his country was on the brink of disaster. His announcement came 11 days after a bomb in his charitable cancer hospital killed seven people and injured 35. (*Daily Telegraph*, April 26)

Emma Liddell, a 15-year-old Sydney schoolgirl, took ten for nought for Metropolitan East against Metropolitan West. All her victims were bowled. (*Bombay Times*, May 8)

Dave Stock and his 17-year-old son Peter, who both play for the Lords Wood club in Kent, were run out for 99 in successive weeks. (*Daily Telegraph*, May 18)

Due to a computer error, a press release for the Brian Johnston Memorial Trust listed "Sir Colin Cowardly" as one of the patrons. (*Daily Telegraph*, May 18)

A cage had to be erected on the square of the Earl of Bessborough's ground, Stansted Park in Sussex, to protect a green-winged orchid, one of only 13 specimens known to have grown in England in 1996. (*Daily Telegraph*, May 22)

Tony Cole, 66, completed 50 years as an umpire at Kington Langley, Wiltshire, having never played a single match. (*The Sun,* May 23)

Eight-year-old leg-spinner William Bruce, of King's Junior School, Canterbury, took all ten wickets for 26 against Northbourne Park. (*Kentish Gazette*, May 23)

Gavin Roebuck, who keeps wicket for Darfield in the Barnsley Sunday League, had his elbow broken by team-mates congratulating him for securing a match-winning stumping. (*Daily Express*, June 3)

David Church of the East Woodhay club completed 40 years of club cricket without missing a match through injury. (*Newbury Weekly News*, June 27)

A batsman called Cordingly was recorded as "absent, babysitting" in the match between Cliffe and Yalding in Kent. (*Daily Telegraph*, June 15)

In a prep school match between Northbridge and St Paul's, Northbridge were given an extra "for too much chatter in the short-leg cordon while J. Edwards was bowling his hat-trick ball". (*The Times*, June 15)

Winslow Town from Buckinghamshire turned up to fulfil a fixture at Kempston, Bedfordshire, and began playing the wrong team at the wrong ground. They were supposed to be playing Kempston Ramblers but found themselves playing Kempston Meltis, whose own opponents had failed to turn up. No one realised the mistake until a Ramblers player came looking for the Winslow team, and they were led off to play the right game. "I have played against Ramblers a number of times over the years and I thought all their batsmen must have retired or died off," said Winslow batsman Ron Phillips. (*Buckingham and Winslow Advertiser*, June 28)

Cliff Spinks, batting for Langleybury, Hertfordshire, in a cup-tie against Northwood, decided he had had enough after scoring 31 not out and threw his bat at the stumps. The fielders' appeals were turned down under Law 35, because he had not been playing the ball or attempting a run. Spinks then appealed himself and, when this was rejected, walked off. He was given "retired out" and said: "I have been playing too much cricket." (*Daily Telegraph*, June 29)

Batsman Ray Thorpe, playing for Hampton Hill in the Thames Valley League, punched an Old Latymerians bowler who hit him on the arm with a short-pitched delivery. (*The Sun*, July 1)

Nick Causton, 14, took a double hat-trick for Brooke Under-18 v Loddon in Norfolk, emulating a feat achieved by his late grandfather, Sidney Causton, for another Norfolk team, Mundford, in 1922. Nick kept the ball his grandfather had used on a shelf in his bedroom. (*Daily Express*, July 11)

A fielder who chased a ball hit out of the ground down a steep hill brought it back by bus. Paul Crabb, playing for Ilfracombe Rugby Club in Devon against Woolacombe, caught up with the ball a quarter of a mile from the ground at Hele. When he saw the bus coming, he decided to hop on it. The driver was sporting enough to overlook the fact that he did not have the 46p for his fare. (*North Devon Journal*, July 11)

North Derbyshire team Dronfield protested against Bents Green's domination of the local Midweek Alliance by declaring on nought for nought and then bowling a deliberate no-ball to give Bents Green victory. Dronfield claimed their opponents included star outsiders; the league fined them £25. (*Daily Mirror*, July 16)

Eight male streakers stopped play in the Pembrokeshire League match between Neyland and Lawrenny. They were believed to be guests at a nearby stag party. (*Western Telegraph*, July 17)

Two cricketers were sent off by the umpires in a match between Buckley and Shotton in North Wales. Wicket-keeper Marcel Carrino and batsman Andy Cummings began fighting after Carrino dropped a simple catch and words were exchanged. (*Daily Mail*, July 17)

Alan Drew, 65, and his 14-year-old grandson, James Docherty, shared a century opening stand for Penarth in a Third Eleven fixture against Pontypridd. (*Daily Express*, July 27)

A toast was drunk at Ballynahinch Castle, a hotel in County Galway, to mark the centenary of the Test debut of Ranjitsinhji, who bought the castle and the estate in 1927, six years before his death. (*Daily Telegraph*, July 27)

The Barbados youth team were docked eight points for ball-tampering in the West Indian youth tournament. "Everyone who has seen the ball was shocked," said the West Indian board president Pat Rousseau. "It was terrible." (*Daily Mail*, July 29)

A reunion of members of a family called Alston, at Bere Alston, Devon, included a game between 11 Alstons and the village team. (*Daily Mail*, August 5)

A 15-year-old Calcutta boy, Debashish Sen, confessed to killing his mother, Juthika, by striking her repeatedly with his cricket bat. They had a heated argument after he complained that there was insufficient milk and sugar in his tea. The boy had a history of disturbed behaviour. (*Indian Express*, August 6)

Rob Owens hit a six at Chandler's Ford, Hampshire, and smashed the rear window of his own car. (*Daily Express*, August 15)

A Madras schoolboy, Hemanth Kumar of Santhome A, scored 205 not out and 151 in successive rounds of the Tamil Nadu schools cricket tournament. (*The Hindu*, Madras, August 15)

A former Miss Sri Lanka was caught by security officials hiding in a bush outside the Hotel Lanka Oberoi during the Singer one-day tournament, where unprecedented security was in operation. It was alleged that she had just visited one of the players' bedrooms. (*Divaina*, Colombo, August 29)

Five people were electrocuted after a man in Negombo, Sri Lanka, tried to put up a 42-foot booster aerial to watch the Singer World Series cricket. P. D. Appuhamy, 40, and his wife were killed when the piping containing the antenna fell on an electrical cable. Three neighbours, including two 16-year-old boys, who tried to extricate them were also killed. (*Daily News*, Colombo, August 29)

Seventeen ships were left waiting outside the harbour in Colombo because half the port's 16,000 workers stayed away from work to watch the India v Sri Lanka one-day international. (*Daily News*, Colombo, August 30)

November 14 was officially declared David Boon Day by the Premier of Tasmania, Tony Rundle. Schoolchildren in Launceston were allowed out early to watch an eight-a-side tournament. (*Inside Edge*, Australia, September)

Henderson Wallace, a Barbadian playing as a professional in Ireland, hit seven sixes in an over for Eglinton against Limavady. The over, bowled by the Irish international Desmond Curry, included a no-ball. (*Derry Journal*, September 3)

A Devon homeowner claimed that a cricket stump caused £40,000 damage to his house. John Chalmers of Ashburton said the stump had blocked a pipe outside his cottage, causing sewage to flood back inside. (*Daily Express*, September 4)

Laura Harper, a 12-year-old off-spinner from Penhallow, Cornwall, was chosen for a Cornish schoolboys' Under-13s tour of South Africa. (*Daily Express*, September 5)

John Shaw, 47, died after being struck on the head while batting for Broxtowe against Gladstone in Nottinghamshire. Doctors said a medical condition which meant a rapid rise in blood pressure could prove fatal had contributed to his death, and no inquest was held. (*Sunday Telegraph*, September 8)

Derbyshire County Cricket Club's advert for a new secretary produced 125 replies, mostly from applicants who listed their typing and shorthand speeds. (*Daily Express*, September 9)

The former Government minister John Redwood, who challenged John Major for the Conservative Party leadership in 1995, led a team of "Eurosceptics" to a five-wicket win over a team of "Europhiles", captained by Lord Archer, at Burton's Court, London. (*Daily Express*, September 17)

Craig Scully won the last match of the season for Chipping Sodbury in Gloucestershire with a six and broke his car windscreen. (*Daily Mirror*, September 27)

Philip Halden, a British businessman kidnapped in Colombia and held in the jungle by guerrillas for eight months, taught his captors cricket after carving a bat and wooden balls with a machete. But he said both his kidnappers and his fellow-hostages preferred playing soccer and, when the bat broke, he was not encouraged to carve another one. (*Daily Telegraph*, October 4)

Purdey, a golden retriever, has been made vice-president of Hutton Cranswick Cricket Club in Yorkshire after finding 50 lost balls. (*Wisden Cricket Monthly*, December)

Kyle Kristal took ten for 20 in an under-14 match in Cape Town for Paul Roos Gymnasium against Paarl Boys' High. Two weeks earlier, his brother Sean had taken five for nought for his under-12 side. (*SA Cricket Action*, December)

The Duke of Edinburgh was attacked as "stupid" and "insensitive" by people campaigning for gun control in the wake of the Dunblane primary school massacre when he compared guns to cricket bats. He said on BBC Radio: "If a cricketer, for instance, suddenly decided to go into a school and batter a lot of people to death with a cricket bat, which he could do very easily, I mean, are you going to ban cricket bats?" (*The Guardian*, December 19)

Deepak Choughale, a 12-year-old schoolboy, scored 400 not out in Karnataka's 589 for four against Goa in a two-day match in the Sportstar Under-13 tournament in Madras. He batted 316 minutes, and was given a bicycle as a reward. (*The Hindu*, Madras, December 25)

Contributions from readers for this feature are very welcome, particularly if the items are from local or non-UK newspapers. Please send cuttings to the editor, with the title and date of publication clearly marked.

CRICKET BOOKS, 1996

By SEBASTIAN FAULKS

The 1996 World Cup has changed the way people in England think about cricket. It had been clear for a long time that the game is taken more seriously on the Indian subcontinent than elsewhere, that the financial potential existed to make cricket in some parts of the world the commercial equivalent of football, that the future of international cricket is now irreversibly with the one-day game and that the England side is not able to compete at the highest level. For a time many writers and commentators had, for reasons of their own, been able to deny some or all of these facts, but the brilliant spectacle of Sri Lanka winning the World Cup in India made further self-delusion difficult.

As authors and journalists struggled to come to terms with the new realities, many of the books published in 1996 inevitably lack a sense of perspective. The close relationship between cricketing authorities and the press means that journalists are exceptionally well informed about the frequently trivial detail of team management, but this is not the same thing as having a clear grasp of the game's global development, particularly when the managers themselves are often as far out to sea as the reporters. It is therefore not surprising that, for the time being, most of the more successful books are about the past. The ones that attract most attention, however, are those most connected to the present.

One-Man Committee by Ray Illingworth and Jack Bannister is an account of Illingworth's period as chairman of selectors, and later also manager, of the England side. The book appeared last summer, before the story ended, and is in that sense like Hamlet without the sword fight. But to some extent, the book – and the arguments over Illingworth's right to publish – became part of the story. The most surprising aspect of it is that, despite the telegrams and anger, the tears and the defeats, it often reads like comedy.

Illingworth first gets a call from Sir Lawrence Byford, the president of Yorkshire, in December 1993. Illingworth is surprised, because he is expecting M. J. K. Smith to be the favoured choice as chairman. Hats enter rings; committees divide, then appoint new committees and working parties. Powers of veto are invented, withheld and switched. Illingworth finally gets "the nod" and sets to work. He does not head for the nets; he does not go to watch new talent; he does not meet his captain: first there has to be a committee.

Dennis Amiss, Brian Bolus, Phil Sharpe, Doug Insole, Donald Carr, A. C. Smith, Fred Titmus, Ossie Wheatley, Bob Cottam . . . one could make a strong and rather well-balanced team from the 1960s players whose names flit through these pages: solid men no doubt, though arguably more effective in white flannels than in blazer and tie. Eventually, Illingworth does meet the captain, Mike Atherton, who has just returned from the West Indies (it is by now spring 1994) and thinks he has "quite a decent cricketing brain".

England's expected defeat in the 1994-95 Australia tour is overshadowed here by the sacking of Keith Fletcher. No one, according to Illingworth, quite seemed to know what Fletcher's role was; so various committees (Dennis Silk now to the fore) wield the knife. The world is informed not by Illingworth, Atherton or Silk but by the ubiquitous A. C. Smith, chief executive of the TCCB. Illingworth, who has appeared only briefly to witness England's travails in Australia, now assumes the role of team manager.

In South Africa in 1995-96, the Devon Malcolm problems come to a head. Illingworth's version of events is that he and Peter Lever, the bowling coach, merely tried to get Malcolm to follow through straight, as Michael Holding had also recommended; Lever did not call him a "nonentity" and they did not attempt to remodel his action completely. Rain and Mike Atherton's great match-saving innings at the Wanderers are the most memorable aspects of the tour until Cape Town, when Illingworth tells Malcolm, "You bowled crap and probably cost us the Test match." Although Illingworth and Lever obviously brought out the worst in Malcolm, this account conclusively shows that that was only too easy to do. It was not clever of Malcolm to play the race card, either, particularly as he was then forced to withdraw it. It is interesting that the other bowler Lever tried to help, Peter Martin, improved with every game.

This book did not have time to deal in detail with England's World Cup disasters or Illingworth's disciplinary problems, and subsequent pardon, in the wake of the Malcolm affair, which would have required a sequel. Two things, however, emerge clearly from this collaboration: first, that the administration of English cricket is too complicated and is prone to unnecessary secrecy; and, second, that Illingworth was frustrated as much by that structure as by his own shortcomings from giving all that he could have done to English cricket.

Jack Bannister is a busy man, though why he is the choice of so many cricketers as their ghost or co-author is a mystery, given his limited verbal powers. On the first page of his **Tampering with Cricket**, co-written with umpire Don Oslear, he offers a "pressure-cooker scenario", while page 12 reminds us that great fast bowlers "hunt in pairs". The subject here is ball-tampering, with various other malpractices roped in to make book length. The important ("fateful" to Bannister) incident took place in the Lord's one-day international between England and Pakistan in August 1992. Allan Lamb, who was batting, reported to umpires Ken Palmer and John Hampshire that Wasim and Waqar were interfering with the ball and that it was starting to swing violently. Don Oslear, the third umpire, was shown the scuffed ball at lunch and the match referee, Deryck Murray of West Indies, was called in. Everyone agreed that tampering had taken place, but under pressure from the Pakistan manager, Intikhab Alam, and the captain, Javed Miandad (who at one stage grabbed the ball and started rubbing it on his cycling shorts), Murray was persuaded into a "diplomatic" cover-up, deleting any suggestion of tampering from his statement about the change of ball at lunch time.

Oslear's contemporaneous notes make this version of events unimpeachable, and it is disappointing to think that Murray, outside the English committee structure and from a neutral country, did not feel he could make the facts available. In November 1993, Oslear's evidence was crucial in the libel action brought by Sarfraz Nawaz against Allan Lamb. Richie Benaud's recorded comments on seeing Aqib Javed working on the ball – "Aw, steady on ... Jeesuz" – were also unhelpful to Sarfraz, who dropped the case.

Trouble seems to have followed Don Oslear; and while Jack Bannister praises his integrity with all the eloquence he can muster – "his own man", "without fear or favour" and so on – one can imagine less charitable descriptions. Surrey gave him problems in the person of Waqar again, but the acting-captain Monte Lynch begged him not to report any tampering or he would be sacked. Oslear took pity, partly because he liked Lynch and partly because sending a report to the TCCB is not a very rewarding experience. Over his career Oslear has filed six reports of tampering and five of misconduct: no action has followed, and most of the reports have not even been acknowledged.

Bannister winds up with some depressing stories of how umpires and referees have failed to stop cheating and, in particular, intimidatory bowling. It is inevitable that such a book should end with a chapter called "Towards the Millennium", though here it is called "Whitherwards Authority?" "Whitherwards" is an interesting, Imran-and-Oxford sort of word, though in what respect Bannister imagines its meaning differs from that of its comprehensively educated cousin "whither" is not clear. For all the scuff marks on the surface, Bannister makes his central point well: "An examination of events chronicled in this book suggests it is difficult to refute Don Oslear's belief that the English cricket authorities run for cover whenever an unpleasant issue arises."

The crucial decision by Deryck Murray not to mention that the ball had been tampered with during the Texaco game at Lord's also plays a part in **Allan Lamb: My Autobiography**, a book that begins with fun and games on sunny South African pitches and ends with Lamb's disastrous libel action, with Ian Botham, against Imran Khan last year. We are taken through the whole saga once again by – for it is he – Jack Bannister, who must by now be able to rehearse the events in his sleep, and indeed frequently writes as though half-conscious. He does not consider whether Lamb's successful defence in court against his old team-mate Sarfraz Nawaz encouraged him to bring his preposterous action against Imran, or whether the blame should be placed on whoever advised Lamb and Botham to proceed in the first place. Any cricket lover who read about the grounds of the action on day one could only hang his head and curse the lawyers. "Every bit of advice Ian Botham and I were given was positive and encouraging," writes Lamb innocently – and there you have the whole sad story. There is some inadvertent humour when Bannister/Lamb talks about the Judge and leaves the reader unsure whether he is referring to the witness Robin Smith or His Lordship, but for the rest this is a very depressing book, a cautionary tale in the ways of certain lawyers and a dismal memorial to a man who brought such pugnacity and good humour to playing cricket.

In **Winning Ways**, Dermot Reeve comments that the libel action was "followed closely but not taken too seriously on the county circuit". Reeve's book, co-written with Patrick Murphy, is bustling, lippy, unburdened by natural talent and full of dressing-room gossip. Although he is amusing about Imran Khan's magnificent arrogance – justified by talent but rather less so by intelligence – most of Reeve's stories of sledging, niggling, winding-up and bickering are pathetic.

After all this it is a relief to find some cricket books about batting and bowling. **World Cricketers: A Biographical Dictionary**, compiled by Christopher Martin-Jenkins, aims to be a "readable reference book containing short cricketing biographies of every notable player or influential personality" from the origins of the game to the present day. It succeeds. Such a book must be heavy on fact, but this one does not eschew the colourful detail. Ted Dexter is a "T. E. Lawrence of the cricket field . . . an adventurer who will try anything once" (one may doubt whether he experimented with quite everything Lawrence indulged in); he was "apt to practise golf shots in the outfield", but was a "gifted dilettante . . . a hero too". The only way to evaluate such a book is to examine the entries for the players for whom the reader has a special affection, and this is a test the book passes gracefully. It is also well printed and bound, though why the publisher found it necessary to have four photographs of Wasim Akram on the jacket is not clear.

Alan Lee, cricket correspondent of *The Times*, has written a book called **Raising the Stakes**, subtitled "The Modern Cricket Revolution". Despite its forward-looking, whitherwards sort of title and the unappealing jacket photograph of Dominic Cork imploring the umpire for a decision, this is largely a nostalgic work. By comparing the professional lives of Ray Illingworth, Graham Gooch and Dominic Cork, Lee shows how the game has changed over three playing generations: not much for the better, is his implied conclusion, and it is difficult to disagree.

Gooch and Ken McEwan used to drive a Commer transit van with the team kit to away matches and would always have a drink in the pub with the opposition after play had finished; now the players simply disappear to their hotels in sponsored cars. Alan Lee is not a reactionary, but he is wistfully conservative about the passing of the old ways, particularly as the main force for change has not been any improvement in the game itself but merely the pursuit of cash. Lee would like to see Test cricket played in leagues with at least 12 countries and is cautiously in favour of leading English players being contracted to an international board rather than primarily to their county; the resulting shrinkage of the county scene he regards as inevitable and in some senses desirable. Lee is a much better writer than Jack Bannister, though in *Raising the Stakes* he does not have such a good story, in simple journalistic terms, as Bannister has in his more newsy co-operations.

In journalism, what is old is useless. But the rule of biography is that if a subject has been "done" once, then he is worth doing several times, the second or third attempts often being given spurious justification by supposed "revelations", often of a sexual nature. In **Wally Hammond: The Reasons Why**, David Foot says he has set out not to write a conventional biography but to "interpret the paradoxes and the darker mental caverns which dogged and distracted" the man who was, until Bradman's arrival, the best batsman in the world. Why was this masterful cricketer such a wretched man? Foot's belief is that Hammond suffered from syphilis, which he contracted on a tour of the West Indies in 1925-26. Foot, however, a transparently honourable writer, seems panicked by the tabloid implications of what he has suggested and too gentlemanly to follow his thesis in the detail it requires. What he says is this: "Wretchedly, his body's reaction to the experimental treatment added to the tortures and uncertainties of his protracted recovery. My belief is that it permanently affected his mental make-up, his traits of character and even, up to a point, his career as one of the world's greatest cricketers."

Foot is never more explicit than that. He can produce no evidence that the illness Hammond suffered was syphilis and little medical analysis of how the treatment affected him; it is almost as though he fears the production of hard evidence would be seen as prurient. This is a serious misjudgment. The claim itself is not so terrible – bacteria are no respecters of persons, even masters of the cover-drive – and in a climate where AIDS sufferers are embraced by Hollywood and the Princess of Wales, a dose of syphilis does not seem so very terrible. Without the follow-up documentation, however, Foot's thesis never leaves the plane of conjecture.

There are other feasible explanations of Hammond's character, the most succinct being supplied by his county captain Basil Allen, who was asked by Plum Warner: "That Wally Hammond of yours really is a wonderful chap, isn't he?" and replied: "If you want my honest opinion, Plum, I think he's an absolute shit." The Allen theory was the one most widely held in Hammond's

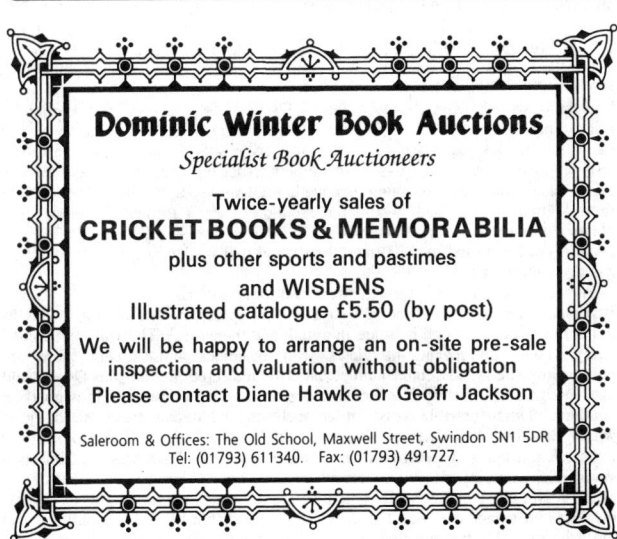

lifetime: although there were players whose awe of Hammond's talent made them uncritically respectful of him as a man, most people found him cold, selfish, surly and ungenerous to those younger or less gifted.

Hammond was a big drinker and a keen womaniser; a smile on his face when he arrived at the county ground was thought to mean he had been in luck the night before; a twirl of his bat when he took guard was taken to be a signal to a watching female; after being dismissed in a Test match he would sit for hours on the boundary looking at the women's enclosure through binoculars, then, his choice made, silently make off. When Eddie Paynter was asked for his reminiscences of the great batsman he thought for a long time before replying: "Wally, well, yes – he liked a shag."

David Foot does not consider the effects of this promiscuity in a man he has diagnosed as syphilitic and his accounts of Hammond's wives and girlfriends do little to illuminate Hammond's "darker mental caverns". Very late in the book Foot also raises the question of Hammond's racial origin. Was there, as one witness so delicately put it, "a touch of the tarbrush"? Again, no evidence is forthcoming; and Foot, having held off for reasons of delicacy about venereal disease, now over-indulges some coarse speculation he might have done better to paraphrase.

And yet, as a conventional biography, as the kind of book Foot did not mean to write, this account is excellent. Away from medical psychology and into cricket, Foot's knowledge of the game and unshakable sympathy for his awkward subject are powerful advantages. Hammond's rise through the professional ranks, his affectations of amateurism (fast cars, coloured handkerchiefs), his place in county folklore, his sadly underused bowling abilities, his ascent to the England captaincy – all these strands of the story are expertly handled, while those too young to have seen Hammond bat can almost picture him from Foot's descriptions. In an essay on Graeme Hick in *Wisden* 1989, Peter Roebuck said he thought Hick might have been a little like Hammond – "authoritative, commanding, civil and durable" – and it is interesting to see from the evidence in David Foot's account that Hammond might indeed have been like Hick on an exceptional day. But Bradman moved like a small, dark cloud across his sky; war came and Hammond aged fast. The last years brought dodgy jobs in the motor trade, emigration to South Africa, drink and penury. When Hammond died, aged only 62, Bradman had to help raise a fund for his widow and three children. As a former Gloucestershire player commented: "Greatest cricketer we'll ever see – but a funny bugger." David Foot has failed to illuminate the second half of that apt judgment, but he has done the first half proud.

Part of Hammond's problem was doubtless the rise and rise of D. G. Bradman. Bradman has attracted two new biographies, neither of which tells us much that is new, though both are thorough and thoughtful. **The Don**, by Roland Perry, draws on recent interviews with Bradman himself, but these are unrevealing; Perry has coaxed no revision or indiscretion from the Don in old age, though he himself goes over the old ground with enthusiasm. He is good on Bradman's unquenchable sense of competition and quotes from the diary in which Bradman recorded his tennis victories on the ship to England in 1930 ("beat Kippax 6–0 in semi-final"). In 1939, when Bradman was working as a stockbroker, he played a bit of squash to keep fit, and reached the final of the South Australian championship, where he met a Davis Cup tennis player. He lost the first two games and was 1–5 down in the third, but he was beginning to get the hang of it. He ground his opponent down to win 10–8 in the fifth.

The glory of Perry's biography is in the photographs. The picture of Bradman leaving the SCG in twilight, bat raised, after his last innings there in 1949 (courtesy of the *Sydney Sun*) and the one of him going out to bat at Leeds in 1938, walking modestly down a gangway of rapt, adoring faces (this one, alas, uncredited) are heart-stopping.

Charles Williams in **Bradman: An Australian Hero** ventures on to more technical ground by trying to analyse why Bradman was so pre-eminent; he looks at stance, grip, stillness of head, follow-through and so on. This is a more successful project than Perry's attempt to show by "biochemical" graphs (the so-called Bell curve) that Bradman was better at cricket than anyone else has ever been at any sport. Charles Williams also goes more deeply into the question of Australian identity and what sort of national need was satisfied by Bradman's pre-eminence in the sporting world; the fact that Bradman sprang from such a decent, modest, archetypically Australian background was ideal for a hero-hungry public in the depressed 1930s, though it made him unpopular with a certain Irish element in the Australian team. Both authors agree, as have their predecessors, on Bradman's shy, private personality, on his honour, determination and self-discipline; both are tactful to the point of reticence on the extent to which his illnesses in the war years were of physical or partly psychological origin; but Williams, formerly the biographer of de Gaulle, is the subtler. His book is also well illustrated (it includes the farewell to the SCG picture) and it is shorter – not a bad thing in a well-known story. Neither of these new biographies, however, replaces the gripping *Don Bradman's Book* (1930) on the stump-and-tennis-ball years (Williams has it in his bibliography; Perry does not), or Irving Rosenwater's *Sir Donald Bradman* (1978) for the mature years.

Peter May, meanwhile, has found a diligent and sympathetic biographer in Alan Hill, whose authorised life, entitled simply **Peter May**, has a foreword by Sir Colin Cowdrey. May's story, from Charterhouse prodigy to uneasy committee man, is pretty well known, but Hill has brought an impressive number of witnesses to his account of it. At the heart of May's character was a remarkable self-possession, which some saw as coldness, and Hill is anxious to bring the evidence of his friends, particularly J. J. Warr, to demonstrate that in family life or with a small circle of friends May was amusing and warm-hearted. In fact a certain ruthlessness was essential to May's success as a batsman and as a captain; it was this that won him the respect of the opposition, particularly the Australians who could scent the weakness in less decisive England captains. His habitual modesty and self-effacing manner did not inhibit his domineering attitude to bowlers; he feared no one, and Hill admirably evokes the power of his on- and straight-driving. Peter May seems to have undertaken the chairmanship of the selectors more from a sense of duty than of enjoyment, and was not unnaturally stung by coarse and uninformed press comment. Hill aptly quotes *Wisden's* obituary of this remarkable cricketer: "His gifts were sublime, indeed mysterious, and he bore them with honour, modesty and distinction."

The biographies of current players seem small beer by comparison, and it is interesting that the most popular account of a cricketing man has been that of an umpire, Harold Bird. There is not in fact very much to say about Dickie Bird, though what there is has been said with admirable concision by David Hopps in **Free as a Bird: The Life and Times of Harold "Dickie" Bird**. He is a moaner and a worrier; he was too nervous to be a successful batsman with Yorkshire and Leicestershire, though he had some talent; he found his *métier*, somewhat improbably, as an umpire, where he has been almost universally liked and respected. "For eccentricity and authority to go together is rare enough," Hopps writes. "To combine them in such quantity as Bird has is arguably unique."

Anyway, that is the Bird story, and the rest is anecdote. Hopps thinks Bird's disinclination to give lbw decisions in the bowler's favour may have stemmed from conversations with Johnny Wardle, who made him understand how many balls delivered from wide of the crease would miss the stumps. In the final of the NatWest Trophy at Lord's in 1995, Bird took this scepticism beyond the bounds of plausibility when Anil Kumble of Northamptonshire continually struck Dermot Reeve of Warwickshire on the shin with straight top-spinners but still failed to extract a decision. No one, however, has ever suggested that Bird is less than scrupulous, or scrupulously honest; and while his on-field flapping may have annoyed spectators, people who know him are certain that it was due to genuine anxiety rather than any cheap desire for attention. A second book about Bird, **Dickie: A Tribute to Umpire Harold Bird**, edited by Brian Scovell, has contributions from many players which, though uniformly affectionate in tone, are anecdotally limp. Many of them appear anyway in David Hopps's biography.

Robert Winder's **Hell for Leather: A Modern Cricket Journey** stands out from the other books under review, initially because it is of a different genre. The back of the (extremely garish) jacket calls it "a personal view of the 'cricketing experience' seen from the hurly-burly of the 1996 World Cup". This is apt as far as it goes, though the book seems really to be attempting three things: to report on the World Cup, both on and off the pitch; to relate this narrative to the personal experience of the author both as traveller in India and club cricketer at home; and most importantly to try to throw off all received ideas about cricket – Test, one-day and amateur – and the way it is thought about and reported, and analyse afresh its nature, its appeal, and its future.

In other words, this is an ambitious book, especially when you consider that its far-reaching concerns have been kept down to a very reasonable 270 pages and are expressed in a lively, conversational style. As straight reporting, *Hell for Leather* is outstanding; Winder's description of Tendulkar facing Ambrose evokes the brilliance of both players, while his evocations of the rhythm of a one-day match unfolding are acute and dramatic. It helps that he likes the one-day game and does not view it as a perversion or travesty; one-day cricket, after all, *is* cricket as experienced by the great majority of people who play the game.

On the journalistic background to the tournament, Winder is depressingly good. How does an England press conference in which routine questions are boringly and routinely answered by the captain and manager turn into a tabloid sensation the next morning? The answer is by all the tabloid reporters getting together and working out how some innocuous "quote" can be flammed up into a "rift" or "shock". They must all have the same "shock" too, or they might be disturbed over dinner by their editors in London asking them to match another paper's story. Although tabloid readers probably discount about half of what they read as being unreliable, it is only people who work with the relevant reporters who know that readers should actually discount twice that amount. The autobiographical element is also well handled and extremely funny.

Winder is merciless on England's shortcomings, as players and as people. "It's amazing how much they hate us," Graham Thorpe remarks, but Winder's comparison of other countries' elementary courtesy compared to England's ignorance and surliness shows that it is not amazing at all, while his account of

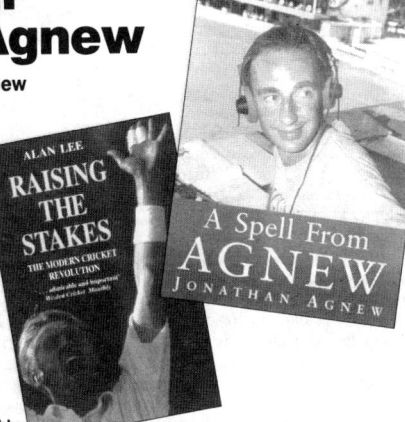

an England practice session is enough to make one weep. The future is with the subcontinent, inevitably, it appears: that is where the money and the enthusiasm are. As far as England are concerned, Winder agrees with Alan Lee in suggesting a contraction of the county scene, which will have to go semi-pro, in order to give more competition to the best players; he speculates on teams of London versus the North and points out that there are only about 30 full-time professionals in Australia.

Winder does not have all the answers, but at least he has asked the questions; that, and the excellence of the reporting (the Australia–Sri Lanka final in particular), make this the outstanding book of the season. This is bad luck on Mike Marqusee, whose alternative view of the World Cup, **War Minus the Shooting**, might otherwise seem even more interesting than it is. Marqusee is an American socialist (says his publisher) based in London, who is fascinated by cricket both as a game and as a political and cultural force. He has gone deeply into the questions of race, caste and religious division that divide the game on the subcontinent; he shows how the game of cricket is for millions in this part of the world both an escape from, and a metaphorical enactment of, historic and national rivalries: it is not like a Sunday slog at Chelmsford. This is not a comfortable book to read, but nor is it meant to be. Marqusee has a similar view to Robert Winder of the English side's hopeless lack of education, self-awareness and public relations skills (especially compared to the South Africans), but is more critical of attitudes (from all countries) he believes to be racist. This is a challenging and dignified book, though it is not for those who want more detail of whether Roger Twose was provoked by Dermot Reeve to tell David Capel he was ugly.

Admirers of E. W. Swanton will be pleased by **Last Over**, which contains many of Swanton's greatest hits and some real curiosities, with linking commentaries by David Rayvern Allen and Swanton himself. Allen talks of Swanton's "balanced, reasoned, constructive, sometimes portentous but always well-informed accounts", and all those qualities are on show here, though the book's scope goes beyond cricket to include a letter to the *Spectator* criticising Enoch Powell in 1968 and memories of life on the Burma-Siam railway as a POW. There is also a fascinating letter to Swanton from Field Marshal Montgomery in 1968 which criticises Colin Cowdrey's captaincy of England and stresses the importance of boldness – from which flows luck, the vital ingredient – in leadership, and an extraordinary letter written by Swanton to Alec Bedser, then a selector, arguing the case for Tony Greig's selection in 1970. There is curiously little development of style in the journalism; Swanton seems to have been born oracular. But readers of his autobiography *Sort of a Cricket Person* need not feel that they will be familiar with the material here; on the contrary, *Last Over* is a rather frisky and surprising complement.

In **Uncorked!** Dominic Cork shares his thoughts on the 1995 and 1995-96 seasons, in which time he moved from uncapped player to England's fieriest performer, collecting a hat-trick against West Indies on the way. To begin with it is all frustration as he keeps hoping for "the nod" from the selectors, but when it finally comes for the one-dayers, life soon becomes sweet: "After the match I drove to London on my own and checked in at the Conrad Hotel in Chelsea Harbour. It's a top spot. The lads have no complaint about staying there." At Trent Bridge for the Fifth Test he goes out to join Geoffrey Boycott and Brian Lara. Boycott says to Lara: "Don't let that little twat get you out. With his pace he'll never get you going back. Get a hundred against him." Cork likes a bit of confrontation, however: his favourite opponents being the ex-Derbyshire batsmen Peter Bowler and Daryll Cullinan. Cork's angle on the Devon Malcolm–Ray Illingworth problems in South Africa is cautiously pro-Malcolm, though he points out that "Plank" (Peter Lever) called him (Cork) a "pillock" for his bowling at Lord's. When he rings home and his baby son says "Dada" for the first time, Cork remarks that he appears to be the only person in the Derby area who hasn't commented on Malcolm. Cork's most admired batsman is "Judgey" (Robin Smith), though he is also keen on "Winker", "Daffy" and "Digger". The publisher has provided a glossary.

It is a mistake to read Cork's book after **Pod Almighty: The Dave Podmore Story** as told to Christopher Douglas, Nick Newman and Andrew Nickolds. Although it won't, this pitiless spoof should be enough to deter all future recollections of life on the circuit. Pod, a seam bowler, is always hoping for "the nod" from the selectors after 23 years of keeping it there or thereabouts, particularly in what he calls a "diarrhoea finish". He gets a sniff of the nod quite early on, or at least he feels he is in with a shout of a sniff of the nod; but many curries, panatellas and car sponsorship deals have gone under the bridge before the nod itself comes for an injury-affected Indian tour. Dysentery makes it a tricky trip. On the first day of the Second Test in Bombay, Pod reflects: "To be fair, Reevesie's mum is the only one of us in any serious nick at the moment." The final chapter is called "Towards the Millennium" – though it could equally have been called "Whitherwards Authority?" – and Pod's main recommendation is automatic weapons for the figures in authority, or as he puts it "Tool up the Umps". This book is very funny, but you should not read it if you ever intend to take a real cricket memoir seriously again.

Sebastian Faulks is an author, journalist and enthusiastic village cricketer. Among his novels is the international best-seller Birdsong.

BOOKS RECEIVED IN 1996

GENERAL

Bassano, Brian **South African Cricket 1947-1960** (Cricket Connections International, 15 Hylands Road, Epsom, Surrey KT19 7ED, £14.50 paperback, £19.50 hardback; p&p extra for overseas orders)

Booth, Keith **Atherton's Progress: From Kensington Oval to Kennington Oval** (Clifford Frost Publications; from the author, 6 Kingswood Drive, Sutton, Surrey SM2 5NB, £9.95 + £1.55 p&p)

Christen, Richard **Some Grounds to Appeal: The Australian Venues for First-Class Cricket** (from the author, PO Box 762, Parramatta, NSW 2150, $A50, £25 in UK)

Craven, Nico **A Moveable Feast** Foreword by Scyld Berry (from the author, The Coach House, Ponsonby, Seascale, Cumberland CA20 1BX, £5.55)

Dexter, Ted with Ralph Dellor **Ted Dexter's Little Cricket Book: A Collection of Inspirational Anecdotes** (Bloomsbury, £12.99)

Douglas, Christopher, Newman, Nick and Nickolds, Andrew **Pod Almighty: The Dave Podmore Story** (Simon & Schuster, £9.99)

Freddi, Cris **The Guinness Book of Cricket Blunders** (Guinness Publishing, £9.99)

Falkenmire, David ed. **At Last! The Quest for the Shield 1926-1995** (The Dell Partnership, 48 Jephson Street, Toowong, Queensland 4066, $A35 + $10 p&p to UK; leather-bound edition signed by every member of Queensland team that won the Sheffield Shield, $A300)

Greenway, Harry MP ed. **Electing to Bat: Tales of glory and disaster from the Palace of Westminster** (Lennard/Queen Anne, £12.99)

Illingworth, Ray and Bannister, Jack **One-Man Committee: The controversial reign of England's cricket supremo** (Headline, £17.99)

Knott, Richard comp. **Cricket: Wit, Wickets and Wisdom** (Running Press, miniature edition, £3.50)

Lee, Alan **Raising the Stakes: The Modern Cricket Revolution** (Gollancz, £16.99)

McLellan, Alistair ed. **Nothing Sacred: The New Cricket Culture** (Two Heads, £7.99)

Marqusee, Mike **War Minus the Shooting: A journey through South Asia during Cricket's World Cup** (William Heinemann, £12.99)

Meher-Homji, Kersi **Hat-Tricks** (Kangaroo Press, PO Box 6125, Dural Delivery Centre, NSW 2158, $A14.95 + $5.30 air mail p&p; in UK from Hi Marketing, 38 Carver Road, London SE24 9LT, £7.99)

Meher-Homji, Kersi **Six Appeal: On Soaring Sixes and Lusty Six-Hitters** Foreword by Doug Walters (Kangaroo Press, $A16.95, £9.45 in UK)

Oslear, Don and Bannister, Jack **Tampering with Cricket** (Collins Willow, £14.99)

Rayvern Allen, David ed. **In the Covers: The Best Cricket Writing of the Year** (Headline, £15.99)

Scovell, Brian ed. **Dickie: A Tribute to Umpire Harold Bird** (Partridge Press, £12.99)

Shuja Ud-Din Butt with Salim Parvez **Babes of Cricket to World Champion: A History of Pakistan Cricket 1947-1996** Foreword by Zaheer Abbas (from the authors at 32 E Askari Apartments III, School Road, Karachi Cantonment, Karachi, Pakistan or 31 Cambridge Road, Hounslow, Middlesex TW4 7BT, R150 or £15.99)

Smith, Nigel **Kiwis Declare: Players tell the story of New Zealand cricket** (Random House New Zealand; in UK from Sportspages, 94-96 Charing Cross Road, London WC2H 0JG and Barton Square, St Ann's Square, Manchester M2 7HA, £19.95)

Sobers, Sir Garfield with Ivo Tennant **The Changing Face of Cricket** (Ebury Press, £16.99)

Swanton, E. W. with David Rayvern Allen **Last Over: A Life in Cricket** (Richard Cohen Books, £18.99)

Willis, Bob with Pat Gibson **Cricket: Six of the Best** Foreword by Allan Border (Hodder & Stoughton, £14.99)

Winder, Robert **Hell for Leather: A Modern Cricket Journey** (Gollancz, £17.99)

AUTOBIOGRAPHY

Cork, Dominic with David Norrie **Uncorked! Diary of a Cricket Year** (Richard Cohen Books, £15.99)

Lamb, Allan with Jack Bannister **My Autobiography** (Collins Willow, £15.99)

Reeve, Dermot with Patrick Murphy **Winning Ways** (Boxtree, £15.99)

Smith, David with Paul Newman **Larger than Life: The David Smith Story** Foreword by Micky Stewart (Two Heads, £14.99)

BIOGRAPHY

Foot, David **Wally Hammond: The Reasons Why** (Robson Books, £17.95)

Gunasekara, Channa **The Willow Quartette: A Study of Four Former Cricket Stalwarts of Ceylon 1930-1965** (Sumathi Publishers; from N. Sivasambu, Palmyrah Beddagama, 28 Tavistock Place, London WC1H 9RE, £3.50 + 26p p&p)

Hearne, Jack **Wheelwrights to Wickets: The Story of the Cricketing Hearnes** Foreword by E. W. Swanton (Boundary Books, Southlands, Sandy Lane, Goostrey, Cheshire CW4 8NT, £13.95. Limited edition of 50, £65)

Hill, Alan **Peter May: A Biography** Foreword by Sir Colin Cowdrey (Andre Deutsch, £15.99)

Hopps, David **Free as a Bird: The Life and Times of Harold "Dickie" Bird** Foreword by Geoffrey Boycott (Robson Books, £14.95)

Narinesingh, Clifford **Gavaskar: Portrait of a Hero** (Royards Publishing, Union Village, Claxton Bay, Trinidad; in UK from Chris Lloyd Sales, 463 Ashley Road, Parkstone, Dorset BH14 0AX, £14.95, hardback; £9.95, paperback)

Perry, Roland **The Don** Based on interviews with cricket legend Sir Donald Bradman (Sidgwick & Jackson, £25)

Phillips, Barry **Arthur Wellard: No Mere Slogger** Foreword by Harold Pinter (Leisuresolve, 13 Hawthorn Ave, Headington, Oxford OX3 9JQ, £15.99)

Piesse, Ken **Warne: Sultan of Spin: An Unauthorised Biography** (Modern Publishing, PO Box 126, Baxter, Victoria 3911, $A19.95, paperback; in UK from Sportspages, 94-96 Charing Cross Road, London WC2H 0JG and Barton Square, St Ann's Square, Manchester M2 7HA, £13.50)

Williams, Charles **Bradman: An Australian Hero** (Little, Brown, £20)

PICTORIAL

Jenkins, Viv **Fields of Glory: A Celebration of Cricket in Australia** Foreword by Richie Benaud (Harper Sports, Australia; in UK from Sportspages, 94-96 Charing Cross Road, London WC2H 0JG and Barton Square, St Ann's Square, Manchester M2 7HA, $A29.95, £19.95)

Levine, Emma **Cricket: A Kind of Pilgrimage** (Local Colour, Hong Kong, £17.50)

Powell, William A. **Cricket Phone Cards** (Cricket Memorabilia Society, 29 Highclere Road, Crumpsall, Manchester M8 4WS, £6·99)

Powell, William A., comp. **Surrey County Cricket Club: The archive photographs series** (Chalford Publishing, St Mary's Mill, Chalford, Glos GL6 8NX, £9.99)

Speight, Martin **A Cricketer's View: A Collection of Paintings** (Two Heads, £9.99)

TECHNICAL

Gough, Darren with David Hopps **Darren Gough's Book for Young Cricketers: My Guide to Your Success** Foreword by Ian Botham (Hodder & Stoughton, £14.99)

Tuffery, Alan **Thinking About Cricket Umpiring: An Aid for Aspiring Umpires** (from the author, 9 Grange Park Avenue, Raheny, Dublin 5, Ireland, £4.99 + 50p p&p to UK)

REFERENCE

Martin-Jenkins, Christopher **World Cricketers: A Biographical Dictionary** (Oxford University Press, £25)

STATISTICAL

Bailey, Philip comp. **First-Class Cricket Matches 1901** (ACS, 3 Radcliffe Road, West Bridgford, Nottingham NG2 5FF, £13.99)

Bailey, Philip comp. **Important Match Scores 1801-1819** and **1820-29** (ACS, address as above, £8.99 and £9.99 respectively)

Bailey, Philip, Lane, Bill and Thorn, Philip comp. **Jamaica Cricketers 1894-95 – 1994-95** (ACS, address as above, £3)

Bailey, Philip comp. **Sri Lanka First Class Matches 1991-92** (ACS, address as above, £4.99)

Clayton, Howard, Griffiths, Peter and Sederman, Derek **England Under-19 Test Matches and One-day Internationals** (ACS, address as above, £9.99)

Dyson, Paul E. comp. **Benson and Hedges Cup Record Book 1972-1995** (ACS, address as above, £8.99)

Griffiths, Peter and Wynne-Thomas, Peter **Complete First-Class Match List Volume 1 1801-1914** (ACS, address as above, £7.99)

Heald, Brian ed. **Statistical Survey 1872** (ACS, address as above, £4.99)

Isaacs, Vic **Hampshire County Cricket Club One-Day Records 1963-1995** (Limlow Books, Blue Bell House, 2-4 Main Street, Scredington, Sleaford, Lincs NG34 0AE, £8.50 + 50p p&p)

Isherwood, Robin and Bailey, Philip comp. **Western Province Cricketers 1889-90 – 1995-96** (ACS, address as above, £3.99)

Johns, Nigel **Somerset County Cricket Club First-Class Records 1882-1995** (Limlow Books, address as above, £9 + 50p p&p)

Ledbetter, Jim ed. **First-Class Cricket: A Complete Record 1934** (Limlow Books, address as above, £15.95 + £1.50 p&p)

Lodge, Derek **D. G. Bradman** His Record Innings-by-Innings (ACS, address as above, £4.99)

Menon, Mohandas **World Cup Cricket '96: A Statistical Survey 1975-1992** (Marine Sports, 63a Gokhale Road (North), Dadar, Bombay 400 028, R100)

Salim Parvez **Hanif Mohammed** His Record Innings-by-Innings (ACS, address as above, £4.99)

Sandiford, Keith **Clyde Walcott** His Record Innings-by-Innings (ACS, address as above, £4.99)

Walmsley, Keith **Clem Hill** His Record Innings-by-Innings (ACS, address as above, £6.99)

Ward, John comp. **Zimbabwe First Class Matches 1995-96** (ACS, address as above, £3.99)

Wynne-Thomas, Peter **Nottinghamshire County Cricket Club First-Class Records 1826-1995** (Limlow Books, address as above, £8.50 + 50p p&p)

FIRST-CLASS COUNTY YEARBOOKS, 1996

Derbyshire (£4.50), Durham (£6), Essex (£6), Glamorgan (£5.50), Gloucestershire (£3), Hampshire (£6), Kent (£4.99), Lancashire (£6), Leicestershire (£4.95), Middlesex (£8), Northamptonshire (£7), Nottinghamshire (£4.50), Somerset (£6.50), Surrey (£5), Sussex (£6), Warwickshire (£4.50), Worcestershire (£4), Yorkshire (£9.50). 1997 prices may change. Some counties may add charges for p&p.

CLUB CRICKET

Collis, G. R. **The Jack of Clubs** (Pentland Press, 1, Hutton Close, South Church, Bishop Auckland, Co. Durham DL14 6XB, £5.99)

Fairbank, David and Ulyatt, Mike, comp. **The Pen Pushers of High Street: A Centenary History of Hull Zingari** (from Mike Ulyatt, 28 Blackthorn Lane, Willerby, Hull HU10 6RD, £9.95)

The Forty Club **Diamond Anniversary Brochure** (The Forty Club, 113 Palace View, Bromley, Kent BR1 3EP, £2.50)

Redbourn, Dick **Cricket at the grassroots: Humorous memories of the Sussex club game** (SB Publications, 19 Grove Road, Seaford, East Sussex BN25 1TP, £10.50)

OTHER HANDBOOKS AND ANNUALS

Bader, Nauman ed. **PCB Wills Cricket Annual 1995-96** (from Limlow Books, Blue Bell House, 2-4 Main Street, Scredington, Sleaford, Lincs NG34 0AE, £21 inc. p&p)

Bailey, Philip comp. **ACS International Cricket Year Book 1996** (ACS, 3 Radcliffe Road, West Bridgford, Nottingham NG2 5FF, £9.99)

Berry, Mike ed. **Minor Counties Cricket Annual and Official Handbook 1996** (ACS, address as above, £4.99)

Bryden, Colin ed. **Protea Assurance South African Cricket Annual 1996** (UCBSA/Protea Assurance, PO Box 646, Cape Town 8000, no price given)

Il Cricket Italiano (from Associazione Italiana Cricket, Via S. Ignazio 9, 00186 Roma)

The Cricketers' Who's Who, 1996 Statistics by Richard Lockwood (Lennard/Queen Anne Press, £12.99)

Frindall, Bill ed. **NatWest Playfair Cricket Annual 1996** (Headline, £4.99)

Hatton, Les comp. **ACS First Class Counties Second Eleven Annual** (ACS, address as above, £4.99)

Lemmon, David ed. **Benson and Hedges Cricket Year Fifteenth Edition** Foreword by David Lloyd (Bloomsbury, £20)

Miller, Allan ed. **Allan's Australian Cricket Annual 1995-96** (from Allan Miller, PO Box 974, Busselton, WA 6280, $A37.95; in UK from Sport in Print, 3 Radcliffe Road, West Bridgford, Nottingham NG2 5FF, £17.50 inc. p&p)

National Association of Young Cricketers 1996 Year Book (NAYC, £3)

FICTION

Botham, Ian and Coath, Dennis **Deep Cover** (Harper Collins, £5.99, paperback)

CHILDREN'S FICTION

Cattell, Bob **The Big Test** and **World Cup Fever** (Julia Macrae Books, £8.99 each hardback, Red Fox, £2.99 each paperback)
Hardcastle, Michael **The Fastest Bowler in the World** (Faber & Faber, £9.99)

VERSE

Shakespeare, Colin **22 Cricket Poems** (Oak Press, PO Box 16, Birkenshaw, Bradford BD11 2YX, £6.50 inc. p&p)

MONOGRAPHS AND PAMPHLETS

Baloch, Khadim Hussain **Wallis Mathias: A Memorial – The Life and Times of a Gentleman Cricketer** (from Martin Wood, 2 St John's Road, Sevenoaks, Kent TN13 3LW, £1.75 + 26p p&p UK, 76p overseas surface mail)
Clements, Roy **A Short History of Irish Cricket with Literary Connections** (from J. W. MacKenzie, 12 Stoneleigh Park Road, Ewell, Surrey KT19 0QT)
Engel, Matthew ed. **Thirty Obituaries from Wisden** (Penguin, 60p)
Heavens, Roger **Cricket's Other Chronicler: Arthur Haygarth 1825-1903** (from the author, 2 Lowfields, Little Eversden, Cambs CB3 7HJ, £1)
Hit Racism For Six: Race and Cricket in England Today (Centre for Sport Development Research, Dept of Sport Studies, Roehampton Institute, London SW15 3SN, £2.50)
West, William T. **Gentlemen and Players: The First Seventy Years** (from the author, "Lindis", Roundhay Road, Bridlington, Yorks YO15 3JZ, no price given)

REPRINTS AND UPDATES

Atherton, Mike with Pat Gibson **A Test of Cricket: Know the Game** Updated 1996 edition (Hodder & Stoughton, £8.99)
Benaud, Richie **The Appeal of Cricket: The Modern Game** Updated paperback (Coronet, £7.99)
Berkmann, Marcus **Rain Men** Paperback edition (Abacus, £6.99)
Bhogle, Harsha **Azhar** Revised and updated edition (Penguin India R150; in UK from Sportspages, 94-96 Charing Cross Road, London WC2H 0JG and Barton Square, St Ann's Square, Manchester M2 7HA, £6.95)
Frindall, Bill **The Guinness Book of Cricket Facts and Feats** Fourth Edition (Guinness Publishing, £13.99)
Grayson, Edward **Corinthians and Cricketers and Towards a New Sporting Era** Updated version of 1995 book with new foreword by Gary Lineker (Yore Publications, 12 The Furrows, Hatfield, Middlesex UB9 6AT, £9.95)
Arthur Haygarth's Scores and Biographies Volume One 1746-1826 (Facsimile edition, from Roger Heavens, 2 Lowfields, Little Eversden, Cambs CB3 7HJ, £50 + £3.50 p&p (UK), £4.50 (elsewhere). Volumes Two and Three scheduled for 1997)
Holmes, Bob and Marks, Vic **Fifty Cricket Stars describe My Greatest Game** Paperback edition (Mainstream, £9.99)
Lee, Alan **Lord Ted: The Dexter Enigma** Paperback edition (Vista, £6.99)
James Lillywhite's Cricketers' Annual 1896 Facsimile edition (Cricket Lore, 22 Grazebrook Road, London N16 0HS, £11.95 UK, £13.95 overseas inc. p&p)
Murphy, Colm **Catalogue of Cricket Philately** Second edition (from the author, 7 St Bartholomew's Terrace, Rochester, Kent ME1 1BX, £6)
Rosenwater, Irving comp. **500 Notable Cricket Quotations** Paperback edition (Andre Deutsch, £6.99)
Ryder, Rowland **Cricket Calling** Paperback edition (Faber & Faber, £7.99)
John Wisden's Cricketers' Almanacks for 1900 and 1901 Facsimile edition (Willows Publishing, 17 The Willows, Stone, Staffs ST15 0DE, £44 (1900), £46 (1901) inc. p&p UK, £2 extra overseas; £5 extra for version with facsimile of original hard cloth cover)

PERIODICALS

Cricket Digest (scheduled for three issues a year, 13 Wynter St, London SW11 2TZ, £2.50 or £7.50 per year)

The Cricketer International (monthly) editorial director Richard Hutton (Beech Hanger, Ashurst, Tunbridge Wells, Kent TN3 9ST, £2.50)

The Cricketer Quarterly: Facts and Figures ed. Richard Lockwood (The Cricketer International, address as above, £2.80)

Cricket Lore (ten per volume, frequency variable) ed. Richard Hill (Cricket Lore, 22 Grazebrook Road, London N16 0HS, £35 per volume)

The Cricket Statistician (quarterly) ed. Philip J. Bailey (ACS, 3 Radcliffe Road, West Bridgford, Nottingham NG2 5FF, £1.50, free to ACS members)

Cricket World (most months) editorial director Michael Blumberg (157 Praed Street, London W2 1RL, £2.35)

Howzat (irregular, "at least quarterly") editor-in-chief Olisa Egwuatu (c/o David Jay Communications, PO Box 2653, Ikeja, Lagos State, Nigeria 100 Naira)

Inside Edge (Australia, monthly) managing editor Norman Tasker (ACP Publishing, 54 Park Street, Sydney, NSW 2000, $A5.20)

Inside Edge (UK, monthly in summer) ed. Alastair McLellan (PO Box 10006, London N19 3XG, £1.95)

The Journal of the Cricket Society (twice yearly) ed. Clive W. Porter (from Mr P. Ellis, 63 Groveland Road, Beckenham, Kent BR3 3PX, £5 to non-members)

Minor Counties News (ten issues a year) (from counties or from Mike Berry, Idsworth, 3 Fair Close, Frankton, Rugby, Warwicks CV23 9PL, annual subscription £10)

Red Stripe Caribbean Quarterly ed. Tony Cozier (Cozier Publishing, PO Box 40W, Worthing, Christ Church, Barbados, annual subscription £12 Europe, $BDS22 Barbados, $BDS28/$US14 rest of the West Indies, $US18 US, $Can24 Canada, $US24 elsewhere)

SA Cricket Action (eight issues a year) (Cricket Action Subscriptions, PO Box 2735, Cape Town 8000, R9.50)

Wisden Cricket Monthly ed. Tim de Lisle (25 Down Road, Merrow, Guildford, Surrey GU1 2PY, £2.50)

INDEX

Heavens, Roger **An Index to Frederick Lillywhite's/Haygarth's Cricket Scores and Biographies of Celebrated Cricketers Volumes One to Ten, 1746-1868** (Roger Heavens, 2 Lowfields, Little Eversden, Cambs CB3 7HJ, £4.95 each inc. p&p)

COMPUTER DATABASE

Test Cricket Database (Ric Finlay, 214 Warwick Street, West Hobart, Tasmania 7000 $A50, £30 in UK airmail + £30 subscription for annual updates)

THE CRICKET SOCIETY LITERARY AWARD

The Cricket Society Literary Award has been presented since 1970 to the author of the cricket book judged as best of the year. The 1997 award went to Charles Williams for **Bradman: An Australian Hero**.

CRICKET VIDEOS, 1996

By STEVEN LYNCH

A famous name made an unheralded appearance on the video shelves during 1996. Twentieth Century Fox, traditionally associated with Hollywood blockbusters, turned its attention to cricket and, in association with Sky TV, produced **Atherton's Innings**, a look at the England captain's great rearguard action at Johannesburg. The tension is not quite the same when you know the outcome, but it is none the less a fitting memento of a monumental innings. The same company also released a two-hour review of the 1996 English season, **Ultimate Cricket '96**.

The small pool into which Fox is dipping its paw contains one big fish. **Cover Point** continued to release their increasingly authoritative monthly video magazine, in which elusive footage of overseas Tests is a particular delight. They also produced an end-of-season round-up, and an entertaining World Cup review. Cover Point catered for the county supporter in 1996 as well, releasing titles of special interest to Kent, Lancashire and Yorkshire followers. Their new **Superstars of Cricket** series saw five of England's finest talking to Patrick Murphy of BBC Radio, an experienced and sympathetic interviewer. His chat with Mike Atherton was the pick of the programmes, which all last about 45 minutes, though England's poor Test performances led to some comment about the use of the word "superstar".

Comedy came in the form of two tapes from the ITV comedy **Outside Edge**, one including the whole second series, and the other following the club's annual tour. Most weekend cricketers will recognise some of the stereotypes on view, from the star player to the captain's much put-upon wife. More laddish humour was available in a longer and less vigorously edited version of the BBC's **They Think It's All Over** comedy quiz. The cricket content is supplied by the presence of David Gower.

VIDEOS RECEIVED IN 1996

Atherton's Innings (Twentieth Century Fox; £12.99)

Benson and Hedges "King Side": The Lancashire Triumphs of 1995 and '96 (Cover Point; £13.99)

Cover Point Video magazine (Cover Point Cricket Ltd, 113 Upper Tulse Hill, London SW2 2RD; ten issues per year for £89.99 in UK)

The Cricketing Cowdreys Presented by Cliff Morgan (Cover Point; £16.45)

Lombard Official History of Kent CCC (Cover Point; £12.99)

Outside Edge: Series Two and The Corfu Tour (Carlton; £10.99 each)

Superstars of Cricket: Interviews with Mike Atherton, Dominic Cork, Darren Gough, Graeme Hick, Graham Thorpe (Cover Point; £8.99 each)

They Think It's All Over No Holds Barred (BBC; £12.99)

Ultimate Cricket '96 (Twentieth Century Fox; £12.99)

Yorkshire – Gathering Pace The Story of the 1996 Season. Presented by Michael Parkinson. (Cover Point; £12.99)

Prices shown are Recommended Retail Prices.

CRICKET AND THE MEDIA IN 1996

By DAVID McKIE

What with the European Soccer Championships, staged in England, and the Atlanta Olympics to add to all its other familiar summer competitors, cricket got rather squeezed in the summer of 1996 – despite the expansion of sports pages for what newspapers, sensing that sport was now selling papers as never before, had designated the "Summer of Sport".

Pages assigned to Fantasy Cricket appeared to be sacrosanct, but elsewhere the game, as they say in newspaper offices when editorial space is fought over, had to "take its chance". Still, given some of the coverage which English cricket did come in for, this was perhaps a mercy. "They were as solid as 11 jellies in a hurricane," Geoffrey Boycott wrote in *The Sun* after the final Test against Pakistan under the headline: "ATHERS FLOPS ARE SPINELESS NO-HOPERS". But the paper's leader writers were too busy with Charles and Camilla to spare a word for The Oval. And no one, for once, got compared to a turnip.

The two scheduled big events of the summer programme – England v India, England v Pakistan – were hardly a match for the great off-pitch battles: Devon Malcolm v Raymond Illingworth, and Ian Botham and Allan Lamb v Imran Khan. Families, friends, offices, pubs, even his native county of Yorkshire, quarrelled over the Illingworth issue almost as much as they did over Princess Di. Few fought the Yorkshireman's corner as doughtily as Michael Parkinson (Barnsley and the *Daily Telegraph*). Illy's error, he argued, was not to say what he had about Malcolm – "in my view he lets the player off lightly" – but to publish when he did, thus strengthening the hands of his enemies at Lord's, a significant number of whom, it appeared, were called Smith. If Illingworth went, Parkinson warned, the replacement might be A. C., "a thought too terrible to contemplate". More awful still would be the enthronement as permanent chairman of the selectors of M. J. K. – "a risk to our good name and national standing far worse than dodgy beef or gay priests".

These sentiments earned an official rebuke from his *Telegraph* colleague Christopher Martin-Jenkins. Writing more in sorrow than anger, he seemed less pro-Malcolm than anti-pro-Illingworth, deploring especially those who tried to defend their hero by casting doubt on Smiths who had worked no less hard than Illingworth for the good of English cricket. Ian Wooldridge in the *Daily Mail* was less temperate. He said Lord's should have fired Illingworth as soon as they saw his book.

Meanwhile, in the Strand, the Shane Warne of litigation, George Carman QC, was spinning Imran Khan back from what some had assumed was likely to be an innings defeat. "No one can deny," Carman was reported as saying, "that this case is emotionally charged. Issues of race, class and country move in and out of it like black clouds" – a diagnosis which acres of newspaper coverage did much to support.

Even the women's pages took up the theme with profiles of the wives: Jemima Khan, Kathy Botham and Lindsay Lamb in their moments of Gethsemane. Occasionally, the newspapers even explored the effects of this case on cricket. It was all too likely, they warned, to stoke up the animosities which had for so long defaced England–Pakistan series. Remember Donald Carr and the soaking of Idris Begh? Mike Gatting and Shakoor Rana? As the season advanced, it was clear that the truth was the opposite.

The series was virtually free from hostilities – largely because, the newspapers later concluded, Mike Atherton and his Lancashire colleague Wasim Akram were such good friends. Unfortunately, the lack of on-pitch or off-pitch punch-ups made the series, in terms of tabloid coverage, boring, and the space allotted suffered accordingly.

There was a good deal of grumbling – about the England team, naturally, the grounds, especially Edgbaston and Headingley, and the umpiring. But that at least could now frequently be blamed on foreigners. Imran Khan, whose Carman-like advocacy had helped establish the case for neutral umpires in the first place, drew a different conclusion from most: "I just hope the umpiring is better than what we have seen so far," he wrote in the *Daily Telegraph* after the Trent Bridge Test. "Thank God for the neutral umpire, otherwise it would have been like the 1980s when hardly a series was played where touring teams did not blame biased home umpiring for their misfortunes." As Mike Selvey pointed out in *The Guardian*, the instant scrutiny to which modern Test umpires were subjected appeared to be having an adverse effect: "Direct television replays and the new giant screens are stripping them bare in front of the crowd and the players".

It wasn't all negative. The game still has its heroes, commemorated richly and generously in the media. To have missed Tendulkar's innings at Edgbaston, said Stephen Fay in the *Independent on Sunday*, would have been like missing Agincourt. "One of the greatest innings played in Test cricket," said Peter Roebuck in the *Sunday Times*. The resurrection of Nasser Hussain and Alec Stewart caused general pleasure, even if E. W. Swanton found Stewart's celebration of his Headingley hundred displeasingly over the top: "Am I being irritatingly square," he inquired, "to plead once more for some restraint in moments of achievement?" And of course there was Dickie Bird at Lord's making his last tear-stained appearance and, to common astonishment, crowning the day with an lbw verdict. "Bird had entered the field a good two minutes after a respectful PA announcement," wrote David Hopps in *The Guardian* beneath a picture of Dickie, handkerchief at the ready, "making one wonder whether he had paused for a last visit to the loo. He walked, back slightly bent, through a guard of honour formed by two applauding teams. As he headed for the square, he turned to deliver a wave that needed only the addition of a pipe and a Gannex raincoat to look the very spit of Harold Wilson." How Wilson would have savoured that comparison!

Some predicted heroes crumbled. Hick's 215 from 195 balls off the Indians at Worcester brought lip-smacking prophecies of Test match carnage to come. By mid-July, he was failing time and again even in county matches: "performing like a lost soul," wrote Alan Lee in *The Times*. Dominic Cork, firmly installed at the start of the season as the greatest England fast-bowling find since, well, Darren Gough, was written off in the tabloids by the end of it, whereas Gough was reinstated as the new, well, Dominic Cork. Alistair Brown of Surrey, hustled on to the international stage for the one-day matches amid a chorus of adulatory profiles, was forgotten by August, when Chris Lewis, also saluted in spring, was being absolutely vilified. By then the talk had turned to the two Surrey Hollioakes, especially Adam, the older, picked to captain England A on their winter tour and profiled with much the same adulatory awe as his colleague Brown a mere four months earlier. "A lot of the guys on this tour know me only as this lunatic opponent who comes charging down the pitch swearing at them, with his eyes on stalks,'' Hollioake confided to Derek Pringle of *The Independent*.

This fascination with once great names in decline and new talents expected soon to be blazing across the firmament extended beyond the Test match and county circuit. In May, Bill Day of the *Mail on Sunday* went to watch Lashings, a team representing a restaurant, rather than a town or village, easing their way to a nine-wicket victory over Hempstead in the Medway League. It all started badly: Hempstead had not brought an umpire and Lashings' skipper Nigel Sharp had forgotten to bring the stumps. But none of this discommoded the former West Indian captain Richie Richardson, signed in a £20,000 deal, and – against the backdrop of traffic hurtling down the M20 – he made the first of many big scores on the way to taking Lashings to the league title, little noticed by anyone outside the area. If only cricket were that easy when the media are there in force.

David McKie is a columnist on The Guardian.

CRICKET AND THE LAW IN 1996

The following cricket-related court cases were reported during 1996:

BOTHAM & LAMB v KHAN

After a 13-day trial at Court 13 of the High Court in London, two former England captains, Ian Botham and Allan Lamb, lost the libel case they had brought against the former Pakistan captain Imran Khan. Botham and Lamb claimed that Imran had (a) called them racists and said they lacked education and class in an article in *India Today* magazine and (b) branded Botham a cheat in *The Sun*.

After hearing from a list of witnesses that read like a Who's Who of English Cricket, the jury of seven men and five women found for Imran by a majority verdict, which means 10-2 or 11-1. Botham and Lamb later said they intended to appeal. The case was estimated to have cost them at least £250,000 each. The trial, piquantly, clashed with the Lord's Test between England and Pakistan, which was expected to start another bitter series between the two sides. In fact, there was unexpected good feeling on the field. This did not spread to Court 13.

Botham denied emphatically that he was a racist, citing his friendship with Viv Richards, and said he had been stung by the allegations that he had no class. Lamb said he had left South Africa because he was against apartheid. Their counsel, Charles Gray QC, then showed the court two TV clips from England Tests in 1982 which the defence had intended to introduce as evidence that Botham had cheated, by being associated with ball-tampering.

In one clip Botham threw the ball to wicket-keeper Bob Taylor, who worked on the ball with his gloves; in the other Botham was seen pressing the ball with his thumbs. Botham said he had thrown the ball to Taylor to dry it and that, on the other occasion, he had simply been trying to get it back into shape. Imran later withdrew any suggestion of cheating after hearing a stream of further witnesses for the plaintiffs: John Emburey, Bob Taylor, Gladstone Small, Robin Smith, David Gower and the two wives, Kathy Botham and Lindsay Lamb.

However, Imran's counsel, George Carman QC, insisted to the court that Imran had been misquoted and had never called either of them a cheat or a racist in the first place. He also said that his client had been trying to settle the case for two years but that Botham and Lamb had refused all attempts at apologies. "In your search for the truth," he said to the jury, "remember this. Who offered the hand of friendship and who spurned it?"

Mike Atherton and David Lloyd, the England captain and coach, had to attend court on the eve of the Test to give evidence for Imran. His other witnesses were Derek Pringle, Christopher Martin-Jenkins, Tony Lewis and Geoff Boycott, who provided a bizarre interlude by arriving jacketless from Lord's, wearing a shirt with a sponsor's name, and brandishing a boot in the witness box to try to make a point unconnected with the case. He was silenced by the judge, Mr Justice French.

Before the trial, the Court of Appeal had refused to strike out part of the claim against Imran. His lawyers had argued that his comments to *The Sun* could not have been defamatory because Imran had gone on to say seam-lifting was not cheating. But the Appeal Court said that if the person reading the comments might disagree, they were potentially libellous.

An industrial tribunal at Bedford ruled that Tony Pocock, former head groundsman at Cambridge University's ground, Fenner's, had not been unfairly dismissed.

The tribunal heard that the pitches at Fenner's had begun to attract criticism (*Wisden* had mentioned "the declining standard"). After the match between Combined Universities and the New Zealanders in 1994, the TCCB inspector, Harry Brind, was called in and said the wickets should be relaid. Pocock went on sick leave and later retired through ill health. He claimed the university had effectively dismissed him by trying to force him to take another job away from the cricket ground, which he loved, at an indoor sports centre. He told the tribunal the problems with the square were caused by a dreadfully wet spring. His counsel, Ingrid Simla, said: "They decided to use Mr Pocock as a scapegoat."

Tony Lemons, the university's director of physical education, said he thought Pocock might want to move away from the "immense pressure" at Fenner's, and offered him a better-paid job. "It is bewildering why he has misunderstood the situation," he said. The tribunal ruled that the university had acted "inconsiderately" but said its behaviour did not amount to constructive dismissal.

A 21-year-old fruitpicker was fined $NZ250 for hurling a water bomb at New Zealand Test batsman Mark Greatbatch, who was fielding on the boundary during a Shell Cup match at Alexandra, Otago, on New Year's Day, 1996. Timothy William Colin Cooney pleaded guilty to a charge of disorderly behaviour likely to cause violence. Police said Cooney and his friends had been drinking heavily.

Justin Nutter, 23, of Colne, Lancashire, got drunk when his match was rained off during a tour of Devon and bared his backside at passing drivers, including two policemen in an unmarked car. He admitted being drunk and disorderly and was fined £60 in Torquay.

A change of mind by the Ministry of Agriculture prevented a possible court case involving cricket-bat manufacturers. The Government had ruled that many types of trees could be cut down only with 28 days notice. This would have made it difficult for batmakers to obtain supplies of willow, which are often grown in the middle of cultivated fields and can be cut only in the short interval between harvesting and replanting. The manufacturers successfully lobbied for cricket-bat willows to be exempt.

CRICKETANA IN 1996

By DAVID FRITH

If 1996 was an unremarkable year for English cricket, this was not the case in memorabilia trading. It was the year of the Big Names. Record prices were paid for books, bats and letters, all with highly important associations, while the staple fare of *Wisdens*, autographs, postcards and photographs continued to swell in value.

The most desirable *Wisdens* ever offered inspired frenzied bidding at Bearne's, Exeter in July. They once belonged to W. G. Grace, who had signed many of them. The run, from the 1864 first edition to 1915, the year of W.G.'s death, went to a collector from Maidenhead who paid £94,100 (all prices include premium) and excitedly proclaimed, unchallengeably, that W.G. and *Wisden* were cricket's ultimate combination. Over 100 lots were contested by eager collectors and dealers, the spectacular realisations justifying the auctioneers' decision to abstain from publishing estimates.

Phillips had no such scruples. Before their London sale in May, they estimated an inscribed bat used by Don Bradman to score 212 at Adelaide in the 1936-37 Test series at £500-700. It fetched £23,525, more than twice the sum – £10,586 – paid by a telephone bidder at Christie's in October for the bat used by Jack Hobbs in 1925 to equal and then break W.G.'s record of 126 centuries. It made one of Wally Hammond's bats, sold a week earlier at Phillips, seem a remarkable bargain, for only £2,117 was needed to secure the willow with which the master batsman scored 251 for England at Sydney in 1928-29. It was sold by an Australian whose grandfather had relieved Hammond of this piece of history for a mere ten shillings. The preceding lot had been the bat with which Herbert Sutcliffe scored twin centuries in the Melbourne Test of January 1925. It made only £1,035 because the back was patterned with woodworm holes. "Makes it easier to pick up," suggested the auctioneer helpfully.

Knight's of Norwich ventured to Melbourne to stage a sale, the outstanding items being a bat used by Joe Darling at the turn of the century (£1,069), one of Graham Gooch's England caps (£506), and an indulgence of £180 for a signed photograph of Bradman's dismissal by Hollies in his final Test.

All kinds of other cricketana came on to the market. Vennett-Smith of Nottingham came up with a letter from George Parr, written in 1868 on All England XI notepaper. Unremarkable of content and consisting of only 53 words, it went for £1,732, which made the significant William Lillywhite letter (1837) on roundarm bowling, sold for £1,035 at Phillips, seem cheap. Gubby Allen's gold watch, presented to him by the Board of Control during the 1930 Lord's Test, and still in working order, changed hands for £450 at a premium-free Cricket Memorabilia Society sale. And elsewhere, purchasers thrilled to such gems as Hammond's wallet (£69), Colin Milburn's Northamptonshire sweater (£135), Geoff Boycott's panama hat (£150), the gloves worn by Brian Lara during his 375 (£551) and the Nawab of Pataudi's delectable gold cigarette-case (£2,837).

Phillips sold the late Brian Johnston's collection, which included his MCC tie (£600) and Colin McDonald's Australian cap (£917). Later in the same sale, there was a ball used in the Brisbane tied Test of 1960, once the property of Johnny Martin, and signed by Worrell, Hall and Alexander. It fetched a breath-taking £3,919.

None of the literary items from the collection of the late Jim Coldham went cheaply, underlining yet again that the auction-houses, in spite of the daunting buyer's premium, probably remain the most lucrative area for vendors. As by-products, many of the illustrated catalogues themselves have been collectable.

In the autumn of a memorable year for cricketana, the most diminutive Big Name of them all, A. P. "Tich" Freeman, appeared. Never had so many notable cricket balls been on offer at once. Top price was £1,412 for one presented to him by John Wisden & Co to mark his incredible 304 wickets in 1928. At least this treasure remained in the family. It was bought by the cricketer's great-nephew.

Another gigantic bid emerged in Allan Lamb's testimonial auction at Knight's when Allan Border's Australian cap fetched £1,687. And while Alan Wells understandably got rid of his maiden-Test duck-making bat (£292), items such as Dermot Reeve's Test cap (£202) and the ball with which Courtney Walsh took his 300th Test wicket (£371) underlined what an unsentimental breed are many of the cricketers of today.

CRICKET EQUIPMENT IN 1996

By NORMAN HARRIS

The biggest non-issue of the 1996 English season turned out to be balls. Nevertheless, throughout the Test series it was thought so important that the English and Pakistani captains seemingly placed as much importance on the toss for the ball as they did on the toss for innings.

Pakistan won this toss in all three Tests and opted to play with the Reader ball, their favourite because they believed it to be responsive, after a certain stage of an innings, to "reverse swing". England's preference for the Dukes ball was based on the belief that it allowed more conventional swing early in the innings. Did the Reader ball perform up to expectation for the tourists? The frequency with which the shape of the ball was questioned – allowing a replacement, if the umpires agreed – suggests it did not.

Such questioning was a considerable irritation to the company who make the Reader ball. Their managing director, Mark Wellbelove, made a point of inspecting the five balls that were changed at Lord's, and maintained that only one had lost its shape. He was also at a loss to know why his product might be more responsive to the charms of reverse swing. "There's nothing you can do to make it swing more."

The makers of the alternative ball, Dukes, were equally mystified. Both have to conform to the specifications of the relevant British Standard, which prescribes the height of the seam, the number of stitches, the number of strands in the thread (nine), and the thread material (linen). Equally, both agree that small variations are inevitable in a man-made product which uses an organic material. But any differences are likely to be as much between balls as between brands.

Both makers were also sceptical about the growing practice of cricket managers, or even fast bowlers, going to the factory to select the county's supply of balls for the season. "They're all looking for something that feels comfortable in the hand," said Dilip Jajodia of Dukes. "They like to think that it feels small, which really is a nonsense, with the very tight parameters on size and weight. And they like a dark red colour. Small and dark is the flavour of the moment."

Meanwhile, the seed of a bigger issue than this was starting to germinate. Buried beneath high-profile decisions (or non-decisions) at the midsummer meeting of the International Cricket Council was an item that promised much anguish for bat makers and administrators – but joy for players and their agents. Commercial logos (as distinct from the maker's own branding) will in future be allowed on the front and back of bats.

For some time the pressure had been growing. It had been resisted by international legislators and by some national bodies. In England, the TCCB kept a list of "recognised" bat makers, and had stopped at least one overseas player using, in county cricket, an Indian-made bat which appeared to bear the name of a cigarette company.

The matter came to a head with the use by Sachin Tendulkar of a bat bearing the letters MRF. Madras Rubber Factory is a well-known Indian tyre manufacturer and a big sponsor of cricket. The company had, evidently for promotional purposes, also set up as a bat maker. Tendulkar's use of the bat in an international one-day tournament brought a threat that he might be banned.

Consequently, his bat was plain throughout the 1996 World Cup, and in the early stages of last summer's Indian tour of England.

But lawyers for the player and for MRF were at work, and a legal letter evidently persuaded ICC that Tendulkar's bat did not breach their own regulations. Meanwhile, other Indian (and Pakistani) batsmen were using bats bearing the names of cigarette brands, underlining the urgent need for decision making.

In the event, the administrators from the subcontinent won the day. Their view was that it was reasonable to limit the area covered by logos, but not to try to differentiate between various commercial interests. One argument was that, given that the bat market is relatively small, makers could no longer pay the sort of money star players could command: commercial ''sponsorship'' was the obvious solution.

A compromise emerged as ICC worked on the detail of the new arrangement. The area available for a commercial logo would be nine inches on the front of the bat – as at present – and nine inches also on the back, instead of an unlimited area. Anticipating that the pressure would come from players, the new rules said that such deals could be done only on the expiry of players' present contracts with bat makers.

Naturally, the larger bat makers were alarmed. They could see players cutting them out completely: buying the bat of their choice for, say, £150 and then replacing the maker's livery with the logo of the sponsor with whom they have made a deal for, say, £15,000.

National governing bodies would be entitled to maintain their own rules in domestic cricket – which is what the South Africans soon decided to do. But the situation for Test matches is far from clear. England's team, for example, have been sponsored by a brewery, their home Tests by an insurance company. What if a player – from either side – uses a bat bearing the logo of a rival beer or insurance company? The old TCCB was inclined to believe that, since they ran these Tests, they could, and should, veto this. And what about the political and moral sensitivities aroused by extending the promotion of tobacco and alcohol?

The problems that loom have the potential to be very messy indeed. The issue of ball changing, even ball tampering, may yet pall in comparison.

UMPIRING IN 1996

By JACK BAILEY

All the signs are that Dickie Bird's retirement from Test match cricket could turn out to have been a pretty shrewd move. The large slices of income the TCCB received from television companies were bound to have had their price, and umpires are the sufferers. The boundaries have been altered: quite literally during a Sunday League match at Cardiff, when the TCCB gave permission for a TV camera on the playing area.

Meanwhile, the pitch inspection and toss for innings before a Test match are accompanied by an array of television personnel; and instant replays of possible run-outs appear on the big screen before the third umpire has had the chance to make a ruling. It must be hell to have to adjudicate on a close call with the roar of the crowd in your ears.

We have also seen slow left-armers bowling interminably over the wicket – a negative tactic which brought from Warwickshire's Dermot Reeve a similarly negative response. Rather than run the risk of being caught by the ball running off the inevitable pad thrust at the ball, and thence on to the hand holding the bat, he jettisoned the bat, letting it fall where it may, to the consternation of the close fielders.

Reeve's protest had its merits. But under Law 37, the umpire has redress if he thinks such an action constitutes "wilful obstruction" of the opposing side. Yet apart from the problems associated with the need to decide what is "wilful", a more effective way of preventing the disturbing trend towards negative bowling may have to be found. In England in 1997 there will be two runs for a wide and bowlers will aim outside leg stump at their peril.

Umpires are still likely to spend a great deal of their time studying balls that have apparently gone out of shape. The constant stoppages are depriving spectators of action in a game already loaded with long static periods. At Old Trafford, in the NatWest semi-final, the ball split in two, which could have been an added complication. In such circumstances the Laws permit the umpire to call and signal "dead ball"; in this case, presumably, licence would be given to make that "dead balls".

There has been no further development with the move to make Law 42.8, governing the bowling of bouncers, applicable at international level once again. It was reported in last year's *Wisden* that the umpires wanted to use the Law as it stands, without recourse to the need for being told, as in the ICC regulations, what constitutes intimidation. Watch this space, but don't hold your breath.

CRICKET GROUNDS IN 1996

The fantasy of a new Test ground in England, for the first time in almost a hundred years, moved into the realms of possibility, and maybe even probability, in 1996 after Yorkshire announced plans to leave Headingley for a new stadium at Wakefield at the start of the new millennium.

Yorkshire, long jealous of other counties with their own homes, found themselves chafing more and more against their problems as tenants of Headingley. And the sudden availability of funding from the National Lottery made the move feasible. The county investigated one site within Leeds, at Parlington, where the M1 and A1 are due to link up. But officials were quickly seduced by a campaign to woo them by Wakefield, West Yorkshire's county town. Wakefield Council promised the club a site just by Junction 39 of the M1, the main railway line (a new station will be built) and the River Calder ("You could even arrive by boat," said the promotional video), set in countryside between a country park and a golf course. There would be room for at least 25,000 spectators, and all the ancillary services the cricket club might desire. Since Wakefield is a "regeneration area" and is allowed European Union funds that would be denied to Leeds, the council said it was confident the £50 million project would not cost Yorkshire a penny.

The Wakefield plan was due to be put to club members in March 1997. Apart from turning the promise of funding into reality, the main problem, if the members approved, concerned the lease at Headingley. Yorkshire's landlords, the Leeds Cricket, Football and Athletic Co. – effectively the rugby league club – have been taken over by a property developer, Paul Caddick, who has been anxious to prevent the move to Wakefield. Yorkshire signed a 99-year lease in 1982 and appeared to face difficult negotiations.

Crowd trouble at Headingley Tests has done much to diminish public affection for the ground. And the advent of summer rugby league – both the Leeds and Bramley clubs now play at Headingley – has increased the technical difficulties of playing there. Surprisingly, though, Yorkshire simultaneously decided to scrap four of their five out-grounds, ending county cricket at Bradford, Harrogate, Sheffield, and Middlesbrough, and sparing only Scarborough. In the short term, this will lead to a greater concentration of cricket than ever before at what may become an increasingly run-down Headingley. All Second Eleven and Academy matches have been moved elsewhere.

This short term is certain to last at least three years. Early in 1997 Yorkshire were hoping they might be able to lay the Wakefield square in 1998, with a view to playing cricket in 1999 and the first Test in 2000. But experience suggests delays are probable; and Durham's difficulties in getting the Chester-le-Street pitch to settle down would make Lord's officials wary about granting Wakefield a Test match prematurely.

The fashion for new grounds may be catching. The lottery has enabled Hampshire to re-focus on their plans for a new stadium, and they hope to move to their new ground in 2001. Landscaping work is due to start this spring. And the Somerset committee has been considering the possibility of leaving their cramped but much loved County Ground at Taunton. This move, however, may well run into more resistance from members than the others: Somerset have now abandoned their festival at Weston-super-Mare.

CHARITIES IN 1996

THE LORD'S TAVERNERS distributed more than £1.7 million during 1996. The overall aim is "to give young people, particularly those with special needs, a sporting chance". Half the money was sent direct to grassroots cricket via the National Cricket Association and the English Schools Cricket Association. The other half was used to provide 25 New Horizons minibuses, bringing the total presented to schools and care organisations since 1980 to 412.

The year saw the inauguration of the Under-16 Inner Cities Cup at Arundel, sponsored by Britvic Soft Drinks. The Lord's Taverners were once again the nominated charity of the *Daily Telegraph* Fantasy Cricket League, and an awards dinner in London helped to raise over £25,000. The now traditional Long Room Concert was held in October, featuring Julian Lloyd-Webber. The soprano, Lesley Garrett, has agreed to perform in 1997. In November, former President Sir Tim Rice nominated the Taverners as the major beneficiary of the gala preview of *Jesus Christ Superstar*, which raised more than £27,000.

The Director: Patrick Shervington, The Lord's Taverners, 22 Queen Anne's Gate, London SW1H 9AA. Telephone: 0171-222 0707.

THE JOHN ARLOTT MEMORIAL TRUST was launched in 1993 to help provide affordable housing and improve recreational facilities in rural areas. Events in 1996 included the Sphere Drake England Seniors XI match at Dunsfold, Surrey, and the John Arlott Rioja Dinner. The Trust also entered a team of runners for the London Marathon. There will be another Rioja Dinner in 1997.

Janet Hart, John Arlott Memorial Trust, Prince Consort House, 27–29 Albert Embankment, London SE1 7TJ. Telephone: 0171-793 8144.

THE BRIAN JOHNSTON MEMORIAL TRUST was launched in 1995. Its aims are to foster cricket (a) for young people, (b) in the community, and (c) for players with disabilities. Brian Johnston Scholarships are available for young cricketers of potential who are in need of financial help, and Brian Johnston Awards are given to inner city schools which present projects to establish cricket in their area. The Johnners Cricket Week is to be held from June 21 to 29, 1997, and clubs everywhere are invited to participate and raise funds for themselves and the Trust.

Chief Executive: Michael Elmitt, PO Box 3897, Lord's Cricket Ground, London NW8 8QG. Telephone: 0171-224 1005. Fax: 0171-224 0431.

THE PRIMARY CLUB, one of the favourite charities of the late Brian Johnston, raises money for sporting and recreational facilities for the blind and partially sighted. Membership is nominally restricted to players who have been dismissed first ball in any form of cricket. Started in 1955, the club raises money by donations and a wide variety of members' activities. Lately, a regiment in Worcester has run a sponsored net. The Dorton House School swimming pool for kindergarten children was completed in June, and officially opened by the club's new patron, Derek Underwood.

Hon. Secretary: Robert Fleming, 5 South Villas, Camden Square, London NW1 9BS. Telephone: 0171-267 3316. Fax: 0171-485 6808.

THE HORNSBY PROFESSIONAL CRICKETERS FUND was established in 1928, from the estate of J. H. J. Hornsby, who played for Middlesex, MCC and the Gentlemen. It provides money to assist "former professional cricketers [not necessarily first-class] or their wives, widows until remarriage, children and other dependents, provided the persons concerned shall be in necessitous circumstances". Assistance is given by monthly allowances, special grants or, in certain cases, loans. Donations, requests for help or information about potential recipients are all welcome.

Clerk to the Trustees: A. K. James, "Dunroamin", 65 Keyhaven Road, Milford-on-Sea, Lymington, Hampshire SO41 0QX. Telephone: 01590-644720.

THE CRICKETERS ASSOCIATION CHARITY was founded in 1983 to relieve financial hardship amongst present or former members of the Association, anyone who has played cricket for a first-class county or their "wives, widows, children, parents and dependents". It is becoming the custom for cricketers in their benefit year to donate half of one per cent of their proceeds to the fund. Donations are welcome; also requests for help and information about cricketers who may be in need.

Chairman of the Trustees: Harold Goldblatt, 60 Doughty Street, London WC1N 2LS. Telephone: 0171-405 9855.

GRANT AID FOR CRICKET, 1996

By the end of 1996, Britain's National Lottery had contributed £23.7 million towards cricket since the first hand-outs took place in 1995. The total costs of those projects amounted to £47.6 million; applicants are required to provide at least 35 per cent of the overall budget for themselves. The biggest grant was £7.2 million awarded to Hampshire in June, to help them with their projected £16 million move to a new ground. Lancashire received £600,000 towards a new indoor cricket school, and Durham £458,000 for ground development at Chester-le-Street. But most of the beneficiaries were small community clubs, such as Darwen, in Lancashire, which received £6,919 for artificial pitches, or Horningsham, in Wiltshire, which got £3,841. For first-class clubs, there were further bonuses from the Sports Grounds Initiative, launched by the Foundation for Sports and the Arts in the autumn of 1995, which gave £250,000 each to Durham, Lancashire and Somerset. For further information on these and other potential donors – several of which will consider grants for much smaller projects – consult the booklet *Sources of Grant Aid for Cricket*, which is available from the ECB at Lord's. Mike Turner, author of the booklet, is available to give advice to clubs on 0116-283 1615.

BLIND CRICKET IN 1996

Representatives of seven countries met in New Delhi in September 1996 and agreed to hold the first Blind Cricket World Cup. It is to be staged in New Delhi in November 1998.

Seven of the Test-playing countries had delegates at the meeting – the exceptions being West Indies and Zimbabwe. It was organised by George Abraham, the driving force behind Indian blind cricket, who first conceived the idea of a World Cup in 1993.

The delegates first had to agree a set of rules, because every country played the game differently. Most played with a small ball, bowling underarm. Pakistan used a hard ball. The Australian game was a mixture of cricket and baseball. In India there were some idiosyncratic rules about who could catch whom. Sight categorisation was also a problem, as different countries had different standards about who could compete.

Finally, it was agreed that a hard, plastic white ball should be used, with underarm bowling. Abraham was elected chairman of the new World Blind Cricket Council, with Tony Hegarty of England as secretary.

Tony Hegarty, 8 Rockells Place, Forest Hill Road, London SE22 0RT.
British Blind Sport, 67 Albert Street, Rugby, Warwickshire CV21 2SN.

CRICKET IN THE CLASSROOM IN 1996

By PETER MASON

A ruler and a serviceable Biro may have been essential prerequisites for school exams of the past; now you must take along a decent piece of willow and a pair of whites. Studying cricket at A-level may once have seemed a fanciful schoolkid's dream, but now it is reality.

The first cricket A-level courses began in September 1996, with the first examinations due in 1998. They are not devoted entirely to cricket, and go under the general heading of Physical Education, but they do offer a new-look syllabus which allows 15 per cent of all marks to be devoted to practical performance in the summer game. There will be no questions about the origin of the Ashes or the size of The Oval boundary, and no last-minute cramming on Test averages, but cricket is at last on the academic map.

The game owes its new-found status to a thorough review of the PE syllabus carried out by the Guildford-based Associated Examining Board (which pioneered the subject at A-level), and by the Oxford & Cambridge Examination & Assessment Council. Their lead is almost certain to be followed by other boards around Britain.

Seventy per cent of the marks on the AEB course are for deskbound examinations on anatomical, historical, cultural and psychological aspects of sport. But 30 per cent will be for practical exams in individual and team games, which means 15 per cent will hinge on cricket for anyone who chooses it as their option.

Cricketers will be assessed in three sections: on their personal performance, on their skill at demonstrating elements of the game, and on their ability to observe and analyse. They need not only to show they can play but that they can correct their faults. Students will be tested, in both the nets and in a real match, on their ability to play the on- and off-drives, and forward and backward defensives, to bowl swing and seam, and to field close or in the deep. Those who are unorthodox will not be marked down as long as they show they have the potential to achieve results and – most importantly – to understand what they are doing and why.

After playing, candidates must then be questioned on their understanding of what has happened. Being bowled first ball is not ideal, but a student who points out why he or she went so quickly – perhaps by playing back instead of forward to a pitched-up ball on a low-bouncing pitch – has the power to rescue the situation.

The Oxford & Cambridge practical exams have a more flexible format, but essentially it is the same as the AEB's course. Those who have set up the syllabuses say ability at cricket will not necessarily guarantee a pass, nor will studying the game necessarily turn anyone into a decent cricketer. But the new option has already helped to increase the number of people taking PE at A-level: around 14,000 students began studying it from September 1996, compared with 10,000 a year earlier. The AEB says that despite the traditional emphasis on sport in public schools there is equal, if not more, interest from state schools in the new syllabus.

Studying A-level PE with cricket is unlikely to help anyone directly find a job in the game, even with an A grade. But course organisers say that only four per cent of those studying PE express a desire to go into sports-related industries anyway. Most just take it as an interesting third subject, which may at last show that A-levels can be fun.

CRICKET AND BETTING IN 1996

By PAUL HAIGH

Cricket is split on betting. On one side are people who think the excitement of gambling can only be beneficial to a sport which in Britain attracts a significantly older following than most. On the other side are the traditionalists, their ranks swelled after the problems caused by the Salim Malik Affair and the rumours of match fixing in Asia. They remain convinced that gambling can only corrupt and must eventually damage the spirit of the game – if it hasn't done so already.

Both sides have gained a new weapon for their arguments. The thrills – and the spills – of cricket betting have been dramatically enhanced by the seductive and dangerous form of gambling known as "spread betting".

This was devised in the late 1980s by a group of Stock Exchange traders, who realised there was no need for them to speculate on anything as tedious as company performances; the same principles could be applied just as easily to sport. The essence of spread betting is that the investor takes a position on the success or failure of teams and individuals, just like buying a share. If he believes they will outperform the expectation of the betting firm's market framer, he will buy. If he believes they will do worse than expected, he will sell. The buying price will be higher than the selling price, as on the stock market; and the discrepancy between the two prices is, theoretically, where the spread firm makes its profit.

The great attraction of spread betting is that the more right you are, the more you win. Before the 1993-94 West Indies v England series, several firms estimated Brian Lara's total runs at 340-360. Those satisfied that his double-century against Australia a year earlier was not a flash in the pan bought, some for as much as £100 a run. There were few sellers at 340. Lara totalled 798. The spread firms lost heavily, even though many investors took their profit before Lara scored his 375 in Antigua.

The unfortunate corollary of all this is that the more wrong you are, the more you lose – as, for example, those who thought Graeme Hick might finally establish himself as a Test batsman against India and Pakistan in 1996 will readily testify. The risks are obvious. If your batsman is dropped from the team, your shares are worthless, just as the shares in Lara would have been useless if, say, he had broken his arm in the first over he faced at Sabina Park.

At the moment, football attracts most spread betting, a fact which reflects its popularity. But football is far from being an ideal medium for punters, who are often reduced to such idiocies as gambling on the time in seconds of the first throw-in or on the number of corners in a match. Cricket – because of its scoring system and because whole games can turn on a single over – is recognised as the most appropriate, as well as the most frightening medium for spread betting. The question, though, is whether a game which has always depended on the integrity and sportsmanship of its players and officials can withstand the pressures which must result if heavy gambling takes hold.

In 1996 Wally Pyrah of the spread betting firm Sporting Index estimated that 39 per cent of his company's trading was on football, and 36 per cent horse racing. Cricket at nine per cent came third. In 1997, an Ashes year, that gap may be expected to close. If it does, there will be some who will regret it – both among those who don't bet and among those who do.

CRICKET PEOPLE IN 1996

By SIMON BRIGGS

When the Lord's Grand Stand was knocked down in the autumn of 1996, among the casualties was the famous old print shop, which had clattered away on the ground floor throughout the stand's 70-year life. The demolition coincided with the retirement of MCC's head printer, VINCE MILLER, who went to Lord's in 1955, and lived through an era in which – in his domain – things changed remarkably little. The Lord's scorecard, printed on a Heidelberg letterpress, was a thing of beauty and could be updated with remarkable speed. One of Miller's predecessors, for a bet, managed to print an up-to-date version before the dismissed batsman had made it back to the dressing-room. The tradition of amending the card after every wicket was abandoned in 1978, but Miller continued to reprint at lunch and tea. The old ways may not be gone forever: the traditional scorecards were said to be confusing the new computer printers in close-season experiments conducted in the new print shop in the tennis-court building. The Heidelberg has found a home in what was the sweet shop under the Mound Stand and will be there in case of emergency.

June saw the retirement of Lancashire's cricket secretary, ROSE FITZGIBBON, who in 1991 had become the first woman in Britain to hold such a post. She celebrated by flying to the USA to judge an Irish dancing contest. "I've not missed the job," she said, six months later. "It was becoming too stressful, what with 20 full-time staff to look after, and the ECB reforms coming in." FitzGibbon began her Lancashire career as a humbler kind of secretary in 1956, when the offices were manned by a workforce of five, with the First Eleven scorer helping out when he could. She stopped sneaking into the pavilion via the back staircase when promoted to assistant cricket secretary, although she was occasionally refused entrance at the front door – Lancashire was, in 1990, the last county to admit women to the pavilion. Nevertheless, she feels that her gender often worked in her favour. "I got a lot of respect from players and at TCCB meetings, and perhaps got away with a few things as a result."

A £50 bet was the beginning of an epic journey for JASON BARRY, a PE teacher from Leicester. Over a pint at the local cricket club, Barry idly proposed a world tour punctuated by a few cricket matches – 52 matches in 52 countries in 52 weeks, in fact. The idea turned into a challenge, which Barry narrowly failed to complete when he contracted bilharzia in Borneo and was forced to return, having ticked off 43 countries. He is not dispirited, however, and has plans to continue his odyssey in 1997, aiming first to pass 50 countries, and then to reach 100 by the end of the millennium. He has already raised close to £10,000 for Save the Children, and sponsors are easier to find now that his determination has been proved beyond doubt. Other setbacks that Barry has overcome include a broken foot sustained while playing on coconut matting in the South of France, and two nights in prison cells: first in Moscow, where he broke an airport window with a cricket ball, and then in Colombia, after a misunderstanding with a customs official.

In April, the Army cricket ground at Aldershot bade farewell to Frank Vincent, its groundsman for over 40 years. The heavy roller was passed on to his assistant, MARILYN AVERY, who had served her apprenticeship on the military's football pitch. At first, Avery was worried that she didn't have enough cricketing experience, although she felt better after attending a day course in Surrey. "I discovered that I already knew most of the things they were telling us. That was after they asked me if I was there to do the refreshments." According to the Army cricket secretary, Major Rupert Ross-Hurst, her wickets have been "first-rate", and visiting players have been highly impressed.

There was an England call-up for seam bowler SARAH-JANE COOK, who played in one Test and one limited-overs international against New Zealand. Cook's achievement is all the more impressive because she is both deaf and dumb. Using sign language and the help of her mother, she explained to *The Sun's* John Etheridge: "I can communicate with the rest of the team by waving my arms about and using facial expressions. I also lip read quite well and can certainly make myself understood when I need to." England team-mate Barbara Daniels describes her as an aggressive bowler who enjoys digging the ball in, and a particularly forceful appealer. "It's definitely an experience playing with Sarah. I've captained her in the past, and sometimes you have to write things down for her beforehand, but she's an excellent fielder and has a good understanding of the game." Cook's season was curtailed by a persistent back complaint, but she has since returned to the England training squad, and is fighting for a place in the 1997 series against South Africa.

Former Derbyshire batsman JIM HUTCHINSON celebrated an unusual century on November 29, when he became only the seventh first-class cricketer known to have reached his 100th birthday. The others, in chronological order, are G. O. Deane of Hampshire, J. Wheatley of Canterbury, E. A. English of Hampshire, G. R. U. Harman of Dublin University, R. de Smidt of Western Province and D. B. Deodhar of Maharashtra. De Smidt lived longest, reaching 102 years and 252 days. Hutchinson, who is rated by Derbyshire's official history as the finest cover fielder to represent the county, was aware of that record, and keen to surpass it.

JOHN STEPHENSON, the captain of Hampshire, founded a particularly exclusive club. To qualify for entrance, you needed to have played one Test for England – and one Test only. Eighteen living players met this criterion, from H. D. "Hopper" Read, who made his appearance in 1935, to Alan Wells, whose first innings against the 1995 West Indians brought him a golden duck. Other members of the One Test Wonders club included Norman Mitchell-Innes, who withdrew from what would have been his second Test in 1935 with "a chronic asthmatic allergy", and Dennis Brookes, still Northamptonshire's leading run-scorer, who appeared once in the West Indies in 1947-48. Stephenson hoped to see some of the younger generation turn out for the club in a few charity matches in 1997, perhaps accompanied by the president of the One Test Wonders, Graham Gooch. Gooch, of course, holds the record for England caps with 118.

The founder members of the One Test Wonders were: Joey Benjamin, Mark Benson, Dennis Brookes, Alan Butcher, Alec Coxon, Andy Lloyd, Norman Mitchell-Innes, Charles Palmer, Ken Palmer, Paul Parker, Tony Pigott, H. D. "Hopper" Read, Dick Richardson, Arnie Sidebottom, John Stephenson, Alan Wells, James Whitaker and Neil Williams.

DIRECTORY OF BOOK DEALERS

AARDVARK BOOKS, "Copperfield", High Street, Harmston, Lincoln LN5 9SN. Tel: 01522-722671. Peter Taylor specialises in Wisdens. Send SAE for list. Wisden cleaning and repair service available. Wisdens purchased, *any* condition.

TIM BEDDOW, 62a Stanmore Road, Edgbaston, Birmingham B16 9TB. Tel: 0956-456112 (mobile); fax: 0121-770 9645. Visit my stall at Edgbaston. New books from £1.00. Large selection of Wisdens available. Open every first-team game.

BOUNDARY BOOKS, Southlands, Sandy Lane, Goostrey, Cheshire CW4 8NT. Tel: 01477-533106; fax 01477-544529. Second-hand and antiquarian cricket books and autographs. Catalogues issued. Viewing by appointment at Stockport offices.

PETER BRIGHT, 11 Ravens Court, Ely, Cambridgeshire CB6 3ED. Tel: 01353-661727. Antiquarian and second-hand cricket books bought and sold. Occasional catalogues. Representative stock held at **The Bookshop, 24 Magdalene Street, Cambridge**.

IAN DYER, 29 High Street, Gilling West, Richmond, North Yorkshire DL10 5JG. Wisdens, antiquarian, second-hand, printed ephemera bought/sold. **Tel/fax: 01748-822786; e-mail: iandyercricketbooks@btinternet.com. Catalogue also at www.j15.com/iandyer.**

E. O. KIRWAN, 3 Pine Tree Garden, Oadby, Leicestershire LE2 5UT. Tel: 0116-271 4267 (evenings and weekends only). Second-hand and antiquarian cricket books, Wisdens, autograph material and cricket ephemera of all kinds.

J. W. McKENZIE, 12 Stoneleigh Park Road, Ewell, Epsom, Surrey KT19 0QT. Tel: 0181-393 7700; fax: 0181-393 1694. Specialists in antiquarian second-hand cricket books, particularly Wisdens, since 1969. Books and collections bought. Catalogues sent on request. Publishers of rare cricket books. Shop premises open regular business hours.

ROGER PAGE, 10 Ekari Court, Yallambie, Victoria 3085, Australia. Tel: (03) 9435 6332; fax: (03) 9432 2050. Dealer in new and second-hand cricket books. Distributor of overseas cricket annuals and magazines. Agent for Cricket Statisticians and Cricket Memorabilia Society.

RED ROSE BOOKS, 196 Belmont Road, Astley Bridge, Bolton BL1 7AR. Tel/fax: 01204-598080. Specialist in antiquarian and second-hand cricket books. Catalogue available on request. Collections purchased.

CHRISTOPHER SAUNDERS, Orchard Books, Kingston House, High Street, Newnham on Severn, Gloucestershire GL14 1BB. Tel: 01594-516030; fax: 01594-517273. Office/bookroom by appointment. Second-hand/antiquarian cricket books and memorabilia bought and sold. Full-time bookseller for 16 years.

SOUTHERN BOOKSELLERS, 76 Norman Road, St Leonards-on-Sea, East Sussex TN38 0EJ. Tel/fax: 01424-428565. Over 30 years personal service in supply of new, second-hand, antiquarian books and ephemera. Lists, catalogues issued.

SPORTSPAGES, Caxton Walk, 94-96 Charing Cross Road, London WC2H 0JG. Tel: 0171-240 9604; fax 0171-836 0104. Barton Square, St Ann's Square, Manchester M2 7HA. Tel: 0161-832 8530; fax 0161-832 9391. New cricket books, audio and videotapes, including imports, especially from Australasia; retail and mail order service.

STUART TOPPS, 40 Boundary Avenue, Wheatley Mills, Doncaster, South Yorkshire DN2 5QU. Tel: 01302-366044. Our 80-page catalogue of cricket books, Wisdens and brochures is always available.

WISTERIA BOOKS, Wisteria Cottage, Birt Street, Birtsmorton, Malvern WR13 6AW. Tel: 01684-833578. Visit our family-run stall at county grounds for new, second-hand, antiquarian cricket books and ephemera, or contact Grenville Simons at the address above. Send SAE for catalogue.

MARTIN WOOD, Dept WIS, 2 St John's Road, Sevenoaks, Kent TN13 3LW. Tel: 01732-457205. Martin Wood has been dealing in cricket books for 28 years, in which time he has sent 24,000 parcels worldwide. For a copy of his 1997 catalogue, please send 26p stamp to the above address.

AUCTIONEERS

CHRISTIE'S inaugural cricket sale was the MCC Bicentenary Sale of 1987. Since then sales have been held on a regular basis at London, South Kensington, with 18 June and 20 August as the planned dates for this year's sales.

DOMINIC WINTER, Specialist Book Auctioneers & Valuers, The Old School, Maxwell Street, Swindon SN1 5DR. Tel: 01793-611340; fax: 01793-491727. Twice-yearly auction sales of sports books and memorabilia, including Wisdens.

KNIGHT'S SPORTING MEMORABILIA AUCTIONS. Quarterly auctions specialising in cricket. Free valuation and collection. Auctions January, April, June, October. Commission 12.5% including insurance. **Fox Cottage, Aldborough, Norfolk NR11 7AA. Tel: 01263-768051.**

PHILLIPS have held specialised cricket auctions since 1978, highlighted by the celebrated Hal Cohen Collection in 1995. Free valuations and collection undertaken by Mike Ashton on **01222-396453**.

T. VENNETT-SMITH, 11 Nottingham Road, Gotham, Nottinghamshire NG11 0HE. Tel: 0115-983 0541. Auctioneers and valuers. Twice-yearly auctions of cricket and sports memorabilia. The cricket auction run by cricketers for cricket lovers worldwide.

DIRECTORY OF CRICKET SUPPLIERS

CRICKET EQUIPMENT

CLASSIC BAT CO., 53 High Street, Keynsham, Bristol BS18 1DS. Tel: 0117-986 2714; fax: 0117-986 1753. Hand-made bats, balls, pads, gloves, helmets, coffins and clothing. Free colour catalogue available. Sponsorships for Young Players, Schools, Clubs, Coaches.

DUNCAN FEARNLEY, 17 Vigo Place, Brickyard Road, Aldridge, Walsall WS9 8UG. Tel: 01922 57733; fax: 01922 52659. Makers of the finest hand-made English willow bats, and suppliers of a complete range of cricket equipment, including pads, gloves, clothing, footwear and accessories.

GUNN & MOORE LTD, 119/121 Stanstead Road, Forest Hill, London SE23 1HJ. Tel: 0181-291 3344; fax: 0181-699 4008. Gunn & Moore, established in 1885, are the world's most comprehensive provider of cricket bats, equipment, footwear and clothing.

LARA INTERNATIONAL, Whitwell Way, Coton, Cambridge CB3 7PW. Tel: 01223-893330; fax: 01223-893337. A new range of cricket equipment, including hand-made bats, gloves, leg-guards, protective equipment, bags, clothing and balls, designed by Brian Lara in recognition of his record-breaking achievements.

NOMAD BOX CO LTD. Custom-made coffins available to order. 10 different colours from stock. Umpires' and youths' coffins also available. Special club rates apply. **Nomad Box Co. Ltd, Rockingham Road, Market Harborough, Leicestershire. Tel: 01858-464878.**

READERS – The largest UK manufacturers of leather and plastic cricket balls. Distributors of Albion C & D cricket helmets. Contact Graham Brown for more information. **Invicta Works, Teston, Maidstone, Kent ME18 5AW. Tel: 01622 812230.**

SLAZENGER, PO Box 8, Wakefield 41, West Yorkshire WF2 0XB. Tel: 01924 880000; fax: 01924 888231. Top-quality cricket equipment for all levels of play. English-made handcrafted bats, together with a comprehensive range of protective equipment, clothing, luggage and balls.

BOWLING MACHINES

JUGS, 53 High Street, Keynsham, Bristol BS18 1DS. Tel: 0117-986 9519; fax: 0117-986 1753. The *original* bowling machine company. New machines from £995 + VAT. Used by Lancashire, Hampshire, Gloucestershire. Free colour catalogue and video available.

STUART & WILLIAMS (BOLA), 6 Brookfield Road, Cotham, Bristol BS6 5PQ; e-mail info@bola.co.uk; web site http://www.bola.co.uk. Manufacturers of bowling machines and ball throwing machines for all sports. Machines for recreational and commercial application. UK and overseas.

CLOTHING

BOLLÉ SUNGLASSES LTD, Westmead House, 123 Westmead Road, Sutton, Surrey SM1 4JH. Tel: 0181-770 1766. Quality performance sporting sunglasses providing 100% UV protection. As worn by professional cricketers worldwide.

CLASSIC CLUBWEAR, 53 High Street, Keynsham, Bristol BS18 1DS. Tel: 0117-986 9519; fax: 0117-986 1753. Fast, efficient embroidery and screenprinting service on cricket shirts, wool or acrylic sweaters, caps, sweatshirts, leisurewear. Free colour catalogue available.

LUKE EYRES, Freepost, Denny Industrial Estate, Pembroke Avenue, Waterbeach, Cambridge CB5 8BR. Tel: 01223-440501. 100% wool, cotton or acrylic sweaters as supplied to major county clubs, international cricket teams and schools.

JOHN GOULD NECKWEAR, Marash House, 2-5 Brook Street, Tring HP23 5ED. Tel: 01442-890706; fax: 01442-890769. Club ties in silk or polyester, also blazer badges and scarves. Supplier to TCCB. Free design service.

McLELLAN SPORTS, 94-96 Moorside Road, Swinton, Manchester M27 0HJ. Tel: 0161-794 1169. Cricket caps, shirts, sweaters and tracksuits made to your design. Full range of embroidered leisurewear. Catalogue available.

FANTASY CRICKET

MMM FANTASY CRICKET LEAGUES, PO Box 11, Whaley Bridge, Stockport SK12 7NY. Tel: 01663-733945; e-mail: mikem@mmmfcl.prestel.co.uk. Independent Fantasy Cricket competitions, comprehensive, challenging and entertaining.

GAMES AND VIDEOS

FSH MARKETING, PO Box 71217, Ocala, Florida 34471, USA. Tel: (001) 800-529 3500; fax: (001) 352-694 9696; e-mail: cliffmay@praxis.net. Cricket videos catalogue, including Golden Greats of Cricket, Exciting Test Match Series, Great One-Day Internationals, Cricket Legend Series, World Cup Matches at $US29.95 each (NTSC only).

"THE FIRST XI" cricket game system enables enthusiasts to conduct own Test, county and one-day series. Produces realistic scores and results. Allows choice of scoring rates and team/player ratings. **TULLAMORE GAMES, 3 Fauna Avenue, Longbeach 2536, NSW, Australia. Fax 044-728040**

LIMITED EDITION PRINTS

DD DESIGNS, 40 Willowbank, Tamworth, Staffordshire B78 3LS. Tel: 01827 69950. Specialists in signed limited edition prints. Official producer of Wisden's "Cricketers of the Year" sets and other art portfolios. Advertisement page 169.

MAIL ORDER/RETAIL CRICKET SPECIALISTS

FORDHAM SPORTS CRICKET EQUIPMENT SPECIALIST, 81 Robin Hood Way, Kingston Vale, London SW15. Largest range of branded stock in UK at discount prices. 1,000 bats in stock. **Free catalogue 0181-974 5654.**

ROMIDA SPORTS. Now 3 retail branches: **18 Shaw Road, Newhey, Rochdale OL16 4LT; tel: 01706 882444; Wakefield Road, Brighouse, West Yorkshire; tel/fax: 01484 401193; 70 Kingston Road, Leatherhead, Surrey; tel: 01372 363737.**

PAVILION AND GROUND EQUIPMENT

E. A. COMBS LIMITED, Pulteney Works, London E18 1PS. Tel: 0181-530 4216. Pavilion clocks for permanent and temporary siting. Wide choice of sizes and styles to suit any ground.

COURTYARD DESIGNS – CLASSIC PAVILIONS, Suckley, Worcester WR6 5EH. Tel/fax: 01886-884640/884444. Designers, makers and erectors of beautiful, traditional timber pavilions. Request our brochure, together with prices and testimonials.

ST JOHN'S SECURITY SYSTEM. Tel: 01932-341319. Cricket-square protection incorporating plastic-dipped post and chain system, removable when wicket in use. For more information or quotation contact Graham Pope.

J. M. SMITH, Saw Mill Yard, Bobbins Mill Close, Steeton, West Yorkshire BD20 6PZ. Manufacturer of mobile wicket covers, portable and static net frames. Installer and supplier of artificial surfaces. **Tel: 01535-654520.**

THE SPORTING BENCH COMPANY, Pardlestone Farm, Pardlestone Lane, Kilve, Somerset TA5 1SQ. Tel/fax: 01278-741664. Unique oak cricket benches, featuring carved cricket balls, bats, stumps and relief carved centre "panel". Ring for colour brochure.

STADIA SPORTS INTERNATIONAL LTD, Ely, Cambridgeshire CB6 3NP, England. Tel: 01353-668686. Manufacturers of quality sightscreens, scoreboxes and faces, net cages, synthetic wickets and wicket covers. Full colour catalogue available.

TILDENET LTD, Longbrook House, Ashton Vale Road, Bristol BS3 2HA. Tel: 0117-966 9684; fax: 0117-923 1251. Mobile and static practice nets, perimeter and ballstop, netting, sightscreens, raincovers, germination sheets and a complete range of other sports products.

PITCHES (NON-TURF)

CARPETITION LTD, 14 Kaffir Road, Edgerton, Huddersfield HD2 2AN. Tel: 01484-428777; fax: 01484-423251. Manufacturers of "Tufturf" artificial grass match and practice wickets in lengths to suit requirements.

CLUB SURFACES LIMITED, Bisham Grange, Marlow, Buckinghamshire SL7 1RS. Tel: 01628-485969; fax: 01628-471944. ClubTurf, world-leading pitch since 1978, with 4,500 installations. Chosen for ICC World Cup (Malaysia) 1997 and Commonwealth Games 1998.

PITCHES (TURF)

C. H. BINDER LTD, Moreton, Ongar, Essex CM5 0HY. Tel: 01277-890246; fax: 01277-890105. Sole suppliers nationwide of ONGAR LOAM for cricket squares, grass seed, fertilisers etc. Collections available.

SOCIETIES

CRICKET MEMORABILIA SOCIETY. Hon. Secretary, Tony Sheldon, 29 Highclere Road, Crumpsall, Manchester M8 4WH. Tel: 0161-740 3714. For collectors worldwide – meetings, speakers, auctions, magazines, directory, merchandise, but most of all friendship.

CRICKET TOURS (OVERSEAS)

ALL-WAYS PACIFIC TRAVEL, 4 The Green, Chalfont St Giles, Buckinghamshire HP8 4QF. Tel: 01494-875757; fax: 01494-874747. Specialist tour operators to the South Pacific. Worldwide cricket supporters' tours include Australia, New Zealand and South Africa.

MIKE BURTON SPORTS TRAVEL, Bastion House, Brunswick Road, Gloucester GL1 1JJ. Tel: 01452-412444; fax: 01452-527500. The number 1 in cricket, specialist in the arrangement of inbound and outbound sports tours for supporters, clubs and schools.

GULLIVERS SPORTS TRAVEL, Fiddington Manor, Tewkesbury, Gloucestershire GL20 7BJ. Tel: 01684-293175; fax: 01684-297926. The best-value, quality cricket tours for supporters, clubs and schools.

SPORT ABROAD, the official travel agent for the ECB, are the acknowledged experts in arranging cricket supporters' tours (West Indies v England 1998), corporate hospitality and club and school tours, at home and overseas. **Tel/fax: 01306-744345/744380.**

SUN LIVING, 10 Milton Court, Ravenshead, Nottingham NG15 9BD. Tel: 01623-795365; fax 01623-797421. Worldwide specialists in cricket tours for all levels and ages, plus our ever popular supporters' tours. ABTA and ATOL bonded.

SUNSPORT TOURS, Hamilton House, 66 Palmerston Road, Northampton NN1 5EX. Tel: 01604-31626; fax: 01604-31628. Fully bonded tour operator. England supporter tours – Caribbean January to April 1998. Club, school playing tours and business travel, worldwide.

CRICKET TOURS (UK)

MIKE BURTON SPORTS TRAVEL, Bastion House, Brunswick Road, Gloucester GL1 1JJ. Tel: 01452-412444; fax: 01452-527500. (Incorporating 3-D UK CRICKET TOURS) Specialist department in UK and Ireland. Cricket tours arranged, fixtures arranged, matches, hotels, transport, fixture bureau etc.

CLIFF VIEW HOTEL, Ventnor, Isle of Wight PO38 1SQ. Tel: 01983-852226. Hotel with coastal views and beach close by. Long experience with touring sides, open ended bar – evening bar snacks.

OBITUARY

ANDREW, FREDERICK JAMES, died suddenly on July 15, 1996, aged 59, at the annual Sir Garfield Sobers schools tournament in Barbados, an event he helped found. Jim Andrew was a fast-medium bowler who had a lengthy career with Gloucestershire but played only 21 first-class matches. He took five for eight, and ten for 91 in the match, against Kent at Dartford in 1962. But Andrew found his *métier* when he followed Reg Sinfield as cricket professional at Clifton College, where he spent 30 years and became an institution, insisting on the highest standards of play, dress and behaviour. According to the Old Cliftonian Society annual report: "His tall, impressive and bronzed figure at the controls of tractor or mower, and his piercing whistle, were a forbidding warning to any real or imagined malefactors trespassing on his precious Close."

BOSE, BISMAL KRISHNA, who died on May 20, 1996, was Bihar's most successful Ranji Trophy bowler, taking 205 wickets at 16.59. He played for his state in 38 matches from 1940-41 to 1957-58, and captained the team for several seasons.

BOYCE, KEITH DAVID, who died on October 11, 1996, his 53rd birthday, played in 21 Test matches for West Indies in the early 1970s but was better-known for being one of the most exciting and successful imports into county cricket. He spent 12 years with Essex from 1966 to 1977, and it was appropriate – and maybe no coincidence – that these were years when Essex won nothing but had an enormous amount of fun.

Boyce started in Barbados as a leg-spinner, but had to open the bowling in a match against the International Cavaliers in 1964-65. Trevor Bailey was so impressed that he signed him for Essex before he had even watched him bat. Boyce had to spend two years qualifying, but when he made his English first-class debut (after just the one appearance for Barbados), he took nine for 61 against Cambridge. When he was allowed to play competitive matches, Boyce became an instant star. He was an uncomplicated, aggressive fast bowler, sometimes slowed down by no-ball problems, and – though Bailey did not know it at first – an equally aggressive if not always disciplined batsman, whose *tours de force* were all the more memorable for their irregularity. He was an obvious power in one-day cricket and was the first player to reach the 1,000 runs/100 wickets double in the Sunday League. But he occasionally translated his methods into Championship cricket: he scored a hundred in 58 minutes against Leicestershire in their Championship year of 1975, with no contrivance involved whatever. He then took 12 for 73 in the match. Perhaps only Essex of the 1970s could have failed to win such a contest. Boyce was a spectacular fielder, who could throw accurately on the turn, and an all-round enthusiast.

He seemed to fit rather less well into West Indian teams than he did at Essex, but played a vital role in the recapture of the Wisden Trophy in 1973, with match figures of 11 for 147 at The Oval and eight for 99 at Lord's. Boyce became one of *Wisden's* Five Cricketers in 1974, and had another triumph in the first World Cup final a year later, when he scored a rapid late-order 34 and took four Australian wickets, alongside one for Clive Lloyd and five run-outs. However, he faded out of Test cricket after being part of the team slaughtered in Australia in 1975-76. In his penultimate Test, at Adelaide, he was left stranded on 95 and was destined never to make a Test century. By now his heavy workload was beginning to have its effect on his knees and he retired, after a tearful public farewell at Chelmsford in 1977. Boyce was known as a prodigious drinker and went through some difficult years after his return to Barbados: his marriage broke up and his house was blown away in a hurricane. However, he had settled down and had a job running the Barbados Cricket Association lottery when he collapsed. The archetypal Boyce story came when he was supposed to be blocking, and got out attempting a huge hit. He said blithely that he thought it would waste more time if the fielders had been forced to go and look for the ball.

BROUGHTON, SHAUN WALTER, died of viral encephalitis on his 20th birthday, May 1, 1996. He was a right-handed opening batsman who played two first-class matches for Natal B in 1995-96.

BUSH, RONALD GEORGE, who died on May 10, 1996, aged 87, was one of two men (along with Alan Clark of Wellington) to have played in winning teams in both New Zealand's traditional inter-provincial cricket and rugby competitions: the Plunket Shield and the Ranfurly Shield. He was a seam bowler who played ten first-class matches for Auckland in the 1930s. During a rugby tour of Japan, he is said to have given his boots to the son of the Tokyo University captain, who later became commandant of a POW camp in Malaya. When an officer answered "Yes" to the question "You know Ron Bush?" conditions in the camp improved immediately.

CLIFT, PATRICK BERNARD, died of bone marrow cancer on September 2, 1996, aged 43. Paddy Clift played Currie Cup cricket for Rhodesia before being recommended to Leicestershire by his compatriot, Brian Davison. He spent a year qualifying before making an astonishing impact in Leicestershire's match against MCC as champion county in April 1976. Against a team containing nine past or future England players, he took eight for 17 – five bowled and three lbw. Clift said he just bowled straight. In the next five sessions, only three wickets fell. He played for the county until 1987 without ever doing anything quite as spectacular, though his cricket was often dramatic. He took two hat-tricks, and one of his two centuries, made in 50 minutes at Hove in 1983, was the fastest ever made for Leicestershire. Since his batting was powerful, his seam bowling accurate with cunning changes of pace, and he was an athletic fielder, he was a natural one-day cricketer. This reputation tended to overshadow his first-class performances. In 1980 he moved his winter home to Natal, captained their Currie Cup team and settled in Durban with his family to work as a banker. He was an affable, popular, family man and his death cast a pall over Leicestershire's 1996 Championship celebrations.

COLDWELL, LEONARD JOHN, died suddenly on August 6, 1996, aged 63. Len Coldwell had his finest hour at Lord's in 1962 when he bowled England to a nine-wicket victory over Pakistan on his Test debut in front of a 20,000 Saturday crowd. But he played only seven Tests in all, and was never really a man for the grand occasion. In county cricket, however, he was one of the most effective fast bowlers of the 1960s, and he battled on undemonstratively through a succession of injuries. What made him special was the partnership he formed with Jack Flavell. Together they took Worcestershire to the brink of the County Championship in 1962, and then to the club's first ever titles in 1964 and 1965. It was a classic pairing – Flavell bowling out-swing, Coldwell bowling in-swing – and enabled Worcestershire to supplant Yorkshire as the most feared team in the country. Coldwell was a Devonian who made his debut for Worcestershire in 1955. He developed slowly for a fast bowler, but in 1961 he took 140 wickets, and in 1962 he took 152 – a figure surpassed only once, by Derek Underwood in 1966, in the 34 seasons since then, and now unthinkable. That summer he bowled 1,103 overs, an extraordinary workload for someone never wholly confident of the sturdiness of his hips and knees. According to Basil D'Oliveira, Coldwell would work out exactly where to bowl to each individual opponent: sometimes he would aim straight at the stumps, sometimes he would use the extreme edge of the crease. His methods proved less effective at the highest level. Success against Pakistan got him on to the 1962-63 tour of Australasia, but conditions there were less helpful and the batsmen less easy to think out. He returned for the first two Tests against Australia in 1964, was obliged to bowl a 100-minute spell in conditions which *Wisden* said would have been far more responsive to spin, and was never chosen again. Coldwell played on for Worcestershire until 1969 but then retired in mid-season and returned to Devon; in later years, he helped run a seaside cafe and became captain of Teignmouth Golf Club. His comradeship with Flavell lasted way beyond cricket. The two of them were firm friends as well as partners in the fast bowling business, and the families spent their holidays with each other. Coldwell had been looking forward to a hip replacement operation and getting rid of some of the pain that had bothered him since his playing days.

COLDWELL, WILLIAM RODNEY, died in late 1995, aged 63. Bill Coldwell played two first-class matches for MCC in 1954 and 1955. He was later general manager of Birmingham City Football Club, and team manager for three matches in 1991. He is believed to be the only Birmingham manager in history with an unbeaten record.

COOK, CECIL, died on September 4, 1996, aged 75. "Sam" Cook epitomised everything that has traditionally been considered best about county cricketers in general, and West Country cricketers in particular. He was a phlegmatic, humorous, locally-rooted man who loved a wry laugh, a pint and the life he led, and made friends everywhere he played. He was also a naturally gifted, slow left-arm bowler who could drop the ball on a length, without bothering to practise, and keep it there all season, with enough flight and variation to outwit the best batsmen in the game. After training as a plumber and serving in the war, Sam arrived at the Bristol nets in 1946, and announced himself as "Cook of Tetbury, sir". He immediately impressed Wally Hammond, took a wicket with his first ball in first-class cricket, and 133 in the first season. A year later he was preferred to Doug Wright for the Trent Bridge Test against South Africa, but he tried too hard on a docile pitch, returned horrid figures and was never picked again. He still kept bowling and bowling for Gloucestershire and took 1,782 wickets over 19 years, putting him 49th on the all-time list. He remained "Cook of Tetbury", never gave himself airs or took anything too seriously, certainly not his batting: his runs (1,965) just exceeded his wickets. David Foot tells how he arrived at the crease once, and whispered to Andy Wilson what looked like an important instruction. "How are yer onions this year, Andy?" he said. From 1971 to 1986 Sam Cook was a first-class umpire. It was universally understood that, unlike his colleagues, he took pity on suffering bowlers and would give batsmen out lbw on the sweep; tyros learned this as an unwritten regulation of county cricket. After his funeral at Tetbury parish church, Arthur Milton saw that Sam's grave was in a distant corner and remarked: "See they've got you down at third man again, old son."

CREED, LEONARD GOLLEDGE, died on June 3, 1996, aged 79. Len Creed was the Bath bookmaker and Somerset committee member whose holiday in Antigua in 1973 led to the county signing Viv Richards. He was Somerset chairman in 1977 and 1978.

CROWTHER, LESLIE DOUGLAS SARGENT, CBE, who died on September 28, 1996, aged 63, was a well-known TV comedian and game show host with a passion for cricket. He was a tireless worker for the Lord's Taverners, and president in 1991 and 1992.

DARE, JOHN ST FELIX, who died on February 10, 1996, aged 90, played ten matches for British Guiana between 1924-25 and 1929-30. He was President of the West Indies Cricket Board of Control between 1960 and 1966, having been secretary in the 1930s.

DOYLE, SISTER MARY PETER, who died in Upper Hutt, New Zealand, on April 17, 1996, aged 109, attributed her longevity to her faith in God and her interest in cricket. She was believed to be the oldest Sister of Mercy in the world.

FISHER, FREDERICK ERIC, died on June 19, 1996, aged 71. Eric Fisher was a left-arm swing bowler who was picked for New Zealand against South Africa at Wellington in 1952-53. He struggled as a bowler and dropped Jackie McGlew twice during his unbeaten innings of 255. Figures of eight for 34 for Wellington against Canterbury had got him into the team, and he continued to be an effective Plunket Shield bowler, but he was surprisingly omitted from the tour to South Africa a year later and never played Test cricket again. The selectors apparently took against him, and several others, for being a bit rotund at a time when the South Africans had made athletic fielding fashionable. Fisher went to England to become professional for Rochdale. He also played three matches for Central Districts, but dropped out of the first-class game two years after his Test.

FOTHERGILL, DESMOND HUGH, died on March 16, 1996, aged 75. Des Fothergill was a batsman and occasional leg-spinner who played 27 matches for Victoria from 1938-39 to 1948-49, scoring 102 against South Australia at Adelaide in November 1947. He was better known as an Australian Rules footballer for Collingwood, but knee trouble forced him to retire aged 27 and he played little cricket after that either.

GOMEZ, GERALD ETHRIDGE, died from a heart attack when playing tennis in Trinidad on August 6, 1996, aged 76. Gerry Gomez was a major figure in West Indian cricket for more than half a century, as a player, manager, selector, administrator, commentator and finally elder statesman. In an emergency, at Georgetown in 1964-65, he even umpired a Test match. He made his name as a batsman, scoring 161 not out for Trinidad against Jamaica when he was still a teenager, and earning selection for the 1939 tour of England, though his achievements there did not match his promise. By the time West Indies resumed Test cricket almost nine years later he was senior enough to take over the captaincy for one match, but – as all white West Indians were to find – his place in the team was being challenged by the emergence of new talent. Gomez adapted: he dropped down the order, provided dogged counterpoint to the genius of the three Ws and developed into a gifted swing bowler. From quiet beginnings, he matured enough to take seven for 55 at Sydney in 1951-52. He still played important innings, including his only Test century in West Indies' first match against India, at Delhi in 1948-49, but usually he was either in a supporting role or – as happened regularly in Australia – in charge of repairs. Gomez captained the team on only the one occasion; his compatriot and contemporary Jeff Stollmeyer overtook him. But his leadership qualities came through later. When he was appointed manager for the 1960-61 tour of Australia, C. L. R. James said it was "a brilliant selection . . . Gerry is popular at home and in Australia, knowledgable and tough." The tour was a triumph and Gomez was an important behind-the-scenes influence in ensuring harmony. He was a longstanding member of the West Indies Board, and president for 30 years of the West Indies Cricket Umpires' Association, which he welded together. Gomez played football for Trinidad, and became a vice-president of the country's football and tennis associations, an executive member of the Olympic Association, president of the Boy Scouts' movement and chairman of the annual music festival. He was a holder of Trinidad's Humming Bird Medal (Gold), for services to sport. When he died, he was president of the Queen's Park Cricket Club.

HALFYARD, DAVID JOHN, who died suddenly on August 23, 1996, aged 65, had a remarkable, indeed eccentric, career which was supposed to have ended after a serious road accident in 1962. But he returned to the first-class game six years later and was still taking wickets for Tiverton Heathcoat in the Devon Premier League a few weeks before he died. Dave Halfyard came to prominence as a tireless seamer for Kent in the late 1950s, and took 135 wickets in 1958. After his accident he kept trying to make a comeback, but failed, and in 1967 went on to the first-class umpires' list. However, Nottinghamshire saw him bowling in the nets – in itself not normal practice for an umpire – and decided to sign him, although almost the entire committee had to watch him for two hours before they were convinced of his fitness. He thus became perhaps the only umpire to retire and return to playing. Bowling more sedately but even more craftily than he did for Kent, he spent three productive years at Nottinghamshire, bringing his total of first-class wickets to 963 before finally leaving the first-class game in 1970. Even while with Nottinghamshire he would slip away on his days off to bowl leg-breaks for club sides. Over the next 12 years he had spells as professional with Durham, Northumberland and Cornwall and had another period as an umpire. While with Cornwall, he took all 16 Devon wickets to fall in a match at Penzance. Halfyard's zest for displaying the tricks of his trade before audiences others might have thought unworthy made him in that sense comparable to Sydney Barnes. His pride and joy was a camper van with almost 400,000 miles on the clock; his cricket had the same improbable durability.

HOUGHTON, WILLIAM ERIC, died on May 1, 1966, aged 85. Eric Houghton played seven matches as a batsman for Warwickshire in 1946 and 1947. He was better known as an outside-left for Aston Villa, Notts County and England. It was said he could hit a dead ball harder than any of his contemporaries and once smashed the crossbar with a free kick.

HURST, ROBERT JACK, who died on February 10, 1996, aged 62, was a tall, slow left-arm bowler with a good action, who played 100 matches for Middlesex between 1954 and 1961. Bob Hurst was successful in 1956 and 1957, and received his cap, but was inclined to be short of confidence and never fully established himself at a time when Lord's pitches were becoming less helpful to spin. He returned to club cricket with Teddington, where he was a major force. Hurst was a popular dressing-room figure; his red hair earned him the nickname "Bloodnut".

JEGANATHAN, SRIDHARAN, who died on May 14, 1996, aged 44, was the first Sri Lankan Test player to die. Jeganathan was a left-arm spinner and lower-order batsman who played in two Tests in New Zealand in 1982-83. He was recalled to play in the 1987 World Cup and dismissed Graham Gooch, Tim Robinson, Mansoor Akhtar and Richie Richardson. He later became Malaysia's national coach.

JOHNSON, JOHAN ECKARD, who died in a car crash on February 9, 1996, aged 24, was a fast-medium bowler and useful tail-end batsman for Griqualand West and Orange Free State. He topped the Griquas' bowling averages in 1993-94 with 19 wickets at 22.94, then moved up to play Castle Cup cricket for Free State. His appearances were restricted because of back trouble and he moved back to Griqualand West the following year. He had been due to play the day he died, but an injury had forced him to withdraw.

JONES, WILLIAM EDWARD, died on July 25, 1996, aged 79. Willie Jones was a left-handed batsman of fatalistic temperament who played 340 matches for Glamorgan between 1937 and 1958, as an amateur before the war and then as a professional. "Little Willie" scored two double-centuries in a fortnight in Glamorgan's Championship year, 1948. After the first, he received a heap of telegrams, opened some and stuffed the rest into his bag. Asked why, he said: "I'll open those when I have a bad day." The bad days would have come less often had he been less dependent on his wristy square-cut, but he played the shot so effectively it brought him a stack of runs. He was a gifted slow left-armer, with a nice action but not enough confidence, and an athletic outfielder. Jones was a fly-half for Penarth, Neath and Gloucester and played in a wartime rugby international for Wales.

JORDAN, FRANK SLATER, who died on October 22, 1995, aged 90, was in the New South Wales team along with Don Bradman in Bradman's debut match at Adelaide in 1927-28. Jordan was a fast-medium bowler who played in five other games for the state, with match figures of eight for 43 against Tasmania in 1928-29.

KANNAYIRAM N., who died on January 1, 1996, aged 70, was an all-rounder who played for Madras and Tamil Nadu. He toured the West Indies in 1952-53, but did not play in a Test match.

KARDAR, ABDUL HAFEEZ, who died on April 21, 1996, aged 71, may be regarded as the father figure of Pakistani cricket and, as such, an important character in the history of the country as a whole. He captained Pakistan in their first Test match in 1952 and was at the forefront of events from then until he resigned from the Pakistani Board in 1977 in protest against Government interference. But he was a Test cricketer before Pakistan even existed, playing for India on the 1946 tour of England under the name Abdul Hafeez. After the tour he added the family name Kardar, stayed in England and went to Oxford to read PPE and enhance his reputation as an idiosyncratic and fearless cricketer: a left-handed batsman, whose response to any bowler or situation was to dance down the track first ball and slam it back over the bowler's head, and a left-arm medium-paced bowler, economical on a good pitch, devastatingly effective on a bad one. Kardar had a couple of productive seasons with Warwickshire, where his successes included marrying the club chairman's daughter, then returned to Pakistan to take on the captaincy. He had learned well under Martin Donnelly and Tom Dollery and, as Test cricket's newcomers, Pakistan at once made themselves worthy of respect rather than anyone's sympathy. In 23 matches as captain, Kardar led his team to victory over all the then Test-playing countries except South Africa, whom they never met. He then became chairman of selectors, and president of Pakistan's Board of Control from 1972 to 1977. In all his positions of authority, he was inclined to be dictatorial and quickly angered, especially by any hint of criticism. In some ways, his prickly brilliance has become characteristic of his country's cricket. But he was also a visionary. He ruthlessly modernised the organisation of the Pakistani game, and many of the themes he was advocating in the 1970s have become common currency among modern administrators: the need to do away with unwieldy committees, to break the post-imperial dominance of Lord's, and to expand the game in Asia. He was an early advocate of neutral umpires. Little of this was well received by his colleagues on ICC at the time. In later years he removed himself from cricket and his last public role was as Pakistan's ambassador to Switzerland. Diplomacy may not have come easily to him. Imran Khan said: "After Kardar's retirement, Pakistan cricket was thrown to the wolves, the cricket bureaucrats whose progeny still rule the game."

KENNY, CHARLES JOHN MICHAEL, who died in September 1996, aged 67, was a right-arm medium-pace bowler who won a Cambridge Blue in 1952; at Lord's he had Colin Cowdrey stumped for seven. He played 18 matches for Essex and also appeared for Ireland.

KENYON, DONALD, died on November 12, 1996, aged 72, after being taken ill when he was about to show a film at a members' evening at Worcester, the ground he adorned for so long. Don Kenyon was almost synonymous with Worcestershire cricket in the two decades after the war. In the words of his old team-mate, George Chesterton, Worcester was the only place in the cricket world where "Don" did not immediately

[*Popperfoto*

Don Kenyon: giant of Worcestershire cricket.

conjure up Bradman. Kenyon was born in Staffordshire, played for Stourbridge and was taken on the county staff in 1946, when he scored a century against them for Combined Services. Then he embarked on a career of run-accumulation that hardly ever wavered, and opposing bowlers could only stand despairingly as this broad-shouldered figure boomed the ball past mid-on or extra cover. He was helped by the friendliness of the New Road pitch; when he played for England, his trumpet sounded far more uncertainly. He is said to have been incurably homesick in India in 1951-52, and was quickly blown away by the Australian fast bowlers when chosen to open with Hutton in two Tests in 1953. Two years later he finally did himself justice with 87 at Trent Bridge against South Africa, but after failing in the next two Tests disappeared from international cricket. At county level, he remained a giant. He is still Worcestershire's leading scorer, with 33,490 runs for the county, and passed 2,000 seven times. In 1959, he became Worcestershire captain and led the team to its first two County Championships and two of the first four Gillette Cup finals. Don Kenyon was never a talkative or, perhaps, imaginative man but his natural seriousness, authority and example made his captaincy successful. He was also a good listener, ready to take advice. Between 1965 and 1972, he was an England selector and he became county president when Worcestershire were champions again in 1988 and 1989. His greatest pleasure in later years was bowling to his young grandson in the nets at New Road.

KERSEY, GRAHAM JAMES, died in hospital in Western Australia on January 1, 1997, aged 25, after being injured in a car crash on Christmas Eve. Kersey was a wicket-keeper who played occasionally for Kent in 1991 and 1992 before moving to Surrey the following year. He quickly established himself at The Oval as the first-choice keeper, except on the big one-day occasions when the captain, Alec Stewart, did the job. Kersey was not an especially stylish keeper – apart from anything else, his cap regularly fell off – but he rarely dropped catches, and was a battling batsman who could irritate opposing bowlers with effective use of the sweep. Above all, he was a dedicated team man whose cheerful attitude and combative approach were an important part of Surrey's revival in 1996. Stewart described him as "the most popular member of the staff – a true player's player". The Surrey vice-captain Adam Hollioake said: "You could rely on him totally. You could get the best wicket-keeper in the world, but he couldn't possibly fill the gap."

KUMAR, SIVA SHANTHI, was shot dead while playing golf at the Royal Colombo club on December 7, 1996, aged 53. Two gunmen climbed a wall and fired six shots at him on the 12th green. Shanthi Kumar was captain of the Tamil Union team in the early 1970s.

LANGLEY, JOHN DOUGLAS ALGERNON, who died on April 27, 1996, aged 78, was an aggressive right-hand batsman who won a Cambridge Blue in 1938 after scoring a century, described by *Wisden* as a "brilliant exhibition of driving", against Glamorgan. He also played once for Middlesex. Langley was an excellent golfer, and played in three Walker Cup matches, the first in 1936 within a few weeks of leaving Stowe School. He was English champion in 1950, having been runner-up while still at Stowe.

LAWTON, THOMAS, died on November 6, 1996, aged 77. Tommy Lawton was one of the best-known forwards in English soccer during the early post-war years and won 23 England caps, scoring 22 goals. As a teenager, he played Lancashire League cricket for Burnley and hit Learie Constantine for two successive sixes.

LAY, RONALD SAMUEL MARSHALL, died on November 9, 1996, aged 79. Ron Lay was one of the successful and respected county umpires who had not played first-class cricket. He emerged from officiating in local cricket round Northamptonshire via the Minor Counties, and joined the first-class list in 1956, staying on until 1968. He missed much of the 1964 season because Ted Dexter lashed a straight drive on to his foot.

LINDWALL, RAYMOND RUSSELL, MBE, died on June 23, 1996, aged 74. Ray Lindwall was undeniably one of the great fast bowlers, arguably the greatest of all the Australian practitioners, and perhaps the man who established fast bowling's role in the modern game. In the 1930s the game had been dominated by batsmen, with the brief, unacceptable, interlude of Bodyline. Lindwall began a new era in which bat and ball were more evenly matched, when the bouncer (or "bumper" as it was then called) was an accepted weapon, provided it was not overused. He bowled the bumper sparingly but brilliantly, and the mere possibility of it made batsmen uneasy. He thus paved the way for all the other great fast bowlers of the post-war era, from Trueman to Ambrose. But in fact more than two-fifths of Lindwall's 228 Test victims were bowled.

Ray was a Sydney boy and watched Larwood during the Bodyline series. He played with other kids on patches of green and in the streets, choosing – it is said – the street down which the great leg-spinner Bill O'Reilly walked home in the hope of catching his eye. He was also a promising batsman, scoring a double-century and a century in different junior matches on the same day. At the St George club, he came under the wing of O'Reilly, who used the novel technique of photography to help the lad correct his faults. But Lindwall was a smart learner and dedicated to practice; during the war, when he was in the South Pacific and suffered horribly from tropical diseases, he marked out his run-up between the palm trees and got his bowling into a beautiful groove. Halfway through the home 1946-47 series against England, he and Keith Miller emerged as the undisputed leaders of Australia's attack; on top of that Lindwall actually beat Miller to a Test century, scoring 100 at the MCG in the New Year Test of 1947, batting at No. 9. At Sydney two months later, Lindwall took seven for 63 and, after getting seven for 38 against India in 1947-48, came to England in 1948 an established star.

On that tour, he rose to even greater fame as the leader of the attack in Australia's 4-0 triumph. And though Bradman used him carefully, his very presence dictated the terms. Lindwall was injured during the First Test, but in three of the subsequent four he was devastating, reaching his peak at The Oval when he took six for 20 as England were bowled out for 52. He had a clever slower ball (which would have stood him in good stead in modern one-day cricket) and, though his arm was too low to satisfy the sternest purists, he was close to being the complete fast bowler. The low arm meant his bowling had a skidding effect, which made the bouncers all the more fearsome. Sir Pelham Warner once exclaimed "Poetry!" and Lindwall, watching himself on film, discovered that all the effort and pain failed to transmit itself to anyone else. "I don't look tired," he murmured with surprise.

Lindwall never quite reached such a peak after 1948, but he played Test cricket for more than another decade. Jack Fingleton said Lindwall never liked bowling much, and always preferred batting, but he was opening Australia's attack as late as January 1960, when he was 38, and played the last of his 61 Tests a few weeks later. Lindwall simply would not go away. Inevitably, his shock effect had declined by then but, like his eventual heir Dennis Lillee, he compensated by his canniness, mastery of technique – he began to use the in-swinger far more – and utter determination. He captained Australia once and, for several seasons, Queensland, having moved from New South Wales, before finishing with 228 Test wickets at 23.03 and 794 first-class wickets at 21.35.

He was a much liked man but not a flamboyant character like Miller. Cardus rated Lindwall alongside Ted McDonald as "the most hostile and artistic fast bowlers I have ever seen" – but preferred to write about Miller, who was better copy. Lindwall was a quieter man, whose strongest adjective was his own concoction, "blooing". He was a phenomenal all-round sportsman: had he not played cricket, Lindwall could easily have been a rugby league international, and he ran 100 yards in 10.6 seconds. But when he retired he ran a flower shop with his wife in the centre of Brisbane. If anyone in Australia ever imagined floristry was unmanly, his presence in the shop provided an answer, though he concentrated on the figures, and his assistant claimed he could not tell a rose from a dandelion.

While still playing for New South Wales, he once saw the young Alan Davidson bowl a bouncer at an opposing No. 8. "You've just insulted all fast bowlers," Lindwall told him. "You've admitted No. 8 can bat better than you can bowl. Get into the nets and learn how to bowl." And he took him there, and taught him.

LODGE, DEREK HARRY ALAN, who died on July 10, 1996, aged 67, was a civil servant and a cricket statistician with an unusually lateral cast of mind. His 1982 book *Figures on the Green* tried to offer answers to questions usually considered beyond statisticians' reach, such as What Was the Greatest Innings Ever Played? (Jessop's 104 at The Oval, 1902, suggested Lodge). He was vice-chairman of the Cricket Society and a keen long-distance runner.

LOMAX, IAN RAYMOND, who died on July 31, 1996, aged 65, was a tall, powerful Etonian cricketer with an Edwardian sense of style and 18th century zest. He played only six matches for Somerset, but his performances included 83 in 64 minutes against Hampshire in 1962. There were committee members who would have liked him to have taken over the captaincy, but he played most of his cricket for the grander wandering clubs and Wiltshire, for whom he was Man of the Match in a Gillette Cup tie with Essex in 1969. He hit 63, including 16 in one over off Robin Hobbs; Lomax smashed the ball hard whoever was bowling. Increasingly, though, he devoted himself to horses, and was Master of the Craven Farmers' Hunt. His first wife, Rosemary, was a racehorse trainer. To get round Jockey Club rules which barred women, he held the licence for many years.

McGILVRAY, ALAN DAVID, AM, MBE, who died on July 16, 1996, aged 86, was the voice of Australian cricket. He first commentated on an Ashes series in 1938, sitting in Sydney and interpreting cables from England accompanied by sound effects such as a pencil on the tabletop to simulate bat on ball. He retired at The Oval in 1985, after 225 Tests, including more than a hundred between Australia and England. His popularity was such that in the midst of the schism between Kerry Packer and official cricket, the ABC advertised traditional cricket with a jingle, The Game Is Not the Same Without McGilvray. Alan McGilvray was a fine left-hand batsman and sturdy right-arm medium-pacer himself, playing 18 games for New South Wales. In 13 of those games he was captain, starting in only his third match in February 1934. He took over again when Bert Oldfield was with Australia in South Africa in 1935-36, and continued when Stan McCabe was playing against England the following year. However, when New South Wales dropped him, he changed direction and became the exemplar of the Australian style of radio commentary: precise, factual and statistically oriented with only faint traces of humour. In England, amid the sometimes irrelevant hilarity of the BBC commentary box, he could sound a rather po-faced, disapproving, guest and he often saved his best anecdotes for the evenings. The nearest thing he had to a catchphrase was a firm: "That's by the by, as Lillee [or whoever] comes in to bowl . . ." His greatest professional disaster was when he flew home early from the Tied Test at Brisbane in 1960-61, believing Australia were certain to lose. It was an aberration. His professional standards were exceptionally high. He expected the same of the game

[*Hulton Getty*

Ray Lindwall in action for Australia at the Oval Test, 1948: "The man who paved the way for modern fast bowling."

he loved, and was often appalled by sloppy dress or bad behaviour. But he still had Australian tastes. There is a story that during a one-day international in 1983, a brewery donated two dozen cans of beer to the ABC commentary team, who agreed to save them until after the match. No one remembered to tell McGilvray, though. He drank 23 of the cans – and never slurred a word. "His presence and style were what we all aspired to," said his fellow-commentator Neville Oliver.

McINNES, MELVILLE JAMES, OAM, died on July 23, 1996, aged 80. Mel McInnes umpired 16 Tests in Australia in the 1950s, including all five Tests of the 1954-55 Ashes series. He won a solid reputation for his judgment, impartiality and bearing, but became mired in controversy on the 1958-59 tour when he was blamed by the English press after some bad decisions and for not stamping out throwing and dragging among Australian fast bowlers.

McKENNA, DONALD CHARLES, died in Australia, where he was born, on September 4, 1995, aged 51. He was a left-handed batsman who made 35 first-class appearances in South Africa for Border in the old Currie Cup B section between 1973-74 and 1979-80, usually keeping wicket. He made 69 on debut against Orange Free State and his only century, 129 not out, against the same opposition a year later.

MICHAEL, LEONARD, who died on March 16, 1996, aged 74, was a wicket-keeper who played 21 matches for South Australia, starting in 1939-40, though he did not make his Shield debut for another eight years. He saved a match against Victoria in 1949-50 by scoring 85 and sharing a last-wicket stand of 104 with Ernie Pynor.

MILLER, LAWRENCE SOMERVILLE MARTIN, died on December 17, 1996, aged 73. Lawrie Miller was a left-handed batsman who played 13 Tests for New Zealand, not making his debut until just before his 30th birthday. His career was held up because he came from rural Taranaki. He failed to pass 50 in Tests; indeed, in South Africa in 1953-54, he made four successive Test ducks, a sequence ended only by a fairly inglorious two. But he played some important little innings, and his 47 and 25 in the low-scoring match against West Indies at Auckland in 1955-56 were instrumental in securing New Zealand's first Test win. He was often prolific in provincial cricket: at one stage of the 1952-53 season he had scored 397 for Central Districts without being dismissed. Miller later moved to Wellington. He also played first-class rugby.

MILLER, ROLAND, died on May 7, 1996, aged 55. Ron Miller was an all-rounder from County Durham who played 133 matches for Warwickshire between 1961 and 1968, best known for his left-arm spin and close catching. His application never quite matched his natural gifts, and Warwickshire barred him from the night-watchman's job after he was caught, hooking Fred Trueman.

MITCHELL, THOMAS BIGNALL, who died on January 27, aged 93, was the oldest surviving England Test cricketer and the last man alive from Douglas Jardine's Bodyline party of 1932-33. The pictures of Tommy Mitchell, in his spectacles, make him look an improbable cricketer. He was actually one of the best leg-spinners England ever produced, who might have played far more than his five Tests had he possessed a more equable temperament. R. C. Robertson-Glasgow described him as "one of the great bowlers, a master of flight and variety. But he only does it when he feels like it . . . There is something of Donald Duck about him. No cricketer so conveys to the spectators the perplexities and frustration of man at the mercy of malignant fate. He has much in common with that golfer who missed short putts because of the uproar of the butterflies in the adjoining meadows."

Mitchell's cricket career came out of adversity. He was spotted by Derbyshire during the General Strike when the captain, Guy Jackson, took a team to play striking miners at Creswell Colliery, where he was a faceworker. Characteristically, he held out for £4 a week rather than £3 before he would leave the pit. By 1929 he had taken 100 wickets for the first time, a habit he kept up for the next nine years. He had also established himself on the circuit as a popular figure among professionals, who enjoyed his humour, and the spectators, who enjoyed his bowling, if less so amongst the administrators, who were wary of his bluntness. Mitchell went on the Bodyline tour only because Walter Robins turned it down, and his one match of the Test series was at Brisbane, where he dismissed Woodfull twice. He never played Test cricket again after getting into an argument with his captain, Bob Wyatt, during the Lord's Test of 1935 and telling him, "You couldn't captain a box of bloody lead soldiers." Perhaps his major contribution to Test match history was that he lent Wally Hammond his bat to score his 336 not out in New Zealand. But Mitchell remained a dominating bowler on the circuit, taking 171 wickets in 1935, and 121 in Derbyshire's Championship year of 1936, when he was the essential foil for Bill Copson and Alf Pope. However, he decided to return to the pit after the war and thus lost the benefit that had become due in 1940. He bamboozled league cricketers, playing for Hickleton Main, well into his fifties. As a nine-year-old, he had sung "Oh, for the Wings of a Dove" before King George V and Queen Mary. In old age, he seemed contented, and surrounded by great-grandchildren.

MODI, RUSI SHERIYAR, who died on May 17, 1996, aged 71, was an Indian Test batsman, writer and all-round enthusiast for the game. Modi made his reputation when he hit centuries in seven consecutive Ranji matches for Bombay in the Indian seasons of 1943-44 and 1944-45. He scored three double-centuries in 1944-45, when he became the first batsman to make 1,000 in a Ranji Trophy season, and a fourth the following year against the Australian Services team on their way back from England, which Modi regarded as his best-ever innings. He was still only 21 when he came to England in 1946, and John Arlott was quick to notice the contrast between Modi off the field, "tall, painfully thin, grey of face and huddled into an overcoat, tending to tremble", and the confident, controlled batsman. Modi made 57 not out on his Test debut, at Lord's, and went on to play ten Tests, contributing crucial innings in the two games at Brabourne Stadium, Bombay, against West Indies in 1948-49: 112, his only Test century, in the Second, and 86 in the Fifth, when India almost snatched victory. Later he became aide-de-camp to the Governor of Bombay and one of India's most thoughtful and influential cricket writers. He died of a heart attack in the Cricket Club of India pavilion at the Brabourne, scene of his great triumphs. Initial reports said, erroneously, that he had fallen to his death from the third floor.

MORGAN, GRACE A., who died on October 22, 1996, aged 87, was reserve wicket-keeper on the English tour to Australasia in 1934-35 which included the first women's Test. She played only two Tests herself, but became a prominent administrator.

NAZAR MOHAMMAD, who died on July 12, 1996, aged 75, faced the first ball received by a Pakistani in Test cricket, at Delhi in 1952-53, and in the next match became the country's first Test centurion. On a matting wicket at Lucknow, he carried his bat for 124 not out in eight hours 35 minutes and set up an innings victory; he was the first player to be on the field throughout a Test. He also made 55 and 47 in the final Test but, soon afterwards, a domestic accident damaged his arm and ended his career. He became a coach, selector and one of Pakistan's best cricketing raconteurs. His son, Mudassar Nazar, played 76 Tests.

NEWMAN, SIR JACK, the world's senior Test player, died on September 23, 1996, aged 94. Jack Newman was a left-arm medium-pace bowler who played in three Tests for New Zealand, against South Africa in 1931-32, and against England a year later. He was the first New Zealand Test player to emerge from outside the big cities. He came from Nelson and was unable to get a game in first-class cricket between his debut for

Canterbury in February 1923 and being picked by Wellington eight years later. Against England, he had to bowl to Wally Hammond on the way to his world record 336 not out, and was hit for three successive sixes. Newman became a selector and, from 1965 to 1967, president of the New Zealand Cricket Council. He was a legend in Nelson cricket, and played for the team from teenage years until he was past 50. He also turned the small family business he joined even before he became a Test player into a major national company, and its airline division became Ansett New Zealand. In the week Sir Jack died, this was sold to Rupert Murdoch. On his death, the senior Test cricketer became Lionel Birkett of West Indies, born in 1904.

NUTTER, ALBERT EDWARD, died on June 3, 1996, aged 82. Bert Nutter was an all-rounder who played for Lancashire before the war and then accompanied his friend Buddy Oldfield both into League cricket and to Northamptonshire, where they shared a testimonial. The two men died within seven weeks of each other. Nutter bowled accurately at good pace, and regularly scored middle-order runs in pleasant style. In 1938 he came close to the double, but just missed his 100 wickets, a mark he did pass in his first season with Northamptonshire ten years later. After retirement, he emigrated to South Africa.

OLDFIELD, NORMAN, died on April 19, 1996, aged 84. "Buddy" Oldfield was less than 5ft 3in tall and extremely nervous, but he was one of the best, and bravest, English batsmen of the 1930s, who delighted Cardus with his wristy strokeplay and said he enjoyed receiving bouncers. Oldfield played in one Test – against West Indies at The Oval in 1939 – and scored a much praised 80. But war broke out a fortnight later, and he never had another opportunity: he remains the top scorer among the 80-plus players who have appeared in only one Test for England. Oldfield came from Dukinfield on the outskirts of Manchester and spent six years on the Lancashire staff before becoming an overnight success. *Wisden* described his debut season, 1935, as "sensational" and Cardus began comparing him to J. T. Tyldesley: "If this young man does not go to the top of his calling, there will be a scandalous interference with destiny." He scored 1,066 runs that year, maintained his form for the next two years and then raised his game. He scored 1,812 runs in 1938 and 1,922 in 1939, and there was some surprise that he was not chosen for England earlier. But the really scandalous interference with his destiny came from Hitler. When peace returned, Oldfield, then 35, fell out with Lancashire over terms and went to play League cricket. He returned to the county game with Northamptonshire in 1948 and remained for seven years, playing a major part in the county's rise from the cellar: in 1949, the county's best year since 1913, Oldfield passed 2,000. After leaving Lancashire, he was banned from Old Trafford except when Northamptonshire were playing there: in 1951 he dealt with this situation in the traditional manner, and scored hundreds against his old county in the next two years as well. But he came to regret his decision to leave Lancashire, and believed in old age that it had cost him the chance of another Test cap. Oldfield was a first-class umpire from 1955 to 1965 and stood in two Tests, but he said he never really enjoyed the job: "I wanted to be one of the lads and you just can't be. I didn't like giving people out either." He was nervy in that job too and often explained his decisions to the players. Lancashire then forgave him enough to appoint him their coach from 1968 to 1972. It was said he never ate breakfast for fear of vomiting when he batted. According to Frank Tyson, when Oldfield was next in he sat by the window "padded up and fully prepared, smoking cigarette after cigarette and blinking furiously".

PALSULE, SADASHIV GOPAL, who died on February 19, 1996, aged 77, played three matches for Maharashtra, and hit 97 out of 604 in the second innings when his team lost the 1948-49 Ranji Trophy semi-final against Bombay in which a world record 2,376 runs were scored. He was later a journalist.

PEACH, FRANCIS GEORGE, died on February 3, 1996, aged 84. Frank Peach was Derbyshire's statistician and co-founded the club yearbook in 1954. He played an important role in fundraising as a member of the Supporters' Club during some trying years for the county.

PETER, RAJESH, who was found dead in his flat in New Delhi in suspicious circumstances early in 1996, aged 36, played for Delhi in the Ranji Trophy. He was a fast bowler, but was best-known for scoring 67 not out in a ninth-wicket partnership of 118 with Rakesh Shukla in the 1981-82 Trophy final against Karnataka, when both sides passed 700.

PIGOT, DAVID RICHARD, who died on June 8, 1996, aged 66, was a batsman who played 44 times for Ireland, although he did not win his first cap until he was 37; his last came when he was 46. His father also appeared for Ireland and his grandfather was president of the Irish Cricket Union.

POOLE, CYRIL JOHN, who died on February 11, 1996, aged 74, was a splendidly entertaining member of the Nottinghamshire side of the 1950s. He made three Test appearances on the "second-string" MCC tour of the subcontinent in 1951-52 and scored half-centuries in both innings on his debut in Calcutta. But he did not have enough application to be a serious contender for a home Test place in such a strong era, and instead acquired a reputation as one of the most gifted and audacious left-handed batsmen on the circuit, and a great fielder. Poole, from the mining area round Mansfield, started as a footballer and, at 15, became Mansfield Town's youngest-ever player before going on to Gillingham and Wolves. He did not make his first-class debut until he was 27, in 1948, but thereafter became a steady county run-scorer, passing 1,000 regularly, and making 1,860 in 1961 when he was already 40. There was about him the vague hint of the chancer off the field. He would regularly borrow any bat that was lying around the dressing-room, never worrying about the weight or other technicalities. It is said his team-mates tried to cure him with a trick bat, which was merely a shell filled with sawdust. He scored about 70 with it and apparently never noticed.

POPE, ALFRED VARDY, died on May 11, 1996, aged 86. Alf Pope was a Derbyshire stalwart of the 1930s, alongside his younger brother George (and, on one occasion, his youngest brother Harold). He was a fast-medium bowler who came to Derbyshire via the classic route: he began work as a coal miner at 14 but left during the General Strike of 1926 and joined Sam Cadman's nursery at the County Ground. He was a tall man, a touch quicker than George but less overtly aggressive, who could move the ball sharply off the seam, especially on Derbyshire's responsive pitches. His best year was the county's Championship year of 1936, when he compensated for George's absence through injury by taking 99 wickets. Arthur Richardson, the captain, would warn him he might have to bowl until close of play, and would get the cheery response: "I like bowling, skipper." Alf Pope was also a very useful late-order bat and scored a century against Warwickshire when promoted to No. 4 at Edgbaston in 1938. In 1941 he re-created his Championship-winning partnership with Bill Copson to take Saltaire to the Bradford League title. Later, he was a roving professional and coach before settling to spend 20 years as coach and groundsman at Berkhamsted School. He played until he was 69 and gave up umpiring only the summer before his death.

PUNA, NAROTAM, died on June 7, 1996, aged 66. "Tom" Puna was a highly regarded off-spinner and the first migrant from Asia to be capped for New Zealand, playing in the three Tests against England in 1965-66. His family emigrated from Bombay when he was eight and he got into the Northern Districts team as a batsman and occasional seamer. He turned to off-breaks as a last resort in a match against

Central Districts in 1957-58, and promptly took four for two to win the match. By the time Puna retired in 1969, he had become the team's leading wicket-taker with 223. He took 34 wickets in 1965-66 at an average of just over 13, and was a natural choice for the Test team. In the three Tests against England he got only four wickets, but some of those present still believe that, had he been given more overs in the final innings at Auckland, New Zealand might have won. He later ran a greengrocer's shop in Hamilton, but was still playing just before he died; two of his three sons have also represented Northern Districts.

RICHARDS, DICK STANLEY, who died on November 13, 1995, aged 87, played 18 matches in the Sussex middle order between 1927 and 1935. He coached at Rossall School from 1937 to 1982.

ROBERTS, ALPHONSO THEODORE, died of cancer on July 24, 1996, aged 58. Alfie Roberts was the first Test player from any of the Leeward and Windward Islands which have become so influential in modern West Indian cricket. Roberts came from St Vincent and was picked to go to New Zealand in 1955-56, aged only 18, on the basis of a couple of promising innings and the recommendation of Everton Weekes. He made 28 and 0 in his only Test and was never picked again. A job was arranged for him in Trinidad to try and give him more cricketing opportunities, but he failed in his only first-class match there, and was criticised by locals who objected to a ''small islander'' being picked ahead of native Trinidadians. He scored only 1 and 0 for the Windwards against MCC – on a matting pitch in terrible conditions – in 1959-60. Roberts subsequently emigrated to Canada, where he obtained a degree and worked in Montreal. He is believed to have played only one friendly game there – against a touring Vincentian XI in 1966 – scoring a brilliant 50 before tossing his wicket away.

ROBERTS, Air Vice-Marshal JOHN FREDERICK, CB, CBE, FCA, died on April 20, 1996, aged 83. ''Robbie'' Roberts was a left-hand batsman who played five times for Glamorgan before the war and three first-class matches for Combined Services afterwards. He rose to be the RAF's Director-General of Ground Training.

ROBERTSON, JOHN DAVID BENBOW, died on October 12, 1996, aged 79. Jack Robertson was the under-stated, under-rated Middlesex opening batsman who laid the groundwork for Compton and Edrich in what was perhaps the greatest batting line-up county cricket has seen. His own chances of the highest honours were largely blocked by the presence of Hutton and Washbrook. He won only 11 caps for England, nine of them abroad on the second-rank tours of West Indies and India, and never played against Australia at all. There was a perception, strengthened by his failures for MCC and Middlesex against the 1948 Australians, that he was vulnerable against the highest pace. Others thought he was vulnerable to leg-spin. A career record of almost 32,000 runs suggests he cannot have been all that vulnerable to anything.

Robertson came from Turnham Green in West London, and his father played for the local club. The son went into the Middlesex Second Eleven at 15, got a chance in the Championship at 21, and a year later won his cap. Unfortunately, this was 1939 and the opening partnership he had already formed with Sid Brown could not re-convene for seven long years. But in 1947 Middlesex blossomed with a glorious luxuriance. Robertson and Brown not merely paved the way for Compton and Edrich but often reached the destination themselves. In successive matches they shared stands of 310 against Nottinghamshire and 222 against Yorkshire. Robertson scored 2,760 runs in 1947, more than anyone else in the country excluding the big two, and was included in the team for the Oval Test. He scored 133 for England in the Port-of-Spain Test the following winter and 121 against New Zealand at Lord's in 1949. Both innings were match-savers but he was playing at Lord's only because Washbrook was unfit, and he was promptly dropped again.

He seemed to be a player whose triumphs never quite had happy endings. Four weeks later at Worcester he scored 331 not out in a day, still the highest for Middlesex and then the biggest score in England since Hutton's 364. He would ruefully tell how the day ended with his car getting a flat tyre; only Worcestershire players were around to help and they were not feeling very compassionate. His batting, even when less overwhelming, was always stylish; he was said to be one of the few batsmen Denis Compton would go on the balcony to watch. Robertson was responsible for a famous act of defiance at Lord's in 1944 when a flying-bomb stopped play and the players hurled themselves to the ground as it exploded nearby; then he hooked Bob Wyatt's next ball for six. In all other circumstances, he was soft-spoken, kindly, unfailingly polite and uncynical. He was a teetotaller and lived in a house called Stickiwickits. For some years he ran a small hotel in Cornwall and cricketers often went there for gentle pre-season training and, in some cases, on honeymoon. A number, however, were rather shocked on discovering it was unlicensed.

ROBINSON, THOMAS LLOYD, died on August 2, 1996, aged 83. Lloyd Robinson was a fast-medium bowler who played four matches for Warwickshire as an amateur in 1946. He later captained the Second Eleven, and was president of Gloucestershire in 1980. Robinson was a successful businessman and, from 1974 to 1977, chairman of the Dickinson Robinson Group.

ROGERS, REX ERNEST, who died on May 22, 1996, aged 79, was a left-handed bat who scored steadily for Queensland before and after the war. His family moved to Brisbane when a cyclone destroyed their home in Cairns, and he made his state debut in 1935-36. He gained a regular place the following season and stayed in the team until he retired 12 years later, often captaining the side after the war. He scored eight centuries and made 3,382 runs at 35.97. Against South Australia at Adelaide over Christmas 1937, Rogers scored 181 in just 231 minutes, an innings described as "especially brilliant" by *Wisden*. The war ruined his chance of Test cricket.

ROWAN, COLIN MACDONALD, died on February 23, 1996, aged 53. Don Rowan had a collection of 1,500 cricketing interviews on tape, especially with players of the 1950s.

RUDD, CLIFFORD ROBIN DAVID, died in September 1996, aged 67. Robin Rudd was a South African-born batsman who captained Eton in 1946 and won an Oxford Blue as a freshman in 1949. He subsequently played for a number of gentlemanly teams and worked for the Anglo-American Corporation, mostly in Bulawayo.

RUSHTON, WILLIAM GEORGE, who died on December 11, 1996, aged 59, was a well-known TV and radio humorist and a passionate follower of cricket. He regularly drew cartoons for *The Cricketer* – including the January 1997 cover illustration – and his novels included *W. G. Grace's Last Case*, a fantasy in which W.G. and Dr Watson foil a plot to take over the world by the Martians.

RYDER, ROWLAND, who died on February 13, 1996, aged 81, was a schoolmaster and cricket writer, who virtually grew up at Edgbaston, where his father was Warwickshire secretary for almost half a century. His work included biographies of Edith Cavell and Sir Oliver Leese, the soldier and MCC president. Both father and son had articles published in *Wisden*. Ryder's final book, *Cricket Calling*, an evocation of the game and his connection with it, was published to widespread acclaim a year before his death. "Cricket is not so much a game," he wrote, "as an extension of being English: a gallimaufry of paradoxes, contradictions, frightening logic and sheer impossibilities, of gentle courtesy and rough violence."

SANDERS, HAZEL MARY, who died on December 29, 1995, aged 69, played in 12 women's Test matches for England between 1949 and 1958. She was a defensive bat and a brilliant close fielder.

SARGENT, EDWARD ROTAN, died on January 28, 1996, aged 81. "Tanny" Sargent was responsible, in 1974, for restarting cricket at the once-famous Merion College in Philadelphia, fifty years after it disappeared. He was one of the few American members of MCC and between 1970 and 1984 was curator of the C. C. Morris Cricket library at Haverford College, reputedly the finest in North America.

SCAIFE, JOHN WILLIE, who died on October 27, 1995, aged 86, was a Lancashire-born batsman who played 42 matches for Victoria between the wars, often scoring useful runs after the state's great batting stars – headed by Woodfull and Ponsford – had had their fill. Scaife earned a Test trial in 1928-29 but did not hit his best form until after he had regained his place in the state side in 1933-34. He scored 573 runs at 52.09 in 1935-36. The following year he played for Europeans in the Bombay Quadrangular, becoming an unlikely team-mate of Harold Larwood.

SHENTON, PETER ANTHONY, who died on January 13, 1996, aged 59, was a Yorkshire-born batsman and off-spinner who played once for Northamptonshire in 1958 and seven times for Kent in 1960. Later, he was a successful and nomadic professional for various Yorkshire clubs.

SIMONS, DOROTHY EDITH, OBE, died on September 13, 1996, aged 84. Dot Simons was a pioneer of women's cricket in New Zealand and bowled left-arm spin for Wellington. In 1934 she became the first secretary of the NZ Women's Cricket Council, and was president of the International Women's Cricket Council from 1966 to 1969. She was a successful sports journalist.

SMITH, RAYMOND, who died on February 21, 1996, aged 81, was an all-rounder who, with his cousin Peter, almost had to carry the Essex attack in the years after the war. Luckily, he loved bowling. Ray Smith often opened the attack, with his sleeves rolled up, bowling huge in-swingers at a fair pace; then with cap on and sleeves rolled down – as though he was someone else entirely – he would return to purvey somewhat less effective off-breaks. His batting, when it came off, was thunderous. He scored only eight first-class centuries, but three of them were the fastest of the season: 63 minutes against Derbyshire in 1948; 70 minutes against the South Africans in 1951, when he went on to 147; and 73 minutes against Northamptonshire in 1955. He was especially harsh on off-spinners and once reduced even Jim Laker to standing, despairingly, with hands on hips. He did the double three times, even though his appeals – contrary to fast-bowling tradition – were always whispered, in a surprisingly upper-crust voice. He retired in 1956, seven years before the introduction of one-day cricket, at which he would have excelled. By then he had embarked on a long career coaching at Felsted. But he achieved one ambition; in his last home match Essex beat Yorkshire for the first time since the war, something for which he had been known to say he would give either a month or a year's salary. Smith scored the winning runs off Trueman. For many years he ran a restaurant outside Birmingham.

SMITH, THOMAS EDWARD, MBE, who died on December 14, 1996, aged 87, was revered throughout English umpiring circles. Tom Smith called the meeting in 1953 that led to the foundation of the Association of Cricket Umpires, and became the general secretary for its first 25 years. He served on countless committees dealing with the Laws, and worked closely with Billy Griffith, the MCC secretary, to produce the 1980 code. He took over R. S. Rait-Kerr's book, *Cricket Umpiring and Scoring*, which, if not quite cricket's bible, is regarded by many officials as the essential commentary on it. Unusually for a figure little known to the public, he was made an honorary life member of MCC.

STOCKS, FREDERICK WILFRED, died on February 23, 1996, aged 77. Freddie Stocks was a Nottinghamshire all-rounder who never achieved the classic double, but instead managed a unique one: a century in his first match and a wicket with his first ball. Yorkshire-born but Nottinghamshire-raised, Stocks played a few wartime games for the county and was picked for the first game after the war, against Kent. He came to the crease with the score 66 for five and hit 114. It was six weeks and ten games before he was given a bowl, at Old Trafford, but he immediately had Winston Place caught at the wicket. By then he had already played in a Test trial at Lord's, but he made just 19 and Stocks became one of only three players in that match never to play Test cricket. He settled into a career of playing fighting middle-order innings for his county, and switched from bowling medium pace to off-spin. Ten years after his sensational entry, and close to his exit, he had one more brilliant day, scoring 171 against the 1956 Australians, the highest score ever for Nottinghamshire against the Australians.

TEBAY, KEVAN, who died on August 13, 1996, aged 60, played 15 matches for Lancashire between 1961 and 1963. He rescued the county from 14 for four by scoring 106 against Hampshire in 1962, and shared century stands with Brian Booth in both innings against Worcestershire the following year. However, he quickly returned to the Bolton League where he became a local legend, mainly as a batsman for Egerton. His three sons all followed him into the League.

THOMAS, CECIL H., died on September 1, 1996, aged 69. "Bruiser" Thomas represented British Guiana as an all-rounder throughout the early 1950s and later became chairman of selectors and Guyana's representative on the West Indies Board. He was also one of Guyana's best-known radio personalities, acting as summariser on cricket commentaries and hosting the weekly programme Sports Action Line.

THOMAS, DILLWYN, who died on August 27, 1996, aged 91, was a medium-pacer who played just two matches for Glamorgan in 1939, but took a match-winning five for 64 at Ilford on his debut.

TICKOO, R. C., died on November 15, 1995, aged 88. "Ramjoo" Tickoo was regarded as the father of cricket in Jammu and Kashmir. He was a founder of the Jammu Cricket Club, the Kashmir Cricket Club and the joint Cricket Association, which first entered the Ranji Trophy in 1959-60 with Tickoo, then 53, as player-manager. He was a fast-medium bowler in his youth and took all ten wickets in a non-first-class match against a visiting Bombay side in 1935.

TYLER, Professor CYRIL, who died on January 25, 1996, aged 84, played 16 matches for Gloucestershire between 1936 and 1938, bowling off-spin and, occasionally, leg-spin. He was an agricultural chemist and became deputy vice-chancellor of Reading University from 1968 to 1976.

WARNER, JOHN EDWIN, who died on October 31, 1995, aged 84, umpired two Tests in South Africa in the 1960s. The second, against England at Cape Town, was dominated by two disputes about his decisions regarding close catches: Eddie Barlow stood his ground when given not out and went on from 41 to 138; Ken Barrington walked.

WATERMAN, ALFRED GEORGE, died on March 27, 1996, aged 84. "Tiny" Waterman (who was 6ft 2in) was an all-rounder who made ten appearances as an amateur for Essex in 1937 and 1938, taking four for 79, bowling fast-medium, on debut against Yorkshire, and scoring a match-winning 103 at Bath the following year. He then devoted himself to club cricket and the timber trade, but returned to Essex to exercise fierce financial control as treasurer when the club contemplated extinction in 1967. A decade later he became chairman and was able to enjoy the team's first trophies.

WATT, LESLIE, died on November 15, 1996, aged 72. Les Watt had a very brief Test career, scoring 0 and 2 in his only match for New Zealand, against England on his home ground at Dunedin in 1954-55. This contrasted with his usual performances: he was a defensive batsman who for a long while opened the innings for Otago with Bert Sutcliffe, whose left-handed dash received the ideal back-up from Watt's right-handed solidity. Against Auckland in 1950-51 they shared what is still the highest opening partnership in New Zealand, 373. Sutcliffe had 258 by the last over of the day; Watt had just 96 and was caught off the last ball. His first-class career lasted from 1942-43 (when he represented South Island Army) until 1962-63.

WELBY-EVERARD, Major-General CHRISTOPHER EARLE, KBE, CB, who died on May 10, 1996, aged 86, played six times for Lincolnshire in the 1930s. He was the last British General to command the Nigerian army.

WERAPITIYA, T. B., died on May 18, 1996, aged 71. "Tissa" Werapitiya was president of the Sri Lankan Cricket Board between 1979 and 1981, when the country was elevated to Test status. He later became Minister of Internal Defence. Werapitiya was an all-round sportsman who scored 96, 100 and 143 in successive years for St Anthony's College against Trinity in Kandy's big schools match. He was also a successful bowler in Ceylonese club cricket; while playing for Police against a touring Indian army team he returned figures of 10.5–7–8–9.

WHITFIELD, EDWARD WALTER, died on August 10, 1996, aged 85. Ted Whitfield was an orthodox, skilful but rather diffident batsman who played more than 100 games for Surrey between 1930 and 1939, and passed 1,000 runs in 1938 when he hit 198 against Cambridge. He played for Northamptonshire in 1946 before becoming games master and coach at St Paul's School.

WILMOT, KILBURN, who died in April 1996, aged 85, was a swing bowler who played 75 matches for Warwickshire between 1931 and 1939. He played professional football for Coventry City and Walsall.

YOUNG, DOUGLAS EDMUND, who died on December 27, 1995, aged 78, was a leg-spinning all-rounder who won an Oxford Blue in 1938. He took six for 58 against Lancashire that year. In the 1950s he played for Berkshire.

CAREER FIGURES OF TEST CRICKETERS WHO DIED IN 1996

	Tests				*First-class*			
	Runs	*Avge*	*Wkts*	*Avge*	*Runs*	*Avge*	*Wkts*	*Avge*
Boyce, K. D.	657	24.33	60	30.01	8,800	22.39	852	25.02
Coldwell, L. J.	9	4.50	22	27.72	1,474	5.96	1,076	21.18
Cook, C.	4	2.00	0	–	1,965	5.41	1,782	20.52
Fisher, F. E.	23	11.50	1	78.00	485	21.08	53	23.24
Gomez, G. E.	1,243	30.31	58	27.41	6,764	43.63	200	25.26
Jeganathan, S.	19	4.75	0	–	437	13.65	49	31.61
Kardar, A. H.	927	23.76	21	45.42	6,832	29.83	344	24.55
Kenyon, D.	192	12.80	–	–	37,002	33.63	1	187.00
Lindwall, R. R.	1,502	21.15	228	23.03	5,042	21.82	794	21.35
Miller, L. S. M.	346	13.84	0	–	4,777	37.61	3	25.00
Mitchell, T. B.	20	5.00	8	62.25	2,431	7.97	1,483	20.59
Modi, R. S.	736	46.00	0	–	7,529	53.02	32	38.31
Nazar Mohammad	277	39.57	0	–	2,484	40.06	5	49.80
Newman, J.	33	8.25	2	127.00	206	8.95	69	24.76
Oldfield, N.	99	49.50	–	–	17,811	37.89	2	60.50
Poole, C. J.	161	40.25	0	–	19,364	32.54	4	86.75
Puna, N.	31	15.50	4	60.00	1,305	14.81	229	24.43
Roberts, A. T.	28	14.00	–	–	153	13.90	–	–
Robertson, J. D.	881	46.36	2	29.00	31,914	37.50	73	34.73
Watt, L.	2	1.00	–	–	1,972	23.47	0	–

INDEX TO TEST MATCHES

Page

PAKISTAN v SRI LANKA, 1995-96

September 8	Peshawar	Pakistan won by an innings and 40 runs	1089
September 15	Faisalabad	Sri Lanka won by 42 runs	1090
September 22	Sialkot	Sri Lanka won by 144 runs	1092

ZIMBABWE v SOUTH AFRICA, 1995-96

October 13	Harare	South Africa won by seven wickets	1106

INDIA v NEW ZEALAND, 1995-96

October 18	Bangalore	India won by eight wickets	1099
October 25	Madras	Drawn	1100
November 8	Cuttack	Drawn	1101

AUSTRALIA v PAKISTAN, 1995-96

November 9	Brisbane	Australia won by an innings and 126 runs	1114
November 17	Hobart	Australia won by 155 runs	1115
November 30	Sydney	Pakistan won by 74 runs	1117

SOUTH AFRICA v ENGLAND, 1995-96

November 16	Centurion	Drawn	1058
November 30	Johannesburg	Drawn	1060
December 14	Durban	Drawn	1063
December 26	Port Elizabeth	Drawn	1065
January 2	Cape Town	South Africa won by ten wickets	1068

AUSTRALIA v SRI LANKA, 1995-96

December 8	Perth	Australia won by an innings and 36 runs	1128
December 26	Melbourne	Australia won by ten wickets	1129
January 25	Adelaide	Australia won by 148 runs	1130

NEW ZEALAND v PAKISTAN, 1995-96

December 8	Christchurch	Pakistan won by 161 runs	1118

NEW ZEALAND v ZIMBABWE, 1995-96

January 13	Hamilton	Drawn	1137
January 20	Auckland	Drawn	1138

WEST INDIES v NEW ZEALAND, 1995-96

April 19	Bridgetown	West Indies won by ten wickets	1149
April 27	St John's	Drawn	1151

ENGLAND v INDIA, 1996

June 6	Birmingham	England won by eight wickets	379
June 20	Lord's	Drawn	383
July 4	Nottingham	Drawn	387

ENGLAND v PAKISTAN, 1996

July 25	Lord's	Pakistan won by 164 runs	402
August 8	Leeds	Drawn	407
August 22	The Oval	Pakistan won by nine wickets	411

INDEX OF UNUSUAL OCCURRENCES

Ball splits in two ... 712
Batsman reaches Test fifty during tea interval ... 403
Batsman repeatedly throws bat away ... 653
Bogus batsman faces ball ... 765
Dispute over toss causes loss of morning's play ... 1252
England match abandoned through boredom ... 1062
Father and son play first-class match together ... 1289
Four foot eight inch tall 14-year-old plays for Yorkshire ... 911
Hat-tricks by same player in consecutive matches ... 533
Hot coals used to dry pitch ... 1084
Hundred in one-day international by player yet to appear in first-class cricket ... 1093
Muntjac fawn in members' enclosure ... 473
Paper cup bowled in one-day international ... 1109
Player takes tea in middle ... 625
Result reversed when scores were corrected ... 1206
Roebuck stops play ... 681
Shout of "Bowler's mother's maiden name?" ... 879
Soccer stops play at Lord's ... 384
Team forfeits match claiming opponents had secretly changed ball ... 1259
Thirty-five runs in an over ... 1238
Triple-century on losing side ... 546
Twelve players take field ... 769
Twins each dislocate shoulder in same match ... 968
Two hat-tricks in a match and three by same player in a season ... 537
Two sets of brothers in same county team ... 632, 834
Umpire suffers fractured skull ... 911
Wicket-keeper breaks world record and scores two 99s in match ... 1288

TEST MATCHES, 1996-97

Full details of these Tests, and others too late for inclusion, will appear in the 1998 edition of *Wisden.*

SRI LANKA v ZIMBABWE

First Test: At R. Premadasa Stadium, Colombo, September 11, 12, 13, 14. Sri Lanka won by an innings and 77 runs. Toss: Sri Lanka. Sri Lanka 349 (A. P. Gurusinha 52, P. A. de Silva 35, A. Ranatunga 75, R. S. Kaluwitharana 71, H. D. P. K. Dharmasena 42 not out, W. P. U. J. C. Vaas 34; H. H. Streak three for 54, P. A. Strang five for 106); Zimbabwe 145 (G. J. Whittall 39, C. B. Wishart 51; W. P. U. J. C. Vaas four for 73, K. J. Silva three for ten) and 127 (M. Muralitharan five for 33, K. J. Silva four for 25).

Sri Lanka won a Test by an innings for the first time. In his 13th match, Vaas became the fifth Sri Lankan to take 50 Test wickets. Left-arm spinner Silva returned match figures of 33.4–21–35–7. Zimbabwe's 127 was their lowest total in Tests to date.

Second Test: At Sinhalese Sports Club, Colombo, September 18, 19, 20, 21. Sri Lanka won by ten wickets. Toss: Zimbabwe. Zimbabwe 141 (G. W. Flower 52, A. D. R. Campbell 36; M. Muralitharan four for 40, K. J. Silva four for 16) and 235 (A. H. Shah 62, A. Flower 31, P. A. Strang 50; M. Muralitharan three for 94); Sri Lanka 350 for eight dec. (S. T. Jayasuriya 41, A. P. Gurusinha 88, H. P. Tillekeratne 126 not out; B. C. Strang three for 63, P. A. Strang four for 66) and 30 for no wkt.

Shah played his first Test since Zimbabwe's inaugural season of 1992-93 and made a maiden fifty. Tillekeratne's unbeaten 126 was his fifth Test century and his first at home. Sri Lanka took the series 2-0.

INDIA v AUSTRALIA

Only Test: At Delhi, October 10, 11, 12, 13. India won by seven wickets. Toss: Australia. Australia 182 (M. J. Slater 44; A. Kumble four for 63) and 234 (M. A. Taylor 37, S. R. Waugh 67 not out, M. G. Bevan 33; B. K. V. Prasad three for 18, A. Kumble five for 67); India 361 (N. R. Mongia 152, S. C. Ganguly 66, R. Dravid 40; P. R. Reiffel three for 35, P. E. McIntyre three for 103) and 58 for three.

Mongia scored his maiden Test century in his 14th Test. Sachin Tendulkar won his first Test as captain, despite scoring ten and nought, ensuring that India remained unbeaten in a home series since 1986-87 and claiming the newly created Border-Gavaskar Trophy.

PAKISTAN v ZIMBABWE

First Test: At Sheikhupura, October 17, 18, 19, 20, 21. Drawn. Toss: Zimbabwe. Zimbabwe 375 (G. W. Flower 110, D. L. Houghton 43, P. A. Strang 106 not out, B. C. Strang 42, Extras 34; Shahid Nazir five for 54, Saqlain Mushtaq three for 126) and 241 for seven (G. W. Flower 46, D. L. Houghton 65, G. J. Whittall 32; Saqlain Mushtaq four for 75); Pakistan 553 (Aamir Sohail 46, Saeed Anwar 51, Salim Malik 52, Wasim Akram 257 not out, Saqlain Mushtaq 79; P. A. Strang five for 212).

The Sheikhupura Stadium became Test cricket's 77th venue and the 16th in Pakistan. Paul Strang was the 18th player to score a hundred and take five wickets in an innings in the same Test. Wasim's unbeaten 257 was the highest score ever made by a Test No. 8; he hit 12 sixes, another Test record, and 22 fours in 370 balls and eight hours. His partnership of 313 with Saqlain was the highest eighth-wicket stand for any country in Tests and rescued Pakistan from 237 for seven. Grant Flower became the third Zimbabwean to reach 1,000 Test runs, in his 19th match.

Second Test: At Faisalabad, October 24, 25, 26. Pakistan won by ten wickets. Toss: Zimbabwe. Zimbabwe 133 (A. Flower 61; Wasim Akram six for 48) and 200 (D. L. Houghton 74, A. D. R. Campbell 51; Wasim Akram four for 58, Waqar Younis four for 54); Pakistan 267 (Saeed Anwar 81, Wasim Akram 35, Moin Khan 58; B. C. Strang three for 53) and 69 for no wkt (Saeed Anwar 50 not out).

Wasim took ten wickets in a Test for the fourth time. Pakistan debutant Hassan Raza's birth certificate claimed he was 14 years and 227 days old, and thus the youngest Test player ever; later, the Pakistan board disputed this on the basis of a bone scan of his wrist. He scored 27. Pakistan took the series 1-0 after winning in two and a half days.

INDIA v SOUTH AFRICA

First Test: At Ahmedabad, November 20, 21, 22, 23. India won by 64 runs. Toss: India. India 223 (S. V. Manjrekar 34, S. R. Tendulkar 42, M. Azharuddin 35; A. A. Donald four for 37) and 190 (R. Dravid 34, V. V. S. Laxman 51, A. Kumble 30 not out; A. A. Donald three for 32, P. R. Adams three for 30); South Africa 244 (D. J. Cullinan 43, P. L. Symcox 32, P. S. de Villiers 67 not out; S. B. Joshi four for 43) and 105 (W. J. Cronje 48 not out; J. Srinath six for 21, A. Kumble three for 34).

Srinath took five in an innings for the first time in his 22 Tests to give India their first Test victory over South Africa. South Africa left the field for ten minutes on the third afternoon after Adams was struck by two missiles from the crowd.

Second Test: At Calcutta, November 27, 28, 29, 30, December 1. South Africa won by 329 runs. Toss: South Africa. South Africa 428 (A. C. Hudson 146, G. Kirsten 102, H. H. Gibbs 31, D. J. Cullinan 43, D. J. Richardson 36 not out, Extras 39; B. K. V. Prasad six for 104) and 367 for three dec. (G. Kirsten 133, D. J. Cullinan 153 not out, W. J. Cronje 34); India 329 (N. R. Mongia 35, R. Dravid 31, M. Azharuddin 109, A. Kumble 88; A. A. Donald three for 72) and 137 (M. Azharuddin 52; L. Klusener eight for 64).

Kirsten became the third South African to score two centuries in a Test; his partnership of 212 with Cullinan in the second innings was a South African second-wicket record. This was the first time South Africa had scored four hundreds in a Test. Azharuddin reached 100 in 74 balls, equalling the fourth-fastest Test century recorded in balls, despite having briefly retired hurt when six. In the second innings, Klusener returned the third-best analysis for South Africa, and the fourth-best for any country on debut.

Third Test: At Kanpur, December 8, 9, 10, 11, 12. India won by 280 runs. Toss: India. India 237 (N. R. Mongia 41, W. V. Raman 57, S. C. Ganguly 39, S. R. Tendulkar 61; P. R. Adams six for 55) and 400 for seven dec. (A. Kumble 42, S. C. Ganguly 41, S. R. Tendulkar 36, M. Azharuddin 163 not out, R. Dravid 56); South Africa 177 (G. Kirsten 43; J. Srinath three for 42, A. Kumble four for 71) and 180 (A. C. Hudson 31, W. J. Cronje 50, L. Klusener 34 not out; J. Srinath three for 38, S. B. Joshi three for 66).

India took the series 2-1, extending their unbeaten run at home to ten series (including one-off Tests). It was South Africa's first series defeat since they lost a one-off Test to West Indies in 1991-92 on their return to Test cricket.

PAKISTAN v NEW ZEALAND

First Test: At Lahore, November 21, 22, 23, 24. New Zealand won by 44 runs. Toss: New Zealand. New Zealand 155 (A. C. Parore 37; Waqar Younis four for 48, Mushtaq Ahmed four for 59) and 311 (B. A. Young 36, S. P. Fleming 92 not out, C. L. Cairns 93; Mushtaq Ahmed six for 84); Pakistan 191 (Moin Khan 59; S. B. Doull five for 46, J. T. C. Vaughan four for 27) and 231 (Mohammad Wasim 109 not out, Moin Khan 38; S. B. Doull three for 39, D. N. Patel four for 36).

New Zealand's victory was their first in 16 Tests since November 1994 and their first in Pakistan for 27 years. Mohammad Wasim was the fourth Pakistani to score a century on Test debut. Umpires Shakoor Rana and Russell Tiffin gave 15 lbw decisions – the second-most in any Test.

Second Test: At Rawalpindi, November 28, 29, 30, December 1. Pakistan won by an innings and 13 runs. Toss: Pakistan. New Zealand 249 (B. A. Young 39, S. P. Fleming 67, L. K. Germon 55; Mohammad Zahid four for 64, Mushtaq Ahmed six for 87) and 168 (B. A. Young 61; Mohammad Zahid seven for 66); Pakistan 430 (Saeed Anwar 149, Ijaz Ahmed, sen. 125, Mushtaq Ahmed 42, Salim Malik 78; C. L. Cairns five for 137).

The match was delayed on the opening morning because the ball provided was not of Test standard. Mushtaq took his 100th Test wicket in his 26th match; by the end of the game, he had taken 63 in his last eight Tests. Zahid became the first Pakistani to take ten wickets on Test debut; his eventual 11 for 130 represented the seventh-best match figures by any debutant. Umpires Lloyd Barker and Javed Akhtar awarded a further 13 lbws. The series was drawn 1-1.

AUSTRALIA v WEST INDIES

First Test: At Brisbane, November 22, 23, 24, 25, 26. Australia won by 123 runs. Toss: West Indies. Australia 479 (M. A. Taylor 43, R. T. Ponting 88, M. E. Waugh 38, S. R. Waugh 66, I. A. Healy 161 not out, Extras 33; C. A. Walsh four for 112, I. R. Bishop three for 105) and 217 for six dec. (M. A. Taylor 36, M. E. Waugh 57, I. A. Healy 45 not out; I. R. Bishop three for 49); West Indies 277 (C. L. Hooper 102, S. Chanderpaul 82; P. R. Reiffel four for 58) and 296 (S. L. Campbell 113, B. C. Lara 44; G. D. McGrath four for 60, M. G. Bevan three for 46).

Healy's unbeaten 161 was the highest Test score by an Australian wicket-keeper. In their first innings, West Indies' last seven fell for 28; by the end of the match, they had gone ten successive innings since they last reached 300 against Australia.

Second Test: At Sydney, November 29, 30, December 1, 2, 3. Australia won by 124 runs. Toss: Australia. Australia 331 (G. S. Blewett 69, I. A. Healy 44; C. A. Walsh five for 98, I. R. Bishop three for 55) and 312 for four dec. (M. T. G. Elliott 78 retired hurt, M. E. Waugh 67, M. G. Bevan 52, G. S. Blewett 47 not out); West Indies 304 (S. L. Campbell 77, R. G. Samuels 35, S. Chanderpaul 48, J. C. Adams 30, I. R. Bishop 48; G. D. McGrath four for 82, S. K. Warne three for 65) and 215 (C. L. Hooper 57, S. Chanderpaul 71; G. D. McGrath three for 36, S. K. Warne four for 95).

Australia became the first team to open up a two-Test lead in a series against West Indies since they themselves did it in 1975-76.

Third Test: At Melbourne, December 26, 27, 28. West Indies won by six wickets. Toss: Australia. Australia 219 (S. R. Waugh 58, G. S. Blewett 62, I. A. Healy 36; C. E. L. Ambrose five for 55) and 122 (S. R. Waugh 37; C. E. L. Ambrose four for 17, K. C. G. Benjamin three for 34, C. A. Walsh three for 41); West Indies 255 (S. Chanderpaul 58, J. C. Adams 74 not out, J. R. Murray 53; G. D. McGrath five for 50, S. K. Warne three for 72) and 87 for four (S. Chanderpaul 40; G. D. McGrath three for 41).

McGrath took his 100th wicket in his 23rd Test and his 200th in first-class cricket. The crowd on the first day was 72,821, the highest for a Test in Australia since Boxing Day 1975, when 85,596 watched the same teams at the same venue.

Fourth Test: At Adelaide, January 25, 26, 27, 28. Australia won by an innings and 183 runs. Toss: West Indies. West Indies 130 (J. R. Murray 34; M. G. Bevan four for 31, S. K. Warne three for 42) and 204 (B. C. Lara 78, C. L. Hooper 45; M. G. Bevan six for 82, S. K. Warne three for 68); Australia 517 (M. L. Hayden 125, M. E. Waugh 82, G. S. Blewett 99, M. G. Bevan 85 not out, Extras 41).

Australia ensured they would retain the Frank Worrell Trophy 48 minutes into the fourth morning. It was their first home series win over West Indies since 1975-76. West Indies had suffered only two heavier innings defeats.

Fifth Test: At Perth, February 1, 2, 3. West Indies won by ten wickets. Toss: Australia. Australia 243 (M. E. Waugh 79, M. G. Bevan 87 not out; C. E. L. Ambrose five for 43, I. R. Bishop three for 54) and 194 (M. L. Hayden 47, S. K. Warne 30, Extras 38; C. A. Walsh five for 74); West Indies 384 (R. G. Samuels 76, B. C. Lara 132, C. L. Hooper 57, Extras 44; P. R. Reiffel five for 73) and 57 for no wkt (R. G. Samuels 35 not out).

Walsh pulled a hamstring and left the field in the first innings; Ambrose and Bishop bowled alternate overs from one end to conserve their strength in heat of 108°F. Mark Waugh reached 4,000 runs in his 60th Test. Lara scored 132 out of 208 for the third wicket with Samuels. Warne finished with 229 wickets, passing Ray Lindwall to become Australia's fifth leading wicket-taker. In the second innings, Walsh bowled his 20 overs unchanged for fear of seizing up. West Indies maintained their 100 per cent record at Perth, in their fifth Test there, but Australia took the series 3-2.

ZIMBABWE v ENGLAND

First Test Match

At Bulawayo, December 18, 19, 20, 21, 22. Drawn. Toss: Zimbabwe.

Zimbabwe

G. W. Flower c Hussain b Silverwood	43	– lbw b Gough	0
S. V. Carlisle c Crawley b Gough	0	– c Atherton b Mullally	4
*A. D. R. Campbell c Silverwood b Croft	84	– b Croft	29
D. L. Houghton c Stewart b Croft	34	– c Croft b Tufnell	37
†A. Flower c Stewart b Tufnell	112	– c Crawley b Tufnell	14
A. C. Waller c Crawley b Croft	15	– c Knight b Gough	50
G. J. Whittall c Atherton b Silverwood	7	– (8) c Croft b Tufnell	56
P. A. Strang c Tufnell b Silverwood	38	– (9) c Crawley b Croft	19
H. H. Streak b Mullally	19	– (10) not out	8
B. C. Strang not out	4	– (7) c Mullally b Tufnell	3
H. K. Olonga c Knight b Tufnell	0	– c Stewart b Silverwood	0
L-b 4, w 3, n-b 13	20	B 4, l-b 6, w 2, n-b 2	14
1/3 2/130 3/136 4/206 5/235 6/252 7/331 8/372 9/376	376	1/6 2/6 3/57 4/82 5/103 6/111 7/178 8/209 9/233	234

Bowling: *First Innings*—Mullally 23–4–69–1; Gough 26–4–87–1; Silverwood 18–5–63–3; Croft 44–15–77–3; Tufnell 26.5–4–76–2. *Second Innings*—Gough 12–2–44–2; Mullally 18–5–49–1; Croft 33–9–62–2; Silverwood 7–3–8–1; Tufnell 31–12–61–4.

England

N. V. Knight lbw b Olonga	56	– run out	96
*M. A. Atherton lbw b P. A. Strang	16	– b Olonga	4
†A. J. Stewart lbw b P. A. Strang	48	– c Campbell b P. A. Strang	73
N. Hussain c B. C. Strang b Streak	113	– c Carlisle b P. A. Strang	0
G. P. Thorpe c Campbell b P. A. Strang	13	– (6) c Campbell b Streak	2
J. P. Crawley c A. Flower b P. A. Strang	112	– (5) c Carlisle b Whittall	7
R. D. B. Croft lbw b Olonga	7		
D. Gough c G. W. Flower b Olonga	2	– (7) not out	3
C. E. W. Silverwood c Houghton b P. A. Strang	0		
A. D. Mullally c Waller b Streak	4		
P. C. R. Tufnell not out	2		
B 4, l-b 4, w 1, n-b 24	33	B 2, l-b 13, w 3, n-b 1	19
1/48 2/92 3/160 4/180 5/328 6/340 7/344 8/353 9/378	406	1/17 2/154 3/156 4/178 5/182 6/204	(6 wkts) 204

Bowling: *First Innings*—Streak 36–8–86–2; B. C. Strang 17–5–54–0; P. A. Strang 58.4–14–123–5; Olonga 23–2–90–3; Whittall 10–2–25–0; G. W. Flower 7–3–20–0. *Second Innings*—Streak 11–0–64–1; Olonga 2–0–16–1; P. A. Strang 14–0–63–2; G. W. Flower 8–0–36–0; Whittall 2–0–10–1.

Umpires: R. S. Dunne (New Zealand) and I. D. Robinson. Referee: Hanumant Singh (India).

This Test was the first ever to end in a draw with the scores level, though there had been two ties (scores level and the side batting last all out). England needed 205 from 37 overs to win and 13 from the final over. Knight hit Heath Streak's third ball for six, but was run out off the last ball attempting a third run for victory. Atherton captained England for their 36th successive Test, beating Peter May's record. Campbell became the fourth Zimbabwean to reach 1,000 Test runs, in his 21st match, and Stewart reached 4,000 for England in his 59th Test.

ZIMBABWE v ENGLAND

Second Test Match

At Harare, December 26, 27, 28, 29, 30. Drawn. Toss: Zimbabwe.

England

N. V. Knight c A. Flower b Olonga	15	– c Campbell b Strang	30
*M. A. Atherton c Campbell b Whittall	13	– c Campbell b Streak	1
†A. J. Stewart c G. W. Flower b Streak	19	– not out	101
N. Hussain c A. Flower b Streak	11	– c Houghton b Strang	6
G. P. Thorpe c Dekker b Streak	5	– not out	50
J. P. Crawley not out	47		
C. White c Campbell b Whittall	9		
R. D. B. Croft c G. W. Flower b Whittall	14		
D. Gough b Strang	2		
A. D. Mullally c and b Whittall	0		
P. C. R. Tufnell b Streak	9		
B 1, l-b 5, w 1, n-b 5	12	L-b 5, w 1, n-b 1	7
1/24 2/50 3/50 4/65 5/73 6/94 7/128 8/133 9/134	156	1/7 2/75 3/89	(3 wkts) 195

Bowling: *First Innings*—Streak 24.1–7–43–4; Brandes 16–6–35–0; Olonga 9–1–23–1; Whittall 16–5–18–4; Strang 18–7–31–1. *Second Innings*—Streak 18–5–47–1; Brandes 21–6–45–0; Olonga 7–0–31–0; Whittall 14–6–16–0; Strang 26–6–42–2; G. W. Flower 7–2–9–0.

Zimbabwe

G. W. Flower c Crawley b Gough	73
M. H. Dekker c Stewart b Mullally	2
*A. D. R. Campbell c Thorpe b White	22
D. L. Houghton c Stewart b Gough	29
†A. Flower lbw b Gough	6
A. C. Waller lbw b Tufnell	4
G. J. Whittall b Gough	1
P. A. Strang not out	47
H. H. Streak c Crawley b Croft	7
E. A. Brandes c Gough b Croft	9
H. K. Olonga c Hussain b Croft	0
L-b 8, w 1, n-b 6	15
1/5 2/46 3/110 4/131 5/136 6/138 7/159 8/197 9/211	215

Bowling: Mullally 23–7–32–1; Gough 26–10–40–4; Croft 15–2–39–3; White 16–4–41–1; Tufnell 25–3–55–1.

Umpires: K. T. Francis (Sri Lanka) and R. B. Tiffin. Referee: Hanumant Singh (India).

England's first-innings 156 was the second-lowest Test total against Zimbabwe (after Pakistan's 147 at Lahore in 1993-94). Stewart scored his ninth Test hundred, and his first as a wicket-keeper, reaching 793 Test runs in 1996, more than any other player. Rain prevented any play on the final day.

SOUTH AFRICA v INDIA

First Test: At Durban, December 26, 27, 28. South Africa won by 328 runs. Toss: India. South Africa 235 (A. C. Hudson 80, B. M. McMillan 34; B. K. V. Prasad five for 60) and 259 (A. C. Hudson 52, A. M. Bacher 55, B. M. McMillan 51 not out; J. Srinath three for 80, B. K. V. Prasad five for 93); India 100 (A. A. Donald five for 40) and 66 (A. A. Donald four for 14, S. M. Pollock three for 25).

India's two innings lasted a combined 73.2 overs; their second-innings 66 was the lowest total ever made against South Africa, under-cutting Australia's 75 on the same ground in 1949-50.

Second Test: At Cape Town, January 2, 3, 4, 5, 6. South Africa won by 282 runs. Toss: South Africa. South Africa 529 for seven dec. (G. Kirsten 103, D. J. Cullinan 77, W. J. Cronje 41, B. M. McMillan 103 not out, D. J. Richardson 39, L. Klusener 102 not out; J. Srinath three for 130, B. K. V. Prasad three for 114) and 256 for six dec. (A. C. Hudson 55, D. J. Cullinan 55, B. M. McMillan 59 not out, S. M. Pollock 40 not out; J. Srinath three for 78); India 359 (S. R. Tendulkar 169, M. Azharuddin 115) and 144 (S. C. Ganguly 30, V. V. S. Laxman 35 not out; A. A. Donald three for 40, P. R. Adams three for 45).

South Africa reached 500 for the first time since their return to Test cricket in 1992, thanks to an unbroken stand of 147 between McMillan and Klusener, a South African eighth-wicket record. India were 58 for five in reply before Tendulkar and Azharuddin added 222 in 40 overs. Richardson made his first stumping in his 33rd Test; he had taken 119 catches.

Third Test: At Johannesburg, January 16, 17, 18, 19, 20. Drawn. Toss: India. India 410 (R. Dravid 148, S. R. Tendulkar 35, S. C. Ganguly 73, J. Srinath 41; A. A. Donald three for 88, L. Klusener three for 75) and 266 for eight dec. (V. Rathore 44, N. R. Mongia 50, R. Dravid 81, S. C. Ganguly 60; A. A. Donald three for 38, P. R. Adams three for 80); South Africa 321 (D. J. Cullinan 33, W. J. Cronje 43, B. M. McMillan 47, S. M. Pollock 79; J. Srinath five for 104) and 228 for eight (D. J. Cullinan 122 not out, L. Klusener 49; A. Kumble three for 40).

Set 356 to win, South Africa were 76 for five before lunch on the final day, when a thunderstorm caused the second serious hold-up of the match. The aggregate attendance of 192,256 was a record for a three-Test series in South Africa.

NEW ZEALAND v ENGLAND

First Test Match

At Auckland, January 24, 25, 26, 27, 28. Drawn. Toss: England.

New Zealand

B. A. Young lbw b Mullally	44	– (2) c Hussain b Cork	3
B. A. Pocock lbw b Gough	70	– (1) lbw b Gough	20
A. C. Parore c Stewart b Cork	6	– st Stewart b Tufnell	33
S. P. Fleming c and b Cork	129	– c Crawley b Tufnell	9
N. J. Astle c Stewart b White	10	– (6) not out	102
J. T. C. Vaughan lbw b Cork	3	– (7) lbw b Tufnell	2
C. L. Cairns c Stewart b White	67	– (8) b Mullally	7
*†L. K. Germon c Stewart b Gough	14	– (5) run out	13
D. N. Patel lbw b Gough	0	– lbw b Mullally	0
S. B. Doull c Knight b Gough	5	– b Gough	26
D. K. Morrison not out	6	– not out	14
B 5, l-b 12, w 2, n-b 17	36	L-b 11, n-b 8	19
1/85 2/114 3/193 4/210 5/215 6/333 7/362 8/362 9/380	390	1/17 2/28 3/47 4/88 5/90 6/92 7/101 8/105 9/142 (9 wkts)	248

Bowling: *First Innings*—Cork 32.5–8–96–3; Mullally 27–11–55–1; Gough 32–5–91–4; Tufnell 25–5–80–0; White 15–3–51–2. *Second Innings*—Cork 16–3–45–1; Mullally 26–11–47–2; White 10–2–26–0; Gough 22–3–66–2; Tufnell 40–18–53–3.

England

N. V. Knight lbw b Doull	5	D. Gough c Germon b Morrison	2
†M. A. Atherton c and b Patel	83	A. D. Mullally c Germon b Morrison	21
†A. J. Stewart c and b Doull	173	P. C. R. Tufnell not out	19
N. Hussain c Flemming b Patel	8	B 2, l-b 12, w 2, n-b 2	18
G. P. Thorpe hit wkt b Cairns	119		
J. P. Crawley run out	14	1/18 2/200 3/222	521
C. White lbw b Vaughan	0	4/304 5/339 6/339	
D. G. Cork c Young b Morrison	59	7/453 8/471 9/478	

Bowling: Morrison 24.4–4–104–3; Doull 39–10–118–2; Cairns 30–3–103–1; Astle 14–3–33–0; Vaughan 36–10–57–1; Patel 44–10–92–2.

Umpires: S. A. Bucknor (West Indies) and R. S. Dunne. Referee: P. J. Burge (Australia).

Despite having dislocated a finger while keeping, Stewart made 173, the highest score by an England wicket-keeper, beating Les Ames's 149 against West Indies in 1929-30. Thorpe scored his third hundred in 35 Tests, having reached 50 on 19 other occasions. On the final day, New Zealand were 142 for nine – just 11 ahead – 37 minutes after lunch. But Morrison, the world record-holder for Test ducks with 24, batted for 166 minutes, scoring 14 and sharing an unbroken last-wicket stand of 106 with Astle to save the match.

NEW ZEALAND v ENGLAND

Second Test Match

At Wellington, February 6, 7, 8, 9, 10. England won by an innings and 68 runs. Toss: New Zealand.

New Zealand

B. A. Young c Stewart b Gough	8	– (2) c Stewart b Tufnell	56
B. A. Pocock c Cork b Caddick	6	– (1) c Knight b Gough	64
A. C. Parore c Stewart b Gough	4	– lbw b Croft	15
S. P. Fleming c and b Caddick	1	– c and b Croft	0
N. J. Astle c Croft b Gough	36	– (7) c Stewart b Gough	4
C. L. Cairns c Hussain b Gough	3	– (8) c Knight b Caddick	22
*†L. K. Germon c Stewart b Caddick	10	– (6) b Gough	11
D. N. Patel c Cork b Caddick	45	– (5) lbw b Croft	0
S. B. Doull c Stewart b Gough	0	– c Knight b Gough	0
G. I. Allott c Knight b Cork	1	– b Caddick	2
D. L. Vettori not out	3	– not out	2
L-b 5, n-b 2	7	B 5, l-b 4, n-b 6	15
1/14 2/18 3/19 4/19 5/23	124	1/89 2/125 3/125 4/125 5/161	191
6/48 7/85 8/85 9/106		6/164 7/175 8/175 9/182	

Bowling: *First Innings*—Cork 14–4–34–1; Caddick 18.3–5–45–4; Gough 16–6–40–5. *Second Innings*—Cork 10–1–42–0; Caddick 27.2–11–40–2; Croft 20–9–19–3; Gough 23–9–52–4; Tufnell 23–9–29–1.

England

N. V. Knight c Patel b Doull	8	D. Gough c Fleming b Doull	18
*M. A. Atherton lbw b Doull	30	A. R. Caddick c Allott b Vettori	20
†A. J. Stewart c Fleming b Allott	52	P. C. R. Tufnell not out	6
N. Hussain c Young b Vettori	64		
G. P. Thorpe st Germon b Patel	108	B 3, l-b 9, n-b 2	14
J. P. Crawley c Germon b Doull	56		
D. G. Cork lbw b Astle	7	1/10 2/80 3/106 4/213 5/331	383
R. D. B. Croft c Fleming b Doull	0	6/331 7/331 8/357 9/357	

Bowling: Doull 28–10–75–5; Allott 31–6–91–1; Vettori 34.3–10–98–2; Cairns 4–2–8–0; Astle 14–5–30–1; Patel 24–6–59–1; Pocock 2–0–10–0.

Umpires: S. A. Bucknor (West Indies) and D. B. Cowie. Referee: P. J. Burge (Australia).

Daniel Vettori became New Zealand's youngest Test player at 18 years 10 days; it was his third first-class match. Overnight rain prevented play before tea on the opening day, when New Zealand were reduced to 23 for five. Thorpe scored his second hundred in successive Test innings. More rain washed out the first two sessions of the fourth day, but England won half an hour after lunch on the final day.

NEW ZEALAND v ENGLAND

Third Test Match

At Christchurch, February 14, 15, 16, 17, 18. Toss: England.

New Zealand

B. A. Young b Cork	11	– (2) c Knight b Tufnell	49
B. A. Pocock c Atherton b Croft	22	– (1) b Cork	0
M. J. Horne c Thorpe b Gough	42	– (8) c Stewart b Caddick	13
*S. P. Fleming st Stewart b Croft	62	– c Knight b Tufnell	11
N. J. Astle c Hussain b Croft	15	– c Hussain b Croft	5
†A. C. Parore c Hussain b Croft	59	– (3) c Stewart b Gough	8
C. L. Cairns c Stewart b Caddick	57	– (6) c Knight b Tufnell	52
S. B. Doull run out	1	– (7) c Knight b Croft	5
D. L. Vettori run out	25	– not out	29
H. T. Davis c Hussain b Croft	8	– b Gough	1
G. I. Allott not out	8	– c Stewart b Gough	1
B 1, l-b 16, n-b 19	36	L-b 8, n-b 4	12
1/14 2/78 3/106 4/137 5/201 6/283 7/288 8/310 9/337	346	1/0 2/42 3/61 4/76 5/80 6/89 7/107 8/178 9/184	186

Bowling: *First Innings*—Cork 20–3–78–1; Caddick 32–8–64–1; Gough 21–3–70–1; Croft 39.1–5–95–5; Tufnell 16–6–22–0; Thorpe 1–1–0–0. *Second Innings*—Cork 6–2–5–1; Caddick 10–1–25–1; Croft 31–13–48–2; Gough 13.3–5–42–3; Tufnell 28–9–58–3.

England

N. V. Knight c Fleming b Allott	14	– c Davis b Vettori	29
*M. A. Atherton not out	94	– c Parore b Astle	118
†A. J. Stewart c sub (C. Z. Harris) b Allott	15	– c Pocock b Vettori	17
N. Hussain c Parore b Cairns	12	– (5) c Fleming b Vettori	33
G. P. Thorpe b Astle	18	– (6) c and b Vettori	2
J. P. Crawley c Parore b Allott	1	– (7) not out	40
D. G. Cork c Parore b Davis	16	– (8) not out	39
R. D. B. Croft c Davis b Astle	31		
D. Gough b Vettori	0		
A. R. Caddick c sub (C. Z. Harris) b Allott	4	– (4) c Fleming b Doull	15
P. C. R. Tufnell c Young b Doull	13		
L-b 4, w 1, n-b 5	10	B 2, l-b 8, w 1, n-b 3	14
1/20 2/40 3/70 4/103 5/104 6/145 7/198 8/199 9/210	228	1/64 2/116 3/146 4/226 5/226 6/231	(6 wkts) 307

Bowling: *First Innings*—Allott 18–3–74–4; Doull 17.4–3–49–1; Davis 18–2–50–1; Vettori 12–4–13–1; Cairns 8–5–12–1; Astle 11–2–26–2. *Second Innings*—Allott 12.4–2–32–0; Davis 18–6–43–0; Doull 21–8–57–1; Vettori 57–18–97–4; Cairns 10–1–23–0; Astle 28–10–45–1.

Umpires: D. B. Hair (Australia) and R. S. Dunne. Referee: P. J. Burge (Australia).

Stephen Fleming became New Zealand's youngest Test captain at 23 years 319 days when Lee Germon withdrew with a groin strain on the morning of the match. Atherton was the seventh England player to carry his bat in a Test and remained on the field for 26 and a half hours. In New Zealand's second innings, Young at first refused to walk when given out; referee Burge accepted that he had not seen umpire Hair signal his verdict. It was the second time England had passed 300 in the fourth innings to win a Test; they took the series 2-0, their first overseas series win since they beat New Zealand in 1991-92.

FIXTURES, 1997

** Indicates Sunday play.* † *Not first-class.*

All County Championship matches are of four days' duration. Other first-class matches are of three days' duration unless stated.

Tuesday, April 15

Cambridge	Cambridge U. v Derbys
Oxford	Oxford U. v Durham

Wednesday, April 16

Leeds	Yorks v Lancs ("friendly" match, 4 days)

Friday, April 18

Birmingham*	England A v The Rest (4 days)
Cambridge*	Cambridge U. v Leics
Oxford	Oxford U. v Hants

Wednesday, April 23

Chelmsford	Essex v Hants
Cardiff	Glam v Warwicks
Canterbury	Kent v Derbys
Manchester	Lancs v Durham
Leicester	Leics v Glos
Nottingham	Notts v Worcs
The Oval	Surrey v Somerset
Hove	Sussex v Northants
Cambridge	Cambridge U. v Middx
Oxford	Oxford U. v Yorks

Saturday, April 26

Oxford	†British Univs v Yorks (1 day)

Monday, April 28

†Benson and Hedges Cup (1 day)

Chelmsford	Essex v Glam
Bristol	Glos v British Univs
Dublin (Castle Avenue)	Ireland v Middx
Manchester	Lancs v Yorks
Leicester	Leics v Scotland
Lakenham	Minor Counties v Derbys
Nottingham	Notts v Durham
The Oval	Surrey v Kent
Hove	Sussex v Hants
Worcester	Worcs v Warwicks

Wednesday, April 30

†Benson and Hedges Cup (1 day)

Cambridge	British Univs v Sussex
Chester-le-Street	Durham v Northants
Bristol	Glos v Surrey
Canterbury	Kent v Hants
Manchester	Lancs v Derbys
Leicester	Leics v Notts
Lord's	Middx v Essex
Taunton	Somerset v Glam
Birmingham	Warwicks v Minor Counties
Leeds	Yorks v Worcs

Friday, May 2

†Benson and Hedges Cup (1 day)

Derby	Derbys v Yorks
Cardiff	Glam v Middx
Southampton	Hants v Glos
Canterbury	Kent v Sussex
Nottingham	Notts v Northants
Forfar	Scotland v Durham
Taunton	Somerset v Ireland
The Oval	Surrey v British Univs
Birmingham	Warwicks v Lancs
Worcester	Worcs v Minor Counties

Sunday, May 4

Lord's	†MCC v Wales (2 days)

Monday, May 5

†Benson and Hedges Cup (1 day)

Derby	Derbys v Worcs
Chester-le-Street	Durham v Leics
Chelmsford	Essex v Somerset
Cardiff	Glam v Ireland
Southampton	Hants v Surrey
Canterbury	Kent v British Univs
Walsall	Minor Counties v Lancs
Northampton	Northants v Scotland
Hove	Sussex v Glos
Birmingham	Warwicks v Yorks

Wednesday, May 7

Derby	Derbys v Surrey
Hartlepool	Durham v Notts
Bristol	Glos v Hants
Lord's	Middx v Sussex
Northampton	Northants v Somerset

Worcester Worcs v Leics
Leeds Yorks v Glam
Cambridge Cambridge U. v Essex
Oxford Oxford U. v Warwicks

Monday, May 12

†**Benson and Hedges Cup** (1 day)

Oxford British Univs v Hants
Derby Derbys v Warwicks
Bristol Glos v Kent
Downpatrick Ireland v Essex
Manchester Lancs v Worcs
Lord's Middx v Somerset
Northampton Northants v Leics
Glasgow (Titwood) Scotland v Notts
The Oval Surrey v Sussex
Leeds Yorks v Minor Counties

Wednesday, May 14

Chelmsford Essex v Durham
Southampton Hants v Leics
Canterbury Kent v Glam
Manchester Lancs v Notts
Lord's Middx v Derbys
Taunton Somerset v Sussex
The Oval Surrey v Glos
Birmingham Warwicks v Yorks
Cambridge Cambridge U. v Northants
Oxford Oxford U. v Worcs

Thursday, May 15

Arundel †Duke of Norfolk's XI v Australians (1 day)

Saturday, May 17

Northampton †Northants v Australians (1 day)
Cambridge †Cambridge U. v Oxford U. (1 day)

Sunday, May 18

Worcester †Worcs v Australians (1 day)

Tuesday, May 20

Chester-le-Street †Durham v Australians (1 day)

Wednesday, May 21

Chester-le-Street Durham v Worcs
Cardiff Glam v Hants
Gloucester Glos v Essex
Manchester Lancs v Northants
Leicester Leics v Surrey
Nottingham Notts v Derbys
Taunton Somerset v Yorks
Horsham Sussex v Kent
Birmingham Warwicks v Middx

Thursday, May 22

Leeds †ENGLAND v AUSTRALIA (1st 1-day Texaco Trophy)

Saturday, May 24

The Oval †ENGLAND v AUSTRALIA (2nd 1-day Texaco Trophy)

Sunday, May 25

Lord's †ENGLAND v AUSTRALIA (3rd 1-day Texaco Trophy)

Tuesday, May 27

†**Benson and Hedges Cup – Quarter-finals** (1 day)

Bristol or Hove Glos or Sussex v Australians

Or Surrey if both Glos and Sussex in B&H Cup quarter-finals.

Thursday, May 29

Ilford Essex v Yorks
Cardiff Glam v Durham
Southampton Hants v Warwicks
Leicester Leics v Lancs
Lord's Middx v Northants
Nottingham Notts v Kent
Worcester Worcs v Somerset

Friday, May 30

Oxford Oxford U. v Sussex

Saturday, May 31

Derby* Derbys v Australians

Wednesday, June 4

Chesterfield Derbys v Hants
Chester-le-Street Durham v Sussex
Tunbridge Wells Kent v Warwicks
Lord's Middx v Leics
Northampton Northants v Notts
Taunton Somerset v Lancs
The Oval Surrey v Essex
Leeds Yorks v Glos

Thursday, June 5

Birmingham*	ENGLAND v AUSTRALIA (1st Cornhill Test, 5 days)
Oxford	Oxford U. v Glam

Monday, June 9

Harrogate	†Costcutter Cup (3 days)

Tuesday, June 10

†Benson and Hedges Cup – Semi-finals (1 day)

Wednesday, June 11

Northampton or Nottingham	Northants or Notts v Australians

Or Durham if both Northants and Notts in B&H Cup semi-finals.

Thursday, June 12

Cardiff	Glam v Middx
Bristol	Glos v Worcs
Basingstoke	Hants v Somerset
Manchester	Lancs v Kent
The Oval	Surrey v Yorks
Hove	Sussex v Essex
Birmingham	Warwicks v Derbys

Saturday, June 14

Leicester*	Leics v Australians
Cambridge*	Cambridge U. v Durham
Oxford	Oxford U. v Notts

Wednesday, June 18

Derby	Derbys v Sussex
Darlington	Durham v Kent
Bristol	Glos v Middx
Liverpool	Lancs v Glam
Northampton	Northants v Hants
Nottingham	Notts v Yorks
Bath	Somerset v Leics
Worcester	Worcs v Surrey

Thursday, June 19

Lord's*	ENGLAND v AUSTRALIA (2nd Cornhill Test, 5 days)

Friday, June 20

Chelmsford*	Essex v Oxford U.

Tuesday, June 24

†NatWest Trophy – First Round (1 day)

Beaconsfield	Bucks v Essex
Wisbech	Cambs v Hants
Barrow	Cumb v Northants
Exmouth	Devon v Leics
Cardiff	Glam v Beds
Bristol	Glos v Scotland
Manchester	Lancs v Berks
Lincoln Lindum	Lincs v Derbys
Lord's	Middx v Kent
Nottingham	Notts v Staffs
Taunton	Somerset v Herefords
The Oval	Surrey v Durham
Hove	Sussex v Salop
Birmingham	Warwicks v Norfolk
Worcester	Worcs v Holland
Leeds	Yorks v Ireland

Wednesday, June 25

Oxford	British Univs v Australians

Thursday, June 26

Southend	Essex v Derbys
Swansea	Glam v Sussex
Leicester	Leics v Warwicks
Luton	Northants v Glos
Worcester	Worcs v Lancs
Leeds	Yorks v Middx
Lord's	†MCC v Melbourne Cricket Club (1 day)

Friday, June 27

The Oval	*Surrey v Notts
Lord's	†Eton v Harrow (1 day)

Saturday, June 28

Southampton*	Hants v Australians
Canterbury*	Kent v Cambridge U.
Taunton*	Somerset v Oxford U.

Wednesday, July 2

Chester-le-Street	Durham v Hants
Chelmsford	Essex v Somerset
Swansea	Glam v Glos
Maidstone	Kent v Northants
Leicester	Leics v Yorks
Uxbridge	Middx v Lancs
Arundel	Sussex v Worcs
Birmingham	Warwicks v Surrey
Nottingham	Notts v Pakistan A
Lord's	Oxford U. v Cambridge U.

Thursday, July 3

Manchester*	ENGLAND v AUSTRALIA (3rd Cornhill Test, 5 days)

Saturday, July 5

Derby*	Derbyshire v Pakistan A

Tuesday, July 8

Jesmond	†Minor Counties v Australians (1 day)

Wednesday, July 9

†NatWest Trophy – Second Round
(1 day)

Marlow or Chelmsford	Bucks or Essex v Worcs or Holland
Wisbech or Southampton	Cambs or Hants v Glam or Beds
Exmouth or Leicester	Devon or Leics v Yorks or Ireland
Lincoln Lindum or Derby	Lincs or Derbys v Cumb or Northants
Uxbridge or Canterbury	Middx or Kent v Glos or Scotland
The Oval or Chester-le-Street	Surrey or Durham v Notts or Staffs
Hove or St Georges, Telford	Sussex or Salop v Lancs or Berks
Birmingham or Lakenham	Warwicks or Norfolk v Somerset or Herefords
Shenley Park	MCC v Pakistan A

Saturday, July 12

Lord's	†BENSON AND HEDGES CUP FINAL (1 day)
Edinburgh (Grange CC)	†Scotland v Australians (1 day)
Scarborough	†Yorks v Durham (Northern Electric Trophy, 1 day)

Sunday, July 13

Walsall	†ECB XI v Pakistan A (1 day)

Monday, July 14

Scarborough	†Yorks v The Yorkshiremen (1 day)

Tuesday, July 15

Lord's	†MCC v MCC Schools (1 day)

Wednesday, July 16

Cheltenham	Glos v Derbys
Canterbury	Kent v Leics
Manchester	Lancs v Sussex
Northampton	Northants v Essex
Nottingham	Notts v Warwicks
Guildford	Surrey v Hants
Scarborough	Yorks v Durham
Cardiff	Glam v Australians
Worcester	Worcs v Pakistan A
Lord's	†MCC Schools v NAYC (1 day)

Thursday, July 17

Lord's	†NCA Young Cricketers v Combined Services (1 day)

Saturday, July 19

Lord's*	Middx v Australians
Taunton*	Somerset v Pakistan A

Tuesday, July 22

Cheltenham	†Glos v Pakistan A (1 day)

Wednesday, July 23

Chesterfield	Derbys v Glam
Chelmsford	Essex v Worcs
Cheltenham	Glos v Durham
Southampton	Hants v Lancs
Leicester	Leics v Notts
Lord's	Middx v Kent
Northampton	Northants v Surrey
Birmingham	Warwicks v Somerset
Birmingham area	†Triple Crown Tournament (3 days)

Thursday, July 24

Leeds*	ENGLAND v AUSTRALIA (4th Cornhill Test, 5 days)
Hove*	Sussex v Pakistan A (4 days)

Tuesday, July 29

†NatWest Trophy – Quarter-finals
(1 day)

Cardiff or Southampton	†Glam or Hants v Pakistan A (1 day)

Thursday, July 31

Chester-le-Street	Durham v Derbys
Colchester	Essex v Leics
Colwyn Bay	Glam v Notts
Birmingham	Warwicks v Sussex
Worcester	Worcs v Kent
Leeds	Yorks v Northants
Swansea	†Wales v Pakistan A (1 day)

Friday, August 1

Taunton*	Somerset v Australians (4 days)
Bristol*	Glos v Pakistan A (4 days)
Hove	†England Under-19 v Zimbabwe Under-19 (1st 1-day)

Monday, August 4

Southampton	†England Under-19 v Zimbabwe Under-19 (2nd 1-day)

Wednesday, August 6

Canterbury	Kent v Essex
Blackpool	Lancs v Warwicks
Lord's	Middx v Hants
Northampton	Northants v Worcs
Taunton	Somerset v Glos
The Oval	Surrey v Durham
Eastbourne	Sussex v Leics

Thursday, August 7

Nottingham*	ENGLAND v AUSTRALIA (5th Cornhill Test, 5 days)
Leeds*	Yorks v Pakistan A (4 days)
Birmingham*	†England Under-19 v Zimbabwe Under-19 (1st Unofficial Test, 4 days)

Saturday, August 9

Dublin (Malahide)*	Ireland v Scotland

Monday, August 11

†NAYC Under-19 One-Day Cup (6 days)

Tuesday, August 12

†NatWest Trophy – Semi-finals (1 day)

Derby or Northampton	†Derbys or Northants v Pakistan A (1 day)

Friday, August 15

Derby*	Derbys v Lancs
Portsmouth*	Hants v Yorks
Lord's*	Middx v Surrey
Nottingham*	Notts v Somerset
Hove*	Sussex v Glos
Worcester*	Worcs v Glam
Chelmsford*	First-class Counties Select XI v Pakistan A (4 days)

Saturday, August 16

Canterbury*	Kent v Australians

Monday, August 18

†Bain Hogg Insurance Trophy Semi-finals (1 day)

Tuesday, August 19

†Bain Hogg Insurance Trophy Semi-finals (1 day) (if not played on August 18)

Wednesday, August 20

Chester-le-Street	Durham v Middx
Abergavenny	Glam v Northants
Leicester	Leics v Derbys
Worksop	Notts v Essex
Taunton	Somerset v Kent
Birmingham	Warwicks v Worcs
Scarborough	Yorks v Sussex

Thursday, August 21

The Oval*	ENGLAND v AUSTRALIA (6th Cornhill Test, 5 days)
Northampton*	†England Under-19 v Zimbabwe Under-19 (2nd Unofficial Test, 4 days)
Lord's	†MCC v Ireland (2 days)

Wednesday, August 27

Derby	Derbys v Somerset
Chelmsford	Essex v Warwicks
Bristol	Glos v Notts
Portsmouth	Hants v Kent
Manchester	Lancs v Yorks
Leicester	Leics v Glam
Northampton	Northants v Durham
Hove	Sussex v Surrey
Kidderminster	Worcs v Middx
Lord's	†Minor Counties Knockout Final (1 day)

Thursday, August 28

Canterbury*	†England Under-19 v Zimbabwe Under-19 (3rd Unofficial Test, 4 days)

Friday, August 29

Lord's	†National Club Championship Final (1 day)

Sunday, August 31

Lord's	†National Village Championship Final (1 day)

Tuesday, September 2

Derby	Derbys v Northants
Chester-le-Street	Durham v Warwicks
Canterbury	Kent v Glos
Manchester	Lancs v Essex
Nottingham	Notts v Hants
Taunton	Somerset v Middx
The Oval	Surrey v Glam
Leeds	Yorks v Worcs

Saturday, September 6

Lord's	†NATWEST TROPHY FINAL (1 day)

Monday, September 8

†Bain Hogg Insurance Trophy Final (1 day)

Wednesday, September 10

Chester-le-Street	Durham v Somerset
Cardiff	Glam v Essex
Southampton	Hants v Sussex
Lord's	Middx v Notts
Northampton	Northants v Leics
The Oval	Surrey v Lancs
Birmingham	Warwicks v Glos
Worcester	Worcs v Derbys
Leeds	Yorks v Kent

Thursday, September 18

Derby*	Derbys v Yorks
Chelmsford*	Essex v Middx
Bristol*	Glos v Lancs
Southampton*	Hants v Worcs
Canterbury*	Kent v Surrey
Leicester*	Leics v Durham
Taunton*	Somerset v Glam
Hove*	Sussex v Notts
Birmingham*	Warwicks v Northants

AUSTRALIAN TOUR, 1997

MAY

15	Arundel	†v Duke of Norfolk's XI (1 day)
17	Northampton	†v Northants (1 day)
18	Worcester	†v Worcs (1 day)
20	Chester-le-Street	†v Durham (1 day)
22	Leeds	†v ENGLAND (1st 1-day Texaco Trophy)
24	The Oval	†v ENGLAND (2nd 1-day Texaco Trophy)
25	Lord's	†v ENGLAND (3rd 1-day Texaco Trophy)
27	Bristol or Hove	v Glos or Sussex

Or Surrey if both Glos and Sussex in B&H Cup quarter-finals.

31	Derby*	v Derbys

JUNE

5	Birmingham*	v ENGLAND (1st Cornhill Test, 5 days)
11	Northampton or Nottingham	v Northants or Notts

Or Durham if both Northants and Notts in B&H Cup semi-finals.

14	Leicester*	v Leics
19	Lord's*	v ENGLAND (2nd Cornhill Test, 5 days)
25	Oxford	v British Universities
28	Southampton*	v Hants

JULY

3	Manchester*	v ENGLAND (3rd Cornhill Test, 5 days)
8	Jesmond	†v Minor Counties (1 day)
12	Edinburgh (Grange CC)	†v Scotland (1 day)
16	Cardiff	v Glam
19	Lord's*	v Middx
24	Leeds*	v ENGLAND (4th Cornhill Test, 5 days)

AUGUST

1	Taunton*	v Somerset (4 days)
7	Nottingham*	v ENGLAND (5th Cornhill Test, 5 days)
16	Canterbury*	v Kent
21	The Oval*	v ENGLAND (6th Cornhill Test, 5 days)

PAKISTAN A TOUR, 1997

JULY

2	Nottingham	v Notts
5	Derby*	v Derbys
9	Shenley Park	v MCC
13	Walsall	†v ECB XI (1 day)
16	Worcester	v Worcs
19	Taunton*	v Somerset
22	Cheltenham	†v Glos (1 day)
24	Hove*	v Sussex (4 days)
29	Cardiff or Southampton	†v Glam or Hants (1 day)
31	Swansea	†v Wales (1 day)

AUGUST

1	Bristol*	v Glos (4 days)
7	Leeds*	v Yorks (4 days)
12	Derby or Northampton	†v Derbys or Northants (1 day)
15	Chelmsford*	v First-class Counties Select XI (4 days)

†AXA LIFE LEAGUE, 1997

All matches are of one day's duration.

APRIL

27–Essex v Hants (Chelmsford); Glam v Warwicks (Cardiff); Kent v Derbys (Canterbury); Lancs v Durham (Manchester); Leics v Glos (Leicester); Notts v Worcs (Nottingham); Surrey v Somerset (The Oval); Sussex v Northants (Hove).

MAY

4–Derbys v Lancs (Derby); Essex v Middx (Chelmsford); Hants v Yorks (Southampton); Kent v Surrey (Canterbury); Somerset v Glam (Taunton); Sussex v Notts (Hove); Warwicks v Northants (Birmingham).

11–Derbys v Surrey (Derby); Durham v Notts (Hartlepool); Glos v Hants (Bristol); Middx v Sussex (Lord's); Northants v Somerset (Northampton); Worcs v Leics (Worcester); Yorks v Glam (Leeds).

18–Essex v Durham (Chelmsford); Hants v Leics (Southampton); Kent v Glamorgan (Canterbury); Lancs v Notts (Manchester); Middx v Derbys (Lord's); Somerset v Sussex (Taunton); Surrey v Glos (The Oval); Warwicks v Yorks (Birmingham).

25–Durham v Worcs (Chester-le-Street); Glam v Hants (Cardiff); Glos v Essex (Gloucester); Lancs v Northants (Manchester); Leics v Surrey (Leicester); Notts v Derbys (Nottingham); Somerset v Yorks (Taunton); Sussex v Kent (Horsham); Warwicks v Middx (Birmingham).

JUNE

1–Essex v Yorks (Ilford); Glam v Durham (Pontypridd); Hants v Warwicks (Southampton); Leics v Lancs (Leicester); Middx v Northants (Lord's); Notts v Kent (Nottingham); Worcs v Somerset (Worcester).

8–Derbys v Hants (Chesterfield); Durham v Sussex (Chester-le-Street); Kent v Warwicks (Tunbridge Wells); Middx v Leics (Lord's); Northants v Notts (Campbell Park, Milton Keynes); Somerset v Lancs (Taunton); Surrey v Essex (The Oval); Yorks v Glos (Leeds).

15–Glam v Middx (Cardiff); Glos v Worcs (Bristol); Hants v Somerset (Basingstoke); Lancs v Kent (Manchester); Surrey v Yorks (The Oval); Sussex v Essex (Hove); Warwicks v Derbys (Birmingham).

22–Derbys v Sussex (Derby); Durham v Kent (Darlington); Glos v Middx (Bristol); Lancs v Glam (Manchester); Northants v Hants (Northampton); Notts v Yorks (Nottingham); Somerset v Leics (Bath); Worcs v Surrey (Worcester).

26–Surrey v Notts (The Oval; evening fixture).

29–Essex v Derbys (Southend); Glam v Sussex (Swansea); Leics v Warwicks (Leicester); Northants v Glos (Luton); Worcs v Lancs (Worcester); Yorks v Middx (Leeds).

JULY

6–Durham v Hants (Chester-le-Street); Essex v Somerset (Chelmsford); Glam v Glos (Swansea); Kent v Northants (Maidstone); Leics v Yorks (Leicester); Middx v Lancs (Uxbridge); Sussex v Worcs (Arundel); Warwicks v Surrey (Birmingham).

13–Derbys v Yorks (Derby); Durham v Warwicks (Chester-le-Street); Hants v Worcs (Southampton); Notts v Somerset (Nottingham); Sussex v Glos (Hove). *Note: Matches involving B&H Cup finalists to be played on July 15.*

20–Glos v Derbys (Cheltenham); Kent v Leics (Canterbury); Lancs v Sussex (Manchester); Northants v Essex (Northampton); Notts v Warwicks (Nottingham); Surrey v Hants (Guildford); Worcs v Glam (Worcester); Yorks v Durham (Scarborough).

27–Derbys v Glam (Chesterfield); Essex v Worcs (Chelmsford); Glos v Durham (Cheltenham); Hants v Lancs (Southampton); Leics v Notts (Leicester); Middx v Kent (Lord's); Northants v Surrey (Northampton); Warwicks v Somerset (Birmingham).

AUGUST

3–Durham v Derbys (Chester-le-Street); Essex v Leics (Colchester); Glam v Notts (Colwyn Bay); Middx v Surrey (Lord's); Warwicks v Sussex (Birmingham); Worcs v Kent (Worcester); Yorks v Northants (Leeds).

10–Kent v Essex (Canterbury); Lancs v Warwicks (Manchester); Middx v Hants (Lord's); Northants v Worcs (Northampton); Somerset v Glam (Taunton); Surrey v Durham (The Oval); Sussex v Leics (Eastbourne).

24–Durham v Middx (Chester-le-Street); Glam v Northants (Cardiff); Glos v Lancs (Bristol); Leics v Derbys (Leicester); Notts v Essex (Nottingham); Somerset v Kent (Taunton); Worcs v Warwicks (Worcester); Yorks v Sussex (Scarborough).

31–Derbys v Somerset (Derby); Essex v Warwicks (Chelmsford); Glos v Notts (Bristol); Hants v Kent (Portsmouth); Lancs v Yorks (Manchester); Leics v Glam (Leicester); Northants v Durham (Northampton); Sussex v Surrey (Hove); Worcs v Middx (Worcester).

SEPTEMBER

7–Derbys v Northants (Derby); Kent v Glos (Canterbury); Lancs v Essex (Manchester); Leics v Durham (Leicester); Notts v Hants (Nottingham); Somerset v Middx (Taunton); Surrey v Glam (The Oval); Yorks v Worcs (Leeds). *Note: Matches involving NWT finalists to be played on September 9.*

14–Durham v Somerset (Chester-le-Street); Glam v Essex (Cardiff); Hants v Sussex (Southampton); Middx v Notts (Lord's); Northants v Leics (Northampton); Surrey v Lancs (The Oval); Warwicks v Glos (Birmingham); Worcs v Derbys (Worcester); Yorks v Kent (Leeds).

†MINOR COUNTIES CHAMPIONSHIP, 1997

All matches are of two days' duration.

MAY

25–Cumb v Beds (Askam); Devon v Wales (Sidmouth); Dorset v Herefords (Sherborne); Lincs v Herts (Sleaford); Oxon v Berks (Challow & Childrey).

JUNE

4–Bucks v Staffs (Beaconsfield).

8–Beds v Suffolk (Dunstable); Cheshire v Wilts (Neston); Dorset v Wales (Dean Park, Bournemouth); Lincs v Bucks (Bourne); Northumb v Norfolk (Jesmond); Oxon v Salop (Challow & Childrey).

10–Berks v Salop (Hurst CC).

15–Beds v Staffs (Bedford Town); Bucks v Northumb (High Wycombe); Wales v Oxon (Swansea); Wilts v Herefords (Westbury).

16–Cheshire v Cornwall (New Brighton); Cumb v Lincs (Netherfield).

17–Herts v Northumb (St Albans).

18–Cambs v Norfolk (Saffron Walden); Salop v Cornwall (Newport).

29–Herefords v Berks (Dales, Leominster); Lincs v Suffolk (Cleethorpes); Oxon v Dorset (Banbury CC); Salop v Devon (Bridgnorth); Wales v Wilts (Newport, Panteg).

JULY

1–Cheshire v Devon (Toft); Northumb v Suffolk (Jesmond).

2–Staffs v Cambs (Cannock).

6–Berks v Dorset (Reading CC); Bucks v Cumb (Aylesbury); Wilts v Devon (South Wilts CC).

7–Staffs v Northumb (Stone).

8–Cambs v Beds (Fenner's, Cambridge); Herts v Cumb (Hertford).

13–Beds v Lincs (Southill Park); Herts v Norfolk (Radlett); Northumb v Cambs (Tynemouth); Salop v Wales (Oswestry); Wilts v Cornwall (Marlborough CC).

15–Cumb v Cambs (Carlisle); Dorset v Cornwall (Weymouth).

22–Herefords v Cheshire (Brockhampton).

24–Herts v Staffs (Bishop's Stortford).

27–Devon v Berks (Torquay); Herefords v Salop (Colwall); Herts v Beds (Shenley Park); Norfolk v Cumb (Lakenham); Oxon v Wilts (Thame); Suffolk v Bucks (Ransomes, Ipswich); Wales v Cheshire (Pontypridd).

29–Cornwall v Berks (Falmouth); Norfolk v Bucks (Lakenham); Suffolk v Cumb (Mildenhall).

30–Cambs v Lincs (Fenner's, Cambridge).

AUGUST

3–Oxon v Cheshire (Rover, Cowley); Wales v Herefords (Pontarddulais).

4–Norfolk v Staffs (Lakenham).

5–Berks v Cheshire (Finchampstead).

6–Cambs v Herts (March); Norfolk v Beds (Lakenham); Suffolk v Staffs (Bury St Edmunds).

10–Berks v Wilts (Falkland CC); Bucks v Cambs (Slough); Cornwall v Oxon (St Austell); Norfolk v Suffolk (Lakenham); Northumb v Lincs (Jesmond); Salop v Dorset (Wellington).

12–Cheshire v Dorset (Bowdon); Devon v Oxon (Bovey Tracey).

17–Cornwall v Wales (Camborne); Cumb v Northumb (Barrow); Devon v Herefords (Exmouth).

18–Suffolk v Herts (Ipswich School).

19–Cornwall v Herefords (Truro); Staffs v Lincs (Brewood).

24–Beds v Bucks (Wardown Park); Dorset v Devon (Dean Park, Bournemouth); Wilts v Salop (Trowbridge).

31–Bucks v Herts (Marlow); Devon v Cornwall (Instow); Dorset v Wilts (Dean Park, Bournemouth); Herefords v Oxon (Kington); Lincs v Norfolk (Lincoln Lindum); Northumb v Beds (Jesmond); Salop v Cheshire (Shifnal); Staffs v Cumb (Longton); Suffolk v Cambs (Ransomes, Ipswich); Wales v Berks (Colwyn Bay).

SEPTEMBER

14–Final.

†MCC TROPHY KNOCKOUT COMPETITION, 1997

All matches are of one day's duration.

Preliminary Round

May 18 Berks v Salop (Finchampstead); Herefords v Cornwall (Brockhampton); Herts v Lincs (Shenley Park); Suffolk v Staffs (Copdock CC).

First Round

June 1 Berks or Salop v Herefords or Cornwall (Finchampstead or Wellington); Cambs v Cheshire (March); Cumb v Dorset (Penrith); Devon v Wales (Exmouth); Herts or Lincs v Suffolk or Staffs (Shenley Park or Grantham); Northumb v Bucks (Jesmond); Oxon v Beds (Thame); Wilts v Norfolk (Corsham).

Quarter-finals to be played on June 22.

Semi-finals to be played on July 20.

Final to be played on August 27 at Lord's.

†SECOND ELEVEN CHAMPIONSHIP, 1997

Unless otherwise stated, matches are of three days' duration.

APRIL

23–Middx v Notts (Uxbridge CC); Somerset v Sussex (Taunton); Worcs v Leics (Worcester).

30–Essex v Glam (Chelmsford); Kent v Yorks (Eltham); Leics v Notts (Hinckley Town CC); Surrey v Middx (Cheam).

MAY

7–Essex v Durham (Chelmsford); Glam v Yorks (Pontypridd); Hants v Worcs (Southampton); Leics v Kent (Leicester); Notts v Lancs (Nottingham); Somerset v Glos (Taunton); Surrey v Derbys (The Oval); Sussex v Northants (Eastbourne).

13–Notts v Derbys (Nottingham; 4 days); Sussex v Surrey (Hove; 4 days).

14–Durham v Hants (Felling CC); Kent v Essex (Maidstone); Lancs v Glam (Fleetwood); Somerset v Leics (North Perrott); Yorks v Warwicks (Bingley).

21–Essex v Sussex (Saffron Walden); Glam v Kent (Pontarddulais); Glos v Derbys (Bristol); Hants v Notts (Southampton); Middx v Leics (Uxbridge CC); Northants v Somerset (Northampton); Surrey v Yorks (Oxted); Warwicks v Lancs (Stratford-upon-Avon); Worcs v Durham (Worcester).

28–Derbys v Lancs (Cheadle CC, Staffs); Durham v Glam (Stockton CC); Kent v Somerset (Ashford); Leics v Glos (Hinckley Town CC); Northants v Worcs (Campbell Park, Milton Keynes); Warwicks v Hants (Knowle & Dorridge); Yorks v Essex (Elland).

JUNE

3–Worcs v Somerset (Kidderminster; 4 days).

4–Derbys v Sussex (Abbotsholme School, Rocester); Essex v Warwicks (Ilford); Glam v Northants (Swansea); Glos v Yorks (Tuffley Park, Gloucester); Hants v Surrey (Southampton); Middx v Durham (Lensbury CC).

11–Derbys v Middx (Abbotsholme School, Rocester); Essex v Leics (Wickford); Glam v Notts (Ammanford); Hants v Northants (Finchampstead); Lancs v Glos (Southport); Surrey v Worcs (Cheam); Warwicks v Durham (Griff & Coton); Yorks v Sussex (York).

17–Essex v Middx (Coggeshall; 4 days).

18–Glam v Glos (Swansea); Kent v Derbys (Canterbury); Lancs v Northants (Middleton); Leics v Surrey (Hinckley Town CC); Somerset v Durham (Taunton); Sussex v Warwicks (Horsham); Yorks v Worcs (Middlesbrough).

25–Derbys v Glam (Belper Meadows); Durham v Surrey (Boldon CC); Glos v Northants (Shirehampton CC); Kent v Worcs (Sittingbourne); Leics v Hants (Kibworth CC); Notts v Yorks (Collingham CC); Somerset v Lancs (North Perrott); Warwicks v Middx (Moseley).

JULY

1–Derbys v Leics (Chesterfield; 4 days).

2–Glos v Surrey (Bristol); Middx v Sussex (Harrow CC); Northants v Kent (Wardown Park); Notts v Essex (Worksop CC); Somerset v Glam (Taunton); Worcs v Warwicks (Worcester); Yorks v Durham (Todmorden).

8–Northants v Essex (Northampton; 4 days).

9–Derbys v Durham (Chesterfield); Lancs v Kent (Haslingden); Notts v Surrey (Nottingham); Somerset v Hants (Clevedon); Sussex v Glos (Horsham); Yorks v Middx (Harrogate).

15–Somerset v Warwicks (Taunton; 4 days); Surrey v Kent (The Oval; 4 days).

16–Durham v Leics (South Shields); Essex v Lancs (Chelmsford); Hants v Yorks (Southampton); Middx v Glos (Southgate CC); Northants v Notts (Wellingborough); Sussex v Glam (Hove); Worcs v Derbys (Halesowen).

22–Durham v Notts (Chester-le-Street; 4 days); Glam v Hants (Pontypridd; 4 days).

23–Kent v Middx (Canterbury); Northants v Derbys (Dunstable); Surrey v Somerset (The Oval); Warwicks v Glos (Solihull); Worcs v Essex (Worcester).

29–Glam v Surrey (Usk); Lancs v Durham (Ramsbottom; 4 days).

30–Kent v Warwicks (Folkestone); Middx v Hants (Harrow CC); Notts v Worcs (Nottingham High School); Sussex v Leics (Hastings); Yorks v Somerset (Marske-by-Sea).

AUGUST

5–Hants v Glos (Southampton; 4 days); Warwicks v Glam (Studley; 4 days).

6–Durham v Kent (Seaton Carew); Leics v Northants (Lutterworth CC); Middx v Lancs (Southgate CC); Notts v Somerset (Worksop College); Surrey v Essex (Oxted); Worcs v Sussex (Barnt Green).

12–Leics v Yorks (Oakham School; 4 days).

13–Derbys v Hants (Chesterfield); Durham v Northants (Chester-le-Street); Glos v Notts (Hatherley & Reddings CC, Cheltenham); Surrey v Warwicks (Guildford); Sussex v Lancs (Middleton-on-Sea); Worcs v Middx (Ombersley).

20–Derbys v Somerset (Derby); Glos v Essex (Bristol); Lancs v Hants (Manchester);

Middx v Glam (Lensbury CC); Northants v Yorks (Campbell Park, Milton Keynes); Notts v Kent (Nottingham); Sussex v Durham (Hove); Warwicks v Leics (Walmley).

26–Kent v Sussex (Tunbridge Wells; 4 days); Middx v Northants (Vine Lane, Uxbridge; 4 days); Yorks v Lancs (Park Avenue, Bradford; 4 days).

27–Derbys v Warwicks (Chesterfield); Durham v Glos (Sunderland); Glam v Worcs (Panteg); Hants v Essex (Southampton).

SEPTEMBER

2–Warwicks v Notts (Birmingham); Yorks v Derbys (Castleford).

3–Essex v Somerset (Colchester); Glos v Kent (Bristol); Leics v Glam (Hinckley Town CC); Northants v Surrey (Northampton); Sussex v Hants (Hove); Worcs v Lancs (Worcester).

9–Glos v Worcs (Bristol; 4 days).

10–Essex v Derbys (Chelmsford); Hants v Kent (Bournemouth SC); Lancs v Surrey (Manchester); Notts v Sussex (Nottingham); Somerset v Middx (Taunton); Warwicks v Northants (Kenilworth Wardens).

15–Lancs v Leics (Liverpool).

†BAIN HOGG INSURANCE TROPHY, 1997

All matches are of one day's duration.

APRIL

28–Yorks v Lancs (Bradford).

29–Durham v Lancs (Boldon CC).

MAY

6–Notts v Lancs (Mansfield); Somerset v Hants (Taunton); Surrey v MCC Young Cricketers (The Oval); Warwicks v Middx (Leamington).

12–Hants v Somerset (Portsmouth); Lancs v Durham (Urmston); Leics v Middx (Leicester); Worcs v Glos (Worcester).

13–Glos v Glam (Old Bristolians, Westbury); Kent v Essex (Maidstone).

19–Hants v Glam (Southampton); Kent v MCC Young Cricketers (Canterbury); Minor Counties v Warwicks (Leek); Yorks v Derbys (Park Avenue, Bradford).

20–Essex v Sussex (Saffron Walden); Minor Counties v Leics (Leek).

27–Derbys v Lancs (Glossop).

JUNE

2–Glam v Hants (Christ College, Brecon); MCC Young Cricketers v Surrey (Shenley Park); Minor Counties v Northants (North Runcton); Yorks v Notts (Park Avenue, Bradford).

3–Derbys v Notts (Eyes Meadow, Duffield); Essex v Kent (Chelmsford); Leics v Minor Counties (Egerton Park, Melton Mowbray).

5–Lancs v Notts (Manchester).

9–Lancs v Yorks (Manchester); Sussex v Kent (Eastbourne); Warwicks v Leics (Aston Unity).

10–Glam v Somerset (Ebbw Vale); MCC Young Cricketers v Essex (Shenley Park); Minor Counties v Middx (Sleaford); Notts v Durham (Worksop College).

16–Hants v Worcs (Southampton); Kent v Surrey (Canterbury); MCC Young Cricketers v Sussex (Shenley Park).

17–Lancs v Derbys (Wigan).

23–Durham v Derbys (Bishop Auckland); Essex v Surrey (Chelmsford); Hants v Glos (Southampton); Middx v Northants (Southgate CC).

24–Notts v Yorks (Farnsfield CC); Sussex v MCC Young Cricketers (Haywards Heath).

30–Middx v Warwicks (Harrow CC); Somerset v Worcs (King's College, Taunton).

JULY

1–Glos v Somerset (Bristol); Surrey v Kent (The Oval); Yorks v Durham (Park Avenue, Bradford).

7–MCC Young Cricketers v Kent (Shenley Park); Middx v Leics (Harrow CC); Northants v Warwicks (Northampton); Somerset v Glam (Taunton).

8–Derbys v Durham (Dunstall); Glos v Hants (Bristol); Worcs v Glam (Worcester).

10–Warwicks v Minor Counties (West Bromwich, Dartmouth).

14–Durham v Yorks (Benwell Hill); Glam v Worcs (Llanarth); Somerset v Glos (Taunton).

15–Essex v MCC Young Cricketers (Chelmsford); Glos v Worcs (Bristol); Notts v Derbys (Welbeck CC).

21–Derbys v Yorks (Belper Meadows); Durham v Notts (Chester-le-Street); Leics v Warwicks (Leicester); Northants v Minor Counties (Campbell Park, Milton Keynes); Surrey v Sussex (The Oval); Worcs v Somerset (Bromsgrove CC).

22–Kent v Sussex (Canterbury); Middx v Minor Counties (Uxbridge CC); Northants v Leics (Bedford School).

28–Glam v Glos (Newport); Sussex v Surrey (East Grinstead); Warwicks v Northants (Leamington); Worcs v Hants (Kidderminster).

29–Sussex v Essex (Hastings).

AUGUST

1–Surrey v Essex (The Oval).

4–Northants v Middx (Tring).

5–Leics v Northants (Leicester).

Semi-finals to be played on August 18 or 19.

Final to be played on September 8 (reserve day September 9).

†WOMEN'S CRICKET, 1997

JULY

26	Cambridge	Area Championship (5 days)

AUGUST

15	Bristol	ENGLAND v SOUTH AFRICA (1st one-day international)
17	Taunton	ENGLAND v SOUTH AFRICA (2nd one-day international)
20	Lord's	ENGLAND v SOUTH AFRICA (3rd one-day international)
27	Hinckley	ENGLAND v SOUTH AFRICA (4th one-day international)
30	Milton Keynes (Campbell Park)	ENGLAND v SOUTH AFRICA (5th one-day international)

SEPTEMBER

7	Milton Keynes (Campbell Park)	National League final
14	Cannock	Tilney National Club Knockout final

†WOMEN'S WORLD CUP, 1997

All fixtures subject to confirmation.

Group A

DECEMBER

11–Australia v Ireland (Madras); Denmark v Pakistan (Bangalore); England v South Africa (Vijayawada).

13–Australia v South Africa (Madras); Denmark v Ireland (Bangalore); England v Pakistan (Hyderabad).

15–Australia v Pakistan (Hyderabad); Denmark v England (Bombay); Ireland v South Africa (Pune).

17–Australia v Denmark (Bombay); England v Ireland (Pune); Pakistan v South Africa (Goa).

19–Australia v England (Nagpur); Denmark v South Africa (Bombay); Ireland v Pakistan (Ahmedabad).

Group B

DECEMBER

10–Canada v New Zealand (Delhi); Holland v West Indies (Delhi); India v Japan (Gauhati).

12–Holland v New Zealand (Chandigarh); India v Canada (Faridabad); Japan v West Indies (Delhi).

14–Canada v Holland (Ghaziabad); India v West Indies (Gwalior); Japan v New Zealand (Jalandhar).

16–Canada v Japan (Jaipur); India v Holland (Ghaziabad); New Zealand v West Indies (Agra).

18–Canada v West Indies (Lucknow); Holland v Japan (Mohali); India v New Zealand (Indore).

Quarter-finals to be played at Patna and Pune on December 21 and at Hyderabad and Lucknow on December 22.

Semi-finals to be played at Gauhati on December 24 and Madras on December 26.

Final to be played at Calcutta on December 28.